The tithe surveys of mid-nineteenth-century England and Wales marked a new departure in government-sponsored, cadastral surveying of the nation's land. The 11,800 large-scale, detailed maps which they comprise are recognised as one of the most important sets of manuscript historical sources used by historical geographers and economic, social and local historians, by lawyers representing clients in property and rights of way disputes, and by county and local planning offices. Despite the much acknowledged value of tithe surveys, historians are not well-served with indexes, descriptive catalogues or indications of tithe map coverage. A first object of this book is to provide a standard work of reference which will be an essential research tool for users of tithe maps. The database from which this reference work is compiled has also been analysed to make an original contribution to knowledge by revealing more about the general cartographic characteristics of this internationally important government survey.

THE TITHE MAPS OF ENGLAND AND WALES

Frontispiece: Robert Kearsley Dawson, assistant tithe commissioner and superintendent of the tithe surveys, pictured in about 1841. Reproduced from a miniature in the possession of G. A. Dawson with his kind permission.

THE TITHE MAPS OF ENGLAND AND WALES

A cartographic analysis and county-by-county catalogue

ROGER J. P. KAIN AND
RICHARD R. OLIVER

University of Exeter

with contributions from

Rodney E. J. Fry, *University of Exeter*
and Sarah A. H. Wilmot, *University of Lancaster*

Published by the Press Syndicate of the University of Cambridge
The Pitt Building, Trumpington Street, Cambridge CB2 1RP
40 West 20th Street, New York, NY 10011-4211, USA
10 Stamford Road, Oakleigh, Victoria 3166, Australia

First published 1995

Printed in Great Britain at the University Press, Cambridge

A catalogue record for this book is available from the British Library

Library of Congress cataloguing in publication data
Kain, R. J. P. (Roger J. P.)
The tithe maps of England and Wales: a cartographic analysis and county-by-county catalogue/Roger J. P. Kain and Richard R. Oliver; with contributions from Rodney E. J. Fry and Sarah A. H. Wilmot.
p. cm.
Includes index.
ISBN 0 521 44191 9
1. Tithes – England – History – Maps. 2. Tithes – Wales – History – Maps. 3. Cartography – England – History. 4. Cartography – Wales – History. I. Oliver, Richard R. II. Fry, Rodney E. J. III. Wilmot, Sarah A. H. IV. Title.
G1816.E423K35 1994
336.2′00942022 – dc20 93–44929 CIP

ISBN 0 521 44191 9 hardback

Contents

List of figures — *page* xii
List of tables — xvii
Preface — xxiii

Introduction — 1
  Tithe and tithe commutation — 1
  Establishing tithe districts — 2
  Corn rent conversions — 3
  Exemptions from tithe — 5
  Tithe agreements and awards: assistant tithe commissioners — 6
  Apportioning tithe rent-charge: tithe valuers — 7
  The boundaries of tithe districts — 17
  The tithe survey database and county-by-county catalogues — 17
  Explanatory key to the county tithe survey catalogues — 19

County-by-county catalogues and analyses of the tithe surveys — 29
  Arrangement of text, tables, and catalogues — 29
1 Bedfordshire — 30
2 Berkshire — 36
3 Buckinghamshire — 46
4 Cambridgeshire — 55
5 Cheshire — 63
6 Cornwall — 85
7 Cumberland — 98
8 Derbyshire — 109
9 Devonshire — 122
10 Dorset — 145
11 Durham — 158
12 Essex — 174
13 Gloucestershire — 194
  Hampshire (see 31 Southampton)

14 Herefordshire 206
15 Hertfordshire 219
16 Huntingdonshire 228
17 Kent 234
18 Lancashire 256
19 Leicestershire 277
20 Lincolnshire 287
21 Middlesex 306
22 Monmouthshire 313
23 Norfolk 322
24 Northamptonshire 350
25 Northumberland 359
26 Nottinghamshire 384
27 Oxfordshire 394
28 Rutland 405
29 Shropshire 410
30 Somerset 428
31 Southampton (Hampshire) 450
32 Staffordshire 466
33 Suffolk 480
34 Surrey 503
35 Sussex 513
36 Warwickshire 530
37 Westmorland 540
38 Wiltshire 548
39 Worcestershire 562
40 York City and Ainsty 572
41 Yorkshire, East Riding 576
42 Yorkshire, North Riding 588
43 Yorkshire, West Riding 608
44 Anglesey 631
45 Breconshire 637
46 Cardiganshire 644
47 Carmarthenshire 650

48 Carnarvonshire 656
49 Denbighshire 662
50 Flintshire 670
51 Glamorganshire 675
52 Merionethshire 684
53 Montgomeryshire 689
54 Pembrokeshire 695
55 Radnorshire 703

The tithe maps of England and Wales: a 'national' survey? 708
First-class and second-class tithe maps 708
New surveys and maps based on existing surveys 712
Map-makers 717
Tithe map scales 726
Manuscript and printed tithe maps 732
The chronology of tithe map production 742
Topographic content of the tithe surveys 744
Borders and cartouches 787
Legends, explanations and tabulated information 789
Decoration on tithe maps 789
Altered tithe apportionments and maps 793
Original and statutory copies of tithe maps 802
A quintessential tithe map? 808

Appendices 820
1 Assistant tithe commissioners and local tithe agents of England and Wales 820
2 Tithe district boundaries on the maps of PRO IR 105 and the Ordnance Survey 'Index to Tithe Survey' 827
3 Tithe map-makers of England and Wales 831
4 Map-makers who made twenty-five or more tithe maps in England and Wales 855

Place-name index 857

Figures

Frontispiece: Robert Kearsley Dawson, assistant tithe commissioner and superintendent of the tithe surveys. *page* iv
1 England and Wales: counties as defined by the Tithe Commission. 4
2 England and Wales: tithe districts where corn rent annuities were confirmed in lieu of tithes. 5
3 Brighton, Sussex: tithe map, 1852. 7
4 Upper Heyford tithable to Flore, Northamptonshire: tithe apportionment, 1848. 9
5 Bedford, Lancashire: tithe apportionment, 1846. 10
6 England and Wales: tithe apportionments which list crops under 'state of cultivation'. 11
7 Whittle, Northumberland: tithe apportionment, 1843. 12
8 Cowley, Gloucestershire: tithe apportionment, 1841. 13
9 England and Wales: tithe districts where tithe was apportioned on holdings rather than field-by-field. 14
10 Llandefailog, Carmarthenshire: tithe apportionment, 1842. 15
11 Horn, Rutland: tithe map, 1838. 16
12 A map extract from Public Record Office class IR 105. 18
13 Bedfordshire: tithe district boundaries. 31
14 Berkshire: tithe district boundaries. 37
15 Buckinghamshire: tithe district boundaries. 47
16 Cambridgeshire: tithe district boundaries. 56
17 Cheshire: tithe district boundaries. 64
18 Cornwall: tithe district boundaries. 86
19 Cumberland: tithe district boundaries. 99
20 Derbyshire: tithe district boundaries. 110
21 Devon: tithe district boundaries. 124
22 Dorset: tithe district boundaries. 146
23 Durham: tithe district boundaries. 159
24 Essex: tithe district boundaries. 176
25 Gloucestershire: tithe district boundaries. 195
26 Herefordshire: tithe district boundaries. 207
27 Hertfordshire: tithe district boundaries. 220
28 Huntingdonshire: tithe district boundaries. 229
29 Kent: tithe district boundaries. 235
30 Lancashire: tithe district boundaries. 257
31 Leicestershire: tithe district boundaries. 278
32 Lincolnshire: tithe district boundaries. 288
33 Middlesex: tithe district boundaries. 307
34 Monmouthshire: tithe district boundaries. 314
35 Norfolk: tithe district boundaries. 324
36 Northamptonshire: tithe district boundaries. 351
37 Northumberland: tithe district boundaries. 361

38 Nottinghamshire: tithe district boundaries. 385
39 Oxfordshire: tithe district boundaries. 395
40 Rutland: tithe district boundaries. 406
41 Shropshire: tithe district boundaries. 411
42 Somerset: tithe district boundaries. 430
43 Southampton (Hampshire): tithe district boundaries. 451
44 Staffordshire: tithe district boundaries. 467
45 Suffolk: tithe district boundaries. 482
46 Surrey: tithe district boundaries. 504
47 Sussex: tithe district boundaries. 514
48 Warwickshire: tithe district boundaries. 531
49 Westmorland: tithe district boundaries. 541
50 Wiltshire: tithe district boundaries. 549
51 Worcestershire: tithe district boundaries. 563
52 York City and Ainsty: tithe district boundaries. 573
53 Yorkshire, East Riding: tithe district boundaries. 577
54 Yorkshire, North Riding: tithe district boundaries. 589
55 Yorkshire, West Riding: tithe district boundaries. 610
56 Anglesey: tithe district boundaries. 632
57 Breconshire: tithe district boundaries. 638
58 Cardiganshire: tithe district boundaries. 645
59 Carmarthenshire: tithe district boundaries. 651
60 Carnarvonshire: tithe district boundaries. 657
61 Denbighshire: tithe district boundaries. 663
62 Flintshire: tithe district boundaries. 671
63 Glamorganshire: tithe district boundaries. 676
64 Merionethshire: tithe district boundaries. 685
65 Montgomeryshire: tithe district boundaries. 690
66 Pembrokeshire: tithe district boundaries. 696
67 Radnorshire: tithe district boundaries. 704
68 The Tithe Commission's official seal which denotes a first-class map. 710
69 England and Wales: first-class tithe maps. 711
70 Wacton, Norfolk: original tithe map at one inch to three chains, 1840. 713
71 Wacton, Norfolk: statutory copy of tithe map at one inch to six chains, 1840. 714
72 Aston, Cheshire: tithe map, 1846. 715
73 South Cliffe, East Riding of Yorkshire: tithe map, 1775. 716
74 Buslingthorpe, Lincolnshire: tithe map, 1838. 716
75 Caerwys, Flintshire: tithe map, 1849. 717
76 Alderley, Gloucestershire: tithe map, 1838. 718
77 R. K. Dawson's instructions for setting out tithe map construction lines. 719
78 England and Wales: second-class tithe maps with construction lines. 720
79 Week St Mary, Cornwall: tithe map, 1839. 721
80 Capel le Fern, Kent: tithe map, 1840. 722
81 Boughton Aluph, Kent: tithe map, 1839. 723
82 Great Mongeham, Kent: tithe map, *circa* 1841. 724
83 Ripon, West Riding of Yorkshire: tithe map, 1839. 725
84 Troed yr Aur, Cardiganshire: tithe map, 1840. 726
85 Some tithe map-makers and the extent of their practices. 727
86 Barton, Lancashire: tithe map, 1847. 728
87 Extract from Ordnance Survey six-inch map, Lancashire sheet 53, published 1848. 729
88 England and Wales: tithe maps at a scale of one inch to three chains. 730
89 England and Wales: tithe maps at a scale of one inch to four chains. 731
90 England and Wales: tithe maps at a scale of one inch to six chains. 732
91 England and Wales: tithe maps at scales of one inch to eight chains and smaller scales. 733
92 Widworthy, Devon: manuscript tithe map, 1839. 734
93 Widworthy, Devon: lithographed tithe map, 1839. 735

94 Nantglyn, Denbighshire: tithe map, 1840. 736
95 England and Wales: lithographed tithe maps. 737
96 Polesworth, Warwickshire: tithe map, 1850. 738
97 West Orchard, Dorset: tithe map, *circa* 1841. 739
98 Brighstone, Hampshire: tithe map, 1840. 740
99 Bridge and Patrixbourne, Kent: tithe map, 1838. 741
100 Gargrave, West Riding of Yorkshire: tithe map, 1839. 743
101 England and Wales: tithe maps dated 1836-39. 744
102 England and Wales: tithe maps dated 1840-41. 745
103 England and Wales: tithe maps dated 1842-45. 746
104 England and Wales: tithe maps dated 1846-83. 747
105 Linstead Magna, Suffolk: tithe map, 1842. 748
106 Thrybergh, West Riding of Yorkshire: tithe map, 1840. 749
107 Capel le Fern, Kent: tithe map, 1840. 750
108 Barnby in the Willows, Nottinghamshire: tithe map, 1840. 752
109 Kington, Worcestershire: tithe map, *circa* 1848. 753
110 Gargrave, West Riding of Yorkshire: tithe map, 1839. 754
111 Lower Mitton, Worcestershire: tithe map, *circa* 1849. 755
112 Lakenheath Fen Lands, Suffolk: tithe map, 1854. 756
113 Gwennap, Cornwall: tithe map, 1839. 758
114 Waterfall, Staffordshire: tithe map, 1846. 759
115 Grey's Forest, Northumberland: tithe map, 1845. 760
116 Leckford, Hampshire: tithe map, 1840. 761
117 Capel le Fern, Kent: tithe map, 1840. 762
118 St Mary Magdalene, Cornwall: tithe map, 1839. 763
119 Whitehaven, Cumberland: tithe map, 1847. 764
120 Swansea, Glamorgan: tithe map, *circa* 1842. 765
121 St Mary Magdalene, Lincolnshire: tithe map, 1851. 766
122 Gargrave, West Riding of Yorkshire: tithe map, 1839. 767
123 England and Wales: tithe maps which distinguish houses from other buildings. 768
124 Knaresdale, Northumberland: tithe map, *circa* 1838. 769
125 Holy Trinity Kingston upon Hull, East Riding of Yorkshire: tithe map, *circa* 1848. 770
126 Cocklaw, Northumberland: tithe map, *circa* 1839. 771
127 North Clifton, Nottinghamshire: tithe map, 1845. 772
128 Melton Mowbray, Leicestershire: tithe map, 1843. 773
129 R. K. Dawson's system of conventional signs for tithe maps. 774
130 Madeley, Shropshire: tithe map, 1848. 775
131 Raby and Keverstone, Durham: tithe map, *circa* 1839. 776
132 England and Wales: tithe maps which distinguish arable and grass. 778
133 Whitcliffe with Thorpe, West Riding of Yorkshire: tithe map, 1839. 779
134 Aller, Somerset: tithe map, *circa* 1838. 780
135 Bridge and Patrixbourne, Kent: tithe map, 1838. 781
136 Folkington, Sussex: tithe map, 1838. 782
137 Seaton, Rutland: tithe map, 1847. 783
138 Seaton, Rutland: altered tithe apportionment map, 1862. 784
139 England and Wales: tithe maps which record the ownership of field boundaries. 785
140 England and Wales: tithe maps with field names. 786
141 Southwell, Nottinghamshire: tithe map, 1840. 788
142 Gargrave, West Riding of Yorkshire: tithe map, 1839. 790
143 Denbury, Devon: tithe map, 1839. 791
144 Draycott Foliatt, Wiltshire: tithe map, 1838. 792
145 Elstob, Durham: tithe map, 1837. 793
146 Charlbury, Oxfordshire: tithe map, 1848. 794
147 Gargrave, West Riding of Yorkshire: tithe map, 1839. 795
148 Pitsea, Essex: tithe map, 1845. 796
149 Pooley, Warwickshire: tithe map, 1849. 797

150 England and Wales: tithe maps which use colour to distinguish features other than buildings, roads and water. 798
151 Faversham, Kent: tithe map, *circa* 1842. 799
152 Brauncewell, Lincolnshire: tithe map, 1845. 800
153 Burgh Castle, Suffolk: tithe map, 1842. 801
154 Barwick, Somerset: tithe map, 1837. 802
155 Lanhydrock, Cornwall: tithe map, 1841. 803
156 Sithey, Cornwall: tithe map, 1841. 804
157 Tywardreath, Cornwall: tithe map, *circa* 1839. 805
158 Box, Wiltshire: tithe map, 1839. 806
159 Holton-le-Moor, Lincolnshire: tithe map, 1838. 806
160 Bratton Clovelly, Devon: tithe map, 1845. 807
161 Northam, Devon: tithe map, 1839. 808
162 Eccles next the Sea, Norfolk: tithe map, 1839. 809
163 Winchelsea, Sussex: tithe map, 1842. 810
164 Whittington, Shropshire: altered tithe apportionment map, 1871. 811
165 Barwick, Somerset: altered tithe apportionment map, 1908. 812
166 Gwythrania, Tre Llan and Tan y Bedwal, Denbighshire: altered tithe apportionment map, 1924. 813
167 Morthoe, Devon: tithe map, 1840. 814
168 West Wratting, Cambridgeshire: tithe map, *circa* 1852. 815
169 Winlaton, Durham: tithe map, 1838. 816
170 Martindale, Westmorland: tithe map 'taken in September 1838'. 817
171 Titlington, Northumberland: tithe map, *circa* 1842. 818
172 Gwythrania, Tre Llan and Tan y Bedwal, Denbighshire: tithe map, *circa* 1840. 819

Tables

1.1 Agreements and awards for commutation of tithes in Bedfordshire 32
1.2 Tithe valuers and tithe map-makers in Bedfordshire 32
1.3 The tithe maps of Bedfordshire: scales and classes 33
1.4 The tithe maps of Bedfordshire: dates 33
2.1 Agreements and awards for commutation of tithes in Berkshire 38
2.2 Tithe valuers and tithe map-makers in Berkshire 39
2.3 The tithe maps of Berkshire: scales and classes 39
2.4 The tithe maps of Berkshire: dates 39
3.1 Agreements and awards for commutation of tithes in Buckinghamshire 48
3.2 Tithe valuers and tithe map-makers in Buckinghamshire 49
3.3 The tithe maps of Buckinghamshire: scales and classes 49
3.4 The tithe maps of Buckinghamshire: dates 49
4.1 Agreements and awards for commutation of tithes in Cambridgeshire 57
4.2 Tithe valuers and tithe map-makers in Cambridgeshire 58
4.3 The tithe maps of Cambridgeshire: scales and classes 58
4.4 The tithe maps of Cambridgeshire: dates 58
5.1 Agreements and awards for commutation of tithes in Cheshire 66
5.2 Tithe valuers and tithe map-makers in Cheshire 67
5.3 The tithe maps of Cheshire: scales and classes 67
5.4 The tithe maps of Cheshire: dates 68
6.1 Agreements and awards for commutation of tithes in Cornwall 87
6.2 Tithe valuers and tithe map-makers in Cornwall 87
6.3 The tithe maps of Cornwall: scales and classes 88
6.4 The tithe maps of Cornwall: dates 88
7.1 Agreements and awards for commutation of tithes in Cumberland 100
7.2 Tithe valuers and tithe map-makers in Cumberland 101
7.3 The tithe maps of Cumberland: scales and classes 101
7.4 The tithe maps of Cumberland: dates 101
8.1 Agreements and awards for commutation of tithes in Derbyshire 111
8.2 Tithe valuers and tithe map-makers in Derbyshire 112
8.3 The tithe maps of Derbyshire: scales and classes 112
8.4 The tithe maps of Derbyshire: dates 112
9.1 Agreements and awards for commutation of tithes in Devon 123
9.2 Tithe valuers and tithe map-makers in Devon 124
9.3 The tithe maps of Devon: scales and classes 124
9.4 The tithe maps of Devon: dates 124
10.1 Agreements and awards for commutation of tithes in Dorset 147
10.2 Tithe valuers and tithe map-makers in Dorset 147
10.3 The tithe maps of Dorset: scales and classes 148
10.4 The tithe maps of Dorset: dates 148
11.1 Agreements and awards for commutation of tithes in Durham 160
11.2 Tithe valuers and tithe map-makers in Durham 161
11.3 The tithe maps of Durham: scales and classes 161

11.4 The tithe maps of Durham: dates 162
12.1 Agreements and awards for commutation of tithes in Essex 175
12.2 Tithe valuers and tithe map-makers in Essex 178
12.3 The tithe maps of Essex: scales and classes 178
12.4 The tithe maps of Essex: dates 179
13.1 Agreements and awards for commutation of tithes in Gloucestershire 196
13.2 Tithe valuers and tithe map-makers in Gloucestershire 197
13.3 The tithe maps of Gloucestershire: scales and classes 197
13.4 The tithe maps of Gloucestershire: dates 197
14.1 Agreements and awards for commutation of tithes in Herefordshire 208
14.2 Tithe valuers and tithe map-makers in Herefordshire 209
14.3 The tithe maps of Herefordshire: scales and classes 209
14.4 The tithe maps of Herefordshire: dates 209
15.1 Agreements and awards for commutation of tithes in Hertfordshire 221
15.2 Tithe valuers and tithe map-makers in Hertfordshire 222
15.3 The tithe maps of Hertfordshire: scales and classes 222
15.4 The tithe maps of Hertfordshire: dates 222
16.1 Agreements and awards for commutation of tithes in Huntingdonshire 230
16.2 Tithe valuers and tithe map-makers in Huntingdonshire 230
16.3 The tithe maps of Huntingdonshire: scales and classes 231
16.4 The tithe maps of Huntingdonshire: dates 231
17.1 Agreements and awards for commutation of tithes in Kent 236
17.2 Tithe valuers and tithe map-makers in Kent 237
17.3 The tithe maps of Kent: scales and classes 237
17.4 The tithe maps of Kent: dates 238
18.1 Agreements and awards for commutation of tithes in Lancashire 259
18.2 Tithe valuers and tithe map-makers in Lancashire 260
18.3 The tithe maps of Lancashire: scales and classes 261
18.4 The tithe maps of Lancashire: dates 261
19.1 Agreements and awards for commutation of tithes in Leicestershire 279
19.2 Tithe valuers and tithe map-makers in Leicestershire 280
19.3 The tithe maps of Leicestershire: scales and classes 280
19.4 The tithe maps of Leicestershire: dates 280
20.1 Agreements and awards for commutation of tithes in Lincolnshire 290
20.2 Tithe valuers and tithe map-makers in Lincolnshire 291
20.3 The tithe maps of Lincolnshire: scales and classes 292
20.4 The tithe maps of Lincolnshire: dates 292
21.1 Agreements and awards for commutation of tithes in Middlesex 308
21.2 Tithe valuers and tithe map-makers in Middlesex 308
21.3 The tithe maps of Middlesex: scales and classes 309
21.4 The tithe maps of Middlesex: dates 309
22.1 Agreements and awards for commutation of tithes in Monmouthshire 315
22.2 Tithe valuers and tithe map-makers in Monmouthshire 316
22.3 The tithe maps of Monmouthshire: scales and classes 316
22.4 The tithe maps of Monmouthshire: dates 316
23.1 Agreements and awards for commutation of tithes in Norfolk 326
23.2 Tithe valuers and tithe map-makers in Norfolk 326
23.3 The tithe maps of Norfolk: scales and classes 327
23.4 The tithe maps of Norfolk: dates 327
24.1 Agreements and awards for commutation of tithes in Northamptonshire 352
24.2 Tithe valuers and tithe map-makers in Northamptonshire 352
24.3 The tithe maps of Northamptonshire: scales and classes 353
24.4 The tithe maps of Northamptonshire: dates 353
25.1 Agreements and awards for commutation of tithes in Northumberland 362
25.2 Tithe valuers and tithe map-makers in Northumberland 362
25.3 The tithe maps of Northumberland: scales and classes 363

25.4 The tithe maps of Northumberland: dates 363
26.1 Agreements and awards for commutation of tithes in Nottinghamshire 387
26.2 Tithe valuers and tithe map-makers in Nottinghamshire 387
26.3 The tithe maps of Nottinghamshire: scales and classes 388
26.4 The tithe maps of Nottinghamshire: dates 388
27.1 Agreements and awards for commutation of tithes in Oxfordshire 397
27.2 Tithe valuers and tithe map-makers in Oxfordshire 397
27.3 The tithe maps of Oxfordshire: scales and classes 398
27.4 The tithe maps of Oxfordshire: dates 398
28.1 Agreements and awards for commutation of tithes in Rutland 406
28.2 Tithe valuers and tithe map-makers in Rutland 407
28.3 The tithe maps of Rutland: scales and classes 407
28.4 The tithe maps of Rutland: dates 407
29.1 Agreements and awards for commutation of tithes in Shropshire 413
29.2 Tithe valuers and tithe map-makers in Shropshire 413
29.3 The tithe maps of Shropshire: scales and classes 414
29.4 The tithe maps of Shropshire: dates 414
30.1 Agreements and awards for commutation of tithes in Somerset 429
30.2 Tithe valuers and tithe map-makers in Somerset 432
30.3 The tithe maps of Somerset: scales and classes 432
30.4 The tithe maps of Somerset: dates 433
31.1 Agreements and awards for commutation of tithes in Southampton (Hampshire) 453
31.2 Tithe valuers and tithe map-makers in Southampton (Hampshire) 453
31.3 The tithe maps of Southampton (Hampshire): scales and classes 454
31.4 The tithe maps of Southampton (Hampshire): dates 454
32.1 Agreements and awards for commutation of tithes in Staffordshire 469
32.2 Tithe valuers and tithe map-makers in Staffordshire 469
32.3 The tithe maps of Staffordshire: scales and classes 470
32.4 The tithe maps of Staffordshire: dates 470
33.1 Agreements and awards for commutation of tithes in Suffolk 484
33.2 Tithe valuers and tithe map-makers in Suffolk 484
33.3 The tithe maps of Suffolk: scales and classes 485
33.4 The tithe maps of Suffolk: dates 485
34.1 Agreements and awards for commutation of tithes in Surrey 505
34.2 Tithe valuers and tithe map-makers in Surrey 506
34.3 The tithe maps of Surrey: scales and classes 506
34.4 The tithe maps of Surrey: dates 506
35.1 Agreements and awards for commutation of tithes in Sussex 515
35.2 Tithe valuers and tithe map-makers in Sussex 516
35.3 The tithe maps of Sussex: scales and classes 516
35.4 The tithe maps of Sussex: dates 516
36.1 Agreements and awards for commutation of tithes in Warwickshire 532
36.2 Tithe valuers and tithe map-makers in Warwickshire 532
36.3 The tithe maps of Warwickshire: scales and classes 533
36.4 The tithe maps of Warwickshire: dates 533
37.1 Agreements and awards for commutation of tithes in Westmorland 542
37.2 Tithe valuers and tithe map-makers in Westmorland 542
37.3 The tithe maps of Westmorland: scales and classes 543
37.4 The tithe maps of Westmorland: dates 543
38.1 Agreements and awards for commutation of tithes in Wiltshire 550
38.2 Tithe valuers and tithe map-makers in Wiltshire 550
38.3 The tithe maps of Wiltshire: scales and classes 551
38.4 The tithe maps of Wiltshire: dates 551
39.1 Agreements and awards for commutation of tithes in Worcestershire 564
39.2 Tithe valuers and tithe map-makers in Worcestershire 564
39.3 The tithe maps of Worcestershire: scales and classes 565

39.4 The tithe maps of Worcestershire: dates 565
40.1 Agreements and awards for commutation of tithes in York City and Ainsty 573
40.2 Tithe valuers and tithe map-makers in York City and Ainsty 574
40.3 The tithe maps of York City and Ainsty: scales and classes 574
40.4 The tithe maps of York City and Ainsty: dates 574
41.1 Agreements and awards for commutation of tithes in Yorkshire, East Riding 578
41.2 Tithe valuers and tithe map-makers in Yorkshire, East Riding 579
41.3 The tithe maps of Yorkshire, East Riding: scales and classes 579
41.4 The tithe maps of Yorkshire, East Riding: dates 579
42.1 Agreements and awards for commutation of tithes in Yorkshire, North Riding 590
42.2 Tithe valuers and tithe map-makers in Yorkshire, North Riding 591
42.3 The tithe maps of Yorkshire, North Riding: scales and classes 591
42.4 The tithe maps of Yorkshire, North Riding: dates 592
43.1 Agreements and awards for commutation of tithes in Yorkshire, West Riding 612
43.2 Tithe valuers and tithe map-makers in Yorkshire, West Riding 612
43.3 The tithe maps of Yorkshire, West Riding: scales and classes 613
43.4 The tithe maps of Yorkshire, West Riding: dates 613
44.1 Agreements and awards for commutation of tithes in Anglesey 632
44.2 Tithe valuers and tithe map-makers in Anglesey 633
44.3 The tithe maps of Anglesey: scales and classes 633
44.4 The tithe maps of Anglesey: dates 633
45.1 Agreements and awards for commutation of tithes in Breconshire 639
45.2 Tithe valuers and tithe map-makers in Breconshire 639
45.3 The tithe maps of Breconshire: scales and classes 639
45.4 The tithe maps of Breconshire: dates 640
46.1 Agreements and awards for commutation of tithes in Cardiganshire 646
46.2 Tithe valuers and tithe map-makers in Cardiganshire 646
46.3 The tithe maps of Cardiganshire: scales and classes 646
46.4 The tithe maps of Cardiganshire: dates 646
47.1 Agreements and awards for commutation of tithes in Carmarthenshire 652
47.2 Tithe valuers and tithe map-makers in Carmarthenshire 652
47.3 The tithe maps of Carmarthenshire: scales and classes 652
47.4 The tithe maps of Carmarthenshire: dates 652
48.1 Agreements and awards for commutation of tithes in Carnarvonshire 658
48.2 Tithe valuers and tithe map-makers in Carnarvonshire 658
48.3 The tithe maps of Carnarvonshire: scales and classes 658
48.4 The tithe maps of Carnarvonshire: dates 658
49.1 Agreements and awards for commutation of tithes in Denbighshire 664
49.2 Tithe valuers and tithe map-makers in Denbighshire 664
49.3 The tithe maps of Denbighshire: scales and classes 665
49.4 The tithe maps of Denbighshire: dates 665
50.1 Agreements and awards for commutation of tithes in Flintshire 672
50.2 Tithe valuers and tithe map-makers in Flintshire 672
50.3 The tithe maps of Flintshire: scales and classes 672
50.4 The tithe maps of Flintshire: dates 672
51.1 Agreements and awards for commutation of tithes in Glamorganshire 677
51.2 Tithe valuers and tithe map-makers in Glamorganshire 678
51.3 The tithe maps of Glamorganshire: scales and classes 678
51.4 The tithe maps of Glamorganshire: dates 678
52.1 Agreements and awards for commutation of tithes in Merionethshire 686
52.2 Tithe valuers and tithe map-makers in Merionethshire 686
52.3 The tithe maps of Merionethshire: scales and classes 686
52.4 The tithe maps of Merionethshire: dates 686
53.1 Agreements and awards for commutation of tithes in Montgomeryshire 691
53.2 Tithe valuers and tithe map-makers in Montgomeryshire 691
53.3 The tithe maps of Montgomeryshire: scales and classes 691

53.4 The tithe maps of Montgomeryshire: dates 691
54.1 Agreements and awards for commutation of tithes in Pembrokeshire 697
54.2 Tithe valuers and tithe map-makers in Pembrokeshire 697
54.3 The tithe maps of Pembrokeshire: scales and classes 697
54.4 The tithe maps of Pembrokeshire: dates 697
55.1 Agreements and awards for commutation of tithes in Radnorshire 705
55.2 Tithe valuers and tithe map-makers in Radnorshire 705
55.3 The tithe maps of Radnorshire: scales and classes 705
55.4 The tithe maps of Radnorshire: dates 705

Preface

This work derives from a five-year research project funded by The Leverhulme Trust and sponsored by the Public Record Office and is conceived as a sequel to two previous studies published by Cambridge University Press. In *The tithe surveys of England and Wales*, 1985, Roger Kain and Hugh Prince provide a general handbook to the tithe surveys which reviews the nature of tithes, the process of tithe commutation, the documents produced, and how these can be used to reconstruct components of past rural landscapes, economies and social structures. *An index and atlas of the tithe files of mid-nineteenth-century England and Wales*, 1986, by Roger Kain and others at the University of Exeter contains first, a cartographic reconstruction of the agricultural geography of England and Wales in the mid-nineteenth century based on data in the tithe files and second, provides a detailed index of the contents of these files.

The mid-nineteenth-century tithe surveys are among the most important manuscript sources used by English historical geographers and economic historians researching questions concerning landownership, management and use, whereas to local historians concerned with the history of particular places, tithe maps provide early, large-scale maps for about three-quarters of England and Wales. In area covered, scale of compilation, and detail of content, these English and Welsh tithe surveys marked a new departure in government-sponsored cadastral surveying of the nation's land. A recent Public Record Office annual report records that 'tithe maps and related records continue to be the single most popular category of cartographic record for written enquiries and personal searches'. Notwithstanding these facts which render the tithe surveys such an important quarry of historical evidence, the potential user is not well served with descriptive indexes or coverage maps of tithe surveys. One of the objects of this book is to provide an essential research tool for users of tithe maps. Of particular value in this respect are the detailed coverage maps for each county which show the precise boundaries of tithe districts.

Previous research has told us much about the way in which the tithe surveys of England and Wales were organised, how the map specifications were drawn up, and how the land surveys and map compilation were accomplished, but many questions remained unanswered at the commencement of this project. These concern matters such as map scale, particularly in relation to terrain character and cadastral complexity; the use of conventional symbols to record topographic and tenurial detail such as woodland, crops, settlements, buildings, fields and farm and estate boundaries; the extent of individual surveyor's practices; and regional patterns of map and apportionment characteristics. To provide some measure of all these we have recorded in addition to the cartobibliographic data in the county-by-county catalogues, a broad range of information about the areal coverage, cartographic characteristics, and topographic content of tithe maps and apportionments. A database of more than a million items has been compiled by inspecting every tithe map and apportionment in the Public Record Office and analysis of these data has revealed much that is new about the general cartographic characteristics of this important body of manuscript maps.

In the research and writing of this book we have been given much help which it is our pleasure to acknowledge. We have received financial support from The Leverhulme Trust and the University of Exeter for which we are most grateful. The staff of the Public Record Office, particularly Geraldine Beech and Margaret Condon, have been unstinting of their time and assistance as we inspected every tithe map in the Public Record Office collection. We would also like to thank the archivists of our local Devon and Cornwall Record Offices, Marjery Rowe and Christine North, and Robert Davies of the National Library of Wales for their helpful advice at a number of stages of the work. Andrew Teed made all the photographic illustrations and the products of his work much enhance both the appearance and utility of this book. George Foot provided much help and advice relating to the design of the database and Jennifer Baker, Christopher Hammond, and David Fletcher assisted with proof-reading the database. The first two of the five years of primary research were conducted largely by Sarah Wilmot when she was full-time research fellow on the project. We are delighted to acknowledge this major contribution on the title page as also that of our cartographer, Rodney Fry, for the set of tithe district coverage maps published in this book.

Introduction

Tithe and tithe commutation

Tithe surveys derive from the Tithe Commutation Act of 1836 which reformed the way in which the established Church was financed by a tax (the tithe) on local agricultural output. A tithe survey of a *tithe district* (usually a parish in southern England and the Midlands and a township in the North) consists of three related documents: *tithe apportionments* are the legal instruments which specify the amount of the reformed tax (tithe rent-charge) apportioned to the owners of particular land parcels (tithe areas), *tithe maps* identify these tithe areas (usually individual enclosed fields, strips in open-field parishes, houses, gardens and other land parcels) and provide a record of their boundaries, and *tithe files* contain the locally generated papers from the process of tithe commutation such as minutes of meetings between tithe owners and tithe payers and reports from assistant tithe commissioners or local tithe agents.

It is not clear exactly when the Church began collecting tithes, the traditional tenth of a farmer's produce given to support the Church, but by the nineteenth century there was certainly great confusion about the manner of payment. This was made locally by each farmer who gave tithe to support his own priest. Over the centuries, the peculiarities, ambiguities and irregularities of local custom multiplied. Precedent was piled upon precedent and fresh complications were caused by the dissolution of the monasteries and the enclosure of open fields. By the beginning of the nineteenth century it was no longer possible to discern even the vaguest outlines of a system amongst a host of local practices and customary arrangements. The courts sanctioned both gross oppressions by the Church and flagrant evasions by tithe payers. Discontent over tithe payment erupted into violence before a remedy was found in the Tithe Commutation Act of 1836. The essence of the settlement was the substitution of a money payment, fluctuating from year to year in accordance with the price of wheat, barley and oats, in place of all customary payments whether in kind (as, for example, sheaves from the corn field, hay from the meadows, apples from the orchard, piglets from the litter) or in cash. This rent-charge was fixed initially by the actual value of tithes collected in a tithe district and was apportioned among its farmers according to the type and value of land which they occupied. All of this necessitated a detailed field survey of parishes and townships from which tithes were payable.[1] The rural

[1] The nature of tithes, the manner of their payment, and the aggravation and dispute occasioned by their payment are reviewed in E. J. Evans' seminal work, *The contentious tithe. The tithe problem and English agriculture, 1750-1850* (London, Routledge and Kegan Paul, 1976) and also in his excellent summary, *Tithes: maps,*

landscape of England and Wales and the townscapes of some urban settlements are depicted exactly in these field-by-field tithe surveys. The enquiries of the Tithe Commission covered that three-quarters of the country where some tithe remained payable in 1836.

The maps drawn for each parish or township show the boundaries of fields, woods, roads, streams, the position of buildings and often much else of local topographical interest, and the accompanying schedules of apportionment give the names of the owners and occupiers of each tithe area, describe and name the property, and list the state of cultivation (land use) and statute acreage of each tithe area. Parish tithe files often contain descriptions of local landscapes and farming practices and statistics on crops, yields and livestock numbers. In total, the amount of information which the tithe surveys can provide about land tenure, field systems, land use and farming is unequalled by any other series of documents. Their accuracy is sufficient to warrant their continued use in courts of law and their comprehensiveness and uniformity is surpassed only by enquiries such as the Land Utilisation Survey of Great Britain undertaken in the 1930s. Indeed, the tithe surveys rank as the most complete record of the agrarian landscape at any period.[2]

Establishing tithe districts

One of the first tasks of the three tithe commissioners appointed by the Tithe Commutation Act was to ascertain where tithe was still paid and to establish the boundaries of every district in which tithes were paid separately to a particular incumbent or lay impropriator.[3] They found 14,829 tithe districts which contain in total 36.2 million statute acres. The Tithe Commission's enquiries revealed that in 3044 of these districts tithes had either never been paid, or had already been commuted, or were to be merged in the land.[4] In thirty-nine tithe districts corn rents agreed in lieu of tithes before 1836 were converted after 1862 into corn rent annuities (see next section). Places where corn rent annuities were confirmed are listed among Public Record Office classes IR29 and IR30 (the tithe surveys) so there are 11,785 districts with tithe surveys proper, and these extend over some 27.2 million acres in total which is about 75 per cent of England and Wales by area.

A majority of tithe districts are either parishes or townships; the latter are usual in north-east Wales and in most of England on the north and west side of the Trent. A few are classed as hamlets, and other descriptions include chapelry, division, liberty, lordship, manor, rectory and tithing; some are extra-parochial and a few tithe districts enjoyed separate existence only for tithe commutation purposes. Tithe commutation was

apportionments and the 1836 Act (Chichester, British Association for Local History, 1993). Consummate accounts of the process of tithe commutation in Derbyshire and Nottinghamshire have been written by J. V. Beckett: 'Tithe commutation in Nottinghamshire in the 1830s and 1840s', *Transactions of the Thoroton Society*, 96 (1992), 146-65 and (with J. E. Heath) 'Derbyshire tithe files', *Derbyshire Record Society*, forthcoming. The passage of the 1836 Tithe Commutation Act through parliament, its amendments, and the way that the tithe surveys were made are reviewed in R. J. P. Kain and H. C. Prince, *The tithe surveys of England and Wales* (Cambridge, Cambridge University Press, 1985), pp. 28-119.

2 Tithe surveys as historical sources and especially the evidence they contain on field systems, land use, farming, landowners, and rural social structure are reviewed in Kain and Prince, *The tithe surveys of England and Wales*, pp. 148-251.

3 Kain and Prince, *The tithe surveys of England and Wales*, pp. 41-3.

4 Mergers were effected after purchase of the tithes by the landowner or where the land owner and tithe owner were one and the same person. See E. J. Evans, *The contentious tithe . . .*, pp. 35-6.

organised on a county basis and the county divisions employed by the Tithe Commission and used to structure our county-by-county catalogue and for statistical purposes in this book are identified on Fig. 1.

Corn rent conversions

Before 1836 some tithe had been commuted in the course of parliamentary enclosure. This was effected in three main ways: by a single cash payment, by allotment of land, or by a 'corn rent', which was a continuing money payment. Corn rents were fixed by reference to the local price of grain and could be varied periodically, usually every twenty-one years. Such corn rents anticipated the method used for tithe commutation after 1836 but lacked the mechanism for automatic annual review of tithe rent-charge which was a central tenet of the 1836 Tithe Commutation Act. The Tithe Amendment Act of 1860 enabled pre-1836 corn rents to be converted into tithe rent-charges on application by either those paying the corn rent or those entitled to receive it.[5]

To judge from the infrequency with which this facility was used (only thirty-nine conversions were effected between 1862 and 1929), there was no great enthusiasm for the process. The first conversion of a corn rent to a tithe rent-charge was at Scartho in Lincolnshire in 1862 where one of the principal landowners was the Earl of Yarborough. As Charles Anderson-Pelham he had been a leading mover for general enclosure legislation in 1844-45 and it is possible that he envisaged a corresponding general conversion of corn rents. He died in 1862 and any enthusiasm for corn rent conversion seems to have died with him. There were only five further conversions in Lincolnshire and none was on the Yarborough estates. In national terms, the peak was in 1919-22 when ten conversions were effected (Fig. 2). The last corn rent conversion was that of Ruislip in Middlesex, in 1929.[6]

Corn rent conversions are usually accompanied by a schedule of the lands affected, though this often omits occupier and land use details. In a number of cases schedules are direct transcripts from enclosure awards. There is usually a map (in five cases this was dispensed with) and, though the maps tend to reflect the same pattern of development as altered apportionment maps with an increasing Ordnance Survey contribution from the later nineteenth century (see pp. 720-29), there are some notable differences. At Willesden, Middlesex where the corn rent was converted to tithe rent-charge in 1887, a commercial firm undertook a thorough revision of the published Ordnance Survey 1:2500 map. In other cases enclosure maps were copied for corn rent conversion purposes.[7] The availability of published Ordnance Survey maps did not supplant entirely the re-use of older maps. At Boultham, Lincolnshire the Ordnance Survey 1:2500 was used in 1920 but at nearby South Hykeham the corn rent conversion map is a copy of the 1803 enclosure map.

[5] Tithe Amendment Act, 1860, (23 and 24 Vict., cap. 93).

[6] Four other 'tithe cases' in Middlesex were corn rent conversion *sui generis*. One was the merger of moduses at Hornsey and three others were the reapportionment of rent-charges in the City of London: Allhallows the Less, Bishopgate St Helen, and St Lawrence Poultney. The St Laurence Poultney map and apportionment are actually located in PRO MAF 8/22.

[7] Compare, for example, the corn rent conversion map of Charlton Adam and Charlton Mackrell in Somerset (PRO IR30 30/97) with the original in the Somerset Record Office (Q/RDe 92).

Fig. 1 England and Wales: counties as defined by the Tithe Commission.

Fig. 2 England and Wales: tithe districts where corn rent annuities were confirmed in lieu of tithes.

Exemptions from tithe

The reasons for exemption from tithe were particular to each tithe district and are normally stated in the agreement or award for tithe apportionment. These reasons for tithe exemption have been recorded in our database as deposited at the ESRC Data Archive at the University of Essex and are thus available for analysis, though for reasons of space they are not listed in our county-by-county catalogue.[8] The general picture of tithe exemption is well known and is confirmed by our detailed district-by-district recording.[9] In many districts in midland England tithe had been commuted for money payments or extinguished

[8] Requests for extracts from, or copies of, the database should be addressed to The Director, ESRC Data Archive, University of Essex, Wivenhoe Park, Colchester, Essex CO4 3SQ.

[9] Kain and Prince, *The tithe surveys of England and Wales*, pp. 112-13.

by award or exchange of lands in the course of parliamentary enclosure. Elsewhere, the existence of moduses (small customary payments in lieu of tithe) was the most common reason for exemption. Moduses were particularly common in Wales and in northern England where they often applied over whole districts; elsewhere their application might be more limited, sometimes to only a few fields or to particular agricultural products. Other important reasons for exemption from tithe included crown land, former manorial or monastic land, the merger of tithes in the land, exemption by custom or prescription, exemption of land agriculturally unproductive, for example roadside waste and foreshore, or *de facto* exemption because of an agreement between landowners and tithe owners to apportion tithe rent-charge on some lands but not on others. This last was particularly common where a modus covered a large area and had the practical effect from a tithe owner's point of view of converting a small sum per acre which was expensive to collect from extensive tracts into a larger sum per acre levied on a limited area. Other reasons for tithe exemption are of local rather than general significance. In some districts there was no agistment tithe on pasture or tithe of woodland; in some counties all beech woods were tithe free and all woodland in the Weald of Kent, Surrey and Sussex was exempt from tithe. Some districts were exempt from paying the great (rectorial) or small (vicarial) tithes; in yet others, cottage gardens, commons, moorland and forests might not be tithed. Agriculturally unproductive built-up areas were usually wholly tithe free or were subject only to residual tithes; the tithing of cows at Brighton, Sussex is an example (Fig. 3). In practice it was not unusual for cottage gardens and other plots which generated only minute amounts of tithe to be treated as tithe free when tithe was apportioned, although they are not specified as tithe free in the tithe agreement or award.

There was no need to survey tithe free land in a tithe district but many tithe surveys do map tithe free properties, though information on these may well be absent in the schedule of tithe apportionment. Where tithable and tithe-free land was much intermixed in a district or where the tithe map was compiled from existing surveys, it could be easier and more economical to include all properties in the tithe map. The entry for each tithe survey in our county-by-county catalogue specifies the number of acres surveyed in each tithe district.

Tithe agreements and awards: assistant tithe commissioners

Under the Tithe Commutation Act of 1836 it was envisaged that a compulsory award would be imposed in those districts where no agreement between landowners and tithe owners had been reached after two years. In practice the tithe commissioners were unwilling to impose a compulsory award if this could be avoided and in the event only 43 per cent of districts were subject to awards. The acreage of England and Wales subject to awards was proportionately rather less than this figure as in districts where most tithe had been extinguished at some earlier date, there was little incentive for landowners and tithe owners to commute the remaining, usually small and untroublesome payments. The national extremes are represented by Denbighshire, where only 13 per cent of districts were subject to awards, and Leicestershire, where awards were imposed in nearly 78 per cent of districts. In England, Kent is unusual in that 49 per cent of districts were subject to awards,

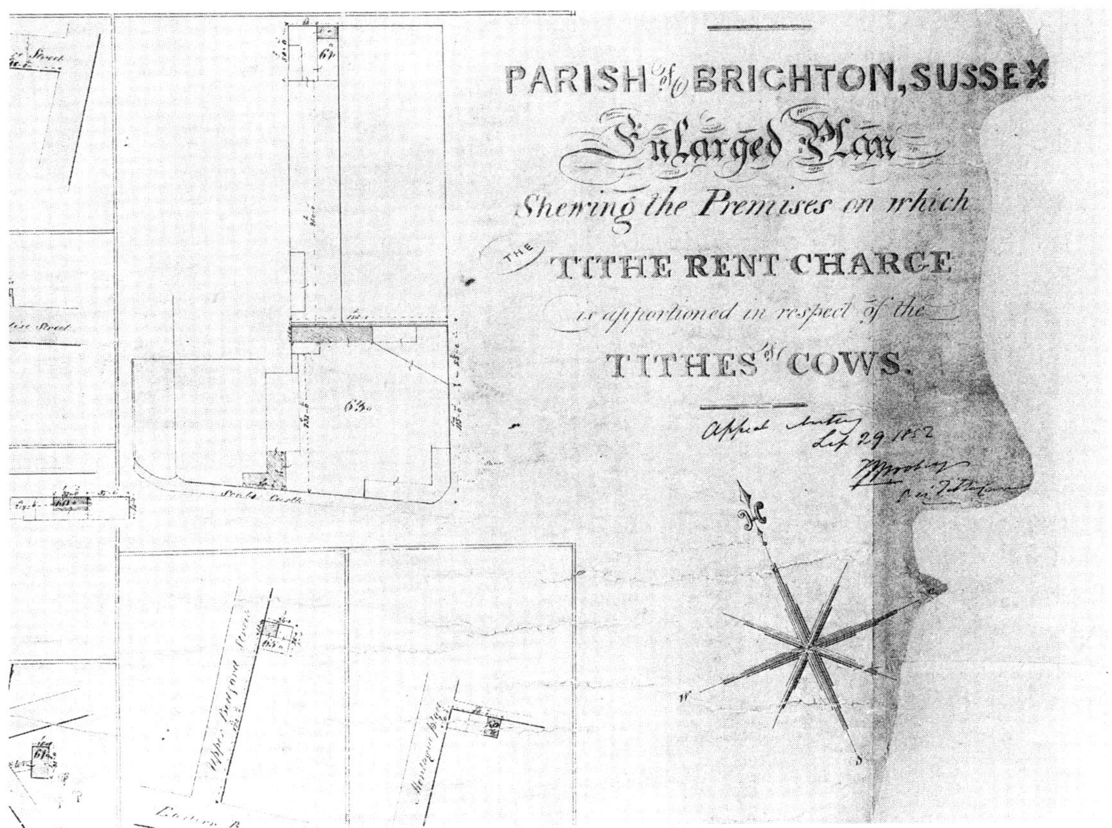

Fig. 3 Brighton, Sussex, 1852. The only tithable properties in this district at this time were a few cow houses; the manner in which they were mapped is unique amongst tithe maps. The measurements stated on the map imply that it is more diagrammatic than planimetric. Source: PRO IR30 35/45. Photograph reproduced by kind permission of the Keeper of the Public Record Office.

a fact probably related to the continued payment of tithes in kind which generated particular acrimony in this county.

Appendix 1 lists the assistant tithe commissioners and the local tithe agents who worked in England and Wales. Both categories reported on agreements but the more difficult process of imposing an award was the province of assistant tithe commissioners. These men were usually barristers or experienced land agents.[10]

Apportioning tithe rent-charge: tithe valuers

Once an agreement had been reached or an award had been imposed and the settlement confirmed by the tithe commissioners, the next stage was to prepare a draft apportionment of the rent-charge between the owners of tithable properties. A great majority of tithe rent-charges were apportioned on a field-by-field basis and the schedules of tithe

[10] See, for example, the biographical notes on Joseph Townsend in Kain and Prince, *The tithe surveys of England and Wales*, pp. 35-41 and on Henry Pilkington in Harriet M. E. Holt, 'Assistant commissioners and local agents: their role in tithe commutation', *Agricultural History Review*, 32 (1984), 189-200.

apportionment in which the division of tithe rent-charge is recorded set out the names of the owner and occupier of each land parcel which is then described and named, and the state of cultivation (land use) and acreage in statute measure are each recorded. Tithe apportionments are the legal documents in which the terms of a local tithe commutation are set down; the tithe map of a district is simply a visual illustration and a graphic record of the settlement designed to obviate disputes over rent-charge payments in the future. By comparison with tithe maps, tithe apportionments are remarkably homogeneous in format. Almost all apportionments are written in manuscript usually on pre-printed sheets of vellum with standardised headings (Fig. 4). A few tithe apportionments, some 381 in all, are printed from letterpress on vellum. Most of these are to be found in Cornwall (103), Devon (80), and Suffolk (82), with lesser concentrations of fifteen in Monmouthshire and nineteen in Somerset.

Occasionally descriptions of the properties and state of cultivation are omitted from the schedules or are incomplete for all parcels. This is particularly the case in Wales and to a lesser extent in the fens of eastern England. In some districts the omission of field names may be simply because the fields did not have a name but a few valuers, for example Charles Etheredge of Starston in Norfolk, systematically omitted to record field names. Property descriptions are occasionally idiosyncratic. In the district of Upper Heyford tithable to Flore in Northamptonshire illustrated in Fig. 4, the apportionment contains sale lot numbers instead of field names. In Wales field names are sometimes descriptions which might belong more properly in the state of cultivation column, for example 'Rhos' (moor) or 'Ty y gardd' (cottage and garden). Land use information is often omitted where all the land in a parish was wholly arable or wholly pasture or was cultivated alternately as arable or grassland, a practice widespread in Cornwall and the Fens. On the other hand, descriptions such as 'arable and pasture' probably indicate that part of a field was under one cultivation and part under the other. Grassland for meadow and grassland for pasture are usually distinguished in state of cultivation entries as the produce of mown meadows was usually classified as a great or rectorial tithe, but the agistment of pasture was generally a small, or vicarial, tithe. Occasionally, notably in south-west Wales, more precise descriptions may be employed; for example, at Lawrenny, Pembrokeshire the descriptions 'moory pasture' and 'clover pasture' are used, and in other places rotation grasses are sometimes named. A small number of apportionments, 195 in total, record the actual crops grown on the arable land field-by-field (Fig. 5). This practice is heavily concentrated in Cheshire and the surrounding counties of Denbighshire, Derbyshire, Flintshire, Lancashire and Staffordshire where about 80 per cent of apportionments with cropping information are to be found (Fig. 6). Although this is clearly a regional phenomenon, it is also a personal one; most of the apportionments with cropping information in Derbyshire and Staffordshire, for example, are of districts valued by Joseph Bennett Hankin Bennett of Tutbury in Staffordshire. Hop grounds and market gardens attracted enhanced or extraordinary tithe rent-charge and are usually carefully identified in state of cultivation columns. References to infield–outfield systems are also recorded occasionally (Fig. 7) as are acreages in both local and statute measures (Fig. 8).

In 744 districts (6 per cent), tithe was apportioned on holdings or estates so that tithe areas are farms or estates rather than fields or other individual land parcels. Although most

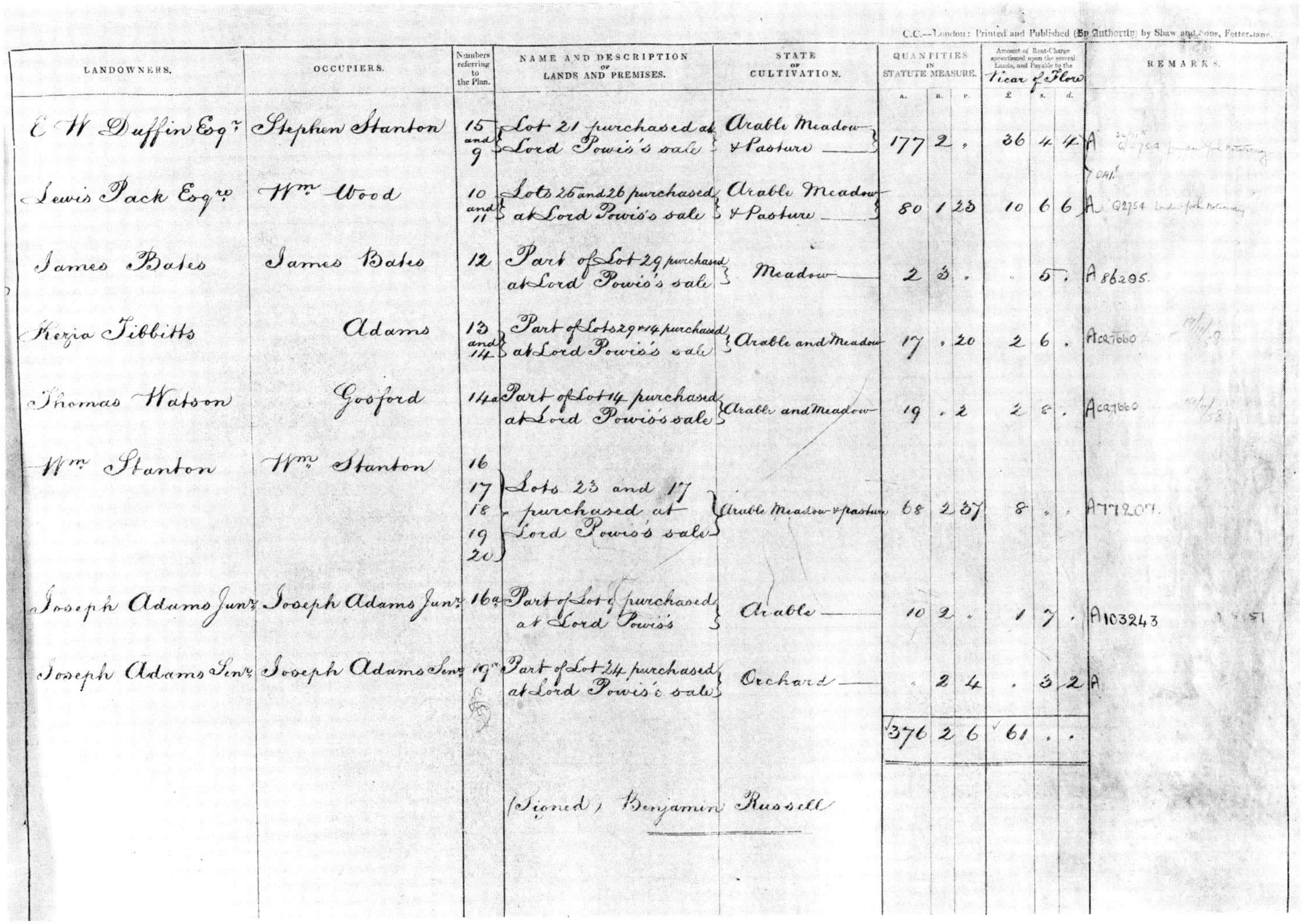

C.C.—London: Printed and Published (By Authority) by Shaw and Sons, Fetter-lane.

LANDOWNERS.	OCCUPIERS.	Numbers referring to the Plan.	NAME AND DESCRIPTION OF LANDS AND PREMISES.	STATE OF CULTIVATION.	QUANTITIES IN STATUTE MEASURE. A.	R.	P.	Amount of Rent-Charge apportioned upon the several Lands, and Payable to the Vicar of Flore £	s.	d.	REMARKS.
E W Duffin Esq.r	Stephen Stanton	15 and 9	Lot 21 purchased at Lord Powis's sale	Arable Meadow & Pasture	177	2	.	36	4	4	A
Lewis Pack Esq.re	Wm. Wood	10 and 11	Lots 26 and 26 purchased at Lord Powis's sale	Arable Meadow & Pasture	80	1	23	10	6	6	A
James Bates	James Bates	12	Part of Lot 29 purchased at Lord Powis's sale	Meadow	2	3	.	.	5	.	A 86295.
Kezia Tibbitts	Adams	13 and 14	Part of Lots 29 & 14 purchased at Lord Powis's sale	Arable and Meadow	17	.	20	2	6	.	Acq7660
Thomas Watson	Gosford	14a	Part of Lot 14 purchased at Lord Powis's sale	Arable and Meadow	19	.	2	2	8	.	Acq7660
Wm. Stanton	Wm. Stanton	16 17 18 19 20	Lots 23 and 17 purchased at Lord Powis's sale	Arable Meadow & pasture	68	2	37	8	.	.	A 77207.
Joseph Adams Junr.	Joseph Adams Junr.	16a	Part of Lot 9 purchased at Lord Powis's	Arable	10	2	.	.	1	7	A 103243
Joseph Adams Senr.	Joseph Adams Senr.	19a	Part of Lot 24 purchased at Lord Powis's sale	Orchard	.	2	4	.	3	2	A
					376	2	6	61	.	.	

(Signed) Benjamin Russell

Fig. 4 Upper Heyford, tithable to Flore, Northamptonshire, 1848. The three divisions of Upper Heyford are apportioned by sale-lot numbers. Source: PRO IR29 24/72. Photograph reproduced by kind permission of the Keeper of the Public Record Office.

C.C.—London: Printed and Published By Authority by Shaw and Sons, Fetter-lane

OCCUPIERS.	Numbers referring to the Plan.	NAME AND DESCRIPTION OF LANDS AND PREMISES.	STATE OF CULTIVATION.	QUANTITIES IN STATUTE MEASURE. A.	R.	P.	Amount of Rent-Charge apportioned upon the several Lands, and Payable to George William Dumbell £	s.	d.	REMARKS.
		Lands in Schedule C								
Richard Shuttleworth	741	House Garden fold Lane to Pasture field & Orchard		1		33				
	745	Barn field	Water Meadow	2	3	15		2		A
	740	Little Meadow	Meadow	2		26		3	5	A
	739	Great Meadow	do	3	3	9		6	1	A
	742	Big high field	Wheat Oats & Beans	3	2	32		5	11	A
	738	Twin field	Peas	2		14		3	4	CRC 40
	737	Little High field	Wheat & Potatoes	2		19		3	10	A
	743	Scotch Heys	Pasture	3	1	37		5	6	A
				21	1	25	1	10	1	
George Blackburne	607	House Outbuildings Road Garden Orchard & Fold		1	1	37				
	606	Half Acre	Turnips	1	1	3		2	4	A CR 6373
	608	Little Acre	Water Meadow	2		27		1	5½	A
	610	Great Meadow	do	8	3	26		6		A OA1
	609	Coppy	do	1	1	1		1	1½	A
	611	Rye field	Wheat	4	3	25		7	9	A
	613	Big Isabel Close	Beans & Peas	2	2	25		4	3	A CRC87
	612	Little Isabel Close	Peas & Oats	1	1	24		2	3	A
	627	Little Broken Earth	Potatoes & Fallow	2	1	12		4	3	A.A.I.
	624	Big Parlour field	Meadow	5	2	21		8	10	
	626	Big Broken Earth	Pasture	4	1	31		6	6	
	625	Little Parlour field	Clover	4	1	31		6	6	
	652	Big Bents	Pasture	4	1	31		6	1	A CRC87
	657	Middle & little Bents	do	4	2	16		5	3	A
				49	3	30	3	2	7	
John Wood	795	House & Garden				27				
	794	Croft	Meadow		1	34			9	A
	796	Moss field	Clover		2	21		1		A
	793	ditto	Meadow	1	2	8		2	1	A CR.
	797	ditto	Wheat & Potatoes	1	2	36		2	3½	A
	792	ditto	Clover	1	1			1	1½	A
	[illegible]	Plantation		8		11				

Fig. 5 Bedford, Lancashire, 1846. This is one of the 195 tithe apportionments which list crops under 'state of cultivation'. Unfortunately, as here, the year to which the cropping information relates is rarely stated. Source: PRO IR29 18/28. Photograph reproduced by kind permission of the Keeper of the Public Record Office.

Fig. 6 England and Wales: tithe apportionments which list crops under 'state of cultivation'.

counties contain a few districts where tithe was apportioned by holding, there is a strong regional concentration in the north-eastern counties of Northumberland (356 districts) and Durham (47 districts), and in Wales in Anglesey, Carnarvonshire, Merionethshire, and Carmarthenshire with 58, 19, 10 and 18 districts respectively (Fig. 9). The concentrations of apportionment by holding in the North East and in parts of Wales are related to the prevalence of modus payments and a preference for distributing the consequentially small rent-charges amongst the occupiers rather than concentrating these on a few specific parcels of land as was often the practice with small rent-charges elsewhere.

The practical result of apportionment by holding is that schedules of tithe apportionment lack information on field names, acreages, and states of cultivation for individual land parcels (Fig. 10). Where rent-charge is apportioned on estates rather than holdings, then

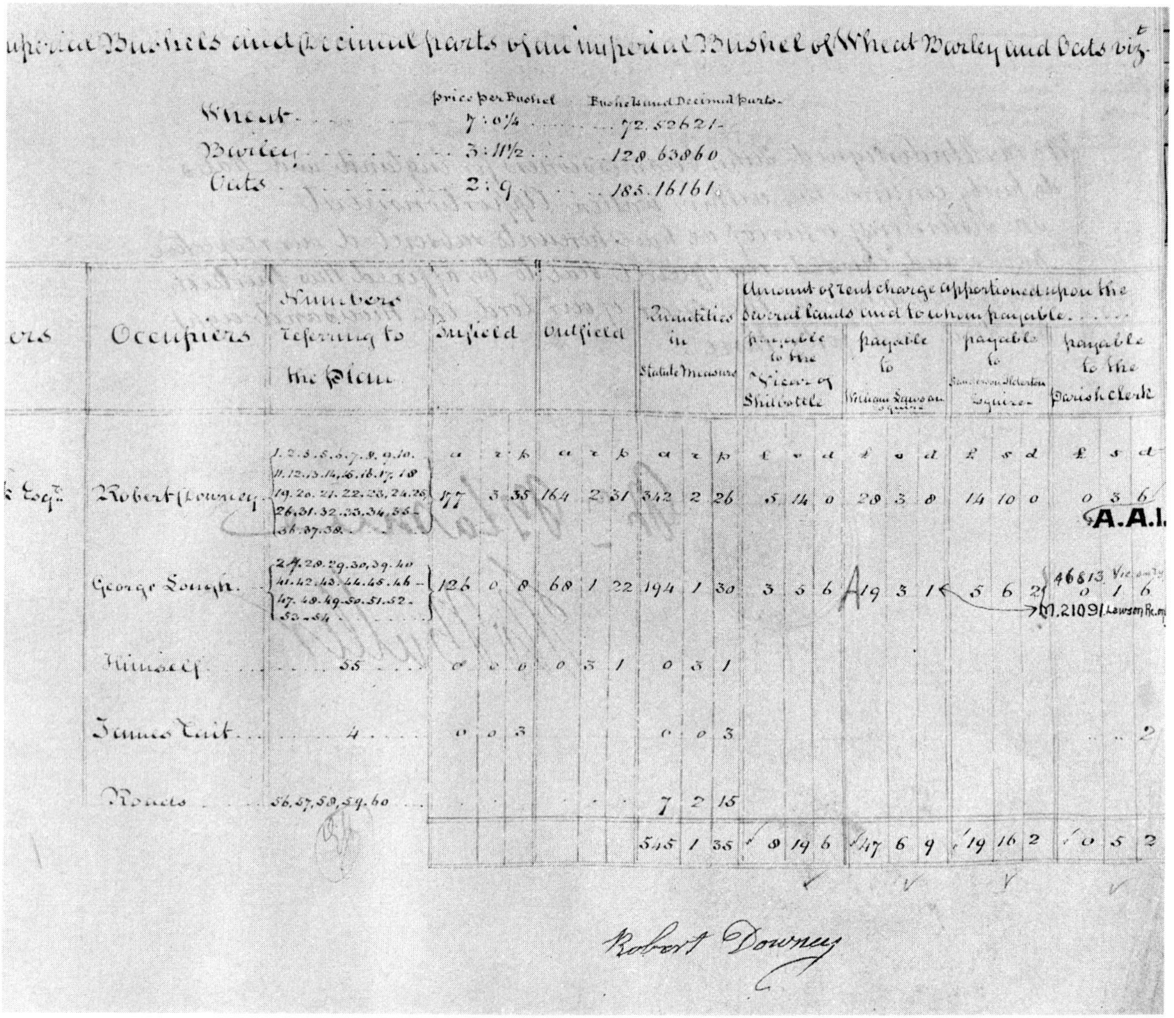
...perial Bushels and Decimal parts of an imperial Bushel of Wheat Barley and Oats viz[t]

	Price per Bushel	Bushels and Decimal parts
Wheat	7:0¼	72.52621
Barley	3:11½	128.63960
Oats	2:9	185.16161

Occupiers	Numbers referring to the Plan	Infield a r p	Outfield a r p	Quantities in Statute Measure a r p	payable to the Vicar of Shilbottle £ s d	payable to William Lawson Esquire £ s d	payable to Sanderson Ilderton Esquire £ s d	payable to the Parish Clerk £ s d
Robert Downey	1.2.3.5.6.7.8.9.10. 11.12.13.14.15.16.17.18 19.20.21.22.23.24.25 26.31.32.33.34.35 36.37.38	177 3 35	164 2 31	342 2 26	5 14 0	28 3 8	14 10 0	0 3 6
George Lough	27.28.29.30.39.40 41.42.43.44.45.46 47.48.49.50.51.52 53.54	126 0 8	68 1 22	194 1 30	3 5 6	19 3 1	5 6 2	0 1 6
Himself	55	0 0 0	0 3 1	0 3 1				
James Tait	4	0 0 3		0 0 3				2
Roads	56.57.58.59.60			7 2 15				
				545 1 35	9 19 6	47 6 9	19 16 2	0 5 2

Robert Downey

Fig. 7 Whittle, Northumberland, 1843. Tithe apportionments such as this one which list infield and outfield acreages are most unusual. Source: PRO IR29 25/477. Photograph reproduced by kind permission of the Keeper of the Public Record Office.

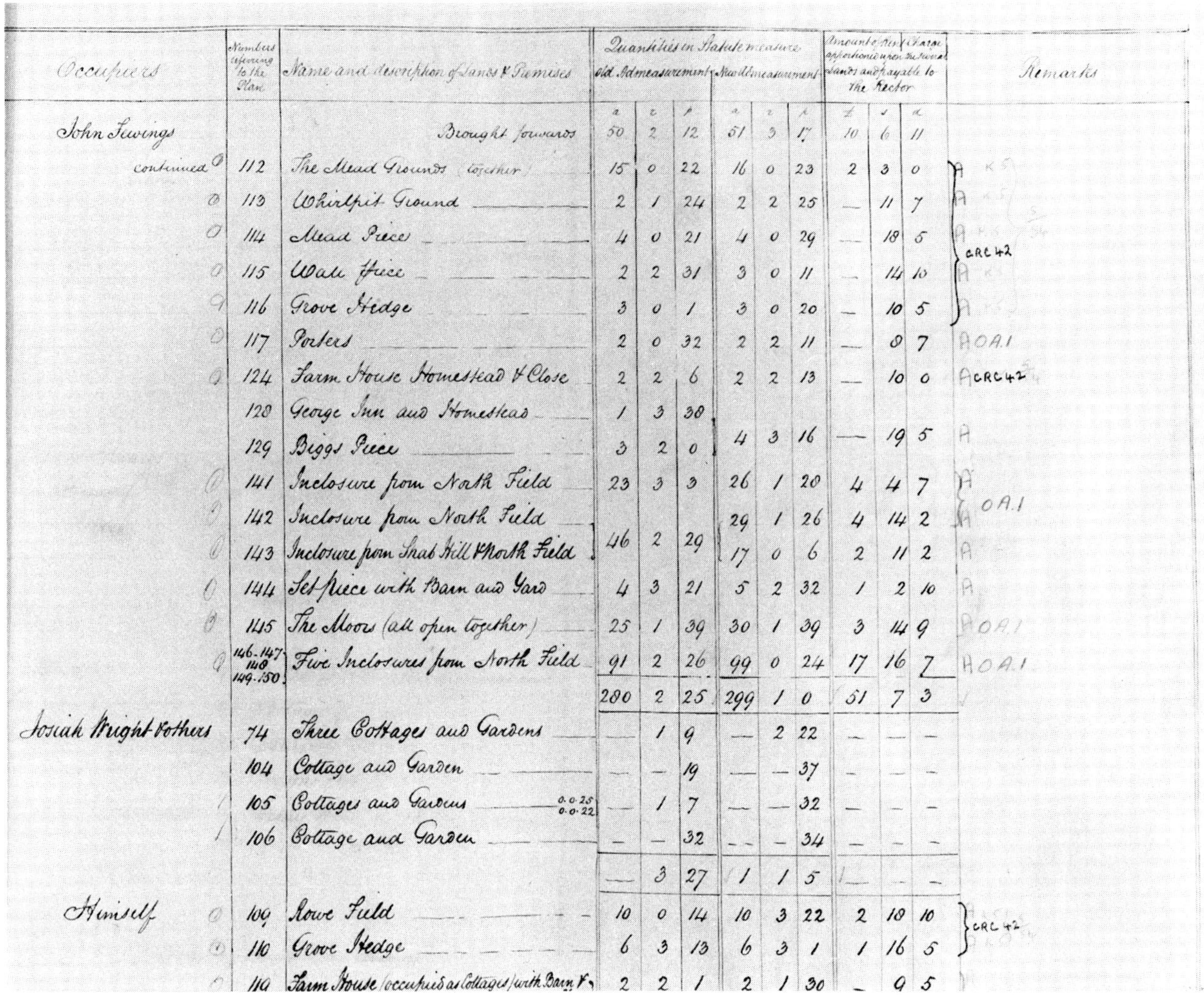

Occupiers	Numbers referring to the Plan	Name and description of Lands & Premises	Old Admeasurement a	r	p	New Admeasurement a	r	p	Amount of Rent Charge apportioned upon the several Lands and payable to the Rector £	s	d	Remarks
John Sewings		Brought forwards	50	2	12	51	3	17	10	6	11	
continued	112	The Mead Grounds (together)	15	0	22	16	0	23	2	3	0	
	113	Whirlpit Ground	2	1	24	2	2	25	—	11	7	
	114	Mead Piece	4	0	21	4	0	29	—	18	5	
	115	Wall Piece	2	2	31	3	0	11	—	14	10	
	116	Grove Hedge	3	0	1	3	0	20	—	10	5	
	117	Porters	2	0	32	2	2	11	—	8	7	
	124	Farm House Homestead & Close	2	2	6	2	2	13	—	10	0	
	128	George Inn and Homestead	1	3	38							
	129	Biggs Piece	3	2	0	4	3	16	—	19	5	
	141	Inclosure from North Field	23	3	3	26	1	20	4	4	7	
	142	Inclosure from North Field				29	1	26	4	14	2	
	143	Inclosure from Snab Hill & North Field	46	2	29	17	0	6	2	11	2	
	144	Set Piece with Barn and Yard	4	3	21	5	2	32	1	2	10	
	145	The Moors (all open together)	25	1	39	30	1	39	3	14	9	
	146.147 148 149.150	Five Inclosures from North Field	91	2	26	99	0	24	17	16	7	
			280	2	25	299	1	0	51	7	3	
Josiah Wright & others	74	Three Cottages and Gardens	—	1	9	—	2	22	—	—	—	
	104	Cottage and Garden	—	—	19	—	—	37	—	—	—	
	105	Cottages and Gardens 0.0.25 0.0.22	—	1	7	—	—	32	—	—	—	
	106	Cottage and Garden	—	—	32	—	—	34	—	—	—	
			—	3	27	1	1	5	—	—	—	
Himself	109	Rowe Field	10	0	14	10	3	22	2	18	10	CRC 42
	110	Grove Hedge	6	3	13	6	3	1	1	16	5	
	110	Farm House (occupied as Cottages) with Barn &c	2	2	1	2	1	30	—	9	5	

Fig. 8 Cowley, Gloucestershire, 1841. The separate columns for quantities in old and new measurement are very unusual. Source: PRO IR29 13/59. Photograph reproduced by kind permission of the Keeper of the Public Record Office.

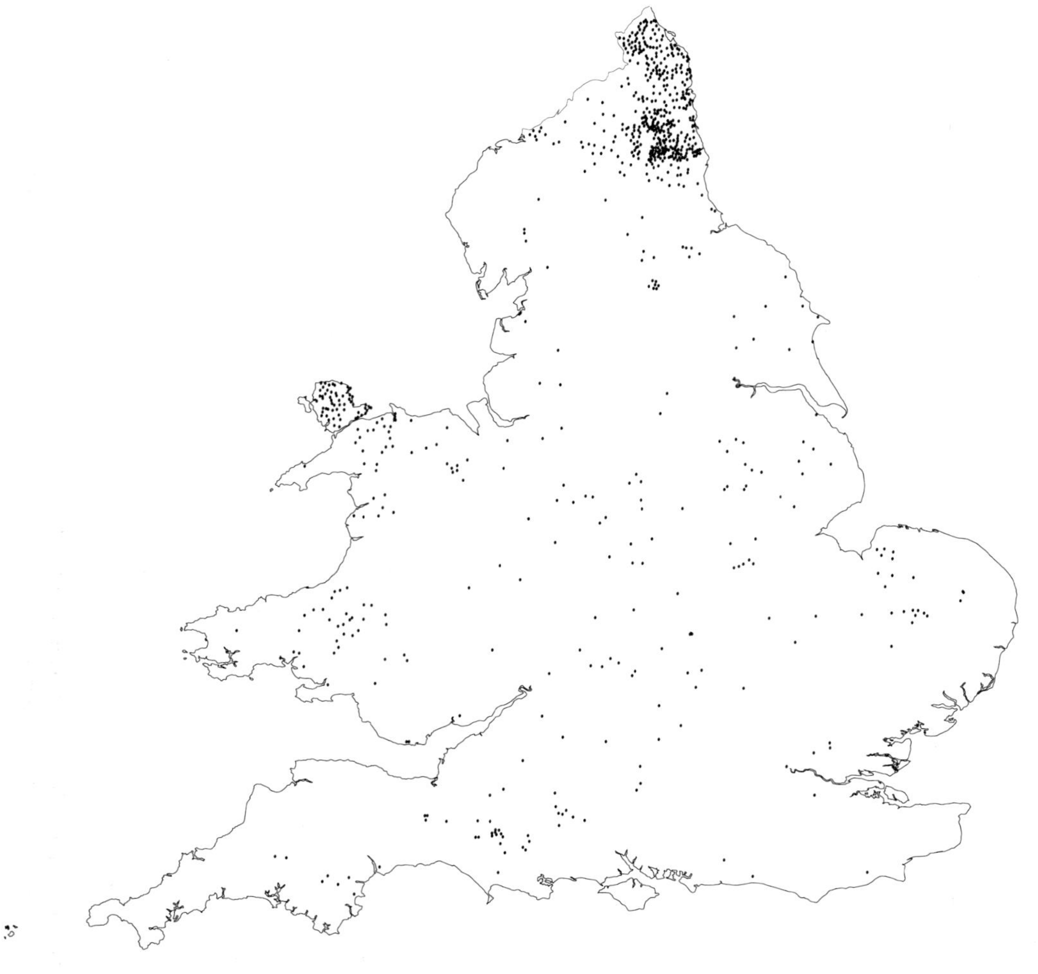

Fig. 9 England and Wales: tithe districts where tithe was apportioned on holdings rather than field-by-field.

information on occupiers may also be incomplete. The tithe survey of Horn in Rutland is an extreme case of such a method of apportionment as the whole district is designated a single tithe area (Fig. 11).

The work of apportioning tithe rent-charge as agreed or awarded was undertaken by men known as tithe valuers. Usually one valuer was appointed for a district, sometimes there were two with one to represent the landowners and one the tithe owners, and occasionally there were three valuers, with the third acting as umpire. Tithe valuers could be almost anyone from a local farmer or the parish schoolmaster to a London-based specialist; a majority were local men who regularly undertook land agency work. Some valuers also made tithe maps and some men who were primarily land surveyors also undertook tithe valuations but usually an individual specialised in one or the other task. The extent of valuation practices varied as much as did the men themselves. Very many

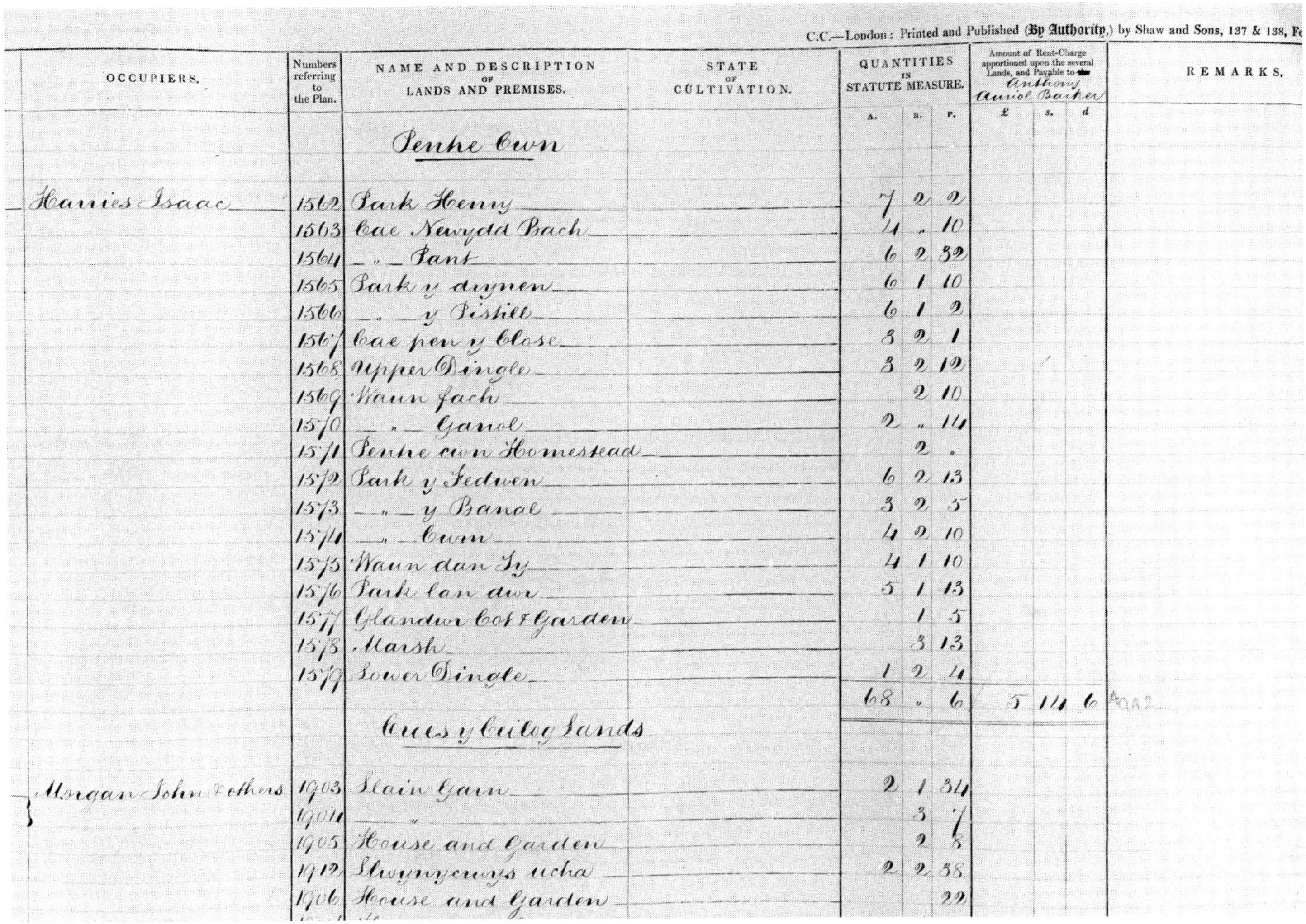

C.C.—London: Printed and Published (By Authority,) by Shaw and Sons, 137 & 138, Fe

OCCUPIERS.	Numbers referring to the Plan.	NAME AND DESCRIPTION OF LANDS AND PREMISES.	STATE OF CULTIVATION.	QUANTITIES IN STATUTE MEASURE. A.	R.	P.	Amount of Rent-Charge apportioned upon the several Lands, and Payable to Anthony Auriol Barker £	s.	d	REMARKS.
		Penhe Cwn								
Harries Isaac	1562	Park Henry		7	2	2				
	1563	Cae Newydd Bach		4	„	10				
	1564	„ Pant		6	2	32				
	1565	Park y dynen		6	1	10				
	1566	„ y Pistill		6	1	2				
	1567	Cae pen y Close		3	2	1				
	1568	Upper Dingle		3	2	12				
	1569	Waun fach			2	10				
	1570	„ Ganol		2	„	14				
	1571	Penhe cwn Homestead			2	.				
	1572	Park y Fedwen		6	2	13				
	1573	„ y Banal		3	2	5				
	1574	„ Cwm		4	2	10				
	1575	Waun dan Ty		4	1	10				
	1576	Park lan dwr		5	1	13				
	1577	Glandwr Cot & Garden			1	5				
	1578	Marsh			3	13				
	1579	Lower Dingle		1	2	4				
				68	„	6	5	14	6	AQA2
		Cwes y Ceilog Lands								
Morgan John & others	1903	Llain Garn		2	1	34				
	1904	„			3	7				
	1905	House and Garden			2	8				
	1912	Llwynycrwys ucha		2	2	38				
	1906	House and Garden				22				

Fig. 10 Llandefailog, Carmarthenshire, 1842. In this part of the tithe district, tithe is apportioned on holdings and the state of cultivation column is characteristically left blank. Source: PRO IR29 47/28. Photograph reproduced by kind permission of the Keeper of the Public Record Office.

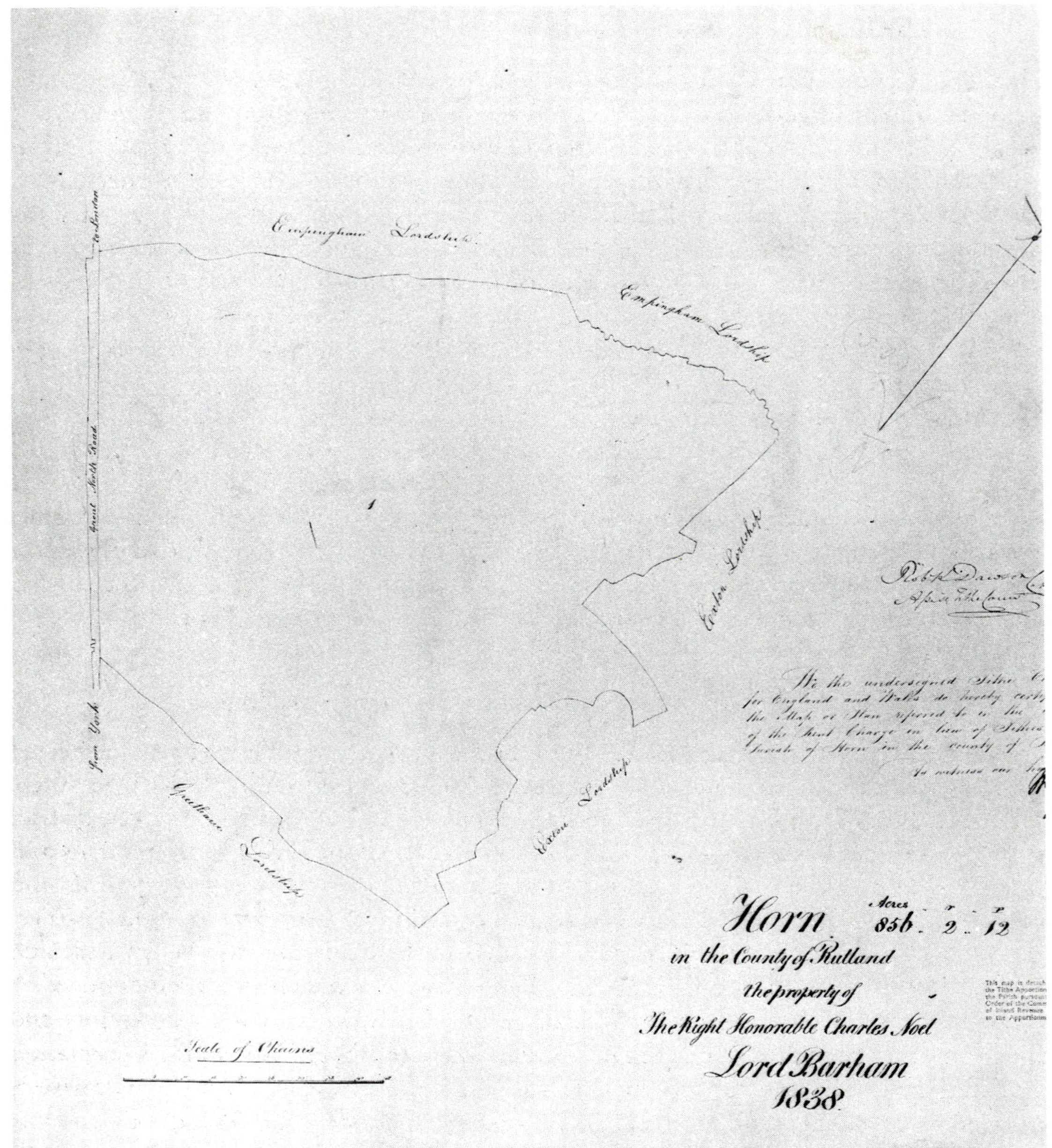

Fig. 11 Horn, Rutland, 1838. Where tithe was apportioned on holdings there was no need to map individual fields; this tithe map represents the extreme case where the whole district is designated a single tithe area for apportionment of tithe rent-charge. Source: PRO IR30 28/16. Photograph reproduced by kind permission of the Keeper of the Public Record Office.

valuers worked only in their home parish whereas others were employed over wide areas. Some experienced valuers, such as Robert Pratt of Norwich, who valued 121 districts in Norfolk and Suffolk, or Morris and William Sayce, who valued 83 districts in and around the Welsh borders, must at times have been engaged on tithe work almost to the exclusion of everything else.

The boundaries of tithe districts

Obtaining accurate boundaries of parishes and townships in England and Wales in the period before the large-scale maps of the Ordnance Survey were produced, is an exercise fraught with difficulties. The second half of the nineteenth century was a period of significant boundary reform, particularly affecting parishes adjoining, or affected by, urban development. Tithe maps largely pre-date these changes and as such are one of the best sources for the boundaries of 'ancient' parishes. Our county-by-county catalogue of the tithe maps of each county is accompanied by a map which shows the boundaries of tithe districts in that county. Each tithe district is identified on these maps by its Public Record Office reference number which also links districts on the map to the county-by-county catalogue entries.

Boundaries of tithe districts for most of the country are available as manuscript additions to a set of Old Series Ordnance Survey one-inch maps now held in the Public Record Office in class IR 105 (Fig. 12).[11] These maps were marked up with tithe district boundaries in 1849-50 in preparation for the publication of the more familiar published series of one-inch maps known as the 'Index to Tithe Survey'. The provenance of these two series of maps and the way we have used them to compile the maps of tithe district boundaries for each county of England and Wales are discussed in Appendix 2.

The tithe survey database and county-by-county catalogues

Every tithe map and apportionment held in the Public Record Office has been inspected and data from each entered into a database.[12] The database used is Prime Computers INFORMATION and it is organised county-by-county and tithe district-by-tithe district in the precise order of the class list of PRO IR29 and IR30, the tithe apportionments and tithe maps respectively.[13] Data for each tithe district are organised in seventy fields and were recorded on data sheets before editing and entry into the database. As noted earlier, the entire contents of the database are deposited in the Economic and Social Research Council Data Archive at the University of Essex from where copies can be obtained.[14]

The database has been edited and rearranged to constitute the county-by-county and tithe district-by-tithe district catalogue as published in this book. Not all the information extracted from the tithe apportionments and entered for analysis into the database is included in the county-by-county catalogue as some is of only marginal interest to most users of tithe apportionments and maps. This includes the names and addresses of tithe valuers (field 9) and the various reasons cited for tithe exemptions (field 13). These and other additional data can be obtained from the database deposited with the ESRC Data Archive.

[11] These maps were transferred from the Tithe Redemption Commission to the Public Record Office and are catalogued under PRO IR 105.

[12] A small number of tithe maps (fewer than ten) were unavailable for inspection at the time of data transcription and in these cases copies were examined in the respective county record offices.

[13] These catalogues have been published by the List and Index Society, viz. *Inland Revenue tithe maps and apportionments*, London, Swift (P. and D.), 68 and 83 (1971 and 1972).

[14] Requests should be addressed to The Director, ESRC Data Archive, University of Essex, Wivenhoe Park, Colchester, Essex CO4 3SQ.

Fig. 12 PRO class IR 105 contains a set of Ordnance Survey Old Series one-inch maps to which tithe district boundaries have been added in the office of the Tithe Commission. Photograph reproduced by kind permission of the Keeper of the Public Record Office.

Each tithe apportionment (PRO IR29) and each tithe map (PRO IR30) is identified in the Public Record Office holdings by a reference number with two components: first a county number and second, a tithe district number. This county-by-county catalogue follows the arrangement of the PRO IR29 and IR30 catalogues in that it is arranged in alphabetical order of English and then Welsh counties with counties numbered exactly as in PRO IR29 and IR30. For example, Hampshire and the Isle of Wight are listed together as 'Southampton' and Monmouthshire is listed as an English county by the Public Record Office. Within counties, our county-by-county catalogue numbering follows that of the Public Record Office which is a generally alphabetic ordering by name of tithe district.

The counties and their identifying reference numbers are listed below.

1 Bedfordshire
2 Berkshire
3 Buckinghamshire
4 Cambridgeshire
5 Cheshire
6 Cornwall
7 Cumberland
8 Derbyshire
9 Devon
10 Dorset
11 Durham
12 Essex
13 Gloucestershire
14 Herefordshire
15 Hertfordshire
16 Huntingdonshire
17 Kent
18 Lancashire
19 Leicestershire
20 Lincolnshire
21 Middlesex
22 Monmouthshire
23 Norfolk
24 Northamptonshire
25 Northumberland
26 Nottinghamshire
27 Oxfordshire
28 Rutland
29 Shropshire
30 Somerset
31 Hampshire (Southampton)
32 Staffordshire
33 Suffolk
34 Surrey
35 Sussex
36 Warwickshire
37 Westmorland
38 Wiltshire
39 Worcestershire
40 York City and Ainsty
41 Yorkshire, East Riding
42 Yorkshire, North Riding
43 Yorkshire, West Riding
44 Anglesey
45 Breconshire
46 Cardiganshire
47 Carmarthenshire
48 Carnarvonshire
49 Denbighshire
50 Flintshire
51 Glamorganshire
52 Merionethshire
53 Montgomeryshire
54 Pembrokeshire
55 Radnorshire

Explanatory key to the county tithe survey catalogues

The following two entries in the county-by county catalogue are used as examples in this explanation of the contents and layout of each of the county catalogues:

20/291 Saltfleet cum Skidbrook (parish) TF 452941
Apt 27.06.1837; 2081a (3455); Map 1838?, 3 chns, 1st cl, by Chas Cave Jno. Orme; construction lines, waterbodies, houses, plantations, arable (col), gardens, marsh/bog, heath/moor (col), hedge ownership, fence ownership, field gates, windmill (by symbol), boundary post, sandhills (col), saltmarsh (col), drains, beach (col); red lines could represent later additions. Apt omits most field names, and omits land use for fields laid out at enclosure.

30/201 St Benedict and St John, Glastonbury (parish) ST 500385 [Glastonbury]
Apt 15.12.1840; 7083a (7083); Map 1844, 6 chns, in 23 parts, by Thomas Hawkes, Williton, Taunton, Somerset, (includes town separately at 3 chns and four 3-chn enlargements of detail, and 17 3-chn enlargements of common fields in manuscript), litho (Standidge); waterbodies, houses (by shading), woods, plantations, orchards, open fields, fences, decoy, tor, abbey buildings.

Heading line or lines

The heading is printed in bold typeface at the opening of each catalogue entry as in the following two examples:

20/291 Saltfleet cum Skidbrook (parish) TF 452941

30/201 St Benedict and St John, Glastonbury (parish) ST 500385 [Glastonbury]

Public Record Office tithe district reference number

This is in two parts: first the county number and second the tithe district number, separated by a '/'. To requisition an apportionment the tithe district reference number should be prefixed by 'IR 29', to requisition a map the prefix is 'IR 30'. Thus for district 20/291 the tithe apportionment is IR29 20/291 and the tithe map for 30/201 is IR30 30/201.
It should be noted that these reference numbers do not apply to the tithe records held in local record offices which each have their own system of listing.

Tithe district name

This is in the form as given in the tithe apportionment, the legal instrument of tithe commutation. These names can differ from those on the tithe maps, from those in current use, and from those in the Public Record Office IR29 and IR30 catalogues.

Category of tithe district

This is in ( ) brackets. Most tithe districts are parishes in southern England and in Wales or townships in northern England.

National Grid reference

A six-figure full National Grid reference is given to the approximate centroid of the tithe district.

Modern form of tithe district name

Where the form given in the tithe apportionment differs from that listed in the Ordnance Survey Gazetteer of Great Britain (Southampton and London, 1987) the latter is given in [ ] brackets. A significant minority of tithe district names are not in use today; where a name does not appear in the Gazetteer, this is signalled by the entry: '[Not listed]'. If one component of a multiple name tithe district, for example 'Saltfleet cum Skidbrook' is the same as in the Ordnance Survey Gazetteer, there is no entry in [ ] brackets.

Main entry

This is printed in ordinary typeface and contains information on the following:

The tithe apportionment – date and coverage
The tithe map and its technical characteristics
The topographical etc content of the tithe map
Nature and content of the tithe apportionment

The tithe apportionment – date and coverage

The first part of the Main Entry relates to the tithe apportionment, for example:

20/291 Saltfleet cum Skidbrook (parish) **TF 452941**
...............Apt 27.06.1837; 2081a (3455);

30/201 St Benedict and St John, Glastonbury (parish) **ST 500385 [Glastonbury]**
...............Apt 15.12.1840; 7083a (7083);

'Apt', followed by date as day.month.year
This is the date when the tithe commissioners confirmed the agreement or award for commutation of tithes.

Acreage
This is the total acreage covered by the apportionment and is expressed by a figure in statute acres followed by the abbreviation: 'a'. Tithe maps do in some cases cover a more extensive area than tithe apportionments, particularly where there were large tracts of tithe-free land or land the tithes of which had been commuted at enclosure. Where it is stated in the tithe apportionment that the whole tithe district is liable to tithe, the acreage is followed by the word: 'all'. Where it is not clear from the tithe apportionment whether a whole tithe district is tithable or where it is explicitly stated that part was tithe free, the acreage of the tithe district as listed in the published tables of the 1851 census of population is given in ( ) brackets. Where it is known that part of a tithe district is tithe free but it is not possible to trace an acreage for an equivalent district in the census tables, a '?' appears. The purpose of listing these census-derived acreages is to give users a guide as to the completeness of a particular tithe survey. The acreages listed in the 1851 census were supplied to the Registrar General by the Tithe Commission from its tithe surveys. There are known to be small discrepancies between the census of population acreages and those published later by the Ordnance Survey, that the census acreage is occasionally slightly less than the tithe apportionment acreage due to rounding and that for tithe districts adjoining estuaries or open sea the apportionment acreage is sometimes substantially less than the census acreage which usually includes land below high water normally excluded from tithe apportionments.

The tithe map and its technical characteristics

A majority of the entries in the county-by county catalogue relate to the cartographic characteristics and topographic and other content of tithe maps. The first set of entries as in the following examples relate to map technical details:

20/291 Saltfleet cum Skidbrook (parish) TF 452941
..........Map 1838?, 3 chns, 1st cl, by Chas Cave Jno. Orme;

30/201 St Benedict and St John, Glastonbury (parish) ST 500385 [Glastonbury]
..........Map 1844, 6 chns, in 23 parts, by Thomas Hawkes, Williton, Taunton, Somerset, (includes town separately at 3 chns and four 3-chn enlargements of detail, and 17 3-chn enlargements of common fields in manuscript), litho (Standidge);

Map date

Where a date is not stated explicitly on the map, the date is that of the earliest Tithe Commission receipt stamp on the map; in a few cases there is no legible receipt stamp and the map is listed as 'Not dated'.

Scale

Scale of the map is given as the number of chains on the ground to an inch on the map followed by the abbreviation: 'chns'. In a very few instances scales not related to chains were used, and in these cases a representative fraction is listed as well as a chain scale. Scales obtained by comparative measurement where no scale is given on the map are given in square brackets: [ ]. Uncertain scales are identified by the symbol: '?'. The representative fractions for the most commonly encountered chain scales of tithe maps are:

1 chain	1:792	6 chains	1:4752
2 chains	1:1584	8 chains	1:6336
3 chains	1:2376	10 chains	1:7920
4 chains	1:3168	12 chains	1:9504
5 chains	1:3960		

First-class maps

The Tithe Act Amendment Act of 1837 introduced two classes of tithe maps, known as first and second class. First-class maps are noted by the entry '1st cl' immediately following the scale.

Map-maker's name and address

These are listed exactly as stated on the map; they have not been edited into consistent forms. In those cases where authorship is inferred (either on grounds of style or from an ambiguous signature), the map-maker's name is preceded by the symbol: '?'. Where there is information on the map as to the circumstances of its construction such as: 'surveyed', 'revised', 'copied' or 'compiled' etc., this is also noted.

Tithable parts only

Where a map is of only the tithable parts of a tithe district, this is noted at this point.

Tinted
Coloured maps, that is those where the whole district has a coloured ground tint, are identified by the word: 'tinted'.

Number of parts and enlargements
These are noted in ( ) brackets. A 'part' is defined as either a separate map of a detached tithable area not linked to the main map by construction lines, roads or other detail, or a separate enlargement of detail which also appears on the main map. Not included in the count of parts are those instances where one map is drawn on a number of sub-sheets or has been cut into separate pieces at some later date.

Printed maps
Those maps lithographed or engraved are identified together with the name and address of the lithographer except that those by Standidge and Co. of 77 Cornhill, London are abbreviated to 'Standidge'.

A semi-colon now follows in all entries to separate the entries on technical details from those which summarise the topographic and other content of the tithe map.

The topographical and other content of the tithe map

All tithe maps derive from the same piece of national legislation and all have the same purpose: to serve as a record of the apportionment of tithe rent-charge as set out in the schedule of tithe apportionment. Both general and specific advice on the nature and content of tithe maps were given to surveyors by the centralised, London-based Tithe Commission. Notwithstanding all these influences towards homogeneity, our analysis of the database to produce these catalogues reveals that as a body the tithe maps are an extremely heterogeneous class of map. This fact is underscored by the variation of map content listed in this section of the main catalogue entry.

This section of the county-by-county catalogue gives users an impression of the detail of topographical and other content communicated by each tithe map. However, omission of a particular feature on a tithe map does not mean that the feature was not present on the ground at the time the map was compiled. One of the reasons for this is related to the purpose of the tithe maps. The direct and immediate purpose of tithe maps is quite clear; they were to serve as an official record of the boundaries of all tithe areas (usually fields or other similar land parcels) on which tithe rent-charge was apportioned in the schedule of tithe apportionment. The portrayal of other features incidental to the purpose of tithe commutation is very variable. Advice to the privately commissioned surveyors of tithe maps was itself imprecise. The official instructions required that surveyors should include such other detail on their maps as it is usual to find on estate maps, though there was no statutory requirement to do this and in this respect the instructions ran counter to other advice from the Tithe Commission that 'plain working plans' with construction lines and little else constituted the preferred specification for first-class maps (see pp. 708–17).

Most of the entries in the county-by-county catalogue relating to map content, are, as in the two specimens below, reasonably self-explanatory.

20/291 Saltfleet cum Skidbrook (parish) TF 452941
...................construction lines, waterbodies, houses, plantations, arable (col), gardens, marsh/bog, heath/moor (col), hedge ownership, fence ownership, field gates, windmill (by symbol), boundary post, sandhills (col), saltmarsh (col), drains, beach (col); red lines could represent later additions.

30/201 St Benedict and St John, Glastonbury (parish) ST 500385 [Glastonbury]
...................waterbodies, houses (by shading), woods, plantations, orchards, open fields, fences, decoy, tor, abbey buildings.

General conventions

The following general conventions are employed:

Where a feature is coloured '(col)' is added after the name of a feature viz.: 'sandhills (col)';

Where a feature such as a church is represented by a pictogram, '(pictorial)' is added after the name of the feature;

Where a feature is represented by a conventional symbol, '(by symbol)' is added after the name of the feature viz.: 'windmill (by symbol)'.

Where land use is depicted on the face of the map it is usually by colour-tint and/or symbol; occasionally it is shown 'by annotation'. The county-by-county catalogue indicates which of these methods was used and also those cases where the symbols used on the map are the same as the conventional signs recommended in 1837 by Lieutenant Robert Kearsley Dawson, the officer seconded from the Royal Engineers to superintend tithe commutation mapping.

Some particularly obscure local terms for features listed in these entries are explained within [ ] brackets.

Specific interpretations and conventions

There are several hundred separate categories of features noted on tithe maps and listed in the county-by-county catalogue; the overwhelming majority are straightforward, can be recognised unequivocally on the maps, and the entries by name of feature in this catalogue require no explanation. However, for the accurate interpretation of some twenty-five categories, an understanding of our working definitions and conventions is essential. These are as follows:

Hill-shading

Denotes the physical form of the land as indicated by hachures or brush-shading. Hill-shading on tithe maps is very rarely as complete as on Ordnance Survey maps; sometimes it is no more than the depiction of bluffs or river-cliffs.

Waterbodies

Includes all rivers, streams, lakes and ponds identified as such, usually by the use of blue colouring or water-lining.

Roads

Roads are usually shown on tithe maps as they normally bounded individual tithe areas.

Only very rarely is their status as public or private indicated with any certainty, though the general convention of colour filling public roads in sienna is often followed.

Foot/bridleways
These are sometimes explicitly annotated as such, but more usually they are indicated by single or double pecked lines. Only very occasionally are foot/bridleways described on the maps as rights of way.

Turnpike roads
Turnpikes may be distinguished either by colour, by edging, by annotation, or by the presence of a toll gate.

Houses
On those maps which differentiate houses from other buildings, the usual practice was to colour inhabited buildings in pink (though red, brown, and orange were all used) and to colour uninhabited buildings in grey (though purple, blue, and black are also encountered). On uncoloured maps the usual practice was to make houses more prominent than other buildings, variously by heavier shading, solid black filling or by the addition of a dot within their outline.

Farmyards
These are sometimes highlighted in colour, usually the same colour as is used to tint roads.

Woods and plantations
Both are commonly shown either by symbol or by tint or by a combination of the two methods and this practice in severalty or combination is noted in the county-by-county catalogue. Where both woods and plantations or plantations only are mentioned then it can be assumed that the map-maker was making a conscious distinction between 'ancient' and 'planted' woodland. Where only the general category of 'woods' is employed on a map then it is less clear whether 'ancient' woodland is being explicitly recorded, or whether the map-maker is merely indicating a parcel of land with trees. Reference must be made to the tithe apportionment to clarify this issue. Plantations are usually depicted by either more regular symbols than other woodland, or by 'conifer-like' symbols. It should not be assumed, however (cf. later Ordnance Survey maps), that use of a 'conifer' symbol necessarily indicates coniferous planting.

Osiers
These are sometimes shown by distinctive symbol, though often are subsumed in 'woods'.

Parkland
This is sometimes shown by use of a particular colour but more usually by the distinctive grouping of trees and patterns of avenues.

Arable land
Arable is usually shown by brown tint, though red, pink, yellow and grey were all occasionally used.

Grassland
Grass as depicted on the maps normally includes both meadow (for hay) and pasture (for grazing animals), and is usually shown by green tint; occasionally different shades of green are used for meadow and pasture. Although green is the usual colour, blue is occasionally used.

Orchards
These are usually shown by regular symbol.

Hops
Hops are usually shown by a symbol characterised by an 'S' twining round an upright. Very often hops are listed as a state of cultivation in an apportionment but are not distinguished by symbol on the accompanying map.

Gardens
As a general rule these are gardens attached to cottages: larger ornamental gardens are either explicitly noted as such or are treated as parkland. The three main methods of showing gardens are: by multi-coloured stripes, by stipple accompanied by conventional 'bushes', and by a pattern of rectangular paths. Occasionally cottage gardens are subsumed in, and coloured as, arable land; market gardens are not distinguished from arable land on tithe maps.

Heath/moor
This includes all uncultivated land which is not wetland. It is usually shown either by symbol or by a colour distinctive from that used for cultivated land.

Marsh/bog
Includes all wetland and may be shown either by a colour distinctive from that used for cultivated land or by 'marshy' symbol.

Hedges and fences: hedge and fence ownership
Hedges and fences are shown usually by pictorial symbols; ownership is shown normally by the symbol lying 'on its side' with its head towards the property of the hedge owner. Hedges are shown sometimes by 'bushes' at intervals rather than by a continuous symbol.

Open/enclosed fields
In compiling the county-by-county catalogue it has been assumed that all solid lines bounding tithe areas on tithe maps represent boundaries marked on the ground by physical features (enclosed fields) and that all broken lines represent tithe areas without such marks (open fields). The entry 'open fields' in the catalogue does not, therefore, carry any implication of the existence of common rights or husbandry practices.

Field boundary ownerships
This entry is only used when hedges or fences are not shown representationally; field boundary ownerships may be shown either by a 'T' symbol or by a band of colour to the side of the owner to whom the field boundary belongs.

Field gates
This entry is not used where the only gates on a map are those across roads, paths and tracks.

Field acreages
These are given sometimes on tithe maps; they are not always complete, and they are often struck through.

Field names
These are also given occasionally on tithe maps themselves; again they are not always complete, and also are often struck through. Tithe apportionments do, of course, contain an unparalleled record of field names.

Building names and road names
Naming of buildings and roads usually is less complete than on later Ordnance Survey maps; often only two or three buildings or roads are named on an individual tithe map.

Landownership
Usually the only landowners named are those owning land surrounding the tithe district, and particularly those surrounding detached tithable parts. The owners of tithable lands are, of course, stated in the apportionment.

Churches
Unless noted otherwise it can be assumed that Anglican churches or chapels are indicated distinctively, either by colour, name or by a cross. Churches and chapels of other denominations and sects are listed in the county-by-county catalogue where these are identified on the map.

Decorative features
These are listed in the county-by-county catalogue after the content of mapped topographical and other features.

Nature and content of tithe apportionments

Tithe apportionments are much more standardised in format and content than tithe maps but any variations from the general rule are noted in this final section of the county-by-county catalogue entries. Generally speaking, apportionment was on a field-by-field basis with a schedule of tithe apportionment providing details of landowner, land occupier, name and description of each tithe area, the state of cultivation in general categories such as arable, grass, wood etc., the acreage of each tithe area in statute measure, and the amount of tithe rent-charge apportioned to each tithe area. Sometimes, particularly in upland districts, tithe rent-charge was apportioned on a holding or ownership basis, and thus details of individual fields are omitted or given in generalised form with states of cultivation recorded as, for example, 'arable, pasture, etc.'. Sometimes field-by-field apportionments omit land use or field names and in others the crops grown on the arable are specified. Where variations such as these occur, they are noted in the county-by-county catalogue. For example:

20/291 Saltfleet cum Skidbrook (parish) **TF 452941**
.........Apt omits most field names, and omits land use for fields laid out at enclosure.

County-by-county catalogues and analyses

Arrangement of text, maps, tables and catalogue

In this, the largest part of the book in terms of length, we provide for each of the fifty-five counties of England and Wales which the Tithe Commission recognised, the following descriptive and analytical materials:

1 A short text which discusses tithe and tithe commutation and the characteristics and contents of the tithe maps of each county;

2 A map which identifies the boundaries of tithe districts and indicates tithable and tithe-free districts. Reference numbers on these maps are the Public Record Office press marks of the tithe surveys of the county and relate tithe districts on the map to entries in the catalogue of that county.

The following conventions are used on the maps:

grey tone highlights districts with tithe surveys; white areas are tithe-free districts; horizontal line shading identifies insets drawn for clarity at a larger scale;

numerals in ordinary upright typeface indicate that the tithe district boundary is taken from PRO IR 105 maps (but from Ordnance Survey maps north of the Hull–Preston line where IR 105 is not extant, see Appendix 2 pp. 827–30);

numerals in bold italic are used where IR 105 is deficient and boundaries have been taken from an Ordnance Survey source south of Hull-Preston;

underlining is used to highlight those reference numbers placed outside their respective tithe districts;

a reference number within square brackets and with a county identifier as well as a piece number indicates that the district is listed in the catalogue of another county;

where a tithe district straddles a county boundary this is indicated by a 'S' brace;

pecked lines link detached parts of tithe districts.

3 Tables which list the assistant tithe commissioners, local tithe agents, valuers of tithe rent-charge, and map-makers who worked in that county, and which summarise the scales, classes, and dates of the tithe maps;

4 The catalogue entries arranged tithe district-by-tithe district as described in the previous section.

Reference is made in the county texts to a large number of particular tithe apportionments and maps. It is not considered necessary to cite the Public Record Office press mark of these documents in addition to the name of the tithe district; these references can be obtained by taking the name of a tithe district to the entry for that place in the county catalogue.

The Index at the end of this book is to help identify first, those tithe districts no longer known by the name used in the tithe survey and second, those places which the Tithe Commission amalgamated with others in a single tithe district.

Bedfordshire

PRO IR29 and IR30 1/1–64

128 tithe districts: 299,943 acres
58 tithe commutations: 105,891 acres
24 voluntary agreements, 34 compulsory tithe awards,
6 corn rent annuities

Tithe and tithe commutation

Bedfordshire on the south-eastern margins of the English Midlands conforms very much to the midland pattern of extensive parliamentary enclosure accompanied by commutation of tithe. In 1836, 45 per cent of tithe districts (35 per cent of the county by area) remained subject to tithes but only twenty districts were wholly tithable (Fig. 13). In addition to commutation at the time of enclosure, the main causes of tithe exemption in Bedfordshire were modus payments in lieu of tithes and exemption by prescription.

Assistant tithe commissioners and local tithe agents who worked in Bedfordshire are listed in Table 1.1 and the valuers of the county's tithe rent-charge in Table 1.2. All Bedfordshire tithe rent-charges were apportioned field-by-field so that the record of property and field names is unusually complete. In two tithe apportionments land use information is omitted, though that for Totternhoe is exceptional for a midland district as it lists the crops grown in each field.

Tithe maps

Bedfordshire is also a typical midland county as only 5 per cent of its tithe maps are first class. The precise number of maps derived from earlier surveys is unknown but it is probable that enclosure maps were used as a basis for tithe maps in those districts where much tithe had been commuted by enclosure act.

The scales used for Bedfordshire tithe maps range from one inch to three chains to one inch to twelve chains. Exactly half the maps are in the recommended scale range of one inch to three to four chains and all but three of the others are at the widely favoured six-chain scale (Table 1.3).

The tithe maps of Bedfordshire are variable records of land use: 60 per cent of the maps depict woodland and 22 per cent portray parks but only one map distinguishes arable and grass and only five show orchards. Twelve maps (20 per cent) depict open-field strips and many have either washes of colour or colour bands to show tithe-free land or the extent of

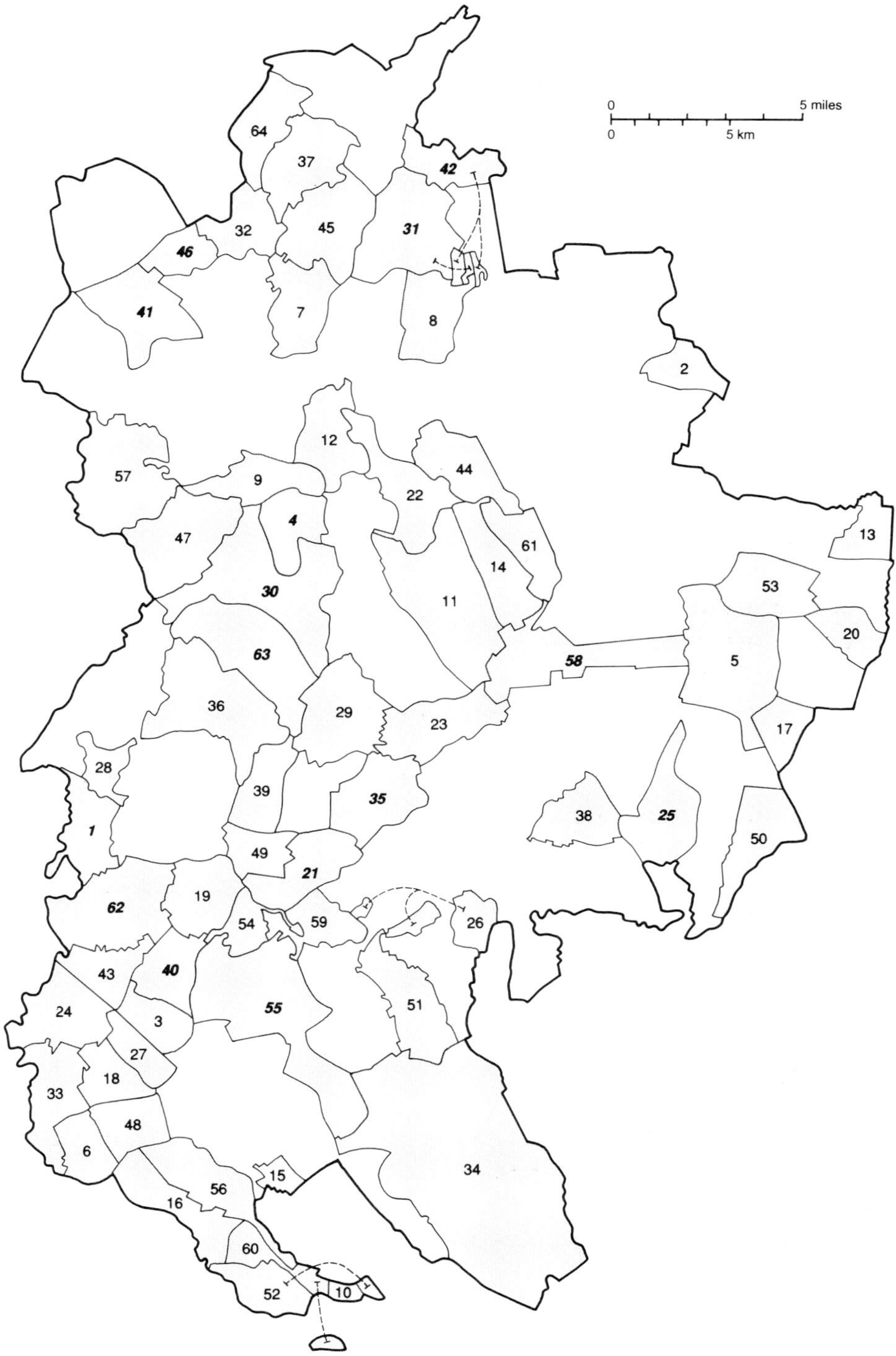

Fig. 13 Bedfordshire: tithe district boundaries.

holdings. Field boundary ownership is indicated on 20 per cent of maps and field gates on 10 per cent. No Bedfordshire map has any decorative embellishment.

Only twenty-four Bedfordshire tithe maps (41 per cent) in the Public Record Office collection can be attributed to a particular map-maker (Table 1.2). William Heard who made two maps in Bedfordshire was also active in this and many other counties as an assistant tithe commissioner.

Table 1.1. *Agreements and awards for commutation of tithes in Bedfordshire*

Assistant commissioner/ local tithe agent	*Number of agreements**	*Number of awards*
Francis Offley Martin	0	20
Thomas Smith Woolley	5	7
John Maurice Herbert	0	5
John Pickering	5	0
F. Browne Browne	4	0
John West	3	0
William Heard	2	0
Thomas James Tatham	0	2
Joseph Townsend	2	0
Edward Greathed	1	0
Roger Kynaston	1	0

*Computed from the number of extant reports on tithe agreements in the tithe files [PRO IR 18].

Table 1.2. *Tithe valuers and tithe map-makers in Bedfordshire*

Name and address (in Bedfordshire unless indicated)	*Number of districts*	*Acreage*
Tithe valuers		
Thomas Bloodworth, Kimbolton, Huntingdonshire	6	7,689
Thomas Bennett, Park Farm Office, Woburn	6	5,987
Michael Rowed, Flamstead, Hertfordshire	3	4,390
Matthew Reynolds, Old Warden	3	3,226
William Golding, Biddenham	3	967
Others [22]	37	83,632
Attributed tithe map-makers		
Matthew Reynolds, Old Warden	5	8,688
William Heard, St Margarets, Ware, Hertfordshire	2	6,281
J. Bailey Denton, Gray's Inn, London	2	4,610
Charles Day, Colleyweston, Northamptonshire	2	2,550
Keen and Son, Parliament Street, Westminster	2	2,508
Others [11]	11	32,933

Table 1.3. *The tithe maps of Bedfordshire: scales and classes*

Scale in chains/inch	*All maps*		*First Class*		*Second Class*	
	Number	*Acreage*	*Number*	*Acreage*	*Number*	*Acreage*
3	20	27,990	3	6,269	17	21,721
4	9	27,377	0	0	9	27,377
4.5, 5.5	2	4,405	0	0	2	4,405
6	26	45,239	0	0	26	45,239
12	1	880	0	0	1	880
TOTAL	58	105,891	3	6,269	55	99,622

Table 1.4. *The tithe maps of Bedfordshire: dates*

	1837	*1838*	*1839*	*1840*	*1841*	*1842*	*1843*	*1844*	*1845*	*1846*	*1847*	*1848*	*1849*	*1850*	*>1850*
All maps	1	7	8	5	6	4	4	3	3	1	3	2	5	1	5
1st class	0	0	1	0	0	0	0	0	0	0	0	1	1	0	0
2nd class	1	7	7	5	6	4	4	3	3	1	3	1	4	1	5

Bedfordshire

1/1 Aspley Guise (parish) SP 942365
Apt 29.11.1845; 407a (1936); Map 1849, 6 chns (tithable parts only); waterbodies, building names, landowners.

1/2 Little Barford (parish) TL 188565
Apt 13.09.1844; 1188a (1188); Map 1840, 6 chns; waterbodies, houses, woods, plantations.

1/3 Battlesden (parish) SP 967284
Apt 31.03.1847; 1123a (all); Map 1845, [6 chns], by Keen and Son, 2, Parliament Street, Westminster; waterbodies, houses, woods, plantations, parkland (in great detail).

1/4 Biddenham (parish) TL 023500
Apt 29.09.1851; 21a (1760); Map 1852?, 3 chns, (tithable part only). Apt omits land use.

1/5 Biggleswade (parish) TL 203440
Apt 27.06.1837; 4311a (all); Map 1838, 3 chns; canal, waterbodies, houses, woods, parkland (named), open fields, field boundary ownerships, field gates, building names, road names, workhouse, mill, brick kilns, common (named), tithe-free land, public roads.

1/6 Billington (hamlet in parish of Leighton Buzzard) SP 940228
Apt 29.11.1845; 1196a (1196); Map 1847, 6 chns; railway, waterbodies, building names.

1/7 Bletsoe (parish) TL 027591
Apt 10.05.1839; 2240a (2239); Map 1840?, 4.5 chns; pictorial church; land belonging to Bletsoe poor named.

1/8 Bolnhurst (parish) TL 080588
Apt 19.10.1846; 979a (2160); Map 1846?, 4 chns (tithable parts only); foot/b'way, waterbodies, woods, field gates.

1/9 Bromham (parish) TL 009515
Apt 16.01.1844; 1798a (all); Map 1843?, 6 chns; foot/b'way.

1/10 Buckwood Stubbs (district in parish of Houghton Regis) TL 045165 [Buckwood Stubs]
Apt 19.03.1842; 258a (all); Map 1841, 6 chns, revised and corrected by John Griffin, H.Hempstead; woods, field gates.

1/11 Cardington (parish) TL 088464
Apt 18.06.1840; 5170a (all); Map 1840?, [4 chs]; waterbodies, houses, woods, plantations, orchard, ornamental gardens.

1/12 Clapham (parish) TL 038537
Apt 04.02.1843; 1984a (1982); Map 1839, 3 chns, 1st cl, by M. Reynolds, Bedford; construction lines, foot/b'way, waterbodies, houses, woods (named), plantations (named), parkland, field boundary ownerships.

1/13 Cockayne Hatley (parish) TL 260496
Apt 15.02.1839; 1156a (1161); Map 1848?, 6 chns; foot/b'way, waterbodies, houses, woods (named), parkland, lawn (named), field boundary ownerships; the map is described as a map of the property of the Honble and Revd Henry Cockayne Cust, reduced to one half the size of the original map made in 1826 by Charles Oakden, surveyor.

1/14 Cople (parish) TL 107480
Apt 11.06.1842; 2109a (all); Map 1838, 6 chns, by M. Reynolds; foot/b'way, turnpike roads, waterbodies, houses, woods (col, named), field boundary ownerships, building names, landowners, toll bar, mills.

1/15 Dunstable (parish) TL 021217
Apt 29.11.1839; 302a (390); Map 3 chns, surveyed by John Durham 1822 and revised 1840 by Joseph Mead; foot/b'way, waterbodies, houses, parkland (col), field boundary ownerships, road names, windmill.

1/16 Eaton Bray (parish) SP 982202
Apt 04.07.1848; 2336a (2650); Map 1849, 3 chns, 1st cl, by Wm Phi. Heard, Hitchin, Herts; construction lines, waterbodies, houses, open fields.

1/17 Edworth (parish) TL 224412
Apt 28.02.1838; 1099a (all); Map 1839, 3 chns; foot/b'way, waterbodies, houses, woods, gravel pit, parsonage; colour bands may indicate field boundary ownerships.

1/18 Eggington (hamlet in parish of Leighton Buzzard) SP 952259
Apt 27.10.1840; 1336a (all); Map 1841, 6 chns; waterbodies.

1/19 Eversholt (parish) SP 986335
Apt 13.07.1837; 2119a (2119); Map 1838, 6 chns, litho (Standidge); foot/b'way, waterbodies, woods, plantations, parkland, building names, field names, landowners.

1/20 Eyeworth (parish) TL 255453
Apt 14.02.1839; 1229a (all); Map 1842?, 6 chns, by M. Reynolds; foot/b'way, waterbodies, woods (col).

1/21 Flitwick (parish) TL 032345
Corn rent conversion, 1901; 0a (1700); Map 1900, OS 1:2500 annotated with tithe areas.

1/22 Goldington (parish) TL 067518
Apt 11.07.1842; 2530a (2735); Map 1843, 6 chns, by Charles Day, Colleyweston; canal, waterbodies, woods, marsh/bog, open fields, common.

1/23 Hawnes (parish) TL 088413 [Haynes]
Apt 09.05.1840; 2561a (2561); Map 1839, 4 chns, by P. Peachey, 17 Salisbury Square, London; foot/b'way, waterbodies, houses, woods, plantations, parkland (in detail), open fields (named), building names.

1/24 Heath and Reach (chapelry in parish of Leighton Buzzard) SP 932285
Apt 30.01.1841; 2396a (2396); Map 1841, 6 chns; foot/b'way, waterbodies, woods, plantations, common.

1/25 Henlow (parish) TL 177378
Apt 02.06.1852; 2a (2450); Map 1853?, 3 chns (tithable parts only).

1/26 Higham Gobion (parish) TL 099325
Apt 12.09.1837; 1288a (all); Map 1838, 6 chns, by W.G. Wallace; foot/b'way, turnpike roads, waterbodies, houses, farmyards, woods, arable (col), grassland (col), heath/moor, hedges, field boundary ownerships, building names; map is described as reduced from the original plan by direction of a meeting of the Higham tithe proprietors held 12 June 1838.

1/27 Hockcliffe (parish) SP 963269 [Hockliffe]
Apt 26.09.1845; 1021a (1021); Map 1839, 3 chns, by J. Witty; foot/b'way, turnpike roads, waterbodies, woods (sketchy), field gates, tollbar.

1/28 Holcut (parish) SP 947393 [Not listed]
Apt 24.10.1848; 880a (880); Map 1849?, 12 chns, by J. Palmer, Bedford; waterbodies, woods; map is described as a plan of an estate, the property of the Rev. B. Smith and others in Holcut parish. Apt omits land use.

1/29 Houghton Conquest (parish) TL 045415
Apt 31.07.1843; 3345a (all); Map 1843, 6 chns, by Richard Allerton; turnpike roads, toll gate, waterbodies, houses, farmyards, woods (named), parkland (in detail), road and riverside waste (col), building names, road names, brick kiln, ruins of mansion, milestone, smithy, pound, tithe barn, windmill, chapels (named).

1/30 Kempstone (parish) TL 011469 [Kempston]
Apt 23.11.1848; 66a (5160); Map 1849?, 3 chns, in 2 parts (tithable part only, with 6-chain location diagram); waterbodies, woods (named), landowners, tithe-free land.

1/31 Keysoe (parish) TL 074628
Apt 21.03.1840; 427a (3564); Map 1844, 6 chns (tithable parts only); woods (named), landowners.

1/32 Knotting (parish) TL 005625
Apt 22.04.1839; 1724a (1724); Map [6 chns] surveyed 1822, copied and corrected 1838 by M. Reynolds; foot/b'way, waterbodies, houses,

woods (named), field boundary ownerships, building names, private roads.

1/33 Leighton Buzzard (township) SP 927250
Apt 21.03.1840; 2315a (2315); Map 1841?, 3 chns; waterbodies, houses, farmyards, heath (named), field gates, building names, road names, workhouse, windmills (pictorial); field pattern is a mass of tiny enclosed strips. Scale bar is not figured.

1/34 Luton (parish) TL 096220
Apt 14.02.1842; 15232a (15750); Map 1842, 4 chns, in 2 parts, (urban part also at 1.5 chns) by Henry Davies, Kimpton; foot/b'way, waterbodies, houses, woods, plantations, parkland, open fields, building names, road names, windmill (pictorial), hamlet boundaries.

1/35 Maulden (parish) TL 059378
Corn rent conversion, 1874; 592a (2574); Map 1874?, 6 chns; foot/b'way, waterbodies, woods (named), building names.

1/36 Marston Mortaine (parish) SP 995420
Apt 23.09.1840; 4172a (4171); Map 're-surveyed' in 1837, 3 chns, by Glenister, Tring; waterbodies, field boundary ownerships, building names, woods (by name).

1/37 Melchbourne (parish) TL 029655
Apt 29.01.1841; 2574a (2574); Map 1847?, 6 chns; waterbodies, field gates.

1/38 Meppershall (parish) TL 143373
Apt 23.09.1845; 1949a (1949); Map 1848?, 3 chns, 1st cl; waterbodies, houses, woods, plantations, open fields (named), field boundary ownerships, building names, mill.

1/39 Millbrook (parish) TL 011385
Corn rent conversion, 1878; 749a (1450); Map 1878?, 6 chns; railways, gravel pit.

1/40 Milton Bryant (parish) SP 975304 [Milton Bryan]
Corn rent conversion, 1901; 1510a (1480); Map 1901, OS 1:2500 annotated with tithe areas.

1/41 Odell (parish) SP 960590
Apt 25.06.1851; 296a (2980); Map 1851?, 4 chns (tithable parts only); building names, road names, field names, landowners; map has small drawing of church in margin.

1/42 Pertenhall (parish) TL 087655
Apt 23.11.1838; 244a (1805); Map 1839, 3 chns; private road.

1/43 Potsgrove (parish) SP 947302
Apt 31.03.1847; 1385a (1385); Map 1845, 6 chns, by Keen and Son, 2 Parliament Street, Westminster; foot/b'way, waterbodies, houses, woods, plantations, parkland, orchard, fence.

1/44 Renhold (parish) TL 098524
Apt 07.12.1838; 2165a (all); Map 1839?, 5.5 chns; foot/b'way, turnpike roads, waterbodies, houses, woods, plantations, parkland, orchard, open fields; bridge named; map is described as produced at 'the Appeal Meeting' held 25 July 1839, countersigned by Assistant Tithe Commissioner Roger Kynaston.

1/45 Riseley (parish) TL 040627
Apt 19.10.1846; 252a (2980); Map 1847?, 3 chns; waterbodies.

1/46 Souldrope (parish) SP 978615 [Souldrop]
Apt 22.02.1842; 268a (1290); Map 1842, 4 chns, (tithable parts only); waterbodies, woods, landowners, glebe; 'Old inclosures formerly belonging to the Duke of Bedford' are not mapped.

1/47 Stagsden (parish) SP 979490
Apt 12.11.1839; 3387a (3386); Map 1839? [6 chns]; building names.

1/48 Stanbridge (chapelry in parish of Leighton Buzzard) SP 959237
Apt 17.04.1841; 1490a (all); Map 1841?, 6 chns; waterbodies.

1/49 Stepingley (parish) TL 012355 [Steppingly]
Corn rent conversion, 1872; 1252a (1060); Map undated, 6 chns; railway, waterbodies, houses, woods, building names, glebe. Apt omits land use.

1/50 Stotfold (parish) TL 211360
Apt 20.01.1847; 2323a (2323); Map 1849, 6 chns, in 2 parts, by J. Bailey Denton, Graveley, Herts, (including 4-chn enlargement of detail); waterbodies, houses, woods, marsh/bog, field boundary ownerships, building names, road names, landowners, mill, public drains and gravel pit, private roads; colours show types of tithe-free land.

1/51 Streatley (parish) TL 078282
Apt 22.02.1843; 2287a (2287); Map 1844, 3 chns, by I. Bailey Denton, Grays Inn, London; turnpike roads, waterbodies, houses, woods, open fields, building names.

1/52 Studham (parish) (partly in Herts) TL 020158
Apt 31.12.1851; 1738a (3100); Map 1852, 3 chns, by James Louis Atty, Ashridge, Herts; hill-drawing, waterbodies, houses, woods, plantations, orchard, open fields, sand or stone pits.

1/53 Sutton (parish) TL 220475
Apt 26.08.1839; 207a (2230); Map 1838, 3 chns; foot/b'way, waterbodies, woods, field boundary ownerships, landowners, tithe-free land; map is described as 'of the Park and other Land at Sutton in the County of Bedford being part of the Estate of Sir John Montagn Burgoyne Bart, taken for the commutation of Tithe'.

1/54 Tingrith (parish) TL 004324
Apt 22.11.1838; 946a (all); Map 1839, 4 chns; open fields, detached portions of adjoining districts.

1/55 Toddington (parish) TL 018283
Corn rent conversion, 1911; 2079a (5390); Map 1901, OS 1:2500 annotated with tithe areas.

1/56 Totternhoe (parish) SP 995207
Apt 16.02.1841; 2394a (2394); Map 1840, 3 chns, by J.O. Brown (for John Griffin of Hemel Hempstead); hill-drawing, waterbodies, houses, woods, orchard, heath/moor, open fields (with balks), building names, road names, field names, quarries (in detail), water mill, military station 1823, tumuli, commons, roadside waste (col); map heavily annotated and coloured. Apt has cropping information.

1/57 Turvey (parish) SP 956522
Apt 13.06.1837; 3945a (3944); Map 1843, 6 chns, in 2 parts, by Wm Thomas Heard, Saint Margarets, Ware, (including 3-chn enlargement of detail); foot/b'way, waterbodies, woods (named), parkland, heath/moor, field names, mill, modus land (col).

1/58 Old Warden (parish) TL 140442
Apt 03.05.1849; 13a (3350); Map 1850?, 4 chns (tithable part only); road names, landowners.

1/59 Westoning (parish) TL 033322
Apt 13.11.1839; 1683a (all); Map 1841, 6 chns.

1/60 Whipsnade (parish) TL 020177
Apt 10.02.1842; 1205a (1205); Map 1844?, 3 chns; foot/b'way, waterbodies, houses, woods (col), plantations (col), parkland (col), hedges.

1/61 Willington (parish) TL 121489
Apt 20.08.1839; 1642a (all); Map [6 chns] surveyed 1822 and copied and corrected 1838, by M. Reynolds; foot/b'way, waterbodies, woods (col, named), field boundary ownerships, building names, glebe, mill.

1/62 Woburn (parish) SP 950333
Apt 29.10.1850; 85a (3200); Map 1851, 3 chns (tithable parts only, tinted); foot/b'way, waterbodies, building names, road names.

1/63 Wootton (parish) TL 010444
Apt 26.11.1844; 20a (3711); Map 1845, 6 chns, by Charles Day, Colleyweston, (tithable part only); milestone.

1/64 Yelden (parish) TL 011665
Apt 17.08.1842; 1912a (1912); Map 1842?, 4 chns; waterbodies, open fields, common.

Berkshire

PRO IR29 and IR30 2/1–157

188 tithe districts: 459,622 acres
157 tithe commutations: 375,578 acres
96 voluntary tithe agreements, 61 compulsory tithe awards

Tithe and tithe commutation

Some 84 per cent of Berkshire tithe districts were subject to payment of tithes in 1836 and fifty-five districts were wholly tithable at this date (Fig. 14). The main causes of tithe exemption in Berkshire were commutation at the time of enclosure, modus payments in lieu of tithes, exemption of former manorial, monastic, or Crown land, merger of tithes in the land, and exemption by prescription.

Assistant tithe commissioners and local tithe agents who worked in Berkshire are listed in Table 2.1. In contrast to the adjoining county of Hampshire, the work of valuing tithe rent-charge in Berkshire was not dominated by any one tithe valuer. Seven individuals or partnerships valued the tithe rent-charge of five or more districts but no fewer than forty-six others valued tithes in this county (Table 2.2). All but thirteen Berkshire tithe valuers were resident in the county or adjoining counties; twelve came from in or near London and one (W. T. Heard) from near Hertford.

Tithe maps

About 8 per cent of Berkshire's 157 tithe maps are sealed as first class. Only two second-class maps carry construction lines and it may be surmised that a majority of this county's tithe maps are derived from earlier surveys, though copying is explicitly acknowledged on only six maps. Berkshire tithe maps are drawn at scales ranging from one inch to one chain to one inch to twelve chains. Just under half of the maps are in the recommended scale range of one inch to three to four chains, and 42 per cent are at the six-chain scale (Table 2.3).

Woodland is portrayed on 69 per cent of the county's tithe maps, parkland on 36 per cent, marsh and bog on 13 per cent and heath and moor on 12 per cent. On the other hand, agricultural land use is less well mapped; only 13 per cent of maps depict arable and grass and less than 4 per cent show gardens. Field boundary ownership is indicated on 27 per cent of the maps and some are coloured to indicate estate boundaries or lands subject to modus.

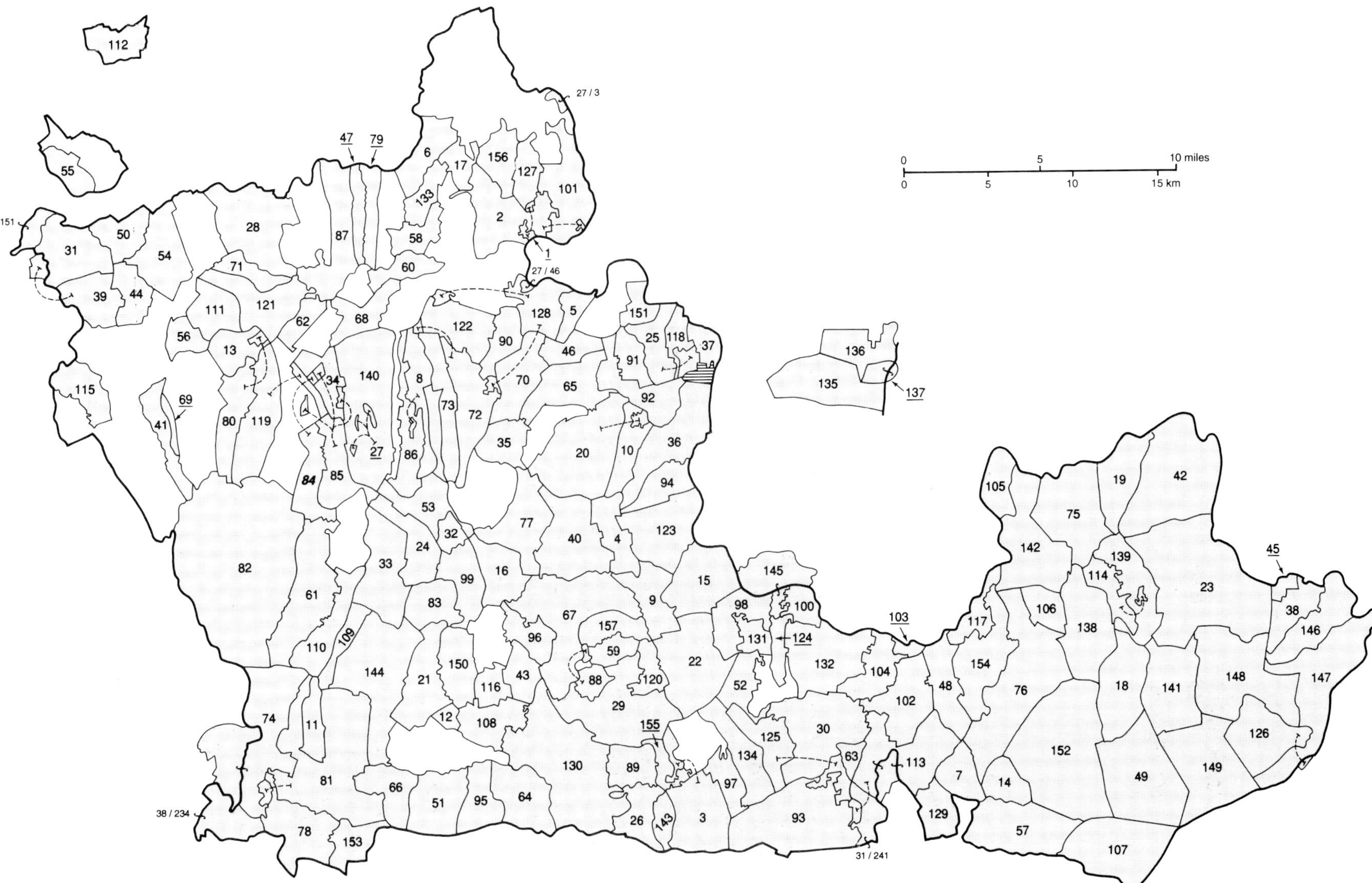

Fig. 14 Berkshire: tithe district boundaries.

Ninety-five Berkshire tithe maps can be attributed to a particular map-maker; the most prolific were William Baillie of Newbury, Messrs Phillips and Westbury of Andover, Hampshire, and William Fuller of Reading (Table 2.2). Six of the unattributed maps are possibly by Daniel Trinder of Cirencester as they use colour bands to show both cultivation and field boundary ownership, a characteristic of the 'Cirencester school' of tithe map-makers (see Wiltshire). Only one Berkshire map has any decorative embellishment: on the East Shefford map a bird is pictured holding the scale bar in its talons.

Table 2.1. *Agreements and awards for commutation of tithes in Berkshire*

Assistant commissioner/ local tithe agent	*Number of agreements**	*Number of awards*
Thomas Clements Parr	35	0
Francis Offley Martin	0	25
Thomas James Tatham	0	20
Joseph Townsend	10	2
F. Browne Browne	10	1
Roger Kynaston	10	0
Thomas Smith Woolley	9	1
Horace William Meteyard	7	0
John Mee Mathew	6	1
John Maurice Herbert	0	5
Henry Jemmett	5	0
John Pickering	5	0
William Wakeford Attree	0	3
William Heard	3	0
Frederick Leigh	0	1
John Penny	0	1
Charles Pym	1	0
Tithe Commissioners	0	1

*Computed from the number of extant reports on tithe agreements in the tithe files [PRO IR 18].

Table 2.2. *Tithe valuers and tithe map-makers in Berkshire*

Name and address (in Berkshire unless indicated)	*Number of districts*	*Acreage*
Tithe valuers		
Thomas Edward Washbourne, Newbury	10	32,833
Francis Hawkes, Reading	8	19,977
William Ellis, Stratfield Mortimer	7	21,822
John Terry, Maidenhead	6	26,640
Daniel Trinder, Cirencester, Gloucestershire	5	11,334
William Trumper, Dorney, Buckinghamshire	5	20,319
William Dodd, Peppard, Oxfordshire	5	4,749
Others [46]	111	237,904
Attributed tithe map-makers		
William Baillie, Newbury	8	28,202
Phillips and Westbury, Andover, Hampshire	8	20,803
William Henry Fuller, Reading	8	16,408
Hawkes and Sons, Reading	7	18,675
Daniel Trinder, Cirencester, Gloucestershire	6	15,569
Joseph Dymock	5	7,275
Others [32]	52	126,495

Table 2.3. *The tithe maps of Berkshire: scales and classes*

Scale in chains/inch	*All maps*		*First Class*		*Second Class*	
	Number	*Acreage*	*Number*	*Acreage*	*Number*	*Acreage*
>3	1	36	0	0	1	36
3	65	161,683	11	36.022	54	125,661
4	12	22,220	1	2,850	11	19,370
5	4	10,119	0	0	4	10,119
6	67	159,461	0	0	67	159,461
<6	9	22,059	0	0	9	22,059
TOTAL	157	375,578	12	38,872	145	336,706

Table 2.4. *The tithe maps of Berkshire: dates*

	1837	*1838*	*1839*	*1840*	*1841*	*1842*	*1843*	*1844*	*1845*	*1846*	*1847*	*1848*	*1849*	*1850*	*>1850*
All maps	3	9	21	33	27	14	14	2	6	3	5	3	9	3	4
1st class	0	1	2	3	2	1	0	0	2	0	0	0	1	0	0
2nd class	3	8	19	30	25	13	14	2	4	3	5	3	8	3	4

Berkshire

2/1 Abingdon St Nicholas (parish) SU 500971 [Not listed]
Apt 10.03.1842; 177a (177); Map 1842, 6 chns, in 2 parts; waterbodies, plantations, road names; built-up part generalised (col).

2/2 Abingdon St Helen (parish) SU 490981 [Not listed]
Apt 10.03.1842; 3109a (3184); Map 1842, 6 chns; waterbodies, woods, plantations.

2/3 Aldermaston (parish) SU 596645
Apt 06.05.1839; 1441a (3669); Map 1841?, 3 chns; foot/b'way, canal, waterbodies, houses, woods (col), plantations (col), parkland (in detail, col), building names, mill, osiers.

2/4 Aldworth (parish) SU 549800
Apt 08.06.1840; 1786a (1960); Map 1840, 3 chns, by Hawkes and Son, Reading; foot/b'way, waterbodies, houses, woods (named, col), plantations (named), hedge ownership, field gates, building names, roadside waste (col).

2/5 Appleford (hamlet in parish of Sutton Courtenay) SU 525928
Apt 22.04.1839; 844a (all); Map 1839, 6 chns; waterbodies, hedge ownership.

2/6 Appleton (parish) SP 440017
Apt 08.06.1840; 1992a (all); Map 1840, 6 chns, in 2 parts, by John Hardy, Oxford, (including enlargement of common fields, 3 chns, 1843); open fields, building names.

2/7 Arborfield (parish) SU 753668
Apt 11.06.1841; 1467a (all); Map 1839, 3 chns, by William Henry Fuller, Reading; foot/b'way, waterbodies, houses, woods (named), plantations (named), parkland (named), hedge ownership, fence ownership, field gates, building names, road names, field names, gravel pit, brick kiln, well, osiers, boundary post, pound, mill.

2/8 Ardington (parish) SU 433885
Apt 08.07.1842; 1776a (all); Map 1840, 6 chns, by Phillips and Westbury, Andover; railway, foot/b'way, canal, waterbodies, houses, woods, plantations, parkland, arable (col), grassland (col), gardens, building names, road names, mill, fish pond, barns, downs.

2/9 Ashampstead (parish) SU 570764
Apt 11.09.1844; 2057a (2057); Map 1845, 6 chns, by Phillips and Westbury, Andover; foot/b'way, waterbodies, houses, woods, plantations, parkland, arable (col), grassland (col), orchards, open fields.

2/10 Aston Tirrold (parish) SU 558850
Apt 16.05.1840; 1674a (1674); Map 1840?, 6 chns; hedge ownership, field names, tithe-free land (col), glebe.

2/11 Avington (parish) SU 366700
Apt 26.02.1839; 1143a (all); Map 1838, 12 chns; houses, farmyards, woods, arable (col), grassland (col), hedge ownership, fences, field acreages.

2/12 Bagnor (tithing in parish of Speen) SU 449697
Apt 18.02.1848; 437a (?); Map 1848, 6 chns.

2/13 Balking otherwise Baulking (hamlet in parish of Uffington) SU 324912
Apt 21.11.1838; 1443a (1443); Map 1839, 6 chns; railway, foot/b'way, waterbodies, houses, woods, field boundary ownerships, field gates.

2/14 Barkham (parish) SU 780664
Apt 01.02.1840; 1358a (all); Map copied and revised 1839, 6 chns; woods (named), building names, field names, heath (named), Crown allotments; the map is described as 'map of the parish of Barkham, part of the late Forest of Windsor...as copied in the Year of Our Lord 1839 from the map accompanying the Award which was made Anno Domini 1821 and altered to the state of the parish at the present time'.

2/15 Basildon (parish) SU 603776
Apt 27.08.1838; 3083a (all); Map 1839, 6 chns, by Phillips and Westbury, Andover; railway, foot/b'way, waterbodies, houses, woods, plantations, parkland, heath/moor, building names.

2/16 Beedon (parish) SU 480781
Apt 28.08.1841; 2004a (2004); Map 1841, 6 chns, ? by Daniel Trinder; waterbodies, houses, woods, plantations, arable (col), grassland (col), field boundary ownerships, building names; colour bands show arable, grass and field boundary ownership.

2/17 Besselsleigh (parish) SP 458013
Apt 14.07.1841; 893a (all); Map 1842?, 6 chns; waterbodies, houses, woods, plantations, parkland, arable, grassland, gardens.

2/18 Binfield (parish) SU 850720
Apt 22.11.1837; 3208a (all); Map 1838?, 6 chns; waterbodies, woods (named), parkland, building names, road names, field names, windmill.

2/19 Bisham (parish) SU 850833
Apt 24.02.1851; 2485a (2520); Map 1845, 4 chns; waterbodies, houses, open fields.

2/20 Blewberry (parish) SU 530843
Apt 31.01.1839; 6814a (6814); Map 1838, 6 chns, from award and other maps; foot/b'way, turnpike roads, private roads, waterbodies, hedge ownership, building names, road names, hamlet boundaries, common. (Map in PRO IR 30 is a copy; original is in PRO IR 77/1.)

2/21 Boxford (parish) SU 433720
Apt 12.01.1838; 2769a (2769); Map 1840?, 6 chns; foot/b'way, woods, plantations, heath/moor, road names.

2/22 Bradfield (parish) SU 595728
Apt 13.11.1846; 4384a (all); Map 1847, 8 chns; waterbodies, woods, parkland, osier beds.

2/23 Bray (parish) SU 901775
Apt 20.01.1843; 9102a (9102); Map 1840, 3 chns, in 2 parts, by James Richardson, West Middx Water Works, New Road, surveyor and engineer; construction lines, railway, foot/b'way, waterbodies, woods, marsh/bog, fences, building names, tithing boundaries, gravel pits, occupation roads, public drain, ditch; woodland indicated by name. (Map in PRO IR 30 is a copy; original is in PRO IR 77/2.)

2/24 Brightwaltham (parish) SU 432800 [Brightwalton]
Apt 14.03.1838; 2039a (all); Map 1840, 4 chns, by William Baillie, C.E., Newbury, for Thomas E. Washbourne; foot/b'way, waterbodies, houses, woods, plantations, hedge ownership, field boundary ownerships.

2/25 Brightwell (parish) SU 575905
Apt 08.06.1840; 2024a (2024); Map 1841?, 6 chns; waterbodies, woods, orchards, open fields.

2/26 Brimpton (parish) SU 563645
Apt 07.06.1839; 1036a (1692); Map 1841, 3 chns; waterbodies, woods, plantations, arable (col), orchards, hedge ownership, fences.

2/27 Bryants Fee (tything in parish of Wantage) SU 407867 [Not listed]
Apt 01.02.1844; 173a (?); Map 1844, [6 chns], by Neighbour and Son, Oxford; waterbodies, road names.

2/28 Buckland (parish) SU 340985
Apt 19.11.1839; 4434a (4434); Map 1842, [6 chns]; foot/b'way, canal, waterbodies, bridle road, township or tithing boundary.

2/29 Bucklebury and Hawkeridge (tithing in parish of Bucklebury) SU 552702
Apt 29.12.1840; 5252a (5252); Map 1842?, 3 chns, in 3 parts, litho; foot/b'way, waterbodies, woods, plantations, parkland, open fields, fences, field gates. (Map in PRO IR 30 is a copy; original is in PRO IR 77/3.)

2/30 Burghfield (parish) SU 673690
Apt 14.11.1842; 4237a (all); Map 1839, 6 chns, by Hawkes and Son, Reading; hill-drawing, foot/b'way, canal, waterbodies, houses, woods (named), marsh/bog, hedge ownership, fences, field gates, building names, field names, common; hills named.

2/31 Buscot (parish) SU 229966
Apt 07.05.1839; 2856a (all); Map 1839, 4 chns, by John Hardy, Oxford; canal, houses, parkland, road names, landowners, weirs, wharf and pound; bridges named.

2/32 Catmore (parish) SU 450804
Apt 06.06.1846; 697a (all); Map 1846?, 6 chns; waterbodies, woods, plantations, hedge ownership, fences, field gates, private road.

2/33 Chaddleworth (parish) SU 412788
Apt 24.02.1841; 3344a (3319); Map 1840, 7 chns, ? by Daniel Trinder; foot/b'way, waterbodies, houses, woods, plantations, parkland, arable (col), grassland (col), field boundary ownerships, building names, tithe barn.

2/34 Challow East (hamlet in parish of Letcombe) SU 382892
Apt 31.10.1846; 1297a (1297); Map 1847, 6 chns; waterbodies, houses, building names.

2/35 Chilton (parish) SU 484856
Apt 23.04.1840; 1416a (all); Map 1840, 3 chns, by Joseph Dymock; foot/b'way, waterbodies, arable (by annotation), grassland (by annotation), building names, down.

2/36 Cholsey (parish) SU 590855
Apt 13.12.1841; 2827a (4447); Map 1842, 3 chns, 1st cl, surveyed by William Baillie, C.E., Newbury, for Thomas E. Washbourne, (tithable parts only); railway, foot/b'way, waterbodies, houses, woods, orchards, hedges, building names, field names, common; colour bands may show land or tithe ownership.

2/37 Clapcot and Queen's Arbour (liberty and extra-parocial district in parish of Wallingford, Allhallows) SU 606909 [Not listed]
Apt 13.09.1839; 822a (821); Map 1837, 3 chns; turnpike roads, canal, waterbodies, houses, woods, plantations, orchards, marsh/bog, building names, road names, ferry, infants school, keepers house, mill, towpath, tithe ownership boundary.

2/38 Clewer (parish) SU 946755 [Clewer Green]
Apt 14.11.1839; 1666a (1666); Map 1839, 3 chns, by H. Walter, Windsor; construction lines, foot/b'way, waterbodies, houses, woods, parkland, hedges, fences, field gates, building names, road names, cavalry barracks, gravel pits, gas works, gaol, boundary stones. (Map in PRO IR 30 is a copy; original is in PRO IR 77/4.)

2/39 Coleshill (parish) SU 245941
Apt 21.12.1840; 2301a (2301); Map 1841?, 8 chns, by F.J. Kelsey, Salisbury; waterbodies, houses, building names.

2/40 Compton (parish) SU 522799
Apt 21.10.1840; 3795a (all); Map 1841, 6 chns, surveyed by William Baillie, C.E., Newbury, for T.E. Washbourne; foot/b'way, waterbodies, houses, woods, plantations, hedges.

2/41 Compton Beauchamp (parish) SU 284857
Apt 18.05.1838; 1454a (all); Map 1838, 8 chns, in 2 parts, by Chapman Son and Webb, Arundel St, Strand, (including 4-chn enlargement of village); foot/b'way, canal, waterbodies, houses, farmyards, woods, plantations, parkland, orchards, building names, road names, sand and stone pits, mere stones; meaning of colour bands is unclear.

2/42 Cookham (parish) SU 885835
Apt 22.08.1843; 6509a (6509); Map 1843, 3 chns; canal, waterbodies, houses, open fields, commons (col).

2/43 Courage (tithing in parish of Chieveley) SU 492722 [Curridge]
Apt 26.08.1839; 1273a (1273); Map 1840?, 3 chns; foot/b'way, waterbodies, houses, woods, plantations, parkland, heath/moor, field gates.

2/44 Great Coxwell (parish) SU 268944
Apt 08.03.1843; 1410a (1410); Map 1843?, 4 chns, by F.J. Kelsey, Salisbury; foot/b'way, waterbodies, houses.

2/45 Dedworth (hamlet in parish of New Windsor) SU 945773
Apt 03.03.1848; 347a (347); Map 1848, 3 chns, by William Trumper, Dorney; foot/b'way, waterbodies, houses, building names, boundary stones.

2/46 Didcot (parish) SU 530905
Apt 13.02.1840; 1094a (all); Map 1841?, 6 chns; railways, foot/b'way, waterbodies, field boundary ownerships, field gates, building names; private and public footpaths and roads are shown.

2/47 Draycott Moor (township in parish of Longworth) SU 399984 [Not listed]
Apt 07.04.1842; 1042a (1041); Map 1842, 3 chns, by J. Dymock; waterbodies, houses.

2/48 Earley (liberty in parish of Sonning) SU 744718
Apt 27.10.1840; 2223a (?); Map 1843?, 3 chns, by Hawkes and Sons, Reading; railway, foot/b'way, waterbodies, houses, woods, parkland, building names, road names, botanic gardens.

2/49 Easthampstead (parish) SU 863663
Apt 15.06.1841; 5187a (5186); Map 1841, 6 chns; foot/b'way, waterbodies, houses, woods, plantations, parkland (in detail), heath/moor, building names, brick kiln, fuel allotment, workhouse; colours show tithing practices. (Apt in PRO includes a 9-chn map of the district.)

2/50 Eaton Hastings (parish) SU 260975
Apt 07.04.1842; 1487a (1330); Map 1842, 4 chns, by Anthony Fidel, Faringdon, Berks; foot/b'way, plantations (by annotation).

2/51 Enbourne (parish) SU 440652
Apt 22.04.1840; 2486a (all); Map 1840, 3 chns, 1st cl, by William Baillie, C.E., Newbury; construction lines, canal, houses, hedge ownership, fences.

2/52 Englefield (parish) SU 624720
Apt 20.10.1840; 1427a (all); Map 1843, 6 chns; foot/b'way, waterbodies, houses, woods (col), plantations (col), parkland (col), marsh/bog.

2/53 Farnborough (parish) SU 438820
Apt 28.12.1838; 1844a (1844); Map 1839, 6 chns, ? by Daniel Trinder, Cirencester; waterbodies, woods (col), arable (col), grassland (col), field boundary ownerships, building names; colour bands show arable, grass and field boundary ownership.

2/54 Farringdon (parish) SU 284963 [Faringdon]
Apt 06.06.1848; 3235a (6910); Map 1849-50, 3 chns, 1st cl, in 3 parts, by J.Bravender and Trinder, Cirencester, (tithable parts only: Westbrook and Port at 6 chns; Wadley, Littleworth and Thrupp at 3 chns; including 12-chn index); construction lines, foot/b'way, waterbodies, houses, woods, arable (col), grassland (col), open fields, field boundary ownerships, field gates, building names, landowners, gravel pit, weir, lodge, common; colour bands show arable, grass and field boundary ownership.

2/55 Little Farringdon (hamlet in parish of Langford) SP 228014 [Little Faringdon]
Apt 28.10.1840; 1123a (?); Map 1841, 9 chns, ? by Richard Hall; foot/b'way, woods, arable (col), grassland (col), orchards, field boundary ownerships; colour bands show arable, grass and field boundary ownerships.

2/56 Fernham (hamlet in parish of Shrivenham) SU 295918
Apt 07.10.1841; 1013a (all); Map 1842?, 3 chns, by Anthony Fidel, Farringdon, Berks; waterbodies, woods, hedges, fences, field gates, bridle road, stone walls.

2/57 Finchampstead (parish) SU 790638
Apt 03.01.1844; 3926a (3926); Map 1841, 3 chns; waterbodies, houses, woods, plantations, parkland, orchards; map has note of acceptance by landowners.

2/58 Frilford (hamlet in parish of Marcham) SU 438972
Apt 31.12.1850; 1217a (all); Map 1853, 6 chns, by W.H. Davies, Abingdon; foot/b'way, turnpike roads, waterbodies, open fields, building names, toll gate.

2/59 Frilsham (parish) SU 548735
Apt 10.05.1839; 990a (all); Map 1839, 3 chns, by John Harris, Thatcham; foot/b'way, brick kiln, common; woodland shown by name.

2/60 Garford (hamlet in parish of Marcham) SU 426955
Apt 21.12.1850; 1024a (?); Map 1852, 6 chns, by W.H. Davies, Abingdon; building names.

2/61 East Garston (parish) SU 366768
Apt 30.06.1841; 4342a (4342); Map 1840, 4 chns, surveyed by William

Baillie, C.E., Newbury, for Thomas E. Washbourne; foot/b'way, waterbodies, houses, woods (col), plantations (col), hedges.

2/62 Goosey (township in parish of Stanford in the Vale) SU 366926
Apt 11.01.1848; 959a (958); Map 1847, 6 chns, by William Bryan Wood, Barnbridge, Chippenham; foot/b'way, waterbodies, houses, building names.

2/63 Grazely (hamlet or township) SU 695675
Apt 06.06.1846; 521a (520); Map 1847, 3 chns, by Francis Hawkes, Reading; railway, waterbodies, houses, woods, hedge ownership, building names, pound.

2/64 Greenham (tithing in parish of Thatcham) SU 494651
Apt 18.06.1840; 2531a (2531); Map 1840, 3 chns, 1st cl; construction lines, foot/b'way, turnpike roads, canal, waterbodies, houses, woods, plantations, open fields, hedges, fences, field gates, building names, seed mill, towpath.

2/65 Hagbourne (parish) SU 523885 [Not listed]
Apt 15.06.1841; 2756a (2755); Map 1840, 6 chns, railway, open fields; double lines may show balks.

2/66 Hamstead Marshall (parish) SU 415668
Apt 02.04.1840; 1840a (1839); Map 1840, 3 chns, 1st cl, surveyed by William Baillie, C.E., Newbury, for Thomas E. Washbourne; construction lines, canal, waterbodies, houses, woods, hedges.

2/67 Hampstead Norris (parish) SU 520750 [Hampstead Norreys]
Apt 08.06.1839; 5769a (5769); Map 1842?, 8 chns, ? by U.B. Vines; foot/b'way, waterbodies, houses, woods, parkland, hedges, field boundary ownerships, building names, road names, cattle road, glebe (col).

2/68 West Hanney and North Denchurch and Ploughley or Filberts (township and tithings in parish of West Hanney) SU 400925
Apt 11.05.1842; 1698a (1990); Map 1842, 6 chns, by Joseph Dymock; foot/b'way, waterbodies, houses, hedges, fences, field gates, building names, field names; field boundaries are edged with curious symbols which may indicate hedges, fences or both.

2/69 Hardwell (district in parish of Uffington) SU 288872 [Not listed]
Apt 30.06.1848; 345a (all); Map 1849, 8 chns, ? by John Bravender; waterbodies, houses, woods, plantations, arable, grassland; colour bands show arable, grass and field boundary ownership.

2/70 Harwell (parish) SU 494890
Apt 30.07.1839; 2424a (2482); Map 1840, 6 chns, by Richard Davis, Banbury; railways, turnpike roads, waterbodies, road names.

2/71 Hatford (parish) SU 336954
Apt 16.05.1839; 999a (999); Map 1840?, [?4 chns], by John Morton; field gates, bridle road, glebe; buildings are shown by sketchy pictograms.

2/72 East Hendred (parish) SU 465875
Apt 09.01.1840; 3100a (3099); Map 1841, 3 chns, 1st cl, in 2 parts, by William Baillie, C.E., Newbury, (including 3-chn enlargement of meadow); construction lines, hill-drawing, railway, canal, waterbodies, houses, woods, plantations, hedge ownership, tumulus, common.

2/73 West Hendred (parish) SU 449877
Apt 08.04.1841; 1974a (1973); Map 1841, 6 chns, in 2 parts, by Joseph Dimock, (including location diagram); waterbodies, houses, grassland (col), fences, road names, field names; symbols along field boundaries may be fences.

2/74 Hungerford (parish) (partly in Wilts) SU 340685
Apt 08.05.1848; 3908a (6940); Map 1849, 6 chns, (tithable parts only); railway, foot/b'way, canal, waterbodies, woods (col), plantations, building names. Apt omits land use.

2/75 Hurley (parish) SU 822818
Apt 26.01.1843; 4098a (4097); Map 1843, 3 chns; foot/b'way, canal, waterbodies, houses, woods (col), plantations (col), parkland (col), orchard (col), marsh/bog (col).

2/76 Hurst (parish) (including the hamlet of Broad Hinton in Wilts) SU 798722
Apt 28.01.1841; 6846a (6845); Map 1840, 6 chns, by W.H. Fuller, Reading; railway, waterbodies, houses, woods, plantations, parkland (in detail), marsh/bog, common.

2/77 East Ilsley (parish) SU 493810
Apt 13.04.1839; 2980a (all); Map 1839?, 5 chns, by G.H. Eliot, 39 Great Marlborough St, London; foot/b'way, turnpike roads, waterbodies, houses, woods (named), open fields, hedges, field boundary ownerships, building names, road names, field names, windmill, milestone, chalk pit, downs, (named, with boundaries, col), farm names.

2/78 Inkpen (parish) SU 362638
Apt 02.02.1841; 2850a (2850); Map 1841, 4 chns, 1st cl, in 3 parts, by P. Cassidy, London, (includes 'the weir', around the canal, 4 chns, 1842, by William Baillie, C.E., Newbury, and a further sketch of 'the weir' on the main map); construction lines, canal, waterbodies, houses, heath/moor (col), hedges, field boundary ownerships, building names.

2/79 Kingston Bagpuize (parish) SU 407984
Apt 26.11.1844; 1098a (all); Map 1845, 3 chns; turnpike roads, waterbodies, woods (col), hedge ownership, field gates.

2/80 Kingstone Lisle and Fawler (hamlet in parish of Sparsholt) SU 321870 [Kingston Lisle]
Apt 08.06.1840; 2154a (2060); Map 1843, 3 chns, by Wm Thos Heard, St Margarets, Ware; railway, canal, waterbodies, houses, woods, plantations, parkland (in detail), building names.

2/81 Kintsbury (parish) SU 380667 [Kintbury]
Apt 15.07.1841; 7645a (7645); Map 1842?, 3 chns, in 2 parts; foot/b'way, canal and bank, waterbodies, houses, woods, plantations, parkland, hedge ownership, fences, field gates, road names, boundary posts, footbridge (named); meaning of land-use symbols is unclear.

2/82 Lambourne (parish) SU 325785 [Lambourn]
Apt 03.06.1848; 14830a (14830); Map 1845, 3 chns, 1st cl, in 3 parts, by William Bryan Wood, Barnbridge, Chippenham; construction lines, waterbodies, houses, open fields, hedge ownership, building names.

2/83 Leckhampstead (chapelry and tithing in parish of Chieveley) SU 439764
Apt 07.09.1841; 1742a (1742); Map 1841?, 3 chns, by Henry Adams, Chieveley, Berks; foot/b'way, waterbodies, houses, woods, heath/moor, field gates, sand or stone pits.

2/84 Letcombe Bassett, otherwise Upper Letcombe (parish) SU 369835
Apt 17.04.1850; 30a (1260); Map 1851?, 6 chns, (tithable parts only).

2/85 Letcombe Regis (parish) SU 383844
Apt 18.02.1841; 2424a (2424); Map 1841, 6 chns, ? by Daniel Trinder, Cirencester; foot/b'way, waterbodies, houses, woods, plantations, parkland, arable (col), grassland (col), hedges; colour bands show arable, grass and field boundary ownerships.

2/86 East Lockinge (parish) SU 425870
Apt 28.10.1840; 2822a (2822); Map 1840, 6 chns, by Phillips and Westbury, Andover; railway, foot/b'way, canal, waterbodies, houses, woods, plantations, parkland, arable (col), grassland (col), gardens (col), field boundary ownerships, building names, road names, field names, kitchen gardens, down. Colour bands show arable, grass and field boundary ownerships.

2/87 Longworth and Charney (hamlet and chapelry in parish of Longworth) SU 390975
Apt 01.07.1845; 3374a (3374); Map 1846, 6 chns, by Wm Bryan Wood; waterbodies, houses, building names.

2/88 Marlston otherwise Martleston (tithing in parish of Bucklebury) SU 532719 [Not listed]
Apt 08.06.1839; 756a (?); Map 1840, 6 chns; waterbodies, houses, woods, parkland, open fields.

2/89 Midgham (chapelry or tithing in parish of Thatcham) SU 558672
Apt 02.09.1841; 1430a (1430); Map 1839, 3 chns, 1st cl, by John Harris,

Thatcham, Berks; construction lines, canal; woodland indicated by name.

2/90 Milton (parish) SU 485915
Apt 08.06.1840; 1431a (all); Map 1841, 5 chns, 'copied from the Award Map of the Parish' by John Harris, Thatcham, Berks; railway, foot/b'way, waterbodies, building names, mill.

2/91 North Moreton (parish) SU 560904
Apt 11.08.1842; 1103a (1103); Map 1845, 3 chns, 1st cl, by Wm Bryan Wood, Barnbridge, Chippenham; construction lines, houses.

2/92 South Moreton (parish) SU 562882
Apt 27.09.1849; 326a (1470); Map 1849, 3 chns, by Washbourne and Keen, 8 Cannon Row, Westminster; railway, foot/b'way, waterbodies, houses, field road; map is described as a map of Fulscote farm in South Moreton parish. District is apportioned by holding.

2/93 Mortimer (parish) SU 655642
Apt 27.03.1838; 5953a (all); Map 1838, 6 chns, by Phillips and Westbury, Andover; foot/b'way, waterbodies, houses, woods (named), plantations (named), parkland, arable (col), grassland (col), gardens, heath/moor, building names, road names, field names, poor's allotment.

2/94 Moulsford (chapelry or parish) SU 577833
Apt 24.11.1840; 1430a (1429); Map 1841?, 6 chns, ? by Henry Dixon, Oxford; turnpike roads, waterbodies, woods (named), orchards, heath/moor, hedge ownership, building names, road names, barns, common.

2/95 Newbury (parish) SU 465655
Apt 30.06.1840; 1722a (1722); Map 1839, 3 chns, 1st cl, ? by Cornelius B. Davis, The Hitchen, East Woodhay; construction lines, waterbodies, houses, woods, plantations, open fields, hedges, fences, field gates, field names; one farm not mapped in detail.

2/96 Oare (chapelry in parish of Chieveley) SU 496747
Apt 08.05.1839; 1429a (1421); Map 1840?, 3 chns, (tithable parts only); hill-drawing, foot/b'way, waterbodies, houses, woods, plantations, heath/moor, field gates, building names, landowners, quarry or sandstone pit, lodges.

2/97 Padworth (parish) SU 618663
Apt 11.03.1838; 1176a (all); Map 1840, 6 chns, by Phillips and Westbury, Andover; canal, waterbodies, houses, woods, plantations, parkland, marsh/bog, heath/moor, building names, mill, lodge, wharf, boundary posts, brewery, fish pond.

2/98 Pangbourn (parish) SU 619760 [Pangbourne]
Apt 06.04.1839; 1926a (1925); Map 1839, 3 chns; railway, waterbodies, houses, woods, plantations, parkland, hedge ownership, fences, field gates, building names, sand or stone pits, marsh (col, named).

2/99 Peasemore (parish) SU 461774
Apt 28.04.1838; 2048a (all); Map 1840?, 6 chns; foot/b'way, waterbodies, houses, woods, parkland, field boundary ownerships, field gates, road names, sand or stone pit.

2/100 Purley (parish) SU 660763
Apt 07.08.1839; 877a (all); Map 1840, 3 chns, by W.H. Fuller; hill-drawing, railway, canal, waterbodies, houses, woods, plantations, parkland, open fields, fences, building names, field names, osiers, lodges, garden paths.

2/101 Radley (parish) SU 524998
Apt 22.05.1849; 2994a (2994); Map 1849?, 3 chns; railway, foot/b'way, waterbodies, houses, woods (col, named), parkland (named), hedges, fences, building names, ferry, lodge, shrubberies, osiers; areas belonging to other parishes coloured.

2/102 Saint Giles Reading (parish) SU 719714 [Not listed]
Apt 26.02.1839; 2539a (2538); Map 1840, 3 chns, by W.H. Fuller, Reading; foot/b'way, canal with lock, waterbodies, houses, woods, plantations, parkland, marsh/bog, open fields, field gates, building names, road names, field names, brewery, kiln, mill, hospital, tollgate, common.

2/103 Saint Laurence Reading (parish) SU 722739 [Not listed]
Apt 10.07.1847; 315a (315); Map 1848, 4 chns; railways and station, waterbodies, building names, road names, market place, county gaol, tithable meadows (col); built-up part is generalised.

2/104 Saint Mary Reading (parish) SU 705733 [Not listed]
Apt 04.04.1838; 1846a (1846); Map 1838, 4 chns, by Hawkes and Son, Reading; foot/b'way, turnpike roads, turnpike gate, canal, dock, waterbodies, houses, woods, plantations, parkland, hedge ownership, fences, building names, road names, brick kilns, mill; built-up part is generalised.

2/105 Remenham (parish) SU 776835
Apt 30.06.1840; 1591a (1590); Map 1841?, 4 chns; waterbodies, houses, woods, plantations, parkland, marsh/bog, water mill; map has note of acceptance by landowners.

2/106 Ruscombe (parish) SU 804763
Apt 21.07.1840; 1250a (all); Map 1840, 6 chns, revised by W.H. Fuller, Reading; railway, turnpike roads, waterbodies, houses, woods, plantations, parkland, heath/moor, building names, road names, quarries, stone or sand pits, osiers, roadside waste (col).

2/107 Sandhurst (parish) SU 845625
Apt 04.03.1842; 4563a (4562); Map 1839, 3 chns, (tinted); foot/b'way, woods, parkland (col, in detail), building names, road names, landowners, Royal Military College, tollbar.

2/108 Shaw-cum-Donnington (parish) SU 474696
Apt 24.03.1838; 1990a (1989); Map 1838, 3 chns, by John Harris, Thatcham, Berks; foot/b'way, hedges, field gates, building names, castle remains, well, brick kiln, ice house, waterhouse, boat house, common, glebe (col). Apt is by holding and omits land use.

2/109 East Shefford (parish) SU 386743 [Not listed]
Apt 05.06.1845; 1042a (all); Map 1843, 6 chns; foot/b'way, waterbodies, woods, plantations; bird of prey with outstretched wings holds in its feet draped scale bar.

2/110 Great Shefford otherwise West Shefford (parish) SU 380755
Apt 30.11.1838; 2196a (all); Map 1841?, 8 chns, in 2 parts, by U.B. Vines, Newbury, (including 4-chn enlargement of village); waterbodies, houses, woods, glebe (col); gardens and homesteads generalised (col).

2/111 Shellingford (parish) SU 313933
Apt 11.09.1840; 1718a (all); Map 1840, 6 chns, by Daniel Trinder; foot/b'way, waterbodies, houses, woods, plantations, arable (col), grassland (col), field boundary ownerships, building names; colour bands show arable, grass and field boundary ownerships.

2/112 Shilton (parish) SP 260087
Apt 13.04.1839; 36a (1595); Map 1841?, [? 1 chn]; turnpike roads, open fields, building names, road names, weir, turnpike house (pictorial), road and riverside waste (col); there is a note about landmark stones in a meadow.

2/113 Shinfield (parish) (partly in Wilts) SU 723683
Apt 21.11.1838; 4504a (4514); Map 1837, 3 chns, 'copied from the original survey' by Hawkes and Sons, Reading; foot/b'way, waterbodies, houses, woods (named), plantations (named), parkland, heath/moor, open fields (named), hedges, fences, field gates, building names, road names, mill, common (col), roadside waste (col); Wilts part is tinted; other colours may show tithe-free land.

2/114 Shottesbrook (parish) SU 845769 [Not listed]
Apt 29.08.1843; 1316a (1316); Map 1843, 6 chns, by Little and Weaver, Chippenham, Wilts; railway, waterbodies, houses, woods, plantations, parkland, orchards, building names, osiers, spoil heaps.

2/115 Shrivenham (tithing in parish of Shrivenham) SU 237888
Apt 30.11.1843; 1856a (?); Map 1844, 6 chns, by Phillips and Westbury, Andover; railway with station, foot/b'way, canal, waterbodies, houses, woods, plantations.

2/116 Snelsmore (tithing in parish of Chieveley) SU 474717 [Not listed]
Apt 26.08.1839; 870a (870); Map 1840?, 3 chns; foot/b'way, waterbodies, houses, woods, plantations, heath/moor, open fields, fences, field boundary ownerships, field gates.

2/117 Sonning Town (district in parish of Sonning) SU 763762 [Sonning]
Apt 27.05.1851; 16a (?); Map 1851?, 6 chns, (tithable parts only).

2/118 Sotwell (parish) SU 587912 [Not listed]
Apt 03.11.1838; 702a (701); Map 1840?, 3 chns; waterbodies, houses, woods, marsh/bog.

2/119 Sparsholt (parish) SU 340872
Apt 22.12.1838; 3694a (6340); Map 1843, 3 chns, by Wm Thos Heard, St Margarets, Ware; railway, foot/b'way, turnpike roads, canal, waterbodies, woods, plantations, parkland, tithe-free land.

2/120 Stanford Dingley (parish) SU 570725
Apt 12.10.1838; 918a (914); Map 1838, 3 chns, 1st cl, by Cornelius B. Davis, The Hitchens, East Woodhay; waterbodies, houses (cross-hatched), woods, plantations, open fields; boundaries show land belonging to adjacent parishes.

2/121 Stanford in the Vale (except Goosey) (parish) SU 344934
Apt 06.06.1846; 2871a (all); Map 1837, 3 chns; woods (col), orchards, bridle road.

2/122 Steventon (parish) SU 456923
Apt 07.12.1842; 2382a (2382); Map 1843, 6 chns, by J. Neighbour and Son, Oxford; railway, canal, waterbodies, open fields.

2/123 Streatley (parish) SU 577803
Apt 28.01.1841; 386a (1500); Map 1841?, 3 chns, in 2 parts, by J.B. Clary, Reading, (tithable parts only); landowners; second part is of lands belonging to Thomas Bowles Esq., who is not mentioned in the apportionment schedule.

2/124 Sulham (parish) SU 646740
Apt 23.09.1840; 696a (all); Map 1840, 6 chns, by W.H. Fuller, Reading; railway, turnpike roads, waterbodies, houses, woods, plantations, hedges, fences, field gates, building names, workhouse, sand or stone pit.

2/125 Sulhampstead Abbotts, Sulhampstead Bannister and Sulhampstead, Upper End (parish or townships) SU 643687 [Sulhampstead Abbots and Sulhampstead Bannister]
Apt 02.04.1846; 2431a (all); Map 1846, 3 chns, in 2 parts, by W.H. Fuller, Reading; railway, foot/b'way, canal, waterbodies, houses, woods, plantations, parkland, marsh/bog, heath/moor, building names, mill, osiers; meaning of colours is unclear.

2/126 Sunning Hill (parish) SU 932688 [Sunninghill]
Apt 01.05.1840; 3174a (3173); Map 1839, 3 chns, by Henry Walter; foot/b'way, waterbodies, houses, woods, plantations, parkland, hedge ownership, fences, field boundary ownerships, field gates, building names, road names, brick kiln, heath.

2/127 Sunningwell (parish) SP 498005
Apt 22.01.1841; 1298a (1298); Map 1838, 3 chns, by Benjamin Reed, Old Broad Street, London; canal, waterbodies, houses, woods (col, named), hedges (col); single and double hedges appear to be shown.

2/128 Sutton Courtney (parish) SU 505930 [Sutton Courtenay]
Apt 23.4.1840; 2091a (2091); Map 1840?, 6 chns, in 3 parts; canal, waterbodies, hedge ownership, private roads, bridle roads.

2/129 Swallowfield (parish) (partly in Wilts) SU 729647
Apt 13.08.1846; 1515a (3712); Map 1847?, 3 chns, by T.A. Readwin, Wokingham; foot/b'way, waterbodies, houses, woods, plantations, parkland, marsh/bog, fences, road names.

2/130 Thatcham Borough, Henwick, Colthrop, Awbery Street and Crookham (hamlets or tithings in parish of Thatcham) SU 522675
Apt 28.08.1841; 7773a (7773); Map 1840, 3 chns, surveyed by William Baillie, Newbury, for T.E. Washbourne; waterbodies, houses, woods, plantations, parkland, heath/moor, building names, mills, wharf, malthouse, common (col), greens (col, named); bridge named.

2/131 Tidmarsh (parish) SU 632746
Apt 13.04.1839; 779a (779); Map 1840?, 3 chns; waterbodies, houses, woods, plantations, marsh/bog; map has note of acceptance by landowners.

2/132 Tilehurst (parish) SU 677735
Apt 03.03.1843; 5164a (5164); Map 1844?, 6 chns; railway, waterbodies, houses, woods, plantations, parkland, marsh/bog, sand or stone pit, quarry.

2/133 Tubney (parish) SU 440995
Apt 08.06.1840; 1145a (1144); Map 1841, 3 chns, by Joseph Dymock; waterbodies, houses, woods (named), plantations (named), arable (by annotation), grassland (by annotation), open fields, hedges, field gates, building names, field names, pound, milestone, fishponds, heath.

2/134 Ufton Nervet (parish) SU 625682
Apt 30.07.1842; 2080a (all); Map 1843, 6 chns, by Phillips and Westbury, Andover; foot/b'way, canal, waterbodies, houses, woods (named), plantations (named), marsh/bog, heath/moor, building names.

2/135 Saint Leonard in the Borough of Wallingford (parish) SU 599891 [Not listed]
Apt 19.01.1847; 211a (211); Map 1849?, 3 chns, (tithable parts only); open fields; orchards, garden, farm premises, yard and pleasure grounds shown by annotation.

2/136 Saint Mary the More in the Borough of Wallingford (parish) SU 603898 [Not listed]
Apt 25.05.1847; 94a (93); Map 1850?, 3 chns; waterbodies, woods, building names, workhouse.

2/137 Saint Peter in Wallingford (parish) SU 606893 [Not listed]
Apt 18.02.1848; 10a (10); Map 1850?, 3 chns, by W.C. Vine; turnpike roads, waterbodies, toll house.

2/138 Waltham Saint Laurence (parish) SU 832753
Apt 25.03.1839; 3469a (3468); Map 1839?, 6 chns; railway, waterbodies, woods, parkland, building names; bridges named.

2/139 White Waltham (parish) SU 860775
Apt 28.08.1843; 2576a (2576); Map 1843, 6 chns, by Little and Weaver, Chippenham, Wilts; railway, turnpike roads, waterbodies, houses, woods (col), plantations (col), parkland, arable (col), grassland (col), orchards, building names, lodge, spoil heaps; bridges named.

2/140 Wantage (except Briants Fee) (parish) SU 403873
Apt 30.06.1843; 5750a (?); Map 1841, 6 chns; railway, foot/b'way, canal, waterbodies, houses, woods, open fields, building names, road names, mills, down.

2/141 Warfield (parish) SU 877715
Apt 25.06.1841; 3240a (3239); Map 1843, 6 chns, copied from enclosure award map by H. Walter, Windsor; waterbodies, houses, hedge ownership, building names, road names.

2/142 Wargrave (parish) SU 796803
Apt 21.03.1840; 4315a (4314); Map 1839, 5 chns, by F.W. Dibbin, Chiswick; railway, foot/b'way, waterbodies, houses, woods, plantations, parkland, orchards, marsh/bog, building names, road names, withy beds, chalk pit, druids' temple; legend explains depiction of buildings, roads, waterbodies and land use.

2/143 Wasing (parish) SU 575642
Apt 03.11.1848; 682a (all); Map 1849, 3 chns, taken from a survey by Wm Baillie by Chas Sanderson, Reading; waterbodies, houses, farmyards, woods, plantations, parkland, building names.

2/144 Welford (parish) SU 409727
Apt 30.12.1837; 5173a (all); Map 1839?, 6 chns; waterbodies, houses, woods, plantations, parkland, marsh/bog, sand or stone pit.

2/145 Whitchurch (parish) SU 646780
Apt 31.07.1839; 302a (2070); Map 1839, 6 chns, by W.H. Fuller, Reading, (tithable parts only, tinted); railway, waterbodies, houses, woods, plantations, field gates, building names, lodge.

2/146 New Windsor (except Dedworth) (parish) SU 962748 [Windsor]
Apt 07.11.1848; 2434a (2890); Map 1850, 3 chns, by E. and G.N. Driver; railway with terminus, foot/b'way, waterbodies, houses, woods, plantations, parkland (in detail), field gates, building names, road names, cavalry barracks, castle, dairy, aviary, kennel, private roads.

2/147 Old Windsor (parish) SU 960702
Apt 08.01.1842; 5262a (5401); Map 1842, 6 chns, by E. and G.N. Driver, London; foot/b'way, canal, waterbodies, houses, woods (named), plantations (named), parkland (in detail, with ornamental features), orchards, marsh/bog, field gates, building names, road names, sand or stone pit, mill, lodge, deer pen, workhouse, brick kiln, mills, woodland.

2/148 Winkfield (part of) North District (parish) SU 915725
Apt 31.07.1839; 4360a (?); Map 1839, 6 chns; foot/b'way, waterbodies, houses, woods, plantations, parkland, arable, grassland, orchards, gardens, marsh/bog, heath/moor, road names, sand or stone pit. Apt says that it omits certain numbers on the map as they are Crown property.

2/149 Winkfield (part of) South District (parish) SU 900672
Apt 03.06.1848; 4623a (?); Map 1849, 6 chns, by C.P. Dyke; foot/b'way, houses.

2/150 Winterbourne (tithing in parish of Chieveley) SU 454730
Apt 05.05.1840; 2085a (2085); Map 1841?, 3 chns; by Henry Adnams, Chieveley, Berks; foot/b'way, waterbodies, houses, woods, plantations, heath/moor, field boundary ownerships, field gates, sand or stone pit.

2/151 Little Wittenham (parish) SU 565933
Apt 30.06.1843; 871a (all); Map 1841, 6 chns; hill-drawing, waterbodies, houses, woods, arable (col), grassland (col), marsh/bog, field boundary ownerships, tumulus; colour bands show arable, grass and field boundary ownership.

2/152 Wokingham (parish) (partly in Wilts) SU 818677
Apt 24.09.1839; 8131a (8131); Map '1825' (1841?), 3 chns; waterbodies, houses, farmyards, woods (col, named), coppice (col), plantations (col, named), parkland (col), arable (col), grassland (col), orchard (col), gardens (col), hedges, fences, building names, road names, field names, landowners, windmill, town hall, field acreages, county boundary; many of the areas appear to have been renumbered.

2/153 West Woodhay (parish) SU 392630
Apt 30.04.1840; 1407a (all); Map 1841, 3 chns, by Cornelius B. Davis, The Hitchen, East Woodhay; foot/b'way, woods, plantations, parkland, field gates, road names.

2/154 Woodley and Sandford (liberty in parish of Sonning) SU 767733
Apt 16.11.1840; 3558a (?); Map 1843, 3 chns, by Hawkes and Sons, Reading; railway, waterbodies, houses, heath/moor, road and riverside waste (col).

2/155 Woolhampton (parish) SU 575672
Apt 16.03.1842; 694a (all); Map 1842?, 3 chns; foot/b'way, canal, waterbodies, houses, woods, parkland, hedge ownership, fences, field gates.

2/156 Wootton (parish) SP 483017
Apt 13.02.1849; 1558a (?); Map 1849, 6 chns, in 2 parts, by W.H. Davies, Abingdon, (including location diagram); waterbodies, houses, woods, plantations, field boundary ownerships, building names, limekilns, boundary stones, osiers, brick kiln, wells.

2/157 Yattendon (parish) SU 545752
Apt 28.03.1844; 1393a (all); Map 1845?, 5 chns, in 2 parts, (including 3-chn enlargement of part of district); waterbodies, houses, woods (col), osiers, parkland, open fields, pound; enlargement is described as a supplementary map deposited for inspection of the landowners.

Buckinghamshire

PRO IR29 and IR30 3/1–131

214 tithe districts: 473,362 acres
130 tithe commutations: 228,452 acres
57 voluntary tithe agreements, 73 compulsory tithe awards,
1 corn rent annuity

Tithe and tithe commutation

The lowland part of Buckinghamshire was subject to extensive parliamentary enclosure accompanied by commutation of tithe and thus it is no surprise to find that by 1836 only 61 per cent of the county's tithe districts (48 per cent of the county by area) were subject to tithes (Fig. 15). Twenty-seven districts were wholly tithable at this date and the main causes of tithe exemption elsewhere were commutation at the time of enclosure (in 36 per cent of the partially exempt districts), modus payments in lieu of tithes, the merger of tithes in the land, exemption by prescription, and exemption of some woodland.

Assistant tithe commissioners and local tithe agents who worked in Buckinghamshire are listed in Table 3.1. The tithes of eight Buckinghamshire tithe districts were valued by the Tithe Commission in default of a valuation being lodged by the landowners within the statutory six months after the confirmation of the agreement or award (Table 3.2).

Tithe maps

The upland, southern part of Buckinghamshire is 'south-eastern' in character with a relatively high proportion of first-class maps, but the tithe surveys of the northern part of the county are essentially 'midland' in nature. Overall, first-class maps are 15 per cent of the total and are generally of districts which were wholly tithable, a pattern which has parallels in Sussex (Table 3.3). As in some other midland counties, there were two peaks of map production, a first in 1838–40, and a second in 1848–50. Fifteen maps date from as late as 1850–59 due in part to the presence of districts with only small residual tithable tracts left in the wake of enclosure. The disproportionate cost of these small commutations meant that there was often little incentive for landowners to initiate the commutation process (Table 3.4).

The scales of Buckinghamshire tithe maps vary from one inch to one chain to one inch to nine chains; 53 per cent of maps are in the recommended scale range of one inch to three to four chains (Table 3.3).

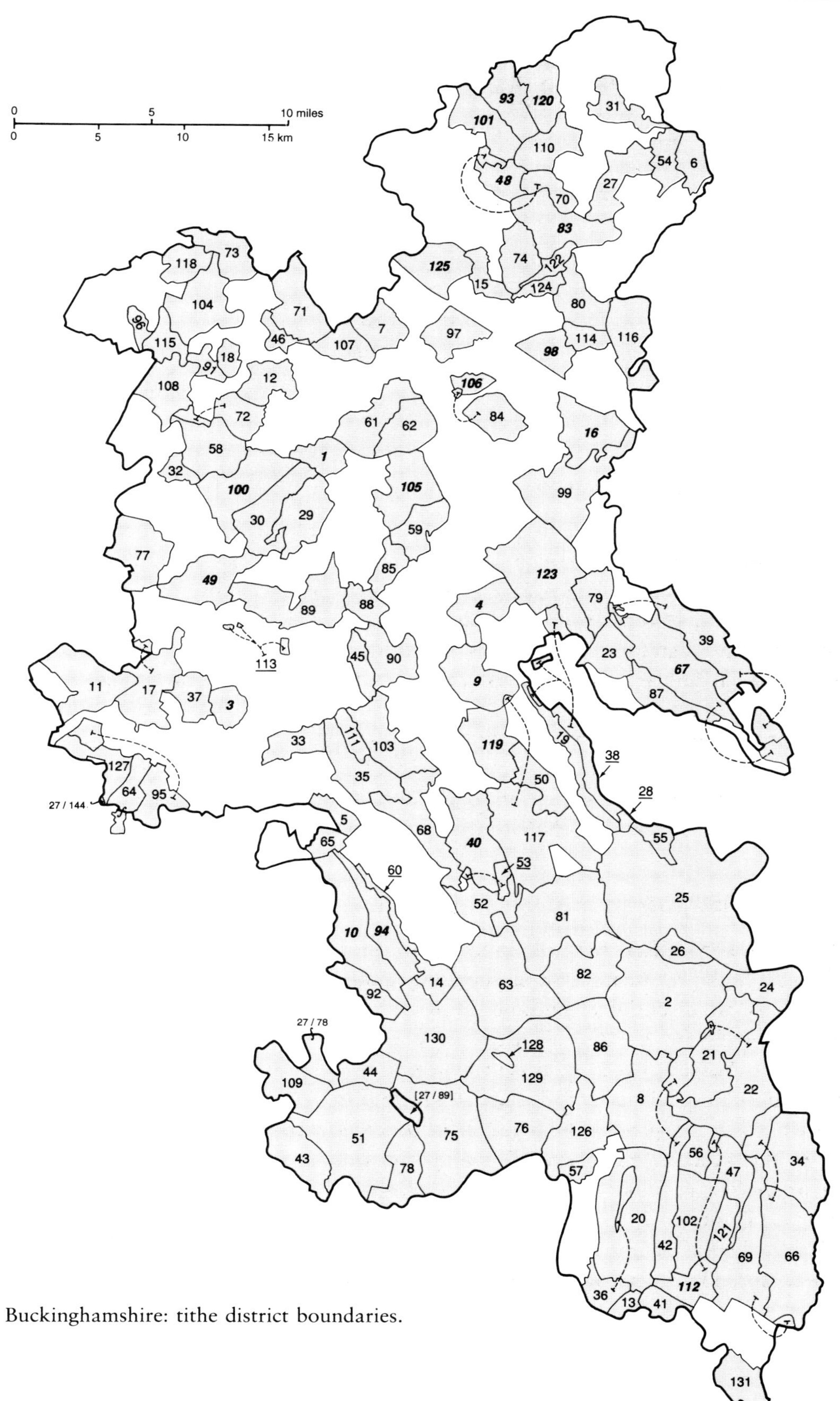

Fig. 15 Buckinghamshire: tithe district boundaries.

Woodland is indicated on 62 per cent of Buckinghamshire tithe maps, and parks on 17 per cent. Parkland is shown in particular detail at Middle Claydon, Hedgerley, and Stowe. On the other hand, agricultural land use is poorly recorded and only a very few maps depict arable, grass, gardens and orchards. Residual open fields appear on 23 per cent of Buckinghamshire tithe maps and indications of field boundary ownership on 36 per cent of maps.

Eighty-four Buckinghamshire tithe maps in the Public Record Office collection can be attributed to a particular map-maker (Table 3.2); the most prolific was William Brown of Tring, Hertfordshire, who produced fifteen maps. Five maps were produced by London surveyors and three more by map-makers from well outside the county: H. and F. Hitchens of Brighton, Sussex, Messrs Gilbert and Tayspill of Colchester, Essex, and W. Brown of Tonbridge, Kent.

Buckinghamshire tithe maps are essentially functional rather than ornamental and only three have decorative embellishments. Two of these, Lower Boveney and Dorney, are by W. T. Buckland of Wraysbury and picture his name on a slab of stone resting against a tree trunk.

Table 3.1. *Agreements and awards for commutation of tithes in Buckinghamshire*

Assistant commissioner/ local tithe agent	*Number of agreements**	*Number of awards*
F. Browne Browne	19	0
Thomas James Tatham	0	18
William Wakeford Attree	0	17
Francis Offley Martin	0	17
Joseph Townsend	13	0
John Maurice Herbert	0	11
Thomas Smith Woolley	9	5
John West	5	0
Horace William Meteyard	4	0
John Mee Mathew	3	1
John Pickering	3	0
John Job Rawlinson	1	0
Henry Jemmett	2	0
John Coldridge	0	1
Roger Kynaston	1	0

*Computed from the number of extant reports on tithe agreements in the tithe files [PRO IR 18].

Table 3.2. *Tithe valuers and tithe map-makers in Buckinghamshire*

Name and address (in Buckinghamshire unless indicated)	*Number of districts*	*Acreage*
Tithe valuers		
John Rolfe, Beaconsfield	23	89,137
John King, Winslow	13	14,919
Tithe Commissioners	8	3,619
John Durham, Stony Stratford	7	6,251
Others [55]	79	114,526
Attributed tithe map-makers		
William Brown, Tring, Hertfordshire	15	17,563
John Durham, Stony Stratford	8	6,990
John King, Winslow	7	7,236
William Hussey and son, High Wycombe	6	30,504
Richard Davis, Banbury, Oxfordshire	5	11,877
W.T. Buckland, Wraysbury	5	6,122
John Rolfe Glenister, Tring, Hertfordshire	4	3,653
Others [25]	34	86,485

Table 3.3. *The tithe maps of Buckinghamshire: scales and classes*

Scale in chains/inch	*All maps*		*First Class*		*Second Class*	
	Number	*Acreage*	*Number*	*Acreage*	*Number*	*Acreage*
>3	2	912	0	0	2	912
3	51	94,904	19	52,444	32	42,460
4	18	26,834	0	0	18	26,834
5	4	6,462	0	0	4	6,462
6	42	87,046	0	0	42	87,046
<6	13	12,294	0	0	13	12,294
TOTAL	130	228,452	19	52,444	111	176,008

Table 3.4. *The tithe maps of Buckinghamshire: dates*

	1838	*1839*	*1840*	*1841*	*1842*	*1843*	*1844*	*1845*	*1846*	*1847*	*1848*	*1849*	*1850*	*>1850*
All maps	15	13	16	9	7	7	6	3	8	9	3	9	8	15
1st class	4	2	3	4	1	2	1	0	0	0	0	0	1	1
2nd class*	11	11	13	5	6	5	5	3	8	8	3	9	7	14

*Two second-class tithe maps of Buckinghamshire in the Public Record Office collection are undated.

Buckinghamshire

3/1 Addington (parish) SP 749288
Apt 29.04.1852; 13a (1320); Map 1854, 4 chns, (tithable parts only); railway, waterbodies.

3/2 Agmondesham or Amersham (parish) (partly in Herts) SU 959969
Apt 26.10.1837; 7735a (10544); Map 1838, 6 chns, by James Stratford, Amersham; foot/b'way, waterbodies, woods, plantations, parkland, building names, sand or stone pit, mills, paths, brewery, kennel, rectory, county boundary. (The map in PRO IR 30 is a copy; original is in PRO IR 77/6.)

3/3 Ashenden (parish) SP 703132 [Ashendon]
Apt 28.02.1848; 961a (1790); Map 1849?, 4 chns, by Henry Howard, Winchester; waterbodies, houses, woods, plantations, open fields, hedge ownership, fence ownership, ownership boundaries (col); map is titled: 'Plan of the hamlets of Great and Little Pollicott, Ashenden, Bucks, belonging to the Duke of Buckingham and Lincoln College'.

3/4 Aston Abbotts (parish) SP 843201
Apt 22.11.1850; 599a (2180); Map 1850, 4 chns, by G.M. Thompson, 9 Grays Inn Square; waterbodies, houses, woods.

3/5 Aston Sandford (parish) SP 770072
Apt 23.02.1839; 670a (669); Map 1838?, 6 chns; waterbodies, parkland, orchard, processioning crosses; meaning of colours is unclear; map is described as being of 'the Estates of Mrs Susannah Barber'.

3/6 Astwood (parish) SP 952475
Apt 17.04.1839; 1259a (1259); Map 1839, 6 chns, ? by Thomas Bloodworth; waterbodies, woods.

3/7 Beachampton (parish) SP 779367
Apt 04.08.1839; 1492a (all); Map 1839, 6 chns, in 3 parts, (including two 3-chn enlargements of open fields); waterbodies, woods, open fields, glebe.

3/8 Beaconsfield (parish) SU 949897
Apt 13.04.1844; 4541a (all); Map 1846, 6 chns, by Keen and Son, 2, Parliament Street, Westminster; foot/b'way, waterbodies, houses, woods (named), plantations, coppice (named), parkland (named), heath/moor, fences, building names, sand or stone pits, turnpike gate.

3/9 Bierton with Broughton (parish) SP 842152
Apt 24.04.1850; 77a (2470); Map 1850, 3 chns, by W. Brown, Tring, Herts, (tinted); foot/b'way, public bridle and drift way, canal, waterbodies, woods, hedges, landowners.

3/10 Bledlow (parish) SU 777999
Apt 04.03.1843; 52a (4130); Map 1851, 8 chns, by Robt G. Murray, (tithable parts only, tinted); map is titled: 'Woodland in the parish of Bledlow grubb'd between 1812 and 1843, copied from the Bledlow Award'.

3/11 Boarstall (parish) SP 625142
Apt 31.10.1850; 3043a (3080); Map 1851, 6 chns, by W. Brown, Tring; foot/b'way, waterbodies, houses, woods (named), parkland, field boundary ownerships, building names, boundary stones, osiers.

3/12 Bourton (hamlet in parish of Buckingham) SP 713333
Apt 21.01.1848; 1433a (?); Map 1849, 3 chns, by Henry Howard, Winchester; foot/b'way, waterbodies, houses, woods, hedge ownership, Lammas land (with acreage).

3/13 Lower Boveney (hamlet or liberty in parish of Burnham) SU 940780 [Not listed]
Apt 26.08.1843; 480a (480); Map 1842, 3 chns, 1st cl, by W.T. Buckland, Wraysbury, Bucks; construction lines, waterbodies, houses, open fields, hedge ownership, river lock, common; surveyor's name is on a stone tablet resting against a wall, decorated with grass and ivy.

3/14 Bradenham (parish) SU 828976
Apt 26.05.1846; 1001a (1001); Map 1847, 3 chns, by Dredge and Mead, West Wycombe; waterbodies, woods, open fields.

3/15 Bradwell (parish) SP 834399
Apt 18.07.1839; 892a (892); Map 1839, 3 chns, by John Durham, jnr; foot/b'way, waterbodies, hedge ownership, field boundary ownerships, field gates, river embankment; colours show tithing practice.

3/16 Great Brickhill (parish) SP 901309
Apt 26.08.1839; 364a (2370); Map 1840, 6 chns, by John Durham, (tithable parts only, tinted); waterbodies, woods, plantations, landowners, private road; pictorial church.

3/17 Brill (parish) SP 659142
Apt 21.07.1851; 3089a (2600); Map 1850, 3 chns, 1st cl, by Davis and Saunders, Banbury and Oxford; construction lines, foot/b'way, waterbodies, houses, woods (col), hedge ownership, fences, field boundary ownerships, field gates.

3/18 Buckingham (except Lenbro' and Bourton hamlets) (parish) SP 693343
Apt 25.05.1847; 520a (?), (tithable parts only); Map 1847, 3 chns, waterbodies, houses, building names, road names, landowners, gaol, brewery.

3/19 Buckland (parish) SP 902102
Apt 04.03.1843; 1544a (1544); Map 1843, 4 chns, by W. Brown, Tring; foot/b'way, turnpike roads, canal, waterbodies, houses, woods, plantations, hedges, field boundary ownerships, field gates, building names, road names.

3/20 Burnham (except Lower Boveney hamlet) (parish) SU 940834
Apt 04.04.1839; 6251a (6250); Map 1841, 3 chns, 1st cl, by Joseph Witty; construction lines, railway, waterbodies, houses, woods, plantations, parkland, open fields, hedge ownership, fences, field gates, building names, road names, quarry, sand or stone pits, chapel, vicarage, boundary marks, common; colour bands may show liberty boundaries. (The map in PRO IR 30 is a copy; original is in PRO IR 77/7.)

3/21 Chalfont Saint Giles (parish) SU 990942
Apt 17.12.1838; 3642a (3641); Map 1840?, 6 chns, in 2 parts, (including unenclosed lands at 3 chns); construction lines, open fields.

3/22 Chalfont Saint Peter (parish) TQ 008912
Apt 01.03.1843; 4718a (4717); Map 1840, 3 chns, 1st cl, 'made under the authority of the Poor Law Commissioners' by James Nightingale, Kingston, Surrey, and James Stratford, Amersham, Bucks; waterbodies, houses, woods (named), plantations (named), parkland (named), open fields, hedge ownership, building names, field names, boundary stones, kilns, common.

3/23 Cheddington (parish) SP 918175
Apt 08.06.1840; 1386a (1398); Map 1842, 3 chns, by William Andrews; railways, canal, waterbodies, open fields, field gates, road names, field names; areas not mapped in detail are tinted.

3/24 Chenies (parish) TQ 016978
Apt 16.01.1838; 1744a (1744); Map 1838, [3 chns], 1st cl, by M. Reynolds, Old Warden, Beds; construction lines, waterbodies, houses, woods (col), plantations (col), field boundary ownerships, building names, almshouses; field acreages given along district boundary only; map bears the endorsement of the landowners.

3/25 Chesham (parish) SP 963029
Apt 26.01.1843; 12657a (12657); Map 1843, 6 chns, in 3 parts, by Hussey and Son, Wycombe, (including enlargements of detail and of Chesham town at 3 chns), litho (Standidge); waterbodies, woods, plantations, parkland, orchard, open fields, fences, building names, market house, mills, paper mill, hamlet boundaries.

3/26 Chesham Bois (parish) SU 963998
Apt 30.04.1838; 906a (905); Map 1838, 3 chns, 1st cl, by Glenister, Tring; construction lines, waterbodies, houses, woods, plantations, field boundary ownerships, road names, disused road.

3/27 Chicheley (parish) SP 912467
Apt 28.04.1849; 2073a (1620); Map 1851?, 3 chns, 1st cl; construction lines, foot/b'way, waterbodies, houses, woods, plantations, parkland.

3/28 Cholesbury (parish) SP 930070
Apt 07.02.1838; 176a (176); Map 1838, 3 chns, by Glenister, Tring; waterbodies, houses, woods, plantations, parkland, hedge ownership, building names, lawn, garden, rickyard, common (col).

3/29 East Claydon (parish) SP 739252
Apt 05.11.1857; 2252a (2160); Map 1858?, 8 chns. District is apportioned by holding and fields are not shown.

3/30 Middle Claydon (parish) SP 714250
Apt 06.12.1839; 2586a (all); Map 1840?, 6 chns; waterbodies, plantations (named), parkland (in detail), hedges, porter's lodge. Apt omits some land use.

3/31 Clifton Reynes (parish) SP 911502
Apt 30.01.1841; 1444a (1444); Map 1841, 3 chns, 1st cl; construction lines, foot/b'way, waterbodies, houses, woods (col), field boundary ownerships, tithe-free land (col).

3/32 Cowley (hamlet in parish of Preston Bissett) SP 667276 [Not listed]
Apt 24.08.1839; 589a (?); Map 1839, 3 chns, by John King, Winslow, Bucks; waterbodies, houses.

3/33 Cuddington (parish) SP 743111
Apt 08.06.1840; 1281a (1281); Map 1844, 6 chns, in 2 parts, ? by Henry Dixon, Oxford, (including Cuddington village at 3 chns); foot/b'way, hedge ownership.

3/34 Denham (parish) TQ 036870
Apt 09.05.1840; 3905a (3905); Map 1841, 3 chns, 1st cl, by Jas Richardson, 5 Bickford Place, Kennington; construction lines, waterbodies, houses, woods (by name), plantations, open fields, fences, field boundary ownerships, building names, private road, osiers, springs; physical features named.

3/35 Donnington otherwise Dinton (parish) SP 779095
Corn rent conversion, 1921; 352a (4100); Map 1921?, 7.5 chns, copied from enclosure map; foot/b'way, waterbodies, open fields, field boundary ownerships; Apt is copy of enclosure award.

3/36 Dorney (parish) SU 927789
Apt 03.12.1844; 1550a (1550); Map 1840, 3 chns, 1st cl, in 2 parts, by W.T. Buckland, Wraysbury, (including 80-chn location diagram); construction lines, foot/b'way, waterbodies, houses, woods, open fields, hedge ownership, building names, sand or stone pits, public road, common; surveyor's name is on a plaque resting against a tree trunk.

3/37 Dorton (parish) SP 682135
Apt 19.10.1848; 1431a (all); Map 1849?, 6 chns; woods.

3/38 Drayton Beauchamp (parish) SP 908108
Apt 27.09.1838; 1874a (1874); Map 1838, 3 chns, 1st cl, by Glenister, Tring; construction lines, turnpike roads, canal, waterbodies, houses, woods, marsh/bog, heath/moor, open fields, field boundary ownerships, building names, road names, old rag pit.

3/39 Edlesborough and part of Cheddington (parish) SP 979179
Apt 07.08.1839; 4593a (4579); Map 1840?, 3 chns, in 5 parts, by William Andrews; railway, canal, waterbodies, houses, woods, plantations, heath/moor, open fields, hedges, road names, field names, landowners, sand or stone pits or quarries; pictorial church; the various parts are drawn in different styles, and are evidently the work of several draughtsmen.

3/40 Ellesborough (parish) SP 845060
Apt 06.05.1848; 415a (3310); Map 1847, 8 chns, by Wm Brown, Tring, Herts, (tithable parts only, tinted); waterbodies, woods, building names; pictorial church.

3/41 Eton (parish) SU 960782
Apt 12.10.1839; 784a (783); Map 1843, 2 chns, by H. Walter, Windsor; canal with towpath, waterbodies, houses, woods, marsh/bog, open fields (named), hedges, building names, road names, weir, mill, Eton College, osiers, common.

3/42 Farnham Royal (parish) SU 962849
Apt 28.07.1840; 1257a (2910); Map 1841?, 4 chns; waterbodies, houses, woods, open fields, hedges, building names, road names, landowners, gravel pit; colour bands may show property ownerships; unnumbered areas are left uncoloured.

3/43 Fawley (parish) SU 755865
Apt 21.04.1840; 2216a (?); Map 1840?, 4 chns; foot/b'way, waterbodies, woods, plantations, parkland.

3/44 Fingest (parish) SU 788919
Apt 06.04.1839; 1305a (1304); Map 1838, 4 chns, by William Peacock, Great Marlow; foot/b'way, waterbodies, houses, woods, plantations, building names, road names, well, spring, pits, boundary marks, church lands, poor lands, common, lammas land.

3/45 Fleet Marston (parish) SP 778160 [Not listed]
Apt 06.07.1842; 930a (all); Map 1842, 6 chns, by W. Brown, Tonbridge, Kent; waterbodies, building names.

3/46 Foscott (parish) SP 722358 [Foscote]
Apt 09.01.1840; 715a (714); Map 1840, 3 chns, by John King, Winslow, Bucks; canal, waterbodies, houses, woods, plantations, field gates, private road.

3/47 Fulmer (parish) SU 998857
Apt 18.04.1843; 1886a (all); Map 1843, 3 chns, 1st cl, by Michael Fitzgerald; construction lines, waterbodies, houses, woods (col), park, field boundary ownerships, field gates, building names, boundary points and well, common.

3/48 Gothurst otherwise Gayhurst (parish) SP 845549
Apt 17.05.1850; 22a (840); Map (drawn on Apt) 1850?, 9 chns, (tithable parts only); foot/b'way, woods.

3/49 Grendon Underwood (parish) SP 685209
Apt 31.07.1843; 488a (3670); Map 1844, 6 chns, by J. King, Winslow, (tithable parts only); foot/b'way, waterbodies, houses, woods, field gates, road names, landowners, private roads.

3/50 Halten (parish) SP 882094 [Halton]
Apt 19.10.1848; 1453a (1452); Map 1840, 5 chns, by William Brown, Tring, Herts; foot/b'way, waterbodies, woods, plantations. Apt omits land use.

3/51 Hambledon (parish) SU 783880 [Hambleden]
Apt 16.01.1838; 6616a (6615); Map 1843, 3 chns, by H. and F. Hitchins, Brighton, Sussex; foot/b'way, woods (col), open fields.

3/52 Great Hampden (parish) SP 851021
Apt 29.06.1839; 1711a (all); Map 1839, 8 chns; foot/b'way, hedge ownership; woodland and avenues of trees are indicated by pecked dotted lines. Apt omits land use.

3/53 Little Hampden (parish) SP 863036
Apt 27.07.1840; 509a (508); Map 1840, 4 chns; foot/b'way.

3/54 Hardmead (parish) SP 937475
Apt 04.04.1838; 1113a (all); Map 1838?, 5 chns; foot/b'way, waterbodies, field boundary ownerships, glebe (col).

3/55 Hawridge (parish) SP 948062 [Not listed]
Apt 16.01.1838; 697a (696); Map 1838, 3 chns, 1st cl, by Glenister, Tring; construction lines, hill-drawing, waterbodies, houses, woods, field boundary ownerships, building names, sand or stone pit or quarry, ancient tumulus, moat, common.

3/56 Hedgerley (parish) SU 977872
Apt 26.01.1841; 1065a (all); Map 1838, 3 chns, by Wm Francis, Great Marlow; construction lines, hill-drawing, foot/b'way, waterbodies, houses, woods, plantations, parkland, heath/moor, fences, ornamental gardens; whole district is parkland; mapmaker notes: 'Bulstrode Park wall bounds the parish on the North, the Middle of the Roads, as far as they go, on the East, South and West, dotted lines and fences in other parts. The hills delineated upon this plan have been reduced to and measured on the horizontal plane'.

3/57 Hedsor (parish) SU 911863
Apt 07.06.1838; 527a (all); Map 1839, 4 chns, in 2 parts, by W. Brown,

Tring; foot/b'way, waterbodies, woods, plantations, parkland, arable (col), grassland (col), hedge ownership.

3/58 Hillsden (parish) SP 685291 [Hillesden]
Apt 30.04.1846; 2577a (2150); Map 1846, 6 chns; foot/b'way, waterbodies, houses, woods.

3/59 Hoggeston (parish) SP 805245
Apt 19.05.1847; 1527a (1526); Map 1847, 4 chns, by W. Brown, Tring; waterbodies.

3/60 Horsendon (parish) SP 800018 [Horsenden]
Apt 25.02.1839; 518a (517); Map 1838, 3 chns, by William Brown, Tring; foot/b'way, turnpike roads, waterbodies, houses, woods, parkland, arable (col), grassland (col).

3/61 Great Horwood (parish) SP 777309
Apt 18.01.1842; 2389a (all); Map 1842, 6 chns; waterbodies.

3/62 Little Horwood (parish) SP 795308
Apt 22.05.1849; 233a (1950); Map 1850, 6 chns, (tithable parts only); railway, foot/b'way, waterbodies, houses, landowners.

3/63 Hughendon otherwise Hitchenden (parish) SU 865973 [Not listed]
Apt 26.01.1843; 5752a (5751); Map 1844?, 3 chns, 1st cl, by Wm Hussey and Son, Wycombe; construction lines, foot/b'way, waterbodies, houses, open fields, hedge ownership, fences, heath.

3/64 Ickford (parish) (partly in Oxon) SP 650075
Apt 03.07.1845; 1249a (1249); Map 1845, 3 chns; waterbodies, houses.

3/65 Illmire (parish) SP 762057 [Ilmer]
Apt 10.09.1839; 674a (all); Map 1839, 4 chns; waterbodies, hedge ownership, fences, building names; map has schedule of owners, occupiers, description of property, acreage and amount apportioned to tithe. Apt omits land use.

3/66 Iver (parish) TQ 034812
Apt 22.06.1844; 3697a (6149); Map not dated, 6 chns, in 2 parts, litho (T. Savill, Sible Hedingham); turnpike roads, toll gate, rights of way, waterbodies, woods (named), plantations (named), parkland (named), heath/moor, building names, park lodge.

3/67 Ivinghoe (parish) SP 962162
Apt 14.05.1840; 235a (5260); Map 1842, 3 chns, by William Andrews, Ivinghoe, Bucks; canal, waterbodies, open fields, field gates, field names.

3/68 Great Kimble (parish) SP 821061
Apt 28.09.1839; 2473a (2473); Map 1840, 8 chns; open fields, hedge ownership, fences, stone pits, gardens.

3/69 Langley Marish (parish) TQ 010825 [Langley]
Apt 28.05.1844; 3895a (3895); Map 1846?, 6 chns, in 2 parts, award map 'amended' by W.T. Buckland, Wraysbury, Bucks, (including enlargement of Colnbrook at 3 chns); railway, foot/b'way, waterbodies, houses, woods (named), plantations (named), parkland (named), orchard, open fields, building names, road names, field names, weirs, occupation and private roads.

3/70 Lathbury (parish) SP 872458
Apt 21.05.1841; 1294a (1294); Map 1843, 3 chns, in 2 parts; foot/b'way, waterbodies, woods.

3/71 Leckhampstead (parish) SP 730376
Apt 13.04.1839; 2522a (2522); Map 1839, 3 chns, 1st cl, by John Williams, Bicester; construction lines, foot/b'way, waterbodies, houses, woods, plantations, orchard, gardens, marsh/bog, hedge ownership, fences, field gates.

3/72 Lenbro' (hamlet in parish of Buckingham) SP 700311 [Lenborough]
Apt 25.02.1847; 1644a (?); Map 1847, 6 chns, by Davis and Saunders, Banbury; railway, foot/b'way, public roads and ways, waterbodies, houses, woods (col), hedges, fences, field boundary ownerships, field gates.

3/73 Lillingstone Dayrell (parish) SP 693405
Apt 16.11.1837; 1583a (2223); Map 1839, 4 chns, in 2 parts, by John King, Winslow, Bucks, (tithable parts only); foot/b'way, waterbodies, houses, woods, plantations.

3/74 Great Linford (parish) SP 857412
Apt 30.04.1840; 1788a (1787); Map 1841?, 6 chns; turnpike roads, canal, waterbodies, houses, woods.

3/75 Great Marlow (parish) SU 841881 [Marlow]
Apt 19.07.1841; 6152a (6152); Map 1841, 3 chns, 1st cl, by J. Eivers and M. FitzGerald; construction lines, foot/b'way, waterbodies, houses, woods, marsh/bog, open fields, building names, road names, paper mills, chalk pit, workhouse, common; built-up part generalised.

3/76 Little Marlow (parish) SU 876887
Apt 10.06.1844; 3347a (3346); Map 1846, 3 chns, by W. Hussey and Son, Wycombe; foot/b'way, waterbodies, houses.

3/77 Marsh Gibbon (parish) SP 648224
Apt 05.06.1839; 2753a (2752); Map 1846, 6 chns, in 12 parts, by Henry Dixon, Oxford, (including eleven 1-chn enlargements of detail, tinted on main map); foot/b'way, waterbodies, road names, public drains, freeboard.

3/78 Medmenham (parish) SU 812860
Apt 03.01.1839; 2421a (2420); Map 1840, 3 chns, 1st cl, by Wm Hussey and Son, Wycombe; construction lines, foot/b'way, private roads, public footpaths, houses, open fields, field boundary ownerships, building names, mill, abbey, embankments.

3/79 Mentmore (parish) SP 908208
Apt 12.05.1851; 1524a (1240); Map 1852, 6 chns, by John King, Winslow; railway, waterbodies, houses, woods, plantations.

3/80 Middleton otherwise Milton Keynes (parish) SP 892387
Apt 11.07.1837; 1843a (1842); Map undated, 7.5 chns; foot/b'way, waterbodies, glebe (col).

3/81 Great Missenden (parish) SP 900015
Apt 27.02.1841; 5732a (5731); Map 1839, 4 chns, by W. Brown, Tring; foot/b'way, waterbodies, woods (col), plantations (col), heath/moor (col), open fields, field boundary ownerships, building names.

3/82 Little Missenden (parish) SU 910982
Apt 15.03.1843; 3173a (3173); Map 1845, 3 chns, by Keen and Son, 2 Parliament Street, Westminster; waterbodies, houses, woods (col), building names, watermill, windmill, greens (named), heath.

3/83 Newport Pagnell (parish) SP 882432
Apt 31.07.1843; 194a (3220); Map 1844, 6 chns, by John Durham, Stony Stratford, (tithable parts only, tinted); waterbodies, hedge ownership, field names, landowners.

3/84 Newnton Longueville otherwise Newton Longville (parish) SP 848315
Apt 13.06.1844; 1719a (1718); Map 1844, 6 chns, in 2 parts, by H. Churchill, Aylesbury; foot/b'way, waterbodies, hedges, field gates, road names, private road. Apt omits land use.

3/85 Oving (parish) SP 790223
Apt 21.02.1846; 972a (all); Map 1846, 3 chns, by Willm Brown, Tring, Herts; foot/b'way, waterbodies, houses.

3/86 Penn (parish) SU 921940
Apt 30.11.1838; 3889a (4270); Map 1839?, [5 chns]; foot/b'way, waterbodies, woods, open fields, green, heath; hills named.

3/87 Pightleshorne or Pitstone (parish) SP 950148
Apt 12.07.1838; 374a (2836); Map 1838, 4 chns, in 2 parts, (tithable parts only, tinted); hill-drawing, railway, canal, waterbodies, houses, woods (named), plantations (named), parkland (col, named), open fields, field boundary ownerships, building names, road names, field names, landowners, sheepwalk, greens, sand or stone pit, hills.

3/88 Pitchcot (parish) SP 778198 [Pitchcott]
Apt 26.05.1846; 925a (all); Map 1846, 3 chns, by W. Brown, Tring; foot/b'way, waterbodies, houses.

3/89 Quainton (parish) SP 739189
Apt 17.09.1842; 5369a (5368); Map 1842, 4 chns, in 2 parts, by Richard Davis, Banbury, (including Shipton Lee at 5 chns); foot/b'way, waterbodies, houses, woods, hedge ownership, fences, field boundary ownerships, courses of piped water, springs.

3/90 Quarrendon (hamlet) SP 792165
Apt 25.05.1847; 1922a (all); Map 1848, 3 chns, by Willm Brown, Tring, Herts; foot/b'way, waterbodies, houses, woods, marsh/bog, field gates, building names, osier beds.

3/91 Radclive (parish) SP 679340
Apt 21.03.1840; 522a (all); Map 1840, 4 chns; woods; meaning of colour bands is unclear. District is apportioned by holding; Apt omits land use and field names.

3/92 Radnage (parish) SU 791970
Apt 29.07.1841; 1353a (all); Map 1842, 3 chns, by G.R. New, High Wycombe; construction lines, foot/b'way, waterbodies, houses, woods, hedge ownership, field gates, road names, wells, boundary marks, common, greens (named); many field boundaries are shown with double lines; meaning of cross symbols on boundaries is unclear.

3/93 Ravenstone (parish) SP 846505
Apt 17.04.1850; 22a (2230); Map (drawn on Apt) 1850?, 8 chns, (tithable parts only).

3/94 Saunderton (parish) SP 795010
Apt 24.05.1847; 9a (1590); Map (drawn on Apt) 1847?, 9 chns, (tithable parts only); woods, landowners; pictorial church.

3/95 Shabbington (parish) SP 670075
Apt 06.05.1839; 2139a (2138); Map 1840, 3 chns, in 3 parts, by T. Read and H. Cooling, (including 10-chn location diagram); foot/b'way, waterbodies, houses, woods, orchard, gardens, marsh/bog, hedge ownership, fences, field gates, building names, private roads, spring; clouds surround map title.

3/96 Shalston otherwise Shaldeston (parish) SP 640362 [Shalstone]
Apt 26.02.1850; 437a (1320); Map 1850?, 6 chns; foot/b'way, waterbodies, woods, heath/moor. Apt omits land use.

3/97 Shenley (parish) SP 820366 [Not listed]
Apt 13.08.1840; 1910a (2900); Map 1840, 6 chns, by John Durham; foot/b'way, waterbodies, field boundary ownerships, public and carriage roads.

3/98 Simpson (parish) SP 877355
Apt 15.07.1858; 7a (1330); Map (drawn on Apt) 1858?, 5 chns, (tithable parts only); building names, field names, landowners.

3/99 Soulbury (parish) SP 889269
Apt 24.11.1846; 472a (4460); Map 1847, 6 chns, in 4 parts, (tithable parts only; including 26.67 chn location diagram); canal, waterbodies, woods, building names, landowners, mill lodge, dirt house, tithe-free land, heath.

3/100 Steeple Claydon (parish) SP 701265
Apt 31.12.1850; 64a (3270); Map 1851?, 6 chns, (tithable parts only); field names and acreages.

3/101 Stoke Goldington (parish) SP 832493
Apt 31.10.1846; 1003a (2061); Map 1847, 3 chns; foot/b'way, rights of way, waterbodies, woods (named), parkland (named), open fields, hedge ownership, fences; map is carefully drawn and coloured according to Dawson's conventions.

3/102 Stoke Poges (parish) SU 980832
Apt 03.05.1842; 653a (2500); Map 1839, 4 chns, by H. Walter; railway, foot/b'way, waterbodies, houses, farmyards, woods, parkland, arable (col), grassland (col), orchard, gardens, building names, road names, field names, common.

3/103 Stone (parish) SP 793111
Apt 24.11.1846; 51a (2590); Map 1847, 6 chns, (tithable parts only, tinted); woods, hedge ownership, fences, landowners.

3/104 Stowe (parish) SP 675375 [Not listed]
Apt 14.10.1850; 3012a (3460); Map 1845, 6 chns; waterbodies, houses, woods (col), parkland (in great detail).

3/105 Swanbourne (parish) SP 798269
Apt 14.02.1851; 45a (2510); Map (drawn on Apt) 1852?, 3 chns, (tithable parts only).

3/106 Tattenhoe (parish) SP 832335
Apt 23.04.1857; 96a (690); Map (drawn on Apt) 1858?, 6 chns, (tithable parts only); waterbodies, houses, woods, plantations, fences.

3/107 Thornton (parish) SP 759366
Apt 22.04.1840; 1332a (1332); Map 1841?, 9 chns, by J. King; waterbodies, houses, freeboard. District is apportioned by holding; Apt omits land use.

3/108 Tingewick (parish) SP 656326
Apt 21.01.1848; 306a (2290); Map 1848, 9 chns, 'copied from a map of the property of the Warden and Scholars of New College, Oxford' by Davis and Saunders, (tithable parts only); woods, hedge ownership, field gates, field names, landowners, tithe and poors' allotments.

3/109 Turville (parish) SU 750910
Apt 08.03.1843; 2315a (2315); Map 1843?, 3 chns, 1st cl; foot/b'way, waterbodies, houses, woods, plantations, heath.

3/110 Tyringham-cum-Filgrave (parish) SP 869480
Apt 07.07.1838; 1737a (1736); Map 1838, [3 chns], by John Durham, Stony Stratford; waterbodies, field boundary ownerships, glebe (col).

3/111 Upton (hamlet in parish of Dinton) SP 773115
Apt 22.01.1841; 739a (all); Map 1849, 3 chns, by Willm Brown, Tring, Herts; foot/b'way, waterbodies, houses, woods, plantations, field gates.

3/112 Upton-cum-Chalvey (parish) SU 973790 [Chalvey]
Apt 23.12.1851; 268a (1950); Map 1852, 3 chns, in 3 parts, by Buckland, surveyors, Windsor, (tithable parts only, tinted, including two parts at 6 chns); railway and station, foot/b'way, waterbodies, park; built-up part generalised.

3/113 Waddesden (parish) SP 733170 [Waddesdon]
Apt 03.02.1859; 317a (6010); Map 1859, 6 chns, by W. Brown, Tring, (tithable parts only, tinted); waterbodies, building names, road names, landowners.

3/114 Walton (parish) SP 898365
Apt 11.03.1839; 758a (all); Map 1838, 3 chns, by John Durham junr; foot/b'way, waterbodies, houses, open fields, hedge ownership, glebe (col), commoners' land (col).

3/115 Water Stratford (parish) SP 656353
Apt 30.04.1839; 1082a (1082); Map 1838, 3 chns, by John Durham junior; foot/b'way, waterbodies, houses, hedges, fences, glebe (col).

3/116 Wavenden (parish) SP 920364 [Wavendon]
Apt 27.10.1840; 2665a (all); Map 1839, 3 chns, 1st cl, by Joseph Tween, Knebworth, Herts; construction lines, foot/b'way, waterbodies, houses, woods (col), plantations (col), parkland, field boundary ownerships, building names, freeboard.

3/117 Wendover (parish) SP 880065
Apt 10.06.1842; 852a (5719); Map 1841, 9 chns, by W. Brown, Tring, (tithable parts only); canal, waterbodies, woods, plantations, arable (col), grassland (col), hedges, building names, landowners; pictorial church.

3/118 Westbury (parish) SP 665401
Apt 11.09.1843; 1038a (2547); Map 1844, 6 chns, in 2 parts, by Keen and Son, 2 Parliament Street, Westminster; waterbodies, field boundary ownerships, landowners; green band shows modus land.

3/119 Weston Turville (parish) SP 854115
Apt 06.05.1848; 24a (2450); Map (drawn on Apt) 1849?, 3 chns, (tithable parts only); plantations, hedges, road names.

3/120 Weston Underwood (parish) SP 865510
Apt 29.06.1850; 53a (1300); Map 1850, 6 chns, by John Durham, Stony Stratford, (tithable parts only, tinted).

3/121 Wexham (parish) SU 995827 [Not listed]
Apt 20.03.1848; 29a (670); Map 1849, 6 chns, by Buckland, Windsor and Wraysbury, (tithable parts only); waterbodies, houses, road names, field acreages.

3/122 Willen (parish) SP 878410
Apt 21.07.1850; 658a (450); Map 1851?, 6 chns; canal, waterbodies.

3/123 Wing (parish) SP 878221
Apt 11.02.1850; 1005a (5310); Map 1851, 7 chns, by John King, Winslow, (tithable parts only); waterbodies, woods, landowners.

3/124 Little Wolstone (parish) SP 870396 [Woolstone]
Apt 30.06.1845; 614a (613); Map 1846, 3 chns; foot/b'way, canal with towpath, waterbodies, houses, woods, plantations, marsh/bog.

3/125 Wolverton (parish) SP 810406
Apt 31.10.1850; 23a (2260); Map 1851, 6 chns, (tithable parts only).

3/126 Wooburn (parish) SU 911885
Apt 24.05.1847; 117a (2850); Map 1848, 6 chns, (tithable parts only, tinted); building names, osiers (col), furze (col); map has note that lands have become tithable since enclosure, as a result of grubbing woodland.

3/127 Worminghall (parish) SP 639095
Apt 23.07.1841; 1469a (all); Map 1841, 4 chns, by R. Davis, Banbury; foot/b'way, waterbodies, houses, woods, hedge ownership, fences, field boundary ownerships, field gates, private roads.

3/128 Chipping or High Wycombe (except Borough of Wycombe) (parish) SU 868930
Apt 24.11.1848; 6199a (6198); Map 1849?, 6 chns, by W. Hussey and Son, Wycombe; foot/b'way, waterbodies, houses, open fields, building names, road names, landowners, abbey, farm boundaries, park.

3/129 High Wycombe (borough in parish of Chipping Wycombe) SU 883923
Apt 24.11.1848; 128a (all); Map 1849, 1 chn, by Thomas Wooster Hussey, High Wycombe, litho (by Robt Newberry, Percy St, Tottenham Court Road, London); foot/b'way, waterbodies, woods, open fields, abbey.

3/130 West Wycombe (parish) SU 826942
Apt 07.04.1847; 6382a (6340); Map 1849, 6 chns, by Rd Dredge, West Wycombe; foot/b'way, waterbodies, woods, parkland, common.

3/131 Wyrardisbury otherwise Wraysbury (parish) TQ 009733
Apt 22.04.1839; 1656a (1656); Map 1840, 6 chns, by Gilbert and Tayspill, Colchester; canal with towpath, waterbodies, woods, plantations, parkland, open fields, osiers, weir, paper mill, tithe-free land; some field boundaries are shown with double lines.

Cambridgeshire

PRO IR 29 and IR30 4/1–93

177 tithe districts: 560,707 acres
93 tithe commutations: 349,720 acres
70 voluntary tithe agreements, 23 compulsory tithe awards

Tithe and tithe commutation

Although usually regarded as an eastern county, the pattern of tithe commutation in Cambridgeshire has more in common with the counties of the Midlands than of East Anglia. In 1836 tithe was still payable in 52 per cent of Cambridgeshire tithe districts and most of the thirty-eight wholly tithe-free districts are in the southern, higher part of the county where there was most parliamentary enclosure and associated tithe commutation (Fig. 16). In addition to commutation at the time of enclosure, the main causes of tithe exemption in Cambridgeshire were modus payments in lieu of tithes, exemption of former Crown, manorial or monastic land, merger of tithes in the land, exemption by prescription, and exemption of common land in some districts. Cambridgeshire has a number of very small tithe districts and indeed West Wratting with just one mill property of 0.02 acres tithable is the smallest of all English and Welsh tithe districts.

Assistant tithe commissioners and local tithe agents who worked in Cambridgeshire are listed in Table 4.1. As in Essex, two valuers undertook a disproportionately large amount of tithe rent-charge valuation in Cambridgeshire but, unusually, both were resident a short way outside the county: Anthony Jackson at Barkway, Hertfordshire and James Jones at Ramsey, Huntingdonshire. In five districts rent-charge was valued by the Tithe Commission in default of a valuation being undertaken by the landowners within the statutory period of six months following the confirmation of an agreement or award (Table 4.2).

Tithe maps

As in many counties in which there had been extensive enclosure, there are very few first-class tithe maps in Cambridgeshire (Table 4.3). In this respect, Cambridgeshire is similar to the counties to the west and north but very different from the pattern in the counties to the south and east. The re-use of older survey material is explicitly acknowledged on nine maps but it is very likely that many more Cambridgeshire tithe maps were produced by compilation rather than from new fieldwork. Construction lines, probably the most certain evidence of new work, are present on just one second-class map.

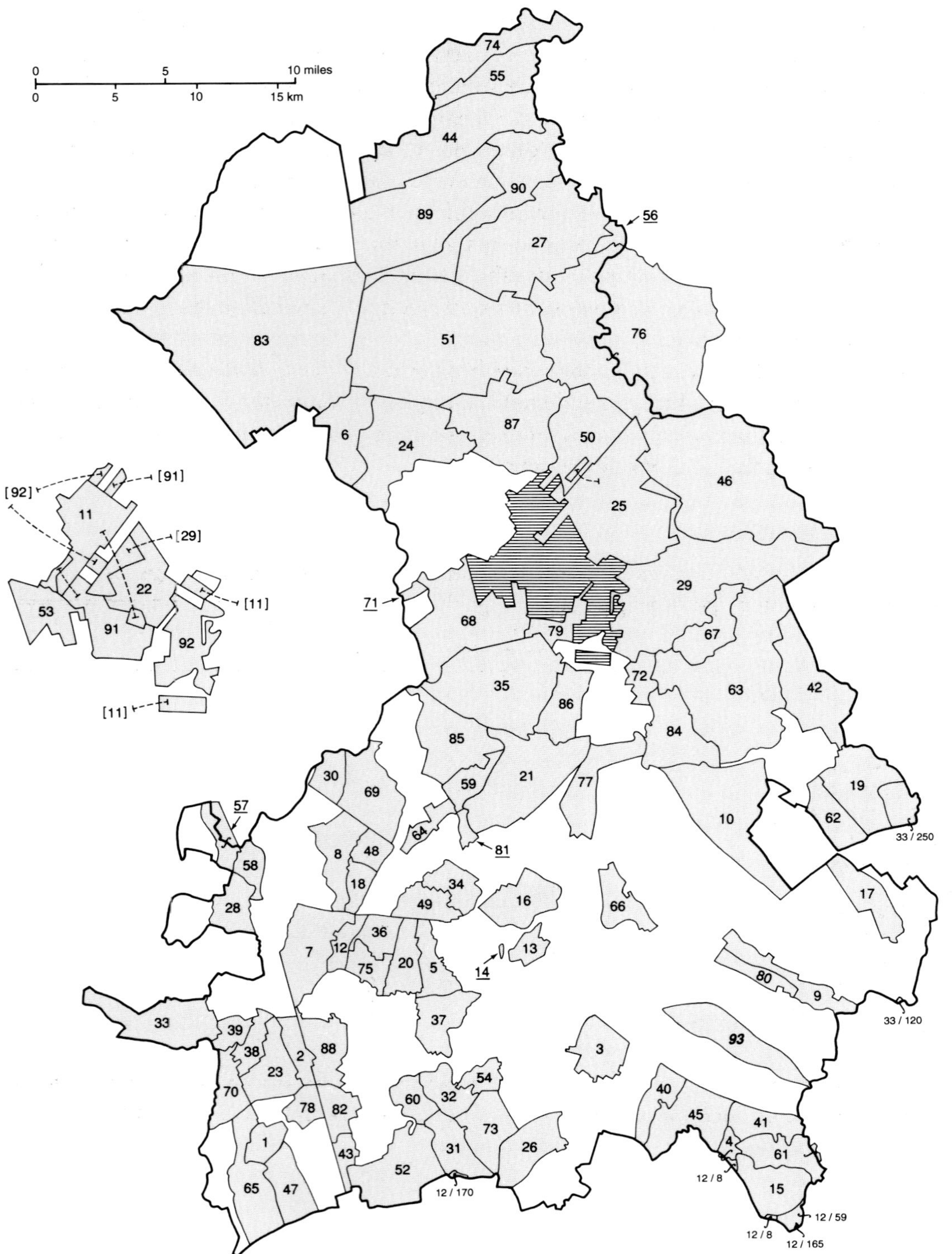

Fig. 16 Cambridgeshire: tithe district boundaries.

Cambridgeshire maps are drawn at a variety of scales from one inch to 0.6 chain to one inch to 12 chains. Only 22 per cent of maps are in the officially recommended scale range of one inch to three to four chains and 55 per cent of maps are at the six-chain scale (Table 4.3).

Cambridgeshire maps follow the national pattern in that they usually portray woodland (on 59 per cent of maps) and parkland (on 20 per cent of maps) but are uninformative about most agricultural land uses. Residual open fields, some very extensive, appear on 20 per cent of this county's tithe maps and the mapping of field boundary ownership is quite widespread (on 31 per cent of the maps). Many fenland maps depict an extensive network of drainage channels. Not one Cambridgeshire tithe map in the Public Record Office collection has any decorative embellishment, though on several maps churches and windmills are shown pictorially.

Fifty-two Cambridgeshire tithe maps can be attributed to a particular map-maker. Alexander Watford of Cambridge produced the largest number (ten maps) but the eight maps by Joseph Jackson of March covered more than twice Watford's acreage as the Fenland parishes where he worked are much larger.

Table 4.1. *Agreements and awards for commutation of tithes in Cambridgeshire*

Assistant commissioner/ local tithe agent	*Number of agreements**	*Number of awards*
Henry Bertram Gunning	17	0
William Heard	11	0
F. Browne Browne	10	0
Thomas Smith Woolley	6	4
Francis Offley Martin	0	7
James Drage Merest	0	5
John Pickering	5	0
John Maurice Herbert	0	4
? Mears	4	0
William Wakeford Attree	3	0
Anthony Jackson	3	0
Joseph Townsend	3	0
John Mee Mathew	3	0
Horace William Meteyard	2	0
Roger Kynaston	2	0
Henry Dixon	1	0

*Computed from the number of extant reports on tithe agreements in the tithe files [PRO IR 18].

Table 4.2. *Tithe valuers and tithe map-makers in Cambridgeshire*

Name and address (in Cambridgeshire unless indicated)	*Number of districts*	*Acreage*
Tithe valuers		
Anthony Jackson, Barkway, Hertfordshire	12	33,366
James Jones, Ramsey, Huntingdonshire	11	76,488
Martin Nockolds, Saffron Walden, Essex	6	15,202
Joseph Jackson, March	5	40,238
John Cross, West Walton, Norfolk	5	31,768
Alexander Watford, Cambridge	5	22,763
Thomas Utton, Brome, Norfolk	5	12,899
Tithe Commissioners	5	2,799
Others [26]	39	114,197
Attributed tithe map-makers		
Alexander Watford, Cambridge	8	25,823
Joseph Jackson, March	8	58,084
John King and Son, Saffron Walden, Essex	7	15,150
Charles M. Bidwell, Ely	5	46,783
Richard Harwood, Cambridge	5	5,744
Lenny and Croft, Bury St Edmunds, Suffolk	4	47,478
Richard Freeman, Wisbech	3	16,386
Others [8]	10	81,184

Table 4.3. *The tithe maps of Cambridgeshire: scales and classes*

Scale in chains/inch	*All maps*		*First Class*		*Second Class*	
	Number	*Acreage*	*Number*	*Acreage*	*Number*	*Acreage*
>3	2	1,077	0	0	2	1,077
3	16	46,217	2	3,780	14	42,437
4	5	23,070	0	0	5	23,070
5	2	2,816	0	0	2	2,816
6	51	214,448	0	0	51	214,448
7.5	1	2,332	0	0	1	2,332
8	9	27,007	0	0	9	27,007
<8	7	32,751	0	0	7	32,751
TOTAL	93	349,720	2	3,780	91	345,940

Table 4.4. *The tithe maps of Cambridgeshire: dates*

	1837	*1838*	*1839*	*1840*	*1841*	*1842*	*1843*	*1844*	*1845*	*1846*	*1847*	*1848*	*1849*	*1850*	*>1850*
All maps	1	5	12	19	19	9	3	4	1	3	2	3	1	2	9
1st class	0	0	0	1	1	0	0	0	0	0	0	0	0	0	0
2nd class	1	5	12	18	18	9	3	4	1	3	2	3	1	2	9

Cambridgeshire

4/1 Abington Pigotts (parish) TL 305448
Apt 23.11.1838; 1215a (1237); Map 1838?, 8 chns; woods.

4/2 Arrington (parish) TL 321507
Apt 26.12.1837; 1381a (all); Map 1853?, 4 chns; turnpike roads, tollhouse, waterbodies, woods, building names, church pit, glebe (col); pictorial church.

4/3 Babraham (parish) TL 511512
Apt 09.06.1845; 2306a (2350); Map 1851, 6 chns; field boundary ownerships, building names.

4/4 Bartlow (parish) TL 591455
Apt 05.02.1845; 371a (all); Map 1848, 3 chns, by John King and Son, Saffron Walden, Essex; waterbodies, houses, plantations, parkland, heath/moor, open fields, building names, pound, roadside and riverside waste (col); strip-field boundaries are red.

4/5 Barton (parish) TL 403567
Apt 19.10.1841; 1812a (all); Map 1841?, 6 chns, by Alexander Watford, Cambridge; waterbodies, field boundary ownerships.

4/6 Benwick (township and hamlet in parish of Doddington) TL 342905
Apt 02.05.1839; 3097a (3096); Map 1840?, 8 chns, by Joseph Jackson; heath/moor, building names, windmills (pictorial), roadside and riverside waste (col); fenland named. Apt notes all tithable lands are 'Fen or Marsh lands and cultivated in some years as arable lands and in other years as lands laid down in grass seeds and cultivated as grass lands'.

4/7 Bourn (parish) TL 329573
Apt 27.01.1842; 4066a (all); Map 1841?, 6 chns, by R. Whittet; woods, arable, grassland, hedge ownership, field gates, building names, private roads.

4/8 Boxworth (parish) TL 344632
Apt 04.10.1838; 2521a (all); Map 1841?, 6 chns; turnpike roads.

4/9 Burrough Green (parish) TL 626564
Apt 27.06.1837; 2218a (2217); Map 1838?, 12 chns, in 3 parts, (including two settlements separately at 3 chns); turnpike roads, waterbodies, woods, plantations, field boundary ownerships, building names, field names, windmill (by symbol), brick kiln, green (col), former common lands; pictorial church.

4/10 Burwell (parish) TL 588665
Apt 18.08.1841; 4717a (7232); Map 1842, 6 chns, by John King and Son, Saffron Walden; waterbodies, houses, woods, heath/moor, building names, waste (col); double lines may be drains.

4/11 Byall Fen, West Fen, Hale Fen and Grunty Fen (extra-parochial place) TL 457857
Apt 31.07.1840; 3435a (all); Map 1840, 3 chns, 1st cl, in 5 parts, by Chas M. Bidwell, Ely, (includes 30-chn index); construction lines, foot/b'way, waterbodies, houses, woods, plantations, heath/moor, fence, field boundary ownerships, building names, mills (by symbol), public drains, dam, flying bridge, waste (col); double lines may be drains.

4/12 Caldecott (parish) TL 350577 [Caldecote]
Apt 22.05.1844; 931a (all); Map 1851, 6 chns; foot/b'way, waterbodies.

4/13 Cambridge, St Andrew the Less otherwise Barnwell (parish) TL 466578 [Barnwell]
Apt 18.06.1847; 103a (?); Map 1856, 3 chns, amended by Rd Harwood from an original survey, (tithable parts only, tinted); railways, open fields, hedge ownership, road names, landowners, common.

4/14 Cambridge, Little St Mary (parish) TL 446576 [Not listed]
Apt 31.12.1851; 2a (?); Map 1852, 3 chns, by Rd Harwood, (tithable parts only); road names, weir; table lists owners, occupiers, lands and acreages.

4/15 Castle Camps (parish) TL 622428
Apt 09.05.1840; 2704a (2703); Map 1840?, 4 chns; waterbodies, woods, parkland, heath/moor, open fields (pink, named), building names, lodge, roadside waste (col).

4/16 Chesterton (parish) TL 459607
Apt 05.03.1839; 2730a (2729); Map 1840, 6 chns, by Rd Harwood, Cambridge; waterbodies, field boundary ownerships, windmill (pictorial).

4/17 Cheveley (parish) TL 676617
Apt 31.01.1839; 2528a (2527); Map 1840?, 6 chns, by R. and V.H. Wyatt, copied from a map in the possession of His Grace John Henry Duke of Rutland made in the year 1817; foot/b'way, waterbodies, houses, woods, parkland, heath/moor, road names, limekiln, gravel pit, glebe (col), green (col), roadside waste.

4/18 Childerly (parish) TL 357615
Apt 20.08.1849; 1052a (1052); Map 1850?, 8 chns; waterbodies.

4/19 Chippenham (parish) TL 666687
Apt 16.05.1839; 4205a (4205); Map 1842, 6 chns, copied from an 'Old Map' by J. King and Son, Saffron Walden; waterbodies, houses, woods, plantations, parkland (in detail), building names.

4/20 Comberton (parish) TL 389569
Apt 19.11.1839; 1925a (1925); Map 1840, 6 chns, by Richd Harwood, Cambridge; waterbodies, field boundary ownerships, field gates.

4/21 Cottenham (parish) TL 460687
Apt 17.12.1838; 7107a (7107); Map 1848, 6 chns; waterbodies, open fields, fen engines, ferry, tithe-free land (pink); some field boundaries are pink.

4/22 Coveney (parish) TL 485828
Apt 10.06.1842; 2482a (2481); Map 1840, 6 chns, by Chas M. Bidwell, Ely; waterbodies, houses, woods, osiers, fences, field boundary ownerships, building names, road names.

4/23 Croydon cum Clapton (parish) TL 307495
Apt 14.02.1839; 2711a (2711); Map 1839, 8 chns; waterbodies, woods, orchard, heath/moor, field boundary ownerships.

4/24 Doddington (township in parish of Doddington) TL 378903
Apt 04.05.1839; 7159a (7159); Map 1839, 8 chns, in 2 parts, by Joseph Jackson, (includes enlargement of village at 4 chns); foot/b'way, turnpike roads, waterbodies, houses, heath/moor, road names, roadside waste (col), intercommon land, windmills (pictorial); colours may show property ownerships.

4/25 Downham (parish) TL 510872
Apt 08.06.1838; 9789a (9789); Map 1838, 6 chns, by Lenny and Croft, Bury St Edmund's; turnpike roads, waterbodies, houses, woods, osiers, parkland, open fields (named), fen common, building names, road names, brick kiln, windmills (by symbol), extra parochial land boundary; strip field boundaries are in colour.

4/26 Duxford St Peter and Duxford St John (parish) TL 466450 [Duxford]
Apt 07.03.1840; 1567a (all); Map 1841?, 6 chns; waterbodies, houses, woods, plantations, parkland, building names.

4/27 Elm and part of Outwell (parish) TF 454034
Apt 25.03.1840; 11105a (11105); Map 1841, 6 chns, in 2 parts, by Joseph Jackson, (one part at 9 chns); turnpike roads, canal, waterbodies, houses, building names, road names, former open field names, windmills (pictorial); colours may show property ownerships; north is pointed to by a hand.

4/28 Eltisley (parish) TL 280600
Apt 10.09.1841; 1922a (1922); Map 1841, 3 chns; waterbodies, woods, heath/moor, open fields, hedge ownership, fence, field gates, greens (col), waste (col).

4/29 Ely, Holy Trinity and St Mary (parish) TL 559820 [Not listed]
Apt 02.06.1843; 13909a (?); Map 1846, 6 chns, in 3 parts, by Chas M. Bidwell, Ely and I. Bailey Denton, 9 Grays Inn Square, London, (includes 30-chn index); railways, turnpike roads, toll bar, waterbodies, houses, woods, plantations, field boundary ownerships, building names, road names, brick kiln, mills, steam engine.

4/30 Fendrayton (parish) TL 339685 [Fen Drayton]
Apt 28.10.1840; 1497a (1496); Map 1840, 6 chns, by Joseph Jackson; foot/b'way, turnpike roads, waterbodies, houses, road names, field names, windmill (pictorial), ferry, public drains, common; pictorial church; meaning of colours is unclear.

4/31 Foulmire (parish) TL 420448 [Fowlmere]
Apt 31.03.1845; 2212a (all); Map 1847, 6 chns; waterbodies, houses, woods, field boundary ownerships, private road.

4/32 Foxton (parish) TL 415482
Apt 05.09.1837; 1691a (all); Map 1839, 6 chns; waterbodies, woods.

4/33 Gamlingay (parish) TL 237522
Apt 31.12.1849; 4359a (4143); Map 1850?, 6 chns, in 2 parts; waterbodies, houses, woods.

4/34 Girton (parish) TL 418617
Apt 28.08.1841; 1674a (all); Map 1842?, 6 chns, by Alexander Watford, Cambridge; waterbodies, woods.

4/35 Haddenham (parish) TL 442748
Apt 26.06.1844; 8846a (8912); Map 1846, 6 chns, by Lenny and Croft, Bury St Edmunds; waterbodies, houses, woods, parkland, building names, road names, steam engine, tithe-free land.

4/36 Hardwick (parish) TL 370583
Apt 17.12.1836; 1410a (all); Map 1837, 6 chns, by Alexander Watford, Cambridge; foot/b'way, waterbodies, woods (named), grassland (col), hedge ownership, landowners, field acreages.

4/37 Haslingfield (parish) TL 409528
Apt 09.03.1842; 2527a (2527); Map 1844?, 6 chns; waterbodies, grassland (col). Apt omits some field names.

4/38 East Hatley (parish) TL 295509
Apt 16.11.1842; 1177a (all); Map 1840, 8 chns; waterbodies, woods, field boundary ownerships.

4/39 Hatley St George (parish) TL 280515
Apt 23.05.1838; 1000a (all); Map 1839, 6 chns, reduced to one half the size of the originals in the possession of the proprietors by Charles Oakden; waterbodies, woods, field boundary ownerships.

4/40 Hildersham (parish) TL 544482
Apt 05.09.1837; 1500a (all); Map 1840?, [4 chns]; waterbodies, woods (named), parkland, grassland (col), heath/moor, open fields, hedge ownership, field gates, road names, field names, mill, sandpits, field acreages.

4/41 Horseheath (parish) TL 613471
Apt 24.12.1839; 1850a (all); Map 1841, 5 chns, litho; waterbodies, woods, plantations, parkland, open fields (named), building names, windmill (pictorial).

4/42 Isleham (parish) TL 637754
Apt 25.09.1847; 5211a (5211); Map 1848, 6 chns, by Chas M. Bidwell, Ely; foot/b'way, waterbodies, houses, woods, plantations, field boundary ownerships, building names, road names, windmill (by symbol).

4/43 Kneesworth (hamlet in parish of Bassingbourn) TL 354441
Apt 26.08.1839; 248a (948); Map 1840?, 3 chns; waterbodies, houses, woods, chalk pit.

4/44 Leverington (parish) TF 402101
Apt 15.07.1842; 7878a (all); Map 1843, 4 chns, by J. Lehair, Leverington; turnpike roads, waterbodies, houses, marsh/bog, road names, former open field names, private roads.

4/45 Linton (parish) TL 569474
Apt 10.09.1839; 3776a (3775); Map 1841, 6 chns, by Alexander Watford, Cambridge; waterbodies, woods.

4/46 Littleport (parish) TL 583878
Apt 05.03.1839; 16137a (16136); Map 1839, 6 chns, by Lenny and Croft, Bury Saint Edmunds; turnpike roads, tollgate, waterbodies, housekland, fence, field gates, building names, road names, field names, brick kilns, windmills (by symbol); colour may show allotments.

4/47 Litlington (parish) TL 318420
Apt 15.09.1841; 2099a (all); Map 1841?, 4 chns, by Alexander Watford, Cambridge; waterbodies, woods, windmill (pictorial).

4/48 Lolworth (parish) TL 365638
Apt 22.01.1841; 1076a (all); Map 1842?, 2 chns; foot/b'way, woods, fence, field gates, former open field names, common.

4/49 Madingley (parish) TL 400605
Apt 12.05.1842; 1763a (all); Map 1849, 6 chns; foot/b'way, waterbodies, woods, parkland.

4/50 Manea (parish) TL 492911
Apt 03.08.1844; 4769a (4768); Map 1846, 6 chns; railway, waterbodies, woods, steam engine, tithe-free land (col).

4/51 March (township and hamlet in parish of Doddington) TL 400969
Apt 04.05.1839; 19141a (19141); Map 1840, 10 chns, in 2 parts, by Joseph Jackson, March, (includes town at 4 chns); turnpike roads, houses, road names, ferry, windmills (pictorial), church, district boundaries; fens named; pictorial church; meaning of colour tints is unclear.

4/52 Melbourn (parish) TL 386432
Apt 31.01.1839; 4688a (all); Map 1842?, 6 chns, by Alexander Watford, Cambridge; waterbodies, woods, marsh/bog, landowners.

4/53 Mepal (parish) TL 437817
Apt 27.04.1838; 1525a (1452); Map 1840, 6 chns, in 3 parts, by Joseph Jackson, March, (includes 3-chn enlargements of detail and of open fields); turnpike roads, canal, waterbodies, houses, heath/moor, common (col), open fields, road names, windmills (pictorial), steam engine (pictorial), private roads.

4/54 Newton (parish) TL 438493
Apt 07.09.1841; 984a (all); Map 1841, 3 chns, by Richard Harwood, Cambridge; waterbodies, open fields, hedge ownership, field gates.

4/55 Newton (Isle of Ely) (parish) TF 428140
Apt 20.05.1841; 3057a (3056); Map 1838, 3 chns, surveyed for tithe commutation by J. Leahair, Leverington; hill-drawing, waterbodies, marsh/bog, field gates, road names, former open field names, Roman embankment, drainage embankments; open field boundaries are shown as red pecked lines.

4/56 Outwell (parish) TF 505040
Apt 18.06.1840; 345a (?); Map 1841, 3 chns, 1st cl, by Richard Freeman, Wisbech; construction lines, canal, houses, field gates, corn mill, boundary of lands paying tithe to Elm and rates to Outwell.

4/57 Papworth St Agnes (parish) TL 267645
Apt 25.05.1839; 1291a (all); Map 1839?, [4 chns]; woods, field names, field acreages.

4/58 Papworth St Everard (parish) TL 289624 [Papworth Everard]
Apt 22.01.1841; 1091a (all); Map 1841?, 9 chns, copied from a map dated 1825 by Newton and Berry, 66 Chancery Lane; foot/b'way, waterbodies, woods, parkland, field boundary ownerships, milestones, field acreages. District is apportioned by holding; Apt omits land use.

4/59 Rampton (parish) TL 426686
Apt 06.08.1842; 1312a (1312); Map 1844, 6 chns, by Alexander Watford, Cambridge; waterbodies, woods, former open field names, commons, tithe-free land, possible former open field boundaries.

4/60 Shepreth (parish) TL 395476
Apt 16.10.1840; 1269a (all); Map 1843?, 6 chns; foot/b'way, turnpike roads, waterbodies, houses, farmyards, woods, plantations, parkland, grassland, orchard, gardens, heath/moor, hedge ownership, field boundary ownerships, road names, field names, mill, public drain; pictorial church; bridge named.

4/61 Shudy Camps (parish) TL 624451
Apt 20.10.1841; 2332a (2332); Map 1842, 7.5 chns, by J. King and Son,

Saffron Walden; waterbodies, houses, woods, plantations, parkland, open fields (named), possible open field boundaries, building names; open strips have solid red boundaries.

4/62 Snailwell (parish) TL 653668
Apt 30.10.1839; 2014a (2014); Map 1842, 6 chns, copied from an old map and corrected by J. King and Son, Saffron Walden; waterbodies, houses, woods, parkland.

4/63 Soham (parish) TL 589751
Apt 12.06.1837; 12706a (12706); Map 1841, 6 chns, in 5 parts, by Lenny and Croft, Bury St Edmunds, (includes four 3-chn enlargements of detail); waterbodies, houses, woods, parkland, open fields (named), hedges, fence ownership, field gates, building names, road names, field names, watermill, windmills (by symbol), weir, ferry, embankments, tunnels, brick kiln, common; fenland named.

4/64 Long Stanton St Michael and part of Long Stanton All Saints (parish) TL 401654 [Longstanton]
Apt 17.03.1847; 885a (?); Map 1847, 6 chns, 'revised' by J. King and Son, Saffron Walden; railway, waterbodies, houses, woods.

4/65 Steeple Morden (parish) TL 295418
Apt 26.02.1839; 3767a (3767); Map 1839, 6 chns; waterbodies, houses, woods, open fields (col, with acreages), field boundary ownerships, building names, mills, public gravel pit.

4/66 Stow-cum-Quy (parish) TL 521608 [Stow cum Quy]
Apt 6.9.1838.; 1820a (1820); Map 1839, 3 chns; waterbodies, houses, woods, parkland, building names, water mill, boundary posts.

4/67 Stuntney (hamlet in parish of Ely Trinity) TL 574785
Apt 30.03.1838; 2598a (all); Map 1839?, [3 chns]; foot/b'way, waterbodies, houses, woods, plantations, open fields, fence ownership, field boundary ownerships, field gates, building names, field names, milestone.

4/68 Sutton (parish) TL 425790
Apt 17.04.1838; 6970a (6970); Map 1840, 10 chns, in 2 parts, by Joseph Jackson, March (includes enlargement of village at 5 chns); turnpike roads, houses, building names, road names, windmills (pictorial), counter wash drain; fen names; a hand points to north.

4/69 Swavesey (parish) TL 364679
Apt 20.03.1838; 3892a (3891); Map 1840?, 6 chns, by Alexander Watford, Cambridge; waterbodies, field boundary ownerships, windmill (pictorial), recreation ground, ruin; pictorial church.

4/70 Tadlow (parish) TL 280481
Apt 27.08.1842; 1717a (1717); Map 1840, 8 chns, ? by Chas Oakden; waterbodies, woods, field boundary ownerships.

4/71 The Adventurer's Hall Wood (district in parish of Chatteris) TL 387808 [Not listed]
Apt 12.08.1851; 233a (?); Map 1852?, 12 chns; turnpike roads, toll gate, field gates. Apt omits land use.

4/72 Thetford (hamlet) TL 532753 [Little Thetford]
Apt 28.02.1838; 1042a (1630); Map 1839?, 3 chns; foot/b'way, waterbodies, houses, woods, marsh/bog, open fields (named), field boundary ownerships, field gates, ferry, mill, common; fenland named.

4/73 Thriplow (parish) TL 440460
Apt 19.09.1840; 2489a (all); Map 1841, 6 chns, in 2 parts, by Alexander Watford, Cambridge, (including lands tithable to Newton at 3 chns); waterbodies, woods, windmill (pictorial), private road.

4/74 Tid St Giles (parish) TF 426160 [Tydd St Giles]
Apt 06.09.1843; 4792a (4991); Map 1844, 6 chns, by F.J. Utting, Wisbech; turnpike roads, toll bar, canal, houses, road names, field names, ferry.

4/75 Toft (parish) TL 364562
Apt 22.05.1844; 1243a (all); Map 1845, 6 chns; foot/b'way, waterbodies, woods, windmills (by symbol); map is described as of the parish 'as altered since the Inclosure Survey of 1820'.

4/76 Upwell cum Welney (parish) (partly in Norfolk) TL 499980
Apt 10.10.1842; 21746a (21764); Map 1839-42, 3 chns, in 4 parts: Upwell by C. Mumford, Downham, and Welney by C.M. Bidwell, Ely, (includes 30-chn index); waterbodies, houses, woods, plantations, marsh/bog, building names, road names, suspension bridge, pigeon house, fishpond, sluice, windmills (by symbol).

4/77 Waterbeach (parish) TL 496684
Apt 10.12.1838; 692a (5556); Map 1841?, 9 chns; building names; table lists owners and acreages. Apt generalises land use and omits occupiers.

4/78 Wendye (parish) TL 329472 [Wendy]
Apt 28.11.1850; 966a (947); Map 1851?, 5 chns.

4/79 Wentworth (parish) TL 482787
Apt 25.03.1840; 1438a (all); Map 1840, 6 chns; turnpike roads, tollgate, occupation and public roads, houses, woods, embankments; pictorial church.

4/80 Westley Waterless (parish) TL 607565
Apt 07.01.1838; 1102a (all); Map 1843?, 6 chns; waterbodies, houses, woods, plantations.

4/81 Westwick (hamlet in parish of Oakington) TL 423655
Apt 31.03.1838; 326a (all); Map 1839?, 3 chns; waterbodies, grassland (col), open fields (named), field gates, road names.

4/82 Whaddon (parish) TL 349467
Apt 28.02.1842; 1463a (all); Map 1841, 6 chns; waterbodies, woods, parkland.

4/83 Whittlesey St Mary and Whittlesey St Andrew (parish) TL 295962 [Whittlesey]
Apt 08.02.1841; 25856a (25131); Map 1841, 6 chns, in 4 parts, ? by R.J. Wright, Norwich, (includes enlargements of Whittlesey town and of Eastrea and Coates at 3 chns); waterbodies, houses, marsh/bog, building names, road names, pump, market.

4/84 Wicken (parish) TL 553719
Apt 06.08.1842; 1626a (?); Map 1844, 6 chns, by John King and Son, Saffron Walden, Essex; waterbodies; pictorial church; double lines may be drains.

4/85 Willingham (parish) TL 417711
Apt 26.09.1837; 4663a (4663); Map 1841, 6 chns; waterbodies, houses, marsh/bog, open fields (named), field boundary ownerships, building names, road names, windmills (by symbol), sluice, common.

4/86 Wilburton (parish) TL 484736
Apt 31.03.1838; 1784a (2233); Map 1840?, 3 chns; foot/b'way, waterbodies, houses, woods, marsh/bog, open fields (named), fence, field boundary ownerships, field gates, road names, ferry; double lines may be drains.

4/87 Wimblington (township and hamlet in parish of Doddington) TL 445915
Apt 04.05.1839; 7590a (7589); Map 1840, 8 chns, in 2 parts, by Joseph Jackson, March, (includes enlargement of Wimblington village at 4 chns); turnpike roads, tollbar, houses, building names, farm names and boundaries, common, windmills (pictorial); fenland named; meaning of colour tints is unclear. Apt generalises land use.

4/88 Wimpole (parish) TL 340508 [Not listed]
Apt 26.09.1837; 2406a (all); Map 1851?, 8.3 chns; waterbodies, woods, parkland.

4/89 Wisbech St Mary (parish) TF 391052
Apt 11.10.1838; 9607a (9606); Map 1838, 4 chns, in 2 parts, copied and enlarged from Wattes survey by Richard Freeman, Wisbech; turnpike roads, waterbodies, building names, road names, former open field names, counterdrain, embankment.

4/90 Wisbech St Peters (parish) TF 430055 [Wisbech]
Apt 29.01.1841; 6434a (all); Map 1842, 3 chns, in 2 parts, by R. Freeman, Wisbech; construction lines, turnpike roads, canal, road names, former open field names, watermill steam engine, old river bed, toll gate, canal sluice.

4/91 Witcham (parish) TL 466808
Apt 09.03.1840; 2671a (all); Map 1841, 6 chns, in 2 parts, by Alexander Watford, Cambridge, (including 10-chn location diagram); waterbodies, recreation ground.

4/92 Witchford (parish) TL 503799
Apt 27.07.1839; 2376a (2376); Map 1839, 6 chns, in 3 parts, by Henry Grounds, Cambridge; foot/b'way, waterbodies, embankment.

4/93 West Wratting (parish) TL 600520
Apt 12.09.1848; 1a (3441); Map (drawn on Apt) 1852?, 0.6 chns (1:480), (tithable parts only); waterbodies, landowners, occupation road, mill; only 0a 0r 3p remains tithable.

Cheshire

PRO IR29 and IR30 5/1–452

477 tithe districts: 657,123 acres
452 tithe commutations: 588,866 acres
239 voluntary tithe agreements, 213 compulsory tithe awards

Tithe and tithe commutation

In the county of Cheshire some 95 per cent of tithe districts remained subject to payment of tithes in 1836 and eighty-three districts were wholly tithable (Fig. 17). As in other counties with predominantly pastoral agriculture, modus payments in lieu of tithes were the main cause of tithe exemption.

Assistant tithe commissioners and local tithe agents who worked in Cheshire are listed in Table 5.1 and the valuers of the county's tithe rent-charge in Table 5.2. Cheshire tithe apportionments are distinguished by the comparatively large number (11 per cent) which list the crops grown in each field under 'state of cultivation' (see also Lancashire and Staffordshire).

Tithe maps

About 7 per cent of Cheshire's 452 tithe maps are sealed as first class. The proportion of districts mapped to this standard is comparable to Lancashire but is markedly greater than in any of the surrounding counties. This is all the more surprising as considerable tracts of land were subject to small modus payments rather than a full tithe, a fact which elsewhere was not conducive to high-quality mapping. Construction lines are present on 9 per cent of second-class maps which suggests that these were also new surveys. On twenty-seven maps copying is explicitly acknowledged, though a considerable proportion of these maps are by Henry White of Warrington who was particularly diligent in acknowledging his sources.

Map production in Cheshire follows the usual pattern through time with a noticeable peak in 1840 but, as Table 5.4 shows, output thereafter remained quite steady throughout the 1840s. Cheshire maps are drawn at a variety of scales from one inch to two chains to one inch to twenty chains and 58 per cent are in the recommended scale range of one inch to three to four chains. The most popular scale in this county was the six-chain which was employed for 30 per cent of tithe districts, but in large districts, the eight-chain scale was favoured. Two maps are certainly drawn to a scale of one inch to 4.4 statute chains which is the equivalent of one inch to three Cheshire chains of 32 yards and it is possible that

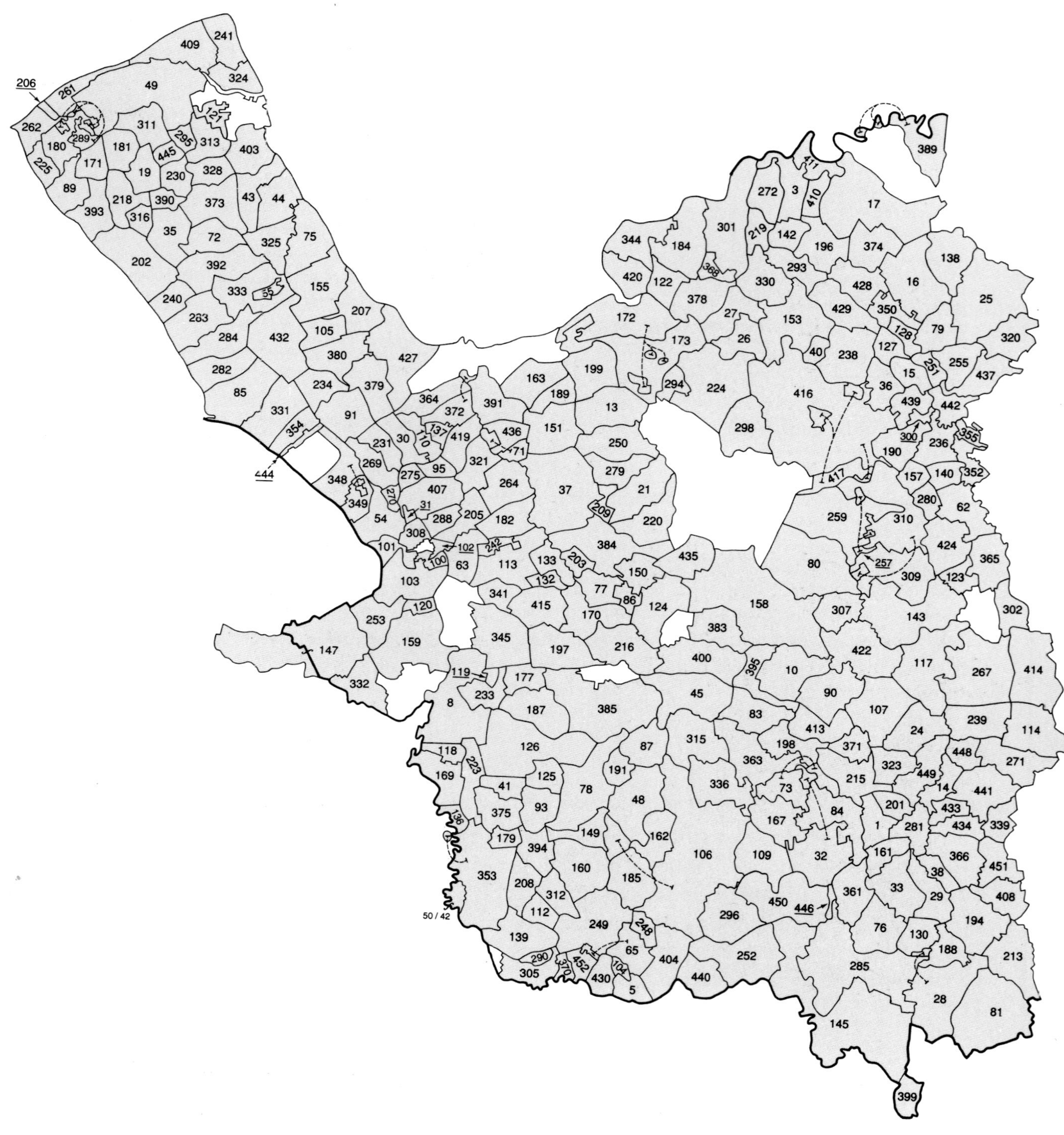

Fig. 17 Cheshire: tithe district boundaries.

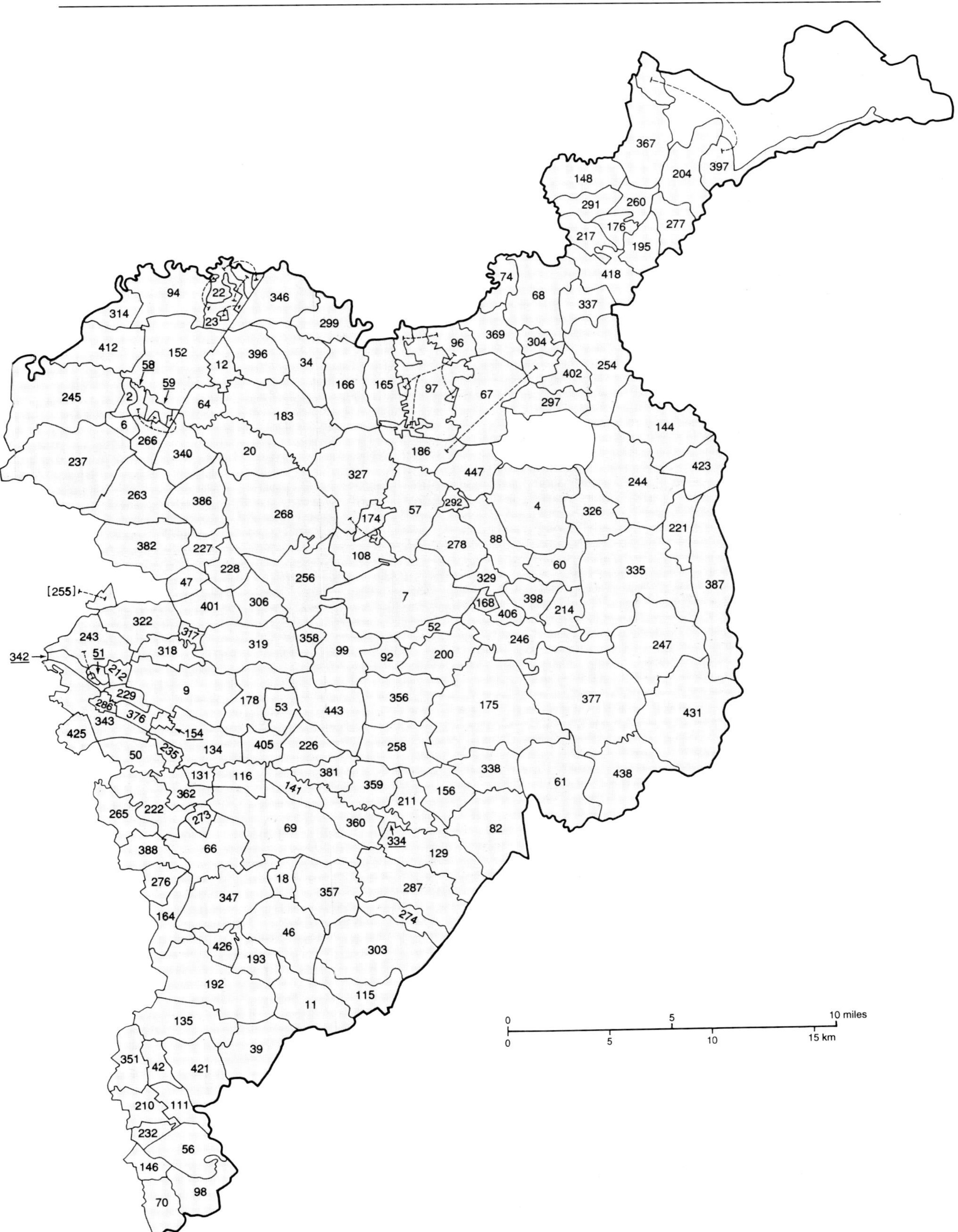
367
397
204
148
291
260
176
277
217
195
418
74
68
337
94
22
346
314
23
299
96
369
304
412
152
58
12
396
34
402
254
59
2
166
165
97
67
245
64
183
297
6
144
266
20
186
340
237
447
423
327
263
386
292
244
268
174
57
4
326
221
382
227
278
88
108
228
60
335
256
47
329
[255]
387
7
401
306
398
168
214
406
322
52
317
243
358
246
319
99
92
200
247
342
51
318
212
9
229
178
53
356
377
286
443
175
431
376
343
154
425
405
226
258
134
50
235
338
438
61
131
116
381
141
359
156
362
211
265
222
273
360
82
69
334
388
66
129
18
276
287
357
347
274
164
46
426
303
193
192
11
115
135
39
351
42
421
210
111
232
56
146
98
70
0 5 10 miles
0 5 10 15 km

paper distortion masks the fact that a number of maps recorded at scales of one inch to 4.3, 4.5 and 9 chains were in fact drawn to Cheshire chain-related scales of one inch to 4.4 and 8.8 statute chains (3 and 6 Cheshire chains respectively).

As records of land use, Cheshire tithe maps have some similarities with Welsh tithe maps in that woodland (on 86 per cent of maps) and parkland (on 28 per cent) are well recorded but other agricultural land uses are rarely depicted. None shows arable or grass and few depict gardens or orchards. Only 16 per cent of the maps record inhabited houses but 48 per cent identify foot or bridle paths and an unusually high proportion of 12 per cent show turnpike roads.

It was quite usual in Cheshire for the same man to value the tithes of a district and also to make the tithe map. Thus it is no surprise that the two most prolific valuers, James Cawley of Macclesfield and John Davies of Great Mollington also head the list of surveyors in Table 5.2.

Cheshire maps as a whole are very much 'plain working plans' in appearance. A notable exception is the map of Weaverham on which a bird of prey holds the scale bar by its beak. Colour is used on a number of Cheshire maps to emphasise parkland and demesne land or to indicate tithe-free land. A few maps, such as that of Brereton cum Smethwick are very finely drawn whereas at least four maps are noted in the catalogue of Cheshire tithe maps as little more than rough sketches.

Table 5.1. *Agreements and awards for commutation of tithes in Cheshire*

Assistant commissioner/ local tithe agent	*Number of agreements**	*Number of awards*
John Holder	132	0
John Job Rawlinson	0	130
Thomas Sudworth	54	0
Richard Burton Phillipson	43	0
Charles Howard	6	19
John Mee Mathew	1	24
John Maurice Herbert	0	15
Thomas Martin	12	1
George Wingrove Cooke	0	12
John Penny	11	0
Thomas Hoskins	10	0
John Strangeways Donaldson Selby	0	10
Henry Pilkington	8	0
George Bolls	0	1
Horace William Meteyard	1	0
Thomas Smith Woolley	0	1

*Computed from the number of extant reports on tithe agreements in the tithe files [PRO IR 18].

Table 5.2. *Tithe valuers and tithe map-makers in Cheshire*

Name and address (in Cheshire unless indicated)	*Number of districts*	*Acreage*
Tithe valuers		
John Davies, Great Mollington	43	43,610
James Cawley, Macclesfield	38	67,198
Samuel Harding, Alpraham	28	38,392
Henry White, Warrington, Lancashire	27	38,744
John Johnstone, Sandbach	20	49,471
Charles Brittain, Everton, Liverpool, Lancashire	20	15,464
Daniel Shaw, Cheadle	16	33,091
Richard Trim Beckett, Oulton Farm	13	23,910
Thomas Burgess, Norton, Runcorn	13	20,006
William Worrall, Chester	13	9,751
George Cawley, Tabley Superior	11	9,269
John Palin, Denbighshire/Flintshire	10	9,586
Others [78]	200	230,374
Attributed tithe map-makers		
James Cawley and others, Macclesfield	35	63,926
John Davies, Mollington	33	40,518
Henry White, Warrington, Lancashire	28	38,465
George Cawley, Tabley, Knutsford	24	24,007
Samuel Harding, Alpraham	18	24,883
William Worrall, Chester	17	12,725
Thomas Burgess and Richard Owen	11	22,721
Thomas Greaves, Hale, Altrincham	8	12,938
Others [49]	95	130,892

Table 5.3. *The tithe maps of Cheshire: scales and classes*

Scale in chains/inch	*All maps*		*First Class*		*Second Class*	
	Number	*Acreage*	*Number*	*Acreage*	*Number*	*Acreage*
>3	6	4,771	1	2,890	5	1,881
3	130	165,574	27	45,526	103	120,048
3.3	1	803	1	803	0	0
4	68	83,562	4	5,833	64	77,729
4.3, 4.4, 4.5, 4.75	7	13,272	0	0	7	13,272
5	23	21,479	0	0	23	21,479
6	148	183,304	0	0	148	183,304
7, 7.5	4	15,957	0	0	4	15,957
8	32	61,260	0	0	32	61,260
9	23	22,857	0	0	23	22,857
<9	10	16,027	0	0	10	16,027
TOTAL	452	588,866	33	55,052	419	533,814

Table 5.4. *The tithe maps of Cheshire: dates*

	<1837	*1837*	*1838*	*1839*	*1840*	*1841*	*1842*	*1843*	*1844*	*1845*	*1846*	*1847*	*1848*	*>1848*
All maps	2	8	34	76	46	41	21	20	29	31	24	41	32	41
1st class	0	1	3	1	5	7	1	1	1	1	1	2	0	4
2nd class*	2	7	31	75	41	34	20	19	28	30	23	39	32	37

*Three second-class tithe maps of Cheshire in the Public Record Office collection are undated.

Cheshire

5/1 Acton (township in parish of Acton) SJ 631526
Apt 16.10.1841; 722a (722); Map 1842?, 3 chns; hill-drawing, foot/b'way, canal, waterbodies, woods, parkland, building names.

5/2 Acton otherwise Agden (township in parish of Bowdon) SJ 719867 [Not listed]
Apt 25.04.1839; 203a (1139); Map 1839, 3 chns, by Thomas Greaves, Altringham; canal, waterbodies, woods.

5/3 Acton Grange (township in parish of Runcorn) SJ 588854 [Not listed]
Apt 22.07.1843; 1004a (1004); Map 1841, 6 chns, by H. White, Warrington; railways, foot/b'way, turnpike roads, canal, waterbodies, houses, woods (col), parkland (col), marsh/bog (col), building names, sand or stone pit, mill.

5/4 Adlington (township in parish of Prestbury) SJ 918804
Apt 08.05.1848; 3899a (all); Map 1850, 3 chns, 1st cl, by Cawley and Firth, Macclesfield; hill-drawing, railway, foot/b'way, canal, waterbodies, houses, woods, plantations, parkland, fences, milestone, boundary markers, well; compass rose has motto 'Ich Dien'.

5/5 Agden (township in parish of Malpas) SJ 510440 [Not listed]
Apt 20.07.1838; 548a (548); Map 1839?, 3 chns, 1st cl, 'rough draught' ? by Saml Rowe; construction lines, waterbodies, woods, field acreages.

5/6 Agden (township in parish of Rostherne) SJ 717855 [Not listed]
Apt 19.06.1848; 379a (all); Map 1848, 3 chns, by John Myatt, Congleton; foot/b'way, canal, waterbodies, woods, fences, field boundary ownerships, boathouse, ornamental gardens.

5/7 Alderley (parish) SJ 851761 [Alderley Edge]
Apt 23.12.1841; 6173a (6173); Map 1842, 7 chns, in 4 parts, by J. Cawley, Macclesfield; (one part at 6 chns; index at 18 chns); railway, foot/b'way, waterbodies, woods, plantations, parkland, field boundary ownerships, demesne lands (col).

5/8 Aldford (parish) SJ 420585
Apt 27.04.1837; 2633a (2633); Map 1838, 3 chns, 1st cl, by John Davies, Mollington near Chester; construction lines, waterbodies, houses, woods, plantations, parkland, field gates, building names, training ground, mill, lodge, school, quarry.

5/9 Allostock (township in parish of Great Budworth) SJ 743718
Apt 15.01.1845; 2925a (2924); Map 1847, 12 chns, by H. White, Warrington; foot/b'way, turnpike roads, waterbodies, woods, plantations, orchards, field gates, building names, Unitarian Chapel, mill; bridge named. Apt has cropping information.

5/10 Alphraham (township in parish of Bunbury) SJ 587604
Apt 06.06.1840; 1596a (1596); Map 1841?, 6 chns, by Samuel Harding; railway, foot/b'way, canal, waterbodies, woods (named), parkland, heath/moor, building names. Apt omits land use.

5/11 Alsager (township in parish of Barthomley) SJ 794555
Apt 27.03.1839; 2184a (2184); Map 1838, 6 chns, by Charles Heaton, Enden near Leek; foot/b'way, turnpike roads, waterbodies, woods (col, named), plantations (col), open fields, field gates, building names, lodge, school, marl pit, mill, toll bar.

5/12 Altrincham (township in parish of Bowdon) SJ 768883
Apt 21.11.1838; 657a (657); Map 1835, 3 chns, by John Crampton; foot/b'way, canal, waterbodies, plantations, moss (named); built-up part generalised.

5/13 Alvanley (township in parish of Frodsham) SJ 498739
Apt 01.11.1844; 1501a (1532); Map 1839, 5 chns, by Sam. Harding; waterbodies, woods, field boundary ownerships, building names, mill. Apt omits land use.

5/14 Alvaston (township in parish of Nantwich) SJ 664543
Apt 08.04.1841; 611a (all); Map 1839, 3 chns, by Sam. Harding; waterbodies, woods.

5/15 Anderton (township in parish of Great Budworth) SJ 648757
Apt 29.10.1844; 481a (481); Map 1845, 4 chns; foot/b'way, waterbodies, woods. Apt omits land use.

5/16 Antrobus (township in parish of Great Budworth) SJ 646806
Apt 29.10.1844; 2087a (2086); Map 1847, 6 chns, by H. White, Warrington; foot/b'way, waterbodies, woods, plantations, parkland, orchards, heath/moor, building names, Methodist Chapel, pump house, rough land (named); colours may show property ownerships. Apt has cropping information.

5/17 Appleton (township in parish of Great Budworth) SJ 632840 [Appleton Park]
Apt 31.12.1844; 3325a (3324); Map 1847, 8 chns, by H. White, Warrington; hill-drawing, foot/b'way, turnpike roads, canal, waterbodies, woods, plantations, parkland, field gates, building names; mapmaker notes: 'This plan is principally compiled from Estate Plans of landowners but all that part north of the Duke of Bridgewater's Canal and a part immediately on the south side of Do. is from an actual survey made in 1845'. Apt has cropping information.

5/18 Arclid (township in parish of Sandbach) SJ 785618 [Not listed]
Apt 29.06.1839; 539a (538); Map 1840?, 3 chns; foot/b'way, turnpike roads, waterbodies, houses, woods, road names, toll bar, green. Apt omits land use.

5/19 Arrow (township in parish of Woodchurch) SJ 268863 [Arrowe Hill]
Apt 24.03.1846; 752a (752); Map 1846, 6 chns; foot/b'way, waterbodies, woods, parkland, fences, field gates.

5/20 Ashley (township in parish of Bowdon) SJ 777840
Apt 21.11.1838; 2174a (2173); Map 1838, 6 chns; waterbodies, woods, parkland, building names, mill.

5/21 Ashton (township in parish of Tarvin) SJ 513695
Apt 21.11.1838; 1303a (1303); Map 1839, 6 chns, by Geo. Cawley, Tabley; foot/b'way, waterbodies, farmyards, woods (col), parkland (col), building names. Apt omits land use.

5/22 Ashton upon Mersey (township in parish of Ashton upon Mersey) SJ 769918 [Ashton Upon Mersey]
Apt 27.08.1847; 831a (831); Map 1847?, 3 chns, 1st cl; foot/b'way, waterbodies, houses, woods (col), plantations (col), heath/moor (col); map also covers district 5/23.

5/23 Ashton upon Mersey (township in parish of Bowdon) SJ 772909 [Ashton Upon Mersey]
Apt 21.11.1838; 780a (780); Map 1847?, 3 chns, 1st cl; foot/b'way, waterbodies, houses, woods (col), plantations (col), heath/moor (col); map also covers district 5/22.

5/24 Aston (township in parish of Acton) SJ 649572 [Aston juxta Mondrum]
Apt 14.01.1842; 1255a (1255); Map 1839, 4 chns; railway, canal, waterbodies, farmyards, woods.

5/25 Aston (township in parish of Great Budworth) SJ 684797 [Not listed]
Apt 01.11.1844; 2860a (2859); Map 1846, 9 chns, surveyed for tithe commutation by H. White, Warrington; foot/b'way, waterbodies, woods, parkland, building names, road names; demesne lands (green), tithe-free lands (purple); bridge named; mapmaker notes: 'This plan is compiled from old estate plans of R.E.E. Warburton Esq and Lord de Tabley with the exception of Arley Park and the Estate belonging to Mrs Forrest which are from recent survey'. Apt has cropping information.

5/26 Aston Grange (township in parish of Runcorn) SJ 563778
Apt 26.04.1843; 438a (437); Map 1844, 4 chns; foot/b'way, waterbodies, woods, field boundary ownerships.

5/27 Aston by Sutton (township in parish of Runcorn) SJ 556786 [Aston]
Apt 26.04.1843; 1013a (1012); Map 1844, 6 chns, by R. Stelfox, Allesley; railways, foot/b'way, turnpike roads and gate, canal, waterbodies, woods, parkland, building names, road names, lodges, dog kennel, tunnel mouth.

5/28 Audlem (township in parish of Audlem) SJ 663437
Apt 27.07.1839; 2358a (2358); Map 1842, 8 chns, in 3 parts, (includes Audlem town at 4 chns); foot/b'way, canal, waterbodies, woods, fences, building names, moss (named).

5/29 Austerson (township in parish of Acton) SJ 662498 [Not listed]
Apt 31.08.1841; 899a (899); Map 1842?, 8 chns, by John Gregory, Adderley, Salop; foot/b'way, waterbodies, woods, fence.

5/30 Backford (township in parishes of Backford and Stoke) SJ 398723
Apt 28.02.1839; 750a (749); Map 1842?, 5 chns, by John Davies, Mollington near Chester; turnpike roads, canal, waterbodies, woods, parkland, building names, road names, quarry, tollgate.

5/31 Bache (township in parish of Chester St Oswald) SJ 400683 [Not listed]
Apt 23.11.1844; 94a (94); Map 1845?, 3 chns, by C. Brittan; waterbodies, woods, parkland, field gates.

5/32 Baddiley (parish) SJ 604508 [Not listed]
Apt 18.12.1839; 1962a (1962); Map 1839, 8 chns, in 2 parts, by Sam. Harding; canal, waterbodies, woods (col), building names, mill, greens. Apt omits land use.

5/33 Baddington (township in parish of Acton) SJ 643493 [Not listed]
Apt 31.08.1841; 1402a (1401); Map 1841?, 6 chns, by John Gregory, Adderley, Salop; canal, waterbodies, woods.

5/34 Baguley (township in parishes of Bowdon and Northen) SJ 808887
Apt 21.11.1838; 1769a (1769); Map 1838, 4 chns, 'copied, valued and apportioned' by James Cawley and Son, Tabley; foot/b'way, turnpike roads, waterbodies, woods, building names, road names, mill, moor. Apt omits land use.

5/35 Barnston (township in parish of Woodchurch) SJ 281827
Apt 24.03.1846; 1068a (1068); Map 1847?, 9 chns, by J. Palin, Christleton, litho (by Evans and Howarth, Chester); waterbodies, woods, tilery.

5/36 Barnton (township in parish of Great Budworth) SJ 633753
Apt 29.10.1844; 751a (751); Map 1843, 3 chns, 1st cl, 'made for the commutation of the tithes', copied from the original plan made by John Beckett for Henry White, Warrington; foot/b'way, turnpike roads, canal, waterbodies, houses, woods, orchards, open fields, field gates, building names, road names, weir, rope walk, salt works, Methodist Chapel, sand or stone pits. Apt has cropping information.

5/37 Barrow (parish) SJ 475696 [Not listed]
Apt 12.04.1838; 2916a (2916); Map 1839?, 6 chns; foot/b'way, waterbodies, woods, building names. Apt omits land use.

5/38 Bartherton (township in parish of Wybunbury) SJ 662500 [Not listed]
Apt 28.05.1838; 404a (all); Map 1839?, 5 chns; waterbodies, gardens.

5/39 Barthomley (township in parish of Barthomley) SJ 767530
Apt 27.03.1839; 1872a (1982); Map 1838, 12 chns; waterbodies, woods.

5/40 Bartington (township in parish of Great Budworth) SJ 599770 [Not listed]
Apt 20.02.1841; 307a (306); Map 1841, 6 chns, made for the commutation of tithes from an original survey by J. Eagle in 1822 by H. White, Warrington; canal, waterbodies, woods, boundary stones, demesne lands. Apt has cropping information.

5/41 Barton (township in parish of Farndon) SJ 447542
Apt 16.04.1840; 511a (511); Map 1840?, 9 chns, by W. Worrall, Chester; waterbodies, woods, parkland, fences, field gates. Apt omits land use.

5/42 Basford (township in parish of Wybunbury) SJ 718523 [Not listed]
Apt 28.05.1838; 643a (all); Map 1839?, 5 chns; railways, waterbodies, woods, gardens, sandpit.

5/43 Higher Bebbington (township in parish of Bebbington) SJ 319850 [Higher Bebington]
Apt 25.07.1843; 899a (all); Map 1844, 6 chns; railway (named), waterbodies, woods, parkland, landowners, hotels, ferry, baths.

5/44 Lower Bebbington (township in parish of Bebbington) SJ 335846 [Lower Bebington]
Apt 25.07.1843; 1053a (all); Map 1844, 6 chns, in 3 parts, by C. Brittain, (includes parts of villages at 3 chns); railways (named), foot/b'way, waterbodies, woods, parkland, building names, quarry, quay.

5/45 Beeston (township in parish of Bunbury) SJ 537592
Apt 06.03.1846; 1957a (1957); Map 1846?, 3 chns, 1st cl, by Samuel Harding; hill-drawing, railway with cuttings, waterbodies, woods.

5/46 Betchton (township in parish of Sandbach) SJ 786589 [Not listed]
Apt 28.11.1840; 2594a (2594); Map 1841?, 4 chns; hill-drawing, foot/b'way, canal, aqueduct, waterbodies, woods, building names, landowners, malt kilns, salt works, sand hole, ownership boundaries (col). Apt omits land use.

5/47 Bexton (township in parish of Nether Knutsford) SJ 746773 [Not listed]
Apt 27.08.1847; 621a (all); Map 1847, 3 chns, by G.H. Davenport, Knutsford; foot/b'way, waterbodies, farmyards, woods, building names.

5/48 Bickerton (township in parish of Malpas) SJ 511535
Apt 29.11.1838; 1755a (1755); Map 1839?, 4 chns; waterbodies, plantations; uplands named. Apt omits land use.

5/49 Bidston (parish) SJ 266904
Apt 01.09.1838; 4207a (4248); Map 1842?, 3 chns, in 5 parts, by John Davies, Mollington near Chester, (includes index); turnpike roads and gate, toll gate, waterbodies, woods, plantations, open fields, building names, road names, coastal embankment, lighthouse, smithy, quarries, windmill, boundary stones, common, moss. Apt has cropping information.

5/50 Biley cum Yatehouses (township in parish of Middlewick) SJ 714685 [Byley]
Apt 14.09.1842; 1030a (1030); Map 1843?, 4 chns; foot/b'way, waterbodies.

5/51 Birches (township in parish of Great Budworth) SJ 699728 [Not listed]
Apt 31.12.1844; 158a (157); Map 1845, 3 chns, by G. Cawley; foot/b'way, waterbodies, farmyards, field gates.

5/52 Birtles (township in parish of Prestbury) SJ 864742 [Not listed]
Apt 07.07.1848; 160a (460); Map 1849?, 4 chns, ? by E.W. Wilmot; waterbodies, woods.

5/53 Blackden (township in parish of Sandbach) SJ 788704 [Not listed]
Apt 31.10.1840; 736a (all); Map 1841?, 6 chns, by James Cawley, Macclesfield; foot/b'way, waterbodies, woods, plantations, orchards, field boundary ownerships; colour bands may show property ownerships

5/54 Blacon with Crabhall (township in parish of Chester Holy Trinity and St Oswalds) SJ 384685
Apt 28.10.1843; 1115a (1115); Map 1847?, 8 chns; waterbodies, woods, gardens, hedges, field gates.

5/55 Blakely Brow and Hargreave (district in parish of Neston) SJ 331797 [Not listed]
Apt 28.03.1845; 275a (?); Map 1847?, 4 chns, by John Davies, Mollington near Chester; hill-drawing, foot/b'way, waterbodies, woods, field gates.

5/56 Blakenhall (township in parish of Wybunbury) SJ 730479
Apt 26.11.1842; 1544a (1544); Map 1843?, 5 chns; railways, waterbodies, woods, fences, building names.

5/57 Bollin Fee (township in parish of Wilmslow) SJ 862806 [Not listed]
Apt 05.02.1840; 2664a (2664); Map 1841, 4 chns, 1st cl, by J. Cawley, Macclesfield; railway, waterbodies, houses, plantations.

5/58 Bollington (township in parish of Rostherne) SJ 727867
Apt 19.06.1848; 330a (all); Map 1848, 4 chns, by G.H. Davenport, Knutsford; hill-drawing, canal with embankment, waterbodies, houses, farmyards, woods, plantations, field gates, building names.

5/59 Bollington (township in parish of Bowdon) SJ 732864
Apt 25.04.1839; 303a (631); Map 1839, 4 chns, by R. Thornton, Manchester; foot/b'way, canal, waterbodies, woods (col). Apt omits land use.

5/60 Bollington (township in parish of Prestbury) SJ 930773
Apt 07.07.1848; 875a (1184); Map 1848, 6 chns, by Cawley and Firth, Macclesfield, (tithable parts only); foot/b'way, canal, waterbodies, woods, plantations, parkland, heath/moor; colour bands may show property ownerships.

5/61 Bosley (township in parish of Prestbury) SJ 921661
Apt 27.07.1848; 3073a (all); Map 1850, 8 chns, by George Lamb, Derby; waterbodies, plantations.

5/62 Bostock (township in parish of Davenham) SJ 674688 [Bostock Green]
Apt 11.05.1838; 1112a (1111); Map 1839, 3 chns, by Burgess and Owen; waterbodies, woods, parkland, building names, lodge, boat house, dog kennel, ox house. Apt omits land use.

5/63 Great Boughton (township in parish of Chester St Oswald) SJ 427662 [Boughton]
Apt 23.11.1844; 760a (760); Map 1846?, 6 chns, by W. Worrall; railways, canal, waterbodies, woods, fences, field gates. Apt omits land use.

5/64 Bowdon (township) SJ 757866
Apt 21.11.1838; 829a (828); Map 1839, 4 chns, by R. Thornton, Manchester; foot/b'way, waterbodies, woods, building names.

5/65 Bradley (township in parish of Malpas) SJ 510459 [Bradley Green]
Apt 21.07.1838; 887a (887); Map 1839?, 3 chns, 1st cl, by Robert Cotgreave for Saml Rowe; foot/b'way, waterbodies, woods, landowners, field acreages.

5/66 Bradwall (township in parish of Sandbach) SJ 752634 [Bradwall Green]
Apt 29.06.1839; 2063a (2063); Map 1839?, 4 chns; foot/b'way, waterbodies, houses, woods, parkland, gardens (col), building names. Apt omits land use.

5/67 Bramall (township in parish of Stockport) SJ 894859 [Bramhall]
Apt 25.05.1849; 2890a (3250); Map 1841 and 1842, 2 chns, 1st cl, by Thomas Hill, Ashton-under-Lyne; construction lines, railway with station, foot/b'way, turnpike roads, waterbodies, woods, plantations, parkland, building names, toll bar; legend explains boundaries.

5/68 Bredbury (township in parish of Stockport) SJ 925914
Apt 25.10.1842; 2522a (2521); Map 1841, 3 chns, 1st cl, by Willm Dabbs, Leicester; construction lines, turnpike roads, canal, waterbodies, houses, woods, parkland, fences, field boundary ownerships, building names, brick kiln, gravel, mills, factory, toll bar.

5/69 Brereton cum Smethwick (parish) SJ 789642 [Brereton Green, Smethwick Green]
Apt 29.05.1847; 4501a (all); Map 1848, 3 chns, surveyed for the commutation of tithes by J. Beckett, Oulton Farm; railway, foot/b'way, waterbodies, woods (named), parkland, building names, mill.

5/70 Bridgmere (township in parish of Wybunbury) SJ 718450 [Not listed]
Apt 21.11.1842; 1097a (1097); Map 1843, 8 chns, by R. Owen; foot/b'way, waterbodies, woods, parkland, field gates.

5/71 Bridge Trafford (township in parish of Plemondstall) SJ 453716
Apt 07.03.1838; 402a (401); Map 1840?, 6 chns; waterbodies, woods. Apt omits land use.

5/72 Brimstage (township in parish of Bromborough) SJ 302827
Apt 26.01.1841; 1013a (1012); Map 1842?, 9 chns.

5/73 Brindley (township in parish of Acton) SJ 585541
Apt 16.10.1841; 1090a (1090); Map 1839, 6 chns, by Samuel Harding; waterbodies, woods, building names.

5/74 Brinnington (township in parish of Stockport) SJ 909919
Apt 25.10.1842; 783a (783); Map 1842, 3 chns, by Thomas Hill, Ashton under Lyne; hill-drawing, foot/b'way, turnpike roads, waterbodies, farmyards, woods, parkland, field gates, pound.

5/75 Bromborow (township in parish of Bromborow) SJ 351823 [Bromborough]
Apt 27.03.1839; 1511a (2600); Map 1840?, [6 chns]; railway, foot/b'way, waterbodies, woods, parkland, low and high water marks. Apt omits land use.

5/76 Broomhall (township in parish of Acton) SJ 633472 [Broomhall Green]
Apt 31.08.1841; 1291a (1291); Map 1842?, 6 chns; foot/b'way, canal, waterbodies, woods.

5/77 Bruen Stapleford (township in parish of Tarvin) SJ 492645 [Not listed]
Apt 21.11.1838; 744a (744); Map 1838, 5 chns, ? by George Ruce; foot/b'way, waterbodies, woods. Apt omits land use.

5/78 Broxton (township in parish of Malpas) SJ 488545
Apt 18.09.1838; 2129a (2128); Map 1839?, 3 chns; waterbodies, woods, parkland. Apt omits land use.

5/79 Great Budworth (township in parish of Great Budworth) SJ 659779
Apt 01.11.1844; 875a (875); Map 1841, 6 chns, in 2 parts, by H. White, Warrington, (includes enlargement of Great Budworth village at 2 chns); foot/b'way, waterbodies, woods, parkland, field gates, building names, pump. Apt has cropping information.

5/80 Little Budworth (parish) SJ 598657
Apt 08.02.1839; 2764a (2762); Map 1840?, 9 chns; building names. Apt omits land use.

5/81 Buerton (township in parish of Audlem) SJ 688428 [Not listed]
Apt 17.10.1843; 2954a (2953); Map 1844, 6 chns, by John Myatt, Buerton near Audlem, Cheshire; foot/b'way, waterbodies, houses, woods (named), field boundary ownerships, field gates, building names, windmill, sand or stone pits, moss (named).

5/82 Buglawton (township in parish of Astbury) SJ 888638
Apt 14.05.1840; 2853a (2852); Map 1839, 3 chns, in 2 parts, by J.P. Lofthouse, Hopton, litho; turnpike roads, toll gate, canal, waterbodies, woods (col), plantations, parkland, common, building names, mill, tan yard, tan house, quarries, boundary stones; part of the map is titled 'enlargements on the three chain scale', although this part is at the same scale as the main map.

5/83 Bunbury (township in parish of Bunbury) SJ 571581
Apt 06.06.1840; 1141a (1140); Map 1839, 6 chns, by Sam. Harding; railway, waterbodies, woods. Apt omits land use.

5/84 Burland (township in parish of Acton) SJ 620529
Apt 16.10.1841; 1520a (1520); Map 1842?, 8 chns, (tinted); foot/b'way, canal, waterbodies, woods, heath/moor, field gates, windmill.

5/85 Burton (township in parish of Burton) SJ 319744
Apt 29.07.1843; 1858a (all); Map 1847?, 6 chns, by John Davies, Mollington, Chester; waterbodies, woods, plantations, parkland, building names, road names, well, mill. Apt has cropping information.

5/86 Burton (township in parish of Tarvin) SJ 508641
Apt 21.11.1838; 324a (324); Map 1839, 4 chns, by George Cawley, Tabley; waterbodies, farmyards, woods (col); map is signed by landowners. Apt omits land use.

5/87 Burdwardsley (township in parish of Bunbury) SJ 516564 [Burwardsley]
Apt 06.06.1840; 1020a (1039); Map 1842, 6 chns, by William Worrall, Chester; hill-drawing, waterbodies, woods, heath/moor, building names, sand pits, well, trig. point.

5/88 Butley (township in parish of Prestbury) SJ 901786 [Butley Town]
Apt 08.05.1848; 1810a (all); Map 1849, 3 chns, 1st cl, by Cawley and Firth, Macclesfield; railway, foot/b'way, waterbodies, houses, woods, plantations, parkland, field gates.

5/89 Caldy (township in parish of West Kirby) SJ 231854
Apt 03.01.1844; 747a (all); Map 1844, 6 chns, by Charles Brittain; waterbodies, houses, woods, rock outcrops, building names, high water mark.

5/90 Calveley (township in parish of Bunbury) SJ 608594
Apt 22.12.1848; 1517a (1517); Map 1849, 6 chns, by R. Owen; foot/b'way, railway with station, canal, waterbodies, woods, parkland, field boundary ownerships, field gates, building names, sand or stone pit.

5/91 Capenhurst (township in parish of Capenhurst) SJ 368735
Apt 28.03.1839; 1174a (1173); Map 1840, 6 chns; railway, turnpike roads, waterbodies, woods, windmill, toll gate.

5/92 Capesthorne (township in parish of Prestbury) SJ 841728
Apt 31.07.1848; 749a (all); Map 1849?, 6 chns, ? by E.W. Wilmot; foot/b'way, waterbodies, woods, parkland (in detail), field gates, building names.

5/93 Carden (township in parish of Tilston) SJ 464531 [Not listed]
Apt 06.06.1840; 802a (802); Map 1839, 9 chns, by William Worrall, Chester; waterbodies, woods (col), parkland (col), building names. Apt omits land use.

5/94 Carrington (township in parish of Bowdon) SJ 742922
Apt 21.11.1838; 2334a (2333); Map 1841, 3 chns, 1st cl, by James Cawley, Macclesfield; construction lines, waterbodies, houses, plantations, moss (named).

5/95 Caughall (township in parish of Backford) SJ 413707 [Not listed]
Apt 17.04.1838; 328a (328); Map 1839?, 6 chns, by John Davies, Mollington, Chester; canal, waterbodies.

5/96 Cheadle Bulkeley (township in parish of Cheadle) SJ 883892 [Not listed]
Apt 23.09.1844; 1790a (1842); Map 1845, 3 chns, by John Taylor, Ollerset near Stockport, 'copied from a map belonging to the Guardians of the Stockport Union, which was tested by the Commissioners in the year 1842'; railways with station, foot/b'way, turnpike roads, waterbodies, farmyards, building names, road names, print works, township boundary (col); legend explains boundaries.

5/97 Cheadle Moseley (township in parish of Cheadle) SJ 872869 [Not listed]
Apt 23.09.1844; 2652a (2652); Map 1845, 3 chns, by John Taylor, Ollerset near Stockport, 'copied from a map belonging to the Guardians of the Stockport Union which was tested by the Commissioners in the year 1842'; railways, foot/b'way, turnpike roads, waterbodies, farmyards, building names, road names, tan pits, pumphouse, mills, print works, toll house, township boundaries (col); legend explains boundaries.

5/98 Checkley cum Wrinehill (township in parish of Wybunbury) SJ 736456
Apt 26.11.1842; 1433a (1433); Map 1843?, 6 chns; railway, foot/b'way, waterbodies, woods, plantations, heath/moor, landowners, moss (named).

5/99 Chelford (township in parish of Prestbury) SJ 821735
Apt 05.01.1848; 234a (290); Map 1848?, 4 chns, copied 'from a map made by Thomas Hale of Darnhall in the year 1789' by John Beckett, Oulton Farm; turnpike roads, waterbodies, woods, field acreages, landowners, bowling green (?); heath land is annotated 'lately enclosed'; table lists area numbers, description of property and acreages; map is subtitled 'late belonging to Robert Salisbury Brooke Esq and now to Miss F.D. Furnivall'. Apt omits land use.

5/100 Chester St Bridget with St Martin, St Peter and St Olave with St Michael (parishes) SJ 414660 [Not listed]
Apt 27.10.1845; 202a (201); Map 1848?, 3 chns, by John Davies, Mollington, Chester; hill-drawing, railways, waterbodies, field gates, building names, road names, weir, mills, city walls, exchange, infirmary, boundary stone, parish boundaries; built-up part generalised.

5/101 Chester Holy and Undivided Trinity (parish) SJ 393667 [Not listed]
Apt 24.04.1838; 269a (all); Map 1838?, 4 chns; canal, waterbodies, houses, woods, road names, water tower, river embankment, infirmary, city gaol, workhouse.

5/102 Chester St John the Baptist (parish) SJ 418668 [Not listed]
Apt 14.10.1845; 115a (all); Map 1848, 2 chns; railways, canal, road names, lead works; built-up part mostly generalised.

5/103 Chester St Mary on the Hill (parish) SJ 402648 [Not listed]
Apt 29.06.1839; 1449a (1441); Map 1842?, 6 chns, in 2 parts, by John Davies, Mollington, Chester, (includes enlargement of town at 2 chns); hill-drawing, waterbodies, woods, field gates, building names, road names, weir, boundary stones, city wall, lodges, toll gates, maypole, poor house, mills, castle, barracks, gaol, courts, esplanade. Apt has some cropping information.

5/104 Chidlow (township in parish of Malpas) SJ 504450 [Not listed]
Apt 01.01.1841; 153a (152); Map 1840?, 3 chns, by John Davies, Mollington, Chester; foot/b'way, waterbodies, field gates.

5/105 Childer Thornton (township in parish of Eastham) SJ 357777
Apt 26.02.1839; 724a (723); Map 1847?, 6 chns; railway with station, turnpike roads and gate, waterbodies, woods, road names.

5/106 Cholmondeley, Bickley, Bulkeley and Larkton (township in parish of Malpas) SJ 549510
Apt 21.01.1839; 5962a (6322); Map 1839, 6 chns, in 5 parts, by Burgess and Owen, (Bickley at 8 chns; includes index); foot/b'way, canal, waterbodies, houses, parkland (in detail), field gates, building names, kitchen garden, dog kennels, castle, common. Apt has cropping information.

5/107 Cholmondeston (township in parish of Acton) SJ 632584 [Not listed]
Apt 18.03.1843; 1747a (all); Map 1843, 8 chns, by J. Cawley, Macclesfield; railway, canal, plantations, field boundary ownerships.

5/108 Chorley (township in parish of Wilmslow) SJ 835782 [Not listed]
Apt 05.02.1840; 1358a (1357); Map 1841, 4 chns, 1st cl, by J. Cawley, Macclesfield; railway, waterbodies, houses, woods, plantations.

5/109 Chorley (township in parish of Acton) SJ 574506
Apt 16.10.1841; 1381a (1381); Map 1841, 6 chns, by T. Burgess and Owen; foot/b'way, waterbodies, building names, green. Apt omits land use.

5/110 Chorlton (township in parish of Backford) SJ 406725 [Not listed]
Apt 11.02.1847; 527a (527); Map 1849?, 6 chns, by John Davies, Mollington, Chester; canal, waterbodies, woods, plantations, parkland, field gates, building names, quarry. Apt has some cropping information.

5/111 Chorlton (township in parish of Wybunbury) SJ 729501
Apt 26.11.1842; 811a (810); Map 1843?, 6 chns; railway, waterbodies, woods.

5/112 Chorlton (township in parish of Malpas) SJ 466477 [Not listed]
Apt 28.02.1838; 461a (460); Map 1837, 6 chns; foot/b'way, waterbodies, woods, parkland, field gates.

5/113 Christleton (township) SJ 451659
Apt 23.11.1844; 1465a (all); Map 1847?, 6 chns, in 2 parts, by John Davies, (includes enlargement of village at 3 chns); railway, turnpike roads, turnpike gate, canal, waterbodies, woods, building names, road names, mill.

5/114 Church Coppenhall (township in parish of Coppenhall) SJ 707574
Apt 08.06.1841; 1531a (1530); Map 1840, 6 chns, by Sam. Harding; hill-drawing, railways with embankments, waterbodies, woods, building names, glebe (green).

5/115 Church Lawton (parish) SJ 820556 [Coppenhall]
Apt 09.02.1839; 1452a (1452); Map 1839, 6 chns, by Thomas Heaton, Endon near Leek; railway, foot/b'way, turnpike roads, tollgate, canal, waterbodies, woods (col, named), plantations, parkland (col), building names, road names, salt works, park lodges, occupation road.

5/116 Church Hulme (township in parish of Sandbach) SJ 765672 [Not listed]
Apt 06.06.1840; 864a (864); Map 1840?, 3 chns; hill-drawing, railway, foot/b'way, waterbodies, houses, woods, gardens; colours may show property ownerships. Apt omits land use.

5/117 Church Minshull (township in parish of Church Minshull) SJ 655607
Apt 28.05.1838; 2287a (2286); Map 1838, 5 chns; foot/b'way, canal, waterbodies, woods; tree symbols are drawn upside down or at right angles.

5/118 Churton by Farndon (township in parish of Farndon) SJ 418560
Apt 01.11.1839; 432a (432); Map 1840, 6 chns; waterbodies, woods. Apt omits field names.

5/119 Churton Heath otherwise Churton on the Heath (township in parish of Chester St Oswald) SJ 440600 [Not listed]
Apt 28.02.1839; 130a (129); Map 1838, 3 chns, made for the commutation of tithes by William Worrall, Chester; foot/b'way, waterbodies, woods, parkland, field gates, field names.

5/120 Claverton (township in parish of Chester St Mary on the Hill) SJ 405636 [Not listed]
Apt 11.10.1838; 253a (252); Map 1842?, 8 chns, by John Davies, Mollington near Chester; waterbodies, woods, road names.

5/121 Claughton cum Grange (township in parish of Woodchurch) SJ 305891
Apt 30.07.1846; 43a (436); Map 1850, 2 chns, ? by Edward Mills; plantations, parkland, road names.

5/122 Clifton otherwise Clifton with Rocksavage (township in parish of Runcorn) SJ 526802
Apt 04.07.1844; 625a (624); Map 1845, 6 chns, by Henry White, Warrington; hill-drawing, foot/b'way, occupation road, canal, wharf, waterbodies, woods, field acreages. Apt has cropping information.

5/123 Clive (township in parish of Middlewich) SJ 671653
Apt 8.6.1841; 458a (457); Map 1841?, 3 chns; hill-drawing, railway, foot/b'way, canal, waterbodies, houses, woods, land liable to flooding. Apt omits land use.

5/124 Clotton Hoolfield (township in parish of Tarvin) SJ 521635 [Clotton]
Apt 21.11.1838; 1539a (1539); Map 1840, 6 chns, surveyed for commutation of tithes; waterbodies, woods. Apt has cropping information.

5/125 Clutton (township in parish of Farndon) SJ 467546 [Not listed]
Apt 08.08.1840; 604a (609); Map 1840?, 9 chns, by W. Worrall, Chester; waterbodies, woods, parkland, school. Apt omits land use.

5/126 Coddington (parish) SJ 462564
Apt 07.03.1838; 2957a (2957); Map 1839, 8 chns, in 3 parts; waterbodies, woods (named), parkland, waste (named), landowners, tithe ownership boundaries (col); legend explains boundaries; '8 chains to an inch' is written in pencil. Apt omits land use.

5/127 Cogshall (township in parish of Great Budworth) SJ 635771 [Not listed]
Apt 01.11.1844; 517a (517); Map 1844, 3 chns, by 'copied from one made by H. White for the overseers of Cogshall in 1842', by H.White, Warrington; foot/b'way, waterbodies, houses, woods, parkland (in detail), field gates, building names. Apt has cropping information.

5/128 Comberbatch (township in parish of Great Budworth) SJ 645775 [Comberbach]
Apt 13.02.1845; 362a (362); Map 1845?, 4 chns; waterbodies, woods. Apt has cropping information.

5/129 Congleton (township in parish of Astbury) SJ 862628
Apt 30.10.1843; 2564a (2564); Map 1845, 3 chns, 1st cl, in 2 parts, (includes enlargement of town at 1 chn); hill-drawing, foot/b'way, turnpike roads, toll gate, canal, waterbodies, woods (named), plantations (named), field boundary ownerships, field gates, building names, road names, schools, factory, silk factory, Wesleyan Chapel, cemetery, Roman Catholic Chapel, post office, rope walk, moss (named).

5/130 Coole Pilate (township in parish of Acton) SJ 653466 [Not listed]
Apt 31.08.1841; 685a (685); Map 1838, 4.5 chns, by [Saml H. Ashdown], Uppington, Shrewsbury; foot/b'way, canal, waterbodies, houses, woods, field boundary ownerships, building names, brine pits; part of mapmaker's name is lost.

5/131 Cotton (township in parish of Sandbach) SJ 746673 [Not listed]
Apt 26.06.1839; 356a (355); Map 1839?, 3 chns; hill-drawing, waterbodies, houses, woods, building names. Apt omits land use.

5/132 Cotton Abbott (township in parish of Christleton) SJ 467649 [Cotton Abbotts]
Apt 23.11.1844; 312a (311); Map 1847?, 6 chns, by John Davies, Mollington, Chester; foot/b'way, waterbodies, woods, field gates, mill, township boundaries.

5/133 Cotton Edmunds (township in parish of Christleton) SJ 471658 [Not listed]
Apt 23.11.1844; 595a (595); Map 1847?, 6 chns; foot/b'way, waterbodies, woods, field gates, mill; map includes a large part of Cotton Abbott (5/132). Apt has some cropping information.

5/134 Cranage (township in parish of Sandbach) SJ 749690
Apt 27.05.1844; 1876a (1876); Map 1844?, 4 chns; waterbodies. Apt omits land use.

5/135 Crewe (township in parish of Barthomley) SJ 737546 [Crewe Green]
Apt 27.03.1839; 1950a (1993); Map 1840, 12 chns; railways, waterbodies, woods, parkland.

5/136 Crewe (township in parish of Farndon) SJ 424527
Apt 23.11.1844; 279a (279); Map 1840, 6 chns; waterbodies, woods. Apt omits some field names.

5/137 Croughton (township in parish of Chester St Oswald) SJ 415725 [Not listed]
Apt 20.03.1849; 276a (all); Map 1850?, 9 chns, (tinted); hill-drawing, canal, waterbodies, farmyards, woods, parkland, hedge.

5/138 Crowley (township in parish of Great Budworth) SJ 664815 [Not listed]
Apt 29.10.1844; 1385a (1384); Map 1846, 9.75 chns, by H. White, Warrington, 'made from one in the possession of R.E.E. Warburton Esqr (the principal landowner) with the exception of 1 or 2 small estates which are from actual Survey'; foot/b'way, waterbodies, woods, heath/moor (named), occupation roads. Apt has cropping information.

5/139 Cuddington (township in parish of Malpas) SJ 454465 [Cuddington]
Apt 20.07.1838; 1347a (1347); Map 1838, 3 chns, 1st cl, by Robert Cotgreave; construction lines, foot/b'way, waterbodies, woods, field acreages; scale is noted in pencil.

5/140 Davenham (township in parish of Davenham) SJ 663707
Apt 11.05.1838; 479a (479); Map 1839, 3 chns; foot/b'way, waterbodies, farmyards, woods, parkland, building names. Apt omits land use.

5/141 Davenport (township in parish of Astbury) SJ 792664 [Not listed]
Apt 31.01.1839; 755a (755); Map 1839?, 6 chns; waterbodies, woods, fences, field boundary ownerships.

5/142 Daresbury (township in parish of Runcorn) SJ 585828
Apt 22.07.1843; 599a (599); Map 1844, 3 chns, 'corrected from an original survey made by James Cowley in 1831', by Henry White, Warrington; foot/b'way, private road, turnpike roads, waterbodies, woods, parkland, field gates, building names, quarry, sand or stone pits, school, demesne land boundary (col). Apt has cropping information.

5/143 Darnhall (township in parish of Whitegate) SJ 649632 [Not listed]
Apt 17.11.1846; 10a (1700); Map 1849?, 3 chns, by J. Roberts; foot/b'way, waterbodies.

5/144 Disley (township in parish of Stockport) SJ 983843
Apt 25.05.1849; 2611a (2700); Map 1851?, 6 chns; canal, waterbodies, woods, plantations, rock outcrops.

5/145 Dodcott cum Wilksley (township in parishes of Acton and Audlem) SJ 604423 [Not listed]
Apt 17.12.1842; 5671a (5956); Map 1843, 7 chns; foot/b'way, waterbodies, woods, parkland (in detail), park wall, building names; legend explains boundaries. Apt omits land use.

5/146 Doddington (township in parish of Wybunbury) SJ 712472 [Not listed]
Apt 21.11.1842; 589a (588); Map 1843?, 5 chns; waterbodies, woods, parkland (in detail), building names, lodge, old castle, garden, osiers.

5/147 Dodleston (parish) SJ 342616
Apt 09.02.1839; 4014a (all); Map 1840?, 3 chns, 1st cl, by John Davies, Mollington near Chester; foot/b'way, waterbodies, woods, parkland, building names, road names, boundary stones, moat, chapel, well, smithy, quarry, township boundaries. Apt has cropping information.

5/148 Duckinfield (township in parish of Stockport) SJ 950976 [Dukinfield]
Apt 25.05.1849; 469a (?); Map 1850, 3 chns, 'copied' by Thos Hill, Ashton under Lyne; railways, foot/b'way, canal, waterbodies, farmyards, woods, plantations, parkland, building names, road names, school, chapels, stone quarry, stone pits, foundry, new pits, collieries, brick kilns, boiler works, dye works, mill.

5/149 Duckington (township in parish of Malpas) SJ 486517
Apt 15.09.1838; 666a (666); Map 1839?, 3 chns, 1st cl; construction lines, waterbodies, woods. Apt omits land use.

5/150 Duddon (township in parish of Tarvin) SJ 513654
Apt 21.11.1838; 661a (661); Map 1840, 6 chns, by Thomas Hitchen; waterbodies, woods, hedge ownership.

5/151 Dunham (township in parish of Thornton in the Moors) SJ 469729 [Dunham-on-the-Hill]
Apt 02.09.1843; 1370a (1458); Map 1844, 9 chns; waterbodies, woods.

5/152 Dunham Massey (township in parish of Bowdon) SJ 742887 [Not listed]
Apt 21.11.1838; 3471a (3470); Map 1841?, 4 chns, by R. Thornton, Manchester; canal, waterbodies, woods, parkland, building names. Apt omits land use.

5/153 Dutton (township in parishes of Great Budworth and Runcorn) SJ 588783
Apt 19.02.1841; 2076a (2076); Map 1841, 6 chns, made for tithe commutation by H. White, Warrington, 'taken from a reduced plan (of 9 chns to an Inch) made by J. Dunn in 1821. Corrected up to this present time'; railway, viaduct, tunnel mouth, foot/b'way, turnpike roads, canal, waterbodies, woods, field gates, building names, road names, weir, sand or stone pits, demesne land boundary. Apt has cropping information.

5/154 Earnshaw Hall Farm (district in parish of Sandbach) SJ 729700 [Earnshaw House Farm]
Apt 21.06.1841; 126a (?); Map 1841?, 3 chns; waterbodies, houses, woods, gardens, building names. Apt omits land use.

5/155 Eastham (township in parish of Eastham) SJ 360801
Apt 26.02.1839; 1451a (2036); Map 1840, 4 chns; railway, waterbodies, woods, road names, glebe (col); map is subtitled 'belonging to Sir S.M. Stanley Bart'; scale on map is in Cheshire chains of 32 yards each. Apt omits land use.

5/156 Eaton (township in parish of Astbury) SJ 867657
Apt 23.08.1839; 1224a (?); Map 1840, 6 chns; foot/b'way, turnpike roads, tollgate, waterbodies, woods, parkland, building names.

5/157 Eaton (township in parish of Davenham) SJ 648704 [Not listed]
Apt 11.05.1838; 431a (431); Map 1843?, 4 chns; railway, waterbodies, woods, occupation road; scale has been corrected from 6 to 4 chns in pencil. Apt omits land use.

5/158 Eaton, Ukinton and Rushton (township in parish of Tarporley) SJ 574634
Apt 18.01.1838; 4914a (4913); Map 1837, 3 chns, in 3 parts, by Thos Burgess and Rd Owen; foot/b'way, waterbodies, houses, woods, plantations, parkland, rock outcrops, field gates, building names, flax yards.

5/159 Eccleston (parish) SJ 402616
Apt 07.02.1837; 2403a (all); Map 1839?, 12 chns, by John Davies, Mollington, Chester; turnpike roads and gate, waterbodies, woods, parkland, building names, road names.

5/160 Edge (township in parish of Malpas) SJ 485502 [Not listed]
Apt 14.09.1838; 1573a (1572); Map 1839, 3 chns, 1st cl, ? by Thomas Fenna, Cherry Hill nr Malpas; construction lines, waterbodies, woods, field gates.

5/161 Edleston (township in parish of Acton) SJ 636508 [Not listed]
Apt 16.10.1841; 618a (617); Map 1841?, 6 chns, by Burgess and Owen; canal, waterbodies, building names, road names. Apt omits land use.

5/162 Egerton (township in parish of Malpas) SJ 523515 [Egerton Green]
Apt 07.09.1838; 912a (911); Map 1839?, 4 chns; waterbodies, woods. Apt omits land use.

5/163 Elton (township in parish of Thornton in the Moors) SJ 460754
Apt 23.10.1838; 1090a (1090); Map 1840, 6 chns; waterbodies.

5/164 Elton (township in parish of Warmingham) SJ 727602 [Not listed]
Apt 31.12.1838; 1028a (1027); Map 1840?, 4 chns; foot/b'way, canal, waterbodies, woods. Apt omits land use.

5/165 Etchells (township in parish of Stockport) SJ 848871 [Not listed]
Apt 26.06.1839; 1582a (1582); Map 1839, 3 chns, by Charles Laing, 14, Charlotte Street, Manchester, surveyor and architect; construction lines, hill-drawing, waterbodies, woods, orchards, landowners.

5/166 Etchells (township in parish of Northern otherwise Northenden) SJ 829872 [Not listed]
Apt 06.11.1841; 2283a (2282); Map 1830, 3 chns, by Thomas Greaves, Hale, Altringham; hill-drawing, foot/b'way, waterbodies, houses, woods, plantations, building names, moss (named).

5/167 Faddiley (township in parish of Acton) SJ 581526
Apt 16.10.1841; 1199a (1199); Map 1839, 9 chns; waterbodies, building names, greens.

5/168 Fallibroome (township in parish of Prestbury) SJ 892754 [Not listed]
Apt 31.07.1848; 241a (all); Map 1848, 3 chns, by Cawley and Firth, Macclesfield; foot/b'way, waterbodies, plantations, field boundary ownerships, ownership boundaries.

5/169 Farndon (township in parish of Farndon) SJ 419546
Apt 09.05.1840; 1026a (1025); Map 1840, 6 chns; waterbodies, stone quarry, common.

5/170 Faulk Stapleford (township in parish of Tarvin) SJ 487628 [Not listed]
Apt 21.11.1838; 1322a (1321); Map 1840?, 3 chns, 1st cl; construction lines, waterbodies, woods, building names, mill, ford.

5/171 Frankby (township in parish of West Kirby) SJ 242865
Apt 03.04.1844; 559a (all); Map 1844, 6 chns, by C. Brittain; waterbodies, houses, woods.

5/172 Frodsham (township in parish of Frodsham) SJ 509785
Apt 06.11.1844; 2256a (2256); Map 1838, 6 chns, by J. Cawley and Son, Tabley; waterbodies.

5/173 Frodsham Lordship (township in parish of Frodsham) SJ 515765 [Not listed]
Apt 06.11.1844; 2594a (3524); Map 1838, 6 chns, in 2 parts, by J. Cawley and Son, Tabley, (including open fields at 3 chns, by George Cawley, Knutsford, 1846?); waterbodies, woods, plantations, parkland, open fields.

5/174 Fulshaw (township in parish of Wilmslow) SJ 839802 [Not listed]
Apt 05.02.1840; 451a (all); Map 1841, 4 chns, 1st cl, by J. Cawley, Macclesfield; railway, waterbodies, houses, woods.

5/175 Gawsworth (parish) SJ 889702
Apt 17.09.1847; 5423a (all); Map 1849, 8 chns; railway, waterbodies, woods, plantations.

5/176 Godley (township in parish of Mottram in Longdendale) SJ 965949
Apt 14.10.1845; 640a (639); Map 1846, 4 chns, by Joseph Tinker, Hyde; hill-drawing, railways, foot/b'way, turnpike roads, waterbodies, houses, farmyards, woods, building names, road names, mill.

5/177 Golborne David (township in parish of Handley) SJ 456600 [Not listed]
Apt 23.11.1844; 642a (642); Map 1845, 4 chns; turnpike roads, toll bar, waterbodies, plantations, parkland, field gates.

5/178 Goostrey cum Barnshaw (township in parish of Sandbach) SJ 775712
Apt 29.11.1838; 1698a (1697); Map 1839, 6 chns, by George Cawley, Tabley; foot/b'way, waterbodies, woods, field gates, building names, township boundaries.

5/179 Grafton (township in parish of Grafton) SJ 446515 [Not listed]
Apt 14.03.1845; 384a (384); Map 1847?, 8 chns; table lists occupiers and holding acreages. District is apportioned by holding and fields are not shown. [The map in PRO IR 30 is a photocopy of the Diocesan copy.]

5/180 Grange (township in parish of West Kirby) SJ 229878
Apt 03.01.1844; 907a (all); Map 1847?, 6 chns; waterbodies, woods, plantations, building names, road names, common.

5/181 Greasby (township in parish of West Kirby) SJ 255872
Apt 03.01.1844; 742a (all); Map 1848?, 3 chns; waterbodies, woods, building names, windmill, common. Apt omits land use.

5/182 Guilden Sutton (parish) SJ 448680
Apt 31.12.1844; 935a (934); Map 1848?, 6 chns, by W. Worrall; foot/b'way, waterbodies, woods. Apt omits land use.

5/183 Hale (township in parish of Bowdon) SJ 794859
Apt 21.11.1838; 3679a (3679); Map 1841, 3 chns, by E. Nicholson, Manchester; hill-drawing, waterbodies, houses, woods (named), building names, road names, mill, poorhouse. Apt omits land use.

5/184 Halton (township in parish of Runcorn) SJ 535823
Apt 26.04.1843; 1779a (1779); Map 1845, 3 chns, by Henry White, Warrington, from 'Sir R. Brooke's old map' and 'tithe plan of Runcorn town'; hill-drawing, foot/b'way, turnpike roads, canal, waterbodies, houses, woods, plantations, orchards, field gates, building names, landowners, castle, free grammar school, public library, Wesleyan Chapel, waste, common; boundaries are annotated with reference to the maps from which the tithe map was compiled. Apt has cropping information.

5/185 Hampton (township in parish of Malpas) SJ 510495 [Hampton Green]
Apt 22.02.1838; 1219a (1219); Map 1837, 6 chns, ? by Jos Lee; foot/b'way, waterbodies, woods, field gates, sand or stone pits. Apt has cropping information.

5/186 Handforth cum Bosden (township in parish of Cheadle) SJ 864835
Apt 23.09.1844; 1781a (1781); Map 1844, 3 chns, in 2 parts, by John Taylor, Ollerset, near Stockport; railway, foot/b'way, turnpike roads, toll bar, waterbodies, farmyards, building names, road names, print works, mill; legend explains symbols.

5/187 Handley (township in parish of Handley) SJ 463582
Apt 31.12.1838; 1334a (1334); Map 1839, 6 chns; foot/b'way, waterbodies, woods, field gates; map is signed by landowners. Apt omits land use.

5/188 Hankelow (township in parish of Audlem) SJ 667458
Apt 15.03.1838; 650a (all); Map 1838, [4.5 chns]; construction lines, foot/b'way, waterbodies, woods, plantations, mill; map is upside down to title.

5/189 Hapsford (township in parish of Thornton in the Moors) SJ 471745
Apt 10.04.1838; 531a (531); Map 1839, 6 chns; waterbodies. Apt omits land use.

5/190 Hartford (township in parish of Great Budworth) SJ 642722
Apt 15.01.1845; 929a (1102); Map 1846?, 4 chns, by G. Cawley, Knutsd; railway with station, turnpike roads, toll bar, waterbodies, farmyards, woods, parkland.

5/191 Harthill (parish) SJ 503551
Apt 31.12.1838; 482a (all); Map 1839?, [12 chns]. Apt has cropping information.

5/192 Haslington (township in parish of Barthomley) SJ 747566
Apt 27.07.1840; 3670a (3670); Map 1839, 4 chns, by George Cawley, Tabley; foot/b'way, waterbodies, farmyards, woods, parkland, heath/moor, field gates, building names, moss (named).

5/193 Hassall otherwise Little Hassall (township in parish of Sandbach) SJ 769577
Apt 25.03.1840; 1025a (1024); Map 1839, 3 chns; hill-drawing, canal, waterbodies, woods, parkland, field gates, building names, sand or stone pits, reservoir. Apt omits some land use.

5/194 Hatherton (township in parish of Wybunbury) SJ 682474
Apt 21.11.1842; 1632a (1632); Map 1843, 6 chns, by Rd Owen; waterbodies, woods, plantations, parkland, fences, field boundary ownerships, building names.

5/195 Hattersley (township in parish of Mottram in Longdendale) SJ 979940
Apt 04.09.1839; 1073a (all); Map 1840, 3 chns, 1st cl, 'draught' by W. Gregson, Kirkham near Preston, Lancs; construction lines, railway, foot/b'way, turnpike roads, waterbodies, woods (col), building names.

5/196 Hatton (township in parish of Runcorn) SJ 602821
Apt 26.04.1843; 1020a (1020); Map 1844, 6 chns, by Henry White, Warrington, 'chiefly made from a number of Estate plans which have been reduced to the above scale and fitted together. A few small Estates are from new surveys.'; foot/b'way, waterbodies, woods, field gates. Apt has cropping information.

5/197 Hatton (township in parish of Waverton) SJ 474613 [Not listed]
Apt 23.01.1838; 1380a (1381); Map 1838?, 4 chns; waterbodies, houses, building names. Apt omits land use.

5/198 Haughton (township in parish of Bunbury) SJ 590564 [Not listed]
Apt 14.12.1839; 1079a (1079); Map 1840?, 3 chns; construction lines, foot/b'way, waterbodies, woods, building names.

5/199 Helsby (township in parish of Frodsham) SJ 489758
Apt 06.11.1844; 1262a (1261); Map 1845?, 6 chns; waterbodies, woods.

5/200 Henbury with Pexall (township in parish of Prestbury) SJ 869728
Apt 27.07.1848; 565a (1400); Map 1849, 6 chns, by Cawley and Firth, Macclesfield; foot/b'way, waterbodies, houses, woods, plantations, field boundary ownerships; colour bands may show property ownerships.

5/201 Henhull (township in parish of Acton) SJ 641534 [Not listed]
Apt 20.11.1839; 494a (494); Map 1839, 3 chns, by Samuel Harding; foot/b'way, turnpike roads, canal with towpath and aqueduct, waterbodies, woods, building names, wharf, brick yard, whitning yard. Apt omits land use.

5/202 Heswall (parish) SJ 265815
Apt 30.04.1849; 2022a (all); Map 1851?, [6 chns], by John Davies, Mollington near Chester; waterbodies, woods, building names, township boundaries.

5/203 Hockenhall (township in parish of Tarvin) SJ 482659 [Not listed]
Apt 16.03.1839; 331a (330); Map 1839?, 7 chns; woods, gardens, building names, mill. Apt omits land use.

5/204 Hollingworth (township in parish of Mottram in Longdendale) SJ 999977
Apt 14.10.1845; 2041a (2041); Map 1846, 3 chns, surveyed for tithe commutation by J. Beckett, Oulton Farm; hill-drawing, foot/b'way, waterbodies, woods, plantations, parkland, building names, sand or stone pits, reservoirs, green, moorland.

5/205 Hoole (township in parishes of Plemondstall and St John) SJ 429681
Apt 04.04.1838; 744a (743); Map 1839?, 9 chns; waterbodies, woods. Apt omits land use.

5/206 Hoose (township in parish of West Kirby) SJ 221893 [Not listed]
Apt 27.03.1844; 98a (all); Map 1844, 3 chns, by John Parkin, New House, Upton, Birkenhead.

5/207 Hooton (township in parish of Eastham) SJ 372790
Apt 26.02.1839; 1113a (2443); Map 1850?, 6 chns; railway with station, waterbodies, woods, parkland (in detail), building names, kennels, keepers lodge, bathing house. Apt omits land use.

5/208 Horton (township in parish of Tilston) SJ 455492 [Horton Green]
Apt 10.12.1838; 801a (800); Map 1838, 6 chns, by Jos Fenna; waterbodies, woods, open fields, field gates.

5/209 Horton cum Peele (township and district in parish of Tarvin) SJ 496691 [Not listed]
Apt 17.09.1846; 334a (240); Map 1850, 6 chns, by John Davies, Mollington near Chester; foot/b'way, waterbodies, woods, building names.

5/210 Hough (township in parish of Wybunbury) SJ 710502
Apt 12.07.1838; 980a (all); Map 1839, [?9 chns]; waterbodies, woods (col), plantations (col), sand or stone pit.

5/211 Hulmewalfield (township in parish of Astbury) SJ 849652 [Hulme Walfield]
Apt 31.10.1840; 1048a (1047); Map 1840, 6 chns, by Geo. Harding, Maerfield near Newcastle, Staffs; foot/b'way, waterbodies, woods, heath/moor, field gates, building names.

5/212 Hulse (township in parish of Great Budworth) SJ 709727 [Not listed]
Apt 15.01.1845; 296a (295); Map 1841, 3 chns, by G. Cawley; foot/b'way, waterbodies, woods (col).

5/213 Hunsterson (township in parish of Wybunbury) SJ 699454 [Not listed]
Apt 21.11.1842; 1510a (1510); Map 1843?, 5 chns; waterbodies, woods, parkland, sand or stone pits.

5/214 Hurdsfield (township in parish of Prestbury) SJ 932748
Apt 07.07.1848; 386a (860); Map 1848, 6 chns, by Cawley and Firth, Macclesfield, (tithable parts only in detail); foot/b'way, canal, waterbodies, houses, plantations, parkland.

5/215 Hurleston (township in parish of Acton) SJ 618547 [Not listed]
Apt 16.10.1841; 1358a (1357); Map 1839, 8 chns; canal, waterbodies, woods, reservoir. Apt omits land use.

5/216 Huxley (township in parish of Waverton) SJ 505616
Apt 23.01.1838; 1502a (1501); Map 1837, 8 chns; canal, waterbodies, woods, field gates, building names. Apt has cropping information.

5/217 Hyde (township in parish of Stockport) SJ 952944
Apt 07.08.1839; 890a (all); Map 1841, 2 chns, by Joseph Tinker, Hyde; construction lines, hill-drawing, foot/b'way, occupation road, turnpike roads, canal, waterbodies, houses, woods (col), building names, road names, mills, coal works, corn mill, reservoir, print works, gas well, lime kilns; built-up part generalised.

5/218 Irby (township in parish of Woodchurch) SJ 258846
Apt 24.03.1846; 575a (574); Map 1848?, 9 chns; waterbodies, woods, road names; colour bands may show township and parish boundaries.

5/219 Keckwick (township in parish of Runcorn) SJ 572829
Apt 16.05.1844; 523a (522); Map 1844, 6 chns, by H. White, Warrington, litho (Standidge); railway, foot/b'way, canal, waterbodies, plantations, field gates; colour bands may show property ownerships; mapmaker notes: 'This plan was lithographed at the time the Estate was sold in 1843, and has been corrected by H. White of Warrington in 1844. The width of the Railway is incorrectly shown, but the quantity as shown in the Reference Book is right'. Apt has cropping information.

5/220 Kelsall on the Hill (township in parish of Tarvin) SJ 522683 [Kelsall]
Apt 21.11.1838; 1223a (1223); Map 1838, 3 chns, by Marker Gaze, Chester; waterbodies, road names.

5/221 Kettleshulme (township in parish of Prestbury) SJ 989788
Apt 07.07.1848; 735a (1207); Map 1849?, 6 chns, ? by James Cawley and Thomas Dyson Firth; foot/b'way, waterbodies, woods, plantations.

5/222 Kinderton cum Hulme (township in parish of Middlewich) SJ 723659 [Not listed]
Apt 14.09.1842; 402a (1637); Map 1842?, 6 chns; turnpike roads, toll house, waterbodies, houses, woods, building names; colour bands may show property ownerships. Apt omits land use.

5/223 Kingsmarsh (extra-parochial place) SJ 430546 [Not listed]
Apt 19.05.1847; 822a (all); Map 1847, 6 chns, by C. Brittain, Liverpool; foot/b'way, waterbodies, woods, plantations, field gates.

5/224 Kingsley (township in parish of Frodsham) SJ 550752
Apt 06.11.1844; 2601a (2606); Map 1845, 6 chns, in 3 parts, by Thomas Gerrard, Kingsley, (includes 3-chn enlargements of detail); waterbodies, houses, woods, marl pit, awarded land. Apt omits land use.

5/225 West Kirby (township in parish of West Kirby) SJ 217864
Apt 30.04.1844; 441a (all); Map 1844, 3 chns; foot/b'way, waterbodies, road names, lime kiln, beach.

5/226 Kermincham (township in parish of Swettenham) SJ 800685 [Not listed]
Apt 26.06.1839; 1209a (1209); Map 1839, 4.75 chns; waterbodies, woods. Apt omits land use.

5/227 Nether Knutsford (township in parish of Nether Knutsford) SJ 755787 [Knutsford]
Apt 27.08.1847; 757a (all); Map 1848?, 3 chns, by G.H. Davenport, Knutsford; hill-drawing, waterbodies, houses, woods, parkland, heath/moor, building names, prison, race course, garden allotments, pits.

5/228 Over Knutsford (township in parish of Nether Knutsford) SJ 767779
Apt 27.08.1847; 943a (all); Map 1847?, 4 chns, by G.H. Davenport, Knutsford; foot/b'way, waterbodies, houses, woods, plantations, parkland, building names, obelisk, mill.

5/229 Lache Dennis (township in parish of Great Budworth) SJ 714715 [Lach Dennis]
Apt 15.01.1845; 384a (406); Map 1845?, 4 chns; waterbodies; colour bands may show property ownerships. Apt omits land use.

5/230 Landican (township in parish of Woodchurch) SJ 283856
Apt 24.03.1846; 606a (605); Map 1847?, 5 chns; foot/b'way, woods, stone quarry. Apt has cropping information.

5/231 Lea (township in parish of Backford) SJ 388718 [Not listed]
Apt 28.02.1839; 684a (684); Map 1839?, 6 chns; foot/b'way, canal, waterbodies. Apt omits land use.

5/232 Lea (township in parish of Wybunbury) SJ 714488 [Not listed]
Apt 28.05.1838; 405a (all); Map not dated, 5 chns; foot/b'way, waterbodies, woods, orchard.

5/233 Lea Newbold (township in parish of Chester, St Oswald) SJ 438589 [Not listed]
Apt 16.07.1839; 723a (723); Map 1839?, 6 chns; waterbodies, woods. Apt omits land use.

5/234 Ledsham (township in parish of Neston) SJ 356748
Apt 25.03.1840; 803a (803); Map 1839, 4.3 chns; railway, foot/b'way, waterbodies, woods, orchard. Apt omits land use.

5/235 Lees (township in parish of Sandbach) SJ 732685 [Not listed]
Apt 27.01.1842; 386a (386); Map 1842?, 4 chns; waterbodies, houses; colours may show property ownerships.

5/236 Leftwich (township in parish of Davenham) SJ 660724
Apt 31.10.1840; 972a (972); Map 1840, 3 chns, 1st cl, by James Cawley, Macclesfield; construction lines, canal, waterbodies.

5/237 High Leigh (township in parish of Rostherne) SJ 691837
Apt 27.08.1847; 4257a (all); Map 1848, 8 chns, by Henry White, Warrington; foot/b'way, waterbodies, woods, plantations, parkland, building names, road names; meaning of pink tint is unclear; mapmaker notes: 'This plan is compiled from the old Estate plans of the Landowners with corrections up to the present time. Where no alterations had been made in the fences the old quantities were for the most part adopted'. Apt has cropping information.

5/238 Little Leigh (township in parish of Great Budworth) SJ 616768
Apt 21.02.1840; 1530a (1529); Map 1841?, 6 chns; foot/b'way, canal, waterbodies, woods, waste lot. Apt omits land use.

5/239 Leighton (township in parish of Nantwich) SJ 681578
Apt 10.05.1845; 1244a (1244); Map 1845?, 4 chns; colour bands may show property ownerships. Apt omits land use.

5/240 Leighton (township in parish of Neston) SJ 284794 [Not listed]
Apt 27.07.1843; 610a (all); Map 1847, 6 chns; foot/b'way, waterbodies, woods, plantations, building names, boathouse.

5/241 Liscard (township in parish of Wallasey) SJ 310929
Apt 30.11.1839; 897a (4236); Map 1841?, 4 chns; hill-drawing, waterbodies, woods, parkland, gardens, building names, road names, ferry, hotel, coastline.

5/242 Littleton (township in parish of Christleton) SJ 443669
Apt 23.11.1844; 258a (257); Map 1847?, 3 chns, by W. Worrall, Chester; foot/b'way, waterbodies, woods, parkland, field gates.

5/243 Lostock Graham (township in parish of Great Budworth) SJ 693743
Apt 15.01.1845; 1707a (1706); Map 1845, 4 chns, by G. Cawley, Tabley; canal, waterbodies, farmyards, woods.

5/244 Lyme Handley (township in parish of Prestbury) SJ 967817 [Not listed]
Apt 19.06.1848; 3782a (all); Map 1850, 7.5 chns, made for tithe commutation, litho; foot/b'way, canal, waterbodies, woods (named), plantations (named), parkland (in detail), mill.

5/245 Lymm (parish) SJ 685872
Apt 26.09.1837; 4284a (4284); Map 1837, 3 chns, by J. Cawley, Macclesfield; foot/b'way, canal with towpath, waterbodies, houses, woods, plantations, parkland, orchard. (The map in PRO IR 30 is a copy; original is in PRO IR 77/8.)

5/246 Macclesfield (township in parish of Prestbury) SJ 917735
Apt 27.07.1848; 1626a (2410); Map 1849, 6 chns, by Cawley and Firth, Macclesfield; foot/b'way, canal, waterbodies, houses, woods, plantations, parkland, gardens, field boundary ownerships; built-up part mostly generalised; colour bands may show property ownerships.

5/247 Macclesfield Forest (township in parish of Prestbury) SJ 973729
Apt 03.06.1848; 3378a (all); Map 1849, 4.4 chns, 'taken from the Original Map belonging to the Earl of Derby revised and corrected for the commutation of the tithes'; foot/b'way, turnpike roads, toll bar, woods, plantations, building names, sand or stone pits.

5/248 Macefen (township in parish of Malpas) SJ 516470 [Not listed]
Apt 30.12.1837; 329a (329); Map 1838?, 5 chns; foot/b'way, waterbodies, landowners. Apt omits land use.

5/249 Malpas (township in parish of Malpas) SJ 491472
Apt 26.02.1839; 1998a (?); Map 1840?, 3 chns, ? by Robert Cotgreave; waterbodies, woods, building names, landowners, waterworks.

5/250 Manley (township in parish of Frodsham) SJ 501721
Apt 06.11.1844; 1327a (1326); Map 1840, 3 chns, 1st cl; hill-drawing, waterbodies, woods, parkland, heath/moor, building names, toll bar, stone quarries, boundary stones, common; some physical features named.

5/251 Marbury (township in parish of Great Budworth) SJ 656761 [Not listed]
Apt 01.11.1844; 362a (362); Map 1843, 3 chns, by G. Cawley; foot/b'way, canal with towpath, waterbodies, farmyards, woods, parkland, building names, ownerships (col).

5/252 Marbury cum Quoisley (township in parish of Marbury) SJ 564456
Apt 08.12.1837; 2106a (2105); Map 1839, 6 chns, by Thomas Fenna; foot/b'way, canal, waterbodies, woods.

5/253 Marlston cum Lache (township in parish of Chester St Mary on the Hill) SJ 381631
Apt 11.05.1843; 975a (975); Map 1844?, 6 chns, by John Davies, Mollington near Chester; turnpike roads and gate, waterbodies, woods, building names, road names; bridge named.

5/254 Marple (township in parish of Stockport) SJ 958874
Apt 25.05.1849; 3017a (3210); Map 1850, 6 chns; foot/b'way, canal, aqueduct, waterbodies, farmyards, building names, road names, lime kilns.

5/255 Marston (township in parish of Great Budworth) SJ 671764
Apt 15.01.1845; 1045a (1045); Map 1846?, 4 chns, by Geo. Cawley; canal with towpath, waterbodies, woods, plantations.

5/256 Marthall and Little Warford (township in parish of Rostherne) SJ 806771
Apt 21.08.1847; 1774a (all); Map 1848, 4 chns, by J. Beckett, Oulton Farm; foot/b'way, waterbodies, woods, road names. Apt omits land use.

5/257 Marton (township in parish of Over) SJ 622666
Apt 27.02.1846; 122a (?), (tithable parts only, tinted); Map 1846?, 3 chns, in 2 parts, by G. Cawley, Knutsford, (includes 8-chn index); waterbodies, building names, lodge.

5/258 Marton (township in parish of Prestbury) SJ 848682
Apt 19.06.1848; 1948a (all); Map 1849, 8 chns, ? by Edwd Woollett Wilmot; foot/b'way, waterbodies, woods, field gates.

5/259 Marton (township in parish of Whitegate) SJ 611684
Apt 06.08.1846; 2562a (2684); Map 1847, 3 chns, surveyed for tithe commutation by J. Beckett, Oulton Farm; foot/b'way, waterbodies, woods, plantations, building names, sand or stone pit. Apt omits land use.

5/260 Matley (township in parish of Mottram Longdendale) SJ 975963
Apt 27.02.1840; 701a (all); Map 1842, 2 chns, by Thomas Hill, Ashton; hill-drawing, foot/b'way, turnpike roads, toll bar, waterbodies, woods, building names, sand or stone pits, quarries, mill, 'Improved common'.

5/261 Great Meolse (township in parish of West Kirby) SJ 241909 [Meols]
Apt 27.03.1844; 684a (all); Map 1844, 6 chns; lighthouse, embankment.

5/262 Little Meolse (township in parish of West Kirby) SJ 215884 [Not listed]
Apt 27.03.1844; 652a (all); Map 1844, 6 chns, by F.M. Sarsfield, Birkenhead; boundary posts, coastline. Apt omits land use.

5/263 Mere (township in parish of Rostherne) SJ 725821
Apt 27.08.1847; 2438a (all); Map 1848, 12 chns, 'copied and corrected from one made by Mr Dunn in 1828' by Henry White, Warrington; foot/b'way, waterbodies, woods, plantations, parkland, building names.

5/264 Mickle Trafford (township in parish of Plemondstall) SJ 448698
Apt 10.03.1838; 1143a (1143); Map 1839, 9 chns; foot/b'way, mill, glebe. Apt omits land use.

5/265 Middlewich and Newton (township in parish of Middlewich) SJ 705655
Apt 31.08.1846; 530a (?); Map 1847?, 3 chns; canal, waterbodies, fence; built-up part generalised. Apt omits land use.

5/266 Millington (township in parish of Rostherne) SJ 729847 [Not listed]
Apt 27.08.1847; 737a (all); Map 1847, 6 chns, by Thomas Greaves, Hale; waterbodies, woods.

5/267 Minshul Vernon (township in parish of Middlewich) SJ 682606 [Not listed]
Apt 06.03.1846; 2657a (2753); Map 1846?, 6 chns; railway, waterbodies, woods. Apt omits land use.

5/268 Mobberley (parish) SJ 792807
Apt 30.12.1847; 5139a (5138): Map 1839, 4 chns, by Thomas Wainwright, Manchester; construction lines, hill-drawing, foot/b'way, waterbodies, woods (named), fences, building names, road names, mills, reservoir, cotton mill, sand pits, clay pit, school, Methodist Chapel, Calvinist Chapel, Quaker burial ground; physical features named.

5/269 Great Mollington (township in parish of Backford) SJ 381710 [Mollington]
Apt 17.04.1838; 822a (821); Map 1839?, 6 chns; canal, waterbodies, woods. Apt omits land use.

5/270 Little Mollington (township in parish of Chester St Mary on the Hill) SJ 392692 [Not listed]
Apt 21.1.1839; 249a (248); Map 1845?, 3 chns, by John Davies, Mollington near Chester; hill-drawing, canal, road and canal embankments, waterbodies, woods, field gates.

5/271 Monks Coppenhall (township in parish of Coppenhall) SJ 697557 [Not listed]
Apt 15.12.1840; 1319a (1318); Map 1840, 6 chns, by Samuel Harding; railway, waterbodies, woods, building names.

5/272 Moor (township in parish of Runcorn) SJ 575850 [Moore]
Apt 26.04.1843; 901a (901); Map 1845, 3 chns, by Henry White, Warrington; railway, foot/b'way, canal, waterbodies, houses, woods, osiers, field gates, road names, Wesleyan Chapel; mapmaker notes: 'this plan is copied from one made some years ago, at the time of the Inclosure of the moss - by Mr Moorhouse with corrections up to the present time - 1845'. Apt has cropping information.

5/273 Moorsbarrow with Parm (township in parish of Middlewich) SJ 746650 [Not listed]
Apt 06.03.1846; 404a (425); Map 1846?, 3 chns; waterbodies, fence; colour bands may show property ownerships. Apt omits land use.

5/274 Moreton cum Alcumlow (township in parish of Astbury) SJ 843596 [Not listed]
Apt 21.01.1839; 1100a (1100); Map 1838, 5 chns, by W.S. Cope, Milton; canal, waterbodies. Apt omits land use.

5/275 Moston (township in parish of Chester St Mary on the Hill) SJ 401703
Apt 29.09.1838; 273a (273); Map 1839?, [5 chns]; railway, waterbodies, houses, woods, parkland.

5/276 Moston (township in parish of Warmingham) SJ 725619 [Moston Green]
Apt 23.01.1839; 679a (678); Map 1840?, 3 chns; canal, waterbodies, woods. Apt omits some land use.

5/277 Mottram in Longdendale (township in parish of Mottram in Longdendale) SJ 994952
Apt 14.10.1845; 1080a (1079); Map 1847, 3 chns; hill-drawing, railway with embankments and station, foot/b'way, turnpike roads, toll house, milestones, waterbodies, woods, plantations, parkland, field boundary ownerships, building names, print works, mill, weir, quarry.

5/278 Mottram St Andrew (township in parish of Prestbury) SJ 880786
Apt 27.07.1848; 400a (1600); Map 1848, 4 chns, (tithable parts only, tinted); foot/b'way, waterbodies, woods, building names, common.

5/279 Mouldsworth (township in parish of Tarvin) SJ 503707
Apt 21.11.1838; 880a (879); Map 1839?, 6 chns; waterbodies, woods, quarry; map is signed by the landowners. Apt omits land use.

5/280 Moulton (township in parish of Davenham) SJ 655692
Apt 31.10.1840; 483a (483); Map 1841?, 3 chns, by Geo. Cawley, Tabley; railway, foot/b'way, waterbodies, farmyards, woods, parkland, gardens (col), field gates, building names.

5/281 Nantwich (township in parish of Nantwich) SJ 651522
Apt 11.07.1845; 696a (696); Map 1846?, 6 chns; hill-drawing, foot/b'way, canal with embankments, waterbodies, woods, parkland, fences, building names, road names, heath; built-up part generalised.

5/282 Ness (township in parish of Neston) SJ 308759
Apt 27.03.1839; 2376a (?); Map 1845, 3 chns; waterbodies, farmyards, woods, heath/moor, field boundary ownerships, building names, colliery, brickyard, limekilns.

5/283 Great Neston (township in parish of Neston) SJ 295784 [Neston]
Apt 31.05.1845; 1304a (2563); Map 1847, 6 chns; waterbodies, woods, plantations, parkland, building names, racecourse, old quay.

5/284 Little Neston (except Blakeley Brow and Hargreave) (township in parish of Neston) SJ 308773
Apt 31.05.1845; 1113a (1993); Map 1847, 6 chns; foot/b'way, waterbodies, woods, field gates, well. Apt omits land use.

5/285 Newhall (township in parishes of Acton and Audlem) SJ 622452
Apt 17.12.1842; 4033a (4033); Map 1843?, 6 chns; canal, waterbodies, woods, building names, parish boundaries. Apt omits land use.

5/286 Newall (township in parish of Davenham) SJ 700712 [Not listed]
Apt 15.05.1838; 234a (234); Map 1840?, 3 chns, ? by Jas Cawley; waterbodies, farmyards, woods, field gates, landowners. Apt omits land use.

5/287 Newbold Astbury (township in parish of Astbury) SJ 849608 [Astbury]
Apt 31.01.1839; 2731a (2730); Map 1838, 4 chns, 'plan'd and corrected' by T. Burgess and Owen; foot/b'way, canal, waterbodies, houses, woods, building names.

5/288 Newton (township in parish of Chester St Oswald) SJ 416679
Apt 18.06.1840; 423a (423); Map 1841?, 6 chns; waterbodies, woods, field boundary ownerships, building names.

5/289 Newton (township in parish of West Kirby) SJ 238878
Apt 03.04.1844; 488a (all); Map 1847?, 6 chns, by John Davies, Mollington near Chester, (tinted); waterbodies, woods, building names, road names.

5/290 Newton (township in parish of Malpas) SJ 465455 [Not listed]
Apt 24.10.1838; 211a (210); Map 1839?, [3 chns]; waterbodies, field gates, road names, field acreages; map is subtitled 'The property of Thomas Tyrwhitt Drake Esqre'.

5/291 Newton (township in parish of Mottram in Longdendale) SJ 954961
Apt 14.10.1845; 869a (868); Map 1847, 3 chns, by J. Tinker, Hyde; railway, foot/b'way, canal with towpath, waterbodies, houses, farmyards, building names, road names, cotton mills, print works.

5/292 Newton (township in parish of Prestbury) SJ 881809 [Not listed]
Apt 08.05.1848; 268a (all); Map 1850, 3 chns, 1st cl, by Cawley and Firth, Macclesfield; foot/b'way, waterbodies, houses, woods, field gates.

5/293 Newton by Daresbury (township in parish of Runcorn) SJ 589812 [Not listed]
Apt 26.04.1843; 759a (758); Map 1844?, 6 chns; waterbodies, woods. [There is no copy of this map in PRO IR 30: details are from Diocesan copy, Cheshire Record Office EDT 295.]

5/294 Newton by Frodsham (township in parish of Frodsham) SJ 529752 [Newton]
Apt 06.11.1844; 416a (416); Map 1845?, 3 chns, by Thos Gerrard, Kingsley; waterbodies, woods, meeting house, marlpit, wasteland, bog. Apt omits land use.

5/295 Noctorum (township in parish of Woodchurch) SJ 286879
Apt 08.04.1846; 327a (326); Map 1844, 5 chns, by Henry White, Warrington, litho; foot/b'way, waterbodies, houses, woods, building names, landowners, quarry, spring. [There is no copy of this map in PRO IR 30: details are from Diocesan copy, Cheshire Record Office EDT 299.]

5/296 Norbury (township in parish of Marbury) SJ 557476
Apt 30.12.1837; 1534a (1533); Map 1838, 5 chns, by Thomas Fenna; foot/b'way, waterbodies, woods, field gates. Apt has cropping information.

5/297 Norbury (township in parish of Stockport) SJ 929860 [Norbury Moor]
Apt 25.05.1849; 1231a (1410); Map 1850, 6 chns, made for tithe commutation; foot/b'way, waterbodies, woods, plantations, heath/moor, building names, road names, mill.

5/298 Norley (township in parish of Frodsham) SJ 565729
Apt 06.11.1844; 1368a (1367); Map 1845?, 8 chns; waterbodies, woods, parkland, building names. Apt omits land use.

5/299 Northen otherwise Northenden (township in parish of Northen otherwise Northenden) SJ 824903
Apt 06.11.1841; 1404a (1434); Map 1839, 3 chns, by Thomas Greaves, near Altrincham, Cheshire; construction lines, hill-drawing, waterbodies, houses, woods, plantations, building names, boat house, mill.

5/300 Northwich and Northwich Castle (township in parish of Great Budworth) SJ 653737
Apt 15.01.1845; 132a (300); Map 1849?, 2 chns; foot/b'way, canal, waterbodies, woods, timber yard. District is apportioned by holding.

5/301 Norton (township in parish of Runcorn) SJ 555834
Apt 26.08.1843; 2180a (2469); Map 1844, 4 chns, 'a copy of one made by Mr Dunn about 40 years ago, with additions and corrections up to the present time' by Henry White, Warrington; railway, foot/b'way, canal with towpath, waterbodies, houses, woods, parkland, field gates, building names, sand or stone pits, embankment, brick wall, ferry, pinfold.

5/302 Occlestone (township in parish of Middlewich) SJ 697638 [Occlestone Green]
Apt 28.11.1845; 151a (721); Map 1848?, 3 chns, (tithable parts only); waterbodies, houses, woods, landowners, turnpike. [There is no copy of this map in PRO IR 30: details are from Diocesan copy, Cheshire Record Office EDT 308/2.]

5/303 Odd Rode (township in parish of Astbury) SJ 829579 [Not listed]
Apt 26.02.1839; 3693a (3692); Map 1838, 3 chns; construction lines, foot/b'way, canal, waterbodies, building names. Apt omits land use.

5/304 Offerton (township in parish of Stockport) SJ 924889 [Offerton Green]
Apt 25.05.1849; 626a (730); Map 1850, 3 chns, 1st cl, copied from a plan made for the Poor Law Commissioners in 1848, by E. Nicholson, Architect, Surveyor and Valuer, 28, Princess Street, Manchester; foot/b'way, turnpike roads, toll house, old roads and highways, waterbodies, farmyards, woods, plantations, building names.

5/305 Old Castle (township in parish of Malpas) SJ 461447 [Not listed]
Apt 22.02.1838; 836a (835); Map 1838?, 6 chns; foot/b'way, waterbodies, woods. [There is no copy of this map in PRO IR 30: details are from Diocesan copy, Cheshire Record Office EDT 311.]

5/306 Ollerton (township in parish of Nether Knutsford) SJ 781762
Apt 27.08.1847; 1216a (all); Map 1848, 3 chns, surveyed for tithe commutation by John Beckett, Oulton Farm; foot/b'way, waterbodies, woods, plantations, parkland, common. Apt omits land use.

5/307 Oulton Low (township in parish of Over) SJ 611635 [Oultonlowe Green]
Apt 27.01.1845; 938a (937); Map 1845?, 4 chns, ? by Richd T. Beckett; waterbodies, woods, building names. Apt omits land use.

5/308 St Oswald (township in parish of Chester St Oswald) SJ 403674 [Not listed]
Apt 23.11.1844; 426a (425); Map 1847, 5 chns, by W. Worrall, Chester; railways with tunnels, canal with towpath, waterbodies, woods, building names, infirmary.

5/309 Over (township in parish of Over) SJ 639657
Apt 24.10.1845; 1796a (4578); Map 1846, 5 chns, in 2 parts, by G. Cawley, (includes 3-chn enlargement of open fields); hill-drawing, waterbodies, open fields, quarry.

5/310 Over (township in parish of Whitegate) SJ 645691
Apt 16.02.1846; 2782a (?); Map 1846?, 6 chns, by G. Cawley, Knutsford; railway, waterbodies, woods (col), parkland, building names.

5/311 Overchurch or Upton (parish) SJ 269884
Apt 08.12.1837; 930a (929); Map 1839?, 3 chns, by John Davies, Mollington, Chester; turnpike roads, waterbodies, woods, plantations, parkland, building names, road names, smithy. Apt has cropping information.

5/312 Overton (township in parish of Malpas) SJ 473487 [Not listed]
Apt 28.02.1839; 709a (708); Map 1839?, 6 chns; foot/b'way, waterbodies, woods, field gates. Apt omits land use.

5/313 Oxton (township in parish of Woodchurch) SJ 300877
Apt 24.03.1846; 802a (802); Map 1847?, 4 chns; foot/b'way. Apt omits land use.

5/314 Partington (township in parish of Bowden) SJ 719914
Apt 21.11.1838; 803a (803); Map 1841, 3.3 chns, 1st cl, by Wm Whitehead, Altrincham; construction lines, waterbodies, houses, woods (col), plantations (col), boundary stones.

5/315 Peckforton (township in parish of Bunbury) SJ 539567
Apt 16.02.1846; 1730a (1729); Map 1846, 6 chns; hill-drawing, foot/b'way, waterbodies, woods, field gates, building names, mill, quarries.

5/316 Pensby (township in parish of Woodchurch) SJ 266835
Apt 24.03.1846; 336a (355); Map 1849?, 9 chns; woods. [There is no copy of this map in PRO IR 30: details are from Diocesan copy, Cheshire Record Office EDT 321.]

5/317 Peover Inferior otherwise Little Peover (township in parish of Great Budworth) SJ 746745
Apt 01.11.1844; 279a (278); Map 1841, 3 chns, by Geo. Cawley, Tabley; waterbodies, farmyards, gardens (col).

5/318 Nether Peover (township in parish of Great Budworth) SJ 733737 [Not listed]
Apt 01.11.1844; 915a (914); Map 1841, 4 chns, by Geo. Cawley, Tabley; waterbodies, plantations.

5/319 Over Peover otherwise Peover Superior (township in parish of Rostherne) SJ 778739 [Peover Heath]
Apt 27.08.1847; 2930a (all); Map 1841, 3 chns, by Thomas Greaves; construction lines, railway, waterbodies, woods, plantations.

5/320 Pickmere (township in parish of Great Budworth) SJ 697777
Apt 29.10.1844; 1045a (1045); Map 1841, 6 chns, by Geo. Cawley, Tabley; waterbodies, woods (col).

5/321 Picton (township in parish of Plemonstall) SJ 433709
Apt 04.04.1838; 844a (844); Map 1838, [10 chns], by John Davies, Mollington near Chester; waterbodies, woods; map is described as 'copied from an existing map belonging to the Rector of Plemondstall. The particulars compared with the Landowners acreages'. Apt has cropping information.

5/322 Plumley (township in parish of Great Budworth) SJ 722753
Apt 01.11.1844; 1622a (1622); Map 1841, 4 chns, by Geo. Cawley, Tabley; waterbodies, farmyards, woods (col), moss (named).

5/323 Poole (township in parish of Acton) SJ 638554 [Not listed]
Apt 18.05.1842; 771a (770); Map 1840, 3 chns, by Geo. Cawley, Tabley; canal with towpath, waterbodies, farmyards, woods (col), parkland, building names.

5/324 Poolton cum Seacombe (township in parish of Wallasey) SJ 316907 [Poulton]
Apt 19.11.1839; 669a (1069); Map 1841?, 4 chns; foot/b'way, waterbodies, field gates, road names, coastline, hotel, ferry. Apt omits land use.

5/325 Poolton cum Spittle (township in parish of Bebbington) SJ 332824 [Poulton]
Apt 29.04.1843; 954a (954); Map 1845?, 6 chns, by John Davies, Mollington, Chester; railway, turnpike roads and gate, waterbodies, woods, building names. workhouse.

5/326 Pot Shrigley (township in parish of Prestbury) SJ 946805 [Pott Shringley]
Apt 19.06.1848; 1720a (all); Map 1848, 6 chns, by Cawley and Firth, Macclesfield; canal with towpath, waterbodies, woods, plantations, parkland, field boundary ownerships; colour bands may show property ownerships.

5/327 Pownall Fee (township in parish of Wilmslow) SJ 834826 [Not listed]
Apt 25.02.1840; 3557a (3556); Map 1839, 3 chns; foot/b'way, occupation roads, waterbodies, houses, woods, plantations, parkland, orchards, unenclosed marsh, landowners, demesne lands (col); map is subtitled 'belonging to Sir Thomas S.M. Stanley Bart', and his ownership of a deer leap is noted.

5/328 Prenton (township in parish of Woodchurch) SJ 303860
Apt 27.03.1845; 629a (all); Map 1845, 6 chns, by W. Blakeway; foot/b'way, waterbodies, plantations, boundary stones.

5/329 Prestbury (township in parish of Prestbury) SJ 895767
Apt 08.05.1848; 746a (all); Map 1849, 3 chns, 1st cl, by Cawley and Firth, Macclesfield; railway, foot/b'way, waterbodies, houses, woods, plantations.

5/330 Preston on the Hill (township in parish of Runcorn) SJ 575806
Apt 26.04.1843; 1122a (1122); Map 1843?, 6 chns, by William Worrall, Chester; railway, canal with tunnel, waterbodies, woods, plantations.

5/331 Puddington (township in parish of Burton) SJ 335736
Apt 26.06.1839; 1360a (1359); Map 1841, 4 chns, 1st cl, by J. Cawley, Macclesfield; railway, waterbodies, houses, woods, plantations, parkland, moss (named). Apt omits land use.

5/332 Pulford (parish) SJ 375595
Apt 27.02.1837; 2567a (2567); Map 1837, [3 chns], by John Davies, Mollington; foot/b'way, turnpike roads, waterbodies, woods, plantations, parkland (named), field gates, building names, school, smithy, lodge, deer house, brick yard, township boundaries. Apt has incomplete cropping information.

5/333 Raby (township in parish of Neston) SJ 315798
Apt 27.07.1843; 1472a (1472); Map 1845?, 9 chns; waterbodies, woods, building names, water mill. Apt omits land use.

5/334 Radnor (township in parish of Astbury) SJ 840645 [Not listed]
Apt 23.05.1842; 252a (252); Map 1840, 6 chns, by J. Cawley, Macclesfield; waterbodies, woods, plantations, parkland. Apt has cropping information.

5/335 Rainow (township in parish of Prestbury) SJ 965768
Apt 07.07.1848; 3838a (?); Map 1850?, 8 chns, 'copied' by Cawley and Firth, Macclesfield; foot/b'way, waterbodies, woods, plantations, sand or stone pit.

5/336 Ridley (township in parish of Bunbury) SJ 552544
Apt 06.06.1840; 1419a (all); Map 1839, 6 chns; hill-drawing, foot/b'way, turnpike roads, toll gate, waterbodies, woods, field gates, building names. Apt omits land use.

5/337 Romiley (township in parish of Stockport) SJ 949909
Apt 25.05.1849; 1187a (2290); Map 1849, 3 chns; hill-drawing, railways, foot/b'way, canal, waterbodies, farmyards, building names, road names, field acreages, aqueduct, print works, moor.

5/338 North Rode (township in parish of Prestbury) SJ 888668
Apt 27.07.1848; 1557a (1520); Map 1848, 8 chns, by Cawley and Firth, Macclesfield; railway, foot/b'way, waterbodies, houses, woods, plantations, parkland, field boundary ownerships.

5/339 Rope (township in parish of Wybunbury) SJ 692528 [Not listed]
Apt 28.05.1838; 573a (all); Map not dated, 5 chns; waterbodies, woods, gardens, waste.

5/340 Rostherne (township in parish of Rostherne) SJ 745840
Apt 27.08.1847; 1513a (all); Map 1848, 6 chns, 'copied and part surveyed' by Thomas Greaves; waterbodies, woods, plantations.

5/341 Rowton (township in parish of Christleton) SJ 442643
Apt 23.11.1844; 563a (563); Map 1847, 3 chns, by W. Worrall, Chester; railway, foot/b'way, canal, waterbodies, parkland, fences, field gates.

5/342 Rudheath (township in parish of Great Budworth) SJ 690730
Apt 21.10.1845; 393a (?); Map 1846?, 4 chns, in 2 parts, by G. Cawley, Knutsford, (includes 8-chn index); canal with towpath, waterbodies, woods.

5/343 Rudheath (lordship in parish of Davenham) SJ 691711
Apt 16.01.1841; 1569a (1961); Map 1842, 6 chns, by Sam. Harding, Alpraham; canal, waterbodies, woods, plantations, field gates, road names.

5/344 Runcorn (township in parish of Runcorn) SJ 512826
Apt 26.04.1843; 950a (1490); Map 1844?, 4 chns; foot/b'way, canal, waterbodies, woods, field boundary ownerships; built-up part generalised.

5/345 Saighton (township in parish of Chester St Oswald) SJ 442621
Apt 21.03.1840; 1721a (1720); Map 1840, 4.5 chns, by W. Worrall, Chester; foot/b'way, waterbodies, farmyards, woods, field gates, building names, lodge, smithy, nursery, school; colours may show property ownerships. Apt omits land use.

5/346 Sale (township in parish of Ashton upon Mersey) SJ 793915
Apt 20.04.1844; 1981a (1981); Map 1844?, [6 chns], 1st cl, by Thomas Greaves, Altrincham; construction lines, railways, waterbodies, woods, plantations.

5/347 Sandbach (township) SJ 757608
Apt 14.12.1840; 2584a (2584); Map 1841?, 8 chns, in 2 parts, by J. Johnstone, (includes enlargement of village at 4 chns), litho (by J. Bell, Liverpool); foot/b'way, canal, waterbodies, woods, plantations, parkland, building names, common, tithing boundaries. Apt omits land use.

5/348 Great Saughall (township in parish of Shotwick) SJ 369713 [Saughall]
Apt 18.03.1843; 1201a (1200); Map 1848?, 6 chns, by John Davies, Mollington near Chester; waterbodies, woods, building names, road names, windmill.

5/349 Little Saughall (township in parish of Shotwick) SJ 373692 [Not listed]
Apt 11.05.1843; 457a (456); Map 1843?, 9 chns; building names, windmill.

5/350 Seven Oaks (township in parish of Great Budworth) SJ 639787 [Not listed]
Apt 29.10.1844; 602a (601); Map 1845?, 3 chns, by Thos Burgess; waterbodies, houses, woods.

5/351 Shavington cum Gresty (township in parish of Wybunbury) SJ 705526
Apt 15.02.1839; 1132a (all); Map 1839?, [5 chns]; waterbodies, plantations (col).

5/352 Shipbrooke (township in parish of Davenham) SJ 674713 [Not listed]
Apt 11.05.1838; 539a (539); Map 1840?, 3 chns; hill-drawing, foot/b'way, canal, waterbodies, woods, field gates. Apt omits land use.

5/353 Shocklach (parish) SJ 436500
Apt 21.01.1839; 2871a (2261); Map 1839, 8 chns, in 3 parts, by Joseph Gregory, Worthenbury, (Church Shocklach and Shocklach Oviat 'from a map and survey made in the year 1787' by Saml Botham revised

and corrected in 1839 by Joseph Gregory); foot/b'way, waterbodies, houses, woods, open fields. Apt omits land use.

5/354 Shotwick (township) SJ 342727
Apt 18.03.1843; 570a (570); Map 1847?, 3 chns, by John Davies, Mollington, Chester; foot/b'way, turnpike roads, waterbodies, woods. Apt has cropping information.

5/355 Shurlach (township in parish of Davenham) SJ 676726 [Higher Shurlach]
Apt 16.01.1841; 312a (312); Map 1841, 3 chns, by Geo. Cawley, Tabley; canal, waterbodies.

5/356 Siddington (township in parish of Prestbury) SJ 846707
Apt 31.07.1848; 2142a (all); Map 1849?, 6 chns, ? by Edward Woollett Wilmot; foot/b'way, waterbodies, woods, parkland, field gates.

5/357 Smallwood (township in parish of Astbury) SJ 807609
Apt 31.01.1839; 2133a (2133); Map 1839?, 4 chns; hill-drawing, foot/b'way, waterbodies, woods, open fields, building names, moss (named). Apt omits land use.

5/358 Snelson (township in parish of Rostherne) SJ 804740 [Not listed]
Apt 27.08.1847; 427a (all); Map 1847?, 3 chns, by G.H. Davenport, Knutsford; railway, foot/b'way, waterbodies, houses, woods, heath/moor.

5/359 Somerford Booths (township in parish of Astbury) SJ 832662 [Not listed]
Apt 23.08.1839; 1274a (1274); Map 1839, 8 chns; foot/b'way, waterbodies, woods, parkland, building names, mill.

5/360 Somerford Radnor (township in parish of Astbury) SJ 823645 [Not listed]
Apt 23.05.1842; 1204a (1203); Map 1843, 6 chns, by J. Cawley, Macclesfield; waterbodies, woods, plantations, parkland. Apt has cropping information.

5/361 Sound (township in parish of Acton) SJ 620489
Apt 15.12.1841; 1068a (1067); Map 1839, 6 chns, by Samuel Harding; waterbodies, woods, heath/moor (col).

5/362 Sproston (township in parish of Middlewich) SJ 735666 [Sproston Green]
Apt 26.06.1839; 847a (846); Map 1839?, 3 chns; hill-drawing, foot/b'way, waterbodies, woods, building names.

5/363 Spurstow (township in parish of Bunbury) SJ 568557
Apt 06.06.1840; 1798a (all); Map 1839, 6 chns, by Sam. Harding; waterbodies, woods, building names, mill pool, mill.

5/364 Little Stanney (township in parish of Stoke) SJ 412743
Apt 31.12.1844; 798a (797); Map 1845?, 4 chns, by W. Worrall, Chester; foot/b'way, canal, waterbodies, woods. Apt omits land use.

5/365 Stanthorne (township in parish of Davenham) SJ 687660
Apt 16.01.1841; 1062a (1062); Map 1841, 4 chns; railway, canal and towpath, waterbodies, woods (col), parkland (col).

5/366 Stapeley (township in parish of Wybunbury) SJ 672508 [Not listed]
Apt 12.07.1838; 1198a (1198); Map 1839, 3 chns; foot/b'way, waterbodies.

5/367 Stayley (township in parish of Mottram Longdendale) SJ 984997 [Stalybridge]
Apt 25.03.1840; 2330a (all); Map 1850, 3 chns, 1st cl, by Joseph Tinker, Hyde; construction lines, foot/b'way, turnpike roads, canal and towpath, waterbodies, building names, road names, mill, moor.

5/368 Stockham (township in parish of Runcorn) SJ 550807 [Not listed]
Apt 26.04.1843; 328a (328); Map 1843, 4 chns, by Henry White, Warrington; foot/b'way, turnpike roads, waterbodies, houses, woods, field gates, building names; mapmaker notes 'This plan is copied from Sir Richd Brooke's Estate Plan (made several years ago by Joseph Dunn) with corrections up to the present time'. Apt has cropping information.

5/369 Stockport (township in parish of Stockport) SJ 904893
Apt 25.05.1849; 1317a (1740); Map 1850?, 3 chns, by E. Nicholson, Architect and Surveyor, 28 Princess St, Manchester; railways and tunnel, waterbodies, fences, building names, road names, reservoir, water works, barrack yard, borough cemetery, ropery; built-up part generalised.

5/370 Stockton (township in parish of Malpas) SJ 477451 [Not listed]
Apt 30.12.1837; 264a (263); Map 1838?, 4 chns; foot/b'way, waterbodies, woods. Apt omits land use.

5/371 Stoke (township in parish of Acton) SJ 619564 [Not listed]
Apt 16.10.1841; 665a (665); Map 1840, 4 chns, by G. Cawley, Tabley; canal, reservoir, embankment, waterbodies, woods (col), parkland, building names.

5/372 Stoke with Ince (township in parish of Stoke) SJ 421737 [Not listed]
Apt 22.11.1844; 707a (706); Map 1845?, 4 chns, by William Worrall; foot/b'way, canal, waterbodies, woods, building names. Apt omits land use.

5/373 Storeton (township in parish of Bebbington) SJ 304842
Apt 27.03.1839; 1298a (1298); Map 1840, 4 chns; railway, waterbodies, houses, plantations, landowners; coach road along boundary noted as belonging to Sir T.S.M. Stanley Bt. Apt omits land use.

5/374 Stretton (township in parish of Great Budworth) SJ 626822
Apt 01.07.1845; 1137a (1118); Map 1846, 6 chns, made from actual survey by Joseph Okell for H. White, Warrington, litho; foot/b'way, waterbodies, woods, orchards, heath/moor, building names, schools, moss (named). Apt has cropping information.

5/375 Stretton (township in parish of Tilson) SJ 444530
Apt 16.05.1840; 901a (900); Map 1840?, 9 chns, by W. Worrall, Chester; foot/b'way, waterbodies, woods (col), parkland (col), field gates. Apt omits land use.

5/376 Stublach and Lees (township in parish of Middlewich) SJ 717704 [Not listed]
Apt 21.01.1848; 471a (471); Map 1848?, 6 chns; waterbodies; colour bands may show property ownerships.

5/377 Sutton (township in parish of Prestbury) SJ 941703 [Sutton Lane Ends]
Apt 31.03.1849; 3517a (4460); Map 1850, 6 chns, by Cawley and Firth, Macclesfield; foot/b'way, canal with towpath, waterbodies, woods, plantations, open fields, field boundary ownerships; built-up part generalised; colour bands may show property ownerships. Apt omits some land use.

5/378 Sutton (township in parish of Runcorn) SJ 544796 [Sutton Weaver]
Apt 22.07.1843; 1182a (1181); Map 1844, 6 chns, by R. Stelfox, Allesley; foot/b'way, turnpike roads and gate, canal with towpath, waterbodies, woods, orchards, building names, road names, dockyard, wharf, mill, weir, lock house, town pit.

5/379 Great Sutton (township in parish of Eastham) SJ 381752
Apt 01.08.1843; 1142a (1142); Map 1845?, 8 chns, by John Davies, Mollington; Chester; foot/b'way, waterbodies, woods, field gates, road names, tithe ownership (green). Apt has cropping information.

5/380 Little Sutton (township in parish of Eastham) SJ 365766
Apt 09.08.1843; 1121a (1120); Map 1847?, 8 chns; railway, foot/b'way, waterbodies, woods, building names, tithe-free area (col).

5/381 Swettenham (township) SJ 811671
Apt 26.06.1839; 949a (991); Map 1839, 4 chns; waterbodies, woods, plantations, parkland, gardens. Apt omits land use.

5/382 Over Tabley otherwise Tabley Superior (township in parish of Rostherne) SJ 724793
Apt 27.08.1847; 2660a (all); Map 1849?, 4 chns, by G.H. Davenport, Knutsford; foot/b'way, waterbodies, houses, farmyards, woods, parkland, field gates, building names. Apt has cropping information.

5/383 Tarporley (township in parish of Tarporley) SJ 553626
Apt 18.01.1838; 1145a (all); Map 1837, 3 chns, by Thos Burgess and Rd Owen; foot/b'way, waterbodies, houses, woods, field gates.

5/384 Tarvin (township in parish of Tarvin) SJ 499667
Apt 21.11.1838; 2007a (2007); Map 1838, 3 chns, by Marker Gaze; construction lines.

5/385 Tattenhall (parish) SJ 491585
Apt 31.01.1838; 4136a (4134); Map 1837, 3 chns, 1st cl, surveyed for Saml Rowe by Sam. Hughes and Robt Cotgreave; construction lines, foot/b'way, canal, waterbodies, woods, parkland (named), field boundary ownerships, field acreages, field gates, building names, smithy, mill. Apt omits land use.

5/386 Tatton (township in parish of Rostherne) SJ 756817 [Not listed]
Apt 27.08.1847; 1887a (all); Map 1848, 6 chns, by Thomas Greaves; hill-drawing, waterbodies, farmyards, woods, plantations, parkland (in detail). District is apportioned by holding.

5/387 Taxal (township in parish of Taxal) SK 005760
Apt 01.04.1844; 3718a (3718); Map 1844?, 8 chns; waterbodies, woods, plantations, parkland, field boundary ownerships, glebe (yellow), demesne (green); map also includes Yeardsley cum Whaley (5/423).

5/388 Tetton (township in parish of Warmingham) SJ 720631 [Not listed]
Apt 31.12.1838; 997a (997); Map 1840?, 4 chns; foot/b'way, canal with towpath, waterbodies, woods, building names; colour bands may show property ownerships. Apt omits land use.

5/389 Thelwall (township in parish of Runcorn) SJ 653871
Apt 26.04.1843; 1417a (1417); Map 1845, 3 chns, by Henry White, Warrington; hill-drawing, foot/b'way, turnpike roads, canal, waterbodies, houses, woods, parkland, field gates, building names, road names, powder mills, pinfold, quay; mapmaker notes: 'the principal part of this plan is compiled from Estate Plans of the different owners, the remainder is from actual survey'. Apt has cropping information.

5/390 Thingwell (township in parish of Woodchurch) SJ 280847 [Thingwall]
Apt 24.03.1846; 371a (371); Map 1848?, 3 chns, by John Davies, Mollington, Chester; hill-drawing, foot/b'way, waterbodies, woods, field gates, building names, folly, well, mill, quarries, common. Apt omits land use.

5/391 Thornton (township in parish of Thornton in the Moors) SJ 438744 [Thornton-le-Moors]
Apt 10.04.1838; 1214a (1213); Map 1841, 6 chns, by John Davies, Mollington, Chester; waterbodies, woods, field gates, building names, school, mill. Apt has cropping information.

5/392 Thornton Hough (township in parish of Neston) SJ 307812
Apt 27.07.1843; 1482a (1481); Map 1847, 6 chns; hill-drawing, waterbodies, woods, plantations, parkland, building names, workhouse.

5/393 Thurstaston (parish) SJ 244842
Apt 31.12.1847; 1247a (2762); Map 1848?, 9 chns, by John Davies, Mollington near Chester; hill-drawing, waterbodies, woods, plantations, building names, mill, lime kiln, township boundaries (col). Apt omits land use.

5/394 Tilston (township) SJ 463511
Apt 16.05.1840; 758a (758); Map 1840?, 6 chns, by W. Worrall, Chester; waterbodies, woods.

5/395 Tilstone (township in parish of Bunbury) SJ 569595 [Not listed]
Apt 14.12.1839; 864a (864); Map 1838, 9 chns, by Sam. Harding; canal, waterbodies, woods, parkland, building names. Apt omits land use.

5/396 Timperley (township in parish of Bowdon) SJ 784888
Apt 21.11.1838; 1629a (1628); Map 1838, 3 chns, 1st cl, by Thos Smith, Dunham Massey; construction lines, foot/b'way, turnpike roads, toll bar, canal with towpath, waterbodies, woods, parkland, field boundary ownerships, field gates, building names, road names, quarry, slush pits, field acreages. Apt omits land use and occupation information.

5/397 Tintwistle (township in parish of Mottram in Longdendale) SK 017976
Apt 14.10.1845; 3000a (?); Map 1847, 4 chns, in 3 parts, (one part at 3 chns); canal, waterbodies, woods, building names, mills.

5/398 Titherington (township in parish of Prestbury) SJ 917755 [Tytherington]
Apt 31.07.1848; 934a (all); Map 1849, 6 chns, by Cawley and Firth, Macclesfield; railway, foot/b'way, canal with towpath, waterbodies, woods, plantations, parkland, field boundary ownerships, field gates.

5/399 Tittenley (township in parish of Audlem) SJ 649387 [Not listed]
Apt 26.03.1846; 562a (525); Map 1846?, 6 chns; waterbodies, farmyards, woods, parkland.

5/400 Tiverton (township in parish of Bunbury) SJ 543610
Apt 14.12.1839; 1658a (1657); Map 1840?, 8 chns, by Samuel Harding; railway, canal, waterbodies, woods, building names, mills. Apt omits land use.

5/401 Toft (township in parish of Nether Knutsford) SJ 756760 [Not listed]
Apt 27.08.1847; 1298a (all); Map 1847?, 3 chns, by G.H. Davenport, Knutsford; foot/b'way, waterbodies, houses, farmyards, woods, plantations, parkland, field gates, building names.

5/402 Torkington (township in parish of Stockport) SJ 943872
Apt 25.05.1849; 819a (820); Map 1840, 3 chns, by W. Dabbs, Leicester; hill-drawing, foot/b'way, waterbodies, houses, woods, hedge ownership, fence ownership, building names, boundary stones, site of Roman camp.

5/403 Tranmore (township in parish of Bebbington) SJ 321869 [Tranmere]
Apt 25.07.1843; 1174a (all); Map 1843, 6 chns, in 3 parts, (includes 3-chn enlargements of detail); hill-drawing, railways, waterbodies, woods, building names, road names, ferries, hotels, sand or stone pits.

5/404 Tushingham cum Grindley (township in parish of Malpas) SJ 527453 [Not listed]
Apt 15.06.1838; 1292a (1292); Map 1838, 6 chns, litho (by J. Bell, Liverpool); foot/b'way, canal, waterbodies, woods, plantations, parkland, fences, field gates. Apt has cropping information.

5/405 Twemlow (township in parish of Sandbach) SJ 781688 [Twemlow Green]
Apt 29.06.1839; 929a (928); Map 1839?, 3 chns; foot/b'way, turnpike roads, toll bar, waterbodies, houses, woods, parkland, gardens, building names; colour bands may show property ownerships.

5/406 Upton (township in parish of Prestbury) SJ 902748 [Not listed]
Apt 31.07.1848; 478a (all); Map 1848, 3 chns, by Cawley and Firth, Macclesfield; foot/b'way, waterbodies, houses, woods, plantations, parkland, field boundary ownerships, field gates.

5/407 Upton (township in parish of Chester St Mary on the Hill and St Oswald) SJ 411693
Apt 09.07.1839; 1106a (1106); Map 1839, [20 chns]; railways, waterbodies, woods; colours may show property ownerships. Apt omits land use.

5/408 Walgherton (township in parish of Wybunbury) SJ 693488
Apt 26.11.1842; 838a (838); Map 1844?, 5 chns; waterbodies, woods, parkland, building names, sheep walk.

5/409 Wallasey (township in parish of Wallasey) SJ 285925
Apt 16.02.1841; 1542a (12470); Map 1841?, 4 chns; foot/b'way, waterbodies, woods, parkland, open fields, building names, high water mark, embankment, private road, sandhills 'to be left uninclosed'.

5/410 Higher Walton (township in parish of Runcorn) SJ 599849
Apt 26.04.1843; 424a (424); Map 1845, 9 chns, by H. White, Warrington; turnpike roads, canal, waterbodies, woods, parkland, pinfold; mapmaker notes: 'The plan is copied from Mr Brooke's Estate Plan and from reduced plans of other Estates, part actually surveyed. The whole corrected up to the present time'. Apt has cropping information.

5/411 Lower Walton (township in parish of Runcorn) SJ 599861
Apt 26.04.1843; 538a (537); Map 1844, 9 chns, in 2 parts, by Henry White, Warrington, ('part copied from estate plans of landowners and part is from new surveys'; includes 2-chn enlargement of detail); railway, foot/b'way, turnpike roads, canal, waterbodies, woods, open fields. Apt has cropping information.

5/412 Warburton (parish) SJ 710895
Apt 26.09.1837; 1747a (1747); Map 1838?, 4 chns, ? by Joseph Dunn; foot/b'way, waterbodies, woods, plantations, field gates, field names, moss (named); scale is pencilled in.

5/413 Wardle (township in parish of Bunbury) SJ 603572
Apt 06.06.1840; 1037a (1036); Map 1839, 8 chns, by Sam. Harding; hill-drawing, railway, canal, waterbodies, woods. Apt omits land use.

5/414 Warmingham (township in parish of Warmingham) SJ 707605
Apt 31.12.1838; 2029a (2028); Map 1840?, 4 chns; hill-drawing, railway, foot/b'way, waterbodies, woods, building names, mill; colour bands may show property ownerships. Apt omits land use.

5/415 Waverton (township in parish of Waverton) SJ 463637
Apt 27.04.1837; 1146a (all); Map 1839?, 6 chns, by John Davies, Mollington, Chester; canal with towpath, waterbodies, heath/moor, building names, road names, quarry, smithy, common.

5/416 Weaverham (parish) SJ 608730
Apt 02.07.1839; 6730a (7634); Map 1838, 3 chns, in 6 parts, by Cawleys, Tabley, (includes one part at 4 chns and 12-chn index); railway with station, foot/b'way, waterbodies, woods, plantations, parkland, heath/moor, field gates, building names, mills, windmill, viaduct, paper mill, waste. Apt omits land use.

5/417 Weaverham (township in parish of Whitegate) SJ 609704
Apt 6.8.1846; 999a (?); Map 1845-6, 3 chns, in 3 parts; surveyed for tithe commutation by John Beckett; railway, foot/b'way, waterbodies, woods, parkland, building names, kennels, sand or stone pit; a large coloured bird of prey holds the scale bar suspended from its beak by a chain. Apt omits land use.

5/418 Werneth (township in parish of Stockport) SJ 955923 [Not listed]
Apt 26.06.1839; 1561a (1560); Map 1840?, 3 chns, by Saml Taylor, Manchester; hill-drawing, foot/b'way, turnpike roads, canal, waterbodies, woods, plantations, field boundary ownerships, building names, road names, landowners, mills, school, weir, smithy; bands may show property ownerships.

5/419 Wervin (township in parish of Chester St Oswald) SJ 425722
Apt 20.03.1849; 709a (all); Map 1850?, 9 chns, by William Worrall; canal, waterbodies, woods, hedge ownership.

5/420 Weston (township in parish of Runcorn) SJ 506807
Apt 17.03.1846; 868a (1282); Map 1847, 3 chns, made for tithe commutation by H. White, Warrington; hill-drawing, foot/b'way, canal, waterbodies, houses, woods, heath/moor, garden (by annotation), field gates, chemical works, stone quarries, spoil, village cross. Apt has cropping information.

5/421 Weston (township in parish of Wybunbury) SJ 738522
Apt 14.10.1845; 1837a (1851); Map 1847, 5 chns; hill-drawing, waterbodies, woods, field boundary ownerships, building names, mill.

5/422 Wettenhall (township in parish of Over) SJ 622614
Apt 15.02.1844; 1955a (1954); Map 1839, 6 chns, by Sam. Harding; waterbodies, woods, building names, mill.

5/423 Whaley with Yeardsley (township in parish of Taxal) SK 002822 [Whaley Bridge]
Apt 01.04.1844; 1305a (all); Map 1844?, 8 chns, in 2 parts, (including small part separately at a larger scale); canal, woods, plantations, field boundary ownerships.

5/424 Wharton (township in parish of Davenham) SJ 664670
Apt 15.05.1838; 1225a (1224); Map 1841?, 3 chns; railway, waterbodies, farmyards, woods, building names, well.

5/425 Whatcroft (township in parish of Davenham) SJ 687695 [Not listed]
Apt 02.08.1838; 642a (641); Map undated, 12 chns; canal with towpath, waterbodies, woods, hedge ownership. Apt omits land use.

5/426 Wheelock (township in parish of Sandbach) SJ 753585
Apt 29.06.1839; 667a (666); Map 1839?, 3 chns; foot/b'way, turnpike roads and gate, canal, waterbodies, houses, farmyards, woods, parkland, field gates, building names, sunken park fences, salt works, sluice, mill, sand hole, pound, gardens. Apt omits land use.

5/427 Whitby Over Pool and Nether Pool (township in parishes of Eastham and Stoke) SJ 399764 [Whitby]
Apt 27.09.1837; 2104a (3370); Map 1839?, 6 chns, in 3 parts, by John Davies, Mollington near Chester, (includes 12-chn index); foot/b'way, canal with towpath, waterbodies, woods, plantations, rock outcrops, building names, landowners, high water mark, tile yard, township boundaries.

5/428 Higher Whitley (township in parish of Great Budworth) SJ 618804
Apt 29.10.1844; 1011a (1011); Map 1842, 3 chns, by Henry White, Warrington; hill-drawing, foot/b'way, waterbodies, houses, woods, heath/moor, field gates, building names, school, mills, Methodist Chapel, town pit, sand or stone pits.

5/429 Lower Whitley (township in parish of Great Budworth) SJ 613790
Apt 02.07.1845; 1118a (1118); Map 1847, 6 chns, by H. White, Warrington; foot/b'way, waterbodies, woods, building names, mill, occupation road; mapmaker notes: 'This plan is principally compiled from Estate Plans reduced to one scale, but parts are from actual survey. The whole has been examined and corrected up to the present time'. Apt has cropping information.

5/430 Wigland (township in parish of Malpas) SJ 495447 [Not listed]
Apt 30.08.1838; 562a (562); Map 1838, 6 chns; hill-drawing, foot/b'way, waterbodies, woods, field gates, sand or stone pits. Apt has cropping information.

5/431 Wildboarclough (township in parish of Prestbury) SJ 989692
Apt 03.06.1848; 4826a (all); Map 1849, 4.4 chns, from a map belonging to Earl of Derby, 'revised and corrected'; hill-drawing, waterbodies, woods (named), plantations, common, moor, building names, toll bar, collieries, quarry, factory, slate quarry; mapmaker notes the original survey was taken with the Cheshire Chain of 32 yards and laid down to the scale of 3 chns or 96 yards to the inch.

5/432 Willaston (township in parish of Neston) SJ 331775
Apt 27.07.1843; 1941a (1941); Map 1848, 6 chns; railway, foot/b'way, waterbodies, woods. Apt omits some land use.

5/433 Willaston (township in parish of Nantwich) SJ 665533
Apt 11.07.1845; 407a (?); Map 1846?, 6 chns; waterbodies, woods, orchards, building names, mill.

5/434 Willaston (township in parish of Wybunbury) SJ 671524
Apt 08.07.1845; 563a (?); Map 1846?, 8 chns; waterbodies, woods, plantations, fences, building names.

5/435 Willington (extra-parochial place) SJ 536661 [Willington Corner]
Apt 31.12.1849; 366a (910); Map 1850, 3 chns, in 2 parts, surveyed for tithe commutation by William Vernon, Willington; hill-drawing, foot/b'way, waterbodies, woods, plantations, building names, mills, sand or stone pits, tithe-free lands.

5/436 Wimbolds Trafford (township in parish of Thornton in the Moors) SJ 449726 [Not listed]
Apt 19.11.1839; 574a (574); Map 1840, 6 chns; waterbodies, woods, parkland.

5/437 Wincham (township in parish of Great Budworth) SJ 682755
Apt 29.10.1844; 942a (941); Map 1841, 4 chns, by G. Cawley, Tabley; railway, canal with towpath, waterbodies, woods, field gates.

5/438 Wincle (township in parish of Prestbury) SJ 956662
Apt 07.07.1848; 2014a (1980); Map 1848, 6 chns, by Cawley and Firth, Macclesfield; foot/b'way, waterbodies, houses, woods, plantations, field boundary ownerships, field gates.

5/439 Winnington (township in parish of Great Budworth) SJ 646743
Apt 29.10.1844; 597a (597); Map 1845, 8 chns, ? by Robert Simpson; foot/b'way, waterbodies, woods, parkland. Apt omits land use.

5/440 Wirswall (township in parish of Whitchurch) SJ 544445
Apt 08.12.1837; 972a (971); Map 1840, 6 chns, by Bate and Timmis; foot/b'way, canal with towpath, waterbodies, woods, parkland, field gates, building names.

5/441 Wistaston (parish) SJ 682541
Apt 25.10.1839; 1466a (1465); Map 1839, 3 chns; waterbodies, woods, parkland, building names.

5/442 Witton cum Twambrook (township in parish of Prestbury) SJ 665741 [Not listed]
Apt 15.01.1845; 588a (588); Map 1846, 4 chns, by G. Cawley; hill-drawing, foot/b'way, waterbodies, woods, quarries.

5/443 Lower Withington (township in parish of Great Budworth) SJ 815705 [Withington]
Apt 03.06.1848; 1599a (2265); Map 1848, 6 chns, by Cawley and Firth, Macclesfield; railway, foot/b'way, waterbodies, houses, woods, plantations, field boundary ownerships; colour bands may show property ownerships.

5/444 Woodbank (township in parish of Shotwick) SJ 346723
Apt 18.06.1840; 175a (175); Map 1843?, 3 chns; foot/b'way, turnpike roads and gate, waterbodies, woods, plantations, building names, boundary stones. Apt has cropping information.

5/445 Woodchurch (township) SJ 278869
Apt 27.03.1846; 331a (331); Map 1848?, 5 chns, by John Davies, Mollington near Chester; hill-drawing, foot/b'way, waterbodies, woods, field gates.

5/446 Woodcote (township in parish of Acton) SJ 609483 [Not listed]
Apt 31.08.1841; 153a (152); Map 1841?, 6 chns; canal, waterbodies.

5/447 Woodford (township in parish of Prestbury) SJ 889825
Apt 19.06.1848; 1449a (all); Map 1849, 8 chns, ? by E.W. Wilmot; foot/b'way, waterbodies.

5/448 Woolstanwood (township in parish of Nantwich) SJ 673563 [Not listed]
Apt 09.06.1839; 609a (all); Map 1838, 3 chns, by Sam. Harding; railway, waterbodies, woods.

5/449 Worleston (township in parish of Acton) SJ 656551
Apt 26.01.1843; 1123a (1122); Map 1842, 6 chns, in 2 parts, by Sam. Harding, (including open fields at 3 chns); hill-drawing, railway with embankment and viaduct, waterbodies, woods, parkland, open fields, fences, field gates, building names.

5/450 Wrenbury cum Firth (township in parish of Acton) SJ 586484
Apt 31.08.1841; 2074a (2078); Map 1842?, 6 chns, by J. Gregory, Adderley; canal with towpath, waterbodies, woods, field gates.

5/451 Wybunbury (township in parish of Wybunbury) SJ 691504
Apt 14.10.1845; 811a (810); Map 1846?, 6 chns; waterbodies, open fields, fences.

5/452 Wychough (township in parish of Malpas) SJ 485453
Apt 26.06.1839; 323a (?); Map 1838?, 6 chns; waterbodies, woods; there is a note as to the meeting at which the map was adopted for voluntary tithe commutation by the parish landowners and signed by the chairman, Samuel Brittain.

Cornwall

PRO IR29 and IR30 6/1–212

212 tithe districts: 869,224 acres
212 tithe commutations: 848,875 acres
116 voluntary tithe agreements, 92 compulsory tithe awards

Tithe and tithe commutation

All Cornish tithe districts were subject to payment of some tithes in 1836 though 114 districts contained some tithe-free land (Fig. 18). The main causes of exemption were moduses in lieu of some tithes, merger of tithes in the land, exemption by prescription, and the exemption of woodland in some districts.

Assistant tithe commissioners and local tithe agents who worked in Cornwall are listed in Table 6.1 and the valuers of the county's tithe rent-charge in Table 6.2. The tithe apportionments of 103 (48 per cent) of Cornwall tithe districts are lithographed, the highest proportion of any county. Cornwall is a county where grassland leys were occasionally broken up for arable cultivation for a year or two and the conventional arable/pasture distinction in the 'state of cultivation' column of the tithe apportionment is often replaced by descriptions such as 'occasionally arable', 'converting to arable', and 'improving pasture'. In the tithe apportionment for Braddock it is noted that 'the custom of Cornwall is to sow grass seeds with the second corn crop and to plough up again after two years.'

Tithe maps

A very high proportion of Cornwall tithe maps (33 per cent) are sealed as first class. Furthermore, about a quarter of the second-class maps carry construction lines which are often a sign of putative first-class status. Map scales vary from one inch to between one and twelve chains but 92 per cent are drawn within the recommended scale range of one inch to three to four chains (Table 6.3).

The portrayal of industrial activity is quite remarkable on Cornwall tithe maps; the principal industries shown are china clay extraction and non-ferrous metal mining and smelting. Some forty tithe maps depict mine shafts, adits, winding engines and spoil heaps. Field boundary ownership is recorded on a similar number of maps and many others use colour bands to indicate the extent of estates. Ancient earthworks and similar archaeological features are commonly recorded on Cornish tithe maps.

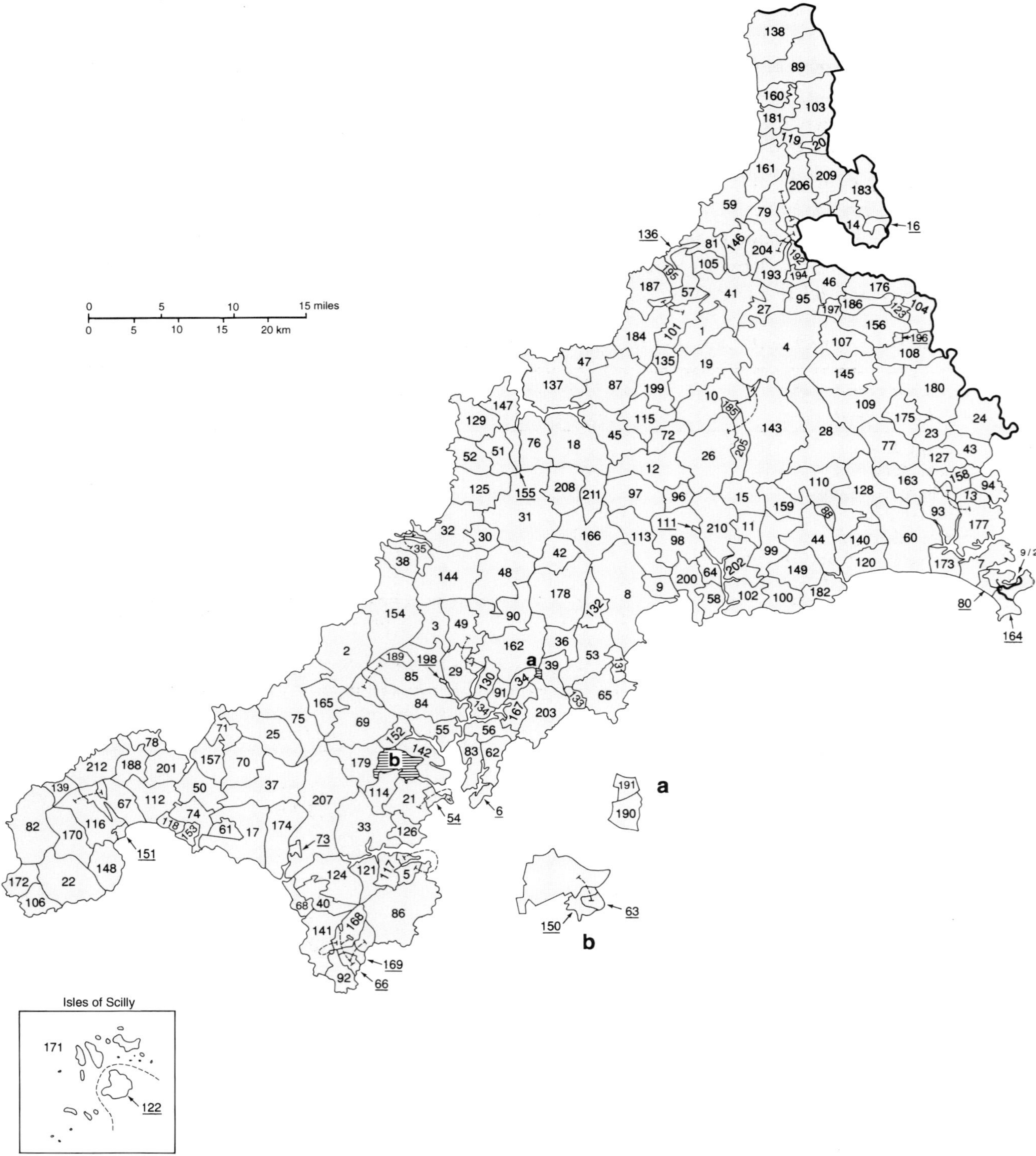

Fig. 18 Cornwall: tithe district boundaries.

An unusually large proportion of Cornwall tithe maps in the Public Record Office collection can be attributed to a particular map-maker. The most prolific was the Woodmass partnership of Chudleigh and Ivybridge in Devon which produced fifteen maps. Second in numerical rank are Henry and Robert Badcock of Launceston who produced twelve maps distinguished by an economical style and the use of stamped lettering (Table 6.2).

The tithe maps of Cornwall are above average in decorative embellishment; for example, fifteen have decorated cartouches, a concentration unmatched elsewhere. At Lanhydrock the cartouche depicts the mansion, that on the Tywardraeth map is composed of various mythical elements, and those on the maps of Sithney and St Winnow depict rural harmony and leisure and convey a direct message of peace and prosperity.

Table 6.1. *Agreements and awards for commutation of tithes in Cornwall*

Assistant commissioner/ local tithe agent	*Number of agreements**	*Number of awards*
George Louis	2	90
James Jerwood	61	0
William Glasson	44	0
Charles Pym	6	0
Frederick Leigh	2	0
George Hammond Whalley	0	2
William Richards	1	0

* Computed from the number of extant reports on tithe agreements in the tithe files [PRO IR 18]

Table 6.2. *Tithe valuers and tithe map-makers in Cornwall*

Name and address (in Cornwall unless indicated)	*Number of districts*	*Acreage*
Tithe valuers		
Thomas Bishop, Tintagel	30	127,207
Henry Badcock, Launceston	23	105,499
William Searle, Lanreath	14	62,557
Jonathan Kittow, North Petherwin	11	29,556
William Richards, Penzance	9	34,090
Robert Coad, Liskeard	8	43,388
Richard Rosewarne, Phillack	8	33,031
Others [54]	109	413,547
Attributed tithe map-makers		
Woodmass and others, Ivybridge, Devon	15	61,796
Henry and Robert Badcock, Launceston	12	36,559
Christopher Bennison, London/Liverpool	9	36,592
John Thompson, Newlyn	9	36,006
John Sandercock and Sons, Altarnun	8	49,317
Robert Symons, Truro	8	46,313
Hans W. Allen	7	33,852
J. S. Olver, Falmouth	7	36,738
Jonathan Kittow, North Petherwin	7	19,589
Others [49]	98	395,046

Table 6.3. *The tithe maps of Cornwall: scales and classes*

Scale in chains/inch	*All maps*		*First Class*		*Second Class*	
	Number	*Acreage*	*Number*	*Acreage*	*Number*	*Acreage*
>3	6	10,348	1	6,192	5	4,156
3	103	371,351	36	156,552	67	214,799
4	86	386,325	35	166,403	51	219,922
4.5	1	735	0	0	1	735
6	10	47,222	0	0	10	47,222
<6	6	32,894	0	0	6	32,894
TOTAL	212	848,875	72	329,147	140	519,728

Table 6.4. *The tithe maps of Cornwall: dates*

	1838	*1839*	*1840*	*1841*	*1842*	*1843*	*1844*	*1845*	*1847*
All maps	7	37	54	54	32	14	7	1	2
1st class*	1	14	17	14	14	10	1	0	0
2nd class*	6	23	37	40	18	4	6	1	2

*One first-class and two second-class tithe maps of Cornwall in the Public Record Office collection are undated.

Cornwall

6/1 Advent (parish) SX 126825 [Not listed]
Apt 09.03.1841; 4059a; Map 1841, 4 chns, 1st cl, by H. and R. Badcock, Launceston; construction lines, building names, triangulation points; names and numbers stamped.

6/2 St Agnes (parish) SW 724485
Apt 22.04.1842; 8294a (all); Map 1841, [8 chns], by R. Symons, Truro; waterbodies, houses, building names, harbour, mines, British School, common, coast features named; colour bands may indicate property boundaries.

6/3 St Allen (parish) SW 818514
Apt 29.12.1840; 3502a (all); Map 1841, 3 chns, by Charles Williams and Richard Reed; construction lines, waterbodies, houses, building names, mill; colour bands may indicate field boundary ownership.

6/4 Alternun (parish) SX 203798 [Altarnun]
Apt 22.07.1841; 15015a (all); Map 1843, 4 chns, 1st cl, by J. and Robert Sandercock, Altarnun near Launceston; foot/b'way, houses, building names, moors.

6/5 St Anthony in Meneage (parish) SW 780245 [St Anthony-in-Meneage]
Apt 31.12.1840; 1510a (all); Map 1840, 3 chns, 'surveyed and laid down' by Charles B. Evans and Christopher Hannan, Helston, Cornwall under the direction of Hughbert Baker, land surveyor, Helston, Cornwall; construction lines, waterbodies, building names.

6/6 St Anthony in Roseland (parish) SW 862323 [St Anthony]
Apt 13.06.1839; 682a (1117); Map 1840, 4 chns, by Nichs Whitley, Truro; foot/b'way, waterbodies, houses, woods, parkland, arable (col), grassland (col), heath/moor, rock outcrops, building names, rocky foreshore, harbour, lighthouse, mills; forelands named; pink tint may indicate tithe-free land. Apt omits land use.

6/7 Anthony in the East (parish) SX 401545 [Anthony]
Apt 21.12.1841; 3222a (?); Map 1840, 4 chns, by Eastcott and Frise, Devonport; hill-drawing, foot/b'way, turnpike roads, waterbodies, houses, woods, plantations, parkland, orchards, heath/moor, coastline, quarries, sand or stone pits, ferry landing.

6/8 St Austell (parish) SX 020550
Apt 11.04.1839; 12126a (12125); Map 1842, 3 chns, 1st cl, in 4 parts, by Murray Vicars, St Austell; construction lines, hill-drawing, railways, foot/b'way, waterbodies, commons, rock outcrops, fences, field boundary ownerships, building names, road names, mines, engine houses, gunpowder magazine, mills, limekilns, blowing houses, burial ground, coastline, foundry, naptha works, clayworks, iron mine; coast features named; it is unclear what the colouring of some buildings denotes; grey may indicate industrial waste land.

6/9 Saint Blazey (parish) SX 060539
Apt 31.10.1839; 1797a (1797); Map 1840, 3 chns, 1st cl, by John Wallis Barnicoat, Falmouth and John James Gummoe, Saint Austell; turnpike roads, canal, waterbodies, houses, fences, field boundary ownerships, property boundaries, building names, road names, mines, engine houses, smith shop, boundary posts, steam whim, mill, high water mark; furze, plantations, orchards, woodland and moorland are shown by annotation; bridges named; legend explains boundary symbols; map is decorated with a drawing of the parish church.

6/10 Blisland (parish) SX 124744
Apt 15.08.1839; 6339a (6338); Map 1840, 4 chns; construction lines, hill-drawing, railway, foot/b'way, waterbodies, field boundary ownerships, mill, common, downland; tors and bridges named.

6/11 Boconnoc (parish) SX 156600
Apt 28.11.1837; 2003a (2003); Map 1838, 6 chns; foot/b'way, waterbodies, woods, parkland (col, in detail), orchards, gardens, hedges, fences, building names, field names, bowling green, manorial boundaries, pheasantry, farm acreages and paths; colour bands may indicate land use as well as boundaries; fleur-de-lys and leaf border surround map title.

6/12 Bodmin (borough and parish) SX 055679
Apt 20.11.1840; 6192a (6191); Map 1841, 2 chns, 1st cl, by Robert Hodge; hill-drawing, railway, turnpike roads and gate, waterbodies, houses, farmyards, woods (col), plantations (col), orchards, rock outcrops, building names, mills, sand wharf, quarries, gaol, county house, market house, tumuli, lunatic asylum.

6/13 Botus Fleming (parish) SX 400620 [Botusfleming]
Apt 21.09.1843; 1138a (all); Map 1844, 4 chns, by R. Polgreen, St Germans; construction lines, foot/b'way, waterbodies, houses; compass, pen and ruler surround the scale bar; scroll on pedestal bears mapmaker's name and details.

6/14 Boyton (except Bradridge) (parish) SX 308925
Apt 14.03.1842; 3426a (?); Map 1843, 4 chns, 1st cl, by Jonathan Kittow, North Petherwin, Launceston; construction lines, foot/b'way, building names, mill.

6/15 Braddock (parish) SX 155633
Apt 28.11.1837; 3367a (?); Map 1838, 3 chns; hill-drawing, turnpike road ('newly made'), waterbodies, houses, woods (col, named), parkland (col), heath/moor (col, named), landowners, tumuli, tollgate, mill, milestones; colours may indicate property ownership or land use.

6/16 Barton of Bradridge (district in parish of Boyton) SX 320934 [Not listed]
Apt 04.05.1842; 728a (?); Map 1843, 4 chns, 1st cl, by Jonathan Kittow, North Petherwin; foot/b'way, building names.

6/17 Breage (parish) SW 606297
Apt 21.07.1842; 7057a (7161); Map 1839, 4 chns, by R. Symons, Truro; foot/b'way, turnpike roads, waterbodies, houses, woods, plantations, rock outcrops, building names, rocky foreshore, mines, sand or stone pits, beach, downland; colour bands may indicate property and manorial boundaries.

6/18 St Breock (parish) SW 980700
Apt 30.04.1841; 8018a (all); Map 1842, 3 chns, 1st cl, by Robert Hodge; railway, waterbodies, houses, farmyards, rock outcrops, building names, path to market, druids' altar, mill, boundary posts, common; names and numbers stamped.

6/19 St Breward otherwise Simonward (parish) SX 126786
Apt 30.06.1843; 9238a (9237); Map 1840, 6 chns, by Nichs Whitley, Truro; foot/b'way, building names, boundary marks, tors (named), downs (named).

6/20 West Bridgerule (parish) SS 267020 [Not listed]
Apt 06.04.1842; 1010a (1010); Map 1842, 3 chns, 1st cl, by Thomas Shearm; construction lines, canal, fences, building names.

6/21 Budock (parish) SW 782320 [Not listed]
Apt 30.06.1843; 3919a (4214); Map 1840, 4 chns, by J.S. Olver; turnpike roads and gate, waterbodies, houses, plantations, rock outcrops, field boundary ownerships, building names, building grounds, hotel, burial grounds, garrison, harbour, high and low water marks, forelands, mills, ropewalk, limekiln.

6/22 St Buryan (parish) SW 414252
Apt 30.11.1838; 6965a (6964); Map 1840, 4 chns, surveyed by R. Henwood for Mr J.H. Rutger; hill-drawing, foot/b'way, waterbodies, farmyards (col), woods, plantations, parkland, orchards, heath/moor (col), rock outcrops, building names, rocky foreshore, coves (named).

6/23 Callington (parish) SX 360696
Apt 16.04.1841; 2493a (all); Map 1841, 3 chns, by Messrs Woodmass and Co; construction lines, waterbodies, houses, field boundary ownerships, building names, road names, mill; depiction of buildings, boundaries and waterbodies explained in legend, which describes the construction lines on the map as 'chain lines'.

6/24 Calstock (parish) SX 413706
Apt 10.09.1839; 6133a (6133); Map 1840, 4 chns, in 3 parts, surveyed for tithe commutation by T. Woodmass and Co, (with 2-chn enlargements of Gunnislake and Calstock); construction lines, foot/b'way, waterbodies, houses, field boundary ownerships, weir, ferry landing.

6/25 Camborne (parish) SW 636404
Apt 11.03.1840; 6744a (6744); Map 1841, 4 chns, by J.S. Olver; railways, foot/b'way, turnpike roads, waterbodies, woods, heath/moor,

field gates, building names, road names, boundary stones, market house, mines, park lodges, mills, commons, foreshore.

6/26 Cardynham (parish) SX 121679 [Cardinham]
Apt 13.05.1839; 9534a (9534); Map 1840, 3 chns, in 2 parts; foot/b'way, waterbodies, houses, farmyards, woods (col), parkland, tumuli or barrows, quarries, well.

6/27 St Cleather (parish) SX 192845 [St Clether]
Apt 03.09.1840; 2961a (2960); Map 1841, 3 chns, 1st cl, by John Sandercock and Sons, Altarnun; construction lines, houses, woods, orchards, building names, mill.

6/28 St Cleer (parish) SX 248703
Apt 27.02.1840; 11263a (11263); Map 1843, 4 chns, 1st cl, in 2 parts, by Chris. Bennison; foot/b'way, waterbodies, woods, plantations, parkland, rock outcrops, building names, mine, mill, common, marsh (by annotation), tors (named, prominent).

6/29 St Clements (parish) SW 847455 [St Clement]
Apt 11.09.1840; 3495a (3494); Map 1842, 3 chns, 1st cl, surveyed for tithe commutation by John Thompson, Civil Engineer, Newlyn; houses.

6/30 Colan, otherwise Little Colan (parish) SW 874605
Apt 07.06.1841; 1395a (1545); Map 1841, 3 chns, tithable part surveyed for tithe commutation by Charles Williams and Richard Reed, Civil Engineers, Grampond; construction lines, foot/b'way, waterbodies, houses, field boundary ownerships.

6/31 St Columb Major (parish) SW 921634
Apt 22.01.1840; 12697a (all); Map 1840, 4 chns, in 2 parts, by Hughbert Baker; construction lines, turnpike roads, waterbodies, marsh/bog, heath/moor, rock outcrops, fences, field gates, field acreages, building names, tumulus or ancient castle, quarry, mines and shafts, engine shaft, stamp mill, steam workers excavations, boundary stones, barrows, ice house, commons; some land use shown by annotation, e.g. 'marshy', 'heathy sedgy moor', 'partially reclaimed'.

6/32 St Minor Columb (parish) SW 840617
Apt 31.12.1840; 5563a (?); Map 1839, 3 chns, by George S. and John S. Body, St Germans, Cornwall; construction lines, houses; scrolls surround map title.

6/33 Constantine (parish) SW 734291
Apt 19.03.1842; 7909a (8179); Map 1841, 4 chns, 'surveyed and laid down' by Jno. King and C.B. Evans for H. Baker, Land surveyor, Helston; waterbodies, building names, coastline. Apt omits some land use.

6/34 Cornelly (parochial chapelry) SW 908445 [Not listed]
Apt 14.09.1844; 1348a (1348); Map undated, 6 chns, by Nichs Whitley, Truro; waterbodies, houses, woods, plantations, parkland, heath/moor, rock outcrops, building names, weir, quarry.

6/35 Crantock (parish) SW 805597
Apt 22.02.1840; 2458a (all); Map 1839, 3 chns, by Alexander Withers; construction lines, hill-drawing, foot/b'way, waterbodies, houses, woods, orchards, foreshore, rock outcrops, hedges, building names, road names, well, mill, smelting house, shipyard, river steps, old entrenchments, tumuli, quarry; headlands and coves named; colour bands may indicate property boundaries.

6/36 Creed (parish) SW 951485
Apt 06.11.1840; 2810a (all); Map 1841, 3 chns, surveyed for tithe commutation by Charles Williams and Richard Reed; construction lines, foot/b'way, waterbodies, houses, building names, mill, double hedge.

6/37 Crowan (parish) SW 638343
Apt 22.07.1841; 7240a (7239); Map 1840, 4 chns, by J.H. Rutger, Marazion; waterbodies, woods (by annotation), plantations (by annotation), common, down, rock outcrops, building names, burrow or tumulus, mines, boundary posts, land unproductive of tithe (col).

6/38 Cubert (parish) SW 785586
Apt 03.11.1840; 2443a (all); Map 1842?, 4 chns, surveyed for tithe commutation by John Thompson, C.E., Newlyn; construction lines.

6/39 Cuby (parish) SW 940451 [Not listed]
Apt 10.02.1841; 2300a (2300); Map 1841, 3 chns, 1st cl, by Michael FitzGerald; construction lines, turnpike roads and gate, waterbodies, houses, farmyards, woods, plantations, orchards, building names, mills, smithy.

6/40 Cury (parish) SW 691213
Apt 12.10.1839; 2770a (2845); Map 1840?, 3 chns; hill-drawing, foot/b'way, waterbodies, woods, parkland, orchards, fences, building names, barrows, kennel, boundary trench; farms are named and colour bands may indicate their boundaries.

6/41 David Stowe (parish) SX 160864 [Davidstow]
Apt 07.12.1838; 6757a (6756); Map 1839, 4 chns, 1st cl, by H. and R. Badcock, Launceston; construction lines, foot/b'way, building names, moor (named); names and numbers stamped.

6/42 St Dennis (parish) SW 952580
Apt 31.12.1840; 1960a (all); Map 1838, 3 chns, ? by Wm Geo. Sheringham, Truro; foot/b'way, waterbodies, houses, farmyards, woods, gardens, rock outcrops, clayworks.

6/43 St Dominick (parish) SX 401674
Apt 08.05.1841; 3127a (3226); Map 1842, 4 chns, 'trignometrical survey' by Messrs Robinson and Morgan; construction lines, waterbodies, houses, quarry.

6/44 Duloe (parish) SX 227586
Apt 15.05.1841; 5845a (5844); Map 1841, 3 chns, by A. Heathman, Duloe, J. Rutger, Marazion, and R. Henwood, Penzance; foot/b'way, waterbodies, farmyards, woods, plantations, parkland, orchards, building names; beige wash adjoining river may indicate land not producing tithe; map uses Dawson's symbols.

6/45 Egloshayle (parish) SX 025711
Apt 29.01.1840; 5619a (5748); Map 1840, 4 chns, surveyed by R. Hodge for H. Crispin junr, land agent; railways, foot/b'way, turnpike roads and gate, waterbodies, woods (named), plantations (named), parkland (in detail), orchards, gardens, ornamental gardens (in detail), rock outcrops, field boundary ownerships, building names, tumulus, mill (by symbol), quarries, sand and mudbanks; it is unclear what colours in Egloshayle village mean. Apt omits some land use.

6/46 Egloskerry (parish) SX 265869
Apt 17.10.1838; 3236a (3235); Map 1839, 4 chns, 1st cl, by H. and R. Badcock, Launceston; construction lines, foot/b'way, waterbodies, woods, plantations, parkland, orchards, heath/moor, field gates, building names; names and numbers are stamped.

6/47 Endellion (parish) SX 001799 [St Endellion]
Apt 10.09.1841; 3730a (3729); Map 1839, 3 chns, 1st cl, by Henry Coom, Bodmin; construction lines, foot/b'way, waterbodies, houses, rock outcrops, hedges, field boundary ownerships, building names, coastline.

6/48 St Enoder (parish) SW 899565
Apt 30.12.1839; 7038a (all); Map 1840, 3 chns, surveyed for tithe commutation by C. Williams and S.S. Bassett; construction lines, foot/b'way, waterbodies, houses, field boundary ownerships.

6/49 St Erme (parish) SW 848514
Apt 11.03.1840; 4507a (all); Map 1840, 3 chns, by Thomas Woodmass, John Thompson, John Huddleston and John Woodmass, Chudleigh, Devon; construction lines, foot/b'way, houses, field boundary ownerships, burrow, boundary stones.

6/50 St Erth (parish) SW 566344
Apt 14.07.1842; 4093a (4092); Map 1840, 3 chns, constructed from 'ancient and modern maps' by John Rundle, Hayle; waterbodies, houses, rock outcrops, fences, field gates, building names, road names, woods (by annotation), tumuli, glebe; colour bands may indicate property ownership; compass rose is decorated with rose and thistle and fleur-de-lys. Apt omits land use.

6/51 St Ervan (parish) SW 896700
Apt 08.07.1841; 3108a (3218); Map 1842, 3 chns, surveyed for tithe commutation by E. and J. Hocking, Tregony; foot/b'way, waterbodies, houses, heath/moor, building names, mill.

6/52 St Eval (parish) SW 866698
Apt 16.11.1841; 2886a (all); Map 1842, 4 chns, by John Thompson C.E., Newlyn; construction lines, foot/b'way, houses, open fields.

6/53 St Ewe (parish) SW 982468
Apt 13.04.1839; 5935a (all); Map 1839, 3 chns, by Richard Carveth and John J. Gummoe, St Austell and John W. Barnicoat, Falmouth; railway, foot/b'way, turnpike roads, waterbodies, houses, field boundary ownerships, building names, mine, quarries, almshouses, adits, shafts, engine house, compting house, embankments, mill, poor house, common; furze, waste, copse, marsh, orchard and plantation shown by annotation; a note explains boundary symbols.

6/54 Falmouth (parish) SW 808322
Apt 10.02.1841; 735a (989); Map 1841, 4.5 chns, by Richard Thomas; rock outcrops, road names, quarry, pier, low water mark, coast features, old line of fortifications, earthworks, rope walk, market; colours may indicate property ownership.

6/55 Feock (parish) SW 816394
Apt 24.06.1841; 3090a (3765); Map 1842, 3 chns; foot/b'way, building names, creeks, down.

6/56 Filley otherwise Philleigh (parish) SW 872395 [Not listed]
Apt 24.08.1840; 2377a (all); Map 1841, 3 chns, surveyed for tithe commutation by John Thompson, Thomas Woodmass, John Huddleston and John Woodmass; foot/b'way, houses, building names.

6/57 Forrabury (parish) SX 100915 [Not listed]
Apt 07.08.1839; 508a (all); Map 1842, 4 chns, 1st cl, by C. Bennison; waterbodies, houses, woods, open fields, building names, quarry, summer house, down.

6/58 Fowey (parish) SX 113523
Apt 12.02.1838; 1895a (1945); Map 1839, 3 chns, by John Bowen; construction lines, waterbodies, woods (named), plantations (named), parkland, orchards, gardens, rock outcrops, hedges, building names, field names, field acreages, landowners, coast features, quarry, castle, fort, quay, dog kennel, rope walk, custom house, corn mill, old windmill tower, tithe-free land; colours may show ownerships; map includes notes on determination of parish boundaries and on leasing and purchase of land.

6/59 St Gennis (parish) SX 160964 [St Gennys]
Apt 11.04.1839; 5487a (all); Map 1839, [4 chns], 1st cl, by J. Kittow, Northpetherwin, Devon; construction lines, building names, mill.

6/60 St Germans (parish) SX 331569
Apt 30.01.1843; 9998a (10317); Map 1843, 4 chns, 1st cl, by Eastcott and Pollgreen; foot/b'way, waterbodies, houses.

6/61 Germoe (parish) SW 586298
Apt 14.04.1841; 1288a (all); Map 1841?, 3 chns; foot/b'way, waterbodies, orchards, building names, boundary stones, china clay works, tumuli, commons.

6/62 Gerrans (parish) SW 872350
Apt 22.04.1841; 2656a (all); Map 1841, 3 chns, 1st cl, by Messrs Woodmass and Co, Chudleigh, Devon; construction lines, foot/b'way, houses, field boundary ownerships.

6/63 St Gluvias (parish) SW 785349
Apt 10.12.1844; 2575a (2574); Map 1844, 3 chns, by J.S. Olver; turnpike roads, waterbodies, building names, area dry at low water, powder mill, glebe, woodland (by annotation).

6/64 Golant otherwise St Sampsons (parish) SX 112556
Apt 27.07.1839; 1470a (1470); Map '1840-3', 4 chns, by John Bowen; foot/b'way, waterbodies, houses, woods (col, named), parkland (named), building names, public highway, coastline, earth works; map is coloured in an idiosyncratic 'artistic' fashion; map title is enclosed within a decorative leaf border.

6/65 St Gorran (parish) SW 997425 [Gorran Churchtown]
Apt 22.04.1841; 4726a (?); Map 1842, 3 chns, waterbodies, woods, plantations, parkland, orchards, heath/moor, building names, lodge, mill; bays and other coast features named.

6/66 Grade (parish) SW 713148
Apt 10.02.1841; 1943a (1981); Map 1843?, 4 chns, in 4 parts, compiled from surveys by Moody Prisk etc, by H. Baker; foot/b'way, waterbodies, building names, mill, coastline, glebe, property ownership, common (named), down (named).

6/67 Gulval (parish) SW 479339
Apt 02.02.1843; 4357a (4547); Map 1844?, 3 chns, by R. Pentreath, Penzance; foot/b'way, public roads ('PR'), waterbodies, houses, woods, parkland, rock outcrops, field boundary ownerships, building names, landowners, mill, well, shoreline, high and low water marks (col), boundary marks, cairns, burrows, mines. Apt distinguishes moorland under improvement.

6/68 Gunwalloe (parish) SW 661221
Apt 30.10.1839; 1429a (all); Map 1838, 3 chns, by I.H. Rutger, Marazion; construction lines, hill-drawing, waterbodies, woods, rock outcrops, field gates, building names, capstans, castle, sandy foreshore, coast features (in detail), high and low water marks, coves (named), beaches (annotated as accessible or inaccessible), commons; colours may indicate property ownership; bridges named; pictorial church (outside district).

6/69 Gwennap (parish) SW 742415
Apt 17.08.1838; 6565a (6565); Map 1839, 4 chns, by Robert Symons, Truro; hill-drawing, railway, turnpike roads, waterbodies, houses, woods, parkland, heath/moor, fences, field gates, building names, tumuli, marl pit, mills, engine, pound, account house, mines, manorial boundaries, commons (col); colours may indicate property ownership. Apt notes that a large proportion of the common land is totally destroyed by the working of the mines.

6/70 Gwinear (parish) SW 611371
Apt 29.03.1841; 4611a (4611); Map 1839, 3 chns, by Richard Thomas, Falmouth; hill-drawing, railway and embankment, waterbodies, woods, plantations, heath/moor, building names, tumuli, ancient fort, mines, mills, foundry; colour bands and tints may indicate property ownership.

6/71 Gwithian (parish) SW 591409
Apt 17.08.1838; 2318a (2633); Map 1839, 4 chns, waterbodies, boundary marks; stipple may be woods or rock. Apt omits some land use.

6/72 Helland (parish) SX 078707
Apt 30.06.1840; 2475a (2475); Map 1840, 4 chns, 1st cl, by John Sandercock and Sons, Alternun near Launceston; construction lines, railway, woods, field boundary ownerships.

6/73 Helston (parish) SW 660274
Apt 21.11.1838; 292a (291); Map 1838, 2 chns, by J.H. Rutger, Marazion, Cornwall; hill-drawing, foot/b'way, turnpike roads, waterbodies, woods, plantations, parkland, orchards, gardens, hedges, fences, field gates, road names, public buildings (col, named), guildhall, workhouse, chapels, bowling green, meeting house, mills, quarry, gas works, burial ground, commercial school, national school, prison; map is described as of the townlands within the Borough of Helston.

6/74 St Hilary (parish) SW 555316
Apt 11.02.1841; 2786a (all); Map 1842?, 4 chns; waterbodies, heath/moor (col), rock outcrops, building names, coastline, boundary posts.

6/75 Illogen (parish) SW 672421 [Illogan]
Apt 22.04.1840; 8273a (8317); Map 1840, 4 chns, by J.S. Olver, Falmouth; railway, foot/b'way, carriage road, waterbodies, park (named), heath/moor, rock outcrops, building names, boundary ownerships, boundary stones, burrow, mines, workhouses, mill, park lodges, monument, castle, embankments, coast features (named), common (col); tithe-merged and possibly tithe-free land coloured. Apt omits land use.

6/76 St Issey (parish) SW 934704
Apt 26.11.1840; 4720a (all); Map 1841, 3 chns, 'rough plan' by R. Symons, Truro; foot/b'way, turnpike roads, waterbodies, houses, woods, plantations, heath/moor, building names, boundary stone, mill, mill pool.

6/77 St Ive (parish) SX 316682
Apt 16.11.1840; 5781a (5780); Map 1840, 3 chns, by John Moorshead,

South-hill; foot/b'way, waterbodies, houses, woods, plantations, parkland, orchards.

6/78 St Ives (parish) SW 505400
Apt 14.12.1839; 1876a (all); Map 1841, 3 chns; foot/b'way, plantations, rock outcrops, building names, road names, sandy coves; coastline shown in detail.

6/79 Jacobstow (parish) SX 204955
Apt 23.04.1839; 4554a (all); Map 1839, 4 chns, 1st cl, by John Saundercock and sons, Altarnun near Launceston; construction lines, foot/b'way, woods, parkland.

6/80 St John (parish) SX 404521
Apt 30.06.1840; 699a (all); Map 1840, 3 chns, by Eastcott and Frise, Devonport; construction lines, foot/b'way, waterbodies, houses, woods, open fields, field boundary ownerships, shoreline; tithe area numbers are stamped.

6/81 St Juliott (parish) SX 135920 [Not listed]
Apt 28.10.1840; 2674a (all); Map 1842?, 3 chns, 1st cl, by Chrisr Bennison, London; construction lines, building names, mills, coastline.

6/82 St Just in Penwith (parish) SW 375315 [St Just]
Apt 12.05.1843; 7391a (7421); Map 1841, 4 chns, in 2 parts, by R. Henwood; hill-drawing, waterbodies, rock outcrops, building names, commons, mills, mines, stamping mill, fire whan, fire stamps and draft engine, boat house, coast (in detail); physical and coast features named.

6/83 St Just in Roseland (parish) SW 853360
Apt 04.02.1841; 2602a (4192); Map 1840, 6 chns, by Nichs Whitley; foot/b'way, farmyards, heath/moor (col), rock outcrops, building names, ferry landing, cliffs, mill, fortification or ornamental feature.

6/84 Kea (except the Manor of Tregavethan) (parish) SW 802421
Apt 06.05.1842; 6938a (all); Map 1843, 4 chns, 1st cl, by John Thompson C.E., Newlyn; construction lines, foot/b'way, waterbodies.

6/85 Kenwyn (parish) SW 800460
Apt 29.12.1840; 8997a (all); Map 1840, 8 chns, in 2 parts 'compiled from surveys by R. Thomas, corrected etc by F.L. Turner under the directions of H. Baker', (including several 2-chn enlargements of detail); turnpike roads, road names, quays, ssmelting house, manorial boundaries.

6/86 St Keverne (parish) SW 770200
Apt 30.06.1842; 10158a (10173); Map 1840, 4 chns, by Bushell and Vine; waterbodies, houses, woods, plantations, marsh/bog, building names, mill, common.

6/87 St Kew (parish) SX 022769
Apt 31.12.1840; 7515a (7514); Map 1844?, 4 chns, surveyed for tithe commutation by John Thompson, C.E., Newlyn; construction lines, field boundary ownerships, boundary stones, tumulus.

6/88 St Keyne (parish) SX 243609
Apt 12.11.1840; 945a (944); Map 1840, 3 chns, by John Bowen; foot/b'way, canal, waterbodies, woods, parkland, hedges, field gates, well, parsonage grounds (col); map title surrounds a compass intersected by the scale bar.

6/89 Kilkhampton (parish) SS 250109
Apt 02.11.1840; 8078a (8272); Map 1839, 3 chns, 1st cl, in 2 parts, by Charles Cooper, Alverdiscott, Bideford, Devon, (partly from a survey by Mr Thomas Shearm of Launceston in 1826 and laid down at a scale of 4 chains); construction lines, houses, field boundary ownerships, building names.

6/90 Ladock (parish) SW 890514
Apt 11.04.1839; 5691a (all); Map 1839, 3 chns, by Thomas Woodmass, John Thompson, John Huddleston and John Woodmass, Teignmouth, Devon; foot/b'way, waterbodies, houses, field boundary ownerships.

6/91 Lamorran (parish) SW 883432
Apt 05.02.1840; 1234a (1234); Map 1840, 8 chns; foot/b'way, waterbodies, woods, plantations, orchards, field boundary ownerships. Apt omits land use.

6/92 Landewednack (parish) SW 701135 [Lizard]
Apt 29.03.1841; 1999a (1999); Map 1839, 3 chns, 'rough plan' by F. Carter, William Thomas and S. Hendy; construction lines, foot/b'way, houses, woods, rock outcrops, building names, windmill, lighthouses (pictorial), coast features (in detail), sands (col), manorial boundaries, downland.

6/93 Landrake and St Erney (parish) SX 370602
Apt 01.12.1841; 3541a (3745); Map 1842, 4 chns, 1st cl, 'trigonometrical survey' by Messrs Robinson and Morgan, Civil Engineers, Dublin; waterbodies, houses, farmyards, building names.

6/94 Landulph (parish) SX 426300
Apt 12.08.1841; 2086a (2686); Map 1841?, 3 chns, by John Woodmass, Alston, Cumberland; foot/b'way, waterbodies, houses, field boundary ownerships, building names; legend explains depiction of buildings, waterbodies and boundaries.

6/95 Laneast (parish) SX 235850
Apt 05.02.1840; 2487a (2485); Map 1840, 3 chns, by W. Brock, Launceston, Cornwall; construction lines, foot/b'way, houses, farmyards, woods, plantations, parkland (named), orchards, heath/moor, building names, mill, common.

6/96 Lanhydrock (parish) SX 085638 [Not listed]
Apt 05.02.1840; 1756a (1755); Map 1841, 4 chns; waterbodies, houses, parkland (in detail), fences, field boundary ownerships, building names, boundary stones, mill; above the title is a semicircular watercolour of a mansion and church in parkland.

6/97 Lanivet (parish) SX 040640
Apt 15.08.1839; 5396a (all); Map 1840, 3 chns, 1st cl, by Messrs Woodmass and Co, Chudleigh, Devon; construction lines, waterbodies, houses, field boundary ownerships.

6/98 Lanlivery (parish) SX 081593
Apt 26.01.1841; 6791a (6790); Map 1839, 4 chns, in 3 parts, by Chrisr Bennison, Civil Engineer and Surveyor, Liverpool (including two 1.3 chn enlargements of detail); railway, foot/b'way, waterbodies, woods, plantations, parkland, rock outcrops, building names, tramroad, tors, castle, mill, boundary stones.

6/99 Lanreath (parish) SX 180580
Apt 07.03.1842; 4878a (4878); Map 1842, 3 chns, 1st cl, by I. Woodmass; construction lines ('chain lines'), foot/b'way, waterbodies, houses, field boundary ownerships; legend explains depiction of buildings, waterbodies and boundaries.

6/100 Lansallos (parish) SX 188520
Apt 16.10.1840; 2985a (all); Map 1843?, 4 chns, 1st cl, by George S. Body; construction lines, houses, farmyards.

6/101 Lanteglos by Camelford (parish) SX 101837 [Lanteglos]
Apt 09.03.1841; 3951a (3951); Map 1841, 4 chns, 1st cl, by H. and R. Badcock, Launceston; construction lines, foot/b'way, woods, building names, quarry; names and numbers are stamped.

6/102 Lanteglos by Fowey (parish) SX 148521 [Not listed]
Apt 07.08.1839; 3196a (3320); Map 1845?, 6 chns, in 2 parts, (village at 3 chns); foot/b'way, waterbodies; map title and the enlargement have leafy surround.

6/103 Launcells (parish) SS 262062
Apt 08.08.1840; 6179a (6179); Map 1840, 4 chns, 1st cl, in 2 parts, by Hans W. Allen; construction lines, waterbodies, houses, building names.

6/104 Lawhitton (parish) SX 359826
Apt 12.10.1840; 2629a (2629); Map 1839, 4 chns, 1st cl, by H. and R. Badcock, Launceston; construction lines, hill-drawing, foot/b'way, waterbodies, woods, parkland, orchards, building names; names and numbers stamped.

6/105 Lesnewth (parish) SX 135899
Apt 14.12.1841; 2028a (all); Map 1842, 4 chns, 1st cl, by Chrisr Bennison; construction lines, woods, building names, barrow, mill.

6/106 St Levan (parish) SW 378232
Apt 30.11.1838; 2328a (2328); Map 1841?, 4 chns; hill-drawing, foot/b'way, waterbodies, orchards, heath/moor, rock outcrops, building names, cliffs, coast features (named), waste (col), common; hills and tors named.

6/107 Lewannick (parish) SX 274800
Apt 22.04.1841; 4001a (4000); Map 1839, 4 chns, 1st cl, by H. and R. Badcock, Launceston; construction lines, foot/b'way, waterbodies, woods, plantations, parkland, orchards, building names; names and numbers stamped.

6/108 Lezant (parish) SX 343788
Apt 03.09.1840; 4561a (4560); Map 1841, 3 chns, 1st cl, by Carlos and FitzGerald; construction lines, waterbodies, houses, farmyards, woods (named), plantations (named), orchards, heath/moor, common, building names, mills, quarry, ruins of ancient chapel, mine; green bands may indicate coppice.

6/109 Linkinhorne (parish) SX 294730
Apt 17.07.1839; 7894a (7894); Map 1841, 3 chns, 1st cl, in 3 parts, by George Conroy, (including construction line diagram); construction lines, trigonometrical stations, hill-drawing, waterbodies, houses, woods, plantations, parkland, orchards, gardens, marsh/bog, heath/moor (col), rock outcrops, field boundary ownerships, building names, landowners, tors, boundary marks; colour bands may indicate estate or farm boundaries; incomplete table lists acreages, and is decorated with a drawing of a tor in elevation with shepherd and sheep standing beneath.

6/110 Liskeard (parish) SX 242625
Apt 30.08.1842; 8129a (8129); Map 1840, 4 chns, 1st cl, by Carlos and FitzGerald, Hanover Chambers, Buckingham St, Adelphi, London; construction lines, canal, waterbodies, houses, farmyards, plantations (named), parkland, ornamental gardens, building names, road names, site of castle, school house, mills, quarries, kilns.

6/111 Lostwithiel (parish) SX 105600
Apt 18.07.1839; 111a (110); Map 1844?, 4 chns, by John Parkin junr, Lostwithiel; built-up parts are generalised.

6/112 Ludgvan (parish) SW 505331
Apt 27.03.1839; 4544a (4584); Map 1838, 3 chns, by J.H. Rutger, Marazion; construction lines, hill-drawing, foot/b'way, waterbodies, woods, plantations, heath/moor (named), rock outcrops, coast features (named), sands, cliff, high and low water marks, carn, boundary stones, ancient fort, account house, engine house, mines, waste (col); colours may indicate property ownership. Apt distinguishes 'improved arable'.

6/113 Luxulian (parish) SX 045588 [Luxulyan]
Apt 22.04.1839; 5355a (5354); Map 1840, 3 chns, 1st cl, by Murray Vicars, Exeter; construction lines, hill-drawing, foot/b'way, turnpike roads, toll-gate, canal, waterbodies, woods (named), plantations, parkland, gardens, field boundary ownerships, building names, mills, tumulus, viaduct, ancient castle, barrows, moor (named); map has long note about boundaries and boundary ownership.

6/114 Mabe (parish) SW 754333 [Mabe Burnthouse]
Apt 17.12.1839; 2569a (all); Map 1840, 3 chns, by Richd Thomas, Falmouth; hill-drawing, foot/b'way, turnpike roads, waterbodies, woods, parkland, orchards, heath/moor, rock outcrops, field gates, building names, quarries, cairns, mill; physical features named; colours may indicate property ownerships; note explains boundary depiction.

6/115 St Mabyn (parish) SX 056727
Apt 24.08.1839; 4068a (all); Map 1840, 3 chns, 1st cl, surveyed by John Woodmass pro Messrs Woodmass, Thompson and Co.; construction lines, foot/b'way, waterbodies, houses, field boundary ownerships; legend explains depiction of buildings, boundaries and water bodies.

6/116 Madron (parish) SW 442316
Apt 28.01.1841; 5476a (5991); Map 1839, 3 chns; hill-drawing, foot/b'way, waterbodies, woods, plantations, parkland, orchards, gardens, rock outcrops, open fields, fences, building names, mills, workhouse, tors, standing stones, commons; hills named; colours may indicate property ownership or manorial divisions.

6/117 Manaccan (parish) SW 756248
Apt 19.12.1840; 1719a (all); Map 1840, 3 chns, by W.H. Fortesque and Christ. Hannan; construction lines, foot/b'way, waterbodies, houses, building names, mill, harbour, custom house. Apt omits land use.

6/118 Marazion (parish) SW 524310
Apt 11.04.1839; 681a (all); Map 1840, 2 chns, by J.H. Rutger, Marazion, Cornwall; foot/b'way, waterbodies, woods, plantations, parkland, orchards, rock outcrops, field gates, building names, road names, coastline, sandy foreshore, mines, market house, beacon; physical features named.

6/119 Marhamchurch (parish) SS 229031
Apt 13.09.1839; 2646a (2720); Map 1840?, 3 chns, 1st cl, by George Cooper and Son, Alverdiscott, Bideford, Devon; construction lines, foot/b'way, canal, rock outcrops, hedge ownership, field gates, coastline, cliffs.

6/120 Saint Martins otherwise Saint Kaynne near Looe (parish) SX 282552 [St Martin]
Apt 13.09.1839; 3069a (3199); Map 1839, 2 chns, by Simon Hill, Saint Martins near Looe; foot/b'way, houses, field gates, building names, road names, watchhouse, mill.

6/121 St Martin in Meneage (parish) SW 734239 [St Martin]
Apt 22.10.1841; 2295a (2369); Map 1840, 4 chns, by H. Baker; foot/b'way, building names; colour bands may indicate property boundaries or tithing practices.

6/122 Island of St Mary (district in parish of Scilly Isles) SV 920111 [St Mary's]
Apt 27.01.1847; 1529a (all); Map 1847?, 12 chns; waterbodies, building names, castle, quay, coastline, large pond (named); whole island is treated as a single tithe area and no fields or other features are shown. Apt omits land use and field names.

6/123 St Mary Magdalene (parish) SX 334831 [Not listed]
Apt 26.01.1842; 1105a (?); Map 1839, 4 chns, by H. and R. Badcock, Launceston; farmyards, woods, orchards, building names, workhouse, castle (in detail), castle gates, ornamental planting; names and numbers stamped.

6/124 Mawgan in Meneage (parish) SW 700245 [Mawgan]
Apt 22.03.1841; 5274a (5273); Map undated, 4 chns; hill-drawing, foot/b'way, waterbodies, woods (col), coppice (sym), parkland, orchards, building names, farm names, coastline, boundary stones; colour bands may indicate farm boundaries.

6/125 Mawgan-in-Pyder (parish) SW 872659 [St Mawgan]
Apt 31.01.1840; 5468a (all); Map 1841, 3 chns, 1st cl, by Chrisr. Bennison; construction lines, foot/b'way, waterbodies, woods, open fields, building names, road names, nunnery, mills.

6/126 Mawnan (parish) SW 778287
Apt 06.04.1839; 2059a (2258); Map 1839?, 3 chns; construction lines, hill-drawing, foot/b'way, waterbodies, houses, farmyards, woods, plantations, heath/moor (col), rock outcrops, building names, coast features (named), cliffs, beach, watermills, downland; colour bands may indicate property boundaries.

6/127 St Mellion (parish) SX 368665
Apt 17.11.1840; 2985a (all); Map 1840, 4 chns, 1st cl, 'trigonometrical survey' by Hans W. Allen (tinted); houses, woods. Apt omits land use and most field-names.

6/128 Menheniot (parish) SX 288638
Apt 03.11.1840; 6998a (all); Map 1841, 3 chns, 1st cl, by Henry Crispin junr and Richard Davie Gould; construction lines, waterbodies, houses, field boundary ownerships, building names.

6/129 St Merryn (parish) SW 874737
Apt 16.02.1841; 3799a (3928); Map 1841, 3 chns, surveyed for tithe commutation by John Thompson, Civil Engineer, Newlyn; open fields, field boundary ownerships.

6/130 Merther (parish) SW 867448
Apt 17.01.1844; 1727a (1726); Map 1844, 4 chns; foot/b'way, waterbodies,

woods (col), plantations (col), orchard (col), marsh/bog (col), building names.

6/131 Mevagissey (parish) SX 013453
Apt 09.03.1841; 1345a (1344); Map 1842, 3 chns, by John Andrewartha, Truro; hill-drawing, foot/b'way, waterbodies, houses, building names, coastline.

6/132 St Mewan (parish) SW 990526
Apt 11.08.1838; 2632a (all); Map 1838, 3 chns, 1st cl, by Richard Carveth, Saint Austell; construction lines, hill-drawing, foot/b'way, turnpike roads, waterbodies, houses, heath/moor, rock outcrops, field boundary ownerships, field gates, greenstone quarry, mines, engine house, chimney, shafts, china clay works, spoil banks, clay pits, quarries, whim, adits, flat rods, elvan pits, account house, meeting house, stamps, Quakers' burial ground, boundary posts; some land use indicated by annotation, e.g. trees and waste, furze; a note explains boundary depiction.

6/133 St Michael Carhayes (parish) SW 965423 [St Michael Caerhays]
Apt 31.12.1840; 871a (all); Map 1841, 3 chns; construction lines, hill-drawing, foot/b'way, waterbodies, houses, rock outcrops, building names, cliffs, look-out house, limekiln, mills (Dawson's symbol), lodge, old watercourse, poor house, coast features (named).

6/134 St Michael Penkevil (parish) SW 860415
Apt 21.02.1840; 1189a (1189); Map 1840, 8 chns; foot/b'way, waterbodies, woods, plantations, parkland (in detail), orchards, coastline; colour bands may indicate property boundaries. Apt omits land use.

6/135 Michaelstow (parish) SX 080790
Apt 11.07.1842; 1618a (1617); Map 1842, 4 chns, 1st cl, by H. and R. Badcock, Launceston; construction lines, hill-drawing, foot/b'way, waterbodies, building names, earthworks; names and numbers stamped.

6/136 Minster (parish) SX 112880 [Not listed]
Apt 07.08.1839; 3322a (all); Map 1843, 4 chns, 1st cl, by C. Bennison; houses, farmyards, plantations, building names, machine house, downland (named).

6/137 St Minver (parish) SW 961770
Apt 12.04.1838; 7579a (8683); Map 'purveyed' in 1838 and 1839 under the Tithe Act for the parishioners, 3 chns, 1st cl, in 2 parts, by Murray Vicars, Paul Street, Exeter; construction lines, hill-drawing, foot/b'way, waterbodies, woods, plantations, parkland, orchards, heath/moor, furze, rock outcrops, field boundary ownerships, field gates, building names, quarries, mills, coastline, castle; physical features named; note explains boundary symbols.

6/138 Moorwinstow (parish) SS 231149 [Morwenstow]
Apt 06.02.1840; 7927a (7956); Map 1840, 4 chns, 1st cl, in 2 parts, by Hans W. Allen; construction lines, base line, triangulation points (named), foot/b'way, houses.

6/139 Morvah (manor) SW 411353
Apt 20.08.1839; 1227a (all); Map 1840, 3 chns, by R. Pentreath and G. Hosken; construction lines, foot/b'way, public roads ('PR'), waterbodies, heath/moor, rock outcrops, building names, ancient castle, quoit, boundary stones, cairns, coastline, cliffs, mills, tin mines, shaft, whims, stamps, barrow, gurgos; coast features named.

6/140 Morval (parish) SX 280580
Apt 30.09.1845; 3562a (3562); Map 1842, 3 chns, 1st cl, by Messrs H. Crispin junr and Rd Davie Gould; construction lines, houses, building names.

6/141 Mullion (parish) SW 683174
Apt 12.12.1840; 4786a (all); Map 1841, 4 chns, by F. Carter, W. Thomas and S. Hendy; construction lines, foot/b'way, waterbodies, houses, rock outcrops, open fields, building names, coastline, cliffs, boundary stones; colouring and names written across map may indicate property ownership. Apt omits land use.

6/142 Mylor (parish) SW 804363 [Mylor Churchtown]
Apt 14.12.1839; 3562a (5002); Map 1842?, 3 chns; hill-drawing, foot/b'way, waterbodies, woods, plantations, parkland (in detail), orchards, heath/moor (col), rock outcrops, field boundary ownerships, field gates, building names, coastline, cliffs, quays, quarries, ferries, wharf, timber pond, tide mill, dockyard, weir; coast features named; colours may indicate property ownership boundaries.

6/143 St Neot (parish) SX 191701
Apt 08.12.1842; 13997a (all); Map 1844, 4 chns, 1st cl, by John Sandercock and Sons, Altarnun near Launceston; waterbodies, farmyards, woods, orchards, building names, mills; bridges named.

6/144 Newlyn (parish) SW 839564 [St Newlyn East]
Apt 04.11.1840; 8020a (8010); Map 1840, 3 chns, by Thomas Woodmass, John Thompson, John Huddleston and John Woodmass, Chudleigh, Devon; foot/b'way, houses, field boundary ownerships.

6/145 North-Hill (parish) SX 268765 [North Hill]
Apt 12.10.1840; 5877a (all); Map 1841, 3 chns, 1st cl, of the 'inclosed' lands, by Thomas Suter, Exeter; construction lines, foot/b'way, canal, waterbodies, houses, woods, plantations, parkland, rock outcrops, fence ownership, field gates, building names, tors, quarry.

6/146 Otterham (parish) SX 164912
Apt 13.09.1841; 3262a (all); Map 1840, 4 chns, 1st cl, by H. and R. Badcock, Launceston; construction lines, foot/b'way, woods, plantations, orchards, building names; names and numbers stamped.

6/147 Padstow (parish) SW 906753
Apt 19.12.1840; 3239a (3864); Map 1841, 3 chns, 1st cl, by Chrisr Bennison, London; construction lines, foot/b'way, waterbodies, woods, plantations, parkland, rock outcrops, building names, cliffs, smithy, custom house, hotel, market house, chapels, flagstaff, coastguard house, windmill.

6/148 Paul (parish) SW 458268
Apt 11.09.1840; 3433a (all); Map 1843, 3 chns, 1st cl, by John Thompson, C.E., Newlyn; construction lines, waterbodies, houses.

6/149 Pelynt (parish) SX 209550
Apt 10.09.1840; 4683a (all); Map 1840, 3 chns, by John Wallis Barnicoat, Falmouth and John James Gummoe, St. Austell; construction lines, hill-drawing, foot/b'way, waterbodies, houses, farmyards, woods, plantations, orchards, gardens, heath/moor, fence ownership, field boundary ownerships, field gates, building names, wirehouse, wharf, limekiln, mills, quarry, Methodist meeting houses, ancient forts; plantation, coppice, woodland, furze, garden, orchard and common indicated by annotation; map is decorated with detailed drawing of church.

6/150 Penryn (borough) SW 778348
Apt 10.12.1844; 291a (325); Map 1841, 3 chns; turnpike roads, toll-gate, toll-bar, waterbodies, houses, building names, road names, dock, bowling green, town hall, boundary stones.

6/151 Penzance (parish) SW 470306
Apt 15.05.1841; 401a (all); Map 1841, 4 chns, by J.S. Olver; hill-drawing, houses, rock outcrops, fences, building names, road names, coastline, pier, beach, baths, battery, cliffs, market house, town hall, chapel, ancient castle, boundary stones.

6/152 Perranarworthal (parish) SW 775395
Apt 17.01.1842; 1797a (all); Map 1840, 4 chns, by J.S. Olver, Falmouth; hill-drawing, turnpike roads, canal, waterbodies, woods, plantations, heath/moor (col), field boundary ownerships, building names, wharf, timber ponds, arsenic mill, weir, limekilns, mill, commons, intertidal area, glebe.

6/153 Perran Uthnoe (parish) SW 546299 [Perranuthnoe]
Apt 12.02.1841; 1128a (1182); Map 1841?, 4 chns; hill-drawing, foot/b'way, woods, plantations, rock outcrops, field gates, boundary stones, building names, pits, mines, cliffs, beach, low water mark; colour bands may indicate property boundaries; symbols may indicate mine winding gear. Apt omits land use.

6/154 Perranzabuloe (parish) SW 778528
Apt 27.08.1841; 10955a (all); Map 1840, 8 chns, by R. Symons, Truro; heath/moor (col), rock outcrops, building names, cliffs, beach, barrows, ancient castle, mill, mines, almshouse, commons.

6/155 Little Petherick (parish) SW 916701
Apt 16.02.1841; 1216a (1215); Map 1842, 3 chns, 1st cl, surveyed for tithe commutation by John Thompson C.E., Newlyn; construction lines.

6/156 South Petherwin (parish) SX 310819
Apt 04.03.1841; 5064a (all); Map 1841, 4 chns, 1st cl, by Jonathan Kittow, North Petherwin; construction lines, foot/b'way, building names.

6/157 Phillack (parish) SW 574378
Apt 31.05.1842; 2907a (all); Map 1842, 3 chns, constructed from 'ancient and modern maps' by John Rundle, Hayle; hill-drawing, railway, foot/b'way, waterbodies, houses, heath/moor, field boundary ownerships, field gates, building names, quarries, sand or stone pits, quay, ancient castle, coastline, boundary stones, common, towans, coastline royalty ownership; colour bands may indicate property boundaries.

6/158 Pillaton (parish) SX 384640
Apt 16.04.1841; 2458a (2478); Map 1841, 3 chns, by Messrs Robinson and Morgan, Civil Engineers; construction lines, triangulation points and poles (named), houses.

6/159 St Pinnock (parish) SX 200624
Apt 30.01.1841; 3488a (all); Map 1841, 3 chns, by John Woodmass and Co; construction lines ('chain lines'), waterbodies, houses, field boundary ownerships, building names, mill; legend explains building depiction, boundaries and waterbodies.

6/160 Poughill (parish) SS 218080
Apt 18.01.1840; 1847a (1947); Map 1840, 3 chns, 1st cl, by George Braund and Henry Hearn, Exeter; construction lines; scale bar is surrounded by quill pen, ruler, charcoal holder, and pair of compasses.

6/161 Poundstock (parish) SX 202998
Apt 31.12.1840; 4625a (4810); Map 1840, 3 chns, 1st cl, surveyed for tithe commutation by George Braund and Henry Hearn, Exeter; construction lines.

6/162 Probus (parish) SW 900479
Apt 06.04.1843; 8113a (all); Map 1840, 6 chns, in 2 parts, by R. Symons, Truro, (including 3-chn enlargement of village); foot/b'way, turnpike roads, waterbodies, houses, farmyards, woods, plantations, parkland, heath/moor, building names, mill; colour bands may indicate property boundaries.

6/163 Quethiock (parish) SX 325640
Apt 06.04.1842; 4531a (all); Map 1840, 4 chns, 1st cl, by Hans W. Allen; construction lines, triangulation points (named), houses.

6/164 Rame (parish) SX 426501
Apt 11.09.1840; 1187a (all); Map 1843?, 3 chns; foot/b'way, grotto (pictorial), pier, headland, coastline; built-up parts generalised. Apt includes some cropping information, and records acreage under hedges.

6/165 Euny Redruth otherwise Redruth (parish) SW 701430
Apt 16.07.1841; 3907a (3907); Map 1841, 3 chns, by John Rowe; railways and embankments, foot/b'way, field boundary ownerships, building names, commons.

6/166 Roche (parish) SW 992602
Apt 16.04.1838; 6441a (all); Map 1839, 3 chns, 1st cl, by Bushell and Vine; construction lines, hill-drawing, commons, turnpike roads, houses, building names, beacon, tor, chapel, engine house, mine, mill, dye house, workhouse, clayworks; map has note: 'This plot has been carefully divided into squares, the intersections of which are shown in blue ink, and from which the tracings of the fair copies have been taken. The Base Lines were all laid down on this Plot in one day, and stations described at every forty chains. The contractions will be seen'; map is decorated with a feather below the title and a coloured drawing of Roche Rock in centre of map.

6/167 Ruan Lanyhorne (parish) SW 900425 [Ruanlanihorne]
Apt 14.04.1842; 2251a (all); Map 1842, 3 chns, surveyed for tithe commutation by Messrs Woodmass and Co, Ivey Bridge, Devon; construction lines, foot/b'way, waterbodies, houses, field boundary ownerships, building names; legend explains depiction of buildings, boundaries and waterbodies; map is also signed by John Huddleston, surveyor.

6/168 Ruan Major (parish) SW 715185
Apt 20.04.1838; 2471a (2470); Map 1839, 4 chns, by Wm George Sheringham, Truro; foot/b'way, waterbodies, houses, farmyards, woods, orchards, gardens, building names, marl pit, quarries, barrows, glebe (col).

6/169 Ruan Minor (parish) SW 717159
Apt 15.05.1841; 658a (all); Map 1842, 3 chns, by R. Symons junr, Truro; waterbodies, houses, rock outcrops, building names, coastline, cliffs; colours may indicate property ownership.

6/170 Sancreed (parish) SW 419301
Apt 14.12.1839; 4471a (all); Map 1842?, 4 chns, by R. Pentreath, W. Marrack and G. Hosking; construction lines, foot/b'way, waterbodies, houses, woods, rock outcrops, field boundary ownerships, building names, cairns, ancient tumulus, boundary stones, mill, beacon, burrows.

6/171 Scilly Isles (except Island of St Mary) (district) SV 895142 [Isles of Scilly]
Apt 27.01.1847; 696a (all); Map 1847?, 12 chns; waterbodies, building names, coastline, battery, harbour; whole island is treated as a single tithe area and no fields or other features are shown. Apt omits land use and field names.

6/172 Sennen (parish) SW 363255
Apt 30.11.1838; 2230a (2300); Map 1839, 3 chns; hill-drawing, foot/b'way, waterbodies, woods, plantations, rock outcrops, field gates, building names, road names, boundary stones, Quakers' burial ground, coast features (named), common.

6/173 Sheviock (parish) SX 365550
Apt 18.11.1841; 2282a (all); Map 1841, 4 chns, by Eastcott and Frise, Devonport; waterbodies, houses, woods (col), plantations (col), orchards (col), coastline; ruler, quill pen, charcoal holders, pair of compasses and leaf border surround scale bar; pedestal and scroll bear surveyors' names; barley forms a small cartouche in corner.

6/174 Sithney (parish) SW 645289
Apt 22.02.1842; 5833a (5898); Map 1841, 3 chns, by Joseph Reed junr, Tregathenan, Sithney near Helston, Cornwall; foot/b'way, waterbodies, houses, woods, plantations, parkland, orchards, marsh/bog, rock outcrops, cliffs, low water mark, beach, shaft, mines, harbour, pier, standing stone, tumulus, downland; map is decorated with a small pastoral scene with a cow in background, and trees in the distance; in foreground two trees border a lake, on one side of which a man is climbing a tree, with his hat and stick left below, and on the other side two men are fishing.

6/175 South Hill (parish) SX 335715
Apt 16.04.1841; 3460a (all); Map 1841, 3 chns, surveyed for tithe commutation by T. Woodmass and Co; construction lines, waterbodies, houses; legend explains depiction of buildings, boundaries and water bodies; construction lines are described as 'chain lines'. Border lettering is surrounded by ornate scrolling, including a bird shape.

6/176 St Stephen's by Launceston (parish) SX 320860 [St Stephens]
Apt 28.07.1840; 3906a (3905); Map 1839, 4 chns, 1st cl, by H. and R. Badcock, Launceston; construction lines, foot/b'way, woods, plantations, parkland, orchards, building names, mills, quarry; names and numbers stamped.

6/177 St Stephens by Saltash (parish) SX 408589 [St Stephens]
Apt 22.04.1841; 5701a (6901); Map 1841, 3 chns, by [cropped], Devonport; foot/b'way, waterbodies, houses, farmyards, woods, parkland, orchards, marsh/bog, fences, coastline.

6/178 St Stephens in Branwell (parish) SW 955545 [St Stephen]
Apt 22.08.1838; 9002a (9002); Map 1839, 6 chns; hill-drawing, foot/b'way, waterbodies, houses, farmyards, woods (col), grassland (col), rock outcrops, building names, field names, landowners, ancient castle, mill, china clay works, quarries and factory, virginia clay works, beacon, downland, pleasure grounds; grey may indicate industrial spoilheaps or rough land.

6/179 Stithians (parish) SW 735365
Apt 06.11.1840; 4292a (all); Map 1841?, 3 chns, by Messrs Woodmass and Co, Chudleigh, Devon; construction lines, foot/b'way, waterbodies, houses, field boundary ownerships.

6/180 Stoke Climsland (parish) SX 368743
Apt 12.09.1840; 8732a (8732); Map 1841, 4 chns, by I. Mason, Hornacott, Lanson; hill-drawing, foot/b'way, farmyards, woods, plantations, parkland (in detail), orchards, heath/moor, rock outcrops, field boundary ownerships, building names, windmill, mill, mines; physical features named.

6/181 Stratton (parish) SS 230060
Apt 31.08.1840; 2618a (2837); Map 1840, 3 chns, 1st cl, in 2 parts, by Hans W. Allen, (including 1-chn enlargement of town); construction lines, triangulation points (named), canal, rock outcrops; physical features named.

6/182 Talland (parish) SX 230524 [Not listed]
Apt 14.12.1839; 2666a (all); Map 1840, 3 chns, 1st cl, by Benjn S.W. Cotton, West Pennard, Somerset; construction lines, waterbodies.

6/183 North Tamerton (parish) SX 301970
Apt 31.07.1841; 5262a (5261); Map 1842, 4 chns, by Isaac Mason, Hornacott, Launceston; construction lines, foot/b'way, canal, waterbodies, houses, fences, building names, mill.

6/184 St Teath (parish) SX 059821
Apt 19.06.1841; 5839a (5899); Map 1843, 4 chns, 1st cl, by J. and Robt Sandercock, Altarnun near Launceston; construction lines, houses, farmyards, woods, orchards, building names, coastline, mill.

6/185 Temple (parish) SX 146733
Apt 29.01.1841; 843a (all); Map 1839, 3 chns, by John and Richard Stephens; houses, boundary stones. Apt omits land use.

6/186 St Thomas the Apostle (parish) SX 295844 [Not listed]
Apt 16.12.1841; 519a (1817); Map 1842, 4 chns, by Jn Kittow, North Petherwin, Devon; turnpike roads, National School, mill.

6/187 Tintagel (parish) SX 070874
Apt 05.08.1841; 4281a (4350); Map 1842, 3 chns, 1st cl, surveyed for tithe commutation by John Thompson C.E., Newlyn; open fields, tithe-free areas.

6/188 Towednack (parish) SW 486376
Apt 08.07.1841; 2795a (2794); Map 1839, 3 chns, by Wm Marrack, Rd Pentreath and George Hosken; hill-drawing, foot/b'way, waterbodies, woods, heath/moor, rock outcrops, field boundary ownerships, building names, coastline, cliffs, boundary stones, burrows, whims, engine, drains, mine, gurgo. Apt distinguishes partly enclosed and improved land.

6/189 Manor of Tregavethan (district in parish of Kea) SW 773479 [Tregavethan Manor]
Apt 31.03.1842; 1007a (1007); Map 1842, 4 chns, by Nichs Whitley, Truro; farmyards, woods, orchards, building names, barrows, spring, downland.

6/190 Tregony (borough and town) SW 925449
Apt 11.02.1841; 63a (all); Map 1841, 2 chns, by John Andrewartha, Gwinear near Camborne; hill-drawing, houses, ancient castle, school room and playground.

6/191 St James Tregony (parish) SW 925455 [Not listed]
Apt 11.02.1841; 60a (69); Map 1841, 3 chns, by Michael FitzGerald; waterbodies, building names, mill; district is desribed as 'the property of Henry Dungey'.

6/192 Tremayne (parish) SX 230900 [Tremaine]
Apt 23.10.1838; 1046a (1045); Map 1839, 4 chns, 1st cl, by H. and R. Badcock, Launceston; construction lines, foot/b'way, woods, plantations, orchards, heath/moor, field boundary ownerships, field gates, building names, mill; names and numbers stamped.

6/193 Treneglos (parish) SX 203880
Apt 14.12.1839; 2731a (2730); Map 1841, 4 chns, 1st cl, by John Sandercock and Sons, Altarnun; construction lines, houses, woods, orchards, building names, mill.

6/194 Tresmeer (parish) SX 235879
Apt 12.09.1839; 1345a (all); Map 1839, 3 chns, 1st cl, by John Sandercock and Son, Altarnun, Launceston; construction lines, foot/b'way, field gates.

6/195 Trevalga (parish) SX 093890
Apt 30.06.1841; 1299a (all); Map not dated, 4 chns, 1st cl, by Chrisr Bennison, London; construction lines, waterbodies, building names, barrow, mill. Apt omits land use.

6/196 Trewarlet (hamlet in parishes of Lezant and South Petherwin) SX 336812 [Trewarlett]
Apt 20.10.1840; 263a (all); Map 1841, 3 chns, by Jonathan Kittow, North Petherwin, Devon. Apt omits land use.

6/197 Trewenn (parish) SX 261839 [Trewen]
Apt 14.02.1843; 989a (all); Map 1842, 4 chns, 1st cl, by H. and R. Badcock, Launceston; construction lines, waterbodies, farmyards, heath/moor, building names, sand or stone pit or quarry; names and numbers stamped.

6/198 St Marys Truro (parish) SW 825450 [Truro]
Apt 30.09.1840; 51a (all); Map 1841, 2 chns, by R. Symons, Truro; turnpike roads, waterbodies, houses, woods, rock outcrops, hedge ownership, fences, road names, landowners, ancient castle, quarries, quays, chapels, West Briton Office, hotels, market place, coinage hall, town hall, poor house, almshouse; areas not built over are coloured green.

6/199 St Tudy (parish) SX 075761
Apt 20.08.1839; 3257a (all); Map 1840, 3 chns, 1st cl, by Henry Coom, Bodmin; construction lines, foot/b'way, waterbodies, houses, fence ownership, field boundary ownerships, building names.

6/200 Tywardreath (parish) SX 090542
Apt 20.07.1839; 3252a (3252); Map undated, 4 chns; hill-drawing, foot/b'way, turnpike roads, canal, waterbodies, woods, parkland, heath/moor, rock outcrops, fences, road names, landowners, shafts, mines, cobbing house, clock, counting house, timber yard, engine, tunnel, coastline, cliffs, beaches, pier; colours may indicate property ownership; map has notes on scales and purchase activity on land taken up by canal and mining tunnel; above the scale-bar is a landscape including a church and a ship; beneath are winged lions and horses, a trident, a scallop shell, chains, floral and fruit border and cornucopia; at the base a plaque carries the title.

6/201 Uny Lelant (parish) SW 525375 [Lelant]
Apt 07.11.1839; 3758a (all); Map 1839, 4 chns, by J.H. Rutger, Marazion, Cornwall; hill-drawing, foot/b'way, turnpike roads, waterbodies, woods, plantations, parkland, orchards, heath/moor (col), rock outcrops, fences, field gates, building names, hills, tors, low water mark, cliffs, sands (col), dock, quay, embankment, mine, boundary stones, stamps, downland.

6/202 St Veep (parish) SX 142559
Apt 30.08.1839; 3146a (3146); Map 1842?, 4 chns; hill-drawing, foot/b'way, waterbodies, woods, rock outcrops, building names, coastline, cliffs; colours may indicate property boundaries or tithing practice.

6/203 Veryan (parish) SW 932410
Apt 18.06.1840; 5593a (all); Map 1841, 6 chns, by Nichs Whitley, Truro; hill-drawing, foot/b'way, waterbodies, farmyards, heath/moor, rock outcrops, open fields, building names, cliffs, coast features (named).

6/204 Warbstow (parish) SX 199911
Apt 10.09.1840; 4102a (all); Map 1841, 4 chns, by Jonathan Kittow, North Petherwin; hill-drawing, building names, road names, ancient earthworks, tucking mill.

6/205 Warleggan (parish) SX 155685
Apt 07.08.1839; 2056a (all); Map 1839, 4 chns, by John and Richard Stephens, Cardinham; foot/b'way, houses, fence. Apt omits land use.

6/206 Week St Mary (parish) SX 240972
Apt 13.02.1840; 5825a (5824); Map 1839, 3 chns, 1st cl, in 2 parts, by Hans W. Allen; houses, construction lines, triangulation points (named), and construction diagram, with red lines denoting the calculated and chained sides of the triangles and blue lines those formed by calculation and used in scoring the triangles.

6/207 Wendron (parish) SW 694322
Apt 27.12.1841; 13029a (13029); Map 1843, 4 chns, in 2 parts, surveyed by H. Baker and revised by J.S. Olver, (including some 2-chn enlargements of detail); waterbodies, building names, coastline, boundary stones, mill, old mine, mines, downland.

6/208 St Wenn (parish) SW 965656
Apt 22.03.1841; 4546a (all); Map 1841, 3 chns, by J. and R. Stephens, Cardinham; foot/b'way, waterbodies, houses, farmyards, fences, building names. Apt omits land use.

6/209 Whitstone (parish) SX 269986
Apt 29.12.1840; 3787a (3787); Map 1839, 4 chns, compiled from original surveys and for the use of the landowners by Hans W. Allen; canal, houses, building names; colour bands may indicate property ownerships.

6/210 St Winnow (parish) SX 125603
Apt 10.10.1839; 6137a (6137); Map 1842?, 6 chns; hill-drawing, foot/b'way, waterbodies, houses, woods, parkland, rock outcrops, hedge ownership, building names, landowners, beacon, coastline, cliffs, mill, ancient castle, gamekeeper's lodge, deer lodge, downland, manorial boundaries; allotment of Duchy Waste; colours may indicate property ownership; map has circular cartouche divided into two hemispheres by the scale bar: the top hemisphere contains the compass rose and the bottom hemisphere a riverside scene with people at leisure, including a church, woodland, fishermen and boatmen.

6/211 Withiel (parish) SW 998650
Apt 12.08.1841; 3006a (all); Map 1840, 3 chns, by J. and R. Stephens, Cardinham; foot/b'way, waterbodies, houses, farmyards. Apt omits land use.

6/212 Zennor (parish) SW 452378
Apt 13.12.1839; 4229a (all); Map 1841, 3 chns, by Rd Pentreath and G. Hosken; hill-drawing, foot/b'way, waterbodies, heath/moor, rock outcrops, open fields, field boundary ownerships, building names, cliffs, coastline, boundary stones, well, gurgos, cairns, old engine, mills, stamps, beacon, common.

Cumberland

PRO IR29 and IR30 7/1–188

247 tithe districts: 970,161 acres
188 tithe commutations: 435,110 acres
51 voluntary tithe agreements, 137 compulsory tithe awards

Tithe and tithe commutation

In 1836, 76 per cent of the tithe districts of Cumberland by number but only about 45 per cent of the county by area were still subject to the payment of tithes (Fig. 19). More than fifty districts had been exempted in the course of parliamentary enclosure, only one district was wholly tithable, and in 92 per cent of tithe districts modus payments applied in lieu of tithes. Other significant reasons for exemptions from tithe in Cumberland were the merger of tithes in the land and exemption by prescription.

Assistant tithe commissioners and local tithe agents who worked in Cumberland are listed in Table 7.1 and the valuers of the county's tithe rent-charge in Table 7.2. Nine Cumberland tithe apportionments (5 per cent) are lithographed which is an unusually high proportion for northern and north-western England. The tithes of eleven districts are apportioned on holdings which is low by comparison with Northumberland and Durham. As in Northumberland, several apportionments describe moduses in considerable detail and that of Sebergham is unique in that it lists landowners in both 1771 and 1849.

Tithe maps

Uncharacteristically for a northern county, Cumberland is distinguished by a relatively high proportion of first-class maps: 18 per cent by number and 21 per cent by area. Additionally three second-class maps have construction lines and probably approach first-class standards. Furthermore, a very high proportion of the county, 87 per cent of its area, is mapped at the one inch to three- and four-chain scales (Table 7.3). This is quite unlike the pattern in any of the adjoining counties where the expense of new surveys was usually avoided and also different from midland counties with similarly extensive enclosure but very few first-class maps. Rather, Cumberland tithe maps are more like those of the south-east or south-west of England.

There was not the usual marked peak of map production around 1840 in Cumberland but instead the output of maps was fairly steady between 1838 and 1850 (Table 7.4). The county's tithe maps are drawn at scales ranging from one inch to one chain to one inch to

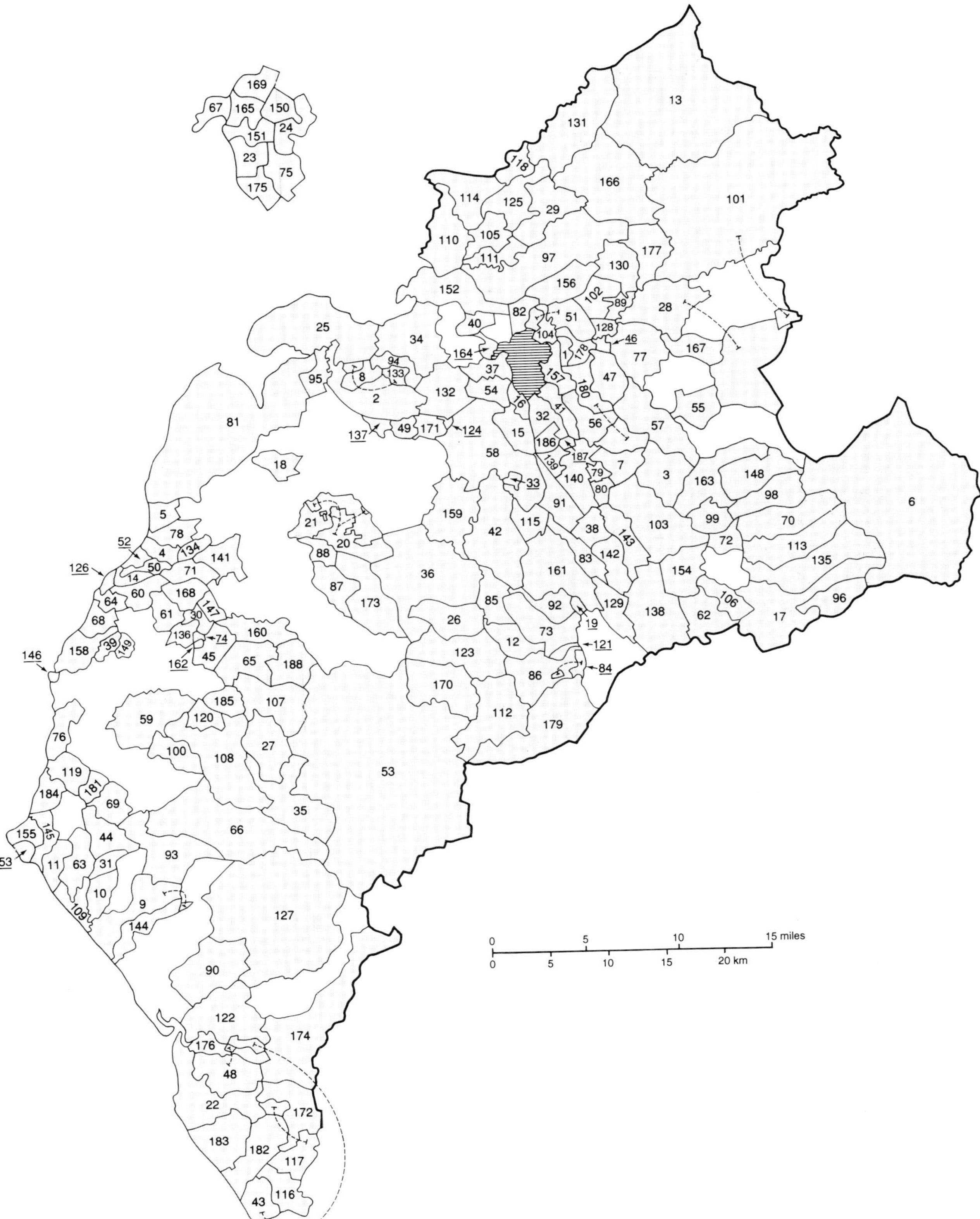

Fig. 19 Cumberland: tithe district boundaries.

fifteen chains but 80 per cent are in the recommended scale range of one inch to three to four chains. Only 10 per cent are at the scale of one inch to six chains which was much favoured elsewhere in northern England.

As in other counties with good first-class tithe map coverage, Cumberland tithe maps are poor records of agricultural land use. Woodland is recorded on 62 per cent of maps, parkland on 13 per cent, 12 per cent depict orchards, but none records arable or grass, and fewer than 4 per cent show heath and moor. Only 19 per cent of maps distinguish houses from other buildings but 20 per cent show industrial features, including extraction of lead, stone, slate, coal and iron ore, and tile-works, potteries, breweries, cotton and paper mills. A number of maps show Roman and pre-Roman (usually 'Druidical') archaeological features and appropriately for an 'upland' county, 23 per cent of maps depict slopes. The tithe map of Whitehaven portrays the streets and buildings of the town in great detail.

About a half of Cumberland tithe maps in the Public Record Office collection can be attributed to a particular map-maker. The most prolific was Richard Asquith of Carlisle who produced sixteen maps covering about 9 per cent of the tithable land in the county. His nearest rival was Thomas Woodmass of Alston who made seven maps; Woodmass sometimes worked with John Huddleston of Newborough, Northumberland and their maps have a stylistic affinity to the Woodmass and Huddleston maps of Devon and Cornwall (Table 7.2).

Table 7.1. *Agreements and awards for commutation of tithes in Cumberland*

Assistant commissioner/ local tithe agent	*Number of agreements**	*Number of awards*
John Job Rawlinson	24	81
John Strangeways Donaldson Selby	2	33
Henry Pilkington	13	0
Charles Howard	2	7
George Wingrove Cooke	0	8
Thomas Smith Woolley	0	8
Thomas Martin	6	0
Richard Atkinson	1	0
John Mee Mathew	1	0
Richard Burton Phillipson	1	0

*Computed from the number of extant reports on tithe agreements in the tithe files [PRO IR 18].

Table 7.2. *Tithe valuers and tithe map-makers in Cumberland*

Name and address (in Cumberland unless indicated)	*Number of districts*	*Acreage*
Tithe valuers		
Richard Asquith, Carlisle	22	47,574
William Dickinson, North Mosses	16	38,274
John Studholme, Morton, Carlisle	11	16,831
Richard Atkinson, Assenthwaite Halls	9	63,815
Thomas Woodmass, Maryport	7	13,707
John Barker, Greystoke	7	12,788
William Hetherington, Cockermouth	6	13,666
John Coulson, Cumwhinton	5	13,982
John Huddleston, Newborough, Northumberland	5	8,239
Others [67]	100	206,234
Attributed tithe map-makers		
Richard Asquith, Carlisle	16	37,953
Thomas Woodmass, Alston	7	20,293
William Gaythorp, Whitehaven	5	11,347
William Robinson, Hesket-new-market	5	10,775
George Larmer, Carlisle	5	9,646
George Robinson	5	6,891
John Huddleston, Newborough, Northumberland	4	5,687
John Watson junior, Kendal	4	18,164
Sylvanus Miller, Durham	4	17,121
Thomas Bouch	4	7,639
John Salkeld, Melmerby	4	7,529
Others [30]	44	120,651

Table 7.3. *The tithe maps of Cumberland: scales and classes*

Scale in chains/inch	*All maps*		*First Class*		*Second Class*	
	Number	*Acreage*	*Number*	*Acreage*	*Number*	*Acreage*
>3	3	904	0	0	3	904
3	82	175,490	24	56,254	58	119,236
4	68	203,418	10	35,430	58	167,988
5	3	6,655	0	0	3	6,655
6	19	22,670	0	0	19	22,670
8	8	17,228	0	0	8	17,228
<8	5	8,745	0	0	5	8,745
TOTAL	188	435,110	34	91,684	154	343,426

Table 7.4. *The tithe maps of Cumberland: dates*

	1837	*1838*	*1839*	*1840*	*1841*	*1842*	*1843*	*1844*	*1845*	*1846*	*1847*	*1848*	*1849*	*1850*	*>1850*
All maps	3	15	20	17	18	14	13	18	16	5	17	9	11	7	5
1st class	1	2	4	0	2	6	7	3	5	1	0	1	1	0	1
2nd class	2	13	16	17	16	8	6	15	11	4	17	8	10	7	4

Cumberland

7/1 Aglionby (township in parish of Warwick) NY 446570
Apt 31.12.1840; 560a (559); Map 1841, 4 chns, 1st cl, by Richd Asquith, Carlisle; hill-drawing, woods, building names.

7/2 Aikton Biglands, Gamelsby, Wampool and Wiggonby (township in parish of Aikton) NY 274534 [Aikton]
Apt 07.07.1842; 6155a (6157); Map 1843, 3 chns, 1st cl, in 2 parts, by John Watson junr, Kendal; construction lines, foot/b'way, waterbodies, woods, plantations, orchards, open fields, building names, windmill. Apt has cropping information.

7/3 Ainstable (parish) NY 529455
Apt 24.08.1841; 4178a (4178); Map 1840, 4 chns, 'copied'; hill-drawing, foot/b'way, woods, plantations, parkland, rock outcrops, building names, mill, druids stone circle, sandbanks, gravel pit, seat; physical features named.

7/4 Allerby (township in parish of Aspatria) NY 088399
Apt 22.01.1846; 1198a (?); Map 1845, 3 chns, 1st cl, by John Huddleston, Newborough, Northumberland; construction lines, foot/b'way, houses, farmyards.

7/5 Allonby (township in parish of Bromfield) NY 091435
Apt 07.08.1845; 1221a (?); Map 1846, 6 chns, ? by Thomas Woodmass; waterbodies, open fields.

7/6 Alston (parish) NY 739425
Apt 24.04.1841; 28a (35060); Map 1841, 15 chns, in 2 parts, (main map is location map of enlargements of tithable parts); foot/b'way, field gates, building names, field names, landowners, common, field acreages, manor boundaries; map is described as 'sketches of each of the leasehold estates situate within the manor of Tynehead'; ownership of estates is tabulated.

7/7 Armathwaite, Nunclose and Aiket Gate (townships in parish of Hesket in the Forest) NY 492464 [Armathwaite]
Apt 05.04.1845; 2243a (?); Map 1844, 4 chns, in 2 parts, (including Armathwaite at 1.33 chns); foot/b'way, waterbodies, woods, building names, tile kiln, quarry, township boundaries.

7/8 Little Bampton (township in parish of Kirkbampton) NY 268554
Apt 25.10.1839; 1338a (1337); Map 1839, 3 chns, 1st cl, by George Larmer, Carlisle; construction lines, foot/b'way, waterbodies, open fields, building names, tileworks, parish boundaries; map covers the whole parish of Kirk Bampton.

7/9 St Bridgets Beckermont (parish) NY 049068 [Beckermet]
Apt 18.06.1844; 292a (5025); Map 1848, 3 chns; building names; the roads are at 6 chns and the fields at 3 chns.

7/10 St John's Beckermont (parish) NY 019085 [Beckermet]
Apt 06.06.1844; 138a (2752); Map 1848, 4 chns; building names, mill, field acreages.

7/11 St Bees (township in parish of St Bees) NX 978115
Apt 22.06.1838; 1758a (1945); Map 1840?, 5 chns, in 2 parts, (including 3 chn enlargement of village); hill-drawing, waterbodies, houses, woods, open fields, building names, road names, pinfold, mill, public watering places.

7/12 Berrier and Murrah (township in parish of Greystoke) NY 390304
Apt 29.10.1846; 2501a (2604); Map 1847, 4 chns, by Wm Robinson, Hesket-new-market.

7/13 Bewcastle (parish) NY 546797
Apt 11.09.1839; 528a (30000); Map 1839, 2 chns, in 5 parts, by William Steele, (including 8-chn index); building names, landowners, mill, quarter boundaries, public roads. District is apportioned by holding.

7/14 Birkby (township in parish of Cross Canonby) NY 060375
Apt 16.04.1844; 729a (871); Map 1844, 3 chns, by T. Woodmass, Alston; construction lines, railway, foot/b'way, houses.

7/15 Blackhall, High Quarter (township in parish of Carlisle St Cuthbert) NY 402502 [Not listed]
Apt 15.04.1840; 2460a (2459); Map 1840, 8 chns, 'copied'; hill-drawing, woods, plantations, building names.

7/16 Blackhall Low Quarter (township in parish of St Cuthberts Carlisle) NY 404526 [Not listed]
Apt 25.01.1847; 942a (941); Map 1847, 8 chns; railways, foot/b'way, woods, building names, school.

7/17 Blencarn, Culgaith and Skirwith (township in parish of Kirkland) NY 631327
Apt 31.10.1850; 6370a (?); Map 1851, 3 chns, in 4 parts, by Watson and Hoggarth, Kendal, (including 10-chn index); hill-drawing, foot/b'way, waterbodies, woods, plantations, parkland, gardens, open fields, building names, mills, smithy, schools, tile kilns, Wesleyan Chapels.

7/18 Blencogo (township in parish of Bromfield) NY 191477
Apt 15.08.1840; 1698a (1697); Map 1838, 3 chns; foot/b'way, woods, plantations, open fields, field gates, building names, public watering place.

7/19 Blencow (township in parish of Greystoke) NY 447334 [Not listed]
Apt 29.10.1846; 323a (324); Map 1847, 4 chns, by Wm Robinson, Hesket-new-market.

7/20 Bolton High Side Quarter (township in parish of Bolton) NY 249398 [Not listed]
Apt 18.04.1840; 3876a (3875); Map 1844, 3 chns, 1st cl, in 2 parts, by R.H. Watson, Bolton Park; turnpike roads, waterbodies, woods, plantations, orchards, building names, mill, toll bar, quarter boundaries (col).

7/21 Bolton Lowside Quarter (township in parish of Bolton) NY 244440 [Not listed]
Apt 18.04.1840; 4570a (4570); Map 1844, 3 chns, 1st cl, by John Watson junr, Kendal; foot/b'way, turnpike roads, toll bar, waterbodies, woods, plantations, orchards, building names, smithy, limekiln, mill, coal pit, township boundaries; bridges named.

7/22 Bootle (parish) SD 094893
Apt 15.11.1848; 6652a (7146); Map 1837, 3 chns, 1st cl, in 4 parts, by Geo. and John Robinson; construction lines, foot/b'way, waterbodies, woods, rock outcrops, field gates, building names, well, crags, mill, coastline, landmark, poor house, common; land not mapped is coloured green.

7/23 Botchardgate (township in parish of St Cuthbert's Carlisle) NY 406549 [Not listed]
Apt 20.09.1847; 346a (346); Map 1848, 4 chns; railways with stations, turnpike roads, toll bar, waterbodies, building names, road names, factory, gaol; built-up part generalised.

7/24 Botcherby (township in parish of St Cuthbert's Carlisle) NY 425564
Apt 25.01.1847; 496a (495); Map 1848, 4 chns; mill, toll bar.

7/25 Bowness (parish) NY 227601 [Bowness-on-Solway]
Apt 28.03.1839; 8261a (17947); Map 1838, 4 chns, in 2 parts, by David Browne, (including ancient inclosures in Anthorn township copied by J. Watson junior, 1839, 6 chns); canal, waterbodies, woods, plantations, building names, road names, marlpit, windmill, public drain, warehouses, site of Roman wall, pottery, steam packet berths, pier, schools, township boundaries (col); field acreages in tithable parts only.

7/26 Bowscale and Mossdale (township in parish of Greystoke) NY 336325
Apt 29.10.1846; 136a (2560); Map 1850, 3 chns, by J. Barker; common.

7/27 Brackenthwaite (township in parish of Brigham) NY 169212
Apt 22.06.1844; 2477a (2478); Map 1845, 4 chns, by Wm Hodgson; foot/b'way, building names, mill.

7/28 Brampton (parish) NY 533611
Apt 10.03.1849; 8a (16970); Map 1850, 10 chns, in 63 parts, by Wm Salkeld, (including 62 1-chn and 2-chn enlargements of detail); railways with stations, foot/b'way, turnpike roads, toll bar, waterbodies, woods, plantations, rock outcrops, building names, road names, haha,

National School, market place, brewery, old brewery, limekilns, quarry, gas works, zinc works, mills, tile works, workhouse, township boundaries; no fields are shown. Apt omits land use.

7/29 Breckonhill Quarter (township or quarter in parish of Arthuret) NY 438700 [Not listed]
Apt 18.07.1849; 1130a (4535); Map 1849, 6 chns, by Richard Asquith, Carlisle; building names, workhouse. District is apportioned by holding and fields are not shown.

7/30 Bridekirk (township in parish of Bridekirk) NY 121337
Apt 14.06.1844; 916a (916); Map 1842, 4 chns, by Soddrel; foot/b'way, turnpike roads, waterbodies, woods (col), parkland (col), hedges, building names, watering place, mill.

7/31 Briscoe (district in parish of St Johns Beckermont) NY 024114
Apt 31.10.1840; 1072a (?); Map 1841?, 4 chns, by Jonathan Stanwix; waterbodies, woods, building names, mills; bridge named; blue bands show 'shares' in wasteland.

7/32 Brisco (township in parish of St Cuthbert Carlisle) NY 427514
Apt 27.06.1839; 1904a (1904); Map 1840?, 4 chns; hill-drawing, foot/b'way, woods, plantations, parkland, building names.

7/33 Broadfield (district in parish of Dalston) NY 395453 [Not listed]
Apt 20.07.1840; 704a (?); Map 1848?, 8 chns; field gates, building names.

7/34 Burgh by Sands (parish) NY 313594
Apt 13.07.1843; 477a (7839); Map 1844?, 6 chns; canal, waterbodies, woods, building names, mill, windmill, coastline, marshland; built-up part generalised. Apt omits land use.

7/35 Buttermere (township in parish of Brigham) NY 182164
Apt 17.06.1844; 4399a (4398); Map 1845, 3 chns, in 4 parts, by J.N. Dickinson, (one part at 10 chns; includes 80-chns location diagram); waterbodies, houses, building names, common.

7/36 Caldbeck (parish) NY 322368
Apt 31.01.1851; 6226a (24280); Map 1852, 3 chns, 1st cl, in 2 parts, by Daniel Jennings; construction lines, hill-drawing, foot/b'way, waterbodies, woods, plantations, orchards, open fields, hedges, field gates, building names, Friends Meeting House, mills, boundary stones, Wesleyan Chapel, school, river weirs, quarry, factory, tile kiln, common.

7/37 Caldewgate (township in parish of St Mary Carlisle) NY 377556 [Not listed]
Apt 12.04.1841; 1564a (1564); Map 1842?, 3 chns; canal with towpath, waterbodies, woods, building names, road names, pinfold, infirmary, steam engine; built-up part generalised.

7/38 Calthwaite (hamlet in parish of Hesket in the Forest) NY 464405
Apt 31.05.1844; 1876a (1876); Map 1844, 4 chns; railway, foot/b'way, waterbodies, woods, parkland, building names, tile kiln, mill.

7/39 Camerton (township in parish of Camerton) NY 038313
Apt 07.06.1841; 788a (788); Map 1841?, 4 chns, copied, ? by W. Gaythorn and W. Dickinson; hill-drawing, foot/b'way, houses, woods, plantations, parkland, gardens, building names, pits.

7/40 Cargo (township in parish of Stanwix) NY 367598
Apt 16.10.1839; 1121a (1196); Map 1839, 3 chns; turnpike roads, toll bar, waterbodies, building names, willow bed.

7/41 Carleton (township in parish of St Cuthberts Carlisle) NY 443517
Apt 14.09.1846; 811a (?); Map 1847, 8 chns; foot/b'way, woods, open fields, building names, common, leasehold land.

7/42 Castle Sowerby (parish) NY 378406 [Not listed]
Apt 25.05.1849; 23a (7940); Map 1850?, 4 chns; landowners.

7/43 Chapel Sucken (township in parish of Millom) SD 145799 [Not listed]
Apt 29.10.1846; 2054a (2054); Map 1848, 3 chns, 1st cl; waterbodies, houses, building names, stunted pasture; field acreages given along boundary only.

7/44 Cleator (parish) NY 023142
Apt 31.05.1841; 2844a (2844); Map 1839, 4 chns, copied from enclosure plans with necessary alterations; waterbodies, houses, woods, plantations, gardens, heath/moor, mills, forge, tithe barn.

7/45 Cockermouth (township in parish of Brigham) NY 132308
Apt 31.03.1840; 2327a (2326); Map 1840?, 3 chns, in 2 parts, (including Cockermouth town at 1 chn); turnpike roads, toll-bar, waterbodies, woods, field gates, building names, road names, landowners, Quaker Chapel, market, Sunday school, Independent Chapel, paper mills, tan yards, brewery, house of correction, post office, castle, lord of manor's allotment; tinting may indicate modus land; wasteland named.

7/46 Little Corby (township in parish of Hayton) NY 479574
Apt 10.08.1839; 352a (352); Map 1839, 3 chns, 1st cl, by Wm Morley, Corby; construction lines, houses, woods, orchards, field gates, building names, fishery, field acreages, occupation roads.

7/47 Corby and Warwick Bridge (township in parish of Wetherall) NY 482547
Apt 31.12.1840; 2748a (2747); Map 1843, 4 chns, 1st cl, by Rd Asquith, Carlisle; hill-drawing, railway with embankments, foot/b'way, waterbodies, woods, parkland, open fields, building names, river coops, cells, well, quarry, mill.

7/48 Corney (parish) SD 122918
Apt 17.11.1842; 2743a (?); Map 1843, 3 chns, 1st cl, in 3 parts, by M. and J. Turner, Lyth; construction lines, waterbodies, woods, plantations, orchards, building names, iron ore pits.

7/49 Crofton (township in parish of Thursby) NY 303507
Apt 08.04.1845; 976a (975); Map 1844, 3 chns, by Thomas Bouch; foot/b'way, waterbodies, woods, parkland, building names.

7/50 Crosby (township in parish of Cross Canonby) NY 073385
Apt 16.04.1844; 1042a (1041); Map 1844, 3 chns, by T. Woodmass, Alston; construction lines, railway, houses.

7/51 Crosby upon Eden (parish) NY 454600 [Crosby-on-Eden]
Apt 22.01.1857; 2844a (3590); Map 1857, 6 chns, by Richard Asquith, Carlisle; foot/b'way, waterbodies, woods, parkland, fences, building names.

7/52 Cross Canonby (township in parish of Cross Canonby) NY 066393 [Crosscanonby]
Apt 16.04.1844; 580a (1093); Map 1845?, 3 chns, 1st cl, by T. Woodmass, Alston; construction lines, houses. Apt omits land use.

7/53 Crosthwaite (parish) NY 265190 [Not listed]
Apt 11.11.1840; 38888a (58330); Map 1841-3, 4 chns, in 9 parts, surveyed for tithe commutation by D.W. Rome, Alston, (including Keswick township at 3 chns and enlargement of town at 1 chn, and 30 chn index); foot/b'way, turnpike roads, toll bar, waterbodies, woods, building names, slate quarries, stone landmark, public quarry, black lead mine, mill; fells and moss named; some field boundaries are blue.

7/54 Cummersdale (township in parish of St Mary Carlisle) NY 379539 [Not listed]
Apt 18.08.1840; 1911a (1911); Map 1841, 3 chns, ? by John Studholme, Carlisle; foot/b'way, waterbodies, woods, building names, mill.

7/55 Cumrew (parish) NY 557513
Apt 13.03.1838; 2695a (2694); Map 1839?, 3 chns, by John Studholme; hill-drawing, foot/b'way, woods, plantations, building names, field names, landowners, standing stone, boundary features, field acreages; physical features named.

7/56 Cumwhinton and Coathill (township in parish of Wetheral) NY 459513
Apt 31.12.1840; 2550a (2549); Map 1842, 4 chns, 1st cl, by Rd Asquith, Carlisle; hill-drawing, waterbodies, woods, open fields, building names, quarries, school, mossland.

7/57 Cumwhitton (parish) NY 527502
Apt 27.10.1838; 5401a (5400); Map 1838, 4 chns, by George Larmer,

Carlisle; waterbodies, open fields, building names, quarries, school house, chapel, well, old enclosures. First page of Apt omits land use.

7/58 Dalston (parish) NY 387475
Apt 26.07.1849; 11732a (10890); Map 1850, 3 chns, in 16 parts, copied by R. Asquith, (including 20-chn index); railways with cutting, foot/b'way, waterbodies, woods, building names, castle, mills, factories, old brewery, brewery, forge, park lodge, ford, windmill.

7/59 Dean (parish) NY 070252
Apt 22.05.1849; 54a (6360); Map 1850, 3 chns; coal pit; there is a note as to the distances of tithable lands from certain reference points.

7/60 Dearham (township in parish of Dearham) NY 069363
Apt 27.07.1839; 2154a (2153); Map 1838, 4 chns, surveyed for tithe commutation by Wm Gaythorp, Whitehaven; construction lines, hill-drawing, railway, foot/b'way, waterbodies, houses, woods (col), plantations (col), orchards, field gates, building names, former open field names, landowners, watermills (by symbol), pottery, public quarry, quarry, Methodist Chapel.

7/61 Dovenby (district or hamlet in parish of Bridekirk) NY 088345
Apt 13.12.1838; 1721a (?); Map 1838?, 4 chns, ? by William Hetherington and William Dickinson; hill-drawing, waterbodies, woods, plantations, parkland, building names, colliery, spring, common.

7/62 Edenhall (parish) NY 556317
Apt 30.09.1841; 3354a (3354); Map 1841, 3 chns, by Sylvanus Miller, Durham; hill-drawing, waterbodies, woods, parkland (col), orchards, hedges, fences, building names, boundary stones.

7/63 Egremont (parish) NY 002114
Apt 31.05.1841; 2708a (2708); Map 1842?, 4 chns, in 2 parts, (including village at 1 chn); waterbodies, woods, parkland, orchards, open fields, building names, paper mill, mill; built-up part partly generalised.

7/64 Ellenborough and Unerigg (township in parish of Dearham) NY 043354
Apt 16.04.1844; 975a (1224); Map 1844, 3 chns; railway, waterbodies, rock outcrops, open fields, field gates, building names, school, pits, coastline, piers, quay, well, dog kennel, harbour, dock.

7/65 Embleton (township in parish of Brigham) NY 157296
Apt 21.08.1839; 3870a (?); Map 1841?, 4 chns; waterbodies, woods, building names, tile kilns, well, mill; legend explains distinction between ancient inclosures and former common.

7/66 Ennerdale (township in parish of St Bees) NY 141134 [Ennerdale Bridge]
Apt 23.04.1844; 16998a (17782); Map 1845, 3 chns, in 2 parts; waterbodies, woods, building names, mill, school, smithy, lake island, moor.

7/67 Etterby (township in parish of Stanwix) NY 388574
Apt 16.10.1839; 297a (297); Map 1839, 3 chns; hill-drawing, waterbodies, building names; table gives cultivated and wasteland acreage.

7/68 Flimby (parish) NY 031338
Apt 16.04.1844; 100a (1842); Map 1847, 4 chns; railway, turnpike roads, woods, building names, landowners. Apt omits land use.

7/69 Frizington (township in parish of Arlecdon) NY 032169
Apt 20.09.1845; 1235a (?); Map 1839, 3 chns, 'Plan of the Ancient Inclosures' surveyed for tithe commutation; waterbodies, houses, woods, plantations, orchards, gardens, heath/moor, building names, quarries, medicinal well, common.

7/70 Gamblesby (township in parish of Addingham) NY 636405
Apt 24.08.1839; 1486a (4783); Map 1841?, 3 chns; houses, commons, undivided common.

7/71 Gilcrux (parish) NY 112378
Apt 31.05.1841; 1965a (1964); Map 1843?, 3 chns; woods, churchyard, boundary stones; colours may show property ownerships.

7/72 Glassonby (township in parish of Addingham) NY 579387
Apt 13.09.1841; 1643a (1643); Map 1843?, 3 chns, 1st cl; hill-drawing, foot/b'way, waterbodies, houses, woods, field gates, free stone quarry.

7/73 Greystoke (township in parish of Greystoke) NY 417313
Apt 05.03.1839; 4539a (4538); Map 1839, [5 chns]; village cross, castle, mill, park.

7/74 Hameshill (hamlet in parish of Bridekirk) NY 119319 [Not listed]
Apt 13.12.1838; 166a (?); Map 1838, 4 chns; hill-drawing, foot/b'way, woods, plantations, quarry.

7/75 Harraby (township in parish of St Cuthberts Carlisle) NY 421545
Apt 20.11.1846; 605a (604); Map 1847, 8 chns; railways, woods, building names, cotton works.

7/76 Harrington (parish) NX 991238
Apt 29.08.1843; 2339a (2790); Map surveyed for tithe commutation, 1844, 3 chns, in 2 parts, (including 1-chn enlargement of village); woods, building names, road names, windmill, mill, pits.

7/77 Hayton, Fenton and Faugh (district in parish of Hayton) NY 508571
Apt '31.06.1841' (? 01.07.1841); 4929a (?); Map 1839, 3 chns, by Robert and James Nixon, Sandy Syke near Longtown and Thomas Smith, Whitebeck near Bewcastle; hill-drawing, railway with cutting and station, turnpike roads, toll bar, waterbodies, houses, woods (col), parkland, orchards, gardens (col), field gates, building names, water mills, mill, hotel, workhouse, lodge, field acreages.

7/78 Hayton and Melay (township in parish of Aspatria) NY 103415
Apt 05.04.1845; 1847a (1971); Map 1845?, 3 chns, 1st cl; construction lines, waterbodies, houses, open fields; lettering and numbering on map are stamped.

7/79 Nether Hesket (district in parish of Hesket-in-the-Forest) NY 71458 [Low Hesket]
Apt 28.11.1842; 528a (?); Map 1842, 4 chns, 1st cl, by W. Carr; building names.

7/80 Upper Hesket (township or quarter in parish of Hesket-in-the-Forest) NY 474441 [High Hesket]
Apt 31.05.1844; 781a (?); Map 1844, 4 chns, foot/b'way, waterbodies, woods, marsh/bog, building names, school.

7/81 Holme Cultram (parish) NY 161509 [Not listed]
Apt 31.12.1847; 18611a (38962); Map 1849, 4 chns, 1st cl, in 5 parts (including index); West Division surveyed by P. Kendall, Whitehaven; Abbey Division and East Waver Division surveyed by Richard Asquith, Carlisle; Northern Division surveyed by Daniel Jennings, Carlisle; construction lines, foot/b'way, waterbodies, houses, woods, plantations, orchards, open fields, building names; some built-up parts generalised.

7/82 Houghton (township in parish of Stanwix) NY 409605
Apt 16.10.1839; 1449a (1478); Map 1841?, 3 chns; waterbodies, woods, parkland, building names; some field boundaries are double blue lines.

7/83 Hutton (parish) NY 452387 [Hutton End]
Apt 25.01.1840; 2300a (2300); Map 1840?, 4 chns; waterbodies, woods, open fields, building names, mill.

7/84 Hutton John (township in parish of Greystoke) NY 448276
Apt 06.07.1838; 665a (665); Map 1838, [6 chns], by John Barker; woods, building names. District is apportioned by holding; Apt omits land use.

7/85 Hutton Roof (township in parish of Greystoke) NY 373345
Apt 29.10.1846; 2505a (2505); Map 1847, 4 chns, by Wm Robinson, Hesket-new-market; foot/b'way, building names; bridge named.

7/86 Hutton Soil (township in parish of Greystoke) NY 416276 [Not listed]
Apt 29.10.1846; 4271a (5111); Map 1847, 4 chns, by John Salkeld; foot/b'way, waterbodies, woods, mill race; compass rose and scale bar coloured.

7/87 High Ireby (township in parish of Ireby) NY 239361
Apt 30.11.1844; 2702a (2701); Map 1845, 3 chns, 1st cl, surveyed for tithe commutation by John Huddleston, Newbrough; construction lines, waterbodies, houses.

7/88 Low Ireby (township in parish of Ireby) NY 227396 [Ireby]
Apt 16.05.1844; 832a (831); Map 1844, 3 chns, 1st cl, surveyed for tithe commutation by J. Huddleston, Newborough; construction lines, houses.

7/89 Irthington (township in parish of Irthington) NY 494612
Apt 16.06.1845; 290a (947); Map 1847?, 4 chns; hill-drawing, foot/b'way, waterbodies, woods, field gates, landowners, Roman walls, mill, road destinations; colours may show property ownerships.

7/90 Irton (parish) NY 114015 [Not listed]
Apt 10.10.1839; 2021a (5270); Map surveyed for tithe commutation 1840, 3 chns; waterbodies, houses, woods (col), orchards, building names.

7/91 Itonfield (township in parish of Hesket in the Forest) NY 434441 [Not listed]
Apt 07.05.1845; 2940a (2940); Map 1846, 8 chns; foot/b'way, woods, parkland, building names, smithy, school house, boundary markers.

7/92 Johnby (township in parish of Greystoke) NY 415335
Apt 29.10.1846; 2119a (2119); Map 1847, 4 chns, by Wm Robinson, Hesket-new-market; occupation roads.

7/93 Kinnyside (township in parish of St Bees) NY 080120 [Not listed]
Apt 23.04.1844; 1547a (11950); Map 1845?, 3 chns, in 2 parts; building names, common.

7/94 Kirkbampton (township in parish of Kirkbampton) NY 301566
Apt 18.06.1840; 118a (1260); Map 1839, 3 chns, 1st cl, by George Larmer, Carlisle; building names.

7/95 Kirkbride (parish) NY 232557
Apt 29.01.1841; 732a (1654); Map 1841, 3 chns; waterbodies, building names, school, rectory, guide post, meeting house, old river course, mill, mill race.

7/96 Kirkland (township in parish of Kirkland) NY 669330
Apt 27.09.1850; 1069a (?); Map 1851, 3 chns, by Watson and Hoggarth, Kendal; foot/b'way, woods, plantations, Roman station.

7/97 Kirklinton (parish) NY 429655
Apt 26.06.1839; 495a (7800); Map 1839?, 6 chns, in 3 parts, (tinted); waterbodies, building names, road names, field names, occupation roads, glebe, field acreages. Apt omits land use.

7/98 Kirkoswald High Quarter (township in parish of Kirkoswald) NY 618428 [Not listed]
Apt 07.10.1843; 1294a (?); Map 1843, 3 chns, 1st cl, by John Salkeld, Melmerby; construction lines, foot/b'way, houses, watermill.

7/99 Kirkoswald Lower Quarter (township in parish of Kirkoswald) NY 568409 [Not listed]
Apt 07.10.1843; 272a (?); Map 1844, 3 chns, by John Salkeld, Melmerby; construction lines, foot/b'way, common.

7/100 Lamplugh (parish) NY 093210
Apt 15.06.1837; 6354a (6354); Map 1838, 3 chns, surveyed for tithe commutation by Wm Gaythorp, Whitehaven; hill-drawing, foot/b'way, waterbodies, houses, woods (col), plantations (col), parkland, orchards, marsh/bog, heath/moor, rock outcrops, open fields, field gates, building names, tithe barn, sandstone pits, quarries, iron deposits (by Dawson's symbol); watermills, cliffs, limekilns, old quern, sheepfolds, forge, pinfold, tors, smithy, common, demesne; physical features named.

7/101 Lanercost (parish) NY 598713
Apt 18.05.1849; 115a (36510); Map 1851, 10 chns, in 2 parts, by Wm Salkeld, (including 2-chn enlargement of tithable fields); woods, plantations, building names.

7/102 Laversdale (township in parish of Irthington) NY 471620
Apt 16.06.1845; 685a (3415); Map 1847?, 3 chns, in 4 parts, by Robt Bell Nook, (including 10-chn index); foot/b'way, waterbodies, houses, farmyards, woods, building names, landowners, Roman Wall, road destinations, occupation roads; colours may show property ownerships.

7/103 Lazonby (township in parish of Lazonby) NY 518409
Apt 24.08.1844; 8155a (8154); Map 1845, 10 chns, in 2 parts, by S. Miller, Durham (including Lazonby village at 3 chns); hill-drawing, waterbodies, woods (named), marsh/bog, open fields, weir, boundary stones, churchyard, well, vicarage; colours may show property ownerships.

7/104 Linstock (township in parish of Stanwix) NY 430593
Apt 25.08.1840; 1133a (1133); Map 1841?, 3 chns; waterbodies, woods, building names.

7/105 Longtown Quarter (township or quarter in parish of Arthuret) NY 382681 [Longtown]
Apt 18.07.1849; 571a (all); Map 1849, 6 chns, by Richard Asquith, Carlisle; waterbodies, woods, building names; built-up part generalised. District is apportioned by holding; Apt omits land use.

7/106 Longwathby (parish) NY 577336 [Langwathby]
Apt 09.04.1839; 1987a (1987); Map 1839, 3 chns, by Sylvanus Miller, Durham; hill-drawing, woods, weir.

7/107 Lorton (township) NY 179257 [Not listed]
Apt 12.11.1840; 5239a (5264); Map 1841?, 4 chns, in 2 parts; foot/b'way, waterbodies, woods, building names; colours may show property ownerships.

7/108 Loweswater (township in parish of St Bees) NY 131201
Apt 10.10.1839; 6474a (?); Map 1843?, 4 chns, in 4 parts, (including 80-chn index); hill-drawing, foot/b'way, waterbodies, houses, woods (col), orchards, gardens, building names, sheepfold, school house, boundary stones, old quern, common.

7/109 Lowside Quarter (township in parish of St Bees) NY 002076 [Not listed]
Apt 22.06.1838; 1941a (2666); Map 1838, 3 chns, in 2 parts, by William Mitchell; construction lines, hill-drawing, foot/b'way, waterbodies, woods, plantations, marsh/bog, field gates, building names, summer house, mill, paper mill, castle, moor; bridge named; arable or meadow indicated by annotation in a few fields; built-up part generalised.

7/110 Low Quarter (township or quarter in parish of Kirkandrews on Esk) NY 347687 [Not listed]
Apt 18.07.1849; 1195a (3852); Map 1849?, 6 chns; railway and station, waterbodies, building names, mill, school. District is apportioned by holding; Apt omits land use.

7/111 Lyneside Quarter (township or quarter in parish of Arthuret) NY 389659 [Not listed]
Apt 18.07.1849; 342a (1444); Map 1849, 6 chns, by Richard Asquith, Carlisle; turnpike roads, toll bar, waterbodies, building names, smiths shop, tile works, school. District is apportioned by holding and fields are not shown.

7/112 Matterdale (township in parish of Greystoke) NY 373233 [Matterdale End]
Apt 29.10.1846; 7313a (7313); Map 1847, 4 chns, by Thomas Woodmass, Alston and John Huddleston, Newborough; construction lines, foot/b'way.

7/113 Melmerby (parish) NY 644382
Apt 18.12.1839; 1692a (4496); Map 1840, 3 chns, by John Salkeld; construction lines, foot/b'way, building names, watermill, moor; fells named. Map title is enclosed within a shield-shaped cartouche with leaves on top.

7/114 Middle Quarter (township or quarter in parish of Kirkandrews on Esk) NY 365716 [Not listed]
Apt 18.07.1849; 607a (4531); Map 1849, 6 chns, by Richard Asquith, Carlisle; turnpike roads, toll bar, waterbodies, woods, building names. District is apportioned by holding and fields are not shown.

7/115 Middlesceugh (hamlet in parish of St Mary Carlisle) NY 410415
Apt 04.09.1844; 2010a (2010); Map 1847?, 4 chns; waterbodies, plantations (col), occupation roads.

7/116 Lower Millom (township in parish of Millom) SD 167807 [Not listed]
Apt 31.03.1848; 78a (?); Map 1848, 6 chns, in 2 parts, by G. Robinson, (tithable parts only; including 30-chn location diagram); woods, building names.

7/117 Upper Millom or Millom Above (township in parish of Millom) SD 179837 [Not listed]
Apt 31.03.1848; 46a (?); Map 1848, 6 chns, in 2 parts, by Geo. Robinson, (tithable parts only; including 24-chn location diagram); building names, deer park.

7/118 Moat Quarter (township or quarter in parish of Kirkandrews on Esk) NY 409741 [Not listed]
Apt 18.07.1849; 197a (1581); Map 1849, 6 chns, by Richard Asquith, Carlisle; woods, building names, mill, saw mill. District is apportioned by holding and fields are not shown.

7/119 Moresby (parish) NX 999201
Apt 21.06.1838; 2135a (2187); Map 1838, 4 chns, surveyed for tithe commutation by Wm Gaythorp; hill-drawing, foot/b'way, turnpike roads, turnpike road 'now in progress', toll bar, milestones, waterbodies, houses, woods, parkland, field gates, building names, landowners, quarries, pinfold, pit, tile works, mill, smithy, coal deposits (by Dawson's symbol), trig points, coastline, boundary stone, demesne.

7/120 Mosser (township in parish of Brigham) NY 118243
Apt 21.05.1841; 1018a (1018); Map surveyed for tithe commutation 1839, 3 chns; construction lines, hill-drawing, houses, woods (col), plantations (col), orchards, gardens (col), open fields, field gates, building names, tile works, watermill.

7/121 Motherby and Gill (township in parish of Greystoke) NY 433293
Apt 05.03.1839; 447a (446); Map 1842?, 4 chns; no buildings are shown.

7/122 Muncaster (parish) SD 120971 [Not listed]
Apt 31.12.1842; 5051a (5166); Map surveyed for tithe commutation 1843, 3 chns; houses, woods, orchards, building names, school, boat house, mill.

7/123 Mungrisdale (township in parish of Greystoke) NY 343296
Apt 29.10.1846; 6730a (6729); Map 1847, 4 chns, by Thomas Woodmass, Alston and John Huddleston, Newborough; construction lines, foot/b'way, boundary stones.

7/124 Nealhouse (township in parish of Thursby) NY 340509
Apt 05.09.1844; 214a (?); Map 1843, 3 chns, 1st cl, by T. Bouch; construction lines, foot/b'way, waterbodies, building names.

7/125 Netherby Quarter (township or quarter in parish of Arthuret) NY 404716 [Netherby]
Apt 18.07.1849; 1525a (?); Map 1849, 6 chns, by Richard Asquith, Carlisle; woods, building names, mill, sawmill. District is apportioned by holding and fields are not shown.

7/126 Netherhall otherwise Maryport (township in parish of Cross Canonby) NY 041373
Apt 16.04.1844; 26a (906); Map 1844, 3 chns; hill-drawing, rock outcrops, building names, quays, dock, ship building yard, mill, pier, supposed Roman camp, foreshore, well; built-up part generalised.

7/127 Netherwasdale, Eskdale and Wasdale (township in parish of St Bees) NY 177062 [Nether Wasdale]
Apt 20.08.1839; 439a (30000); Map 1840, 12 chns, in 6 parts, by Jonathan Stanwix, Egremont, (including three enlargements); turnpike roads, waterbodies, building names, landowners, synagogue, mills, school, church house, lodge, carding mill, common, high roads.

7/128 Newby (township in parish of Irthington) NY 482592 [Not listed]
Apt 23.12.1842; 14a (807); Map 1849?, 4 chns. Apt has cropping information.

7/129 Newton (parish) NY 479327 [Newton Reigny]
Apt 10.09.1838; 2714a (?); Map 1837, 3 chns, by George Larmer, Carlisle; hill-drawing, waterbodies, woods (col), plantations (col), orchards, heath/moor, field gates, building names, sand or stone pit, school house. Modus land is apportioned by holding.

7/130 Newton (township in parish of Irthington) NY 494647 [Not listed]
Apt 23.09.1842; 216a (?); Map 1843, 3 chns, by George Hetherington and George Carruthers; foot/b'way, occupation roads, woods, road names, landowners, wall, site of Roman wall, mill race, freehold and common land; mapmakers' names are on a scroll resting against a pillar, with a wheatsheaf at the base. District is partly apportioned by holding.

7/131 Nicholforest (township or quarter in parish of Kirkandrews on Esk) NY 462781 [Not listed]
Apt 13.04.1849; 218a (7302); Map 1850, 6 chns, by Robert Graham; building names, mill; colours may show property ownerships; compass rose and scale bar are brightly coloured.

7/132 Orton (parish) NY 341538 [Not listed]
Apt 05.10.1847; 4277a (4277); Map 1843, 3 chns, 1st cl, by T. Bouch; construction lines, waterbodies, woods, building names.

7/133 Oughterby (township in parish of Kirkbampton) NY 298555
Apt 18.06.1840; 75a (905); Map 1839, 3 chns, by George Larmer, Carlisle; waterbodies, building names, tile works.

7/134 Oughterside (township in parish of Aspatria) NY 117401
Apt 05.04.1845; 955a (2466); Map 1845, 3 chns, 1st cl, by John Huddleston, Newborough, Northumberland; construction lines, railway, waterbodies, houses, farmyards.

7/135 Ousby (parish) NY 655359
Apt 08.02.1843; 2172a (6000); Map 1842, 3 chns, 1st cl, by Bouch and Carr, Thursby near Carlisle, (tithable parts only); construction lines, waterbodies, woods, building names, quarry.

7/136 Papcastle (township in parish of Bridekirk) NY 105321
Apt 28.11.1838; 1127a (1216); Map 1839?, 4 chns; hill-drawing, woods, hedges, building names, pinfold, weirs, quarries, common.

7/137 Parton and Micklethwaite (township in parish of Thursby) NY 281508
Apt 20.11.1844; 628a (627); Map 1845?, 3 chns; woods, open fields, building names, mill.

7/138 Penrith (parish) NY 513326
Apt 14.03.1843; 7352a (7664); Map 1849?, 6 chns, in 2 parts, (including 3-chn enlargement of town of Penrith); railway, turnpike roads, toll bars, milestone, waterbodies, woods, plantations (named), parkland, building names, road names, mills, tithe barn, castle, nursery ground, race ground, grandstand, markets, fair ground, quarries, moss.

7/139 Petteril Crooks (township in parish of Hesket in the Forest) NY 433471 [Not listed]
Apt 19.11.1839; 929a (?); Map 1839, 3 chns, by J. Brown, Oughterside; woods, plantations, building names; colours may show property ownerships.

7/140 Petteril Crooks (township in parish of Hesket in the Forest) NY 452452 [Not listed]
Apt 30.09.1846; 3651a (?); Map 1845, 4 chns; railway, waterbodies, woods, plantations, orchards, building names, mills, public quarry.

7/141 Plumbland (parish) NY 144390
Apt 08.03.1850; 2552a (2970); Map 1850, 3 chns; railway, woods, plantations, limekilns.

7/142 Plumpton Street (township in parish of Hesket in the Forest) NY 483368 [Plumpton]
Apt 06.09.1845; 2678a (2677); Map 1846, 4 chns, 1st cl, by T. Woodmass, Maryport; construction lines, railway, houses, building names.

7/143 Plumpton Wall (district in parish of Lazonby) NY 496392 [Not listed]
Apt 24.08.1844; 3021a (3021); Map 1844?, 4 chns, by Machell, Carlisle; hill-drawing, foot/b'way, waterbodies, woods, weir, boundary stones.

7/144 Ponsonby (parish) NY 055055
Apt 11.04.1844; 77a (2265); Map 1845, 4 chns; building names.

7/145 Preston Quarter (township in parish of St Bees) NX 976137 [Not listed]
Apt 23.04.1844; 9a (2699); Map 1846, 4 chns; hill-drawing, building names, limekilns.

7/146 Priestgate (district in parish of Workington) NX 989288 [Not listed]
Apt 19.04.1844; 438a (?); Map 1845?, 3 chns; pier.

7/147 Redmain (township in parish of Isell) NY 129343
Apt 16.11.1837; 960a (?); Map 1837, 4 chns, by Jonathan Stanwix; foot/b'way, woods, landowners (col).

7/148 Renwick (parish) NY 613452
Apt 14.12.1842; 4220a (4220); Map 1844?, 4 chns; houses, woods, plantations.

7/149 Ribton (township in parish of Bridekirk) NY 054312 [Not listed]
Apt 28.08.1840; 16a (596); Map 1840?, 4 chns, by W. Gaythorp; houses, woods, plantations, orchards, field gates, building names, field names; field acreages given for tithable areas only.

7/150 Rickerby (township in parish of Stanwix) NY 419573
Apt 16.10.1839; 561a (560); Map 1839, 3 chns; waterbodies, woods, building names, mill.

7/151 Rickergate (township in parish of St Mary Carlisle) NY 408562 [Not listed]
Apt 07.12.1842; 291a (290); Map 1844, 4 chns, by Richard Asquith, Carlisle; hill-drawing, turnpike roads, toll bar, waterbodies, woods, building names, road names, cattle market, grand stand, racecourse, mill, gaol, court houses, castle, boundary stones; built-up part generalised.

7/152 Rockcliff (parish) NY 352632 [Rockcliffe]
Apt 07.12.1842; 5438a (6572); Map 1843, 4 chns, in 3 parts, by Richd Asquith, Carlisle, (one part at 8 chns); hill-drawing, foot/b'way, turnpike roads, toll bar, canal, waterbodies, woods, parkland, building names, boathouse, embankment, sandbed.

7/153 Rottington (township in parish of St Bees) NX 955129
Apt 23.04.1844; 330a (735); Map 1845, 3 chns; houses, woods, rock outcrops, reservoir.

7/154 Great Salkeld (parish) NY 542365
Apt 31.03.1842; 3725a (3724); Map 1840, 3 chns, by Sylvanus Miller, Durham; hill-drawing, waterbodies, woods, parkland, boundary stones.

7/155 Sandwith (township in parish of St Bees) NX 956146
Apt 19.12.1838; 1345a (1406); Map 1838, 3 chns; hill-drawing, foot/b'way, waterbodies, houses, woods (col), orchards, heath/moor, field gates, building names, landowners, lighthouse, high water mark, coal yard, boundary stones, stone quarries, wells, reservoir, National School, guide post; coast features named.

7/156 Scaleby (parish) NY 449631
Apt 16.07.1839; 254a (3100); Map 1842?, 3 chns, waterbodies, woods, building names, castle, moat, smith shop, mill, tile works.

7/157 Scotby (township in parish of Wetheral) NY 435553
Apt 31.12.1840; 1672a (1672); Map 1842, 4 chns, 1st cl, by Rd Asquith, Carlisle; hill-drawing, railway, foot/b'way, waterbodies, woods, building names.

7/158 Seaton (township in parish of Cammerton) NY 017314
Apt 24.06.1841; 2597a (2939); Map 1841, 4 chns, ? by [name lost], Colliery Office, Whitehaven; hill-drawing, foot/b'way, turnpike roads, houses, woods, heath/moor, open fields, field gates, building names, quays, pier, beach, oyster bank, high water mark, reservoirs, tile works, iron works, quarry, brick works, mill race, lime kiln, rabbit warren, rubbing house, school, smithies, river coops; company owning tile and brick works named.

7/159 Sebergham (parish) NY 342427
Apt 17.03.1849; 182a (5890); Map 1849, 3 chns, in 2 parts, by 'G.M.C.' [George McCall, Bromfield, Cumberland, Land Surveyor], (residual modus lands only); building names, landowners, mill, well, limekiln, public well.

7/160 Setmurthy (township in parish of Brigham) NY 165322 [Not listed]
Apt 18.06.1840; 2579a (2579); Map 1840?, 4 chns; woods, parkland, building names, school; colours may show property ownerships.

7/161 Skelton (parish) NY 429366
Apt 31.12.1841; 3327a (6326); Map 1842?, 4 chns, by Wm Robinson, Gillfoot, Caldbeck, Cumberland; waterbodies, woods (col), open fields, building names; buildings at edge of district are annotated with distance from parish church.

7/162 Soulfitts, Pallett Wythes, Michael Brows, Sandair and Goat (district in parish of Bridekirk) NY 119310 [Not listed]
Apt 25.07.1845; 90a (?); Map 1846, 4 chns, by C. Hodgson; foot/b'way, woods, plantations, weirs, sand bank.

7/163 Staffield (township in parish of Kirkoswald) NY 569459
Apt 07.10.1843; 5473a (5472); Map 1842, 4 chns, in 3 parts, by D.W. Rome, Alston; construction lines, waterbodies, houses.

7/164 Stainton (township in parish of Stanwix) NY 378576
Apt 16.10.1839; 586a (585); Map 1840?, 3 chns; hill-drawing, foot/b'way, waterbodies, field gates, public gravel bed, common.

7/165 Stanwix (township in parish of Stanwix) NY 405574
Apt 16.10.1839; 425a (425); Map 1840?, 3 chns; hill-drawing, waterbodies, woods, building names.

7/166 Stapleton (parish) NY 492727
Apt 25.07.1845; 259a (11335); Map 1844?, 2 chns, in 5 parts, (including 8-chn index); waterbodies, field gates, building names, wells, mill race, common allotments, public and private roads.

7/167 Talkin (township in parish of Hayton) NY 556570
Apt 29.10.1839; 964a (?); Map 1840?, 4 chns; railway, woods, plantations, building names, school house.

7/168 Tallantire (township in parish of Bridekirk) NY 108359
Apt 11.07.1838; 1913a (1913); Map 1838?, 4 chns; waterbodies, woods, parkland, building names, public quarry; some field boundaries are double solid lines.

7/169 Tarraby (township in parish of Stanwix) NY 411583
Apt 16.10.1839; 484a (484); Map 1840?, 3 chns; foot/b'way, waterbodies, woods, orchards, field gates, building names, mill.

7/170 Threlkeld (township in parish of Greystoke) NY 331262
Apt 12.01.1849; 2128a (4710); Map 1838, 3 chns, in 2 parts, by Wm Hodgson and Wm Atkinson, Bassenthwaite; woods, parkland, building names, road names.

7/171 Thursby (township in parish of Thursby) NY 326505
Apt 31.10.1840; 1166a (2984); Map 1841?, 4 chns; field gates, building names, mill.

7/172 Thwaites (township in parish of Millom) SD 189881 [Not listed]
Apt 31.03.1848; 43a (?); Map 1848, 6 chns, in 2 parts, by Geo. Robinson, (including 24-chn location diagram); building names, Druid's temple.

7/173 Uldale (parish) NY 267349
Apt 16.11.1840; 2340a (5500); Map 1841?, 3 chns, in 2 parts; hill-drawing, waterbodies, woods, open fields, building names, tumulus, mill.

7/174 Ulpha (township in parish of Millom) SD 212972
Apt 23.07.1847; 72a (?); Map 1847, 6 chns, in 2 parts, by G. Robinson, (including 24-chn location diagram); building names.

7/175 Upperby (township in parish of St Cuthbert Carlisle) NY 409537
Apt 02.07.1839; 450a (449); Map 1842?, 8 chns; building names, mill, workhouses, township boundaries.

7/176 Waberthwaite (parish) SD 117940
Apt 17.11.1842; 920a (1901); Map 1838, 3 chns, 1st cl, by John Robinson, Bootle; construction lines, building names, mill, common.

7/177 Walton (parish) NY 524662
Apt 19.09.1839; 3592a (3592); Map 1840?, 6 chns; hill-drawing, woods, parkland, building names, property names, churchyard, moss, undivided common, disputed property; meaning of colouring is unclear. District is apportioned by holding and not all fields are shown; Apt omits land use.

7/178 Warwick (township in parish of Warwick) NY 456579
Apt 31.12.1840; 1287a (1286); Map 1841, 4 chns, 1st cl, by R. Asquith, Carlisle; hill-drawing, foot/b'way, waterbodies, woods, parkland, building names, river coops.

7/179 Watermillock (chapelry in parish of Greystoke) NY 407213
Apt 30.09.1841; 8316a (9336); Map 1843?, 8 chns; woods, building names, tower, public quarries, coastline, waterfall; legend explains boundary depiction. Apt omits land use.

7/180 Wetheral (township in parish of Wetheral) NY 461535
Apt 31.12.1840; 4459a (4458); Map 1842-3, 4 chns, 1st cl, in 2 parts, by Richd Asquith, Carlisle; hill-drawing, railway, foot/b'way, waterbodies, woods, plantations, building names, ford, river coops, cells, abbey, boundary stones.

7/181 Wheddicar (township in parish of St Bees) NY 018184 [Not listed]
Apt 23.04.1844; 49a (926); Map 1847, 4 chns, foot/b'way, woods, building names, field names, landowners, mill, quarry, field acreages; occupier given for each field.

7/182 Whicham (parish) SD 144843
Apt 29.11.1838; 2500a (7502); Map 1838, 3 chns, 1st cl, by John Robinson, Bootle; construction lines, farmyards, building names, mill, coastline; surveyer notes that one of the construction lines has been measured since 'the return of plan'.

7/183 Whitbeck (parish) SD 119859
Apt 10.12.1838; 1036a (5372); Map 1839, 3 chns, 1st cl, by John Robinson, Bootle; construction lines, waterbodies, building names, landowners; some field boundaries are shown with double solid lines; surveyor has added notes on the placing of triangulation lines in some cases, and that 'morass' was 'not possible to chain'.

7/184 Whitehaven (township in parish of St Bees) NX 978179
Apt 23.04.1844; 117a (267); Map 1847, 1 chn; turnpike roads, waterbodies, building names, road names, castle, castle gardens, manufactories, granary yard, workhouse, High Meeting House, market places, hot baths, old and new quays, piers, harbour, timber slip, steps, marine school, jetties, patent slip, ship building yard, ore yard, lodge; map is extremely detailed. Apt omits land use.

7/185 Whinfell (township in parish of St Bees) NY 136256 [Not listed]
Apt 27.07.1840; 1723a (1723); Map 1841?, 3 chns; woods, building names; boundaries may show property ownerships.

7/186 Wreay (township or chapelry in parish of St Mary's Carlisle) NY 427490
Apt 19.11.1839; 358a (1088); Map 1839?, [5 chns]; school.

7/187 Wreay Hall (district in parish of Hesket in the Forest) NY 446487
Apt 16.11.1842; 337a (?); Map 1842, 4 chns, 1st cl, by W. Carr; construction lines, waterbodies, woods, building names, mill, weir; legend explains boundary depiction.

7/188 Wythop (township in parish of Brigham) NY 198289 [Not listed]
Apt 22.06.1844; 2998a (3013); Map 1845, 4 chns, by Wm Lw Newby, Burrowdale; foot/b'way, waterbodies, woods (named), orchards, heath/moor, building names, road names, stone quarries, mill, gravel pit, peat moss (col).

Derbyshire

PRO IR29 and IR30 8/1–240

316 tithe districts: 658,874 acres
240 tithe commutations: 384,777 acres
86 voluntary tithe agreements, 154 compulsory tithe awards

Tithe and tithe commutation

The proportion of tithable districts in Derbyshire (76 per cent) is similar to Staffordshire but a much smaller proportion of the total area of the county (58 per cent) was still subject to payment of tithes in 1836 (Fig. 20). Twenty-two districts were wholly tithable and as usual in counties with predominantly upland terrain and pastoral agriculture, modus payments in lieu of tithes were the main cause of tithe exemption. Other important reasons for exemption were commutation at the time of enclosure, the merger of tithes in the land, and exemption by prescription.

Assistant tithe commissioners and local tithe agents who worked in Derbyshire are listed in Table 8.1 and the valuers of tithe rent-charge in Table 8.2. Twenty-two Derbyshire tithe districts (9 per cent) have field-by-field records of crops listed under 'state of cultivation'. As in Staffordshire, the valuer J. B. H. Bennett was responsible for most of the tithe apportionments which include this information.

Tithe maps

Derbyshire has very little first-class tithe mapping; only 3 per cent of the county's 240 maps are sealed as first class (Table 8.3). The temporal pattern of map production in Derbyshire is unusual with three peaks: in 1839, in 1843–44, and in 1847–50 (Table 8.4). Derbyshire tithe maps are drawn at a variety of scales from one inch to 2 chains to one inch to 12 chains and a significant number are at irregular scales such as one inch to 3.75 chains and one inch to 6.25 chains, perhaps the result of working to scales in local customary measure which have been converted to statute measure. The most favoured scale in Derbyshire was one inch to six chains which was used in 53 per cent of tithe districts. Only 23 per cent of maps are in the recommended scale range of one inch to three to four chains. Twenty-one maps are at the five-chain scale which was not much used outside the Midlands (Table 8.3).

Derbyshire conforms to a common pattern in that its tithe maps have a generally good record of woodland (on 84 per cent of maps) and parkland (on 24 per cent and in detail on five maps) but are a poor source of information on agricultural land uses. None records

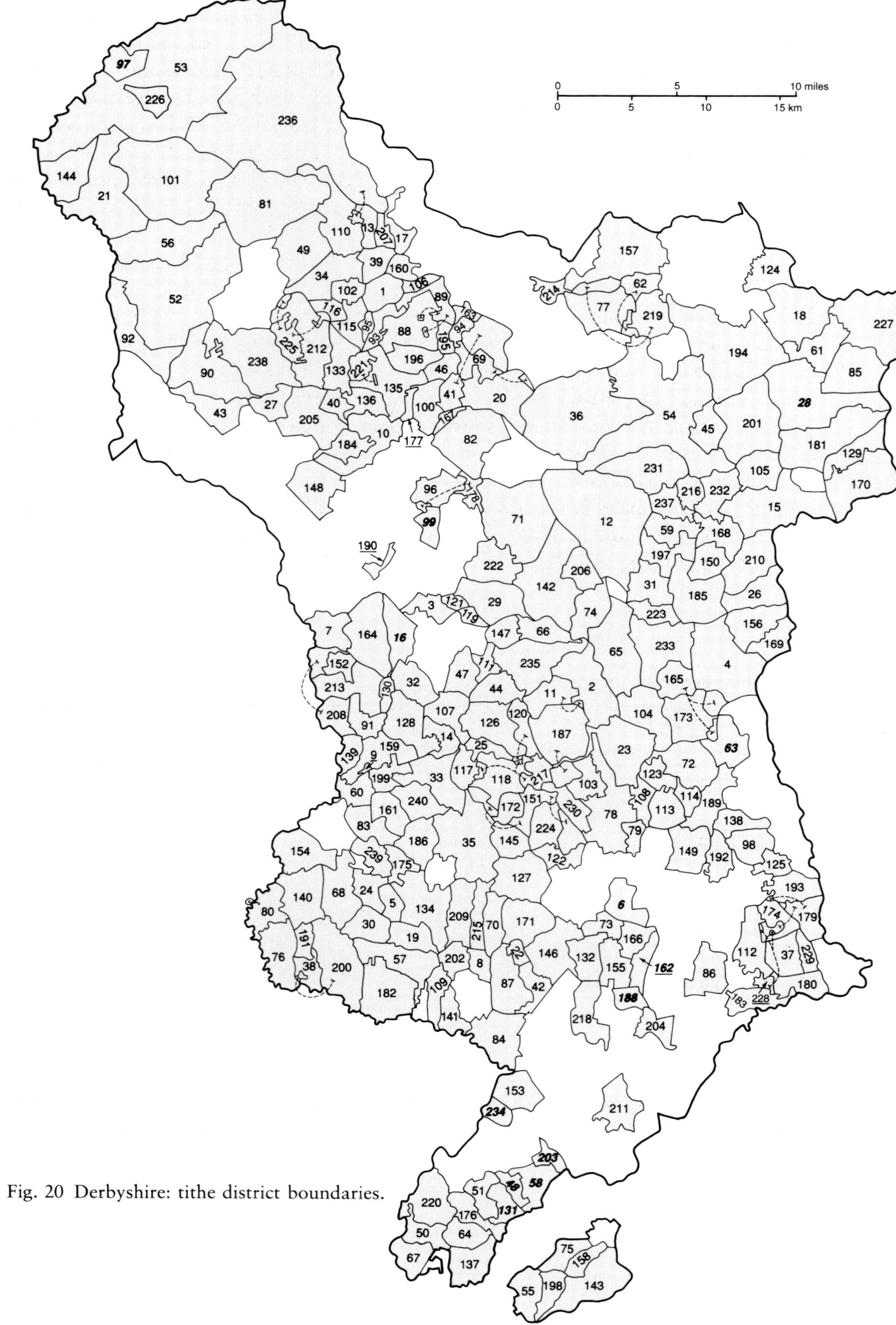

Fig. 20 Derbyshire: tithe district boundaries.

arable or grass and only a few show gardens, heath and moor, marsh or bog, or orchards. There is also little information on field boundary ownership or on hedges and fences. The mapping of industry is more complete and extraction of slate, lime, lead and coal, metal smelting, the milling of paper, flax, silk and cotton, gunpowder manufacture and marble, iron and bleach works are among activities recorded. Urban land use is less well recorded with many built-up areas either not mapped in detail or not mapped at all. At Matlock the spa and various ancillary buildings are depicted and three maps show castles and ancient earthworks. The map of Hazlewood shows tenurial status (freehold and copyhold 'fine certain' and 'fine uncertain') by different colours.

Some 153 Derbyshire tithe maps in the Public Record Office collection can be attributed to a particular map-maker; the most prolific were John and Robert Bromley of Derby, who produced nineteen and fifteen maps respectively in plain, straightforward styles. Most map-makers were drawn from within or close to the county (Table 8.2). Some tithe districts which comprised a number of townships were mapped by different surveyors in different styles; the map of Chesterfield is an extreme example of this.

There is not a great deal of decorative embellishment on Derbyshire tithe maps but four maps have ornamental cartouches. The most distinctive is that on the map of Holbrooke which includes two snakes and a bird of prey. That for Atlow has an elaborate leafy surround and several maps have borders which are more than functional, though perhaps not strictly decorative, and several maps have ornamental compass roses and scale bars. The standard of drawing varies from the amateurish on South Normanton to very good on at least eight maps.

Table 8.1. *Agreements and awards for commutation of tithes in Derbyshire*

Assistant commissioner/ local tithe agent	*Number of agreements**	*Number of awards*
John Job Rawlinson	4	77
George Wingrove Cooke	0	40
Joseph Townsend	0	24
Richard Burton Phillipson	21	0
Thomas Martin	20	0
John Holder	12	0
John Pickering	12	0
John Mee Mathew	0	9
Roger Kynaston	8	0
Edward Greathed	7	0
Thomas Smith Woolley	5	3
Horace William Meteyard	4	0
Henry Pilkington	1	0
Charles Pym	0	1
Thomas Sudworth	1	0

*Computed from the number of extant reports on tithe agreements in the tithe files [PRO IR 18].

Table 8.2. *Tithe valuers and tithe map-makers in Derbyshire*

Name and address (in Derbyshire unless indicated)	*Number of districts*	*Acreage*
Tithe valuers		
Joseph Bennett Hankin Bennett, Tutbury, Staffordshire	28	33,209
Robert Cresswell, Idridgehay, Wirksworth	23	47,534
John Bromley, Derby	19	29,449
Mansfeldt Forster Mills, Chesterfield	17	14,077
John Chambers, Tibshelf	11	13,443
George Lamb, Derby	11	11,266
John Wright, Romely, Chesterfield	9	47,577
Henry Roper, Craske, Etwall	9	11,789
Robert Bromley, Derby	8	14,967
John Taylor, Low Leighton near Ollerset	7	20,427
John Harrison, Bakewell	7	17,700
Others [48]	91	123,339
Attributed tithe map-makers		
John Bromley, Derby	19	30,225
Robert Bromley, Derby	15	25,971
George Lamb, Derby	13	17,889
John Parkin, Idridgehay, Wirksworth	15	22,182
Joseph Gratton, Timberfield, Chesterfield	11	17,183
George Unwin	10	39,087
Joseph Bennett Hankin Bennett, Tutbury, Staffordshire	10	7,406
Mansfeldt F. Mills and Smithers, Chesterfield	8	5,001
Others [31]	52	74,030

Table 8.3. *The tithe maps of Derbyshire: scales and classes*

Scale in chains/inch	*All maps*		*First Class*		*Second Class*	
	Number	*Acreage*	*Number*	*Acreage*	*Number*	*Acreage*
>3	8	2,895	2	1,712	6	1,183
3	30	45,683	6	16,037	24	29,646
3.75	1	1,009	0	0	1	1,009
4	23	33,077	0	0	23	33,077
4.5	1	1,828	0	0	1	1,828
5	21	23,205	0	0	21	23,205
6	128	221,697	0	0	128	221,697
<6	28	55,383	0	0	28	55,383
TOTAL	240	384,777	8	17,749	232	367,028

Table 8.4. *The tithe maps of Derbyshire: dates*

	<1838	*1838*	*1839*	*1840*	*1841*	*1842*	*1843*	*1844*	*1845*	*1846*	*1847*	*1848*	*1849*	*1850*	*>1850*
All maps	3	9	18	13	15	6	25	17	6	6	31	28	33	21	7
1st class	1	1	1	2	0	1	0	1	1	0	0	0	0	0	0
2nd class	2	8	17	11	15	5	25	16	5	6	31	28	33	21	7

Derbyshire

8/1 Abney and Abney Grange (township in parish of Hope) SK 196796
Apt 02.10.1847; 1330a (1331); Map 1849, 4 chns, by John Parkin, Idridgehay near Wirksworth; foot/b'ways, woods, plantations, building names, well, boundary marks, common.

8/2 Alderwasley (township in parish of Wirksworth) SK 331522
Apt 27.02.1841; 3108a (3108); Map 1841, 6 chns, by Robert Bromley, Derby; railway, foot/b'ways, turnpike roads, toll bar, waterbodies, houses, woods, plantations, parkland, marsh/bog, field gates, building names, ironworks, corn mill, smelting mills, mill, dog kennels, deer cote, school.

8/3 Aldwark (township in parish of Bradborne) SK 226580
Apt 24.02.1848; 945a (945); Map 1849, 6.25 chns; woods, grange. Apt is by holding and omits land use.

8/4 Alfreton (parish) SK 419537
Apt 26.04.1847; 270a (4550); Map 1850?, 4 chns, (including index to various parts); railway, canal with towpath, waterbodies, woods.

8/5 Alkmonton (township in parish of Longford) SK 198374
Apt 23.01.1839; 717a (?); Map 1839, 6 chns, by J.B.H. Bennett, Tutbury; foot/b'ways, waterbodies, woods, building names, meer stones, smithy, site of paper mill. Apt includes cropping information.

8/6 St Alkmunds (township in parish of St Alkmunds) SK 354373 [Not listed]
Apt 11.02.1850; 21a (?); Map 1850, 6 chns, by J. Clarke, Higham Cliff; railways and station, canal.

8/7 Alsop le Dale (township in parish of Ashbourne) SK 155563 [Alsop en le Dale]
Apt 05.02.1846; 1524a (?); Map 1846, 5 chns, by John Bromley, Derby; foot/b'ways, waterbodies, houses, woods, building names.

8/8 Ash (township in parish of Sutton on the Hill) SK 257332 [Not listed]
Apt 15.02.1839; 692a (?); Map 1839, 6 chns; foot/b'ways, waterbodies, woods, building names. Apt includes cropping information.

8/9 Ashbourne (township) SK 179468
Apt 28.05.1846; 60a (?); Map 1849?, 2 chns, by John Shaw, (tithable parts and streets only); waterbodies, woods, ecclesiastical building names, road names, market place.

8/10 Ashford (township in parish of Bakewell) SK 194693 [Ashford in the Water]
Apt 01.05.1847; 2561a (?); Map 1847, 6 chns, by B. Grove, Birmingham; waterbodies, building names, toll bar, marble works, mine, sand or stone pits.

8/11 Ashleyhay (township in parish of Wirksworth) SK 303517 [Not listed]
Apt 21.05.1841; 1438a (1438); Map 1842, 6 chns, by John Bromley, Derby; hill-drawing, foot/b'ways, waterbodies, houses, woods, plantations, field gates, building names, boundary stones, stone or sand pits or quarries, Ordnance picket.

8/12 Ashover (township in parish of Ashover) SK 341640
Apt 30.03.1849; 8865a (9180); Map 1851?, 6 chns, in 2 parts (including 3-chn enlargements of built-up parts); waterbodies, woods, parkland, building names, windmill, cupola, hut bar.

8/13 Aston (township in parish of Hope) SK 188842
Apt 24.08.1847; 715a (714); Map 1849, 3 chns; hill-drawing, foot/b'ways, waterbodies, houses, woods, heath/moor, field gates, building names, mill, weir, Ordnance station, common.

8/14 Atlow (township in parish of Bradborne) SK 236489
Apt 04.05.1838; 890a (1433); Map 1839?, [8 chns], ? by J. Craner; hill-drawing, foot/b'ways, woods, road names, landowners; map is titled 'A plan of the Estate of Edwd Walhonje Okeover Esq and other lands' and is dated 1775; honeysuckle and ribbons, coloured, surround map title. Apt omits land use.

8/15 Ault Hucknall (parish) SK 457646
Apt 11.07.1838; 4293a (3730); Map 1839, 6 chns, by George Unwin; waterbodies, woods, parkland; colours show tithe-free and modus land.

8/16 Ballidon (township in parish of Bradborne) SK 205560
Apt 22.11.1847; 108a (?); Map 1850, 6 chns, by J.B.H. Bennett, Tutbury; foot/b'ways, landowners.

8/17 Bamford (township in parish of Hathersage) SK 207836
Apt 24.07.1840; 868a (1456); Map 1842, 3 chns, by Josiah Fairbank; hill-drawing, turnpike roads, tollbar, woods, plantations (named), field gates, building names, road names, mill, moorland; bridges named. The district is tinted, except for woodland which is left uncoloured; no woodland symbols are used.

8/18 Barlborough (parish) SK 475776
Apt 28.03.1839; 3305a (3220); Map 1839?, 8 chns; waterbodies, houses, woods (named), plantations (named), parkland, ornamental gardens (col), road names; colours may indicate ownerships.

8/19 Barton Blount (parish) SK 212350 [Not listed]
Apt 26.05.1849; 60a (1150); Map 1850, 4 chns, by Henry C. Roper, Uttoxeter; waterbodies, woods, marsh/bog, boundary stones.

8/20 Baslow (township in parish of Bakewell) SK 274725
Apt 27.04.1847; 3009a (?); Map 1848, 6 chns; foot/b'ways, waterbodies, plantations, parkland, moorland. Apt includes cropping information.

8/21 Beard, Ollerset, Whittle and Thornset (township in parish of Glossop) SK 007866
Apt 25.06.1841; 5044a (5044); Map 1841, 4 chns, by John Taylor, Ollerset near Stockport; foot/b'ways, turnpike roads, toll bar, waterbodies, farmyards, woods, building names, mills, bleach works, quarries or stone pits, tan pits, hamlet boundaries; legend explains depiction of roads, water courses and buildings.

8/22 Bearward Cote (township in parish of Etwall) SK 282339 [Not listed]
Apt 07.05.1847; 20a (?); Map 1848, 3 chns, by Henry C. Roper, Etwall; foot/b'ways, waterbodies, woods, plantations, road names.

8/23 Belper (township in parish of Duffield) SK 352481
Apt 17.11.1842; 3078a (3078); Map 1844, 6 chns, in 2 parts, (Belper mapped separately at 3 chns); railway and station, foot/b'ways, waterbodies, plantations, building names, artificial river features.

8/24 Bentley (township in parish of Longford) SK 180385 [Not listed]
Apt 16.10.1839; 1074a (?); Map 1839, 6 chns; waterbodies, woods, building names, boundary stones, smithy, spring. Apt includes cropping information.

8/25 Biggin (township in parish of Wirksworth) SK 262481
Apt 18.02.1841; 595a (595); Map 1843, 8 chns; woods, plantations, orchards, building names, mill.

8/26 Blackwell (parish) SK 442586
Apt 28.03.1839; 1716a (?); Map 1839, 5 chns, by George Unwin; woods, glebe (col).

8/27 Blackwell (township in parish of Bakewell) SK 120720
Apt 14.08.1847; 1071a (1071); Map 1847, 6 chns (tinted); waterbodies, woods, rock outcrops, building names, road names, mill. Apt omits land use.

8/28 Bolsover (township in parish of Bolsover) SK 477717
Apt 11.10.1848; 42a (5340); Map 1849, 2 chns, by Charles J. Neale, Mansfield; hill-drawing, foot/b'ways, woods, open fields, field gates, windmill (pictorial); shading may indicate waste.

8/29 Bonsall (parish) SK 266584
Apt 05.12.1846; 2465a (2464); Map 1848, 3 chns, surveyed by John Parkin, Idridgehay, for Robert Cresswell; foot/b'ways, waterbodies, woods, plantations, open fields, building names.

8/30 Boylston (parish) SK 182359 [Boyleston]
Apt 07.05.1847; 73a (1360); Map 1848, 6 chns, by J.B.H. Bennett, Tutbury; foot/b'ways, building names, road names, landowners. Apt includes cropping information.

8/31 Brackenfield and Woolley (township in parish of Morton) SK 372594
Apt 19.06.1839; 1557a (1557); Map 1840, 3 chns, 1st cl, by Robert Bromley, Derby; construction lines, railway, foot/b'ways, waterbodies, houses, woods (named), plantations (named), parkland, field boundary ownerships, building names, pound, mill, old river course, green (col).

8/32 Bradbourne (township in parish of Bradborne) SK 212526
Apt 02.08.1841; 1433a (?); Map 1840, 4 chns, by Robert Bromley junr, Derby; foot/b'ways, waterbodies, plantations, parkland, field gates, building names, sand or stone pits or quarries, mill.

8/33 Bradley (parish) SK 228461
Apt 21.06.1838; 2375a (all); Map 1839, 8 chns, foot/b'ways, turnpike roads, toll bar, private roads, waterbodies, woods (named), building names, road names, folly, gravel pits, mill dam, old lime quarries, kennels, park. Apt includes cropping information.

8/34 Bradwell (township in parish of Hope) SK 158809
Apt 26.08.1843; 2158a (2158); Map 1845?, 3 chns; waterbodies, woods, road names, mill dam; gardens shown by annotation; scale statement and graduation do not agree.

8/35 Brailsford (parish) SK 249418
Apt 29.07.1837; 4296a (4296); Map 1837, 3 chns, 1st cl, by John Bromley, Derby; foot/b'ways, turnpike roads, waterbodies, houses, woods, parkland, orchards, gardens, field boundary ownerships, field gates, building names, mill.

8/36 Brampton (parish) SK 322709
Apt 21.01.1839; 7915a (8820); Map 1840, 6 chns, by George Unwin; foot/b'ways, waterbodies, woods, building names.

8/37 Breaston (township in parish of Wilne) SK 460338
Apt 16.02.1841; 1484a (?); Map 1840?, 3 chns, facsimile 'of the original plan corrected to the present time' by Granville Smith, Castle Donington, land agent and surveyor; railway, foot/b'ways, occupation roads, canal with towpath, woods, boundary stones, tithe barn, tithe-free land (col). The map is signed by 26 landowners, signifying its adoption. Apt omits land use.

8/38 West Broughton (township in parish of Doveridge) SK 142329
Apt 29.11.1842; 746a (?); Map 1843, 6.25 chns; foot/b'ways, turnpike roads, waterbodies, woods, building names, weir, township boundaries, field acreages. Compass rose and scale bar are unusually combined into one.

8/39 Brough and Shatton (township in parish of Hope) SK 192818
Apt 26.08.1843; 987a (987); Map 1844, 4 chns, by John Parkin, (reduced from Mr J. Bainbrigge's original plotting of the township at a scale of 2 chns in 1825); waterbodies, woods, plantations, building names, boundary marks, common.

8/40 Brushfield (township in parish of Bakewell) SK 163720
Apt 01.05.1847; 657a (?); Map 1847, 6 chns (tinted); waterbodies.

8/41 Bubnell (township in parish of Bakewell) SK 241727
Apt 25.03.1840; 2489a (?); Map 1847, 6 chns; turnpike roads, plantations, building names, moorland; bridge named. Apt includes cropping information.

8/42 Burnaston (township in parish of Etwall) SK 297316
Apt 31.03.1848; 975a (?); Map 1849, 6 chns, by Henry C. Roper, junr, Uttoxeter; foot/b'ways, waterbodies, woods.

8/43 Buxton (township in parish of Bakewell) SK 083716
Apt 10.08.1847; 1828a (1827); Map 1848, 4.5 chns, by John Taylor, Low Leighton, nr Stockport; foot/b'ways, waterbodies, woods, parkland, field gates, building names, mill, crescent of buildings, stables; legend explains depiction of roads, waterbodies and houses.

8/44 Callow (township in parish of Wirksworth) SK 268522
Apt 18.02.1841; 1257a (1257); Map 1844, 5 chns, by John Parkin; foot/b'ways, waterbodies, woods, plantations, building names, mill.

8/45 Calow (township in parish of Chesterfield) SK 414700
Apt 30.12.1848; 1281a (?); Map 1849?, 6 chns, ? by Edw. Woollett Wilmot; woods.

8/46 Calver (township in parish of Bakewell) SK 237744
Apt 27.04.1847; 765a (?); Map 1847, 6 chns, by M.F. Mills, Chesterfield; hill-drawing, waterbodies, woods, limekilns, mill.

8/47 Carsington (parish) SK 245532
Apt 04.05.1838; 1118a (1118); Map 1839, 2 chns, 1st cl, by John Wheatcroft, Wirksworth; construction lines, railway, foot/b'ways, waterbodies, woods, parkland, hedges, building names, road names, kennels, boundary posts, sand or stone pit, milestone; tor (named).

8/48 Castle Gresley (township in parish of Gresley) SK 280180
Apt 21.04.1849; 9a (?); Map (drawn on Apt) 1849?, 3 chns; waterbodies, building names.

8/49 Castleton (township in parish of Castleton) SK 142828
Apt 23.06.1840; 2875a (2875); Map 1841?, 6 chns, in 2 parts (including enlargements of village and open fields); hill-drawing, waterbodies, woods, rock outcrops, open fields, building names, castle, mill stream, tor, mine.

8/50 Catton (township in parish of Croxall) SK 216151 [Not listed]
Apt 09.05.1840; 1065a (1064); Map 1839, 6 chns; waterbodies, woods, parkland, fence. Apt omits land use.

8/51 Cauldwell (township in parish of Stapenhill) SK 256174 [Caldwell]
Apt 18.12.1839; 1041a (all); Map 1839, 6 chns; waterbodies, woods, field gates.

8/52 Chapel-en-le-Frith (parish) SK 055797
Apt 31.12.1846; 52a (13220); Map 1847, 10 chns, (tinted); waterbodies, woods, parkland, building names, mills, limestone quarries, reservoir, silk mill, paper mill, moss (named).

8/53 Charlesworth and Chisworth Chunall, Dinting, Glossop, Ludworth, Padfield and Simmondley (hamlets and townships in parish of Glossop) SK 054952
Apt 18.05.1849; 1182a (?); Map 1852, 3 chns, (tinted); waterbodies, woods, plantations, building names, cotton factory.

8/54 Chesterfield, Brimington, Hasland, Newbold, Tapton, Temple Normanton and Walton (townships in parish of Chesterfield) SK 390710
Apt 30.12.1848; 10170a (?); Map 1849, 6 chns, in 7 parts, by Geo. Unwin; J. Ashton, Chesterfield; J. Clarke, Higham Cliff, near Alfreton; Smithers and Mills, Chesterfield; railway and station, foot/b'ways, canal and wharf, waterbodies, woods, plantations, parkland, orchards, open fields, building names, road names, malthouse, iron foundry, tramway, market place, vicarage, bowling green, house of correction, workhouse, reservoir; the various parts, by the map are by different makers, with variations in scale, style and content: Part 1 of Chesterfield Borough is tinted and is at 2 chns; part 2 is of Newbold Township at 6 chns; part 3 is of Brimington Township at 6 chns by G. Unwin and contains an enlargement of town of Brimington at 3 chns; part 4 of Tapton Township by J. Ashton is at 5 chns with park in detail and with enlargements of open fields at 2 chns; part 5 of Hasland Township is at 6 chns by J. Clarke with an enlargement of the village at 3 chns; part 6 is of Walton Township at 6 chns; part 7 is of Temple Normanton Township at 6 chns by Smithers and Mills.

8/55 Chilcote (township in parish of Clifton Campville) SK 288112
Apt 22.03.1843; 1325a (1325); Map 1843, 6 chns, by J.B.H. Bennett, Tutbury; foot/b'ways, turnpike roads, toll gate, waterbodies, woods, plantations, building names, road names, heath.

8/56 Chinley, Bugsworth and Brownside (townships in parish of Glossop) SK 051833
Apt 25.06.1841; 3806a (3805); Map 1841, 3 chns, by J. Broadhurst and J. Braddock, Bugsworth near Chapel-en-le-Frith; hill-drawing, foot/b'ways, waterbodies, houses, woods, plantations, rock outcrops, building names, tithe barn, mill, limekilns, quarries, slate brecks; legend explains depiction of roads, stone quarries, waterbodies, limekilns, buildings and township boundaries. Apt omits cropping information.

8/57 Church Broughton (parish) SK 205335
Apt 05.02.1847; 637a (2272); Map 1847, 6 chns; foot/b'ways, turnpike roads, waterbodies, woods, building names, road names, mill, sand or stone pits; colours may indicate manorial and hamlet divisions; compass rose is combined with the scale bar.

8/58 Church Gresley (township in parish of Gresley) SK 294183
Apt 31.12.1849; 3a (6700); Map 1850, 2.5 chns; waterbodies, common.

8/59 Clay lane (township in parish of Northwingfield) SK 382631 [Clay Cross]
Apt 21.05.1841; 1292a (1292); Map 1841, 6 chns, in 2 parts, by W.H. Wilson (with 3-chn enlargements of details); railway and tunnel, foot/b'ways, waterbodies, woods, building names, mills, windmill (pictorial).

8/60 Clifton (township in parish of Ashbourn) SK 170451
Apt 05.02.1846; 1016a (1016); Map 1846, 4 chns; foot/b'ways, turnpike roads, toll gates, waterbodies, woods, parkland, building names, road names, weir, mill.

8/61 Clown (parish) SK 489752 [Clowne]
Apt 26.02.1839; 1859a (all); Map 1839, 6 chns, in 2 parts; waterbodies, woods, landowners.

8/62 Coal Aston (township in parish of Dronfield) SK 367798
Apt 21.07.1847; 1258a (?); Map 1850, 6 chns; waterbodies, woods, plantations, building names.

8/63 Codnor and Loscoe (township in parish of Heanor) SK 422482
Apt 25.10.1851; 7a (?); Map 1854, 3 chns; turnpike roads, waterbodies, woods, school.

8/64 Coton in the Elms (township in parish of Lullington) SK 245150
Apt 21.08.1840; 1176a (all); Map 1839, 6 chns, (including index to detached parts); waterbodies.

8/65 Crich (township in parish of Crich) SK 347547
Apt 23.07.1847; 3585a (3770); Map 1849, 6 chns, in 2 parts, ? by Richard Heyward, (including village at 3 chns); railway, foot/b'ways, canal, waterbodies, woods (named), plantations (named), rock outcrops, building names, quarries (extensive), limekiln, tramway.

8/66 Cromford (township in parish of Wirksworth) SK 296560
Apt 25.03.1840; 1320a (?); Map 1840?, 5 chns, in 2 parts, by J. Gratton, (including village at 2.5 chns); railway, foot/b'ways, canal with towpath, waterbodies, woods, parkland, hedges, building names; leaf borders surround map and also map title.

8/67 Croxall (township in parish of Croxall) SK 207134
Apt 01.03.1843; 1277a (1221); Map 1843?, 6 chns, ? by Thos Longhurst, Alrewas; waterbodies, glebe (col), school land.

8/68 Cubley (parish) SK 162382 [Cubley Common]
Apt 17.12.1839; 2254a (2254); Map 1844, 6 chns, by Robert Bromley; foot/b'ways, waterbodies, houses, woods, plantations, heath/moor, building names.

8/69 Curbar (township in parish of Bakewell) SK 260750
Apt 27.04.1847; 1117a (?); Map 1848, 6 chns; waterbodies, woods, corn mill. Apt includes cropping information.

8/70 Dalbury otherwise Dalbury Lees (parish) SK 266361
Apt 28.02.1838; 1172a (1172); Map 1839, 6 chns, by John Bromley, Derby; foot/b'ways, waterbodies, houses, woods, parkland, heath/moor, hedges, field gates, green (named).

8/71 Darley and Little Rowsley (township and lordship in parish of Darley) SK 284639 [Darley Dale]
Apt 05.03.1839; 4945a (4945); Map 1838, 6 chns; hill-drawing, foot/b'ways, waterbodies, woods, parkland, building names, paper mill, flax mills, flash dam; bridge named; leaf pattern surrounds title.

8/72 Denby (parish) SK 398469
Apt 16.05.1843; 2396a (2395); Map 1845, 5 chns; foot/b'ways, waterbodies, houses, woods, field boundary ownerships, building names, collieries, tram road, common.

8/73 St Werburgh (parish) SK 341359 [Not listed]
Apt 22.11.1843; 594a (?); Map 1844, 2 chns, 1st cl, by John Bromley, Derby; waterbodies, houses, plantations, fences, field boundary ownerships, field gates, road names, cemetery, gaol, mill dam.

8/74 Dethick and Lea with Holloway (townships in parish of Ashover) SK 332574
Apt 26.10.1848; 34a (2110); Map 1849?, 6 chns, by Joseph Gratton; waterbodies, woods, landowners; leaf design forms border.

8/75 Donisthorpe (township in parish of Measham and Gresley) SK 312136
Apt 22.11.1843; 575a (all); Map 1843, 8 chns, by Robt Bromley, Derby; foot/b'ways, canal with towpath, waterbodies, plantations, open fields, field gates; colours show to which parishes areas belong.

8/76 Doveridge (township in parish of Doveridge) SK 120342
Apt 29.11.1842; 2199a (4278); Map 1843, 6 chns, by John Bromley, Derby; foot/b'ways, turnpike roads, toll-gate, waterbodies, woods, parkland, glebe, tithe-free land, manorial boundary.

8/77 Dronfield (township in parish of Dronfield) SK 344782
Apt 29.07.1847; 329a (?); Map 1850, 6 chns, by Edmd C. Bright, Sheffield; waterbodies, woods, plantations, building names, hamlet boundary (col); built-up part generalised.

8/78 Duffield (township) SK 343438
Apt 21.01.1839; 3416a (?); Map 1840, 3 chns, 1st cl, by Robert Bromley, Derby; construction lines, railway and tunnel, foot/b'ways, waterbodies, houses, plantations, parkland, fences, field boundary ownerships, field gates, road names, road earthworks, waste.

8/79 Little Eaton (township in parish of St Alkmund) SK 360421
Apt 06.07.1850; 314a (490); Map 1850, 4 chns, by John Bromley, Derby; foot/b'ways, turnpike roads, canal, waterbodies, woods, parkland, building names, tramway, pound, paper mill, weirs, sand or stone pit.

8/80 Eaton and Sedsall (township in parish of Doveridge) SK 112372
Apt 29.11.1842; 1334a (?); Map 1843, 6 chns; foot/b'ways, waterbodies, woods (named), building names; field boundary shown with double solid lines. Apt includes cropping information.

8/81 Edale (township in parish of Castleton) SK 117858
Apt 23.06.1840; 7171a (7171); Map 1839, 4 chns; hill-drawing, foot/b'ways, waterbodies, farmyards, woods, rock outcrops, building names, tors, mill, peat pits, stone quarry, moorland; physical features named and prominent; legend explains depiction of roads, water courses and woodland.

8/82 Edensor (township in parish of Edensor) SK 254696
Apt 26.01.1841; 7a (4382); Map 1843, 6 chns, by George Unwin (tinted); waterbodies, woods, landowners.

8/83 Edlaston (parish) SK 180425
Apt 17.08.1846; 1356a (1360); Map 1848, 5 chns, by George Lam; waterbodies, plantations, parkland.

8/84 Egginton (parish) SK 268283
Apt 24.10.1848; 2290a (2289); Map 1849, 6 chns, by J.B.H. Bennett, Tutbury; railways with station, foot/b'ways, turnpike roads, canal with towpath, waterbodies, woods, parkland, marsh/bog, building names, mills, weir.

8/85 Elmton (parish) SK 510736
Apt 08.11.1849; 1172a (2970); Map 1850?, 6 chns; foot/b'ways, waterbodies, woods, plantations, building names, stone quarry.

8/86 Elvaston (parish) SK 410324
Apt 14.10.1852; 2571a (2760); Map 1852, 5 chns, by George Lamb, Derby; foot/b'ways, waterbodies, woods, plantations, parkland (in detail).

8/87 Etwall (township in parish of Etwall) SK 274319
Apt 05.05.1848; 1781a (?); Map 1849, 7.5 chns, by Henry C. Roper junr; foot/b'ways, waterbodies, woods, parkland, field gates, building names, sand or stone pit, osiers.

8/88 Eyam (township) SK 217774
Apt 20.08.1839; 2395a (2395); Map 1842?, 3 chns, in 2 parts; construction lines, hill-drawing, foot/b'ways, waterbodies, houses, woods, parkland, gardens (col), willow beds, field gates; Foolow tithing and Eyam Woodland tinted; a pair of compasses straddle the scale bar.

8/89 Eyam Woodland (township in parish of Eyam) SK 233797 [Not listed]
Apt 20.08.1839; 1051a (1051); Map 1844, 9 chns, in 2 parts, by Paul Bright, Sheffield, (including 3-chn enlargement of detail); foot/b'ways, waterbodies, woods (col), plantations (col), parkland, field gates, building names, road names, boundary points, tombs; area covered by enlargement is tinted purple on main map.

8/90 Fairfield (township in parish of Hope) SK 072744
Apt 24.08.1841; 3915a (3914); Map 1841, 6 chns, by John Taylor, Ollerset near Stockport, (tinted); foot/b'ways, turnpike roads, toll bar, waterbodies, woods, building names, mills, housing crescent, race stand; tors named; legend explains depiction of roads, water bodies and buildings.

8/91 Fenny Bentley (parish) SK 177498
Apt 02.08.1841; 1037a (1036); Map 1841, 6 chns, by Robert Bromley junr, Derby; foot/b'ways, waterbodies, houses, woods, plantations, field gates, mill.

8/92 Fernilee (township in parish of Hope) SK 022769
Apt 15.08.1848; 65a (2240); Map 1849, 10 chns (tinted); railway, woods, parkland, building names, gunpowder works, moss (named); bridge named. Blue tint indicates lands on which the rent-charge is specially apportioned.

8/93 Foolow (township in parish of Eyam) SK 193776
Apt 20.08.1839; 980a (980); Map 1842?, 3 chns, (tinted); construction lines, hill-drawing, foot/b'ways, waterbodies, houses, woods (col), field gates, industrial waste.

8/94 Froggatt (township in parish of Bakewell) SK 248771
Apt 27.04.1847; 421a (?); Map 1849?, 6 chns, woods. Apt includes cropping information.

8/95 Grindlow (township in parish of Hope) SK 185776
Apt 20.03.1849; 16a (16); Map 1850?, 5 chns, by Pickering and Smith, 14, Whitehall Place; road names. Apt omits land use.

8/96 Nether Haddon (township in parish of Bakewell) SK 232661 [Not listed]
Apt 06.05.1848; 4a (?); Map 1848, 6 chns, by Smithers and Mills, Chesterfield; waterbodies, woods, parkland, building names.

8/97 Hadfield (township in parish of Glossop) SK 023958
Apt 18.05.1849; 136a (?); Map 1852?, 3 chns; railways, plantations, building names; bridge named.

8/98 West Hallam (parish) SK 438414
Apt 27.09.1837; 1324a (1323); Map 1838, 5 chns, by Robert Bromley, Derby; foot/b'ways, canal with towpath, waterbodies, woods, plantations, parkland, gardens, field gates, quarry, well, limekilns; district is described as 'The Property of Francis Newdigate Esq.' Apt omits land use.

8/99 Harthill otherwise Hartle (township in parishes of Bakewell and Youlgreave) SK 225635 [Not listed]
Apt 29.04.1847; 15a (?); Map 1849, 6 chns, by Smithers and Mills, Chesterfield; woods, landowners; colours show occupiers. Apt omits land use.

8/100 Hassop (township in parish of Bakewell) SK 224718
Apt 27.04.1847; 93a (?); Map 1847, 6 chns, by M.F. Mills, Chesterfield (tinted); foot/b'ways, waterbodies.

8/101 Hayfield (township in parish of Glossop) SK 053877
Apt 18.05.1849; 7891a (?); Map 1851, 6 chns, by 'G.T.'; hill-drawing, foot/b'ways, waterbodies, woods, plantations, parkland, rock outcrops, building names, printworks, mills, tors, peaks, Ordnance station, shooters refectory, smithy, stone or sand pits, hamlet boundaries (col), moorland (named); physical features prominent and named.

8/102 Hazlebache (township in parish of Hope) SK 172798 [Not listed]
Apt 24.08.1847; 62a (62); Map 1848, 6 chns, by Smithers and Mills, Chesterfield; woods. Apt omits land use.

8/103 Hazlewood (township in parish of Duffield) SK 331457 [Hazelwood]
Apt 22.03.1843; 1330a (?); Map 1844?, 6 chns, in 3 parts, by G.H. Hopkins, Belper, auctioneer and surveyor, (includes Walstone at 8 chns and property at Milford at 2 chns); foot/b'ways, waterbodies, woods, orchards, hedge ownership, building names, landowners; colours show freehold property, copyhold 'fine certain' and copyhold 'fine uncertain'. Map and title borders are decorative.

8/104 Heage (township in parish of Duffield) SK 369505
Apt 19.11.1842; 2332a (?); Map 1843, 6 chns, in 8 parts, by Robert [Bromley?] (including 3-chn enlargements of settlements); railway and station, foot/b'ways, turnpike roads, toll-bar, canal, waterbodies, woods, field gates, building names, road names, iron foundry, Quakers Hospital lands (col); green tint may indicate gardens.

8/105 Heath (parish) SK 446670
Apt 04.05.1838; 1611a (1611); Map 1838, 6 chns, ? by George Unwin; waterbodies, woods; colours may indicate ownerships.

8/106 Highlow (township in parish of Hope) SK 222802 [Not listed]
Apt 14.08.1847; 422a (422); Map 1849, 6 chns; foot/b'ways, turnpike roads, toll bar, waterbodies, woods, field gates, weir.

8/107 Hognaston (township or chapelry) SK 237507
Apt 13.12.1844; 1385a (1384); Map 1846, 4 chns, by John Parkin, Idridgehay, for Robert Cresswell; foot/b'ways, waterbodies, plantations, field gates, building names.

8/108 Holbrooke (township in parish of Duffield) SK 366446 [Holbrook]
Apt 18.01.1840; 859a (?); Map 1841, 5 chns, in 2 parts, by Frederick Simpson, Derby, (Holbrooke village also at 2.5 chns); hill-drawing, railway, foot/b'ways, waterbodies, woods (named), parkland, building names, quarry, spring, coal pit, wells; compass rose is decorated with wings of birds of prey, below which two snakes are entwined, facing each other.

8/109 Hoon (township in parish of Marston upon Dove) SK 225310 [Not listed]
Apt 16.07.1846; 67a (?); Map 1847, 6 chns, by J.B.H. Bennett, Tutbury; turnpike roads, waterbodies, building names. Apt includes cropping information.

8/110 Hope (township) SK 167845
Apt 24.08.1847; 2673a (?); Map 1848?, 6 chns; foot/b'ways; map title is in style of a plaque.

8/111 Hopton (township in parish of Wirksworth) SK 261539
Apt 18.02.1841; 643a (643); Map 1846, 6 chns, by Edwin Heaton, Leek; railway, waterbodies, parkland, building names, road names, Roman road. Apt is by holding and fields are not mapped.

8/112 Hopwell (hamlet in parish of Wilne) SK 438344 [Not listed]
Apt 03.12.1846; 20a (?); Map 1850, 2.5 chns, by T. Miles, Leicester; hill-drawing, waterbodies, woods, building names, landowners.

8/113 Horsley (township in parish of Horsley) SK 381439
Apt 30.06.1843; 1255a (all); Map 1844, 6 chns, in 3 parts, by John Bromley, Derby (including Coxbench and Horsley at 3 chns); railway, foot/b'ways, waterbodies, houses, woods (named), plantations (named), building names, road names, castle earthworks.

8/114 Horsley Woodhouse (township in parish of Horsley) SK 397447
Apt 30.06.1843; 622a (all); Map 1843, 5 chns, by George Lamb, Derby.

8/115 Great Hucklow (township in parish of Hope) SK 175776
Apt 14.08.1847; 1088a (1088); Map 1849, 6 chns, by John Parkin,

Idridgehay near Wirksworth; foot/b'ways, waterbodies, woods, plantations, building names; map has note: 'This plan is made from the Township Plan dated 1811 and from sundry Estate Plans upon various scales and degrees of accuracy and is adopted by the landowners'.

8/116 Little Hucklow (township in parish of Hope) SK 161786
Apt 02.09.1847; 564a (564); Map 1848, 6 chns, by John Parkin, Idridgehay; waterbodies, woods, road names.

8/117 Hulland (township in parish of Ashbourne) SK 244467
Apt 21.05.1846; 948a (?); Map 1847, 4 chns, in 2 parts, by John Parkin, Idridgehay; foot/b'ways, waterbodies, woods, plantations, parkland, heath/moor, field gates, mill, mossland (named).

8/118 Hulland Ward and Hulland Ward Intakes (township and hamlet) SK 272459
Apt 20.11.1846; 455a (1871); Map 1847, 3 chns; foot/b'ways, houses, field gates, building names.

8/119 Ible (township in parish of Wirksworth) SK 252572
Apt 18.02.1841; 421a (421); Map 1843?, 3 chns, by Edwd Kirk; waterbodies.

8/120 Idridgehay and Alton (township in parish of Wirksworth) SK 285494
Apt 18.02.1841; 993a (993); Map 1836, 4 chns, in 2 parts, by Edmund Greatorex; foot/b'ways, waterbodies, woods, building names, mill.

8/121 Ivenbrook Grange (township in parish of Wirksworth) SK 242583 [Not listed]
Apt 21.05.1841; 12a (?); Map 1843, 9 chns, by J. Clarke, Newton; waterbodies, building names, mill.

8/122 Kedleston (parish) SK 309404
Apt 31.07.1848; 950a (950); Map 1849, 4 chns, by J. Clarkes, Higham Cliff near Alfreton; waterbodies, woods, parkland (in detail), building names, rectory, lodges, baths, boat house, common, tithe-free land named.

8/123 Kilburn or Kilbourn (township in parish of Horsley) SK 374462
Apt 30.06.1843; 917a (all); Map 1844, 6 chns. in 2 parts, by John Bromley, Derby, (village also at 3 chns); railway, foot/b'ways, turnpike roads, toll-house, waterbodies, houses, woods, plantations, marsh/bog, building names, road names.

8/124 Killamarsh (parish) SK 458807
Apt 18.10.1844; 1647a (1646); Map 1847?, 6 chns; railways, canal with towpath, waterbodies, woods, building names.

8/125 Kirkhallam (parish) SK 456403 [Kirk Hallam]
Apt 13.05.1846; 727a (all); Map 1848, 6 chns, by Robert Bromley, Derby; foot/b'ways, canal, woods, building names.

8/126 Kirk Ireton (parish) SK 267499
Apt 20.11.1846; 2291a (2290); Map 1848, 6 chns, in 2 parts, by John Parkin, Idridgehay, for Robert Cresswell, (with 3-chn enlargement of village); foot/b'ways, waterbodies, woods, plantations, parkland, building names, windmill.

8/127 Kirk Langley with Meynell Langley (parish) SK 285392
Apt 13.07.1843; 1516a (2900); Map 1847?, 5 chns, in 2 parts, by Robert Bromley, Derby, (including Meynell Langley at 6 chns); foot/b'ways, waterbodies, houses, woods, heath/moor, field gates.

8/128 Kniveton (parish) SK 208498
Apt 17.12.1847; 550a (2240); Map 1850, 6 chns, by John Shaw, Derby; foot/b'ways, waterbodies, woods, building names, quarries, mill.

8/129 Upper Langwith (parish) SK 509680
Apt 31.12.1838; 1515a (1600); Map 1839, 6 chns, by George Unwin; woods, glebe (col).

8/130 Lea Hall (hamlet in parish of Bradborne) SK 194519
Apt 13.12.1848; 450a (450); Map 1849?, 9 chns; building names, landowners, mill; fields are not mapped; table lists landowners and acreages. Apt omits land use.

8/131 Linton (township in parish of Gresley) SK 273172
Apt 21.04.1849; 22a (?); Map 1849?, 3 chns; foot/b'ways, road names.

8/132 Littleover (township in parish of Mickleover) SK 329336
Apt 07.07.1848; 928a (?); Map 1849?, 5 chns, by George Lamb, Derby; woods.

8/133 Litton (township in parish of Tideswell) SK 167750
Apt 26.04.1847; 1638a (?); Map 1847, 3 chns; hill-drawing, foot/b'ways, turnpike roads, toll bar, private and occupation roads, waterbodies, houses, woods (named), parkland, rock outcrops, fences, building names, road names, landowners, mills, marble quarry, lead mines, village cross; physical features named.

8/134 Longford (township in parish of Longford) SK 218374
Apt 31.01.1839; 2919a (?); Map 1840, 6 chns; foot/b'ways, waterbodies, woods (named), parkland, heath/moor, building names, terrace, fish pond, dam, mill, boundary stones, ice house, almshouses. Apt includes cropping information.

8/135 Great Longstone (township in parish of Bakewell) SK 199734
Apt 24.12.1846; 3005a (?); Map 1847, 6 chns, by Smithers and Mills; hill-drawing, foot/b'ways, turnpike roads, waterbodies, woods, osiers, parkland, orchards, heath/moor, field gates, building names, road names, quarries, fire house, lead mines.

8/136 Little Longstone (township in parish of Bakewell) SK 183723
Apt 24.12.1846; 1030a (?); Map 1847, 6 chns, by Smithers and Mills, litho; foot/b'ways, turnpike roads, waterbodies, woods (named), gardens, heath/moor, fences, field gates, building names, road names, Dutch barn, mill.

8/137 Lullington (township in parish of Lullington) SK 248128
Apt 20.11.1846; 1808a (2983); Map 1847, 9 chns, ? by Joshua Hanning, Rosliston; foot/b'ways; few fields and no individual buildings are shown. Apt is by holding.

8/138 Mapperley (parish) SK 429431
Apt 14.12.1842; 972a (972); Map 1843, 6 chns; foot/b'ways, waterbodies, woods.

8/139 Mappleton (parish) SK 169477 [Mapleton]
Apt 12.10.1848; 778a (778); Map 1849, 6 chns; foot/b'ways, waterbodies, houses, woods, plantations, orchards, field gates, building names.

8/140 Marston Montgomery (parish) SK 135380
Apt 21.09.1839; 2472a (2471); Map 1838, 3 chns, 1st cl, by J. Treasure, Newport, Salop; construction lines, waterbodies, woods, plantations, orchards, field gates, building names, sand or stone pits.

8/141 Marston upon Dove (township in parish of Marston upon Dove) SK 235296 [Marston on Dove]
Apt 23.06.1840; 975a (4775); Map 1840, 6 chns; foot/b'ways, turnpike roads, woods, building names, mill stream. Apt includes cropping information.

8/142 Matlock (parish) SK 302595
Apt 12.04.1847; 4514a (3960); Map 1849, 3 chns, by Joseph Gratton, Timberfield near Chesterfield; railway with stations, foot/b'ways, turnpike roads, toll bar, waterbodies, woods, building names, boat house, caverns, tower, villas, baths, temple, tor; bridges named; map title has leafy surround.

8/143 Measham (township in parish of Measham) SK 334114
Apt 31.07.1850; 43a (1490); Map 1850, 5 chns; canal, building names, road names.

8/144 Mellor (township in parish of Glossop) SJ 984882
Apt 18.05.1849; 2352a (2352); Map 1849, 3 chns, 'copied and corrected' by John Taylor, New Mills, Derbyshire, from a survey dated 1836 by J. Treasure, Uttoxeter, Staffordshire; hill-drawing, foot/b'ways, waterbodies, woods, parkland, building names, tan yard, mill, stone pit.

8/145 Mercaston (township in parish of Muggington) SK 276418
Apt 10.03.1847; 1121a (1120); Map 1848, 8 chns; turnpike roads. District is apportioned by holding and no fields are shown.

8/146 Mickleover (township in parish of Mickleover) SK 306343
Apt 23.01.1840; 2326a (?); Map 1840, 6 chns, by George Lamb, Derby; waterbodies, plantations (col), osiers.

8/147 Middleton by Wirksworth (township in parish of Wirksworth) SK 273560 [Middleton]
Apt 18.02.1841; 1006a (1006); Map 1843, 2 chns, by John Bromley, Derby; hill-drawing, railway, foot/b'ways, occupation roads, turnpike roads, toll bar, waterbodies, houses, woods (named), field gates, building names, road names, mines, engine house, coal deposits (by Dawson's symbol), paper mill, village tap, spring, Roman road.

8/148 Monyash (township in parish of Bakewell) SK 148665
Apt 01.05.1847; 2267a (?); Map 1848, 4 chns, by Richard Heyward; waterbodies, houses, plantations, building names, toll bar.

8/149 Morley (parish) SK 398410
Apt 30.11.1843; 1811a (3513); Map 1843, 7 chns; hill-drawing, foot/b'ways, waterbodies, woods, quarries.

8/150 Morton (parish) SK 410608
Apt 17.03.1843; 1252a (?); Map 6 chns, in 2 parts, surveyed in 1837 by W.H. Wilson, revised in 1843, by Joseph Gratton, Timberfield (tinted; one part litho); railway with tunnel, foot/b'ways, waterbodies, houses, woods (named), plantations (named), colliery; leafy borders surround map and title.

8/151 Mugginton (township in parish of Mugginton) SK 291441
Apt 29.05.1847; 2195a (2195); Map 1848, 6 chns, by Robert Bromley, Derby; foot/b'ways, turnpike roads, waterbodies, woods (named), plantations (by annotation), parkland (in detail), fox covert, building names, road names, limekiln, stone quarry, sand or stone pits, gothic temple, kitchen garden, well, windmill, boat house, deer house, lodge.

8/152 Newton Grange (township in parish of Ashbourne) SK 163538
Apt 05.02.1846; 44a (?); Map 1846?, 4 chns, in 2 parts, (tithable part only; includes 80-chn (1:63,360) location diagram); woods, building names, field names, landowners.

8/153 Newton Solney (parish) SK 283248
Apt 21.03.1846; 655a (1280); Map 1850, 6 chns, by J. Bromley, Derby; foot/b'ways, waterbodies, woods, marsh/bog, ferry and ford.

8/154 Norbury and Roston (parish) SK 135409
Apt 18.01.1844; 1356a (2242); Map 1844, 6 chns; foot/b'ways, turnpike roads, waterbodies, woods (named), common, building names, school, rectory, meadow (named), glebe (col), tithe-free land.

8/155 Normanton (township in parish of St Peter) SK 348328
Apt 31.07.1846; 1363a (1362); Map 1847, 6 chns, by George Lamb, Derby; railway, foot/b'ways, waterbodies, woods.

8/156 South Normanton (parish) SK 441566
Apt 09.01.1840; 1916a (1730); Map 1842?, 3 chns, 1st cl, (including small enlargements of detail); foot/b'ways, turnpike roads, waterbodies, houses, woods, plantations, parkland, rock outcrops, fences, field boundary ownerships, field gates, building names, road names, colliery, engine, quarry. Overall appearance of the map is amateurish. Some of the names are stamped.

8/157 Norton (parish) SK 359820
Apt 28.09.1842; 4330a (?); Map 1845, 12 chns, in 7 parts, by Paul Bright, Sheffield (including six 6-chn enlargements of detail); foot/b'ways, waterbodies, woods (col).

8/158 Oakthorpe (township) SK 324131
Apt 29.09.1843; 778a (all); Map 1844, 6 chns; foot/b'ways, turnpike roads, toll gate, canal with towpath, village pump.

8/159 Offcote Underwood (township in parish of Ashbourne) SK 190480 [Not listed]
Apt 21.05.1846; 1774a (?); Map 1847, 4 chns, by George Lamb, Derby; woods.

8/160 Offerton (township in parish of Hope) SK 209813 [Not listed]
Apt 26.08.1847; 659a (659); Map 1848, 6 chns, by John Parkin, Idridgehay; waterbodies, plantations, common.

8/161 Osmaston (parish) SK 196438
Apt 29.07.1837; 1254a (1254); Map 1838, 6 chns, by J.B.H. Bennett, Tutbury; foot/b'ways, turnpike roads, waterbodies, woods, field gates, building names, road names, boat house, glebe (col); compass rose is combined with scale bar. Apt includes cropping information.

8/162 Osmaston next Derby (parish) SK 368333 [Osmaston]
Apt 12.06.1849; 71a (?); Map 1850, 7.5 chns, by John Parkin, Idridgehay, Wirksworth; foot/b'ways, turnpike roads, toll gate, canal with towpath, road names, landowners, osiers (col).

8/163 Nether Padley (township in parish of Hope) SK 251783
Apt 24.08.1841; 296a (296); Map 1842, 9 chns; turnpike roads, woods, road names, landowners, well; bridge named.

8/164 Parwich (parish) SK 182560
Apt 01.03.1843; 3248a (3247); Map 1844, 6 chns, in 2 parts, by John Bromley, Derby (village also at 3 chns); hill-drawing, railway, foot/b'ways, waterbodies, houses, woods, plantations, building names, Roman station.

8/165 Pentrich (township in parish of Pentrich) SK 391526
Apt 27.07.1843; 1375a (?); Map 1848, 5 chns, by John Bromley, Derby; foot/b'ways, turnpike roads, toll bar, waterbodies, woods, plantations, building names, mill, reservoir.

8/166 St Peters and Litchurch (township in parish of St Peters) SK 362350 [Not listed]
Apt 06.05.1846; 826a (?); Map 1847, 4 chns, in 2 parts, by Robert Bromley, Derby; railways with station, foot/b'ways, canal with towpath, waterbodies, woods, plantations, parkland, road names, osiers; built-up parts generalised.

8/167 Pilsley (township in parish of Edensor) SK 237709
Apt 19.04.1841; 96a (447); Map 1847, 6 chns, by George Unwin; hill-drawing, foot/b'ways, waterbodies, woods.

8/168 Pilsley (township in parish of Northwingfield) SK 419627
Apt 21.05.1841; 1554a (1554); Map surveyed in 1828 and revised in 1841, 6 chns, by W.H. Wilson, Pilsley; foot/b'ways, waterbodies, woods (named), plantations, sand or stone pit.

8/169 Pinxton (parish) SK 454553
Apt 31.12.1838; 1242a (?); Map 1838, 3 chns, by Geo. Sanderson, Mansfield, Notts; construction lines, railway, foot/b'ways, canal, waterbodies, parkland, field boundary ownerships, building names, road names, field names, old engine, wharves, collieries, pits, field acreages, tithe-free land; gardens, orchards, plantations and stackyards are sometimes indicated by annotation.

8/170 Pleasley (parish) SK 513661
Apt 13.05.1843; 3184a (3750); Map 1841, 6 chns, in 4 parts, by John Bromley, Derby (including index); foot/b'ways, waterbodies, woods (named), building names.

8/171 Radbourne (parish) SK 287362
Apt 23.06.1846; 2034a (2034); Map 1848, 7.5 chns, by Robert Bromley, Derby; waterbodies. District is apportioned by holding and fields are not shown.

8/172 Ravensdale Park (township in parish of Muggington) SK 277439 [Not listed]
Apt 26.11.1846; 629a (629); Map 1847, 4 chns, by J. Clarke, Higham Cliff near Alfreton; houses, woods (named), building names.

8/173 Ripley (township in parish of Pentrich) SK 397500
Apt 02.08.1843; 1329a (?); Map 1847, 6 chns, by John Bromley, Derby; railway, foot/b'ways, canal with towpath, waterbodies, houses, woods.

8/174 Risley (township in parishes of Wilne and Sandiacre) SK 457364
Apt 19.11.1839; 1148a (?); Map 1838, 3 chns, by Thomas A. Campbell, Nottingham; construction lines, foot/b'ways, turnpike roads, toll bar, waterbodies, houses, woods, hedge ownership, field gates, building names, schools; colour bands may indicate parish boundaries. Apt omits land use.

8/175 Rodsley (township in parish of Longford) SK 202401
Apt 23.01.1839; 809a (?); Map 1840, 6 chns; foot/b'ways, waterbodies, woods (named), plantations (named), building names, Wesleyan chapel. Apt has cropping information.

8/176 Rostliston (parish) SK 249163 [Rosliston]
Apt 15.04.1840; 1197a (1197); Map 1839, 6 chns, foot/b'ways, waterbodies, woods, fences, building names; map notes that Coton Park Farm is copied from an old plan.

8/177 Rowland (township in parish of Bakewell) SK 213720
Apt 27.04.1847; 27a (?); Map 1847, 6 chns, by M.F. Mills, Chesterfield, (tinted); foot/b'ways, waterbodies. Apt omits land use.

8/178 Great Rowsley (township in parish of Bakewell) SK 252658 [Rowsley]
Apt 30.12.1846; 681a (?); Map 1848, 6 chns, in 2 parts; woods, plantations, mill.

8/179 Sandiacre (township in parish of Sandiacre) SK 473365
Apt 30.11.1844; 39a (1420); Map 1848, 9 chns, by John Bromley, Derby; foot/b'ways, canal with towpath, woods, field gates, road names, toll gate, mill.

8/180 Sawley (township in parish of Sawley) SK 471318
Apt 10.07.1846; 4a (1915); Map 1849, 6 chns, by George Lamb, Derby; canal.

8/181 Scarcliffe (parish) SK 489688
Apt 12.10.1848; 1438a (3674); Map 1849?, 6 chns; foot/b'ways, waterbodies, woods (col, named); meaning of colours is uncertain.

8/182 Scropton (parish) SK 195315
Apt 02.09.1846; 1106a (3340); Map 1847, 6 chns; foot/b'ways, turnpike roads, waterbodies, woods, fences, building names, road names, landowners, gravel pits, site of Foston Hall ('burnt down').

8/183 Shardlaw and Great or Far Wilne (township in parish of Aston) SK 443307
Apt 31.10.1849; 251a (1580); Map 1850, 5 chns, by George Lamb, Derby; canal with towpath, weir, waterbodies, woods, plantations, osiers.

8/184 Sheldon (township in parish of Bakewell) SK 171692
Apt 19.10.1847; 1062a (?); Map 1847, 6 chns, by B. Grove, Birmingham; turnpike roads, toll bar, waterbodies, rock outcrops, building names, mine, quarry.

8/185 Shirland (parish) SK 401584
Apt 18.12.1839; 1441a (?); Map 1843?, 5 chns, by Joseph Gratton, Timberfield, litho; railway, waterbodies, woods, plantations, building names, mill, tithe-free land; map title has leafy surround.

8/186 Shirley (township in parish of Shirley) SK 216417
Apt 27.02.1837; 1599a (?); Map 1838, 6 chns; foot/b'ways, waterbodies, woods (named), parkland, heath/moor, building names, mill, fish ponds; colours may indicate tithing practice. Apt includes cropping information.

8/187 Shottle and Postern (township in parish of Duffield) SK 312486
Apt 13.05.1843; 3741a (3741); Map 1848, 6 chns, by John Bromley, Derby; foot/b'ways, houses, woods (named), plantations, building names, sand or stone pits, mineral spring. Scrolls decorate border corners.

8/188 Sinfin Moor (extra-parochial place) SK 357308
Apt 12.06.1849; 52a (?); Map 1850, 2.5 chns, by John Shaw, Derby; woods, landowners, moorland (named).

8/189 Smalley (township in parish of Morley) SK 412444
Apt 19.12.1840; 1703a (all); Map 1844?, 6 chns, by George Lamb, Derby; foot/b'ways, waterbodies, woods.

8/190 Smerill (township in parish of Youlgreave) SK 194608 [Not listed]
Apt 09.01.1840; 428a (?); Map 1843, 6 chns. Apt omits land use.

8/191 Somershall Herbert otherwise Church Somershall (parish) SK 136349 [Somersal Herbert]
Apt 26.11.1842; 698a (all); Map 1843, 6 chns, by J.B.H. Bennett, Tutbury; foot/b'ways, turnpike roads, waterbodies, woods, building names, road names, mill, mill dam, public carriage road.

8/192 Stanley (township in parish of Spondon) SK 418405
Apt 28.11.1846; 294a (1470); Map 1847?, 5 chns, by Henry C. Roper, Etwall; foot/b'ways, waterbodies, woods, field gates.

8/193 Stanton Juxta Dale Abbey (parish) SK 466385 [Stanton-by-Dale]
Apt 19.04.1844; 1412a (1412); Map 1844, 6 chns; canal with towpath, waterbodies, woods, plantations.

8/194 Staveley (parish) SK 428753
Apt 26.02.1839; 6682a (6682); Map 1841, 6 chns, by George Unwin; railway, canal with towpath, waterbodies, woods (col), demesne boundary.

8/195 Stoke (township in parish of Hope) SK 237765 [Not listed]
Apt 15.08.1848; 536a (536); Map 1850, 6.5 chns (tinted); foot/b'ways, waterbodies, woods, building names.

8/196 Stoney Middleton (township in parish of Hathersage) SK 216750
Apt 01.05.1847; 1193a (?); Map 1847, 3 chns; hill-drawing, foot/b'ways, turnpike roads, waterbodies, houses, parkland, heath/moor, fences, building names, road names, cupolas, limekilns, mine, sand or stone pits, lead mine, mill, mill dam.

8/197 Stretton (township in parish of North Wingfield) SK 382613
Apt 21.05.1841; 1562a (1562); Map 1843?, 6 chns, by Joseph Gratton, litho; railway and station, foot/b'ways, waterbodies, woods, plantations, parkland, building names, mill; leafy borders surround map and title.

8/198 Stretton en le Field (township in parish of Stretton en le Field) SK 304110
Apt 13.03.1844; 1009a (all); Map 1838, 3.75 chns; foot/b'ways, turnpike roads, toll gate, waterbodies, field gates.

8/199 Sturston (township in parish of Ashbourne) SK 192463 [Not listed]
Apt 21.05.1846; 932a (?); Map compiled from old maps adopted by the landowners, 1848, 4 chns, by John Bromley; foot/b'ways, waterbodies, woods, building names, mill; built-up parts generalised.

8/200 Sudbury (parish) SK 161336
Apt 30.04.1845; 3603a (3603); Map 1845, 9 chns; foot/b'ways, turnpike roads, waterbodies, woods, parkland (in detail), building names, road names, deer cote, buck pool, caves, sand or stone pit, drain, rectory, public carriage road, rectorial glebe (col); bridge named.

8/201 Sutton cum Duckmanton (parish) SK 441704
Apt 27.02.1837; 4297a (4296); Map 1837, 6 chns, by George Lamb, Derby; foot/b'ways, waterbodies, woods (col), plantations, parkland, road names; legend explains colouring of school and glebe lands, but not what the colour bands denote; the district is described as 'the property of Richard Arkwright Esqre'. Apt omits land use.

8/202 Sutton on the Hill (township in parish of Sutton on the Hill) SK 240335
Apt 15.02.1839; 856a (3233); Map 1839, 6 chns, by J.B.H. Bennett, Tutbury (tithable parts only); foot/b'ways, waterbodies, woods, building names, mill dam, mill. Apt includes cropping information.

8/203 Swadlincote (township in parish of Gresley) SK 299202
Apt 14.08.1850; 8a (?); Map 1850, 4 chns, (tithable parts only); building names, common.

8/204 Swarkeston (parish) SK 376289 [Swarkeston]
Apt 31.07.1846; 37a (943); Map 1849, 6 chns, by Henry C. Roper junr,

Uttoxeter; foot/b'ways, canal with towpath, waterbodies, woods, field gates; bridge named.

8/205 Taddington and Priestcliffe (township in parish of Bakewell) SK 144711
Apt 01.05.1847; 2969a (?); Map 1847, 6 chns, litho; foot/b'ways, turnpike roads, toll bar, waterbodies, fences, building names; scale-bar is ruler-like; border has geometrical corners.

8/206 Tansley (township in parish of Crich) SK 325604
Apt 16.09.1845; 1146a (1150); Map 1846, 4 chns, by Jno. Wheatcroft?; foot/b'ways, waterbodies, woods, parkland.

8/207 Thornhill (township in parish of Hope) SK 196836
Apt 24.08.1847; 590a (589); Map 1848, 4 chns; foot/b'ways, woods, field gates, weir; bridges named.

8/208 Thorpe (parish) SK 158509
Apt 30.12.1848; 1777a (1400); Map 1850, 6 chns, by John Parkin, Idridgehay, near Wirksworth; foot/b'ways, waterbodies, woods, plantations, building names, mills.

8/209 Thurvaston, Oslaston and Cropper (township in parish of Sutton on the Hill) SK 244366
Apt 27.05.1840; 1688a (?); Map 1840, 6 chns, by Dickinson Ward, Tutbury; hill-drawing, foot/b'ways, waterbodies, woods, building names, road names, boundary marks, sand or stone pits.

8/210 Tibshelf (parish) SK 438607
Apt 29.07.1844; 2380a (2280); Map 1845, 3 chns, 1st cl; foot/b'ways, waterbodies, houses, woods, orchards, building names, windmill (pictorial), quarry.

8/211 Ticknall (parish) SK 351236
Apt 29.04.1843; 1867a (1867); Map 1843, 6 chns, in 2 parts, by J. Topliss, Ticknall, (including enlargement of detail); foot/b'ways, waterbodies, osiers, woods, parkland, building names, tram road, parsonage, old church ruins, lime works.

8/212 Tideswell (township in parish of Tideswell) SK 150765
Apt 26.05.1841; 3036a (?); Map 1844, 7.5 chns, in 2 parts, by John Parkin, (including Tideswell village at 2.5 chns); woods, plantations, road names.

8/213 Tissington (parish) SK 174522
Apt 05.03.1842; 2316a (2316); Map 1844, 6 chns, in 2 parts, by John Parkin, (village at 3 chns); foot/b'ways, waterbodies, woods, plantations, parkland, field gates, building names, cotton mill.

8/214 Totley (township in parish of Dronfield) SK 309797
Apt 31.07.1839; 581a (?); Map 1840, 6 chns, in 3 parts, by Geo. Sanderson, Mansfield, Notts (includes 3 chn enlargements of village); foot/b'ways, waterbodies, field gates.

8/215 Trusley (parish) SK 256363
Apt 28.11.1838; 1078a (1078); Map 1839, 7 chns; waterbodies, woods, building names, tithe-free land (col, numbered in red), glebe (col). Apt omits land use.

8/216 Tupton (township in parish of North Wingfield) SK 398657
Apt 21.05.1841; 724a (724); Map 1843?, 6 chns, by Joseph Gratton; railway and station, waterbodies, woods, parkland, building names, colliery.

8/217 Turnditch (township in parish of Duffield) SK 297463
Apt 17.11.1842; 1007a (?); Map 1844, 6 chns, in 6 parts, by John Bromley, Derby, (including three 6-chn and one 3-chn enlargements of detail, and 36-chn index); hill-drawing, foot/b'ways, waterbodies, houses, woods, plantations, field gates, building names, sand or stone pits, quarries.

8/218 Twyford and Stenson (township in parish of Barrow upon Trent) SK 325297
Apt 19.12.1848; 1702a (1800); Map 1849, 5 chns; railway, foot/b'ways, canal, waterbodies, woods, landowners; colour bands show property ownership.

8/219 Unstone (township in parish of Dronfield) SK 373776
Apt 12.08.1847; 290a (?); Map 1850, 6 chns; foot/b'ways, turnpike roads, waterbodies, woods, plantations, road names.

8/220 Walton upon Trent (parish) SK 223174 [Walton-on-Trent]
Apt 10.08.1839; 2310a (all); Map 1841, 6 chns; foot/b'ways, turnpike roads, toll gate, waterbodies, woods (named), osiers, parkland, building names, road names, weir, ford, rectory; bridge named; compass rose is combined with scale bar. Apt includes cropping information.

8/221 Wardlow (township in parishes of Bakewell and Hope) SK 180747
Apt 23.02.1847; 629a (629); Map 1848, 6 chns; waterbodies, houses, woods.

8/222 Wensley and Snitterton (township in parish of Darley) SK 266610
Apt 26.04.1847; 2005a (2005); Map 1849, 6 chns, in 2 parts, by John Parkin, Idridgehay near Wirksworth, (including 3-chn enlargement of village); foot/b'ways, waterbodies, woods, plantations, building names.

8/223 Wessington (township in parish of Crich) SK 374573
Apt 30.09.1845; 958a (958); Map 1848?, 6 chns, by Joseph Gratton; railway, waterbodies, woods, building names, mill, green (named); leafy borders surround map and title. Apt includes cropping information.

8/224 Weston Underwood (township in parish of Mugginton) SK 300428
Apt 26.11.1846; 1382a (1382); Map 1847, 6 chns, in 2 parts, by J. Clarke, Higham Cliff near Alfreton, (including 3-chn enlargement of village); waterbodies, houses, woods, plantations, building names.

8/225 Wheston (township in parish of Tideswell) SK 132765
Apt 17.03.1841; 1370a (?); Map 1841?, (dated 1819), 7.5 chns, in 2 parts; turnpike roads, waterbodies, woods, road names, landowners, mineral rakes, field acreages.

8/226 Whitfield (township in parish of Glossop) SK 042932 [Not listed]
Apt 18.05.1849; 418a (?); Map 1852?, 3 chns; foot/b'ways, turnpike roads, waterbodies, woods, building names, mill; built-up parts generalised.

8/227 Whitwell (parish) SK 528770
Apt 29.09.1838; 5082a (4880); Map 1839, 6 chns, by George Unwin; waterbodies, woods (col). Meaning of colours is uncertain.

8/228 Wilne Church and Draycott (liberty in parish of Wilne) SK 448317
Apt 10.07.1846; 92a (?); Map 1848?, 5 chns, by George Lamb, Derby; foot/b'ways, woods, landowners, weir, mill dam.

8/229 Wilsthorpe (hamlet in parish of Sawley) SK 475338
Apt 10.07.1846; 602a (all); Map 1847, 5 chns, by George Lamb, Derby; foot/b'ways, field gates.

8/230 Windley (township in parish of Duffield) SK 318441
Apt 12.11.1840; 1149a (?); Map 1841, 6.25 chns, by Frederick Simpson, Derby; foot/b'ways, waterbodies, woods, parkland, building names, farm boundaries.

8/231 Wingerworth (parochial chapelry) SK 373672
Apt 29.10.1842; 2906a (2906); Map 1843, 6 chns, by Joseph Gratton, Timberfield; hill-drawing, railway, foot/b'ways, waterbodies, woods (named), plantations (named), parkland (in detail), building names, mill, park gates, fish house, saw mills, malthouse; leafy borders surround map and title.

8/232 North Wingfield (township) SK 417656
Apt 18.11.1842; 1425a (1425); Map 1843?, 6 chns, by Joseph Gratton, litho; railway, foot/b'ways, waterbodies, woods, building names; leafy borders surround map and title.

8/233 South Wingfield (parish) SK 377552
Apt 16.12.1843; 1637a (3308); Map 1845, 6 chns, by Robert Bromley, Derby; hill-drawing, railway with station and embankments, foot/b'ways, waterbodies, woods, plantations, park (named), gardens, fences, field gates, building names, road names, wire mill, coal pit, moorland (named), modus lands (col); compass rose is combined with scale bar.

8/234 Winshill (township in parish of Burton upon Trent) SK 268233
Apt 07.12.1847; 18a (1150); Map 1848, 3 chns, by J.B.H. Bennett, Tutbury; building names, landowners.

8/235 Wirksworth (township in parish of Wirksworth) SK 289539
Apt 31.03.1848; 2960a (2960); Map 1849, 4 chns; railway, foot/b'ways, waterbodies, woods, plantations, parkland, building names, windmill, tape mill, mill.

8/236 Woodlands (township in parish of Hope) SK 131912 [Not listed]
Apt 26.08.1847; 20259a (20259); Map 1849?, 12 chns; hill-drawing, foot/b'ways, woods (col), rock outcrops, building names, boundary points, tower; physical features named.

8/237 Woodthorpe (township in parish of North Wingfield) SK 383649 [Not listed]
Apt 21.05.1841; 1047a (1047); Map 1843?, 6 chns, by Joseph Gratton; railway, foot/b'ways, waterbodies, woods, plantations, orchards, building names, collieries, mill; leafy borders surround map and title.

8/238 Wormhill (township in parish of Tideswell) SK 113754
Apt 29.07.1847; 4683a (?); Map 1849, 6 chns; hill-drawing, foot/b'ways, waterbodies, woods, plantations, parkland, building names; physical features named. Apt includes cropping information.

8/239 Yeaveley (township in parish of Shirley) SK 185407
Apt 14.08.1839; 1006a (?); Map 1840, 6 chns; foot/b'ways, woods, building names, road names. Apt includes cropping information.

8/240 Yieldersley (township in parish of Ashbourne) SK 215445 [Not listed]
Apt 08.12.1840; 1468a (?); Map 1841, 6 chns; foot/b'ways, waterbodies, woods, building names, road names, spring. Apt includes cropping information.

Devon

PRO IR29 and IR30 9/1-466

478 tithe districts: 1,659,423 acres
466 tithe commutations: 1,536,422 acres
252 voluntary tithe agreements, 214 compulsory tithe awards

Tithe and tithe commutation

Although only the third largest historical county, Devon contained the largest extent of tithable land of any county in 1836. Some 97 per cent of its tithe districts and about 92 per cent of its land area remained subject to payment of tithes and 278 districts were wholly tithable (Fig. 21). The main causes of tithe exemption in Devon were modus payments in lieu of tithes, mergers of tithes in the land (usually where the landowner and tithe owner were one and the same), and exemption by prescription. The assistant tithe commissioners and local tithe agents who officiated in Devon are listed in Table 9.1 and the valuers of the county's tithe rent-charge in Table 9.2.

No fewer than eighty (17 per cent) of Devon tithe apportionments are lithographed, a proportion only exceeded in the adjoining county of Cornwall. As in Cornwall the practice of intermittently ploughing up long ley grassland results in entries such as 'arable occasionally', 'arable and pasture', 'arable and furze' and 'pasture and furze' in the state of cultivation columns of Devon's tithe apportionments.

Tithe maps

Exactly one-fifth of Devon's 466 tithe maps are sealed as first class (Table 9.3). Construction lines appear on the very high proportion of 37 per cent of second-class maps and it is likely that at least some of these aspired to first-class status. Scales vary from one inch to one chain to one inch to nine chains but 83 per cent of maps are in the recommended scale range of one inch to three to four chains. Four second-class maps are lithographed and the Public Record Office collection contains both manuscript and lithographed versions of the Widworthy map. Very few maps contain a record of arable and grass, but 33 per cent show orchards, the highest proportion in any county, and 46 per cent depict woodland.

A very large number of Devonshire tithe maps in the Public Record Office collection can be attributed to a particular map-maker. The most prolific was the partnership of George Braund and Henry Hearn of Exeter, who together or separately produced twenty-four maps, the partnership of Luckraft, Warren, Reaney and Warren of Crediton, who together or separately made twenty-one maps, the Woodmass partnership of Ivybridge who were responsible for nineteen maps, and the Badcocks of Launceston, who produced sixteen maps, characterised by stamped lettering. Six maps were made by men resident well outside the county: four by Robert Park of London, and one each by Alexander Doull (Chatham, Kent), and B. H. Galland (Suffolk). Other map-makers tended to work within their home localities, for example, Thomas Lock of Instow, Charles Cooper of Bideford and George Northcote of Barnstaple.

Unusual information on Devon tithe maps includes details of the ownership of coastal royalties at Morthoe and drainage and sewerage at Stoke Damerel. The nature of Devon's terrain occasioned perjorative remarks from a number of surveyors. At Holcombe Burnell the surveyor was so exasperated by the 'Hill and Dale' and its effect on the accuracy of his measurements that he remarked on this on the map. At Lynton the map made by Suffolk-based surveyor, B. H. Galland, carries such comments as 'very steep Ang[le] 60 d[egree]s' and 'steep rocky pasture'.

There are rather more decorative embellishments than usual on Devon tithe maps. There are a number of ornamental cartouches, drawing instruments appear on eleven maps, four maps contain pictorial allegories of political harmony, and two maps show ships in the sea. Several others have decorative north pointers and map titles; at Honeychurch a snake is woven into the map title.

Table 9.1. *Agreements and awards for commutation of tithes in Devon*

Assistant commissioner/ local tithe agent	*Number of agreements**	*Number of awards*
George Louis	3	191
James Jerwood	122	1
Frederick Leigh	73	0
Charles Pym	11	4
Robert Page	9	0
Tithe Commissioners	0	9
Aneurin Owen	2	5
George Wingrove Cooke	0	3
John Coldridge	2	0

*Computed from the number of extant reports on tithe agreements in the tithe files [PRO IR 18].

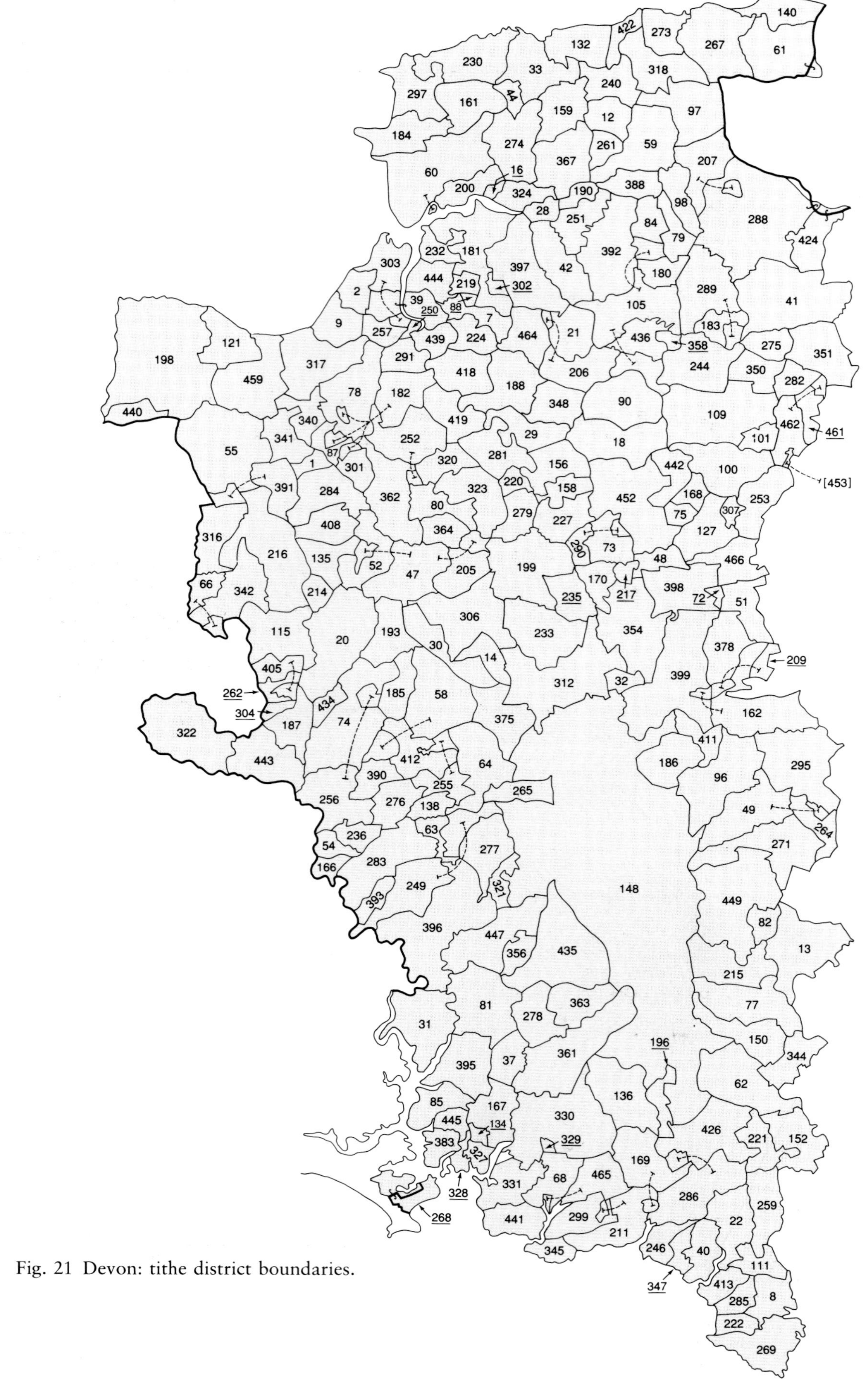

Fig. 21 Devon: tithe district boundaries.

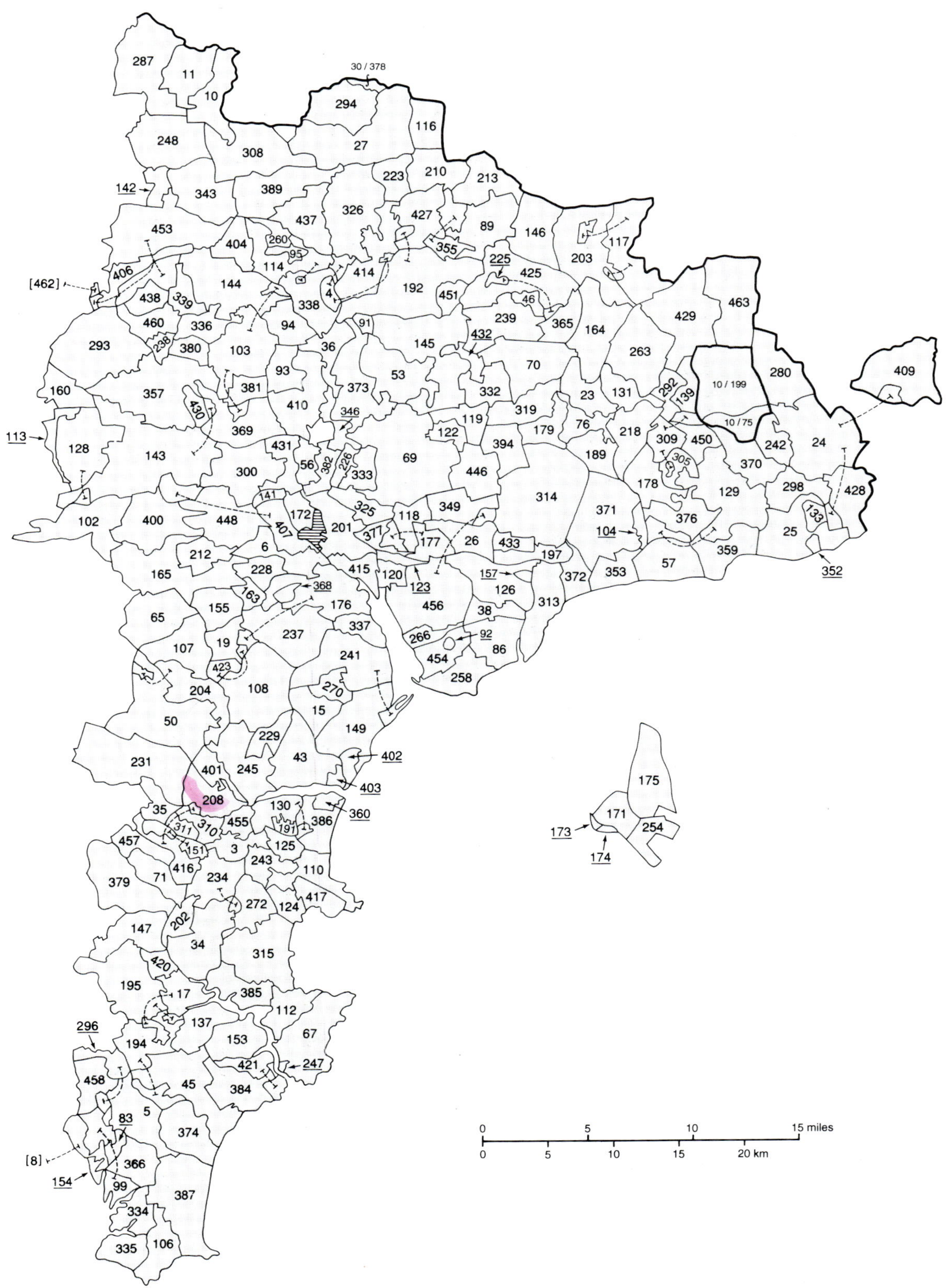
0 5 10 15 miles
0 5 10 15 20 km

Table 9.2. *Tithe valuers and tithe map-makers in Devon*

Name and address (in Devon unless indicated)	*Number of districts*	*Acreage*
Tithe valuers		
George Cooper, Alverdiscott	25	70,760
Henry and Robert Badcock, Launceston, Cornwall	23	85,930
Jon Hooper, Chagford	21	42,673
Joseph Risdon, Speccott	20	69,776
Charles John Cutcliffe, South Molton	15	80,213
John Mallet, Great Torrington	14	49,080
Thomas Lock, Instow	14	37,608
Peter Gillard, Stokeham	13	48,967
Henry Ellis, Sampford Peverell	13	39,517
John Coldridge, Exeter	13	21,069
Others[97]	295	1,040,829
Attributed tithe map-makers		
George Braund and Henry Hearn, Exeter	24	75,617
Luckraft, Warren, Reaney and Warren, Crediton	21	81,921
Woodmass and others, Ivybridge	19	68,176
Henry and Robert Badcock, Launceston, Cornwall	16	60,442
Henry Crispin, Chulmleigh / South Molton	13	56,132
William Richards, Tiverton	13	46,526
John Grant, Ugborough	13	36,562
Hugh Ballment, Barnstaple	13	31,605
Others [100]	334	847,804

Table 9.3. *The tithe maps of Devon: scales and classes*

Scale in chains/inch	*All maps*		*First Class*		*Second Class*	
	Number	*Acreage*	*Number*	*Acreage*	*Number*	*Acreage*
>3	4	2,999	0	0	4	2,999
3	279	933,377	66	264,128	213	669,249
4	107	341,774	27	106,898	80	234,876
4.75, 5.5	2	2,232	0	0	2	2,232
6	61	206,225	0	0	61	206,225
<6	13	49,815	0	0	13	49,815
TOTAL	466	1,536,422	93	371,026	373	1,165,396

Table 9.4. *The tithe maps of Devon: dates*

	<1837	*1837*	*1838*	*1839*	*1840*	*1841*	*1842*	*1843*	*1844*	*1845*	*1846*	*1847*	*1848*	*>1848*
All maps	1	3	20	78	106	71	74	59	27	11	10	2	2	1
1st class	0	0	3	17	22	9	3	17	7	2	3	0	0	1
2nd class*	1	3	17	61	84	62	71	42	20	9	7	2	2	0

*One second-class tithe map of Devon in the Public Record Office collection is undated.

Devonshire

9/1 Abbotts Bickington (parish) SS 378134 [Abbots Bickington]
Apt 04.11.1839; 1079a (all); Map 1839, 3 chns, by Robert Heard, Dulverton, Somerset; construction lines, foot/b'way, houses, woods, orchards.

9/2 Abbotsham (parish) SS 418272
Apt 28.11.1840; 1758a (1758); Map 1840?, 3 chns; construction lines.

9/3 Abbotskerswell (parish) SX 859685
Apt 12.01.1839; 1461a (all); Map 1839, 4 chns, 1st cl, in 2 parts, by H. Symons, Fancy, Plymouth, (including 2-chn enlargement of detail); construction lines, waterbodies, building names; bridge named.

9/4 All Fours (district in parish of Tiverton) SS 946108 [Not listed]
Apt 30.09.1841; 1155a (?); Map 1842, 6 chns, by William Richards junr; weir, quarry, district boundaries (col).

9/5 East Allington (parish) SX 778481
Apt 28.09.1839; 3647a (3646); Map 1840, 3 chns, by William Jarvis, Kingsbridge; construction lines, foot/b'way, farmyards, parkland, hedges, fences, field gates.

9/6 Alphington (parish) SX 899911
Apt 10.11.1841; 2472a (all); Map 1842?, 4 chns, by Robert Dymond; foot/b'way, canal and towpath, waterbodies, houses, farmyards, fences, weir, quarries, milestones.

9/7 Alverdiscott (except Bulworthy) (parish) SS 515250
Apt 12.11.1840; 2023a (2273); Map 1839, 3 chns, 'partially survey'd and copied' by Chas Cooper, Alverdiscott, Bideford, Devon; waterbodies, farmyards, woods, plantations, parkland, orchards.

9/8 West Alvington (parish) SX 723428
Apt 11.10.1839; 4021a (4110); Map 1841, 3 chns, by W. Jarvis; construction lines, foot/b'way, parkland, fences, field gates, glebe named.

9/9 Alvington (parish) SS 404246 [Alwington]
Apt 28.09.1837; 2655a (2655); Map 1838, 3 chns, by Wm Collard Cox, Williton, Somerset; waterbodies, hedge ownership.

9/10 East Anstey (parish) SS 864265
Apt 16.09.1842; 3245a (all); Map 1844?, 3 chns, by H. Crispin Junr, South Molton; construction lines, waterbodies.

9/11 West Anstey (parish) SS 846280
Apt 25.11.1839; 3009a (3008); Map 1839, 4 chns, by H. and R.L. Badcock, Launceston; farmyards, building names, mill; valley named; names and numbers are stamped.

9/12 Arlington (parish) SS 624406
Apt 06.05.1842; 2536a (all); Map 1844, 3 chns, by Thos Lock Jr, Instow; waterbodies, woods, plantations, parkland (in detail), orchards, fences.

9/13 Ashburton (parish) SX 754716
Apt 09.05.1840; 6937a (6936); Map 1840, [3 chns], by Wm Norris, Exeter; waterbodies, woods (by name), houses, building names, road names, limekilns, mill, tin mines.

9/14 Ashbury (parish) SX 514962
Apt 10.03.1842; 1701a (all); Map 1842, 3 chns, by Geo. Gould junr, Okehampton; construction lines, waterbodies, houses, farmyards, woods, plantations, parkland (in detail), ornamental gardens (in detail), fences, field gates, building names, glebe, farm names; colour bands may show holdings.

9/15 Ashcombe (parish) SX 922789
Apt 11.08.1840; 1933a (all); Map 1840, 3 chns, by Robert Dymond, Exeter; hill-drawing, waterbodies, houses, farmyards, woods, plantations, arable (col), grassland (col), orchards, gardens, heath/moor, fences, field gates, barrow, milestone, ancient fortification, tower, sand or stone pits, limekilns, stucco sand pit, glebe; hill-drawings suggest river incision.

9/16 Ashford (parish) SS 533349
Apt 14.02.1842; 360a (all); Map 1842, 3 chns, by G. Braund and H. Hearn; construction lines.

9/17 Ashprington (parish) SX 814573
Apt 30.11.1842; 2646a (all); Map 1843, 3 chns, 1st cl, by Woodmass and Co; construction lines, foot/b'way, waterbodies, houses, field boundary ownerships, building names; legend explains depiction of buildings, boundaries and waterbodies; ruler, pair of compasses and quill pen surround map scale.

9/18 Ashreigney otherwise Ringsash (parish) SS 622139
Apt 12.07.1838; 5664a (all); Map 1841?, 6 chns; waterbodies, building names, mills.

9/19 Ashton (parish) SX 855842 [Higher and Lower Ashton]
Apt 17.05.1839; 1710a (1709); Map 1840, 3 chns, by John Widdicombe, Ugborough; foot/b'way, waterbodies, woods, plantations, orchards, heath/moor, fences, field gates, building names, limekiln, watermill; bridge named; some field boundaries are shown as double lines; scrolls carry scale and mapmaker's name, and clouds (?) surround map title.

9/20 Ashwater (parish) SX 397982
Apt 02.08.1842; 8588a (all); Map 1843, 4 chns, 1st cl, by H. and R.L. Badcock, Launceston; construction lines, waterbodies, farmyards, building names, glebe; tithe area numbers are stamped.

9/21 Atherington (parish) SS 591232
Apt 18.03.1839; 3326a (all); Map 1840?, 3 chns, by George Northcote, Barnstaple; construction lines, waterbodies, houses, woods (col), fences, boundary stone.

9/22 Aveton Gifford (parish) SX 691485
Apt 30.06.1840; 3953a (all); Map 1841, 3 chns, by Humphrey and Garland; foot/b'way, waterbodies, houses, farmyards, woods, plantations, coppices (grey stipple), orchards, field gates, avenue of trees; colour bands may show property ownerships; zig-zag lines indicate brake or waste in arable fields.

9/23 Awliscombe (parish) ST 130026
Apt 02.09.1840; 2569a (2569); Map 1840, 3 chns, by Summers and Slater, Ilminster; fences, building names.

9/24 Axminster (parish) SY 299985
Apt 27.09.1838; 7637a (7637); Map 1842?, 6 chns; foot/b'way, turnpike roads, waterbodies, woods, plantations, parkland, orchards, heath/moor, fences, building names, mill; bridge named; tithe-free land is not mapped in detail; public buildings are coloured.

9/25 Axmouth (parish) SY 285915
Apt 02.04.1842; 4534a (4723); Map 1846?, 4 chns, 1st cl; hill-drawing, waterbodies, woods, plantations, orchards, heath/moor, hedges, building names, embankment, pier head, low and high water marks, flag staff, cliffs, sand or stone pits, quarry, chasm.

9/26 Aylesbeare (parish) SY 039910
Apt 10.08.1841; 2948a (2948); Map 1842, 3 chns, by John Doherty; waterbodies, houses, woods, plantations, orchards, heath/moor, fences, building names, road names, mill, factory, common.

9/27 Bampton (parish) SS 972220
Apt 12.06.1843; 7785a (7785); Map 1842, 6 chns, in 2 parts, by E. Browne, (including 3-chn enlargement of Bampton town); waterbodies, houses, farmyards, building names, road names; bridge named.

9/28 Barnstaple (parish) SS 569334
Apt 21.12.1841; 1103a (1102); Map 1844?, 3 chns, by R.D. Gould; construction lines, waterbodies, houses, woods, plantations, orchards, tumulus; bridge named; built-up part generalised.

9/29 Beaford (parish) SS 553151
Apt 27.07.1839; 3203a (all); Map 1840, 3 chns, by George Arnold junr; waterbodies, houses, woods, orchards, heath/moor, building names, mills, weir.

9/30 Beaworthy (parish) SX 477967
Apt 31.12.1841; 3806a (all); Map 1842, 3 chns, by William Gould, Okehampton; waterbodies, houses, ancient castle mound, sand or stone pit.

9/31 Beerferris (parish) SX 452658 [Bere Ferrers]
Apt 28.02.1842; 5888a (all); Map 1844?, 6 chns, in 3 parts, (including Beer Town and Beer Alston at 3 chns); hill-drawing, foot/b'way, waterbodies, woods (named), orchards, cherry orchards, gardens, marsh/bog, heath/moor, landowners, ferry, mill, quay, schoolhouse, spoil heaps.

9/32 Belstone (parish) SX 621940
Apt 23.12.1841; 1136a (all); Map 1842, 3 chns, by William Gould, Okehampton; construction lines, waterbodies, houses, field boundary ownerships, line of trees.

9/33 Berrynarbor (parish) SS 565450
Apt 20.09.1839; 4958a (4958); Map 1840, 3 chns, 1st cl, by George Northcote, Barnstaple; construction lines, foot/b'way, waterbodies, houses, woods (col), fences, field gates, building names, coastline, boundary stones, limekilns, glebe.

9/34 Berry Pomeroy (parish) SX 835616
Apt 30.03.1841; 4525a (4525); Map 1841, 4 chns, by Sawdye and Taperell, Ashburton; houses, fences; colour bands may show property ownerships.

9/35 Bickington (parish) SX 802722
Apt 03.01.1840; 1375a (all); Map 1841, 3 chns, 1st cl, 'from an actual survey' by T. Irish and A.S. Parker, Scoriton near Buckfastleigh, Devon; construction lines, houses, farmyards, hedge ownership, fences, building names, limekiln.

9/36 Bickleigh [Hayridge Hundred] (parish) SS 944060
Apt 09.11.1842; 1835a (all); Map 1842, 3 chns, by John Coldridge; foot/b'way, waterbodies, houses, farmyards, woods, orchards, fences, field gates, building names, six oaks, mill; mapmaker's name is on a ribbon, surmounted by a shield, coloured.

9/37 Bickleigh [Roborough Hundred] (parish) SX 518627
Apt 28.09.1839; 2324a (2323); Map 1840, 4 chns, by H. Symons, Fancy, Plymouth; construction lines, waterbodies, houses, woods, plantations, orchards, heath/moor, hedges, fences.

9/38 Bicton (parish) SY 059858 [Not listed]
Apt 13.09.1839; 1294a (1294); Map 1844?, 3 chns; hill-drawing, foot/b'way, waterbodies, houses, farmyards, parkland (in detail), orchards (col), heath/moor, fences, field gates, manor pound, quarry, common.

9/39 Bideford (parish) SS 460260
Apt 10.10.1839; 3196a (3196); Map 1841?, 3 chns, by George Braund and Henry Hearn, Exeter; foot/b'way; built-up part generalised.

9/40 Bigbury (parish) SX 667470
Apt 26.10.1842; 2903a (all); Map 1843, 3 chns, by John Huddleston, Plymstock, Devon; construction lines, waterbodies, houses, field boundary ownerships, coastline; legend explains depiction of buildings, waterbodies and boundaries.

9/41 Bishops Nympton (parish) SS 766255 [Bishop's Nympton]
Apt 27.03.1841; 9580a (9570); Map 1840, 3 chns, 1st cl, in 2 parts, by H. Crispin jnr, Chulmleigh, (includes enlargement of village at 1.5 chns); rock outcrops, building names, mills, parsonage, weir.

9/42 Bishops Tawton (parish) SS 582287 [Bishop's Tawton]
Apt 04.09.1843; 4264a (all); Map 1844?, 3 chns; construction lines, waterbodies, houses, woods, rock outcrops, mill, cherry orchards.

9/43 Bishopsteignton (parish) SX 907754
Apt 18.01.1840; 4706a (4748); Map 1839, 4 chns, by Thomas Woodmass, John Thompson, John Huddleston and John Woodmass; foot/b'way, waterbodies, houses, limekiln and quarry; colour bands may show property ownerships.

9/44 Bittadon (parish) SS 546427
Apt 12.01.1839; 1018a (all); Map 1840, 3 chns, by Chas Cooper, Alverdiscott, Bideford, Devon; construction lines, waterbodies.

9/45 Blackawton (parish) SX 812502
Apt 11.10.1839; 5586a (5646); Map 1840, 4 chns, by John Grant, Ugborough; hill-drawing, foot/b'way, waterbodies, houses, woods, marsh/bog, rock outcrops, fences, field gates, building names, sand or stone pits, quarry, cliffs, beach, gun boundary mark; colour bands may show property ownerships; some field boundaries are double lines which may indicate hedges; rose, thistle, shamrock, wheat, barley and vegetation are grouped above map title, below which a ribbon bears the motto 'union, peace and plenty'.

9/46 Blackborough (parish) ST 096097
Apt 11.12.1845; 508a (all); Map 1844, 3 chns, by G. Braund; construction lines.

9/47 Blacktorrington (parish) SS 455042 [Black Torrington]
Apt 31.07.1843; 6595a (7200); Map 1840, 3 chns, 1st cl, in 2 parts, by H.W. Bushell, 40, Upper Charlotte St, Fitzroy Square, London; construction lines, waterbodies, houses, woods (named), fences, field gates, building names, weirs, mills, rectory, chapel.

9/48 Bondleigh (parish) SS 655043
Apt 30.05.1842; 1784a (all); Map 1843, 3 chns, by Messrs Huddleston and White, Plymtree, Devon; houses, farmyards.

9/49 North Bovey (parish) SX 716833
Apt 27.07.1839; 5655a (all); Map 1841?, 3 chns, by W. Gould, Okehampton; construction lines, houses; colours may show property ownerships. Apt omits land use and observes that 'common land is chiefly covered with furze and heath which is occasionally cut for fuel and occasionally burnt where growing in order to improve the pasture and the whole is depastured in the summer season with sheep and other cattle...'

9/50 Bovey Tracey (parish) SX 811787 [Bovey Tracy]
Apt 25.03.1839; 7262a (7262); Map 1841, 3 chns, in 2 parts, by Sawdye and Taperell, Ashburton, (includes enlargement of Bovey Tracey town at 1.5 chns); waterbodies, houses, fences, sand or stone pit, coal pit, ornamental gate, boundary landmarks; colour bands may show property ownerships; bridge named; table summarises land use; 62 acres outside the district are mapped.

9/51 Bow otherwise Nymet Tracey (parish) SX 725996
Apt 30.11.1840; 2963a (all); Map 1841, 3 chns, 1st cl, by H. Crispin Junr, Chulmleigh; construction lines, foot/b'way, waterbodies, houses, farmyards, fences, building names, rectory, mill, moor; colour bands may show property ownerships.

9/52 Bradford (parish) SS 430055
Apt 14.04.1840; 3468a (3468); Map 1840?, 4 chns, by Hughbert Baker, Parliament St, Westminster, London; waterbodies, farmyards, building names, mills, farm names.

9/53 Bradninch (parish) SS 993046
Apt 07.11.1838; 4351a (4351); Map 1839, 3 chns, by Wm Collard Cox, Sampford Brett, Somerset; waterbodies, hedge ownership; map carries recital of proceedings for its adoption by the landowners.

9/54 Bradstone (parish) SX 382809
Apt 18.12.1839; 1258a (all); Map 1840?, 3 chns; waterbodies, plantations, fences, building names, well, mill, barton lands boundary, farm names.

9/55 Bradworthy (parish) SS 312147
Apt 06.04.1842; 9587a (9586); Map 1843, 3 chns, 1st cl, in 4 parts, by G. Braund and H. Hearn, Exeter; waterbodies.

9/56 Brampford Speke (except Cowley) (parish) SX 924982
Apt 30.06.1842; 1151a (all); Map 1843, 3 chns, surveyed for tithe commutation by E. Browne; railway, foot/b'way, houses, farmyards, building names.

9/57 Branscombe (parish) SY 185896
Apt 18.11.1841; 3423a (3487); Map 1840, 6 chns, by Jno. Coldridge; foot/b'way, waterbodies, houses, woods, plantations, rock outcrops, building names, cliffs, beach, preventive buildings, limekilns, farm names.

9/58 Bratton Covelly (parish) SX 471936
Apt 30.04.1845; 8316a (all); Map 1845, 4 chns, in 3 parts, by John Palmer, Devonport, (including 16 chn outline plan of district by H. and R.L. Badcock); foot/b'way, houses; charcoal holders, a pair of compasses,

a quill pen, a ruler and leaves surround the scale; Palmer's name is on a scroll draped over a pedestal with ears of barley and vegetation at the base.

9/59 Bratton Fleming (parish) SS 656381
Apt 18.12.1839; 5846a (all); Map 1840, 3 chns, in 2 parts, by Chas Cooper, Alverdiscott, Bideford, Devon; construction lines, trig points (named), waterbodies, houses. Apt omits some land use.

9/60 Braunton (parish) SS 487376
Apt 19.11.1840; 10474a (all); Map 1840, 3 chns, 1st cl, in 2 parts, by Alexr Doull, L.S., Chatham; construction lines, foot/b'way, waterbodies, houses, woods (col), orchards, rock outcrops, open fields (named), fences, field gates, building names, road names, sand or stone pit, marsh, lighthouse, fish weirs, site of old chapel, sluice, limekiln, old kiln, watermill; downs, watercourses, coastal features and Braunton Burrows named; colour bands may show property ownerships.

9/61 Brendon (parish) SS 766463
Apt 27.07.1839; 6733a (all); Map 1840, 3 chns, 1st cl, by John Wiggins, 30, Tavistock Place, London, surveyor and land agent; construction lines, foot/b'way, houses, field boundary ownerships, building names, road names, parsonage, abbey, mill; hills and bridge named.

9/62 South Brent (parish) SX 713599
Apt 11.10.1839; 6313a (9374); Map 1841, 3 chns, 'working plan', in 2 parts, by Gould and Taperell, Ashburton, Devon, (includes South Brent town separately at 0.75 chn); construction lines, foot/b'way, waterbodies, houses, farmyards, fences, field gates, tithe-free land (col); some field boundaries are shown as double lines.

9/63 Brentor (parish) SX 468820
Apt 26.10.1842; 1212a (1212); Map 1844, 3 chns; hill-drawing, turnpike roads, toll bar, milestone, houses, woods, plantations, orchards, heath/moor, fences, commons, green. District is apportioned by holding.

9/64 Bridestowe (parish) SX 506876
Apt 22.09.1841; 5661a (5661); Map 1844, 4 chns, 1st cl, by Henry and R.L. Badcock, Launceston; construction lines, waterbodies, fences, building names, mill; area numbers are stamped.

9/65 Bridford (parish) SX 807866
Apt 30.06.1840; 4115a (4114); Map 1840, 3 chns, from a trignometrical survey by Luckraft, Warren, Reaney and Warren, Crediton; foot/b'way, waterbodies, houses, woods, plantations, orchards, marsh/bog, heath/moor, rock outcrops (named), field gates, building names, mill, lime kiln, weir, sand or stone pit; colour bands may show property ownerships. Apt omits land use.

9/66 East Bridgrule (parish) SS 284029 [Bridgerule]
Apt 08.07.1842; 2209a (3219); Map 1843, 4 chns, 1st cl, in 2 parts, by Chapple and Oliver; construction lines, waterbodies, building names, mill.

9/67 Brixham (parish) SX 910536
Apt 05.06.1840; 5596a (all); Map 1838, 3 chns, by Henry Andrews, Modbury and John Grant, Ugborough; construction lines, hill-drawing, woods, plantations, rock outcrops, fences, field gates, building names, cliffs, beach, low water mark, floating bridge, harbour, limekiln, limestone quarries; single red lines may be walls; some boundaries are shown with double lines; coastal features named, and shown in detail.

9/68 Brixton (parish) SX 552528
Apt 21.10.1840; 2914a (2999); Map 1839, 6 chns, by John Grant, Ugborough; foot/b'way, waterbodies, houses (by hatching), woods, plantations, parkland, orchards, hedges, fences, field boundary ownerships, field gates, quarries, sand or stone pits, coastline, limekilns; headland named.

9/69 Broadclist (parish) SX 999985 [Broadclyst]
Apt 22.07.1841; 9188a (9188); Map 1842, 6 chns, in 2 parts, surveyed by Messrs Drew and Cox, and drawn by R.P. Frise, Williton, Somerset, (includes Broadclist village separately at 3 chns); waterbodies, woods, parkland, orchards, fences.

9/70 Broadhembury (parish) ST 094049
Apt 29.11.1841; 4704a (4703); Map 1843?, 8 chns, taken fron old surveys, by John Easton; waterbodies, houses, plantations, building names, ornamental ground.

9/71 Broadhempston (parish) SX 801665
Apt 08.07.1841; 2047a (all); Map 1841, 4 chns, 1st cl, by H. Symons, Fancy, Plymouth; construction lines, houses, fences, field boundary ownerships, building names.

9/72 Broadnymet (parish) SS 703008 [Broadnymett]
Apt 17.03.1841; 458a (all); Map 1845, 3 chns; waterbodies, old bank.

9/73 Broadwoodkelly (parish) SS 612059
Apt 30.11.1839; 2666a (all); Map 1842?, 3 chns, 1st cl; construction lines, trig points (named), houses, woods, plantations, orchards, building names; colour bands may show property ownerships.

9/74 Broadwoodwidger (parish) SX 402922
Apt 09.12.1841; 8781a (all); Map 1842, 3 chns, by J. Kittow, North Petherwin; foot/b'way, waterbodies, fences, building names, mill.

9/75 Brushford (parish) SS 671078
Apt 26.10.1842; 895a (894); Map 1843?, 3 chns; construction lines, waterbodies, houses, farmyards, building names, road names, mill; colour bands may show property ownerships.

9/76 Buckerell (parish) ST 124005
Apt 07.09.1842; 1560a (1559); Map 1845?, 9 chns; waterbodies, building names; colours show detached parts of other districts.

9/77 Buckfastleigh (parish) SX 710670
Apt 25.05.1839; 5928a (5928); Map 1843?, 3 chns, ? by Peter Gillard and James Elliott; construction lines, waterbodies, houses, building names, mills, vicarage, abbey; bridge named; compass rose is in the form of a globe with true and magnetic north shown. Apt omits land use.

9/78 Buckland Brewer (parish) SS 415189
Apt 29.07.1841; 6158a (all); Map 1842, 4 chns, by Warren, Reaney and Warren; foot/b'way, waterbodies, houses, woods, plantations, parkland, orchards, heath/moor, building names, mill, castle; colour bands may show property ownerships.

9/79 East Buckland (parish) SS 675315
Apt 19.04.1837; 755a (1385); Map 1838, 3 chns, by Hugh Ballment, Barnstaple; hill-drawing, foot/b'way, waterbodies, coppice and woodland (by name), building names, road names, field names, landowners, quarry, boundary features, smithy, glebe, barton lands; map has schedule which has been pasted over.

9/80 Buckland Filleigh (parish) SS 481091
Apt 27.10.1842; 3038a (3037); Map 1843, 3 chns, 1st cl, by George Braund junr; construction lines.

9/81 Buckland Monachorum (parish) SX 500676
Apt 09.06.1842; 6838a (6338); Map 1842?, 4 chns, by Messrs Woodmass and Co, Ivy Bridge, Devon; construction lines, waterbodies, houses. Apt omits land use.

9/82 Buckland-on-the-Moor (parish) SX 725736 [Buckland in the Moor]
Apt 31.08.1840; 1459a (all); Map 1840?, 4 chns; houses, building names, beacon, limekiln, common, downland, woodland (by name). Apt omits land use.

9/83 Buckland Tout Saints (parish) SX 758460 [Buckland-tout-Saints]
Apt 31.07.1839; 529a (all); Map 1840?, 4 chns, ? by Henry Andrews; foot/b'way, waterbodies, woods, parkland, field boundary ownerships, field gates, sand or stone pit; bridge named.

9/84 West Buckland (parish) SS 657322
Apt 20.11.1839; 1773a (all); Map 1840?, 3 chns, by Thos Lock jr, Instow; construction lines, foot/b'way, waterbodies, woods, coppice, plantation.

9/85 St Budeaux (parish) SX 461592
Apt 31.12.1842; 2507a (all); Map 1840, 4 chns, in 2 parts, by H. Symons, Fancy near Plymouth, (including 2-chn enlargements of detail); hill-drawing, foot/b'way, waterbodies, houses, woods, plantations, orchards, marsh/bog, building names, sand or stone pits, quarries, coastline, road embankments. Apt omits land use.

9/86 East Budleigh (parish) SY 055838
Apt 19.04.1842; 3238a (all); Map 1845?, 3 chns; hill-drawing, waterbodies, houses, woods (named), plantations (named), orchards, heath/moor, rock outcrops, fences, field gates, boundstones, beach, cliffs, coastguard station, limekilns, chapel, manor pound, well, ornamental gates, river embankments, tithing divisions.

9/87 Bulkworthy (parish) SS 389142
Apt 30.06.1841; 1115a (all); Map 1842, 4 chns, by Warren, Reaney and Warren, Crediton; foot/b'way, houses, woods, plantations, orchards, heath/moor, building names, mill, weir; colour bands may show arable.

9/88 Bulworthy (hamlet in parish of Alverdiscott) SS 510261
Apt 06.04.1842; 251a (all); Map 1843, 3 chns, by Chas Cooper, Alverdiscott, Bideford; woods, heath/moor; there are two scale bars, one being combined with the direction pointer.

9/89 Burlescombe (parish) ST 065159
Apt 12.01.1837; 3768a (3768); Map 1840?, 6 chns, ? by Chas Bailey and Thos Wright; foot/b'way, canal and towpath, waterbodies, houses, woods, plantations, arable (col), grassland (col), orchards, gardens, rock outcrops, building names, limekilns, quarries, abbey; uncoloured land could be meadow.

9/90 Burrington (parish) SS 629175
Apt 07.05.1838; 5331a (all); Map 1840, 3 chns, by Chas Cooper, Alverdiscott, Bideford, Devon; construction lines, foot/b'way, waterbodies, houses, flying bridge; map carries recital of proceedings for its adoption.

9/91 Butterleigh (parish) SS 972085
Apt 14.10.1837; 479a (all); Map 1839, 3 chns, by G.A. Boyce; foot/b'way, waterbodies, houses, field gates, building names, parsonage, mill.

9/92 Bystock (district in parish of Colaton Raleigh) SY 022835
Apt 21.06.1841; 172a (all); Map 1841?, 3 chns; woods, field gates, building names, park lodges. District is apportioned by holding and fields are not shown; Apt generalises land use.

9/93 Cadbury (parish) SS 911051
Apt 06.05.1842; 1899a (1899); Map 1842, 3 chns, by Messrs Warren; hill-drawing, waterbodies, houses, woods, plantations, parkland, orchards, fences, building names, ancient castle, trig point, vicarage, mill, school, sand or stone pit; bridge named; colour bands may show property ownerships.

9/94 Cadeleigh (parish) SS 912087
Apt 22.07.1840; 2191a (2191); Map 1840, 6 chns, by William Richards, Tiverton; foot/b'way, waterbodies, houses, building names, mill; border corners have floral decorations; map carries summary of proceedings for its adoption.

9/95 Calverleigh (parish) SS 915145
Apt 31.01.1838; 502a (all); Map 1839, 4 chns; waterbodies, houses, parkland, fences.

9/96 Chagford (parish) SX 691861
Apt 07.01.1840; 7492a (all); Map 1840-1, 3 chns, 1st cl, in 4 parts, by Messrs Luckraft, Warren, Reaney and Warren, Crediton; construction lines, trig points (named), waterbodies, houses, woods, plantations, orchards, building names, factory, mills, rectory; colour bands may show property ownerships.

9/97 Challacombe (parish) SS 690412
Apt 31.01.1839; 5343a (all); Map 1840, 6 chns, by Hugh Ballment, Barnstaple; foot/b'way, boundstones, well, castle, burrows, standing stone, common; valleys and a field named; pictorial church, with gravestones; colour bands may show property ownerships.

9/98 Charles (parish) SS 682337
Apt 06.04.1842; 2432a (all); Map 1842, 3 chns, by H. Crispin junr, South Molton; construction lines, foot/b'way, houses, building names, mill, quarries, woodland (by name); colour bands may show property ownerships.

9/99 Charleton (parish) SX 756427 [East and West Charleton]
Apt 24.12.1839; 2380a (2779); Map 1840, 3 chns, by John Andrew, Plympton, Devon; hill-drawing, foot/b'way, turnpike roads, waterbodies, woods, plantations, orchards, heath/moor, field boundary ownerships, coastline, coastal embankment, limekilns, quarry, tumuli, private and public roads; pictorial church; bridges named.

9/100 Chawley (parish) SS 711118 [Chawleigh]
Apt 20.04.1848; 5481a (all); Map 1849?, 3 chns, 1st cl; waterbodies, woods, plantations, parkland, building names, parsonage, mills, dog kennel, weirs, deer park, old river course; bridge named; PRO copy has a note that this copy has been compared with the offical map.

9/101 Cheldon (parish) SS 738138
Apt 15.09.1837; 1108a (all); Map 1838, 3 chns, by William Collard Cox, Williton, Somerset; foot/b'way, waterbodies, houses, hedge ownership, fences, field gates.

9/102 Cheriton Bishop (parish) SX 757937
Apt 22.09.1838; 4866a (all); Map 1840, 3 chns, by J. Philp; foot/b'way, woods, plantations, orchards, heath/moor, field boundary ownerships, milestone.

9/103 Cheriton Fitzpaine (parish) SS 881069
Apt 30.04.1838; 5383a (all); Map 1839, 6 chns, in 2 parts, by William Richards, Tiverton, (including small inset at 4 chns added in 1841); construction lines, foot/b'way, waterbodies, houses, building names, roadside cross, mill, woodland (by name).

9/104 Chilston (district in parish of Salcombe Regis) SY 166923 [Chelson]
Apt 15.01.1845; 602a (?); Map 1845, 3 chns, by Messrs Blackmore, Churchingford; foot/b'way, field gates.

9/105 Chittlehampton (parish) SS 638252
Apt 10.11.1842; 8720a (8720); Map 1840?, 3 chns, 1st cl, in 4 parts, by H. Crispin, South Molton, (including 80-chn index); construction lines, foot/b'way, waterbodies, houses, woods, plantations, parkland (col), orchards, rock outcrops, building names, quarry, parsonage, mill; colour bands may show property ownerships.

9/106 Chivelstone (parish) SX 787378
Apt 18.08.1842; 2696a (2806); Map 1842, 3 chns, 1st cl, by Frederick H.E. Drayson; construction lines, waterbodies, houses, building names, coastline, broken fence; boundaries near coast are annotated 'continuing straight down rocks'; headland named.

9/107 Christow (parish) SX 825840
Apt 11.09.1841; 3219a (3218); Map 1841, 4 chns, by E. Browne; waterbodies, houses, farmyards, building names. Apt omits land use.

9/108 Chudleigh (parish) SX 880810
Apt 13.06.1838; 6037a (6037); Map 1841, 3 chns, by T. Woodmass and Co; foot/b'way, waterbodies, houses, fences.

9/109 Chulmleigh (parish) SS 703160
Apt 31.03.1840; 8815a (8815); Map 1841?, 3 chns; construction lines, trig points, waterbodies, woods, plantations, parkland, orchards, heath/moor, building names, rectory, moor; bridge named; colours may show property ownerships; map has recital of adoption proceedings together with 18 landowners' signatures.

9/110 St Mary Church (parish) SX 914665 [St Marychurch]
Apt 30.06.1841; 2590a (2589); Map 1840, 3 chns, copied from a survey by H. Symons, Fancy, Plymouth made in 1838, by John Grant, Ugborough; foot/b'way, waterbodies, woods, rock outcrops, field boundary ownerships, building names, cliffs.

9/111 Churchstow (parish) SX 712453
Apt 15.06.1839; 1877a (all); Map 1841, 3 chns, by Wm Collard Cox, Williton, Somerset; waterbodies, hedge ownership, fences, building names, workhouse; meaning of green tint is unclear.

9/112 Churston Ferrers (parish) SX 895559
Apt 20.10.1840; 2528a (2777); Map 1839, 3 chns, by John Grant, Ugborough; hill-drawing, foot/b'way, woods, rock outcrops, fences, field boundary ownerships, field gates, building names, limestone

quarries, sandbank, low water mark, limekilns, windmill; red field boundaries may be walls; some field boundaries are shown by double lines; compass rose is drawn in the shape of a globe with magnetic and true north shown; roses, thistle, wheat, barley and scallop shell surround title.

9/113 Clannaborough (parish) SS 736001 [Not listed]
Apt 07.07.1838; 875a (all); Map 1839, 3 chns, 1st cl, by Wm Collard Cox, Williton near Taunton, Somerset; construction lines, foot/b'way, fences.

9/114 Clare (district in parish of Tiverton) SS 903133 [Not listed]
Apt 06.08.1841; 3550a (all); Map 1844, 6 chns, in 2 parts, by William Richards junr, (including 3-chn enlargement of detail); foot/b'way, canal, waterbodies, building names, weir, mill.

9/115 Clawton (parish) SX 346993
Apt 02.08.1842; 5358a (5358); Map 1843, 4 chns, 1st cl, by Henry and R.L. Badcock, Launceston; construction lines, waterbodies, houses, building names; tithe area numbers are stamped.

9/116 Clayhanger (parish) ST 019235
Apt 05.06.1840; 2083a (all); Map 1837, 3 chns, from an actual survey by Wm Collard Cox, Williton, Somerset; foot/b'way, waterbodies, hedge ownership, fences.

9/117 Clayhidon (parish) ST 160132
Apt 10.01.1838; 5090a (5089); Map 1838, 3 chns, by Messrs Blackmore, Churchingford; hill-drawing, foot/b'way, waterbodies, woods, plantations, arable (col), grassland (col), orchards, gardens, marsh/bog, heath/moor, hedges, field gates; legend explains cultivation symbols, including nurseries, coppice, ozier beds, undivided common land, allotments for stone and sand and roadside waste; some of Dawson's symbols are used; scroll suggesting birds of prey is drawn above the scale and legend; map title is surrounded by a decorative pagoda.

9/118 Clist Honiton (parish) SX 993934 [Clyst Honiton]
Apt 22.11.1839; 1725a (all); Map 1839, 4 chns, by Henry and R.L. Badcock, Launceston; foot/b'way, waterbodies, woods, parkland, orchards, building names; names and tithe area numbers are stamped.

9/119 Clisthydon (parish) ST 042013 [Clyst Hydon]
Apt 10.03.1841; 1725a (all); Map 1840, 4 chns, surveyed for John Drew, Peamore Cottage near Exeter, by Jno. Grant; construction lines, foot/b'way, waterbodies, houses, farmyards, hedge ownership, field gates, building names; legend explains boundary depiction.

9/120 Clist St George (parish) SX 982892 [Clyst St George]
Apt 22.03.1839; 1041a (all); Map 1839, 4 chns, surveyed for John Drew by by Jno. Grant; construction lines, turnpike roads, waterbodies, houses, farmyards, woods, hedge ownership, building names, mill, rectory, milestones, toll house, limekilns; bridge named; woodland is shown by crosses; legend explains boundary depiction.

9/121 Clovelly (parish) SS 315235
Apt 20.08.1839; 3503a (3502); Map 1840, 4 chns, by T. Woodmass and Co; hill-drawing, waterbodies, houses, ancient earthworks, beach; legend explains boundary depiction, buildings and waterbodies; leaves surround map title.

9/122 Clyst St Lawrence (parish) ST 031001
Apt 09.11.1842; 1060a (all); Map 1844, 3 chns, 1st cl, by G. Braund, Exeter.

9/123 Clyst St Mary (parish) SX 987902
Apt 14.08.1838; 583a (all); Map 1839, 3 chns, by Jno. Coldridge; construction lines, foot/b'way, waterbodies, woods, heath/moor, fences, field gates, building names, mill, parsonage, lodge, schoolhouse, weirs, glebe boundary, riverside wasteland; built-up part generalised.

9/124 Cockington (parish) SX 894638
Apt 07.03.1842; 1016a (all); Map 1846, 8 chns, by J. Andrew, Plympton, Devon. District is apportioned by holding and some fields and land use are omitted.

9/125 Coffinswell (parish) SX 895685
Apt 02.12.1842; 1126a (1126); Map 1841, 3 chns, by George Braund and Henry Hearn, Exeter; construction lines.

9/126 Colaton Raleigh (parish) SY 059879
Apt 14.04.1842; 3758a (all); Map 1842, 3 chns, by John Doherty; waterbodies, houses, farmyards, woods, plantations, parkland, orchards, gardens, heath/moor, fences, field gates, common.

9/127 Coldridge (parish) SS 693065
Apt 02.12.1844; 3670a (3670); Map 1839, 3 chns, by Hugh Ballment, Barnstaple; waterbodies, building names, weir.

9/128 Colebrook (parish) SX 760995 [Colebrooke]
Apt 24.02.1845; 4990a (all); Map 1846, 4 chns, 1st cl, by Henry and R.L. Badcock, Launceston; construction lines, waterbodies, woods, plantations, orchards, heath/moor, building names, mill; names are stamped.

9/129 Colyton (parish) SY 234946
Apt 11.09.1841; 7196a (7196); Map 1843, 6 chns, in 2 parts, (including 3-chn enlargement of meadow); waterbodies, houses, woods, plantations, orchards, heath/moor, fences, building names, mills, green, district boundaries (col); some hills and rough land named.

9/130 Combeintinhead (parish) SX 890712 [Combeinteignhead]
Apt 08.11.1837; 2217a (2407); Map 1839, 4 chns, in 2 parts, by Sawdye and Taperell, Ashburton, (includes enlargement of village at 2 chns); foot/b'way, waterbodies, houses, marsh/bog (col), rock outcrops, fences, field gates, boundary stones, limekiln, ornamental gardens, cliffs, sandbanks (col), downland; legend explains the total measurements of estates, roads, cottages etc in the district.

9/131 Combe Raleigh (parish) ST 166023
Apt 14.04.1840; 1747a (all); Map 1840, 4 chns, by Augustus Henry Warmington, Honiton, Devon; hill-drawing, waterbodies, houses, woods, plantations, osiers, parkland, orchards, hedge ownership, fences, field gates; hedges and lands belonging to adjacent districts coloured.

9/132 Combmartin (parish) SS 601471 [Combe Martin]
Apt 25.10.1842; 3816a (all); Map 1843, 3 chns, by A. Rowe, Barnstaple; construction lines, waterbodies, houses, building names, parsonage, boundary stones.

9/133 Combpyne (parish) SY 295926
Apt 28.06.1844; 797a (796); Map 1842, 3 chns, by Jas Alex. Knight; foot/b'way, waterbodies, woods (col), plantations (col), parkland (col), orchards (col), quarries, mills; colour bands may show property ownerships.

9/134 Compton Gifford otherwise Efford (tithing in parishes of Plymouth, St Andrew and Charles the Martyr) SX 492566 [Compton]
Apt 21.10.1840; 641a (641); Map 1839, 3 chns, 1st cl, by J. Kittow, Northpetherwin; construction lines, foot/b'way.

9/135 Cookbury (parish) SS 385050
Apt 26.10.1842; 2711a (2710); Map 1843, 4 chns, 1st cl, by Henry and R.L. Badcock, Launceston; construction lines, hamlet names; names are stamped.

9/136 Cornwood (parish) SX 609599
Apt 30.06.1842; 6004a (10680); Map 1842, 4 chns, by John Grant, Ugborough; construction lines, hill-drawing, waterbodies, houses, woods, fences, field boundary ownerships, building names, old river course, mill, mill leat, vicarage, clay mines, clay pans, downland; red lines may be walls; mapmaker's name is on decorative ribbon beneath title.

9/137 Cornworthy (parish) SX 826546
Apt 22.09.1843; 1723a (2721); Map 1844, 3 chns, 1st cl, by Thos Cutmore and Son; waterbodies, houses, farmyards, fences, field boundary ownerships.

9/138 Coryton (parish) SX 463841
Apt 06.08.1841; 1335a (all); Map 1842, 4 chns, by Edward Sawdye, Ashburton; waterbodies, fences.

9/139 Cotleigh (parish) ST 211032
Apt 13.04.1840; 1218a (all); Map 1840, 4 chns, by Wm Dawson, Exeter; woods, arable (col), grassland (col), orchards, gardens.

9/140 Countisbury (parish) SS 761491
Apt 20.03.1839; 2942a (all); Map 1841?, 6 chns, in 2 parts, (includes enlargement of Countisbury village at 3 chns), litho (by Day and Haghe, Lithographers to the Queen); hill-drawing, waterbodies, houses, woods, rock outcrops, building names, cliffs, beach, burrow, mill; physical features named.

9/141 Cowley (hamlet in parish of Brampford Speke) SX 896957
Apt 10.03.1842; 493a (all); Map 1842, 3 chns, by G. Braund and H. Hearn; construction lines; map carries recital of procedure for its adoption by the landowners.

9/142 Creacombe (parish) SS 824193
Apt 31.07.1839; 1050a (1050); Map 1840?, 3 chns, 1st cl, by Messrs Luckraft, Warren, Reaney and Warren, Crediton; construction lines, houses, woods, plantations, orchards, building names, parsonage.

9/143 Crediton otherwise Kyrton (parish) SX 804982
Apt 26.02.1839; 12309a (12309); Map 1839, 3 chns, in 3 parts, by Messrs Luckraft, Warren, Reaney and Warren; foot/b'way, turnpike roads and gate, waterbodies, houses, woods, plantations, parkland, orchards, marsh/bog, heath/moor, fences, building names, road names, vicarage, meeting house, Unitarian Chapel, mills, quarry, workhouse; bridges named; colour bands may show property ownerships.

9/144 Cruwys Morchards (parish) SS 875117
Apt 15.07.1839; 5766a (5766); Map 1840, 3 chns, by Luckraft, Warren, Reaney and Warren; waterbodies, houses, woods, plantations, parkland, orchards, heath/moor, building names, tithing house, parsonage.

9/145 Cullompton (district in parish of Cullompton) ST 022061
Apt 22.02.1839; 7370a (7370); Map 1841, 6 chns, in 3 parts, by G.A. Boyce, Tiverton, (including 3-chn enlargement of gardens in Cullompton); foot/b'way, waterbodies, houses, building names, landowners, mills, mill leat, paper mills.

9/146 Culmstock (parish) ST 100154
Apt 27.03.1841; 3494a (all); Map 1841, 6 chns, in 2 parts, by Robert Fry, Culmstock, (includes enlargement of Culmstock and Millmoor villages at 3 chns); woods, plantations, orchards, hedge ownership, building names, farm names, moor; hills named.

9/147 Dartington (parish) SX 775625
Apt 30.09.1839; 3249a (all); Map 1840, 3 chns, by Thos Cutmore, Halwell near Totnes; hill-drawing, waterbodies, houses, farmyards, woods, plantations, parkland, orchards, fences, watermill, boundstones, weir.

9/148 Dartmoor Forest (district in parish of Lydford) SX 623760
Apt 18.12.1839; 4037a (54241); Map 1840, 8 chns, (tithable parts only); railways, waterbodies, plantations, rock outcrops, building names, landowners, stone circle, well, prison of war, barracks, cross, childs tomb, mines, pound, white works, Wesleyan Chapel, tors (pictorial, col, named); some field boundaries shown as double lines; bridges named; colours may show property ownerships.

9/149 Dawlish (parish) SX 953779
Apt 29.06.1839; 5017a (5512); Map 1840, 3 chns, in 3 parts, by Luckraft, Warren, Reaney and Warren; construction lines, trig points (named), waterbodies, houses, woods, plantations, parkland, orchards, heath/moor, building names, limekiln, lodge, mill, chapel, common; hill land named; colours may show property ownerships; one part, with field acreages, maps the boundary between Dawlish and Kenton across Cockwood marshes and is signed by Robert Dymond and Peter Gillard.

9/150 Dean Prior (parish) SX 701649
Apt 16.04.1839; 4165a (all); Map 1840, 4 chns; construction lines, hill-drawing, waterbodies, woods, heath/moor, rock outcrops, hedges, fences, field gates, building names, ditch, boundary features, boundary stones, road embankments, sand or stone pits.

9/151 Denbury (parish) SX 828684
Apt 20.03.1839; 1068a (1068); Map 1839, 3 chns, by S.W. Adams, Newton Ferrers; construction lines, foot/b'way, private and parish roads, waterbodies, houses, woods, plantations, orchards, gardens, ornamental gardens, heath/moor, rock outcrops, fences, field boundary ownerships, field gates, road names, limekilns, quarries, slate quarry, public watering place, conduit; legend explains depiction of gardens, waterbodies, roads, boundaries, and buildings; some field boundaries are shown as double lines, those in red being walls.

9/152 Diptford (parish) SX 749557
Apt 05.10.1838; 4145a (4154); Map 1841?, 4 chns, by Jno. Thos Tucker; construction lines, waterbodies, woods, plantations, heath/moor, hedges, fences, building names, sand or stone pit; bridge named.

9/153 Dittisham (parish) SX 853536
Apt 30.11.1839; 3098a (3438); Map 1840, 4 chns, by Thomas Cutmore, Halwell; foot/b'way, waterbodies, houses, woods, plantations, orchards, heath/moor, fences, field boundary ownerships, field gates, high and low water marks, sand or mud flats, ferry, limekiln.

9/154 Dodbrook (parish) SX 738439 [Dodbrooke]
Apt 10.10.1839; 359a (464); Map 1843?, 3 chns; colour bands may show property ownerships; map title is surrounded by drawings of birds, greek urns and flowers.

9/155 Doddiscombsleigh (parish) SX 851870
Apt 27.09.1838; 2391a (2391); Map 1841?, 4 chns, ? by Geo. W. Cumming; foot/b'way, woods, plantations, orchards, building names, rectory, holdings (col); bridge named. Apt omits land use.

9/156 Dolton (parish) SS 572124
Apt 24.10.1842; 3553a (all); Map 1842, 3 chns, by G. Arnold, Dolton; waterbodies, houses, fences, building names, parsonage, weir.

9/157 Dolton (extra-parochial manor) SY 082887 [Not listed]
Apt 06.05.1842; 214a (214); Map 1842, 3 chns, by John Doherty; houses, building names, mill.

9/158 Dowland (parish) SS 579102
Apt 03.01.1839; 1755a (all); Map 1841?, 6 chns; waterbodies, woods, plantations, field boundary ownerships.

9/159 East Down (parish) SS 589415
Apt 26.02.1841; 3644a (3643); Map 1842, 3 chns, 1st cl, by John Woodmass; construction lines, foot/b'way, waterbodies, houses; legend explains depiction of buildings and waterbodies.

9/160 Down St Mary (parish) SS 743042
Apt 06.05.1842; 2230a (all); Map 1843, 3 chns, 1st cl, in 3 parts, (including 80-chn index); waterbodies, houses, woods, plantations, orchards, heath/moor, building names, mill; colour bands may show property ownerships.

9/161 West Down (parish) SS 515423
Apt 15.03.1841; 4059a (4059); Map 1842?, 3 chns; construction lines, houses, farmyards, orchards, field boundary ownerships.

9/162 Drewsteignton (parish) SX 722915
Apt 03.01.1839; 6938a (6937); Map 1840, 4 chns, in 2 parts, by William Joll, Plymouth, and Geo. Murphy; construction lines, hill-drawing, foot/b'way, turnpike roads, waterbodies, houses, farmyards, woods, orchards, hedges, field gates, building names. Apt omits land use.

9/163 Dunchideock (parish) SX 875880
Apt 09.11.1842; 950a (all); Map 1843, 3 chns, by J. Philp; foot/b'way, houses, woods, plantations, heath/moor, field boundary ownerships, boundary posts, quarries, old limekiln, old quarry; map is signed by landowners.

9/164 Dunkeswell (parish) ST 142076
Apt 16.05.1844; 1159a (5160); Map 1844?, 3 chns, in 2 parts; foot/b'way, turnpike roads, waterbodies, woods, plantations, orchards, building names, landowners, sand or stone pits, chapel.

9/165 Dunsford (parish) SX 824896
Apt 15.09.1837; 5949a (5948); Map 1838, 3 chns, by J. Philp, Moretonhampstead; construction lines, waterbodies, woods, plantations, parkland, orchards, heath/moor, field boundary ownerships, building names; legend explains boundary depiction.

9/166 Dunterton (parish) SX 380793
Apt 31.05.1842; 1161a (all); Map 1844, 3 chns, houses, building names, glebe.

9/167 Eggbuckland (parish) SX 504584
Apt 28.01.1839; 3204a (all); Map 1840, 3 chns, by J. Andrew, Plympton, Devon; hill-drawing, railways, foot/b'way, turnpike roads, private and public roads, waterbodies, woods, plantations, willows, parkland, orchards, fences, field boundary ownerships, quarry, limekilns; bridge named; a pair of compasses straddles the scale bar.

9/168 Eggesford (district) SS 684096 [Not listed]
Apt 24.03.1848; 1085a (all); Map 1840, 3 chns, by Luckraft, Warren, Reaney and Warren; waterbodies, houses, woods, plantations, orchards, heath/moor, building names, weir; bridge named; colour band may indicate Eggesford Barton lands, which are not part of the district. Apt omits land use.

9/169 Ermington (parish) SX 622544
Apt 30.01.1841; 4952a (4952); Map 1841, 3 chns, in 2 parts, by T. Woodmass and Co; construction lines, waterbodies, houses, field boundary ownerships, boundary stone; legend explains depiction of buildings, boundaries and water bodies.

9/170 Exbourne (parish) SS 603021
Apt 28.03.1840; 2121a (all); Map 1840, 4 chns, 1st cl, 'working plan' by H.W. Allen; construction lines, trig points (named), foot/b'way, houses.

9/171 Exeter, Holy Trinity (parish) SX 919926 [Not listed]
Apt 17.11.1842; 5a (?); Map 1848?, 4 chns, by G. Anstice, (tithable parts only, tinted); building names, road names, hospital, burial ground.

9/172 Exeter, St David (parish) SX 916946 [Not listed]
Apt 10.03.1842; 1154a (all); Map 1842, 3 chns, by M. and W.T. Warren, Crediton; turnpike roads, waterbodies, woods, plantations, orchards, marsh/bog, fences, building names, road names, road embankments, reservoir, county gaol, bridewell, city prison, barracks, weir, turnpike gates; colour bands may show property ownerships.

9/173 Exeter, St Edmund (parish) SX 915923 [Not listed]
Apt 28.09.1843; 1a (?); Map 1846, 1 chn, by Geo. H. Julian, Exeter; fences, building names, road names, weirs, mills, cattle market, Exe Island; built-up part generalised; the only tithable properties in the district are three mills.

9/174 Exeter, St Mary Steps (parish) SX 917922 [Not listed]
Apt 09.11.1840; 1a (?); Map 1843?, 1 chn; road names, quay, leats; the only tithable properties in the district are the mills.

9/175 Exeter, St Sidwell (parish) SX 928934 [Not listed]
Apt 10.03.1842; 387a (all); Map 1842, 3 chns, by George Braund; built-up part generalised.

9/176 Exminster (parish) SX 935879
Apt 19.07.1839; 5448a (5817); Map 1842?, 4 chns, in 4 parts, by Robert Dymond, Exeter, (including 80-chn index); hill-drawing, foot/b'way, canal with embankments, waterbodies, houses, farmyards, woods, plantations, osiers, parkland, gardens, marsh/bog, heath/moor, fences, field gates, sand or stone pit, limekilns, drawbridge.

9/177 Farringdon (parish) SY 015913
Apt 07.06.1838; 2015a (all); Map 1839, 3 chns, ? by Jno. Coldridge and Wm Dawson, Exeter; construction lines, waterbodies, fences, building names, road names, mill, manor pound, boundstones, weir.

9/178 Farway (parish) SY 176955
Apt 30.08.1838; 2578a (all); Map 1839, 3 chns, by Wm Dawson, Exeter; waterbodies, houses, pit. Apt describes common as tithable but 'now uncultivated and overgrown for the most part with furze'.

9/179 Feniton (parish) ST 101001
Apt 28.01.1839; 1822a (1822); Map 1839, 3 chns, 1st cl, by Wm Dawson; construction lines, hill-drawing, foot/b'way, houses, fences, field gates, weir, boundary trees, burrows, ornamental ground; bridge named.

9/180 Filleigh (parish) SS 661278
Apt 19.04.1837; 431a (2038); Map 1838, 3 chns, 1st cl, in 2 parts, by Hugh Ballment, Barnstaple, Devon, (including glebe 'copied from a map by Mr Wm Gliddon about 1816', at 5 chns); construction lines, hill-drawing, turnpike roads, waterbodies, woods, parkland, orchards, hedge ownership, building names, road names, field names, quarries, well, mill, smithy, triumphal arch, dog kennel, 'tee house', castle, lodge; bridge named; gardens and woodland shown by annotation; colours may show tithe-free land; part showing glebe has table of land use and acreages.

9/181 Fremington (parish) SS 516296
Apt 18.09.1838; 6811a (all); Map 1840, 3 chns, 1st cl, by George Northcote, Barnstaple; construction lines, foot/b'way, waterbodies, houses, woods (col), field gates, building names, coastline, fish weir, quarry.

9/182 Frithelstock (parish) SS 453186
Apt 07.07.1838; 3567a (4382); Map 1838, 6 chns, by J. Risdon, Speccott, Merton, Devon; hill-drawing, foot/b'way, woods, orchards, building names, watermill; ruler, a pair of compasses, charcoal holders and leaves surround scale; mapmaker's name is on a scroll, resting against a pedestal, with wheatears and leaf decoration.

9/183 George Nympton (parish) SS 708238
Apt 01.09.1842; 1684a (all); Map 1843, 3 chns, by H. Crispin jr, South Molton; construction lines, foot/b'way, waterbodies, houses, farmyards, rock outcrops, building names, parsonage, stone pits, mill; colour bands may show property ownerships.

9/184 Georgeham (parish) SS 459401
Apt 23.04.1839; 4060a (4229); Map 1840?, [3 chns]; houses (by cross-hatching), woods, building names, free school, coastline, mill, downland; sands and headland named.

9/185 Germansweek (parish) SX 442944
Apt 10.03.1842; 2595a (all); Map 1842, 4 chns, by Messrs Robinson and Morgan; houses, building names, mills,

9/186 Gidley (parish) SX 654876 [Gidleigh]
Apt 04.09.1843; 3449a (all); Map 1841?, 3 chns, 1st cl, 'from an actual survey made in 1841' by T.B. Irish and A.S. Parker, Winkleigh, Devon; construction lines, waterbodies, houses, farmyards, building names, mill, boundary features; colour bands may show property ownerships.

9/187 St Giles on the Heath (parish) SX 359912 [St Giles-on-the-Heath]
Apt 31.12.1840; 3045a (3044); Map 1840, 4 chns, by J. Kittow, Northpetherwin, Devon; construction lines, hamlet names; map title is on shield.

9/188 St Giles in the Wood (parish) SS 534193
Apt 11.03.1842; 4827a (4827); Map 1842, 3 chns, by G. Braund and H. Hearn; construction lines, foot/b'way. Apt omits details of modus lands.

9/189 Gittisham (parish) SY 139980
Apt 26.06.1838; 2068a (all); Map 1838, 6 chns, by E. Watts, Yeovil; foot/b'way, waterbodies, houses, woods, plantations, parkland, arable (col), grassland (col), orchards, heath/moor, hedge ownership, fences, field gates, building names, field names, parsonage; bridge and hill named.

9/190 Goodleigh (parish) SS 599346
Apt 20.11.1839; 1167a (1167); Map 1839, 3 chns, 1st cl, by George Northcote, Barnstaple; construction lines, foot/b'way, waterbodies, houses, woods (col), fences, field gates. Apt omits land use.

9/191 Haccombe (parish) SX 895700
Apt 03.02.1842; 364a (363); Map 1846, 3 chns, by James Taperell; construction lines, waterbodies, houses, farmyards, parkland (col), fences, field gates, quarry.

9/192 Halberton (parish) ST 003114
Apt 19.06.1840; 7592a (5755); Map 1838, 8 chns, by W. Richards, Tiverton; foot/b'way, canal with towpath, waterbodies, hamlet names; border corners have floral decoration.

9/193 Halwell [Black Torrington Hundred] (parish) SX 432989 [Halwill] Apt 31.05.1842; 3427a (all); Map 1843, 4 chns, 1st cl, by Henry and R.L. Badcock, Launceston; construction lines, building names, mill, glebe; names and tithe area numbers are stamped.

9/194 Halwell [Coleridge Hundred] (parish) SX 781535
Apt 15.08.1839; 3667a (all); Map 1842, 8 chns, in 9 parts, by Wm Collard Cox, Williton, Somerset, (including 2-chn enlargements of settlements); foot/b'way, waterbodies, fences.

9/195 Harberton (parish) SX 774584
Apt 30.04.1842; 5756a (all); Map 1842, 3 chns, 1st cl, in 2 parts, by G. Braund and H. Hearn; construction lines.

9/196 Harford (parish) SX 639586
Apt 02.02.1838; 1571a (2050); Map 1838, 3 chns, by John Grant, Ugborough; construction lines, trig points, hill-drawing, waterbodies, houses, woods, plantations, orchards, marsh/bog, heath/moor, rock outcrops, hedge ownership, field gates, watermill, stone circles, hill fort, archaelogical features, boundstones, weir, ownership boundaries (col), tors (named); north pointer is in the form of a globe with magnetic and true north.

9/197 Harpford (parish) SY 088905
Apt 11.03.1839; 1518a (all); Map 1839, 3 chns, by Jno. Coldridge; construction lines, foot/b'way, turnpike roads, toll houses, milestones, waterbodies, houses, fences, building names, road names, bound post, woodland (by name); hills and bridge named.

9/198 Hartland (parish) SS 259228
Apt 11.05.1842; 16701a (16700); Map not dated, 4 chns; foot/b'way, waterbodies, houses (depiction inconsistent), woods, plantations, orchards, heath/moor, building names, abbey, quay, coastline, mills, quarry; bridges and headland named.

9/199 Hatherleigh (parish) SS 548042
Apt 25.03.1841; 7049a (7048); Map 1839, 4 chns, 1st cl, by H. and R. Badcock, Launceston; construction lines, foot/b'way, woods, plantations, orchards, field gates, building names, glebe, moor; names and tithe area numbers are stamped.

9/200 Heanton Punchardon (parish) SS 509352
Apt 17.12.1838; 3021a (all); Map 1840?, 3 chns, 1st cl, by George Northcote, Barnstaple; construction lines, waterbodies, houses, fences, building names, coastline.

9/201 Heavitree (parish) SX 945929
Apt 23.3.1842; 3469a (all); Map 1843, 3 chns, by Irish and Parker, Buckfastleigh; construction lines, waterbodies, houses, farmyards, fences, building names, vicarage, old abbey, barracks, irrigation channels.

9/202 Little Hempston otherwise Hempston Arundell (parish) SX 816631 [Littlehempston]
Apt 23.06.1838; 1271a (all); Map 1841?, 4 chns; hill-drawing, foot/b'way, waterbodies, woods, marsh/bog, field gates, building names, weir, boundstones, mill leat, mill, sand or stone pits.

9/203 Hemyock (parish) ST 136129
Apt 03.12.1841; 5438a (all); Map 1843, 3 chns, by Messrs Blackmore, Clayhidon; foot/b'way, waterbodies, houses, field gates, building names, castle.

9/204 Hennock (parish) SX 843805
Apt 15.11.1838; 3469a (3469); Map 1839, 4 chns, 1st cl, by Thos Cutmore, Halwell near Totnes, Devon; construction lines, foot/b'way, waterbodies, houses, farmyards, woods, plantations, parkland, orchards, heath/moor, rock outcrops, fences, field gates, bound posts, ownership boundaries (col).

9/205 Highampton (parish) SS 494036
Apt 25.07.1842; 3039a (all); Map 1843, 3 chns, by J.H. Cotterell, Bath; houses, building names, road names, mill, pound, glebe, moor; bridge named. PRO copy is described as the 'Tithes Commissioners' Copy'.

9/206 Highbickington (parish) SS 595198 [High Bickington]
Apt 21.07.1840; 4195a (all); Map 1840, 3 chns, in 2 parts, by Hugh Ballment, Barnstaple; construction lines, waterbodies, building names, mill, weir, old river course, parsonage; map has recitial of proceedings for its adoption.

9/207 Highbray (parish) SS 702363 [High Bray]
Apt 19.12.1838; 4274a (all); Map 1838, 4 chns, 1st cl, by George Nortcote, Barnstaple; construction lines, waterbodies, houses, building names, mill, common, downland, farmyards.

9/208 Highweek (parish) SX 843724
Apt 16.05.1840; 2423a (all); Map 1842, 3 chns, 1st cl, in 2 parts, by James Taperell, Ashburton, (includes village at 1.5 chns); construction lines, waterbodies, houses, rock outcrops, fences, field gates, sand or stone pits, quarries, weirs, boundstones; pictorial church; colour bands may show property ownerships.

9/209 Hittisleigh (parish) SX 734954
Apt 09.11.1841; 1156a (1155); Map 1841, 3 chns, by George Braund and Henry Hearn, Exeter; construction lines.

9/210 Hockworthy (parish) ST 030202
Apt 08.03.1842; 2526a (2526); Map 1842?, 6 chns; foot/b'way, waterbodies, houses, woods (col), plantations (col), orchards (col), rock outcrops, building names, quarries, downland.

9/211 Holbeton (parish) SX 600482
Apt 28.12.1839; 4623a (all); Map 1842, 3 chns, by J.W. Adams, Newton Ferrers; foot/b'way, waterbodies, houses, rock outcrops, fences, ownership boundaries (col), limekilns, quarry, cliffs, beach, sands (named); bridge named; some field boundaries shown as double lines; legend explains depiction of buildings and boundaries.

9/212 Holcombe Burnell (parish) SX 842912 [Not listed]
Apt 10.10.1839; 1836a (all); Map 1841, 3 chns, by J. Philp, Exeter; construction lines, woods, plantations, orchards, heath/moor, quarry, ford; the surveyor notes: 'The land which this map represents is nothing scarcely but Hill and Dale - hence many of the lines will not prove to that degree of accuracy which they would if the ground was level'.

9/213 Holcombe Rogus (parish) ST 065190
Apt 21.07.1840; 3024a (3024); Map 1840, [3 chns], by James Hellings, Lea Wellington, Somerset; construction lines, canal with towpath, waterbodies, houses, woods, rock outcrops, hedges, fences, building names, quarries, limekilns; colour bands may show property ownerships.

9/214 Hollacombe (parish) SS 378027
Apt 16.01.1844; 1218a (all); Map 1842, 4 chns, 1st cl, by Henry and R.L. Badcock, Launceston; construction lines, building names; tithe area numbers are stamped.

9/215 Holne (parish) SX 698696
Apt 10.09.1838; 2300a (4197); Map 1839?, 9 chns, copied by H.C. Creach, Ash[burton?]; hill-drawing, waterbodies, woods (named), orchards, heath/moor, boundstone, tors, well, common; colours may show property ownerships; physical features and bridge named. Apt omits land use.

9/216 Holsworthy (parish) SS 346062
Apt 26.04.1842; 8836a (all); Map 1843, 3 chns, 1st cl, in 4 parts, by G. Braund and H. Hearn, Exeter, (part 1 by Braund, parts 2-4 by Braund and Hearn); canal.

9/217 Honey Church (parish) SS 626036 [Honeychurch]
Apt 27.10.1838; 607a (all); Map 1839, 3 chns, 1st cl, by I. Mallett; construction lines; a snake is entwined with 'Honeychurch' in the map title.

9/218 Honiton (parish) SY 162994
Apt 09.07.1842; 3047a (all); Map 1843, 3 chns, in 2 parts, by Wm Dawson, Exeter, (includes enlargement of Honiton town at 1.5 chns); foot/b'way, waterbodies, houses, fences, field gates, building names, road names, weir; bridge and waste named.

9/219 Horwood (parish) SS 509275
Apt 21.03.1840; 867a (all); Map 1841, 3 chns, by Hugh Ballment, Barnstaple; waterbodies, building names, parsonage.

9/220 Huish (parish) SS 538110
Apt 07.07.1838; 987a (all); Map 1838, 4 chns; hill-drawing, waterbodies, woods, plantations, osiers, parkland, orchards, gardens, hedge ownership, fences, building names, rectory; bridges named; colour bands may

show property ownerships; border is leafy; map is described as 'combined from the original plans of the Right Honourable Lord Clinton, (including the Glebe lands) and of Onesiphorus Saunders Esqr and corrected according to the present state of the Fences'.

9/221 North Huish (parish) SX 716558
Apt 15.04.1840; 2663a (all); Map 1839, 3 chns, by Wm Snell, Stonehouse, Devon; construction lines, houses.

9/222 South Huish (parish) SX 692407
Apt 19.12.1840; 1150a (1150); Map 1842, 3 chns, by Wm Jarvis; foot/b'way, coastline; colour bands may show property ownerships; wavy lines may be hedges.

9/223 Huntsham (parish) SS 995199
Apt 28.10.1840; 1876a (all); Map 1841, 6 chns, by Edwin Palmer, Stawley; waterbodies, houses, woods (col), plantations (col), parkland (col), orchards (col), heath/moor (col), building names, glebe.

9/224 Huntshaw (parish) SS 509234
Apt 20.03.1839; 2051a (2050); Map 1841, 4 chns, 'partially surveyed and copied' by Chas Cooper, Alverdiscott, Bideford, Devon; woods, plantations, building names, parsonage, mill; colour bands may show property ownerships.

9/225 Lands of Richard Hurley Esquire (district in parish of Uffculme) ST 068117 [Not listed]
Apt 06.11.1840; 664a (all); Map 1840, 6 chns, by R.D. Bevan; foot/b'way, waterbodies, houses, building names, landowners, ownership boundaries (col); mapmaker's name is on compass rose.

9/226 Huxham (parish) SX 951977
Apt 15.09.1837; 762a (all); Map 1841, 4 chns, by Robert Park, 8 Geo. St, Euston Square, London; waterbodies, houses, farmyards, woods, plantations, hedges, building names, mills, parsonage; legend explains boundary depiction.

9/227 Iddesleigh (parish) SS 575075
Apt 23.12.1842; 2952a (all); Map 1843, 3 chns, by G. Arnold junr, Dolton; construction lines, waterbodies, houses, fences, building names, mill, weir, glebe.

9/228 Ide (parish) SX 885897
Apt 06.05.1842; 1436a (all); Map 1843?, 4 chns; waterbodies, circle of trees.

9/229 Ideford (parish) SX 886769
Apt 15.02.1839; 1472a (1471); Map 1839?, 4 chns, in 2 parts, by Thomas Woodmass, Alston, (includes village separately at 2 chns); construction lines, waterbodies, houses; pictorial church.

9/230 Ilfracombe (parish) SS 514461
Apt 23.04.1839; 5583a (5583); Map 1840, 3 chns, 1st cl, by James Webb, Worcester; construction lines, foot/b'way, turnpike roads, turnpike gate, waterbodies, houses, open fields (named), field gates, building names, harbour, headlands, bays, limekilns, vicarage; physical features named; colour bands may show property ownerships.

9/231 Ilsington (parish) SX 790757
Apt 07.06.1838; 7563a (7563); Map 1839, 3 chns, by John Dawe, Witheycombe Rawleigh, Exmouth; construction lines, hill-drawing, foot/b'way, waterbodies, houses, woods, plantations, parkland, orchards, heath/moor, hedge ownership, fences, tors (named), quarries, old lime kiln, boundstones; bridges, rocks and boundary features named; birds of prey are entwined with map title.

9/232 Instow (parish) SS 488305
Apt 17.03.1842; 1632a (all); Map 1841, 3 chns, by Thos Lock jr, Instow; waterbodies, woods, orchards, coastline.

9/233 Inwardleigh (parish) SX 560985
Apt 26.10.1842; 6281a (all); Map 1843, 3 chns, by T. Woodmass; foot/b'way, waterbodies, houses; colour bands may show property ownerships.

9/234 Ipplepen (parish) SX 842661
Apt 15.07.1839; 3070a (3069); Map 1842, 3 chns, 1st cl, 'working plan' in 3 parts, by Gould and Taperell, Okehampton, (includes Ipplepen village at 1.5 chns); hill-drawing, waterbodies, houses, farmyards, rock outcrops, fences, quarries, limekilns, road embankments; colour bands may show property ownerships.

9/235 Jacobstow (parish) SS 581014 [Jacobstowe]
Apt 05.12.1838; 2836a (all); Map 1839, 3 chns, by Hugh Ballment, Barnstaple; building names, churchyard; colour bands may show property ownerships; map has note: 'the property of Charles F. Burton Esqr is copied from a map made by Mr John Wills in 1825, and all other Estates are delineated from actual measurements now taken'.

9/236 Kelly (parish) SX 403818
Apt 31.10.1838; 1722a (all); Map 1839, 4 chns; waterbodies, houses, woods, parkland, orchards, gardens, hedge ownership, ownership boundaries (col); table lists property names. Apt omits land use.

9/237 Kenn (parish) SX 904852
Apt 06.03.1841; 5413a (5412); Map 1841, 6 chns, in 3 parts, by Robert Dymond, Exeter, (including index); hill-drawing, waterbodies, houses, woods (col), plantations (col), parkland (col), arable (col), grassland (col), orchards (col), alders (col), fences, sand or stone pits, racecourse, tithe-free land.

9/238 Kennerleigh (parish) SS 819075
Apt 20.08.1839; 733a (all); Map 1841?, 3 chns; turnpike roads, waterbodies, houses, woods, orchards, heath/moor, building names, toll house; colour bands may show property ownerships.

9/239 Kentisbeare (parish) ST 070085
Apt 31.08.1841; 3721a (3720); Map 1842, 6 chns, by G. Braund and H. Hearn.

9/240 Kentisbury (parish) SS 626436
Apt 20.07.1839; 3129a (all); Map 1840, 4 chns, by G. Northcote, Barnstaple; houses, woods (col), field gates, building names, glebe, farmyard.

9/241 Kenton (parish) SX 945830
Apt 30.01.1840; 5882a (6811); Map 1840, 4 chns, in 2 parts, by Robert Dymond; hill-drawing, foot/b'way, turnpike roads, waterbodies, houses, farmyards, gardens, rock outcrops, fences, field gates, lagoons, cliffs, sand banks, sand or stone pits, boundstones, millstones, toll-bar, river incision.

9/242 Kilmington (parish) SY 268985
Apt 28.08.1838; 1761a (all); Map 1840?, 6 chns, by W. Pickering; waterbodies, houses, woods, plantations, parkland, orchards, building names.

9/243 Kingkerswell (parish) SX 881672 [Kingskerswell]
Apt 31.03.1841; 1744a (all); Map 1838, 3 chns, surveyed for the Newton Abbott Union Board of Guardians by H. Symons, Fancy, Plymouth; waterbodies, houses, woods, willows, plantations, orchards, building names; colour bands may show property ownerships.

9/244 Kingsnympton (parish) SS 691204 [King's Nympton]
Apt 12.07.1842; 5539a (all); Map 1843, 6 chns, in 2 parts, by H. Crispin, South Molton, (includes enlargement of village at 1.5 chns); foot/b'way.

9/245 Kingsteignton (parish) SX 866745
Apt 14.04.1840; 3984a (all); Map 1840, 3 chns, 1st cl, by W. Norris, Exeter; construction lines, waterbodies, houses, fences; colour bands may show property ownerships.

9/246 Kingston (parish) SX 632479
Apt 18.11.1841; 2233a (all); Map 1839, 3 chns, by S.W. Adams, Newton Ferrers; waterbodies, houses, woods (named), plantations (named), orchards (named), heath/moor (named), rock outcrops, field boundary ownerships, field gates, cliffs, beach, mill leat, limekilns, ownership boundaries (col); coast features named; legend explains depiction of buildings, waterbodies and boundaries; rose, thistle, clover and leaves decorate title.

9/247 Kingswear (parish) SX 885511
Apt 14.05.1840; 108a (152); Map 1841, 3 chns, by John Grant, Ugborough; hill-drawing, houses, woods, orchards, gardens, rock outcrops, field gates, boundary post, ferries, cliffs, low water mark,

creek, castle; red lines may be stone walls; some field boundaries are shown with double lines; colour bands may show property ownerships; table gives owners, occupiers, land use and acreage of fields. Apt distingushes types of garden: 'kitchen', 'herbs', 'potatoe', 'fruit'.

9/248 Knowstone (parish) SS 832227
Apt 28.01.1841; 4990a (4989); Map 1842, 3 chns, by George Braund and Henry Hearn; construction lines.

9/249 Lamerton (parish) SX 442768
Apt 03.11.1840; 7232a (7232); Map 1842, 3 chns, by William Gould, Okehampton; waterbodies, houses, fences, building names, landowners, tor, mine, mill, ownership boundaries (col).

9/250 Landcross (parish) SS 462239
Apt 27.09.1838; 332a (all); Map 1839?, 4 chns, ? by George Doe; foot/b'way, houses, woods (col), orchards (col), hops (col), gardens (col), field gates, building names, mills, limekilns, downland, glebe.

9/251 Landkey (parish) SS 598323
Apt 06.09.1845; 3162a (all); Map 1846, 3 chns, by Abiezer Rowe, Barnstaple; construction lines, waterbodies, houses, building names, weir, lime quarry.

9/252 Langtree (parish) SS 454150
Apt 07.07.1838; 4595a (all); Map 1841?, 4 chns; foot/b'way, houses, woods, plantations, orchards, heath/moor, field gates, building names, moor.

9/253 Lapford (parish) SS 734091
Apt 28.03.1840; 3820a (3819); Map 1841?, 3 chns, 1st cl, in 2 parts, by G. Braund and H. Hearn, Exeter; construction lines; map also includes Nymet Rowland.

9/254 St Leonard (parish) SX 926920 [Not listed]
Apt 28.09.1839; 173a (172); Map 1840, 2 chns, by Geo. W. Cumming, Exeter, (tinted); foot/b'way, waterbodies, houses, building names, landowners, Artillery Barracks, factory, weir, deaf and dumb institution, school, glebe.

9/255 Lewtrenchard (parish) SX 474859
Apt 20.07.1839; 2819a (2818); Map 1839, [4 chns], by A.B. Gould, Lieut, Madras Artillery; construction lines, turnpike roads, woods, plantations, orchards, downland, building names, mill, mines, lime and slate quarries, rectory; colour bands may show property ownerships; names are stamped; map has recital of proceedings for its adoption.

9/256 Lifton (parish) SX 387849
Apt 24.08.1840; 5982a (5982); Map 1840, 3 chns, 1st cl, in 2 parts, by T. Lancaster, Lifton; construction lines, waterbodies, houses, building names, quarry; colour bands may show property ownerships.

9/257 Littleham (parish) SS 438237
Apt 20.07.1839; 1250a (1250); Map 1840, 3 chns, copied from a map made by William Bear, Bideford, by Thos Lock jr, Instow; waterbodies, woods, plantations, orchards, fences, building names, parsonage, ownership boundaries (col).

9/258 Littleham and Exmouth (parish) SY 029809
Apt 02.08.1842; 3012a (3651); Map 1844, 3 chns, by John Doherty; hill-drawing, foot/b'way, waterbodies, houses, woods, rock outcrops, field gates, building names, cliffs, beach (col), market house, hotel, pound.

9/259 Loddiswell (parish) SX 720497
Apt 30.06.1838; 3568a (3568); Map 1839, 3 chns, by W. Jarvis; waterbodies, farmyards, boundstones; wavy lines may be hedges or woodland edges; colour bands may show property ownerships.

9/260 Loxbear (parish) SS 910157 [Loxbeare]
Apt 15.2.1842; 761a (all); Map 1843, 4.75 chns, ? by Thos Heathfield; foot/b'way, waterbodies, building names, mill.

9/261 Loxhore (parish) SS 623383
Apt 06.05.1842; 1531a (all); Map 1843?, 3 chns; construction lines, waterbodies, houses, farmyards, building names, glebe; colour bands may show property ownerships.

9/262 Luffincot (parish) SX 336939 [Luffincott]
Apt 26.10.1842; 971a (all); Map 1842, 4 chns, by Henry and R.L. Badcock, Launceston; foot/b'way, houses, woods, plantations, orchards, marsh/bog, building names, glebe; names and tithe area numbers are stamped.

9/263 Luppitt (parish) ST 172058
Apt 19.09.1840; 4294a (4293); Map 1843?, 3 chns, by Messrs Blackmore, Clayhidon; hill-drawing, foot/b'way, waterbodies, houses, woods, plantations, orchards, field gates, sand or stone pits or quarries, tithe-free lands.

9/264 Lustleigh (parish) SX 770820
Apt 10.06.1837; 2939a (2939); Map 1838, 3 chns, by R. Luscombe, Torquay; foot/b'way, waterbodies, woods, plantations, orchards, heath/moor, fences, building names, rectory, mill, boundary marks; scale is graduated in poles, chains, furlongs and miles.

9/265 Old Lydford (district in parish of Lydford) SX 534855 [Not listed]
Apt 08.05.1846; 2093a (all); Map 1846, 4 chns, 1st cl, by W.F. Cotterell [and son?] Bath; construction lines, houses, woods, building names, moor; boundary features named.

9/266 Lympston (parish) SY 010842 [Lympstone]
Apt 17.05.1839; 1121a (all); Map 1840, 3 chns, by Wm Norris, Exeter; waterbodies, houses.

9/267 Lynton (parish) SS 712469
Apt 20.07.1839; 7163a (all); Map 1840, 4 chns, in 2 parts, by Bland Hood Galland, C.E. and D. Vaughan, (includes Lynton and Lynmouth at 2 chns by 'D. Vaughan for B.H. Galland'); hill-drawing, foot/b'way, waterbodies, woods (col), plantations (col), parkland (col), orchards (col), heath/moor (col), rock outcrops, hedges, field gates, building names, road names, field names, landowners, bowling green, barrow, waterfall, limekilns, cliffs, beach, pier, summer houses, clubhouse, school, quarry, offices, hotels, trig points (named), Danish fort, castles, boundstones, salmon weir, parsonage, commons, downland, ownership boundaries (col), glebe; physical features named and mapped in detail, and map is annotated with comments such as 'very steep Ang. 60 dgs', 'steep rocky pasture', etc; on top of the title of the enlargement a plover holds a flag, on top of which a smaller plover is perched.

9/268 Maker (parish) SX 423518 [Not listed]
Apt 28.07.1840; 2465a (3204); Map 1841, 4 chns, by John Andrew, Plympton, Devon; waterbodies, woods, plantations, parkland (in detail, named), orchards, building names, batteries, coastline, ferry, quarry; built-up part generalised; pictorial church.

9/269 Malborough (parish) SX 712385
Apt 21.05.1841; 4890a (5310); Map 1841, 3 chns, by Wm Jarvis; coast features; headland, creeks, sands and coves named.

9/270 Mamhead (parish) SX 933805 [Not listed]
Apt 29.09.1838; 1165a (1165); Map 1839, 3 chns, by Robert Dymond, Exeter; hill-drawing, waterbodies, houses, woods (col), plantations (col), parkland (in detail, col), arable (col), grassland (col), orchards (col), gardens (in detail, col), heath/moor (col), hedge ownership, fences, field gates, sand or stone pits; colour bands may show property ownerships.

9/271 Manaton (parish) SX 725808
Apt 05.03.1842; 6393a (all); Map 1842, 3 chns, by Irish and Parker; construction lines, waterbodies, houses, farmyards, plantations, fences, building names, rectory. Apt omits land use.

9/272 Marldon (parish) SX 872636
Apt 24.09.1839; 2333a (all); Map 1839, 4 chns, 1st cl, by H. Symons, Fancy near Plymouth; construction lines, foot/b'way, waterbodies, building names, castle. Apt omits land use.

9/273 Martinhoe (parish) SS 670479
Apt 30.04.1841; 2549a (all); Map 1842, 3 chns; woods (col), orchards (col), building names, mill, coastline, limekiln, commons, downland; physical features named.

9/274 Marwood (parish) SS 549385
Apt 13.12.1843; 5396a (all); Map 1840, 3 chns, by F. Cattlin, 39 Ely

Place, Holborn, London; foot/b'way, waterbodies, houses, building names, mills, woodland (by name), downland.

9/275 Maryansleigh (parish) SS 748217 [Mariansleigh]
Apt 31.07.1839; 1964a (all); Map 1839, 3 chns, by Hugh Ballment, Barnstaple; foot/b'way, sand or stone pit; map has note: 'This map as far as Sir H.P. Davies property is copied from Mr Robt Ballment's map made in 1794-95, except the village, which, with the remainder of the map, is delineated from measurements now taken'.

9/276 Marystow (parish) SX 436846
Apt 15.07.1839; 2895a (all); Map 1839, 4 chns, 1st cl, by Henry and R.L. Badcock, Launceston; construction lines, foot/b'way, waterbodies, woods, plantations, parkland, orchards, building names; names and tithe area numbers are stamped.

9/277 Marytavy (parish) SX 507805 [Mary Tavy]
Apt 04.08.1843; 4180a (all); Map 1841, 4 chns, 1st cl, by H. Symons, Fancy near Plymouth; construction lines, houses.

9/278 Meavy (parish) SX 540663
Apt 12.11.1839; 3289a (3289); Map 1840, 3 chns, compiled from 'original surveys'; hill-drawing, railway, waterbodies, woods, plantations, parkland, orchards, marsh/bog, heath/moor, rock outcrops, building names, tors (named), leats, sand or stone pits, downland; bridges named; colour bands may show property ownerships.

9/279 Meeth (parish) SS 542081
Apt 30.04.1839; 2479a (all); Map 1839, 3 chns, by H. Crispin junr, Chulmleigh; foot/b'way, woods, plantations, parkland, orchards, field gates, building names, parsonage, mill leat; colours may show property ownerships.

9/280 Membury (parish) ST 277032
Apt 21.07.1840; 4090a (4089); Map 1843?, 6 chns, in 2 parts; hill-drawing, foot/b'way, waterbodies, houses, woods (col, named), plantations (col, named), orchards (col), heath/moor (col), field gates, building names, mill, castle; bridge named.

9/281 Merton (parish) SS 526134
Apt 26.03.1841; 3738a (3738); Map 1842, 6 chns, copied from old maps in the possession of the landowners by Joseph Risdon, Speccott; houses, building names, mill; title is decorated with oak leaves and acorns and leaves decorate borders.

9/282 Meshaw (parish) SS 764188
Apt 24.10.1838; 1752a (all); Map 1838, 3 chns, by Henry Crispin junr, Chulmleigh, Devon; foot/b'way, houses, farmyards, woods (col), plantations (col), orchards, heath/moor, field gates, building names, mill.

9/283 Milton Abbott (parish) SX 422800 [Milton Abbot]
Apt 18.12.1839; 6618a (6617); Map 1840, 4 chns, 1st cl, by H. Symons, Fancy near Plymouth; construction lines, waterbodies, houses, fences, building names, boundary posts, sand or stone pits.

9/284 Milton Damarel (parish) SS 387109
Apt 26.08.1840; 4252a (all); Map 1840, 3 chns, by Mr Robert Heard, Dulverton, Somerset; woods (col).

9/285 South Milton (parish) SX 696426
Apt 11.10.1839; 1557a (all); Map 1843?, 3 chns; foot/b'way, waterbodies, woods, plantations, rock outcrops, fences, field boundary ownerships, beach (col), cliffs, sand or stone pits, quarry; colour bands may show property ownerships.

9/286 Modbury (parish) SX 664518
Apt 29.01.1841; 6234a (6258); Map 1841, 3 chns, by Thomas Suter, Exeter; construction lines, waterbodies, houses, woods, plantations, field gates, building names, glebe; colour bands may show property ownerships.

9/287 Molland (parish) SS 811283
Apt 24.06.1841; 6168a (6168); Map 1842, 3 chns; waterbodies, woods (col), orchards (col), building names, field names, mill.

9/288 North Molton (parish) SS 737320
Apt 13.04.1840; 14351a (14351); Map 1842, 8 chns, in 15 parts, by Wm Collard Cox, Williton, Somerset, (including 14 enlargements of settlements at 2 chns); waterbodies.

9/289 South Molton (parish) SS 698266
Apt 05.12.1839; 6265a (all); Map 1844?, 3 chns, 1st cl, by H. Crispin junr, Chulmleigh; construction lines, waterbodies, woods, rock outcrops, building names, road names, weir, mills, gas works, limekiln, quarries, lines of trees; bridge named; built-up part generalised; colour bands may show property ownerships.

9/290 Monkokehampton (parish) SS 584055
Apt 16.02.1845; 1488a (all); Map 1845, 3 chns, in 3 parts; foot/b'way, waterbodies, houses, building names, mill.

9/291 Monkleigh (parish) SS 455218
Apt 25.05.1839; 2177a (2177); Map 1840, 3 chns, by Chas Cooper, Alverdiscott, Bideford, Devon; construction lines, trig points, waterbodies, houses; colour bands may show property ownerships.

9/292 Monkton (parish) ST 188025
Apt 09.09.1842; 1233a (all); Map 1842, 3 chns, by Wm Dawson; foot/b'way, waterbodies, houses, building names.

9/293 Morchards Bishop (parish) SS 774075
Apt 03.05.1838; 7089a (all); Map 1840, 3 chns, 1st cl, surveyed for Mr Jos. Risdon, land surveyor by Wm and Geo. Graham; construction lines, waterbodies, weir.

9/294 Morebath (parish) SS 960252
Apt 26.01.1838; 3449a (3449); Map 1838, 3 chns; waterbodies, houses, hedges, sand or stone pits; hedges may show property boundaries.

9/295 Moretonhampstead (parish) SX 758869
Apt 03.05.1839; 7656a (all); Map 1840, 3 chns, by George Murphy and Jno. Germon; construction lines, trig points (named), turnpike roads, turnpike house, waterbodies, houses, woods, plantations, parkland, orchards, building names, road names, mills, tan yard, ownership boundaries (col), glebe; bridge named; legend explains depiction of buildings and boundaries on map. Apt omits land use and some field names.

9/296 Morley (parish) SX 753527 [Moreleigh]
Apt 09.06.1842; 1488a (1487); Map 1843, 3 chns, 1st cl, by Thos Cutmore, Halwell nr Totnes, Devon; waterbodies, houses, farmyards, weir, property boundaries.

9/297 Morthoe (parish) SS 468435 [Mortehoe]
Apt 16.10.1840; 4246a (4621); Map 1840, 3 chns, by Hugh Ballment, Barnstaple; waterbodies, building names, landowners, high and low watermarks, parsonage, lodge; coast is annotated with details of ownership of royalties; roads not belonging to the parish are distinguished; map has recital of proceedings for its adoption.

9/298 Musbury (parish) SY 284950
Apt 18.12.1839; 2178a (all); Map 1839, 3 chns, by Wm Dawson, Exeter; construction lines, hill-drawing, turnpike roads, waterbodies, houses, farmyards, fences, field gates, boundstones, turnpike gate, tumulus; bridge named.

9/299 Newton Ferrers (parish) SX 569496
Apt 30.09.1839; 2991a (3191); Map 1839, 4 chns, by John Andrew, Plympton St Mary, Devon; foot/b'way, waterbodies, woods, plantations, parkland, orchards, field gates, quarry; bridge named.

9/300 Newton St Cyres (parish) SX 877976
Apt 03.02.1842; 4305a (4305); Map 1843, 4 chns, by E. Browne; houses, woods, plantations, orchards, heath/moor, building names; bridge named.

9/301 Newton St Petrock (parish) SS 413126
Apt 27.07.1840; 1557a (all); Map 1840?, 6 chns; houses, woods, building names, mill, glebe; ruler, pair of compasses, charcoal holder and quill pen surround scale.

9/302 Newton Tracey (parish) SS 530272
Apt 21.03.1840; 336a (all); Map 1841, 3 chns, by Hugh Ballment, Barnstaple; building names; north pointer has unusual floral decoration.

9/303 Northam (parish) SS 446293
Apt 30.11.1838; 2194a (4190); Map 1839, 3 chns, by B. Herman, Northam; hill-drawing, foot/b'way, houses, woods, plantations, parkland, orchards, marsh/bog (col), rock outcrops, hedge ownership, fences, field gates, building names, beach (col), limekilns, harbour walks, cliffs, watermill; church, Kenwith Lodge and houses surrounding church are shown pictorially; coast features named; sea is decorated with several vessels in sail with coloured flags and rowing boats with oarsmen; pair of compasses, charcoal holders, quill pen and ruler surround scale bar.

9/304 Northcot (hamlet in parish of Boyton) SX 341928 [Not listed]
Apt 05.02.1841; 803a (802); Map 1841, 3 chns, 1st cl, by Jonathan Kittow, North Petherwin; construction lines, building names, mill.

9/305 Northleigh (parish) SY 197968
Apt 11.03.1839; 994a (all); Map 1839, 3 chns, by Wm Dawson, Exeter; houses, waste. Common is described in Apt as 'subject to tithes but now uncultivated and overgrown for the most part with furze'.

9/306 Northlew (parish) SX 500999
Apt 31.12.1841; 7248a (all); Map 1843, 3 chns, by George Gould junr, Okehampton; waterbodies, houses, fences, glebe (col); colour bands may show property ownerships.

9/307 Nymet Rowland (parish) SS 715083
Apt 26.01.1842; 595a (all); Map 1840, 3 chns, 1st cl, by G. Braund and H. Hearn, Exeter.

9/308 Oakford (parish) SS 895222
Apt 11.06.1840; 5464a (all); Map 1841?, 3 chns; construction lines, trig points (named), waterbodies, woods, plantations, orchards, heath/moor, building names, lodge, mill stream, downland.

9/309 Offwell (parish) SY 189988
Apt 26.10.1842; 2207a (all); Map 1843, 3 chns, by John Taperell; hill-drawing, waterbodies, houses, woods, plantations, orchards, fences, building names, parsonage, common, ornamental ground; colours may show property ownerships.

9/310 East Ogwell (parish) SX 834703
Apt 23.10.1841; 1249a (1249); Map 1844, 3 chns, by John Widdicombe, Ugborough; waterbodies, rock outcrops, field gates, quarries, limekilns, watermill; red lines may be stone walls; some field boundaries are shown as double lines; mapmaker's name is on ribbon beneath map title.

9/311 West Ogwell (parish) SX 821701
Apt 10.09.1838; 684a (683); Map 1839, 3 chns, by John Widdicombe, Ugborough; foot/b'way, waterbodies, houses, woods, plantations, orchards, fences, field gates, sand or stone pits, ownership boundaries (col).

9/312 Okehampton (parish) SX 573943
Apt 19.04.1839; 9553a (9552); Map 1841, 3 chns, by Wm Morris, Bristol; hill-drawing, waterbodies, houses, farmyards (col), woods (col), plantations (col), parkland (col), orchards (col), building names, direction posts, boundstones, quarry, vicarage, farm names, downland, hospital lands (col), borough boundary.

9/313 Otterton (parish) SY 092857
Apt 18.09.1843; 3479a (all); Map 1844, 3 chns, by John Doherty; hill-drawing, waterbodies, houses, woods, heath/moor, bound stones, beach, cliffs, common.

9/314 Ottery St Mary (parish) SY 096949
Apt 14.04.1842; 9945a (9942); Map 1845?, 3 chns, in 2 parts, by W. Morris, Bristol; foot/b'way, waterbodies, houses, building names; bands may show property ownerships.

9/315 Paington (parish) SX 872603 [Paignton]
Apt 22.07.1840; 5093a (all); Map 1841, 3 chns, 1st cl, in 2 parts, by Luckraft, Warren and Company, Crediton; construction lines, trig points (named), houses, woods, plantations, orchards, heath/moor, building names; colour bands may show property ownerships.

9/316 Pancraswike (parish) SS 299078 [Pancrasweek]
Apt 31.12.1841; 3783a (all); Map 1842, 3 chns, 'compiled partly from old surveys' by Henry and R.L. Badcock, Launceston; foot/b'way, canal, farmyards, building names, sand or stone pit, glebe; names and tithe area numbers are stamped.

9/317 Parkham (parish) SS 387216
Apt 08.06.1840; 5808a (all); Map 1840, 3 chns, by Chas Cooper, Alverdiscott, Bideford; waterbodies, woods, plantations.

9/318 Parracombe (parish) SS 667446
Apt 15.05.1838; 4363a (all); Map 1839, 3 chns; foot/b'way, turnpike roads, waterbodies, woods, plantations, parkland, orchards, fences, building names, road names, barrows, ancient castle and ditch, parsonage, mill, ownership boundaries (col).

9/319 Payhembury (parish) ST 089017
Apt 29.10.1839; 2699a (2698); Map 1839, 6 chns, by G.A. Boyce, Tiverton; hill-drawing, foot/b'way, waterbodies, houses, building names, Roman entrenchment, mill.

9/320 Peters Marland (parish) SS 483129
Apt 16.12.1839; 2238a (all); Map 1840?, 3 chns, 1st cl, by Henry Hearn, Shebbear and George Braund junr, Exeter; construction lines, houses (by shading).

9/321 Petertavy (parish) SX 512780 [Peter Tavy]
Apt 04.04.1839; 2770a (3500); Map 1841?, 3 chns, by Eastcott and Frise, Devonport; construction lines, waterbodies, houses, farmyards, woods, plantations, orchards, fences, boundary trees.

9/322 North Pertherwin (parish) SX 268910 [North Petherwin]
Apt 06.08.1842; 8160a (8157); Map 1840, 4 chns, 1st cl, by J. Kittow, North Petherwin; construction lines, building names; names are stamped.

9/323 Petrockstow (parish) SS 516098 [Petrockstowe]
Apt 07.07.1838; 4001a (4000); Map 1840?, 4 chns; foot/b'way, waterbodies, houses, woods (col), plantations (col), orchards (col), gardens (col), marsh/bog (col), field gates, parsonage, farm and property names, ornamental ground; bridge named; colour bands may show property ownerships.

9/324 Pilton (parish) SS 553348
Apt 31.05.1842; 835a (1861); Map 1843, 4 chns, by Hugh Ballment, Barnstaple, (tithable parts only, tinted); turnpike roads, tollhouse, houses, building names; map has recital of proceedings for its adoption.

9/325 Pinhoe (parish) SX 956944
Apt 26.02.1839; 1735a (1735); Map 1839, 6 chns, by Wm Norris, Exeter; waterbodies, houses (by shading), hedge ownership.

9/326 Pitt (district in parish of Tiverton) SS 966173
Apt 04.08.1841; 5840a (5840); Map 1842, 6 chns, in 4 parts, by William Richards junr, (including three 2-chn enlargements of detail); foot/b'way, canal, waterbodies, building names, weir, rectory, chapel, mill, fishponds, district boundaries.

9/327 Plymouth, Charles the Martyr (parish) SX 493548 [Not listed]
Apt 10.12.1844; 688a (1116); Map 1846, 4 chns, by John Eastridge Adams and William Rowden Sanders, 57, York Street, Plymouth; railways, waterbodies, rock outcrops, road names, pier, reservoirs, exchange; bridge named; built-up part generalised.

9/328 Plymouth, St Andrew (parish) SX 477552 [Not listed]
Apt 06.06.1845; 240a (519); Map 1846, 4 chns, by William Snell, Chapel Street, Stonehouse; waterbodies, building names, road names, pier, docks, old victualling office, citadel, hotel, chapel, Athenaeum, market, guildhall, hospital, burial ground, parade; chapels and public buildings coloured; built-up part generalised.

9/329 Plympton Maurice (parish) SX 547557 [Plympton]
Apt 23.12.1841; 203a (all); Map 1843, 3 chns, by John Andrew, Plympton, Devon; foot/b'way, waterbodies, tumulus, embankments.

9/330 Plympton St Mary (parish) SX 559575 [Plympton]
Apt 29.12.1840; 9984a (9983); Map 1841, 3 chns; hill-drawing, railway, turnpike roads, canal with towpath, waterbodies, woods, plantations, parkland, orchards, field gates, quarries, ampitheatre, boundstones,

burrows, tor; boundary features and gates, bridge and private drive named. (Part of the PRO copy is a modern redrawing.)

9/331 Plymstock (parish) SX 518527
Apt 14.04.1842; 3550a (all); Map 1842, 3 chns, by Messrs Woodmass and Co, Ivy Bridge, Devon; construction lines, houses, farmyards, field boundary ownerships, building names; legend explains depiction of buildings, waterbodies and boundaries; John Huddleston, one of the Woodmass partnership, has signed the map and may have been particularly responsible for it; a tree design is incorporated into the map title.

9/332 Plymtree (parish) ST 060033
Apt 06.05.1842; 2185a (2185); Map 1843?, 3 chns, by Thomas Woodmass, John Huddlestone, John Thompson, John Woodmass, Alston; waterbodies, houses, road names; title is surrounded by leaf border, with red and white roses on top.

9/333 Poltimore (parish) SX 965972
Apt 15.09.1837; 1711a (all); Map 1841?, 4 chns, by Robert Park, 8 Geo. St, Euston Square, London; waterbodies, houses, farmyards, plantations, parkland, hedge ownership, building names, sand or stone pit, stables, rectory; hedges show property boundaries.

9/334 South Pool (parish) SX 770407
Apt 20.10.1840; 1930a (2289); Map 1840, 3 chns, by W. Jarvis; coastline; creeks named; colour bands may show property ownerships; wavy lines may show hedges or woodland edges.

9/335 East Portlemouth (parish) SX 758379
Apt 14.12.1839; 1973a (2143); Map 1840, 4 chns, by Hans W. Allen; construction lines, houses, open fields.

9/336 Poughill (parish) SS 854086
Apt 22.05.1839; 1663a (1663); Map 1840, 6 chns, by Joseph Risdon, Torrington; hill-drawing, waterbodies, houses, woods, building names; pair of compasses, quill pen, charcoal holder and ruler suround scale.

9/337 Powderham (parish) SX 958851
Apt 02.02.1838; 1188a (all); Map 1839, 4 chns, by Robert Dymond, Exeter; hill-drawing, turnpike roads, toll house, waterbodies, woods (col), plantations (col), parkland (in detail, col), arable (col), grassland (col), orchards (col), gardens (col), marsh/bog (col), hedge ownership, building names, dovecot, boat house, limekiln, river embankment, drains; hill named.

9/338 Priors (district in parish of Tiverton) SS 932105 [Not listed]
Apt 21.09.1841; 3185a (all); Map 1842, 6 chns, by William Richards junr, Tiverton; canal, waterbodies, building names, weirs, parks (named); districts named.

9/339 Puddington (parish) SS 835110
Apt 30.04.1838; 1362a (all); Map 1839, 3 chns, 1st cl, 'draft plan'; construction lines, waterbodies, sand or stone pit; colour bands may show property ownerships.

9/340 East Putford (parish) SS 376172
Apt 08.07.1841; 2380a (all); Map 1842, 4 chns, by Warren, Reaney and Warren, Crediton; foot/b'way, waterbodies, houses, woods, plantations, orchards, heath/moor, building names, common; colour bands may show property ownerships.

9/341 West Putford (parish) SS 353155
Apt 07.11.1838; 2621a (2620); Map 1840, 3 chns, by Mr Robt Heard, Dulverton, Somerset; construction lines, foot/b'way, houses, woods (col).

9/342 Pyworthy (parish) SS 314028
Apt 30.08.1838; 5022a (all); Map 1840, 4 chns, by Isaac Mason, Hornacott, Launceston; construction lines, building names; colour bands may show property ownerships.

9/343 Rackenford (parish) SS 856188
Apt 11.08.1842; 3939a (all); Map 1843, 3 chns, by H. Crispin junr, South Molton; rock outcrops, building names, stone pits or quarries, parsonage, mill.

9/344 Rattery (parish) SX 746624
Apt 31.12.1841; 2824a (all); Map 1843, 2 chns, by Irish and Parker, Buckfastleigh; construction lines, waterbodies, houses, farmyards, fences, building names, mill, stables, vicarage.

9/345 Revelstoke (parish) SX 548467 [Not listed]
Apt 28.01.1841; 1471a (1478); Map 1841, 5.5 chns, by S.W. Adams, Newton Ferrers; foot/b'way, waterbodies, woods, plantations, orchards, heath/moor, coastline; headland named.

9/346 Rewe (parish) SS 946008
Apt 26.10.1837; 1341a (all); Map 1839, 6 chns, ? by John Drew and Thos Wright; watermill; border corners have floral decoration and there is a bird-shaped scroll above the scale.

9/347 Ringmore (parish) SX 648470
Apt 11.06.1840; 1129a (all); Map 1841, 4 chns, by S.W. Adams, Newton Ferrers; foot/b'way, waterbodies, houses, woods (col), plantations (col), orchards (col), rock outcrops, field gates, cliffs, limekilns, property boundaries, glebe; coast features named; some field boundaries are shown with double lines; legend explains depiction of buildings, boundaries and waterbodies.

9/348 Roborough (parish) SS 574174
Apt 08.06.1840; 3115a (all); Map 1840, 6 chns, by Geo. Copland; foot/b'way, waterbodies, parkland (in detail); colours may show property ownerships.

9/349 Rockbeare (parish) SY 039941
Apt 27.09.1843; 2375a (2375); Map 1844, 3 chns, by D. Climie; waterbodies, houses, farmyards.

9/350 Romansleigh (parish) SS 736197
Apt 18.12.1839; 2492a (all); Map 1840?, 4 chns, by Thomas Woodmass and Co; construction lines, houses; map has recital of proceedings for its adoption.

9/351 Rose Ash (parish) SS 791209
Apt 01.09.1842; 5082a (all); Map 1844, 3 chns, by H. Crispin junr, South Molton; waterbodies, houses, farmyards, building names, parsonage, mill.

9/352 Rousdon St Pancras (parish) SY 295905 [Rousden]
Apt 10.04.1844; 254a (?); Map 1843?, 7 chns; hill-drawing, waterbodies, woods.

9/353 Salcombe Regis (except Chilstone) (parish) SY 146888
Apt 04.12.1839; 1963a (2605); Map 1839, 6 chns, by Jno. Coldridge; hill-drawing, waterbodies, houses, woods, plantations, heath/moor, fences, building names, beach, cliffs, farm and property names, roughland, glebe; bridge named; colour bands may show property ownerships.

9/354 Sampford Courtney (parish) SX 627986 [Sampford Courtenay]
Apt 16.02.1842; 7962a (all); Map 1843, 3 chns, 1st cl, by T. Woodmass and Co; construction lines, waterbodies, houses.

9/355 Sampford Peverell (parish) ST 035143
Apt 08.03.1844; 2000a (2000); Map 1844, 6 chns, in 2 parts, by W. Richards, Tiverton, (includes enlargement of village at 3 chns); railway, foot/b'way, canal with towpath, waterbodies, houses, farmyards, building names, quarrying or mining (by symbol).

9/356 Sampford Spiney (parish) SX 530718
Apt 21.12.1841; 1721a (all); Map 1842, 4 chns, 1st cl, by J. Palmer, 23 James Street, Devonport; construction lines, waterbodies, houses, farmyards, fences, boundary stones; pair of compasses, quill pen, charcoal holder, ruler and leaves surround scale; surveyor's name is on scroll draped over pedestal, with wheat at base.

9/357 Sandford (parish) SS 815040
Apt 26.02.1839; 7793a (7793); Map 1841?, 3 chns, in 3 parts; foot/b'way, waterbodies, houses, woods, plantations, parkland (named), orchards, heath/moor, rock outcrops, fences, building names, mills, stone pits, quarries, park lodges; bridge named; colour bands may show property ownerships.

9/358 Satterleigh (parish) SS 667225
Apt 03.04.1839; 515a (all); Map 1839?, [3 chns], 1st cl, by Geo.

Northcote, Barnstaple; construction lines, waterbodies, houses, field gates, building names.

9/359 Seaton and Beer (parish) SY 233904
Apt 10.09.1839; 2767a (all); Map 1840, 4 chns, in 2 parts, by Wm Collard Cox, Williton, Somerset, (includes towns of Seaton and Beer at 2 chns, banded on part 1); waterbodies, rock outcrops, fences, cliffs, coastline, quarries.

9/360 St Nicholas Shaldon (parish) SX 927718 [Shaldon]
Apt 31.07.1839; 446a (?); Map 1843, 3 chns, 1st cl, surveyed for Messrs George Braund and Henry Hearne, Surveyors, Exeter by James McNair Harkness and Henry O'Hagan; field boundary ownerships. Apt omits land use.

9/361 Shaugh (parish) SX 572639 [Shaugh Prior]
Apt 26.04.1842; 8707a (all); Map 1841, 3 chns, by John Andrew, Plympton, Devon; hill-drawing, foot/b'way, waterbodies, woods, plantations, orchards, fences, building names, boundary stones, burrows, tors (named), mill, clayworks, leat; bridges and rough land named.

9/362 Shebbeare (parish) SS 439106 [Shebbear]
Apt 02.08.1842; 5827a (all); Map 1844, 3 chns, 1st cl, by G. Braund, Exeter; construction lines.

9/363 Sheepstor (parish) SX 579672
Apt 23.09.1842; 3595a (3595); Map 1843, 3 chns, by Thomas Woodmass, Ivy Bridge; construction lines, foot/b'way, waterbodies, houses, farmyards, building names, watermills.

9/364 Sheepwash (parish) SS 480074
Apt 27.07.1839; 1972a (all); Map 1839, 4 chns, by Henry and R.L. Badcock, Launceston; foot/b'way, waterbodies, field gates, building names; names and tithe area numbers are stamped; map has recital of proceedings for its adoption.

9/365 Sheldon (parish) ST 118084
Apt 16.05.1839; 1682a (1681); Map 1840, 6 chns, ? by Wm Summers, litho (Standidge); waterbodies, woods, plantations, orchards, avenue of trees.

9/366 Sherford (parish) SX 772444
Apt 30.12.1842; 2326a (2326); Map 1843, 3 chns, 1st cl, by Thos Cutmore and Son, Halwell Nr Totnes, Devon; construction lines, foot/b'way, waterbodies, houses, fences, field gates, watermill, farm boundaries.

9/367 Sherwill (parish) SS 588375 [Shirwell]
Apt 21.11.1838; 4763a (all); Map 1839, 3 chns, by Chas Cooper, Alverdiscott, Bideford, Devon; construction lines, waterbodies, woods, plantations.

9/368 Shillingford (parish) SX 905880 [Shillingford Abbot]
Apt 20.06.1839; 398a (397); Map 1839?, 4 chns, by Robert Dymond, Exeter; foot/b'way, waterbodies, houses, woods (col), parkland (col), arable (col), grassland (col), orchards (col), gardens (col), marsh/bog (col), hedge ownership, fences, field gates.

9/369 Shobrook (parish) SS 873009 [Shobrooke]
Apt 20.10.1841; 3836a (all); Map 1841, 3 chns, by Warren and Company, Crediton; construction lines, trig points (named), waterbodies, houses, woods, plantations, parkland, orchards, heath/moor, building names, old bank; colour bands may show property ownerships.

9/370 Shute (parish) SY 251970
Apt 05.02.1842; 2738a (2738); Map 1844, 6 chns; hill-drawing, waterbodies, houses, woods (col), plantations (col), parkland (in detail, col), orchards (col), fences, building names, road embankments, sand or stone pits, mill.

9/371 Sidbury (parish) SY 142926
Apt 28.04.1840; 6828a (all); Map 1840, 3 chns, 1st cl, in 4 parts, by Luckraft, Warren and Co, Crediton; construction lines, trig points (named), houses, woods, plantations, orchards, building names, sand or stone pit; colour bands may show property ownerships.

9/372 Sidmouth (parish) SY 121889
Apt 27.05.1840; 1540a (1600); Map 1839, 3 chns, by Robert Dymond; foot/b'way, waterbodies, houses, woods (col), plantations (col), parkland (col), arable (col), grassland (col), orchards (col), gardens (col), heath/moor (col), rock outcrops, hedge ownership, fence ownership, cliffs, coastline, sand or stone pits or quarries, brickfield.

9/373 Silverton (parish) SS 960044
Apt 14.04.1842; 4714a (all); Map 1842, 4 chns, by John Grant; waterbodies, houses, farmyards, hedge ownership, building names, mill, rectory; hedges may show property boundaries.

9/374 Slapton (parish) SX 810466
Apt 14.03.1844; 317a (3430), (tithable parts only); Map 1845, 3 chns, by Thos Cutmore and Son; waterbodies, houses, fences.

9/375 Sourton (parish) SX 526915
Apt 21.09.1841; 5019a (all); Map 1844, 4 chns, 1st cl, by Henry and R.L. Badcock, Launceston; houses, farmyards, building names; bridge named; tithe area numbers are stamped.

9/376 Southleigh (parish) SY 200930
Apt 08.02.1841; 2580a (2579); Map 1842?, 3 chns, ? by Henry Ellis; houses, woods, plantations, orchards, heath/moor, building names, boundposts, parsonage, tower, trig point. Apt omits land use for modus lands.

9/377 Sowton (parish) SX 979920
Apt 21.04.1837; 1095a (all); Map 1837, 3 chns, by Wm Dawson, Exeter; construction lines, turnpike roads and gate, milestones, waterbodies, houses, woods, parkland, arable (col), grassland (col), orchards, gardens, hedge ownership, fences, building names, mill, parsonage, lodge, glebe; bridge named.

9/378 Spreyton (parish) SX 704967
Apt 04.08.1841; 3606a (3606); Map 1842, 3 chns, 1st cl, by George Braund and Henry Hearn, Exeter; construction lines.

9/379 Staverton (parish) SX 776654
Apt 17.05.1842; 5357a (5356); Map 1845, 3 chns, 1st cl; construction lines, building names; colour bands may show property ownerships.

9/380 Stockley English (parish) SS 845070 [Stockleigh English]
Apt 10.10.1839; 1110a (all); Map 1840, 3 chns, by Luckraft, Warren, Reaney and Warren, Crediton; construction lines, trig points (named), waterbodies, houses, woods, plantations, orchards, heath/moor, building names, parsonage, ornamental ground; colour bands may show property ownerships.

9/381 Stockley Pomeroy (parish) SS 880039 [Stockleigh Pomeroy]
Apt 19.10.1841; 1240a (1239); Map 1842, 3 chns, by M. and W.T. Warren, Crediton; foot/b'way, woods, plantations, orchards, heath/moor, building names, mill.

9/382 Stoke Canon (parish) SX 937975
Apt 05.06.1840; 1217a (all); Map 1839, 4 chns; turnpike roads, waterbodies, houses, woods, plantations, field boundary ownerships, building names, road names, mill, property and farm names; pictorial church.

9/383 Stoke Damerel (parish) SX 462555 [Not listed]
Apt 21.10.1840; 897a (2380); Map 1842, 6 chns, in 2 parts, by I.H. Rutger, (including two 3-chn enlargements of detail), litho (Standidge); hill-drawing, foot/b'way, turnpike roads, milestones, waterbodies, woods, plantations, orchards, gardens, rock outcrops, fences, building names, road names, docks, slips, basins, timber sheds, saw pits, mast houses, yarn houses, rope walks, boat stores, warehouses, barracks, officers buildings, guard rooms, smiths, millwrights, joiners, steam engine house, coal yards, kiln, laboratory, batteries, government buildings, Ordnance land and offices, telegraph, cranes, powder magazines, ferry, sewers and drainage leats, bastion, government ground, military hospital, market place, cliffs, chapels (with denominations), glebe, rectory, toll houses, school, mills, slate quarry, water supply pipes, reservoir, tide marks, weir, fortifications, baths. Apt omits land use.

9/384 Stoke Fleming (parish) SX 851495
Apt 04.11.1840; 3332a (all); Map 1841, 3 chns, by John Grant, Ugborough; hill-drawing, waterbodies, houses, woods, parkland, orchards, gardens, rock outcrops, fences, field gates, building names, coastline (in detail), cliffs, beach, mills, sand or stone pits, property boundaries; red lines may be walls; some field boundaries are shown with double lines; title is on shield crowned with fleur de lys and flanked by crowned lion and unicorn, with 'Honi soit qui mal y pense' beneath.

9/385 Stoke Gabriel (parish) SX 856576
Apt 02.07.1839; 2595a (all); Map 1840, 4 chns, by T. Woodmass and Co; waterbodies, houses, field boundary ownerships, coastline, limekilns, ornamental gardens; pair of compasses, quill pen, ruler and leaves surround scale.

9/386 Stokeinteignhead (parish) SX 926701
Apt 26.10.1842; 2484a (all); Map 1843, 3 chns, 1st cl, surveyed for Messrs George Braund and Henry Hearne, Exeter by James McNair Harkness and Henry O'Hagan; fences, field boundary ownerships, building names, parsonage; colour bands may show property ownerships.

9/387 Stokenham (parish) SX 802418
Apt 03.02.1843; 5901a (6011); Map 1841, 4 chns, 1st cl, by Thos Cutmore, Halwell near Totnes, Devon; construction lines, foot/b'way, houses, rock outcrops, fences, cliffs, lagoon, boundstone; headland named; colour bands may show property ownerships.

9/388 Stoke Rivers (parish) SS 645350
Apt 05.02.1842; 2426a (all); Map 1842, 3 chns, by Irish and Parker; construction lines, waterbodies, houses, farmyards, fences; colour bands may show property ownerships.

9/389 Stoodleigh (parish) SS 915192
Apt 22.03.1841; 4336a (4336); Map 1841, 4 chns, by William Richards, Tiverton; foot/b'way, waterbodies, houses, farmyards, building names, rectory, mill; bridge named.

9/390 Stowford (parish) SX 418868
Apt 06.09.1838; 2066a (all); Map 1839, 4 chns, 1st cl, by H. and R. Badcock, Launceston; construction lines, hill-drawing, foot/b'way, woods, plantations, parkland, orchards, field gates, building names, mill, tumuli, quarry, glebe; names and tithe area numbers are stamped; colour bands may show property ownerships.

9/391 Sutcombe (parish) SS 352115
Apt 19.08.1842; 3593a (3593); Map 1844, 3 chns, 1st cl, by Abiezer Rowe, Barnstaple; construction lines, foot/b'way, waterbodies, houses, building names, mill.

9/392 Swimbridge (parish) SS 621299
Apt 13.08.1845; 7062a (all); Map 1846, 3 chns, 1st cl, in 2 parts, by Abiezer Rowe, Barnstaple, (including two 80-chn construction line diagrams for Swimbridge and Landkey); construction lines, waterbodies, houses, building names; surveyor notes on part 2 that contraction is about one perch per acre.

9/393 South Sydenham (parish) SX 418765 [Sydenham Damerel]
Apt 14.11.1840; 1413a (1413); Map 1841, 3 chns, by N. Cuming, Tavistock; construction lines, foot/b'way, waterbodies, houses, fences, building names, mills, parsonage, sand or stone pits, mines.

9/394 Talaton (parish) SY 072986
Apt 04.11.1839; 2365a (all); Map 1840, 3 chns, by Wm Dawson, Exeter; waterbodies, woods, plantations, parkland, arable (col), grassland (col), orchards, gardens, fences, building names, weir, parsonage, common, old river course.

9/395 Tamerton Foliott (parish) SX 481626 [Tamerton Foliot]
Apt 15.06.1839; 4691a (5150); Map 1840, 4 chns, in 2 parts, by H. Symons, Fancy, Plymouth, (includes enlargement of part of village at 2 chns); construction lines, waterbodies, houses, woods, plantations, parkland, orchards, heath/moor, fences, building names, sand or stone pit.

9/396 Tavistock (parish) SX 471745
Apt 08.04.1843; 3152a (10700); Map 1842, 3 chns, 1st cl, in 4 parts, by Michael FitzGerald, (including two indexes, one at 30 chns); construction lines, canal, waterbodies, houses, woods (named), building names, mill, quay.

9/397 Tawstock (parish) SS 552284
Apt 29.01.1842; 6582a (6582); Map 1842, 3 chns, by George Harkness, Barnstaple; foot/b'way, waterbodies, houses, woods (col), heath/moor, field gates, building names, road names, boundstones, chapel, sand or stone pits or quarries, wells, seats; bridge named; colour bands may show property ownerships.

9/398 North Tawton (parish) SS 670015
Apt 05.06.1844; 5357a (all); Map 1847?, 9 chns; houses (depiction incomplete), building names.

9/399 South Tawton (parish) SX 666949
Apt 01.02.1844; 10880a (all); Map 1847?, 3 chns; hill-drawing, houses, building names, boundstones, tor, mill, quarry, lime quarries; colour bands may show property ownerships.

9/400 Tedburn St Mary (parish) SX 810941
Apt 24.03.1838; 4433a (all); Map 1839, 3 chns, in 2 parts, by J. Philp, Exeter, (including 1.5 chn enlargements of detail); construction lines, foot/b'way, woods, plantations, orchards, heath/moor, building names, manor pound, bound posts, roadside boundary ownership, farm boundaries.

9/401 Teigngrace (parish) SX 850741
Apt 16.02.1838; 1330a (all); Map 1838, 8 chns, by E.S. Bearne, Teigngrace, Newton Abbot, Devon; railway, canal, waterbodies, building names, clay cellars, stables, ownerships (col), glebe; legend explains property colouring. District is apportioned by holding and fields are not shown.

9/402 East Teignmouth (parish) SX 944743 [Teignmouth]
Apt 21.04.1840; 671a (all); Map 1839, 3 chns, by Thomas Woodmass, John Thompson, John Huddleston, John Woodmass; construction lines, foot/b'way, waterbodies, houses, field boundary ownerships, coastline; built-up part generalised.

9/403 West Teignmouth (parish) SX 935735 [Teignmouth]
Apt 20.08.1839; 403a (all); Map 1840, 3 chns, by T. Woodmass and Co; construction lines, waterbodies, houses, field boundary ownerships.

9/404 Templeton (parish) SS 877149
Apt 26.04.1842; 1892a (all); Map 1842, 3 chns, by Thos B. New, Worcester; construction lines, foot/b'way, waterbodies, houses, farmyards, woods, plantations, heath/moor (named), rock outcrops, fences, field gates, building names, watermills, rectory, weir, boundary trees, well, quarry; bridge named; colour bands may show property ownerships; north pointer is decorated with coloured shield design and fleur de lys.

9/405 Tetcott (parish) SX 345962
Apt 21.04.1837; 2181a (2181); Map '1832', (1837?), 4 chns, by Taperell and Son; waterbodies, houses, woods, plantations, parkland (in detail), orchards, heath/moor (named), fences, field gates, building names, glebe; colour bands may show arable, pasture and meadow; district is described as 'the property of Sir William Molesworth Bart'. Apt omits land use.

9/406 Thelbridge (parish) SS 806134 [Not listed]
Apt 11.10.1843; 2240a (all); Map 1841, 6 chns, in 2 parts, by William Richards, Tiverton, (including 3-chn enlargement of detail); foot/b'way, waterbodies, houses, building names, rectory.

9/407 St Thomas the Apostle (parish) SX 904932 [St Thomas]
Apt 19.12.1838; 2922a (3700); Map 1839, [4 chns], in 2 parts, by Robert Park, 8 Geo. St, Euston Sq, London; construction lines, foot/b'way, canal, waterbodies, houses, woods (named), plantations (named), orchards, gardens, heath/moor, hedge ownership, field boundary ownerships, building names, road names, field names, chapel, weirs, gas works, priory, quarries, workhouse, Devon ward; woodland shown by cross symbols; some field boundaries are red; some plantations, gardens, orchards and nurseries are shown by annotation; bridge named; public buildings coloured; colours may show property ownerships.

9/408 Thornbury (parish) SS 387080
Apt 20.07.1839; 2772a (all); Map 1840, 3 chns, by Mr Robt Heard, Dulverton, Somerset; construction lines, waterbodies, houses, woods

(col), orchards (col), heath/moor (col, named); map title has geometric decoration.

9/409 Thorncombe (parish) ST 364035
Apt 03.11.1841; 4892a (4896); Map 1840?, 3 chns, 1st cl, in 3 parts, by Thomas Woodmass, John Thompson, John Huddleston, John Woodmass, (includes enlargements of Thorncombe village at 1.5 chns); construction lines, foot/b'way, waterbodies, houses, property boundaries, factories (by heavy shading); legend explains depiction of buildings and boundaries.

9/410 Thorverton (parish) SS 931032
Apt 18.08.1840; 4037a (all); Map 1841, 3 chns, by George Braund and Henry Hearn, Exeter; construction lines.

9/411 Throwley (parish) SX 680896 [Throwleigh]
Apt 08.12.1840; 1943a (1943); Map 1840, 3 chns, copied by Chas Cooper from a survey made by George Murphy and Jno. Germon; woods, plantations, orchards.

9/412 Thrushelton (parish) SX 454885
Apt 18.12.1839; 3715a (all); Map 1840, 3 chns, by Hugh Ballment, Barnstaple; foot/b'way, building names, lime quarries, mills.

9/413 Thurleston (parish) SX 680440 [Thurlestone]
Apt 03.11.1840; 1763a (1898); Map 1842?, 3 chns, by John Thomas Tucker, Bridgetown; construction lines, foot/b'way, houses (depiction incomplete), plantations, heath/moor, rock outcrops, hedge ownership, building names, cliffs, coastline, sands, mud, high and low water marks, 'Brake' land.

9/414 Tidcombe (district in parish of Tiverton) SS 983139 [Not listed]
Apt 18.11.1841; 3920a (all); Map 1842, 6 chns, in 2 parts, by William Richards junr, (including 2-chn enlargement of detail); foot/b'way, canal with towpath, waterbodies, building names, weir, chapel, rectory, district boundaries (col); built-up part generalised.

9/415 Topsham (parish) SX 960889
Apt 25.10.1842; 1570a (all); Map 1843?, 6 chns; houses, woods, plantations, orchards, building names, weir; built-up part generalised.

9/416 Torbrian (parish) SX 812691 [Torbryan]
Apt 28.09.1839; 2011a (all); Map 1845?, 4 chns, by John Thomas Tucker, Totnes; waterbodies, boundstones.

9/417 Tormoham (parish) SX 918643 [Torquay]
Apt 15.11.1847; 729a (1560); Map 1848?, 8 chns; waterbodies, landowners, coastline; built-up part generalised; lands belonging to H.S.S. Cary Esqre are shown in colour. Apt omits land use.

9/418 Great Torrington (parish) SS 501204
Apt 16.09.1842; 3456a (all); Map 1843, 6 chns, by G. Braund, Exeter; foot/b'way, weir.

9/419 Little Torrington (parish) SS 489167
Apt 09.05.1838; 2881a (all); Map 1839, 6 chns, by Joseph Risdon, Speccott, Merton, Devon; hill-drawing, foot/b'way, woods, plantations, fences, building names, churchyard; charcoal holders, pair of compasses, quill pen and leaves surround scale.

9/420 Totnes (parish) SX 798600
Apt 14.04.1842; 1040a (1043); Map 1842, 3 chns, by G. Braund and H. Hearn; construction lines, foot/b'way; built-up part generalised; map carries recital of its adoption by the landowners.

9/421 Townstall (parish) SX 859516 [Not listed]
Apt 11.03.1840; 1689a (1758); Map 1841, 3 chns, by John Grant, Ugborough; hill-drawing, foot/b'way, waterbodies, houses, woods, orchards, rock outcrops, fences, field gates, building names, road names, lodges, quay, coastline, cliffs, limekilns, watermill, sand or stone pits, quarries; some field boundaries shown with double lines; red lines may be walls; colour bands may show property ownerships; north pointer has floral decoration.

9/422 Trentishoe (parish) SS 634476
Apt 26.05.1841; 1572a (all); Map 1842, 3 chns, by G.P. Williams; woods (col), orchards (col), building names, boundstones, coastline, common.

9/423 Trusham (parish) SX 854822
Apt 02.10.1838; 749a (749); Map 1839, [4 chns], 1st cl, by Robert Park, 8 Geo. St, Euston Sq, London; construction lines, waterbodies, houses, woods, field boundary ownerships, building names; woodland shown by cross symbols; surveyor notes that corrections to field boundaries are drawn in red ink.

9/424 Twitchen (parish) SS 783306
Apt 13.04.1840; 2918a (all); Map 1841?, 8 chns, in 2 parts, (includes enlargements of settlements at 4 chns).

9/425 Uffculme (except Hurley) (parish) ST 083117
Apt 20.08.1839; 5459a (6122); Map 1840, 6 chns, in 3 parts, by Richard Dunstanne Bevan, Uffculme, (includes enlargement of Uffculme and Ashill at 3 chns); foot/b'way, waterbodies, houses, fences, building names, mills, parsonage; map has schedule of the lands owned by Richard Hurley which are to be considered a separate tithe district.

9/426 Ugborough (parish) SX 673570
Apt 31.08.1842; 2760a (8659); Map 1843, 4 chns, by John Grant, Ugborough, (tithable parts only); waterbodies, houses, woods, rock outcrops, fences, field gates, building names, quarries, mill; red lines may be walls; some field boundaries are shown with double lines; colour bands may show property ownerships.

9/427 Uplowman (parish) ST 015165
Apt 19.10.1841; 2913a (all); Map 1843?, 6 chns; foot/b'way, waterbodies, houses, woods (col), plantations (col), orchards (col), building names, rectory, mills.

9/428 Uplyme (parish) SY 320935
Apt 30.08.1838; 3150a (all); Map 1839, 6 chns, in 2 parts, ? by W. Pickering, (including 3 chn enlargements of detail); hill-drawing, foot/b'way, turnpike roads and gate, waterbodies, houses, woods, plantations, parkland, orchards, heath/moor, building names, coastline, low water mark, sand or stone pits or quarries, parsonage, factory; rough land named.

9/429 Upottery (parish) ST 208083
Apt 17.11.1840; 5831a (5830); Map 1841, 3 chns, by Wm Dawson, Exeter; foot/b'way, turnpike roads, toll gate, old toll house, building names, road names, parsonage, smithy, pound, old mill, mill, linhays, common; rough land named.

9/430 Upton Hellions (parish) SS 846027
Apt 27.05.1840; 820a (all); Map 1841?, 3 chns, by Luckraft, Warren, Reaney and Warren; construction lines, houses, woods, plantations, orchards, building names, parsonage, mill; colour bands may show property ownerships.

9/431 Upton Pyne (parish) SX 911975
Apt 10.01.1838; 1853a (all); Map 1838?, 4 chns, by Edward Brown, Newton St Cyres, Devon; woods (col), parkland (col), orchards (col), building names, mills, engine and mill streams, farm boundaries (col) and names, glebe.

9/432 Upton Weaver (district in parish of Cullompton) ST 050054 [Not listed]
Apt 31.12.1840; 863a (?); Map 1841, 6 chns, by G.A. Boyce, Tiverton; waterbodies, houses, building names.

9/433 Venn Ottery (parish) SY 072912
Apt 18.05.1839; 919a (918); Map 1839, 4 chns, by Robert Dymond, Exeter; foot/b'way, waterbodies, houses, woods (col), plantations (col), arable (col), grassland (col), orchards (col), gardens (col), boundary stones.

9/434 Virginstow (parish) SX 383932
Apt 17.05.1839; 1275a (all); Map 1840, 4 chns, by J. Kittow, North Pertherwin; construction lines, building names, parsonage; title is in shield-shaped cartouche; names are stamped.

9/435 Walkhampton (parish) SX 565725
Apt 28.09.1839; 10541a (10540); Map 1840, 6 chns, in 3 parts, (includes enlargement of Walkhampton village at 1 chn and various fields at 2 chns); hill-drawing, railway, foot/b'way, turnpike roads, waterbodies,

woods, plantations, orchards, rock outcrops, building names, tors (named), leats, copper mine, vicarage, mill, downland.

9/436 Warkleigh (parish) SS 644227
Apt 31.08.1841; 2452a (all); Map 1841, 3 chns, by Henry Crispin, junr, Chulmleigh; construction lines, waterbodies, houses, farmyards, woods (col, named), plantations (col, named), orchards, building names, hotel, parsonage; colour bands may show property ownerships; map carries recital of its adoption.

9/437 Washfield (parish) SS 931169
Apt 17.01.1838; 3319a (all); Map 1840, 6 chns, by William Richards junr, Tiverton, Devon; waterbodies, houses, farmyards, building names, rectory, mill, boundary features.

9/438 Washford Pyne (parish) SS 811109
Apt 31.07.1839; 1141a (all); Map 1839, 3 chns, 1st cl, by Lieut Luckraft, R.N., M. Warren, W. Reaney and W.T. Warren; construction lines, houses, woods (named), orchards, heath/moor (named), building names, trig points (named), parsonage; colour bands may show property ownerships.

9/439 Wear Gifford (parish) SS 481229 [Weare Giffard]
Apt 03.10.1837; 1587a (1587); Map 1839, 3 chns, by J. Risdon, Speccott, near Great Torrington; houses (by shading), woods, plantations, building names, watermill, locks; mapmaker's name is on scroll draped over pedestal, decorated with ears of wheat and leaf border, and a pair of compasses, quill pen, charcoal holder, ruler and leaves surround scale.

9/440 Welcomb (parish) SS 238182 [Welcombe]
Apt 21.12.1841; 1752a (1751); Map 1842, 3 chns, by J. Woodmass; construction lines, houses, building names, mill; legend explains depiction of buildings, boundaries and waterbodies.

9/441 Wembury (parish) SX 519496
Apt 05.06.1838; 2625a (3205); Map 1839?, 6 chns, litho (by G.S. Lee, Plymouth); building names, coastline, pier, mill, reservoir, farm names; headlands and bay named.

9/442 Wembworthy (parish) SS 673112
Apt 10.01.1838; 2412a (all); Map 1838, 3 chns, 1st cl, by Hugh Ballment, Barnstaple, Devon; construction lines, hill-drawing, waterbodies, woods, rock outcrops, field gates, building names, field names, lodge, brickyard, stables, quarries, parsonage; colour bands may show property ownerships.

9/443 Werrington (parish) SX 332886
Apt 13.05.1839; 4212a (5000); Map 1843, 3 chns, by Wm Brock, Launceston; turnpike roads, turnpike house, canal, canal pool, wharf, houses, farmyards, woods (col), plantations (col), orchards, building names.

9/444 Westleigh (parish) SS 479279
Apt 19.12.1840; 2457a (all); Map 1842?, 3 chns, by George Braund and Henry Hearn, Exeter; construction lines.

9/445 Weston Peveral otherwise Pennycross (tithing in parish of Pennycross) SX 476576
Apt 19.12.1840; 1232a (1281); Map 1839, 4 chns, by H. Symons, Fancy, Plymouth; waterbodies, fences, building names, mill. Apt omits land use.

9/446 Whimple (parish) SY 047970
Apt 30.04.1842; 3019a (3019); Map 1834, 6 chns, by I. Poole, Sherborne, Dorset; waterbodies, houses, woods, plantations, arable (col), grassland (col), orchards, building names, disappearing streams.

9/447 Whitchurch (parish) SX 514733
Apt 26.09.1843; 5980a (all); Map 1843, 4 chns, 1st cl, by John Palmer, 22 James Street, Devonport; construction lines, waterbodies, houses, plantations, rock outcrops, fences, tor (named).

9/448 Whitestone (parish) SX 863942
Apt 22.02.1840; 4077a (all); Map 1841?, 4 chns; waterbodies, houses, farmyards, woods (named), orchards, building names, road names, rectory; border corners have floral decoration.

9/449 Widdecombe in the Moor (parish) SX 703754 [Widecombe in the Moor]
Apt 18.09.1843; 10614a (all); Map 1844, 3 chns, 1st cl, by Irish and Parker; construction lines, building names, vicarage; beacons and tors used as reference points are named.

9/450 Widworthy (parish) SY 215987
Apt 24.10.1838; 1437a (1437); Map 1839, 6 chns, by Summers and Slater; woods, parkland, orchards, fences, quarries; coppice, orchards and plantations are shown by annotation. PRO IR 30 also contains a Standidge litho version of 1839 on which orchards, woodland and plantation symbols are used and park is shown in detail.

9/451 Willand (parish) ST 034105
Apt 29.01.1841; 990a (989); Map 1839, 3 chns, 1st cl, by Thomas Parker, Willand, Devon; construction lines, waterbodies, houses, woods, plantations, orchards, hedge ownership, building names, mills; bridge and cross-roads named.

9/452 Winkleigh (parish) SS 631091
Apt 12.05.1846; 9118a (9118); Map 1843, 3 chns, 1st cl, by Irish and Parker; construction lines, waterbodies, houses, farmyards, fences, building names, mill.

9/453 Witheridge (parish) SS 823162
Apt 20.10.1837; 9048a (all); Map 1839, 3 chns, in 5 parts, by Luckraft, Warren, Reaney and Warren, Crediton, (including index); construction lines, trig points (named), waterbodies, houses, woods, plantations, parkland, orchards, heath/moor, building names, downland; bridge named; colour bands may show property ownerships.

9/454 Withycombe Rawleigh (parish) SY 018827 [Withycombe Raleigh]
Apt 31.01.1838; 1983a (2617); Map 1839?, 3 chns, by Wm Dawson, Exeter; construction lines, hill-drawing, waterbodies, houses, woods, parkland, orchards, gardens, fences, field gates, quarry, direction and boundary posts, estuary, sand or stone pit; channels may indicate water meadows.

9/455 Wolborough (parish) SX 861703
Apt 26.04.1844; 1231a (all); Map 1845?, 4 chns, by Robert Dymond; waterbodies, houses, rock outcrops, building names, quarries; built-up part generalised; colour bands may show property ownerships.

9/456 Woodbury (parish) SY 012873
Apt 11.10.1839; 7305a (7804); Map 1841?, 3 chns, ? by Wm Norris, (including location diagram); waterbodies, houses, building names, high and low water marks, parsonage, road embankments.

9/457 Woodland (parish) SX 791689
Apt 23.01.1838; 1606a (1606); Map 1840, 6 chns, by Wm Norris, 59, High Street, Exeter; waterbodies, houses (by shading). Apt omits land use.

9/458 Woodleigh (parish) SX 745508
Apt 16.03.1842; 2319a (2319); Map 1842, 3 chns, 1st cl, by Thos Cutmore, Halwell near Totnes, Devon; construction lines, waterbodies, houses, farmyards, weir.

9/459 Woolfardisworthy (Hartland Hundred) (parish) SS 333202
Apt 28.12.1838; 5798a (all); Map 1841, 3 chns, by Benjamin Herman and William Blake, Bideford; houses, woods, orchards, heath/moor, rock outcrops, building names, coastline, cliffs, mills, limekiln, watermill, ownership boundaries; sea decorated with ships with sailors on board; pair of compasses, quill pen, charcoal holders and ruler surround scale.

9/460 Woolfardisworthy (Witheridge Hundred) (parish) SS 812090
Apt 31.12.1840; 1815a (all); Map 1841?, 6 chns, by William Richards, Tiverton; foot/b'way, hedges, building names, rectory, mill; hedges show property boundaries; border corners have leaf decoration.

9/461 East Worlington (parish) SS 775159
Apt 28.01.1839; 2363a (all); Map 1839, 3 chns, 1st cl, by W. and C. Graham; construction lines.

9/462 West Worlington (parish) SS 760152
Apt 23.12.1841; 2684a (all); Map 1842?, 6 chns; foot/b'way, field acreages; colour bands may show property ownerships.

9/463 Yarcombe (parish) ST 245090
Apt 30.12.1842; 578a (4689); Map 1844, 6 chns, by W. Pickering; waterbodies, houses, building names, mills, sand or stone pit.

9/464 Yarnscombe (parish) SS 554229
Apt 22.04.1840; 3047a (all); Map 1840?, 6 chns; waterbodies, houses, woods; ruler, quill pen and pair of compasses surround scale.

9/465 Yealmpton (parish) SX 586530
Apt 29.11.1841; 3433a (3537); Map 1843, 3 chns, by Irish and Parker, Winkleigh; construction lines, waterbodies, houses, farmyards, fences, building names, waterwheels, mills, quay, coastline, limekilns.

9/466 Zeal Monachorum (parish) SS 715041
Apt 21.07.1840; 3265a (3264); Map 1840, 3 chns, 1st cl, in 2 parts, by Luckraft, Warren, Reaney and Warren, Crediton; construction lines, houses (depiction incomplete), woods, plantations, orchards; colour bands may show property ownerships.

Dorset

PRO IR29 and IR30 10/1-270

283 tithe districts: 631,107 acres
269 tithe commutations: 554,811 acres
185 voluntary tithe agreements, 84 compulsory tithe awards,
1 corn rent annuity

Tithe and tithe commutation

Some 95 per cent of Dorset tithe districts by number and about 88 per cent of the county area were subject to payment of tithes in 1836 (Fig. 22). The main causes of tithe exemption by this date were modus payments in lieu of tithe, merger of tithes in the land, and exemption by prescription. Although parliamentary enclosure was quite extensive in Dorset, it was not usually accompanied by commutation of tithe.

The assistant tithe commissioners and local tithe agents who officiated at Dorset commutations are listed in Table 10.1 and the valuers of the county's tithe rent-charge in Table 10.2. Fifteen tithe districts in Dorset were apportioned by holding rather than field-by-field. Two apportionments give details of land tenure and four list common rights.

Tithe maps

Only 3 of the 269 tithe maps of Dorset are sealed as first class. This is the lowest proportion in any county south of a line through the River Severn to the Wash and is similar to that in those counties which had undergone extensive parliamentary enclosure. Less than 2 per cent of second-class maps carry construction lines and it may well be that many Dorset tithe maps were based on copies of earlier surveys, notably those made for enclosure, though only one map, that of Horton with Woodlands explicitly acknowledges copying. Map scales used in Dorset vary from one inch to one chain to one inch to twelve chains with 24 per cent of maps in the recommended scale range of one inch to three to four chains (Table 10.3).

Dorset maps are more than usually informative about land use. About 19 per cent show arable and grass, 30 per cent depict orchards, 15 per cent map parkland, and 58 per cent identify woodland. Map-makers' names are recorded on 156 Dorset tithe maps in the Public Record Office collection (Table 10.2). Map quality varies from highly detailed maps, for example that of Corfe Castle, to some minimalist maps, for example Folke and Wareham Lady St Mary. Dorset tithe maps have an overall plain appearance. Thirteen do

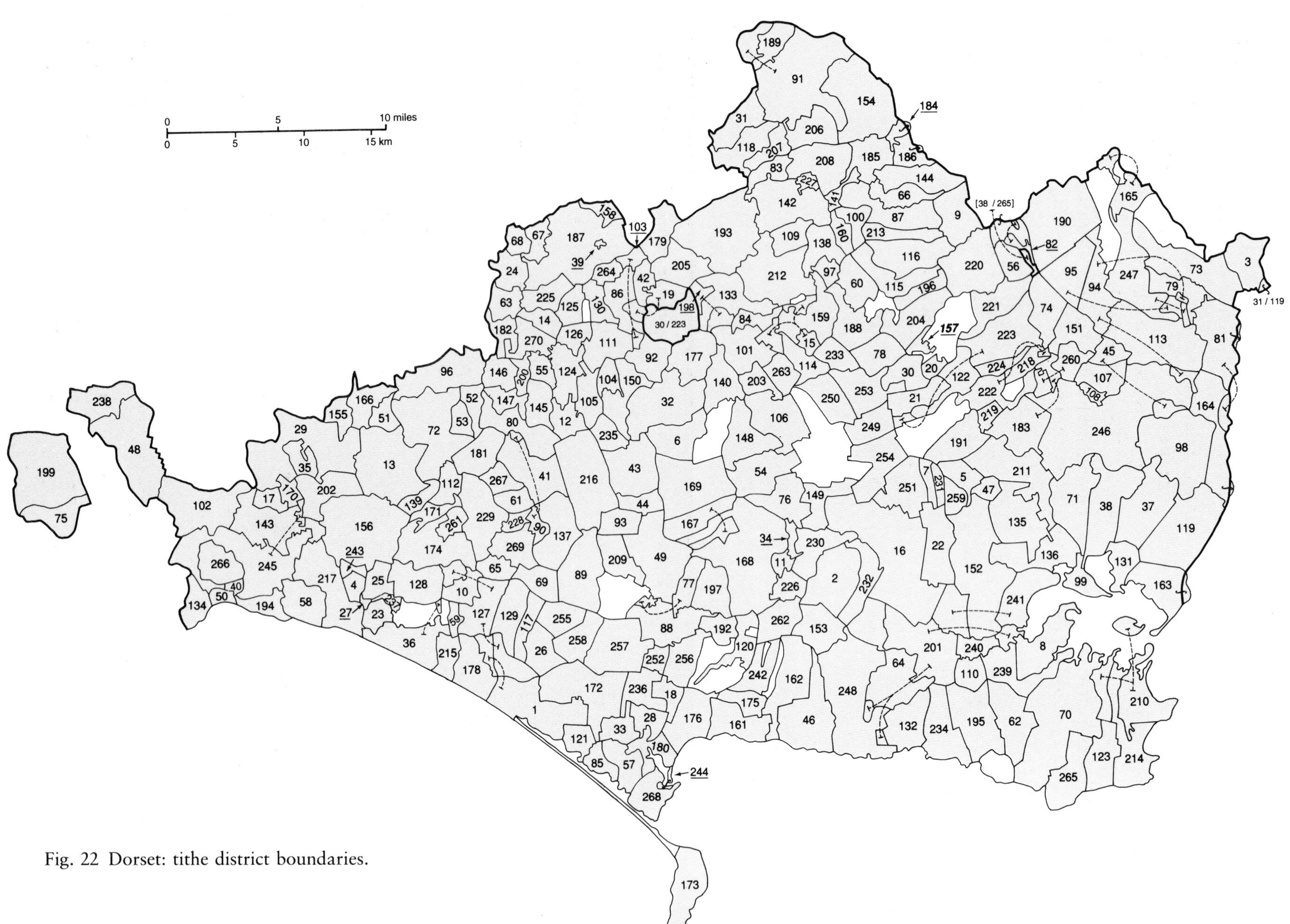

Fig. 22 Dorset: tithe district boundaries.

show churches pictorially and at Charmouth local renown as a fossil collector's Mecca is acknowledged by fossil and shell decorations in the map borders. On the map of Osmington a field contains a picture of a man on horseback and on the map of Worth Matravers a ship is illustrated in the sea. These and similar features underscore the county's ambivalent cartographic nature. It adjoins Devon, a county of decorated maps, and Wiltshire, with tithe maps more characteristic of a midland county.

Table 10.1. *Agreements and awards for commutation of tithes in Dorset*

Assistant commissioner/ local tithe agent	*Number of agreements**	*Number of awards*
George Bolls	116	0
Aneurin Owen	5	78
James Jerwood	22	0
George Louis	17	2
Robert Page	8	0
John Milner	7	0
George Wingrove Cooke	0	2
Thomas Phippard	1	0
Charles Pym	0	1
John J. Rawlinson	0	1

*Computed from the number of extant reports on tithe agreements in the tithe files [PRO IR 18].

Table 10.2. *Tithe valuers and tithe map-makers in Dorset*

Name and address (in Dorset unless indicated)	*Number of districts*	*Acreage*
Tithe valuers		
John Martin, Evershot	39	73,359
John Baverstock Knight, Puddlehinton	25	61,575
John Raymond, Shaftesbury	20	45,824
John Symonds, Broadwindsor	17	45,141
James Poole, Sherborne	15	29,299
Charles Gearing, Kilmiston/Redbridge, Hants	12	41,920
George Easton, Oakley, Wimborne	12	25,910
Levi Luckham, Broadway	11	47,951
Others [49]	118	183,832
Attributed tithe map-makers		
John Martin, Evershot	27	55,018
John Baverstock Knight, Puddlehinton	20	46,516
James Poole, Sherborne	18	39,810
John Raymond, Shaftesbury	13	32,686
George Easton, Oakley, Wimborne	10	17,842
Others [31]	68	150,788

Table 10.3. *The tithe maps of Dorset: scales and classes*

Scale in chains/inch	*All maps*		*First Class*		*Second Class*	
	Number	*Acreage*	*Number*	*Acreage*	*Number*	*Acreage*
>3	1	398	0	0	1	398
3	43	59,687	3	7187	40	52,500
4	22	32,138	0	0	22	32,138
4.5, 5	7	9,128	0	0	7	9,128
6	135	320,818	0	0	135	320,818
6.67, 7, 7.5	6	8,003	0	0	6	8,003
8	36	88,408	0	0	36	88,408
9	14	29,776	0	0	14	29,776
<9	5	6,455	0	0	5	6,455
TOTAL	269	554,811	3	7187	266	547,624

Table 10.4. *The tithe maps of Dorset: dates*

	<1837	*1837*	*1838*	*1839*	*1840*	*1841*	*1842*	*1843*	*1844*	*1845*	*1846*	*1847*	*>1847*
All maps	1	5	30	50	58	29	19	18	24	16	9	6	4
1st class	0	0	0	0	1	0	0	2	0	0	0	0	0
2nd class	1	5	30	50	57	29	19	16	24	16	9	6	4

Dorset

10/1 Abbotsbury (parish) SY 584845
Apt 30.06.1841; 735a (5616); Map 1844, 6 chns, in 4 parts, by John Martin, Evershot, (includes enlargement of Abbotsbury village at 3 chns and 12-chn index); waterbodies, houses, farmyards, woods (named), plantations (named), withy beds, arable (col), grassland (col), orchards, building names, landowners, beach, lagoon, chapel, mill, churchyard, glebe; pictorial church.

10/2 Affpuddle (parish) SY 808925
Apt 13.12.1838; 3819a (3818); Map 1839, 8 chns; waterbodies, houses, woods (named), plantations (named), heath/moor, building names, field names, mill, chalk pit, glebe (col), farm names, manor names.

10/3 Alderholt otherwise Aldershott (tithing in parish of Cranborne) SU 119127
Apt 11.12.1845; 2122a (?); Map 1845, 8 chns, in 2 parts, (including 3 chn enlargement of detail); foot/b'way, waterbodies, houses, plantations, common.

10/4 Allington (parish) SY 458939
Apt 02.05.1839; 595a (594); Map 1840?, 3 chns, by John Martin; hill-drawing, turnpike roads and gates, waterbodies, houses, woods, arable (col), grassland (col), orchards, factory, willow bed; hill named in ornate lettering.

10/5 Almer and Mapperton (parish) SY 903992
Apt 26.03.1844; 1161a (1161); Map 1845, 6 chns, by Henry Richards, Abbotts Court Farm, Dorset; waterbodies, houses, building names; woodland (by name).

10/6 Alton Pancras (parish) ST 703029
Apt 17.07.1839; 2244a (2243); Map 1841, 6 chns; waterbodies, woods, plantations, withy beds, parkland, fence.

10/7 Anderson (parish) SY 879988
Apt 23.06.1837; 571a (all); Map 1839?, [8 chns], ? by John Baverstock Knight; foot/b'way.

10/8 Arne (chapelry) SY 963872
Apt 09.05.1842; 2617a (all); Map 1844, 9 chns; waterbodies, open fields, high water mark, moor, heath; coast features named.

10/9 Ashmore (parish) ST 907174
Apt 05.01.1842; 2335a (all); Map 1842, 3 chns; foot/b'way, waterbodies, woods, plantations, toll house, heath/moor, open fields (named), field gates, sand or stone pit, commons (col, named); pictorial church.

10/10 Askerswell (parish) SY 536932
Apt 31.10.1845; 1161a (1161); Map 1846, 3 chns, by Richard James, Chideock, Dorset; waterbodies, open fields, fences, chalk pit.

10/11 Athelhampton (parish) SY 769937
Apt 14.05.1840; 472a (471); Map 1841, 6 chns; waterbodies, building names.

10/12 Batcombe (parish) ST 618047
Apt 23.02.1839; 1109a (all); Map 1838, 3 chns, by J. Martin, Evershot, Dorset; hill-drawing, waterbodies, houses, farmyards, woods (named), arable (col), grassland (col), orchards, road names, standing stone, pound, waste, common; hill named.

10/13 Beaminster (parish) ST 488023
Apt 26.01.1842; 5119a (5118); Map 1842?, 6 chns, by James Oliver, Beaminster, (includes enlargement of Beaminster town at 3 chns); waterbodies, houses, woods, parkland, orchards, fences, building names, downland.

10/14 Beerhackett (parish) ST 604118 [Beer Hackett]
Apt 10.10.1839; 904a (all); Map 1840?, 3 chns, 1st cl; construction lines, foot/b'way, field gates.

10/15 Belchalwell (parish) ST 797091
Apt 19.06.1840; 1308a (all); Map 1841?, 5 chns, ? by John Martin; turnpike roads, turnpike gate, waterbodies, farmyards, woods, plantations, arable (col), grassland (col), orchards, building names, landowners, common; pictorial church; hill named.

10/16 Bere Regis (parish) SY 855939
Apt 11.04.1842; 8895a (8894); Map 1844, 6 chns, in 2 parts, (includes enlargement of Bere Regis village at 3 chns); foot/b'way, waterbodies, fences, pound; scale and border coloured.

10/17 Bettiscombe (parish) ST 401001
Apt 15.02.1839; 668a (all); Map 1839, 6 chns, in 2 parts; waterbodies, houses, woods, gardens, glebe.

10/18 Bincombe (parish) SY 686847
Apt 03.07.1838; 954a (all); Map 1837, 6 chns, by J. Martin, Evershot, Dorset; hill-drawing, waterbodies, arable (col), grassland (col), hedges, fences, field gates, field names, stone pits, quarries, common, farm names, field acreages; map is subtitled 'the property of Gonville and Caius College, Cambridge'.

10/19 Bishop's Caundle (parish) ST 695130
Apt 26.11.1841; 1398a (all); Map 1842, 4.5 chns, by J. Poole, Sherborne, Dorset; houses, fence.

10/20 Blandford Forum (parish) ST 887066
Apt 20.07.1837; 863a (all); Map 1838, 10 chns, by George Easton, Great Canford; woods, arable (col), grassland (col), hedge ownership, fences, weir, waste, farm names; one field named.

10/21 Blandford St Mary (parish) ST 874045
Apt 30.12.1837; 1583a (all); Map 1840, 5 chns; waterbodies, houses.

10/22 Bloxworth (parish) SY 884946
Apt 20.01.1845; 2777a (all); Map 1845, 6 chns; foot/b'way, waterbodies, houses, woods, plantations, parkland, road names.

10/23 Bothenhampton (parish) SY 475917
Apt 02.09.1844; 823a (823); Map 1845, 6 chns; waterbodies, quarries, harbour.

10/24 Bradford Abbas (parish) ST 584153
Apt 30.06.1838; 1139a (all); Map 1838, 9 chns in 2 parts, (includes enlargement of Bradford Abbas village at 3 chns), litho (by J.R. Jobbins, Warwick Court, Holborn); woods.

10/25 Bradpole (parish) SY 476942
Apt 27.11.1844; 966a (966); Map 1845, 3 chns, by Richard James, Chideock, Dorset; waterbodies.

10/26 Little Bredy (parish) SY 589888 [Littlebredy]
Apt 12.11.1841; 1593a (1636); Map 1842, 3 chns, by Humphrey and John Knight; waterbodies, woods, plantations, parkland, tumuli, sand or stone pits.

10/27 Bridport (parish) SY 465927
Apt 24.11.1842; 62a (62); Map 1845, 3 chns, by R. James, Chideock, Dorset; foot/b'way, fences, building names, road names, town hall.

10/28 Broadway (parish) SY 667835 [Broadwey]
Apt 03.06.1837; 1029a (all); Map 1841?, 3 chns; houses, sand or stone pit.

10/29 Broadwindsor (parish) ST 422047
Apt 23.01.1839; 6215a (all); Map 1840, 6 chns; waterbodies, houses.

10/30 Bryanston (parish) ST 865064
Apt 30.01.1837; 1512a (1512); Map 1837, 9 chns; woods, plantations, arable (col), grassland (col), hedges, road names, landowners; map is described as 'of Bryanston, the property of The Right Honourable Lord Portman'. District is apportioned by holding; Apt omits land use.

10/31 Buckhorn Weston (parish) ST 757247
Apt 20.09.1838; 1633a (1632); Map 1838, 4 chns, by William Raymond; woods, orchards, building names, road names, common pit; pictorial church.

10/32 Buckland Newton (parish) ST 689054
Apt 14.08.1838; 6018a (all); Map 1840, 8 chns, in 2 parts, by John Baverstock Knight; houses.

10/33 Buckland Ripers (parish) SY 644827
Apt 09.10.1837; 1238a (1237); Map 1840?, 3 chns; waterbodies, houses, quarry, stone or sand pits.

10/34 Burlestone (parish) SY 777955 [Burleston]
Apt 12.06.1843; 350a (all); Map 1843, 4 chns; houses, arable (col), grassland (col), open fields, field names; a different 'arable' tint is used to distinguish the open fields.

10/35 Burstock (parish) ST 423026
Apt 28.08.1840; 914a (913); Map 1839, 3 chns, by Norris and Dickinson, Wincanton; foot/b'way, waterbodies, houses, building names, mill, grange, common; some field boundaries are shown as double lines with grey tint between, which may indicate hedges.

10/36 Burton Bradstock (parish) SY 497896
Apt 26.01.1841; 4054a (2680); Map 1839, 6 chns, in 2 parts, by John Martin; waterbodies, houses, woods, arable (col), grassland (col), orchards, rock outcrops, cliffs, beach, harbour.

10/37 Great Canford (Middle Division) (parish) SZ 033963 [Canford Magna]
Apt 16.12.1841; 1480a (?); Map 1843, 3 chns, by George Easton, Oakley near Wimborne; foot/b'way, houses, woods (col), parkland; copy in PRO IR 30 is accompanied by what appears to be an earlier draft of part of the map.

10/38 Great Canford (Western Division) (parish) SZ 004961 [Canford Magna]
Apt 16.12.1841; 1724a (?); Map 1845, 9 chns, in 2 parts, by George Easton, Oakley, nr. Wimborne; foot/b'way, waterbodies, houses, woods, gardens.

10/39 Castleton (parish) ST 648168 [Not listed]
Apt 16.11.1841; 70a (all); Map 1844?, 3 chns, by William Tooks; waterbodies, houses, old castle.

10/40 Catherston Lewston (parish) SY 371942 [Catherston Leweston]
Apt 04.01.1844; 248a (248); Map 1847, 3 chns, by Wm Dawson, Exeter; foot/b'way, turnpike roads, toll gate, houses, woods, orchards, building names, chapel.

10/41 Cattistock (parish) ST 591011
Apt 21.03.1839; 3009a (3009); Map 1838, 6 chns, by Geo. Easton, Wimborne; foot/b'way, woods.

10/42 Caundle Marsh (parish) ST 682140
Apt 07.06.1837; 792a (792); Map 1838, 6 chns, by J. Poole, Sherborne, Dorset; woods, orchards, tithe-free lands, ownerships (col), common. District is apportioned by holding and fields are not shown.

10/43 Cerne Abbas (parish) ST 664011
Apt 08.08.1844; 781a (3063); Map 1844, 6 chns, by J. Poole, Sherborne, Dorset; foot/b'way, waterbodies, houses, disappearing streams; built-up part generalised.

10/44 Nether Cerne (parish) SY 668984
Apt 16.11.1841; 845a (all); Map 1839, 7 chns; houses, woods.

10/45 Chalbury (parish) SU 013074
Apt 11.11.1840; 1344a (all); Map 1840, 8 chns, in 3 parts, compiled from various maps by R.C. Gale, Winchester, (including 80-chn index); waterbodies, houses, woods, plantations, building names, common.

10/46 Chaldon Herring (parish) SY 784828
Apt 22.12.1841; 130a (2981); Map 1841, 6 chns, by Henry Hyde, Lulworth, Dorset, land, timber and house surveyor; foot/b'way, open fields, sand or stone pits; built-up part generalised.

10/47 Charborough (parish) SY 921981 [Not listed]
Apt 06.06.1848; 685a (all); Map 1849, 6 chns; foot/b'way, waterbodies, houses.

10/48 Chardstock (parish) ST 305039
Apt 06.11.1839; 5800a (all); Map 1841?, 6 chns, in 2 parts; foot/b'way, turnpike roads, waterbodies, houses, woods, plantations, orchards, building names, mill, downs.

10/49 Charminster (parish) SY 679946
Apt 09.10.1837; 4095a (4095); Map 1839, 6 chns; foot/b'way, houses, woods, arable (col), grassland (col), county asylum, farm names.

10/50 Charmouth (parish) SY 359935
Apt 05.06.1840; 433a (all); Map 1841, 3 chns; hill-drawing, waterbodies, houses, woods, plantations, parkland, orchards, rock outcrops, fences, coastline (in detail), undercliff, lime kiln; border has shell or fossil shapes decorating map corners.

10/51 Cheddington (parish) ST 487056 [Chedington]
Apt 30.08.1838; 774a (773); Map 1839?, 3 chns, by J. Martin; houses, woods (named), plantations (named), parkland, arable (col), grassland (col), orchards, building names; map carries recital of proceedings for its adoption.

10/52 East Chelborough (parish) ST 551057
Apt 09.02.1839; 948a (all); Map 1839, 3 chns; houses, woods, plantations, arable (col), grassland (col), orchards, gardens, building names, ornamental gardens; map carries recital of the proceedings for its adoption.

10/53 West Chelborough (parish) ST 541051
Apt 05.03.1839; 579a (all); Map 1839, 6 chns; hill-drawing, foot/b'way, waterbodies, houses, woods, arable (col), grassland (col), orchards, gardens, field gates, building names, limekilns, sand or stone pits.

10/54 Cheselbourne (parish) ST 759001
Apt 20.07.1839; 2581a (2580); Map 1841?, 7 chns, by John Martin; houses, woods, arable (col), grassland (col), orchards, heath/moor, open fields (named), sand or stone pits, common, downland.

10/55 Chetnole and Yetminster (chapelry and hamlet in parish of Yetminster) ST 603082
Apt 30.06.1840; 878a (877); Map 1840, 6 chns, by E. Watts, Yeovil; houses, farmyards, woods, plantations, arable (col), grassland (col), orchards, hedge ownership, fences, field names; pictorial church (col).

10/56 Chettle (parish) ST 947139
Apt 17.09.1839; 1114a (1113); Map 1839, [8 chns]; waterbodies.

10/57 Chickerell (parish) SY 648806
Apt 31.01.1839; 1812a (1812); Map 1839, 3 chns, surveyed for John Taperell, C.E., by John Doherty; foot/b'way, waterbodies, houses, fences, coastline, beach, lagoon, boundary stones.

10/58 Chideock (parish) SY 421929
Apt 08.07.1841; 1983a (2052); Map 1842?, 3 chns; waterbodies, houses, building names, coastline, disappearing stream.

10/59 Chilcombe (parish) SY 529912
Apt 28.08.1840; 466a (all); Map 1840?, 4 chns; houses, woods, avenue of trees.

10/60 Child Okeford (parish) ST 832133
Apt 04.05.1839; 1752a (1752); Map 1840, 6 chns, in 2 parts; waterbodies, woods, arable (col), grassland (col), open fields, common, common meadow; hills named; pictorial church.

10/61 Chilfrome (parish) SY 578992
Apt 14.04.1842; 940a (940); Map 1844?, 6 chns, by John Martin; foot/b'way, waterbodies, houses, woods (col), plantations (col), orchards, field boundary ownerships.

10/62 Church Knowle (parish) SY 933818
Apt 27.10.1842; 2920a (2920); Map 1843, 3 chns, 1st cl, by Harry Holloway, Ringwood; construction lines, railway 'to the claypits', foot/b'way, waterbodies, houses.

10/63 Clifton Maybank (parish) ST 579132
Apt 20.09.1838; 1255a (all); Map 1839, 9 chns; foot/b'way, waterbodies, woods (named), parkland, church land.

10/64 Coombe Keynes with Wool (parochial chapelry) SY 847860
Apt 10.09.1839; 4555a (4554); Map 1840, 6 chns, in 2 parts, by Henry Hyde, Lulworth, Dorset, land, timber and house surveyor; foot/b'way, waterbodies, houses, sand or stone pits or quarries, ornamental gardens; bridge named.

10/65 Compton Abbas (parish) SY 561943
Apt 08.07.1841; 846a (all); Map 1842, 3 chns; waterbodies, field gates.

10/66 Compton Abbas (parish) ST 873188
Apt 10.06.1842; 1516a (1516); Map 1844, 6 chns, in 2 parts, by William Painter, Stower Provost, Dorset, (including 3 chn enlargement of open fields); foot/b'way, waterbodies, houses (by shading), woods, orchards, open fields (named), fences, field gates, road names, boundary stones, farm names.

10/67 Nether Compton (parish) ST 602171
Apt 07.07.1838; 892a (892); Map 1839, 6 chns, by E. Watts, Yeovil; waterbodies, houses, woods (col), plantations (col), arable (col), grassland (col), orchards (col), open fields, hedge ownership, fences, field gates, building names, road names, field names, lime kiln, lodge, water mill, glebe.

10/68 Over Compton (parish) ST 587173
Apt 14.08.1838; 789a (788); Map 1847, 4 chns, by Edward Thos Percy; railway, foot/b'way, waterbodies, houses, woods, plantations, parkland, orchards, fences, glebe.

10/69 Compton Vallence (parish) SY 589934 [Compton Valence]
Apt 06.03.1839; 1297a (all); Map 1840, 8 chns, by John Martin; woods (col), plantations (col), parkland, arable (col), grassland (col), orchards, osiers, fences, field gates; pictorial church.

10/70 Corfe Castle (parish) SY 970820
Apt 24.02.1843; 8809a (9884); Map 1844, 6 chns, by John Martin; hill-drawing, railway, waterbodies, houses, woods, plantations, parkland, rock outcrops, fences, field boundary ownerships, field gates, building names, islands, coastline, cliffs, castle ruins, tumulus, parsonage, clay pits, mill, common, downland, heath, osiers; physical features named.

10/71 Corfe Mullen (parish) SY 979967
Apt 12.01.1839; 3086a (3086); Map 1840, 9 chns; waterbodies, woods, hedge ownership, field boundary ownerships.

10/72 Corscombe (parish) ST 522046
Apt 06.09.1838; 5003a (5003); Map 1840, 6 chns, by William Richards, Tiverton; hill-drawing, foot/b'way, waterbodies, houses, woods (named), plantations, orchards, heath/moor, building names, sand or stone pits, quarries, osiers.

10/73 Cranborne and Holwell (tithing) SU 062131
Apt 03.09.1846; 4072a (13730); Map 1844, 8 chns, in 2 parts, (includes enlargement of village at 4 chns); houses, woods, plantations, common.

10/74 Long Critchell (parish) ST 970104 [Long Crichel]
Apt 31.12.1842; 1869a (1869); Map 1846?, 10 chns.

10/75 Dalwood (parish) SY 245998
Apt 14.08.1845; 1710a (1709); Map 1840, 6 chns, by G. Anstice, Stockland; foot/b'way, waterbodies, houses, woods, plantations, orchards, heath/moor, field gates, building names; bridge named.

10/76 Dewlish (parish) SY 774982
Apt 08.11.1844; 2091a (2090); Map 1845?, 6 chns, ? by John B. Knight and John Martin; waterbodies, woods (named), plantations (named), orchards, field boundary ownerships, churchyard, foreshore to vicar.

10/77 Dorchester, Holy Trinity with Froome Whitfield (parish) SY 698923 [Frome Whitfield]
Apt 11.03.1840; 1370a (1369); Map 1840, 6 chns; woods, plantations, arable (col), grassland (col), field names, county gaol, pits, milestone, tithe-free areas, friary lands, common, glebe, avenue of trees; furlongs named; strips within furlongs, which are unnumbered, are shown with red solid boundaries.

10/78 Durweston (parish) ST 846079
Apt 30.01.1837; 1764a (1763); Map 1837, [12 chns]; colours show glebe, in-hand lands and farm lands, as explained in legend; map is described as of the Manor of Durweston belonging to the Right Honourable Lord Portman. District is apportioned by holding; Apt omits land use.

10/79 Edmondsham (parish) SU 068114
Apt 19.12.1838; 1672a (1671); Map 1840, 8 chns, by R.C. Gale, Winchester; waterbodies, woods (col), plantations (col), houses (depiction inconsistent).

10/80 Evershot and Frome St Quintin (parish) ST 585042
Apt 21.11.1838; 2435a (2434); Map 1838, 6 chns, in 2 parts, by J. Martin; foot/b'way, waterbodies, houses, woods, plantations, arable (col), grassland (col), orchards, churchyard, pound, willows, farm names; map carries recital of adoption proceedings, with landowners' signatures.

10/81 Fairwood (tithing in parish of Cranborne) SU 095076 [Verwood]
Apt 22.01.1846; 2323a (?); Map 1847, 6 chns; foot/b'way, waterbodies, houses, building names, road names, castle, common, tithe-free land; copses, heath and hills named.

10/82 Farnham (parish) ST 952148
Apt 17.09.1842; 402a (all); Map 1843, 7 chns, by John Raymond; fences, field gates, common, downland; coppice named.

10/83 Fifehead Magdalen (parish) ST 773211
Apt 08.05.1839; 967a (976); Map 1839, 6 chns, by H. Bennett; foot/b'way, waterbodies, houses, woods, withy beds, parkland, orchards, mill.

10/84 Fifehead Neville (parish) ST 764108
Apt 28.04.1842; 791a (791); Map 1842, 8 chns.

10/85 Fleet (parish) SY 633803
Apt 22.09.1838; 845a (1385); Map 1839?, 6.67 chns; foot/b'way, houses, coastline, beach, lagoon; colours show West and East Fleet; scale is stated as 1 inch to 27 perches [i.e. 6.67 chns or 1 inch to 1 foot (1:5280)].

10/86 Folke (parish) ST 659127
Apt 23.09.1840; 1723a (1722); Map 1840, 6 chns, by J. Poole, Sherborne, Dorset; waterbodies, houses. District is apportioned by holding and fields are not shown.

10/87 Fontmell Magna (parish) ST 860173
Apt 08.06.1837; 2853a (2853); Map 1839, 6 chns, by John Raymond, Shaftesbury, Dorset; hill-drawing, foot/b'way, waterbodies, houses, woods, orchards, heath/moor, open fields (named), fences, building names, milestones, mills, chapels, common, downland, glebe.

10/88 Fordington (parish) SY 687898 [Not listed]
Apt 18.06.1841; 2749a (2749); Map 1843?, 6 chns, in 2 parts, by John Martin, Evershot, Dorset, (includes enlargement of Fordington at 3 chns); turnpike roads, turnpike gates, houses, plantations, hedge ownership, fences, field gates, building names, road names, field names, barracks, tumulus, pummery, old bridge, parish and ward names, downland, common; built-up part generalised; map is dominated by strip-like fields drawn with solid boundaries.

10/89 Frampton (parish) SY 623940
Apt 07.08.1839; 3509a (3508); Map 1839, 6 chns, in 4 parts; foot/b'way, turnpike roads, waterbodies, houses, woods, plantations, parkland, rock outcrops, building names, road names, sand or stone pits or quarries, glebe (col).

10/90 Frome Vauchurch (parish) SY 594974
Apt 19.04.1838; 615a (all); Map 1838, 3 chns, in 2 parts; hill-drawing, foot/b'way, houses, woods, plantations, arable (col), grassland (col), orchards, fences, building names, road names, weir house, parsonage, poor houses, pit, pound, osiers, wasteland; cow leazes named; map carries a recital of the procedures for its adoption by the landowners.

10/91 Gillingham (parish) ST 799269
Apt 13.09.1839; 8355a (8355); Map 1841, 8 chns, in 3 parts, by John Raymond, Shaftesbury, (includes enlargement of Gillingham town at 4 chns); building names, mills, Crown lands, forest land; pictorial church; most farm buildings appear to be omitted.

10/92 Glanvilles Wootton (parish) ST 684087
Apt 15.05.1838; 1665a (1665); Map 1839, 4 chns; woods, parkland, orchards, field boundary ownerships; colour bands may show property ownerships.

10/93 Godmanstone (parish) SY 654971
Apt 26.11.1838; 1154a (1154); Map 1839, 6 chns, by John Baverstock Knight; waterbodies, houses, plantations, orchards.

10/94 Gussage All Saints (parish) SU 006125
Apt 18.08.1841; 2997a (2907); Map 1843, 9 chns, in 4 parts, (including 80-chn index); woods, plantations, parkland.

10/95 Gussage St Michael (parish) ST 990130
Apt 07.12.1842; 2883a (2882); Map 1841, 9 chns, in 3 parts, by H. Holloway, Ringwood; foot/b'way, waterbodies, houses, woods, plantations, building names; pictorial church.

10/96 Halstock (parish) ST 530081
Apt 11.04.1842; 3182a (all); Map 1845?, 6 chns, by W. Pickering; waterbodies, houses, woods (col), plantations (col), orchards (col), heath/moor (col), building names, factory, sand or stone pit.

10/97 Hammoon (parish) ST 815140
Apt 19.03.1838; 677a (all); Map 1839?, [4 chns].

10/98 Hampreston (parish) SU 070005
Apt 30.06.1837; 1116a (4948); Map 1838, 10 chns, by George Easton, Oakley, Wimborne; woods.

10/99 Hamworthy (parish) SY 990910
Apt 19.12.1838; 1032a (all); Map 1838, 8 chns, by Wm Baker, Oakley near Wimborne; foot/b'way, woods (col), hedge ownership, road names, landowners, coast features (named), harbour; built-up part generalised.

10/100 Hartgrove otherwise East Orchards (parish) ST 836171
Apt 04.02.1846; 825a (?); Map 1846, 6 chns, by W. Painter; foot/b'way, waterbodies, houses (by shading), woods, orchards, fences, field gates, building names, farm names.

10/101 Hazelbury Bryan (parish) ST 749089
Apt 14.09.1838; 2359a (?); Map 1838, 6 chns, by J. Poole, Sherborne, Dorset; foot/b'way, woods, orchards, building names, disappearing stream, common.

10/102 Hawkchurch (parish) ST 357001
Apt 07.10.1842; 4130a (4130); Map 1842, 3 chns, by J. Woodmass and Co; foot/b'way, waterbodies, houses, field boundary ownerships; legend explains depiction of buildings, waterbodies and boundaries.

10/103 Haydon (parish) ST 672155
Apt 18.05.1839; 633a (all); Map 1840, 6 chns, by J. Poole, Sherborne, Dorset; houses. District is apportioned by holding; Apt omits land use.

10/104 Hermitage (parish) ST 650076
Apt 22.07.1840; 752a (751); Map 1845?, 8 chns.

10/105 Hillfield (parish) ST 635061 [Hilfield]
Apt 28.10.1843; 1585a (1584); Map 1844?, 6 chns, by John Martin; woods, arable (col), grassland (col), orchards, landowners, chalk pit, common.

10/106 Hilton (parish) ST 770039
Apt 23.09.1842; 2974a (2974); Map 1842?, 6 chns; foot/b'way, waterbodies, disappearing streams.

10/107 Hinton Martel (parish) SU 008056 [Hinton Martell]
Apt 19.12.1838; 1535a (1534); Map 1840, 8 chns, by R.C. Gale, Winchester; waterbodies, houses (depiction inconsistent), woods (col), road names.

10/108 Hinton Parva (parish) ST 999045
Apt 27.05.1841; 440a (all); Map 1845?, 6 chns; foot/b'way, waterbodies, woods, hedge ownership.

10/109 Hinton St Mary (parish) ST 787165
Apt 26.11.1841; 983a (982); Map 1843, 4 chns, (including 2-chn enlargement of detail); foot/b'way, houses, woods, orchards, withy bed.

10/110 East Holme (parish) SY 904854
Apt 30.07.1841; 406a (1200); Map 1841, 6 chns, by Henry Hyde, Lulworth, Dorset, land, timber and house surveyor; foot/b'way, houses, fences.

10/111 Holnest (parish) ST 650098
Apt 12.06.1843; 2063a (all); Map 1844?, 8 chns; waterbodies, houses, pound, waste.

10/112 Hook (parish) ST 533004 [Hooke]
Apt 06.03.1839; 1238a (1237); Map 1839?, 6 chns; hill-drawing, waterbodies, houses, woods, arable (col), grassland (col), orchards, willow beds.

10/113 Horton with Woodlands (parochial chapelry) SU 048082
Apt 23.09.1840; 5302a (5301); Map 1841, 8 chns, in 2 parts, by R.C. Gale, Winchester; waterbodies, houses, woods (col), plantations (col); Gale notes that tithe areas 1-12 and 49-64 were taken from a map made by F Webb.

10/114 Ibberton (parish) ST 788080
Apt 07.10.1839; 1384a (1383); Map 1840, 9 chns, by J. Poole, Sherborne, Dorset; foot/b'way, houses, disappearing stream.

10/115 Iwerne Courtney with Farringdon (parochial chapelry) ST 861124
Apt 12.09.1838; 1954a (1953); Map 1838, 6 chns, by E. Watts, Yeovil; waterbodies, houses, woods, plantations, parkland, arable (col), grassland (col), orchards, heath/moor, hedge ownership, fences, field gates, road names, field names, keeper's house, bull pit, brick kiln, chapel, mill, downland, common named.

10/116 Iwerne Minster (parish) ST 872145
Apt 16.11.1841; 2949a (2949); Map 1838, 6 chns, by Raymond, Shaftesbury, Dorset; hill-drawing, woods, plantations, orchards, open fields, building names, common, downland.

10/117 Kingston Russell (parish) SY 581903 [Not listed]
Apt 14.09.1838; 1148a (1147); Map 1839, 8 chns, by Humphrey Evans Knight; foot/b'way, woods, plantations, parkland.

10/118 Kington Magna (parish) ST 759226
Apt 08.04.1846; 1891a (1891); Map 1846, 6 chns, by Raymond and Son, Shaftesbury; turnpike roads, toll bar, fences, field gates, pound.

10/119 Kinson (tithing or chapelry in parish of Great Canford) SZ 066953
Apt 09.02.1839; 1589a (4715); Map 1839, 9 chns; woods.

10/120 West Knighton (parish) SY 728876
Apt 21.04.1843; 1157a (2339); Map 1843?, 6 chns; waterbodies, houses, road names, landowners, springs, water mill, boundstones, tithe-free land, heath, ownerships (col); built-up part generalised.

10/121 Langton Herring (parish) SY 614821
Apt 30.10.1841; 902a (1202); Map 1837, 3 chns, by Geo. Moss, Crewkerne, Somerset; hill-drawing, foot/b'way, waterbodies, houses, woods, plantations, parkland, orchards, heath/moor, hedges, fences, walls (double solid lines), field gates, preventive houses, garden allotments, flag mast, sand or stone pit, lime kilns, coastline; legend explains depiction of buildings, boundaries and land-use symbols.

10/122 Langton Long Blandford (parish) ST 903056
Apt 21.03.1839; 1808a (all); Map 1841, 6 chns, by John Baverstock Knight; foot/b'way, waterbodies, orchards, fences, field gates, ornamental gardens.

10/123 Langton Matravers (parish) SY 998788
Apt 30.06.1840; 2250a (all); Map 1841, 8 chns, in 2 parts, by George Easton, (including open fields at 3 chns); construction lines, hill-drawing, foot/b'way, waterbodies, houses, woods, parkland, rock outcrops, open fields, field gates, coastline, cliffs; enlargement has construction lines.

10/124 Leigh (chapelry in parish of Yetminster) ST 619075
Apt 31.08.1840; 1984a (1984); Map 1840, 6 chns, by E. Watts, Yeovil; houses, farmyards, woods, plantations, arable (col), grassland (col), orchards, hedge ownership, field gates, building names, field names, mill; pictorial church.

10/125 Lillington (Inner District) (parish) ST 626127
Apt 16.01.1841; 873a (873); Map 1843, 6 chns, in 2 parts, by J. Poole, Sherborne, Dorset, (including 3-chn enlargement of detail); foot/b'way, houses, landowners, disappearing stream; scrolling forms cartouche.

10/126 Lillington (Outer District) (parish) ST 628105
Apt 16.01.1841; 934a (934); Map 1843, 6 chns; foot/b'way, disappearing stream.

10/127 Litton Cheney (parish) SY 551917
Apt 31.06.1839; 3818a (3817); Map 1840, 6 chns, ? by John Baverstock Knight and Levi Luckham; foot/b'way, waterbodies, houses, sand or stone pit.

10/128 Loders (except West End) (parish) SY 504937
Apt 07.11.1845; 2242a (2241); Map 1846, 3 chns, by Richard James, Chideock, Dorset; foot/b'way, open fields.

10/129 Longbredy (parish) SY 567909 [Long Bredy]
Apt 07.10.1839; 2118a (all); Map 1840, 8 chns, by John Baverstock Knight; foot/b'way, waterbodies, houses, woods, plantations, orchards, heath/moor.

10/130 Longburton (parish) ST 645129
Apt 30.11.1842; 1026a (1025); Map 1843, 6 chns, by J. Poole, Sherborne, land and timber surveyor; waterbodies, houses, fences, disappearing stream, common.

10/131 Longfleet (tithing in parish of Great Canford) SZ 018924 [Longfleet]
Apt 27.07.1843; 923a (1458); Map 1844, 6 chns, by George Easton, Oakley, Wimborne; waterbodies, woods, parkland.

10/132 East Lulworth (parish) SY 856821
Apt 10.09.1839; 2284a (?); Map 1840, 6 chns, by Henry Hyde, Lulworth, Dorset, land, timber and house surveyor; foot/b'way, waterbodies, houses, woods, rock outcrops, open fields, fences, quarries, coastline, cliffs, beach, sand or stone pits, steps to house.

10/133 Lydlinch (parish) ST 743127
Apt 19.06.1840; 2447a (all); Map 1841, 6 chns, by J. Poole, Sherborne; waterbodies, houses, disappearing stream.

10/134 Lyme Regis (parish) SY 344933
Apt 08.01.1842; 1389a (1499); Map 1841, 3 chns; hill-drawing, foot/b'way, waterbodies, houses, woods (named), plantations (named), orchards, heath/moor, rock outcrops, fences, building names, road names, coastline (in detail), cliffs, beach, harbour, mill, common.

10/135 Lytchett Matravers (parish) SY 941957
Apt 01.06.1837; 3330a (all); Map 1838, 9 chns, by George Easton, Wimborne, Dorset; waterbodies, woods, sand or stone pit; physical features named.

10/136 Lytchet Minster (parish) SY 961934 [Lytchett Minster]
Apt 12.11.1838; 3173a (3344); Map 1838, 9 chns; foot/b'way, woods (col), fences, coastline, common, greens (named); bridges named.

10/137 Maiden Newton (parish) SY 611969
Apt 30.12.1837; 2854a (2853); Map 1838, 6 chns, by John Martin, Evershot, Dorset; foot/b'way, houses, arable (col), grassland (col), farm names; colour bands may show property ownerships; map carries recital of procedure for its adoption.

10/138 Manston (parish) ST 813157
Apt 14.11.1839; 1323a (all); Map 1840, 9 chns; woods, arable (col), grassland (col), orchards, open fields.

10/139 Mapperton (parish) SY 511996
Apt 09.10.1837; 804a (804); Map 1839?, 3 chns; foot/b'way, waterbodies, houses, woods (col), parkland (col), arable (col), grassland (col), orchards (col), gardens (col), hedge ownership, field gates, landowners.

10/140 Mappowder (parish) ST 733069
Apt 28.05.1841; 1887a (all); Map 1842?, 6 chns; waterbodies, houses, woods (named), arable (col), grassland (col), orchards, heath/moor, field boundary ownerships, disappearing stream, willows.

10/141 Margaret Marsh (parish) ST 826196
Apt 18.01.1843; 525a (525); Map 1843, 6 chns, by John Raymond; foot/b'way, waterbodies, fences, field gates, building names, poor house; pictorial church.

10/142 Marnhull (parish) ST 787188
Apt 26.01.1838; 3751a (all); Map 1838, 3 chns; waterbodies, houses, woods, open fields, hedge ownership, fences, field gates.

10/143 Marshwood (parish) SY 401984
Apt 12.07.1843; 3397a (3396); Map 1844, 6 chns, by Richard James, Chideock, Dorset; foot/b'way, waterbodies, houses.

10/144 Melbury Abbas (parish) ST 882201
Apt 19.03.1838; 2277a (all); Map 1838, 6 chns; building names, mills; one field named.

10/145 Melbury Bubb (parish) ST 599056
Apt 14.02.1839; 1227a (1227); Map 1840?, 6 chns; turnpike roads, toll bar, waterbodies, houses, woods, plantations, parkland, arable (col), grassland (col), building names, spring, willow beds; pictorial church; map carries recital of proceedings for its adoption.

10/146 Melbury Osmond (parish) ST 572081
Apt 27.11.1838; 1193a (all); Map 1839?, 4 chns, by John Martin, Evershot, Dorset; waterbodies, houses, woods, arable (col), grassland (col), orchards, fences; pictorial church; map carries recital of proceedings for its adoption.

10/147 Melbury Sampford (parish) ST 576062
Apt 28.11.1838; 1025a (1024); Map 1838, 4 chns, by John Martin; waterbodies, houses, woods (col), plantations (col), parkland (col, named), fences, field boundary ownerships, building names; map has note of adoption proceedings.

10/148 Melcombe Horsey (parish) ST 746027 [Not listed]
Apt 12.01.1841; 2152a (2151); Map 1839, 6 chns; houses, woods. Apt omits land use.

10/149 Milborne St Andrew (parish) SY 797979
Apt 17.12.1839; 1717a (1717); Map 1840?, 6 chns; foot/b'way, waterbodies, houses.

10/150 Mintern Magna (parish) ST 662059 [Minterne Magna]
Apt 30.08.1843; 2064a (2064); Map 1844, 8 chns; hill-drawing, foot/b'way, waterbodies, houses, woods, parkland, building names; red lines show stone walls.

10/151 Moore Critchell (parish) ST 988090 [Moor Crichel]
Apt 28.10.1843; 1705a (1705); Map 1845?, 6 chns; waterbodies.

10/152 Morden (parish) SY 907930
Apt 02.09.1846; 6574a (6574); Map 1847?, 6 chns, by H. Richards; waterbodies, disappearing stream; some field boundaries are shown with double solid lines.

10/153 Moreton (parish) SY 796891
Apt 07.11.1838; 2312a (2311); Map 1839, 8 chns, by J. Raymond; hill-drawing, waterbodies, houses, woods, plantations, fences, field gates, field names, barrow, glebe (col); hill named.

10/154 Motcombe (parish) ST 847255
Apt 28.09.1838; 4841a (all); Map 1840?, 6 chns, in 2 parts, by J. Raymond, (including Enmore Green at 3 chns); foot/b'way, turnpike roads, tollgate, waterbodies, houses, woods (named), plantations (named), parkland, fences, field gates, building names, sand or stone pit, allotment.

10/155 Mosterton (parish) ST 455058
Apt 17.08.1838; 958a (958); Map 1838, 3 chns; waterbodies, houses, woods, plantations, arable (col), grassland (col), orchards, building names, mill pond, willow beds; legend explains colours and depiction of buildings and water bodies; map carries a recital of proceedings for its adoption.

10/156 Netherbury (parish) SY 467976
Apt 20.8.1839; 6225a (6225); Map 1835, 6 chns, in 2 parts, by J. Poole,

Sherborne, Dorset, (includes enlargement of village at 3 chns), litho (by Porter, Sloane St), with hand-colour; houses (by shading), woods (named), arable (col), grassland (col), orchards, building names; hills named.

10/157 Nutford (tithing in parish of Pimperne) ST 878085 [Not listed]
Apt 06.02.1846; 19a (?); Map 1847, 4 chns.

10/158 Oborne (parish) ST 651191
Apt 30.06.1838; 593a (all); Map 1838, 6 chns, by R.J. Wright, Norwich; houses, woods, arable (col), grassland (col), orchards, hedge ownership, glebe (col).

10/159 Okeford Fitzpaine (parish) ST 800108
Apt 28.05.1838; 2569a (2633); Map 1839, 8 chns, in 2 parts, by J. Poole, Sherborne, Dorset, (includes enlargement of village at 3 chns); waterbodies, houses, woods, disappearing streams, sand or stone pit; pictorial church.

10/160 West Orchard (parish) ST 826166
Apt 02.06.1840; 618a (617); Map 1841?, 6 chns; woods, orchards, hedge ownership, fences, field gates, road names, field names; names are stamped; map shows signs of later alterations.

10/161 Osmington (parish) SY 733827
Apt 11.11.1837; 2182a (all); Map 1839, 6 chns, by John Taperell; hill-drawing, foot/b'way, waterbodies, houses, field gates, coastline, sand or stone pits; colours may show property ownerships; in one field there is a sketch of a man on a horse.

10/162 Ower Moigne (parish) SY 772852 [Owermoigne]
Apt 21.02.1840; 3271a (3271); Map 1838, 3 chns, by Thos Newbery, (including construction line diagram); construction lines, foot/b'way, houses, woods, barrow, beach, high and low water mark, chalk pits, limekiln.

10/163 Parkstone (tithing in parish of Great Canford) SZ 048905
Apt 27.07.1843; 842a (3513); Map 1844, 6 chns, in 2 parts, by George Easton, Oakley, Wimborne; houses, woods, plantations, parkland, coastline.

10/164 West Parley (parish) SU 091008
Apt 10.10.1839; 3407a (3407); Map 1839, 3 chns, by James Roger Bramble, Devizes; construction lines, waterbodies, houses, woods, plantations, fences, field boundary ownerships.

10/165 Pentridge (parish) SU 035183
Apt 17.12.1838; 1764a (1764); Map 1839, 9 chns, in 2 parts, by Harry Holloway, near Lyndhurst; hill-drawing, foot/b'way, waterbodies, houses.

10/166 South Perrott (parish) ST 472066
Apt 10.05.1838; 1452a (1451); Map 1839?, 6 chns; foot/b'way, houses (by shading), disappearing stream.

10/167 Piddlehinton (parish) SY 715973
Apt 19.03.1838; 2264a (2264); Map 1840?, 6 chns, waterbodies, houses, fences.

10/168 Piddletown (parish) SY 745941 [Puddletown]
Apt 04.12.1839; 7653a (7653); Map 1842, 8 chns, by E.T. Percy, Sherborne; waterbodies, open fields, building names, road names, field names, disappearing stream, common meadows; heathland and woodland indicated by name.

10/169 Piddletrenthide (parish) SY 706997
Apt 20.09.1838; 4488a (4487); Map 1840, 6 chns; foot/b'way, waterbodies, woods, parkland, tithing boundaries.

10/170 Pilsdon (parish) ST 414006
Apt 22.12.1841; 648a (648); Map 1841, 6 chns; houses, woods, arable (col), grassland (col), orchards.

10/171 North Poorton (parish) SY 519985
Apt 30.12.1837; 664a (664); Map 1838?, 6 chns; houses, woods, arable (col), grassland (col), orchards; colours show lands belonging to other districts; map carries recital as to its adoption.

10/172 Portisham (parish) SY 622858
Apt 04.08.1859; 1584a (4540); Map 1860, 6 chns, (tithable parts only, tinted); foot/b'way, houses, field gates, building names, landowners, mill, field acreages.

10/173 Portland (parish) SY 689711 [Isle of Portland]
Apt 07.11.1839; 2343a (3555); Map 1841, 4 chns, by John Taperell; hill-drawing, railways, waterbodies, houses, heath/moor, rock outcrops, open fields (named), fences, road names, lighthouse (pictorial), piers, cliffs, high and low water marks, battery, well, castles, beach, signal station, limekilns, old church, wasteland, quarry, quarried land, quarry rubble, common (col).

10/174 Powerstock with West Milton (parochial chapelry) SY 520959
Apt 22.02.1839; 3317a (?); Map 1839, 6 chns, in 3 parts, by James Oliver, Beaminster, (includes enlargement of villages at 3 chns); houses, arable (col), grassland (col), disappearing stream.

10/175 Poxwell (parish) SY 737844
Apt 21.02.1840; 888a (887); Map 1839, 3 chns, by John Doherty; foot/b'way, waterbodies, houses, field gates, sand or stone pits, springs, milestones; map is subtitled 'the property of Revd George Pickard'.

10/176 Preston and Sutton Pointz (parish) SY 698831
Apt 25.10.1838; 2610a (all); Map 1838, 6 chns, litho (Standidge); hill-drawing, foot/b'way, waterbodies, woods, plantations, parkland, individual trees, rock outcrops, cliffs, beach, sluice, water pipes, ice house, quarry, tumuli, stone pits, meeting house, drains.

10/177 Pulham (parish) ST 714086
Apt 27.09.1838; 2370a (2370); Map 1838, 8 chns, by J. Poole, Sherborne; waterbodies, disappearing stream, glebe, rack-rent estate boundaries. District is apportioned by holding.

10/178 Puncknoll (parish) SY 537874 [Puncknowle]
Apt 05.12.1839; 1882a (all); Map 1841, 3 chns; foot/b'way, waterbodies, houses, woods, orchards, field gates, building names, beach, boundstone, limekilns, osiers; pictorial church.

10/179 Purse Caundle (parish) ST 695173
Apt 07.11.1838; 1471a (all); Map 1838, 6 chns, by J. Poole, Sherborne, Dorset; foot/b'way, waterbodies, houses, ownerships (col). Apt omits land use.

10/180 Radipole (parish) SY 667816
Apt 17.10.1837; 1308a (all); Map 1839, 6 chns, litho (Standidge); foot/b'way, waterbodies, houses (by shading), woods, individual trees, rock outcrops, fences, building names, embankment, beach, quays, ice house, kilns, spas, boundary post.

10/181 Rampisham (parish) ST 556025
Apt 07.10.1839; 2030a (2030); Map 1840?, 6 chns; woods, plantations, arable (col), grassland (col), orchards.

10/182 Ryme Intrinseca (parish) ST 578109
Apt 07.12.1839; 1004a (1003); Map 1840, 6 chns, by R.F. Hearle, Sherborne; waterbodies, houses, building names, landowners; bridge named. Apt omits land use.

10/183 Shapwicke (parish) ST 954032 [Shapwick]
Apt 14.09.1848; 3057a (3670); Map 1849, 6 chns; woods, plantations.

10/184 Shaston, Holy Trinity with St Peter, St Martin and St Lawrence (parishes) ST 866232 [Not listed]
Apt 03.04.1840; 398a (?); Map 1845, 1 chn, in 3 parts, by J. Raymond and Son, Shaftesbury; hill-drawing, foot/b'way, turnpike roads, toll gate, waterbodies, houses, woods, plantations, parkland, park wall (pictorial), fences, field gates, building names, road names, field names, boundary stones, women's almshouse, infant school, chapels, town hall, schools.

10/185 Shaston St James (parish) ST 848216 [Not listed]
Apt 11.11.1840; 1773a (?); Map 1838, 6 chns, by S. Stephens, 180, High Street, Southampton, litho (Standidge); foot/b'way, waterbodies, houses (by shading), woods, plantations, gardens, heath/moor, fences, building names, mill, ancient cold bath, sand or stone pit, commons.

10/186 Shaston St Rumbold otherwise Cann (parish) ST 875217
Apt 16.11.1840; 931a (930); Map 1841, 6 chns, by J. Raymond; foot/b'way, waterbodies, houses, disappearing stream. (The map in PRO IR 30 is a copy of 1925.)

10/187 Sherborne (parish) ST 633168
Apt 16.09.1842; 6467a (6467); Map 1842, 6 chns, by E.T. Percy, Sherborne, Dorset; waterbodies, houses, woods, orchards, open fields, castle; built-up part generalised.

10/188 Shillingstone or Shilling Okeford (parish) ST 830103
Apt 21.07.1838; 2224a (2223); Map 1839, 8 chns, by John Baverstock Knight; waterbodies, woods, plantations, orchards, heath/moor, open fields, disappearing stream.

10/189 Silton (parish) ST 779296
Apt 30.12.1837; 1257a (all); Map 1837, 4 chns; houses, woods, plantations, orchards, road names, landowners, commons.

10/190 Sixpenny Handley (parish) ST 983167
Apt 15.06.1841; 5928a (5928); Map 1841?, 6 chns; foot/b'way, waterbodies, houses; hamlets named.

10/191 Spetisbury (parish) ST 899014
Apt 20.09.1838; 1742a (2148); Map 1839, 8 chns, ? by John Baverstock Knight and George Easton; foot/b'way, waterbodies, woods, tithe-free land, Spetisbury Rings.

10/192 West Stafford (parish) SY 723895
Apt 07.11.1838; 984a (all); Map 1839, 4.5 chns; foot/b'way, turnpike roads, waterbodies, field gates, landowners, ownership boundaries (col); legend explains ownership colours. District is apportioned by holding and fields are not shown.

10/193 Stalbridge (parish) ST 741171
Apt 26.02.1839; 5682a (all); Map 1839, 6 chns, by J.R. Jobbins, draughtsman and lithographer, Warwick Court, Holborn, litho (Standidge); woods, plantations, parkland, avenues of trees, orchards, hedges, field gates, building names, obelisk, mill; bridge named.

10/194 Stanton St Gabriel (parish) SY 389929 [Not listed]
Apt 16.05.1840; 1053a (1242); Map 1840, 4 chns, by Woodmass, Thompson and Co; hill-drawing, waterbodies, houses, field boundary ownerships, building names, beach, cliffs, farm names and boundaries; legend explains depiction of buildings, streams and boundaries.

10/195 Steeple (parish) SY 908818
Apt 27.10.1842; 3363a (3362); Map 1843, 3 chns, 1st cl, by Harry Holloway, Ringwood; construction lines, foot/b'way, houses, parkland, building names, disappearing streams.

10/196 Steepleton Preston (parish) ST 881121 [Not listed]
Apt 21.02.1839; 773a (all); Map 1840, 6 chns, by J. Poole, Sherborne, Dorset; waterbodies, houses, woods, plantations, parkland, field gates, downland; coppice named. District is apportioned by holding; Apt omits land use.

10/197 Stintsford (parish) SY 718921 [Stinsford]
Apt 30.11.1838; 2000a (1999); Map 1839, 6 chns, by John Baverstock Knight; foot/b'way, waterbodies, woods, plantations, parkland, orchards, sand or stone pit.

10/198 Stock Gaylard (parish) ST 721131 [Not listed]
Apt 07.01.1842; 849a (all); Map 1841, 6 chns, by J. Poole, Sherborne, Dorset; houses. District is apportioned by holding and fields are not shown.

10/199 Stockland (parish) ST 238034
Apt 21.12.1844; 5850a (5849); Map 1840, 6 chns, in 2 parts, by G. Anstice, Stockland, (includes 3-chn enlargement of detail); foot/b'way, waterbodies, houses, woods, orchards, marsh/bog, building names, mill, turbary.

10/200 Stockwood (parish) ST 589079
Apt 14.02.1839; 693a (692); Map 1839, 6 chns, by J. Martin; foot/b'way, waterbodies, houses, woods, plantations, arable (col), grassland (col), orchards, fences, common; map has recital of the procedure for its adoption.

10/201 East Stoke (parish) SY 872877
Apt 28.10.1843; 3234a (3273); Map 1844, 6 chns, in 7 parts, (includes 30-chn index); foot/b'way, waterbodies, houses, open fields, field gates, building names.

10/202 Stoke Abbott (parish) ST 441005
Apt 24.12.1839; 2304a (2303); Map 1840, [4 chns]; foot/b'way, houses.

10/203 Stoke Wake (parish) ST 758066
Apt 10.09.1839; 1039a (all); Map 1841, 4 chns, by John Baverstock Knight; foot/b'way, woods; pictorial church.

10/204 Stourpain (parish) ST 878104 [Stourpaine]
Apt 05.06.1840; 2305a (all); Map 1841, 6 chns, by George Easton; hill-drawing, foot/b'way, waterbodies, houses, woods (col), heath/moor, open fields, hedges, fences, waste.

10/205 Stourton Caundle (parish) ST 709149
Apt 10.10.1839; 170a (1975); Map 1840, 8 chns, by J. Poole, Sherborne, Dorset; houses, common. District is apportioned by holding; Apt omits land use.

10/206 East Stower (parish) ST 807236 [East Stour]
Apt 22.07.1842; 1675a (all); Map 1842, 6 chns; turnpike roads, houses (by shading), fences, building names, field names, parish pound.

10/207 West Stower (parish) ST 778223 [West Stour]
Apt 02.05.1842; 1016a (all); Map 1842, 6 chns, by J. Raymond, Shaftesbury; foot/b'way, houses (by shading), building names.

10/208 Stower Provost (parish) ST 814213 [Stour Provost]
Apt 26.11.1841; 2777a (2777); Map 1842, 6 chns, in 2 parts, (includes 3-chn enlargement of open fields); waterbodies, woods (named), orchards, willow bed, open fields, building names; bridge named.

10/209 Stratton (parish) SY 650946
Apt 12.04.1838; 1683a (1683); Map 1838, 6 chns, by J. Martin, Evershot, Dorset; turnpike roads, toll bar, houses, arable (col), grassland (col), open fields, farm names and boundaries, downland, waste, inclosures; map carries a recital of adoption proceedings, with 23 landowners' signatures.

10/210 Studland (parish) SZ 025835
Apt 11.07.1839; 2137a (7814); Map 1840, 8 chns; foot/b'way, plantations, coastline, beach, castle.

10/211 Sturminster Marshall (parish) SY 946995
Apt 14.02.1839; 3852a (3851); Map 1844, 6 chns; waterbodies, woods, fences, field boundary ownerships; colour bands may show property ownerships.

10/212 Sturminster Newton Castle and Bagber (parish and tithing) ST 777138 [Sturminster Newton]
Apt 06.04.1839; 4229a (4229); Map 1840, 8 chns, in 2 parts, by J. Raymond, (includes enlargement of town at 3 chns); hill-drawing, turnpike roads, toll gates, waterbodies, woods (named), plantations (named), open fields, fences, field gates, building names, field names, mills, workhouse, common; pictorial church (with gravestones).

10/213 Sutton Waldron (parish) ST 869159
Apt 01.05.1845; 1014a (1013); Map 1847?, 12 chns; open fields, church walls; scale has been corrected from 6 to 12 chns in pencil. District is apportioned by holding.

10/214 Swanage (parish) SZ 013809
Apt 16.05.1839; 2923a (3163); Map 1840, 6 chns; waterbodies, woods, gardens, rock outcrops, open fields, building names, cliffs, coastline, boundstones, hotel; headlands and bays named; gardens indicated by annotation.

10/215 Swyre (parish) SY 522886
Apt 03.07.1838; 1081a (1146); Map 1839, 8 chns, by John Baverstock Knight; houses, woods, orchards, coastline, beach.

10/216 Sydling St Nicholas (parish) ST 631003
Apt 11.07.1839; 5029a (5028); Map 1841?, 6 chns, by John Martin and John Baverstock Knight; waterbodies, houses, woods, plantations, arable (col), grassland (col), building names, chalk pit, parish pound, ornamental garden.

10/217 Symmondsbury (parish) SY 445936 [Symondsbury]
Apt 07.10.1839; 3925a (3925); Map 1843?, 6 chns, by John Martin; foot/b'way, houses, woods (col), plantations (col), orchards (col), withy beds, rock outcrops, building names, harbour, wharves, coastline, beach, cliffs, downland, ewe leaze; hills named.

10/218 Tarent Rushton (parish) ST 951065 [Tarrant Rushton]
Apt 31.12.1842; 843a (1221); Map 1844?, 10 chns; the only building shown is the church.

10/219 Tarrant Crawford (parish) ST 922031
Apt 16.03.1850; 21a (600); Map 1850, 6 chns, by H. Richards; mill; bridge named; pictorial church.

10/220 Tarrant Gunville (parish) ST 918138
Apt 22.11.1839; 3425a (3425); Map 1840, 4 chns, by John Baverstock Knight; foot/b'way, waterbodies, woods, plantations, parkland, field gates, downland (col).

10/221 Tarrant Hinton (parish) ST 934112
Apt 12.09.1839; 2279a (all); Map 1840, 3 chns, by John Baverstock Knight; foot/b'way, waterbodies, houses, plantations, field names, parsonage, bog, kennel, tumulus, field acreages; enclosures adjoining downland named, with arable/pasture annotations; names are stamped.

10/222 Tarrant Keinston (parish) ST 930043 [Tarrant Keyneston]
Apt 20.09.1838; 1962a (1962); Map 1840, 6 chns; houses, road names, landowners.

10/223 Tarrant Monkton and Tarrant Launceston (parish) ST 934089
Apt 21.03.1839; 3819a (all); Map 1840, 6 chns, by John Baverstock Knight; foot/b'way, waterbodies, houses.

10/224 Tarrant Rawston (parish) ST 934066
Apt 20.09.1838; 697a (all); Map 1840, 3 chns; waterbodies, houses.

10/225 Thornford (parish) ST 610133
Apt 21.03.1843; 1408a (1407); Map 1846, 6 chns, by E.T. Percy; houses.

10/226 Tincleton (parish) SY 774921
Apt 08.01.1846; 886a (885); Map 1844, 3 chns; hill-drawing, foot/b'way, waterbodies, houses, woods, plantations, osiers, parkland, orchards, fences, field gates, building names, stone pits, tumuli, spring; colours may show property ownerships.

10/227 Todber (parish) ST 802202
Apt 23.04.1840; 385a (all); Map 1839, 4.5 chns; waterbodies, woods, orchards.

10/228 Toller Fratrum (parish) SY 579976
Apt 29.07.1841; 501a (500); Map 1841?, 6 chns, by J. Martin, Evershot; waterbodies, houses, woods, plantations, withy beds, arable (col), grassland (col), orchards, milestone.

10/229 Toller Porcorum (parish) SY 556981
Apt 07.08.1843; 3144a (3143); Map 1844?, 6 chns, by John Martin; foot/b'way, woods, plantations, withy beds, orchards, field boundary ownerships.

10/230 Tolpuddle (parish) SY 790945
Apt 30.06.1841; 2040a (2039); Map 1842, 6 chns, by John Baverstock Knight; hill-drawing, waterbodies, woods, orchards, heath, osiers.

10/231 Tomson (parish) SY 885986 [Not listed]
Apt 03.07.1838; 475a (all); Map 1838, 8 chns, surveyed for T.G. Robson by W. Kemp; plantations, road names.

10/232 Toners Puddle (parish) SY 829917 [Not listed]
Apt 13.12.1838; 1984a (?); Map 1839, 8 chns, by J. Raymond; hill-drawing, waterbodies, woods, plantations, heath/moor, fences, field gates, building names, boundary stone, private roads, glebe (col); one field named.

10/233 Turnworth (parish) ST 815080
Apt 19.06.1840; 1445a (1560); Map 1842?, 6 chns, in 2 parts; foot/b'way, houses, building names.

10/234 Tyneham (parish) SY 880817
Apt 23.04.1840; 2138a (2915); Map 1840, 6 chns, by Henry Hyde, Lulworth, Dorset, land, timber and house surveyor; foot/b'way, waterbodies, houses, rock outcrops, fences, coastline, cliffs.

10/235 Up Cerne (parish) ST 648033
Apt 04.05.1839; 1104a (all); Map 1840, 6 chns; foot/b'way, waterbodies, houses, arable (col), grassland (col).

10/236 Upwey (parish) SY 661853
Apt 19.03.1838; 1785a (1785); Map 1840?, 6 chns, by John Baverstock Knight; woods.

10/237 Walditch (parish) SY 483927
Apt 04.10.1838; 286a (285); Map 1841?, 4 chns; foot/b'way, houses, woods, orchards, field gates, osiers.

10/238 Wambrook (parish) ST 282081
Apt 23.10.1844; 1857a (1857); Map 1845, 6 chns; waterbodies.

10/239 Wareham, Holy Trinity (parish) SY 948843 [Not listed]
Apt 20.03.1843; 2520a (2670); Map 1845, 8 chns, by Humphry Evans Knight; foot/b'way, waterbodies, tumuli, water meadow channels.

10/240 Wareham, Lady St Mary (parish) SY 910871 [Not listed]
Apt 24.01.1843; 824a (823); Map 1846?, 4 chns; railway, waterbodies, houses, disappearing streams; some built-up parts generalised.

10/241 Wareham, St Martin (parish) SY 940905 [Not listed]
Apt 09.05.1842; 4034a (all); Map 1843, 4 chns, by John Baverstock Knight; hill-drawing, waterbodies, houses, coastline, sand or stone pits.

10/242 Warmwell (parish) SY 749861
Apt 25.02.1841; 1531a (1531); Map 1844?, 6 chns, in 2 parts, (includes 3-chn enlargement of open fields); construction lines, turnpike roads, waterbodies, woods, plantations, arable (col), grassland (col), orchards, open fields (named), field acreages, hedges, boundary markers, chalk pits, tumuli, glebe; pictorial church; crossroads named.

10/243 West End (hamlet in parish of Loders) SY 458950 [Not listed]
Apt 20.08.1845; 321a (?); Map 1846, 3 chns, by Richard James, Chideock, Dorset; foot/b'way, waterbodies, fences.

10/244 Weymouth (parish) SY 677786
Apt 20.12.1839; 52a (all); Map 1842, 3 chns, by John Taperell; hill-drawing, houses, fences, field boundary ownerships, building names, road names, coal yard, brewery, burial ground, shipwrights yards, barracks quay, embankment, gas works, town hall, chapel, workhouse, waste; built-up part generalised.

10/245 Whitchurch Canonicorum (parish) SY 396955
Apt 12.07.1843; 6113a (6113); Map 1844, 6 chns, by Richard James, Chideock, Dorset; foot/b'way, waterbodies, houses, quarries, tunnel, hamlet names; hill named; legend explains depicition of buildings, roads, water bodies and boundaries.

10/246 Wimborne Minster (parish) SU 010024
Apt 21.11.1845; 11967a (?); Map 1846, 6 chns, in 2 parts, by J. Poole, Sherborne, Dorset, (includes town separately at ?3 chns); foot/b'way, waterbodies, houses, building names, disappearing stream, woods and coppices (by name), downland, park.

10/247 Wimborne, St. Giles and All Hallows (parish) SU 029126
Apt 19.12.1838; 3978a (11966); Map 1839, 8 chns, by R.C. Gale, Winchester; waterbodies, houses, woods (col), plantations (col), parkland (in detail, col), building names.

10/248 Winfrith Newburgh and West Lulworth (parish) SY 813837
Apt 20.03.1843; 7053a (?); Map 1843, 6 chns, in 2 parts, by Henry Hyde, Ringwood, Hants, land, timber and house surveyor, (includes 3-chn enlargement of open fields); hill-drawing, waterbodies, houses, rock outcrops, open fields, cliffs, beach, sand or stone pit, heath, common.

10/249 Winterborne Clenstone (parish) ST 838030 [Winterborne Clenston]
Apt 21.03.1839; 1407a (all); Map 1839?, 7 chns; disappearing stream.

10/250 Winterborne Houghton (parish) ST 809050
Apt 26.11.1838; 1923a (1923); Map 1839?, 7.5 chns; foot/b'way.

10/251 Winterborne Kingston (parish) SY 862987
Apt 16.09.1842; 2508a (2508); Map 1843?, 6 chns; waterbodies, open fields, disappearing streams; map has note of adoption proceedings.

10/252 Winterborne Monkton (parish) SY 676875
Apt 21.03.1839; 631a (631); Map 1840, 3 chns, by J. Martin, Evershot; hill-drawing, foot/b'way, waterbodies, houses, woods, plantations, arable (col), grassland (col), orchards, heath/moor, road embankments.

10/253 Winterborne Stickland (parish) ST 834052
Corn rent conversion, 1919; ?a (1340); no map.

10/254 Winterborne Whitchurch (parish) ST 843004 [Winterborne Whitechurch]
Apt 27.03.1839; 2841a (2841); Map 1839?, 6 chns; foot/b'way, waterbodies, houses, disappearing streams.

10/255 Winterbourne Abbas (parish) SY 607908
Apt 07.10.1839; 1500a (all); Map 1840, 3 chns; foot/b'way, waterbodies, houses.

10/256 Winterbourne Came (parish) SY 698875 [Winterborne Came]
Apt 14.11.1843; 1971a (1970); Map 1844?, 6 chns; foot/b'way, turnpike roads, turnpike gate, waterbodies, houses, fences, ancient barrows, church ruins; colours may show property ownerships.

10/257 Winterbourne Martin (parish) SY 648886 [Martinstown]
Apt 17.07.1841; 3503a (3503); Map 1844?, 4 chns; hill-drawing, foot/b'way, waterbodies, houses, fences, field gates, tumuli, hill fort or castle.

10/258 Winterbourne Steepleton (parish) SY 619893
Apt 17.07.1839; 1783a (1783); Map 1840, 8 chns, by John Martin; waterbodies, woods, arable (col), grassland (col), orchards, open fields, field names, pound; pictorial church.

10/259 Winterbourne Zelstone (parish) SY 897977 [Winterborne Zelston]
Apt 06.03.1839; 824a (823); Map 1840, 4.5 chns, by John Baverstock Knight; woods, orchards, gardens, stone pits; pictorial church.

10/260 Witchampton (parish) ST 984066
Apt 05.04.1838; 1481a (1481); Map 1840?, 4 chns; waterbodies, woods, parkland, orchards, hedge ownership, field gates, landowners, sand or stone pits, glebe (col); colour bands may show property ownerships. Apt omits field names.

10/261 Witherstone (parish) SY 533975 [Not listed]
Apt 09.01.1840; 762a (?); Map 1840, 6 chns; woods, plantations, arable (col), grassland (col), orchards.

10/262 Woodsford (parish) SY 765898
Apt 21.02.1840; 1742a (all); Map 1842?, 8 chns; woods, plantations, arable (col), grassland (col), building names, weirs, heath, boundary between Higher and Lower Woodsford.

10/263 Woolland (parish) ST 777071
Apt 26.11.1839; 14a (1098); Map 1845, 6? chns, ? by G. Symonds; field gates; scale is written as 15 chns, but a later amendment suggests 6 chns.

10/264 North Wootton (parish) ST 654147
Apt 31.12.1842; 619a (619); Map 1843?, 3 chns; woods, plantations. District is apportioned by holding.

10/265 Worth Matravers (parish) SY 974776
Apt 28.09.1839; 2646a (2645); Map 1840, 5 chns, by John Baverstock Knight; foot/b'way, waterbodies, woods, withy beds, rock outcrops, field gates, coastline, cliffs; sailing ship is drawn in sea.

10/266 Wotton Fitzpaine (parish) SY 362957 [Wootton Fitzpaine]
Apt 08.02.1842; 1680a (1679); Map 1838, 3 chns, by John Martin, Evershot, Dorset; railway with tunnel, waterbodies, houses, woods (named), plantations, parkland, arable (col), grassland (col), marsh/bog (named), building names, road names, spring, mill; hills and bridge named.

10/267 Wraxall (parish) ST 568007
Apt 07.10.1839; 952a (all); Map 1840?, 6 chns, by J. Martin, Evershot; foot/b'way, woods, plantations, osiers, arable (col), grassland (col), orchards.

10/268 Wyke Regis (parish) SY 665780
Apt 01.05.1839; 1623a (all); Map 1841, 6 chns, in 4 parts, by John Taperell, (includes four 1.5-chn enlargements of detail); hill-drawing, houses, woods, plantations, parkland, orchards, rock outcrops, building names, limekiln, rectory gardens, churchyard, castle, rope walk, beach, coastline, cliffs; colours may show property ownerships.

10/269 Wynford Eagle (parish) SY 578959
Apt 19.04.1839; 1789a (all); Map 1839, 4 chns, by Summers and Slater, Ilminster, Somerset; waterbodies, plantations, line of trees.

10/270 Yetminster (tithing in parish of Yetminster) ST 594103
Apt 30.06.1840; 1460a (1460); Map 1840, 6 chns, by E. Watts, Yeovil; foot/b'way, waterbodies, houses, woods, plantations, arable (col), grassland (col), orchards, hedge ownership, building names, field names, limekilns; pictorial church.

Durham

PRO IR29 and IR30 11/1-293

313 tithe districts: 701,196 acres
293 tithe commutations: 562,423 acres
197 voluntary tithe agreements, 96 compulsory tithe awards

Tithe and tithe commutation

Until 1844 the administrative county of Durham included three outliers in other counties: Norhamshire, Islandshire, and Bedlingtonshire in Northumberland, and Craike in the North Riding of Yorkshire. Nearly 94 per cent of the tithe districts of this historic County Durham by number and about 80 per cent of the county by area were subject to payment of tithes in 1836 (Fig. 23). Only thirty-six districts remained wholly subject to tithe, and fully two-thirds of districts were partially covered by modus payments in lieu of tithes. Other significant reasons for tithe exemption in Durham were the merger of tithes in the land, exemption by prescription, and exemption of some agistment tithes.

The assistant tithe commissioners and local tithe agents who officiated at Durham tithe commutations are listed in Table 11.1 and the valuers of the county's tithe rent-charge in Table 11.2. A significant number of Durham tithe districts (forty-seven) are apportioned by holding and thus the schedules of tithe apportionment of these districts lack information on field names and land use. By contrast, three apportionments record the actual crops grown on the arable.

Tithe maps

Durham resembles Northumberland and much of the North Riding of Yorkshire in that there are no first-class maps and no maps with construction lines. Probably the prevalence of moduses and the paucity of wholly tithable districts discouraged the making of expensive new surveys. Copying of earlier work is specifically acknowledged on twenty-three maps and it may be suspected that there was relatively little wholly new tithe survey mapping in this county. Evidence for this conjecture includes the fact that thirty-two of the forty-seven maps of districts apportioned by holdings portray individual field boundaries, although such detailed mapping was not required when tithe was apportioned by holdings. Further evidence of copying is the map of Fenham which covers a much larger area than the apportionment and also includes tables of acreages not needed for tithe commutation purposes.

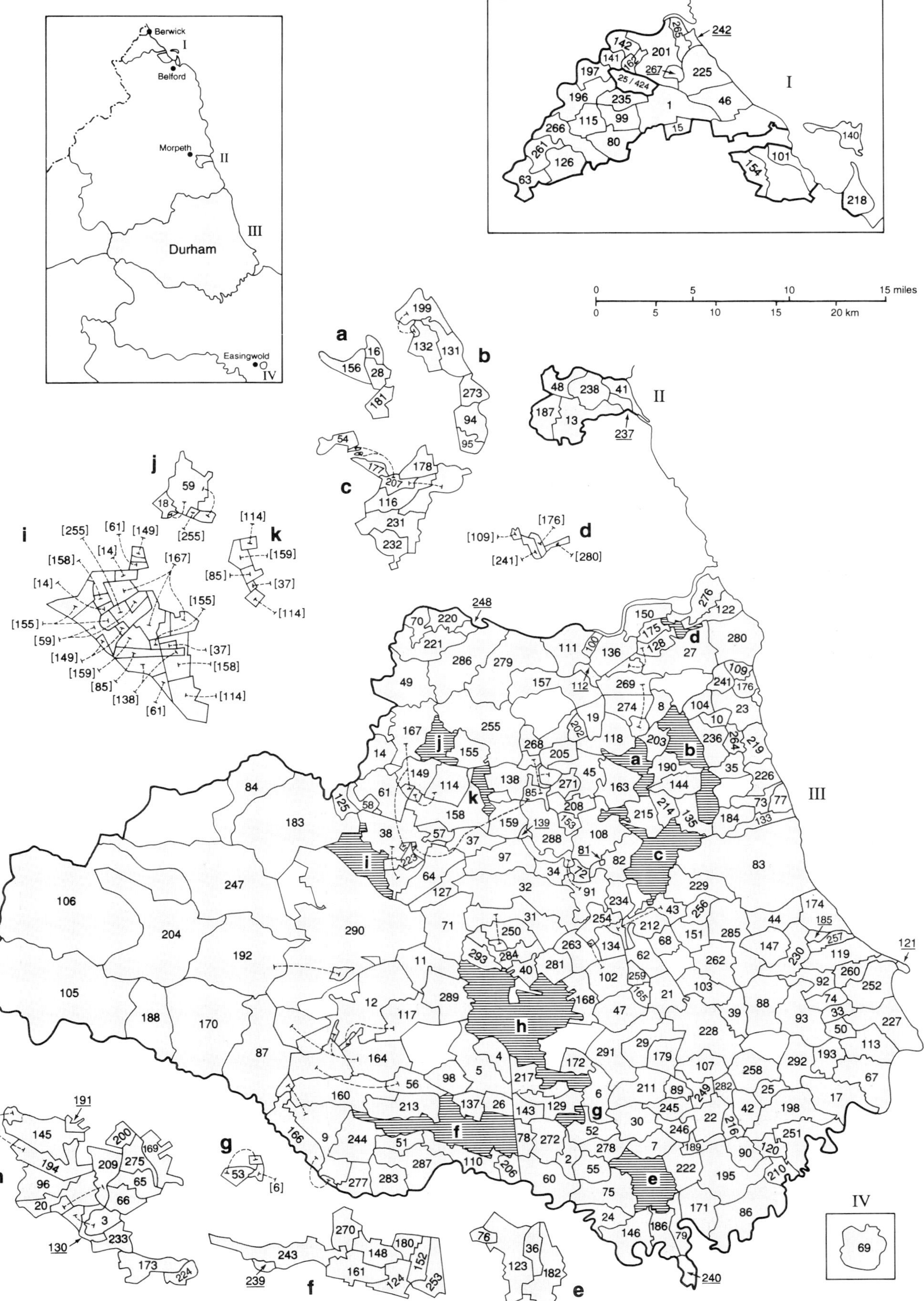

Fig. 23 Durham: tithe district boundaries.

The scales of Durham tithe maps range from one inch to two chains to one inch to twenty chains. A little more than half the county's maps are in the recommended scale range of one inch to three to four chains, though as in Northumberland there was a marked preference for the smaller scale. Some 29 per cent of maps are at the six-chain scale and 11.5 per cent at the eight-chain scale (Table 11.3).

The depiction of agricultural land use on Durham tithe maps is poor, though 84 per cent show woodland and 15 per cent depict parks, occasionally in considerable detail. Given the extensive tracts of uncultivated land in parts of the county, it is notable that this category of land is depicted on only 8 per cent of the maps. A significant minority of Durham maps (about 15 per cent) name landowners. In contrast, the physical features of the county are recorded more thoroughly than in most other counties: 34 per cent of Durham maps indicate some slopes, though only 5 per cent show rock outcrops. The industrial nature of Durham is better recognised than its agriculture, with 18 per cent of maps depicting some industry. This includes quarrying, coal mining, lead, iron and steel works, engineering, tanning, brick and tile-making, potteries, paper and bone mills and bleach, alkali, and salt works. Communications are often recorded in detail, including waggonways, railways, occupation roads, private roads and foot and bridle paths. Miscellaneous features include castles (seven maps), windmills (seven maps), standing and other notable stones and mounds (four maps) and enclosure or encroachment boundaries (four maps).

Only 153 Durham tithe maps in the Public Record Office collection can be attributed to a particular map-maker; the most prolific was Thomas Davison of Durham, who was also the most widely employed valuer of tithe rent-charge (Table 11.2). The Bell partnership of Newcastle contributed sixteen maps in a distinctive style with an emphasis on the detail of railways and industry. Frederick Laycock of Lanchester, who produced three maps, describes himself as a 'teacher'.

Quite a number of Durham's tithe maps are particularly crude in appearance, and only a few are noted in the catalogue as 'carefully drawn'. There is little ornamental decoration on Durham tithe maps apart from seven which have north pointers embellished with acorn and oak-leaf motifs.

Table 11.1. *Agreements and awards for commutation of tithes in Durham*

Assistant commissioner/ local tithe agent	*Number of agreements**	*Number of awards*
Henry Pilkington	101	0
John Job Rawlinson	7	85
Charles Howard	41	0
Richard Burton Phillipson	27	0
John Story Penleaze	13	0
Tithe Commissioners	0	7
John Strangeways Donaldson Selby	5	1
John Penny	4	0
George Louis	1	2
John B. Neal	3	0
Joseph Townsend	0	1

*Computed from the number of extant reports on tithe agreements in the tithe files [PRO IR 18].

Table 11.2. *Tithe valuers and tithe map-makers in Durham*

Name and address (in Durham unless indicated)	*Number of districts*	*Acreage*
Tithe valuers		
Thomas Davison, Durham	26	54,813
George Young Wall, Durham	21	24,564
Robert Rayson, Stockton upon Tees	12	16,374
Edward Grace, Wallsend, Northumberland	11	33,248
Andrew Stoddart, South Shields	11	20,159
William Lowrey, Barmoor	11	16,366
John Lee, Bishop Auckland	11	16,060
Matthew Ryle, Houghton-le-Spring	11	10,047
Robert Darling, Plawsworth	9	26,316
Thomas Peacock, Bishop Auckland	9	14,230
John Machell, Carlisle, Cumberland	8	32,556
William Lax, Darlington	8	9,445
James Rutherford, Bowes House	8	4,628
Richard William Matthews, Beamish Park	7	10,842
George Trotter, Tunstall	7	8,708
Others [61]	133	264,067
Attributed tithe map-makers		
Thomas Davison, Durham	18	36,738
Thomas Bell and Sons, Newcastle, Northumberland	16	39,075
John Turner junior, Durham	13	31,180
Otley and William Lax, Darlington	13	19,799
John Lee, Bishop Auckland	10	14,885
George Young Wall, Durham	9	16,727
John Machell, Carlisle, Cumberland	7	36,077
John Laverick, Durham	7	12,433
Andrew Stoddart, South Shields	7	11,534
Others [24]	43	88,761

Table 11.3. *The tithe maps of Durham: scales and classes*

Scale in chains/inch	*All maps*		*First Class*		*Second Class*	
	Number	*Acreage*	*Number*	*Acreage*	*Number*	*Acreage*
>3	4	1,112	0	0	4	1,112
3	21	31,066	0	0	21	31,066
4	133	220,178	0	0	133	220,178
5, 5.5	4	5,624	0	0	4	5,624
6	84	199,714	0	0	84	199,714
6.5, 6.67	2	2,219	0	0	2	2,219
8	34	89,063	0	0	34	89,063
<8	11	13,447	0	0	11	13,447
TOTAL	293	562,423	0	0	293	562,423

Table 11.4. *The tithe maps of Durham: dates*

	<1837	*1837*	*1838*	*1839*	*1840*	*1841*	*1842*	*1843*	*1844*	*1845*	*1846*	*1847*	*1848*	*1849*	*>1849*
2nd class*	1	6	42	72	32	18	16	19	18	14	12	24	6	3	9

*One second-class tithe map of Durham in the Public Record Office collection is undated.

Durham

11/1 Ancroft (township in parish of Ancroft) NT 992457
Apt 10.06.1844; 3642a (10210); Map 1845, 8 chns; waterbodies, woods, building names, mills; colours may show property ownerships. District is apportioned by holding and fields are not shown.

11/2 Archdeacon Newton (township in parish of Darlington) NZ 253177
Apt 30.04.1847; 1041a (1040); Map 1847, 5 chns, 'redrawn' by T. Dixon, Darlington; foot/b'way, turnpike roads, waterbodies, building names, tollbar; colours may show property ownerships.

11/3 St Andrew Auckland (township in parish of St Andrew Auckland) NZ 216276 [Not listed]
Apt 04.02.1843; 872a (1186); Map 1843, 3 chns, by John Lee, Bp Auckland, (tithable parts only); woods, building names, mill.

11/4 St Helens Auckland (township in parish of St Andrew Auckland) NZ 198262 [St Helen Auckland]
Apt 21.07.1840; 1481a (1480); Map 1840, 4 chns, by T. Dixon, Darlington; railways, foot/b'way, waterbodies, woods, sand or stone pits; colours may show property ownerships.

11/5 West Auckland (township in parish of St Andrew Auckland) NZ 177256
Apt 18.05.1843; 1731a (3720); Map 1849?, 8 chns, in 2 parts, (tithable parts only; including town of West Auckland at 2 chns); railways, school.

11/6 Great Aycliffe (township in parish of Aycliffe) NZ 276233 [Aycliffe]
Apt 25.09.1838; 2135a (2134); Map 1838, 4 chns, by George Young Wall, Durham, litho (Standidge); hill-drawing, railways, woods, building names, field acreages.

11/7 Barmpton (township in parish of Haughton-le-Skerne) NZ 320186
Apt 02.02.1843; 1521a (1520); Map 1843, 6 chns; hill-drawing, foot/b'way, waterbodies, woods, building names.

11/8 Barmston (township in parish of Washington) NZ 330563
Apt 21.10.1840; 893a (all); Map 1840?, 4 chns; railway, waterbodies, woods, road names, landowners, boreholes; colours may show property ownerships.

11/9 Barnard Castle (township in parish of Gainford) NZ 054189
Apt 24.08.1840; 4008a (4007); Map 1839, 4 chns, in 2 parts by Machell; hill-drawing, foot/b'way, woods, rock outcrops, field gates, road names, weirs, stone pits, market place, market cross, township boundaries; built-up part generalised.

11/10 High and Low Barnes (district in parish of Bishop Wearmouth) NZ 373555 [Not listed]
Apt 13.03.1844; 726a (?); Map 1845?, 2.5 chns, railways, waterbodies, landowners, township boundaries. Apt omits some field names.

11/11 North Bedburn (township in parish of St Andrew Auckland) NZ 135350 [Not listed]
Apt 08.03.1844; 2036a (2036); Map 1845, 3 chns, by John Lee, Bp Auckland, (tithable parts only); hill-drawing, railway, woods, building names; lettering and numbers are stamped.

11/12 South Bedburn (township in parish of Auckland St Andrew) NZ 090312 [Bedburn]
Apt 20.06.1844; 740a (6765); Map 1847, 4 chns, in 2 parts by John Lee, Bp Auckland, (tithable parts only; including 48-chn location diagram); hill-drawing, woods, building names, landowners.

11/13 Bedlington (township) NZ 259821
Apt 10.12.1838; 2468a (9011); Map 1839, 6 chns, by John Laverick, Durham; hill-drawing, foot/b'way, waterbodies, woods, staiths, waggon ways.

11/14 Benfieldside (township in parish of Lanchester) NZ 099524
Apt 25.05.1843; 1834a (1834); Map 1845, 4 chns, in 6 parts, (including 1:84,480 location diagram); turnpike roads, waterbodies, woods, building names, road names, weir, paper mills, toll bar, school; colours may indicate quarries and waste.

11/15 Berrington Law (hamlet in parish of Kyloe Parochial Chapelry) NT 989438 [Berringtonlaw]
Apt 05.02.1840; 661a (?); Map 1840, [4 chns]; houses, rock outcrops, landowners, limestone quarry, limekiln; map is subtitled 'belonging to Prideaux John Selby Esqr'. Apt omits land use.

11/16 South Biddick otherwise Biddick Waterville (township in parish of Houghton le Spring) NZ 314529 [Not listed]
Apt 21.09.1841; 343a (343); Map 1847?, 10 chns; railway, waterbodies, woods, building names.

11/17 Billingham (township) NZ 468228
Apt 16.05.1838; 2771a (3139); Map 1838, 6 chns; railway, foot/b'way, turnpike roads, toll bar, woods, building names, mill, port, coal staiths, coal depot, old river channel, field acreages.

11/18 Billingside (township in parish of Lanchester) NZ 136527 [Not listed]
Apt 29.01.1844; 288a (288); Map 1844, 4 chns, by I. Turner junr; woods, building names; boundary may indicate modus land.

11/19 Birtley (township in parish of Chester-le-Street) NZ 275558
Apt 31.10.1846; 1393a (1392); Map 1846?, 4 chns; hill-drawing, foot/b'way, turnpike roads, toll bar, waterbodies, woods (col), building names, landowners, iron factory, salt works, ownership boundaries (col). Apt omits some field names.

11/20 Bishop Auckland otherwise Bondgate in Auckland (township in parish of St Andrew Auckland) NZ 198293
Apt 20.03.1844; 1175a (1919); Map 1839, 3 chns, by Wm Thompson, Bishop Auckland; railways, woods, building names, weir, township boundaries, mill; bridge named; gardens shown by annotation; built-up part generalised.

11/21 Bishop Middleham (township) NZ 331318
Apt 18.12.1839; 2023a (2023); Map 1839, 6 chns, by Thomas Davison, Durham; hill-drawing, foot/b'way, turnpike roads, toll bar, waterbodies, woods, building names, drains. Apt omits some field names.

11/22 Bishopton (township in parish of Bishopton) NZ 367211
Apt 16.07.1839; 2102a (2102); Map 1840, 6 chns, 'made from estate plans upon various scales' by A. and R. Reed, Stockton upon Tees; foot/b'way, waterbodies, woods, plantations, building names, mill, mill race, vicarage.

11/23 Bishop Wearmouth (except Barnes) (township in parish of Bishop Wearmouth) NZ 393569 [Not listed]
Apt 12.05.1843; 1751a (?); Map 1846?, 4 chns, by Andrew Stoddart, South Shields; hill-drawing, railway, woods, building names, quarry; built-up part generalised; colours may show property ownerships.

11/24 Blackwell (township in parish of Darlington) NZ 283125
Apt 30.04.1847; 1500a (1499); Map 1847, 4 chns; railway, waterbodies, woods, parkland; colours may show property ownerships.

11/25 Blakiston (lordship in parish of Norton) NZ 415234 [Not listed]
Apt 28.06.1844; 774a (all); Map 1846, 3 chns; waterbodies, building names, mill.

11/26 Bolam (township in parish of Gainford) NZ 194223
Apt 29.01.1841; 989a (989); Map 1839, 4 chns, ? by Thos Peacock; hill-drawing, foot/b'way, turnpike roads, toll bar, woods, well.

11/27 Boldon (parish) NZ 346613
Apt 20.09.1838; 3956a (?); Map 1839?, 8 chns; hill-drawing, railway, foot/b'way, turnpike roads, toll bar, milestones, waterbodies, woods, building names, landowners (col), tyle sheds, rectory, mills, tanyard, glebe; hill named. Apt omits land use.

11/28 Bourn Moor (township in parish of Houghton le Spring) NZ 315516 [Bournmoor]
Apt 21.09.1841; 54a (500); Map 1847?, 4 chns; woods, building names.

11/29 Bradbury (township in parish of Sedgefield) NZ 318278
Apt 31.01.1838; 2043a (2043); Map 1838, 6 chns, by Thos Davison, Durham; railway, railway depot, foot/b'way, waterbodies, woods, heath/moor, building names, field acreages.

11/30 Brafferton (township in parish of Aycliffe) NZ 308207
Apt 21.07.1840; 2312a (2409); Map 1841, 6 chns, compiled from various estate plans 'upon various scales and degrees of accuracy' by A. and R. Reed, Stockton upon Tees; foot/b'way, woods, plantations, building names, mill.

11/31 Brancepeth (township in parish of Brancepeth) NZ 214390
Apt 07.07.1838; 4516a (4515); Map 1839, 6 chns, by W.J. Ware; hill-drawing, foot/b'way, waterbodies, woods, plantations, parkland, ford.

11/32 Brandon and Byshottles (township in parish of Brancepeth) NZ 217412
Apt 23.06.1838; 6726a (6726); Map 1839, 6 chns, by J. Turner junr; hill-drawing, waterbodies, woods, plantations, building names, quarry, mills.

11/33 Brearton (township in parish of Stranton) NZ 472300 [Brierton]
Apt 31.05.1842; 748a (all); Map 1842, 3 chns, by George Peirson, Guisbrough.

11/34 Broom (township in parish of Durham, St Oswalds) NZ 239425 [Not listed]
Apt 25.09.1838; 1030a (1029); Map 1838, [6.67 chns]; waterbodies, woods, plantations, building names.

11/35 Burdon (township in parish of Bishop Wearmouth) NZ 388513
Apt 27.11.1839; 1110a (1109); Map 1840?, 4 chns; hill-drawing, railway, waterbodies, woods, building names, sand or stone pits.

11/36 Burdon (township in parish of Haughton le Skerne) NZ 322161 [Not listed]
Apt 21.07.1838; 589a (588); Map 1838, 4 chns, by George Young Wall, Durham, litho (Standidge); railway, field acreages.

11/37 Burnhope and Hamsteels (township in parish of Lanchester) NZ 178451
Apt 14.10.1839; 1703a (2027); Map 1840, 4 chns, by I. Turner junr; woods, building names, sand or stone pit.

11/38 East Butsfield, West Butsfield and Steely (district in parish of Lanchester) NZ 109454
Apt 31.10.1840; 1422a (1422); Map 1840, 4 chns, by I. Turner junr; waterbodies, woods, plantations, heath/moor, building names.

11/39 Butterwick and Old Acres (township in parish of Sedgefield) NZ 389299
Apt 07.07.1838; 1496a (1495); Map 1838, 6 chns, by Thomas Davison, Durham; foot/b'way, waterbodies, woods, building names, road names, field acreages.

11/40 Byers Green (township) NZ 219338
Apt 30.12.1843; 997a (997); Map 1847?, 4 chns, in 2 parts, (including one part at 5 chns); railway, turnpike roads, toll bar, waterbodies, woods, colliery, bog.

11/41 Camboise (township in parish of Bedlington) NZ 306837 [Cambois]
Apt 19.09.1845; 960a (?); Map 1846, 8 chns; hill-drawing, landowners, high and low water marks at spring tides. District is apportioned by holding and fields are not shown.

11/42 Carlton (township in parish of Redmarshall) NZ 398218
Apt 12.09.1839; 1453a (all); Map 1840?, 4 chns; railway, woods.

11/43 Cassop (township in parish of Kelloe) NZ 332394
Apt 28.08.1840; 1622a (1622); Map 1840, 6 chns, by G.Y. Wall; hill-drawing, railway, foot/b'way, waterbodies, woods, heath/moor, building names, quarry, mill. Apt omits some field names.

11/44 Castle Eden (parish) NZ 422381
Apt 30.06.1840; 1936a (all); Map 1845?, 4 chns, ? by I.T.W. Bell; railway, foot/b'way, turnpike roads, toll bar, waterbodies, woods, building names, castle.

11/45 Chester le Street (township in parish of Chester le Street) NZ 272509 [Chester-le-Street]
Apt 31.10.1846; 2666a (2666); Map 1846?, 4 chns; hill-drawing, railways, foot/b'way, woods.

11/46 Cheswick (township in parish of Ancroft) NU 029462
Apt 03.08.1841; 1876a (?); Map 1841, 8 chns; woods (col), landowners; colours may show property ownerships.

11/47 Chilton (township in parish of Merrington) NZ 295301
Apt 23.11.1838; 2340a (2339); Map 1838, 6 chns, by Thomas Davison, Durham; railway, foot/b'way, waterbodies, woods, building names; double wavy lines may be hedges or drains.

11/48 Choppington (township in parish of Bedlington) NZ 247847
Apt 30.12.1842; 41a (?); Map 1845?, 4 chns; ownership boundaries (col). Apt omits land use.

11/49 Chopwell (township in parish of Winlaton) NZ 125589
Apt 13.03.1844; 744a (3150); Map 1852, 12 chns, 'compiled from various plans' by Thomas Bell and Sons; building names, landowners (col), tithe-free land. District is apportioned by holding and fields are not shown.

11/50 Claxton (township in parish of Greatham) NZ 476285 [Not listed]
Apt 06.09.1843; 866a (all); Map 1841, 3 chns, by A. and R. Reed, Stockton upon Tees; foot/b'way, waterbodies, houses, woods, plantations, field gates, building names, grange. Apt has cropping information.

11/51 Cleatlam (township in parishes of Gainford, Staindrop and Winston) NZ 116191
Apt 16.12.1841; 1097a (1097); Map 1842?, 6 chns, by Machell, Carlisle; foot/b'way, turnpike roads, toll bar, waterbodies, woods, building names, quarries.

11/52 Coatham Mundeville (township in parish of Haughton le Skerne) NZ 273200
Apt 31.07.1838; 1518a (1517); Map 1838, 6 chns; railway, waterbodies, woods, building names, field acreages.

11/53 Coats-a-Moor (township in parish of Heighington) NZ 251209 [Coatsay Moor]
Apt 26.11.1844; 434a (all); Map 1845, 4 chns; waterbodies, woods, building names; colours may show property ownerships.

11/54 Cocken (township in parish of Houghton-le-Spring) NZ 289476 [Not listed]
Apt 21.09.1841; 437a (437); Map 1846?, 6 chns, (tinted); hill-drawing, woods, building names, ford. District is apportioned by holding and fields are not shown.

11/55 Cockerton (except 239 acres) (township in parish of Darlington) NZ 271167 [Not listed]
Apt 31.03.1847; 1509a (1509); Map 1847, 6 chns, by William Lax, Darlington; foot/b'way, waterbodies, woods.

11/56 Cockfield (parish) NZ 127242
Apt 07.06.1838; 4416a (4416); Map 1837, 4 chns, in 2 parts by Machell, Carlisle; hill-drawing, railway, foot/b'way, occupation roads, woods, landowners, public quarry, quarry, tithe-free land, township boundary; physical features named.

11/57 Coldpighill (district in parish of Lanchester) NZ 149459 [Colepike Hall]
Apt 21.01.1839; 764a (all); Map 1838, 4 chns, by John Turner junr; woods, heath/moor, building names, field acreages.

11/58 Cold Rowley (township in parish of Muggleswick) NZ 082485 [Not listed]
Apt 21.10.1840; 518a (?); Map 1841, 6 chns, by I. Coulson; railway, building names, landowners, mill; colours may show property ownerships. District is apportioned by holding and fields are not shown.

11/59 Collierley and Pontop (township in parish of Lanchester) NZ 150539
Apt 28.09.1843; 1056a (?); Map 1844, 4 chns, 'copied from various

surveys and plans' by Frederick James Laycock, Lanchester; railways, foot/b'way, waterbodies, woods, field gates, building names, road names, landowners, common quarry, pit heap, encroachments; colours may show property ownerships; bird-shaped scroll decorates north pointer. Apt omits land use.

11/60 Coniscliffe (parish) NZ 233160 [Not listed]
Apt 19.02.1841; 3008a (3008); Map 1841, 6 chns, by J. Humphries, Ripon; waterbodies, woods, limekilns, ford; colours may show property ownerships.

11/61 Conside with Knitsley (township in parish of Lanchester) NZ 107491
Apt 22.02.1843; 386a (2617); Map 1848, 4 chns; railway, foot/b'way, woods, plantations, heath/moor, building names. Apt has cropping information.

11/62 Cornforth (township in parish of Bishop Middleham) NZ 313352
Apt 26.06.1839; 1689a (1689); Map 1839, 6 chns, by Thomas Davison, Durham, (drawn by J.Raine); hill-drawing, railway, foot/b'way, waterbodies, woods, building names, mills, mill dam, tilery, tile sheds, limekilns, pottery.

11/63 Cornhill (township in parish of Cornhill) NT 863395 [Cornhill-on-Tweed]
Apt 24.05.1843; 1163a (4746); Map 1843?, 5.5 chns; waterbodies, woods (col), gardens, building names, landowners, glebe; pictorial church; colours may show holdings. District is apportioned by holding and fields are not shown.

11/64 Cornsay (township in parish of Lanchester) NZ 141422
Apt 14.10.1839; 3404a (3404); Map 1840, 6 chns, by J. Turner junr; woods, plantations, open fields, building names, landowners, almshouses, mill, common, boundary of lands belonging to Sir Thomas Cavering, Bart; fell named.

11/65 Coundon (township in parish of St Andrew Auckland) NZ 240298
Apt 14.11.1843; 585a (584); Map 1844, 3 chns, by John Lee, Bishop Auckland; hill-drawing, foot/b'way, turnpike roads, toll bar, open fields, field gates, building names, quarry, well, school.

11/66 Coundon Grange (township in parish of St Andrew Auckland) NZ 230287
Apt 11.01.1840; 615a (615); Map 1839, 4 chns; hill-drawing, railway, foot/b'way, woods, building names, quarry, pits.

11/67 Cowpen Bewley (township in parish of Billingham) NZ 499244
Apt 07.07.1838; 1639a (4594); Map 1838, 6 chns, litho (Standidge); foot/b'way, embankment, defaced hedges, field acreages, marsh (named), spring tide mark, old river course, muddy ground, sand.

11/68 Coxhoe (township in parish of Kelloe) NZ 331362
Apt 01.02.1842; 1056a (1055); Map 1842?, 4 chns; hill-drawing, railway, waterbodies, woods, parkland, building names, pit, limekilns, colliery.

11/69 Craike (parish) SE 564710 [Crayke]
Apt 27.03.1839; 2780a (all); Map 1840, 6 chns, by Henry Scott, Oulston; hill-drawing, foot/b'way, waterbodies, woods, field boundary ownerships, castle, pinfold.

11/70 Crawcrook (township in parish of Ryton) NZ 133639
Apt 05.03.1840; 1136a (1158); Map 1841?, 6 chns, by Thomas Bell; railway and station, foot/b'way, turnpike roads, toll bar, waterbodies, woods, parkland, hedges, field gates, building names, landowners, mill, dam, pinfold, quarry, old quarry, ford, old waggon ways, gravel bed; colours may show property ownerships. District is apportioned by holding; Apt omits land use.

11/71 Crook and Billy Row (township in parish of Brancepeth) NZ 156375
Apt 11.07.1838; 4008a (4008); Map 1839, 6 chns, by J. Roddam, Stanhope; foot/b'way, waterbodies, woods, building names, corn mill.

11/72 Crossgate (township in parish of Durham, St Oswalds) NZ 263421 [Not listed]
Apt 30.07.1838; 386a (454); Map 1838, 4 chns, by John Turner, Junr; hill-drawing, waterbodies, woods, gardens, heath/moor, building names, quarry, churchyard, tithe-free land, waste ground.

11/73 Dalton-le-Dale (township in parish of Dalton-le-Dale) NZ 414482
Apt 23.02.1843; 797a (797); Map 1843, 4 chns; hill-drawing, railway, foot/b'way, waterbodies, woods, building names, quarries or pits, vicarage.

11/74 Dalton Piercy (township in parish of Hart) NZ 465310
Apt 14.10.1839; 988a (987); Map 1839?, 4 chns, by George Trotter, Tunstall; woods, field boundary ownerships.

11/75 Darlington (township in parish of Darlington) NZ 283145
Apt 18.03.1847; 2869a (3569); Map 1847, 4 chns, by Wm Greenwell Lax, Darlington; foot/b'way, waterbodies, woods, parkland, road names, chapels; glebe not mapped; built-up part generalised.

11/76 Darlington and Cockerton (township in parish of Houghton le Skerne) NZ 293170
Apt 22.11.1838; 412a (?); Map 1839, 6 chns; turnpike roads, toll bar, woods, building names, road names, field acreages.

11/77 Dawdon (township in parish of Dalton le Dale) NZ 428483
Apt 27.06.1850; 1081a (all); Map 1850, 4 chns, ? by John Gibson; railway, waterbodies, woods, rock outcrops, building names, road names, Wesleyan Chapel, coastline, cliffs, harbour, entrance basin, parapet wall, wet dock, coal depots, engine, wagon way for ballast transport, ropery, pottery, stables; coast features named. Apt omits some field names.

11/78 Denton (township in parish of Gainford) NZ 216194 [Not listed]
Apt 21.01.1839; 966a (966); Map 1839?, 4 chns; foot/b'way, waterbodies, woods, road names, quarry.

11/79 Dinsdale (parish) NZ 337116 [Not listed]
Apt 17.12.1839; 1150a (1150); Map 1840, 4 chns, by Otley and Lax, Darlington; hill-drawing, railway, railway depots, foot/b'way, waterbodies, woods, building names, rectory, fish locks, hotel, baths. Apt omits some field names.

11/80 Duddo (township in parish of Norham) NT 936426
Apt 02.01.1844; 1651a (1651); Map 1844, 8 chns; hill-drawing, waterbodies; colours may show property ownerships. District is apportioned by holding and fields are not shown.

11/81 Durham, Magdalen Close or the Chapelry of St Mary Magdalene (parish or extra-parochial district) NZ 282429 [Not listed]
Apt 23.12.1851; 27a (all); Map 1852?, 4 chns, foot/b'way.

11/82 Durham, St Giles (parish) NZ 296434 [Not listed]
Apt 01.08.1844; 1661a (1661); Map 1845?, 4 chns; hill-drawing, railways, waterbodies, woods, extra parochial land; colours may show property ownerships. Apt omits some field names.

11/83 Easington (parish) NZ 404431
Apt 23.11.1838; 13244a (all); Map 1839?, 6 chns, in 5 parts, (including 12-chn index); hill-drawing, railway, turnpike roads, waterbodies, woods (col), building names, landowners, beach, coal pits, mills, mill dam. District is apportioned by holding.

11/84 Edmondbyers (parish) NY 989489 [Not listed]
Apt 13.11.1840; 2169a (4880); Map 1841, 8 chns, 'drawn from original plans and recent surveys' by Henry Roodham; building names, boundary stones, standing stone, currocks, commons, encroachments. Apt omits some field names.

11/85 Edmondsley (township in parish of Chester le Street) NZ 229492
Apt 31.10.1846; 1964a (1964); Map 1847?, 4 chns, in 2 parts; hill-drawing, railway, foot/b'way, woods, building names. Apt omits some field names.

11/86 Egglescliffe (parish) NZ 395127
Apt 02.02.1838; 4821a (4821); Map 1841?, 4 chns; railways and railway depots, waterbodies, woods, plantations, building names, ornamental ground; built-up part generalised. Apt omits some field names.

11/87 Egleston (township in parish of Middleton in Teesdale) NZ 003272 [Eggleston]
Apt 09.11.1849; 7919a (7919); Map 1850?, 4 chns, in 2 parts; hill-drawing, waterbodies, woods, building names, currocks, common, ornamental ground; physical features named; acorn and leaves decorate north pointer.

11/88 Elmeden otherwise Emelden otherwise Embleton (township in parish of Sedgefield) NZ 414309
Apt 07.07.1838; 3357a (3356); Map 1837, 4 chns, by Robert Robson and Matthew Ryle junr; woods, building names, field acreages, glebe, holding boundaries (col); legend explains estate boundary colours.

11/89 Elstob (township in parish of Great Stainton) NZ 341237
Apt 24.08.1838; 734a (all); Map 1837, 4 chns, by Edmd Bowman; railway, foot/b'way, waterbodies, woods, plantations, orchards, field gates, field names, field acreages, holding boundaries (col) and names. Table lists farms and acreages.

11/90 Elton (parish) NZ 395180
Apt 07.07.1838; 1419a (all); Map 1839?, 4 chns; waterbodies, woods, parkland (in detail), orchards.

11/91 Elvet (township in parish of Durham, St Oswald) NZ 272406 [Elvet Hill]
Apt 12.07.1838; 1374a (3800); Map 1838?, [8 chns], in 2 parts; foot/b'way, waterbodies, woods, plantations, parkland, old river course.

11/92 Elwick (township in parish of Hart) NZ 455332
Apt 20.03.1845; 1501a (1500); Map 1839, 4 chns, by George Trotter, Tunstall; foot/b'way, woods, field gates, field acreages.

11/93 Elwick Hall (parish) NZ 443297 [Not listed]
Apt 24.12.1839; 4322a (4321); Map 1839, 6 chns, by Thos Davison, Durham, (? drawn by J. Raine); hill-drawing, foot/b'way, waterbodies, woods, building names, occupation and carriage roads; hill named.

11/94 Great Eppleton (township in parish of Houghton-le-Spring) NZ 369484
Apt 21.06.1838; 696a (695); Map 1838, 4 chns, by Robert Robson and Matthew Ryle junr; hill-drawing, railway, woods, building names, field acreages, pit; colours may show property ownerships.

11/95 Little Eppleton (township in parish of Houghton-le-Spring) NZ 366471 [Not listed]
Apt 24.08.1839; 335a (335); Map 1839?, 4 chns; foot/b'way, field gates.

11/96 Escomb (township in parish of St Andrew Auckland) NZ 184299
Apt 26.08.1845; 295a (840); Map 1848, 3 chns, by John Lee, (tithable parts only); railway. Apt omits some field names.

11/97 Eshe, otherwise Ashe (township in parish of Lanchester) NZ 196434 [Esh]
Apt 12.09.1839; 3016a (3016); Map 1839, 4 chns; woods.

11/98 Evenwood (township in parish of St Andrew Auckland) NZ 156246
Apt 26.09.1843; 5336a (?); Map 1844, 4 chns, by John Lee, Bp Auckland; railway, woods, building names, mill, ford.

11/99 Felkington (township in parish of Norham) NT 942445
Apt 27.07.1844; 1431a (1431); Map 1843, 5 chns; hill-drawing, turnpike roads, toll-bar, woods (col), building names, limekiln, limestone quarry, collieries; colours may show property ownerships. District is apportioned by holding and fields are not shown.

11/100 Felling (township or district in parish of Jarrow) NZ 275621
Apt 06.05.1844; 362a (?); Map 1850?, 8 chns; railways, turnpike roads, toll gate, waterbodies, woods, building names, tube pit, colliery; built-up part generalised.

11/101 Fenham (township in parish of Holy Island) NU 084407
Apt 31.12.1842; 40a (?); Map 1827, 12 chns; hill-drawing, foot/b'way, waterbodies, orchards, marsh/bog, field gates, building names, road names, landowners, quarries, coastline, ford, wells, mill, mill race, field acreages, limekiln, stile; colours may show property ownerships; orchards, bog, marshy land and salt grass indicated by annotation; map includes schedule of field names and acreages and farm acreages, and covers a much larger district than is included in Apt, which omits land use.

11/102 Ferry Hill (township in parish of Merrington) NZ 286331 [Ferryhill]
Apt 21.11.1838; 2495a (2495); Map 1838, 6 chns, by John Laverick, Durham; hill-drawing, railways, foot/b'way, waterbodies, woods, building names, quarries, limekilns, well, field acreages; bridge named.

11/103 Fishburn (township in parish of Sedgefield) NZ 365321
Apt 07.02.1838; 2082a (all); Map 1839?, 4 chns; hill-drawing, waterbodies, woods, plantations, quarries, field acreages.

11/104 Ford (township in parish of Bishop Wearmouth) NZ 362570 [Not listed]
Apt 13.03.1844; 192a (1000); Map 1844, 4 chns, by Mattw Bowser, Thornaby Grange; hill-drawing, foot/b'way, building names, landowners; map is titled a map of lands 'belonging to George John Scurfield Esq and now occupied by Mr Ralph Lawson'.

11/105 Forest and Frith (township in parish of Middleton in Teesdale) NY 839324 [Not listed]
Apt 21.08.1846; 17270a (17270); Map 1840, 8 chns, by Machell, Carlisle; hill-drawing, waterbodies, rock outcrops, building names, sod and rock currocks, dams, shafts, quarry, river cut, waterfall, boundary cairns; physical features named. District is apportioned by holding.

11/106 Forest Quarter (district in parish of Stanhope) NY 846394 [Not listed]
Apt 04.11.1841; 13062a (20000); Map 1842, 4 chns, by A. and R. Reed, 'made partly from new surveys by us, and partly from existing estate plans by sundry persons upon various scales and degrees of accuracy'; foot/b'way, woods, plantations, building names, smelt mill, common.

11/107 Foxton cum Shotton (township in parish of Sedgefield) NZ 362255
Apt 31.01.1838; 1787a (1787); Map 1838, 6 chns, 'copied from plans dated 1769 and 1801; Corrected and Reduced in 1838', by W.J. Ware, Skirpenbeck near York; hill-drawing, railway, foot/b'way, waterbodies, woods, plantations, road names.

11/108 Framwellgate (township in parish of Durham, St Oswald) NZ 281456 [Framwellgate Moor]
Apt 13.07.1838; 3279a (3467); Map 1838, 4 chns, by John Turner junr; hill-drawing, waterbodies, woods, parkland, gardens, heath/moor, building names, road names, quarry, common quarries, gas works, mills, field acreages, ornamental ground; one estate named.

11/109 Fulwell (township in parish of Monkwearmouth) NZ 395598
Apt 13.03.1844; 741a (all); Map 1845?, 4 chns, by Andrew Stoddart; beach.

11/110 Gainford (township) NZ 165179
Apt 08.07.1841; 2275a (2274); Map 1840, 3 chns, by Otley and Lax, Darlington; waterbodies, woods, plantations, parkland, building names, mills. Apt omits some field names.

11/111 Gateshead (parish) NZ 256618
Apt 12.06.1838; 2296a (?); Map 1838, 4 chns, by Andrew Stoddart, South Shields; hill-drawing, railways, foot/b'way, turnpike roads, milestones, waterbodies, woods, field gates, field acreages, building names, road names, sand or stone pits or quarries, dam, forge dam, quays, coal staiths; colours may show property ownerships.

11/112 Gateshead Fell (parish) NZ 271603 [Not listed]
Apt 09.06.1840; 577a (?); Map 1844, 4 chns, by John Bell, Gateshead; hill-drawing, railways, turnpike roads, toll gate, milestone, waterbodies, building names, road names, pottery, quarries (extensive), colliery, engine, bound stones, mill, reservoir, windmill, mill, pits, school, burial ground, rectory, chapel, Methodist meeting house; built-up part generalised.

11/113 Greatham (township in parish of Greatham) NZ 500274
Apt 22.04.1839; 1817a (?); Map 1840, 6 chns, by A. and R. Reed, Stockton upon Tees; waterbodies, building names, tidal areas; coast features and bridges named.

11/114 Greencroft (township in parish of Lanchester) NZ 157500
Apt 14.06.1840; 3051a (3050); Map 1842, 8 chns, in 6 parts, 'reduced from various surveys and plans' by Thomas Bell and Sons, Newcastle; foot/b'way, private roads, turnpike roads, woods, parkland, field gates, building names, road names, landowners, mill, quarry, leasehold ground, common, encroachments; colours may show property ownerships. District is apportioned by holding; Apt omits land use.

11/115 Grindon (township in parish of Norham) NT 916445
Apt 22.05.1843; 1475a (1475); Map 1843?, 10 chns; colours may show property ownerships. District is apportioned by holding and no buildings or fields are shown.

11/116 Hall Garth (district in parish of Pittington) NZ 328439 [Hallgarth]
Apt 08.03.1844; 700a (?); Map 1844?, 4 chns; hill-drawing, railway, foot/b'way, waterbodies, woods, building names, colliery, mill, quarry, vicarage.

11/117 Hamsterley (township in parish of St Andrew Auckland) NZ 118301
Apt 14.03.1843; 3581a (4003); Map 1848, 6 chns, by Wm Greenwell Lax, Darlington, (including 20-chn location diagram); hill-drawing, railway, canal, farmyards, field gates. Apt omits some field names.

11/118 Harraton (township in parish of Chester le Street) NZ 295540 [Not listed]
Apt 31.10.1846; 2300a (2394); Map 1846?, 4 chns; railway, woods (col), plantations (col), parkland, building names, pits.

11/119 Hart (township in parish of Hart) NZ 471349
Apt 24.04.1839; 2366a (2589); Map 1840?, 8 chns; railway, foot/b'way, turnpike roads, woods, field gates, building names, field names, beach, churchyard, glebe, farm names; colours may show property ownerships or holdings. District is apportioned by holding; Apt omits land use.

11/120 East Hartburn (township in parish of Stockton) NZ 419184 [Not listed]
Apt 19.04.1839; 1021a (1020); Map 1839, 4 chns, by George Trotter, Tunstall; field acreages.

11/121 Hartlepool (township in parish of Hart) NZ 527340
Apt 28.06.1844; 136a (990); Map 1840, 2 chns, by J.T.W. Bell; hill-drawing, waterbodies, docks; colours may show holdings; built-up part generalised.

11/122 Harton (township in parish of Jarrow) NZ 371648
Apt 23.11.1838; 1393a (1537); Map 1839, 8 chns, by Andrew Stoddart, South Shields; foot/b'way, waterbodies, woods, field gates, road names, field acreages.

11/123 Haughton-le-Skerne (township in parish of Haughton-le-Skerne) NZ 310155 [Haughton Le Skerne]
Apt 23.09.1838; 1899a (1898); Map 1838, 6 chns; railway, turnpike roads, toll bars, waterbodies, woods, parkland, orchards, building names, field acreages.

11/124 Headlam (township in parish of Gainford) NZ 183190
Apt 29.01.1841; 780a (780); Map 1839, 3 chns, by Otley and Lax, Darlington; foot/b'way, waterbodies, woods, limekilns, stone pit or quarry, fox cover.

11/125 Healey Field (township in parish of Lanchester) NZ 069484 [Healeyfield]
Apt 13.05.1843; 977a (1221); Map 1843?, 4 chns; hill-drawing, railway, foot/b'way, waterbodies, woods, building names. Apt omits some field names.

11/126 Heaton (township in parish of Cornhill) NT 895408 [Not listed]
Apt 18.06.1843; 1895a (?); Map 1843?, 8 chns; woods, holding boundaries (col) and names. District is apportioned by holding and fields are not shown.

11/127 Hedley Hope (township in parish of Lanchester) NZ 152407 [Not listed]
Apt 18.06.1840; 104a (1506); Map 1840?, 4 chns; landowners.

11/128 Hedworth (township in parish of Jarrow) NZ 314614
Apt 04.07.1848; 1572a (?); Map 1850?, 6 chns; railway with station, waterbodies, woods, building names.

11/129 Heighington (township) NZ 239223
Apt 13.10.1838; 1743a (1743); Map 1838, 6 chns, in 2 parts; waterbodies, woods, building names, landowners, sand or stone pit, field acreages.

11/130 Henknowle and Coppycrooks (district in parish of St Andrew Auckland) NZ 208274 [Not listed]
Apt 21.08.1839; 313a (?); Map 1839?, 3 chns; woods, building names, estate boundaries (col).

11/131 East and Middle Herrington (township in parish of Houghton le Spring) NZ 358531
Apt 25.07.1846; 1003a (all); Map 1847, 4 chns; hill-drawing, railway, waterbodies, woods, building names. Apt omits some field names.

11/132 West Herrington (township in parish of Houghton-le-Spring) NZ 342531
Apt 08.07.1842; 970a (969); Map 1847, 4 chns; railway, woods (named), building names, mill, engine; colours may show property ownerships.

11/133 Heseldon (township in parish of Dalton le Dale) NZ 411467 [Cold Hesledon]
Apt 27.07.1844; 994a (?); Map 1844?, 4 chns, (tinted); railway, plantations (col), field boundary ownerships, landowners, field acreages. Apt omits some field names.

11/134 Hett (township in parish of Merrington) NZ 287361
Apt 26.11.1838; 1257a (1256); Map 1838, 6 chns, by John Laverick, Durham; hill-drawing, foot/b'way, waterbodies, woods, building names, road names, paper mills, field acreages.

11/135 Hetton-le-Hole (township in parish of Houghton-le-Spring) NZ 352470 [Hetton-Le-Hole]
Apt 20.07.1838; 1598a (?); Map 1839, 4 chns, by John Laverick, Durham; hill-drawing, railway and tunnel, foot/b'way, waterbodies, woods, field acreages, building names, quarry, mill, colliery, limekiln, stables, engine, office.

11/136 Heworth (except Felling) (chapelry in parish of Jarrow) NZ 291616
Apt 01.05.1844; 2425a (2853); Map 1850?, 8 chns; railways, waterbodies, building names, quay, reservoir, pit.

11/137 Hilton (township in parish of Staindrop) NZ 173223
Apt 17.12.1838; 1093a (1092); Map 1839, 3 chns, by Otley and Lax, Darlington; waterbodies, woods, building names. Apt omits some field names.

11/138 Holmside (district in parish of Lanchester) NZ 212507
Apt 02.02.1843; 2604a (2860); Map 1843, 6 chns, by I. Turner junr; railway, waterbodies, woods, heath/moor, building names, road names, pit, engine, colliery, common quarries, common, tithe-merged land.

11/139 Holmside (township in parish of Lanchester) NZ 219459
Apt 05.05.1843; 257a (?); Map 1847?, 6 chns; woods, plantations, building names.

11/140 Holy Island (township in parish of Holy Island) NU 126433
Apt 02.02.1843; 5a (8296); Map 1850?, 2 chns; hill-drawing, gardens, field gates, building names, road names, field names, landowners, old fort, chapel, market place, market cross, well, old cathedral, churchyard, shop, herring houses; hill named; tithable lands tinted.

11/141 Horncliffe (township in parish of Norham) NT 936498
Apt 21.11.1840; 606a (606); Map 1844?, 8 chns; woods (col), parkland, building names, mill; colours may show property ownerships. District is apportioned by holding and fields are not shown.

11/142 Horncliffe Loanend (township in parish of Norham) NT 944511 [Loanend]
Apt 18.08.1841; 833a (833); Map 1844?, 8 chns; woods, building names; colours may show property ownerships; bridge named. District is apportioned by holding and fields are not shown.

11/143 Houghton-le-Side (township in parish of Gainford) NZ 219217
Apt 28.10.1840; 1061a (1060); Map 1840, 4 chns, by Otley and Lax, Darlington; foot/b'way, occupation roads, turnpike roads, toll bar, waterbodies, woods, plantations, building names, fox cover.

11/144 Houghton le Spring (township in parish of Houghton le Spring) NZ 342499 [Houghton-le-Spring]
Apt 12.11.1841; 1475a (1475); Map 1838, 4 chns; railway, foot/b'way, waterbodies, woods, heath/moor, landowners, colliers' houses, pits, rectory, windmill (by symbol), field acreages; built-up part generalised.

11/145 Hunwick and Helmington (township in parish of St Andrew Auckland) NZ 185331
Apt 04.02.1843; 468a (1560); Map 1843, 3 chns, by John Lee; woods, building names, mill, mill race, furnace.

11/146 Hurworth (township in parish of Hurworth) NZ 302109 [Hurworth-on-Tees]
Apt 29.09.1838; 2355a (2355); Map 1839, 3 chns, by Otley and Lax, Darlington; hill-drawing, railway and railway depot, foot/b'way, waterbodies, woods, parkland, gardens, building names, grange, fox cover. Apt omits some field names.

11/147 Hutton Henry (township in parish of Monk Heselden) NZ 417359
Apt 08.12.1837; 1947a (all); Map 1838, [6 chns]; woods, building names, field acreages. Apt omits some field names.

11/148 Ingleton (township in parish of Staindrop) NZ 171205
Apt 12.02.1838; 814a (all); Map 1838?, 4 chns; foot/b'way, waterbodies, field gates, well.

11/149 Iveston (township in parish of Lanchester) NZ 131509
Apt 09.05.1840; 1926a (1925); Map 1842?, 6 chns, in 9 parts, 'copied from various surveys and plans' by Thomas Bell; railway and depot, foot/b'way, waterbodies, woods, field gates, building names, road names, landowners, chapel, pits, engine, quarry, encroachments, colliery housing; colours may show property ownerships; one part shows copyhold and freehold land. District is apportioned by holding; Apt omits land use.

11/150 Jarrow and Hebburn (townships or hamlets in parish of Jarrow) NZ 312648
Apt 23.10.1847; 897a (?); Map 1850?, 8 chns; woods, building names, pit.

11/151 Kelloe (township in parish of Kelloe) NZ 355368
Apt 25.09.1839; 1370a (1592); Map 1842, 4 chns; waterbodies, woods (col), building names, landowners.

11/152 Killerby (township in parish of Heighington) NZ 197200
Apt 27.02.1838; 605a (605); Map 1839?, 4 chns; foot/b'way, woods, road names, rights of way.

11/153 Kimblesworth (parish) NZ 255467
Apt 22.11.1844; 571a (all); Map 1847?, 12 chns; woods. Apt omits land use.

11/154 Kyloe (township in parish of Kyloe) NU 052399 [Not listed]
Apt 12.07.1843; 1478a (all); Map 1848, 4 chns; hill-drawing, waterbodies, woods (col), building names, parsonage, farm boundaries (col), old turnpike road. District is apportioned by holding and fields are not shown.

11/155 Kyo (except Tanfield Moor) (township in parish of Lanchester) NZ 174528 [Not listed]
Apt 18.05.1843; 480a (1230); Map 1845, 4 chns, (tinted); railway, old railway, foot/b'way, woods, building names, landowners, pits, quaking house; colours may show property ownerships.

11/156 Lambton (township in parish of Chester le Street) NZ 298521 [Not listed]
Apt 15.05.1846; 21a (652); Map 1847?, 4 chns; woods.

11/157 Lamesley (chapelry in parish of Chester le Street) NZ 245590
Apt 15.05.1846; 7016a (7016); Map 1847?, 8 chns, in 2 parts by Thomas Bell and Sons, Newcastle, (including enlargment of Eighton Banks village at 2 chns); railway, foot/b'way, turnpike roads, toll bars, occupation roads, waterbodies, woods, parkland, field gates, building names, road names, landowners, boundary stones, grange, pit, mill, dam, park lodges, National School, Methodist Chapel; colours may show property ownerships. District is apportioned by holding; Apt omits land use.

11/158 Lanchester, otherwise Lanchester Proper (township, hamlet or district in parish of Lanchester) NZ 157474
Apt 04.02.1843; 4266a (4266); Map 1843, 6 chns, 'reduced from various surveys and plans' by Frederick James Laycock, Teacher, Lanchester; turnpike roads, turnpike gates, waterbodies, woods, parkland, field gates, building names, landowners, deanery, toll bar, common quarries, windmill. Apt omits land use.

11/159 Langley (township in parish of Lanchester) NZ 205471
Apt 18.05.1843; 2378a (all); Map 1846?, 12 chns, in 2 parts; woods, building names, road names, mill. District is apportioned by holding and fields are not shown.

11/160 Langleydale and Shotton (township in parish of Staindrop) NZ 067237 [Not listed]
Apt 19.06.1840; 4686a (4685); Map 1841?, 8 chns; hill-drawing, woods, rock outcrops, building names, road names, mill, old park wall; rock named; acorn and leaves decorate north pointer. District is apportioned by holding and fields are not shown.

11/161 Langton (township in parish of Gainford) NZ 160195
Apt 07.11.1838; 1062a (1061); Map 1839, 4 chns, by Otley and Lax, Darlington; foot/b'way, woods, parkland, building names, grange, keepers house, coach roads. Apt omits some field names.

11/162 Longridge (township in parish of Norham) NT 954498 [West Longridge]
Apt 28.05.1841; 559a (558); Map 1843?, 6 chns; turnpike roads, road names; colours may show property ownerships. District is apportioned by holding and fields are not shown.

11/163 Great and Little Lumley (township in parish of Chester-le-Street) NZ 297500
Apt 19.06.1840; 2411a (2410); Map 1840, 4 chns, by Thomas Davison, Durham; hill-drawing, railway, waterbodies, building names, ford, forge, mill, castle.

11/164 Lynesack and Softley (township in parish of St Andrew Auckland) NZ 097264
Apt 30.06.1843; 838a (5946); Map 1847, 6 chns, by John Lee, Bp Auckland; building names, mill, lead yard, tithe-merged land. Apt omits some field names.

11/165 Mainsforth (township in parish of Bishop Middleham) NZ 313316
Apt 19.07.1844; 628a (627); Map 1843, 6 chns, by I. Turner junr; railway, waterbodies, woods, plantations, parkland, heath/moor, building names; double lines may indicate hedges.

11/166 Marwood (township in parish of Gainford) NZ 033195 [Not listed]
Apt 11.07.1842; 3671a (3671); Map 1842?, 4 chns; hill-drawing, foot/b'way, waterbodies, woods, weirs, wells, quarry; built-up part generalised; acorn and oak leaves decorate compass.

11/167 Medomsley (except Tanfield Moor) (township in parish of Medomsley) NZ 124546
Apt 29.10.1847; 4824a (4823); Map 1842, 6 chns, in 2 parts by I. Turner junr; railway, waterbodies, woods, plantations, parkland, building names, lime depot, engine, pits, quarry, forge, abbey.

11/168 Merrington (township in parish of Merrington) NZ 267314 [Kirk Merrington]
Apt 24.07.1840; 1934a (1934); Map 1839, 6 chns, by John Laverick, Durham; hill-drawing, railway, foot/b'way, waterbodies, woods, building names, mill, quarries, defaced hedges; colours may show property ownerships.

11/169 Middlestone (township in parish of St Andrew Auckland) NZ 250310
Apt 04.02.1843; 879a (all); Map 1843?, 4 chns; hill-drawing, railway, foot/b'way, waterbodies, woods, colliery.

11/170 Middleton in Teesdale (township in parish of Middleton in Teesdale) NY 958291
Apt 07.05.1842; 10434a (10434); Map 1840, 4 chns, in 2 parts; hill-drawing, foot/b'way, waterbodies, woods, boundary stones, sheep fold, currocks.

11/171 Middleton St George (parish) NZ 358132
Apt 07.02.1838; 2050a (2050); Map 1838?, 6 chns; railway, foot/b'way, woods, gardens, building names, farm boundary names and hedges, glebe.

11/172 Midridge (township in parish of St Andrew Auckland) NZ 261258 [Middridge]
Apt 08.03.1844; 1119a (1118); Map 1844?, 4 chns; hill-drawing, railway, waterbodies, building names, quarry. Apt omits some field names.

11/173 Middridge Grange (township in parishes of St Andrew Auckland and Heighington) NZ 244245
Apt 20.11.1843; 928a (923); Map 1844, 4 chns, by J. Marley, Shildon; railway, foot/b'way, waterbodies, building names, landowners, mill race, corn mill, old quarry, engine building shops, old pit, gate house.

11/174 Monk Heselden (township in parish of Monk Heselden) NZ 462382 [Monk Hesleden]
Apt 08.12.1837; 2453a (2937); Map 1838, [6 chns]; hill-drawing, railway, woods, building names, field acreages. Apt omits some field names.

11/175 Monkton (township in parish of Jarrow) NZ 324634
Apt 28.11.1838; 766a (?); Map 1839, 6 chns, by Thomas Davison, Durham; hill-drawing, railway, woods, well.

11/176 Monkwearmouth (township in parish of Monkwearmouth) NZ 401584
Apt 22.02.1840; 548a (616); Map 1839, 4 chns, by Thomas Davison, Durham; hill-drawing, railways, foot/b'way, waterbodies, woods, building names, grange, road names, colliery, shipbuilding yards, banks and quay, battery, quay, cliffs, mill, boundary posts.

11/177 Moorhouse (township in parish of Houghton le Spring) NZ 310459 [Not listed]
Apt 21.09.1841; 273a (272); Map 1846?, 4 chns; railways, woods, building names. Apt omits land use and some field names.

11/178 Moorsley (township in parish of Houghton-le-Spring) NZ 343461 [High and Low Moorsley]
Apt 21.06.1838; 588a (588); Map 1838?, 4 chns; hill-drawing, railway, foot/b'way, occupation and public roads, waterbodies, woods, quarries, limekilns, colliery, springs, field acreages, defaced hedge.

11/179 Morden (township in parish of Sedgefield) NZ 331265 [Mordon]
Apt 02.02.1838; 1538a (1537); Map 1837, 4 chns, made for tithe commutation by Thomas Davison, Durham; hill-drawing, railway, foot/b'way, occupation roads, waterbodies, woods, heath/moor, hedge ownership, building names, well, field acreages.

11/180 Morton (township in parish of Gainford) NZ 188210 [Morton Tinmouth]
Apt 20.02.1841; 399a (399); Map 1841?, 4 chns, by William Lax, Darlington; foot/b'way, woods, township boundaries (col).

11/181 Morton Grange (township in parish of Houghton le Spring) NZ 316499 [Morton Grange Farm]
Apt 21.09.1841; 34a (505); Map 1847?, 4 chns; railway, woods, plantations, building names, grange.

11/182 Morton Palmes (township in parish of Houghton le Skerne) NZ 333149 [Not listed]
Apt 13.10.1838; 750a (1316); Map 1838?, 4 chns; railway, waterbodies, woods, arable, grassland, landowners, field acreages, farm names, tithe-free land; colours may show holdings.

11/183 Muggleswick (township in parish of Muggleswick) NZ 029466
Apt 13.03.1844; 32a (7098); Map 1845, 4 chns, by I. Coulson; building names, landowners, chapel; colours may show property ownerships.

11/184 Murton (township in parish of Dalton-le-Dale) NZ 388469
Apt 15.02.1843; 1466a (1466); Map 1843, 4 chns; hill-drawing, railway, foot/b'way, waterbodies, woods, building names, colliery.

11/185 Nesbit, otherwise Nesbit Hall (township in parish of Hart) NZ 456367 [Nesbitt Hall]
Apt 17.09.1839; 327a (326); Map 1839, [?20 chns]; woods. Apt has cropping information.

11/186 Nesham (township in parish of Hurworth) NZ 328111 [Neasham]
Apt 09.07.1838; 1576a (1575); Map 1839?, 4 chns; waterbodies, woods, plantations.

11/187 Netherton (township in parish of Bedlington) NZ 236820 [Not listed]
Apt 10.12.1838; 1469a (?); Map 1838, 12 chns, 'taken from the original plan ... by White of York with corrections &c by E. Bowman'; railway, foot/b'way, turnpike roads, toll bar, milestones, woods, building names; bridge named. Apt omits land use.

11/188 Newbiggin (township in parish of Middleton in Teesdale) NY 912299
Apt 07.05.1842; 4628a (4627); Map 1840, 3 chns, in 2 parts by Machell; hill-drawing, foot/b'way, waterbodies, woods, rock outcrops, building names, shops, sheep fold, trig points, currocks, dams, sod cabin, slate quarry; physical features named.

11/189 Newbiggin (township in parish of Bishopton) NZ 362186 [East and West Newbiggin]
Apt 26.04.1839; 831a (846); Map 1840, 6 chns, 'from Estate Plans upon various scales' by A. and R. Reed, Stockton upon Tees; foot/b'way, woods, plantations, building names, cart roads.

11/190 Newbottle (township in parish of Houghton-le-Spring) NZ 335514
Apt 21.06.1838; 1389a (1388); Map 1838, 4 chns, by Robert Robson and Matthew Ryle junr; railway, waterbodies, woods, marsh/bog, rock outcrops, building names, quarries, tile sheds, mill, pits or limekilns, field acreages; built-up part generalised; colours may show property ownerships. Apt omits some field names.

11/191 Newfield (township in parish of St Andrew Auckland) NZ 205335
Apt 05.02.1840; 200a (199); Map 1840, 4 chns, by G.Y. Wall, Durham; foot/b'way, woods. Apt omits some field names.

11/192 Newslandside Quarter (district in parish of Stanhope) NY 986354 [Not listed]
Apt 04.11.1841; 3816a (?); Map 1842, 4 chns; foot/b'way, turnpike roads, woods, plantations, building names, mills, lodge, lime kilns, smelt mill.

11/193 Newton Bewley (township in parish of Billingham) NZ 465261
Apt 07.07.1838; 1552a (1562); Map 1838, 6 chns, by George Young Wall, Durham, litho (Standidge); hill-drawing, foot/b'way, waterbodies, woods, building names, gravel holes, mill, grange, field acreages, defaced hedges.

11/194 Newton Cap (township in parish of St Andrew Auckland) NZ 189311 [Not listed]
Apt 25.09.1846; 939a (939); Map 1847?, 3 chns, by John Lee, Bp Auckland; hill-drawing, waterbodies, woods, building names. Apt omits most field names.

11/195 Long Newton (parish) NZ 382157 [Longnewton]
Apt 03.07.1837; 4544a (4544); Map 1837, 6 chns, made for tithe commutation by Thomas Davison, Durham; hill-drawing, railway, woods, arable, grassland, gardens, heath/moor, hedge ownership, building names, quarries; red lines may indicate stone walls.

11/196 Norham (township in parish of Norham) NT 907466
Apt 18.08.1841; 2343a (2717); Map 1842, 8 chns, in 2 parts; waterbodies, woods (col), gardens, landowners, churchyard, well, farm names and boundaries; colours may show property ownerships. District is apportioned by holding.

11/197 Norham Mains (township in parish of Norham) NT 917487 [Norham West Mains]
Apt 05.02.1840; 1051a (1051); Map 1841?, 11 chns; hill-drawing, waterbodies, woods, building names, landowners, castle, fishery boundaries in river; colours may show property ownerships. District is apportioned by holding; Apt omits land use.

11/198 Norton (except Blakiston) (parish) NZ 431218 [Not listed]
Apt 01.02.1842; 3841a (4614); Map 1842, 4 chns; woods, drains.

11/199 Offerton (township in parish of Houghton le Spring) NZ 344556
Apt 05.07.1842; 810a (809); Map 1847, 8 chns, 'copied from Sundry Surveys' by Thomas Bell and Sons; woods, building names, landowners; colours may show property ownerships. Apt omits some field names.

11/200 Old Park (township) NZ 233326 [Not listed]
Apt 13.03.1844; 394a (401); Map 1845, [4 chns]; railway, woods, parkland, building names.

11/201 Ord (except Unthank) (township in parish of Tweedmouth) NT 977501 [Not listed]
Apt 17.01.1844; 1913a (2568); Map 1847?, 8 chns; woods (col); colours may show property ownerships. District is apportioned by holding.

11/202 Ouston (township in parish of Chester le Street) NZ 262548
Apt 15.05.1846; 636a (636); Map 1847, 8 chns; railway, foot/b'way, woods, building names, landowners, quarry, collieries, stack yard, pit. District is apportioned by holding; Apt omits land use.

11/203 Painshaw (township in parish of Houghton-le-Spring) NZ 326536 [Penshaw]
Apt 12.07.1842; 1066a (1066); Map 1848, 4 chns; hill-drawing, railway, foot/b'way, waterbodies, woods, rock outcrops, building names, quarries, foundry, pit, stables, engine, staiths, windmill.

11/204 Park Quarter (district in parish of Stanhope) NY 930379 [Not listed]
Apt 04.11.1841; 9718a (12190); Map 1842, 4 chns, by A. and R. Reed, 'made partly from new surveys by us, and partly from existing estate plans by sundry persons upon various scales and degrees of accuracy'; foot/b'way, turnpike roads, toll bar, woods, plantations, building names, common.

11/205 Pelton (township in parish of Chester-le-Street) NZ 247527
Apt 31.10.1846; 1101a (1109); Map 1846?, 4 chns; railway, foot/b'way, woods, building names, landowners, grange. Apt omits some field names.

11/206 Piersbridge (township in parish of Gainford) NZ 203168 [Piercebridge]
Apt 07.11.1838; 920a (920); Map 1839, 6 chns, by Otley and Lax, Darlington; woods (named), heath/moor (named), building names, grange, mill.

11/207 Pittington (except Hall Garth) (township in parish of Pittington) NZ 324448
Apt 15.12.1840; 1853a (2552); Map 1841?, 6 chns, by I. Raine; hill-drawing, railways, foot/b'way, waterbodies, woods, parkland, building names, collieries; built-up part generalised. Apt omits some field names.

11/208 Plawsworth (township in parish of Chester le Street) NZ 259481
Apt 16.11.1846; 782a (1224); Map 1848, 4 chns; turnpike roads, toll bar, waterbodies, woods, building names, mill; colours may show property ownerships. District is apportioned by holding.

11/209 Pollards Lands (township in parish of St Andrew Auckland) NZ 212305 [Not listed]
Apt 04.02.1843; 132a (458); Map 1844?, 4 chns; railway, foot/b'way, woods, building names, road names, landowners, mill, market place, school.

11/210 Preston (township in parish of Stockton) NZ 426162 [Preston-on-Tees]
Apt 11.10.1838; 1077a (1108); Map 1839?, 4 chns; foot/b'way, waterbodies, woods (col), parkland, arable (col), grassland (col), landowners, quarry, tile sheds. Apt omits some field names.

11/211 Preston-le-Skerne (township in parish of Aycliffe) NZ 313235
Apt 12.07.1838; 2610a (2610); Map 1839?, 4 chns; railway, woods (col), building names, landowners, bleach mill, factory, waste, field acreages, drains; bridge named; some buildings drawn in elevation.

11/212 Quarrington (township in parish of Kelloe) NZ 318378 [Not listed]
Apt 28.08.1839; 1589a (1589); Map 1839, 6 chns, by 'J.R.'; hill-drawing, railway, foot/b'way, woods, building names Apt omits some field names.

11/213 Raby and Keverstone (township in parish of Staindrop) NZ 118221 [Not listed]
Apt 30.11.1838; 2753a (2752); Map 1839?, 4 chns, hill-drawing, foot/b'way, coach and occupation roads, waterbodies, woods, parkland (in detail), heath/moor, rock outcrops, building names, dog kennel, brick dams, quarries, castle, bath, haysheds, barns, lodges, summerhouse, stables, folly, spring; acorn and oak leaves decorate north pointer.

11/214 East Rainton (township in parish of Houghton-le-Spring) NZ 334480
Apt 31.01.1839; 1065a (1065); Map 1839, 4 chns, by John Laverick, Durham; hill-drawing, railways, foot/b'way, waterbodies, building names, collieries, quarry, defaced hedges, field acreages.

11/215 West Rainton (township in parish of Houghton-le-Spring) NZ 317471
Apt 26.02.1839; 1616a (1788); Map 1838, 4 chns, by John Laverick, Durham; hill-drawing, railways, foot/b'way, waterbodies, woods, building names, engines, stables, pits, chimney, well, old pit, field acreages, defaced hedges.

11/216 Redmarshall (township in parish of Redmarshall) NZ 385207
Apt 12.09.1839; 859a (all); Map 1840?, 6 chns; waterbodies, woods.

11/217 Redworth (township in parish of Heighington) NZ 224239
Apt 10.12.1838; 1840a (1840); Map 1839?, 4 chns; railway, foot/b'way, turnpike roads, tollbar, woods (col), parkland, heath/moor, building names, field acreages.

11/218 Ross (township in parish of Belford) NU 135375
Apt 20.10.1842; 1500a (3598); Map 1843, 8 chns; hill-drawing. District is apportioned by holding and fields are not shown.

11/219 Ryhope (township in parish of Bishop Wearmouth)NZ 408532
Apt 18.06.1840; 1569a (1876); Map 1843?, 6 chns, by Andrew Stoddart; hill-drawing, railways, waterbodies, woods, foreshore.

11/220 Ryton (township in parish of Ryton) NZ 156644
Apt 05.03.1840; 1203a (1302); Map 1841?, 4 chns, by Thos Bell; hill-drawing, railway and station, foot/b'way, turnpike roads, waterbodies, woods, parkland, heath/moor, field gates, building names, road names, landowners, manufactory, old pits, river shoals, reservoirs, rectory, school, quarry, milestone, village cross, embankments, glebe, waste; a few fields named; colours may show property ownerships; types of road indicated. District is apportioned by holding.

11/221 Ryton Woodside (township in parish of Ryton) NZ 148623
Apt 05.03.1840; 2802a (2802); Map 1843?, 6 chns, by Thomas Bell and Sons; railway, foot/b'way, turnpike roads, waterbodies, woods, field gates, building names, road names, landowners, firebrick factory, mills, pit, engine, mill dam; colours may show property ownerships. District is apportioned by holding; Apt omits land use.

11/222 Sadberge (township in parish of Haughton le Skerne) NZ 346170
Apt 15.02.1839; 2050a (2050); Map 1839?, 6 chns; woods, building names, grange.

11/223 Satley (hamlet in parish of Lanchester) NZ 119432
Apt 21.12.1846; 901a (all); Map 1847?, 4 chns, in 2 parts, by Frederick James Laycock, Lanchester, Durham, (one part at 8 chns); foot/b'way,

turnpike roads, waterbodies, woods, building names, road names, landowners; colours may show property ownerships. Apt omits land use.

11/224 School Aycliffe (township in parish of Heighington) NZ 262240
Apt 20.09.1838; 525a (524); Map 1838?, 4 chns; railway, woods (col), building names, field acreages. North pointer is coloured and decorated with oak leaves.

11/225 Scremerston (township in parish of Holy Island) NU 010485
Apt 15.02.1839; 2859a (?); Map 1839?, [12 chns], by Nich. Weatherly, 1824, (engraved by J. Walker); hill-drawing, foot/b'way, waterbodies, woods, rock outcrops, field names, landowners, limekiln, colliery, kilns, sea links, quarries, working pit, engine banks, wells, field acreages, farm names, fishery boundaries, common, common quarry; coast features named; map is described as of land belonging to the Commissioners and Governors of Greenwich Hospital; there are two scale bars, one saying 'Scale 2 chains', the other indicating 16 chns; comparision with Ordnance Survey 1:63,360 indicates 12 chns to be correct. District is apportioned by holding.

11/226 Seaham (parish) NZ 414504
Apt 03.08.1841; 2871a (3079); Map 1839, 4 chns, by J. Turner junr; railways, waterbodies, woods, plantations, parkland, building names, mill, engines, grange, foreshore.

11/227 Seaton Carew (township in parish of Stranton) NZ 517294
Apt 12.09.1839; 1877a (4885); Map 1840?, 4 chns; woods, plantations; built-up part generalised. Apt omits some field names.

11/228 Sedgefield (township in parish of Sedgefield) NZ 365287
Apt 31.01.1838; 5171a (5171); Map 1838, 6 chns, in 2 parts by Thomas Davison, Durham, (including 2-chn enlargement of Sedgefield town), litho (Standidge); foot/b'way, occupation roads, turnpike roads, toll bar, waterbodies, woods, parkland, building names, road names, rectory, pump, dog kennels, temple, garden house, mill, field acreages.

11/229 Shadforth (township in parish of Pittington) NZ 364411
Apt 14.07.1838; 2872a (2872); Map 1838, 6 chns; railway, woods, quarry, field acreages.

11/230 Sheraton and Hulam (townships in parish of Monk Heselden) NZ 439348
Apt 11.04.1839; 2257a (2256); Map 1839, 6 chns, by Thomas Davison, Durham, (? drawn by I. Raine); hill-drawing, foot/b'way, woods, building names, granges, public roads, township boundaries. Apt omits some field names.

11/231 Sherburn (township in parish of Pittington) NZ 322423
Apt 03.06.1838; 1303a (1303); Map 1838?, 6 chns, by Geo. Y. Wall, Durham; railways, woods, quarry, field acreages, waste.

11/232 Sherburn House (district) NZ 319409 [Not listed]
Apt 03.07.1848; 731a (730); Map 1849?, 4 chns; railways, foot/b'way, waterbodies, woods, parkland, building names, colliery, mill, chapel.

11/233 Shildon (township in parish of St Andrew Auckland) NZ 225263
Apt 02.12.1840; 321a (552); Map 1839, 4 chns; railways with tunnel, foot/b'way, road names, boundary stones, pits; colours may show property ownerships.

11/234 Shincliffe (township in parish of Durham, St Oswald) NZ 296399
Apt 29.06.1839; 1303a (1303); Map 1839?, 6 chns; hill-drawing, waterbodies, woods, ornamental ground.

11/235 Shoreswood (township in parish of Norham) NT 944463
Apt 04.12.1841; 1201a (all); Map 1839, 4 chns, by Nichs Weatherly, Newcastle upon Tyne; foot/b'way, waterbodies, woods, building names, colliery; colours may show property ownerships. District is apportioned by holding.

11/236 Silksworth (township in parish of Bishop Wearmouth) NZ 375541
Apt 03.11.1838; 1989a (1988); Map 1841?, 5 chns, by Andrew Stoddart, South Shields; railway, foot/b'way, waterbodies, woods, parkland, building names, sand or stone pit.

11/237 East Sleekburn (township in parish of Bedlington) NZ 296835
Apt 10.12.1838; 850a (?); Map 1839?, 4 chns; hill-drawing, foot/b'way, private and public carriage roads, waterbodies, woods, building names, fords, grange, muddy ground dry at low water, field acreages.

11/238 West Sleekburn (township in parish of Bedlington) NZ 271845
Apt 10.12.1838; 1604a (?); Map 1839, 6 chns, surveyed by Thomas Davison; foot/b'way, waterbodies, woods, building names, pit; Davison is described as author in map title, but in bottom right hand corner is 'surveyed April 1839. Jno. Laverick. Copied by RaR' (or RaK).

11/239 Snotterton (township in parish of Staindrop) NZ 108199 [Not listed]
Apt 30.11.1838; 217a (all); Map not dated, 4 chns; hill-drawing, foot/b'way, woods, building names, quarries; acorn and oak leaves decorate north pointer.

11/240 Sockburn (township) NZ 350077
Apt 22.02.1840; 517a (all); Map 1840, 4 chns; site of old churchyard, glebe. District is apportioned by holding; Apt omits some field names.

11/241 Southwick (township in parish of Monkwearmouth) NZ 381591
Apt 29.01.1840; 1018a (1018); Map 1839, 4 chns; hill-drawing, railway, foot/b'way, waterbodies, woods, building names, patent slip.

11/242 Spittle (township in parish of Tweedmouth) NU 004513 [Spittal]
Apt 12.07.1843; 245a (244); Map 1844?, 2 chns; common quarry, sands; colours may show property ownerships. District is apportioned by holding.

11/243 Staindrop (township in parish of Staindrop) NZ 115206
Apt 30.11.1838; 1751a (1751); Map 1838, 4 chns, by Machell; hill-drawing, foot/b'way, waterbodies, woods, heath/moor, rock outcrops, building names, quarries, lodges, township boundaries; acorn and oak leaves decorate north pointer.

11/244 Stainton and Streatlam (township in parish of Gainford) NZ 080195
Apt 08.07.1841; 2907a (2907); Map 1840, 3 chns, in 2 parts by Machell, Carlisle; hill-drawing, foot/b'way, waterbodies, woods, parkland (in detail), rock outcrops, building names, gamekeepers house, hinds house, old mill, farm house, quarries, stewards house, pumps, lodges, castle, old mill, stone post, troughs, wells, limekiln; acorn and oak leaves decorate north pointer. Apt omits some field names.

11/245 Stainton-le-Street (township in parish of Great Stainton) NZ 335220 [Great Stainton]
Apt 18.01.1839; 1215a (1214); Map 1839, 6 chns, by William Simpson, Pinchingthorpe near Guisbrough; woods, churchyard, glebe, fox cover.

11/246 Little Stainton (township in parish of Bishopton) NZ 343200
Apt 26.04.1839; 1083a (1083); Map 1839, 6 chns, by William Simpson, Pinchingthorpe near Guisbrough; woods.

11/247 Stanhope Quarter (district in parish of Stanhope) NY 962426 [Not listed]
Apt 04.11.1841; 3749a (13000); Map 1842, 4 chns, by A. and R. Reed, 'made partly from the new surveys by us, and partly from existing estate plans by sundry persons upon various scales and degrees of accuracy'; railway, foot/b'way, waterbodies, woods, plantations, parkland, heath/moor, building names, chapels, rectory, castle, lime kilns, smelt mill, waste land; chapels, church, rectory and castle are named using ornate lettering.

11/248 Stella (township in parish of Ryton) NZ 172636
Apt 23.11.1838; 141a (319); Map 1839, 4 chns, by Thomas Bell; railway, turnpike roads, waterbodies, woods, road names, landowners, reservoir, park, farm, glebe; colours may show property ownerships.

11/249 Stillington (township in parish of Redmarshall) NZ 361234
Apt 22.11.1839; 1104a (1104); Map 1841?, 6 chns, by I. Raine; railway, foot/b'way, woods, building names.

11/250 Stockley (township in parish of Brancepeth) NZ 205372
Apt 07.07.1838; 1333a (?); Map 1839, 6 chns, by W.J. Ware; hill-drawing, foot/b'way, waterbodies, woods, plantations, ford.

11/251 Stockton (township in parish of Stockton on Tees) NZ 443196 [Stockton-on-Tees]
Apt 26.12.1843; 2810a (3032); Map 1844, 6 chns, in 2 parts by A. and R. Reed, Stockton upon Tees; railway, foot/b'way, waterbodies, woods, plantations, parkland, field gates, building names, granges, churchyard, tile sheds, mill; built-up part not mapped; bridges named; colours may indicate tithing practice. Apt omits some field names.

11/252 Stranton (township in parish of Stranton) NZ 504325 [Not listed]
Apt 27.03.1839; 2775a (3695); Map 1839, 6 chns, by George Young Wall, Durham; foot/b'way, waterbodies, building names. Apt omits some field names.

11/253 Summerhouse (township in parish of Gainford) NZ 205193
Apt 21.01.1839; 809a (809); Map 1839?, 4 chns; foot/b'way, turnpike roads, toll bar, waterbodies, road names.

11/254 Sunderland Bridge (township in parish of Croxdale) NZ 275379
Apt 04.12.1839; 1377a (1376); Map 1842?, 6 chns; turnpike roads, toll bar, waterbodies, woods, parkland, building names, mills.

11/255 Tanfield (and part of Tanfield Moor) (township in parish of Chester-le-Street) NZ 186553
Apt 26.07.1844; 7072a (7072); Map 1847?, 8 chns, in 8 parts by Thomas Bell and Sons, Newcastle, (including five 5-chn enlargements of detail); railways, foot/b'way, public and occupation roads, turnpike roads, waterbodies, woods, field gates, building names, road names, landowners, ford, waterfall, paper mill, school, quarries, pit, railway cottages, colliery stables, colliery, engine, mills, boundary of recent enclosure; colours may show property ownerships. District is apportioned by holding; Apt omits land use.

11/256 Thornley (township in parish of Kelloe) NZ 361391
Apt 08.03.1844; 1108a (1107); Map 1845?, 4 chns; hill-drawing, railway, woods, pit.

11/257 Thorpe Bulmer (township in parish of Hart) NZ 469364 [Not listed]
Apt 16.11.1837; 827a (?); Map 1838?, 4 chns; railway, waterbodies, woods.

11/258 Thorpe, otherwise Thorpe Thewles (township in parish of Grindon) NZ 403252
Apt 05.02.1842; 3447a (?); Map 1844?, 6 chns; waterbodies, woods, parkland (in detail), sand or stone pit.

11/259 Thrislington (township in parish of Bishop Middleham) NZ 309332
Apt 12.11.1839; 582a (592); Map 1840?, 8 chns, 'copied from an old survey' by Thomas Bell; foot/b'way, woods, field gates, road names, quarry.

11/260 Throston (township in parish of Hart) NZ 492338 [Not listed]
Apt 17.09.1839; 1471a (1575); Map 1840?, 8 chns; railway, foot/b'way, woods, field gates, building names, farm boundaries (col) and names, foreshore; one field named.

11/261 Tilmouth (township in parish of Cornhill) NT 873420 [Not listed]
Apt 17.11.1841; 1189a (?); Map 1841?, 6.5 chns; waterbodies, woods (col), building names; colours may show property ownerships. District is apportioned by holding.

11/262 Trimdon (parish) NZ 375343
Apt 17.12.1839; 2281a (2280); Map 1839, 4 chns, by J. Turner junr; hill-drawing, railway, waterbodies, woods, plantations, heath/moor, building names, landowners, quarries, sand or stone pits, engine, grange, tithe-merged land.

11/263 Tudhoe (township in parish of Brancepeth) NZ 263355
Apt 21.07.1838; 1700a (1699); Map 1839?, 6 chns, by Robt J. Allen, Durham; railway, foot/b'way, occupation roads, waterbodies, woods, gardens, field boundary ownerships, building names, ford; colours may show property ownerships.

11/264 Tunstall (township in parish of Bishop Wearmouth) NZ 390537
Apt 03.11.1838; 801a (801); Map 1838, 6 chns, by Thomas Davison, Durham, litho (Standidge); field acreages.

11/265 Tweedmouth (township in parish of Tweedmouth) NT 994516
Apt 28.12.1843; 731a (2328); Map 1847?, 3 chns; foot/b'way, plantations (col), road names, quarry; colours may show property ownerships; built-up part generalised. District is apportioned by holding.

11/266 Twisel (township in parish of Norham) NT 905426 [Not listed]
Apt 15.02.1840; 2190a (2190); Map 1840?, 15 chns; foot/b'way, woods (col); colours may show holdings. District is apportioned by holding.

11/267 Unthank (hamlet in parish of Tweedmouth) NT 989485 [Not listed]
Apt 31.07.1839; 656a (all); Map 1839, [6 chns]; woods, rock outcrops, limestone quarry; map is described as of lands 'belonging to Prideaux John Selby Esqr'.

11/268 Urpeth (township in parish of Chester-le-Street) NZ 244540 [High Urpeth]
Apt 31.10.1846; 1667a (1671); Map 1846?, 8 chns, 'reduced from various surveys' by Thomas Bell and Sons; railway, foot/b'way, waterbodies, woods, field gates, building names, landowners, oil mill, corn mill, iron forge; colours may show holdings. District is apportioned by holding; Apt omits land use.

11/269 Great Usworth, Little Usworth and North Biddick (township in parish of Washington) NZ 304588 [Usworth]
Apt 01.08.1844; 2548a (2548); Map 1849?, 8 chns, in 4 parts, (including 16 chn index); railway, foot/b'way, waterbodies, woods, parkland, building names, road names; colours may show property ownerships. District is apportioned by holding; Apt omits land use.

11/270 Wackerfield (township in parish of Staindrop) NZ 154219
Apt 17.12.1838; 745a (744); Map 1839, 3 chns, by Otley and Lax, Darlington; turnpike roads, toll bar, waterbodies, woods, building names.

11/271 Waldridge (township in parish of Chester le Street) NZ 254499
Apt 19.06.1840; 732a (795); Map 1839, 4 chns, by Thomas Davison, Durham; hill-drawing, railway, foot/b'way, carriage roads, woods, parkland, building names, boundary stones. Apt omits some field names.

11/272 Walworth (township in parish of Heighington) NZ 236192
Apt 04.10.1838; 2133a (2132); Map 1837, 4 chns, by Thos Dixon, Darlington; hill-drawing, foot/b'way, waterbodies, woods, parkland (in detail), hedge ownership; scattered numbers may be connected with construction of map.

11/273 Warden Law (township in parish of Houghton-le-Spring) NZ 369503
Apt 21.09.1841; 518a (518); Map 1844?, 8 chns. District is apportioned by holding; Apt omits land use and field names.

11/274 Washington (township in parish of Washington) NZ 304566
Apt 02.03.1843; 1894a (all); Map 1843?, 8 chns; railway, waterbodies, woods, building names; colours may show property ownerships. Apt omits land use.

11/275 Westerton (township in parish of St Andrew Auckland) NZ 235313
Apt 24.07.1840; 697a (697); Map 1839, 4 chns, by Thomas Davison, Durham; hill-drawing, turnpike roads, toll bar, woods, quarries.

11/276 Westoe (township in parish of Jarrow) NZ 362655
Apt 27.11.1838; 1795a (2070); Map 1840?, 8 chns, by Andrew Stoddart, South Shields; railway, waterbodies, woods, quarry.

11/277 Westwick (township in parish of Gainford) NZ 082161
Apt 29.07.1844; 1445a (1445); Map 1841, 6 chns; woods, plantations, building names; bridge named; colours may show holdings. District is described as 'belonging to Frederick Webb Esquire'.

11/278 Whessoe (township in parish of Haughton-le-Skerne) NZ 283184 [Not listed]
Apt 21.07.1838; 1412a (1412); Map 1838, 6 chns; railway, woods, heath/moor, building names, field acreages. Apt omits some field names.

11/279 Whickham (except part of Tanfield Moor) (parish) NZ 199603
Apt 18.02.1840; 5906a (5993); Map 1842?, 6 chns, by Thomas Bell; railway, foot/b'way, turnpike roads, toll bar, occupation and carriage roads, waterbodies, woods, parkland (in detail), hedges, field gates, building names, road names, landowners, sandbanks, mill dams, mills, coal staith, old pits, chapel, quarries, fishpond, ford, grange, rectory, monument (pictorial), stables, banqueting house, lodges, allotments; colours may show property ownerships. District is apportioned by holding; Apt omits land use.

11/280 Whitburn (parish) NZ 392628
Apt 31.01.1840; 4185a (4594); Map 1839, 4 chns, by John Bell, Gateshead; hill-drawing, railway, foot/b'way, turnpike roads, milestones, waterbodies, woods, parkland, rock outcrops, field gates, building names, rectory, road names, quarries, mills, old quarries, limekilns, tile sheds, coastline, tidal areas. Apt omits some field names.

11/281 Whitworth (township in parish of Whitworth) NZ 242343 [Not listed]
Apt 13.01.1844; 1465a (1465); Map 1845?, 6 chns; railway, woods, parkland, pit. Apt omits some field names.

11/282 Whitton (township in parish of Grindon) NZ 380237
Apt 20.12.1839; 742a (741); Map 1839, 4 chns; railway, foot/b'way, woods, building names. Apt omits some field names.

11/283 Whorlton (township in parish of Gainford) NZ 106161
Apt 08.06.1850; 1926a (1760); Map 1841, 4 chns, 'corrected and in part surveyed' by T. Dixon, Darlington; foot/b'way, waterbodies, woods, plantations, field gates; colours may show property ownerships.

11/284 Willington (township in parish of Brancepeth) NZ 201351
Apt 11.07.1838; 1485a (1485); Map 1839, 6 chns, by W.J. Ware; hill-drawing, foot/b'way, waterbodies, woods, plantations.

11/285 Wingate (township in parish of Kelloe) NZ 392360
Apt 21.07.1840; 4155a (4154); Map 1839, 8 chns, by George Young Wall, Durham, (drawn by 'J.R.'); woods, building names, foot/b'way, occupation and carriage roads.

11/286 Winlaton (township in parish of Winlaton) NZ 169606
Apt 26.09.1837; 5029a (5111); Map 1838, 4 chns, 'surveyed by, and partly taken from old surveys by Thomas Bell, Newcastle'; hill-drawing, railway and railway depot, foot/b'way, turnpike roads, toll bars, waterbodies, woods, parkland (in detail), hedge ownership, fences, field gates, building names, road names, landowners, alkali factory and bleach ground, weirs, corn mills, clay works, old pit, reservoir, forge and foundry, limekiln, sal ammoniac factory, coal staiths, steel furnace, quarries, quays, working pits, mills, coke factory, bone mill, fire brick factories, sandbanks, embankment, lodge, allotments, farm names; colours may show holdings; bridges named. Apt omits land use.

11/287 Winstone (township in parish of Winstone) NZ 127174 [Winston]
Apt 18.05.1841; 2961a (2961); Map 1839, 4 chns, 'made from plans in the possession of the landowners'; hill-drawing, foot/b'way, waterbodies, building names, landowners, ownership boundaries (col), glebe, field acreages; some field boundaries appear to have been altered after the map was originally drawn.

11/288 Witton Gilbert (township in parish of Durham, St Oswald) NZ 236462
Apt 20.07.1838; 1756a (2535); Map 1839, 6 chns, by Thomas Davison, Durham; hill-drawing, foot/b'way, woods, parkland, building names, landowners, quarries, boundary stones, parsonage, tithe-free lands. Apt omits some field names.

11/289 Witton-le-Wear (township in parish of Auckland St Andrew) NZ 152319
Apt 17.04.1844; 2776a (2955); Map 1846, 3 chns, by John Lee, Bp Auckland; railway, woods, parkland, building names, castle, tithe-merged land. Apt omits field names.

11/290 Wolsingham (parish) NZ 082374
Apt 13.02.1838; 17371a (20403); Map 1838, 6 chns, by Jonathan Roddam, Stanhope; hill-drawing, foot/b'way, waterbodies, woods, building names, coal pit, quarries, lead mine. Apt omits some field names.

11/291 Woodham (township in parish of Aycliffe) NZ 285273
Apt 25.09.1838; 3705a (3705); Map 1839, 3 chns, 'chiefly made from Estate plans furnished by the Landowners, upon various scales and degrees of accuracy &c' by A. and R. Reed, Stockton upon Tees; railway, woods, plantations, orchards, field gates, building names, grange, mill.

11/292 Woolviston (township in parish of Billingham) NZ 440256 [Wolviston]
Apt 30.04.1838; 2396a (2396); Map 1838, 6 chns, by George Young Wall, Durham, litho (Standidge); foot/b'way, private carriage road, woods, building names, grange, pottery, tile sheds, mill, defaced hedges, field acreages.

11/293 Helmington Row (township in parish of Brancepeth) NZ 181351
Apt 11.07.1838; 1234a (1244); Map 1839, 6 chns, by Robt J Allen, Durham; foot/b'way, turnpike roads, toll bar, woods, building names, quarry; grey stipple may indicate gardens; colours may show property ownerships.

Essex

PRO IR29 and IR30 12/1-397

418 tithe districts: 986,047 acres
397 tithe commutations: 938,457 acres
291 voluntary tithe agreements, 106 compulsory tithe awards

Tithe and tithe commutation

In 1836 about 95 per cent of Essex tithe districts were subject to payment of tithes and 223 tithe districts were wholly tithable (Fig. 24). The main causes of exemption in Essex tithe districts were modus payments in lieu of tithes, exemption of former Crown, manorial or monastic land, the merger of tithes in the land, and exemption by prescription.

Assistant tithe commissioners and local tithe agents who worked in Essex are listed in Table 12.1 and the valuers of tithe rent-charge in Table 12.2. In three districts tithe was apportioned on holdings and thus the schedules of apportionment omit details of field names and land use, as also do a number of apportionments made in the normal way on a field-by-field basis. At Prittlewell mussel beds were tithable, the apportionments for Witham and Woodham Walter include details of 'forecropping', and that for Ugley refers to the colouring scheme of the tithe map.

Tithe maps

Fewer than 9 per cent of the 397 Essex tithe maps are sealed as first class. Such a proportion is characteristic of those counties which had undergone extensive parliamentary enclosure, a process by no means widespread in Essex. However, construction lines are present on 13 per cent of second-class maps and some of these were doubtless submitted for first-class status. Taken together, first-class maps and second-class maps with construction lines cover about a fifth of the county and this is very similar to the proportion of first-class maps in Suffolk. As in Suffolk and Norfolk, first-class maps are mainly on the seaward side of the county, with particular concentrations in Essex in the Tendring and Shoebury peninsulas. Many of the maps in the Shoebury area are the work of one particular surveyor, Alexander Doull of Chatham, Kent, and formerly of the Ordnance Survey of Ireland.

Tithe commutation proceeded very expeditiously in Essex and the peak of tithe map production was as early as 1838-39 (Table 12.4). Essex tithe maps are drawn at a variety of scales from one inch to one chain to one inch to twelve chains and 66 per cent are within the recommended scale range of one inch to three to four chains. Most of the remainder are at the six-chain scale (Table 12.3).

Essex tithe maps are less informative about agricultural than about non-agricultural land uses. Only five maps indicate arable and grass, 4 per cent show gardens, and 9 per cent depict orchards. Eleven maps detail hops; the map of Colne Engaine is unusual in that different symbols are used for young and old hops. Common pasture adjoining rivers is often distinguished on Essex tithe maps and four depict substantial areas of open field. Non-agricultural land use is better mapped: 16 per cent show parks (depicted in exceptional detail on seven maps), 5 per cent map heath and moor, 7 per cent distinguish marsh or bog, and 78 per cent portray woodland. Village greens are often mapped and emphasised in colour, and maps of the lower lying districts in the county often show drainage channels and sluices and sea defences. Windmills appear on about 10 per cent of the maps and miscellaneous features depicted on Essex tithe maps include a tithe barn and various monastic remains.

Some 281 Essex tithe maps in the Public Record Office collection (71 per cent) can be attributed to a particular map-maker, a figure which is well above the national average (Table 12.3). Essex maps display a considerable diversity of style and content, though not many are decorated. There are cartouches on seven maps, three of which are embellished with drawing instruments and two with acorns and oak leaves. The cartouche on the map of Great Holland is gilded. Churches and windmills are occasionally shown pictorially but this practice is by no means as widespread in Essex as in Norfolk or Suffolk.

Table 12.1. *Agreements and awards for commutation of tithes in Essex*

Assistant commissioner/ local tithe agent	*Number of agreements**	*Number of awards*
Thomas James Tatham	6	106
Roger Kynaston	63	0
William Heard	49	0
John Mee Mathew	45	0
Edward Young Hancock	34	0
John Pickering	20	0
Joseph Townsend	17	0
F. Browne Browne	16	0
Thomas Smith Woolley	9	2
William Downes	10	0
Henry Dixon	7	0
Francis Offley Martin	0	6
John Maurice Herbert	0	5
Henry Pilkington	5	0
Horace William Meteyard	5	0
Charles Pym	4	0
Edward Greathed	3	0
William Wakeford Attree	0	2
Arthur Biddell	1	0
James Drage Merest	1	0
Thomas Sutton	1	0

*Computed from the number of extant reports on tithe agreements in the tithe files [PRO IR 18].

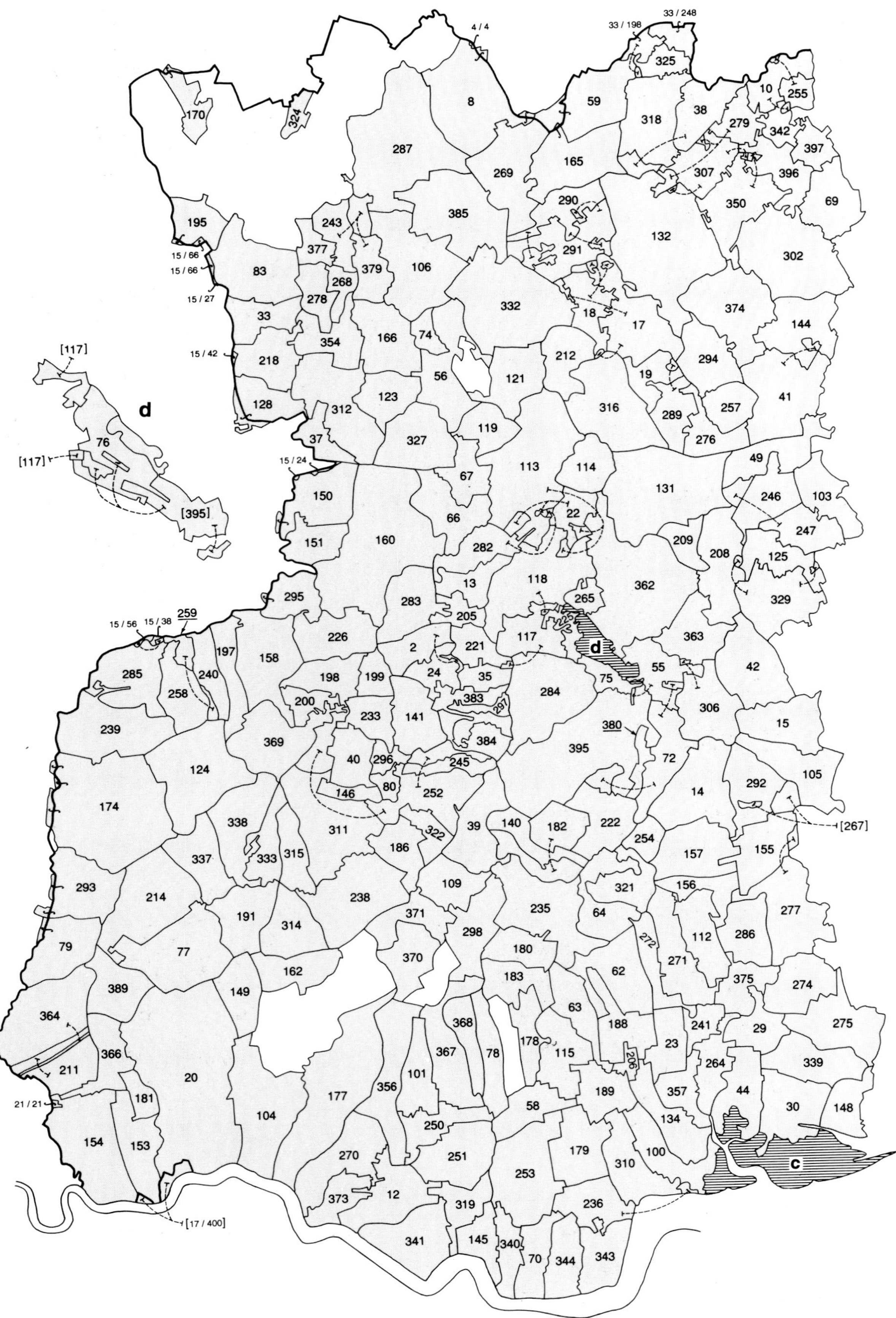

Fig. 24 Essex: tithe district boundaries.

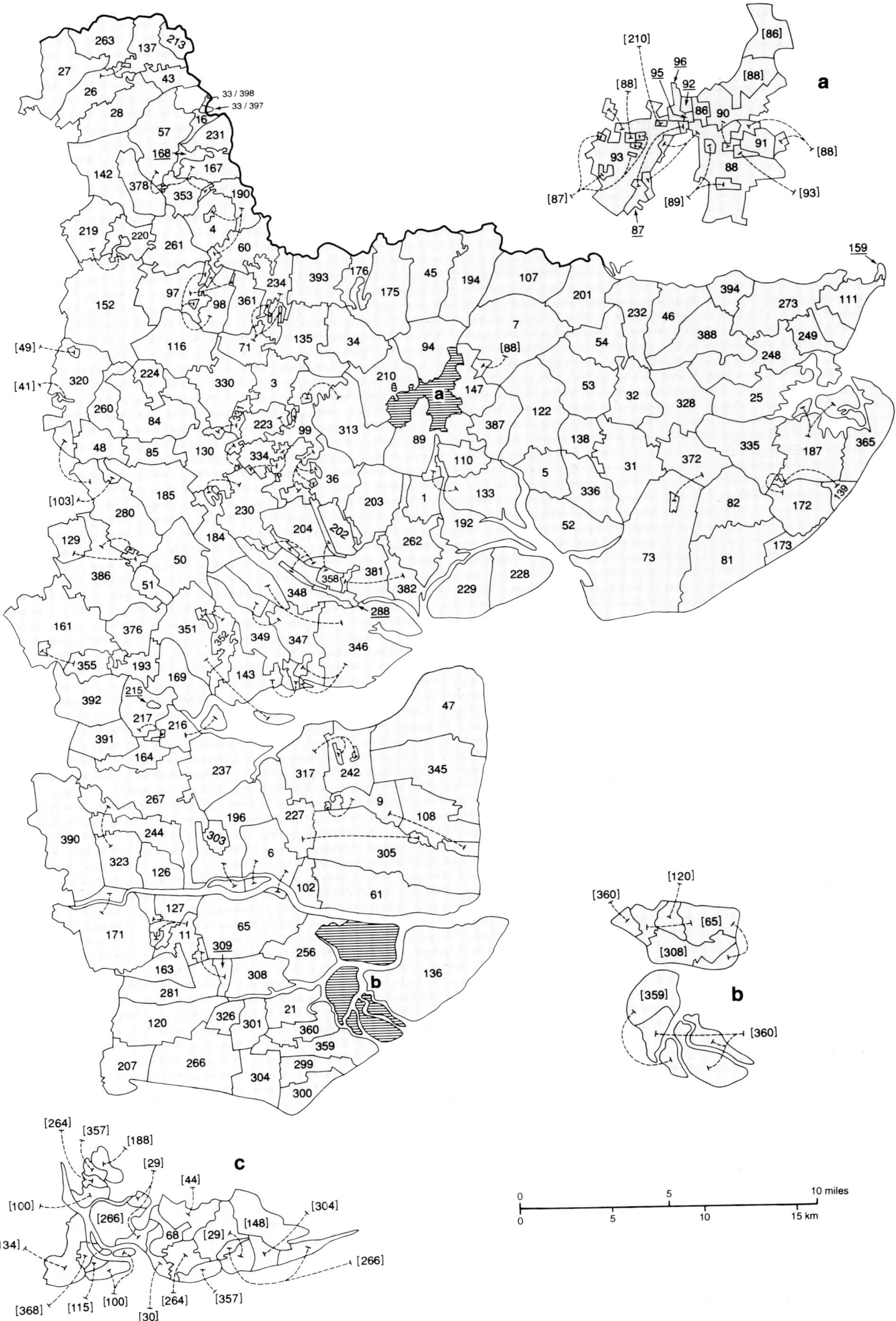

263
137
213
27
26
43
28
33 / 398
33 / 397
16
57
231
168
142
167
378
353
190
4
219
220
261
60
393
176
175
45
194
107
201
152
97
98
361
234
394
232
46
273
111
159
7
54
388
249
116
71
135
34
94
[88]
248
[49]
[41]
320
224
330
3
210
a
147
53
32
328
25
260
84
223
99
313
89
122
387
48
85
130
331
334
36
110
138
365
335
187
[103]
185
280
230
1
133
5
336
31
372
82
172
139
203
202
192
52
129
184
204
262
73
173
81
386
50
51
358
381
382
229
228
161
376
348
288
351
352
349
347
346
355
193
143
169
392
215
217
216
391
164
47
237
317
242
345
267
9
108
390
244
303
196
227
6
305
323
126
102
61
127
171
11
65
309
256
163
308
136
281
b
120
326
301
21
360
359
207
266
299
304
300
[210]
[86]
96
95
92
[88]
86
90
93
91
[87]
88
[93]
[89]
87
[360]
[120]
[65]
[308]
[359]
[264]
[357]
[188]
[29]
c
[44]
[100]
[266]
68
[148]
[304]
[134]
[368]
[115]
[30]
0
5
10 miles
15 km

Table 12.2. *Tithe valuers and tithe map-makers in Essex*

Name and address (in Essex unless indicated)	*Number of districts*	*Acreage*
Tithe valuers		
Robert Baker, Writtle	61	157,039
Robert Franklin, Thaxted	33	98,779
Henry Crawter, Southampton Buildings, London	20	74,059
William Kendall Dawson, Colchester	19	37,399
Martin Nockolds, Saffron Walden	17	37,725
Robert Hardy, Tendring	16	35,714
Edward Cook, Stratford St Mary, Suffolk	15	37,593
James Beadel, Witham	14	25,056
Joseph Smith Surridge, Coggeshall	13	23,362
John Issacson, Clare, Suffolk	13	22,185
Henry Clayton, Ingatestone	12	28,908
Samuel Baker, Hawkwell	11	34,579
John Austin Nockolds, Stansted Mountfitchet	10	28,278
Charles Matson, Great Baddow	10	25,503
Thomas Chapman, Arundel Street, London	10	25,234
Others [52]	123	247,047
Attributed tithe map-makers		
Robert Baker, Writtle	45	104,053
Gilbert and Tayspill, Colchester	36	64,028
Messrs Crawter, London/Cheshunt, Hertfordshire	20	71,508
John King and Son, Saffron Walden	18	40,015
Henry Clayton, Ingatestone	12	28,851
Alexander Doull, Chatham, Kent	11	35,913
James Beadel, Witham	11	33,887
Joseph Smith Surridge, Coggeshall	9	17,702
Others [54]	119	266,978

Table 12.3. *The tithe maps of Essex: scales and classes*

Scale in chains/inch	*All maps*		*First Class*		*Second Class*	
	Number	*Acreage*	*Number*	*Acreage*	*Number*	*Acreage*
>3	8	10,123	1	5,069	7	5,054
3	191	404,611	34	88,308	157	316,303
3.5	1	2,985	0	0	1	2,985
4	70	150,582	0	0	70	150,582
4.5, 5	3	6,994	0	0	3	6,994
6	106	305,201	0	0	106	305,201
7	2	8,836	0	0	2	8,836
8	12	41,516	0	0	12	41,516
<8	4	7,609	0	0	4	7,609
TOTAL	397	938,457	35	93,377	362	845,080

Table 12.4. *The tithe maps of Essex: dates*

	<1837	*1837*	*1838*	*1839*	*1840*	*1841*	*1842*	*1843*	*1844*	*1845*	*1846*	*1847*	*1848*	*>1848*
All maps	7	9	82	95	62	39	23	14	4	13	13	9	16	11
1st class	0	2	9	8	8	3	0	0	1	1	1	1	1	0
2nd class	7	7	73	87	54	36	23	14	3	12	12	8	15	11

Essex

12/1 Abberton (parish) TL 999191
Apt 21.11.1838; 1067a (all); Map 1839, 3 chns, by Gilbert and Tayspill, Colchester; foot/b'way, waterbodies, woods, plantations, heath/moor, building names, gravel pit, rectory. Apt omits land use.

12/2 Abbotts Roothing (parish) TL 566114 [Abbess Roding]
Apt 24.08.1842; 1602a (all); Map 1838, 3 chns, 1st cl, by Robert Burton, Hatfield Broad Oak; construction lines, foot/b'way, waterbodies, houses, woods (named), orchards (by annotation), hedge ownership, fences, field gates, building names, field names, field acreages, rectory.

12/3 Aldham (parish) TL 911256
Apt 25.10.1839; 1825a (all); Map 1841?, 6 chns, in 2 parts, by Gilbert and Tayspill, Colchester, (includes Ford Street separately at 3 chns); waterbodies, woods (named), heath/moor, building names, waste.

12/4 Alphamstone (parish) TL 878354
Apt 08.06.1840; 1558a (all); Map 1840?, 3 chns, ? by J.S. Surridge; waterbodies, houses, woods, hops, hedge ownership, building names; Lamarsh parsonage land is not mapped.

12/5 Alresford (parish) TM 068205
Apt 25.11.1843; 1509a (all); Map 1839, 6 chns, by Gilbert and Tayspill, Colchester; waterbodies, woods, plantations, parkland, building names, watermill, ford, low water mark, parsonage, glebe.

12/6 Althorne (parish) TQ 910990
Apt 25.04.1838; 2251a (all); Map 1839, 3 chns, by Thomas Bygrave, Clements Inn; waterbodies, houses, woods, drains.

12/7 Ardleigh (parish) TM 048288
Apt 29.05.1843; 4906a (4905); Map 1842, 6 chns, in 2 parts, (includes town separately at 3 chns); waterbodies, woods, plantations, parkland, sand or stone pit.

12/8 Ashdon (parish) TL 585420
Apt 05.02.1845; 4969a (all); Map 1848, 6 chns; waterbodies, houses, woods, parkland, building names, rectory.

12/9 Asheldham (parish) TL 972014
Apt 14.09.1838; 1699a (all); Map 1839?, 4 chns; foot/b'way, waterbodies, woods, field gates, coastline, drains.

12/10 Ashen or Esse (parish) TL 755435 [Not listed]
Apt 04.10.1838; 1499a (all); Map 1839, 3 chns, by J. Hasell; foot/b'way, houses, fences, field gates, boundary trees, mill, windmill (pictorial), floodgate; pictorial church.

12/11 Ashingdon (parish) TQ 868938 [Ashington]
Apt 19.03.1838; 1165a (all); Map 1839?, 3 chns, 1st cl, construction lines, waterbodies, houses, woods (col). Apt omits land use.

12/12 Aveley (parish) TQ 565805
Apt 05.06.1839; 2935a (all); Map 1839, 6 chns, by Gilbert and Tayspill, Colchester; waterbodies, woods, plantations, field gates, sea wall.

12/13 Aythorpe Roding (parish) TL 596149
Apt 15.07.1846; 1395a (all); Map 1845, 3 chns, 1st cl, by R. Burton, Dunmow; construction lines, waterbodies, houses, woods, plantations, fences, building names.

12/14 Great Baddow (parish) TL 725035
Apt 27.10.1838; 3620a (all); Map 6 chns, 'surveyed by Messrs Chapman and Black in 1815, corrected... 1838' by Robert Baker, Writtle; waterbodies, woods, plantations, open fields, road names, common. (The map in PRO IR 30 is a copy; original is in PRO IR 77/9.)

12/15 Little Baddow (parish) TL 772077
Apt 07.05.1839; 2739a (all); Map 1843?, 4 chns, by Robt Baker, Writtle, Essex; waterbodies, woods (named), open fields, building names, paper mill, mill; coloured and named fields are open pasture.

12/16 Ballingdon (hamlet) TL 864405
Apt 15.12.1845; 366a (366); Map 1847?, 3 chns, by J. Hasell, Sudbury; waterbodies, woods, plantations, gardens, road names, windmills (pictorial), limekilns, drains.

12/17 Great Bardfield (parish) TL 683296
Apt 20.07.1842; 3689a (3689); Map 1835, 3 chns, by James Beadel, Witham; waterbodies, woods (col), parkland, open fields (named), building names, road names, vicarage, pound, mill (possibly windmill), watermill, greens (col), common.

12/18 Little Bardfield (parish) TL 659309
Apt 13.06.1839; 1710a (all); Map 1838, 3 chns, by James Beadel junr, Witham; construction lines, waterbodies, houses, woods (col, named), plantations (col), fences, field boundary ownerships, building names, windmills (pictorial), rectory.

12/19 Bardfield Saling (parish) TL 690270
Apt 06.12.1844; 1114a (all); Map 1845, 3 chns, by J.S. Surridge, Coggeshall, Essex; waterbodies, houses, woods, windmill, greens (col).

12/20 Barking (parish) TQ 450870
Apt 14.10.1844; 12517a (12741); Map 1846, 6 chns, in 3 parts, by Messrs Crawter, Cobham, Surrey and Southampton Buildings, Chancery Lane, London, (tithable parts only; includes towns of Ilford and Barking separately at 3 chns); railways, waterbodies, woods (col), parkland, drains, township boundary. (The map in PRO IR 30 is a copy; original is in PRO IR 77/10.)

12/21 Barling (parish) TQ 930899
Apt 03.11.1838; 1259a (all); Map 'field map' 1839, 3 chns; construction lines, waterbodies, building names (in gothic), gaol, vicarage, mill (possibly windmill). Apt omits land use.

12/22 Barnston (parish) TL 650195
Apt 28.12.1838; 1443a (1442); Map 1838, 6 chns, in 2 parts, by Arthur Barfield, Great Dunmow, (includes village separately at 3 chns); waterbodies, houses, woods, plantations, parkland, sand or stone pit.

12/23 Basildon (parish) TQ 715898
Apt 11.01.1838; 1628a (all); Map 1841?, 3 chns, by Robt Baker, Writtle, Essex; waterbodies, houses, woods (by annotation).

12/24 Beauchamp Roothing (parish) TL 598102 [Beauchamp Roding]
Apt 31.12.1840; 1259a (1311); Map 1841, 3 chns, by Robert G. Palmer; waterbodies, houses, woods (col).

12/25 Beaumont (parish) TM 191253
Apt 19.12.1838; 3047a (all); Map 1839, 3 chns, by G.R. Jay and W. Ruffell; woods (named), building names, rectory, churchyard, brickyard, marsh. Apt omits land use.

12/26 Belchamp Otten (parish) TL 802419
Apt 04.09.1839; 1694a (1693); Map 1839?, 3 chns; woods, plantations, orchards, gardens, fences, building names, field name, boundary trees, rectory, windmill (pictorial), common; pictorial church; ruler, quill pen, charcoal holders and pair of compassses surround scale-bar.

12/27 Belchamp St Pauls (parish) TL 789435 [Belchamp St Paul]
Apt 08.06.1840; 2557a (2557); Map 1839, 3 chns, by J. Hasell, Sudbury; woods, plantations, orchards, gardens, fences, building names, boundary trees, windmill (pictorial), rectory, school; pictorial church, (with gravestones); ruler, quill pen, charcoal holders and pair of compasses surround scale-bar.

12/28 Belchamp Walter (parish) TL 823408
Apt 03.07.1846; 2125a (all); Map 1839, 3 chns, by George Dring, Melford, Suffolk; foot/b'way, waterbodies, houses, woods, plantations, parkland (in detail), orchards, gardens (col), field boundary ownerships, building names, gravel pit, water meadows (col).

12/29 North Bemfleet (parish) TQ 764904 [North Benfleet]
Apt 30.04.1840; 2418a (all); Map 1839, 3 chns, in 2 parts, by Messrs Crawter, (includes index); hill-drawing, foot/b'way, waterbodies, houses, woods, marsh/bog, building names, ditch or embankment, rectory, boundary trees, drains.

12/30 South Bemfleet (parish) TQ 781866 [South Benfleet]
Apt 18.01.1840; 3056a (all); Map 1841?, 3 chns, by John Hills, Billericay, Essex; construction lines, waterbodies, houses, woods (col), plantations (col), parkland (col), gardens (col), heath/moor, field boundary ownerships, field gates, drains, ditches, embankments,

saltings, low water mark. Apt omits some field names. (The map in PRO IR 30 is a copy; original is in PRO IR 77/11.)

12/31 Great Bentley (parish) TM 114213
Apt 31.12.1840; 3188a (3188); Map 1838, 3 chns, by S.L. Bransby, Ipswich; waterbodies, houses, woods, building names, windmill (pictorial), green (col); pictorial church. Apt omits land use.

12/32 Little Bentley (parish) TM 120250
Apt 30.11.1839; 2012a (2012); Map 1841?, 4 chns; waterbodies.

12/33 Berden (parish) TL 475295
Apt 17.02.1838; 1772a (1771); Map 1839, 6 chns; waterbodies, houses, woods, building names, priory, greens.

12/34 West Bergholt (parish) TL 957282
Apt 18.05.1843; 2274a (all); Map 1843?, 3 chns; construction lines, rectory, wood (by annotation), heath.

12/35 Berners Roothing (parish) TL 606096 [Berners Roding]
Apt 22.04.1839; 1035a (1050); Map 1839, 4 chns, copied from a map made in 1772 by R. Baker, Writtle; waterbodies, houses, woods, plantations.

12/36 Great and Little Birch (parish) TL 941198 [Birch]
Apt 13.04.1842; 3070a (all); Map 1842?, 6 chns, by Gilbert and Tayspill, Colchester, and Alfred Rush, Messing; waterbodies, houses, woods, building names, church ruins, rectory.

12/37 Birchanger (parish) TL 509228
Apt 25.10.1839; 1052a (all); Map 1838, 6 chns, by Nockolds and Son, Stansted, Essex; waterbodies, houses, woods, plantations, field boundary ownerships, building names; bridge named.

12/38 Birdbrook (parish) TL 713412
Apt 27.06.1839; 2387a (all); Map 1835, 6 chns, by J. King and Son; waterbodies, houses, woods, parkland, building names, rectory.

12/39 Blackmore (parish) TL 602017
Apt 11.12.1845; 2576a (2576); Map 1847, 4 chns, by Robert Baker, Writtle, Essex; waterbodies, houses, woods, plantations, tithe-free lands.

12/40 Bobbingworth (parish) TL 533049
Apt 07.07.1837; 1628a (1628); Map 1837, 3 chns, by J. Lewis, Walter End Farm, 'assisted by' Fk F. Cattlin; construction lines, foot/b'way, building names, rectory, poorhouse, springs, windmill (pictorial), milestone, gamekeeper's cottage, woods and plantations (by annotation); springs and bridges named.

12/41 Bocking (parish) TL 765261
Apt 30.05.1838; 4578a (4607); Map 1840, 3 chns, 1st cl, by J. King and Son, Saffron Walden; construction lines, foot/b'way, waterbodies, houses, woods (col), field boundary ownerships, building names, road names, windmill (pictorial), mill, boundary trees, workhouse, silk mill, deanery; it is unclear what the various road colours mean.

12/42 Boreham (parish) TL 745102
Apt 02.06.1838; 3740a (3739); Map 1841?, 3 chns; foot/b'way, waterbodies, houses, woods (named), parkland (in detail), open fields, fences, field boundary ownerships, field gates, building names, road names, field names, coal wharf, paper mill, vicarage, rectory, vicarial and rectorial glebe; one owner's land is coloured.

12/43 Borley (parish) TL 848429
Apt 16.03.1839; 776a (all); Map 1840?, 3 chns, by Henry Clayton; waterbodies.

12/44 Bowers Gifford (parish) TQ 756872
Apt 25.08.1842; 2607a (all); Map 1843, 3 chns, in 2 parts, by Messrs Crawter, (includes index); foot/b'way, waterbodies, houses, woods, marsh/bog, building names, vicarage, parsonage, drains.

12/45 Boxtead (parish) TL 999325
Apt 22.11.1838; 3083a (3082); Map 1838, 6 chns; waterbodies, houses, woods, building names, mill, drains. Apt omits land use.

12/46 Bradfield (parish) TM 144299
Apt 19.11.1842; 2119a (2719); Map 'copied from a survey taken in 1818 and corrected to 1838', 3 chns; waterbodies, building names, glebe.

12/47 Bradwell near the Sea (parish) TM 010070 [Bradwell-on-Sea]
Apt 13.01.1837; 4734a (all); Map 1838, 3 chns, 'copied from a Survey made by Mr Thomas Bygrave, 1826', by Baker, Writtle; foot/b'way, waterbodies, houses, woods (col), plantations, building names, windmill (pictorial), sea wall, coastline, drains, glebe, chapel.

12/48 Bradwell next Coggeshall (parish) TL 816220 [Bradwell]
Apt 27.02.1841; 1161a (1161); Map 1842?, 3 chns; foot/b'way, waterbodies, houses, hedge ownership, fences, field gates, building names, road names, parsonage, mill, wood (by annotation), greens (col); hamlets named.

12/49 Braintree (parish) TL 759230
Apt 11.12.1845; 2242a (2242); Map 1847?, 6 chns, in 2 parts, (includes town at 1.5 chns), zincographed (by Shaw and Sons, 137 Fetter Lane, London); foot/b'way, waterbodies, houses (by shading), woods, plantations, orchards, churchyard.

12/50 Great Braxted (parish) TL 858156
Apt 28.02.1838; 2632a (2631); Map 1839, [3 chns], by James Beadel, Witham; construction lines, waterbodies, houses, woods (col), parkland, fences, building names.

12/51 Little Braxted (parish) TL 839140
Apt 20.09.1841; 563a (all); Map 1842?, 3 chns; foot/b'way, waterbodies, woods, heath/moor, field gates.

12/52 Brightlingsea (parish) TM 083177
Apt 31.01.1839; 3090a (3560); Map 1840?, 6 chns, in 2 parts, by Gilbert and Tayspill, Colchester, (includes town separately at 3 chns); waterbodies, woods, building names, sand or stone pit or quarry, Methodist Chapel, green, drains.

12/53 Great Bromley (parish) TM 089253
Apt 09.01.1844; 2677a (all); Map 1839, 3 chns, 1st cl, by C.R. Jay; waterbodies, woods (named), parkland, greens, heath.

12/54 Little Bromley (parish) TM 101283
Apt 06.05.1839; 1841a (all); Map 1841?, 6 chns, by Gilbert and Tayspill, Colchester; waterbodies, woods, plantations. Apt omits land use.

12/55 Broomfield (parish) TL 702102
Apt 12.10.1844; 2215a (all); Map 1845, 3 chns, by Robert Baker, Writtle, Essex; foot/b'way, waterbodies, houses, woods (col), plantations (col), marsh/bog, sand or stone pit.

12/56 Broxted (parish) TL 579260
Apt 08.03.1839; 3149a (3149); Map 1839, 6 chns, 'revised' by J.S. Surridge, Feering, Sx [Essex]; foot/b'way, waterbodies, houses, woods, plantations, heath/moor, fences, building names.

12/57 Bulmer (parish) TL 842398
Apt 05.05.1840; 2779a (all); Map 1840, 3 chns, by Richard Peyton, Cooks Court, Carey Street, London; construction lines, foot/b'way, waterbodies, houses, woods (named), plantations, parkland (in detail), hedge ownership, fence ownership, field gates, building names, sand or stone pits or quarries, cold bath, lodge, windmills (by symbol); bridge named.

12/58 Bulpham (parish) TQ 640860 [Bulphan]
Apt 04.10.1837; 1667a (all); Map 1838, 4 chns, by Henry Clayton; waterbodies, orchards, building names, parsonage. Apt omits some field names.

12/59 Bumpsted Helion (parish) (partly in Cambs) TL 655420 [Helions Bumpstead]
Apt 05.12.1840; 3191a (3191); Map 1841?, 8 chns; foot/b'way, waterbodies, woods, parkland, building names, parsonage, county boundary.

12/60 Bures Hamlet (parish) TL 897338 [Not listed]
Apt 28.02.1838; 1589a (?); Map 1840?, 6 chns, by Gilbert and Tayspill, Colchester; waterbodies, houses, woods, building names, parsonage.

12/61 Burnham (parish) TQ 975965 [Burnham-on-Crouch]
Apt 02.04.1845; 2504a (5523); Map 1849?, 6 chns, in 3 parts, by Messrs Baker and Son, Writtle, Essex, (includes 24-chn index); foot/b'way, waterbodies, houses, plantations, marsh/bog, building names, gravel pit, vicarage, modus lands, tithe-free lands, drains; built-up parts generalised.

12/62 Great Burstead (parish) TQ 690930
Apt 08.03.1839; 1781a (3502); Map 1840?, 3 chns; foot/b'way, waterbodies, houses, field boundary ownerships, field gates, landowners, windmills (by symbol).

12/63 Little Burstead (parish) TQ 668906
Apt 11.01.1838; 1829a (1829); Map 1838, 4 chns, by M.J. Mason, Foxboro; construction lines, waterbodies, woods, orchards, boundary trees.

12/64 Buttsbury (parish) TQ 670970 [Not listed]
Apt 26.02.1839; 2117a (2116); Map 1839, 4 chns, by Henry Clayton; waterbodies, woods, tithe-free lands (col).

12/65 Canewdon (parish) TQ 900946
Apt 14.05.1840; 5509a (4071); Map 1839, 3 chns, 1st cl, by Alexdr Doull, Chatham; construction lines, waterbodies, houses, fences, field gates, sea wall, drains.

12/66 Great Canfield (parish) TL 589186
Apt 08.05.1846; 2472a (2472); Map 1839, 3 chns; waterbodies, houses, woods (col), building names.

12/67 Little Canfield (parish) TL 591209 [Not listed]
Apt 23.03.1842; 1480a (1479); Map 1838, 3 chns, by Messrs Nockolds and Son, Stansted, Essex; hill-drawing, waterbodies, houses, woods, plantations, hedge ownership, fence ownership, field gates, sand or stone pits, quarry.

12/68 Canvey Island (district in parish of Prittlewell) TQ 775835
Apt 28.08.1839; 616a (all); Map 1839, [? 9 chns]; drains. Apt omits some field names and gives only holding acreages.

12/69 Castle Hedingham (parish) TL 787366
Apt 27.07.1844; 2429a (all); Map 1841?, 3 chns; waterbodies, houses, woods, parkland (in detail), orchards, hops, building names, castle.

12/70 Chadwell (parish) TQ 645778 [Chadwell St Mary]
Apt 17.05.1839; 1818a (?); Map 1840?, 4 chns; hill-drawing, waterbodies, embankment, drains. Apt omits some field names.

12/71 Chapel or Chapple otherwise Pontesbright (parish) TL 894277 [Chappel]
Apt 12.10.1841; 1147a (all); Map 1840, 4 chns, 'copied from an old survey and modernized' by Gilbert and Tayspill; foot/b'way, waterbodies, woods (named), plantations, orchards, building names, field names, landowners, glebe; meadows named.

12/72 Chelmsford (parish) TL 701059
Apt 22.01.1841; 2841a (2841); Map 1843?, 3 chns, by Robt Baker, Writtle, Essex; railway, turnpike roads, waterbodies, houses, woods (named); built-up parts generalised.

12/73 Chick St Osyth (parish) TM 124157 [St Osyth]
Apt 31.01.1839; 2344a (9671); Map 1840?, 4 chns, 'copied from the original in the possession of F. Nassau Esqr'; foot/b'way, waterbodies, woods, plantations, parkland, gardens, marsh/bog, building names, sea wall, sandbank, high water mark, sluices, towers, telegraph, farm boundaries and names, drains. Apt omits land use.

12/74 Chickney (parish) TL 569285
Apt 24.12.1838; 701a (all); Map 1838, 3 chns, by John King and Son, Saffron Walden; waterbodies, houses, woods, building names; it is unclear what the various road colours mean.

12/75 Great Chignal or Chignal St James (parish) TL 675100 [Chignall St James]
Apt 11.12.1845; 909a (all); Map 1846?, 4 chns, in 2 parts, 'sketch from Chapman and Andres' Map' by Robert Baker, Writtle, Essex, (includes index); waterbodies, building names.

12/76 Little Chignal, otherwise Chignal Smeeley (parish) TL 668117 [Chignall Smealy]
Apt 18.03.1847; 476a (all); Map 1848, 3 chns, by Robt Baker, Writtle, Essex; foot/b'way, waterbodies, houses, woods.

12/77 Chigwell (parish) TQ 443937
Apt 21.04.1838; 3819a (4522); Map 1839?, 6 chns, by Robt Baker, Writtle; foot/b'way, waterbodies, houses, woods, ford, boundary marks.

12/78 Childerditch (parish) TQ 615891
Apt 28.02.1839; 1615a (1614); Map 1839, 3 chns, by Michl Jno. Mason; construction lines, waterbodies, houses, woods, plantations, parkland, orchards. Apt omits details of tithe-free lands.

12/79 Chingford (parish) TQ 382939
Apt 30.05.1838; 2766a (2766); Map 1838, 6 chns, in 2 parts, (includes 3-chn enlargement of land subject to river course changes); construction lines, foot/b'way, waterbodies, houses, woods, heath/moor, open fields, field boundary ownerships, avenue of trees, glebe.

12/80 Chipping Ongar (parish) TL 555035
Apt 28.02.1838; 509a (all); Map 1841?, [1.5 chns]; construction lines, hill-drawing, foot/b'way, waterbodies, houses, woods, plantations, hedge ownership, fence ownership, field gates, earthworks.

12/81 Great Clacton (parish) TM 177165
Apt 01.06.1841; 4046a (4280); Map 1839, 3 chns, by W. Ruffell; woods, drains, coastline; colours may show property ownerships.

12/82 Little Clacton (parish) TM 172190
Apt 18.11.1840; 2967a (2966); Map 1838, 3 chns, by S.L. Bransby, Ipswich; waterbodies, houses, woods; pictorial church. Apt omits land use.

12/83 Clavering (parish) TL 468322
Apt 17.07.1839; 3799a (3798); Map 1840, 3 chns, by J. King and Son, Saffron Walden; waterbodies, houses, woods, plantations, open fields (named), building names, greens (col); it is unclear what the various road colours mean.

12/84 Great Coggeshall (parish) TL 840237 [Coggeshall]
Apt 28.02.1851; 2609a (2770); Map 1853?, 3 chns, by J.S. Surridge and Son, Inworth and Halstead, Essex; waterbodies, houses, woods (col), plantations (col), parkland (col), marsh/bog, building names, vicarage; pictorial church.

12/85 Little Coggeshall (parish) TL 840216 [Coggeshall Hamlet]
Apt 28.02.1851; 996a (830); Map 1851, 3 chns, by J.S. Surridge and Son, Inworth Hall, and Halstead; waterbodies, houses, woods (col), plantations (col), building names, mills, avenue of trees.

12/86 Colchester, All Saints (parish) TM 001053
Apt 26.04.1838; 281a (?); Map 1837, 3 chns, by Gilbert and Tayspill, Colchester; construction lines, foot/b'way, waterbodies, woods, plantations, building names, road names, castle, town wall, avenue of trees, field acreages.

12/87 Colchester, Holy Trinity (parish) TL 987238 [Not listed]
Apt 02.05.1845; 99a (?); Map 1846?, 6 chns; road names.

12/88 Colchester, St Botolph (parish) TM 007241 [Not listed]
Apt 08.11.1838; 881a (?); Map 1838, 4 chns, 'copied from a book of old surveys' by Gilbert and Tayspill, Colchester; foot/b'way, waterbodies, woods, building names, road names, milestone, workhouse, waterworks, mill, lock, ruins of priory, distillery; bridge named; built-up parts generalised.

12/89 Colchester, St. Giles (parish) TL 992221 [Not listed]
Apt 09.10.1838; 590a (?); Map 1839, 3 chns, by Gilbert and Tayspill, Colchester; hill-drawing, foot/b'way, woods, marsh/bog, road names, river embankment, gravel pit.

12/90 Colchester, St James (parish) TM 005257 [Not listed]
Apt 11.12.1845; 207a (?); Map 1846?, 6 chns; waterbodies, fences, building names, road names, gaol; built-up parts generalised.

12/91 Colchester, St Leonard (parish) TM 012248 [Not listed]
Apt 11.12.1845; 83a (all); Map 1846?, 3 chns; foot/b'way, waterbodies, road names, quay; built-up parts generalised.

12/92 Colchester, St Martin (parish) TL 997252 [Not listed]
Apt 26.03.1849; 3a (all); Map 1850?, 1.5 chns; road names.

12/93 Colchester, St Mary at the Walls (parish) TL 981241 [Not listed]
Apt 25.05.1845; 486a (?); Map 1846?, 6 chns; woods, plantations, road names.

12/94 Colchester, St Michael Mile End (parish) TL 999274 [Not listed]
Apt 28.11.1842; 2343a (?); Map 1842, 6 chns, in 2 parts, by Gilbert and Tayspill, Colchester, (including 3-chn enlargement of meadow); waterbodies, woods, field names.

12/95 Colchester, St Nicholas (parish) TL 999251 [Not listed]
Apt 26.03.1849; 13a (all); Map 1850?, 1.5 chns; road names, tithe-free land; built-up parts generalised.

12/96 Colchester, St Peter (parish) TL 993252 [Not listed]
Apt 11.12.1845; 26a (all); Map 1848, 1 chn, by William A. Bowler, Colchester; waterbodies, road names; built-up parts generalised; bridge named; meaning of colours is unclear.

12/97 Colne Engaine (parish) TL 851305
Apt 23.11.1838; 2444a (all); Map 1840?, 4 chns; waterbodies, houses, woods (named), plantations, old and young hops (by symbol), hedge ownership, fences, field gates, building names, field names, sheds, stables, greens.

12/98 White Colne (parish) TL 880300
Apt 12.07.1838; 1468a (all); Map 1840, 4 chns; waterbodies, houses, woods (col), pits, meadows (col).

12/99 Copford (parish) TL 928233
Apt 07.10.1839; 2398a (all); Map 8 chns, 'copied from an ancient survey and modernized to the year 1839' by Gilbert and Tayspill, Colchester; waterbodies, woods, plantations.

12/100 Corringham (parish) TQ 712834
Apt 18.03.1839; 2857a (3536); Map 1840, 6 chns, by Messrs Crawter; foot/b'way, waterbodies, woods (col), building names, road names, oil mill, drains.

12/101 Cranham (parish) TQ 575868
Apt 31.10.1839; 1875a (1875); Map 1840, 3 chns; foot/b'way, waterbodies, woods (named), plantations, building names, road names, rectory, boundary posts.

12/102 Creeksea or Crixeth (parish) TQ 930971
Apt 14.01.1845; 855a (985); Map 1844, 3 chns, by Thomas Bygrave, Clement Inn; hill-drawing, waterbodies, houses, woods, field gates, building names, ferry, sand or stone pit, drains.

12/103 Cressing (parish) TL 789205
Apt 31.12.1838; 2358a (2357); Map 1841?, 4 chns, in 2 parts, (includes index); foot/b'way, waterbodies, woods, building names.

12/104 Dagenham (except part of Hainault Forest) (parish) TQ 498844
Apt 22.03.1841; 5069a (all); Map 1844?, 2.5 chns, 1st cl, (tithable parts only); railway, foot/b'way, waterbodies, houses, woods, plantations, open fields, building names, road names, mill, stone windmills (by symbol), drains, heath, levels.

12/105 Danbury (parish) TL 783051
Apt 10.05.1839; 2951a (all); Map 1840, 3 chns, 1st cl, by Richd and John Bevan, Whiteheads Grove; construction lines, foot/b'way, waterbodies, houses, woods (col, named), parkland (named), marsh/bog, heath/moor (col), fences, field gates, building names, green; colours may show property ownerships.

12/106 Debden (parish) TL 560327
Apt 12.12.1842; 4405a (all); Map 1843, 6 chns; waterbodies, houses, woods, parkland (in detail), building names, rectory; it is unclear what the various road colours mean.

12/107 Dedham (parish) TM 054322
Apt 29.11.1841; 2551a (2551); Map 1838, 3 chns, by S.W. Parkes, Ipswich; turnpike roads, tollgate, waterbodies, houses, woods (col), plantations (col), parkland (in detail), orchards, gardens, building names, school, assembly room, widows' asylum, almshouses, drains.

12/108 Dengie (parish) TM 005005
Apt 21.01.1839; 2306a (all); Map 1838, 4 chns; construction lines, hill-drawing, waterbodies, houses, woods, orchards, drains.

12/109 Doddinghurst (parish) TQ 568982
Apt 11.12.1845; 1893a (all); Map 1846, 3 chns, by Moses Dodd, 16 New Broad Street, London; waterbodies, houses, woods.

12/110 East Donyland (parish) TM 021214 [Not listed]
Apt 05.03.1840; 1067a (1067); Map 1839, 3 chns, 'working plan' by Messrs Sheldrake and McLachlan; construction lines, foot/b'way.

12/111 Dovercourt (parish) TM 241309
Apt 17.02.1842; 1747a (2966); Map 1840, 3 chns, by T.C. Harris, Great Bromley; hill-drawing, waterbodies, houses, orchards, ditches or embankments, coastline, drains.

12/112 Downham (parish) TQ 730952
Apt 30.09.1842; 2224a (all); Map 1843, 4 chns, by John Hills, Billericay, Essex; waterbodies, houses, woods (col), parkland.

12/113 Great Dunmow (parish) TL 628218
Apt 09.06.1840; 6747a (6746); Map 1842?, 6 chns, in 2 parts; foot/b'way, waterbodies, houses, woods, plantations, parkland, building names, road names.

12/114 Little Dunmow (parish) TL 658218
Apt 30.11.1839; 1715a (1715); Map 1839, 6 chns; foot/b'way, waterbodies, houses, woods, marsh/bog.

12/115 Dunton (parish) TQ 653887
Apt 26.12.1837; 2339a (all); Map 1838, 4 chns, by Henry Clayton; hill-drawing, waterbodies, plantations, marsh/bog, boundary trees, low water mark, drains. Apt omits some field names.

12/116 Earls Colne (parish) TL 860280
Apt 21.01.1838; 2959a (2959); Map 1839, 6 chns, by James Beadel jr, 1835, litho (Standidge); waterbodies, woods (named), hops, heath/moor, building names, mill, priory.

12/117 Good Easter (parish) TL 634120
Apt 04.05.1840; 2082a (2081); Map 1839, 3 chns, by Robert Burton, Dunmow; construction lines, waterbodies, houses, woods, plantations, hedge, fences, gate, building names, parsonage, osier ground, ornamental ground.

12/118 High Easter (parish) TL 625150
Apt 19.05.1848; 4726a (4725); Map 1848, 6 chns, by J. Savill, Sible Hedingham, litho (by S. Straker, 80 Bishopgate St, London); foot/b'way, waterbodies, woods, plantations, building names, parsonage.

12/119 Little Easton (parish) TL 604235
Apt 31.10.1838; 1549a (1548); Map 1802?, 4 chns, by A. Baker; foot/b'way, waterbodies, woods (col), parkland (in detail, named), grassland (col), hedge ownership, fences, field gates, field names, field acreages; church, mansion and park buildings are shown pictorially; title is on shield surrounded by ribbon and leaves.

12/120 Eastwood (parish) TQ 850890
Apt 22.06.1840; 3201a (all); Map 1839, 3 chns, 1st cl, by Alexr Doull, Chatham; construction lines, waterbodies, houses, building names, road names, drains.

12/121 Great Eiston (parish) TL 620260 [Great Easton]
Apt 12.06.1839; 2533a (?); Map 1839, 3 chns, by William Cheffins, Bishop Stortford; waterbodies, houses, woods, plantations, parkland, arable (col), grassland (col), orchards, gardens, hedges, building names, parsonage.

12/122 Elmstead (parish) TM 063240
Apt 02.01.1844; 3645a (3644); Map 1841, 3 chns, 1st cl, by G.R. Jay; waterbodies, woods; colours may show property ownerships.

12/123 Elsenham (parish) TL 547251
Apt 31.10.1839; 1829a (all); Map 1840, 6 chns, by J.A. Nockolds, Stansted, Essex; waterbodies, houses, woods, parkland, green.

12/124 Epping (parish) TL 450040
Apt 28.11.1838; 5282a (5281); Map 1839, 6 chns, in 2 parts, by Messrs Crawter, (includes town separately at 3 chns); waterbodies, houses, woods, building names, forest, commons, greens.

12/125 Fairsted (parish) TL 768167 [Fairstead]
Apt 29.03.1837; 1854a (all); Map 1838?, 4 chns, by Robt Baker, Writtle; waterbodies, woods (col, named), building names, rectory.

12/126 North Fambridge (parish) TQ 852978
Apt 08.06.1840; 1249a (all); Map 1839?, 3 chns, 1st cl, by Frederick F. Cattlin, Danbury; construction lines, hill-drawing, foot/b'way, waterbodies, woods, fences, field gates, building names, well, ferry, walls, drains, saltings, glebe.

12/127 South Fambridge (parish) TQ 859950
Apt 12.09.1837; 1235a (all); Map 1838, 3 chns, 1st cl, by Gilbert and Tayspill, Colchester; construction lines, foot/b'way, waterbodies, low water mark, drains. Apt omits land use.

12/128 Farnham (parish) TL 472246
Apt 31.10.1839; 1966a (all); Map 1842?, 6 chns; waterbodies, houses, woods (named).

12/129 Faulkbourn (parish) TL 793166 [Faulkbourne]
Apt 21.11.1838; 1152a (all); Map 1838, 3 chns, by Robert Baker, Writtle, Essex; foot/b'way, waterbodies, houses, woods (named), plantations, parkland, orchards, marsh/bog.

12/130 Feering (parish) TL 875212
Apt 23.09.1840; 3230a (all); Map 1843, 6 chns, in 2 parts, by Joseph S. Surridge, Feering and Coggeshall, (includes 12-chn index); railway, waterbodies, houses, woods (col), plantations (col), grassland (col), building names, mill, old mill, pit.

12/131 Felsted (parish) TL 700206
Apt 30.03.1844; 6247a (6247); Map 1837, 6 chns, by Messrs Savill and Son, litho (by John Savill, Sible Hedingham); foot/b'way, waterbodies, woods, plantations, building names, mills, priory, vicarage, greens.

12/132 Finchingfield (parish) TL 692339
Apt 21.03.1840; 8387a (8387); Map 1834, 6 chns, in 2 parts, by James Beadle, Witham, (includes enlargement of village at 3 chns); waterbodies, woods, parkland (in detail), building names, field name, sand or stone pit.

12/133 Fingringhoe (parish) TM 034196
Apt 24.08.1842; 2863a (all); Map 1842, 6 chns; waterbodies, woods, plantations.

12/134 Fobbing (parish) TQ 717852
Apt 30.05.1840; 2654a (all); Map 1839, 6 chns, by Messrs Crawter; hill-drawing, waterbodies, houses, woods, intended dock site, sluice, wharf, drains.

12/135 Fordham (parish) TL 930280
Apt 31.08.1837; 2518a (2517); Map 1838, 6 chns, by Gilbert and Tayspill, Colchester; waterbodies, houses, woods, plantations, building names, parsonage, open meadows (named), farm names.

12/136 Foulness Island (district) TR 010924
Apt 12.07.1850; 6310a (28505); Map 1847, 6 chns, by Herbert Mew, Canewdon, Essex, corrected to August 22nd 1850 by Benjamin Pickever Wilme, 15, Featherstone Bldgs, Bedford Row, London; foot/b'way, houses, woods, field gates, building names, sea wall, ferry, gutters, sheep pounds, sheep folds, school, windmill (by symbol), drains, ornamental gardens.

12/137 Foxearth (parish) TL 836448
Apt 01.05.1839; 1640a (1640); Map 1840?, 3 chns; woods, plantations, orchards, gardens, marsh/bog, building names, mill, boundary marks, glebe; scrolling surrounds title and ruler, pair of compasses, quill pen and charcoal holders surround scale bar.

12/138 Frating (parish) TM 087227
Apt 08.03.1842; 1237a (all); Map 1840?, 3 chns; construction lines, waterbodies, houses, woods.

12/139 Frinton (parish) TM 223198 [Frinton-on-Sea]
Apt 31.03.1840; 480a (all); Map 1839, 6 chns, by Gilbert and Tayspill, Colchester; construction lines, waterbodies, houses, rock outcrops, coastline, cliffs.

12/140 Fryerning (parish) TL 632010
Apt 12.05.1843; 1370a (all); Map 1842, 4 chns, by Henry Clayton; railway, waterbodies, woods.

12/141 Fyfield (parish) TL 564074
Apt 22.01.1841; 2451a (2450); Map 1839, 3 chns, by J. Bailey Denton, 9 Grays Inn Square; foot/b'way, waterbodies, houses, woods, plantations, field boundary ownerships, building names, rectory, brick ground, waste.

12/142 Gestingthorpe (parish) TL 810380
Apt 03.11.1838; 2610a (2630); Map 1838, 4 chns, 'copied from a survey made by Mr Isaac Johnson in the year 1804, the property placed to the present Proprietors in the year 1838'; woods (named), plantations, building names, field names, foundry; colour bands may show property ownerships.

12/143 Goldhanger (parish) TL 900087
Apt 05.03.1839; 2134a (2724); Map 1841?, 6 chns; foot/b'way, waterbodies, farmyards, woods, building names, river walls, drains, saltings.

12/144 Gosfield (parish) TL 774297
Apt 30.06.1841; 2991a (2990); Map 1841, 8 chns; waterbodies, houses, woods, plantations, building names, vicarage.

12/145 Grays Thurrock (parish) TQ 628781 [Grays]
Apt 07.12.1841; 1874a (1634); Map 1840, 3 chns, by Messrs Crawter; hill-drawing, foot/b'way, waterbodies, houses, woods, plantations, building names, wharves, brickfields, gravel pit, ditch or embankment, chalk pits, chapel, limekilns, drains.

12/146 Greenstead (parish) TL 534028 [Greensted]
Apt 15.06.1839; 1499a (1498); Map 1838, 6 chns, by Gilbert and Tayspill, Colchester; foot/b'way, waterbodies, building names, park, woods (by name).

12/147 Grinstead (parish) TM 028250 [Greenstead]
Apt 18.07.1839; 675a (?); Map 1838, 3 chns, 1st cl, by E. Corfield; construction lines, waterbodies, houses, woods, gardens, building names, green, ornamental ground.

12/148 Hadleigh (parish) TQ 810869
Apt 15.07.1846; 2679a (2679); Map 1847?, 3 chns, 1st cl, by Alexander Doull; construction lines, waterbodies, houses, fences, field gates, old castle, drains. Apt omits some field names.

12/149 Hainault Forest (part of) (district in parish of Dagenham) TQ 478920
Apt 31.12.1851; 1524a (?); Map 1854?, 12 chns, by Pickering and Smith, 14, Whitehall Place; waterbodies, building names, road names, heath, farm. District is apportioned by holding; Apt omits land use.

12/150 Great Hallingbury (parish) TL 511196
Apt 04.05.1838; 2652a (2651); Map 1838, ?6 chns; waterbodies, houses, woods, parkland (in detail), green; scale has been corrected in pencil from 3 chns.

12/151 Little Hallingbury (parish) TL 509171
Apt 26.04.1838; 1612a (1612); Map 1838, 6 chns, by Chapman Son and Webb, 3 Arundel St, Strand; waterbodies, houses, woods (named), open fields, building names.

12/152 Halsted (parish) TL 815300 [Halstead]
Apt 06.09.1838; 5634a (all); Map 1840?, 4 chns; waterbodies, houses, woods, plantations, parkland, orchards, hops, heath/moor, field gates, building names, road names, mill, workhouse, greens; pictorial church.

12/153 East Ham (parish) TQ 427832
Apt 26.04.1838; 2455a (all); Map 1838, 8 chns, by Chapman Son and Webb, Arundel St, Strand; waterbodies, houses, woods, drains.

12/154 West Ham (parish) TQ 402826
Apt 06.03.1852; 4390a (5390); Map 1852, 2 chns, in 2 parts, ? by William Dean, Stratford, (includes index); railways, waterbodies, houses, drains; bridge named; built-up parts generalised. (The map in PRO IR 30 is a copy; original is in PRO IR 77/12.)

12/155 East Hanningfield (parish) TL 768015
Apt 11.06.1840; 2446a (2446); Map 1840, 4 chns, by Mich. Jno. Mason; waterbodies, houses, woods, common.

12/156 South Hanningfield (parish) TQ 735985
Apt 03.05.1837; 1527a (all); Map 1843, 4 chns, in 2 parts, by Robt Baker, Writtle, Essex, (including index, from Chapman and Andre's map of Essex); foot/b'way, waterbodies, houses, plantations (col, named), heath/moor, sand or stone pits.

12/157 West Hanningfield (parish) TL 731003
Apt 20.08.1844; 2819a (2818); Map 1845, 4 chns, by Robert Baker, Writtle, Essex; foot/b'way, waterbodies, houses, woods (col), plantations (col).

12/158 Harlow (parish) TL 480110
Apt 19.05.1848; 4000a (all); Map 1849?, 6 chns, in 2 parts, (includes town separately at 3 chns); railway, foot/b'way, waterbodies, houses, woods, plantations, parkland, building names, road names, green.

12/159 Harwich, St Nicholas (parish) TM 261326 [Harwich]
Apt 22.02.1843; 57a (all); Map 1843, 2 chns, by E. and G.N. Driver, Parliament St, London; hill-drawing, foot/b'way, waterbodies, houses, building names, road names, circular redoubt, magazine, ordnance depot, light houses, guard house, batteries, cement factory, drains, high water marks, jetties, esplanade.

12/160 Kings Hatfield, otherwise Hatfield Broadoak (parish) TL 545165 [Hatfield Broad Oak]
Apt 22.12.1838; 8760a (8810); Map 1838, 6 chns; waterbodies, houses, woods, parkland, open fields, fences, building names, heath, green.

12/161 Hatfield Peverel (parish) TL 794119
Apt 22.01.1841; 4729a (all); Map 1841?, 6 chns; foot/b'way, waterbodies, houses, woods (col), parkland.

12/162 Havering, and part of Romford (parish) TQ 510930 [Havering-atte-Bower]
Apt 11.05.1844; 7840a (9173); Map 1845, 6 chns, by Messrs Crawter, Cobham, Surrey and Southampton Buildings, Chancery Lane; waterbodies, houses, woods, parkland, building names.

12/163 Hawkwell or Hackwell (parish) TQ 854918
Apt 25.09.1838; 1354a (1353); Map 1838, 3 chns, 1st cl, by Gilbert and Tayspill, Colchester; construction lines, foot/b'way, waterbodies, houses, woods, plantations.

12/164 Hazeleigh (parish) TL 836039
Apt 27.07.1844; 974a (all); Map 1845, 6 chns, 'corrected Map from a survey made by J. Polley junr in 1814' by Robt Baker, Writtle, Essex; waterbodies, houses, woods (named), plantations.

12/165 Hempsted (parish) TL 646386 [Hempstead]
Apt 03.05.1842; 3566a (all); Map 1842?, 5 chns; waterbodies, houses, woods (col).

12/166 Henham (parish) TL 545285
Apt 21.03.1840; 2958a (2958); Map 1840, 3 chns, by J. King and Son, Saffron Walden; waterbodies, houses, woods, open fields (named), building names, vicarage, windmill (pictorial), greens (col); mapmaker notes that the dotted lines show the balks in the common fields.

12/167 Great Henny (parish) TL 871379
Apt 26.11.1840; 1096a (1120); Map 1840?, 4 chns, by H. Coates, 12, Duke Street, Portland Place, London; houses, woods, open fields, field boundary ownerships, drains.

12/168 Little Henny (parish) TL 860385 [Not listed]
Apt 10.05.1839; 410a (all); Map 1839?, 4 chns, made in 1808 and 1810 and copied by J. Hasoll, Sudbury; waterbodies, woods (named), parkland, boundary trees, glebe; table lists owners, occupiers, property names and acreages. Apt omits some field names.

12/169 Heybridge (parish) TL 860083
Apt 18.05.1843; 2013a (all); Map 1846?, 6 chns, in 2 parts, (includes village separately at 3 chns); waterbodies, houses, woods.

12/170 Heydon (parish) TL 432410
Apt 26.04.1838; 1226a (2470); Map 1839, [8 chns]; waterbodies, woods, plantations, church yard, gravel pit, ornamental ground.

12/171 Hockley (parish) TQ 826942
Apt 12.05.1843; 4614a (all); Map 1840, 3 chns, 1st cl, in 2 parts, by A. Doull, Chatham, (includes index); waterbodies, houses, field gates, building names, vicarage, drains. Apt omits some field names.

12/172 Great Holland (parish) TM 216191
Apt 23.06.1838; 2064a (all); Map 1839, [3 chns]; by Alfred Rush, Messing; waterbodies, woods (col); compass rose is tinted gold; oak branches, oak leaves, acorns and ribbon, with gilding, appear beneath title.

12/173 Little Holland (parish) TM 202163 [Holland-on-Sea]
Apt 27.06.1839; 647a (all); Map 1840, 6 chns; hill-drawing, waterbodies, field gates, coastline, coastal embankments, drains, church ruins.

12/174 Holyfield, Upshire and Waltham (township and hamlet in parish of Waltham Holy Cross) TL 405015
Apt 24.02.1841; 7893a (?); Map 3 chns, surveyed in the year 1823-4 'and corrected according to the several alterations up to the year 1842', by H. Crawter and Sons, Cheshunt, Herts; canal, waterbodies, houses, open fields, road names, boundary trees, woods (by name), greens, warren.

12/175 Great Horkesley (parish) TL 977312
Apt 27.05.1840; 3084a (all); Map 1840?, 6 chns, by Gilbert and Tayspill, Colchester; waterbodies, houses, woods, plantations, building names, parsonage. Apt omits land use.

12/176 Little Horkesley (parish) TL 959323
Apt 11.12.1845; 1030a (all); Map 1848?, 4 chns, in 2 parts (including common meadows at 3 chns); waterbodies, houses, woods, common meadows (named).

12/177 Hornchurch and Romford (part of) (parish) TQ 532858
Apt 05.12.1848; 6659a (6799); Map 1849?, 6 chns, in 3 parts, by Washbourne and Keen, 8 Cannon Row, Westminster, (includes enlargement of Romford town at 1 chn and village of Hornchurch at 2 chns); railways, foot/b'way, waterbodies, houses, open fields, building names. (The map in PRO IR 30 is a copy; original is in PRO IR 77/13.)

12/178 East Horndon (parish) TQ 637896
Apt 11.12.1845; 1477a (all); Map 1846?, 4 chns; waterbodies, woods, parkland, windmill (pictorial), churchyard.

12/179 Horndon on the Hill (parish) TQ 669837
Apt 30.12.1840; 2635a (2634); Map 1839, 6 chns; proposed railway, foot/b'way, waterbodies, houses, woods, building names.

12/180 Hutton (parish) TQ 632945
Apt 19.04.1838; 1699a (all); Map 1838, 8 chns, by Robt Baker, Writtle, Essex; waterbodies, woods (col), building names, poorhouse, rectory, avenues of trees.

12/181 Little Ilford (parish) TQ 427860
Apt 28.02.1839; 764a (all); Map 1839, 3 chns, by James Renshaw, 8 Union Court O.B.S; railway, foot/b'way, waterbodies, building names, drains.

12/182 Ingatestone (parish) TQ 633993
Apt 21.02.1839; 2678a (2678); Map 1839, 4 chns, by Henry Clayton; foot/b'way, waterbodies, ornamental ground. Apt omits some field names.

12/183 Ingrave (parish) TQ 633926
Apt 30.04.1839; 1793a (all); Map 1839, 3 chns, by M.J. Mason; waterbodies, houses, woods, plantations, parkland, orchards.

12/184 Inworth (parish) TL 879169
Apt 07.05.1838; 1555a (all); Map 1838, 4 chns, by A. Rush, Messing, Essex; construction lines, waterbodies, houses, woods (col), boundary trees.

12/185 Kelvedon (parish) TL 854187
Apt 31.01.1838; 3168a (all); Map 1839, 6 chns; foot/b'way, waterbodies, houses, field boundary ownerships, building names, woods (by name); meadows named.

12/186 Kelvedon Hatch (parish) TQ 565995
Apt 09.03.1837; 1666a (1665); Map 1837?, 8 chns, 'compiled from the plans of the landowners' ? by John Prujean; foot/b'way, woods; colours may show property ownerships. District is apportioned by holding; Apt omits land use.

12/187 Kirby le Soken (parish) TM 219208 [Kirby-le-Soken]
Apt 30.04.1840; 4758a (all); Map 1841, 3 chns, by Jay and Ruffell; waterbodies; pecked lines appear inside some field perimeters, possibly indicating ploughing margins or space taken by hedges or ditches; colours may show property ownerships.

12/188 Laindon (parish) TQ 687899
Apt 23.01.1838; 2373a (all); Map 1840?, 3 chns, in 4 parts, by John Hills, Billericay, Essex; construction lines, waterbodies, houses, field boundary ownerships, field gates, drains.

12/189 Laindon Hills (parish) TQ 680870 [Not listed]
Apt 30.04.1841; 1776a (all); Map 1840, 4 chns, by Thomas Bird; waterbodies, woods.

12/190 Lamarsh (parish) TL 888358
Apt 20.08.1839; 1246a (all); Map 1839, 4 chns, by J.S. Surridge, Feering; Essex; waterbodies, woods, plantations, open fields.

12/191 Lambourne (parish) TQ 480960
Apt 20.05.1841; 2441a (2440); Map 1841?, 6 chns, in 2 parts, (includes village at 3 chns); foot/b'way, waterbodies, houses, woods, plantations, osiers.

12/192 Langenhoe (parish) TM 019174
Apt 19.12.1838; 2104a (all); Map 1841?, 6 chns; waterbodies, houses, woods, field boundary ownerships, building names, parsonage, drains.

12/193 Langford (parish) TL 838090
Apt 31.01.1838; 1076a (all); Map 1839?, 3 chns, by Robert Baker, Writtle, Essex; foot/b'way, waterbodies, houses, woods (col, named), orchards, marsh/bog, building names, parsonage, osiers.

12/194 Langham (parish) TM 024318
Apt 28.04.1838; 2896a (2896); Map 1838, 6 chns, in 2 parts, by Gilbert and Tayspill, Colchester, (including 'lands subject to modus' at 3 chns); waterbodies, woods, plantations, open fields, field names. Apt omits land use.

12/195 Langley (parish) TL 438345
Apt 25.04.1838; 1618a (all); Map 1838, 6 chns, 'copied from a plan made in the year 1783 belonging to the Governors of Christ Hospital'; waterbodies, woods, heath/moor (col), open fields (col), building names, field names, green.

12/196 Latchingdon cum Lawling (parish) TQ 893993
Apt 05.03.1839; 3672a (all); Map 1841?, 3 chns, ? by Robert Baker; construction lines, waterbodies, houses, woods (col), plantations (col), sluice, drains.

12/197 Latton (parish) TL 468095 [Latton Bush]
Apt 17.12.1838; 1606a (all); Map 1839, 3 chns, by Gabriel Fleck; foot/b'way, turnpike roads, cart roads, carriage roads, waterbodies, common, houses, building names, road names, priory, assembly rooms, vicarage, ice cellar, mill.

12/198 High Laver (parish) TL 522092
Apt 17.03.1847; 1894a (all); Map 1848?, 6 chns; waterbodies, houses (by shading), woods, building names, rectory, old workhouse, green.

12/199 Little Laver (parish) TL 545095
Apt 17.03.1847; 968a (all); Map 1848, 3 chns, by H. Crawter and Sons, Cheshunt, Herts; waterbodies, houses, woods.

12/200 Magdalen Laver (parish) TL 510080
Apt 17.03.1847; 1229a (all); Map 1847, 3 chns, by H. Crawter and Sons, Cheshunt, (tinted); waterbodies, houses.

12/201 Lawford (parish) TM 090310
Apt 15.06.1839; 2679a (all); Map 1839, 6 chns, in 2 parts, by Gilbert and Tayspill, Colchester, (includes Manningtree town at 3 chns); waterbodies, woods, parkland, sand or stone pit, drains; bridge named.

12/202 Layer Breton (parish) TL 945186
Apt 24.08.1842; 955a (all); Map 1842, 3 chns, by Gilbert and Tayspill, Colchester; waterbodies, houses, heath; scale is not figured.

12/203 Layer-de-la-haye (parish) TL 970190 [Layer de la Haye]
Apt 27.03.1838; 2577a (2577); Map 1838, 3 chns, by Gilbert and Tayspill, Colchester; waterbodies, woods, heath/moor.

12/204 Layer Marney (parish) TL 933173
Apt 20.09.1838; 1973a (1973); Map 1838, 3 chns, compiled partly from old surveys, by Gilbert and Tayspill, Colchester; foot/b'way, waterbodies, woods, plantations, orchards, heath/moor, building names, parsonage, gravel pit, glebe, green.

12/205 Leaden Roothing (parish) TL 594132 [Leaden Roding]
Apt 30.04.1846; 907a (all); Map 1839, 3 chns, by J. Bailey Denton, 9 Grays Inn Square; waterbodies, houses, woods, field gates, building names, rectory, pound.

12/206 Lee Chapel (extra-parochial place) TQ 691881
Apt 03.07.1846; 482a (all); Map 1846, 3 chns, by John Hills, Billericay; waterbodies, houses, woods.

12/207 Leigh (parish) TQ 837867 [Leigh-on-Sea]
Apt 15.07.1846; 2297a (all); Map 1839, 3 chns, 1st cl, by Alex. Doull, Chatham; construction lines, waterbodies, houses, fences, field gates, rectory, drains.

12/208 Great Leighs (parish) TL 735161
Apt 18.05.1838; 3126a (3125); Map 1839?, 4 chns; foot/b'way, waterbodies, woods (named), plantations, building names.

12/209 Little Leighs (parish) TL 715171
Apt 22.12.1838; 1080a (all); Map 1839?, 3 chns, by Rt Baker, Writtle; foot/b'way, waterbodies, houses, woods, plantations, building names, parsonage, priory.

12/210 Lexden (parish) TL 972254
Apt 30.04.1838; 2312a (?); Map 1839?, 4 chns, 'copy from an old survey 1821' by Gilbert and Tayspill, Colchester; hill-drawing, foot/b'way, houses, woods, plantations, building names, road names, mound, park.

12/211 Leyton (parish) TQ 388875
Apt 02.11.1839; 2241a (2241); Map 1841?, 3 chns, 1st cl, by Carlos and Fitzgerald, Hanover Chambers, Buckingham St, Adelphi; construction lines, railways, waterbodies, houses, woods, parkland, open fields, building names, workhouse, nursery, green. (The map in PRO IR 30 is a copy; original is in PRO IR 77/14.)

12/212 Lindsell (parish) TL 644276
Apt 24.06.1845; 1959a (all); Map 1838, 3 chns, by John King and Son, Saffron Walden; construction lines, waterbodies, houses, woods, plantations, hedge ownership, fence ownership, building names, green.

12/213 Liston (parish) TL 851449
Apt 13.04.1839; 632a (all); Map 1841?, 3 chns; waterbodies, open fields.

12/214 Loughton (parish) TQ 428968
Apt 21.02.1850; 3944a (3170); Map 1850, 4 chns; hill-drawing, foot/b'way, waterbodies, woods, parkland, field boundary ownerships, building

names, road names, sand or stone pits, milestones, quarries, green; physical features and bridge named; colour bands may relate to glebe land and tithing practice. Apt has incomplete cropping information.

12/215 Maldon, All Saints (parish) TL 848070 [Not listed]
Apt 21.01.1848; 56a (all); Map 1848, 1 chn, by N.L. Valpy, Chelmsford; waterbodies, woods, plantations, orchards, building names, road names, landowners, town hall, churchyard, pump, public pond, pound, yards, gardens (by annotation). Apt omits some field names.

12/216 Maldon, St Mary (parish) TL 859058 [Not listed]
Apt 31.07.1843; 1348a (1827); Map 1843, 4 chns, by Robt Baker, Writtle, Essex; waterbodies, houses, low water mark, saltings, drains, high water mark spring tides, mudflats; built-up parts generalised.

12/217 Maldon, St Peter (parish) TL 838065 [Not listed]
Apt 22.02.1840; 1627a (1626); Map 1838, 3 chns, by James Beadel, Witham; hill-drawing, foot/b'way, waterbodies, houses, woods, plantations, building names, pound, grange, mill, river embankments, abbey, sand or stone pit, artificial drainage channels, rope walk, Quaker Meeting House, meeting house, windmill.

12/218 Manuden (parish) TL 480270
Apt 03.06.1839; 2488a (2486); Map 1840, 6 chns, by J.A. Nockolds, Stansted, Essex; waterbodies, woods, plantations, building names, green.

12/219 Great Maplestead (parish) TL 817345
Apt 30.04.1840; 1901a (1929); Map 1840?, 3 chns, by H. Coates, 12 Duke Street, Portland Place, London; waterbodies, houses, woods, plantations, hops, field boundary ownerships, building names.

12/220 Little Maplestead (parish) TL 830340
Apt 16.05.1839; 1063a (1062); Map 1840?, 6 chns; waterbodies, houses, woods, hops, building names.

12/221 Margaret Roothing (parish) TL 597117 [Margaret Roding]
Apt 14.01.1845; 1222a (all); Map 1844?, 3 chns; waterbodies, houses, woods, plantations.

12/222 Margaretting (parish) TL 677022
Apt 19.12.1837; 2260a (2259); Map 1838?, 3 chns, by Baker, Writtle; waterbodies, woods, plantations, building names, parsonage.

12/223 Marks Tey (parish) TL 907232
Apt 24.07.1841; 1214a (1214); Map 1838, 6 chns, by Gilbert and Tayspill, Colchester; railway, waterbodies, woods, building names.

12/224 Marks Hall (parish) TL 841255 [Markshall]
Apt 03.12.1839; 805a (all); Map 1842, 3 chns; foot/b'way, waterbodies, houses, woods, plantations, parkland (in detail), fence ownership, field boundary ownerships, field gates, building names, gravel pit, brick kiln, rectory, dog kennel, chapel, ice house, deer leap, kitchen garden, trig. points, avenue of trees.

12/225 Mashbury (parish) TL 651119
Apt 15.07.1846; 816a (all); Map 1847?, 3 chns, by Robt Baker, Writtle, Essex; waterbodies, houses, woods (col).

12/226 Matching (parish) TL 522118
Apt 12.11.1840; 2385a (all); Map 1840, 3 chns; waterbodies, houses, woods (col), plantations (col), parkland, hedge ownership, greens.

12/227 Mayland (parish) TL 922010
Apt 21.10.1837; 2030a (2030); Map 1838, 3 chns, in 2 parts, corrected from a survey made in 1813; waterbodies, houses, woods, windmill (pictorial).

12/228 East Mersea (parish) TM 041146
Apt 02.11.1837; 1958a (3857); Map 1838, 4 chns, compiled from old surveys by Gilbert and Tayspill, Colchester; waterbodies, woods, plantations, building names, parsonage, drains coastline, embankments, 'church land'. Apt omits land use.

12/229 West Mersea (parish) TM 024142
Apt 27.12.1839; 3365a (4415); Map 1838, 3 chns, 1st cl, by W. Ruffell; woods, plantations, field names, marshland, saltings; colours may show property ownerships; map has note of adoption with landowners' signatures. (The map in PRO IR 30 is a copy; original is in PRO IR 77/15.)

12/230 Messing (parish) TL 897183
Apt 12.06.1839; 2550a (2549); Map 1839, 3 chns, by Alfred Rush, Messing; waterbodies, woods (col), waste, heath.

12/231 Middleton (parish) TL 872396
Apt 30.10.1839; 875a (all); Map 1840?, 3 chns, by H. Coates, 12 Duke Street, Portland Place, London; foot/b'way, waterbodies, houses, woods, open fields, field boundary ownerships, road names, landowners, boundary posts, greens; colours may show property ownerships.

12/232 Mistley (parish) TM 112300
Apt 30.11.1841; 2116a (2115); Map 1843?, 3 chns; foot/b'way, waterbodies, houses, woods (col), parkland, building names, road names, workhouse, old church ruins, glebe; some built-up parts generalised.

12/233 Moreton (parish) TL 544073
Apt 30.11.1838; 1421a (all); Map 1839, 3 chns, surveyed by Messrs Clayton of Ingatestone and copied by Robt Baker, Writtle; waterbodies, houses, woods (col), plantations (col).

12/234 Mount Bures (parish) TL 910320
Apt 09.10.1838; 1386a (1404); Map 1839?, [4 chns], ? by S.L. Bransby, Ipswich; waterbodies, houses, woods, arable (col), grassland (col), open fields, windmill (pictorial); pictorial church. Apt omits land use.

12/235 Mountnessing (parish) TQ 649966
Apt 12.09.1838; 941a (4005); Map 1840?, 4 chns; waterbodies, road names, churchyard. Apt omits some field names.

12/236 Mucking (parish) TQ 682810
Apt 02.04.1845; 2146a (all); Map 1846, 6 chns, in 3 parts, by Messrs Crawter, Cobham, Surrey and Southampton Buildings, Chancery Lane, London, (includes index); waterbodies, houses, woods, building names, drains, heath.

12/237 Mundon (parish) TL 887032
Apt 05.12.1839; 3761a (4295); Map 1840, 4 chns, by Robt Baker, Writtle, Essex; construction lines, waterbodies, houses, woods, plantations, grassland (col), marsh/bog (col), building names, vicarage, parsonage, drains, embankment wall.

12/238 Navestock (parish) TQ 540970 [Not listed]
Apt 21.07.1838; 4329a (all); Map 1838, 4 chns, by T. and H. Crawter; foot/b'way, waterbodies, woods, plantations, parkland; bridge named.

12/239 Nazeing (parish) TL 403062
Apt 17.03.1847; 3894a (3893); Map 1848, 3 chns, by H. Crawter and Sons, Cheshunt, Herts; waterbodies, houses, woods, open fields.

12/240 Netteswell (parish) TL 460095
Apt 18.08.1837; 1360a (1521); Map 1840?, 3 chns; foot/b'way, waterbodies, houses, woods, plantations, open fields, field boundary ownerships, building names, road names, field name, mill, rectory, bury, common, green.

12/241 Nevendon (parish) TQ 731904
Apt 16.05.1842; 992a (all); Map 1841?, 3 chns, by John Hills, Billericay, Essex; construction lines, waterbodies, houses, woods (col), field boundary ownerships, field gates.

12/242 Newland, St Lawrence (parish) TL 959042 [St Lawrence]
Apt 28.04.1837; 2032a (all); Map 1838?, 3 chns, by Robt Baker, Writtle; waterbodies, woods (col), plantations (col), building names, old sea walls, drains, rectory, saltings.

12/243 Newport (parish) TL 519341
Apt 14.12.1839; 1714a (1714); Map 1840, 3 chns, by J. King and Son, Saffron Walden; foot/b'way, waterbodies, woods, parkland, open fields (named), building names, vicarage, windmill (pictorial), common; open strip boundaries are solid green; green tint may show tithe-free land.

12/244 Cold Norton (parish) TL 843001
Apt 23.02.1839; 1651a (1651); Map 1839?, 6 chns, by Walter J. Ray; waterbodies, houses, woods, hedge ownership, fence ownership, field gates, building names, rectory, glebe boundary; colours may show property ownerships.

12/245 Norton Mandeville (parish) TL 590048
Apt 20.04.1847; 757a (757); Map 1847, 4 chns, based on a 'copy of map made by T. Skinner in 1840 with alterations and corrections...in 1847', by R. Baker, Writtle, Essex; turnpike roads, tollbar, waterbodies, houses, woods, plantations, building names, heath.

12/246 Black Notley (parish) TL 759202
Apt 11.10.1837; 1937a (all); Map 1838, 4 chns, by Robt Baker, Writtle, Essex; foot/b'way, waterbodies, woods (named), orchards, building names.

12/247 White Notley (parish) TL 781186
Apt 15.08.1839; 2228a (2228); Map 1840?, 4 chns; foot/b'way, turnpike roads, waterbodies, woods (col, named), building names.

12/248 Great Oakley (parish) TM 195275
Apt 15.02.1842; 3050a (3049); Map 1841, 3 chns, 1st cl, by Bowron and Harris; construction lines, foot/b'way, waterbodies, houses. Apt omits land use.

12/249 Little Oakley (parish) TM 219288
Apt 29.06.1839; 1029a (all); Map 1838, 3 chns, by John Bull, 16 Tavistock St, Covent Garden, London; construction lines, foot/b'way, waterbodies, houses, woods, plantations, hedge ownership, field gates, building names, road names, sluice, saltings, kiln, ornamental ground; bridge named.

12/250 North Ockendon (parish) TQ 588849
Apt 27.07.1840; 1698a (all); Map 1841, 3 chns, by Messrs Crawter; construction lines, hill-drawing, foot/b'way, waterbodies, houses, woods, building names, ornamental ground.

12/251 South Ockenden (parish) TQ 600830
Apt 04.11.1839; 2907a (all); Map 1840, 6 chns, in 2 parts, by Gilbert and Tayspill, Colchester, (includes village separately at 3 chns); waterbodies, woods, plantations, marsh/bog.

12/252 High Onger (parish) TL 580030 [High Ongar]
Apt 21.01.1848; 4510a (all); Map 1848, 3 chns, by Jonathan Lewis and Son, Bobbingworth, Essex; construction lines, waterbodies, houses, field gates, building names, rectory, mill, 'clap gates', green, common.

12/253 Orsett (except Orsett Hamlet) (parish) TQ 641823
Apt 19.11.1839; 4134a (all); Map 1840?, 6 chns; waterbodies, woods, plantations. Apt omits land use.

12/254 Orsett (hamlet in parish of Orsett) TL 696010 [Not listed]
Apt 18.05.1849; 850a (?); Map 1849?, 6 chns; waterbodies, woods, building names, common.

12/255 Ovington (parish) TL 768424
Apt 23.11.1838; 705a (all); Map 1839, 6 chns, by J. Hasell, Sudbury; waterbodies, houses, fences, building names, boundary trees; pictorial church.

12/256 Paglesham (parish) TQ 930930 [Paglesham Churchend]
Apt 09.03.1838; 2129a (all); Map 1838, 3 chns, by James Beadel, Witham; construction lines, waterbodies, houses, woods, fences, field boundary ownerships, building names, brick kiln, parsonage, embankment, drains.

12/257 Panfield (parish) TL 736252
Apt 10.09.1838; 1476a (all); Map 1838, 4 chns, by John King and Son, Saffron Walden; construction lines, waterbodies, houses, woods, hops, field boundary ownerships, building names, rectory, priory.

12/258 Great Parndon (parish) TL 435085
Apt 14.03.1844; 2211a (all); Map 1845?, 4 chns, construction lines, trig points, waterbodies, houses, woods, plantations, open fields.

12/259 Little Parndon (parish) TL 445110
Apt 31.08.1841; 522a (all); Map 1841, 3 chns, by Gabriel Fleck; railway, waterbodies, houses, building names, road names, rectory, mill.

12/260 Pattiswick (parish) TL 816240
Apt 08.02.1842; 1297a (1297); Map 1842, 3 chns, 'copied from an old Survey and Modernized' by J.S. Surridge, Coggeshall; foot/b'way, waterbodies, woods, plantations.

12/261 Pebmarsh (parish) TL 853336
Apt 23.01.1839; 2023a (all); Map 1839, 6 chns, litho (Standidge); waterbodies, building names.

12/262 Peldon (parish) TL 993163
Apt 26.02.1840; 2187a (all); Map 1838, 3 chns, by R.E. Sheldrake, Colchester; construction lines, trig points, foot/b'way, waterbodies, marsh/bog, boundary posts, drains.

12/263 Pentlow (parish) TL 810450
Apt 20.09.1838; 1847a (1847); Map 1839?, 3 chns; foot/b'way, woods, plantations, parkland, orchards, gardens, fences, field gates, building names, road names, boundary trees, rectory, drains.

12/264 Pitsea (parish) TQ 737881
Apt 25.11.1847; 2043a (all); Map 1845, 3 chns, in 4 parts, by John Hills, Billericay, (includes 40-chn index, 'taken from the Ordnance Map'); construction lines, foot/b'way, waterbodies, houses, woods (col), field boundary ownerships, field gates, building names, sluice, windmill (by symbol), mill, walls, wharf, drains.

12/265 Pleshey (parish) TL 661142
Apt 15.07.1846; 726a (all); Map 1848, 6 chns, litho (by S. Straker, 80, Bishopsgate St, London); waterbodies, woods, building names.

12/266 Prittlewell (except Canvey Island) (parish) TQ 876868
Apt 19.11.1840; 6591a (?); Map 1840?, 3 chns, 1st cl, by A. Doull; construction lines, waterbodies, houses, fences, field gates, building names, road names, hotel, windmill, drains; pictorial church (The map in PRO IR 30 is a copy; original is in PRO IR 77/16.)

12/267 Purleigh (parish) TL 840020
Apt 21.03.1846; 5579a (all); Map 1848, 8 chns, in 2 parts, by Robt Baker, Writtle, Essex, (includes 40-chn index taken from Chapman and Andre's map of Essex); hill-drawing, waterbodies, houses, woods, plantations, embankments, drains, commons, marshes.

12/268 Quendon (parish) TL 519312
Apt 21.01.1839; 644a (all); Map 1838, 3 chns, by John King and Son, Saffron Walden; construction lines, turnpike roads, toll bar, waterbodies, houses, woods, plantations, parkland (in detail), orchards, hedge ownership, fence ownership, building names, road names, rectory, churchyard.

12/269 Radwinter (parish) TL 610376
Apt 10.12.1838; 3803a (3802); Map 1839, 3 chns, by J. King and Son, Saffron Walden; waterbodies, houses, woods, building names, tile kiln, rectory, grange, green.

12/270 Rainham (parish) TQ 541829
Apt 31.12.1838; 3197a (3312); Map 1839, 4 chns; waterbodies, drains.

12/271 Ramsden Bellhouse (parish) TQ 713950
Apt 31.10.1839; 2686a (2685); Map 1839, 3 chns, by John Hills, Billericay, Essex; construction lines, foot/b'way, waterbodies, houses, woods (col), field boundary ownerships, field gates, windmill (by symbol).

12/272 Ramsden Crays (parish) TQ 705936 [Not listed]
Apt 09.06.1845; 1454a (all); Map 1845, 3 chns, by John Hills, Billericay; construction lines, foot/b'way, waterbodies, houses, woods, field boundary ownerships, field gates.

12/273 Ramsey (parish) TM 2103341
Apt 22.07.1845; 5238a (6693); Map 'working plan', 1846?, 3 chns, 1st cl, in 3 parts, by G.R. Jay; construction lines, waterbodies, woods, plantations, building names, drains.

12/274 Rawreth (parish) TQ 783932
Apt 24.04.1838; 2377a (2377); Map surveyed in 1830 and revised in 1838, 3 chns, 1st cl; construction lines, foot/b'way, waterbodies, houses, field boundary ownerships, field gates, commons.

12/275 Rayleigh (parish) TQ 806910
Apt 16.10.1840; 2874a (all); Map 1839, 3 chns, 1st cl, by Alex. Doull, Chatham; construction lines, waterbodies, houses, building names, road names, windmill, mound.

12/276 Rayne (parish) TL 723233
Apt 12.09.1837; 1676a (all); Map 1838, 3 chns, by J. King and Son, Saffron Walden; waterbodies, houses, woods, hops, building names; part of wood is noted as claimed as extra-parochial by the owner.

12/277 Rettendon (parish) TQ 780970
Apt 12.11.1838; 3933a (all); Map 1838, 3 chns, 1st cl, by William Browne for R.J. Wright, Norwich; construction lines, waterbodies, houses, woods, field gates, building names, rectory, windmill (by symbol), commons.

12/278 Rickling (parish) TL 503310
Apt 17.02.1838; 1332a (all); Map 1839, 6 chns, by Messrs Nockolds and Son, Stansted, Essex; foot/b'way, waterbodies, houses, woods, plantations, building names, green.

12/279 Ridgewell (parish) TL 735410
Apt 23.04.1839; 1717a (1717); Map 1840, 6 chns; waterbodies, woods, building names, road names, vicarage, windmill (pictorial), greens; pictorial church.

12/280 Rivenhall (parish) TL 823186
Apt 28.02.1838; 3590a (3589); Map 1839, 3 chns, by Alfred Rush, Messing; railway, waterbodies, woods (col), plantations (col); scale statement is on ribbon.

12/281 Rochford (parish) TQ 865905
Apt 22.06.1838; 1856a (all); Map 1840?, 3 chns, 1st cl, by Alex. Doull; construction lines, waterbodies, houses, fences.

12/282 High Roothing (parish) TL 602170 [High Roding]
Apt 12.06.1839; 1803a (1803); Map 1838, 3 chns, 1st cl, by Robert Burton, Hatfield Broad-Oak; construction lines, trig points, waterbodies, houses, woods, hedges, fences, building names, green; mapmaker notes amendments to boundaries following boundary disputes with neighbouring parishes.

12/283 White Roothing and Morrell (parish) TL 565137
Apt 03.06.1839; 2521a (all); Map 1837, 3 chns, 1st cl, by Robert Burton; construction lines, foot/b'way, waterbodies, woods (named), fences, field gates, building names, field names, ruin, rectory, village barn, school, property names, orchards (by annotation), gardens (by annotation), barns, glebe.

12/284 Roxwell (parish) TL 640090
Apt 21.03.1839; 4755a (4755); Map 1842?, 4 chns; waterbodies, woods (named), parkland, building names, greens.

12/285 Roydon (parish) TL 412092
Apt 25.07.1843; 2996a (2995); Map 1839, 3 chns, by John Doyley Senr, Belgrave Str, New Road; railway, foot/b'way, canal with lock, waterbodies, houses, woods, open fields (named), field gates, building names, road names, mill, weir, drains, common, green, hamlet boundary.

12/286 Runwell (parish) TQ 760960
Apt 10.06.1845; 2059a (all); Map 1845, 3 chns, in 3 parts, by Messrs Crawter, Cobham, Surrey and Southampton Buildings, Chancery Lane, London, (includes index); waterbodies, houses, woods, hedge ownership, building names, road names.

12/287 Saffron Walden (parish) TL 550390
Apt 06.04.1842; 7417a (7416); Map 1843, 8 chns; waterbodies, houses, woods, parkland, building names, museum, castle; built-up parts generalised.

12/288 Salcott (parish) TL 951135
Apt 08.09.1840; 256a (all); Map 1839, 3 chns, by Robt E. Sheldrake, Colchester; waterbodies, houses, road names.

12/289 Great Saling (parish) TL 707250
Apt 26.03.1839; 1651a (all); Map 1838, 3 chns, by John King and Son, Saffron Walden; foot/b'way, waterbodies, houses, woods, plantations, hops, building names, vicarage, osiers.

12/290 Great Sampford (parish) TL 640360
Apt 03.05.1842; 2225a (all); Map 1836, 6 chns, by John King and Son, Saffron Walden; foot/b'way, waterbodies, houses, woods, building names, osiers, drains.

12/291 New Sampford (parish) TL 653333 [Little Sampford]
Apt 23.04.1839; 2778a (all); Map 1839, 6 chns, by John King and Son, Saffron Walden; waterbodies, houses, woods, parkland, building names, rectory.

12/292 Sandon (parish) TL 754038
Apt 03.02.1843; 2278a (all); Map 1842?, 4 chns, by Robert Baker, Writtle, Essex; waterbodies, woods, plantations, parkland (named), sand or stone pit.

12/293 Sewardstone (hamlet in parish of Waltham Holy Cross) TQ 405989
Apt 17.03.1847; 2985a (?); Map 3.5 chns, 'surveyed in the years 1823-4 and corrected according to the several alterations up to the year 1847' by H. Crawter and Sons, Cheshunt, Herts; waterbodies, houses, open fields, forest.

12/294 Shalford (parish) TL 720280
Apt 13.07.1846; 2456a (2455); Map 1846, 6 chns, by John Savill, Sible Hedingham, and litho (by S. Straker, 80 Bishopgate St. Within); waterbodies, woods, plantations, parkland (named), building names, mill, parsonage.

12/295 Sheering (parish) TL 503142
Apt 30.04.1840; 1628a (1628); Map 1840?, 3 chns; railway, foot/b'way, waterbodies, houses, woods, plantations, open fields, hedges, field gates.

12/296 Shelley (parish) TL 554050
Apt 28.02.1837; 600a (600); Map '1814', (1839?), 3 chns, by J. Barnard, Dunmow, Essex; waterbodies, woods, heath/moor, common (col); colours may show property ownerships; the name Revd H. Soames appears in the title.

12/297 Shellow Bowells (parish) TL 601080
Apt 20.05.1837; 457a (457); Map 1837, 3 chns, by E. Corfield; waterbodies, houses, woods, plantations, orchards, field boundary ownerships; bridge named.

12/298 Shenfield (parish) TQ 605955
Apt 07.06.1838; 2398a (all); Map 1837, 3 chns; construction lines, hill-drawing, foot/b'way, waterbodies, building names, common.

12/299 North Shoebury (parish) TQ 940866
Apt 19.06.1838; 1087a (all); Map 1838, 3 chns, by Edwd Flowers; waterbodies, building names, tithe barn, vicarage.

12/300 South Shoebury (parish) TQ 939851 [Shoeburyness]
Apt 22.05.1838; 1011a (all); Map 1840?, 3 chns, 1st cl, by Alex. Doull; construction lines, waterbodies, houses, field gates, drains.

12/301 Shopland (parish) TQ 904888 [Not listed]
Apt 27.06.1839; 1040a (all); Map 1838, 3 chns, by E. Flowers; waterbodies, building names.

12/302 Sible Hedingham (parish) TL 765340
Apt 16.10.1839; 5395a (all); Map 1840?, 4 chns; waterbodies, houses, woods, hops, osiers, ornamental ground; it is unclear why some plots are numbered, coloured or outlined in red.

12/303 Shoreham (parish) TQ 881997
Apt 30.06.1841; 399a (all); Map 1840?, 3 chns, by Robert Baker, Writtle, Essex; foot/b'way, waterbodies, houses, plantations.

12/304 South Church (parish) TQ 910860 [Southchurch]
Apt 11.07.1838; 1880a (all); Map 1839, 3 chns, 1st cl, in 2 parts, by J. King and Son, Saffron Walden; construction lines, waterbodies, building names, rectory, spring, post, drains. (The map in PRO IR 30 is a copy; original is in PRO IR 77/17.)

12/305 Southminster (parish) TQ 980990
Apt 19.03.1842; 6262a (7701); Map 1842, 6 chns, in 2 parts, ? by Walter J. Ray, (includes village at 3 chns); foot/b'way, waterbodies, houses, orchards, fences, field boundary ownerships, field gates, building names, road names, embankment, saltings, vicarage, windmills (by symbol), pump, drains.

12/306 Springfield (parish) TL 728084 [Not listed]
Apt 09.01.1840; 2878a (2878); Map 1842?, 3 chns, by Robert Baker, Writtle; canal, waterbodies, houses, woods, plantations, osiers, marsh/bog, building names, convict goal.

12/307 Stambourne (parish) TL 715385
Apt 18.05.1843; 1842a (all); Map 1838, 6 chns, by Messrs Savill and Son, litho (by S. Straker, 118 Bishopgate Street); foot/b'way, waterbodies, woods, plantations, parkland, building names, rectory.

12/308 Great Stambridge (parish) TQ 910917
Apt 07.05.1840; 2545a (all); Map 1840, 3 chns, 1st cl, by Alex. Doull, Chatham; construction lines, waterbodies, houses, fences, field gates, boundary posts, drains; mapmaker notes that 'neither Roads, Lanes, nor Drains, included in the Fields'.

12/309 Little Stambridge (parish) TQ 888920 [Not listed]
Apt 08.11.1837; 600a (all); Map 1838, 3 chns, 1st cl, by Gilbert and Tayspill, Colchester; construction lines, waterbodies, building names, farm and property names, glebe.

12/310 Stanford-le-hope (parish) TQ 690830 [Stanford-le-Hope]
Apt 26.06.1840; 2415a (2984); Map 1839, 4 chns; waterbodies, houses, woods, heath/moor, building names, wharf, river embankments, sand or stone pit, green, drains.

12/311 Stanford Rivers (parish) TL 524013
Apt 31.01.1838; 4387a (4386); Map 1839, 3 chns, by Robert Hale; foot/b'way, waterbodies, houses, farmyards, woods (col, named), plantations (col), parkland, orchards, open fields, hedge ownership, building names, road names, workhouse, rectory, mill, windmill (by symbol); scale is stated in poles; tithe areas were originally lettered rather than numbered.

12/312 Stansted Mountfitchett and part of Ugley (parish) TL 520250 [Stansted Mountfitchet]
Apt 21.06.1842; 4193a (4193); Map 1843, 6 chns; waterbodies, houses, woods, plantations, parkland.

12/313 Stanway (parish) TL 952236
Apt 08.01.1840; 3368a (3368); Map 10 chns, surveyed by Messrs King and Cole in 1807 and 1808 and revised in 1839 by R.E. Sheldrake, Colchester; foot/b'way, turnpike roads, tollbar, waterbodies, houses, woods, plantations, parkland; bridge named.

12/314 Stapleford Abbotts (parish) TQ 503957
Apt 08.05.1844; 2332a (2331); Map 1845, 6 chns; waterbodies, houses, woods, plantations, osiers, marsh/bog, windmill (by symbol); bridge named.

12/315 Stapleford Tawney (parish) TQ 515993
Apt 23.08.1837; 1633a (all); Map 1838, 6 chns; waterbodies, woods, plantations, parkland, sand or stone pit, mill, common; bridge named.

12/316 Stebbing (parish) TL 673251
Apt 21.01.1839; 4301a (all); Map 1839?, 3 chns; waterbodies, woods, orchards, heath/moor, field boundary ownerships, building names, windmill (pictorial).

12/317 Steeple (parish) TL 933034
Apt 25.10.1839; 2804a (3434); Map 1839, 4 chns; foot/b'way, waterbodies, houses, woods, orchards, marsh/bog, field gates, building names, grange, abbey, bars, drains.

12/318 Steeple Bumpstead (parish) TL 689408
Apt 11.10.1839; 3296a (all); Map 1840, 3 chns, by J. Hasell, Sudbury; foot/b'way, waterbodies, houses, woods, plantations, parkland, orchards, field gates, building names, boundary trees, post, windmills (pictorial), brick kiln, green; pictorial church.

12/319 Stifford (parish) TQ 604803
Apt 22.12.1838; 1548a (all); Map 1838, 4 chns, by Messrs Crawter; foot/b'way, waterbodies, woods, osiers, marsh/bog, field gates, road names, landowners, sand or stone pit, quarry.

12/320 Stisted (parish) TL 800252
Apt 05.06.1840; 2912a (2967); Map 1839, 6 chns, by Newton and Woodrow, Norwich; foot/b'way, turnpike roads, waterbodies, houses, woods, plantations, parkland (in detail), fences, landowners; detached portions have location descriptions, signed by J.S. Surridge; pictorial church.

12/321 Stock (parish) TQ 687981
Apt 21.05.1841; 1849a (all); Map 1841, 4 chns, by Henry Clayton; foot/b'way, waterbodies, woods. Apt omits some field names.

12/322 Stondon Massey (parish) TL 582008
Apt 21.01.1848; 1121a (all); Map 1848, 3 chns, 1st cl, by J. Lewis and Son, Bobbingworth, Essex; construction lines, waterbodies, houses, woods (col), plantations (col).

12/323 Stowe Maries (parish) TQ 831982 [Stow Maries]
Apt 26.02.1839; 2445a (all); Map 1839?, 4 chns, by Robert Baker, Writtle, Essex; waterbodies, plantations (col, named), sea wall, high and low water marks, mudflats, saltings, drains.

12/324 Streethall (parish) TL 491405 [Not listed]
Apt 19.05.1848; 607a (all); Map 1848, 3 chns; waterbodies, houses, woods, open fields (named); open strips are shown with solid red lines.

12/325 Sturmer (parish) TL 692442
Apt 30.10.1839; 946a (945); Map 1841?, 6 chns, 'revised' by J. Hasell, Sudbury; waterbodies, houses, woods, plantations, orchards, gardens, marsh/bog, open fields, building names, boundary trees, green; pictorial church; colours may indicate land use.

12/326 Sutton (parish) TQ 890893 [Not listed]
Apt 26.05.1838; 721a (all); Map 1838?, 3 chns, by R.H. Jago, 74, Great Queen Street; construction lines, hill-drawing, waterbodies, houses, farmyards, woods, orchards, hedge ownership, fence ownership, field gates, embankments, trig points, boundary marks, farm and property names. Apt omits some field names.

12/327 Takeley (parish) TL 565223
Apt 27.07.1839; 3155a (all); Map 1838, 6 chns; foot/b'way, waterbodies, woods (named), plantations, hedge ownership, building names, landowner, greens.

12/328 Tendring (parish) TM 145245
Apt 27.02.1841; 2828a (2827); Map 1842?, 6 chns; foot/b'way, waterbodies.

12/329 Terling (parish) TL 768149
Apt 09.03.1842; 3206a (3205); Map 1843?, 4 chns, by Robert Baker, Writtle, Essex; hill-drawing, waterbodies, houses, woods (col), plantations (col), orchards, sand or stone pits.

12/330 Great Tey (parish) TL 884252
Apt 23.10.1838; 2503a (all); Map 1839, 4 chns, by J.S. Surridge, surveyor and auctioneer; waterbodies, woods, plantations, field boundary ownerships, road names, green; colours may show property ownerships; title is surrounded by acorns, oak branches and leaves.

12/331 Little Tey (parish) TL 892237
Apt 26.01.1841; 486a (all); Map 1840, 6 chns, by Gilbert and Tayspill, Colchester; waterbodies, woods, plantations.

12/332 Thaxted (parish) TL 615305
Apt 12.12.1842; 6219a (6219); Map 1844, 6 chns; waterbodies, woods, open fields, building names, windmills (pictorial), greens.

12/333 Theydon Mount (parish) TL 492002
Apt 23.08.1837; 1501a (all); Map 1838, 7 chns; waterbodies, woods (named), parkland, building names, common; hall named ornately.

12/334 Easthorpe (parish) TL 908213
Apt 31.12.1840; 909a (all); Map 1841?, [4 chns]; waterbodies, houses, woods (named), building names, rectory.

12/335 Thorpe le Soken (parish) TM 181222 [Thorpe-le-Soken]
Apt 01.09.1840; 3191a (all); Map 1841?, 3 chns; building names, greens, sand or stone pits, windmill (by symbol); colour bands may show property ownerships.

12/336 Thorrington (parish) TM 097197
Apt 18.05.1843; 1931a (all); Map 1841?, 6 chns; waterbodies, waste.

12/337 Thoydon Bois (parish) TQ 453990 [Theydon Bois]
Apt 13.02.1849; 2177a (all); Map 1848, 6 chns; waterbodies, houses, woods, open fields, sand or stone pit, green, avenues of trees, common, osiers.

12/338 Thoydon Garnon otherwise Theydon Gernon (parish) TL 473012 [Theydon Garnon]
Apt 17.01.1838; 3161a (3161); Map 1838, 6 chns, in 2 parts, by Chapman, Son and Webb, Arundel St, StrandIV, (includes Epping Backstreet village at 3 chns); foot/b'way, turnpike roads, toll bar, waterbodies, houses, woods, plantations, hedge ownership, building names, rectory, workhouse.

12/339 Thundersley (parish) TQ 794889
Apt 19.03.1838; 2500a (2499); Map 1838, 4 chns, by Henry Clayton; waterbodies. Apt omits some field names.

12/340 Little Thurrock (parish) TQ 630778
Apt 06.11.1840; 1336a (all); Map 1840, 6 chns, by Messrs Crawter; foot/b'way, waterbodies, woods, brick fields, wharf, tramway, sand or stone pits, drains.

12/341 West Thurrock (parish) TQ 580780
Apt 28.04.1837; 2907a (3607); Map 1838?, 3 chns, ? by Henry Clayton; hill-drawing, waterbodies, woods, marsh/bog, embankment, drains; bridge named. Apt omits some field names.

12/342 Tilbury juxta Clare (parish) TL 758405 [Not listed]
Apt 05.02.1839; 946a (?); Map 1841?, 3 chns; turnpike roads, waterbodies, houses, woods, landowners, green.

12/343 East Tilbury (parish) TQ 683779
Apt 11.04.1839; 2113a (all); Map 1838, 4 chns, copied from a survey and map made by Robert Hale in 1836 by Henry Clayton; landowners, greens, common saltings, drains. Apt omits some field names.

12/344 West Tilbury (parish) TQ 662775
Apt 07.08.1839; 1832a (all); Map 1838, 4 chns; hill-drawing, waterbodies, woods, plantations, fort, embankments, drains, commons.

12/345 Tillingham (parish) TM 010038
Apt 08.11.1837; 4136a (all); Map 1838, 4 chns, by Thomas Bygrave, Clements Inn; foot/b'way, waterbodies, houses, woods, field gates, building names, glebe, gravel pit, drainage outfalls, decoys, drains, 'extraordinary rise of tide', high water mark, sea wall; legend explains depiction of buildings, watercourses and boundaries; colour bands may show property ownerships.

12/346 Tollesbury (parish) TL 960107
Apt 02.05.1839; 7919a (10638); Map 1840, 3 chns, by A. Rush, Messing; construction lines, waterbodies, woods, field boundary ownerships, field gates, drains, embankment; offshore islands named.

12/347 Tolleshunt D'Arcy (parish) TL 929112
Apt 06.02.1840; 3142a (3371); Map 1840?, 3 chns, by Robt Baker, Writtle, Essex; construction lines, waterbodies, woods (col, named), building names.

12/348 Tolleshunt Knights (parish) TL 918144
Apt 29.01.1840; 2080a (all); Map 1839, 3 chns, by Alfred Rush, Messing; waterbodies, woods (col).

12/349 Tolleshunt Major (parish) TL 899120
Apt 21.01.1848; 2184a (all); Map 1848?, 8 chns; waterbodies, woods, field gates, building names; map has note of adoption proceedings and nineteen signatures.

12/350 Toppesfield (parish) TL 735367
Apt 22.03.1839; 3238a (all); Map 1840, 6 chns, litho (Standidge); waterbodies, building names, field names, field acreages, rectory, windmill (by symbol), glebe, common, gardens (by annotation), orchards (by annotation).

12/351 Great Totham (parish) TL 865110
Apt 03.02.1843; 4321a (5363); Map 1839, 3 chns, in 3 parts, by James Beadel, Witham, (includes two small enlargements of detail); construction lines, hill-drawing, waterbodies, houses, woods (col), field boundary ownerships, field gates, building names, mill, salt works, embankments.

12/352 Little Totham (parish) TL 885104 [Not listed]
Apt 05.03.1839; 1265a (all); Map 1839, 3 chns, by James Beadel, Witham; construction lines, foot/b'way, waterbodies, houses, woods, heath/moor, field boundary ownerships, field gates, building names, common (col).

12/353 Twinsted (parish) TL 857363 [Twinstead]
Apt 30.04.1840; 1009a (all); Map 1840?, 3 chns, by H. Coates, 12, Duke Street, Portland Place, London; waterbodies, houses, woods, plantations, parkland, field boundary ownerships, boundary trees.

12/354 Ugley (part of) (parish) TL 518285
Apt 04.06.1839; 2038a (all); Map 1839?, 8 chns; waterbodies, woods, plantations, open fields (named), hedge ownership, boundary of small tithe ownership. Apt refers to colours on map.

12/355 Ulting (parish) TL 810091
Apt 31.01.1838; 1148a (all); Map 1841?, 3 chns, in 2 parts, by Robert Baker, Writtle, Essex; canal, waterbodies, houses, plantations (col), building names.

12/356 Upminster (parish) TQ 560868
Apt 10.03.1842; 3374a (all); Map 1841, 3 chns, by Messrs Crawter; construction lines, hill-drawing, railway, foot/b'way, waterbodies, houses, woods (col), plantations (col), marsh/bog, building names, osiers, commons.

12/357 Vange (parish) TQ 731878
Apt 25.03.1839; 1701a (all); Map 1841?, 3 chns, in 2 parts, by Robert Baker, Writtle, Essex; hill-drawing, waterbodies, houses, building names, sea wall, drains, saltings.

12/358 Virley (parish) TL 945145
Apt 05.02.1839; 632a (all); Map 1838, 6 chns, by Gilbert and Tayspill, Colchester; waterbodies, woods.

12/359 Great Wakering (parish) TQ 953878
Apt 12.06.1838; 2784a (all); Map 1840?, 3 chns, by Robert Baker, Writtle, Essex; foot/b'way, waterbodies, houses, woods (col), plantations (col), building names, sea wall, high and low water mark, saltings, mud, ferries, drains, spring tide mark. (The map in PRO IR 30 is a copy; original is in PRO IR 77/18.)

12/360 Little Wakering (parish) TQ 938887
Apt 12.03.1841; 2736a (all); Map 1840, 3 chns, 1st cl, by A. Doull; construction lines, waterbodies, houses, field gates, drains. Apt omits some field names.

12/361 Wakes Colne (parish) TL 896301
Apt 26.08.1839; 1926a (all); Map 1839, 6 chns, by Newton and Woodrow, Norwich; foot/b'way, waterbodies, houses, woods, plantations, open fields, windmill (by symbol), sand or stone pit. Apt omits land use.

12/362 Great Waltham (parish) TL 692150
Apt 29.05.1839; 7335a (7335); Map 1839, 7 chns, by Henry Clayton; foot/b'way, waterbodies, open fields, building names, mill.

12/363 Little Waltham (parish) TL 721126
Apt 11.07.1837; 2228a (all); Map 1838, 5 chns, in 2 parts, copied from a survey made by Messrs I. and H. Clayton, 1812 by Robert Baker, Writtle, Essex, (includes village separately at 1.5 chns); waterbodies, houses, woods (col), building names, watermill, rectory, glebe.

12/364 Walthamstow (parish) TQ 372898
Apt 16.04.1842; 4355a (4436); Map 1842?, 6 chns; railway, foot/b'way, waterbodies, woods (col), parkland, orchards, open fields, building names, road names, ferry.

12/365 Walton (parish) TM 253221 [Walton-on-the-Naze]
Apt 08.02.1840; 2600a (3260); Map 1841, 6 chns, in 2 parts, (includes town separately at 3 chns); waterbodies, houses, woods, marsh/bog, rock outcrops, building names, road names, cliffs, embankments,

tower, mill, library, preventive station, jetty; tithe areas marked 'a' are tithe free.

12/366 Wanstead (parish) TQ 410880
Apt 01.03.1841; 2004a (2004); Map 1840?, 3 chns, by Geo. Richd Noble, Woodford, Essex; waterbodies, building names, road names, glebe boundary; bridge named.

12/367 Great Warley (parish) TQ 590900
Apt 23.06.1837; 2793a (all); Map 1838?, 3 chns, by Gilbert and Tayspill, Colchester; waterbodies.

12/368 Little Warley (parish) TQ 601895
Apt 23.06.1837; 1651a (all); Map 1838, 3 chns, by Gilbert and Tayspill, Colchester, Essex; waterbodies, woods (named), building names, barracks, drains.

12/369 North Weald Bassett (parish) TL 498051
Apt 17.10.1838; 3378a (all); Map 1838, 3 chns, by Gabriel Fleck; construction lines, waterbodies, houses, building names, milestones, common.

12/370 South Weald (Vicar's Division) (parish) TQ 570940
Apt 16.01.1838; 2937a (2937); Map 1838?, 6 chns, by S.J. King, Saffron Walden, Essex; waterbodies, houses, woods, plantations, parkland, heath/moor, road names, magazine, gravel pit, windmill (pictorial), greens (col), common, new enclosures, rabbit warren; bridge named.

12/371 South Weald (Impropriate Rectors Division) (parish) TQ 571966
Apt 16.05.1839; 2101a (2101); Map 1839, 9 chns, by Mich. Jno. Mason; waterbodies, building names, road names, landowners, vicarage, glebe; bridge named; colour bands may show property ownerships. District is apportioned by holding and fields are mostly not shown.

12/372 Weeley (parish) TM 152217
Apt 05.03.1840; 2087a (all); Map 1840?, 6 chns, by Gilbert and Tayspill, Colchester; foot/b'way, waterbodies, woods, plantations.

12/373 Wennington (parish) TQ 537807
Apt 17.09.1839; 1286a (1570); Map 1839, 4 chns; waterbodies, drains, disputed land.

12/374 Wethersfield (parish) TL 736307
Apt 14.09.1842; 4213a (all); Map 1841, 6 chns, by Savil and Son, Sible Hedingham, litho (by S. Straker, 118 Bishopgate St, London); waterbodies, woods (named), plantations, building names, mill, parsonage, green.

12/375 Wickford (parish) TQ 752938
Apt 03.04.1839; 1759a (all); Map 1841?, 4 chns; waterbodies.

12/376 Wickham Bishops (parish) TL 834115
Apt 30.06.1841; 1535a (all); Map 1835, 3 chns, by James Beadel, Witham; waterbodies, woods (named), field boundary ownerships, building names, workhouse, mill, well, parsonage, boundary trees.

12/377 Wickham Bonhunt otherwise Wicken Bonant (parish) TL 502334 [Wicken Bonhunt]
Apt 31.08.1841; 841a (all); Map 1842, 3 chns, by J. King and Son, Saffron Walden; waterbodies, houses, woods, heath/moor, open fields and meadows (named), building names, rectory, roadside waste (col); open strip boundaries are solid, in colour.

12/378 Wickham St Pauls (parish) TL 830368 [Wickham St Paul]
Apt 12.02.1838; 1183a (all); Map 1839?, 4 chns; waterbodies, houses, farmyards, woods (col, named), arable (col), grassland (col), gardens (col), hedge ownership, fences, field gates, building names, field names, boundary trees, green.

12/379 Widdington (parish) TL 535322
Apt 02.06.1838; 2008a (2028); Map 4 chns, 'copied from a plan made in the year 1795 by Daniel Mumford and revised and corrected' in 1839 by John King and Son, Saffron Walden; waterbodies, houses, woods, plantations, open fields (named), building names, rectory; open strip boundaries are solid, in colour.

12/380 Widford (parish) TL 693053
Apt 25.04.1838; 692a (all); Map 1841?, 3 chns, by Robt Baker, Writtle, Essex; waterbodies, houses, woods (col), plantations (col), parkland (named), building names.

12/381 Great Wigborough (parish) TL 969147
Apt 26.11.1844; 2586a (all); Map 1845?, 6 chns, copied from a survey by Henry Clayton made in 1833 by John J. Bird, Boughton Monchelsea; waterbodies, woods, boundary trees, glebe (col), property and farm names, heath. Apt omits some field names.

12/382 Little Wigborow (parish) TL 983147 [Little Wigborough]
Apt 19.12.1838; 1169a (1168); Map 1838, 6 chns, in 2 parts, by Walter J. Ray; foot/b'way, waterbodies, houses, woods (col), arable (col), grassland (col), gardens (col), marsh/bog, hedge ownership, fences, field gates, building names, mudflats, embankments, drains, rectory.

12/383 Willingale Doe (parish) TL 594065 [Willingale]
Apt 20.05.1837; 1740a (1739); Map 1837, 3 chns, 1st cl, by E. Corfield; construction lines, hill-drawing, foot/b'way, waterbodies, houses, woods, plantations, hedge ownership, sand or stone pits or quarries, greens, common meadow; bridge named.

12/384 Willingale Spain (parish) TL 608060 [Not listed]
Apt 19.09.1837; 1200a (1200); Map 1832, 4.5 chns, by J. and H. Clayton; waterbodies, woods, orchards, gardens, hedge ownership, field gates, landowners, milestone, glebe, farm and property names, green; bridge named; colours may show property ownerships; map title is on a coloured background of rock, bushes and trees.

12/385 Wimbish cum Thunderley (parish) TL 584360
Apt 23.04.1839; 4862a (all); Map 1840?, 6 chns, by Messrs King and Nockolds, Saffron Walden and Stansted; waterbodies, houses, woods, building names, windmill (pictorial), vicarage, greens.

12/386 Witham (parish) TL 820150
Apt 22.04.1839; 3633a (3633); Map 1839, 3 chns, by James Beadel, Witham; construction lines, railway, waterbodies, houses, woods (col, named), open fields, field boundary ownerships, building names, school, vicarage, mills, brick kiln, pit, gravel pit; bridge named.

12/387 Wivenhoe (parish) TM 040234
Apt 17.12.1838; 1572a (1597); Map 1838, 3 chns, by Gilbert and Tayspill, Colchester; waterbodies, woods, plantations, parkland, marsh/bog, building names, gravel pit, river embankments, clay pit, glebe, drains.

12/388 Wix (parish) TM 158288
Apt 04.02.1843; 2179a (3090); Map 1837, 3 chns, by R.E. Sheldrake, Colchester; waterbodies, houses, woods, arable (col), grassland (col), orchards, gardens, building names, abbey, windmill (by symbol); colour bands may show property ownerships.

12/389 Woodford (parish) TQ 408918
Apt 24.04.1838; 2149a (all); Map 1839?, 3 chns; building names, road names, rectory, National School, glebe (col); bridge named.

12/390 Woodham Ferris (parish) TQ 798995 [Woodham Ferrers]
Apt 06.05.1839; 4481a (4481); Map 1842?, 3 chns, by Robt Baker, Writtle, Essex; construction lines, hill-drawing, foot/b'way, waterbodies, woods (col, named), plantations (col), building names, river embankments, windmill (pictorial), priory arch (pictorial), fens, drains; bridge named.

12/391 Woodham Mortimer (parish) TL 818050
Apt 25.04.1838; 1381a (1380); Map 1838, 3 chns, by Robert Baker, Writtle, Essex; construction lines, hill-drawing, waterbodies, houses, woods, field gates.

12/392 Woodham Walter (parish) TL 810070
Apt 12.10.1844; 1758a (2421); Map 1845, 4 chns, by Robt Baker, Writtle, Essex; waterbodies, houses, woods (col), plantations (col), marsh/bog, sand or stone pit, common.

12/393 Wormingford (parish) TL 936319
Apt 27.03.1838; 2332a (all); Map 1838, [6 chns]; waterbodies, woods, plantations, building names.

12/394 Wrabness (parish) TM 174312
Apt 29.05.1841; 1077a (all); Map 1839, 3 chns, by J.C. Harris; construction lines, waterbodies, houses.

12/395 Writtle (parish) TL 650050
Apt 22.04.1839; 8672a (8672); Map 1842?, 8 chns, in 3 parts, by Robt Baker, Writtle, Essex, (includes enlargement of village at 4 chns and index from Chapman and Andre's map of Essex); waterbodies, houses, woods, plantations, parkland, sand or stone pits.

12/396 Great Yeldham (parish) TL 760382
Apt 13.11.1840; 1793a (1820); Map 1839, 3 chns, in 2 parts, by S. Parkinson; construction lines, waterbodies, houses, glebe.

12/397 Little Yeldham (parish) TL 776393
Apt 24.11.1840; 926a (938); Map 1841?, 3 chns, by H. Coates, 12, Duke Street, Portland Place, London; waterbodies, houses, woods (col), field boundary ownerships, landowners, extra parochial land (col).

Gloucestershire

PRO IR29 and IR30 13/1-229

349 tithe districts: 802,332 acres
229 tithe commutations: 472,544 acres
139 voluntary tithe agreements, 90 compulsory tithe awards,
4 corn rent annuities

Tithe and tithe commutation

Considerable tracts of Gloucestershire were subject to parliamentary enclosure with the result that by 1836 only 65 per cent of its tithe districts (59 per cent of the county area) remained subject to payment of tithes (Fig. 25). Eighty-six districts were wholly tithable; the main causes of partial exemption in the remainder were commutation at the time of enclosure, modus payments in lieu of tithes, exemption of former Crown, manorial or monastic land, merger of tithes in the land, and exemption by prescription.

Assistant tithe commissioners and local tithe agents who officiated in Gloucestershire are listed in Table 13.1. As in most counties, a majority of the valuations of tithe rent-charge were undertaken by valuers based in, or close to, the county. Notable exceptions include four districts valued by London-based men (three by John Clutton), and one each by Edward Sacheverall Gisborne of Hay, Breconshire, Francis Attwood of Salisbury, William Hussey of High Wycombe, Buckinghamshire, and Richard Lumbert of Burghfield, Berkshire (Table 13.2).

Tithe maps

Some 16 per cent of Gloucestershire tithe maps are sealed as first class. Many second-class maps are of residual tithable lands in predominantly tithe-free districts. Construction lines are present on five per cent of second-class maps indicating that these were new surveys, and a further 9 per cent acknowledge copying from existing surveys dating from 1805 onwards. Gloucestershire maps are drawn at a variety of scales from one inch to half a chain to one inch to twelve chains; just over half the maps are within the recommended scale range of one inch to three to four chains (Table 13.3). The complicated intermixing of districts which was particularly common around Stroud sometimes results in land outside a tithe district being mapped, as, for example at Alderley.

The mapping of land use in Gloucestershire is rather more thorough than the average: about 27 per cent of maps show arable and grass, 19 per cent depict gardens, 19 per cent

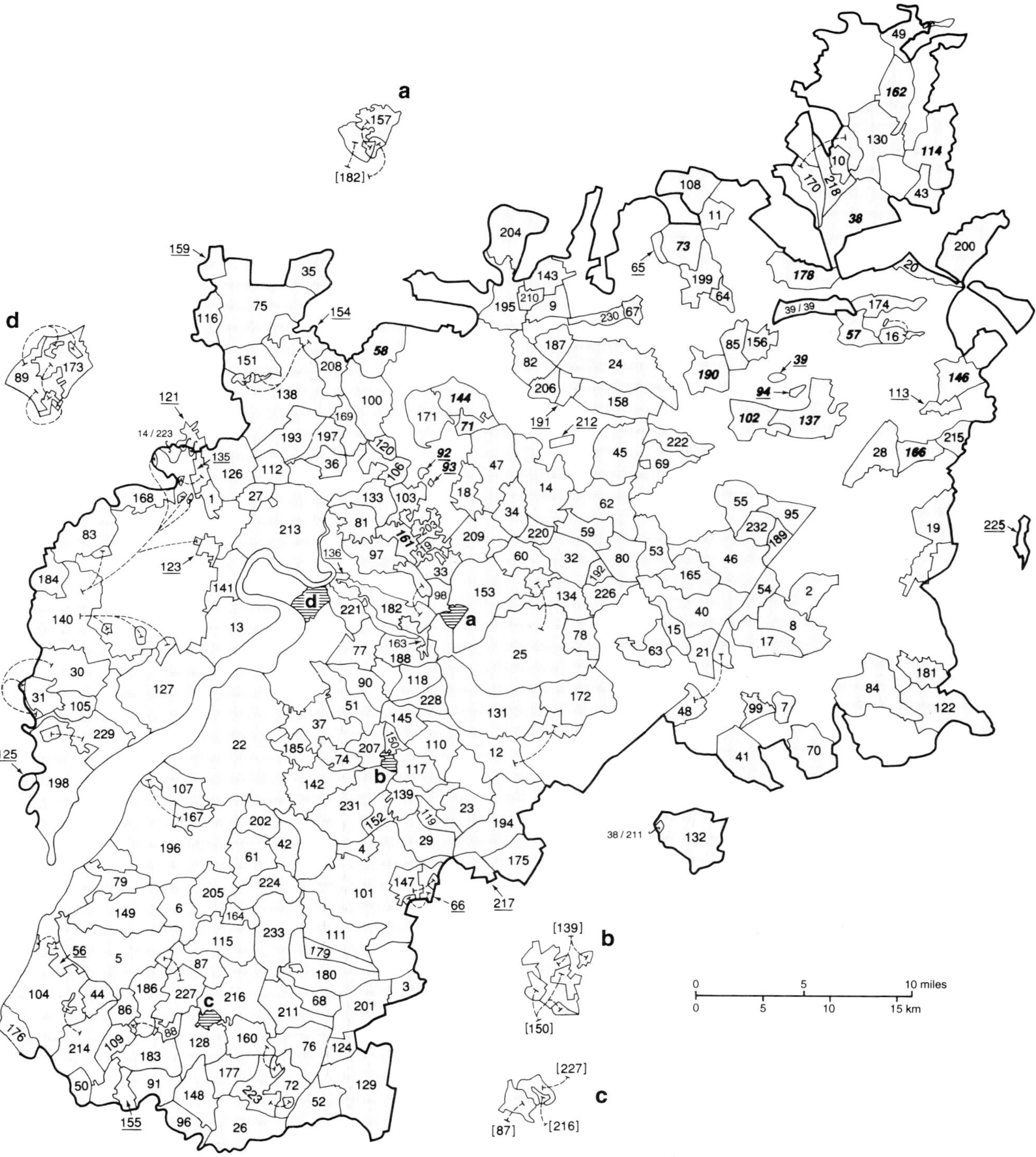

Fig. 25 Gloucestershire: tithe district boundaries.

map parks, 7 per cent show marsh or bog, 30 per cent indicate orchards, and 63 per cent depict woodland. The Cirencester surveyors Hall and Trinder frequently used colour bands to show both cultivation and field-boundary ownership. Although parliamentary enclosure was significant in Gloucestershire, residual open fields appear on 16 per cent of the county's maps. Gloucestershire maps also contain considerable evidence of industrial activities, including quarrying, saw, snuff, paper and pepper mills, iron works, coal mining, brick works and tan yards. Castles appear on four maps, and ancient earthworks on eight. A 'glebe barn', presumably a tithe barn, appears on the map of Bishops Cleeve; tithe barns are rarely identified on tithe maps.

Some 148 Gloucestershire tithe maps in the Public Record Office collection can be attributed to a particular map-maker (Table 13.2); Cirencester was the main centre of the profession from where Richard Hall (thirty-two maps) and Daniel Trinder (ten maps) operated. Bristol was the second centre for the county's tithe map-makers, exemplified by Young and Jacob Player Sturge (fourteen maps), James Marmont (four maps), Thomas Ward (three maps) and Daniel Horwood (two maps). A few maps were made by surveyors based well outside the county, notably two by William Hussey of High Wycombe in Buckinghamshire, one by Long and Taylor of Wolverhampton and one each by William Clutton and John Hosmer of London.

There is little decoration on Gloucestershire maps; an unusual exception is a display of farm tools on the map of Oldland. Five other maps have minor decorative features and that of Old Sodbury has an ornate coloured compass rose.

Table 13.1. *Agreements and awards for commutation of tithes in Gloucestershire*

Assistant commissioner/ local tithe agent	*Number of agreements**	*Number of awards*
Charles Pym	31	76
George Bolls	37	0
Thomas Hoskins	27	0
Robert Page	23	0
Aneurin Owen	0	10
George Louis	4	0
George Wingrove Cooke	0	3
Tithe Commissioners	0	1

*Computed from the number of extant reports on tithe agreements in the tithe files [PRO IR 18].

Table 13.2. *Tithe valuers and tithe map-makers in Gloucestershire*

Name and address (all in Gloucestershire)	*Number of districts*	*Acreage*
Tithe valuers		
Richard Hall, Cirencester	36	72,952
Daniel Trinder, Cirencester	19	73,939
Jacob Player Sturge, Bristol	15	51,988
Josiah Castree, Gloucester	15	21,057
James Croome, Berkeley	10	30,265
Young Sturge, Bristol	10	25,556
Charles Baker, Painswick	9	11,916
Others [61]	115	185,111
Attributed tithe map-makers		
Richard Hall, Cirencester	32	45,535
Young and Jacob Player Sturge, Bristol	14	39,564
Daniel Trinder, Cirencester	10	35,778
Charles Baker, Painswick	8	20,923
Others [45]	84	171,425

Table 13.3. *The tithe maps of Gloucestershire: scales and classes*

Scale in chains/inch	*All maps*		*First Class*		*Second Class*	
	Number	*Acreage*	*Number*	*Acreage*	*Number*	*Acreage*
>3	4	1,859	1	1,059	3	800
3	93	193,741	34	80,207	59	113,534
3.5	1	208	0	0	1	208
4	25	48,027	1	2,984	24	45,043
5	12	6,825	0	0	12	6,825
6	75	192,765	0	0	75	192,765
<6	19	29,119	0	0	19	29,119
TOTAL	229	472,544	36	84,250	193	388,294

Table 13.4. *The tithe maps of Gloucestershire: dates*

	1837	*1838*	*1839*	*1840*	*1841*	*1842*	*1843*	*1844*	*1845*	*1846*	*1847*	*1848*	*1849*	*1850*	*>1850*
All maps	4	30	45	38	26	25	21	6	5	5	11	4	2	3	4
1st class	0	6	11	8	5	1	2	1	0	1	0	0	0	0	0
2nd class	4	24	34	30	21	24	19	5	5	4	11	4	2	3	4

Gloucestershire

13/1 Abinghall (parish) SO 672173 [Abenhall]
Apt 23.05.1838; 752a (all); Map 1839?, 3 chns; foot/b'way, waterbodies, houses, building names, boundary trees.

13/2 Ablington (tithing in parish of Bibury) SP 114093
Apt 11.06.1840; 1755a (all); Map 1840, 6 chns, by Richard Hall, Cirencester; woods, arable (col), grassland (col), gardens (col).

13/3 Acton Turville (parish) ST 812807
Apt 15.02.1839; 1009a (all); Map 1838, 1st cl, 3 chns, by W.B. Wood, Barnbridge, Chippenham, Wilts; construction lines, foot/b'way, waterbodies, houses, hedge ownership.

13/4 Alderley (parish) ST 775910
Apt 30.07.1838; 899a (898); Map 1838, 9 chns, in 2 parts, by Y. and J.P. Sturge, (tinted; includes skeletal details of land outside district); foot/b'way, waterbodies, woods (named), plantations, open fields.

13/5 Almondsbury (parish) ST 599832
Apt 02.02.1838; 6928a (6927); Map 1839?, 6 chns; foot/b'way, waterbodies, woods (col), parkland (in detail), orchards, building names.

13/6 Alveston (parish) ST 642863
Apt 05.06.1839; 2519a (all); Map 1840, 3 chns, 1st cl, ? by Geo. Osbourne, Elberton; construction lines, hill-drawing, foot/b'way, waterbodies, houses, woods (named), plantations, parkland, orchards, fences, field boundary ownerships, field gates, building names, road names, pounds, quarry, milestones, green, mead, moor, withy beds.

13/7 Ampney St Peter (parish) SP 090007
Apt 15.04.1842; 154a (533); Map 1842, 3 chns; waterbodies, houses, arable (col), grassland (col), road names, landowners.

13/8 Arlington and Winson (hamlet in parish of Bibury) SP 103070
Apt 30.11.1839; 2766a (?); Map 1840, 6 chns, ? by Daniel Trinder; waterbodies, houses, woods (col), plantations, arable (col), grassland (col), marsh/bog, building names, withy beds.

13/9 Ashchurch (except Northway and Newton) (parish) SO 922312
Apt 10.03.1841; 1349a (?); Map 1842, 4 chns, 'revised and corrected' by James Webb, Worcester 'from an old survey of William Hensley's'; railway, waterbodies, houses.

13/10 Ashton Underhill (parish) SP 137418 [Aston Subedge]
Apt 01.09.1841; 67a (1300); Map 1843, 4 chns; foot/b'way, houses, woods (named), orchards, field boundary ownerships, field gates, field names, landowners.

13/11 Aston Somerville (parish) SP 045383
Apt 07.07.1837; 978a (all); Map 1837?, 6 chns; foot/b'way, waterbodies, houses, hedge ownership, field gates, glebe boundary; map is subtitled 'the property of the Right Honourable Mark Lord Somerville' and has table of tithe area numbers, names and acreages.

13/12 Avening (parish) ST 872980
Apt 27.09.1838; 4429a (4428); Map 1839, 6 chns, by C. Baker, Painswick; foot/b'way, waterbodies, houses, woods, field gates, building names, mills, iron mills, sawing mills; two farms named.

13/13 Awre (parish) SO 690080
Apt 13.02.1840; 4081a (6115); Map 1840?, 7 chns; waterbodies, building names, coast, vicarage, paper mill, green; scale incorrectly figured.

13/14 Badgeworth and Shurdington Magna (parish) SO 913178
Apt 16.01.1838; 4310a (4310); Map 1838, 6 chns; railway, foot/b'way, waterbodies, houses, woods (named), building names, landowners, glebe, common, Roman encampment, manor bush, manor stone, yew tree, well; colours may show property ownerships.

13/15 Bagendon (parish) SP 007070
Apt 18.09.1838; 1106a (all); Map 1839?, 8 chns; foot/b'way, waterbodies, houses, woods, arable (col), grassland (col).

13/16 Banks Fee (hamlet in parish of Longborough) SP 178284
Apt 14.04.1842; 696a (?); Map 1845?, 5 chns; foot/b'way, waterbodies, houses, woods (col), hedge ownership, fence ownership, field gates, landowners, ornamental ground.

13/17 Barnsley (parish) SP 075050
Apt 30.11.1841; 2090a (all); Map 1840, 6 chns, by Daniel Trinder; waterbodies, houses, woods, plantations, parkland, arable (col), grassland (col), orchard.

13/18 Barnwood (parish) SO 859178
Apt 21.11.1838; 1472a (all); Map 1840?, 6 chns, ? by Richard Hall; railways, waterbodies, houses, woods, arable (col), grassland (col), orchards, gardens, building names, road names.

13/19 Great Barrington (parish) (partly in Berks) SP 210140
Apt 25.02.1841; 2984a (2983); Map 1841, 4 chns, 1st cl, by P. Cassidy; construction lines, trig points, houses, woods (col), field gates, building names, waste; band may show boundaries of modus lands.

13/20 Batsford (parish) SP 193336
Apt 18.01.1839; 932a (all); Map 1841?, 6 chns; railway, foot/b'way, woods, plantations, parkland, marsh/bog, hedge ownership, field gates.

13/21 Baunton (parish) SP 030050
Apt 29.09.1849; 1340a (1340); Map 1849, 6 chns, ? by John Bravender; foot/b'way, waterbodies, houses, plantations, arable (col), grassland (col), building names.

13/22 Berkeley (parish) ST 686989
Apt 18.01.1839; 13420a (15740); Map 1839, 4 chns, in 5 parts, by Long and Taylor, Wolverhampton, (includes 2-chn enlargement of town and 18-chn index); foot/b'way, turnpike roads and gate, canal, waterbodies, woods, plantations, parkland, open fields (named), fences, building names, castle, headland, mills, summerhouse, pound, tithing boundaries (col), greens; bridges named.

13/23 Beverstone (parish) ST 858940 [Beverston]
Corn rent conversion, 1927; 1948a (2360); Map 1927?, [10 chns], ('correct tracing' of enclosure map of 1804); foot/b'way, turnpike roads, waterbodies, houses, road names, field names, field acreages, landowners; map has table of owners and acreages. Apt is based on the enclosure award of 1804.

13/24 Bishops Cleeve and Southam, Brockhampton and Woodmancote (township and hamlet in parish of Bishops Cleeve) SO 972262 [Bishop's Cleeve]
Apt 31.01.1839; 5883a (6819); Map 1841, 6 chns, ? by Richard Hall; hill-drawing, railway, waterbodies, houses, woods, arable (col), grassland (col), orchards, gardens (col), building names, rectory, glebe barn, chapel ruin, race course, grandstand, pit, ornamental ground.

13/25 Bisley (parish) SO 897052
Apt 19.08.1841; 11844a (8033); Map 1842, 6 chns, in 2 parts, ? by Daniel Trinder; railway, foot/b'way, canal, waterbodies, houses, woods, plantations, arable (col), grassland (col), building names, reservoir, mills, greens, commons.

13/26 Bitton (hamlet in parish of Bitton) ST 688707
Apt 09.10.1841; 3355a (?); Map 1842?, 6 chns, in 2 parts, by Thomas Ward, Bristol, (includes town separately at 3 chns), litho (by A. Pocock, Bristol); railway, turnpike roads, waterbodies, houses, woods, plantations, orchards, open fields (named), building names, mill, coalworks, brewery, commons.

13/27 Blaisdon (parish) SO 705174
Apt 28.08.1839; 900a (900); Map 1840?, 3 chns, in 2 parts.

13/28 Bourton on the Water including Clapton on the Hill (parish and hamlet) SP 168201 [Bourton-on-the-Water]
Apt 12.06.1846; 812a (2282); Map 1842, 6 chns, (tithable parts only in detail; other parts tinted); woods, orchards, churchyard; bridge named.

13/29 Boxwell and Leighterton (parish) ST 823917
Apt 11.08.1838; 2267a (all); Map 1838, 4 chns; hill-drawing, turnpike roads and gate, waterbodies, houses, woods, plantations, orchards, field gates, sand or stone pit, glebe.

13/30 St Briavels (parish) SO 567043
Apt 03.01.1840; 3795a (5104); Map 1842?, 3 chns; construction lines, houses, field boundary ownerships, building names, mill, common, extra-parochial land; map has recital of adoption proceedings.

13/31 St Briavels Common, the Lower Mean, the fences, the Forest fences, Mawkins, Hazel, Brockwear Common and Bearse Common (extra-parochial) SO 542022
Apt 20.09.1850; 134a (?); Map 1852?, 5 chns; houses, field gates, woods (by name); bridge named; pictorial church.

13/32 Brimsfield (parish) SO 935124 [Brimpsfield]
Apt 26.10.1837; 2612a (2611); Map 1838, 4 chns, ? by Rich. Hall; waterbodies, houses, woods (named), plantations, arable (col), grassland (col), orchards, gardens, open fields, parkland (by name); land use is not shown in open fields.

13/33 Brockthorp (parish) SO 841118 [Brookthorpe]
Apt 18.02.1841; 1009a (all); Map 1843?, 3 chns, by William Hussey, Wycombe; railway, waterbodies, houses, woods, orchards, field boundary ownerships, building names.

13/34 Brockworth (parish) SO 893160
Apt 25.10.1841; 1847a (1847); Map 1841, 8 chns; waterbodies, houses, building names.

13/35 Bromsberrow (parish) SO 744339
Apt 30.12.1837; 1803a (all); Map 1838?, 1st cl, [3 chns]; construction lines, hill-drawing, foot/b'way, turnpike roads, waterbodies, woods, plantations, parkland, orchards, hedge ownership, fences, field gates, building names, boundary stones, peppermill, keepers house, rick yard, heath; physical features named.

13/36 Bulley (parish) SO 759199
Apt 31.05.1839; 951a (all); Map 1838, 3 chns, 1st cl; construction lines, foot/b'way, waterbodies, houses, woods, arable (col), grassland (col), orchards, gardens, fences, building names, field names; land use is shown by both colour-bands and annotation.

13/37 Cam (parish) SO 753002
Apt 19.02.1839; 2946a (2946); Map 1841?, 4 chns; waterbodies, woods, open fields, building names, road names, mill, common, inter-common land, green; physical features and bridge named. (The map in PRO IR 30 is a copy; original is in PRO IR 77/19.)

13/38 Campden (parish) SP 148383 [Chipping Campden]
Apt 13.03.1845; 32a (?); Map 1850, 4 chns, by John Kettle, (tithable parts only); turnpike roads, toll gate, field gates, building names, road names, landowners, Wesleyan Chapel, town hall, corn hall, almshouses, courthouse.

13/39 Castlett (hamlet in parish of Lower Guiting) SP 091258 [Not listed]
Apt 08.03.1842; 228a (?); Map 1848, 5 chns; waterbodies, field gates, landowners.

13/40 North Cerney (parish) SP 030080
Apt 30.12.1837; 4158a (4158); Map 1842?, 6 chns, ? by Richard Hall; foot/b'way, waterbodies, woods, arable (col), grassland (col), gardens (col), building names, rectory, ornamental ground.

13/41 South Cerney (parish) SU 057971
Corn rent conversion, 1863; 2184a (3100); Map in 2 parts: part 1 traced from a map annexed to an enclosure award dated November 11th 1814; part 2 prepared for corn rent conversion, 1863, 6 chns; foot/b'way, turnpike roads, canal, waterbodies, houses, road names. Apt omits land use.

13/42 Charfield (parish) ST 721913
Apt 23.04.1839; 1370a (all); Map 1839, 3 chns, 1st cl, ? by James Croome; construction lines, waterbodies, houses, woods, plantations, orchards, hedge ownership, fences, field gates.

13/43 Charingworth (hamlet in parish of Ebrington) SP 202395
Apt 28.03.1844; 1028a (?); Map 1847?, 4 chns; construction lines, foot/b'way, waterbodies, plantations, field boundary ownerships, building names, road names, landowners, green.

13/44 Charlton (township in parish of Henbury) ST 585806 [Not listed]
Apt 31.08.1840; 1121a (?); Map 1841, 6 chns, in 3 parts, by J.P. Sturge and J. Marmont, litho (by Day and Haghe); woods, orchards, heath/moor.

13/45 Charlton Kings (parish) SO 974205
Apt 02.09.1844; 1054a (3170); Map 1848, 6 chns, in 2 parts, by Hall and Crouch, Cirencester, (including common fields at 3 chns); waterbodies, woods, open fields (named).

13/46 Chedworth (parish) SP 050120
Apt 23.06.1842; 4689a (all); Map 1843, 6 chns; foot/b'way, waterbodies, houses, woods, arable (col), grassland (col), orchards, gardens (col), marsh/bog, building names, mill, chapel; bridge named.

13/47 Churchdown (parish) SO 880195
Apt 03.11.1840; 4076a (4076); Map 1842, 6 chns, in 2 parts, by Richard Hall; railway, turnpike roads, toll bar, waterbodies, houses, woods, arable (col), grassland (col), orchards, gardens (col), building names, road names, milestone, green; bridge named.

13/48 Cirencester (parish) SP 023005
Apt 28.09.1838; 1389a (5000); Map 1839, 6 chns, in 2 parts, by Rd Hall, Cirencester; hill-drawing, foot/b'way, waterbodies, woods, arable (col), grassland (col), orchards, gardens, building names, road names, abbey, market place.

13/49 Clifford Chambers (parish) SP 190498
Apt 20.04.1842; 133a (2500); Map 1845?, 12 chns; waterbodies, field gates, landowners.

13/50 Clifton (parish) ST 570735
Apt 19.04.1842; 740a (740); Map 1844, 2 chns, by J. Marmont, Bristol; turnpike roads, toll bars, ferry, building names, road names, observatory, hotel, zoological gardens, river basin and harbour, wells, 'collonade', quarry, downs; some built-up parts generalised; tithable areas tinted.

13/51 Coaley (parish) SO 772017
Apt 30.08.1839; 2463a (2463); Map 1841?, 4 chns, by Jas Croome, (transcribed from a map belonging to Lord Segrave); waterbodies, houses, woods, plantations, open fields, chapel.

13/52 Cold Ashton (parish) ST 743722
Apt 18.08.1841; 2300a (all); Map 1842, 3 chns, by Thomas Weaver, Bath; waterbodies, houses, open fields, building names; scale bar is combined with north pointer and is surrounded by a decorative ribbon.

13/53 Colesborne (parish) SO 999129 [Colesbourne]
Apt 30.09.1839; 2201a (2200); Map 1839, 6 chns, by Daniel Trinder; waterbodies, houses, woods, plantations, parkland, arable (col), grassland (col), clump of trees (named).

13/54 Coln Rogers (parish) SP 073090
Apt 08.04.1839; 1508a (1508); Map 1839, 5 chns, ? by Daniel Trinder; waterbodies, woods (col), arable (col), grassland (col).

13/55 Compton Abdale (parish) SP 062163
Apt 18.07.1842; 2174a (2215); Map 1843, 6 chns, by Richard Hall; waterbodies, houses, woods, plantations, arable (col), grassland (col), gardens (col).

13/56 Compton Greenfield (parish) ST 556830
Apt 27.05.1840; 650a (all); Map 1841?, 3 chns, by Geo. Osborne; turnpike roads, waterbodies, houses, woods, plantations, orchards, building names, common, green.

13/57 Condicote (parish) SP 145289
Apt 13.11.1856; 55a (890); Map (drawn on Apt) 1856?, 5 chns, (tithable parts only); plantations, building names.

13/58 Corse (parish) SO 798282 [Not listed]
Corn rent conversion, 1890; 883a (2190); Map 1890, 1:2500; foot/b'way, waterbodies, building names, road names, vicarage, kennels, Methodist Chapel, smithy; map appears to be derived from Ordnance Survey.

13/59 Cowley (parish) SO 946145
Apt 05.05.1841; 1834a (1834); Map 1847, 6 chns, by Richard Hall,

Cirencester; waterbodies, woods, plantations, heath/moor, common (col); meaning of colours is unclear. Apt omits land use, and has separate columns for 'quantities in old admeasurement' and 'quantities in new admeasurement'.

13/60 Cranham (parish) SO 898125
Apt 23.05.1838; 1860a (1859); Map 1838, 6 chns, by Richard Hall, Cirencester; foot/b'way, waterbodies, houses, woods, arable (col), grassland (col), orchards, gardens (col), building names, common.

13/61 Cromhall (parish) ST 697906
Apt 07.08.1839; 2579a (2579); Map 1838, 6 chns, by Y. and J.P. Sturge, Bristol; turnpike roads, waterbodies, houses, woods (named), plantations, parkland, marsh/bog, building names, chapel, pound, coal works, mill, rectory, quarries, boat house, ancient yew tree, common, meads, withy beds; hills and bridge named.

13/62 Cubberley otherwise Coberley (parish) SO 962165
Apt 27.09.1838; 3422a (all); Map 1838, 8 chns; turnpike roads, toll bars, waterbodies, houses, field gates, building names, springs, Roman encampment, mills.

13/63 Daglinworth (parish) SO 995050 [Daglingworth]
Apt 18.02.1837; 1885a (all); Map 1837, 3 chns, by Richard Hall; construction lines, foot/b'way, waterbodies, houses, woods, plantations, arable (col), grassland (col), orchards, gardens, heath/moor, hedge ownership, field gates, pits.

13/64 Didbrook (parish) SP 049318
Apt 22.06.1847; 928a (2578); Map 1847?, 6 chns, 'copied for Mr Pryce' by W. Shuter; houses.

13/65 Didcote (hamlet in parish of Beckford) SP 002356 [Not listed]
Apt 24.11.1840; 274a (all); Map 1843, 5 chns, by T. Yells, Bengeworth; waterbodies, landowners.

13/66 Didmarton (parish) ST 827879
Apt 28.08.1838; 720a (all); Map 1839, 1st cl, [3 chns], 'copied' by E. and S. Rich, Didmarton; foot/b'way, waterbodies, houses, woods, plantations, parkland, fences, road names, drains.

13/67 Dixton (hamlet in parish of Alderton) SO 982308
Apt 31.03.1838; 542a (all); Map 1839?, 6 chns, by J. Plumley, Bristol; hill-drawing, foot/b'way, waterbodies, houses, woods, orchards, gardens, hedge ownership (col), field gates.

13/68 Dodington (parish) ST 747798
Apt 03.01.1839; 1473a (all); Map 1839, 4 chns, by Edwd Dowding and Thos Chapman; foot/b'way, waterbodies, woods, parkland, orchards; colour bands show glebe (red), parkland (green) and 'pleasure grounds' (yellow); north pointer has leaf decoration.

13/69 Dowdeswell (parish) SP 001192
Apt 31.03.1838; 2246a (2246); Map 1838, 6 chns, by Richd Hall, Cirencester; foot/b'way, waterbodies, houses, woods (named), plantations, parkland (named), arable (col), grassland (col), orchards, gardens (col), building names, mearstones.

13/70 Down Ampney (parish) SU 111973
Apt 19.05.1843; 2496a (2510); Map 1842, 8 chns, by Daniel Trinder; waterbodies, houses, woods, plantations, arable (col), grassland (col).

13/71 Down Hatherley (parish) SO 868225
Apt 31.12.1850; 15a (930); Map 1851?, 6 chns; wood (named). District is apportioned by holding.

13/72 Doynton (parish) ST 722739
Apt 10.08.1839; 1703a (1703); Map 1839, 3 chns, 1st cl; construction lines, foot/b'way, waterbodies, houses, woods, plantations, orchards, field gates, building names, quarry, park (named), ancient boundary.

13/73 Dumbleton (District within) (parish) SP 021355
Apt 16.01.1844; 220a (all); Map 1846, 4 chns, in 2 parts, (including glebe at 12 chns); houses, hedge ownership, landowners.

13/74 Dursley (parish) ST 762978
Apt 29.11.1845; 1059a (1059); Map 1844, 2 chns, 1st cl, by R.C. Herbert, Worcester; construction lines, foot/b'way, turnpike roads, waterbodies, houses, rock outcrops, field boundary ownerships, building names, road names, mills, quarries, gas works.

13/75 Dymock (parish) SO 710316
Apt 11.03.1848; 1269a (6875); Map 1847, 3 chns, by James Webb; hill-drawing, canal, waterbodies, houses, open fields, building names, mills, tumulus, woods (by name), heath.

13/76 Dyrham cum Hinton (parish) ST 737764
Apt 23.12.1841; 3006a (3005); Map 1843, 6 chns, by Y. Sturge and J. Marmont, Bristol; waterbodies, houses, woods (named), plantations, parkland (named), orchards.

13/77 Eastington (parish) SO 782058
Apt 07.08.1839; 2043a (?); Map 1839, 3 chns, in 2 parts; foot/b'way, canal, waterbodies, houses, woods, plantations, parkland, arable (col), grassland (col), orchards, gardens (col), open fields, field boundary ownerships, building names; colour bands show both land use and field boundary ownership.

13/78 Edgeworth (parish) SO 941063
Apt 30.07.1839; 1566a (all); Map 1838, 6 chns, by Richard Hall, Cirencester; waterbodies, houses, woods, plantations, arable (col), grassland (col), orchards, gardens (col).

13/79 Elberton (parish) ST 601887
Apt 08.01.1840; 1524a (1673); Map 1840?, 4 chns; foot/b'way, waterbodies, woods, plantations, orchards, fences, road names; red lines may show walls.

13/80 Elkstone (parish) SO 973121
Apt 30.07.1841; 2058a (all); Map 1843, 6 chns, by Daniel Trinder; waterbodies, houses, woods, arable (col), grassland (col).

13/81 Elmore (parish) SO 782153
Apt 18.02.1841; 1486a (all); Map 1841, 6 chns; foot/b'way, waterbodies, houses, woods, building names, landowners, avenue of trees.

13/82 Elmstone Hardwick (hamlet) SO 908273 [Elmstone Hardwicke]
Apt 18.09.1838; 1732a (all); Map 1838, 3 chns, ? by Josiah Castree; foot/b'way, waterbodies, houses, woods, grassland (dark green), orchards, gardens (light green), open fields (named), field boundary ownerships, field gates.

13/83 English Bicknor (parish) SO 578151
Apt 19.04.1838; 2377a (all); Map 1839?, 4 chns; waterbodies, houses, woods, plantations, gardens, hedges, building names, common.

13/84 Fairford (parish) SP 157019
Apt 05.02.1840; 3879a (all); Map 1841, 6 chns, ? by Daniel Trinder; waterbodies, houses, woods, plantations, parkland, arable (col), grassland (col), marsh/bog.

13/85 Farmcote (hamlet in parish of Lower Guyting) SP 059281
Apt 22.06.1847; 1267a (?); Map 1847, 6 chns, copied for Mr Pryce by W. Shuter; houses.

13/86 Filton (parish) ST 602792
Apt 07.03.1838; 1030a (1030); Map 1838, 4 chns, 'copied from the parochial map made in 1825', by J. Marmont, Bristol; turnpike roads, houses, open fields.

13/87 Frampton Cotterell (parish) ST 620824
Apt 07.12.1840; 2121a (2120); Map 1840, 6 chns, in 3 parts, (includes 2-chn enlargement of detail); waterbodies, houses, plantations, parkland, building names, factories, chapels, mills, windmill, quarries, rectory, coal pit, moorland, common, greens; bridges named.

13/88 St John the Baptist, Frenchay (parish) ST 681777 [Frenchay]
Apt 30.12.1842; 551a (all); Map 1844, 6 chns, in 2 parts, by J.P. Sturge and Co, Bristol; waterbodies, woods, building names, iron mill; bridge named.

13/89 Fretherne (parish) SO 739090
Apt 23.11.1838; 566a (all); Map 1842, 6 chns, ? by Chas Baker; canal, waterbodies, houses, arable (col), grassland (col), building names.

13/90 Frocester (parish) SO 783032
Apt 07.08.1839; 1833a (1833); Map 1840, 3 chns, 1st cl, by T. Ward, Guildhall Chambers, Bristol; construction lines, houses.

13/91 St George (parish) ST 625736
Apt 29.07.1842; 1832a (all); Map 1844?, 3 chns, by D. Horwood, Bristol; railways, turnpike roads with gates, waterbodies, houses, building names, road names, field name, coal works, factory, cotton factory, fire engine, dam, poor house; hills named.

13/92 St Catherine, Gloucester (parish) SO 827191 [Not listed]
Apt 31.12.1850; 55a (200); Map 1851, 3 chns, (tithable parts only, tinted); railways, foot/b'way, building names, road names, landowners, school, churchyard, Bishop's palace, field acreages, freehold land.

13/93 St Michael, Gloucester (parish) SO 832183 [Not listed]
Apt 08.07.1841; 3a (500); Map 1850, 0.5 chns, in 2 parts, ? by J. Castree, (tithable parts only; includes 3-chn index).

13/94 Guiting Grange (hamlet in parish of Guiting Power) SP 103246 [Not listed]
Apt 26.10.1842; 6a (?); Map (drawn on Apt) 1848?, 9 chns, (tithable parts only); building names.

13/95 Hampnett (parish) SP 097156
Apt 21.02.1842; 1406a (all); Map 1843?, 8 chns; foot/b'way, houses, building names, prison.

13/96 Hanham (hamlet in parish of Bitton) ST 647706
Apt 09.10.1841; 1213a (?); Map 1842, 4 chns, by Cotterells and Cooper, Bath; railway, open fields (named), common, building names, wharf, coal wharf, mills, weir, factory.

13/97 Hardwicke (parish) SO 792127
Apt 24.08.1839; 2378a (all); Map 1839, 6 chns, in 2 parts, by Richard Hall, Cirencester; foot/b'way, canal, waterbodies, houses, woods (named), parkland, arable (col), grassland (col), orchards, gardens (col).

13/98 Harescomb (parish) SO 839098
Apt 24.08.1839; 479a (478); Map 1838, 3 chns, by Hussey, Wycombe; canal, waterbodies, houses, orchards, fence ownership, field boundary ownerships, field names; bridge named.

13/99 Harnhill (parish) SP 068007
Apt 03.01.1839; 689a (all); Map 1839, 3 chns; waterbodies, houses.

13/100 Hartpury (parish) SO 790240
Apt 13.04.1840; 3619a (3618); Map 1839, 3 chns; woods, plantations, parkland, field boundary ownerships, building names, vicarage, 'persh bed' (by symbol).

13/101 Hawkesbury (parish) ST 777873
Apt 27.01.1841; 9771a (9770); Map 1840, 6 chns, by Wm Bryan Wood, Barnbridge, Chippenham; foot/b'way, waterbodies, houses, woods, plantations, arable (col), grassland (col), open fields, field boundary ownerships, field gates; colour bands show both land use and field boundary ownership.

13/102 Hawling (parish) SP 070225
Apt 25.10.1842; 14a (1846); Map 1843?, 10 chns.

13/103 Hempstead and South Hamlet (parish and extra-parochial district) SO 813170 [Hempsted]
Apt 07.08.1839; 995a (1311); Map 1840, 3 chns, (tithable parts only, tinted); foot/b'way, canal, canal basin, waterbodies, houses, woods, plantations, parkland, orchards, gardens, open fields, fences, field gates, building names, field names, abbeys, tithe-free area, common meadow; bridge named.

13/104 Henbury except Charlton (parish) ST 540810
Apt 03.06.1839; 8469a (15409); Map 1839, 6 chns, ? by Jacob P. Sturge and J. Marmont; hill-drawing, waterbodies, houses, woods, plantations, parkland, building names, cliff (named), pier, dock, castle.

13/105 Hewelsfield (parish) SO 572021
Apt 30.12.1839; 1189a (all); Map 1841?, 3 chns; waterbodies, houses, common; map title has floral decoration.

13/106 Highnam, Over and Linton (hamlet in parish of Churchham) SO 799199 [Highnam]
Apt 03.01.1844; 1100a (?); Map 1846, 6 chns, ? by Richd Hall; foot/b'way, canal, waterbodies, farmyards (col), woods, arable (col), grassland (col), orchards, gardens (col), field boundary ownerships, building names; bridge named; colour bands show both land use and field boundary ownership.

13/107 Hill (parish) ST 647956
Apt 24.02.1841; 1966a (2476); Map 1840?, 4 chns, 'Transcribed from a map belonging to Miss Fust'; hill-drawing, waterbodies, houses, woods, parkland, orchards, building names, fishery, sea wall, vicarage, greens, common; map has leafy border.

13/108 Hinton on the Green (parish) SP 029402
Apt 10.09.1841; 2259a (all); Map 1841, 6 chns, by C. Cull; waterbodies, houses, woods, plantations. District is apportioned by holding; Apt omits land use and field names.

13/109 Horfield (parish) ST 597770
Apt 29.07.1840; 1287a (1287); Map 1843?, 6 chns, by J.M. Tucker; waterbodies.

13/110 Horsley (parish) ST 832983
Apt 28.04.1840; 541a (4082); Map 1841, 6 chns, by Richard Hall, (tithable parts only); waterbodies, woods, arable (col), grassland (col), gardens (col).

13/111 Horton (parish) ST 760847
Apt 21.11.1838; 3541a (3540); Map 1839, 6 chns; waterbodies, houses, woods (named), plantations, parkland, building names, road names.

13/112 Huntley (parish) SO 717194
Apt 03.05.1838; 1409a (all); Map 1841?, 3 chns; construction lines, waterbodies, houses, woods, plantations, field gates, building names. Apt omits some field names.

13/113 Icomb (parish) SP 212231
Apt 24.02.1842; 57a (970); Map 1842?, 2 chns, by W. Mitchell, (tithable parts only); foot/b'way, hedges, field gates; map is accompanied by schedule of owners, occupiers, land use and field names.

13/114 Ilmington (parish) (partly in Warwickshire) SP 212428
Apt 14.05.1845; 79a (4000); Map 1846?, 6 chns, (tithable parts only); foot/b'way, turnpike roads, waterbodies, woods, hedge ownership, field gates.

13/115 Iron Acton (parish) ST 678843
Apt 22.03.1839; 2927a (2927); Map 1840, 3 chns, 1st cl, surveyed for Messrs Sturge by J. Millard; construction lines, waterbodies, houses, building names, sand or stone pit.

13/116 Kempley (parish) SO 671308
Apt 22.02.1840; 1565a (1564); Map 1839, 3 chns, 1st cl, by Lakin and Giles, Worcester; construction lines, waterbodies, houses, woods, fences, field boundary ownerships, field gates, building names.

13/117 Kingscote (parish) ST 819965
Apt 27.04.1838; 1811a (1810); Map 1838, 3 chns, by Charles Hyde, Horsley, Gloucestershire; waterbodies, woods, parkland, arable (col), grassland (col), gardens (pink), fences, field gates, landowners, windmill (by symbol), hamlet names.

13/118 King Stanley (parish) SO 821032 [King's Stanley]
Apt 22.04.1839; 1680a (1679); Map 1838, 6 chns; hill-drawing, waterbodies, woods (col), plantations (col), parkland, arable (col), grassland (col), orchards, open fields (named), fences, landowners, quarry; hills named.

13/119 Lasborough (parish) ST 828932
Apt 17.03.1849; 1054a (all); Map 1849, 3 chns, by S. Rich, Didmarton; waterbodies, houses, woods, plantations, parkland, arable (col), grassland (col), gardens, field boundary ownerships; colour bands show both land use and field boundary ownership.

13/120 Lassington (parish) SO 799210
Apt 30.09.1839; 535a (535); Map 1840, 5 chns; canal, waterbodies,

houses, woods, plantations, arable (col), grassland (col), orchards, marsh/bog, 'Persh bed'.

13/121 Lea (parish) (partly in Herefordshire) SO 658217
Apt 09.05.1840; 703a (?); Map 1841, 3 chns, 1st cl, by William Price, Ross; construction lines, foot/b'way, turnpike roads, toll bar, waterbodies, houses, hedge ownership, building names, boundary stones and trees, milestones; woods are shown by annotation.

13/122 Lechlade (parish) SP 205005
Apt 09.04.1838; 3542a (3542); Map 1839, 6 chns; foot/b'way, turnpike roads and gate, canal, waterbodies, houses, arable (col), grassland (col), building names.

13/123 Littledean (parish) SO 671138
Apt 28.08.1839; 459a (510); Map 1839?, 4 chns; foot/b'way, waterbodies, woods, arable, grassland, orchards; land use is indicated by annotation; scale bar is combined with north pointer.

13/124 West Littleton (parish) ST 762762
Apt 26.02.1840; 1010a (all); Map 3 chns, surveyed by T. Weaver, Bath, 'revised' in 1840; houses.

13/125 Lancaut (parish) ST 533966
Apt 28.01.1839; 199a (all); Map 1840?, 4 chns; houses, woods, plantations, orchards.

13/126 Longhope (parish) SO 689194
Apt 23.05.1838; 3070a (all); Map 1840?, 3 chns; construction lines, foot/b'way, waterbodies, houses, woods (named), plantations, field boundary ownerships, field gates, building names, parsonage, common.

13/127 Lydney with Aylburton (parochial chapelry) SO 633032 [Lydney]
Apt 23.09.1840; 6724a (?); Map 1840, 3 chns, by John Hosmer, 105, Camden Road Villas, Camden Town, London; construction lines, foot/b'way, canal, waterbodies, houses, woods, plantations, avenue of trees, field boundary ownerships, extra parochial land, forest land, parish and chapelry boundaries.

13/128 Mangotsfield (parish) ST 655768
Apt 02.08.1844; 766a (2591); Map 1845?, 6 chns; railway with tunnel, waterbodies, houses, woods, plantations, orchards, building names; hill named.

13/129 Marshfield (parish) ST 782737
Apt 13.04.1840; 5846a (5845); Map 1840, 3 chns, by T. Weaver, Bath; waterbodies, houses.

13/130 Mickleton (parish) SP 169440
Apt 30.06.1841; 3767a (3766); Map 1840, 7.5 chns, 'compiled from various plans'; foot/b'way, waterbodies, building names.

13/131 Minchinhampton and Rodborough (parish) SO 870010
Apt 14.09.1839; 6205a (6205); Map 1839, in 2 parts: Rodborough at 3 chns ? by Chas Baker, Painswick; Minchinhampton at 6 chns by Y. and J.P. Sturge; canal, waterbodies, houses, woods (named), plantations, parkland, marsh/bog, open fields (named), fences, building names, school, fort, mills, iron mill, commons (col, named).

13/132 Minety (parish) (partly in Wilts) SU 023912
Apt 03.01.1839; 3547a (all); Map 1840, 6 chns, by Daniel Trinder; railway, foot/b'way, waterbodies, houses, woods, plantations, arable (col), grassland (col).

13/133 Minsterworth (parish) SO 791171
Apt 15.07.1839; 1828a (1938); Map 1839?, 4 chns; waterbodies, open fields, field names, landowners, fishery ownership.

13/134 Miserdine otherwise Miserden (parish) SO 918092
Apt 12.10.1838; 2435a (2434); Map 1840, 6 chns; waterbodies, houses, woods, plantations, arable (col), grassland (col), orchards, building names.

13/135 Mitcheldean (parish) SO 665193
Apt 15.07.1839; 620a (all); Map 1839?, 5 chns; waterbodies, houses, woods, orchards, gardens, rock outcrops, hedge ownership, fence ownership, field names, stone pits, forest land; woods are indicated by name, and former woodland, since cleared, is also indicated.

13/136 Moreton Valence (parish) SO 787087
Apt 29.01.1840; 1400a (all); Map 1840, 6 chns, by Richard Hall, litho (Standidge); foot/b'way, waterbodies, woods, orchards, pound, tithings.

13/137 Naunton (parish) SP 120230
Apt 30.06.1841; 617a (3106); Map 1840, 5 chns, by William Mitchell, (tithable parts only); foot/b'way, houses (incompletely shown), field gates, landowners, farm names, allotment in lieu of glebe; hills named; map is described as 'the outlines or a draught of all the tithable land in the parish of Naunton... also the Allotment in lieu of Glebe. Likewise showing the situation of the Rectory and Church, taken from the Award'.

13/138 Newent (parish) SO 721253
Apt 23.05.1838; 7804a (7803); Map 1840, 6 chns, by Richard Hall, Cirencester; canal, waterbodies, houses, woods (named), parkland, arable (col), grassland (col), orchards, gardens (col), building names, mill.

13/139 Newington Bagpath (parish) ST 816948
Apt 21.03.1839; 2131a (2131); Map 1839, 6.5 chns, by Chas Baker, Painswick; waterbodies, houses (incompletely shown), woods, arable (col), grassland (col), gardens (col), building names, road names, fishpond.

13/140 Newland (parish) SO 560080
Apt 20.10.1840; 8744a (?); Map 1842?, 3 chns, in 2 parts; construction lines, foot/b'way, waterbodies, houses, building names, road names, vicarage, brickyard, gasworks, skin-house, camp, mill, forest lands; bridge named; decorative compass roses.

13/141 Newnham (parish) SO 683113
Apt 21.08.1839; 1891a (2105); Map 1839, 3 chns, 1st cl, by Charles Hyde and Son, Horsley near Stroud, Gloucs; construction lines, waterbodies, houses, building names, modus land boundary.

13/142 North Nibley (parish) ST 743958
Apt 07.12.1846; 3245a (3245); Map 1847, 6 chns, in 2 parts, by J.P. Sturge and Son, Bristol, (includes 3-chn enlargements of detail); waterbodies, building names, greens, wood (by name).

13/143 Northway and Newton (tithing in parish of Ashchurch) SO 921331
Apt 09.02.1842; 1430a (?); Map 1841, 4 chns, 'compiled from a survey taken by W. Hensley', by James Webb, Worcester; railway, waterbodies, houses.

13/144 Norton (parish) SO 858240
Apt 22.07.1840; 208a (1870); Map 1841?, 3.5 chns; turnpike roads.

13/145 Nymphsfield (parish) SO 809003 [Nympsfield]
Apt 29.08.1838; 1072a (1472); Map 1839?, 8 chns; field gates.

13/146 Oddington (parish) SP 230260
Corn rent conversion, 1892; 656a (1660); Map 1892, 1:2500; railway, waterbodies, woods, building names, rectory; map is presumably copied from Ordnance Survey.

13/147 Oldbury on the Hill (parish) ST 812882
Apt 10.09.1838; 1343a (all); Map 1839, [3 chns], 1st cl, by E. and S. Rich, Didmarton; waterbodies, houses, woods, plantations, fences.

13/148 Oldland (hamlet in parish of Bitton) ST 660730
Apt 18.11.1841; 2589a (2589); Map 1843, 3 chns, 'copied' by John Beard Carruthers, Willsbridge, Bitton, Gloucs; hill-drawing, railway, waterbodies, houses, open fields, building names, road names, field names, school, mills, coal wharf, quarries, chapel, coal pit, intermixed lands (col), common meadows; physical features named; plough, scythe, rake, pitchfork, spade, trowel and billhook appear above the compass rose.

13/149 Olveston (parish) ST 602868
Apt 17.09.1839; 4787a (all); Map 1840, 6 chns, in 3 parts, by Y. and J.P. Sturge, (includes 3-chn enlargements of detail); turnpike roads, waterbodies, woods, plantations, marsh/bog, heath/moor, building names, road names, pound, mill, quarry, commons (col, named), withy beds.

13/150 Owlpen (parish) ST 802987
Apt 04.07.1838; 720a (720); Map 1839, 3 chns, in 2 parts, by Chas Baker, Painswick; hill-drawing, foot/b'way, turnpike roads, waterbodies, houses, farmyards, woods, plantations, arable (col), grassland (col), orchards, gardens, marsh/bog, open fields, building names, landowners, withy beds.

13/151 Oxenhall (parish) SO 705274
Apt 05.11.1841; 1887a (all); Map 1842?, 6 chns, by Richard Hall; canal, waterbodies, houses, woods, arable (col), grassland (col), orchards, gardens (col).

13/152 Ozleworth (parish) ST 792936
Apt 02.05.1838; 1114a (1114); Map 1838, 3 chns, by John Croome; waterbodies, houses, farmyards, woods, parkland, arable (col), grassland (col), gardens (col), field gates, glebe boundary, tithe-free land.

13/153 Painswick (parish) SO 870095
Apt 04.12.1839; 5569a (5815); Map 1839-41, 6 chns, in 3 parts, by Charles Baker, Painswick, (includes enlargements of town at 2 chns and open fields at 3 chns); construction lines, hill-drawing, foot/b'way, waterbodies, woods (named), plantations, parkland, orchards, arable (col), grassland (col), gardens, ornamental gardens, heath/moor (col), open fields, hedges, fences, building names, field names, mills, vicarage; hills and bridge named.

13/154 Pauntley (parish) SO 746293 [Not listed]
Apt 09.02.1839; 1968a (all); Map 1840, 3 chns, 1st cl, in 2 parts, by Henry Lakin junr, Worcester; construction lines, canal with towpath, waterbodies, houses, woods (named), fences, field boundary ownerships, field gates, building names, mills, park (named).

13/155 St Philip and Jacob (parish) ST 603733 [Not listed]
Apt 29.07.1842; 535a (?); Map 1847?, 3 chns, by W. Hicks Townsend, Bristol; railways, railway yard, canal, lock, waterbodies, building names, road names, toll gate, prison, mills, gas works, iron factories, cotton factory; bridge named.

13/156 Pinnock and Hyde (parishes) SP 078282
Apt 03.03.1847; 1050a (1050); Map 1847, 6 chns, 'copied for Mr Pryce' by W. Shuter; hill-drawing, houses, sand or stone pits, parish boundary.

13/157 Pitchcombe (parish) SO 852083
Apt 30.08.1838; 218a (all); Map 1838, 3 chns, 1st cl, by Richard Hall, Cirencester; construction lines, foot/b'way, waterbodies, houses, woods, plantations, arable (col), grassland (col), orchards, gardens (col).

13/158 Prestbury (parish) SO 972241
Apt 10.01.1838; 3022a (3022); Map 1840?, 3 chns, 1st cl, ? by H. Croome, Tewkesbury; construction lines, turnpike roads, toll bar, waterbodies, houses, woods, plantations, parkland, withy beds, marsh/bog, field boundary ownerships, field gates, building names, quarry, stone quarry, grandstand.

13/159 Preston (parish) SO 675349
Apt 20.09.1842; 885a (884); Map 1843, 3 chns, by Robert Jones, Ledbury; waterbodies, houses, building names, vicarage.

13/160 Pucklechurch (parish) ST 693770
Apt 24.02.1841; 2428a (2428); Map 1843, 6 chns, in 2 parts, by J. Marmont, Bristol; railway, houses (incompletely shown), building names, vicarage, woods (by name), glebe, common; some buildings are indicated by annotation but are not mapped.

13/161 Quedgley (parish) SO 812139 [Quedgeley]
Apt 07.08.1839; 439a (1453); Map 1839, 3 chns, in 3 parts, by Arthur Causton, Berkeley Street, Gloucester; foot/b'way, canal, waterbodies, houses, farmyards, woods, arable (col), grassland (col), orchards, field boundary ownerships, field gates, building names, landowners.

13/162 Quinton (parish) SP 183470 [Lower and Upper Quinton]
Apt 30.08.1839; 320a (4800); Map 1840?, 4 chns; foot/b'way, waterbodies, houses, woods (col), plantations (col), hedge ownership, field gates.

13/163 Randwick (parish) SO 828068
Apt 18.02.1841; 581a (all); Map 1842, 6 chns, by Chas Baker; railway, canal, waterbodies, houses, woods, rock outcrops, open fields, building names, detached field names, landowners, chapels, brewery, stone quarry.

13/164 Rangeworthy (chapelry) ST 689860
Apt 24.04.1844; 890a (?); Map 1844, 3 chns, by J.P. Sturge and Co, Bristol; waterbodies, houses.

13/165 Rendcomb (parish) SP 022105
Apt 14.08.1837; 2532a (2532); Map 1837, 8 chns, by Robt Jackman, Gloucs; foot/b'way, waterbodies, houses, woods, plantations, parkland (named, in detail).

13/166 Little Risington (parish) SP 192198 [Little Rissington]
Apt 11.03.1843; 29a (1300); Map 1846?, 3 chns, (tithable parts only in detail); foot/b'way, hedges, landowners.

13/167 Rockhampton (parish) ST 651935
Apt 13.11.1839; 1207a (all); Map 1839?, 3 chns; hill-drawing, waterbodies, houses, woods (col), orchards (col), common building names, sea wall.

13/168 Ruardean (parish) SO 621177
Apt 19.01.1847; 1591a (1590); Map 1840, 3 chns, 1st cl, by W. Fosbrooke, Hereford; construction lines, foot/b'way, waterbodies, houses, woods, field boundary ownerships, field gates, building names, road names. Apt omits some field names.

13/169 Rudford (parish) SO 776222
Apt 26.09.1837; 1205a (1204); Map 1837, 3 chns: Rudford Manor by Thomas Wakeman and Robert Jackman, 1829 and Hamlet of Highleadon by Arthur Causton; foot/b'way, canal with towpaths, waterbodies, houses, woods, orchards, marsh/bog, open fields, field boundary ownerships, field gates, manor and hamlet boundaries.

13/170 Saintbury (parish) SP 116402
Apt 31.08.1841; 1336a (all); Map 1842?, 6 chns; foot/b'way, waterbodies, woods (col), hedge ownership, field gates.

13/171 Sandhurst (parish) SO 828234
Apt 21.06.1839; 2227a (2227); Map 1839, 3 chns, by Josiah Castree, Gloucester; foot/b'way, waterbodies, houses, woods, plantations, orchards, marsh/bog, 'persh bed', heath/moor, open fields, field boundary ownerships, field gates, building names, road names, field names, landowners, greens, vicarage, pound, ferry; bridge named; field names may relate to an earlier field pattern; meaning of colours is unclear.

13/172 Saperton (parish) SO 939018 [Sapperton]
Apt 15.04.1842; 400a (3908); Map 1843, 8 chns, by Richard Hall; woods, arable (col), grassland (col), building names.

13/173 Saul (parish) SO 751096
Apt 26.06.1838; 565a (all); Map 1841?, 6 chns, by Richard Hall; canal, waterbodies, houses, arable (col), grassland (col), orchards, gardens (col), building names, chapel.

13/174 Sezincote (parish) SP 173310
Apt 24.02.1842; 1414a (1413); Map 1843?, 5 chns; foot/b'way, turnpike roads, road names. District is apportioned by holding and fields are not shown.

13/175 Shipton Moyne (parish) ST 890900
Apt 21.07.1838; 2299a (2298); Map 1838?, 9 chns; waterbodies, houses.

13/176 Shirehampton (tithing in parish of Westbury-on-Trym) ST 526776
Apt 05.03.1840; 1437a (all); Map 1840, 6 chns, in 3 parts, 'corrected from the parochial map' by Y. and J.P. Struge; hill-drawing, waterbodies, woods, plantations, park (named), building names, road names, Friends' Meeting House, chapel, ferry, sea banks, lighthouse, old battery, powder magazine; hill named; meaning of green tinting is unclear.

13/177 Siston (parish) ST 682750
Apt 31.01.1839; 1827a (1827); Map 1839, 3 chns, 1st cl, by J. Marmont; construction lines, trig points, waterbodies, houses.

13/178 Snowshill (parish) SP 112335
Apt 14.09.1839; 295a (2294); Map 1842?, 5 chns, by J. Kettle; foot/b'way, waterbodies, houses, building names, road names, landowners; plantations and coppice are shown by annotation.

13/179 Little Sodbury (parish) ST 759831
Apt 28.01.1839; 1071a (1071); Map 1838, 3 chns, by Henry Smith, Bath; hill-drawing, foot/b'way, waterbodies, houses, woods (col), plantations (col), fences, field gates, ancient camp, common; legend explains symbols.

13/180 Old Sodbury (parish) ST 749818
Apt 11.06.1839; 3618a (3637); Map 1839, 3 chns, by Henry Smith, Bath, (borough of Chipping Sodbury not mapped); hill-drawing, waterbodies, houses, woods (col), plantations (col), parkland, field gates, quarries, limekilns, common, private road; legend explains symbols; the 'Ridings' named on the map are areas of land subject to a modus for small tithes and exempt from great tithes; ornate coloured compass rose. (The map in PRO IR 30 is a copy; original is in PRO IR 77/20, and has additional colouring.)

13/181 Southrop (parish) SP 195030
Apt 26.09.1840; 1453a (1453); Map 1843, 4 chns, by Richard Hall; waterbodies, houses, woods, plantations, arable (col), grassland (col), orchards, gardens (col).

13/182 Standish (parish) SO 801085
Apt 21.11.1839; 3389a (3388); Map 1842, 6 chns, in 3 parts, by Daniel Trinder; railways, canal, waterbodies, houses, woods, plantations, arable (col), grassland (col), building names, vicarage.

13/183 Stapleton (parish) ST 626764
Apt 23.09.1842; 2554a (2554); Map 1839, 3 chns, by Daniel Horwood, Bristol; railway, waterbodies, houses, field boundary ownerships, building names, road names, 'Late' French prison, mills, snuff mills, park (named).

13/184 Staunton (parish) SO 550122
Apt 28.03.1844; 1517a (all); Map 1845, 3 chns, by W.H. Apperley, Hereford; hill-drawing, foot/b'way, turnpike roads, toll bar, waterbodies, houses, rock outcrops, building names, mill, limekilns, boundary trees, brewery, pump, milestone, spring, quarry, pound, school, village cross; boundary and landmark trees are described, (e.g. 'ash', 'beech', 'yew').

13/185 Stinchcombe (parish) ST 734981
Apt 07.08.1839; 1465a (1464); Map 1846?, 3 chns, 1st cl, by Jas Croome; construction lines, waterbodies, houses, woods, parkland, orchards, open fields, hedge ownership, field gates.

13/186 Stoke Gifford (parish) ST 621803
Apt 26.07.1842; 115a (2065); Map 1847, 6 chns; waterbodies, houses, orchards, building names.

13/187 Stoke Orchard (hamlet in parish of Bishops Cleeve) SO 927287
Apt 07.07.1837; 1331a (all); Map 1838, 3 chns, by Richard Hall; foot/b'way, waterbodies, houses, woods, plantations, arable (col), grassland (col), orchards, gardens (col); colour bands may show property ownerships.

13/188 Stonehouse (parish) SO 815055
Apt 18.07.1839; 1626a (all); Map 1839, 3 chns; hill-drawing, foot/b'way, canal, waterbodies, houses, woods, plantations, fences, field gates; areas belonging to other districts are tinted.

13/189 Stowell (parish) SP 089134
Apt 07.11.1842; 823a (all); Map 1843?, 8 chns, ? by Wm Clutton, 8 Parliament Street; waterbodies, houses, building names.

13/190 Sudeley Manor and the Abbey Demesnes, Langley Sudeley Tenements, and Coates in the parish of Winchcombe (parish and hamlet) SP 040260 [Not listed]
Apt 09.01.1844; 451a (?); Map 1848, 9 chns, by Richard Storr, Cirencester; woods, plantations, arable (col), grassland (col), road names, landowners.

13/191 Swindon (parish) SO 932251
Apt 05.09.1839; 722a (721); Map 1841, 3 chns, 1st cl, by Chas Baker, Painswick; railways, foot/b'way, waterbodies, houses, field gates.

13/192 Syde (parish) SO 956111
Apt 21.04.1838; 614a (614); Map 1838, 6 chns, by Richd Hall, Cirencester; waterbodies, woods, arable (col), grassland (col), gardens, field boundary ownerships, glebe (pink).

13/193 Taynton (parish) SO 730217
Apt 02.09.1840; 2501a (all); Map 1841?, 3 chns, 1st cl, by Richard Hall, Cirencester; construction lines, waterbodies, houses, arable, pasture, orchards, woods (named), field boundary ownerships, building names, quarry, boundary trees; land use is shown by annotation.

13/194 Tetbury (parish) ST 883928
Apt 27.09.1838; 4582a (4582); Map 1839, 3 chns, 1st cl, by Richard Hall; waterbodies, woods, plantations, parkland, arable (col), grassland (col), orchards, gardens (col), building names, gas works, market house, Independent meeting house, National schools, Baptist chapel.

13/195 Tewkesbury (parish) SO 890319
Apt 14.07.1842; 459a (2333); Map 1843, 6 chns, by W. Croome, Tewkesbury; waterbodies, houses, open fields (named), field boundary ownerships, road names, landowners; built-up part generalised.

13/196 Thornbury (except Rangeworthy) (parish) ST 642908
Apt 20.08.1839; 10509a (?); Map 1841?, 3 chns, 1st cl, in 4 parts; construction lines, hill-drawing, waterbodies, houses, woods (named), plantations, orchards, marsh/bog, withy beds, heath, common, hedge ownership, field gates, field acreages, building names, road names, ancient encampments, well, pounds, register office, town hall, Friends house, Independent and Baptist chapels, National School, Free School, British School, steam mill, mills, tan yard, castle. (There is another copy of the map in PRO IR 77/96, which is unfit for production.)

13/197 Tibberton (parish) SO 752217
Apt 17.10.1838; 1400a (all); Map 1839, 3 chns; construction lines, foot/b'way, waterbodies, houses, woods, plantations, parkland, orchards, open fields, field boundary ownerships, field gates, field acreages, building names, poorhouse, mill.

13/198 Tidenham (parish) ST 555965
Apt 30.10.1843; 6217a (9527); Map 1843?, 3 chns, 1st cl, in 3 parts, by James Peachy Williams, Bridgewater; construction lines, hill-drawing, waterbodies, houses, woods (named), plantations, parkland, orchards, field boundary ownerships, field gates, building names, landowners, schools, cliffs, hamlet boundaries (col); physical features and bridge named.

13/199 Toddington (parish) SP 037333
Apt 17.08.1847; 1857a (1857); Map 1847, 6 chns, 'copied for Mr Pryce' by W. Shuter; foot/b'way, houses, ornamental ground.

13/200 Todenham (parish) SP 230350
Apt 28.07.1840; 2478a (2477); Map 1843?, 6 chns; railway, foot/b'way, waterbodies, houses, woods (col), hedge ownership, fences, field gates; band may indicate tithe-free land.

13/201 Tormarton (parish) ST 777792
Apt 15.02.1839; 2645a (all); Map 1839, [3 chns], 1st cl, by Wm Bryan Wood, Barnbridge, Chippenham; construction lines, foot/b'way, waterbodies, houses, hedge ownership, field names; land use is incompletely shown by annotation.

13/202 Tortworth (parish) ST 702932
Apt 06.07.1842; 1551a (all); Map 1843?, 3 chns, 1st cl, by Jas Croome; construction lines, waterbodies, houses, woods, plantations, parkland, orchards, hedge ownership, fences, field boundary ownerships, field gates, brick walls (solid red lines).

13/203 Tuffley (hamlet in parish of St Mary de Lode) SO 831151
Apt 12.05.1840; 771a (?); Map 1839, 3 chns, in 2 parts; canal, waterbodies, houses, arable (col), grassland (col), orchards, heath/moor, open fields (named), field gates, landowners; bridge named.

13/204 Twyning (parish) SO 896369
Apt 20.11.1840; 3155a (3155); Map 1841, 3 chns, by James Webb, Worcester; construction lines, hill-drawing, foot/b'way, waterbodies, houses, open fields (col, named), fence ownership, field boundary ownerships, field gates, building names, quarry, commons (col), green.

13/205 Tytherington (parish) ST 669880
Apt 21.07.1838; 2218a (2100); Map 1838, 3 chns, surveyed by Y. Sturge in 1805 and 'corrected' by Y. and J.P. Struge; waterbodies, woods, open fields, field boundary ownerships, field gates, building names, road names, field names, churchyard, pound, moor, 'the castle'; hills named.

13/206 Uckington (hamlet in parish of Elmstone Hardwicke) SO 915255
Apt 31.01.1839; 881a (all); Map 1840?, 3 chns; waterbodies, houses, woods, open fields (named), field boundary ownerships, field gates; bridges named.

13/207 Uley (parish) ST 788981
Apt 07.12.1838; 1493a (1492); Map 1840, 3 chns, 1st cl, by Cotterells and Cooper, Bath; construction lines, hill-drawing, foot/b'way, turnpike roads, toll bar, waterbodies, woods, plantations, fences, field gates, avenue of trees.

13/208 Upleadon (parish) SO 762268
Apt 02.09.1840; 1208a (all); Map 1842, 6 chns; foot/b'way, waterbodies, houses, woods, arable (col), grassland (col), orchards, building names.

13/209 Upton St Leonards (parish) SO 867141
Apt 28.03.1840; 2976a (2975); Map 1841, 3 chns, in 2 parts; waterbodies, houses, woods (named), plantations, arable (col), grassland (col), gardens, heath/moor, open fields (named), field boundary ownerships, field gates, building names, parsonage, mills.

13/210 Walton Cardiff (parish) SO 905323
Apt 30.06.1842; 449a (650); Map 1842, 5 chns, by W. Croome, Tewkesbury; waterbodies, houses, field boundary ownerships, field gates; map has note of adoption proceedings.

13/211 Wapley cum Codrington (parish) ST 724791
Apt 04.12.1839; 2449a (all); Map 1840, 4 chns, by Dowding and Chapman; road names.

13/212 Westall, Naunton and Sandford (hamlets in parish of Cheltenham) SO 930215 [Not listed]
Apt 31.10.1849; 131a (?); Map 1850, 3 chns, by G.J. Engall, Cheltenham; waterbodies, woods, building names, road names, landowners; built-up part generalised; table gives field acreages.

13/213 Westbury upon Severn (parish) SO 730150 [Westbury-on-Severn]
Apt 21.10.1839; 8026a (8695); Map 1842, 3 chns, by Jackman and Strode; waterbodies, houses, woods (named), coppice (named), plantations, orchards, marsh/bog, 'persh bed', open fields (named), field boundary ownerships, field gates, building names, watermill (by symbol), green, common; colour bands may show property ownerships; meaning of other colours is unclear.

13/214 Westbury and Stoke Bishop (tithing in parish of Westbury upon Trym) ST 572763 [Westbury on Trym]
Apt 06.08.1842; 3800a (?); Map 1841, 6 chns, in 6 parts, by Y. and J.P. Sturge, (includes three enlargements of Cotham and Bristol, Redland and Westbury at 2 chns); hill-drawing, waterbodies, houses, woods, parkland, orchards, building names, road names, mills, quarries, folly, chapel, pound, castle, priory, college, tithing boundaries (col); physical features named.

13/215 Westcote (parish) SP 222207
Apt 05.02.1840; 1503a (1503); Map 1840?, 3 chns; houses, field gates.

13/216 Westerleigh (parish) ST 682802
Apt 24.02.1840; 3959a (4009); Map 1845, 6 chns, by W. Hicks Townsend, Bristol; railway, waterbodies, houses, woods, plantations.

13/217 Weston Birt (parish) ST 863893 [Westonbirt]
Apt 02.04.1839; 850a (?); Map 1839, 1st cl, [3 chns], by E. and S. Rich, Didmarton; construction lines, waterbodies, houses, parkland (col), gardens (col), hedges, fences.

13/218 Weston Subedge (parish) SP 130400 [Weston-sub-Edge]
Apt 30.11.1839; 2632a (all); Map 1840, 3 chns, in 2 parts, 'compiled from various plans', (including one part at 8 chns); turnpike roads, houses, parkland, open fields (named), field boundary ownerships, field gates, building names; hills named.

13/219 Whaddon (parish) SO 833137
Apt 01.02.1841; 727a (all); Map 1842, 3 chns; waterbodies, houses, woods, plantations, orchards, open fields, fences, field gates, avenue of trees.

13/220 Great Witcomb (parish) SO 912145 [Great Witcombe]
Apt 16.08.1837; 918a (918); Map 1838, 4 chns, by Rich. Hall; foot/b'way, woods (col), plantations (col), parkland, arable (col), grassland (col), gardens, field boundary ownerships, field gates, building names.

13/221 Whitminster otherwise Wheatenhurst (parish) SO 772085
Apt 21.10.1837; 1238a (all); Map 1838, 3 chns, by Richd Hall, Cirencester; foot/b'way, canal, waterbodies, houses, woods, plantations, parkland, arable (col), grassland (col), orchards, gardens, marsh/bog, withy beds, open fields, fences.

13/222 Whittington (parish) SP 014209
Apt 11.08.1838; 1422a (1422); Map 1838, 3 chns; woods, parkland, field acreages, field boundary ownerships, building names, mill, boundaries of the estate of William Gracchus Peachey Esqre.

13/223 Wick cum Abson (parish) ST 710730
Apt 24.02.1841; 2315a (2315); Map 1842, 3 chns, 1st cl, in 2 parts, by Thomas Ward, Bristol and Edmd Troy, Tytherton, Chippenham; construction lines, waterbodies, houses, building names, iron works.

13/224 Wickwar (parish) ST 707882
Apt 21.04.1838; 2308a (all); Map 1838, [3 chns], 1st cl; construction lines, foot/b'way, waterbodies, houses, woods, open fields, hedge ownership, field gates, building names, road names, castle, rectory, school, town hall, well, coal works, milestone, field acreages; bridges named.

13/225 Widford (parish) SP 271129
Apt 18.01.1839; 564a (all); Map 1841?, 3 chns; houses, hedge ownership, field gates, building names, chapel.

13/226 Winstone (parish) SO 962094
Apt 26.03.1842; 1438a (1437); Map 1842, 6 chns, by Richard Hall; waterbodies, houses, woods, plantations, arable (col), grassland (col), orchards, gardens (col).

13/227 Winterbourne (parish) ST 647804
Apt 16.11.1842; 2620a (all); Map 1844, 6 chns, in 3 parts, 'copied from J. Dymock's map of 1824' by J.P. Sturge and Co; building names, road names, rectory, commons; bridges named.

13/228 Woodchester (parish) SO 833021
Apt 19.04.1838; 1203a (1203); Map 1838, 3 chns, by Richard Hall, Cirencester; hill-drawing, waterbodies, houses, woods, parkland, arable (col), grassland (col), gardens.

13/229 Woolastone (parish) ST 585995 [Woolaston]
Apt 05.06.1838; 4376a (5416); Map 1840?, 3 chns, 1st cl, by E.S. Gisborne; construction lines, waterbodies, houses, field boundary ownerships, building names, parsonage, grange.

13/230 Woolstone (parish) SO 961302
Apt 10.09.1838; 787a (787); Map 1838, 3 chns, 1st cl, by R.C. Herbert, Worcester; construction lines, foot/b'way, turnpike roads, toll gate, waterbodies, fences, field boundary ownerships, field acreages, road names.

13/231 Wootton under Edge (parish) ST 770940 [Wotton-under-Edge]
Apt 15.11.1842; 4881a (4880); Map 1847, 3 chns, 1st cl, by George Garner, Wotton-under-Edge; railway, waterbodies, houses, woods, plantations, parkland, orchards, rock outcrops, hedges, field gates, building names, sand or stone pit, mills, quarry; hills named.

13/232 Yanworth (parish) SP 074142
Apt 28.01.1839; 1228a (all); Map 1841?, [10 chns]; foot/b'way, woods, hedge ownership.

13/233 Yate (parish) ST 715849
Apt 30.11.1838; 4042a (4042); Map 1839, 3 chns, 1st cl, in 4 parts, by J.P. Sturge and J. Marmont, Bristol, (includes index); construction lines, houses, building names, common.

Herefordshire

PRO IR29 and IR30 14/1-239

252 tithe districts: 544,387 acres
238 tithe commutations: 502,932 acres
157 voluntary tithe agreements, 81 compulsory tithe awards,
1 corn rent annuity

Tithe and tithe commutation

Some 94 per cent of the tithe districts of Herefordshire were subject to payment of tithes in 1836 and 138 districts were wholly tithable (Fig. 26). The main causes of tithe exemption in this county were modus payments in lieu of tithes, the merger of tithes in the land, and exemption by prescription.

Assistant tithe commissioners and local tithe agents who officiated in Herefordshire are listed in Table 14.1. Most Herefordshire tithe valuers were resident in or close to the county; notable exceptions were Richard Allerton from London (four districts), Oliver Stubbs, of Hinton St George, Somerset, and George Ashdown from Staffordshire (one district each) (Table 14.2).

Tithe maps

Herefordshire is similar to Monmouthshire in that it has an exceptionally large proportion of first-class tithe maps (37 per cent). Construction lines are present on 8 per cent of second-class maps and doubtless some of these were offered as first-class maps but failed to pass the Tithe Commission's tests. Copying is acknowledged on eight maps but was probably much more widespread. The acreages recorded in the tithe apportionment of Garway are, for example, said to have been taken from a survey of 1784. Scales employed on Herefordshire tithe maps range from one inch to three chains to one inch to twelve chains; 62 per cent of maps are in the recommended scale range of one inch to three to four chains and 29 per cent are at the six-chain scale (Table 14.3).

The preponderance of plain, first-class 'working plans' results in a sparse record of land use on Herefordshire tithe maps: about 44 per cent show woodland (an exceptionally low proportion), 4 per cent depict arable and grass, 6 per cent gardens, and 13 per cent parks. Orchards appear on 20 per cent of Herefordshire maps and hops on eleven maps (5 per cent). The mapping of hops in Herefordshire is even more deficient than in Kent, as hop growing is mentioned in sixty-six schedules of tithe apportionment. Residual open fields

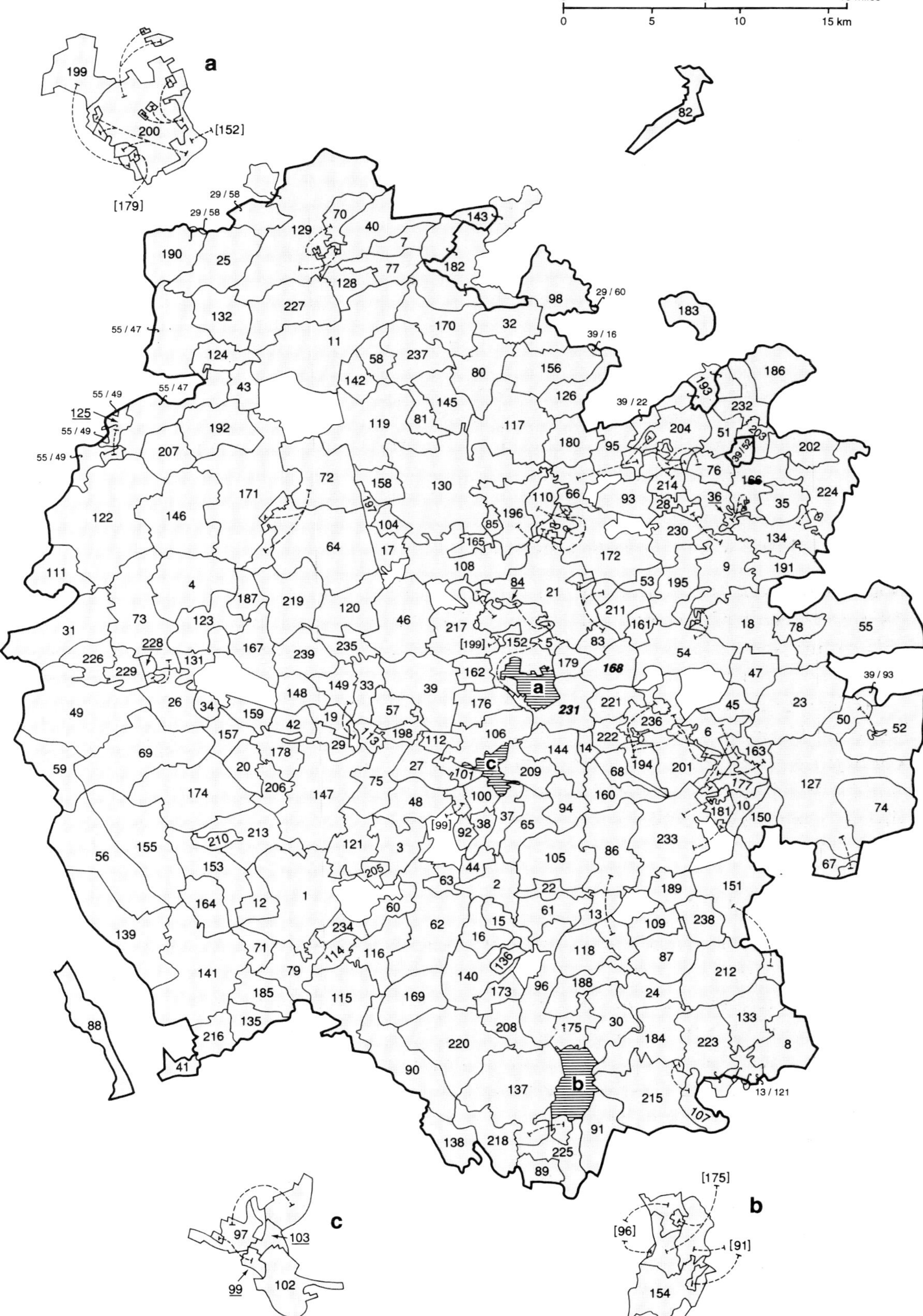

Fig. 26 Herefordshire: tithe district boundaries.

appear on 12 per cent of Herefordshire tithe maps and as in Monmouthshire, the mapping of field boundary ownership is more comprehensive than usual and occurs on 43 per cent of maps. Roads on some Herefordshire tithe maps are occasionally coloured to distinguish turnpike, public and private roads, as at Cradley. The map for Upper Sapey most unusually identifies buildings by naming owners rather than the buildings. A number of Herefordshire tithe maps depict antiquities, including castles (six maps), Roman roads (three maps), and various ruins and earthworks (fifteen maps). The townscape of the city of Hereford is mapped in particular detail. Tithe barns, a rarity on tithe maps, appear on the maps of Orcop and St Weonards.

Some 175 Herefordshire tithe maps in the Public Record Office collection can be attributed to a particular map-maker; the most prolific was William Fosbrooke who produced thirty-three maps (four of them jointly with others), covering 17 per cent of the area of the county. This is an unusually high proportion for a single map-maker. Four maps are definitely the work of men from well outside the county; two of these are by Richard Allerton from London (Table 14.2).

Unlike Monmouthshire, where the high proportion of first-class maps is complemented by a dearth of decoration, a number of Herefordshire maps are ornamented. Ten have decorative borders (often with floral or leaf motifs), nine have cartouches, and several have decorated direction pointers.

Table 14.1. *Agreements and awards for commutation of tithes in Herefordshire*

Assistant commissioner/ local tithe agent	*Number of agreements**	*Number of awards*
Thomas Hoskins	103	0
John Johnes	2	74
Charles Pym	27	2
George Bolls	16	0
Robert Page	6	0
George Wingrove Cooke	0	1
Aneurin Owen	0	1
John Job Rawlinson	0	1
Thomas Smith Woolley	0	1
Tithe Commissioners	0	1

*Computed from the number of extant reports on tithe agreements in the tithe files [PRO IR 18].

Table 14.2. *Tithe valuers and tithe map-makers in Herefordshire*

Name and address (in Herefordshire unless indicated)	*Number of districts*	*Acreage*
Tithe valuers		
William Fosbrooke, Hereford	61	132,595
William Price, Ross	27	56,908
William Havard Apperley	23	38,492
Morris and William Sayce, Kington	17	43,674
John, Richard and Walter Tench, Hereford	16	33,991
Thomas Blashill, Kings Acre	14	18,001
Thomas Henry Davis, Orleton, Worcestershire	10	19,966
Others [31]	70	159,305
Attributed tithe map-makers		
William Fosbrooke, Hereford	33	85,406
William Price, Ross	27	56,653
William Havard Apperley, Hereford	21	36,146
Morris and William Sayce, Kington	16	39,216
James Webb, Worcester	12	26,596
Edward Sacheverall Gisborne, Huntingdon	6	15,825
James Cranston, Kings Acre	6	6,963
Others [30]	54	111,484

Table 14.3. *The tithe maps of Herefordshire: scales and classes*

Scale in chains/inch	*All maps*		*First Class*		*Second Class*	
	Number	*Acreage*	*Number*	*Acreage*	*Number*	*Acreage*
3	130	240,350	86	179,382	44	60,968
3.5	2	5,710	0	0	2	5,710
4	16	30,667	1	7,078	15	23,589
4.5, 5	2	2,558	0	0	2	2,558
6	72	181,145	0	0	72	181,145
8	14	38,091	0	0	14	38,091
<8	2	4,411	0	0	2	4,411
TOTAL	238	502,932	87	186,460	151	316,472

Table 14.4. *The tithe maps of Herefordshire*: dates

	1837	*1838*	*1839*	*1840*	*1841*	*1842*	*1843*	*1844*	*1845*	*1846*	*1847*	*1848*	*1849*	*>1849*
All maps	2	24	46	49	25	23	20	18	11	8	8	2	1	1
1st class	1	11	20	18	12	8	5	7	3	0	2	0	0	0
2nd class	1	13	26	31	13	15	15	11	8	8	6	2	1	1

Herefordshire

14/1 Abbey Dore (parish) SO 395325
Apt 15.07.1839; 5391a (all); Map 1840, 6 chns; waterbodies, houses, building names; bridge named.

14/2 Aconbury (parish) SO 515334
Apt 27.07.1842; 39a (1591); Map 1847?, 6 chns; woods (named). District is apportioned by holding and fields are not shown.

14/3 Allensmore (parish) SO 455357
Apt 01.09.1840; 2007a (all); Map 1839, 3 chns, 1st cl, by W. Fosbrooke, Hereford; construction lines, turnpike roads, toll bar, waterbodies, houses, field boundary ownerships, building names.

14/4 Almeley (parish) SO 337520
Apt 18.07.1839; 3353a (3352); Map 1840, 6 chns, ? by Morris and Wm Sayce; turnpike roads, waterbodies, woods, plantations, open fields (named), building names, road names, tramroad, common, greens.

14/5 Amberley (parish) SO 547479
Apt 30.04.1841; 377a (377); Map 1841?, 6 chns; foot/b'way, waterbodies, houses, orchards, fences, building names, folly; bridge named.

14/6 Ashperton (parish) SO 642420
Apt 16.06.1838; 1741a (all); Map 1838, 3 chns, 1st cl, in 2 parts, by W. Fosbrooke; construction lines, houses, field boundary ownerships, field gates, building names, castle, field acreages; woodland and parkland are shown by annotation.

14/7 Aston (parish) SO 465720
Apt 04.04.1845; 920a (all); Map 1846?, 8 chns; waterbodies, houses, woods (col), plantations (col).

14/8 Aston Ingham (parish) SO 681232
Apt 28.09.1838; 2378a (all); Map 1839, 3 chns, 1st cl, by William Price, Ross; construction lines, foot/b'way, waterbodies, houses, hedge ownership, fences, building names, mills, rectory; hills named; woods and coppices are shown by annotation.

14/9 Avenbury (parish) SO 651521
Apt 27.07.1840; 3234a (3233); Map 1840, 6 chns; waterbodies, houses, building names, limekiln.

14/10 Aylton (parish) SO 663377
Apt 30.12.1840; 825a (all); Map 1839, 3 chns, 1st cl, by W. Fosbrooke; construction lines, foot/b'way, waterbodies, houses, field boundary ownerships, field gates.

14/11 Aymestry (parish) SO 425665 [Aymestrey]
Apt 30.09.1842; 6350a (6349); Map 1843?, 6 chns, by Richard Allerton, Norfolk St, Strand; waterbodies, houses, woods, plantations, parkland, field gates, building names, township boundaries (col), common; hills named.

14/12 Bacton (parish) SO 373327
Apt 04.12.1839; 1155a (1155); Map 1842, 4 chns; houses, building names, mill. Apt omits some field names.

14/13 Ballingham (parish) SO 574318
Apt 16.11.1842; 888a (901); Map 1839, 6 chns, by William Price, Ross; foot/b'way, waterbodies, houses, woods.

14/14 Bartestree (chapelry in parish of Dormington) SO 570411
Apt 02.11.1839; 410a (all); Map 1839, 3 chns, by George Stokes, Hereford; foot/b'way, waterbodies, houses, farmyards, woods, plantations, parkland, arable (col), grassland (col), orchards, gardens (col), ornamental gardens, rock outcrops, field boundary ownerships, field gates, stiles, quarry; hops are shown by annotation over orchard symbols.

14/15 Little Birch (parish) SO 518311
Apt 21.01.1840; 967a (967); Map 1840, 3 chns, by W.H. Apperley, Hereford; foot/b'way, waterbodies, houses, fences, field boundary ownerships, field gates, building names, rectory, boundary stones; green tint may show tithe-free land.

14/16 Much Birch (parish) SO 506304
Apt 09.08.1843; 1288a (1287); Map 1840, [3 chns], by W.H. Apperley, Hereford; construction lines, waterbodies, woods, fences, field boundary ownerships, field gates, building names.

14/17 Birley (parish) SO 454538
Apt 21.11.1837; 1004a (all); Map 1840?, 6 chns, ? by Morris and Wm Sayce; foot/b'way, waterbodies, woods (named), orchards, gardens, heath/moor, building names, chapel, common; hill named.

14/18 Bishops Froome otherwise Froome Bishop (parish) SO 667481 [Bishops Frome]
Apt 28.10.1843; 4016a (4550); Map 1844, 3 chns, 1st cl, by Henry Lakin, Worcsr; hill-drawing, waterbodies, houses, woods, plantations, orchards, hops, fences, field boundary ownerships, building names, sand or stone pits, quarry, boundary trees; colours may show tithe exemptions and tithing practice.

14/19 Bishopstone (parish) SO 418432
Apt 31.07.1839; 777a (all); Map 1840, 3 chns, by James Cranston; construction lines, waterbodies, houses.

14/20 Blakemore (parish) SO 363409 [Blakemere]
Apt 13.12.1843; 1128a (all); Map 1847, 3 chns, 1st cl, by W. Fosbrooke, Hereford; waterbodies, houses, field boundary ownerships, building names.

14/21 Bodenham (parish) SO 550510
Corn rent conversion, 1928; 1613a (5260); there is no map, and Apt omits field names, occupiers and land use.

14/22 Bolston (parish) SO 546327 [Bolstone]
Apt 12.11.1840; 657a (all); Map 1839, 6 chns, by William Price, Ross; waterbodies, houses, woods (named), plantations, orchards, fences.

14/23 Bosbury (parish) SO 695435
Apt 10.10.1839; 4769a (4769); Map 1841, 3 chns, 1st cl, by Robert Jones; canal, waterbodies, houses, open fields, building names, vicarage, mill.

14/24 Brampton Abbotts (parish) SO 602265
Apt 15.11.1838; 1452a (1452); Map 1838, [6 chns], by William Price, Land Agent and Surveyor, Ross; waterbodies, woods (col), open fields.

14/25 Brampton Brian (parish) SO 361713 [Brampton Bryan]
Apt 18.05.1839; 2926a (?); Map 1839, 4 chns, by Walter Tench, Hereford; foot/b'way, waterbodies, houses, farmyards (col), woods (col), plantations (col), parkland (named; in detail), orchards, gardens (col), meadows (col), fences, field gates, building names, woodkeeper's lodge, keeper's lodge, castle, hall; above the north pointer is a hat with 'libertas' on the hat-band.

14/26 Bredwardine (parish) SO 329448
Apt 24.02.1841; 2246a (all); Map 1840, 3 chns, 1st cl, by W. Fosbrooke; construction lines, turnpike roads, toll bar, houses, field boundary ownerships, building names, vicarage.

14/27 Breinton (parish) SO 471402 [Not listed]
Apt 12.11.1840; 1629a (all); Map 1839, 3 chns, 1st cl, by William Fosbrooke; construction lines, houses, field boundary ownerships, building names.

14/28 Bridenbury or Bredenbury (parish) SO 618563
Apt 14.11.1839; 546a (all); Map 1839, 3 chns, 1st cl, by Richd Philtt Porter; construction lines, foot/b'way, waterbodies, houses, fences, field boundary ownerships, field gates, building names.

14/29 Bridge Sollers (parish) SO 421419
Apt 24.12.1842; 768a (all); Map 1842, 3 chns; waterbodies, woods, orchards, ferry.

14/30 Bridstow (parish) SO 582246
Apt 10.09.1839; 592a (all); Map 1839, 6 chns, in 2 parts, by William Price, Ross; waterbodies, houses, woods, parkland, common, estate names; colours may show property ownerships.

14/31 Brilley (parish) SO 261492
Apt 15.12.1840; 3793a (all); Map 1841, 8 chns, by Walter Tench, Hereford; waterbodies, houses, woods, plantations, orchards, building names; leaves surround map title.

14/32 Brimfield (parish) SO 528670
Apt 16.11.1840; 1842a (1842); Map 1840, 6 chns, 'compiled from an old survey' by James Webb, Worcester; hill-drawing, turnpike roads, toll bars, canal, waterbodies, houses, building names, commons; hills are drawn in elevation, with one crowned by an oak tree.

14/33 Brinsop (parish) SO 441451
Apt 13.12.1843; 1364a (all); Map 1843, 6 chns, 'compiled from old surveys' by Hy Lakin junr, Worcester; waterbodies, houses, woods (col, named), field boundary ownerships, building names, mill, vicarage.

14/34 Brobury (parish) SO 345443
Apt 31.05.1839; 508a (all); Map 1839, 3.5 chns; waterbodies, woods, orchards, glebe (col).

14/35 Brockhampton (parish) SO 688557
Apt 23.09.1840; 786a (all); Map 1840, 3 chns, 1st cl, by James Webb, Worcester; construction lines, foot/b'way, waterbodies, houses, woods, fences, field boundary ownerships, field gates.

14/36 Bromyard (Town Parish of) (district in parish of Bromyard) SO 655542
Apt 13.12.1843; 261a (8611); Map 1844, 3 chns, 1st cl, in 2 parts; construction lines, field boundary ownerships, building names, road names, field names; built-up part generalised.

14/37 Lower Bullingham (township in parish of Hereford St Martin) SO 515376
Apt 11.11.1846; 1109a (all); Map 1840, 3 chns, by William Price, Ross; waterbodies, houses, woods (by name), open fields, building names, sand or stone pit, ford.

14/38 Over Bullinghope, otherwise Upper Bullingham (parish) SO 506365 [Bullinghope]
Apt 03.04.1843; 698a (all); Map 1844, 3.5 chns, (tinted); waterbodies, woods, orchards, open fields, building names.

14/39 Burghill (parish) SO 479451
Apt 16.07.1846; 3704a (3704); Map 1847, 4 chns; waterbodies, houses, woods (by name), open fields, fences, building names, brick kiln, Roman road; physical features named.

14/40 Burrington (parish) SO 445725
Apt 08.11.1841; 2581a (2580); Map 1845?, 8 chns; waterbodies, houses, woods, plantations, parkland, hedges, field gates, building names, forge, mill.

14/41 Bwlch Trewyn (township in parish of Cwmyoy) SO 325231 [Tre-wyn]
Apt 04.12.1839; 636a (635); Map 1840, 3 chns, surveyed for Robert Gabb by John Davies; construction lines, waterbodies, building names, sheds.

14/42 Byford (parish) SO 396432
Apt 25.06.1842; 903a (all); Map 1842, 3 chns; foot/b'way, turnpike roads, waterbodies, woods, parkland, orchards, building names, road names, ferry, terrace, lodge, glebe; park and house lying outside district are mapped.

14/43 Byton (parish) SO 372636
Apt 11.11.1842; 946a (all); Map 1843, 8 chns, in 3 parts, ? by Morris and Wm Sayce, (includes two 3-chn enlargements of common fields); waterbodies, woods, plantations, orchards, open fields, building names, moors; hills named.

14/44 Callow (parish) SO 500345
Apt 13.04.1840; 622a (621); Map 1840, 3 chns, by William Price, Ross; foot/b'way, waterbodies, houses, woods, building names.

14/45 Canon Frome (parish) SO 653435
Apt 27.06.1838; 1023a (1023); Map 1838, 5 chns; waterbodies, houses.

14/46 Canon Pion (parish) SO 465492 [Canon Pyon]
Apt 24.03.1842; 3707a (all); Map 1841, 3 chns, 1st cl, by W. Fosbrooke; construction lines, foot/b'way, waterbodies, houses, open fields, field boundary ownerships, field gates, building names.

14/47 Castle Froome (parish) SO 669454
Apt 31.10.1840; 1512a (all); Map 1841, 4 chns, by Robert Jones; foot/b'way, waterbodies, houses, field gates, building names, mill, parsonage.

14/48 Clehonger (parish) SO 465381
Apt 24.08.1840; 1889a (all); Map 1839, 6 chns; foot/b'way, waterbodies, houses, woods, plantations, parkland, orchards, fences, field boundary ownerships.

14/49 Clifford (parish) SO 262444
Apt 30.04.1846; 6522a (6522); Map 1842, 3 chns, 1st cl, by W. Fosbrooke, Hereford; hill-drawing, foot/b'way, waterbodies, houses, field boundary ownerships, field gates, building names, priory, vicarage, mill, fort, common, boundary trees, township boundaries (col); hill named. Apt omits some field names.

14/50 Coddington (parish) SO 724423
Apt 24.03.1838; 1077a (all); Map 1838, 3 chns, by Robert Jones; waterbodies, houses, woods, arable (col), grassland (col), orchards, gardens, field boundary ownerships, building names, rectory.

14/51 Collington (parish) SO 645602
Apt 31.08.1840; 985a (all); Map 1840, 3 chns, by James Webb, Worcester; construction lines, waterbodies, houses, fences, field boundary ownerships, field gates, building names, parsonage.

14/52 Colwall (parish) SO 750420
Apt 01.05.1840; 3772a (3771); Map 1841, 3 chns, 1st cl, in 2 parts, by Arthur Causton, Clarence Street, Gloucester, (includes six 1-chn enlargements of detail); construction lines, hill-drawing, waterbodies, houses, woods, plantations, parkland, orchards, hops, fences, field boundary ownerships, field gates, building names, chapel, school, sand or stone pit, tan house, mill; beacon named.

14/53 Little Cowarn (parish) SO 605510 [Little Cowarne]
Apt 21.04.1840; 697a (all); Map 1840, 3 chns, by Walter Pitt; construction lines, waterbodies, houses, woods (named), building names, mill, pound.

14/54 Much Cowarne (parish) SO 626470
Apt 20.04.1847; 3707a (3706); Map 1848, 8.5 chns, 'compiled from the Inclosure Award plan' by W.H. Apperley, Hereford; hill-drawing, foot/b'way, turnpike roads, waterbodies, woods, plantations, building names, quarries, clay pits, vicarage, parsonage, toll bar, mill, tan house, blacksmith's shop; bridge named.

14/55 Cradley (parish) SO 720480
Apt 29.11.1838; 5967a (5966); Map 1839, 3 chns, by William Jones, Cradley; turnpike roads (orange), toll bar, parish roads (yellow), occupation roads (uncoloured), waterbodies, woods (by name), common, houses, building names, quarries, mills, weir; hills named; legend explains symbols.

14/56 Upper and Lower Crasswell (township in parish of Clodock) SO 282359 [Craswall]
Apt 04.08.1843; 5204a (5204); Map 1840, 3 chns, 1st cl, surveyed for W. Fosbrooke, Hereford, by J.J. Haslett and Michael O'Rourke; construction lines, houses, woods, plantations, orchards, field boundary ownerships, building names, mill, chapel, abbey tan yard. Apt omits some field names.

14/57 Credenhill (parish) SO 451438
Apt 24.05.1842; 1225a (all); Map 1843, 6 chns; waterbodies, houses.

14/58 Croft (township in parish of Croft) SO 450655
Apt 30.04.1842; 1058a (all); Map 1839, 4 chns; hill-drawing, foot/b'way, waterbodies, houses, woods, plantations, parkland, orchards, fence ownership, field boundary ownerships, field gates, building names, castle, boundary stones, quarries, limekiln, lodge; north pointer is decorated with acorn and oak leaves, there is leaf decoration beneath the map title, and the border has geometrical patterns with floral corners.

14/59 Cusop (parish) SO 247414
Apt 30.04.1840; 2295a (all); Map 1839, 3 chns, by Walter Tench, Hereford; waterbodies, houses, rock outcrops, building names, quarries, mill, commons; compass rose is coloured with gold leaf and north pointer tip is a star. Apt omits some field names.

14/60 St Devereux (parish) SO 450321 [Not listed]
Apt 11.01.1838; 1095a (all); Map 1839, 3 chns, 1st cl, by W. Fosbrooke; construction lines, waterbodies, houses, field boundary ownerships, field acreages, building names, road names, tramroad.

14/61 Little Dewchurch (parish) SO 546317
Apt 22.12.1838; 1653a (all); Map 1839, 6 chns, in 2 parts, 'compiled from an Old Survey' by William Price, Ross; township boundaries (col). District is apportioned by holding.

14/62 Much Dewchurch (parish) SO 475310
Apt 13.03.1846; 4879a (all); Map 1841, 6 chns, by William Price, Ross; foot/b'way, waterbodies, houses, woods (named), plantations, park (named), marsh/bog, building names, tram house, tram road, boundary stones, vicarage, commons; bridge named.

14/63 Dewsall (parish) SO 483334 [Not listed]
Apt 31.08.1840; 677a (all); Map 1840, 3 chns, by William Price, Ross; waterbodies, houses, woods, building names, boundary trees and stones, rectory.

14/64 Dilwyn (parish) SO 419545
Apt 03.07.1837; 6068a (all); Map 1838?, 6 chns, in 2 parts, ? by Morris Sayce, (includes village separately at 3 chns); hill-drawing, waterbodies, woods, plantations, ornamental ground (col), orchards (by annotation), open fields, building names, tumulus, common; bridge named. Apt omits land use.

14/65 Dinedor (parish) SO 535370
Apt 30.09.1846; 1679a (all); Map 1840, 3 chns, 1st cl, by William Price, Ross; construction lines, waterbodies, houses, hedge ownership, building names, mills, boundary trees, garrison, school, park (named) glebe.

14/66 Docklow (parish) SO 564575
Apt 30.01.1841; 1715a (1715); Map 1841, 3 chns, by Francis Harris, Leominster; foot/b'way, waterbodies, houses, woods, plantations, parkland, orchards, gardens (col), fences.

14/67 Donnington (parish) SO 711341
Apt 30.06.1837; 809a (all); Map 1837, 3 chns; construction lines, canal, field boundary ownerships, building names, coppice (by annotation).

14/68 Dormington (parish) SO 587399
Apt 06.02.1843; 971a (1381); Map 1842, 3 chns, 1st cl, surveyed for Mr W.H. Apperley by H.J. Clarke, Hereford; construction lines, foot/b'way, waterbodies, houses, woods, plantations, rock outcrops, fence ownership, field boundary ownerships, field gates, building names, limekilns, mill, boundary trees and stones, flood gate, stone quarry, vicarage, stone walls (by annotation).

14/69 Dorstone (parish) SO 314418
Apt 15.12.1840; 5386a (5385); Map 1840, 8 chns, by Thomas Bate, Brecon; hill-drawing, waterbodies, woods, building names, boundary stones, mill, lodge, vicarage, hamlet boundaries (col), parks (named); hills named; map title is framed by border incorporating Tudor roses. Apt omits some field names.

14/70 Downton (parish) SO 437748 [Not listed]
Apt 15.05.1847; 1202a (all); Map 1847?, 8 chns; hill-drawing, waterbodies, houses, woods (col), plantations (col), hedges, field gates, building names, sand or stone pit, avenue of trees.

14/71 Dulas (parish) SO 372295 [Not listed]
Apt 11.03.1845; 845a (845); Map 1843?, 3 chns, by W. Croome, Tewkesbury; foot/b'way, waterbodies, houses, woods, orchards, field boundary ownerships, field gates, stiles.

14/72 Eardisland (parish) SO 419589
Apt 28.10.1842; 4455a (all); Map 1844, 3 chns, 1st cl, in 4 parts, (includes index); waterbodies, woods (by annotation), plantations (by annotation), orchards, open fields, hedges, building names, glebe, common, mills, ancient fortress (moat), court house, tan yard; meadow named; bridge named.

14/73 Eardisley (parish) SO 307503
Apt 23.01.1839; 4534a (4455); Map 1840?, 6 chns; hill-drawing, railway, foot/b'way, waterbodies, houses, woods, plantations, parkland, hops (col), fences, building names, chapel, castle.

14/74 Eastnor (parish) SO 740370
Apt 20.03.1838; 3186a (all); Map 1840, 3 chns, 1st cl, by Robert Jones; construction lines, waterbodies, houses, field boundary ownerships, building names, mill, castle.

14/75 Eaton Bishop (parish) SO 441391
Apt 21.01.1840; 2229a (all); Map 1840, 3 chns, 1st cl, by Willm Fosbrooke, Hereford; waterbodies, houses, field boundary ownerships, field gates, building names, mills, common.

14/76 Edwin Ralph (parish) SO 642580 [Edwyn Ralph]
Apt 13.04.1840; 1591a (all); Map 1840, 3 chns, 1st cl, by W. Fosbrooke, Hereford; foot/b'way, waterbodies, houses, woods (by name), field boundary ownerships, field gates, building names, mill, rectory.

14/77 Elton (parish) SO 457706
Apt 18.09.1845; 1470a (1470); Map 1846, 8 chns; woods, plantations, building names.

14/78 Evesbatch (parish) SO 699481
Apt 31.12.1841; 973a (all); Map 1839, 3 chns, 1st cl, by W.H. Apperley; construction lines, waterbodies, houses, woods, fences, field boundary ownerships, field gates, parsonage, boundary trees.

14/79 Ewias Harold (parish) SO 389285 [Ewyas Harold]
Apt 02.02.1844; 1838a (1838); Map 1844, 3 chns, 1st cl, by W. Fosbrooke, Hereford; construction lines, waterbodies, houses, woods (by name), rock outcrops, field boundary ownerships, building names, site of castle, quarry, mill, common; bridge named.

14/80 Eye, Moreton and Ashton (township in parish of Eye) SO 510640
Apt 30.06.1843; 2577a (2577); Map 1844, 8 chns, in 2 parts, (includes 3-chn enlargement of lands of the poor of Laysters); foot/b'way, canal with towpath, waterbodies, woods, plantations, parkland, orchards, field boundary ownerships, building names, landowners, boathouse, lodge, glebe.

14/81 Eyton (parish) SO 476618
Apt 30.12.1842; 964a (964); Map 1843, 6 chns, compiled by James Webb, Worcester from an old survey taken by William Galliers; waterbodies, fences, building names, mill, common; bridge named.

14/82 Farlow (chapelry) SO 640805
Apt 06.09.1844; 1440a (all); Map 1845, 8 chns; waterbodies, woods, field boundary ownerships, building names.

14/83 Felton (parish) SO 575480
Apt 31.12.1841; 1341a (1699); Map 1842, 6 chns, in 2 parts, by W.H. Apperley, Hereford, (includes index); waterbodies, houses, woods, plantations, parkland, rock outcrops, building names, landowners, quarry, vicarage, estate boundary (red), public roads.

14/84 Fenn and Fern, otherwise Venn and Vern (part of tithing in parish of Bodenham) SO 526504 [The Vern]
Apt 22.08.1840; 484a (?); Map 1844, 6 chns; waterbodies, houses, landowners.

14/85 Fordsbridge, otherwise The Ford (extra-parochial place) SO 514554 [Ford]
Apt 07.09.1842; 325a (324); Map 1843, 3 chns, in 2 parts; woods, plantations, orchards, hops, building names, chapel; bridge named.

14/86 Fownhope (parish) SO 584350
Apt 18.01.1843; 4724a (4723); Map 1843, 3 chns, 1st cl, in 2 parts, by W. Fosbrooke and W.H. Apperley, Hereford; waterbodies, houses, woods (by name), open fields, fences, field boundary ownerships, building names, mills, brewery, chapel.

14/87 Foy (parish) SO 611287
Apt 29.11.1838; 2323a (all); Map 1838, 6 chns; turnpike roads, toll bar, waterbodies, houses, building names.

14/88 Fwddog (township in parish of Cwmyoy) SO 267258 [Not listed]
Apt 24.04.1845; 2082a (all); Map 1843?, 3 chns, 1st cl, in 2 parts, by James Nunan; construction lines. Apt omits some field names.

14/89 Ganerew (parish) SO 532165 [Ganarew]
Apt 31.05.1842; 835a (all); Map 1842, 6 chns, by W.H. Apperley, Hereford; waterbodies, houses, woods, heath/moor, building names, boundary trees.

14/90 Garway (parish) SO 468226
Apt 23.09.1840; 3525a (3625); Map 1840, 3 chns, 1st cl, by William Price, Ross; construction lines, turnpike roads, toll bar, waterbodies, houses, heath/moor, rock outcrops, hedge ownership, building names, boundary stones and trees, quarries, sand or stone pits, mills, pigeon house, chapels, pound; bridge named. Apt uses a survey of 1784 by Matthew Williams for its summary acreages.

14/91 Goodrich (parish) SO 570188
Apt 10.01.1838; 2422a (all); Map 1838, 3 chns, 1st cl, by William Price, Ross; construction lines, hill-drawing, foot/b'way, turnpike roads, waterbodies, houses, woods, fences, building names, road names, landowners, field boundary ownerships, parish boundary wall, boundary stones, dole stones, vicarage, priory, stone quarry, ferries, ferry house, field acreages, glebe; bridge named.

14/92 Grafton (township in parish of Hereford St Martin) SO 496365
Apt 29.11.1845; 425a (all); Map 1846, 3 chns; waterbodies, building names.

14/93 Grendon Bishop (parish) SO 595564
Apt 29.12.1840; 1689a (all); Map surveyed in 1845, 3 chns, by Philip Baylis; construction lines, waterbodies.

14/94 Hampton (township in parish of Hampton Bishop) SO 558378 [Hampton Bishop]
Apt 12.10.1841; 1330a (1330); Map 1842, 3 chns, 1st cl, by W. Fosbrooke; construction lines, waterbodies, houses, open fields, field boundary ownerships.

14/95 Hatfield (parish) SO 586594
Apt 06.11.1843; 1529a (?); Map 1844, 6 chns; waterbodies, woods, orchards, building names, spring, mill.

14/96 Hentland (parish) SO 533262
Apt 31.03.1841; 2906a (all); Map 1839, 3 chns, 1st cl, by William Price, Ross, Land Agent; construction lines, waterbodies, houses, gardens, hedge ownership, fences, field gates, field acreages, building names, boundary trees, horse ferry (by symbol), glebe; colour bands show land belonging to other districts.

14/97 Hereford, All Saints (parish) SO 520410 [Not listed]
Apt 06.03.1841; 342a (341); Map 1841, 3 chns, ? by Thomas Blashill, Kings Acre; foot/b'way, turnpike roads, toll gates, waterbodies, woods, parkland, orchards, building names, road names, field names, burial ground, old race course, mill, tithe-free lands (pink).

14/98 Little Hereford (parish) SO 552696
Apt 28.08.1845; 3550a (3550); Map 1845, 3 chns, 1st cl, by W. Herbert, Worcester; foot/b'way, turnpike roads, canal with aqueduct and towpath, waterbodies, houses, field boundary ownerships, field gates, building names, boundary trees, mill, vicarage, sand or stone pit.

14/99 Hereford, St John the Baptist (parish) SO 511398 [Not listed]
Apt 30.01.1841; 436a (436); Map 1840, 3 chns, by Walter Tench, Hereford; railway, foot/b'way, waterbodies, houses, woods, plantations, orchards, hops, fences, field gates, building names, road names, milestone, boundary trees, burial ground, town hall, college, castle?, Nelson's monument, infirmary, Cathedral, county hall, city and county gaols, Catholic chapel, Bishop's palace, hospital gardens; border has floral corners; north pointer has acorn and oak leaf decoration.

14/100 Hereford, St Martin (parish) SO 506383 [Not listed]
Apt 12.06.1843; 805a (770); Map 1844, 3 chns; building names, road names, tramroad.

14/101 Hereford, St Nicholas (township) SO 497399 [Not listed]
Apt 28.12.1842; 555a (all); Map 1843, 3 chns; turnpike roads, toll bar, waterbodies, building names, road names.

14/102 Hereford, St Owen (township) SO 518392 [Not listed]
Apt 15.03.1845; 256a (all); Map 1843, 3 chns, ? by Morris Sayce; foot/b'way, turnpike roads and gate, waterbodies, houses, woods, plantations, parkland, orchards, fences, field boundary ownerships, field gates, building names, road names, bone mill, boundary stones, lunatic asylum, infirmary, workhouse, scutt mill, mill, castle moat, burial ground, drainage ditch; built-up part generalised; compass rose has a floral boss and an axe above the north pointer.

14/103 Hereford, St Peter (parish) SO 514402 [Not listed]
Apt 02.04.1844; 44a (60); Map 1843, 3 chns, ? by Morris Sayce; foot/b'way, waterbodies, houses, woods, orchards, fences, field boundary ownerships, field gates, building names, road names, mill, gas works, infant school, town hall, county hall, workhouse, county and old and new city prisons, drainage ditch, boundary stones; built-up part mostly generalised.

14/104 Upper Hide (township in parish of Leominster) SO 455555 [Not listed]
Apt 22.04.1841; 663a (?); Map 1841, 3 chns, 1st cl, by W. Fosbrooke; construction lines, foot/b'way, houses, field boundary ownerships, field gates, building names. Apt omits some field names.

14/105 Holme Lacy (parish) SO 552346
Apt 12.11.1840; 3192a (all); Map 1840, 6 chns, by William Price, Ross, land agent and surveyor; foot/b'way, waterbodies, houses, woods, plantations, parkland, building names, limekiln, ferry.

14/106 Holmer (except Huntingdon) (parish) SO 515420
Apt 28.04.1840; 2514a (?); Map 1844, 3 chns, 1st cl, by W. Fosbrooke, Hereford; construction lines, turnpike roads and gate, canal, waterbodies, houses, fences, field boundary ownerships, building names, racecourse, common; bridge named. Apt omits some field names.

14/107 Hope Mansell (parish) SO 626196
Apt 25.01.1840; 1174a (1173); Map 1840, 3 chns, 1st cl, by Chas. Baker, Painswick; construction lines, hill-drawing, foot/b'way, waterbodies, houses, woods, hedge ownership, fences, field gates, boundary trees, glebe.

14/108 Hope under Dinmore (parish) SO 497525
Apt 04.05.1844; 3797a (3796); Map 1845, 6 chns; hill-drawing, foot/b'way, turnpike roads, toll gate, waterbodies, woods, plantations, parkland, orchards, hops, building names, saw mills, quarry; hills named.

14/109 How Caple (parish) SO 607306
Apt 03.06.1839; 1016a (all); Map 1839, 3 chns, 1st cl, by William Price, Ross; construction lines, waterbodies, houses, woods (by names), field boundary ownerships, building names, rectory.

14/110 Humber (parish) SO 541563
Apt 21.06.1844; 1498a (1494); Map 1843, 3 chns, 1st cl, by W. Fosbrooke, Hereford; waterbodies, houses, field boundary ownerships, building names, ancient camp, mill; bridge named.

14/111 Huntingdon (parish) SO 257530 [Huntington]
Apt 26.03.1844; 1938a (all); Map 1844, 6 chns, ? by Morris and Wm Sayce; waterbodies, houses, woods (named), plantations, building names, mills, school; bridge named.

14/112 Huntingdon (township in parish of Holmer) SO 484419 [Huntington]
Apt 25.03.1840; 545a (all); Map 1840, 3 chns, 1st cl, by William Price, Ross; construction lines, waterbodies, houses, hedge ownership, fences, field names, field acreages, old Roman road.

14/113 Kenchester (parish) SO 440423
Apt 23.11.1842; 534a (all); Map 1843, 4 chns, by W.H. Apperley, Hereford; waterbodies, houses, building names, lodge, vicarage.

14/114 Kenderchurch (parish) SO 416296 [Not listed]
Apt 15.08.1843; 174a (783); Map 1846, 6 chns; turnpike roads, waterbodies, building names, tramroad.

14/115 Kentchurch (parish) SO 421267
Apt 15.02.1840; 3285a (all); Map 1839, 3 chns, 1st cl, by E.S. Gisborne; construction lines, waterbodies, houses, woods, plantations, parkland, orchards, heath/moor, field boundary ownerships, building names, school, watermill (by symbol). Apt omits some field names.

14/116 Kilpeck (parish) SO 442298
Apt 18.03.1846; 2135a (all); Map 1846, 6 chns; foot/b'way, waterbodies, building names, priory, mill.

14/117 Kimbolton (parish) SO 529614
Apt 16.11.1840; 4061a (all); Map 1842, 6 chns, ? by Morris Sayce; foot/b'way, canal, waterbodies, houses, woods, plantations, orchards, open fields, fences, building names; map date and scale are on drape ground.

14/118 King's Caple (parish) SO 564290
Apt 08.10.1839; 1697a (1697); Map 1839, 4 chns, by William Price, Ross; waterbodies, houses, woods, parkland, orchards, fences, building names, road names, mill, ferries, circle of trees ('tump').

14/119 Kingsland (parish) SO 447613
Apt 01.09.1841; 4735a (4735); Map 1841, 8 chns, by Richard Allerton, Norfolk Street, Strand; hill-drawing, foot/b'way, waterbodies, woods, plantations, parkland, building names, rectory, mill, ?cairn; bridge named.

14/120 King's Pyon (parish) SO 431503
Apt 05.06.1838; 2408a (2407); Map 1839?, 6 chns, ? by Morris and Wm Sayce; hill-drawing, foot/b'way, waterbodies, woods, open fields (named), building names, boundary trees, quarries; hill named. Apt omits land use.

14/121 Kingstone (parish) SO 428356
Apt 23.09.1840; 1992a (1991); Map 1842, 6 chns; waterbodies, houses, building names, mill, commons.

14/122 Kington (parish) SO 285565
Apt 30.06.1843; 8314a (all); Map 1845, 6 chns, by W. Fosbrooke; waterbodies, houses, building names, road names, woods (by name), pound, mills, foundry, workhouse, tram road; hills named; built-up part generalised.

14/123 Kinnersley (parish) SO 344497
Apt 11.06.1840; 2200a (all); Map 1839, 4 chns, by Thomas Blashill, land agent and surveyor; turnpike roads, waterbodies, woods, parkland, orchards, hops, heath/moor, open fields, building names, road names, field names, castle, parsonage, common.

14/124 Upper Kinsham (parish) SO 358657
Apt 04.11.1858; 168a (1243); Map 1859, 6 chns; waterbodies, landowners, quarry.

14/125 Knill (parish) SO 293613
Apt 01.04.1844; 798a (all); Map 1844, 4 chns, ? by Morris Sayce and Wm Sayce; waterbodies, houses, woods (named), plantations, parkland, field boundary ownerships, building names; pictorial church.

14/126 Laysters (parish) SO 565630 [Not listed]
Apt 15.04.1843; 1989a (1989); Map 1842, 3 chns, 1st cl, by R.C. Herbert, Worcester; waterbodies, houses, fences, field boundary ownerships, building names, vicarage, boundary trees, sand or stone pit.

14/127 Ledbury (parish) SO 703384
Apt 14.12.1839; 8195a (8194); Map surveyed in 1837 and 1838, 3 chns, in 2 parts, (includes Borough of Ledbury separately at 2 chns); turnpike roads, toll bars, canal, navigation yard, waterbodies, houses, woods, plantations, parkland, arable (col), grassland (col), orchards, gardens, field boundary ownerships, building names, road names, hotels, workhouse, mill; ornate compass rose has flower and leaf decoration.

14/128 Leinthall Starks (parish) SO 435698 [Leinthall Starkes]
Apt 23.10.1844; 991a (all); Map 1847?, 8 chns; waterbodies, houses, woods, field gates.

14/129 Leintwardine (parish) SO 415735
Apt 06.05.1846; 8106a (8576); Map 1847?, 8 chns, in 3 parts, (tithable parts only; includes small enlargements of detail, and common fields at 3 chns); turnpike roads and gate, waterbodies, woods, plantations, open fields (named), building names, ancient camp.

14/130 Leominster (except Upper Hide) (parish) SO 490570
Apt 06.05.1848; 6783a (?); Map 1849, 6 chns, in 3 parts, by W.H. Apperley, (includes two 3-chn enlargements of open fields); turnpike roads, waterbodies, houses, open fields, building names, road names, field names, mill; bridge named.

14/131 Letton (parish) SO 336470
Apt 12.11.1840; 1197a (all); Map 1840, 3 chns, 1st cl, by James Cranston; construction lines, waterbodies, houses, field boundary ownerships, building names, boundary trees, parsonage, common. Apt omits some field names.

14/132 Lingen (parish) SO 362676
Apt 23.09.1840; 2283a (2283); Map 1840?, 8 chns; waterbodies, woods; pictorial church.

14/133 Linton (parish) SO 656250 [Not listed]
Apt 09.12.1839; 2775a (all); Map 1839, 3 chns, 1st cl, by James Webb, Worcester; construction lines, foot/b'way, waterbodies, houses, woods (by name), fences, field boundary ownerships, field gates, building names, mills.

14/134 Linton (township in parish of Bromyard) SO 680535
Apt 28.02.1842; 2433a (all); Map 1841, 3 chns, 1st cl, in 2 parts, surveyed for W. Fosbrooke, Hereford by M. Smith; construction lines, foot/b'way, turnpike roads and gate, field boundary ownerships, field gates, building names, mills, workhouse, downs, common.

14/135 Llancillow (parish) SO 366256
Apt 06.03.1841; 1086a (1085); Map 1839, 4 chns, by E.S. Gisborne; hill-drawing, ancient fort, forge, old roads; one old road is annotated 'impassable'.

14/136 Llandinabo (parish) SO 519287 [Not listed]
Apt 10.11.1842; 495a (all); Map 1842, 3 chns, by W.H. Apperley, Hereford; construction lines, foot/b'way, turnpike roads, toll bar, waterbodies, houses, woods, fences, field boundary ownerships, field gates, building names.

14/137 Llangarren (parish) SO 528208 [Llangarron]
Apt 04.07.1840; 5606a (all); Map 1842, 3 chns, 1st cl, by William Fosbrooke and William Price; construction lines, foot/b'way, waterbodies, houses, woods (by name), open fields, hedge ownership, field boundary ownerships, building names, rectory, mills, chapels, vicarage, sand or stone pit, workhouse.

14/138 Llanrothal (parish) SO 481186
Apt 22.07.1840; 1631a (all); Map 1840, 3 chns, 1st cl, by R.N. Purchas, Chepstow; construction lines, waterbodies, houses, rock outcrops, building names, quarry, corn mill, boundary trees, ruin, glebe (yellow), farm names; meaning of green band is unclear.

14/139 Llanveynol (township in parish of Clodock) SO 300306
Apt 29.03.1841; 4610a (4610); Map 1840, 6 chns; building names, chapel; mountain named. Apt omits some field names.

14/140 Lanwarne (parish) SO 496278 [Llanwarne]
Apt 26.05.1841; 2469a (all); Map 1840, 6 chns, by William Price, Ross; waterbodies, houses, woods, building names, rectory, smith shop; hill named.

14/141 Longtown (township in parish of Clodock) SO 345285
Apt 08.04.1841; 6275a (6275); Map 1840, 6 chns, by E.S. Gisborne; building names, vicarage. Apt omits some field names.

14/142 Lucton (parish) SO 437642
Apt 12.11.1842; 1018a (all); Map 1845?, 4 chns; foot/b'way, waterbodies, houses, farmyards, woods, plantations, parkland, orchards, gardens (col), heath/moor, fences.

14/143 Ludford (parish) (partly in Shropshire) SO 523735
Apt 03.12.1846; 1868a (1867); Map 1847?, 6 chns; turnpike roads, toll gates, waterbodies, houses, woods, plantations, orchards, ornamental ground, field gates, building names, mills, paper mill.

14/144 Lugwardine (parish) SO 555405
Apt 31.07.1839; 2098a (2097); Map 1839, 3 chns, 1st cl, by William Fosbrooke; construction lines, turnpike roads, toll bar, waterbodies, open fields, field boundary ownerships, building names.

14/145 Luston (township in parish of Eye) SO 488626
Apt 14.02.1842; 1732a (1732); Map 1840, 3 chns, 1st cl, surveyed by John Powell, Marden, Herefordshire, (apparently for Walter Tench); construction lines, foot/b'way, waterbodies, houses, fences, field boundary ownerships, field gates.

14/146 Lyonshall (parish) SO 331561
Apt 25.03.1840; 4659a (all); Map 1840, 6 chns, ? by Morris Sayce; railway, waterbodies, woods, plantations, parkland, open fields (named), building names, mills.

14/147 Madley (parish) SO 410390
Apt 21.06.1842; 5361a (all); Map 1840, 3 chns, 1st cl, by William Price, Ross; construction lines, foot/b'way, waterbodies, houses, gardens, hedge ownership, fences, building names, lunatic asylum, mill, tuck mill, boundary trees, township boundaries (col).

14/148 Mansell Gamage (parish) SO 400449
Apt 21.06.1842; 1323a (all); Map 1842, 4 chns; foot/b'way, waterbodies, woods, parkland, orchards, hops, building names, terrace, mill.

14/149 Mansel Lacy (parish) SO 426452 [Mansell Lacy]
Apt 07.04.1842; 1547a (1547); Map 1843, 3 chns, 1st cl, by W.H. Apperley, Hereford; construction lines, foot/b'way, waterbodies, houses, fences, field boundary ownerships, field gates, building names, vicarage, mill, parsonage.

14/150 Little Marcle (parish) SO 671369
Apt 11.01.1838; 1219a (all); Map 1838, 3 chns; waterbodies, houses, farmyards, rickyards, plantations, arable (col), grassland (col), orchards, hops, gardens, hedge ownership, fences, field gates, building names, road names, field names, glebe.

14/151 Much Marcle (parish) SO 653327
Apt 27.07.1839; 3960a (6349); Map 1839, 6 chns, in 2 parts, 'compiled from the Maps accompanying the Award for Henry Burgum Esq' by James Webb, Worcester; waterbodies, houses, woods (named), arable (col), grassland (col), building names.

14/152 Marden (parish) SO 531480
Apt 31.05.1842; 3671a (4048); Map 1842, 6 chns, by W.H. Apperley, Hereford; waterbodies, building names, school; bridges named; a flag decorates the north pointer.

14/153 St Margaret (parish) SO 352340 [St Margarets]
Apt 11.08.1843; 2583a (all); Map 1844, 3 chns, by W.H. Apperley, Hereford; waterbodies, houses, field boundary ownerships, field gates, building names, tan house.

14/154 Marstow (parish) SO 552198
Apt 18.01.1839; 810a (all); Map 1838, 3 chns, 1st cl, by William Price, Ross; construction lines, foot/b'way, waterbodies, houses, fences, field boundary ownerships, field acreages, building names, glebe.

14/155 Michaelchurch Eskley (parish) SO 310357 [Michaelchurch Escley]
Apt 13.12.1843; 4567a (all); Map 1844, 6 chns; waterbodies, houses, building names, school house, common. Apt omits some field names.

14/156 Middleton on the Hill (parish) SO 550650
Apt 25.03.1840; 2922a (2921); Map 1841, 3 chns, by Francis Harris, Leominster; foot/b'way, waterbodies, houses, orchards, field gates, stiles.

14/157 Moccas (parish) SO 356427
Apt 29.06.1837; 1163a (all); Map 1838?, 6 chns, by Wm Fosbrooke, Hereford; waterbodies, houses.

14/158 Monkland (parish) SO 451579
Apt 23.09.1840; 1079a (1079); Map 1841, 3 chns, by Francis Harris, Leominster; foot/b'way, waterbodies, houses, orchards, gardens; compass rose is marked 'polar star'.

14/159 Monnington on Wye (parish) SO 370438
Apt 29.06.1837; 1011a (all); Map 1837, 3 chns, 1st cl, by James Webb, Worcester; hill-drawing, foot/b'way, waterbodies, houses, woods (named), arable (col), grassland (col), hedge ownership, fences, field boundary ownerships, field gates, building names, rectory, ferries, ford, boundary trees; table lists landowners with acreages.

14/160 Mordiford (parish) SO 581384
Apt 16.04.1840; 1478a (?); Map 1841, 6 chns; waterbodies.

14/161 Morton Jeffries (parish) SO 606482 [Moreton Jeffries]
Apt 15.04.1843; 704a (all); Map 1846, 12 chns; waterbodies, woods, plantations, orchards.

14/162 Morton on Lugg (parish) SO 502462 [Moreton on Lugg]
Apt 22.05.1846; 885a (all); Map 1845, 3 chns, 1st cl, by William Fosbrooke, Hereford; construction lines, turnpike roads and gate, milestone, waterbodies, houses, field boundary ownerships.

14/163 Munsley (parish) SO 664408
Apt 30.12.1837; 1229a (all); Map 1839?, 3 chns; construction lines, waterbodies, woods (named), hops, field boundary ownerships, building names, school house, smiths shop, glebe.

14/164 Newton (township in parish of Clodock) SO 340340
Apt 24.04.1841; 1743a (1743); Map 1840, 3 chns, 1st cl, surveyed for W. Fosbrooke, Hereford by J.J. Haslett and Michael O'Rourke; construction lines, waterbodies, houses, woods, plantations, orchards, field boundary ownerships, building names, chapel. Apt omits some field names.

14/165 Newton (township in parish of Croft) SO 503440 [Not listed]
Apt 14.08.1838; 508a (all); Map 1839, 6 chns; turnpike roads, woods, plantations, orchards, building names, field names. Apt omits land use.

14/166 Norton (township in parish of Bromyard) SO 668570 [Not listed]
Apt 23.01.1838; 1708a (all); Map 1839, 4 chns; foot/b'way, waterbodies, houses, woods, plantations, parkland (in detail), orchards, downs, building names, mill, racecourse; scale statement is on floral and ribbon background.

14/167 Norton Canon (parish) SO 375480
Apt 12.09.1840; 2111a (all); Map 1841?, 6 chns, ? by Jas Cranston; waterbodies, houses (depiction incomplete), building names, common.

14/168 Ocle Pitchard (parish) SO 582462 [Ocle Pychard]
Apt 27.01.1842; 1132a (1507); Map 1842, 3 chns, 1st cl, by W.H. Apperley, Hereford; construction lines, waterbodies, houses, fences, field boundary ownerships, field gates, building names, vicarage, milestone, canal, common, tithe-merged lands (col).

14/169 Orcop (parish) SO 463263
Apt 30.11.1842; 2403a (2403); Map 1843, 6 chns; waterbodies, building names, tithe barn, mill, limits of hill and common land (red). Apt omits some field names.

14/170 Orleton (parish) SO 487673
Apt 20.11.1840; 2604a (2603); Map 1840, 3 chns, 1st cl, by James Webb, Worcester; construction lines, foot/b'way, canal with tunnel, waterbodies, houses, fences, field boundary ownerships, field gates, building names, boundary trees, quarries; one estate named.

14/171 Pembridge (parish) SO 378575
Apt 27.02.1841; 7078a (7077); Map 1841, 4 chns, 1st cl, by James Webb, Worcester; construction lines, waterbodies, houses, woods (by name), open fields, field boundary ownerships, field gates, building names, mill, weir, common.

14/172 Pencombe (parish) SO 580530
Apt 21.11.1837; 3955a (all); Map 1839?, 6 chns, in 2 parts, ? by Morris Sayce, (includes village separately at 3 chns); waterbodies, woods, plantations, heath/moor, building names, parsonage, chapel, mill. Apt omits land use.

14/173 Pencoyd (parish) SO 514268
Apt 19.04.1839; 879a (all); Map 1838, 3 chns, 1st cl, by W. Fosbrooke; construction lines, waterbodies, houses, field boundary ownerships, field gates, building names, boundary trees.

14/174 Peterchurch (parish) SO 339389
Apt 30.04.1845; 5089a (5089); Map 1845, 6 chns, in 3 parts, by W. Fosbrooke and W.H. Apperley, Hereford, (including open fields at 3 chns); open fields, building names, road names, field names, old chapel, chapel, castle, mills, parsonage, commons.

14/175 Peterstow (parish) SO 557242
Apt 18.06.1840; 1544a (all); Map 1839, 3 chns, 1st cl, by William Price, Ross; construction lines, waterbodies, houses, woods, gardens, hedge ownership, fences, field boundary ownerships, field gates, building names, rectory, boundary trees, common.

14/176 Pipe and Lyde (parish) SO 509440
Apt 09.06.1838; 1620a (all); Map 1838, 3 chns, 1st cl, in 3 parts, by William Fosbrooke; construction lines, waterbodies, houses, field boundary ownerships, field acreages.

14/177 Pixley (parish) SO 660389
Apt 05.10.1838; 656a (all); Map 1838, 3 chns, 1st cl, by Robert Jones; turnpike roads, toll bar, waterbodies, houses, woods, plantations, arable (col), grassland (col), orchards, gardens, building names, glebe.

14/178 Preston on Wye (parish) SO 385415
Apt 24.02.1844; 1379a (all); Map 1844, 3 chns, 1st cl, by Wm Fosbrooke, Hereford; waterbodies, houses, field boundary ownerships, building names.

14/179 Preston Wynn (parish) SO 558467 [Preston Wynne]
Apt 22.11.1839; 876a (876); Map 1839, 3 chns, 1st cl, in 2 parts, by W.H. Apperley, Hereford; construction lines, waterbodies, houses, fences, field boundary ownerships, field gates, building names.

14/180 Pudlestone (parish) SO 560599 [Pudleston]
Apt 14.02.1842; 1743a (all); Map 1842, 3 chns; waterbodies, woods, plantations, parkland, orchards, building names.

14/181 Putley (parish) SO 646374
Apt 11.07.1839; 589a (589); Map 1838, 3 chns, 1st cl, in 3 parts; construction lines, waterbodies, houses, fences, field boundary ownerships, field gates, building names, common.

14/182 Richards Castle (parish) (partly in Shropshire) SO 497697
Apt 14.08.1839; 4872a (4871); Map 1840?, 6 chns, ? by Oliver Stubbs; canal, waterbodies, plantations, disappearing streams.

14/183 Rochford (parish) SO 632677
Apt 27.03.1841; 1379a (1379); Map 1841, 3 chns, 1st cl, by James Webb, Worcester; construction lines, waterbodies, houses, fences, field boundary ownerships, field gates; part of the parish boundary is annotated: 'accepted line of Boundary from Mr Cookes Map'.

14/184 Ross (parish) SO 605242 [Ross-on-Wye]
Apt 14.09.1843; 3118a (all); Map 'corrected' to 1840, 6 chns, in 2 parts, by William Price, Ross, (includes enlargement of town at 3 chns); waterbodies, building names, road names, market place, tan yard, gated road; bridge named.

14/185 Rowlstone (parish) SO 375270 [Rowlestone]
Apt 23.11.1842; 1679a (1678); Map 1839, 4 chns; houses, building names, mills.

14/186 Upper Sapey (parish) SO 687642
Apt 28.08.1838; 2191a (2190); Map 1847?, 3 chns, 1st cl, by Robert Massey, Birmingham; foot/b'way, waterbodies, houses, woods (col), orchards, field boundary ownerships, building names, landowners, Poors Land, charity lands (in pink); many buildings are named by the owner or occupier rather than by farm or house name.

14/187 Sarnesfield (parish) SO 371509
Apt 01.04.1844; 1256a (all); Map 1842, 6 chns, by James Cranston; waterbodies, houses, building names, common.

14/188 Sellack (parish) SO 562273
Apt 21.07.1840; 1540a (all); Map 1839, 6 chns, by William Price, Ross; waterbodies, houses, fences.

14/189 Sollars Hope (parish) SO 618328 [Sollers Hope]
Apt 22.05.1839; 1153a (all); Map 1839, 3 chns, 1st cl, by William Price, Ross; construction lines, waterbodies, houses, woods (by name), field boundary ownerships, building names.

14/190 Stanage (township in parish of Brampton Brian) SO 332717 [Not listed]
Apt 19.04.1845; 2388a (?); Map 1841?, 6 chns; turnpike roads, toll gate, waterbodies, houses, field gates, building names. District is apportioned by holding and most fields are omitted; Apt omits land use.

14/191 Stanford Bishop (parish) SO 685519
Apt 19.03.1838; 1471a (1471); Map 1838, 3 chns, 1st cl, by Edward Sacheverell Gisborne; construction lines, waterbodies, building names, common.

14/192 Stanton upon Arrow (parish) SO 354612 [Staunton on Arrow]
Apt 31.01.1840; 2925a (all); Map 1839, 3 chns, 1st cl, by W.H. Apperley, Hereford; construction lines, waterbodies, houses, woods, fences, field boundary ownerships, field gates, building names, tan house.

14/193 Stoke Bliss (parish) (partly in Worcestershire) SO 640623
Apt 12.09.1839; 2078a (all); Map 1840, 3 chns, 1st cl, by James Bourn junr, Cleobury Mortimer, Salop; construction lines, turnpike roads, tollgate, waterbodies, houses, woods, plantations, heath/moor.

14/194 Stoke Edith (parish) SO 601402
Apt 14.08.1839; 1661a (1661); Map 1839, 8 chns, by Bate, Brecon; turnpike roads, waterbodies, building names, mill.

14/195 Stoke Lacy (parish) SO 623507
Apt 19.11.1841; 2006a (2005); Map 1842, 3 chns, 1st cl, by W. Fosbrooke; construction lines, foot/b'way, waterbodies, houses, open fields, fences, field boundary ownerships, building names, rectory, mill.

14/196 Stoke Prior (parish) SO 529559
Apt 16.07.1842; 2570a (?); Map 1843, 6 chns, by F. Harris; foot/b'way, waterbodies, houses, open fields, field gates.

14/197 Stretford (parish) SO 443565
Apt 14.08.1838; 425a (all); Map 1838, 6 chns, by J. Blashill, land agent; foot/b'way, woods, orchards, building names; bridge named; an eagle surmounts the north pointer.

14/198 Stretton Sugwas (parish) SO 462425
Apt 28.03.1840; 780a (all); Map 1840, 3 chns, by Thomas Blashill, Kings Acre near Hereford; construction lines, foot/b'way, turnpike roads, toll gates (named), milestone, occupation roads, waterbodies, woods, orchards, old Roman road, boundary trees.

14/199 Sutton St Michael (parish) SO 526460
Apt 12.05.1843; 479a (679); Map 1843, 6 chns, by W.H. Apperley, Hereford; houses, building names.

14/200 Sutton St Nicholas (parish) SO 540450
Apt 11.09.1843; 722a (all); Map 1844, 3 chns, 1st cl, by W.H. Apperley, Hereford; construction lines, canal, waterbodies, houses, fences, field boundary ownerships, building names, chapel, rectory; bridge named.

14/201 Tarrington (parish) SO 621403
Apt 22.05.1839; 2225a (all); Map 1838, 3 chns, 1st cl, by E.S. Gisborne; construction lines, waterbodies, woods (by annotation), plantations, hops (by annotation), rock outcrops, quarries, school house, vicarage, pound, tan house, commons.

14/202 Tedstone Delamere (parish) SO 699590
Apt 24.02.1841; 1677a (all); Map 1840, 6 chns, 'compiled from old surveys of different Persons' by James Webb, Worcester; waterbodies, houses, building names, parsonage, mill.

14/203 Tedstone Wafer (parish) SO 675597

Apt 07.02.1838; 684a (all); Map 1838, 3 chns, by William Fosbrooke, Hereford; waterbodies, houses, field boundary ownerships, building names, chapel.

14/204 Thornbury (parish) SO 627600
Apt 17.02.1843; 2131a (2130); Map 1843, 3 chns, 1st cl, by R.C. Herbert, Worcester; construction lines, waterbodies, field boundary ownerships, building names, parsonage.

14/205 Thruxton (parish) SO 439344
Apt 22.05.1839; 437a (all); Map 1839, 3 chns, 1st cl, by Wm Fosbrooke; construction lines, houses, field boundary ownerships, field acreages, field gates, boundary trees.

14/206 Tibberton (parish) SO 380390 [Tyberton]
Apt 05.05.1842; 1112a (all); Map 1844?, 6 chns; waterbodies, houses, woods, plantations, building names.

14/207 Titley (parish) SO 321605
Apt 13.08.1842; 1876a (all); Map 1842, 3 chns, 1st cl, in 2 parts: part 1 by Wm Sayce, Kington; part 2 by Richd Galliers, Ledbury; construction lines, hill-drawing, turnpike roads, toll bar, waterbodies, houses, woods, plantations, parkland, building names, brickyard, kennel, quarry.

14/208 Tretire with Michaelchurch (parish) SO 518248
Apt 30.01.1840; 1356a (all); Map 1839, 6 chns, by W. Fosbrooke, Hereford; waterbodies, houses, building names, rectory, mill stream; red band indicates land belonging to Benjamin Mayo.

14/209 Tupsley (township in parish of Hampton Bishop) SO 535395
Apt 07.10.1841; 1516a (1516); Map 1839, 3 chns, by W. Fosbrooke; construction lines, turnpike roads and gate, waterbodies, houses, open fields, fences, field boundary ownerships, building names, scut mill. Apt omits some field names.

14/210 Turnastone (parish) SO 349365
Apt 15.06.1841; 530a (all); Map 1842, 6 chns, by W.H. Apperley, Hereford; houses, woods, fences, building names.

14/211 Ullingswick (parish) SO 591500
Apt 17.01.1838; 1245a (all); Map 1839, 3 chns, 1st cl, in 2 parts, by Samuel Barnett, St Johns, Worcester, (including detached parts at 4 chns); construction lines, turnpike roads, waterbodies, houses, woods (named), open fields, fences, field boundary ownerships, field gates, building names, field names, landowners, pound.

14/212 Upton Bishop (parish) SO 648276
Apt 12.05.1840; 3391a (all); Map 1842, 6 chns; building names, vicarage.

14/213 Vowchurch (parish) SO 376363
Apt 15.12.1843; 2690a (all); Map 1845, 6 chns, by W.H. Apperley, Hereford; hill-drawing, foot/b'way, waterbodies, houses, plantations, fences, field gates, building names, chapel house, mill, tumulus, dog kennel, sand or stone pits; hill named.

14/214 Wacton (parish) SO 619572
Apt 26.06.1838; 1002a (all); Map 1840, 3 chns, by Joseph Powell, Sutton, near Hereford; waterbodies.

14/215 Walford (parish) SO 601203
Apt 06.09.1843; 4242a (all); Map 1840, 3 chns, 1st cl, by William Price, Ross; waterbodies, houses, woods (by name), fences, field boundary ownerships, field gates, building names.

14/216 Walterstone (parish) SO 340250
Apt 08.07.1841; 1242a (all); Map 1842, 3 chns, surveyed for W.H. Apperley, Hereford by H.J. Clarke and J. Powell; construction lines, foot/b'way, waterbodies, houses, woods, fences, field boundary ownerships, field gates, building names, tump and moat, ancient camp.

14/217 Wellington (parish) SO 494484
Apt 17.01.1842; 2538a (2538); Map 1843?, 6 chns; waterbodies, houses, woods, orchards, field gates; bridge named.

14/218 Welsh Newton (parish) SO 507180
Apt 29.11.1844; 401a (1821); Map 1846, 3 chns, by William Havard Apperley; foot/b'way, waterbodies, houses, rock outcrops, field gates, stiles, building names, boundary stones and trees, quarry, mill, bathing pool; a flag decorates the north pointer.

14/219 Weobley (parish) SO 398514
Apt 12.01.1838; 3310a (all); Map 1838?, 6 chns, in 2 parts, ? by Morris and Wm Sayce, (includes Weobley village separately at 3 chns); hill-drawing, foot/b'way, turnpike roads (named), toll bars, waterbodies, woods, plantations, parkland, open fields (named), building names, road names, quarries, workhouse, lodge. Apt omits land use.

14/220 St Weonards (parish) SO 488240
Apt 03.01.1840; 4537a (all); Map 1839, 3 chns, 1st cl, by William Price, Ross; construction lines, hill-drawing, foot/b'way, waterbodies, houses, woods (by name), gardens, rock outcrops, hedge ownership, building names, chapels, milepost, tithe barn, tump (tumulus), mill, quarries, boundary stones and markers.

14/221 Westhide (parish) SO 589439
Apt 15.06.1839; 1191a (1191); Map 1838, 4 chns, by J. Cranston, Kings Acre, near Hereford; houses.

14/222 Weston Beggard (parish) SO 582418
Apt 20.07.1839; 934a (934); Map 1838, 3 chns, 1st cl, by Bate, Brecon; construction lines, foot/b'way, waterbodies, woods, building names, field acreages; bridge named.

14/223 Weston under Penyard (parish) SO 640230
Apt 17.01.1838; 3142a (all); Map 1838, 3 chns, 1st cl, by William Fosbrooke, Hereford; construction lines, foot/b'way, waterbodies, houses, field boundary ownerships, field acreages, field gates, building names, boundary stones, mills, rectory, park (named).

14/224 Whitbourne (parish) SO 713564
Apt 16.11.1839; 3056a (3056); Map 1838, 3 chns; turnpike roads, waterbodies, arable (col), grassland (col), building names, common; map title is with roses and leaves, and compass rose is ornamented with leaves.

14/225 Whitchurch (parish) SO 550170
Apt 31.10.1844; 1957a (all); Map 1848, 3 chns; foot/b'way, turnpike roads, toll bars, waterbodies, houses, woods (by name), field gates, stiles, building names, limekilns, iron mines, shaft, vicarage, boundary trees, well, limestone rocks.

14/226 Whitney (parish) SO 275476 [Whitney-on-Wye]
Apt 11.07.1839; 1483a (all); Map 1840, [6 chns], by E.S. Gisborne; turnpike roads, waterbodies, building names, tramroad; pictorial church.

14/227 Wigmore (parish) SO 405685
Apt 01.06.1844; 3441a (3441); Map 1841, 3 chns, ? by Morris Sayce; foot/b'way, waterbodies, houses, woods, plantations, parkland, fences, building names, castle ruins, coal pits (by symbol), chapel, watermill (by symbol); the decorative compass rose is placed in the centre of the map.

14/228 Willersley (parish) SO 309471
Apt 08.07.1841; 231a (all); Map 1841, 3 chns, 1st cl, by James Cranston, Kings Acre, near Hereford; construction lines, houses.

14/229 Winforton (parish) SO 295470
Apt 21.02.1839; 1099a (all); Map 1839, 6 chns, by Wm Sayce; waterbodies, woods, building names, tramroad, parsonage, court, woods (by name), common. Apt omits land use.

14/230 Winslow (township in parish of Bromyard) SO 634544
Apt 20.03.1838; 3107a (all); Map 1841, 3 chns, 1st cl, by W. Fosbrooke, Hereford; construction lines, waterbodies, houses, field boundary ownerships, building names, abbey, mills, Poor's land.

14/231 Withington (parish) SO 562432
Apt 13.08.1840; 1514a (1514); Map 1841, 3 chns, 1st cl, in 3 parts, by W. Fosbrooke; construction lines, waterbodies, houses, field boundary ownerships, building names, road names, forge, school, vicarage, common.

14/232 Wolferlow (parish) SO 668618
Apt 27.11.1839; 1535a (1535); Map 1840, 4.5 chns, 'compiled from

different surveys' by James Webb, Worcester; waterbodies, houses, arable (col), grassland (col), building names, park (named); north pointer has floral decoration.

14/233 Woolhope (parish) SO 616361
Apt 02.05.1843; 4653a (all); Map 1844, 6 chns, by W. Fosbrooke and W.H. Apperley, Hereford; waterbodies, houses, open fields, building names, camp, commons.

14/234 Wormbridge (parish) SO 420311
Apt 13.07.1839; 720a (all); Map 1839, 3 chns, 1st cl, by W. Fosbrooke, Hereford; construction lines, foot/b'way, waterbodies, houses, field boundary ownerships, field gates.

14/235 Wormesley (parish) SO 430480 [Wormsley]
Apt 14.04.1845; 1233a (1233); Map 1846?, 6 chns; hill-drawing, waterbodies, houses, woods, field gates, building names, sand or stone pits.

14/236 Yarkhill (parish) SO 610430
Apt 23.05.1844; 1667a (1666); Map 1845, 3 chns, 1st cl, by W.H. Apperley, Hereford; construction lines, canal, waterbodies, houses, fences, field boundary ownerships, building names, mill, vicarage, boundary trees, school house, commons.

14/237 Yarpole (parish) SO 472657
Apt 05.02.1842; 2523a (2523); Map 1841, 3 chns, 1st cl, surveyed for Walter Tench of Hereford by Caleb Cull and Henry Clarke; construction lines, foot/b'way, waterbodies, houses, woods (by name), open fields, fences, field boundary ownerships, field gates, watermill; a flag decorates the north pointer.

14/238 Yatton (township in parish of Much Marcle) SO 630309 [Not listed]
Apt 21.07.1840; 1410a (all); Map 1840, 6 chns, in 3 parts, (including open fields separately at 3 chns); waterbodies, houses, woods (by name), open fields, field boundary ownerships, building names, field names.

14/239 Yazor (parish) SO 405475
Apt 27.07.1840; 2051a (2051); Map 1841, 3 chns, 1st cl, by W. Fosbrooke; construction lines, foot/b'way, waterbodies, houses, woods (by name), plantations, field boundary ownerships, field gates, building names.

Hertfordshire

PRO IR29 and IR30 15/1-117

138 tithe districts: 404,732 acres
117 tithe commutations: 327,148 acres
84 voluntary tithe agreements, 33 compulsory tithe awards

Tithe and tithe commutation

In its pattern of tithes and tithe commutation, most of Hertfordshire shows some affinity with the south-eastern and East Anglian counties characterised by substantial proportions of tithable land. However, northern Hertfordshire has much in common with those midland counties where there was much tithe commutation at the time of enclosure (Fig. 27). In 1836 Hertfordshire still had considerable tracts of tithable open-field arable. Overall, tithes were still paid in 85 per cent of Hertfordshire tithe districts; by comparison 95 per cent of Essex districts remained subject to tithe but only 35 per cent of Bedfordshire and 62 per cent of Cambridgeshire. Fifty-one Hertfordshire districts were wholly subject to tithe; the main causes of partial tithe exemption elsewhere were commutation at the time of enclosure, modus payments in lieu of tithes, exemption of former Crown, manorial or monastic land, merger of tithes in the land, exemption by prescription, and exemption of some woodland.

The assistant tithe commissioners and local tithe agents who officiated in Hertfordshire are listed in Table 15.1. All but one of the county's tithe valuers were based in or near Hertfordshire, though as in Essex, a considerable number of valuers gave London addresses (Table 15.2). Hertfordshire shares with Bedfordshire the unusual attribute that none of its tithe districts is apportioned by holding and thus the record of ownership, occupation, land use and field names in the tithe apportionments is unusually complete.

Tithe maps

Some 14 per cent of the 117 tithe maps of Hertfordshire are sealed as first class, a proportion similar to that of other south-eastern and East Anglian counties. As in Essex, construction lines which are evidence of new survey rather than re-use of former maps, occur on the high proportion of 13 per cent of second-class maps in the Public Record Office collection. First-class maps and second-class maps with construction lines together cover a quarter of Hertfordshire tithe districts, a proportion broadly in line with the first-class mapping of Suffolk. Twenty-one maps (18 per cent) explicitly acknowledge

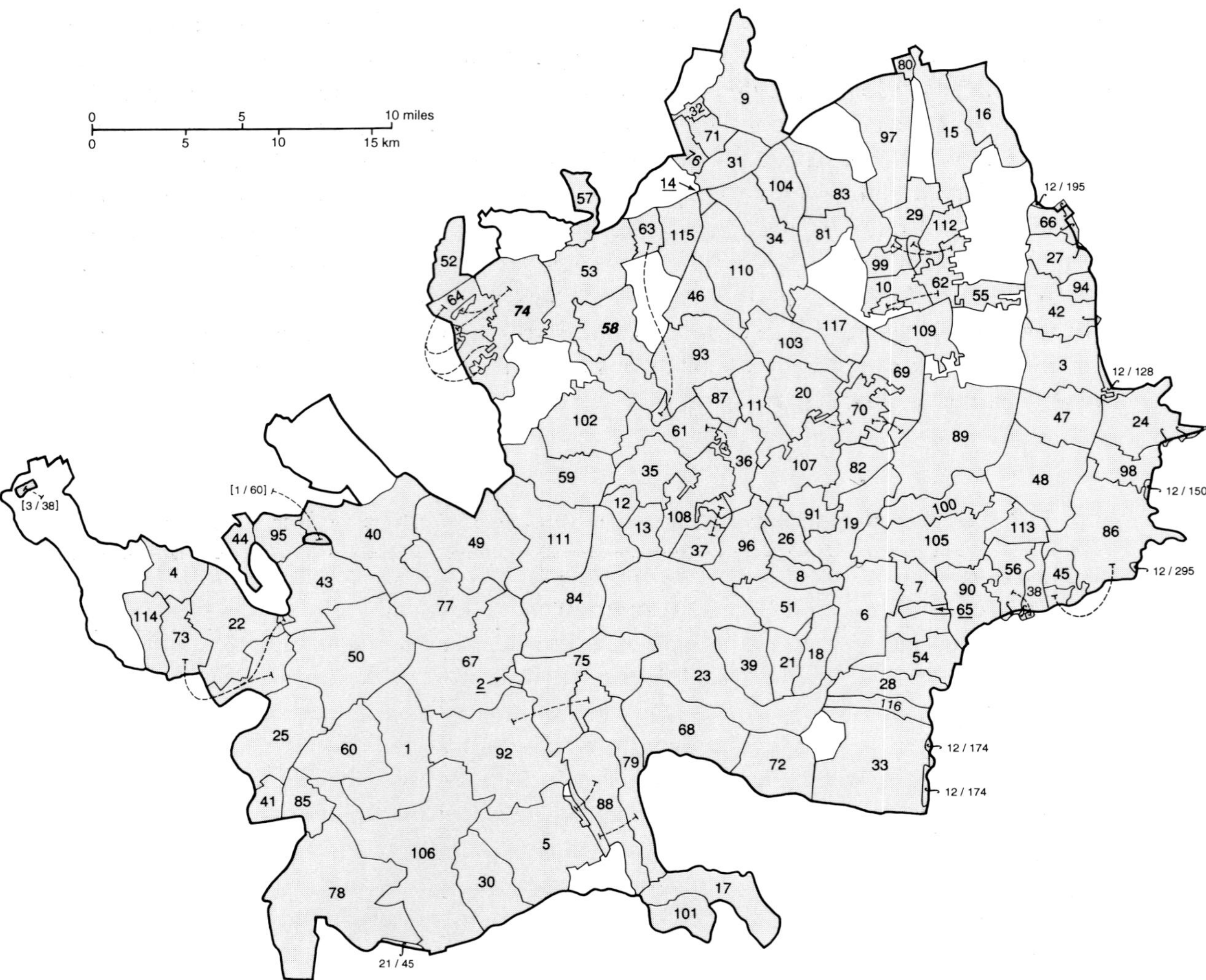

Fig. 27 Hertfordshire: tithe district boundaries.

copying from earlier sources. This again is an unusually high proportion. The variety of scales used for Hertfordshire tithe maps is not as great as in many counties with a range from one inch to two chains to one inch to nine chains; 61 per cent of maps are at the recommended scales of one inch to three to four chains. As in Essex, most of the remainder are at the six-chain scale (Table 15.3).

The record of land use on Hertfordshire maps is somewhat idiosyncratic. Arable and grass (4 per cent) and gardens (6 per cent) are not much recorded and the orchards shown (on 10 per cent of the maps) are far short of their real extent. Fifty-two maps (44 per cent) show residual open-field farming and some maps include detail on small open-field landscape features such as balks. Field names appear on a quarter of the county's tithe maps, usually in association with open-field farming. Woodland is depicted on 89 per cent of the maps (often emphasised by the use of colour) but it is rare for so high a proportion as half of a county's tithe maps to show parkland, and thirteen Hertfordshire maps portray parks in great detail. The 19 per cent of maps depicting uncultivated ground is also high, in part due to inclusion of village greens as 'uncultivated'. Field boundary ownership is also recorded to an unusual extent in Hertfordshire (on half the maps) and the proportion of maps distinguishing houses from other buildings is likewise high at 79 per cent.

A rather higher than average proportion of Hertfordshire tithe maps in the Public Record Office collection (67 per cent) can be attributed to a particular map-maker. No one map-maker was outstandingly productive in Hertfordshire; the most prolific surveyor was John Godman of St Albans but he made only seven maps (Table 15.2).

On the whole, Hertfordshire tithe maps are rather more colourful than those of many other counties but they carry no cartouches or decorative borders and only three maps have decorative compass roses.

Table 15.1. *Agreements and awards for commutation of tithes in Hertfordshire*

Assistant commissioner/ local tithe agent	*Number of agreements**	*Number of awards*
William Heard	37	0
Thomas Smith Woolley	9	12
William Wakeford Attree	0	13
Joseph Townsend	13	0
Edward Greathed	8	0
F. Browne Browne	4	0
John Maurice Herbert	0	4
John Mee Mathew	3	0
John Pickering	3	0
Francis Offley Martin	0	2
Thomas James Tatham	0	2
Anthony Jackson	1	0
Roger Kynaston	1	0

*Computed from the number of extant reports on tithe agreements in the tithe files [PRO IR 18].

Table 15.2. *Tithe valuers and tithe map-makers in Hertfordshire*

Name and address (in Hertfordshire unless indicated)	*Number of districts*	*Acreage*
Tithe valuers		
Anthony Jackson, Barkway	24	65,558
John Horner Rumball, St Albans	16	64,102
Edward Lewis, Bayford	9	26,926
John Sedgwick, Rickmansworth	8	23,954
Thomas Boyn Mallam, Paddington, London	7	14,614
William Heard, St Margarets, Ware	6	7,881
Others [26]	47	124,113

Table 15.2 . (*cont.*) *Tithe valuers and tithe map-makers in Hertfordshire*

Name and address (in Hertfordshire unless indicated)	*Number of districts*	*Acreage*
Attributed tithe map-makers		
John Godman, St Stephens, St Albans	7	36,770
John Horner Rumball, St Albans	7	22,871
Henry Davis, Kimpton	7	17,710
Messrs Crawter, Cheshunt/London/Cobham, Surrey	6	13,489
John Griffin, Hemel Hempstead	5	11,059
Charles F. Adams, Barkway	5	8,147
Others [24]	42	119,205

Table 15.3. *The tithe maps of Hertfordshire: scales and classes*

Scale in chains/inch	*All maps*		*First Class*		*Second Class*	
	Number	*Acreage*	*Number*	*Acreage*	*Number*	*Acreage*
>3	2	306	0	0	2	306
3	59	164,388	16	62,698	43	101,690
3.5	2	5,710	0	0	2	5,710
4	12	22,093	0	0	12	22,093
6	37	107,977	0	0	37	107,977
<6	5	26,674	0	0	5	26,674
TOTAL	117	327,148	16	62,698	101	264,450

Table 15.4. *The tithe maps of Hertfordshire: dates*

	1837	*1838*	*1839*	*1840*	*1841*	*1842*	*1843*	*1844*	*1845*	*1846*	*1847*	*1848*	*1849*	*>1849*
All maps	4	16	25	18	15	9	4	5	6	2	5	2	2	3
1st class	2	4	1	4	3	2	0	0	0	0	0	0	0	0
2nd class*	2	12	24	14	12	7	4	5	6	2	5	2	2	3

*One second-class tithe map of Hertfordshire in the Public Record Office collection is undated.

Hertfordshire

15/1 Abbots Langley (parish) TL 085012
Apt 29.07.1841; 5213a (5213); Map 1839, 3 chns, 1st cl, by J. Godman, St Stephen, St Albans; construction lines, railway with tunnel mouth and earthworks, canal, waterbodies, houses, woods, parkland, field boundary ownerships, building names, mills, burys, parsonage farm. (The map in PRO IR 30 is a copy; original is in PRO IR 77/21.)

15/2 St Albans (parish) TL 146070
Apt 02.04.1846; 165a (all); Map 1847, 2 chns, 'revised' by J.H. Rumball, St Albans; foot/b'way, waterbodies, houses, building names, cotton mill, silk mill, abbey.

15/3 Albury (parish) TL 442250
Apt 09.05.1842; 3183a (all); Map 1841, 6 chns; foot/b'way, waterbodies, houses, woods, open fields, fences, field boundary ownerships, building names, sand or stone pits, heath, greens.

15/4 Aldbury (parish) SP 958122
Apt 04.09.1840; 2024a (2071); Map 1840, 3 chns, by W. Brown, Tring; railway, foot/b'way, canal with towpath, waterbodies, houses, woods (col), plantations (col), parkland, heath/moor (col), open fields, hedge ownership, building names, field names, monument, ornamental gardens; hills and bridge named.

15/5 Aldenham (parish) TQ 165975
Apt 27.07.1840; 3762a (5840); Map 1839, 3 chns, by John Godman, St Stephens; waterbodies, houses, woods, parkland, heath/moor, field boundary ownerships, building names, abbey, hamlet names, greens; hill named.

15/6 All Saints and St John and Brickendon and Little Amwell (parish or liberty in parishes of All Saints and St John) TL 339114
Apt 13.08.1846; 2067a (4025); Map 1847, in 5 parts: St Johns, 8 chns, 'compiled and revised' in 1847; Brickenden Liberty, 7 chns, 'revised'; All Saints, no scale, 1848, ? by D. Hollingsworth, Hertford; Little Amwell and Ball's Park, 3 chns; railway, waterbodies, canal with towpath, houses, woods (named), parkland, heath/moor, open fields, building names, road names, field names, churchyard, town hall, school, watercourse, common, greens (col), parish and liberty boundaries; built-up part generalised.

15/7 Great Amwell (parish) TL 370120
Apt 23.02.1839; 2437a (all); Map 1839, 6 chns, ? by E.W. Mylne; foot/b'way, canal, waterbodies, woods, plantations, heath/moor, open fields, hedge ownership, building names, field names, East India College, heath, drains, marsh; built-up part generalised.

15/8 St Andrew (parish) TL 300130 [Not listed]
Apt 20.10.1838; 1143a (1143); Map 1838, 4 chns, by W. Wilds, Hertford; foot/b'way, waterbodies, woods, parkland, arable (col), grassland (col), orchards, gardens, field boundary ownerships, road names, drains.

15/9 Ashwell (parish) TL 263394
Apt 21.03.1840; 3852a (3852); Map 1841, 6 chns, by J. Bailey Denton, 9, Grays Inn Square; hill-drawing, waterbodies, houses, woods, plantations, heath/moor, rock outcrops, open fields, field boundary ownerships, building names, road names, field names, quarries (col), tumulus, vicarage, bury, cow common (col), green ways (col), common, village greens; some physical features named; double lines may be balks.

15/10 Aspeden (parish) TL 350289 [Aspenden]
Apt 22.06.1843; 1351a (1351); Map 1845, 6 chns, in 2 parts, by Adams and Sibley, Buntingford, (includes 3-chn enlargement of open fields); foot/b'way, waterbodies, houses, woods, parkland (named), open fields, field boundary ownerships, field gates, building names, field names, green.

15/11 Aston (parish) TL 278219
Apt 31.01.1839; 2053a (all); Map 1840, 3 chns, 'by Mallam', 'copy from his original'; foot/b'way, waterbodies, houses, woods, plantations, heath/moor, open fields (named), field gates, boundary posts, roadside waste, glebe.

15/12 Ayot St Lawrence (parish) TL 202165
Apt 09.02.1846; 748a (all); Map 1848?, 4 chns; foot/b'way, houses, woods, park.

15/13 Ayott St Peter (parish) TL 220148 [Ayot St Peter]
Apt 26.06.1838; 1100a (all); Map 1838, 3 chns, by J.H. Rumball, St Albans; construction lines, foot/b'way, turnpike roads, waterbodies, houses (by shading), woods (named), plantations, hedge ownership, fence ownership, field gates, building names, rectory, sand or stone pits or quarries, lodge, green; table lists owners, occupiers, land use and acreages.

15/14 Baldock (parish) TL 247338
Apt 17.12.1850; 141a (all); Map 1851?, 2 chns.

15/15 Barkway (parish) TL 380380
Apt 13.02.1849; 32a (5060); Map 1849?, 6 chns, by Chas F. Adams, Barkway, Herts, (tithable parts only, tinted); field boundary ownerships, landowners.

15/16 Barley (parish) TL 399389
Apt 15.02.1839; 2648a (2648); Map 1841, 6 chns; waterbodies, woods, plantations, building names, rectory, folly, gravel pit, tithe-free lands (col), ornamental ground; pictorial church.

15/17 East Barnet cum Chipping Barnet (parish) TQ 255958
Apt 16.05.1840; 3186a (3185); Map 1840, 3 chns, 1st cl, by Duckworth and Taplin, Barnet; construction lines, foot/b'way, waterbodies, houses (by shading), woods, plantations, parkland, orchards (by annotation), garden (by annotation), grass (by annotation), hedge ownership, fence ownership, field boundary ownerships, field gates; 'Middle of Brook' denotes limit of some tithe areas; there is a note that obliterated lengths of boundary have been taken from Barnet Common Enclosure Act; compass rose is decorated with flowers and leaves. (The map in PRO IR 30 is a copy; original is in PRO IR 77/22.).

15/18 Bayford (parish) TL 310090
Apt 17.02.1838; 1608a (all); Map not dated, 3 chns; foot/b'way, waterbodies, houses, woods (col), plantations (col), parkland (in detail), marsh/bog, field boundary ownerships, boundary trees and posts, sand or stone pit; colour bands may show property ownerships.

15/19 Bengeo (parish) TL 326152
Apt 16.09.1841; 3048a (3047); Map 1842?, 3 chns; construction lines, foot/b'way, waterbodies, houses, woods, plantations, open fields (named), field boundary ownerships, field gates, building names, mills, vicarage, boundary posts, chalk pit, marsh; double lines may be balks.

15/20 Bennington (parish) TL 298232 [Benington]
Apt 31.01.1838; 2909a (2908); Map 1840, 3 chns, by Mallam; foot/b'way, waterbodies, houses, woods, plantations, parkland, open fields with balks.

15/21 Little Berkhampstead (parish) TL 293093 [Little Berkhamstead]
Apt 14.03.1838; 1690a (1689); Map 1843?, 3 chns, 'revised copy of Woodcock's map' by Mallam; foot/b'way, waterbodies, houses, woods, osiers, plantations, parkland, marsh/bog, spring.

15/22 Berkhamstead, St Peter (parish) SP 989091 [Berkhamsted]
Apt 14.08.1839; 4341a (4250); Map 1840?, 4 chns, 'The Town with other parts surveyed, the remainder copied, revised and corrected' by John Griffin, Hemel Hempsted, Herts; hill-drawing, railway, waterbodies, canal with towpath, houses, woods, plantations, parkland (named), building names, ancient castle, sand or stone pits, field acreages, common, bounds of old park, greens.

15/23 Bishops Hatfield (parish) TL 230090 [Hatfield]
Apt 31.01.1839; 12620a (12619); Map 'revised' 1838, 8 chns; foot/b'way, waterbodies, houses, woods, parkland, open fields (named), sand or stone pit. Apt omits land use.

15/24 Bishops Stortford (parish) TL 486214 [Bishop's Stortford]
Apt 25.03.1839; 3115a (all); Map 1839, 6 chns; waterbodies, houses, woods, plantations, windmill (by symbol); built-up part generalised.

15/25 Bovingdon (parish) TL 020037
Apt 10.09.1838; 3956a (all); Map 1841, 3 chns, 1st cl, by J.O. Browne,

8 Furnival's Inn; construction lines, railway, foot/b'way, canal with toll house, waterbodies, houses, woods (mostly by annotation), fences, field boundary ownerships, field gates, building names, lawns (by annotation), pleasure gardens (by annotation), parkland (by annotation), moor, common, greens.

15/26 Bramfield (parish) TL 292150
Apt 04.07.1838; 1540a (1540); Map 1838, 6 chns, 'copied from a Plan of 6 chains to an inch. Surveyed in 1804', and 'revised' by T. Sawyer; waterbodies, woods, field boundary ownerships, sand or stone pits.

15/27 Brent Pelham (parish) TL 436304
Apt 26.09.1837; 1601a (1601); Map 1839, 3 chns, waterbodies, houses, woods, open fields, hedge ownership, building names, windmill; double lines may be balks.

15/28 Broxborne (except Hoddesdon) (parish) TL 350069 [Broxbourne]
Apt 19.12.1840; 1923a (1923); Map 1839, 3 chns, by H. Crawter and Sons, Cheshunt, Herts; canal, waterbodies, houses, woods, parkland, open fields, road names, landowners, river towpath, drains, green, common.

15/29 Buckland (parish) TL 361334
Apt 14.09.1838; 1553a (all); Map 1844, 3 chns; waterbodies, houses, woods, open fields (named); double lines may be balks.

15/30 Bushey (parish) TQ 138948
Apt 12.11.1840; 3189a (3188); Map 1840, 4 chns, by Thos Lavender, Watford, Herts; railway, foot/b'way, waterbodies, houses, woods, plantations, parkland, heath/moor (col), building names, quarries, granges.

15/31 Bygrave (parish) TL 259356
Apt 29.11.1845; 1810a (1809); Map 1847, 3 chns, by W.T. Heard, Hitchin; foot/b'way, waterbodies, houses (by shading), woods, parkland, open fields, road names, sand or stone pit, Icknield Way, glebe (pink).

15/32 Caldecott (parish) TL 236385 [Caldecote]
Apt 28.02.1838; 319a (all); Map 1841, 3 chns; foot/b'way, waterbodies, houses, woods, building names, rectory.

15/33 Cheshunt (parish) TL 350030
Apt 14.07.1841; 4772a (8493); Map 1842, 3.5 chns, 'corrected for the purposes of the Tithe Commutation' by H. Crawter and Sons, Cheshunt, Herts; railway, foot/b'way, canal, waterbodies, woods (by annotation), houses, drains, field gates, 'New Enclosures', 'exempt by prescription', 'tithe free old inclosures'.

15/34 Clothall (parish) TL 279315
Apt 22.02.1843; 3444a (all); Map 1842, 6 chns; foot/b'way, waterbodies, houses, woods, plantations, open fields (named), field boundary ownerships, building names, bury; double lines may be balks.

15/35 Codicote (parish) TL 219187
Apt 17.09.1842; 2516a (2671); Map 1842?, 3 chns, by Henry Davies, Kimpton, Herts; construction lines, waterbodies, houses, woods, plantations, field boundary ownerships.

15/36 Datchworth (parish) TL 270190
Apt 13.02.1838; 1862a (all); Map 1839, 6 chns, 'copied' from an existing map at 6 chns by T. Sawyer; waterbodies, woods, heath/moor, open fields, building names, greens (col).

15/37 Digswell (parish) TL 245145
Apt 26.05.1841; 1618a (all); Map 1841, 4 chns, 'A revised copy by Mallam (as to Fences) 1841 of a compiled map dated 1822'; waterbodies, farmyards, woods, parkland (in detail), heath/moor, open fields, fences.

15/38 Eastwick (parish) TL 431130
Apt 08.07.1845; 811a (810); Map 1839, 3 chns, by Gabriel Fleck; waterbodies, houses, building names, road names, river towpath, rectory.

15/39 Essendon (parish) TL 273079
Apt 17.02.1838; 2304a (2303); Map 1838, 3 chns, 1st cl, by J.H. Rumball, St Albans; construction lines, foot/b'way, waterbodies, houses, woods, parkland, hedge ownership, fence ownership, field gates, boundary trees and posts, waste.

15/40 Flamsted (parish) TL 072142 [Flamstead]
Apt 30.11.1838; 5930a (5929); Map 1843?, 6 chns; waterbodies, woods, plantations, parkland (named), open fields, building names (in gothic), road names, bury, boundary trees.

15/41 Flaunden (hamlet or township in parish of Hemel Hempsted) TL 012001
Apt 14.07.1838; 900a (all); Map 1838, 3 chns, 1st cl, by John Griffin, Hemel Hempsted, Herts; construction lines, hill-drawing, foot/b'way, waterbodies, houses, woods, plantations, orchards, gardens, heath/moor, hedge ownership, fence ownership, field gates, building names, sand or stone pits, roadside waste (col).

15/42 Furneux Pelham (parish) TL 438273
Apt 31.08.1837; 2535a (2535); Map 1840, 6 chns; foot/b'way, waterbodies, houses, woods, plantations, building names.

15/43 Great Gaddesden (parish) TL 042122
Apt 05.02.1839; 4075a (all); Map 1838, 6 chns, by John Godman, St Stephens, Herts; waterbodies, houses, woods, parkland (in detail), building names, mill, parsonage; meaning of pink tint is unclear.

15/44 Little Gaddesden (parish) SP 998138
Apt 31.01.1839; 925a (all); Map 1838, 4 chns, 'revised and corrected' by John Griffin, Hemel Hempsted, Herts; waterbodies, woods (named), plantations, heath/moor.

15/45 Gilston (parish) TL 442134 [Not listed]
Apt 09.02.1846; 981a (all); Map 1839, 3 chns, by Gabriel Fleck; waterbodies, houses, woods, parkland, building names, road names, landowners, river towpath, rectory, acreages of parts not mapped in detail.

15/46 Gravely cum Chisfield (parish) TL 242277 [Graveley]
Apt 09.02.1839; 1815a (1817); Map 1838, 3 chns, 1st cl, by M. Reynolds, Old Warden, Beds; construction lines, waterbodies, houses, woods (col), plantations (col), parkland, open fields (named), field boundary ownerships, building names, windmills (pictorial), boundary trees, common.

15/47 Little Hadham (parish) TL 440220
Apt 25.07.1843; 3068a (all); Map 1844, 3 chns, by C.F. Adams, Buntingford; foot/b'way, waterbodies, houses, woods, open fields (named), field boundary ownerships, building names, brick kiln, bury, parsonage, greens, avenue of trees; double lines may be balks.

15/48 Much Hadham (parish) TL 433189
Apt 04.04.1838; 4385a (all); Map 1838, 6 chns, by Lenny and Croft, Bury St Edmunds; waterbodies, houses, parkland (in detail), open fields, building names, road names, rectory, greens; bridge named.

15/49 Harpenden (parish) TL 126138
Apt 31.07.1839; 5061a (all); Map 1840, 3 chns, 1st cl, by John Godman, St Stephens, St Albans; construction lines, waterbodies, houses, woods, parkland, open fields (named), field boundary ownerships, building names, field names, bury, mills, common land, greens.

15/50 Hemel Hempsted (parish) TL 055075 [Hemel Hempstead]
Apt 02.02.1843; 7137a (7136); Map surveyed 1840-1, 3 chns, 1st cl, surveyed for John Griffin by George Alexander Smith; construction lines, hill-drawing, railway with station, canal with towpath and locks, foot/b'way, turnpike roads, green lanes or waste (col), waterbodies, houses, woods (col), plantations (col), parkland (in detail), orchards, common, field gates, building names (some in gothic), sand or stone pits or quarries; scale bar has the names Troughton and Simms, London although Smith is clearly stated as surveyor below map title. (The map in PRO IR 30 is a copy; original is in PRO IR 77/23.)

15/51 Hertingfordbury (parish) TL 297115
Apt 17.02.1838; 2587a (all); Map 1838, 3 chns, by Henry Davies, Kimpton, Herts; construction lines, waterbodies, houses, woods, plantations, parkland, fences, field boundary ownerships.

15/52 Hexton (parish) TL 106302
Apt 14.08.1837; 1453a (1453); Map 1837, 3 chns, by John Willding; foot/b'way, waterbodies, houses, woods, plantations, parkland (named, in gothic), arable (col), grassland (col), gardens, hedge ownership,

fence ownership, field gates, building names (in gothic), gravel pit, barrow, common; red boundaries may be stone walls; land use is shown using Dawson's symbols.

15/53 Hitchin (parish) TL 180290
Apt 29.11.1841; 6400a (6457); Map 1844, 6 chns, in 5 parts, by J. Bailey Denton, Grays Inn, London, (includes enlargement of town at 2 chns); hill-drawing, waterbodies, houses, woods (named), plantations, parkland (named), orchards, open fields, building names, road names, meeting houses, priory, Friends Meeting House, infirmary, school, brewery, market place, mills, town hall, brick kiln, windmill (pictorial), sand or stone pits, workhouse, chapel, common land.

15/54 Hoddesdon (hamlet in parish of Broxborne) TL 360090
Apt 27.03.1841; 2482a (2583); Map 1842, 3 chns, 'surveyed in the year 1819 and corrected according to the several alterations up to the year 1842' by H. Crawter and Sons, Cheshunt, Herts; railways, waterbodies, houses, open fields, road names, drains, commons, greens, woodlands (by name).

15/55 Little Hormead (parish) TL 399285
Apt 25.05.1839; 1042a (1041); Map 1844, 3 chns; foot/b'way, waterbodies, houses, woods, open fields (named), field boundary ownerships, field gates, building names, rectory, bury; double lines may be balks.

15/56 Hunsdon (parish) TL 413133
Apt 22.11.1837; 1929a (1928); Map 1842, 6 chns, in 2 parts, (includes 3-chn enlargement of open meadows); construction lines, canal, waterbodies, houses, woods, plantations, parkland (in detail), open fields, field boundary ownerships, building names, mill, gravel pit, rectory.

15/57 Ickleford (parish) TL 184332
Apt 04.09.1840; 258a (1007); Map 1841, 3 chns; foot/b'way, waterbodies, houses, farmyards, woods, arable (col), grassland (col), orchards, gardens, marsh/bog, hedge ownership, field gates, building names, landowners, rectory, churchyard, green, drains.

15/58 Ippolitts (parish) TL 196269 [St Ippollitts]
Apt 29.11.1845; 305a (2970); Map 1847, 6 chns, by W.T. Heard, (tithable parts only, tinted); waterbodies, woods (named), parkland, building names, sand or stone pit.

15/59 Kimpton (parish) TL 172182
Apt 10.03.1837; 3580a (3579); Map 1837, 3 chns, 1st cl, by Henry Davies, Kimpton; construction lines, waterbodies, houses, woods, fence ownership, field boundary ownerships, building names (in gothic), greens, glebe.

15/60 King's Langley (parish) TL 060027 [Kings Langley]
Apt 08.02.1838; 3461a (all); Map 1839, 3 chns, by John Griffin, Hemel Hempsted, Herts; hill-drawing, foot/b'way, canal with towpath, waterbodies, houses, woods, plantations, parkland, orchards, field gates, building names, sand or stone pits, mill, commons, ornamental ground.

15/61 Knebworth (parish) TL 230210
Apt 10.06.1845; 2697a (all); Map 1845, 6 chns, by Henry Davies, Kimpton; waterbodies, houses, woods, plantations, parkland (in detail), building names.

15/62 Layston (parish) TL 372292 [Not listed]
Apt 01.02.1842; 2209a (2208); Map 1838, 6 chns, in 2 parts, by C.F. Adams, (includes enlargement of Buntingford town at 3 chns); waterbodies, houses, woods, parkland, open fields (named), field boundary ownerships, building names, road names, lime pit, green.

15/63 Letchworth (parish) TL 215315
Apt 07.08.1839; 884a (1027); Map 1845?, 3 chns; foot/b'way, waterbodies, houses, woods (col), plantations (col), sand or stone pit.

15/64 Lilley (parish) TL 120270
Apt 08.09.1847; 1822a (all); Map 1848, 6 chns, by W.T. Heard, Hitchin; foot/b'way, waterbodies, woods, building names.

15/65 St Margarets (parish) TL 370115
Apt 20.04.1837; 383a (all); Map 1838, 3 chns, by W. Wilds; turnpike roads, waterbodies, houses, farmyards, woods (col, named), parkland, arable (col), meadow (dark green), pasture (light green), orchards, gardens, hedge ownership, field names, field acreages, drains.

15/66 Meesden (parish) TL 432325
Apt 17.02.1838; 983a (all); Map 1840, 6 chns; waterbodies, woods, plantations, building names, rectory.

15/67 St Michaels (parish) TL 118078
Apt 30.06.1843; 6462a (?); Map 1840, 3 chns, 'revised and corrected' by John Godman, St Stephens, St Albans, Herts; turnpike roads, toll bar, waterbodies, houses, woods, parkland (in detail), heath/moor, field boundary ownerships, building names, road names, mills, pond yards, bury, silk mill, workhouse, greens; bridge named.

15/68 North Mimms (parish) TL 231042 [Not listed]
Apt 14.05.1844; 4926a (4925); Map 1839-44, 3 chns, in 2 parts, by J.H. Rumball; construction lines, foot/b'way, waterbodies, houses (by shading), woods, plantations, parkland, heath/moor, open fields, hedge ownership, fence ownership.

15/69 Great Munden (parish) TL 357238
Apt 29.11.1841; 3352a (3352); Map 1840, 6 chns; waterbodies, houses, woods, plantations, heath/moor, open fields.

15/70 Little Munden (parish) TL 335219 [Not listed]
Apt 31.12.1840; 2205a (2204); Map 1842, 3 chns, 1st cl, in 2 parts; construction lines, waterbodies, houses, woods, heath/moor, open fields, hedge ownership, fence ownership, field boundary ownerships, building names, greens, windmill, bury; map also covers Great Munden (15/69). (The map in PRO IR 30 is a copy; original is in PRO IR 77/24.)

15/71 Newnham (parish) TL 248376
Apt 25.05.1842; 949a (951); Map 1842, 6 chns; waterbodies, houses, woods, plantations, building names, rectory.

15/72 Northaw (parish) TL 282028
Apt 20.01.1849; 1173a (3180); Map 1849, 3 chns, 'corrected ... according to the several alterations from the original survey made in the year 1838 by J.H. Rumball' by H. Crawter and Sons, Cheshunt, (tithable parts only); waterbodies, houses.

15/73 Northchurch (parish) SP 969081
Apt 05.05.1840; 3881a (all); Map 1839, 6 chns, in 2 parts, by Glenister, Tring and Griffin, Hemel Hempsted; hill-drawing, railway with cutting, foot/b'way, canal, waterbodies, woods (named), plantations, parkland, heath/moor, open fields (named), building names, road names, rectory, churchyard, heath, greens.

15/74 Offley (parish) TL 145265
Apt 02.04.1846; 12a (5160); Map 1850, 4 chns, by Wm Thos Heard, Hitchin, (tithable parts only, tinted); woods, building names; pictorial church; map is described as of the 'temple lands'.

15/75 St Peters (parish) TL 183077
Apt 21.11.1840; 5745a (5745); Map 'revised in 1843', 6 chns, in 2 parts, by J.H. Rumball, (includes 3 -chn enlargement of common fields); construction lines, waterbodies, houses, open fields.

15/76 Radwell (parish) TL 238360
Apt 15.02.1837; 743a (748); Map 1837, 3 chns, 1st cl, by M. Reynolds, Old Warden, Beds; hill-drawing, foot/b'way, waterbodies, houses, farmyards, woods, plantations, parkland (in detail), gardens, marsh/bog, hedge ownership, fences, field gates, road embankments.

15/77 Redbourn (parish) TL 105115
Apt 30.06.1843; 4515a (4515); Map 1841, 3 chns, 1st cl; construction lines, waterbodies, houses, woods, field boundary ownerships, building names, bury, common.

15/78 Rickmansworth (parish) TQ 050950
Apt 14.03.1838; 9938a (9937); Map 1839, 3 chns, by John Sedgwick and Son, Rickmersworth; construction lines, hill-drawing, foot/b'way, canal with towpath, waterbodies, houses, woods, plantations, parkland (named), orchards, marsh/bog, heath/moor, hedge ownership, fence ownership, field boundary ownerships, field gates, building names, old toll bar, copper mills, mills, parsonage, sand or stone pits, drains, stone

walls, greens. (The map in PRO IR 30 is a copy; original is in PRO IR 77/25, and is unfit for production.)

15/79 Ridge (parish) TL 211010
Apt 29.06.1839; 3607a (3607); Map 1838, 9 chns, 'partly revised and partly measured' by J.H. Rumball; waterbodies, houses, woods, plantations, parkland, orchards, hedge ownership, building names, ownerships (col); table lists owners, properties, land use and acreages.

15/80 Royston (parish) (partly in Cambs) TL 358408
Apt 19.10.1850; 323a (320); Map 1851, 6 chns; waterbodies, houses, woods, building names, priory.

15/81 Rushden (parish) TL 311319
Apt 23.09.1845; 1487a (1486); Map 1846, 6 chns, by Charles F. Adams, Barkway, Herts; waterbodies, houses, woods, tithe-free woods (col), parkland (named), greens.

15/82 Sacomb (parish) TL 332191 [Sacombe]
Apt 12.09.1837; 1511a (all); Map 1839, 3 chns, by Henry Davies, Kimpton, Herts; construction lines, waterbodies, houses, woods, plantations, parkland, fence ownership, field boundary ownerships, waste. Apt omits some land use.

15/83 Sandon (parish) TL 320350
Apt 05.05.1840; 3943a (3943); Map 1841, 6 chns, by J. Bailey Denton, 9 Grays Inn Square; foot/b'way, waterbodies, houses, woods (named), plantations, orchards, fence ownership, field boundary ownerships, building names, vicarage, bury, common land, greens named.

15/84 Sandridge (parish) TL 168102
Apt 28.08.1843; 5766a (5766); Map 1844?, 9 chns, in 2 parts, (includes Sandridge village separately at 3 chns); waterbodies, heath/moor (col), greens (col); pictorial church.

15/85 Sarratt (parish) TQ 034996
Apt 31.12.1840; 1551a (1550); Map 1840, 3 chns, 1st cl, by Thos Lavender, Watford, Herts; construction lines, hill-drawing, waterbodies, houses, woods, plantations, parkland, heath/moor, building names, vicarage, sand or stone pits or quarries, mill, pound, greens (col).

15/86 Sawbridgeworth (parish) TL 470153
Apt 12.11.1838; 6606a (all); Map 1839, 3 chns, by John King Doyley, No 1, South Square, Grays Inn, London; construction lines, hill-drawing, railway with station, foot/b'way, canal, waterbodies, houses, farmyards (in detail), woods (col, named), plantations, parkland (in detail), arable (by annotation), meadow (by annotation), pasture (by annotation), grass (by annotation), orchards (by annotation), gardens, marsh/bog, nurseries (by annotation), open fields (named, with boundary marks), hedges, fence ownership, field boundary ownerships, field gates, building names, road names, Independent Meeting House, vicarage, lodge, school house, boundary trees, gravel pits, mill, commons, greens, drains. (The map in PRO IR 30 is a copy; original is in PRO IR 77/26.)

15/87 Sheephall (parish) TL 260230 [Shephall]
Apt 23.09.1845; 1143a (all); Map 1846, 3 chns, by William Thomas Nash, Royston, Herts; foot/b'way, waterbodies, farmyard (by annotation), woods, plantations, parkland, open fields (named), field boundary ownerships, field gates, building names, stone walls, greens; double lines may be balks.

15/88 Shenley (parish) TQ 200997
Apt 28.08.1840; 4056a (4056); Map 1839, 3 chns, by John Godman; waterbodies, houses, woods, plantations, parkland (in detail), field boundary ownerships, building names, bury, rectory, green.

15/89 Standon (parish) TL 390210
Apt 22.11.1838; 7521a (7520); Map 1839, 6 chns; waterbodies, houses, woods (named), plantations, parkland (named), hedge ownership, building names, road names, mill, sand or stone pit, windmill.

15/90 Stanstead Abbott (parish) TL 395121 [Stanstead Abbotts]
Apt 19.04.1839; 2595a (2594); Map 1840, 4 chns; waterbodies, woods (named), open fields (named), building names, bury, boundary posts, drains, avenue of trees.

15/91 Stapleford (parish) TL 308168
Apt 03.10.1837; 1319a (all); Map 1839, 3 chns, by Henry Davies, Kimpton, Herts; construction lines, waterbodies, houses, woods, field boundary ownerships.

15/92 St Stephen (parish) TL 140030 [St Stephens]
Apt 16.01.1838; 8141a (8140); Map 1838, 3 chns, 1st cl, in 2 parts, by J. Godman, St Stephens, St Albans; construction lines, turnpike roads, toll bar, waterbodies, woods (col, named), parkland, open fields (named), field boundary ownerships, building names, road names, abbey, ruins, mill, gas works, greens.

15/93 Stevenage (parish) TL 240245
Apt 22.11.1837; 4309a (4434); Map 1839?, 6 chns, by James Richardson, Cambridge; foot/b'way, turnpike roads, toll bar, waterbodies, farmyards, woods (col, named), parkland (named), avenue of trees, grassland (col), open fields (named), fence ownership, field names, field boundary ownerships, building names, 'pest house', six ancient tumuli, winding balks, windmill (pictorial), National School, rectory, keeper's lodge, brick kilns, glebe (with acreages), greens; public houses named in detail.

15/94 Stocking Pelham (parish) TL 450290
Apt 05.09.1837; 629a (all); Map 1839, 3 chns; waterbodies, houses, woods, open fields (named), hedge ownership, building names, green; double lines may be balks.

15/95 Studham (part of) (parish) TL 018158
Apt 15.07.1839; 1432a (all); Map 1839, 4 chns, 'revised and corrected' by John Griffin, Hemel Hempsted; waterbodies, woods (col), plantations (col), open fields (named), sand or stone pit, common.

15/96 Tewin (parish) TL 271146
Apt 29.09.1838; 2614a (all); Map 1838, 8 chns, 'copied from a map of 8 chains' and 'revised' by Thomas Sawyer, land and timber surveyor, Hertford; hill-drawing, waterbodies, houses, woods, parkland (in detail), heath/moor, field boundary ownerships, greens (col), waste (col).

15/97 Therfield (parish) TL 345368
Apt 21.03.1840; 4277a (all); Map 1843, 6 chns; waterbodies, houses, woods, building names, bury; waste named.

15/98 Thorley (parish) TL 475190
Apt 04.06.1845; 1516a (all); Map 1845, 6 chns, by Arthur Nockolds, Stansted, lithographed; waterbodies, woods, plantations, open fields.

15/99 Throcking (parish) TL 345302
Apt 16.01.1842; 903a (all); Map 1841, 3 chns, in 2 parts; foot/b'way, waterbodies, houses, woods, open fields (named), field boundary ownerships, field gates, building names, rectory; double lines may be balks.

15/100 Thundridge (parish) TL 373169
Apt 21.04.1845; 2201a (all); Map 1845, 3 chns, by Messrs T. and H. Crawter, Cobham, Surrey and Southampton Buildings, Chancery Lane, London; hill-drawing, waterbodies, houses, woods, parkland, sand or stone pits, chalk pit, green.

15/101 Totteridge (parochial chapelry) TQ 242943
Apt 08.09.1840; 1598a (1597); Map 1840, 3 chns, 1st cl, by Duckworth and Taplin, Barnet; construction lines, foot/b'way, waterbodies, houses (by shading), fences, field boundary ownerships, field gates, sand or stone pits.

15/102 St Pauls Walden (parish) TL 182212 [St Paul's Walden]
Apt 11.09.1841; 3678a (3678); Map 1840, 3 chns; construction lines, foot/b'way, waterbodies, houses, woods, plantations, parkland, open fields, fence ownership, field boundary ownerships, building names.

15/103 Walkern (parish) TL 292262
Apt 03.11.1838; 2925a (2924); Map 1841?, 3 chns; waterbodies, houses, woods, parkland, open fields (named), building names, watermill, windmill (by symbol), rectory.

15/104 Wallington (parish) TL 290340
Apt 16.05.1839; 1951a (all); Map 1839, 4 chns; waterbodies, houses, woods, open fields, road names, well, bound crosses, common, avenue of trees; double lines may be balks; a road called 'The Forty Feet High

Way' is annotated: 'It is now reduced to twenty, the Parish of Sandon having ploughed up their half'.

15/105 Ware (parish) TL 375155
Apt 21.04.1845; 4701a (4700); Map 1845, 6 chns, in 2 parts, by J.S. Surridge, Coggeshall, Essex, (includes manuscript enlargement of town at 1.5 chns), litho (by Shaw and Sons, Fetter Lane, London); hill-drawing, railway with station and platform, canal with locks, waterbodies, houses, woods, plantations, parkland (in detail), orchards, marsh/bog, open fields, building names, workhouse, hotel, priory, sand or stone pits, post office, town hall, burial ground, gas works, churchyard (col), burial ground (col).

15/106 Watford (parish) TQ 100970
Apt 20.03.1844; 10793a (10792); Map 1842, 3 chns, 1st cl, by Thomas Lavender; railway with viaduct and station, foot/b'way, canal, waterbodies, houses, common wood, common moor, greens, woods, plantations, parkland, open fields, building names, road names, sand or stone pits, mill, silk mill, workhouse, tithe-merged land (yellow), tithe-free land (red).

15/107 Watton (parish) TL 302190 [Watton at Stone]
Apt 22.11.1837; 3500a (all); Map 1839, 3 chns, by Henry Davies, Kimpton, Herts; foot/b'way, waterbodies, houses, woods, plantations, parkland, marsh/bog, heath/moor, fence ownership, field boundary ownerships, building names, common.

15/108 Welwyn (parish) TL 240170
Apt 31.08.1837; 2952a (2987); Map 1837, 4 chns, 'revised for the purposes of the Tithe Apportionment' ? by J. Tootel; turnpike roads, toll bar, waterbodies, building names, workhouse, bury, rectory, green; pictorial churches.

15/109 Westmill (parish) TL 368266
Apt 27.09.1838; 2138a (all); Map 1841, 6 chns; waterbodies, houses, woods, parkland (named), building names, gravel pit, rectory.

15/110 Weston (parish) TL 262302
Apt 19.11.1845; 405a (4530); Map 1847, 6 chns, ? by J. Bailey Denton; waterbodies, houses, woods, plantations, building names, landowners.

15/111 Whethampstead (parish) TL 162148 [Wheathampstead]
Apt 21.07.1840; 5034a (5033); Map 1840, 6 chns, in 2 parts, 'revised and corrected' by John H. Rumball, St Albans, (includes 3-chn enlargement of common fields); construction lines, open fields, field boundary ownerships, building names, field names, mill, woods (by name), common, heath.

15/112 Widdial (parish) TL 375319 [Wyddial]
Apt 15.05.1841; 1187a (all); Map 1840, 4 chns; waterbodies, houses, woods, parkland (named), open fields (named), field boundary ownerships, field gates, building names, road names, boundary trees, rectory; double lines may be balks.

15/113 Widford (parish) TL 420160
Apt 21.01.1839; 1134a (all); Map 1840?, 3 chns; foot/b'way, waterbodies, houses, woods, plantations, open fields (named), building names, rectory; bridge named.

15/114 Wigginton (parish) SP 943093
Apt 12.05.1842; 1662a (1662); Map 1841, 6 chns, by I.G. Glenister, Tring; canal, waterbodies, houses, woods, heath/moor, building names, common (col), greens (col), woods (by name).

15/115 Willian (parish) TL 228312
Apt 22.11.1837; 1855a (all); Map 1839, 3 chns; foot/b'way, waterbodies, houses, woods, plantations, parkland, open fields, fence ownership, field boundary ownerships, building names, road names, rectory, vicarage, Icknield Way; meadow named; double lines may be balks.

15/116 Wormley (parish) TL 345060
Apt 26.06.1840; 938a (940); Map 1841, 3.5 chns, 'surveyed in the year 1826, and corrected according to the several alterations up to the year 1841' by H. Crawter and Sons; railway, foot/b'way, canal, waterbodies, houses, woods, plantations, parkland, open fields, fence ownership, field gates, road names, landowners, greens, drains, 'Emmanuel Pollard's waste'.

15/117 Yardley (parish) TL 310270 [Ardeley]
Apt 30.10.1839; 2405a (2405); Map 1839, 3 chns; waterbodies, houses, open fields, field gates, building names, bury, sand or stone pit, windmill (by symbol), greens; bridge named.

Huntingdonshire

PRO IR29 and IR30 16/1-62

112 tithe districts: 235,054 acres
60 tithe commutations: 83,515 acres
31 voluntary tithe agreements, 29 compulsory tithe awards,
2 corn rent annuities

Tithe and tithe commutation

The pattern of tithe commutation in Huntingdonshire is characteristic of midland rather than eastern counties. In 1836 only 53 per cent of Huntingdonshire tithe districts by number and 35 per cent of the county by area remained subject to tithe (Fig. 28). Twenty-one districts were still wholly tithable; elsewhere the main causes of tithe exemption were commutation at the time of enclosure and modus payments in lieu of tithes.

Assistant tithe commissioners and local tithe agents who worked in Huntingdonshire are listed in Table 16.1. Although the three most prolific Huntingdonshire tithe valuers, James Jones, Charles Bloodworth and Thomas Lovell, all resided in the county, Huntingdonshire is exceptional in that eleven districts were valued by men based some distance away (Table 16.2). Two tithe districts in Huntingdonshire are apportioned wholly or partly by holding and a further two apportionments omit land use and some field names. The apportionment for Somersham has field-by-field cropping information which is very rare in this part of England. Three apportionments are unusual in that they include explicit agreements to adopt surveys of 1775 and 1802 for tithe commutation.

Tithe maps

Huntingdonshire follows the usual midland pattern in that only two of its sixty maps are sealed as first class. Two maps are acknowledged copies of earlier material but the copying of existing surveys was probably much more widespread, particularly in districts where little tithe remained payable. As in most counties with much parliamentary enclosure, there were two peaks of map production in Huntingdonshire, in 1839 and 1851, though the latter was mainly the result of mapping residual tithable tracts of very small extent (Table 16.4). Huntingdonshire tithe maps are drawn at a wide variety of scales from one inch to 1.1 chains to one inch to 16 chains. Only 27 per cent of maps are in the recommended scale range of one inch to 3 to 4 chains, whereas 43 per cent are at the six-chain scale (Table 16.3).

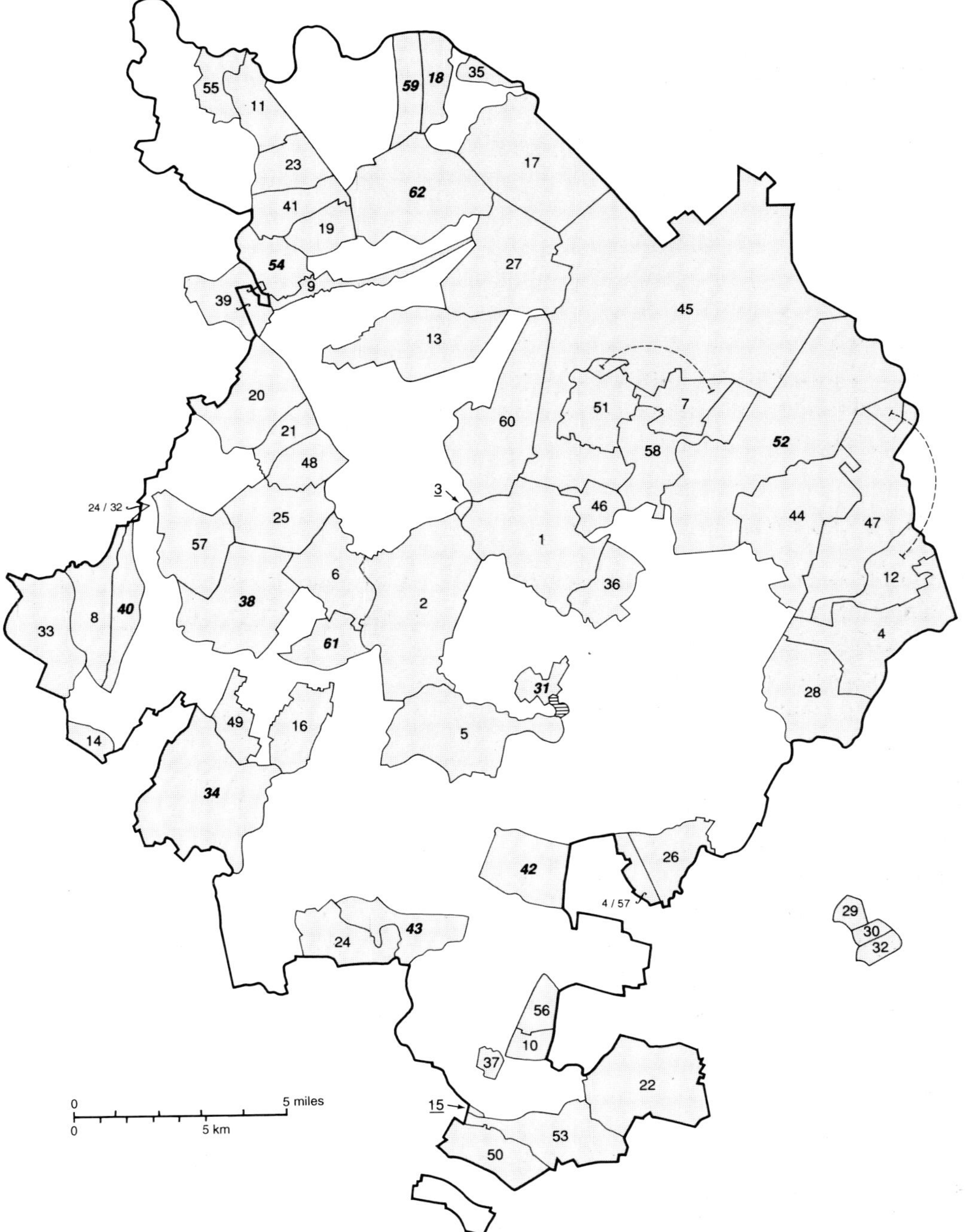

Fig. 28 Huntingdonshire: tithe district boundaries.

About a half of Huntingdonshire tithe maps in the Public Record Office collection can be attributed to a particular map-maker (Table 16.2). The most prolific of these was Charles Bidwell of Ely who produced seven maps, neatly executed and unremarkable but for the use of Dawson's recommended symbol for wooden windmills and windpumps.

None of the tithe maps of Huntingdonshire is decorated, though that of Tetworth is unusually colourful and is the only map in the county to depict agricultural land use. The map of the small district of Lansbury is unique among tithe maps as it is drawn on an octagonal-shaped piece of parchment.

Table 16.1. *Agreements and awards for commutation of tithes in Huntingdonshire*

Assistant commissioner/ local tithe agent	*Number of agreements**	*Number of awards*
Francis Offley Martin	0	18
Thomas Smith Woolley	7	4
John West	9	0
William Wakeford Attree	0	5
Joseph Townsend	5	0
John Pickering	3	0
Henry Bertram Gunning	2	0
William Heard	2	0
John Maurice Herbert	0	2
? Mears	2	0
F. Browne Browne	1	0

*Computed from the number of extant reports on tithe agreements in the tithe files [PRO IR 18].

Table 16.2. *Tithe valuers and tithe map-makers in Huntingdonshire*

Name and address (in Huntingdonshire unless indicated)	*Number of districts*	*Acreage*
Tithe valuers		
James Jones, Ramsey	11	34,013
Charles Bloodworth, Kimbolton	8	4,326
Thomas Lovell, Huntingdon	6	2,082
Charles Paul Berkeley, Oundle, Northamptonshire	3	6,264
William Peppercorn, St Neots	3	3,288
Robert Wright, Norwich, Norfolk	4	8,585
Others [19]	25	24,957
Attributed tithe map-makers		
Charles M. Bidwell, Ely, Cambridgeshire	7	24,026
Charles Bloodworth, Kimbolton	5	1,873
Thomas Lovell, Huntingdon	4	540
Others [13]	14	24,459

Table 16.3. *The tithe maps of Huntingdonshire: scales and classes*

Scale in chains/inch	*All maps*		*First Class*		*Second Class*	
	Number	*Acreage*	*Number*	*Acreage*	*Number*	*Acreage*
>3	3	24	0	0	3	24
3	9	10,435	2	5,752	7	4,683
4	7	14,137	0	0	7	14,137
5	3	2,064	0	0	3	2,064
6	27	39,773	0	0	27	39,773
8	1	2,150	0	0	1	2,150
9	7	10,294	0	0	7	10,294
<9	3	4,638	0	0	3	4,638
TOTAL	60	83,515	2	5,752	58	77,763

Table 16.4. *The tithe maps of Huntingdonshire: dates*

	1837	*1838*	*1839*	*1840*	*1841*	*1842*	*1843*	*1844*	*1845*	*1846*	*1847*	*1848*	*1849*	*1850*	*>1850*
All maps	1	4	11	7	4	3	2	2	2	0	2	1	3	3	15
1st class	0	0	2	0	0	0	0	0	0	0	0	0	0	0	0
2nd class	1	4	9	7	4	3	2	2	2	0	2	1	3	3	15

Huntingdonshire

16/1 Abbotts Ripton (parish) TL 232783 [Abbots Ripton]
Apt 31.12.1841; 3956a (3956); Map 1843, 6 chns, ? by Charles Bidwell, Ely, Cambs; waterbodies, houses, woods (named), parkland, orchards, building names, farm names, road names, glebe, green, notable tree; pictorial church.

16/2 Alconbury cum Alconbury Weston (parish) TL 183771
Apt 30.01.1849; 1187a (4240); Map 1851, 6 chns, ? by Charles Bloodworth, Kimbolton, Hunts (tithable parts only); waterbodies, private roads (uncoloured).

16/3 Bevills Wood (extra-parochial place) TL 204794 [Bevill's Wood]
Apt 31.12.1851; 87a (?); Map 1852, 6 chns, ? by Charles Bloodworth, Kimbolton, Hunts; woods.

16/4 Bluntisham with Earith (parish) TL 366746
Apt 30.06.1843; 3424a (all); Map 1844, 6 chns, by Chas M. Bidwell, Ely; railway, waterbodies, houses, woods, osiers, field boundary ownerships, rectory, chapel, sluice, embankments; watercourses named.

16/5 Brampton (parish) TL 202705
Apt 14.09.1839; 819a (2411); Map 1841?, 9 chns, in 2 parts, (tithable parts only, tinted; most fields mapped separately at 3 chns); woods (col, named), sluice; former open meadow and hedge bordering wood named. Apt is partly by holding.

16/6 Buckworth (parish) TL 150770
Apt 03.01.1839; 1900a (1950); Map 1839?, [? 9 chns]; waterbodies, woods; unnumbered fields tinted light blue may be tithe-free; other tithable areas are tinted light yellow; it is unclear why some fields are tinted pink.

16/7 Bury (parish) TL 290832
Apt 30.09.1845; 1645a (1645); Map 1841, 6 chns, by C. M. Bidwell, Ely, Cambs; foot/b'way, waterbodies, houses, woods, field boundary ownerships, building names, road names, roadside waste (col); watercourses named; map was revised after drawing, by scraping out some field boundaries.

16/8 Bythorn (parish) TL 058757
Apt 15.06.1839; 196a (1503); Map 1839?, [4 chns], in 2 parts, (tithable parts only, tinted); foot/b'way, turnpike roads, private road, waterbodies, landowners.

16/9 Caldecot (parish) TL 164883 [Caldecote]
Apt 08.02.1847; 779a (all); Map 1847, 9 chns, by Cuming and Hill, Easton, Stamford; waterbodies, woods, glebe (col); former open fields and fen named.

16/10 Caldecote (hamlet in parish of Eynesbury) TL 226583 [Not listed]
Apt 22.03.1839; 426a (all); Map 1839, 6 chns; waterbodies, woods, field boundary ownerships; owner named in title; private roads uncoloured.

16/11 Chesterton (parish) TL 125952
Apt 28.03.1837; 1331a (1330); Map 1838, 6 chns, by R. Hayward and Son, Thorpe Malsor, Northants; foot/b'way, turnpike roads, waterbodies, houses, woods, glebe (col); streams named.

16/12 Colne (parish) TL 378765
Apt 28.04.1838; 2012a (all); Map 1839, 3 chns, 1st cl, in 6 parts, by Chas M. Bidwell, Ely, Cambs; construction lines, foot/b'way, turnpike roads, waterbodies, houses, woods, osiers, boundary stones (by symbol), windmill (by symbol).

16/13 Connington (parish) TL 182862 [Conington]
Apt 17.03.1841; 3090a (all); Map 'sketch of the Parish', 1840?, 12 chns; foot/b'way, waterbodies, woods, windpumps (pictorial); pictorial church; watercourses named; the owner is named in the title, but this has been struck through.

16/14 Covington (parish) TL 056704
Apt 31.10.1846; 231a (1290); Map 1851, 3 chns, ? by Charles Bloodworth, Kimbolton, Hunts, (tithable parts only).

16/15 Drewells (district in parish of Eynesbury) TL 203568 [Not listed]
Apt 19.10.1850; 29a (all); Map 1852, 6 chns, ? by Charles Bloodworth, Kimbolton, Hunts.

16/16 Easton (parish) TL 139712
Apt 12.09.1842; 302a (1310); Map 1844?, 6 chns, (tithable parts only in detail); woods (named).

16/17 Farcet (parish) TL 235925
Apt 29.10.1839; 3408a (3408); Map 1840, 6 chns, by Chas. H. Bidwell, Ely; woods, field boundary ownerships, building names, private roads (uncoloured), windpumps (by symbol); watercourses named.

16/18 Fletton (parish) TL 195967 [Old Fletton]
Apt 19.12.1849; 8a (780); Map 1853?, 1.1 chns (1 inch to 72 feet, 1:864), (tithable part only); railways, public drift road.

16/19 Folksworth (parish) TL 149903
Apt 29.10.1847; 194a (867); Map 1848, 5 chns, by R.D. Miles, Leicester (tithable parts only); foot/b'way, occupation roads, waterbodies, woods.

16/20 Great Gidding (parish) TL 121838
Apt 25.02.1843; 2349a (2050); Map 1849, 4 chns, ? by Wm Heard, Hitchin; waterbodies, woods, open fields (named), building names, field names; agreement concludes with agreement to 'abide by the Survey of Thomas Thorp, Land Surveyor' made in 1802. Apt omits land use and some field names.

16/21 Little Gidding (parish) TL 135824
Apt 29.04.1847; 714a (all); Map 1849, 3 chns, by Charles Day, Colleyweston, Stamford; waterbodies, woods, ownership of field boundaries along district boundary.

16/22 Great Gransden (parish) TL 273567
Apt 30.01.1843; 3365a (3364); Map 1845, 6 chns, by John King and Son, Saffron Walden, Essex; foot/b'way, waterbodies, woods, former open field names.

16/23 Haddon (parish) TL 135930
Apt 28.03.1837; 1214a (1214); Map 1838, 6 chns, by R. Hayward and Son, Thorpe Malsor, Northants; foot/b'way, turnpike roads, waterbodies, houses, woods, building names, landowners, glebe (col); stram named.

16/24 Hailweston (parish) TL 157625 [Hail Weston]
Apt 08.06.1837; 1553a (all); Map 1838, 3 chns, ? by Robert Wright, junior, Norwich; foot/b'way, waterbodies, houses, woods (named), building names, field names, landowners (col), pond, brick kiln, pit.

16/25 Hamerton (parish) TL 130792
Apt 05.05.1838; 2150a (all); Map 1840?, 8 chns; houses, building names. Apt is partly by holding.

16/26 Hilton (parish) TL 285657
Apt 30.10.1839; 1280a (all); Map 1839, 6 chns; foot/b'way, private roads, turnpike roads, waterbodies, houses, woods, parkland, green (col).

16/27 Holme Fern (district in parish of Holme) TL 225891 [Holme Fen]
Apt 01.09.1840; 4055a (all); Map 1841, 9 chns; waterbodies, woods, decoy, mills (by symbol); watercourses named (in gothic).

16/28 Holywell cum Needingworth (parish) TL 344721
Apt 30.05.1851; 21a (3290); Map (drawn on Apt) 1851?, 6 chns, (tithable parts only); railway.

16/29 All Saints, Huntingdon (parish) TL 238718 [Not listed]
Apt 05.05.1848; 10a (all); Map 1850?, 2 chns, ? by Thos. Lovell, Huntingdon, Hunts; foot/b'way, road names, churchyard, market place.

16/30 St Benedicts, Huntingdon (parish) TL 241716 [Not listed]
Apt 05.05.1848; 6a (all); Map 1851?, 2 chns, in 2 parts, ? by Thos. Lovell, Huntingdon, Hunts (tithable parts only); road names, churchyard.

16/31 St John, Huntingdon (parish) TL 233723 [Not listed]
Apt 07.11.1848; 444a (?); Map 1849?, 4 chns, in 2 parts, ? by Thomas Lovell, Huntingdon, Hunts; railway, waterbodies, open fields, road names, spring, pest house, churchyard, glebe (col), corporation land (col).

16/32 St Marys, Huntingdon (parish) TL 242714 [Not listed]
Apt 29.06.1850; 80a (?); Map 1851?, 4 chns, ? by Thomas Lovell, Huntingdon, Hunts (tithable parts only); railway, road names, landowners, mills, gas works, vicarage.

16/33 Keyston (parish) TL 038755
Apt 23.11.1838; 2535a (2535); Map 1839, 6 chns; waterbodies, open fields, waste (named).

16/34 Kimbolton (parish) TL 101683
Apt 05.05.1847; 339a (5061); Map 1847?, 6 chns, ? by Thomas Bloodworth, Kimbolton, Hunts, (tithable parts only); foot/b'way, toll gate, waterbodies, windmill (pictorial), stiles.

16/35 Kings Delph and Eight Roods (district in parish of Stanground and Farcet) TL 210968 [King's Delph]
Apt 16.03.1850; 536a (?); Map 1840, 6 chns, by Chas M. Bidwell, Ely; houses, field boundary ownerships, building names. Fields numbered 401 upwards are tinted pink: it is unclear why.

16/36 Kings Ripton (parish) TL 261764
Apt 04.11.1850; 1a (1210); Map 1852?, 6 chns, (tithable parts only).

16/37 Lancelynsbury or Lansbury (hamlet in parish of Eynesbury) TL 211586 [Not listed]
Apt 12.05.1843; 214a (all); Map 1845?, 4 chns; waterbodies, woods, hedge ownership (col), landowners; the map is drawn on an octagonal-shaped piece of parchment.

16/38 Leighton Bromswold (parish) TL 116758
Apt 30.05.1851; 1006a (2770); Map 1851?, 5 chns; waterbodies, woods, vicarage. District is apportioned by holding and no fields are shown.

16/39 Lutton (parish) (partly in Northants) TL 112876
Apt 24.05.1842; 1479a (1509); Map 1842, 6 chns; waterbodies, houses, open fields, field names, 'Old Inclosures'; pictorial church; agreement concludes with agreement to abide by Thomas Thorpe's survey of 1802.

16/40 Molesworth (parish) TL 071753
Apt 03.01.1839; 346a (1710); Map 1838? (copied from the enclosure map of 1799), [6 chns], (tithable parts only, tinted); turnpike roads, woods.

16/41 Morborne (parish) TL 139915
Apt 21.01.1839; 1174a (all); Map 1839?, [9 chns], (tinted); foot/b'way, woods, glebe (col).

16/42 Offord Darcey (parish) TL 227656 [Offord D'Arcy]
Apt 14.12.1841; 312a (1827); Map 1841, 9 chns, (tithable parts only).

16/43 Little Paxton (parish) TL 181632
Apt 07.03.1850; 85a (2040); Map 1850?, 3 chns; pictorial church.

16/44 Pidley cum Fenton (parish) TL 332786
Apt 13.07.1839; 3740a (3739); Map 1839, [3 chns], 1st cl, surveyed for R.J. Wright, Norwich by William Browne; construction lines, waterbodies, houses, woods, building names, road names, bank, drain mill, drainage ditches.

16/45 Ramsey (parish) TL 280870
Apt 28.04.1838; 9045a (16196); Map 1839, 4 chns, in 3 parts, by C.M. Bidwell, Ely, Cambs, and J. Bailey Denton, 9 Grays Inn Square, London, (tithable parts only); construction lines, houses, woods, osiers, open fields, building names, landowners, drainage ditches, drainage pumps (by symbol), embankment, mill; fen and bridge named. Agreement notes that 'fen' land is arable in some years and grass in others.

16/46 Little Raveley (parish) TL 257757
Apt 21.06.1848; 723a (760); Map 1852?, 6 chns; woods (col), private roads (uncoloured).

16/47 Somersham (parish) TL 363787
Apt 30.04.1838; 2868a (4121); Map 1839, 6 chns, in 2 parts, by Joseph Jackson, March, (tithable parts only in detail; including 2-chn enlargement of village); turnpike roads, toll bar, milestones, houses (village only), woods, orchards, field boundary ownerships, road names, windmills (pictorial), modus land (pink), 'highland' (green), 'lowland' (brown); pictorial church; some watercourses named; scale bars are ruler-like. Apt has cropping information.

16/48 Steeple Gidding (parish) TL 140812
Apt 27.03.1841; 1091a (all); Map 1840?, 6 chns, in 2 parts; waterbodies, woods, landowners; owner named in title; pictorial church.

16/49 Stow (parish) TL 112711 [Stow Longa]
Apt 30.11.1839; 815a (1480); Map 1841?, 6 chns; waterbodies.

16/50 Tetworth (hamlet in parish of Everton cum Tetworth) (partly in Beds and/or Cambs) TL 220540
Apt 19.09.1839; 1447a (all); Map 1839, 3 chns; waterbodies, houses, farmyards (col), woods (col), plantations (col), arable (col), grassland (col), gardens (col), hedge ownership, decoy; only the part of the district in the main part of Hunts is mapped.

16/51 Upwood (parish) TL 261832
Apt 19.12.1837; 1809a (1809); Map 1842, 4 chns; foot/b'way, waterbodies, houses, woods, open fields (named), common; schedule to agreement includes agreement to abide by the survey by William Elstobb of 1775.

16/52 Warboys (parish) TL 315815
Apt 26.10.1838; 1536a (8100); Map 1840?, [12 chns], (tithable parts only); windmill (pictorial), boundary stone; pictorial church.

16/53 Waresley (parish) TL 239548
Apt 23.10.1841; 1980a (all); Map 1842, 6 chns, ? by Charles Oakden, Waresley, Hunts; waterbodies, woods (named), field boundary ownerships, meerway, glebe, garden, rickyard, 'pleasure ground', kitchen gardens.

16/54 Washingley (parish) TL 130890 [Not listed]
Apt 21.06.1848; 42a (1260); Map 1850?, 3 chns, in 2 parts, by Thomas Miles, Leicester (tithable part only; including 9 chns location diagram); woods, landowners.

16/55 Water Newton (parish) TL 105960
Apt 29.11.1837; 864a (863); Map 1843?, 5 chns; waterbodies.

16/56 Weald (hamlet in parish of Eynesbury) TL 232599
Apt 22.03.1839; 611a (all); Map 1837, 3 chns, by Charles Oakden; waterbodies, woods, osiers, building names, landowners, private road.

16/57 Old Weston (parish) TL 097776
Apt 12.11.1840; 2012a (?) Map 1841, 6 chns; there is some evidence of field boundaries scraped out.

16/58 Wistow (parish) TL 278815
Corn rent conversion, 1862; 4647a (2070); Map (traced from enclosure award) 1862?, 6 chns; foot/b'way, turnpike roads, woods (named), field boundary ownerships, road names, former open field names, landowners, private roads (col); pictorial church. Apt omits land use.

16/59 Woodstone (parish) TL 185965 [Woodston]
Corn rent conversion, 1881; 1028a (1050); Map 1881?, 6 chns, ? by Tithe Commission; railways, foot/b'way.

16/60 Woodwalton (parish) TL 220826 [Wood Walton]
Apt 22.10.1839; 3719a (all); Map compiled from owners' maps, 1840, 6 chns, by Thos Hatchard, Godmanchester, Hunts; woods, plantations, windmill (pictorial), glebe.

16/61 Woolley (parish) TL 152742
Apt 19.10.1851; 12a (1420); Map (drawn on Apt) 1851?, 16 chns, (tithable part only).

16/62 Yaxley (parish) TL 190920
Apt 31.12.1849; 1255a (4290); Map 1851?, 9 chns, (tithable parts only, tinted); railway, woods, drove names, steam engine; mere and some water courses named.

Kent

PRO IR29 and IR30 17/1-407

417 tithe districts: 999,210 acres
407 tithe commutations: 975,829 acres
206 voluntary tithe agreements, 201 compulsory tithe awards

Tithe and tithe commutation

Kent ranks second to Cornwall in the proportion of tithable land in 1836; about 99 per cent of Kent tithe districts by number and 97 per cent of the county by area were subject to payment of tithes at this time (Fig. 29). Some 162 districts were wholly tithable; elsewhere the main causes of partial exemption were modus payments in lieu of tithes, the merger of tithes in the land (usually where the landowner and the tithe owner were one and the same), exemption by prescription, and exemption of some woodland. As in Surrey and Sussex, all woodland in the Weald was tithe free.

Assistant tithe commissioners and local tithe agents who worked in Kent are listed in Table 17.1 and the valuers of the county's tithe rent-charge in Table 17.2. An unusual characteristic of Kent tithe apportionments is that in some schedules field acreages are divided into 'in-bounds' and 'out-bounds', that is the acreage under cultivation and the acreage including that occupied by hedges, ditches and other 'waste'.

Tithe maps

No fewer than 55 per cent of Kent tithe maps are sealed as first class, a proportion only exceeded in Monmouthshire. Of second-class maps, 14 per cent carry construction lines and some of these may well be 'failed' first-class maps. Scales employed on Kent tithe maps vary from one inch to one chain to one inch to eighteen chains; 82 per cent are in the recommended scale range of one inch to three to four chains (Table 17.3).

Kent tithe maps are generally uninformative about agricultural land use: about 5 per cent show arable and grass, 12 per cent depict gardens, and 51 per cent map woodland. Symbols representing hop grounds appear on 21 per cent of maps, a proportion greater than in any other county but still an understatement of the true extent of hop cultivation which is recorded in 62 per cent of tithe apportionments.

Some 363 Kent tithe maps in the Public Record Office collection can be attributed to a particular map-maker (Table 17.2); the most prolific of these was Thomas Thurston of Ashford, who produced sixty maps, thirty-six of them first class and the remainder mostly

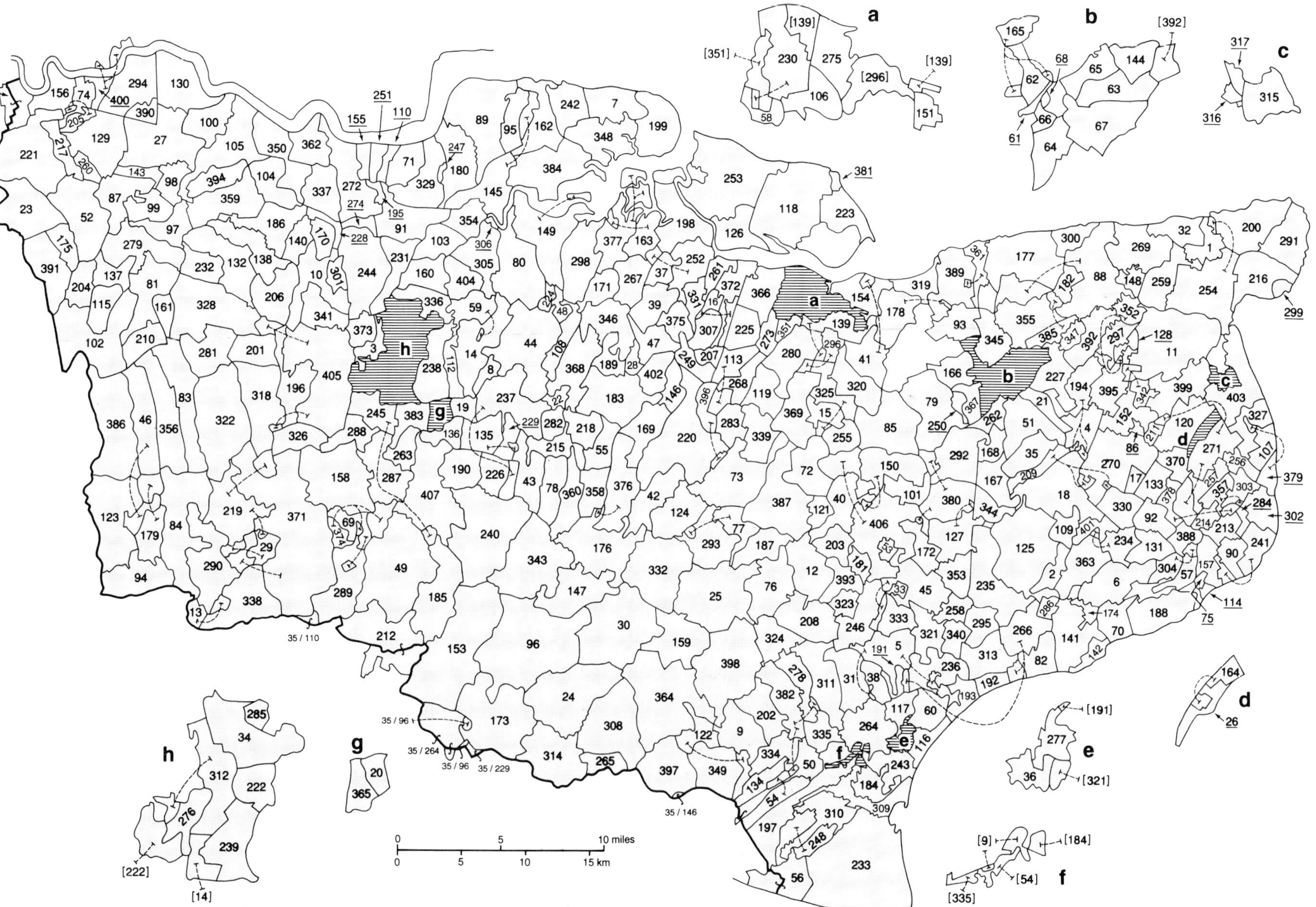

Fig. 29 Kent: tithe district boundaries.

six-chain scale reworkings of earlier surveys of Romney Marsh. Thurston's maps are distinguished by neat linework and a very consistent style, content and finish; his lettering is a modern-looking sans-serif and his woods are shown in green wash. Alexander Doull of Chatham produced thirty-one maps, twenty-seven of them first class. Doull was employed earlier on the Ordnance Survey of Ireland and most of his maps show an Ordnance Survey stylistic influence, though he introduced a number of personal features, such as a distinctive method of 'bracing' parcels by asterisks and bars. Thomas White Collard of Canterbury produced twenty-seven maps, twenty of them first class. Some of Collard's maps show parish churches by small neat drawings rather than in the more usual plan form. Frederick and Henry E. Drayson of Faversham produced twenty-six maps, twenty-four of them first class. The Drayson maps are mostly 'plain working plans' without land use information, though their map of Faversham is embellished by a neat drawing of a smock mill. The maps of the other ninety-one known map-makers are variable in quality; some of those of East Kent parishes and especially of districts around Dover are rather sketchy in appearance. Most surveyors tended to work locally and produced a small quantity of maps, but the proximity of London encouraged a considerable number of metropolitan surveyors to tender for work in this county.

Only two Kent maps in the Public Record Office collection have decorated cartouches and seven others have lithographed cartouches and scale bars, a feature rarely encountered on tithe maps outside this county. Unusual maps include Tonge which shows haystacks pictorially and is also endorsed with the signature of all three Tithe Commissioners. The colourful map of Stourmouth is dated 1820 and was originally sectioned as for a library.

Table 17.1. *Agreements and awards for commutation of tithes in Kent*

Assistant commissioner/ local tithe agent	*Number of agreements**	*Number of awards*
Thomas Smith Woolley	144	46
Thomas P. Hilder	0	39
Horace William Meteyard	0	28
Roger Kynaston	0	27
Thomas James Tatham	19	0
Joseph Townsend	15	1
John Mee Mathew	0	16
Henry Gilbert	0	13
John Maurice Herbert	11	0
F. Browne Browne	0	10
Francis Offley Martin	9	0
Charles Wilson	0	5
A. O. Baker	0	4
John Pickering	0	4
John Farncome	0	2
William W. Attree	1	0
Tithe Commissioners	1	0
Thomas Neve	0	1
John J. Rawlinson	1	0

*Computed from the number of extant reports on tithe agreements in the tithe files [PRO IR 18].

Table 17.2. *Tithe valuers and tithe map-makers in Kent*

Name and address (all in Kent)	*Number of districts*	*Acreage*
Tithe valuers		
Thomas Coleman, Ash	32	72,028
William Murton, Tunstall	24	47,233
Robert Lake, Milton near Canterbury	22	48,330
John Stevens, Pluckley	18	74,173
John Coleman, Kearsney, Dover	18	23,155
James Stevens, Willesborough	15	39,465
Frederick Neame, Selling	15	31,783
John Vinson, Borden	15	27,075
William Hubble, Northfleet	13	40,397
Henry Morris, Maidstone	13	24,550
James Russell, Horton Kirby	12	32,000
John Staples, Sutton at Hone	11	28,397
Walter Murton, Ashford	11	22,319
John Selby, Birling	10	20,811
Others [71]	178	443,813
Attributed tithe map-makers		
Thomas Thurston, Ashford	60	159,713
Alexander Doull, Chatham	31	68,705
Thomas White Collard, Canterbury	27	59,253
Frederick and Henry E. Drayson, Faversham	26	54,136
Thomas Cooper, Canterbury	16	18,430
John Adams, Hawkhurst	14	25,697
J. M. Davey, Canterbury	11	25,031
Small and Son, Buckland, Dover	10	16,735
William Huntly, Dover	9	13,805
Others [70]	159	412,497

Table 17.3. *The tithe maps of Kent: scales and classes*

Scale in chains/inch	*All maps*		*First Class*		*Second Class*	
	Number	*Acreage*	*Number*	*Acreage*	*Number*	*Acreage*
>3	11	10,257	3	2,163	8	8,094
3	309	709,503	221	532,539	88	176,964
3.5	2	9,185	0	0	2	9,185
4	22	66,467	1	3,280	21	63,187
6	56	167,989	0	0	56	167,989
<6	7	12,428	0	0	7	12,428
TOTAL	407	975,829	225	537,982	182	437,847

Table 17.4. *The tithe maps of Kent: dates*

	<1837	*1837*	*1838*	*1839*	*1840*	*1841*	*1842*	*1843*	*1844*	*1845*	*1846*	*1847*	*1848*	*>1848*
All maps	3	10	59	88	78	44	43	37	25	3	6	2	1	6
1st class*	0	3	37	60	44	24	24	13	11	2	4	1	1	0
2nd class*	3	7	22	28	34	20	19	24	14	1	2	1	0	6

*One first-class tithe map and one second-class tithe map of Kent in the Public Record Office collection are undated.

Kent

17/1 Acol (parish) TR 325677
Apt 30.10.1839; 1421a (all); Map 1832, 4 chns, by George Grist, Canterbury; foot/b'way, houses, building names, watch house, holdings (col).

17/2 Acrise (parish) TR 202429 [Not listed]
Apt 05.06.1839; 1033a (all); Map 1837-8, 3 chns, 1st cl, by John Adams, Hawkhurst; construction lines, waterbodies, houses, woods, building names, rectory.

17/3 Addington (parish) TQ 651590
Apt 05.12.1843; 935a (all); Map 1842, 3 chns, 1st cl, in 2 parts, by James Renshaw, 8 Union Court, Old Broad Street, London, (including 15-chn construction line diagram); construction lines, houses, woods, plantations, osiers, orchards (by annotation), hops (by annotation), gardens (by annotation), building names, road names, field names, milestone, oast houses, pound, village green, sheepfold, Druidical Temple, 'Druid Piles', dog kennel.

17/4 Adisham (parish) TR 225539
Apt 15.08.1840; 1815a (all); Map [3 chns], in 2 parts, 'By G. Hailey, 1826 - Enlarged and copied by J.M. Davey, Canterbury, 1839'; foot/b'way, waterbodies, houses, building names, road names, ancient fort, park.

17/5 Aldington (parish) TR 072364
Apt 20.01.1842; 3576a (3576); Map 1842, 3 chns, 1st cl, in 5 parts, by S.H. Perkins, Faversham, (includes index); construction lines, railway, foot/b'way, canal with towpath, houses, building names (in red), mill, sheep pound, waste.

17/6 Alkham (parish) TR 251422
Apt 18.08.1840; 3199a (3200); Map 1838, 3 chns, 1st cl, by Jno. Adams, Hawkhurst and Dover; construction lines, foot/b'way, waterbodies, houses, field gates, building names, green, churchyard; it is unclear why some fields are tinted pink.

17/7 Allhallows (parish) TQ 838777
Apt 19.02.1841; 2460a (all); Map 1839, 3 chns, 1st cl, in 2 parts, by S. Elliott; construction lines, foot/b'way, waterbodies, houses, field gates, building names, sea wall, ownership of creeks, gravel-pit.

17/8 Allington (parish) TQ 742573
Apt 30.06.1843; 612a (all); Map 1843, 3 chns, 1st cl, by R. Summerfield, Maidstone; construction lines, waterbodies, houses, locks, weir.

17/9 Appledore (parish) TQ 954303
Apt 11.09.1841; 3001a (3001); Map 1841, 3 chns, 1st cl, in 5 parts, by J.S. Thomson, Tenterden, (includes index); construction lines, foot/b'way, canal, waterbodies, houses, woods, fences, field boundary ownerships, field gates; north pointer and scale bar are combined on one part.

17/10 Ash (parish) TQ 603644
Apt 19.04.1839; 3020a (all); Map 1838, 3 chns, 'Enlarged and Corrected' from a survey made by T. Fulljames in 1792, 'In compliance with an order given by the landowners on the 2nd of May 1838' by William Hodsell; foot/b'way, waterbodies, houses, woods, plantations, arable (col), grassland (col), orchards, hops, gardens, heath/moor, hedge ownership, fence ownership, field names, pit, schools, private road, stackyards; shell, bowl and grapes surround the title; the border is multi-colour dicing.

17/11 Ash next Wingham (parish) TR 294605 [Ash]
Apt 22.07.1840; 7028a (6871); Map 1843, 3 chns, 1st cl, 'Copied' by Fred. R. Davey, Canterbury; foot/b'way, waterbodies, houses, building names, mills, parsonage, churchyard, ferry, castle ruins, tithery boundary; yellow-filled double field boundaries may be sewers.

17/12 Ashford (parish) TR 004429
Apt 08.08.1842; 2785a (2786); Map 1843, 6 chns, 'Copied and corrected' from a survey of 1818 by James Gouge of Sittingbourne, in 4 parts, by Thomas Thurston, Ashford, (includes three 3-chn enlargements of detail); railways and station, foot/b'way, waterbodies, houses, woods (col), field gates, building names, field names, parsonage, stiles, footbridges; built-up parts generalised.

17/13 Ashurst (parish) TQ 513387
Apt 20.10.1843; 891a (891); Map 1842, 3 chns, 1st cl, by E. Sheridan; construction lines, waterbodies, houses, 'Undefined boundary', boundary trees, shed, gate, oasthouse.

17/14 Aylesford (parish) TQ 731595
Apt 16.04.1841; 4391a (all); Map 1840, 3 chns, 1st cl, in 2 parts, by Thomas White Collard, Canterbury and Harry Finnet, Maidstone; construction lines, hill-drawing, waterbodies, woods (by name), building names, road names, quarries, river towpath, antiquity (pictorial).

17/15 Badlesmere and Leveland (parishes) TR 015545
Apt 29.06.1839; 1151a (all); Map 1840, 6 chns, in 2 parts, litho (Standidge); waterbodies, woods, orchards, hops, building names, pit.

17/16 Bapchild (parish) TQ 927629
Apt 26.04.1839; 1058a (all); Map 1838, 3 chns, 1st cl, by A. Doull, Chatham; construction lines, waterbodies, houses, building names, road names, boundary posts and trees, chalk pit, spring (named, in gothic).

17/17 Barfrestone (parish) TR 266499
Apt 07.02.1843; 500a (all); Map 1843, 3 chns, 1st cl, by Thomas W. Collard, St Georges Place, Canterbury; construction lines, waterbodies, houses, woods.

17/18 Barham (parish) TR 202492
Apt 26.09.1842; 4646a (4600); Map 1844, 3 chns, 1st cl, by Thomas Cooper, Canterbury; construction lines, hill-drawing, waterbodies, houses, woods (named), hops, building names, windmills (pictorial), park, chalk pit.

17/19 East Barming (parish) TQ 725546
Apt 11.02.1840; 749a (all); Map 1841, 4 chns; waterbodies, houses, hedges (col), field boundary ownerships, windmill (pictorial); pictorial church.

17/20 West Barming (extra-parochial place) TQ 708545 [Not listed]
Apt 24.02.1844; 331a (all); Map 1844, 3 chns, 1st cl, by Richard Summerfield, Maidstone; construction lines, waterbodies, houses.

17/21 Beaksbourne (parish) TR 195555 [Bekesbourne]
Apt 26.09.1840; 1114a (all); Map 1839, 3 chns, 1st cl, in 4 parts, by Thomas Cooper, Canterbury, (including location diagram); construction lines, foot/b'way, waterbodies, houses, woods, plantations, hops, building names, vicarage, parsonage, kennel, mill, glebe.

17/22 Bearsted (parish) TQ 798553
Apt 19.04.1842; 610a (all); Map 1842, 3 chns, 1st cl, by Henry Cobb, Lincolns Inn Fields; construction lines, hill-drawing, waterbodies, houses, building names, road names, wells, vicarage, school, turnpike gate, green, road earthworks, glebe (green band).

17/23 Beckenham (parish) TQ 377690
Apt 19.12.1838; 3875a (all); Map 1840?, 3 chns, 1st cl, by Frederick and Henry E. Drayson; construction lines, hill-drawing, railway, waterbodies, houses, field boundary ownerships, building names, park; 'Terminates' is shown at extremity of a stream or drain; a field is annotated 'Half of carways inch'; many area numbers are given twice, once in black and once in blue. (The map in PRO IR 30 is a copy; original is in PRO IR 77/27.)

17/24 Benenden (parish) TQ 810329
Apt 26.08.1839; 6508a (6508); Map 1840?, 4 chns, 'From a Survey by Josh. Hodskinson, 1777', by T.D.W. Beard, Architect and Surveyor, Cranbrook; waterbodies, woods, plantations, fences, field gates, park (in detail). Apt omits land use.

17/25 Bethersden (parish) TQ 926405
Apt 08.03.1839; 6345a (6345); Map 1839, 6 chns, by G. Durey, Great Chart; railway, foot/b'way, waterbodies, woods, orchards, vicarage; pictorial church. Apt has in-bound and out-bound quantities.

17/26 Betshanger (parish) TR 321531 [Betteshanger]
Apt 19.04.1844; 397a (all); Map 'Surveyed October 1838', 3 chns, 1st cl,

by William Huntley, 4 Lauriston Place, Dovor; foot/b'way, houses, boundary tree.

17/27 Bexley (parish) TQ 477742
Apt 17.07.1839; 5287a (all); Map surveyed in 1838-9, 3 chns, 1st cl, by G. Darbyshire and Sons, Brompton; construction lines, chainages, foot/b'way, waterbodies, houses, fences, field boundary ownerships, building names, market place, chapel, footbridges, pound, 'Undefined' boundary. (The map in PRO IR 30 is a copy; original is in PRO IR 77/28.)

17/28 Bicknor (parish) TQ 859584
Apt 09.06.1842; 631a (all); Map 1842?, 3 chns, by Henry Cobb, 18 Lincoln Inn, Fields, London; foot/b'way, houses, woods, orchards, hops, gardens, building names.

17/29 Bidborough (parish) TQ 568436
Apt 21.01.1839; 1300a (1299); Map 1839, 6 chns, by Messrs Crawter; foot/b'way, waterbodies, woods (named), pit, hops (by annotation).

17/30 Biddenden (parish) TQ 849382
Apt 19.12.1837; 7208a (7208); Map 1838, 3 chns, 1st cl, in 5 parts, by Thomas Thurston, Ashford, (including construction line diagram: part surveyed by G.T. Cloutt, part by Mr Thomson of Tenterden, part by Jno. Arnott, and part by Thurston in 1821, 'but examined and checked with the remainder of the plans'); construction lines, foot/b'way, turnpike roads, toll gates, waterbodies, houses, woods (col, named), hops, fences, field boundary ownerships, field gates, building names, mill, boundary trees, workhouse, windmill (by symbol), rectory; bridge named; a drain across a field is shown by double pecked lines; one construction line is annotated 'On Pluckley Church'; there are notes on paper contraction on each part, and that acreages have been compensated accordingly; pecked lines within field perimeters may be evidence of ploughing margins or of inbound-outbound. Apt has in-bound and out-bound quantities.

17/31 Bilsington (parish) TR 039347
Apt 12.11.1840; 2844a (2843); Map 1840, 3 chns, 1st cl, in 3 parts, by Thomas Thurston, Ashford, (including 30-chn construction line diagram); construction lines, foot/b'way, right of road, canal with towpath, waterbodies, houses, woods (col), hops, field boundary ownerships, field gates, building names, obelisk (named, pictorial), stiles, footbridges, drains; double-pecked lines indicate drains across fields.

17/32 Birchington (parish) TR 298691
Apt 18.01.1840; 1680a (all); Map 1840-1, 3 chns, by William Edmunds, Margate; foot/b'way, waterbodies, houses, woods, plantations, orchards, farm name, park.

17/33 Bircholt (parish) TR 075414 [Bircholt Forstal]
Apt 02.03.1843; 298a (all); Map 1839, 3 chns, 1st cl, by J.M. Davey, Canterbury; foot/b'way, waterbodies, houses, farmyards (by annotation), woods, arable (by annotation), grassland (by annotation), orchards (by annotation), hops, gardens (by annotation), hedges, building names; map has a note, 'This map has been compared with the Orgl. Map - Correct'.

17/34 Birling (parish) TQ 679610
Apt 26.12.1837; 1884a (1883); Map 1840, 3 chns, 1st cl, in 2 parts 'Surveyed under the Poor Law and Tithe Commutation Acts' by Thomas Thurston, Ashford, (including 30-chn construction line diagram); construction lines, hill-drawing, foot/b'way, waterbodies, houses, woods (col), hops, field boundary ownerships, field gates, building names, stiles, vicarage, right of road, sand pit, quarry, tithery boundary; double-pecked lines indicate drains across fields.

17/35 Bishopbourn (parish) TR 181519 [Bishopsbourne]
Apt 27.10.1840; 2002a (all); Map 1839, 3 chns, 1st cl, by Thomas Cooper, Canterbury; construction lines, foot/b'way, waterbodies, houses, woods (named), plantations, orchards, hops, fences, building names, field names, warren, allotments, grandstand, rectory, wilderness, glebe, pit; meaning of pink tint is unclear.

17/36 Blackmanstone (parish) TR 075293 [Not listed]
Apt 06.03.1844; 294a (293); Map 1843, 6 chns, from the Survey by Ts. Hogben, with alterations surveyed by Thomas Thurston, Ashford; waterbodies, drains.

17/37 Bobbing (parish) TQ 884652
Apt 13.05.1839; 1072a (1071); Map 1840?, 3 chns, 1st cl, by Alexander Doull; construction lines, foot/b'way, waterbodies, houses, building names, windmill, boundary stones.

17/38 Bonnington (parish) TR 059343
Apt 08.04.1842; 1109a (1109); Map 1839, 3 chns, 1st cl, in 2 parts, by Thomas Thurston, Ashford, (including 30-chn construction line diagram); construction lines, foot/b'way, canal with towpath, waterbodies, houses, woods (col), hops, field boundary ownerships, field gates, building names, road names, parsonage, boundary posts, trees and stones, 'Pinn Oaks', drains; drains across fields are shown by double pecked lines; primary construction lines sighted on objects outside the parish are annotated e.g 'On Eastbridge Tower'; pecked lines within field perimeters may be ploughing margins or evidence of inbound-outbound. Apt has in-bound and out-bound quantities.

17/39 Borden (parish) TQ 876624
Apt 26.08.1839; 2133a (2132); Map 1838, 3 chns, 1st cl, by Alexander Doull; construction lines, foot/b'way, waterbodies, houses, field gates, building names, road names, boundary stones and trees, windmills, chalk pits, pond, parsonage, graveyard, milestone; one construction line is noted as sighted on Bobbing church, in a district also mapped by Doull.

17/40 Boughton Aluph (parish) TR 029476
Apt 31.05.1839; 2419a (2418); Map 1839, 3 chns, 1st cl, in 2 parts, by Thomas Thurston, Ashford, (including 30-chn construction line diagram); construction lines, hill-drawing, foot/b'way, waterbodies, houses, woods (col), hops, field gates, building names, boundary trees, coach road, carriage road, old turnpike road, chalk pit, milestones (by symbol), rectory; primary construction line sightings are noted, e.g. 'On Boughton Church'. Apt has in-bound and out-bound quantities.

17/41 Boughton under Blean (parish) TR 050588 [Boughton Street]
Apt 31.07.1840; 2353a (all); Map 1840?, 3 chns, 1st cl, in 2 parts, by Frederick and Henry Drayson; construction lines, foot/b'way, waterbodies, houses, chalk pit.

17/42 Boughton Malherbe (parish) TQ 877481
Apt 07.03.1838; 2699a (2699); Map 1839, 3 chns, 1st cl, in 2 parts, by Thomas Thurston, Ashford, (including 30-chn construction line diagram); construction lines, foot/b'way, waterbodies, houses, woods (col, named), hops, fences, field boundary ownerships, field gates, building names, rectory, mills, boundary stones, drains; drains across fields are shown by double pecked lines; colour band surrounds one estate; pecked lines within field perimeters may be ploughing margins or evidence of inbound-outbound. Apt has in-bound and out-bound quantities.

17/43 Boughton Monchelsea (parish) TQ 777498
Apt 30.09.1842; 2295a (2296); Map 1843, 4 chns, by John Jackson Bird; waterbodies, woods.

17/44 Boxley (parish) TQ 774595
Apt 19.12.1849; 5783a (5745); Map 1844, 3 chns, 1st cl, by Thomas White Collard, Westgate, Canterbury, Kent; waterbodies, building names, boundary trees, posts, and stones, towpath, mills, woods (by name); pink band surrounds an estate; it is unclear what green tint means.

17/45 Brabourne (parish) TR 093420
Apt 20.05.1841; 3500a (3499); Map 1841, 3 chns, 1st cl, in 2 parts, by J.M. Davey, Canterbury; railway, foot/b'way, waterbodies, houses, building names, road names, woods (by name), vicarage, parsonage, pound, chapel, water mill, chalk pits.

17/46 Brasted (parish) TQ 472528
Apt 23.07.1844; 4383a (4456); Map 1845?, 6 chns, by D. Booth, Sundridge, Kent; railway, waterbodies, common mead; colour bands may show property ownerships.

17/47 Bredgar (parish) TQ 876598
Apt 05.12.1839; 1727a (all); Map 1838, 3 chns, 1st cl, by Alexander Doull; construction lines, waterbodies, houses, road names, boundary trees and stones, chalk pit.

17/48 Bredhurst (parish) TQ 798622
Apt 13.03.1839; 600a (all); Map 1839, 3 chns, 1st cl, by A. Doull, Chatham; construction lines, waterbodies, houses, chalk pit, boundary trees; some field boundaries may be later additions, as the linework is much rougher.

17/49 Brenchley (parish) TQ 674423
Apt 16.12.1842; 7794a (7780); Map 1843, 3 chns, 1st cl, in 4 parts, 'Surveyed for... the Poor Rate Assessment Act' by Thomas Thurston, Ashford, (including 30-chn construction line diagram); construction lines, railway with station and platform, foot/b'way, waterbodies, houses, woods (col), hops, field boundary ownerships, field gates, school, mill, 'right of road', green, tollgate; pecked lines within field perimeters may be ploughing margins or evidence of inbound-outbound; drains across fields are shown by double-pecked lines. Apt has in-bound and out-bound quantities.

17/50 Brenzett (parish) TR 001271
Apt 26.02.1844; 1822a (1802); Map 1843, 6 chns, with alterations surveyed by Thomas Thurston, Ashford, with the Walland Marsh portion surveyed by Netlam and Francis Giles in 1812-13, and the Romney Marsh portion surveyed by Thos Hogben; foot/b'way, waterbodies, houses, building names, road names, drainage walls, banks, footbridges, toll bridge, drains, windmill (by symbol); bridges named.

17/51 Bridge and Patrixbourn (parish) TR 179544
Apt 08.03.1839; 2798a (all); Map 1838, 3 chns, 1st cl, in 2 parts, by J.M. Davey, Canterbury; construction lines, foot/b'way, waterbodies, houses, farmyards (by annotation), woods, arable (by annotation), grassland (by annotation), orchards (by annotation), hops (by annotation), building names, lodges, kennel, lime works, chalk pit, turnpike, brick kiln, workhouse, grandstand, glebe, waste; each part has two cartouches, lithographed, pasted on, one with the map title, the other with the acreages, and a gummed-on scale bar, in imitation of a foot ruler.

17/52 Bromley (parish) TQ 418688
Apt 21.01.1841; 4646a (4646); Map 1840, 3 chns, 'Revised and Enlarged' by Francis Fuller, Croydon, Surrey; waterbodies, houses, woods, building names, college, churchyard, park, woods (by name). (The map in PRO IR 30 is a copy; original is in PRO IR 77/29.)

17/53 Brooke (parish) TR 066444 [Brook]
Apt 26.12.1837; 582a (582); Map 1840, 3 chns, by William Williams, Ashford; construction lines, foot/b'way, waterbodies, woods (col), arable (col), grassland (col), hops (by annotation), gardens (col), fences, windmill; north pointer has rope-weave decoration; one construction line is annotated 'Line upon Kennington windmill'.

17/54 Brookland (parish) TQ 983255
Apt 26.02.1844; 1883a (1833); Map 1843, 6 chns, Romney Marsh part surveyed by Thomas Hogben, and Walland Marsh part surveyed in 1812-13 by Netlam and Francis Giles, 'with alterations...surveyed' by Thomas Thurston, Ashford; foot/b'way, waterbodies, houses, field boundary ownerships, building names, road names, drainage wall; drains across fields are shown by double-pecked lines.

17/55 Broomfield (parish) TQ 835517
Apt 30.06.1843; 1430a (1430); Map 1843, 6 chns, 'From No. 95 to 170 Surveyed by T. Thurston, Ashford; The Remainder revised from a Map made in 1825'; foot/b'way, waterbodies, houses, woods (col), field boundary ownerships, field gates, building names, park with pale.

17/56 Broomhill or Roomhill (parish) (partly in Sussex) TQ 990194 [Not listed]
Apt 26.12.1843; 3323a (3580); Map 1843, 6 chns, the Walland Marsh portion surveyed in 1812-13 by N. and F. Giles, and the remainder for tithe purposes by Thomas Thurston, Ashford; foot/b'way, waterbodies, houses, building names, blockade stations, kettle nets, sea walls, sluice, site of church, beached boat, single beach (col), high and low water marks at spring tides. Apt has in-bound and out-bound quantities.

17/57 Buckland (parish) TR 308426
Apt 03.08.1840; 978a (978); Map 1841, 3 chns, 1st cl, 'Working Plan' by Messrs Small and Son, Buckland, Dovor; construction lines, foot/b'way, waterbodies, houses, building names, boundary stones and tree, workhouse, hospital, mill, tithery boundaries.

17/58 Buckland next Faversham (parish) TQ 980618 [Not listed]
Apt 18.08.1843; 336a (all); Map 1838, 3 chns, by Frederick and Henry E. Drayson; construction lines, foot/b'way, houses, woods, orchards, gardens, quarry.

17/59 Burham (parish) TQ 730623
Apt 02.05.1842; 1737a (1737); Map 1842, 3 chns, 1st cl, in 2 parts, by R. Summerfield, Maidstone; construction lines, waterbodies, houses; pecked lines within field perimeters may be ploughing margins or evidence of inbound-outbound.

17/60 Burmarsh (parish) TR 102321
Apt 06.03.1844; 1796a (1796); Map 1843, 6 chns, from a survey by Thomas Hogben of 1760-65, with 'alterations' by Thomas Thurston, Ashford; waterbodies, houses, field boundary ownerships, building names, road names, drains.

17/61 Holy Cross Westgate, Canterbury (parish) TR 139575 [Not listed]
Apt 31.12.1851; 30a (103); Map 1852, 3 chns, by Collard and Ashendon, Canterbury, (tithable parts only in detail, tinted); railway with station, houses, road names; lands tithable to Eastbridge hospital are tinted green.

17/62 St Dunstan, Canterbury (parish) TR 138587 [Not listed]
Apt 31.12.1851; 151a (365); Map 1852, 3 chns, compiled from a survey by Thomas and Henry Cooper, by Collard and Ashendon, Surveyors, (tithable parts only in detail); railway with station, foot/b'way, waterbodies, houses, woods, building names; lands tithable to Eastbridge hospital are tinted green.

17/63 St Martin, Canterbury (parish) TR 174583 [Not listed]
Apt 26.08.1839; 628a (627); Map 1839?, 3 chns, 1st cl, by Thomas Cooper, Canterbury; construction lines, foot/b'way, turnpike roads, waterbodies, houses, woods, grassland (col), gardens (col), field gates, turnpike gate, windmill (pictorial), gravel pit, boundary stones; pictorial church, with gravestones; a small hand points the way to Deal; scale bar is ruler-like, but no values are written to the divisions.

17/64 St Mary Bredin, Canterbury (parish) TR 149562 [Not listed]
Apt 29.04.1852; 729a (707); Map 1839, 3 chns, 1st cl, by T. Cooper, Canterbury; construction lines, foot/b'way, water-bodies, houses, woods, orchards, hops, building names, limekiln, chalk pits (col), city wall, windmill (pictorial); charity lands, gardens, glebe and a nursery are shown by annotation.

17/65 St Mary Northgate, Canterbury (parish) TR 162589 [Not listed]
Apt 19.09.1851; 135a (all); Map 1851, 3 chns, by T. and H. Cooper, Canterbury, (tithable parts only); waterbodies, houses, road names, mill, right of way, kiln, barracks, hospital, gate.

17/66 St Mildred, Canterbury (parish) TR 142570 [Not listed]
Apt 31.12.1851; 54a (?); Map 1851, 3 chns, by Thomas Henry Cooper, (tithable parts only); houses; built-up parts generalised and tinted.

17/67 St Paul, Canterbury (parish) TR 168570 [Not listed]
Apt 31.12.1851; 828a (963); Map 1839, 3 chns, 1st cl, by T. Cooper, Canterbury; construction lines, foot/b'way, waterbodies, houses, woods, orchards, hops, hedges, fences, building names, road names, windmill (pictorial), gaol, vicarage, hospital, churchyard, chalk pit, limekilns, glebe, charity lands; meaning of green and yellow tints is uncertain.

17/68 St Peter, Canterbury (parish) TR 146579 [Not listed]
Apt 24.06.1852; 16a (59); Map 1852, 3 chns, by Collard and Ashenden, Canterbury, (tithable parts only in detail, tinted); houses, road names, tithe-free land (green).

17/69 Capel (parish) TQ 637457
Apt 30.06.1843; 1569a (1568); Map 1843, 6 chns, in 2 parts, by M. Brady, 55 Chester Road, Kennington Lane; railway, waterbodies, houses, woods (col), orchards (col), building names, quarry, waste (col); colour bands may show property ownerships.

17/70 Capel le Fern (parish) TR 251393 [Capel-le-Ferne]
Apt 31.10.1842; 1636a (1736); Map 1840, 3 chns, 1st cl, in 2 parts, 'Surveyed under the direction of the Board of Guardians of the Dover Union for the purposes of the Poor Law Assessment Act' by Thomas Thurston, Ashford, (including 30-chn construction line diagram);

construction lines, hill-drawing, railway with earthworks, foot/b'way, right of road, turnpike roads, waterbodies, houses, woods (col), rock outcrops, field boundary ownerships, field gates, building names, beached ship, cliffs, high and low water marks at spring tides, beach (col); black figures of uncertain meaning are placed alongside most field boundaries; drains across fields are shown by double pecked lines.

17/71 Chalk (parish) TQ 677729
Apt 24.02.1841; 1941a (2246); Map 1840, 4 chns, in 2 parts, by Messrs Crawter; canal with towpath, waterbodies, woods (col), building names, turnpike gate, canal; pictorial church.

17/72 Challock (parish) TR 000503
Apt 30.06.1841; 2837a (2837); Map 1840, 3 chns, 1st cl, in 2 parts, by Thomas Thurston, Ashford, (including 30-chn construction line diagram); construction lines, waterbodies, houses, woods (col), plantations (col), heath/moor (col), field boundary ownerships, field gates, building names, road names, limekiln, windmills (by symbol), park, quarries, pits; small black numbers of uncertain purpose appear on each side of most field boundaries. Apt has in-bound and out-bound quantities.

17/73 Charing (parish) TQ 940495
Apt 22.10.1839; 4551a (4551); Map 1840, 6 chns, in 2 parts, (includes 4-chn enlargement of detail), litho (Standidge); foot/b'way, waterbodies, woods, orchards, building names, heath, tithe-free land.

17/74 Charlton (parish) TQ 416778
Apt 13.06.1838; 1174a (all); Map 1839, 8 chns, in 2 parts, by G.H. Graham, Woolwich, (one part at 3 chns); waterbodies, boundary stones and drains, park, Dover Road.

17/75 Charlton next Dover (parish) TR 319424 [Not listed]
Apt 03.03.1843; 235a (381); Map 1842, 3 chns, in 3 parts, by William Huntley, 4 Lauriston Place, Dovor, (includes built-up parts separately at 2 chns); turnpike roads, houses.

17/76 Great Chart (parish) TQ 974415
Apt 15.06.1839; 3281a (3281); Map 1839, 3 chns, 1st cl, by G. Durey, Chart Magna; construction lines, foot/b'way, waterbodies, houses, hops (by annotation), woods (by name), hedge ownership, building names, rectory; pecked lines within field perimeters may be evidence of either ploughing margins or of inbound-outbound. Apt has in-bound and out-bound quantities.

17/77 Little Chart (parish) TQ 946459
Apt 28.11.1840; 1578a (1578); Map 1839, 3 chns, 1st cl, in 2 parts, by Thomas Thurston, Ashford, (including 30-chn construction line diagram); construction lines, railway, foot/b'way, waterbodies, houses, woods (col), field boundary ownerships, field gates, building names, right of road, mills, rectory, boundary trees, tithe-free land (col, with stamped annotation), park, stiles.

17/78 Chart Sutton (parish) TQ 795486
Apt 19.10.1842; 2175a (2073); Map 1843, 6 chns, by R. Summerfield, Maidstone; foot/b'way, waterbodies, houses. Apt has in-bound and out-bound quantities.

17/79 Chartham (parish) TR 106553
Apt 21.09.1842; 4530a (4530); Map 1839, 3 chns, 1st cl, by Thos W. Collard, 1 Bridge Street, Canterbury; construction lines, waterbodies, woods (col), orchards, gardens, building names, field boundary stones, parish boundary trees; meaning of green banding is unclear.

17/80 Chatham (parish) TQ 767649
Apt 31.12.1841; 4135a (4273); Map 1842, 3 chns, 1st cl, in 2 parts, by R.B. George, Rochester, (includes town separately at 1.5 chns); houses, woods (col), plantations (col), arable (col), grassland (col), heath/moor, building names, road names, chapel, windmill, boundary marks and trees, school, burial ground, wharf, barracks, hospital, dockyard.

17/81 Chelsfield (parish) TQ 471636
Apt 31.12.1838; 3280a (all); Map 1840?, 4 chns, 1st cl; construction lines, foot/b'way, waterbodies, woods, building names, turnpike.

17/82 Cheriton (parish) TR 191362
Apt 05.03.1840; 1786a (1861); Map '1828' (?1841), 3 chns, 1st cl, in 2 parts, by John Adams, Hawkhurst, (includes Sandgate town at 1.5 chns); railway, foot/b'way, canal, waterbodies, woods (col), building names, camp ground, cavalry barracks, grand redoubt, churchyard, kiln, hospital, extraordinary high water mark, low water neap tides; colour bands may show property ownerships.

17/83 Chevening (parish) TQ 504543
Apt 08.01.1840; 2900a (3773); Map 1839, 8 chns, by Dixon and Maitland, 21 John St, Bedford Row; woods, heath/moor, Old Pilgrim Road.

17/84 Chiddingstone (parish) TQ 496455
Apt 27.05.1838; 5979a (5979); Map 3 chns, in 3 parts: part 1 by D.A. Nicholson, 1839; part 2 by Charles Doubell, 1840; construction lines, hill-drawing, railway, waterbodies, houses, landowners, pit; pecked lines within field perimeters may be evidence of ploughing margins or of inbound-outbound.

17/85 Chilham (parish) TR 067538
Apt 04.08.1840; 4332a (all); Map 1839, 3 chns, 1st cl, by Thos W. Collard, Canterbury; construction lines, foot/b'way, waterbodies, houses (by 'plus' sign), woods (col), plantations, orchards, parkland (in detail), gardens (in detail), hops (by annotation), fences, field gates, building names, castle, sundial; meaning of red band is unclear.

17/86 Chillenden (parish) TR 269538
Apt 14.02.1843; 196a (all); Map 1837, 3 chns, by Thomas W. Collard, Canterbury and J.M. Davey; railway, waterbodies, houses, landowners, windmill (by symbol); meaning of green bands is unclear.

17/87 Chiselhurst (parish) TQ 444706 [Chislehurst]
Apt 15.12.1843; 2739a (2738); Map 1844, 3 chns, 1st cl, in 2 parts, by Thomas Thurston, Ashford, (including 30-chn construction line diagram); foot/b'way, waterbodies, houses, woods (col), greens, commons, field boundary ownerships, field gates, stiles, building names, rectory, windmill, cricket ground; figures of uncertain meaning are written alongside field boundaries.

17/88 Chislet (parish) TR 236653
Apt 29.11.1841; 6675a (6835); Map 1838, 3 chns, in 2 parts, by Thomas W. Collard, Prospect House, Herne, Surveyor and Estate Agent; foot/b'way, waterbodies, woods (col), orchards, hops, gardens, hedges, field gates, building names, droveway, drains.

17/89 Cliffe (parish) TQ 736766
Apt 19.12.1840; 5661a (7830); Map 1839, 3 chns, 1st cl, in 2 parts, by Alexander Doull, Chatham; construction lines, waterbodies, houses, field gates, house name, coastguard station.

17/90 West Cliffe (parish) TR 344444
Apt 21.03.1840; 1169a (1194); Map 1840, 3 chns, by E.P. Coleman, Dover; waterbodies, houses, woods, hedges, field gates, field acreages, high and low water marks, cliff edge; it is unclear why some field boundaries are in red.

17/91 Cobham (parish) TQ 674685
Apt 05.06.1845; 3016a (all); Map 1838, 3 chns, 1st cl, by James Renshaw, 8 Union Court, Old Broad St, London; construction lines, foot/b'way, waterbodies, woods, plantations, parkland (in detail), orchard (by annotation), garden (by annotation), building names, road names, field names, boundary stones (by symbol), parsonage, college, mausoleum, avenue.

17/92 Coldred (parish) TR 277472
Apt 30.06.1843; 1533a (1532); Map 1844, 3 chns, 1st cl, by John Cheesman, Charlton, near Dover; construction lines, foot/b'way, houses, woods.

17/93 Saints Cosmus and Damian in the Blean (parish) TR 124615 [Blean]
Apt 18.06.1839; 1789a (2260); Map 1840, 6 chns, litho (Standidge); railway with engine house and locomotive shed, foot/b'way, waterbodies, houses (by shading), woods, orchards, hops, building names, landowners, 'Coal Duty Toll Gate'.

17/94 Cowden (parish) TQ 465415
Apt 26.04.1842; 3232a (3232); Map 1841, 3 chns, by William Saxby, Edenbridge, Kent; waterbodies, houses; pecked lines within field

perimeters may be ploughing margins, or evidence of inbound-outbound; mapmaker's name is on scroll.

17/95 Cowling or Cooling (parish) TQ 759763
Apt 02.06.1841; 1544a (all); Map 1839, 3 chns, 1st cl, by Samuel Elliott; construction lines, foot/b'way, waterbodies, houses, woods, boundary trees (by symbol) and stones, drainage ditches with ownerships.

17/96 Cranbrook (parish) TQ 777367
Apt 31.10.1839; 9862a (9862); Map 1840, 6 chns, in 2 parts: part 1, whole district, surveyed by T. Brown of Maidstone in 1811-12, and corrected in 1840; part 2, 2 chns, of Cranbrook town, surveyed by T.D.W. Dearn in 1840; colour on part 2 may indicate ownerships. Apt omits land use.

17/97 St Mary Cray (parish) TQ 492676
Apt 30.06.1843; 2017a (2010); Map surveyed in 1841, 3 chns, 1st cl, by W. Roberts, 68 Chancery Lane; construction lines, hill-drawing, foot/b'way, waterbodies, houses, building names, paper mill, boundary trees, quarry.

17/98 North Cray (parish) TQ 490718
Apt 11.07.1837; 1443a (all); Map 1837, 3 chns; waterbodies, woods (named), building names, mill, lodge, pits, boundary trees, shed, weirs, rectory, tithe barn, steps to houses.

17/99 St Pauls Cray (parish) TQ 472692 [St Paul's Cray]
Apt 03.05.1839; 1651a (all); Map 1840, 3 chns, 1st cl, by C.H. Tripp; construction lines, hill-drawing, foot/b'way, houses, woods, plantations, hedge ownership, fence ownership, field gates, ornamental gardens, rectory, boundary post and trees, disputed boundary, mill, mill race, weirs; meaning of green banding is uncertain.

17/100 Crayford (parish) TQ 520759
Apt 12.11.1839; 2384a (all); Map 1841, 3 chns, 1st cl, by F. and H.E. Drayson; construction lines, waterbodies, building names; a note says that half the drains are included in each field through which they run.

17/101 Crundale (parish) TR 083488
Apt 08.03.1839; 1587a (all); Map 1839, 3 chns, 1st cl, in 3 parts, by Thomas Thurston, Ashford, (including construction line diagram); construction lines, foot/b'way, waterbodies, houses, woods (col), field boundary ownerships, field gates, building names, rectory, tithery boundary (yellow); numerals appear alongside some field boundaries, of uncertain purpose (ploughing margins?); pecked lines within field perimeters may be evidence of ploughing margins or of inbound-outbound. Apt has in-bound and out-bound quantities.

17/102 Cudham (parish) TQ 430588
Apt 25.07.1843; 5869a (all); Map 1844?, 3 chns; construction lines, houses, woods (by name); pecked lines within field boundaries may be evidence of ploughing margins or of inbound-outbound.

17/103 Cuxton (parish) TQ 704672
Apt 12.05.1842; 1686a (1756); Map 1839, 3 chns, by James Renshaw, No. 8, Union Court, Old Broad Street, London; waterbodies, woods, building names, rectory, chalk pit, churchyard.

17/104 Darenth (parish) TQ 566714
Apt 26.09.1840; 2188a (all); Map surveyed 1833, 6 chns, by William Hubbard, Dartford; foot/b'way, woods (col, named), field boundary ownerships, field gates, building names, mills; colour bands may show farm ownership.

17/105 Dartford (parish) TQ 539739
Apt 21.07.1840; 4101a (all); Map 1838, 3 chns, in 2 parts, (including 'The Common Marshes', 'Surveyed by W. Hubbard, Dartford, June 1841'); hill-drawing, foot/b'way, waterbodies, houses, woods (named), orchards, field gates, building names, road names, field names, farm boundaries, mill, magazine, dusting house, charcoal works, powder mills, zinc works, pits, workhouse, limekilns, gas works, foundry, chapels, pound, barn, wharves, burial ground, parsonage, summer house, turnpike gate, milestone, gravel pit, common (col), osiers, waste, saltings, river wall.

17/106 Davington (parish) TR 004622
Apt 22.05.1844; 538a (537); Map 1845?, 3 chns, 1st cl; powder works, waterbodies, foot/b'way.

17/107 Deal (parish) TR 373525
Apt 07.02.1843; 1153a (1217); Map 1843, 2 chns, 1st cl, by W. Holtum, Walmer; construction lines, foot/b'way, waterbodies, houses, road names, castles, naval yard, high and low water marks, 'Stones Foot' (? limit of shingle), pier, gas works, chapel, water works; built-up parts generalised.

17/108 Debtling (parish) TQ 802596 [Detling]
Apt 22.11.1838; 1576a (all); Map 1839, 3 chns, by R. Summerfield, Maidstone; houses.

17/109 Denton (parish) TR 211462
Apt 30.01.1843; 1193a (all); Map 1842, 3 chns, 1st cl, by Thomas W. Collard, St George Place, Canterbury; construction lines, waterbodies, houses.

17/110 Denton (parish) TQ 659729
Apt 29.10.1845; 434a (all); Map 1846, 3 chns, 1st cl; construction lines, railway, canal with towpath, waterbodies, woods, building names, boundary stones, ruins of church, pit.

17/111 St Nicholas Deptford and St Paul Deptford (parishes) (partly in Surrey) TQ 364771 [Deptford]
Apt 04.11.1842; 1340a (all); Map 1844, 2.62 chns; railways, foot/b'way, canal, waterbodies, road names, Royal Dock Yard, boundary stones and posts, dock, victualling office, river stairs, pump, watch house, water works, reservoir, schools, chapel, workhouse, windmill, 'Comical House', parish and county boundaries.

17/112 Ditton (parish) TQ 713578
Apt 31.07.1841; 1075a (1075); Map 1840, 3 chns, 1st cl, by Murrell R. Robinson, Otford, near Sevenoaks; construction lines, waterbodies, houses, farmyards, woods, plantations, parkland (col), hops (col), park fences, building names, common (col), green (col).

17/113 Doddington (parish) TQ 942582
Apt 30.08.1839; 1918a (1918); Map 1838, 3 chns, 1st cl, by Frederick and Henry E. Drayson; construction lines, foot/b'way, waterbodies, houses, woods (col, named), orchards, hops, gardens, building names, windmill, pits; Dawson's conventions are used for land use; construction-line sightings are given.

17/114 St James the Apostle, Dover (parish) TR 324416 [Not listed]
Apt 31.12.1842; 56a (all); Map 1844, 2 chns, by William Huntly; houses; mapmaker's name is damaged. Apt omits most land use.

17/115 Down (parish) TQ 434617 [Downe]
Apt 27.05.1841; 1654a (all); Map 1840, 6 chns, by Newton and Woodrow, Norwich; waterbodies, houses, woods, plantations, carriage drives; pictorial church.

17/116 Dymchurch (parish) TR 102298
Apt 03.11.1843; 1534a (1534); Map 1842, 3 chns, 1st cl, by Thomas Thurston, Ashford; construction lines, foot/b'way, waterbodies, houses, field boundary ownerships, field gates, footbridges, stiles, martello towers, sea wall, high water springs and low water ordinary and spring tides, drains; there is a note that 'The sewers which are coloured Blue are not scaled into the Fields'; numerals of uncertain purpose appear alongside some field boundaries.

17/117 Eastbridge (parish) TR 078322 [Not listed]
Apt 23.03.1847; 1136a (1135); Map 1843, 6 chns, taken from Thomas Hogben's survey, with alterations surveyed by Thomas Thurston, Ashford; drains, foot/b'way, waterbodies, houses, building names.

17/118 Eastchurch (parish) TQ 985702
Apt 15.06.1842; 7511a (8621); Map 1842?, 3 chns, 1st cl, by Alexander Doull, Chatham; construction lines, foot/b'way, waterbodies, houses, field gates, boundary posts and trees, farm boundaries and names; there is a note that drains and roads are excluded from adjoining field acreages.

17/119 Eastling (parish) TQ 965564
Apt 30.07.1842; 1914a (all); Map 1842, 6 chns, in 2 parts, (includes enlargement of village at 3 chns), litho (Standidge); foot/b'way, waterbodies, houses (by shading), woods; marginal distances are given in furlongs and poles.

17/120 Eastry (parish) TR 305543
Apt 12.10.1839; 2715a (all); Map 1841, 3 chns, by Thomas W. Collard, St Georges Place, Canterbury; foot/b'way, waterbodies, houses, woods (col), orchards, gardens (col), building names, park.

17/121 Eastwell (parish) TR 011471 [Not listed]
Apt 08.11.1838; 894a (894); Map 1838, 3 chns, 1st cl, in 3 parts, by Thomas Thurston, Ashford, (including 30-chn construction line diagram); construction lines, foot/b'way, turnpike roads, waterbodies, houses, woods (named), orchards, hops, arable (by annotation), field gates, building names, rectory, boundary trees, chalk pits, well, in- and out-bound field acreages, park, paths and drives. Apt has in-bound and out-bound quantities.

17/122 Eboney (parish) TQ 919301 [Not listed]
Apt 24.02.1844; 2209a (2209); Map 1843, 3 chns, 1st cl, in 2 parts, by Thomas Thurston, Ashford, (including 30-chn construction line diagram); construction lines, foot/b'way, right of road, canal, waterbodies, houses, woods (col), hops, field boundary ownerships, field gates, building names, pit or quarry (col); drains across fields are shown by double pecked lines; bridge named; there is a note, 'The Marsh Sewers are coloured Blue, and are not scaled into the Fields - The Red dotted Line... shows the extent of the Marsh Lands'. Apt has in-bound and out-bound quantities.

17/123 Edenbridge (parish) TQ 443460
Apt 28.03.1844; 5293a (7020); Map 1844, 6 chns, by William Saxby, Edenbridge, Kent; railway with station, waterbodies, houses, woods, building names, field names, park.

17/124 Egerton (parish) TQ 897467
Apt 22.09.1843; 2779a (2780); Map 1841, 3 chns, 1st cl, in 2 parts, by Thomas Thurston, Ashford, (including 30-chn construction line diagram); construction lines, foot/b'way, waterbodies, houses, woods (col), hops, field gates, building names, tenter well; drains across fields are shown by double pecked lines; numerals of uncertain meaning appear on each side of some fences; pecked lines within field perimeters may be evidence of either ploughing margins or of inbound-outbound. Apt has in-bound and out-bound quantities.

17/125 Elham (parish) TR 178446
Apt 20.04.1844; 6492a (6570); Map 1844, 3 chns, 1st cl, by Thos W. Collard, Surveyor and Estate Agent, St George's Place, Canterbury; foot/b'way, waterbodies, woods (col), building names, parsonage; there is a note that reference numbers have been compared with the original map; pecked lines within field perimeters may be evidence of ploughing margins or of inbound-outbound.

17/126 Elmley (parish) TQ 942684 [Elmley Island]
Apt 29.08.1843; 1761a (all); Map 1844, 8 chns, by Frederick Drayson; sea wall, ferry, salts.

17/127 Elmsted (parish) TR 120456 [Not listed]
Apt 30.06.1841; 2692a (2692); Map 1840, 3 chns, 1st cl, in 2 parts, by George Durey, Great Chart, (including 30-chn construction line diagram); construction lines, foot/b'way, waterbodies, houses, field boundary ownerships, building names, field names, boundary trees (by symbol), greens (col), commons (col), woods (by name), park.

17/128 Elmstone (parish) TR 258602
Apt 29.01.1842; 432a (all); Map 1842, 3 chns, by George Quested, Ash; waterbodies, fences.

17/129 Eltham (parish) TQ 431743
Apt 26.04.1844; 3713a (all); Map 1839, 4 chns, by E. and G.N. Driver; foot/b'way, waterbodies, houses, woods (named), building names, road names, gravel pit, lodges, milestones, pond, conduit, reservoir, common, park.

17/130 Erith (parish) TQ 494787
Apt 12.07.1843; 3851a (4585); Map 1843, 3 chns, by H. Adams, 3 Church Court, Clements Lane, City; houses, building names, wells.

17/131 Ewell (parish) TR 282498 [Not listed]
Apt 08.08.1842; 1590a (1590); Map 1841, 3 chns; construction lines, foot/b'way, waterbodies, houses, field gates, stiles.

17/132 Eynesford (parish) TQ 542657 [Eynsford]
Apt 07.04.1842; 3503a (all); Map not dated, 4 chns; foot/b'way, waterbodies, houses, woods, hedges, fences, field gates, glebe, churchyard paths.

17/133 Eythorne (parish) TR 282498
Apt 07.04.1842; 1318a (all); Map 1840, 3 chns, by J.M. Davey, Canterbury; waterbodies, houses, building names, ice house, waste, 'Clerk's Acre', chalk pit; plain cartouches and a scale-bar styled like a ruler are lithographically printed and pasted on.

17/134 Fairfield (parish) TQ 970264
Apt 26.12.1843; 1204a (1203); Map 1842, 6 chns, surveyed by Netlam and Francis Giles in 1812-13, with alterations surveyed by Thomas Thurston, Ashford; foot/b'way, waterbodies, houses, building names, footbridges, drainage embankments, drains.

17/135 East Farleigh (parish) TQ 738527
Apt 27.05.1841; 2023a (2023); Map 1842, 3 chns, 1st cl, by John Adams, Hawkhurst; construction lines, waterbodies, houses, river lock, woods (by name). Apt has in-bound and out-bound quantities.

17/136 West Farleigh (parish) TQ 713526
Apt 18.08.1843; 1106a (1010); Map 1844, 3 chns, 1st cl, by Joseph Tootell, Maidstone; construction lines, waterbodies, houses, field boundary ownerships, boundary stones and tree; below the scale bar is a note: 'Contraction 10 links in 30 chains'.

17/137 Farnborough (parish) TQ 441641
Apt 15.05.1841; 1412a (1412); Map 1840, 7 chns, by S. Rhodes, 2 Bow Churchyard, London; railway, waterbodies, woods, plantations, orchards, hops, well, stiles, pond, pound, stiles, common.

17/138 Farningham (parish) TQ 557669
Apt 22.10.1840; 2709a (all); Map 1840, 3 chns, by D. Booth, Sundridge; waterbodies, houses, woods (col), field boundary ownerships, road cutting, pit; colour bands may show farm boundary ownership.

17/139 Faversham (parish) TR 028613
Apt 30.09.1839; 2269a (2469); Map 1842?, 3 chns, 1st cl, in 3 parts, by F. and H.E. Drayson; construction lines, waterbodies, houses, building names, workhouse, boundary stones, windmill (by symbol), school, market house, coal yard, crane, breweries, Wesleyan Chapel; in one corner is a large neat drawing of a smock mill with furled sails. (The map in PRO IR 30 is a copy; original is in PRO IR 77/30.)

17/140 Fawkham (parish) TQ 591671 [Fawkham Green]
Apt 22.11.1838; 1195a (all); Map '1831' (? 1839), 4 chns; waterbodies, houses, woods (named), orchards, gardens, building names, field names, field boundary ownerships, stiles, rectory; colour bands may show estate or farm ownerships.

17/141 Folkestone (parish) TR 216374
Apt 24.06.1841; 1109a (?); Map 1840, 6 chns, by H.S. Tiffen, Hythe, (tithable parts only in detail); hill-drawing, turnpike roads, waterbodies, woods (col), arable (col), grassland (col), orchards (col), gardens (col), hedge ownership, building names, cherry garden, mill, tile kiln, pit.

17/142 Folkstone (township and liberty) TR 233364
Apt 14.02.1843; 186a (?); Map 1843, 3 chns, by John Cheesman, Buckland, (tithable parts only); railways, foot/b'way, waterbodies, houses, plantations, stiles; scale-bar is ruler-like.

17/143 Foots Cray (parish) TQ 463724
Apt 03.07.1838; 799a (all); Map 1840, 3 chns, 1st cl, by R.P. Browne, Greenwich; construction lines, waterbodies, houses, woods (named), building names, paper mill, school, lodge, milestones (by symbol), garden paths.

17/144 Fordwich (parish) TR 181594
Apt 22.10.1841; 459a (all); Map 1839, 3 chns, by Thomas Cooper, Canterbury; construction lines, foot/b'way, houses, woods, hops, hedges, field names, pits; meaning of green and pink tint is uncertain; map has note that it was 'Approved and Adopted' at a meeting of landowners on 20 August 1841.

17/145 Frindsbury (parish) TQ 748710
Apt 31.08.1841; 3595a (3765); Map 1839, 3 chns, 1st cl, in 2 parts, by Alexander Doull, Chatham; construction lines, foot/b'way, waterbodies, houses, woods (named), building names, road names, magazine, castle (named, in gothic), marsh.

17/146 Frinstead (parish) TQ 893564 [Frinsted]
Apt 09.05.1840; 1273a (1273); Map 1839?, 3 chns, 1st cl, by Frederick and Henry E. Drayson; construction lines, houses.

17/147 Frittenden (parish) TQ 817409
Apt 08.08.1837; 3319a (3318); Map 4 chns, surveyed in 1806 by J. Grist, and corrected to June 1839; waterbodies, woods (named), limekiln, clay pit, marl pit, glebe, charity land; pictorial church; north pointer has tassle decoration.

17/148 St Gyles or Sarr (parish) TR 262652 [Sarre]
Apt 29.07.1841; 653a (653); Map 1842?, 6 chns; fences, chalk pit; colours may show property ownerships.

17/149 Gillingham (parish) TQ 790675
Apt 24.11.1840; 4273a (6683); Map 3 chns, 1st cl, in 2 parts: part 1 by George Darbyshire and George C. Darbyshire, Brompton, 1838; part 2 by John and George C. Darbyshire, Brompton, 1839; construction lines, foot/b'way, waterbodies, houses, marsh/bog (col), building names, road names, tower, fort, barracks, chapel, stile, ramparts, washouse yard; meaning of purple band is unclear. (The map in PRO IR 30 is a copy; original is in PRO IR 77/31.)

17/150 Godmersham (parish) TR 068507
Apt 30.11.1839; 3077a (3077); Map 1839, 6 chns, surveyed by James Gouge of Sittingbourne in 1815, with 'Alterations' by Thomas Thurston, Ashford; waterbodies, houses, woods (col), hops, building names, tower, vicarage, temple, park.

17/151 Goodnestone next Faversham (parish) TR 043615 [Goodnestone]
Apt 26.12.1837; 334a (all); Map 1837, 3 chns, 1st cl, by George Quested, Ash next Wingham, Kent; construction lines, tidal land, field acreages; table lists land use; there is a note about the main construction line in relation to certain trees.

17/152 Goodnestone next Wingham (parish) TR 262548 [Goodnestone]
Apt 25.02.1843; 461a (1864); Map 1844, 3 chns, by George Quested, Ash, (tithable parts only); foot/b'way; legend explains symbols for unfenced parish and property boundaries.

17/153 Goudhurst (parish) TQ 720363
Apt 17.01.1842; 9685a (9685); Map 1840, 3 chns, in 2 parts, by J. and P. Payte, J. Gill and W. Gibson; construction lines, foot/b'way, waterbodies, houses, woods (col), building names, mills, village pond, vicarage; meaning of yellow band is unclear; pecked lines within field perimeters may be ploughing margins or evidence of inbound-outbound. Apt has in-bound and out-bound quantities.

17/154 Graveney (parish) TR 044636
Apt 18.01.1842; 2002a (3722); Map 1842, 6 chns, in 4 parts, litho (Standidge); waterbodies, houses (by shading), sand hole, ponds.

17/155 Gravesend (parish) TQ 643733
Apt 01.12.1840; 569a (683); Map 1841, 2 chns, by Richard B. George; construction lines, waterbodies, houses, field gates, road names, cemetery paths, urban sidewalks, chalk cliff.

17/156 Greenwich (parish) TQ 397780
Apt 20.05.1843; 1549a (2013); Map 1844, 4 chns, by Messrs Crawter, Southampton Buildings, Chancery Lane and Cobham, Surrey, (tithable parts only in detail); railway, waterbodies, woods, road names, gravel pits, observatory, burial ground, Naval Asylum, college, workhouse, boundary stones and trees, ranger's house; meaning of green band is unclear. (The map in PRO IR 30 is a copy; original is in PRO IR 77/98, and is unfit for production.)

17/157 Guston (parish) TR 326439
Apt 09.04.1842; 1401a (1421); Map 1840, 3 chns, 1st cl, by William Huntley, Dover; construction lines, foot/b'way, houses, building names, pottery, pits, beach, low water mark, boundary trees; plain cartouches with title and summary acreages and ruler-style scale bar are pre-printed and pasted on.

17/158 Hadlow (parish) TQ 625492
Apt 04.08.1841; 5856a (5856); Map 1842, 6 chns, in 2 parts, by W. Brown, Tonbridge, (includes village separately at 1 chn); waterbodies, houses, building names, cricket ground, boundary trees and stones, mill, chapels; green tint indicates lands belonging to adjoining districts.

17/159 Halden (parish) TQ 899374 [High Halden]
Apt 13.07.1837; 3753a (3753); Map 1837, 3 chns, 1st cl, in 2 parts, by Thomas Thurston, Ashford, (including construction line diagram); construction lines, foot/b'way, right of road, turnpike roads and gate, waterbodies, houses, woods (col), field boundary ownerships, field gates, building names, pot kilns, rectory, crock kilns, chapel, windmill (by symbol), stiles, drains; drains across fields are shown by double-pecked lines; numerals of uncertain purpose appear beside some field boundaries; pecked lines within field perimeters may be ploughing margins or evidence of inbound-outbound. Apt has in-bound and out-bound quantities.

17/160 Halling (parish) TQ 694646
Apt 05.06.1840; 1847a (all); Map 1843?, 3 chns, 1st cl, by Alexander Doull; construction lines, waterbodies, houses, field gates.

17/161 Halstead (parish) TQ 486615
Apt 22.02.1840; 919a (all); Map 1840?, 3 chns; foot/b'way, waterbodies, houses, woods (col), plantations (col).

17/162 High Halstow (parish) TQ 783761
Apt 06.04.1842; 3190a (4244); Map 1839, 3 chns, 1st cl, by S. Elliott; construction lines, hill-drawing, waterbodies, houses, boundary posts, embankments, ditch ownerships.

17/163 Lower Halstow (parish) TQ 868677
Apt 18.01.1842; 1612a (1891); Map 1838, 3 chns, in 2 parts, by Alexander Doull; construction lines, waterbodies, houses, building names, ponds, boundary stones.

17/164 Ham (parish) TR 329548
Apt 07.02.1843; 321a (all); Map 'Surveyed October 1838', 3 chns, by William Huntly, 4 Lauriston Place, Dovor; houses; map has note that tithe areas exclude bounding roads and ditches.

17/165 Harbledown, St Comus and Damian in the Blean, Hackington or St Stephens, Thannington, St Dunstan, Holy Cross, Westgate (district) TR 133601
Apt 06.09.1845; 427a (5884); 'Reduced Map' 1846, 18 chns, in 6 parts, by Thomas Cooper, Canterbury, (includes two parts at 6 chns and three parts at 5 chns); railway, engine house, houses, woods, hops, gardens, building names; map is titled 'Eastbridge Hospital, Canterbury'; it is unclear why some fields are coloured; scale bars have coloured dicing.

17/166 St Michael Harbledown (parish) TR 120582 [Harbledown]
Apt 15.06.1837; 1676a (1670); Map 1841, 3 chns, 1st cl, by J.M. Davey, Canterbury; construction lines, waterbodies, houses, woods (by name), arable (by annotation), grassland (by annotation), orchards (by annotation), hops (by annotation), osiers, hospital, quarry, vicarage, brick field, mill.

17/167 Great Hardres (parish) TR 154498
Apt 04.05.1839; 2038a (?); Map 1842, 3 chns, 1st cl, by J.M. Davey, Canterbury; waterbodies, woods (by name), houses, building names, road names, pits.

17/168 Lower Hardres (parish) TR 154524
Apt 28.03.1839; 1176a (all); Map 'Working Plan', 1840, 3 chns, 1st cl, by Small and Son, Buckland, Dover; construction lines, houses, building names, boundary stones and trees, way post, field acreages; PRO IR 30 also contains a 'Copy', without field acreages, and with the boundary less completely drawn.

17/169 Harrietsham (parish) TQ 869532
Apt 09.01.1840; 2464a (2464); Map 1839, 3 chns, 1st cl, by G. Durey, Great Chart, Kent; construction lines, waterbodies, houses, building names, stiles, rectory, heath, woods, estate boundary (yellow).

17/170 Hartley (parish) TQ 611672
Apt 20.05.1844; 1179a (all); Map 1839?, 3 chns, 1st cl, by Frederick and Henry E. Drayson; construction lines, waterbodies, houses, woods (col, named), building names, parsonage, field acreages.

17/171 Hartlip (parish) TQ 835639
Apt 11.06.1840; 1413a (all); Map 1840?, 3 chns, 1st cl, by Alexander Doull; construction lines, waterbodies, houses, building names, road names, boundary stones and trees, chalk pits, gravel pits.

17/172 Hastingleigh (parish) TR 096446
Apt 22.01.1841; 1498a (1498); Map 1839, 3 chns, by W. Williams, Ashford; construction lines, foot/b'way, waterbodies, houses, woods (col), arable (col), grassland (col), hops, gardens (col), farm names, stiles, chalk pit; north pointer has a rope-weave centre.

17/173 Hawkhurst (parish) (partly in Sussex) TQ 754309
Apt 20.11.1840; 6495a (6494); Map 1838, 3 chns, by Messrs Martyr and Wright, Greenwich; foot/b'way, waterbodies, woods, plantations, orchards, field boundary ownerships, building names, churchyard, gardens mound, wood gate, garden mound, mill stream ownership; relationship of parish boundaries to the centre or sides of streams is carefully noted. Apt has in-bound and out-bound quantities.

17/174 Hawkinge (parish) TR 230400
Apt 17.02.1843; 521a (all); Map 1842, 3 chns, 1st cl, 'From an actual Survey' by John Adams, Hawkhurst, Kent; construction lines, foot/b'way, waterbodies, houses, stiles; some pecked boundaries are annotated 'Laid off from Lord Radnor's Map' or 'Mr Kelcey's Old Map'.

17/175 Hayes (parish) TQ 404664
Apt 18.01.1839; 1272a (all); Map 1839?, 3 chns, 1st cl, by Murrell R. Robinson, Otford Castle, nr Sevenoaks; construction lines, foot/b'way, waterbodies, houses, woods, building names, parsonage, common (col), windmill (pictorial).

17/176 Headcorn (parish) TQ 834442
Apt 06.09.1841; 5011a (5011); Map 1843?, 3 chns, 1st cl, by Frederick and Henry E. Drayson, Faversham; construction lines, railway, waterbodies, houses, woods (col); several fields are annotated as to whether they include roads and ponds.

17/177 Herne (parish) TR 172664
Apt 24.02.1840; 4829a (5399); Map 1839, 4 chns, by Thomas W. Collard, Canterbury; foot/b'way, woods, orchards, hops, building names, road names, field names, workhouse, common. (The map in PRO IR 30 is a copy; original is in PRO IR 77/33.)

17/178 Hernhill (parish) TR 072620
Apt 28.09.1839; 2817a (2816); Map 1839?, 3 chns, 1st cl, in 2 parts, by Frederick and Henry E. Drayson; construction lines, waterbodies, houses, building names; several construction lines are annotated to show which points they lead to outside the tithe-district.

17/179 Hever (parish) TQ 475448
Apt 24.11.1840; 2608a (2608); Map 1841, 3 chns, 1st cl, by Richard Peyton, Cooks Court, Lincolns Inn; construction lines, hill-drawing, railway, foot/b'way, waterbodies, houses, woods (named), hops, hedges, fences, field gates, building names, limekilns. Apt has in-bound and out-bound quantities.

17/180 Higham (parish) TQ 719731
Apt 22.10.1841; 2965a (3155); Map 1841, 3 chns, by Henry Cobb, 18 Lincolns Inn Fields; hill-drawing, waterbodies, woods, hops, building names, road names, canal with towpath and entrance to tunnel, Roman road, road cutting, mill.

17/181 Hinxhill (parish) TR 044432
Apt 08.06.1839; 663a (all); Map '1823', (1840?), 3 chns, by Thomas Kennett, Wye; waterbodies, houses, woods, plantations, gardens, hedges, field gates, building names, road names, boundary stone and trees, rectory; north pointer has oak leaf and acorn decoration.

17/182 Hoath (borough and parish) TR 209649
Apt 24.05.1839; 898a (898); Map 1839, 3 chns, by Thos W. Collard, Bridge St, Canterbury; railway, waterbodies, houses (light pink), woods (col), plantations (col), gardens, heath/moor, hedges, building names, park.

17/183 Hollingbourne (parish) TQ 846556
Apt 04.09.1840; 4560a (all); Map 3 chns, 1st cl, surveyed by John and George C. Darbyshire, Brompton, 1839, and 'Finished and Corrected as to Leaseholds' by Henry Cobb, Surveyor, 18 Lincolns Inn Fields, 1841; construction lines, foot/b'way, waterbodies, houses, field boundary ownerships, building names, workhouse, paper mills; it is unclear why some land is tinted pink.

17/184 Hope All Saints (parish) TR 058263 [Not listed]
Apt 08.12.1842; 1464a (1464); Map 1843, 6 chns, taken from Thomas Hogben's survey, with alterations by Thomas Thurston, Ashford; foot/b'way, waterbodies, houses, field boundary ownerships, building names, brick kilns, chapel ruins.

17/185 Horsmonden (parish) TQ 706401
Apt 28.04.1840; 4517a (4517); Map 1842?, 3 chns; foot/b'way, waterbodies, woods, building names, parsonage, mill, garden paths.

17/186 Horton Kirby (parish) TQ 570682
Apt 11.06.1844; 2811a (all); Map 1842, 4 chns, by W. Hodsell, South Ash; waterbodies, houses, farmyards (col), woods (col), orchards, hops, gardens (col), hedge ownership, field gates, pits; scale-bar and north pointer are tinted.

17/187 Hothfield (parish) TQ 965444
Apt 16.05.1843; 1810a (1777); Map 1843, 6 chns, 'Corrected and Copied' from a survey of 1819 by J. Gouge, Sittingbourne, by Thomas Thurston, Ashford; railway, foot/b'way, waterbodies, houses, woods (col), field boundary ownerships, field gates, building names, stiles, parsonage, heath. Apt has in-bound and out-bound quantities.

17/188 Hougham (parish) TR 288401 [Church Hougham and West Hougham]
Apt 02.02.1843; 2995a (all); Map 1841, 3 chns, 1st cl, in 2 parts, by John Cheesman, Buckland, (includes 1.5-chn enlargement of detail); foot/b'way, waterbodies, houses, field boundary ownerships, spout, stiles; colour bands show leasehold and tithing boundaries.

17/189 Hucking (parish) TQ 839582
Apt 14.04.1841; 1188a (all); Map 1839, 3 chns, 1st cl, by John and George C. Darbyshire, Brompton; construction lines, waterbodies, houses, building names, field acreages.

17/190 Hunton (parish) TQ 723500
Apt 13.10.1838; 2062a (2061); Map 1837-8, 3 chns, by R.A. Ranger, Tunbridge Wells; foot/b'way, houses, woods (by name), field boundary ownerships, building names, road names, mill; area numbers are in red.

17/191 Hurst (parish) TR 076345 [Not listed]
Apt 06.03.1844; 460a (459); Map 1843, 3 chns, 1st cl, in 3 parts, by Thomas Thurston, Ashford, (including 30-chn construction line diagram); construction lines, right of road, canal bank and towpath, waterbodies, houses, woods (col), field boundary ownerships, field gates, building names, site of chapel; there is a note, 'The Marsh Sewers are coloured Blue, and are not scaled into the Fields. The Red Dotted Line shows the extent of the Lands scotted to Romney Marsh'; numerals of uncertain meaning are written alongside some field boundaries.

17/192 St Leonards Hythe (parish) TR 154344 [Hythe]
Apt 21.09.1841; 882a (all); Map 1842, 2 chns, 1st cl, by Thomas Thurston, Ashford; construction lines, foot/b'way, right of road, canal, waterbodies, houses, woods (col), field boundary ownerships, field gates, road names, forts, martello towers, flagstaffs (by symbol), boundary trees and stones (by symbol), high and low ordinary and spring tide marks, stairs (by symbol), windmills (by symbol).

17/193 West Hythe (parish) TR 134334
Apt 30.05.1842; 1254a (1423); Map 1839, 3 chns, 1st cl, in 2 parts, by Thomas Thurston, Ashford, (including 30-chn construction line diagram); construction lines, foot/b'way, canal, waterbodies, houses, fence ownership, field gates, building names, martello towers, redoubt, Dymchurch Wall, fort, boundary posts and trees, wreck, cross, low water mark ordinary and spring tides, Roman ruins, sands (col); there are long notes on Shepway Cross and the wreck of a Dutch warship.

17/194 Ickham and Well (parish) TR 222570
Apt 20.03.1841; 2441a (all); Map 1838-9, 3 chns, 1st cl, in 5 parts, surveyed by Thomas Cooper for Thomas W. Collard, Canterbury, (includes 18-chn index); construction lines, foot/b'way, waterbodies, houses, woods (col, named), plantations (col), hops, building names, field names, ruined chapel, boundary trees, downs; pictorial church.

17/195 Ifield (parish) TQ 657706 [Not listed]
Apt 26.08.1839; 312a (312); Map 1839, 3 chns, 1st cl, by Alexander Doull, Chatham; construction lines, houses, farmyards, chalk pit.

17/196 Ightham (parish) TQ 589562
Apt 18.09.1839; 2540a (2540); Map 1839, 3 chns, 1st cl, in 2 parts, by Richard Dixon, 21 John Street, Bedford Row, (includes 1-chn enlargement of detail); construction lines, waterbodies, houses, field boundary ownerships; meaning of green-banding of roads is unclear.

17/197 Ivychurch (parish) TQ 999251
Apt 07.03.1842; 4541a (4542); Map 1842, 6 chns, by Thomas Thurston, Ashford, from the surveys of Romney Marsh of 1760-5 by Thomas Hogben and of Walland Marsh of 1812-13 by Netlam and Francis Giles, London; foot/b'way, waterbodies, houses, field boundary ownerships, building names, marsh walls, ownerships (col).

17/198 Iwade (parish) TQ 896692
Apt 22.01.1841; 3373a (3762); Map 1838, 3 chns, 1st cl, by Alexr Doull, L.S.; construction lines, waterbodies, farmyards, building names, boundary stones, coastguard station; two construction lines are noted as 'From the Milton Plan'.

17/199 St James, Grain (parish) TQ 877759 [Grain]
Apt 02.05.1842; 3281a (all); Map 1839, 3 chns, 1st cl, by Samuel Elliott; construction lines, waterbodies, houses, fences, field gates, sea wall.

17/200 St John the Baptist (parish) TR 353696 [Not listed]
Apt 11.06.1840; 3802a (all); Map 1841, 3 chns, by William Edmunds, Surveyor, Margate; hill-drawing, waterbodies, houses, woods, orchards, building names, road names, pits, bays, windmills, building land, brewery, baths, pleasure gardens, 'Building Land'; bays named; built-up parts generalised; red and yellow bands indicate boundary between small-tithe owners.

17/201 Kemsing (parish) TQ 560589
Apt 02.02.1841; 1867a (1867); Map 'Surveyed October 1839', 3 chns, 1st cl, in 2 parts, by William Cronk, Seal, Kent; construction lines, foot/b'way, waterbodies, houses.

17/202 Kennardington (parish) TQ 971320 [Kenardington]
Apt 18.06.1839; 2160a (2160); Map 1839, 3 chns, 1st cl, in 2 parts, by J.S. Thomson, Tenterden; construction lines, foot/b'way, canal, waterbodies, houses, woods, orchards, fences, field boundary ownerships, field gates, boundary stones (by symbol); scale-bar and decorative north pointer are combined.

17/203 Kennington (parish) TR 024446
Apt 08.12.1840; 1380a (1380); Map 1840, 3 chns, 1st cl, in 2 parts, by Thomas Thurston, Ashford, (including construction line dia-gram); construction lines, foot/b'way, right of road, waterbodies, houses, woods (col), hops, field boundary ownerships, building names, road names, obelisk, mill, boundary trees (by symbol), vicarage, windmill (by symbol); numerals of uncertain meaning appear alongside field boundaries; drains across fields are shown by double pecked lines. Apt has in-bound and out-bound quantities.

17/204 Keston (parish) TQ 416635
Apt 26.05.1838; 1474a (all); Map 1841?, 3 chns, 1st cl; hill-drawing, waterbodies, houses, woods, field boundary ownerships, field gates, building names, road names, mills, post office, pits, toll bar, well head, heath, green.

17/205 Kidbrook (extra-parochial place) TQ 412760 [Kidbrooke]
Apt 29.06.1850; 756a (755); Map 1844, 6 chns; waterbodies, houses, arable (col), grassland (col), building names, milestone, green.

17/206 Kingsdown (parish) TQ 572628 [West Kingsdown]
Apt 29.07.1841; 2781a (2780); Map 1840, 6 chns, by W. Hodsoll, South Ash; hill-drawing, foot/b'way, waterbodies, houses, woods (col), orchards, hops, hedge ownership (col), chalk pit, 'hole'.

17/207 Kingsdown (parish) TQ 922589 [Not listed]
Apt 27.08.1839; 696a (all); Map 1839?, 3 chns, 1st cl, by Alexander Doull; construction lines, waterbodies, houses, road names.

17/208 Kingsnorth (parish) TR 003391
Apt 02.12.1839; 3245a (all); Map 1839, 3 chns, 1st cl, in 2 parts, by Thomas Thurston, Ashford, (including construction line diagram); construction lines, foot/b'way, waterbodies, houses, woods (col), hops, fences, field boundary ownerships, building names, stiles, rectory; numerals of uncertain meaning appear alongside field boundaries; drains across fields are indicated by double-pecked lines.

17/209 Kingstone (parish) TR 190507 [Kingston]
Apt 01.09.1840; 1525a (all); Map 1839, 3 chns, 1st cl, in 3 parts, by Thomas Cooper, Canterbury; construction lines, foot/b'way, waterbodies, houses, woods (named), plantations, hops, fences, building names, rectory, chalk pit, glebe.

17/210 Knockholt (parish) TQ 469595
Apt 22.06.1843; 1684a (all); Map 1841, 3 chns, 1st cl, by W. Roberts, 68 Chancery Lane; construction lines, foot/b'way, waterbodies, houses, woods, pit.

17/211 Knowlton (parish) TR 281536
Apt 17.09.1842; 429a (all); Map 1841, 3 chns, 1st cl, by Thomas W. Collard; construction lines, foot/b'way, waterbodies, woods (named), gardens (col), rock outcrops, field boundary ownerships, pits, glebe (green); it is unclear why one field is tinted yellow.

17/212 Lamberhurst (parish) (partly in Sussex) TQ 669368
Apt 20.02.1841; 5430a (5390); Map 1839, 3 chns, 1st cl, 'Surveyed under the Poor-Rate Assessment Act' by Robert B. Phillips, 78 King William St, London Bridge; hill-drawing, foot/b'way, waterbodies, houses, woods (col), plantations (col), hops, field boundary ownerships, field gates, building names, quarries, stiles, farm names and boundaries (col), windmill (pictorial); numerals of uncertain purpose appear alongside field boundaries. Apt has in-bound and out-bound quantities.

17/213 East Langdon (parish) TR 338463
Apt 10.12.1841; 1065a (1065); Map 1842, 3 chns, 1st cl, by John Cheesman, Buckland, Kent; construction lines, foot/b'way, waterbodies, houses, windmill, tithe-merged land (green).

17/214 West Langdon (parish) TR 325472
Apt 29.01.1841; 698a (698); Map 1840, 3 chns, by E.P. Coleman, Dover; foot/b'way, waterbodies, houses, woods, hedges, field gates, stiles.

17/215 Langley (parish) TQ 799516
Apt 24.02.1844; 1474a (all); Map 1843, 3 chns, 1st cl, by J. Tootell, Maidstone; construction lines, waterbodies, houses, building names, rectory, boundary trees and stones, chapel.

17/216 Saint Lawrence (parish) TR 362662
Apt 22.10.1840; 3247a (all); Map 1839, 3 chns, 1st cl, by William Roberts, 68 Chancery Lane; construction lines, waterbodies, houses; some pecked boundaries may be marked at angles by boundary stones.

17/217 Lee (parish) TQ 401736
Apt 02.07.1839; 1210a (all); Map 1840?, 3 chns, by Richard Martyr, Greenwich; waterbodies, houses, woods, road names, school and playground.

17/218 Leeds (parish) TQ 820531
Apt 04.05.1844; 1240a (1610); Map 1843, 3 chns, areas 1 to 242 surveyed by Joseph Tootell, Maidstone, and the rest 'copied from old Surveys and revised'; castle named in gothic.

17/219 Leigh next Tonbridge (parish) TQ 538468
Apt 05.12.1840; 4660a (4660); Map 1840, 3.5 chns, in 3 parts, (including 2 parts at 3 chns); construction lines, railway, foot/b'way, waterbodies, houses, woods, plantations, arable (by annotation), grassland (by annotation), orchards, hops, marsh/bog, heath/moor, field gates, building names, weir, quarry, boundary trees and stones, sundial, 'Ha! Ha!', pound, windmill.

17/220 Lenham (parish) TQ 901521
Apt 31.10.1839; 6963a (6963); Map 1838, 3 chns, 1st cl, in 2 parts, made for Tithe and Poor Law Assessment purposes by Thomas Thurston, Ashford, (including 40-chn construction line diagram, which includes Boughton Malherbe and Ulcomb); construction lines, foot/b'way, right of road, waterbodies, houses, woods (col, named), hops, field boundary ownerships, field gates, building names, windmill (by symbol), stiles, vicarage, tanyard, head of the River Stour, heaths; numerals of uncertain purpose appear alongside field boundaries; drains across fields are shown by double-pecked lines. Apt has in-bound and out-bound quantities.

17/221 Lewisham (parish) TQ 376733
Apt 07.02.1843; 5710a (5789); Map 1845?, 3 chns, 1st cl; railway, foot/b'way, waterbodies, houses, woods (col). (The map in PRO IR 30 is a copy; original is in PRO IR 77/34.)

17/222 Leybourne (parish) TQ 686591
Apt 25.10.1842; 1510a (1510); Map 1842, 3 chns, 1st cl, in 2 parts, by Harry Finnis, Leybourne Castle, Maidstone; construction lines, waterbodies, houses, orchards, hops, hedges, fences, boundary trees (by symbol), garden paths.

17/223 Leysdown (parish) TR 028699 [Leysdown on Sea]
Apt 14.04.1841; 2183a (all); Map 1839, 3 chns, 1st cl, in 2 parts, by Thomas Thurston, Ashford, (including 30-chn construction line diagram); construction lines, foot/b'way, right of road, waterbodies, houses, woods (col), field boundary ownerships, field gates, building names, blockade stations, signal mast (by symbol), limekiln, boundary posts and stones, vicarage, pump, navigation beacon (by symbol), embankments; numerals of uncertain purpose appear alongside field boundaries; drains across fields are shown by double-pecked black lines. Apt has in-bound and out-bound quantities.

17/224 Lidsing ('vill' in parish of Gillingham) TQ 789629
Apt 16.09.1841; 439a (479); Map 1841?, 3 chns; foot/b'way, waterbodies, houses, woods (col, by Dawson's symbol, and named), orchards, hops, field names, chalk pit, boundary marks, pits.

17/225 Linstead (parish) TQ 950608 [Lynsted]
Apt 25.03.1840; 1806a (all); Map 1839?, 3 chns, 1st cl, by Frederick and H. E. Drayson; construction lines, waterbodies, houses, heath/moor, rabbit warren.

17/226 Linton (parish) TQ 749497
Apt 04.09.1840; 1383a (1383); Map 1840, 3 chns, 1st cl, by John Adams, Hawkhurst; construction lines, waterbodies, houses, building names, workhouse, stiles, parsonage; one pecked boundary is noted as taken from an old plan, there being now 'no vestiges of division upon the ground'. Apt has in-bound and out-bound quantities.

17/227 Littlebourn (parish) TR 201578 [Littlebourne]
Apt 04.09.1840; 2102a (2102); Map 1841?, [3 chns], 1st cl, by Thomas Cooper, Canterbury; construction lines, waterbodies, houses, woods (by name), plantations, hops, marsh/bog (by annotation), heath/moor, downs, building names, gravel pit, gorse, fox covert, charity land; pictorial church.

17/228 Longfield (parish) TQ 618685
Apt 23.05.1844; 582a (all); Map 1847?, 3 chns, 1st cl, by Frederick and Henry E. Drayson; construction lines, waterbodies, houses, pit or quarry (col).

17/229 Loose (parish) TQ 761522
Apt 31.10.1840; 960a (all); Map 3 chns, 'Revised and corrected...for the year 1840' by J. Quested; hill-drawing, foot/b'way, waterbodies, woods (col), arable (col), grassland (col), orchards, gardens, hedge ownership, fence ownership, boundary stones, garden walls. Apt has in-bound and out-bound quantities.

17/230 Luddenham (parish) TQ 990639 [Not listed]
Apt 24.11.1840; 1323a (1438); Map 1841?, 3 chns, 1st cl, in 4 parts, by Frederick and Henry E. Drayson; construction lines, houses, orchards, building names, spring.

17/231 Luddesdown (parish) TQ 671647
Apt 30.06.1841; 1983a (all); Map 1841?, 3 chns, by A. Doull; construction lines, waterbodies, houses, building names, field names, woods (by name), hops (by annotation); it is unclear why some fields are coloured yellow.

17/232 Lullingstone and Lullingstaine (consolidated parishes) TQ 516650 [Not listed]
Apt 04.09.1843; 1531a (all); Map 1840?, 6 chns; waterbodies, park, glebe. District is almost all apportioned by holding and fields are not shown.

17/233 Lydd (parish) TR 050203
Apt 05.09.1837; 11788a (all); Map 1838?, 6 chns, surveyed by Netlam and Francis Giles in 1812-13, and drawn by Thomas Giles of Salisbury Street, Adelphi, London, in 1817; farmyards (col), woods (col), arable (col), grassland (col), building names, field acreages, spring tide marks, wells, forts, redoubt, signal house, lighthouse, pits, kettle nets, post office, custom house, boundary stones (by symbol) and posts, sheep houses, brick kilns, pest house, limekilns, beach (col), marsh boundaries (col), unproductive land (grey or yellow); ditches across fields are indicated by double pecked lines with grey infill.

17/234 Lydden (parish) TR 254452
Apt 11.03.1840; 1422a (all); Map 1841, 3 chns, 1st cl, by John Cheesman, Buckland, Kent; construction lines, foot/b'way, waterbodies, houses, building names, stiles.

17/235 Lyminge (parish) TR 146419
Apt 06.11.1840; 4595a (4594); Map 1837, 3 chns, 1st cl, by John Adams, Hawkhurst and Dover; construction lines, foot/b'way, waterbodies, houses, gardens, building names, woods (by name), Roman road, workhouse, rectory, pits and quarries, brick kiln.

17/236 Lympne (parish) TR 107355
Apt 24.09.1841; 2658a (all); Map 1839, 3 chns, 1st cl, by E. Sheridan; construction lines, canal, waterbodies, houses, woods (col), hops, building names, Romney Marsh boundary; drains are shown by double blue lines without colour-fill.

17/237 Maidstone (parish) TQ 762551
Apt 16.05.1843; 4232a (4632); Map 1843, 3 chns, 1st cl, in 3 parts, by Harry Finnis, Leybourne Castle, (includes town at 1.5 chns); construction lines, railway, waterbodies, houses (not in town), building names, road names, milestone, boundary stones, posts and other markers, paper mills, gaol, sessions house, corn exchange, town hall, gas works, cavalry barracks, park, borough boundary.

17/238 East Malling (parish) TQ 699575
Apt 08.03.1839; 2765a (2765); Map 1840, 3 chns, 1st cl, by Carrington and Robinson, Sevenoaks; construction lines, foot/b'way, waterbodies, houses, building names; yellow bands may indicate partial exemption from tithe.

17/239 West Malling (parish) TQ 677566
Apt 06.11.1840; 1366a (1366); Map 1840, 3 chns, 1st cl, by Alexander Doull, Chatham; construction lines, waterbodies, houses, road names, boundary trees and stones.

17/240 Marden (parish) TQ 746449
Apt 08.01.1841; 7608a (7607); Map 1841, 6 chns, in 2 parts, surveyed by John Adams in 1818-19, with alterations and corrections by Thomas Thurston, Ashford, (includes enlargement of Marden village at 3 chns); waterbodies, houses, woods (col), building names, road names, parsonage, vicarage, notable grave, tithe-free land (col). Apt has in-bound and out-bound quantities.

17/241 St Margarets at Cliff (parish) TR 366447 [St Margaret's at Cliffe]
Apt 16.05.1840; 1759a (all); Map 1840, 3 chns, in 2 parts, by George Quested, Ash, being a copy of an original by him of 1825; foot/b'way, turnpike roads, waterbodies, beach, high water mark, lighthouse sites, churchyard, sheep droves, free downs.

17/242 St Mary, Hoo (parish) TQ 803774 [St Mary Hoo]
Apt 06.02.1841; 2196a (2866); Map 1839, 3 chns, 1st cl, in 4 parts, by S. Elliott; construction lines, waterbodies, houses, woods (col), field gates, gravel pit (col), embankments; multi-colour bands may show leased tithes.

17/243 St Mary, Romney Marsh (parish) TR 075281 [St Mary in the Marsh]
Apt 08.12.1842; 1936a (2051); Map 1843, 6 chns, copied from the map by Thomas Hogben of 1760-5 with 'alterations' by Thomas Thurston, Ashford; foot/b'way, waterbodies, houses, field boundary ownerships, building names, road names, brick kilns, foreshore.

17/244 Meopham (parish) TQ 646650
Apt 26.03.1841; 4693a (all); Map 1840, 3 chns, 1st cl, by William Roberts, 68 Chancery Lane; construction lines, hill-drawing, waterbodies, houses, woods, orchards, greens.

17/245 Mereworth (parish) TQ 653541
Apt 07.12.1840; 2373a (2374); Map 1838, 3 chns, in 3 parts, by John Budgen, Tunbridge; waterbodies, houses, boundary trees and stones (by symbol), steps (by symbol), pits.

17/246 Mersham (parish) TR 048390
Apt 05.02.1841; 2674a (all); Map 1840, 3 chns, 1st cl, in 2 parts, by Thomas Thurston, Ashford, (including 30-chn construction line diagram); construction lines, railway, foot/b'way, right of road, waterbodies, houses, woods (col), field boundary ownerships, field gates, building names, boundary trees and stones, chapel, rectory, stiles, mills; numerals of uncertain meaning appear alongside field boundaries; drains across fields are shown by double-pecked lines. Apt has in-bound and out-bound quantities.

17/247 Merston (parish) TQ 704722 [Not listed]
Apt 11.08.1842; 159a (all); Map 1842, 3 chns, 1st cl, by A. Doull; construction lines, woods, boundary trees, chalk pit; it is unclear why some fields are colour-edged.

17/248 Midley (parish) TR 014221 [Not listed]
Apt 08.12.1842; 2153a (2153); Map 1842, 6 chns, surveyed by Netlam and Francis Giles of London in 1812-13, with 'alterations' by Thomas Thurston, Ashford; waterbodies, houses, building names, road names, site of chapel, embankments.

17/249 Milstead (parish) TQ 908580
Apt 01.09.1840; 1217a (all); Map 1838, 3 chns, 1st cl, by Alexander Doull; construction lines, waterbodies, houses, boundary trees, stones and posts.

17/250 Milton (parish) TR 123555 [Not listed]
Apt 03.09.1840; 399a (all); Map 1838, 3 chns, 1st cl, by Thomas Collard, 1 Bridge St, Canterbury; construction lines, waterbodies, houses, woods (named), hops, boundary trees (by symbol) and markers, bridle gate, pit.

17/251 Milton next Gravesend (parish) TQ 653731 [Milton]
Apt 08.06.1840; 703a (all); Map 1840?, 3 chns, by R.B. George; hill-drawing, foot/b'way, canal with locks and basin, waterbodies, houses, woods (col), parkland (col), grassland (col), gardens (col), road names, fort, windmill (by symbol); hill named.

17/252 Milton next Sittingbourne (parish) TQ 910658 [Not listed]
Apt 27.12.1839; 2557a (2566); Map 1838, 3 chns, 1st cl, in 3 parts, by Alexander Doull, Chatham; construction lines, waterbodies, houses, building names, road names, 'Ship' [?graving dock], workhouse, quay.

17/253 Minster, in Sheppey (parish) TQ 942719 [Minster]
Apt 22.04.1841; 10129a (11035); Map 1842, 3 chns, 1st cl, by R.B. George; cliffs, waterbodies, houses, woods (col), building names, road names, guard house, magazines, workhouse; dockyard and garrison areas are not mapped in detail. (The map in PRO IR 30 is a copy; original is in PRO IR 77/36.)

17/254 Minster, in Thanet (parish) TR 324645 [Minster]
Apt 30.06.1842; 5570a (6170); Map 1839, 3 chns, 1st cl, in 2 parts, by William Huntly, 4 Lauriston Place, Dover; construction lines, hill-drawing, foot/b'way, turnpike roads, waterbodies, houses, road names, road cutting, river cut, mills, milestone, high water mark, ferry, tithe ownership boundaries; hill named; there is a note that streams and ditches are included in the area of waste; cartouches containing title and acreages and the ruler-style scale-bar are pre-printed and pasted on. (The map in PRO IR 30 is a copy; original is in PRO IR 77/38.)

17/255 Molash (parish) TR 028526
Apt 15.06.1841; 1449a (1449); Map 1839, 3 chns, 1st cl, by Thomas W. Collard, Canterbury; construction lines, waterbodies, woods (col), orchards, hops, gardens (col), building names, boundary posts and trees, windmill (by symbol); Apt contains a 12-chn reduction of the main map.

17/256 Great Mongeham (parish) TR 354512
Apt 18.06.1839; 874a (all); Map 1841?, 3 chns, in 2 parts, 'Copy of Map' by Messrs Small and Son, Dover; foot/b'way, waterbodies, houses, windmill (pictorial); there is a note, 'Note - We could not extend the Lines Nos. 57 and 69 to the out Bounds of the Parish so as to take in the Triangle D, it being very dangerous'.

17/257 Little Mongeham (parish) TR 327499
Apt 14.02.1843; 1145a (1160); Map 1840, 3 chns, 1st cl, by Fred. R. Davey, Canterbury; construction lines, waterbodies, houses, building names, occupation road, bush, tithery boundaries, boundary bush (by symbol).

17/258 Monks Horton (parish) TR 124400 [Not listed]
Apt 29.01.1840; 1079a (1079); Map 1840, 3 chns, 1st cl, by Small and Son, Buckland, Dover; construction lines, foot/b'way, waterbodies, houses, building names, boundary trees and stones, stiles; PRO IR 30 contains two copies, a 'Working Plan', with construction lines, and a 'Copy'; farms are named only on the copy.

17/259 Monkton (parish) TR 284652
Apt 05.06.1840; 2365a (all); Map 1838, 3 chns, 1st cl, by William Huntly, Dover; construction lines, foot/b'way, waterbodies, pits, parsonage, sea mark, milestones; there is a note that ditches in the marshes are included in the area of waste; title and summary of contents and ruler-style scale-bar are all pre-printed and pasted on; map is decorated bottom right with a pen and wash drawing of 'Sea Mark'.

17/260 Mottingham (extra-parochial place) TQ 420724
Apt 10.11.1842; 639a (all); Map 1843, 3 chns, foot/b'way, waterbodies, houses, woods, building names, boundary trees (by symbol) and post, milestone.

17/261 Murston (parish) TQ 926654
Apt 16.01.1840; 1318a (1462); Map 1838, 3 chns, 1st cl, in 3 parts, by Alexander Doull, Chatham; construction lines, waterbodies, houses, coastguard station, rectory, boundary stones and trees.

17/262 Nackington (parish) TR 155548
Apt 21.03.1843; 450a (906); Map 1842, 3 chns, 1st cl, by Thomas W. Collard, Canterbury; construction lines, foot/b'way, waterbodies, houses, woods (col), gardens (col), ornamental gardens (col), building names, parsonage, boundary trees and stones, castle ruins, municipal boundary.

17/263 Nettlestead (parish) TQ 679512
Apt 31.07.1843; 1442a (1441); Map 1846, 3 chns, 1st cl, in 4 parts, by R. Summerfield, Maidstone; construction lines, railway, foot/b'way, turnpike roads, waterbodies, houses, boundary stones.

17/264 Newchurch (parish) TR 054311
Apt 07.06.1841; 3121a (3122); Map 1839, 3 chns, 1st cl, in 2 parts, made under the Parochial Assessment Act by Thomas Thurston, Ashford, (including 30-chn construction line diagram); construction lines, foot/b'way, right of road, waterbodies, houses, field boundary ownerships, field gates, building names, rectory, footbridges, steps (by symbol), boundary posts, mound; drains are uncoloured, and drains across fields are shown by double pecked lines; numerals of uncertain meaning appear against field boundaries.

17/265 Newenden (parish) TQ 842280
Apt 08.05.1839; 1044a (1044); Map 1838, 3 chns, 1st cl, by John Adams, Hawkhurst and Dover; construction lines, foot/b'way, waterbodies, houses, building names, field acreages. Apt has in-bound and out-bound quantities.

17/266 Newington next Hythe (parish) TR 180383 [Newington]
Apt 05.03.1840; 3134a (3194); Map '1832', (1839?), 3 chns, 1st cl, in 5 parts, by John Adams, Hawkhurst, (includes index); construction

lines, foot/b'way, canal with towpath, waterbodies, landowners, fort, martello tower, sea walls, low water mark, military road, shingle, waste; alpha-numerical parcel numbers have been struck through and replaced by ordinary numbering. Apt has in-bound and out-bound quantities.

17/267 Newington (parish) TQ 860645
Apt 06.07.1840; 2103a (all); Map 1840, 3 chns, 1st cl, by A. Doull; waterbodies, houses, boundary trees and stones, pools, windmill (by symbol).

17/268 Newnham (parish) TQ 948570
Apt 14.07.1841; 1293a (1293); Map 1838, 3 chns, 1st cl, by Frederick and Henry E. Drayson; construction lines, woods, plantations, orchards, hops, windmill (by symbol) on mound.

17/269 St Nicholas at Wade (parish) TR 266676
Apt 10.10.1839; 3441a (3660); Map 1839, 6 chns, in 4 parts, by John Quested, Maidstone; foot/b'way, waterbodies, houses, building names, charity lands, sea wall, sluice, pits; names in gothic writing indicate importance rather than antiquity.

17/270 Nonington and Wimblingswold or Womenswold (parish) TR 250517 [Womenswold]
Apt 12.06.1839; 5092a (5091); Map 1839, 6 chns, 'constructed from several plans belonging to the Landowners' by George Quested, Ash; foot/b'way.

17/271 Northbourne (parish) TR 329524
Apt 26.09.1843; 3629a (3628); Map 1841, 3 chns, 1st cl, in 3 parts, by Thomas W. Collard, Canterbury; waterbodies, woods, plant-ations, hops, gardens (col), building names, telegraph, pits, private roads (col).

17/272 Northfleet (parish) TQ 631716
Apt 23.02.1839; 3908a (4313); Map 1838, 4 chns, by Paul Padley, London; waterbodies, houses, woods, orchards, building names, pound, mills, dock yard, pits, greens. (The map in PRO IR 30 is a copy; original is in PRO IR 77/39.)

17/273 Norton (parish) TQ 969603 [Not listed]
Apt 26.08.1839; 902a (902); Map 1838, 3 chns, 1st cl, by Frederick and Henry E. Drayson; construction lines, foot/b'way, waterbodies, houses, farmyards, woods, plantations, parkland, orchards, hops, gardens, building names, rectory, pit; church roof-ridges are indicated.

17/274 Nursted (parish) TQ 643684 [Not listed]
Apt 15.02.1839; 510a (all); Map 1838, 3 chns, by Richard Smirke Martyr; waterbodies, houses, woods (col), arable (col), grassland (col), orchards (col), hops (col), gardens (col), field gates, building names, quarry, glebe.

17/275 Oare (parish) TR 010638
Apt 26.08.1839; 686a (all); Map 1838, 3 chns, 1st cl, in 2 parts, by Frederick and Henry E. Drayson; construction lines, foot/b'way, houses, farmyards (col), woods, gardens, orchards, building names, sea wall, ferry, high and low water marks.

17/276 Offham (parish) TQ 656575
Apt 20.04.1844; 707a (707); Map 1844, 3 chns, 1st cl, ? by Thomas W. Collard, Canterbury; construction lines, waterbodies, houses, building names, boundary trees and markers.

17/277 Orgarswick (parish) TR 084306 [Not listed]
Apt 28.10.1843; 392a (392); Map 1843, 6 chns, copied from Thomas Hogben's survey of 1760-5, with alterations by Thomas Thurston, Ashford; waterbodies, houses, site of chapel; drains are uncoloured.

17/278 Orlestone (parish) TR 001345
Apt 08.03.1839; 1825a (1825); Map 1839, 3 chns, 1st cl, in 2 parts, by Thomas Thurston, Ashford, (including 20-chn construction line diagram); construction lines, foot/b'way, right of road, turnpike roads, canal, waterbodies, houses, woods (col, named), hops, field boundary ownerships, field gates, building names, green, stiles, boundary trees (by symbol), Romney Marsh boundary; numerals of uncertain purpose appear alongside field boundaries. Apt has in-bound and out-bound quantities.

17/279 Orpington (parish) TQ 461666
Apt 30.06.1843; 3477a (3477); Map 1841, 3 chns, 1st cl, by W. Roberts, 68 Chancery Lane; construction lines, waterbodies, houses, woods, building names, boundary tree (by symbol), mill.

17/280 Ospringe (parish) TQ 989590
Apt 24.11.1840; 2798a (all); Map 1839?, 3 chns, 1st cl, by Frederick H. E. Drayson; construction lines, waterbodies, houses, woods (col), parkland (col), gardens, building names, pool, vicarage, old track of stream, quarries; it is unclear why some fields are tinted.

17/281 Otford (parish) TQ 526586
Apt 15.11.1844; 2772a (2852); Map 1841, 3 chns, by E.E. and G. Cronk, Seal; construction lines, foot/b'way, waterbodies, houses, building names, 'Pilgrim Road', well, chalk pit, limekiln, mill, glebe; map has a note 'All Woodlands below the Pilgrim Road are not tithable'.

17/282 Otham (parish) TQ 795535
Apt 16.05.1838; 947a (all); Map 1838, 3 chns, by J. Walker, Maidstone; hill-drawing, foot/b'way, waterbodies, houses, woods, boundary trees and stones, toll gate, kiln.

17/283 Otterden (parish) TQ 939538 [Not listed]
Apt 08.06.1839; 1434a (all); Map 1839, 8 chns, by George Grist, litho (Standidge); foot/b'way, waterbodies, woods, building names, land-owner, field names, garden (by annotation).

17/284 Oxney (parish) TR 355466 [Not listed]
Apt 05.06.1839; 313a (313); Map 'Copy from an Old Survey', 1840, 4 chns; houses, plantations, orchards.

17/285 Paddlesworth (parish) TQ 685621
Apt 08.03.1839; 349a (349); Map 1842?, 3 chns, 1st cl, in 3 parts; construction lines, waterbodies, woods, chapel ruins, chalk pit.

17/286 Paddlesworth (parish) TR 198402
Apt 22.11.1838; 557a (all); Map 1838, 3 chns, 1st cl, by John Adams, Hawkhurst; construction lines, foot/b'way, waterbodies, houses, building names.

17/287 East Peckham (parish) TQ 665494
Apt 30.09.1841; 3358a (3358); Map 1842, 6 chns, surveyed by John Adams of Hawkhurst in 1822, with 'alterations and corrections' by Thomas Thurston, Ashford; foot/b'way, waterbodies, houses, woods (col), hops, field boundary ownerships, building names, river locks, weirs, wharf, oil mills, vicarage, parsonage.

17/288 West Peckham (parish) TQ 637527
Apt 22.11.1841; 1583a (1583); Map 1839, 3 chns, 1st cl, by John and George C. Darbyshire, Brompton; construction lines, waterbodies, houses, building names, field acreages, old water course, well house, boundary trees; a 'covered' section of parish boundary is shown in blue.

17/289 Pembury (parish) TQ 634406
Apt 23.05.1844; 3482a (3481); Map 1848?, 3 chns, 1st cl; waterbodies, houses, fences, field gates, building names, boundary trees (by symbol), mill, Queen Anne's Bounty land, park, woods (by name), glebe.

17/290 Penshurst (parish) TQ 527423
Apt 27.05.1838; 4525a (4526); Map 1838-40, 3.5 chns, in 2 parts, by Geo. Prickett, Highgate, and 12 Southampton Buildings; railway, waterbodies, houses, woods (named), plantation (by annotation), park (by annotation), orchards (by annotation), gardens, greens, building names, farm names, boundary trees and marks, boat house, private carriage road, mill, paper mills; map has a note, 'When this Plan left my Office it was perfectly clean and unsoiled. George Prickett'.

17/291 St Peter, Thanet (parish) TR 385686 [St Peters]
Apt 22.04.1839; 1841a (all); Map 1838, 3 chns, 1st cl, by William Huntly, Dover; construction lines, foot/b'way, building names, monument, navigation beacons (by symbol), low water mark, lighthouse, tithery boundaries (col); title and ruler-like scale bar are printed and pasted on. (The map in PRO IR 30 is a copy; original is in PRO IR 77/41.)

17/292 Petham (parish) TR 123527
Apt 30.06.1837; 3235a (all); Map 1838, 3 chns, in 2 parts, by Small and Son, Buckland; foot/b'way, houses, woods (col), arable (col), grassland

(col), hops, gardens (col), hedge ownership, fence ownership, building names, boundary trees, tithery boundaries, pits; names at the 'top' (to the title) of the map are written upside down; 'Unproductive' woodland is shown by brown flecks added to the usual green.

17/293 Pluckley (parish) TQ 925446
Apt 26.12.1837; 3047a (3047); Map 1838, 3 chns, surveyed by John Adams in 1817, with 'alterations' by Thomas Thurston, Ashford; construction lines, waterbodies, woods, hops, field gates, building names, windmill, rectory, in- and out-bound field acreages. Apt has in-bound and out-bound quantities.

17/294 Plumstead (parish) TQ 455787
Apt 22.08.1842; 3372a (3715); Map 1842, 3 chns, by A. Doull; waterbodies, houses, woods (col), parkland (col), orchards (col), gardens, hedges, fences, building names, Royal Arsenal (in detail), rifle butts, boundary stones and tree, chapel, boundary walls (red).

17/295 Postling (parish) TR 145390
Apt 07.02.1843; 1561a (all); Map 1838, 3 chns, 1st cl, by John Adams, Hawkhurst; railway, foot/b'way, waterbodies, houses, woods, orchards, hops, gardens, building names.

17/296 Preston (parish) TR 021596
Apt 08.06.1840; 1547a (1547); Map 1840?, 3 chns, 1st cl, in 3 parts, by Frederick and Henry E. Drayson; construction lines, waterbodies, houses, woods, orchards, hops, building names, paper mill, gunpowder works, windmill (by symbol), chalk pit (by symbol).

17/297 Preston next Wingham (parish) TR 247609 [Not listed]
Apt 05.08.1840; 1478a (all); Map 1840, 3 chns, copied from one of 1826 by George Quested, Ash; waterbodies.

17/298 Rainham (parish) TQ 815659
Apt 31.05.1838; 3609a (all); Map 1840?, [3 chns], 1st cl, by Alexander Doull; construction lines, waterbodies, houses, building names, road names, cage, pound, chalk pits, 'Gillingham Station', boundary tree, ruins, ponds, park.

17/299 St George Ramsgate (parish) TR 381649 [Ramsgate]
Apt 30.06.1843; 176a (all); Map 1843, 2.75 chns, (tithable parts only, tinted); arable (col), grassland (col), hedges, road names, post and smock windmills (by symbol), sea-shore; streets laid out for building are superimposed on some fields, the original boundaries of which are indicated by vignetting. Apt omits most land use.

17/300 Reculver (parish) TR 213682
Apt 20.06.1839; 1249a (1653); Map 1839, 3 chns, by Thomas W. Collard, Canterbury; foot/b'way, waterbodies, orchards, gardens (col), walls.

17/301 Ridley (parish) TQ 621646
Apt 19.04.1839; 814a (all); Map 1838, 4 chns, by W. Hodsoll, made by order of the landowners, 1 November 1838; foot/b'way, waterbodies, houses, farmyards, woods (col, named), plantations, arable (col), grassland (col), orchards, hops (col), gardens (col), hedges, field names, pond, pits, churchyard; pears, grapes, shell and rushes surround map title; border and scale bar are both diced brown.

17/302 Ringwould (parish) TR 369479
Apt 13.05.1839; 1600a (1710); Map 1840?, 3 chns, 1st cl, by William Henry (?) Gilbert, Sibertswold; construction lines, waterbodies, houses, beach; PRO IR 30 contains two copies, one of which omits the construction lines.

17/303 Ripple (parish) TR 353494
Apt 30.04.1840; 1012a (1134); Map 1840, 3 chns, by Small and Son, Dovor; waterbodies, houses, building names, windmill (by symbol); some names are written upside down.

17/304 River (parish) TR 294434
Apt 04.03.1843; 1199a (all); Map 1844, 3 chns, 1st cl, by Small and Son, Dover; construction lines, foot/b'way, waterbodies, houses, boundary trees and stones, stiles; tithe area numbers in the upper part of the map are written 'upside down'; meaning of green band is uncertain.

17/305 St Margaret, Rochester (parish) TQ 736664 [Not listed]
Apt 30.05.1842; 2828a (?); Map 1842, 3 chns, 1st cl, in 2 parts, by Alexander Doull, Chatham, (includes town separately at 1 chn); construction lines, turnpike roads, waterbodies, houses, woods (named), garden (col), building names, road names, forts, hospital, turnpike gate, boundary trees and stones, chapels.

17/306 St Nicholas, Rochester (parish) TQ 746687 [Not listed]
Apt 28.10.1841; 91a (?); Map 1841, 2 chns, (tithable parts only); waterbodies, road names, embankment, saltings, castle, custom house, gas works, garden; map has a scribbled note that it was revised by A. Doull, Chatham, in 1842.

17/307 Rodmersham (parish) TQ 919608
Apt 26.04.1839; 1231a (all); Map 1839, 3 chns, 1st cl, by Alexander Doull, Chatham; construction lines, waterbodies, houses, building names, road names, windmill, ponds, green, chalk pit.

17/308 Rolvenden (parish) TQ 849309
Apt 14.02.1839; 5622a (5622); Map 'constructed' from J. Adams' survey of 1828, and 'Corrected to June 1839', 6 chns, in 2 parts, (includes enlargement of village at 3 chns); foot/b'way, woods, park. Apt omits land use.

17/309 New Romney (parish) TR 045251
Apt 14.09.1842; 2919a (2919); Map 1841, 3 chns, 1st cl, in 2 parts, by Thomas Thurston, Ashford, (including 30-chn construction line diagram); construction lines, foot/b'way, waterbodies, houses, field boundary ownerships, field gates, building names, road names, boundary stones (by symbol), blockade station, high and low spring tide marks, well, workhouse, old churchyards; numerals of uncertain meaning appear alongside field boundaries; drains are uncoloured, and covered drains are shown by double pecked lines; red band may indicate either the limits of Romney Marsh, or else be connected with the moduses.

17/310 Old Romney (parish) TR 025244
Apt 14.02.1843; 2536a (2535); Map 1842, 6 chns, surveyed in 1812-13 by Netlam and Francis Giles of London, with 'alterations' by Thomas Thurston, Ashford; foot/b'way, waterbodies, woods, houses, building names, road names, site of chapel, footbridges, embankments; drains are uncoloured.

17/311 Ruckinge (parish) TR 019342
Apt 23.08.1839; 3445a (3445); Map 1838, 3 chns, 1st cl, by J.S. Thomson, Tenterden; construction lines, foot/b'way, canal, waterbodies, woods, orchards, fence ownership, field boundary ownerships, field gates, stiles.

17/312 Ryarsh (parish) TQ 670591
Apt 27.10.1840; 1551a (all); Map 1840, 3 chns, 1st cl, in 2 parts, by Murrell R. Robinson, Otford Castle, Seven Oaks; construction lines, waterbodies, houses, fences, building names; it is unclear why some land is tinted brown.

17/313 Saltwood (parish) TR 151364
Apt 21.09.1841; 2600a (all); Map 1842, 6 chns, 'corrected and copied' from one by John Adams of Hawkhurst and Dover of 1833 by Thomas Thurston, Ashford; railway, waterbodies, houses, woods (col), building names, stiles, castle, garden paths.

17/314 Sandhurst (parish) TQ 800284
Apt 23.01.1838; 4382a (4382); Map '1826' (1838?), 2 chns, in 3 parts, by Thomas Gibson, Robertsbridge; turnpike roads, waterbodies, road names, weir, windmill. Apt omits land use.

17/315 St Clements, Sandwich (parish) TR 339576 [Not listed]
Apt 04.09.1844; 541a (540); Map 'Copied 1842', 2 chns, by W. Woodland, Ramsgate; hedge ownership (col), fences, field boundary ownerships, road names, prison, windmill (by symbol), ownerships (col).

17/316 Sandwich St Marys (parish) TR 327577 [Not listed]
Apt 31.12.1842; 128a (127); Map 1846, 1 chns, 1st cl, by Thomas W. Collard, Canterbury; construction lines, railway, waterbodies, houses, field gates, road names, grammar school, tanyard. Apt omits most land use.

17/317 Sandwich St Peters (parish) TR 328583 [Not listed]
Apt 19.11.1857; 20a (36); Map 1858, 3 chns, by Michael Warren, Winchester St, Pimlico, London, (tithable parts only); railway, houses, rope walk, cattle market, ownerships (col). Apt omits land use.

17/318 Seal (parish) TQ 564549
Apt 06.03.1841; 4374a (4374); Map 1839, 3 chns, by John Quested, Maidstone; foot/b'way, waterbodies, houses, greens, commons; some buildings are uncoloured.

17/319 Seasalter (parish) TR 091644
Apt 19.06.1841; 1451a (3171); Map 1840, [3 chns], 1st cl; construction lines, waterbodies, houses, marsh/bog, 'Cliff Station', boundary stones, embankments, drains (uncoloured).

17/320 Selling (parish) TR 041569
Apt 01.09.1840; 2463a (2463); Map 1840, 6 chns, litho (Standidge); waterbodies, houses (by shading), woods, orchards, hops, building names, landowners, vicarage, windmill.

17/321 Sellinge (parish) TR 102381 [Sellindge]
Apt 16.06.1840; 2055a (2055); Map 1838, 3 chns, 1st cl, in 2 parts, by John Adams, Hawkhurst; construction lines, waterbodies, houses, building names, woods (by name), windmill (by symbol); there is a note that fields are 'scaled' to the centre of streams, that some detail is from Adams' recent plan of Aldington, and that the construction lines were laid down on 9 August 1838.

17/322 Seven Oaks (parish) TQ 533534 [Sevenoaks]
Apt 21.11.1838; 4830a (6000); Map 1839, 6 chns, by D. Booth, Sundridge; waterbodies, woods, field gates, building names, rectory, chapel, inn, parsonage, turnpike gate, gas house, park wall, common, modus land; colour bands may show property ownerships; built-up parts generalised; north pointer has Prince of Wales' feathers.

17/323 Sevington (parish) TR 033402
Apt 30.04.1838; 833a (all); Map 1838, 3 chns, 1st cl, in 3 parts, by Thomas Thurston, Ashford, (including 30-chn construction line diagram with pictorial churches); construction lines, foot/b'way, waterbodies, houses, woods (col), field gates, building names, mill, site of mote house, rectory, boundary stones and trees (by symbol), stiles; hops are shown outside the distrct; numerals of uncertain purpose appear alongside field boundaries; drains are uncoloured, and drains across fields are shown by double pecked lines; there is a note, 'In taking the direction of a church, the vane is always taken'.

17/324 Shadoxhurst (parish) TQ 977375
Apt 10.07.1841; 1931a (1932); Map 1839, 3 chns, 1st cl, by G. Durey, Great Chart; construction lines, waterbodies, houses, field names, woods (by name), churchyard (col), green; a field belonging to another district is tinted; meaning of green band is unclear.

17/325 Sheldwich (parish) TR 015563
Apt 29.07.1841; 1898a (all); Map 1842, 6 chns, in 3 parts, (includes 1.5-chn enlargement of detail), litho (Standidge); houses (by shading), woods, orchards, hops, building names, gardens.

17/326 Shipborne (parish) TQ 592522 [Shipbourne]
Apt 10.06.1845; 1906a (1906); Map 1846, 3 chns, by E.E. and G. Cronk, Seven Oaks; construction lines, waterbodies, houses, greens (col).

17/327 Sholden (parish) TR 352545
Apt 09.01.1840; 1881a (1985); Map 'Surveyed 1838', 3 chns, by Elias Pym Fordham, Dover; foot/b'way, turnpike roads, houses, road names, high and low water marks, castle (in detail), battery, sea walls.

17/328 Shoreham (parish) TQ 520621
Apt 24.02.1843; 5506a (all); Map 1840, 3 chns, in 2 parts, by D. Booth, Sundridge; construction lines, waterbodies, houses, woods.

17/329 Shorne (parish) TQ 694715
Apt 21.12.1842; 3050a (all); Map 1842, 3 chns, 1st cl, by Alexander Doull, Chatham; construction lines, foot/b'way, canal, waterbodies, houses, woods (named), plantations, orchards, hops, building names, boundary trees and stones, heath.

17/330 Sibertswould (parish) TR 255480 [Shepherdswell]
Apt 17.05.1839; 1835a (all); Map 1840, 3 chns, 1st cl, by Thomas W. Collard, Bridge St, Canterbury; construction lines, waterbodies, houses, woods (col), field boundary ownerships, building names, occupation road; meaning of red band is unclear.

17/331 Sittingbourne (parish) TQ 910631
Apt 12.11.1840; 1008a (1008); Map 1838, 3 chns, 1st cl, by A. Doull, Chatham; construction lines, waterbodies, wood (by name), houses, springs, milestone, vicarage, post office, boundary stones and trees, inns, sea wall.

17/332 Smarden (parish) TQ 882427
Apt 17.06.1841; 5380a (5380); Map 1838, 3 chns, 1st cl, made under the Poor Law Assessment Act by Thomas Thurston, Ashford; construction lines, railway, right of road, waterbodies, houses, woods (col), hops, field boundary ownerships, field gates, building names, road names, limekiln, chapel, rectory. Apt has in-bound and out-bound quantities.

17/333 Smeeth (parish) TR 074394
Apt 06.06.1840; 1612a (all); Map 1840, 3 chns, 1st cl, in 2 parts, surveyed under the Poor Rate Assessment Act by Thomas Thurston, Ashford, (including 30-chn construction line diagram); construction lines, railway, foot/b'way, waterbodies, houses, woods (col), fence ownership, field boundary ownerships, field gates, building names, mill, rectory, footbridges, boundary and isolated trees (by symbol); numerals of uncertain purpose are written alongside field boundaries; drains are uncoloured, and drains across fields are shown by double pecked lines.

17/334 Snargate (parish) TQ 983289
Apt 24.02.1844; 1591a (1591); Map 1843, 6 chns, taken from Thomas Hogben's survey of Romney Marsh of 1780-5 (sic) and Netlam and Francis Giles' survey of Walland Marsh of 1812-13 with 'alterations' by Thomas Thurston, Ashford; foot/b'way, waterbodies, houses, field boundary ownerships, building names, road names, windmill (by symbol), footbridges, embankments.

17/335 Snave (parish) TR 016301
Apt 24.02.1844; 1481a (1494); Map 1843, 6 chns, in 2 parts, taken from the survey of Romney Marsh by Thomas Hogben, and of Walland Marsh by Netlam and Francis Giles of London of 1812-13, with 'alterations' by Thomas Thurston, Ashford; foot/b'way, waterbodies, houses, field boundary ownerships, building names, road names, footbridges.

17/336 Snodland (parish) TQ 695626
Apt 24.02.1844; 1517a (all); Map 1844, 3 chns, by Henry Finnis, Leybourne Castle, Maidstone, Kent; construction lines, waterbodies, houses, building names, paper mill, ferry, chapel, turnpike, boundary stones and trees, wharf.

17/337 Southfleet (parish) TQ 611709
Apt 27.02.1841; 2340a (2340); Map '1839-40', 3 chns, 1st cl, by W. Hubbard, Dartford; construction lines, foot/b'way, waterbodies, houses, woods, gardens, stiles, pits, windmill (by symbol).

17/338 Speldhurst (parish) TQ 553396
Apt 27.03.1841; 3947a (3947); Map 1840, 3 chns, 1st cl, by Alexander Doull, Chatham; construction lines, waterbodies, houses, building names, mill pond, hop kiln, hotels, 'parade', woods (by name), green, commons, quarry.

17/339 Stalisfield (parish) TQ 964530
Apt 05.02.1840; 2227a (all); Map 1841?, 3 chns, 1st cl, by Frederick and Henry E. Drayson; construction lines.

17/340 Standford (parish) TR 124379 [Stanford]
Apt 31.10.1838; 1182a (1181); Map 1839, 6 chns, by John Adams, Hawkhurst and Dover, 1835, litho (Standidge); waterbodies, houses, woods, gardens, fences, common; fields are identified by ownership letters and parcel numbers.

17/341 Stansted (parish) TQ 607617 [Stanstead]
Apt 19.07.1841; 1956a (all); Map 1841, 4 chns, by William Hodsoll, South Ash; foot/b'way, waterbodies, houses, woods (col), orchards

(col), hops (col), gardens (col), hedges (col), building names, turnpike gate, pits; colour bands may show property ownerships.

17/342 Staple (parish) TR 274567
Apt 04.01.1840; 1010a (1009); Map 1837-41, 3 chns, 1st cl, in 2 parts, by J.M. Davey, Canterbury; construction lines, foot/b'way, waterbodies, houses, building names, chalk pit, mill.

17/343 Staplehurst (parish) TQ 782430
Apt 11.08.1838; 5737a (5737); Map '1838 and 1839', 3 chns, 1st cl, in 2 parts, by Tootell, Maidstone; railway, waterbodies, field boundary ownerships, building names, boundary marks, rectory, woods (by name); there is a note on paper contraction.

17/344 Stelling (parish) TR 148476 [Stelling Minnis]
Apt 07.07.1837; 1325a (all); Map 1837, 3 chns, by Small and Son, Dover; construction lines, foot/b'way, waterbodies, houses, building names; some names are written sideways on or upside down.

17/345 St Stephens, or Hackington (parish) TR 152602
Apt 03.07.1839; 1985a (1984); Map 1839, [3 chns], 1st cl, in 2 parts, by Thomas W. Collard, Canterbury; construction lines, railway with sidings and earthworks, waterbodies, woods (col), plantations (col), parkland (in detail), orchards (col), hops, gardens (col), building names; fields also included in Apt for 'Harbledown, Saint Cosmos, etc.' are tinted pink.

17/346 Stockbury (parish) TQ 842612
Apt 11.09.1840; 2940a (2940); Map 1839, 3 chns, 1st cl, by S. Elliott; construction lines, waterbodies, houses, field gates, tithing boundaries; north pointer has crown and plumes.

17/347 Stodmarsh (parish) TR 215610
Apt 22.10.1840; 169a (695); Map 1838, 3 chns, by Thomas Cooper, Canterbury; construction lines, houses, woods, plantations, orchards, hops, field boundary ownerships, field gates, building names, landowners; colour bands show tithe-free, glebe and church land.

17/348 Stoke (parish) TQ 832750
Apt 27.05.1841; 3564a (all); Map 1839, 3 chns, 1st cl, by Saml Elliott; construction lines, waterbodies, houses, embankments; colour bands may show property ownerships.

17/349 Stone (parish) TQ 935274 [Not listed]
Apt 22.10.1839; 3042a (3042); Map 1841, 6 chns, 'Revised and Copied' by J.S. Thomson, Tenterden; foot/b'way, canal with towpath, waterbodies, woods (col), arable (col), grassland (col), orchards, fences, footbridges. Apt omits land use.

17/350 Stone (parish) TQ 580736
Apt 08.08.1837; 3000a (all); Map surveyed in 1838-9, 3 chns, in 2 parts; construction lines, foot/b'way, right of way, waterbodies, houses, woods, orchards, building names, road names, boundary trees and markers, Roman road, chalk pits, saltings.

17/351 Stone next Faversham (parish) TQ 986610 [Not listed]
Apt 22.07.1840; 753a (753); Map 1840?, 3 chns, 1st cl, in 2 parts, by Frederick and Henry E. Drayson; construction lines, waterbodies, houses, building names.

17/352 Stourmouth (parish) TR 260629 [East and West Stourmouth]
Apt 27.06.1837; 878a (all); Map 1820, 6 chns, surveyed in 1819 by Peter Potter, Kentish Town, Maidstone; foot/b'way, waterbodies, farmyards (col), woods (col), arable (col), grassland (col), orchards, gardens (col), hedges, fences, building names, glebe and common field names, sluice, ferry house, pit, stop gate, drains, embankments, field acreages; map was originally sectioned, and appears to be an original of 1820.

17/353 Stowting (parish) TR 124426
Apt 19.10.1842; 1624a (all); Map 1837, 3 chns, by John Adams, Hawkhurst and Dover, Kent; foot/b'way, waterbodies, houses, woods, plantations, orchards, hops, gardens, building names, stiles, rectory, [Roman] causeway, common; north pointer has Prince of Wales' feathers. Apt has in-bound and out-bound quantities.

17/354 Strood (parish) TQ 726690
Apt 19.04.1844; 1488a (all); Map 1844, 3 chns; foot/b'way, waterbodies, woods (named), hops, fences, building names, windmills (pictorial), milestone, boundary trees and marks, Giants Grave, mill pond; there are notes in red about a tithe owner.

17/355 Sturry (parish) TR 175620
Apt 31.12.1840; 3089a (3089); Map 1841, 3 chns, 1st cl; construction lines, foot/b'way, waterbodies, houses, woods (named), hops, building names, milestone; scale-bar is ruler-like.

17/356 Sundridge (parish) TQ 489534
Apt 05.05.1840; 4041a (4041); Map 1839-40, 3 chns, 1st cl, by D. Booth, Sundridge, Kent; construction lines, waterbodies, houses.

17/357 Sutton (parish) TR 334493
Apt 30.10.1839; 1055a (all); Map 1839, 4 chns, in 2 parts, by W. Holtum, Walmer; foot/b'way, waterbodies, houses, woods (col), plantations (col), arable (col), grassland (col), orchards, gardens (col), hedges (col), pits.

17/358 East Sutton (parish) TQ 831486 [Not listed]
Apt 25.07.1843; 1592a (1590); Map 1843, 3 chns, 1st cl, by Thomas Thurston, Ashford; construction lines, foot/b'way, waterbodies, houses, woods (col), hops, field boundary ownerships, field gates, building names, workhouse, parsonage, boundary trees (by symbol); numerals of uncertain meaning appear along field boundaries; drains across fields are shown by double pecked lines. Apt has in-bound and out-bound quantities.

17/359 Sutton at Hone (parish) TQ 533699
Apt 31.10.1840; 3588a (3587); Map 1834, 4 chns, by Thomas Adams, Dartford; foot/b'way, waterbodies, houses, woods, plantations, farm names, pit or quarry, mills, college, malthouse; colour bands may show property ownerships or holdings; scale-bar is ruler-like.

17/360 Sutton Valence (parish) TQ 811478
Apt 15.05.1841; 2156a (2132); Map 1840, 3 chns, 1st cl, by J.M. Davey, Canterbury; construction lines, waterbodies, houses, woods, arable (by annotation), grassland (by annotation), hops (by annotation), gardens (by annotation), building names, turnpike gate, parsonage, vicarage, castle; green band may show tithe-free land; scale bar and title and acreage summary cartouches are litho-printed and glued on.

17/361 Swalecliffe (parish) TR 141654
Apt 23.02.1837; 962a (all); Map 1837, 3 chns, by G. Grist, Canterbury; construction lines, foot/b'way, waterbodies, houses, woods (by name), field gates, building names, watch house, footbridges, cliffs.

17/362 Swanscombe (parish) TQ 601742
Apt 28.10.1843; 2188a (2593); Map 1844, 3 chns, foot/b'way, waterbodies, houses.

17/363 Swingfield (parish) TR 224433 [Swingfield Minnis]
Apt 25.09.1841; 2638a (all); Map 1840, 3 chns, 1st cl, in 2 parts, 'Surveyed for... the Inclosure and Commutation' by Thomas Thurston, Ashford, (including 30-chn construction line diagram); construction lines, hill-drawing, foot/b'way, right of road, waterbodies, houses, woods (col), field boundary ownerships, field gates, building names, pits or quarries, boundary stones (by symbol); numerals of uncertain purpose appear along field boundaries.

17/364 Tenterden (parish) TQ 890328
Apt 18.04.1843; 8394a (8300); Map 1843, 6 chns, in 4 parts, by Thomas Thurston, Ashford, (includes three enlargements of town and built-up areas at 2 chns; town and adjacent lands mapped by Thurston, and the remainder 'altered' from a map made by John Adams, Senior, in 1822); foot/b'way, right of road, waterbodies, houses, woods (col), hops, field boundary ownerships, field gates, building names, windmills, water mill, vicarage, turnpike, stiles; drains are uncoloured; drains across fields are shown by pecked double lines.

17/365 Teston (parish) TQ 704536
Apt 23.05.1844; 517a (491); Map 1844, 3 chns, 1st cl, by R. Summerfield, Maidstone; construction lines, railway, water-bodies, houses, weir.

17/366 Teynham (parish) TQ 964638
Apt 05.12.1839; 2439a (2648); Map 1839?, 3 chns, 1st cl, by Frederick and Henry E. Drayson; construction lines, foot/b'way, waterbodies,

houses, building names, high and low water marks, Queen Anne's Bounty lands.

17/367 Thanington (parish) TR 135558
Apt 07.04.1838; 1212a (1212); Map surveyed in 1838, 3 chns, 1st cl, by Thomas W. Collard, Canterbury; construction lines, foot/b'way, woods (col), orchards, hops, gardens (col), marsh/bog, hedge ownership, fence ownership, field gates, building names, castle ruins, boundary stones and trees.

17/368 Thornham (parish) TQ 813580 [Thurnham]
Apt 26.09.1840; 3320a (all); Map 1841?, 8 chns, surveyed in 1825 by Thomas Brown, Maidstone; hill-drawing, turnpike roads and gate, waterbodies, woods, arable, orchards, heath/moor, building names, gardens (col); meaning of colours is unclear.

17/369 Throwley (parish) TQ 991549
Apt 01.06.1841; 3180a (3180); Map 1841, 6 chns, litho (Standidge); waterbodies, houses (by shading), woods, hops, building names.

17/370 Tilmanstone (parish) TR 299515
Apt 15.02.1840; 1140a (all); Map 1838, 3 chns, by J.M. Davey, Canterbury; foot/b'way, waterbodies, houses, woods (by annotation), arable (by annotation), grassland (by annotation), hops (by annotation), gardens (by annotation), park, building names, quarries or pits; title and acreage summary cartouches and ruler-style scale bar are litho-printed and pasted on.

17/371 Tonbridge (parish) TQ 597447
Apt 03.03.1841; 15235a (15235); Map 1838, 4 chns, in 8 parts, by W. Brown, Tonbridge, (including two urban parts at 1 chn and four indexes); waterbodies, building names, road names, mills, brick yard, river lock, wharf, pot kiln, powder mills, turnpike gates. (The map in PRO IR 30 is a copy; original is in PRO IR 77/42.)

17/372 Tonge (parish) TQ 938634 [Not listed]
Apt 23.12.1836; 1619a (all); Map 1837?, 3 chns, by William Huntly, Dovor; construction lines, foot/b'way, waterbodies, farmyards (col), woods (col), arable (col), grassland (col), orchards (col), hops (col), gardens (col), hedge ownership, fence ownership, sea wall, rickyard, boundary tree; north pointer has sketchy plumes and oak-leaf boss; a rickyard is depicted with haystacks.

17/373 Trotterscliffe (parish) TQ 644603 [Trottiscliffe]
Apt 22.10.1841; 1160a (all); Map 1841, 3 chns, 1st cl, by James Renshaw, 8 Union Court, Old Broad St; construction lines, foot/b'way, waterbodies, woods (by name), plantations, building names, 'Temple of the Druids', chalk pits, prominent tree (by symbol).

17/374 Tudeley (parish) TQ 629448
Apt 30.06.1843; 1592a (1605); Map 1844, 4 chns, in 4 parts, by M. Brady, 55 Chester St, Kennington Lane, London, (includes index); railway with bridge earthworks, turnpike roads and gate, waterbodies, houses, woods (col), orchards (col), gardens (col), pit, glebe, farm names; colours may show property ownerships or holdings.

17/375 Tunstall (parish) TQ 897614
Apt 12.11.1839; 1196a (all); Map 1838, 3 chns, 1st cl, in 2 parts, by Alexander Doull; construction lines, foot/b'way, waterbodies, houses, building names, boundary trees and marks, chalk pit, gatehouse, pond, stile, woods (by name), park.

17/376 Ulcomb (parish) TQ 853487 [Ulcombe]
Apt 11.08.1838; 3520a (3529); Map 1838, 3 chns, 1st cl, in 2 parts, by Thomas Thurston, Ashford, (including 40-chn construction line diagram); construction lines, foot/b'way, waterbodies, houses, hops, field boundary ownerships, field gates, field acreages, building names, boundary trees (by symbol), stiles, rectory; drains across fields are shown by pecked double lines. Apt has in-bound and out-bound quantities.

17/377 Upchurch (parish) TQ 852689
Apt 31.12.1841; 3619a (all); Map 1843?, 3 chns, 1st cl, by Alexander Doull; construction lines, waterbodies, houses, road names, grave yard, drains, sea wall, boundary stones, windmill, sand pit, navigation beacon, pools.

17/378 Waldershare (parish) TR 293484 [Not listed]
Apt 30.06.1843; 999a (1242); Map 1844, 3 chns, 1st cl, in 2 parts, by John Cheesman, Charlton; construction lines, foot/b'way, waterbodies, houses.

17/379 Walmer (parish) TR 374504
Apt 07.02.1843; 939a (1079); Map 1844, 2 chns, in 2 parts, by William Holtum, Walmer; foot/b'way, houses, woods, plantations, gardens, hedge ownership, castle, ancient encampment, ruins, pound, hospital, barracks, pit, high and low water marks, 'Stones Foot' (on beach), capstans, sea cliffs, foreshore rocks.

17/380 Waltham (parish) TR 115484
Apt 14.11.1840; 3215a (3215); Map 1840, 3 chns, in 4 parts, by Small and Son, Dovor; foot/b'way, waterbodies, houses, building names, boundary trees (col); some names are written upside down; meaning of 'L' in some fields is uncertain.

17/381 Warden (parish) TR 019718
Apt 03.02.1846; 257a (all); Map 1846, 3 chns, 1st cl, by Thomas W. Collard, Canterbury; waterbodies, woods, gardens, pier or jetty.

17/382 Warehorne (parish) TQ 989331
Apt 02.03.1843; 2869a (2870); Map 1842, 3 chns, 1st cl, in 3 parts, by Thomas Thurston, Ashford, (including 30-chn construction line diagram); construction lines, foot/b'way, canal with embankment, waterbodies, houses, woods (col), field boundary ownerships, field gates, building names, boundary trees (col), rectory, windmill (by symbol), footbridges; drains are uncoloured, and drains across fields are shown by pecked double lines; numerals of uncertain purpose appear alongside field boundaries; there is a note that marsh sewers are coloured blue 'and are not measured into the fields' and that red bands show boundary of Romney Marsh. Apt has in-bound and out-bound quantities.

17/383 Wateringbury (parish) TQ 685536
Apt 05.03.1840; 1420a (all); Map 1839, 6 chns, in 2 parts, surveyed by Thomas Brown in 1828, and revised by Henry Williams, 19 Romney Place, Maidstone.

17/384 St Werneth, or Hoo (parish) TQ 791728
Apt 18.01.1840; 4822a (6032); Map 1839, 3 chns, 1st cl, by Samuel Elliott; construction lines, waterbodies, houses, woods, windmill, high water mark, embankments, gravel pit.

17/385 Westbere (parish) TR 198610
Apt 22.06.1837; 1185a (1185); Map surveyed in 1838, 3 chns, 1st cl, by George Hurst, Canterbury; construction lines, foot/b'way, waterbodies, houses, farmyards (col), woods (col), arable (col), grassland (col), orchards (col), hops (col), marsh/bog (col), hedge ownership, field gates, stiles, pits (col), garden walls (red), drains (uncoloured).

17/386 Westerham (parish) TQ 450525
Apt 19.10.1843; 5677a (5676); Map 1844?, 6 chns, waterbodies, building names, turnpike gate, Pilgrim Road.

17/387 Westwell (parish) TQ 979476
Apt 25.09.1841; 5199a (5199); Map not dated, 3 chns, 1st cl, in 2 parts, by Thomas Thurston, Ashford, (including 30-chn construction line diagram); construction lines, hill-drawing, foot/b'way, waterbodies, houses, woods (col, named), hops, field gates, building names, lime kilns, 'Pilgrims Path', chalk pits, chapel, workhouse, windmill, boundary stones (by symbol), water mill and wheel, heath; drains across fields are shown by double-pecked lines; numerals of uncertain purpose appear alongside field boundaries.

17/388 Whitfield (parish) TR 305459
Apt 14.02.1843; 893a (all); Map 1842, 4 chns, by John Cheesman, Buckland, copied from map made in 1824; foot/b'way, waterbodies, houses, woods, plantations, field gates, stiles, turnpike gates.

17/389 Whitstable (parish) TR 122647
Apt 19.06.1840; 3610a (4075); Map 1842?, 3 chns, 1st cl, in 3 parts, by Frederick and Henry E. Drayson; construction lines, railway, waterbodies, houses; colours are used to brace tithe areas; meaning of colour-tinted fields is uncertain.

17/390 East Wickham (parish) TQ 467765
Apt 10.11.1842; 885a (all); Map 1838, 3 chns, 1st cl, by W. Hubbard, Dartford; construction lines, foot/b'way, waterbodies, houses, woods

(col), parkland (col), orchards, gardens (col, some by Dawson's symbol), fences, field boundary ownerships, milestone, springs, stiles, green; colours may show property ownerships.

17/391 West Wickham (parish) TQ 395646
Apt 22.12.1838; 2645a (all); Map 1840, 3 chns, 1st cl, by Murrell R. Robinson, Otford Castle, nr 7 Oaks; construction lines, hill-drawing, turnpike roads, waterbodies, houses, woods, building names, parsonage, pits, tree at road junction.

17/392 Wickhambreux (parish) TR 231608
Apt 24.04.1838; 2310a (2310); Map 1839, 3 chns, in 2 parts, copied with renumbered fields from a map by J. Grist of 1828, by George Quested, Ash; foot/b'way, waterbodies, field gates, building names, ferry.

17/393 Willesborough (parish) TR 030422
Apt 29.08.1839; 1457a (all); Map 1837, 3 chns, by William Williams, Ashford; construction lines, foot/b'way, waterbodies, houses, farmyards (col), woods (col), plantations (col), arable (col), grassland (col), orchards (col), hops (col), gardens (col), heath/moor (col), hedge ownership, fence ownership, field gates, pits or quarries, workhouse; ash plantations are shown with a special 'spreading tree' symbol. Apt has in-bound and out-bound quantities.

17/394 Wilmington (parish) TQ 526717
Apt 11.09.1841; 1715a (all); Map 1840?, 3 chns, 1st cl, by F. and H.E. Drayson; construction lines, waterbodies, houses, heath, common; it is unclear why some fields are tinted.

17/395 Wingham (parish) TR 247572
Apt 11.06.1840; 2642a (2641); Map 1840, 3 chns, by Small and Son, Buckland, Dovor; waterbodies, houses, building names; some names are written upside down.

17/396 Witchling (parish) TQ 916552 [Wichling]
Apt 31.12.1841; 1310a (all); Map 1841, 3 chns, by Jas Drewry; construction lines, waterbodies, houses, building names, parsonage, churchyard.

17/397 Wittersham (parish) TQ 894275
Apt 27.09.1838; 3601a (3601); Map 1839, 3 chns, 'Copied' by J.S. Thomson, Tenterden; waterbodies, farmyards (col), woods (col), arable (col), grassland (col), orchards (col), fences, field gates; combination of orchard with brown or green tint may show dual land use.

17/398 Woodchurch (parish) TQ 941354
Apt 19.12.1838; 6949a (6949); Map surveyed in 1839, 3 chns, 1st cl, in 5 parts, by J. McLachlan, Stowmarket, Suffolk; construction lines, foot/b'way, turnpike roads and gate, waterbodies, houses, building names, road names, boundary trees and posts, rectory, green, windmills (by symbol), chapel, park, woods (by name); colour bands may show property ownerships; pecked lines within field perimeters may indicate either ploughing margins or inbound-outbound. Apt has in-bound and out-bound quantities.

17/399 Woodnesborough (parish) TR 304571
Apt 26.09.1840; 2944a (all); Map 1841?, 3 chns, 1st cl, by Thomas White Collard, Canterbury; construction lines, waterbodies, houses, woods, orchards, building names, drains (uncoloured).

17/400 Woolwich (parish) TQ 431785
Apt 30.09.1846; 1116a (1596); Map 1847?, 3 chns, by George Hudson, Woolwich, (tithable parts only in detail); waterbodies, woods (col), field gates, building names, road names, spring, barracks, battery, observatory, rotunda, repository, landmark trees.

17/401 Wootton (parish) TR 235465
Apt 22.01.1841; 1020a (1019); Map 1840, 3 chns, 1st cl, by Thomas Cooper, Canterbury; construction lines, foot/b'way, waterbodies, houses, woods (named), plantations, hops, building names, rectory, limekiln, windmill (pictorial), pound, glebe, park; cross-hatching may show a glass-house.

17/402 Wormshill (parish) TQ 877575
Apt 27.06.1839; 1467a (all); Map 1840?, 3 chns, 1st cl, by Frederick and Henry E. Drayson; construction lines, chalk pit.

17/403 Worth (parish) TR 358571
Apt 10.01.1840; 6147a (7431); Map 1843?, 3 chns; foot/b'way, houses, high water mark, battery, sea and river banks (yellow).

17/404 Wouldham (parish) TQ 723642
Apt 19.04.1842; 1532a (all); Map 1838, 3 chns, by Alexander Doull; construction lines, waterbodies, houses, building names, wharf, ferry, parsonage, boundary trees and post, chalk pits, ancient fort (named in gothic), smithy, woods (by name), saltings, common, glebe; meaning of colour-bands is unclear.

17/405 Wrotham (parish) TQ 621571
Apt 06.03.1841; 8878a (8878); Map 1839?, 3 chns, 1st cl, in 4 parts; construction lines, foot/b'way, waterbodies, houses, woods (some col), building names, mill, paper mill, boundary trees and stones, garden paths, tithe-free areas, glebe (pink); meaning of multi-colour bands is unclear. (One part of the map in PRO IR 30 is a copy; original is in PRO IR 77/99, and is unfit for production.)

17/406 Wye (parish) TR 057463
Apt 15.06.1841; 7282a (7282); Map 1840, 3 chns, 1st cl, in 2 parts, by J.M. Davey, Canterbury; foot/b'way, waterbodies, woods (by name), houses, building names, road names, chalk pits, limekiln, well, mill, windmill (by symbol), college, dog kennel, Giants Grave, Roman camp, tithery boundaries, boundary trees (by symbol); plain oval cartouche containing summary acreages and a ruler-style scale bar have been printed separately and pasted on.

17/407 Yalding (parish) TQ 698479
Apt 23.05.1844; 5812a (5804); Map 1840, 3 chns, 1st cl, by F. and H.E. Drayson; railway, foot/b'way, waterbodies, building names; rivers are identified by letter rather than by name.

Lancashire

PRO IR29 and IR30 18/1-354

469 tithe districts: 1,207,594 acres
354 tithe commutations: 763,265 acres
198 voluntary tithe agreements, 156 compulsory tithe awards

Tithe and tithe commutation

In 1836, 75 per cent of Lancashire tithe districts by number, though less than two thirds of the county by area, were subject to payment of tithes (Fig. 30). Only sixty-four districts were wholly tithable; as elsewhere in northern England, the main cause of exemption was a modus payment in lieu of tithes (in 66 per cent of districts). Other reasons for exemption were the merger of tithes in the land, exemption by prescription, and exemption of some woodland.

Assistant tithe commissioners and local tithe agents who worked in Lancashire are listed in Table 18.1 and the valuers of tithe rent-charge in Table 18.2. No one tithe valuer was particularly dominant and most came from within the county or close to it. Exceptionally, five valuations were by James Birrell of Gretna, Dumfriesshire, two were by John Lawrence of Leicester, and ten by the Tithe Commission. These last were undertaken in default of valuations being lodged by landowners within the statutory six-month period and are mostly commutations of residual tithable lands in what were substantially tithe-free districts.

Lancashire is on the northern fringe of the main concentration of tithe apportionments which include field-by-field records of crops grown on the arable land; crops are recorded in a substantial proportion (13 per cent) of the county's apportionments. Lancashire tithe apportionments are also somewhat more informative than the average on other land uses; descriptions of grassland include, for example, 'old meadow', 'clover', 'rye grass', 'vetches', 'meadow and oats', 'old convertible pasture', and 'clover arable'. Unusual land uses or descriptions include accommodation land at Ardwick, 'woody pasture' at Caton, and 'rabbit pasture' at Formby. The apportionment for Over Wyersdale is divided into vacheries which are defined on the tithe map.

Tithe maps

About one-sixth of the 354 tithe maps of Lancashire are sealed as first-class and construction lines are present on 6 per cent of the second-class maps. The proportion of

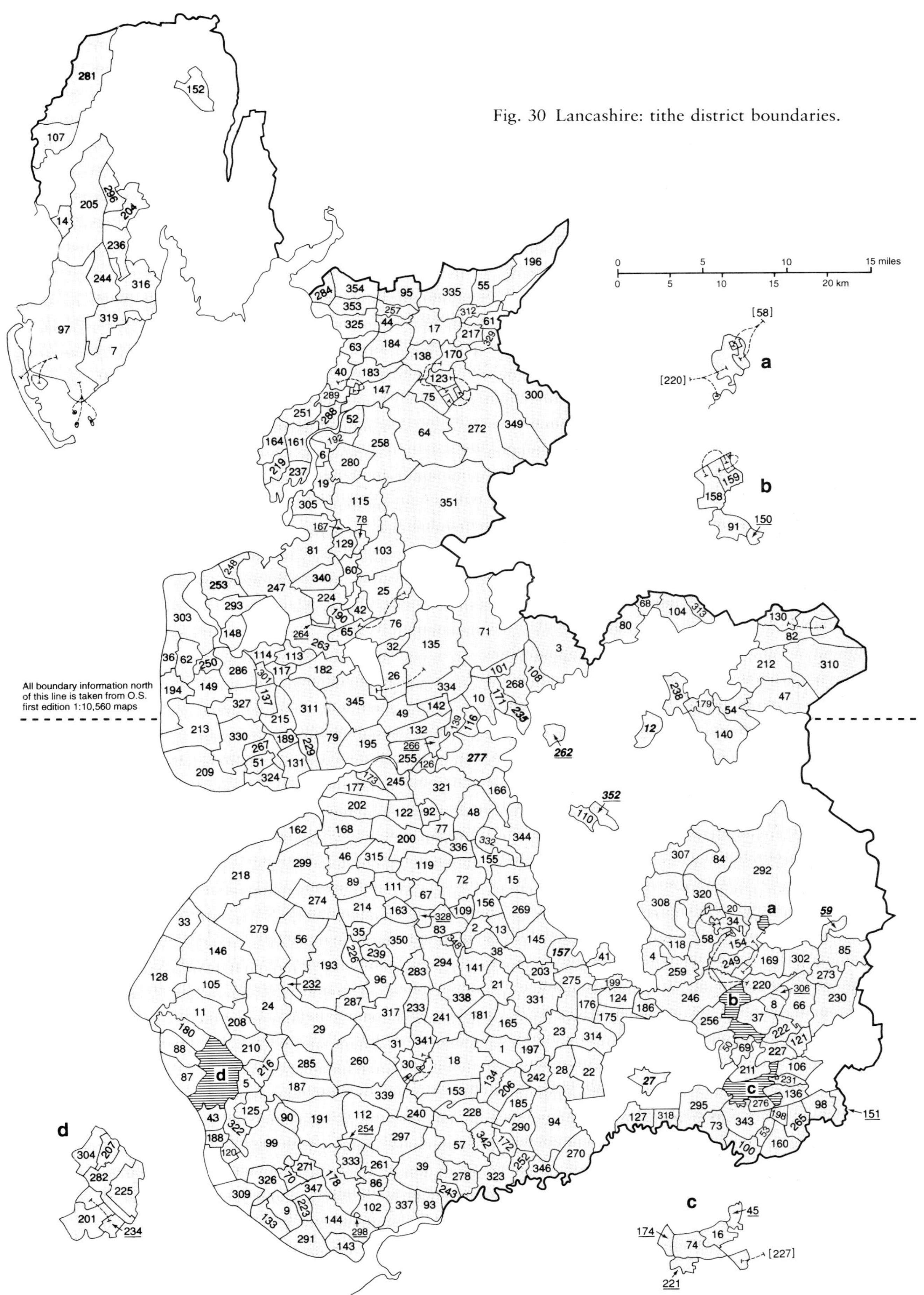

Fig. 30 Lancashire: tithe district boundaries.

first-class maps is unusually high and can be explained partially by the fact that some maps in this county were made by the Ordnance Survey between 1842 and 1846 and are all first class. If these maps produced by Ordnance Survey surveyors are discounted, the proportion of first-class maps is about 8 per cent, a figure comparable with the adjoining county of Cheshire. There was a peak of tithe map production in Lancashire in 1839 and periods of heightened activity in 1846 and 1849; the last map was not received until 1874 and is the third from last of all English and Welsh tithe maps (Table 18.4).

It was alleged by contemporaries that a good deal of copying and enlarging of Ordnance Survey material was done by tithe map-makers but if the number of Lancashire tithe maps at inch-related rather than chain-related scales is any guide, the practice was not very usual. Only fifteen maps, less than 5 per cent of the total, are at inch-related scales. With some maps, however, an Ordnance Survey derivation is quite clear. At Little Bolton a published map has been annotated and at Barton a careful transcript was made and acknowledged.

Other of the county's tithe map-makers include a number of civil engineers, for example J. F. Bateman of Manchester, who noted on his first-class plan of Alkrington that 'trial lines were run in testing the accuracy of an existing plan, and then formed the base lines of the new survey'.

Scales of Lancashire tithe maps vary from one inch to 1.33 chains (the Ordnance Survey standard of five feet to one mile), to one inch to 13.33 chains (the Ordnance Survey standard of six inches to one mile). Three fifths are in the recommended scale range of one inch to three to four chains. Three maps are at the scale of one inch to 4.4 chains (one inch to three Cheshire chains of 32 yards). It is possible that other maps recorded in the catalogue of Lancashire tithe maps at the 4.5 chain scale were in fact drawn at one inch to 4.4 chains but have been affected by subsequent paper shrinkage. Eleven Lancashire tithe maps are at the little-used five-chain scale (Table 18.3).

Lancashire tithe maps, in common with those of other northern counties, are more satisfactory as records of industrial than of agricultural land use. The Ordnance Survey tithe maps record no land use at all and in that respect are inferior to the published six-inch maps. Ordnance Survey tithe maps are distinguished by the way that they depict small details such as sun-dials, pumps and sheepfolds which otherwise are rarely recorded on tithe maps. About 26 per cent of Lancashire tithe maps record industrial land use and a number record industrial waste such as the 'pit hills' on the map of Wigan. Turnpike roads appear on nearly 19 per cent of Lancashire tithe maps, a very high proportion even allowing for the fact that this industrialised county would have had a rather higher mileage of turnpikes than more agricultural counties. The mapping of woodland, on 77 per cent of maps, and of parkland, on 28 per cent, is also a high proportion especially considering the systematic omission of this information from the Ordnance Survey tithe maps. Unusual features on Lancashire tithe maps include coastal reclamation at Warton with Lindeth, the dating of the survey of high water mark at Formby, the racecourse at Aintree, and a maypole at Scarisbrick.

Some 279 Lancashire tithe maps in the Public Record Office collection can be attributed to a particular map-maker. The Ordnance Survey supplied three-chain mapping of about 8 per cent of the county and the most prolific private surveyor was Andrew Halliday of

Preston, who produced fifteen maps (Table 18.2). Ordnance Survey work was concentrated in particular areas; for example, its surveyors mapped seven of the ten townships in the parish of Standish but made no maps at all in Furness or the Fylde.

Lancashire tithe maps, with the exception of those by the Ordnance Survey, are notable for their decoration; some 14 per cent have decorative borders, sometimes with leaf motifs or floral corners, and a number have decorated compass roses and cartouches.

Table 18.1. *Agreements and awards for commutation of tithes in Lancashire*

Assistant commissioner/ local tithe agent	*Number of agreements**	*Number of awards*
John Job Rawlinson	18	73
Thomas Martin	82	0
Joseph Townsend	0	61
Henry Martin	32	0
John Penny	30	0
Charles Howard	11	17
Richard Burton Phillipson	24	0
Horace William Meteyard	0	3
Thomas Sudworth	2	0
George Wingrove Cooke	0	1
John Mee Mathew	0	1
John Selby Donaldson Selby	1	0

*Computed from the number of extant reports on tithe agreements in the tithe files [PRO IR 18].

Table 18.2. *Tithe valuers and tithe map-makers in Lancashire*

Name and address (in Lancashire unless indicated)	*Number of districts*	*Acreage*
Tithe valuers		
Joseph Newton, Preston	24	66,917
William Rothwell, Winwick	16	28,360
Reuben Ledger, West Derby	13	18,812
William Talbot, Burton in Kendal, Westmorland	10	23,292
Thomas Wilcock, Hothersal	10	19,209
Tithe Commissioners	10	5,557
Henry Fisher, Carleton	9	24,388
Richard Thornton, Manchester	9	19,823
Henry Atkinson, Hutton le Hay, Westmorland	8	27,876
Andrew Halliday, Preston	8	22,444
Henry White, Warrington	8	18,818
William Lamb, Hay Carr, Ellel	8	15,311
John Watson junior, Kendal, Westmorland	8	11,118
John Young, Liverpool	7	26,589
Jonathan Bennison, Liverpool	7	20,466
William Benson, Bury	5	18,198
James Birrell, Gretna, Dumfriesshire	5	16,060
James Woods, Liverpool	5	13,130
Barton Fletcher Allen, Preston	5	12,236
Alexander Bannerman, Chorley	5	7,945
Charles Robert Brady, Stockport, Cheshire	5	2,963
Others [105]	169	345,753
Attributed tithe map-makers		
Ordnance Survey*	28	70,367
Andrew Halliday, Preston	15	29,371
John Watson junior, Kendal, Westmorland	13	25,167
Charles Birket	12	38,562
William Rothwell, Winwick	10	20,579
Richard Thornton, Manchester	9	18,091
Phillip Park, Preston	9	14,615
William Bell, Manchester	8	23,438
Jonathan Bennison, Liverpool	7	15,740
Robert Dobson, Preston	7	3,213
John Young, Liverpool	6	23,968
Henry White, Warrington	6	20,244
John Robinson, Keldray, near Ulverston	6	13,962
Thomas Addison junior, Preston	6	13,440
Others [69]	127	260,715

*The total for the Ordnance Survey includes only manuscript maps of undoubted Ordnance Survey provenance; it does not include maps by other authors based on OS work.

Table 18.3. *The tithe maps of Lancashire: scales and classes*

Scale in chains/inch	*All maps*		*First Class*		*Second Class*	
	Number	*Acreage*	*Number*	*Acreage*	*Number*	*Acreage*
>3	6	7,572	1	1,858	5	5,714
3	171	354,153	51	121,954	120	232,199
3.6, 3.75	2	2,968	0	0	2	2,968
4	39	85,879	4	16,468	35	69,411
4.4, 4.5	14	37,335	0	0	14	37,335
5	11	26,499	0	0	11	26,499
5.45	1	2,324	0	0	1	2,324
6	65	157,310	0	0	65	157,310
6.67	5	1,000	0	0	5	1,000
8	18	50,737	0	0	18	50,737
<8	22	37,488	0	0	22	37,488
TOTAL	354	763,265	56	140,280	298	622,985

Table 18.4. *The tithe maps of Lancashire: dates*

	<1837	*1837*	*1838*	*1839*	*1840*	*1841*	*1842*	*1843*	*1844*	*1845*	*1846*	*1847*	*1848*	*1849*	*>1849*
All maps	1	11	31	51	38	15	19	16	16	26	34	22	17	30	26
1st class	0	0	1	4	2	3	8	3	2	12	11	3	2	2	3
2nd class*	1	11	30	47	36	12	11	13	14	14	23	19	15	28	23

*One second-class tithe map of Lancashire in the Public Record Office collection is undated.

Lancashire

18/1 Abram (township in parish of Wigan) SD 615010
Apt 28.02.1839; 1966a (all); Map 1844, 3 chns, 1st cl, by R. Kellet, Wigan; construction lines, railways, foot/b'way, canal with towpath, waterbodies, houses, woods, plantations, parkland, orchards, building names, drains.

18/2 Adlington (township in parish of Standish) SD 598130
Apt 30.09.1842; 1062a (1062); Map 1842, 3 chns, 1st cl, by Ordnance Survey; construction lines, railway, foot/b'way, canal with towpath, waterbodies, houses, rock outcrops, fences, building names, road names, garden paths, school house, National School, Methodist Chapel, toll bar, print works, village pump, quarries, blacking mills, aqueduct, well; bridges named.

18/3 Aighton, Bailey and Chaighley (townships in parish of Mitton) SD 685405 [Not listed]
Apt 24.06.1846; 49a (5780); Map 1850, 3 chns, by E.J. Welch, Whalley (tithable parts only; includes index); foot/b'way, woods, plantations, field gates, building names, landowners; bridge named.

18/4 Ainsworth (township in parish of Middleton) SD 762097
Apt 27.03.1839; 1296a (all); Map 3 chns, surveyed in 1838 for James Whitehead, Tipping Place, (Little) Bolton, by Thos Bird, 8 Chatham Street, Picadilly, Manchester; hill-drawing, foot/b'way, turnpike roads, toll bar, waterbodies, woods, building names, mill, lodge, new mill, old mill, quarry and limekilns.

18/5 Aintree (township in parish of Sefton) SJ 378985
Apt 07.03.1843; 826a (825); Map 1845, 6 chns, 'reduced from one made by Mr Henry Singleton of Liverpool in 1838, with corrections up to the present time' ? by R. Ledger; foot/b'way, turnpike roads, canal with towpath, waterbodies, woods, building names, road names, mill, wharves, cock pit, stands, grand stand, stables. Apt has cropping information.

18/6 Aldcliffe (township in parish of Lancaster) SD 464602
Apt 12.06.1843; 13a (652); Map 1847, 2 chns, in 5 parts, by John Watson junr, Kendal, (including 16-chn index); waterbodies, houses, arable (yellow), grassland (pink), orchards, gardens (green), landowners; north pointer has Prince of Wales feathers.

18/7 Aldingham (parish) SD 270710
Apt 22.01.1846; 4694a (4694); Map 1846, 3 chns, by John Huddleston, Pewborough; construction lines, waterbodies, houses, open fields, drains, coastline; legend explains depiction of buildings and boundaries; map title has leafy surround.

18/8 Alkrington (township in parish of Prestwich cum Oldham) SD 872048 [Not listed]
Apt 17.12.1838; 191a (788); Map 1840, 4 chns, 1st cl, by J.F. Bateman; construction lines, waterbodies, woods, field boundary ownerships, moss (col), field acreages, ownership boundaries (col); there is a note: 'Trial lines were run in testing the accuracy of an existing plan, and then formed the base lines of the new survey'.

18/9 Allerton (township in parish of Childwall) SJ 402865
Apt 13.02.1840; 1531a (all); Map 1839, 3.75 chns, by Edwd Eyes, Junr, Liverpool; waterbodies, woods, parkland (in detail), gardens, building names, road names, priory, obelisk, stone quarry, lodges. Apt has cropping information.

18/10 Alston (within Alston with Hathersall) (township in parish of Ribchester) SD 610350 [Not listed]
Apt 20.07.1837; 1989a (all); Map 1837, 6 chns; hill-drawing, railway, foot/b'way, waterbodies, woods, plantations, parkland, orchards, building names, ford, chapels. Apt has cropping information.

18/11 Altcar (parish) SD 338058 [Great Altcar]
Apt 06.06.1848; 4079a (4284); Map 1848?, 8 chns, in 2 parts, (including eight 3-chn enlargements of detail); foot/b'way, waterbodies, houses, woods (named), open fields, building names, road names, drains, schools, sand pit, kennel, quarry, pinfold, smithy; bridges, moss, sandy waste and marshland named. Apt has cropping information.

18/12 Altham (township in parish of Whalley) SD 769319
Apt 26.04.1842; 8a (1406); Map 1847?, 3 chns; turnpike roads, toll bar, field gates, building names, field names, landowners.

18/13 Anderton (township in parish of Standish) SD 622127
Apt 13.04.1843; 1175a (1175); Map 1844, 6 chns, by A. Halliday, Preston; waterbodies, woods, quarry. Apt omits some field names.

18/14 Angerton (extra-parochial place) SD 222838
Apt 30.06.1840; 773a (?); Map 1840?, 3 chns, 'copied... from a plan surveyed by Mr Gibson 1806' by J.V. Higgin; hill-drawing, foot/b'way, field boundary ownerships, building names, landowners (col), limekiln, marsh and moss (by annotation). Apt omits land use.

18/15 Anglezark (township in parish of Bolton le Moors) SD 631166 [Not listed]
Apt 23.11.1844; 110a (1279); Map 1849, 13.33 chns, by R.W. Dobson, Preston (tithable parts only); waterbodies, woods, building names, mill, moor.

18/16 Ardwick (township in parish of Manchester) SJ 861972
Apt 29.11.1844; 338a (all); Map 1846, 3 chns, 1st cl, by Ordnance Survey (tithable parts only); construction lines, trig points, railways, tram ways, turnpike roads, toll bar, waterbodies, drains, building names, road names, weir, bowling green, garden paths, summer house, greenhouse, steel yards, weigh houses, brick kilns, firebrick and chimmey pot factory, rope walks, factory, chemical works, weighing machines, engine house, ventilation shaft, chimney, shafts, spindle works, lime kilns, powder magazine, lamp, well, cemetery, tombs, ruins, school. Apt omits land use.

18/17 Arkholme with Cawood (township in parish of Melling) SD 573722
Apt 06.05.1848; 3022a (3022); Map 'surveyed in 1848, and the Dales staked out on the ground in April and May 1849', 6 chns, in 2 parts, by Geo. Wolfenden, Kirkby Lonsdale, ('Dales and c' on Arkholme Wastes at 3 chns); foot/b'way, waterbodies, farmyards, woods, plantations, marsh/bog, building names, road names, waste, moor; bridge named.

18/18 Ashton within Mackerfield (township in parish of Winwick) SD 570003 [Ashton-in-Makerfield]
Apt 09.07.1838; 5558a (5557); Map 1838, 4.5 chns, 'copied from a map in the possession of Sir John Gerard Bart with amendments', by Jonn. Binns, Lancaster; foot/b'way, waterbodies, woods, plantations, parkland, mill dam, demesne lands (col), heath; houses and gardens unnumbered, and possibly tithe-free. Apt has cropping information.

18/19 Ashton with Stodday (township in parish of Lancaster) SD 466573 [Not listed]
Apt 20.10.1840; 147a (1439); Map 1842, 6 chns, by Jonn. Binns, Lancaster; foot/b'way, canal with towpath, waterbodies, woods, plantations, parkland (in detail), deer park, marsh/bog, sand banks (by symbol), building names, green; double lines may be walls; note explains that tithable lands are red, and the Duke of Hamilton's tithe-merged lands are uncoloured.

18/20 Ashworth (township in parish of Middleton) SD 841137 [Not listed]
Apt 27.06.1839; 68a (all); Map 1840, 2 chns, by Samuel Taylor, 30, Cooper Street, Manchester; construction lines, hill-drawing, foot/b'way, waterbodies, woods (named), plantations, building names, field names, landowners, smithy, Sunday School; map is described as of the lands 'belonging to Wilbraham Egerton Esq'.

18/21 Aspull (township in parish of Wigan) SD 617073
Apt 27.06.1839; 1879a (1879); Map 1840, 6 chns, by R. Thornton; canal, waterbodies, woods, heath/moor, building names, road names, green, moated houses.

18/22 Astley (township in parish of Leigh) SJ 700990
Apt 31.12.1845; 2628a (2628); Map 1846?, 3 chns; railway, foot/b'way, canal with towpath, waterbodies, houses, woods.

18/23 Atherton (township in parish of Leigh) SD 670030
Apt 03.01.1839; 2324a (2323); Map 1839, 1 inch to 120 yards, (5.45 chns, 1:4320), litho (by Bolton, Warrington); railway, foot/b'way, waterbodies, woods, parkland (in detail), building names, coal pit, demesne lands (col); built-up part hand-coloured and unnumbered. Apt omits land use.

18/24 Aughton (parish) SD 398068
Apt 29.09.1843; 4463a (4462); Map 1848, 3 chns, by J. Young; hill-drawing, railway, waterbodies, woods, plantations, building names, road names, Roman Catholic Chapels, brewery, mill, road embankments, sand or stone pits, tithe-free moss and hill pasture (by annotation), greens; bridge named; double lines may be stone walls.

18/25 Barnacre (hamlet in parish of Garstang) SD 520457 [Not listed]
Apt 26.08.1839; 3396a (3395); Map 1839, 5 chns; hill-drawing, railway, foot/b'way, canal with towpath, waterbodies, woods, plantations, orchards, field gates, building names, mill, stone quarry; colours may show ownership or tithable status. Apt has cropping information.

18/26 Barton (township in parish of Preston) SD 525375
Apt 10.09.1846; 203a (2536); Map 1847, 13.33 chns, 'copied from the Ordnance Plans' by Thornbarrow and Singleton, Preston; railway, viaduct, foot/b'way, waterbodies, woods, plantations, parkland (named), orchards, gardens, building names, road names, landowners, chapel, manor house, ulverts, brick pit, tile kiln, tan pits, wells, weir, smithy, pipes, ruins, fords, corn mill, mill race, sand pits, swallow holes; tithable lands are numbered and tinted, and tithe-free land is not; legend explains symbols, and gives ownership, acreage and tithable value of tithable lands.

18/27 Barton upon Irwell (township in parish of Eccles) SJ 757973 [Barton Upon Irwell]
Apt 30.06.1849; 70a (10530); Map 1852?, 14 chns; canal (named), aqueduct, building names, road names, tramroad. Apt has cropping information and refers to colour coding on the map.

18/28 Bedford (township in parish of Leigh) SJ 675985
Apt 13.03.1846; 2439a (2438); Map 1847, 13.33 chns (tithable parts only); railway, foot/b'way, canal with towpath, waterbodies, woods, tithe-free land (col). Apt has cropping information and refers to colouring on the map.

18/29 Bickerstaffe (township in parish of Ormskirk) SD 450040
Apt 27.06.1839; 6354a (6353); Map 1838, 4.5 chns, copied by Wm Benson, Bury, land and mine surveyor; foot/b'way, waterbodies, woods, marsh/bog, road names, windmill (pictorial); hill named.

18/30 Billinge, Chapel End (township in parish of Wigan) SJ 529999 [Billinge]
Apt 04.10.1838; 1129a (all); Map 1842, 3 chns, by R. Thornton; hill-drawing, foot/b'way, waterbodies, woods (col), orchards, heath/moor, building names, road names, beacon, parsonage, Catholic Chapel, chapel.

18/31 Billinge, Higher End (township in parish of Wigan) SD 521017 [Billinge]
Apt 04.10.1838; 1550a (all); Map 1842, 3 chns, by R. Thornton; foot/b'way, waterbodies, woods (col), parkland, orchards, heath/moor (col), rock outcrops, building names, road names, school, quarry, moss (col).

18/32 Bilsborough (township in parish of Garstang) SD 527403 [Bilsborrow]
Apt 26.06.1840; 842a (all); Map 1841, 3 chns, by T. Howson, Blackburn; hill-drawing, railway with embankments, foot/b'way, waterbodies, woods, orchards, hedges, field gates; road destinations given.

18/33 Birkdale (township in parish of North Meols) SD 325145
Apt 27.03.1845; 2236a (all); Map 1845, 3 chns, 1st cl, by A. Halliday and H. Hyde; construction lines, hill-drawing, foot/b'way, waterbodies, woods, common, high water mark 19th August 1845, sand hills (by annotation), rabbit warrens.

18/34 Birtle cum Bamford (township in parish of Middleton) SD 834129
Apt 15.01.1845; 1389a (1388); Map 1846, 4 chns, by William Rothwell, Winwick; foot/b'way, waterbodies, woods, building names, weirs (named), war office.

18/35 Bispham (township in parish of Croston) SD 486129 [Bispham Green]
Apt 19.06.1840; 926a (926); Map 1845, 3 chns, 1st cl, in 2 parts, by Ordnance Survey (including 6-inch (13.33 chn, 1:10,560) triangulation diagram); construction lines (on diagram only), foot/b'way, waterbodies, houses, field gates, building names, road names, draw well, well, free grammar school, green; bridges named.

18/36 Bispham with Norbreck (township in parish of Bispham) SD 315405
Apt 16.07.1847; 1639a (2624); Map 1848, 3 chns, in 3 parts, by W. Gregson, Kirkham, Lancs, (including 6-inch (13.33 chn, 1:10,560) index, tinted); construction lines, hill-drawing, railway and station, foot/b'way, waterbodies, woods, building names, coastline, milestone, school; double lines may be drains.

18/37 Blackley, otherwise Blakeley (township in parish of Manchester) SD 855035
Apt 10.12.1844; 1765a (all); Map 1846?, 3 chns; foot/b'way, waterbodies, woods, plantations, parkland, field gates, building names, site of old mill, mills, reservoirs, Methodist Chapel, print works, bleach works, workhouse, chapel, well, weir; bridges named; legend explains depiction of roads, buildings, waterbodies and footpaths.

18/38 Blackrod (township in parish of Bolton le Moors) SD 620100
Apt 16.07.1839; 2368a (2367); Map 1840, 3 chns, by T. Addison; hill-drawing, railway, foot/b'way, waterbodies, woods, parkland, orchards, gardens (sketchy), heath/moor, building names, bowling green, sand or stone pits, bleach works, moss (col); double lines may be drains.

18/39 Bold (township in parish of Prescot) SJ 540900 [Bold Heath]
Apt 16.04.1840; 4339a (4338); Map 1840, 8 chns; foot/b'way, waterbodies, woods, parkland, building names, smithy, windmill, moated houses, heath. Apt has cropping information.

18/40 Bolton le Sands (township in parish of Bolton le Sands) SD 482679 [Bolton-le-Sands]
Apt 06.03.1845; 1572a (1571); Map 1846, 6 chns, in 2 parts, 'corrected' by J.F. Clarkson, (village at 3 chns); hill-drawing, railway, foot/b'way, turnpike roads, canal with towpath, waterbodies, woods, parkland, building names, road names, coastline, cliffs, pound, vicarage, tithe barn, school, summer house, mill, mill dam, tan yard, cinder ovens, roads passable at low water; lands coloured green are tithe-free when in the hands of the owner.

18/41 Little Bolton (manor in parish of Bolton-le-Moors) SD 715097 [Not listed]
Apt 30.01.1845; 443a (1450); Map part of published Ordnance Survey 1:10,560 sheet Lancashire sheet 87, surveyed 1844-7, with tithe area annotations. Apt is by holding and omits land use.

18/42 Bonds (township in parish of Garstang) SD 499442
Apt 12.03.1846; 921a (921); Map 1846, 4 chns, by Willm Lamb; railway with embankments, foot/b'way, turnpike roads, canal with towpath, waterbodies, woods, orchards, building names, castle, mill, drains. Apt omits some land use.

18/43 Bootle cum Linacre (township in parish of Walton on the Hill) SJ 342955
Apt 30.11.1839; 1171a (1781); Map 1839, 4.5 chns, compiled from 'Plans in the possession of Lord Derby; and the Additions and Alterations surveyed at the present time' by Jonn. Bennison, Liverpool; turnpike roads, toll bar, canal with towpath, waterbodies, woods, building names, road names, priory, waterworks, hotel; bridge named.

18/44 Borwick (township in parish of Warton) SD 532730
Apt 14.06.1845; 836a (836); Map 1846, 3 chns, 'copied and revised' by John Watson junr, Kendal; hill-drawing, foot/b'way, turnpike roads, canal, waterbodies, woods, plantations, parkland, orchards, building names, road names, lodge, boathouse, public stone quarry, boundary stone, drains.

18/45 Bradford (township in parish of Manchester) SJ 872986
Apt 29.11.1844; 280a (all); Map 1845, 3 chns, by T. Gaskell; canal with towpath, waterbodies, woods, parkland, public houses, public park and walks (col) named and highlighted in colour.

18/46 Bretherton (township in parish of Croston) SD 479207
Apt 30.11.1838; 2405a (2405); Map 1838, 3 chns, by J.J. Myres, Preston, copied by R. James; hill-drawing, waterbodies, woods, parkland, orchards; double lines may be drains; meadow land is divided into strips.

18/47 Briercliffe with Extwisle (township in parish of Whalley) SD 893346 [Not listed]
Apt 26.04.1842; 4269a (4180); Map 1850, 3 chns, 1st cl, by William Bell and Henry O'Hagan; construction lines, foot/b'way, waterbodies, building names, factories.

18/48 Brindle (parish) SD 600243
Apt 04.10.1838; 2936a (all); Map 1838, 8 chns, litho (Standidge) with MS additions; hill-drawing, foot/b'way, canal, waterbodies, woods, parkland. Apt has cropping information.

18/49 Broughton (township in parish of Preston) SD 540340
Apt 10.10.1839; 2347a (2346); Map 1839?, 3 chns, by James Carter Bibby, 28, Butlers Court, Fishergate, Preston; hill-drawing, foot/b'way, turnpike roads, waterbodies, woods, plantations, parkland, orchards, field gates, turnpike gate, pinfold; legend explains symbols; decorative border.

18/50 Broughton with Kersall (township in parish of Manchester) SD 829011
Apt 29.11.1844; 170a (960); Map 1849?, 6.67 chns, by Edward Wollett Wilmot, surveyor and land agent, Congleton, (tithable parts only in detail, tinted); waterbodies, woods, parkland, field boundary ownerships, building names, old race course, dye works, moor.

18/51 Bryning with Kellamergh (township in parish of Kirkham) SD 397298
Apt 27.06.1839; 1043a (1043); Map 1839, 3 chns, copied by A. Halliday; hill-drawing, foot/b'way, waterbodies, orchards, field gates, drains.

18/52 Bulk (township in parish of Lancaster) SD 493633 [Not listed]
Apt 22.03.1843; 1147a (1147); Map 1843, 4 chns; hill-drawing, foot/b'way, turnpike roads, canal with towpath, aqueduct, waterbodies, houses, woods (col), plantations (col), orchards, building names, road names, weirs; one owner signs, adopting the map. Apt has cropping information.

18/53 Burnage (township in parish of Manchester) SJ 865925
Apt 29.11.1844; 659a (all); Map 1845, 4 chns, by Charles Robert Brady, Castle Farm, Stockport; foot/b'way, waterbodies, woods, orchards, open fields, building names, road names, guide post.

18/54 Burnley (township in parish of Whalley) SD 845325
Apt 26.04.1842; 1785a (1839); Map 1844, 4 chns, by H. Merryweather, Burnley; foot/b'way, turnpike roads, toll bar, canal with towpath, waterbodies, woods (named), plantations (named), parkland (in detail), field gates, building names, road names, free grammar school, new market place, waterworks reservoir, parsonage, Wesleyan Chapel, gas works, print works, dock, mill, keepers lodge, fish pond, ropewalk; bridge named; colours may show land ownership or tithable status.

18/55 Burrow (township in parish of Tunstall) SD 628768 [Nether Burrow and Over Burrow]
Apt 31.12.1850; 2371a (all); Map 1849, 6 chns, 'corrected to the present date and copied' by Geo. Wolfenden, Kirkby Lonsdale; waterbodies, woods, plantations, parkland (named), hedges, building names, corn mill, ford, tithe barn, barns; colour bands may be property boundaries.

18/56 Burscough (township in parish of Ormskirk) SD 428128
Apt 28.03.1845; 4959a (4959); Map 1846?, 3 chns, 1st cl, in 3 parts, by Ordnance Survey; railway, foot/b'way, turnpike roads, toll bar, milestone, finger post, canal with towpaths, waterbodies, houses, field gates, building names, road names, tithe barn, abbey house, priory ruins, old quarry, school, pinfold, wells, pumps, boundary stones, kennel, drains, mills, wind mill; bridges named; double lines may be drains; woodland and moss are named. Apt has cropping information.

18/57 Burtonwood (township in parish of Warrington) SJ 578918
Apt 23.09.1837; 4145a (4144); Map 1838, 3 chns, made for tithe commutation by H. White and R. Ledger, Warrington; railways, foot/b'way, canal, waterbodies, woods, plantations, field gates, building names, pottery, chapel. Apt has cropping information.

18/58 Bury (township) SD 809107
Apt 10.10.1837; 2307a (2370); Map 1840?, 3 chns, by Wm Burton, Bury, Lancs; foot/b'way, turnpike roads, toll bars, waterbodies, woods, plantations, parkland, orchards, rock outcrops, fences, building names, weirs, quarries, Unitarian Chapel, pottery, workhouse, mills, colliery, gas works; bridges named; built-up parts not mapped. Legend explains symbols.

18/59 Butterworth (township in parish of Rochdale) SD 932120 [Not listed]
Apt 17.09.1846; 1248a (?); Map 1851?, 6 chns, in 2 parts, (including Milnrow at 3 chns); railway, foot/b'way, turnpike roads, canal with towpath, waterbodies, woods (col), plantations (col), building names, road names, reservoir, mills, school, bleach works, colliery, lordship/freehold boundary. Apt omits land use and some field names, and summary uses customary measure.

18/60 Cabus (and part of Nether Wyersdale) (township in parish of Garstang) SD 488478
Apt 03.11.1843; 2309a (?); Map 1844, 3 chns, by John Lawson; hill-drawing, railway, canal with towpath, waterbodies, woods, orchards, building names, factory, smithy, chapel, school, township boundaries; district is described as 'the Tithes of which belongs to Charles Standish Esqre and Thomas Butler Cole Esqre'.

18/61 Cantsfield (township in parish of Tunstal) SD 627730
Apt 24.01.1845; 1222a (1221); Map 1845?, 3 chns, 1st cl, in 3 parts, by Ordnance Survey; construction lines, trig points, turnpike roads, toll gate, milestones, waterbodies, houses, building names, road names, castle, malt kiln, mill, drains, boundary trees and stones, weir, moat, watering trough, old lime kiln, wells, saw pit, tithe barn, school, pump, pump boiler, waterfalls; bridges and plantation named.

18/62 Carleton (township in parish of Poulton le Fylde) SD 333397
Apt 30.08.1839; 1973a (1979); Map 1838, 3 chns, by Lovat; foot/b'way, waterbodies, woods, field gates, building names, road names, landowners; title is surrounded by drawing of stone column and woodland.

18/63 Carnforth (township in parish of Warton) SD 500704
Apt 14.06.1845; 1454a (1492); Map 1846, 6 chns, by John Watson junr, Kendal; hill-drawing, railway, foot/b'way, canal, waterbodies, woods, plantations, building names, tithe barn, post office, coastline, boundary stones, drains; hill named.

18/64 Caton (township in parish of Lancaster) SD 560620
Apt 30.05.1843; 8374a (8373); Map 1843, 3 chns, 1st cl, in 6 parts, by Ordnance Survey; construction lines, trig points (named), turnpike roads, waterbodies, houses, rock outcrops, field gates, building names, road names, school, post office, summer house, arbour, parsonage, Wesleyan Chapel, Calvinist Chapel, chapel, cotton mills, warehouse and school, silk mills, bobbin mill, forge, old flag quarry, freestone quarry, quarries, slate quarry, old slate quarries, coal shafts, threshing mill, mill, barns, sheep folds, pump, waterfalls, springs, cairns, boundary marks, pinfold, ruin, turf bog, green, poor's land and houses; woodland, moss and marsh are indicated by name; bridges and physical features named.

18/65 Catteral (township in parish of Garstang) SD 489422 [Catterall]
Apt 30.09.1845; 1733a (1733); Map 1846 (Higher Division), 1847 (Lower Division), 3 chns, 1st cl, in 2 parts, by R.W. Dobson, Preston; construction lines, hill-drawing, railway, foot/b'way, waterbodies, woods, orchards, building names, ruins, cotton factory, worsted mill, saw mill, mill dam, stone quarries; bridges named; double lines may be drains.

18/66 Chadderton (township in parish of Prestwich cum Oldham) SD 900060
Apt 28.09.1839; 2978a (2978); Map 1840, 3 chns, in 2 parts, by Henry Wood, Brown Lodge nr Rochdale; railway, canal, waterbodies, woods, heath/moor, fences, building names, reservoir, mill.

18/67 Charnock Richard (township in parish of Standish) SD 552162
Apt 30.09.1842; 1949a (1948); Map 1842, 3 chns, 1st cl, by Ordnance Survey; construction lines, railway, waterbodies, houses, rock outcrops, building names, road names, quarries, coal works; bridges named.

18/68 Chatburn (township in parish of Whalley) SD 772445
Apt 19.06.1845; 21a (720); Map 1852?, 3 chns; railway, foot/b'way, turnpike roads, woods, building names, field names and acreages. Apt omits land use.

18/69 Cheetham (township in parish of Manchester) SD 844007
Apt 29.11.1844; 919a (all); Map 1846?, 3 chns, 1st cl, by Ordnance Survey; construction lines, trig points (named), turnpike roads, toll bars, milestones, waterbodies, houses, fences, building names, road names, chapels, Presbyterian Churches, grave yards, schools, brewery, corn mill, paper mill, dye works, gasometer, rope walks, brick kilns, water wheel, bowling greens, wire works, print works, pump, reservoirs, weir, wells, culverts, sheds, palings (by annotation); bridge named. Apt omits land use.

18/70 Childwall (township in parish of Childwall) SJ 417892
Apt 13.03.1845; 828a (all); Map 1846, 3 chns, 1st cl, by James Woods, Liverpool; construction lines, railway, waterbodies, woods, parkland, orchards, heath/moor, boundary stones.

18/71 Chipping (parish) SD 615415
Apt 27.06.1839; 8757a (8756); Map 1840, 6 chns, in 2 parts, by Chas Birket; hill-drawing, foot/b'way, waterbodies, woods, heath/moor.

18/72 Chorley (township in parish of Chorley) SD 585175
Apt 29.09.1843; 3571a (3571); Map 1839, 3 chns, in 2 parts, by Wm Forshaw, (including Chorley town at 1.5 chns); railway, foot/b'way, canal, waterbodies, woods, parkland, road names, market place.

18/73 Chorlton cum Hardy (township in parish of Manchester) SJ 819932 [Chorlton-cum-Hardy]
Apt 21.02.1845; 1266a (all); Map 1847, 4 chns, by William Rothwell, Winwick; foot/b'way, waterbodies, woods, plantations, parkland, building names.

18/74 Chorlton on Medlock (township in parish of Manchester) SJ 845965 [Not listed]
Apt 29.11.1844; 297a (all); Map 1849, 6.67 chns, (12-inch; 1:5280), 'enlarged from the Ordnance Map of six inches to a mile' by E. Nicholson, 18 Princess Street, Manchester, architect and surveyor, and examined by C.R. Brady, land valuer and agent, Mile End, Stockport; waterbodies, building names, road names, union chapel and school.

18/75 Claughton (parish) SD 569656
Apt 26.06.1846; 1550a (all); Map 1847?, 6 chns, 'compiled from Plans of Estates'; foot/b'way, woods, heath/moor, building names, corn mill, school.

18/76 Claughton (township in parish of Garstang) SD 526425
Apt 27.03.1838; 3701a (3700); Map 1838, 6 chns, by William Lamb; hill-drawing, railway, foot/b'way, turnpike roads, turnpike house, canal with towpath, waterbodies, woods, parkland (in detail), gardens, field gates, building names (some in gothic), chapel, school, factory, workhouse, quarry. Apt has cropping information.

18/77 Clayton le Woods (township in parish of Leyland) SD 569228 [Clayton-le-Woods]
Apt 27.06.1838; 1450a (1450); Map 1838, 5 chns, by A. Halliday; foot/b'way, waterbodies, woods, orchards, building names.

18/78 Cleveley (township in parishes of Garstang and Cockerham) SD 500513 [Not listed]
Apt 11.12.1844; 202a (597); Map 1844, 3 chns, by Willm Lamb; hill-drawing, railway, turnpike roads, waterbodies, woods, orchards, building names, mill, chapel, weir, school, drains; colour bands may indicate tithable status.

18/79 Clifton with Salwick (township in parish of Kirkham) SD 467312
Apt 10.08.1839; 3411a (3776); Map 1840?, 9 chns; railway, foot/b'way, canal, waterbodies, woods, building names, mill, sand (by annotation); scale is stated to be 6 chns, but has been corrected in pencil.

18/80 Clitheroe (township in parish of Whalley) SD 745422
Apt 29.10.1842; 2324a (2324); Map 1847?, 6 chns, in 2 parts, (built-up parts at 1.5 chns); foot/b'way, waterbodies, woods, plantations, building names, factory, barns; bridges and park named.

18/81 Cockerham (township in parish of Cockerham) SD 459509
Apt 08.05.1848; 105a (4860); Map 1850, 4 chns, by Willm Lamb; waterbodies, woods, orchards, building names, field names, landowners, drains. Apt omits some field names.

18/82 Colne (township in parish of Whalley) SD 915415
Apt 26.04.1842; 4575a (4575); Map 1845?, 6 chns, in 22 parts, (town at 1 chn; other enlargements at 1, 1.5 and 3 chns); canal, waterbodies, building names, mills, brewery, old engine houses, lock house, reservoir, barns; a note says the dimensions of a large reservoir are taken from an old map made before the reservoir was constructed.

18/83 Coppul (township in parish of Standish) SD 564139 [Coppull]
Apt 30.09.1842; 2279a (2279); Map 1842, 3 chns, 1st cl, by Ordnance Survey; construction lines, railway, waterbodies, houses, building names, road names, wells; woodland and bridges named.

18/84 Cowpe Lenches, New Hall Hey and Hall Carr (township in parish of Bury) SD 825189 [Cowpe]
Apt 07.02.1840; 1546a (1545); Map 1839, 3 chns, 'copied... from the original survey taken 1835 by Messrs Lowe and Bake, Ashton-under-Lyne' by Thomas Wainwright; hill-drawing, foot/b'way, waterbodies, farmyards, woods, plantations, common, rock outcrops, building names, reservoirs, mills, stone quarries, old stone quarries, engine; red lines may be stone walls.

18/85 Crompton (township in parish of Prestwich cum Oldham) SD 941096 [Not listed]
Apt 06.11.1845; 2865a (2864); Map 1847, 3 chns, 1st cl, in 2 parts, by Ordnance Survey; construction lines, turnpike roads, toll gates (named), waterbodies, building names, bowling green, grand stand, parsonage, Methodist Chapel, Refuge Chapel, Ebenezer Chapel, chapels, National Schools, workhouse, mills, thread mill, old mill, gas works, warehouse, collieries, old colliery.

18/86 Cronton (township in parish of Prescot) SJ 495885
Apt 16.04.1840; 1122a (1121); Map 1843, 8 chns, revised from a map by Jno. Maughan, 1808, by John Daglish, land and mine surveyor, St Helens; waterbodies, woods, building names, sand or stone pit, quarry, old tanhouse.

18/87 Great Crosby (township in parish of Sefton) SJ 319996
Apt 18.05.1843; 2119a (5267); Map 1844, 3 chns; foot/b'way, waterbodies, woods, building names, road names, hotel, boundary marks.

18/88 Little Crosby (township in parish of Sefton) SD 314019
Apt 07.03.1843; 1812a (6241); Map 1844, 3 chns, by James Woods; foot/b'way, waterbodies, plantations, parkland, field gates, building names, light house, boys and girls schools, museum, folly, dog kennels, chapel; meaning of colours is unclear.

18/89 Croston (township in parish of Croston) SD 490180
Apt 09.04.1838; 2344a (2343); Map 1837, 3 chns, by W. Forshaw; hill-drawing, foot/b'way, turnpike roads, waterbodies, woods, osiers, parkland, field gates, building names, road names, corn mill, river embankments, old river courses, rectory, school, dungeon, property boundaries (col); legend explains some symbols. Apt has cropping information.

18/90 Croxteth Park (district) SJ 418949
Apt 17.10.1838; 953a (953); Map 1838, 6 chns; foot/b'way, waterbodies, woods, plantations, parkland, building names, road names, mill, dog kennel, ice house, water pipes to Croxteth Hall; map is described as of land 'belonging to the Rt Hon The Earl of Sefton'.

18/91 Crumpsall (township in parish of Manchester) SD 843023
Apt 29.11.1844; 733a (all); Map 1846, 3 chns, 1st cl, by Ordnance Survey; construction lines, foot/b'way, turnpike roads, toll bar, milestones, direction posts, waterbodies, houses, fences, field gates, building names, road names, lodge, weirs, sluice, reservoirs, drains, smithy, print works, bleach works, cotton mill, dye works, office, bleaching ground, sheds, pumps, wells, culverts, nursery, bowling green, schools, chapel, burial ground, Wesleyan Methodist Chapels, palings (by annotation).

18/92 Cuerden (township in parish of Leyland) SD 560246 [Not listed]
Apt 12.04.1838; 800a (800); Map 1839, 5 chns, by A. Halliday; foot/b'way, waterbodies, woods, parkland, building names. Apt gives summary acreages in customary measure.

18/93 Cuerdley (township in parish of Prescot) SJ 544863 [Cuerdley Cross]
Apt 16.04.1840; 1538a (1717); Map 1842, 4.5 chns, partly surveyed by Henry White, Warrington; hill-drawing, foot/b'way, canal, waterbodies, houses, woods, field gates, building names, road names, embankment, wharf, marsh (by name); scale is also given as 1 inch to 3 Cheshire chns; there is a note: 'This map is made from one in the possession of Sir Richard Brooke Bart dated 1804, with corrections up to the present time, - excepting the Marsh, Canal, River and Doe Green, which parts are from actual Survey by H. White in 1842, and excepting fields above the canal which were formerly part of the Marsh which are taken from a plan made a few years ago by Mr Taylor of Holywell'. Apt has cropping information.

18/94 Culcheth (township in parish of Winwick) SJ 653942
Apt 30.04.1838; 5362a (5361); Map 1838, 4 chns, by R. Thornton, Manchester; railway, foot/b'way, waterbodies, woods (col), parkland, orchards, heath/moor, moss (named), building names, chapel.

18/95 Dalton (township in parish of Burton) SD 550760
Apt 24.05.1837; 2136a (2135); Map 1839?, 6 chns; foot/b'way, turnpike roads, canal, woods, parkland, building names, road names, barn, tithe barn, mill.

18/96 Dalton (township in parish of Wigan) SD 493083
Apt 28.02.1839; 2091a (2090); Map 1842, 3 chns, by T. Addison junr; hill-drawing, foot/b'way, waterbodies, woods, plantations, parkland, orchards, heath/moor, building names, beacon, quarries, sand or stone pits, green (col).

18/97 Dalton in Furness (parish) SD 220730 [Dalton-in-Furness]
Apt 30.12.1840; 13059a (16364); Map 1842, 3 chns, in 7 parts, by John Robinson, Dalton (including index); construction lines, foot/b'way, turnpike roads, toll bar, waterbodies, woods (named), plantations, parkland, open fields, field gates, building names, mill, mine works, tile works, smithy, abbey ruins, parsonage, chapel, school, castle ruins, lighthouse, manor, rabbit warren, common, tithe barn; islands and marshes named; there is a note that unnumbered areas belong to the Rt Hon William Earl of Burlington.

18/98 Denton (township in parish of Manchester) SJ 914949 [Not listed]
Apt 29.11.1844; 1647a (all); Map 1849, 4.5? chns, by William Rothwell, Winwick, surveyor, valuer and land agent; railways, foot/b'way, waterbodies, plantations, fences, building names, road names, chapel; scale is written in yards (10 per inch), with '4.5' added later in pencil.

18/99 West Derby (township in parish of Walton on the Hill) SJ 400930
Apt 27.03.1839; 6124a (6123); Map 'surveyed in 1835 and corrected to Novr. 1838', 3 chns, in 2 parts, by Jonathan Bennison, Liverpool; railway, foot/b'way, waterbodies, woods, parkland, gardens, zoological and botanical gardens, building names, road names, chapels, Liverpool parliamentary boundary; bridge named. Apt omits land use.

18/100 Didsbury (township in parish of Manchester) SJ 848912
Apt 22.02.1845; 1527a (1527); Map 1848?, 4 chns, by F. Tinker, Hyde; waterbodies, woods, plantations, building names, road names, weir, college; bridge named.

18/101 Dilworth (township in parish of Ribchester) SD 627380 [Not listed]
Apt 17.04.1838; 1226a (1226); Map 1837, 3 chns, by P. Park, Preston; hill-drawing, railway, foot/b'way, waterbodies, woods, plantations, building names, factory, quarry.

18/102 Ditton (township in parish of Prescot) SJ 498859
Apt 23.06.1842; 1883a (2072); Map 1844, 3 chns, 1st cl, by Joseph Barwise; foot/b'way, waterbodies, woods, parkland, field gates, building names, road names, 'Line for a new road but now laid aside'; goblet surmounts map title. Apt omits some field names.

18/103 Dolphinholme House, Scabgill, Foxhouses, Gregories, Birkenhead and Bournes in the township of Nether Wyersdale (district in parish of Garstang) SD 517500 [Dolphinholme]
Apt 15.12.1838; 2766a (?); Map 1839, 6 chns (tithable parts only); hill-drawing, foot/b'way, waterbodies, woods, plantations, parkland, building names, mill, bobbin mill, district or tithery boundaries (col); some physical features named. Apt omits land use.

18/104 Downham (township in parish of Whalley) SD 798437
Apt 18.02.1850; 39a (1870); Map 1852?, 6 chns; building names. Apt omits some land use.

18/105 Downholland (township in parish of Halsall) SD 355075 [Downholland Cross]
Apt 07.08.1844; 3474a (all); Map 1843?, 3 chns, 1st cl, in 3 parts, by Ordnance Survey; hill-drawing, canal with towpath, waterbodies, houses, rock outcrops, field gates, building names, road names, river embankments, pounds, wells, weighing machines, pipes, forges, sandstone quarry, old quarry, pumps, saw pit, milestone, boundary stones; hill and bridges named.

18/106 Droylsden (township in parish of Manchester) SJ 896989
Apt 29.11.1844; 1611a (1611); Map 1847, 4 chns; railways and station house, foot/b'way, turnpike roads, toll house, canal with towpath, waterbodies, building names, road names, colliery, dye works, cotton mills, print works, weir, tithable status boundary.

18/107 Dunnerdale (township in parish of Broughton in Furness) SD 212921
Apt 03.03.1846; 174a (?); Map 1849, 6 chns, in 2 parts, by Geo. Robinson, (tithable parts at 6 chns, location map at 24 chns); foot/b'way, woods, building names.

18/108 Dutton (township in parish of Ribchester) SD 659377 [Not listed]
Apt 19.12.1838; 1810a (1809); Map 1837, 8 chns; foot/b'way, waterbodies, woods, plantations. (The map in PRO IR 30 is a photocopy of Diocesan copy.) Apt has cropping information.

18/109 Duxbury (township in parish of Standish) SD 585150 [Not listed]
Apt 30.09.1842; 1012a (1011); Map 1842, 3 chns, 1st cl, by Ordnance Survey; construction lines, railway, waterbodies, houses, corn mill, smithy, building names, collieries, forge, sand or stone pits, print works, fences (by annotation); bridges named.

18/110 Eccleshill (township in parish of Blackburn) SD 702232 [Not listed]
Apt 24.11.1843; 792a (792); Map 1843?, 3 chns; foot/b'way, waterbodies; double lines may be walls.

18/111 Eccleston (township) SD 522173
Apt 18.05.1841; 2085a (2085); Map 1841, 3 chns, 1st cl, by Messrs Watson and Turner, Kendal; construction lines, foot/b'way, turnpike roads, toll bar, waterbodies, woods, orchards, building names, rectory, ornamental ground.

18/112 Eccleston (township in parish of Prescot) SJ 486950
Apt 07.05.1840; 3312a (3387); Map 1842?, 8 chns, litho (by T. Bolton); canal, waterbodies, woods, building names, road names, copper works.

18/113 Great Eccleston (township in parish of St Michael on Wyre) SD 435401
Apt 24.10.1838; 1413a (1412); Map 1839?, 6 chns; foot/b'way, waterbodies, woods, building names, Catholic Chapel, chapel, school.

18/114 Little Eccleston with Larbreck (township in parish of Kirkham) SD 408405
Apt 14.08.1839; 1108a (1198); Map 1839, 6 chns, by Alexr Bannerman; foot/b'way, waterbodies, gardens, building names, mill, mill site; acorn and oak leaf decorate north pointer.

18/115 Ellel (township in parish of Cockerham) SD 501547
Apt 12.12.1844; 2648a (5620); Map 1845, 4 chns, in 3 parts, by Willm Lamb, (includes Dolphinholme at 1 chn and Galgate at 2 chns); hill-drawing, railway and embankments, canal with towpath, waterbodies, woods, plantations, building names, landowners, mill, school, chapel, grange; colour bands may show ownerships. Apt omits some land use.

18/116 Elston (township in parish of Preston) SD 600326
Apt 16.11.1837; 934a (934); Map 1837, 6 chns, 'compiled from the estate maps of the Land Owners' by P. Park, Preston; foot/b'way, waterbodies, woods, plantations, gardens, building names (ornate); red band shows gardens. Apt has cropping information.

18/117 Elswick (township in parish of St Michael on Wyre) SD 422384
Apt 27.06.1839; 984a (1009); Map 1839?, 6 chns; foot/b'way, waterbodies, woods, parkland, building names, sand hole.

18/118 Elton (township in parish of Bury) SD 790115
Apt 12.04.1838; 2522a (2521); Map 1840?, 3 chns, in 2 parts, by Wm Benson, Bury, Lancs, (including enlargements of detail); hill-drawing, foot/b'way, turnpike roads, toll bar, canal, waterbodies, woods, plantations, fences, building names, reservoir, weir, mill, stone quarries, workhouse; bridge named; legend explains symbols; table summarises land-use acreages.

18/119 Euxton (township in parish of Leyland) SD 553193
Apt 08.10.1846; 2927a (2924); Map 1847, 3 chns, by Thomas Addison junr, Preston; hill-drawing, railway with stations and embankments, foot/b'way, waterbodies, woods, parkland, orchards, building names, cotton mill, sand or stone pits.

18/120 Everton (chapelry in parish of Walton on the Hill) SJ 360920
Apt 01.05.1845; 246a (700); Map 1846, 2 chns, from 'actual survey' by James Woods, Liverpool; waterbodies, woods, plantations, parkland (in detail), gardens (in detail), rock outcrops, building names, road names, Roman Catholic Church, Methodist Chapels, bowling green, bridewell, post office, tax office, collegiate institution, workhouse, quarries, reservoirs; meaning of pink tint is unclear; elaborate leafy border surrounds map.

18/121 Failsworth (township in parish of Manchester) SD 900012
Apt 29.11.1844; 1064a (all); Map 1847, 4 chns, by F. Tinker, Hyde; foot/b'way, turnpike roads, canal with towpath, waterbodies, building names, road names, print works, mill, pole, Roman road.

18/122 Farington (township in parish of Penwortham) SD 535245
Apt 07.07.1842; 1787a (1786); Map 1839, 6 chns; railway, foot/b'way, occupation roads, waterbodies, woods, plantations, parkland.

18/123 Farleton (township in parish of Melling) SD 581672
Apt 16.05.1848; 1036a (1036); Map 1849?, 5 chns; turnpike roads, turnpike house, woods, plantations, building names, Roman camp (named in gothic).

18/124 Farnworth (township in parish of Deane) SD 730058
Apt 11.03.1845; 52a (1450); Map 1850, 13.33 chns, by Geo. Piggot, Bolton, (tithable parts only); railway, turnpike roads, toll bar, waterbodies, woods, building names, road names, National School; bridge named. Colours may be owners.

18/125 Fazakerley (township in parish of Walton on the Hill) SJ 383963
Apt 01.05.1845; 1688a (1688); Map 1846, 6 chns, by H. White, Warrington; railways, foot/b'way, waterbodies, woods, plantations, parkland, orchards, building names, road names, school, pinfold; bridge named. There is a note, 'This plan is partly compiled from Estate Plans, reduced to one uniform scale, and corrected up to the present time - and partly from Actual Survey'.

18/126 Fishwick (township in parish of Preston) SD 561293
Apt 24.11.1843; 673a (672); Map 1843, 3 chns, 'copied' by P. Park, Preston; waterbodies, woods, plantations, building names, road names; bridges named.

18/127 Flixton (township) SJ 742945
Apt 13.08.1842; 1576a (1575); Map 1843, 3 chns, 1st cl, by W. Gregson, Kirkham, Lancs; construction lines, foot/b'way, waterbodies, building names, parsonage, new parsonage, chapel, workhouse, beershops, mill, rafts, river locks, tan house; bridge named.

18/128 Formby (township in parish of Walton on the Hill) SD 300090
Apt 04.04.1845; 6704a (15264); Map 1845, 3 chns, 1st cl, by A. Halliday and H. Hyde; construction lines, foot/b'way, water-bodies, woods, parkland, open fields, building names, ancient Catholic burying ground, Catholic Chapel, windmill, brewery, pinfold, coastline, headland, boat house, flag post, high water mark August 1845, sand hills (by annotation), rabbit warren; double lines may be drains.

18/129 Forton (part of) (township) SD 490510
Apt 23.10.1844; 271a (1278); Map 1846, 4 chns, by Willm Lamb, (tithable lands only); turnpike roads, canal with towpath, waterbodies, woods, orchards, building names, landowners, chapel, lime kilns.

18/130 Foulridge (township in parish of Whalley) SD 893427
Apt 25.02.1842; 2451a (2450); Map 1846, 3 chns, 1st cl, in 2 parts, by Whitle and Dawson, Whalley near Preston, (including Foulridge at 1.5 chns); construction lines, foot/b'way, canal, waterbodies, field gates, building names, reservoirs, distillery, corn mill, stone quarry; bridge named; double lines may be drains; a boundary running through a reservoir is noted as taken from Mr Greenwood's plan of Colne township.

18/131 Freckleton (township in parish of Kirkham) SD 432295
Apt 27.06.1839; 1775a (all); Map 1838, 3 chns, by P. Park, Preston; hill-drawing, foot/b'way, waterbodies, woods, field gates, building names.

18/132 Fulwood (township in parish of Lancaster) SD 549322
Apt 13.05.1847; 2078a (2077); Map 1847, 3 chns; railway, waterbodies, woods, plantations, orchards, Board of Ordnance lands (col). Apt omits some field names.

18/133 Garston (township in parish of Childwall) SJ 395850
Apt 07.03.1842; 1628a (3293); Map 1840, 3 chns, 1st cl, by Jonn. Bennison; construction lines, foot/b'way, waterbodies, woods, parkland (in detail), building names, road names, Methodist Chapel, Catholic Chapel, mill dam, salt works, lodges.

18/134 Golborne (township in parish of Winwick) SJ 609983
Apt 28.04.1837; 1634a (1634); Map 1838, 3 chns, by Charles Mawson, Warrington; hill-drawing, railways, waterbodies, houses, woods, parkland (named), building names, road names, field names, landowners, mills, green, walled garden; colours show property ownership.

18/135 Goosnargh with Newsham (township in parish of Kirkham) SD 565405
Apt 19.12.1848; 8643a (9290); Map 1849, 4 chns, 1st cl, by William Bell and Henry O'Hagan, Resident Engineer, Bolton, Blackburn, Clitheroe and West Yorkshire Railway, Blackburn; construction lines, railway, foot/b'way, canal with towpath, waterbodies, building names, corn mills, hospital, Independent Chapel, Roman Catholic Chapel.

18/136 Gorton (township in parish of Manchester) SJ 884962
Apt 29.11.1844; 1429a (all); Map 1846?, 4 chns; railways, turnpike roads, canal with towpath, waterbodies, woods, building names, road names, race ground, crescent, chapel, bleach works, factory; bridge named. Apt omits land use.

18/137 Greenalgh (hamlet in parish of Kirkham) SD 407356 [Greenhalgh]
Apt 27.06.1839; 1147a (all); Map 1838, 3 chns, by W. Gregson and G. Garlick, Greenalgh; foot/b'way, waterbodies; legend explains symbols.

18/138 Gressingham (township in parish of Lancaster) SD 568695
Apt 16.09.1844; 1934a (1934); Map 1845, 6 chns; waterbodies, woods, plantations.

18/139 Grimsargh with Brockhole (township in parish of Preston) SD 587340
Apt 19.04.1842; 1945a (1945); Map 1841, 3 chns, in 3 parts, by H. Bibby, (including 6-chn index); hill-drawing, railway, foot/b'way, turnpike roads, toll bar, waterbodies, woods, parkland, orchards, field gates, building names, quarry; legend explains symbols.

18/140 Habergham Eaves (township in parish of Whalley) SD 840310
Apt 26.04.1842; 4007a (4007); Map 1844, 9 chns, by Richd Holden, Burnley, land agent and surveyor; hill-drawing, foot/b'way, canal with towpath, woods, plantations, parkland, field gates, building names, racecourse, chapels, barracks, old turnpike, gas works, lime kiln, mills, school, quarry; bridges named; colours may indicate property ownership.

18/141 Haigh (township in parish of Wigan) SD 593089
Apt 22.09.1838; 2110a (all); Map 1840?, 5 chns, 'copied by R. Thornton

from a survey taken by James Leigh, 1796'; canal, building names, mill, iron works, ford; Apt is by holding and no fields are shown.

18/142 Haighton (township in parish of Preston) SD 565345 [Haighton Green]
Apt 10.10.1839; 1054a (1054); Map 1840, 6 chns, by A. Halliday, Preston; waterbodies, woods, building names, chapel.

18/143 Hale (township in parish of Childwall) SJ 465825
Apt 21.04.1841; 1626a (?); Map 1843?, 6 chns, (including enlargement of detail); hill-drawing, waterbodies, woods (col, named), parkland, building names, road names, bowling green, bathing house, decoy, dungeon, salt works, windmill, glebe (col); meaning of colour bands is unclear. Apt has cropping information.

18/144 Halewood (township in parish of Childwall) SJ 460850
Apt 09.03.1840; 3760a (3759); Map 1843, 6 chns, 'corrected from plans in the possession of the landowners' by John Young, Liverpool; hill-drawing, foot/b'way, waterbodies, woods, building names, road names, workhouse, brewery; bridges named.

18/145 Halliwell and Horwich (townships in parish of Deane) SD 655115
Apt 28.11.1845; 183a (2320); Map 1851, 14 chns, by R.W. Dobson, Preston, (tithable parts only, tinted); turnpike roads, waterbodies, building names, road names, print works. Apt omits some field names.

18/146 Halsall (township in parish of Halsall) SD 350120
Apt 30.08.1844; 6997a (all); Map 1843, 3 chns, 1st cl, in 6 parts, by Ordnance Survey; construction lines, hill-drawing, canal with towpath, waterbodies, houses, fences, building names, road names, old stone cross, windmill, pound, smithies, school house, finger post, rectory, quarry; bridges named.

18/147 Halton (parish) SD 522665
Apt 28.03.1838; 3738a (3738); Map 1839, 3 chns, by J. Tayler; foot/b'way, canal with towpath, waterbodies, woods (col), building names, chapel, school, furnace, aqueduct, limekilns; bridge named; meaning of colours is uncertain.

18/148 Hambleton (township in parish of Kirkham) SD 378424
Apt 18.11.1839; 1323a (1603); Map 1839, 3 chns, by Rob. Jervis; foot/b'way, waterbodies, modus meadow (col); legend explains symbols.

18/149 Hardham with Newton (township in parish of Poulton) SD 351370
Apt 18.10.1839; 2605a (2605); Map 1838, 4 chns, by Thos Hull; construction lines, railway, waterbodies; legend explains symbols.

18/150 Harpurhey (township in parish of Manchester) SD 859015
Apt 29.11.1844; 193a (all); Map 1846, 3 chns, 1st cl, by Ordnance Survey; construction lines, turnpike roads, turnpike house, waterbodies, houses, fences, building names, road names, post office, reservoirs, cotton mills, print works, print shop, offices, sheds, machines, drying shed, bleaching ground, wells, pumps, bowling green, graveyard, boatshed, ruin, fences (by annotation), wooden bridge.

18/151 Haughton (township in parish of Manchester) SJ 932948 [Haughton Green]
Apt 29.11.1844; 887a (all); Map 1845, 3 chns, 1st cl, by Ordnance Survey; construction lines, foot/b'way, waterbodies, houses, marsh/bog, building names, road names, milestone, hat factories, dyewood factory, gasometer, old coal pits, cotton mills, weighing machine, rope walk, collieries, pumps, sluices, school, quarry, weir, wells, graveyard, Wesleyan Methodist Chapel; bridges and woodland named.

18/152 Hawkshead (township) SD 350966
Apt 14.07.1846; 126a (3732); Map 1847, 3 chns, by John Robinson, Dalton; waterbodies, building names; small occupations tinted blue.

18/153 Haydock (township in parish of Winwick) SJ 562970
Apt 30.04.1838; 2362a (2362); Map 1838, 6 chns, by Charles Mawson, Warrington; railways, canal, waterbodies, houses, woods (named), building names, road names, colliery, dams, lodge.

18/154 Heap (township in parish of Bury) SD 848107 [Heap Bridge]
Apt 12.04.1838; 2934a (2934); Map 1840?, 3 chns, by Wm Benson, Bury, Lancs; hill-drawing, foot/b'way, turnpike roads, waterbodies, woods, plantations, building names, chapel, war office, workhouse, paper mills, water mill, weirs, quarries, colleries, mills, dye house; bridge named; legend explains symbols; Heywood town is not mapped.

18/155 Heapy (township in parish of Leyland) SD 610196 [Heapey]
Apt 03.11.1845; 1456a (1456); Map 1848?, 8 chns; hill-drawing, canal with towpath, waterbodies.

18/156 Heath Charnock (township in parish of Standish) SD 610150
Apt 30.09.1842; 1597a (1596); Map 1842, 3 chns, 1st cl, by Ordnance Survey; construction lines, railway, turnpike roads, toll bar, canal with towpath, aqueduct, waterbodies, houses, building names, saw mill, firebrick works, engine house, colliery, smithy, moat (named in gothic), school, sand pit, viaduct; bridges named.

18/157 Heaton (township in parish of Deane) SD 670110
Apt 26.04.1845; 7a (1630); Map 1852?, scale 'sixty poles, eight yards each' [about 1 inch to 12 poles: 4.5 chns added in pencil]; foot/b'way, occupation road, turnpike roads, waterbodies, woods, field gates, building names, landowners; district is described as 'belonging to L.G.N. Starkie Esqr.'.

18/158 Great Heaton (township in parish of Prestwich cum Oldham) SD 831052 [Not listed]
Apt 28.02.1839; 866a (866); Map 1839, 5 chns, 'copied' by W. Bell, Manchester; hill-drawing, waterbodies, woods, parkland (in detail; named), field boundary ownerships, field gates, building names, milestone, lodges, weirs; meaning of colour bands is unclear.

18/159 Little Heaton (township in parish of Prestwich cum Oldham) SD 839053 [Not listed]
Apt 23.01.1845; 509a (509); Map 1846, 3 chns, by W. Bell, Manchester; hill-drawing, foot/b'way, waterbodies, farmyards, woods, plantations, parkland (named), field boundary ownerships, building names, road names, fish pond, lodge, weir, reservoir, boundary stones, property boundaries (col), green; there are two scale bars, in statute and Cheshire chains. Apt has cropping information.

18/160 Heaton Norris (township in parish of Manchester) SJ 878912
Apt 29.11.1844; 2109a (2108); Map 1848, 3 chns, 1st cl, by Charles E. Cawley, civil engineer, Manchester, (tithable parts only); construction lines, railways with viaduct and station, foot/b'way, waterbodies, woods, parkland, building names, pottery, tythe barn, rope walk; leaves decorate north pointer.

18/161 Heaton with Oxcliffe (township in parish of Lancaster) SD 441613
Apt 29.03.1838; 1979a (1977); Map 1840?, 6 chns; waterbodies, woods, mere stones.

18/162 Hesketh with Becconsall (parish) SD 435235
Apt 27.06.1839; 1947a (3632); Map 1839, 1 inch to 200 ft (3 chns), by J.R. Allen; waterbodies, woods, building names, chapel, mill, moss, marsh, inclosed marsh (col).

18/163 Heskin (township in parish of Eccleston) SD 527151 [Heskin Green]
Apt 18.05.1841; 1235a (1235); Map 1837, 3 chns, by Robt Kellett, Wigan; construction lines, foot/b'way, waterbodies, houses (hatched), woods, building names, school, mill dam, sand pit, lodge, dog kennels, coal pit, stone quarries.

18/164 Heysham (parish) SD 417612
Apt 15.06.1838; 1704a (all); Map 1838, 3 chns, by A. and R. Reed, Stockton upon Tees; waterbodies, woods, plantations, open fields, building names, field acreages; double lines may be drains.

18/165 Hindley (township in parish of Wigan) SD 623043
Apt 28.02.1839; 2522a (2522); Map 1840?, ?3 chns, by S. Williamson, Wigan; railways, tram roads, foot/b'way, waterbodies, woods, plantations, building names, ornamental ground, pits (? coal); scale is one inch to '2 chains of 32 yards each' [i.e. Cheshire chns], which has been altered by another hand to 3 chns.

18/166 Hoghton (township in parish of Leyland) SD 627258
Apt 08.08.1845; 2227a (2227); Map 1841, 6 chns, by Chas Birket; railway, foot/b'way, canal with towpath, waterbodies, woods.

18/167 Holleth (and part Forton) (township in parishes of Garstang and Cockerham) SD 481524 [Not listed]
Apt 02.12.1839; 362a (?); Map 1839, 3 chns; hill-drawing, canal with towpath, waterbodies, woods, plantations, orchards, building names.

18/168 Hoole (parish) SD 480230 [Much Hoole]
Apt 13.11.1841; 2854a (2923); Map 1839, 3 chns, in 2 parts: Much Hoole 'enlarged and copied' from 'the survey made by the late Mr John Clifton' by Miller and Hunter; Little Hoole 'copied from a survey made in the year 1774 showing the alterations and additions', by John J. Myres; foot/b'way, waterbodies, woods, heath/moor, building names, pinfold, uncultivated mossland (by symbol), modus land (col), changes in river course; leafy border surrounds Much Hoole; Little Hoole has leaf-decorated north pointer.

18/169 Hopwood (township in parish of Middleton) SD 870089
Apt 27.03.1839; 2043a (all); Map 1840, 3 chns, by Hy H. Fishwick, Rochdale; railway, canal with towpath, waterbodies, woods, building names, smithy. Apt omits land use.

18/170 Hornby (township in parish of Melling) SD 593697
Apt 06.05.1848; 2116a (2115); Map 1849?, 5 chns, in 2 parts; waterbodies, woods, plantations, building names, castle, Roman Camp (named in gothic), priory.

18/171 Hothersall (township in parish of Ribchester) SD 625355 [Not listed]
Apt 17.04.1838; 1033a (all); Map 1838, 6 chns, 'compiled in part from the Estate Maps of the landowners' by P. Park, Preston; foot/b'way, waterbodies, woods, plantations, field gates, sand or stone pits.

18/172 Houghton, Middleton and Arbury (township in parish of Winwick) SJ 615922 [Houghton Green]
Apt 30.04.1838; 840a (839); Map 1838, 5 chns, by Richard Thornton, Manchester; foot/b'way, waterbodies, woods (col), gardens, building names, township boundaries (col).

18/173 Howick (township in parish of Penwortham) SD 505278 [Howick Cross]
Apt 20.02.1840; 749a (879); Map 1840, 6 chns, by A. Halliday, Preston; foot/b'way, waterbodies, woods (named), plantations (named), parkland, orchards, field gates, building names, sand or stone pits, school, sand bank.

18/174 Hulme (township in parish of Manchester) SJ 830970
Apt 29.11.1844; 8a (all); Map 1854, 60 inches to 1 mile [1:1056; 1.33 chns], in 2 parts 'copied from Ordnance plans' by E. Nicholson, 28, Princess Street, Manchester, architect, surveyor and valuer, (tithable parts only, tinted); railways, foot/b'way, canal with towpath, waterbodies, building names, road names, Manchester Commercial School, Baptist Chapel, Apostolic Chapel, Roman Catholic Chapel, Zion Chapel, Wesleyan Methodist Chapel, burial ground, school, glass works, mill, cotton mill, factory, chimney, timberyard, workhouse, Bridgewater trustees office, towns office, weighing machine, reservoir, hotel, stone yard, cavalry barracks; gardens and bridge named; double lines may be walls.

18/175 Little or Red Hulton (township in parish of Deane) SD 722038
Apt 28.11.1844; 24a (1470); Map 1851?, 6 chns, (tithable parts only in detail, tinted); railway, colliery railway, building names, road names, mill, parsonage, chapel, colliery, limekilns, moss (named), 'Peel Hall (1668)'.

18/176 Middle Hulton (township in parish of Deane) SD 702053 [Not listed]
Apt 28.11.1844; 214a (1280); Map 1851?, 6-inch (1:10,560; 13.33 chns), (tithable part only in detail); foot/b'way, waterbodies, building names, road names, green; colours show property ownership.

18/177 Hutton (township in parish of Penwortham) SD 490270
Apt 30.09.1846; 143a (2683); Map 1874, 8.5 chns, 'copied' by A. Halliday; foot/b'way.

18/178 Huyton (township) SJ 459888
Apt 12.05.1848; 1751a (1630); Map 1850, 4 chns, by Edwd Eyes junr; railway with stations, turnpike roads, toll bars, waterbodies, woods, plantations, parkland, gardens, rock outcrops, building names, road names, vicarage, school, limekiln, mill, collieries, stone quarry; bridges named.

18/179 Ightonhill Park (township in parish of Whalley) SD 820342 [Not listed]
Apt 30.04.1838; 753a (752); Map 1839, 6 chns, by C. Birket; railway, tram roads, waterbodies, woods, rock outcrops, building names, quarry, coal pits.

18/180 Ince Blundell (township in parish of Sefton) SD 320039
Apt 07.03.1843; 2259a (2258); Map 1844, 4.5 chns, by James Wood; waterbodies, woods, plantation (by name), parkland (in detail), building names, road names, lighthouse, tower, school, village cross (pictorial). Apt has cropping information.

18/181 Ince within Mackerfield (township in parish of Wigan) SD 598044 [Ince-in-Makerfield]
Apt 27.06.1839; 2314a (2314); Map 1840, 3 chns, by T. Addison junr; railway, turnpike roads, canal with towpath, waterbodies, woods, parkland, orchards, heath/moor, building names, road names, moss (named).

18/182 Inskip with Sowerby (township in parish of St Michael on Wyre) SD 467382
Apt 30.11.1839; 2888a (2888); Map 1839, 8 chns, by C. Birket; waterbodies, woods. Apt omits land use.

18/183 Nether Kellet (township in parish of Bolton by the Sands) SD 502682
Apt 05.02.1840; 2019a (2018); Map 1840, 6 chns, by Hodgson and Watson, Lancaster; hill-drawing, waterbodies, woods (col), building names, road names, rock outcrop, millstone quarry, public quarry, quarry, lime kilns, mill, old lime kilns, pinfold.

18/184 Over Kellet (parochial chapelry) SD 534708
Apt 09.03.1847; 3203a (3208); Map 1847?, 6 chns, by Hodgson and Watson, Lancaster; hill-drawing, foot/b'way, canal with towpath, waterbodies, woods (col), parkland (col), field boundary ownerships, building names, gamekeeper's house, gardeners house, lodge, chapel, stone quarries, limekilns, mill, former monastic land (col).

18/185 Kenyon (township in parish of Winwick) SJ 632957
Apt 30.04.1838; 1598a (1596); Map 1839, 4.5 chns, 'copied' by William Bell, Manchester; hill-drawing, railways with embankments, foot/b'way, waterbodies, woods, plantations, field boundary ownerships, field gates, building names, ornamental ground; some houses are drawn in elevation; colours may show property ownership. Apt has cropping information.

18/186 Kersley (township in parish of Deane) SD 752048 [Kearsley]
Apt 28.11.1844; 331a (900); Map 1853, 13.33 chns; hill-drawing, railway with embankments, tunnel and station, waterbodies, building names, moss (named).

18/187 Kirkby (township in parish of Walton on the Hill) SJ 421982
Apt 16.07.1839; 3921a (3920); Map 1839, 8 chns; foot/b'way, canal, building names, road names, quarry, chapel; plantations and woodlands shown by name; bridges named. Apt has cropping information.

18/188 Kirkdale (township in parish of Walton on the Hill) SJ 347935
Apt 30.11.1839; 703a (1132); Map 1839, 3 chns, by J. Bennison; canal with towpath, waterbodies, woods, building names, road names, prison, factory, cemetery, mill.

18/189 Kirkham (township in parish of Kirkham) SD 413320
Apt 27.06.1839; 840a (840); Map 1837, 3 chns, by P. Park; hill-drawing, railway, foot/b'way, waterbodies, woods, orchards, field gates, building names, road names; double lines may be walls.

18/190 Kirkland (township in parish of Garstang) SD 478438 [Churchtown]
Apt 23.11.1843; 9a (894); Map 1848, 13.33 chns [6-inch; 1:10,560], by R.W. Dobson, Preston, (tithable parts only); hill-drawing, woods, building names, chapel, vicarage, Sunday school.

18/191 Knowsley (township in parish of Huyton) SJ 445945
Apt 10.07.1847; 5056a (4750); Map 1849, 4.5 chns, 'copied' by James Green junr, Manchester, land and mine surveyor; hill-drawing, foot/b'way, turnpike roads, waterbodies, woods, parkland (in detail, parts named), building names, pinfold, windmill (pictorial), sand or stone pit, tannery, octagon, lodge, tower, school, parsonage, stone quarry; bridge named.

18/192 Lancaster (township in parish of Lancaster) SD 468615
Apt 06.02.1845; 61a (1240); Map 1845, 4 chns, (tithable parts only); waterbodies, woods, road names, landowners, sand or stone pit. Apt omits land use and some field names.

18/193 Lathon (except Newburgh) (township in parish of Ormskirk) SD 462092 [Not listed]
Apt 29.06.1839; 7578a (?); Map 1841, 3 chns, 1st cl, in 4 parts, by John Young, Liverpool, (including index); construction lines, foot/b'way, canal with towpath, waterbodies, woods, parkland, building names, road names, windmill, distillery, mill, lodges, dairy, free school, chapel; bridges and moss named. (PRO IR 30 also contains a plan of the whole township, 8 chns, 1846, lithographed by G.J. Poore, printer, Liverpool.)

18/194 Layton with Warbreck (township in parish of Bispham) SD 310360
Apt 19.06.1840; 2401a (3241); Map 1838, 3 chns, by A. Halliday; hill-drawing, waterbodies, woods, plantations, building names, coastline, ordinary high tide mark, sand or stone pits, ornamental ground.

18/195 Lea, Ashton, Ingol and Cotton (townships in parish of Preston) SD 500310
Apt 13.02.1838; 3347a (3522); Map 1838, 6 chns, in 4 parts: by P. Park, Preston, (Ashton, 4 chns, 'compiled from the Estate Maps of the Land Owners') and W. Miller, (other parts, also 9-chn index); hill-drawing, railway, foot/b'way, turnpike roads, toll bar, canal with towpath, waterbodies, woods, plantations, parkland, hedges, field gates, building names, landowners, wharves, slipways, parsonage, sand or stone pits, marsh (by name). Apt has cropping information.

18/196 Leck (township in parish of Tunstal) SD 660780
Apt 24.01.1845; 4637a (all); Map 1845?, 3 chns, 1st cl, in 4 parts, by Ordnance Survey; construction lines, trig points, hill-drawing, turnpike roads, waterbodies, houses, field gates, building names, road names, caverns, sheep folds, drains, parsonage, mill, springs, pumps, ruins, wells, hot house, summer houses, sun dial, watering troughs, boiler, old lime kiln, school, waterfall, lime kiln, cistern, limestone quarries, tithe barn, thrashing mill, cairns, swallow holes.

18/197 West Leigh (township in parish of Leigh) SD 645010 [Westleigh]
Apt 15.10.1846; 1895a (all); Map 1848?, 3 chns, by William Rothwell, Winwick; construction lines, railway with station, foot/b'way, canal with towpath, waterbodies, woods, plantations, parkland (in detail), orchards, gardens, hedges, building names, road names, bone and size works, bone works, colleries, National School, mills, chemical works, common, heath (named); bridge named.

18/198 Levenshulme (township in parish of Manchester) SJ 879942
Apt 29.11.1844; 606a (all); Map 1845?, 3 chns, 1st cl, by Ordnance Survey; construction lines, railways with station, turnpike roads, waterbodies, houses, marsh/bog, building names, road names, milestone, school, reservoirs, bleach works, print works, cotton mill, ticking factory, Wesleyan Methodist Chapel; ornamental ground indicated by paths.

18/199 Great Lever (township in parish of Middleton) SD 722072
Apt 15.01.1845; 16a (770); Map 1850, 14 chns, by Geo. Piggot, Bolton (tithable parts only, tinted); railway, waterbodies, woods, building names. Apt omits land use.

18/200 Leyland (township) SD 531220
Apt 30.03.1838; 3652a (3651); Map 1838, 3 chns, by T. Addison; hill-drawing, railway with embankments, foot/b'way, waterbodies, woods, parkland, orchards, gardens, heath/moor, building names, gravel pits, obelisk, drains; legend explains symbols.

18/201 Litherland (township in parish of Sefton) SJ 337975
Apt 07.03.1843; 1179a (1914); Map 1845, 3 chns; foot/b'way, canal with towpath, waterbodies, woods, plantations, parkland, building names, road names, schools. Apt has cropping information.

18/202 Longton (township in parish of Penwortham) SD 490250
Apt 09.04.1838; 3132a (3692); Map 1839, 3 chns, by A. Halliday; foot/b'way, waterbodies, woods, orchards, building names, mill. Apt has cropping information.

18/203 Lostock (township in parish of Bolton le Moors) SD 658085
Apt 30.11.1839; 207a (1426); Map 1849, 14 chns, by R.W. Dobson, (tithable parts only); railway, foot/b'way, waterbodies, woods, building names, well, sandstone quarry, mill, plantation (by name).

18/204 Lowick (township in parish of Ulverstone) SD 287847
Apt 18.11.1847; 144a (1900); Map 1849, 3 chns, by John Robinson, Keldray near Ulverston, (tithable parts only); foot/b'way, waterbodies, houses, building names, chapel, green, common; bridge named.

18/205 Low Quarter, Middle Quarter and Heathwaite and Woodland (townships in parish of Kirkby Ireleth) SD 247855
Apt 26.05.1845; 5496a (?); Map 1842, 4 chns, in 2 parts; hill-drawing, railway, foot/b'way, waterbodies, woods, plantations, parkland, orchards, building names (in ornate gothic), quarries.

18/206 Lowton (township in parish of Winwick) SJ 620980
Apt 30.04.1837; 1825a (1824); Map 1838, 3 chns, by R. Thornton; railway, foot/b'way, waterbodies, woods (col), orchards (col), heath/moor, building names, stone pits.

18/207 Lunt (township in parish of Sefton) SD 350018
Apt 07.03.1843; 477a (476); Map 'copied from one made for Tithe Commutation purposes by the Board of Ordnance in 1844, with a few additions as to the divisions of Property', 1845, 3 chns, by R. Ledger; foot/b'way, waterbodies, houses, open fields, building names, road names, boundary stones; bridge named.

18/208 Lydiate (township in parish of Halsall) SD 372050
Apt 17.08.1844; 1996a (all); Map 1845?, 3 chns, 1st cl, in 5 parts, by Ordnance Survey (including 40-chn (1:31,680) index); construction lines, hill-drawing, canal with towpath and embankments, waterbodies, houses, field gates, building names, road names, boilers, smithy, mill, windmill, school, abbey (named in gothic), Methodist meeting house, Roman Catholic Chapel, boundary stones, cross, pipes, wells, pump, sun dials, milestone, culverts, finger post, sand pit, old sand pit; bridges and woodland named.

18/209 Lytham (township in parish of Lytham) SD 345290
Apt 26.09.1839; 5177a (?); Map 1840, 6 chns, by C. Birket; hill-drawing, waterbodies, woods, mill dams.

18/210 Maghull (township in parish of Halsall) SD 375020
Apt 27.06.1839; 2073a (2073); Map 1839, 3 chns, 1st cl, by Jonathan Bennison, Liverpool; construction lines, canal with towpath, waterbodies, woods, building names, road names, schools, chapel, drains.

18/211 Manchester and Beswick (district in parish of Manchester) SJ 852988
Apt 29.11.1844; 232a (?); Map 1849, 'Enlarged from the Ordnance map of 6 inches to a mile' to 12 inches to a mile (1:5280, 6.67 chns), by E. Nicholson, 18, Princess St, Manchester and 'Examined by C.R. Brady, land valuer and agent, Mile End, Stockport', (tithable parts only in detail); foot/b'way, waterbodies, rock outcrops, building names, road names, quarry, cemetery, rope walk; park and estate named; pink band shows modus lands.

18/212 Great and Little Marsden (township in parish of Whalley) SD 885375
Apt 26.04.1842; 4711a (4360); Map 1849, 3 chns, 1st cl, by P. Roberts, Burnley; construction lines, railway, foot/b'way, waterbodies, building names, monuments, pinfold, collieries, sand or stone pits, limekilns, coal pits, mills, flour mill, brewery, parsonage, Quaker Chapel, Independent Chapel, Primitive Methodist Chapel, bridge named; ornamental ground.

18/213 Marton (township in parish of Poulton le Fylde) SD 340335 [Not listed]
Apt 08.02.1839; 4647a (5452); Map 1839, 4 chns, in 2 parts, 'enlarged

and copied' by Miller and Hunter; waterbodies, woods, plantations, orchards, coastlines, sand hills; meaning of green tint is unclear; both parts have border with floral corners; part 2 has cartouches decorated with a stylised bird below the map title, and by a highly stylised marine creature wound around a rope and anchor.

18/214 Mawdesley (township in parish of Croston) SD 492152
Apt 26.08.1839; 2888a (2887); Map 1837, 4 chns, by W. Thornborrow, Broughton; foot/b'way, waterbodies, woods, orchards, field gates, building names, sand or stone pit, chapel, school, green, moor.

18/215 Medlar with Wesham (township in parish of Kirkham) SD 420338
Apt 24.01.1840; 1971a (1971); Map 1839, 3 chns, by W. Gregson and G. Garlick; railway, foot/b'way, waterbodies, woods (col), plantations (col), building names, windmill (pictorial); pink bands may indicate tithable status. Scale bar is decorated with scallop design.

18/216 Melling cum Cunscough (township in parish of Halsall) SD 400004
Apt 22.04.1839; 2120a (2120); Map 1839, 3 chns, 1st cl, by Jonathan Bennison, Liverpool; construction lines, foot/b'way, canal with towpath, waterbodies, woods, building names, road names, chapel, quarries, school.

18/217 Melling with Wrayton (township in parish of Melling) SD 607716
Apt 06.05.1848; 1052a (1120); Map 1849, 3 chns, by Geo. Wolfenden, Kirkby Lonsdale; hill-drawing, waterbodies, woods, plantations, orchards, gardens, building names, quarry, green, moor.

18/218 North Meols (township in parish of North Meols) SD 365185 [Not listed]
Apt 26.09.1839; 8067a (18871); Map 3 chns, 'surveyed in chief by Thomas Maddock', Southport, in 1839 and 'completed by Henry White', Warrington, in 1840; hill-drawing, foot/b'way, canal, waterbodies, woods, plantations, orchards, building names, National and Sunday School, schools, boarding school, Quakers' Meeting House, Roman Catholic Chapel, Primitive and Wesleyan Methodist Chapels, Wesleyan Chapel, Independent Chapels, rectory, old baths, baths, hotels, market place, post office, round house, assembly and news rooms, dispensary, toll house, coastline, coastal embankments, mill, sheepfold, drains.

18/219 Middleton (township in parish of Lancaster) SD 421595
Apt 28.10.1843; 1230a (1229); Map 1844, 8 chns, in 2 parts, by J. Watson, Lancaster, (including village at 4 chns); foot/b'way, waterbodies, woods (col), orchards, building names, coastline, drains. Apt omits some land use.

18/220 Middleton (township in parish of Middleton) SD 864066
Apt 27.03.1839; 1908a (all); Map 1839, 3 chns, by Benson Smith; railway, foot/b'way, canal, waterbodies, woods. Apt omits land use.

18/221 Moss Side (township in parish of Manchester) SJ 840958
Apt 28.02.1845; 248a (430); Map 1849, 12 inches to 1 mile, (6.67 chns, 1:5280), 'Enlarged from the Ordnance Map of six inches to a mile', by E. Nicholson, architect and surveyor, 18, Princes Street, Manchester, and 'examined by C.R. Brady, land valuer and agent, Mile End, Stockport'; waterbodies, building names, road names. Apt omits some land use.

18/222 Moston (township in parish of Manchester) SD 880020
Apt 29.11.1844; 1272a (all); Map 1848, 3 chns, by Taylor and Lawton; hill-drawing, railways with embankments, foot/b'way, canal, waterbodies, woods (col), moss (named), field boundary ownerships, field gates, building names, road names, side cutting, weir, schools, colliery, sand or stone pit, green; bridge named.

18/223 Much Woolton, otherwise Great Woolton with Thingwall (township in parish of Childwall) SJ 427862 [Woolton]
Apt 26.05.1842; 930a (930); Map 1840, 4 chns, in 3 parts, by Edward Eyes junr, (including location map); railway, foot/b'way, occupation roads, waterbodies, woods, plantations, parkland, orchards, gardens, building names, road names, mill, school, workhouse, quarry, chapels, boundary stones, village cross. Apt has cropping information.

18/224 Nateby (township in parish of Garstang) SD 465455
Apt 30.10.1843; 2031a (2030); Map 1844, 4 chns, by Willm Lamb; hill-drawing, canal with towpath, waterbodies, woods, building names, drains, 'improved top moss'.

18/225 Netherton (township in parish of Sefton) SJ 362995
Apt 07.03.1843; 1093a (1093); Map 'copied from one made by Mr James Bennett junr of Melling in 1843 with corrections up to the present time', 1845, 4 chns; foot/b'way, turnpike roads, canal with towpath, waterbodies, woods, open fields, field gates, building names, road names, green; bridge named. Apt has cropping information.

18/226 Newburgh (hamlet in parish of Ormskirk) SD 479104
Apt 04.04.1845; 1074a (all); Map 1845, 3 chns, 1st cl, by Ordnance Survey; canal with towpath, waterbodies, houses, woods, building names, road names, bowling green, milestones, water trough, pound, gravel pit, weir, drains, wells, coal shafts, old coal shafts, malt kiln, springs, independent chapel, saw pits, old stone cross (named, in gothic), school; bridges named and types of bridge distinguished. Apt has cropping information.

18/227 Newton (township in parish of Manchester) SD 874001 [Newton Heath]
Apt 29.11.1844; 1585a (all); Map 1846, 3 chns, 1st cl, in 2 parts, by Ordnance Survey; construction lines, railways and station, viaduct, turnpike roads, canal with towpath and locks, waterbodies, weirs, houses, fences, building names, road names, Methodist New Connexion Sabbath School, National School, school, graveyard, parsonage, museum, post office, match and pill box factory, corn mill, cotton and worsted mill, bleach works, mill, cotton mills, silk dye works, silk mills, steel works, chemical works, rope walks and works, dye works, glass works, sandstone quarry, coal pits, tannery, foundry, breweries, smithies, platting house, sheds, reservoirs, pipes, culverts, pumps, wells, summer houses, bowling greens, toll houses, fences (by annotation); bridges named and types of bridge distinguished; pleasure grounds and garden named. Apt omits land use.

18/228 Newton within Mackerfield (township in parish of Winwick) SJ 590950 [Newton-le-Willows]
Apt 28.04.1838; 2693a (2692); Map 1838, 6? chns, by Charles Mawson, Warrington; railways, viaduct, foot/b'way, canal with towpath and locks (named), waterbodies, houses, woods, building names, road names, landowners, foundries, mill, vitriol works, glass works, workhouse, race course, grand stand, parsonage, property boundaries (col), common, moor. Apt omits cropping information.

18/229 Newton with Scales (township in parish of Kirkham) SD 347307 [Not listed]
Apt 27.06.1839; 1230a (1525); Map 1838, 3 chns, by P. Park, Preston; waterbodies, marsh (named); double lines may be drains.

18/230 Oldham (township in parish of Prestwich cum Oldham) SD 936051
Apt 06.11.1845; 4618a (4617); Map 1848, 4 chns, by William Rothwell, Winwick, (tithable parts only); foot/b'way, canal with towpath, waterbodies, plantations, parkland (in detail), building names, road names, workhouse, corn mill, mills, colleries, reservoir, school, chapel.

18/231 Openshaw (township in parish of Manchester) SJ 885973
Apt 29.11.1844; 572a (all); Map 1846, 3 chns, by William Rothwell, Winwick; railways, foot/b'way, canal with towpath, waterbodies, farmyards (col), gardens (col), building names, road names, dye works.

18/232 Ormskirk (township in parish of Ormskirk) SD 421082
Apt 28.03.1845; 573a (all); Map 1846?, 3 chns, 1st cl, by Ordnance Survey; railway, foot/b'way, waterbodies, houses, fences, field gates, building names, road names, boundary stones, smithy, wells, dispensary, police station, model schools, windmill, independent chapel; some field boundaries are in red. Apt has cropping information.

18/233 Orrell (township in parish of Wigan) SD 540055
Apt 24.09.1838; 1542a (1542); Map 1840?, 4.5 chns, by R. Thornton; waterbodies, woods, building names, Catholic Chapel, coal pits.

18/234 Orrell and Ford (township in parish of Sefton) SJ 350970
Apt 07.03.1843; 729a (728); Map 1845, 3 chns, in 2 parts; foot/b'way, occupation roads, canal with towpath, waterbodies, houses, woods,

building names, road names, quarry, boundary stones, well. Apt has cropping information.

18/235 Osbaldestone (township in parish of Blackburn) SD 643337 [Osbaldeston]
Apt 21.01.1845; 39a (980); Map 1850, 3 chns, by E.T. Welch, Whalley; turnpike roads, waterbodies, field gates, building names, landowners, Roman Catholic Chapel.

18/236 Osmotherley (township in parish of Ulverstone) SD 277812 [Not listed]
Apt 18.11.1847; 147a (1140); Map 1849, 3 chns, by John Robinson, Keldray near Ulverston, (tithable lands only); foot/b'way, waterbodies, field gates, building names, school, commons; bridge named; some houses are shown.

18/237 Overton (township in parish of Lancaster) SD 431579
Apt 29.04.1844; 6315a (6314); Map 1844, 4 chns, by J. Watson, Lancaster; foot/b'way, waterbodies, woods, rock outcrops, building names, road names, drains, harbours, docks, fisheries, ferry, fish holds, stone quarries, chapel, dog kennel; marsh, sandbanks, headlands and pools are shown by annotation. Apt omits some land use.

18/238 Padiham (township in parish of Whalley) SD 795353
Apt 15.05.1838; 1917a (1917); Map 1839, 6 chns, by C. Birkett; foot/b'way, waterbodies, woods, plantations, building names.

18/239 Parbold (township in parish of Eccleston) SD 500110
Apt 08.05.1841; 1166a (1165); Map 1837, 3 chns, by Robt Kellett, Wigan; construction lines, foot/b'way, canal with towpath, waterbodies, houses (hatched), woods, marsh/bog, field gates, building names, old mill, stone quarries, reform pillar, tan house, windmill; bridges named.

18/240 Parr (township in parish of Prescot) SJ 533962
Apt 08.06.1840; 1601a (1601); Map 1841, 4 chns; railway, canal, waterbodies, woods, moss (named), coal pits, coalpit brows (i.e. spoiltips; by symbol); legend explains symbols.

18/241 Pemberton (township in parish of Wigan) SD 559047
Apt 04.07.1844; 2868a (2868); Map 1847, 3 chns, 1st cl, by William Rothwell, Winwick; construction lines, railway, foot/b'way, green, waterbodies, farmyards, woods, fences, building names, road names, mill, stone quarries, colliery, colliery and quarry waste (col); bridge named; tree, bird and bell, crudely drawn, surround map date. Apt has cropping information.

18/242 Penington (township in parish of Leigh) SJ 652988
Apt 09.02.1846; 1438a (all); Map 1847, 6-inch (1:10,560, 13.33 chns), in 2 parts, (including Leigh at 1 inch to 120 yards, 1:4320); railway, foot/b'way, canal with towpath, waterbodies, woods, building names.

18/243 Penketh (township in parish of Prescot) SJ 562877
Apt 16.04.1840; 1048a (1048); Map 1840, 3 chns, by John Laurance, Leicester; construction lines, canal, waterbodies, building names, chapel, ferry, school, Friends Meeting House, windmill, heath. Apt omits some field names.

18/244 Pennington (parish) SD 262788
Apt 27.07.1839; 2767a (2767); Map 1840, 6 chns, by J. Bintley, (tinted); woods, building names, watering place, quarries.

18/245 Penwortham (township in parish of Penwortham) SD 524276
Apt 28.03.1838; 2277a (2277); Map 1838, 3 chns, 1st cl, by N. Lea, Birmingham; construction lines, hill-drawing, railway, waterbodies, woods, parkland (with land-use annotations), fences, building names, bowling green, wharves, ferry house, grand bank, sands; hill and marsh named.

18/246 Pilkington (township in parish of Prestwich cum Oldham) SD 792054 [Not listed]
Apt 26.01.1841; 5379a (5378); Map 1841?, 2.5 chns, in 3 parts, by Wm Benson, Bury, Lancashire; hill-drawing, railway, tramway, foot/b'way, turnpike roads, canal with towpath, locks (named) and aqueduct, wharf, waterbodies, woods, parkland, orchards, heath/moor, building names, road names, mills, cotton factory, colliery, weirs, pinfold, print works, water works, workhouse, chapels, parsonage, school, spring, lodges; bridges named; legend explains symbols; leaves decorate north pointer.

18/247 Pilling (township in parish of Garstang) SD 420470
Apt 11.04.1844; 8017a (8017); Map 1845, 5 chns; waterbodies, woods, building names, road names, landowners, pinfold; sands and moss named; colours may show property ownerships.

18/248 Pilling Lane (hamlet in parish of Lancaster) SD 377487
Apt 24.10.1845; 805a (?); Map 1847, 3 chns, 1st cl, by R.W. Dobson, Preston; construction lines, foot/b'way, waterbodies, woods, orchards, field gates, building names, coastline, marsh (named). Apt omits some field names.

18/249 Pilsworth (township in parish of Middleton) SD 835091 [Not listed]
Apt 27.03.1839; 1478a (all); Map 1838, 6 chns; foot/b'way, waterbodies, woods, plantations, field boundary ownerships, quarry waste, property ownerships; bridge named. Apt has cropping information.

18/250 Poulton (township in parish of Poulton) SD 353393 [Poulton-le-Fylde]
Apt 30.08.1839; 900a (900); Map 1839, 3 chns, by H. Bibby, Preston; hill-drawing, railway, foot/b'way, waterbodies, woods, orchards, gardens; double lines may show drains; legend explains symbols.

18/251 Poulton, Bare and Torrisholme (township in parish of Lancaster) SD 445645
Apt 11.04.1839; 1642a (1641); Map 1840?, 3 chns; foot/b'way, waterbodies, woods, building names, road names, township boundaries (col). Apt has cropping information.

18/252 Poulton with Fearnhead (township in parish of Warrington) SJ 630900
Apt 24.06.1840; 1234a (1233); Map 1841, 6 chns, by T. Burgess; canal, waterbodies, woods, field boundary ownerships.

18/253 Preesall with Hackensall (excepting Pilling Lane) (township in parish of Lancaster) SD 364472
Apt 30.06.1840; 2091a (?); Map 1839, 3 chns, by T. Hull; waterbodies, woods, plantations, parkland, orchards; legend explains symbols.

18/254 Prescot (township) SJ 467927
Apt 21.12.1841; 270a (270); Map 1847, 4 chns; waterbodies, woods, plantations, building names, vicarage, graveyard; built-up parts generalised; there is a note as to township boundaries demarcated by Act of Parliament.

18/255 Preston (township in parish of Preston) SD 541299
Apt 27.06.1839; 1437a (2081); Map 1840, 1 inch to 80 yards (1:2880, 3.6 chns), by J.J. Myres, litho; hill-drawing, railways, foot/b'way, canal, waterbodies, woods, plantations, parkland, arable (hatched), orchards, gardens, building names, road names, bowling greens, milestone, Unitarian and Independent chapels, Wesleyan Chapel, Roman Catholic Church, chapels, burial grounds, schools, baths, institution, court house, stamp office, corn exchange, fish stones, market place, market cross, cattle market, slaughter houses, packet house, house of recovery, prison, workhouses, quay, slip, wharves, warehouses, old water works, gas works, machine shops, starch houses, coal yards, steam sawmill, foundries, scavengers yard, flax mills, foundry and machine shop, cotton mills, timber yards, rope walk, lime kilns, tanning works, nurseries (by annotation); bridge, marsh and estates named; leaves decorate north pointer.

18/256 Prestwick (township in parish of Prestwick cum Oldham) SD 817033 [Prestwich]
Apt 28.02.1839; 1906a (1906); Map 1839, [3 chns], 1st cl, by William Bell, Manchester; construction lines, hill-drawing, railway, foot/b'way, turnpike roads, canal with towpath, waterbodies, woods, parkland (named), gardens (col), field boundary ownerships, building names, road names, rectory, bleach and dye works, printworks, racecourse, grandstand, embankments, field acreages; bridge named. Colours may show property ownership.

18/257 Priest Hutton (township in parish of Warton) SD 538739
Apt 14.06.1845; 1069a (1068); Map 1846, 4 chns, by John Watson junr,

Kendall; foot/b'way, canal, waterbodies, woods, plantations, parkland (in detail), orchards, building names; north pointer has Prince of Wales' feathers.

18/258 Quernmore (township in parish of Lancaster) SD 526606
Apt 26.04.1843; 518a (6593); Map 1844, 9 chns; waterbodies, woods, plantations, building names, field acreages; colours may show property ownership; map has six signatures, approving it for tithe commutation.

18/259 Radcliffe, otherwise Ratcliffe Tower (parish) SD 783080
Apt 03.12.1839; 2466a (2466); Map 1841, 3 chns, by W. Bell, Manchester; foot/b'way, canal with towpath, waterbodies, woods (col), plantations, gardens (col), field boundary ownerships, building names, road names, reservoirs, ford, weir, print works, bleach works, colliery, workhouse, barracks, rectory, parsonage, Old Roman Road. Apt has cropping information.

18/260 Rainford (township in parish of Prescot) SD 485005
Apt 16.04.1840; 5803a (5803); Map 1841, 8 chns, by J. Young, Liverpool; foot/b'way, waterbodies, woods (col).

18/261 Rainhill (township in parish of Prescot) SJ 497905
Apt 19.06.1840; 1642a (1642); Map 1843, 4 chns, by John Daglish, St Helens; railway, waterbodies, woods.

18/262 Ramsgrave (township in parish of Blackburn) SD 677316 [Not listed]
Apt 24.12.1846; 53a (757); Map 1849, 6.67 chns, (tithable parts only, tinted); turnpike roads, toll house, building names, landowners. Apt is by holding and omits land use.

18/263 Upper Rawcliffe, with Tarnicar (part of) (township in parish of St Michaels upon Wyre) SD 455420 [Not listed]
Apt 14.05.1840; 1360a (?); Map 1840, 6 chns, by C. Birket; waterbodies, woods, heath/moor.

18/264 Rawcliffe with Tarnacre (part of) (township in parish of Garstang) SD 463429 [Not listed]
Apt 22.11.1847; 190a (?); Map 1846, 3 chns, by Willm Lamb; hill-drawing, waterbodies, orchards; hatched boundaries appear to show 'turbary dales'.

18/265 Reddish (township in parish of Manchester) SJ 895933
Apt 29.11.1844; 1542a (all); Map 1846, 3 chns, 1st cl, by Ordnance Survey; railways, canal with towpath, waterbodies, houses, fences, field gates, building names, road names, priory, smithies, old marl pits, reservoirs, tank, pumps, bleach mills, weighing machine, gasometer, pumping engine, sand pit, brickfields, brick kiln, shed, saw pit, wells, boundary stones, gatehouses, pipes, moat (named, in gothic), fences (by annotation), drains, culverts; ornamental ground is indicated by paths only.

18/266 Ribbleton (township in parish of Preston) SD 569317
Apt 10.11.1843; 744a (?); Map 1843?, 3 chns; waterbodies, woods, plantations, parkland, orchards, gardens, building names, bowling green, common; common and hall named in gothic.

18/267 Ribby with Wrea (township in parish of Kirkham) SD 402313
Apt 27.06.1839; 1366a (1366); Map 1839, 3 chns, by A. Halliday, Preston; hill-drawing, foot/b'way, waterbodies, woods, parkland, orchards, building names, mill, drains, green.

18/268 Ribchester (township and hamlet in parish of Ribchester) SD 643365
Apt 17.04.1838; 2094a (2093); Map 1838, 8 chns, in 2 parts, by Willm Harper, (including Ribchester at 1 chn); hill-drawing, foot/b'way, waterbodies, woods, plantations, orchards, building names, school, embankments, mill. There is a note as to proceedings for the adoption of the map.

18/269 Rivington (township in parish of Bolton le Moors) SD 640140
Apt 30.01.1845; 166a (2630); Map 1850, 9 chns, by R.W. Dobson, Preston; hill-drawing, waterbodies, woods, orchards, gardens, building names, moor.

18/270 Rixton cum Glazebrook (township in parish of Warrington) SJ 683907
Apt 24.06.1840; 2841a (2840); Map undated, 6 chns, ? by T. Burgess; hill-drawing, waterbodies, woods, field boundary ownerships, moss (named).

18/271 Roby (township in parish of Huyton) SJ 431903
Apt 14.07.1847; 1013a (all); Map 1849, 4.4 chns, by J. Young, Liverpool; hill-drawing, railway, foot/b'way, waterbodies, woods, plantations, parkland.

18/272 Roeburndale (township in parish of Melling) SD 611622 [Not listed]
Apt 16.05.1848; 8845a (8845); Map 1849, 6 chns, by D. McCay; woods.

18/273 Royton (township in parish of Prestwick cum Oldham) SD 925075
Apt 07.08.1845; 1352a (1352); Map 1847, 3 chns, by William Rothwell, Winwick; foot/b'way, waterbodies, plantations, building names, road names, mills, workhouse, Quakers' Chapel, colliery; built-up parts generalised; bridge named.

18/274 Rufford (parish) SD 451162
Apt 27.06.1839; 3102a (3102); Map 1839, 3 chns, surveyed by J.J. Myres and copied 'showing the alterations and additions' by James Crompton; foot/b'way, canal with towpath, waterbodies, woods, plantations, parkland (in detail), estate boundary; scale is given in statute and in '32 yard' [i.e. Cheshire] chains.

18/275 Rumworth (township in parish of Deane) SD 695078 [Not listed]
Apt 01.05.1845; 48a (1300); Map 1849, 3 chns, by Thomas Young, Humshaugh, Hexham, (tithable parts only); railway, foot/b'way, turnpike roads, toll gate, waterbodies, houses, woods, plantations, field boundary ownerships, building names, road names, sand or stone pits or quarry.

18/276 Rushulme (township in parish of Manchester) SJ 861953 [Rusholme]
Apt 29.11.1844; 956a (all); Map 1848, 3 chns, by Joseph Butterworth, Manchester; hill-drawing, railway with embankments, foot/b'way, old footpaths, turnpike roads, toll bar, intended roads, old watercourses, waterbodies, woods, marsh/bog, building names, road names, chapels, lodge, old green boundary.

18/277 Samlesbury (township in parish of Blackburn) SD 609297
Apt 23.02.1849; 1212a (4270); Map 1849, 6 chns, by E.G. Melling, Preston; foot/b'way, turnpike roads, toll bar, waterbodies, woods, rock outcrops, building names, landowners, cotton factory, quarry; scale wrongly numbered.

18/278 Great Sankey (township in parish of Prescot) SJ 577888
Apt 16.04.1840; 1909a (1909); Map 1839, 3 chns, by I. Laurance, Leicester; construction lines, canal with towpath, waterbodies, woods, plantations, building names, field names, schools, chapel, rope walk, mill, heath; meadows named.

18/279 Scarisbrick (with Hamlet of Snape) (township in parish of Ormskirk) SD 400140
Apt 02.11.1839; 8376a (8377); Map 1839, 3 chns, by Robt Kellett, Wigan; construction lines, foot/b'way, canal with towpath, waterbodies, houses (hatched), woods (named), parkland (in detail), orchard (by annotation), marsh/bog, heath/moor, field boundary ownerships, field gates, building names, road names, chapels, school, maypole, boundary stones, limekiln, coal yard, quarry, stone quarry, windmills, lodges, bowling greens, hamlet boundary (col), greens; bridge named; double lines may be drains; 'Martin Mere' may be reclaimed land.

18/280 Scotforth (township in parish of Lancaster) SD 490590
Apt 02.05.1844; 2764a (2764); Map 1844, 3 chns, by Willm Lamb; hill-drawing, railway, canal with embankments, waterbodies, woods, parkland, building names, fell (named). Apt omits some land use.

18/281 Seathwaite (township in parish of Kirkby Ireleth) SD 248985
Apt 07.05.1840; 153a (?); Map 1839, 3 chns, in 2 parts, by Geo. Robinson, (including location map); hill-drawing, foot/b'way, water-bodies, field gates, building names; physical features named.

18/282 Sefton (township in parish of Sefton) SJ 346999
Apt 07.03.1843; 1234a (1233); Map 1845?, 3 chns, in 3 parts; foot/b'way, canal with towpath, waterbodies, houses, woods, rock outcrops, building names, road names, quarry, old moat, rectory, mill race, school, marl pit, green; bridges named. Apt has cropping information.

18/283 Shevington (township in parish of Standish) SD 542090
Apt 28.09.1842; 1707a (1706); Map 1843, 3 chns, by A. Halliday, Preston; canal with towpath, waterbodies, woods.

18/284 Silverdale (township in parish of Warton) SD 469759
Apt 14.06.1845; 1145a (1145); Map 1846, 5 chns, by John Watson junr, Kendal; foot/b'way, waterbodies, woods, plantations, parkland, orchards, rock outcrops, building names, chapel, coastline, quarry.

18/285 Simonswood (district) SD 433006 [Not listed]
Apt 05.03.1840; 2862a (2862); Map 1841?, 6 chns; foot/b'way, building names, road names; plantations and moss shown by name. Apt has cropping information.

18/286 Great and Little Singleton (township in parish of Kirkham) SD 380383 [Singleton]
Apt 16.07.1839; 2635a (2860); Map 1839, 6 chns, by C. Birkett; waterbodies, woods, windmill (pictorial).

18/287 Skelmersdale (township in parish of Ormskirk) SD 478060
Apt 19.12.1838; 1921a (1920); Map 1839, 3 chns, 1st cl, by Jonathan Bennison, Liverpool; construction lines, waterbodies, woods, building names, road names, quarries, chapel, school, corn mill, smithy, carpenters shop, occupation roads; there is a note that several of the construction lines are continued in the survey of Lathom.

18/288 Skerton (township in parish of Lancaster) SD 473636
Apt 24.03.1838; 1160a (1186); Map 1841, 6 chns; turnpike roads, toll gate, canal with towpath, woods, building names, road names, mill, ruins of old bridge, limekilns.

18/289 Slyne with Hest (township in parish of Bolton le Sands) SD 474658
Apt 14.03.1845; 1115a (1114); Map 1846, 9 chns, in 2 parts, by Wm Talbot, Lane House, (includes Slyne village at 3 chns); railway, canal, waterbodies, woods, plantations, building names; areas coloured green are tithe-free when owner-occupied.

18/290 Southworth with Croft (township in parish of Winwick) SJ 632936
Apt 30.04.1837; 1852a (1851); Map 1842?, 3 chns; waterbodies, woods.

18/291 Speke (township in parish of Childwall) SJ 430832
Apt 25.02.1842; 2473a (5492); Map 1844, 8 chns, 'copied from one made by J. Bennison in 1825 with corrections up to the present time', by Henry White, Warrington; foot/b'way, waterbodies, woods, field gates, building names, salt works, demesne boundary. Apt has cropping information.

18/292 Spotland (township in parish of Rochdale) SD 850200 [Not listed]
Apt 26.09.1845; 2940a (?); Map 1852?, 6 chns, ? by Geo. Greenwood; foot/b'way, turnpike roads, waterbodies, woods (named), building names, road names, field names, reservoirs, well, ruin, mills, collieries, coal pits, coal staiths, quarry, township divisions (col, named); pasture lands, some fields and some physical features named. Apt omits land use.

18/293 Stalmine with Staynall (township in parish of Lancaster) SD 375450
Apt 30.06.1840; 2153a (2138); Map 1839, 3 chns, by Robert Jervis and James Bradshaw; waterbodies, woods (col), plantations (col), road destinations; red band may show tithe-free land.

18/294 Standish with Langtree (township in parish of Standish) SD 562099
Apt 30.09.1842; 3258a (3257); Map 1842, 3 chns, 1st cl, by Ordnance Survey; construction lines, railway, canal with towpath, waterbodies, houses, rock outcrops, building names, quarries, Sunday Free School, National School, Quakers' Meeting House, rectory, glebe; internal boundary may be that between Standish and Langtree.

18/295 Stretford (township in parish of Manchester) SJ 799952
Apt 28.02.1839; 3140a (3140); Map 1838, 3 chns, by W. Forshaw, Manchester; construction lines, turnpike roads, toll bar, canal with towpath, waterbodies, woods, parkland, orchards, building names, road names, landowners; bridges named. Apt omits land use.

18/296 Subberthwaite (township in parish of Ulverstone) SD 268865 [Not listed]
Apt 18.11.1847; 37a (1246); Map 1849, 3 chns, by John Robinson, Keldray near Ulverston; waterbodies, woods, field gates, building names, mill, stone dykes, slate quarries, rubbish heaps, commons; bridge named.

18/297 Sutton (township in parish of Prescot) SJ 520930
Apt 16.04.1840; 3616a (3616); Map 1843, 8 chns, copied by Jno. Daglish, St Helens; railway, canal, waterbodies, woods, parkland, building names, road names, plate glass factory, pottery, copper works, dock yard, heath; some gardens named; green may show lands exempt from tithe.

18/298 Tarbock (township in parish of Huyton) SJ 481851 [Tarbock Green]
Apt 10.07.1847; 2447a (2447); Map 1849?, 8 chns, in 5 parts, (including four 3-chn enlargements of detail); foot/b'way, waterbodies, houses, woods, building names, brewery, sandstone quarries, marl pit, brick and tile works, green; bridges and park named. Apt has cropping information.

18/299 Tarleton (parish) SD 430200
Apt 30.09.1845; 5405a (5405); Map 1839, 4.4 chns, 'copied from a survey made in the year 1811, showing the alterations and additions', by John J. Myres; canal with towpath, waterbodies, woods, plantations, orchards, building names, parsonage; scale is given in statute chns (1 inch to 4.4 chns) and in [Cheshire] chns of 32 yards (1 inch to 3 Cheshire chns).

18/300 Tatham (parish) SD 658658
Apt 14.10.1848; 8501a (8501); Map 1848, 6 chns, by James Scally; waterbodies, woods, orchards, building names, boundary features, chapel, commons, moor; fells named.

18/301 Thistleton (hamlet in parish of Kirkham) SD 404379
Apt 27.06.1839; 676a (?); Map 1838, 3 chns, by W. Gregson and G. Garlick, Greenalgh; foot/b'way, waterbodies, woods (col); legend explains some symbols.

18/302 Thornham (township in parish of Middleton) SD 900090
Apt 27.03.1839; 1998a (all); Map 1839, 3 chns, by Benson Smith; railway, foot/b'way, canal, waterbodies, woods, arable (col), grassland (col); table lists land use for each owner. Apt omits land use.

18/303 Thornton (township in parish of Poulton) SD 325455
Apt 19.06.1840; 2248a (9730); Map 1839, 4 chns, by Thos Hull; railway, waterbodies; legend explains some symbols, including 'Occupation' and 'Highway' roads.

18/304 Thornton (township in parish of Sefton) SD 338015
Apt 07.03.1843; 774a (773); Map 1845, 3 chns; foot/b'way, waterbodies, houses, farmyards, plantations, open fields, building names, road names, boundary stones, green. Apt has cropping information.

18/305 Thurnham (township in parishes of Lancaster and Cockerham) SD 453551 [Lower and Upper Thurnham]
Apt 13.11.1841; 775a (1470); Map 1843, 6 chns, by J. Watson, Lancaster; foot/b'way, canal with towpath, waterbodies, woods (col), plantations (col), parkland, field gates, building names, road names, school house, drains. Apt has cropping information.

18/306 Tonge (township in parish of Prestwick cum Oldham) SD 881058 [Not listed]
Apt 17.12.1838; 368a (367); Map 1839, 3 chns, by Fishwick; railway, canal with towpath, waterbodies, woods, building names, brewery, school, boundary stone. Apt omits land use.

18/307 Tottington Higher End (township in parish of Bury) SD 797195 [Tottington]
Apt 17.12.1838; 3677a (3686); Map 1840?, 3 chns, by J. Whitle; hill-drawing, foot/b'way, waterbodies, woods, plantations, rock outcrops, field gates, building names, weirs, tunnel, chapel, boundary markers, stone quarries, springs, 'ancient cross', common; bridge named.

18/308 Tottington Lower End (township in parish of Bury) SD 770150 [Tottington]
Apt 17.12.1838; 4297a (5038); Map 1842?, 3 chns, surveyed by Thomas Bird, Chatham Street, Manchester, for James Whitehead, Tipping Place, Bolton-le-Moors; construction lines, hill-drawing, waterbodies, woods, plantations, building names, weir.

18/309 Toxteth Park (extra-parochial place) SJ 368878 [Toxteth]
Apt 31.03.1845; 2333a (3768); Map 1847, 4.5 chns, by Henry White, Warrington; foot/b'way, turnpike roads, toll bar, waterbodies, woods, parkland (named, in detail), building names, road names, high water mark, quarry, gas works, docks, windmill, Unitarian Chapel, Independent Chapel, school; built-up part generalised; park named; 'This Plan is... partly compiled from Estate Plans of the landowners and part from actual Survey by Mr John Young of Liverpool. This Plan is drawn at The Office of the Apportioner'.

18/310 Trawden (township in parish of Whalley) SD 935375
Apt 26.04.1842; 6686a (2510); Map 1850, 3 chns, 1st cl; foot/b'way, fences, building names, boundary stones, mills.

18/311 Treales, Roseacre and Wharles (townships in parish of Kirkham) SD 446347
Apt 27.06.1839; 3983a (all); Map 1840, 6 chns, by C. Birket; railway, foot/b'way, waterbodies, woods, hamlet boundaries and names.

18/312 Tunstal (township in parish of Tunstal) SD 615739
Apt 24.01.1845; 1077a (1077); Map 1845, 3 chns, 1st cl, in 2 parts, by Ordnance Survey; construction lines, hill-drawing, foot/b'way, waterbodies, houses, field gates, building names, road names, drain, springs, swallows, stile, walks, sundial, smithy, trough, pump, gravel pit, saw pits, graveyard, vicarage, school, milestone, boundary stones, foot stick, stepping stones.

18/313 Twiston (township in parish of Whalley) SD 813438
Apt 23.08.1843; 9a (849); Map 1849?, 4 chns; foot/b'way, waterbodies, woods, building names, landowners, spring, well, lime kiln, mills.

18/314 Tyldesley cum Shakerley (township in parish of Leigh) SD 705025
Apt 06.05.1846; 2474a (2474); Map 1847, 3 chns, by William Rothwell, Winwick; foot/b'way, waterbodies, woods, plantations, parkland, orchards, building names, road names, quarry, colliery, cotton mill, corn mill, tannery, Sunday School, township boundary, projected streets; bridge named. Apt has cropping information.

18/315 Ulnes Walton (township in parish of Croston) SD 509201 [Not listed]
Apt 30.03.1838; 2088a (2087); Map 1837, 3 chns, by T. Addison; construction lines, hill-drawing, foot/b'way, occupation roads, turnpike roads, toll gate, waterbodies, plantations, orchards, heath/moor, field gates, building names, 'Pits growing Arable', malt kiln; one symbol used for both orchards and gardens; legend explains certain symbols.

18/316 Ulverston (township in parish of Ulverston) SD 293773
Apt 12.07.1849; 449a (2900); Map 1850, 3 chns, in 2 parts, by John Robinson, Keldray near Ulverston; foot/b'way, canal with towpath, waterbodies, building names, Meeting House, school, mills, sands; bridge named; built-up part generalised.

18/317 Upholland (township in parish of Wigan) SJ 515050 [Up Holland]
Apt 01.08.1844; 4453a (4452); Map 1845, 4 chns, 1st cl, by E. Geo. Melling, Winstanley, Wigan; hill-drawing, foot/b'way, waterbodies, woods, marsh/bog, building names, quarries, old coal pit.

18/318 Urmston (township in parish of Flixton) SJ 773944
Apt 13.08.1842; 974a (974); Map 1845, 3 chns, 1st cl, by Richard Warburton, Flixton; foot/b'way, waterbodies, building names.

18/319 Urswick (parish) SD 265745 [Great and Little Urswick]
Apt 05.08.1848; 4016a (4100); Map 3 chns, 'Copied from the Survey of 1839 and Corrected to Sept. 1849', by J. Bolton, Ulverston; hill-drawing, foot/b'way, houses, field gates, beacon, ancient earthwork, sands, hamlet boundaries; legend explains boundary colours; lettering is stamped; area numbers are handwritten.

18/320 Walmersley cum Shuttleworth (township in parish of Bury) SD 810154
Apt 12.04.1838; 5056a (5056); Map 1840?, 3 chns, in 2 parts, by William Benson, Bury, Lancashire; hill-drawing, foot/b'way, turnpike roads, toll bars, waterbodies, woods, plantations, parkland, rock outcrops, building names, road names, aqueduct, weirs, mills, cotton mill, paper mill, spindle mill, school, old engine, print works, stone quarries, chapels, Tabernacle, dog kennels, reservoirs; moor and hills named; legend explains some symbols; north pointer has leafy decoration.

18/321 Walton le Dale (township in parish of Blackburn) SD 572268 [Walton-le-Dale]
Apt 21.02.1839; 4631a (4630); Map 1839, 6 chns, copied by C. Birket; hill-drawing, railway, foot/b'way, waterbodies, woods, plantations.

18/322 Walton on the Hill (township in parish of Walton on the Hill) SJ 368945 [Walton]
Apt 04.04.1845; 1887a (1886); Map 1847, 9 chns; hill-drawing, railway, foot/b'way, turnpike roads, toll bar, waterbodies, woods, parkland, building names, road names, priory, stone quarries. Apt has cropping information.

18/323 Warrington (township in parish of Warrington) SJ 610890
Apt 31.03.1838; 2508a (2507); Map 1837, 3 chns, by John Laurence, Leicester; railways, foot/b'way, canal with towpath, waterbodies, woods, building names, road names, quay, dock works, weir, mills, obelisk (named in gothic), drains; park and bridge named; built-up part is generalised. Apt has cropping information.

18/324 Warton (township in parish of Kirkham) SD 405282
Apt 08.05.1841; 1535a (all); Map 1839, 3 chns, copied by A. Halliday, Preston; waterbodies, woods, orchards, building names, mill, sea wall, occupation roads, drains.

18/325 Warton with Lindeth (township in parish of Warton) SD 487724
Apt 14.06.1845; 2924a (2924); Map 1846, 4 chns, 'Copied and revised' by John Watson junr, Kendal; hill-drawing, railway, foot/b'way, turnpike roads, toll bar, canal with towpath, waterbodies, woods, plantations, parkland, orchards, rock outcrops, building names, Wesleyan Chapel, vicarage, springs, hotel, coastline and coastal embankments, drains; part of the foreshore has been staked out and is possibly in the process of reclamation.

18/326 Wavertree (township in parish of Childwell) SJ 398888
Apt 13.03.1845; 1797a (1796); Map 1846, 3 chns, by James Woods, Liverpool; railway, waterbodies, woods, plantations, parkland (in detail), orchards, gardens, rock outcrops, quarries; legend explains land-use symbols.

18/327 Weeton with Preese (township in parish of Kirkham) SD 378353
Apt 27.06.1839; 2876a (2876); Map 1840, 6 chns, by C. Birket; hill-drawing, railway, foot/b'way, waterbodies, woods, sand or stone pits, township boundary.

18/328 Welch Whittle (township in parish of Standish) SD 546147 [Not listed]
Apt 28.03.1842; 595a (594); Map 1843, 3 chns, by Robt Kellett, Wigan; construction lines, hill-drawing, foot/b'way, turnpike roads, toll bar, waterbodies, woods, plantations, orchards, field gates, stocks, wells.

18/329 Wennington (township in parish of Melling) SD 624705
Apt 06.05.1848; 976a (830); Map 1849, 3 chns, by Geo. Wolfenden, Kirkby Lonsdale; railway, waterbodies, woods, plantations, parkland, field gates, building names, drains.

18/330 Westby with Plumpton (township in parish of Kirkham) SD 377320
Apt 10.08.1839; 3427a (3426); Map 1840, 6 chns, by A. Bannerman; railway, foot/b'way, waterbodies, field gates, sand or stone pits.

18/331 Westhoughton (township in parish of Deane) SD 650060
Apt 21.03.1846; 3441a (4460); Map 1850, 9 chns; railway, foot/b'way, waterbodies, woods, landowners, tithe-free land (col).

18/332 Wheelton (township in parish of Leyland) SD 613211
Apt 07.08.1845; 1669a (1669); Map 1846, 6 chns, 'copied'; foot/b'way, canal with towpath, waterbodies, woods, plantations.

18/333 Whiston (township in parish of Prescot) SJ 471907
Apt 19.06.1840; 1776a (1793); Map 1842, 3 chns, 1st cl, by Jno. Daglish, St Helens, land and mine surveyor; railway, waterbodies, houses, woods, parkland (in detail), building names, smithies, coal pit (with Dawson's symbol).

18/334 Whittingham (township in parish of Kirkham) SD 575365 [Not listed]
Apt 12.01.1849; 3181a (?); Map 1850, 4 chns, 1st cl, by William Bell, Goosnargh; construction lines, waterbodies, building names, parsonage.

18/335 Whittington (parish) SD 590760
Apt 11.05.1848; 4322a (4322); Map 1849?, 6 chns, in 2 parts; hill-drawing, foot/b'way, waterbodies, woods, plantations, parkland, building names, school, rectory, quarry, limekiln, mill, river banks, townships.

18/336 Whittle le Woods (township in parish of Leyland) SD 581209 [Whittle-le-Woods]
Apt 07.08.1845; 1358a (1357); Map 1840, 3 chns, by Charles Birket; hill-drawing, foot/b'way, canal with towpath, waterbodies, woods, parkland, orchards, quarries.

18/337 Widnes (township in parish of Prescot) SJ 512872
Apt 16.04.1840; 3000a (3330); Map 1842, 8 chns, by Jno. Daglish, St Helens, land and mine surveyor; railway, canal, waterbodies, woods, drains.

18/338 Wigan (township in parish of Wigan) SD 582065
Apt 14.02.1839; 1858a (2161); Map 1848, 2 chns, 1st cl, by Thomas Young, Humshaugh, Hexham, (tithable parts only); construction lines, hill-drawing, railways with station and goods station, tramways, foot/b'way, turnpike roads, toll bar, canal with towpath and warehouse, waterbodies, houses, woods, plantations, parkland, field boundary ownerships, field gates, building names, road names, monument, reservoirs, factory, mills, pepper mill, pottery, foundries, chemical works, gas works, forge, sand pit, colleries, 'pit hills', quarry; bridges named.

18/339 Windle (township in parish of Prescot) SJ 509973 [Not listed]
Apt 16.04.1840; 2907a (2907); Map '1808' (? 1842), 8 chns, in 2 parts, by Jno. Maughan, (including 1 chn enlargements of detail; tithable parts only); waterbodies, woods, industrial spoil.

18/340 Winmarleigh (township in parish of Garstang) SD 463475
Apt 21.11.1838; 1304a (2282); Map 1849, 8 chns, by Jonn. Binns, Lancaster; canal, moss (named); colours may show owners. Apt is by holding.

18/341 Winstanley (township in parish of Wigan) SD 542021
Apt 31.10.1838; 1854a (all); Map 1841?, 4.4 chns, in 2 parts, by R. Thornton; hill-drawing, foot/b'way, waterbodies, woods, parkland (in detail), building names, sand or stone pit or quarry, chapel. Apt omits land use.

18/342 Winwick with Hulme (township in parish of Winwick) SJ 600925
Apt 16.08.1838; 1432a (1431); Map 1839?, 4 chns; railway, foot/b'way, canal, waterbodies, woods, parkland (in detail), field boundary ownerships, property ownership. Apt has cropping information.

18/343 Withington (township in parish of Manchester) SJ 850930
Apt 21.02.1845; 2498a (2498); Map 1848, 4 chns, by William Rothwell, (tithable parts only); foot/b'way, waterbodies, plantations, parkland, orchards, gardens, hedges, field gates, building names, road names, Independent college. Apt has cropping information.

18/344 Withnell (township in parish of Leyland) SD 640220
Apt 08.08.1845; 3557a (3557); Map 1840, 9 chns, in 4 parts, by P. Park, Preston, (including built-up parts at 3 chns); hill-drawing, canal with towpath, waterbodies, woods, plantations, building names (some in gothic), engine house, quarries, school, moor. Apt omits field names.

18/345 Woodplumpton (township in parish of St Michael upon Wyre) SD 490350
Apt 27.06.1839; 4723a (4722); Map 1840?, 5 chns, railway, canal with towpath, waterbodies, woods, building names, road names, workhouse, chapels, tithe barn, hamlet or district boundaries, green.

18/346 Woolston with Martinscroft (township in parish of Warrington) SJ 648896
Apt 24.06.1840; 1445a (1444); Map 1841, 6 chns, by T. Burgess; canal with towpath, waterbodies, woods, field boundary ownerships, moss named; tithe-free land not mapped in detail.

18/347 Little Woolton (township in parish of Childwall) SJ 431892 [Not listed]
Apt 13.06.1845; 1351a (1200); Map 1848, 3 chns, 'revised from a former survey' by John Young, Liverpool; foot/b'way, waterbodies, woods, plantations, parkland, orchards, building names, quarries, school; bridge named.

18/348 Worthington (township in parish of Standish) SD 577117 [Not listed]
Apt 30.09.1842; 657a (657); Map 1842, 3 chns, 1st cl, by Ordnance Survey; construction lines, trig points, railway, waterbodies, houses, fences, building names, weir, sluice, wells, milestone, water troughs, paper mill, coal pits, engine house ruins.

18/349 Wray with Botton (township in parish of Melling) SD 643638
Apt 06.05.1848; 6507a (6506); Map 1849, 6 chns, by D. McCay; railway, waterbodies, woods.

18/350 Wrightington (township in parish of Eccleston) SD 528120 [Not listed]
Apt 08.05.1841; 3876a (3876); Map 1841, 3 chns, by A. Halliday, Preston; construction lines, hill-drawing, canal, waterbodies, woods, plantations, parkland (in detail), orchards, building names, chapel, school, tithe barn, mill, sand or stone pit, old mine; mansions named in gothic lettering; bridge and hills named.

18/351 Over Wyersdale (township in parish of Lancaster) SD 570540 [Not listed]
Apt 30.05.1843; 16939a (16938); Map 1848, 12 chns; foot/b'way, waterbodies, building names, chapel house, sheep fold, fells (named), vaccary boundaries (col, named), stone marked 'HSCC 1692'. Apt omits land use and some field names.

18/352 Yate and Pickup Bank (township in parish of Blackburn) SD 725229
Apt 31.12.1851; 75a (1360); Map 1852, 3 chns, woods, building names. Apt omits land use.

18/353 Yealand Conyers (township in parish of Warton) SD 502744
Apt 13.08.1845; 1578a (1577); Map 1846, 3 chns, by Ordnance Survey and 'revised and corrected' by J. Watson Jnr, Kendal for the ratepayers, (i.e. parochial assessment); railway, foot/b'way, canal, waterbodies, woods, plantations, parkland (in detail), orchards, rock outcrops, building names, pound, post office, gravel pit, boundary stones and trees, National School, Friends School, Friends Meeting House, R.C. Chapel, monument, summer house, rustic houses, cemetery, lock house, limekilns, engine house, shafts, mining shafts, pumps, wells; the map appears to have been drawn by the Ordnance Survey and subsequently amended by Watson, e.g. the Lancaster and Carlisle Railway has been added, and the original detail scraped out.

18/354 Yealand Redmayne (township in parish of Warton) SD 500763
Apt 13.08.1845; 2099a (2099); Map 1846, 4 chns, 'copied and revised' by John Watson junr, Kendal; railway, foot/b'way, canal with towpath, waterbodies, woods, plantations, orchards, building names, gravel pit, National School, watering place, furnance.

Leicestershire

PRO IR29 and IR30 19/1-168

353 tithe districts: 527,119 acres
167 tithe commutations: 157,271 acres
37 voluntary tithe agreements, 130 compulsory tithe awards,
1 corn rent annuity

Tithe and tithe commutation

The proportion of land in Leicestershire exonerated from tithe commutation at the time of parliamentary enclosure is exceeded only by that in Huntingdonshire and Northamptonshire. As in other midland counties the enclosure process left a number of pockets of residual tithable land within otherwise tithe-free districts so that, although some tithe remained payable in 47 per cent of tithe districts, less than 30 per cent of the area of the county remained tithable (Fig. 31). Like Nottinghamshire, Leicestershire straddles the division between that part of England dominated by parishes (54 per cent of Leicestershire tithe districts) and that dominated by townships (38 per cent of Leicestershire tithe districts).

Assistant tithe commissioners and local tithe agents who worked in Leicestershire are listed in Table 19.1. Leicestershire is unusual in the relatively large number of valuations of tithe rent-charge made by outsiders. Ten districts were valued by men from London, including eight by Frederick Thynne, and one district was valued by William Lancaster from the North Riding of Yorkshire. Eight districts were valued by the Tithe Commission in default of the landowners arranging for a valuation within the statutory six-month period (Table 19.2).

Tithe maps

About 7 per cent of Leicestershire's 167 tithe maps are sealed as first class. These first-class maps are based on either new survey or a thorough overhaul of older work but as always it is impossible to say how many second-class maps were produced in this way. No Leicestershire second-class map carries construction lines but on only three maps is copying acknowledged explicitly. The phrase '...the property of...' in the titles of ten maps probably indicates copying from estate maps. Characteristic of Leicestershire and other 'enclosure' counties is that the nominal peak of map production is at the end rather than the beginning of the 1840s, though by that time most maps are of small pockets of residual tithable land (Table 19.4).

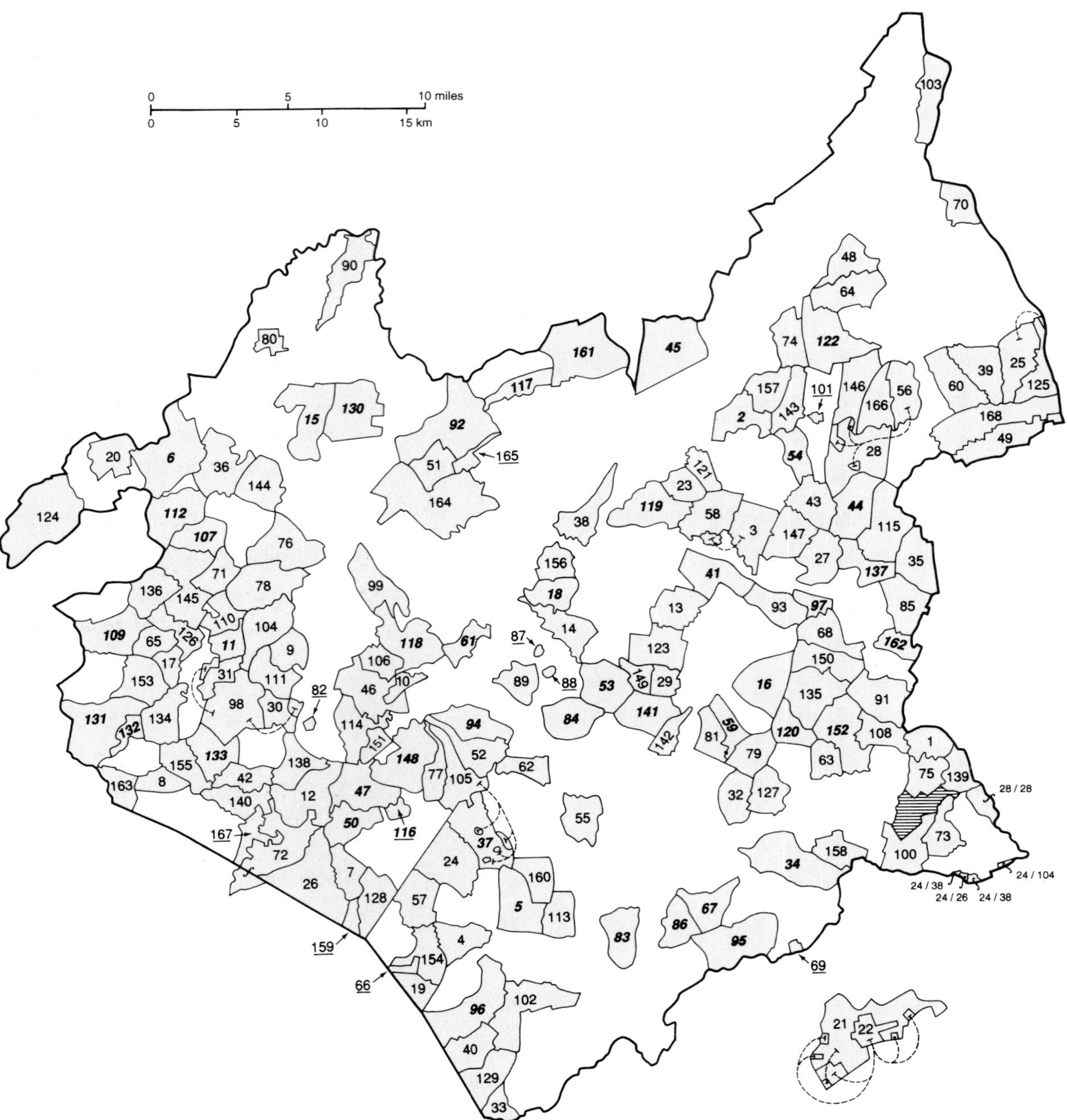

Fig. 31 Leicestershire: tithe district boundaries.

Leicestershire tithe maps are drawn at a wide variety of scales, from one inch to 1.5 chains to one inch to 18 chains; 31 per cent are in the recommended scale range of one inch to 3 to 4 chains. Maps at the six-chain scale are most numerous and this scale was employed in 42 per cent of districts. In common with some other midland counties, significant use was also made of the five-chain scale (15 per cent of maps).

Leicestershire tithe maps usually record woodland (on 67 per cent of the maps) and some parkland (on 12 per cent, though only on two maps in any detail) but they constitute a poor record of other land uses; only one map distinguishes arable and grass, six depict gardens, and eight map orchards. The progress of enclosure in Leicestershire was such that only two maps show residual open-field farming. Non agricultural land use is understated with, for example, no hint of the coalfield in the north-west of the county. Most urban areas in Leicestershire were tithe free; Melton Mowbray is a partial exception and its tithe map depicts numerous public buildings and lists these and important private residences in tables. Tithe-free areas are often coloured on Leicestershire tithe maps, archaeological features appear on a few maps, notably an 'encampment' at Ratby, and seven maps show churches by pictorial symbols.

Only half the Leicestershire tithe maps in the Public Record Office collection can be attributed to a particular map-maker. By far the most productive of these was R. D. Miles of Leicester who produced twenty maps in a straightforward, unadorned style. Two maps were made by men from well outside the county, one by G. B. Lancaster from the North Riding of Yorkshire and another by Robert Booth from Wainfleet, Lincolnshire.

Leicestershire maps have little decoration apart from some minor embellishments of borders, scale bars and north pointers. The map of Little Ashby has drawing instruments around the scale bar, a motif more common in Devon than the Midlands. The map-maker seems to have intended a legend for the map of Horninghold but only its floral surround was drawn.

Table 19.1. *Agreements and awards for commutation of tithes in Leicestershire*

Assistant commissioner/ local tithe agent	*Number of agreements**	*Number of awards*
John Job Rawlinson	1	49
Thomas Smith Woolley	13	36
George Wingrove Cooke	0	29
John Pickering	17	0
Edward Greathed	5	0
Charles Howard	0	5
Joseph Townsend	1	4
Charles Pym	0	4
Richard Burton Phillipson	3	0
Henry Pilkington	2	0
John Mee Mathew	0	2
George Louis	0	1
Horace William Meteyard	1	0

*Computed from the number of extant reports on tithe agreements in the tithe files [PRO IR 18].

Table 19.2. *Tithe valuers and tithe map-makers in Leicestershire*

Name and address (in Leicestershire unless indicated)	*Number of districts*	*Acreage*
Tithe valuers		
Thomas Miles, Keyham	36	45,244
John Thorpe, Shenton, near Hinckley	11	9,692
Nathaniel C. Stone, Rowley Fields, Leicester	9	4,652
Frederick Thynne	8	5,374
Tithe Commissioners	8	579
Thomas S. Woolley junior, South Collingham, Nottinghamshire	7	4,746
Others [54]	88	86,984
Attributed tithe map-makers		
R. D. Miles, Leicester	20	26,053
Samuel Morris, Sutton Cheney	7	9,549
John Bromley, Derby	7	6,327
Thomas Miles, Leicester	6	5,315
Robert Bromley, Derby	4	6,001
R. Hayward and Son, Northampton	4	3,596
Walker and Goodacre, Leicester	4	1,048
Others [25]	32	33,862

Table 19.3. *The tithe maps of Leicestershire: scales and classes*

Scale in chains/inch	*All maps*		*First Class*		*Second Class*	
	Number	*Acreage*	*Number*	*Acreage*	*Number*	*Acreage*
>3	8	794	1	29	7	765
3	38	33,213	10	12,181	28	21,032
4	13	14,998	0	0	13	14,998
4.5	1	1,000	0	0	1	1,000
5	25	22,532	0	0	25	22,532
5.5	1	2,998	0	0	1	2,998
6	70	70,967	0	0	70	70,967
<6	11	10,769	0	0	11	10,769
TOTAL	167	157,271	11	12,210	156	145,061

Table 19.4. *The tithe maps of Leicestershire: dates*

	1838	*1839*	*1840*	*1841*	*1842*	*1843*	*1844*	*1845*	*1846*	*1847*	*1848*	*1849*	*1850*	*1851*	*>1851*
All maps	7	9	11	5	8	5	9	6	6	16	16	21	13	18	17
1st class	0	2	1	1	0	0	1	0	0	0	0	0	1	2	1
2nd class	7	7	10	4	8	5	8	6	6	16	16	21	12	16	16

Leicestershire

19/1 Alexton (parish) SP 814996 [Allexton]
Apt 06.05.1846; 1000a (all); Map 1847, 4.5 chns, by R.D. Miles, Leicester; foot/b'way, waterbodies, woods, plantations, parkland.

19/2 Asfordby (parish) SK 705195
Apt 08.07.1851; 6a (1210); Map 1851?, 10 chns, (tithable parts only, tinted); field names, landowners, field acreages.

19/3 Ashby Folville (township in parish of Ashby Folville) SK 710129
Apt 20.02.1847; 1984a (1983); Map 1848, 6 chns, by R.D. Miles, Leicester; foot/b'way, waterbodies, woods, fences.

19/4 Little Ashby (township) SP 530886 [Ashby Parva]
Apt 29.07.1847; 1357a (all); Map 1848, 4 chns, by H. Tarry; foot/b'way, turnpike roads, houses, woods, gardens, field gates, road names; mapmaker's name is on scroll; pair of compasses, quill pen, charcoal holders and ruler surround the scale bar.

19/5 Ashby Magna (township) SP 567906
Apt 29.11.1849; 227a (1720); Map 1850?, 3 chns; waterbodies, woods. Apt omits some field names.

19/6 Ashby de la Zouch (township in parish of Ashby de la Zouch) SK 369178 [Ashby-de-la-Zouch]
Apt 06.02.1846; 6a (6980); Map 1852?, 6 chns, (tithable parts only); foot/b'way, building names, road names, theatre. District is apportioned by holding; Apt omits land use.

19/7 Aston Flamville (parish) SP 464926
Apt 11.02.1850; 962a (4670); Map 1851, 6 chns, by Thomas Miles, Leicester; foot/b'way, waterbodies, woods, field gates, glebe (with acreages).

19/8 Atterton (township in parish of Witherley) SP 353982
Apt 15.02.1848; 639a (all); Map 1848, 3 chns, by Samuel Morris and William Thorpe; foot/b'way, waterbodies, plantations.

19/9 Barlestone (township in parish of Market Bosworth) SK 434061
Apt 10.03.1849; 1040a (1039); Map 1849, 5 chns, foot/b'way, waterbodies, woods.

19/10 Barrons Park (township in parish of Desford) SK 502041 [Not listed]
Apt 03.09.1844; 419a (?); Map 1849, 5 chns, by R.D. Miles, Leicester; railway, foot/b'way, waterbodies, woods, plantations, building names.

19/11 Barton in the Beans (part of) (hamlet in parish of Shackerston) SK 394065
Apt 10.06.1844; 103a (all); Map 1848?, 3 chns; foot/b'way.

19/12 Barwell (parish) SP 441970
Apt 08.11.1838; 2321a (3950); Map 1838, 3 chns, in 3 parts, by John Lane, Stony Stanton near Hinckley, (includes two enlargements of village at 1.5 chns); waterbodies, houses, woods, road names, ownership boundaries (col), glebe (green).

19/13 Beeby (parish) SK 663082
Apt 26.02.1839; 1418a (all); Map 1839, 3 chns, 1st cl, by John Bromley, Derby; construction lines, foot/b'way, waterbodies, houses, woods, parkland, fence, field boundary ownerships, field gates. Apt has cropping information.

19/14 Belgrave (parish) SK 600070
Apt 12.09.1845; 1553a (all); Map 1846, 5 chns; railway, foot/b'way, waterbodies, woods, field gates; churches and chapels are black.

19/15 Belton (parish) SK 450200
Apt 23.02.1852; 50a (1900); Map 1852, 6 chns, by Thomas Miles, Leicester; turnpike roads, toll bar, tithe-free land.

19/16 Billesdon (township) SK 716033
Apt 18.02.1847; 61a (?); Map 1850?, 5 chns, foot/b'way, waterbodies, woods, building names, road names, chapel, vicarage, brickyard.

19/17 Bilstone (township in parishes of Market Bosworth and Norton juxta Twycross) SK 362051
Apt 25.01.1849; 693a (all); Map 1851?, 6 chns; foot/b'way, waterbodies, woods, plantations, orchards, marsh/bog, osiers. Apt omits land use.

19/18 Birstall (chapelry in parish of Belgrave) SK 592091
Apt 12.09.1845; 85a (?); Map 1850, 4 chns, by Thomas Miles, Leicester; foot/b'way, waterbodies, woods, plantations, landowners, tithe-free land, field acreages.

19/19 Bittesby (hamlet in parish of Claybrook) SP 501856
Apt 22.12.1842; 746a (all); Map 1843, 6 chns, by R. Stelfox, Allesley; railway, waterbodies, houses, woods, building names, road names, ornamental ground.

19/20 Blackfordby and Boothorpe (township in parish of Ashby de la Zouch) SK 327178
Apt 31.03.1842; 335a (1117); Map 1842, 6 chns, by Joseph Kidger, Ashby-de-la-Zouch; foot/b'way, waterbodies, woods, field boundary ownerships, field acreages.

19/21 St Giles in Blaston (parish) SP 800956 [Not listed]
Apt 30.11.1839; 927a (all); Map 1840, 6 chns; waterbodies, woods, field gates, cow pasture with note of 'cow commons'; colours show detached parts of other districts.

19/22 St Michaels in Blaston (parish) SP 807955 [Not listed]
Apt 18.11.1842; 340a (all); Map 1843, 6 chns, by G. Cuming, Easton, Northamptonshire, (tinted); waterbodies, cow pasture with note of 'cow commons'.

19/23 Brookesby (parish) SK 673155 [Brooksby]
Apt 02.11.1847; 861a (all); Map 1848, 6 chns, by R.D. Miles, Leicester; railway, foot/b'way, waterbodies, woods, fences.

19/24 Broughton Astley and part of Croft (parish) SP 537921
Apt 22.11.1844; 2506a (all); Map 1845, 3 chns, 1st cl, by William Phillips, Coventry; construction lines, railway with station, foot/b'way, waterbodies, houses, woods, osiers, parkland, orchards, marsh/bog, hedge ownership, fences, field gates, building names, road names, mills, rectory, windmill, chapel, Roman road; bridge named.

19/25 Buckminster (except Sewsterne) (parish) SK 864224
Apt 27.01.1841; 1796a (1796); Map 1842?, 6 chns, in 2 parts, (including 2-chn plan of Lord Dysart's house and grounds); landowners.

19/26 Burbage (parish) SP 443922
Apt 29.01.1840; 2952a (?); Map 1838, 3 chns, by Joseph Hanson, Caldecote, Architect and Surveyor; foot/b'way, turnpike roads, toll gate, canal with towpath, waterbodies, houses, farmyards, woods, plantations, orchards, gardens, heath/moor, fences, field boundary ownerships, road names, ornamental ground, Roman road.

19/27 Burrow or Burrough (parish) SK 752107 [Not listed]
Apt 30.06.1843; 1566a (all); Map 1839, 3 chns, by R.D. Miles, Leicester; hill-drawing, foot/b'way, waterbodies, woods, tumulus.

19/28 Burton Lazaars (part of) (township and hamlet in parish of Melton Mowbray) SK 779170 [Burton Lazars]
Apt 19.10.1848; 2462a (2060); Map 1850, 7 chns, by Thomas Miles, Leicester, (tithable parts only in detail); railway, foot/b'way, waterbodies, woods, plantations, landowners.

19/29 Bushby (part of) (township in parish of Thurnby) SK 660040
Apt 16.07.1845; 661a (2740); Map 1846, 3 chns, by R.D. Miles, Leicester; foot/b'way, waterbodies, woods, field gates.

19/30 Cadeby (except East Osbaston) (parish) SK 426022
Apt 24.01.1840; 797a (all); Map 1840, 6 chns; foot/b'way, turnpike roads, toll gate, waterbodies, woods, field gates.

19/31 Carlton (township in parish of Market Bosworth) SK 391047
Apt 25.01.1849; 726a (all); Map 1849, 6 chns, 'copied' by S. Morris and W. Thorpe; foot/b'way, canal with towpath, waterbodies.

19/32 Carlton Curlieu (township in parish of Carlton Curlieu) SP 699968
Apt 12.08.1850; 1292a (2970); Map 1851, 6 chns, by Robt Bromley, Derby; foot/b'way, waterbodies, woods (named), parkland, building names, road names, sand or stone pit, glebe, Roman road.

19/33 Catthorpe (parish) SP 552788
Apt 26.01.1846; 625a (625); Map 1846?, 2.5 chns, ? by T.W. Martin, Dunchurch; foot/b'way, waterbodies, woods (col), field boundary ownerships, road names, Roman road.

19/34 Church Langton (parish) SP 732921
Corn rent conversion, 1920; ?a (4280); there is no map.

19/35 Cold Overton (parish) SK 810100
Apt 18.10.1838; 507a (1657); Map 1840?, 6 chns; foot/b'way, waterbodies, woods, parkland, field names, field acreages, glebe; map is titled 'Estate belonging to T. Frewen Esqr'.

19/36 Coleorton (parish) SK 393171
Apt 30.12.1841; 1999a (1999); Map 1842, 6 chns; waterbodies, woods, plantations, parkland, sand or stone pit or quarry, township boundaries, rectorial lands, tithe-free land; map date is on red ribbon draped across the north pointer.

19/37 Cosby (parish) SP 545944
Apt 31.12.1850; 8a (2550); Map 1853?, 4 chns, (tithable parts only). Apt omits land use.

19/38 Cossington (parish) SK 612136
Apt 01.08.1842; 1551a (1551); Map 1842, 6 chns, by John Bromley, Derby; railway, foot/b'way, canal, lock house, waterbodies, houses, woods, plantations, building names, road names, mills, Roman road.

19/39 Coston (parish) SK 852218
Apt 12.10.1844; 1724a (all); Map 1845?, 6 chns; foot/b'way, waterbodies, woods (col), parkland, building names, rectory, glebe (col); meaning of yellow tint is unclear.

19/40 Cottesbach (parish) SP 537820 [Cottesbach]
Apt 17.08.1848; 1228a (all); Map 1849?, 6 chns, (surveyed in 1804 by J. Eagle); foot/b'way, woods, plantations, orchards; map is subtitled 'the property of the Revd James Powell Marriott'.

19/41 South Croxton (parish) SK 688102
Apt 10.06.1844; 455a (1760); Map 1852, 5 chns, by Thomas Miles, Leicester; foot/b'way, waterbodies, woods, landowners.

19/42 Dadlington (chapelry in parish of Hinckley) SP 403982
Apt 12.06.1843; 1022a (all); Map 1843?, 6 chns; foot/b'way, canal with towpath.

19/43 Great Dalby (parish) SK 748140
Apt 12.11.1840; 2295a (2328); Map 1841, 8 chns; foot/b'way, woods.

19/44 Little Dalby (parish) SK 775135
Apt 07.12.1846; 496a (1848); Map 1848?, 5 chns, in 2 parts, (including enlargement of glebe); foot/b'way, private road, turnpike roads, waterbodies, woods, plantations, building names, landowners, vicarage; map is titled 'the property of E.B. Hartopp Esqre.'

19/45 Old Dalby (extra-parochial place) SK 664236
Apt 20.04.1849; 80a (?); Map 1852?, 6 chns, (tithable parts only); landowners.

19/46 Desford (township in parish of Desford) SK 480032
Apt 27.03.1845; 867a (?); Map 1845, 5 chns; railway, foot/b'way, waterbodies, woods (named), field gates, building names, landowners, mill, freeboard, tithe-free land.

19/47 Earl Shilton (township in parish of Kirkby Mallory) SP 471975
Apt 30.06.1849; 67a (920); Map 1856, 6 chns; churchyard.

19/48 Eastwell (parish) SK 775285
Apt 03.09.1846; 1347a (all); Map 1847, 5 chns; foot/b'way, waterbodies, field boundary ownerships.

19/49 Edmondthorpe (parish) SK 865171
Apt 22.10.1841; 1753a (1753); Map 1842, 6 chns, in 5 parts, by Jno. Brereton, Melton Mowbray, (includes four 1-chn enlargements of detail); canal, waterbodies, woods (col).

19/50 Elmsthorpe (parish) SP 463958
Apt 08.06.1850; 319a (1650); Map 1851, 3 chns, 1st cl, by Walker and Goodacre, Leicester; construction lines, foot/b'way, waterbodies, houses, field boundary ownerships, field gates.

19/51 Emmanuel (except Woodthorpe) (parish) SK 533165 [Not listed]
Apt 10.01.1849; 1151a (?); Map 1849, 6 chns, by John Bromley, Derby; foot/b'way, waterbodies, woods, plantations, building names, road names.

19/52 Enderby (township in parish of Enderby) SP 523996
Apt 16.01.1849; 1661a (all); Map 1849, 5 chns, in 3 parts, by R.D. Miles, Leicester, (including Ratby Meadow separately at 3 chns, and Enderby village separately at 2.5 chns); foot/b'way, waterbodies, woods, plantations (named), parkland, heath/moor, fox covert, open fields, road names, boundary stones.

19/53 Evington (parish) SK 625030
Apt 28.02.1850; 168a (1360); Map 1851, 6 chns, by Robt Bromley, Derby; foot/b'way, waterbodies, woods.

19/54 Eye Kettleby (township in parish of Melton Mowbray) SK 737168 [Not listed]
Apt 03.02.1844; 5a (?); Map 1848?, 9 chns; railway, building names, mill.

19/55 Foston (parish) SP 605954
Apt 12.02.1850; 1317a (all); Map 1850, 6 chns, by R.S. Booth, Wainfleet; foot/b'way, turnpike roads, toll bar, milestone, canal, waterbodies, houses, woods, plantations, field boundary ownerships, field gates, building names.

19/56 Freeby and part of Burton Lazaars (township) SK 203204
Apt 03.02.1844; 1651a (1546); Map 1844, 5 chns, in 2 parts, by R.D. Miles, Leicester; foot/b'way, canal, waterbodies, woods, landowners.

19/57 Frolesworth (parish) SP 504906
Apt 23.01.1838; 1496a (all); Map 1838, 3 chns, by John Lane, Stony Stanton near Hinckley; waterbodies, houses, woods, hedge ownership, fences.

19/58 Gaddesby (parochial chapelry) SK 689135
Apt 02.07.1846; 1657a (1657); Map 1847, 6 chns, by R.D. Miles, Leicester; foot/b'way, waterbodies, woods, parkland, fences.

19/59 Galby (township in parish of Galby) SK 698009
Apt 20.11.1849; 253a (?); Map 1850, 6 chns, by Robert Bromley, Derby; foot/b'way, waterbodies, woods.

19/60 Garthorpe (parish) SK 833209
Apt 16.04.1839; 1714a (all); Map 1839?, 6 chns; waterbodies, field names. District is apportioned by holding.

19/61 Glenfield (parish) SK 540062
Apt 21.10.1852; 594a (all); Map 1853, 5 chns, in 2 parts; railway, foot/b'way, waterbodies, woods.

19/62 Little Glenn (hamlet in parish of Aylestone) SP 570989 [Glen Parva]
Apt 12.09.1839; 811a (all); Map 1840, 3 chns, 1st cl, by John Laurance, Leicester; turnpike roads, canal with towpath, wharf, waterbodies, field gates, building names, road names, mill, mill dam. Apt omits some field names.

19/63 Goadby (township in parish of Billesdon) SP 752987
Apt 02.03.1847; 947a (?); Map 1847, 5 chns, by R.D. Miles, Leicester; waterbodies, woods.

19/64 Goadby Marwood (parish) SK 777264
Apt 13.07.1839; 1619a (1618); Map 1840, 4 chns, by G.B. Lancaster, Marderby Grange, nr Thirsk; foot/b'way, waterbodies, woods, parkland, stone pit.

19/65 Gopsall Hall (extra-parochial place) SK 349067 [Gopsall Hall Farm]
Apt 31.01.1850; 731a (all); Map 1850?, 11 chns; waterbodies, woods, ornamental ground.

19/66 Gores Land (district in parish of Monks Kirby) SP 491866 [Not listed]
Apt 05.05.1843; 203a (all); Map 1842, 6 chns, by R. Stelfox, Allesley; railway, waterbodies, woods, field boundary ownerships, road names, Roman road.

19/67 Gumley (parish) SP 700900
Apt 15.10.1850; 31a (1550); Map 1852, 2.5 chns; waterbodies, woods, field names, landowners.

19/68 Halstead (township in parish of Tilton-on-the-Hill) SK 754061
Apt 21.11.1845; 1432a (1432); Map 1847, 6 chns, by R.D. Miles, Leicester; foot/b'way, waterbodies, woods, fences; compass rose is decorated with flowers and leaves.

19/69 Harborough (township in parish of Bowden Magna) SP 732875 [Market Harborough]
Apt 24.08.1844; 48a (all); Map 1852, 1.5 chns, by Messrs Hayward, Northampton, copied from a plan of the township 'furnished by the Landowners'.

19/70 Harston (parish) SK 841316
Apt 21.07.1840; 1009a (1009); Map 1840, 3 chns, by W.B. Collingwood; waterbodies, houses, woods, arable (col), gardens, heath/moor, hedges, field names.

19/71 Heather (parish) SK 391109
Apt 27.10.1845; 1015a (all); Map 1847?, 4 chns; foot/b'way, waterbodies, woods, parkland.

19/72 Hinckley (township in parish of Hinckley) SP 423925
Apt 28.03.1844; 746a (?); Map 1844, 6 chns, in 2 parts, (tithable parts only; includes town separately at 3 chns); foot/b'way, waterbodies, private road.

19/73 Holt and Bradley (parish) SP 824939 [Nevill Holt]
Apt 01.08.1846; 1166a (all); Map 1850, 4 chns, by J. Crookes and Son, Leeds; foot/b'way, waterbodies, woods (named), plantations, parkland, arable (by annotation), grassland (by annotation), gardens, fences, field gates, building names, road names, field names, landowners, chapel; map is subtitled as a map of 'the property of Cosmo Charles George Neville Esqre.'

19/74 Holwell (township in parish of Abkettleby) SK 735236
Apt 31.08.1849; 1233a (?); Map 1850, 6 chns, by John Bromley, Derby; hill-drawing, foot/b'way, waterbodies, houses, woods, sand or stone pits or quarries.

19/75 Horninghold (parish) SP 812974
Apt 30.06.1849; 1205a (1205); Map 1849?, 4 chns; foot/b'way, waterbodies, woods, field gates; map has floral surround to what was evidently to be the legend.

19/76 Hugglescote and Donnington (township in parish of Ibstock) SK 431126
Apt 20.02.1838; 1833a (2589); Map 1838, 5 chns; railway, churchyard, greens, 'Rectory land'.

19/77 Huncote (township in parish of Narborough) SP 517989
Apt 28.10.1840; 903a (?); Map 1840, ?4 chns, by 'A.R.S.'; foot/b'way, turnpike roads, woods, field boundary ownerships, field gates, windmill (pictorial), boundary trees, gardens (by annotation), orchards (by annotation).

19/78 Ibstock (township or liberty in parish of Ibstock) SK 420100
Apt 20.02.1838; 120a (2257); Map 1838?, 3 chns; waterbodies, woods, fences, field acreages, boundary of tithable lands.

19/79 Ilston (township in parish of Carlton Curlieu and Noseley) SP 710992 [Illston on the Hill]
Apt 11.02.1848; 1354a (all); Map 1849, 6 chns, by R.D. Miles, Leicester; foot/b'way, waterbodies, woods, plantations, building names, road names.

19/80 Isley Walton (township and district) SK 425250
Apt 19.12.1840; 471a (all); Map 1840, 3 chns; turnpike roads, toll gate, waterbodies, houses, woods, gardens (col).

19/81 Kings Norton (parish) SK 683002 [King's Norton]
Apt 23.02.1847; 989a (1990); Map 1847, 5 chns; foot/b'way, waterbodies, woods, heath/moor, field gates.

19/82 Kirkby Mallory (township in parish of Kirkby Mallory) SK 454003
Apt 26.02.1850; 168a (2190); Map 1850, 3 chns, 1st cl, by Walker and Goodacre, Leicester; construction lines, foot/b'way, waterbodies, houses, field boundary ownerships, field gates.

19/83 Knaptoft (parish) SP 626887
Apt 26.08.1858; 47a (4940); Map 1859?, 2.5 chns, (tithable parts only); foot/b'way, waterbodies, woods, churchyard.

19/84 Knighton (chapelry or township in parish of Leicester, St Margarets) SK 602013
Apt 11.02.1850; 29a (1020); Map 1851, 3 chns, by Saml Harris, Leicester, (tithable parts only); canal with towpath; meadows named.

19/85 Knossington otherwise Knawston (parish) SK 804079
Apt 30.04.1847; 1443a (1443); Map 1848?, 6 chns; foot/b'way, waterbodies, houses, woods (col, named), plantations (col), marsh/bog, field names, 'Abbey Lands', glebe.

19/86 Laughton (parish) SP 662892
Apt 26.06.1839; 383a (1109); Map 1840, 3 chns; foot/b'way, waterbodies, woods, plantations, field boundary ownerships, road names, landowners; village generalised.

19/87 Leicester, St Leonard (parish) SK 580060 [Not listed]
Apt 13.11.1850; 29a (?); Map 1851, 2 chns, 1st cl, by Walker and Goodacre, Leicester, (tithable parts only); construction lines, waterbodies, houses, field boundary ownerships.

19/88 Leicester, St Margaret (parish) SK 588058 [Not listed]
Apt 11.02.1850; 100a (?); Map 1851, 3 chns, by Saml Jn Harris, Leicester, (tithable parts only); foot/b'way, canal, building names, road names, cattle market, school, prebend land, Abbey Meadows; built-up part generalised.

19/89 Leicester, St Mary including Bromkingsthorpe and West Cotes (township) SK 573035 [Not listed]
Apt 29.09.1849; 940a (?); Map 1851, 5 chns, by Saml Jh Harris, Leicester, (tithable parts only); railways with station, foot/b'way, turnpike roads, canal, waterbodies, woods, parkland; built-up part generalised.

19/90 Lockington (parish) SK 471289
Apt 28.11.1848; 1713a (2135); Map 1849, 18 chns, (tithable parts only); foot/b'way, canal, waterbodies, woods.

19/91 Loddington (parish) SK 789024
Apt 07.07.1846; 1840a (all); Map 1847, 6 chns, by R.D. Miles, Leicester; foot/b'way, waterbodies, woods, field gates.

19/92 Loughborough (parish) SK 537197
Apt 10.01.1849; 59a (?); Map 1849, 3 chns, by John Bromley, Derby, (tithable parts only); railway, canal with towpath, waterbodies, houses, road names, tithe-free land.

19/93 Lowesby (parish) SK 722080
Apt 04.12.1849; 187a (2350); Map 1851, 5 chns; foot/b'way, waterbodies, woods, field names, landowners, ownership boundaries (col).

19/94 Lubbesthorpe (township or chapelry in parish of Aylestone) SK 540012 [Not listed]
Apt 29.03.1848; 16a (1200); Map 1849, 5 chns, (tithable parts only); canal, landowners.

19/95 Lubbenham (township in parish of Lubbenham) SP 688876 [Lubenham]
Apt 06.03.1845; 90a (2400); Map 1852, 8 chns, (tithable parts only in detail, tinted). Apt omits land use.

19/96 Lutterworth (parish) SP 539843
Apt 12.01.1849; 141a (1890); Map 1853, 3 chns, (tithable parts only); houses, building names, water mill; built-up part generalised.

19/97 Marefield (township in parish of Tilton on the Hill) SK 750079
Apt 21.11.1845; 170a (170); Map 1847, 6 chns; foot/b'way, woods; colours show tithe ownership.

19/98 Market Bosworth (township in parish of Market Bosworth) SK 401029
Apt 19.07.1847; 2998a (6410); Map 1848, 5.5 chns, in 2 parts, by R.D. Miles, Leicester; foot/b'way, canal with towpath, waterbodies, woods, plantations, ornamental ground.

19/99 Markfield (parish) SK 487098
Apt 11.02.1846; 1209a (2534); Map 1847, 6 chns; foot/b'way, woods, farm names, farm and property boundaries (col).

19/100 Medbourn (parish) SP 799929 [Medbourne]
Apt 22.09.1846; 1828a (all); Map 1847, 6 chns, by R. Hayward and sons, Northampton; foot/b'way, waterbodies, houses, plantations, field boundary ownerships, building names, windmill.

19/101 Melton Mowbray (township in parish of Melton Mowbray) SK 752190
Apt 28.11.1842; 102a (?); Map 1843, 3 chns, in 32 parts, (including 'the Framlands' at 6 chns and 30 enlargements of detail at 1 inch to 80 feet (1:960); tinted); canal, waterbodies, houses, building names, road names, landowners, Methodist Chapel, Primitive Methodist Chapel, Independent Chapel, Catholic Chapel, vicarage, charity house, bedehouse, almshouses, free schools, county bridewell, old club house, bank, town hall, mills, timber, stable and hotel yards, coal yards, toll house, garden ground measurements (in yards); table lists public buildings and important private residences.

19/102 Misterton and Poultney (hamlet in parish of Misterton) SP 560845
Apt 30.05.1838; 2566a (all); Map 1839?, 8 chns; woods (col), hedges (col), field gates, road names, glebe, manorial lands; pictorial church. District is apportioned by holding and fields are not shown.

19/103 Muston (parish) SK 827382
Apt 30.03.1849; 1624a (1623); Map 1849, 5 chns; waterbodies, canal with towpath.

19/104 Nailstone with Barton in the Beans except Normanton on the Heath (parish) SK 416073
Apt 30.06.1840; 2486a (all); Map 1840, 3 chns, in 2 parts, by S. and R. Morris, Sutton Cheney; foot/b'way, waterbodies, woods.

19/105 Narborough (township) SP 535981
Apt 20.05.1846; 773a (?); Map 1846, 6 chns, litho (by Lane and Penny, 126, Chancery Lane, London); railway, foot/b'way, waterbodies, woods, plantations, field gates, landowners; villages generalised; bridge named.

19/106 Newtown Unthank and Newtown Botcheston (township in parish of Ratby) SK 489050
Apt 08.11.1847; 367a (all); Map 1848?, 4 chns, railway, waterbodies, woods.

19/107 Normanton le Heath (township in parish of Nailstone) SK 382127
Apt 30.06.1841; 104a (1320); Map 1851?, 5 chns; built-up part generalised. Apt omits land use.

19/108 East Norton (parish) SK 748002
Apt 21.02.1839; 1113a (1390); Map 1841?, 4 chns; foot/b'way, waterbodies, woods, heath/moor; pictorial church.

19/109 Norton juxta Twycross (parish) SK 321070 [Norton-Juxta-Twycross]
Apt 12.10.1844; 12a (2340); Map 1848?, 3 chns, (tithable parts only, tinted); waterbodies, building names, road names, National School, pinfold.

19/110 Odestone (township in parish of Shackerston) SK 392082 [Odstone]
Apt 10.06.1844; 733a (all); Map 1849?, 8 chns; foot/b'way, waterbodies, landowners; colours may show property ownerships; The Earl Howe's lands are described as 'free' and are not mapped in detail. Apt omits land use.

19/111 Osbaston (township in parishes of Market Bosworth and Cadeby) SK 442042
Apt 14.02.1850; 1301a (all); Map 1850, 6 chns, by Thomas Miles, Leicester; foot/b'way, waterbodies, woods, plantations, parkland, building names; map has note as to the parish boundary, signed by the rectors.

19/112 Packington with Snibstone (parish) SK 364144
Apt 31.08.1849; 229a (2020); Map 1850, 6 chns; building names, parsonage.

19/113 Peatling Parva (parish) SP 590899
Apt 15.10.1850; 940a (all); Map 1851, 5 chns; foot/b'way, waterbodies, woods, plantations, parkland.

19/114 Peckleton (township in parish of Peckleton-cum-Tooley) SK 470010
Apt 13.07.1846; 1555a (all); Map 1847, 3 chns, by Samuel Morris, Sutton Cheney, Leics, litho (by Lane and Penny, 126 Chancery Lane, London); foot/b'way, waterbodies, building names, mill dam, manor house, rectory, brick kiln, freeboard, common.

19/115 Pickwell and Leesthorpe (parish) SK 792122
Apt 20.11.1843; 2358a (all); Map 1844, 3 chns, 1st cl; construction lines, hill-drawing, foot/b'way, waterbodies, houses, woods, plantations, parkland (in detail), field gates, boundary stones, sand or stone pit. Apt omits field names.

19/116 Potters Marston (township in parish of Barwell) SP 497962
Apt 26.01.1852; 8a (280); Map 1852, 8 chns, (tithable parts only); foot/b'way, waterbodies, building names, field name and acreage, landowners, chapel; map is subtitled 'The property of the Revd Robert Boothby Heathcote'.

19/117 Prestwold (township in parish of Prestwold) SK 575215
Apt 22.12.1848; 7a (?); Map 1849?, 3 chns; foot/b'way, woods, hedges, field gates, building names, landowners.

19/118 Ratby (township in parish of Ratby) SK 505065
Apt 10.05.1847; 764a (5410); Map 1847, 6 chns, by R.D. Miles, Leicester; hill-drawing, waterbodies, woods, building names, encampment.

19/119 Rearsby (parish) SK 652143
Apt 31.07.1848; 25a (1800); Map 1851, 3 chns, by J. Tyres, (tithable parts only, tinted); railway, foot/b'way, woods, hedge ownership, field gates, landowners, churchyard.

19/120 Rollestone (township in parish of Billesdon) SK 703003 [Rolleston]
Apt 17.04.1850; 178a (?); Map 1851?, 5 chns, (tithable parts only in detail); foot/b'way, waterbodies, woods, landowners.

19/121 Rotherby (parish) SK 682162
Apt 08.04.1846; 766a (all); Map 1845, 6 chns, by J. Tyres, Thrussington; railway, foot/b'way, waterbodies, woods; pictorial church.

19/122 Scalford (parish) SK 759239
Apt 09.09.1846; 72a (2520); Map 1847, 3 chns; foot/b'way, waterbodies, landowners.

19/123 Scraptoft (parish) SK 653057
Apt 26.02.1850; 1679a (1450); Map 1850, 6 chns, by R.D. Miles, Leicester; foot/b'way, waterbodies, woods, plantations.

19/124 Seal (parish) SK 280142 [Not listed]
Apt 14.12.1842; 4388a (4890); Map 1843, 4 chns, in 4 parts, by Robt Bromley, Derby, (one part tinted; includes parts at 8 chns and 9 chns);

foot/b'way, canal with towpath, waterbodies, woods (named), plantations (named), parkland, rock outcrops, open fields, field gates, stone pit or quarry.

19/125 Sewsterne (township in parish of Buckminster) SK 884210 [Sewstern]
Apt 27.01.1841; 1257a (1257); Map 1842?, 6 chns.

19/126 Shackerstone (township) SK 338097
Apt 27.01.1851; 1055a (1920); Map 1851?, 3 chns; foot/b'way, waterbodies, canal with towpath.

19/127 Shankton and Shangton (parish) SP 719971 [Shangton]
Apt 06.04.1842; 1250a (all); Map 1842?, 5 chns: waterbodies, houses, woods, plantations, field boundary ownerships, road names.

19/128 Sharnford (parish) SP 480910
Apt 29.10.1850; 6a (740); Map 1852, 2.5 chns, by Richd Holyoak, (tithable parts only, tinted); road names, Roman road, landowners; table lists owners and acreages.

19/129 Shawell (parish) SP 545802
Apt 30.06.1840; 1408a (1407); Map 1839, 3 chns, 1st cl, by Jos. Gilbert, Welford, Northamptonshire; construction lines, waterbodies, houses, woods.

19/130 Sheepshead (parish) SK 471200 [Shepshead]
Apt 14.04.1847; 199a (5280); Map 1849, 6 chns, by R.D. Miles, Leicester; foot/b'way, canal, building names, road names.

19/131 Sheepey Magna (township in parish of Sheepey) SK 318012 [Sheepy Magna]
Apt 10.06.1844; 493a (2650); Map 1847, 6 chns, (tithable parts only); turnpike roads and gate, waterbodies, glebe, 'Rector's Allotments', 'Mythe land', 'North Mediety Glebe' (yellow), 'South Mediety Glebe' (green).

19/132 Sheepey Parva (township in parish of Sheepey) SK 333012 [Sheepy Parva]
Apt 10.06.1844; 105a (600); Map 1847, 6 chns; field names, landowners, 'Glebe S.M.' and 'Glebe N.M.' (col).

19/133 Shenton (township) SP 385999
Apt 25.01.1849; 1534a (all); Map 1849, 6 chns, by Samuel Morris and William Thorpe; foot/b'way, canal with towpath, waterbodies, woods, plantations, parkland (in detail).

19/134 Sibson (township in parish of Sibson) SK 355021
Apt 12.11.1847; 473a (?); Map 1849?, 6 chns, in 2 parts; foot/b'way, waterbodies, field gates; part 2 is 'Plan of land belonging to Lady Noel Byron'.

19/135 Skeffington (parish) SK 747027
Apt 05.04.1843; 797a (2132); Map 1844, 6 chns, in 2 parts; woods. Apt omits some field names.

19/136 Snareston (parish) SK 351103 [Snarestone]
Apt 11.04.1843; 1296a (1325); Map 1839, 6 chns; canal with towpath, waterbodies, houses, woods (col).

19/137 Somerby (parish) SK 775105
Apt 20.04.1847; 7a (1000); Map 1852?, 3 chns; waterbodies, road names.

19/138 Stapleton (parish or township) SP 435990
Apt 31.10.1838; 1326a (all); Map 1838, 3 chns, by S. and R. Morris; foot/b'way, waterbodies, woods; a sketch of a bird decorates one corner.

19/139 Stockerstone (parish) SP 832978 [Stockerston]
Apt 21.01.1840; 973a (all); Map 1841?, 6 chns; foot/b'way, woods, plantations (by annotation), ownership boundaries (col), glebe (yellow); pictorial church.

19/140 Stoke Golding (parish) SP 400970
Apt 23.08.1844; 1283a (all); Map 1844, 6 chns, by John Thorpe, Shenton and S. and R. Morris, Sutton Cheney, Leics; canal with towpath.

19/141 Stoughton (township in parish of Thurnby) SK 649021
Apt 12.09.1845; 716a (?); Map 1849, 6 chns, by John Bromley, Derby; foot/b'way, waterbodies, woods, road names, stone pit or quarry.

19/142 Great Stretton (township in parish of Great Glenn) SK 657006
Apt 30.07.1849; 690a (?); Map 1849, 5 chns, by R.D. Miles, Leicester; foot/b'way, waterbodies, houses, woods, road names.

19/143 Sysonby (hamlet in parish of Melton Mowbray) SK 739200 [Not listed]
Apt 30.06.1843; 1210a (980); Map 1845?, 8 chns; waterbodies, woods, field names, landowners, tithe-free land (yellow); table lists field names and acreages; colour bands and prefixes 'b' and 'm' to tithe area numbers indicate Lord Besborough's Estate and Lord Viscount Melbourne's Estate; map is subtitled a map of their property.

19/144 Swannington (township) SK 415163
Apt 16.05.1844; 1550a (all); Map 1844?, 6 chns.

19/145 Swepstone (parish) SK 370100
Apt 31.12.1840; 2288a (all); Map 1839, 6 chns, in 5 parts, (includes four small enlargements of detail); foot/b'way, waterbodies, woods.

19/146 Thorpe Arnold (parish) SK 772210
Apt 13.05.1848; 1743a (1742); Map 1848, 6 chns; railway, canal with towpath, waterbodies.

19/147 Thorpe Satchville (township in parish of Twyford) SK 735121
Apt 01.12.1843; 1320a (all); Map 1844, 5 chns, by R.D. Miles, Leicester; foot/b'way, waterbodies, woods (named), parkland, field gates.

19/148 Thurlaston (parish) SP 502995
Apt 24.01.1851; 532a (2980); Map 1852, 3 chns, 1st cl, by Walker and Goodacre, architects and surveyors, Leicester, (tithable parts only); construction lines, foot/b'way, waterbodies, houses, field boundary ownerships, field gates, building names, landowners, rectory.

19/149 Thurnby and part of Bushby (hamlet in parish of Thurnby) SK 640041
Apt 16.09.1845; 599a (?); Map 1846?, 4 chns; foot/b'way, waterbodies, woods (col), glebe.

19/150 Tilton on the Hill (except Halstead, Marefield, Whatborough or Woodborough) (parish) SK 752050
Apt 12.09.1839; 1510a (1510); Map 1841, 3 chns, 1st cl, by George Lamb, Derby; construction lines, foot/b'way, waterbodies, field boundary ownerships, field gates.

19/151 Tooley (hamlet in parish of Peckleton-cum-Tooley) SK 479001 [Not listed]
Apt 26.02.1850; 610a (?); Map 1851, 6 chns, ? by Messrs Hayward, Northampton; foot/b'way, waterbodies, houses, plantations, parkland, field boundary ownerships.

19/152 Tugby including Keythorpe (parochial chapelry) SK 765005
Apt 04.08.1849; 2a (1830); Map (drawn on Apt) 1852?, 2.25 chns, (tithable parts only).

19/153 Twycross (parish) SK 343043
Apt 31.01.1850; 1574a (all); Map 1851?, 6 chns; waterbodies, plantations.

19/154 Ullesthorpe (hamlet in parish of Claybrook) SP 510872
Apt 02.02.1843; 1266a (?); Map 1839, 3 chns, by W. Dabbs, Leicester; hill-drawing, railway with cutting, foot/b'way, waterbodies, houses, woods, plantations, fences, field boundary ownerships, field gates; north pointer has Prince of Wales's feathers.

19/155 Upton (township in parish of Sibson) SP 365995
Apt 19.07.1847; 1320a (?); Map 1848, 6 chns, by W. Thorpe; foot/b'way, waterbodies, woods, plantations, orchards, fences.

19/156 Wanlip (parish) SK 591109
Apt 26.10.1838; 953a (all); Map 1839, 6 chns; foot/b'way, waterbodies, houses, woods, parkland (in detail), orchards, gardens, fences.

19/157 Welby (lordship or hamlet in parish of Melton Mowbray) SK 726211
Apt 20.03.1838; 1173a (?); Map 1838, 4 chns, by S.H. Surplice, Beeston, Notts, (tinted); waterbodies, woods; pictorial church; map title is on a scroll held aloft by a hand, with subtitle 'belonging to Edward Godfrey Esq'.

19/158 Welham (parish) SP 759926
Apt 21.06.1844; 1110a (all); Map 1844, 6 chns, by R. Hayward and Son; foot/b'way, waterbodies, houses.

19/159 Wigston Parva otherwise Little Wigston (hamlet in parish of Claybrook) SP 467900
Apt 02.02.1843; 386a (?); Map 1845, 6 chns, by R. Stelfox, Allesley; foot/b'way, waterbodies, woods, orchards, road names, Roman road.

19/160 Willoughby Waterless (parish) SP 578921 [Willoughby Waterleys]
Apt 18.02.1846; 1151a (all); Map 1846, 3 chns, 1st cl, by William Phillips, Coventry; construction lines, foot/b'way, waterbodies, houses, woods, orchards, hedge ownership, fences, field gates, road names, rectory.

19/161 Wimeswold (parish) SK 613137 [Wymeswold]
Apt 01.03.1847; 6a (4220); Map 1848, 2.5 chns, (tithable parts only, tinted); road names, field names, landowners.

19/162 Withcote (parish) SK 799059 [Not listed]
Apt 19.12.1846; 274a (777); Map 1848?, 6 chns; map is subtitled 'the Property of The Revd Henry Palmer'.

19/163 Witherley (township in parish of Witherley) SP 330980
Apt 15.02.1848; 842a (?); Map 1848, 3 chns; foot/b'way, waterbodies, plantations, field gates.

19/164 Woodhouse, Woodhouse Eaves and Beau Manor (township and district) SK 524146
Apt 16.05.1840; 320a (3980); Map 1841, 6 chns, in 2 parts, (tithable parts only in detail; includes 12 chn index); woods (named), parkland; hills, farms and manors named; table on map repeats information in Apt, which omits some field names.

19/165 Woodthorpe (hamlet or township in parish of Emmanuel) SK 540171
Apt 10.01.1849; 199a (?); Map 1849, 6 chns, by John Bromley, Derby; foot/b'way, canal with towpath, waterbodies, building names.

19/166 Wyfordby cum Brentingby (township in parish of Wyfordby) SK 789200
Apt 21.11.1848; 1370a (all); Map 1849, 5 chns, by R.D. Miles, Leicester; railway, foot/b'way, canal, waterbodies, woods (named), plantations, field gates.

19/167 Wykin (hamlet in parish of Hinckley) SP 405950
Apt 23.03.1844; 935a (all); Map 1844, 6 chns, by John Thorpe, Shenton, Leics; canal with towpath, waterbodies, woods.

19/168 Wymondham (parish) SK 858188
Apt 16.03.1842; 2853a (all); Map 1840, 6 chns; canal with towpath, waterbodies, houses (by shading), woods, building names; pictorial church.

Lincolnshire

PRO IR29 and IR30 20/1-382

757 tithe districts: 1,693,547 acres
376 tithe commutations: 632,105 acres
185 voluntary tithe agreements, 191 compulsory tithe awards, 6 corn rent annuities

Tithe and tithe commutation

Although Lincolnshire is the second largest historic county and contains the largest number of tithe districts of any county, it ranks only tenth in the number of districts still subject to tithe in 1836. Tithe commutation in association with parliamentary enclosure was extensive; indeed the area north and west of Boston was the largest tract of tithe-free land in England and Wales at the time of the Tithe Commutation Act (Fig. 32). In addition to commutation at enclosure, the main reasons for tithe exemption in Lincolnshire were modus payments in lieu of tithes, the merger of tithes in the land, and exemption by prescription.

Many Lincolnshire tithe districts contained only small tracts of tithable land comprising a few old enclosures or a mill; the extreme was Mumby at 0.04 acre. The settlement of some Lincolnshire tithe awards was very protracted, a few continued on after 1855, and the Moulton award was the last but one English and Welsh tithe award to be confirmed (1880). The delay at Moulton was due to uncertainties as to the extent of tithable land in the parish and the disinclination of landowners to trust the tithe map; one boundary was castigated as 'a fancy line drawn by Mr Millington the Valuer without sufficient information.' 'The case appears to be exceptional', observed the assistant tithe commissioner in 1866![1]

Assistant tithe commissioners and local tithe agents who worked in Lincolnshire are listed in Table 20.1. At 143, the number of tithe rent-charge valuers in Lincolnshire is the largest of any county. In eleven tithe districts, all but ten of them residuals from enclosure, landowners failed to appoint a valuer within the statutory six-month period and so the Tithe Commission undertook the valuation itself (Table 20.2).

Rent-charge was apportioned by holdings in thirteen Lincolnshire tithe districts and at Utterby the tithe apportionment has several unorthodox descriptions of land use, including 'garden, pigs and poultry', 'willow poles' and 'vegetables'. At Wroot almost all the land is described as 'alternately arable, meadow and pasture.'

[1] PRO IR18 5145

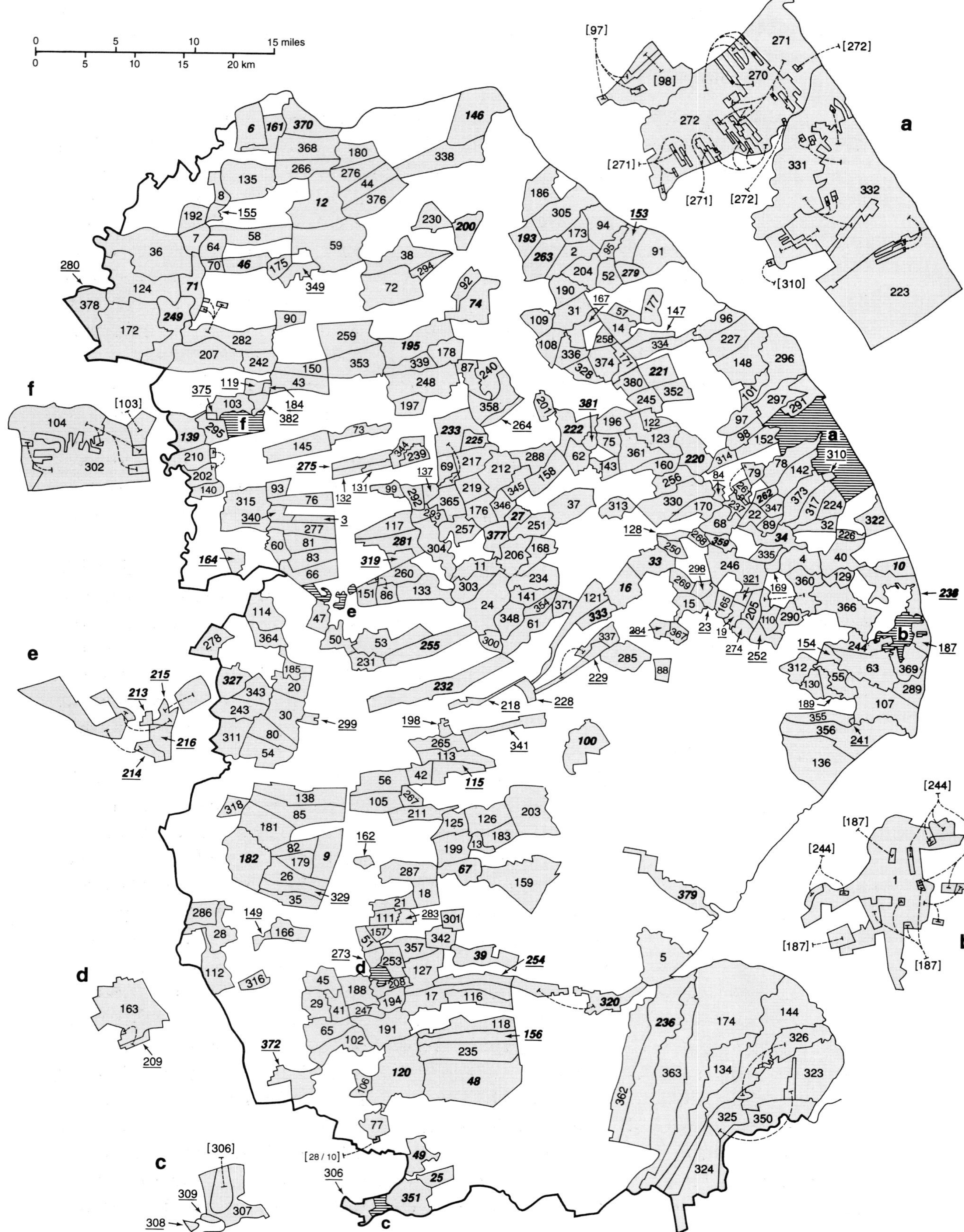

Fig. 32 Lincolnshire: tithe district boundaries.

Tithe maps

Although not recognised by the Tithe Commission, Lincolnshire is often divided into the three divisions of Lindsey, Kesteven and Holland and these divisions are of some help in analysing the tithe mapping of the county. As usual in counties with much enclosure, less than 5 per cent of the 376 tithe maps of Lincolnshire are sealed as first class. Fourteen of these are in Lindsey. Kesteven has two first-class maps and Holland only one, similar to adjoining parts of Norfolk and Cambridgeshire which also have little first-class mapping. As in most counties with extensive enclosure, there were two peaks of map production, in 1838-41 and in 1848-50. The second of these high points is represented by maps of those many districts in which only small pieces of land remained tithable such that landowners and tithe owners had little incentive to effect an early settlement (Table 20.4).

Lincolnshire tithe maps are drawn at a wide variety of scales, ranging from one inch to one chain to one inch to twenty-four chains. About 26 per cent are in the officially recommended scale range of one inch to three to four chains, 38 per cent are at the six-chain scale, and 15 per cent are at the eight-chain scale (Table 20.3). An above average proportion of Lincolnshire tithe maps explicitly acknowledges copying earlier work. The extreme example of this, both in the county and nationally, is the map of Buslingthorpe based on a map of 1653.

The mapping of land use on Lincolnshire tithe maps is above average; woodland is shown on 60 per cent of the maps, about 6 per cent depict arable and grass, 6 per cent map gardens, 6 per cent show parks, 5 per cent plot orchards, and one map, that of Denton, depicts hops. On the other hand, Lincolnshire tithe maps are a poor source for names of buildings. Unusual features shown on Lincolnshire tithe maps include a note on water abstraction for Grimsby Haven, a 'Priests House' at Irnham, and a samphire bed at Wyberton. Although there is comparatively little urban tithe mapping in this county, there are detailed maps of three Lincoln city parishes.

Some 232 Lincolnshire tithe maps in the Public Record Office collection can be attributed to a particular map-maker; the most prolific was Charles Cave John Orme of Louth who produced 33 maps covering about 9 per cent of the tithable area of the county. Most of his tithe maps are unremarkable but his map of Saltfleet and Skidbrook is one of the very few maps in the whole country which approaches Robert Kearsley Dawson's specification for an ideal tithe map. It is a first-class map and one which also shows land use by colour. The second most productive map-makers were Samuel Hill and Son of Croft, near Wainfleet. Like several Lindsey map-makers, the Hills usually tinted the tithable parts of their maps and they occasionally used scale bars graduated with a 'battlement' effect, as at Gunby. Frederick Talbot of Brocklesby or Caistor produced a number of finely-drawn, distinctive maps of districts mainly owned by the Earl of Yarborough whose family seat was at Brocklesby. Landowner influence (of Lord Willoughby de Eresby) is probably also a reason why three districts were mapped by Henry Kennedy of Chancery Lane, London.

The quality of Lincolnshire maps varies widely in both standard of execution and in content. A few tithe maps of places apportioned on a field-by-field basis show no buildings other than the church as, for example, those of Aswarby and North Owersby. In common with tithe maps elsewhere in eastern England, Lincolnshire tithe maps often portray churches and windmills pictorially. Three maps include pictures which are wholly decorative: the maps of Asgarby and Brauncewell include neat wash drawings of the parish churches and that of Holton le Moor includes a scene of rural life.

Table 20.1. *Agreements and awards for commutation of tithes in Lincolnshire*

Assistant commissioner/ local tithe agent	*Number of agreements**	*Number of awards*
John Job Rawlinson	5	113
Charles Howard	27	50
John Pickering	63	0
Thomas Smith Woolley	58	4
Richard Burton Phillipson	14	0
John Mee Mathew	0	12
Joseph Townsend	1	6
George Wingrove Cooke	0	4
Edward Greathead	4	0
George Louis	3	1
John Penny	4	0
Thomas Hoskins	2	0
Henry Pilkington	2	0
James Drage Merest	1	0
Charles Pym	1	0
John Strangeways Donaldson Selby	1	0
Thomas Sudworth	1	0
Tithe Commissioners	0	1

*Computed from the number of extant reports on tithe agreements in the tithe files [PRO IR 18].

Table 20.2. *Tithe valuers and tithe map-makers in Lincolnshire*

Name and address (all in Lincolnshire)	*Number of districts*	*Acreage*
Tithe valuers		
John Higgins, Alford	21	41,594
Robert John Atkinson, Haxey/Brocklesby	19	32,453
William Smith, West Rasen	14	28,250
Edward Arden, Morton	14	26,494
William Bartholemew, Goltho	13	17,393
Tithe Commissioners	11	3,069
Samuel Vessey, Halton Holegate	9	27,068
Samuel Hill, Croft	8	10,232
Edward Betham, Lincoln	8	6,219
Edward Millington, Fleet	7	59,919
Thomas Wyles, Little Ponton	7	19,317
Thomas Bartholemew, Langton by Wragby	7	9,263
Charles Cave John Orme, Louth	7	8,998
James Sandby Padley, Lincoln	7	7,576
William Hudson, Epworth	7	6,940
Others [129]	216	327,320
Attributed tithe map-makers		
Charles Cave John Orme, Louth	33	54,555
Samuel Hill and Son, Croft	25	39,027
Frederick C. Talbot, Brocklesby/Caistor	14	27,266
James Sandby Padley, Lincoln	13	18,678
Robert Coddington Moore, Harmston	12	19,737
Thomas Bartholemew, Langton by Wragby	8	12,586
William Hudson, Epworth	8	11,998
Makin Durham, Thorne	7	12,863
Joseph Silvester Langwith, Grantham	7	7,812
Edward Betham and Son, Lincoln	6	3,078
Robert Stapleton Booth, Wainfleet	5	14,685
William Hardy, Lincoln	5	3,895
Others [56]	89	153,330

Table 20.3. *The tithe maps of Lincolnshire: scales and classes*

Scale in chains/inch	*All maps*		*First Class*		*Second Class*	
	Number	*Acreage*	*Number*	*Acreage*	*Number*	*Acreage*
>3	8	439	0	0	8	439
3	60	81,840	17	40,287	43	41,553
4	37	36,816	0	0	37	36,816
5	6	9,167	0	0	6	9,167
6	143	241,443	0	0	143	241,443
6.67, 7, 7.5	5	6,374	0	0	5	6,374
8	57	117,871	0	0	57	117,871
9	22	47,379	0	0	22	47,379
10	10	14,285	0	0	10	14,285
12	16	49,481	0	0	16	49,481
<12	12	27,010	0	0	12	27,010
TOTAL	376	632,105	17	40,287	359	591,818

Table 20.4. *The tithe maps of Lincolnshire: dates*

	1837	*1838*	*1839*	*1840*	*1841*	*1842*	*1843*	*1844*	*1845*	*1846*	*1847*	*1848*	*1849*	*1850*	*>1850*
All maps	4	38	46	40	35	26	24	10	10	10	10	36	24	22	40
1st class	1	3	4	3	2	0	1	0	0	0	1	1	0	0	1
2nd class*	3	35	42	37	33	26	23	10	10	10	9	35	24	22	39

*One second-class tithe map of Lincolnshire in the Public Record Office collection is undated.

Lincolnshire

20/1 Addlethorpe (parish) TF 547690
Apt 12.06.1843; 2007a (2006); Map 1842, 6 chns, by S. Hill and Son, Croft, (tinted); building names, gowt, Roman bank, sepulchre, pound, chapel.

20/2 Ailsby (parish) TA 198070 [Aylesby]
Apt 30.06.1840; 2112a (all); Map 1839, 9 chns, by T. Bartholemew; foot/b'way, waterbodies, osiers (by symbol), ownerships (col).

20/3 Aisthorpe (parish) SK 951802
Apt 30.06.1842; 803a (all); Map 1843?, 4 chns; foot/b'way, waterbodies, road names, churchyard, milestone (by symbol, with distance).

20/4 Alford with Tothby and Rigsby with Ailby (parishes and hamlets) TF 439765
Apt 12.07.1838; 2128a (2450); Map 1839?, 4 chns, in 2 parts; footpath destinations, foot/b'way, waterbodies, field boundary ownerships, field gates.

20/5 Algarkirk cum Fosdyke (parish) TF 310350
Apt 30.12.1837; 4727a (all); Map 1838, 3 chns, 1st cl, by S. Hill and Son, Croft; turnpike roads, waterbodies, road names, ice house, wash dike, Roman bank, wood mill, sea bank, bede house, pound, chapel, mill; bridge named, as are larger water courses.

20/6 Alkborough (parish) SE 880205
Apt 30.06.1841; 447a (2875); Map 1850, 4 chns, 'Drawn' by Thomas Laughton, Brigg, (tithable parts only); waterbodies, plantations, heath/moor, building names, road names; land tinted pink is old enclosure, and land tinted green is modus land. Apt omits most land use.

20/7 Althorpe, including Althorpe and Derrythorpe (township with hamlets in parish of Althorpe) SE 825091
Apt 01.11.1842; 164a (?); Map 1843, 4 chns, by J. Alexander, Doncaster, (tithable parts only); grassland (col), orchards, open fields (named), road names, warping drain, drains (named), embankment.

20/8 Amcotts (district in parish of Althorpe) SE 850148
Apt 26.08.1839; 55a (?); Map 1840?, 3 chns, in 2 parts, by M. Durham, Thorne, (tithable parts only, tinted); landowners. There are two versions of this map; the foregoing description applies to that in PRO IR 29; the map in PRO IR 30 contains the same basic information, but is uncoloured and has a table listing owners and a note of its adoption by the landowners.

20/9 Ancaster (parish) SK 975445
Apt 30.05.1846; 3a (2800); Map 1849?, 6 chns, ? by Tithe Commission (tithable parts only); woods, roads names.

20/10 Anderby (parish) TF 538758
Apt 11.09.1858; 61a (1845); Map 1858, 6 chns, by John Hill, Croft, (tithable parts only, tinted); landowners, Roman bank.

20/11 Apley (parish) TF 117754
Apt 30.04.1849; 1336a (1658); Map 1849, 9 chns, in 4 parts, (includes three 4.5-chn enlargements of detail); woods.

20/12 Appleby (parish) SE 958128
Apt 17.12.1847; 797a (6164); Map 1848, 6 chns, in 4 parts, by M. Brady, Brigg, (tithable parts only); houses, Roman road, mill, ownerships (col); watercourses named.

20/13 Asgarby (parish) TF 126454
Apt 04.08.1846; 839a (all); Map 1846, 6 chns, by Robt C. Moore, Harmston, near Lincoln; foot/b'way, waterbodies, houses, farmyards (col), woods (col), arable (col), grassland (col), gardens (col), field boundary ownerships, building names, banks, engine; drains named; map is decorated with a grey wash drawing of the parish church, with name 'R.P. Wright'.

20/14 Ashby cum Fenby (parish) TA 253007
Apt 12.07.1843; 1676a (1675); Map 1840, 3 chns, 1st cl, by C. Cave J. Orme, Louth; construction lines, waterbodies, houses, fences, field boundary ownerships.

20/15 Ashby Puerorum (parish) TF 331717
Apt 20.07.1849; 1329a (1620); Map 1850?, 6.6 chns; foot/b'way, houses, woods (col).

20/16 West Ashby (parish) TF 267733
Apt 21.04.1853; 11a (?); Map 1853, 8 chns, (tithable parts only, tinted); road names, landowners, field acreages; pictorial church; north pointer has yellow boss and grey shading.

20/17 Aslackby (parish) TF 088298
Apt 16.11.1846; 3183a (3934); Map 1847?, 8 chns; turnpike roads, waterbodies, houses, woods, mill-dam, decoy; lode named; pictorial church.

20/18 Aswarby (parish) TF 076404
Apt 27.06.1837; 1548a (all); Map 1838?, [6 chns], by J. Tomlinson, Sleaford; foot/b'way, field names, field acreages; the only building shown is the hall, unnamed. Apt omits land use.

20/19 Aswardby (parish) TF 378703
Apt 12.07.1843; 742a (all); Map 1844, 6 chns; waterbodies, houses, woods.

20/20 Auborn (parish) SK 930620
Apt 30.10.1848; 2109a (2109); Map 1848, 6 chns; foot/b'way, waterbodies, houses, modus land boundary; fen named.

20/21 Aunsby (parish) TF 040393
Apt 02.02.1838; 1183a (all); Map 1838, 6 chns, 'compiled' by J.S. Langwith; field names, field acreages, well.

20/22 Authorpe (parish) TF 398807
Apt 24.09.1838; 921a (all); Map 1838, 12 chns, copied with 'the alterations' added by Chas Cave Jno. Orme, Louth; woods (col), landowners, pit, glebe boundary.

20/23 Bag Enderby (parish) TF 352722
Apt 05.05.1838; 618a (617); Map 1839?, 4 chns; woods (col), ford.

20/24 Bardney (parish) TF 124712
Apt 14.07.1841; 1235a (4800); Map 1842, 6 chns, ? by T. Bartholemew; foot/b'way, woods (col), osiers (by symbol), common field (named), ferry, windmill (pictorial), common (col), common meadow.

20/25 Barholm cum Stow (parish) TF 095108
Apt 12.07.1843; 363a (1585); Map 1843, 6 chns, by Charles Day, Land surveyor etc, Collyweston, (tithable parts only); foot/b'way, houses.

20/26 Barkston (parish) SK 940420
Apt 02.02.1838; 2083a (2083); Map 1838, 6 chns, copied from a plan by J. Hudson of Louth, 1763, with 'Additions' by J.S. Langwith, Grantham; houses; pictorial church.

20/27 West Barkwith (parish) TF 154805
Apt 08.11.1849; 288a (500); Map 1850, 6 chns, (tithable parts only); waterbodies, houses, landowners.

20/28 Barrowby (parish) SK 861362
Apt 29.03.1848; 2305a (4462); Map 1848, 5 chns, in 3 parts, (tithable parts only; includes village and surrounding fields at 2.5 chns and 10-chn index); foot/b'way, waterbodies, landowners, canal with towpath and locks.

20/29 Basingthorpe and Westby (parish) SK 962287
Apt 17.04.1839; 1789a (all); Map 1840?, 6 chns; foot/b'way, waterbodies, district boundary.

20/30 Bassingham (parish) SK 927591
Apt 25.06.1851; 3015a (all); Map 1852, 8 chns; foot/b'way, waterbodies, woods, road names.

20/31 Beelsby (parish) TA 210020
Apt 03.06.1846; 2189a (all); Map 1848, 6 chns; woods, plantations, heath/moor, building names, mill.

20/32 Beesby (parish) TF 458799
Apt 29.01.1840; 1170a (1180); Map 1839, 6 chns; houses, arable (col), grassland (col), field gates, occupation road; legend explains colours.

20/33 Belchford (parish) TF 295755
Apt 30.06.1849; 10a (2390); Map 1850, 6 chns, copied from the enclosure award by J. Parkinson, (tithable parts only); road names, landowners.

20/34 Belleau and Aby (parish) TF 409782
Apt 08.12.1848; 918a (2016); Map 1849?, 6 chns, 'Revised and Drawn' by R.S. Booth, Wainfleet, (tithable parts only); railway, waterbodies, houses, woods (named), osiers (by symbol), field boundary ownerships, tomb, gravel pit, chalk pit.

20/35 Belton (parish) SK 937398
Apt 30.08.1837; 1709a (all); Map 1839?, 6 chns, ? by J.S. Langwith; waterbodies, houses, farmyards (col), woods (col), parkland (col), arable (col), grassland (col), gardens (col), hedges, field acreages, 'Pleasure Ground' (in detail).

20/36 Belton in Axholme (parish) SE 782081 [Belton]
Apt 16.09.1842; 5058a (8530); Map 1843, 8 chns, by W. Hudson, Epworth, (tithable parts only); foot/b'way, waterbodies, woods, plantations, parkland, open fields, building names, tithe-free land boundary, former commons; watercourses and bridge named. Apt omits most field names.

20/37 Benniworth or Benningworth (parish) TF 210816
Apt 19.10.1847; 9a (2994); Map 1849?, 9 chns, (tithable parts only); woods, field names; pictorial church.

20/38 Bigby (parish) TA 039074
Apt 19.06.1840; 3480a (all); Map 1840, 10 chns, in 2 parts, by Frs. Bennet, (includes 4-chn enlargement of built-up part); foot/b'way, waterbodies, landowners (col), hamlet names and boundaries; pictorial church.

20/39 Billingborough (parish) TF 128338
Apt 05.05.1848; 3a (2020); Map (drawn on Apt) 1852?, 8 chns, (tithable parts only); road names, landowners, ownership boundaries; pictorial church.

20/40 Bilsby (parish) TF 479765
Apt 12.01.1841; 2820a (2820); Map 1841, 6 chns, by William Bourne; foot/b'way, waterbodies, houses, plantations, building names, former open field names, vicarage; drain named; there are two versions in PRO IR 30, one dated 1841, uncoloured, with pink band showing one hamlet, on tracing paper, and the other undated and coloured, and with a number of other differences.

20/41 Bitchfield (parish) SK 989285
Apt 25.10.1842; 1344a (1344); Map 1843, 6 chns; foot/b'way, waterbodies, woods, osiers (by symbol), ownerships (col).

20/42 Bloxholm (parish) TF 067530
Apt 04.10.1837; 1390a (1298); Map 1837, 6 chns; foot/b'way, waterbodies, houses, woods, parkland, building names, coach road, rectory, walls; map is signed by principal landowner, expressing satisfication as to accuracy.

20/43 Blyborough (parish) SK 933942
Apt 21.11.1838; 2249a (all); Map 1839?, [13.33 chns], by G. Empringham; foot/b'way, waterbodies, woods (col), grassland (col), holding boundaries (col).

20/44 Bonby (parish) TA 002154
Apt 16.02.1841; 2410a (2410); Map 1839, 8 chns, in 2 parts, 'Revised and Copied' by F.C. Talbot, Brocklesby, (includes enlargement of part of village at 4 chns); waterbodies, woods, road names, glebe (col).

20/45 Boothby Pagnell (parish) SK 972308
Apt 04.04.1838; 1795a (1794); Map 1838?, 4 chns, by George Hardwick, Valuer; foot/b'way, waterbodies, houses (stippled), woods (named), hedge ownership, field names, field acreages, landowners (col), oxwell; pictorial church.

20/46 Bottesford and Yaddlethorpe (township and hamlet in parish of Bottesford) SE 883070
Corn rent conversion, 1904; 273a (?); Map 1904, OS 1:2500, surveyed 1885, annotated with tithe areas; map and Apt apply only to the former parish of Yaddlethorpe.

20/47 Boultham or Boltham (parish) SK 960695
Corn rent conversion, 1920; 118a (1210); Map 1920, OS 1:2500, surveyed 1905, annotated with tithe areas. Apt omits land use and field names.

20/48 Bourne (parish) TF 125205
Apt 17.12.1847; 1063a (9352); Map 1848, 6 chns, in 2 parts, by Cuming and Hill, Easton, Stamford, (tithable parts only); woods (named); fen, drain and bank named.

20/49 Braceborough (parish) TF 078132
Corn rent conversion, 1881; 1693a (2230); there is no map. Apt omits land use.

20/50 Bracebridge (parish) SK 975675
Apt 10.03.1842; 1482a (1482); Map 1842, 6 chns, by William Hardy, Lincoln; foot/b'way, waterbodies, houses, woods, plantations, gardens (col), field boundary ownerships, building names, churchyard, vicarage; bridge named.

20/51 Braceby (parish) TF 016354
Apt 03.03.1838; 903a (all); Map 1838?, 3 chns; waterbodies, houses, arable (col), grassland (col), heath/moor (col), hedge ownership, field names, field acreages, pit.

20/52 Bradley (parish) TA 246055
Apt 26.06.1839; 1524a (all); Map 1839?, [5 chns]; foot/b'way, waterbodies, woods, stiles.

20/53 Branston (parish) TF 030670
Apt 23.02.1847; 852a (5389); Map 1849, 8 chns, (tithable parts only in detail); houses, woods (named), parkland; pictorial church.

20/54 Brant Broughton (parish) SK 909549
Apt 06.07.1838; 2933a (2932); Map 1838, 3 chns, by W.H. Wright; waterbodies, houses, plantations; map cartouche is oval, with rectangular surround propping up a tree stump, and an urn on top, and another tree in the background.

20/55 Bratoft (parish) TF 483640
Apt 26.05.1841; 1815a (1814); Map 1843, 6 chns, by S. Hill and Son, Croft; waterbodies, field boundary ownerships, pound, mill, moated site; drain named; meaning of pink band is unclear.

20/56 Brauncewell (parish) TF 032519
Apt 06.06.1850; 2674a (?); Map 1845, 6 chns, by Robt C. Moore, Harmston, near Lincoln; foot/b'way, waterbodies, houses, plantations (col, by Dawson's symbol), arable (col), grassland (col), orchards, field boundary ownerships, building names, well, stone pits; meaning of pink tint is unclear; map is decorated with a grey wash drawing of the parish church, with top-hatted shirt-sleeved figure, evidently digging grave.

20/57 Brigsley (parish) TA 265016
Apt 03.05.1850; 924a (860); Map 1850, 6 chns, surveyed by Edward Micklethwait, Great Grimsby, (tinted); foot/b'way, waterbodies, woods, gardens, field boundary ownerships, road names, pound, glebe (green). Apt omits field names.

20/58 Bromby (township in parish of Frodingham) SE 882096 [Brumby]
Apt 30.06.1843; 3009a (?); Map 1843, 6 chns, in 5 parts, by W. Rawson, (includes four 3-chn enlargements of detail, 1844); foot/b'way, waterbodies, houses (by shading), woods, embankment, lodge.

20/59 Broughton (parish) SE 965087
Apt 19.10.1841; 6919a (all); Map 1842, 8 chns, in 4 parts, (includes two 4-chn and one 1.5-chn enlargements of detail), litho (Standidge); turnpike roads, waterbodies, woods, lodges; dot-dash pecked lines are used between owners in woods.

20/60 Broxholme (parish) SK 917773
Apt 22.02.1840; 1298a (all); Map 1842, 8 chns, by 'Lowdham'; hedge ownership.

20/61 Bucknall (parish) TF 170690
Apt 24.08.1839; 2472a (all); Map 1840, 6 chns, by T. Bartholemew; foot/b'way, 'Cottage Pasture' (yellow), meadows (green), glebe (grey); pictorial church.

20/62 Burgh cum Girsby (parish) TF 213862 [Burgh on Bain]
Apt 22.01.1844; 1561a (all); Map 1838, 6 chns; hill drawing, waterbodies, woods (col), plantations (col), parkland, gardens, hedges (col), fence, mill, vicarage, springs, mansion (col, named), glebe (yellow).

20/63 Burgh le Marsh (parish) TF 512652
Apt 01.11.1841; 4233a (4233); Map 1842, 8 chns, in 2 parts, 'Revised and Drawn' by R.S. Booth, Wainfleet, (includes enlargement of town at 4 chns); foot/b'way, waterbodies, houses, road names, windmill (pictorial), tumulus (named), hall; drains named, 'gateroom' (? pasture access lane).

20/64 Burringham (township in parish of Bottesford) SE 845087
Apt 15.07.1841; 1542a (?); Map 1842?, 5 chns, in 2 parts, by W. Rawson, Land Surveyor and Valuer, Barton, (includes 3-chn enlargement of common fields); houses, waterbodies, woods, road names, warping drain, embankment, ferry, brick works; drains named.

20/65 Burton Coggles (parish) SK 975260
Apt 26.02.1839; 2677a (2676); Map 1839?, 6 chns, ? by Frans. Musson, Valuer, etc; waterbodies, houses, woods (col, named), arable (col), grassland (col), gardens (col), road names, field names, glebe; pictorial church; the owner is named in the title; some land outside the district is mapped and tinted pink. The glebe is apportioned by field, with land use; the rest of the district is apportioned as a single unit; Apt generalises land use and omits occupiers.

20/66 Burton by Lincoln (parish) SK 952742 [Burton]
Apt 29.07.1847; 2326a (all); Map 1848, 8 chns, by S. Hill and Son, Croft; canal with towpath, woods, road names, pound, windmill (pictorial), glebe (col), hall; drains named.

20/67 Burton Pedwardine (parish) TF 110428
Apt 10.07.1850; 28a (2580); Map 1852, 2 chns, in 2 parts, by Robt C. Moore, Harmston, near Lincoln, (tithable parts only; including 4-chn location diagram, with pictorial churches and sightings thereto); waterbodies, houses, field gates, landowners.

20/68 Burwell (parish) TF 360800
Apt 17.12.1850; 2000a (all); Map 1851?, 10 chns; waterbodies, woods (named), hall; pictorial church. District is apportioned by holding and most fields are not shown; Apt omits occupiers.

20/69 Buslingthorpe (parish) TF 087852
Apt 24.12.1838; 1096a (1096); Map 1838, 6 chns, 'Revised from a Survey taken in the Year 1653' by J. S. Padley, Lincoln; foot/b'way, waterbodies, houses, woods (col).

20/70 East Butterwick (township in parish of Bottesford) SE 847066
Apt 11.11.1841; 604a (?); Map 1842, 6 chns, by J. Alexander, Doncaster, (tinted); plantations, gardens, heath/moor, embankments, common; stream named.

20/71 West Butterwick with Kelfield (township in parish of Owston) SE 824052
Apt 29.06.1850; 1363a (?); Map 1851, 3 chns, by Makin Durham, Thorne, (tithable parts only); foot/b'way, open fields (named), building names, road names; drains named.

20/72 Cadney cum Howsham with Newstead (parish with extra-parochial hamlet) TA 028048
Apt 16.11.1844; 4860a (4860); Map 1844, 8 chns, in 3 parts, (includes two 2-chn enlargements of detail), litho (Standidge); foot/b'way, waterbodies, woods, osiers (by symbol), plantations, heath/moor, building names, school, canal with towpath, hamlet boundary; watercourses named.

20/73 Caenby (parish) TF 001897
Apt 30.04.1844; 1431a (1430); Map 1843, 12 chns, 'Copied' by Chas Cave Jno. Orme, Louth; woods.

20/74 Caistor (parish) TA 117027
Apt 30.09.1839; 2006a (?); Map 1841, 9 chns, by Fred. C. Talbot, Caistor, (tithable parts only); hill drawing, waterbodies, woods, building names, landowners, spa spring, toll bar, hamlet boundaries (col); pictorial church.

20/75 Calcethorpe (parish) TF 248884
Apt 11.07.1849; 1088a (all); Map 1849, 8 chns, by J.S. Padley, Lincoln; turnpike roads, houses, drains, holding boundaries. District is apportioned by holding and fields are not shown.

20/76 Cammeringham (parish) SK 940822
Apt 19.10.1847; 1806a (1806); Map 1848, 6 chns, by S. Hill and Son, Croft; waterbodies, woods, fish pond, stone pit (col), pound, roads names.

20/77 Careby (parish) TF 028162
Apt 31.03.1838; 1454a (all); Map 1838, 6 chns, 'Copied' by S. Hill and Son, Croft; woods, field acreages, ownerships (col); pictorial church.

20/78 Great Carlton (parish) TF 425866
Apt 28.03.1839; 251a (2190); Map 1839, 8 chns, 'Copied and the alterations added' by Chas Cave Jno. Orme, Louth, (tithable parts only). Apt omits field names.

20/79 Little Carlton (parish) TF 393855
Apt 19.06.1840; 1024a (1006); Map 1840, 3 chns, 1st cl, by S. Hill and Son, Croft; construction lines, woods, building names, road names, pound, mill pond, horse bridge, windmill (pictorial), milestone. Apt omits most land use.

20/80 Carlton le Moorland (parish) SK 911572 [Carlton-le-Moorland]
Apt 29.09.1849; 2237a (2610); Map 1848-9, 6 chns, surveyed by H.M. Wood; foot/b'way, waterbodies, field boundary ownerships; tithable land is finely stippled.

20/81 North Carlton (parish) SK 947777
Apt 23.10.1844; 1795a (1795); Map 1847?, 8 chns; woods (col), road names, tithe ownership boundary [deserted village]; drain named.

20/82 Carlton Scroope (parish) SK 940449 [Carlton Scroop]
Apt 30.06.1837; 1342a (1342); Map 1837, 4 chns, by John Wood; foot/b'way, waterbodies, houses, woods (col), osiers (by symbol, col), arable (col), grassland (col), orchards (col), gardens (col), hedges, field names, quarry, rectory, ownership boundaries (col).

20/83 South Carlton (parish) SK 952762
Apt 04.09.1844; 1910a (1910); Map 1845, 8 chns, in 4 parts, by S. Hill and Son, Croft, (includes three 2-chn enlargements of detail); waterbodies, woods, heath/moor, field boundary ownerships, pound, road names; drain named.

20/84 Little Cawthorpe (parish) TF 359832
Apt 27.03.1838; 460a (460); Map 1838, 6 chns, by W. Upton; foot/b'way, houses; uninhabited buildings are shown in outline only, without infill.

20/85 Caythorpe cum Friston (parish) SK 939486
Apt 29.10.1844; 4211a (all); Map 1845, 6 chns; foot/b'way, houses, woods (col).

20/86 Cherry Willingham (parish) TF 027721
Apt 12.11.1849; 1092a (980); Map 1850, 6 chns, by Wm Hardy, Lincoln; railway, foot/b'way, waterbodies, houses, woods, field boundary ownerships, occupation roads, bank, cess [overflow channel]; pictorial church; dyke named.

20/87 Claxby by Normanby (parish) TF 109947 [Claxby]
Apt 26.06.1847; 1690a (all); Map 1848?, 6 chns, in 2 parts, (includes 3-chn enlargement of detail), litho (Standidge); railway, waterbodies, woods, plantations, chapel, pound, glebe.

20/88 Claxby Pluckacre (parish) TF 307644
Apt 11.04.1839; 848a (all); Map 1839, 3 chns; foot/b'way, waterbodies, houses, woods, hedge ownership, fence ownership, field gates; owner is named in title: 'Henry Dymoke Esqre., The Honorable The Queen's Champion'.

20/89 Claythorpe (hamlet in parish of Belleau) TF 410795
Apt 26.06.1839; 766a (all); Map 1840, 6 chns, by Chas Cave Jno. Orme, Louth; waterbodies, woods, osiers (by symbol); buildings are shown in outline only, without infill. Apt omits field names.

20/90 Cleatham (township in parish of Manton) SE 927013
Apt 14.01.1845; 1063a (all); Map 1845, 4 chns, by Joseph Cross, Wisbech; woods; scale-bar is ruler-like, but is not figured. Apt omits field names.

20/91 Clee (parish) TA 295085
Apt 30.06.1843; 2234a (9790); Map 1843, 6 chns, in 3 parts, by R. Smith, York, (tinted; includes enlargements of villages at 3 chns); foot/b'way, waterbodies, road names, windmill (pictorial), recreation ground; drain named.

20/92 Clixby (parish) TA 100043
Apt 13.07.1839; 1142a (?); Map 1845, 6 chns, by William Rawson, Barton upon Humber; foot/b'way, houses, woods (col), arable (col), grassland (col), field boundary ownerships; pictorial church; tithe-free land is mapped but not numbered or coloured.

20/93 Coates (parish) SK 913833
Apt 31.12.1849; 984a (950); Map 1851, 4 chns; woods.

20/94 Great Coates (parish) TA 239107
Apt 19.04.1839; 2606a (4480); Map 1840, 9 chns, copied from map of 1829 by Paul Bausor, Southwell; waterbodies, houses, woods, glebe, building names, cloughs; drains named; a river has a note about water abstraction for Grimsby Haven. District is apportioned by holding, though fields are numbered separately; Apt generalises land use and omits field names, and only certain tenants are named; acreages are for land use rather than for holdings.

20/95 Little Coates (parish) TA 249091
Apt 22.11.1844; 1024a (all); Map 1844?, 8 chns; the only building shown is the church. Apt omits land use.

20/96 North Coats (parish) TA 358011 [North Cotes]
Apt 24.08.1841; 2062a (all); Map 1842, 9 chns, litho (Standidge); canal, road names; pictorial church.

20/97 North Cockerington (parish) TF 380909
Apt 18.06.1840; 81a (1750); Map 1844, 18 chns, by Joseph Gace, Louth, (tithable parts only in detail, tinted); landowners.

20/98 South Cockerington or Cockerington St Leonard (parish) TF 385895
Apt 21.11.1845; 154a (1880); Map 1846?, 18 chns, copied from a map in the possession of the lord of the manor in 1839 ? by Chas Cave Jno. Orme, (tithable parts only in detail, tinted).

20/99 Cold Hanworth (parish) TF 030833
Apt 31.07.1847; 707a (all); Map 1848, 6 chns, by J.S. Padley, Lincoln; foot/b'way, waterbodies, houses, woods, field gates; streams across fields are shown discontinuously.

20/100 Coningsby (parish) TF 227563
Apt 25.08.1852; 3a (5560); Map 1853?, 12 chns, (tithable parts only); railway with station, windmill (pictorial).

20/101 Conisholme (parish) TF 391943
Apt 21.10.1839; 1195a (1195); Map 1839, 6 chns; houses, field boundary ownerships; drains and fen named. Apt omits field names.

20/102 Corby (parish) SK 997254 [Corby Glen]
Apt 04.03.1841; 1160a (2726); Map 1841?, 8 chns, (tithable parts only in detail); woods (by name, with acreages), waterbodies, glebe; it is unclear what pecked dot-dash line denotes; scale-bar is ruler-like.

20/103 Great Corringham (hamlet or division) SK 872918 [Corringham]
Apt 20.08.1840; 1889a (?); Map 1842, 4 chns, in 3 parts, ? by W. Hudson, Epworth; foot/b'way, waterbodies, houses, woods, heath/moor (col), open fields, road names, field names, ownerships (col); scale is on a background of trees and heathland.

20/104 Little Corringham (hamlet or division in parish of Corringham) SK 870910 [Not listed]
Apt 23.10.1838; 988a (?); Map 1842, 4 chns, by W. Hudson, Epworth; foot/b'way, waterbodies, open fields, hedges, field names, deer leap, glebe (yellow), modus land (pink).

20/105 Cranwell (parish) TF 024498
Apt 15.01.1846; 2523a (all); Map 1846, 6 chns, by James Dunn; foot/b'way, waterbodies, woods (col), field boundary ownerships, fox cover, green lanes (col).

20/106 Creeton (parish) TF 013200
Apt 25.03.1841; 1004a (all); Map 1841, 4 chns, 'Revised and Copied' by R.S. Booth, Wainfleet; foot/b'way, waterbodies, houses, woods, field boundary ownerships, field gates, occupation road; pictorial church.

20/107 Croft and Bamburgh Field (parish and hamlet) TF 530610
Apt 01.08.1846; 5474a (all); Map 1847, 3 chns, 1st cl, by S. Hill and Son, Croft; construction lines, gowt, sluice, coastline, chapel, mill, clough, sand hills, outmarsh, private roads (uncoloured), hamlet boundary; drain named.

20/108 Croxby (parish) TF 185986
Apt 24.04.1837; 1628a (all); Map 1838, 8 chns, by F.C. Talbot, Brocklesby; hill drawing, waterbodies, woods, osiers (by symbol), decoy. Apt omits some field names.

20/109 Cuxwold (parish) TA 175009
Apt 31.10.1838; 1564a (1563); Map 1839, 9 chns, by Fred. C. Talbot, Brocklesby, (tinted); hill drawing, woods (col), glebe (col); pictorial church.

20/110 Dalby (except Dexthorpe) (parish) TF 410700
Apt 28.03.1842; 931a (all); Map 1842, 6 chns, by J.S. Padley, Lincoln; foot/b'way, waterbodies, houses, woods, osiers (by symbol), parkland, field boundary ownerships, field gates, hall, chalk pit, tumulus.

20/111 Dembleby (parish) TF 036379
Apt 07.10.1837; 1071a (all); Map 1838?, 8 chns; turnpike roads, woods (col), arable (col), grassland (col).

20/112 Denton (parish) SK 862328
Apt 16.07.1839; 2601a (2600); Map 1838, 3 chns, surveyed by W.B. Collingwood; waterbodies, houses, farmyards (col), woods (col), plantations (col), arable (col), grassland (col), hops (col), gardens (col), heath/moor (col), hedge ownership, field names, reservoir, canal with towpath, windmill (by symbol), watermill (by symbol). Apt omits field names for some holdings.

20/113 Digby (parish) TF 090550
Apt 09.12.1839; 2383a (all); Map 1841?, 7.5 chns; buildings are shown in outline only, without fill. District is apportioned by holding, though fields are numbered separately; acreages are for land use and no occupation information is given.

20/114 Doddington (district in parish of Doddington) SK 903700
Apt 17.07.1849; 2372a (all); Map 1849, 13.33 chns; woods, hall, glebe, (col, with acreage); pictorial church. District is apportioned as a single holding and fields are not shown.

20/115 Dorrington (parish) TF 095535
Apt 27.05.1851; 142a (680); Map 1851, 3 chns, by Robt C. Moore, Harmston, Lincoln, (tithable parts only); field boundary ownerships, road names, aqueduct; drains named.

20/116 Dowsby (parish) TF 128295
Apt 30.12.1837; 1809a (1809); Map 1838?, 8 chns; waterbodies, woods, boundary of tithe-free land; pictorial church.

20/117 Dunholm (parish) TF 023792 [Dunholme]
Apt 24.01.1844; 2190a (all); Map 1844, 6 chns, 'Corrected and Copied' from a survey of 1838 by R.T. Blyth; foot/b'way, woods (col), stone pit (col).

20/118 Dunsby (parish) TF 121267
Apt 10.09.1839; 251a (?); Map 1840, 6 chns, in 2 parts, (tithable parts only); woods; pictorial church.

20/119 Dunstall and Bonsdale (hamlet or division in parish of Corringham) SK 891839
Apt 23.10.1838; 701a (?); Map 1840, 6 chns, by W. Hudson, Epworth; waterbodies, houses, woods (col), orchards, Roman camp, field boundary ownership, ownerships (col).

20/120 Edenham (parish) TF 055220
Apt 15.12.1845; 23a (6844); Map 1848, 8 chns, by Cuming and Hill, Easton, Stamford, (tithable parts only, tinted); waterbodies, landowners.

20/121 Edlington (parish) TF 219705
Apt 17.07.1849; 2683a (all); Map 1850, 6 chns; foot/b'way, waterbodies, woods (col).

20/122 North Elkington (parish) TF 289908
Apt 08.05.1838; 992a (all); Map 1839, 9 chns, ? by C.C.J. Orme; hill drawing, waterbodies, houses, woods.

20/123 South Elkington (parish) TF 296887
Apt 28.03.1839; 3049a (3049); Map 1840, 9 chns, by Chas Cave Jno. Orme; waterbodies, houses, woods, parkland, building names, toll bar, paper mill.

20/124 Epworth (parish) SE 762039
Apt 23.10.1847; 64a (8140); Map 1848?, 4 chns, (tithable parts only, tinted); open fields.

20/125 Evedon (parish) TF 095475
Apt 29.03.1845; 1624a (all); Map 1845, 6 chns, by Charles Day, Collyweston; houses, woods, canal with locks; pictorial church.

20/126 Ewerby (parish) TF 133481
Apt 26.02.1850; 2904a (2520); Map 1851?, 3 chns, 1st cl; foot/b'way, houses, woods, plantations, field boundary ownerships, windmills or windpumps (by symbol), occupation road.

20/127 Falkingham and Laughton (parish) TF 073324 [Folkingham]
Apt 31.10.1839; 2998a (all); Map 1841, 6 chns, in 3 parts, (includes enlargement of Falkingham town at 3 chns); turnpike road, houses, gaol, windmill (pictorial); pictorial church. [The map in PRO IR 30 is a copy of 1923].

20/128 Farforth (parish) TF 317787
Apt 04.07.1844; 543a (all); Map 1843, 3 chns, 1st cl, by Saml Hill and Son, Croft; construction lines, waterbodies, houses, woods, field gates, stone pit, glebe.

20/129 Farlsthorpe (parish) TF 482744 [Farlesthorpe]
Apt 20.10.1840; 1043a (1043); Map 1838, 6 chns; foot/b'way, houses, woods (col), orchards, field boundary ownerships, field gates, old decoy, earthwork, hall; drains named.

20/130 Firsby (parish) TF 460630
Apt 07.10.1839; 1093a (910); Map 1840, 6 chns, in 3 parts, by S. Hill and Son, Croft, (includes 3-chn enlargement of 'mixed tithe'); waterbodies, field boundary ownerships, windmill (pictorial), chapel; scale is graduated with 'battlement' effect.

20/131 East Firsby (hamlet or division in parish of Firsby) TF 016857
Apt 28.11.1839; 536a (?); Map 1840, 6 chns, by Wm Hudson, Epworth; foot/b'way, waterbodies, houses, plantations, orchards, field boundary ownerships; owner of district is named in title.

20/132 West Firsby (parish) SK 985849
Apt 19.06.1840; 664a (?); Map 1840, 6 chns, by Robt C. Moore, Harmston, near Lincoln; houses, farmyards, woods (col), plantations (col, by Dawson's symbol), orchards (col), gardens (col), arable (col), grassland (col), field boundary ownerships.

20/133 Fiskerton (parish) TF 063726
Apt 09.07.1850; 767a (2040); Map 1850, 9 chns, (tithable parts only in detail); foot/b'way, waterbodies, houses, woods, field boundary ownerships, building name.

20/134 Fleet (parish) TF 354203
Apt 28.03.1839; 6667a (all); Map 1839, 12 chns; waterbodies, woods, building names, decoy, Roman bank, windmill (pictorial), workhouse; pictorial church. Apt omits field names.

20/135 Flixborough and Normanby (parish and hamlet) SE 880163
Apt 05.02.1840; 2899a (?); Map 1840?, 9 chns, in 2 parts; foot/b'way, woods, holding boundaries (col); tithe-free parts are unnumbered, and no buildings are shown.

20/136 Friskney (parish) TF 364547
Apt 18.01.1840; 7004a (13083); Map 1840, 3 chns, 1st cl, in 2 parts, by R.S. Booth, Wainfleet, (including construction line diagram); construction lines, foot/b'way, waterbodies, houses, woods, plantations, field boundary ownerships, field gates, landowners, embankment, residual channels, stiles, decoy, rectory, glebe.

20/137 Fristhorpe (parish) TF 069829 [Friesthorpe]
Apt 23.02.1847; 586a (586); Map 1847, 9 chns, in 2 parts, copied from a map of 1816 owned by Lord Brownlow, with alterations as necessary by Betham and Son, Lincoln, (including open meadow at 3 chns, dated 1848, and claimed to be 'from actual survey'); waterbodies, houses, woods.

20/138 Fulbeck (parish) SK 947503
Corn rent conversion, 1898; 3076a (3900); Map 1898, OS 6-inch, with village at 1:2500, surveyed 1886, annotated with tithe areas.

20/139 Gainsborough (township in parish of Gainsborough) SK 822882
Apt 06.07.1850; 14a (7210); Map 1852, 7.5 chns, (tithable parts only, tinted).

20/140 Gate Burton (parish) SK 842832
Apt 12.09.1848; 1108a (all); Map 1850, 12 chns; railway, foot/b'way, woods, parkland, field boundary ownerships, embankment. Apt omits land use.

20/141 Gautby (parish) TF 172722
Apt 27.03.1839; 1444a (1444); Map 1838, 6 chns, by Fred. C. Talbot, Brocklesby; waterbodies, woods (col); pictorial church; glebe is pink and rest of district is green or yellow, but it is unclear why.

20/142 Gayton le Marsh (parish) TF 434851
Apt 30.12.1839; 2167a (2166); Map 1839, 6 chns, by Fras. W. Mager, Louth; foot/b'way, houses, arable (col), grassland (col), field acreages, 'Poor Plot', old and new rectories, tunnel, footbridge; drains named; legend explains colours; scale is combined with north pointer.

20/143 Gayton le Wold (parish) TF 244856
Apt 07.05.1840; 1140a (1139); Map 1838, 12 chns, copied and alterations added by Chas Cave Jno. Orme, Louth; hill drawing, woods, churchyard (col). Apt omits field names.

20/144 Gedney (parish) TF 408333
Apt 02.11.1841; 12377a (25257); Map 1842?, 9 chns; turnpike roads, waterbodies, road names, sea banks, sluices; land in Lutton is tinted pink and unnumbered; no buildings are shown. Apt omits field names. [The map in PRO IR 30 is a copy of 1920.]

20/145 Glentworth (parish) SK 941880
Apt 03.03.1842; 3044a (3043); Map 1842?, 8 chns, 'Sketch', '1813', by Edwd Gee; waterbodies, fences, field boundary ownerships, fish pond, heath, cliff, Roman road. Apt omits land use and some field names.

20/146 Goxhill (parish) TA 117230
Apt 26.06.1847; 15a (8790); Map 1852, 4 chns, in 3 parts, by Henry Bake, Barton, (tithable parts only, tinted); road names, landowners; table summarises details of lands.

20/147 Grainsby (parish) TF 283996
Apt 08.06.1840; 1168a (1167); Map 1843, 8 chns, 'Revised and Copied' by Chas Cave Jno. Orme, Louth; waterbodies, woods.

20/148 Grainthorpe (parish) TF 380970
Apt 15.03.1845; 3968a (4955); Map 1845, 8 chns; road names; drains named.

20/149 Grantham (parish) SK 908354
Apt 02.11.1847; 335a (?); Map 1848?, 3 chns, compiled from a survey in January 1838 by J.S. Langwith, (tithable parts only in detail); houses, landowners, canal with towpath; built-up parts generalised.

20/150 Grayingham (parish) SK 937959
Apt 12.11.1845; 1675a (all); Map 1848?, 6 chns, copied from a map of 1805 with additions in 1838 by J.S. Langwith, Grantham; waterbodies, houses; pictorial church.

20/151 Greetwell (parish) TF 008721
Apt 03.03.1847; 1113a (all); Map 1848, 6 chns, by Edward Betham and Son, Lincoln; construction lines, railway, foot/b'way, waterbodies, houses, woods, plantations, toll bar. Apt omits field names.

20/152 Grimoldby (parish) TF 396883
Apt 08.04.1846; 149a (1729); Map 1848?, 12 chns, (tithable parts only in detail); landowners.

20/153 Great Grimsby (parish) TA 267091 [Grimsby]
Apt 30.06.1842; 477a (2748); Map 1842, 3 chns, in 5 parts, by John Lusby, (tithable parts only; including one part at 6 chns); waterbodies, landowners, toll bar, locks, haven, occupation road; the only building mapped is the church. Apt omits most land use.

20/154 Gunby (parish) TF 473662
Apt 31.01.1839; 667a (all); Map 1837, 6 chns, by S. Hill and Son, Croft, (tinted); waterbodies, houses, lodge, glebe, park; scale bar has 'battlement' graduations.

20/155 Gunhouse (township in parish of West Halton) SE 845115 [Gunness]
Apt 14.02.1838; 501a (?); Map 1840, 6 chns, by William Rawson; waterbodies, houses, woods; pecked lines are between ownerships and dot-dash lines are within holdings.

20/156 Hacconby (parish) TF 120255 [Haconby]
Apt 01.03.1847; 1a (3220); Map (drawn on Apt) 1852?, 3 chns, (tithable parts only); the map shows a mill, which is the only remaining tithable land. Apt omits land use.

20/157 Haceby (parish) TF 030361
Apt 26.07.1837; 706a (all); Map 1838?, 3 chns; turnpike road (col), houses, woods (col, named), arable (col), grassland (col), orchards, hedge ownership, field names, field acreages, pits; glebe is not mapped in detail.

20/158 Hainton (parish) TF 188849
Apt 20.03.1843; 2307a (2306); Map 1843, 12 chns, 'Revised and Copied' by Chas Cave Jno. Orme, Louth; waterbodies, woods.

20/159 Great Hale (parish) TF 173416
Apt 28.02.1850; 6166a (5110); Map 1843, 6 chns, by Robt C. Moore, Harmston, near Lincoln; foot/b'way, waterbodies, houses, woods, orchards, drove names, windmills (pictorial), embankments; watercourses named.

20/160 Hallington (parish) TF 299858
Apt 31.12.1850; 1498a (all); Map 1852, 8 chns, by W. Upton; foot/b'way, road names; streams named,; owner is named in title.

20/161 West Halton (township in parish of West Halton) SE 905200
Apt 18.01.1838; 1017a (?); Map not dated, 8 chns, in 2 parts, (tithable parts only; one part at 12 chns); woods, building names, holding boundaries (col).

20/162 Hanbeck (hamlet in parish of Wilsford) TF 011433 [Not listed]
Apt 09.12.1839; 370a (?); Map 1839, 8 chns, 'Compiled' by J.S. Langwith, Grantham; houses.

20/163 Hanby (hamlet in parish of Lavington or Lenton) TF 028320
Apt 30.11.1847; 706a (all); Map 1848, 6 chns; waterbodies; scale-bar is ruler-like.

20/164 Hardwick (township in parish of Torksey) SK 872754
Apt 08.07.1851; 221a (?); Map 1852, 3 chns, by Willm Hardy, Lincoln, (tithable parts only); foot/b'way, canal, waterbodies, houses, woods (named), field boundary ownerships, landowners, ferries.

20/165 Harrington (parish) TF 365715
Apt 30.12.1837; 1053a (all); Map 1839?, 3 chns; waterbodies, houses, woods (col), hedges, spring; scale-bar is ruler-like. Apt omits land use.

20/166 Harrowby (township in parish of Grantham) SK 935361
Apt 09.12.1839; 1485a (all); Map 1841?, 6 chns, by George Hardwick; foot/b'way, waterbodies, heath, Roman road, field names, field acreages; colours show land ownership and tithable status.

20/167 Hatcliffe (parish) TA 214001
Apt 27.03.1839; 1371a (all); Map 1839, 3 chns, 1st cl, by Chas Cave Jno. Orme, Louth; construction lines, houses, field boundary ownerships, Roman road.

20/168 Hatton (parish) TF 175765
Apt 17.12.1847; 1831a (all); Map 1848, 9 chns, ? by T. Bartholemew; woods, plantations, pit, glebe.

20/169 Haugh (extra-parochial township) TF 417758
Apt 06.07.1850; 26a (640); Map (drawn on Apt) 1852?, 10 chns, (tithable parts only); foot/b'way, woods, chapel. Apt omits land use.

20/170 Haugham (parish) TF 338816
Apt 29.12.1840; 1907a (1907); Map 1840?, 16 chns, in 2 parts, by W. Upton, (includes enlargement of village at 8 chns); foot/b'way, woods (named), field boundary ownerships, tumuli, pit, houses.

20/171 Hawerby cum Beesby (parish) TF 261964
Apt 31.03.1838; 1179a (1179); Map 1838, 15 chns, by Chas Cave Jno. Orme, Louth; hill drawing, woods (col), hedge ownership (col), churchyard (col); table summarises acreages.

20/172 Haxey (parish) SK 764998
Apt 20.02.1847; 3860a (8470); Map 1848, 3 chns, in 5 parts, by Makin Durham, Thorne, (tithable parts only; includes one part at 8 chns and 24-chn index); foot/b'way, waterbodies, woods (col), open fields, brickyard, embankment, windmill (by symbol).

20/173 Healing (parish) TA 213101
Apt 09.07.1839; 1328a (all); Map 1840, 6 chns, surveyed by Chas Cave Jno. Orme; waterbodies, houses, woods, fences. Apt omits field names.

20/174 Holbeach (parish) TF 359248
Apt 04.06.1839; 20981a (all); Map 1840?, 12 chns, in 2 parts, (includes town at 2.5 chns); turnpike roads, waterbodies, road names, sea banks (col), Roman bank (col); pink bands show ownerships to seaward of the Roman bank. Apt omits field names.

20/175 Holme (township in parish of Bottesford) SE 913067
Apt 15.07.1841; 1067a (?); Map 1847?, 6 chns; woods.

20/176 Holton with Beckering (parish) TF 118810
Apt 12.07.1843; 745a (1862); Map 1843, 3 chns, by Geo. Park, (tithable parts only); waterbodies, houses, woods.

20/177 Holton le Clay (parish) TA 290023
Apt 05.02.1840; 325a (1430); Map 1841?, 4 chns, (tithable parts only in detail, tinted); field acreages.

20/178 Holton le Moor (parish) TF 082978
Apt 12.09.1838; 1812a (all); Map 1838, 6 chns, by Waite, Haxey; waterbodies, woods, ownerships (col); cartouche has map title on an angled 'tablet', propped against a tree stump, on top of which is a bird, being looked at by a boy in gaiters with a gun, and a dog sitting on a stool; in the background a courting couple are sitting on a stile. Apt omits land use.

20/179 Honington (parish) SK 945435
Apt 28.02.1839; 1454a (1454); Map 1841, 3 chns; foot/b'way, woods.

20/180 Horkstowe (parish) SE 988185 [Horkstow]
Apt 14.01.1841; 2085a (all); Map 1840, 8 chns, by F.C. Talbot, Brocklesby; canal, waterbodies, woods, parkland, glebe (col), ancient road.

20/181 Hough on the Hill (parish) SK 911471
Apt 08.05.1850; 3992a (3600); Map 1850, 6 chns, by J.H. Hutchinson, Grantham; waterbodies, houses, woods, plantations, parkland, orchards, townships (col); legend explains township colours.

20/182 Hougham and Marston (united parishes) SK 890440
Apt 29.04.1852; 418a (2590); Map 1852, 8 chns, revised by John Hardwick, (tithable parts only); railway, foot/b'way, woods, field names, field acreages, ownerships (col); pictorial churches.

20/183 Howell (parish) TF 151465
Apt 09.06.1849; 1454a (1650); Map 1849, 6 chns, ? by John Parkinson; waterbodies, houses.

20/184 Huckerby (hamlet or division in parish of Corringham) SK 902938
Apt 23.10.1838; 184a (all); Map 1840, ?4 chns, by Wm Hudson, Epworth; waterbodies, houses, plantations (col), orchards (col), field boundary ownership; owner is named in title. Apt omits field names.

20/185 South Hykeham (parish) SK 935645
Corn rent conversion, 1920; 0a (1160); Map 1920?, 9 chns, from enclosure award map of 1803; houses, woods, landowners, field boundary ownerships; table gives details of allotments and owners in 1803.

20/186 Immingham (parish) TA 178142
Apt 15.12.1842; 3195a (3715); Map 1841, 9 chns, in 2 parts, by F.C. Talbot, Caistor; waterbodies, houses, woods, landowners, cloughs, glebe (col); pictorial church.

20/187 Ingoldmells (parish) TF 562690
Apt 28.03.1844; 1407a (all); Map 1842, 6 chns, by S. Hill and Son, Croft, (tinted); waterbodies, coal yard, hotel, outfall, Roman bank, chapel, tumulus (pictorial).

20/188 Ingoldsby (parish) TF 008302
Apt 22.11.1847; 2238a (all); Map 1848, 6 chns, by Cuming and Hill, Easton, Stamford; woods, parsonage, brickyard, windmill (by symbol), glebe (col), cottagers' pasture (col), manor house; pecked lines are used between holdings and dot-dash lines within holdings.

20/189 Irby (parish) TF 470630 [Irby in the Marsh]
Apt 20.03.1841; 756a (1090); Map 1840, 6 chns, 'modernised' by S. Hill and Son, Croft, (tinted); waterbodies, field boundary ownerships, chapels, pound; scale bar has 'battlement' graduations, glebe (pink); bridge and watercourses named.

20/190 Irby or Irby upon Humber (parish) TA 201044
Apt 30.05.1837; 1812a (1811); Map 1837, 3 chns, 1st cl, by Fred. C. Talbot; construction lines, hill drawing, foot/b'way, waterbodies, woods, osiers (by symbol), field boundary ownerships, field gates, spring, stone pits (col), moated site, stiles, green lane; scale-bar is ruler-like.

20/191 Irnham (parish) TF 032262
Apt 21.01.1839; 3731a (3520); Map 1841?, 8 chns; field names, school, priest's house, park, woods (by annotation); names and tithe area numbers are stamped.

20/192 Keadby (township in parish of Althorpe) SE 823116
Apt 31.01.1850; 1544a (?); Map 1850, 6 chns, by Makin Durham, Thorne, (tinted); canal with towpath and locks, warping drain, embankments; drains named; it is unclear why most buildings are grey but some are hatched. Apt does not give individual acreages for groups of tithe-free fields.

20/193 Keelby (parish) TA 165095
Apt 14.01.1845; 76a (1861); Map 1845, 3 chns, by F.C. Talbot, Caistor, (tithable parts only); waterbodies, landowners, windmill (pictorial).

20/194 Keisby (hamlet in parish of Lavington or Lenton) TF 045295
Apt 30.11.1847; 1246a (all); Map 1848, 6 chns; waterbodies.

20/195 South Kelsey (parish) TF 045985
Apt 12.10.1847; 329a (4980); Map 1848?, 10 chns, by Wm Lawrence, South Kelsey, (tithable parts only, tinted); foot/b'way, waterbodies, woods (col), building names, road names, landowners. Apt omits field names.

20/196 Kelstern (hamlet in parish of Kelstern) TF 253903
Apt 12.11.1849; 1745a (?); Map 1850?, 8 chns; waterbodies, woods (col), parkland, road name.

20/197 Kingerby (parish) TF 048921
Apt 31.05.1842; 1436a (1435); Map 1842, 8 chns, surveyed by William Bentley; foot/b'way, canal, waterbodies, houses, woods (col).

20/198 Kirkby Green (parish) TF 087579
Apt 12.08.1840; 438a (437); Map 1840, 6 chns, ? by James Sandby Padley; foot/b'way, waterbodies, windmill (pictorial); pictorial church, which resembles an ordinary house.

20/199 Kirkby Lathorpe (parish) TF 100453 [Kirkby la Thorpe]
Apt 26.09.1850; 2565a (all); Map 1851, 6 chns, by Robt C. Moore, Harmston, near Lincoln; foot/b'way, waterbodies, houses, woods (col), plantations (col), orchards, fox cover; 'Old Place', outside district, is named in gothic; it is the valuer's own residence.

20/200 Kirmington (parish) TA 102108
Apt 15.07.1841; 15a (1815); Map 1843?, 8 chns, (tithable parts only).

20/201 Kirmond le Mire (parish) TF 183920
Apt 19.04.1839; 1051a (1051); Map 1839?, [10 chns]; foot/b'way, woods (col). District is apportioned by holding and fields are not shown; Apt generalises land use.

20/202 Knaith (parish) SK 837845
Apt 21.03.1848; 1465a (all); Map 1850?, 12 chns; railway, foot/b'way, woods, parkland, field boundary ownerships. Apt omits land use.

20/203 South Kyme (parish) TF 177498
Apt 29.04.1847; 4869a (all); Map 1848, 6 chns; drove names. District is apportioned by holding and fields are not shown; Apt generalises land use.

20/204 Laceby (parish) TA 222062
Apt 19.06.1840; 2038a (all); Map 1840, 6 chns, by F.C. Talbot, Caistor; woods, windmill (pictorial), glebe (col).

20/205 Langton (parish) TF 397718
Apt 06.07.1838; 1292a (all); Map 1838?, [4 chns]; waterbodies, woods (col), marsh/bog, fish pond; owner is named in title and signs the map, adopting it.

20/206 Langton (parish) TF 151765 [Langton by Wragby]
Apt 20.06.1844; 1984a (2249); Map 1839, 5 chns, ? by Thomas Bartholemew; foot/b'way, waterbodies, woods (col), modus lands (greenish-yellow), glebe (grey), ownership boundary; pictorial church.

20/207 Laughton with Wildsworth (parish) SK 838972
Apt 10.02.1847; 4598a (4598); Map 1848?, 6 chns; foot/b'way, waterbodies (named), building names, moor, warren. Apt omits field names for a few holdings.

20/208 Lavington or Lenton (hamlet in parish of Lavington or Lenton) TF 041308
Apt 12.08.1843; 1095a (all); Map 1844?, 6 chns; waterbodies, houses (by shading), woods, tithe-free land; pictorial church.

20/209 Lavington or Lenton, certain lands (district in parish of Lavington or Lenton) TF 032310
Apt 26.03.1849; 55a (all); Map 1849?, 3 chns.

20/210 Lea (parish) SK 831867
Apt 10.01.1838; 2149a (2149); Map 1838, [8 chns]; holding boundaries; the only building shown is the church. District is apportioned by owner and fields are not shown; Apt generalises land use.

20/211 South Leasingham (parish) TF 062487 [Not listed]
Apt 14.12.1839; 2050a (all); Map 1840?, 6 chns, by R.C. Moore, Harmston, near Lincoln; turnpike roads (col), canal with haling path and locks, waterbodies, houses, woods (col), plantations (col), arable

(col), grassland (col), orchards (col), vegetable gardens, ornamental gardens (col), road names, water mill, gravel; pictorial church.

20/212 Legsby (parish) TF 135852
Apt 15.12.1845; 2887a (2886); Map 1846, 6 chns, 'Copied from plans made by J. Ayer, etc, dated 1811 etc'; foot/b'way, waterbodies, houses, woods, osiers (by symbol), hamlet boundaries (col), glebe, nursery.

20/213 Lincoln, St Mary Magdalene (parish) SK 977719 [Not listed]
Apt 26.09.1850; 13a (?); Map 1851, 1 chn, ? by Edward Betham, Lincoln; Cathedral (in detail), chapter residences, gate, assembly rooms, judge's lodgings, club house, building names, property boundary ownerships, including leasehold/freehold division; lilac shows public buildings and inns. Apt omits land use.

20/214 Lincoln, St Mary le Wigford (parish) SK 965710 [Not listed]
Apt 26.08.1850; 243a (?); Map 1851, 2 chns, by Wm Hardy, Lincoln, (tithable parts only in detail); railways, canal, waterbodies, houses, osiers (by symbol), road names, gas tank, race course, grand stand, pound, wharf, common.

20/215 Lincoln, St Peter in Eastgate (parish) SK 983721 [Not listed]
Apt 19.10.1848; 23a (?); Map 1849, 6 chns, 'Copied from the Inclosure Award, 1805; with additions where requisite, 1849', by Betham and Son, Lincoln, (tithable parts only); pictorial church.

20/216 Lincoln, St Swithin (parish) SK 982711 [Not listed]
Apt 29.10.1850; 82a (?); Map 1851, 2 chns, ? by Edward Betham, Lincoln, (tithable parts only in detail); foot/b'way, waterbodies, houses, field boundary ownerships, road names, lock, dock, ropery, burial ground, police station (in detail, not named); bridge named. Apt omits most land use.

20/217 Linwood (parish) TF 113864
Apt 16.04.1839; 2317a (all); Map 1842?, 8 chns, copied by C.C.J. Orme, Louth; houses, woods, landowners.

20/218 Linwood (hamlet in parish of Blankney) TF 122608
Apt 17.12.1847; 336a (?); Map 1848, 3 chns, 1st cl, by Wm Skill, Lincoln; construction lines, foot/b'way, waterbodies, houses, woods, plantations, parkland, field boundary ownerships, field gates, hall, occupation road, hauling path, bank; the whole district is mapped and numbered, but only the tithable parts are apportioned.

20/219 Lissington (parish) TF 109833
Apt 20.08.1839; 1527a (all); Map 1840, 3 chns, surveyed by Rd Iveson, Hedon; construction lines, waterbodies, houses, hedge ownership; it is unclear why some roads are coloured and some are not.

20/220 Louth (parish) TF 331875
Apt 02.07.1846; 121a (3620); Map 1849, 3 chns, in 5 parts, (tithable parts only); canal with locks, road names, windmills (by symbol), railway; built-up parts generalised and very few buildings are shown. Apt omits most land use.

20/221 Ludborough (parish) TF 295960
Apt 28.11.1850; 14a (2250); Map 1851, 4 chns, (tithable parts only); foot/b'way, landowners; pictorial church; table gives details of lands.

20/222 Ludford Magna (parish) TF 209897 [Ludford]
Apt 19.04.1849; 63a (?); Map 1852?, 6 chns, 'Drawn' by Maughan and Fowler, Surveyors, Louth, (tithable parts only); field names, field acreages, landowners.

20/223 Mablethorpe St Mary (parish) TF 495845 [Mablethorpe]
Apt 15.05.1847; 1892a (2221); Map 1847, 4 chns, in 2 parts; waterbodies, hall, sea bank; drain, bridge, 'hurn' and 'nook' named.

20/224 Maltby le Marsh (parish) TF 472816
Apt 26.02.1839; 1377a (all); Map 1840?, 6 chns; houses, field gates; scale is combined with north pointer.

20/225 Market Rasen (parish) TF 114887
Apt 10.07.1850; 5a (1220); Map 1852?, 3 chns, (tithable parts only); hedges (col), trees (col), fences, road names, mills, mill dam, landowners, gardens, paddocks, orchards. Apt omits land use.

20/226 Markby (parish) TF 489788
Apt 26.06.1839; 652a (652); Map 1839, 3 chns, 1st cl, by S. Hill and Son, Croft; construction lines, waterbodies, residual open fields (named), pound, chapel; drain named.

20/227 Marsh Chapel (parish) TF 370990 [Marshchapel]
Apt 20.08.1839; 3068a (all); Map 1841, 6 chns; canal, houses.

20/228 Martin Dales (township or district in parish of Timberland) TF 170622
Apt 24.11.1842; 604a (all); Map 1848, 5 chns, by John Bromley, Derby; waterbodies, osiers, milestones, ferry, engine, drains; it is unclear why both dot-dash and pecked lines are used.

20/229 Martin (parish) TF 240665
Apt 12.09.1839; 765a (all); Map 1839, 3 chns, 1st cl, by S. Hill and Son, Croft; construction lines, canal with lock, waterbodies, woods, orchards, tower, occupation road, fish pond, pound, moor.

20/230 Melton Ross (parish) TA 069117
Apt 11.05.1848; 1755a (all); Map 1849, 6 chns; railway, waterbodies, houses, woods (col), osiers (by symbol).

20/231 Mere (parish) TF 007650
Apt 31.12.1850; 1410a (all); Map 1852, 6 chns, by Robt C. Moore, Harmston, near Lincoln; waterbodies, houses, plantations, heath/moor, field boundary ownerships, quarries.

20/232 Metheringham (parish) TF 080622
Apt 13.02.1847; 9a (4590); Map 1847, 9 chns, by William Peart, (tithable parts only); pictorial church.

20/233 Middle Rasen (township in parish of Middle Rasen Tupholme and Middle Rasen Drax) TF 090895
Apt 30.03.1849; 356a (3470); Map 1849, 3 chns, in 2 parts, by John H. Hutchinson, Grantham, (tithable parts only); waterbodies, houses, plantations; pictorial churches, with gravestones.

20/234 Minting (parish) TF 178738
Apt 22.02.1843; 2543a (2543); Map 1841, 6 chns, by Percy W. Brackenbury, Wellow House, Ollerton; foot/b'way, waterbodies, houses, woods (col, named).

20/235 Morton (parish) TF 118238
Apt 01.03.1847; 1a (3390); Map 1851?, 8 chns, (tithable parts only); road names; pictorial church.

20/236 Moulton (parish) TF 307242
Apt 31.01.1850; 817a (13785); Map 1880?, 6 chns, (tithable parts only); sea banks.

20/237 Muckton (parish) TF 378818
Apt 31.01.1839; 1025a (all); Map 1841, 6 chns; waterbodies, woods; pictorial church.

20/238 Mumby (parish) TF 522743
Apt 27.06.1850; 1a (2620); Map 1850, 10 chns, (tithable parts only); windmills (pictorial); pictorial church; only the mills are tithable. Apt omits land use.

20/239 Newton next Toft (parish) TF 053870 [Newton by Toft]
Apt 08.02.1841; 1004a (all); Map 1843, 8 chns, copied by Chas Cave Jno. Orme.

20/240 Normanby on the Wolds (parish) TF 123958 [Normanby le Wold]
Apt 26.06.1847; 1950a (all); Map 1848, 6 chns, in 2 parts, (includes 3-chn enlargement of detail), litho (Standidge); foot/b'way, waterbodies, woods, mill, glebe.

20/241 Northolme or Wainfleet St Thomas (parish) TF 499593 [Not listed]
Apt 31.01.1850; 25a (all); Map 1850, 2 chns, by S. Hill and Son, Croft, (tinted); street name, churchyard, hall.

20/242 Northorpe (parish) SK 895967
Apt 04.10.1838; 1817a (all); Map 1839, 6 chns; waterbodies, glebe.

20/243 Norton Disney (parish) SK 880595
Apt 01.11.1839; 1706a (2305); Map 1839, 6 chns, by Thomas Davison, Durham, (tithable parts only); woods, holding boundaries (col). District is apportioned by holding; Apt omits land use.

20/244 Orby in the Marsh (parish) TF 503673 [Orby]
Apt 06.02.1843; 2089a (2088); Map 1843, 10 chns; woods.

20/245 North Ormsby (parish) TF 283930
Apt 08.07.1842; 1708a (1707); Map 1843, 6 chns; waterbodies, houses, woods.

20/246 South Ormsby cum Ketsby with Calceby and Driby (united rectory with vicarage and rectory) TF 380753
Apt 11.01.1840; 4334a (4333); Map 1840, 13.33 chns, 'Copied and Revised' by Chas Cave Jno. Orme, Louth; waterbodies, woods (col), parish boundaries.

20/247 Osgodby (township in parish of Lavington or Lenton) TF 017283 [Not listed]
Apt 19.06.1840; 1094a (?); Map 1840, 6 chns; waterbodies, houses (by shading), woods.

20/248 Owersby (parish) TF 058946 [North Owersby]
Apt 18.12.1839; 4718a (4718); Map 1840, [?13.33 chns]; foot/b'way; pictorial church; no other buildings are shown. Apt omits occupancy and field details for tithe-merged land.

20/249 Owston (township in parish of Owston) SE 808002
Apt 29.06.1850; 3307a (?); Map 1851, 3 chns, in 3 parts, by Makin Durham, Thorne, (tithable parts only, tinted; including open fields at 3 chns); waterbodies, woods, open fields (named), motte; drains named.

20/250 Oxcomb (parish) TF 313772 [Oxcombe]
Apt 12.02.1842; 1022a (all); Map 1840, 9 chns; waterbodies, ridgeway; owner is named in title.

20/251 Panton (parish) TF 172795
Apt 13.07.1838; 1997a (1996); Map 1839, [6 chns]; woods (col), glebe (pink); green is land not owned by the main owner. District is apportioned by holding and fields are not shown; Apt generalises land use.

20/252 Partney (parish) TF 410681
Apt 28.03.1839; 920a (all); Map 1839, 3 chns, by Henry Kennedy, 100 Chancery Lane, London; foot/b'way, waterbodies, houses, woods, arable (col), grassland (col), field boundary ownerships, field gates, guide post (pictorial), stiles (pictorial), churchyard.

20/253 Pickworth (parish) TF 042331
Apt 31.05.1844; 1474a (all); Map 1845, 6 chns; foot/b'way, waterbodies, houses, woods.

20/254 Pointon (township in parish of Sempringham) TF 123313
Apt 17.09.1849; 191a (?); Map 1852?, 10 chns, by Parker Smith, Caythorpe, near Grantham, (tithable parts only); road names, landowners.

20/255 Potter Hanworth (parish) TF 072674 [Potterhanworth]
Apt 19.10.1848; 253a (4150); Map 1849, 4 chns, in 2 parts, by W. Bartholemew, Goltho, near Wragby, (tithable parts only); woods, road names, landowners, field acreages; pictorial church.

20/256 Raithby with Maltby (parish) TF 316849
Apt 31.12.1850; 1877a (1930); Map 1851, 8 chns, by W. Upton; foot/b'way, turnpike roads and gate, waterbodies, gardens, landowners, springs, glebe, hamlet boundary; pictorial church; north pointer has plumes and 'Ich Dien'.

20/257 Rand with Fulnetby (parish) TF 102792
Apt 25.10.1841; 2085a (all); Map 1842, 6 chns; waterbodies, houses, woods.

20/258 East Ravendale or Great Ravendale (parish) TF 241992
Apt 31.05.1842; 812a (all); Map 1842, 6 chns, by Henry Teal, Junr, Leeds; waterbodies. Apt omits field names.

20/259 Redbourne (parish) SK 987992
Apt 12.08.1841; 3919a (3919); Map 1841, 6 chns, by R. Smith, York; foot/b'way, waterbodies, woods (col), parkland (col), building names, Roman road, pits, glebe (col); map title is on 'sky' background.

20/260 Repham (parish) TF 040743 [Reepham]
Apt 09.02.1842; 1836a (1430); Map 1851?, 3 chns, surveyed by W.H. Wright; houses, woods.

20/261 North Reston (parish) TF 384837
Apt 27.06.1839; 703a (all); Map 1841?, 3 chns; foot/b'way, houses, woods, hedge ownership, field gates.

20/262 South Reston (parish) TF 404830
Apt 12.08.1850; 23a (710); Map 1851?, 2 chns, (tithable parts only); gardens, road names, landowners.

20/263 Riby (parish) TA 182078
Apt 28.08.1839; 2749a (2749); Map 1839, 12 chns, by F.C. Talbot, Brocklesby, (tithable parts only, tinted); woods (col), landowners.

20/264 Risby (township in parish of Walesby) TF 142913
Apt 19.08.1852; 710a (?); Map 1853?, 6 chns; woods.

20/265 Roulston (parish) TF 083565 [Rowston]
Apt 07.08.1843; 1872a (all); Map 1841, 4 chns, by Robt C. Moore, Harmston, nr Lincoln; foot/b'way, waterbodies, houses, farmyards (col), woods (col), osiers (by symbol), coppice (col, by Dawson's symbol), plantations (col), arable (col), grassland (col), orchards (col), gardens (col), heath/moor (col), field boundary ownerships, field gates, building names, stiles, vicarage, cross, holy well, encroachments; drain named.

20/266 Roxby cum Risby (parish) SE 941172
Apt 15.04.1841; 2656a (4784); Map 1841, 16 chns, in 2 parts, 'Revised and Copied' by F.C. Talbot, Caistor, (includes Roxby village at 8 chns); woods, Roman road, glebe (pink); pictorial church.

20/267 Roxholm (township or parish) TF 053502 [Not listed]
Apt 13.04.1840; 909a (all); Map 1840, 6 chns, 'Copied' by Robt C. Moore, Harmston, near Lincoln; foot/b'way, private road, waterbodies, houses, farmyards (col), plantations (col), arable (col), grassland (col), orchards (col), gardens (col), heath/moor (col), field boundary ownerships, field gates, stiles, milestone (pictorial).

20/268 Ruckland (parish) TF 339785
Apt 04.07.1844; 713a (all); Map 1844?, 8 chns; woods, glebe.

20/269 Salmonby (parish) TF 324734
Apt 29.07.1841; 992a (all); Map 1841, 6 chns, surveyed by C.C.J. Orme, Louth; waterbodies, houses, woods.

20/270 Saltfleetby All Saints (parish) TF 455904
Apt 17.07.1839; 1169a (1169); Map 1841, 6 chns, surveyed by C.C.J. Orme, Louth; waterbodies, houses, road names, drains. Apt omits field names.

20/271 Saltfleetby St Clement (parish) TF 460918
Apt 27.08.1839; 1030a (all); Map 1841, 6 chns, surveyed by C.C.J. Orme, Louth; houses, road names, drains. Apt omits field names.

20/272 Saltfleetby St Peters (parish) TF 432893
Apt 14.12.1840; 2004a (all); Map 1841, 6 chns, surveyed by C.C.J. Orme, Louth; waterbodies, houses, road names, drains. Apt omits field names.

20/273 Sapperton (parish) TF 022337
Apt 30.12.1848; 656a (all); Map 1849, 4 chns, surveyed by W.B. Collingwood; waterbodies, houses, woods (col), orchards (col), gardens (col), arable (col), grassland (col), field names.

20/274 Sausthorpe (parish) TF 387690
Apt 27.03.1839; 728a (all); Map 1839, 3 chns, by S. Hill and Son, Croft, (tinted); woods (col), parkland, building names, marl pit (col), ford, school, pound, spring, glebe (col).

20/275 Saxby in Aslacoe (parish) TF 004864 [Saxby]
Apt 31.01.1850; 84a (2322); Map 1850, 4 chns, by Henry Ellison, Stone, (tithable parts only, tinted); woods, road names.

20/276 Saxby (parish) SE 992167 [Saxby All Saints]
Apt 22.11.1837; 2323a (all); Map 1838, 4 chns; waterbodies, woods; pictorial church.

20/277 Scampton (parish) SK 943795
Apt 18.01.1849; 2148a (all); Map 1849, 6 chns, by Robert Banks, Scampton; churchyard, glebe.

20/278 North Scarle (parish) SK 850670
Apt 12.09.1839; 1956a (all); Map 1840, 6 chns, by J.S. Padley, Lincoln; foot/b'way, waterbodies, houses, plantations, road names, brick yard, windmill (by symbol); drains named.

20/279 Scartho (parish) TA 266071
Corn rent conversion, 1862; 1136a (1390); Map 1862?, [6 chns], (tithable parts only). Apt omits land use and field names.

20/280 Skate Intack and Wroot Acres (district in parish of Wroot) SE 715042 [Not listed]
Apt 02.09.1847; 88a (all); Map 1847, 4 chns, by M. Durham, Thorne, (tinted); engine, old river course; drain named.

20/281 Scothern or Scothorn (parish) TF 035775
Apt 31.01.1850; 53a (2500); Map 1850, 3 chns, by J.S. Padley, Lincoln, (tithable parts only); foot/b'way, waterbodies, houses, field boundary ownerships, field gates, field acreages. Apt omits land use.

20/282 Scotton (parish) SK 869991
Apt 23.01.1838; 4358a (all); Map 1839, 6 chns, in 3 parts; waterbodies (named), woods (col), building names, residual open fields, former open field names, landowners, glebe (col), commons; legend explains colours.

20/283 Scot Willoughby (parish) TF 056380 [Scott Willoughby]
Apt 21.03.1838; 557a (all); Map 1838, [3 chns], by J.S. Langwith, copy of the map adopted at the meeting in November 1837; pictorial church.

20/284 Scrafield (parish) TF 303689
Apt 06.06.1840; 670a (all); Map 1841?, 3 chns; foot/b'way, waterbodies, houses, woods, field boundary ownerships, glebe.

20/285 Scrivelsby and Dalderby (united parishes) TF 267661
Apt 22.08.1849; 2833a (?); Map 1850, 4 chns, in 2 parts; foot/b'way, canal and locks, waterbodies, houses, woods (named), hedge ownership, fence ownership, field acreages, landowners, churchyard, glebe, footbridge; owner is named in title: 'Henry Dymoke Esqre., The Honorable The Queen's Champion'.

20/286 Sedgebrook (parish) SK 848380
Apt 02.11.1847; 1642a (all); Map 1848, 6 chns, in 2 parts, by James Dunn, (including 'Cottagers' Pastures' at 3 chns); railway, foot/b'way, waterbodies, houses, woods (col), field boundary ownerships, common waste (col).

20/287 Silk Willoughby (parish) TF 058427
Apt 11.04.1839; 24a (all); Map 1839?, 8 chns; houses, field acreages. Apt omits some field names.

20/288 Sixhills (parish) TF 171869
Apt 17.12.1847; 1962a (all); Map 1848?, 12 chns; woods.

20/289 Skegness (parish) TF 560628
Apt 17.07.1849; 1644a (2474); Map 1849, 6 chns, by S. Hill and Son, Croft; waterbodies, hotel, coal yards, lifeboat station, Roman bank, pound, chapel, sandhills.

20/290 Skendleby (parish) TF 433702
Apt 27.05.1846; 1526a (1710); Map 1846, 6 chns, in 2 parts, revised by R.S. Booth, Wainfleet, (tinted); foot/b'way, waterbodies, houses, woods, parkland, field boundary ownerships, field gates, landowners, vicarage, occupation roads, chalk pit, stiles, swamp.

20/291 Saltfleet cum Skidbrook (parish) TF 452941
Apt 27.06.1837; 2081a (3455); Map 1838?, 3 chns, 1st cl, by Chas Cave Jno. Orme; construction lines, waterbodies, houses, plantations, arable (col), gardens, marsh/bog, heath/moor (col), hedge ownership, fence ownership, field gates, windmill (by symbol), boundary post, sandhills (col), saltmarsh (col), drains, beach (col); red lines could represent later additions. Apt omits most field names, and omits land use for fields laid out at enclosure.

20/292 Snarford (parish) TF 053825
Apt 06.06.1848; 1144a (all); Map 1851, 7 chns; waterbodies, woods.

20/293 Snelland (parish) TF 073806
Apt 09.07.1839; 1261a (all); Map 1839, 4 chns, 'enlarged' by George Betham; houses, churchyard, hamlet name and boundary; route of River Snart to sea is described.

20/294 Somerby (parish) TA 064064
Apt 07.07.1847; 977a (1940); Map 1848, 6 chns, by M. Brady, Brigg; waterbodies, houses, farmyards (col), woods (col), parkland (col), orchards (col), gardens (col), stone pit (col); pink band shows glebe and boundary of old warren; meaning of green band is unclear.

20/295 Somerby (hamlet or division) SK 851895
Apt 23.10.1838; 1569a (?); Map 1840, 8 chns, by Wm Hudson, Epworth, Lincs; waterbodies, houses, woods (col), field boundary ownerships, toll bar; owner is named in title.

20/296 North Somercotes (parish) TF 421975
Apt 29.10.1840; 4753a (8622); Map 1841, 6 chns, by Chas Cave Jno. Orme, Louth; waterbodies, houses, coastal creeks. Apt omits field names.

20/297 South Somercotes (parish) TF 418933
Apt 10.10.1839; 2598a (2597); Map 1840?, 6 chns, ? by C.C.J. Orme; waterbodies, houses. Apt omits field names.

20/298 Somersby (parish) TF 342729
Apt 05.05.1838; 601a (600); Map 1838?, 4 chns, ? by T. Bartholemew; foot/b'way, woods (col); owner is named in title.

20/299 Somerton Castle (manor in parish of Boothby Graffoe) SK 949590
Apt 31.03.1842; 418a (?); Map 1842, 3 chns, by Robt C. Moore, Harmston, near Lincoln; foot/b'way, waterbodies, houses, woods, osiers (by symbol), reeds, landowners, moat, castle; scale and north pointer are combined.

20/300 Southrey (hamlet in parish of Bardney) TF 133671
Apt 17.07.1841; 690a (690); Map 1841, 6 chns, by Chas Cave Jno. Orme; waterbodies, houses.

20/301 Spanby (parish) TF 102379
Apt 29.07.1841; 1009a (all); Map 1841, 8 chns, 'Copied' by S. Hill and Son, Croft, (tinted); foot/b'way, waterbodies, woods, field boundary ownerships, road name.

20/302 Springthorpe (parish) SK 880899
Apt 30.04.1838; 1073a (1072); Map 1841, 4 chns, by William Hudson, Epworth; foot/b'way, waterbodies, open fields (named), commons; the map has an explanation about intermixed lands.

20/303 Stainfield (parish) TF 110729
Apt 23.10.1847; 2098a (all); Map 1848, 9 chns, ? by T. Bartholemew; waterbodies, woods, embankment (col).

20/304 Stainton by Langworth (parish) TF 072772
Apt 20.07.1843; 3021a (3021); Map 1839, 16 chns, 'Newbold, Surveyed by J.S. Padley, 1824. Stainton, Copied from an Old Plan'; foot/b'way, waterbodies, woods, milestone, tumuli, earthwork, hamlet names and boundaries, hall; bridge named.

20/305 Stallingborough (parish) TA 200120
Apt 26.08.1842; 2968a (5792); Map 1844, 6 chns, by R. Smith, York, (tinted); foot/b'way, waterbodies, woods (col), field boundary ownerships, embankment; pecked lines are within holdings and dot-dash lines are between holdings.

20/306 Stamford, All Saints with St Peters (parish) TF 017075 [Not listed]
Apt 16.04.1841; 1320a (?); Map 1842, 8 chns, (tithable parts only); waterbodies, open fields (named).

20/307 Stamford, St George with St Paul annexed (parish) TF 041074 [Not listed]
Apt 04.12.1841; 337a (?); Map 1842, 4 chns; turnpike roads, open fields, infirmary, stone pits, locks.

20/308 Stamford, St John with St Clements (parish) TF 024073 [Not listed]
Apt 19.02.1847; 3a (?); Map 1848, 1 chn, by Cuming and Hill, Easton, Stamford, (tithable parts only); parkland, building names, road names; tithable buildings are pink and others grey.

20/309 Stamford, St Michael with St Stephen's and St Andrews annexed (district) TF 033074 [Not listed]
Apt 19.02.1847; 22a (?); Map 1847, 2 chns, (tithable parts only); road names, glebe.

20/310 Stane or Stain (parish) TF 467848
Apt 05.10.1847; 254a (all); Map 1847, 6 chns, by W. Barker.

20/311 Stapleford (parish) SK 872569
Apt 30.04.1849; 2644a (2930); Map 1846, 6 chns, by H.M. Wood, Nottingham; woods, heath/moor; colours show smaller owners. District is apportioned by holding and fields are not shown; Apt generalises land use, and no individual occupancy or acreages information is given for most of the district.

20/312 Great Steeping (parish) TF 443644
Apt 18.08.1841; 1724a (1724); Map 1839, 3 chns, 'Taken by order of the Proprietors', by Henry Kennedy, 100 Chancery Lane, London; waterbodies, houses, woods, residual open fields, field boundary ownerships, field gates, embankments, pound, tithe-free land, land tithable elsewhere (with acreages); bridges named.

20/313 Stenigot (parish) TF 255815
Apt 09.04.1840; 1321a (1321); Map 1841, 9 chns, 'Revised and copied' by Chas Cave Jno. Orme; hill drawing, houses.

20/314 Stewton (parish) TF 361867
Apt 23.09.1837; 972a (all); Map 1838, 16 chns, copied with 'the alterations' added by Chas Cave Jno. Orme, Louth; hedges (col), occupation road, glebe (col); stream named.

20/315 Stowe (parish) SK 885814 [Stow]
Apt 13.07.1839; 4752a (4620); Map surveyed 1838, 6 chns, by J.S. Padley, Land Valuer and Surveyor, Lincoln; foot/b'way, waterbodies, houses, woods (col), orchards, heath/moor, field boundary ownerships, building names, road names, landowners (col), site of bishop's palace, brick kiln, stiles, township names and boundaries (col); drains named; tables list small owners and plots in the villages; legend explains field boundary ownership symbols.

20/316 Stroxton (parish) SK 902313
Apt 24.04.1849; 969a (all); Map 1850?, 4 chns, by W.B. Collingwood; waterbodies, houses, gardens (col), plantations (col), arable (col), grassland (col), field names.

20/317 Strubby with Woodthorpe (parish) TF 453819
Apt 29.07.1842; 2076a (2075); Map 1842, 9 chns, 'Surveyed and Mapped' by Chas Cave Jno. Orme, Louth; waterbodies, houses, woods.

20/318 Stubton (parish) SK 875490
Apt 27.04.1837; 1159a (all); Map 1838?, 6 chns; foot/b'way, private road, houses, woods (by Dawson's symbol), plantations (by Dawson's symbol), parkland, gardens (col); pictorial church.

20/319 Sudbrooke (parish) TF 039761
Apt 04.05.1838; 226a (1000); Map 1838, 3 chns, in 3 parts, by J.S. Padley, (tithable parts only); foot/b'way, coach road, waterbodies, houses, woods, plantations, parkland, field boundary ownerships, field gates, building names, landowners.

20/320 Surfleet (parish) TF 260295
Apt 02.04.1846; 232a (3500); Map 1846?, 6 chns, ? by Edward Millington, Fleet, (tithable parts only); sea bank, hauling paths, sluice.

20/321 Sutterby (parish) TF 386723
Apt 11.03.1839; 472a (471); Map 1840, 10 chns, copied and alterations added by Chas Cave Jno. Orme; hill drawing, foot/b'way, woods, glebe (col).

20/322 Sutton in the Marsh (parish) TF 517806 [Sutton on Sea]
Apt 12.09.1839; 1666a (all); Map 1840?, 6 chns; arable (col), grassland (col), former common field names; sea bank; drain, drainage outfalls and tunnels named.

20/323 Sutton St Mary or Long Sutton or Sutton in Holland (parish) TF 445223
Apt 13.08.1842; 9373a (?); Map 1845?, 6 chns, in 2 parts; waterbodies, houses, landowners, lighthouses, sluices; drain and bridge named. Apt omits land use.

20/324 Sutton St Edmunds with commons in Long Sutton (chapelry) TF 362118 [Sutton St Edmund]
Apt 13.09.1843; 5473a (?); Map 1844, 8 chns, in 5 parts, 'Copy Survey' by Joseph Cross, (includes two 3-chn enlargements of detail); road names; drains named.

20/325 Sutton St James with common in Long Sutton (hamlet) TF 388178
Apt 13.08.1842; 2946a (?); Map 1844?, 6 chns, ? by Edward Millington, Fleet; waterbodies; drains named; cartouche has a leopard/human face at the top. Apt omits land use.

20/326 Sutton St Nicholas or Lutton (parish) TF 446255
Apt 13.08.1842; 3845a (?); Map 1843, 8 chns, ? by Edward Millington, Fleet; turnpike roads, waterbodies, road names, Roman bank, sea banks, sluices, windmills (by symbol); drains named; field acreages appear to have been scraped out; lands belonging to other districts are pink. Apt omits field names.

20/327 Swinderby (parish) SK 870630
Apt 12.08.1850; 612a (1640); Map 1851, 6 chns, by J.S. Padley, Lincoln, (tithable parts only); railway with station, foot/b'way, turnpike roads, waterbodies, houses, woods, field boundary ownerships, road names, milestones, toll house.

20/328 Swinhop (parish) TF 221960 [Swinhope]
Apt 19.12.1842; 1308a (1307); Map 1842, 6 chns, 'Surveyed and Mapped' by Chas Cave Jno. Orme, Louth; foot/b'way, waterbodies, houses, woods, building names.

20/329 Syston (parish) SK 934408
Apt 30.06.1849; 35a (1613); Map 1849?, 3 chns, by John Hardwick, (tithable parts only, tinted); woods (col), field names, field acreages.

20/330 Tathwell (parish) TF 314820
Apt 16.07.1846; 4274a (4314); Map 1846, 8 chns; foot/b'way, waterbodies, houses, woods (named), plantations, field boundary ownerships, field gates, blue stone, tumuli, encampment, lodge, hamlet boundary.

20/331 Theddlethorpe All Saints (parish) TF 463882
Apt 22.11.1838; 1780a (all); Map 1841, 3 chns, 1st cl, by S. Hill and Son, Croft, (tinted); private roads (uncoloured), woods, field boundary ownerships, sandhills, island, school, pound, gowts; drains and some bridges and outfalls named; map is certified as compared with original. Apt omits some land use.

20/332 Theddlethorpe St Helen with Mablethorpe St Peter (parish) TF 485875
Apt 19.05.1843; 2852a (5112); Map 1841, 3 chns, 1st cl, in 2 parts, by S. Hill and Son, Croft; construction lines, woods, lifeboat station, chapel, windmill (pictorial); banks, bridges and drains named; the map also covers the whole of 20/331, Theddlethorpe All Saints.

20/333 Thimbleby (parish) TF 242705
Apt 21.03.1853; 3a (1770); Map (drawn on Apt) 1853, 6 chns, (tithable parts only). Apt omits field names.

20/334 North Thoresby (parish) TF 294985
Apt 29.06.1839; 2485a (2485); Map 1839, [4 chns]; canal, waterbodies, woods, windmill (pictorial); pictorial church. Apt omits most field names.

20/335 South Thoresby (parish) TF 407769
Apt 19.12.1848; 931a (all); Map 1849?, 3 chns; waterbodies, woods, glebe boundary.

20/336 Thorganby (parish) TF 205976
Apt 09.02.1842; 1569a (1568); Map 1841, 12 chns; waterbodies, woods; pictorial church.

20/337 Thornton (parish) TF 233661
Apt 23.04.1839; 1738a (1755); Map 1839, 3 chns, in 2 parts; waterbodies, houses, woods, hedge ownership, field gates, landowners, canal with towpath and locks; owner is named in title: 'Henry Dymoke Esqre., The Honorable The Queen's Champion'.

20/338 Thornton Curtis (parish) TA 072181
Apt 06.11.1849; 4836a (4610); Map 1850, 6 chns, by Abraham Atkinson, Langholme; foot/b'way, waterbodies, woods, osiers (by symbol), plantations, parkland, orchards, abbey ruins.

20/339 Thornton le Moor (parish) TF 048962
Apt 15.02.1843; 1504a (all); Map 1839, [?7.5 chns]; foot/b'way, waterbodies, woods, ownerships (col); legend explains colours.

20/340 Thorpe in the Fallows or West Thorpe (parish) SK 916804 [Thorpe le Fallows]
Apt 31.01.1850; 857a (640); Map 1850, 4 chns, by Wm Hardy, Lincoln; foot/b'way, waterbodies, houses, woods, gardens, field boundary ownerships, glebe (col, with acreage).

20/341 Thorpe Tilney (township in parish of Timberland) TF 140580
Apt 12.11.1840; 1070a (all); Map 1841?, 6 chns; waterbodies, bank; drains and fens named.

20/342 Threekingham with Stow (parish) TF 091358
Apt 30.05.1846; 449a (2270); Map 1846?, 3 chns, (tithable parts only); foot/b'way, turnpike roads, houses, road names; pictorial church.

20/343 Thurlby (parish) SK 898615
Apt 19.12.1838; 1803a (all); Map 1838, 8 chns, by J.S. Padley, Lincoln; foot/b'way, turnpike roads, waterbodies, woods, plantations, field boundary ownerships, halfway stone, glebe; pictorial church; legend explains field boundary ownership symbols.

20/344 Toft next Newton (parish) TF 038872
Apt 20.03.1844; 1294a (all); Map 1843, 8 chns, by J. Gace, Louth; woods.

20/345 East Torrington (parish) TF 154838
Apt 13.05.1848; 1498a (1498); Map 1849, 4 chns; houses.

20/346 West Torrington (parish) TF 139813
Apt 26.08.1839; 1110a (1109); Map 1849, 8 chns; foot/b'way, woods (col).

20/347 Tothill (parish) TF 417816
Apt 19.12.1848; 854a (all); Map 1849, 6 chns, by J.H. Hutchinson, Grantham; waterbodies, woods, ownership boundaries (col); pictorial church; border has small wheatsheaves in corners.

20/348 Tupholme (parish) TF 149697 [Not listed]
Apt 17.12.1847; 1795a (all); Map 1848, 8 chns; foot/b'way, waterbodies, woods.

20/349 Twigmoor (township in parish of Manton) SK 928062
Apt 25.07.1851; 94a (?); Map 1851, 24 chns, by Thomas Laughton, Brigg, (tithable parts only in detail, tinted).

20/350 Tyd St Mary (parish) TF 423180 [Tydd St Mary]
Apt 10.05.1838; 4646a (all); Map 1839, 10 chns, 'Copied from the Parish Survey and Amended' by Joseph Jackson, March, Cambs; waterbodies, arable (col), grassland (col), road names, engine, windmills (pictorial), public pond, boundary of old and new enclosure; pictorial church; drains named; scale-bar is ruler-like; map title is on scroll resting on column.

20/351 Uffington (parish) TF 063085
Apt 04.08.1839; 105a (3996); Map 1841?, 6 chns, (tithable parts only); turnpike roads, woods; pictorial church.

20/352 Utterby (parish) TF 310940
Apt 10.01.1838; 1565a (1564); Map 1839, 3 chns, 1st cl, surveyed in 1836 and 1837 by Chas Cave Jno. Orme, Louth; construction lines, foot/b'way, turnpike roads, waterbodies, houses, woods (col), hedge ownership, fence ownership, field gates, field acreages, building names, road names, churchyard (col); streams and bridge named.

20/353 Waddingham (township in parish of Waddingham) SK 993965
Apt 26.09.1837; 3721a (all); Map 1838, 3 chns, 1st cl, surveyed by Chas Cave Jno. Orme, Louth; construction lines, hill drawing, foot/b'way, waterbodies, houses, plantations (col), heath/moor (col), walls, hedge ownership (col), fence ownership, field boundary ownerships, field acreages, glebe boundary, building names, road names, toll bar, canal with locks, towpaths and embankments, windmill (by symbol); drains named; map uses Dawson's symbols, and some are explained in legend, which includes hedges measured to the roots and hedges measured to the ditches.

20/354 Waddingworth (parish) TF 181711
Apt 16.11.1837; 925a (all); Map 1838, 3 chns; waterbodies, houses, woods, hedge ownership, fence ownership, field gates, glebe.

20/355 Wainfleet All Saints (parish) TF 473597
Apt 10.05.1838; 1598a (1598); Map 1838, [4 chns]; foot/b'way, pasture droves (col, named); drains appear to have been superimposed on an earlier survey.

20/356 Wainfleet St Mary (parish) TF 498576
Apt 25.08.1841; 2103a (13019); Map 1839, 8 chns, (tithable parts only); embankments (col, named); bridge named.

20/357 Walcot (parish) TF 061349
Apt 01.02.1841; 1748a (1747); Map 1841?, 6 chns; houses (by shading), tithe-merged land (col); pictorial church.

20/358 Walesby and Otby (townships or hamlets in parish of Walesby) TF 135925
Apt 13.12.1847; 2874a (all); Map 1848?, 8 chns; houses, glebe (col). Apt omits field names.

20/359 Walmsgate (parish) TF 363780
Apt 26.08.1850; 293a (920); Map 1852, 3 chns, (tithable parts only); woods (col); the minority owner's land is pink.

20/360 Well, with Dexthorpe and Claxby (district) TF 446731
Apt 26.06.1839; 3018a (?); Map 1838, 8 chns, copied by J.S. Padley, Lincoln; foot/b'way, waterbodies, houses, woods (col), parkland, building names, toll bar, parish/hamlet boundaries.

20/361 Welton on the Wold (parish) TF 273870 [Welton le Wold]
Apt 30.04.1849; 74a (2520); Map 1849, 4 chns, (tithable parts only).

20/362 Weston (parish) TF 285235
Apt 10.04.1838; 5386a (5386); Map 1839?, 4 chns, by Jno. Rooe; waterbodies, houses, woods (col), arable (col), grassland (col), gardens (col), road names, field acreages, modus land boundary; drains named; tithe-free areas are numbered but are not apportioned.

20/363 Whaplode (parish) TF 328197
Apt 26.01.1845; 10165a (10164); Map 1843, 8 chns, ? by Edw. Millington, Fleet, (tithable parts only in detail); waterbodies, road names, tithe-free land (col), Roman bank; drains named; meaning of building shading is unclear. Apt omits field names.

20/364 Whisby (township in parish of Doddington) SK 908674
Apt 14.02.1839; 1635a (all); Map 1839, 6 chns, 'Revised and Copied' by Fred. C. Talbot, Brocklesby, (tinted); woods, moor (brown), glebe (pink).

20/365 Wickenby cum Westlaby (parish) TF 090820
Apt 21.06.1842; 1998a (all); Map 1842, 9 chns, by J.S. Padley; houses, woods; pictorial church.

20/366 Willoughby with Sloothby (parish) TF 483712
Apt 10.01.1838; 5062a (all); Map 1839?, 3 chns, 'Taken by Order of the Proprietors' by Henry Kennedy, 100 Chancery Lane, London; foot/b'way, waterbodies, houses, woods (named), osiers (by symbol), field boundary ownerships, field gates, road names, field names, rectory, old road, windmill (by symbol); hamlets, bridges and drains named.

20/367 Winceby (parish) TF 319683
Apt 18.01.1839; 843a (842); Map 1838, 3 chns, by T.F. Blundy; woods (col), churchyard (col), glebe (col for arable/grass); pictorial church.

20/368 Winterton (parish) SE 940191
Apt 08.05.1841; 271a (3628); Map 1843?, 6 chns, (tithable parts only); waterbodies, houses, woods, parkland; map title is in centre of map, in tithe-free area. Apt omits land use.

20/369 Winthorpe (parish) TF 554652
Apt 01.08.1846; 2339a (2339); Map 1846, 6 chns, by S. Hill and Son, Croft, (tinted); Roman bank, pound.

20/370 Wintringham (parish) SE 939216
Apt 26.02.1863; 46a (5675); Map 1863?, 8 chns, (tithable parts only, tinted); table lists field names and acreages.

20/371 Wispington (parish) TF 204716
Apt 26.06.1839; 1208a (1570); Map 1839?, [?5 chns]. District is apportioned by owner and fields are not shown; Apt generalises land use and gives holding acreages.

20/372 North Witham (parish) SK 951205
Apt 25.09.1847; 1666a (2373); Map 1848?, 8 chns, (tithable parts only); road names.

20/373 Withern (parish) TF 440830
Apt 25.09.1838; 2415a (2415); Map surveyed in 1839, 12 chns, by Chas Cave Jno. Orme; waterbodies, woods; drain named. Apt omits field names.

20/374 Wold Newton (parish) TF 240968
Apt 18.05.1843; 1968a (all); Map 1843, 12 chns, by F.C. Talbot, Caistor; waterbodies, woods; pictorial church.

20/375 Woodhouse Farm (hamlet or division in parish of Corringham) SK 847908
Apt 09.02.1839; 150a (?); Map 1843?, 4 chns; houses, woods, plantations, landowner.

20/376 Worlaby (parish) TA 011137
Apt 23.11.1843; 3211a (3210); Map 1840, 6 chns, by J. Humphries, Ripon, Yorks; woods; colouring of fields is ornamental.

20/377 Wragby (parish) TF 136780
Apt 05.10.1847; 230a (1594); Map 1848, 3 chns, in 3 parts, (tithable parts only); woods, mud fang [freeboard or deer leap].

20/378 Wroot (parish) SE 720020
Apt 28.03.1840; 2646a (3158); Map 1841, 12 chns, by M. Durham, Thorne, (tithable parts only, tinted); woods, road names, drains.

20/379 Wyberton (parish) TF 325412
Apt 19.06.1840; 163a (3231); Map 1840, 6 chns, by S. Hill and Son, Croft, (tithable parts only, tinted); waterbodies, field boundary ownerships, samphire bank, embankments, Roman bank; scale bar has 'battlement' graduations.

20/380 Wyham with Cadeby (parish) TF 270950
Apt 23.02.1849; 1464a (all); Map 1848, 9 chns, by Edward Micklethwait, Grimsby; waterbodies, woods, parkland, gardens, building names (in two styles of writing), rectory.

20/381 East Wykeham (parish) TF 229882
Apt 12.07.1850; 68a (560); Map 1850, 3 chns, (tithable parts only, tinted); turnpike roads, waterbodies, field acreages.

20/382 Yawthorpe (hamlet in parish of Corringham) SK 896923
Apt 18.01.1839; 712a (?); Map 1839?, [6 chns], ? by William Chafer; woods, private road. Apt omits land use, and though occupiers are named it is not apparent who occupies which parcels.

Middlesex

PRO IR29 and IR30 21/1-56

102 tithe districts: 181,297 acres
50 tithe commutations: 78,410 acres
18 voluntary tithe agreements, 32 compulsory tithe awards,
6 corn rent annuities

Tithe and tithe commutation

Only 49 per cent of Middlesex tithe districts by number and about 43 per cent of the county by area were still subject to payment of tithes in 1836 (Fig. 33). Fifteen districts were wholly tithable; elsewhere the main causes of exemption were commutation at the time of enclosure, modus payments in lieu of tithes, the merger of tithes in the land, and exemption by prescription. Assistant tithe commissioners and local tithe agents who worked in Middlesex are listed in Table 21.1 and the valuers of the county's tithe rent-charge in Table 21.2.

Tithe maps

Exactly 14 per cent of Middlesex's fifty tithe maps are sealed as first class. One second-class map carries construction lines and eight second-class plans explicitly acknowledge copying from earlier surveys. In contrast to many counties, there was no peak of map-making around 1840 but rather output was fairly steady between 1838 and 1845 (Table 21.4).

Middlesex tithe maps are drawn at a variety of scales, ranging from one inch to 1.21 chains to one inch to 10 chains: 56 per cent of maps are in the recommended scale range of one inch to 3 to 4 chains. The county is exceptional in that seven maps (14 per cent) are at the two-chain scale; three of these are sealed as first class, all are on the fringes of London, and the larger than usual scale is justified by the cadastral complexity of these places. On the other hand, the one ten-chain scale plan is of Chelsea, a district so built up that use of a larger scale might have been expected (Table 21.3).

Middlesex is the only south-eastern county whose tithe maps portray extensive non-agricultural development: 14 per cent depict industrial activity. At Ealing this includes a pottery, distillery and soap works; brickworks appear on several maps, notably on that of Northolt. Railways are depicted on 34 per cent of maps, though rarely more than a boundary fence is shown; the inclusion of rails on the map of Hammersmith is exceptional.

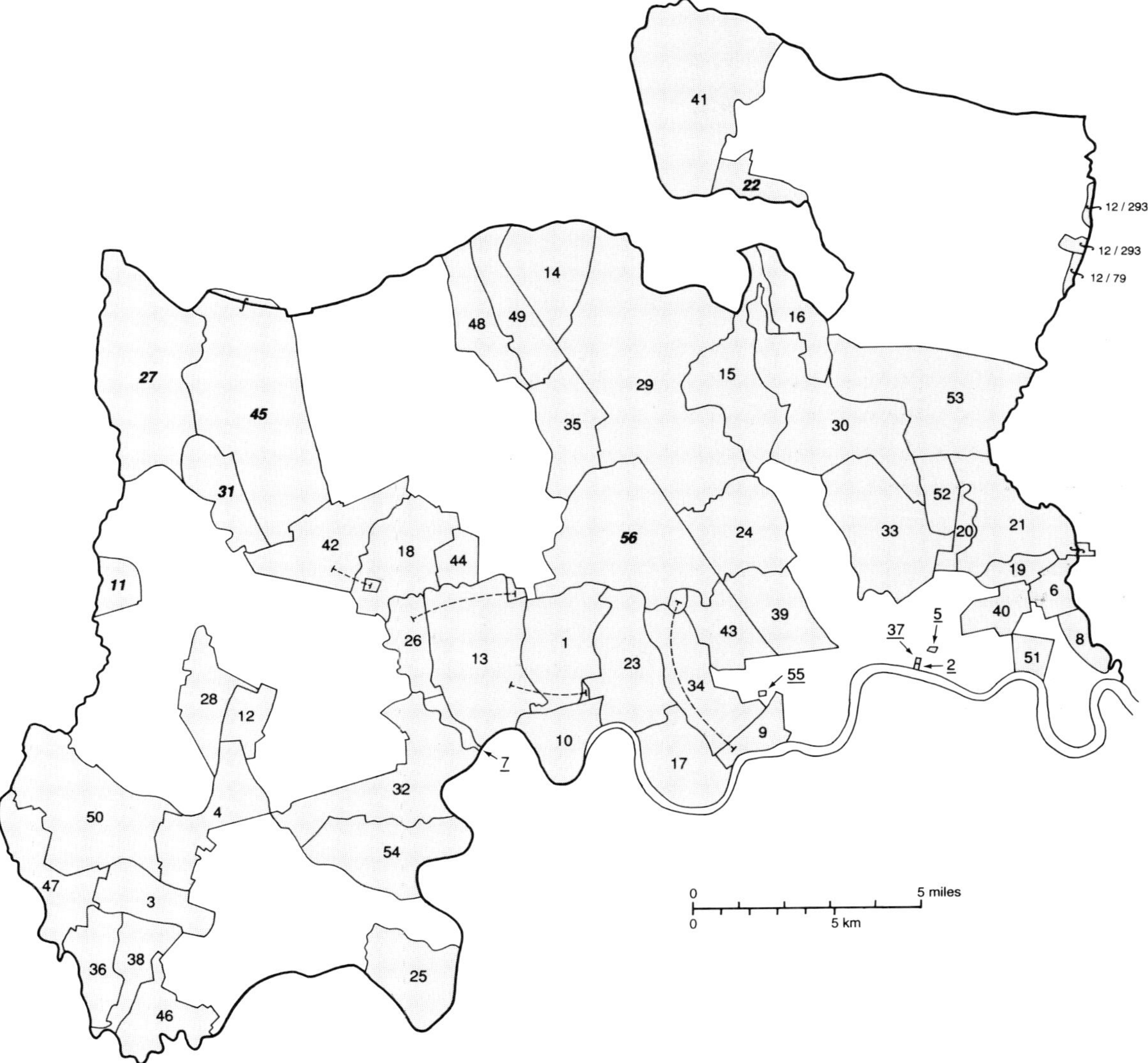

Fig. 33 Middlesex: tithe district boundaries.

Somewhat less than a half of Middlesex maps portray woodland and agricultural land use in general is mapped only fragmentarily: just 4 per cent of maps distinguish arable and grass, 8 per cent show gardens, 24 per cent portray parks, and 10 per cent depict orchards. There is little evidence on the maps of the extensive market gardens of this county, although nurseries are shown on the maps of New Brentford and South Mimms. The map of Hendon is most unusual in that not only is the map coloured by owners but each estate is numbered in Roman numerals.

Thirty-two Middlesex tithe maps in the Public Record Office collection can be attributed to a particular map-maker; the most prolific was Joseph Tootell of Maidstone, Kent, who made four maps of parishes close to each other. The quality of Middlesex maps ranges from very ordinary on the clay lands of the south-west of the county to the very colourful and finely executed maps of New Brentford and Northolt. One of the most elaborate maps in the county, and the only one with decorative embellishments, is that of Hadley. This covers only a small part of the whole parish but is distinguished by its use of colourful tree symbols and an elaborate compass rose with oak-leaf decoration.

Table 21.1. *Agreements and awards for commutation of tithes in Middlesex*

Assistant commissioner/ local tithe agent	*Number of agreements**	*Number of awards*
Francis Offley Martin	0	16
John Maurice Herbert	0	11
Thomas James Tatham	1	4
John Mee Mathew	4	0
F. Browne Browne	3	0
Horace William Meteyard	3	0
Roger Kynaston	2	0
Edward Greathed	1	0
William Heard	1	0
John Pickering	1	0
Charles Pym	1	0
Thomas Smith Woolley	0	1

*Computed from the number of extant reports on tithe agreements in the tithe files [PRO IR 18].

Table 21.2. *Tithe valuers and tithe map-makers in Middlesex*

Name and address (in Middlesex unless indicated)	*Number of districts*	*Acreage*
Tithe valuers		
John Pickering, 2 Derby St, Westminster	5	6,635
Moses Adams, Isleworth	4	7,328
Tithe Commissioners	4	2,258
William Tress, Finsbury Square	3	8,118
James Trumper, Southall	3	6,783
Others [26]	31	47,288
Attributed tithe map-makers		
Joseph Tootell, Maidstone, Kent	4	6,739
William Sherborn, Bedfont	3	10,084
William Tress, Finsbury Square	3	8,111
Moses Adams, Isleworth	3	5,079
Others [15]	19	23,824

Table 21.3. *The tithe maps of Middlesex: scales and classes*

Scale in chains/inch	*All maps*		*First Class*		*Second Class*	
	Number	*Acreage*	*Number*	*Acreage*	*Number*	*Acreage*
>2	2	329	1	314	1	15
2	7	6,155	3	3087	4	3,068
2.7	1	173	0	0	1	173
3	22	39,275	3	5,083	19	34,192
3.5	2	5,446	0	0	2	5,446
4	4	2,075	0	0	4	2,075
4.5, 5, 5.5	4	11,977	0	0	4	11,977
6	7	12,593	0	0	7	12,593
<6	1	387	0	0	1	387
TOTAL	50	78,410	7	8,484	43	69,926

Table 21.4. *The tithe maps of Middlesex: dates*

	1837	*1838*	*1839*	*1840*	*1841*	*1842*	*1843*	*1844*	*1845*	*1846*	*1847*	*1848*	*1849*	*>1849*
All maps	1	6	4	6	2	3	6	2	4	2	1	3	2	6
1st class	0	1	0	0	0	1	3	1	0	0	0	1	0	0
2nd class*	1	5	4	6	2	2	3	1	4	2	1	2	2	6

*Two second-class tithe maps of Middlesex in the Public Record Office collection are undated.

Middlesex

21/1 Acton (parish) TQ 202812
Apt 07.12.1842; 2286a (2286); Map 1842, 3 chns, 1st cl, by William Tress, Wilson St, Finsbury Square; railway, foot/b'way, canal with towpath, waterbodies, houses, woods, open fields, fences, field boundary ownerships, field gates, building names, road names, field names, sewer, parish boundary posts, culvert, 'Island' pond, mill, boundary stones, greens, commons. (The map in PRO IR 30 is a copy; original is in PRO IR 77/43.)

21/2 Allhallows the Less (parish) TQ 328807 [Not listed]
Apportionment of rentcharge, 1891; 2a (5); Map 1891?, 1 inch to 5 feet (1:1056; 1.33 chns); brewery, printing works, school, boundary posts, archways; map appears to be a straightforward copy of the Ordnance Survey 1:1056. (Map and apportionment are combined, and located at PRO MAF 8/19.)

21/3 Ashford (parish) TQ 071713
Apt 03.12.1839; 1378a (1378); Map 1840?, 6 chns; waterbodies, houses, woods, parkland, road names, milestones.

21/4 Bedfont (parish) TQ 083736
Apt 10.10.1839; 1867a (all); Map 1840, 6 chns, by Wm Sherburn, Bedfont; houses, woods, plantations, fences, tithing boundary.

21/5 Bishopgate St Helen (parish) TQ 330812 [Not listed]
Apportionment of rentcharge, 1927; ?a (9); no map; Apt (at PRO MAF 8/20) only lists addresses, and does not give acreages.

21/6 Bow, St Mary Stratford (parish) TQ 369848 [Bow]
Apt 27.07.1844; 377a (809); Map 1849, 2 chns; railways, canal with towpath, locks and feeder, waterbodies, houses, building names, road names, rope-walk, reservoirs, gas works, water works, public park.

21/7 New Brentford (parish) TQ 168779 [Brentford]
Apt 27.10.1838; 179a (220); Map 1838, 2 chns, 'Corrected Survey' by W.T. Warren, Isleworth; canal with towpath and locks, waterbodies, houses, woods (col), osier bed, parkland (col, in detail, named), notable tree, arable (col), grassland (col), orchards (col), gardens (col), marsh/bog (col), nursery (by symbol), hedge ownerships, fence ownerships, field boundary ownerships, field gates, building names, road names, field names, schools, tan yard, iron bridge, old workhouse, post office, old river course; lake named; this is one of the most beautifully produced and 'artistic' of all the tithe maps. Apt omits land use.

21/8 Bromley, St Leonard (parish) TQ 379820 [Bromley]
Apt 01.08.1848; 267a (619); Map 1848?, 3 chns, by M. Adams, Isleworth and T. Tyerman, 14 Parliament St, Westminster; railways, waterbodies, houses, road names.

21/9 Chelsea (parish) TQ 273821
Apt 29.11.1845; 387a (865); Map 1846?, 10 chns, in 2 parts, ? by Nathaniel Handford, Chelsea; railway, hedges, building names, road names, rectory, burial ground, Chelsea Hospital, botanic garden, Royal Military Asylum; park named.

21/10 Chiswick (parish) TQ 208775
Apt 02.04.1846; 1311a (1311); Map 1847, 4 chns, by John Pyne; railway, proposed railway, foot/b'way, waterbodies, houses, woods, parkland (in detail), fences, building names, road names, horticultural gardens, osier beds.

21/11 Cowley (parish) TQ 055820
Apt 19.10.1850; 126a (300); Map 1851?, 4 chns, (tithable parts only); canal with towpath and dock, waterbodies, houses, building names.

21/12 Cranford (parish) TQ 100780
Apt 26.04.1838; 721a (all); Map 1838?, 4.5 chns; waterbodies, field acreages; pictorial church.

21/13 Ealing (parish) TQ 179812
Apt 13.06.1840; 3815a (all); Map 1839, 3 chns, in 2 parts, by William Tress, No 1 Princes St, Wilson Street, Finsbury Square; railway with station, foot/b'way, canal with towpath and docks, waterbodies, houses, building names, road names, field names, osier beds, boundary stones, water works, clay ponds, pottery, lock-up house, milestone, ferry, timber depots, distillery, soap factory, barracks, pound, chapels, almshouses, vicarage, green, commons; parks named. (The map in PRO IR 30 is a copy; the original is in PRO IR 77/44.)

21/14 Edgware (parish) TQ 192935
Apt 26.02.1845; 1980a (1979); Map 1845, 3 chns, 'Revised and corrected' by J. Tootell, Maidstone; waterbodies.

21/15 Finchley (parish) TQ 263902
Apt 27.11.1839; 2427a (2899); Map 'Rough Plan', 1840, 3 chns, in 3 parts, (tithable parts only); construction lines, houses, farmyards, woods, plantations, fences, field boundary ownerships, field gates, building names, road names, turnpike gate, glebe; meaning of yellow band is unclear. (The map in PRO IR 30 is a copy; the original is in PRO IR 77/100, and is unfit for production.)

21/16 Friern Barnet (parish) TQ 276924
Apt 20.11.1844; 1293a (1292); Map 1845?, 3 chns, by A. Jack? [? Jackson]; foot/b'way, waterbodies, houses, woods, orchards, building names, toll house, almshouses.

21/17 Fulham (parish) TQ 252772
Apt 24.03.1843; 1684a (1834); Map 1843, 3 chns, by M. Adams, Isleworth; waterbodies, houses, road names, turnpike gate.

21/18 Great Greenford (parish) TQ 152843 [Greenford]
Apt 31.01.1840; 2010a (all); Map 1840, 5.5 chns, 'Revised plan' by William Tress, No 1 Princes St, Wilson St, Finsbury Square, London; foot/b'way, canal with towpath, woods (col, named), parkland (in detail), hedge ownership, fence ownership, road names; there is a note, 'Note - the number is sometimes repeated, where it seems necessary to describe, what is comprised by it' (sic).

21/19 Hackney St John (part of) or Hackney Rectory (parish) TQ 358840 [Not listed]
Apt 16.09.1845; 2072a (2346); Map 1843, 2 chns, 1st cl, surveyed by Michael Fitzgerald for Mr Pickering, 2 Derby Street, Westminster; construction lines, foot/b'way, canal with towpath and bank, waterbodies, houses, field boundary ownerships, building names, road names, field names, boundary stones and posts, chapel, old tower, workhouse, mill, spring. (The map in PRO IR 30 is a copy; the original is in PRO IR 77/45.)

21/20 Hackney St John (part of) or West Hackney (parish) TQ 339858 [Not listed]
Apt 22.02.1843; 314a (472); Map 1843, 1 inch to 80 feet (1:960; 1.21 chns), 1st cl; construction lines, foot/b'way, canal with towpath, houses, road names, toll gates, rectory, chapels, schools, dispensary, commons, green. Not all areas shown on the map appear in detail in Apt. (The map in PRO IR 30 is a copy; the original is in PRO IR 77/46.)

21/21 South Hackney (parish) TQ 355855
Apt 30.01.1843; 403a (?); Map 1843?, 2 chns, 1st cl, surveyed by Michael Fitzgerald for Mr Pickering, 2 Derby Street, Westminster; construction lines, canal with towpath, waterbodies, houses, road names, Jews' burial ground, school, chapel, well.

21/22 Hadley or Monken Hadley (parish) TQ 258972
Apt 12.10.1848; 240a (2530); Map 1851?, 3 chns, by John Duckworth, Barnet, (tithable parts only); railway, waterbodies, woods (col); railway appears to be a later addition; compass rose is elaborate, with oak-leaf in centre.

21/23 Hammersmith (parish) TQ 229811
Apt 21.11.1845; 2293a (all); Map 1846?, 2 chns, in 22 parts (including 21 0.5 chn enlargements of detail); railways, canal with towpath, waterbodies, houses, woods, plantations, osiers (by symbol), parkland, orchards, building names, road names, post, covered drain, defaced boundary; some built-up parts generalised. (The map in PRO IR 30 is a copy; original is in PRO IR 77/47.)

21/24 St John Hampstead (parish) TQ 261851 [Hampstead]
Apt 26.08.1839; 1237a (2252); Map 1838, 3 chns, 1st cl, by J. Richardson, (tithable part only); construction lines, railway, waterbodies, field boundary ownerships, boundary posts; double lines may show walls.

21/25 Hampton (parish) TQ 168690
Apt 25.10.1849; 1756a (3190); Map 1850, 3 chns, by E. and G.N. Driver;

foot/b'way, waterbodies, houses, woods, plantations, osiers (by symbol), parkland (in detail), marsh/bog, field boundary ownerships, building names, landowners, maze, ice house, pavilion, keeper's cottage, brewhouse, bath, cascade, boundary stones, stile, lodge, tennis court, barracks, ferry, estate boundary.

21/26 Hanwell (parish) TQ 157812
Apt 19.05.1837; 1042a (all); Map 'altered in 1837 from the Inclosure Map', 3.5 chns, in 2 parts; railway and viaduct, foot/b'way, canal with towpath and lock, waterbodies, houses, field gates, road names, toll gate; colour bands may show ownerships.

21/27 Harefield (parish) TQ 060900
Apt 28.05.1845; 428a (4513); Map 1846?, 6 chns, (tithable part only); foot/b'way, canal, waterbodies, woods, plantations, osiers and bogs.

21/28 Harlington (parish) TQ 088785
Apt 09.07.1839; 1414a (all); Map 1840?, 4.5 chns, in 2 parts, (including 2-chn enlargement of village centre); railway.

21/29 Hendon (parish) TQ 222900
Apt 13.06.1842; 7832a (8250); Map 1840, 5 chns, in 3 parts 'Revised, corrected and in part resurveyed in 1840' by James Bocock Holbrook, Lower Hale, Hendon, Middx, and Richard Dent, Camden Town, Middx, (including two enlargements of built-up parts); hill-drawing, foot/b'way, waterbodies, houses, woods, plantations, parkland (in detail), field boundary ownerships, building names, road names, field names, toll bar, milestone, greens; hills named; colours show ownerships, with Roman numerals; there is a note as to parish boundaries following brooks. (The map in PRO IR 30 is a copy; the original is in PRO IR 77/49.)

21/30 Hornsey (parish) TQ 304892
A series of mergers of moduses, circa 1880 onwards, accompanied by three printed Ordnance Survey 6-inch sheets of circa 1865 (Middlesex sheets 7, 11, 12) acting as index sheets to plans of isolated areas accompanying the apportionment.

21/31 Ickenham (parish) TQ 082856
Apt 08.03.1839; 165a (1400); Map 1841?, 4 chns, in 2 parts, (tithable parts only); waterbodies, landowners, green (named).

21/32 Isleworth (parish) TQ 162758
Apt 11.03.1840; 3128a (3128); Map 1839, 3 chns, 'enlarged and corrected' from the 6-chn scale enclosure plan of 1819 by M. Adams, Isleworth; foot/b'way, waterbodies, building names, road names, rectory, gravel pit, parks (by name), greens, glebe. (The map in PRO IR 30 is a copy; the original is in PRO IR 77/50.)

21/33 Islington, St Mary (parish) TQ 308857 [Islington]
Apt 09.06.1848; 1955a (3127); Map undated, 3 chns, (tithable parts only); railway, projected railway, foot/b'way, canal, waterbodies, college; pictorial church. (The map in PRO IR 30 is a copy; the original is in PRO IR 77/101, and is unfit for production.)

21/34 Kensington (parish) TQ 250810
Apt 21.08.1843; 1560a (1942); Map 1844, 3 chns, 1st cl, (tithable parts only); construction lines, railway, canal with towpaths, waterbodies, houses, boundary stones.

21/35 Kingsbury (parish) TQ 207889
Apt 22.03.1839; 1766a (all); Map 1839, 3 chns, 'Copied from the Original and revised' by Jos. Tootell, Maidstone; waterbodies.

21/36 Laleham (parish) TQ 056688
Apt 02.08.1844; 1209a (1214); Map 1845, 6 chns, by J.M. Sanderson, Sunbury; waterbodies, field gates.

21/37 St Lawrence Pountney (parish) TQ 328809 [Not listed]
Apportionment of rentcharge, 1884; 2a (all); Map 'Enlarged from the Ordnance Map', 1886, 1 inch to 44 feet (1:528; 0.67 chns); churchyard, wharf, pier, archways. Map and apportionment are combined and located at MAF 8/22.

21/38 Littleton (parish) TQ 070695
Apt 13.05.1848; 1017a (all); Map 1848, 6 chns; waterbodies, woods (col), parkland, heath/moor, common, recreation allotment, manorial allotment.

21/39 St Marylebone (parish) TQ 272822 [Marylebone]
Apt 10.03.1841; 12a (1509); Map 1851, 3 chns, by E. and G.N. Driver, 5 Whitehall, London; canal with towpath, waterbodies, parkland, field gates, road names, landowners, zoological and botanical gardens, boundary stones, gymnasium; map is described as 'part of Regents Park... in... St Marylebone', and the mapped area considerably exceeds the tithable portion.

21/40 St Matthew, Bethnal Green (parish) TQ 350830
Apt 30.04.1846; 173a (760); Map 1850?, 2.7 chns, by E.C. Duncombe, Guildford, (tithable parts only); railways, turnpike roads, toll gates, canal with towpaths and locks, houses, road names, public park.

21/41 South Mimms (parish) TQ 232999
Apt 02.12.1841; 5153a (5153); Map 1842, 6 chns, by William Sherborn, Bedfont, Middx; waterbodies, woods (col), parkland, orchards (col), field boundary ownerships, building names, turnpike gate, chase boundary (col), nurseries (by symbol).

21/42 Northolt, or Northalt or Northaw (parish) TQ 130840
Apt 23.12.1836; 2193a (all); Map 1838?, 3 chns, in 2 parts; hill-drawing, foot/b'way, canal and towpath, 'civil engineer' (by canal), waterbodies, houses, farmyards (col), woods, arable (col), grassland (col), orchards, gardens, hedge ownership, fence ownership, field gates, building names, road names, landowners, rectory, churchyard, school, brickfields (by symbol); arable and grass parts within single tithe areas are carefully distinguished.

21/43 Paddington (parish) TQ 261819
Apt 22.03.1844; 473a (1277); Map 1842, 4 chns, in 5 parts, by George Oakley Lucas; railway, foot/b'way, turnpike roads, turnpike gate, canals and towpaths, waterbodies, houses, plantations, post offices, chapel, schools, stone yard, vestry room, parsonage, almshouse, reservoirs, glebe (col), square gardens (col); main 4 chn index plan has a note that the numbers on the map do not refer to the apportionment; there are also four detail plans: 1, part of the parish, 4 chns, 1842; 2, Westbourne Grove, 1 inch to 100 ft (1:1200), by Lucas, 1845; 3, Dorchester Gardens, no scale, ?1846; 4, Uxbridge Gardens and St Petersburgh Place, no scale, ?1846.

21/44 Perivale (parish) TQ 170835
Apt 25.02.1839; 626a (all); Map 1839, 3 chns, by James Trumper, Southall, Middlesex; foot/b'way, canal with towpath, waterbodies, woods, orchards, gardens, field boundary ownerships, field gates, rectory, green (named).

21/45 Ruislip (parish) TQ 100880
Corn rent conversion, 1929; 16a (6260); no map.

21/46 Shepperton (partly in Surrey) (parish) TQ 079672
Apt 26.09.1842; 1541a (1541); Map 1843, 6 chns, by I.M. Sanderson, Sunbury, Land and Timber Surveyor; waterbodies, houses.

21/47 Staines (parish) TQ 033717
Apt 24.08.1842; 1844a (1844); Map 1843, 3 chns; foot/b'way, waterbodies, houses, road names, field names, lock, towpath, 'City stone', footbridges (by symbol); moor and various common fields and allotments named.

21/48 Great Stanmore (parish) TQ 168922 [Stanmore]
Apt 29.09.1838; 1441a (1441); Map 1838, 3 chns, 'Copied from the Original Plan and revised' by J. Tootell, Maidstone; foot/b'way, waterbodies, woods, plantations, parkland, gardens (col).

21/49 Little Stanmore, or Whitchurch (parish) TQ 182922 [Not listed]
Apt 17.12.1838; 1552a (1552); Map 1838, 3 chns, 'Copied from the Original Plotted Plan and Revised' by J. Tootell, Maidstone; waterbodies.

21/50 Stanwell (parish) TQ 041744
Apt 31.03.1843; 3964a (3963); Map 1841, 3 chns, by Wm Sherborn, Bedfont, Middlesex; foot/b'way, turnpike roads, turnpike gate, canal with towpath, waterbodies, building names, road names, paper mills; park named.

21/51 Stepney (parish) TQ 362812
Apt 21.06.1848; 219a (901); Map 1849, 2 chns, ? by John Eivers, 12 Buckingham Street, Adelphi, (tithable parts only); railway, canal with towpath, houses, building names, road names, Jews burial grounds, gas works, hospital, cemeteries, almshouses, workhouse.

21/52 Stoke Newington (parish) TQ 333873
Apt 10.12.1847; 612a (all); Map 1848, 2 chns, 1st cl, by Richard Allerton, James Renshaw, John Doyley; construction lines, foot/b'way, waterbodies, houses, woods, parkland, building names, road names, reservoir, lunatic asylum, milestone, boundary stones, cemetery, catacombs, Unitarian Chapel, Friends Meeting House, almshouses, reservoir engine house, sidewalks, pound, statue, modus boundary (col); under the title the map is described as 'Surveyed by Richard Allerton'; under the scale bar it is described as 'Surveyed by James Renshaw and John Doyley'.

21/53 Tottenham (parish) TQ 333898
Apt 16.05.1843; 4404a (all); Map 1844, 3.5 chns; railway with station, foot/b'way, canal with towpath and lock, waterbodies, houses, woods, plantations, marsh/bog, building names, road names, turnpike, tile kilns, boundary stones, greens. (The map in PRO IR 30 is a copy; the original map is in PRO IR 77/52.)

21/54 Twickenham (parish) TQ 151741
Apt 24.05.1845; 2249a (all); Map not dated, 3 chns, by William Thomas Warren, Isleworth; foot/b'way, waterbodies, houses. (The map in IR 30 is a copy; the original is in PRO IR 77/54.)

21/55 St Margaret Westminster, detached lands near Kensington (district in parish of St Margaret Westminster) TQ 271796 [Not listed]
Apt 30.12.1854; 15a (657); Map 1856?, 1 inch to 105 feet (1:1260; 1.6 chns), (tithable parts only); turnpike roads, road names, ornamental garden. Apt omits land use.

21/56 Willesden (parish) TQ 222848
Corn rent conversion, 1887; 4147a (4190); Map 1887, 1:2500 (3.16 chns), revised from Ordnance Survey with some omissions by H.M. and W. Grellier, 17 Abchurch Lane, E.C.; railways (coloured by company) and stations, railway signal works, canal with towpath, building names, road names, cemeteries, school; PRO IR 18/5554 contains an earlier draft, including houses, and also a detailed breakdown of the cost of making the map.

Monmouthshire

PRO IR29 and IR30 22/1-130

144 tithe districts: 340,849 acres
130 tithe commutations: 326,160 acres
71 voluntary tithe agreements, 59 compulsory tithe awards

Tithe and tithe commutation

About 90 per cent of Monmouthshire tithe districts by number and 96 per cent of the county by area were subject to payment of tithes in 1836 (Fig. 34). Sixty-six districts were wholly tithable; elsewhere the main reasons for exemption were modus payments in lieu of tithes, the merger of tithes in the land, and exemption by prescription. Monmouthshire contains the last complete parish to have its tithe commuted, Llangunnock, which 'from its small extent' (157 acres) was apparently overlooked until 1864.[2]

Assistant tithe commissioners and local tithe agents who worked in Monmouthshire are listed in Table 22.1. Although most of the valuers of tithe rent-charge employed in Monmouthshire were resident either within the county or in adjoining counties, nine came from the far side of the River Severn. Unusually, no London-based valuer was employed, although two districts were valued by the Tithe Commission in default of action by landowners.

Monmouthshire tithe apportionments are not as informative as those of most English counties. Field names are often omitted and land-use entries such as 'arable and grass', and 'meadow, arable and brake' are encountered often. Unusual apportionments include Aberystruth and Mynyddislwyn which record industrial waste and Trevethin which distinguishes freehold and copyhold land.

Tithe maps

Monmouthshire has the highest proportion of first-class maps of any county (60 per cent). Even more maps probably aspired to first-class status as construction lines are present on 15 per cent of second-class maps. On only one map, that of Tregare, is copying explicitly acknowledged. More Monmouthshire tithe maps (92 per cent) are in the recommended scale range of three to four chains than are those of any other county. The only lithographed Monmouthshire tithe map in the Public Record Office collection is a six-chain reduction of the three-chain, first-class original map of Undy.

[2] PRO IR18 5617.

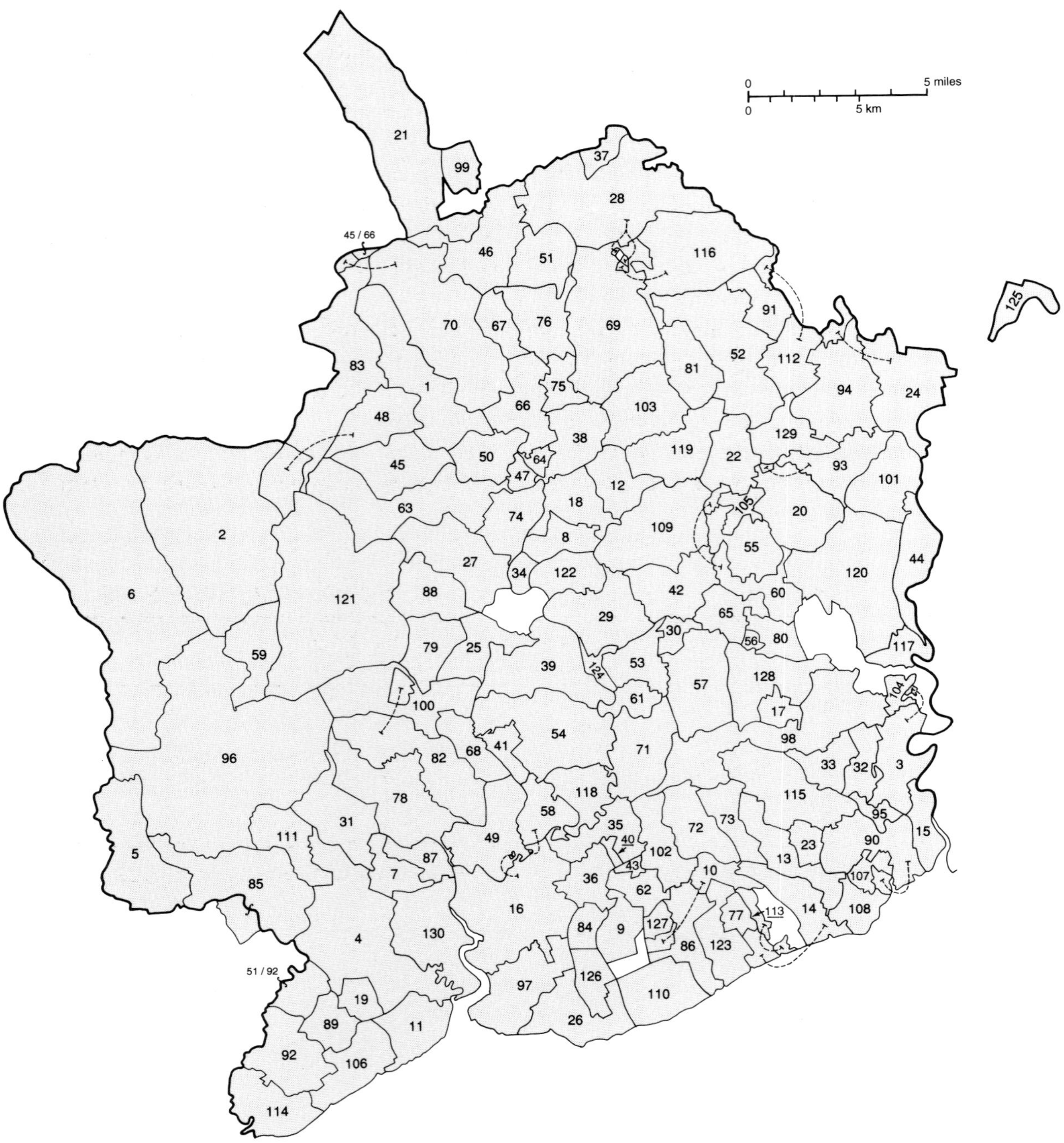

Fig. 34 Monmouthshire: tithe district boundaries.

Although Monmouthshire maps may be the most planimetrically accurate of tithe maps and, therefore, in that regard atypical of neighbouring Welsh tithe maps, they are similar to Welsh maps in that they are generally uninformative about land use; only 25 per cent show woodland, and only between 3 and 5 per cent depict arable, grass, gardens, parks, or heath and moor, though 16 per cent show orchards.

Monmouthshire tithe maps are more satisfactory as records of industry, which appears on 11 per cent of the maps. Industries recorded include the extraction of coal, gravel and stone, various metallurgical industries (particularly at Bedwellty), brewing, acid-making, potteries, and paper milling, as well as the associated infrastructure of canals, tramways, docks, wharves and reservoirs.

Some 115 Monmouthshire tithe maps in the Public Record Office collection can be attributed to a particular map-maker; the most prolific was Thomas Morris of Newport who produced thirty-seven maps extending over about a quarter of the county by area. Five maps were produced by map-makers from well outside the county, including three by George Taylor of Huddersfield. Many of the first-class maps are subtitled 'working plans' and indeed Monmouthshire tithe maps are on the whole plain and undecorated in appearance.

Table 22.1. *Agreements and awards for commutation of tithes in Monmouthshire*

Assistant commissioner/ local tithe agent	*Number of agreements**	*Number of awards*
John Johnes	12	54
Thomas Hoskins	56	0
Aneurin Owen	0	3
Charles Pym	3	0
George Wingrove Cooke	0	1
Tithe Commissioners	0	1

*Computed from the number of extant reports on tithe agreements in the tithe files [PRO IR 18].

Table 22.2. *Tithe valuers and tithe map-makers in Monmouthshire*

Name and address (in Monmouthshire unless indicated)	*Number of districts*	*Acreage*
Tithe valuers		
Thomas Morris, Newport	37	82,168
Robert Gabb, Abergavenny	13	25,390
Robert Whittlesey Purchas, Pilstone	9	26,539
William Jones, Mount Pleasant, Brecon	7	38,357
James White, Coleford, Gloucestershire	7	19,629
William Metcalf, Monmouth	7	17,794
James Peachy Williams, Bristol*	7	10,432
Others [22]	43	105,848
Attributed tithe map-makers		
Thomas Morris, Newport	37	81,313
James Nunan, Abergavenny	9	23,237
James Peachy Williams, Bristol/Bridgwater, Somerset*	9	12,083
Robert Nathaniel Purchas, Chepstow	7	16,291
William Bryan Wood, Chippenham, Wiltshire	7	12,357
William Jones, Brecon	6	33,190
Edward Sacheverall Gisborne	4	21,995
William Havard Apperley, Hereford	4	15,677
William Metcalf	4	13,398
Others [21]	28	65,685

*Although J. P. Williams gives Bristol as his address on his Monmouthshire valuations, he gives variously Bridgwater and Bristol on his Monmouthshire maps, and Bridgwater on all his Somerset work.

Table 22.3. *The tithe maps of Monmouthshire: scales and classes*

Scale in chains/inch	*All maps*		*First Class*		*Second Class*	
	Number	*Acreage*	*Number*	*Acreage*	*Number*	*Acreage*
3	93	243,361	73	203,230	20	40,131
4	27	51,140	5	8,266	22	42,874
6	9	24,821	0	0	9	24,821
8	1	6,838	0	0	1	6,838
TOTAL	130	326,160	78	211,496	52	114,664

Table 22.4. *The tithe maps of Monmouthshire: dates*

	1837	*1838*	*1839*	*1840*	*1841*	*1842*	*1843*	*1844*	*1845*	*1846*	*1847*	*1848*	*>1848*
All maps	1	2	20	20	19	17	14	9	5	8	7	4	3
1st class	1	1	14	16	14	8	11	3	2	4	0	3	1
2nd class*	0	1	6	4	5	9	3	6	3	4	7	1	2

*One second-class tithe map of Monmouthshire in the Public Record Office collection is undated.

Monmouthshire

22/1 Abergavenny (parish) SO 301144
Apt 01.09.1843; 4229a (4229); Map 1845, 3 chns, 1st cl, by James Todd, Abergavenny; waterbodies, houses; built-up part generalised. Apt omits some field names.

22/2 Aberystruth (parish) SO 200080 [Not listed]
Apt 20.10.1840; 11788a (all); Map 1841, 3 chns, 1st cl, in 2 parts, by E.S. Gisborne; waterbodies, fences; green bands may show woodland.

22/3 St Arvans (parish) ST 520960
Apt 20.11.1845; 2309a (2309); Map 1847, 6 chns, by James P. Williams, Bristol; waterbodies, houses, woods, building names.

22/4 Bassalleg (parish) ST 270870 [Bassaleg]
Apt 08.02.1841; 6955a (6955); Map 1842, 3 chns, 1st cl, in 2 parts, by William Jones, Brecon; construction lines, waterbodies, woods, plantations, parkland (in detail), orchards, building names, works; double lines may be drains.

22/5 Bedwas (parish) ST 162907
Apt 11.06.1840; 4208a (all); Map 1841, 3 chns, by W. Jones; construction lines, waterbodies, houses, building names; bridge named.

22/6 Bedwellty (parish) SO 165035
Apt 31.07.1839; 16211a (16210); Map 1840, 3 chns, 1st cl, in 3 parts, by W. Jones; construction lines, waterbodies, houses, woods, plantations, parkland, building names, road names, iron works, colliery, old mill, mills, coke yard, commons; bridge named.

22/7 Bettws (near Newport) (parish) ST 288908
Apt 08.02.1841; 1132a (all); Map 1840, 3 chns, 1st cl, by Thos Morris, Newport; construction lines, canal, waterbodies, houses, building names; woodland named. Apt omits some field names.

22/8 Bettws Newydd (parish) SO 365063
Apt 26.10.1842; 1123a (1122); Map 1843, 3 chns, 1st cl, by Wm Bryan Wood, Barnbridge, Chippenham; construction lines, foot/b'way, waterbodies, houses, building names.

22/9 Bishton (parish) ST 392876
Apt 21.11.1845; 1212a (1211); Map 1847, 4 chns; houses, building names, moor, drains. Apt omits some field names.

22/10 St Brides Netherwent including the Hamlet of Landevenny (parish) ST 438903 [St Bride's Netherwent]
Apt 20.12.1839; 1033a (1032); Map 'working plan', 1839, 3 chns, 1st cl, in 2 parts, by Thos Morris, Newport; construction lines, turnpike roads, waterbodies, houses, open fields, building names, field names, mill, common. Apt omits some field names.

22/11 St Brides (Wentlooge) (parish) ST 296827 [St Brides Wentlooge]
Apt 31.05.1842; 1904a (all); Map 1842, 4 chns, by Thomas Morris, Newport; orchards, building names, chapel, lighthouse. Apt omits some field names.

22/12 Bryngwin (parish) SO 392092 [Bryngwyn]
Apt 24.09.1839; 1484a (1484); Map 1839, 3 chns, by - Hand, Llandenny, Nr Ragland, Monmouthshire; construction lines, turnpike roads, building names.

22/13 Caerwent (parish) ST 467908
Apt 20.07.1843; 1963a (1962); Map 1841, 4 chns, 1st cl, by Jas P. Williams, B'Water; construction lines, foot/b'way, houses, field boundary ownerships; woodland named.

22/14 Caldicott (parish) ST 479888 [Caldicot]
Apt 23.06.1842; 1938a (all); Map 1842?, 3 chns; construction lines, foot/b'way, waterbodies, houses, open fields, field boundary ownerships, commons.

22/15 Chepstow (parish) ST 537921
Apt 21.02.1846; 1163a (1282); Map 1846, 3 chns, by James P. Williams, Bristol, (tithable parts only in detail); railway, waterbodies, houses, woods, plantations, orchards, field gates, building names, road names, Castle, workhouse; built-up part generalised.

22/16 Christchurch (parish) ST 338882
Apt 11.06.1839; 5758a (5757); Map 'working plan', 1840, 3 chns, 1st cl, by Thomas Morris, Newport; construction lines, waterbodies, houses, field gates, building names, common; woodland and bridge named. Apt omits some field names.

22/17 Cilgwrrwg otherwise Kilgwrrwg (parish) ST 466981 [Not listed]
Apt 05.10.1845; 660a (all); Map 1846, 3 chns, 1st cl, by Christopher Heydon, Shirenewton; construction lines, waterbodies, houses, boundary stones, chapel; woodland named. Apt omits some field names.

22/18 Clytha (hamlet in parish of Llanarth) SO 376086 [Not listed]
Apt 26.10.1842; 1842a (1841); Map 1843?, 3 chns, 1st cl, in 2 parts, ? by J. Nunan, Abergavenny; construction lines, watermill (by symbol). Apt omits some field names.

22/19 Coedkernew (parish) ST 271839
Apt 23.05.1843; 765a (all); Map 1840, 3 chns, 1st cl, by Thos Morris, Newport; construction lines, houses, building names; map is described as a 'working plan'. Apt omits some field names.

22/20 Cwmcarvon (parish) SO 474078 [Cwmcarvan]
Apt 17.03.1843; 2875a (2875); Map 1842?, 4 chns, by Wm Metcalf; waterbodies, houses, boundary trees and stones, hamlet or chapelry boundary. Apt omits some field names.

22/21 Cwmyoy, Upper and Lower Divisions (parish) SO 297260
Apt 26.09.1850; 8270a (10366); Map 1851, 3 chns, 1st cl, in 2 parts, by W.H. Apperley, Hereford; construction lines, hill-drawing, foot/b'way, waterbodies, houses, fences, field boundary ownerships, field gates, building names, abbey, boundary stones, quarries. Apt omits some field names.

22/22 Dingestow (parish) SO 449106
Apt 30.01.1841; 1930a (all); Map 1841, 4 chns, by Wm Metcalf; waterbodies, houses (by shading), woods, plantations, building names.

22/23 Dinham (hamlet in parish of Llanvaer Discoed) ST 480920 [Not listed]
Apt 10.10.1839; 671a (all); Map 1840?, 3 chns, by Thomas D. Barry; construction lines, houses, glebe.

22/24 Dixton (parish) SO 532135
Apt 16.05.1843; 3849a (3848); Map 1844?, 4 chns, by Wm Metcalf; turnpike roads and gate, waterbodies, houses, building names, foundry, vicarage, boundary trees, mill; bridge named.

22/25 Glascoed (hamlet in parish of Usk) SO 332017
Apt 23.04.1840; 1732a (all); Map 1842, 3 chns, by R.N. Purchas, Chepstow; construction lines, waterbodies, houses, pound, commons.

22/26 Goldcliff (parish) ST 370830
Apt 29.08.1840; 2198a (14262); Map 1842, 4 chns, by Thomas Morris, Newport; orchards, heath/moor, building names, road names, sea walls, roadside waste (col), common (col). Apt omits some field names.

22/27 Goytrey (parish) SO 318053 [Not listed]
Apt 14.02.1838; 3333a (all); Map 1839, 3 chns, by David Thomas; waterbodies, houses, woods, plantations, orchards, field gates, building names, mill.

22/28 Grosmont (parish) SO 395232
Apt 30.07.1841; 6838a (6838); Map 1841, 8 chns, in 2 parts, by T. Bate, Brecon; waterbodies, building names. Apt omits some field names.

22/29 Gwehellog (hamlet in parish of Usk) SO 385031 [Gwehelog]
Apt 18.06.1842; 2819a (all); Map 1843, 3 chns, 1st cl, by Morris, Thomas; Newport; construction lines, turnpike roads, waterbodies, houses, field gates, building names, castle, common. Apt omits some field names.

22/30 Gwernesney (parish) SO 418022
Apt 30.05.1842; 543a (all); Map 1842, 3 chns, 1st cl, by Wm Bryan Wood, Barnbridge, Chippenham; construction lines, foot/b'way, houses, hedge ownership, field gates, building names, rectory.

22/31 Henllis (parish) ST 260958 [Henllys]
Apt 17.03.1843; 2623a (all); Map 1842, 3 chns, 1st cl, by Williams Jones, Brecon; construction lines, waterbodies, woods, plantations, orchards, building names, mill, boundary stones, pound, limekiln.

22/32 Howick (parish) ST 503955
Apt 20.04.1850; 635a (635); Map 1850, 6 chns, by J.P. Williams, Bristol; waterbodies, woods, orchards, building names.

22/33 Itton (parish) ST 490953
Apt 16.05.1843; 1103a (1103); Map 1844, 3 chns, by James Peachy Williams, Bristol; foot/b'way, waterbodies, houses, woods, plantations, parkland, building names, tuck mill, lime kilns, disappearing stream, commons. Apt omits some field names.

22/34 Kemeys Commander (parish) SO 350049
Apt 11.08.1838; 501a (all); Map 1839, 3 chns, 1st cl, by H. Williams, Newport; construction lines, waterbodies, houses, woods, plantations, orchards, building names, parsonage, boundary stones, springs.

22/35 Kemeys Inferior (parish) ST 383924
Apt 26.06.1846; 1676a (1676); Map 1846, 3 chns, 1st cl, by Thomas Morris, Newport; construction lines, waterbodies, houses, field gates, well, boundary trees, folly, ruin. Apt omits some field names.

22/36 Langstone (except Llandbedr) (parish) ST 375900
Apt 12.08.1844; 1139a (all); Map 1846, 4 chns; waterbodies, disappearing streams, drains.

22/37 Langua (parish) SO 392252 [Llangua]
Apt 29.06.1837; 696a (all); Map 1838, 6 chns, by Edward Sacheverell Gisborne; railway, turnpike roads, woods, orchards, building names, road names; woodland named.

22/38 Llanarth (except Clytha) (parish) SO 375116
Apt 11.09.1843; 1953a (1952); Map 1844?, 3 chns, 1st cl, ? by James Nunan, Abergavenny; construction lines, building names, Roman Catholic Chapel, vicarage. Apt omits some field names.

22/39 Llanbaddock (parish) SO 359008 [Llanbadoc]
Apt 11.09.1843; 3466a (3465); Map 'working plan', 1843, 3 chns, 1st cl, by Thomas Morris, Newport; construction lines, houses, building names, wells, chapel. Apt omits some field names.

22/40 Llanbedr (hamlet in parish of Langstone) ST 388912 [Llanbeder]
Apt 08.10.1846; 175a (all); Map 1848, 3 chns, 1st cl, by Thomas Morris, Newport; construction lines, turnpike roads, houses, field gates. Apt omits some field names.

22/41 Llandegfydd otherwise Llandegveth (parish) ST 340962 [Llandegveth]
Apt 10.05.1838; 789a (789); Map 1840, 3 chns, by Richd Hall, Cirencester; waterbodies, houses, woods, arable, grassland, orchards, gardens (col), building names, rectory. Apt omits some field names.

22/42 Llandenny (parish) SO 421042
Apt 22.04.1840; 2228a (all); Map 1843?, 3 chns, 1st cl, in 2 parts, by Charles Harry Bate; construction lines, foot/b'way, waterbodies, woods, building names, wells, quarries, chapel. Apt omits some field names.

22/43 Llandevaud (hamlet in parish of Llanmartin) ST 396917
Apt 27.06.1846; 172a (all); Map 1847, 3 chns, by Thomas Morris, Newport; waterbodies, houses, building names, chapel, school, mill. Apt omits some field names.

22/44 Llandogo (parish) SO 532050
Apt 03.08.1844; 1844a (1843); Map 1845?, 3 chns, by Purchas, Pilstone; foot/b'way, waterbodies, houses, plantations, heath/moor, building names, chapel, boundary stones, may pole, ornamental ground, common (col).

22/45 Llanellan (parish) SO 293102 [Llanellen]
Apt 27.09.1843; 2536a (all); Map 1846?, 3 chns, 1st cl, ? by James Nunan, Abergavenny; construction lines, boundary marks. Apt omits some field names.

22/46 Llanfihangel Crucorney (parish) SO 331202 [Llanvihangel Crucorney]
Apt 07.04.1842; 3264a (3264); Map 1848?, 3 chns, 1st cl, ? by James Nunan, Abergavenny; construction lines, building names, post office. Apt omits some field names.

22/47 Llanfihangel-juxta-Usk (parish) SO 348098 [Llanvihangel Gobion]
Apt 02.12.1842; 385a (all); Map 1843, 3 chns, 1st cl, surveyed for Messrs Gabb and Price by Richd Budgen, Abergavenny; construction lines, waterbodies, houses, gardens, hedge ownership, fences, building names, mill.

22/48 Llanfoist (parish) SO 282127
Apt 07.04.1843; 3289a (all); Map 1844, 6 chns, by Robert Gabb, Abergavenny, Land agent and Surveyor; waterbodies, building names, rectory, wells, boundary marks, brewery, limekiln.

22/49 Llangattock juxta Caerleon (parish) ST 334917 [Caerleon]
Apt 31.05.1839; 2938a (all); Map 'working plan', 1840, 3 chns, 1st cl, by Thos Morris, Newport; turnpike roads, houses, building names, amphitheatre, castle mount, priory, tin and wire works, township boundary; double lines may shown drains. Apt omits some field names.

22/50 Llangattock juxta Usk (parish) SO 34100 [Not listed]
Apt 27.07.1840; 1613a (1613); Map 1840, 3 chns, 1st cl, surveyed for Mr Robt Gabb, Abergavenny by George Taylor, South Parade, Huddersfield; construction lines, waterbodies, field gates, building names.

22/51 Llangattock Lingoed (parish) SO 360200
Apt 02.05.1843; 1927a (1926); Map 1843?, 3 chns, 1st cl, by J. Nunan, Abergavenny; construction lines, building names. Apt omits some field names.

22/52 Llangattock-vibon-Avel (parish) SO 450158 [Llangattock-Vibon-Avel]
Apt 11.08.1838; 4194a (4194); Map 1842?, 3 chns, by White and Reid; construction lines, foot/b'way, waterbodies, houses, field gates, building names, mill, spring. Apt omits some field names.

22/53 Llangeview (parish) SO 403007
Apt 30.05.1842; 1454a (1454); Map 1842, 3 chns, 1st cl, by Wm Bryan Wood, Barnbridge, Chippenham; construction lines, houses, hedge ownership, building names.

22/54 Llangibby (parish) ST 365969 [Not listed]
Apt 10.05.1838; 4444a (4443); Map 1839?, 3 chns, 1st cl; construction lines, waterbodies, houses, woods, plantations, parkland, arable (by annotation), grassland (by annotation), orchards, gardens, fences, building names, field names, landowners, mear stones, boundary trees, chapel, church lands; woodland named; map also covers district 22/41. Apt omits land use.

22/55 Llangoven (parish) SO 453062 [Llangovan]
Apt 27.03.1841; 1889a (all); Map 1841?, 3 chns, 1st cl, by P.E. Wanklyn, Amberley Nr Monmouth; construction lines, foot/b'way, waterbodies, houses, woods, plantations, arable (by annotation), grassland (by annotation), orchards, field boundary ownerships, field gates, building names, field acreages; woodland named.

22/56 Llangunnock (parish) SO 456014 [Llangunnog]
Apt 04.11.1864; 157a (?); Map 1866, 3 chns, by Christopher Heydon, Shirenewton, Chepstow, Monsh; construction lines, waterbodies, houses, woods, plantations, building names, church ruins, quarry, boundary stones and trees, spring, well.

22/57 Llangwm Issaf and Llangwn Uchaf (parish) SO 431007 [Llangwm]
Apt 07.11.1845; 3159a (all); Map 1848?, 3 chns, 1st cl, by J. and M. Nunan, Abergavenny; construction lines, turnpike roads, waterbodies, road destinations. Apt omits some field names.

22/58 Llanhenock (parish) ST 358931 [Llanhennock]
Apt 28.01.1839; 1506a (all); Map 1840, 3 chns, 1st cl, by Thomas Morris, Newport; construction lines, waterbodies, houses, field gates, building names, mills, parsonage.

22/59 Llanhilleth (parish) SO 223011
Apt 26.02.1840; 2014a (all); Map 'working plan', 1841, 3 chns, 1st cl, by

Thos Morris, Newport; construction lines, tramroad, inclined planes, canal, waterbodies, houses, building names. Apt omits some field names.

22/60 Llanishen (parish) SO 458048
Apt 10.09.1840; 1743a (1742); Map 1840, 3 chns, 1st cl, in 2 parts, by Wm Bryan Wood, Barnbridge, Chippenham; construct-ion lines, foot/b'way, waterbodies, houses, hedge ownership, field gates, building names.

22/61 Llanllowell (parish) ST 398988 [Llanllowel or Llanllywel]
Apt 30.12.1837; 797a (all); Map 1837, 3 chns, 1st cl, by Thomas Morris, Newport; construction lines, hill-drawing, foot/b'way, houses, woods (col), arable (col), grassland (col), orchards, gardens (col), building names, field acreages; woodlands named.

22/62 Lanmartin (parish) ST 396896 [Llanmartin]
Apt 18.12.1839; 941a (941); Map 1839, 3 chns, 1st cl, by Thos Morris, Newport; construction lines, waterbodies, houses, building names, castle, common. Apt omits some field names.

22/63 Llanover (parish) SO 293083
Apt 02.09.1843; 4744a (all); Map 1840?, 3 chns, in 2 parts, by Wm Metcalf; hill-drawing, waterbodies, houses, fences, field gates, building names, forge, cairn, furnaces, lodge.

22/64 Llansaintfraed (parish) SO 358101 [Not listed]
Apt 26.10.1842; 290a (all); Map 1843, 3 chns, 1st cl, by H. Price; construction lines, boundary features, milestone.

22/65 Llansoy (parish) SO 448028
Apt 19.11.1841; 1410a (all); Map 1842, 3 chns, 1st cl, by Wm Bryan Wood, Barnbridge, Chippenham; construction lines, waterbodies, houses, hedge ownership, building names.

22/66 Llanthewy Rytherch (parish) SO 350130 [Llanddewi Rhydderch]
Apt 31.07.1840; 2187a (2187); Map 1840, 3 chns, 1st cl, surveyed for Mr Robert Gabb, Abergavenny by George Taylor, South Parade, Huddersfield; construction lines, foot/b'way, waterbodies, field gates.

22/67 Llanthewy Skirrid (parish) SO 341142 [Llanddewi Fach]
Apt 16.09.1839; 1061a (all); Map 1842?, 3 chns, 1st cl, by J. Nunan; construction lines, building names, mill, blacksmith shop. Apt omits some field names.

22/68 Llanthewy Vach (parish) ST 327963
Apt 18.11.1842; 1350a (all); Map 'working plan', 1842, 3 chns, 1st cl, by Thomas Morris, Newport; construction lines, houses, building names, chapel. Apt omits some field names.

22/69 Llantillio Crossenny (parish) SO 395165 [Llantilio Crossenny]
Apt 25.07.1843; 6025a (5951); Map 1843, 6 chns, by P. McCormick; waterbodies, houses, fences, building names, Free School. Apt omits some field names.

22/70 Llantillio Pertholey (parish) SO 315172 [Llantilio Pertholey]
Apt 30.10.1839; 6859a (6859); Map 1847?, 6 chns, in 2 parts; hill-drawing, railway, waterbodies, building names, mill; mountain named. Apt omits some field names.

22/71 Llantrissent (parish) ST 400966 [Llantrisant]
Apt 20.07.1839; 2762a (2762); Map 'working plan', 1840, 3 chns, 1st cl, by Thos Morris, Newport; construction lines, waterbodies, houses, building names, vicarage. Apt omits some field names.

22/72 Llanvaches (parish) ST 429921
Apt 11.11.1842; 2108a (2108); Map 1840, 3 chns, 1st cl, by Thos Morris, Newport; construction lines, turnpike roads, toll gates, milestone, houses, field boundary ownerships, building names, boundary trees, common.

22/73 Llanvair Discoed (except Dinham) (parish) ST 445925 [Llanvair-Discoed]
Apt 19.06.1846; 1316a (1316); Map 1847, 6 chns, by Wm Jones; hill-drawing, waterbodies, woods, plantations, orchards, building names, ruins, boundary marks, castle; hill named. Apt omits some field names.

22/74 Llanvair Kilgeddin (parish) SO 345075 [Llanfair Kilgeddin]
Apt 23.04.1841; 1801a (1801); Map 1838, 4 chns, 1st cl, by E.S. Gisborne; construction lines, turnpike roads, waterbodies, woods (named), parkland, orchards, field boundary ownerships, building names, parsonage; bridge named. Apt omits some field names.

22/75 Lanvapley (parish) SO 366141 [Llanvapley]
Apt 07.06.1838; 820a (all); Map 1839?, 3 chns; construction lines, waterbodies, houses, building names, rectory, grist mill. Apt omits some field names.

22/76 Llanvetherine (parish) SO 361171
Apt 07.11.1839; 2154a (all); Map 1841?, [3 chns], 1st cl, surveyed for Mr Robert Gabb, surveyor, Abergavenny by James Nunan; construction lines, building names, road names, parsonage; bridge named. Apt omits some field names.

22/77 Llanvihangel juxta Roggett otherwise Roggiett (parish) ST 448882 [Llanfihangel Rogiet]
Apt 30.10.1839; 557a (all); Map 1840, 3 chns, 1st cl, by Thomas Morris, Newport; construction lines, waterbodies, houses; woodland named. Apt omits some field names.

22/78 Llanvihangel Llantarnam (parish) ST 295937 [Llantarnam]
Apt 17.02.1844; 4093a (4092); Map 1843, 3 chns, 1st cl, by Thomas Morris, Newport; construction lines, turnpike roads, tramroads, canal, waterbodies, houses, building names, chapel, abbey (named in gothic), fishpond; map is described as 'working plan'. Apt omits some field names.

22/79 Llanvihangel Pontymoil (parish) SO 306012 [Llanvihangel Pontymoel]
Apt 07.06.1839; 89a (1651); Map 1839, 3 chns, 1st cl; construction lines, foot/b'way, canal with towpath, houses, field gates, building names. Apt omits some field names.

22/80 Llanvihangel Torymynydd (parish) SO 465015 [Not listed]
Apt 12.01.1839; 1032a (all); Map 1840?, 3 chns, 1st cl, by R.N. Purchas, Chepstow; construction lines, houses.

22/81 Llanvihangel Yesterne Llewerne (parish) SO 426127 [Llanfrechfa]
Apt 16.10.1839; 1864a (all); Map 1841?, 3 chns, 1st cl, surveyed for Mr Robert Gabb, Abergavenny by Robt Armstrong; construction lines, turnpike roads, building names, parsonage. Apt omits field names.

22/82 Llanvrechva (parish) ST 308952
Apt 30.06.1840; 4184a (4320); Map 1840, 3 chns, in 2 parts, by Robert Nathaniel Purchas, Chepstow; construction lines, tramroads, tunnel, canal with towpath, waterbodies, houses, woods, plantations, orchards, building names, spring, factories, workhouse, colliery, field acreages.

22/83 Llanwenarth (parish) SO 272146
Apt 23.11.1842; 5341a (all); Map 1843?, 3 chns, 1st cl, in 2 parts, by J. Nunan, Abergavenny and H. Price, Abergavenny; construction lines, hill-drawing, canal, balance lift, tunnel mouths, level, feeder, reservoir, waterbodies, rock outcrops, building names, forge and mills, springs, gravel pit; some physical features named. Apt omits some field names.

22/84 Llanwern (parish) ST 374876
Apt 18.05.1838; 701a (701); Map 1839?, 4 chns; woods, parkland, field gates, building names, limekilns, spring, field acreages; pictorial church; double lines may be drains. District is apportioned by holding; Apt omits land use.

22/85 Machen (parish) (partly in Glamorganshire) ST 228900
Apt 03.01.1839; 5167a (all); Map 1841?, 4 chns, surveyed for W. Jones by J. Prujean; construction lines, waterbodies, houses, woods, plantations, rock outcrops, building names, forge, factory, tucking mill, ornamental ground.

22/86 Magor (parish) ST 422874
Apt 17.09.1846; 1891a (2720); Map 1847, 4 chns, by Thomas Morris, Newport; waterbodies, houses, open fields (named), building names, sea walls, mill, commons, drains (named). Apt omits some field names.

22/87 Malpas (parish) ST 304908
Apt 30.07.1839; 989a (all); Map 1839, 3 chns, 1st cl, by Thos Morris,

Newport; construction lines, canal, waterbodies, houses, building names. Apt omits some field names.

22/88 Mamhilad (parish) SO 305039
Apt 26.08.1839; 1987a (1987); Map 1841, 3 chns, 1st cl, by Henry Williams, Newport, Mommouthshire; construction lines, canal with towpath, waterbodies, houses, building names, mill.

22/89 Marshfield (parish) ST 255828
Apt 08.02.1841; 1270a (all); Map 'working plan', 1840, 3 chns, 1st cl, by Thos Morris, Newport; construction lines, foot/b'way, houses, field gates, vicarage, mill. Apt omits some field names.

22/90 Mathern and Runston (parish) ST 512919
Apt 27.11.1844; 2851a (3281); Map 1839, 4 chns, 1st cl, by James Peachy Williams, Bridgewater; waterbodies, houses, fishpond; three fuchsia flowers decorate title.

22/91 St Maughan (parish) SO 465198 [St Maughans]
Apt 26.10.1842; 1305a (1304); Map 1843, 6 chns, by Purchas, Pilstone; waterbodies, houses, building names, maypole, nunnery; woodland, orchard and plantation are shown by annotation.

22/92 St Mellons (parish) ST 234811
Apt 15.09.1845; 2574a (all); Map 1841, 3 chns, 1st cl, by Thomas Morris, Newport; construction lines, houses, building names, mill.

22/93 Mitchel Troy (parish) SO 500100
Apt 24.02.1841; 2000a (2000); Map 1841, 3 chns, 1st cl, by Wm Bryan Wood, Barnbridge, Chippenham; construction lines, waterbodies, houses, hedge ownership, building names.

22/94 Monmouth (parish) SO 500130
Apt 22.05.1843; 3421a (3420); Map 1844, 3 chns, 1st cl, by W.H. Apperley, Hereford; construction lines, waterbodies, houses, field boundary ownerships, building names; built-up part generalised; some of the boundaries have been endorsed by the agent to the Duke of Beaufort.

22/95 Mounton (parish) ST 512931
Apt 29.06.1846; 408a (407); Map 1846, 4 chns, by Jas Peachy Williams, Bristol; waterbodies, houses.

22/96 Mynddysllwyn (parish) ST 215955 [Mynyddislwyn]
Apt 22.04.1839; 15939a (15938); Map 1841, 3 chns, 1st cl, in 4 parts, by Thos Morris, Newport; construction lines, canal, waterbodies, houses, woods (by name), field gates, building names, field names, landowners, school, reservoir, iron works, mills, acid works, tramroads (named), collieries, spelter works; bridges named. Apt omits some field names.

22/97 Nash (parish) ST 350840
Apt 29.08.1840; 2739a (3563); Map 1842, 4 chns, by Thomas Morris, Newport; houses, orchards, heath/moor, building names, decoy pool, common (col). Apt omits some field names.

22/98 Newchurch East and West (parish) ST 470970 [Newchurch]
Apt 06.06.1840; 5434a (all); Map 1839, 3 chns, 1st cl, in 2 parts; construction lines, hill-drawing, turnpike roads, toll-gate, waterbodies, houses, field boundary ownerships, building names, mill, boundary trees and marks, wells, quarry. Apt omits some field names.

22/99 Old Castle (parish) SO 323244 [Oldcastle]
Apt 16.09.1839; 923a (922); Map 1839, 4 chns; field boundary ownerships.

22/100 Panteague (parish) ST 300985 [Panteg]
Apt 26.12.1837; 3455a (all); Map 1839, 3 chns, in 2 parts, by D. Thomas; waterbodies, houses, field gates, building names, workhouse, pump, rickyard, chapel, reservoir, dam, spring, tin works, factory; woodland named.

22/101 Penallt (parish) SO 520090
Apt 04.07.1844; 1554a (2284); Map 1847, 4 chns; waterbodies, houses, building names, limekilns, school, mills. Apt omits some field names.

22/102 Penhow (parish) ST 408913
Apt 19.05.1843; 1784a (1784); Map 1842, 3 chns, surveyed for Edmund Scott Barber of Newport, Monmouth by George Taylor, Brecon; construction lines, foot/b'way, waterbodies, plantations, field gates, building names, rectory, parish pound. Apt omits some field names.

22/103 Penrose (parish) SO 406128 [Penrhos]
Apt 08.03.1844; 2696a (2695); Map 1846, 3 chns, 1st cl, by P. McCormick, Grosmont; construction lines, waterbodies, houses, fences, building names, boundary trees. Apt omits some field names.

22/104 Penterry (parish) ST 521989 [Not listed]
Apt 26.10.1842; 479a (all); Map 1844, 3 chns, ? by William Jane, Chepstow; houses, woods, orchard.

22/105 Peny-clawdd (parish) SO 450080 [Pen-y-clawdd]
Apt 27.03.1841; 614a (all); Map 1841, 4 chns; waterbodies, houses.

22/106 Peterstone (parish) ST 270810 [Peterstone Wentlooge]
Apt 26.03.1841; 2135a (all); Map 1844, 4 chns, by T. Morris, Newport; building names, road names, sluice house, wharf, drains (named). Apt omits some field names.

22/107 St Pierre (parish) ST 508902
Apt 19.12.1838; 592a (all); Map 1839, 4 chns, 1st cl, by Jas Peachy Williams, Bridgwater; foot/b'way, waterbodies, houses.

22/108 Portskewett and Southbrook (parish) ST 505885
Apt 18.01.1839; 1059a (all); Map 1839, 4 chns, 1st cl, by Jas Peachy Williams, Bridgwater; foot/b'way, waterbodies, houses.

22/109 Ragland (parish) SO 413071 [Raglan]
Apt 30.04.1840; 4084a (4083); Map 1841, 3 chns, 1st cl, by Wm Bryan Wood, Barnbridge, Chippenham; construction lines, foot/b'way, waterbodies, houses, hedge ownership, field gates, building names, castle.

22/110 Redwick (parish) ST 412846
Apt 23.08.1844; 2234a (7794); Map 1846, 4 chns, by Thomas Morris, Newport; houses, orchards, open fields (named), building names, road names, wharves, commons, drains (named). Apt omits some field names.

22/111 Risca (parish) ST 240920
Apt 17.03.1843; 1877a (all); Map 1843, 3 chns, by William Jones, Brecon; construction lines, canal, woods (col), plantations (col), building names, factory, ornamental ground.

22/112 Rockfield (parish) SO 475152
Apt 15.05.1841; 1993a (1993); Map 1842, 4 chns, by P.E. Wanklyn, Monmouth; foot/b'way, waterbodies, houses, field boundary ownerships, field gates, building names, paper mill; bridge named.

22/113 Roggett otherwise Roggiett (parish) ST 455879 [Rogiet]
Apt 30.07.1839; 400a (all); Map 1840, 3 chns, 1st cl, in 2 parts, by Thomas Morris, Newport; construction lines, houses, field gates, commons, drains; woodland named.

22/114 Rumney (parish) ST 220790
Apt 16.09.1843; 2215a (3375); Map 1845, 4 chns, by Thomas Morris; waterbodies, houses, building names, field names, wharves, drains. Apt omits some field names.

22/115 Shirenewton (parish) ST 470940
Apt 18.02.1841; 3545a (all); Map 1840?, 3 chns, 1st cl, by R.N. Purchas, Chepstow; construction lines, waterbodies, houses, rock outcrops, building names, mills, limekiln, quarry, common.

22/116 Skenfrith (parish) SO 440200
Apt 04.05.1843; 4720a (4720); Map 1842, 3 chns, 1st cl, by P.M'Cormick, Grosmont; waterbodies, houses, building names. Apt omits some field names.

22/117 Tintern Parva (parish) SO 525010
Apt 17.01.1844; 828a (827); Map 1844, 3 chns, 1st cl, surveyed for P.E. Wanklyn, Monmouth by T. M'Grane; construction lines, waterbodies, houses, field boundary ownerships, building names, boundary trees.

22/118 Tredynog otherwise Tredunnock (parish) ST 363943
Apt 29.11.1838; 1394a (all); Map 'working plan', 1839, 3 chns, 1st cl, by Thos Morris, Newport; construction lines, waterbodies, houses, plantations, building names, avenues of trees; bridge named.

22/119 Tregare (parish) SO 420107
Apt 19.10.1843; 2387a (all); Map 1844, 6 chns, by W.H. Apperley, Hereford; turnpike roads, toll bar, waterbodies, houses, building names, mill; mapmaker notes: 'This plan is partly complied from old Estate Maps for the correctness of which I am not responsible'.

22/120 Trellock (parish) SO 507049 [Trelleck]
Apt 11.03.1845; 3270a (5287); Map 1848?, 4 chns; waterbodies, houses, building names, mills, churchyard, well; woodland named. Apt omits some field names.

22/121 Trevethin (parish) SO 265050
Apt 31.07.1839; 7674a (all); Map 1841 and 1843, 3 chns, 1st cl, in 3 parts, by E.S. Gisborne; construction lines, canal, waterbodies, fences, field boundary ownerships, building names, shops, stone quarry, furnaces. Apt omits some field names.

22/122 Trostrey (parish) SO 370047 [Not listed]
Apt 28.09.1839; 1255a (all); Map 'original or working plan', 1839, 3 chns, 1st cl, by Thos Morris, Newport; construction lines, waterbodies, houses, woods, building names, mill and fish weir, mill, sand or stone pits, avenue of trees.

22/123 Undy (parish) ST 439871
Apt 18.01.1840; 1718a (3717); Map 1839, 3 chns, 1st cl, by Thomas Morris, Newport; construction lines, waterbodies, houses, open fields (named), building names, wharf, chapel, commons, drains. [PRO IR 30 also contains a 6-chn version litho by Standidge, 1842.]

22/124 Usk (except Gwehellog) (parish) SO 380005
Apt 11.09.1843; 405a (404); Map 1843, 3 chns, 1st cl, by Thomas Morris, Newport; construction lines, turnpike roads, waterbodies, houses, building names, new bridewell, priory, mill.

22/125 Welsh Bicknor (parish) SO 585179
Apt 29.05.1838; 850a (all); Map not dated, 4 chns; houses, woods, orchards, gardens, hedges.

22/126 Whitson (parish) ST 377855
Apt 02.05.1844; 1073a (all); Map 1845, 4 chns; heath/moor, building names, decoy pool, common (col).

22/127 Wilcrick (parish) ST 410880
Apt 07.01.1840; 407a (406); Map 1839, 3 chns, 1st cl, by Thos Morris, Newport; construction lines, waterbodies, houses, building names, field name.

22/128 Woolvesnewton (parish) ST 461997 [Wolvesnewton]
Apt 04.04.1839; 2649a (all); Map 1841?, 3 chns, 1st cl, by Robert N. Purchas; construction lines, foot/b'way, houses, woods (named), orchards, field boundary ownerships, field gates, field acreages.

22/129 Wonastow (parish) SO 476113
Apt 08.03.1844; 1599a (1599); Map 1845?, 3 chns, 1st cl, by W.H. Apperley, Hereford; construction lines, waterbodies, houses, field boundary ownerships, building names, vicarage.

22/130 St Woollos (parish) ST 309874 [Not listed]
Apt 19.08.1841; 3584a (all); Map 1841, 3 chns, 1st cl, by Thomas Morris, Newport; construction lines, hill-drawing, turnpike roads, toll house, canal, waterbodies, houses, plantations, field gates, building names, road names, site of intended barracks, fort, new powder magazine, castle, watch house, union poorhouse, sand or stone pits or quarries, docks, wharves, factory, pottery, weighing machine, common; park and bridges named; built-up part generalised. Apt omits some field names.

Norfolk

PRO IR29 and IR30 23/1-669

732 tithe districts: 1,300,183 acres
669 tithe commutations: 1,206,892 acres
488 voluntary tithe agreements, 181 compulsory tithe awards

Tithe and tithe commutation

Although only fifth in size of the historic counties of England and Wales, Norfolk is second only to Devon in tithable acreage, second only to Lincolnshire in number of tithe districts, and itself has the largest number of tithable districts of any county (Fig. 35). In 1836 tithes were still paid in respect of 91 per cent of Norfolk tithe districts. Though there had been some limited parliamentary enclosure in the western half of the county, 336 Norfolk districts were still wholly tithable. The main causes of tithe exemption elsewhere in Norfolk were commutation at the time of enclosure, modus payments in lieu of tithes, the merger of tithes in the land, and exemption by prescription.

Assistant tithe commissioners and local tithe agents who worked in Norfolk are listed in Table 23.1. Very little tithe valuation work was undertaken by men residing even a short distance outside Norfolk's county boundary, which makes the eleven districts valued by men from London and Nottinghamshire all the more remarkable. The most prolific valuer of tithe rent-charge both in Norfolk and in England and Wales as a whole, was Robert Pratt of Norwich whose ninety-seven valuations extend over about 15 per cent of the tithable land of the county (Table 23.2).

In twenty-two Norfolk tithe districts tithes are apportioned by holding and so the schedules of tithe apportionment of these districts lack information on field names and land use. Some apportionments made on a field-by-field basis are also deficient in this respect; Charles Etheredge of Starston made twenty-six valuations but usually entered the general term 'Field' in the 'Names and Descriptions' columns of his tithe apportionments.

Tithe maps

Although it also adjoins Lincolnshire and Cambridgeshire, Norfolk's tithe survey cartography more closely resembles that of Suffolk. About 11 per cent of the 669 tithe maps of Norfolk are sealed as first class, a proportion which is somewhat below the national average and is less than half the proportion of Suffolk but twice the proportion of Cambridgeshire and Lincolnshire. By contrast to Suffolk, construction lines are present on only 2 per cent of Norfolk second-class maps; from this fact and from the small number of first-class maps it can be inferred that in Norfolk there was probably both less of a desire to commission surveys intended to reach first-class standards and a greater re-use of older surveys.

Scales used for Norfolk maps range from one inch to two chains to one inch to twelve chains; only 34 per cent of maps are in the recommended scale range of one inch to three to four chains, whereas the six-chain scale was used for 50 per cent of the maps. In this last respect Norfolk resembles Lincolnshire rather than Suffolk. Eleven second-class maps in the Public Record Office collection are lithographed; some of these are by Joseph Manning of Norwich who offered both a map-making and a map-printing service.

The mapping of land use on Norfolk tithe maps is somewhat similar to that of Suffolk. About 5 per cent of maps show arable and grass, 16 per cent depict gardens, 16 per cent map parks, 5 per cent portray heath and moor, and 8 per cent distinguish orchards. Marl and other pits appear in their hundreds on Norfolk maps and are usually stippled. Windmills are also common; they are usually shown pictorially rather than by symbol and often post mills and tower mills are distinguished. At Castle Acre, the first-class map includes careful depictions of both the castle and the priory ruins.

Some 481 Norfolk maps in the Public Record Office collection can be attributed to a particular map-maker; at nearly 72 per cent this figure is rather above the national average and neatly epitomises the county's tithe survey position between Lincolnshire and Suffolk, with more attributable maps than the former and fewer than the latter. In so large a county it would have been hard for any one map-maker to be dominant but Pratt and Sons of Norwich did map nearly 9 per cent of Norfolk, albeit mostly to second-class standards. James Wright of Aylsham mapped a rather smaller area but produced a number of first-class maps and was usually careful to acknowledge his sources when reworking earlier material. His style varies but is usually a straightforward one at the three- or four-chain scale with uncoloured roads, though around Felbrigg he executed a group of nine-chain maps which differ somewhat from his usual style and have attractive, grey-tinted woods. Norfolk maps tend not to be particularly colourful but W. G. Bircham of Fakenham enlivened the north-west of the county with thirty-one maps, many of which show landownership by colour. A group of thirteen maps in the south of the county are variously signed by Henry Calver and C. S. Alger, both of Diss, but in a common style with bright red buildings and pale blue borders. A group of five maps east of Norwich were made by J. P. Luckraft and Co., a name more usually associated with Devon.

Apart from the pictorial windmills, Norfolk maps generally eschew decoration. A notable exception is the pictorial depiction of churches, a characteristic of the tithe maps of eastern England and one which reaches its high point in this county. Pictorial churches appear on over 28 per cent of Norfolk maps and vary from stylised pictograms to neat, plausible-looking drawings. Outstanding examples include Osmondeston with overflying birds and Empingham which includes a man and woman walking towards the church. At Eccles the ruined church tower destroyed by the sea in 1895 is rather overshadowed by a neat drawing of a paddle-steamer.

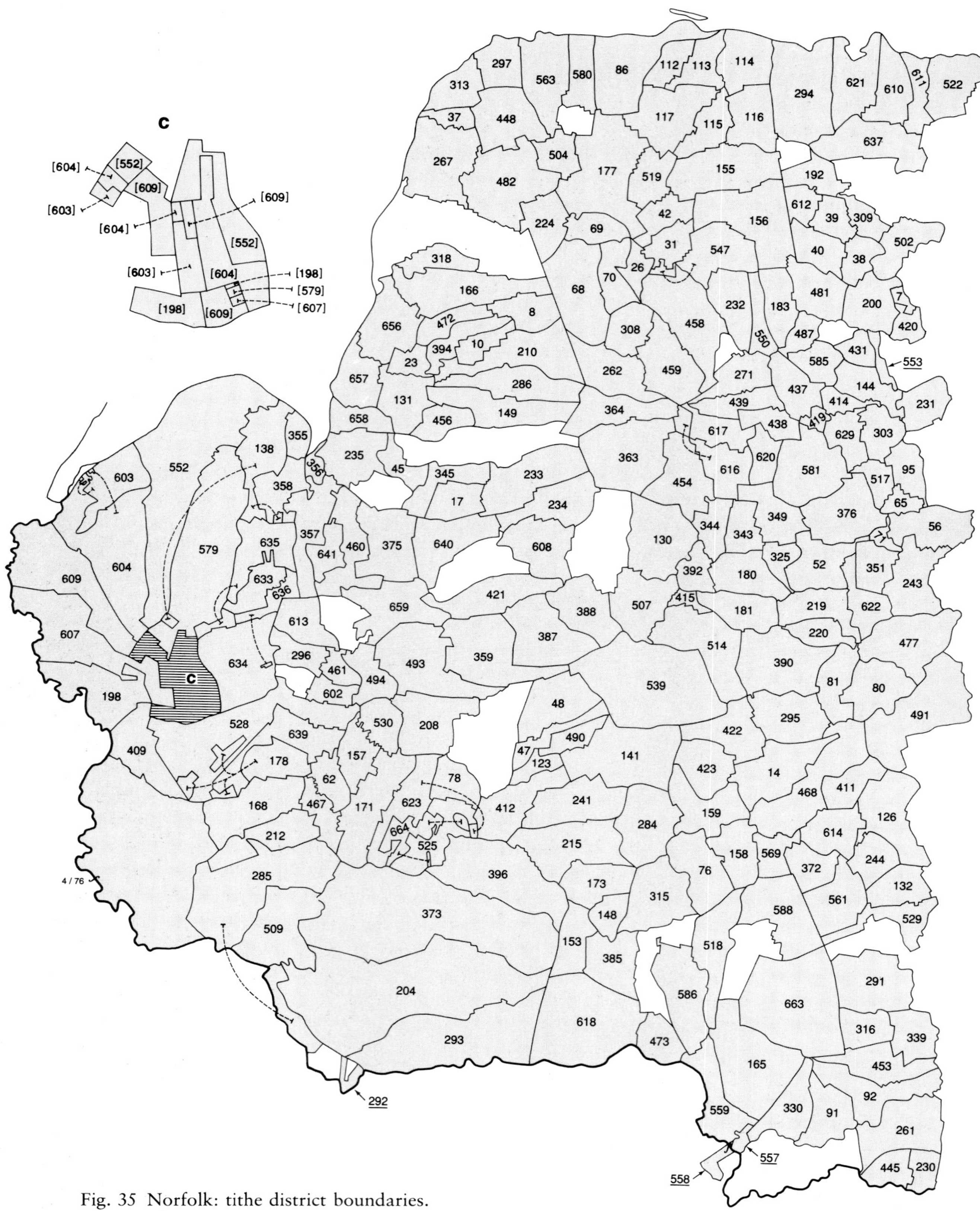

Fig. 35 Norfolk: tithe district boundaries.

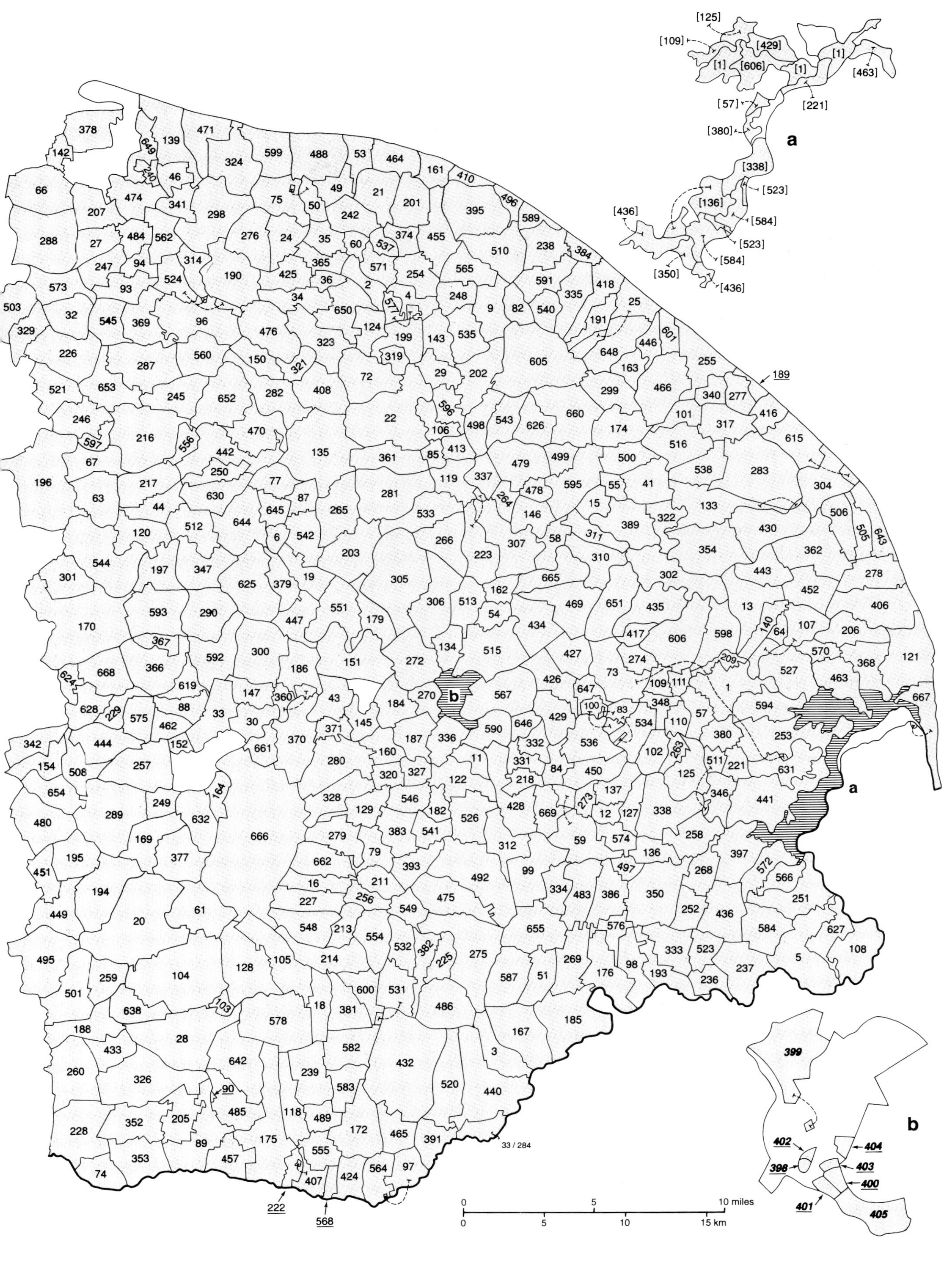

Table 23.1. *Agreements and awards for commutation of tithes in Norfolk*

Assistant commissioner/ local tithe agent	*Number of agreements**	*Number of awards*
James Drage Merest	161	154
Henry Bertram Gunning	109	0
? Mears	81	0
Horace William Meteyard	42	0
Thomas Sutton	31	0
William Heard	20	0
Thomas Smith Woolley	14	1
Francis Offley Martin	0	14
John Mee Mathew	9	2
John Maurice Herbert	0	7
Roger Kynaston	6	0
Thomas Turner	5	0
John Pickering	3	0
Arthur Biddell	0	1
John Job Rawlinson	0	1
Thomas Sudworth	1	0
Joseph Townsend	1	0
Tithe Commissioners	0	1

*Computed from the number of extant reports on tithe agreements in the tithe files [PRO IR 18].

Table 23.2. *Tithe valuers and tithe map-makers in Norfolk*

Name and address (in Norfolk unless indicated)	*Number of districts*	*Acreage*
Tithe valuers		
Robert Pratt, Norwich	97	180,450
John Beck, Congham, Norfolk	40	88,914
Thomas Salter, Attleborough	36	79,815
William Salter Millard, Sprowston	30	44,541
William Beck, Mileham	28	50,634
William Newton, Norwich	28	44,869
Charles Etheredge, Starston	26	46,962
Edward Seppings, Swaffham	22	39,947
James Wright, Aylsham	22	24,891
Robert Wright, Norwich	20	39,135
John Warnes, Aylsham	16	25,557
Thomas Burton, Langley	15	20,286
Thomas Edwards, Hapton	14	23,245
William Atkins, Coston	13	24,041
Charles Burcham, Kings Lynn	12	24,101
Thomas Pooly, Northwold	11	36,720
William Robberds Woodrow, Norwich	11	21,749
John Reeve, Little Walsingham	11	19,498
Samuel Lock, Barton Bendish	10	19,000
William Barcham, Mundesley	10	15,242
Tithe Commissioners	10	94
Others [93]	182	337,201

Table 23.2. *(cont.)*

Name and address (in Norfolk unless indicated)	*Number of districts*	*Acreage*
Attributed tithe map-makers		
Pratt and Son, Norwich	59	108,709
James Wright, Aylsham/Brixton Road, London	57	79,592
Newton and Woodrow, Norwich	39	68,897
W. G. Bircham, Fakenham	31	57,950
William Drane, Norwich	25	35,986
Joseph Manning, Norwich	21	35,020
Edwin Durrant, Kings Lynn	21	53,798
William Salter Millard and Son, Norwich	21	33,164
James Utting, Kings Lynn	19	40,612
Lenny and Croft, Bury St Edmunds, Suffolk	15	59,807
Thomas Burton junior, Langley	14	17,331
Adam Taylor Clarke, Norwich	11	15,321
Charles Burcham, Kings Lynn	10	19,421
Others [49]	138	284,763

Table 23.3. *The tithe maps of Norfolk: scales and classes*

Scale in chains/inch	*All maps*		*First Class*		*Second Class*	
	Number	*Acreage*	*Number*	*Acreage*	*Number*	*Acreage*
>3	5	2,459	1	140	4	2,319
3	201	290,107	70	120,078	131	170,029
4	28	54,261	1	4,986	27	49,275
4.5	11	11,706	0	0	11	11,706
5	12	17,868	0	0	12	17,868
6	336	677,202	1	2,238	335	674,964
6.67, 7, 7.5	10	17,622	0	0	10	17,622
8	21	43,820	0	0	21	43,820
9	28	59,471	0	0	28	59,471
10	4	8,422	0	0	4	8,422
12	13	23,954	0	0	13	23,954
TOTAL	669	1,206,892	73	127,442	596	1,079,450

Table 23.4. *The tithe maps of Norfolk: dates*

	<1837	*1837*	*1838*	*1839*	*1840*	*1841*	*1842*	*1843*	*1844*	*1845*	*1846*	*1847*	*1848*	*>1848*
All maps	1	25	149	156	97	60	47	22	27	28	21	9	2	23
1st class	0	7	18	13	12	9	5	1	2	2	1	1	1	1
2nd class*	1	18	131	143	85	51	42	21	25	26	20	8	1	22

*Two second-class tithe maps of Norfolk in the Public Record Office collection are undated.

Norfolk

23/1 Acle (parish) TG 402100
Apt 07.04.1838; 3210a (3209); Map 1838, 6 chns, (includes enlargement of town at 3 chns, by Issac Lenny, Norwich); turnpike roads, waterbodies, houses, woods (col), arable (col), grassland (col), orchards (col), gardens (col), fences, field gates, road names, drains, decoy, direction post, mile irons [mileposts], toll gate, brick ground, parsonage, stackyards, ferry, drainage wall, steam engine, private roads; various 'gates' named; enlargement of town has combined scale and north pointer.

23/2 Alborough (parish) TG 173345 [Aldborough]
Apt 12.06.1839; 788a (788); Map surveyed in 1838, 3 chns, by George F. Playford, North Repps; construction lines, foot/b'way, waterbodies, houses, woods, field boundary ownerships, mill dam, boundary tree, green.

23/3 Alburgh (parish) TM 274872
Apt 10.06.1842; 1512a (all); Map 1843, 6 chns, in 2 parts, by Newton and Woodrow, Norwich, (includes 3-chn enlargement of detail, by Pratt and Son, Norwich); waterbodies, houses, windmill (pictorial); pictorial church.

23/4 Alby (parish) TG 203335 [Not listed]
Apt 31.10.1838; 811a (811); Map 1841, 6 chns; waterbodies; buildings are shown in outline only, without fill.

23/5 Aldeby (parish) TM 447938
Apt 26.11.1840; 3057a (3056); Map 1841, 6 chns, in 3 parts, by Pratt and Son, Norwich, (includes two 3-chn enlargements of detail); waterbodies, houses, woods, orchards, drains.

23/6 Alderford (parish) TG 122188
Apt 09.06.1840; 432a (all); Map 1842, 5 chns; foot/b'way, houses, woods, hops.

23/7 Alethorpe (parish) TF 950310 [Not listed]
Apt 11.09.1843; 239a (all); Map 1838, 3 chns, by W.G. Bircham, Fakenham; waterbodies, houses, plantations (col), arable (col), grassland (col), field boundary ownerships, landowners, pit, glebe (uncoloured); a table summarises ownerships.

23/8 Anmer (parish) TF 738297
Apt 31.01.1839; 1360a (1420); Map 1842, 5 chns; foot/b'way, waterbodies, road names, field names, Roman Road, pits, ownerships (col), common, 'Present Roads' (sienna), 'Roads stoped up' (dark blue); pictorial church; no other buildings are shown. District is apportioned by holding; Apt generalises land use and omits field names.

23/9 Antingham St Mary and Antingham St Margaret (incorporated parishes) TG 254334 [Antingham]
Apt 09.02.1839; 1510a (all); Map surveyed in 1830 and corrected in 1839, 3 chns, by James Wright, 2 Grove Place, Buxton Rd, London, and Aylsham, Norfolk; foot/b'way, waterbodies, houses, woods, field boundary ownerships, pit; pictorial churches.

23/10 Appleton (parish) TF 713276 [Not listed]
Apt 06.05.1839; 876a (875); Map 1839, 6 chns, by Pratt and Son, Norwich; foot/b'way, waterbodies, houses; north pointer has plumes and diadem.

23/11 Arminghall or Armeringhall (parish) TG 246052
Apt 22.03.1839; 651a (all); Map 1838, 3 chns; waterbodies, houses, woods, gardens, pits, driftways (col); bridge named.

23/12 Ashby (parish) TG 330019 [Ashby St Mary]
Apt 25.10.1839; 488a (all); Map 1840, 3 chns, by Thos Burton Junr, Langley; foot/b'way, waterbodies, houses, woods, parkland, gardens, pit; pictorial church.

23/13 Ashby, Oby and Thurne (parishes) TG 413154
Apt 22.11.1841; 2068a (all); Map 1842, 3 chns, 1st cl, by James Wright, Aylsham; construction lines, foot/b'way, waterbodies, houses, field boundary ownerships, building names, road names, pit, stiles, parish boundaries.

23/14 Ashill (parish) TF 888043
Apt 31.10.1838; 2990a (2990); Map 1839, 3 chns, 1st cl, by Pratt and Son, Norwich; construction lines, houses, field boundary ownerships.

23/15 Ashmanhaugh (parish) TG 316203
Apt 27.01.1841; 666a (665); Map 1841, 3 chns, by James Wright, Aylsham; foot/b'way, waterbodies, houses, woods; map title has leafy lettering, with sky background.

23/16 Ashwellthorpe (parish) TM 151978
Apt 20.10.1841; 979a (all); Map 1842, 3 chns, by W.S. Millard and Son, Norwich; waterbodies, houses, woods.

23/17 Ashwicken (parish) TF 701188
Apt 21.06.1842; 1282a (all); Map 1842?, 6 chns, copied by E. Durrant, Lynn; waterbodies, houses.

23/18 Aslacton (parish) TM 155903
Apt 01.05.1839; 1194a (1194); Map 1838, 3 chns, by Samuel Colman, Norwich; foot/b'way, waterbodies; pictorial church. Apt omits most field names.

23/19 Attlebridge (parish) TG 135168
Apt 13.07.1837; 1267a (1267); Map 1837, 6 chns, by Pratt and Son, Norwich; houses, woods, glebe.

23/20 Attleburgh (parish) TM 041953 [Attleborough]
Apt 23.05.1838; 5261a (5260); Map 1838, 6 chns, 'Corrected from the Map of the Parish' by J. Eaton, Old Buckenham; waterbodies, houses, arable (col), grassland (col).

23/21 Aylmerton (parish) TG 182401
Apt 07.11.1842; 1679a (1679); Map 1842, 9 chns, by James Wright, Aylsham; hill-drawing, foot/b'way, waterbodies, houses, woods, heath/moor (col), road names, cross, pit; valleys named; pictorial church.

23/22 Aylsham (parish) TG 195263
Apt 25.04.1838; 4309a (4308); Map 1839?, 3 chns, 1st cl, by James Wright, Aylsham; construction lines, waterbodies, houses, field boundary ownerships, building names, road names, brickworks.

23/23 Babingley (parish) TF 671263
Apt 24.04.1838; 850a (849); Map 1838, 7.5 chns, by Edwin Durrant, Kings Lynn; foot/b'way, waterbodies, arable (col), grassland (col).

23/24 Baconsthorpe (parish) TG 137382
Apt 13.06.1840; 1360a (all); Map 1838, 3 chns, by Wm Drane, Norwich; foot/b'way, waterbodies, houses, woods, plantations, pits.

23/25 Bacton (parish) TG 337337
Apt 13.12.1844; 1601a (all); Map 1845?, 3 chns; foot/b'way, canal with towpath, waterbodies, houses, woods (named).

23/26 Bagthorp (parish) TF 796323 [Bagthorpe]
Apt 24.04.1838; 751a (all); Map 1838?, [12 chns], by R. Cartwright, 1 Warwick Place, Bedford Row, litho; woods (named), plantation (by annotation), gardens, orchards (by annotation), lawn (by annotation), heath/moor, field names; map has manuscript additions; one wood is annotated 'Planted in 1836'; table lists field names and acreages.

23/27 Bale (parish) TG 010368
Apt 26.04.1838; 1042a (1041); Map 1838, 6 chns; waterbodies, houses, woods, pits, modus land boundary, driftways (col).

23/28 Banham (parish) TM 066880
Apt 22.04.1845; 3964a (all); Map 1846, 6 chns, by C.S. Alger, Diss; waterbodies, houses, woods, plantations, orchards, gardens, brickworks, pits, windmills (pictorial).

23/29 Banningham (parish) TG 220291
Apt 15.06.1842; 909a (920); Map 1839, 3 chns, by Wm Drane, Norwich; waterbodies, houses, woods, parkland; pictorial church.

23/30 Barford (parish) TG 110077
Apt 31.01.1839; 1053a (all); Map 1838, 5 chns, by Adam Taylor Clarke, Norwich; waterbodies, houses, woods, orchards, landowners (col); pictorial church.

23/31 Barmer (parish) TF 813337
Apt 21.02.1846; 552a (890); Map 1850?, 6 chns, (tithable parts only); waterbodies, woods (col), pits, brick ground, limekiln, ownerships (col); table gives acreages. Apt gives quantities to the nearest acre.

23/32 Barney (parish) TF 995325
Apt 24.04.1838; 1390a (1389); Map 1838, 6 chns; waterbodies, houses, woods, plantations, landowners, boundary of tithe-free land, driftways (col).

23/33 Barnham Broom and Bickerstone (parish and parish or hamlet) TG 085078
Apt 16.04.1846; 1776a (all); Map 1846, 6 chns, by W.S. Millard and Son, Norwich; foot/b'way, waterbodies, houses, woods, parkland, orchards, pits.

23/34 Little Barningham (parish) TG 136332
Apt 20.10.1838; 1225a (all); Map 1839, 6 chns, by W.G. Bircham, Fakenham; waterbodies, houses, woods, landowners (col), pit, boundary tree; pictorial church.

23/35 Barningham Norwood (parish) TG 150372 [Not listed]
Apt 20.08.1844; 835a (all); Map 1844, 3 chns, 1st cl, by John F. Deyns; construction lines, waterbodies, houses, field boundary ownerships.

23/36 Town Barningham (parish) TG 147357 [Not listed]
Apt 25.03.1839; 834a (833); Map 1842?, 6 chns; waterbodies, houses, woods, gardens; pictorial church.

23/37 Barrett Ringstead (parish) TF 686402 [Not listed]
Apt 26.03.1844; 631a (all); Map 1844, 12 chns, in 2 parts, (includes 4-chn enlargement of detail); woods, beach (col).

23/38 East Basham (parish) TF 921333 [East Barsham]
Apt 04.04.1838; 1168a (all); Map 1838, 6 chns; waterbodies, houses, plantations, pit, driftways (col).

23/39 North Basham (parish) TF 905335 [North Barsham]
Apt 13.06.1839; 1016a (all); Map 1839, 6 chns, ? by Edwin Durrant; waterbodies, houses, green way.

23/40 West Barsham (parish) TF 899337
Apt 31.05.1845; 1571a (1571); Map 1844, 6 chns, by A.T. Clarke, Norwich; waterbodies, houses, plantations, orchards, pits, hall, notable oaks; north pointer has diadem and plumes, and there are small north pointers at each end of the scale bar.

23/41 Barton Turf (parish) TG 351224
Apt 26.11.1838; 1599a (1599); Map surveyed in 1835, and corrected in 1839, 6 chns, by James Wright, Aylsham, Norfolk, and 2, Grove Place, Brixton Rd, London; foot/b'way, waterbodies, houses, woods, osiers (by symbol), field boundary ownerships, building names, stiles, windmill (pictorial).

23/42 Barwick (parish) TF 807351 [Not listed]
Apt 09.02.1846; 1279a (1278); Map 1846?, 6 chns; waterbodies, woods (col), township boundaries.

23/43 Bawburgh (parish) TG 160090
Apt 05.06.1839; 1404a (1440); Map 1839, 6 chns, by Pratt and Son, Norwich; waterbodies, houses, glebe.

23/44 Bawdeswell (parish) TG 046206
Apt 31.07.1844; 1197a (1196); Map 1844, 6 chns, by Pratt and Son, Norwich; houses, woods.

23/45 Bawsey (parish) TF 664204
Apt 23.06.1837; 1090a (all); Map 1839?, 6 chns, copied by J. Utting, Lynn Regis; foot/b'way, warren.

23/46 Bayfield (parish) TG 060410 [Not listed]
Apt 16.03.1839; 780a (all); Map 1838, 4.5 chns, by W.G. Bircham, Fakenham; houses, woods (col), plantations (col), arable (col), grassland (col), field names, landowners, pit, driftways (col), hall.

23/47 Beachamwell All Saints (parish) TF 761059 [Beachamwell]
Apt 22.07.1845; 1023a (?); Map 1845, 12 chns; foot/b'way, waterbodies.

23/48 Beachamwell St Mary and Beachamwell St John with part of Barton Bendish (united parishes) TF 762074 [Beachamwell]
Apt 22.07.1845; 3061a (?); Map 1845, 12 chns, by Edwin Durrant, Kings Lynn; foot/b'way, waterbodies; the map also includes the district mapped in 23/47.

23/49 East Beckham (parish) TG 158403
Apt 07.07.1848; 782a (782); Map 1848?, 9 chns, ? by John F. Deyns; foot/b'way, waterbodies, houses, woods, pits.

23/50 West Beckham (parish) TG 143397
Apt 22.04.1844; 785a (all); Map 1844, 3 chns, 'Copy of a Map of the Parish' by James Wright, Aylsham, (tinted); foot/b'way, waterbodies, houses, woods, road names, pits, stiles.

23/51 Bedingham (parish) TM 289920 [Bedingham green]
Apt 23.01.1840; 1340a (1340); Map 1839, 3 chns, by Geo. Baker, Bungay; hill-drawing, waterbodies, houses, woods (col), plantations (col), parkland (col), arable (col), grassland (col), orchards (col), gardens (col), heath/moor (col), hedges with trees, fences, field gates, road names, windmill (by symbol), pound, greens, common; colour bands show tithe-free land (red), and ownership of great tithes (green).

23/52 Beeston next Mileham (parish) TF 905157 [Beeston]
Apt 27.05.1838; 2073a (2073); Map 1838, 5 chns; waterbodies, houses, woods, brickworks, windmill (pictorial).

23/53 Beeston Regis (parish) TG 170420
Apt 22.09.1838; 823a (all); Map 1839, 3 chns, 1st cl, by Pratt and Son, Norwich; construction lines, houses; there is a note, 'Restoration in red, made by means of tracings prepared from the Map, prior to the confirmation of the apportionment.'

23/54 Beeston St Andrew (parish) TG 257142 [Not listed]
Apt 28.04.1842; 625a (all); Map 1842, 6 chns, by Pratt and Sons, Norwich; waterbodies, houses, woods, parkland, gardens, fences, avenue of trees.

23/55 Beeston St Lawrence (parish) TG 329221
Apt 27.05.1838; 519a (519); Map surveyed in 1834, and corrected in 1839, 3 chns, by James Wright, Aylsham, Norfolk, and 2 Grove Pl, Brixton Rd, Kennington, London; foot/b'way, waterbodies, houses, woods, plantations, field boundary ownerships, building names, road names, driftway, churchyard.

23/56 Beetley and part of Great Bittering (district) TF 969180
Apt 30.09.1843; 2187a (all); Map 1844, 6 chns; waterbodies, houses, woods, road names, pits; pictorial church. Apt omits some land use.

23/57 Beighton (parish) TG 385082
Apt 29.06.1839; 1015a (1015); Map surveyed May 1839, 3 chns, in 2 parts, by T. M'Grane; construction lines, waterbodies, houses, pits, glebe (col).

23/58 Belaugh (parish) TG 292186
Apt 28.03.1839; 855a (854); Map 1839, 6 chns, by Pratt and Son, Norwich; waterbodies, houses, woods; north pointer has diadem and plumes.

23/59 Bergh Apton and Holveston (parish) TG 310010
Apt 29.06.1839; 2287a (2100); Map 1839, [3 chns], 1st cl, in 2 parts, by W.G. Jones, Loddon and Thos Burton Junr, Langley, Norfolk; construction lines, waterbodies, houses, woods, fences, field boundary ownerships, holding boundaries (col), modus land (green band); yellow bands are used for some bracing of farmyards etc.

23/60 Bessingham (parish) TG 168369
Apt 30.04.1839; 515a (all); Map 1841, 3 chns, by James Wright, Aylsham; foot/b'way, waterbodies, houses, woods, pit; pictorial church with tombstones.

23/61 Besthorpe (parish) TM 078961
Apt 11.03.1845; 2164a (2164); Map 1846, 3 chns, by J. Faxton, Attleburgh; railway; buildings are shown in outline only, without fill.

23/62 Bexwell (parish) TF 635025
Apt 31.01.1839; 1178a (1177); Map 1838, 9 chns, by Lenny and Croft,

Bury St Edmunds; turnpike roads, waterbodies, houses, woods, parkland, building names, pits, rectory.

23/63 Billingford (parish) TG 011212
Apt 18.08.1837; 1795a (1820); Map 1837, 6 chns, by Pratt and Son, Norwich; waterbodies, houses.

23/64 Billockby (parish) TG 431135
Apt 31.03.1838; 390a (all); Map 1838, [4 chns]; houses; table lists owners and occupiers.

23/65 East Bilney (parish) TF 952193
Apt 04.10.1838; 544a (all); Map 1838, 4.5 chns; waterbodies, houses, woods (col), plantations (col), parkland (col), arable (col), grassland (col), orchards (col), field names, field acreages.

23/66 Binham (parish) TF 975400
Apt 16.06.1838; 2243a (2242); Map 1838, 6 chns, in 2 parts, by W.G. Bircham, Fakenham, (includes enlargement of village at 3 chns); waterbodies, houses, woods, landowners (col), pit; tithe-free land is not coloured or numbered; north pointer has plumes and diadem.

23/67 Bintry (parish) TG 010234 [Bintree]
Apt 26.02.1844; 1456a (all); Map 1844, 6 chns, by Pratt and Son, Norwich; waterbodies, houses, woods, fox-coverts.

23/68 Great Bircham (parish) TF 765313
Apt 18.05.1838; 3607a (all); Map 1838, 12 chns; waterbodies, woods. Apt omits land use.

23/69 Bircham Newton (parish) TF 770345
Apt 11.05.1838; 1129a (all); Map 1838, 12 chns; waterbodies. Apt omits land use.

23/70 Bircham Tofts (parish) TF 782318
Apt 05.06.1838; 1432a (all); Map 1838, 12 chns; waterbodies, woods. Apt omits land use.

23/71 Little Bittering (parish) TF 942172 [Bittering]
Apt 14.09.1838; 398a (all); Map 1839, 4 chns, copied from the map by Bailey Bird dated 1797 by Thomas Bradfield, Litcham; houses, farmyards, plantations (col), arable (col), grassland (col); table lists field names and acreages.

23/72 Blickling (parish) TG 179288
Apt 10.05.1839; 2114a (2123); Map 1840, 3 chns, 1st cl, by Newton and Woodrow, Norwich; construction lines, waterbodies, houses, fences, field boundary ownerships, field gates, boundary trees, ice house, pits.

23/73 Blofield (parish) TG 330105
Apt 15.03.1845; 2334a (2334); Map 1845, 6 chns, in 3 parts, (includes enlargement of village at 3 chns); foot/b'way, waterbodies, houses, woods, parkland, private or occupation roads (uncoloured).

23/74 Blo Norton (parish) TM 019798 [Blo' Norton]
Apt 24.03.1838; 1132a (1132); Map 1838, 3 chns, surveyed in 1820 for enclosure purposes and revised by R. Payne; foot/b'way, waterbodies, houses, woods, building names, road names, meeting houses, windmill (pictorial), footbridge.

23/75 Bodham (parish) TG 123392
Apt 17.01.1842; 1688a (all); Map 1841, 3 chns, 1st cl, by James Wright, Aylsham; construction lines, waterbodies, houses, woods, osiers (by symbol), field boundary ownerships.

23/76 Bodney (parish) TL 850980
Apt 28.12.1839; 2571a (2605); Map 1842?, 6 chns; waterbodies, houses, woods (col), parkland (col), arable (col), grassland (col), building names, road names, wash pit, notable bushes.

23/77 Booton (parish) TG 121222
Apt 31.05.1839; 1041a (1040); Map 1839, 4.5 chns, by W.G. Bircham, Fakenham; waterbodies, houses, woods.

23/78 Boughton (parish) TF 705025
Apt 21.06.1842; 1324a (1323); Map 1840, 6 chns, by Charles Mumford, Downham Market, Norfolk; waterbodies; bridge named.

23/79 Bracon Ash (parish) TM 185997
Apt 20.09.1842; 975a (974); Map 1838, 3 chns, 1st cl, by William Drane, Norwich; construction lines, foot/b'way, waterbodies, houses, woods, fences, field boundary ownerships, field gates, avenue of trees, signpost (by symbol); grey-green bands are used for some bracing; detail in blue may be later correction.

23/80 East Bradenham (parish) TF 943088 [Bradenham]
Apt 31.03.1838; 2340a (2340); Map 1838, 6 chns, corrected from the enclosure survey of 1814 by W.G. Bircham, Fakenham; waterbodies, houses, woods, orchards, landowners (col), modus lands (col).

23/81 West Bradenham (parish) TF 918091 [Bradenham]
Apt 07.06.1838; 1683a (1682); Map 1838, 6 chns, by John Browne, Norwich; foot/b'way, waterbodies, houses, woods (col), plantations (col), parkland (col), park fence, arable (col), grassland (col), orchards (col), gardens (col), hedges, field boundary ownerships, landowners, gravel pit (col).

23/82 Bradfield (parish) TG 268302
Apt 21.10.1839; 757a (all); Map 1840, 3 chns, by Jame Wright, Aylsham; foot/b'way, waterbodies, houses, woods, field boundary ownerships, pits, stiles.

23/83 Bradiston (parish) TG 335086 [Not listed]
Apt 24.10.1844; 516a (all); Map 1845, 4.5 chns, by Pratt and Son, Norwich; railway, waterbodies, houses.

23/84 Bramerton (parish) TG 298048
Apt 12.04.1838; 729a (728); Map 1838, 3 chns, 1st cl, by William Drane, Norwich; construction lines, waterbodies, houses, woods, plantations, parkland, orchards, gardens, fences, field boundary ownerships, avenue of trees, boundary trees, pit; it is unclear what blue band means.

23/85 Brampton (parish) TG 219239
Apt 02.11.1837; 521a (521); Map 1837, 3 chns, by James Harford, Bristol; construction lines, waterbodies, houses, woods (col), osiers (by symbol, col), arable (col), grassland (col), orchards (col), gardens (col), hedges, fences, boundary tree, mill, glebe.

23/86 Brancaster (parish) TF 793443
Apt 27.03.1841; 3672a (all); Map 1841?, 6 chns, in 2 parts, by Edwin Durrant, Kings Lynn; waterbodies, houses, commons, marshes; creeks named.

23/87 Brandeston (parish) TG 139219 [Brandiston]
Apt 03.09.1841; 765a (764); Map 1841, 6 chns; waterbodies, woods; buildings are shown in outline only, without fill. Apt omits some field names.

23/88 Brandon Parva (parish) TG 066086
Apt 31.03.1838; 979a (all); Map 1838, 6 chns, by Newton and Woodrow, Norwich; waterbodies, houses, woods; pictorial church; north pointer has diadem and plumes.

23/89 Bressingham (parish) TM 082822
Apt 21.06.1842; 2354a (2354); Map 1841, 6 chns, by Henry Calver; waterbodies, woods, parkland, orchards, gardens, windmills (pictorial); map also includes district 23/90. Apt omits most land use.

23/90 Bressingham (district in parish of Bressingham) TM 088845
Apt 21.08.1847; 33a (all); Map (drawn on Apt) 1851?, 6 chns.

23/91 Brettenham (parish) TL 925845
Apt 12.09.1837; 1981a (all); Map 1838, 3 chns, 1st cl, by Thomas Burton Junr, Langley, Norfolk; construction lines, houses, woods, gardens, field boundary ownerships.

23/92 Bridgham (parish) TL 958862
Apt 17.02.1838; 2693a (2692); Map 1838, 6 chns, revised from the Award Map, as agreed by the landowners, by J. Eaton, Old Buckenham; waterbodies, houses, farmyards (col), woods (col), plantations (col), osiers (by symbol, col), arable (col), grassland (col), gardens (col), heath/moor, landowners, chalk pit, windmill; meaning of pink band is unclear.

23/93 Brinningham (parish) TG 030340
Apt 16.04.1838; 1202a (all); Map 1839, 6 chns, by Wm Glenister, Norwich; waterbodies, houses (by shading), woods, building names, windmills (pictorial), heath/moor.

23/94 Brinton (parish) TG 038358
Apt 12.04.1838; 626a (all); Map 1838, 6 chns, by Wm Glenister, Norwich; waterbodies, houses (by shading), woods, parkland.

23/95 Brisley (parish) TF 953212
Apt 11.03.1840; 1202a (all); Map 1838, 3 chns, in 2 parts, by Wm Glenister, Norwich; waterbodies, houses, woods, parkland, orchards, field boundary ownerships, rectory, cricket ground, commons (col), greens (col); bridge named.

23/96 Briston (parish) TG 067321
Apt 31.10.1844; 2751a (all); Map 1843, 6 chns, by C. Burcham, Lynn; waterbodies, houses, common (col).

23/97 Brockdish (parish) TM 209801
Apt 20.09.1838; 1070a (all); Map 1839, 6 chns, by Fredk W. Etheredge; waterbodies, woods, plantations, osiers (by symbol), gardens, drains; it is unclear why one glebe area is green.

23/98 Brome (parish) TM 348925
Apt 09.01.1840; 1443a (1442); Map 1840, 6 chns, by Pratt and Son, Norwich; gravel pit; pictorial church.

23/99 Brooke (parish) TM 285989
Apt 29.06.1839; 2135a (all); Map 1839, 6 chns; waterbodies, houses, woods, parkland. Apt omits some field names.

23/100 Brundall (parish) TG 321085
Apt 25.04.1838; 545a (544); Map 1838, 6 chns, by Pratt and Son, Norwich; waterbodies, houses, woods, parkland.

23/101 Brunstead (parish) TG 369268 [Not listed]
Apt 21.06.1842; 790a (all); Map 1840, 3 chns, 1st cl, by James Wright, Aylsham; construction lines, foot/b'way, waterbodies, houses, field boundary ownerships.

23/102 Buckenham (parish) TG 359058
Apt 22.07.1837; 931a (931); Map 1838?, 3 chns; waterbodies, houses, windmill (pictorial), pit, ferry; pictorial church.

23/103 New Buckenham (parish) TM 093903
Apt 18.02.1848; 53a (324); Map 1850, 4 chns, (tithable parts only); turnpike roads, houses, landowners, milestone, market cross.

23/104 Old Buckenham (parish) TM 069919
Apt 26.05.1841; 4986a (4986); Map 1842, 4 chns, 1st cl, by J. Eaton, Attleburgh; construction lines; buildings are shown in outline only, without infill.

23/105 Bunwell (parish) TM 131930
Apt 24.12.1838; 2443a (2470); Map 1839?, 6 chns; woods; buildings are shown in outline only, without infill. Apt omits most field names.

23/106 Burgh next Aylsham (parish) TG 219251
Apt 07.08.1839; 789a (789); Map 1839, 6 chns, by Pratt and Son, Norwich; waterbodies, houses, woods, orchards, gardens, pit, boundary stump.

23/107 Burgh or Burgh St Margaret and Burgh St Mary (parish) TG 448141 [Burgh St Margaret (Fleggburgh)]
Apt 04.10.1837; 1655a (1655); Map 1838, 3 chns, by J.T. Brown and Josh. Manning, Norwich; waterbodies, houses, woods (col), parkland (col), grassland (col), gardens, windmills (pictorial), ruined church (pictorial), drains. Apt omits some field names.

23/108 Burgh St Peter (parish) TM 482938
Apt 29.11.1838; 2042a (2041); Map 1843?, 3 chns, 1st cl, by Richd Barnes, Lowestoft; construction lines, waterbodies, ferry; pictorial church; buildings and ponds are shown in outline only, without infill.

23/109 Burlingham St Andrew (parish) TG 361102 [Not listed]
Apt 03.05.1839; 751a (all); Map 1838, 3 chns, surveyed by J.P. Luckraft and Co; waterbodies, houses, woods, orchards, gardens, parsonage, pit.

23/110 Burlingham St Edmund (parish) TG 372079 [Not listed]
Apt 03.05.1839; 661a (661); Map 1839?, 3 chns, in 2 parts; waterbodies, houses, woods, orchards, gardens, pits, boundary post; one detached portion is mapped both in situ and independently.

23/111 Burlingham St Peter (parish) TG 372101 [Not listed]
Apt 10.03.1841; 405a (all); Map 1838, 3 chns, surveyed by J.P. Luckraft and Co; waterbodies, houses, woods, plantations, parkland, orchards, gardens, hall.

23/112 Burnham Deepdale (parish) TF 809438
Apt 29.05.1845; 1061a (all); Map 1840, 3 chns, by J. Manning, 64 Bethel St, Norwich; waterbodies, houses, woods, pits, embankment; pictorial church.

23/113 Burnham Norton (parish) TF 827438
Apt 19.06.1838; 3227a (all); Map 1839?, 6 chns; waterbodies, houses, sea bank, sluices.

23/114 Burnham Overy (parish) TF 851441 [Burnham Overy Town]
Apt 19.06.1838; 2299a (2548); Map 1840?, 6 chns; foot/b'way, waterbodies, houses, sluice, old and new channels, harbour, beach, salt marsh, tithe ownership boundary.

23/115 Burnham Sutton or Sutton cum St Andrew (parish) TF 833410 [Not listed]
Apt 19.06.1838; 1453a (1452); Map 1840?, 10 chns; waterbodies, houses, woods, pit, glebe, ownership boundaries (col); pictorial church.

23/116 Burnham Thorpe (parish) TF 857412
Apt 11.05.1838; 2329a (3228); Map 1838?, [9 chns]; houses, woods (col), parkland (col), ownership boundaries (col), glebe, modus land; pictorial church.

23/117 Burnham Westgate (parish) TF 816412 [Not listed]
Apt 15.09.1837; 3048a (3047); Map 1837, 4 chns, by J.T. Brown, Norwich; principal construction lines, woods, windmill (pictorial), pits; pictorial church; buildings are shown in outline only.

23/118 Burston (parish) TM 137840
Apt 09.07.1839; 1400a (all); Map 1839, [6 chns], by Fredk W. Etheredge; waterbodies. Apt omits most field names.

23/119 Buxton (parish) TG 231226
Apt 03.09.1841; 1274a (1274); Map 1842, 6 chns, by Newton and Woodrow, Norwich; waterbodies, houses, woods, vicarage; pictorial church.

23/120 Bylaugh (parish) TG 035190 [Not listed]
Apt 22.01.1841; 1543a (1546); Map 1842?, 6 chns; houses, driftway, lodge, hall, heath, drains; pictorial church.

23/121 Caister (parish) TG 511122 [Caister-on-Sea]
Apt 18.08.1841; 2926a (all); Map 1842?, 9 chns, in 2 parts, (includes 3-chn enlargement of detail); pictorial church; buildings are shown in outline only, without infill.

23/122 Caister St Edmunds with Marketshall (parish with hamlet) TG 238039 [Caistor St Edmund]
Apt 14.07.1838; 1593a (all); Map 1838, 3 chns, 1st cl, in 2 parts; construction lines, waterbodies, houses, woods, parkland, building names, landowners, hamlet boundary.

23/123 Caldecot (parish) TF 752036 [Not listed]
Apt 24.01.1851; 50a (930); Map 1851?, 4 chns, (surveyed in 1722 by Philip Wissiter); woods, field gates, road names, field names; buildings are shown by outline elevation drawings; a scale of perches has been struck through, and one of chains added; tithable lands are numbered and tinted; table lists acreages. Apt omits land use.

23/124 Calthorpe (parish) TG 180318
Apt 31.10.1839; 1048a (1048); Map 1840, 6 chns, by Newton and Woodrow, Norwich; waterbodies, houses, woods, pound; bridge named; pictorial church.

23/125 Cantley (parish) TG 380044
Apt 03.07.1837; 1850a (1850); Map 1837, 6 chns; waterbodies, houses, drains, modus land (col); pictorial church.

23/126 Carbrooke (parish) TF 951018
Apt 07.01.1840; 3033a (3033); Map 1839, 3 chns; woods (col), orchards, road names, mills, holding and ownership boundaries (col); pictorial church.

23/127 Carleton (parish) TG 344023 [Carleton St Peter]
Apt 10.09.1838; 773a (772); Map 1839, 4 chns, copied by Thos Burton Jun, Langley, Norfolk; waterbodies, houses, ferry, cross (pictorial); pictorial church.

23/128 Carleton Rode (parish) TM 106930
Apt 21.01.1839; 2631a (all); Map 1839, 3 chns, by John Eaton, Old Buckenham; waterbodies, houses, private roads (col). Apt omits most field names.

23/129 Carleton St Mary and Carleton St Peter (district) TG 177020 [East Carleton]
Apt 20.12.1848; 1213a (?); Map 1850, 3 chns, 1st cl, by Willm Drane, Norwich; construction lines, foot/b'way, right of way, waterbodies, houses, parkland, fences, field boundary ownerships, pound, ice house, pit, lodge, glebe.

23/130 Castleacre (parish) TF 815165 [Castle Acre]
Apt 10.09.1838; 3249a (3249); Map 1837, 1st cl, [3 chns]; construction lines, houses, field names, landowners, castle with earthworks, priory ruins, modus lands, water meadows; 'TWC' in fields indicates Earl of Leicester's property.

23/131 Castle Rising (parish) TF 668246
Apt 09.08.1837; 2097a (all); Map 1838, 6 chns; houses, woods, parkland, gardens, building names, castle with earthworks, keep, pit, windmill (pictorial); pictorial church, drains. Apt omits some land use.

23/132 Caston (parish) TL 960977
Apt 20.04.1847; 1557a (all); Map 1847, 6 chns; houses; uninhabited buildings are shown in outline only.

23/133 Catfield (parish) TG 399215
Apt 16.10.1840; 2393a (2393); Map 1840, 6 chns, in 2 parts, by Newton and Woodrow, Norwich; waterbodies, houses, woods, windpump (pictorial), private road; dyke named.

23/134 Catton (parish) TG 230121 [Old Catton]
Apt 12.06.1843; 925a (895); Map 1843, 6 chns, by W.S. Millard and Son; houses, woods, parkland.

23/135 Cawston (parish) TG 149240
Apt 24.11.1843; 4297a (all); Map 1840, 9 chns, in 2 parts, (includes enlargement of village at 3 chns); houses.

23/136 Chedgrave (parish) TM 361995
Apt 19.12.1838; 1433a (1432); Map 1838, 3 chns, in 2 parts, by Thos Burton Junr, Langley, Norfolk; construction lines, waterbodies, houses, cross (pictorial); colour bands show modus and tithe-free land.

23/137 Claxton (parish) TG 336036
Apt 11.02.1846; 992a (all); Map 1846, 3 chns, ? by Thos Burton Junr, Langley, Norfolk; waterbodies, houses, woods, abbey (named in gothic); pictorial church.

23/138 Clenchwarton (district) TF 588203
Apt 15.12.1843; 2115a (3505); Map 1844, 6 chns, in 3 parts, by Edwin Durrant, Kings Lynn, (tithable parts only); waterbodies, houses, roadside common (col), tithe-free land (red). Apt omits most field names.

23/139 Cley next the Sea (parish) TG 053433
Apt 22.11.1838; 2199a (all); Map 1841, 6 chns, in 2 parts, (includes enlargement of village at 2 chns); woods, limekiln; buildings are shown in outline only, without infill.

23/140 Clippesby (parish) TG 426135
Apt 12.06.1839; 861a (all); Map 1838, 8 chns, 'Revised and Drawn' by Issac Lenny, Norwich; foot/b'way, waterbodies, houses, woods (col), parkland (col), arable (col), grassland (col), gardens (col), field gates, building names, former common field name, mile iron, stiles; pictorial church. Apt omits land use other than arable.

23/141 All Saints and St Peters, Cockley Cley (parishes) TF 800046 [Cockley Cley]
Apt 27.01.1841; 4312a (4312); Map 1845, 6 chns; waterbodies, woods, field names, mansion house, cottages, gamekeeper's house, field acreages, parish boundary; pictorial church. Apt omits land use and field names.

23/142 Cockthorpe (parish) TF 985422
Apt 08.03.1839; 514a (514); Map 1841, 6 chns; waterbodies, houses, woods, plantations, orchards, osiers (by symbol); pictorial church.

23/143 Colby (parish) TG 221311
Apt 12.06.1839; 1115a (all); Map 1839, 3 chns, surveyed and corrected by James Wright, Aylsham; foot/b'way, waterbodies, houses, woods, field boundary ownerships, stiles.

23/144 Colkirk (parish) TF 930260
Apt 19.06.1838; 1482a (1482); Map 1840, 6 chns, by W.G. Bircham, Fakenham; waterbodies, houses, woods, plantations, commons; pictorial church.

23/145 Colney (parish) TG 178077
Apt 31.05.1839; 948a (948); Map 1839?, 5 chns; woods, parkland, landowners; pictorial church; scale is graduated in poles. Apt omits most field names.

23/146 Coltishall, and parts of Sco Ruston and Scottow (parish) TG 279202
Apt 05.02.1840; 1218a (1180); Map 1841, 3 chns; waterbodies, houses, gardens, residual open fields, road names, mills, river lock; pictorial church; some uninhabited buildings are grey and some are brown.

23/147 Colton (parish) TG 106093
Apt 25.07.1846; 912a (all); Map 1846, 6 chns, by John Atmore, Barford; waterbodies, houses, woods; pictorial church; scale has miniature north pointers at each end.

23/148 Colvestone (parish) TL 794957 [Not listed]
Apt 20.09.1843; 861a (all); Map 1842, 6 chns, by Lenny and Croft, Bury St Edmunds; waterbodies, houses, woods, parkland, gardens, field gates, building names, brick kiln, footbridges, pit, boat house, signpost, heath.

23/149 Congham (parish) TF 721238
Apt 08.12.1837; 2851a (2850); Map 1838, 6 chns, by Newton and Woodrow, Norwich; hill-drawing, waterbodies, houses, woods, parkland, landowners (col), tithe owners (in red), pits, windmill (pictorial); hill named.

23/150 Corpusty (parish) TG 101295
Apt 11.06.1838; 1019a (1018); Map 1839, 6 chns; waterbodies, houses, pits; pictorial church.

23/151 Costessy (parish) TG 171115
Apt 18.01.1840; 3041a (3040); Map 1839, 6 chns, by J. Manning, Surveyor and Lithographer, Norwich, litho; hill-drawing, woods, parkland; pictorial church.

23/152 Coston (parish) TG 063062
Apt 16.05.1842; 343a (all); Map 1842?, 4 chns; waterbodies, houses, woods (col), arable (col), grassland (col), gardens (col).

23/153 Cranwick (parish) TL 777945 [Cranwich]
Apt 15.02.1838; 1824a (all); Map 1843, 6 chns, by Lenny and Croft, Bury St Edmunds; waterbodies, houses, plantations, parkland, heath/moor, fences, boundary stones (by symbol), Devils Dyke, hall, rectory, sluices, glebe.

23/154 Cranworth (parish) TF 982047
Apt 16.6.1838; 1127a (1126); Map '1838-9', 6 chns, by Issac Lenny, Norwich; foot/b'way, waterbodies, houses, orchards, gardens, landowners, post, direction post (by symbol), boundary tree, rectory; lawns, stackyard, garden, orchards and osiers are shown by annotation.

23/155 North Creake (parish) TF 843382
Apt 20.03.1839; 3602a (3601); Map 1839, 6 chns, by W.G. Bircham, Fakenham; waterbodies, houses, woods, gardens, pit; pictorial church; north pointer has diadem and plumes.

23/156 South Creake (parish) TF 861357
Apt 07.07.1838; 4146a (all); Map 1839, 6 chns, by W.G. Bircham, Fakenham; waterbodies, houses, woods, windmill (pictorial), commons.

23/157 Great Cressingham (parish) TF 852018
Apt 26.02.1839; 2424a (all); Map 1839, 3 chns, by J. Utting, Lynn Regis; waterbodies, houses; scale-bar is ruler-like.

23/158 Little Cressingham (parish) TL 867990
Apt 12.07.1843; 1826a (all); Map 1843?, 6 chns; waterbodies, houses, ford; pictorial church; colours show lands tithable to another district, and glebe.

23/159 Crimplesham (parish) TF 648040
Apt 31.10.1839; 1623a (all); Map 1840?, 6.67 chns, by Edwin Durrant, Kings Lynn; waterbodies, private roads (col).

23/160 Cringleford (parish) TG 191058
Apt 01.02.1842; 981a (all); Map 1842?, 6 chns; waterbodies, woods.

23/161 Cromer (parish) TG 214416
Apt 19.05.1843; 851a (all); Map 1844, 3 chns, 1st cl, by John F. Deyns, North Walsham; construction lines, waterbodies, houses, field boundary ownerships.

23/162 Crostwick (parish) TG 261157
Apt 04.10.1837; 691a (all); Map 1839?, 3 chns, by W.S. Millard, Norwich; waterbodies, houses, woods, toll gate, common; pictorial church.

23/163 Crostwight or Crostwick (parish) TG 336288
Apt 11.06.1838; 777a (777); Map 1838?, 6 chns; waterbodies, houses (dark grey), grassland (col).

23/164 Crownthorpe (parish) TG 088030
Apt 20.05.1841; 685a (696); Map 1841, 9 chns, by A.T. Clarke, Norwich; waterbodies, houses; modus land is not mapped; north pointer has plumes and diadem and scale-bar has miniature north pointers at each end.

23/165 Croxton (parish) TL 875875
Apt 20.03.1844; 4610a (all); Map 1845?, 9 chns; houses. Apt omits land use.

23/166 Darsingham (parish) TF 702302 [Dersingham]
Apt 03.04.1840; 3473a (3472); Map 1839, 6 chns; hill-drawing, waterbodies, houses, woods, pit, embankments.

23/167 Denton (parish) TM 280885
Apt 24.05.1839; 2437a (all); Map 1839, [6.67 chns], by Fredk Wm Etheredge; waterbodies, houses, woods, parkland, fords. Apt omits some field names.

23/168 Denver (parish) TF 595007
Apt 12.04.1838; 3150a (all); Map 1837, 4 chns, 'Copied and Corrected from Old Survey' by Charles Mumford, Downham; waterbodies, houses, woods (col), plantations (col), landowners, pound, moat, sluices, drift, rough pasture, church land; fens and drove named. Apt has a note, 'The great quantity of Fen Land which lays as pasture three or four years and then corn cropped again renders it impossible to return the correct proportion of Arable and Pasture.'

23/169 Deopham (parish) TG 050005
Apt 25.06.1842; 1647a (all); Map 1843, 6 chns, by W.S. Millard and Son, Norwich; waterbodies, houses, woods, pits.

23/170 East Dereham with Dillington (parish and hamlet) TF 999131
Apt 11.07.1838; 5223a (5222); Map 1838, 6 chns, in 4 parts, by Pratt and Son, Norwich; houses, (includes town separately at 1.5 chns and 12-chn index); moor, green; on the main map, uninhabited buildings are shown in outline only, without infill.

23/171 West Dereham (parish) TF 662015
Apt 14.08.1845; 3272a (3440); Map 1845, 6 chns, by C. Burcham, Lynn; waterbodies, houses.

23/172 Dickleburgh (parish) TM 178828
Apt 11.03.1840; 2344a (all); Map 1843, 6 chns, in 2 parts, by Wm Browne, Surveyor and Lithographer, Norwich, (includes enlargement of village at 3 chns), litho; waterbodies, houses, woods, parsonage, pound, greens, common, moor; houses and roads are hand-coloured.

23/173 Didlington (parish) TL 789971
Apt 19.09.1843; 1854a (1854); Map 1844, 6 chns, by W.S. Millard and Son, Norwich; waterbodies, houses, woods, parkland, avenue of trees.

23/174 Dilham (parish) TG 332260
Apt 11.06.1838; 1563a (all); Map 1840, 3 chns, 1st cl, by James Wright, Aylsham; construction lines, waterbodies, houses, woods, field boundary ownerships, canal with locks and towpath, brickworks.

23/175 Diss (parish) TM 124832
Apt 16.08.1837; 3628a (3627); Map 1838, 6 chns, by Henry Calver; waterbodies, woods, windmills (pictorial).

23/176 Ditchingham (parish) TM 332921
Apt 26.08.1839; 2083a (all); Map 1839?, 8 chns, by Geo. Baker, Bungay; foot/b'way, waterbodies, pits; buildings and ponds are shown in outline only, without infill.

23/177 Docking (parish) TF 770370
Apt 19.11.1840; 5114a (all); Map 1843?, 6 chns, by Josh. Manning, Norwich; foot/b'way, waterbodies, houses, woods, road names, windmills (pictorial), workhouse, pit.

23/178 Downham Market (parish) TF 610030
Apt 03.09.1840; 2491a (2490); Map 1841, 6 chns, by Charles Mumford, Downham Market; workhouse, windmill (by symbol).

23/179 Drayton (parish) TG 185135
Apt 13.04.1839; 1332a (1332); Map 1839, 6 chns, by Robert Pratt, Norwich; waterbodies, houses; north pointer has diadem and plumes.

23/180 Great Dunham (parish) TF 868150
Apt 27.02.1838; 1968a (1968); Map 1838, 6 chns, by Newton and Woodrow, Norwich; houses, woods, ownerships (col), field names, hall.

23/181 Little Dunham (parish) TF 861132
Apt 16.05.1838; 1837a (all); Map 1838, 3 chns, by J. Utting, Lynn Regis; waterbodies, houses.

23/182 Dunston (parish) TG 224024
Apt 13.11.1846; 617a (all); Map 1849, 5 chns, by Willm Drane, Norwich; railway, turnpike roads, waterbodies, ownerships (col); pictorial church; owners are named in table. District is apportioned by holding and fields are not shown; Apt generalises land use.

23/183 Dunton (parish) TF 880308
Apt 13.07.1837; 1721a (1721); Map 1838, [3 chns], 1st cl; construction lines, waterbodies, houses, woods, osiers (by symbol), field boundary ownerships, field names, pits, footbridge, boundary stone, wash pot.

23/184 Earlham St Mary Norwich (parish) TG 199086 [Earlham]
Apt 26.08.1845; 1255a (all); Map 1846, 6 chns; foot/b'way, turnpike roads, waterbodies, houses, woods, toll gate; pictorial church.

23/185 Earsham (parish) TM 310894
Apt 08.03.1839; 3052a (3052); Map 1840, 5 chns, by Geo. Baker, Bungay; waterbodies, houses, private roads (uncoloured).

23/186 Easton (parish) TG 138109
Apt 12.06.1843; 1576a (1576); Map 1844?, 6 chns, in 6 parts, (includes five 3-chn enlargement of detail by Newton and Woodrow, Norwich, ?1844); turnpike roads, canal, old canal, waterbodies, houses, woods, plantations, orchards, building names, road names; colours may show tithable status.

23/187 Eaton (parish) TG 210063
Apt 05.06.1839; 1290a (?); Map 1838, 3 chns, by Joseph Manning, Norwich; construction lines, houses.

23/188 Eccles (parish) TM 011891 [Eccles Road]
Apt 27.03.1838; 1685a (?); Map 1838?, [6 chns]; waterbodies, houses, woods (col), plantations (col), arable (col), grassland (col), orchards (col), gardens (col), landowners, glebe (lilac); table lists field names and acreages. Apt omits land use.

23/189 Eccles next the Sea (parish) TG 414288
Apt 12.11.1840; 297a (all); Map 1839, 6 chns; waterbodies, houses, cart gap; pictorial ruined church; sea is decorated with a neat drawing of a paddle-steamer, with lifeboat and plumes of smoke.

23/190 Edgefield (parish) TG 095348
Apt 02.11.1844; 2436a (all); Map 1845, 6 chns, by C. Burcham, Kings Lynn; foot/b'way, waterbodies, houses (black), woods, pits, droves (col); pictorial church. Apt omits most field names.

23/191 Edingthorpe (parish) TG 315323
Apt 06.04.1839; 710a (all); Map 1840, 6 chns, by James Wright, Aylsham; waterbodies, houses, woods, pits; church and churchyard are shown pictorially, with sky background.

23/192 Egmere (parish) TF 896376
Apt 31.03.1838; 1238a (1237); Map 1838, 3 chns, 1st cl, by Pratt and Son, Norwich; construction lines, houses, field boundary ownerships.

23/193 Ellingham (parish) TM 362923
Apt 09.01.1840; 1338a (1379); Map 1840, 9 chns; waterbodies, houses, woods, osiers (by symbol), parkland, mills, pits; pictorial church; scale has miniature north pointers at each end.

23/194 Great Ellingham (parish) TM 021972
Apt 16.12.1843; 2670a (2670); Map 1844?, 6 chns, by Pratt and Son, Norwich; waterbodies, houses, tithe ownerships (col).

23/195 Little Ellingham (parish) TM 002990
Apt 31.05.1839; 1540a (all); Map 1840, 6 chns, by A.T. Clarke, Norwich; waterbodies, houses, woods, common; north pointer has plumes.

23/196 North Elmham (parish) TF 979222
Apt 29.09.1838; 4631a (4631); Map 1839, 6 chns, by Wm Glenister, Norwich; waterbodies, houses (by shading), woods, plantations, parkland, gardens, marsh/bog, windmill (pictorial), hall, keeper's lodge, holly bush; scale-bar is ruler-like.

23/197 Elsing (parish) TG 051166
Apt 31.01.1839; 1420a (all); Map 1841?, 6 chns, in 5 parts, (includes three 3-chn enlargements of detail); waterbodies, houses, mill, hall, commons, heath, green; bridge named; pictorial church.

23/198 Emneth (parish) TF 501074
Apt 02.01.1844; 3449a (3449); Map 1844, 6 chns; turnpike roads, waterbodies, houses, drains; bridge named.

23/199 Erpingham (parish) TG 198302
Apt 10.05.1839; 1386a (1381); Map 1839, 3 chns, by William Drane, Norwich; waterbodies, houses, windmill (pictorial); pictorial church, with a man and a woman walking towards it.

23/200 Fakenham (parish) TF 932311
Apt 25.08.1843; 2209a (2208); Map 1844, 6 chns, by F. Tinkley, Fakenham, (includes enlargement of town at 3 chns); waterbodies, houses, woods, osiers (by symbol), rectory, churchyard, market place, commons, windmill; orange-brown band shows land which in practice pays no tithe.

23/201 Felbrigg (parish) TG 201395
Apt 07.11.1842; 1558a (1557); Map 1843, 9 chns, by James Wright, Aylsham; foot/b'way, waterbodies, houses (dark grey), woods, parkland, orchards, gardens, heath/moor, pits, modus lands; pictorial church.

23/202 Felmingham (parish) TG 249290
Apt 31.10.1839; 1887a (all); Map 1840, 3 chns, 1st cl, by James Wright, Aylsham; construction lines, foot/b'way, waterbodies, houses, woods, field boundary ownerships, stiles.

23/203 Felthorpe (parish) TG 165177
Apt 28.04.1840; 2286a (2286); Map 1840, 6 chns; houses, sand pit.

23/204 St Mary and St Nicholas in Feltwell (parish) TL 687910 [Feltwell]
Apt 09.08.1837; 13200a (14060); Map 1837, 6 chns, by Lenny and Croft, Bury St Edmunds; turnpike roads, waterbodies, houses, woods, parkland, gardens, heath/moor, fences, avenues of trees, lodge, pits, mere pits, rectory, pound, notable oak (pictorial), windmills (pictorial), windpumps (pictorial), drove names, church dedications, commons.

23/205 Fersfield (parish) TM 068831
Apt 16.05.1839; 1386a (1386); Map 1840, 6 chns, by Lenny and Croft, Bury St Edmunds; waterbodies, houses, woods, parkland, orchards, fences, windmill (pictorial).

23/206 Filby (parish) TG 477134
Apt 13.07.1837; 1425a (1425); Map 1838, 2 chns, surveyed by J. Manning, 64 Bethel St, Norwich; construction lines, foot/b'way, waterbodies, houses, woods, plantations, alder cars, field boundary ownerships. Apt omits most field names.

23/207 Field Dalling (parish) TG 009389
Apt 31.10.1839; 1620a (all); Map 1840, 3 chns, 1st cl, by James Wright, Aylsham; construction lines, waterbodies, houses, woods, road names.

23/208 Fincham St Michael and Fincham St Martin (parish) TF 693058 [Fincham]
Apt 30.05.1840; 2969a (2968); Map 1839, 6 chns; waterbodies, houses, private roads (uncoloured).

23/209 Fishley (parish) TG 399115
Apt 12.03.1841; 476a (all); Map 1838, 3 chns; turnpike roads, waterbodies, houses, woods (col), arable (col), grassland (col), gardens (col), fences, field gates, pits, drainage mill (by symbol), glebe.

23/210 Flitcham (parish) TF 723268
Apt 24.08.1838; 3325a (3325); Map 1838, 6 chns, by Pratt and Son, Norwich; waterbodies, houses, footbridges, common.

23/211 Flordon (parish) TM 190977
Apt 23.02.1843; 930a (all); Map 1842, 6 chns, in 4 parts, by Pratt and Sons, Norwich, (including three 3-chn enlargements of residual open fields); buildings are shown in outline only, without infill.

23/212 Fordham (parish) TL 595995
Apt 11.03.1840; 2205a (all); Map 1839, 6 chns; houses, drainage mills (by symbol), riverside towpath, drains.

23/213 Forncett St Mary (parish) TM 168952
Apt 23.10.1840; 729a (all); Map 1841?, 3 chns; waterbodies, houses; pictorial church. Apt omits most field names.

23/214 Forncett St Peter (parish) TM 150931
Apt 23.10.1840; 1829a (all); Map 1839, 6 chns, by Newton and Woodrow, Norwich; waterbodies, houses, woods, private roads (uncoloured); pictorial church.

23/215 Foulden (parish) TL 770992
Apt 17.09.1839; 3396a (3395); Map 1838, 3 chns; waterbodies, houses, woods, plantations, osiers (by symbol), parkland, gardens, heath/moor, building names, road names, fish ponds, drainage banks, water mill, gravel pit.

23/216 Foulsham (parish) TG 040249
Apt 07.12.1838; 3226a (3226); Map 1838, 6 chns, by John Wright, Aylsham; foot/b'way, waterbodies, houses, woods (col), arable (col), grassland (col), gardens (col), windmills (by symbol), private roads (uncoloured), modus lands.

23/217 Foxley (parish) TG 041221
Apt 11.03.1839; 1620a (1620); Map 1840?, 6 chns; waterbodies, houses, common, former park.

23/218 Framingham Pigot (parish) TG 279040
Apt 06.02.1841; 608a (all); Map 1840, 6 chns, by A.T. Clarke, Norwich; waterbodies, houses, woods, plantations, parkland, residual open fields, pits; pictorial church.

23/219 Great Fransham (parish) TF 906133
Apt 27.09.1838; 1882a (all); Map 1838, 6 chns, by W.G. Bircham, Fakenham; houses, woods, gardens, landowners, avenue of trees, windmill (pictorial); pictorial church. Apt omits land use.

23/220 Little Fransham (parish) TF 905121
Apt 26.04.1838; 1030a (all); Map 1838, [6 chns]; waterbodies, houses, woods; pictorial church.

23/221 Freethorpe (parish) TG 409053
Apt 08.06.1840; 869a (869); Map 1841, 4.5 chns, by Pratt and Sons, Norwich; foot/b'way, waterbodies, houses, woods, building names, boundary trees, brickworks.

23/222 Frenze (parish) TM 140800
Apt 13.06.1839; 399a (399); Map 1839, 6 chns; waterbodies, woods, osiers (by symbol), parkland; pictorial church; bridge named.

23/223 Frettenham and Stanninghall (parish) TG 246184
Apt 24.01.1840; 1896a (1904); Map 1840, 3 chns, by James Wright, Aylsham; foot/b'way, waterbodies, houses, woods, field boundary ownerships, pits, township boundary.

23/224 Fring (parish) TF 741345
Apt 09.06.1840; 1710a (all); Map 1838, 6 chns; waterbodies, houses, woods, parkland, pits.

23/225 Fritton (parish) TM 229931
Apt 20.09.1838; 820a (all); Map 1839, 6 chns, by Pratt and Son, Norwich; foot/b'way, waterbodies, houses, woods, orchards, fences, field names, boundary trees, common (col); pictorial church; it is unclear why some fields are pink.

23/226 Fulmodeston with Croxton (parish) TF 992301
Apt 12.09.1837; 2334a (2333); Map 1838?, 6 chns, in 3 parts, by Pratt and Son, Norwich; waterbodies, houses, windmill (pictorial).

23/227 Fundenhall (parish) TM 147963
Apt 18.06.1840; 1348a (1347); Map 1840, 6 chns; waterbodies, houses, woods; pictorial church.

23/228 Garboldisham (parish) TM 005823
Apt 18.01.1840; 2705a (all); Map 1842, 5 chns; waterbodies; churches are shown by name, but the buildings are not mapped.

23/229 Garvestone (parish) TG 027085
Apt 26.08.1839; 802a (802); Map 1839, 6 chns, by Newton and Woodrow, Norwich; waterbodies, houses; pictorial church.

23/230 Gasthorpe (parish) TL 981817
Apt 09.06.1840; 864a (864); Map 1838, 6 chns; houses, woods, plantations, pits; as well as the main feathery north pointer, there are similar smaller ones at each of the scale-bar.

23/231 Gateley (parish) TF 961252
Apt 11.03.1840; 1490a (all); Map 1839, 6 chns; waterbodies, houses (by shading), common, woods, osiers (by symbol), orchards, gardens; scale-bar is ruler-like.

23/232 Gatesend or Tattersett (parish) TF 855301
Apt 13.07.1839; 1758a (all); Map 1839, 6 chns, by W.G. Bircham, Fakenham; waterbodies, houses, plantations, hops, gardens, building names, ford.

23/233 Gayton (parish) TF 740200
Apt 13.04.1839; 3273a (all); Map 1839, 6 chns; waterbodies, houses, droveways (col).

23/234 Gayton Thorpe (parish) TF 751185
Apt 22.09.1842; 2356a (2355); Map 1840, 6 chns, by Wm Drane, Norwich; waterbodies, houses, woods, osiers (by symbol, col), plantations, heath/moor; pictorial church.

23/235 Gaywood (parish) TF 640207
Apt 23.07.1838; 2335a (all); Map 1838, 6 chns, in 3 parts, (includes enlargement of village at 3 chns); turnpike roads, waterbodies, houses, woods, osiers (by symbol), plantations, embankment, toll bars.

23/236 Geldeston (parish) TM 396921
Apt 07.02.1838; 821a (820); Map not dated, [6 chns]; modus lands.

23/237 Gillingham All Saints and Gillingham St Mary (parish) TM 415926 [Gillingham]
Apt 26.11.1844; 2008a (all); Map 1840, 6 chns; foot/b'way, waterbodies, houses, woods, parkland, gardens, windmill (pictorial); pictorial churches.

23/238 Gimingham (parish) TG 285371
Apt 06.05.1839; 1471a (1491); Map 1839, 3 chns, by James Wright, Aylsham; foot/b'way, waterbodies, houses, woods, osiers (by symbol), pits; north pointer has crown; 'A Map' in leafy letters in map title is on sky background.

23/239 Gissing (parish) TM 150855
Apt 14.12.1839; 1981a (1981); Map 1840, 6 chns, by W.S. Millard and Son, Norwich; houses.

23/240 Glandford (parish) TG 043411
Apt 16.03.1839; 364a (all); Map 1838, 4.5 chns; waterbodies, houses, woods (col), plantations (col), arable (col), grassland (col), field names, landowners, gravel pit, churchyard, ford, footbridge, glebe; north pointer has plumes; fields are either named or else have the owner named.

23/241 Gooderstone (parish) TL 779995
Apt 11.03.1840; 2782a (all); Map 1838, 3 chns, 1st cl; construction lines, waterbodies, houses, woods, field boundary ownerships, public drain, windmill, pound, pit, bank, fences, windmill (by symbol).

23/242 Gresham (parish) TG 167385
Apt 07.11.1842; 1304a (all); Map 1842, 9 chns, by James Wright, Aylsham, (tinted); waterbodies, woods (col); pictorial church.

23/243 Gressenhall and part of Great Bittering (district) TF 959155
Apt 30.08.1843; 2541a (all); Map 1844, 8 chns, by Mann and Son, Norwich, litho (by R.B. Coe, Norwich); waterbodies, workhouse.

23/244 Griston (parish) TL 943992
Apt 16.01.1840; 1360a (1360); Map 1840, 5 chns, copied from the enclosure award map by W. Fendick; pictorial church. Apt omits field names.

23/245 Guestwick (parish) TG 055275
Apt 19.02.1847; 1646a (1646); Map 1845, [6 chns], by Sands, Reepham; waterbodies, houses.

23/246 Guist (parish) TG 001261
Apt 15.05.1845; 1674a (1674); Map 1846, 6 chns, by Newton and Woodrow, Norwich; waterbodies, houses, woods, plantations, pits.

23/247 Gunthorpe (parish) TG 013351
Apt 31.10.1838; 1087a (1087); Map 1838, 6 chns; foot/b'way, waterbodies, houses, woods, parkland, gardens, pits, hall, land tithable elsewhere, droveways (col); pictorial church.

23/248 Gunton (parish) TG 232338 [Not listed]
Apt 23.05.1838; 945a (all); Map surveyed in 1830, with 'The Alterations taken and Maps adjusted to' 1839, 3 chns, by James Wright, 2 Grove Place, Brixton Rd, Kennington, London, and Aylsham, Norfolk; foot/b'way, waterbodies (named), houses, woods, parkland, gardens, building names, chapel, lodges.

23/249 Hackford (parish) TG 056026
Apt 23.11.1839; 754a (all); Map 1840, 3 chns, by W.S. Millard and Son, Norwich; houses. Apt omits some field names.

23/250 Hackford next Reepham (parish) TG 085227 [Not listed]
Apt 28.03.1844; 816a (all); Map 1844, 6 chns, in 2 parts, ? by Sands, Reepham, (includes enlargement of village at 3 chns); foot/b'way, waterbodies, houses.

23/251 Haddiscoe (parish) TM 446970
Apt 09.06.1840; 2072a (2071); Map 1841, 6 chns, by Thomas Barton Junr, Langley, Norfolk; houses, plantations, parkland (col), orchards (col), gardens (col), pits, droves or driftways (col); pictorial church.

23/252 Hales (parish) TM 381963
Apt 17.10.1838; 980a (980); Map 1839, 6 chns, by Richd Barnes, Lowestoft; foot/b'way, waterbodies, houses, woods; pictorial church.

23/253 Halvergate (parish) TG 435065
Apt 08.01.1840; 2666a (2675); Map surveyed 1839, 3 chns, 1st cl, by T. M'Grane; construction lines, waterbodies, houses, woods, parkland, gardens, hall, rectory, boundary trees, old drain, mill, pits, smithies (by Dawson's symbol), sheds; yellow-green bands are used for some bracing.

23/254 Hanworth (parish) TG 206349
Apt 31.01.1839; 1347a (1347); Map 1840, 3 chns, by James Wright, Aylsham; foot/b'way, turnpike roads, waterbodies, houses, woods, hall, pit; north pointer has plumes and visored helment; 'A Map' in title is on cloud background.

23/255 Happisburgh (parish) TG 383299
Apt 21.07.1840; 1953a (all); Map 1840, 3 chns, 1st cl, by James Wright, Aylsham; construction lines, foot/b'way, waterbodies, houses, woods, field boundary ownerships, road names, stiles, cart gap.

23/256 Hapton (parish) TM 182966
Apt 16.11.1847; 696a (all); Map 1846, 6 chns, by Willm Drane, Norwich; foot/b'way, waterbodies, houses, woods, gardens, heath/moor, residual open fields (named), building names, sluice, stiles, pits, private roads (uncoloured), common (col); pictorial church; meaning of yellow band is unclear.

23/257 Hardingham (parish) TG 041048
Apt 02.09.1840; 2415a (all); Map 1841, 8 chns, by Wm Drane, Norwich; waterbodies, houses, woods, osiers (by symbol), plantations, parkland, gardens, pits; pictorial church.

23/258 Hardley (parish) TG 383006 [Hardley Street]
Apt 27.06.1839; 1462a (1469); Map 1840, 8 chns, by Thos Burton Junr, Langley, Norfolk; houses, woods, pits; pictorial church.

23/259 Hargham (parish) TM 022915 [Not listed]
Apt 26.11.1838; 1081a (all); Map 1838?, 6 chns, copied by James Drane, Norwich; turnpike roads, holding names; no buildings are shown; a table of acreages, etc, has been scraped out. District is apportioned by holding and fields are not shown.

23/260 East Harling (parish) TM 002860
Apt 23.10.1844; 2573a (2572); Map 1845, 8 chns, (includes enlargement of village at 4 chns); waterbodies, woods, private roads (uncoloured); pictorial church; buildings are shown in outline only, without infill.

23/261 West Harling (parish) TL 958842 [Not listed]
Apt 07.02.1838; 3034a (all); Map 1837?, 6 chns; houses, building names, holding names, gallop, glebe (pink); only a few buildings are shown. District is apportioned by holding.

23/262 Harpley (parish) TF 789261
Apt 11.05.1838; 2193a (all); Map 1840?, 12 chns, by Edwin Durrant, Kings Lynn; foot/b'way, houses, woods; green tinted land is tithable; other land is tinted pink, orange and yellow; north pointer is arrow-like. Apt omits land use.

23/263 Hassingham (parish) TG 370059
Apt 22.07.1837; 575a (574); Map 1838?, 3 chns, by Thos Burton Junr, Langley, Norfolk; waterbodies, houses, gardens, gravel pit (col); pictorial church.

23/264 Great Hautbois (parish) TG 264212 [Not listed]
Apt 08.02.1838; 611a (610); Map 1838, [6 chns]; turnpike roads, waterbodies, houses, woods; pictorial church.

23/265 Haveringland (parish) TG 159202 [Not listed]
Apt 09.06.1840; 2062a (2062); Map 1840?, 6 chns; waterbodies, entrance gate (pictorial); buildings and ponds are shown in outline only, without infill.

23/266 Haynford (parish) TG 230187 [Hainford]
Apt 09.08.1837; 1790a (1600); Map 1837, [3 chns], 1st cl; construction lines, turnpike roads, houses, woods (named), field boundary ownerships, road names, field names, churchyard, boundary tree; bridge named.

23/267 Heacham (parish) TF 683379
Apt 25.05.1842; 3554a (4853); Map 1839, 6 chns, by J. Utting, Lynn Regis; foot/b'way, waterbodies, houses, beach, common; scale-bar is ruler-like.

23/268 Heckingham (parish) TM 388989
Apt 17.10.1838; 1102a (1102); Map 1838, 6 chns; waterbodies, houses, woods (col); pictorial church; stylised leaf surmounts title.

23/269 Hedenham (parish) TM 310930
Apt 26.02.1839; 1771a (all); Map 1839?, 10 chns, by Geo. Baker, Bungay; foot/b'way, waterbodies, pits.

23/270 Heigham (parish) TG 219089 [Not listed]
Apt 08.06.1840; 814a (?); Map 1842, 6 chns, by Newton and Woodrow, Norwich, (tithable parts only in detail); waterbodies, houses, woods, city gates, gaol, pit.

23/271 Helhoughton (parish) TF 852262
Apt 21.03.1840; 1638a (1637); Map 1839, 6 chns, by W.G. Bircham, Fakenham; houses, woods, plantations, ford, footbridge; pictorial church.

23/272 Hellesdon (parish) TG 207113
Apt 26.04.1839; 2014a (?); Map 1839, 6 chns, by Pratt and Son, Norwich; houses, mills, turnpike.

23/273 Hellington (parish) TG 315029
Apt 16.04.1839; 516a (516); Map 1841?, 3 chns; houses.

23/274 Hemblington (parish) TG 347116
Apt 07.12.1840; 739a (all); Map 1838, 3 chns, by J.P. Luckraft and Co; waterbodies, houses, woods, plantations, gardens, pits, avenue of trees.

23/275 Hempnall (parish) TM 250936
Apt 22.01.1841; 3626a (all); Map 1842, 6 chns, in 2 parts, by Pratt and Son, Norwich, (includes enlargement of village at 2 chns); houses; pictorial church.

23/276 Hempstead (parish) TG 105371
Apt 10.09.1839; 1756a (all); Map 1841, 6 chns, copied by Pratt and Son, Norwich; waterbodies, houses, woods, old decoy, green.

23/277 Hempstead (parish) TG 405281
Apt 28.01.1841; 907a (907); Map 1841, 3 chns, by James Wright, Aylsham; waterbodies, houses, woods; pictorial church.

23/278 Hemsby (parish) TG 490171
Apt 14.12.1839; 1744a (1785); Map 1838, 3 chns, by J.T. Brown and J. Manning, Surveyors, Bethel St, Norwich, litho (by J. Manning); waterbodies, houses, woods, windmill (by symbol), sand hills (named); it is unclear why certain fields are tinted green; buildings and water are hand-coloured. Apt omits field names.

23/279 Hethel (parish) TG 163009
Apt 30.09.1840; 1429a (all); Map 1842, 6 chns, by Wm Drane, Norwich; waterbodies, houses, woods, plantations.

23/280 Hethersett (parish) TG 155045
Apt 25.07.1846; 2675a (2674); Map 1846, 6 chns, by Wm Drane, Norwich; railway, waterbodies, houses, woods, parkland, park fences, gravel pits (col); farm named; pictorial church.

23/281 Hevingham (parish) TG 195215
Apt 25.04.1838; 2856a (2855); Map 1838, 3 chns, surveyed by James Hartford, Bristol; foot/b'way, turnpike roads, waterbodies, woods (col), plantations (col), arable (col), grassland (col), orchards (col), road names, sand and marl allotments, brick works, rectory, windmill, communal land (yellow), hall, glebe.

23/282 Heydon (parish) TG 113276
Apt 08.06.1840; 1912a (1942); Map 1841, 9 chns, by Alexander Sa...[damaged]; waterbodies, houses, woods (col), parkland (col), arable (col), grassland (col).

23/283 Hickling (parish) TG 415235
Apt 18.01.1842; 4335a (all); Map 1842, 6 chns, by Pratt and Son, Norwich; waterbodies, houses, road names; bridge named.

23/284 Hilborough (parish) TF 815008
Apt 05.09.1845; 3101a (all); Map 1843, 6 chns, by Pratt and Son, Norwich; foot/b'way, waterbodies, houses.

23/285 Hilgay (parish) TL 598968
Apt 08.09.1840; 7861a (7860); Map 1839, 3 chns, surveyed by Richard Freeman, Wisbech; waterbodies, houses, building names, fen names, drove names, steam engine. Apt generalises field names.

23/286 Hillington (parish) TF 726254
Apt 04.10.1838; 2529a (2529); Map 1838, 12 chns, by J. Utting, Lynn Regis; building names, rectory, churchyard; few buildings are shown.

23/287 Hindolveston (parish) TG 038293
Apt 05.09.1839; 2490a (2490); Map 1839, 6 chns, by W.G. Bircham, Fakenham; waterbodies, houses, woods (named), plantations; pictorial church.

23/288 Hindringham (parish) TF 978368
Apt 22.11.1838; 3314a (all); Map 1838, 6 chns, by W.G. Bircham, Fakenham; waterbodies, houses, woods, plantations, landowners (col), windmills (pictorial); pictorial church.

23/289 Hingham (parish) TG 021018
Apt 31.12.1840; 3649a (all); Map 1841, 6 chns, in 2 parts, by A.T. Clarke, Norwich, (includes enlargement of town at 3 chns); waterbodies, houses, woods, parkland, pits, market place, fairstead, private roads (uncoloured). Apt omits some field names.

23/290 Hockering (parish) TG 080138
Apt 30.05.1838; 1931a (1931); Map 1838, 6 chns; waterbodies, houses, woods, windmill (pictorial); pictorial church, with gravestones. Apt omits some land use.

23/291 Great and Little Hockham (parish) TL 950922
Apt 12.09.1837; 3407a (3406); Map 1840, 4.5 chns; landowners, sand pit, holding boundaries (col); pictorial church; no buildings or water are shown. District is apportioned by holding and fields are not shown.

23/292 Hockwold (district in parish of Hockwold) TL 655855 [Not listed]
Apt 21.05.1841; 307a (all); Map 1842?, 6 chns; landowners, farm house, pumping engine. District is apportioned by holding.

23/293 Hockwold cum Wilton (parish) TL 703877
Apt 22.05.1839; 4617a (7171); Map 1838, 6 chns, by Lenny and Croft, Bury St Edmunds; turnpike roads, waterbodies, houses, woods, parkland, heath/moor, building names, road and drove names, former open field names, fen names, lode, suspension bridge, cross, limekiln, brick kiln, rectory, Devils Dyke, chapel, pits, pound, well, steam engine. Apt omits some field names.

23/294 Holkham (parish) TF 888428
Apt 31.01.1839; 5209a (5973); Map 1839, 6 chns, by Pratt and Son, Norwich; waterbodies, houses, woods, plantations, parkland, gardens, heath/moor, rock outcrops, beacons (named, pictorial), lime pits; pictorial church.

23/295 Holme Hale (parish) TF 891070
Apt 30.10.1839; 2602a (2601); Map 1839, 3 chns, by Bradfield, Litcham, Norfolk; waterbodies, houses, driftways (col); pictorial church; colour bands show modus lands.

23/296 Holme or Runcton Holme (parish) TF 616094 [Runcton Holme]
Apt 15.02.1839; 1096a (1096); Map 1839?, 3 chns; waterbodies, houses, drains; pictorial church.

23/297 Holme next the Sea (parish) TF 710433
Apt 26.03.1844; 1648a (all); Map 1844, 6 chns, by W.S. Millard and Son, Norwich; waterbodies, houses, beach.

23/298 Holt (parish) TG 082386
Apt 31.10.1839; 2991a (2991); Map 1839, 3 chns, by J.D. Hawkes, Holt; waterbodies, houses, woods, plantations, gardens, heath/moor, pits, lime pit. Apt omits some field names.

23/299 Honing (parish) TG 327280
Apt 29.12.1843; 1400a (all); Map 1841, 3 chns, 1st cl, by James Wright, Aylsham; construction lines, foot/b'way, waterbodies, houses, woods, canal with towpaths and locks; green band shows 'Common Severals'.

23/300 Honingham (parish) TG 110116
Apt 15.12.1840; 2563a (all); Map 1839, 6 chns, by Wm Drane, Norwich; waterbodies, houses, woods, osiers (by symbol), plantations, parkland, hops, marsh/bog, pits; pictorial church.

23/301 Hoo (parish) TF 992163 [Hoe]
Apt 02.07.1846; 1400a (1400); Map 1847, 6 chns, by Thos Bradfield, Lund; railway, waterbodies, houses, farmyards, woods, plantations, parkland, orchards, footbridge, ford; pictorial church; railway was added after the rest of the map had been drawn.

23/302 Horning (parish) TG 363168
Apt 05.06.1839; 2567a (2567); Map 1839, 6 chns; houses; pictorial church; colours show modus and tithe-free land.

23/303 Horningtoft (parish) TF 937233
Apt 21.03.1840; 1406a (1405); Map 1839, 5 chns, by Thos Bradfield, Litcham; foot/b'way, waterbodies, houses, woods, pit, driftways (col), occupation roads (col); pictorial church; the symbols of a recently-felled wood have been scraped out; scale-bar is ruler-like.

23/304 Horsey (parish) TG 457228
Apt 22.11.1838; 1812a (1880); Map 1840, 9 chns; waterbodies, windmills (pictorial); pictorial church. Apt omits land use.

23/305 Horsford (parish) TG 200160
Apt 31.08.1841; 4178a (4177); Map 1841, 4 chns; waterbodies, houses, woods, plantations, parkland, orchards, gravel pit, boundary of tithe-free land, private roads (uncoloured).

23/306 Horsham St Faith and Newton St Faith (parish and hamlet) TG 221151
Apt 20.05.1841; 2341a (2340); Map 1841, 6 chns; waterbodies, houses, woods, road names, private roads (uncoloured).

23/307 Horstead (parish) TG 267186 [Not listed]
Apt 26.08.1845; 2420a (all); Map 1846, 6 chns; foot/b'way, waterbodies, houses, woods, parkland, pits, avenue of trees, drains; pictorial church.

23/308 Houghton (parish) TF 792285 [Not listed]
Apt 30.04.1839; 1496a (1495); Map 1840?, 12 chns, 'Copied' by Edwin Durrant, Kings Lynn; lodge; only a few buildings are shown. District is apportioned by holding and fields are not shown.

23/309 Houghton next Walsingham (parish) TF 923357 [Houghton St Giles]
Apt 12.04.1838; 978a (978); Map 1838, 3 chns; private roads (uncoloured).

23/310 Hoveton St John (parish) TG 318172 [Hoveton]
Apt 19.10.1841; 1542a (1541); Map 1840, 8 chns, 'Copied' by Pratt and Son, Norwich; foot/b'way, waterbodies, woods, parkland, hall, lawn, drains; some physical features named; meaning of grey band is unclear.

23/311 Hoveton St Peter (parish) TG 317193 [Hoveton]
Apt 22.01.1840; 952a (952); Map 1841, 6 chns, by Pratt and Son, Norwich; waterbodies, houses, woods, parkland, avenue of trees. [The map in PRO IR 30 is a copy of 1919.]

23/312 Howe and West or Little Porringland (parishes) TG 270001
Apt 08.11.1838; 1415a (all); Map 1838, 3 chns, 1st cl, by W.G. Jones, Loddon; construction lines, waterbodies, houses, field boundary ownerships, parish boundary. Apt omits most field names.

23/313 Hunstanton (parish) TF 690420
Apt 02.04.1844; 1499a (all); Map 1844, 12 chns; waterbodies, woods, parkland, beach (col), common; smaller buildings are omitted.

23/314 Hunworth (parish) TG 070351
Apt 06.04.1839; 838a (838); Map 1838, 3 chns, surveyed and lithographed by Joseph Manning, 64 Bethel St, Norwich; hill-drawing, woods, osiers (by symbol), heath/moor, chapel; hill named; buildings are shown in outline only.

23/315 Igborough and Langford (parishes) TL 823965 [Ickburgh]
Apt 13.05.1839; 2979a (3004); Map 1839, 4 chns, taken from maps in the possession of the landowners by W. Fend...[cropped]; woods (col), parish boundaries.

23/316 Illington (parish) TL 943896
Apt 12.09.1842; 1280a (all); Map 1842, 6 chns, by Newton and Woodrow, Norwich; foot/b'way, waterbodies, houses, woods, plantations, pits, avenue of trees.

23/317 Ingham (parish) TG 399261
Apt 30.06.1841; 1504a (1503); Map 1842, 6 chns, by James Wright, Aylsham; waterbodies, woods, osiers (by symbol), windmill (pictorial); pictorial church; district name in title is on sky background.

23/318 Ingoldisthorpe (parish) TF 683325
Apt 08.03.1839; 1395a (all); Map 1839, 6 chns; waterbodies, houses, woods, osiers (by symbol), reeds (by symbol), heath/moor, gardens, building names, milestone, parsonage.

23/319 Ingworth (parish) TG 194301
Apt 08.03.1839; 505a (512); Map 1839, 6 chns, 'Corrected to the present time' by James Wright, Aylsham, Norfolk, and 2 Grove Place, Brixton Rd, London; waterbodies, woods, road names; pictorial church.

23/320 Intwood (parish) TG 193042
Apt 16.05.1839; 616a (all); Map 1839, 3 chns, by Samuel Colman, Norwich; glebe; pictorial church.

23/321 Irmingland (parish) TG 130293 [Not listed]
Apt 30.05.1840; 704a (714); Map 1839, [9 chns], surveyed and lithographed by Josh Manning, 64 Bethel St, Norwich; waterbodies, houses (black), woods, pit, glebe.

23/322 Irstead (parish) TG 363201
Apt 27.05.1838; 1065a (1065); Map 1839, 3 chns, surveyed in 1835, 'the Alterations and Quantities adjusted to the present time', by James Wright, 2 Grove Place, Kennington, London, and Aylsham, Norfolk, (tinted); waterbodies, houses, woods, field boundary ownerships.

23/323 Itteringham with Mannington (parish) TG 141309
Apt 25.04.1838; 1991a (1990); Map 1839, 6 chns, by Newton and Woodrow, Norwich; waterbodies, houses, woods, osiers (by symbol), road names, mills, pits, township boundary; pictorial church.

23/324 Kelling (parish) TG 092420
Apt 22.11.1838; 2179a (2211); Map 1838, 3 chns, by Edwd Houghton, Wells; waterbodies, houses, woods, plantations, grassland (col), heath/moor (col), tidal mud (col), marsh/bog (col), shrubbery (by symbol), windmill (pictorial); heath is variously brown and blue, according to ownership and use.

23/325 Kempstone (parish) TF 883171 [Not listed]
Apt 10.09.1838; 810a (814); Map 1838, [3 chns], 1st cl; construction lines, waterbodies, houses, woods, plantations, parkland, orchards, gardens, field boundary ownerships, road names, field names, pit, conspicuous oak (pictorial); pictorial church.

23/326 Kenninghall (parish) TM 050852
Apt 04.08.1842; 3601a (3600); Map 1840, 6 chns; waterbodies, woods, workhouse, windmills (pictorial), pit; pictorial church.

23/327 Keswick (parish) TG 211042
Apt 31.10.1846; 729a (all); Map 1847, 6 chns; waterbodies, houses, gardens, brick ground, railway; pictorial church, with windswept churchyard.

23/328 Ketteringham (parish) TG 163027
Apt 16.01.1849; 1594a (all); Map 1850?, 6 chns; railway with station, foot/b'way, waterbodies, houses, woods, osiers (by symbol), plantations, parkland, orchards, kitchen and ornamental gardens (by symbol), building names, school, avenues of trees; pictorial church.

23/329 Kettlestone (parish) TF 966315
Apt 02.07.1839; 1169a (all); Map 1839?, 4.5 chns; waterbodies; pictorial church.

23/330 Kilverstone (parish) TL 900950 [Not listed]
Apt 27.08.1842; 2027a (all); Map 1839, 4 chns, by Philip James Cowell, Thetford; boundary of tithe-free lands and glebe; very few buildings are shown. Apt omits field names.

23/331 Kirby Bedon St Andrew (parish) TG 277054 [Kirby Bedon]
Apt 20.05.1841; 624a (all); Map 1841?, 6 chns; houses, pit, wood (by name); pictorial churches.

23/332 Kirby Bedon St Mary (parish) TG 283062 [Kirby Bedon]
Apt 30.05.1861; 1a (625); Map (drawn on Apt) 1862?, 2 chns, (tithable parts only); field gates, field acreages, landowners. Apt omits land use.

23/333 Kirby Cane (parish) TM 371938
Apt 27.02.1839; 1476a (all); Map 1839?, 6 chns; waterbodies, houses; some roads are coloured and some are not.

23/334 Kirstead (parish) TM 298973 [Kirstead Green]
Apt 18.03.1842; 1011a (all); Map 1842, 6 chns, by Newton and Woodrow, Norwich; foot/b'way, waterbodies, houses, woods.

23/335 Knapton (parish) TG 302338
Apt 05.11.1839; 1481a (all); Map 1840, 3 chns, by James Wright, Aylsham; foot/b'way, waterbodies, houses, woods, canal with towpath; bridge named; pictorial church, with gravestones; north pointer has plumes and crown.

23/336 Lakenham (parish) TG 225063
Apt 04.09.1840; 1107a (?); Map 1843?, 6 chns, (tithable parts only in detail); woods, osiers (by symbol), parkland, windmill (by symbol).

23/337 Lamas and Little Hautbois (parishes) TG 250230
Apt 10.05.1839; 811a (829); Map 1840, 6 chns, by Newton and Woodrow, Norwich; waterbodies, houses, woods, parkland, pit, parish boundary; pictorial church.

23/338 Langley (parish) TG 366026 [Not listed]
Apt 11.07.1838; 2224a (2723); Map 1839, 8 chns, by Thomas Burton Junr, Langley; waterbodies, houses, woods, parkland, gardens, building names, cross (pictorial), 'Abbey' (named in gothic), hall; pictorial church.

23/339 Larling (parish) TL 972892
Apt 07.02.1838; 1548a (all); Map 1838, 7.5 chns; waterbodies, houses, woods (col), osiers (by symbol), gardens (col), windmill (pictorial); pictorial church. District is apportioned by holding and fields are not shown; individual acreages are omitted for most holdings.

23/340 Lessingham (parish) TG 389283
Apt 22.01.1841; 640a (639); Map 1840, 3 chns, 1st cl, by James Wright, Aylsham; construction lines, foot/b'way, waterbodies, houses, field boundary ownerships, road names.

23/341 Letheringsett (parish) TG 060392
Apt 17.04.1838; 853a (853); Map 1838?, (surveyed in 1834), 3 chns, by J. Manning, Norwich; waterbodies, houses, woods, osiers (by symbol, col), arable (col), grassland (col), gardens (col), heath/moor, pits, glebe (yellow), driftways (col).

23/342 Letton (parish) TF 976060 [Not listed]
Apt 04.10.1838; 1274a (1274); Map 1838, 6 chns, by Issac Lenny, Norwich; foot/b'way, waterbodies, houses, woods (col), parkland (col), arable (col), grassland (col), gardens (col), fence ownership, field gates, road names, site of gate, boundary trees and marks, pound, green, hall.

23/343 East Lexham (parish) TF 860180
Apt 26.01.1841; 1189a (all); Map 1841, 9 chns, by Pratt and Son, Norwich; houses, woods, pit; meaning of grey bands is unclear.

23/344 West Lexham (parish) TF 843175
Apt 31.01.1838; 1155a (1155); Map 1838, 3 chns, by Pratt and Son, Norwich; construction lines, houses, field boundary ownerships; map is dated 1838 in title, and 1837 after mapmaker's name.

23/345 Leziate (parish) TF 688198
Apt 27.05.1840; 1470a (all); Map 1840?, 6 chns; houses.

23/346 Limpenhoe (parish) TG 399032
Apt 24.10.1844; 1075a (all); Map 1845?, 6 chns, by Pratt and Son, Norwich; railway, houses.

23/347 Ling (parish) TG 077169
Apt 14.02.1839; 1900a (1899); Map 1841?, 6 chns, in 3 parts, (includes two 3-chn enlargements of detail); waterbodies, houses, common; hill and hamlets named; pictorial church; pink band shows land tithable to another parish.

23/348 Lingwood (parish) TG 362086
Apt 18.01.1840; 659a (all); Map 1838, 3 chns, surveyed by J.P. Luckraft and Co; waterbodies, houses, woods, plantations, parkland, orchards, gardens, workhouse.

23/349 Litcham (parish) TF 876187
Apt 14.07.1841; 1933a (all); Map 1841, 9 chns, in 2 parts, (includes town separately at 4.5 chns); houses, woods, gardens, commons (col).

23/350 Loddon (parish) TM 360970
Apt 10.10.1838; 3021a (3020); Map 1837, 3 chns, 1st cl, in 2 parts, by W.G. Jones; construction lines, foot/b'way, water-bodies, houses, fences, field boundary ownerships, field gates, common.

23/351 Longham (parish) TF 938158
Apt 10.09.1838; 1304a (1304); Map 1838, 4.5 chns, by Pratt and Son, Norwich; woods, parkland; pictorial church; scale has miniature north pointers at each end.

23/352 North Lopham (parish) TM 040828
Apt 26.07.1845; 1982a (2000); Map 1845, 6 chns, by C.S. Alger, Diss; waterbodies, woods, parkland, gardens.

23/353 South Lopham (parish) TM 044808
Apt 21.03.1846; 1938a (1937); Map 1847, 6 chns, by Lenny and Croft; waterbodies, houses, woods, osiers (by symbol), parkland, building names, road names, windmill (pictorial), avenue of trees, ford, signpost (pictorial); bridge and fen named.

23/354 Ludham (parish) TG 388184
Apt 15.05.1841; 2977a (2977); Map 1840, 6 chns, by Newton and Woodrow, Norwich; waterbodies, houses, woods, windmills (pictorial); pictorial church.

23/355 North Lynn (rectory and liberty) TF 612214 [Not listed]
Apt 16.05.1838; 1726a (1205); Map 1839?, 6 chns, by Edwin Durrant, Kings Lynn; waterbodies, houses, arable (col), grassland (col), salt marsh, fences, ditches, (old) sea bank, sluices, jetty, ferry, wash pit; map also includes part of Clenchwarton (23/138).

23/356 St Margaret, Kings Lynn (parish) TF 620200 [Not listed]
Apt 06.05.1848; 59a (?); Map 1851, 2 chns, ? by Edwin Durrant, Land Surveyor and Valuer, Lynn, (tithable parts only in detail); waterbodies, road names, hospitals, reservoir, railway station, chapel, waterworks, quay; creeks named. Apt omits most land use.

23/357 South Lynn or All Saints, Kings Lynn (parish) TF 621185 [Not listed]
Apt 06.12.1843; 2426a (?); Map 1844, 6 chns, by James Utting, Kings Lynn; waterbodies, town gate, drains (named). Apt omits field names.

23/358 West Lynn St Peter (parish) TF 602189 [West Lynn]
Apt 15.12.1843; 1620a (1619); Map 1843, 6 chns, by J. Utting, Lynn Regis; waterbodies, houses, old river bed, ferry, jetties, hotel, foreshore (col); marsh and banks named.

23/359 Marham (parish) TF 722097
Apt 22.07.1840; 3967a (3966); Map 1840, 6 chns, surveyed by Charles Mumford, Downham; waterbodies, houses, woods (col), plantations (col), windmill (pictorial), droveways.

23/360 Marlingford (parish) TG 131091
Apt 04.10.1838; 675a (all); Map 1839?, 6 chns; waterbodies, houses, woods, parkland, windmill (pictorial), pit; uninhabited buildings are shown in outline only, without infill.

23/361 Marsham (parish) TG 190238
Apt 12.06.1839; 1820a (1819); Map 1840, 3 chns, 1st cl, by James Wright, Aylsham; construction lines, foot/b'way, turnpike roads, waterbodies, houses, woods, field boundary ownerships, road names.

23/362 Martham (parish) TG 454186
Apt 31.12.1841; 2644a (all); Map 1842, 3 chns, 1st cl, by Josh Manning, Norwich; construction lines, houses, reed beds, alders; uninhabited buildings are shown in outline only, without infill. Apt omits some field names.

23/363 Great Massingham (parish) TF 790205
Apt 30.04.1838; 4112a (4112); Map 1838, 8 chns; waterbodies, houses, windmill (pictorial).

23/364 Little Massingham (parish) TF 792241
Apt 17.10.1838; 2278a (all); Map 1838, 9 chns; glebe. District is apportioned by holding and fields are not shown.

23/365 Matlaske (parish) TG 151348
Apt 12.11.1839; 472a (all); Map 1839, 3 chns, 1st cl, by James Wright, Aylsham; construction lines, foot/b'way, waterbodies, houses, woods, stiles.

23/366 Mattinshall (parish) TG 048110 [Mattishall]
Apt 06.09.1838; 2239a (2280); Map 1839, 6 chns, by Newton and Woodrow, Norwich; waterbodies, houses, woods; pictorial church.

23/367 Mattishall Burgh (parish) TG 050122 [Not listed]
Apt 26.10.1837; 604a (all); Map 1840?, 3 chns, by J. Wright, Norwich; waterbodies, houses, woods (col), plantations (col), parkland (col), arable (col), grassland (col).

23/368 Mautby (parish) TG 489114
Apt 07.12.1838; 1660a (1659); Map 1839, 6 chns, revised by Lenny and Croft, Bury St Edmunds; foot/b'way, canal, waterbodies, houses, plantations, cattle swim, windmill (pictorial); pictorial church.

23/369 Melton Constable with Little Burgh annexed (parish) TG 039323
Apt 21.04.1840; 1723a (2710); Map 1850, 6 chns, by J.D. Hawkes, Holt; waterbodies, houses, woods, plantations, parkland, gardens, tithe-free land; pictorial churches.

23/370 Great Melton otherwise Melton St Mary and All Saints (parish) TG 165034
Apt 31.10.1839; 2486a (2485); Map 1840, 6 chns, by Robt Corby; waterbodies, houses; pictorial churches.

23/371 Little Melton (parish) TG 160070
Apt 22.12.1841; 672a (all); Map 1842, 6 chns, by Wm Corby, Witlingham; turnpike roads, waterbodies, houses, woods, parkland; pictorial church.

23/372 Merton (parish) TL 912987
Apt 08.02.1837; 1362a (all); Map 1837, 5 chns, by Chapman, Son and Webb; waterbodies, houses, farmyards (col), woods (col), plantations (col), parkland (col), arable (col), grassland (col), glebe boundary, roadside waste.

23/373 Methwold (parish) TL 685952
Apt 16.06.1840; 13193a (13192); Map 1839, 6 chns, by Lenny and Croft, Bury St Edmunds; foot/b'way, houses, plantations, fences, building names, decoys, green, steam engine, windmills (pictorial); droves and drains named.

23/374 Metton (parish) TG 199372
Apt 07.11.1842; 661a (all); Map 1842, 9 chns, by James Wright, Aylsham; waterbodies, woods; pictorial church.

23/375 Middleton (parish) TF 662160
Apt 27.08.1840; 3029a (all); Map 1838, 6 chns, by J. Utting, Lynn Regis; waterbodies, mansion (pictorial); pictorial church, tithe ownership boundaries; drains named.

23/376 Mileham (parish) TF 920190
Apt 04.09.1840; 2851a (2851); Map 1840, 6 chns, by W.G. Bircham,

Fakenham; waterbodies, houses, woods, osiers, plantations, gravel pits, windmill (pictorial); pictorial church.

23/377 Morley otherwise Morley St Buttolph and Morley St Peter (parish) TM 069993 [Morley St Botolph]
Apt 31.10.1840; 1835a (all); Map 1841, 6 chns, by Newton and Woodrow, Norwich; waterbodies, houses, woods, windmill (pictorial); pictorial churches. Apt omits most field names.

23/378 Morston (parish) TG 006437
Apt 26.11.1838; 2111a (all); Map 1838, 6 chns, by W.G. Bircham, Fakenham; foot/b'way, waterbodies, houses, plantations, heath/moor, landowners (col), pits, high water spring tides, earthwork, embankments.

23/379 Morton (parish) TG 124162
Apt 20.05.1841; 977a (all); Map 1842, 6 chns, by Newton and Woodrow, Norwich; waterbodies, houses, woods, parkland; pictorial church.

23/380 Moulton (parish) TG 402068 [Moulton St Mary]
Apt 06.12.1844; 1019a (1018); Map 1845, 3 chns, 1st cl, in 2 parts, by Adam T. Clarke, Orford Hall, Norwich; construction lines, railway, foot/b'way, waterbodies, houses, woods (named), cement works, stiles, sand pit; yellow bands are used for some bracing.

23/381 Moulton St Michael (parish) TM 169902 [Not listed]
Apt 09.10.1837; 1348a (all); Map 1837, 6 chns; waterbodies, woods, road names, windmill (pictorial), gravel pit; pictorial church; compass rose has leafy ornament in pointers, and there are small north pointers at each end of the scale.

23/382 Mourningthorpe (parish) TM 218929 [Morningthorpe]
Apt 22.11.1838; 1001a (1001); Map 1839, 6 chns, by A.T. Clarke, Surveyor, Norwich; waterbodies, houses, woods, parkland, gardens, road names, parsonage, hall, common, glebe; north pointer has crown and plumes.

23/383 Mulbarton (parish) TG 198008
Apt 12.03.1841; 1348a (all); Map 1840, 3 chns, 1st cl, by Wm Drane, Norwich; construction lines, waterbodies, houses, woods, plantations, orchards, gardens, fences, field boundary ownerships, pit, boundary trees, common.

23/384 Mundesley (parish) TG 305366
Apt 04.10.1838; 574a (674); Map 1839, 3 chns, surveyed 'and corrected to the present time' by James Wright, Aylsham; waterbodies, houses, woods, field boundary ownerships, road names, pit.

23/385 Mundford (parish) TL 802930
Apt 28.03.1842; 2051a (2050); Map 1842, 6 chns, by Lenny and Croft, Bury St Edmunds; waterbodies, houses, plantations, parkland, gardens, heath/moor, building names, pound, cross, lodge, footbridge, pit; bridge named.

23/386 Mundham (parish) TM 333971
Apt 31.01.1839; 1547a (1547); Map 1838, 3 chns, 1st cl, by W.G. Jones, Loddon; waterbodies, houses, windmill (pictorial).

23/387 Narborough or Narburgh (parish) TF 752113
Apt 07.12.1838; 3446a (3545); Map 1837, 3 chns, 'Planned from a Scale of 3 Chains to an Inch' by J. Utting, Lynn Regis; waterbodies, houses, field boundary ownerships, boundary stone; stream across fields is shown by pecked line. Apt omits some field names.

23/388 Narford (parish) TF 774127
Apt 23.01.1840; 2397a (all); Map 1837, 6 chns, surveyed by J. Utting, Lynn Regis; waterbodies, houses, woods (col), osiers (by symbol, col), plantations (col), parkland (col), arable (col), grassland (col), gardens (col), heath/moor (col), hedges, fences, pits.

23/389 Neatishead (parish) TG 337197
Apt 21.07.1840; 1906a (1905); Map 1841, 3 chns, 1st cl, by James Wright, Aylsham; construction lines, foot/b'way, waterbodies, houses, woods, field boundary ownerships, road names, stiles; inhabited buildings are marked with an 'O'.

23/390 Necton (parish) TF 882100
Apt 09.04.1840; 3748a (all); Map 1839, 3 chns, by W.S. Millard and Son, Norwich; houses; table summarises land use with acreages.

23/391 Needham (parish) TM 223917
Apt 07.06.1841; 1128a (all); Map 1841, 6 chns, ? by C.S. Alger, Diss; waterbodies, woods, osiers (by symbol), plantations, pits, boundary trees, drains; pictorial church. Apt omits most field names.

23/392 Newton next Castle Acre (parish) TF 833152 [Newton]
Apt 23.04.1840; 1063a (all); Map 1839, 6 chns, by Lenny and Croft, Bury St Edmunds; waterbodies, houses, woods, building names, road names, pits, churchyard, water mill, signpost (pictorial), commons; hill named.

23/393 Newton Flotman (parish) TM 212988
Apt 26.07.1837; 1173a (all); Map 1838, 6 chns; waterbodies, houses, woods, landowners (col); pictorial church.

23/394 West Newton (parish) TF 695278
Apt 13.07.1838; 1230a (1230); Map 1837, 4.5 chns, 'Copied' by J. Utting, Lynn Regis; waterbodies, houses, windmill (pictorial).

23/395 North Repps (parish) TG 243392 [Not listed]
Apt 11.03.1839; 2731a (all); Map 1840, 3 chns, by James Wright, Aylsham; foot/b'way, turnpike roads, waterbodies, houses, woods, heath/moor, road names, toll gate, pits, churchyard, hall.

23/396 Northwold (parish) TL 730977
Apt 28.11.1837; 5233a (5232); Map 1837, 6 chns, by Lenny and Croft, Bury St Edmunds; waterbodies, houses, plantations, parkland, building names, rectory, water mill, quay, ferry, right of way to glebe, windmills (pictorial), footbridge, Devils Dyke; hills, boundary corners, lode, drove, drains, and some bridges named.

23/397 Norton Subcorse (parish) TM 410996
Apt 18.01.1840; 1858a (1882); Map 1840, 6 chns, by R. Barnes, Lowestoft; waterbodies, houses, woods, ferry, windmills (pictorial); pictorial church. Apt omits most field names.

23/398 Norwich, All Saints (parish) TG 231082 [Not listed]
Apt 17.03.1849; 4a (?); Map 1851, 3 chns, (tithable parts only); road names. Apt omits land use.

23/399 Norwich, St Clement (parish) TG 231000 [Not listed]
Apt 01.07.1845; 165a (all); Map 1846?, 3 chns.

23/400 Norwich, St Etheldred (parish) TG 236080 [Not listed]
Apt 19.09.1848; 4a (?); Map 1851, 3 chns; road names. District is apportioned by holding; Apt omits land use.

23/401 Norwich, St John Sepulchre (parish) TG 234078 [Not listed]
Apt 17.03.1849; 11a (all); Map 1851, 3 chns, (tithable parts only); road names. Apt omits most land use.

23/402 Norwich, St John the Baptist, Timberhill (parish) TG 232084 [Not listed]
Apt 09.12.1848; 2a (?); Map 1851, 3 chns, (tithable parts only); road names. District is apportioned by holding; Apt omits land use.

23/403 Norwich, St Julian (parish) TG 235082 [Not listed]
Apt 03.05.1849; 6a (all); Map 1851, 3 chns, (tithable parts only); road names. District is apportioned by holding; Apt omits land use and some occupiers' names.

23/404 Norwich, St Peter Mountregate (parish) TG 237086 [Not listed]
Apt 09.12.1848; 5a (?); Map 1851, 3 chns, (tithable parts only); road names. Apt omits land use and some occupiers' names.

23/405 Norwich, St Peter Southgate (parish) TG 238077 [Not listed]
Apt 09.12.1848; 7a (?); Map 1851, 3 chns, (tithable parts only); road names. Apt omits land use.

23/406 Ormesby St Margaret and Ormesby St Michael with Scrotby (parishes) TG 486149
Apt 22.09.1838; 2686a (all); Map 1839?, 3 chns; waterbodies, houses, residual open fields; pictorial church, with gravestones.

23/407 Osmondeston or Scole (parish) TM 148795
Apt 15.02.1840; 821a (all); Map 1839, 6 chns, by Henry Calver; waterbodies, woods, parkland, orchards, gardens, windmill (pictorial), pit; bridge named; pictorial church, with tombstones and overflying birds. Apt omits most field names.

23/408 Oulton (parish) TG 146283
Apt 27.11.1839; 1849a (1849); Map 1839, 9 chns, surveyed and lithographed by J. Manning, 64 Bethel St, Norwich; waterbodies, houses (black), woods, pits; pictorial church.

23/409 Outwell and Emneth (parishes) TF 531033
Apt 09.06.1840; 2513a (2512); Map 1841, 3 chns, 1st cl, surveyed by R. Freeman, Wisbech; construction lines, canal with locks, waterbodies, houses, road and drove names, field names, sluice, toll gate, hall.

23/410 Overstrand (parish) TG 238411
Apt 18.03.1839; 438a (all); Map 1838, 3 chns, by George F. Playford, North Repps; foot/b'way, waterbodies, houses, woods (col), osiers (by symbol), gardens (col), lawn (col), heath/moor, field boundary ownerships, lighthouse (pictorial), pit, cliffs.

23/411 Ovington (parish) TF 925031
Apt 20.07.1842; 1497a (1497); Map 1843, 6 chns, by Newton and Woodrow, Norwich; waterbodies, houses, woods, plantations, shrubbery, windmill (pictorial), parsonage, hall; pictorial church.

23/412 Oxborough (parish) TF 741017
Apt 30.06.1845; 2519a (2518); Map 1845?, 10 chns, in 2 parts, (includes enlargement of village centre at 5 chns); waterbodies, houses, woods (col), plantations (col), parkland, avenue of trees, modus lands. Apt omits some land use and some field names.

23/413 Oxnead (parish) TG 231245
Apt 09.01.1840; 645a (644); Map 1839, 6 chns, by Newton and Woodrow, Norwich; waterbodies, houses, woods, plantations, pits; pictorial church.

23/414 Oxwick (parish) TF 914251
Apt 18.06.1840; 720a (719); Map 1840, 6 chns, by Wm Drane, Norfolk; foot/b'way, waterbodies, houses, woods, plantations; pictorial church.

23/415 Palgrave Parva (parish) TF 832136 [Not listed]
Apt 22.12.1838; 454a (all); Map 1838, 3 chns, by J. Utting, Lynn Regis; waterbodies, houses.

23/416 Palling (parish) TG 423269 [Sea Palling]
Apt 16.06.1838; 831a (905); Map 1839, 3 chns, by James Wright, Aylsham; waterbodies, houses, windmills (pictorial); pictorial church.

23/417 Panxworth (parish) TG 344131
Apt 24.05.1839; 577a (all); Map 1838, 6 chns, by Issac Lenny, Norwich; foot/b'way, waterbodies, houses, woods (col), arable (col), grassland (col), gardens (col), fences, field boundary ownerships, field gates, building names, landowners, direction post, old steeple, lodge, leaping bars, windmill (by symbol); bridge named.

23/418 Paston (parish) TG 319341
Apt 22.12.1841; 1375a (1445); Map 1841, 6 chns, in 2 parts, by James Wright, Aylsham, (includes 3-chn enlargement of detail, dated 1842); waterbodies, houses, woods, gardens, road names, canal with towpath; pictorial church.

23/419 Pattisley (parish) TF 899246 [Not listed]
Apt 21.12.1842; 320a (320); Map 1843, 3 chns, by Josh Manning, Norwich; houses, woods.

23/420 Pensthorpe (parish) TF 953298
Apt 30.11.1838; 753a (753); Map 1839, 6 chns, by Edwin Durrant, Kings Lynn; waterbodies, houses; bridge named.

23/421 Pentney (parish) TF 721134
Apt 21.03.1846; 218a (2330); Map 1851?, 6 chns, (tithable parts only); railway, plantations; pictorial church. District is apportioned by holding; Apt generalises land use.

23/422 North Pickenham and Houghton on the Hill (parish) TF 861065
Apt 26.02.1839; 2191a (2191); Map 1839-40, 6 chns, by W.G. Bircham, Fakenham, (including one part at 3 chns); waterbodies, houses, woods, plantations, watch house; pictorial church.

23/423 South Pickenham (parish) TF 846141
Apt 31.12.1841; 1830a (all); Map 1840, 6 chns, by W.G. Bircham, Fakenham; houses, woods, plantations, parkland, pits; pictorial church.

23/424 Pierleston or Billingford (parish) TM 174793
Apt 20.08.1839; 1037a (?); Map 1839, 6 chns, by Henry Calver; waterbodies, woods, windmill (pictorial), glebe; pictorial church.

23/425 Plumstead (parish) TG 128349
Apt 20.11.1839; 1272a (all); Map 1839, 3 chns, 1st cl, by James Wright, Aylsham; construction lines, foot/b'way, waterbodies, houses, woods, field boundary ownerships, pits, stiles; green bands are used for some bracing.

23/426 Great Plumstead (parish) TG 300098
Apt 12.09.1838; 1403a (all); Map 1839, 6 chns, by Pratt and Son, Norwich; houses.

23/427 Little Plumstead (parish) TG 306118
Apt 31.03.1838; 1396a (1395); Map 1839, 6 chns, by Newton and Woodrow, Norwich; waterbodies, houses, plantations, claypit, brickworks; pictorial church, with tombstones.

23/428 East Poringland (parish) TG 271017 [Poringland]
Apt 25.07.1851; 4a (?); Map (drawn on Apt) 1852?, 3 chns, (tithable parts only); road names, landowners, field acreages. Apt describes location of each tithe area.

23/429 Postwick (parish) TG 295080
Apt 26.11.1838; 1426a (1426); Map 1838, 3 chns, 1st cl, (tithable parts only); construction lines, waterbodies, houses, woods, plantations, parkland, gardens, hall, water mill (windpump, by symbol), embankment, ferry, pits, prominent tree (pictorial), drains.

23/430 Potter Heigham (parish) TG 426200
Apt 19.12.1838; 2527a (all); Map 1840, 3 chns, surveyed by Charles William Millard, Norwich; construction lines, houses, field boundary ownerships, drains; principal construction lines have notes of which objects they bear on.

23/431 Pudding Norton (parish) TF 923280 [Not listed]
Apt 21.04.1849; 840a (840); Map 1849?, 9 chns; building names, glebe.

23/432 Pulham St Mary the Virgin and Pulham St Mary Magdalen (parish) TM 205865
Apt 09.08.1837; 5955a (5955); Map 1838?, [6 chns], in 2 parts; buildings are shown in outline only, without infill.

23/433 Quidenham (parish) TM 026872
Apt 31.03.1843; 1116a (1126); Map 1841, 4 chns, by Calver and Alger; waterbodies, houses, woods, gardens with wall, fences, pit (col); pictorial church.

23/434 Rackheath (parish) TG 279136
Apt 26.07.1837; 1980a (all); Map 1837?, 6 chns, surveyed in 1834 by J. Manning, Norwich; waterbodies, houses, woods, parkland (col), gardens (col), fences, pits, glebe, driftways (col).

23/435 Ranworth (parish) TG 353147
Apt 31.01.1839; 1902a (all); Map 1838, 6 chns, by Issac Lenny, Norwich; waterbodies, houses, woods (col), arable (col), grassland (col), gardens (col), field gates, building names, chapel, sheep wash; bridge and dykes named.

23/436 Raveningham (parish) TM 402965
Apt 24.08.1840; 2415a (2415); Map 1839, 7 chns, in 2 parts, by R. Barnes, Lowestoft, (including one part at 10 chns); waterbodies, houses, woods, residual open fields, sluices, windmills (pictorial), canal with towpath. Apt omits most field names.

23/437 East Raynham (parish) TF 886261
Apt 01.05.1839; 1608a (1635); Map 1838, 6 chns, by W.G. Bircham,

Fakenham; waterbodies, houses, woods (col), plantations (col), arable (col), grassland (col), gardens, hall, avenue of trees, ice house, church land.

23/438 South Raynham (parish) TF 877237
Apt 01.05.1839; 1036a (all); Map 1838, 6 chns, by W.G. Bircham, Fakenham; waterbodies, houses, woods, plantations, windmill (pictorial); pictorial church.

23/439 West Raynham (parish) TF 856248
Apt 10.09.1838; 1370a (1370); Map 1838, 6 chns, by W.G. Bircham, Fakenham; waterbodies, houses, woods, landowners (col).

23/440 Redenhall with Harleston and Workwell (parish) TM 259851
Apt 25.05.1838; 3652a (all); Map 1839, 6 chns, in 5 parts, (includes enlargement of Harleston town and other detail at 3 chns and 24-chn index); waterbodies, houses, woods, gardens, windmills (pictorial), site of old rectory, sand pit. Apt omits most field names.

23/441 Reedham (parish) TG 426033
Apt 05.06.1840; 3329a (3328); Map 1841, 6 chns, by Pratt and Son, Norwich; waterbodies, houses, drains, commons (col); uninhabited buildings are shown in outline only, without infill.

23/442 Reifham St Mary with Kerdestone (parish) TG 078248 [Reepham]
Apt 07.06.1844; 2421a (all); Map 1845, 6 chns, in 2 parts, by Newton and Woodrow, Norwich; woods; stream across fields is shown discontinuously.

23/443 Repps with Bastwick (parish) TG 423173
Apt 05.02.1839; 1229a (all); Map 1838, 3 chns, by W.S. Millard, Norwich; waterbodies, houses, boundary of land tithable to Martham.

23/444 Reymerston (parish) TG 018060
Apt 28.11.1838; 1600a (1599); Map 1840?, 6 chns; waterbodies, houses, woods; uninhabited buildings are shown in outline only, without infill; pictorial church.

23/445 Riddlesworth (parish) TL 963816 [Not listed]
Apt 09.06.1840; 1157a (1157); Map 1838, 6 chns; foot/b'way, waterbodies, houses, woods, orchards; scale has north pointer at each end.

23/446 Ridlington (parish) TG 348311
Apt 22.03.1844; 635a (all); Map 1844, 3 chns, by James Wright, Aylsham; foot/b'way, waterbodies, houses, woods, osiers (by symbol), commons; pictorial church, with tombstones.

23/447 Ringland (parish) TG 132140
Apt 12.09.1840; 1211a (1210); Map 1841, 6 chns, by Newton and Woodrow, Norwich; waterbodies, houses, woods, windmill (pictorial); pictorial church.

23/448 Great Ringstead (parish) TF 714403 [Ringstead]
Apt 30.04.1842; 2715a (all); Map 1841, 6 chns, 'Copied' by E. Durrant, Lynn.

23/449 Rockland St Andrew and Rockland All Saints (united parishes) TL 992960 [Not listed]
Apt 20.04.1847; 1682a (all); Map 1846, 6 chns; houses, workhouse.

23/450 Rockland St Mary (parish) TG 320045
Apt 09.07.1839; 1360a (all); Map 1840, 3 chns, by William Jno. Browne, Norwich, 'for Mr. William Drane'; waterbodies, houses, woods, plantations, parkland, fences, field boundary ownerships, field gates, pits, brickworks, fish pond, parsonage, churchyard, brick ground.

23/451 Rockland St Peter (parish) TL 983983
Apt 25.04.1838; 1000a (all); Map 1838, 3 chns, 'Revised from the Award Map' by J. Eaton, Old Buckenham; waterbodies, houses, woods (col), arable (col), grassland (col), road names, land tithable elsewhere, watering pit, chapel, windmill (pictorial); colours may also show owners.

23/452 Rollesby (parish) TG 450160
Apt 18.12.1839; 1683a (1653); Map 1840, 3 chns, by Josh Manning, 64 Bethel St, Norwich; waterbodies, houses, woods, plantations, parkland, gardens, fences, pits; pictorial church; legend explains colours; north pointer has diadem and plumes, and scale has miniature north pointers at each end.

23/453 Roudham (parish) TL 949877 [Not listed]
Apt 24.09.1842; 2085a (2085); Map 1838, 12 chns, 'Revised from the Map of the Parish' by J. Eaton, Old Buckenham; houses, woods (col), heath/moor (col), glebe (pink), ownership boundaries; table summarises acreages.

23/454 Rougham (parish) TF 826205
Apt 18.05.1842; 2630a (2627); Map 1841, 9 chns, 'copied' by E. Durrant, Lynn.

23/455 Roughton (parish) TG 220376
Apt 09.02.1839; 1740a (all); Map 1838, 3 chns, surveyed by G. Pank, Cromer; construction lines, foot/b'way, waterbodies, woods, grassland (by symbol), gardens, heath/moor, hedge ownership, field names, landowners, field acreages.

23/456 Roydon (parish) TF 692229
Apt 09.08.1837; 1117a (all); Map 1838, 6 chns, ? by W.G. Bircham, Fakenham; waterbodies, houses, woods, landowners (col); pictorial church.

23/457 Roydon (parish) TM 097807
Apt 27.03.1839; 1329a (all); Map 1839, 6 chns; waterbodies, woods, orchards, residual open fields, windmill (pictorial); pictorial church; scale has small north pointers at each end. Apt omits most field names.

23/458 East Rudham (parish) TF 834289
Apt 15.02.1839; 3892a (3891); Map 1839, 6 chns, by W.G. Bircham, Fakenham; modus land boundary, windmill (pictorial); pictorial church.

23/459 West Rudham (parish) TF 814274
Apt 21.12.1842; 2836a (all); Map 1842, 6 chns, by W. Bircham, Fakenham; houses, woods, road names, avenue of trees; pictorial church.

23/460 North Runcton with Hardwick and Setch or Setchey (district and hamlet) TF 644160
Apt 13.06.1840; 2239a (2239); Map 1839, 6 chns, by Charles Burcham, Kings Lynn; waterbodies, houses; drains and bridge named.

23/461 South Runcton (parish) TF 636088
Apt 23.11.1838; 831a (831); Map 1838, 3 chns, by Chas Burcham, Kings Lynn; waterbodies, houses; pictorial church.

23/462 Runhall (parish) TG 057072
Apt 14.01.1845; 834a (834); Map 1846, 2 chns, by Mann[ing] and Son, Norwich; waterbodies, houses, woods (named), mills, tithe-free land (yellow), commons; scale has miniature north pointers at each end.

23/463 Runham (parish) TG 471105
Apt 13.07.1839; 1715a (1715); Map 1839, 6 chns, by J. Manning, Surveyor and Lithographer, 64 Bethel St, Norwich; waterbodies, houses, woods, windmills (pictorial); pictorial church; north pointer has plumes. Apt omits field names.

23/464 Runton (parish) TG 196422 [West Runton]
Apt 22.11.1838; 1253a (all); Map 1839, 3 chns, by Pratt and Son, Norwich; waterbodies, houses, residual open fields, field boundary ownerships, landowners, spring, commons; red lines may be walls.

23/465 Rushall (parish) TM 204823
Apt 02.02.1843; 1170a (1170); Map 1841, 6 chns, by Wm S. Millard and Son, Surveyors etc, Norwich; waterbodies, houses, woods.

23/466 East Ruston (parish) TG 358287
Apt 28.01.1841; 2494a (2494); Map 1841, 3 chns, 1st cl, by James Wright, Aylsham; construction lines, foot/b'way, waterbodies, houses, woods, field boundary ownerships; bridge named.

23/467 Ryston and Roxham (parishes) TF 635005 [Not listed]
Apt 11.03.1840; 1199a (all); Map 1839, 6 chns, by Chas Burcham, Kings Lynn; waterbodies, houses, parish boundary.

23/468 Saham Toney (parish) TF 908038
Apt 26.11.1841; 4049a (all); Map 1842, 6 chns; waterbodies, houses, woods, osiers (by symbol).

23/469 Salhouse (parish) TG 303150
Apt 12.09.1842; 2027a (2060); Map 1841, 7 chns; waterbodies, woods, avenue of trees.

23/470 Sall (parish) TG 104255 [Salle]
Apt 10.09.1838; 1803a (all); Map 1840?, 3 chns; houses.

23/471 Salthouse (parish) TG 072433
Apt 22.11.1838; 1537a (1614); Map 1838, 3 chns; waterbodies, houses, grassland (col), heath/moor (col), marsh, windmill (pictorial).

23/472 Sandringham (parish) TF 695287
Apt 20.09.1838; 1172a (1172); Map 1839?, 7.5 chns; very few buildings are shown. District is apportioned by holding and fields are not shown; Apt generalises land use.

23/473 Santon or Santon House (parish) TL 830887 [Not listed]
Apt 02.09.1840; 1500a (all); Map 1849?, 5 chns; foot/b'way, woods, driftway. District is apportioned by holding; Apt generalises land use.

23/474 Saxlingham (parish) TG 035397
Apt 01.06.1844; 1498a (1498); Map 1842, 9 chns; houses.

23/475 Saxlingham Thorpe and Saxlingham Nethergate (parish) TM 233969
Apt 20.04.1841; 2111a (2111); Map 1841, 3 chns, 1st cl, by Willm Drane, Norwich; construction lines, waterbodies, houses (grey), woods, plantations, gardens, fences, field boundary ownerships, field gates, road names, boundary tree, spring, prominent trees (pictorial), greens.

23/476 Saxthorpe (parish) TG 117313
Apt 15.02.1842; 2113a (2113); Map 1842, 9 chns, in 6 parts, by Newton and Woodrow, Norwich, (including five 3-chn plans of 'Unenclosed Lands'); foot/b'way, pit; pictorial church.

23/477 Scarning (parish) TF 958117
Apt 24.03.1846; 3471a (3470); Map 1846, 6 chns, by William Browne, Norwich, for William Corby; turnpike roads, toll bar, waterbodies, houses, woods, building names, road names; pictorial church; bridge named.

23/478 Sco Ruston (district in parish of Sco Ruston) TG 281219
Apt 04.08.1841; 472a (471); Map 1841, 3 chns, 1st cl, by James Wright, Aylsham; construction lines, turnpike roads, waterbodies, houses, field boundary ownerships, road names, churchyard, fields tithable to Coltishall.

23/479 Scottowe (parish) TG 274234 [Scottow]
Apt 05.06.1839; 2105a (2120); Map 1839, 6 chns, by Josh Manning, Surveyor and Lithographer, 64 Bethel St, Norwich, litho; waterbodies, houses, woods, parkland, gardens, heath/moor, brickpits, windmill (pictorial); pictorial church; houses and pond are hand-coloured.

23/480 Scoulton (parish) TF 981010
Apt 20.09.1838; 2193a (2193); Map 1838, 6 chns, by Newton and Woodrow, Norwich; waterbodies, houses, woods, osiers (by symbol), plantations, reeds (by symbol), landowners (col), boundary of tithe-free land.

23/481 Sculthorpe (parish) TF 889312
Apt 12.04.1838; 2056a (all); Map 1838, 6 chns; waterbodies, houses, woods, plantations, pit, mill, driftways (col).

23/482 Sedegford (parish) TF 717366 [Sedgeford]
Apt 13.06.1840; 4181a (4180); Map 1840, 6 chns, by William Newham, Lynn, Norfolk; waterbodies, houses, Roman road.

23/483 Seething (parish) TM 316970
Apt 30.04.1838; 1630a (1630); Map 1838, 3 chns, 1st cl, by W.G. Jones, Loddon; waterbodies, houses; bridge named.

23/484 Sharrington (parish) TG 031370
Apt 10.09.1840; 863a (all); Map 1840?, 6 chns, by Alexr.... [damaged]; waterbodies, houses.

23/485 Shelfanger (parish) TM 100839
Apt 12.05.1843; 1720a (all); Map 1842, 3 chns, 1st cl, by Lenny and Croft, Bury St Edmds; construction lines, waterbodies, houses, woods, open meadows, fences, field boundary ownerships, field gates, building names, road names, rectory, common, greens.

23/486 Shelton and Hardwick (parish) TM 228904
Apt 26.09.1837; 2148a (2147); Map 1838, 3 chns, in 2 parts; waterbodies, houses.

23/487 Shereford (parish) TF 892291
Apt 13.06.1839; 843a (all); Map 1838, 9 chns, by W.G. Bircham, Fakenham; waterbodies, houses, woods, plantations.

23/488 Sheringham (parish) TG 143420
Apt 06.04.1839; 2177a (all); Map 1838, 3 chns, by Wm Drane, Norwich; waterbodies, houses, pit; pictorial church.

23/489 Shimpling (parish) TM 157831
Apt 21.11.1845; 781a (all); Map 1846, 6 chns, in 5 parts, by C.S. Alger, Diss, (includes four 3-chn enlargements of open fields); waterbodies, woods, plantations, parkland, orchards, gardens, ford, footbridge, boundary trees; pictorial church.

23/490 Shingham (parish) TF 772053
Apt 28.12.1839; 935a (935); Map 1840?, 8 chns, by Edwin Durrant, Kings Lynn; glebe; church is only building shown. District is apportioned by holding and fields are not shown; Apt generalises land use, and there are no details of occupiers.

23/491 Shipdham (parish) TF 964074
Apt 02.12.1845; 4560a (4560); Map 1846, 6 chns, by Pratt and Son, Norwich; houses; pictorial church; uninhabited buildings are shown in outline only, without infill.

23/492 Shotisham All Saints, Shotisham St Mary, Shotisham St Botolph, and Shotisham St Martin (parish) TM 249987 [Shotesham]
Apt 19.04.1841; 3440a (all); Map 1841?, 6 chns; waterbodies, houses, woods.

23/493 Shouldham (parish) TF 686089
Apt 24.05.1843; 3889a (3888); Map 1841, 4 chns, surveyed by John Wiggins; waterbodies, houses, woods, osiers (by symbol), warren. Apt omits some field names.

23/494 Shouldham Thorpe (parish) TF 658083
Apt 15.07.1846; 1430a (1430); Map 1847, 4 chns, surveyed by John Wiggins; waterbodies, houses, woods. Apt omits some field names.

23/495 Shropham (parish) TL 983926
Apt 03.11.1838; 2679a (2678); Map 1839, 10 chns, copied by James Drane, Norwich; field boundary ownerships; pictorial church; no other buildings shown; bridge named. District is apportioned by holding and fields are not shown; Apt generalises land use, and only names principal occupiers.

23/496 Sidestrand (parish) TG 263398
Apt 20.06.1838; 445a (560); Map 1838, 3 chns, 1st cl, surveyed by George F. Playford, North Repps; construction lines, waterbodies, houses, field boundary ownerships, field names, cliff, claypit.

23/497 Sisland (parish) TM 342987
Apt 12.04.1838; 466a (466); Map 1838, 3 chns, 1st cl, by W.G. Jones, Loddon; construction lines, foot/b'way, waterbodies, houses, woods, parkland, orchards, gardens, fence ownership, field boundary ownerships, field gates. Apt omits most field names.

23/498 Skeyton (parish) TG 246261
Apt 05.06.1840; 1264a (all); Map 1840, 6 chns; waterbodies, houses, woods.

23/499 Sloley (parish) TG 298241
Apt 13.07.1837; 719a (719); Map 1839, 6 chns, by W.S. Millard, Norwich. Apt omits land use.

23/500 Smallburgh (parish) TG 340240
Apt 27.05.1838; 1248a (all); Map 1840?, 6 chns, in 2 parts, by Robt Corby, (includes 3-chn enlargement of detail); waterbodies, houses, workhouse; bridge named.

23/501 Snetterton (parish) TM 000909
Apt 20.10.1843; 2190a (2189); Map 1844, 6 chns, by W.S. Millard and Son, Norwich; foot/b'way, waterbodies, houses, woods, plantations.

23/502 Great Snoring (parish) TF 945346
Apt 13.06.1840; 1645a (all); Map 1840, 6 chns; waterbodies, houses, woods, plantations, orchards, gardens, workhouse.

23/503 Little Snoring (parish) TF 959328
Apt 06.04.1838; 1525a (all); Map 1838?, 6 chns; houses, windmills (by symbol); pictorial church. Apt omits some land use.

23/504 Somerfield (parish) TF 750385 [Summerfield]
Apt 30.06.1845; 1205a (all); Map 1845, 6 chns; waterbodies, houses.

23/505 East Somerton (parish) TG 482198
Apt 17.12.1839; 798a (798); Map 1840, 3 chns; gardens, hedge ownership, embankment, windmill (pictorial), gates (pictorial).

23/506 West Somerton (parish) TG 470198
Apt 02.12.1840; 1190a (1189); Map 1841?, 3 chns, by Josh Manning, 64 Bethel St, Norwich; waterbodies, houses, woods, plantations, windmill (pictorial), pits; pictorial church.

23/507 Southacre (parish) TF 806132 [South Acre]
Apt 22.11.1837; 2492a (all); Map 1837, 8 chns, surveyed by J. Utting, Lynn Regis; foot/b'way, waterbodies, houses, plantations (col), arable (col), grassland (col), gardens (col), heath/moor (col), hedge ownership, fence ownership, windmill (by Dawson's symbol), pits (col). District is apportioned by holding, though fields are numbered separately; Apt omits land use.

23/508 Southburgh (parish) TG 001050
Apt 24.04.1838; 1216a (1216); Map not dated, 6 chns; foot/b'way, waterbodies, houses, field names; pictorial church.

23/509 Southery (parish) TL 612952
Apt 24.04.1838; 3695a (all); Map 1838, 3 chns, by Lenny and Croft, Bury St Edmunds; turnpike roads, waterbodies, houses, woods, building names, road and drove names, windmills (pictorial, named), ferry, waring pond, rectory, churchyard.

23/510 South Repps (parish) TG 258366 [Southrepps]
Apt 09.07.1839; 2081a (2081); Map 1839, 3 chns, surveyed and corrected by James Wright; foot/b'way, waterbodies, houses, woods, osiers (by symbol), road names, stiles, pits.

23/511 Southwood (parish) TG 394054
Apt 06.05.1845; 482a (all); Map 1845, 4.5 chns, in 2 parts, by Pratt and Son, Norwich; foot/b'way, waterbodies, houses, woods, plantations, pits; pictorial church.

23/512 Sparham (parish) TG 071195
Apt 18.03.1842; 1771a (1770); Map 1841, 6 chns, by Pratt and Son, Norwich; waterbodies, houses, pit.

23/513 Spixworth (parish) TG 241148
Apt 03.07.1837; 1224a (1224); Map 1816, 3 chns, by W.S. Millard, Norwich; waterbodies, houses, woods, boundary tree (pictorial); pictorial church.

23/514 Sporle with Palgrave (parish) TF 849111
Apt 26.06.1838; 3818a (3817); Map 1838, 3 chns, in 2 parts, by J. Utting, Lynn Regis; waterbodies, houses, mill.

23/515 Sprowston (parish) TG 253121
Apt 31.12.1842; 2577a (all); Map 1843, 6 chns, by W.S. Millard and Son, Norwich; foot/b'way, waterbodies, houses, woods.

23/516 Stalham (parish) TG 371251
Apt 22.06.1843; 1792a (1792); Map 1841, 3 chns, 1st cl, by James Wright, Aylsham; foot/b'way, waterbodies, houses, woods, osiers (by symbol), road names.

23/517 Stanfield (parish) TF 938206
Apt 12.09.1838; 903a (all); Map 1839?, [6 chns], by Newton and Woodrow, Norwich; waterbodies, houses, woods, field names.

23/518 Stanford (parish) TL 856937
Apt 20.06.1839; 2608a (all); Map 1839, 8 chns; waterbodies, houses, woods, plantations.

23/519 Stanhoe (parish) TF 800372
Apt 11.05.1838; 1489a (1489); Map 1838, 3 chns, litho, by J.T. Brown and J. Manning, Surveyors, etc, Bethel St, Norwich; waterbodies, woods, parkland, gardens, pits; ponds are hand-coloured. Apt omits some field names.

23/520 Starston (parish) TM 234857
Apt 22.11.1837; 2245a (all); Map 1838, 6 chns, by Henry Calver, Diss; waterbodies, woods; scale has small north pointers at each end.

23/521 Stibbard (parish) TF 985280
Apt 02.12.1843; 1469a (1468); Map 1844, 6 chns; waterbodies, houses, woods (named), plantations, modus land boundary, driftways (col).

23/522 Stiffkey (parish) TF 971431
Apt 30.04.1840; 2227a (all); Map 1840?, 6 chns, by W.G. Bircham, Fakenham; waterbodies, houses, plantations, parkland, heath/moor, landowners (col), cockle strand (col), high water springs, pit, windmill (pictorial), salt marsh; pictorial church; north pointer has diadem and plumes.

23/523 Stockton (parish) TM 389939
Apt 12.02.1846; 1052a (1051); Map 1846, 3 chns, in 2 parts, by Thos Burton Junr; waterbodies, houses, woods, pit; pictorial church.

23/524 Stody (parish) TG 058348
Apt 06.04.1839; 1278a (1277); Map 1839, 6 chns, in 2 parts, by Wm Glenister, Norwich; waterbodies, houses (dashed), plantations (by Dawson's symbol), orchards; scale-bar is ruler-like.

23/525 Stoke Ferry (parish) TL 700995
Apt 29.07.1841; 2060a (2059); Map 1838, 3 chns, by C. Mumford, Downham; foot/b'way, turnpike roads, waterbodies, houses, woods (col), orchards, gardens, field boundary ownerships, road and drove names, towing path, windmills (by symbol).

23/526 Stoke Holy Cross (parish) TG 242019
Apt 20.07.1843; 1660a (all); Map 1843, 6 chns, by Newton and Woodrow, Norwich; waterbodies, houses, windmill (pictorial), mills.

23/527 Stokesby, with Herringby (parish) TG 440108
Apt 04.06.1839; 2110a (2119); Map 1840, 6 chns, by Pratt and Son; waterbodies, houses, woods, reed ground.

23/528 Stow Bardolph (parish) TF 595075
Apt 23.11.1842; 6128a (6127); Map 1840, 4 chns, in 2 parts, surveyed by John Wiggins; waterbodies, woods, osiers (by symbol), road and drove names, drains (col, named), chapel, signpost (pictorial), conspicuous tree (pictorial), kitchen garden, decoy; bridge named; lands in Wimbotsham are coloured green.

23/529 Stow Bedon (parish) TL 955961
Apt 29.08.1845; 1692a (all); Map 1845, 6 chns, by Pratt and Son, Norwich; waterbodies, houses.

23/530 Stradsett (parish) TF 665056
Apt 31.05.1839; 1319a (1318); Map 1840?, 8 chns, copied by Edwin Durrant, Lynn; waterbodies.

23/531 Stratton St Mary (parish) TM 200913 [Not listed]
Apt 16.05.1839; 1518a (1517); Map 1839, 3 chns, 1st cl, by R. Hotson, Long Stratton; construction lines, foot/b'way, turnpike roads, waterbodies, houses, woods, plantations, parkland, field boundary ownerships, field acreages, road names, glebe; table summarises acreages. Apt omits most field names.

23/532 Stratton St Michael (parish) TM 204938
Apt 12.06.1839; 1050a (1050); Map 1838, 6 chns, in 2 parts, by Adam Taylor Clarke, Norwich, (includes 3-chn enlargement of detail); foot/b'way, turnpike roads, waterbodies, houses, woods, parkland, orchards, gardens, mills, milestones, pit, green (col), glebe.

23/533 Stratton Strawless (parish) TG 213203
Apt 04.04.1838; 1583a (1582); Map 1838, 3 chns, by James Harford, Bristol; foot/b'way, turnpike roads, waterbodies, woods (col, named), osiers (by symbol), parkland (col), arable (col), grassland (col), orchards (col), gardens, building names, road names, old gravel pits, lodges, icehouse, laundry, bleach ground, milestone.

23/534 Strumpshaw (parish) TG 347070
Apt 24.10.1844; 1337a (all); Map 1846, 6 chns; railway, waterbodies, houses, drains.

23/535 Suffield (parish) TG 238313
Apt 23.05.1838; 1458a (all); Map 1838, 3 chns, surveyed in 1830 and corrected by James Wright, 2 Grove Place, Brixton Rd, London, and Aylsham, Norfolk; waterbodies, houses, woods, orchards, field boundary ownerships, building names, lodge, pits; pictorial church.

23/536 Surlingham St Mary and Surlingham St Saviour (parishes) TG 317058
Apt 01.08.1843; 1768a (all); Map 1839, 3 chns, 1st cl, by John Wright, Foulsham; construction lines, houses, field boundary ownerships. Apt says that the precise boundary between the two parishes is at present unknown.

23/537 Sustead (parish) TG 187369
Apt 12.05.1848; 522a (522); Map 1847, 3 chns, 1st cl, by John F. Deyns, North Walsham; construction lines, waterbodies, houses, field boundary ownerships.

23/538 Sutton (parish) TG 386237
Apt 04.09.1840; 1373a (all); Map 1841?, 6 chns, by Pratt and Son, Norwich; waterbodies, houses, woods, staith, windmill (pictorial).

23/539 Swaffham (parish) TF 808090
Apt 04.11.1840; 7433a (all); Map 1840, 3 chns, 1st cl, by Newton and Woodrow, Norwich; construction lines, waterbodies, houses, field boundary ownerships, pit, glebe.

23/540 Swafield (parish) TG 286331
Apt 06.04.1839; 827a (all); Map 1839, 3 chns, surveyed by George F. Playford; foot/b'way, canal with locks and towpath, waterbodies, houses, woods.

23/541 Swainsthorpe (parish) TG 221008
Apt 26.07.1837; 819a (all); Map 1837, [6 chns]; waterbodies, houses, woods, workhouse, ownerships (col).

23/542 Swannington (parish) TG 139190
Apt 02.11.1841; 1433a (all); Map 1842, 3 chns, by Wm Drane, Norwich; waterbodies, houses, residual open fields; pictorial church. Apt omits field names for some smaller tithe areas.

23/543 Swanton Abbott (parish) TG 263264
Apt 22.11.1838; 1131a (1130); Map 1839, 6 chns, by Pratt and Son, Norwich; waterbodies, houses, avenue of trees, tithe-free land (col).

23/544 Swanton Morley and Worthing (district) TG 010172
Apt 06.05.1846; 3520a (all); Map 1847, 6 chns, in 2 parts, by William Browne, for William Corby, Norwich; waterbodies, bridleway (col), houses, woods, building names, mills, pit, windmill (pictorial); pictorial church.

23/545 Swanton Novers (parish) TG 017321
Apt 30.05.1838; 1316a (1315); Map 1838, 6 chns, by W.G. Bircham; houses, woods (named), pit, landowners (col); pictorial church; north pointer has diadem and plumes.

23/546 Swardeston (parish) TG 205028
Apt 03.09.1846; 933a (all); Map 1846, 3 chns, 1st cl, by Wm Drane, Norwich; construction lines, foot/b'way, turnpike roads, waterbodies, houses, woods, parkland, gardens, field boundary ownerships, field gates, pound, boundary tree, pit, commons.

23/547 Syderstone (parish) TF 841335
Apt 30.06.1845; 2518a (all); Map 1845?, 12 chns.

23/548 Tacolneston (parish) TM 143951
Apt 15.11.1844; 1581a (1580); Map 1845, 6 chns, in 2 parts, by Adam Taylor Clarke, Wymondham, (including open fields at 3 chns); turnpike roads, waterbodies, houses, woods, open fields, building names, boundary of tithe-free land.

23/549 Tasburgh (parish) TM 208960
Apt 08.09.1840; 917a (all); Map 1840, 6 chns, by Pratt and Son, Norwich; turnpike roads, waterbodies, houses, road names; pictorial church.

23/550 Tatterford (parish) TF 864295
Apt 12.06.1839; 960a (all); Map 1839, 6.67 chns, by W.G. Bircham, Fakenham; waterbodies, houses, woods, footbridge, ford, common; pictorial church.

23/551 Taverham (parish) TG 162147
Apt 02.11.1844; 2100a (all); Map 1845, 8 chns; waterbodies, houses, woods; uninhabited buildings are shown in outline only, without infill.

23/552 Terrington St Clements and Terrington St Johns (consolidated parishes) TF 550190 [Terrington St Clement]
Apt 06.02.1841; 11432a (34236); Map 1840?, 9 chns, in 5 parts, by E. Durrant, Kings Lynn, (including Terrington St Johns at 8 chns); turnpike roads, waterbodies, building names, road names, road junction names, marshes (col), Roman bank, sea bank, samphire marsh, wall. Apt omits most field names.

23/553 Testerton (parish) TF 936273 [Not listed]
Apt 28.02.1849; 36a (?); Map 1849?, 3 chns, (tithable parts only); houses, building names.

23/554 Tharston (parish) TM 185945
Apt 22.04.1839; 1572a (1582); Map 1839, 6 chns, by Newton and Woodrow, Norwich; houses, woods, residual open fields.

23/555 Thelveton (parish) TM 155812
Apt 15.02.1839; 1051a (all); Map 1839, [3 chns], 1st cl; construction lines, waterbodies, houses, woods (named), parkland, gardens, fences, ford, footbridge, boundary post, milestone, field acreages; pictorial churches; meaning of grey edging is unclear; map also includes whole of 23/424, Pierlestown.

23/556 Themelthorpe (parish) TG 061245
Apt 30.05.1838; 652a (652); Map 1839?, 3 chns, by Pratt and Warren; waterbodies, houses, glebe (pink), modus land boundary; north pointer has diadem and plumes.

23/557 St Cuthbert in Thetford (parish) TL 877832 [Not listed]
Apt 31.03.1845; 247a (260); Map 1846, 3 chns, (tithable parts only in detail); road names, common.

23/558 St Mary Thetford (parish) (partly in Suffolk) TL 860820 [Not listed]
Apt 30.06.1845; 263a (3960); Map 1849?, 3 chns, by C.S. Morris, Thetford, (tithable parts only); turnpike roads, houses, plantations, mill, Roman Catholic Chapel, gas works. Apt omits field names.

23/559 St Peter and St Nicholas in Thetford (parishes) TL 852855 [Not listed]
Apt 04.09.1843; 2036a (2240); Map 1843, 8 chns, (tithable parts only in detail); parish boundary; buildings are shown in outline only, without infill.

23/560 Thirning (parish) TG 075298 [Thurning]
Apt 13.07.1837; 1565a (1584); Map 1837, 3 chns, 1st cl, by W.S. Millard, Norwich; construction lines, waterbodies, houses, field boundary ownerships.

23/561 Thompson (parish) TL 922969
Apt 21.04.1845; 87a (2890); Map 1845, 3 chns, 'Copied' by Salter and Son, Attleboro', (tithable parts only); woods.

23/562 Thornage (parish) TG 052371
Apt 16.04.1838; 1267a (all); Map 1838, 3 chns, by Wm Glenister, Norwich; construction lines, waterbodies, houses, woods, field boundary ownerships, green.

23/563 Thornham (parish) TF 740428
Apt 27.03.1841; 2154a (all); Map 1842, 8 chns, partly copied and partly surveyed by Wm S. Millard and Son; waterbodies, woods, parkland.

23/564 Thorpe Abbots (parish) TM 191798 [Thorpe Abbotts]
Apt 20.10.1840; 1123a (all); Map 1839, 6 chns, by Henry Calver; waterbodies, woods, 'vale formerly a fence', boundary trees, windmill (pictorial); pictorial church with grassy churchyard and birds in flight. Apt omits most field names.

23/565 Thorpe Market (parish) TG 238356
Apt 07.05.1838; 1309a (all); Map 1839, 3 chns, surveyed in 1830 and corrected by James Wright, 2 Grove Place, Brixton Road, Kennington, London and Aylsham, Norfolk; foot/b'way, waterbodies, houses, woods, building names, chapel yard, lodge, tower, green; hill named.

23/566 Thorpe next Haddiscoe (parish) TM 435982 [Thorpe]
Apt 15.02.1839; 825a (all); Map 1839, 6 chns, by Thos Burton Junr, Langley, Norfolk; houses, windmills (pictorial); pictorial church.

23/567 Thorpe next Norwich with Thorpe (parish with hamlet) TG 262089 [Thorpe St Andrew]
Apt 12.05.1841; 2525a (all); Map 1841?, 6 chns, in 4 parts, (includes three 3-chn enlargements of detail); houses, woods, osiers (by symbol), building names, pits, asylum, gasworks, drains; bridge named.

23/568 Thorpe Parva (parish) TM 162793 [Not listed]
Apt 03.02.1842; 350a (349); Map 1844, 6 chns, by C.S. Alger, Diss; waterbodies, houses, woods, orchards, gardens, ruin (pictorial), gravel pit.

23/569 Threxton (parish) TL 888994 [Not listed]
Apt 11.07.1837; 1097a (all); Map 1839?, 4 chns; waterbodies, houses, woods (col), arable (col), grassland (col), gardens (col).

23/570 Thrigby (parish) TG 458124
Apt 19.12.1837; 576a (575); Map 1839, [4 chns]; waterbodies, woods (col), parkland (col), grassland (col), gardens (col), marsh/bog, hedges, fences, landowners, windmill (pictorial). Apt omits field names.

23/571 Thurgarton (parish) TG 181356
Apt 19.11.1839; 962a (961); Map 1840, 6 chns, by James Wright, Aylsham; waterbodies, houses, woods, park (named), windmill (pictorial), pit; pictorial church.

23/572 Thurlton (parish) TM 424990
Apt 16.10.1838; 1170a (1170); Map 1840?, 8 chns; foot/b'way, houses, windmill (pictorial); pictorial church.

23/573 Thursford (parish) TF 985342
Apt 11.08.1842; 1350a (all); Map 1843, 6 chns, by W.S. Millard and Son, Norwich; waterbodies, houses, woods, parkland.

23/574 Thurton (parish) TG 337004
Apt 16.06.1838; 772a (771); Map 1838, 4 chns, 'copied' by Thos. Burton Junr, Langley, Norfolk; waterbodies, houses, cross (pictorial, named in gothic); pictorial church.

23/575 Thuxton (parish) TG 040078
Apt 22.03.1844; 1103a (all); Map 1845, 6 chns, by William Corby; waterbodies, houses, plantations, parkland, orchards, pit; pictorial church.

23/576 Thwaite (parish) TM 335950 [Thwaite St Mary]
Apt 27.01.1841; 677a (all); Map 1838, 3 chns, 1st cl, by W.G. Jones, Loddon, Norfolk; construction lines, waterbodies, houses, field boundary ownerships.

23/577 Thwaite All Saints (parish) TG 192331
Apt 15.05.1841; 602a (all); Map 1841, 3 chns, by James Wright, Aylsham; foot/b'way, waterbodies, houses, woods, churchyard. [The map in PRO IR 30 is a copy of 1926.]

23/578 Tibenham (parish) TM 125893
Apt 16.01.1840; 3286a (3286); Map 1840, [8 chns], by Newton and Woodrow; waterbodies, houses, woods, parkland, gardens, hall.

23/579 Tilney All Saints, Tilney St Lawrence and Islington (district) TF 560153
Apt 24.06.1842; 7506a (7511); Map 1840, 6 chns, in 13 parts, by E. Durrant, Kings Lynn, and J. Utting, Lynn Regis, (includes 10-chn index); waterbodies, houses, tithe barn, old river bed, former open field boundaries; bridge named. Apt omits most field names.

23/580 Titchwell (parish) TF 758433
Apt 26.02.1839; 1452a (1627); Map 1838, 9 chns, by Edwin Durrant, Kings Lynn; foot/b'way, old creek, sea bank (col); pictorial church.

23/581 Tittleshall cum Godwick (parish) TF 898213
Apt 02.11.1837; 3365a (3364); Map 1837, 3 chns, 1st cl, by Pratt and Son, Norwich; construction lines, houses, woods (named), field boundary ownerships, building names, field names, boundary tree, pound, fox covert, glebe, township boundary.

23/582 Tivetshall St Margaret (parish) TM 172876
Apt 31.01.1839; 1632a (1668); Map 1839, [8 chns]; foot/b'way, waterbodies. Apt omits most field names.

23/583 Tivetshall St Mary (parish) TM 171852
Apt 21.01.1839; 1096a (1125); Map 1839?, [8 chns]; waterbodies. Apt omits most field names.

23/584 Toft Monks (parish) TM 428953
Apt 06.11.1840; 2238a (2238); Map 1840, 6 chns, 1st cl, in 4 parts, by W.G. Jones, Loddon, and T. Burton, Junr, Langley, (including detached parts at 3 chns); construction lines, waterbodies, houses, woods, gardens, fences, field boundary ownerships, field gates, windmill (pictorial); yellow bands are used for some bracing.

23/585 Tofttrees (parish) TF 901273
Apt 01.05.1839; 1195a (all); Map 1838, 9 chns, by W.G. Bircham, Fakenham; waterbodies, houses, woods, plantations; scale has small north pointers at each end.

23/586 West Tofts (parish) TL 841911
Apt 31.07.1844; 3052a (all); Map 1845, 6 chns; waterbodies, houses, woods, gardens, pits, fox covert, drove road.

23/587 Topcroft (parish) TM 270920
Apt 26.08.1839; 1875a (1875); Map 1840, 7 chns, by Geo. Baker, Bungay; waterbodies, residual open fields.

23/588 Tottington (parish) TL 897958
Apt 11.02.1846; 3179a (all); Map 1847?, 8 chns; waterbodies, houses, woods, plantations.

23/589 Trimingham (parish) TG 279388
Apt 04.10.1838; 525a (all); Map 1838, 3 chns, 'Surveyed and Mapped' by George F. Playford, North Repps; foot/b'way, waterbodies, houses, woods, heath/moor, field boundary ownerships, cliffs, sea; pink band shows land tithable to Sidestrand.

23/590 Trowse Newton and Trowse Millgate (parish and hamlet) TG 253069
Apt 26.03.1844; 1164a (1153); Map 1844, 6 chns; waterbodies, woods, osiers (by symbol), plantations, common.

23/591 Trunch (parish) TG 286351
Apt 24.12.1839; 1353a (1353); Map 1839, 3 chns, by James Wright, Aylsham; waterbodies, houses, woods, osiers (by symbol), field boundary ownerships, pit.

23/592 East Tuddenham (parish) TG 086115
Apt 12.06.1839; 2066a (2065); Map 1839, 6 chns, by Wm Drane, Norwich; waterbodies, houses, woods, plantations, parkland; pictorial church.

23/593 North Tuddenham (parish) TG 061137
Apt 26.02.1839; 2270a (2270); Map 1842, 6 chns, by Pratt and Son, Norwich; foot/b'way, waterbodies, houses; bridges named.

23/594 Tunstall (parish) TG 425085
Apt 03.03.1848; 1611a (1612); Map 1847, 6 chns, by Wm Drane, Norwich; foot/b'way, waterbodies, houses, woods, gardens, toll house, windmills (pictorial), pit, marked tree, ditches; dyke and drains named; pictorial church.

23/595 Tunstead (parish) TG 306226
Apt 20.08.1841; 2291a (2291); Map 1841, 3 chns, 1st cl, by James Wright, Aylsham; construction lines, foot/b'way, waterbodies, houses, woods, field boundary ownerships, road names.

23/596 Tuttington (parish) TG 229271
Apt 27.07.1839; 831a (all); Map 1839, 3 chns, 1st cl, by James Wright, 2 Grove Place, Brixton Rd, London, and Aylsham, Norfolk; waterbodies, houses, woods.

23/597 Twyford (parish) TG 015245
Apt 30.05.1838; 529a (all); Map 1838, 3 chns, 1st cl, by John Wright, Foulsham; construction lines, waterbodies, houses, woods, gardens (col), field boundary ownerships.

23/598 Upton (parish) TG 393127
Apt 12.06.1839; 1693a (1693); Map 1839?, 3 chns, 1st cl, by Thomas Burton Junr, Langley, Norfolk; construction lines, waterbodies, houses, field boundary ownerships, windmills (pictorial), pit; colour bands show land tithable elsewhere.

23/599 Waborne or Waybourne (parish) TG 115428 [Weybourne]
Apt 08.03.1839; 1618a (1680); Map 1839, [6 chns], by Edward Houghton, Wells; waterbodies, houses, woods (col), heath, gravel pit, windmill (pictorial), field boundary ownerships, ownerships (col).

23/600 Wacton Magna et Parva (parish) TM 184908 [Wacton]
Apt 25.03.1839; 1044a (all); Map 1840, 3 chns, 1st cl, in 2 parts, by Richard Hotson, Long Stratton; construction lines, foot/b'way, waterbodies, houses, road names, windmill (by symbol), glebe; yellow bands are used for some bracing. (PRO IR30 also contains a 6-chn reduction, by Hotson, including woods.) Apt omits most field names.

23/601 Walcot (parish) TG 361318 [Walcott]
Apt 30.11.1839; 686a (735); Map 1839, 3 chns, 1st cl, by James Wright, Aylsham; construction lines, foot/b'way, waterbodies, houses, woods, field boundary ownerships; pictorial church; green bands are used for some bracing.

23/602 Wallington (parish) TF 633076 [Not listed]
Apt 13.06.1840; 797a (?); Map 1840, 4 chns, by John Wiggins; foot/b'way, waterbodies, woods, plantations, park (named), building names, landowners, remains of church (pictorial, named in gothic), pit, ice house, chase, milestone, keepers lodge.

23/603 Walpole St Andrew (parish) TF 508190
Apt 23.09.1840; 2364a (3494); Map 1839, 6 chns, in 4 parts, by J. Utting, Lynn Regis, (includes 13.5-chn index, 1840); waterbodies, houses, former open field names and boundaries (col), marsh, Roman bank, toll gate, sea bank.

23/604 Walpole St Peter (parish) TF 515138
Apt 05.06.1839; 6982a (6982); Map 1839, 6 chns, in 7 parts, by J. Utting, Lynn Regis, (includes 13.5-chn index, 1840); waterbodies, houses, road names, former open field names and boundaries (col), Roman bank, marsh; drains and lodes named.

23/605 North Walsham (parish) TG 280300
Apt 01.02.1842; 4253a (all); Map 1842, 3 chns, by James Wright, Aylsham, (includes enlargement of town at 1 chn); foot/b'way, turnpike roads, waterbodies, houses (dark grey), woods, heath/moor, road names, canal with locks and towpath.

23/606 South Walsham St Lawrence and South Walsham St Mary (parishes) TG 370130 [South Walsham]
Apt 17.09.1839; 3150a (3149); Map 1838, 3 chns, 1st cl, in 2 parts, by J.P. Luckraft and Co.; construction lines, waterbodies, houses, woods, plantations, gardens, pits, old tower, parish boundary, drains.

23/607 Walsoken (parish) TF 495095
Apt 19.04.1842; 4656a (4656); Map 1842, 3 chns, 1st cl, by F.J. Utting, Wisbech for Charles Mumford, Downham.; construction lines, canal, waterbodies, houses, building names, road names, former open field names.

23/608 East Walton (parish) TF 747161
Apt 27.08.1841; 2660a (2659); Map 1840, 6 chns, by Wm Drane, Norwich; foot/b'way, waterbodies, houses, woods, plantations, heath/moor, pit; pictorial church.

23/609 West Walton (parish) TF 491130
Apt 12.06.1839; 5219a (all); Map 1839, 6 chns, in 4 parts, by J. Utting, Lynn Regis, (includes 13.5-chn index, 1840); former open field names, road names, Roman bank, drains (named), tithe ownership boundaries.

23/610 Warham All Saints (parish) TF 953431 [Not listed]
Apt 04.04.1838; 1164a (1774); Map 1838, 6 chns, by Pratt and Son, Norwich; waterbodies, houses, sandhills, beach, boundary posts (pictorial), beach.

23/611 Warham St Mary Magdalen and St Mary the Virgin (parish) TF 940428 [Not listed]
Apt 07.07.1837; 2056a (3066); Map 1837, 6 chns, by Pratt and Son, Norwich; waterbodies, houses, woods (col), arable (col), grassland (col), heath/moor, Roman camp, sandhills, beach, tides meet [in creek], embankments, sea wall, beach.

23/612 Waterden (parish) TF 889362
Apt 13.07.1837; 794a (763); Map 1837, 3 chns, 1st cl, by Pratt and Son, Norwich; construction lines, houses, woods.

23/613 Watlington (parish) TF 620110
Apt 07.11.1838; 1709a (1709); Map 1839, 4 chns; waterbodies, houses, drains (named), driftway (col).

23/614 Watton (parish) TF 921008
Apt 02.09.1841; 1808a (1807); Map 1839, 4 chns; waterbodies, houses, windmill (pictorial); land tinted pink is tithe-free; land tinted yellow is problematic. Apt omits most field names.

23/615 Waxham (parish) TG 442251
Apt 11.06.1838; 1963a (2087); Map corrected to 1839, 3 chns, in 2 parts, by James Wright, 2 Grove Place, Brixton Rd, London, and Aylsham, Norfolk; foot/b'way, waterbodies, houses, woods, hedges, windmills (pictorial), copper, boundary posts, landowners, field acreages; pictorial church.

23/616 Weasenham All Saints (parish) TF 852212
Apt 03.12.1839; 1988a (1988); Map 1840, 6 chns, by Pratt and Son, Norwich; houses, gravel pit.

23/617 Weasenham St Peter (parish) TF 846227
Apt 14.12.1839; 1423a (1423); Map 1840, 6 chns, by Pratt and Son, Norwich; houses, gravel pit.

23/618 Weeting (parish) TL 780900
Apt 19.04.1849; 6188a (6187); Map 1845, 6 chns, by Lenny and Croft; railway, waterbodies, houses, woods, parkland, gardens, fences, school, castle, rectory; drove named.

23/619 Welborne (parish) TG 068099
Apt 11.12.1838; 732a (all); Map 1838, 6 chns; waterbodies, houses, woods, milestone.

23/620 Wellingham (parish) TF 871222
Apt 19.02.1838; 1067a (1066); Map 1837, 3 chns, 1st cl, by Pratt and Son, Norwich; construction lines, houses, field boundary ownerships.

23/621 Wells next the Sea (parish) TF 916432 [Wells-next-the-Sea]
Apt 08.08.1844; 2691a (4510); Map 1843, 4 chns, by Edwd Houghton, Wells; waterbodies, houses, plantations (col), grassland (col), sandhills, windmills (pictorial), rectory, salt marshes, tidal mud (col). Apt omits some field names.

23/622 Wendling (parish) TF 931136
Apt 11.03.1840; 1436a (1436); Map 1841?, 6 chns. District is apportioned by holding and fields are not shown.

23/623 Wereham (parish) TF 679014
Apt 31.08.1841; 2232a (2231); Map 1840, 6 chns, by Newton and Woodrow, Norwich; waterbodies, houses; there is a verbose note about the location of a detached portion.

23/624 Westfield (parish) TF 995098
Apt 28.11.1838; 569a (569); Map 1839, 6 chns, by Newton and Woodrow, Norwich; waterbodies, houses, woods, pit; pictorial church.

23/625 Weston Longville (parish) TG 107159
Apt 22.01.1841; 2737a (2737); Map 1841, 6 chns, by Pratt and Son, Norwich; waterbodies, houses, woods.

23/626 Westwick (parish) TG 280260
Apt 15.09.1837; 1044a (1043); Map 1844, 4 chns, copied by Wm Drane, Norwich; waterbodies, mansion (pictorial), roadside waste (col); pictorial church. Apt omits field names.

23/627 Wheatacre All Saints (parish) TM 465950 [Wheatacre]
Apt 18.06.1840; 1164a (1163); Map 1840, 6 chns, by Wm Drane, Norwich; waterbodies, houses, woods, plantations, parkland, gardens, fences, pit, windmills (pictorial); pictorial church.

23/628 Whinbergh (parish) TG 007083 [Not listed]
Apt 15.06.1839; 1241a (1241); Map 1839, 3 chns, by Newton and Woodrow, Norwich; waterbodies, houses, modus land boundary; pictorial church; north pointer has diadem and plumes.

23/629 Whissonsett (parish) TF 911232
Apt 07.06.1842; 1345a (1344); Map 1838, 6 chns, by W.G. Bircham, Fakenham; waterbodies, houses, woods, windmills (pictorial), pit; pictorial church.

23/630 Whitwell (parish) TG 087214 [Not listed]
Apt 08.03.1844; 1512a (all); Map 1845?, 6 chns; waterbodies, houses.

23/631 Wickhampton (parish) TG 441050
Apt 08.04.1842; 1602a (1605); Map 1842, 3 chns; waterbodies, houses, woods, osiers (by symbol), windmill (pictorial).

23/632 Wicklewood (parish) TG 077016
Apt 27.12.1843; 1564a (1564); Map 1843, 6 chns, by A.T. Clarke, Norwich; waterbodies, houses, woods, plantations, pit, house of industry; north pointer has diadem and plumes.

23/633 Wiggenhall St Germans (parish) TF 587129
Apt 21.11.1838; 1215a (all); Map 1839?, 6 chns, by Charles Burcham, Kings Lynn; waterbodies. Apt omits most field names.

23/634 Wiggenhall St Mary Magdalen (parish) TF 580084
Apt 22.08.1840; 4248a (4248); Map 1840, 4 chns, by Edwin Durrant, Kings Lynn; waterbodies, houses; drains, hooks and headings (all watercourses) are named.

23/635 Wiggenhall St Mary the Virgin (parish) TF 586150
Apt 06.09.1838; 2807a (2807); Map 1839, 6 chns, in 3 parts, by Charles Burcham, Kings Lynn, (includes 30-chn index); waterbodies, houses, saltmarsh (col), banks (col), roadside waste (col); blue field boundaries may be ditches; index shows and names former open fields. Apt omits some field names.

23/636 Wiggenhall St Peters (parish) TF 600120
Apt 26.02.1839; 945a (944); Map 1839, 6 chns, in 2 parts, by Charles Burcham. Apt omits field names.

23/637 Wighton (parish) TF 925400
Apt 14.09.1839; 2932a (2934); Map 1839?, 6 chns, by Pratt and Son, Norwich; waterbodies, houses.

23/638 Wilby (parish) TM 043897
Apt 26.03.1839; 1396a (1400); Map 1838, 4 chns, copied by William Drane, Norwich; glebe, warren (col); no buildings are shown. District is apportioned by holding and fields are not shown.

23/639 Wimbotsham (parish) TF 622047
Apt 09.02.1843; 2015a (2015); Map 1840, 4 chns, in 2 parts, surveyed by John Wiggins; waterbodies, woods, sluice, modus land (pink); bridge and some drains named.

23/640 East Winch (parish) TF 698164
Apt 17.07.1838; 2531a (2530); Map 1838, 6 chns, by J. Utting, Lynn Regis; foot/b'way, waterbodies, houses, common.

23/641 West Winch (parish) TF 629152
Apt 21.07.1840; 1170a (all); Map 1838, 4 chns, by J. Utting, Lynn Regis; waterbodies, houses, common; drain named.

23/642 Winfarthing (parish) TM 107864
Apt 08.06.1840; 2620a (2620); Map 1841, 6 chns, by Henry Calver; waterbodies, woods (col), orchards, gardens, windmill (pictorial), notable trees (pictorial), boundary trees; pictorial church.

23/643 Winterton (parish) TG 491205 [Winterton-on-Sea]
Apt 26.09.1844; 1296a (all); Map 1845, 3 chns, 1st cl, by James Wright, Aylsham; construction lines, waterbodies, houses, woods, field boundary ownerships, decoy, lookout, flagstaff, boundary posts.

23/644 Great Witchingham (parish) TG 100198
Apt 03.09.1841; 2245a (2245); Map 1842, 6 chns, by W.S. Millard and Sons, Norwich; waterbodies, houses, woods.

23/645 Little Witchingham (parish) TG 120205 [Not listed]
Apt 20.03.1844; 738a (all); Map 1844?, 6 chns, by W.S. Millard and Son, Norwich; waterbodies, houses, woods.

23/646 Witlingham (parish) TG 275075 [Not listed]
Apt 05.02.1841; 543a (542); Map 1842, 6 chns, by Robt Corby; houses, woods, marlpits, boundary posts; pictorial church.

23/647 Witton (parish) TG 314095
Apt 20.06.1838; 577a (587); Map 1840?, 3 chns, by John T. Brown, and J. Manning, Norwich; foot/b'way, waterbodies, houses, woods (col), parkland (col), grassland (col), gardens, windmill (pictorial).

23/648 Witton (parish) TG 331310 [Witton Bridge]
Apt 27.03.1839; 1746a (1746); Map 1841, 3 chns, by James Wright, Aylsham; foot/b'way, waterbodies, houses (dark grey), woods, windmills (pictorial), canal towpath and locks, churchyard, water mill, pit.

23/649 Wiveton (parish) TG 040428
Apt 20.07.1842; 1042a (1042); Map 1842, 6 chns, by W.G. Bircham, Fakenham; houses, woods, hall, heath/moor, windmills (pictorial), pit.

23/650 Wolterton and Wickmore or Wolterton cum Wickmore (parish or respective parishes) TG 163329
Apt 24.02.1840; 1697a (1697); Map 1840, 6 chns, by Newton and Woodrow, Norwich; foot/b'way, waterbodies, houses, woods, plantations, parkland, gardens.

23/651 Woodbastwick (parish) TG 330150
Apt 31.12.1838; 2163a (all); Map 1839, 3 chns, surveyed in 1832 and corrected by Thos. Hornidge, 10 Mitre Court Chambers, Temple; foot/b'way, waterbodies, houses (by shading), woods, orchards, sink well.

23/652 Wooddalling (parish) TG 089273 [Wood Dalling]
Apt 23.01.1839; 2444a (2444); Map 1840?, 9 chns, surveyed in 1834 and lithographed by Joseph Manning, Bethel St, Norwich, litho; foot/b'way, waterbodies, woods; pictorial church.

23/653 Wood Norton (parish) TG 013280
Apt 26.07.1842; 1726a (1726); Map 1842, 6 chns, by Chas Burcham, Kings Lynn; waterbodies, houses, woods, boundary stone.

23/654 Woodrising (parish) TF 989031
Apt 17.07.1838; 1364a (1363); Map 1839?, 6 chns, by Newton and Woodrow, Norwich; foot/b'way, waterbodies, houses, woods, plantations, parkland, arable (col), grassland (col), gardens, landowners (col); pictorial church.

23/655 Woodton (parish) TM 285950
Apt 22.01.1841; 2125a (2124); Map 1841, 6 chns; waterbodies, houses, woods, plantations, parkland, orchards, gardens, road names, windmill (pictorial), parsonage; pictorial church.

23/656 Woolferton (parish) TF 660283 [Wolferton]
Apt 24.04.1838; 2715a (5634); Map 1838, 7.5 chns, by Edwin Durrant, Kings Lynn; waterbodies, grassland (col), embankment (col), salt marsh, warren.

23/657 North Wootton (parish) TF 641251
Apt 09.08.1837; 1844a (all); Map 1838, 6 chns; waterbodies, houses, woods, embankment, windmill (pictorial); pictorial church.

23/658 South Wootton (parish) TF 645231
Apt 24.11.1843; 1370a (all); Map 1844?, 3 chns; waterbodies, houses, field boundary ownerships, field gates, clay pits, rectory, milestone, bank, green, common, waste, sands.

23/659 Wormegay (parish) TF 671125
Apt 03.05.1838; 2789a (2788); Map 1838, 6 chns; waterbodies, houses, drains named; pictorial churches.

23/660 Worstead (parish) TG 304266
Apt 29.03.1843; 2603a (all); Map 1843, 6 chns, by Pratt and Son, Norwich, (includes village separately at 1.5 chns); waterbodies, houses, woods, parkland; pictorial church.

23/661 Wramplingham (parish) TG 116060
Apt 11.06.1838; 845a (all); Map 1839, 3 chns, copy of the map used for enclosing the parish, revised and corrected by Issac Lenny, Norwich; foot/b'way, turnpike roads, waterbodies, houses, woods (col), osiers (by symbol, col), parkland (col), arable (col), grassland (col), orchards (col), gardens (col), road names, field names, occupiers, boundary trees, parsonage, signpost, churchyard, fosse, carriage drive, gravel pit, stackyard, bleach [ground].

23/662 Wreningham (parish) TM 149989
Apt 08.06.1839; 1528a (1528); Map 1838, 3 chns, by Samuel Colman, Norwich; foot/b'way, tithe-free land (green), glebe (yellow). Apt omits most field names.

23/663 East and West Wretham (parish) TL 900906 [Wretham]
Apt 09.01.1840; 6443a (6442); Map 1840, 6 chns, surveyed by Hopcraft, Son and Hemingway in 1811, and copied by Richard Payne; waterbodies (named), houses, plantations (col, named), building names, glebe (green) ruined church (pictorial), pits (named), estate boundary; red band divides East and West Wretham. District is apportioned by holding and fields are not shown; Apt generalises land use, and only principal occupiers are named.

23/664 Wretton (parish) TL 686998
Apt 15.02.1839; 1155a (1154); Map 1838, 3 chns, surveyed by Charles Mumford, Downham, Norfolk; foot/b'way, waterbodies, houses, woods, field boundary ownerships, road and drove names, church path; drains named.

23/665 Wroxham (parish) TG 300170
Apt 26.08.1839; 1489a (1489); Map 1840, 6 chns, by Newton and Woodrow, Norwich; waterbodies, houses, woods, pit.

23/666 Wymondham (parish) TM 115999
Apt 18.06.1839; 10559a (10613); Map 1839, 6 chns, (includes town separately at 3 chns); houses, parkland, gardens, cross; modus land is not mapped in detail. Apt omits field names.

23/667 Great Yarmouth (parish) TG 526081
Apt 24.11.1846; 140a (1510); Map 1848, 2 chns, 1st cl, by William Browne, Norwich, for Robert Wright and Son (tithable parts only); construction lines, foot/b'way, road names, waterbodies, houses, pumps, milestones, embankment, town wall, tower, churchyard. Apt omits land use for houses and gardens.

23/668 Yaxham (parish) TG 017105
Apt 08.11.1838; 1596a (1596); Map 1839, 6 chns, by Newton and Woodrow, Norwich; waterbodies, houses, woods, plantations. Apt omits some field names.

23/669 Yelverton and Alpington (parishes) TG 293021
Apt 13.07.1838; 1069a (all); Map 1838, 3 chns, 1st cl, by Thos Burton Junr, Langley, Norfolk; construction lines, houses, field boundary ownerships, parish boundary.

Northamptonshire

PRO IR29 and IR30 24/1-144

340 tithe districts: 641,159 acres
144 tithe commutations: 148,184 acres
47 voluntary tithe agreements, 97 compulsory tithe awards

Tithe and tithe commutation

By 1836 more tithe had been commuted in association with parliamentary enclosure in Northamptonshire than in any other county. Enclosure commutation usually affected only those parts of a parish enclosed by the parliamentary award and so left as tithable any small tracts of early enclosed land. As a result tithes were still paid in 42 per cent of the county's tithe districts but only 23 per cent of the county area remained tithable (Fig. 36).

Assistant tithe commissioners and local tithe agents who worked in Northamptonshire are listed in Table 24.1. An unusually high proportion of Northamptonshire tithe districts (13 per cent) was valued by men based some distance outside the county; most of these were from London (Table 24.2). The tithe apportionments for the three divisions of Upper Heyford are unusual in having sale-lot numbers in place of field-names.

Tithe maps

Only 6 per cent of Northamptonshire maps are first class. Six maps are acknowledged copies of earlier work and many of the large number of maps of very small residual tracts of tithable land are probably based on enclosure maps. As in some other counties where much tithe had already been commuted by 1836, the chronology of Northamptonshire mapping is somewhat irregular with peaks of activity around 1839, 1845 and 1849 (Table 24.4). The scales used on the maps vary from one inch to one chain to one inch to twelve chains; 41 per cent use the officially recommended scale-range of one inch to three to four chains. As elsewhere in the Midlands, the six-chain scale was the most widely used (in 42 per cent of districts) (Table 24.3).

Northamptonshire tithe maps contain a better record of land use than do those of many tithe districts in the Midlands, though the proportion of maps showing woodland, at 61 per cent, is rather below the average. Field boundary ownership is indicated on the high proportion of 45 per cent of the maps. Fifteen maps show churches by pictorial symbols which, though stylised, compare well with Ordnance Survey mapping of church steeples.

Eighty-three Northamptonshire tithe maps in the Public Record Office collection can be

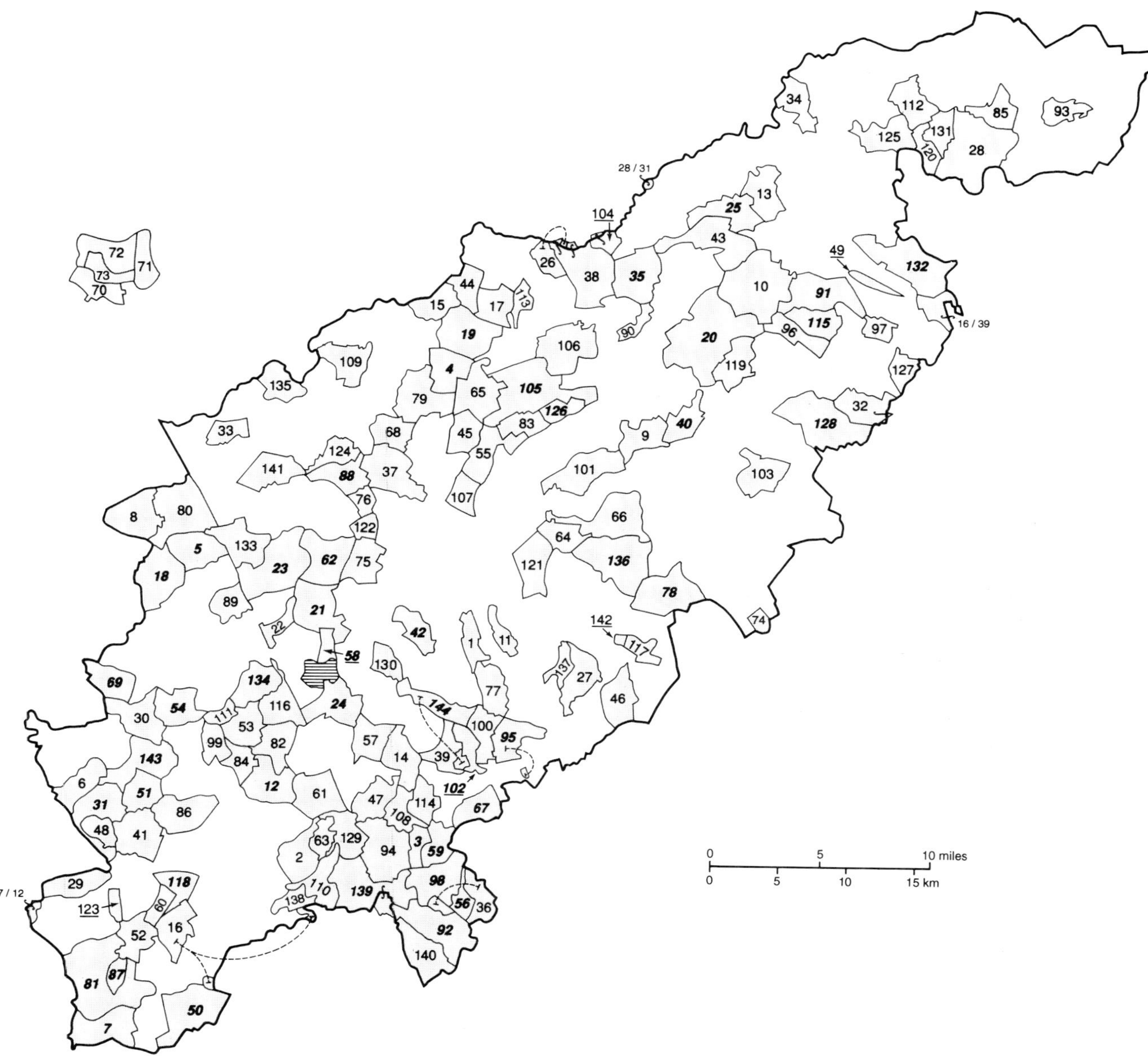

Fig. 36 Northamptonshire: tithe district boundaries.

attributed to a particular map-maker; the most prolific were Messrs Hayward of Northampton. Neatness and fairly fine linework characterise the work of these surveyors and of most of the other more prolific map-makers working in Northamptonshire. A few map-makers came from well outside the county, notably Thomas Mulliner from London, who produced four very colourful maps with 'billowy' woodland symbols. Colour and decoration are used on Northamptonshire tithe maps to a greater extent than in other midland counties. Visually the most striking map is that of Brockhall which has a system of colouring which indicates both land use and landownership; the colouring of landownership and tithable status is a common feature on Northamptonshire tithe maps. The map of Easton Maudit has leaves, a coronet, a robe and other objects decorating the title, and the maps of Preston Deanry and Rushton have banner-and-belt decoration. The Rushton map also has a coat of arms and a motto.

Table 24.1. *Agreements and awards for commutation of tithes in Northamptonshire*

Assistant commissioner/ local tithe agent	*Number of agreements**	*Number of awards*
Thomas Smith Woolley	9	68
Francis Offley Martin	0	18
John West	16	0
F. Browne Browne	7	0
John Maurice Herbert	0	6
John Pickering	4	0
Henry Pilkington	3	0
William Wakeford Attree	0	2
Thomas James Tatham	0	2
Joseph Townsend	1	0
Tithe Commissioners	1	0

*Computed from the number of extant reports on tithe agreements in the tithe files [PRO IR 18].

Table 24.2. *Tithe valuers and tithe map-makers in Northamptonshire*

Name and address (in Northamptonshire unless indicated)	*Number of districts*	*Acreage*
Tithe valuers		
Charles Paul Berkeley, Oundle	16	17,165
John Durham, Stony Stratford, Buckinghamshire	13	7,232
Richard Francis Hayward, Northampton	8	9,599
John Davis, Banbury, Oxfordshire	8	8,877
John Breasley, Chapel Brampton	6	7,066
John West, Little Bowden	5	7,557
Others [56]	88	90,688
Attributed tithe map-makers		
Messrs Hayward, Northampton	15	18,524
John Durham, Stony Stratford, Buckinghamshire	14	13,896
Richard Davis, Banbury	9	5,633
G. Smith, Oundle/Market Deeping, Lincolnshire/Stamford, Lincolnshire	8	5,546
Charles Day, Colleyweston	4	8,260
Joseph Gilbert, Welford	4	4,160
Others [21]	29	35,107

Table 24.3. *The tithe maps of Northamptonshire: scales and classes*

Scale in chains/inch	*All maps*		*First Class*		*Second Class*	
	Number	*Acreage*	*Number*	*Acreage*	*Number*	*Acreage*
>3	4	293	0	0	4	293
3	46	46,101	8	9,756	38	36,345
4	13	13,011	1	2,422	12	10,589
5	5	3,396	0	0	5	3,396
6	61	73,720	0	0	61	73,720
<6	15	11,663	0	0	15	11,663
TOTAL	144	148,184	9	12,178	135	136,006

Table 24.4. *The tithe maps of Northamptonshire: dates*

	1837	*1838*	*1839*	*1840*	*1841*	*1842*	*1843*	*1844*	*1845*	*1846*	*1847*	*1848*	*1849*	*>1849*
All maps	1	8	19	15	5	7	6	7	15	14	5	8	14	23
1st class	0	2	1	0	0	0	1	1	1	0	1	2	0	0
2nd class*	1	6	18	15	5	7	5	6	14	14	4	6	14	23

*One second-class tithe map of Northamptonshire in the Public Record Office collection is undated.

Northamptonshire

24/1 Abington (parish) SP 777620
Apt 26.08.1840; 1113a (1112); Map 1841, 6 chns, surveyed by William Bonsor, Clipston; foot/b'way, waterbodies, houses, woods, parkland, gardens, field boundary ownerships; green tint shows glebe and Crown land.

24/2 Abthorpe (parish) SP 654457
Apt 26.02.1839; 1920a (all); Map 1839, 3 chns, by John Durham, Junior, Stony Stratford; foot/b'way, waterbodies, hedge ownership, fence ownership; it is unclear why some glebe land is tinted.

24/3 Alderton (parish) SP 741468
Apt 24.11.1853; 48a (910); Map (drawn on Apt) 1853?, 6 chns, (tithable parts only).

24/4 Arthingworth (parish) SP 752819
Apt 6.2.1847; 10a (2030); Map 1851, 3 chns, by Washbourne and Keen, Cannon Row, Westminster, (tithable parts only); waterbodies, houses, farmyards, arable (col), grassland (col).

24/5 Ashby St Ledgers (parish) SP 571685
Apt 16.01.1849; 58a (2050); Map 1850, 5 chns, in 4 parts, by Thomas Smith, Rugby, (tithable parts only; includes 80-chn index, from Ordnance Survey); foot/b'way, turnpike roads, waterbodies, woods, hedge ownership, field gates, field names, landowners, windmill (by symbol), milestone; scale says 4 chns, but is graduated for 5 chns.

24/6 Aston-le-Walls (parish) SP 493507 [Aston le Walls]
Apt 09.08.1850; 1533a (1270); Map 1851?, 3 chns; foot/b'way, waterbodies, houses, woods, plantations, fence, field gates, stiles.

24/7 Aynhoe (parish) SP 518332 [Aynho]
Apt 21.03.1846; 260a (2330); Map 1846, 3 chns, (tithable parts only); canal, farmyards (col), woods (col), arable (col), grassland (col), field boundary ownerships; colour bands show both land use and field boundary ownership.

24/8 Barby (parish) SP 527708
Apt 10.12.1844; 1625a (2535); Map 1845, 3 chns, by R. Stelfox, Allesley, (tithable parts only in detail); foot/b'way, canal with towpath, waterbodies, woods, plantations, orchard; pink band separates glebe and tithe-free lands. Apt omits land use and field names for glebe.

24/9 Barton Seagrave (parish) SP 897774
Apt 26.04.1842; 1782a (all); Map 1842, 6 chns, by Thomas Miles, Leicester; foot/b'way, waterbodies, woods, plantations, freeboard.

24/10 Upper and Lower Benefield (parish) SP 977890
Apt 26.08.1848; 394a (5100); Map 1850?, 12 chns, (tithable parts only in detail); waterbodies, woods, building names, landowners, brickfield, rectory, stone pits, old stone pit.

24/11 Little Billing (parish) SP 801624
Apt 05.03.1840; 857a (all); Map 1840?, 3 chns; foot/b'way, waterbodies, houses, woods (col), osiers (by symbol), field boundary ownerships, glebe (col).

24/12 Blakesley, including Woodend, Foxley, Seywell and Kirby (parish) SP 630513
Apt 26.06.1840; 781a (2840); Map 1839, 3 chns, in 5 parts, 'Surveyed and Planned' by J. Durham; waterbodies, houses, field boundary ownerships, landowners; map has landowners' signatures, including a charity's seal, signifying its adoption.

24/13 Blatherwycke (parish) SP 979955
Apt 22.01.1846; 1858a (1975); Map 1847, 6.67 chns; waterbodies, woods (named), parkland (in detail), gardens, deer park, drying yard, fountain, statue (by symbol), summer house, boat house, mill, trap, racecourse, deer hovel, freeboard, milestone, glebe; hill named.

24/14 Blisworth (parish) SP 727535
Apt 22.04.1845; 68a (1980); Map 1846?, 3 chns, by John Durham, Junr, Stony Stratford, (tithable parts only, tinted); hedge ownership.

24/15 Little Bowden (parish) SP 746866
Apt 15.01.1845; 17a (1670); Map 1845?, 4 chns, (tithable parts only); waterbodies, field boundary ownerships.

24/16 St Peter Brackley (parish) SP 566404 [Brackley]
Apt 19.12.1840; 2092a (3717); Map 1839, 6 chns, in 2 parts; waterbodies, woods (col, named), landowners, college chapel, freeboard; pictorial church, with gravestones.

24/17 Brampton Ash (parish) SP 785867
Apt 14.08.1844; 1153a (?); Map 1839, 6 chns, by W. Bonsor, Clipston, Market Harborough; foot/b'way, waterbodies, houses, field boundary ownerships, rectorial land, wood (by annotation); most of the writing is gothic.

24/18 Braunceston (parish) SP 544665 [Braunston]
Apt 17.08.1842; 785a (3930); Map 1842, 8 chns, (tithable parts only); canal, waterbodies, estate boundary.

24/19 Braybrooke (parish) SP 765847
Apt 16.01.1845; 132a (3060); Map 1849?, 3 chns, (tithable parts only); arable (col), grassland (col), hedge ownership.

24/20 Brigstock (parish) SP 944851
Apt 12.01.1846; 85a (5900); Map 1850?, 4 chns, (tithable parts only); landowner.

24/21 Brington (parish) SP 661641 [Great Brington]
Apt 18.06.1839; 1002a (3761); Map 1840, 4 chns, (tithable parts only); township names (in gothic); Earl Spencer's lands are yellow and other lands green.

24/22 Brockhall (parish) SP 636627
Apt 21.01.1839; 862a (861); Map 1839, 6 chns; railway with cutting, canal with towpath, waterbodies, woods (col), parkland, grassland (col), gardens, hedge ownership, fence ownership, glebe (pink); land use is shown by rulings on top of colours showing owners.

24/23 Long Buckby (parish) SP 634671
Apt 28.07.1845; 81a (3900); Map 1845?, 2 chns, 'Copy' by Stephen St Peter Langton, Teeton, Northampton, (tithable parts only); woods, hedge ownership.

24/24 Bugbrook (parish) SP 679573 [Bugbrooke]
Apt 20.03.1849; 193a (2420); Map 1850, 6 chns, (tithable parts only, tinted); foot/b'way, waterbodies, field boundary ownerships, mill.

24/25 Bulwick (parish) SP 956944
Apt 13.05.1845; 138a (1910); Map 1845, 3 chns, by G. Smith, Market Deeping, (tithable parts only); houses, plantations, building names.

24/26 East Carlton (parish) SP 822901
Apt 15.01.1845; 623a (all); Map 1845, 6 chns, (tithable parts only, tinted); waterbodies, woods, glebe (pink).

24/27 Castle Ashby (parish) SP 861592
Apt 13.06.1840; 1926a (1926); Map 1840?, 6 chns, by R.F. Hayward; waterbodies, houses, woods, plantations, modus land (pink), glebe (green); map is dated 1841 but there is a receipt date stamp, 26 Nov 1840.

24/28 Castor and Ailesworth (district in parish of Castor) TL 132995
Apt 29.01.1844; 4867a (?); Map 1846, 3 chns, by Charles Day, Colleyweston; railway, waterbodies, woods, open fields (named), park, windmill (pictorial); pictorial church; both dot-dash and pecked field boundaries are used.

24/29 Chacombe (parish) SP 494436
Apt 31.10.1839; 1694a (1694); Map 1840, 3 chns, by Richard Davis, Banbury; construction lines, foot/b'way, waterbodies, houses, woods, plantations, parkland, gardens, orchards (by annotation), hedge ownership, fence ownership, field boundary ownerships, field gates, stiles.

24/30 Charwelton (parish) SP 535557
Apt 01.03.1847; 2332a (all); Map 1847, 6 chns, by J. Payn, Fawsley; foot/b'way, waterbodies, houses, woods, osiers (by symbol), plantations, fence, building names, windmills, mill.

24/31 Chipping Warden (parish) SP 503492
Apt 26.10.1838; 179a (1987); Map 1837, 3 chns, in 4 parts, by Richard Davis, Banbury, (tithable parts only; including 6-chn location map); waterbodies, houses, woods, hedge ownership, field gates, landowners.

24/32 Clapton (parish) TL 060802 [Clopton]
Apt 20.08.1839; 1946a (1946); Map 1840, 6 chns; foot/b'way, waterbodies, woods, building names, pound, notable oak.

24/33 Clay Coton (parish) SP 594772
Apt 11.04.1839; 974a (all); Map surveyed in March and April 1839, 3 chns, by C. Walker, Swinford; foot/b'way, houses, woods, plantations, hedges, fences, field gates, stiles; churchyard has tombstone symbols.

24/34 Collyweston (parish) SK 998025
Apt 18.07.1839; 1549a (all); Map 1842?, 6 chns, in 2 parts, by George Canning, (includes 3-chn enlargement of detail); foot/b'way, waterbodies, woods (col); map is dated 1842 and 1843 in different places; it is unclear why some land is tinted green.

24/35 Corby (parish) SP 889892
Apt 16.01.1844; 1259a (2800); Map 1844?, 6 chns, (tithable parts only).

24/36 Cosgrove (parish) SP 786426
Apt 13.05.1845; 172a (1760); Map 1840, 6 chns, by John Durham, (tithable parts only); hedge ownership, landowners.

24/37 Cottesbrooke (parish) SP 711745
Apt 23.04.1841; 2781a (2780); Map 1839, 3 chns, by Thomas Mulliner, 37 Old Broad St, London; foot/b'way, turnpike roads, waterbodies, houses, woods, plantations, parkland, field boundary ownerships, field gates, landowners, hospital [almshouses], mansion, lodges, freeboard, roadside verge (col).

24/38 Cottingham cum Middleton (parish) SP 854894
Apt 15.12.1843; 3287a (3286); Map 1844, 6 chns, in 2 parts, (tithable parts only in detail; includes village separately at 3 chns); waterbodies, houses, woods, orchard, field boundary ownerships, township boundary; it is unclear why some areas are tinted green or what a blue band signifies.

24/39 Courteenhall (parish) SP 762538
Apt 03.11.1838; 1331a (1330); Map not dated, 6 chns, in 2 parts 'Surveyed and Planned' by John Durham, Stony Stratford; waterbodies, hedge ownership, fence ownership.

24/40 Cranford St Andrew (parish) SP 928786
Apt 27.07.1844; 133a (?); Map 1849, 4 chns, copied from a plan of the parish belonging to the Duke of Buccleuch, by Messrs Hayward, Northampton, (tithable parts only); waterbodies, woods, hedges.

24/41 Culworth (parish) SP 536474
Apt 16.11.1839; 2246a (all); Map 1839, 3 chns, by T. Collins, Culworth; foot/b'way, waterbodies, houses, woods (col), osiers (by symbol), hedge ownership, mill.

24/42 Dallington (parish) SP 735630
Apt 17.07.1845; 53a (1520); Map 1846?, 6 chns, by John Durham, (tithable parts only in detail, tinted); waterbodies, field boundary ownerships, landowners.

24/43 Deene with Deenethorpe (district) SP 949925
Apt 02.10.1847; 3152a (3152); Map 1846, 6 chns, by R. Hayward and Sons; foot/b'way, waterbodies, houses, woods, osiers (by symbol), plantations, footbridges, township boundaries.

24/44 Dingley (parish) SP 766882
Apt 24.04.1837; 1318a (1317); Map 1838, 6 chns, by R. Hayward and Son, Thorpe Malsor, Northants; waterbodies, houses, woods, plantations, gardens, landowners, turnpike gate, glebe (col), ownerships (col).

24/45 Draughton (parish) SP 766773
Apt 04.04.1837; 1474a (1477); Map 1838, 6 chns, by R. Hayward and Son, Thorpe Malsor, Northants; foot/b'way, waterbodies, houses, woods, plantations, landowners, glebe (col).

24/46 Easton Maudit (parish) SP 889579
Apt 15.04.1840; 1765a (1764); Map 1840, 6 chns; foot/b'way, waterbodies, houses, woods, plantations, arable (col), grassland (col), private carriage road, vicarage lands; owner is named in the title, which is on a plinth with a robe and crown or coronet above, with various leaves scattered below; plumes decorate the scale bar.

24/47 Easton Neston with Hulcote (parish) SP 708500
Apt 17.01.1844; 1703a (all); Map 1849, 6 chns, by John Durham, Stony Stratford; foot/b'way, waterbodies, woods, plantations, parkland, hedge ownership, fence ownership.

24/48 Edgcott (parish) SP 508475 [Edgcote]
Apt 22.10.1840; 1345a (all); Map 1841?, 4 chns; foot/b'way, houses, mill, stiles, road gates. District is apportioned by owner and fields are not shown; Apt generalises land use and only names one occupier.

24/49 Elmington (hamlet in parish of Oundle) TL 058891 [Not listed]
Apt 16.02.1838; 516a (?); Map 1838, 6 chns, by R. Hayward and Son, Thorpe Malsor, Northants, (tithable parts only in detail); landowners, tithe-free land (green), ownership boundaries (col). Tithe-free part is apportioned by holding, with land use omitted.

24/50 Evenley (parish) SP 580345
Apt 05.09.1839; 1160a (3104); Map 1840?, 6 chns, by R. Russel, Brackley, (tithable parts only); foot/b'way, turnpike roads, waterbodies, woods, hedge ownership, landowners, holding boundaries (col); owner is named in title.

24/51 Eydon (parish) SP 538502
Apt 13.05.1845; 44a (1620); Map 1846, 3 chns, in 3 parts, by Thomas Collins, Culworth, (tithable parts only; includes 6.67 chn 'Skeleton Road Map'); foot/b'way, houses, hedge ownership, rickyard, mill, landowners.

24/52 Farthinghoe (parish) SP 538399
Apt 29.12.1840; 1472a (all); Map 1841, 6 chns, by R. Russel, Brackley; waterbodies, woods; pictorial church.

24/53 Farthingston (parish) SP 614552 [Farthingstone]
Apt 16.05.1845; 222a (1820); Map 1846?, 8 chns, (tithable parts only in detail); woods, arable (col), grassland (col), gardens (col), landowners; pictorial church.

24/54 Fawsley (parish) SP 560566 [Not listed]
Apt 24.01.1851; 34a (1550); Map 1851, 6 chns, (tithable parts only); houses; owner is named in the title.

24/55 Faxton Cum Mawsley (parish) SP 782762
Apt 10.01.1840; 2259a (2120); Map 1839, 3 chns, ? by Thomas Mulliner, 37 Old Broad St, London; foot/b'way, waterbodies, houses, woods, plantations, field boundary ownerships, field gates, building names, dams, pits, roadside waste (col).

24/56 Furtho (parish) SP 774428
Apt 21.10.1850; 288a (480); Map 1850, 4 chns, copied from a plan belonging to the trustees of Arnold's Charity by Messrs Hayward, Northampton, (tithable parts only); foot/b'way, waterbodies, houses, woods, plantations, hedge ownership, fence ownership, private road.

24/57 Gayton (parish) SP 705546
Apt 28.07.1840; 1712a (all); Map 1840?, 6 chns; railway, canal with towpath, foot/b'way, waterbodies, houses, woods, orchard, hedge ownership, fence ownership, field gates, road names, pit, spring.

24/58 Glasthorpe (township in parish of Flore) SP 669616 [Not listed]
Apt 30.11.1849; 571a (?); Map 1850, 10 chns; ownership boundaries (col); buildings are shown in outline.

24/59 Grafton Regis (parish) SP 756468
Apt 24.11.1853; 65a (1510); Map (drawn on Apt) 1853?, 9 chns, (tithable parts only).

24/60 Greatworth (parish) SP 556421
Apt 13.05.1845; 869a (all); Map 1845, 3 chns, 1st cl, by James Saunders, Oxford; construction lines, foot/b'way, waterbodies, houses, woods (col), heath/moor, hedge ownership, stiles; double lines may show walls.

24/61 Greens Norton (hamlet or township in parish of Greens Norton) SP 666504
Apt 16.05.1845; 854a (2490); Map 1848, 9 chns, (tithable parts only, tinted); waterbodies, landowners.

24/62 East Haddon (parish) SP 668678
Apt 02.03.1842; 223a (2572); Map 1849, 6 chns, by Davis and Saunders, Banbury, Oxon, (tithable parts only); woods, hedge ownership, landowners.

24/63 Handley (township in parish of Towcester) SP 673471 [Not listed]
Apt 28.02.1849; 893a (all); Map 1849, 6 chns; foot/b'way, waterbodies, woods.

24/64 Hardwick (parish) SP 843697
Apt 20.08.1839; 1260a (all); Map surveyed 1839, [3 chns], 1st cl, by Jos. Gilbert, Welford, Northants; construction lines, waterbodies, houses, woods, field boundary ownerships, stone pit.

24/65 Harrington (parish) SP 774802
Apt 26.04.1839; 2519a (2519); Map 1839?, [6 chns]; woods (col), arable (col), grassland (col), field boundary ownerships.

24/66 Harrowden Magna or Great Harrowden and Harrowden Parva or Little Harrowden (parish and hamlet or township) SP 877714
Apt 06.03.1844; 1502a (2895); Map 1848?, 8 chns, in 2 parts, (tithable parts only); waterbodies.

24/67 Hartwell (parish) SP 787498
Apt 26.02.1850; 9a (1850); Map 1850, 3 chns, by Richard P. Tallis, (tithable parts only, tinted); road names, field names, landowners, field acreages.

24/68 Hazelbeech (parish) SP 714774 [Not listed]
Apt 23.04.1840; 1649a (all); Map 1840, 3 chns; foot/b'way, waterbodies, woods.

24/69 Helmdon (parish) SP 586430
Apt 17.07.1845; 191a (3560); Map 1846?, 4 chns, in 2 parts, (tithable parts only); waterbodies, road names, landowners; pictorial church.

24/70 Lower Heyford (hamlet or township in parish of Lower Heyford or Nether Heyford) SP 660586 [Nether Heyford]
Apt 24.10.1848; 169a (1690); Map 1849, 3 chns, in 2 parts, (tithable parts only in detail); foot/b'way, waterbodies, houses, village green.

24/71 Upper Heyford, tithable to Bugbrook (district) SP 676595
Apt 24.10.1848; 350a (?); Map 1845, 10 chns; mill; map also covers those parts of the parish tithable elsewhere, (24/72, 24/73); district is apportioned by holding and no buildings are shown. Apt has sale lot numbers in place of field names and generalises land use.

24/72 Upper Heyford, tithable to Flore (district) SP 667597
Apt 24.10.1848; 377a (?); Map 1845, 10 chns; mill; map also covers those parts of the parish tithable elsewhere, (24/71, 24/73); district is apportioned by holding and no buildings are shown. Apt has sale lot numbers in place of field names and generalises land use.

24/73 Upper Heyford, tithable to Lower Heyford (district) SP 665591
Apt 09.06.1849; 158a (?); Map 1850?, 10 chns; mill; map also covers those parts of the parish tithable elsewhere, (24/71, 24/72); district is apportioned by holding and no buildings are shown. Apt has sale lot numbers in place of field names and generalises land use.

24/74 Higham Park (extra-parochial place) SP 990641
Apt 31.01.1839; 597a (all); Map 1839?, (surveyed in 1794), 6 chns, litho (by Geo. Masser, 166 Bro-gate, Leeds); waterbodies, field gates, field names, landowners, orchard (by annotation), yard; owner is named in the title; table lists acreages.

24/75 Holdenby (parish) SP 695678
Apt 18.01.1842; 1856a (all); Map 1842, 3 chns, by Richard Davis, Banbury; foot/b'way, waterbodies, houses, hedge ownership, fence ownership, field gates.

24/76 Hollowell (township in parish of Guilsborough) SP 695722
Apt 02.09.1847; 664a (?); Map 1848, 6 chns, in 2 parts, by Messrs Hayward, Northampton, (tithable parts only in detail); foot/b'way, waterbodies, houses, field boundary ownerships.

24/77 Great Houghton (parish) SP 795584
Apt 23.11.1838; 1783a (all); Map 1839?, 6 chns, in 2 parts; turnpike roads, waterbodies, woods, toll bar.

24/78 Irchester (parish) SP 922657
Apt 29.04.1845; 178a (1980); Map 1845, 2 chns, in 3 parts, by William Whitten, (tithable parts only, including two parts at 3.75 chns); foot/b'way, woods (col), parkland, arable (col), grassland (col), orchard, gardens (col), hedge ownership, road names, landowners; legend explains symbols.

24/79 Kelmarsh (parish) SP 732798
Apt 24.07.1837; 2751a (2751); Map 1838?, 10 chns; waterbodies, woods; pictorial church.

24/80 Kilsby (parish) SP 561715
Apt 19.06.1845; 10a (3200); Map 1846?, 2.5 chns, (tithable parts only); railway, waterbodies, landowners; scale-bar is ruler-like.

24/81 Kings Sutton (parish) SP 510366
Apt 10.06.1845; 329a (3850); Map 1847, 3 chns, 1st cl, by Davis and Saunders, Banbury, (tithable parts only); construction lines, foot/b'way, waterbodies, houses, woods, hedge ownership, field gates.

24/82 Litchborough (parish) SP 636544
Apt 28.10.1843; 1705a (1704); Map 1843, 5 chns, by G. Smith, Oundle; foot/b'way, waterbodies.

24/83 Loddington (parish) SP 807780
Apt 13.11.1841; 1225a (all); Map 1842?, 6 chns, by R.F. Hayward; waterbodies, houses, woods, parkland, field boundary ownerships, avenue of trees.

24/84 Maidford (parish) SP 610527
Apt 13.02.1846; 133a (1930); Map 1846, 8 chns, (tithable parts only in detail); landowners, woods, arable (col), grassland (col), windmills (pictorial); pictorial church.

24/85 Marham or Marholme (parish) TF 147023 [Marholm]
Apt 30.12.1857; 1357a (all); Map 1858, [6 chns]; railways, houses, woods; pictorial church.

24/86 Morton Pinckney (parish) SP 568488 [Moreton Pinkney]
Apt 14.07.1847; 2422a (2422); Map 1848, 4 chns, 1st cl, by Messrs Hayward, Northampton; main and subsidiary construction lines, foot/b'way, waterbodies, houses, field boundary ownerships, windmill.

24/87 Newbottle (parish) SP 527369
Apt 02.11.1844; 930a (2990); Map 1844, 3 chns, (tithable parts only); foot/b'way, waterbodies, woods, plantations, landowners; church is shown pictorially, with gravestones, but other buildings appear to be omitted.

24/88 Nortoft (township in parish of Guilsborough) SP 680740 [Not listed]
Apt 10.07.1850; 1535a (?); Map 1848, 6 chns, ? by Messrs Hayward; foot/b'way, waterbodies, houses, woods, hedge ownership, fence ownership.

24/89 Norton (parish) SP 597644
Apt 25.11.1848; 1947a (3260); Map 1849?, 6 chns, in 2 parts, (tithable parts only); railway, foot/b'way, canal, reservoir, waterbodies, houses, woods, parkland, building names, windmill (pictorial), Roman road, hamlet names.

24/90 Little Oakley (parish) SP 892854
Apt 14.04.1845; 110a (724); Map 1847, 3 chns, by Richd Hayward, (tithable parts only); woods, road names.

24/91 Oundle (parish) TL 024885
Apt 25.03.1845; 57a (?); Map 1845, 3 chns, by G. Smith, Market Deeping, (tithable parts only); houses.

24/92 Passenham (parish) SP 767403
Apt 30.08.1844; 833a (2230); Map 1845?, 5 chns, in 3 parts, by John

Durham, Stony Stratford, (tithable parts only); foot/b'way, hedge ownership, canal with towpath.

24/93 Paston with Gunthorpe (parish) TF 191027
Apt 23.09.1840; 1146a (?); Map 1841?, 6 chns; waterbodies, houses (by shading), woods, parkland, road names, boundary of Gunthorpe; pictorial church.

24/94 Paulerspury (parish) SP 718466
Apt 12.02.1842; 2961a (2961); Map 1839, 3 chns, 'Surveyed and Planned' by John Durham, Stony Stratford; foot/b'way, private road, toll bar, waterbodies, woods, hedge ownership, fence ownership. Apt has incomplete cropping information.

24/95 Piddington and Hackleton (parish and township or hamlet) SP 809550
Apt 30.01.1849; 558a (1980); Map 1850?, 6 chns, (tithable parts only, tinted); waterbodies, hedge ownership, landowners.

24/96 Pilton (parish) TL 006853
Apt 02.02.1838; 1473a (1473); Map 1838, 6 chns, by Hayward and Son, Thorpe Malsor, Kettering; waterbodies, woods, landowners, ownership boundaries (col); tithe-free land (col).

24/97 Polebrook (parish) TL 066860
Apt 21.02.1846; 834a (2730); Map 1846, 9 chns, by G. Smith, Market Deeping, (tithable parts only); foot/b'way, waterbodies, woods.

24/98 Potterspury (parish) SP 758442
Apt 22.04.1845; 436a (2820); Map 1846?, 6 chns, by Jno. Durham, (tithable parts only, tinted); foot/b'way, waterbodies, field boundary ownerships, landowners, wood (by name).

24/99 Little Preston (hamlet or district in parish of Preston Capes) SP 588542
Apt 07.02.1838; 1115a (all); Map 1838, 3 chns, 1st cl, by H.W. Bushell; waterbodies, farmyards (col), woods (col), plantations (col), arable (col), grassland (col), orchards (col), gardens (col), hedge ownership (col), walls (red); border has ball-and-trefoil decoration. Apt omits land use.

24/100 Preston Deanry (parish) SP 789554 [Preston Deanery]
Apt 24.12.1839; 1471a (1470); Map surveyed in 1840, 6 chns, by R.P. Coles; foot/b'way, turnpike roads, waterbodies, houses, woods (col), plantations (col), arable (col), grassland (col), gardens (col), road names; scale-bar is ruler-like; north pointer and title are decorated with banner and belt, north pointer has tassle, and title is on a scroll.

24/101 Pytchley (parish) SP 855747
Apt 31.08.1842; 2834a (2833); Map 3 chns, surveyed by Messrs Bonsor and Gilbert, 1840 and 1843; foot/b'way, waterbodies, field boundary ownerships.

24/102 Quinton (parish) SP 778542
Apt 29.03.1851; 183a (1170); Map 1851, 6 chns, in 2 parts, by Washbourne and Keen, (tithable parts only); waterbodies, woods, field boundary ownerships.

24/103 Ringstead (parish) SP 987748
Apt 24.10.1838; 1982a (1981); Map 1840, 6 chns.

24/104 Rockingham (parish) SP 867916
Apt 22.02.1842; 449a (890); Map 1849, 6 chns, ? by Wm Th. Heard, Hitchin, Herts, (tithable parts only in detail); woods, castle, windmill.

24/105 Rothwell or Rowell and Orton (district) SP 814807
Apt 15.11.1844; 68a (4070); Map 1844, 6 chns, in 2 parts, by G. Smith, Oundle, (tithable parts only); woods, landowners.

24/106 Rushton (parish) SP 840837
Apt 31.05.1842; 2820a (2960); Map 1849?, 4 chns; foot/b'way, waterbodies, woods (named) with rides (col), osiers (by symbol), plantations, parkland (in detail, col), gardens, rock outcrops, field gates, building names, field names, landowners, statue, kennel, poultry yard, rickyard, spring, rectory, pound, hovel, stiles, quarries, limestone quarry and kiln, fossil site, labyrinth, Triangular Lodge, parterre, ice house, lodges, windmill, holding boundaries (col), glebe; pictorial church; title cartouche is formed of very stylised leaves, with tassle at the bottom, and is surmounted by coloured coat of arms with motto 'Orbe fracto spec illaesa'.

24/107 Scaldwell (parish) SP 768728
Apt 29.04.1845; 57a (1060); Map 1850?, 6 chns, (tithable parts only in detail); houses, field boundary ownerships.

24/108 Shutlanger (hamlet in parish of Stoke Bruern) SP 726493
Apt 29.11.1842; 1250a (1250); Map 1843?, 6 chns; waterbodies, houses, woods, avenue of trees, modus lands (pink).

24/109 Sibbertoft (parish) SP 682823
Apt 29.01.1841; 2048a (2048); Map 1841, 6 chns, copied by Thomas Mulliner, 37 Old Broad St, London; foot/b'way, waterbodies, woods, field boundary ownerships, field gates, stiles.

24/110 Silverston (hamlet in parish of Greens Norton) SP 672442 [Silverstone]
Apt 13.05.1845; 59a (2110); Map 1851?, 3 chns, in 3 parts, (tithable parts only); chapel. Apt omits most land use.

24/111 Snorscombe (hamlet in parish of Everdon) SP 596560 [Snorscomb]
Apt 13.06.1839; 639a (all); Map 1851?, (surveyed by John Upton, 1816), 4 chns, foot/b'way, waterbodies, woods, freeboards (coloured according to width).

24/112 Southorpe with Walcot (township in parish of Barnack) TF 085025
Apt 12.08.1839; 1857a (all); Map 1843, 6 chns; foot/b'way, waterbodies, woods, grassland (col), hall.

24/113 Stoke Albany (parish) SP 806872
Apt 14.09.1841; 507a (1661); Map 1839, 3 chns, in 2 parts, by R. Hayward and Son, (tithable parts only); waterbodies, houses, woods (col), arable (col), grassland (col), landowners, modus lands (pink, without land use), glebe (blue).

24/114 Stoke Bruern (district in parish of Stoke Bruern) SP 746500 [Stoke Bruerne]
Apt 29.11.1842; 1319a (1319); Map 1843?, 6 chns, by Chas Day, Colleyweston; foot/b'way, canal with towpath and locks, waterbodies, houses, woods, parkland, avenue of trees, modus land boundary; map also covers hamlet of Shutlanger (24/108).

24/115 Stoke Doyle (parish) TL 022862
Apt 30.04.1845; 450a (1500); Map 1848?, 5 chns, (tithable parts only); foot/b'way, waterbodies, woods; pictorial church.

24/116 Stowe Nine Churches (parish) SP 638570 [Church Stowe]
Apt 26.08.1839; 1866a (1865); Map 1839, 6 chns, 'Revised' by C. Oakley; railway, foot/b'way, turnpike roads, canal with towpath, waterbodies, woods, field boundary ownerships.

24/117 Strixton (parish) SP 904616
Apt 30.06.1843; 890a (889); Map surveyed in 1843, 3 chns, 1st cl, in 2 parts, by Joseph Gilbert, Welford; railway, foot/b'way, waterbodies, houses, field boundary ownerships; owner is named in the title.

24/118 Stutchbury (parish) SP 570437 [Stuchbury]
Apt 22.04.1845; 114a (1007); Map 1845, 3 chns, by Davis and Saunders, Banbury, (tithable parts only); foot/b'way, waterbodies, hedge ownership, field names, landowners, stiles, field acreages.

24/119 Sudborough (parish) SP 964829
Apt 28.02.1838; 1781a (1781); Map 1839, 6 chns, by R. Hayward and Son; houses, farmyards, woods, landowners (col), glebe (col).

24/120 Sutton (township in parish of Castor) TL 098992
Apt 14.11.1843; 889a (all); Map 1845, 6 chns, by Charles Day, Colleyweston; railway, woods, open fields (named), common.

24/121 Sywell (parish) SP 822677
Apt 27.05.1843; 2032a (all); Map surveyed in 1844, 3 chns, 1st cl, in 4 parts, by Joseph Gilbert, Welford; waterbodies, houses, woods with rides (col), plantations, gardens, field boundary ownerships, poor allotments.

24/122 Teeton (hamlet in parish of Ravensthorpe) SP 695704
Apt 22.11.1842; 681a (681); Map 1842, 4 chns, by Richd Davis, Banbury; foot/b'way, waterbodies, houses, hedge ownership, fence ownership, field boundary ownerships, field gates, ford with footbridge.

24/123 Thenford (parish) SP 522420
Apt 21.10.1850; 350a (890); Map 1851, 5 chns, 'Copied' by Davis and Saunders, Banbury and Oxford, (tithable parts only); waterbodies, houses, woods (col), heath/moor, hedge ownership, field gates, tithe-free land (green).

24/124 Thornby (parish) SP 674758
Apt 30.04.1841; 1212a (1212); Map 1840, 4 chns, 'Surveyed and Planned' by J. Durham; waterbodies, houses, field boundary ownerships.

24/125 Thornhaugh and Wansford (parish) TF 067003
Apt 15.02.1839; 2176a (2175); Map 1838, 4 chns; turnpike roads, waterbodies, houses (by shading), woods, plantations, hedge, building names, road names, field names, landowners, pump, mill dam, toll bar, township boundary, glebe (blue); pictorial churches; one owner is named in the title.

24/126 Thorpe Malsor (parish) SP 835791
Apt 31.08.1842; 53a (680); Map 1842, 3 chns, by Edward Fisher, Little Bowden, (tithable parts only); houses, woods, landowners.

24/127 Thurning (parish) (partly in Hunts) TL 086828
Apt 12.01.1838; 1000a (all); Map 1839, 6 chns.

24/128 Titchmarsh (parish) TL 029791
Apt 14.12.1844; 133a (4480); Map 1845, 3 chns, in 2 parts, by G. Smith, Market Deeping, (tithable parts only); railway, waterbodies, houses, woods, landowners, ownership boundaries (col).

24/129 Towcester (parish) SP 689476
Apt 19.10.1843; 374a (2790); Map 1844, 6 chns, by John Durham, Stony Stratford, (tithable parts only in detail, tinted); foot/b'way, waterbodies, woods, hedge ownership, landowners; scale is graduated as 3 chns, but has been corrected in pencil to 6 chns.

24/130 Upton (parish) SP 714605
Apt 08.09.1847; 980a (all); Map 'Working Plan', surveyed in January 1848, 3 chns, 1st cl, by Joseph Gilbert, Mkt Harborough; construction lines, waterbodies, houses, field boundary ownerships, mill dam and pond, garden (by annotation).

24/131 Upton (township in parish of Castor) TF 105008
Apt 14.11.1843; 1185a (all); Map 1850, 6 chns, by Charles Day, Colleyweston, Stamford; woods.

24/132 Warmington (parish) TL 092907
Apt 08.04.1846; 78a (3150); Map 1846?, 3 chns, (tithable parts only); waterbodies, woods, parkland, spring.

24/133 Watford (parish) SP 608689
Apt 06.02.1849; 1440a (3080); Map 1847, 6 chns, in 2 parts, by G. Smith, Stamford, (tithable parts only); railway, foot/b'way, canal, waterbodies, houses, woods, landowners, Roman road.

24/134 Weedon Beck (parish) SP 620587 [Weedon Bec]
Apt 16.08.1844; 24a (1710); Map 1845, 1 chn, (tithable parts only); railway, road names. Apt omits land use.

24/135 Welford (parish) SP 632807
Apt 03.08.1844; 1171a (3650); Map 1844, 6 chns, by G. Smith, Oundle, (tithable parts only); foot/b'way, canal with towpath, waterbodies; pictorial church.

24/136 Wellingborough (parish) SP 886682
Apt 19.01.1847; 89a (4490); Map 1848, 3 chns, in 5 parts, (tithable parts only; includes 20-chn index); waterbodies, road names, mills, mill heads; three detached areas are framed on 'scrolls'; buildings are shown in outline only, without hatching. Apt omits most land use.

24/137 Whiston (parish) SP 848603
Apt 05.09.1839; 809a (all); Map 1840?, 9 chns; foot/b'way, waterbodies, woods, hedge ownership, fence, field boundary ownerships, field gates; pictorial church; owner is named in the title.

24/138 Whitfield (parish) SP 600390
Apt 08.07.1845; 637a (1210); Map 1846?, 6 chns, (tithable parts only in detail); turnpike roads, waterbodies, landowners.

24/139 Whittlebury (township in parish of Greens Norton) SP 709435
Apt 29.03.1851; 310a (2870); Map 1861?, 6 chns, in 2 parts, (tithable parts only in detail, tinted); foot/b'way, waterbodies, woods, hedge ownership, fence ownership, field names, landowners, tithe-free land (yellow). Apt omits land use.

24/140 Wicken (parish) SP 750388
Apt 28.02.1838; 2281a (all); Map 1838, 3 chns, 1st cl, by John Bromley, Derby; construction lines; foot/b'way, turnpike roads, milestone, canal with towpath, waterbodies, houses, woods, plantations, parkland, orchard, field gates, building names, freeboards, rectory, notable tree, stone pit, green lanes.

24/141 Winwick (parish) SP 623745
Apt 18.09.1839; 2038a (all); Map 1839, 3 chns, 'Surveyed and Planned' by John Durham Junr; road and path widths, foot/b'way, canal with towpath, waterbodies, houses, field boundary ownerships.

24/142 Wollaston Lodge Farm (district in parish of Wollaston) SP 888623 [Not listed]
Apt 23.09.1848; 110a (?); Map 1850, 3 chns, by Wm Whitten, Wellingborough; waterbodies, woods, hedge ownership, landowners. 'Names and Descriptions' column in Apt gives verbal description of field abutments.

24/143 Woodford cum Membris (parish) SP 539527 [Woodford Halse]
Apt 10.01.1840; 207a (2655); Map 1840, 3 chns, in 2 parts, by Richard Davis, Banbury, (tithable parts only); waterbodies, woods, hedge ownership, fence ownership, field boundary ownerships, field gates, landowners, quarry (col), tithe-free land (red).

24/144 Wootton (parish) SP 758567
Apt 20.03.1849; 14a (1420); Map 1849, 3 chns, by John Durham, Stony Stratford; waterbodies, woods, hedge ownership, field names, field acreages, landowners; tithable lands are tinted yellow; owner is named in the title.

Northumberland

PRO IR29 and IR30 25/1-493

548 tithe districts: 1,282,287 acres
492 tithe commutations: 1,042,097 acres
269 voluntary tithe agreements, 223 compulsory tithe awards

Tithe and tithe commutation

Until 1844 Northumberland included three districts, Norhamshire, Islandshire and Bedlingtonshire, which were administratively part of County Durham. Most of the tithe commutations in these outliers were completed before 1844 and the Tithe Commission treated them as part of County Durham for tithe purposes (Fig. 37). Northumberland tithe districts varied enormously in size. Although a few were of under 100 acres, some were very large and four were over 20,000 acres, covering 14 per cent of the county. Elsdon at 74,918 acres is the largest of all English and Welsh tithe districts.

The tithe surveys of Northumberland are among the most impoverished of the whole country; only those of Anglesey are less informative. As in Anglesey this is due in large measure to the prevalence of apportionment by holdings rather than field-by-field. Thus for 77 per cent of the tithable acreage of the county the tithe survey does not extend beyond generalised information for holdings; in a few instances the whole district is 'apportioned' as a single unit.

In 1836, 90 per cent of the tithe districts of Northumberland by number and about 81 per cent of the county by area remained subject to payment of tithes. Only thirty-nine districts were wholly tithable; the most usual cause of tithe exemption was the existence of modus payments in lieu of tithes. These affected 423 districts (86 per cent of tithable districts), a fact which doubtless contributed to apportionment by holding rather than by field.

Assistant tithe commissioners and local tithe agents who worked in Northumberland are listed in Table 25.1 and the valuers of tithe rent-charge in Table 25.2. As a result of all the apportionment by holdings, Northumberland tithe apportionments are poor records of field names and of cultivation, with the latter sometimes further generalised as 'arable, pasture, etc.'. The apportionment for Brunton is exceptional in that it includes cropping information for fields. However, many apportionments describe moduses in considerable detail.

Tithe maps

In keeping with the large extent of the county apportioned by holding, Northumberland does not contain a single first-class map, nor one with construction lines. Although copying is rarely acknowledged, one may suspect that it was widespread, particularly as field boundaries are shown on almost three-quarters of the maps of districts apportioned by holding; it is hard to believe that unnecessary field boundaries would have been surveyed and mapped had wholly new tithe surveys been made for these places.

Only 222 Northumberland tithe maps (45 per cent) in the Public Record Office collection can be attributed to a particular map-maker; the most prolific was Thomas Bell and Sons of Newcastle who produced eighty-nine maps covering 18 per cent of Northumberland tithe districts by number and area. Even allowing for the fact that many of these maps are copies and at comparatively small scales, it is a very impressive achievement. Bell maps are characterised by a high standard of linework, sans-serif lettering, and woodland shown by densely-packed symbols. In addition they often show railway track layouts in detail and slopes by grey wash. There is an interesting group of some thirty maps around Newcastle which are anonymous but are clearly the work of one map-maker with distinguishing features which include tithe areas numbered in red, buildings infilled in grey, owners' names written across holdings, and blue rails on railways and waggonways. These maps correlate closely with valuations by the partnership of Edward, Nathaniel and William Grace and may well be their work.

Northumberland tithe maps are drawn to the widest range of scales of any county and vary from one inch to two chains to one inch to thirty chains; 25 per cent are in the recommended scale range of one inch to three to four chains. The six-chain scale, which is the most favoured 'small' scale in most other counties, is 'large-scale' by Northumberland standards and is used for only 17 per cent of the maps. The most favoured scale was the eight-chain, used for 39 per cent of the districts. Northumberland is the only English county where significant use was made of the ten-, twelve- and sixteen-chain scales; together these account for 13 per cent of districts.

Northumberland maps are not good sources for land-use information, nor are they at all informative about field boundary ownership or buildings, and only on 3 per cent of maps are houses distinguished from other buildings. By contrast, the naming of landowners (on 37 per cent of maps), the highlighting of holding boundaries in colour, and the recording of boundary stones and cairns are quite usual. The rugged nature of much of the landscape is reflected by the 10 per cent of maps which indicate rock outcrops and the 20 per cent which show some slopes. In the south-east of the county, particularly on maps produced by the Bells and the Graces, railways and waggonways are usually portrayed. Industry is also extensively recorded in Northumberland and includes many collieries, quarries and spoil heaps, and iron works on Tyneside.

The standard of draughtmanship of Northumberland maps is somewhat below average. The maps of Edington, Elwick, Harnham, and Thockrington are notably crude in appearance. Decoration is almost unknown on Northumberland tithe maps: Shawdon has a leafy cartouche and a few others have simple circular or oblong surrounds to the map title.

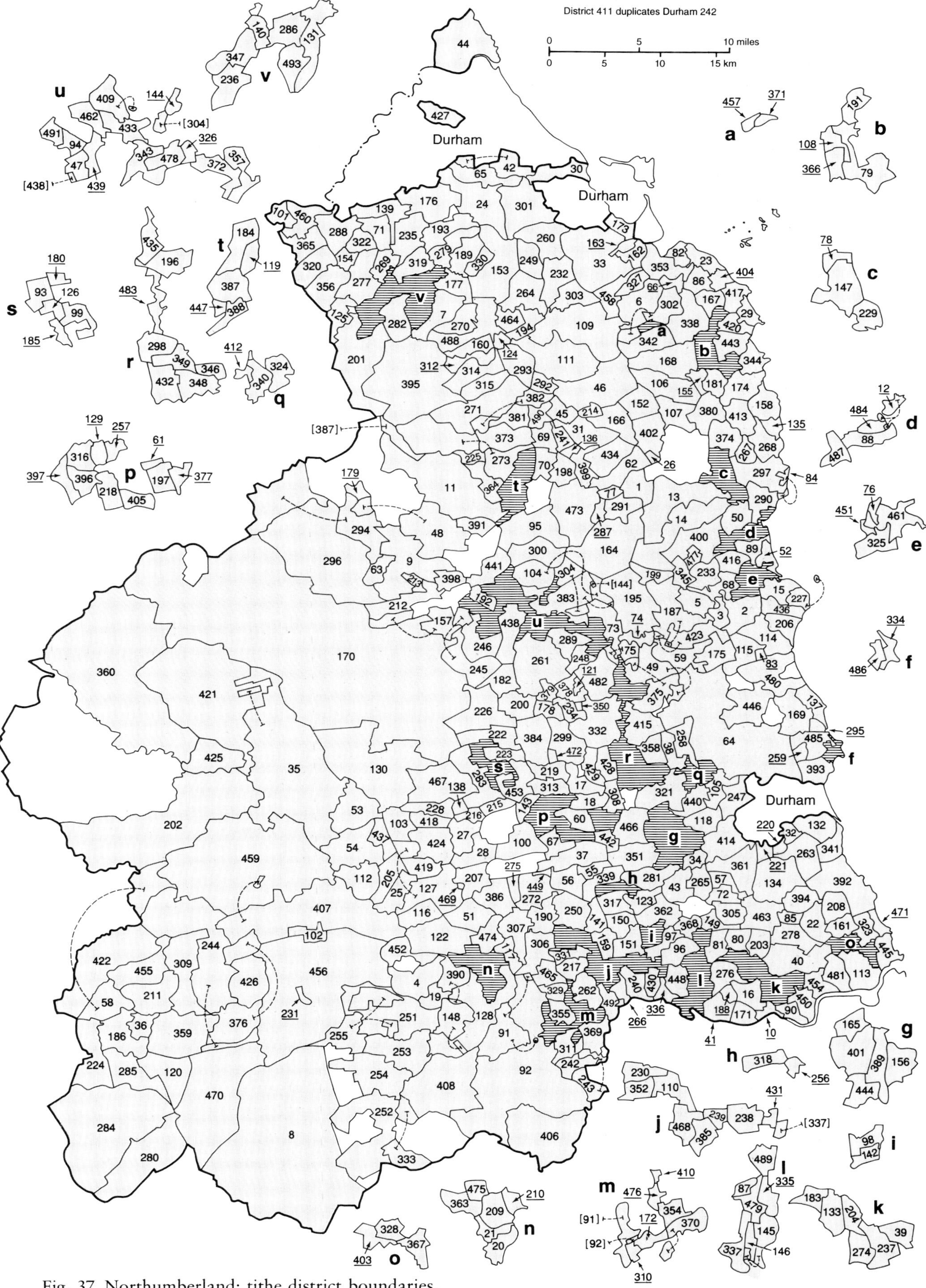

Fig. 37 Northumberland: tithe district boundaries.

Table 25.1. *Agreements and awards for commutation of tithes in Northumberland*

Assistant commissioner/ local tithe agent	*Number of agreements**	*Number of awards*
Henry Pilkington	173	0
John Job Rawlinson	7	133
John Strangeways Donaldson Selby	51	54
Richard Burton Phillipson	38	0
Joseph Townsend	0	15
Charles Howard	0	11
John B. Neal	3	0
John Penny	1	0

*Computed from the number of extant reports on tithe agreements in the tithe files [PRO IR 18].

Table 25.2. *Tithe valuers and tithe map-makers in Northumberland*

Name and address (in Northumberland unless indicated)	*Number of districts*	*Acreage*
Tithe valuers		
Thomas Bell, Newcastle upon Tyne	39	44,112
William Lowrey, Barmoor	28	66,902
Edward Grace, Wallsend	27	64,434
William Winship, Kirkhill	19	22,524
Thomas Tate, Bilton	14	120,950
Daniel Turner, Blagdon	13	17,978
Joseph Snowball, Netherwitton	11	19,110
William Grace, Saltwick	11	11,936
Andrew Ker Moffat, Beanley	10	14,222
William Dickson, Alnwick	10	11,587
Robert Dand, Field House	9	15,048
John James Thompson, Alnwick	9	14,060
Henry Turner, Killingworth	9	10,684
Joseph Storey, Wark	8	102,389
Thomas Burdus, Coalpits	8	33,083
William Sample, Matfen	8	13,314
Matthew Ryle, Herrington Hall, Durham	8	13,051
Thomas Duncan, Alnwick	8	10,527
Others [102]	243	436,236
Attributed tithe map-makers		
Thomas Bell and Sons, Newcastle upon Tyne	89	195,193
I. Coulson	29	125,999
Edmund Bowman, Newcastle upon Tyne	29	51,949
John Bourne, Newcastle upon Tyne	19	23,530
James Watson, Rothbury	13	32,420
Others [23]	43	84,160

Table 25.3. *The tithe maps of Northumberland: scales and classes*

Scale in chains/inch	All maps		First Class		Second Class	
	Number	Acreage	Number	Acreage	Number	Acreage
>3	2	571	0	0	2	571
3	10	6,108	0	0	10	6,108
4	112	137,335	0	0	112	137,335
5	11	20,553	0	0	11	20,553
6	82	106,002	0	0	82	106,002
6.5, 7, 7.5	5	9,250	0	0	5	9,250
8	194	460,321	0	0	194	460,321
9	6	7,442	0	0	6	7,442
10	19	35,075	0	0	19	35,075
10.5	1	1,594	0	0	1	1,594
12	24	162,182	0	0	24	162,182
15	3	3,174	0	0	3	3,174
16	20	45,846	0	0	20	45,846
<16	3	46,644	0	0	3	46,644
TOTAL	492	1,042,097	0	0	492	1,042,097

Table 25.4. *The tithe maps of Northumberland: dates*

	<1837	1837	1838	1839	1840	1841	1842	1843	1844	1845	1846	1847	1848	1849	1850	>1850
2nd class*	1	1	12	58	55	82	49	52	41	32	27	32	14	23	6	5

*Two second-class tithe maps of Northumberland in the Public Record Office collection are undated.

Northumberland

25/1 Abberwick (township in parish of Edlingham) NU 133135
Apt 30.03.1844; 1674a (1673); Map 1845, 8 chns, in 3 parts, by E. Bowman, (including two 3-chn enlargements); woods, parkland, building names. Apt omits land use.

25/2 Acklington (township in parish of Warkworth) NU 227017
Apt 09.02.1839; 2072a (2072); Map 1839, 9 chns, by Thomas Bell; hill-drawing, foot/b'way, woods, heath/moor, building names, landowners, collieries, old pits, quarries, old engine, fords, ferry, holding boundaries (col). Apt omits land use.

25/3 Acklington Park (parish) NU 209012
Apt 09.02.1839; 766a (766); Map 1839, 6 chns, by Thomas Bell; foot/b'way, plantations, heath/moor, building names, road names, dam, woollen factory, mill race, fords, well, boundary stones (by symbol), holding boundaries (col). Apt omits land use.

25/4 Acomb (township in parish of St John Lee) NY 938667
Apt 31.12.1838; 2690a (2745); Map 1838, 8 chns, by I. Coulson; building names, road names, landowners (col), public quarries, ford, toll bar, field acreages. Apt omits land use.

25/5 Acton and Old Felton (township in parish of Felton) NU 185025
Apt 02.02.1842; 209a (1244); Map 1842, 4 chns, (tithable parts only). District is apportioned as a single holding; Apt omits land use.

25/6 Adderstone (township in parish of Bamburgh) NU 131306 [Not listed]
Apt 31.12.1842; 2604a (2603); Map 1846?, 5 chns, ? by William Nelson; foot/b'way, waterbodies, building names, landowners, holding boundaries (col). District is apportioned by holding; Apt omits land use.

25/7 Akeld (township in parish of Kirknewton) NT 954291
Apt 18.01.1840; 2203a (2208); Map 1840?, 8 chns; waterbodies, woods (col), building names, holding boundaries (col). Apt omits land use.

25/8 Allendale (parish) NY 830520 [Allendale Town]
Apt 01.05.1847; 18309a (37267); Map 1847, 8 chns, in 9 parts, by I. Coulson, (including six parts at 8 chns, two at 2 chns, and index at 24 chns); building names, toll bars, chapels, quarries, school house, mills, stinted pasture, springs; streams named. Apt omits some land use.

25/9 Allenton (township in parish of Allenton) NT 930055 [Alwinton]
Apt 19.11.1844; 33a (1550); Map 1845, 2 chns, (tithable parts only); holding boundaries (col).

25/10 All Saints (township in parish of St Nicholas, Newcastle upon Tyne) NZ 252641 [Not listed]
Apt 20.09.1843; 264a (?); Map 1839, 4 chns, drawn by Thomas Oliver; railway, road names, burying ground. District is apport-ioned by holding; Apt omits land use.

25/11 Alnham (township in parish of Alnham) NT 957136
Apt 23.09.1843; 9535a (9535); Map 1845, 8 chns, in 2 parts, by Thomas Bell and Sons, (enclosed parts at 6 chns); hill-drawing, footbridge, foot/b'way, occupation roads, plantations, rock outcrops, building names, ford, sheepfolds, quarries, crags, dam, well, old quarry, holding boundaries (col); streams named. Apt omits land use.

25/12 Alnmouth (township in parish of Lesbury) NU 250110
Apt 09.09.1841; 579a (579); Map 1841, 4 chns, in 3 parts, by Thomas Reay, (including 2-chn enlargement of Alnmouth town); hill-drawing, waterbodies, woods (col), high and low water marks, foreshore (col), old river course, well, ownership boundaries (col). Apt omits land use. (PRO IR 30 also has a lithographed copy, by Lamberts, with coloured water, but without property colouring.)

25/13 Alnwick (township in parish of Alnwick) NU 160120
Apt 09.11.1842; 4605a (4604); Map 1846?, 4 chns, in 2 parts, by Thomas Bell and Sons, (including detached part at 12 chns); hill-drawing, railway, plantations, building names, road names, landowners, monumental columns, castle, dam, toll bar, quarries, ownership boundaries (col); built-up part generalised. Apt omits land use.

25/14 Alnwick South Side (township in parish of Alnwick) NU 167104 [Not listed]
Apt 18.11.1839; 2668a (4760); Map 1839, 10 chns; waterbodies, building names, landowners, well, boundary cairns; colours show holdings, (also listed in table). District is apportioned by holding; Apt omits land use.

25/15 Amble (township in parish of Warkworth) NU 262038 [Amble-by-the-Sea]
Apt 12.08.1841; 1143a (1142); Map 1842, 8 chns; foot/b'way, building names, high and low water marks, holding boundaries (col). District is apportioned by holding and fields are not shown.

25/16 St Andrew (chapelry in parish of Newcastle upon Tyne) NZ 243658 [Not listed]
Apt 01.11.1844; 1262a (?); Map 1849, 8 chns, by W. Crozier, (tithable parts only, tinted); railways, waterbodies, road names, baths, barracks, quarry, race course, grand stand, cricket ground, moors; hill named. District is apportioned by holding; Apt omits land use.

25/17 High Angerton (township in parish of Hartburn) NZ 088852
Apt 04.05.1843; 1232a (1232); Map 1843, 12 chns; woods, building names; colour bands show holdings. District is apportioned by holding; Apt omits land use.

25/18 Low Angerton (township in parish of Hartburn) NZ 096835
Apt 04.05.1843; 1040a (1040); Map 1843, 12 chns; waterbodies, building names, holding boundaries (col). District is apportioned by holding; Apt omits land use.

25/19 Anick (township in parish of St John Lee) NY 958653
Apt 26.02.1839; 451a (451); Map 1838, 8 chns, in 2 parts, by I. Coulson; woods, building names, landowners, holding boundaries (col). District is apportioned by holding; Apt omits land use.

25/20 Aydon (township in parish of Corbridge) NZ 001663
Apt 26.07.1842; 750a (750); Map 1844?, 8 chns; woods, building names, lime kiln, quarry, holdings (col). District is apportioned by holding; Apt omits land use.

25/21 Aydon Castle (township in parish of Corbridge) NZ 002668
Apt 26.07.1842; 394a (393); Map 1843?, 4 chns; woods, building names. Apt omits land use.

25/22 Backworth (district in parish of Earsdon) NZ 298723
Apt 30.11.1843; 1361a (1360); Map 1844, 8 chns, by Thomas Bell and Sons; railways, houses, parkland, building names, collieries, stationary engines, old quarries, reservoir, spoil heap, holding boundaries (col). District is apportioned by holding; Apt omits land use.

25/23 Bamburgh (township in parish of Bamburgh) NU 185345
Apt 31.12.1842; 1243a (1242); Map 1846?, 4 chns, in 2 parts, by Thomas Bell and Sons, (including enlargement of village); hill-drawing, plantations, gardens, rock outcrops, open fields, building names, flag staff, boat house, foreshore (col), wells, occupation roads, quarries, ownership boundaries (col); hill named. Apt omits land use.

25/24 Barmoor (township in parish of Lowick) NT 986398 [Not listed]
Apt 13.02.1840; 4120a (?); Map 1840, 6 chns; hill-drawing, woods, plantations (col), landowners, lime kilns, quarries, holding boundaries (col). District is apportioned by holding; Apt generalises land use.

25/25 Barrasford (township in parish of Chollerton) NY 922749
Apt 30.08.1839; 1395a (1394); Map 1840, 8 chns, copied from a survey of 1813 by John Bell and Son, by Thomas Bell; woods, rock outcrops, building names, crags (named), well, dam, mill, mill race, sheepfold, holding boundaries (col). District is apportioned by holding, though fields are numbered separately; Apt omits land use.

25/26 Bassington (township in parish of Eglingham) NU 142162
Apt 15.07.1839; 234a (234); Map 1839?, 4 chns; landowners, park wall,

holding boundaries (col). District is apportioned by holding; Apt omits land use.

25/27 Great Bavington (township in parish of Kirk Whelpington) NY 981801
Apt 30.10.1839; 1561a (1565); Map 1841?, 12 chns, in 2 parts, (including 3-chn enlargement of village); hill-drawing, waterbodies, woods, rock outcrops, building names, property ownerships (col). District is apportioned by holding; Apt omits land use.

25/28 Little Bavington (township in parish of Thockrington) NY 992785
Apt 30.09.1844; 513a (1702); Map 1844?, 10 chns, by William Arthur, Little Bavington, Land Surveyor; plantations, building names, tithe-free land. Map is more diagramatic than planimetric. District is apportioned by holding; Apt omits land use.

25/29 Beadnell (township in parish of Bamburgh) NU 227295
Apt 29.05.1841; 744a (743); Map 1841?, 4 chns; foot/b'way, waterbodies, woods (col), building names, kilns, harbour, herring houses, holding boundaries (col). District is apportioned by holding; Apt omits land use.

25/30 Beal and Lowlin (township in parish of Kyloe) NU 055425
Apt 17.09.1846; 1980a (?); Map 1847?, 4 chns; woods (col). District is apportioned by holding and fields are not shown.

25/31 Beanley (township in parish of Eglingham) NU 084184
Apt 05.02.1840; 2253a (2341); Map 1843?, 10 chns, 'Copied from an Old Survey' by Thos Bell and Sons; foot/b'way, plantations, building names, moor, moss, holding boundaries (col). District is apportioned by holding; Apt omits land use.

25/32 Bebside (township in parish of Woodhorn) NZ 272809
Apt 03.11.1843; 523a (464); Map 1850?, 6 chns; waterbodies, woods, mill, property ownership boundaries (col). District is apportioned by holding and fields are not shown.

25/33 Belford (township in parish of Belford) NU 090350
Apt 20.10.1842; 2698a (2698); Map 1842, 10 chns; waterbodies, rock outcrops, building names, mill, brick kilns, tile works, crag, 'Rogues Road'; streams named. District is apportioned by holding, fields are not shown, and no holding acreages are given.

25/34 Bellasis (township in parish of Stannington) NZ 189782 [Not listed]
Apt 13.11.1841; 534a (all); Map 1844?, 8 chns; plantations, building names, landowners, ownership boundaries (col).

25/35 Bellingham (parish) NY 825875
Apt 29.03.1843; 20212a (20211); Map 1845?, 8 chns, in 6 parts, (including Bellingham village at 3 chns, and 24 chns index); building names, coal pit, rectory, ford, mills, holding boundaries (col); streams named. District is apportioned by holding and fields are not shown.

25/36 Bellister (township in parish of Haltwhistle) NY 693622 [Not listed]
Apt 18.04.1840; 830a (988); Map 1842?, 4 chns; foot/b'way, houses, woods, building names, riverside cliff; streams named.

25/37 Belsay (township in parish of Bolam) NZ 083785
Apt 24.04.1839; 2496a (2516); Map 1840?, [5 chns]; waterbodies, woods, parkland, building names, holdings (col). District is apportioned by holding; Apt generalises land use.

25/38 Benridge (township in parish of Mitford) NZ 167877 [Not listed]
Apt 18.01.1839; 1007a (1085); Map 1841, 18 chns, by E. Bowman, Newcastle on Tyne; woods, building names, wells, pits, holding boundaries. District is apportioned by holding; Apt omits land use.

25/39 Little Benton (township in parish of Long Benton) NZ 277671 [Not listed]
Apt 16.02.1842; 574a (?); Map 1842?, 8 chns; railways, waterbodies, woods, parkland, building names, colliery, holding boundaries (col). District is apportioned by holding; Apt omits land use.

25/40 Long Benton (township in parish of Long Benton) NZ 280690 [Longbenton]
Apt 16.02.1842; 3301a (?); Map 1842, 8 chns; railways, waterbodies, woods, parkland, building names, collieries, mill, holding and ownership boundaries (col). District is apportioned by holding; Apt omits land use.

25/41 Benwell (township in parish of St Nicholas, Newcastle upon Tyne) NZ 211643
Apt 05.08.1841; 1346a (1346); Map 1843, 6 chns, in 3 parts, by E. Bowman, Newcastle upon Tyne, (including two 3-chn enlargements); railway, turnpike roads, old turnpike road, toll bar, waterbodies, woods, parkland, building names, paper mill, ownership boundaries (col). District is apportioned by holding; Apt omits land use.

25/42 Berrington (except Berrington Law) (district in parish of Kyloe) NU 009431
Apt 17.09.1846; 1912a (?); Map 1847, 8 chns; tithe-free land, plantations (col), building names, mills; meaning of pink band is uncertain. District is apportioned by holding; Apt omits land use.

25/43 Berwick Hill (township in parish of Ponteland) NZ 176756
Apt 16.06.1840; 1594a (1604); Map 1841?, 10.5 chns; foot/b'way, waterbodies, woods, marsh/bog, rock outcrops, building names, mill dam; streams named. District is apportioned by holding; Apt omits land use.

25/44 Berwick upon Tweed (parish) NT 969545 [Berwick-upon-Tweed]
Apt 10.07.1847; 5607a (6195); Map 1850?, 4 chns; railway, foot/b'way, waterbodies, woods, parkland, open fields, building names, road names, town walls, mills, toll gates, high and low water marks, mole, fords, snuff mill, ownership boundaries (col); built-up part generalised.

25/45 New Bewick (township in parish of Eglingham) NU 062202
Apt 20.11.1839; 1125a (1125); Map 1839, 8 chns. District is apportioned by holding and fields are not shown.

25/46 Old Bewick (township in parish of Eglingham) NU 100230
Apt 09.01.1840; 5487a (5487); Map 1839, 16 chns; building names, mill. District is apportioned by holding and fields are not shown.

25/47 Bickerton (township in parish of Rothbury) NY 999996
Apt 25.11.1842; 503a (505); Map 1843?, 4 chns, by Thos Duncan, Alnwick; woods (col). Apt omits land use and some field names.

25/48 Biddleston (township in parish of Allenton) NT 953085 [Biddlestone]
Apt 29.10.1844; 124a (?); Map 1849, 3 chns, by Thos Fenwick, Morpeth, (tithable parts only); plantations, field names and acreages; a 'Table of Contents' duplicates the information on the map.

25/49 Bigges Quarter (township in parish of Longhorsley) NZ 145965 [Not listed]
Apt 17.09.1846; 2869a (2869); Map 1846, 8 chns, in 2 parts, by I. Coulson; building names, mill, holding boundaries (col); streams named. Apt omits land use.

25/50 Bilton (township in parish of Lesbury) NU 221107
Apt 09.03.1840; 1361a (?); Map 1840?, 8 chns, in 2 parts copied by Thomas Bell from a survey of 1807 by John Bell, (including 2 chn enlargement of detail); foot/b'way, waterbodies, woods, building names, landowners, mill, fords, quarry, old quarries, limekiln, holding boundaries (col). Apt omits land use.

25/51 Bingfield (chapelry in parish of St John Lee) NY 983725
Apt 30.08.1839; 2048a (2047); Map 1838, 'Constructed from various plans as stated in the schedule of contents and reduced to a scale of 3 chns' by James Milne; woods, field gates, building names, road names, landowners, chapel, limekiln, wells, quarry, holding boundaries (col). District is apportioned by holding and fields are not shown.

25/52 Birling (township in parish of Warkworth) NU 250071
Apt 09.02.1839; 827a (826); Map 1840?, 9 chns; holding boundaries. District is apportioned by holding; Apt omits land use.

25/53 Birtley, High Division (district in parish of Chollerton) NY 883825 [Birtley]
Apt 22.07.1845; 3113a (?); Map 1848, 8 chns, by Thomas Bell and Sons;

woods, field gates, building names, fords, dams, mills, earthworks, peel tower, quarries, mill race, holding boundaries (col); streams named. District is apportioned by holding; Apt omits land use.

25/54 Birtley, Low Division (district in parish of Chollerton) NY 885791 [Birtley]
Apt 01.07.1845; 3607a (?); Map 1847?, 12 chns, in 2 parts, by Thomas Bell and Sons, (including 'Birtley Village and Cottager's Lands' at 4 chns); hill-drawing, woods (col), plantations (uncoloured), building names, limekilns, quarry waste, mill, crags, holding boundaries (col). District is apportioned by holding; Apt omits land use.

25/55 Bitchfield (township in parish of Stamfordham) NZ 099774
Apt 27.07.1839; 717a (717); Map 1839, 4 chns; woods; streams named.

25/56 Black Heddon (township in parish of Stamfordham) NZ 077761
Apt 29.05.1846; 1620a (1619); Map 1839, 4 chns; woods. District is apportioned by holding, though fields are numbered separately; Apt omits land use.

25/57 Blagdon (township in parish of Stannington) NZ 221763 [Not listed]
Apt 26.09.1845; 887a (?); Map 1846, 8 chns; foot/b'way, turnpike roads, building names, garden house.

25/58 Blenkinsopp (township in parish of Haltwhistle) NY 668646 [Not listed]
Apt 18.04.1840; 4920a (4919); Map 1841, 6 chns, in 2 parts, by John Morton, Studholme, Carlisle, (part 2 at 12 chns); railway, woods, building names, lodge, school, colliery; streams named. District is apportioned by holding; Apt omits land use.

25/59 Bockenfield (township in parish of Felton) NZ 175975
Apt 20.07.1843; 2325a (all); Map 1844, 8 chns, by I. Coulson; building names, mill, holding boundaries (col). District is apportioned by holding; Apt omits land use.

25/60 Bolam (township in parish of Bolam) NZ 084821
Apt 24.04.1839; 1117a (1119); Map 1840?, 8 chns; hill-drawing, waterbodies, woods, parkland, building names, landowners, pond, quarry, old camp, slate quarry, holding boundaries (col). District is apportioned by holding; Apt generalises land use.

25/61 Bolam Vicarage (township in parish of Bolam) NZ 099828 [Not listed]
Apt 12.11.1839; 130a (130); Map 1840?, 8 chns; woods. District is apportioned by holding; Apt generalises land use.

25/62 Bolton (township in parish of Edlingham) NU 118144
Apt 31.12.1845; 2049a (2048); Map 1847?, 8 chns; woods, building names, landowners, ford, holdings (col). Apt omits land use.

25/63 Borrowden (township in parish of Alwinton) NT 902050 [Not listed]
Apt 10.09.1846; 1538a (all); Map 1846, 6 chns, by Jas Watson; foot/b'way, woods (col), building names, pit, holding boundaries (col).

25/64 Bothal (parish) NZ 210890
Apt 28.01.1837; 15290a (7593); Map 1837, 12 chns, 'constructed from Authentic Maps and Plans of Estates within the Parish and from Recent Surveys' by Edmd Bowman; turnpike roads, woods, building names, landowners, rectory, quarry, mill, windmill (by symbol), school, castle, fords, holding boundaries (col); each holding has a miniature essay giving the owner, the acreage, and the moduses. District is apportioned by holding, with fields listed, but not numbered separately; Apt omits land use.

25/65 Bowsdon (township in parish of Lowick) NT 988420
Apt 02.07.1846; 1988a (?); Map 1846, 8 chns; hill-drawing, foot/b'way, woods, quarries, limekilns, holding boundaries (col). Apt generalises land use.

25/66 Bradford (township in parish of Bamburgh) NU 159323
Apt 07.05.1841; 528a (528); Map 1841?, 4 chns; building names. District is apportioned by holding and fields are not shown.

25/67 Bradford (township in parish of Bolam) NZ 064795
Apt 24.04.1839; 1033a (1033); Map 1839?, 6 chns; woods, holding boundaries (col); scale is stated to be 4 chns, but in fact is 6 chns. Apt generalises land use.

25/68 Brainshaugh (extra-parochial place) NU 210040
Apt 30.12.1837; 677a (?); Map 1838?, 6 chns; landowners, (col); streams named; table lists areas and owners. District is apportioned by holding; Apt omits land use.

25/69 Brandon (township in parish of Eglingham) NU 047178
Apt 10.02.1849; 1080a (?); Map 1851?, 6 chns; woods, building names, mill race, well, ford, holding boundaries. District is apportioned by holding; Apt omits land use.

25/70 Branton (parish) NU 049152
Apt 08.01.1840; 1147a (1147); Map 1840?, 6 chns; landowners, holding boundaries (col); owner is named in plain cartouche; acreages summaried below title. Apt omits land use.

25/71 Branxton (parish) NT 897368
Apt 16.11.1841; 1487a (1487); Map 1842, 8 chns, by J. Bourne, Newcastle; waterbodies, woods, building names, holding boundaries (col). District is apportioned by holding; Apt omits land use but says that 'is wholly cultivated in what is termed the five course rotation'.

25/72 Brenkley (township in parish of Ponteland) NZ 217751
Apt 16.06.1840; 886a (885); Map 1841?, 8 chns; waterbodies, woods (col), property boundaries (col). District is apportioned by holding; Apt omits land use.

25/73 Brinkburn High Ward (township in parish of Brinkburn) NU 114002 [Not listed]
Apt 26.07.1844; 1846a (1846); Map 1844, 10 chns, by Edmund Bowman, Newcastle on Tyne; woods, building names, ford. District is apportioned by owner, with no information about individual holdings.

25/74 Brinkburn Low Ward (township in parish of Brinkburn) NZ 136988 [Not listed]
Apt 26.07.1844; 567a (all); Map 1849, 4 chns; hill-drawing, foot/b'way, woods, field gates, building names, ford, holding boundaries (col).

25/75 Brinkburn South Side (township in parish of Brinkburn) NZ 127980 [Not listed]
Apt 20.09.1844; 965a (965); Map 1845, 8 chns, by I. Coulson; building names, landowners (col). District is apportioned by holding; Apt omits land use.

25/76 Brotherwick (township in parish of Warkworth) NU 229058
Apt 09.02.1839; 184a (184); Map 1839, 10 chns; woods. The map is drawn in blue ink. Apt omits land use.

25/77 Broome Park (township in parish of Edlingham) NU 108125
Apt 04.07.1844; 461a (460); Map 1845, 4 chns, by E. Bowman; woods, parkland, building names. Apt omits land use.

25/78 Broxfield (township in parish of Embleton) NU 203167
Apt 21.11.1839; 314a (315); Map 1848, 6 chns.

25/79 Brunton (township in parish of Embleton) NU 202248
Apt 21.11.1839; 962a (238); Map 1839?, 8 chns; railway, woods, limestone quarry, ownership boundaries (col). Apt has cropping information.

25/80 East Brunton (township in parish of St Nicholas) NZ 229708
Apt 05.02.1840; 954a (953); Map 1841, 8 chns; railway, foot/b'way, waterbodies, woods, property ownerships (col). District is apportioned by holding; Apt omits land use.

25/81 West Brunton (township in parish of St Nicholas) NZ 211704 [Not listed]
Apt 05.02.1840; 1135a (1134); Map 1841, 8 chns; waterbodies, woods, building names, mill, lodge, property ownerships (col). District is apportioned by holding; Apt omits land use.

25/82 Budle (township in parish of Bamburgh) NU 164350
Apt 27.12.1842; 725a (724); Map 1843, 4 chns; rock outcrops, building names, quay, harbour, rocks, granary, ownership boundaries (col). District is apportioned by holding and fields are not shown.

25/83 Bullocks Hall (township in parish of Warkworth) NZ 244976 [Bullock's Hall]
Apt 23.08.1839; 206a (205); Map 1843, 4 chns; building names, holding boundaries. District is apportioned by holding and fields are not shown.

25/84 Boulmer and Seaton House (township in parish of Longhoughton) NU 265144
Apt 18.11.1839; 392a (391); Map 1840, 8 chns, in 2 parts, (including 4 chns enlargement of village); building names, holding boundaries (col). Apt omits land use.

25/85 Burradon (township in parish of Earsdon) NZ 275729
Apt 09.01.1840; 536a (all); Map 1840, [4 chns]; foot/b'way, hedge ownership, field names, borehole, quarry, stackyards, wells. Cartouche, surmounted by stag, has elaborate scallop ornament, and includes the name of the owner of the township, and the date 1804; a small note, bottom right, says that it is a copy of 1840.

25/86 Burton (township in parish of Bamburgh) NU 182326
Apt 31.12.1842; 1050a (1050); Map 1843, 6 chns; well; stream named; meaning of colour bands is uncertain. District is apportioned by holding; Apt omits land use.

25/87 Butterlaw (township in parish of Newburn) NZ 186693
Apt 13.07.1843; 250a (250); Map 1847?, 3 chns, by Thomas Bell and Sons; hill-drawing, waterbodies, woods, whinstone quarry, holding boundaries (col); stream named. Apt omits land use.

25/88 High Buston (township in parish of Warkworth) NU 234088
Apt 09.02.1839; 707a (706); Map 1840?, 6 chns, 'Reduced' from a survey by John Bell of 1807 by Thomas Bell; foot/b'way, waterbodies, road names, landowners, holding boundaries (col). Apt omits land use.

25/89 Low Buston (township in parish of Warkworth) NU 235075
Apt 05.02.1840; 870a (870); Map 1841?, 8 chns; building names, mill, holding boundaries (col). District is apportioned by holding and fields are not shown.

25/90 Byker (township in parish of St Nicholas) NZ 278672
Apt 11.12.1843; 916a (687); Map 1845, 4 chns, by Thomas Oliver; railways, foot/b'way, turnpike roads, building names, ferry landing, pottery, quarries, dock, holding boundaries (col). District is apportioned by holding and fields are not shown.

25/91 Bywell St Andrew (parish) NZ 002618 [Bywell]
Apt 19.06.1840; 3512a (3512); Map 1842?, 8 chns, in 7 parts (mostly copies) by Thomas Bell, (including one part at 6 chns, and index at 30 chns); hill-drawing, railway with depot and station, foot/b'way, turnpike roads, toll bar, waterbodies, woods, parkland, field gates, building names, road names, landowners, mill, ford, haha, drift, holding boundaries (col). District is apportioned by holding; Apt omits land use.

25/92 Bywell St Peter (parish) NZ 053585 [Bywell]
Apt 09.02.1839; 17785a (17784); Map 1840?, 8 chns, in 14 parts (some copied) by Thomas Bell, (part 11, at 10 chns, engraved by J. Walker; one part at 4 chns, one at 14 chns, two at 12 chns, and index at 30 chns); railway and station, foot/b'way, private road, turnpike roads, waterbodies, woods (col), parkland, hedge ownership, building names, road names, landowners (col), mills, mill race, salmon lock, boundary of old enclosures, quarries, limekilns, tithe-free areas, holding boundaries (col); streams named. District is apportioned by holding; fields are numbered separately, but no details are given in Apt.

25/93 Catcherside (township in parish of Kirkwhelpington) NY 991882
Apt 30.10.1839; 593a (593); Map 1840?, [10 chns]; woods (col), landowners. District is apportioned by holding; Apt omits land use.

25/94 Caistron (township in parish of Rothbury) NT 994004
Apt 30.11.1844; 400a (400); Map 1845, 3 chns, by J. Watson; fords, holding and ownership boundaries (col). Apt omits land use.

25/95 Callaley and Yetlington (townships in parish of Whittingham) NU 037093 [Callaly]
Apt 26.05.1842; 3970a (3970); Map 1842, 8 chns, by J. Watson; hill-drawing, foot/b'way, waterbodies, woods (col), orchards, gardens (col), rock outcrops, building names, boundary stones, cairns, mill, crags, ruins, private road, castle, fords. District is apportioned by holding and fields are not shown.

25/96 Black Callerton (township in parish of Newburn) NZ 176698
Apt 13.07.1843; 1377a (1377); Map 1844, 8 chns; foot/b'way, woods, building names, pits; scale-bar is ruler-like; owner's name is given in the title, holding boundaries (col). District is apportioned by holding; Apt omits land use.

25/97 High Callerton (township in parish of Ponteland) NZ 163702
Apt 16.06.1840; 793a (798); Map 1841?, 8 chns; building names, mill; holding boundaries (col), ownerships (col). District is apportioned by holding and fields are not shown.

25/98 Little Callerton (township in parish of Ponteland) NZ 155719 [Not listed]
Apt 16.06.1840; 574a (573); Map 1840?, 8 chns, by Thomas Bell; landowners; river named. District is apportioned by holding; very little detail is shown apart from some buildings.

25/99 Cambo (township in parish of Hartburn) NZ 018867
Apt 04.05.1843; 630a (630); Map 1844, 16 chns. District is apportioned by holding; very little detail is shown apart from some buildings.

25/100 Capheaton (township in parish of Kirkwhelpington) NZ 035800
Apt 27.07.1840; 2214a (2213); Map 1840?, 9 chns, (tinted); building names, landowners, mill. District is apportioned by holding; map only shows some buildings.

25/101 Carham (township in parish of Carham) NT 805379
Apt 24.11.1843; 972a (?); Map 1842, 6 chns; waterbodies, houses, woods (col), building names, toll gate, churchyard, glebe (col). District is apportioned by holding; Apt generalises land use.

25/102 Carrow (hamlet in parish of Warden) NY 845707 [Not listed]
Apt 16.02.1846; 967a (?); Map 1845, 8 chns, by I. Coulson, (tinted); waterbodies, houses, building names; stream named. District is apportioned by holding and fields are not shown.

25/103 Carry Coats (township in parish of Thockington) NY 921811 [Not listed]
Apt 30.09.1844; 1799a (all); Map 1849, 8 chns; building names, well, holding boundaries (col); streams named. District is apportioned by holding and fields are not shown.

25/104 Cartington (township in parish of Rothbury) NU 041049
Apt 14.08.1839; 1913a (1912); Map 1840, 8 chns, by John Bourne, Newcastle on Tyne; hill-drawing, marsh/bog (col), building names, landowners, castle ruins, holding boundaries (col); streams named. District is apportioned by holding and fields are not shown.

25/105 Catchburn, Morpeth Castle, Parkhouse and Stob Hill (townships in parish of Morpeth) NZ 209855 [Stobhill]
Apt 28.02.1849; 1491a (1491); Map 1849, 4 chns, by E. Bowman; railway with viaduct and station, waterbodies, woods, building names, mills, rectory, toll bar, staith, pit, waggon way; meaning of colour bands is unclear. Apt omits land use.

25/106 North Charlton (township in parish of Ellingham) NU 158226
Apt 08.12.1842; 2731a (2731); Map 1843, 8 chns, by J. Watson; hill-drawing, waterbodies, woods (col), marsh/bog, building names, quarry, limekilns, boundary stones (by symbol), holding boundaries (col). Apt generalises land use.

25/107 South Charlton (township in parish of Ellingham) NU 164202
Apt 17.12.1842; 1866a (1866); Map 1844?, 6 chns; foot/b'way,

waterbodies, building names, park wall, wells, mill, holdings (col). District is apportioned by holding and fields are not shown.

25/108 Chathill (parish) NU 185269
Apt 10.09.1842; 349a (349); Map 1843, 5 chns, by J. Watson; foot/b'way; stream named. Apt omits land use.

25/109 Chatton (township in parish of Chatton) NU 085280
Apt 21.12.1842; 6462a (?); Map 1844?, 4 chns, in 3 parts, by Thomas Bell and Sons, (including one part at 12 chns); foot/b'way, waterbodies, woods, parkland, marsh/bog, moss, field gates, building names, landowners, fords, ox-bow lake, mill, footbridge, ruins, quarry, old quarries, limestone quarries, toll gate, boundary stones, currocks, vicarage, glebe (col), holding boundaries (col). District is mostly apportioned by holding; Apt omits land use.

25/110 Cheeseburn Grange (township in parish of Stamfordham) NZ 095705
Apt 30.11.1839; 796a (795); Map 1839, 4 chns; waterbodies, woods, parkland, gardens, field gates, building names, road names, landowners, quarry, limekilns, farm boundaries (col), garden (by annotation); streams named. Fields are numbered separately, but no further individual details are given; Apt omits land use.

25/111 Chillingham (parish) NU 065250
Apt 30.12.1837; 4930a (4929); Map 1838, 6 chns; hill-drawing, woods, parkland, gardens, marsh/bog, heath/moor, building names, landowners, disputed boundary, earthwork, township boundaries (col), holding boundaries (col). District is apportioned by holding and fields are not shown.

25/112 Chipchase (township in parish of Chollerton) NY 890760 [Not listed]
Apt 19.09.1845; 116a (?); Map 1845, 4 chns, by I. Coulson; woods, parkland, building names, landowners (col), chapel. Apt omits land use.

25/113 Chirton (district in parish of Tynemouth) NZ 339681
Apt 16.03.1843; 818a (?); Map 1845, 8 chns, by J. Bourne, Newcastle; hill-drawing, railways, foot/b'way, waterbodies, woods, parkland, building names, mill, property ownerships (col). District is apportioned by holding; Apt omits land use.

25/114 East Chivington (township in parish of Warkworth) NZ 248996 [Not listed]
Apt 21.04.1841; 2226a (2225); Map 1844?, 8 chns; woods (col), rock outcrops, foreshore (col), building names, holding boundaries (col); streams named. District is apportioned by holding and fields are not shown.

25/115 West Chivington (township in parish of Warkworth) NZ 230977 [West Chevington]
Apt 15.10.1840; 1804a (1804); Map 1841?, 8 chns; woods (col), building names, holding boundaries (col); stream named. District is apportioned by holding and fields are not shown.

25/116 Chollerton (township in parish of Chollerton) NY 945730
Apt 11.03.1840; 1464a (2817); Map 1840?, 8 chns; houses, woods (col), building names, field names, landowners (col), Roman road, modus land boundary (col), glebe, holding boundaries (col); church and two houses are shown pictorially.

25/117 Clarewood (township in parish of Corbridge) NZ 025695
Apt 26.07.1842; 806a (805); Map 1843, 4 chns; woods, building names. Apt omits land use and field names.

25/118 Clifton and Coldwell (township in parish of Stannington) NZ 200820
Apt 02.04.1846; 1422a (?); Map 1846, 12 chns, in 2 parts, by Thos Fenwick, Morpeth, (including 3 chn enlargement of detail); projected railway, foot/b'way, woods, building names, frontages (col), holding boundaries (col). Apt omits land use.

25/119 Clinch (hamlet in parish of Ingram) NU 035145
Apt 20.11.1839; 416a (?); Map 1841?, 6 chns, 'Copied from an old Survey' by Thomas Bell; hill-drawing, woods, marsh/bog, field gates, building names, well, moor; streams named. Apt omits land use.

25/120 Coanwood (township in parish of Haltwhistle) NY 720680
Apt 18.04.1840; 1243a (2042); Map 1842?, 3 chns; waterbodies, houses; green band may indicate modus lands.

25/121 Coat Yards (township in parish of Nether Witton) NZ 083944 [Not listed]
Apt 06.02.1845; 227a (235); Map 1845?, 6 chns, by W.E. Cochrane; woods (col), building names. District is apportioned by holding.

25/122 Cocklaw (township in parish of St John Lee) NY 965709 [Not listed]
Apt 21.01.1839; 3667a (3666); Map 1839?, 8 chns; road names, holding acreages; houses are shown by large stylised pictorial symbols, and other buildings, not drawn to scale, are either hatched or open. District is apportioned by holding and fields are not shown.

25/123 Coldcoats (township in parish of Ponteland) NZ 144742 [Not listed]
Apt 16.06.1840; 1055a (1060); Map 1841?, 8 chns; turnpike roads, woods, building names, landowners, mill race, holding boundaries (col); streams named. District is apportioned by holding; Apt generalises land use.

25/124 Coldmurton (township in parish of Chatton) NU 008268 [Coldmartin]
Apt 31.12.1841; 392a (?); Map 1842, 4 chns; holding boundaries (col). District is apportioned by holding and fields are not shown.

25/125 Coldsnouth and Thompson's Walls (township in parish of Kirknewton) NT 861291 [Not listed]
Apt 02.02.1842; 1415a (1415); Map 1842?, 8 chns; building names, holding boundaries (col); streams named. District is apportioned by holding and fields are not shown.

25/126 Coldwell (township in parish of Kirk whelpington) NZ 002872
Apt 07.10.1839; 295a (295); Map 1839?, 4 chns, by Thomas Bell, Newcastle; building names, landowners, spring. Apt omits land use.

25/127 Colwell and Great Swinburne (townships in parish of Chollerton) NY 955755
Apt 03.03.1843; 4432a (4432); Map 1842, 8 chns, by I. Coulson; waterbodies, woods, building names, Roman road, lodge, mill, toll bar, wells, ownership boundaries (col); streams named. District is apportioned by holding; Apt omits land use.

25/128 Corbridge and Thornborough (townships in parish of Corbridge) NY 996648
Apt 16.07.1839; 5213a (5213); Map 1840?, 6 chns, in 4 parts, (including 3-chn enlargement of Corbridge village); hill-drawing, railway with tunnel, foot/b'way, turnpike roads, waterbodies, woods, rock outcrops, building names, road names, landowners (col), wells, mill, quarry, ravines, river shoals (col). District is mostly apportioned by holding and fields are not shown.

25/129 Corridge (township in parish of Hartburn) NZ 065835
Apt 28.04.1843; 329a (329); Map 1843?, 8 chns, (tinted); woods, holding boundaries. District is apportioned by holding; Apt omits land use.

25/130 Corsenside (parish) NY 905865
Apt 29.06.1839; 11133a (11132); Map 1839, 4 chns, in 2 parts, by Nichs Weatherly, Newcastle upon Tyne; hill-drawing, foot/b'way, private road, woods, marsh/bog, rock outcrops, crags, building names, road names, township boundaries (col), limestone quarries (col), quarries (col), kiln, wells, spring, stell, statue, old park wall, fords; streams, hills and pikes named.

25/131 Coupland (township in parish of Kirknewton) NT 940310
Apt 04.08.1841; 1428a (1428); Map 1841, 8 chns; waterbodies, woods (col); rivers named. District is apportioned by holding; Apt generalises land use.

25/132 Cowpen (township in parish of Woodhorn) NZ 300814
Apt 21.02.1842; 1708a (1707); Map 1842, 8 chns, in 3 parts, by

J. Bourne, Newcastle, (including two small 4 chn enlargements); hill-drawing, farmyards, building names, mills, colliery, holding boundaries (col). Apt omits land use.

25/133 Coxlodge (township in parish of St Nicholas) NZ 237682
Apt 05.02.1840; 809a (?); Map 1841?, 8 chns, (including 3-chn enlargement of detail); hill-drawing, waterbodies, woods, parkland, building names, landowners, colliery, spoil heaps, toll bar, grand stand, holding boundaries (col). District is apportioned by holding; Apt omits land use.

25/134 Cramlington (parochial chapelry) NZ 263767
Apt 26.06.1839; 3493a (all); Map 1839, 8 chns, by John Bourne, Newcastle; railway, building names, holding boundaries (col). District is apportioned by ownerships and fields are not shown.

25/135 Craster (township in parish of Embleton) NU 252190
Apt 07.05.1841; 633a (796); Map 1842?, 5 chns; hill-drawing, rock outcrops, building names, foreshore (col), holding boundaries (col). District is apportioned by holding; Apt omits land use.

25/136 Crawley (township in parish of Eglingham) NU 072168 [Not listed]
Apt 18.11.1839; 314a (314); Map 1840?, 8 chns; building names, holding boundaries (col); stream named. District is apportioned by holding and fields are not shown.

25/137 Cresswell (township in parish of Woodhorn) NZ 293931
Apt 20.05.1846; 1079a (1078); Map 1846, 8 chns, by E. Bowman; building names, holding boundaries (col). District is apportioned by holding and fields are not shown.

25/138 Crookdean (township in parish of Kirkwhelpington) NY 978830 [Crookdene]
Apt 11.11.1843; 355a (354); Map 1843, 4 chns, copied from map of 1811 by T. Robson, Cambo, by T. Arkle; foot/b'way, waterbodies, private road.

25/139 Crookham (township in parish of Ford) NT 903388
Apt 21.12.1848; 2056a (?); Map 1839, 4 chns; foot/b'way, waterbodies, woods (col), building names, holding boundaries (col). District is apportioned by holding; Apt omits land use.

25/140 Crookhouse (township in parish of Kirknewton) NT 908318
Apt 07.08.1841; 476a (467); Map 1841?, 8 chns; woods (col). District is apportioned by holding and fields are not shown.

25/141 Dalton (township in parish of Newburn) NZ 103729
Apt 23.08.1839; 1036a (1035); Map 1841?, 6 chns; foot/b'way, waterbodies, woods, marsh/bog, building names, landowners (col), quarry, mill race, dam, chapel, stiles, holding boundaries (col). District is apportioned by holding; Apt omits land use, though fields are numbered individually.

25/142 Darras Hall (township in parish of Ponteland) NZ 151707
Apt 16.06.1840; 425a (425); Map 1841?, 8 chns; landowners. District is apportioned by holding; Apt omits land use.

25/143 Deanham (township in parish of Hartburn) NZ 035832 [Old Deanham]
Apt 28.04.1843; 741a (740); Map 1843?, 8 chns; hill-drawing, waterbodies, woods, building names, landowners, holding boundaries (col). District is apportioned by holding; Apt generalises land use.

25/144 Debdon (township in parish of Rothbury) NU 059039
Apt 30.11.1844; 289a (?); Map 1851?, 4 chns, in 3 parts, by Thomas Bell and Sons, (including 48 chn index); hill-drawing, building names, road names, landowners, well, crag, sheep bridges; tadpole-like symbols could be trees, heath or boulders. Apt omits land use.

25/145 East Denton and Sugley (townships in parish of Newburn) NZ 200660
Apt 13.07.1843; 810a (809); Map 1844, 4 chns; woods, building names, copperas works, Wesleyan Chapel, holding boundaries (col). District is apportioned by holding; Apt omits land use.

25/146 West Denton (township in parish of Newburn) NZ 190657
Apt 13.07.1843; 530a (329); Map 1848?, 4 chns, 'Reduced from Various Surveys' by Thomas Bell and Sons; turnpike roads, woods, building names, landowners, holding boundaries (col). District is apportioned by holding, though fields are numbered separately; Apt omits land use.

25/147 Denwick (township in parish of Alnwick) NU 205145
Apt 30.10.1839; 1550a (1550); Map 1840?, 8 chns, by Thomas Bell, Newcastle; turnpike roads, woods, building names, landowners, mills, dam, mill race; streams named; colour bands may indicate tithe-merged areas. District is apportioned by holding and fields are not shown.

25/148 Dilston (township in parish of Corbridge) NY 972632
Apt 18.08.1849; 1320a (2904); Map 1851?, 10 chns, by D.W. Rome; railway, houses, woods (col), demesne lands (col), holding boundaries (col); stream named. District is apportioned by holding.

25/149 Dinnington (township in parish of Ponteland) NZ 211722
Apt 16.06.1840; 775a (812); Map 1841, 10 chns, in 2 parts, (including 2 chns enlargement of village); hill-drawing, railway, foot/b'way, waterbodies, woods, building names, road names, landowners, cutting or hollow way, holding boundaries (col). District is apportioned by holding; Apt omits land use.

25/150 North Dissington (township in parish of Newburn) NZ 124726 [Not listed]
Apt 23.08.1839; 1141a (1140); Map 1841?, 8 chns, copied from one by the late John Bell by Thomas Bell; woods, building names, fox cover, garden (by annotation), holding boundaries (col). District is apportioned by holding; Apt omits land use.

25/151 South Dissington (township in parish of Newburn) NZ 135707
Apt 23.08.1839; 1343a (1342); Map 1841?, 8 chns, copied from a survey by E. Grace by Thomas Bell; woods, hedges, building names, road names, landowners, holding boundaries (col). District is apportioned by holding; Apt omits land use.

25/152 Ditchburn (township in parish of Eglingham) NU 137211 [Not listed]
Apt 02.03.1840; 1521a (1520); Map 1840?, [10 chns]; foot/b'way, holding boundaries (col). District is apportioned by holding and fields are not shown.

25/153 Doddington (township in parish of Doddington) NU 008344
Apt 20.04.1849; 4798a (4798); Map 1849?, 8 chns; waterbodies, plantations (col), glebe (col), boundary stones and cairns, holding boundaries (col); wooden bridges are shown by Dawson's symbol. District is apportioned by holding and fields are not shown.

25/154 Downham (township in parish of Carham) NT 865342
Apt 14.12.1839; 717a (all); Map 1839, 8 chns; landowners, old course of river. District is apportioned by holding; Apt omits land use.

25/155 Doxford (township in parish of Ellingham) NU 184233 [Not listed]
Apt 07.12.1842; 612a (612); Map 1843, 6 chns; foot/b'way, waterbodies, woods (col, named), hedges, field names, freestone quarry, well, limestone quarry, holding boundaries (col), field acreages. District is apportioned by holding, though fields are numbered individually; Apt omits land use.

25/156 Duddo (township in parish of Stannington) NZ 188801 [Not listed]
Apt 31.12.1842; 1128a (all); Map 1843, 6 chns; building names. District is partly apportioned by holding; Apt omits most land use.

25/157 Dueshill (parish) NY 960999 [Not listed]
Apt 17.09.1846; 2506a (2505); Map 1847, 8 chns, in 2 parts; hill-drawing, woods (col), landowners, boundary marks, farm names, holding boundaries (col). District is apportioned by holding; Apt omits land use.

25/158 Dunston (township in parish of Embleton) NU 243211 [Dunstan]
Apt 21.11.1839; 1664a (1663); Map 1841?, 8 chns; waterbodies, woods (col), rock outcrops (col), landowners, foreshore (col), holding boundaries (col).

25/159 Eachwick (township in parish of Heddon on the Wall) NZ 111704
Apt 06.11.1844; 985a (985); Map 1847, 8 chns, by Thomas Bell and Sons; woods, parkland, building names, lodge, holding boundaries (col). District is apportioned by holding, though fields are numbered individually; Apt omits land use.

25/160 Earle or Yearle (township in parish of Doddington) NT 979258
Apt 20.04.1849; 1240a (1240); Map 1849, 4 chns; hill-drawing, turnpike roads, toll bar, waterbodies, woods (col), building names, landowners, mill, furze (col); streams named. Colour bands show estates, as explained by legend.

25/161 Earsdon (district in parish of Earsdon) NZ 311721
Apt 05.02.1840; 791a (?); Map 1841?, 6 chns, by Thomas Bell; woods, plantations, field gates, building names, road names, landowners, well, toll bar, ford, ownership boundaries (col). District is apportioned by holding; Apt omits land use.

25/162 Easington (township in parish of Belford) NU 122350
Apt 03.10.1842; 848a (848); Map 1842, 10 chns; landowners, holdings (col, named) with acreages; streams named. District is apportioned by holding and fields are not shown.

25/163 Easington Grange (township in parish of Belford) NU 116358
Apt 03.10.1842; 394a (547); Map 1842, 10 chns; waterbodies, building names, mill, holding boundaries (col) and acreages. District is apportioned by holding and fields are not shown.

25/164 Edlingham (township in parish of Edlingham) NU 110080
Apt 18.09.1844; 5634a (5636); Map 1845?, 16 chns; hill-drawing, turnpike roads and old turnpike road, waterbodies, woods (col), marsh/bog (col), rock outcrops, building names, landowners, mill, mill race, ford, vicarage, school, wells, boundary marks, castle, crags, holdings (col, named); physical features named. District is apportioned by holding; Apt generalises land use.

25/165 Edington (township in parish of Mitford) NZ 157827 [Not listed]
Apt 11.03.1839; 631a (631); Map 1842, [6 chns], (tinted); field gates. Border is diced blue. District is apportioned by holding; Apt generalises land use.

25/166 Eglingham (township in parish of Eglingham) NU 111193
Apt 19.04.1842; 1946a (1946); Map 1842, 8 chns; waterbodies, woods (col), building names, old road, holding boundaries (col); pictorial church; stream and lough named. District is apportioned by holding and fields are not shown.

25/167 Elford (township in parish of Bamburgh) NU 192306
Apt 31.12.1842; 84a (1062); Map 1844?, 6 chns; foot/b'way, waterbodies, houses, woods, gardens, rock outcrops, field names, limestone quarries, limekilns, colliery, engine, wells, ownership boundaries (col); whole district is mapped, with tithe area acreages in the tithable part only. District is apportioned by holding; Apt omits land use.

25/168 Ellingham (township in parish of Ellingham) NU 160250
Apt 30.12.1840; 3110a (3109); Map 1843, 8 chns; foot/b'way, waterbodies, building names, churchyard, boundary marks, holding boundaries (col). District is apportioned by holding and fields are not shown.

25/169 Ellington (township in parish of Woodhorn) NZ 275920
Apt 19.04.1839; 2189a (2189); Map 1840, 8 chns, by Edmund Bowman, Newcastle on Tyne; waterbodies, woods, building names, mill race, mill, holding boundaries (col); streams named. District is apportioned by owner, with no holding acreages; Apt omits land use.

25/170 Elsdon (parish) NY 950920
Apt 31.01.1839; 74918a (74917); Map 1839, 12 chns, in 7 parts, 'Copied from old Plans' by Thomas Arkle, High Carrick, (including 80-chn index); hill-drawing, waterbodies, marsh/bog, rock outcrops, crags (named), building names, boundary stones and cairns (by symbol), springs, toll bars, camps, Roman road, cauldron pot, school, hilltop cross (by symbol), holding boundaries (col). District is apportioned by holding; Apt omits land use.

25/171 Elswick and Westgate (district in parish of Newcastle) NZ 232639
Apt 14.05.1844; 808a (1012); Map 1852, 4 chns, by Thos Oliver, 3 Picton Place, Newcastle; hill-drawing, railways, turnpike roads, waterbodies, woods, parkland, gardens, rock outcrops, building names, road names, workhouse, cemetery, reservoirs, lead works, copperas works, mills, coal depot, quarries, factory chimneys, ownership boundaries (col). District is apportioned by holding; Apt omits land use and some holding acreages.

25/172 Eltringham (township in parish of Ovingham) NZ 077627
Apt 22.02.1840; 320a (320); Map 1841?, 6 chns, by Thomas Bell; railway, turnpike roads, woods, field gates, building names, landowners, holding boundaries (col). District is apportioned by holding; Apt omits land use.

25/173 Elwick (township in parish of Belford) (partly in Durham) NU 112375
Apt 31.01.1839; 819a (819); Map 1840?, 8 chns; field names and acreages, county boundary; buildings shown in outline only. District is apportioned by holding; Apt omits land use.

25/174 Embleton (township in parish of Embleton) NU 226227
Apt 21.11.1839; 1977a (2394); Map 1841?, 6 chns; hill-drawing, waterbodies, woods (col), orchard (col), foreshore (col). District is apportioned by holding; Apt generalises land use.

25/175 Eshot (township in parish of Felton) NZ 206977 [Eshott]
Apt 04.12.1841; 1775a (all); Map 1842, 12 chns, in 2 parts; building names, holdings (col). District is apportioned by holding and fields are not shown.

25/176 Etal (township in parish of Ford) NT 945395
Apt 17.11.1848; 3345a (?); Map 1849, 8 chns; woods (col), holding boundaries (col); village not mapped in detail. District is apportioned by holding and fields are not shown.

25/177 Ewart (township in parish of Doddington) NT 952322 [Not listed]
Apt 20.04.1849; 1572a (1512); Map 1849, 4 chns; waterbodies, woods (col), holding boundaries (col). District is apportioned by holding and fields are not shown.

25/178 Ewesley (township in parish of Netherwitton) NZ 061921
Apt 28.01.1845; 933a (932); Map 1847?, 6 chns, copied from a plan by J. Robertson by Thomas Bell; turnpike roads; stream named. District is apportioned by holding and fields are not shown.

25/179 Fairhaugh (township in parish of Allenton) NT 880125
Apt 13.11.1844; 95a (all); Map 1844?, 6 chns, (tinted); hill-drawing, waterbodies, drove road, wells, field acreages; streams and hills named; table lists holding acreages. District is apportioned by holding; Apt omits land use.

25/180 Fairnley (township in parish of Hartburn) NZ 006889
Apt 28.04.1843; 203a (203); Map 1844?, 16 chns; streams named; owner is named in title. District is apportioned by holding and fields are not shown; Apt generalises land use.

25/181 Falloden (township in parish of Embleton) NU 200231 [Not listed]
Apt 21.11.1839; 1025a (1024); Map 1839, 4 chns, copied from a plan of 1804 by Thomas Arkle, Elsdon; foot/b'way, footbridges (by symbol), waterbodies, woods, plantations, parkland, gardens, marsh/bog, field boundary ownerships, field gates, building names, landowners, limestone quarries, limekiln, wells, watermill (by symbol), coal drift.

25/182 Fallowlees (township in parish of Rothbury) NZ 014948
Apt 17.04.1841; 1548a (1547); Map 1843?, 16 chns, in 2 parts (including location diagram); holding acreages; owner is named in title; streams named. District is apportioned by holding and fields are not shown; Apt generalises land use.

25/183 Fawden (township in parish of St Nicholas) NZ 225693 [Fawdon]
Apt 05.02.1840; 522a (522); Map 1841, 8 chns, in 2 parts; railway,

waterbodies, woods, building names, landowners, collieries, mill, holdings (col). District is apportioned by holding; Apt omits land use.

25/184 Fawdon (vill or hamlet in parish of Ingram) NU 029154
Apt 23.06.1840; 1086a (?); Map 1848?, 8 chns, in 2 parts, by Thomas Bell and Sons, (including 4 chn enlargement of detail); marsh/bog, field gates, mill races, gravel beds (col), old weir, boundary stones (by symbol), ownership boundaries (col). District is apportioned by holding; Apt omits land use.

25/185 Fawns (township in parish of Kirkwhelpington) NZ 006853
Apt 30.10.1839; 269a (all); Map 1840?, 6 chns, (tinted); waterbodies, building names. District is apportioned by holding; Apt omits land use.

25/186 Featherstone (township in parish of Haltwhistle) NY 680610 [Not listed]
Apt 18.04.1840; 2844a (2844); Map 1840?, 6 chns; railway, houses, woods (col), ford, holding boundaries (col).

25/187 Felton (township in parish of Felton) NU 164019
Apt 21.05.1845; 1599a (1528); Map 1846, 8 chns, in 4 parts, by I. Coulson, (including 2 chn enlargement of village); building names, vicarage. District is apportioned by holding; Apt omits land use.

25/188 Fenham (township in parish of St Nicholas, Newcastle upon Tyne) NZ 220658
Apt 05.08.1841; 421a (420); Map 1842, 6 chns, by Edmund Bowman; turnpike roads, waterbodies, woods, parkland, building names, road names, ownership boundaries (col). District is apportioned by holding.

25/189 Fenton (township in parish of Wooler) NT 971348
Apt 14.10.1848; 1720a (1720); Map 1849?, 12 chns, copied by Thomas Bell and Sons, Newcastle; building names, burying ground (col). District is apportioned by holding and fields are not shown; Apt generalises land use.

25/190 Fenwick (township in parish of Stamfordham) NZ 055729
Apt 23.08.1839; 1635a (1634); Map 1839, 4 chns; woods (col); pink tint may indicate modus lands.

25/191 Fleetham (township in parish of Bamburgh) NU 199292 [Not listed]
Apt 31.12.1842; 563a (562); Map 1844, 4 chns, by Thomas Bell and Sons; foot/b'way, waterbodies, woods, building names, landowners, mill, mill race, old quarry, sheepfold, holding boundaries (col). Apt omits land use.

25/192 Flotterton (township in parish of Rothbury) NT 994007
Apt 31.08.1839; 769a (768); Map 1840?, 4 chns, surveyed by E. Smith in 1832; waterbodies, woods (col), gardens (col), hedge ownership (col), field gates, holdings and ownerships (col).

25/193 Ford (township in parish of Ford) NT 953372
Apt 21.12.1848; 2004a (?); Map 1849, 4 chns; woods (col), gardens, colliers' house, castle, common (col), holding boundaries (col), glebe. District is apportioned by holding; Apt omits land use.

25/194 Fowberry (township in parish of Chatton) NU 032287 [Not listed]
Apt 16.05.1840; 1224a (?); Map 1840, 4 chns; woods (col), building names, landowners, holding boundaries (col). District is apportioned by holding; Apt generalises land use.

25/195 Long Framlington (chapelry in parish of Felton) NU 132023 [Longframlington]
Apt 29.06.1842; 4962a (4962); Map 1840, 8 chns, in 2 parts, by Thomas Arkle, Carrick, (including enlargement of detail); foot/b'way, turnpike roads, old turnpike road, building names, cairn (by symbol), well, boundary stones, holdings (col). Apt omits land use.

25/196 Freeholders quarter (township in parish of Longhorsley) NZ 132938 [Not listed]
Apt 26.06.1840; 900a (899); Map 1839, 5 chns, in 2 parts 'Compiled... from various Surveys and Plans' by E. Bowman, (including 2 chns enlargement of detail); turnpike roads, waterbodies, woods, building names, holding boundaries (col), glebe, common. District is apportioned by owner, without holding acreages; Apt omits land use.

25/197 Gallowhill (township in parish of Bolam) NZ 105815
Apt 24.04.1839; 604a (603); Map 1840?, 8 chns; hill-drawing, woods, building names, landowners, quarry, holdings (col). District is apportioned by holding; Apt generalises land use.

25/198 Glanton (township in parish of Whittingham) NU 064148
Apt 08.06.1841; 1330a (1329); Map 1841?, 5 chns; building names, field names, landowners, holding boundaries (col). District is apportioned by holding and only a few fields are shown; Apt omits land use.

25/199 Greens and Glantlees (township in parish of Felton) NU 142053
Apt 15.08.1839; 971a (979); Map 1840?, 8 chns; hill-drawing, waterbodies, woods, building names, holdings (col); stream named. District is apportioned by holding; Apt omits land use.

25/200 Greenleighton (township in parish of Hartburn) NZ 032925
Apt 04.05.1843; 1572a (1572); Map 1844?, 16 chns; landowners, tithe-free land (col); stream named. District is apportioned by holding and fields are not shown; Apt omits land use.

25/201 Grey's Forest (township in parish of Kirknewton) NT 880240 [Not listed]
Apt 27.09.1841; 6615a (6615); Map 1845, 12 chns, partly 'laid down from old Surveys' by E.W. Griffiths; hill-drawing, woods, building names, landowners (col), camp, boundary stones and cairn, mill; hills named; some houses are shown by realistic-looking pictorial drawings. Scale-bar is ruler-like. District is apportioned by holding; Apt omits land use.

25/202 Greystead (parish) NY 720810
Apt 12.07.1843; 18003a (18003); Map 1842, 12 chns, 'Copied from old Plans'; rock outcrops, building names, drove road, pikes (by symbol); physical features named. District is apportioned by holding; Apt omits land use.

25/203 North Gosforth (township in parish of St Nicholas) NZ 249708
Apt 05.02.1840; 1067a (1066); Map 1841?, 8 chns; turnpike roads, waterbodies, woods, parkland, building names, landowners, old churchyard, lodge, carriage road, holdings (col). District is apportioned by holding; Apt omits land use.

25/204 South Gosforth (township in parish of St Nicholas) NZ 250680
Apt 05.02.1840; 437a (436); Map 1841?, 8 chns; railway, turnpike roads, waterbodies, woods, building names, landowners, colliery, spoil heaps, toll bar, mill, holdings (col). District is apportioned by holding; Apt omits land use.

25/205 Gunnerton (township in parish of Chollerton) NY 914762
Apt 07.02.1842; 2657a (?); Map 1841, 8 chns, by I. Coulson; building names, Roman road, ownership boundaries (col). District is apportioned by holding; Apt omits land use.

25/206 Hadston (township in parish of Warkworth) NU 266005
Apt 09.02.1839; 1169a (1165); Map 1839, 6 chns, by Edmund Bowman; foot/b'way, waterbodies, building names, high water mark, links. District is apportioned as an single tithe area, and no acreages or land use are given for holdings. (PRO IR 30 contains two similar copies, one on paper and one on parchment.)

25/207 Hallington (parish) NY 990760
Apt 12.08.1851; 321a (?); Map 1851?, 4 chns; hill-drawing, woods (col), garden (by annotation), building names, wells; stream named. District is apportioned by holding; Apt omits land use.

25/208 Halliwell (township in parish of Earsdon) NZ 313740 [Holywell]
Apt 05.02.1840; 1353a (1180); Map 1840, 6 chns, by J. Bourne, Newcastle; hill-drawing, woods, building names, holding boundaries (col). District is apportioned by holding; Apt omits land use.

25/209 Halton (township in parish of Corbridge) NZ 003681
Apt 30.07.1842; 799a (798); Map 1843?, 4 chns; woods, building names, chapel and burial ground. Apt omits land use and field names.

25/210 Halton Shields (township in parish of Corbridge) NZ 015688
Apt 26.07.1842; 443a (442); Map 1843?, 4 chns; woods, building names. Apt omits land use and field names.

25/211 Haltwhistle (township in parish of Haltwhistle) NY 702651
Apt 18.04.1840; 1609a (2759); Map 1844?, 4 chns; railway and station, open fields, road names, common; map looks like a draft rather than a finished copy.

25/212 Halystone (township in parish of Halystone) NT 928020 [Holystone]
Apt 17.09.1846; 2906a (2906); Map 1841, 4 chns; hill-drawing, woods, building names, boundary stones and cairns, remains of old camp, mill, well, churchyard, holding boundaries (col), common, disputed ground; physical features named. District is apportioned by holding; Apt omits land use.

25/213 Harbottle (township in parish of Holystone) NT 937041
Apt 15.08.1839; 110a (?); Map 1843, 8 chns, in 2 parts, by J. Bourne, Newcastle, (tithable parts only); woods, building names, castle, ford, holding and ownership boundaries (col). District is apportioned by holding; Apt omits land use.

25/214 Harup (township in parish of Eglingham) NU 090204 [Harehope]
Apt 30.10.1839; 566a (all); Map 1839, 4 chns; landowners; streams named; buildings shown in outline only. District is apportioned by holding and fields are not shown.

25/215 Littleharle (township in parish of Kirkwhelpington) NZ 012831 [Not listed]
Apt 26.06.1839; 702a (701); Map 1841?, 6 chns; hill-drawing, woods, parkland, gardens, building names, landowners. District is apportioned by owner; Apt omits land use and holding acreages.

25/216 Westharle (township in parish of Kirkwhelpington) NY 982822 [West Harle]
Apt 26.06.1839; 662a (661); Map 1841?, 6 chns; hill-drawing, woods, rock outcrops, building names, landowners, quarry, limekiln, whinstone outcrops; stream named. District is apportioned by holding; Apt omits land use.

25/217 Harlow Hill (township in parish of Ovingham) NZ 080682
Apt 23.06.1840; 994a (993); Map 1841?, 6 chns, by Thomas Bell; turnpike roads, woods, landowners, holding boundaries (col), farm names. District is apportioned by holding and fields are not shown.

25/218 Harnham (township in parish of Bolam) NZ 071810
Apt 12.11.1839; 680a (679); Map 1841?, 4 chns; woods, ownership boundaries (col); stream named. District is apport-ioned by holding; Apt generalises land use.

25/219 Hartburn Grange (township in parish of Hartburn) NZ 060862
Apt 30.08.1838; 1157a (1157); Map 1839?, 16 chns, (engraved by J. Walker); hill-drawing, foot/b'way, turnpike roads, woods (named), field names, landowners, mill, ford, field acreages. District is apportioned by holding; Apt omits land use.

25/220 East Hartford (township in parish of Woodhorn) NZ 266792
Apt 19.04.1839; 304a (303); Map 1839?, 4 chns, foot/b'way, woods, orchards, landowners. District is apportioned by holding; Apt generalises land use.

25/221 West Hartford (township in parish of Woodhorn) NZ 251791 [Not listed]
Apt 27.07.1839; 522a (521); Map 1838, 6 chns; woods, road names, landowners, holdings (col), field acreages.

25/222 Hartington (township in parish of Hartburn) NZ 010896 [Not listed]
Apt 28.04.1843; 1935a (1935); Map 1844?, 16 chns; woods (col, with acreages), landowners; streams named; blue band shows tithable part. District is apportioned by holding; Apt omits land use.

25/223 Hartington Hall (township in parish of Hartburn) NZ 020880
Apt 02.04.1842; 1005a (1005); Map 1844?, 16 chns; landowners; streams named. District is apportioned by holding; Apt generalises land use.

25/224 Hartley Burn (township in parish of Haltwhistle) NY 652598 [Not listed]
Apt 18.04.1840; 1274a (2676); Map 1841?, 3 chns; houses, building names, fords, engine house; streams named.

25/225 Hartside (hamlet in parish of Ingram) NT 982158
Apt 27.04.1842; 583a (?); Map 1842?, 6 chns; foot/b'way, waterbodies, woods, building names, mill, fold. District is apportioned by holding; Apt omits land use.

25/226 Harwood (township in parish of Hartburn) NY 998918
Apt 02.04.1842; 3795a (3795); Map 1844?, 16 chns; a stream is named, but little else is shown. District is apportioned by owner, without holding acreages; Apt generalises land use.

25/227 Hauxley (township in parish of Warkworth) NU 279031 [Not listed]
Apt 21.10.1840; 748a (748); Map 1842?, 8 chns; building names, holdings (col). District is apportioned by holding and fields are not shown.

25/228 Hawick (township in parish of Kirkharle) NY 952828 [Not listed]
Apt 04.05.1847; 1150a (1150); Map 1847?, 8 chns; waterbodies, landowners. District is apportioned by holding and fields are not shown.

25/229 Hawkhill (township in parish of Lesbury) NU 222129
Apt 11.02.1840; 723a (all); Map 1840, 8 chns; buildings shown in outline only; bridge shown pictorially. District is apportioned by holding and fields are not shown.

25/230 Hawkwell (township in parish of Stamfordham) NZ 072714
Apt 07.05.1840; 568a (567); Map 1839, 4 chns; woods.

25/231 Haydon (chapelry in parish of Warden) NY 837649
Apt 31.01.1839; 13688a (13688); Map 1839, 8 chns, 'Copied and reduced from Various Plans' by Nicholas Weatherley, Newcastle upon Tyne; railway with station, waterbodies, building names, reservoir, public quarries, lead mills, mill, toll gate, holding boundaries (col). District is apportioned by holding; Apt omits land use.

25/232 Hazleridge (township in parish of Chatton) NU 058326 [Not listed]
Apt 09.06.1842; 2185a (?); Map 1842, 8 chns; waterbodies, rock outcrops, crags (named), building names, landowners, quarry, limekiln, boundary stone and cairn, holding boundaries (col). District is apportioned by holding; Apt omits land use.

25/233 Hazon and Hartlaw (townships in parish of Shilbottle) NU 195051
Apt 27.03.1839; 1409a (1409); Map 1839, 8 chns, by Andrew Rotson; hill-drawing, foot/b'way, woods (col), building names, field names, landowners, holding boundaries (col). Sketchy leaves form cartouche.

25/234 Healey and Combhill (township in parish of Netherwitton) NZ 079920
Apt 28.01.1845; 866a (866); Map 1845?, 8 chns, by Thomas Bell; foot/b'way, turnpike roads, woods, building names, landowners, mill, holding boundaries (col). District is apportioned by holding; Apt omits land use.

25/235 Heatherslaw and Hodden (townships in parish of Ford) NT 922363
Apt 21.12.1848; 2305a (?); Map 1849, 4 chns; waterbodies, woods (col), building names, mill, hill forts, tile works, holding boundaries (col); hills and bridge named. District is apportioned by holding; Apt generalises land use.

25/236 Heathpool (township in parish of Kirknewton) NT 891281 [Hethpool]
Apt 29.09.1841; 1038a (1037); Map 1841?, 8 chns; streams named; hills

are shown side-on, 'molehill' style. District is apportioned by holding and fields are not shown.

25/237 Heaton (township in parish of All Saints, Newcastle upon Tyne) NZ 271660
Apt 28.05.1841; 911a (911); Map 1841?, 8 chns; foot/b'way, woods, building names, ford, holding boundaries (col), ownerships (col). District is apportioned by holding and fields are not shown.

25/238 East Heddon (township in parish of Heddon on the Wall) NZ 141688
Apt 22.07.1844; 759a (758); Map 1844, 8 chns; building names, landowners. District is apportioned by holding and fields are not shown.

25/239 West Heddon (township in parish of Heddon on the Wall) NZ 122688 [Not listed]
Apt 18.07.1844; 338a (338); Map 1845, 6 chns, by I. Coulson; building names, holding boundaries (col). District is apportioned by holding and fields are not shown.

25/240 Heddon on the Wall (township in parish of Heddon on the Wall) NZ 136669 [Heddon-on-the-Wall]
Apt 18.07.1844; 1154a (1190); Map 1848?, 8 chns, by Thomas Bell and Sons, (including 3-chn enlargement of village); railway, foot/b'way, turnpike roads, waterbodies, woods, quarries, mill, mill dam, stiles, watering place, holding and ownership boundaries (col). District is apportioned by holding; Apt omits land use.

25/241 Hedgeley (township in parish of Eglingham) NU 065175 [Not listed]
Apt 07.02.1840; 700a (700); Map 1839, 9 chns, ? by Andrew Rotson; hill-drawing, waterbodies, woods (col), hedge ownership, fence ownership, building names, landowners, well; bridges named. District is apportioned by holding; Apt omits land use.

25/242 Hedley (township in parish of Ovingham) NZ 088594 [Hedley on the Hill]
Apt 27.09.1843; 1254a (1399); Map 1845?, 6 chns, 'Reduced from a Survey made by George Laws' by Thomas Bell and Sons; railway, waterbodies, woods, heath/moor, rock outcrops, building names, landowners, colliery, quarry, quarry waste, pinfold, chapel, old pit, holding boundaries (col). District is apportioned by holding, though fields are numbered separately; Apt omits land use.

25/243 Hedley Woodside (township in parish of Ovingham) NZ 099573 [Not listed]
Apt 27.09.1843; 1364a (1364); Map 1845?, 8 chns, by Thomas Bell and Sons; foot/b'way, woods, heath/moor, building names, landowners, gravel bed, mill, holding boundaries (col). District is apportioned by holding; Apt omits land use.

25/244 Henshaw (township in parish of Haltwhistle) NY 760700
Apt 18.04.1840; 11255a (11255); Map 1841, 8 chns, in 2 parts, by I. Coulson; railway with station, waterbodies, building names, Roman wall, military road, wells, mills, pinfold, road names; steams named. Apt omits land use.

25/245 Hepple (township in parish of Rothbury) NT 979009
Apt 25.11.1843; 3610a (3874); Map 1843, 8 chns, by J. Watson; hill-drawing, waterbodies, woods (col), marsh/bog, building names, fords, crags, cairns and pikes, boundary stones, holding boundaries (col). District is apportioned by holding; Apt omits land use.

25/246 Hepple Demesne (township in parish of Rothbury) NY 987992 [Not listed]
Apt 25.11.1843; 1534a (1534); Map 1843, 8 chns, by J. Watson; waterbodies, woods (col), marsh/bog, building names, boundary stones and cairns, hill fort, fords, crags, holding boundaries (col); stream named. District is apportioned by holding; Apt omits land use.

25/247 Hepscott (township in parish of Morpeth) NZ 227841
Apt 26.09.1842; 1595a (1594); Map 1843, 4 chns, by Edmund Bowman, Newcastle upon Tyne; railway, foot/b'way, waterbodies, woods, building names, engine house, ford, holding boundaries (col). Apt omits land use.

25/248 Hesleyhurst (township in parish of Rothbury) NZ 086983 [Not listed]
Apt 30.11.1844; 659a (659); Map 1843, 4 chns, by Thomas Bell and Son; foot/b'way, waterbodies, woods, rock outcrops, crag, field gates, building names, road names, landowners, collieries, limestone quarries, old quarries, limekiln, springs, old pits, wells, waterfall, stiles, guide post, holding boundaries (col); streams named. Apt omits land use.

25/249 Hetton (township in parish of Chatton) NU 030342 [Not listed]
Apt 18.11.1839; 1491a (?); Map 1840?, 8 chns, 'Extracted from a Plan by John Baily, 1798'; landowners, holdings (col). District is apportioned by holding; Apt omits land use.

25/250 Heugh (township in parish of Stamfordham) NZ 082733
Apt 23.08.1839; 2205a (all); Map 1839, 4 chns.

25/251 Hexham (township in parish of Hexham) NY 920638
Apt 28.08.1839; 4776a (4775); Map surveyed 1839-40, 4 chns, by Wylam Walker; hill-drawing, railway with station, waterbodies, woods, plantations, coppice, building names, landowners, mill; built-up part generalised. Apt omits some field names.

25/252 High quarter of Hexhamshire (township in parish of Hexham) NY 905515 [Not listed]
Apt 28.08.1839; 8773a (8773); Map 1839, 8 chns, by I. Coulson; building names, stinted pasture, mill, ownership boundaries (col); streams named. District is apportioned by holding and some fields are not shown; Apt omits land use.

25/253 Low quarter of Hexhamshire (township in parish of Hexham) NY 923601 [Not listed]
Apt 07.10.1839; 3608a (3608); Map 1839, 8 chns, by I. Coulson; building names, fulling mill, mills, dye house, holding boundaries (col). District is apportioned by holding and some fields are not shown; Apt omits land use.

25/254 Middle quarter of Hexhamshire (township in parish of Hexham) NY 910580 [Not listed]
Apt 24.08.1839; 5700a (5700); Map 1839, 8 chns, by I. Coulson; building names, chapel (pictorial), mill, stinted pasture, public quarry, holding boundaries (col). District is apportioned by holding and some fields are not shown; Apt omits land use.

25/255 West quarter of Hexhamshire (township in parish of Hexham) NY 879616 [Not listed]
Apt 07.10.1839; 5118a (5117); Map 1839, 8 chns, in 3 parts, by I. Coulson; railway, building names, stinted pasture, holding boundaries (col). District is apportioned by holding and fields are not shown.

25/256 Higham Dykes (township in parish of Ponteland) NZ 135755
Apt 16.06.1840; 219a (219); Map 1840?, 4 chns; woods; buildings are shown in outline only. District is apportioned by holding though fields are numbered separately; Apt omits land use.

25/257 Highlaws (township in parish of Hartburn) NZ 076839 [High Highlaws]
Apt 28.04.1843; 295a (295); Map 1843, 4 chns, by E. Bowman; field names. District is apportioned by holding; Apt omits land use.

25/258 High and Low Highley (township in parish of Mitford) NZ 178890
Apt 27.07.1839; 1334a (1357); Map 1840, 12 chns, by Edmund Bowman, Newcastle on Tyne; woods, building names, toll bar, holding boundaries (col). District is apportioned by holding and fields are not shown; numbering is by ownerships, but acreages are by holdings.

25/259 Hirst (township in parish of Woodhorn) NZ 281883
Apt 20.05.1846; 395a (395); Map 1848?, 4 chns, by W. and T. Sample; foot/b'way, waterbodies, woods, building names, stile. Apt omits land use and field names.

25/260 Holborn (township in parish of Lowick) NU 047360 [Holburn]
Apt 25.07.1846; 2413a (?); Map 1847?, 6 chns; rock outcrops, building names, landowners, boundary stones, dam, mill, cave, holding names and boundaries (col), crags (named); acreages are tabulated. District is apportioned by owner and fields are not shown.

25/261 Hollinghill (township in parish of Rothbury) NZ 050968 [Not listed]
Apt 30.11.1844; 5264a (5264); Map 1847?, 8 chns, by Thomas Bell and Sons; hill-drawing, foot/b'way, woods, marsh/bog, heath/moor, rock outcrops, building names, landowners, waterfall, quarries, old quarries, sheep folds, wells, ruins, footbridge, boundary stones and marks, ford, wash pool, toll gate, ruined inn, holding boundaries (col), gardens (by annotation); streams named. Apt omits land use and some field names.

25/262 Horsley (township in parish of Ovingham) NZ 095662
Apt 13.07.1839; 1478a (1478); Map 1841?, 8 chns, by Thomas Bell; foot/b'way, turnpike roads, woods, building names, landowners, quarry, holding boundaries (col). District is apportioned by holding, though fields are numbered separately; Apt omits land use.

25/263 Horton (township in parish of Woodhorn) NZ 289786 [Not listed]
Apt 17.09.1846; 2280a (2555); Map 1847, 8 chns; waterbodies, woods, building names, holding boundaries (col). District is apportioned by holding; Apt omits land use.

25/264 Horton (township in parish of Chatton) NU 028310 [Not listed]
Apt 31.12.1841; 2365a (?); Map 1842?, 8 chns; building names, holding boundaries (col). District is apportioned by holding and fields are not shown.

25/265 Horton Grange (township in parish of Ponteland) NZ 197762
Apt 16.06.1840; 1222a (1222); Map 1840?, 8 chns; building names, holding boundaries (col). District is apportioned by holding and fields are not shown.

25/266 Houghton and Close House (township in parish of Heddon on the Wall) NZ 122662
Apt 22.06.1844; 597a (597); Map 1847?, 8 chns, by Thomas Bell and Sons; railway, foot/b'way, turnpike roads, toll bar, waterbodies, woods, parkland, building names, landowners, school, lodges, holding boundaries (col). District is apportioned by holding; Apt omits land use.

25/267 Little Houghton (township in parish of Longhoughton) NU 229166
Apt 15.09.1841; 753a (753); Map 1844?, 12 chns; holdings (col). District is apportioned by holding; Apt omits land use.

25/268 Howick (parish) NU 247178
Apt 26.07.1837; 1535a (1692); Map 1839, 8 chns; landowners, foreshore (col), holding acreages; table summarises land use. District is apportioned by holding and fields are not shown.

25/269 Howtell (township in parish of Kirknewton) NT 900338 [Howtel]
Apt 12.11.1847; 1146a (1145); Map 1848, 4 chns; waterbodies, woods (col), farm names, holding boundaries (col); colour bands show their extent. District is apportioned by holding; Apt omits land use and some fields.

25/270 Humbleton (township in parish of Doddington) NT 971285
Apt 22.05.1849; 1514a (784); Map 1849, 4 chns, in 2 parts, (including 2 chns enlargement of village); hill-drawing, waterbodies, houses, woods (col), building names, mill, ancient earthwork, burying ground, holding boundaries (col); burying ground is shown with boulderlike grave-stones. District is apportioned by holding; Apt generalises land use.

25/271 Ilderton (township in parish of Ilderton) NT 990200
Apt 31.03.1849; 4816a (?); Map 1850?, 16 chns; waterbodies, rock outcrops, building names, boundary stones, holding boundaries (col), glebe (col). District is apportioned by holding; Apt generalises land use.

25/272 Ingher (township in parish of Stamfordham) NZ 048758 [Ingoe]
Apt 25.03.1840; 2113a (2165); Map 1839, 4 chns.

25/273 Ingram, Linhope and Greenshawhill (townships in parish of Ingram) NU 010150
Apt 15.12.1842; 6882a (all); Map 1843?, 10 chns; hill-drawing, foot/b'way, rock outcrops, building names, landowners, old camp, stells, sheep folds, rectory, holding boundaries (col); streams named. District is apportioned by holding; Apt omits land use.

25/274 Jesmond (township in parish of St Andrew, Newcastle upon Tyne) NZ 259660
Apt 05.02.1840; 655a (654); Map 1844?, 4 chns; hill-drawing, foot/b'way, turnpike roads, waterbodies, woods (col), parkland, building names, old chapel, cemetery, lodges, old pit, mill, holding boundaries (col). District is apportioned by holding; Apt omits land use.

25/275 Kearsley (township in parish of Stamfordham) NZ 028755
Apt 12.09.1839; 506a (605); Map 1839, 4 chns; plantations.

25/276 Kenton (township in parish of St Nicholas) NZ 220676
Apt 05.02.1840; 1437a (1436); Map 1841?, 8 chns; turnpike roads, toll bar, waterbodies, rock outcrops, building names, quarries, holding boundaries (col). District is apportioned by holding; Apt omits land use.

25/277 Kilham (township in parish of Kirknewton) NT 881326
Apt 22.12.1841; 2855a (2855); Map 1842?, 7.5 chns; holding boundaries (col). District is apportioned by holding and fields are not shown.

25/278 Killingworth (township in parish of Long Benton) NZ 280713
Apt 29.06.1839; 1656a (?); Map 1843?, 8 chns, in 2 parts, (including 2 chn enlargement of detail); hill-drawing, railway, woods, building names, colliery, holding boundaries (col). District is apportioned by holding; Apt omits land use.

25/279 Kimmerston and Broomridge (townships in parish of Ford) NT 960360
Apt 21.12.1848; 1755a (?); Map 1849, 4 chns; waterbodies, woods (col), building names, holding boundaries (col); bridge named. District is apportioned by holding; Apt omits land use.

25/280 Kirkhaugh (parish) NY 699495
Apt 29.10.1840; 6665a (6665); Map 1841, 4 chns, in 2 parts, by D.W. Rome, Alston; tithe area numbers are stamped. District is apportioned by holding; Apt omits land use.

25/281 Kirkley (township in parish of Ponteland) NZ 150764 [Not listed]
Apt 16.06.1840; 1816a (1816); Map 1841?, 6 chns; woods, parkland, building names, landowners, mill, holding boundaries (col). District is apportioned by holding; Apt generalises land use.

25/282 Kirknewton (township in parish of Kirknewton) NT 912285
Apt 02.03.1843; 2218a (2217); Map 1843, 12 chns; woods, mill.

25/283 Kirkwhelpington (township in parish of Kirkwhelpington) NY 999850
Apt 11.11.1843; 2778a (2778); Map 1844?, 8 chns, by Thomas Bell and Sons; hill-drawing, foot/b'way, turnpike roads, woods, marsh/bog, building names, road names, landowners, mill, mill race, boundary stones and marks, holding and ownership boundaries (col); streams named. District is apportioned by holding; Apt omits land use.

25/284 Knaresdale (parish) NY 660520 [Knarsdale]
Apt 28.02.1837; 2212a (7144); Map 1838?, [4 chns]; building names; streams named; map is very crude with buildings indicated by small open circles.

25/285 Lambley (parish) NY 687580
Apt 07.12.1838; 1855a (2698); Map 1839?, [4 chns]; fords, chapel; streams named.

25/286 Lanton (township in parish of Kirknewton) NT 930320
Apt 24.12.1841; 984a (983); Map 1842?, 4 chns; woods (col), building names, mill, ford, holding boundaries (col); streams named. District is apportioned by owner, with holding acreages; Apt omits land use.

25/287 Learchild (township in parish of Edlingham) NU 100107 [Not listed]
Apt 28.10.1843; 460a (460); Map 1839, 4 chns; building names, holding boundaries (col). District is apportioned by holding and fields are not shown.

25/288 Learmouth (township in parish of Carham) NT 857367 [Not listed]
Apt 07.03.1843; 2605a (?); Map 1842, 8 chns, in 2 parts; common and

holding boundaries (col). District is apportioned by holding; Apt omits land use.

25/289 Lee Ward (township in parish of Rothbury) NZ 073987 [Not listed]
Apt 30.11.1844; 1793a (1793); Map 1847?, 4 chns, by Thomas Bell and Sons; hill-drawing, foot/b'way, turnpike roads, waterbodies, woods, marsh/bog, rock outcrops, building names, road names, landowners, hill fort, sheep washing pool, stone circles, ruins, footbridge, quarries, guide post, old pit, holding boundaries (col); streams named; garden and nursery shown by annotation. District is apportioned by holding; Apt omits land use and most field names.

25/290 Lesbury (township in parish of Lesbury) NU 245121
Apt 30.06.1841; 1653a (?); Map 1844?, 6 chns, in 2 parts, by Thomas Bell and Sons, (village separately at 3 chns); waterbodies, woods, parkland, building names, landowners, mill, dam, toll bar, vicarage, poorhouse, occupation road, ford, stepping stones, holding boundaries (col). Apt omits land use.

25/291 Lemmington (township in parish of Edlingham) NU 118111 [Not listed]
Apt 26.09.1845; 2071a (2071); Map 1839, 5 chns; landowners, holding boundaries (col); no buildings shown. District is apportioned by holding and fields are not shown.

25/292 East Lilburn (township in parish of Eglingham) NU 044229
Apt 09.12.1839; 868a (868); Map 1839, 4 chns; landowners, holding boundaries (col) and acreages. District is apportioned by holding and fields are not shown.

25/293 West Lilburn (township in parish of Edlingham) NU 024248 [Not listed]
Apt 18.11.1839; 1966a (all); Map 1840, 7 chns; landowners, holding boundaries (col); buildings shown in outline only; farms named in table. District is apportioned by holding and fields are not shown.

25/294 Linbriggs (township in parish of Allenton) NT 888090
Apt 27.11.1844; 2800a (9500); Map 1846?, 8 chns, in 3 parts; hill-drawing, building names, ancient camps, Roman road, well, cairns, holding boundaries; physical features named. District is apportioned by holding with acreages in round hundreds, and fields are not shown.

25/295 Linemouth (township in parish of Woodhorn) NZ 295908 [Lynemouth]
Apt 29.01.1845; 315a (315); Map 1845, 10 chns, by E. Bowman; sands. District is apportioned by holding and fields are not shown.

25/296 Linsheeles (township in parish of Halystone) NT 850070 [Linshiels]
Apt 17.09.1846; 1233a (?); Map 1846?, 12 chns; hill-drawing, building names, landowners, oxbow lake; streams named. District is apportioned by holding and land use and some fields are not shown.

25/297 Longhoughton (township in parish of Longhoughton) NU 240150
Apt 12.02.1842; 2748a (2969); Map 1844?, 8 chns, in 2 parts, by Thomas Bell and Sons, (including village separately at 4 chns); hill-drawing, foot/b'way, waterbodies, woods, rock outcrops, building names, road names, landowners, quarries, old quarries, limekiln, vicarage, stiles, holding boundaries (col), tithe ownerships (col). Apt omits land use.

25/298 Longshaws (township in parish of Longhorsley and Hartburn) NZ 122885
Apt 10.07.1847; 767a (767); Map 1848, 9 chns.

25/299 Longwitton (district in parish of Hartburn) NZ 073888
Apt 28.04.1843; 2246a (2247); Map 1844?, 16 chns; landowners; one holding coloured, with acreage; no buildings shown. District is apportioned by holding and fields are not shown; Apt generalises land use.

25/300 Lorbottle (township in parish of Whittingham) NU 047070
Apt 29.01.1845; 2410a (2409); Map 1845, 8 chns; plantations, landowners, quarry, boundary markers, moss.

25/301 Lowick (township in parish of Lowick) NU 022390
Apt 05.06.1846; 3998a (?); Map 1846, 8 chns, in 2 parts, (including village at 4 chns); hill-drawing, foot/b'way, waterbodies, woods, pits, Meeting House, holding boundaries (col). District is apportioned by holding.

25/302 Lucker and Hoppen (township in parish of Bamburgh) NU 157300
Apt 31.12.1842; 1809a (2042); Map 1846?, 8 chns, in 3 parts, by Thomas Bell and Sons, (including Lucker village separately at 4 chns); foot/b'way, turnpike roads, woods, building names, stiles, limekiln, holding boundaries (col). Apt omits land use.

25/303 Lyham (township in parish of Chatton) NU 070310 [Not listed]
Apt 02.12.1839; 1704a (?); Map 1841?, 8 chns, copied from a survey by Thomas Wilkin by Thos Bell; hill-drawing, woods, marsh/bog (col), rock outcrops, crags, building names, landowners, spring, well, dam, mill, camp, ford, boundary marks; physical features named. Apt omits land use.

25/304 Manorial Allotment (district in parish of Rothbury) NU 082052 [Not listed]
Apt 16.09.1845; 1515a (all); Map 1843, 8 chns, by Thomas Bell and Sons; hill-drawing, foot/b'way, private road, waterbodies, marsh/bog (col), rock outcrops, landowners. District is apportioned by holding; Apt omits land use.

25/305 Mason (township in parish of Ponteland) NZ 219734
Apt 16.06.1840; 1158a (1165); Map 1841?, 8 chns; waterbodies, woods, building names, landowners, quarry, holding boundaries (col) and names. District is apportioned by holding; Apt omits land use.

25/306 East Matfen (township in parish of Stamfordham) NZ 050698
Apt 27.07.1839; 2067a (2067); Map 1839, 4 chns; woods.

25/307 West Matfen (township in parish of Stamfordham) NZ 031715
Apt 27.07.1839; 1834a (1905); Map 1839, 4 chns; woods.

25/308 Meldon (township) NZ 116840
Apt 21.04.1849; 994a (all); Map 1849, 6 chns; building names, mill, mill race. District is apportioned by holding; Apt omits land use and some fields.

25/309 Melkridge (township in parish of Haltwhistle) NY 735670
Apt 18.04.1840; 4451a (4451); Map 1842, 8 chns, in 2 parts, by I. Coulson; railway, building names, quarries, toll bar, Roman wall, ford, holding boundaries (col); streams named. District is mostly apportioned by holding; Apt omits land use.

25/310 Maryshields (township in parish of Ovingham) NZ 063619 [Merry Shield]
Apt 05.08.1841; 14a (?); Map 1841?, 4 chns, in 2 parts, by Thomas Bell; railway, turnpike roads, landowners, boundary stones. District is apportioned by holding; Apt omits land use.

25/311 Mickley (township in parish of Ovingham) NZ 074610 [Not listed]
Apt 11.03.1840; 1189a (1188); Map 1841?, 6 chns, in 2 parts 'Copied from sundry surveys and plans' by Thomas Bell, (including one part at 8 chns); foot/b'way, turnpike roads, toll bar, stiles, woods, building names, road names, landowners, chapel, quarries, holding boundaries (col). District is apportioned by holding; Apt omits land use.

25/312 Middleton Hall (township in parish of Ilderton) NT 988252
Apt 22.03.1849; 1101a (1101); Map 1849, 16 chns; waterbodies, woods, landowners, ford, pools, crags, well, cairn; streams named. Apt omits land use.

25/313 North Middleton and Todridge (township in parish of Hartburn) NZ 060850
Apt 28.04.1843; 1128a (1128); Map 1844, 8 chns, by Thos Fenwick, Morpeth; landowners, mill, well, holding boundaries (col) and acreages; stream named. District is apportioned by holding and fields are not shown.

25/314 North Middleton (township in parish of Ilderton) NT 981238
Apt 22.03.1849; 2102a (2102); Map 1849?, 8 chns; waterbodies, woods

(col), boundary markers. District is apportioned by holding; Apt generalises land use and omits some fields.

25/315 South Middleton (township in parish of Ilderton) NT 993229
Apt 22.03.1849; 1609a (1609); Map 1849?, 8 chns; waterbodies, woods (col), boundary markers (pictorial). District is apportioned by holding; Apt generalises land use.

25/316 South Middleton (township in parish of Hartburn) NZ 052832
Apt 05.05.1843; 609a (609); Map 1843?, 8 chns; woods, building names, holding boundaries (col). District is apportioned by holding and fields are not shown.

25/317 Milbourne (township in parish of Ponteland) NZ 118741
Apt 17.04.1841; 1217a (1216); Map 1841?, 4 chns; waterbodies, woods, gardens, building names, landowners, holding boundaries (col). District is apportioned by holding; Apt generalises land use.

25/318 Milbourne Grange (township in parish of Ponteland) NZ 115758
Apt 16.06.1840; 630a (629); Map 1841?, 8 chns; woods, building names, landowners, holding boundaries (col). District is apport-ioned by holding; Apt omits land use.

25/319 Milfield (township in parish of Kirknewton) NT 930339
Apt 04.08.1841; 1471a (1471); Map 1841?, 8 chns; woods (col), holding boundaries (col); stream named. District is apportioned by holding and fields are not shown.

25/320 Mindrum (township in parish of Carham) NT 835335
Apt 05.03.1839; 1955a (?); Map 1840?, 8 chns; hill-drawing, landowners, holding boundaries (col) and names; very little internal detail is shown; table summarises acreages and land use. District is apportioned by holding and fields are not shown.

25/321 Mitford and Moleston (townships in parish of Mitford) NZ 168847
Apt 25.05.1843; 2558a (all); Map 1843, 12 chns, in 2 parts, by Edmund Bowman, (including 4 chn enlargement of detail); woods, building names; colour bands may show tithe ownerships. District is apportioned by holding and fields are not shown.

25/322 Moneylaws (township in parish of Carham) NT 880358 [Not listed]
Apt 21.05.1845; 861a (?); Map 1845, 8 chns; holding boundaries (col). District is apportioned by holding and fields are not shown; Apt generalises land use.

25/323 Monkseaton (township in parish of Tynemouth) NZ 343719
Apt 21.06.1844; 1087a (1087); Map 1845, 8 chns, by J. Bourne, Newcastle; foot/b'way, field gates, building names, holding boundaries (col). District is apportioned by holding; Apt omits land use.

25/324 Morpeth (township in parish of Morpeth) NZ 199866
Apt 26.09.1842; 538a (537); Map 1843, 2 chns, by E. Bowman; woods, building names, mill, ownerships (col); built-up part is not mapped.

25/325 Morrick (township in parish of Warkworth) NU 232037
Apt 09.02.1839; 734a (734); Map 1841, 5 chns; woods (col), mill, holding boundaries (col). District is apportioned by holding; Apt omits land use.

25/326 Mount Healey (township in parish of Rothbury) NU 069006 [Not listed]
Apt 30.11.1844; 442a (442); Map 1843, 4 chns, by Thomas Bell and Sons; hill-drawing, foot/b'way, turnpike roads, toll bar, waterbodies, woods, marsh/bog, heath/moor, rock outcrops, building names, road names, landowners, mill dams, mills, holding boundaries (col). Apt omits land use.

25/327 Mousen (township in parish of Bamburgh) NU 122320
Apt 31.12.1842; 753a (752); Map 1843?, 6 chns. District is apportioned by holding; Apt omits land use.

25/328 Murton (district in parish of Tynemouth) NZ 330708
Apt 28.08.1840; 444a (?); Map 1841, 8 chns, by J. Bourne, Newcastle; foot/b'way, holding boundaries (col). District is apportioned by holding; Apt omits land use.

25/329 Nafferton (township in parish of Ovingham) NZ 065660 [Not listed]
Apt 13.07.1839; 773a (773); Map 1841, 6 chns, 'Copied from a Survey by William Bates' by Thomas Bell; foot/b'way, turnpike roads, woods, field gates, building names, road names; stream named. District is apportioned by holding; Apt omits land use.

25/330 Nesbit (township in parish of Doddington) NT 988342
Apt 20.04.1849; 776a (776); Map 1849?, 6 chns; building names. District is apportioned by holding and fields are not shown.

25/331 Nesbitt (township in parish of Stamfordham) NZ 080698 [Not listed]
Apt 28.11.1839; 844a (843); Map 1839, 4 chns, ? by Thomas Bell; woods, field gates, building names, landowners, quarry, kiln, holding boundaries (col). District is apportioned by holding; Apt omits land use.

25/332 Netherwitton (township in parish of Netherwitton) NZ 104908
Apt 03.02.1845; 3915a (3914); Map 1845?, 12 chns, by Thomas Bell; waterbodies, woods, building names, parsonage, holding boundaries (col), demesne land boundary. District is apportioned by holding and fields are not shown.

25/333 Newbiggen (township in parish of Shotley) NY 933501 [Newbiggin]
Apt 20.04.1844; 877a (2056); Map 1845?, 8 chns, in 2 parts, 'Reduced from sundry surveys and plans' by Thomas Bell and Sons; foot/b'way, woods, building names, road names, landowners, fords, holding boundaries (col). District is apportioned by holding; Apt omits land use.

25/334 Newbiggin (chapelry or township in parish of Woodhorn) NZ 316883 [Newbiggin-by-the-Sea]
Apt 29.01.1845; 324a (all); Map 1847?, 4 chns; holding boundaries (col).

25/335 Newbiggin (township in parish of Newburn) NZ 202683 [Not listed]
Apt 13.07.1843; 520a (519); Map 1843, 6 chns, by J. Bourne, Newcastle; waterbodies, woods, building names, holding boundaries (col). District is apportioned by holding and fields are not shown.

25/336 Newburn (township in parish of Newburn) NZ 160660
Apt 23.08.1845; 635a (790); Map 1849?, 6 chns, in 2 parts, by Thomas Bell and Sons, (including village at 2 chns); railway, turnpike roads, woods, building names, pinfold, vicarage, sand and gravel beds, holding boundaries (col), glebe (col). District is apportioned by holding; Apt omits land use.

25/337 Newburn Hall (township in parish of Newburn) NZ 180650 [Not listed]
Apt 13.07.1843; 876a (876); Map 1848?, 6 chns, in 2 parts; railway, foot/b'way, waterbodies, woods, rock outcrops, building names, road names, coal staiths, ferry landing, quarries, old quarry, holding boundaries (col). District is apportioned by holding; Apt omits land use.

25/338 Newham (township in parish of Bamburgh) NU 176291
Apt 31.12.1842; 2569a (2568); Map 1846?, 8 chns, by Thomas Bell and Sons, (including village at 2 chns); foot/b'way, waterbodies, woods, marsh/bog, fox cover, building names, tile works, footbridge, mill, dam, holding boundaries (col). District is apportioned by holding; Apt omits land use.

25/339 Newham (township in parish of Whalton) NZ 106766 [Not listed]
Apt 29.06.1839; 1322a (1321); Map 1840?, 8 chns; building names, landowners, holding boundaries (col). District is apportioned by holding; Apt omits land use.

25/340 Newminster Abbey (township in parish of Morpeth) NZ 189860
Apt 22.12.1841; 718a (717); Map 1842, 4 chns, by Edmund Bowman, Newcastle on Tyne; foot/b'way, woods, fence, building names, ford, mill, weir, holding boundaries (col). District is apportioned by holding; Apt omits land use.

25/341 Newsham and South Blyth (township in parish of Earsdon) NZ 313796
Apt 05.02.1840; 1181a (all); Map 1840?, [6 chns]; road names, ropery, chapel, tile shed, foreshore; streams named; buildings are shown by pecked lines, in outline only. District is apportioned by owner, no holding acreages are given and fields are not shown.

25/342 Newstead (township in parish of Bamburgh) NU 141268
Apt 31.12.1842; 1988a (1988); Map 1846?, 8 chns, in 2 parts, by Thomas Bell and Sons; foot/b'way, occupation road, turnpike roads, waterbodies, woods, building names, road names, landowners, holding boundaries (col), moss. District is apportioned by holding; Apt omits land use.

25/343 Newtown (township in parish of Rothbury) NZ 038996
Apt 30.11.1844; 951a (951); Map 1848?, 8 chns; hill-drawing, occupation road, foot/b'way, woods, marsh/bog, rock outcrops, crags, building names, boundary stones, old limestone quarry, ruined farms, mill, limekiln, ruined boundary, ancient camp, spring, mill race, old quarries, holding boundaries (col), moss; streams named. District is apportioned by holding; Apt omits land use.

25/344 Newton by the Sea (township in parish of Embleton) NU 235232 [High and Low Newton-by-the-Sea]
Apt 21.11.1839; 1412a (1411); Map 1841?, 8 chns; waterbodies, woods, building names, limekiln, holding boundaries (col). District is apportioned by holding; Apt omits land use.

25/345 Newton Moor (township in parish of Shilbottle) NU 173053 [Not listed]
Apt 26.05.1841; 911a (911); Map 1842, 4 chns, by Andrew Robson; hill-drawing, turnpike roads, woods, gardens, heath/moor, field gates, building names, landowners, stockyard, limestone quarry, limekilns, holy well, well, holding boundaries (col).

25/346 Newton Park (township in parish of Mitford) NZ 157868
Apt 29.06.1839; 341a (all); Map 1840, 6 chns, by Edmund Bowman, Newcastle on Tyne; woods, building names, weir. District is apportioned by holding; Apt generalises land use.

25/347 West Newton (township in parish of Kirk Newton) NT 895303 [Westnewton]
Apt 14.07.1847; 1063a (1063); Map 1849, 4 chns; waterbodies, woods, mill, common. District is apportioned by holding; Apt generalises land use.

25/348 Newton Underwood (township in parish of Mitford) NZ 146860
Apt 30.11.1839; 870a (869); Map 1841?, 7 chns, by Edmund Bowman; foot/b'way, waterbodies, woods, building names, mill, holding boundaries (col), common. District is apportioned by owner, without holding acreages, and fields are not shown; Apt omits land use.

25/349 Nun-Riding (township in parish of Mitford) NZ 134875 [Not listed]
Apt 25.05.1843; 648a (648); Map 1847?, 6 chns; woods, plant-ations.

25/350 Nunnykirk (township in parish of Netherwitton) NZ 084924
Apt 29.01.1845; 111a (111); Map 1847?, 4 chns, 'Copied from Sundry Surveys' by Thomas Bell and Sons; waterbodies, woods, landowners, fish ponds. District is apportioned by holding and fields are not shown.

25/351 Ogle (township in parish of Whalton) NZ 138786
Apt 31.12.1842; 2118a (2117); Map 1844?, 10 chns; waterbodies, woods, building names, landowners, fords, mill, holding boundaries (col). District is apportioned by holding; Apt generalises land use.

25/352 Ouston (township in parish of Stamfordham) NZ 073704
Apt 30.11.1839; 512a (511); Map 1839, 4 chns, ? by Thomas Bell; woods, building names, landowners, holding boundaries (col). District is apportioned by holding, though fields are numbered separately; Apt omits land use.

25/353 Outchester, Spindleston and Glororoum (townships in parish of Bamburgh) NU 150355
Apt 08.03.1839; 1966a (all); Map 1841?, 12 chns, surveyed by Nich. Weatherly, 1824, (engraved by J.Walker, with hand-colour); hill-drawing, foot/b'way, waterbodies, woods, gardens, field names, landowners, wells, tower, Roman fort, quarry, kiln, salt grass, sea banks, field acreages. District is apportioned by township; Apt omits land use.

25/354 Ovingham (township in parish of Ovingham) NZ 089646
Apt 27.07.1839; 510a (all); Map 1841?, 6 chns, in 2 parts, by Thomas Bell, (including 3 chn enlargement of detail); hill-drawing, foot/b'way, woods, orchards, field gates, landowners, holding boundaries (col), tithe-free land; built-up part not mapped. District is apportioned by holding; Apt omits land use.

25/355 Ovington (township in parish of Ovingham) NZ 073640
Apt 22.02.1840; 1104a (1105); Map 1849?, 8 chns, in 4 parts, by Thos Bell and Sons, (village also mapped at 4 chns); foot/b'way, turnpike roads, woods, landowners, mill, school, bleach grounds, ford, ferry, well, military road, stiles, holding boundaries (col), common. District is apportioned by holding; Apt omits land use.

25/356 Paston (township in parish of Kirknewton) NT 847315 [Pawston]
Apt 22.12.1842; 2336a (2336); Map 1845?, 8 chns; woods, landowners, holding boundaries (col). District is apportioned by holding, and buildings and fields are not shown.

25/357 Pauperhaugh (township in parish of Rothbury) NZ 103991
Apt 30.11.1844; 987a (986); Map 1847?, 4 chns, by Thomas Bell and Sons; hill-drawing, foot/b'way, waterbodies, woods, field gates, building names, landowners, springs, old pits, old quarry, footbridges, well, ferry, fords, stepping stones, holding boundaries (col). Apt omits land use.

25/358 Pigdon (township in parish of Mitford) NZ 149885
Apt 23.06.1840; 1084a (all); Map not dated, 8 chns; foot/b'way, woods, building names, landowners, holdings (col). District is apportioned by holding; Apt generalises land use.

25/359 Plainmeller (township in parish of Haltwhistle) NY 731615 [Plenmeller]
Apt 18.04.1840; 4864a (4904); Map 1844?, 16 chns, 'Reduced from several Plans or Surveys' by Thomas Bell and Sons; hill-drawing, woods, building names, landowners, colliery, pit, engine house, rock house, holding boundaries (col), common. District is apportioned by holding; Apt omits land use.

25/360 Plashetts (township in parish of Fallstone) NY 660960
Apt 07.05.1840; 28229a (28225); Map 1841?, 30 chns, in 3 parts, 'Copied from various Surveys and Plans' by Thomas Bell, (including parts at 6 and 12 chns); woods, parkland, building names, farm names, landowners, rectory, fords, crags, peat, moss, chapel, boundary stones, holding boundaries (col); streams named. District is apportioned by holding; Apt omits land use.

25/361 Plessey and Shotton (townships in parish of Stannington) NZ 218777
Apt 07.03.1840; 2674a (?); Map 1840, [8 chns]; turnpike roads, building names, old kennel, mill; bridges named. District is apportioned by owner, without holding acreages, and fields are not shown.

25/362 Ponteland (township in parish of Ponteland) NZ 121735
Apt 17.04.1841; 1661a (1733); Map 1842, 8 chns, in 2 parts, (including enlargement of village at 4 chns); building names, holding boundaries (col), glebe. District is apportioned by holding and fields are not shown.

25/363 Portgate (township in parish of St John Lee) NY 980688
Apt 21.01.1839; 645a (690); Map 1839?, 8 chns; field gates, building names, holding acreages; houses are shown by realistic-looking pictorial symbols; owner is named in the title. District is apportioned by holding and fields are not shown.

25/364 Prendwick (township in parish of Alnham) NT 999129
Apt 23.09.1843; 1612a (1612); Map 1844, 6 chns; waterbodies, houses, woods, plantations, boundary stones (by symbol), holding boundaries (col). District is apportioned by holding; Apt omits land use.

25/365 Pressen (township in parish of Carham) NT 832348
Apt 01.05.1843; 1394a (?); Map 1842, 8 chns; waterbodies, landowners, holding boundaries (col) and names. District is apportioned by holding and fields are not shown.

25/366 Preston (township in parish of Ellingham) NU 186252
Apt 28.05.1841; 457a (457); Map 1841?, 4 chns; woods (col), gardens, landowners, holding boundaries (col). District is apportioned by holding; Apt omits land use.

25/367 Preston (district in parish of Tynemouth) NZ 346696
Apt 15.05.1840; 542a (542); Map 1841, 8 chns, by J. Bourne, Newcastle; waterbodies, woods, parkland, building names, toll bar, holding boundaries (col). District is apportioned by holding; Apt omits land use.

25/368 Prestwick (township in parish of Ponteland) NZ 183720
Apt 17.04.1841; 833a (621); Map 1841, 6 chns, in 2 parts, by J. Bourne, Newcastle, (including 2 chns enlargement of detail); foot/b'way, waterbodies, woods, parkland, holding boundaries (col). District is apportioned by holding; Apt omits land use.

25/369 Prudhoe (township in parish of Ovingham) NZ 102622
Apt 27.09.1843; 1440a (1440); Map 1848, 6 chns, ? by Thomas Bell and Sons; railway, disused waggonway, foot/b'way, turnpike roads, woods, building names, landowners, brick and tile works, ford, ferry, ownership boundaries (col). District is apportioned by holding; Apt omits land use.

25/370 Prudhoe Castle (township in parish of Ovingham) NZ 100637 [Not listed]
Apt 29.06.1839; 719a (all); Map 1839?, 8 chns, 'Complied from various surveys' by Thomas Bell; hill-drawing, railway with station, turnpike roads, woods, building names, landowners, mill, dam, boat house, fords, ferry, holding boundaries (col) and names. District is apportioned by holding; Apt omits land use.

25/371 Ratchwood (township in parish of Bamburgh) NU 143283
Apt 31.12.1842; 152a (155); Map 1846?, 3 chns, by Thomas Bell; foot/b'way, waterbodies, woods, field gates, building names, stiles, holding boundaries (col). District is apportioned by holding; Apt omits land use.

25/372 Raw (township in parish of Rothbury) NZ 090995 [Not listed]
Apt 30.11.1844; 691a (690); Map 1847?, 4 chns, by Thomas Bell and Sons; hill-drawing, foot/b'way, occupation roads, waterbodies, woods, marsh/bog, rock outcrops, field gates, building names, landowners, springs, fords, old camp, crags, wells, holding boundaries (col). Apt omits land use.

25/373 Reaveley (township in parish of Ingram) NU 015175
Apt 30.06.1843; 2340a (all); Map 1843?, 8 chns; hill-drawing, waterbodies, woods, plantations, building names, landowners, old mill, stells, holding boundaries (col); streams named. District is apportioned by holding; Apt omits land use.

25/374 Rennington (township in parish of Embleton) NU 208181
Apt 21.11.1839; 1812a (1812); Map 1846, 8 chns, by Thomas Bell and Sons, (including village separately at 2 chns); foot/b'way, woods, parkland, building names, parsonage, stiles, school, glebe (col); land not owned by the Duke of Northumberland is tinted. Apt omits land use.

25/375 Riddells quarter (township in parish of Longhorsley) NZ 155939 [Not listed]
Apt 17.02.1846; 2146a (2145); Map 1846, 8 chns, in 2 parts, by I. Coulson; houses, building names, mill, holding boundaries (col); streams named. District is apportioned by holding; Apt omits land use.

25/376 Ridley (township in parish of Haltwhistle) NY 779623
Apt 18.04.1840; 4388a (4388); Map 1841, 8 chns, in 2 parts, by T. Sopwith and M. Scott, Arcade, Newcastle; foot/b'way, waterbodies, woods, parkland, rock outcrops, building names, Roman wall, quarries, limekiln, boat house, sheepfold, crags, mill, holding boundaries. District is apportioned by holding; Apt omits land use.

25/377 Riplington (township in parish of Whalton) NZ 116820
Apt 30.10.1839; 378a (377); Map 1840?, [6 chns]; foot/b'way, woods, field gates; houses are shown by 'realistic' pictograms. District is apportioned by holding; Apt omits land use.

25/378 Ritton Colt Park (township in parish of Netherwitton) NZ 077937 [Not listed]
Apt 29.01.1845; 1029a (1029); Map 1845?, 10 chns; woods (col), building names, holding boundaries (col). District is apportioned by holding; Apt omits land use.

25/379 Ritton White House (township in parish of Netherwitton) NZ 058945
Apt 26.09.1845; 637a (636); Map 1847?, 8 chns, by Thomas Bell and Sons, Newcastle; building names, landowners, holding boundaries (col) and names.

25/380 Rock (township in parish of Embleton) NU 193205
Apt 21.11.1839; 1973a (1973); Map 1840?, 16 chns; building names, landowners, mill, holding boundaries (col) and names; buildings are shown without fill. District is apportioned by holding and fields are not shown.

25/381 Roddam (township in parish of Ilderton) NU 022197
Apt 22.03.1849; 1218a (1218); Map 1849, 5 chns; woods (col), building names, landowners, holding boundaries (col). District is apportioned by holding and fields are not shown.

25/382 Rosedon (township in parish of Ilderton) NU 038214 [Roseden]
Apt 31.03.1849; 1580a (?); Map 1850, 16 chns; waterbodies, woods (col), ford, boundary stones and cairns, holding boundaries (col). District is apportioned by holding; tithe areas appear to be numbered within holdings according to land use.

25/383 Rothbury (township in parish of Rothbury) NU 068025
Apt 29.05.1846; 3408a (4923); Map 1848?, 8 chns, in 2 parts, by Thomas Bell and Sons, (including Rothbury town and environs at 4 chns); hill-drawing, foot/b'way, turnpike roads, toll bar, woods, rock outcrops, field gates, building names, road names, landowners, quarries, colliery, fulling mill, gravel beds, fords, girls school, school, workhouse, footbridge, boundary stones, well, dam, holding boundaries (col), moss; streams named. Apt omits land use.

25/384 Rothley (township in parish of Hartburn) NZ 046894
Apt 28.04.1843; 2720a (2720); Map 1844?, 16 chns; waterbodies, landowners, holding boundaries (col); tithable lands tinted. District is apportioned by holding and fields are not shown; Apt generalises land use.

25/385 Rudchester (township in parish of Ovingham) NZ 113675
Apt 26.06.1839; 644a (all); Map 1841?, 6 chns, turnpike roads, waterbodies, field gates, building names, landowners, military road, milestone, ruins, well. District is apportioned by holding; Apt generalises land use.

25/386 Ryal (township in parish of Stamfordham) NZ 012745
Apt 29.05.1846; 2123a (2189); Map 1846, 6 chns; hill-drawing, woods.

25/387 Great Ryle (township in parish of Whittingham) NU 020127
Apt 31.03.1842; 2113a (2113); Map 1842, 8 chns, in 2 parts, by John Craig, Lowick, (including one part at 19 chns); hill-drawing, landowners, holding names, mill, cairn; hills are shown by conical, volcano-shaped, hill-drawing; 'whirligig' hill-drawing may indicate an ancient earthwork. Apt omits land use.

25/388 Little Ryle (township in parish of Whittingham) NU 021107
Apt 07.10.1841; 505a (504); Map 1842, 8 chns, by John Craig, Lowick; woods, building names. Apt omits land use.

25/389 Saltwick (township in parish of Stannington) NZ 175801
Apt 13.07.1839; 918a (?); Map 1840, 15 chns, (tinted); foot/b'way, woods, landowners. District is apportioned by holding; Apt omits land use.

25/390 Sandoe (township in parish of St John Lee) NY 973670 [Sandhoe]
Apt 31.12.1838; 1636a (1648); Map 1838, 4 chns, by I. Coulson; woods,

parkland, gardens, building names, landowners, military road, holding boundaries (col), tithe-free areas. District is apportioned by holding, though fields are numbered separately; Apt omits land use.

25/391 Screnwood (township in parish of Alnham) NT 990095 [Scrainwood]
Apt 29.10.1844; 1070a (1070); Map 1845?, 4 chns; woods (col), field gates, landowners, ford; field boundaries highlighted in colour. Apt omits land use.

25/392 Seaton Delavel and Hartley (townships in parish of Earsdon) NZ 327760
Apt 16.05.1840; 4163a (4219); Map 1840, 10 chns, by J. Bourne, Newcastle; hill-drawing, waterbodies, woods, parkland, building names, mill, colliery, spoil heap, township boundary, holding boundaries (col). District is apportioned by holding; Apt omits land use.

25/393 North Seaton (township in parish of Woodhorn) NZ 298866
Apt 27.06.1846; 1110a (1210); Map 1844, 8 chns, by E. Bowman; woods, building names, tidal areas. District is apportioned as a single tithe area; occupiers are listed, but no further details are given.

25/394 Seghill (township in parish of Earsdon) NZ 286748
Apt 05.02.1840; 1403a (1403); Map 1841?, 8 chns; railways, building names, landowners, colliery, mill, quarry, spoil heap, holding boundaries (col). District is apportioned by holding; Apt omits land use.

25/395 Selby's Forest (township in parish of Kirknewton) NT 930230
Apt 22.12.1841; 11854a (11853); Map 1843, 12 chns, by J. Watson; hill-drawing, rock outcrops, building names, boundary cairns and stones, summit markers, holding boundaries (col); physical features named. District is apportioned by holding and fields are not shown; Apt generalises land use.

25/396 East Shaftoe (township in parish of Hartburn) NZ 059818
Apt 28.04.1843; 602a (602); Map 1843?, 8 chns; hill-drawing, woods, rock outcrops, building names, landowners, beacon, holding boundaries (col). District is apportioned by holding; Apt generalises land use.

25/397 West Shaftoe (township in parish of Hartburn) NZ 043819
Apt 28.04.1843; 489a (489); Map 1843?, 8 chns; hill-drawing, building names, landowners, holding boundaries (col). District is apportioned by holding; Apt generalises land use.

25/398 Sharperton (township in parish of Alwinton) NT 968042
Apt 17.09.1846; 971a (971); Map 1847, 4 chns, by Js. Watson; woods (col), field gates, boundary stones, ownership boundaries (col). District is apportioned by holding; Apt omits land use.

25/399 Shawdon (township in parish of Whittingham) NU 095145 [Not listed]
Apt 28.05.1841; 1056a (1056); Map 1842?, 6 chns; foot/b'way, hedge ownership, field gates, landowners, holding boundaries (col). A note explains about maintenance of boundary fences. Border is yellow with green inner edge; scale is surmounted by dividers; ochre petals and dark green leaves partly frame the title and the note about boundaries, District is apportioned by holding and fields are not shown; Apt generalises land use.

25/400 Shilbottle (township in parish of Shilbottle) NU 190085
Apt 30.06.1840; 2935a (2935); Map 1842?, 12 chns, in 2 parts, (village also at 4 chns); woods, building names, holding boundaries (col); scale statement says 3 chns, but the scale bar and comparative measurement disprove this. Apt omits land use.

25/401 Shilvington (township in parish of Morpeth) NZ 160809
Apt 26.09.1842; 1498a (1497); Map 1843?, 15 chns; woods, building names, landowners, holding boundaries (col). District is apportioned by holding; Apt generalises land use.

25/402 Shipley (township in parish of Eglingham) NU 142182
Apt 07.05.1841; 1991a (1991); Map 1841?, 6 chns; waterbodies, woods (col), building names, landowners, mill. District is apportioned by holding; Apt omits land use.

25/403 Shire Moor (district in parish of Earsdon and Tynemouth) NZ 317702 [Shiremoor]
Apt 21.06.1844; 1182a (?); Map 1845, 8 chns, by J. Bourne, Newcastle; railways, landowners, ownership boundaries (col). District is apportioned by holding; Apt omits land use.

25/404 Shoeston (township in parish of Bamburgh) NU 202328 [Not listed]
Apt 31.12.1842; 670a (669); Map 1845?, 4 chns, by Thomas Bell and Sons; hill-drawing, foot/b'way, woods, parkland, building names, landowners, flagstaff, pits (col), foreshore (col), occupation roads, stiles, ownership boundaries (col). Apt omits land use.

25/405 Shortflatt (township in parish of Bolam) NZ 089805
Apt 24.04.1839; 512a (511); Map not dated, 4 chns; woods, landowners, holding boundaries (col). District is apportioned by holding; Apt generalises land use.

25/406 Shotley Low quarter (township in parish of Shotley) NZ 062525 [Shotleyfield]
Apt 09.04.1844; 6877a (6676); Map 1846?, 6 chns; foot/b'way, waterbodies, woods, building names, toll gate, quarries, mills, lead mill, forge, lodge, school, ford, dog kennel; streams named; meaning of colour bands is unclear. District is apportioned by holding; Apt omits land use.

25/407 Simonburn (parish) NY 850740
Apt 09.05.1840; 13372a (13372); Map 1839, 8 chns, in 6 parts, by I. Coulson; foot/b'way, building names, mills, rectory, sheepfold, pond, paper mill, chapel, old chapel, military road, ownership boundaries (col); streams named. District is apportioned by holding; Apt omits land use.

25/408 Slaley (parish) NY 963573
Apt 12.11.1849; 7430a (7430); Map 1850, 8 chns, by M. Carr and I. Coulson; woods, rock outcrops, building names, quarries, mill, holding boundaries, ownership boundaries (col); streams named. District is apportioned by holding; Apt generalises land use.

25/409 Snitter (township in parish of Rothbury) NU 020040
Apt 07.05.1841; 1084a (1083); Map 1842, 4 chns, by Edward Smith; woods, orchards, marsh/bog, rock outcrops, landowners, mill race, quarries, holding boundaries (col); streams named. Apt omits land use.

25/410 Spital or Spittle (township in parish of Ovingham) NZ 079669
Apt 29.06.1839; 13a (82); Map 1844?, 8 chns, 'Copied from a Survey by the late John Bell' by Thomas Bell and Sons; building names, holding boundaries (col). District is apportioned by holding; Apt omits land use.

25/411 Spittle NU 004513 [Spittal]
This district lies in that part of Northumberland which was formerly in Durham, and the map and apportionment are found under 11/242.

25/412 Spittle Hill (township in parish of Mitford) NZ 175862 [Spital Hill]
Apt 18.01.1839; 160a (160); Map 1840, 4 chns, by Edmund Bowman, Newcastle on Tyne; woods, fence, building names. District is apportioned by holding; Apt generalises land use.

25/413 Stamford (township in parish of Embleton) NU 223199
Apt 21.11.1839; 1602a (1602); Map 1840?, 16 chns; landowners, holding boundaries (col). District is apportioned by holding; Apt omits land use.

25/414 Stannington (township in parish of Stannington) NZ 217798
Apt 11.03.1840; 2522a (?); Map 1840, [10 chns]; turnpike roads, weirs, ownership boundaries (col); stream named. District is apportioned by owner, without holding acreages, and fields are not shown.

25/415 Stanton (township in parish of Long Horsley) NZ 137901
Apt 17.02.1846; 2255a (2254); Map 1847, 4 chns, by John Greenwell, Darlington; woods, building names, mill, limekilns, quarries, weir, gravel bed.

25/416 Sturton Grange (township in parish of Warkworth) NU 216063
Apt 23.06.1840; 1094a (1094); Map 1841, 4 chns; waterbodies, woods (col), plantations (col), owner-occupancies (col, named). District is apportioned by holding; Apt omits land use.

25/417 North Sunderland (township in parish of Bamburgh) NU 213313
Apt 31.12.1842; 1097a (1097); Map 1848?, 8 chns, (including two 3 chn enlargements of settlements); waterbodies, road names, holding boundaries (col); some tithe areas are numbered in blue. District is partly apportioned by holding; Apt omits land use.

25/418 Sweethope (township in parish of Thockrington) NY 952816
Apt 30.09.1844; 1010a (all); Map 1847?, 8 chns; waterbodies, landowners; little else is shown. District is apportioned by holding and fields are not shown.

25/419 Little Swinburne (township in parish of Chollerton) NY 947772
Apt 03.03.1843; 1240a (?); Map 1842, 6 chns, by I. Coulson; waterbodies, building names, Roman road, holding boundaries (col); stream named. District is apportioned by holding; Apt omits land use.

25/420 Swinhoe (township in parish of Bamburgh) NU 217283
Apt 12.06.1838; 1324a (1323);Map 1838?, 6.5 chns; waterbodies, landowners (col); table lists owners and occupiers. District is apportioned by holding and fields are not shown.

25/421 Tarset (township in parish of Thorneyburn) NY 750950 [Not listed]
Apt 30.08.1839; 17408a (17408); Map 1841?, 24 chns, in 3 parts, 'Copied from various plans or surveys' by Thomas Bell, (including parts at 12 chns and 1 chn); woods, building names, landowners (col), boundary cairn, crags, holding boundaries (col); streams named. District is apportioned by holding; Apt omits land use.

25/422 Thirlwall (township in parish of Haltwhistle) NY 655680 [Not listed]
Apt 18.04.1840; 7944a (7944); Map 1842, 5 chns, by I. Coulson; railway with station, foot/b'way, waterbodies, building names, military road, toll bar, mill, holding boundaries (col); streams named. District is apportioned by holding; Apt generalises land use.

25/423 East and West Thirston with Shothaugh (townships in parish of Felton) NZ 187997
Apt 07.05.1841; 1131a (1161); Map 1841, 6 chns, by Wm Harrison; turnpike roads, woods, field gates, landowners, holding boundaries (col). District is apportioned by holding; Apt omits land use and most field names.

25/424 Thockrington (township in parish of Thockrington) NY 955795
Apt 30.09.1844; 2433a (all); Map 1847?, 10 chns; foot/b'way, building names, limekiln; roads are straight single-pecked lines, and buildings are dots; nothing else is shown. District is apportioned by holding and fields are not shown.

25/425 Thorneyburn (township in parish of Thorneyburn) NY 761875 [Not listed]
Apt 30.08.1839; 2726a (2725); Map 1839?, 12 chns, 'Reduced from various Plans or Surveys, made by John Fryer and others' by Thomas Bell; foot/b'way, woods, building names, landowners, quarry, mill, holding boundaries (col). District is apportioned by holding; Apt omits land use.

25/426 Thorngrafton (township in parish of Haltwhistle) NY 791663
Apt 18.04.1840; 3104a (3103); Map 1841, 8 chns, by I. Coulson; railway, building names, road names, Roman wall, military road, holding boundaries (col). District is apportioned by holding and fields are not shown.

25/427 Thornton (township in parish of Norham) NT 952477
Apt 10.07.1846; 1279a (1390); Map 1847?, 8 chns, 'Reduced from an old survey' by Thomas Bell and Sons; building names, engine, holding boundaries (col), tithe ownership boundaries. District is apportioned by holding; Apt omits land use.

25/428 East Thornton (township in parish of Hartburn) NZ 110870
Apt 16.05.1843; 1027a (1026); Map 1850, 6 chns, by Thos Fenwick, North Shields; woods, building names, landowners, holding boundaries (col) and names. Apt omits land use.

25/429 West Thornton (township in parish of Hartburn) NZ 094867 [Not listed]
Apt 28.04.1843; 1047a (1047); Map 1846?, 8 chns, 'Reduced from a survey by J. Dickenson' by Thomas Bell and Sons; hill-drawing, turnpike roads, waterbodies, woods, field gates, building names, landowners, ford, holding boundaries (col). District is apportioned by holding; Apt omits land use.

25/430 Throckley (district in parish of Newburn) NZ 152670
Apt 23.08.1845; 543a (?); Map 1847, 4 chns, by I. Coulson; waterbodies, building names, mill. District is apportioned as one tithe area without holding details, and fields are not shown.

25/431 Throckley Fell (district in parish of Newburn) NZ 156686 [Not listed]
Apt 23.08.1845; 544a (?); Map 1848, 4 chns, 'Reduced from various surveys' by Thomas Bell and Sons; foot/b'way, waterbodies, road names, holding boundaries (col). District is apportioned by holding; Apt omits land use.

25/432 Thropple (township in parish of Mitford) NZ 127859 [Throphill]
Apt 23.06.1840; 862a (862); Map 1840, 9 chns, by E. Bowman; woods, landowners, holding boundaries (col). District is apportioned by holding; Apt generalises land use.

25/433 Thropton (lordship in parish of Rothbury) NU 030023
Apt 09.04.1840; 827a (827); Map 1844, 6 chns, by J. Bourne, Newcastle; woods, building names, quarry, holding and ownership boundaries (col). Apt omits most land use.

25/434 Titlington (township in parish of Eglingham) NU 110160
Apt 29.07.1841; 2235a (2234); Map 1842?, 7 chns; hill-drawing, waterbodies, ownership boundaries (col); almost all lines are drawn with a brush rather than a pen. District is apportioned by holding and fields are not shown.

25/435 Todburn (township in parish of Longhorsley) NZ 121951
Apt 17.02.1846; 700a (699); Map 1847?, 8 chns; woods, holding boundaries (col). District is apportioned by holding and fields are not shown.

25/436 Togston (township in parish of Warkworth) NU 261019
Apt 23.08.1839; 1064a (1063); Map 1841, 8 chns; foot/b'way, building names, holding boundaries (col). District is apportioned by holding and fields are not shown.

25/437 Tone (township in parish of Chollerton) NY 910800 [Not listed]
Apt 10.05.1843; 1121a (?); Map 1843, 4 chns; turnpike roads, woods, gardens, landowners, holding boundaries (col) and names. District is apportioned by holding and fields are not shown; Apt omits land use.

25/438 Great Tosson and Ryehall (townships in parish of Rothbury) NZ 022922
Apt 31.08.1839; 2723a (2760); Map 1840, 4 chns, copied from old plans belonging to the landowners by James Watson, Rothbury; hill-drawing, waterbodies, houses, woods, rock outcrops, field gates, landowners, boundary stones, cairns, and marks, hill fort, fords, cairns, holding boundaries (col). District is apportioned by holding; Apt omits land use.

25/439 Little Tosson (township in parish of Rothbury) NU 008008
Apt 28.08.1840; 518a (518); Map 1841, 8 chns, by J. Bourne, Newcastle on Tyne; woods, holding boundaries (col). District is apportioned by owner, and no holding acreages are given; Apt omits land use.

25/440 Tranwell and High Church (townships in parish of Morpeth) NZ 188837
Apt 31.12.1841; 1220a (1220); Map 1841, 4 chns, by Edward Bowman, Newcastle upon Tyne; waterbodies, woods, building names, wells, toll bar, stiles, holding boundaries (col). Apt omits land use.

25/441 Trewhitt (township in parish of Rothbury) NU 004051 [Not listed]
Apt 07.05.1841; 1653a (1653); Map 1841, 8 chns, copied from old plans belonging to the owners by James Watson; woods, landowners, holdings (col, named). Apt omits land use.

25/442 Trewick (township in parish of Bolam) NZ 111802 [North Trewick]
Apt 27.11.1839; 746a (745); Map 1840?, [12 chns], (tinted); foot/b'way, woods (col). District is apportioned by holding; Apt generalises land use.

25/443 Tughall (township in parish of Bamburgh) NU 213266
Apt 31.12.1842; 1800a (1799); Map 1846, 6 chns, by Thomas Bell and Sons; foot/b'way, woods, field gates, building names, road names, mill, low water mark, holding ownership boundaries (col), foreshore. Apt omits land use.

25/444 Twizell (township in parish of Morpeth) NZ 165785
Apt 26.09.1842; 758a (?); Map 1843?, 15 chns; foot/b'way, woods, building names, landowners, holding boundaries (col). District is apportioned by holding; Apt generalises land use.

25/445 Tynemouth (township in parish of Tynemouth) NZ 361699
Apt 24.07.1844; 357a (1871); Map 1846, 4 chns, in 2 parts, by Thomas Bell and Sons, Newcastle, (tithable parts only, including detached portion at 3 chns); hill-drawing, railways, foot/b'way, turnpike roads, waterbodies, woods, rock outcrops, field gates, building names, road names, landowners, foreshore (col), pond, chapel, stiles, brick garth, mill, old quarry. District is apportioned by holding; Apt omits land use.

25/446 Ulgham (chapelry in parish of Morpeth) NZ 235926
Apt 02.03.1843; 3616a (3615); Map 1843, 8 chns, by E. Bowman, Newcastle on Tyne; woods, building names, ownership boundaries (col); fields not shown in tithe-free part. District is apportioned by holding; Apt omits land use.

25/447 Unthank (township in parish of Alnham) NU 014112
Apt 23.09.1843; 172a (172); Map 1842, 8 chns; waterbodies, woods. Apt omits land use.

25/448 Walbottle (township in parish of Newburn) NZ 177676
Apt 13.07.1843; 1252a (1251); Map 1847?, 6 chns, by Thomas Bell and Sons, (including village separately at 3 chns); hill-drawing, railway, foot/b'way, turnpike roads, waterbodies, woods, parkland, building names, chapel, quarries, old quarries, spoil heaps, colleries, boundary stones, stiles, gardens (by annotation), holding boundaries (col). Apt omits land use.

25/449 Walbridge (township in parish of Stamfordham) NZ 053771 [Wallridge]
Apt 27.07.1839; 148a (all); Map 1839, 4 chns. Apt generalises land use.

25/450 Walker (township in parish of Long Benton) NZ 290650
Apt 16.02.1842; 1109a (?); Map 1843, 8 chns; hill-drawing, railway, wagonways, turnpike roads, waterbodies, woods, building names, mills, factory, ballast heaps, copperas beds, colliery, holding boundaries (col). District is apportioned by holding; Apt omits land use.

25/451 Walkmill (township in parish of Warkworth) NU 227044
Apt 30.06.1843; 123a (123); Map 1845, 3 chns, in 2 parts, by E.W. Griffiths; woods (col), gardens (col), landowners. District is apportioned by holding; Apt omits land use.

25/452 Wall (township in parish of St John Lee) NY 923697
Apt 27.09.1838; 1624a (1623); Map 1838, 8 chns, by I. Coulson; woods, building names, landowners, military road, limekiln, holding boundaries (col). Apt omits land use.

25/453 Wallington (township in parish of Hartburn) NZ 027848
Apt 02.04.1842; 1781a (1781); Map 1844?, 16 chns; landowners. District is apportioned by owner, without holding acreages, and fields are not shown; Apt generalises land use.

25/454 Wallsend (township in parish of Wallsend) NZ 304669
Apt 26.06.1839; 1202a (?); Map 1841, 6 chns, ? by Andrew Stoddart, South Shields; railways, woods, parkland, gardens, tidal areas, colliery, limekilns.

25/455 Wall Town (township in parish of Haltwhistle) NY 700673 [Walltown]
Apt 18.04.1840; 2957a (2956); Map 1843?, 8 chns; waterbodies, woods, rock outcrops, building names, Roman wall, crags; streams named. District is apportioned by holding; Apt omits land use and field names.

25/456 Warden (district) NY 855655
Apt 16.09.1841; 8860a (?); Map 1838, 8 chns, by I. Coulson; railway and station, turnpike roads, building names, road names, pumping engine, mill, military road, township boundaries, ownership boundaries (col). District is apportioned partly by holding; Apt omits land use and field names.

25/457 Warenford (township in parish of Bamburgh) NU 134281
Apt 31.12.1842; 183a (183); Map 1846?, 3 chns, by Thomas Bell and Sons; hill-drawing, foot/b'way, turnpike roads, woods, field gates, building names, road names, stiles, quarry, holding boundaries (col); stream named. Apt omits land use.

25/458 Warenton (township in parish of Bamburgh) NU 102307
Apt 31.12.1842; 118a (1454); Map 1843?, 12 chns; building names; colour bands may show tithable lands. District is apportioned by holding and fields are not shown.

25/459 Wark (parish) NY 780770
Apt 30.11.1838; 22588a (22986); Map 1839, 8 chns, in 11 parts, (including one part at 16 chns, and two versions of 3 chns enlargement of village); hill-drawing, woods, marsh/bog, rock outcrops, building names, quarry, mills, holding and ownership boundaries (col); double field boundaries may indicate stone walls. District is apportioned by holding; Apt omits land use.

25/460 Wark and Sunnilaws (townships in parish of Carham) NT 827377
Apt 28.10.1843; 1736a (?); Map 1842, 8 chns; waterbodies, land-owners, holding boundaries (col) and names. District is apport-ioned by holding and fields are not shown.

25/461 Warkworth (township in parish of Warkworth) NU 243053
Apt 09.02.1839; 1079a (3638); Map 1842?, 6 chns, in 5 parts, 'Copied from Plans by Mr William Barnfather' by Thomas Bell and Sons, (including two 2 chn and two 3 chn enlargements); woods, open fields, building names, road names, landowners, old course of river, fords, castle, holding boundaries (col). Apt omits land use.

25/462 Warton (township in parish of Rothbury) NU 009029
Apt 31.08.1839; 625a (624); Map 1841?, 4 chns, by Edward Smith; waterbodies, woods, orchards, gardens, marsh/bog, field gates, landowners (col), march stone, quarry. Apt omits land use.

25/463 Weetsleet (township in parish of Long Benton) NZ 250730 [Not listed]
Apt 16.02.1842; 2230a (?); Map 1842?, 8 chns; railway, foot/b'way, waterbodies, woods, orchards, building names, colliery, quarry, holding boundaries (col). District is apportioned by holding; Apt omits land use.

25/464 Weetwood (township in parish of Chatton) NU 015287 [Not listed]
Apt 12.04.1847; 1271a (?); Map 1847?, 4 chns, 'Copied from an old Survey'; waterbodies, woods, building names, landowners, ox bow lakes. Apt omits land use.

25/465 Welton (township in parish of Ovingham) NZ 069675 [Not listed]
Apt 13.07.1839; 1183a (1183); Map 1841?, 6 chns, 'Copied from an old Survey' by Thomas Bell; turnpike roads, waterbodies, woods, field gates, building names, landowners, mill, holding boundaries (col), hedgerow trees. District is apportioned by holding; Apt omits land use.

25/466 Whalton (township in parish of Whalton) NZ 132814
Apt 27.07.1840; 2104a (2103); Map 1841?, 6 chns, 'Copied from sundry surveys and plans' by Thomas Bell; woods, building names, landowners,

mill, mill race, rectory, school, holding boundaries (col); streams named. District is apportioned by holding, though fields are numbered separately; Apt omits land use.

25/467 West Whelpington (township in parish of Kirk Whelpington) NY 962850 [Not listed]
Apt 11.11.1843; 3992a (3922); Map 1844, 8 chns, 'Copied from old Plans' by T. Arkle, Carrick; hill-drawing, foot/b'way, waterbodies, rock outcrops, building names, wells, crags, pike, mill, boundary stone, holding boundaries (col); streams named; crags are shown by boulders, and a pike by a conical pictorial symbol. District is apportioned by holding; Apt omits land use.

25/468 Whitchester (township in parish of Heddon on the Wall) NZ 100683
Apt 13.07.1839; 795a (795); Map 1840?, 8 chns; hill-drawing, foot/b'way, waterbodies, woods, building names, landowners (col), military road. District is apportioned by holding; Apt omits land use.

25/469 Whiteside Law (township in parish of Chollerton) NY 979757
Apt 02.03.1843; 90a (?); Map 1843?, 4 chns, (tinted); woods; streams named. District is apportioned by holding; Apt omits land use.

25/470 Whitfield (parish) NY 750550
Apt 15.06.1837; 2703a (12125); Map 1838, 8 chns, by E. Bowman, Newcastle upon Tyne; turnpike roads, woods, parkland, rock outcrops, building names, landowners, boundary marks, old turnpike road, land and tithe ownership boundaries (col) and acreages, glebe (col); a house outside the boundary is shown pictorially, complete with puff of smoke. District is apportioned by holding and fields are not shown.

25/471 Whitley (township in parish of Tynemouth) NZ 354725 [Whitley Bay]
Apt 15.12.1840; 532a (531); Map 1841, 8 chns, by J. Bourne, Newcastle; hill-drawing, railway, woods, colliery, pit, ownership boundaries (col), cliffs. District is apportioned by holding; Apt omits land use.

25/472 Whitridge (township or hamlet in parish of Hartburn) NZ 061877
Apt 28.04.1843; 197a (196); Map 1844?, 16 chns; landowners. District is apportioned by holding; Apt generalises land use.

25/473 Whittingham (township in parish of Whittingham) NU 076112
Apt 07.10.1841; 6054a (6103); Map 1842, 8 chns; waterbodies, woods, building names, mill, glebe. Apt omits land use and field names.

25/474 Great Whittington (township in parish of Corbridge) NZ 006709
Apt 25.07.1842; 1477a (1477); Map 1841, 6 chns, by I. Coulson; waterbodies, building names, mill, well, holding boundaries (col). District is apportioned by holding; Apt omits land use.

25/475 Little Whittington (township in parish of Corbridge) NY 990695
Apt 31.01.1839; 348a (348); Map 1839?, 8 chns; field gates, landowners, Roman road, holding boundaries; houses are shown pictorially. District is apportioned by holding and fields are not shown.

25/476 Whittle (township in parish of Ovingham) NZ 078657 [Not listed]
Apt 27.07.1839; 276a (276); Map 1839?, 8 chns, (engraved by J. Walker); waterbodies, woods, field names and acreages; tithable part is hand-coloured. District is apportioned by owner; Apt omits land use.

25/477 Whittle (township in parish of Shilbottle) NU 182067 [Not listed]
Apt 21.03.1843; 546a (545); Map 1843, 4 chns, by Andrew Robson; hill-drawing, foot/b'way, woods, field gates, landowners, quarry, well, infield and outfield boundaries; streams named. District is apportioned by holding; Apt omits land use, but has columns for infield and outfield acreages.

25/478 Whitton (township in parish of Rothbury) NU 058003
Apt 30.11.1844; 675a (674); Map 1846, 4 chns, by James Watson; foot/b'way, waterbodies, woods (col), field gates, building names, pits, ownership boundaries (col). District is apportioned by holding; Apt omits land use.

25/479 Whorlton (township in parish of Newburn) NZ 191681 [Not listed]
Apt 13.07.1843; 586a (585); Map 1847?, 6 chns, by Thomas Bell and Sons; hill-drawing, foot/b'way, waterbodies, woods, parkland, building names, landowners, quarry, well, pump, old engine, holding boundaries (col). Apt omits land use.

25/480 Widdrington (township or chapelry in parish of Woodhorn) NZ 253960
Apt 06.11.1844; 4530a (4530); Map 1844?, 6 chns, by E. Bowman; hill-drawing, woods, parkland, building names, cliffs, ownership boundaries (col); some field boundaries have been scraped away. The map is dated 1845, bottom right, but carries an 1844 receipt date. Apt omits land use for tithe-free land.

25/481 Willington (township in parish of Wallsend) NZ 327678
Apt 10.12.1838; 1379a (?); Map 1839, 8 chns, by John Bourne; hill-drawing, railways, foot/b'way, waterbodies, building names, landowners (col), colliery, spoil heaps. District is apportioned by holding; Apt generalises land use.

25/482 Wingates (township in parish of Longhorsley) NZ 100950
Apt 17.02.1846; 2643a (2642); Map 1846?, 12 chns, by Thomas Bell; foot/b'way, woods, building names, landowners, spa, holding boundaries (col) and names; streams named. District is apportioned by holding and fields are not shown.

25/483 Witton Shields (township in parish of Longhorsley) NZ 122912
Apt 05.02.1840; 574a (574); Map 1842?, 8 chns, by Thomas Bell; woods, building names, landowners, mill race, mill pond, chapel. District is apportioned by holding, though fields are numbered separately; Apt generalises land use.

25/484 Wooden (township in parish of Lesbury) NU 237097 [Not listed]
Apt 12.09.1845; 274a (?); Map 1845, 5 chns; foot/b'way, field gates, high water mark, foreshore, holding boundaries (col). District is apportioned by holding; Apt omits land use.

25/485 Woodhorn (township in parish of Woodhorn) NZ 296892
Apt 23.01.1847; 1476a (all); Map 1847?, 4 chns, by Wm and T. Sample; woods, building names. Apt omits land use and field names.

25/486 Woodhorne Demesne (township in parish of Woodhorne) NZ 308883 [Not listed]
Apt 14.12.1839; 311a (311); Map 1839, 3 chns, by E. Bowman; foot/b'way, waterbodies, woods, fence, field gates, building names, boundary stone, garden (by annotation); roads only shown where they intersect other features. District is apportioned by holding; Apt omits land use.

25/487 Woodhouse (township in parish of Shilbottle) NU 213081 [Not listed]
Apt 21.02.1839; 542a (572); Map 1839?, 6 chns; building names, landowners, holding boundaries (col); table lists occupiers, with acreages. District is apportioned by holding and fields are not shown.

25/488 Wooler (township in parish of Wooler) NT 980270
Apt 25.10.1842; 3133a (3132); Map 1843, 8 chns; waterbodies, woods (col), boundary marks, holding boundaries (col); built-up part generalised; cauliflower-like objects along the boundary could be cairns or trees. District is apportioned by holding; Apt generalises land use.

25/489 Woolsington (township in parish of Newburn) NZ 197710
Apt 13.07.1843; 621a (?); Map 1843, 6 chns, by J. Bourne, Newcastle; foot/b'way, waterbodies, woods, parkland, gardens, building names, holding boundaries (col). District is apportioned by holding and fields are not shown.

25/490 Wooperton (township in parish of Eglingham) NU 043198
Apt 20.11.1839; 923a (923); Map 1840?, 6 chns, (tinted); woods, landowners. District is apportioned by holding; Apt omits land use.

25/491 Wreigh Hill (township in parish of Rothbury) NT 980020 [Wreighill]
Apt 30.11.1844; 412a (411); Map 1845, 4 chns, by James Watson;

foot/b'way, woods (col), holding boundaries (col). District is apportioned by holding and fields are not shown.

25/492 Wylam (township in parish of Ovingham) NZ 116648
Apt 21.11.1843; 930a (930); Map 1844?, 4 chns, by Thomas Bell and Sons; hill-drawing, railway with station, turnpike roads, toll bar, woods, parkland, field gates, building names, landowners, collieries, iron works, spoil heaps, quarries, holding boundaries (col), public roads; stream named. District is apportioned by holding; Apt omits land use.

25/493 Yeavering (township in parish of Kirknewton) NT 928295
Apt 31.03.1842; 883a (883); Map 1841, 6 chns; hill-drawing, waterbodies. District is apportioned by holding; Apt omits land use.

Nottinghamshire

PRO IR29 and IR30 26/1-137

278 tithe districts: 542,835 acres
137 tithe commutations: 204,618 acres
51 voluntary tithe agreements, 86 compulsory tithe awards

Tithe and tithe commutation

There had been much tithe commutation associated with parliamentary enclosure in Nottinghamshire by 1836 with the result that just 50 per cent of tithe districts were subject to payment of tithes and only forty districts were still wholly tithable (Fig. 38). The main causes of tithe exemption in addition to commutation at the time of enclosure were modus payments in lieu of tithes, the merger of tithes in the land and exemption by prescription.

Assistant tithe commissioners and local tithe agents who worked in Nottinghamshire are listed in Table 26.1 and the valuers of the county's tithe rent-charge in Table 26.2. In five districts tithes were valued by the Tithe Commission in default of action by the landowners within the statutory six-month period (Table 26.2) and in seven districts tithe rent-charge is apportioned by holding and so there is no record of land use or names of fields for these places. The schedules of apportionment of a few other districts either omit all land use, or omit it for tithe-free areas, whereas for four districts there is a record of actual crops grown field-by-field.

Tithe maps

Nottinghamshire's first-class tithe map coverage is exceptional for a county which had already undergone extensive tithe commutation at enclosure; 12 per cent of the 137 maps are sealed as first class, a proportion very close to the national average. Construction lines are present on three second-class maps and may be taken as evidence of either a new survey or the thorough testing of an old one. It is unclear how much wholly new tithe survey mapping there was in this county; very few maps mention copying but it is reasonable to suppose that a majority of the maps of those districts where only small tracts of residual tithable land remained were derived from enclosure surveys.

In contrast to most other counties, tithe mapping in Nottinghamshire proceeded steadily between 1838 and 1850 with a nominal peak right at the end of this period, though by that date most of the mapping was of residual tithable lands of small extent (Table 26.4). Nottinghamshire tithe maps are drawn at a variety of scales from one inch to two

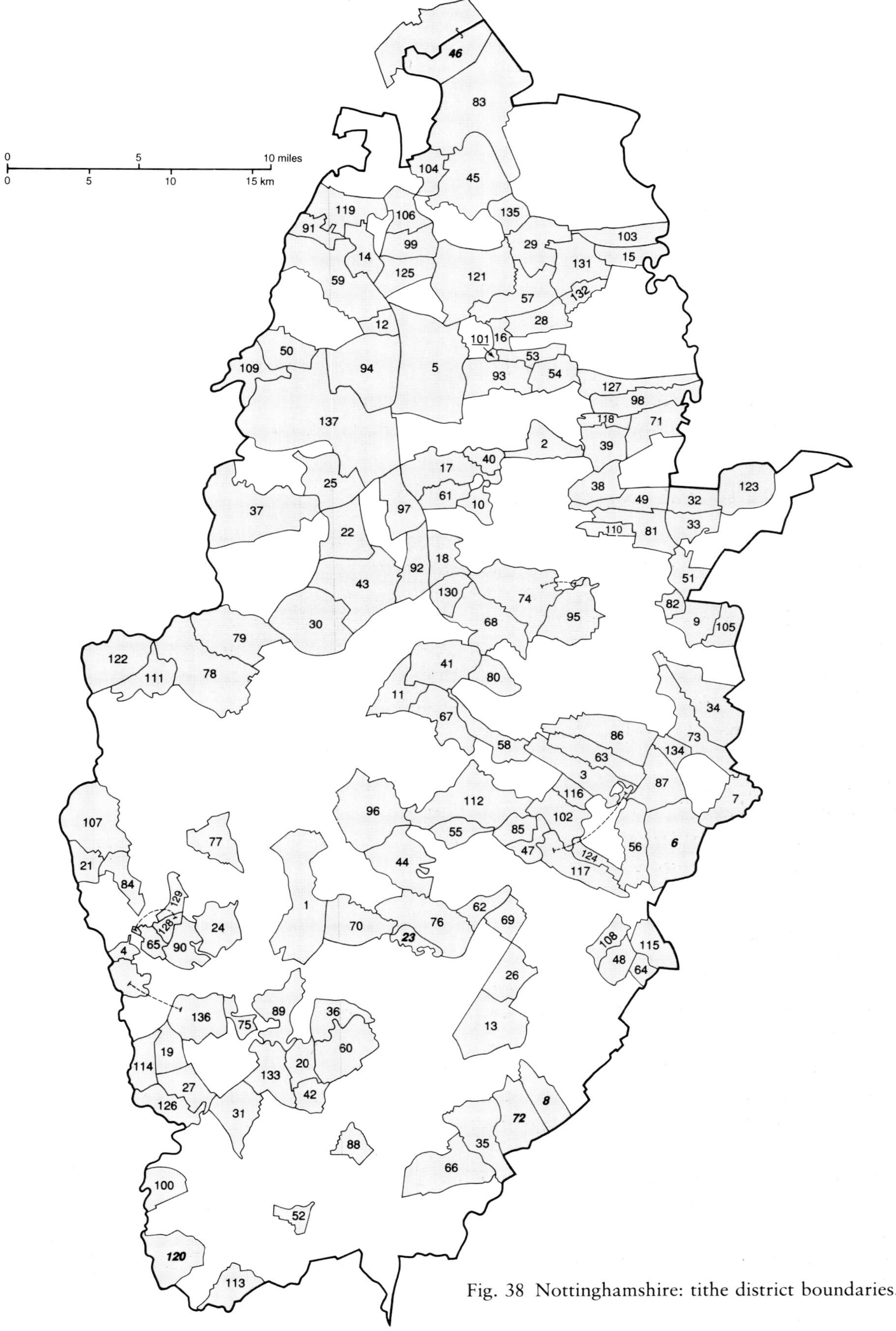

Fig. 38 Nottinghamshire: tithe district boundaries.

chains to one inch to sixteen chains; 32 per cent are in the recommended scale range of one inch to three to four chains. The most favoured scale was the six-chain, used in 40 per cent of districts (Table 26.3).

As records of land use, Nottinghamshire tithe maps conform to the standard pattern by normally depicting woodland (on 67 per cent of maps) and some parkland (on 12 per cent) but they are far less informative about other types of land use. Only two maps distinguish arable and grass and only a few depict orchards and gardens. Around 1840 the north-east of Nottinghamshire was an outpost of hop-growing but although hops are recorded in ten apportionments, they are recorded by symbol only on the map of Southwell. Eight maps, most notably Laxton, portray the open-field cadaster. Southwell and Newark are unusual instances of whole towns mapped to first-class standards; the Newark map is particularly notable for the wide range of chapels and public buildings that it records. Both these maps distinguish houses from other buildings, a relatively uncommon practice in this county and confined to 24 per cent of its tithe maps. The Southwell map is also unusual in showing tenurial status by abbreviated annotations in fields.

Only sixty-eight Nottinghamshire tithe maps in the Public Record Office collection (just under half the total) can be attributed to a particular map-maker (Table 26.2). Sixteen are by Percy Brackenbury, who as a valuer gives his address as Rufford and as a cartographer states that he is from Wellow. His mapping practice was more extensive than his valuation work, though it is likely that his output of maps relies heavily on copying as he uses a variety of scales. Brackenbury is unusual among Nottinghamshire tithe map-makers in that he distinguished inhabited and uninhabited buildings. Most Nottinghamshire map-makers' commissions were very local but Thomas Spenceley of Cottingham, near Hull, would have had to travel over sixty miles to survey his two first-class Nottinghamshire maps. Very different in style is the strange map of the few residual tithable fields at North Clifton which has buildings shown by small pictograms and a schematic road pattern linking the few tithable fields.

There is little decoration on Nottinghamshire tithe maps; a few have cartouches but only the fern-leaf tail of that on the map of Ranskill is really decorative. Nine maps show churches by pictorial symbols, most notably that of Laneham which also pictures the nearby ferry. This map of a few residual tithable lands is the prettiest in the county, and indeed for a long distance around.

Table 26.1. *Agreements and awards for commutation of tithes in Nottinghamshire*

Assistant commissioner/ local tithe agent	*Number of agreements**	*Number of awards*
George Wingrove Cooke	0	23
Thomas Smith Woolley	12	11
Joseph Townsend	0	21
Charles Howard	2	16
John Pickering	17	0
Richard Burton Phillipson	7	0
John Mee Mathew	5	4
John Job Rawlinson	3	9
Horace William Meteyard	2	0
Robert Hart	1	0
John Holder	1	0
George Louis	0	1
Tithe Commissioners	0	1

*Computed from the number of extant reports on tithe agreements in the tithe files [PRO IR 18].

Table 26.2. *Tithe valuers and tithe map-makers in Nottinghamshire*

Name and address (in Nottinghamshire unless indicated)	*Number of districts*	*Acreage*
Tithe valuers		
John Parkinson, Ley Fields, Rufford	16	27,737
Percy William Brackenbury, Rufford	7	11,005
Samuel Abbott, Lowdham	6	5,598
John Dickinson, Austerfield, Yorkshire	5	10,655
George Clark, Barnby Moor	5	9,871
Edward Woollett Wilmot, Etwall, Derbyshire	5	9,678
Tithe Commissioners	5	1,320
Others [49]	88	128,754
Attributed tithe map-makers		
Percy William Brackenbury, Wellow	14	34,503
George Sanderson, Mansfield	10	23,479
Robert Weightman, Torworth	6	11,519
John Hickson, Worksop	4	9,225
Paul Bausor, Southwell	3	4,227
Charles J. Neale, Mansfield	3	3,857
John Bromley, Derby	3	2,507
Others [20]	25	25,442

Table 26.3. *The tithe maps of Nottinghamshire: scales and classes*

Scale in chains/inch	*All maps*		*First Class*		*Second Class*	
	Number	*Acreage*	*Number*	*Acreage*	*Number*	*Acreage*
>3	6	4,149	0	0	6	4,149
3	31	43,523	16	31,230	15	12,293
4	14	9,962	0	0	14	9,962
5	4	2,302	0	0	4	2,302
6	55	105,636	0	0	55	105,636
7	1	2,218	0	0	1	2,218
8	9	10,816	0	0	9	10,816
9	6	5,557	0	0	6	5,557
10	2	1,726	0	0	2	1,726
12	8	18,349	0	0	8	18,349
16	1	380	0	0	1	380
TOTAL	137	204,618	16	31,230	121	173,388

Table 26.4. *The tithe maps of Nottinghamshire: dates*

	1838	*1839*	*1840*	*1841*	*1842*	*1843*	*1844*	*1845*	*1846*	*1847*	*1848*	*1849*	*1850*	*1851*
All maps	6	11	12	9	8	12	11	9	9	14	12	7	15	1
1st class	1	2	3	1	3	0	2	1	0	0	1	0	2	0
2nd classı	5	9	9	8	5	12	9	8	9	14	11	7	13	1

*One second-class tithe map of Nottinghamshire in the Public Record Office collection is undated.

Nottinghamshire

26/1 Arnold (parish) SK 590473
Apt 11.03.1842; 4612a (4670); Map 1842, [3 chns]; construction lines, foot/b'way, waterbodies, houses, woods, plantations, parkland, gardens, fence ownership, field boundary ownerships, building names, road cuttings, turnpike chain, toll bar.

26/2 Askham (parish) SK 740755
Apt 02.09.1844; 1303a (1302); Map 1845, 8 chns, in 4 parts, (includes village separately and enlargements of detail at 2 chns); waterbodies, woods, gardens.

26/3 Averham (parish) SK 755554
Apt 12.06.1838; 2011a (2011); Map 1839?, 3 chns, by W.H. Wright; landowners, holding boundaries (col), mill race, mill, glebe (with acreages). District is apportioned by holding and most fields are not shown; Apt generalises land use.

26/4 Awsworth (hamlet in parish of Nuthall) SK 480441
Apt 13.03.1846; 376a (376); Map 1848, 6 chns, by John Bromley, Derby; railways, foot/b'way, waterbodies, houses, old engine, canal with towpath; stream named.

26/5 Babworth (parish) SK 670804
Apt 31.07.1839; 6166a (6165); Map 1839, 6 chns, 'Compiled' by Percy W. Brackenbury; foot/b'way, canal with towpath and locks, waterbodies, woods, parkland, gardens, field boundary ownerships, field gates, building names, malt kilns, lodges, rectory, toll bar, glebe, ownerships (col), modus lands (col). Apt omits land use for modus lands.

26/6 Balderton (parish) SK 821507
Apt 03.04.1844; 130a (4050); Map 1844?, 12 chns, (tithable parts only); landowners; pictorial church. Apt has cropping information.

26/7 Barnby in the Willows (parish) SK 855527
Apt 22.07.1841; 1704a (1703); Map 1840, 4 chns, by John Paver; foot/b'way, waterbodies, road names, toll bar, occupation roads.

26/8 Barnstone (township or hamlet in parish of Langar cum Barnstone) SK 738351
Apt 29.12.1845; 44a (?); Map 1846, 4 chns, (tithable parts only, tinted); woods, landowners; map also covers Langar (26/72). Apt omits land use.

26/9 Besthorpe (township in parish of South Scarle)SK 833642
Apt 23.11.1838; 1306a (510); Map 1839, 3 chns, 1st cl, by Thos Spenceley, Cottingham, near Hull; construction lines; foot/b'way, waterbodies, plantations, open fields, field boundary ownerships, landowners, landing place; enclosed fields are green; scale-bar is ruler-like.

26/10 Bevercoates (township in parish of West Markham) SK 698717 [Bevercotes]
Apt 31.05.1848; 17a (790); Map 1848?, 9 chns; waterbodies, woods (col); tithable part is tinted pink.

26/11 Bilsthorpe (parish) SK 649595
Apt 26.06.1839; 1572a (1572); Map 1839, 3 chns, 1st cl, by Percy William Brackenbury, Wellow House, Ollerton, Notts; construction lines; hill-drawing, foot/b'way, waterbodies, houses, woods (col), plantations, field boundary ownerships, field gates, building names, landowners, pit, rectory, glebe (pink), tithe-free land (lilac).

26/12 Bilby (township or district in parish of Blyth) SK 639831
Apt 15.04.1841; 65a (?); Map 1844, 6 chns, (tithable parts only); woods.

26/13 Bingham (parish) SK 709392
Apt 31.03.1842; 3054a (all); Map 1840, 8 chns, in 4 parts, by Percy W. Brackenbury, Wellow near Ollerton, (includes enlarge-ment of town at 2 chns and two enlargements of detail at 4 chns); foot/b'way, waterbodies, houses, building names, road names, windmills (by symbol), workhouse, rectory; dike named.

26/14 Blyth (township) SK 628873
Apt 21.05.1842; 1270a (?); Map 1843?, 6 chns; waterbodies.

26/15 Bole (parish) SK 792872
Apt 29.09.1849; 1208a (1250); Map 1850, 2 chns; railway, open fields; dot-dash lines indicate divisions within holdings; pecked lines indicate divisions between holdings.

26/16 Bollam and Moorgate (township in parish of Clarborough) SK 710826 [Not listed]
Apt 29.01.1842; 598a (?); Map 1842?, [4 chns]; canal with towpath; meaning of colour tints is unclear.

26/17 Bothamsall (parish) SK 675738
Apt 13.03.1846; 2297a (all); Map 1847?, 6 chns; foot/b'way, waterbodies, woods, plantations, heath/moor.

26/18 Boughton (parish) SK 677686
Apt 31.05.1845; 1373a (1372); Map 1846, 8 chns, in 3 parts, ? by Percy W. Brackenbury, Wellow House, Ollerton, Notts, (includes two small enlargements of detail); foot/b'way, waterbodies, houses, woods (col).

26/19 Bramcote (parish) SK 510380
Apt 06.06.1845; 746a (1076); Map 1846, 4 chns, by S.H. Surplice, Beeston; foot/b'way, waterbodies, woods, canal with towpath; pictorial church; tithe-free areas are mapped but not numbered; map title is on scroll with wheatears.

26/20 West Bridgeford (township) SK 588374 [West Bridgford]
Apt 10.12.1838; 1096a (all); Map 1839?, 9 chns; foot/b'way, woods (col), hedge ownership, canal with towpath, glebe (col); meaning of pink tint is unclear. Apt omits land use.

26/21 Brinsley (township in parish of Greasley) SK 497452
Apt 24.02.1851; 3a (?); Map 1851, 6 chns, by John Shaw, Derby, (tithable parts only, tinted).

26/22 Budby (township in parish of Edwinstowe) SK 616699
Apt 31.12.1841; 2114a (all); Map 1843, 12 chns, by Percy W. Brackenbury, Wellow House, Ollerton, Notts, (includes three 6-chn enlargements of detail); waterbodies, woods.

26/23 Bulcote (township in parish of Burton Joyce) SK 651446
Apt 18.03.1847; 69a (970); Map 1847?, 4 chns, (tithable parts only); woods, hedge ownership, landowners.

26/24 Bulwell (parish) SK 539458
Apt 27.09.1837; 1629a (1210); Map 1841, 3 chns; foot/b'way, waterbodies, woods, parkland, open fields (named), building names, corn mill, bleach works, cotton mill, mill, quarries, boundary of modus and tithe-free land; some names and most tithe area numbers are stamped; north pointer has crown and plumes.

26/25 Carburton (township in parish of Edwinstowe) SK 605733
Apt 31.12.1841; 2235a (all); Map 1843, 5 chns; waterbodies, woods, plantations, hedge ownership, fence ownership; green band shows Duke of Newcastle's lands.

26/26 Car-Colston (parish) SK 720425
Apt 10.01.1843; 1641a (1200); Map 1842, 3 chns, 1st cl, by Percy William Brackenbury, Wellow House, Ollerton, Notts; construction lines; waterbodies, houses, woods, orchards, field boundary ownerships, field gates, mounds, 'Ring of the Village', green, glebe; stream named.

26/27 Chilwell (hamlet or township in parish of Attenborough) SK 514366
Apt 14.06.1845; 1473a (?); Map 1845, 4 chns, by S.H. Surplice, Beeston; railways, foot/b'way, canal, waterbodies, woods, osiers (by symbol), reeds (by symbol), orchards, fish pond, weir, 'Vicar's Ring' (yellow), modus meadow (pink); pictorial church.

26/28 Clarborough (hamlet in parish of Clarborough) SK 735832
Apt 14.10.1848; 15a (?); Map 1850?, 2 chns, by I.W. Allen, West Retford, (tithable parts only); field boundary ownerships, canal with towpath.

26/29 Clayworth (township in parish of Clayworth) SK 731877
Apt 10.10.1837; 10a (?); Map 1847?, 5 chns, by John Dickinson, Partridge Hill, (tithable parts only in detail); canal with towpath; pictorial church.

26/30 Clipstone (township in parish of Edwinstowe) SK 594648 [Not listed]
Apt 31.12.1841; 4018a (all); Map 1844?, 6 chns.

26/31 Clifton (parish) SK 552341
Apt 29.10.1849; 29a (1980); Map 1847?, 8 chns, by E.S. Gisborne, Nottingham, (tithable parts only in detail, tinted); waterbodies, woods (col), field names, common pasture,.

26/32 North Clifton (township in parish of North Clifton) SK 830720
Apt 31.12.1841; 62a (?); Map 1845, in 2 parts, by J. Squire and J. Williamson, (tithable parts only: vicarial lands at 1 chn and rectorial lands at 4 chns); foot/b'way; on the rectorial part buildings are shown by stylised pictorial symbols, including a house with smoking chimney.

26/33 South Clifton (township in parish of North Clifton) SK 834704
Apt 31.12.1841; 32a (?); Map 1843, 2 chns, (tithable parts only); waterbodies, houses, landowners, ferry.

26/34 South Collingham (parish) SK 840590 [Not listed]
Apt 30.11.1847; 10a (1820); Map 1848, 3 chns, (tithable parts only); field boundary ownerships.

26/35 Colston Basset (parish) SK 702328 [Colston Bassett]
Apt 25.07.1842; 2392a (2391); Map 1843, 6 chns, ? by Joseph Bennett Hankin Bennett, Tutbury; foot/b'way, waterbodies, woods, vicarage, hall; bridge and streams named.

26/36 Colwick (parish) SK 610401
Apt 02.07.1847; 1255a (1255); Map 1848?, 9 chns; foot/b'way, woods, parkland, hedge ownership, hauling path, flood bank, township boundary.

26/37 Cuckney (parish) SK 557712
Apt 26.06.1839; 5157a (5510); Map 1841, 6 chns; waterbodies.

26/38 Darlton (parish) SK 774729
Apt 23.10.1844; 1507a (1507); Map 1845, 3 chns, 1st cl, in 2 parts, by Percy W. Brackenbury, Wellow House, Ollerton, Notts; cons-truction lines; foot/b'way, waterbodies, houses, woods (col), plantations (col), field boundary ownerships, building names, windmill (by symbol), watermill (by symbol).

26/39 East Drayton (parish) SK 756773
Apt 27.11.1844; 1544a (all); Map 1845, 6 chns; foot/b'way, waterbodies, woods.

26/40 West Drayton (parish) SK 702746
Apt 28.02.1850; 654a (all); Map 1850?, 6 chns; waterbodies, woods (col), avenues of trees.

26/41 Eakring (parish) SK 679615
Apt 30.07.1838; 2498a (all); Map 1840, 4 chns, in 2 parts, (including duplicate plan of open fields); waterbodies, woods, open fields (named).

26/42 Edwalton (parish) SK 595351
Apt 15.10.1845; 813a (813); Map 1846?, 6 chns; foot/b'way, woods (col), toll gate; pictorial church.

26/43 Edwinstowe (township in parish of Edwinstowe) SK 626669
Apt 31.12.1841; 6011a (all); Map 1843, 12 chns, in 2 parts, by Percy W. Brackenbury, Wellow House, Ollerton, (includes Edwinstowe village separately at 3 chns); waterbodies, houses, woods (named), plantations, parkland (col), building names, lodges, pillar, notable oak, seat, township boundaries, boundary stones; map also includes Budby (26/22) and Perlethorpe (26/97).

26/44 Epperstone (parish) SK 651495
Apt 27.11.1838; 365a (2300); Map surveyed March 1838, 8 chns, by S. Abbott, (tithable parts only); woods (col, named), hedge ownership, landowners.

26/45 Everton (township in parish of Everton) SK 693923
Apt 31.05.1848; 3631a (?); Map 1848, 6 chns; woods, canal with towpath, 'cutting to make the embankment', river banking.

26/46 Finningley (parish) (partly in Yorks) SK 675985
Apt 03.07.1838; 380a (2360); Map surveyed by Joseph Colbeck in 1818, [16 chns], (tithable parts only); toll bar, field acreages; drain named.

26/47 Fiskerton (township in parish of Rolleston) SK 730502
Apt 06.12.1842; 1043a (1043); Map 1843, 6 chns; foot/b'way, waterbodies, houses, woods, ferry.

26/48 Flawborough (parochial chapelry) SK 782432
Apt 24.04.1849; 966a (all); Map not dated, 6 chns; woods (col), old river course.

26/49 Fledborough cum Woodcoates (parish) SK 792720
Apt 31.01.1839; 1427a (1427); Map 1839, 8 chns, by Geo. Sanderson, Mansfield; foot/b'way, waterbodies, woods, building names, stiles, township boundary (pecked), modus land boundary (stippled), owner-ships (col), hops (by annotation).

26/50 Gateford (township in parish of Worksop) SK 571814
Apt 24.02.1848; 1150a (?); Map 1848, 6 chns, by J. Hickson, Worksop, (tithable parts only); railway, woods, parkland, landowners, pit, private roads (uncoloured).

26/51 Girton (parish) SK 825670
Apt 23.11.1838; 1075a (1075); Map 1841, 3 chns, 1st cl, by Thos. Spenceley, Cottingham, near Hull; construction lines, foot/b'way, waterbodies, woods, open fields (named), field boundary owner-ships, road names, landowners, glebe; green band surrounds enclosed fields; scale-bar is ruler-like. Apt has some rotation information for open fields.

26/52 Grange Leys and High Fields (district in parish of Costock or Cortlingstock) SK 586276
Apt 11.05.1843; 554a (?); Map 1843, 6 chns, by William Roe, Derby; foot/b'way, waterbodies, woods, field boundary ownerships, footbridge, ownerships (col), estate names. Apt omits land use.

26/53 Little Gringley (hamlet in parish of Clarborough) SK 731811
Apt 25.09.1839; 812a (?); Map 1840?, [4 chns]; canal, wood (by name). Apt omits land use.

26/54 Grove (parish) SK 744800
Apt 26.10.1848; 1288a (all); Map 1849?, 12 chns; glebe. District is apportioned by owner and roads, building and fields are omitted; Apt generalises land use.

26/55 Halloughton (parish) SK 685515
Apt 31.05.1848; 977a (977); Map 1841 or 1848, 3 chns, 1st cl, by Paul Bausor, Southwell; construction lines, foot/b'way, waterbodies, field boundary ownerships, stile; map is dated differently in the title and in the margin.

26/56 Hawton (parish) SK 795504
Apt 07.08.1845; 2160a (all); Map 1846, 6 chns; foot/b'way, houses, woods, sconce [earthwork]; streams named.

26/57 Hayton and Tiln (hamlet in parish of Hayton) SK 725845
Apt 12.11.1841; 2393a (2700); Map 1842?, 6 chns, by Geo. Sanderson, Mansfield; foot/b'way, building names, canal with towpath, stiles, township boundaries; streams named; pecked boundaries separate fields within holdings; dot-dash boundaries separate holdings.

26/58 Hockerton (parish) SK 702575
Apt 29.12.1845; 1374a (1373); Map 1847, 6 chns, by Paul Bausor; houses, field boundary ownerships.

26/59 Hodsock (township in parish of Blyth) SK 612855
Apt 21.05.1841; 4110a (?); Map 1841, 6 chns, by Jno. Horncastle Jr, The Yews; waterbodies.

26/60 Holme Pierrepoint, Gamston, Adbolton and Bassingfield (town-ships or districts) SK 620380 [Holme Pierrepont]
Apt 20.08.1839; 2589a (?); Map 1840?, [6 chns]; waterbodies, hedge ownership, lordships (named), canal with towpath; stream named. Apt omits land use.

26/61 Houghton (parochial chapelry) SK 680726 [Haughton]
Apt 26.10.1848; 1002a (?); Map 1850?, 9 chns; waterbodies, houses, woods, plantations, ancient glebe (col).

26/62 Hoveringham (parish) SK 709469
Apt 25.11.1848; 209a (1050); Map 1849, 6 chns, (tithable parts only); woods, ferry house.

26/63 Kelham (parish) SK 772561
Apt 18.10.1844; 1858a (all); Map 1847, 6 chns, in 3 parts, (includes two small enlargements of detail); railway, foot/b'way, waterbodies, houses, gardens.

26/64 Kilvington (parish) SK 800429
Apt 08.06.1850; 486a (900); Map 1850, 3 chns, by C.J. Neale, Mansfield; foot/b'way, waterbodies, woods, field gates, footbridges, former course of stream.

26/65 Kimberley (township in parish of Gresley) SK 500446
Apt 07.07.1846; 688a (?); Map 1848?, 3 chns, (tithable parts only); foot/b'way, landowners, residual open fields.

26/66 Kinoulton (parish) SK 687304
Apt 10.03.1847; 3071a (3070); Map 1847, 6 chns, by Charles J. Neale, Mansfield; foot/b'way, canal with towpath, waterbodies, woods (named), plantations, old church yard; streams named.

26/67 Kirklington (parish) SK 679585
Apt 01.08.1845; 1976a (1976); Map 1846, 6 chns, in 2 parts, ? by Paul Bausor, (one part at 3 chns); foot/b'way, waterbodies, houses, woods, field boundary ownerships, stiles.

26/68 Kneesall and Ompton (townships in parish of Kneesall) SK 705643
Apt 16.10.1839; 2915a (all); Map 1840, 3 chns, 1st cl, by Percy W. Brackenbury, Wellow House, Ollerton, Notts; construction lines, foot/b'way, waterbodies, houses, field boundary ownerships, field gates, building names, brick kiln, occupation roads, green, wood (by annotation), township boundary.

26/69 Kneeton (parish) SK 719469
Apt 16.11.1847; 7a (924); Map (drawn on Apt) 1849?, 5 chns, (tithable parts only); landowners.

26/70 Lambley (parish) SK 625455
Apt 31.12.1841; 2162a (all); Map 1842, 3 chns, 1st cl, by Robert Bromley, Derby; construction lines, foot/b'way, waterbodies, houses, woods, field boundary ownerships, field gates, stiles.

26/71 Laneham (parish) SK 802764
Apt 01.10.1839; 152a (1605); Map 1841, 6 chns, (tithable parts only in detail, tinted); waterbodies, houses, woods, gardens, road names, landowners, sluice, ferry (pictorial); pictorial church with gravestones. Apt omits land use.

26/72 Langar (township in parish of Langar-cum-Barnstone) SK 728342
Apt 29.12.1845; 10a (?); Map 1846?, 4 chns, (tithable parts only, tinted); landowners. Apt omits land use.

26/73 Langford (parish) SK 825575
Apt 08.01.1846; 2182a (all); Map 1847, 6 chns; railway, foot/b'way, waterbodies, woods, parkland, gardens, flood bank.

26/74 Laxton or Lexington (parish) SK 723670
Apt 26.08.1839; 3952a (all); Map 1842, 6 chns; woods, open fields (named), windmill (pictorial), township boundaries; pictorial churches.

26/75 Lenton (parish) SK 551393
Apt 17.09.1846; 14a (5080); Map 1850?, 6 chns, (tithable parts only); woods.

26/76 Lowdham (parish) SK 672459
Apt 10.12.1838; 224a (3010); Map 1839?, 8 chns, (tithable parts only); woods (col, named), hedge ownership, field names, landowners.

26/77 Lyndby (parish) SK 539510 [Linby]
Apt 23.04.1841; 1480a (1190); Map 1842, 8 chns; foot/b'way, waterbodies, woods, landowners (col), glebe (col); pictorial church.

26/78 Mansfield (parish) SK 530610
Apt 12.10.1844; 4444a (all); Map 1845, 6 chns, in 3 parts, by Geo. Sanderson, Mansfield, (tithable parts only; includes two built-up parts separately at 3 chns); foot/b'way, waterbodies, woods, plantations, parkland.

26/79 Mansfield Woodhouse (parish) SK 547635
Apt 12.10.1844; 3188a (all); Map 1845, 6 chns, in 2 parts, by George Sanderson, Mansfield, (tithable parts only; includes enlargement of built-up part at 3 chns); waterbodies, woods, parkland.

26/80 Maplebeck (parish) SK 708609
Apt 19.12.1845; 1137a (all); Map 1847, 9 chns; foot/b'way, woods.

26/81 Marnham (district) SK 807701 [Low Marnham]
Apt 24.01.1844; 1728a (?); Map 1844?, 6 chns; houses, woods, ferry; pictorial church. Apt omits land use for tithe-free lands.

26/82 Mering (extra-parochial place) SK 814655 [Not listed]
Apt 13.03.1846; 37a (458); Map 1848?, 3 chns, (tithable parts only); owner is named in the title.

26/83 Misson (parish) (partly in Lincs) SK 690965
Apt 08.05.1843; 4960a (6129); Map 1844, 3 chns, 1st cl, in 5 parts, by R. Weightman, Torworth, (including enlargement of sluice); construction lines, foot/b'way, waterbodies, drainage bank, sluice, drainage ditches (in detail); dot-dash lines divide holdings, dashed lines are within holdings.

26/84 Moor Green (hamlet in parish of Greasley) SK 483481 [Moorgreen]
Apt 02.04.1846; 18a (?); Map 1850?, 3 chns; railways, foot/b'way, woods (col), arable (col), grassland (col), gardens (col), field gates, building names, landowners, stiles, parsonage, farm names; stream named; land use is only shown in the tithable parts.

26/85 Morton (parish) SK 722515
Apt 30.09.1846; 499a (498); Map 1847, 6 chns; railway, foot/b'way, houses, woods.

26/86 South Muskham (parish) SK 771575
Apt 22.05.1837; 2632a (all); Map 1840, 12 chns, by Geo. Sanderson, Mansfield, Notts; waterbodies, hops (by annotation). District is apportioned by holding and fields are not shown; Apt generalises land use.

26/87 Newark (parish) SK 805545 [Newark-on-Trent]
Apt 07.07.1842; 1889a (1889); Map 1843-4, 3 chns, 1st cl, in 2 parts, by J.S. Padley and George Betham, Lincoln, (includes enlargement of town at 1 chn); construction lines, canal, wharf, hauling path, locks, waterbodies, houses, woods (col), plantations, parkland, field boundary ownerships, field gates, road names, castle, castle ruins, churchyard, Roman Catholic Chapel, Jehovah-Jireh Chapel, Methodist Chapel, Christs Church, infant school, town hall, theatre, cattle market, butchery market, 'Ring of the Town', bowling green (col); meaning of red and yellow bands is unclear. Apt omits land use for lands not producing tithes.

26/88 Normanton on the Woulds (hamlet or district in parish of Plumtree) SK 620321 [Normanton-on-the-Wolds]
Apt 30.10.1839; 790a (?); Map 1838, 3 chns, by Thos A. Campbell, Nottingham; foot/b'way, turnpike roads, waterbodies, woods (named), plantations, avenue of trees, hedge ownership, field gates, building names, road names, landowners, spring, stiles; some land outside the district is mapped, in order to connect a detached part; red band shows area tithable to rector of Clifton; scale-bar is ruler-like.

26/89 St Mary, Nottingham (district in parish of St Mary, Nottingham) SK 578510 [Not listed]
Apt 31.05.1848; 600a (?); Map 1848, 6 chns, by H.M. Wood, Nottingham, (tithable parts only in detail); railways, waterbodies, woods, cemetery, commons.

26/90 Nuthall (township in parish of Nuthall) SK 515445
Apt 13.03.1846; 1269a (all); Map 1848, 6 chns, by E.S. Gisborne, Nottingham; waterbodies, woods, parkland.

26/91 Oldcoates (township) SK 593890 [Oldcotes]
Apt 18.10.1843; 940a (?); Map 1844, 6 chns.

26/92 Ollerton (township in parish of Edwinstowe) SK 658674
Apt 31.12.1841; 1766a (all); Map 1840, 3 chns, 1st cl, in 3 parts, by Percy W. Brackenbury, Wellow House, Ollerton, Notts, (including two small enlargements of detail); construction lines, foot/b'way, houses, woods, field boundary ownerships, field gates, landowners, fox covert, cave; most tithe area numbers are stamped; it is unclear what lilac tint denotes.

26/93 Ordsall (parish) SK 711799
Apt 10.04.1838; 1989a (1989); Map 1839, 6 chns; waterbodies, woods (col), glebe (yellow).

26/94 Osberton, Scofton, and Rayton (township in parish of Worksop) SK 631802
Apt 24.02.1846; 3841a (?); Map 1847, 6 chns, by J. Hickson, Worksop; foot/b'way, canal with towpath, waterbodies, woods, parkland, building names.

26/95 Ossington (parish) SK 757647
Apt 04.07.1844; 54a (2265); Map 1844, 3 chns, by Percy W. Brackenbury, (tithable parts only); field boundary ownerships.

26/96 Oxton (parish) SK 631530
Apt 14.01.1843; 3581a (3580); Map 1842, 3 chns, 1st cl, by Percy W. Brackenbury, Wellow House, Ollerton, Notts; construction lines, hill-drawing, foot/b'way, waterbodies, houses, woods (col, named), parkland, marsh/bog, open fields (named), field boundary ownerships, building names, windmill (by symbol), water mill, mill dam, warren, tumuli, ancient earthwork, road earthworks, stepping stones; some physical features named. (The map in PRO IR 30 is a copy; original is in PRO IR 77/55.)

26/97 Perlethorpe (township in parish of Edwinstowe) SK 650720
Apt 31.12.1841; 1758a (all); Map 1843, 12 chns, by Percy W. Brackenbury, Wellow House, Ollerton, Notts; foot/b'way, waterbodies, houses, woods, plantations.

26/98 Rampton (parish) SK 798782
Apt 18.12.1839; 2156a (2155); Map 1844?, 6 chns, by Geo. Sanderson, Mansfield, (includes enlargement of village at 2 chns); foot/b'way, waterbodies, woods, plantations, former open field names, ferry; meaning of lilac-grey tint is uncertain. Apt omits land use.

26/99 Ranskill (township in parish of Blyth) SK 656880
Apt 07.10.1839; 1266a (all); Map 1840?, 6 chns, ? by Robert Weightman, Torworth; woods; red bands show tithe ownership; cartouche is circular with fern-leaves tail. Apt has detailed cropping information.

26/100 Ratcliff on Soar (parish) SK 507302 [Ratcliffe on Soar]
Apt 16.03.1850; 1098a (all); Map 1850?, 10 chns; foot/b'way, woods, osiers (by symbol), fords. Apt omits land use.

26/101 East Retford (parish) SK 705811
Apt 08.12.1848; 71a (130); Map 1849?, 2 chns, (tithable parts only in detail); woods, road names, town hall, canal with towpath and locks; built-up part generalised.

26/102 Rolleston (township in parish of Rolleston) SK 750524
Apt 12.03.1846; 1662a (all); Map 1847?, 6 chns; railway, foot/b'way, waterbodies, houses, woods, hauling path, old flood bank.

26/103 Saundby (parish) SK 786884
Apt 27.06.1838; 1373a (all); Map 1839, 12 chns, by Geo. Sanderson, Mansfield, Notts. District is apportioned by holding and fields are not shown; Apt generalises land use.

26/104 Scaftworth (township in parish of Everton) SK 670925
Apt 14.10.1848; 1050a (?); Map 1849?, 9 chns; hill-drawing, railway, foot/b'way, waterbodies, woods, plantations, osiers (by symbol), toll bar, embankment, stiles.

26/105 South Scarle (township) SK 850642
Apt 29.09.1838; 1070a (1540); Map 1838, 3 chns, 1st cl, 'Survey'd for Mr Godson' by Fras McWilliam; construction lines, foot/b'way, waterbodies, houses, woods, plantations, parkland, avenue of trees, orchards, stiles.

26/106 Scrooby (parish) SK 651899
Apt 31.05.1848; 384a (1520); Map 1850, 4 chns, in 3 parts, by R. Weightman, Torworth, (tithable parts only); railway, woods, manor house, Great North Road.

26/107 Selston (parish) SK 464525
Apt 02.09.1843; 3257a (2330); Map 1844, 6 chns, in 7 parts, (includes six 3-chn enlargements of detail); railway, foot/b'way, canal and basin, waterbodies, windmill, common; buildings on common are highlighted in red.

26/108 Shelton (parish) SK 779445
Apt 31.03.1848; 844a (740); Map 1850, 3 chns, 1st cl; construction lines, foot/b'way, houses, woods, field boundary ownerships, common sewer.

26/109 Shireoaks and Haggonfield (township in parish of Worksop) SK 560801
Apt 30.04.1846; 1618a (all); Map 1847?, 6 chns, by J. Hickson; railways, canal with towpath and locks, waterbodies, woods.

26/110 Skegby (township in parish of Marnham) SK 779701
Apt 24.04.1849; 616a (?); Map 1849, 3 chns, by John H. Hutchinson, Grantham; waterbodies, houses, plantations (col), orchards (col).

26/111 Skegby (parish) SK 495612
Apt 12.10.1844; 1457a (all); Map 1845, 6 chns; waterbodies, woods, osiers (by symbol).

26/112 Southwell (parish) SK 698536
Apt 26.05.1841; 3882a (4550); Map 1840, 3 chns, 1st cl; construction lines, foot/b'way, turnpike roads, waterbodies, houses, woods, hops, open fields, field boundary ownerships, building names, park, mill, gravel pit, gaol, ownership boundary (yellow); some fields have indications of tenure, e.g. 'C', 'F', 'L-Lives', [copyhold, freehold, lease for lives]; open and former open fields are named.

26/113 Stanford (parish) SK 547232 [Not listed]
Apt 21.01.1839; 628a (1520); Map 1841?, 10 chns; woods, field boundary ownerships; tithe-free parts are not numbered. Apt omits land use.

26/114 Stapleford (parish) SK 490372
Apt 17.05.1850; 83a (1450); Map 1850, 3 chns, 1st cl, by William Edward Brown, Long Eaton, (tithable parts only); construction lines, foot/b'way, turnpike roads, orchards, field boundary ownerships, field gates, road names, landowners, school, chapel, wall, windmill; pictorial church.

26/115 Staunton (parish) SK 807443 [Staunton in the Vale]
Apt 08.06.1850; 300a (1410); Map 1850, 6 chns, by C.J. Neale, Mansfield, (tithable parts only in detail); foot/b'way, waterbodies, woods, building names.

26/116 Staythorpe (township or hamlet) SK 756538
Apt 18.06.1838; 635a (635); Map 1841, 3 chns; foot/b'way, waterbodies, woods. Apt omits land use.

26/117 East Stoke (parish) SK 760491
Apt 10.01.1843; 141a (1730); Map 1844?, 3 chns, (tithable parts only); foot/b'way, windmills (by symbol), locks.

26/118 Stokeham (parish) SK 780770
Apt 13.02.1840; 565a (all); Map 1840?, 4 chns; foot/b'way, houses, arable (col), grassland (col), orchards (col), field boundary ownerships.

26/119 Styrrup with Farworth (township in parish of Blyth and Harworth) SK 616900
Apt 21.05.1841; 2017a (?); Map 1843, 6 chns, by R. Weightman, Torworth; woods.

26/120 Sutton Bonnington St Michaels (parish) SK 505255 [Sutton Bonington]
Apt 11.10.1845; 24a (?); Map 1846?, 3 chns, in 4 parts, (tithable parts only, tinted; includes 24-chn location diagram); railway, road names, landowners, mills; pictorial church; a table summarises owners and acreages.

26/121 Sutton cum Lound (parish) SK 693860
Apt 29.07.1847; 6a (4370); Map 1849?, 4 chns, (tithable parts only). District is apportioned by holding.

26/122 Teversal (parish) SK 476620
Apt 06.06.1840; 2616a (all); Map 1841, 6 chns, by John Hickson; waterbodies, woods (col, named), building names, glebe (yellow).

26/123 Thorney (parish) SK 860730
Apt 17.09.1839; 2218a (4140); Map 1839, 7 chns, (tinted); waterbodies, woods, road names, canal with towpath, glebe (purple); pictorial church with gravestones. District is apportioned by holding and fields are not shown; Apt generalises land use.

26/124 Thorpe (parish) SK 770497
Apt 30.04.1844; 542a (698); Map 1846?, 3 chns, (tithable parts only); turnpike roads, waterbodies, woods (col); some names are stamped.

26/125 Torworth (township in parish of Blyth) SK 652862
Apt 07.10.1839; 1331a (all); Map 1840?, 6 chns, ? by Robert Weightman, Torworth; red band shows tithe ownership. Apt has detailed cropping information.

26/126 Toton (hamlet or township in parish of Attenborough) SK 507343
Apt 06.06.1845; 1371a (?); Map 1850, 6 chns, by John Bromley, Derby; railways, foot/b'way, waterbodies, houses, woods, modus field names and boundary, well, drain, 'Vicar's Ring'.

26/127 Treswell (parish) SK 790795
Apt 01.11.1842; 1561a (1561); Map 1843?, 8 chns, in 2 parts, by R. Weightman, Torworth, (including small enlargement of detail); foot/b'way, woods, road names, flood bank.

26/128 Watnall Cautelupe (township or hamlet in parish of Greasley) SK 505445 [Not listed]
Apt 30.06.1841; 508a (?); Map 1841, 6 chns; waterbodies, woods, orchards, landowners; stream named. Apt has detailed cropping information.

26/129 Watnall Chaworth (township or hamlet in parish of Greasley) SK 410470 [Not listed]
Apt 30.09.1842; 760a (?); Map 1843, 6 chns, by John Bromley, Derby; foot/b'way, waterbodies, woods, parkland, gardens, landowners, mound; stream named

26/130 Wellow (parish) SK 677663
Apt 31.05.1845; 991a (991); Map 1845, 4 chns, by Percy W. Brackenbury, Wellow House, Ollerton, Notts; waterbodies, houses, green, woods (col), with rides; drain named.

26/131 North Wheatley (parish) SK 765869
Apt 15.02.1839; 2181a (2181); Map surveyed in 1837-8, 2.5 chns, by Geo. Sanderson, Mansfield, Notts; construction lines, waterbodies, houses (by shading), woods, field boundary ownerships, building names, road names, field names.

26/132 South Wheatley (parish) SK 765853
Apt 17.04.1839; 642a (all); Map surveyed in 1838, 2.5 chns, by Geo. Sanderson, Mansfield, Notts; construction lines, waterbodies, woods, orchards (by annotation), gardens (by annotation), field boundary ownerships, field gates, field names, field acreages; stream named.

26/133 Wilford (parish) SK 570368
Apt 11.10.1845; 50a (1450); Map 1850, 5 chns, (tithable parts only in detail), tinted); waterbodies, woods, parkland, ford, ferry.

26/134 Winthorpe (parish) SK 815565
Apt 02.03.1846; 5a (680); Map 1848?, 6 chns, (tithable parts only in detail).

26/135 Wiseton (township in parish of Clayworth) SK 718898
Apt 10.10.1837; 1004a (?); Map 1847?, 6 chns, ? by John Dickinson, Austerfield, Yorks; turnpike roads, waterbodies, culvert, canal with towpath, sewers.

26/136 Wollaton cum Cossall (parish) SK 525398
Apt 28.12.1838; 3043a (all); Map 1839, 12 chns, by Geo. Sanderson, Mansfield, Notts; canal with towpath and locks, hall, canal locks. District is apportioned by holding and fields are not shown; Apt generalises land use, and omits occupiers.

26/137 Worksop and Radford (district in parish of Worksop) SK 600770
Apt 21.12.1848; 7671a (?); Map 1850, 6 chns, in 2 parts, (includes enlargement of town at 3 chns); railway with station, woods, plantations (named), building names, vicarage, canal with towpath, notable oaks, sand pit, workhouse; north pointer on enlargement of town has a shell boss.

Oxfordshire

PRO IR29 and IR30 27/1-156

267 tithe districts: 482,933 acres
154 tithe commutations: 214,765 acres
78 voluntary tithe agreements, 76 compulsory tithe awards,
2 corn rent annuities

Tithe and tithe commutation

Although Oxfordshire extends to the Chilterns in the south, it is more 'midland' than 'south-eastern' in terms of its tithe survey characteristics. As there had been extensive parliamentary enclosure and consequent commutation of tithe before 1836, it is unsurprising that only 58 per cent of Oxfordshire tithe districts by number and 44 per cent of the county by area were subject to payment of tithes at this date (Fig. 39). Fifty-nine districts were wholly tithable; in addition to commutation at the time of enclosure the main causes of exemption in others were modus payments in lieu of tithes, exemption by prescription, and exemption of some woodland, particularly beech woods. Assistant tithe commissioners and local tithe agents who worked in Oxfordshire are listed in Table 27.1 and the valuers of tithe rent-charge in Table 27.2.

Tithe maps

For a midland county Oxfordshire has a relatively high proportion (8 per cent) of first-class maps, a figure only exceeded in the Midlands by Nottinghamshire. Only two second-class maps carry construction lines but copying from maps ranging in date from 1786 to 1838 is acknowledged on 6 per cent of second-class maps. The large number of tithe maps of districts where only small tracts of land remained tithable suggests that wholly new tithe survey mapping was probably of limited extent in Oxfordshire.

As in other counties where there was much enclosure, there were two peaks in map production, a first in 1839-40, and a second in 1847-49 (Table 27.4). Twenty-two maps (14 per cent of the total) date from 1850-58 but as they are mostly of residual tithable enclaves in largely tithe-free districts, they are of less than proportional areal extent.

Oxfordshire tithe maps are drawn at a variety of scales from one inch to two chains to one inch to eighteen chains; 60 per cent are in the recommended scale range of one inch to three to four chains and 28 per cent are at the six-chain scale (Table 27.3). Three

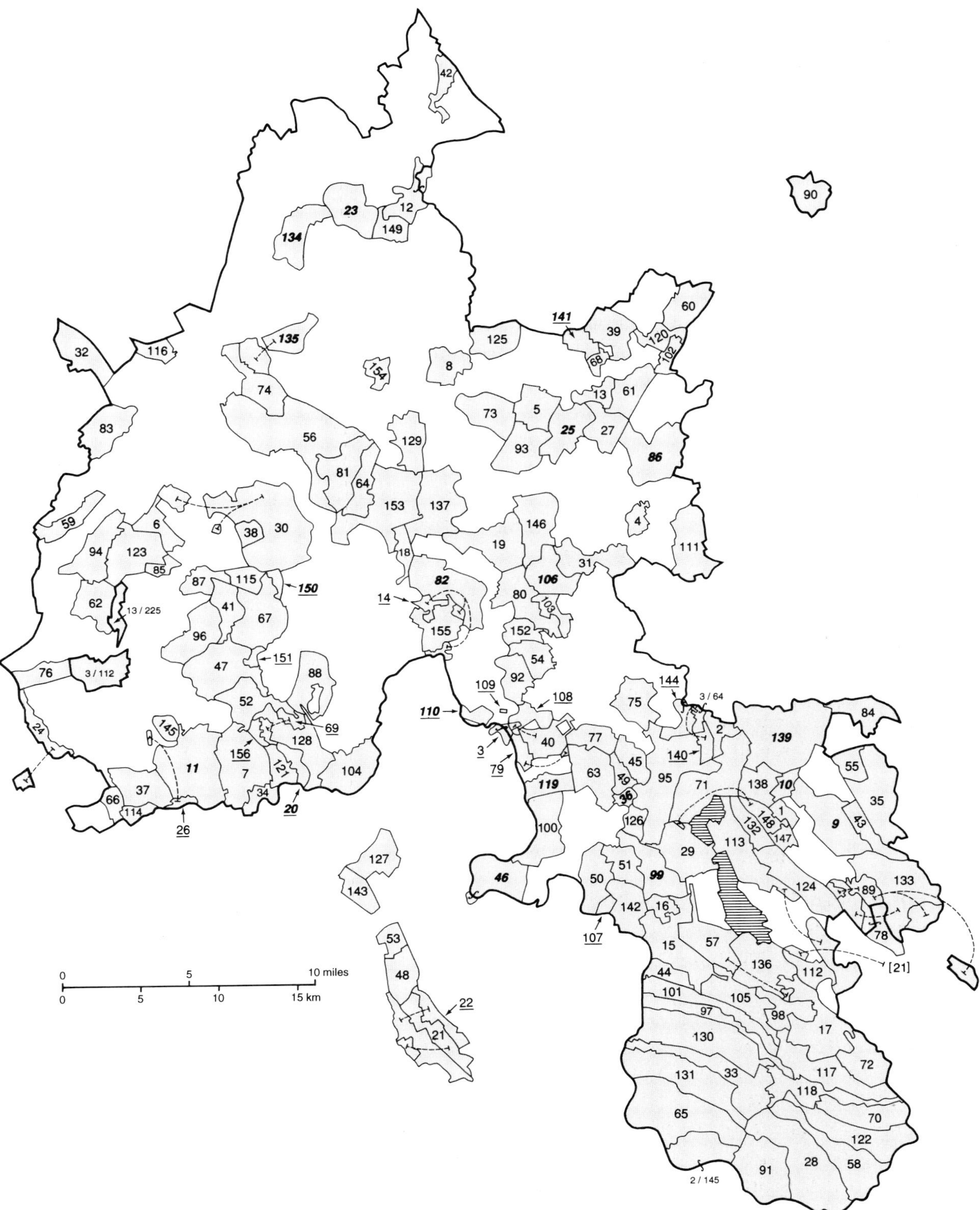

Fig. 39 Oxfordshire: tithe district boundaries.

second-class maps are lithographed and three maps of residual tithable lands are drawn as insets on the folios of the tithe apportionments.

Apart from woodland, which appears on 63 per cent of Oxfordshire tithe maps, parkland (on 11 per cent, and in detail on four maps) and marsh (on 9 per cent), Oxfordshire tithe maps are poor records of land use; arable, grass, gardens and orchards appear on fewer than 4 per cent of maps. Residual open fields are depicted on 20 per cent of Oxfordshire tithe maps; these are usually named and often of considerable extent. As in Buckinghamshire, field boundaries are recorded more consistently than is usual and 42 per cent of maps indicate field boundary ownership and 34 per cent show footpaths or bridleways. Sundry features recorded on Oxfordshire tithe maps include osier beds, drainage channels, archaeological features including earthworks, the Icknield Way (on several maps), a 'Field of Industry' at Bletchington and a tithe barn on the map of Chastleton.

Only eighty-six (56 per cent) of Oxfordshire tithe maps in the Public Record Office collection can be attributed to a particular map-maker; the most prolific of these was John Edward Neighbour of Oxford who produced twenty maps in a distinctive style, often dated with Roman numerals and with a scale bar mounted on a plinth. Thirteen maps were produced by Richard Davis of Banbury, usually in partnership with James Saunders of Oxford, and another nine were produced by Saunders working alone. A higher than average proportion of Oxfordshire tithe maps were the work of men from well outside the county. Five maps were made by London surveyors and two each by William Bryan Wood of Chippenham, Wiltshire and William Thomas Heard of Hitchin, Hertfordshire. S. L. Bransby and B. H. Galland, both based in Suffolk, Francis Kelsey of Salisbury and James Webb of Worcester each mapped one Oxfordshire district.

Oxfordshire tithe maps are of variable quality; twelve are noted in the catalogue of Oxfordshire tithe maps as particularly carefully drawn and five as particularly amateurish. The map of Swerford is especially crude; it is plotted at the eighteen-chain scale and shows only holding boundaries and the locations of two farms. Oxfordshire tithe maps conform to the general trend in central England in their lack of decoration. One map, Newton Purcell, has a decorative cartouche but otherwise embellishment is confined to compass roses and scale bars.

A unique feature of the map of Charlbury is that it is accompanied by an Ordnance Survey one-inch map annotated to show the layout of the various parts of the tithe map.

Table 27.1. *Agreements and awards for commutation of tithes in Oxfordshire*

Assistant commissioner/ local tithe agent	*Number of agreements**	*Number of awards*
Thomas James Tatham	0	47
Thomas Clements Parr	28	0
Henry Jemmett	13	0
Francis Offley Martin	0	11
Joseph Townsend	6	4
Thomas Smith Woolley	7	3
F. Browne Browne	9	0
Roger Kynaston	6	0
William Wakeford Attree	0	5
John Maurice Herbert	0	4
Horace William Meteyard	3	0
William Heard	2	0
John Mee Mathew	2	0
John Pickering	2	0
Charles Pym	2	0
John Job Rawlinson	0	1
Tithe Commissioners	0	1

*Computed from the number of extant reports on tithe agreements in the tithe files [PRO IR 18].

Table 27.2. *Tithe valuers and tithe map-makers in Oxfordshire*

Name and address (all in Oxfordshire)	*Number of districts*	*Acreage*
Tithe valuers		
Edward Lane Franklin, Ascott	18	19,699
William John Dodd, Ipsden	16	34,171
Samuel Druce, Eynsham	14	31,618
James Saunders, Kirtlington, Oxford	9	7,638
Henry Dixon, Oxford	8	13,609
Others [50]	89	108,030
Attributed tithe map-makers		
John Edward Neighbour, Oxford	20	28,930
Davis and Saunders, Banbury and Oxford	13	11,882
James Saunders, Kirtlington, Oxford	8	14,847
Henry Dixon, Oxford	6	9,805
Others [22]	38	57,076

Table 27.3. *The tithe maps of Oxfordshire: scales and classes*

Scale in chains/inch	All maps		First Class		Second Class	
	Number	Acreage	Number	Acreage	Number	Acreage
>3	7	3,304	0	0	7	3,304
3	68	84,978	12	15,129	56	69,849
4	23	33,915	0	0	23	33,915
4.5, 4.75, 5	4	1,624	0	0	4	1,624
6	43	83,584	0	0	43	83,584
<6	9	7,360	0	0	9	7,860
TOTAL	154	214,765	12	15,129	142	200,136

Table 27.4. *The tithe maps of Oxfordshire: dates*

	1837	*1838*	*1839*	*1840*	*1841*	*1842*	*1843*	*1844*	*1845*	*1846*	*1847*	*1848*	*1849*	*>1849*
All maps	1	10	15	23	8	13	9	8	2	6	13	11	11	22
1st class	0	0	5	0	0	1	1	0	0	0	3	1	0	1
2nd class*	1	10	10	23	8	12	8	8	2	6	10	10	11	21

*Two second-class tithe maps of Oxfordshire in the Public Record Office collection are undated.

Oxfordshire

27/1 Adwell (parish) SU 698998
Apt 31.10.1839; 440a (439); Map 1839, 3 chns, 1st cl, 'surveyed under the direction of Mr Benjn Badcock of Oxford' by James Saunders, Kirtlington, Oxon; construction lines, foot/b'way, waterbodies, houses, woods (col), parkland (col, in detail), marsh/bog, hedge ownership, fences, building names, rectory, glebe and church lands; map is subtitled 'the property of Miss Frances Webb'.

27/2 Albury (parish) SP 658051
Apt 26.05.1847; 663a (all); Map 1847?, 3 chns; waterbodies, woods.

27/3 St Aldate (parish) (partly in Berks) SP 515052 [Not listed]
Apt 31.12.1845; 281a (all); Map 1847, 3 chns, by Washbourne and Keen, 2 Parliament Street, Westminster, London; waterbodies, building names, railway station, drains, county boundary.

27/4 Ambrosden (parish) SP 601191
Apt 26.05.1847; 575a (all); Map 1847?, 4.5 chns; foot/b'way, waterbodies, woods.

27/5 Ardley (parish) SP 536263
Apt 18.09.1839; 1469a (all); Map 1839?, 6 chns; foot/b'way, waterbodies, woods (col, named), hedge ownership, freeboard.

27/6 Ascot under Wychwood (parish) SP 300187 [Ascott-under-Wychwood]
Apt 22.07.1840; 957a (1793); Map 1840, 6 chns, by Richard Davis, Banbury; foot/b'way, waterbodies, houses, hedge ownership, field boundary ownerships, landowners, stone pit, glebe. Map has note of adoption proceedings.

27/7 Aston and Coate (hamlet in parish of Bampton) SP 347030
Apt 01.11.1841; 2963a (?); Map 1840, 3 chns, by J. Dymock; waterbodies, houses, grassland (col), open fields, hedge ownership, field gates, building names, field names, pound, moorland, common meadow (col).

27/8 North Aston (parish) SP 478290
Apt 08.05.1843; 1272a (1272); Map 1843, 3 chns; waterbodies, open fields.

27/9 Aston Rowant (parish) SU 720998
Apt 23.01.1840; 755a (2980); Map 1840?, 4 chns; waterbodies, houses, woods, open fields.

27/10 Attington (extra-parochial place) SP 701017
Apt 02.10.1847; 102a (435); Map 1847?, 5 chns; waterbodies, woods.

27/11 Bampton (township) SP 319028
Apt 30.12.1857; 27a (8750); Map 1858, 3 chns, by William Bryan Wood, Chippenham; foot/b'way; bridge named.

27/12 Banbury (except Wickham) (partly in Northants) (parish) SP 454401
Apt 31.12.1850; 1171a (3150); Map 1852, 6 chns, 'copied from old maps' by Davis and Saunders, Banbury and Oxford; railway, foot/b'way, canal with towpath, woods, plantations, hedge ownership, fence; built-up part generalised.

27/13 Baynton (hamlet in parish of Stoke Lyne) SP 580272 [Bainton]
Apt 16.12.1843; 806a (all); Map 1847, 3 chns, 1st cl, by Messrs Davis and Saunders, Banbury and Oxford; construction lines, foot/b'way, waterbodies, houses, woods (col), hedge ownership, field gates, building names, road names.

27/14 Begbrooke (parish) SP 469138 [Begbroke]
Apt 23.06.1840; 623a (623); Map 1844, 6 chns, in 2 parts, ? by Henry Dixon, (including 12-chn skeleton map of district); waterbodies, woods, meadow names.

27/15 Bensington (parish) SU 624921 [Benson]
Apt 26.01.1841; 2922a (all); Map 1841, 6 chns, in 2 parts, by Jno. Edwd Neighbour, St Clement's, Oxford; waterbodies, woods, open fields.

27/16 Berrick Salome (parish) SU 621942
Apt 30.04.1839; 678a (all); Map 1842?, 4 chns, in 2 parts; houses, open fields

27/17 Bix (parish) SU 725865
Apt 03.09.1840; 3075a (3075); Map 1840, 3 chns, by Moses Dodd; waterbodies, houses, woods, plantations, orchards, heath/moor; map has note of adoption proceedings.

27/18 Bladon cum Woodstock (parish) SP 451172
Apt 20.01.1847; 620a (1010); Map 1848, 3 chns; foot/b'way, waterbodies, field gates, building names, road names, borough boundary; built-up part generalised.

27/19 Bletchington (parish) SP 509176 [Bletchingdon]
Apt 30.11.1839; 2654a (2540); Map 1839, 3 chns, 1st cl, in 3 parts, by James Saunders, Kirtlington, Oxon, (including 1.5-chn enlarge-ments of village and 'Lower End'); construction lines, foot/b'way, waterbodies, houses, woods (col), parkland, orchards, marsh/bog, hedge ownership, fences, field gates, building names, field names, landowners, green, roadside waste ownership, charity lands, Rector's lands.

27/20 Brighthampton (hamlet in parish of Bampton) SP 384031
Apt 26.05.1847; 671a (all); Map 1851, 6 chns, by 'A.R.M.'; building names, drains.

27/21 Britwell Prior (parish) SU 671930 [Britwell Priory]
Apt 10.05.1843; 709a (2209); Map 1843, 6 chns, by J. Neighbour and Son, Oxford; woods, plantations.

27/22 Britwell Salome (parish) SU 674937
Apt 10.05.1843; 871a (all); Map 1843, 6 chns, by J. Neighbour and Son, Oxford; woods.

27/23 Broughton (hamlet or township in parish of Broughton) SP 420393
Apt 26.10.1850; 7a (1270); Map (drawn on Apt) 1851?, 2 chns, (tithable parts only).

27/24 Broughton Poggs (parish) SP 221046
Apt 26.08.1839; 1122a (all); Map 1839, 3 chns, in 2 parts; waterbodies, woods (col), plantations (col), arable (col), grassland (col), orchards, marsh/bog, heath/moor.

27/25 Bucknell (parish) SP 555251
Apt 31.03.1849; 7a (1670); Map 1849, 3 chns, (tithable parts only); hedge ownership, building names, landowners; part of the map showing the road to Bucknell church is at 25 chns.

27/26 Burrowey Meadow, Charney Meadow, Norton Meadow, Bourton Meadow and part of Black Bourton parish (district) SP 313007
Apt 22.06.1844; 227a (all); Map 1844, 3 chns, in 2 parts, by G.T. Williams; construction lines, waterbodies, arable (col), grassland (col), orchards, marsh/bog, open fields, field names, landowners, weir.

27/27 Caversfield (parish) SP 583248
Apt 23.03.1854; 1481a (1200); Map 1851, 3 chns, 1st cl, by Davis and Saunders, Banbury and Oxford; construction lines, foot/b'way, waterbodies, houses, woods (col), parkland, hedge ownership, fences, field boundary ownerships, field gates.

27/28 Caversham (parish) SU 711778
Apt 26.04.1845; 4773a (4772); Map 1844, 6 chns; turnpike roads, waterbodies, houses, woods (named), osiers, plantations (named), parkland, marsh/bog, heath/moor, rock outcrops, building names, road names, mill, pit, chalk pit, greens (col), common (col).

27/29 Chalgrove (parish) SU 641969
Apt 26.05.1841; 2364a (all); Map 1840, 3 chns, by Jno. Edwd Neighbour, Oxford; waterbodies, open fields, hedge ownership.

27/30 Charlbury (parish) SP 365195
Apt 26.05.1847; 6108a (11320); Map 1848, 6 chns, in 8 parts; parts 1, 5, 6 and 7 surveyed by W.H. Davies, Abingdon (part 5 at 5 chns); parts 2 and 4 'copied' by Geo. Hewett, Oxford, (part 2 at 4 chns, part 4 at 3 chns); includes Ordnance Survey 1-inch map annotated as index; railways, foot/b'way, waterbodies, houses, woods, plantations, open fields, building names.

27/31 Charlton on Otmoor (parish) SP 571168 [Charlton-on-Otmoor]
Apt 04.09.1840; 1864a (1864); Map 1843?, 6 chns; waterbodies,

grassland (col), gardens (col), open fields, road names, field names, Lammas pasture lands (col), tithe-free land (col); pictorial church.

27/32 Chastleton (parish) SP 248298
Apt 14.09.1843; 1770a (all); Map 1842, 3 chns, 1st cl, by James Webb, Worcester; construction lines, waterbodies, houses, woods, plantations, fences, field boundary ownerships, field gates, building names, sand or stone pit, rectory, tithe barn, ancient barrow.

27/33 Checkendon (parish) SU 658832
Apt 29.06.1839; 3063a (3063); Map 1840, 3 chns, by Moses Dodd; waterbodies, houses, woods, plantations, orchards, heath/moor, open fields; double lines may show walls; meadow named.

27/34 Chimney (hamlet in parish of Bampton) SP 360010
Apt 31.08.1846; 642a (?); Map 1846?, 4.75 chns, by J.B. Clary, Reading; drains.

27/35 Chinnor (parish) SP 757009
Apt 28.01.1841; 2688a (2687); Map not dated, 3 chns; waterbodies, woods, orchards, open fields, road names, pound, green.

27/36 Chippenhurst (hamlet in parish of Cuddesden) SP 598010 [Not listed]
Apt 02.10.1847; 68a (140), (tithable parts only); Map 1851?, 4 chns; woods, building names, weir.

27/37 Clanfield (parish) SP 283013
Apt 31.01.1838; 1621a (1620); Map 1838?, 3 chns, by F.J. Kelsey, Salisbury; foot/b'way, waterbodies, houses.

27/38 Cornbury Park, with Kingsmead, and Bondsmans Mead (extra-parochial place) SP 351181
Apt 27.09.1850; 8a (?); Map 1851?, 2 chns, (tithable parts only, tinted); woods, field names; compass rose and scale bar coloured.

27/39 Cottesford (parish) SP 585315 [Cottisford]
Apt 21.01.1848; 1600a (1520); Map 1855?, 3 chns, by William Keen, 8 Cannon Row, Westminster; waterbodies, houses, woods, plantations, parkland, glebe (col); meaning of colour bands is unclear.

27/40 Cowley (parish) SP 545042
Apt 31.12.1846; 1061a (940); Map 1853, 3 chns; waterbodies, field gates, road names, churchyard, bridge named.

27/41 Crawley (hamlet in parish of Witney) SP 340130
Apt 28.03.1840; 1116a (all); Map 1839, 6 chns, by F. Underwood, Witney; waterbodies, houses, woods, fences, field gates.

27/42 Cropredy (parish) SP 469467
Apt 16.03.1843; 816a (816); Map 1843, 4 chns, by Richard Davis, Bloxham, Oxon; foot/b'way, turnpike roads, canal with towpath, waterbodies, hedge ownership, fences, field boundary ownerships, field gates, landowners, private roads.

27/43 Crowell (parish) SU 756987
Apt 28.08.1839; 988a (987); Map 1840, 3 chns; waterbodies, houses, woods, open fields, hedge ownership.

27/44 Crowmarsh Gifford (parish) SU 628892
Apt 26.07.1845; 662a (all); Map 1841, 6 chns, by Jno. Edwd Neighbour, St Clements, Oxford; road names.

27/45 Cuddesdon (township) SP 602032
Apt 23.06.1840; 962a (1052); Map 1840, 6 chns, by Jno. Edwd Neighbour, Oxford; waterbodies, hedge ownership, fences; compass rose and scale bar coloured.

27/46 Culham (parish) SU 516955
Apt 23.12.1845; 104a (1680); Map 1846?, 3 chns, by W.H. Davies, Abingdon; houses, field boundary ownerships, field gates, gravel pit, drains.

27/47 Curbridge (hamlet in parish of Witney) SP 335092
Apt 13.06.1840; 2952a (2952); Map 1840, 6 chns; waterbodies, houses, drains.

27/48 Cuxham (parish) SU 667953
Apt 13.06.1840; 487a (487); Map 1848?, 3 chns; waterbodies, houses.

27/49 Denton (hamlet or chapelry in parish of Cuddesdon) SP 595022
Apt 28.08.1841; 527a (all); Map 1842, 2.5 chns, by George Francis Davenport, Oxford; waterbodies, houses, open fields.

27/50 Dorchester (parish) SU 576957
Apt 08.04.1846; 1644a (1644); Map 1845, 3 chns, by Neighbour and Son, Oxford; waterbodies, open fields, hedge ownership, river locks.

27/51 Drayton (parish) SU 595967 [Drayton St Leonard]
Apt 16.05.1840; 1260a (1260); Map 1840, 3 chns, by J. Neighbour, St Clements, Oxford; waterbodies, woods, open fields.

27/52 Ducklington (parish) SP 350070
Apt 26.04.1838; 1882a (1881); Map 'copied from the Inclosure Plan', 1838, 6 chns; waterbodies, houses, woods, plantations, building names, road names, chapel, drains.

27/53 Easington (parish) SU 661968
Apt 31.01.1840; 233a (all); Map 1840, 3 chns, by Jno. Edwd Neighbour, Oxford; waterbodies, open fields, hedge ownership.

27/54 Elsfield (parish) SP 538101
Apt 30.07.1840; 1270a (1280); Map 1840?, 6 chns; foot/b'way, hedges, field gates. District is apportioned by holding and fields are not shown.

27/55 Emmington (parish) SP 741029
Apt 22.10.1841; 726a (726); Map 1841, 4 chns; foot/b'way, hedge ownership.

27/56 Enstone (parish) SP 380250
Apt 18.02.1841; 6177a (all); Map 1843, 6 chns, by James Saunders, Kirtlington, Oxon; foot/b'way, private and public roads, turnpike roads, waterbodies, houses, woods, plantations, orchards, heath/moor, hedge ownership, field boundary ownerships, field gates, road names, boundary marks, sand or stone pits, common (col).

27/57 Ewelme (parish) SU 655915
Apt 18.01.1840; 2348a (2376); Map 1840, 4 chns, in 3 parts, by J. Neighbour, St Clements, Oxford; waterbodies, hedge ownership; apparent open strips are bounded by solid lines.

27/58 Eye and Dunsden (liberty in parish of Sonning) SU 730780 [Dunsden Green]
Apt 04.04.1840; 3103a (3102); Map 1841?, 3 chns; hill-drawing, foot/b'way, waterbodies, houses, field gates, sand or stone pits, drains, withies (col), coppice (col).

27/59 Fifield (parish) SP 242191
Apt 28.02.1848; 1149a (all); Map 1846, 6 chns, by B.H. Galland; houses, woods, plantations, road names.

27/60 Finmere (parish) SP 632332
Apt 31.08.1840; 1542a (all); Map 1841?, 6 chns; foot/b'way, waterbodies, plantations, freeboard.

27/61 Fringford (parish) SP 588274
Apt 26.05.1847; 483a (1580); Map 1848?, 4 chns; waterbodies, landowners, freeboard, green; built-up part generalised.

27/62 Fulbrook (parish) SP 258132
Apt 06.02.1849; 101a (1670), (tithable parts only, tinted); Map 1850?, 18 chns; field acreages.

27/63 Garsington (parish) SP 579024
Apt 30.06.1841; 2231a (all); Map 1843?, 6 chns; waterbodies, woods.

27/64 Glympton (parish) SP 424211
Apt 05.09.1837; 1232a (1232); Map 1838, 6 chns, 'copy'd' from a map made by Mr Pratley, 1807, by John Dale, Woolvercott, Oxon; foot/b'way, waterbodies, woods, parkland, gardens, hedge ownership, field names, landowners, glebe, brake, freeboard; woods, park, gardens and meadows indicated by name.

27/65 Goring (parish) SU 630802
Apt 31.12.1846; 1939a (4377); Map 1847?, 6 chns; railways, foot/b'way, waterbodies, houses, woods, plantations, orchards, marsh/bog, building names, mill; north pointer has Prince of Wales Feathers.

27/66 Grafton (township in parish of Langford) SP 269006
Apt 05.02.1840; 611a (all); Map 1844?, 2.5 chns, waterbodies, gardens, weir, drains, green, common.

27/67 Hailey (hamlet in parish of Witney) SP 360120
Apt 08.09.1840; 2827a (all); Map 1839, 6 chns, in 3 parts, by F. Underwood, Witney, (including part of Hailey village at 3 chns and parts at West End and Wood Green at 1.5 chns; waterbodies, houses, woods, plantations, fences.

27/68 Hardwick (parish) SP 576297
Apt 21.01.1848; 359a (?); Map 1849?, 3 chns, ? by Layton Cooke; waterbodies.

27/69 Hardwick (township in parish of Ducklington) SP 383057
Apt 29.09.1849; 670a (all); Map 1851, 6 chns; drains.

27/70 Harpsden cum Bolney (parish) SU 750803
Apt 17.07.1841; 1993a (1460); Map 1842?, 3 chns; foot/b'way, turnpike roads, waterbodies, houses, woods, plantations, orchard.

27/71 Great Haseley (parish) SP 655017
Apt 07.06.1838; 3220a (3219); Map 1837, 3 chns; foot/b'way, turnpike roads, waterbodies, houses, woods, plantations, parkland (in detail), orchards, building names, chapel, pound, tithing boundaries (col, named).

27/72 Henley upon Thames (parish) SU 753836 [Henley-on-Thames]
Apt 26.07.1842; 1737a (1737); Map 1842?, 4 chns; foot/b'way, waterbodies, woods, plantations, drains; double lines may show walls; built-up part generalised; map has note of adoption proceedings.

27/73 Upper Heyford (parish) SP 507258
Corn rent conversion, 1921; 1090a (1300); Map 1922, 6 chns, (tracing of enclosure map of 1842 by James Saunders, Kirtlington, Oxon); foot/b'way, turnpike roads, canal, waterbodies, houses, woods (col, named), hedge ownership, field boundary ownerships, field acreages, road names, landowners, green; map has table of owners, descriptions of property and acreages.

27/74 Heythrop (parish) SP 355276
Apt 24.04.1838; 1664a (all); Map not dated, 18 chns; building names, landowners. District is apportioned by holding and fields are not shown.

27/75 Holton (parish) SP 603067
Apt 26.05.1847; 1595a (all); Map 1846, 4 chns, by John Neighbour and Son, St Clements, Oxford; waterbodies, woods, orchards, freeboard.

27/76 Holwell (hamlet in parish of Broadwell) SP 225088
Apt 11.11.1840; 1045a (all); Map 1840, 6 chns, in 2 parts, (includes 3-chn enlargement of detail), litho (Standidge); foot/b'way, waterbodies, woods, plantations, orchards, gardens, chapel.

27/77 Horsepath (parish) SP 575048
Apt 07.04.1847; 1165a (1164); Map 1848, 3 chns, by Henry Dixon, Oxford; waterbodies, open fields (shown with solid boundaries).

27/78 Ibstone (parish) SU 753937
Apt 22.11.1841; 1113a (1112); Map 1842, 6 chns, ? by Henry Dixon, Oxford, litho (by R. Martin, Long Acre); waterbodies, woods.

27/79 Iffley (parish) SP 529036
Apt 28.09.1839; 679a (679); Map 1847, 3 chns, by Henry Dixon, Oxford; waterbodies, open fields, landowners, old encampment, cricket grounds, stone pit, boundary marks, college lands, green; bridge named; apparent open field strips are shown with solid boundaries.

27/80 Islip (parish) SP 529137
Apt 03.02.1843; 1969a (all); Map 1843, 3 chns, 1st cl, by James Saunders, Kirtlington, Oxon; foot/b'way, waterbodies, houses, woods (col), open fields, hedge ownership (col), fences, building names, mill.

27/81 Kiddington (parish) SP 413218
Apt 26.10.1850; 1877a (2450); Map 'copied... from a map belonging to Mortimer Richards Esq.', 1851, 6 chns, by Davis and Saunders, Banbury and Oxford; foot/b'way, waterbodies, houses, woods (col), hedge ownership.

27/82 Kidlington (including township of Gosford and hamlet of Thrupp, and Water Eaton) (parish) SP 483149
Apt 19.10.1847; 256a (2550); Map 1850, 3 chns, by Wm Th. Heard, Hitchin; railways, foot/b'way, waterbodies, woods, building names, mill.

27/83 Kingham (parish) SP 261248
Apt 11.10.1839; 1878a (1877); Map 1840, 2 chns, by James Saunders, Kirtlington, Oxon; hill-drawing, foot/b'way, waterbodies, houses, woods, open fields, hedge ownership, fences, field gates, gravel pit, ecclesiastical boundaries; map has note of adoption proceedings.

27/84 Kingsey (partly in Bucks) (parish) SP 750070
Apt 02.10.1847; 1405a (all); Map 1848?, 3 chns, in 2 parts; waterbodies, woods, parkland, orchards, open fields, drains.

27/85 Langley without Wychwood Forest (district) SP 302154 [Langley]
Apt 19.06.1846; 300a (all); Map 1845, 8 chns, 'copied and corrected' by James Saunders, Oxford; waterbodies, houses, woods, public carriage road.

27/86 Launton (parish) SP 615235
Apt 05.09.1849; 91a (3550), (tithable parts only); Map 1850, 8 chns, by Davis, Saunders and Hicks; railway, hedge ownership.

27/87 Leafield without Wychwood Forest (district) SP 321148
Apt 04.04.1839; 907a (all); Map 1839, 3 chns, 1st cl, in 2 parts, by James Saunders, Kirtlington, Oxon, (includes 1.5-chn enlargements of detail); construction lines, foot/b'way, waterbodies, houses, woods (col, named), plantations (col, named), hedge ownership (col), fences, field boundary ownerships, field gates, building names, road names, field names, barrow, chapel of ease, 'Field of Industry', leasehold and copyhold land and forest and township boundaries; double lines may indicate walls; map has a note by the surveyor: 'Sept.27th 1839. This sheet of paper has shrunk since the plotting of the work 42 links in 150 chns being 8.75 links in 30 chns which produces a difference of $42/_{4}{}^{5}$ of a pole in an acre. This addition has been made in the Quantities.'

27/88 South Leigh (parish) SP 391083
Apt 26.08.1848; 2020a (all); Map 1849?, 10 chns; waterbodies, woods.

27/89 Lewknor Uphill (parish) SU 740950 [Lewknor]
Apt 12.11.1840; 2003a (2002); Map 1840, 3 chns, in 4 parts, by Joseph Dymock, (includes 12-chn index); foot/b'way, woods (by annotation), arable (by annotation), grassland (by annotation), field gates, building names, chapel.

27/90 Lillingstone Lovell (parish) SP 712405
Apt 27.06.1838; 1270a (all); Map 1839, 4 chns, by S.L. Bransby; waterbodies, woods; pictorial church.

27/91 Mapledurham (parish) SU 684770 [Not listed]
Apt 18.06.1840; 2879a (2878); Map 1841, 6 chns; hill-drawing, waterbodies, houses, woods (named), plantations (named), parkland, marsh/bog, hedges, building names, chalk pit, parsonage, sand or stone pits, school house, green.

27/92 Marston and Whartons Meadow, Kings Mill Ground, Great Kings Mill Ground and part Wilsey Meadow (district) SP 523092
Apt 30.06.1843; 1215a (1212); Map 1843, 3 chns, by John Neighbour, St Clements, Oxford; waterbodies, houses (by shading), osiers, hedge ownership, field gates.

27/93 Middleton (parish) SP 529233 [Middleton Stoney]
Apt 10.12.1841; 1834a (all); Map 1840, 6 chns; turnpike roads, waterbodies, woods, parkland (in detail), engine house, ice house, pound.

27/94 Milton (hamlet in parish of Shipton under Underwood) SP 258173 [Milton-under-Wychwood]
Apt 18.01.1842; 2090a (all); Map 1838, 3 chns, by L. Myers, G. Garlick and I. Reynolds; orchards, open fields, old quarries, heath, 'Poors Allotments'; hill named; map has note of adoption proceedings.

27/95 Great Milton (including Great Milton, Little Milton, Ascot and Chilworth tythings) (parish) SP 627022
Apt 10.10.1838; 4403a (all); Map 1838-43, 4 chns, in 5 parts, (Chilworth at 10 chns; includes index); foot/b'way, waterbodies, houses, woods, plantations, withy bed, parkland (in detail), orchards, gardens, waste, ford; bridges named in gothic.

27/96 Minster Lovell (parish) SP 322112
Apt 21.11.1838; 1939a (1938); Map 1839, 6 chns, by F. Underwood, Witney; waterbodies, houses, woods, plantations.

27/97 Mongewell (parish) SU 648868 [Not listed]
Apt 05.06.1840; 1638a (1638); Map 1840, 4 chns; waterbodies, woods, parkland, fences.

27/98 Nettlebed (parish) SU 702871
Apt 26.04.1842; 1164a (1164); Map 1842, 3 chns, by John Edward Neighbour, Oxford; waterbodies, woods, plantations, hedge ownership, field boundary ownerships, boundary tree; map has note of adoption proceedings.

27/99 Newington (parish) SU 615961
Apt 26.04.1839; 872a (871); Map 1840?, 4 chns, ? by J. Neighbour, St Clements, Oxford; waterbodies, woods, hedge ownership.

27/100 Nuneham Courtenay (parish) SU 545991
Apt 31.12.1838; 2079a (all); Map 1838, 3 chns, by William Y. Freebody, 7 Furnival's Inn, London; foot/b'way, waterbodies, houses, farmyards, woods (col), plantations (col), parkland (in detail), marsh/bog, heath/moor, rock outcrops, hedge ownership (col), fence ownership, field gates, building names, field names, towpath, ox stall, cattle pens, ancient carfax conduit, park lodges, keepers lodge, venison house, deer shed, kitchen garden, brick kilns, barns, gravel pit, pound, ditches, roadside waste (col), glebe (col); legend explains boundary depiction.

27/101 Newnham Murren (parish) SU 657870 [Not listed]
Apt 26.05.1846; 1839a (1830); Map 1847, 4 chns, by Neighbour and Son, St Clements, Oxford; hill-drawing, waterbodies, houses, woods, plantations, building names, gravel pit.

27/102 Newton Purcell (parish) SP 612299
Apt 23.01.1844; 593a (all); Map 1846, 6 chns, by Messrs Davis and Saunders, Banbury; foot/b'way, public roads and paths, turnpike roads, waterbodies, houses, woods, hedge ownership (col), field gates, building names; double lines may indicate walls; coat of arms appears above map title; map has note of adoption proceedings.

27/103 Noke (parish) SP 550130
Apt 10.02.1849; 794a (794); Map 1849?, 3 chns, in 2 parts; waterbodies, houses, woods, plantations, field names, milestone.

27/104 Northmoor (parish) SP 420027
Apt 08.09.1840; 2037a (all); Map 1842, 3 chns, by Joseph Dymock; waterbodies, houses, woods, hedge ownership, field gates, building names, field names, mill; bridge named.

27/105 Nuffield (parish) SU 670880
Apt 07.02.1838; 2077a (2076); Map 1838, 4 chns, by J. Neighbour, St Clements, Oxford; hill-drawing, waterbodies, woods, plantations, hedge ownership, building names, rectory.

27/106 Oddington (parish) SP 548153
Apt 28.02.1848; 387a (1410); Map 1849, 6 chns, by Davis, Saunders and Hicks, Oxford and Banbury; railways, foot/b'way, waterbodies, houses, hedge ownership (col), field gates, landowners.

27/107 Overy (hamlet in parish of Dorchester) SU 584938
Apt 05.09.1839; 260a (?); Map 1839, 3 chns, 'copied, by direction of the landowners, from a map of Dorchester Parish', by J. Neighbour, St Clements, Oxford; waterbodies, houses (by shading), open fields, hedge ownership, field gates, field names, common; bridge named.

27/108 Oxford, St Clements (parish) SP 537061 [Not listed]
Apt 20.01.1849; 258a (all); Map 1853, 2 chns, by William Thomas Heard, Hitchin, Herts; waterbodies, road names, churchyard; bridge named.

27/109 Oxford, St Peters in the East (parish) SP 517063 [Not listed]
Apt 30.06.1851; 15a (?); Map 1852?, 2.5 chns; woods, building names; bridge named.

27/110 Oxford, St Thomas (parish) SP 502061 [Not listed]
Apt 21.03.1846; 566a (?); Map 1847, 3 chns, 1st cl, by W.H. Davies, Abingdon; construction lines, railway, foot/b'way, turnpike roads, field boundary ownerships, field gates, field names, towpath, rickyards, ford, old road, private roads.

27/111 Piddington (parish) SP 637171
Apt 20.01.1847; 2323a (2322); Map 1847, 3 chns, by Frederic Young, Bicester, Oxon; construction lines, waterbodies, woods, field gates.

27/112 Pishill (parish) SU 719896
Apt 19.05.1848; 786a (785); Map 1849?, 3 chns; waterbodies, houses, woods, plantations, heath/moor.

27/113 Pyrton, Golder, Clare and Assenden (townships or liberties in parish of Pyrton) SU 687957
Apt 20.01.1847; 4244a (?); Map 1850?, 4 chns, in 8 parts, (two parts at 3 chns; includes index); foot/b'way, waterbodies, houses, woods, plantations; apparent open field strips are bounded by solid lines.

27/114 Radcot (hamlet in parish of Langford) SU 283996
Apt 28.10.1840; 438a (all); Map 1840, 3 chns, ? by James Fidel; foot/b'way, waterbodies, woods, arable (col), grassland (col), marsh/bog, drains.

27/115 Ramsden (hamlet in parish of Shipton under Wychwood) SP 350150
Apt 22.11.1838; 902a (all); Map 1838, 3 chns, 'surveyed for the purposes of a Rate, made by H. Tuckwell Esq. of Signet', by William Y. Freebody, 7 Furnivals' Inn, London; waterbodies, houses, woods (col, named), plantations (col, named), arable (col), grassland (col), gardens (col), orchards (by annotation), heath/moor (named), rock outcrops, open fields, hedge ownership, fence ownership, field gates, building names, field names, quarries, lodge, rabbit warren; legend explains some symbols; north pointer has Prince of Wales feathers; map has note of adoption proceedings.

27/116 Little Rollright (parish) SP 292303
Apt 12.10.1848; 617a (all); Map 1849, 8 chns; foot/b'way, waterbodies, rock outcrops, standing stones (named); pictorial church.

27/117 Rotherfield Greys (parish) SU 725831
Apt 13.06.1844; 2911a (2910); Map 1844?, 6 chns, in 2 parts, (including Henley town separately at 3 chns); waterbodies, houses, woods, plantations, open fields.

27/118 Rotherfield Peppard (parish) SU 714816
Apt 07.12.1839; 2158a (2158); Map 1840?, 3 chns; waterbodies, houses, woods, common; map has note of adoption proceedings.

27/119 Sandford (parish) SP 545015 [Sandford-on-Thames]
Apt 08.09.1847; 346a (1850); Map 1849?, 3 chns; waterbodies, woods, orchards, building names.

27/120 Shelswell (parish) SP 610309
Apt 23.01.1844; 809a (all); Map 1846, 6 chns, by Messrs Davis and Saunders, Banbury; foot/b'way, turnpike roads, waterbodies, houses, woods, parkland, hedge ownership (col).

27/121 Shifford (hamlet in parish of Bampton) SP 373023
Apt 16.08.1849; 765a (all); Map 1847, 3 chns; foot/b'way, waterbodies, houses, private roads (col).

27/122 Shiplake (parish) SU 745786
Apt 09.01.1840; 2693a (2692); Map 1841?, 6 chns; hill-drawing, waterbodies, houses, woods (col), plantations (col), parkland, marsh/bog (col), building names, quarries, greens (named), heath (col), common (col); church named in gothic; map has note of adoption proceedings.

27/123 Shipton under Wychwood (township) SP 281172 [Shipton-under-Wychwood]
Apt 04.04.1839; 2418a (all); Map 1839, 3 chns; waterbodies, woods (col), plantations (col), parkland, arable (col), grassland (col), orchards,

open fields, road names, field names, open field furlong names; enclosed field boundaries coloured.

27/124 Shirburn (parish) SU 713950
Apt 22.01.1841; 2411a (2411); Map 1842, 4 chns, by G.F. Davenport, Oxford; waterbodies, houses, hedge ownership, road names.

27/125 Souldern (parish) SP 512308
Apt 18.09.1839; 1452a (all); Map 1840, 4 chns, by Richard Davis, Banbury; foot/b'way, canal with towpath, waterbodies, houses, woods, plantations, osiers, open fields, hedge ownership, fence ownership, field boundary ownerships, field gates.

27/126 Stadhampton (parish) SU 604995
Apt 19.09.1848; 621a (620); Map 1849, 3 chns, 'copied from the Parish Plan made 1838'; waterbodies, houses, woods, hedge ownership.

27/127 Standhill (hamlet in parish of Pyrton) SU 647998 [Not listed]
Apt 13.06.1839; 522a (all); Map 1839, 3 chns, 1st cl, 'the property of Jonathan Peel Esq. surveyed under the direction of Mr Bn Badcock, Oxford' by James Saunders, Kirtlington, Oxon; construction lines, foot/b'way, carriage roads, waterbodies, houses, woods (col), marsh/bog, hedge ownership, fence ownership, field gates, building names, boundary posts.

27/128 Standlake (parish) SP 393033
Apt 08.04.1842; 2496a (2495); Map 1841, 3 chns, by Joseph Dymock; waterbodies, houses, woods (named), park (named), open fields, hedge ownership, building names, road names, field names, landowners, weir, mills, pound, chapel, parsonage, gravel pit, keepers lodge, green ways (col), waste (col), orchard (by annotation), nursery (by annotation); unmapped areas are tinted pink.

27/129 Steeple Barton (parish) SP 456242
Apt 03.06.1848; 1625a (2710); Map 1849, 6 chns; foot/b'way, waterbodies, houses, woods (col); sketchy bird surmounts map title.

27/130 North Stoke cum Ipsden (parish) SU 650850
Apt 17.03.1847; 3375a (824); Map 1848, 6 chns, in 2 parts, ? by Henry Dixon; foot/b'way, private roads, waterbodies, woods, road names, heath, common.

27/131 South Stoke cum Woodcote (parish) SU 640820
Apt 26.05.1846; 3291a (3440); Map 1853?, 6 chns; waterbodies, houses, woods.

27/132 Stoke Talmage (parish) SU 681990
Apt 05.02.1840; 230a (859); Map 1842, 4 chns, by G.F. Davenport, Oxford; woods, plantations, hedge ownership. District is apportioned by holding.

27/133 Stokenchurch (parish) SU 775952
Apt 30.03.1844; 4308a (4308); Map 1842, 6 chns, by John Williams, Bicester; foot/b'way, waterbodies, woods, plantations, hedge ownership, fences, windmill (pictorial), sand or stone pit or quarry; adjacent hills and commons named; direction pointer has leafy decoration.

27/134 Swalecliffe (township) SP 380380 [Swalcliffe]
Apt 30.04.1851; 133a (1850); Map 1852, 6 chns; waterbodies, houses, woods (col), hedge ownership, landowners.

27/135 Swerford (parish) SP 370308
Apt 17.06.1842; 773a (4630); Map 1842?, [18 chns], (tithable parts only); farm names. District is apportioned by holding and fields are not shown.

27/136 Swyncombe (parish) SU 688898 [Not listed]
Apt 20.11.1839; 2647a (2646); Map 1839, 4 chns, ? by J. Neighbour, St Clements, Oxford; waterbodies, woods, plantations, parkland, hedge ownership, fence ownership.

27/137 Tackley (parish) SP 476202
Apt 13.04.1839; 2850a (2850); Map 1844, 6 chns, by Henry Dixon; foot/b'way, waterbodies; apparent open field strips are bounded by solid lines.

27/138 Tetsworth (parish) SP 683019
Apt 27.12.1839; 1173a (all); Map 1839, 6 chns; waterbodies, houses, woods; tithing named.

27/139 Thame (parish) SP 700050
Apt 21.08.1847; 830a (5310); Map 1848?, 12 chns; foot/b'way, waterbodies.

27/140 Tiddington (township in parish of Albury) SP 647045
Apt 30.09.1839; 449a (all); Map 1838, 3 chns; foot/b'way, waterbodies, houses, woods, hedge ownership, fences, field boundary ownerships, field gates.

27/141 Tusmore (parish) SP 565307 [Not listed]
Apt 31.12.1850; 71a (?); Map 1851?, 3 chns, (tithable parts only in detail); waterbodies, building names, road destinations. Apt omits some field names.

27/142 Warborough (parish) SU 601936
Apt 22.03.1844; 1673a (1673); Map 1844, 3 chns, by Neighbour and Son, Oxford; waterbodies, open fields.

27/143 Warpsgrove (parish) SU 647982
Apt 19.09.1848; 333a (460); Map 1849, 4 chns, by Moore, Warwick; waterbodies, houses, woods.

27/144 Waterstock (parish) SP 638058
Apt 19.05.1848; 653a (all); Map 1848?, 4 chns; waterbodies, woods.

27/145 Weald (township in parish of Bampton) SP 301055
Corn rent conversion, 1894; 457a (?); Map is undated tracing, 5 chns; turnpike road, road names. Apt omits land use.

27/146 Weston on the Green (parish) SP 539187 [Weston-on-the-Green]
Apt 04.02.1848; 2251a (2466); Map 1848?, 3 chns, 1st cl; construction lines, foot/b'way, public footpaths, hedge ownership, field gates.

27/147 South Weston (parish) SU 701983
Apt 07.04.1847; 478a (all); Map 1847, 3 chns, by Davis and Saunders; foot/b'way, waterbodies, houses, open fields, hedge ownership, fence ownership, field boundary ownerships, field gates, building names, landowners, rectory, mill, windmill.

27/148 Wheatfield (parish) SU 699999
Apt 21.01.1839; 779a (all); Map 1839?, 3 chns, 1st cl; construction lines, hill-drawing, waterbodies, houses, woods, hedge ownership, fence ownership, field gates, building names, rectory (named in gothic), sand or stone pit; some field boundaries appear as double lines.

27/149 Wickham (township in parish of Banbury) SP 440382 [Wykham Park]
Apt 31.12.1851; 964a (?); Map 1852, 12 chns, 'copied from Old Plans' by Davis and Saunders; waterbodies, houses, hedge ownership, fence ownership, field boundary ownerships.

27/150 Wilcote (parish) SP 371149 [Not listed]
Apt 31.10.1850; 308a (all); Map 1851?, 3 chns; woods.

27/151 Witney (except Hailey, Crawley and Curbridge) (parish) SP 357098
Apt 16.06.1840; 189a (all); Map 1840, 3 chns, by J. Underwood, Witney, litho (by R. Martin, 26 Long Acre); waterbodies, houses (by shading), plantations, fence ownership, building names, road names, rectory, grammar school, market place, hotel, staple hall, greens, public roads.

27/152 Woodeaton (parish) SP 531118
Apt 27.09.1837; 640a (639); Map 1838, 4 chns, copied 'from a map made by Bailey Bird of Norwich 1786' by John Dale, Woolvercott, Oxon; hedge ownership, field gates, field names, glebe, freeboard, common; woodland, orchard and gardens indicated by annotation.

27/153 Wootton (parish) SP 441202
Apt 12.01.1842; 984a (3720); Map 1847, 3 chns, 1st cl, by William Bryan Wood, Barnbridge, Chippenham; construction lines, foot/b'way, waterbodies, houses, hedge ownership, building names.

27/154 Over Worton (parish) SP 433286
Apt 23.06.1840; 623a (all); Map 1842?, 3 chns, by G.F. Davenport, Oxford; foot/b'way, landowners, churchyard; map is dated 1827, but may be a later copy, and is subtitled 'the property of the Revd William Wilson'.

27/155 Yarnton (parish) SP 477120
Apt 29.11.1845; 1613a (1613); Map 1844, 3 chns, by Neighbour and Son, Oxford; waterbodies, woods, open fields, hedge ownership, drains.

27/156 Yelford (parish) SP 357049
Apt 20.01.1847; 305a (all); Map 1848?, 5 chns.

Rutland

PRO IR29 and IR30 28/1-37

59 tithe districts: 97,273 acres
36 tithe commutations: 37,725 acres
15 voluntary tithe agreements, 21 compulsory tithe awards,
1 corn rent annuity

Tithe and tithe commutation

The pattern of tithe commutation in Rutland is similar to that of adjoining counties; by 1836 commutation at parliamentary enclosure had reduced the tithable extent of the county to 61 per cent of its tithe districts and about 39 per cent of its area. Although much tithe had either been commuted in the course of enclosure or was suppressed by moduses, twenty districts still remained wholly tithable at this date (Fig. 40).

Assistant tithe commissioners and local tithe agents who worked in Rutland are listed in Table 28.1 and the valuers of the county's tithe rent-charge are in Table 28.2. For a midland county, Rutland has the highest proportion (14 per cent) of districts apportioned by holding and thus without any information in the schedules of tithe apportionment on individual fields and properties. The tithe apportionments of four other districts omit some field names and in one tithe apportionment the state of cultivation column is blank.

Tithe maps

The tithe maps of Rutland are generally similar to those of the adjoining parts of its neighbouring counties and are at best neatly executed but not particularly distinguished. The only first-class map is that of Langham which is unique in that the main map is at a scale of one inch to twelve chains and there are three enlargements of detail at one inch to three chains. It is probable that the first-class seal was really intended for one of the latter. This map embraces the extremes of scale used in the county; a majority of Rutland maps are drawn at the six-chain scale, whereas less than a fifth of the maps have scales in the recommended range of one inch to three to four chains (Table 28.3). Only one map acknowledges copying but there was probably much more. For example, at Lyddington the whole district is mapped, although only a little over a tenth remained subject to tithe; it is likely that the tithe map is a copy of an existing map as it is difficult to see why landowners would have incurred the expense of so much redundant mapping.

Rutland tithe maps follow the usual midland pattern in that they portray little land use

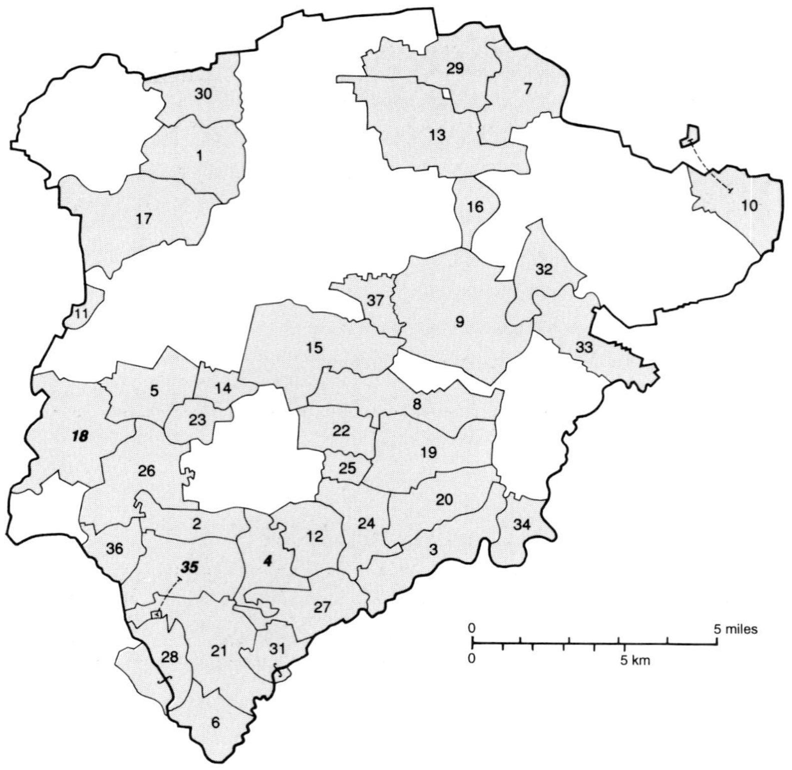

Fig. 40 Rutland: tithe district boundaries.

other than woodland (on 55 per cent of the maps). Open-field farming survived in five districts and the tithe maps of these places are valuable records of the landscape just before belated enclosure.

The only real decorative embellishment on Rutland tithe maps is the representation of some churches by pictorial symbols; these are usually stylised but that on the map of Tinwell has a plausible-looking clerestory roof.

Table 28.1. *Agreements and awards for commutation of tithes in Rutland*

Assistant commissioner/ local tithe agent	*Number of agreements**	*Number of awards*
Joseph Townsend	1	9
John Job Rawlinson	0	9
Edward Greathed	6	0
John Pickering	4	0
George Wingrove Cooke	0	2
Charles Howard	2	0
John Mee Mathew	0	1
Richard Burton Phillipson	1	0

*Computed from the number of extant reports on tithe agreements in the tithe files [PRO IR 18].

Table 28.2. *Tithe valuers and tithe map-makers in Rutland*

Name and address (in Rutland unless indicated)	*Number of districts*	*Acreage*
Tithe valuers		
Edward Arden, Morton, Lincolnshire	6	9,485
George Cuming, Easton, Northamptonshire	6	6,302
John Lacey, Oakham	4	2,151
Others [11]	20	19,787
Attributed tithe map-makers		
Charles Day, Collyweston	4	3,829
George Cuming and - Hill, Easton, Northamptonshire	3	3,458
Others [5]	6	5,066

Table 28.3. *The tithe maps of Rutland: scales and classes*

Scale in chains/inch	*All maps*		*First Class*		*Second Class*	
	Number	*Acreage*	*Number*	*Acreage*	*Number*	*Acreage*
3	4	4,521	0	0	4	4,521
4	3	2,726	0	0	3	2,726
6	21	19,201	0	0	21	19,201
7.5	1	448	0	0	1	448
8	2	3,023	0	0	2	3,023
9	3	3,022	0	0	3	3,022
12	2	4,784	1	2,785	1	1,999
TOTAL	36	37,725	1	2,785	35	34,940

Table 28.4. *The tithe maps of Rutland: dates*

	1837	*1838*	*1839*	*1840*	*1841*	*1842*	*1843*	*1844*	*1845*	*1846*	*1847*	*1848*	*1849*	*1850*	*>1850*
All maps	1	3	3	2	6	1	1	3	5	1	2	2	1	2	3
1st class	0	0	0	0	1	0	0	0	0	0	0	0	0	0	0
2nd class	1	3	3	2	5	1	1	3	5	1	2	2	1	2	3

Rutland

28/1 Ashwell (parish) SK 862137
Apt 26.10.1838; 1800a (all); Map 1838, 4 chns; foot/b'way, waterbodies, houses (by shading), boundary marks; pictorial church.

28/2 Ayston (parish) SK 860010
Apt 21.08.1849; 898a (all); Map 1850, 9 chns; woods, hedge ownership, toll gate; pictorial church; tithe area numbers may be stamped. Apt omits some field names.

28/3 Barrowden (parish) SK 943003
Apt 30.09.1842; 2074a (all); Map 1844, 3 chns; waterbodies, open fields (named).

28/4 Bisbrooke (parish) SP 881998
Apt 02.03.1846; 2a (720); Map (drawn on Apt) 1851?, 6 chns, (tithable parts only); pictorial church.

28/5 Brook (township in parish of Oakham) SK 846057 [Brooke]
Apt 26.03.1841; 1341a (all); Map 1841?, 8 chns; waterbodies, pit, roadside waste; it is unclear why both long and short pecked lines are used.

28/6 Caldecott (parish) SP 870941
Apt 24.08.1844; 63a (1440); Map 1849, 6 chns, copied from the enclosure map by Messrs Hayward, Northampton; foot/b'way, windmill; red band surrounds the tithable parts. Apt omits land use.

28/7 Clipsham (parish) SK 969157
Apt 26.10.1838; 1655a (all); Map 1839?, 6 chns; foot/b'way, waterbodies, woods (col), plantations (col); meaning of pink band is unclear; dot-dash lines indicate boundary between ownerships, dashed lines indicate boundary within ownerships.

28/8 Edith Weston (parish) SK 931051
Apt 28.11.1846; 505a (1723); Map 1847, 6 chns, by Thos S. Cundy, Empingham, Rutland; woods.

28/9 Empingham (parish) SK 950081
Corn rent conversion, 1927; ?a (2780); Map 1927, OS 1:2500 annotated with tithe areas. Apt does not have a schedule of areas.

28/10 Essendine (parish) TF 049126
Apt 19.12.1844; 1527a (all); Map 1845, 6 chns, by Adam Murray and Son; foot/b'way, waterbodies, woods, castle mound.

28/11 Flitteris Park (district in parish of Oakham) SK 825085 [Flitteriss Park Farm]
Apt 24.12.1839; 219a (all); Map 1841?, 6 chns; waterbodies, houses.

28/12 Glaston (parish) SK 901004
Apt 28.08.1840; 1145a (all); Map 1841, 6 chns, by Charles Day, Collyweston; waterbodies, woods, bridle-roads.

28/13 Greetham (parish) SK 940144
Apt 31.10.1838; 448a (2800); Map 1839, 7.5 chns, by John Lacey, (tithable parts only in detail, tinted); foot/b'way, woods, hedge, landowners, windmill (pictorial), toll bar, Great North Road, pit, field acreages, public carriage road; pictorial church. Apt omits some field names.

28/14 Gunthorpe (township in parish of Oakham) SK 870057
Apt 18.05.1843; 463a (all); Map 1844, 6 chns; hedge ownership, field acreages. Apt omits field names.

28/15 Hambleton (parish) SK 900071 [Not listed]
Apt 12.09.1844; 1155a (1154); Map 1845, [6 chns]; foot/b'way, woods, hedge ownership, field gates, landowners, churchyard, township boundary, field acreages; green band surrounds one estate. Apt omits field names.

28/16 Horn (parish) SK 953118 [Not listed]
Apt 31.10.1838; 857a (all); Map 1838, 9 chns; Great North Road; the district is apportioned as a single unit, without any occupation or land use information; the title announces that the district is the property of Lord Barham; the north pointer points south.

28/17 Langham (township in parish of Oakham) SK 843111
Apt 26.03.1841; 2785a (3250); Map 1841?, 12 chns, in 4 parts, (includes three 3-chn enlargements of detail, one of which is 1st cl); waterbodies, houses, fords.

28/18 Leighfield Forest (extra-parochial place) SK 823037 [Not listed]
Apt 13.08.1851; 85a (?); Map 1852, 4 chns, in 2 parts, (tithable parts only); foot/b'way, woods, hedge ownership, field gates, landowners, field acreages; title is on a pre-printed label.

28/19 North Luffenham (parish) SK 943032
Apt 20.08.1844; 1999a (all); Map 1845, 6 chns; open fields (named), mill, well; enclosed land is tinted green.

28/20 South Luffenham (parish) SK 943018
Apt 19.12.1844; 1418a (all); Map 1845, 6 chns; waterbodies, open fields (named), windmill, watermill; enclosed land is tinted green.

28/21 Lyddington (except part of Thorpe by Water) (parish) SP 870970
Apt 05.06.1846; 266a (2020); Map 1848, 6 chns; foot/b'way, waterbodies, stone pit, windmill; tithable lands are tinted red; one tithable and all the unnumbered fields are named; dash-dot boundaries are within holdings, dashed boundaries are between holdings.

28/22 Lyndon (parish) SK 912042
Apt 18.01.1840; 902a (902); Map 1840, 6 chns; waterbodies, woods.

28/23 Martinsthorpe (parish) SK 865045
Apt 30.08.1844; 534a (all); Map 1844, 6 chns, by Charles Day, Collyweston; plantations.

28/24 Morcott (parish) SK 920010
Apt 18.12.1839; 1344a (all); Map 1841, 6 chns, by Cuming and W. Arden; rays on landmarks outside the district.

28/25 Pilton (parish) SK 914030
Apt 13.03.1838; 333a (all); Map 1838, 3 chns; woods, field names, open fields (col), ox-bow lakes, old enclosures (green); pictorial church. Apt omits some field names.

28/26 Ridlington (parish) SK 842055
Apt 27.06.1839; 1999a (2027); Map 1841?, 12 chns; woods, tithe-free lands.

28/27 Seaton (except part of Thorpe by Water) (parish) SP 905982
Apt 22.09.1846; 1434a (?); Map 1847, 3 chns, by Cuming and Hill, Easton, near Stamford; railway, plantations, open fields, field boundary ownerships, field names, rectory, meadow, cow pasture, tithe-free land (yellow), old enclosed land (green); unfenced roads are shown by uncased sienna band.

28/28 Stoke Dry (parish) SP 851961
Apt 11.12.1841; 1419a (?); Map 1842, 6 chns, by Charles Day, Collyweston; waterbodies, woods, milestone (by symbol, with distances), ox-bow lake, ford; tree symbols are 'on their side' relative to the title and writing.

28/29 Stretton (parish) SK 946165
Apt 02.11.1837; 1935a (all); Map 1837, 6 chns; waterbodies, houses (by shading), woods, building names, Great North Road, field acreages; map has signatures adopting it; it is unclear why three fields are tinted pink.

28/30 Teigh (parish) SK 866158
Apt 20.10.1842; 1267a (all); Map 1843, 9 chns; foot/b'way, canal with towpath, ford, glebe (col).

28/31 Thorpe by Water (district in parish of Seaton and Lyddington) SP 891971
Apt 05.06.1846; 680a (?); Map 1848, 3 chns, by Cuming and Hill, Easton, Stamford; railway, waterbodies, open fields, field boundary ownerships, field names; it is unclear why some fields are tinted.

28/32 Tickencote (parish) SK 980098
Apt 07.09.1838; 1257a (1256); Map 1839?, 6 chns; foot/b'way, glebe, woods, mansion house, Great North Road, stiles; pictorial church; map is described as 'Boundary Sketch', and omits fields and some

buildings and roads. District is apportioned by holding; Apt omits land use.

28/33 Tinwell (parish) SK 992072
Apt 19.12.1844; 1682a (1651); Map 1846, 8 chns, by William Higgs, Land Agent, Burghley; woods, road gates, glebe (col); pictorial church; band separates Ingthorpe, which has tithe district numbers but is annotated 'Tithe-free'.

28/34 Tixover (parish) SK 974009
Apt 31.08.1849; 841a (all); Map 1850, 4 chns, by Messrs Hayward, Northampton; foot/b'way, right of road, waterbodies, houses, woods, plantations, parkland, hedge ownership.

28/35 Uppingham (parish) SP 860998
Apt 24.07.1851; 59a (1210); Map 1853?, 6 chns, (tithable parts only); woods.

28/36 Wardley (parish) SK 839003
Apt 03.09.1844; 731a (all); Map 1845, 6 chns, by Charles Day, Collyweston; foot/b'way, woods, tollgate.

28/37 Wing (parish) SK 922088
Apt 03.11.1838; 603a (all); Map 1840?, 6 chns; glebe; map shows field boundaries and roads only. Apt omits some field names.

Shropshire

PRO IR29 and IR30 29/1-369

454 tithe districts: 861,329 acres
369 tithe commutations: 762,812 acres
205 voluntary tithe agreements, 164 compulsory tithe awards

Tithe and tithe commutation

In Shropshire 81 per cent of tithe districts were still subject to payment of tithes in 1836 (Fig. 41). Ninety-eight districts were wholly tithable; as usual in counties where pastoral farming was important, the main reason for tithe exemption (in 58 per cent of districts) was a modus payment in lieu of tithes. Merger of tithes in the land (affecting 21 per cent of tithable districts) and exemption by prescription were also significant in Shropshire.

Assistant tithe commissioners and local tithe agents who worked in Shropshire are listed in Table 29.1 and the valuers of the county's tithe rent-charge in Table 29.2.

The tithe apportionment for Cardiston is most unusual in that it records the occupations of the district's tithe impropriators which include three widows, a mason and an innkeeper, and tells that it was the local custom in tithing wheat to set out every eleventh rather than every tenth stook 'in consideration of the trouble of the farmer in setting it out in stooks and not in single sheaves'.

Tithe maps

The county of Shropshire lies between the large concentration of first-class maps centred on Monmouthshire to the south and a smaller one centred on Lancashire in the north. Only eleven Shropshire maps (3 per cent) are sealed as first class, a proportion similar to Montgomeryshire to the west and Staffordshire to the east. Construction lines have been noted on only two second-class maps, but thirteen maps acknowledge copying. Shropshire tithe maps are drawn at a variety of scales from one inch to two chains to one inch to twelve chains; only 17 per cent are in the recommended scale range of one inch to three to four chains, whereas the most favoured scale in this county was the six-chain (57 per cent of maps). Sixteen second-class maps are lithographed.

Shropshire follows a similar pattern to Cheshire and the adjoining Welsh counties in that woodland (on 87 per cent of maps) and parkland (on 38 per cent) are well recorded but agricultural land uses are poorly depicted; few maps show arable, grass, or gardens, though 16 per cent portray orchards. The Madeley map is unusual in that it records the

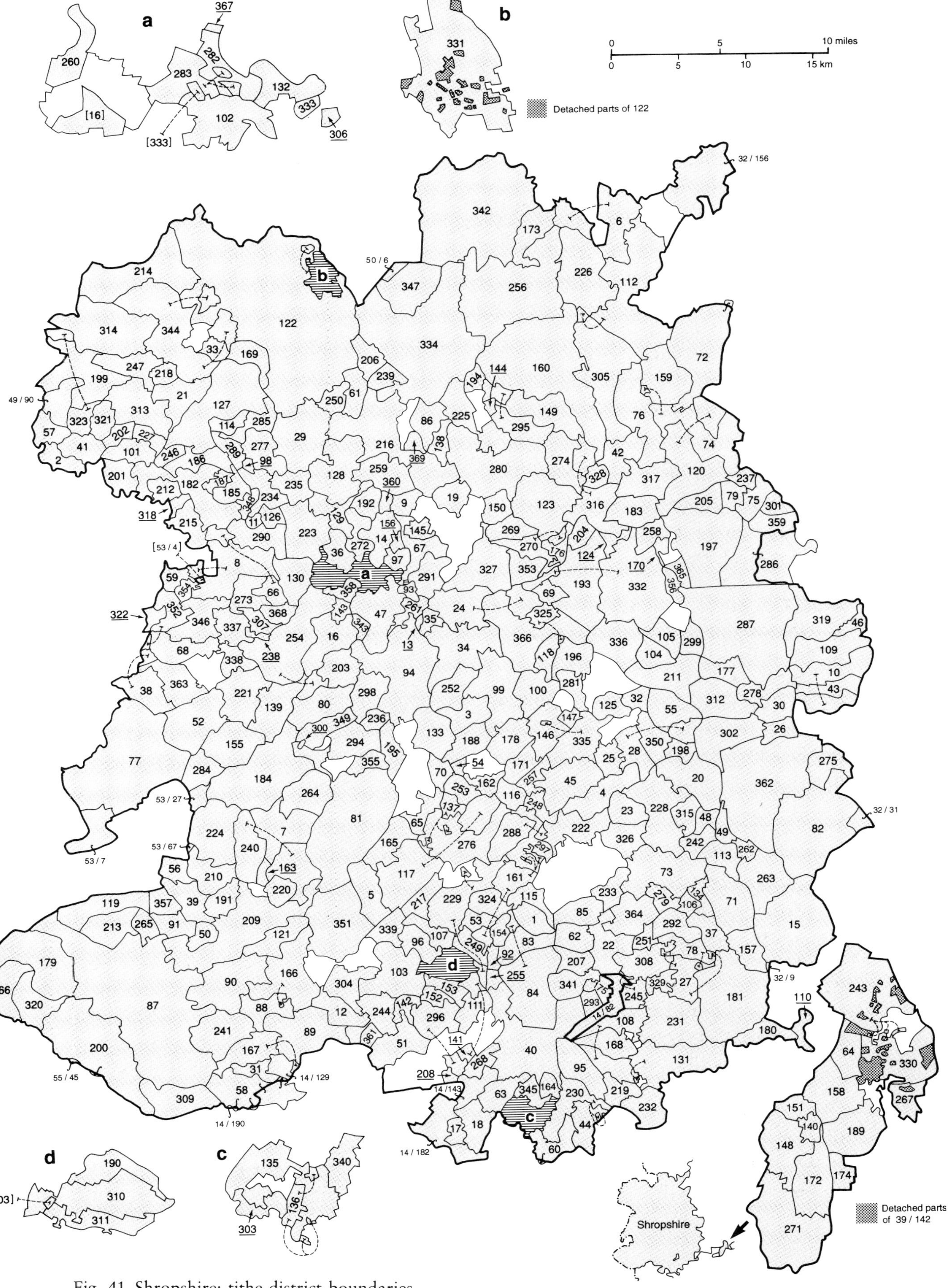

Fig. 41 Shropshire: tithe district boundaries.

species of parkland trees; tree types are normally only noted on tithe maps when they were important landmarks, as for example, on boundaries. Field boundary ownership is recorded better than land use on Shropshire tithe maps (on 17 per cent of maps) and 27 per cent of maps show field gates, a very high proportion. Although Shropshire contained a then heavily industrialised area around Wellington and the Severn gorge, this is only partly reflected on the tithe maps; the apportionment but not the map for Little Dawley records 'ancient coal mounts' and the same applies to the 'furnaces, coke banks, cinder hills, and pit mounts' at Stirchley. The tithe map of Oreton depicts no fewer than forty limekilns! A number of maps record archaeological features, including castles (ten maps), 'camps', (five maps), tumuli (eleven maps), Offa's Dyke and Watling Street.

Only 119 Shropshire tithe maps (32 per cent) in the Public Record Office collection can be attributed to a particular map-maker. The most prolific of these was Samuel Ashdown of Uppington who made thirty maps; his nearest rival, Charles Mickleburgh of Montgomery, produced only eleven. All but two attributed maps are by Shropshire map-makers or by surveyors based within easy reach of the county. The exceptions are maps made by the Reeds of Stockton-on-Tees, Durham, whose work includes the tithe map of the parish of Ellesmere, one of the largest tithe districts in Shropshire.

It was usual in Shropshire for parishes to be divided into townships but often townships were grouped to form single tithe districts so that the 'tithe map' for such districts often consists of one plan for each township, plus an index to the various parts. The extreme example of this is Ellesmere tithe district which consisted of twenty-three townships, each with its own plan. Sometimes the scales of the various plans differ which suggests re-use of earlier maps, whereas sometimes the cartographic style differs, implying mixed authorship within a single district which is again *prima facie* evidence of copying.

Shropshire tithe maps are not particularly decorative or colourful, although colour is sometimes used for woodland, landownership, glebe, and tithe-free land. Four maps have decorated cartouches; that of Baschurch depicts two figures at leisure in the countryside and that of Warley a fish and anchor. A few maps have decorated borders, compass roses and north pointers, the latter often with Prince of Wales's feathers and a diadem.

Table 29.1. *Agreements and awards for commutation of tithes in Shropshire*

Assistant commissioner/ local tithe agent	*Number of agreements**	*Number of awards*
George Wingrove Cooke	0	58
Charles Howard	8	36
George Ashdown	42	0
Gelinger C. Symons	34	0
Charles Pym	5	28
Richard Burton Phillipson	30	0
John Mee Mathew	9	20
Henry Pilkington	20	0
John Job Rawlinson	0	17
John Holder	11	0
Horace William Meteyard	11	0
John Pickering	10	0
Thomas Hoskins	9	0
N. S. Meryweather	5	0
Thomas Sudworth	5	0
Joseph Townsend	0	5
John Penny	4	0
Charles Warner	4	0
James Drage Merest	1	0

*Computed from the number of extant reports on tithe agreements in the tithe files [PRO IR 18].

Table 29.2. *Tithe valuers and tithe map-makers in Shropshire*

Name and address (in Shropshire unless indicated)	*Number of districts*	*Acreage*
Tithe valuers		
William Wyley, The Vineyard, Wellington	55	113,942
Timotheus Bird, Whistone Priory	54	105,706
John Middleton Ashdown, Uppington	34	65,929
John, Robert and Richard Tench, Ludlow	29	46,098
William Eyton, Gonsal, Condover	22	65,514
William Story, Shrewsbury	15	24,376
Thomas Jones Griffithes, Bishops Castle	12	15,472
Jeremiah Mathews, Kidderminster, Worcestershire	11	7,725
Others [63]	137	318,050
Attributed tithe map-makers		
Samuel H. Ashdown, Uppington	30	58,106
Charles Mickleburgh, Montgomery	11	32,176
J. Treasure, Newport	8	30,104
William Story, Shrewsbury	8	14,647
Samuel Groom, Wem	6	20,327
James Bourn junior, Cleobury Mortimer	6	13,463
Issac Porter, Oswestry	5	7,088
Others [30]	45	129,582

Table 29.3. *The tithe maps of Shropshire: scales and classes*

Scale in chains/inch	All maps		First Class		Second Class	
	Number	Acreage	Number	Acreage	Number	Acreage
>3	2	698	0	0	2	698
3	40	120,139	10	29,190	30	90,949
4	22	30,971	1	4,804	21	26,167
5	5	3,459	0	0	5	3,459
6	209	387,392	0	0	209	387,392
6.67, 7, 7.5	4	14,581	0	0	4	14,581
8	25	67,271	0	0	25	67,271
9	46	97,568	0	0	46	97,568
9.5, 10	6	14,354	0	0	6	14,354
12	10	26,379	0	0	10	26,379
TOTAL	369	762,812	11	33,994	358	728,818

Table 29.4. *The tithe maps of Shropshire: dates*

	<1837	1837	1838	1839	1840	1841	1842	1843	1844	1845	1846	1847	1848	>1848
All maps	3	10	28	48	42	27	37	21	20	33	20	27	28	20
1st class	0	0	2	4	1	0	1	0	1	1	0	0	1	0
2nd class*	3	10	26	44	41	27	36	21	19	32	20	27	27	20

*Five second-class tithe maps of Shropshire in the Public Record Office collection are undated.

Shropshire

29/1 Abdon (parish) SO 560860
Apt 06.08.1846; 1134a (all); Map 1848?, 6 chns; hill-drawing, waterbodies, houses, woods, plantations, hedges, field gates, building names.

29/2 Abertanat (township in parish of Llanyblodwel) SJ 233255 [Aber Tanat]
Apt 03.11.1838; 1103a (?); Map 1841, 8 chns; waterbodies, woods, building names.

29/3 Acton Burnell and Acton Pigott (township) SJ 537020
Apt 13.07.1843; 1605a (1605); Map 1845, 6 chns; waterbodies, woods, plantations, parkland, building names, bath, lodge.

29/4 Acton Round (parish) SO 637958
Apt 29.09.1838; 2127a (2126); Map 1839?, 8 chns; foot/b'way, waterbodies, woods, field gates, building names.

29/5 Acton Scott (parish) SO 456890
Apt 20.09.1838; 1889a (1889); Map 1839, 4 chns, by W. Tench, Hereford; hill-drawing, foot/b'way, waterbodies, houses, farmyards, woods, plantations, parkland, orchards, gardens (col), heath/moor, rock outcrops, fences, field boundary ownerships, field gates, building names, quarry, common, glebe (purple). Apt omits some field names.

29/6 Adderley (parish) SJ 665390
Apt 26.10.1837; 3939a (all); Map 1840?, 6 chns; foot/b'way, canal, waterbodies, houses, woods, parkland, marl pits.

29/7 Adston, Medlicott and Wentnor (townships in parish of Wentner) SO 391932 [Adstone]
Apt 22.02.1845; 2886a (?); Map 1846, 6 chns; waterbodies, woods, hedges.

29/8 Alberbury, otherwise Alberbury and Wattlesborough, Eyton, Benthall and Shrawardine (townships in parish of Alberbury) SJ 372147
Apt 26.01.1843; 3144a (?); Map 1842, 6 chns; hill-drawing, foot/b'way, waterbodies, woods, parkland, orchards, fences, fish weir, limekilns, township boundaries (col) and names.

29/9 Albrighton (township in parish of Shrewsbury, St Mary) SJ 810040
Apt 19.04.1844; 755a (750); Map 1845?, 7 chns; waterbodies, woods, orchards, building names.

29/10 Albrighton (parish) SJ 497181
Apt 27.09.1845; 3424a (3424); Map 1846, 9.5 chns, by Geo. Taylor, Wolverhampton; hill-drawing, railway, waterbodies, woods, building names, mill, railway station, brickyard; leaf pattern border.

29/11 Alderton (township in parish of Great Ness) SJ 382173 [Not listed]
Apt 28.02.1849; 196a (?); Map 1850?, 6 chns; waterbodies.

29/12 Aldon and part of Rowton and Broome (township in parish of Stokesay) SO 432798
Apt 29.10.1844; 1632a (?); Map 1845, 6 chns; hill-drawing, woods, limeworks, township boundaries.

29/13 Alkmere (township in parish of Shrewsbury, St Chad) SJ 503092 [Not listed]
Apt 24.04.1844; 212a (all); Map 1845?, 6 chns; woods.

29/14 Almond Park, Great and Little Berwick and Newton (township in parish of Shrewsbury St Mary) SJ 479158
Apt 19.08.1846; 1610a (all); Map 1847, 6 chns; hill-drawing, railway, waterbodies, woods, plantations, parkland, building names, almshouses.

29/15 Alveley (parish) SO 773858
Apt 23.12.1846; 1775a (6788); Map 1849, 6 chns, by John Davies, Stourbridge, (tithable parts only); foot/b'way, waterbodies, building names, landowners, inn, county stone.

29/16 Arscott, the Hamlets (Onslow, Moathall, Woodhall, Panson and Little Hanwood), Cruckmeole, Plealey, Sibberscott and Shorthill (townships in parish of Pontesbury) SJ 435135
Apt 14.10.1837; 2743a (?); Map 1840?, 3 chns, 1st cl, in 2 parts; construction lines, foot/b'way, waterbodies, woods, orchards, hedge ownership, fences, field gates, building names, field acreages.

29/17 Ashford Bowdler (parish) SO 515705
Apt 29.10.1849; 585a (575); Map 1850, 3 chns, by Herbert Evans, Ludlow; foot/b'way, waterbodies, houses, woods, parkland, orchards, field boundary ownerships, field gates, weir.

29/18 Ashford Carbonell (parish) SO 530710
Apt 06.05.1846; 1476a (all); Map 1845?, 6 chns; foot/b'way, waterbodies, houses, woods, parkland, weirs.

29/19 Astley (township or chapelry in parish of Shrewsbury, St Mary) SJ 531186
Apt 16.11.1837; 1196a (all); Map 1837, 6 chns, (tinted); foot/b'way, waterbodies, houses, woods, plantations, parkland, fences, field gates, building names.

29/20 Astley Abbotts (parish) SO 707964 [Astley Abbots]
Apt 13.03.1841; 3228a (3228); Map 1841?, 6 chns; waterbodies, woods (col), plantations (col), parkland, building names, mill, ice house.

29/21 Aston, Hisland and Wotton (township in parish of Oswestry) SJ 328274 [Not listed]
Apt 28.02.1837; 2191a (all); Map 1838?, 12 chns; hill-drawing, canal, waterbodies, woods, building names.

29/22 Aston Botterell (parish) SO 636841
Apt 31.01.1838; 2238a (all); Map 1838, 6 chns, 'from various surveys', by Saml H. Ashdown, Uppington, Shrewsbury; waterbodies, woods.

29/23 Aston Eyre (township in parish of Morville) SO 650940
Apt 30.06.1840; 1300a (?); Map 1841, 6 chns; foot/b'way, waterbodies, houses, woods, plantations, building names.

29/24 Atcham (parish) SJ 534100
Apt 02.07.1846; 3763a (3762); Map 1848?, 6 chns; foot/b'way, canal, waterbodies, houses, farmyards, woods, parkland; urn, sheaf of corn and bird's head appear below title.

29/25 Atterley and Walton (township in parish of Much Wenlock) SO 640980
Apt 31.12.1846; 904a (?); Map 1847, 10 chns; foot/b'way, houses, woods; meaning of green tint is unclear.

29/26 Badger (parish) SO 769998
Apt 17.02.1837; 920a (all); Map 1837, 3 chns, by Billingsley Morris, Birmingham; foot/b'way, waterbodies, houses, woods, plantations, arable, grassland, orchards, gardens, heath/moor, hedge ownership, fences, building names, bird house, boat house, rectory, glebe (with acreages).

29/27 Bardley and Harcourt (township in parish of Stottesdon) SO 691813 [Not listed]
Apt 12.11.1840; 1800a (?); Map 1841, 6 chns, by James Bourn junr, Cleobury Mortimer, Salop, 'copied from maps in the posession of the landowners'; waterbodies, houses, woods, parkland, quarry, field acreages.

29/28 Barrow (parish) SO 656985
Apt 22.11.1838; 1332a (3013); Map 1838, 9 chns; waterbodies, houses, woods, building names, obelisk.

29/29 Baschurch, Boreatton, Birch, Newtown, Marehouse, Stanwardine in the Fields, Weston, Lullingfield and Stanwardine in the Wood (townships in parish of Baschurch) SJ 411242
Apt 11.08.1843; 4837a (?); Map 1844, 6 chns, ? by Wm. Story; canal, waterbodies, woods, field boundary ownerships, field gates, drains, township boundaries (col) and names; below the title is a sketch of a man and woman at leisure in the country.

29/30 Beckbury (parish) SJ 769017
Apt 02.04.1839; 1321a (1343); Map 1839?, 6 chns; waterbodies, woods.

29/31 Bedstone (parish) SO 363759
Apt 08.02.1843; 777a (all); Map 1839, 6 chns; foot/b'way, waterbodies, houses, woods, plantations, arable, grassland, orchards, field gates,

building names, sand or stone pit; decorative coloured compass rose.

29/32 Benthall (parochial chapelry) SJ 661026
Apt 22.03.1844; 819a (824); Map 1844, 6 chns; foot/b'way, waterbodies, woods (named), mill; bridge named.

29/33 Berghill (township in parish of Whittington) SJ 354307
Apt 26.10.1837; 685a (?); Map 1837, 4 chns; canal, waterbodies, woods.

29/34 Berrington (parish) SJ 532070
Apt 09.04.1844; 3521a (3520); Map 1840, 6 chns, in 6 parts, (includes index); hill-drawing, foot/b'way, waterbodies, woods, building names, road names, sand or stone pit, rectory, boundary stones, workhouse, avenue of trees, ornamental ground, Roman road, township boundaries.

29/35 Betton (township in parish of Shrewsbury, St Chad) SJ 512091
Apt 28.01.1842; 500a (all); Map 1843?, 9 chns; waterbodies, woods; scale bar gives the scale as 8 chns, but has been corrected to '9 chains'.

29/36 Bicton cum Calcot (township in parish of Shrewsbury, St Chad) SJ 444147
Apt 31.03.1843; 1147a (all); Map 1845?, 6 chns; foot/b'way, waterbodies, woods, plantations, building names; bridge named.

29/37 Billingsley (parish) SO 715845
Apt 28.02.1839; 1285a (all); Map 1837, 6 chns, by Saml H. Ashdown, Uppington, Shrewsbury; hill-drawing, turnpike roads, waterbodies, woods, plantations, field boundary ownerships, field gates, building names. Apt omits land use.

29/38 Bin Weston (district in parish of Worthen) SJ 299045 [Binweston]
Apt 14.03.1843; 2231a (?); Map 1844, 6 chns; foot/b'way, woods, plantations, hedges, field gates, building names, mill, drains.

29/39 Bishops Castle (borough and township) SO 321886 [Bishop's Castle]
Apt 17.11.1842; 1633a (all); Map 1843, 9 chns, by Charles Mickleburgh, Montgomery; hill-drawing, foot/b'way, turnpike roads (named), waterbodies, houses, woods (named), plantations, fences, field gates, building names, windmill, quarries, dog kennel, tumulus, common; built-up part generalised; hill named.

29/40 Bitterley (parish) SO 571760
Apt 14.02.1839; 6592a (6591); Map 1840?, 7 chns, in 2 parts; hill-drawing, waterbodies, houses, woods, parkland, rock outcrops, field gates, building names, watermills (by symbol), pound, boundary stones, machine, township boundaries (col), tithe-free areas (green), avenue of trees, boundary marks.

29/41 Blodwell (township in parish of Llanyblodwell) SJ 252235 [Not listed]
Apt 10.08.1839; 1680a (?); Map 1840, 6 chns; waterbodies, woods, plantations, building names, landowners, old river course; bridge named.

29/42 Bolas Magna (parish) SJ 660215 [Great Bolas]
Apt 28.02.1837; 1845a (1845); Map 1836, 9 chns; waterbodies, drains. Apt has cropping information.

29/43 Bonninghall (parish) SJ 810028 [Boningale]
Apt 28.09.1837; 1003a (all); Map 1837, 9 chns; hill-drawing, waterbodies, houses, woods, fences, field gates, building names.

29/44 Boraston and Whatmore (township in parish of Burford) SO 613708
Apt 28.03.1840; 1386a (all); Map 1839, 3 chns, 1st cl, by James Webb, Worcester; construction lines, canal with towpath, houses, woods, fences, field boundary ownerships, field gates, building names, mill; map has note that it was exhibited at an apportionment appeal meeting.

29/45 Bourton and Callaughton (township in parish of Much Wenlock) SO 610967
Apt 31.12.1846; 3175a (?); Map 1847, 6 chns; waterbodies, houses, woods (named), field boundary ownerships, building names, township boundary.

29/46 Boscobel (extra-parochial place) SJ 830077 [Not listed]
Apt 18.09.1845; 19a (600); Map 1847, 4 chns; waterbodies, woods, field gates, building names, landowners, 'Royal Oak'.

29/47 Brace Meole otherwise Meole Brace (parish) SJ 474101
Apt 26.01.1844; 2488a (?); Map 1843, 6 chns; hill-drawing, foot/b'way, waterbodies, woods, plantations, parkland, marsh/bog (grey), field gates, building names, mills, boundary stones, ferries, township boundaries (col).

29/48 Bridgnorth, St Leonard (parish) SO 710932 [Not listed]
Apt 05.12.1840; 497a (500); Map 1840, 6 chns; waterbodies, hedges, fences, building names, road names, riverside towpath; built-up part generalised.

29/49 Bridgnorth, St Mary Magdalen (parish) SO 722923 [Not listed]
Apt 25.03.1840; 532a (531); Map 1840, 6 chns; woods, arable, grassland, hedges, building names, road names, mill; built-up part generalised.

29/50 Brockton (township in parish of North Lydbury) SO 330861
Apt 24.08.1840; 700a (all); Map 1841, 6 chns, in 2 parts, (includes 3-chn enlargement of detail); foot/b'way, waterbodies, woods, plantations, hedges, field boundary ownerships, building names, quarries.

29/51 Bromfield (parish) SO 474774
Apt 07.03.1846; 6113a (7174); Map 1846?, 6 chns; waterbodies, houses, woods, field gates, building names, landowners, racecourse, demense lands (pink), township boundaries (col).

29/52 Bromlow (quarter or district in parish of Worthen) SJ 330015
Apt 30.06.1843; 3682a (?); Map 1848?, 3 chns, in 6 parts, (includes 12-chn index); waterbodies, woods, plantations, rock outcrops, field boundary ownerships, field gates, building names, mill.

29/53 Broncroft (township in parish of Diddlebury) SO 544866
Apt 27.09.1841; 795a (?); Map 1843?, 6 chns; waterbodies, houses, woods, orchards, field gates, building names.

29/54 Broome (township and district in parish of Cardington) SO 524981
Apt 13.09.1844; 189a (?); Map 1848, 8 chns; waterbodies, woods.

29/55 Broseley (parish) SJ 688016
Apt 27.04.1838; 1913a (all); Map 1840, 3 chns, litho (by B. Hill, Colemore Row, Birmingham); foot/b'way, turnpike roads, canal with towpath, waterbodies, woods, plantations, orchards, fences, building names, road names, windmill, china factory, ferries, ruins, iron foundry, meeting house, rectory, 'cholera ground', greens; bridge named.

29/56 Broughton (township in parish of Bishops Castle) SO 310910 [Lower Broughton]
Apt 03.12.1846; 855a (?); Map 1847, 6 chns, by Charles Mickleburgh, Montgomery; foot/b'way, turnpike roads and gate, waterbodies, woods, hedges, field boundary ownerships, field gates, building names, pound, boundary trees; scale suggests that map is drawn at both 6 chns and 10 chns; direction pointer has diadem, Prince of Wales' feathers and 'Ich Dien'.

29/57 Bryn (township in parish of Llanyblodwell) SJ 229247
Apt 24.08.1839; 1118a (?); Map 1840, 6 chns; waterbodies, woods. Apt omits some field names.

29/58 Bucknell (parish) SO 350743
Apt 19.06.1840; 3739a (?); Map 1840, 6 chns, by Walter Tench, Hereford; foot/b'way, turnpike roads, toll gate, waterbodies, houses, woods, plantations, orchards, rock outcrops, field boundary ownerships, field gates, building names, quarries, old river course, common; hill named.

29/59 Bulthey (township in parish of Alberbury) SJ 315136 [Bulthy]
Apt 18.12.1839; 720a (?); Map 1840, 6 chns; hill-drawing, waterbodies, woods; hill named.

29/60 Burford (township) SO 591691
Apt 30.06.1840; 1511a (all); Map 1845?, 4 chns; turnpike roads, toll gates, canal with towpath, waterbodies, houses, woods, parkland, orchards, field gates, building names, mill.

29/61 Burlton (township in parish of Loppington) SJ 459264
Apt 12.02.1838; 1324a (?); Map 1840?, 6 chns, by S. Groom; waterbodies, woods, plantations, orchards, drains.

29/62 Burwarton (parish) SO 612850
Apt 17.10.1838; 1240a (all); Map 1841?, 6 chns, in two parts (includes two small enlargements of detail); hill-drawing, waterbodies, woods, parkland, field gates, coal pit.

29/63 Cainham (parish) SO 549731 [Caynham]
Apt 21.12.1846; 2529a (2529); Map 1848?, 6 chns; hill-drawing, railway, turnpike roads, waterbodies, houses, woods, parkland, orchards, field gates, building names, chapel, limeworks, camp, mill, turnpike gates, limekilns, coal mines (?), township boundary.

29/64 Cakemore (township in parish of Halesowen) SO 985865 [Not listed]
Apt 27.02.1841; 548a (?); Map 1845, 6 chns, in 2 parts, (includes 3-chn enlargement of detail); waterbodies.

29/65 Cardington, Lydley, Comley, Botwyle, Enchmarsh and Wilson, otherwise Willstone (townships in parish of Cardington) SO 504951
Apt 02.11.1843; 1519a (?), (tithable parts only); Map 1845, 6 chns; foot/b'way, waterbodies, woods, plantations, orchards, hedges, field gates, glebe.

29/66 Cardiston (parish) SJ 392121 [Cardeston]
Apt 17.09.1846; 2401a (2400); Map 1847?, 6 chns, in 2 parts, (including 2-chn enlargement of glebe); hill-drawing, foot/b'way, waterbodies, houses, woods, plantations, heath/moor, building names, windmill. Apt gives occupations of Impropriators, including three widows, and one each of labourer, mason and innkeeper.

29/67 Castle Ward Within and Castle Foregate (township in parish of Shrewsbury St Mary) SJ 504146
Apt 31.03.1849; 207a (?); Map 1851?, 6 chns, in 2 parts, (includes 3-chn enlargement of detail); hill-drawing, railways and station, foot/b'way, turnpike roads, toll gate, canal, canal buildings, union wharf, waterbodies, building names, road names, Free schools, old factory, tower, castle, castle yard, cattle market, cheese market, infirmary, county goal, tithe-merged land; area covered by enlargement is tinted green on main map, and its scale is erroneously stated as 1 chn.

29/68 Cause, Wallop and Forest (townships in parishes of Westbury, St Julian and St Alkmond) SJ 312075 [Not listed]
Apt 31.07.1839; 1988a (?); Map 1840?, 9 chns; turnpike roads, woods, building names, castle, township boundaries (col).

29/69 Charlton (township in parish of Wrockwardine) SJ 600110
Apt 30.04.1838; 714a (?); Map 1837, 8 chns, by Saml H. Ashdown, Uppington, Shrewsbury.

29/70 Chatwell (township in parish of Cardington) SO 512977 [Not listed]
Apt 30.06.1840; 775a (?); Map 1838, 6 chns; foot/b'way, waterbodies, woods, plantations, quarry.

29/71 Chelmarsh (parish) SO 725871
Apt 09.10.1837; 3260a (all); Map 1838, 9 chns; foot/b'way, waterbodies, houses, woods, orchards, fences, field gates, building names, vicarage, manor house.

29/72 Cheswardine (parish) SJ 725291
Apt 21.03.1842; 5789a (5723); Map 1840, 3 chns, in 5 parts, by J. Treasure, Newport, (includes 21-chn index); foot/b'way, canal with towpath, reservoir, waterbodies, woods, plantations, parkland, heath/moor, building names, mills, drains, common.

29/73 Chetton (except Loughton) (parish) SO 678898
Apt 23.11.1838; 3921a (3921); Map 1838, 6 chns; waterbodies, woods, plantations, orchards, building names, rectory, fountain, sand or stone pit, mill, glebe (col), ownerships (col).

29/74 Chetwynd (parish) SJ 723218 [Not listed]
Apt 09.05.1838; 3803a (3803); Map 1838, 4 chns, in 2 parts, by J. Treasure, Newport; hill-drawing, foot/b'way, canal, waterbodies, plantations, parkland, building names, road names, rectory, mill, National School, drains, heath, common; bridge named.

29/75 Chetwynd Aston (township in parish of Edgmond) SJ 757176
Apt 30.12.1840; 1244a (?); Map 1842, 6.67 chns, by J. Treasure, Newport, Salop; canal, waterbodies.

29/76 Childs Ercall (parish) SJ 675242 [Child's Ercall]
Apt 03.12.1839; 3585a (3633); Map 1840?, 6 chns; waterbodies, woods, plantations.

29/77 Chirbury (parish) SO 280999
Apt 18.10.1843; 11041a (11041); Map 1838, 6 chns, in 11 parts, (includes 24-chn index); hill-drawing, foot/b'way, turnpike roads, toll gates, waterbodies, houses, woods, plantations, orchards, rock outcrops (named), hedges, fences, field boundary ownerships, building names, tumulus, chapel, public watering place, vicarage, quarry, lead works, levels, pits, old pits and levels, steam engine, mills, pinfold, druidical remains, boundary marks, spar works, Offa's Dyke, township boundaries (col), occupation roads, drains, embankments; physical features named.

29/78 Chorley and Northwood (divisions in parish of Stottesdon) SO 696836
Apt 13.03.1841; 1211a (?); Map 1842, 6 chns, 'compiled from old surveys' by Saml H. Ashdown, The Hem, Shiffnal; foot/b'way, waterbodies, houses, woods, hedges, fences, field boundary ownerships, building names.

29/79 Church Aston (township in parish of Edgmond) SJ 741178
Apt 30.12.1840; 710a (?); Map 1842, 6 chns, by J. Treasure, Newport, Salop; waterbodies, woods, building names, drains; leaf and thistle design caps north pointer.

29/80 Church Pulverbatch, Castle Pulverbatch and Wrentnall (townships in parish of Church Pulverbatch) SJ 426031
Apt 28.02.1839; 2360a (all); Map 1839, 6 chns, in 3 parts, (two parts at 7 and 7.5 chns); hill-drawing, foot/b'way, waterbodies, woods, field gates.

29/81 Church Stretton (parish) SO 450940
Apt 07.06.1838; 10718a (10716); Map 1839, 8 chns, in 7 parts, (includes 1.5-chn and 3-chn enlargements of detail); hill-drawing, waterbodies, woods, parkland, fences, building names, road names, mill, rectory, union warehouse, Roman road, drains; internal boundaries may show townships; physical features named. Apt omits land use.

29/82 Claverley (parish) SO 790925
Apt 27.06.1839; 8144a (8143); Map 1840, 9 chns, in 22 parts, (includes 21 3-chn enlargements of detail), litho (by Binns and Clifford, Union St, Birmingham); hill-drawing, foot/b'way, turnpike roads, toll gate, waterbodies, woods, plantations, parkland, fences, building names, tumulus, castle, mill, boundary stones, heath, common.

29/83 St Margaret Clee Brown otherwise St Margaret Clee (parish) SO 571843 [Clee St Margaret]
Apt 11.08.1847; 1590a (1589); Map 1842, 6 chns; foot/b'way, waterbodies, woods, hedges, building names, encampment, well; hill named.

29/84 Clee Stanton, Clee Downton, Moor and Stoke St Milborough (district in parish of Stoke St Milborough) SO 580813 [Cleestanton]
Apt 12.11.1841; 5120a (?); Map 1842?, 9 chns, in 2 parts; hill-drawing, foot/b'way, waterbodies, houses, woods, plantations, orchards, hedges, fences, field gates, building names, boundary stones, mill, glebe (col), Revd Morgan's lands (pink); hill named.

29/85 Cleobury North (parish) SO 619870
Apt 13.11.1846; 1560a (1560); Map 1847?, 6 chns; hill-drawing, turnpike roads, tollgate, waterbodies, houses, woods, field gates, building names, mill.

29/86 Clive and Sansaw (township or chapelry in parish of Shrewsbury St Mary) SJ 512244
Apt 10.11.1842; 1448a (?); Map 1843, 8 chns; hill-drawing, waterbodies, woods, fences, building names; hill named.

29/87 Clun (parish) SO 290800
Apt 08.01.1846; 11882a (19782); Map 1847, 6 chns, in 6 parts, by Chas Mickleburgh, Montgomery, (two parts at 9 chns; includes 18-chn index); hill-drawing, foot/b'way, waterbodies, woods (named), plantations (named), rock outcrops (named), hedges, fences, field gates,

building names, old tile quarry, encampments, tumuli (named), mills, castles, boundary features, quarries, hospital, embankments or dykes, site of church, common; hills named; north pointers have diadem and Prince of Wales' feathers.

29/88 Clunbury and Coston (township in parish of Clunbury) SO 375805
Apt 20.02.1845; 1662a (all); Map 1845, 6 chns.

29/89 Clungunford (parish) SO 405785
Apt 06.12.1845; 3621a (3620); Map 1847?, 6 chns; hill-drawing, waterbodies, houses, woods (named), plantations (named), field gates, building names, mill, weir; bridge named.

29/90 Clunton (township in parish of Clunbury) SO 348828
Apt 14.09.1843; 1974a (?); Map 1844?, 3 chns; hill-drawing, waterbodies, houses, woods (named), plantations, orchards, hedges, fences, field gates, building names, mill, sand or stone pits.

29/91 Colbatch (township in parish of Bishops Castle) SO 300870 [Colebatch]
Apt 31.10.1840; 1130a (all); Map 1841, 6 chns, by Charles Mickleburgh, Montgomery; foot/b'way, waterbodies, woods, plantations, fences, field boundary ownerships, building names, well; north pointer has Prince of Wales' feathers.

29/92 Cold Weston (parish) SO 549833
Apt 08.04.1846; 414a (all); Map 1848?, 6 chns; waterbodies, houses, hedges, field gates.

29/93 Coleham (township and hamlet in parish of Shrewsbury, St Julian) SJ 498115 [Not listed]
Apt 24.02.1845; 318a (?); Map 1848, 6 chns, hill-drawing, foot/b'way, waterbodies, woods, building names, boundary stones, mills; built-up part generalised; north pointer has Prince of Wales' feathers.

29/94 Condover (parish) SJ 490058
Apt 11.04.1839; 7423a (7422); Map 1840, 6 chns, in 3 parts 'corrected and compiled' by Saml H. Ashdown, Uppington, Shrewsbury, (tithable parts only; two parts at 3 chns); foot/b'way, waterbodies, houses, woods, plantations, parkland, fences, building names, lodges, smithy, milestone, greenhouse, boundary stones, chapel; bridge and hill named.

29/95 Coreley (parish) SO 611746
Apt 15.06.1841; 2176a (2175); Map not dated, 6 chns; waterbodies, open fields, building names, rectory, mill. [Map in PRO IR 30 is a copy of 1926; there is no original in PRO IR 77.]

29/96 Corfton (township in parish of Diddlebury) SO 495850
Apt 24.01.1845; 1449a (?); Map 1846?, 4 chns; hill-drawing, waterbodies, houses, woods, plantations, orchards, field gates, building names, township boundaries, tithe-free common boundary, vicar's allotments (yellow).

29/97 Coton (township in parishes of Shrewsbury, St Mary and St Julian) SJ 490140 [Coton Hill]
Apt 30.01.1849; 626a (?); Map 1849?, 6 chns; hill-drawing, railway, foot/b'way, turnpike roads, waterbodies, woods, road names, baths.

29/98 Cotton (township in parish of Ruyton in the Eleven Towns) SJ 379217 [Not listed]
Apt 09.04.1847; 234a (?); Map 1847?, 4 chns; waterbodies, woods (col), orchards (col), building names.

29/99 Cound (except Cressage) (parish) SJ 561039
Apt 19.02.1841; 3675a (?); Map 1842?, 6 chns; waterbodies, woods, plantations, parkland, orchards, marsh/bog, fences, building names, boundary trees and stones, rectory, mill, township boundaries.

29/100 Cressage (township in parish of Cound) SJ 588038
Apt 20.11.1849; 1784a (?); Map 1842, 9 chns, by Saml H. Ashdown, The Hem, Shiffnal; foot/b'way, waterbodies, houses, woods, fences, field boundary ownerships, milestone, boundary stones; bridge named.

29/101 Crickheath (township in parish of Oswestry) SJ 288230
Apt 24.03.1838; 1286a (?); Map 1838, 12 chns, ? by J. Porter, Oswestry; canal with towpath, waterbodies, woods, plantations. [PRO IR 30 has two copies of the map.]

29/102 Crow Meole (township in parish of Shrewsbury, St Chad) SJ 468122 [Not listed]
Apt 17.11.1842; 536a (?); Map 1842, 6 chns; foot/b'way, waterbodies, houses, woods, plantations, parkland, orchards, field gates, building names, boundary stones.

29/103 Culmington (parish) SO 480824
Apt 26.03.1842; 3477a (3476); Map 1842?, 6 chns; hill-drawing, waterbodies, houses, woods, plantations, orchards, field gates, building names, encampment, sand or stone pit.

29/104 Little Dawley (township in parish of Dawley) SJ 678060
Apt 27.06.1839; 931a (?); Map 1840?, 5 chns; railway, foot/b'way, canal with towpaths, waterbodies, woods, plantations, building names, road names, brickworks, furnaces, chapel.

29/105 Dawley Magna or Great Dawley (township) SJ 685075 [Dawley Bank]
Apt 29.03.1843; 997a (?); Map 1845?, 4 chns, (includes numerous 2-chn enlargements of detail); canal with towpath, waterbodies, woods.

29/106 Deuxhill (parish) SO 697870
Apt 23.11.1838; 487a (all); Map undated, 6 chns; foot/b'way, waterbodies, woods, orchards, building names, mill.

29/107 Diddlebury (township) SO 503856
Apt 24.01.1845; 1005a (?); Map 1846?, 6 chns; hill-drawing, waterbodies, houses, woods, plantations, orchards, hedges, field gates, building names, limekiln, mill, township boundaries (col).

29/108 Doddington otherwise Ditton (township in parish of Cleobury Mortimer) SO 647783
Apt 26.08.1839; 2878a (?); Map 1841, 6 chns, 'copied from maps in the possession of the landowners' by James Bourn Junr, Cleobury Mortimer, Salop; waterbodies, houses, woods.

29/109 Donington (parish) SJ 805052
Apt 11.07.1838; 1217a (2641); Map 1842?, 8 chns, waterbodies, building names, rectory.

29/110 Dowles (parish) SO 775770
Apt 28.03.1840; 679a (all); Map 1840, 4 chns, by Willm. Fowler and Son, Brimm.; hill-drawing, foot/b'way, turnpike roads, waterbodies, woods, building names, quay, pound, factory, folly, toll bar, towpath.

29/111 Downton and Hopton (township in parish of Stanton Lacey) SO 528800 [Not listed]
Apt 02.07.1847; 1258a (?); Map 1848?, 6 chns; waterbodies, houses, woods (col), hedges, field gates, building names, sand or stone pit, township boundaries (col).

29/112 Drayton in Hales, part of (parish) SJ 670337 [Market Drayton]
Apt 12.10.1837; 7727a (?); Map 1839?, 3 chns, 1st cl, in 2 parts, by J. Cawley, Macclesfield; construction lines, waterbodies, woods, plantations, orchards, drains.

29/113 Eardington (township in parish of Quatford) SO 723908
Apt 11.03.1842; 1301a (1301); Map 1841?, 6 chns; hill-drawing, foot/b'way, turnpike roads and gate, waterbodies, woods, plantations, orchards, building names, forges, sand or stone pit or quarry, tan house, mill.

29/114 Eardiston (township in parish of Ruyton in the Eleven towns) SJ 365248
Apt 09.04.1847; 705a (?); Map 1846, 3 chns; hill-drawing, waterbodies, woods, parkland, field boundary ownerships, building names, laundry, malthouse, engine house, lodge, smithy.

29/115 Earnestrey Park otherwise Upper Parks (township in parish of Diddlebury) SO 585875 [Upper Earnstrey Park]
Apt 27.11.1841; 1017a (?); Map 1842?, 6 chns; hill-drawing, waterbodies, houses, woods, plantations, hedges, field gates, building names, dyke; hill named.

29/116 Easthope (parish) SO 565955
Apt 30.01.1845; 815a (all); Map 1842, 6 chns; hill-drawing, foot/b'way, waterbodies, woods.

29/117 Eaton (near Church Stretton) (parish)
SO 488905 [Eaton]
Apt 22.09.1841; 6200a (6201); Map 1839, 6 chns, by Chas Evans, Ludlow; hill-drawing, waterbodies, houses, woods (named), plantations, orchards, hedges, field gates, building names, sand or stone pit, limekilns, old mill; meaning of internal divisions is unclear.

29/118 Eaton Constantine (parish) SJ 597061
Apt 30.12.1837; 874a (874); Map 1837, 8 chns, by Saml H. Ashdown, Uppington; woods, field boundary ownerships; bridge named. Apt omits land use.

29/119 Edenhope (township in parish of Mainstone)
SO 271889 [Not listed]
Apt 31.12.1840; 2281a (?); Map 1841, 9 chns, by Charles Mickleburgh, Montgomery; hill-drawing, waterbodies, woods, plantations, rock outcrops, hedges, field boundary ownerships, building names, Offa's Dyke; physical features named; compass rose has Prince of Wales' feathers.

29/120 Edgmond (including Divisions of Adney, Buttery, Calvington, Caynton, Edgmond, Pickstock and Stamford, otherwise Standford) (townships in parish of Edgmond)
SJ 717193
Apt 30.12.1840; 5138a (?); Map 1841, 3 chns, in 6 parts: four parts (one at 6 chns) and 24-chn index by J. Treasure, Newport, Salop, and one part by R. Hammonds; canal with towpath, waterbodies, woods, plantations, orchards, heath/moor, building names, mills, drains, ownership boundaries (col).

29/121 Edgton (parish) SO 387858
Apt 04.09.1839; 1626a (1832); Map 1840?, 8 chns; waterbodies, woods, boundary of extra-parochial land.

29/122 Ellesmere (parish) SJ 410340
Apt 27.06.1839; 25676a (26633); Map 1839, 3 chns, in 25 parts, by A. and R. Reed, Stockton upon Tees, (includes index); hill-drawing, foot/b'way, turnpike roads, toll bars, canal, waterbodies, woods, plantations, parkland (in detail), fences, building names, road names, house of industry, lodge, boundary trees, limekiln, pit, mills, bowling green, brickyard.

29/123 Ercall, Walton, Cotwall, Moortown and Osbaston (townships in parish of High Ercall or Ercall Magna)
SJ 600179 [High Ercall]
Apt 19.04.1839; 4039a (?); Map 1839, 9 chns, by Saml H. Ashdown, Uppington; waterbodies, woods, plantations, field boundary ownerships, building names, mill. Apt has cropping information.

29/124 Eyton upon the Wildmoors (township in parishes of Eyton and Wellington) SJ 650150 [Eyton upon the Weald Moors]
Apt 24.02.1838; 1038a (1038); Map 1839, 8 chns, by Saml H. Ashdown, Uppington, Shrewsbury; waterbodies, woods, field boundary ownerships. Apt omits land use.

29/125 Farley, Wyke and Bradley (townships in parish of Much Wenlock) SJ 640020
Apt 18.06.1847; 960a (?); Map 1848?, 6 chns; hill-drawing, foot/b'way, waterbodies, houses, woods, plantations, fences, field gates, building names, quarry, lime quarry.

29/126 Felton Butler (township in parish of Great Ness)
SJ 393175
Apt 27.02.1846; 527a (all); Map 1844, 8 chns, by Charles Mickleburgh, Montgomery; foot/b'way, waterbodies, woods, plantations. Apt omits land use.

29/127 Westfelton (parish) SJ 360270 [West Felton]
Apt 14.10.1837; 5990a (5991); Map undated, 7.5 chns, in 9 parts, (includes two parts at 6 chns and one at 8 chns and 12-chn index); hill-drawing, canal, waterbodies, woods, parkland, heath/moor, hedges, drains.

29/128 Fennemere, Walford, Eyton, Yeaton and Prescott (townships in parish of Baschurch) SJ 445208
Apt 02.06.1842; 3437a (?); Map 1841, 12 chns, by Saml H. Ashdown, The Hem, Shiffnal; foot/b'way, waterbodies, woods, field boundary ownerships, building names, mills, drains. A quart-er of the district is apportioned by holding.

29/129 Fitz (parish) SJ 445178
Apt 19.12.1837; 1512a (1512); Map 1838, 6 chns, litho (Standidge); foot/b'way, waterbodies, woods, parkland, hedges, building names, boundary stones, field acreages.

29/130 Ford (township in parishes of Ford and Alberbury)
SJ 412130
Apt 17.09.1847; 1773a (1773); Map 1848?, 6 chns; waterbodies, woods, plantations, building names, boundary stones.

29/131 Foreign Liberty otherwise the East Foreign and West Foreign Liberty with the Town Liberty (district in parish of Cleobury Mortimer)
SO 686753 [Cleobury Mortimer]
Apt 06.02.1846; 1896a (?); Map 1846, 6 chns, in 2 parts, by James Bourn junr, (includes enlargement of town); waterbodies, houses, woods, parkland, weir, sand or stone pit. Apt omits some field names.

29/132 Frankwell (township in parish of Shrewsbury, St Chad the Bishop) SJ 480132
Apt 30.01.1849; 271a (all); Map 1851?, 4 chns, in 2 parts, (includes 2-chn enlargement of detail); foot/b'way, waterbodies, houses, woods, plantations, parkland, fences, building names, road names, hospital, boundary stones; bridge named; built-up part generalised.

29/133 Frodesley (parish) SJ 510005
Apt 21.09.1843; 2213a (all); Map 1844, 6 chns; waterbodies, woods, plantations, hedges, field gates, building names; north pointer has diadem and Prince of Wales' feathers; an eagle with outstretched wings holds the scale bar, ornamented with drapery, in its talons.

29/134 Glazeley (parish) SO 706875
Apt 23.11.1838; 633a (all); Map 1838, 8 chns; foot/b'way, waterbodies, houses, woods, parkland, field gates, building names, glebe.

29/135 Greete (parish) SO 575710
Apt 09.09.1844; 1041a (1040); Map 1842, 3 chns, 1st cl, ? by W. Jones, Broseley, Salop; construction lines, hill-drawing, waterbodies, houses, woods, plantations, orchards, hops, fences, field gates, building names, field names, mill, field acreages.

29/136 Greete (part of) (township in parish of Burford) SO 563712
Apt 09.09.1844; 197a (?); Map 1845, 4 chns, 'compiled from Estate Maps' by W. Fosbrooke, Hereford; waterbodies, building names, rectory.

29/137 Gretton (township in parish of Cardington and Rushbury)
SO 519951
Apt 21.05.1844; 809a (?); Map 1846?, 9 chns; foot/b'way, waterbodies, woods, building names, mill.

29/138 Grimshill (parish) SJ 522230 [Grinshill]
Apt 28.12.1838; 828a (827); Map 1835, 9 chns, litho, (by T. Underwood, Birmingham) by W. Bright, Civil Engineer and Land Surveyor, Admaston near Wellington; hill-drawing, foot/b'way, waterbodies, woods, plantations, parkland (named), building names, school, quarries; additional hand-colouring may show property ownerships; hill named.

29/139 Habberley (parish) SJ 390029
Apt 03.07.1838; 795a (all); Map 1839, 3 chns, by Rd. Yates; construction lines, woods.

29/140 Halesowen (township in parish of Halesowen)
SO 968838
Apt 26.11.1844; 131a (?); Map 1845, 2.5 chns, by Oates and Perrens, Stourbridge; waterbodies.

29/141 East Hamlets (township in parish of Stanton Lacey)
SO 526776 [Not listed]
Apt 17.12.1847; 763a (?); Map 1848?, 6 chns; waterbodies, houses, woods, plantations, hedges, field gates, building names.

29/142 West Hamlets (township in parish of Stanton Lacey) SO 480800 [Not listed]
Apt 10.12.1847; 642a (?); Map 1848?, 6 chns; waterbodies, houses, field gates, building names.

29/143 Hanwood otherwise Great Hanwood (parish)
SJ 445102
Apt 30.06.1843; 416a (all); Map 1843, 6 chns; foot/b'way, waterbodies, woods, field gates, building names, mill.

29/144 Harcourt (township in parish of Stanton upon Hine Heath) SJ 568248
Apt 31.07.1839; 235a (?); Map 1839?, 3 chns; foot/b'way, waterbodies, woods, field gates, building names, mill. Apt has cropping information.

29/145 Harlescott (townships in parishes of Shrewsbury, St Alkmond and St Mary) SJ 503163
Apt 30.01.1849; 621a (all); Map 1849, 6 chns, by Saml H. Ashdown, Uppington, Salop; foot/b'way, waterbodies, woods, fences, field boundary ownerships, field gates, boundary stones and trees; north pointer has diadem and Prince of Wales' feathers.

29/146 Harley (parish) SJ 593012
Apt 30.12.1837; 1955a (1955); Map 1841, 6 chns, by Saml H. Ashdown, Uppington, Shrewsbury; foot/b'way, woods, field boundary ownerships, building names, mill, limekilns. Apt omits land use.

29/147 Harley, Wigwig and Homer (township in parish of Much Wenlock) SJ 608015
Apt 31.12.1846; 552a (?); Map 1847, 6 chns, in 2 parts; foot/b'way, waterbodies, houses, fences, common.

29/148 Hasbury (township in parish of Halesowen) SO 958835
Apt 26.11.1844; 863a (?); Map 1845, 5 chns; turnpike roads, waterbodies, woods, building names.

29/149 High Hatton and Booley (township in parish of Stanton on Hine Heath) SJ 606249
Apt 11.04.1839; 1513a (?); Map 1839?, 3 chns; foot/b'way, waterbodies, houses, woods, orchards, fences, building names, sand or stone pit or quarry.

29/150 Haughton and Poynton (townships in parish of High Ercall or Ercall Magna) SJ 565170
Apt 31.07.1839; 989a (?); Map 1840, 9 chns, by Saml H. Ashdown, Uppington, Shrewsbury; foot/b'way, waterbodies, houses, woods, field boundary ownerships, building names, township boundary.

29/151 Hawn (township in parish of Halesowen) SO 961841 [Not listed]
Apt 26.11.1844; 277a (?); Map 1845?, 5 chns, by Oates and Perrens, Stourbridge; railways, waterbodies, woods, building names.

29/152 Lower Hayton (township in parish of Staunton Lacey) SO 503810
Apt 20.05.1846; 524a (?); Map 1848?, 6 chns; foot/b'way, waterbodies, houses, woods, plantations, hedges, field gates.

29/153 Upper Hayton (township in parish of Stanton Lacey) SO 515811
Apt 02.07.1847; 916a (?); Map 1848?, 6 chns; foot/b'way, waterbodies, houses, woods, plantations, hedges, field gates.

29/154 Heath (chapelry in parish of Stoke St Milborough) SO 557857 [Upper Heath]
Apt 21.11.1845; 628a (?); Map 1846?, 6 chns; hill-drawing, waterbodies, houses, woods, plantations, field gates, building names, chapel.

29/155 Heath (quarter or district in parish of Worthen) SJ 361008 [Not listed]
Apt 22.03.1844; 4453a (?); Map 1847, 6 chns, in 4 parts, ? by Wm. Story; hill-drawing, foot/b'way, waterbodies, woods, plantations, rock outcrops (named), field gates, building names, landowners, milestone, mill, ancient [castle] earthworks, wall, chapel, common; physical features named.

29/156 Hencott Grange and Hencott Stye (district in parish of Shrewsbury, St Alkmonds) SJ 487182 [Hencott]
Apt 24.04.1849; 244a (?); Map 1850, 6 chns; railway, foot/b'way, turnpike roads, waterbodies, woods, building names, toll gate.

29/157 Higley (parish) SO 740834 [Highley]
Apt 13.03.1841; 1527a (1527); Map 1839, 4 chns, by Wm. Hill, Cleobury Mortimer, Shropshire; hill-drawing, foot/b'way. Apt omits land use.

29/158 The Hill (township in parish of Halesowen) SO 975848 [Not listed]
Apt 26.11.1844; 856a (?); Map 1845?, 6 chns, in 2 parts, (includes 3-chn enlargement of open fields); canal with towpath, waterbodies, woods, open fields.

29/159 Hinstock (parish) SJ 695269
Apt 08.11.1837; 3036a (3036); Map 1837, 6 chns, surveyed by W. Spendelow in 1802 and 'copied and amended' by Ash and Son; foot/b'way, waterbodies, woods, plantations, parkland, marsh/bog, building names, quarries, marl pits, mill.

29/160 Hodnet (except Moreton Say) (parish) SJ 602287
Apt 08.06.1840; 11595a (16399); Map 1840, 6 chns, in 11 parts, 'copied' by J. Treasure, Newport, (includes five 9-chn parts and 36-chn index); foot/b'way, waterbodies, woods, plantations, parkland, heath/moor, fences.

29/161 Holgate (parish) SO 565898 [Holdgate]
Apt 11.03.1842; 1896a (1896); Map 1842, 6 chns, in 3 parts; hill-drawing, foot/b'way, waterbodies, woods, plantations, open fields, field gates, building names, quarry.

29/162 Holt Preen (township in parish of Cardington) SO 548966 [Holt]
Apt 30.06.1843; 788a (?); Map 1843, 8 chns; waterbodies, woods, hedges, building names, mill.

29/163 Home (township in parish of Wentnor) SO 375905 [Home]
Apt 22.02.1845; 313a (all); Map 1849?, 6 chns; waterbodies, woods; north pointer has Prince of Wales' feathers.

29/164 Hope Bagot (parish) SO 589738
Apt 10.04.1844; 457a (all); Map 1844?, 4 chns; hill-drawing, waterbodies, houses, woods, plantations, field gates, building names, glebe.

29/165 Hope Bowdler (parish) SO 471928
Apt 23.03.1843; 1702a (all); Map 1842, 6 chns; hill-drawing, turnpike roads, toll gate, waterbodies, woods, plantations, building names, quarry.

29/166 Hopesay (parish) SO 391825
Apt 02.12.1840; 4034a (4060); Map 1841?, 8 chns.

29/167 Hopton Castle (parish) SO 358772
Apt 30.10.1840; 2553a (all); Map 1842?, 4 chns, in 2 parts; hill-drawing, waterbodies, houses, woods, plantations, field gates, building names.

29/168 Hopton Wafers (parish) SO 636766
Apt 16.04.1839; 1611a (1610); Map 1839, 3 chns, 1st cl; construction lines, waterbodies, houses, woods, plantations, fences, field boundary ownerships, coal pit (by Dawson's symbol).

29/169 Hordley (parish) SJ 385300
Apt 01.06.1847; 2480a (2479); Map 1847, 6 chns, by Joseph Jones, Oswestry, Salop; canal with towpath, waterbodies, woods, plantations, fences, building names, sand or stone pit, township boundaries.

29/170 Hortons Wood (township in parish of Eyton) SJ 685144 [Hortonwood]
Apt 30.12.1842; 448a (all); Map 1843, 6 chns; foot/b'way, waterbodies, houses.

29/171 Hughley (parish) SO 572980
Apt 30.11.1838; 1102a (1110); Map 1839, 6 chns, by Saml H. Ashdown, Uppington. Shrewsbury; foot/b'way, woods, plantations, heath/moor, field boundary ownerships.

29/172 Hunnington (township in parish of Halesowen) SO 968816
Apt 26.11.1844; 974a (?); Map 1841, 6 chns, litho (Standidge); foot/b'way, waterbodies, woods, building names.

29/173 Ightfield (parish) SJ 594385
Apt 24.01.1845; 1569a (1568); Map 1845?, 6 chns; foot/b'way, waterbodies, woods, fences, building names.

29/174 Illey (township in parish of Halesowen) SO 982818
Apt 26.11.1844; 281a (?); Map 1841, 6 chns, litho (Standidge); waterbodies, woods, building names.

29/175 Ingardine and The Lowe (township in parish of Stottesdon) SO 628810
Apt 25.03.1840; 652a (all); Map 1843?, 6 chns; houses, woods, plantations, field gates, building names, landowners, township boundaries (col). District is apportioned by holding and fields are not shown.

29/176 Isombridge (township in parish of High Ercall or Ercall Magna) SJ 610140
Apt 19.05.1843; 593a (?); Map 1842?, 9 chns, by Saml H. Ashdown, The Hem, Shiffnal; foot/b'way, canal with towpath, waterbodies, houses, field boundary ownerships, building names, mill.

29/177 Kemberton (parish) SJ 730045
Apt 28.02.1839; 1386a (1387); Map 1840?, 6 chns; waterbodies, woods, plantations, open fields.

29/178 Kenley (parish) SO 569996
Apt 30.12.1837; 1898a (1897); Map 1841, 6 chns; foot/b'way, waterbodies, woods, field boundary ownerships, building names, old furnace, boundary stones and trees.

29/179 Kevencalonog (township in parish of Bettws-y-Cruen) SO 211852 [Not listed]
Apt 16.12.1839; 1315a (all); Map 1842, 9 chns, in 2 parts; foot/b'way, waterbodies, woods, hedges, fences, field gates, building names, pound, common.

29/180 Kingswood and Button Oak (township in parish of Stottesdon) SO 751775
Apt 30.04.1849; 1329a (?); Map 1848, 6 chns, by James Bourn jnr, Cleobury Mortimer; waterbodies, houses, woods, sand or stone pit.

29/181 Kinlet (parish) SO 735800
Apt 31.10.1840; 6692a (6692); Map 1840?, 6 chns; waterbodies, woods, parkland, orchards.

29/182 Kinnerley and Argoed, Dovaston, Edgerley and Maesbrook Ucha (townships in parish of Kinnerley) SJ 340200
Apt 05.08.1844; 3646a (?); Map 1845, 6 chns, in 2 parts, (one part at 8 chns); waterbodies, houses (incomplete), woods, plantations, fences, building names, mill, vicarage, township boundaries. Apt omits some field names.

29/183 Kinnersley (parish) SJ 665170 [Kynnersley]
Apt 17.04.1839; 1790a (1789); Map 1840?, 9 chns; waterbodies, woods, plantations, drains.

29/184 Kinnerton and Ritton (township in parish of Wentor) SO 375970
Apt 22.02.1845; 6a (?); Map 1849?, 6 chns, ? by Wm. Story; turnpike roads, building names, rectory.

29/185 Kinton (township in parish of Great Ness) SJ 363195
Apt 28.02.1849; 1164a (?); Map 1850?, 6 chns; woods, plantations, heath/moor, building names.

29/186 Knockin (parish) SJ 342222
Apt 31.10.1838; 1551a (1561); Map 1839, 6 chns; waterbodies, woods.

29/187 Kynaston (township in parish of Kinnerley) SJ 356205
Apt 29.10.1844; 517a (?); Map 1846, 6 chns; waterbodies, woods, plantations.

29/188 Langley and Ruckley (chapelry) SJ 537001
Apt 12.03.1846; 1515a (all); Map 1848?, 6 chns; waterbodies, woods, plantations, orchards, hedges, building names, boundary trees and stones, chapel.

29/189 Lappall (township in parish of Halesowen) SO 980830 [Lapal]
Apt 26.11.1844; 839a (?); Map 1841, 6 chns, litho (Standidge); canal with towpath and tunnel, waterbodies, woods, building names.

29/190 Lawton (township in parish of Diddlebury) SO 519840
Apt 24.01.1845; 460a (?); Map 1848?, 6 chns; waterbodies, houses, hedges, field gates, coppice (named).

29/191 Lea and Oakley (township in parish of Bishops Castle) SO 349889
Apt 15.06.1843; 1062a (all); Map 1843?, 6 chns; waterbodies, houses, woods, plantations, hedges, fences, field gates, building names.

29/192 Leaton (township in parish of Shrewsbury, St Mary) SJ 471187
Apt 18.02.1842; 892a (all); Map 1842, 6 chns; waterbodies, houses (by shading).

29/193 Leaton, Burcott and Cluddley, Wrockwardine including Long Lane, Alscott, Admaston and Bratton (townships in parish of Wrockwardine) SJ 625110
Apt 12.11.1838; 3392a (?); Map 1839, 9 chns, in 2 parts, litho (Standidge); foot/b'way, turnpike roads, toll gate, waterbodies, woods, plantations, building names, workhouse.

29/194 Lee Brockhurst (parish) SJ 549275
Apt 09.04.1847; 375a (664); Map 1847?, 9 chns, (tithable parts tinted); waterbodies, woods, plantations, field gates.

29/195 Leebotwood (parish) SO 479995
Apt 27.06.1839; 590a (1267); Map 1839, 6 chns; hill-drawing, waterbodies, houses, woods, orchards, hedges, field gates, building names, colliery; map includes a number of unnumbered fields which do not appear in Apt.

29/196 Leighton (parish) SJ 615058
Apt 06.05.1846; 2152a (2151); Map 1847?, 6 chns, in 3 parts, (includes index); waterbodies, houses, woods, parkland, fences, building names, mill.

29/197 Lilleshall (parish) SJ 725148
Apt 31.12.1849; 850a (6140); Map 1850?, 9 chns, by G. Hammonds, Adney; railways, canal, waterbodies, woods, plantations, building names. Apt omits land use and field names.

29/198 Linley (parish) SO 692986
Apt 06.05.1846; 33a (628); Map 1846, 6 chns, by Willm. Jones, Salop; foot/b'way, waterbodies, woods, plantations, building names, yew tree.

29/199 Llanforda, Trefardclawdd and Cynynion and Pentregaer (townships in parish of Oswestry) SJ 257297
Apt 18.01.1840; 3853a (?); Map 1838, 6 chns, in 5 parts, (includes 12-chn index); waterbodies, woods, parkland, field gates, building names, racecourse, summer house.

29/200 Llanvair Waterdine (parish) SO 253773 [Llanfair Waterdine]
Apt 10.05.1843; 4758a (7782); Map 1847?, 4 chns; construction lines, hill-drawing, foot/b'way, waterbodies, building names, watermill (by symbol), Offa's Dyke; scale is in pencil. Apt omits some field names.

29/201 Llwyntidman and Trepenal (townships in parish of Llanymynech) SJ 279210
Apt 31.01.1837; 1281a (1281); Map 1838, 6 chns, hill-drawing, canal with towpath, waterbodies, woods, plantations, spoil banks, stone quarries, limekilns, river gravels, township boundaries.

29/202 Llynclys (township in parish of Llanyblodwell) SJ 281242
Apt 03.09.1846; 753a (?); Map 1847, 6 chns, by Joseph Jones, Oswestry; hill-drawing, waterbodies, woods, quarry, limekilns.

29/203 Longden (township in parish of Pontesbury) SJ 451058
Apt 31.12.1840; 1704a (?); Map 1838, [10 chns], 'revised and corrected' by S. Groom; foot/b'way, waterbodies, woods, quarry, sand or stone pit; colours may show property ownerships.

29/204 Longdon upon Tern (parish) SJ 624155 [Longdon on Tern]
Apt 31.01.1839; 796a (all); Map not dated, 9 chns; hill-drawing, canal with towpath, waterbodies, building names, brick kiln, quarry.

29/205 Longford (township) SJ 720170
Apt 06.09.1838; 1258a (?); Map 1838, 3 chns, by J. Treasure, Newport; waterbodies, woods, plantations, parkland, orchards, fences, building names, lodge, rectory, drains.

29/206 Loppington (township in parish of Loppington) SJ 470294
Apt 08.02.1838; 1159a (?); Map 1841?, 3 chns; waterbodies, houses, woods, plantations, parkland, osiers, marsh/bog, heath/moor, drains.

29/207 Loughton (chapelry in parish of Chetton) SO 611830
Apt 19.02.1838; 1015a (all); Map 1837, 6 chns, by Saml H. Ashdown,

Uppington, Shrewsbury; hill-drawing, waterbodies, woods, fences, field boundary ownerships, building names, merestones, embankment (named). Apt omits land use.

29/208 Ludlow, St Lawrence (parish) SO 512748 [Ludlow]
Apt 31.03.1846; 71a (240); Map 1847?, 3 chns, (tithable parts only); hill-drawing, houses, fences, field gates, burial ground, weirs; built-up part mostly generalised.

29/209 Lydbury North (except Brockton) (parish) SO 360865
Apt 01.08.1846; 6819a (all); Map 1846, 6 chns, in 5 parts, by Charles Mickleburgh, Montgomery, (includes 18-chn index); hill-drawing, foot/b'way, turnpike roads and gate, waterbodies, woods (named), plantations, parkland, gardens, rock outcrops, hedges, fences, building names, sand or stone pit, ancient earthworks (named), spring, hermitage, lodge, mills, malthouse, township boundaries (col).

29/210 Lydham (township in parish of Lydham) SO 339906
Apt 29.01.1845; 1869a (all); Map 1847?, 8 chns; waterbodies, houses, woods, plantations, field gates, building names.

29/211 Madeley (parish) SJ 692040 [Not listed]
Apt 11.02.1847; 2810a (2809); Map 1848, 3 chns, 1st cl, in 3 parts, (including one part at 1.5 chns in both manuscript and litho (Standidge) forms); construction lines, hill-drawing, railways, foot/b'way, canal, waterbodies, houses, woods, plantations, parkland, fences, field boundary ownerships, field acreages, field gates, building names, road names, sand pits, Methodist Chapel, chapels, pound, parsonage, hotel, market place, iron bridge, wharf, workhouse, well, furnaces, gas works, engine, shafts, pits, pit mouth, brick and tile works, brick kiln, china works, lime kilns; parkland trees are described ('Beech', 'Hawthorn', 'Sycamore', 'Oak', etc); hills named.

29/212 Maesbrook Issa (township in parish of Kinnerley) SJ 302212 [Maesbrook]
Apt 15.11.1844; 866a (?); Map 1845?, 6 chns; waterbodies, woods, orchards, building names, mill, ford.

29/213 Mainstone and Knuckshadwell (township in parish of Mainstone) SO 272878
Apt 19.12.1848; 1839a (?); Map 1849, [10 chns], by Chas Mickleburgh, Montgomery; hill-drawing, foot/b'way, waterbodies, woods, plantations, building names, township boundaries (col), Offa's Dyke; physical features named.

29/214 St Martins (parish) SJ 305365 [St Martin's]
Apt 10.03.1837; 5315a (all); Map 1838, 3 chns; canal, waterbodies, woods (partly by annotation), plantations, parkland, fences, building names, landowners, lodge, tithing names, tithe owners; colour bands may show tithing boundaries.

29/215 Melverley (parish) SJ 330173
Apt 13.01.1841; 1419a (1418); Map 1840, 6 chns, by Js. Porter, Oswestry; hill-drawing, waterbodies, woods, building names, malthouse.

29/216 Middle (parish) SJ 480230 [Myddle]
Apt 19.02.1838; 6903a (6909); Map 1839, 12 chns, litho (Standidge); hill-drawing, waterbodies, woods, plantations, township boundaries (col), ornamental gardens. Apt has cropping information.

29/217 Middlehope (township in parish of Diddlebury) SO 498885
Apt 05.05.1842; 1091a (?); Map 1843?, [?10 chns]; 'The Tithe Owners Lands'. District is apportioned by holding; Apt omits land use.

29/218 Middleton (township in parish of Oswestry) SJ 317288
Apt 02.05.1838; 641a (?); Map 1839?, 6 chns; woods, hedges, pinfold.

29/219 Milson (parish) SO 641730
Apt 06.05.1846; 1025a (all); Map 1840, 6 chns, by W. Tench, Hereford; foot/b'way, waterbodies, houses, woods, plantations, orchards, hops, field gates, building names, glebe boundary.

29/220 Mindtown (parish) SO 389893 [Myndtown]
Apt 08.03.1842; 908a (908); Map 1845, 6 chns; foot/b'way, waterbodies, woods.

29/221 Minsterley (township in parish of Westbury) SJ 368048
Apt 17.02.1838; 2670a (?); Map 1839?, 6 chns; foot/b'way, waterbodies, houses, woods, plantations, building names, mill.

29/222 Monk Hopton (parish) SO 620930 [Monkhopton]
Apt 16.10.1841; 2209a (2208); Map 1842, 9 chns, by Saml H. Ashdown, The Hem, near Shiffnal; foot/b'way, waterbodies, houses, woods, field boundary ownerships, building names.

29/223 Montford (parish) SJ 420162
Apt 30.06.1843; 2976a (2976); Map 1844, 6 chns, by C. Mickleburgh, Montgomery; foot/b'way, turnpike roads and gate, waterbodies, plantations, heath/moor, hedges, fences, field gates, building names, smithy, vicarage, avenues of trees. Apt omits land use.

29/224 The More (parish) SO 340940 [More]
Apt 27.06.1839; 3502a (3533); Map 1840?, 6 chns; hill-drawing, waterbodies, woods, plantations, parkland, building names, mill; hills named.

29/225 Moreton Corbet (parish) SJ 546240
Apt 07.12.1838; 881a (2140); Map 1839?, 6 chns, in 2 parts, (one part at 12 chns); waterbodies, woods, plantations.

29/226 Moreton Say (chapelry in parish of Hodnet) SJ 630345
Apt 26.07.1837; 4804a (4804); Map 1838, 4 chns, 1st cl, by Samuel Bate; construction lines, foot/b'way, waterbodies, houses, woods, parkland, orchards, hedge ownership, building names, road names, sand or stone pits, field acreages, township boundaries (col), drains.

29/227 Morton (township in parish of Oswestry) SJ 304241
Apt 21.11.1838; 684a (?); Map 1840, 6 chns; railway, canal with towpath, waterbodies, woods, building names, public water place, chapel, gravel pit.

29/228 Morville (township in parish of Morville) SO 674944
Apt 01.11.1844; 3868a (?); Map 1842, 12 chns; foot/b'way, waterbodies, building names, mill, deer park.

29/229 Munslow (parish) SO 523880
Apt 31.12.1841; 3505a (3504); Map 1843, 6 chns, in 4 parts, by Saml H. Ashdown, The Hem, Shiffnal, (includes two 3-chn enlargements of open fields and 40-chn index); foot/b'way, waterbodies, houses, woods, parkland, open fields, fences, field boundary ownerships, building names, ancient castle, mill.

29/230 Nash and Tilsop (township in parish of Burford) SO 600721
Apt 14.03.1844; 2082a (all); Map 1844, 3 chns, 1st cl, by R. C. Herbert, Worcester; construction lines, waterbodies, houses, field boundary ownerships, building names, chapel.

29/231 Neen Savage (parish) SO 682782
Apt 21.11.1838; 3780a (all); Map 1839, 3 chns, 1st cl, by James Bourn junr, Cleobury Mortimer; construction lines, waterbodies, houses, woods, plantations, fences, sand or stone pit.

29/232 Neen Sollars (parish) SO 660720
Apt 08.06.1840; 1780a (all); Map 1841, 6 chns, 'copied from maps in the possession of the landowners' by James Bourn junr, Cleobury Mortimer; waterbodies, houses, woods.

29/233 Neenton (parish) SO 643883
Apt 23.03.1843; 1141a (all); Map 1844, 6 chns; hill-drawing, foot/b'way, waterbodies, woods, plantations, orchards, hedges, field gates.

29/234 Great Ness and Hopton (townships in parish of Great Ness) SJ 390196
Apt 20.02.1845; 1519a (?); Map 1847?, 6 chns; hill-drawing, waterbodies, woods, plantations, heath/moor, building names, cave, boundary stones and trees, avenue of trees; hill named.

29/235 Little Ness (chapelry in parish of Baschurch) SJ 413198
Apt 17.12.1845; 1348a (?); Map 1844, 8 chns, by C. Mickleburgh, Montgomery; foot/b'way, waterbodies, woods, plantations, heath/moor, rock outcrops, hedges, building names, stone pits or quarries, mill, pump, chapel; hill named.

29/236 Netley (township in parish of Stapleton) SJ 465018 [Not listed]
Apt 26.01.1843; 642a (?); Map 1844, 6 chns, ? by Wm. Jones, Pontesbury; foot/b'way, waterbodies, woods, building names, landowners, pound; map is subtitled 'belonging to John Thomas Hope Esq. and Thomas Henry Hope Esq.'

29/237 Newport (parish) SJ 747192
Apt 13.02.1840; 567a (567); Map 1840, 2 chns, by J. Treasure, Newport; canal, waterbodies, woods, drains; churches hatched.

29/238 Newton (township in parish of Westbury) SJ 382086 [Not listed]
Apt 01.03.1842; 221a (?); Map 1842, 9 chns; waterbodies, woods, building names.

29/239 Noneley (township in parish of Loppington) SJ 480280
Apt 08.02.1838; 931a (?); Map 1838, 3 chns, by S. Groom; foot/b'way, waterbodies, houses, woods, plantations, drains.

29/240 Norbury (parish) SO 365926
Apt 29.01.1845; 4585a (all); Map 1846, 6 chns, in 2 parts; waterbodies, woods, fences; hill named. Apt omits some field names.

29/241 Obley (township in parish of Clunbury) SO 344790
Apt 05.05.1842; 1026a (all); Map 1842?, 3 chns; waterbodies, houses, woods, plantations, hedges, field gates, building names. Apt omits land use.

29/242 Oldbury (parish) SO 707918
Apt 18.06.1838; 808a (808); Map 1839?, 6 chns; foot/b'way, waterbodies, woods, orchards, fences, field gates, building names, sand or stone pit.

29/243 Oldbury and Langley (township in parish of Halesowen) SO 990890
Apt 29.01.1841; 1706a (?); Map 1845, 4 chns, by Dugdale Houghton, Birmingham; foot/b'way, canal, waterbodies, open fields (named), fences, building names, green; built-up part generalised.

29/244 Onibury (parish) SO 461795
Apt 27.06.1839; 1939a (all); Map 1839, 6 chns; hill-drawing, foot/b'way, waterbodies, houses, woods, rock outcrops, field gates, road names, boundary trees and stones, common.

29/245 Oreton (hamlet in parish of Stottesdon) SO 657797
Apt 29.10.1844; 580a (?); Map 1845, 6 chns; foot/b'way, waterbodies, houses, woods, hedges, fences, field gates, building names, limekilns, common.

29/246 Osbaston (township in parish of Kinnerley) SJ 321227
Apt 24.12.1844; 559a (?); Map 1839, 3 chns; foot/b'way, waterbodies, woods, plantations, field boundary ownerships. Apt omits some field names.

29/247 Oswestry (liberty in parish of Oswestry) SJ 292297
Apt 08.06.1838; 1833a (?); Map 1838, 3 chns, in 2 parts, ? by Js. Porter, Oswestry; hill-drawing, waterbodies, woods, field gates, road names, town walls, boundary trees and stones; built-up part generalised and tinted; hill named.

29/248 Patten (township in parish of Stanton Long) SO 587948 [Patton]
Apt 23.01.1845; 698a (all); Map 1845, 6 chns, by Samuel Harding Ashdown, The Hem, Shiffnal; foot/b'way, waterbodies, houses, woods, fences, field boundary ownerships, field gates, building names; 'J.B. Script.' appears beneath the map date.

29/249 Peaton (township in parish of Diddlebury) SO 533843
Apt 12.11.1841; 1023a (?); Map 1843?, 8 chns; hill-drawing, foot/b'way, waterbodies, houses, woods, orchards, hedges, field gates.

29/250 Petton (parish) SJ 439262
Apt 15.02.1844; 822a (all); Map 1842, 4 chns, by Groom and Greening; waterbodies, houses, farmyards, woods (col), plantations (col), parkland, hedge ownership, fences, field gates; map subtitled as a map of the parish 'belonging to William Sparling Esq'.

29/251 Pickthorn (hamlet in parish of Stottesdon) SO 661845 [Not listed]
Apt 29.10.1844; 559a (?); Map 1846, 6 chns; foot/b'way, waterbodies, houses, woods, orchards, fences, building names, hut.

29/252 Pitchford (parish) SJ 528040
Apt 19.06.1848; 1646a (1645); Map 1848?, 6 chns; hill-drawing, waterbodies, woods, plantations, parkland, rock outcrops, field gates, building names, stone quarry, sand or stone pit.

29/253 Plaish (township in parish of Cardington) SO 529963
Apt 05.08.1841; 917a (?); Map 1843?, 8 chns; foot/b'way, waterbodies, woods.

29/254 Pontesbury, Asterley, Inwood, Cruckton, Newnham, Sascott, Pontesford, Hinton, Halston, Farley, Edge, Lea and Polmer, Boycott, Malehurst and the Oaks (townships in parish of Pontesbury) SJ 410080
Apt 29.06.1842; 6221a (?); Map 1842, 6 chns, in 37 parts, (in-cludes enlargements of Asterley, Pontesbury, Hinwood, Oakes and Pontesford villages and 31 small enlargements of detail at 3 chns), litho (Standidge); waterbodies, woods (named), plantations, orchards, fences, building names, mills; hills named.

29/255 Great Poston and part of Little Poston (township in parish of Diddlebury) SO 550821 [Greater Poston]
Apt 11.03.1842; 394a (?); Map 1842?, 6 chns; waterbodies, houses, woods, plantations, orchards, building names.

29/256 Prees (except Whixall) (parish) SJ 580335
Apt 31.08.1841; 10097a (?); Map 1838-43, 9 chns, in 11 parts, (one part by T. Fenna, 1838; remaining parts undated (two at 6 chns; Prees village at 4.5 chns); includes 36-chn index of 1843); foot/b'way, turnpike roads, toll gate house, waterbodies, houses, woods, plantations, parkland, field boundary ownerships, field gates, building names, drains; colour bands on one part may show property ownerships.

29/257 Presthope (township in parish of Much Wenlock) SO 580970
Apt 31.12.1846; 743a (all); Map 1847, 9 chns, hill-drawing, foot/b'way, waterbodies, woods, hedge ownership, building names, pound, limekilns, stone pits or quarries.

29/258 Preston (township in parishes of Preston on the Wildmoors and Wellington) SJ 677153 [Preston on the Weald Moors]
Apt 12.12.1842; 1057a (1057); Map 1842, 6 chns; foot/b'way, canal with towpath, waterbodies, houses, woods, building names, hospital, drains; parts in Wellington are green.

29/259 Preston Gubbals (parish) SJ 480207
Apt 11.08.1838; 2281a (2281); Map '1825', 6 chns; hill-drawing, foot/b'way, waterbodies, woods, plantations, orchards, field boundary ownerships, field gates, building names, marl pit, sand or stone pits, green; colours may show exemptions from tithe.

29/260 Preston Montford (township in parish of Shrewsbury, St Alkmond) SJ 430140
Apt 15.01.1849; 270a (all); Map 1850?, 6 chns; waterbodies, woods; bridge named.

29/261 Pulley (part of) (township in parish of Shrewsbury, St Julian) SJ 500103
Apt 13.02.1849; 273a (?); Map 1850?, 6 chns, ? by Wm Story; hill-drawing, waterbodies, woods, building names, boundary stones, ancient encampment.

29/262 Quatford (township in parish of Quatford) SO 743908
Apt 25.01.1845; 513a (512); Map 1846, 6 chns, by Saml H. Ashdown, The Hem, Shiffnal; waterbodies, houses, woods, fences, field boundary ownerships, building names, castle, ferry.

29/263 Quatt (parish) SO 755885
Apt 08.01.1840; 2674a (2674); Map 1840, 6 chns; hill-drawing, foot/b'way, waterbodies, houses, woods, plantations, parkland (in detail), field gates, building names, road names, sand or stone pit.

29/264 Ratlinghope (township in parish of Ratlinghope) SO 411965
Apt 23.08.1845; 2400a (?), (tithable parts only, tinted); Map 1847, 6 chns, by Robert Fowler, Birmingham; hill-drawing, foot/b'way, turnpike roads, waterbodies, houses, woods, building names, road names, tumuli, turnpike gate, mill, boundary marks, Longmynd boundary. District is partly apportioned by holding.

29/265 Reilth (township in parish of Mainstone) SO 286871 [Not listed]
Apt 19.12.1848; 764a (?); Map 1849, 6 chns; foot/b'way, waterbodies, woods, plantations, hedges, field gates, building names, old mill.

29/266 Rhugantin (township in parish of Bettws-y-Cruen) SO 172822 [Not listed]
Apt 17.12.1839; 684a (all); Map 1844, 8 chns, by G. Tayler; foot/b'way, waterbodies, houses, woods, plantations, orchards, hedges, field gates, building names, springs, quarries, mill, boundary stones and marks; north pointer has diadem and Prince of Wales' feathers, in colour. Apt omits some field names.

29/267 Ridgacre (township in parish of Halesowen) SP 006846
Apt 21.02.1844; 550a (?); Map 1844, 6 chns, in 2 parts, (includes 3-chn enlargement of detail); waterbodies, woods.

29/268 Rock and Henley (township in parish of Staunton Lacey) SO 532758
Apt 19.06.1845; 693a (?); Map 1846?, 6 chns; waterbodies, houses, woods, field gates, building names, avenue of trees.

29/269 Roden (township in parish of Ercall Magna) SJ 570160
Apt 06.07.1850; 37a (?); Map 1850, 12 chns, by Saml H. Ashdown, Uppington near Wellington; building names.

29/270 Rodington (parish) SJ 581146
Apt 22.11.1841; 1615a (1615); Map 1842, 6 chns; foot/b'way, canal with towpath, waterbodies, houses, fences, field boundary ownerships, building names, mill, chapel, rectory.

29/271 Romsley (township in parish of Hales Owen) SO 958795
Apt 21.10.1840; 1767a (?); Map 1842, 6 chns, in 4 parts, (includes three 3-chn enlargements of detail), litho (Standidge); waterbodies, woods (named), heath (named), building names, mill, chapel.

29/272 Rossall Up and Down (township in parish of Shrewsbury, St Chad) SJ 457162 [Not listed]
Apt 24.04.1844; 1221a (?); Map 1845?, 6 chns; hill-drawing, foot/b'way, waterbodies, woods, parkland, orchards, hedges, field gates, building names, mill.

29/273 Rowton and Amaston (townships in parish of Alberbury) SJ 370115
Apt 05.09.1843; 1522a (?); Map 1848, 6 chns, ? by Wm. Story; waterbodies, woods, plantations, parkland, building names, lodge, township boundaries.

29/274 Rowton and Ellerdine (townships in parish of High Ercall or Ercall Magna) SJ 640182
Apt 19.04.1839; 2197a (?); Map 1839, 9 chns; waterbodies, woods, field boundary ownerships. Apt omits land use.

29/275 Rudge (township in parish of Pattingham) SO 807976
Apt 11.03.1839; 1567a (1542); Map 1840?, 12 chns; waterbodies, woods, field boundary ownerships, building names.

29/276 Rushbury (except Gretton) (parish) SO 525918
Apt 07.05.1840; 4132a (?); Map 1841, 9 chns; foot/b'way, waterbodies, houses, woods, plantations, hedges, building names.

29/277 Ruyton (township in parish of Ruyton of the Eleven towns) SJ 385229 [Ruyton-XI-Towns]
Apt 26.08.1839; 1715a (?); Map 1838, 3 chns, by S. Groom; hill-drawing, foot/b'way, waterbodies, houses, woods, plantations, osiers, arable, grassland, orchards, gardens, marsh/bog, open fields, fences, drains.

29/278 Ryton (parish) SJ 764030
Apt 11.04.1839; 1443a (1442); Map 1839, 6 chns; foot/b'way, waterbodies, houses, woods, plantations, fences, building names, well, gravel pit.

29/279 Scrivens Middleton otherwise Middleton Scriven (parish) SO 679874
Apt 27.06.1839; 786a (all); Map 1842?, 6 chns; foot/b'way, waterbodies, building names.

29/280 Shawbury (parish) SJ 565206
Apt 04.09.1838; 2721a (7221), (tithable parts only, tinted); Map 1839, 12 chns; waterbodies, woods, building names, hamlet names; built-up parts generalised.

29/281 Sheinton (parish) SJ 614036
Apt 19.02.1841; 947a (all); Map 1839, 6 chns, by Saml H. Ashdown, Uppington, Shrewsbury; hill-drawing, waterbodies, houses, woods, plantations, fences, field boundary ownerships, building names, rectory, boundary stones.

29/282 Shelton (township and district in parish of Shrewsbury, St Julian) SJ 466138
Apt 28.02.1845; 258a (?); Map 1846, 6 chns; hill-drawing, foot/b'way, turnpike roads, toll house, waterbodies, woods, building names, lunatic asylum, pound.

29/283 Shelton and Oxon (township in parish of Shrewsbury, St Chad the Bishop) SJ 464132
Apt 30.06.1843; 341a (?); Map 1844, 6 chns; foot/b'way, waterbodies, woods, building names.

29/284 Shelve (parish) SO 332988
Apt 27.06.1839; 1286a (1285); Map 1840?, 6 chns; hill-drawing, waterbodies, woods, hedges, field gates, building names, boundary marks. Apt omits land use.

29/285 Shelvoke and Wikey (township in parish of Rhyton in the Eleven Towns) SJ 349288 [Shelvock]
Apt 31.07.1839; 1194a (?); Map 1839, 6 chns; waterbodies, woods, field boundary ownerships, building names, drains.

29/286 Sheriffhales (except Woodcote) (parish) SJ 760127
Apt 22.05.1846; 5392a (all); Map 1846, 10 chns, by George Hammonds, Adney near Newport, Salop; woods, plantations, building names.

29/287 Shiffnal (parish) SJ 750075 [Shifnal]
Apt 13.07.1839; 11434a (11441); Map 1840, 6 chns, in 2 parts, by Saml H. Ashdown, Uppington, Shrewsbury, (includes Shiffnal town separately at 2 chns); waterbodies, woods (named), plantations, parkland, fences, field boundary ownerships, building names, road names, mill.

29/288 Shipton (parish) SO 564921
Apt 03.09.1846; 167a (1723); Map 1848, 6 chns, by Saml H. Ashdown, Uppington, Salop; foot/b'way, waterbodies, woods, building names.

29/289 Shotatton (township in parish of Ruyton in the Eleven Towns) SJ 368229
Apt 28.12.1838; 851a (?); Map 1838, 6 chns, by Js. Porter, Oswestry; waterbodies, building names, landowners.

29/290 Shrawardine (parish) SJ 390161
Apt 21.12.1846; 1951a (1951); Map 1844, 6 chns; hill-drawing, foot/b'way, waterbodies, plantations, hedges, field gates, building names, old castle (tumulus). Apt omits land use.

29/291 Shrewsbury, Holy Cross and St Giles (parish) SJ 510126 [Not listed]
Apt 30.10.1840; 1481a (?); Map 1842, 3 chns, in 2 parts; foot/b'way, waterbodies, woods, parkland, building names, depot; bridge named.

29/292 Sidbury (parish) SO 689856
Apt 08.04.1846; 1278a (all); Map 1843, 9 chns; foot/b'way, waterbodies, houses, woods, building names.

29/293 Silvington (parish) SO 620800
Apt 11.02.1846; 494a (all); Map 1847, 9 chns; waterbodies, landowners.

29/294 Smethcott (parish) SJ 459005
Apt 22.03.1844; 2705a (?); Map 1844, 6 chns, in 2 parts; foot/b'way, waterbodies, woods, field gates, building names, boundary stones, common; hamlet of Betchcote is apportioned as one holding.

29/295 Stanton and Moston (townships in parish of Stanton upon Hine Heath) SJ 584235
Apt 27.06.1839; 2338a (?); Map 1839?, 6 chns, in 2 parts, (one part at 9 chns); foot/b'way, waterbodies, houses, woods, heath/moor, field gates, building names.

29/296 Stanton Lacey (township in parish of Stanton Lacey) SO 503792
Apt 02.07.1847; 2321a (?); Map 1848?, 6 chns; waterbodies, houses, woods, plantations, field gates, building names, workhouse, castle, ornamental grounds; bridge named.

29/297 Stanton, Brockton, Weston and Oxenbold (township in parish of Stanton Long) SO 582919 [Stanton Long]
Apt 23.01.1845; 1710a (?); Map 1845, 6 chns, by Saml H. Ashdown, The Hem, Shiffnal; foot/b'way, waterbodies, houses, woods, fences, field boundary ownerships, building names.

29/298 Stapleton with Shadymoor and the Moat (township and hamlet in parish of Stapleton) SJ 462038
Apt 27.11.1838; 1834a (1836); Map 1839, 9 chns, ? by Wm. Story; waterbodies, woods, building names, rectory.

29/299 Stirchley (parish) SJ 705069
Apt 27.06.1839; 833a (833); Map 1838, 6 chns, by Saml H. Ashdown, Uppington, Shrewsbury; canal with towpath, waterbodies, houses, woods, plantations, field boundary ownerships, building names; leaf pattern border.

29/300 Stitt and Gatten (township in parish of Ratlinghope and Pulverbatch) SJ 408002 [Not listed]
Apt 12.01.1846; 16a (?); Map 1845?, 4 chns, (tithable parts only, tinted); building names, field names, landowners, field acreages.

29/301 Stockton (township in parish of Longford) SJ 772169
Apt 30.12.1840; 648a (?); Map 1848, 4 chns, by George Hammonds, Adney, Newport, Salop.

29/302 Stockton (parish) SO 727996
Apt 18.01.1838; 3162a (all); Map undated, 9 chns; foot/b'way, waterbodies, houses, woods, plantations, parkland, building names.

29/303 Stoke (township in parish of Burford) SO 560709 [Not listed]
Apt 09.09.1844; 407a (?); Map 1845, 3 chns, 1st cl, by W. Fosbrooke, Hereford; construction lines, field boundary ownerships.

29/304 Stokesay Newton and Wettleton (township in parish of Stokesay) SO 436818
Apt 21.01.1840; 1936a (?); Map 1840?, [6 chns]; hill-drawing, foot/b'way, turnpike roads, waterbodies, woods (named, shown partly by annotation), rock outcrops, open fields (named), field gates, building names, toll gates, river weir, old river course, limekilns, quarry; bridge named.

29/305 Stoke upon Terne (parish) SJ 645280 [Stoke on Tern]
Apt 26.10.1837; 5603a (5602); Map 1838, [3 chns], 1st cl, in 2 parts, by James Cawley, Macclesfield; construction lines, foot/b'way, waterbodies, houses, woods, plantations, field gates, landowners, township boundaries; some land use is shown by annotation.

29/306 Stone-Ward-Within (district in parish of Shrewsbury, St Chad) SJ 494122 [Not listed]
Apt 15.01.1849; 43a (?); Map 1849, 3 chns, by T. Tisdale, Salop; foot/b'way, waterbodies, fences, building names, ferry, market hall; built-up part generalised and tinted.

29/307 Stony Stretton (township in parish of Westbury) SJ 383096 [Stoney Stretton]
Apt 01.03.1842; 708a (?); Map 1842?, 9 chns, in 2 parts, (includes Stretton village separately at 3 chns); waterbodies, houses, woods, building names, township boundaries, heath.

29/308 Stottesdon, Duddlewick and Hinton (township and hamlet in parish of Stottesdon) SO 663827
Apt 23.11.1844; 1917a (?); Map 1843, 6 chns; foot/b'way, waterbodies, houses, woods, fences, field boundary ownerships, building names.

29/309 Stow (parish) SO 308737 [Stowe]
Apt 05.05.1842; 3724a (all); Map 1839?, 9 chns, ? by Morris and Wm. Sayce; waterbodies, woods, plantations, building names, mill, castle bank, workhouse; built-up part generalised; bridges named; hill named; north pointer has Prince of Wales' feathers.

29/310 Great Sutton (township in parish of Diddlebury) SO 517830
Apt 24.01.1845; 724a (?); Map 1848?, 6 chns; waterbodies, houses, plantations (named), field gates.

29/311 Little Sutton (township in parish of Diddlebury) SO 512824
Apt 24.01.1845; 332a (?); Map 1848?, 6 chns; waterbodies, houses, hedges, field gates.

29/312 Sutton Maddock (parish) SJ 724021
Apt 19.04.1839; 2663a (2662); Map 1840, 9 chns; waterbodies, woods, plantations, orchards, gardens, building names; bridge named.

29/313 Sweeney, Weston Cotton and Maesbury (townships in parish of Oswestry) SJ 296263
Apt 31.01.1837; 3165a (?); Map 1839?, 6 chns, in 3 parts; canal, waterbodies, woods, ownerships (col).

29/314 Sylattyn (parish) SJ 273322 [Selattyn]
Apt 08.06.1838; 5553a (?); Map 1840?, 6 chns; waterbodies, woods, parkland, fences, tumulus.

29/315 Tasley (parish) SO 697938
Apt 30.11.1838; 1032a (all); Map 1839?, [6 chns]; foot/b'way, waterbodies, woods, building names, landowners, boundary trees.

29/316 Tearn, Cold Hatton, Crudgington and Sleap (townships in parish of High Ercall) SJ 631211
Apt 31.07.1839; 2765a (?); Map 1840?, 12 chns; waterbodies, township boundaries (col). District is mostly apportioned by holding.

29/317 Tibberton and Cherrington (township in parish of Edgmond) SJ 687192
Apt 11.04.1839; 2508a (?); Map 1839, 9 chns, in 2 parts; waterbodies, woods, field boundary ownerships, drains.

29/318 Tir-y-coed (township in parish of Kinnerley) SJ 325192
Apt 24.12.1844; 306a (?); Map 1846, 6 chns; waterbodies, building names. Apt omits some field names.

29/319 Tong (parish) SJ 804078
Apt 02.05.1838; 3465a (?); Map 1838, 9 chns, by R. Hammonds, 'from a survey taken by Saml Botham in 1796'; waterbodies, houses, building names, castle.

29/320 Trebrodier (township in parish of Bettws-y-Cruen) SO 195815
Apt 17.12.1839; 910a (all); Map 1845, 8 chns, by - Tayler; foot/b'way, waterbodies, woods, plantations, hedges, building names, springs, common.

29/321 Treflach (township in parish of Oswestry) SJ 270257
Apt 24.08.1839; 1098a (?); Map 1840?, 6 chns, by Js. Porter, Oswestry; woods.

29/322 Trefnant (township in parish of Alberbury) SJ 302103 [Not listed]
Apt 04.12.1842; 528a (?); Map 1843, 6 chns; waterbodies, woods.

29/323 Trefonnen (township in parish of Oswestry) SJ 249255 [Trefonen]
Apt 01.12.1842; 954a (?); Map 1843, 6 chns, in 2 parts, by Saml H. Ashdown, The Hem, Shiffnal, (one part at 3 chns); waterbodies, woods, field boundary ownerships, building names; the name 'John Barber' appears beneath the map date, possibly as draughtsman.

29/324 Tugford (parish) SO 549876
Apt 19.04.1839; 1321a (all); Map 1841?, 6 chns; hill-drawing, houses, woods, plantations, orchards, hedges, field gates, building names, sand or stone pit; bridge named.

29/325 Uppington (parish) SJ 592092
Apt 01.11.1839; 756a (all); Map 1838, 8 chns, by Saml H. Ashdown, Uppington, Shrewsbury; foot/b'way, houses, woods, field boundary ownerships.

29/326 Upton Cressett (parish) SO 651921
Apt 19.02.1841; 1604a (all); Map 1841?, 12 chns; foot/b'way, waterbodies, woods, building names.

29/327 Upton Magna (parish) SJ 552131
Apt 02.02.1845; 3261a (3260); Map 1842, 6 chns, by Saml H. Ashdown, the Hem, Shiffnal; foot/b'way, canal with towpath and tunnel, waterbodies, houses, woods, parkland (named), fences, field boundary ownerships, building names, limekilns.

29/328 Water Upton (parish) SJ 639199 [Waters Upton]
Apt 22.04.1837; 733a (732); Map 1837?, 6 chns, 'from a survey made by Willm Yates'; waterbodies, woods, drains; colours may show property ownerships.

29/329 Walton, Prescott and Bagginswood (township and hamlet in parish of Stottesdon) SO 672812
Apt 01.11.1844; 764a (?); Map 1845, 6 chns, by Saml H. Ashdown, The Hem, Shiffnal; foot/b'way, waterbodies, houses, woods, field boundary ownerships, building names.

29/330 Warley Salop (township in parish of Halesowen) SP 008856 [Not listed]
Apt 15.04.1840; 639a (?); Map 1844?, 6 chns, in 2 parts, (includes 3-chn enlargements of detail); waterbodies, woods, building names, mill, pottery; anchor and stylised fish decorate the north pointer.

29/331 Welchampton (parish) SJ 440359 [Welshampton]
Apt 23.09.1842; 1489a (all); Map 1839, 3 chns, by A. and R. Reed, Stockton upon Tees; hill-drawing, canal and towpath, water-bodies, woods, plantations, building names, township boundaries.

29/332 Wellington (parish) SJ 665115
Apt 15.05.1841; 8758a (8757); Map 1840, 3 chns, in 14 parts, (includes eight manuscript parts at 6 chns and 18-chn index), litho (four parts, by Standidge, one by B. Hill, Colmore Row, Birmm.); hill-drawing, foot/b'way, turnpike roads, canal, wharf, waterbodies, houses, woods, plantations (named), parkland (in detail), fences, field boundary ownerships, building names, road names, iron works, chapel, windmill, furnace, lime works, mill, vicarage, milestone, castle, drains, Roman road, township boundaries (col).

29/333 Welsh Ward (district in parish of Shrewsbury, St Chad) SJ 487124 [Not listed]
Apt 15.01.1849; 24a (?); Map 1849, 3 chns, by T. Tisdale, Salop; hill-drawing, waterbodies, parkland, building names, ferry; bridge named; built-up part generalised and tinted.

29/334 Wem (parish) SJ 510300
Apt 06.11.1841; 13841a (13841); Map 1840-44, 3 chns, in 13 parts, by Groom and Greening and S. Groom, Wem, Salop, (includes 40-chn index 'enlarged from the Ordnance map'); hill-drawing, foot/b'way, canal with towpath, waterbodies, houses, farmyards, woods, plantations, fences, field boundary ownerships, building names, limekilns, embankment, artificial drainage channels, mill dam, tumulus, heath.

29/335 Wenlock (township in parish of Much Wenlock) SO 621998 [Much Wenlock]
Apt 05.01.1848; 2513a (?); Map 1847, 9 chns, in 2 parts, (including one part at 9 chns); hill-drawing, foot/b'way, waterbodies, woods, building names, mill, quarry, lime quarries, windmill, racecourse, township boundaries, common.

29/336 Little Wenlock (parish) SJ 650070
Apt 16.04.1838; 2745a (2745); Map 1839, 6 chns, litho (Standidge); foot/b'way, waterbodies, woods, building names, furnace.

29/337 Westbury (township) SJ 361092
Apt 31.01.1839; 1521a (?); Map 1839, 6 chns; foot/b'way, waterbodies, woods, building names, rectory, coal works.

29/338 Westley (otherwise Westley, Winsley, Lake Hurst and The Hem) (township in parish of Westbury) SJ 362070
Apt 21.10.1840; 1058a (?); Map 1841?, 9 chns, in 2 parts, (includes Westley village at 3 chns); waterbodies, woods, parkland, orchards.

29/339 Westhope (township in parish of Diddlebury) SO 475861
Apt 29.01.1845; 1186a (?); Map 1845?, 6 chns; hill-drawing, waterbodies, houses, woods (named), plantations, rock outcrops, hedges, field gates, building names, sand or stone pits, quarry, chapel; hills named.

29/340 Weston (township in parish of Burford) SO 588720 [Not listed]
Apt 09.09.1844; 301a (?); Map 1846, 3 chns; foot/b'way, waterbodies, woods, orchards, building names.

29/341 Wheathill (parish) SO 606810
Apt 25.09.1838; 1377a (1415); Map 1840, 3 chns, by Walter Tench, Hereford; foot/b'way, waterbodies, houses, woods, plantations, orchards, gardens (col), rock outcrops, field gates, building names, quarries, limekilns, rectory, glebe boundary; border has leafy decoration and compass rose is decorated with leaf and flower design. Apt omits some field names.

29/342 Whitchurch (part of) (township) SJ 550410
Apt 30.12.1837; 14271a (?); Map 1839, 8 chns, in 14 parts, 'corrected and copied' by Bate and Timmis, Whitchurch, Salop, (includes 16-chn index); foot/b'way, turnpike roads, toll gate, canal with towpath, waterbodies, woods, plantations, parkland (in detail), heath (named), field boundary ownerships, building names, road names, rectory, house of industry, moss (named); some built-up parts generalised.

29/343 Whitley and Welbatch (township in parish of Shrewsbury, St Chad) SJ 457089
Apt 18.02.1842; 364a (all); Map 1838, 6 chns; hill-drawing, foot/b'way, waterbodies, woods, orchards, building names, coal pits, sand or stone pits, brick works.

29/344 Whittington, Fernhill, Daywell, Ebnal, Henlle, Hindford, Old Marton and Frankton (townships in parish of Whittington) SJ 325314
Apt 23.09.1837; 7621a (?); Map 1839, 6 chns, in 8 parts, (includes Whittington village at 3 chns and manuscript 18-chn index), litho (Standidge); hill-drawing, foot/b'way, canal with towpath, waterbodies, woods, plantations, parkland, orchards, marsh/bog, building names, castle, gravel hole, sand hole, rectory, drains. Apt omits some field names.

29/345 Whitton (township in parish of Burford) SO 574731
Apt 08.03.1844; 788a (all); Map 1844?, 6 chns; hill-drawing, turnpike roads, waterbodies, houses, plantations, orchards, field gates, building names, chapel, toll gate.

29/346 Whitton, Vennington, Marsh and Wigmore (townships in parish of Westbury) SJ 341096
Apt 21.10.1840; 2233a (?); Map 1841?, 9 chns, in 2 parts, (includes enlargement of Vennington village at 3 chns); waterbodies, woods, building names, windmill, avenue of trees, township boundaries.

29/347 Whixall (township or chapelry in parish of Prees) SJ 505348
Apt 20.02.1847; 3361a (all); Map 1847, 8 chns; foot/b'way, canal with towpaths, waterbodies, woods, road names, moss boundary and name, public drains. Apt omits some field names.

29/348 Wilcott and Nescliffe (township in parish of Great Ness) SJ 378188
Apt 21.01.1848; 461a (?); Map 1848?, 6 chns; waterbodies, woods, plantations, orchards.

29/349 Wilderley and Cothercott (township in parish of Church Pulverbatch) SJ 426012
Apt 07.12.1838; 1705a (all); Map 1839, 9 chns, ? by Wm. Story; hill-drawing, waterbodies, woods.

29/350 Willey (parish) SO 674994
Apt 18.10.1838; 1379a (1390); Map 1838, 9 chns; foot/b'way, waterbodies, houses, woods, plantations, fences, building names, furnace.

29/351 Wistanstow (parish) SO 430865
Apt 08.02.1845; 5124a (all); Map 1845?, 6 chns; waterbodies, houses, woods (named), plantations (named), field gates, building names, mill, sand or stone pits, common.

29/352 Winnington (township in parish of Alberbury) SJ 312107
Apt 03.12.1842; 1605a (?); Map 1843, 6 chns; waterbodies, woods, plantations.

29/353 Withington (parish) SJ 581128
Apt 20.02.1845; 1135a (1135); Map 1841, 9 chns, in 2 parts, (includes 3-chn enlargement of detail), litho (Standidge); foot/b'way, canal, waterbodies, building names.

29/354 Wollaston (township in parish of Alberbury) SJ 327123
Apt 11.06.1847; 496a (?); Map 1842, 6 chns; waterbodies, woods, orchards, building names, chapel.

29/355 Wolstaston (parish) SO 455986
Apt 15.08.1840; 843a (all); Map 1840?, 3 chns; hill-drawing, waterbodies, houses, woods.

29/356 Wombridge (parish) SJ 695110
Apt 25.03.1847; 698a (all); Map 1847, 4 chns; hill-drawing, railway, canal, old and new reservoirs, inclined plane, waterbodies, houses, fences, building names, mill, pit mounts, furnace, ownerships (col); built-up part generalised.

29/357 Woodbatch (township in parish of Bishops Castle) SO 300886
Apt 02.12.1839; 886a (all); Map 1841, 5 chns, by Charles Mickleburgh, Montgomery; foot/b'way, waterbodies, houses, woods (named), plantations, orchards, hedges, field boundary ownerships, field gates, building names; north pointer has diadem and Prince of Wales' feathers.

29/358 Woodcott and Horton (township in parish of Shrewsbury, St Chad) SJ 450119
Apt 18.02.1842; 736a (all); Map 1842?, 6 chns; waterbodies, woods, building names.

29/359 Woodcote (chapelry in parish of Sherriff Hales) SJ 771156
Apt 23.01.1847; 1248a (1248); Map 1848, 4 chns, by George Hammonds, Adney, Newport, Salop; waterbodies, woods, parkland. District is partly apportioned by holding.

29/360 Great and Little Woollascot (township in parish of Shrewsbury, St Mary) SJ 481186
Apt 10.11.1842; 344a (all); Map 1843, 6 chns; waterbodies, woods.

29/361 Wootton (township in parish of Stanton Lacey) SO 453776
Apt 02.07.1847; 501a (all); Map 1848?, 6 chns; waterbodies, houses, fences, field gates, building names, weir.

29/362 Worfield (parish) SO 760960
Apt 15.03.1838; 10321a (10320); Map 1839, 8 chns, litho (Standidge); foot/b'way, waterbodies, woods, plantations, parkland, heath/moor, fences, building names, mills, monument, dog kennel, summer house, quarter boundaries (col).

29/363 Worthen (district in parish of Worthen) SJ 329066
Apt 30.08.1843; 3535a (?); Map 1845?, 6 chns; foot/b'way, waterbodies, woods, plantations, parkland, orchards, hedges, building names, drains, township boundaries (col).

29/364 Wrickton, Newton, Overton and Walkerslow (townships and hamlets in parish of Stottesdon) SO 653863
Apt 18.03.1845; 2184a (?); Map 1845, 9 chns, by T. Branson; foot/b'way, waterbodies, building names, mill, pound.

29/365 Wrockwardine Wood (parish) SJ 703120
Apt 25.05.1847; 502a (502); Map 1847, 5 chns; hill-drawing, canal, woods, fences, building names, inclined plane, mill, glass works, vicarage, chapel, waste, pit mounts.

29/366 Wroxeter (parish) SJ 586076
Apt 23.09.1840; 4775a (4774); Map 1842, 8 chns; foot/b'way, woods, plantations, fences, field boundary ownerships, windmill (by symbol); hills named. Apt omits land use.

29/367 The Yelds (district in parish of Shrewsbury, St Chad) SJ 465145 [Not listed]
Apt 15.01.1849; 17a (all); Map 1850?, 6 chns, ? by Wm Story; woods.

29/368 Yockleton (township in parish of Westbury) SJ 400102
Apt 17.04.1839; 876a (?); Map 1839?, 9 chns, in 2 parts, (includes enlargement of Yockleton village at 4.5 chns); turnpike roads, waterbodies, woods, plantations, building names, pound, mill.

29/369 Yoreton (township in parish of Broughton) SJ 503229 [Yorton]
Apt 18.01.1838; 384a (?); Map 1838, 9 chns; waterbodies, woods; colour bands may show property ownerships. [PRO IR 30 has two copies of the map, one of which omits the putative property boundaries.]

Somerset

PRO IR29 and IR30 30/1-482

501 tithe districts: 1,043,328 acres
476 tithe commutations: 953,256 acres
366 voluntary tithe agreements, 110 compulsory tithe awards, 6 corn rent annuities

Tithe and tithe commutation

In terms of its tithe surveys, Somerset resembles Devon rather than its other adjoining counties in that 95 per cent of its tithe districts were still subject to tithes in 1836 (Fig. 42). Some 153 districts were wholly tithable; the main causes of tithe exemption elsewhere were modus payments in lieu of tithes, merger of tithes in the land (usually where the landowner and tithe owner were one and the same), and exemption by prescription.

Assistant tithe commissioners and local tithe agents who worked in Somerset are listed in Table 30.1. The great majority of tithe valuers came from within or just outside the county (Table 30.2); exceptions are John Baker of Bridgnorth, Shropshire, Thomas Beards from Hampshire, Edward Blackmore from London, and Sanders Pepper from Warwickshire.

Tithe maps

About 11 per cent of the 476 Somerset tithe maps are sealed as first class and these are concentrated in the north-eastern part of the county. Some 3 per cent of second-class maps carry construction lines and thus may have been intended as first-class maps. Scales of Somerset tithe maps vary from one inch to three chains to one inch to twelve chains; 41 per cent of maps are in the recommended scale range of one inch to three to four chains, and 43 per cent are at a scale of one inch to six chains. A particular Somerset characteristic is for the main map of a tithe district to be drawn at a small scale and for this to be supplemented by enlargements of detail. The most extreme example of this practice is Wiveliscombe which consists of two main parts at the six-chain scale and no fewer than forty enlargements of detail! Forty-two second-class maps (10 per cent of the total) are lithographed, which is the highest proportion of any county. For Curry Rivell the Public Record Office collection includes both the manuscript original and a lithographed version. Lithographed maps cluster in the west of the county and as most of them are printed by Standidge the mapping of this area displays an unusual uniformity of style.

Colour is used widely to depict land use on Somerset tithe maps. About 7 per cent of the maps show arable and grass, 9 per cent depict gardens, 38 per cent map orchards, and 48 per cent show woodland. A number of hill-forts are mapped in the south-east of the county, most notably Cadbury Castle. Unusually, a number of Somerset maps carry legends which explain map conventions.

Some 252 Somerset tithe maps in the Public Record Office collection can be attributed to a particular map-maker; the most prolific were Cotterells and Cooper of Bath, who produced nineteen maps with distinctive grey buildings. William Wadman of Martock made fourteen maps, usually with legends. Thomas Player of Pensford (fourteen maps) and James Peachy Williams of Bridgwater (thirteen maps) employed a variety of styles, a response, perhaps, to landowners' demands. William Collard Cox of Williton was responsible for eleven maps, all characterised by black buildings, somewhat rough lettering, and multi-colour parish boundaries. James Poole of Sherborne, Dorset, made eleven maps of ordinary appearance save for scale bars which sometimes are placed on plinths. There is an interesting group of maps which in style and content appear to be by a single author but individual maps are variously signed by S. Court, John Elliott and E. Harris; they are characterised by extensive hachuring and careful depiction of field and farm boundaries. Of anonymous maps, there is a particularly striking group of nine in the south-west of the county which have neat lettering and tree symbols with dark green crowns and are clearly the work of the same hand.

The quality of finish of Somerset maps is very variable. This is particularly apparent around Sedgemoor and the Levels where there is a peculiar mix of first-class maps and neatly drawn second-class maps and others which are very crude. Around Bridgwater and Wedmore there are a number of extremely basic maps which depict the bare minimum of field boundaries but not a single building. Generally, the more 'artistic' maps are to be found in the south west of the county where there is also the greatest variation in style. In contrast to Devon but in conformity with Somerset's other adjoining counties, there is little in the way of decoration on the maps. An interesting exception to this generalisation are a dozen maps which depict churches by pictograms, a method more characteristic of midland and eastern England tithe maps than those of the South West.

Table 30.1. *Agreements and awards for commutation of tithes in Somerset*

Assistant commissioner/ local tithe agent	*Number of agreements**	*Number of awards*
Robert Page	284	0
Charles Pym	37	101
James Jerwood	7	0
George Wingrove Cooke	0	5
Aneurin Owen	1	3
Henry Dixon	2	0
George Louis	1	0
John Milner	1	0
Tithe Commissioners	0	1

*Computed from the number of extant reports on tithe agreements in the tithe files [PRO IR 18].

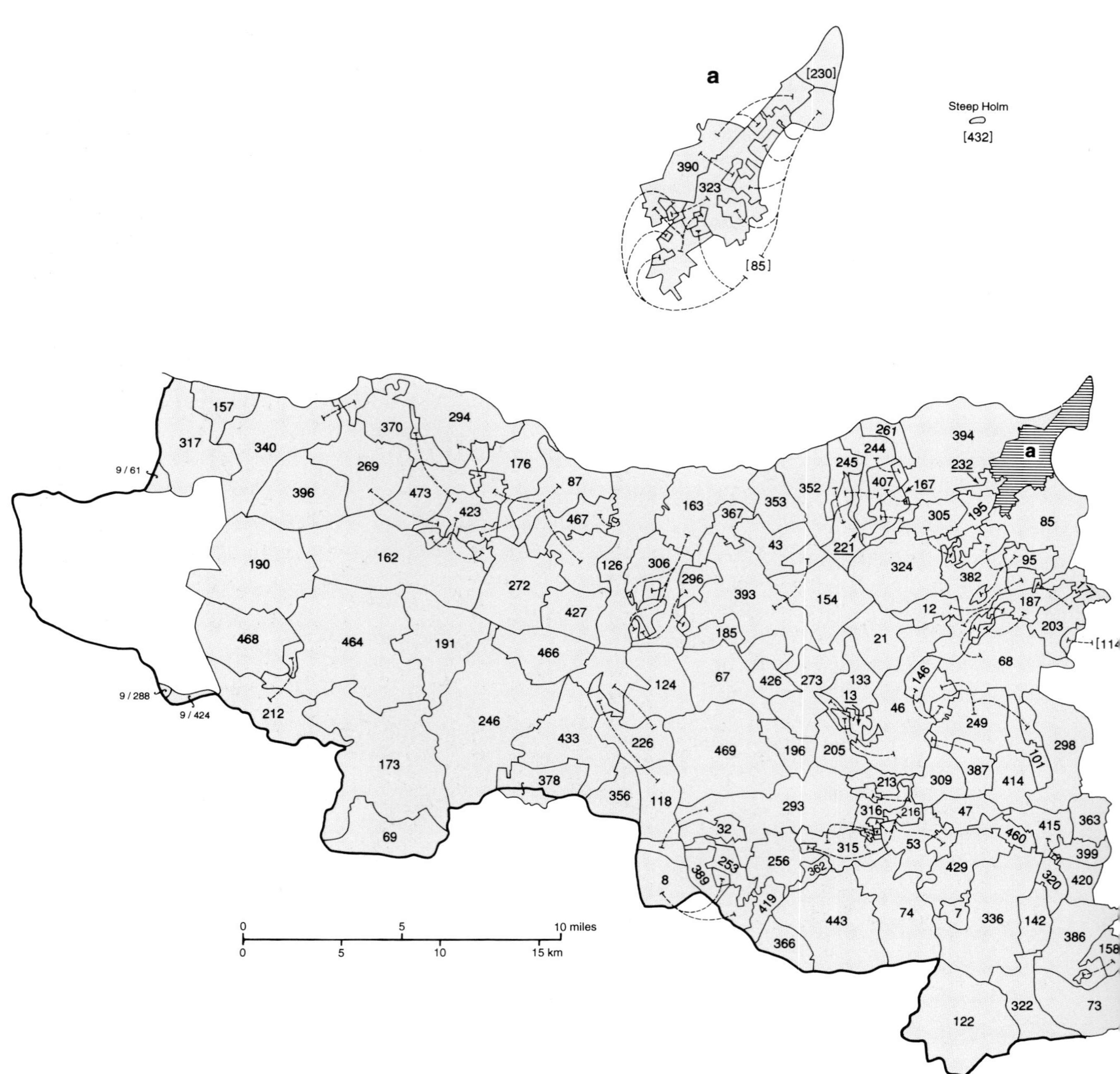

Fig. 42 Somerset: tithe district boundaries.

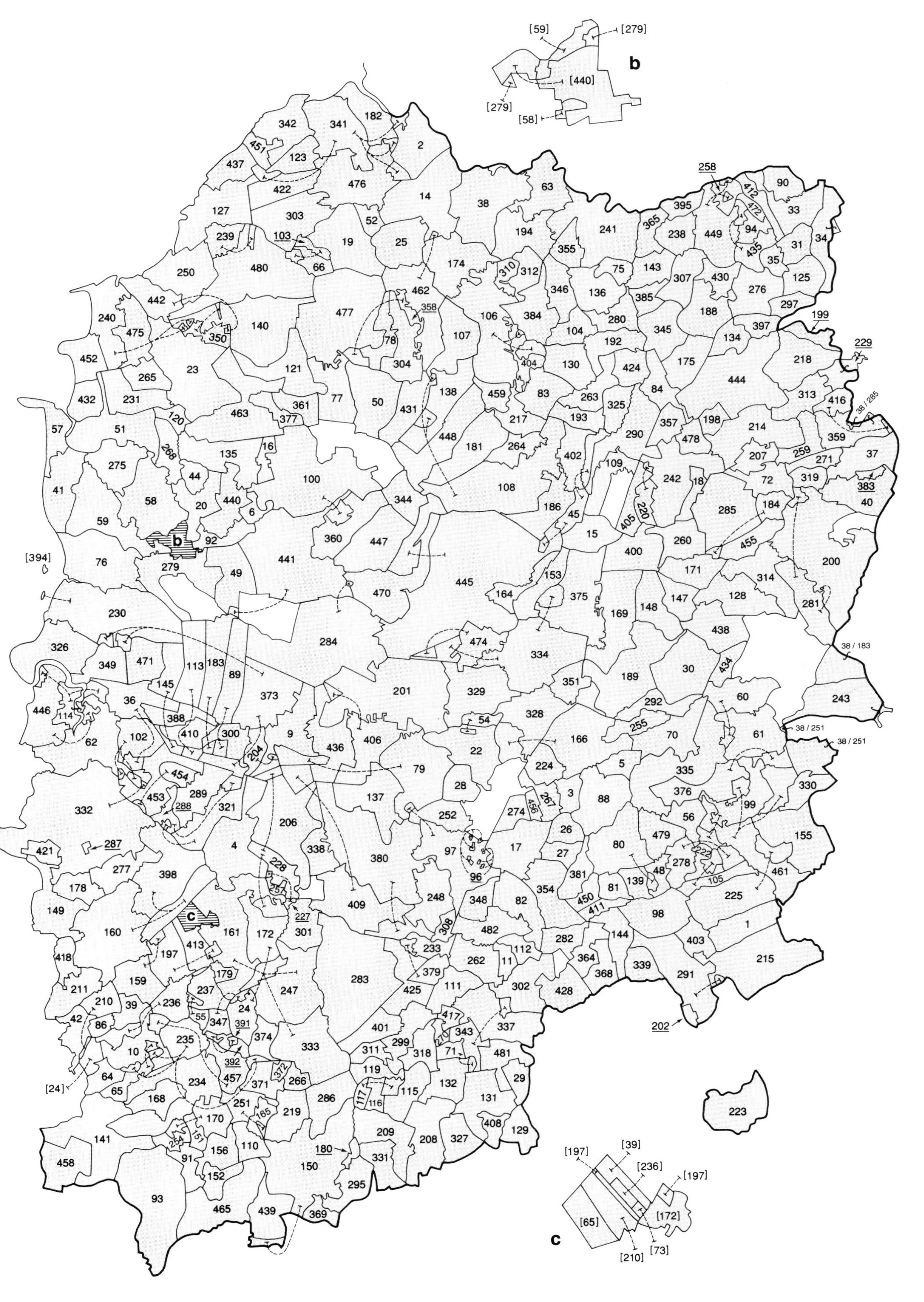

[59]
[279]
b
[440]
[279]
[58]
342
341
182
451
123
2
437
422
476
14
38
63
258
412
90
472
395
33
127
303
52
365
238
449
94
239
103
19
25
194
241
31
34
435
355
35
250
66
174
310
312
143
307
430
125
75
346
136
385
276
480
462
297
442
358
106
384
188
240
477
280
199
475
140
107
104
345
397
229
350
78
192
134
218
452
23
121
304
404
130
424
175
444
265
138
459
83
263
84
313
231
361
77
50
431
325
416
432
120
463
377
193
357
198
38 / 285
217
57
51
448
181
264
290
478
214
359
268
135
16
402
109
37
275
259
271
44
100
108
242
18
207
72
319
41
58
440
220
383
20
6
344
186
405
285
184
40
59
45
15
360
447
b
92
260
455
441
400
200
[394]
76
279
49
153
171
445
164
375
314
470
169
148
147
128
230
281
438
284
474
38 / 183
326
334
349
471
113
183
89
373
201
329
189
30
434
145
351
446
36
243
114
60
328
292
388
54
300
9
255
410
406
166
102
70
61
436
62
204
22
38 / 251
79
224
5
335
38 / 251
454
289
330
137
28
3
88
332
453
376
288
321
274
267
456
99
252
206
56
26
155
17
479
4
338
380
97
27
80
287
421
228
278
222
461
96
354
381
48
139
105
277
398
257
348
82
450
81
225
178
409
248
227
411
149
160
c
161
308
98
172
301
482
144
1
233
282
413
403
418
197
112
364
262
339
215
179
11
159
291
368
211
379
283
111
302
428
210
237
247
425
39
24
42
236
55
391
347
417
343
337
86
202
374
401
333
235
10
[24]
392
311
299
318
71
481
457
372
119
371
29
64
234
266
65
115
132
117
286
168
131
251
116
165
219
170
223
141
408
129
254
209
208
327
151
156
110
91
180
458
150
331
[197]
[39]
152
[236]
[197]
93
295
[172]
465
[65]
439
369
c
[73]
[210]

Table 30.2. *Tithe valuers and tithe map-makers in Somerset*

Name and address (in Somerset unless indicated)	*Number of districts*	*Acreage*
Tithe valuers		
John Hancock, Halse	27	66,495
Henry Fowler Cotterell, Bath	24	38,965
Charles Chilcott, Crowcombe	23	49,980
John Easton, Bradford	17	39,624
Thomas Oatley Bennett, Bruton	17	29,475
John James, Crewkerne	17	28,883
John Martin, Evershot, Dorset	16	27,618
Charles Wainwright, Shepton Mallett	15	28,462
William Summers, Ilminster	14	11,088
John Brown, Brislington	13	23,887
John Millard Tucker, Bristol	11	26,673
George Parsons, West Lambrook	11	13,174
Hezekiah Bartlett Guy, Hinton St George	11	10,996
Edward Watts, Yeovil	10	14,481
Others [101]	250	543,455
Attributed tithe map-makers		
Cotterells and Cooper, Bath	19	28,553
Thomas Player, Pensford	15	17,257
William Wadman, Martock	14	26,734
James Peachy Williams, Bridgwater	13	35,153
William Collard Cox, Williton	11	45,797
James Poole, Sherborne, Dorset	11	18,693
Thomas Oatley Bennett, Bruton	10	18,122
W. Norris and T. F. Dickinson, Wincanton	10	16,851
Edward Watts, Yeovil	10	14,375
Summers and Slater, Ilminster	10	11,727
Others [57]	131	291,621

Table 30.3. *The tithe maps of Somerset: scales and classes*

Scale in chains/inch	*All maps*		*First Class*		*Second Class*	
	Number	*Acreage*	*Number*	*Acreage*	*Number*	*Acreage*
3	128	232,372	47	112,654	81	119,718
3.75	1	5,779	0	0	1	5,779
4	67	107,484	3	5,840	64	101,644
4.5, 5	8	9,246	0	0	8	9,246
6	206	439,654	0	0	206	439,654
6.4, 6.67, 7	4	7,538	0	0	4	7,538
8	50	120,525	0	0	50	120,525
<8	12	30,658	0	0	12	30,658
TOTAL	476	953,256	50	118,494	426	834,762

Table 30.4. *The tithe maps of Somerset: dates*

	<1837	*1837*	*1838*	*1839*	*1840*	*1841*	*1842*	*1843*	*1844*	*1845*	*1846*	*1847*	*1848*	*>1848*
All maps	5	17	79	140	77	55	38	27	14	8	4	3	1	5
1st class	0	2	12	16	14	2	3	1	0	0	0	0	0	0
2nd class*	5	15	67	124	63	53	35	26	14	8	4	3	1	5

*Three second-class tithe maps of Somerset in the Public Record Office collection are undated.

Somerset

30/1 Abbas and Temple Combe or Temple Coombe (parish) ST 714226 [Abbas Combe]
Apt 20.03.1839; 1434a (1850); Map 1839?, 6 chns, 'Surveyed in the Years 1822 and 1823'; foot/b'way, waterbodies, woods, orchards, gardens.

30/2 Abbots Leigh (parish) ST 542741
Apt 17.07.1838; 2228a (2228); Map 'Draft Map, corrected from the map by Richardson and Corfield, 1809', 1838, 7 chns, by Y. and J.P. Sturge; waterbodies, houses, woods (named), plantat-ions, building names, quarries, lodges, park wall; parks are shown by annotation: one is 'PARK, with Inclosures, Plantations etc.'

30/3 Alford (parish) ST 608318
Apt 13.07.1839; 723a (all); Map 1838, 6 chns; foot/b'way, turnpike roads (col), waterbodies, houses, woods, plantations, 'Penny's Grave' (named in gothic).

30/4 Aller (parish) ST 393300
Apt 26.01.1838; 3651a (3651); Map 1838?, 6 chns, surveyed by Richard Dixon, 3 Furnivals Inn, London, in September 1833; waterbodies, woods (col), osiers (by symbol), plantations (col), arable (col), grassland (col), orchards (col), gardens (col), hedges, field boundary ownerships, private roads (green), drains.

30/5 Almsford (parish) ST 644335 [Ansford]
Apt 11.07.1838; 844a (844); Map 1838, 8 chns; foot/b'way, waterbodies, houses, plantations, orchards, building names, keeper's walk, common; bridges named.

30/6 Alston Sutton or Ailiston or Aulston (chapelry in parish of Weare or Over Weare) ST 422515
Apt 27.09.1838; 428a (all); Map 1838?, 3 chns; houses, road names.

30/7 Angersleigh (parish) ST 197194
Apt 15.08.1840; 404a (all); Map 1839, 3 chns, by Frost and Blackmore; farmyards (col), plantations, arable (col), grassland (col), glebe (uncoloured); pictorial church; mapmakers' names are on a streamer interwoven with a combined scale-bar and plumed compass pointer.

30/8 Ashbrittle (parish) ST 047218
Apt 22.04.1839; 2490a (2489); Map 1839, 3 chns, by Cha. Chilcott; canal with locks and towpath, waterbodies, houses, woods, plantations, orchards, rock outcrops, fences, field boundary ownerships, field gates, building names, quarries, weir.

30/9 Ashcott (parish) ST 436370
Apt 13.09.1839; 2218a (2272); Map 1838, 3 chns, in 2 parts, by Jas Peachy Williams, Bridgwater; foot/b'way, houses, remains of old fence.

30/10 Ashill (parish) ST 326176
Apt 26.01.1838; 1790a (1790); Map 1838, 4 chns; spur (by hill-drawing), foot/b'way, canal, waterbodies, houses, woods, parkland, orchards, fence ownership, field gates, building names; bridge named; 'Church' is named but not mapped.

30/11 Ashington (parish) ST 562215
Apt 04.10.1838; 554a (554); Map 1839, 6 chns, in 2 parts, by J. Poole, Sherborne, Dorset; waterbodies, houses; unihabited buildings are shown without infill. District is apportioned by holding; Apt omits land use.

30/12 Asholt (parish) ST 195356 [Aisholt]
Apt 13.08.1842; 1252a (all); Map 1843, 6 chns; houses (grey).

30/13 Ash Priors (parish) ST 150294
Apt 15.09.1837; 613a (635); Map 1838, 8 chns, 'Taken from an old survey'; waterbodies, houses, woods, quarry.

30/14 Long Ashton (parish) ST 544706
Apt 07.06.1845; 1238a (4237); Map 1842, 6 chns, in 2 parts; railway, foot/b'way, waterbodies, houses, building names, old kennel, workhouse, ferry, tidal flats.

30/15 Ashwick (parish) ST 635486
Apt 09.05.1840; 1526a (1525); Map 1841?, 3 chns, by Francis Budd; houses, woods (named), plantations, building names, old road, pound; streams across fields are shown discontinuously.

30/16 Axbridge (parish) ST 431547
Apt 06.11.1839; 468a (540); Map 1839, 3 chns, by Jas Peachy Williams, Bridgwater; houses.

30/17 Babcary (parish) ST 574287
Apt 11.03.1839; 2384a (all); Map 1840?, 3 chns, 1st cl, by Benj. S.W. Cotton, West Pennard, Somerset; construction lines, road names; areas falling outside the parish but inside the primary construction lines are tinted yellow-green; buildings are without infill.

30/18 Babington (parish) ST 704505 [Not listed]
Apt 27.11.1838; 608a (all); Map 1838, 5 chns, by Charles Wainwright; waterbodies, houses, woods; tithe area numbers are stamped.

30/19 Backwell (parish) ST 495680
Apt 05.12.1840; 2902a (2902); Map 1842?, 6 chns; houses, building names, coal works; compass pointer has acorn and oak leaves.

30/20 Badgworth (parish) ST 390523
Apt 09.02.1839; 1815a (all); Map 1839?, 4 chns; houses, road names, droves; the map carries a verbose statement as to its production by the apportioner at a parish meeting.

30/21 West Bagborough (parish) ST 165340
Apt 12.01.1839; 1973a (1972); Map 1838, 8 chns, litho (Standidge); houses (by shading), woods, plantations, orchards, fence ownership, building names, parsonage; some building names appear to be neat manuscript additions.

30/22 Baltonsborough (parish) ST 552348
Apt 24.06.1842; 2473a (2472); Map 1843?, 6 chns; arable (col), grassland (col), orchards (col), gardens (col); colour bands show both field boundary ownership and land use.

30/23 Banwell (parish) ST 388608
Apt 07.07.1837; 4830a (4829); Map 'Copied from the Parish Plan made in 1834', 1838, 9 chns, in 2 parts, by J. Marmont, Bristol, (includes enlargement of village at 3 chns); building names, road names, tithe-free areas (col). Apt omits land use.

30/24 Barrington (parish) ST 392190
Apt 10.10.1839; 1656a (1656); Map 1840, 3 chns, in 2 parts, by Arthur Whitehead, Chard, Somerset; waterbodies, houses, waste.

30/25 Barrow or Barrow Gurney (parish) ST 527678
Apt 06.09.1838; 2027a (all); Map 1839, 6 chns; waterbodies, houses.

30/26 North Barrow (parish) ST 603295
Apt 24.03.1838; 732a (all); Map 1839?, 8 chns; pictorial church; no other buildings are shown; meaning of colours is uncertain.

30/27 South Barrow (parish) ST 600280
Apt 13.08.1842; 753a (all); Map 1843, 7 chns, in 3 parts, by W. Wadman, (including two plans of 'the common Fields'); open fields.

30/28 Barton St David (parish) ST 542326
Apt 28.11.1840; 946a (945); Map 1841, 6 chns; orchards.

30/29 Barwick (parish) ST 563138
Apt 17.02.1838; 785a (all); Map 1837, 6 chns, by E. Watts, Yeovil; foot/b'way, waterbodies, houses, woods, plantations, parkland, arable (col), grassland (col), orchards, hedge ownership, fences, field gates, field names, mill, turnpikes, pigeon house (pictorial), towers (pictorial), glebe; bridge named.

30/30 Batcombe (parish) ST 686394
Apt 03.12.1842; 3229a (3229); Map 1843, 4 chns, by Geo. C. Ashmead, Bristol; waterbodies, houses, woods (named), plantations, orchards, building names, road names, mill.

30/31 Bathampton (parish) ST 776660
Apt 06.09.1844; 931a (931); Map 1845, 3 chns, by Cotterells and Cooper, Bath; railway, canal with towpath and inclined plane, waterbodies, houses (dark grey), quarries (by annotation), sham castle, mill, manor house, suspension bridge.

30/32 Bathealton (parish) ST 072244
Apt 27.07.1840; 941a (941); Map 1841?, 8 chns; waterbodies, houses, woods (col), plantations (col), orchards, building names, quarries; road and field boundary lines are brown, names and symbols are black.

30/33 Bath Easton (parish or district) ST 774681 [Batheaston]
Apt 31.03.1841; 1863a (1863); Map 1840, 3 chns, 1st cl, by Thomas Weaver, Bath; construction lines, waterbodies, houses, woods, plantations, field gates, building names.

30/34 Bathford (parish) ST 792665
Apt 13.04.1839; 1820a (1820); Map 1839, 4 chns, by Cotterells and Cooper, Bath; railway, foot/b'way, waterbodies, houses, woods, plantations, osiers (by symbol), fence, building names, ferry, turnpike gate, lodge, tithing boundaries.

30/35 Bathwick (parish) ST 762651 [Not listed]
Apt 19.12.1838; 573a (573); Map 1840, 3 chns; railway, canal bank and basin, houses (dark grey), woods, plantations, building names, road names, parsonage, churchyard, baths; scale bar is graduated in feet; the title has 'Bathwick, belonging to the Duke of Cleveland'.

30/36 Bawdrip (parish) ST 337395
Apt 17.03.1841; 1826a (1889); Map 1841, 6 chns, in 2 parts, (includes village at 3 chns).

30/37 Beckington (parish) ST 813522
Apt 23.08.1839; 1791a (1830); Map copied 'From an original Map the property of the Parish', 1839, 6 chns, by Dixon and Maitland, 21 John Street, Bedford Row, (tithable parts only in detail); waterbodies, woods, plantations, arable (col), grassland (col), field boundary ownerships.

30/38 Bedminster (parish) (partly in county and city of Bristol) ST 583704
Apt 29.08.1840; 4161a (4161); Map 1841, 3 chns, by Y. and J.P. Sturge; railway, canal, waterbodies, houses, woods, commons (col), building names, school, chapels, coal pits, mill, ferry, docks, locks, turnpike gate, cemetery, county boundary; built-up part generalised; the map makers' names are 'framed' by a ruler-style scale bar.

30/39 Beer Crocombe (parish) ST 324198
Apt 08.11.1837; 871a (871); Map 1839, 6 chns, in 3 parts, by Summers and Slater, Ilminster, litho (Standidge); canal, waterbodies, woods, orchards.

30/40 Berkley (parish) ST 810496
Apt 07.06.1839; 1927a (all); Map 1838, 6 chns; waterbodies, houses, woods, plantations, osiers, glebe (col), shire stone; detached parts of other districts are green.

30/41 Berrow (parish) ST 303536
Apt 20.07.1838; 2153a (6563); Map 1838, 3 chns, 1st cl; construction lines, houses, road names, warren, sea wall, pound, drains, common.

30/42 Bickenhall (parish) ST 288186
Apt 17.02.1838; 1004a (all); Map 1838, 6 chns, by R. Ham, Taunton; hill-drawing, waterbodies, houses, woods (named), plantations, orchards, field boundary ownerships, glebe (col); legend explains colours.

30/43 Bicknoller (parish) ST 113390
Apt 28.05.1838; 1391a (1390); Map 1839, 6 chns, litho (Standidge); houses (by shading), woods, orchards, building names, quarries, common, moors; hill named; there is a verbose declaration as to the map's adoption at a parish meeting.

30/44 Biddisham (parish) ST 385540
Apt 27.09.1838; 574a (all); Map 1838, 3 chns, 1st cl, in 4 parts, by Jas Peachy Williams, Bridgwater; construction lines, foot/b'way, houses, landowners.

30/45 Binegar (parish) ST 623498
Apt 22.02.1840; 1217a (1216); Map 1839, 3 chns, in 2 parts, by Norris and Dickinson, Wincanton; turnpike roads, waterbodies.

30/46 Bishops Lydeard (parish) ST 172295
Apt 21.11.1837; 4687a (4686); Map 1838, 8 chns, in 2 parts, 'Taken from old Surveys'; hill-drawing, waterbodies, houses, mound.

30/47 Bishops Hull (parish) ST 204248 [Bishop's Hull]
Apt 26.08.1842; 1342a (1341); Map 1843?, 6 chns; railway, canal, waterbodies, houses, woods, plantations, parkland, orchards, ownerships (col); map is dated 1835 in the title.

30/48 Blackford (parish) ST 660262
Apt 27.11.1838; 578a (all); Map 1839, 6 chns; houses; pictorial church.

30/49 Blackford (hamlet in parish of Wedmore) ST 410474
Apt 24.03.1840; 1634a (?); Map 1841?, 4 chns, (tithable parts only); foot/b'way, houses (by shading), road names, landowners, rhines.

30/50 Blagdon (parish) ST 502580
Apt 02.06.1842; 3535a (3535); Map 1842, 6 chns, in 2 parts, by Geo. C. Ashmead, Bristol; foot/b'way, waterbodies, houses, woods, plantations, orchards, building names; part 2, of Regilbury, differs in style and possibly authorship from part 1.

30/51 Bleadon (parish) ST 344574
Apt 16.04.1841; 2796a (2795); Map 1843?, 4 chns, in 2 parts; railway.

30/52 Bourton or Flax Bourton (parish) ST 508694
Apt 24.03.1838; 621a (621); Map 1838, 3 chns, ? by John Brown, Brislington, Somerset; construction lines, railway, foot/b'way, waterbodies, houses, woods, hedge ownership, building names, mill, prominent tree (pictorial).

30/53 Bradford (parish) ST 177232 [Bradford-on-Tone]
Apt 12.04.1842; 1782a (1782); Map 1841, 6 chns; canal with towpath, waterbodies, houses, hedge ownership, building names, mill, park.

30/54 West Bradley (parish) ST 557368
Apt 04.05.1842; 626a (625); Map 1843?, 10 chns; waterbodies, woods, arable (col), grassland (col), orchards, pound; bridge named.

30/55 South Bradon (parish) ST 366191 [Not listed]
Apt 04.12.1842; 390a (all); Map 1843?, 3 chns; waterbodies.

30/56 Bratton Seymour (parish) ST 680297
Apt 18.12.1839; 1094a (1093); Map 1840?, 6 chns, 'Copied' by T.F. Dickinson, Wincanton, Somerset.

30/57 Brean (parish) ST 304573
Apt 25.04.1838; 1168a (all); Map 1839?, 6 chns; field gates; hill, crossroads and offshore rock are named.

30/58 East Brent (parish) ST 358526
Apt 18.06.1840; 3038a (3037); Map 1840, in 2 parts: Part 1 by William Body, 4 chns, copied from a map drawn by William Brown in 1804; Part 2 by J.P. Williams, Bridgwater, 6 chns, 'Copied from a reduced plan of Mark Tithe Map'; houses, building names, road names, field names, vicarage, pound; compass pointer and map title are quite ornate, which the map is not.

30/59 South Brent (parish) ST 330518 [Brent Knoll]
Apt 03.02.1842; 3427a (3426); Map 'From a Copy taken in the Year 1811', 1841?, 8 chns, in 2 parts, (includes 2-chn enlargement of detail); hill-drawing, railway, waterbodies; rhines, and a bridge are named; scale statement is framed by two plumed birds.

30/60 North Brewham (parish) ST 720372
Apt 09.05.1840; 2027a (2026); Map 1839, 6 chns, in 2 parts, by Norris and Dickinson, Wincanton, litho (Standidge); waterbodies, woods, coppice, orchards, building names.

30/61 South Bruham (parish) ST 730348 [South Brewham]
Apt 18.09.1839; 2672a (2671); Map 1839, [9 chns]; waterbodies, houses, woods, plantations, tower, ford, quarry.

30/62 Bridgwater (parish) ST 308370
Apt 07.05.1847; 4125a (4315); Map 1847, 10 chns, in 2 parts, (tithable parts only); railway; built-up part generalised.

30/63 Brislington (parish) ST 620707
Apt 21.09.1843; 2304a (2393); Map 1844, 6 chns, in 3 parts, ? by John Brown and Jacob Sturge, (includes two 3-chn enlargements of detail); railway with tunnels with ventilation shafts, canal, inclined plane,

waterbodies, houses (dark grey), woods, plantations, parkland, orchards, building names, burial ground, school, infant school, lodge, spring.

30/64 Broadway, New Enclosed Lands (district in parish of Broadway) ST 303155
Apt 17.09.1844; 779a (?); Map 1845, [9 chns], in 2 parts, (part 2 is at 8 chns).

30/65 Broadway, Old Enclosed Lands (district in parish of Broadway) ST 320154
Apt 17.09.1844; 934a (?); Map 1845, 6 chns, in 5 parts, (including parts at 4 chns and 8 chns and two location diagrams); fences, turnpike gate.

30/66 Brockley (parish) ST 474671
Apt 31.03.1842; 693a (all); Map 1839, 3 chns, by Danl. Horwood, Broad Street, Bristol; construction lines, houses, woods, plantations, field boundary ownerships, field gates, building names; construction lines along a track indicate traversing.

30/67 Brompton Ralph (parish) ST 084322
Apt 08.02.1842; 2691a (2690); Map 1842, 6 chns, in 6 parts, by Thomas Hawkes, Williton, (includes four 1.5-chn enlargements of detail), litho (Standidge); foot/b'way, waterbodies, houses (without infill), woods, plantations, orchards, fences, building names, parsonage, mills, waste; prominent hill named.

30/68 Broomfield (parish) ST 226327
Apt 24.05.1838; 4274a (4274); Map not dated, 12 chns; waterbodies.

30/69 Brushford (parish) SS 904251
Apt 25.05.1839; 2759a (all); Map 1840, 6 chns, by Wm Collard Cox, Williton, Somerset; building names.

30/70 Bruton (parish) ST 678349
Apt 08.12.1841; 634a (3631); Map 1842, 6 chns, in 2 parts, by T.O. Bennett, Bruton, (tithable parts only; 'The Town of Bruton' is mapped separately, at 3-chns); waterbodies, houses, woods, orchards, open fields.

30/71 Brympton (parish) ST 524157 [Brympton D'Everey]
Apt 19.12.1838; 465a (465); Map 1838, 6 chns, by E. Watts, Yeovil; waterbodies, houses, farmyards (col), woods, plantations, parkland, arable (col), grassland (col), orchards, gardens, hedge ownership, field gates, building names; hill named.

30/72 Buckland Dinham (parish) ST 750512
Apt 27.07.1840; 1400a (1399); Map 1841, 6 chns; houses, woods, plantations, orchards, osiers.

30/73 Buckland St Mary (parish) ST 264139
Apt 07.07.1839; 3494a (3494); Map 1841?, 4 chns, in 2 parts; waterbodies, boundary landmarks; pictorial church.

30/74 West Buckland (parish) ST 171198
Apt 11.10.1839; 3672a (3671); Map 1841?, 6 chns; canal with towpath and lock, waterbodies, houses, woods (col), plantations (col), orchards, building names.

30/75 Burnett (parish) ST 664652
Apt 17.10.1838; 609a (608); Map 1838, 4 chns, by Y. and J.P. Sturge; waterbodies, houses, woods, plantations.

30/76 Burnham (parish) ST 325491 [Burnham-on-Sea]
Apt 27.03.1838; 3873a (4302); Map 1838, 3 chns, 1st cl, by James Peachy Williams, Bridgwater; construction lines, railway, foot/b'way, houses, arable (by annotation), orchards (by annotation), field boundary ownerships.

30/77 Burrington (parish) ST 482591
Apt 16.06.1838; 2010a (2009); Map 1839?, 4 chns, in 3 parts; foot/b'way, field gates, road names, boundary stones and marks, well, barrows, fox holes; paths and tracks across fields and downs are shown discontinuously.

30/78 Butcombe (parish) ST 516621
Apt 20.07.1843; 984a (983); Map 1842?, 3 chns, 1st cl, by Thos Ward, Bristol; construction lines, houses; bridge named.

30/79 Butleigh (parish) ST 518337
Apt 30.01.1843; 4467a (4467); Map 1843, 6.4 chns, in 3 parts, by Cha. Wainwright, (including one part at 3 chns with construction lines); waterbodies, houses, woods, plantations, parkland, orchards, fences, drains.

30/80 North Cadbury (parish) ST 637281
Apt 20.10.1837; 2676a (2810); Map 1839, 9 chns; tithing boundaries.

30/81 South Cadbury (parish) ST 631256
Apt 23.06.1842; 712a (all); Map 1839, 4 chns, by Wm Maud, Sherborne; hill-drawing, woods, orchards, fence, hill fort (in detail), parsonage.

30/82 West Camel (parish) ST 571252
Apt 31.05.1839; 1953a (1953); Map 1839?, 6 chns, (tinted); construction lines, waterbodies, houses, woods, plantations, obelisk (pictorial), lime kiln; scale bar is decorated with grey 'spirit-bubbles'.

30/83 Camely (parish) ST 612578
Apt 27.09.1838; 1633a (1633); Map 1839, [3 chns] 1st cl, by J. Marmont, Bristol; construction lines, houses.

30/84 Camerton (parish) ST 684576
Apt 17.07.1844; 1749a (1748); Map 1844, 6 chns; railway, canal; tithable areas are edged in yellow.

30/85 Cannington (parish) ST 257398
Apt 16.08.1839; 4332a (5015); Map 1839, 8 chns; houses (grey); uninhabited buildings are shown in outline only.

30/86 Capland, Old Enclosures (parish) ST 302189
Apt 03.09.1842; 360a (all); Map 1845, 6 chns; common.

30/87 Carhampton (parish) SS 999420
Apt 19.09.1840; 5200a (5724); Map 1839, 8 chns, in 6 parts, by William Collard Cox, Sampford Brett, Somerset, (includes enlargement of Carhampton village at 4 chns and 80-chn index 'from the Ordnance Map'; foot/b'way, fences, lawn; compass is very large, and is integrated into the borders of the detached portions; woodland is indicated by name. Some hills and bridges are named.

30/88 Castle Cary (parish) ST 627312
Apt 18.05.1839; 2573a (2625); Map 1840?, 3 chns; waterbodies, houses, building names, mill.

30/89 Catcott (hamlet in parish of Moorlinch) ST 401402
Apt 08.01.1841; 2256a (2256); Map 1841, 6 chns, in 2 parts; foot/b'way.

30/90 St Catherine or Kattern (hamlet or chapelry) ST 770701
Apt 24.03.1842; 1041a (1040); Map 1840, 3 chns, 1st cl, by T. Weaver, Bath; waterbodies, houses, building names, mills.

30/91 Chaffcombe (parish) ST 354095
Apt 20.03.1839; 999a (999); Map 1840, 6 chns, by Summers and Slater, Ilminster; waterbodies, house names.

30/92 Chapel Allerton (parish) ST 402495
Apt 27.09.1841; 1170a (1169); Map 1837, 3 chns, by John Millard, Bristol; waterbodies, houses, orchards, field boundary ownerships, mill, glebe (col); legend explains some colours; colour bands may show property ownerships.

30/93 Chard (parish) ST 335079
Apt 31.05.1842; 5449a (5449); Map 1841, 6 chns, by Arthur Whitehead, Chard; canal, waterbodies, reservoir; built-up part generalised; streams across fields are shown discontinuously.

30/94 Charlcombe (parish) ST 748672
Apt 18.04.1839; 571a (all); Map 1838, 3 chns; construction lines, foot/b'way, waterbodies, houses, woods, orchards, hedge ownership, fence ownership, boundary stones, milestone.

30/95 Charlinch (parish) ST 243376
Apt 10.05.1837; 1433a (all); Map 1838?, 6 chns; hill-drawing, houses, farmyards, woods (col), arable (col), grassland (col), orchards (col), gardens; map is dated 1831 in the title; legend explains symbols and colours; north pointer has acorn tip.

30/96 Charlton Adam (parish) ST 544285
Apt 14.12.1850; 90a (?); Map 1851?, 6.6 chns; Roman road, road destinations, 'Road not stoned'.

30/97 Charlton Adam and Charlton Mackrell (parish) ST 536281
Corn rent conversion, 1920; ?a (3910); Map 1921, 6.55 chns, in 3 parts, (tracing of 1809 enclosure map); hill-drawing, foot/b'way, houses, woods, gardens, hedge ownership, fence ownership, road names, landowners, footbridge, parish boundaries (col), new enclosues (red); walls are shown by 'battlement' effect. Apt omits land use and acreages.

30/98 Charlton Horethorne (parish) ST 657235
Apt 18.08.1841; 2363a (all); Map 1842, 6 chns by 'J.R. Jobbins, Survr., Draftn., and Lithor., 3 Warwick Ct., Holborn', litho; woods, plantations, orchards.

30/99 Charlton Musgrave (parish) ST 721302 [Charlton Musgrove]
Apt 23.10.1838; 2153a (2153); Map 1839, 6 chns, in 2 parts, by I. Poole, Sherborne, Dorset; houses, building names, brick yard, toll gate, mill, haha; streams across fields are shown discontinuously.

30/100 Cheddar (parish) ST 459531
Apt 21.10.1837; 6998a (6998); Map 1839, 8 chns; houses.

30/101 Cheddon Fitzpaine (parish) ST 235279
Apt 07.06.1837; 945a (960); Map 1837?, 6 chns; canal, waterbodies, houses, woods, hedge ownership.

30/102 Chedzoy (parish) ST 342369
Apt 17.11.1840; 1656a (1655); Map 1836, 6 chns, in 3 parts, by James Peachy Williams, Land Agent and Surveyor, Bridgwater, (includes 3-chn enlargement of detail); foot/b'way, turnpike roads with destinations, waterbodies, houses, farmyards (col), arable (col), grassland (col), orchards (col), gardens (col), open fields (named), hedge ownership, road names, drove names; legend explains symbols; widths are given for some open field access roads. Border has rounded corners.

30/103 Chelvey (parish) ST 472680
Apt 08.12.1837; 442a (1077); Map 1838, 6 chns, by T. Player, Pensford; railway, woods, orchards; field boundaries are highlighted in green.

30/104 Chelwood (parish) ST 633615
Apt 16.11.1837; 1078a (1077); Map 1837, 4 chns, by T. Player, Pensford; woods, arable (col), grassland (col), orchards, gardens; legend explains symbols.

30/105 North Cheriton (parish) ST 698258
Apt 23.10.1838; 1089a (1088); Map 1839, 6 chns; mill, stable, ford, garden (by annotation), house name.

30/106 Chew Magna (parish) ST 584618
Apt 07.06.1839; 5006a (5006); Map 1840, 6 chns, in 8 parts, (includes seven 3-chn enlargements of detail; tithable parts tinted); waterbodies, woods, plantations, building names, road names, well, spring, chapel; bridges and streams are named.

30/107 Chew Stoke (parish) ST 559615
Apt 22.09.1837; 2092a (2092); Map 1839, 3 chns, 1st cl, 'Drawn by Chas F. Humbert, 12/12/39'; waterbodies, building names, snuff mill, Methodist Chapel.

30/108 Chewton Mendip (parish) ST 586518
Apt 16.05.1839; 5810a (5809); Map 1839, 6 chns, in 3 parts; waterbodies, field gates, building names, landowners, milestones, tithe-free wood, recently-enclosed field names.

30/109 Chilcompton (parish) ST 644519
Apt 23.05.1844; 1233a (all); Map 1841, 3 chns, 1st cl, by Alfred T. Beloe; construction lines, hill-drawing, waterbodies, houses, woods, plantations, orchards, earthwork.

30/110 Chillington (parish) ST 393110
Apt 20.03.1839; 882a (881); Map 1839, 6 chns, by George Moss, Crewkerne, Somerset; foot/b'way, woods, orchards, fences, toll gate, nursery; down named.

30/111 Chilthorne Domer (parish) ST 526198
Apt 14.03.1844; 1393a (1392); Map 1844, 6 chns; houses, plantations, orchards.

30/112 Chilton Cantelo (parish) ST 571221
Apt 04.12.1842; 631a (all); Map 1843, 5 chns, by William Wadman; houses, plantations, orchards; bridge named.

30/113 Chilton super Polden (hamlet in parish of Moorlinch) ST 378408 [Chilton Polden]
Apt 20.03.1839; 1857a (1856); Map 1839, 3 chns, in 2 parts; canal with towpath, wooden bridges (by Dawson's symbol).

30/114 Chilton Trinity (parish) ST 299394
Apt 18.03.1839; 1047a (1543); Map 1839, 6 chns, in 9 parts, (includes index); railway, building names.

30/115 East Chinnock (parish) ST 496134
Apt 28.02.1843; 1321a (1320); Map 1844, 6 chns, by Wm Wadman, Martock; waterbodies, woods, plantations, gardens, waste; a stream across fields is shown discontinuously.

30/116 Middle Chinnock (parish) ST 474134
Apt 18.10.1839; 471a (471); Map 1842, 3 chns; arable (col), grassland (col), orchards (col), gardens (col), open fields, ford; pictorial church.

30/117 West Chinnock (parish) ST 467135
Apt 22.10.1839; 642a (642); Map 1842, 3 chns, in 2 parts; waterbodies, woods (col), plantations (col), osiers (col), arable (col), grassland (col), orchards (col), gardens (col); bridge named; pictorial church.

30/118 Chipstable (parish) ST 044262
Apt 16.04.1841; 2253a (2252); Map 1840, 3 chns, by S. Court; hill-drawing, foot/b'way, private roads (uncoloured), waterbodies, houses, woods, plantations, orchards, gardens, hedge ownership, fence ownership, field boundary ownerships, field gates, stone walls, building names, landowners; legend explains symbols and boundaries, though meaning of red band is unclear; north pointer has plumes.

30/119 Chiselborough (parish) ST 473149
Apt 18.10.1839; 790a (all); Map 1842?, 3 chns; waterbodies, woods (col), arable (col), grassland (col), orchards (col), gardens (col); pictorial church.

30/120 Christon (parish) ST 382578
Apt 18.07.1839; 571a (571); Map 1839, 6 chns; houses.

30/121 Churchill (parish) ST 455605
Apt 12.03.1842; 2397a (all); Map 1842, 8 chns; waterbodies.

30/122 Churchstanton (parish) ST 195138
Corn rent conversion, 1920; 3702a (4980); Map 1920, OS 1:2500 of c.1903 annotated with tithe area numbers.

30/123 Clapton, or Clapton in Gordano (parish) ST 465736 [Clapton-in-Gordano]
Apt 21.11.1837; 1066a (all); Map 1838, 3 chns, 1st cl; construction lines, waterbodies, houses, building names, parsonage, drains; scale bar and north pointer are combined.

30/124 Clatworthy (parish) ST 052324
Apt 03.11.1837; 2848a (all); Map 1840, 6 chns, in 12 parts, (includes eleven 2-chn enlargements of detail), litho (Standidge); houses (by shading), woods, plantations, orchards, building names, cross (pictorial).

30/125 Claverton (parish) ST 781640
Apt 22.03.1839; 1229a (1228); Map 8 chns, 'Copied Jan 1840' by Cotterells and Cooper, Bath; canal, weir, holding boundaries (col). District is apportioned by holding.

30/126 Old Cleeve (parish) ST 035395
Apt 11.12.1838; 4793a (5413); Map 1839, 8 chns, in 37 parts, by R. Ham, Taunton, Somerset, (includes 36 4-chn enlargements of detail, in manuscript), litho (Standidge); foot/b'way, turnpike roads, houses (by shading), woods, orchards, rock outcrops, hedge ownership, fence ownership, field boundary ownerships, field gates, building names, quarry, seashore rocks, cliffs, limekiln, mill, pigeon house (pictorial).

30/127 Clevedon (parish) ST 410710
Apt 21.08.1838; 2987a (4067); Map 1839, 3 chns; foot/b'way, waterbodies, houses, footbridges. Apt omits land use.

30/128 Cloford (parish) ST 723438
Apt 28.12.1838; 2244a (2243); Map 1839, 3 chns, 1st cl, by J. Marmont, Bristol; construction lines, waterbodies, houses.

30/129 Closeworth (parish) ST 562105 [Closworth]
Apt 31.01.1837; 1072a (1071); Map 1838, 6 chns; houses, holding boundaries; legend explains holdings; scale bar and compass rose are blue. District is apportioned by holding; Apt omits land use.

30/130 Clutton (parish) ST 627595
Apt 13.11.1837; 1637a (1636); Map 1838, 4 chns, by T. Player, Pensford; waterbodies, woods; field boundaries are highlighted in green; a stream across fields is shown discontinuously; legend explains symbols.

30/131 East Coker (parish) ST 538128
Apt 11.03.1840; 2081a (2121); Map 1839, 6 chns, by William Wadman, Martock; waterbodies, houses, woods, plantations, parkland; legend explains symbols.

30/132 West Coker (parish) ST 520139
Apt 21.07.1838; 1299a (all); Map 1838, 8 chns, surveyed by William Wadman in 1815; waterbodies, houses.

30/133 Coombeflorey (parish) ST 152316 [Combe Florey]
Apt 28.01.1839; 1370a (1369); Map not dated, 8 chns; waterbodies, houses.

30/134 Combhay (parish) ST 733603 [Combe Hay]
Apt 11.06.1839; 994a (1091); Map 1839, 4 chns; canal with towpath and flight of locks, waterbodies, houses, landowners, 'Mansion'; scale-bar is graduated in poles.

30/135 Compton Bishop (parish) ST 410551
Apt 21.07.1838; 2536a (2535); Map 1839, 6 chns, by J.M. Tucker, litho (Standidge); hill-drawing, waterbodies, woods (named), workhouse; physical features named.

30/136 Compton Dando (parish) ST 649640
Apt 11.02.1842; 1974a (1974); Map 1842, 6 chns, in 16 parts, by Thos Player, Pensford, near Bristol, (includes 15 3-chn enlargements of detail).

30/137 Compton Dundon (parish) ST 487323
Apt 18.02.1841; 2571a (2571); Map 1842?, 6 chns; woods, orchards, field boundary ownerships, drove.

30/138 Compton Martin (parish) ST 547578
Apt 24.02.1841; 2315a (2314); Map surveyed in 1840, 3 chns, 1st cl, by W. Morris, Bristol; construction lines, foot/b'way, waterbodies, houses, field boundary ownerships, field gates, ford; compass card is small but distinctive.

30/139 Compton Pauncefoot (parish) ST 646257
Apt 12.01.1839; 672a (all); Map 1839, 3 chns; waterbodies, houses, castle; pictorial church, with gravestones.

30/140 Congresbury (parish) ST 434633
Apt 21.06.1839; 4444a (4443); Map 1840, 3 chns, 1st cl, by Thos Ward, Bristol; construction lines, railway, houses (black), field boundary ownerships.

30/141 Combe St Nicholas (parish) ST 297120
Apt 11.06.1839; 4044a (4203); Map 1840, [6 chns]; waterbodies, glebe (orange), tithe-free land (yellow).

30/142 Corfe (parish) ST 236188
Apt 09.05.1838; 1128a (1127); Map 1839, 8 chns, in 2 parts, litho (Standidge); waterbodies, houses (by shading), woods, plantations, orchards, boundary stones, common.

30/143 Corston (parish) ST 685652
Apt 21.05.1845; 1191a (1190); Map 1843, 6 chns, in 6 parts, by Cotterells and Cooper, Bath, (includes enlargement of village at 2 chns and turnpike gate and other buildings at 3 chns); railway, waterbodies, houses (dark grey), turnpike gate.

30/144 Corton Denham (parish) ST 634223
Apt 14.01.1837; 1371a (1371); Map 1837, 6 chns, by I. Poole, Sherborne, Dorset; landowners, holdings (col); legend explains holding colours; tithe-free land is mapped but not coloured. District is apportioned by holding; Apt omits land use.

30/145 Cossington (parish) ST 366409
Apt 04.06.1839; 1381a (1380); Map 1839?, 3 chns, in 2 parts, by Geo. C. Ashmead, Bristol; canal with towing path, waterbodies, houses, woods, plantations, orchards, drove, decoy pool (in detail), drains, withies.

30/146 Cothelstone (parish) ST 186317
Apt 08.10.1838; 907a (906); Map 1839?, 8 chns; waterbodies, houses.

30/147 East Cranmore (parish) ST 689439
Apt 27.09.1838; 1055a (1054); Map 1839, 4 chns, by J. White, Mells; waterbodies, houses, building names, toll gate. District is apportioned by holding; Apt omits land use.

30/148 West Cranmore (parish) ST 668433 [Cranmore]
Apt 11.06.1840; 1814a (1814); Map 1841?, 6 chns; waterbodies, houses, hedge ownership.

30/149 Creech St Michael (parish) ST 278267
Apt 16.10.1839; 2304a (all); Map 1839, 3 chns, in 2 parts, by R. Hodges, North Petherton, (including Little Creech at 6-chns); foot/b'way, canal with towpath, houses, field gates, weir.

30/150 Crewkerne (parish or district) ST 428094
Apt 03.09.1842; 5331a (5331); Map 1844, 6 chns, in 17 parts, by George Moss, Crewkern, (includes 3-chn enlargement of detail); foot/b'way, turnpike roads, toll gate, waterbodies, houses, open fields, field gates, road names, building names, field names, woods (by name); bridges named.

30/151 Cricket Malherbie (parish) ST 360116
Apt 06.07.1842; 540a (540); Map 1843, 3 chns; canal. Apt omits some land use.

30/152 Cricket St Thomas (parish) ST 373088
Apt 20.07.1838; 297a (875); Map 1840, 3 chns, by Arthur Whitehead, Chard, (tithable parts only); houses.

30/153 Croscombe (parish) ST 602453
Apt 19.12.1838; 1432a (1432); Map 1839?, 6 chns, in 9 parts, by Chas Wainwright; hill-drawing, houses, woods, plantations, orchards, building names, hill fort; tithe area numbers are stamped; mapped areas outside the tithe district are tinted green.

30/154 Crowcombe (parish) ST 138364
Apt 31.05.1842; 3176a (3176); Map surveyed in 1806 and revised in 1842, 8 chns, in 2 parts, by Charles Chilcott, (includes enlargement of village at 3 chns), litho (Standidge); foot/b'way, waterbodies, houses, woods, plantations, orchards, fences, green; legend explains depiction of buildings.

30/155 Cucklington, Stoke and Bayford (parish) ST 749286
Apt 24.03.1838; 2865a (?); Map 1838, 6 chns; waterbodies, woods, orchards, building names, well, parsonage, mill, county boundary, common; buildings are shown without infill.

30/156 Cudworth (parish) ST 373107
Apt 16.07.1841; 1078a (1077); Map 1841, 8 chns, by Arthur Whitehead, Chard; hill-drawing, orchards, pits.

30/157 Culbone or Kitner (parish) SS 825481
Apt 11.08.1838; 1502a (1502); Map 1838, 4 chns; waterbodies, houses, woods, heath/moor, boundary barrow and well, fords; hill named. Apt omits land use.

30/158 Curland (parish) ST 274169
Apt 24.06.1841; 778a (all); Map 1841, 12 chns, in 5 parts, (includes four 4-chn enlargements of detail), litho (Standidge); woods, coppice, orchards, pound.

30/159 Curry Mallet (parish) ST 329220
Apt 12.11.1839; 1651a (1650); Map 1840, 8 chns; waterbodies, building names; pictorial church.

30/160 North Curry (parish) ST 315245
Apt 16.05.1840; 5556a (5556); Map 1840, 3 chns, in 2 parts, by Rd. Hodges, North Petherton, (part 2 at 8 chns); foot/b'way, canal with tunnel, waterbodies, houses, open fields, fences, turnpike gate, drains.

30/161 Curry Rivell (parish) ST 391241 [Curry Rivel]
Apt 13.04.1839; 4108a (4108); Map 1841, 6 chns, in 2 parts; canal with towpath, waterbodies, houses (by shading), woods, parkland, orchards, fences, building names, mills, mill stream, weir, green. (The map in PRO IR 30 is a lithographed copy, possibly by Standidge; the manuscript original is in PRO IR 77/56.)

30/162 Cutcombe (parish) SS 913396
Apt 25.03.1840; 6931a (7231); Map 1841, 6 chns, by Thomas Hawkes, Williton, Somerset; Dunkery Beacon; buildings are shown without infill.

30/163 St Decumans (parish) ST 072416
Apt 29.01.1841; 3762a (4281); Map 1841, 6 chns, in 12 parts, surveyed by Daniel Horwood, Bristol, in 1838 and revised by Thomas Hawkes, Williton in 1841, (including Watchet and Williton and other enlargements of detail at 3 chns), litho (Standidge); waterbodies, houses (by shading), woods, plantations, orchards, open fields, building names, harbour, pier, workhouse.

30/164 Dinder (parish) ST 588452
Apt 16.06.1838; 1071a (all); Map 1838?, 4 chns, in 3 parts, ? by Charles Wainwright, Shepton Mallet, Somerset; hill-drawing, waterbodies, houses, woods, plantations, orchards, hill fort, pit, well; streams named; mapped areas outside the tithe district are tinted pink.

30/165 Dinnington (parish) ST 402125
Apt 26.02.1839; 515a (514); Map 1838, 6 chns; waterbodies, plantations, orchards, field gates, common meadow, glebe.

30/166 Ditcheat (parish) ST 618351
Apt 12.04.1838; 4511a (4511); Map 1838, 6 chns, in 2 parts; houses, orchards, open fields, footbridge, ford, glebe (col), greens, green lanes (uncoloured); bridges named.

30/167 Dodington (parish) ST 174402
Apt 12.01.1839; 543a (all); Map 1838, 4 chns; waterbodies, houses, woods, plantations, coppice, orchards, pit; houses are black and other buildings red.

30/168 Donyatt (parish) ST 337141
Apt 14.03.1838; 1224a (1223); Map 1838, 4 chns, by Summers and Slater, Ilminster; foot/b'way, canal with towpath, waterbodies, fences, field gates, fords, mill.

30/169 Doulting (parish) ST 647427
Apt 25.05.1839; 3526a (3600); Map 1842?, 4 chns, in 2 parts; construction lines, hill-drawing, waterbodies, houses, woods, plantations, orchards, rock outcrops, building names, landmark stone (by symbol), toll gate, quarries, vicarage, water mill (by symbol).

30/170 Dowlish Wake or East Dowlish and West Dowlish (parish) ST 368128
Apt 27.09.1838; 1283a (1282); Map 1840, 6 chns, in 2 parts; canal, building names. (The copy in PRO IR 30 is an uncoloured photocopy of the Diocesan Copy.)

30/171 Downhead (parish) ST 696456
Apt 27.09.1838; 1525a (all); Map 1839?, [6 chns]; foot/b'way, waterbodies, houses, woods, plantations, arable (col), grassland (col). District is apportioned by holding, though fields are numbered separately; Apt omits most land use.

30/172 Drayton (parish) ST 410238
Apt 03.01.1840; 2166a (2165); Map 6 chns, drawn in 1822 by P.B. Ilett, surveyor, Taunton, and corrected to 1840 by J.F.H. Warren, Langport; foot/b'way, canal with towpath and lock, waterbodies, houses (by shading), woods, orchards, building names, field names, obelisk (pictorial).

30/173 Dulverton (parish) SS 904291
Apt 22.11.1839; 8337a (8337); Map 1838, 3 chns, in 2 parts, by E. Harris, (includes Dulverton town separately at 2 chns); hill-drawing, foot/b'way, rights of way, waterbodies, houses, woods, plantations, parkland, orchards, gardens, heath/moor, hedge ownership, fence ownership, building names, road names, landowners, weir, vicarage, Tarr Steps, turnpike gate, farm names and boundaries; bridges are named and shown by Dawson's symbols; hills named; legend explains symbols, including 'Earthern Fences' and 'Stone Walls'.

30/174 Dundry (parish) ST 561663
Apt 07.12.1840; 2800a (2799); Map 1841, 6 chns, in 2 parts, (tinted; includes 3-chn enlargement of detail); waterbodies, houses, woods.

30/175 Dunkerton (parish) ST 704593
Apt 01.09.1840; 1233a (all); Map 1841, 6 chns, in 6 parts, by Cotterells and Cooper, Bath, (includes five 3-chn enlargements of detail), litho (Standidge); canal with towpath and locks, waterbodies, houses (by shading), woods (named), orchards, building names, rectory, quarries, lime kilns, chapel, pumping engine, mill, Roman road; bridge named.

30/176 Dunster (parish) SS 981437
Apt 31.10.1840; 2871a (3455); Map 1842?, 6 chns, in 3 parts, (includes two settlements separately at 3 chns); waterbodies, houses (on enlargements only), fence ownership, pools, well, horse pond, castle earthworks, wooden bridge (by Dawson's symbol).

30/177 Durleigh (parish) ST 272362
Apt 31.05.1839; 887a (all); Map 1839, [6 chns], in 3 parts; turnpike roads; buildings are shown without infill.

30/178 Durston (parish) ST 296279
Apt 21.03.1838; 595a (1022); Map 1838?, 6 chns, in 2 parts; foot/b'way, waterbodies, woods, arable (col), grassland (col), orchards, hedge ownership (col), fence ownership; farm named; pictorial church; land use information is omitted for tithe-free land; map has 'Wm. Summers, Surveyor, 1821' in the title.

30/179 Earnshill (parish) ST 384218 [Not listed]
Apt 27.03.1838; 375a (375); Map 1838, 3 chns, in 2 parts, by Summers and Slater, Ilminster, (detatched parts at 6 chns); waterbodies.

30/180 Easthams (rectory or district in parish of Crewkerne) ST 458099 [Not listed]
Apt 16.05.1840; 205a (?); Map 1839, 5 chns, by Geo. Moss, Crewkerne; foot/b'way, turnpike roads, toll gates, waterbodies, houses, plantations, orchards, field gates, modus land boundary; legend explains symbols.

30/181 East Harptree (parish) ST 564545
Apt 27.11.1838; 2597a (2770); Map 1839?, 6 chns, by J.M. Tucker; waterbodies, field gates, building names; meaning of blue band is unclear.

30/182 Easton in Gordano or St George (parish) ST 515763 [Easton-in-Gordano]
Apt 21.06.1839; 1596a (1931); Map 1840?, 3 chns, 1st cl, by Geo. C. Ashmead, Bristol; construction lines, base line, waterbodies, houses, woods, plantations, parkland, field boundary ownerships, field gates, common, drains; built-up part generalised.

30/183 Edington (hamlet in parish of Moorlinch) ST 391419
Apt 20.07.1838; 2167a (2167); Map 1838?, 6 chns, in 2 parts; canal with towpath, building names, chapels, milestone, sand pit, rhine names.

30/184 Elm (parish) ST 748493 [Great Elm]
Apt 25.10.1839; 893a (all); Map 1840, 6 chns, in 2 parts; foot/b'way, houses, woods, plantations, orchards.

30/185 Elworthy (parish) ST 091336
Apt 11.02.1840; 1635a (all); Map 1840, 6 chns, by R.P. Purssey, Monksilver, litho (Standidge); waterbodies, houses (by shading), woods, plantations, parkland, orchards, fences, building names, ford.

30/186 Emberrow (parish) ST 614505 [Emborough]
Apt 21.03.1839; 2040a (2039); Map 1839?, 4 chns, 1st cl, in 4 parts, by J.M. Tucker, Bristol; construction lines, waterbodies, woods, milestone (by symbol), boundary of areas tithable to vicar and rector.

30/187 Enmore (parish) ST 242352
Apt 06.05.1837; 1113a (1112); Map 1837, 4 chns; waterbodies, houses, woods, orchards, quarry.

30/188 Englishcombe (parish) ST 717620
Apt 06.02.1840; 1852a (all); Map 1840, 6 chns, in 2 parts, by Cotterells and Cooper, Bath, (includes 3-chn enlargement of detail); foot/b'way, houses (black), Roman road.

30/189 Evercreech (parish) ST 653392
Apt 10.01.1838; 4078a (4078); Map 1839, 6 chns, by T.O. Bennett, Bruton; hill-drawing, waterbodies, houses, woods (named), plantations, orchards, building names, mills, hill fort, limekiln, commons.

30/190 Exford (parish) SS 842394
Apt 18.05.1839; 5699a (5699); Map 1840, 3 chns, by John Elliott; hill-drawing, waterbodies, houses, woods, plantations, orchards, gardens, heath/moor, rock outcrops, hedge ownership, fences, field gates, building names, farm names, landowners, boundary mounds and markers; north pointer has plumes; legend explains symbols, including 'Earthen Fences' and walls; a bridge is shown using Dawson's symbol.

30/191 Exton (parish) SS 936353
Apt 30.08.1838; 4046a (all); Map 1840, 6 chns, by I. Keen, Dulverton; building names, ford, pit.

30/192 Farmborough (parish) ST 655605
Apt 05.06.1840; 1494a (1494); Map 1841, 3 chns, 1st cl, by Thos. Player, Pensford, Bristol; construction lines.

30/193 Farrington Gurney (parish) ST 632558
Apt 10.03.1841; 923a (923); Map 1840, 6 chns, by T. Player, Pensford.

30/194 Felton or Whitchurch (parish) ST 603679 [Whitchurch]
Apt 18.01.1839; 2195a (2194); Map 1840, 6 chns; houses, building names, green.

30/195 Fiddington (parish) ST 219403
Apt 15.9.1837; 826a (all); Map 3 chns, surveyed in October 1837 by Alexander King, Nether Stowey; construction lines, base line, foot/b'way, houses, field gates, pit.

30/196 Fitzhead (parish) ST 117286
Apt 11.03.1841; 1208a (all); Map 1840?, 8 chns, litho (by W. Day, 17 Gate Street, Lincolns Inn Fields); waterbodies, woods, parkland, orchards, rock outcrops, building names, boat house, lime kilns.

30/197 Fivehead (parish) ST 352229
Apt 28.12.1838; 1722a (1721); Map '1835' (? 1839), 6 chns, in 2 parts; hill-drawing, foot/b'way, turnpike roads, waterbodies, houses (by shading), woods, plantations, arable, grassland (col), orchards, gardens, hedge ownership, field gates, pits; pictorial church.

30/198 Foxcote (parish) ST 718552
Apt 19.12.1838; 602a (?); Map 1839, 3 chns; foot/b'way, waterbodies, houses, hedge ownership, fence ownership, field gates, mill; some names are written upside down to the title.

30/199 Freshford (parish) ST 782600
Apt 06.05.1837; 562a (561); Map 1838?, 3 chns; foot/b'way, turnpike roads, houses, woods, plantations, parkland, orchards, hedge ownership, fence ownership, field gates.

30/200 Frome Selwood (parish) ST 777462 [Frome]
Apt 13.02.1840; 6932a (7092); Map 1840, 6 chns, by Cruse and Fox; waterbodies, houses, woods (named), field names, forest, workhouse; built-up part generalised; detached parts of other districts are tinted yellow.

30/201 St Benedict and St John, Glastonbury (parish) ST 500385 [Glastonbury]
Apt 15.12.1840; 7083a (7083); Map 1844, 6 chns, in 23 parts, by Thomas Hawkes, Williton, Taunton, Somerset, (includes town separately at 3 chns and four 3-chn enlargements of detail, and 17 3-chn enlargements of common fields in manuscript), litho (Standidge); waterbodies, houses (by shading), woods, plantations, orchards, open fields, fences, decoy, tor, abbey buildings.

30/202 Goathill (parish) ST 674171
Apt 11.06.1839; 300a (all); Map 1840, 6 chns, by J. Poole, Sherborne, Dorset; houses. District is apportioned by holding.

30/203 Goathurst (parish) ST 259343
Apt 29.01.1846; 1438a (1438); Map 1842, 8 chns, in 2 parts; buildings are shown without infill.

30/204 Grenton (parish) ST 414357 [Greinton]
Apt 21.08.1840; 845a (845); Map 1841, 4 chns, by Geoff. Cumming, Exeter; woods (col), orchards (col).

30/205 Halse (parish) ST 138284
Apt 07.09.1840; 1301a (1301); Map 1839, 6 chns, in 2 parts, by Wm Collard Cox, Williton, Somerset, (includes enlargement of village at 3 chns); foot/b'way, waterbodies, hedge ownership, fence ownership, ford; streams across fields are shown by broken lines; it is unclear why some fields are tinted green or pink.

30/206 High Ham (parish) ST 428310
Apt 10.01.1838; 4229a (4229); Map 'September 1832' (? 1838), 6 chns, in 2 parts, by Richard Dixon, 3 Furnivals Inn; waterbodies, houses, farmyards (col), woods (col), plantations (col), arable (col), grassland (col), orchards (col), gardens (col), hedge ownership, field boundary ownerships, avenue of trees, workhouse, drains.

30/207 Hardington (parish) ST 743528
Apt 20.10.1839; 831a (all); Map 1840, 8 chns, by Cotterells and Cooper, Bath; woods.

30/208 Hardington Mandeville (parish) ST 505105
Apt 18.11.1841; 2632a (2631); Map 1843?, 6 chns, in 3 parts, (includes two 3-chn enlargements of detail); foot/b'way, waterbodies, houses, woods (col), plantations (col), arable (col), grassland (col), orchards (col), field names.

30/209 Haselbury Plucknett (parish) ST 486108 [Not listed]
Apt 17.09.1840; 2070a (2069); Map 1841, 6 chns, by J. Poole, Sherborne, Dorset; houses, open fields; streams running through fields are shown discontinuously.

30/210 Hatch Beauchamp (parish) ST 303204
Apt 20.09.1839; 1121a (1120); Map '1834' (? 1839), 4 chns, in 3 parts, by Chas Ilett; foot/b'way, waterbodies, houses (by shading), woods, plantations, parkland, arable, grassland, orchards, gardens, hedge ownership, fence ownership, field gates.

30/211 West Hatch (parish) ST 287212
Apt 15.08.1840; 1682a (1681); Map 1841, [6 chns], in 3 parts, by R. Ham, Taunton, (including one part at 8 chns and a small enlargement at 3 chns), litho (Standidge); fences, drove names.

30/212 Hawkridge (parish) SS 844318
Apt 14.09.1840; 3725a (3725); Map 1841, 6 chns, in 2 parts; woods, plantations, barrows, well, tarr steps, common; meaning of red and blue bands is unclear.

30/213 Heathfield (parish) ST 162267
Apt 28.11.1838; 693a (692); Map 1839, 3 chns, by W. Collard Cox, Williton, Somerset; foot/b'way, waterbodies, hedge ownership, fence ownership.

30/214 Hemington (parish) ST 739545
Apt 23.09.1840; 3047a (all); Map 1840, 8 chns, in 2 parts, by Cotterells and Cooper, Bath, (includes enlargement of Faulkland village at 3 chns); houses (dark grey), open fields, building names.

30/215 Henstridge (parish) ST 723204
Apt 12.01.1839; 4252a (4252); Map 1839, 6 chns, litho (by C.F. Cheffins, 9 Southampton Buildings, Holborn); hill-drawing, turnpike roads, waterbodies, houses (by shading), woods, plantations, orchards, building names, notable tree, quarries.

30/216 Hillfarrance (parish) ST 175248
Apt 17.11.1840; 921a (920); Map 1840, 6 chns, in 8 parts, by William Collard Cox, Williton, (includes 25-chn index); foot/b'way, canal, fences, building names, mill; river named.

30/217 Hinton Blewett (parish) ST 593563
Apt 20.07.1838; 1079a (1102); Map 1838, 4 chns, by William York, Highfield, Compton Martin, Somerset; woods, plantations, osiers, orchards, common.

30/218 Hinton Charterhouse (parish) ST 773586
Apt 16.07.1850; 68a (2890); Map 1851, 4 chns, by John Knapp, (tithable parts only); foot/b'way, woods, plantations, field gates, building names, landowners, malt house, mills, turnpike gate; pictorial church.

30/219 Hinton St George (parish) ST 419124
Apt 20.03.1839; 1500a (1500); Map 1838, 6 chns; foot/b'way, waterbodies, woods, plantations, parkland, orchards, gardens, fence ownership, ornamental statue, road embankment, glebe; only Hinton Park house and a pool are coloured.

30/220 Holcombe (parish) ST 670503
Apt 21.03.1839; 780a (780); Map 1840, 3 chns, in 2 parts, by T.O. Bennett, Bruton; foot/b'way, waterbodies, houses, woods, plantations, building names, brewery.

30/221 Holford (parish) ST 164400
Apt 18.08.1840; 796a (all); Map 1840, 8 chns, litho (Standidge); waterbodies, houses (by shading), woods, plantations, coppice, orchards, boundary land marks.

30/222 Holton (parish) ST 684268
Apt 26.02.1839; 491a (491); Map 1839, 4 chns; houses, lime kiln. Apt omits some land use.

30/223 Holwell (parish) ST 700110
Apt 11.03.1839; 2356a (all); Map 1841?, 4 chns; waterbodies, houses.

30/224 Hornblotton (parish) ST 595336
Apt 29.09.1838; 1082a (all); Map surveyed in 1838, [4 chns], by W. Norris and T.F. Dickinson; construction lines, foot/b'way, waterbodies.

30/225 Horsington (parish) ST 707247
Apt 30.10.1839; 3591a (all); Map surveyed in 1839, 3 chns, 1st cl, in 3 parts, by W. Norris and T.F. Dickinson, Wincanton; construction lines, waterbodies, houses, field boundary ownerships, building names; map has note that it was made under an order of the Poor Law Commissioners of 21 August 1838, and tested by the Tithe Commissioners for the Poor Law Commission-ers, who approved it on 10 February 1842.

30/226 Huish Champflower (parish) ST 037293
Apt 21.08.1839; 2910a (2909); Map 1839, 3 chns, by E. Harris; construction lines, hill-drawing, foot/b'way, waterbodies, houses, woods, plantations, orchards, gardens, heath/moor, hedge ownership, fence ownership, field gates, building names, landowners, pit, parsonage, farm names and boundaries; below the scale is a note on paper distortion; legend explains symbols, including 'Earthen Fences' and stone walls; mapped areas outside the district are tinted pink.

30/227 Huish Episcopi (parish) ST 427260
Apt 04.02.1845; 125a (2314); Map 1845?, 8 chns, (tithable parts only); moor; river named.

30/228 Huish Episcopi (parish) ST 422284
Corn rent conversion, 1914; 2196a (2314); Map 1914, OS 1:2500 of c.1903 annotated with tithe areas.

30/229 Hungerford Farley (parish) ST 799576 [Farleigh Hungerford]
Apt 21.03.1839; 904a (904); Map 1839, 3 chns, by T. Weaver, Bath; waterbodies, houses; reason for tinting some land is unclear; scale-bar (on banner) and compass indicator (with plumes) are combined.

30/230 Huntspill (parish) ST 329452
Apt 27.03.1838; 5944a (9289); Map 1838, 3 chns, 1st cl, in 2 parts, by James Peachy Williams, Bridgwater; construction lines, base line, proof line, foot/b'way, canal with towpath, houses, building names, road names, rectory, turnpike gate, movable bridges; bridges named.

30/231 Hutton (parish) ST 349587
Apt 13.07.1837; 1876a (1876); Map 1838, 3 chns, by J. Marmont, Bristol; construction lines, houses, open fields (named), building names, rhine, road and drove names, moors; hills named; a wood is shown by annotation.

30/232 Idstock and Beere with Habergen (extra-parochial place) ST 226416 [Not listed]
Apt 30.08.1843; 305a (?); Map 1842, 6 chns, by W. Hicks Townsend; waterbodies, houses, woods.

30/233 Ilchester (parish) ST 509228
Apt 25.05.1838; 653a (653); Map 1839, 6 chns; arable (col), grassland (col), orchards; built-up part generalised; bridge and river named.

30/234 Ilminster (parish) ST 362147
Apt 26.10.1837; 4051a (4050); Map 1838, 4 chns; construction lines, canal with towpath and inclined plane, waterbodies, field gates, building names, road names, mill, dye mills, fence.

30/235 Ilton (parish) ST 355175
Apt 22.11.1837; 1719a (1719); Map 1839, 6 chns, litho (Standidge), in 3 parts; canal, waterbodies, woods, osiers, orchards, fences, building names, mill, toll gates, vicarage, quarries, greens; bridges named.

30/236 Isle Abbotts (parish) ST 350200
Apt 02.03.1842; 1936a (1935); Map 1841, 6 chns, in 3 parts; waterbodies, houses, woods, building names; river named; border has shell decoration in each corner.

30/237 Ilebrewers (parish) ST 372206 [Isle Brewers]
Apt 06.03.1841; 1244a (1243); Map 1841?, 6 chns, in 2 parts; waterbodies.

30/238 Kelston (parish) ST 701671
Apt 28.05.1838; 1096a (all); Map 1839?, 6 chns, 'Copied from an Old Map' by R.D. Little, Chippenham; waterbodies, houses, weir, locks.

30/239 Kenn (parish) ST 416690
Apt 17.09.1839; 1019a (1018); Map 1840, 3 chns, 1st cl, in 6 parts, by Danl Horwood, Bristol; construction lines, foot/b'way, houses, woods, plantations, orchards, field boundary ownerships, building names, windmill, decoy pool, rhines (named), drains, drove; rivers named; footpaths are only shown where they cross field boundaries.

30/240 Kewstoke (parish) ST 339638
Apt 28.01.1839; 2426a (4008); Map 1838?, 4 chns, 1st cl, in 3 parts, by J.M. Tucker, (tithable parts only); construction lines, railway, waterbodies, rock outcrops, field gates, coastal rocks, windmill, glebe; hills named.

30/241 Keynsham (parish) ST 658677
Apt 06.06.1840; 4171a (4171); Map 1841, 6 chns, in 2 parts, (includes town separately at 3 chns) railway with station, waterbodies, houses, building names, workhouse, copper works, tan yard, pound, lodge, river locks, weir.

30/242 Kilmersdon (parish) ST 692516
Apt 28.08.1838; 3460a (3460); Map 1839, 6 chns, by T.O. Bennett, Bruton; waterbodies, houses, woods (named), plantations, parkland, orchards, colliery with spoil heap, brewery.

30/243 Kilmington (parish) ST 783367
Apt 07.08.1839; 2746a (2746); Map 1839, 8 chns, ? by T.O. Bennett, Bruton; hill-drawing, turnpike roads and gate, houses, woods (named), plantations, orchards, road names, parsonage.

30/244 Kilton (parish) ST 163427
Apt 19.08.1842; 1552a (1691); Map 1842, 8 chns, by A. King, Nether Stowey; houses, farmyards (col).

30/245 Kilve (parish) ST 150432
Apt 15.08.1839; 1691a (all); Map 1839, 8 chns, litho (Standidge); waterbodies, houses (black), woods (named), orchards, building names, boundary stones, pool, water mill (by symbol), pit, parsonage, kiln, cross, freeboard or deer leap.

30/246 Kingsbrompton (parish) SS 960311 [Not listed]
Apt 17.03.1841; 9080a (8810); Map 1841, 6 chns, by William Collard Cox, Sampford Brett; waterbodies, fords; buildings are shown without infill; bridges are shown by Dawson's symbol, and some are named.

30/247 Kingsbury Episcopi (parish) ST 421206
Apt 13.06.1842; 3648a (3646); Map 1844, 6 chns, in 13 parts, by William

Wadman, Martock, Somerset, (includes 12 3-chn enlargements of detail); hill-drawing, waterbodies, houses, woods, gardens, mill; bridge named.

30/248 Kingsdon (parish) ST 519261
Apt 15.07.1839; 2065a (2064); Map 1839, 6 chns, by E. Watts, Yeovil; houses, woods (col), plantations (col), parkland, arable (col), grassland (col), orchards, furze (col), hedge ownership, fences, field names; streams separating fields are shown by over-sinuous lines.

30/249 Kingston (parish) ST 212296 [Kingston St Mary]
Apt 04.10.1838; 3477a (3477); Map 1838, 3 chns, in 5 parts; foot/b'way, waterbodies, houses, woods, parkland, orchards, heath/moor, rock outcrops, hedge ownership, fences, field gates, pits, tan yards.

30/250 Kingston Seymour (parish) ST 393672
Apt 16.01.1844; 2642a (3422); Map 1846, 8 chns, in 3 parts, by D. Horwood, Broad St, Bristol, (includes two 4-chn enlargements of detail); houses, road names, tidal banks; bridges named.

30/251 Kingstone (parish) ST 391134
Apt 19.01.1842; 983a (?); Map 1841, 6 chns.

30/252 Kingweston (parish) ST 529308
Apt 21.10.1839; 1167a (all); Map 1838, 3 chns, 1st cl, by T.O. Bennett, Bruton; construction lines, hill-drawing, foot/b'way, waterbodies, houses, farmyards, woods (named), plantations, parkland, orchards, gardens, field boundary ownerships, field gates, quarry; landowner is named in title.

30/253 Kittesford (parish) ST 078226 [Kittisford]
Apt 30.06.1842; 952a (952); Map 1843?, 6 chns; canal with towpath, waterbodies, houses, woods (col), plantations, orchards, mill.

30/254 Knowle St Giles (parish) ST 345112
Apt 31.05.1842; 533a (540); Map 1842, 6 chns; waterbodies, canal with towpath.

30/255 Lamyatt (parish) ST 656358
Apt 12.01.1839; 1000a (1000); Map 1839, 6 chns; waterbodies, houses, woods, orchards, building names, lime kiln, pound, parsonage, beacon hill.

30/256 Langford Budville (parish) ST 106228
Apt 08.06.1841; 1853a (1853); Map 1843?, [6 chns]; canal with towpath, waterbodies, houses, woods (col), plantations (col), orchards, building names, mill, pit.

30/257 Langport Eastover (parish) ST 420269 [Langport]
Apt 03.04.1840; 171a (171); Map 1838, 3 chns, by J.F.H. Warren, Langport, Somerset; waterbodies, orchards; PRO IR 30 also contains a lithographed copy, by Standidge, of 1840.

30/258 Langridge (parish) ST 740695
Apt 12.01.1839; 656a (855); Map 1839, [3 chns], 1st cl, by Cotterells and Cooper, Bath; construction lines, hill-drawing, houses, farmyards (col), woods, hedge ownership, fence ownership, field acreages; some fields appear to have been renumbered.

30/259 Laverton (parish) ST 778531
Apt 19.06.1845; 1035a (all); Map 1845, 6 chns, in 2 parts; waterbodies, houses, ford.

30/260 Leigh (parish) ST 691477 [Leigh upon Mendip]
Apt 11.01.1839; 1426a (all); Map 1839, [3 chns], 1st cl, by J. Marmont, Bristol; construction lines, houses.

30/261 Lilstock (parish) ST 179445
Apt 13.08.1842; 54a (1160); Map 1847?, 4 chns, (tithable parts only); houses, fences, building names; map is titled 'Map of the Fairfield Estate in the Parish of Lilstock'.

30/262 Limington (parish) ST 542217
Apt 27.11.1838; 1602a (all); Map 1839, 6 chns, in 2 parts; houses, building names, open fields (named), mill.

30/263 High Littleton (parish) ST 644577
Apt 28.08.1839; 1273a (1273); Map 1839, 3 chns, 1st cl, by Thos. Player, Pensford, Bristol; construction lines.

30/264 Litton (parish) ST 592545
Apt 14.02.1839; 1171a (1171); Map 1840?, 3 chns, 1st cl, in 5 parts, by Geo. Ashmead, Bristol; construction lines, baseline, foot/b'way, waterbodies, houses, woods, plantations, orchards, arable, grassland, marsh (named), field boundary ownerships, field gates, building names, ford, glebe, limekilns; 'Copy' in fields may indicate copyhold tenure.

30/265 Locking (parish) ST 363606
Apt 07.11.1838; 1016a (all); Map 1839, 3 chns; waterbodies, houses, woods, plantations, osiers, orchards, gardens, field gates, drains, farm named.

30/266 Lopen (parish) ST 424147
Apt 20.03.1839; 489a (489); Map 1840?, 3 chns, by Messrs Blackmore, Churchingford; foot/b'way, waterbodies, farmyards, arable (col), grassland (col), orchards, gardens, heath/moor (col), open fields, field gates, bleaching grounds; legend explains symbols and colours; cartouche resembles a summerhouse with a spire.

30/267 Lovington (parish) ST 595314
Apt 11.04.1839; 823a (all); Map 1838, 3 chns, by W. Norris and T.F. Dickinson, Wincanton; waterbodies, holding boundaries (col); river named.

30/268 Loxton (parish) ST 373555
Apt 30.01.1840; 1204a (1203); Map 1840, 3 chns, 1st cl, by T.F. Dickinson, Wincanton; construction lines, foot/b'way, houses, sheep-wash, movable bridges.

30/269 Luckham or Luccombe (parish) SS 902445
Apt 26.06.1840; 4107a (4126); Map 1841, 6 chns, in 7 parts, by William Collard Cox, Williton, Somerset, (includes four 3-chn enlargements of detail); fences; buildings are shown without infill.

30/270 Lufton (parish) ST 517168
Apt 06.09.1838; 293a (all); Map 1840?, 3 chns; houses; a stream running through a field is shown discontinuously.

30/271 Lullington (parish) ST 783522
Apt 19.06.1845; 687a (all); Map 1847?, 6 chns; waterbodies, houses; river named; roads across fields are uncased.

30/272 Luxborough (parish) SS 977380
Apt 27.05.1841; 3740a (3740); Map 1843, 3 chns; hill-drawing, waterbodies, houses, farmyards (col); north pointer has crown and plumes.

30/273 Lydeard St Lawrence (parish) ST 129318
Apt 28.01.1839; 2698a (2697); Map 1839, 6 chns, litho (Standidge); waterbodies, houses (black), woods, plantations, orchards, building names, parsonage, kiln.

30/274 East Lydford (parish) ST 574308
Apt 11.05.1838; 706a (706); Map 1839, 3 chns; waterbodies, churchyard; most of the larger names are stamped; river named.

30/275 Lympsham (parish) ST 339550
Apt 12.01.1839; 1967a (all); Map 1839, 8 chns, (copied from one of 1802); railway, hill-drawing; pictorial church; title is on a scroll with leafy surround.

30/276 Lyncombe and Widcombe (parish) ST 748630 [Not listed]
Apt 11.07.1839; 1846a (1845); Map 4 chns, surveyed in 1836 by T. Weaver and revised in 1839 by Cotterells and Cooper; railway, canal with basins and locks, waterbodies, building names, road names, workhouse, boundary of tithe-free land.

30/277 Lyng (parish) ST 325288
Apt 23.11.1838; 801a (1409); Map 1839, 6 chns, in 3 parts; canal with towpath, tithe-free areas; river named.

30/278 Maperton (parish) ST 674270
Apt 20.03.1839; 1534a (all); Map 1839, 8 chns, in 3 parts; houses,

plantations, parkland with fences, orchards, building names, landowners, brick yard, quarry; pictorial churches.

30/279 Mark (parish) ST 364482
Apt 29.01.1841; 2666a (4354); Map 1839, 3 chns, 1st cl, in 2 parts, by Jas Peachy Williams, Bridgwater; construction lines, foot/b'way, waterbodies, houses, woods, orchards.

30/280 Marksbury (parish) ST 662621
Apt 14.03.1843; 1277a (1277); Map 1843, 6 chns, in 5 parts, by T. Player, Pensford, (including four 3-chn enlargements of detail).

30/281 Marston Bigot (parish) ST 765435
Apt 17.07.1839; 2239a (2238); Map 1839, 6 chns, in 7 parts, (including 2-chn enlargment of a built-up part); foot/b'way, waterbodies, houses, building names, road names, pound, parsonage, boat house, chapel; bridges named.

30/282 Marston Magna (parish) ST 597224
Apt 05.03.1839; 1069a (1068); Map 1838, 6 chns, by J. Poole, Sherborne, Dorset; foot/b'way.

30/283 Martock (parish) ST 463210
Apt 15.05.1841; 7303a (7302); Map 1840, 12 chns, in 11 parts, by William Wadman, Yeovil, Somerset, (includes nine 6-chn enlargements of detail); waterbodies, houses, woods, plantations, landowners; legend explains symbols.

30/284 Meare (parish) ST 459422
Apt 31.12.1842; 8269a (8269); Map 1843, 3 chns, 1st cl, by James Peachy Williams, Bristol; construction lines, waterbodies, houses, woods, plantations, orchards, building names, road names, pound, decoy, chapel, rhines and drains (named), decoy; bridges named. Apt omits some field names.

30/285 Mells (parish) ST 720493
Apt 11.01.1839; 3612a (all); Map 1839?, [3 chns], 1st cl, by J. Marmont, Bristol; construction lines, waterbodies, houses; tithe area numbers are stamped.

30/286 Merriott (parish) ST 445135
Apt 08.12.1842; 1694a (1693); Map 1843, 6 chns, in 3 parts, by Geo. Moss, Crewkerne, Somerset, (includes two 3-chn enlargements of detail); foot/b'way, waterbodies, houses, woods, parkland, orchards, gardens, open fields, fence ownership, field gates, building names, road names, toll gates, mill, open field boundary stones; pond and bridge named; border has four-petalled flower in corners.

30/287 Michael Church or St Michael Church (parish) ST 301303
Apt 28.01.1839; 44a (43); Map not dated, 4 chns; waterbodies, houses.

30/288 Middlezoy (parish) ST 357322
Apt 02.11.1852; 827a (2520); Map 1853, 4 chns, in 2 parts, (tithable parts only); landowners; river and rhine named.

30/289 Middlezoy (parish) ST 374330
Corn rent conversion, 1893; 2234a (2520); Map 1893, OS 1:2500 of c.1885, annotated with tithable areas picked out in red and lilac; all the OS parcel numbers and altitudes have been scraped away, and some distances in links have been added to locate detached tithe areas.

30/290 Midsomer Norton (parish) ST 668548
Apt 15.07.1839; 3920a (3922); Map 1840, 6 chns, in 30 parts, by Cotterells and Cooper, Bath, (including 29 3-chn enlargements of common fields and other detail); railway, waterbodies, houses, building names, road names, college, collieries, Roman road, stall, notable tree, tithing boundaries.

30/291 Milbourne Port (parish) ST 675196 [Milborne Port]
Apt 11.06.1839; 3278a (3277); Map 1839, 4 chns, by T.O. Bennett, Bruton; waterbodies, houses, woods (named), plantations, orchards; north compass pointer has a small crown worked in.

30/292 Milton Clevedon (parish) ST 669370
Apt 06.05.1842; 1221a (1221); Map 1841, 4 chns; foot/b'way, waterbodies, houses, building names, mill, signpost (by symbol), wood (by annotation); hill named.

30/293 Milverton (parish) ST 105253
Apt 08.06.1841; 5475a (all); Map surveyed in 1842, 6 chns, in 3 parts, by Robert Newton and Robert P. Purssey, (including two enlargements of built-up parts at 3-chns and 2-chns), litho (Standidge); foot/b'way, waterbodies, houses (black), woods, plantations, parkland, orchards, fence ownership, building names, mill, lime kilns, common.

30/294 Minehead (parish) SS 948470
Apt 28.12.1842; 3991a (4581); Map 1842, 8 chns, by W.C. Cox, Williton, Somerset, (including four 2-chn enlargements of detail of built-up parts); water mill (by symbol).

30/295 Misterton (parish) ST 457080
Apt 23.09.1840; 1337a (1417); Map 1840, 5 chns, by Geo. Moss, Crewkerne, Somerset; foot/b'way, waterbodies, houses, woods, plantations, orchards, open fields, fences, field gates, toll gate, glebe.

30/296 Monksilver (parish) ST 070378
Apt 15.04.1841; 1006a (all); Map 1841, 4 chns, in 2 parts; houses, woods (col), plantations (col), orchards, rock outcrops, building names, quarries.

30/297 Monkton Combe (parish) ST 774623
Apt 29.03.1851; 684a (720); Map 1851, 4 chns, by J.H. Cotterell, Bath; foot/b'way, canal with aqueduct, waterbodies, houses (dark grey), woods, orchards, building names, mill, old paper mill, infant school, school, chapel, boundary stone, road viaduct, flight of steps.

30/298 West Monkton (parish) ST 258276
Apt 02.11.1840; 3080a (3079); Map 1839, 8 chns; canal with towpath, waterbodies, houses, woods, fences, quarries.

30/299 Montacute (parish) ST 497171
Apt 21.07.1838; 1485a (1485); Map 1838, [6 chns]; woods, orchards, building names, quarry, tithe-free lands (col); streams through fields are shown by pecked lines; buildings are shown in outline only.

30/300 Moorlinch (hamlet in parish of Moorlinch) ST 402365
Apt 02.09.1840; 1122a (1122); Map 1836 (1841?), 3 chns, by Jas P. Williams, Land Agent, Bridgwater; foot/b'way, houses, woods, plantations, field boundary ownerships, field gates, milestone, quarry; land use is shown by annotation, with some tree symbols.

30/301 Muchelney (parish) ST 435246
Apt 08.09.1841; 1566a (1566); Map 1842, 6 chns; waterbodies, houses, drains; north pointer has crown and plumes.

30/302 Mudford (parish) ST 571199
Apt 31.08.1841; 2036a (2035); Map 1838, 6 chns, by E. Watts, Yeovil; waterbodies, houses, farmyards (col), woods (col), plantations (col), arable (col), grassland (col), orchards (col), gardens (col), hedge ownership, fences, building names, field names, brick yard, tithing boundaries; river and bridge named.

30/303 Nailsea (parish) ST 461699
Apt 22.01.1840; 2771a (2771); Map 1843?, 6 chns; waterbodies, houses, woods, building names, drains; north pointer has thistle.

30/304 Nempnett (parish) ST 525615 [Nempnett Thrubwell]
Apt 24.02.1841; 1575a (all); Map 1835 (1842?), 6 chns, by Y. and J.P. Sturge, (tinted); hill-drawing, waterbodies, houses, woods (col), orchards, building names, mill; below the title is: 'N.B. Part of the Regilbury Court and Park Farms are in the parish of Nempnett but the Boundary being unknown they are not included in this Map.'

30/305 Nether Stowey (parish) ST 197397
Apt 13.07.1839; 1215a (1215); Map 1840, 8 chns, in 5 parts, by A. King, Nether Stowey, (including a moor at 3 chns and Nether Stowey town separately at 1.5 chns); houses.

30/306 Nettlecombe (parish) ST 053376 [Not listed]
Apt 26.01.1838; 2801a (2800); Map 1838?, 8 chns, in 2 parts; waterbodies, woods, plantations, parkland, orchards, heath/moor (col), fence ownership, pit.

30/307 Newton St Loe (parish) ST 704644
Apt 18.05.1839; 1579a (1578); Map 1840, 6 chns; railway, waterbodies, houses, kennel, mill; river named.

30/308 Northover (parish) ST 523238
Apt 24.03.1838; 437a (436); Map 1838, [3 chns], by Charles Wainwright; waterbodies, houses, woods, osiers, orchards, Roman road, toll gate (in plan, unnamed); tithe area numbers are stamped.

30/309 Norton Fitzwarren (parish) ST 192265
Apt 15.08.1839; 1308a (1307); Map 1839?, 4 chns, (copy of survey made in 1830 by R. Ham, Taunton); canal with towpath, waterbodies, woods, plantations, orchards.

30/310 Norton Hawkfield (parish) ST 594654
Apt 07.05.1839; 90a (620); Map 1839, 6 chns, by T. Player, Pensford, (tithable parts only, tinted).

30/311 Norton under Hamdon (parish) ST 477161 [Norton Sub Hamdon]
Apt 16.10.1839; 643a (642); Map 1840?, 4 chns; houses; streams through fields are shown discontinuously.

30/312 Norton Malreward (parish) ST 607655
Apt 28.05.1838; 1068a (all); Map 1839?, 3 chns, 1st cl, by J. Marmont, Bristol; houses, fords.

30/313 Norton St Philip (parish) ST 776561
Apt 14.03.1839; 665a (1527); Map 1839, 3 chns, by R.D. Little, Chippenham, (tithable parts only); waterbodies, houses, building names, vicarage, new road.

30/314 Nunney (parish) ST 742450
Apt 13.04.1840; 2421a (all); Map 1839, 8 chns; woods; pictorial church.

30/315 Nynehead (parish) ST 144233
Apt 14.01.1837; 1449a (all); Map 1839?, 6 chns; foot/b'way, canal with towpath and lift, waterbodies, houses, woods (col), plantations (col), parkland, arable (col), grassland (col), orchards (col), gardens (col), fence ownership, building names, mill, school, smith's shop, vicarage; bridges and river named; map has landowners' signatures.

30/316 Oake (parish) ST 159253
Apt 16.04.1839; 866a (865); Map 1821 (1839?), 6 chns, by P.B. Ilett, Taunton; foot/b'way, waterbodies, houses, woods (col), plantations (col), arable (by symbol), grassland (col), hedge ownership, field gates, building names, parsonage, mill, quarry; border has repeated entwined oak-leaf pattern.

30/317 Oare (parish) SS 809464
Apt 22.02.1840; 3100a (all); Map 1842, 6 chns, ? by Edwin Palmer, Stawley; hill-drawing, waterbodies, houses, woods (col, named), plantations (col), orchards, rock outcrops, building names, barrow, foreshore, commons; physical features and bridge named.

30/318 Odcombe (parish) ST 506160
Apt 04.06.1839; 1276a (1276); Map 1839, 6 chns, by William Wadman, Martock; waterbodies, houses, woods, plantations, open fields; legend explains symbols.

30/319 Orchardleigh (parish) ST 774510 [Not listed]
Apt 19.06.1845; 715a (715); Map 1845?, 6 chns, by Henry Mansford, Frome, Somerset, (tinted); foot/b'way, waterbodies, houses, woods, plantations, parkland, gardens, avenue of trees, green lane (named).

30/320 Orchard Portman (parish) ST 246206
Apt 26.01.1838; 636a (635); Map 1837, 5 chns; waterbodies, glebe boundary. District is apportioned by holding; Apt omits land use.

30/321 Othery (parish) ST 382317
Apt 24.06.1841; 1821a (1820); Map 1840, 6 chns, in 2 parts; open field boundary stones; buildings are shown without infill; river named.

30/322 Otterford (parish) ST 230144
Apt 13.03.1843; 2388a (2387); Map 1844, 3 chns, by Messrs Blackmore, Churchingford; hill-drawing, foot/b'way, waterbodies, stiles (by symbol), butts.

30/323 Otterhampton (parish) ST 246430
Apt 12.01.1839; 1018a (1117); Map 1839, 3 chns, 1st cl, in 3 parts, by J.P. Williams, B'Water; construction lines, foot/b'way, houses.

30/324 Overstowey (parish) ST 177378 [Over Stowey]
Apt 20.04.1838; 3648a (3647); Map 1838, 8 chns, in 2 parts, (includes small enlargement of detail), litho (Standidge); hill-drawing, waterbodies, houses (black), woods (named), orchards, building names, mills; water has been hand-coloured, as has one road.

30/325 Paulton (parish) ST 655564
Apt 22.03.1839; 1056a (1056); Map 1838, 3 chns, 1st cl, in 3 parts, by T. Player, Pensford, Bristol, (includes 12-chn index); construct-ion lines, foot/b'way, houses (by black dot).

30/326 Pawlett (parish) ST 294435
Apt 17.02.1838; 2986a (3566); Map 1839?, 8 chns; railway, houses, drains.

30/327 Pendomer (parish) ST 523104
Apt 26.06.1840; 1091a (all); Map 1840, 6 chns, by William Wadman, Martock; foot/b'way, waterbodies, houses, woods, plantations, orchards, gardens, stile (by symbol), waste; legend explains symbols.

30/328 East Pennard (parish) ST 593370
Apt 08.01.1840; 2829a (2829); Map 1842, 6 chns; waterbodies, farmyards (col), houses, woods (col), plantations (col), parkland (col), orchards (col).

30/329 West Pennard (parish) ST 556386
Apt 13.08.1840; 3063a (3063); Map 1841?, 5 chns, by John Beauchamp, Wells; houses.

30/330 Penselwood (parish) ST 757311
Apt 04.05.1842; 1102a (all); Map 1843?, 4.5 chns; waterbodies; streams through fields are shown discontinuously; there is a note that areas 349-53 were erroneously included in map and apportionment of Stourton.

30/331 North Perrott (parish) ST 476091
Apt 16.06.1838; 1249a (1248); Map 1841, 8 chns; foot/b'way; streams through fields are shown discontinuously.

30/332 North Petherton (parish) ST 297318
Apt 02.05.1838; 10331a (10336); Map 1840, 6 chns, surveyed under John Easton's direction; canal with towpath and lock, waterbodies, houses, building names, pits, drains; there is a considerable variety of lettering, according to importance; drain, river and moors are named.

30/333 South Petherton (parish) ST 434169
Apt 11.06.1839; 3311a (3311); Map 1840, 8 chns, in 4 parts, by William Wadman, Martock, (includes three 4-chn enlargements of detail); waterbodies, houses; legend explains symbols, including woodland, which does not appear on the map proper.

30/334 Pilton (parish) ST 589413
Apt 21.11.1838; 5593a (5593); Map 1839, 6 chns, in 4 parts, by I. Poole, Sherborne, Dorset; waterbodies, houses, woods, plant-ations, orchards, osiers, building names; streams across fields are shown discontinuously; hill named.

30/335 Pitcombe (parish) ST 685328
Apt 17.09.1849; 8a (1050); Map 1850, 3 chns, by T.O. Bennett, Bruton, (tithable parts only); turnpike roads, building names, notable tree; river named.

30/336 Pitminster (parish) ST 215190
Apt 15.03.1838; 5120a (5120); Map 1839, 8 chns, litho (Standidge); waterbodies, houses (by shading), woods, plantations, orchards, gardens, fence ownership, building names, commons, green; hill named.

30/337 Pitney (rectory in parish of Yeovil) ST 550173 [Not listed]
Apt 18.03.1846; 524a (all); Map 1846, 12 chns, in 2 parts, by E. Watts, Yeovil, (includes 6-chn enlargement of detail); building names; tithable parts are tinted green.

30/338 Pitney or Pitney Lortie (parish) ST 448298
Corn rent conversion, 1876; 1304a (1500); Map 1876?, 6 chns, in 8 parts; woods, orchards; river and bridge named.

30/339 Pointington (parish) ST 645205 [Poyntington]
Apt 25.08.1840; 1021a (1020); Map 1841, 4 chns, by E.T. Percy, Sherborne; foot/b'way, waterbodies, houses.

30/340 Porlock (parish) SS 852466
Apt 23.09.1840; 5665a (all); Map 1841, 6 chns, in 5 parts, by William Collard Cox, Williton, Somerset, (includes four 3-chn enlargements of detail), litho (Standidge); waterbodies, woods, fences, building names, burrows, mills, high and low water marks.

30/341 Portbury (parish) ST 496753
Apt 24.12.1841; 3719a (3849); Map 1844, 6 chns, in 6 parts, (includes 80-chn index); waterbodies, houses, woods (named), orchards, sea wall.

30/342 Portishead (parish) ST 462757
Apt 07.05.1839; 2093a (all); Map 1840, 3 chns, 1st cl, surveyed by J.S.Cotterell for J. Marmont, Bristol; hill-drawing, foot/b'way, waterbodies, houses, woods, orchards, rock outcrops, cliffs, hedge ownership, school, Friends Meeting House, boundary stones, fort, foreshore, baths, hotel; pond and two nesses named.

30/343 Preston Plucknett (parish) ST 538166
Apt 30.12.1848; 845a (790); Map 1849, 6 chns, by E.B. Watts, Yeovil; railway, houses, building names, workhouse; pictorial church.

30/344 Priddy (parish) ST 520517
Apt 06.03.1839; 1361a (1361); Map 1839, 3 chns, 1st cl, by Geo. C. Ashmead, Bristol; construction lines, waterbodies, houses, plantations, field boundary ownerships, field gates, pound, boundary marks, green.

30/345 Priston (parish) ST 689612
Apt 10.08.1839; 1850a (all); Map 1840, 6 chns; houses.

30/346 Publow (parish) ST 625641
Apt 31.05.1839; 1335a (all); Map 1839, 6 chns, by T. Player, Pensford; field boundaries are highlighted in green.

30/347 Puckington (parish) ST 377189
Apt 31.01.1837; 610a (610); Map 1837, 6 chns, in 7 parts; glebe (col); there is a long note below the title explaining which fields are in which parish. District is apportioned by holding; Apt omits land use.

30/348 Puddimore, or Podymore Milton (parish) ST 545253 [Podimore]
Apt 23.10.1838; 977a (990); Map 1838?, 4 chns, by Charles Wainwright; waterbodies, houses, woods, plantations, orchards, gardens.

30/349 Puriton (parish) ST 324421
Apt 16.02.1842; 1577a (1632); Map 1842, 3 chns, by Jas Peachy Williams, Bridgwater; railway, waterbodies, houses.

30/350 Puxton (parish) ST 405631
Apt 19.02.1839; 614a (all); Map 1840?, 6 chns; foot/b'way; river named; buildings are shown without infill.

30/351 Pylle (parish) ST 613390
Apt 18.02.1837; 1056a (1055); Map 1838, 8 chns; waterbodies, holdings (col); legend explains colours. District is apportioned by holding; Apt omits land use.

30/352 East Quantoxhead (parish) ST 133420
Apt 14.03.1839; 2303a (all); Map 1839?, 4 chns; foot/b'way, waterbodies, woods, plantations, orchards, heath/moor (col), fence ownership, glebe (col). Apt omits land use of 'lots from common'.

30/353 West Quantoxhead (parish) ST 113416
Apt 11.06.1840; 1411a (all); Map 1840, 8 chns, litho (Standidge); waterbodies, houses (black), woods, plantations, orchards, fence ownership, building names.

30/354 Queen Camel or East Camel (parish) ST 590254
Apt 03.02.1842; 2499a (2498); Map 1842, 6 chns, in 2 parts, by J. Poole, Sherborne, Dorset; waterbodies, houses. About half the district is apportioned by owner.

30/355 Queen Charlton (parish) ST 633668
Apt 21.01.1848; 956a (955); Map 1848, 6 chns, by J.P. Sturge and Son, Bristol, copied 'from a Plan and Survey taken by Jno. Hinde A.D. 1760'; road names.

30/356 Raddington (parish) ST 024265
Apt 29.07.1841; 1506a (all); Map 1840, 3 chns, by S. Court; hill-drawing, foot/b'way, private roads (uncoloured), waterbodies, houses, farmyards (col), woods, plantations, coppice, orchards, gardens, heath/moor, hedge ownership, farm names and boundaries, fences, field gates, building names, landowners, mills, old bank; legend explains symbols.

30/357 Radstock (parish) ST 690552
Apt 23.10.1838; 1005a (1005); Map 1839?, 6 chns; railway, Roman road.

30/358 Regilbury (district in parish of Nempnett) ST 527634 [Not listed]
Apt 03.09.1842; 199a (all); Map 1846?, 6 chns.

30/359 Road and Wolverton (parishes) ST 799536 [Woolverton]
Apt 31.05.1839; 1664a (all); Map 1839?, 4.5 chns; foot/b'way, turnpike roads, new turnpike road, waterbodies, woods (col), plantations (col), field gates, pound; Road parish is pink with carmine buildings; Woolverton is yellow with blue buildings; scale bar is combined with banner scale-statement and north pointer with plumes.

30/360 Rodney Stoke (parish) ST 479499
Apt 28.02.1839; 2344a (all); Map 1839, 6 chns, copied from a map made for the landowners in 1821 by Thos Beards; waterbodies, houses, woods, orchards, hedge ownership, fence ownership, field gates, private roads (greenish-grey).

30/361 Rowberrow (parish) ST 457581
Apt 14.07.1843; 954a (all); Map 1844?, 4 chns, ? by Thomas Ward, Bristol; houses, warren.

30/362 Rowington or Runnington (parish) ST 124221
Apt 28.11.1837; 324a (all); Map 1839?, 4 chns, surveyed and drawn under Charles Bailey's direction; foot/b'way, waterbodies, houses, farmyards (col), woods (col), arable (col), grassland (col), orchards (col), gardens (col), rock outcrops, building names, turnpike gate, parsonage, pit, lime kiln; river named.

30/363 Ruishton (parish) ST 267240
Apt 17.05.1842; 1003a (1003); Map 1842, 3 chns; canal with towpath, waterbodies, houses (by shading), woods, plantations, parkland, orchards, fences, building names, old road, boundary tree.

30/364 Rympton (parish) ST 610216 [Rimpton]
Apt 13.02.1840; 1000a (999); Map 1839, 6 chns, by I. Poole, Sherborne, Dorset; foot/b'way, waterbodies, houses; streams across fields are shown discontinuously.

30/365 Saltford (parish) ST 685674
Apt 13.07.1837; 880a (880); Map 1837, 3 chns, 1st cl; construction lines, railway, foot/b'way, turnpike roads, toll gate, waterbodies, houses, woods, osiers, orchards, hedge ownership, mills, brass mills, locks, weir.

30/366 Sampford Arundel (parish) ST 108185
Apt 13.09.1839; 1144a (1144); Map 1840?, 4 chns; waterbodies, houses, farmyards (col), woods (col), plantations (col), orchards, building names.

30/367 Sampford Brett (parish) ST 086403
Apt 10.02.1841; 932a (all); Map 1841, 6 chns, in 2 parts; waterbodies, houses, farmyards.

30/368 Sandford Orcas (parish) ST 621202
Apt 10.01.1838; 1091a (all); Map 'Made in 1837', 3 chns, by T.O. Bennett, Bruton; waterbodies, houses, woods, plantations, parkland, orchards, fence ownership, rectory, pound, ford; roads across fields are shown discontinuously.

30/369 Seaborough (parish) ST 433064
Apt 20.03.1839; 581a (all); Map 1839, 4 chns; waterbodies, houses (by shading); streams through fields are shown discontinuously.

30/370 Selworthy (parish) SS 916467
Apt 18.06.1840; 2219a (2219); Map 1841, 8 chns, litho (Standidge); waterbodies, houses (by shading), woods, plantations, parkland, orchards, fences, lodge, pound, waste, common; river named.

30/371 Sevington St Mary (parish) ST 402147 [Seavington St Mary]
Apt 30.01.1841; 989a (988); Map 1841, 6 chns, in 2 parts; waterbodies, houses; streams through fields are shown discontinuously.

30/372 Seavington St Michael (parish) ST 414152
Apt 20.11.1839; 281a (all); Map 1840, 3 chns; houses (by shading), open fields.

30/373 Shapwick (parish) ST 422391
Apt 19.09.1839; 3781a (3781); Map 1839, 6 chns, in 3 parts; canal with locks and towpath, fences, windmill (by symbol), wood (by annotation); pictorial church; land belonging to another parish is coloured pink.

30/374 Shepton Beauchamp (parish) ST 404174
Apt 15.07.1839; 836a (836); Map 1839, 3 chns, in 3 parts, by Summers and Slater; foot/b'way, waterbodies, open fields, brick yard.

30/375 Shepton Mallet (parish) ST 625445
Apt 13.08.1840; 3572a (all); Map 1841, 4 chns, in 4 parts, (includes 16-chn index); waterbodies, houses, woods, plantations, parkland, orchards, Roman road, churchyard; built-up part generalised.

30/376 Shepton Montague (parish) ST 693315
Apt 27.06.1839; 2424a (2424); Map 1841, 10 chns; waterbodies, houses (black), orchards, landowners; pictorial church.

30/377 Shipham (parish) ST 443576
Apt 13.04.1839; 767a (766); Map 1840?, 4 chns, by J.M. Tucker, Bristol; waterbodies.

30/378 Skilgate (parish) SS 984273
Apt 27.12.1843; 2108a (all); Map surveyed in 1844, 3 chns, in 2 parts, by Robert Newton, (includes enlargement of part of village at 1 chn); foot/b'way, waterbodies, houses (grey), woods, orchards, rock outcrops, quarry, furze.

30/379 Sock Dennis (district) ST 515215 [Not listed]
Apt 15.02.1839; 880a (all); Map 1839, 4 chns, by T.O. Bennett, Bruton; turnpike roads, waterbodies, houses, woods, orchards, road names, private roads (uncoloured).

30/380 Somerton (parish) ST 484286
Apt 24.06.1841; 6925a (6925); Map 1842?, 6 chns, in 2 parts, ? by John Martin; houses, meadow names; the 'link' to one detached portion is at 18-chn scale.

30/381 Sparkford (parish) ST 608265
Apt 31.01.1838; 951a (all); Map 1839, [10 chns]; waterbodies, houses, woods, orchards, water mill (by symbol).

30/382 Spaxton (parish) ST 216354
Apt 02.05.1838; 3388a (all); Map 1839?, 6 chns, in 2 parts, 'Taken in 1824 by W. Downes, Colchester'; waterbodies, woods, orchards, heath/moor, building names; hills named; scale is styled like a measuring rod, with knobs at each end.

30/383 Standerwick (parish) ST 814510
Apt 24.12.1839; 303a (303); Map 1839, 6 chns; waterbodies, houses, woods, plantations, pit, glebe (col).

30/384 Stanton Drew and St Thomas in Pensford (parishes or parish and chapelry) ST 607626
Apt 16.05.1838; 2009a (2075); Map 1842, 3 chns, 1st cl, ? by Thomas Player; waterbodies.

30/385 Stanton Prior (parish) ST 682632
Apt 18.05.1839; 842a (841); Map 1840, 6 chns; waterbodies, houses.

30/386 Staple-Fitz-payne (parish) ST 257178 [Staple Fitzpaine]
Apt 26.01.1838; 2864a (all); Map 1838?, 6 chns, (tinted); hill-drawing, roadside hedges, building names, hill fort, glebe (col). District is apportioned by ownerships and no holding information is given; fields are not shown.

30/387 Staplegrove (parish) ST 211272
Apt 16.02.1837; 1060a (1059); Map 1837?, 6 chns, by John Easton, Taunton; waterbodies, houses, churchyard, waste.

30/388 Stawell (hamlet in parish of Moorlinch) ST 363381
Apt 20.03.1839; 974a (973); Map surveyed in 1833 for poor rate purposes, 4 chns, by Summers and Son; hill-drawing, foot/b'way, waterbodies, farmyards (col), woods (col), arable (col), grassland (col), orchards, hedges, field gates; legend explains symbols.

30/389 Stawley (parish) ST 064223
Apt 23.09.1840; 830a (all); Map 1841?, [6 chns]; waterbodies, houses, woods, plantations, orchards, rock outcrops, building names, quarry; river named.

30/390 Stockland Bristol (parish) ST 240435
Apt 08.11.1837; 1134a (1650); Map 1838, 3 chns, in 3 parts, by J. Marmont, Bristol; houses.

30/391 Stocklinch Magdalen (parish) ST 384175 [Stocklinch St Magdalen]
Apt 05.05.1845; 200a (199); Map 1845, 3 chns; foot/b'way, houses, open fields, fences.

30/392 Stocklinch Ottersey (parish) ST 386169
Apt 12.01.1839; 300a (299); Map 1839, 3 chns, by Summers and Slater, Ilminster, litho (Standidge); waterbodies, woods, orchards, open fields; river named.

30/393 Stogumber (parish) ST 098369
Apt 22.07.1840; 5778a (5777); Map 1842, 8 chns, in 6 parts, (includes Stogumber separately and four enlargements of detail at 2 chns), litho; waterbodies, woods, coppice, plantations, orchards, fences, building names, boundary tree, brewery.

30/394 Stogursey (parish) ST 213441
Apt 18.01.1840; 5854a (8893); Map 1841, 8 chns, in 3 parts, (includes village separately at 2 chns), litho (Standidge); waterbodies, houses (by shading), woods, coppice, orchards, open fields, castle, priory, watermills (by symbol), marshes, commons.

30/395 North Stoke (parish) ST 706688
Apt 07.11.1838; 778a (778); Map 1839?, 6 chns, by F.J. Kelsey; foot/b'way, houses, river locks, stiles, old camp.

30/396 Stoke Pero (parish) SS 866433
Apt 18.05.1839; 3423a (3422); Map 1841, 6 chns, by William Collard Cox, Williton, Somerset; building names, mills; buildings are shown without infill.

30/397 Southstoke (parish) ST 751612
Apt 21.04.1841; 863a (863); Map 1840, 3 chns, 1st cl, by Cotterells and Cooper, Bath; hill-drawing, canal with towpath and locks, old canal, wharf, aqueduct, waterbodies, houses (dark grey), hedge ownership, fence ownership, building names, road cutting, milestone, chapel.

30/398 Stoke St Gregory (parish) ST 358278
Apt 14.09.1838; 3791a (3790); Map surveyed for Poor Rate purposes 1833, 4 chns, in 2 parts, by Summers and Son, (one part at 8 chns); waterbodies, houses, farmyards, open fields, fences, building names, windmill (by symbol); droves, rivers and drains named; legend explains symbols. [Some colours have faded badly on the copy in PRO IR 30.]

30/399 Stoke St Mary (parish) ST 264223
Apt 10.05.1837; 911a (923); Map 1837, 6 chns, 'reduced' from a survey by R. Ham of 1826; waterbodies, houses, woods, plantations, parkland, orchards.

30/400 Stoke St Michael or Stoke Lane (parish) ST 662473
Apt 27.07.1839; 2071a (2071); Map 1841, 3 chns, by Chas Wainwright; foot/b'way, waterbodies, woods, building names, quarry, avenue of trees, limekiln, boundary stones; tithe area numbers are stamped.

30/401 Stoke-under-Hamden (parish) ST 476175 [Stoke Sub Hamdon]
Apt 07.06.1839; 1330a (1330); Map 1840, 4 chns, by William Wadman, Martock; waterbodies, houses, woods, plantations, open fields, fences; streams through fields are shown discontinuously; hill named; legend explains symbols.

30/402 Ston Easton (parish) ST 625536
Apt 21.03.1839; 1374a (1374); Map 1839?, 4 chns, 1st cl, in 3 parts, (including small detached part at 6-chn scale); construction lines, foot/b'way, waterbodies, woods, parkland, field gates, toll gate, milestones, dairy, boundary posts, boundary of lands tithable to vicar and rector.

30/403 Stowell (parish) ST 682219
Apt 31.03.1838; 903a (902); Map 1839?, 6 chns; waterbodies, houses.

30/404 Stowey (parish) ST 595599
Apt 14.02.1839; 815a (814); Map 1839, 6 chns, in 3 parts, by Thos Player, Pensford, near Bristol, (including 12-chn location diagram).

30/405 Stratton on the Foss (parish) ST 661504 [Stratton-on-the-Fosse]
Apt 18.06.1840; 1148a (1148); Map 1840, 4 chns, by Thos Player, Land Surveyor, Pensford.

30/406 Street (parish) ST 485359
Apt 30.01.1841; 2914a (2913); Map 1842, 3 chns, 1st cl, by Cotterells and Cooper, Bath; construction lines, hill-drawing, foot/b'way, droves (named), waterbodies, drains, houses (dark grey), woods (named), plantations, orchards, field gates, building names, turnpike gate, Baptist Chapel, Friends Meeting House, Wesleyan Chapel, National School, British School, site of Roman villa, site of notable tree, mill, quarries; watercourses and bridges are named.

30/407 Stringston (parish) ST 167421
Apt 20.08.1839; 1193a (all); Map 1839, 6 chns, in 2 parts, litho (Standidge); waterbodies, houses (black), woods, parkland, orchards, fences, building names, deer park, hill fort, private road, kiln, spring, hunting path, pits.

30/408 Sutton Bingham (parish) ST 545107
Apt 28.04.1840; 550a (549); Map 1839, 6 chns, by William Wadman, Martock; houses, woods, plantations, orchards, fences; streams across fields are shown discontinuously; legend explains symbols.

30/409 Long Sutton (parish) ST 464261
Apt 02.06.1842; 3865a (3955); Map 1844, 6 chns, in 2 parts; plantations, orchards, field boundary ownerships, fords, pit.

30/410 Sutton Mallett (hamlet in parish of Moorlinch) ST 374371 [Sutton Mallet]
Apt 09.03.1837; 879a (878); Map 1837, 3 chns, 1st cl, by Y. and J.P. Sturge; waterbodies, houses, field gates, pound, chapel, stone quarry, spring.

30/411 Sutton Montis or Sutton Montague (parish) ST 625245
Apt 05.06.1838; 494a (508); Map 1838, 6 chns, by J. Poole, Sherborne, Dorset; waterbodies, houses (black), woods, orchards; a stream across fields is shown discontinuously.

30/412 Swainswick (parish) ST 756689
Apt 28.11.1838; 845a (all); Map 3 chns, by Cotterells and Cooper, Bath; part 1 1839; part 2 surveyed by John Hinde 1775, and corrected by Cotterells in 1839, 5 chns; foot/b'way, waterbodies, houses, building names.

30/413 Swell (parish) ST 366236
Apt 20.07.1838; 891a (all); Map 1838, 4 chns, in 2 parts, by Summers and Slater, Ilminster; waterbodies; rivers named.

30/414 Taunton St James (parish) ST 231262 [Not listed]
Apt 14.03.1839; 1389a (1455); Map 1840, 6 chns, in 2 parts, by Ralph Ham, Taunton, litho (Standidge); canal with towpath, weir, aqueduct, woods, orchards, fences, building names, priory; river named.

30/415 Taunton St Mary, Magdalen (parish) ST 248237 [Not listed]
Apt 15.02.1839; 1195a (1300); Map 1840, 6 chns, by Ralph Ham, Taunton, litho (Standidge); waterbodies, orchards, fences, building names, workhouse, convent, barracks, greens.

30/416 Tellisford (parish) ST 797557
Apt 13.10.1838; 758a (757); Map 1839, 4 chns; waterbodies, houses, woods, plantations, parkland, orchards, gardens, fence, building names, old bath; river named.

30/417 Thorn Coffin (parish) ST 522180 [Thorne Coffin]
Apt 28.12.1842; 411a (all); Map 1843, 3 chns, by William Wadman, Martock; waterbodies, houses, woods, plantations, orchards, gardens, fence ownership.

30/418 Thorn Faulcon (parish) ST 283235 [Thornfalcon]
Apt 14.08.1837; 814a (814); Map 1838, 6 chns, 'Reduced from an Old Survey' by R. Ham, Taunton; canal with locks and towpath, waterbodies, houses, woods, plantations, orchards, glebe (col).

30/419 Thorne St Margaret (parish) ST 097204
Apt 04.11.1840; 806a (all); Map 1840?, 6 chns; canal with towpath and lift, waterbodies, houses, woods (col), plantations (col), orchards, rock outcrops, building names, quarry.

30/420 Thurlbeer (parish) ST 263208 [Thurlbear]
Apt 18.02.1837; 949a (all); Map 1837, 6 chns; houses, holdings (col); uninhabited buildings are shown without infill. District is apportioned by holding; Apt omits land use.

30/421 Thurloxton (parish) ST 276303
Apt 19.12.1838; 552a (551); Map 1838?, 6 chns; waterbodies, houses, boundary hedge.

30/422 Tickenham (parish) ST 456719
Apt 23.11.1841; 1627a (1627); Map 1843?, 4 chns, in 7 parts, (includes six 2-chn enlargements of detail); field gates, hillfort (in detail); wood is shown by name.

30/423 Timberscombe (parish) SS 952416
Apt 10.07.1844; 1902a (all); Map 1843, 6 chns, in 6 parts, (includes enlargement of village at 3 chns), litho (Standidge); foot/b'way, waterbodies, woods, plantations, coppice, orchards, building names, toll house, stiles.

30/424 Timsbury (parish) ST 666589
Apt 05.04.1838; 1149a (1148); Map 1838, 4 chns; canal, waterbodies, houses, plantations, orchards, colleries, spoil heaps, rectory, quarry.

30/425 Tintinhull (parish) ST 498202
Apt 05.10.1838; 1829a (1828); Map 1839, 6 chns, in 2 parts, by William Wadman, Martock, Somerset; waterbodies, houses, fences; a stream across a field is shown discontinuously.

30/426 Tolland (parish) ST 107321
Apt 31.05.1838; 824a (all); Map 1838, 3 chns, by Rt. Purssey; foot/b'way, waterbodies, fords, fences.

30/427 Treborough (parish) ST 005364
Apt 20.11.1840; 1799a (1798); Map 1841, 4 chns; waterbodies, fences, quarries, limekilns.

30/428 Trent (parish) ST 596193
Apt 14.02.1839; 1590a (all); Map 1839, 6 chns, by J. Poole, Sherborne, Dorset; waterbodies, houses, open fields.

30/429 Trull (parish) ST 200219
Apt 12.02.1842; 2234a (all); Map 'Taken from Old Surveys', 1842?, 6 chns; waterbodies, houses, woods, building names; some of the linework is done twice, in pencil and ink.

30/430 Twiverton or Twerton (parish) ST 726641
Apt 27.07.1840; 707a (971); Map 1838, 3 chns, 1st cl, in 2 parts, by Cotterells and Cooper, Bath; railway, waterbodies, houses, orchards, hedge ownership, fence ownership, mill, boundary stones (by symbol), glebe, field acreages; meaning of colour bands round two holdings is unclear.

30/431 Ubley (parish) ST 525573
Apt 30.11.1838; 1811a (1811); Map 1839, 6 chns, by Wm York, Compton Martin, Somerset; waterbodies, houses, woods, plantations, orchards, building names, mill.

30/432 Uphill (parish) ST 323590
Apt 14.02.1842; 1077a (all); Map 1843?, 3 chns; railway, waterbodies; some tithe areas have multiple numbers.

30/433 Upton (parish) ST 000301
Apt 08.05.1838; 3780a (all); Map 1839, 3 chns, by S. Court; hill-drawing, foot/b'way, turnpike roads, waterbodies, houses, woods, plantations, orchards, gardens, heath/moor, hedge ownership, fence ownership, field gates, building names, landowners, farm names and boundaries, chapel; legend explains symbols, including 'earthen' and wooden fences; north pointer has plumes and crown; churchyard is shown with gravestones.

30/434 Upton Noble (parish) ST 713393
Apt 03.12.1842; 677a (all); Map 1843, 3 chns, by Geo. C. Ashmead, Bristol; foot/b'way, waterbodies, houses, woods, plantations, orchards.

30/435 Walcot (parish) ST 749656 [Not listed]
Apt 05.02.1840; 455a (1023); Map 1841, 3 chns, by Cotterells and Cooper, Bath, (tithable parts only), litho (Standidge); waterbodies, woods, plantations, common, park, fences, building names, road names, chapels, turnpike gate; buildings and parish boundary are handcoloured.

30/436 Walton (parish) ST 462362
Apt 31.03.1842; 2502a (2502); Map 1843, 6 chns; houses, decoy, windmill (by symbol), droves (named); hill named; wood is indicated by name.

30/437 Walton in Gordano (parish) ST 425735 [Walton-in-Gordano]
Apt 10.05.1837; 1165a (all); Map 1838, 3 chns; waterbodies, houses, woods (col, named), plantations, orchards, marsh/bog (col), heath/moor (col), rock outcrops, cliffs (col), old church, quarry; hills named.

30/438 Wanstrow (parish) ST 707419
Apt 05.04.1838; 2055a (2054); Map 1838, 6 chns, by E. Watts, Yeovil; waterbodies, houses, woods (col, named), orchards, arable (col), gardens, hedge ownership, field gates, building names, field names, parsonage, commons (col); pictorial church.

30/439 Wayford (parish) ST 401062
Apt 02.09.1842; 1619a (1618); Map 1844, 3 chns, by J. Woodmass; waterbodies, houses.

30/440 Weare (parish) ST 409520
Apt 21.06.1839; 1719a (?); Map 1839?, [8 chns], ? by William Body; houses; fields not part of this tithe district are tinted; farm and river named.

30/441 Wedmore and Northlead (district in parish of Wedmore) ST 438480
Apt 28.12.1838; 5779a (?), (tithable parts only); Map 1839?, 3.75 chns; turnpike roads, droves (named), houses (black), open fields, field names, chapel; plantations are shown by annotation.

30/442 Week St Lawrence (parish) ST 371653 [Wick St Lawrence]
Apt 25.04.1838; 1603a (1900); Map 1838, [3 chns], 1st cl, in 3 parts; construction lines, waterbodies, houses, hedge ownership, field gates, tidal flats.

30/443 Wellington (parish) ST 135194
Apt 06.12.1839; 5196a (5195); Map 1841?, 3 chns, by George Parson, Wellington, Somerset; foot/b'way, canal with towpath, lock and earthworks, wharf, waterbodies, woods, plantations, osiers, parkland, orchards, gardens, hedge ownership (col), building names, road names, mill, quarry, monument, workhouse.

30/444 Wellow (parish) ST 733578
Apt 22.07.1840; 5292a (5292); Map 1839, 3 chns, 1st cl; construction lines, railway with sidings, foot/b'way, canal with wharf, waterbodies, houses, woods, hedge ownership, field gates, building names; meaning of green band is unclear.

30/445 St Cuthbert in Wells (parish) ST 555465 [Wells]
Apt 11.01.1839; 14918a (14918); Map 'working plan', surveyed 1837-8, [3 chns], 1st cl, in 9 parts, (includes 20-chn index); construction lines, offset lines (fragmentary), survey poles (named), waterbodies, drains, houses, woods (col), plantations, coppice, willows, park, orchards, shrubbery, gardens, rock outcrops, fences, field gates, building names, mound, boundary barrows, lodges, summer house, chapel, paper mill, toll house, quarries, hamlet boundaries; some field boundaries lie along construction lines, and are drawn in red; built-up part mostly generalised.

30/446 Wembdon (parish) ST 284393
Apt 05.11.1841; 2463a (2471); Map 1842, 8 chns, (including 3-chn enlargement of Chilton common, in manuscript), litho (Standidge); railway, canal, waterbodies, houses (black), woods, orchards, building names, pound, waste.

30/447 Westbury (parish) ST 499488 [Westbury-sub-Mendip]
Apt 21.07.1838; 2969a (2968); Map 1840?, 3 chns, 1st cl, by Geo. C. Ashmead, Bristol; construction lines, waterbodies, houses, woods, plantations, orchards, field boundary ownerships, field gates, open field (named).

30/448 Westharptree (parish) ST 545552 [West Harptree]
Apt 11.08.1840; 3018a (2850); Map 1841, 6 chns, by Wm York, Compton Martin, Somerset; waterbodies, houses, woods, plantations, building names, vicarage, mills; 'Field gardens' are shown with open strips.

30/449 Weston (parish) ST 725669
Apt 25.09.1844; 1416a (2650); Map 1846, 6 chns, in 3 parts, 'Reduced and Published' by J.H. Cotterell, Bath, (includes two small enlargements of detail), litho (by Hollway, Bath); houses, woods, plantations, building names, road names, college [almshouses], river locks, weirs, turnpike gate, monument; houses hand-coloured; bridge named. Apt omits land use for tithe-free lands and names of small houses and gardens.

30/450 Weston Bampfylde (parish) ST 614253
Apt 16.06.1838; 631a (631); Map surveyed in 1838, 3 chns, by W. Norris and T.F. Dickinson, Wincanton; construction lines; buildings are shown without infill.

30/451 Weston in Gordano (parish) ST 442743 [Weston-in-Gordano]
Apt 19.09.1837; 694a (all); Map 1837, 6 chns; houses, woods, orchards, pound, moor.

30/452 Weston super Mare (parish) ST 327616 [Weston-super-Mare]
Apt 19.09.1837; 1591a (2770); Map 1838, [3 chns], 1st cl, in 2 parts; construction lines, houses.

30/453 Westonzoyland (parish) ST 350345
Apt 11.02.1840; 2730a (2729); Map 1836 (1840?), 6 chns, in 4 parts, by Jas P. Williams, Bridgwater; turnpike roads, droves (col, named), waterbodies, houses, arable (col), grassland (col), orchards (col), gardens (col), hedge ownership, road names, rhines; legend explains symbols.

30/454 Weston Zoyland and Middlezoy (parish) ST 362344
Corn rent conversion, 1893; 495a (5249); Map 1893, 1:2500, in 3 parts, (corn-rented parts only); chapel, pumping engine; some chain distances are given, to locate pecked boundaries; map appears to be a straight copy of the OS 1:2500 of c.1885.

30/455 Whatley (parish) ST 736473
Apt 28.12.1838; 1260a (all); Map 1839, 3 chns, 1st cl, by Joseph White, Mells, Somerset; construction lines, waterbodies, houses, woods, plantations, orchards, gardens, building names, glebe, iron works; bridges named; mapped areas outside the district are tinted pink; some names may be stamped.

30/456 Wheathill (parish) ST 584310
Apt 12.01.1839; 315a (all); Map 1838, 6 chns, by E. Watts, Yeovil; houses, farmyards (col), arable (col), grassland (col), orchards (col), gardens (col), hedge ownership, fences, field gates, field names, glebe; pictorial church; river named.

30/457 White Lackington (parish) ST 382162 [Whitelackington]
Apt 18.09.1838; 1466a (all); Map 1838, 4 chns, in 5 parts, by Summers and Slater, Ilminster, (including one detached part at 8-chns); waterbodies, farmyards (col), field gates, cale; buildings are variously solid red, hatched red and hatched black: it is unclear what, if anything, this signifies.

30/458 Whitestaunton (parish) ST 276104
Apt 18.09.1838; 1937a (1960); Map 1841?, 6 chns; glebe (col).

30/459 Widcombe (tithing in parish of Chewton Mendip) ST 579578 [North Widcombe]
Apt 12.09.1839; 706a (705); Map 1839, 3 chns, by T. Player, Pensford.

30/460 Wilton (parish) ST 225237
Apt 30.07.1839; 539a (700), (tithable parts only); Map 1840, 6 chns, in 2 parts, by Ralph Ham, Taunton, litho (Standidge); waterbodies, houses (by shading), woods, orchards, fence ownership, field boundary ownerships, building names, gaol, toll gate.

30/461 Wincanton (parish) ST 720270
Apt 21.10.1839; 1851a (4130); Map 1840, 8 chns, in 2 parts, by T.F. Dickinson, Wincanton, (includes enlargement of town at 3 chns); houses, woods, orchards, building names, road names, workhouse.

30/462 Winford (parish) ST 542638
Apt 06.11.1838; 2991a (2991); Map 1839, 6 chns, in 2 parts; waterbodies, houses, building names, powder mills, mill pond, tithing or township boundaries (col).

30/463 Winscombe (parish) ST 416577
Apt 12.01.1839; 4140a (?); Map 1840?, 6 chns, ? by J.M. Tucker; waterbodies, mill, boundary between areas tithable to vicar and rector, rhine (named); a wood is shown by name.

30/464 Winsford (parish) SS 885356
Apt 11.08.1838; 8657a (8656); Map 1839?, 6 chns, by Wm Collard Cox, Sampford Brett; waterbodies, castle.

30/465 Winsham (parish) ST 374067
Apt 30.10.1839; 2289a (2953); Map 1840?, [?4 chns]; water-bodies.

30/466 Withiel Florey (parish) SS 990343
Apt 22.04.1839; 2485a (2485); Map 1839, 6 chns, litho (Standidge), by R.P. Purssey, Monksilver; waterbodies, woods, plantations, heath/moor, fence ownership, building names, burrows.

30/467 Withycombe (parish) ST 006411
Apt 17.09.1839; 1788a (all); Map 1839, 6 chns, in 2 parts; foot/b'way, waterbodies, woods (col), plantations (col), field gates, heath (col).

30/468 Withypool (parish) SS 836355
Apt 28.01.1839; 3631a (all); Map 1839?, 4 chns; foot/b'way, houses, woods, plantations, furze, old pit, common, ownership boundaries (col); a bridge is shown using Dawson's symbol.

30/469 Wiveliscombe (parish) ST 079287
Apt 25.08.1840; 5985a (5984); Map 1841, 6 chns, in 42 parts, (includes one large and 40 small 3-chn enlargements of detail), litho (Standidge); foot/b'way, waterbodies, houses (black or by shading), woods, plantations, parkland, orchards, fence ownership, building names, mills, quarries, slate quarry, lime kilns, castle, parsonage.

30/470 Wookey (parish) ST 506459
Apt 20.11.1839; 3421a (all); Map 1839, 4 chns, in 5 parts, 'Copied' by Norris and Dickinson, Wincanton, (including four small 3-chn scale enlargements of common fields); waterbodies, houses, open fields. Apt omits land use.

30/471 Woolavington (parish) ST 349421
Apt 26.01.1842; 1726a (1725); Map 1842?, 3 chns, in 2 parts.

30/472 Woolley (parish) ST 748685
Apt 12.01.1839; 366a (all); Map 1839?, 4 chns; waterbodies, houses; scale bar and north pointer are combined.

30/473 Wootton Courtney (parish) SS 930430
Apt 29.11.1842; 3145a (all); Map 1844, 6 chns; hill-drawing, waterbodies, woods (col), plantations (col), orchards, rock outcrops, building names, mill, quarries, boundary features, barrows, wells, common; hills named.

30/474 North Wootton (parish) ST 562418
Apt 11.02.1840; 1532a (1536); Map 1838, 3 chns, in 2 parts, by Benj. S.W. Cotton, West Pennard; construction lines, hill-drawing, foot/b'way, houses, woods (col), arable (col), grassland (col), orchards, gardens (col), hedge ownership, road names, mill stream, fords; streams named.

30/475 Worle (parish) ST 359619
Apt 11.03.1839; 1811a (1810); Map 1840?, 3 chns, 1st cl, ? by J.M. Tucker; construction lines, railway, waterbodies, quarry; hill named.

30/476 Wraxall (parish) ST 500720
Apt 19.09.1837; 3774a (3773); Map 1837, 3 chns, in 2 parts; foot/b'way, waterbodies, houses, hedge ownership, fence ownership, field boundary ownerships, field gates, building names, rectory, kennels, signpost (by symbol), field acreages, school, lodge, ford; garden and plantation are shown by annotation; scale-bar is concealed in north pointer.

30/477 Wrington (parish) ST 487638
Apt 16.06.1838; 5787a (5786); Map 1839?, 4 chns; field gates, building names, road names, mills, windmill, pit, greens; buildings are shown without infill; woodland is indicated by names. Apt omits land use.

30/478 Writhlington (parish) ST 702541
Apt 23.09.1840; 772a (all); Map 1842?, 3 chns; houses, woods, plantations, orchards, building names, collieries, dried-out ox-bow lakes.

30/479 Yarlington (parish) ST 659288
Apt 23.10.1838; 1208a (all); Map 1840?, 6 chns.

30/480 Yatton (parish) ST 433672
Apt 19.10.1841; 5375a (5374); Map 1840, 3 chns, 1st cl, in 2 parts, by D. Horwood, Bristol; construction lines, railway, houses, field boundary ownerships, woods (by name), osiers, building names, road names, rhines (named), Friends Meeting House; rivers named.

30/481 Yeovil (district in parish of Yeovil) ST 554155
Apt 18.03.1846; 3532a (?); Map 1842, 6 chns, by L.E. Watts, Yeovil; foot/b'way, houses, farmyards (col), woods (col), plantations (col), arable (col), grassland (col), orchards, gardens (col), hedge ownership, fences, field gates, building names, field names, landowners, mills, toll gate, workhouse; legend explains symbols; a note says that some tithe areas appear in the Pitney Apt (30/337).

30/482 Yeovilton (parish) ST 554233
Apt 01.09.1838; 1753a (1753); Map 1838, 6 chns, by Edward Watts, Yeovil; waterbodies, houses, woods (col), plantations (col), arable (col), grassland (col), orchards, open fields (named), hedge ownership, field gates, building names, mill, signposts (by symbol).

Southampton (Hampshire)

PRO IR29 and IR30 31/1-298

354 tithe districts: 1,041,167 acres
298 tithe commutations: 916,722 acres
191 voluntary tithe agreements, 107 compulsory tithe awards

Tithe and tithe commutation

In Hampshire (known by its alternative 'Southampton' to the Tithe Commission), 84 per cent of tithe districts were subject to payment of tithes in 1836 and 147 districts were wholly tithable (Fig. 43). The main causes of tithe exemption in Hampshire were modus payments in lieu of tithes, exemption of former manorial or Crown land, and exemption by prescription.

Assistant tithe commissioners and local tithe agents who worked in Hampshire are listed in Table 31.1. The most prolific tithe valuer was Charles Osborn of Fareham who valued over a quarter of the area of the county and also reported on eighteen tithe commutation agreements; it is unusual for so much of a county's tithe valuation to be undertaken by one person (Table 31.2).

Tithe maps

Some 13 per cent of Hampshire tithe maps are sealed as first class. Construction lines are present on about 9 per cent of second-class maps which suggests that there was a rather greater quantity of original survey in this county than in Wiltshire or Dorset to the west, though still much less than in Surrey or Sussex to the east. The precise extent to which earlier maps were re-used is difficult to judge, though the tithe map of Boarhunt is probably a good example of this practice. In this parish of about 2,000 acres only 357 acres remained tithable. The apportionment lists tithable properties only but the map includes the whole parish.

Hampshire tithe maps are drawn at scales ranging from one inch to 1.33 chains to one inch to 10 chains; 46 per cent are in the recommended scale range of one inch to 3 to 4 chains, 43 per cent are at the six-chain scale, and there is a significant minority of 7 per cent at the eight-chain scale (Table 31.3). The tithe maps of Wootton in the Isle of Wight and Wymering are curiosities in that they are two-chain maps of large rural districts. Ten second-class maps, mostly of districts in the Isle of Wight, are lithographed and that of Arreton was lithographed locally in Newport.

Fig. 43 Southampton (Hampshire): tithe district boundaries.

Hampshire tithe maps portray woodland with unusual thoroughness (on 87 per cent of maps) but agricultural land use is much less consistently depicted. Although only 6 per cent of Hampshire maps show industrial and related features, these include the careful mapping of railway station platforms at Winchfield, several brickworks, (not always named as such), tanyards (for example, Bishops Waltham), salt works at Shalfleet, and the fair ground at Weyhill with its permanent structures mapped in detail. On several maps, for example that of Romsey, distances on milestones are listed; this was usual Ordnance Survey practice but is rarely found on tithe maps.

Some 177 Hampshire tithe maps in the Public Record Office collection can be attributed to a particular map-maker; the most prolific was the partnership of Thomas Phillips and Giles Westbury of Andover who produced twenty-six maps. Their first-class maps are very plain in style but their early second-class maps are more colourful as, for example, that of Longparish. Richard C. Gale of Winchester produced twenty-three maps; his map of Grateley is very colourful but his other maps are more standardised though distinctive in style, with buildings shown variously in red and grey, and black and grey, and with neatly drawn tree-symbols on a green ground. Gale was more careful than most tithe map-makers to acknowledge copying. George Hewett of Elvetham and Oxford produced nine signed maps but may have been responsible for several more with stylistic affinities. His maps are characterised by vivid scarlet buildings and very neat tree symbols and his first-class maps have gothic lettering for house and farm names.

The overall quality of Hampshire tithe maps is very varied. One of the least impressive is that of Sidmonton, a three-chain scale map which contains only holding boundaries. It was produced by Aylwin and May of Newbury whose work in Wiltshire and Berkshire is much more colourful and detailed. By contrast, a number of the tithe maps of the Isle of Wight are nicely finished and coloured, for example Yarmouth. Decorative embellishments, however, are notably lacking on Hampshire maps; that of Bighton has a prettily-coloured cartouche with flowers but this map is very much the exception.

Table 31.1. *Agreements and awards for commutation of tithes in Southampton (Hampshire)*

Assistant commissioner/ local tithe agent	*Number of agreements**	*Number of awards*
Thomas James Tatham	0	63
A. O. Baker	46	0
Roger Kynaston	23	0
Charles Osborn	22	0
William Wakeford Attree	0	19
Joseph Townsend	15	4
F. Browne Browne	18	0
John Mee Mathew	13	0
Thomas Smith Woolley	10	8
Francis Offley Martin	0	10
Horace William Meteyard	9	0
John Farncombe	9	0
William Heard	9	0
Thomas Clements Parr	6	0
John Pickering	6	0
John Maurice Herbert	0	3
Thomas Phippard	3	0

*Computed from the number of extant reports on tithe agreements in the tithe files [PRO IR 18].

Table 31.2. *Tithe valuers and tithe map-makers in Southampton (Hampshire)*

Name and address (in Hampshire unless indicated)	*Number of districts*	*Acreage*
Tithe valuers		
Charles Osborn, Fareham	74	263,554
William Simonds, Winchester	20	81,075
Thomas Hasker, Basingstoke	16	36,780
Charles Gearing, Kilmiston	14	62,420
Thomas Phillips, Andover	13	32,785
James Comely, Winchester	12	42,405
Charles Fielder, Sparsholt	9	31,396
Others [62]	140	366,307
Attributed tithe map-makers		
Richard C. Gale, Winchester	23	124,556
J. W. Blackman, Fareham	17	62,162
George Hewett, Elvetham and Oxford	9	41,801
George Doswell, Southampton	7	23,753
Charles Lewis, Havant	6	15,638
Manwaring Chitty, Farnham, Surrey	5	15,312
Richard Dent, Camden Town, London	5	13,737
Charles Fielder, Sparsholt	5	11,249
Richard and Charles Pink, Hambledon	5	9,548
Others [39]	96	259,087

Table 31.3. *The tithe maps of Southampton (Hampshire): scales and classes*

Scale in chains/inch	*All maps*		*First Class*		*Second Class*	
	Number	*Acreage*	*Number*	*Acreage*	*Number*	*Acreage*
>3	4	845	0	0	4	845
3	107	357,273	40	162,393	67	194,880
4	30	75,401	0	0	30	75,401
4.5, 5	4	7,599	0	0	4	7,599
6	129	406,119	0	0	129	406,119
8	20	47,066	0	0	20	47,066
<8	4	22,419	0	0	4	22,419
TOTAL	298	916,722	40	162,393	258	754,329

Table 31.4. *The tithe maps of Southampton (Hampshire): dates*

	1837	*1838*	*1839*	*1840*	*1841*	*1842*	*1843*	*1844*	*1845*	*1846*	*1847*	*1848*	*1849*	*>1849*
All maps	9	43	58	61	28	31	9	14	13	12	3	3	5	9
1st class	0	8	11	5	5	3	0	3	2	1	0	1	1	0
2nd class	9	35	47	56	23	28	9	11	11	11	3	2	4	9

('Southampton') Hampshire

31/1 Abbotts Ann (parish) SU 326430
Apt 18.07.1839; 3351a (3351); Map 1842, 6 chns, by Phillips and Westbury, Andover; foot/b'way, houses, woods (named), plantations, building names, sedges.

31/2 Aldershott (parish) SU 862515 [Aldershot]
Apt 29.12.1841; 4144a (all); Map 1841, 3 chns, by J. Streat, Ash; construction lines, turnpike roads, canal with towpath and lock, waterbodies, houses, woods, hops, building names, road names, workhouse, brick kilns, stop gate, culvert, vicarage, boundary stones, common; map has a note, bottom left, that it was insured in 1841 for $60.

31/3 New Alresford (parish) SU 584323
Apt 22.08.1842; 684a (all); Map 1843, 3 chns, by R. and C. Pink, Hambledon, (tithable parts only in detail); foot/b'way, houses, woods, plantations, hedge ownership, fence ownership, mill, pit, riverside path, pound, tollgate, boundary tree and post, stiles (by symbol).

31/4 Old Alresford (parish) SU 600357
Apt 24.11.1841; 3609a (3608); Map 1839, 6 chns, 'Compiled from various Maps' by R.C. Gale, Winchester; waterbodies, woods (col); pond named.

31/5 Alton (parish) SU 708394
Apt 06.05.1839; 3897a (all); Map 1842, 6 chns, in 5 parts, (including open fields and town at 3 chns and small enlargements of detail), litho (Standidge); foot/b'way, waterbodies, houses (by shading), woods, hops, open fields, building names, road names, paper mill, turnpike gate.

31/6 Alverstoke (parish) SU 605008
Apt 13.06.1840; 4077a (all); Map 1840, 3 chns, 1st cl, in 2 parts, by Lewis and Walker, Southampton; construction lines, railway, waterbodies, houses, woods, hedge ownership, brickworks.

31/7 Amport (parish) SU 293441
Apt 09.10.1838; 3933a (all); Map 1840, 6 chns, in 3 parts, by Phillips and Westbury, Andover, (includes 24-chn index); foot/b'way, waterbodies, houses, woods (named), plantations, parkland (named), building names.

31/8 Andover cum Foxcott (parish) SU 368481
Apt 19.05.1848; 9554a (8290); Map 1849, 3 chns, 1st cl, in 2 parts: part 1 by Charles Sharp, Ringwood, and part 2 by John Waters, Salisbury; construction lines, railway with earthworks, foot/b'way, canal, woods (col), hedge ownership, fence ownership, building names, road names, turnpike, Roman roads, ladies walk, signpost (by symbol), milestone, almshouses, chapel, workhouse, chalk pit, mills, tan yard, gas works, brick yards, sedge bed; there are differences in style and content between the two parts.

31/9 Appleshaw (parish) SU 305487
Apt 08.06.1839; 697a (697); Map 1838, 3 chns, by Phillips and Westbury, Andover; houses, woods, toll gate.

31/10 Arreton (parish) SZ 524863
Apt 22.08.1842; 8833a (8833); Map 1844?, 8 chn, in 2 parts, by F. and H.E. Draysons, litho (by J. Aresti, 166 High Street, Newport, Isle of Wight); foot/b'way, waterbodies, houses (black), woods, plantations, chapel, glebe, tithe-free areas.

31/11 Ashe (parish) SU 537495
Apt 13.03.1844; 2107a (2107); Map 1846, 6 chns; railway, waterbodies, houses, woods.

31/12 Ashley (parish) SU 394300
Apt 02.06.1840; 1857a (1857); Map 1840, 6 chns, litho (Standidge); foot/b'way, woods, orchard, gardens, boundary tree.

31/13 Ashmansworth (parish) SU 413572 [Ashansworth]
Apt 08.06.1840; 1809a (all); Map 1840, 3 chns, by Cornelius B. Davis, The Hitchen, East Woodhay; construction lines, foot/b'way, waterbodies, houses, woods, plantations, hedge ownership, fence ownership, field gates.

31/14 Avington (parish) SU 535302
Apt 28.11.1838; 1795a (all); Map 1839, 3 chns, in 2 parts, by Thomas Beards, 'Copied from a Map Belonging to His Grace the Duke of Buckingham and Chandos'; foot/b'way, waterbodies, houses, woods, plantations, parkland, hedge ownership, field gates; compass boss is a blank shield. Apt omits land use.

31/15 Basing (parish) SU 670533
Apt 12.10.1841; 5105a (5104); Map 1842, 10 chns; waterbodies, osiers, field boundary ownerships, building names. (The map in PRO IR 30 is a copy; original is in PRO IR 77/57.)

31/16 Basingstoke (parish) SU 625515
Apt 16.06.1840; 4036a (4036); Map 1841?, 6 chns, in 2 parts, (tithable parts only in detail); railway with station, canal with towpath, woods, orchard, rectory, ancient barrow, tollgate, town hall, occupation road.

31/17 Barton Stacey (parish) SU 430403
Apt 05.03.1840; 4943a (4943); Map 1840?, 3 chns, by Charles Fielder, Sparsholt, Winchester; construction lines, waterbodies, houses, woods, parkland, hedge ownership, water meadow channels (in detail).

31/18 Baughurst (parish) SU 575601
Apt 14.02.1839; 1675a (1675); Map 1839, 6 chns, in 2 parts; foot/b'way, waterbodies, woods, stiles (by symbol).

31/19 Beaworth (parish) SU 569251 [Beauworth]
Apt 29.03.1837; 1215a (all); Map 1837, 6 chns, ? by Richard C. Gale, Winchester; foot/b'way, woods (col), plantations, stiles (by symbol).

31/20 Bedhampton (parish) SU 702080
Apt 08.08.1842; 2417a (2606); Map 1844?, 4 chns, in 2 parts; waterbodies, woods, marsh/bog, semaphore, chalk pit.

31/21 Bentley (parish) SU 790449
Apt 27.10.1840; 2288a (2288); Map 1839, 3 chns, 1st cl, by Manwaring Chitty; construction lines, foot/b'way, waterbodies, houses, woods, grassland (by symbol), hops, building names, pits, toll bar, greens.

31/22 Bentworth (parish) SU 666400
Apt 16.06.1840; 3688a (all); Map 1840, 6 chns, litho; waterbodies, woods, building names, pits or quarries, pond; some wood ornament has been added in manuscript.

31/23 Bighton (parish) SU 619349
Apt 26.02.1839; 2094a (2094); Map 1839, 4 chns, by Thomas Beards, 'Copied from an Old Map of the same Scale by direction of the Landowners'; waterbodies, houses, woods, hedge ownership; map has colourful cartouche with flowers, leaves and gold leaf. Apt omits land use.

31/24 Binstead (parish) SZ 546893
Apt 11.01.1848; 259a (1475); Map 1851, 3 chns; woods; table gives field acreages. Apt omits land use.

31/25 Binsted (parish) SU 788412 [Binstead]
Apt 22.10.1841; 6833a (6833), (tithable parts only in detail); Map 1843, 3 chns, by J.M. Sanderson, Sunbury; waterbodies, houses, open fields, tithery boundary.

31/26 Bishopstoke (parish) SU 490188
Apt 26.08.1839; 3318a (3360); Map 1840, 3 chns, copied from the enclosure map by Richard Dixon, Godalming, Surrey; canal with locks, waterbodies, houses, woods, gravel pit, peat ponds.

31/27 Bishops Sutton (parish) SU 612319 [Bishop's Sutton]
Apt 31.12.1847; 3729a (all); Map 1839, 3 chns, by Phillips and Westbury, Andover; foot/b'way, waterbodies, houses, woods (named, shown by Dawson's symbol), osiers, hedge ownership, fence ownership.

31/28 Bishops Waltham (parish) SU 556172 [Bishop's Waltham]
Apt 08.09.1840; 7389a (7388); Map 1839, 3 chns, 1st cl, by I.T. Lewis, Fareham; construction lines, foot/b'way, waterbodies, houses, woods, pits, brickyard, tanyard. (The map in PRO IR 30 is a copy; original is in PRO IR 77/58.)

31/29 Blendworth (parish) SU 719130
Apt 28.01.1841; 2304a (all); Map 1839, 6 chns, by J.W. Blackman, Fareham; foot/b'way, waterbodies, houses, woods, road names, forest gate, tithing boundary, downland.

31/30 Boarhunt (parish) SU 609095
Apt 28.04.1840; 357a (1938); Map 1839, 6 chns, by J.W. Blackman, Fareham; foot/b'way, waterbodies, houses, woods, hedge ownership, building names, road names, monument (by symbol), pit.

31/31 Boldre (parish) SZ 339985
Apt 29.03.1851; 10397a (11950); Map 1841, 3 chns, 1st cl, in 2 parts, by George Doswell, 35 Bernard Street, Southampton; construction lines, foot/b'way, waterbodies, houses (black), woods, plantations, heath/moor, hedge ownership, field boundary ownerships, building names, brick yard, factory, forest gates, ford, stiles (by symbol), crossroads cross, monument, mud flats, chapel, glebe; map has notes 'This Scale was laid off at the commence-ment of laying down the Survey lines', (referring to a 210-chain-long scale), and that 'Mud Land' was surveyed from a boat.

31/32 Bonchurch (parish) SZ 578783
Apt 25.10.1842; 282a (618); Map 1843, 3 chns, by J.F. Tidey, Littlehampton; waterbodies, chine.

31/33 Bossington (parish) SU 328305
Apt 11.04.1837; 616a (all); Map 1837, 4 chns; woods (col), farm buildings, churchyard, pit, private road; individual buildings are not shown.

31/34 St Mary Bourne (parish) SU 415515
Apt 28.04.1840; 7679a (7678); Map 1841, 3 chns; foot/b'way, waterbodies, houses, woods, hedge ownership, weir; it is unclear what the multi-colour bands signify.

31/35 Botley (parish) SU 506124
Apt 25.09.1838; 1818a (1887); Map 1839, 3 chns, 1st cl, by H.C. Wright, 40 Tavistock Street, Covent Garden, London; construction lines, foot/b'way, waterbodies, houses, woods, plantations, fences, field boundary ownerships, building names, parsonage, old church, footbridges (by symbol), pound, common, mud and marsh.

31/36 Brading (parish) SZ 592863
Apt 21.11.1842; 9564a (10107); Map 1840, 3 chns, by Thomas Hellyer, Ryde; construction lines, waterbodies, houses, woods, hedge ownership, high and low water marks, fort.

31/37 Bradley (parish) SU 640420
Apt 15.06.1839; 960a (all); Map 1839?, 8 chns; waterbodies, woods.

31/38 Bramdean (parish) SU 622286
Apt 05.03.1839; 1205a (all); Map 1840, 6 chns, by Henry Howard, St Cross, Winchester; foot/b'way, houses, woods (col).

31/39 Bramley (parish) SU 654595
Apt 10.09.1838; 2256a (all); Map 1840, 6 chns; foot/b'way, open fields, fences, field gates, ford.

31/40 Bramshaw (parish) (partly in Wilts) SU 276157
Apt 16.05.1839; 1804a (3560); Map 1841?, [3 chns], in 2 parts, by Edwd Neale, Southampton, (part 2, of Fritham, is litho (Standidge), 1839); construction lines, waterbodies, houses, woods (named), heath/moor, field gates, landowners, parks, Crown land, heath, waste, county boundary (col); a substantial area outside the tithe district boundary is mapped.

31/41 Bramshott (parish) SU 843329
Apt 15.03.1845; 6677a (all); Map 1846, 6 chns, by George Parson, litho (by Maclure, MacDonald and MacGregor, Lithographers, Draftsmen and Engravers, London, Liverpool and Glasgow); waterbodies, woods, plantations, orchard, building names, boundary landmarks, lime kiln, mill, rectory, county boundary, commons, ponds (named).

31/42 Breamore (parish) SU 152183
Apt 16.03.1840; 2652a (2651); Map 1838, 6 chns, by Phillips and Westbury, Andover; foot/b'way, waterbodies, houses, woods, plantations, orchard, pit, water meadow channels; intermixed tithable land is tinted.

31/43 Brighstone (parish) SZ 433827
Apt 07.07.1838; 3152a (all); Map 1840, 4 chns, in 2 parts, by John Dennett; construction lines, waterbodies, houses, woods, rock outcrops, pit or quarry, tower, cliffs; most area numbers are stamped; many annotated rays from triangulation stations are shown; below the title are the following notes: 'The Lines drawn in Red are measured with a Base chain, double the usual length. Those drawn in Green are measured with the ordinary four pole Chain. The Offsets on both are taken with the usual ten-link staff'.

31/44 Brockenhurst (parish) SU 309012
Apt 03.09.1840; 2858a (2980), (tithable parts only); Map 1848?, 3 chns, 1st cl; waterbodies, houses, woods (col), plantations, field boundary ownerships, ford.

31/45 Brooke (parish) SZ 389843 [Brook]
Apt 16.12.1843; 713a (all); Map 1838, 4 chns, by Jno. Dennett and Son; construction lines, waterbodies, woods (col), osiers (col), arable (col), grassland (col), orchard (col), gardens (col), hedges, cliff, undercliff, beach, chalk pits, tumuli.

31/46 Broughton (parish) SU 308336
Apt 29.08.1837; 3761a (4356); Map 1840?, 3 chns, in 4 parts, (including one part at 8 chns); construction lines, foot/b'way, waterbodies, houses, woods, hedge ownership, former open field names, field gates, pound, turnpike, chalk pit, ford, glebe; hills named; green bands round certain fields are described as 'Water' in Apt.

31/47 Brown Candover (parish) SU 575398
Apt 26.11.1841; 2088a (all); Map 1842, 8 chns; foot/b'way, houses, woods (col), grassland (col), pits.

31/48 Buckholt (extra-parochial place) (partly in Wilts) SU 283325 [Not listed]
Apt 03.12.1839; 1224a (all); Map 1840?, 8 chns, in 4 parts, (includes 24-chn index); waterbodies, houses.

31/49 Bullington (parish) SU 461419 [Not listed]
Apt 22.01.1841; 1624a (1623); Map 1840, 3 chns, 1st cl, by George Hewitt, Elvetham, Hartford; construction lines, woods, hedge ownership, fords.

31/50 Burghclere (parish) SU 471593
Apt 11.01.1838; 5080a (5080); Map 1838?, 3 chns; waterbodies, houses (by shading), woods, plantations; north pointer has rough Prince of Wales' feathers; reason for tinting some land pink is unclear.

31/51 Buriton (parish) SU 740203
Apt 07.09.1841; 6306a (6305); Map 1840, 6 chns, by G. Doswell, Bernard Street, Southampton; hill-drawing, foot/b'way, waterbodies, houses (black), woods (col), hedge ownership, fence ownership, building names, landowners, boundary trees and posts, pits, carriage road, parsonage, down (col), glebe (col), manorial boundaries; hills named.

31/52 Bursledon (parish) SU 487102
Apt 25.03.1840; 795a (905); Map 1839, 3 chns, 1st cl, by R.C. Gale, Winchester; construction lines, waterbodies, houses, woods (col), hedge ownership, fence ownership, road names, mud land.

31/53 Calbourne (parish) SZ 430885
Apt 07.07.1838; 6133a (6397); Map 1840, 4 chns; foot/b'way, waterbodies, houses, woods (named), building names, high water spring tides, salterns, mud, low water mark, pound, mills, fulling mill, school, rectory; most names are stamped; creeks and other coast features are shown in unusual detail.

31/54 Carisbrooke (parish) SZ 480874
Apt 16.12.1843; 7409a (7409); Map 1846?, 4 chns, in 3 parts, 'partly measured and partly complied' by E. Smith and Son; foot/b'way, waterbodies, woods, hedge ownership, fences, boundary stones, pit; built-up part generalised.

31/55 Catherington (parish) SU 693137
Apt 06.01.1842; 5140a (5139); Map 1838, 6 chns, by J.W. Blackman, Fareham; waterbodies, houses, woods, plantations, parkland, building names, sheepwash pond.

31/56 Chale (parish) SZ 484787
Apt 27.07.1844; 2295a (all); Map 1845?, 6 chns, by Fredk. and Henry E.

Drayson, litho; hill-drawing, houses (by shading), waste, high and low water marks, cliffs, hotel, tower; cliffs are shown by an unusual mix of hill-drawing and ledges, giving a vivid suggestion of subsidence.

31/57 Chalton (parish) SU 728160
Apt 26.01.1841; 1723a (all); Map 1838, 6 chns, by J.W. Blackman, Fareham; waterbodies, houses, woods, road names, telegraph, windmill (by symbol), down (col, named).

31/58 South Charford (township or district) SU 170192 [Not listed]
Apt 28.07.1840; 833a (all); Map 1840, 5 chns, by Phillips and Westbury, Andover; foot/b'way, waterbodies, houses, woods (col, named), plantations, building names, pits, water meadow channels.

31/59 Chawton (parish) SU 698370
Apt 15.02.1839; 2663a (all); Map 1838, 3 chns, 1st cl, by Manwaring Chitty, Farnham, Surrey; construction lines, foot/b'way, waterbodies, houses, woods (named), fir and ash plantations, parkland, grassland (by symbol), hops, building names, boundary stones, gravel pit, chalk pits.

31/60 Cheriton (parish) SU 575278
Apt 29.03.1837; 3021a (all); Map 1838, 9 chns, in 2 parts, by R.C. Gale, Winchester, (includes enlargement of village centre at 3 chns); waterbodies, houses, woods (col), road names.

31/61 Chilbolton (parish) SU 407381
Apt 09.10.1838; 3101a (3100); Map 1838, 3 chns, by R.C. Gale, Winchester; construction lines, waterbodies, houses, woods (col), hedge ownership, road names, chalk pit, aqueduct, common, down.

31/62 Chilcomb (parish) SU 505285
Apt 09.05.1838; 2257a (2257); Map 1838, 3 chns, 1st cl, by R.C. Gale, Winchester; construction lines, hill-drawing, canal with locks and towpath, waterbodies, houses, woods (col), plantations (col), hedge ownership, field gates, road names, semaphore, municipal boundary.

31/63 Chilton Candover (parish) SU 592408
Apt 26.11.1841; 1472a (all); Map 1842, 8 chns; waterbodies, houses, woods (col), parkland, grassland (col), pits, avenue of trees.

31/64 Christchurch, or Christchurch Twynham, with Holdenhurst (parish with parish or chapelry) SZ 142942
Apt 18.09.1838; 10605a (32175); Map 1840?-42, 3 chns, in 5 parts, by G.P. Dyke, Christchurch; construction lines, water-bodies, open fields, field boundary ownerships, building names, boundary post (by symbol), tithing boundaries (col). (The map in PRO IR 30 is a copy made in 1928; original is in PRO IR 77/59.)

31/65 Church Oakley (parish) SU 572515
Apt 16.04.1841; 1605a (all); Map 1841, 6 chns; turnpike roads, waterbodies, houses, woods (col), plantations (col), turnpike gate.

31/66 Clanfield (parish) SU 706172
Apt 26.01.1841; 1395a (1395); Map 1838, 6 chns, by J.W. Blackman, Fareham; waterbodies, houses, woods, road names, windmill, lime kiln, house name, down (col); hill named.

31/67 Upper Clatford (parish) SU 348428
Apt 08.06.1840; 2150a (all); Map 1840, 3 chns; hill-drawing, foot/b'way, canal with towpath and lock, waterbodies, houses, woods, plantations, parkland, hedge ownership (with trees), fence ownership, field gates, ford, footbridges (by symbol), ancient earthwork (in detail).

31/68 Cliddesden (parish) SU 642488
Apt 26.07.1842; 1884a (2150); Map 1842, 6 chns; waterbodies, woods, parkland.

31/69 Colemore and Priors Dean (united parishes) SU 711301
Apt 23.09.1840; 3004a (3003); Map 1843?, 6 chns, in 2 parts; foot/b'way, building names, boundary stone, gravel pit, parish boundary; woods named.

31/70 Combe (parish) SU 372606
Apt 14.04.1842; 2227a (all); Map 1843?, 4 chns; foot/b'way, woods, drove way, coppices (named), downs, commons.

31/71 Compton (parish) SU 463255
Apt 27.07.1844; 2100a (all); Map 1846?, 6 chns; railway, foot/b'way, canal with towpath, waterbodies, houses, woods, building names, road names.

31/72 Crondall (parish) SU 809509
Apt 13.03.1844; 9614a (9614); Map 1846, 3 chns, by Messrs G.H. Hewitt, High St, Oxford and Hartford Bridge, Hants; railway, canal with towpath, waterbodies, woods.

31/73 Crawley (parish) SU 429348
Apt 24.07.1837; 3556a (all); Map 1837, 6 chns, by Saml. Stephens, Southampton; foot/b'way, waterbodies, houses, farmyards (col), woods (col), plantations (col), parkland (col), arable (col), grassland (col), building names, brick works.

31/74 Crux Easton (parish) SU 426564
Apt 12.08.1843; 1100a (all); Map 1844, 4 chns; waterbodies, houses, woods, plantations, parsonage.

31/75 East Dean (parish) SU 278263
Apt 05.02.1839; 1060a (1060); Map 1840?, 6 chns; waterbodies, mill.

31/76 Deane (parish) SU 554504
Apt 05.12.1839; 1557a (1557); Map 1839, 6 chns; railway, foot/b'way, houses, woods (col), plantations (col), arable (col), grassland (col), hedge ownership, fence ownership, field gates, churchyard, 'Ha! Ha!'. Apt omits most land use.

31/77 Dibden (parish) SU 409079
Apt 17.03.1842; 2852a (all); Map 1842, 3 chns, 1st cl, by Harry Holloway, Ringwood; construction lines, waterbodies, houses, hedge ownership, field gates, building names, road names, boundary trees and posts, high and low water marks, brick works.

31/78 Dockenfield (tithing) SU 825401
Apt 31.12.1845; 567a (566); Map 1846?, 3 chns, 1st cl, by Henry Hale, Woking, near Ripley, Surrey; construction lines, waterbodies.

31/79 Dogmersfield (parish) SU 774520
Apt 29.03.1837; 1728a (all); Map 1838?, 6 chns; canal with towpaths, waterbodies, houses, woods, plantations, hedge ownership, fence ownership, building names, rectory, dairy, commons (col).

31/80 Droxford (parish) SU 586158
Apt 05.06.1840; 6987a (6986); Map 1841, 6 chns, in 2 parts, by J.W. Blackman, Fareham; waterbodies, houses, woods, heath/moor (named), building names, boundary stones, workhouse, lodge, chase gate, commons (col), greens, high and low water marks.

31/81 Dummer (parish) SU 590458
Apt 31.05.1838; 2181a (2180); Map 1838, 6 chns; foot/b'way, turnpike roads, waterbodies, houses (by shading), woods; red tithe area numbers indicate modus land; uninhabited buildings are shown without colour infill. Apt omits land use.

31/82 Durley (parish) SU 517168
Apt 22.03.1839; 2474a (2474); Map 1840, 3 chns, 1st cl, by Henry Howard, Winchester; construction lines, base-line, foot/b'way, water-bodies, houses, woods, plantations, hedge ownership, fence ownership, boundary marks; there is a long note about the perambulation of a boundary.

31/83 Easton (parish) SU 512308
Apt 09.01.1840; 2735a (2734); Map 1840?, 3 chns, by Thos Beards, copied from map owned by the Duke of Buckingham and Chandos; foot/b'way, houses, woods; scale is styled like a ruler; compass boss is a blank shield.

31/84 Eastrop (parish) SU 644518
Apt 18.01.1839; 438a (438); Map 1839, 6 chns, in 4 parts; canal, houses, woods, landowners, amphitheatre, avenue, nursery; legend explains symbols.

31/85 Ecchinswell (parish) SU 500587
Apt 02.07.1846; 2319a (2319); Map 1846, 3 chns, by Cornelius B. Davis, The Hitchen, East Woodhay; waterbodies, houses (by shading), woods, plantations; two isolated buildings are pink, for no clear reason.

31/86 Up Eldon (parish) SU 366278 [Not listed]
Apt 20.10.1848; 277a (all); Map 1849?, 4 chns; waterbodies, houses, woods.

31/87 Eling (parish) SU 339130
Apt 12.06.1843; 17730a (18459); Map 1842-45, 6 chns, in 8 parts, (including two parts at 3 chns); foot/b'way, waterbodies, houses, building names, magazines, workhouse, brick works; some woods named.

31/88 Ellingham (parish) SU 160079
Apt 27.07.1844; 2545a (2545); Map 1845, 3 chns, 1st cl, by H. Holloway and F.P. Webb; construction lines, foot/b'way, waterbodies, houses, hedge ownership, fence ownership, field gates, building names.

31/89 Elvetham (parish) SU 796570 [Not listed]
Apt 05.02.1839; 3200a (all); Map 1839, 4 chns, in 2 parts ? by George Hewett Jr., Elvetham; railway, foot/b'way, houses, woods (named), plantations, parkland, hops, field gates, building names, brick kiln, milestones, nursery, glebe.

31/90 Empshott (parish) SU 755316
Apt 21.06.1842; 740a (1320); Map 1839, 3 chns, by Jas Harding, Farnham; waterbodies, houses, woods (col, named), parkland (named), grassland (col), orchard, heath/moor, hedges, building names, common, common field, boundary stones.

31/91 Eversley (parish) SU 784608
Apt 04.10.1837; 5224a (all); Map 1838, 3 chns, by Geo. Hewett, Jr; construction lines, waterbodies, woods, plantations, hedge ownership, fence ownership, field gates, flight of steps, boundary trees and marks, tithing boundary; tithe area numbers are written upside-down to the title; map and Apt include the tithing of Bramshill.

31/92 Ewhurst (parish) SU 572571 [Not listed]
Apt 09.02.1843; 479a (all); Map 1842, 4 chns; foot/b'way, waterbodies, woods.

31/93 Exbury (parish) SZ 432998
Apt 23.01.1839; 2406a (all); Map 1838, 6 chns, by J.W. Blackman, Fareham; waterbodies, houses, woods, plantations, hedge ownership, building names, fish ponds, brick yard, watch house and flagstaff (by symbol), quay, high and low water marks, chapel.

31/94 Exton (parish) SU 606216
Apt 13.03.1839; 2465a (2464); Map 1839, 6 chns, by J.W. Blackman, Fareham; waterbodies, houses, woods, plantations, building names, dog kennel, well house.

31/95 Faccombe (parish) SU 390577
Apt 03.09.1839; 2631a (all); Map 1841, 6 chns, by Phillips and Westbury, Andover; waterbodies, houses, woods (named), building names.

31/96 Fareham (parish) SU 575075
Apt 31.10.1840; 6525a (6705); Map 1841, 6 chns, in 2 parts, by J.W. Blackman, Fareham, (includes town at 3 chns); railway with tunnel, foot/b'way, turnpike roads and gates, waterbodies, houses, woods, building names, road names, chapel, school, bathing house, high and low water marks, fish hatches, brick yards, rope walk, mills, mill pond, chalk pit, pottery, kilns.

31/97 Farleigh Wallop (parish) SU 619471
Apt 26.07.1842; 1675a (1675); Map 1842, 6 chns; foot/b'way, waterbodies, woods, plantations; scale appears to be 6 chns, but the scale bar divisions are of unequal length.

31/98 Farley Chamberlayne (parish) SU 396274 [Not listed]
Apt 07.12.1838; 1767a (all); Map 1838, 6 chns, by R.C. Gale, Winchester; waterbodies, houses, woods (col), plantations (col), building names, road names, semaphore, well. Apt omits land use.

31/99 Farlington (parish) SU 682066
Apt 29.06.1839; 2373a (?); Map 1838, 6 chns, 'copied' by Charles Lewis; waterbodies, houses, farmyards (col), woods (col, named), plantations (col), arable (col), grassland (col), gardens (col), building names, boundary stones, rectory, water works, kiln, brick yard.

31/100 Farnborough (parish) SU 874550
Apt 13.07.1839; 2207a (2208); Map 1841?, 6 chns; railway with station, waterbodies, houses.

31/101 Farringdon (parish) SU 703354
Apt 27.04.1839; 2297a (all); Map 1839, 4 chns, by Mainwaring Chitty, Farnham, Surrey; turnpike roads, toll bar, waterbodies, houses, woods, coppice (named), road names, pits (col).

31/102 Fawley (parish) SU 452027
Apt 23.01.1839; 6362a (9722); Map 1838, 6 chns, in 2 parts, by J.W. Blackman, Fareham, (including Hythe at 3 chns); waterbodies, houses, woods, plantations, parkland, heath/moor, hedge ownership, building names, road names, castle, quay, hards, dry dock, gravel pit, mill, mill pond, salterns, forest gates, commons, greens.

31/103 Fordingbridge (parish) SU 155139
Apt 07.01.1840; 6292a (6292); Map 1839, 3 chns, 1st cl, by Samuel Stephens, Southampton; construction lines, foot/b'way, waterbodies, houses, woods, orchard, hedge ownership, field gates, building names, mill, tan yard, schools, chapel, toll gate, stiles (by symbol), tithing boundaries (col), greens; hills named.

31/104 Freefolk (parish) SU 489461
Apt 27.02.1846; 1544a (all); Map 1849?, 4 chns; foot/b'way, turnpike roads, waterbodies, houses, woods, plantations.

31/105 Freshwater (parish) SZ 345872
Apt 23.08.1837; 4961a (all); Map surveyed in 1839, 6 chns, by Richard Dent, 129 High Street, Camden Town, Middlesex, litho ('Drawn on stone' by C.F. Cheffins, 9 Southampton Buildings, Southampton Row, London); foot/b'way, waterbodies, woods, plantations, parkland, marsh/bog, open fields, building names, field names, high and low tide marks, landing places, battery, chines, coast guard stations, beacon, lighthouse, spring, sheep wash, rabbit warren, hotel, rectory, milestones, causeway, windmill, common fields (named), glebe.

31/106 Froxfield (parish) SU 714272 [Froxfield Green]
Apt 20.12.1842; 4899a (all); Map 1839, 3 chns, 1st cl, by S. Stephens, Southampton; construction lines, foot/b'way, waterbodies, houses, woods, plantations, parkland, hedge ownership, fence ownership, field gates, building names, windmill, toll bar, lodge.

31/107 Froyle (parish) SU 754439
Apt 03.02.1846; 3618a (3618); Map 1845, 4 chns, by J.M. Sanderson, Sunbury, Middlesex; waterbodies, houses.

31/108 Fyfield (parish) SU 296481
Apt 24.05.1847; 981a (2210); Map 1849, 6 chns; woods (col).

31/109 Gatcombe (parish) SZ 486854
Apt 05.12.1843; 1392a (all); Map 1843, 4 chns, by Messrs Crawter; waterbodies, houses, woods, osiers, building names, pits or quarries, mill, downs.

31/110 Godshill (parish) SZ 526804
Apt 06.12.1843; 6535a (6535); Map surveyed in 1838-9, 4 chns, in 2 parts, by E. Smith and Son; hill-drawing, foot/b'way, waterbodies, woods, hedge ownership, fence ownership, quarry, cliffs, boundary stones (by symbol).

31/111 Goodworth Clatford (parish) SU 364421
Apt 01.04.1844; 2808a (3390); Map 1845, 6 chns; foot/b'way, canal with towpath, waterbodies, houses, woods, plantations.

31/112 Gratcly (parish) SU 274416 [Grateley]
Apt 05.08.1837; 1541a (all); Map 1837, 6 chns, by R.C. Gale, Winchester; hill-drawing, foot/b'way, waterbodies, houses, woods (col), plantations (col), arable (col), grassland (col), gardens (col), heath/moor (col), hedge ownership, road names, mounds, direction posts, Roman road; 'clumps' named.

31/113 Greatham (parish) SU 776302
Apt 11.05.1842; 2124a (all); Map 3 chns, in 2 parts, by George Doswell, 35 Bernard St, Southampton (1840), and D. Ayling (1841); waterbodies, houses, woods (col), hops (col), hedge ownership, fence ownership,

field gates, building names, old kiln, mill, boundary stones and marks, pound, common.

31/114 Grewell (parish) SU 716513 [Greywell]
Apt 26.09.1840; 860a (all); Map 1842?, 3 chns; canal with towpath and tunnel entrance, waterbodies, woods (named), plantations, orchard, field boundary ownerships, ford.

31/115 Hale (parish) SU 190182
Apt 17.05.1841; 1673a (1672); Map 1841, 6 chns, in 2 parts; waterbodies, houses; map appears originally to have included South Charford tithing, which has been scraped out.

31/116 Hamble or Hamblerice (parish) SU 478067
Apt 06.04.1839; 425a (1319); Map 1839, 3 chns, 1st cl, by T.H. Spencer, 3 Everett Street, Russell Square, London; construction lines, waterbodies, houses, woods, building names, commons, high water mark, saltings; map title and writing are diagonal to the cut of the paper.

31/117 Hambledon (parish) SU 655148
Apt 22.08.1842; 9040a (9040); Map 1844?, 3 chns, 1st cl; foot/b'way, waterbodies, houses, woods, plantations, orchard, hedge ownership, fence ownership, mill pond, boundary stones (by symbol), pits or quarries, downs.

31/118 Hannington (parish) SU 545557
Apt 10.04.1839; 2048a (?); Map 1840, 6 chns, by T. Nation; waterbodies, houses, woods (col), pit.

31/119 Harbridge (parish) SU 126089
Apt 30.06.1841; 4082a (all); Map 1840, 6 chns; waterbodies, houses.

31/120 Hartley Mauditt (parish) SU 746361
Apt 18.01.1840; 1339a (all); Map 1842?, 8 chns; foot/b'way, waterbodies, woods, building names, parsonage.

31/121 Hartley Westpall (parish) SU 700580
Apt 17.12.1838; 1402a (1401); Map 1839, 6 chns, in 3 parts; waterbodies, houses, woods; legend explains symbols.

31/122 Hartley Wintney (parish) SU 763566
Apt 12.06.1843; 2406a (all); Map 1844?, 6 chns; waterbodies, woods.

31/123 Havant (parish) SU 724081
Apt 07.12.1840; 2764a (all); Map 1842, 3 chns, by Charles Lewis, Havant; foot/b'way, waterbodies, houses, woods, building names, mills, obelisk (pictorial), beacon (pictorial), chapel, rectory, lodges, boundary stone, greens, heaths, common.

31/124 Hawkley (parish) SU 752294
Apt 04.11.1850; 1400a (1710); Map 1846, 3 chns; foot/b'way, waterbodies, houses, woods (col).

31/125 North Hayling (parish) SU 727029
Apt 22.02.1843; 1256a (all); Map 1843, 3 chns, by Charles Lewis, Havant; waterbodies, houses, open fields, boundary stones (by symbol), water mill, commons.

31/126 South Hayling (parish) SZ 722998
Apt 11.09.1843; 2501a (8123); Map 1844?, 4 chns, by Charles Lewis, Havant; waterbodies, houses, woods, building names, hotel, mill, chapel, vicarage, coastguard station.

31/127 Headbourne Worthy (parish) SU 471335
Apt 05.09.1837; 1793a (all); Map 1837, 6 chns, by R.C. Gale, Winchester; railway, foot/b'way, waterbodies, houses, woods (col), plantations (col), gardens (col), heath/moor, hedge ownership (col), field boundary ownerships, road names, downs. Apt omits land use.

31/128 Headley (parish) SU 822370
Apt 12.11.1846; 6978a (6977); Map 1847, 3 chns; houses, woods, orchard, furze (by symbol), fences, boundary stones (by symbol); compass has oak leaf boss and acorn pointer.

31/129 Heckfield (parish) SU 728599
Apt 09.07.1839; 3697a (5697); Map 1840, 6 chns; waterbodies, houses, woods, pound, heath, commons.

31/130 St Helens (parish) SZ 619912
Apt 28.04.1840; 1833a (3676); Map 4 chns, surveyed by W. Mortimer and Son, Newport in 1830, and 'corrected' in 1839; foot/b'way, waterbodies, woods (col), parkland (by Dawson's symbol), arable (col), grassland (col), orchard (col), gardens (col), sea mark, tide mill, offshore rocks (col); scale-bar is drawn like a ruler.

31/131 Herriard (parish) SU 670456
Apt 15.02.1839; 2963a (2963); Map 1840, 6 chns, by Phillips and Westbury, Andover; foot/b'way, turnpike roads, waterbodies, houses, farmyards (col), woods (col, named), coppice-with-standards (col), plantations (col), parkland (col), arable (col), grassland (col), gardens (col), building names, pits, dog kennel; land use is shown using Dawson's symbols.

31/132 Highclere (parish) SU 446600
Apt 11.01.1838; 3391a (3391); Map 1839?, 3 chns; waterbodies, woods, plantations; it is unclear what the various tints signify.

31/133 Hinton Ampner (parish) SU 614273
Apt 04.10.1838; 2350a (all); Map 1839, 6 chns, by H. Hyde, Land Surveyor, Architect, etc, Wareham, Dorset; foot/b'way, waterbodies, houses, pit.

31/134 Holybourne (parish) SU 729418
Apt 07.11.1842; 1394a (1394); Map 1842, 4 chns, by J.M. Sanderson, Sunbury; waterbodies, houses.

31/135 Hordle (parish) SZ 273954
Apt 08.02.1843; 3880a (4385); Map 1844?, 3 chns, 1st cl; waterbodies, houses, fences, churchyard, common (col), green (col).

31/136 Houghton (parish) SU 338336
Apt 21.03.1842; 2643a (all); Map 1842, 6 chns, by R.C. Gale, Winchester; foot/b'way, waterbodies, houses, woods (col), plantations (col), ford, weirs, footbridges (by symbol), creep, sedge (by symbol), droves (uncoloured).

31/137 Hound (parish) SU 470092
Apt 08.03.1839; 3657a (4691); Map 1838, 6 chns, by R.C. Gale, Winchester; waterbodies, houses, woods (col), building names, road names, abbey ruins, boundary of tithe-free land, commons (col); ponds named.

31/138 Hunton (parish or chapelry) SU 493417
Apt 07.05.1838; 1033a (all); Map 1837, 3 chns, by Charles Fielder, Sparsholt, nr Winchester; construction lines, foot/b'way, waterbodies, houses, woods, plantations, hedge ownership, fence ownership, milestones (by symbol), boundary stones (by symbol), farm names.

31/139 Hursley (parish) SU 423249
Apt 22.04.1839; 10494a (10493); Map 1839, 9 chns, in 2 parts, by James Fowlie, (includes enlargement of village); waterbodies, houses, woods, hedge ownership, fence ownership, park.

31/140 Hurstbourne Priors (parish) SU 436483
Apt 08.04.1841; 3133a (all); Map 1842, 6 chns, by Phillips and Westbury, Andover; foot/b'way, waterbodies, houses, farmyards, woods (col, named), coppice (col, named), osiers (col), parkland (col), arable (col), grassland (col), gardens (col), building names, road names, field names, landowners, paper mill, well, classical monument, 'Bee House', fords, pound, lodge; land use is mostly shown using Dawson's symbols.

31/141 Hurstbourne Tarrant with Vernham's Dean (parish and chapelry) SU 365550
Apt 17.03.1841; 8723a (8522); Map 1838, 3 chns, in 2 parts, by George Oakley Lucas, Devizes; foot/b'way, waterbodies, houses, woods, hedge ownership, field boundary ownerships, boundary of tithe-free areas, manor boundaries (green); part 2 is uncoloured and shows houses by shading.

31/142 Ibsley (parish) SU 167100
Apt 04.05.1840; 1748a (all); Map 1841?, 6 chns; foot/b'way, waterbodies, houses, ford, footbridge (by symbol), common.

31/143 Idsworth (parish) SU 740133 [Not listed]
Apt 26.01.1841; 1703a (all); Map 1838, 6 chns, by J.W. Blackman, Fareham; foot/b'way, waterbodies, houses, woods, avenue of trees.

31/144 Illsfield (parish) SU 640456 [Ellisfield]
Apt 02.09.1840; 2324a (all); Map 1841, 6 chns, by Phillips and Westbury, Andover; hill-drawing, foot/b'way, waterbodies, houses, woods (by Dawson's symbol), plantations, heath/moor, building names, parsonage, pit, commons, roadside waste (col), glebe, greens; ponds named.

31/145 Itchen Abbas (parish) SU 538345
Apt 28.11.1838; 2100a (all); Map 1839, 3 chns, in 2 parts, by Tho. Beards, copied from one belonging to the Duke of Buckingham and Chandos; foot/b'way, waterbodies, houses, woods; compass boss is a blank shield.

31/146 Itchen Stoke with Abbotstone (parish) SU 562345
Apt 23.07.1838; 2921a (2921); Map 1838?, 8 chns; houses, woods (col), plantations (col), grassland (col), heath/moor, site of garden. Apt omits land use.

31/147 Kilmiston (parish) SU 592257 [Kilmeston]
Apt 24.05.1837; 1913a (all); Map 1838, 6 chns, by Phillips and Westbury, Andover; foot/b'way, waterbodies, houses, farmyards (col), woods (col), plantations (col), arable (col), grassland (col), gardens (col), fences.

31/148 Kimpton (parish) SU 277479
Apt 08.08.1837; 2754a (all); Map 1839, 6 chns, by Phillips and Westbury, Andover; waterbodies, houses, farmyards, woods, plantations, arable (col), grassland (col), gardens (col), building names, road names, turnpike gate.

31/149 Kingsclere (parish) SU 527588
Apt 30.06.1841; 12917a (all); Map 1842, 6 chns; waterbodies, woods, open fields (named), pound, brick kiln, commons.

31/150 Kingsley (parish) SU 791384
Apt 22.10.1841; 1752a (all); Map 1843, 6 chns; waterbodies, woods, hops, building names, mill, pits or quarries, commons.

31/151 Kingsomborne and Little Sombourne (parish) SU 363315 [King's Somborne]
Apt 09.12.1841; 17893a (?); Map 1st cl, in 3 parts: Kingsomborne, 1838, 3 chns; Little Somborne, 1841, 6 chns (2nd cl), (including 3-chn enlargement of village centre); construction lines, hill-drawing, foot/b'way, canal with towpath and locks, waterbodies, houses, woods (col), hedge ownership, field gates, building names, road names, white horse (by symbol); pond named.

31/152 Kingstone (parish) SZ 474812 [Kingston]
Apt 24.12.1838; 884a (all); Map surveyed in 1839, 3 chns, in 3 parts, by Richard Dent; hill-drawing, waterbodies, farmyards (col), woods (col), osiers (col), arable (col), grassland (col), gardens (col), marsh/bog (col), heath/moor (col), hedge ownership, building names, pits.

31/153 Kingsworthy (parish) SU 493342 [Kings Worthy]
Apt 29.05.1838; 2217a (all); Map 1839?, 3 chns, by Charles Fielder, Sparsholt, Winchester; construction lines, railway, foot/b'way, houses, woods, parkland, gardens, ford, boundary stones, water meadows (col); north pointer includes two fox brushes.

31/154 Knights Enham (parish) SU 360478 [Not listed]
Apt 27.06.1838; 788a (all); Map 1839, 3 chns, 1st cl, by Phillips and Westbury, Andover; houses, hedge ownership, fence ownership, milestone (with distances), turnpike gate, boundary stone and trees.

31/155 Lainstone (parish) SU 443317 [Not listed]
Apt 06.07.1850; 117a (110); Map 1851, 3 chns, waterbodies, houses, woods; table on map lists field names, use and acreages.

31/156 Lasham (parish) SU 675428
Apt 24.09.1838; 1769a (all); Map 1838, 3 chns, by R.C. Gale, Winchester; waterbodies, houses, woods (col).

31/157 Laverstoke (parish) SU 495485
Apt 07.08.1851; 1985a (all); Map 1852?, 4 chns; railway, waterbodies, houses, woods, plantations, parkland, field boundary ownerships, Roman road.

31/158 St Lawrence, Isle of Wight (parish) SZ 540769 [St Lawrence]
Apt 12.02.1846; 332a (all); Map 1841, [3 chns]; waterbodies, houses, woods, parkland, orchard, heath/moor, rock outcrops, cliff.

31/159 Leckford (parish) SU 386370
Apt 23.03.1842; 2237a (all); Map 1840, [3 chns], 1st cl, by Richard Nightingale; construction lines, canal with towpath and locks, houses, woods, plantations, orchard, heath/moor, building names, churchyard, water meadow channels (in detail).

31/160 Linkenholt (parish) SU 369581
Apt 24.03.1838; 1074a (all); Map 1838?, 6 chns; waterbodies, woods.

31/161 Liss (parish) SU 783275
Apt 26.07.1842; 3680a (all); Map 1840, 4 chns, 'from Haywood and others', by D. Ayling; foot/b'way, waterbodies, houses, woods, plantations, hops, building names, mill, boundary trees, commons, greens, farm names, glebe.

31/162 Litchfield (parish) SU 469541
Apt 05.03.1839; 1800a (all); Map 1839, [6 chns]; foot/b'way, houses, church lands (col). District is apportioned by holding and fields are not shown.

31/163 Littleton (parish) SU 457328
Apt 11.03.1839; 1294a (1293); Map 1838, 3 chns, 1st cl, by R.C. Gale, Winchester; construction lines, waterbodies, houses, woods (col), plantations (col), hedge ownership, fence ownership, field gates, road names, earthwork, boundary marks, downs.

31/164 Lockerley (parish) SU 300255
Apt 18.06.1840; 1730a (all); Map 1840, 6 chns, 'Compiled from various Maps' by R.C. Gale, Winchester; houses, woods (col).

31/165 Longparish (parish) SU 425447
Apt 02.09.1840; 5251a (5250); Map 1841, 6 chns, by Phillips and Westbury, Andover; foot/b'way, waterbodies, houses, farmyards (col), woods (col, named), plantations (col), coppice (col), parkland (col), arable (col), grassland (col), gardens (col), building names, gravel pits, mills, fords, Roman road, vicarage, dell.

31/166 Longstock (parish) SU 348375
Apt 05.06.1840; 2963a (2962); Map 1839, 3 chns, 1st cl, in 2 parts, by Phillips and Westbury, Andover; construction lines, waterbodies, houses, woods, coppice (named), plantations, sedge beds (by symbol), building names, weirs, ancient moat, pit, mill.

31/167 Lymington (parish) SZ 322954
Apt 23.09.1840; 1497a (all); Map 1842?, 3 chns, 1st cl, in 2 parts, by Richard Nightingale, Lyndhurst, (includes town separately at 1.5 chns); construction lines, turnpike roads, houses, woods.

31/168 Lyndhurst (parish) SU 299076
Apt 11.05.1838; 981a (3618); Map 1838, 3 chns, 1st cl, in 2 parts, by Richard Nightingale, Lyndhurst; construction lines, water-bodies, houses, woods (col), building names, pound.

31/169 Mapplederwell (parish) SU 685516 [Mapledurwell]
Apt 10.10.1839; 818a (818); Map 1840, 6 chns; canal with towpath and cutting, waterbodies, houses, farmyards, woods (col), arable (col), grassland (col), orchard (col), gardens (col), waste, hedge ownership, fence ownership, pit, commons.

31/170 Martyr Worthy (parish) SU 516343
Apt 16.01.1840; 1975a (1974); Map 1841?, 3 chns, by Charles Fielder, Sparsholt, Winchester; construction lines, foot/b'way, houses, woods, osiers, parkland, gardens, water-meadow channels (in detail), fords, pits or quarries; the map has a note, 'Reference - The dotted line in black round the Map, denotes the boundary of the Parish. The small mark such as a Bush, on whichever Side it appears on the boundary line of each field, denotes to which field the fence belongs'; north pointer has fox-brushes decoration, sprouting from an ungraduated scale-bar.

31/171 Medstead (parish) SU 652365
Apt 22.08.1842; 2811a (all); Map 1844?, 6 chns; waterbodies, houses, woods (col), building names, windmill.

31/172 East Meon (parish) SU 689223
Apt 14.03.1851; 8715a (11380), (tithable parts only); Map 1852, 6 chns, by Harry Postlethwaite, 12 Wellington Road, St Johns Wood, London; foot/b'way, waterbodies, houses, woods, building names, brick kilns, mill, chalk pits, lime kilns, pesthouse, vicarage, school, downs, commons, glebe.

31/173 Meonstoke (parish) SU 632196
Apt 22.01.1841; 2053a (2050); Map 1841, 3 chns, 1st cl, by Harry Holloway, Ringwood; construction lines, foot/b'way, waterbodies, houses, hedge ownership, fence ownership, field gates, building names, road names, wells, old entrenchments, stiles (by symbol), weir.

31/174 Millbrook (parish) SU 394140
Apt 04.03.1843; 3017a (3646); Map 1842?, 3 chns, 1st cl, by George Doswell, 35 Bernard Street, Southampton; construction lines, canal with towpath and lock, waterbodies, houses, woods, plantations, marsh/bog (named), fences, building names, iron foundry, 'Unfinished Building District', chapel, common (by Dawson's symbol), warren, spear bed, public gravel pits.

31/175 Milford (parish) SZ 300935 [Milford on Sea]
Apt 27.07.1840; 1536a (5286); Map 1840, 6 chns, in 3 parts, (includes two small enlargements of detail); waterbodies, woods, salterns, mill, tithing boundaries and names, commons.

31/176 Milton (parish) SZ 244952 [Old and New Milton]
Apt 28.08.1841; 6316a (6416); Map 1840, 3 chns, 1st cl, by Harry Holloway, Ringwood; construction lines, foot/b'way, waterbodies, houses, hedge ownership, fence ownership, field gates, building names, road names, marl and gravel pits, boundary trees (by symbol) and markers, mile stone, spring, mill, greens, commons; broken blue appears to show streams across fields. (The map in PRO IR 30 is a copy; original is in PRO IR 77/61.)

31/177 Minestead (parish) SU 278106 [Minstead]
Apt 18.02.1837; 2965a (12800); Map 1838, 3 chns, 1st cl, in 4 parts, by H. Hyde, Wareham, Dorset; construction lines, foot/b'way, waterbodies, houses, woods (col), plantations, waste, fence ownership, field gates, mill pond, mill, fish pond, manor house, manor boundary; 'Lands exchanged for Tithes' are banded yellow, glebe is banded blue, tithe-free land is banded pink; below the title is a table of tithe-free land, and also a note, 'Cadnam and Canterton, being very much intermixed with Bramshaw, was taken up with the Lines of that Parish, both parishes being Surveyed by the same person.'

31/178 Mitcheldever with East and West Stratton and Weston (parish with hamlet or chapelry) SU 523402 [Micheldever]
Apt 12.10.1848; 9702a (9340), (tithable parts only); Map 1848?, 6 chns; railway with station, waterbodies, houses, woods (col), plantations, building names, ford.

31/179 Mitchelmersh (parish) SU 346266 [Michelmersh]
Apt 14.04.1840; 3984a (3983); Map 1840, 8 chns, in 3 parts; foot/b'way, canal with towpath, woods (col), arable (col), grassland (col), orchard, building names, rectory, mill; land use tint is omitted in tithe-free areas; position of the detached portions are described by lengthy notes; map is signed by the landowners to show approval.

31/180 Monk Sherbourne with Ewhurst, Woodgarston and Chineham (parish with tithings) SU 605560 [Monk Sherborne]
Apt 17.09.1839; 3343a (3342); Map 1839, 6 chns, in 6 parts; foot/b'way, carriage road, waterbodies, houses, woods, hedge ownership, fence ownership, field gates, pits or quarries, ring earthwork, churchyard; scale bar is combined with north pointer; there are long notes on the relationship of the detached parts to the main part of the tithe district.

31/181 Monxton (parish) SU 309433
Apt 29.01.1840; 1141a (all); Map 1839, 6 chns, by Phillips and Westbury, Andover; foot/b'way, houses, farmyards (col), woods (col), plantations (col), arable (col), grassland (col), gardens (col), boundary stone.

31/182 Morestead (parish) SU 519262
Apt 10.06.1842; 1520a (1519); Map 1844, 3 chns, 1st cl; waterbodies, Roman road, warren.

31/183 Mottisfont (parish) SU 320272
Apt 16.09.1839; 2740a (2739); Map 1840?, 3 chns; foot/b'way, canal with towpath, waterbodies, houses, fences, field gates, road on causeway, ford, footbridge, boundary stones (by symbol).

31/184 Mottistone (parish) SZ 409836
Apt 12.11.1839; 1107a (1107); Map 1838, 4.5 chns, 'corrected' by W. Mortimer and Son; hill-drawing, foot/b'way, waterbodies, woods, rock outcrops, seashore, quarries, road cuttings, land tithable to Brixton, cliffs, quarries; some names are stamped; scale bar is styled like a ruler.

31/185 Nately Scures (parish) SU 706532
Apt 31.10.1839; 1005a (1004); Map 1842, 6 chns, 'copied' by G.E. Hewett; railway, canal, waterbodies, woods.

31/186 Up Nately (parish) SU 702517
Apt 28.08.1841; 1013a (1013); Map 1841, 3 chns, by Richard and Charles Pink, Hambledon, Hants; hill-drawing, canal with towpath and tunnel entrance, foot/b'way, waterbodies, houses, woods (col), plantations, hedge ownership.

31/187 Newchurch (parish) SZ 565851
Apt 30.06.1843; 8361a (9200), (tithable parts only); Map 1840, 3 chns, by T. Hellyer, Ryde; construction lines, hill-drawing, waterbodies, houses, woods, withy beds; north pointer has plumes.

31/188 Newnham (parish) SU 709539
Apt 05.06.1840; 1009a (1009); Map 1841, 6 chns; railway, waterbodies, woods, field boundary ownerships.

31/189 Newton Valence (parish) SU 712336
Apt 09.02.1843; 2254a (all); Map 1840, 3 chns, by Manwaring Chitty, Farnham, Surrey; waterbodies, houses, woods (col), parkland, grassland (by symbol), hops, building names, rectory, village pond, pit or quarry, milestone, boundary stones, commons; hill named.

31/190 Newtown (parish) SU 475633
Apt 11.01.1838; 476a (?); Map 1839, 3 chns, surveyed for T.E. Washbourne, Newbury by William Baillie, C.E.; foot/b'way, waterbodies, houses, woods (col), gardens (col), hedge ownership (col); colours may show property ownerships.

31/191 Niton (parish) SZ 505766
Apt 23.01.1839; 1338a (all); Map 1840, 4 chns, 'Corrected' by W. Mortimer and Son, Newport, Isle of Wight; hill-drawing, foot/b'way, waterbodies, houses, woods, parkland, open fields, hedge ownership, sea cliffs, quarries, down.

31/192 Northington (parish) SU 553372
Apt 12.07.1849; 3062a (?); Map 1849?, 8 chns; houses, woods (col), parkland (col), grassland (col).

31/193 Northwood (parish) SZ 484939
Apt 29.10.1845; 4647a (all); Map 1844, 6 chns; waterbodies, houses, woods (col), parkland, brick works.

31/194 Nursling (parish) SU 375160
Apt 22.01.1846; 2124a (all); Map 1846, 4 chns; foot/b'way, canal, waterbodies, houses, woods (col), plantations, avenue of trees, water meadow channels (in detail).

31/195 Nutley (parish) SU 609444
Apt 31.01.1839; 1502a (all); Map 1838, 6 chns, by Phillips and Westbury, Andover; foot/b'way, houses, farmyards, woods (col), arable (col), grassland (col), gardens.

31/196 Odiham (parish) SU 741510
Apt 19.11.1840; 7287a (all); Map 1842?, 3 chns, by Geo. Hewett Jr, Hartfordbridge; railway, foot/b'way, canal with towpath, waterbodies, woods, plantations, building names, farm names (in gothic), vicarage, rectory, mill, fulling mill, commons, green, osiers.

31/197 Otterbourne (parish) SU 461225
Apt 02.06.1840; 1508a (1508); Map 1839, 6 chns, 'Compiled from various Maps' by R.C. Gale, Winchester; railway, canal with towpath and lock, waterbodies, houses, woods (col), building names, road names, milestone (with distances), pound, common, boundary of tithe-free lands.

31/198 Overton (parish) SU 514500
Apt 30.12.1843; 6573a (all); Map 1845, 4 chns, in 2 parts, (including open fields at 3 chns); railway, woods (col), plantations, open fields; built-up part generalised.

31/199 Ovington (parish) SU 554295
Apt 02.04.1846; 120a (1270); Map 1848?, 6 chns, (tithable parts only); turnpike roads, warren.

31/200 Owlesbury (parish) SU 515224 [Owslebury]
Apt 08.04.1841; 5332a (all); Map 1840, 6 chns, 'Corrected and Copied from another Map' by R.C. Gale, Winchester; houses, woods (col), heath/moor.

31/201 Pamber (parish) SU 617597 [Pamber Green]
Apt 16.06.1838; 2151a (all); Map 1838, 6 chns, by Phillips and Westbury, Andover; waterbodies, houses, farmyards (col), woods (col), plantations (col), arable (col), grassland (col), heath/moor.

31/202 Penton Mewsey (parish) SU 336476
Apt 02.08.1837; 1045a (all); Map 1837, 3 chns, by Phillips and Westbury, Andover; foot/b'way, waterbodies, houses, farmyards (col), woods (col), plantations (col), parkland (col), arable (col), grassland (col), gardens (col), hedge ownership, fence ownership, field gates, stiles (by symbol).

31/203 Petersfield (parish) SU 747234
Apt 31.08.1841; 234a (234); Map 1840, 2 chns, by George Doswell, 35 Bernard St, Southampton; waterbodies, houses (light grey), woods, heath/moor, hedge ownership, fence ownership, building names, road names, glebe, boundary stone, brewery, workhouse, school; tithe-free areas tinted green; pond named.

31/204 Popham (hamlet or chapelry) SU 557440
Apt 06.05.1846; 1387a (1387); Map 1847, 8 chns; waterbodies, houses, woods.

31/205 Portchester (parish) SU 616057
Apt 09.05.1840; 1374a (2949); Map 1839, 6 chns, by J.W. Blackman, Fareham; waterbodies, houses, woods, heath/moor, powder magazine, castle, chalk pit.

31/206 Portsea (parish) SU 652005
Apt 03.04.1839; 4924a (6891); Map 1838, 3 chns, by Thos E. Owen, Portsmouth; canal with towpath and locks, waterbodies, houses, open fields, fortifications, castle, high and low water marks; built-up part generalised; there are two scale-bars, one for chains and one for feet. (The map in PRO IR 30 is a copy; original is in PRO IR 77/97, and is unfit for production.)

31/207 Preston Candover (parish) SU 612420
Apt 22.03.1839; 3414a (3413); Map 1838, 6 chns, by Phillips and Westbury, Andover; foot/b'way, waterbodies, houses, woods, plantations; pink tint indicates farm exempt from great tithes.

31/208 Privett (parish) SU 674275
Apt 03.07.1845; 1270a (all); Map 1846, 6 chns, by R. and C. Pink, Hambledon; foot/b'way, waterbodies, houses, woods, plantations; pictorial church.

31/209 Quarley (parish) SU 258424
Apt 30.04.1840; 1683a (all); Map 1840, 6 chns; waterbodies, woods.

31/210 Ringwood (parish) SU 158041
Apt 20.03.1844; 10895a (all); Map 1845, 3 chns, 1st cl, in 2 parts: part 1 by Charles Sharp, Ringwood; part 2 by Harry Holloway, Ringwood; construction lines, railway with crossing house, foot/b'way, waterbodies, houses, woods, hedge ownership, fence ownership, field gates, building names, road names, viaducts, toll gate, chapel, mile stone, gravel pit, boundary trees, stones and posts, fish hatches, tithery boundaries.

31/211 Rockbourne (parish) SU 112189
Apt 26.08.1839; 3799a (3798); Map 1840?, 9 chns; foot/b'way, waterbodies, houses, tithing boundary.

31/212 Romsey (parish) SU 359201
Apt 20.03.1844; 7652a (7652); Map 1845, 6 chns, by Charles Sharp, Ringwood, (Romsey Extra 'Copied from the Parish Plans', and Romsey Infra added by Sharp; tithable parts only in detail); railway, foot/b'way, canal with towpath, waterbodies, houses, woods (named), plantations, open fields, building names, road names, mill, milestone (with distances), churchyard, pig market, rookery, division between Extra and Infra.

31/213 Ropley (parish) SU 650323
Apt 25.03.1845; 4596a (all); Map 1839, 6 chns, by Henry Hyde, Wareham, Dorset; foot/b'way, waterbodies, houses, building names, downs.

31/214 Rotherwick (parish) SU 718562
Apt 26.07.1842; 1924a (1924); Map 1841, 8 chns, in 2 parts, by J.W. Blackman, Fareham, (including unenclosed lands at 3 chns); waterbodies, houses, woods, building names, road names, greens, common, moor; part 2 has construction lines.

31/215 Rowner (parish) SU 585015
Apt 14.02.1839; 1192a (all); Map 1840, 6 chns; railway, foot/b'way, waterbodies, houses, woods.

31/216 Selborne (parish) SU 768342
Apt 22.08.1842; 8507a (8506); Map 1842?, 6 chns; waterbodies, woods, plantations, hops, open fields, building names, vicarage, mill.

31/217 Shalden (parish) SU 699420
Apt 27.05.1840; 1510a (all); Map 1841, 6 chns, 'Compiled from various Maps' by R.C. Gale, Winchester; waterbodies, houses (black), woods (col); roads straddling the parish boundary are only coloured for those parts falling within the parish.

31/218 Shalfleet (parish) SZ 397889
Apt 04.07.1844; 6224a (6623); Map surveyed in 1839-40, 6 chns, in 3 parts, by Richard Dent, (includes index), litho (by C.F. Cheffins, Southampton Buildings, Holborn); hill-drawing, waterbodies, woods, building names, cliffs, saltings, brick ground, pits, cow houses, walled garden, salt works, foreshore mud (col); some hand-colour has been added.

31/219 Shanklin (parish) SZ 578804
Apt 22.08.1842; 183a (802); Map 1842, 3 chns, by Lewis and Walker, Southampton, (tithable parts only); hill-drawing, foot/b'way, waterbodies, houses, woods, hedge ownership, cliffs.

31/220 Sheet (tithing in parish of Petersfield) SU 765239
Apt 31.08.1841; 1549a (all); Map 1840, 3 chns, by George Doswell, Southampton; waterbodies, houses, woods (by Dawson's symbol), osiers, plantations, heath/moor (by Dawson's symbol), hedge ownership, ford, common; pond named.

31/221 Sherborne St John (parish) SU 630560
Apt 27.02.1840; 3855a (3885); Map 1840, 6 chns, 'Copied' by Phillips and Westbury, Andover; hill-drawing, waterbodies, houses, woods (named), osiers, plantations, parkland, building names, brick kiln, pits, chalk pits, nursery mills, lodge, park gates, pound; the name 'C. Sharp' appears in the bottom margin.

31/222 Sherfield English (parish) SU 293232
Apt 09.03.1840; 1772a (all); Map 1840, 4 chns; foot/b'way, waterbodies.

31/223 Sherfield upon Loddon (parish) SU 678569 [Sherfield on Loddon]
Apt 24.02.1841; 2236a (2236); Map 1841, 6 chns, waterbodies, houses, woods, plantations, green (col), common (col).

31/224 Shipton, or Shipton Bellinger (parish) SU 240454
Apt 18.03.1841; 2515a (2515); Map 1840, 6 chns, ? by R.C. Gale, Winchester; waterbodies, houses (black), woods (col), plantations.

31/225 Shorwell (parish) SZ 457822
Apt 12.10.1844; 3645a (all); Map 1845?, 3 chns; construction lines,

waterbodies, houses, high and low water marks; one part of the map carries the note, 'This work was surveyed through mistake being in Kingston parish.'

31/226 Sidmonton (parish) SU 488586
Apt 30.04.1846; 2119a (all); Map 1847?, 3 chns, by Aylwin and May, Marlborough and Newbury. District is apportioned by holding and only holding boundaries are shown.

31/227 Silchester (parish) SU 637616
Apt 15.02.1839; 1881a (1881); Map 1841, 6 chns; waterbodies, houses, woods, ford.

31/228 Soberton (parish) SU 617145
Apt 19.09.1840; 5815a (5814); Map 1839, 3 chns, 1st cl, in 2 parts, by Manwaring Chitty, Farnham; construction lines, waterbodies, houses, woods, heath/moor, building names, Catholic Chapel, old telegraph, mills, mill pond, pit or quarry, brick works, heath; boundary alterations are signed by C. Pink of Hambledon and by J.W. Blackman of Fareham.

31/229 Sopley (parish) SZ 161985
Apt 18.06.1839; 3406a (4400); Map 1838, 3 chns, 1st cl, by Richard Nightingale, Lyndhurst, Hants; construction lines, waterbodies, houses, woods (named), field gates, former open field names, fords, boundary marks, gates to commons, commons (col).

31/230 All Saints, Southampton (parish) SU 421124 [Not listed]
Apt 10.03.1853; 124a (?); Map 1853, 1.33 chns, by George Doswell, Southampton, (tithable parts only in detail); hill-drawing, railway with station and 'Tunnell' mouth, waterbodies, houses, woods, plantations, parkland, building names, road names, Ordnance Map Office, chapels, assembly rooms, city gate, gravel pit, weigh bridge; Anglican church names are written in gothic; the actual scale is 1:1056 and the map is evidently a copy of the OS plan of the town on that scale of 1845-6.

31/231 St Marys Extra, Southampton (parish) SU 429124 [Not listed]
Apt 30.05.1851; 2381a (all); Map 1852?, 3 chns, (tithable parts only in detail); waterbodies, houses, woods, plantations, building names, road names, floating bridge, tidal dock, railway station, green, folly temple, toll house, gravel pit, Methodist Chapel; built-up part generalised.

31/232 Southwarnborough (parish) SU 724464 [South Warnborough]
Apt 08.06.1839; 2569a (all); Map 1839, 6 chns, by R.C. Gale, Winchester; waterbodies, houses, woods (col), plantations (col), avenue of trees. Apt has cropping information.

31/233 Southwick (parish) SU 637091
Apt 27.07.1840; 598a (4100); Map 1839, 6 chns, in 2 parts, by J.W. Blackman, Fareham; waterbodies, houses, woods, parkland, heath/moor, building names, road names, chalk pit, ford, commons.

31/234 Sparsholt (parish) SU 431309
Apt 16.12.1843; 3542a (3542); Map 1841, 3 chns, 1st cl, by R.C. Gale, Winchester; construction lines, waterbodies, houses, woods (col), hedge ownership, fences, Roman road, avenues of trees; map includes Lainston, which is treated as a separate tithe district, (see 31/155).

31/235 Steep (parish) SU 746258
Apt 08.07.1841; 2641a (2641); Map 'Principally corrected from an original Survey', 1839, 3 chns; turnpike roads (col), houses, woods (col), plantations (col), hops (col), heath/moor, building names, road names, mill, tan yard, malm pit, commons; hills named.

31/236 Steventon (parish) SU 542469
Apt 13.04.1839; 2101a (2100); Map 1840, 6 chns; railway, foot/b'way, waterbodies, houses, woods (col), plantations (col); north pointer and scale bar are combined.

31/237 Stockbridge (chapelry or parish) SU 366352
Apt 11.12.1841; 1115a (1115); Map 1842, 3 chns; canal with towpath and locks, houses, woods (col), plantations (col), pit, water meadow channels (in detail).

31/238 Stoke Charity (parish) SU 485376
Apt 22.07.1837; 1851a (all); Map 1838, 4 chns; construction lines, railway, waterbodies, houses, woods, hedge ownership, fence ownership; farmland appears to be edged pink and other land green.

31/239 North Stoneham (parish) SU 433179
Apt 24.12.1842; 5011a (5010); Map 1841, 3 chns, 1st cl, in 2 parts, by H.C. Wright, 40 Tavistock St, Covent Garden; construction lines, railway, canal with towpath, waterbodies, houses, woods, plantations, heath/moor, building names, parsonage, turnpike, brick kiln, ford, nursery, garden, grubbed-up field boundaries.

31/240 South Stoneham (parish) SU 470148
Apt 13.03.1844; 8877a (8877); Map 1845?, 6 chns; railway, foot/b'way, canal with towpath, waterbodies, houses, woods (col), plantations (col), building names, workhouse.

31/241 Stratfield Saye and Beech Hill (parish and tithing) (Beech Hill in Berks) SU 686620
Apt 26.02.1839; 3532a (3532); Map 1839, 8 chns; waterbodies, woods, ford, greens.

31/242 Stratfield Turgis (parish) SU 696600
Apt 30.04.1839; 1000a (909); Map 1840?, 6 chns; waterbodies, woods.

31/243 Long Sutton (parish) SU 750468
Apt 31.10.1840; 2267a (all); Map 1841, 3 chns, 1st cl, by George Hewett, Jr, Elvetham, Hartford Bridge; construction lines, waterbodies, woods, heath/moor, hedge ownership, field gates, building names, farm names (in gothic).

31/244 Swarraton (parish) SU 577369
Apt 24.05.1839; 743a (all); Map 1842, 8 chns; houses, woods (col), parkland (col), grassland (col).

31/245 Tadley (parish or township) SU 597608
Apt 23.10.1838; 2047a (all); Map 1840, 6 chns; houses, woods; map has a long note on the position of detached portions.

31/246 Tangley (parish) SU 336530
Apt 02.08.1837; 1561a (all); Map 1837, 3 chns, by Phillips and Westbury, Andover; waterbodies, houses, farmyards (col), woods (col), plantations (col), arable (col), grassland (col), gardens (col).

31/247 South Tedworth (parish) SU 236477 [South Tidworth]
Apt 22.01.1841; 2176a (all); Map 'Surveyed 1840', 4 chns, ? by Thomas Barnes Northeast; field boundary ownerships, field names, woods (col), farm names, glebe (col); no buildings are shown.

31/248 Thorley (parish) SZ 373879
Apt 13.04.1844; 1574a (all); Map 1844?, 6 chns, by Richard Dent, litho (by C.F. Cheffins, 9 Southampton Buildings, Holborn); foot/b'way, waterbodies, woods, heath/moor, building names, toll gate, mill pond, mill, dog kennel, pit.

31/249 Thruxton (parish) SU 267450
Apt 26.02.1839; 1865a (all); Map 1839, 3 chns, in 3 parts, by Phillips and Westbury, Andover, (includes 24-chn index); foot/b'way, waterbodies, houses, woods, plantations, hedge ownership, fence ownership, field gates, building names, wells, 'The Pavement', landmark bushes.

31/250 Tichborne (parish) SU 564287
Apt 05.03.1839; 3300a (all); Map 1844, 6 chns, in 2 parts, by W.T. Heard, St Margarets; waterbodies, woods, parkland, building names, mill; pond named.

31/251 Timsbury (parish) SU 352249
Apt 10.06.1842; 1384a (1411); Map 1843?, 8 chns; canal with lock, woods, orchard, building names, landowners; map carries signatures of approval by the landowners.

31/252 East Tisted (parish) SU 700322
Apt 18.06.1840; 2602a (all); Map 1841, 4.5 chns; foot/b'way, waterbodies, houses, woods, parkland, hedge ownership, pits, avenue of trees; names are stamped; border is a neatly drawn repetition of a pattern of shaded curls and leaves, which appears to have been added by stamping or transfer.

31/253 West Tisted (parish) SU 660293
Apt 07.06.1844; 2268a (all); Map 1845?, 6 chns; woods (named), building names, chalk allotment, semaphore, glebe.

31/254 Titchfield (parish) SU 520060
Apt 18.08.1837; 15408a (17512); Map surveyed 1837-8, 6 chns, in 2 parts, by J.W. Blackman, Fareham, (includes village separately at 3 chns); hill-drawing, foot/b'way, houses, woods (named), parkland, hedge ownership, building names, road names, pest house, lodge, well, sand pit, iron mill, brick works, gravel pits, landmark trees, pound, common gate, windmill (pictorial), flood hatches, high and low water marks, quays, salterns, chapel, tithe-free land, manor boundaries (red), district boundaries (yellow), common (col).

31/255 Tufton (parish) SU 468454
Apt 01.04.1844; 1552a (all); Map 1844?, 6 chns; waterbodies, houses, woods.

31/256 Tunworth (parish) SU 675488
Apt 27.03.1838; 1104a (all); Map 1839?, 6 chns; houses, woods (col), grassland (col).

31/257 Twyford (parish) SU 490244
Apt 26.01.1841; 4220a (all); Map 1840, 6 chns, 'Compiled from various Maps' by R.C. Gale, Winchester; railway, canal with locks and towpath, houses, woods (col), pits (col), brick works.

31/258 East Titherley (parish) SU 299288 [East Tytherley]
Apt 19.09.1851; 61a (1560); Map 1852, 6 chns, by John Waters, Salisbury, (tithable parts only); houses, woods (col), building names, mill.

31/259 West Tytherley (parish) SU 275304
Apt 26.12.1837; 2270a (2270); Map 1839?, 8 chns; foot/b'way.

31/260 Upham (parish) SU 540210
Apt 03.12.1839; 2852a (2852); Map 1838, 3 chns, by R. and C. Pink, Hambledon; construction lines, foot/b'way, waterbodies, houses, woods, plantations, hedge ownership, fence ownership, pits, boundary trees and marks, foot bridge, stiles (by symbol); 'Chalk heaps and a furrow' is written along one boundary.

31/261 Upton Gray (parish) SU 702480
Apt 08.06.1839; 2235a (all); Map 1839, 6 chns; foot/b'way, waterbodies, houses, woods; legend explains symbols; meaning of red band is unclear.

31/262 Nether Wallop (parish) SU 291363
Apt 18.01.1840; 7202a (7201); Map 1840, 6 chns, by Phillips and Westbury, Andover; foot/b'way, waterbodies, houses, woods (named), plantations, building names, racing stables.

31/263 Over Wallop (parish) SU 272393
Apt 30.04.1840; 4632a (all); Map 1840, 6 chns, 'Corrected and Copied from another Map' by R.C. Gale, Winchester; houses (black), woods (col).

31/264 North Waltham (parish) SU 563465
Apt 30.04.1839; 1939a (all); Map 1839, 3 chns; construction lines, foot/b'way, waterbodies, houses, fences, field gates, commons (col), waste (col); uninhabited buildings are shown without infill.

31/265 Warblington (parish) SU 744071
Apt 10.04.1838; 3198a (3848); Map 1841?, 3 chns, by Charles Lewis, Havant; waterbodies, houses, woods, parkland, building names, mill ponds, spring, common, nurseries, county boundary with posts and trees; creeks and large ponds named.

31/266 Warnford (parish) SU 616236
Apt 28.02.1839; 3057a (3057); Map 1839, 5 chns, by J.W. Blackman, Fareham; waterbodies, houses, woods, parkland, heath/moor, building names, parsonage.

31/267 Week (parish) SU 466302
Apt 09.01.1844; 1081a (1080); Map 1840, 3 chns, by Charles Fielder, Sparsholt, Winchester; construction lines, railway, waterbodies, houses, woods (col), hedge ownership, workhouse, borough boundary.

31/268 East Wellow (parish) SU 314204
Apt 20.07.1837; 2374a (2373); Map 1839?, 6 chns, in 3 parts, (includes 18-chn index); waterbodies, woods, plantations, parkland.

31/269 Westmeon (parish) SU 646246 [West Meon]
Apt 14.08.1839; 3729a (all); Map 1839, 3 chns, 1st cl, by R. and C. Pink, Hambledon; construction lines, foot/b'way, waterbodies, houses, woods, hedge ownership, fence ownership, pit, glebe (red band).

31/270 Weston Patrick (parish) SU 695455
Apt 26.07.1842; 1402a (1402); Map 1844, 6 chns, by Phillips and Westbury, Andover; houses, woods, pound.

31/271 Weyhill (parish) SU 320480
Apt 25.03.1840; 1888a (all); Map 1842, 3 chns, in 2 parts; turnpike roads, waterbodies, woods, plantations, parkland, hedge ownership, fence ownership, field gates, road names, avenue of trees, fair ground (in detail).

31/272 Wherwell (parish) SU 377405
Apt 14.09.1841; 3547a (3546); Map 1842?, 6 chns; foot/b'way, canal, houses, woods, plantations, osier and willow beds (by symbol).

31/273 Whippingham (parish) SZ 523927
Apt 13.02.1844; 4629a (5208); Map 1845, 8 chns, in 4 parts, (includes three 2-chn enlargements of built-up parts), litho; foot/b'way, waterbodies, woods, building names, road names, pits or quarries, quay; scale has been corrected by hand from 6 to 8 chns.

31/274 Whitchurch (parish) SU 468495
Apt 09.01.1840; 6143a (all); Map 1840, 6 chns; foot/b'way, woods, glebe.

31/275 Whitsbury (parish) (partly in Wilts) SU 123206
Apt 25.11.1841; 1781a (all); Map 1842, 8 chns; waterbodies, houses, woods, building names, drove (named).

31/276 Whitwell (parish) SZ 520782
Apt 23.01.1844; 1880a (all); Map '1838-39', 4 chns, by E. Smith and Son; waterbodies, woods, parkland, rock outcrops, open fields, hedge ownership, boundary stones (by symbol), pits.

31/277 Wickham (parish) SU 571117
Apt 30.09.1839; 2434a (all); Map 1840, 6 chns, in 2 parts, by J.W. Blackman, Fareham, (includes village separately at 3 chns); turnpike roads and gate, waterbodies, houses, woods, parkland, building names, tan yard, boundary trees, lodge, churchyard, heath, named gates, glebe land (pink band).

31/278 Widley (parish) SU 659072
Apt 30.04.1840; 1091a (all); Map 1840, 4 chns, in 2 parts, by Henry Howard, Winchester; foot/b'way, houses, woods (col), ford.

31/279 Wield (parish) SU 632395
Apt 21.02.1845; 2087a (2087); Map 1839, 6 chns, by Phillips and Westbury, Andover; foot/b'way, waterbodies, houses, woods (col, named), arable (col), grassland (col), gardens (col), chalk pit, pit, meres (named).

31/280 St Bartholemew Hyde, Winchester (parish) SU 482310 [Not listed]
Apt 13.08.1850; 24a (?); Map 1850?, 2 chns; landowners, bound-ary stone, mill stream, droveway.

31/281 St Faith, Winchester (parish) SU 466281 [Not listed]
Apt 25.03.1845; 1169a (?); Map 1846, 6 chns; railway, woods.

31/282 Milland and Seagrims Hill Meadow (vill and close in parish of St Peter Cheesehill) SU 484283 [Not listed]
Apt 31.12.1851; 58a (?); Map 1852, 6 chns; canal, wharves, road names, mill, toll gate.

31/283 Winchfield (parish) SU 768541
Apt 21.09.1842; 1544a (1543); Map 1842, 3 chns, by G. and E. Hewett, Elvetham, Hants; canal with towpath, railway with station, waterbodies, woods.

31/284 Winnall (parish) SU 496300
Apt 09.03.1838; 532a (all); Map 1838, 3 chns; turnpike roads, waterbodies, houses, woods, hedge ownership, turnpike gate, municipal boundary.

31/285 Winslade and Kempshott (parish) SU 661487
Apt 31.01.1839; 1776a (1235); Map 1839, 6 chns, in 2 parts; houses, woods, plantations, parkland.

31/286 Wonston (parish) SU 469394
Apt 26.04.1838; 5470a (?); Map 1838, 3 chns, 1st cl, by Turner P. Clarke, Andover; construction lines, waterbodies, houses, woods (col), plantations (col), hedge ownership.

31/287 East Woodhay (parish) SU 421613
Apt 09.08.1837; 4966a (4966); Map 1837, 3 chns; waterbodies, houses (by shading), woods, plantations, ford, tithe-free land (pink).

31/288 Woodmancott (parish) SU 576423
Apt 14.09.1839; 1396a (all); Map 1838, 6 chns, by R.C. Gale, Winchester; waterbodies, houses, woods (col).

31/289 Woolveston (parish) SU 552576 [Wolverton]
Apt 24.02.1839; 1396a (?); Map 1840, 8 chns; waterbodies, houses, woods, old pit.

31/290 Wootton (parish) SZ 543926 [Wootton Bridge]
Apt 20.04.1844; 463a (1360); Map 1846?, 2 chns, in 5 parts, by C. Smith and Son; waterbodies, houses, woods, hedge ownership, fence ownership, walls.

31/291 Wootton St Lawrence (parish) SU 586522
Apt 13.02.1846; 3957a (3957); Map 1845, 6 chns; railway, waterbodies, houses (black), woods, orchard, building names, chalk pit.

31/292 East Worldham (parish) SU 751380
Apt 01.06.1841; 1687a (1687); Map 1842?, 8 chns; foot/b'way, woods, plantations, orchard, hops, open fields, building names, vicarage, college land.

31/293 West Worldham (parish) SU 737372
Apt 16.04.1841; 450a (all); Map 1842, 8 chns; foot/b'way, woods; map carries Lord Sherborne's signature of approval.

31/294 Worting (parish) SU 600514
Apt 23.01.1838; 1134a (1139); Map 1838, 6 chns; railway with earthworks, waterbodies, houses, farmyards (col), woods (col), parkland (col), arable (col), grassland (col), gardens (col), hedge ownership, fence ownership, landowners, glebe, field gates; land use is shown by Dawson's symbols, although a few fields are left uncoloured; table lists owners and cultivation.

31/295 Wymering (parish) SU 653055
Apt 11.04.1839; 3546a (3907); Map 1838, 2 chns, in 2 parts, by Charles Lewis, Havant; turnpike roads, toll bars, waterbodies, houses, woods (named), building names, boundary stones (by symbol), defensive ditch; pasture apparently covered at high tide is treated as water and coloured blue, with a pecked outer boundary.

31/296 Yarmouth (parish) SZ 356896
Apt 16.12.1843; 94a (all); Map 1840, 3 chns, by Richard Dent; waterbodies, houses, farmyards (col), woods, parkland, grassland (col), gardens (col), fences, pound, common (col), high and low water marks, foreshore (col). Apt omits most land use.

31/297 Yately (parish) SU 840572 [Yateley]
Apt 13.03.1844; 10036a (10036); Map 1845?, 6 chns, by G. and E. Hewett, Elvetham, Hants, and High St, Oxford; railway, canal with towpath, waterbodies, woods, open fields, ford, tithing boundaries.

31/298 Yaverland (parish) SZ 614858
Apt 29.09.1838; 875a (all); Map 1839, 3 chns, by W. Mortimer and Son, Newport, Isle of Wight; construction lines, foot/b'way, waterbodies, houses, woods, orchard, rock outcrops, pits or quarries, high and low water marks, fort, sea cliffs.

Staffordshire

PRO IR29 and IR30 32/1-244

332 tithe districts: 753,327 acres
244 tithe commutations: 533,020 acres
128 voluntary tithe agreements, 116 compulsory tithe awards

Tithe and tithe commutation

In common with Worcestershire to the south-west and Derbyshire to the east, Staffordshire has tithe characteristics of both midland and upland counties. By 1836 a considerable proportion of the county's tithes had already been commuted and only thirty districts were wholly subject to tithe (Fig. 44). The main cause of tithe exemption was the existence of moduses in lieu of tithes which were paid in 66 per cent of tithable districts. Commutation at the time of enclosure, the merger of tithes in the land, exemption of some woodland, and exemption by prescription were also significant in this county.

Assistant tithe commissioners and local tithe agents who worked in Staffordshire are listed in Table 32.1 and the valuers of Staffordshire tithe rent-charge in Table 32.3. No single tithe valuer dominated in Staffordshire but the most prolific was Joseph Bennett Hankin Bennett of Tutbury, a land agent of long and wide experience who wrote a pamphlet on tithe apportionment in 1839. A notable feature of Staffordshire tithe apportionments is that nineteen (about 8 per cent) have field-by-field cropping information; most of these are of districts valued by Joseph B. H. Bennett.

Tithe maps

Staffordshire tithe surveys are similar to those of adjoining counties in that fewer than 3 per cent of the 244 tithe maps are sealed as first class. Though first-class maps are attested as 'accurate' by the Tithe Commission, it is interesting that the first-class map of Colwich has pencil annotations made in the 1950s relating to defects revealed by comparison with later Ordnance Survey maps.

As in many counties with a substantial proportion of tithe-free land, there were two peaks of map production in Staffordshire, a first in 1839 and a second but less marked high point in 1848-50 (Table 32.4).

Staffordshire tithe maps are drawn at a variety of scales from one inch to one chain to one inch to twelve chains; 23 per cent are in the recommended scale range of one inch to three to four chains, half are at the six-chain scale, and there are significant numbers at the

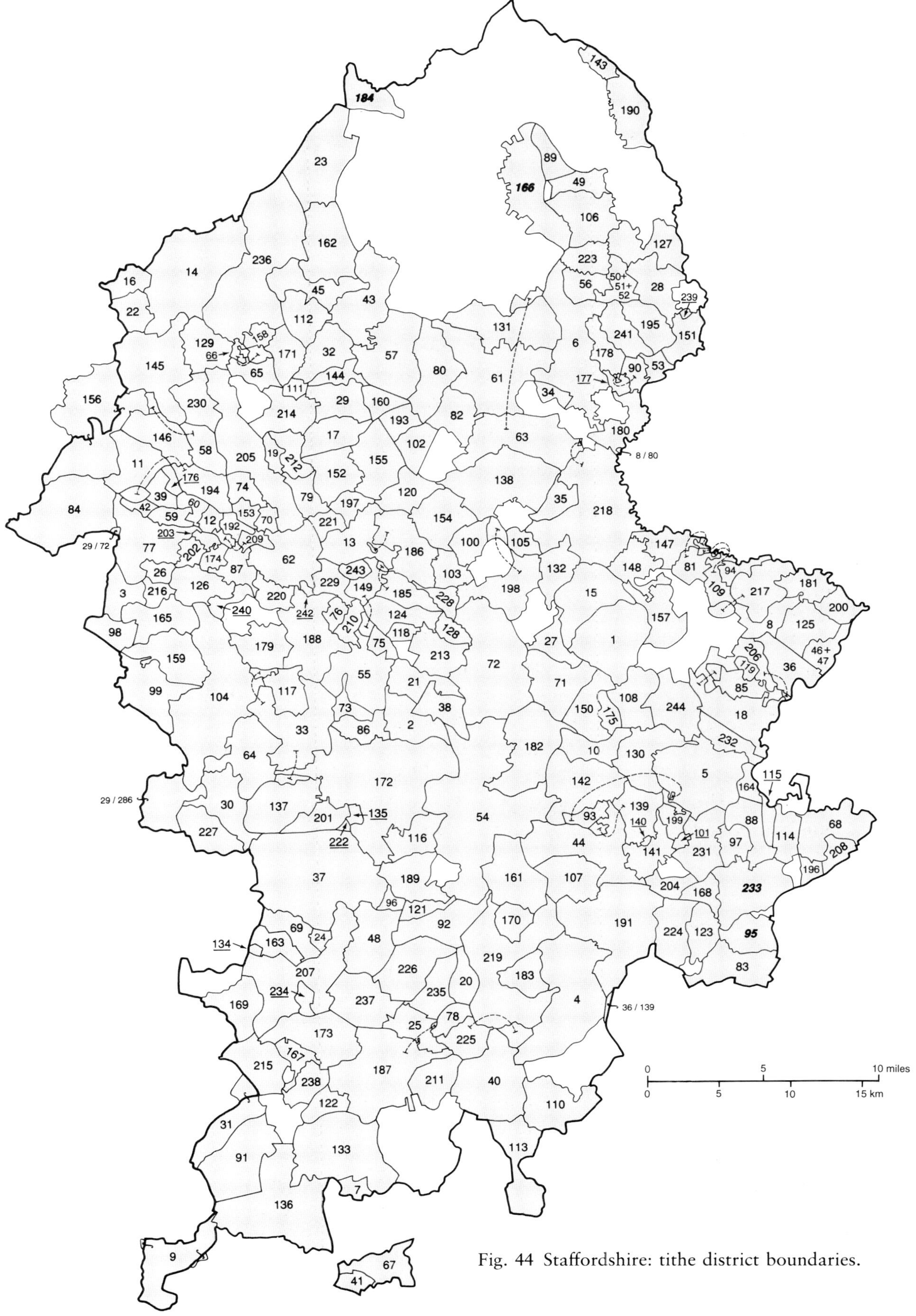

Fig. 44 Staffordshire: tithe district boundaries.

eight- and twelve-chain scales (Table 32.3). Ten second-class maps are lithographed, mainly by Birmingham firms.

Staffordshire maps contain a fairly complete record of woodland (on 87 per cent of maps) and parkland (on 28 per cent) but that of other land uses is less good. Only two maps distinguish arable and grass, 8 per cent show gardens and 7 per cent depict orchards. Industry is recorded on 11 per cent of maps, though the degree of detail varies. In the Black Country it is very comprehensive but on other maps, especially those of districts in the Potteries, there is an unconvincing lack of industrial features. Railways are usually shown by their boundary fences only but waggonways are often depicted in more detail. Many built-up areas are not mapped comprehensively but an exception is the centre of Lichfield. An unusual feature of the Statfold tithe map is the presence of a former right of way stopped up by order of the magistrates. Even more unusually, two maps refer to geology: Bobbington has a 'geological description' and Orton has a peremptory note, 'Geological Character - New Red Sandstone'. The map of Waterfall has elaborate rock-drawing in quarries.

Only 131 Staffordshire tithe maps in the Public Record Office collection, some 53 per cent of the total, can be attributed to a particular map-maker (Table 32.2). The most prolific was J. B .H. Bennett of Tutbury who produced twenty-one maps, few of them signed but all in a very characteristic style with neat copperplate writing and black ruled water. On his map of Tutbury his own house is the only one to be shown with a bay window, though it is unclear whether this is an architectural or a personal statement! Samuel Knutton of Newcastle-under-Lyme produced fourteen maps, mostly of fairly small tithe districts in the Potteries, so that his output by area is only a third that of Bennett. J. P. Lofthouse of Hopton made thirteen maps, mostly in the west of the county and generally unremarkable. Charles Ash of Eccleshall produced nine maps characterised by the use of various shades of grey for woodland, ponds and pits. Some of the neatest maps in the county are three anonymous depictions of Lichfield.

Though no Staffordshire map has an ornamental cartouche, a number of districts around Stafford have borders decorated with a half-ball and half-quatrefoil motif.

Table 32.1. *Agreements and awards for commutation of tithes in Staffordshire*

Assistant commissioner/ local tithe agent	*Number of agreements**	*Number of awards*
Charles Pym	2	32
George Wingrove Cooke	0	33
John Job Rawlinson	0	31
Richard Burton Phillipson	26	0
John Mee Mathew	16	5
George Ashdown	19	0
John Holder	17	0
Charles Howard	5	5
John Pickering	8	0
Henry Pilkington	8	0
Thomas Sudworth	7	0
Edward Greathed	6	0
Thomas Hoskins	5	0
James Drage Merest	4	0
Gelinger C. Symons	4	0
Thomas Smith Woolley	4	2
Joseph Townsend	0	3
Tithe Commissioners	0	3
Roger Kynaston	2	0
N. S. Meryweather	2	0
John Penny	2	0
George Louis	0	1
Horace William Meteyard	0	1

*Computed from the number of extant reports on tithe agreements in the tithe files [PRO IR 18].

Table 32.2. *Tithe valuers and tithe map-makers in Staffordshire*

Name and address (in Staffordshire unless indicated)	*Number of districts*	*Acreage*
Tithe valuers		
Joseph Bennett Hankin Bennett, Tutbury	22	34,031
William Fowler, Birmingham, Warwickshire	14	50,956
Samuel Ginders, Ingestre	13	20,986
Joshua Harding, Rosliston, Derbyshire	13	18,501
Robert Thompson, Walton, near Stone	12	42,642
Thomas Turner, Abbotts Bromley	12	38,771
Tithe Commissioners	12	9,888
James Wyley, High Onn	11	31,952
Joseph Naden, Chesterfield Grange, Shenstone	10	23,628
James Cooke, Longdon	10	20,111
Others [54]	115	241,554
Attributed tithe map-makers		
Joseph Bennett Hankin Bennett, Tutbury	21	24,595
Samuel Bate, Knutton, Newcastle-under-Lyme	14	8,070
J. P. Lofthouse, Hopton	13	25,006
C. B. Ash	9	10,044
George Adie, Rugeley	8	33,951
William Fowler and Son, Birmingham, Warwickshire	6	26,145
Others [38]	60	137,100

Table 32.3. *The tithe maps of Staffordshire: scales and classes*

Scale in chains/inch	*All maps*		*First Class*		*Second Class*	
	Number	*Acreage*	*Number*	*Acreage*	*Number*	*Acreage*
>3	2	211	0	0	2	211
3	42	80,696	7	21,019	35	59,677
4	14	23,233	0	0	14	23,233
5	3	3,361	0	0	3	3,361
6	123	275,448	0	0	123	275,448
8	16	42,103	0	0	16	42,103
9	36	82,110	0	0	36	82,110
10	1	7,728	0	0	1	7,728
12	7	18,130	0	0	7	18,130
TOTAL	244	533,020	7	21,019	237	512,001

Table 32.4. *The tithe maps of Staffordshire: dates*

	1837	*1838*	*1839*	*1840*	*1841*	*1842*	*1843*	*1844*	*1845*	*1846*	*1847*	*1848*	*1849*	*1850*	*>1850*
All maps	4	29	36	14	24	11	14	6	10	16	13	18	14	24	10
1st class	0	2	3	0	0	2	0	0	0	0	0	0	0	0	0
2nd class*	4	27	33	14	24	9	14	6	10	16	13	18	14	24	10

*One second-class tithe map of Staffordshire in the Public Record Office collection is undated.

Staffordshire

32/1 Abbots Bromley and Bromley Hurst (townships in parish of Abbots Bromley) SK 100240
Apt 17.10.1846; 5278a (?); Map 1847, 12 chns, in 2 parts, (tithable parts only; village at 3 chns); foot/b'way, waterbodies, woods.

32/2 Acton Trussel and Bednall (townships in parish of Berkswich) SJ 942178 [Acton Trussell]
Apt 11.12.1848; 2547a (2547); Map 1849, 6 chns; foot/b'way, canal with towpath, waterbodies, woods, reservoir, mill, churchyard (col).

32/3 Adbaston or Adbaston cum Knighton (township in parish of Adbaston) SJ 760278
Apt 29.07.1841; 1639a (1639); Map 1841, 6 chns; waterbodies, woods; pink tint appears to indicate modus lands; tithe-free lands are not given area numbers, but acreages for holdings are given.

32/4 Aldridge (parish) SP 064982
Apt 29.01.1841; 7728a (all); Map 1839-40, 10 chns; railway, canal and towpath, waterbodies, woods, parkland, building names, chapel, beacon hill, pit, canal towpath, rectory, township boundaries (col), pit or quarry.

32/5 Alrewas (parish) SK 159135
Apt 23.06.1840; 3053a (4329); Map 1842?, 9 chns, in 8 parts, (tithable and modus lands only; includes manuscript enlargements of detail), litho (R.B. Moody, 14 Common Street, Birmingham); canal with towpath, waterbodies, woods, building names, road names, field names, reservoir, cotton mill, mill dam, avenue of trees, osiers (by symbol).

32/6 Alton or Alveton (parish) SK 070440
Apt 13.02.1843; 7380a (7379); Map 1843?, 6 chns, in 6 parts, (including four parts at 9 chns and 18-chn index); foot/b'way, canal with towpath and locks, waterbodies, woods, plantations, parkland, orchards, building names, smelting mill, chapel.

32/7 Amblecoat (hamlet in parish of Oldswinford) SO 906861 [Amblecote]
Apt 07.05.1838; 640a (all); Map 1837, 3 chns, by John Davies, Stourbridge; foot/b'way, waterbodies, canal and towpath, woods, building names, avenue of trees, toll bar.

32/8 Anslow (township in parish of Rolleston) SK 210250
Apt 01.11.1844; 1023a (?); Map 1845, 6 chns, ? by J.B.H. Bennett, Tutbury; foot/b'way, turnpike roads, waterbodies, woods, building names, road names, field names, pit, forest gates; tithe-free land is shown by annotation. Apt includes some cropping information but also omits some land use.

32/9 Arley (parish) SO 770805 [Upper Arley]
Apt 17.04.1839; 3912a (3912); Map 1838, 3 chns; waterbodies, houses, parkland, arable (col), grassland (col), gardens, fence, building names, quarry, old quarry, coal pit, toll gate, pound; woods, coppices, commons and quarries are indicated by name; yellow colour bands indicate arable, green bands woods or pasture.

32/10 Armitage (parish) SK 083161
Apt 12.10.1841; 1922a (1921); Map 1842, 6 chns, in 17 parts, (including 16 3-chn enlargements of detail); turnpike roads, canal with towpath, waterbodies, houses, woods, plantations, parkland, heath/moor, building names, road earthworks, osiers.

32/11 Ashley (parish) SJ 760370
Apt 15.03.1838; 2802a (2860); Map 1838, 8 chns, by George Adie, Rugeley; foot/b'way, plantations, building names, rectory.

32/12 Aspley (township in parish of Eccleshall) SJ 812329
Apt 21.11.1838; 564a (564); Map 1838, 3 chns, by C.B. Ash; foot/b'way, heath/moor.

32/13 Aston, Burston, Stoke and Little Aston (district in parish of Stone) SJ 915317
Apt 21.02.1845; 3071a (?); Map 1841, 9 chns; waterbodies, canal with towpath.

32/14 Audley (parish) SJ 800510
Apt 16.08.1837; 8531a (8530); Map 1838, 3 chns, by Allen Booth, Knutton, Staffs; railway, canal with towpath, waterbodies, shed, engine houses, colleries (by symbol); border has quatrefoil and ball decoration. (The map in PRO IR 30 is a copy; original is in PRO IR 77/102, and is unfit for production.)

32/15 Bagots Bromley (township in parish of Abbots Bromley) SK 080280 [Bagot's Bromley]
Apt 19.02.1847; 4110a (?); Map 1848, 12 chns; waterbodies, woods (named), plantations, park (by name); fields are not shown, but fence junctions with roads and holding boundaries are. Some roads are not fully mapped.

32/16 Balterley (township in parish of Barthomley) SJ 755502
Apt 08.04.1839; 1206a (1206); Map 1841?, 3 chns; waterbodies, woods. Apt omits land use.

32/17 Barlaston (parish) SJ 895389
Apt 20.12.1848; 2158a (2157); Map 1849?, 6 chns; foot/b'way, waterbodies, woods, parkland, building names, pit, canal with towpath, common, green.

32/18 Barton under Needwood (township in parish of Tatenhill) SK 188186 [Barton-under-Needwood]
Apt 14.10.1837; 2809a (?); Map 1839, 6 chns, ? by J.B.H. Bennett, Tutbury; railway, foot/b'way, turnpike roads, canal with towpath, waterbodies, woods, plantations, osiers, fences, building names, road names, field names, forest gates, stile, parsonages, brickyard; bridges named. Apt includes cropping information.

32/19 Beech (district in parish of Stone) SJ 851382
Apt 28.11.1845; 163a (?): Map 1849, 6 chns, by Samuel Bate; foot/b'way, waterbodies, woods, landowners, flooded pit; blue band indicates tithe-free areas, fields within which are shown by pecked lines.

32/20 Bentley (township in parish of Wolverhampton) SO 985995
Apt 18.07.1846; 1424a (1650); Map 1847?, 12 chns; foot/b'way, waterbodies, canal with towpath, woods, quarry.

32/21 Berkswick (township in parish of Berkswick) SJ 951211 [Baswich]
Apt 24.06.1846; 1724a (?); Map 1847?, 6 chns, in 2 parts, (detached part at 12 chns); railway, foot/b'way, canal with towpath, waterbodies, woods, plantations, building names; border has ball and half-quatrefoil decoration.

32/22 Betley (parish) SJ 759483
Apt 06.05.1846; 1435a (1435); Map 1842, 4 chns, by J. Myatt, Whitmore near Newcastle, Staffs; foot/b'way, waterbodies, houses, woods (named), parkland, field boundary ownerships, field gates, building names, mill, toll gate, boundary trees, ice houses, vicarage, quarry, road earthworks, stiles.

32/23 Biddulph (parish) SJ 885575
Apt 06.06.1840; 5636a (5635); Map 1840?, 6 chns; foot/b'way, waterbodies (named), woods (named), building names, toll bars and chain, smithies, collieries, mill, silk mills, forge, reservoirs, tower, boundary stones, school, common; some lettering appears to be stamped; border has ball and half-quatrefoil decoration.

32/24 Bilbrooke (township in parish of Tettenhall) SJ 883032 [Bilbrook]
Apt 25.03.1840; 386a (all); Map 1841, 6 chns; waterbodies, canal with towpath.

32/25 Bilston (township in parish of Wolverhampton) SO 951965
Apt 07.04.1845; 1654a (1730); Map 1848, 6 chns, by William Fowler and Son, Birmingham (built-up parts not mapped in detail), litho (T. Underwood, 78$1/_2$ High St, Birmingham); railways, foot/b'way, canal with towpath, waterbodies, woods, road names, furnaces, stone quarries, iron works; roads are hand-coloured.

32/26 Bishops Offley (township in parish of Adbaston) SJ 778298
Apt 13.01.1841; 738a (738); Map 1841?, 6 chns; foot/b'way, waterbodies, woods.

32/27 Blithfield (parish) SK 049238 [Not listed]
Apt 11.12.1845; 3194a (3193); Map ('Skeleton Plan'), 1846, 12 chns; woods, rectory, dairy, mill, township boundaries. District is apportioned by holding, and most fields and all land use are omitted.

32/28 Blore with Swainscoe (township in parish of Blore) SK 131493
Apt 04.12.1844; 1052a (?); Map 1845, 6 chns, by John Parkin, Idridge; waterbodies, woods, building names.

32/29 Blurton and Lightwood Forest (township in parish of Trentham) SJ 904417
Apt 23.12.1845; 169a (?); Map 1847, 9 chns, (tithable parts only, tinted).

32/30 Blymhill (parish) SJ 817129
Apt 21.08.1839; 2926a (2925); Map 1841?, 9 chns; waterbodies, woods, field boundary ownerships, building names; tree symbols look like acorns.

32/31 Bobbington (parish) (partly in Shropshire) SO 815905 [Bobington]
Apt 18.11.1840; 2676a (2676); Map 1839, 9 chns, surveyed 'under the direction of Mr Wyley' by Henry Beckett, Wolverhampton, litho (by B. Hill, Colmore Row, Birmingham); foot/b'way, waterbodies, woods, parkland, orchards, field gates, building names, Methodist Chapel, well, dams, mill, county boundary; the map includes a 'Geological Description'.

32/32 Botteslow, Fenton Vivian and Fenton Culvert (township in parish of Stoke upon Trent) SJ 898448 [Fenton]
Apt 29.11.1849; 786a (?); Map 1850, 6 chns, by S. Bate, Knutton, Newcastle-u-L, (tithable part only); railways, foot/b'way, canal with towpath, waterbodies, woods, building names.

32/33 Bradley (parish) SJ 875180
Apt 22.06.1847; 1083a (3376); Map 1848, 6 chns, in 3 parts; foot/b'way, waterbodies, woods, building names.

32/34 Bradley-in-the-Moors (parish) SK 055415
Apt 30.06.1848; 668a (all); Map 1850?, 6 chns, by C. Smith, Junr, Alton; woods, field gates.

32/35 Bramshall (parish) SK 060339
Apt 31.07.1839; 1276a (1276); Map 1839, [3 chns], by Wm Kendall; waterbodies, spring.

32/36 Branston (township in parish of Burton upon Trent) SK 217217
Apt 10.12.1847; 40a (?); Map 1848, 9 chns, ? by J.B.H. Bennett, Tutbury, (tithable parts only); railway, turnpike roads, canal, osiers.

32/37 Brewood (parish) SJ 881082
Apt 16.10.1840; 11840a (11839); Map 1838, 9 chns, copied by R.H. Walker (town also at 3 chns); railway, foot/b'way, canal with towpath, reservoir and feeder, waterbodies, woods, parkland, heath/moor, building names, road names, mills, avenue.

32/38 Brockton (township in parish of Berkswich) SJ 970193 [Brocton]
Apt 11.06.1847; 2339a (?); Map 1847, 6 chns, in 2 parts; foot/b'way, waterbodies, woods, plantations, parkland, building names, boundary stones; Cannock Chase portion is not mapped in detail; 'Pools' along the boundary and some hills are named.

32/39 Bromley (township in parish of Eccleshall) SJ 784351 [Not listed]
Apt 22.09.1838; 853a (853); Map 1837, 4 chns, by Ash and Son; foot/b'way, waterbodies, woods, gardens, windmill. The district is 'Gerrands-Bromley' in the map title.

32/40 West Bromwich (parish) SP 008928
Apt 09.08.1845; 5126a (5710); Map 1849, 6 chns, by William Fowler and Sons, Waterloo St, Birmingham, litho (by Thos. Radcliffe and Son, 108 New Street, Birmingham); railways with station, foot/b'way, turnpike roads, canal with towpath and earthworks, waterbodies, woods (named), plantations, parkland, building names, iron works, forges, foundries, works, gas works, spoil heap, mills; tithe-free built-up areas are not mapped in detail.

32/41 Broom (parish) SO 902785 [Broome]
Apt 22.12.1838; 717a (716); Map 1838, 3 chns, by J. Matthews, litho (Standidge); foot/b'way, waterbodies, woods, parkland, orchards, building names, mill, field acreages; map is dated 1837 by the maker's name and 1838 in the title.

32/42 Broughton (township in parish of Eccleshall) SJ 763340
Apt 16.08.1845; 466a (466); Map 1847, 4 chns; waterbodies, woods (col), parkland, chapel.

32/43 Bucknall, Bagnall and Eaves (townships, hamlets or districts in parish of Stoke upon Trent) SJ 930490 [Bradley in the Moors]
Apt 29.05.1845; 4250a (?); Map 1846, 6 chns, in 2 parts, (including 2-chn enlargement of detail); canal with towpath, reservoir, waterbodies, woods, parkland, building names, chapel, common; roads across the common are not mapped.

32/44 Burntwood, Edjal, Woodhouse, Pipe Hill and Wall (townships, hamlets or districts in parish of St Michael Lichfield) SK 073090
Apt 15.01.1845; 4753a (?); Map 1847?, 6 chns, in 3 parts; foot/b'way, turnpike roads, canal with towpath, waterbodies, woods, plantations, parkland, building names, road names, parsonage, gravel pit, springs, mills, brick kiln, township boundaries (col).

32/45 Burslem (parish) SJ 872499
Apt 22.01.1844; 1879a (2940); Map 1848, 3 chns, by Ralph Hales, Cobridge, (tithable parts only, tinted); hill-drawing, railways, foot/b'way, canal with towpath and earthworks, waterbodies, houses, woods, building names, mills, shambles, town hall, wharf, colliery, parsonages, bottle kilns; the scale bar is framed, with decoration by what appear to be ungraduated protractors, and has curious graduations: 1,4,9,14,19, etc chains.

32/46 Burton Extra (township in parish of Burton upon Trent) SK 240230 [Not listed]
Apt 10.12.1847; 40a (?); Map 1848, 6 chns, by J.B.H. Bennett, Tutbury, (tithable parts only); railway and station, canal, woods, road names, landowners, windmill.

32/47 Burton upon Trent (township in parish of Burton upon Trent) SK 250230
Apt 10.12.1847; 108a (?); Map 1848, 4 chns, by J.B.H. Bennett, Tutbury, (tithable parts only); railway and station, road names, police station, National Schools. Apt mostly omits land use, but includes a little cropping information.

32/48 Bushbury (township in parish of Bushbury) SJ 921029
Apt 31.07.1847; 3429a (3420); Map 1845, 6 chns; railway, waterbodies, woods, plantations, parkland, building names, canal with towpath, mill.

32/49 Butterton (township in parish of Mayfield) SK 071569
Apt 27.08.1847; 1489a (1940); Map 1848, 3 chns, by William Dykes; foot/b'way, waterbodies, houses, woods, plantations, building names, toll gate, quarries, lime kilns, mine, chapel, school; streams are named.

32/50 Calton (township in parish of Waterfall) SK 101509
Apt 16.12.1844; 583a (?); Map 1848, 6 chns, 'Compiled from Old Maps adopted by the Landowners', by Jno. Bromley, Derby; foot/b'way.

32/51 Calton (township or chapelry in parish of Blore) SK 106489
Apt 04.12.1844; 360a (2480); Map 1848, 6 chns, 'Compiled from Old Maps adopted by the Landowners', by Jno. Bromley, Derby; foot/b'way, waterbodies, woods.

32/52 Calton (township in parish of Mayfield) SK 099488
Apt 22.02.1848; 356a (?); Map 1848, 6 chns, by John Bromley; foot/b'way.

32/53 Calwick (township in parish of Ellaston) SK 128437 [Not listed]
Apt 20.08.1844; 760a (?); Map 1844, 6 chns, by John Parkin, (tithable lands tinted); woods, parkland. Apt omits land use.

32/54 Cannock (parish) SJ 998120
Apt 22.07.1841; 7510a (10775); Map: 5 parts, 1841, 9 chns, by George Adie, (two enlargements of built-up areas at 3 chns); 1 part, 1838, 6 chns, by Long and Taylor of Wolverhampton; foot/b'way, turnpike roads, toll bar and gate, canal with towpath, waterbodies, woods (named), plantations, building names, road names, walk mill, iron works, spoil heaps, gravel pit; the township of Huntington is mapped

separately, at 9 chns, with a border with quatrefoil and ball decoration, and with tithable status by colours, as explained, bottom left.

32/55 Castle Church (parish) SJ 922218 [Not listed]
Apt 23.07.1841; 274a (3774); Map 1842, 6 chns, copied by R.H. Walker, (tithable part only); waterbodies, woods, building names, landowners; border has quatrefoil and ball decoration.

32/56 Cauldon (parish) SK 077495
Apt 30.04.1845; 1459a (1458); Map 1849?, 6 chns.

32/57 Caverswall (parish) SJ 942450
Apt 30.10.1840; 5240a (5300); Map 1841, 6 chns, in 2 parts; foot/b'way, waterbodies, woods, gardens, mill, nunnery, common.

32/58 Chapel-Chorlton and Hill-Chorlton (township in parish of Eccleshall) SJ 810380 [Chapel Chorlton and Hill Chorlton]
Apt 21.06.1838; 1921a (1921); Map 1838, 6 chns, in 2 parts, by Charles Heaton, Endon near Leek; railway, foot/b'way, turnpike roads, waterbodies, woods (col), heath/moor, building names, chapel, Sunday School, Wesleyan Chapel; spinneys are uncoloured.

32/59 Charnes (township in parish of Eccleshall) SJ 799344
Apt 30.09.1845; 837a (837); Map 1845?, 4 chns; waterbodies, woods (col). Apt omits land use.

32/60 Chatcull (township in parish of Eccleshall) SJ 798341
Apt 24.11.1846; 750a (750); Map 1846?, 4 chns; foot/b'way, waterbodies, woods (col), green (named). Apt omits land use.

32/61 Cheadle (parish) SK 015435
Apt 30.06.1842; 6536a (6701); Map 1843?, 6 chns, in 7 parts (including 2-part 18-chn index); railway, foot/b'way, waterbodies, woods, plantations, building names, stiles, mill; Cheadle town is not mapped in detail, and appears to be by a different author; borders have moulding and quatrefoil-and-ball ornament.

32/62 Chebsey (parish) SJ 870300
Apt 06.11.1843; 4172a (4172); Map 1846, 6 chns, by George Adie, Rugeley; railway, foot/b'way, waterbodies, woods, building names, old river course.

32/63 Checkley (parish) SK 029394
Apt 30.11.1841; 6036a (6036); Map 1842?, 6 chns, in 7 parts, (including 2-part 18-chn index); canal with towpath, waterbodies, woods, building names, mill, aqueduct.

32/64 Church Eaton (parish) SJ 839169
Apt 20.09.1838; 4204a (4204); Map 1838, 8 chns, 'from divers Surveys', by R. Hammonds; waterbodies, canal with towpath, woods, plantations.

32/65 Clayton and Seabridge (district in parish of Stoke upon Trent) SJ 849438
Apt 29.11.1849; 710a (?); Map 1850, 6 chns, by S. Bate, Knutton, Newcastle-u-L, (tithable parts only); foot/b'way, waterbodies, woods (col), township boundaries.

32/66 Clayton Griffith (township in parish of Trentham) SJ 849449 [Not listed]
Apt 23.12.1845; 46a (?); Map 1848?, 9 chns, (tithable parts only, tinted). (The copy in PRO IR 30 is a photocopy of the Diocesan copy.)

32/67 Clent (parish) SO 930795
Apt 30.04.1838; 2366a (2365); Map 1838, [5 chns], litho (Standidge); foot/b'way, waterbodies, woods, building names, commons (with acreages).

32/68 Clifton and Haunton (townships in parish of Clifton Campville) SK 251103
Apt 20.02.1838; 3249a (all); Map 1839?, 6 chns, 'from a survey by Mr Robt. H. Wyatt 1810'; waterbodies, woods (col), parkland, gardens. (The map in PRO IR 30 is a photocopy of the Diocesan copy.)

32/69 Codsall (district) SJ 864040
Apt 24.04.1849; 1370a (?); Map 1850, 9 chns, by G. Taylor, Wolverhampton, (tithable parts only); railway, foot/b'way, waterbodies, woods.

32/70 Cold Meece (township in parish of Eccleshall) SJ 853331 [Coldmeece]
Apt 18.09.1845; 569a (all); Map 1839, 3 chns, 1st cl, by Bate and Timmis, Whitchurch, Salop, (tinted); foot/b'way, waterbodies, houses, woods (col), plantations (col), orchards, mill, ford.

32/71 Colton (parish) SK 055205
Apt 07.02.1844; 2552a (3665); Map 1845?, 6 chns, in 3 parts (including 3-chn enlargement of detail); foot/b'way, canal with towpath, aqueduct, wharf, waterbodies, woods, building names, mills.

32/72 Colwich (parish) SK 012226
Apt 04.04.1845; 7551a (7551); Map made [surveyed?] in 1839, 3 chns, 1st cl, in 13 parts, by J.P. Lofthouse, Hopton (tinted); foot/b'way, canal with towpath, aqueduct, waterbodies, woods, plantations, osiers, parkland, gardens (col), lantern, triumphal arch, dog kennel, keepers lodge, mill, boundary stones, nunnery.

32/73 Coppenhall (township in parish of Penkridge) SJ 908197
Apt 28.04.1849; 959a (?); Map 1850?, 6 chns; foot/b'way, waterbodies, woods, heath/moor, building names, mill, earthwork, gravel pit.

32/74 Cotes (township in parish of Eccleshall) SJ 834351
Apt 16.08.1845; 1104a (1104); Map 1843, 3 chns, by Ash and Son; railway, foot/b'way, waterbodies, woods (col), plantations, parkland, chapel, boundary stones.

32/75 Coton (township in parish of St Mary) SJ 929239 [Not listed]
Apt 25.03.1846; 687a (?); Map 1846?, 8 chns, in 2 parts, (includes open fields at 2 chns); foot/b'way, waterbodies, woods. Apt includes cropping information; the main map, at 8 chns, is with Apt in PRO IR 29; a 2 chn enlargement of open fields is in PRO IR 30.

32/76 Creswell (extra-parochial place) SJ 961361 [Not listed]
Apt 11.12.1845; 92a (800); Map 1846?, 4 chns, railway, waterbodies, woods, plantations, parkland, building names, old river course; border has quatrefoil and ball decoration.

32/77 Croxton (township in parish of Eccleshall) SJ 768315
Apt 10.11.1841; 4493a (4493); Map 1839, 3 chns, by C.B. Ash; foot/b'way, waterbodies, woods (named), plantations, open fields, pits, windmill (by symbol), boundary stones, prebend boundaries (col); woods are shown by grey without symbols, plantation by grey with symbols.

32/78 Darlaston (parish) SO 980970
Apt 13.01.1841; 901a (901); Map surveyed in 1842, 3 chns, 1st cl, by John Pickering, (tithable parts only); construction lines, railway with earthworks, foot/b'way, canal with towpath and earthworks, waterbodies, houses, woods, open fields, milepost; scale-bar is ruler-like.

32/79 Darlaston (township in parish of Stone) SJ 881351
Apt 08.01.1846; 1397a (?); Map 1850, 6 chns, by S. Bate, Knutton, Newcastle-u-L, (tithable parts only); railways, woods (col), pit. District is partly apportioned by holding.

32/80 Dilhorn (parish) SJ 973436 [Dilhorne]
Apt 30.04.1838; 3470a (3648); Map 1839, 6 chns, by Binns and Clifford, Birmingham, Surveyors, lithographers and General Draughtsmen; waterbodies, woods, chapel; no buildings are shown and built-up parts are not mapped in detail.

32/81 Draycott, Stubby Lane, and Moreton (township in parish of Hanbury) SK 151289 [Not listed]
Apt 28.05.1838; 1317a (?); Map 1839, 9 chns, ? by J.B.H. Bennett, Tutbury; foot/b'way, turnpike roads, waterbodies, woods, osiers, building names, Methodist Chapel, mill, modus land (col). Apt includes cropping information and some information on crop rotations.

32/82 Draycot in the Moors (parish) SJ 988400 [Draycott in the Moors]
Apt 26.09.1837; 3798a (3690); Map 1853?, 8 chns, (tithable parts only); railway, waterbodies, woods (col, named), holding boundaries (col). District is apportioned by holding, and Apt omits land use and field-names.

32/83 Drayton Bassett (parish) SK 180002
Apt 28.02.1837; 3315a (3315); Map 1838, office copy, corrected as to

fences and occupations, of the Parish Plan of 1832, 8 chns; turnpike roads, canal with towpath, waterbodies, woods (col), parkland, building names; legend explains colouring by tithable status.

32/84 Drayton in Hales (parish) SJ 713340 [Hales]
Apt 23.06.1838; 6475a (6690); Map 1842?, 3 chns, 1st cl, by George Adie, Rugeley; proof construction lines, foot/b'way, canal with towpath and locks, waterbodies, houses, woods, plantations, parkland, field boundary ownerships, field gates, field acreages, building names, paper mills, pits, monument, boundary oak.

32/85 Dunstall (township in parish of Tatenhill) SK 185204
Apt 09.10.1837; 1184a (?); Map 1839, 6 chns, by J.B.H. Bennett, Tutbury; railway, foot/b'way, turnpike roads, canal with towpath and lock, waterbodies, woods, plantations, fences, building names. Apt includes cropping information.

32/86 Dunston (township in parish of Penkridge) SJ 919178
Apt 26.01.1841; 1111a (?); Map 1841?, 9 chns, in 3 parts (including two 3-chn enlargements of detail; tithable lands tinted); railway, waterbodies, woods, landowners. Border has quatrefoil and ball ornament.

32/87 Eccleshall (township in parish of Eccleshall) SJ 830297
Apt 11.03.1839; 1432a (1432); Map 1839, 6 chns, by J.P. Lofthouse, Hopton; foot/b'way, waterbodies, woods, parkland. Buildings in the village are tinted grey; those outside are solid black.

32/88 Elford (parish) SK 195105
Apt 15.10.1841; 332a (2070); Map surveyed 1839, 6 chns, in 2 parts, by Sanders Pepper, (tithable and glebe lands only; including 3-chn enlargement of detail); railway, woods, arable (col), grassland (col), orchards, gardens, landowners, mill, weir, rectory; scale-bar is ruler-like.

32/89 Elkstone (township in parish of Alstonfield) SK 050592 [Lower and Upper Elkstone]
Apt 28.05.1850; 1280a (?); Map 1850, 6 chns, by Edwin Heaton, Leek; foot/b'way, waterbodies, woods, building names.

32/90 Ellaston (township in parish of Ellaston) SK 114434 [Ellastone]
Apt 14.12.1844; 792a (?); Map 1847, 6 chns, by Robert Bromley, Derby; foot/b'way, waterbodies, houses, plantations.

32/91 Enville (parish) SO 829878
Apt 31.12.1840; 4362a (4924); Map 1838, 6 chns, litho (Standidge); foot/b'way, right of road, waterbodies, woods (named), parkland, orchards, building names, mills, park features, spring, lodge, gorse cover, school, rectory, chapel, quarries, commons, greens.

32/92 Essington (township in parish of Bushbury) SJ 971038
Apt 28.11.1839; 2957a (2957); Map 1843, 9 chns; railway, canal with towpath, waterbodies, woods, parkland, hedge ownership, fence ownership, building names, lodge; former uninclosed areas are named; scale bar is ruler-like.

32/93 Farewell (parish) SK 079117
Apt 24.01.1840; 1048a (1049); Map 1838, 3 chns, 1st cl, in 2 parts, by John Brown; construction lines, foot/b'way, waterbodies, houses, woods, parkland, orchards, marsh/bog, heath/moor, hedge ownership, fence ownership, field gates, building names, mills, sheep wash, manorial boundary (col), greens.

32/94 Fauld (township in parish of Hanbury) SK 185290
Apt 30.04.1838; 762a (?); Map 1848, 9 chns, ? by J.B.H. Bennett, Tutbury; railway, foot/b'way, waterbodies, woods, building names, road names, weir, mill stream.

32/95 Fazeley (township in parish of Tamworth) SK 204019
Apt 13.12.1848; 32a (?); Map 1850?, 12 chns, (tithable parts only); canal, waterbodies.

32/96 Featherstone (township in parish of Wolverhampton) SJ 935055
Apt 21.03.1840; 489a (all); Map 1838, 3 chns, 1st cl, by R. Timmis, Wolverhampton; construction lines, waterbodies, woods, field boundary ownerships, boundary tree.

32/97 Fisherwick (township in parish of St Michaels Lichfield) SK 178095 [Not listed]
Apt 25.10.1842; 1289a (all); Map undated, 6 chns; foot/b'way, canal with towpath, waterbodies, woods, plantations, parkland, building names, drift roads, stone quarry, lodge; colours show prebends, as explained in note.

32/98 Flashbrook (township in parish of Adbaston) SJ 741252 [Not listed]
Apt 20.05.1841; 1434a (1434); Map 1838, 6 chns; waterbodies, woods; there are two versions of the map in PRO IR 30; that signed by the Tithe Commissioners is described above: it is uncoloured, with ponds shown by horizontal ruling, and a gorse cover shown by symbol; the second copy is called 'Copy no.3', is by Samuel H. Ashdown, The Hem, Shiffnal, dated 1842, and at same scale; roads and water are coloured, field boundary ownership is shown by lilac bands, and tree symbols have grey 'shadow', the gorse cover being treated as an ordinary wood.

32/99 Forton (parish) SJ 764207
Apt 21.06.1838; 3666a (3718); Map 1838, 6 chns, copied by J. Treasure, Newport, Salop; foot/b'way, canal with towpath, waterbodies, woods, plantations, parkland (in detail), heath/moor, building names, lodge, monument, quarry. Apt omits land use for some modus lands.

32/100 Fradswell (township in parish of Colwich) SJ 992312
Apt 24.06.1841; 1424a (1424); Map 1839, 6 chns, copied by J.P. Lofthouse, Hopton; hill-drawing, foot/b'way, waterbodies, woods (col), parkland, gardens, building names.

32/101 Fulfin (extra-parochial place) SK 144094 [Not listed]
Apt 20.04.1838; 241a (all); Map 1838, 3 chns; canal with towpath, waterbodies, woods, field gates.

32/102 Fulford (township in parish of Stone) SJ 958383
Apt 20.11.1849; 1525a (?); Map 1850, 6 chns, by S. Bate, Knutton, Newcastle-u-L; foot/b'way, waterbodies, woods.

32/103 Gayton (parish) SJ 982290
Apt 19.02.1850; 1479a (all); Map 1850, 6 chns, by J. Wyley, High Onn, Stafford; foot/b'way, waterbodies, woods, open fields (residual).

32/104 Gnosall (parish) SJ 820200
Apt 17.02.1838; 10498a (10497); Map 1839?, 4 chns, in 6 parts; canal with towpath, waterbodies, woods, building names, mill, commons.

32/105 Gratwich (parish) SK 030311
Apt 16.11.1837; 857a (856); Map 1838, 3 chns, by J.P. Lofthouse, Hopton; foot/b'way, waterbodies, woods (col), stiles.

32/106 Grindon (parish) SK 080545
Apt 27.06.1839; 3230a (3229); Map 1840?, 6 chns, by B. Staley, Youlgreave, near Bakewell; hill-drawing, foot/b'way, waterbodies, woods, field gates, building names, mill, ford, green, moor; colours show ownerships; border has quatrefoil and ball decoration.

32/107 Hammerwich (township) SK 063072
Apt 21.09.1843; 1759a (?); Map 1844, 6 chns; hill-drawing, canal with earthworks and feeder, reservoir, dam, waterbodies, houses, woods, plantations, parkland, building names, road names, gravel pit, windmill, boundary stones.

32/108 Hamstall Ridware (parish) SK 110194
Apt 27.03.1839; 1422a (2934); Map 1841, 6 chns; waterbodies, houses, woods, building names, pits, mill, rectory.

32/109 Hanbury, Hanbury Woodend and Coton (township in parish of Hanbury) SK 168280
Apt 30.04.1838; 1254a (?); Map 1839, 9 chns, ? by J.B.H. Bennett, Tutbury; foot/b'way, waterbodies, woods, fence, building names, road names, mill, mill stream, vicarage, pale walk. Apt includes cropping and some rotational information.

32/110 Handsworth (parish) SP 050914
Apt 23.01.1839; 7681a (7680); Map 1840, 3 chns, in 2 parts; hill-drawing, railways, turnpike roads, waterbodies, woods, plantations, parkland, dams, avenue of trees, pits, old college, common.

32/111 Hanford (township in parish of Trentham) SJ 873425
Apt 30.12.1845; 330a (?); Map 1847, 3 chns; foot/b'way, waterbodies.

32/112 Hanley and Shelton (township in parish of Stoke upon Trent) SJ 880477
Apt 29.11.1849; 675a (?); Map 1850, 6 chns, in 2 parts, by S. Bate, Knutton, Newcastle-u-L, (tithable parts only; built-up parts separately at 2 chns); hill-drawing, railways, foot/b'way, canal with towpath, waterbodies, woods, road names, chapel, road embankment.

32/113 Harborne (parish) SP 022856
Apt 27.02.1839; 3265a (3296); Map 1842, 6 chns, corrected 1840 by Saml H. Ashdown, Uppington, Shrewsbury; foot/b'way, canal with towpath and tunnel, reservoir, waterbodies, woods, parkland, building names, forge, foundary, steel works, glass works, spoil heap, rolling mills, workhouse; some bridges are named.

32/114 Harlaston (township in parish of Clifton Campville) SK 217099
Apt 24.03.1843; 1431a (all); Map 1843, 6 chns; railway, foot/b'way, waterbodies, woods, building names, chapel, mill, glebe (col).

32/115 Haslour (lordship) SK 205108 [Not listed]
Apt 21.02.1844; 573a (all); Map 1845, 6 chns, by John Holbeche, Erdington; railway, foot/b'way, waterbodies, woods, pit.

32/116 Hatherton (township) SJ 952099
Apt 26.01.1841; 2001a (?); Map 1840, 6 chns, by Long and Taylor, Wolverhampton; foot/b'way, waterbodies, woods, parkland, gardens, building names, mills, reservoir, ford.

32/117 Haughton (parish) SJ 865205
Apt 14.02.1839; 1860a (1860); Map 1839, 8 chns, copied by J.P. Lofthouse, Hopton; woods, building names, green; the border has quatrefoil and ball decoration.

32/118 Herberton (township in parish of St Mary) SJ 948248 [Not listed]
Apt 25.03.1846; 513a (?); Map 1850?, 8 chns; foot/b'way, waterbodies, woods, building names. Apt includes some cropping information.

32/119 Highlands Park (district in parish of Tatenhill) SK 191219
Apt 09.10.1837; 448a (?); Map 1839, 6 chns, by Jos. B.H. Bennett, Tutbury; foot/b'way, waterbodies, woods (col), building names, landowners, lodge, park pale, sunk fence; park pale is annotated with its width 'from the stools', to accomodate a walk. Apt includes cropping information.

32/120 Hilderstone (township in parish of Stone) SJ 952349
Apt 03.03.1841; 1959a (?); Map 1843, 6 chns, in 2 parts, by Thomas Heaton, Endon, near Leek, (open fields also at 3 chns); foot/b'way, waterbodies, woods, plantations, parkland, gardens, open fields, building names, toll bar, parsonage, stiles; scale bar is ruler-like.

32/121 Hilton (township in parish of Wolverhampton) SJ 953025 [Not listed]
Apt 30.11.1842; 788a (all); Map 1843, 9 chns, copied by R. Timmis, W'Hampton; foot/b'way, waterbodies, woods, plantations, parkland, gardens, field boundary ownerships, building names, tithe-free land (col); border has ball and quatrefoil decoration; scale bar is ruler-like.

32/122 Himley (parish) SO 885913
Apt 11.04.1839; 1186a (all); Map 1841, 8 chns; waterbodies, woods, parkland, building names, fences.

32/123 Hints (parish) SK 158029
Apt 05.02.1847; 1850a (all); Map 1848?, 8 chns; foot/b'way, waterbodies, woods.

32/124 Hopton (township in parish of St Mary's Stafford) SJ 940260
Apt 22.09.1838; 2013a (?); Map 1838, 9 chns, by J.P. Lofthouse, Hopton; foot/b'way, waterbodies, woods (col), plantations (col), parkland, building names, tower; border has ball and quatrefoil decoration.

32/125 Horninglow (township in parish of Burton upon Trent) SK 238248
Apt 31.07.1848; 302a (?); Map 1848, 6 chns, by J.B.H. Bennett, Tutbury, (tithable parts only); railway, foot/b'way, turnpike roads, canal with towpath and lock house, wharf, waterbodies, woods, road names, landowners, workhouse; fence junctions of tithe-free lands are mapped along roads.

32/126 Horseley (township in parish of Eccleshall) SJ 804284 [Not listed]
Apt 30.11.1838; 2212a (2212); Map 1839, 6 chns, by J.P. Lofthouse, Hopton; foot/b'way, waterbodies, woods, osiers, common, building names.

32/127 Ilam (parish) SK 123523
Apt 17.10.1838; 2005a (2939); Map 1839?, 6 chns, by Robert Bromley, Derby; foot/b'way, waterbodies, woods, plantations, parkland, gardens, building names, hotel, fords, weir, stiles, township boundaries (col); woods and plantations are shown by Dawson's symbols.

32/128 Ingestre (parish) SJ 940248
Apt 22.09.1838; 830a (868); Map 1838, 9 chns, by J.P. Lofthouse, Hopton; foot/b'way, waterbodies, woods, parkland (in detail), gardens, field boundary ownerships, building names, pavilion, temple, mill, brine pit; glebe is numbered in red; border has quatrefoil and ball decoration.

32/129 Keele (parish) SJ 810453
Apt 28.11.1845; 2597a (2579); Map 1849, 12 chns; foot/b'way, waterbodies, woods, parkland, building names, toll gate; map is apportioned by holding and only a few fields are shown; scale bar and direction pointer are combined.

32/130 Kings Bromley (parish) SK 115155 [King's Bromley]
Apt 17.09.1849; 3464a (3370); Map 1850, [6 chns], by George Adie, Rugeley; railway, foot/b'way, canal with towpath, wharf, waterbodies, woods (named), building names.

32/131 Kingsley (parish) SK 010460
Apt 27.06.1839; 4717a (4714); Map 1839, 6 chns, in 2 parts, by Sam Harding, Valuer; railway, canal towpath, waterbodies, woods, plantations, building names, brick yard, dog kennel, parsonage, toll gate, copper works, kilns, lime kilns, encroachments (col); a few bridges are named.

32/132 Kingstone (parish) SK 057291
Apt 30.11.1838; 2007a (2009); Map 1837, 9 chns, surveyed by J. Hopton, Lofthouse and made by J. Ginders Junr; foot/b'way, waterbodies, woods (col), field boundary ownerships, building names; red numbers appear to indicate modus lands; scale bar is ruler-like; border has quatrefoil and ball decoration. Apt includes very thorough cropping information.

32/133 Kingswinford (parish) SO 900880
Apt 23.03.1839; 7316a (7315); Map 1839-40, 6 chns, by William Fowler and Son, Waterloo St, Birmingham, litho (by C.F. Cheffins, 9 Southampton Buildings, Holborn); hill-drawing, railway, foot/b'way, canal with towpath and earthworks, waterbodies, woods (named, shown by Dawson's symbol), osiers, plantations (by Dawson's symbol), parkland, heath/moor, building names, reservoirs, iron works, forges, mills, glass works, furnaces, pottery, workhouse, chapel, rectory; one stream has been hand coloured.

32/134 Kingswood (township in parish of Tettenhall) SJ 840026 [Not listed]
Apt 11.03.1840; 139a (all); Map 1841, 6 chns; foot/b'way, waterbodies, woods, field boundary ownerships.

32/135 Kinvaston (township in parish of Wolverhampton) SJ 910116 [Not listed]
Apt 22.10.1846; 234a (all); Map 1847?, 3 chns; railway, foot/b'way, waterbodies, woods, field gates, boundary trees.

32/136 Kinver or Kinfare (parish) SO 861849
Apt 31.12.1850; 634a (8790); Map 1851, 9 chns, by Jno. Davies, Stourbridge, Worcestershire, (tithable parts only); hill-drawing, foot/b'way, canal with towpath, waterbodies, woods, plantations, heath/moor, building names, iron works, mill; colour bands show the various tithes payable, as explained above the scale.

32/137 Lapley (parish) SJ 860130
Apt 09.05.1838; 3475a (3450); Map 1838, 3 chns; foot/b'way, canal with towpath, waterbodies, woods.

32/138 Leigh (parish) SK 020357 [Church Leigh]
Apt 06.06.1840; 6939a (7055); Map 1845?, 6 chns, foot/b'way, waterbodies, woods (col), building names, stiles, township boundaries (col).

32/139 St Chad or Stowe, Lichfield (parish) SK 112112 [Not listed]
Apt 31.07.1848; 2606a (2080); Map 1850?, 4 chns, in 2 parts; railways, foot/b'way, turnpike roads, toll gates, waterbodies, woods, plantations, parkland, orchards, fences, building names, road names, mills, windmill, gas works, chapel, pound.

32/140 St Mary, Lichfield (parish) SK 118098 [Not listed]
Apt 22.02.1848; 60a (all); Map 1849, 1 chn; waterbodies, woods, road names, conduit, market place, market hall, monument, town hall and gaol, National School, Grammar School, Diocesan School, schools, chapels, theatre, barrack yard; numerous inns and pubs are named. Apt omits most land use.

32/141 St Michael (district in parish of St Michael, Lichfield) SK 112085 [Not listed]
Apt 05.06.1847; 1909a (?); Map 1849?, 4 chns; hill-drawing, railways, foot/b'way, turnpike roads, canal with towpath and locks, wharf, waterbodies, woods, plantations, building names, road names, gravel pit, workhouse, mills, Roman Catholic Chapel, county boundary.

32/142 Longdon (parish) SK 078138
Apt 16.06.1843; 4511a (4511); Map 1846?, 6 chns, in 2 parts (including 3-chn enlargement of detail); turnpike roads, toll gate, waterbodies, houses, woods, plantations, parkland, gardens, building names, road names, windmills (by symbol), lodges, mill.

32/143 Longnor (township in parish of Alstonfield) SK 090654
Apt 29.06.1848; 787a (?); Map 1849?, 6 chns, in 2 parts, (village mapped separately at 1.25 chns); foot/b'way, waterbodies, woods, market place, churchyard.

32/144 Longton and Lane End (township in parish of Stoke upon Trent) SJ 906434
Apt 29.11.1849; 646a (?); Map 1850, 6 chns, in 2 parts, by S. Bate, Knutton, Newcastle-u-L, (tithable parts only); railways, canal with towpath, foot/b'way, waterbodies, houses, woods (col), parkland, building names, mills, township boundaries (col).

32/145 Madeley (parish) SJ 772442
Apt 26.08.1839; 5705a (5734); Map 1840, 8 chns, by Allen Booth, (tinted); railway, waterbodies, woods (col), building names, colliery. Apt omits land use.

32/146 Maer (parish) SJ 785391
Apt 24.05.1838; 2736a (2736); Map 1838, 9 chns; waterbodies, woods.

32/147 Marchington (township in parish of Hanbury) SK 135308
Apt 04.12.1842; 1719a (?); Map 1843, 9 chns, in 2 parts, ? by J.B.H. Bennett (meadows at 3 chns); foot/b'way, waterbodies, woods, building names, weir, mill stream, parsonage, tithe-free land.

32/148 Marchington Woodlands (township in parish of Hanbury) SK 106291
Apt 04.12.1842; 1891a (?); Map 1843, 9 chns, in 2 parts, ? by J.B.H. Bennett, Tutbury, (tithable parts only; meadows at 3 chns); foot/b'way, woods, building names.

32/149 Marston (township in parish of St Mary's, Stafford) SJ 922282
Apt 18.09.1838; 1448a (?); Map 1839, 6 chns, by J.P. Lofthouse, Hopton; foot/b'way, waterbodies, woods, plantations, building names, chapel.

32/150 Mavesyn Ridware (parish) SK 078190
Apt 30.11.1838; 2476a (2475); Map 1839, 6 chns, by George Adie, Rugeley; foot/b'way, occupation roads, turnpike roads, toll gate, waterbodies, woods, osiers, heath/moor, building names, mill stream, dam, mill, rectory, footbridge.

32/151 Mayfield (township in parish of Mayfield) SK 150455
Apt 28.12.1848; 1817a (1820); Map 1849, 6 chns, by J.B.H. Bennett, Tutbury; foot/b'way, waterbodies, woods, building names, weirs, cotton mill, footbridge (named), toll gate, schools, hamlet boundaries (col).

32/152 Meaford and Oulton (township in parish of Stone) SJ 905360
Apt 22.09.1842; 2201a (?); Map 1843?, 6 chns, in 2 parts; canal with towpath, waterbodies, woods, mills, tithe-free land.

32/153 Mill Meece (township in parish of Eccleshall) SJ 838332 [Millmeece]
Apt 23.04.1839; 627a (627); Map 1839, 3 chns, by C.B. Ash; railway, foot/b'way, waterbodies, woods, pits.

32/154 Milwich (parish) SJ 978330
Apt 31.12.1838; 2987a (2987); Map 1839, 6 chns, by J.P. Lofthouse, Hopton; foot/b'way, waterbodies, woods (col), plantations (col), building names; border has quatrefoil and ball decoration. Apt includes cropping information.

32/155 Moddershall (township in parish of Stone) SJ 930370
Apt 25.05.1850; 778a (?); Map 1851, 9 chns, 'Taken from the Parish Survey and revised' by Saml Bate, Knutton, Newcastle under Lyme, (tithable parts only); waterbodies, woods, building names.

32/156 Mucclestone (parish) SJ 735405 [Mucklestone]
Apt 15.03.1838; 8532a (8531); Map 1838?, 9 chns; waterbodies, woods, township boundaries (col); buildings are shown in outline only, without fill. Scale bar is ruler-like, without figures; border has quatrefoil and ball decoration.

32/157 Newbro' with Thorney Lanes (township in parish of Hanbury) SK 133257 [Newborough]
Apt 27.09.1838; 2314a (?); Map 1839, 6 chns, by J.B.H. Bennett; foot/b'way, turnpike roads, waterbodies, woods, plantations, parkland, park pale, fences, building names, road names, footway, windmill, brickyard, fishpond; colour bands show tithe-free and modus land. Apt includes cropping information.

32/158 Newcastle-under-Lyme (parish) SJ 849461
Apt 02.09.1841; 151a (554); Map 1841, 2 chns, by Geo. Harding, Maer, Newcastle-under-Lyme, (tithable parts only); hill-drawing, foot/b'way, turnpike roads, toll gates, canal with towpath, waterbodies, houses, woods, parkland, building names, road names, workhouse, rectory, cross, Town Hall, theatre, schools, lime works, rope walk, silk factory, skin yard, stone yard, boundary marks, 'castle bank'; very few buildings are shown.

32/159 Norbury (parish) SJ 786235
Apt 31.07.1839; 3298a (3313); Map 1839, 9 chns in 2 parts, by W. Bright, litho (by B. Hill, Colmore Row, Birmingham); foot/b'way, canal with towpath and locks, waterbodies, houses, woods, fences, field gates, building names, rectory; both parts add hand-colour for houses; part 1 is dated 1835, and shows canal property by green tint; part 2 is dated 1839, and has hand-coloured waterbodies.

32/160 Normicott (township in parish of Stone) SJ 937414 [Normacot]
Apt 15.11.1855; 188a (?); Map 1856?, 3 chns, (tithable parts only); woods, building names, landowners, toll bars.

32/161 Norton Caines or Norton under Cannock (parish) SK 021075 [Norton Canes]
Apt 21.04.1838; 2609a (4077); Map 1840?, [8 chns], surveyed in 1827 by Will. Fowler; railway, foot/b'way, canal with towpath, waterbodies, woods (named), orchards, fences, building names, toll gate, engine, reservoir, pound, boundary trees and stones, well, commons, greens; streams named.

32/162 Norton on the Moors (parish) SJ 895528 [Norton-in-the-Moors]
Apt 09.03.1843; 4235a (4234); Map 1843?, 3 chns; foot/b'way, canal with towpath, waterbodies, woods, building names, chapel, mill, lime kiln; border has quatrefoil and ball decoration.

32/163 Oaken (township in parish of Codsall) SJ 854027
Apt 04.09.1838; 1299a (?); Map 1841, 9 chns; waterbodies, woods.

32/164 Oakley (township in parish of Croxall) SK 193133 [Not listed]
Apt 20.08.1839; 679a (all); Map 1840, 6 chns, ? by J.B.H. Bennett, Tutbury; railway, foot/b'way, turnpike roads and gate, waterbodies, woods, fence, building names, mill, osiers. Apt includes cropping information.

32/165 High Offley (parish) SJ 777261
Apt 29.06.1839; 2727a (2727); Map 1838, 3 chns, by J. Treasure, Newport; foot/b'way, canal with towpath, wharf, waterbodies, woods, building names, mill.

32/166 Onecote (township in parish of Leek) SK 040560
Apt 31.12.1847; 30a (?); Map 1858?, 6 chns, (tithable lands only).

32/167 Orton (township in parish of Wombourn) SO 868950
Apt 29.05.1841; 1129a (?); Map 1840, 9 chns, in 3 parts (two 3-chn enlargements of detail); canal with towpath, waterbodies, woods, orchards, building names, mill; there is a note 'Geological Character - New Red Sand stone'.

32/168 Packington (township in parish of Weeford) SK 158058 [Not listed]
Apt 28.11.1845; 1007a (all); Map 1846?, 6 chns; foot/b'way, turnpike roads, waterbodies, woods, plantations, parkland, building names.

32/169 Pattingham (district in parish of Pattingham) SO 825985
Apt 25.06.1841; 2475a (2500); Map 1843?, 6 chns; waterbodies, woods, field boundary ownerships, building names, mill.

32/170 Pelsall (township in parish of Wolverhampton) SK 021040
Apt 09.05.1840; 993a (all); Map 1840, 6 chns; canal with towpath, woods, open fields, iron works, common (col); yellow vignetting may indicate tithe-free lands.

32/171 Penkhull and Boothen (township in parish of Stoke upon Trent) SJ 870450
Apt 29.11.1849; 644a (?); Map 1850, 6 chns, in 5 parts, by S. Bate, Knutton, Newcastle-u-L, (tithable parts only; including four 2-chn enlargements of detail); waterbodies, canal with towpath, houses, woods, plantations, building names, toll gate.

32/172 Penkridge (district) SJ 930140
Apt 26.01.1841; 2311a (?); Map 1841?, 9 chns, in 4 parts, (tithable parts only, tinted; parts 2, 3 and 4 at 6 chns); railway, foot/b'way, canal with towpath, waterbodies, houses, woods, landowners, township boundary. Borders have quatrefoil and ball decoration.

32/173 Penn (parish) SO 880963
Apt 12.06.1843; 3986a (3986); Map 1839, 3 chns, 1st cl, in 2 parts, by Henry Beckett, Wolverhampton; construction lines, hill-drawing, foot/b'way, canal with towpath, waterbodies, houses (by shading), woods, parkland (in detail), orchards, hedge ownership, fence ownership, field gates, building names, mill, mill stream, dam, boundary trees and stones, open drain, windmill, grotto, lock house, bath house, township boundaries; a few bridges are named; the two parts appear to have been drawn by different hands, though their content is much the same; Part 1 has gummed to it a newspaper clipping of an advertisement of a meeting to make an agreement.

32/174 Pershall (township in parish of Eccleshall) SJ 809312
Apt 06.06.1840; 639a (639); Map 1838, 3 chns, by C.B. Ash; foot/b'way, waterbodies, woods, boat house, pits.

32/175 Pipe Ridware (parish) SK 093183
Apt 03.09.1840; 816a (all); Map 1841, 6 chns; waterbodies, houses, woods, building names, pits.

32/176 Podmore (township in parish of Eccleshall) SJ 784359
Apt 24.12.1838; 404a (404); Map 1837, 3 chns, by Ash and Son; foot/b'way, waterbodies, woods, marsh/bog, old fence.

32/177 Prestwood (township in parish of Ellaston) SK 102421
Apt 21.12.1844; 448a (?); Map 1846?, 6 chns, by C. Smith Jnr, Alton; canal with towpath and locks, waterbodies, woods, orchard.

32/178 Ramshorn (township in parish of Ellaston) SK 091442
Apt 14.09.1847; 1495a (?); Map 1848, 12 chns, by John Bromley, Derby; foot/b'way, waterbodies, woods, plantations, lordship boundaries (col).

32/179 Ranton or Ronton (township in parish of Ranton or Ronton) SJ 850240
Apt 12.09.1849; 738a (?); Map 1850, 4 chns, by S. Bate, Knutton, Newcastle, Staffs; foot/b'way, waterbodies, woods, landowners.

32/180 Rocester (parish) SK 110392
Apt 29.09.1848; 2122a (2105); Map 1849, 9 chns, in 2 parts, by C. Smith Junr, Alton, (tithable parts only; including village separately at 4 chns); foot/b'way, canal with towpath, waterbodies, woods, building names, township boundary.

32/181 Rolleston (township in parish of Rolleston) SK 235274
Apt 26.07.1837; 1528a (?); Map 1838, 6 chns, ? by J.B.H. Bennett, Tutbury, (tithable parts only); foot/b'way, waterbodies, woods, parkland, road names, rectory, lodge, hall, fishpond, osiers; colours apparently show tithe ownership, as explained in a faded note, struck through. Apt includes cropping, apparently for the year 1837.

32/182 Rugeley (parish) SK 038162
Apt 12.12.1840; 3412a (3411); Map 1841, 6 chns, in 4 parts, by George Adie, (tithable parts only; Brereton village at 3 chns, Rugeley town at 2 chns); canal with towpath, aqueduct, waterbodies, woods (named), plantations, parkland, building names, horse fair, furnace pool, mill.

32/183 Rushall (parish) SP 023999
Apt 15.11.1843; 1925a (1924); Map 1844?, 6 chns, in 2 parts (including enlargement of detail); foot/b'way, turnpike roads, toll gate, canal with towpath, waterbodies, woods, plantations, parkland, building names, road names, lime works, iron works, brick kiln, mill, parsonage, notable tree; colours show owners of great tithes.

32/184 Rushton Spencer (township in parish of Leek) SJ 935621
Apt 02.11.1852; 29a (?); Map 1853, 3 chns, by John Leech, Leek, (tithable part only); waterbodies, field boundary ownerships, building names.

32/185 Salt and Enson (township in parish of St Mary Stafford) SJ 952275
Apt 20.04.1838; 1645a (?); Map 1838?, 6 chns; waterbodies, woods, plantations, parkland, stone quarry, avenue of trees; border has quatrefoil and ball and grey dot-dash ornament.

32/186 Sandon (parish) SJ 957306
Apt 31.12.1838; 3640a (3640); Map 1844, 6 chns, by Geo. Adie; foot/b'way, canal with towpath and locks, waterbodies, woods, plantations, parkland, gardens, fence, building names, monument (by symbol), mill, toll gate; streams named.

32/187 Sedgley (parish) SO 920935
Apt 24.07.1845; 7364a (7364); Map 1843, 6 chns, by William Fowler and Son, Birmingham; hill-drawing, foot/b'way, canal with towpath and earthworks, reservoir, waterbodies, woods, building names, boundary stones, iron works, furnaces, mills, Roman Catholic Chapel, graveyard, toll gate; colour tints may indicate tithable status.

32/188 Seighford (parish) SJ 881250
Apt 23.12.1846; 2835a (4451); Map 1839, 6 chns, in 2 parts, (including 3-chn enlargement of detail); railway, foot/b'way, waterbodies, woods, orchards, building names, boundary bushes; tithe-free fields are mapped but not numbered.

32/189 Shareshill (parish) SJ 950070
Apt 26.01.1841; 1985a (1985); Map 1838, 6 chns, surveyed by Thos Peace, W'hampton, (tithable parts only); canal, waterbodies, houses, woods, field boundary ownerships, landowners, mill; colours show ownerships; border includes lattice effect and stiff leaves at corners.

32/190 Sheen (parish) SK 111618
Apt 31.12.1845; 2790a (2790); Map 1847?, 6 chns; woods.

32/191 Shenstone (parish) SK 099035
Apt 26.02.1839; 8452a (8451); Map 1838, 6 chns, by Josh Naden; foot/b'way, turnpike roads, toll gates, canal with towpath, waterbodies,

woods, plantations, parkland, gardens, fence, building names, road names, ice house, pump, gravel pit, pound, brick kiln, vicarage, mill, mill pool, township boundaries (col); streams and artificial channels are named.

32/192 Slindon (township in parish of Eccleshall) SJ 829322
Apt 25.03.1840; 582a (582); Map 1838, 3 chns, by C.B. Ash; railway, waterbodies, woods.

32/193 Stallington (township in parish of Stone) SJ 948400
Apt 16.10.1848; 1066a (?); Map 1850?, 3 chns; building names, windmill. Apt is by holding, and omits land use.

32/194 Standon (parish) SJ 814351
Apt 06.04.1838; 2571a (2570); Map 1839?, 3 chns, in 2 parts; foot/b'way, waterbodies, plantations (col), parkland, gardens, building names, mill.

32/195 Stanton (township in parish of Ellaston) SK 124463
Apt 20.08.1844; 2007a (?); Map 1847, 6 chns, by C. Smith Junr, Alton; waterbodies, woods, building names.

32/196 Statfold (parish) SK 234071 [Not listed]
Apt 19.07.1848; 8a (450); Map 1848?, 4 chns, (tithable part only); field names, 'Site of an ancient Public Carriage Way, Stopped by Order of Magistrates, Confirmed at the General Quarter Sessions'; pictorial church.

32/197 Stone (township in parish of Stone) SJ 912341
Apt 25.03.1846; 35a (?); Map 1851, 6 chns, by Samuel Bate, Newcastle, Staffordshire, (tithable part only); railways, canal with towpath, woods.

32/198 Stowe (parish) SK 024276 [Stowe-by-Chartley]
Apt 21.02.1850; 5133a (7080); Map 1850, 6 chns, by J. Wyley, High Onn, Stafford, (tithable parts only); railway, foot/b'way, canal with towpath, waterbodies, woods (col), marsh/bog (col), building names, castle, chapel.

32/199 Streethay (township in parish of St Michael Lichfield) SK 140109
Apt 26.06.1848; 857a (?); Map 1850?, 4 chns; railways and station, foot/b'way, occupation roads, turnpike roads, canal with towpaths, waterbodies, woods, orchards, gardens, building names, signpost (pictorial), bath.

32/200 Stretton (township in parish of Burton upon Trent) SK 260260
Apt 07.12.1847; 93a (?); Map 1848, 6 chns, ? by J.B.H. Bennett, Tutbury, (tithable parts only); railway, turnpike roads, toll gate, canal with towpath and aqueduct, woods, parkland, building names, weir, mills.

32/201 Stretton (township in parish of Penkridge) SJ 885115
Apt 17.12.1847; 59a (?); Map 1850?, 9 chns, (tithable parts only); woods, canal, aqueduct. Apt omits land use.

32/202 Sugnall Magna (township in parish of Eccleshall) SJ 799309 [Sugnall]
Apt 20.05.1846; 778a (778); Map 1841, 3 chns, by C.B. Ash; foot/b'way, waterbodies, woods, gardens, pits, rock, bath, temple, milestone.

32/203 Sugnall Parva (township in parish of Eccleshall) SJ 809317 [Sugnall]
Apt 07.03.1843; 390a (390); Map 1839, 3 chns, by Bate and Timmis; waterbodies, woods (col), orchard.

32/204 Swinfen (township in parish of Weeford) SK 133060 [Not listed]
Apt 03.12.1844; 1040a (?); Map 1849?, 6 chns; foot/b'way, turnpike roads, waterbodies, woods, plantations, parkland, orchards, fence, building names, avenue of trees.

32/205 Swynnerton (parish) SJ 842368
Apt 15.08.1848; 6529a (6529); Map 1849?, 6 chns, in 2 parts (including 1.5 chn enlargement of detail); railway, foot/b'way, waterbodies, woods (col), plantations (col), parkland, heath/moor, building names, mill; colours show townships.

32/206 Tatenhill and Callingwood (township in parish of Tatenhill) SK 200220
Apt 09.10.1837; 1215a (?); Map 1839, 6 chns, by J.B.H. Bennett, Tutbury; railway, foot/b'way, turnpike roads, canal with lock and towpath, waterbodies, woods, plantations, building names, rectory, mill and dam, glebe (col), township boundaries (col), forest gates. Apt includes cropping information.

32/207 Tettenhall (parish) SJ 870010
Apt 22.03.1849; 85a (7600); Map 1851, 6 chns, (tithable parts only); turnpike roads, waterbodies, woods, landowners.

32/208 Thorpe Constantine (parish) SK 255086
Apt 13.09.1839; 953a (all); Map 1839?, 3 chns; foot/b'way, waterbodies, woods, osiers, parkland, gardens, fence, field names, field acreages, ice house, rectory, mall, cess pool, glebe (col), drain, occupation road; scale-bar is ruler-like; border has ball and quatrefoil decoration.

32/209 Three Farms (township in parish of Eccleshall) SJ 848313 [Not listed]
Apt 12.12.1840; 802a (802); Map 1840, 6 chns; railway, foot/b'way, waterbodies, woods, parkland, pit (col).

32/210 Tillington (township) SJ 913255 [Not listed]
Apt 31.12.1840; 353a (947); Map 1840, 6 chns, by J.P. Lofthouse, (tithable parts only); railway, foot/b'way, ditch (named).

32/211 Tipton or Tibbiston (parish) SO 960930
Apt 30.04.1847; 2076a (3020); Map 1849, 4 chns, by William Fowler and Son, Birmingham, litho (by T. Underwood, Birmingham); hill-drawing, railway, foot/b'way, turnpike roads, canal with towpaths and locks, waterbodies, woods, parkland, iron works, furnaces, galvanised iron works, engine, pound, workhouse; hachured slopes may be spoil heaps. Apt omits most land use.

32/212 Tittensor (township in parish of Stone) SJ 870380
Apt 08.01.1846; 14a (?); Map 1850?, 3 chns, by S. Bate, Knutton, Newcastle-u-L, (tithable parts only, tinted); landowners, (named in title).

32/213 Tixall (parish) SJ 976230
Apt 11.12.1845; 2301a (2352); Map 1846?, 8 chns; hill-drawing, foot/b'way, canal, waterbodies, woods, plantations, parkland, building names, pit, canal with towpath, quarries, boat house, swivel bridge; border has quatrefoil and ball decoration. Apt includes cropping information.

32/214 Trentham (township in parish of Trentham) SJ 868408
Apt 31.12.1845; 6a (?); Map 1847, 9 chns, (tithable part only).

32/215 Trysull and Seisdon (parish) SO 845945
Apt 31.05.1850; 28a (3110); Map 1852, 6 chns, (tithable part only, tinted); field boundary ownerships, mill stream.

32/216 Tunstall (township in parish of Adbaston) SJ 772278
Apt 13.01.1841; 751a (751); Map 1839, 6 chns; waterbodies, woods, pit; woods are depicted by curious dot-like symbols, slightly smudged, and another style of smudging seems to indicate a quarry or pit.

32/217 Tutbury (parish) SK 205275
Apt 03.04.1840; 3227a (4001); Map 1841, 6 chns, ? by J.B.H. Bennett, Tutbury; hill-drawing, foot/b'way, waterbodies, woods (named), building names, road names, castle, vicarage, cotton mills, corn mill, mill stream, mill, dam, notable trees, weir, forest gates, osiers, bay-windows of mapmaker's house (area 39). Apt includes cropping information.

32/218 Uttoxeter (parish) SK 090330
Apt 28.09.1839; 8830a (8973); Map 1843, 6 chns, in 6 parts, by J. Treasure, Newport, Salop, (including 3-chn enlargement of detail, and 18-chn index, dated 1842); foot/b'way, turnpike roads, toll gates, canal with towpath, waterbodies, woods, plantations, parkland, building names, field names, workhouse, vicarage, mills, chapel.

32/219 Walsall (parish) SP 005995
Apt 13.09.1843; 8182a (8182); Map 1845?, 6 chns, in 3 parts (town mapped separately at 3 chns); turnpike roads and gate, canal with towpath and locks, waterbodies, building names, road names, workhouse, collieries (named), steam mill, iron works, gravel pit (by symbol), National School, heaths, commons, borough boundary. (The map in PRO IR 30 is a copy; the original map is in PRO IR 77/62.)

32/220 Walton (township in parish of Eccleshall) SJ 859276
Apt 21.11.1838; 1254a (1254); Map 1842, 6 chns, by J.P. Lofthouse, Hopton; hill-drawing, foot/b'way, waterbodies, woods (col), plantations (col), fences, building names, pits, stiles.

32/221 Walton (township in parish of Stone) SJ 895328
Apt 26.11.1844; 915a (?); Map 1845?, 6 chns, in 2 parts (including 2-chn enlargement of detail).

32/222 Water Eaton (township in parish of Penkridge) SJ 903110 [Not listed]
Apt 17.09.1846; 111a (?); Map 1850, 8 chns, copied by G. Taylor, Deanery, Wolverhampton, (tithable parts only); railway, canal with towpath, woods, heath/moor; tithable buildings are red, others are black.

32/223 Waterfall (parish) SK 081516
Apt 14.12.1844; 1606a (all); Map 1846, 3 chns; hill-drawing, foot/b'way, waterbodies, houses, woods, plantations, osiers, building names, limestone quarries, lime kilns, iron foundaries, paper mills, corn mill, school, pinfold, pit, copper mine shafts; quarries are shown by 'realistic' rock drawing.

32/224 Weeford (township in parish of Weeford) SK 133030
Apt 10.08.1843; 2520a (all); Map 1844, 9 chns; waterbodies, woods, plantations, fences, building names, toll gate, lodge; fields are not mapped, except for their junctions with roads and boundaries; colour bands accentuate areas; roads within holdings appear to be incompletely mapped. Apportionment is by ownerships, and no details are given of holdings, land use or field names, and nearly none of occupiers.

32/225 Wednesbury (parish) SO 987953
Apt 30.10.1844; 2176a (all); Map 1846, 3 chns, by J.G. Weddall, Howden; railways, foot/b'way, canal with towpath, waterbodies, open fields, toll gate.

32/226 Wednesfield (township in parish of Wolverhampton) SJ 958006
Apt 29.10.1840; 3538a (3538); Map 1842, 6 chns; railways and station, foot/b'way, turnpike roads, canal with towpath, waterbodies, woods, building names, chapel.

32/227 Weston under Lizard or Liziard (parish) SJ 808109 [Weston Under Lizard]
Apt 31.01.1839; 2398a (all); Map 1840, 9 chns, by Peter Potter Junr, Gorway House, Walsall; waterbodies, woods, parkland, building names.

32/228 Weston upon Trent (parish) SJ 979271 [Weston-on-Trent]
Apt 26.05.1842; 825a (all); Map 1844, 5 chns, ? by J.B.H. Bennett, Tutbury; foot/b'way, turnpike roads, canal with towpaths, waterbodies, industry, woods, fences, salt works; brooks are named.

32/229 Whitgreave (township in parish of St Mary Stafford) SJ 899289
Apt 11.12.1845; 1198a (?); Map 1846?, 6 chns; foot/b'way, waterbodies, woods (col), field boundary ownerships, toll gate, stiles; scale is ruler-like; border has quatrefoil and ball decoration. Apt includes cropping information.

32/230 Whitmore (parish) SJ 807413
Apt 10.08.1839; 1987a (2023); Map 1839, 6 chns, by Saml H. Ashdown, Uppington, Shrewsbury; railway and station, foot/b'way, waterbodies, houses, woods (named), parkland, gardens, field boundary ownerships, building names, rectory, rookery, boundary stones, heath.

32/231 Whittington (parish) SK 159060
Apt 23.09.1837; 2911a (2921); Map 1839?, 6 chns; foot/b'way, turnpike roads, canal with towpath, waterbodies, woods, fence, building names, road names, gravel pit, milestone, race course, grand stand, winning chair, betting chair, well, mill, heath.

32/232 Wichnor (chapelry in parish of Tattenhill) SK 177165 [Wychnor]
Apt 04.09.1845; 12a (?); Map 1846, 3 chns, by Thos Longhurst, (tithable part only); waterbodies, field names, forge.

32/233 Wigginton, including Cumberford Coton and Hopwas (township and hamlet in parish of Tamworth) SK 209069 [Wiggington]
Apt 24.12.1846; 24a (3470); Map 1850?, 8 chns, in 2 parts, (tithable parts only); railway, canal, landowners.

32/234 Wightwick (township in parish of Tettenhall) SO 870985
Apt 11.03.1840; 497a (all); Map 1841?, 6 chns; waterbodies, woods, canal with towpath.

32/235 Willenhall (township in parish of Wolverhampton) SO 969991
Apt 05.02.1841; 2051a (all); Map 1841, 3 chns, by Henry Beckett, Wolverhampton; hill-drawing, railways with earthworks, foot/b'way, canal with towpath and earthworks, proposed canal, waterbodies, woods, orchards, building names, road names, mills. Apt omits most land use.

32/236 Wolstanton (parish) SJ 850520 [Not listed]
Apt 20.08.1839; 10739a (10739); Map 1841, 8 chns, in 3 parts, (including 3-chn enlargement of detail; Tunstall mapped separately at 4 chns); railway, foot/b'way, canal with towpath, waterbodies, woods (named), houses (Tunstall only), building names, summer house, well, boundary marks, stiles, workhouse, collieries, bottle-kilns, mill, furnace, potteries, toll gate.

32/237 Wolverhampton (township in parish of Wolverhampton) SO 915985
Apt 29.10.1840; 2923a (3008); Map 1842, 6 chns, by Henry Beckett, Wolverhampton, (tithable part only); foot/b'way, canals with towpaths, waterbodies, woods, parkland, building names, road names, workhouse, mills, furnaces, iron works, works lodge, race course, grand stand, distance post, winning chair, deanery, burial ground, Roman Catholic Chapel.

32/238 Wombourn (district) SO 873928 [Wombourne]
Apt 31.10.1840; 1407a (?); Map 1841, 9 chns, 'copied from the Parish Map' by Long and Taylor (village also mapped at 2 chns); hill-drawing, foot/b'way, canal with towpath and locks, waterbodies, woods (col), field boundary ownerships, houses (village only), building names, road names, mills, vicarage, windmill; border has quatrefoil and ball decoration.

32/239 Woodhouses (township in parish of Mayfield) SK 147471 [Not listed]
Apt 07.08.1847; 26a (?); Map 1851?, 6 chns, (tithable part only, tinted).

32/240 Wootton (township in parish of Eccleshall) SJ 828273
Apt 21.11.1838; 785a (785); Map 1839, 6 chns, by J.P. Lofthouse, Hopton; waterbodies, woods, common.

32/241 Wootton (township in parish of Ellaston) SK 104456
Apt 20.08.1844; 1854a (?); Map 1845, 6 chns; hill-drawing, foot/b'way, waterbodies, woods, parkland, field names, hall, pit.

32/242 Worston (liberty in parish of St Mary, Stafford) SJ 879279 [Not listed]
Apt 11.12.1845; 170a (?); Map 1846?, 5 chns; railway, foot/b'way, waterbodies, woods, field boundary ownerships; border has quatrefoil and ball decoration. Apt includes cropping information.

32/243 Yarlet (liberty in parish of St Mary, Stafford) SJ 914293
Apt 11.12.1845; 399a (?); Map 1846, 8 chns; houses, woods, parkland, road cutting.

32/244 Yoxall (parish) SK 140201
Apt 27.06.1839; 3531a (4813); Map 1841?, 9 chns, in 10 parts, (including nine 4.5-chn enlargements of detail); waterbodies, woods, parkland.

Suffolk

PRO IR29 and IR30 33/1-487

522 tithe districts: 951,063 acres
486 tithe commutations: 876,180 acres
363 voluntary tithe agreements, 123 compulsory tithe awards,
1 corn rent annuity

Tithe and tithe commutation

Although there had been a few tithe commutations in association with parliamentary enclosure in the north-western part of Suffolk, 93 per cent of the county's tithe districts remained subject to tithes in 1836 and 209 districts (43 per cent of the total) were wholly tithable (Fig. 45). The main causes of tithe exemption in Suffolk were modus payments in lieu of tithes, the merger of tithes in the land, and exemption by prescription.

Assistant tithe commissioners and local tithe agents who worked in Suffolk are listed in Table 33.1. Arthur Biddell of Playford undertook the greatest number of tithe valuations (sixty-one) in addition to his work as an assistant tithe commissioner (Table 33.2).

Nearly 17 per cent of Suffolk apportionments are lithographed, a proportion only exceeded by Devon and Cornwall and a fact in striking contrast to all the adjoining counties. The influence of particular valuers may be an important explanation as a large number of the apportionments of districts valued by Arthur Biddell are lithographed.

Tithe maps

Suffolk has the highest proportion of first-class tithe maps in eastern England (21 per cent of districts) and construction lines are present on 13 per cent of second-class maps, suggesting that, as in Essex and Hertfordshire, a number of other tithe maps were intended as first-class but failed to pass the Tithe Commission's tests. As in all the east coast counties from the Thames to Flamborough Head, the greatest concentration of first-class maps in Suffolk is in the east of the county.

The progress of Suffolk tithe mapping follows the usual pattern with a peak of map production in 1838-40 (Table 33.4). The very last tithe commutation map is of a Suffolk tithe district. This map of part of Hemingstone is dated 1883 and is the only original tithe map based on Ordnance Survey 1:2500 mapping.

Suffolk tithe maps are drawn at a variety of scales from one inch to two chains to one inch to twelve chains. As in Essex but in contrast to Norfolk, 60 per cent of Suffolk maps are in the recommended scale range of one inch to three to four chains and 28 per cent of maps are at the widely favoured six-chain scale. As Table 33.3 shows, a number of Suffolk maps were drawn at rarely used scales; those at the 6.67-chain scale are drawn to an inch-related rather than a chain-related scale, whereas others may derive from older surveys in customary measure. Fourteen second-class maps are lithographed, including Wickham Market the original of which is sealed as first class.

The mapping of non-agricultural land use is more complete on Suffolk tithe maps than it is on those of many counties. As usual the two land uses most consistently recorded are woodland (on 75 per cent of the maps) and parkland (on 23 per cent). Additionally 6 per cent distinguish arable and grass, 20 per cent depict gardens, 6 per cent show heath and moor and over 25 per cent portray orchards. A few maps show reed beds by distinctive symbol, for example Easton Bavents. The proportion of maps which distinguish houses from other buildings (80 per cent) is unusually high.

Some 394 Suffolk tithe maps in the Public Record Office collection can be attributed to a particular map-maker; this is a proportion of 81 per cent and well above the national average. Lenny and Croft of Bury St Edmunds mapped about an eighth of the county and worked mainly around Bury St Edmunds itself, producing second-class maps, usually at the six-chain scale, in a distinctive style. They also worked south of Lowestoft where they made a number of first-class maps. Richard Barnes was also active around Lowestoft, though mostly to the north of the town and all but two of his twenty-four maps were sealed as first class. His is possibly the most austere style of any of the more prolific first-class surveyors. He often omitted shading for buildings, for example, which can make his maps hard to read. Nearly as prolific, though producing more second-class maps, was Bland Hood Galland of Yoxford, a former employee of the Ordnance Survey of Ireland. His map of Orford is unusual in that the angles of the principal triangles are given on the map. James Smy of Saxmundham produced a number of maps with woods shown by dark blue symbols on a green tint. Smy was one of several Suffolk map-makers who used pink bands rather than conventional braces to link enclosures which were part of a single tithe area.

Suffolk tithe maps are somewhat more decorative than those of counties to the south or west. Many Suffolk maps show churches and wind or drainage mills pictorially and north pointers are sometimes surmounted with plumes or crowns, a feature reminiscent of Welsh maps. A few maps have title decoration: on the map of Burgh a small boy holds a fountain, and on that of Kedington drawing instruments are combined with representations of Britannia and a sheep. On the map of Sternfield there is an insect flying above the title.

Fig. 45 Suffolk: tithe district boundaries.

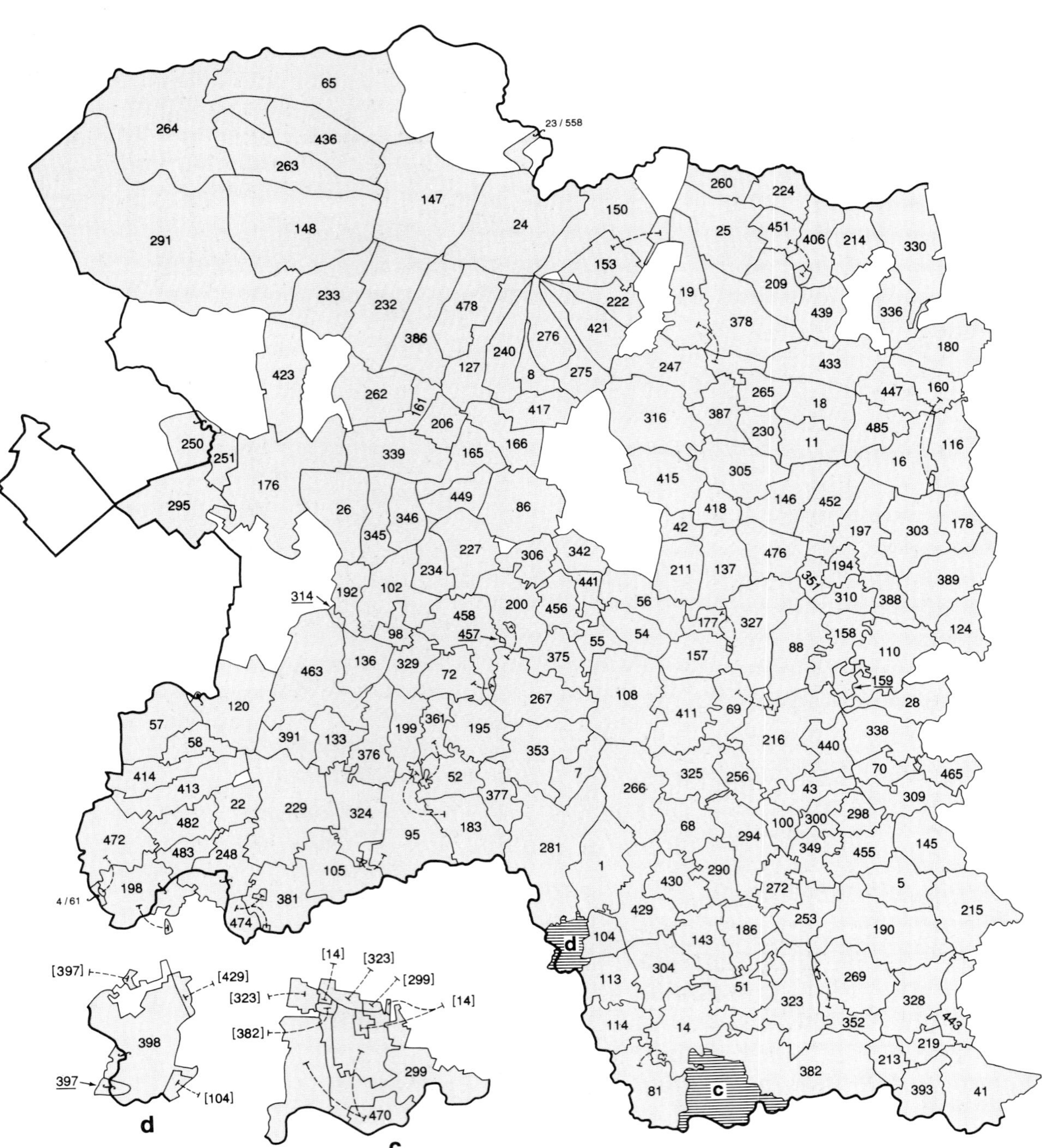

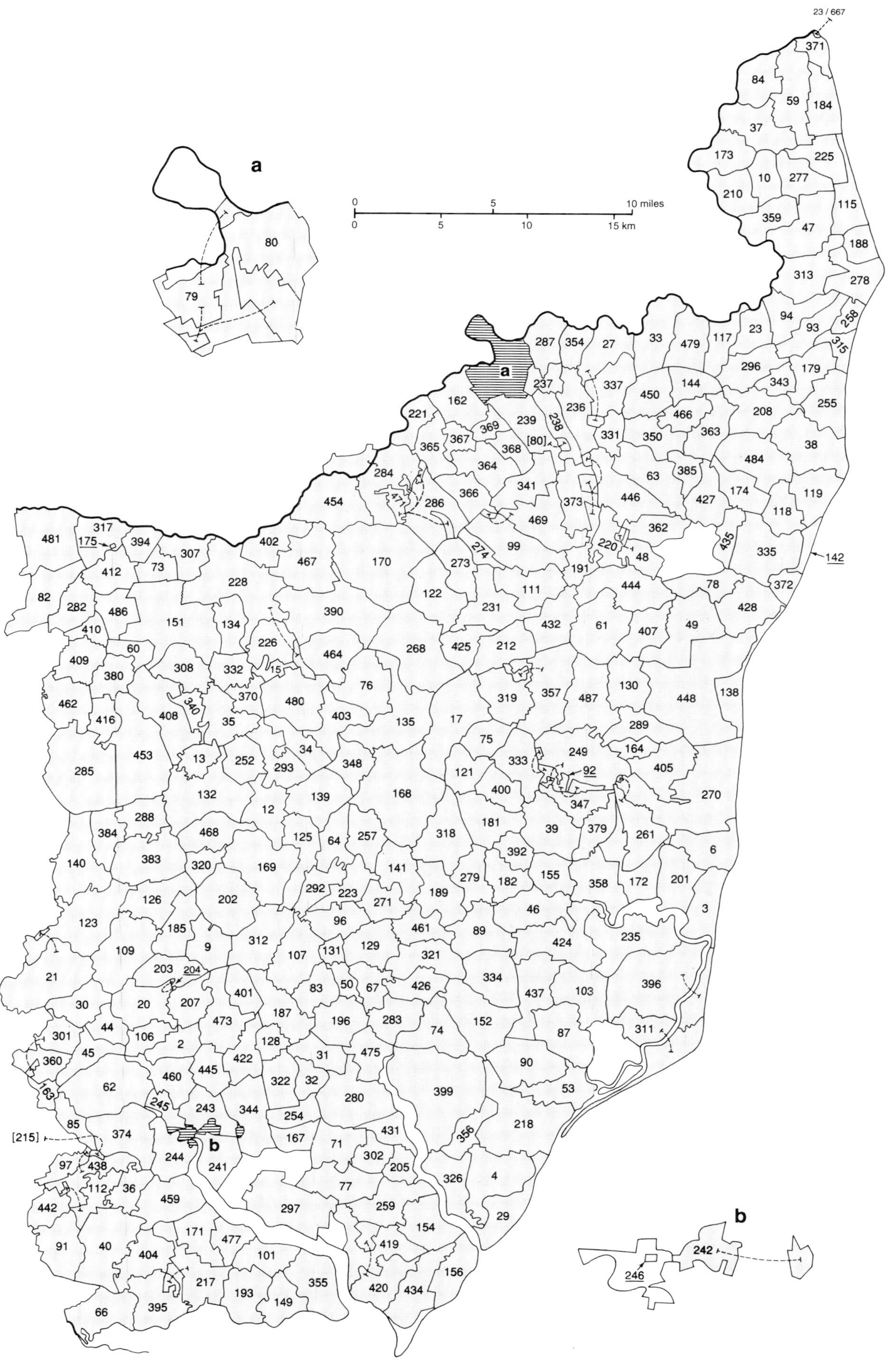
23 / 667
371
84 59 184
37
173 225
10 277
210
115
359
47
188
313
278
a
80
79
0 5 10 miles
0 5 10 15 km
94 93 258
23 315
287 354 27 33 479 117
296 179
a
343
237 337 450 144 255
162 236 208
221 466 363
369 239 238
367 350 38
365 368 [80] 331 484
364 63 385
284 471 286 366 341 373 446 427 174 119
118
454 469 362
99 220 435
481 317 175 394 307 402 467 170 274 48 335
273 142
412 73 228 122 191 444 78
82 231 111 372
282 486 390 428
151 134 432 61 49
410 407
226 268 425 212
60
409 380 308 332 464
15
340 370 480 76 319 357 487 130 448 138
462 416 408 35 403 135 17
289
75 249
453 34 164
13 252 293 348 333 405
285 121 92
132 139 168 400 270
347
12 288
384 468 125 64 257 181 39 379 261
318 6
383 392
140 320 169 141 279 182 155 358 172 201
126 292 223 189
202 271
3
123 185 96 461 46 424 235
9 312 89
109 129
107 131 321
21 203 204 334
83 50 67 426 396
30 20 207 401 437 103
196
473 187 283 152
44 106 74 87
301 311
45 2 128
31 475
360 422
445 90
62 460 322 32
163 280 399
53
245 243 344
85
254
374 218
[215] 167 71
356
b
431
244
302
97 438 241 205
326 4
112 36 77
442 459 297 259
29
b
154
171
91 40 477 419
242
404 101
156
246
217 355
193 420 434
66 395 149

Table 33.1. *Agreements and awards for commutation of tithes in Suffolk*

Assistant commissioner/ local tithe agent	*Number of agreements**	*Number of awards*
James Drage Merest	64	108
Henry Bertram Gunning	86	0
Roger Kynaston	49	0
William Heard	35	0
John Pickering	24	0
Arthur Biddell	21	0
John Mee Mathew	19	0
F. Browne Browne	13	0
Horace William Meteyard	12	0
Thomas Smith Woolley	12	0
Thomas Turner	7	0
Tithe Commissioners	0	7
Thomas Sutton	6	0
Francis Offley Martin	0	5
? Mears	5	0
Henry Dixon	1	0
William Downes	1	0
Charles Howard	0	1
Thomas James Tatham	0	1

*Computed from the number of extant reports on tithe agreements in the tithe files [PRO IR 18].

Table 33.2. *Tithe valuers and tithe map-makers in Suffolk*

Name and address (in Suffolk unless indicated)	*Number of districts*	*Acreage*
Tithe valuers		
Arthur Biddell, Playford	61	104,886
John Medows Rodwell, Little Livermere	28	51,340
William Girling, Peasenhall	28	43,382
James Hillen, Blaxhall	27	46,172
Robert Pratt, Surrey Street, Norwich, Norfolk	24	46,178
John Issacson, Clare	21	40,217
Arthur Blencow, Shimpling	19	29,759
Jonathan Howlett, Wissett	18	29,363
Daniel Riches, Frostenden	18	24,457
William Adams, Great Barton	17	36,894
Charles Etheredge, Starston, Norfolk	17	32,874
Henry Preston, Worlingworth	17	29,394
John Fox, Coddenham	17	24,386
Benjamin Colchester, Ipswich	15	26,656
Edward Cook, Stratford St Mary	14	28,280
John Spurling, Shotley	13	22,825
James Josselyn, Copdock	12	18,101
Others [50]	120	247,016

Table 33.2. *(cont.)*

Name and address (in Suffolk unless indicated)	*Number of districts*	*Acreage*
Attributed tithe map-makers		
Lenny and Croft, Bury St Edmunds	42	71,952
Richard Barnes, Lowestoft	24	34,694
Bland Hood Galland, Yoxford	22	41,564
Benjamin Moulton, Woodbridge	20	35,472
W. and A. Ruffell, Kersey	17	31,513
Spencer L. Bransby, Ipswich	14	24,145
R. E. Sheldrake and J. McLachlan, Colchester, Essex	13	27,012
Richard Payne, Bury St Edmunds	13	23,498
James Smy, Saxmundham	13	20,459
John Stigoll, Bramfield/Linstead Parva	12	24,615
Benjamin Spurling, Burgh	12	18,910
Joseph Manning, Norwich, Norfolk	11	19,777
George Baker and Jno. Crickmay, Bungay	11	13,511
J. Hasell, Sudbury	10	17,666
S. W. Parkes, Ipswich	10	14,209
W. S. Grimwade, Wetheringsett	10	14,030
Others [42]	140	281,645

Table 33.3. *The tithe maps of Suffolk: scales and classes*

Scale in chains/inch	*All maps*		*First Class*		*Second Class*	
	Number	*Acreage*	*Number*	*Acreage*	*Number*	*Acreage*
>3	2	655	1	642	1	13
3	242	371,126	81	129,664	161	241,462
3.16	1	14	0	0	1	14
4	50	90,083	20	36,525	30	53,558
5	10	21,869	1	5,349	9	16,520
5.3	1	1,158	0	0	1	1,158
6	136	250,922	0	0	136	250,922
6.67, 7, 7.2, 7.5	9	23,367	0	0	9	23,367
8	22	58,838	0	0	22	58,838
<8	13	58,148	0	0	13	58,148
TOTAL	486	876,180	103	172,180	383	704,000

Table 33.4. *The tithe maps of Suffolk: dates*

	<1837	*1837*	*1838*	*1839*	*1840*	*1841*	*1842*	*1843*	*1844*	*1845*	*1846*	*1847*	*1848*	*>1848*
All maps	1	27	78	130	80	39	30	21	16	13	24	4	6	14
1st class	0	2	14	31	12	15	9	6	3	4	7	0	0	0
2nd class*	1	25	64	99	68	24	21	15	13	9	17	4	6	14

*Three second-class tithe maps of Suffolk in the Public Record Office collection are undated.

Suffolk

33/1 Acton (parish) TL 892464
Apt 03.04.1839; 2730a (all); Map 1839, 8 chns, in 2 parts, revised by George Dring, Melford; waterbodies, woods, parkland, building names, milestone (pictorial), heath; north pointer has plumes.

33/2 Akenham (parish) TM 156493
Apt 18.08.1837; 999a (all); Map 1837, 3 chns, by Benjn Spurling; waterbodies, houses, woods (col), orchards (col), field boundary ownerships, pit (col), boundary trees.

33/3 Aldborough (parish) TM 459570 [Aldeburgh]
Apt 26.05.1846; 1783a (1832); Map 1846, 3 chns; waterbodies, woods, beach, pits, windmills (by symbol); tithe-free buildings are shown without infill.

33/4 Alderton (parish) TM 340416
Apt 04.05.1840; 2543a (2543); Map 1840, 4 chns, 1st cl, by Benj. Moulton, Woodridge; construction lines, trig points (named), waterbodies, houses, woods, heath/moor, sallows (by symbol).

33/5 Aldham (parish) TM 043451
Apt 31.12.1845; 1745a (1744); Map 1839, [3 chns], in 3 parts surveyed by R.E. Sheldrake, Hadleigh; foot/b'way, waterbodies, houses, woods (col, named), orchards (col), gardens (col), building names, landowners, mill, boundary mereing, trees and stones, rectory.

33/6 Aldringham with Thorpe (parishes) TM 460605
Apt 04.05.1840; 1737a (1783); Map 1839, 3 chns, 1st cl, by James Smy, Saxmundham; construction lines, waterbodies, houses, plantations (col), high water mark, pits, parish boundary; pink banding is used for some bracing.

33/7 Alpheton (parish) TL 884508
Apt 09.02.1839; 1203a (all); Map 1839, 3 chns, surveyed by William Borley; construction lines, waterbodies, houses, woods, plantations, orchards.

33/8 Ampton (parish) TL 864712
Apt 01.05.1839; 737a (all); Map 1840, 6 chns, by Lenny and Croft, Bury St Edmunds; waterbodies, houses, plantations, parkland, gardens, fence ownership, gravel pit, overfall, boundary oak.

33/9 Ashbocking (parish) TM 173545
Apt 20.02.1838; 1409a (all); Map 1838, 4 chns, 'Compiled from Estate Maps' by S.L. Bransby, Ipswich; waterbodies, houses, woods, windmill (pictorial); pictorial church.

33/10 Ashby (parish) TM 492996 [Not listed]
Apt 15.02.1839; 1110a (1109); Map 1843, 3 chns, 1st cl, by Richard Barnes, Lowestoft; houses, boundary trees (pictorial).

33/11 Great Ashfield (parish) TM 003671
Apt 30.12.1845; 1546a (1546); Map 1846, 5 chns, by Lenny and Croft, Bury; waterbodies, houses, woods (named), plantations, parkland, orchards, gardens, fence ownership, building names, road names, private roads, springs, pound, brick kiln.

33/12 Ashfield cum Thorpe (parish) TM 210625
Apt 24.07.1837; 1566a (all); Map 1837, 6 chns, litho (Standidge), by Gilbert and Tayspill, Colchester; foot/b'way, waterbodies, woods, plantations, orchards, building names, ruined church.

33/13 Aspall (parish) TM 172652
Apt 26.03.1842; 835a (all); Map 1838, 3 chns, surveyed by W.S. Grimwade, litho; waterbodies, houses, woods, parkland, orchards; roads, buildings and water are hand coloured.

33/14 Assington (parish) TL 938383
Apt 19.12.1837; 2953a (all); Map 1837, 6 chns, in 3 parts, 'corrected' from the enclosure map by Newton and Woodrow, Norwich, (including one part at 8 chns); waterbodies, houses, woods (named), parkland, gardens, landowners (col); pictorial church. Apt omits land use.

33/15 Athelington or Allington (parish) TM 212708
Apt 31.08.1837; 487a (487); Map 1838, [6 chns]; waterbodies, houses, churchyard, holdings (col).

33/16 Bacton (parish) TM 050670
Apt 12.06.1839; 2205a (2204); Map 1839, 3 chns, by J. Manning, Norwich; waterbodies, houses, woods (col), parkland, arable (col), grassland (col), windmill (pictorial), greens. Apt omits field names.

33/17 Badingham (parish) TM 307678
Apt 10.09.1838; 3172a (3172); Map 1839, 4 chns, surveyed by Bland H. Galland, C.E.; waterbodies, houses, woods.

33/18 Badwell Ash (parish) TM 006690
Apt 02.04.1839; 1860a (1860); Map 1838, 6 chns; woods, holding boundaries (col).

33/19 Bardwell (parish) TL 943748
Apt 25.05.1838; 3143a (3144); Map 1839, 6 chns, litho (Standidge); foot/b'way, turnpike roads, waterbodies, houses, woods, gardens, building names, road names, meeting houses, parsonage, watermill; pictorial church; bridge named; boundary corners are named.

33/20 Barham (parish) TM 137515
Apt 30.03.1844; 1807a (1806); Map surveyed in 1840, 3 chns, 'Working Plan', by Sheldrake and McLachlan, Colchester; construction lines, foot/b'way, turnpike roads and gate, waterbodies, houses, woods, parkland, building names, road names, river locks, workhouse, boundary marks and trees, statue, milestones, green.

33/21 Barking cum Needham and Darmsden (parish) TM 078534
Apt 08.06.1841; 3165a (all); Map surveyed in 1841, 3 chns, in 3 parts, by J. McLachlan, Stowmarket; construction lines, waterbodies, woods (col), boundary trees, fishpond, river locks, ox-bows, hall, tye gate; built-up parts generalised and tinted.

33/22 Barnardiston (parish) TL 715495 [Not listed]
Apt 21.03.1846; 1100a (all); Map 1848, 3 chns, by J. Hasall, Sudbury; foot/b'way, waterbodies, houses, woods (col), plantations (col), gardens (col), field boundary ownerships, building names, marker trees, cross (by symbol); pictorial church.

33/23 Barnby (parish) TM 482908
Apt 22.04.1839; 1100a (1099); Map 1846, 3 chns, 1st cl; construction lines, waterbodies. Apt omits some field names.

33/24 Barnham (parish) TL 860780
Apt 15.07.1837; 5185a (all); Map 1840, 6.67 chns, 'Revised and Drawn' by Sheldrake and McLachlan, Colchester; waterbodies, houses, farmyards, woods (col), plantations (col), parkland, arable (col), grassland (col), orchards, gardens (col), heath/moor (col), hedge ownership, fence ownership, field boundary ownerships, ruined church (named in gothic), windmill (by symbol), pit, drive (col).

33/25 Barnington and Coney Weston (parishes) TL 956779
Apt 08.04.1842; 2927a (all); Map 1843, 6 chns, in 2 parts, by Pratt and Son, Norwich; waterbodies, houses, woods.

33/26 Barrow (parish) TL 770640
Apt 06.04.1839; 2666a (all); Map surveyed in 1839-40, 3 chns, by J.F. Clark, Newmarket; construction lines, waterbodies, woods (col), open fields, field boundary ownerships, field gates, pit (col). Apt omits most field names.

33/27 Barsham (parish) TM 397899
Apt 11.03.1839; 1871a (all); Map 1839, 3 chns, 1st cl, by Chickmay and Beales, Beccles; construction lines, hill-drawing, foot/b'way, waterbodies, houses, woods, orchards, landowners, beer shop, private roads, pit, glebe, 'town land', common.

33/28 Battisford (parish) TM 052542
Apt 30.04.1842; 1543a (1542); Map 1842, 8 chns, from an enclosure survey of 1812, revised by John McLachlan, Stowmarket; waterbodies, building names, grass in mixed-cult-ivation fields (by annotation).

33/29 Bawdsey (parish) TM 349399
Apt 31.03.1843; 1745a (2069); Map 1841, 4 chns, by Benjn Moulton, Woodbridge; construction lines, trig points (named), waterbodies, houses, woods, plantations, martello towers, cliff.

33/30 Baytham (parish) TM 102515 [Baylham]
Apt 22.01.1841; 1332a (1332); Map 1840, 3 chns, by Michl McDermott, Ipswich; canal, waterbodies, houses, woods, residual open fields, mill.

33/31 Great Bealings (parish) TM 238488
Apt 07.10.1839; 1034a (1029); Map 1838, 3 chns, 1st cl, by R.E. Sheldrake and J. McLachlan, Colchester; construction lines, foot/b'way, waterbodies, houses, woods, plantations (by Dawson's symbol), orchards, building names, windmill (by symbol), boundary trees, parsonage, glebe; legend explains use of green bands to brace some farmyards, etc.

33/32 Little Bealings (parish) TM 232473
Apt 16.11.1841; 765a (all); Map 1844?, 3 chns, by S.L. Bransby, Ipswich; waterbodies, houses, woods (col), grassland (col); pictorial church.

33/33 Beccles (parish) TM 430908
Apt 09.05.1840; 948a (1892); Map 1840?, 3 chns, (tithable parts only); waterbodies, houses; yellow bands are used for bracing; map has signatures, signifying adoption.

33/34 Bedfield (parish) TM 227664
Apt 30.06.1841; 1269a (1268); Map 1842?, 6 chns; waterbodies, houses, woods, greens.

33/35 Bedingfeld (parish) TM 183683 [Bedingfield]
Apt 26.02.1839; 1753a (1753); Map 1839?, [6 chns]; waterbodies, houses, greens.

33/36 Belstead (parish) TM 127410
Apt 14.08.1845; 1023a (all); Map 1846, 3 chns, by W.S. Grimwade; railway, foot/b'way, waterbodies, houses, woods (named).

33/37 Belton (parish) TG 485023
Apt 16.04.1839; 2059a (2059); Map 1840, 3 chns; waterbodies, windpumps (by symbol); pictorial church.

33/38 Benacre (parish) TM 517841
Apt 02.05.1840; 2595a (1660); Map 1840, 5 chns, by Lenny and Croft, Bury St Edmds; foot/b'way, turnpike roads and gate, waterbodies, houses, plantations, parkland, heath/moor, fences, building names, sluice, lodge, reeds, beach, drains; pictorial church.

33/39 Benhall (parish) TM 371619 [Benhall Green]
Apt 10.06.1845; 2156a (2156); Map 1846?, 4 chns, 1st cl; waterbodies, houses, brickworks, pits.

33/40 Bentley (parish) TM 118375
Apt 16.02.1838; 2801a (all); Map surveyed November 1836, 4 chns, by John Spurling, Shotley; waterbodies, farmyards (col), woods (col, by Dawson's symbol), arable (col), grassland (col), field boundary ownerships, glebe, windmill (pictorial); pictorial church.

33/41 East Bergholt (parish) TM 085348
Apt 30.12.1837; 3064a (3063); Map 1838, 3 chns, 'enlarged from the original Survey' by John Spurling, Shotley, Suffolk; waterbodies, houses, woods (col), arable (col), grassland (col); pictorial church. Apt omits land use.

33/42 Beyton (parish) TL 938632
Apt 08.06.1837; 600a (625); Map copied 10 March 1837, 3 chns, by P. Baker, Woolpit; construction lines, waterbodies, houses, woods (col), arable (col), grassland (col), orchards, gardens (col), fences, road acreages.

33/43 Bildestone (parish) TL 995495 [Bildeston]
Apt 05.03.1839; 1289a (all); Map 1839, 3 chns, in 2 parts, 'Working Plan' by W. and A. Ruffell; construction lines, waterbodies, houses.

33/44 Great Blakenham (parish) TM 117504
Apt 24.03.1838; 869a (869); Map 1839, 3 chns, by Benjn Spurling; construction lines, waterbodies, houses, woods, field boundary ownerships, river lock, pits.

33/45 Little Blakenham (parish) TM 103485
Apt 12.06.1839; 1054a (1054); Map 1839, 6 chns, by S.W. Parkes, Ipswich; waterbodies, houses, woods, oxbows; leaves and wheatear decorate north pointer.

33/46 Blaxhall (parish) TM 360570
Apt 15.07.1837; 1975a (1975); Map 3 chns, 1st cl, 'Surveyed in December 1838 for J. Smy, Land Surveyor, by Clinton, Dickinson, Purvis and Merrey'; construction lines, trig points (named), waterbodies, houses, woods, fences, fort, pit, defaced boundaries; colour bands may show holdings.

33/47 Blundeston and Flixton (parishes) TM 516966
Apt 31.01.1837; 2176a (2375); Map 1841, 3 chns, 1st cl, by Richard Barnes, Lowestoft; construction lines, parish boundary.

33/48 Blyford (parish) TM 420773
Apt 03.02.1843; 339a (947); Map 1837, 3 chns, 1st cl, by W.G. Jones, Loddon, Norfolk; construction lines, waterbodies, houses, fences, field boundary ownerships, field gates.

33/49 Blythburgh (parish) TM 447741
Apt 01.03.1841; 2578a (?); Map 1841, 8 chns, copied by Pratt and Son, Norwich; houses.

33/50 Boulge (parish) TM 254530
Apt 06.04.1838; 545a (545); Map 1837, 3 chns, by Benjn Moulton, Woodbridge; construction lines, waterbodies, houses (by shading), woods, orchards, gardens, field names, field acreages; there is a note by the valuer about renumbering of some fields following adoption of the map.

33/51 Boxford and Hadleigh (parish and hamlet) TL 962400
Apt 29.12.1841; 1820a (1820); Map 6 chns, in 2 parts, 'Copied from an old Survey and Modernized to the year 1840' by Gilbert and Tayspill, Colchester, (includes 3-chn enlargement of detail); waterbodies, woods, hamlet boundary.

33/52 Boxted (parish) TL 820505
Apt 10.10.1839; 1367a (all); Map 1840, 3 chns, surveyed by William Borley, Alpheton; foot/b'way, waterbodies, houses, woods, plantations, osiers, parkland, orchards, windmill (pictorial), private roads (uncoloured).

33/53 Boyton (parish) TM 380470
Apt 04.04.1843; 1534a (all); Map 1841, 4 chns, 1st cl, 'Surveyed by Henry Battly for J. Smy'; construction lines, waterbodies, houses, pits.

33/54 Bradfield St Clare (parish) TL 914579
Apt 13.06.1840; 1428a (1428); Map 1842?, 6 chns, by William Browne, Norwich; waterbodies, houses, woods, parkland, boundary trees and stones.

33/55 Bradfield Combust (parish) TL 893573
Apt 28.02.1838; 819a (818); Map 1838, 3 chns, in 2 parts; waterbodies, houses, woods (col), parkland, building names, boundary trees and stones, ice house, brick kiln, meeting house, avenue of trees.

33/56 Bradfield St George (parish) TL 919593
Apt 19.04.1844; 1984a (1984); Map 1843, 6 chns, by William Browne, Norwich; waterbodies, houses, woods, plantations, parkland, road names, boundary trees and post, green.

33/57 Great Bradley (parish) TL 677534
Apt 01.08.1842; 2281a (all); Map 1842, 6 chns; waterbodies, houses, woods, field boundary ownerships, hall, mill, greens.

33/58 Little Bradley (parish) TL 688524
Apt 16.01.1840; 958a (957); Map 1839, 3 chns, by John French; foot/b'way, waterbodies, houses, farmyards, orchards (col), gardens (col), field boundary ownerships; north pointer is crimson and yellow.

33/59 Bradwell (parish) TG 506042
Apt 01.05.1839; 2301a (2383); Map 1841, 3 chns, 1st cl, by Richard Barnes, Lowestoft; construction lines, houses, windmill (pictorial); pictorial church.

33/60 Braiseworth (parish) TM 131719
Apt 13.05.1839; 721a (all); Map 1838, 6 chns, by J. Manning; waterbodies, houses, woods, grassland (col), glebe (yellow band).

33/61 Bramfield (parish) TM 399733
Apt 21.03.1840; 2547a (all); Map 1841, 6 chns, by Jno. Stigall, Bramfield; houses, woods, windmill (by symbol).

33/62 Bramford (parish) TM 119468
Apt 23.02.1846; 3225a (3226); Map 1848?, 8 chns; railway, waterbodies, houses, woods (col). Apt omits land use.

33/63 Brampton (parish) TM 427821
Apt 22.02.1839; 2003a (2002); Map 1838, 3 chns, ? by Benjamin Spurling; foot/b'way, houses, farmyards, woods (col), arable (col), grassland (col), gardens, field boundary ownerships.

33/64 Brandeston (parish) TM 246607
Apt 06.03.1844; 1234a (all); Map 1838, 3 chns; waterbodies, woods, orchards, brickworks, sand pit, hall; most buildings are shown in outline only.

33/65 Brandon (parish) TL 752850
Apt 21.08.1838; 6759a (6759); Map 1838, 3 chns, by W.H. Young, Mildenhall; construction lines, turnpike roads, waterbodies, houses, plantations, parkland, orchards, gardens, marsh/bog (col), heath/moor, fence ownership, building names, road names, drainage tunnel, pit, coal yard, roadside waste (col).

33/66 Brantham (parish) TM 116341
Apt 08.12.1837; 1922a (all); Map 1838, 3 chns, by Benjn Spurling, Burgh; waterbodies, houses, woods (col), arable (col), grassland (col), marsh/bog (col), field boundary ownerships, windpump (by symbol), embankment, boundary trees, drains.

33/67 Bredfield (parish) TM 268528
Apt 07.02.1838; 1068a (1067); Map 1838?, 6 chns; waterbodies, houses, woods, parkland, orchards. [The copy in PRO IR 30 was reinked in 1923.]

33/68 Brent Eleigh (parish) TL 939489
Apt 11.05.1838; 1618a (1617); Map 1839, 3 chns, revised by William Borley, Alpheton, Suffolk; waterbodies, houses, woods, plantations, osiers (by symbol), windmill (by symbol). Apt omits land use.

33/69 Brettenham (parish) TL 963539
Apt 12.02.1844; 1559a (all); Map 1844?, 6 chns, by John Barnes; waterbodies, houses, woods, plantations, parkland, orchards, gardens, windmill (pictorial), reeds, avenue of trees, glebe; title and north pointer are brightly coloured.

33/70 Bricett (parish) TM 039506 [Great Bricett]
Apt 29.11.1841; 915a (all); Map surveyed in 1838, 3 chns, by W. Ruffell; waterbodies, woods, estate names and boundaries (col).

33/71 Brightwell (parish) TM 249437
Apt 09.06.1842; 30a (965); Map 1849?, 3 chns, (tithable parts only).

33/72 Brockley (parish) TL 822557 [Brockley Green]
Apt 30.04.1846; 1566a (1565); Map 1845, 3 chns, by W.W. Cawston; waterbodies, houses, woods (col), building names, windmill (by symbol), greens (col), roadside waste (col); hand and arms surmount north pointer.

33/73 Brome (parish) TM 145765 [Not listed]
Apt 07.05.1839; 893a (892); Map 1837, 3 chns, by J. Manning, Norwich; waterbodies, houses, woods, plantations, parkland, orchards, avenue of trees, modus lands (green), glebe (yellow); table summarises contents.

33/74 Bromeswell (parish) TM 310485
Apt 12.04.1843; 1803a (all); Map 1844?, 3 chns, by Michl McDermott; construction lines, houses, woods, boundary trees, osiers (by symbol). Apt omits land use.

33/75 Bruisyard (parish) TM 331666
Apt 22.01.1841; 282a (1126); Map 1839, 8 chns, by Jno. Stigall, (tithable parts only in detail); foot/b'way, houses, windmill (pictorial); the owner is named in the title.

33/76 Brundish (parish) TM 268697
Apt 26.01.1841; 2077a (2077); Map 1840, 6 chns, litho (Standidge); waterbodies, houses (by shading), woods, building names, road names, green.

33/77 Bucklesham (parish) TM 251415
Apt 12.11.1841; 1822a (all); Map 1838, 6 chns; houses, woods, osiers (by symbol), orchards, heath/moor, pits; pictorial church; meaning of green band is uncertain.

33/78 Bulcamp (parish) TM 453763
Apt 30.01.1849; 13a (?); Map 1850, 2 chns, (tithable parts only, tinted); field gate, landowners, workhouse, ford, river lock.

33/79 Bungay St Mary (parish) TM 336899 [Not listed]
Apt 20.10.1848; 596a (758); Map 1847, 6 chns, by Geo. Baker, Bungay, (tithable parts only in detail); foot/b'way, waterbodies, houses, castle, sand pits.

33/80 Bungay Trinity (parish) TM 346890 [Not listed]
Apt 31.07.1844; 1332a (1332); Map 1845?, 6 chns, in 2 parts, by Geo. Baker, Bungay; waterbodies, houses, mills; green bands are used for some bracing.

33/81 Bures St Mary (parish) TL 920350 [Bures]
Apt 28.02.1838; 2543a (?); Map 1837, 3 chns, by John King and Son, Saffron Walden; waterbodies, houses, woods, osiers (by symbol), common meadows (named), hedge ownership, building names, churchyard, green lanes (col).

33/82 Burgate (parish) TM 079751
Apt 26.04.1838; 2076a (2076); Map 1840?, 6 chns; waterbodies, houses, woods (col), orchards (col), glebe (green).

33/83 Burgh (parish) TM 235523
Apt 12.11.1838; 1201a (1201); Map [4 chns], surveyed in May 1823, and 'Resurveyed and Corrected' in January 1839 by B. Spurling; waterbodies, woods (col), field boundary ownerships, road names, windmill (pictorial), glebe; pictorial church; title is in oval cartouche, decorated with leaves and chain and surmounted by a small boy holding a bifurcating jet of water.

33/84 Burgh Castle (parish) TG 482050
Apt 15.07.1840; 1497a (1496); Map 1842, 3 chns, 1st cl, by Richard Barnes, Lowestoft; construction lines, gardens, drainage mill (pictorial); pictorial church; buildings are shown in outline only.

33/85 Burstall (parish) TM 096445
Apt 14.02.1846; 766a (766); Map 1839, 6 chns, by Richard and Frederick Fenning; waterbodies, houses, woods (col), gardens (col), arable (col), grassland (col).

33/86 St Mary and St James, Bury St Edmunds (parishes) TL 860644 [Bury St Edmunds]
Apt 02.04.1845; 1567a (2934); Map 1845, 3 chns; foot/b'way, waterbodies, woods (col), osiers (by symbol), gardens (col), marsh/bog, heath/moor, fence ownership, road names, common meadows (named), botanic gardens, churchyard, chapels, Quaker Meeting House, grammar school, school, hospital, assembly rooms, guildhall, shire hall, theatre, workhouses, gaol, house of correction, pest houses, gasworks, windmills (both pictorially and by symbol), limekiln, pits, boundary stones, parish boundary, footbridge (by Dawson's symbol).

33/87 Butley (parish) TM 378498
Apt 12.08.1845; 1942a (all); Map 1846, 12 chns, 'Revised from Johnson's Survey' by Benj. Moulton; waterbodies, houses, woods; pictorial church.

33/88 Buxhall (parish) TL 999572
Apt 26.07.1837; 2523a (all); Map 1839, 3 chns, 'Surveyed and Mapped' by John Barnes; construction lines, glebe, foot/b'way, waterbodies, houses, woods, drift way, osiers and sallows (by symbol), isolated trees (col), grass in fields of mixed cultivation (by annotation).

33/89 Campsey Ash (parish) TM 330560
Apt 27.09.1838; 1814a (1813); Map 3 chns, 1st cl, 'Working Plan... Surveyed in 1839' by Hayward and Wells; waterbodies, houses, woods, parkland, orchards, gardens, heath/moor, avenue of trees.

33/90 Capel St Andrew (parish) TM 355482
Apt 07.08.1845; 2273a (all); Map 1846, 12 chns; houses, woods, plantations.

33/91 Caple St Mary (parish) TM 091374 [Capel St Mary]
Apt 07.03.1838; 1911a (1910); Map surveyed in 1837, 3 chns, by John Spurling, Shotley, Suffolk; construction lines, foot/b'way, waterbodies, houses, woods (col), parkland, arable (col), grassland (col), field boundary ownerships, windmill (pictorial), pit, glebe; pictorial church.

33/92 Carlton (parish) TM 378646
Apt 03.02.1843; 544a (all); Map 1840, 3 chns, 1st cl, by James Smy, Saxmundham, Suffolk; waterbodies, houses, woods.

33/93 Carlton Colvile (district) TM 516906 [Carlton Colville]
Apt 15.09.1837; 1518a (?); Map 1842, 3 chns, 1st cl, by R. Barnes, Lowestoft; construction lines, houses.

33/94 Carlton Colvile, tithable to lay impropriators (district) TM 503915 [Carlton Colville]
Apt 25.05.1847; 1276a (?); Map 1843, 3 chns, 1st cl, by Richard Barnes, Lowestoft; waterbodies, houses.

33/95 Cavendish (parish) TL 800480
Apt 20.05.1846; 3355a (3354); Map 1848, 7 chns, by J. Hasell, Sudbury; foot/b'way, waterbodies, houses, woods (col), arable (col), grassland (col), field boundary ownerships, building names; pictorial church.

33/96 Charsfield (parish) TM 250564
Apt 02.04.1839; 1300a (1299); Map 1838, 8 chns; waterbodies, houses, woods.

33/97 Chattisham (parish) TM 092422
Apt 28.02.1839; 713a (713); Map 1839, 6 chns, 'Compiled from Original Surveys' by John Spurling, Shotley; houses, windmill (pictorial); pictorial church.

33/98 Chedbury (parish) TL 798580 [Chedburgh]
Apt 30.12.1837; 566a (566); Map 1839, 3 chns, surveyed for enclosure in 1813 and revised by Richard Payne, Bury St Edmunds; waterbodies, houses, woods, parkland, orchards, gardens, road names, school, parsonage, hall, mill, ploughed-up wood; pictorial church.

33/99 Chediston (parish) TM 350780
Apt 12.06.1839; 2378a (2378); Map 1838, 3 chns, by John Stigall, Bramfield, Suffolk; foot/b'way, houses, chapel.

33/100 Chellesworth (parish) TL 984480 [Chelsworth]
Apt 21.03.1838; 862a (all); Map '1831 and 1832', 3 chns, by John Wright; waterbodies, woods (col), plantations (col), arable (col), grassland (col), gardens (col), field names, field acreages, landowners, ownerships (col); curtains and tassles appear above title.

33/101 Chelmondiston (parish) TM 205376
Apt 07.06.1838; 1287a (1627); Map 1837, 3 chns, by S.L. Bransby, Ipswich; houses, woods (col), plantations (col), arable (col), grassland (col), gardens (col), windmill (pictorial), pit; pictorial church. Apt omits land use.

33/102 Chevington (parish) TL 792600
Apt 10.01.1838; 2429a (all); Map 1839, 3 chns, surveyed for enclosure in 1813 and revised by Richard Payne, Bury St Edmunds; foot/b'way, waterbodies, houses, woods, parkland, orchards, gardens, fences, building names, windmill (pictorial), meeting house, pound; pictorial church.

33/103 Chillesford (parish) TM 392522
Apt 07.11.1839; 1806a (all); Map 1838, 6 chns; waterbodies, houses, woods (col), heath/moor (col), watermill, decoy, boundary trees.

33/104 Chilton (parish) TL 893436
Apt 28.03.1839; 979a (all); Map 1840, 6 chns, by James Wright, Aylsham; foot/b'way, waterbodies, woods, gardens, marl pit; pictorial church.

33/105 Clare (parish) TL 764461
Apt 19.10.1847; 2229a (2228); Map 1846, [3 chns], 1st cl, surveyed by William H. Young, Mildenhall; construction lines, foot/b'way, waterbodies, houses, woods, parkland, gardens, hedge ownership, field boundary ownerships, field gates, building names, road names, hamlet boundary, gravel pit, castle, earthworks, windmill (by symbol); fields are dual numbered in black (as in Apt) and in red.

33/106 Claydon (parish) TM 140498
Apt 11.07.1837; 950a (all); Map 1837, 3 chns, by S.W. Parkes and B. Spurling; waterbodies, houses, woods (col), osiers (by symbol), arable (col), grassland (col), residual open fields, field boundary ownerships, windmill (by symbol), boundary trees, chalk and sand pits (col). (PRO IR 30 also contains a 6-chn litho version of 1838, by Standidge).

33/107 Clopton (parish) TM 224546 [Clopton Green]
Apt 05.07.1842; 2074a (all); Map 1840, 6 chns; waterbodies, houses, woods, osiers (by symbol), orchards.

33/108 Cockfield (parish) TL 907543
Apt 12.02.1844; 3626a (all); Map 1843, 6 chns, by Newton and Woodrow, Norwich; waterbodies, houses, woods, parkland, gardens, fences, building names, greens (col); pictorial church.

33/109 Coddenham (parish) TM 130548
Apt 20.06.1839; 2719a (2719); Map 1839?, 3 chns, by Richard Fenning; construction lines, waterbodies, houses, gardens, building names, field names, windmill (by symbol), mill, river lock, boundary trees, churchyard, school.

33/110 Combs (parish) TM 040560
Apt 19.10.1843; 2744a (all); Map 1841, 3 chns, 1st cl, 'Working Plan', surveyed by W. Ruffell; construction lines, woods, plantations, grass in mixed-cultivation fields (by annotation), hops, river lock; bridge named; it is unclear what the large brown letters A to F signify.

33/111 Cookley (parish) TM 358752
Apt 19.02.1845; 1704a (1704); Map 1846, 3 chns, 1st cl, by Jno. Stagoll, Linstead Parva, Suffolk; construction lines, waterbodies, houses, boundary pit, holding boundaries (col); scale bar and north pointer are combined.

33/112 Copdock (parish) TM 114411
Apt 30.04.1838; 955a (954); Map 1839?, 3 chns, by Chapman, Son and Webb, Arundel St, Strand; foot/b'way, waterbodies, houses; wood and arable field shown by annotation.

33/113 Great Cornard (parish) TL 900402
Apt 08.03.1839; 1568a (all); Map 3 chns, in 2 parts, surveyed April-May 1838 and drawn by J. Hasell; foot/b'way, woods, plantations, parkland, orchards, gardens, building names, pot kilns, mill, river locks, brick pits and works; buildings are shown in outline only; pictorial church; pre-printed cartouche has mapmaker's name and map date on a scroll resting on a pillar, with wheat ears in the background.

33/114 Little Cornard (parish) TL 902382
Apt 31.05.1842; 1658a (all); Map 1841, 3 chns, by J. Hasell, Sudbury; foot/b'way, waterbodies, houses, woods, orchards, building names, river locks, footbridge; pictorial church; some names may be stamped.

33/115 Corton (parish) TM 535980
Apt 09.07.1839; 1175a (1495); Map 1842, 3 chns, 1st cl, by Richard Barnes, Lowestoft; construction lines, houses (uncoloured), milestone; pictorial church.

33/116 Cotton (parish) TM 070668
Apt 09.01.1840; 1922a (1921); Map 1840, 8 chns, 'Surveyed and Drawn' by George Drury, Ipswich, Suffolk; foot/b'way, waterbodies, woods, orchards, greens; scale is graduated in rods.

33/117 North Cove (parish) TM 466899
Apt 19.07.1848; 1243a (1242); Map 1848, 6 chns; waterbodies, houses, drainage mills, parish boundary.

33/118 South Cove (parish) TM 502804
Apt 11.07.1838; 1215a (all); Map 'Revised 1838', 6 chns, by Lenny and Croft, Bury St Edmunds and Wrentham; waterbodies, woods, building names; bridge named.

33/119 Covehithe or Northales (parish) TM 519811
Apt 19.06.1840; 1554a (1553); Map 1840, 5 chns, by Lenny and Croft, Bury St Edmds; foot/b'way, waterbodies, houses, woods, orchards, heath/moor, building names, boat house, cliffs, beach.

33/120 Cowlinge (parish) TL 715545
Apt 18.06.1847; 3025a (all); Map 1846, 5 chns, by John Croft, Bury St Edmunds; waterbodies, houses, woods, plantations, gardens, fence ownership, windmill (pictorial).

33/121 Cransford (parish) TM 322648
Apt 22.10.1839; 1190a (all); Map 1840, 4 chns, 1st cl, by Bland H. Galland; construction lines, waterbodies, houses, woods (col), mill, chapel, ownership boundaries (col).

33/122 Cratfield (parish) TM 307753
Apt 22.03.1841; 2123a (2085); Map 1839, 3 chns, 1st cl, by Newton and Woodrow, Norwich; construction lines, foot/b'way, waterbodies, houses, green (col).

33/123 Creeting St Mary, Creeting All Saints and Creeting St Olaves (parish) TM 100567
Apt 31.10.1838; 3116a (all); Map 1838, 3 chns, by W. Ruffell; construction lines, waterbodies, woods, orchards, grass in mixed-cultivation fields (by annotation), windmill (by symbol).

33/124 Creeting St Peters (parish) TM 092568
Apt 12.07.1838; 1337a (all); Map 1838, 3 chns, by John Barnes; waterbodies, houses, woods (col), plantations (col), osiers (by symbol, col), landowners, clay pit (col), boundary trees, churchyard, vicarage.

33/125 Cretingham (parish) TM 223603
Apt 02.12.1841; 1638a (1638); Map 1839, 3 chns, 1st cl, by George Conroy; construction lines, waterbodies, houses, woods (col), parkland, gardens, windmill, sand pit; a table summarises acreages.

33/126 Crowfield (parish) TM 144575
Apt 10.06.1845; 1721a (1721); Map 1845?, 3 chns, surveyed by John McLachlan, Stowmarket; waterbodies, houses, woods, boundary trees, green.

33/127 Culford (parish) TL 836711
Apt 19.06.1840; 2218a (all); Map 1840, 6 chns, by Lenny and Croft, Bury St Edmunds; waterbodies, houses, plantations (named), parkland, heath/moor, fences, building names, churchyard, iron bridge, mills, lodge, brick kiln, pit, windmill (pictorial), river locks, sluice; land tithable to another district is yellow; bridge named.

33/128 Culpho (parish) TM 210493
Apt 16.02.1838; 65a (641); Map 3 chns, surveyed 1837 by S.L. Bransby, Ipswich; woods (col), arable (col), grassland (col); there is a table of field names and acreages.

33/129 Dallinghoo (parish) TM 268550
Apt 31.12.1840; 1530a (all); Map 1840, 6 chns, by Benjamin Moulton, Woodbridge; waterbodies, houses, woods, pit.

33/130 Darsham (parish) TM 418702
Apt 03.02.1843; 1365a (1550); Map 1843, 6 chns, by Jno. Stagoll; waterbodies, houses, woods, green, windmill (pictorial); owner of tithe-free land named; hill named. Apt omits some field names.

33/131 Debach (parish) TM 245545
Apt 25.03.1839; 464a (464); Map 3 chns, 'Surveyed in January 1839 for B. Moulton, Land Surveyor, by M. Clinton and S. Dixon'; construction lines, waterbodies, houses, woods, plantations, holding boundaries (col).

33/132 Debenham (parish) TM 174640
Apt 07.02.1838; 3272a (3271); Map 1837, 6 chns, litho (Standidge); foot/b'way, waterbodies, woods, orchards, building names, avenue of trees.

33/133 Denardiston (parish) TL 764527 [Denston]
Apt 28.11.1850; 51a (1230); Map 1851?, 3 chns, by John Croft, Bury St Edmunds, (tithable parts only); waterbodies, houses, orchards, fences; pictorial church.

33/134 Denham (parish) TM 184738
Apt 08.03.1843; 1268a (all); Map 1838, 8 chns, by J. Manning, Norwich; waterbodies, houses, woods, parkland, arable (by symbol), grassland (by symbol), gardens, glebe (pink), windmill (pictorial); pictorial church.

33/135 Dennington (parish) TM 285680
Apt 30.04.1838; 3263a (3262); Map '1823', (1838?), 3 chns, 1st cl, by Richard Barnes, Lowestoft; construction lines, foot/b'way, field boundary ownerships; buildings are shown in outline only.

33/136 Depden (parish) TL 779563
Apt 31.01.1838; 1596a (1595); Map 1839, 6 chns, by Lenny and Croft, Bury St Edmunds; waterbodies, houses, woods, parkland, fences, pound, windmill (by symbol), green.

33/137 Drinkstone (parish) TL 959611
Apt 31.10.1838; 2172a (2172); Map 1838-9, 6 chns, by Lenny and Croft, Bury St Edmunds; waterbodies, houses, woods, parkland, gardens, fences, road names, rectory, greens, drifts.

33/138 Dunwich (parish) TM 470700
Apt 11.08.1838; 1337a (1465); Map 1838, 5 chns, revised by Lenny and Croft, Bury St Edmunds; hill-drawing, waterbodies, houses, woods, parkland, heath/moor, high and low water marks, watch house, preventive station, duckpond, churchyard, ruin, cliffs, beach, flagstaff (pictorial); colour bands show various categories of tithe-free land.

33/139 Earl Soham (parish) TM 232630
Apt 28.04.1840; 1945a (1944); Map 1840?, [4 chns]; waterbodies, houses, woods, rectory, lodge.

33/140 Earl Stonham (parish) TM 101597 [Earl Stoneham]
Apt 31.10.1838; 2521a (2520); Map 1839, 6 chns, by Newton and Woodrow, Norwich; waterbodies, houses, ownerships (col).

33/141 Easton (parish) TM 285595
Apt 11.07.1838; 1462a (1462); Map 1838, 3 chns; construction lines, foot/b'way, waterbodies, houses, woods, parkland, orchards, gardens, field boundary ownerships, field gates, pound, pits, boundary posts and trees.

33/142 Easton Bavents (parish) TM 513781
Apt 19.07.1848; 381a (all); Map 1849, 5 chns, by Lenny and Croft, Bury St Edmunds; waterbodies, houses, heath/moor, embankment, beach, cliffs, reeds.

33/143 Edwardston (parish) TL 942422 [Edwardstone]
Apt 02.08.1837; 1872a (1872); Map 1838, 3 chns, by William Browne, Norwich; waterbodies, houses, woods, parkland, fence, building names, landowners (col), chapel, poor house, lodge, ice house, vicarage, windmill, watermill.

33/144 Ellough (parish) TM 455875
Apt 06.06.1845; 1098a (all); Map 1846, 3 chns, 1st cl; construction lines, waterbodies, houses, clay pits (col); pink bands are used for bracing.

33/145 Elmsett (parish) TM 057471
Apt 06.01.1842; 1974a (all); Map 'Working Plan' 1838, 3 chns, 1st cl, in 4 parts, surveyed by R.E. Sheldrake, Colchester, (includes 6-chn index); construction lines, foot/b'way, waterbodies, houses, woods, orchards, windmill (by symbol), gravel pit.

33/146 Elmswell (parish) TL 992642
Apt 20.02.1841; 2067a (2066); Map 1842, 12 chns; waterbodies, houses.

33/147 Elvedon (parish) TL 815795 [Elveden]
Apt 09.12.1848; 5479a (5290); Map 1841, 12 chns, surveyed by W.H. Young; foot/b'way, turnpike roads, waterbodies, houses, woods (col, named), plantations (col), parkland (col), gardens (col), heath/moor, building names, road names, field names, landowners, pits, holdings (col).

33/148 Eriswell (parish) TL 751782
Apt 13.05.1839; 6621a (6620); Map 1839, 8 chns; foot/b'way, waterbodies, plantations, heath/moor.

33/149 Erwarton (parish) TM 219349
Apt 21.11.1838; 1319a (2978); Map 1838, 3 chns, by Benjn Spurling,

Burgh; waterbodies, houses, woods (col), osiers (by symbol), arable (col), grassland (col), marsh/bog (col), field boundary ownerships, boundary trees. Apt omits land use.

33/150 Euston (parish) TL 900790
Apt 15.07.1837; 3781a (3780); Map 1840, 6.67 chns, 'Revised and Drawn' by Sheldrake and McLachlan, Colchester; waterbodies, houses, farmyards (col), woods (col), plantations (col), parkland (col), arable (col), grassland (col), gardens (col), heath/moor (col), fences, field boundary ownerships, hall, temple, kennel.

33/151 Eye (parish) TM 153733
Apt 21.06.1841; 4320a (4320); Map 1839, 8 chns, litho, in 2 parts, by Joseph Manning, Land Surveyor and Lithographer, 64 Bethel St, Norwich, (includes enlargement of town at 2 chns); hill-drawing, waterbodies, houses, woods, plantation (named), field names, breweries, workhouse, windmills (pictorial), town hall, theatre, foundry, chapel, green; pictorial church; houses are hand-coloured.

33/152 Eyke (parish) TM 331505
Apt 29.11.1845; 2749a (2749); Map 1842, 4 chns, 1st cl, by Benj. Moulton, Woodbridge; construction lines, waterbodies, houses, pits.

33/153 Great Fakenham (parish) TL 903763 [Not listed]
Apt 02.11.1837; 2155a (2155); Map 1839, 7 chns, 'Revised from a Survey by - Tyson' by Lenny and Croft, Bury St Edmunds; waterbodies, houses, woods (named) with rides (named), parkland, gardens, heath/moor, barn names, road names, marker stones, rectory, limekiln.

33/154 Falkenham (parish) TM 300390
Apt 22.11.1838; 1708a (all); Map 1838, 3 chns, by S.L. Bransby, Ipswich; waterbodies, houses, woods, drains, reeds, estate boundary (pink).

33/155 Farnham (parish) TM 371591
Apt 08.11.1838; 1177a (all); Map 1838, 3 chns, 1st cl, by J. Smy, Saxmundham, Suff.; construction lines, waterbodies, houses, woods, heath/moor, pits; bridge named.

33/156 Felixstow (parish) TM 317366 [Felixstowe]
Apt 15.01.1845; 1924a (all); Map 1845?, 4 chns; waterbodies, houses, woods, battery, (martello) towers, ferry, old hall.

33/157 Felsham St Peter (parish) TL 945565 [Felsham]
Apt 03.07.1837; 1630a (1630); Map 1838, 6 chns, by Lenny and Croft, Bury St Edmunds; waterbodies, houses, woods, parkland, orchards, gardens, fences, building names, mausoleum, rectory, greens.

33/158 Great Finborough (parish) TM 016570
Apt 30.05.1840; 1631a (all); Map 1841, 3 chns; woods, holding boundaries (col).

33/159 Little Finborough (parish) TM 020550
Apt 17.07.1838; 367a (367); Map 1837, 3 chns, in 2 parts, surveyed by W. Ruffell; construction lines, foot/b'way, woods, orchards, field names, landowners (col); part 2 repeats a protruded part of the main map, and carries a note, 'This detached piece is here repeated fearing that it might be lost from its proper situation'.

33/160 Finningham (parish) TM 063699
Apt 12.06.1839; 1243a (all); Map 1839, 6 chns, in 2 parts, by Henry Calver; waterbodies, woods, orchards, avenue of trees.

33/161 Flempton (parish) TL 809698
Apt 24.12.1842; 789a (all); Map 1843, 6 chns, by Lenny and Croft, Bury St Edmunds; waterbodies, houses, woods, plantations, parkland, orchards, fences, watermill, overfall, rectory, hall, pits, staunch, river locks, drainage tunnel; pictorial church.

33/162 Flixton (parish) TM 317862
Apt 03.02.1843; 1762a (1761); Map 1844?, 4 chns, 1st cl, by B.H. Galland, C.E.; waterbodies, houses, farmyards (col), woods (col), drains, disputed boundary; there is a note, '$1/_2$ the drain included in every instance'.

33/163 Flowton (parish) TM 080473
Apt 16.11.1837; 495a (all); Map 1839, 3 chns, by Richard and Fredk Fenning; foot/b'way, waterbodies, houses, glebe.

33/164 Fordley (parish) TM 418667 [Not listed]
Apt 20.09.1838; 604a (all); Map 1839, 3 chns, 1st cl, by James Smy, Saxmundham; foot/b'way, waterbodies, houses, pits; pink bands are used for some bracing.

33/165 Fornham All Saints (parish) TL 838670
Apt 03.03.1838; 1698a (all); Map 1839, 6 chns, by Lenny and Croft, Bury St Edmunds; waterbodies, houses, woods, plantations, gardens, fences, building names, toll gate, rectory, river sluices, overfall, boundary tree, mound, pound, mill, drains.

33/166 Fornham St Martin and Fornham St Genoveve or St Genovieve (parish) TL 853673
Corn rent conversion, 1922; 756a (2020); no map.

33/167 Foxhall (parish) TM 225441 [Not listed]
Apt 18.06.1842; 245a (1872); Map 1842?, 4 chns, (tithable parts only); houses, gravel pit (col).

33/168 Framlingham (parish) TM 285635
Apt 17.03.1842; 4657a (4657); Map 1842?, 3 chns; foot/b'way, waterbodies, houses, woods, orchards, fences, field gates, castle, stiles, windmill (by symbol), boundary trees (pictorial).

33/169 Framsden (parish) TM 206595
Apt 11.03.1839; 2838a (all); Map 1839, 4 chns, by S.L. Bransby, Ipswich; waterbodies, houses, woods, hops, windmill (pictorial); pictorial church with flagpole; uninhabited buildings are shown in outline only.

33/170 Fressingfield (parish) TM 269773
Apt 08.07.1841; 4560a (4560); Map 1838, 6 chns, by Gilbert and Tayspill; waterbodies, heath/moor (col), windmill (by symbol).

33/171 Freston (parish) TM 170384
Apt 18.06.1840; 1413a (all); Map 1839, 3 chns, surveyed by H.T. Ellis, C.E., Ipswich and Wickham Market; construction lines, foot/b'way, waterbodies, houses, woods, osiers (by symbol, col), parkland (col), orchards, gardens (col), field gates, boundary trees and posts, pits (col).

33/172 Friston (parish) TM 418591
Apt 01.03.1847; 1846a (all); Map 1839, 3 chns, 1st cl, in 2 parts, by James Smy, Saxmundham, Suff.; construction lines, foot/b'way, waterbodies, houses, woods (col), pits, decoy; pink band is used for some bracing; part 2 is a repetition of a protrusion at the top.

33/173 Fritton (parish) TG 467005
Apt 19.12.1837; 1563a (1562); Map 1840?, 3 chns, 1st cl, ? by Richard Barnes, Lowestoft; construction lines, stackyard, clay pits; buildings are shown in outline only.

33/174 Frostenden (parish) TM 480813
Apt 06.09.1838; 1311a (1310); Map 1838, 3 chns, 1st cl, by Lenny and Croft, Bury St Edmunds and Wrentham; construction lines, waterbodies, houses, woods, plantations, orchards, gardens, fences, field boundary ownerships, field gates, building names, churchyard, brickworks, lodge.

33/175 Palgrave (district) TM 115777 [Not listed]
Apt 22.11.1849; 6a (all); Map 1850?, 3 chns, (tithable parts only); district is also mapped in 33/317.

33/176 Gazeley (parish) TL 730652
Apt 31.07.1844; 5900a (5899); Map 1840, [6 chns], by Lenny and Croft, Bury St Edmunds; turnpike roads, waterbodies, houses, plantations, orchards, gardens, building names, road names, rectory, vicarage, private roads, brick and lime kilns, beggars bush; bridge named; colours may show tithable status.

33/177 Gedding (parish) TL 948581
Apt 16.03.1842; 522a (all); Map 1838, 3 chns, by W. Chandler; construction lines, foot/b'way, waterbodies, houses, woods, boundary trees, windmill (pictorial), field acreages.

33/178 Gipping (parish) TM 073632
Apt 08.06.1846; 1145a (all); Map 1847?, 6 chns; waterbodies, houses, gardens. Apt omits some land use.

33/179 Gisleham (parish) TM 515885
Apt 15.07.1841; 1344a (1344); Map 1842, 3 chns, 1st cl, by Richard Barnes, Lowestoft; construction lines; pictorial church; buildings are shown in outline only. Apt omits some land use.

33/180 Gislingham (parish) TM 072719
Apt 26.08.1839; 2251a (2251); Map 1840?, [6 chns]; waterbodies, houses, woods.

33/181 Great Glemham (parish) TM 332620
Apt 31.12.1840; 1910a (all); Map 1839, 4 chns, 1st cl, surveyed by Bland Hood Galland, C.E.; construction lines, waterbodies, houses, woods (col, named), plantations, parkland, orchards, gardens, pasture (by annotation), pheasantry, keepers house, ice house, sand pit, pigeon house, hall, boundary post; the map has two ruled 'Standards', one dated 3.9.1839, and the other accompanied by different tables of summary acreages calculated at different times.

33/182 Little Glemham (parish) TM 346588
Apt 30.04.1838; 1273a (all); Map 1842, 6 chns; waterbodies, houses, woods.

33/183 Glemsford (parish) TL 830480
Apt 18.06.1840; 2295a (2295); Map 1838, 3 chns, 'taken' by Wm Borley, Alpheton; waterbodies, houses, woods, osiers (by symbol, col), plantations, orchards, pit (col).

33/184 Gorleston (parish) TG 525038 [Gorleston-on-Sea]
Apt 18.06.1840; 1441a (?); Map 1840, 3 chns, 1st cl, by Richard Barnes, Lowestoft, Suffolk; construction lines, houses, windmill (pictorial); pictorial church. Apt omits most land use.

33/185 Gosbeck (parish) TM 156562
Apt 27.08.1842; 1466a (all); Map 1842, 6 chns, by Richard Fenning; waterbodies, houses.

33/186 Groton (parish) TL 966427
Apt 07.12.1838; 1571a (1571); Map 6 chns, litho 1838 (Standidge), in 2 parts, by Robert Hale and Chas Mumford, 183[2?]; waterbodies, woods, parkland, orchards, garden; scale is graduated in poles.

33/187 Grundisburgh (parish) TM 215514
Apt 25.11.1841; 1898a (1897); Map 1841, 3 chns, 1st cl, by Benj. Spurling, Burgh; waterbodies, houses, woods (col), plantations (col), parkland, orchards, field boundary ownerships, pits.

33/188 Gunton (parish) TM 542957
Apt 31.01.1839; 867a (1072); Map 1844, 6 chns, by Richard Barnes; foot/b'way, houses, woods, parkland, gardens, post; uninhabited buildings are shown in outline only.

33/189 Hacheston (parish) TM 306584
Apt 15.06.1839; 1726a (1726); Map 1839, 8 chns, by Benj. Moulton, Woodbridge; houses, woods, heath/moor.

33/190 Hadleigh (parish) TM 033433
Apt 28.04.1838; 4288a (all); Map 1839, [6 chns], litho (Standidge); foot/b'way, waterbodies, houses (by shading, incomplete), woods (named), building names, road names.

33/191 Halesworth (parish) TM 386774
Apt 18.06.1840; 1446a (all); Map 1840, 3 chns, in 2 parts, by W.G. Jones, Loddon, Norfolk, (includes town separately at 1 chn); foot/b'way, waterbodies, houses, osiers (by symbol, col), plantations, road names, chapel, windmills (pictorial).

33/192 Hargrave (parish) TL 772598
Apt 03.03.1838; 1109a (all); Map 1840?, 6 chns, by W.W. Cawston, Worlington; foot/b'way, waterbodies, houses, woods, orchards.

33/193 Harkstead (parish) TM 198350
Apt 27.02.1839; 1727a (2266); Map 1839, 3 chns, in 2 parts, by H.T. Ellis, Civil Engineer and Surveyor, Ipswich, Suffolk; foot/b'way, waterbodies, houses, woods, orchards, gardens, marsh/bog, boundary trees and marks, gravel, pits, fishpond, clay pit, brick kiln, graveyard, embankment, river cliffs, owners of large houses, public roads. Apt omits land use.

33/194 Harleston (parish) TM 019608
Apt 23.09.1845; 615a (all); Map 1842, 3 chns; waterbodies, houses, woods, green; map is described as 'Revised in the boundary by the Tithe Law Commissioner 1842'.

33/195 Hartest (parish) TL 835525
Apt 30.11.1839; 1964a (all); Map 1839, 3 chns, by Wm Borley, Alpheton, Suffolk; waterbodies, houses, farmyards (col), woods (col), plantations (col), parkland (col), arable (col), grassland (col), orchards, gardens (col), marsh/bog, windmill (by symbol); pictorial church; north pointer has diadem and plumes; title is on scroll, resting on fluted column, with tree behind.

33/196 Hasketon (parish) TM 250505
Apt 21.10.1840; 1665a (1665); Map 3 chns, 1st cl, surveyed October 1838 by Dixon and Maitland, 21 John St, Bedford Row; construction lines, waterbodies, houses, woods, parkland, arable (col), grassland (col), orchards, field boundary ownerships.

33/197 Haughley (parish) TM 030628
Apt 28.05.1844; 2519a (all); Map 1844?, 6 chns, by John Barnes; waterbodies, houses, woods, parkland, orchards, motte and bailey, signpost (pictorial), boundary tree, windmill (by symbol), common.

33/198 Haverhill (parish) (partly in Essex) TL 671455
Apt 22.02.1840; 2507a (all); Map '1826', (1841?), 3 chns; foot/b'way, turnpike roads, waterbodies, houses, woods, parkland, orchards, residual open fields (named), fences, field gates, building names, road names, windmill (pictorial), pound, churchyard, chapel, stiles.

33/199 Hawkedon (parish) TL 799530
Apt 12.10.1839; 1462a (all); Map 1839, 3 chns, surveyed by William Borley, Alpheton; construction lines, waterbodies, houses, woods, orchards; pictorial church.

33/200 Hawstead (parish) TL 855590
Apt 24.03.1842; 2237a (2237); Map 3 chns, surveyed in 1838 by R. Payne, Bury St Edmunds; construction lines, waterbodies, houses, woods, plantations, orchards, building names, pound, green; pictorial church.

33/201 Hazlewood (parish) TM 441590 [Not listed]
Apt 08.06.1846; 1937a (all); Map 1839, 3 chns; waterbodies, houses, woods (col), pit; pink bands are used for some bracing; meaning of other colour bands is unclear.

33/202 Helmingham (parish) TM 187577
Apt 02.07.1839; 2438a (2438); Map 1840, 3 chns, by S.L. Bransby, Ipswich; waterbodies, houses, woods, mound; uninhabited buildings are shown in outline only; pictorial church, with flagpole.

33/203 Hemingstone (parish) TM 152523
Apt 20.07.1837; 1444a (all); Map 1838, 3 chns; turnpike roads, waterbodies, houses, woods (by name), field names, landowners, rectory, churchyard.

33/204 Hemingstone (district in parish of Hemingstone) TM 153524 [Not listed]
Apt 18.10.1883; 14a (?); Map (drawn on Apt) 1883, 3.16 chns (1:2500); district is also mapped in 33/203.

33/205 Hemley (parish) TM 285427
Apt 17.05.1845; 741a (all); Map 1841?, 4 chns; waterbodies, woods, parkland.

33/206 Hengrave (parish) TL 821682
Apt 14.09.1838; 1044a (all); Map 1839, 6 chns, by Lenny and Croft, Bury St Edmunds; waterbodies, houses, woods, parkland, orchards, gardens, fences, building names, mound, almshouses, mills, river sluice and locks, keepers house, pit, brick kiln, bath house; bridge and ornamental ponds named.

33/207 Henley (parish) TM 162516
Apt 31.01.1839; 1233a (all); Map 1838, 3 chns, by S.W. Parkes, Ipswich; waterbodies, houses, woods, plantations, parkland, orchards, windmill (pictorial), gravel pit, sand pit, chapel, boundary trees, vicarage, school; leaves are entwined around north pointer.

33/208 Henstead cum Hulver Street (parish) TM 489859
Apt 21.01.1839; 1906a (1918); Map 1839, 6 chns, ? by Henry Coker; waterbodies, woods, parkland, orchards, glebe; pictorial church.

33/209 Hepworth (parish) TL 986750
Apt 22.04.1845; 1678a (all); Map 1845, 6 chns, by Lenny and Croft, Bury St Edmds; waterbodies, woods, parkland, road names, windmill (pictorial); pictorial church.

33/210 Herringfleet (parish) TM 475985
Apt 31.07.1849; 61a (1720); Map 1849, 6 chns, by Geo. Dowling, Lowestoft; waterbodies, houses, gardens; pictorial church.

33/211 Hessett (parish) TL 938610
Apt 29.11.1837; 1568a (1568); Map 1838, 6 chns, by Lenny and Croft, Bury St Edmunds; waterbodies, houses, woods, plantations, parkland, orchards (col), gardens (col), fences, building names, road names, greens.

33/212 Heveningham (parish) TM 342722
Apt 18.06.1840; 1660a (2855); Map 1840, [6 chns], by Henry Preston, Worlingworth; foot/b'way, waterbodies, houses, woods, pit.

33/213 Higham (parish) TM 036361
Apt 30.04.1838; 881a (880); Map 1839?, 5 chns, surveyed 1833 by John Bransby; foot/b'way, woods, arable (col), grassland (col), field names, landowners, churchyard, park, garden (by annotation); scale is graduated in rods; it is unclear what pink tint signifies. Apt omits land use.

33/214 Hinderclay (parish) TM 025769
Apt 16.11.1843; 1458a (all); Map 1844, 6 chns, by C.S. Alger, Diss; waterbodies, woods, parkland, orchards, gardens, road names, windmill (pictorial), gravel pit, avenue of trees; pictorial church, with flagpole.

33/215 Hintlesham (parish) TM 084435
Apt 12.09.1837; 2761a (2828); Map 1837, 6 chns, surveyed by J.G. Lenny in 1823, and 'Revised and Corrected' by S.L. Bransby; foot/b'way, waterbodies, houses, farmyards (col), woods (col), plantations (col), parkland (col), arable (col), grassland (col), gardens (col), modus lands (blue); pictorial church.

33/216 Hitcham (parish) TL 987525
Apt 18.01.1840; 4118a (4117); Map 1839, 3 chns, surveyed by W. and A. Ruffell; construction lines, waterbodies, houses.

33/217 Holbrook (parish) TM 170360
Apt 19.06.1838; 2203a (3153); Map 1840, 3 chns, by S.L. Bransby, Ipswich; waterbodies, houses, woods (named), reeds (by symbol), green; pictorial church.

33/218 Hollesley (parish) TM 360450
Apt 02.06.1842; 4027a (all); Map 1841, 6 chns, by Pratt and Son, Norwich; waterbodies, houses, woods, orchards, heath/moor, boundary post, pits, boundary trees, drains, high and low water marks, navigation beacons (pictorial), foreshore (col); pictorial church.

33/219 Holton St Mary (parish) TM 056371
Apt 18.10.1838; 838a (all); Map 1839, 6 chns, in 3 parts, by Newton and Woodrow, Norwich; foot/b'way, waterbodies, houses, woods, parkland, orchards, pit, boundary post and trees. Apt omits land use.

33/220 Holton St Peter (parish) TM 402783 [Holton]
Apt 08.05.1841; 1130a (all); Map 1838, 3 chns, by W.G. Jones, Loddon, Norfolk; waterbodies, houses, fences, windmill (pictorial); some measurements are given for unmarked parish boundaries.

33/221 Homersfield (parish) TM 291851
Apt 27.06.1839; 981a (all); Map 1839, 4 chns, 1st cl, surveyed by Bland H. Galland; construction lines, waterbodies, houses, woods, plantations, parkland, gardens, mill, barn, glebe.

33/222 Honington (parish) TL 902742
Apt 04.10.1838; 1203a (1203); Map 1839, 6 chns, by Lenny and Croft, Bury St Edmunds; waterbodies, houses, woods, parkland, orchards, gardens, fences, windmill, private roads, watermill (pictorial).

33/223 Hoo (parish) TM 258587
Apt 29.11.1845; 1186a (all); Map 1846, 4 chns, revised by Benj. Moulton; waterbodies, woods, orchards.

33/224 Hopton (parish) TL 990793
Apt 25.07.1846; 1374a (1373); Map 1846, 6 chns; houses; uninhabited buildings are shown in outline only; pictorial church.

33/225 Hopton (parish) TG 523004 [Hopton on Sea]
Apt 07.06.1844; 1263a (all); Map 1844, 3 chns, 1st cl, ? by Richard Barnes, Lowestoft; construction lines; buildings are shown in outline only; pictorial church.

33/226 Horham (parish) TM 211722
Apt 11.08.1838; 1434a (all); Map not dated, [3 chns]; construction lines, waterbodies, houses, woods (named), gardens, field names, field acreages, orchard (by annotation), glebe.

33/227 Horningsheath (parish) TL 832620 [Horringer]
Apt 29.11.1837; 2201a (all); Map 1839, 3 chns, surveyed for enclosure in 1813, and revised by Richard Payne; waterbodies, houses, woods (named), parkland, orchards, gardens, fences, building names, road names, boundary tree, private road, spring head; pictorial church.

33/228 Hoxne (parish) TM 195760
Apt 12.05.1842; 4228a (4257); Map 1842?, 8 chns, in 2 parts 'Copied and Corrected' by J. Manning, Norwich; waterbodies, houses, woods, parkland, windmill (by symbol); colours may show tithe ownership.

33/229 Hundon (parish) TL 740490
Apt 26.01.1847; 4462a (4461); Map 1846, 3 chns, 1st cl, in 2 parts, by G. Ruffell, Brightlingsea, Essex; construction lines, foot/b'way, waterbodies, houses, woods, plantations, building names.

33/230 Hunston (parish) TL 979678
Apt 08.07.1845; 958a (all); Map 1846, 6 chns, by R. Payne; foot/b'way, waterbodies, houses, woods (col, named), fences, 'Old Water Course now filled up'; pictorial church.

33/231 Huntingfield (parish) TM 337744
Apt 19.02.1845; 2135a (2134); Map 1846, 3 chns, 1st cl, by Jno. Stagoll, Linstead Parva, Suffolk, (tinted); construction lines, waterbodies, houses, woods, osiers (by symbol), windmill (by symbol); scale bar and north pointer are combined.

33/232 Icklingham All Saints (parish) TL 787747 [Icklingham]
Apt 11.03.1839; 3766a (all); Map 1839?, ?8.5 chns; waterbodies, houses, farmyards (col), woods (col), arable (col), grassland (col), heath/moor (col), river locks.

33/233 Icklingham St James (parish) TL 762748 [Icklingham]
Apt 28.02.1839; 2795a (all); Map 1839?, ?8.5 chns; waterbodies, houses, farmyards (col), woods (col), arable (col), grassland (col), heath/moor (col), gravel pit (col).

33/234 Ickworth (parish) TL 813612 [Not listed]
Apt 07.02.1838; 1260a (all); Map 1843?, 6 chns, by Richard Payne, Bury St Edmunds; foot/b'way, waterbodies, houses, woods (col, named), parkland, gardens, building names, pheasantry, ice house, chalk pit (col), glebe; hill named.

33/235 Iken (parish) TM 416558
Apt 02.12.1839; 2597a (all); Map 1839, 4 chns, 1st cl, by Bland H. Galland, C.E.; waterbodies, houses, woods, plantations, decoy, drains, heath; there is a note that ditch centres are taken as property boundaries.

33/236 Ilketshall St Andrew (parish) TM 383862
Apt 21.12.1842; 1695a (1694); Map 1841, 3 chns, 1st cl, by Geo. Baker and Jno. Crickmay, Bungay and Beccles; construction lines, waterbodies, houses, woods, windmills (pictorial), sand pits, green; green bands are used for some bracing.

33/237 St Johns Ilketshall (parish) TM 362875 [Not listed]
Apt 27.07.1839; 743a (742); Map 1839, 3 chns, 1st cl, by Geo. Baker, Bungay; construction lines, waterbodies, houses, woods, sand pits, defaced boundary; pink bands are used for some bracing.

33/238 Ilketshall St Lawrence (parish) TM 371851
Apt 12.08.1847; 1074a (1073); Map 1843, 3 chns, 1st cl, by George Baker, Bungay, and Jno. Crickmay, Beccles; construction lines, turnpike

roads, waterbodies, houses, woods (col), milestones (by symbol), sand pit; green bands are used for some bracing.

33/239 St Margaret in Ilketshall (parish) TM 352855 [Ilketshall St Margaret]
Apt 26.08.1839; 2086a (all); Map 1841?, 6 chns, ? by George Baker, Bungay; foot/b'way, waterbodies, woods, orchards.

33/240 Ingham (parish) TL 853716
Apt 19.06.1840; 1809a (1808); Map 1840, 6 chns, by Lenny and Croft, Bury St Edmunds; waterbodies, houses, plantations, parkland, heath/moor, building names, parsonage, lodge, pits.

33/241 St Clement with Wix Bishop and Wix Ufford, Ipswich (parish with hamlet) TM 181431 [Not listed]
Apt 15.06.1841; 1659a (all); Map 1843?, 3 chns; waterbodies, woods, osiers (by symbol), parkland, orchards, gardens (col), building names, road names, high and low water marks, racecourse, boundary posts, ballast yard, rope walk, pits, brick yards, ship yard.

33/242 St Helen, Ipswich (parish) TM 175447 [Not listed]
Apt 18.10.1843; 228a (all); Map 1843?, 3 chns, in 3 parts, ? by S.S. Gower, Ipswich; hill-drawing, waterbodies, woods, parkland, arable (col), grassland (col), road names, field name, landowner, boundary posts, asylum, chapel, rope walk, gaol, pottery, pound.

33/243 St Margaret, Ipswich (parish) TM 171457 [Not listed]
Apt 08.05.1848; 1289a (?); Map 1849, 4 chns, (tithable parts only); waterbodies, road names; built-up parts generalised; title is framed in square, with single red leaves at corners; scale is graduated in rods. Apt omits some land use.

33/244 St Mary Stoke (parish) TM 145425 [Stoke]
Apt 26.08.1839; 1467a (?); Map 1840, 3 chns, 1st cl, by W.S. Grimwade; construction lines, waterbodies, houses, woods, parkland, orchards, field boundary ownerships; yellow bands are used for some bracing; prolongations of construction lines to landmarks outside the district are given.

33/245 St Matthew, Ipswich (parish) TM 145454 [Not listed]
Apt 06.03.1844; 642a (all); Map 1845, 2 chns, 1st cl, by William Browne, Norwich, and 5 Tavistock Row, Covent Garden, London, (tithable parts only in detail); foot/b'way, waterbodies, houses, woods, parkland, building names, road names, town hall, boundary pollards, milestone, tithe-free land (col).

33/246 St Stephen, Ipswich (parish) TM 163443
Apt 11.01.1848; 5a (?); Map 1849?, 4 chns, (tithable parts only).

33/247 Ixworth (parish) TL 935711 [Not listed]
Apt 08.03.1844; 2249a (all); Map 1840, 7.2 chns, in 3 parts, by Lenny and Croft, Bury St Edmunds, (includes village at 3 chns); turnpike roads, waterbodies, houses, woods, plantations, parkland, orchards, fences, building names, road names, watermill, avenues of trees, pits.

33/248 Kedington (parish) (partly in Essex) TL 709465
Apt 10.03.1841; 2342a (all); Map 1840, 3 chns, by J. Hasell, Sudbury; waterbodies, houses, woods (col, named), plantations (col), parkland, orchards, gardens (col), building names, field names, malting, boundary trees, stackyard, glebe, former commons, county boundary; pictorial church; it is unclear why some fields are tinted; ruler, dividers, quill pen and ruling pens decorate the scale; Brittania points to the mapmaker's name and map date on a plinth surmounted by a vase whilst a sheep looks on.

33/249 Kelsale (parish) TM 383657
Apt 16.03.1843; 3047a (3047); Map 1839, 3 chns, 1st cl, by James Smy, Saxmundham; construction lines, waterbodies, houses, woods (col), pits, brickworks; a note says that the lands in Carlton mapped here appear in that parish's apportionment; pink bands are used for some bracing.

33/250 Kennett (parish) (partly in Cambs) TL 695679
Apt 08.06.1837; 1401a (1425); Map 1838, 9 chns, ? by Lenny and Croft, Bury St Edmunds; turnpike roads, waterbodies, houses, woods, parkland, fences, road names; some physical features named.

33/251 Kentford (parish) TL 709668
Apt 26.03.1841; 799a (798); Map 1842, 3 chns, by Lenny and Croft, Bury St Edmunds; turnpike roads, toll gate, right of way, waterbodies, houses, parkland, chalk pit.

33/252 Kenton (parish) TM 193657
Apt 16.10.1841; 1209a (all); Map 1839, 6 chns, by Henry Calver; waterbodies, woods, orchards, boundary tree; pictorial church.

33/253 Kersey (parish) TL 998438
Apt 23.01.1840; 1511a (1510); Map 1841?, 3 chns, surveyed by W. and A. Ruffell; waterbodies, houses. Apt omits land use.

33/254 Kesgrave (parish) TM 225454
Apt 06.03.1847; 238a (1610); Map 1847?, 4 chns, (tithable parts only); pictorial church.

33/255 Kessingland (parish) TM 528868
Apt 21.03.1839; 1652a (1691); Map 1839, 3 chns, 1st cl; construction lines, hill-drawing, waterbodies, houses, woods, parkland, field boundary ownerships, road names, sluice, coastguard station, pits; pictorial church.

33/256 Kettlebaston (parish) TL 966502
Apt 24.03.1842; 1064a (all); Map 1841, 3 chns, 'Surveyed and Mapped' by John Barnes, Buxhall, Suffolk; waterbodies, houses.

33/257 Kettleburgh (parish) TM 265611
Apt 08.03.1839; 1435a (all); Map surveyed 1838, 3 chns, under the direction of Bland H. Galland, C.E.; waterbodies, houses, woods (col), parkland, orchards, gardens, building names, landowners, sand pit, clay pit, farm boundaries (col).

33/258 Kirtley or Kirkley (parish) TM 539915
Apt 21.11.1838; 540a (579); Map 1841, 3 chns, 1st cl, by Richd Barnes, Lowestoft; construction lines, private roads; most buildings are shown in outline only.

33/259 Kirton (parish) TM 283407
Apt 03.04.1839; 1814a (all); Map 1839?, 7 chns; houses, woods (col), grassland (col), heath/moor, reeds, sluice, clay pit.

33/260 Knettishall (parish) TL 960801
Apt 13.06.1840; 1025a (all); Map 1840, 7.5 chns; foot/b'way, waterbodies, woods, gardens; pictorial church.

33/261 Knoddishall (parish) TM 420610 [Knodishall]
Apt 21.03.1846; 1843a (all); Map 1845, 4 chns, 1st cl, 'Surveyed and Planned' by James Smy, Saxmundham; construction lines, waterbodies, houses, pits.

33/262 Lackford (parish) TL 790700
Apt 04.04.1843; 2344a (all); Map 1842, 6 chns, by J.O. Browne, 8 Furnival's Inn, London; waterbodies, houses, woods (named), heath/moor, building names, green, parsonage, river locks; yellow land is tithable to another district.

33/263 Lakenheath (district) TL 742812
Apt 12.07.1850; 3555a (?); Map 1851, 4 chns, in 2 parts, by W.W. Cawston, (including warren at 8 chns); turnpike roads, waterbodies, houses, plantations, road names, landowners, warren lodge (pictorial), windmill (pictorial); bridge named.

33/264 Lakenheath Fen Lands (district in parish of Lakenheath) TL 685840 [Not listed]
Apt 14.07.1853; 7104a (?); Map 1854, 10 chns, by William Westerman Cawston; railway, foot/b'way, waterbodies, houses, woods, landowner, decoy, sluice, drainage engine, windpump (pictorial), droves (col, named), drains (named); fen named; pictorial church, with weathercock. District is partly apportioned by holding.

33/265 Langham (parish) TL 979699
Apt 07.12.1838; 952a (all); Map 1840?, 6 chns; waterbodies, houses, woods, gardens, road names.

33/266 Lavenham (parish) TL 912502
Apt 12.05.1842; 2788a (all); Map 1841, 6 chns, in 2 parts, surveyed by A. Ruffell, (includes enlargement of town at 3 chns); waterbodies, houses.

33/267 Lawshall (parish) TL 866546
Apt 12.06.1839; 2970a (2969); Map 1842, 6 chns, in 2 parts, by William Browne, Norwich; turnpike roads, waterbodies, houses, woods, parkland, orchards, boundary trees and posts.

33/268 Laxfield (parish) TM 292723
Apt 22.01.1841; 3630a (3630); Map 1840, 6 chns, in 2 parts, by John Stigall, Bramfield, (includes enlargement of village at 2 chns); houses, windmill (pictorial); pictorial church.

33/269 Layham (parish) TM 020404
Apt 24.04.1838; 2488a (all); Map 'Working Plan' 1839, 3 chns, 1st cl, surveyed by Sheldrake and McLachlan, Colchester; construction lines, waterbodies, houses, woods (named), plantations, orchards, building names, brickworks, windmills, rectory, boundary trees.

33/270 Leiston (parish) TM 458628
Apt 14.05.1840; 1919a (4640); Map 1841, 4 chns, 1st cl, by James Smy, Saxmundham, (tithable parts only); construction lines, waterbodies, houses; pink bands are used for some bracing.

33/271 Letheringham (parish) TM 273576
Apt 21.06.1842; 1134a (1134); Map 1842, 8 chns, by Benj. Moulton, Woodbridge; waterbodies, woods.

33/272 Lindsey (parish) TL 982450
Apt 22.06.1838; 1246a (1246); Map 1839, 3 chns, surveyed by W. and A. Ruffell; waterbodies, houses, woods, grass in mixed-use fields (by annotation).

33/273 Linstead Magna (parish) TM 319764 [Not listed]
Apt 22.01.1841; 1304a (all); Map 1842, 3 chns, by Jno. Stagoll, Linstead Parva, (tinted); construction lines, public rights of way, foot/b'way, waterbodies, houses, woods, boundary posts.

33/274 Linstead Parva (parish) TM 330777
Apt 08.09.1840; 554a (554); Map 1840, 6 chns, in 2 parts, by John Stigall, Bramfield, (includes 3-chn enlargement of detail); waterbodies, houses; scale bar and north pointer are combined.

33/275 Great Livermere (parish) TL 888712
Apt 20.01.1847; 1549a (all); Map 1840, 6 chns, by Lenny and Croft, Bury St Edmunds; waterbodies, houses, woods, parkland, gardens, fences, boundary tree, ice house.

33/276 Little Livermere (parish) TL 872728 [Not listed]
Apt 20.01.1847; 1433a (all); Map 1840, 6 chns, by Lenny and Croft, Bury St Edmunds; waterbodies, houses, parkland, fences.

33/277 Lound (parish) TM 510996
Apt 25.09.1838; 1242a (1264); Map 1840, 3 chns, 1st cl, by Richd Barnes, Lowestoft, Suffolk; construction lines, waterbodies, houses.

33/278 Lowestoft (parish) TM 541937
Apt 12.02.1838; 1486a (1685); Map 1841, 3 chns, 1st cl, ? by Richard Barnes, Lowestoft, (tithable parts only in detail); construction lines, houses.

33/279 Marlesford (parish) TM 327587
Apt 09.03.1842; 1278a (all); Map 1841, 4 chns, 1st cl, surveyed by B.H. Galland; construction lines, waterbodies, houses, woods (col), osiers (by symbol), sand pit, stables, glebe, park, garden (by annotation), commons, ownerships (col).

33/280 Martlesham (parish) TM 259461
Apt 18.08.1837; 2560a (2709); Map 1837?, 8 chns, 'Copied from one by Issac Johson, late of Woodbridge, in the year 1832, by Benjn Moulton'; woods (col), heath/moor.

33/281 Long Melford (parish) TL 867470
Apt 13.6.1839; 5185a (5185); Map 1839, 8 chns, 'Revised' by William Borley, Alpheton, Suffolk; waterbodies, houses, woods, parkland, avenue of trees.

33/282 Mellis (parish) TM 098745
Apt 28.12.1839; 1333a (all); Map 1839, 6 chns, litho, by J. Manning, Surveyor and Lithographer, Norwich; foot/b'way, waterbodies, woods, road names, parsonage, pound, meeting house, mill, churchyard, former open field name. Apt omits most field names.

33/283 Melton (parish) TM 282506
Apt 16.08.1837; 1408a (1420); Map 1837, 6 chns, in 3 parts, 'Adjusted and copied from Johnson's Survey and Map made in 1833' by Benj. Moulton, Woodbridge; waterbodies, houses, woods (col), parkland; uninhabited buildings are shown in outline only; bridge named. (The map in PRO IR 30 is a copy.)

33/284 Mendham (parish) (partly in Norfolk) TM 276821
Apt 13.07.1840; 2998a (3144); Map 1840, 6 chns, by S.W. Parkes, Ipswich; foot/b'way, waterbodies, houses, woods, building names, brickworks, mill, county boundary, drains; bridge named.

33/285 Mendlesham (parish) TM 101651
Apt 19.11.1839; 3945a (3944); Map 1839, 6 chns, in 3 parts, by W.S. Grimwade, (includes two 1.5-chn enlargements of detail); waterbodies, houses, woods, milestones.

33/286 Metfield (parish) TM 297802
Apt 06.09.1841; 2162a (2162); Map 1839, 3 chns, 1st cl; waterbodies, houses, woods.

33/287 Mettingham (parish) TM 364900
Apt 25.07.1846; 1387a (1386); Map 1843, 4 chns, surveyed by Richard Barnes of Lowestoft in 1814, and revised by Geo. Baker, Bungay; waterbodies, houses, woods, pit.

33/288 Mickfield (parish) TM 138621
Apt 28.02.1838; 1291a (all); Map 1837, 3 chns, 1st cl; waterbodies, houses, field boundary ownerships, field acreages.

33/289 Middleton (parish) TM 420677
Apt 20.09.1838; 1420a (1420); Map 1839, 3 chns, 1st cl, by James Smy, Saxmundham; construction lines, waterbodies, houses, pits; blue band surrounds Fordley, which is apportioned separately (33/164); pink bands are used for some bracing. Apt omits most field names for tithe-merged land.

33/290 Milden (parish) TL 952458
Apt 30.04.1838; 1339a (all); Map 1839?, 3 chns, 1st cl, surveyed by W. and A. Ruffell, Kersey; construction lines.

33/291 Mildenhall (parish) TL 680780
Apt 19.11.1857; 16770a (13710); Map 1858, 12 chns, by W.W. Cawston, (tithable parts only in detail); barrow, droves (col, named), warren.

33/292 Monewden (parish) TM 238584
Apt 25.09.1838; 1089a (1088); Map 'Content Plan', 1839?, 3 chns; waterbodies, houses, woods, orchards, gardens, hedges, windmill (pictorial), moat, pit, sand pit, holding boundaries (col); a table summarises acreages.

33/293 Monksoham (parish) TM 210655 [Monk Soham]
Apt 28.04.1840; 1570a (1569); Map 1840?, [4 chns]; waterbodies, houses, woods, orchards, green. Apt omits field names.

33/294 Monks Eleigh (parish) TL 970475
Apt 30.09.1842; 2099a (all); Map 1841, 3 chns, 1st cl, in 2 parts, surveyed by W. and A. Ruffell; construction lines; buildings are shown in outline only.

33/295 Moulton (parish) TL 690649
Apt 31.03.1838; 3135a (all); Map 1838, 6 chns, by J. King and Son, Saffron Walden; waterbodies, houses, woods, plantations, building names, former open field names, rectory.

33/296 Mutford (parish) TM 484885
Apt 02.04.1844; 1575a (1574); Map 1843, 3 chns, 1st cl, by Richd Barnes, Lowestoft; construction lines; buildings are shown in outline only.

33/297 Nacton and Levington (parishes) TM 223403
Apt 19.03.1838; 2916a (all); Map 1838, 6 chns, litho (Standidge), surveyed by Benjn Moulton, Woodbridge; waterbodies, houses (by shading), woods, plantations, parkland, heath/moor, avenue of trees, pit, decoy ponds, parish boundary.

33/298 Naughton (parish) TM 026486
Apt 27.08.1841; 855a (all); Map 1839, 3 chns, 1st cl, in 3 parts, by R.E. Sheldrake, Hadleigh, (including 12-chn construction line diagram); construction lines, foot/b'way, waterbodies, houses, woods, boundary posts and trees, windmill (pictorial), glebe.

33/299 Nayland (parish) TL 965345
Apt 06.11.1839; 941a (941); Map 1837, 6 chns, 'Corrected from the Inclosure Survey' by Newton and Woodrow, Norwich; houses, woods (named), osiers (by symbol), landowners (col); pictorial church. Apt omits land use.

33/300 Nedging (parish) TM 008490
Apt 31.03.1838; 837a (837); Map 1838, 3 chns, surveyed by W. and A. Ruffell; houses, landowners (col), glebe.

33/301 Nettlestead (parish) TM 091498
Apt 07.10.1839; 1029a (1028); Map 1839, 3 chns, by S.W. Parkes, Ipswich; construction lines, waterbodies, houses, woods, parkland, orchards, building names, modus land boundary.

33/302 Newbourn (parish) TM 270430 [Newbourne]
Apt 08.06.1846; 897a (all); Map 1846, 3 chns, by W.S. Grimwade; construction lines, waterbodies, houses, wood (by name), field boundary ownerships, craig pits, pits, boundary trees.

33/303 Old Newton (parish) TM 055625
Apt 11.03.1840; 2348a (all); Map 1839, 6 chns, by Henry Calver; waterbodies, houses, woods, orchards, boundary trees and posts, windmill.

33/304 Newton (parish) TL 922410
Apt 20.07.1839; 2198a (2197); Map 'Decr. 1837 and Jany. 1838', 3 chns, by J. Hasell, Sudbury, (including one part at 6 chns); construction lines, fences, road names, boundary trees and mark; buildings are shown in outline only; red and black pecked lines may relate to land ownership.

33/305 Norton (parish) TL 965660
Apt 02.04.1839; 2450a (2449); Map 1840, 6 chns, by W.S. Grimwade; waterbodies, houses, woods (named), pit, pack way, boundary trees, private road; flourishes above title culminate in a bird's head.

33/306 Nowton (parish) TL 864612
Apt 30.05.1842; 1158a (all); Map 1849, 5.3 chns, by John Croft, Bury St Edmunds; turnpike roads, waterbodies, houses, woods, parkland, gardens, fences, road names, pits, hall, greens.

33/307 Oakley (parish) TM 163773
Apt 02.05.1839; 1271a (1288); Map 1839?, 3 chns, by J. Manning, Norwich; waterbodies, houses, woods (col), parkland, grassland (col), orchards, glebe, (yellow), modus land boundary.

33/308 Occold (parish) TM 160707
Apt 28.09.1838; 1480a (1479); Map 3 chns, surveyed 1838 by John Hayward; construction lines, waterbodies, houses, woods, windmill (by symbol); red pecked bands are used for some bracing.

33/309 Offton with Little Bricett (parish) TM 053495
Apt 11.03.1839; 1562a (1561); Map 1840?, 6 chns, ? by S.W. Parkes Ipswich; waterbodies, woods (col), chalk pit, boundary tree; pictorial church; lands in Little Bricett are coloured pink.

33/310 Onehouse (parish) TM 020595
Apt 23.09.1845; 899a (all); Map 1845, 3 chns, 1st cl; construction lines, waterbodies, houses, field boundary ownerships.

33/311 Orford (parish) TM 430502
Apt 22.11.1838; 3400a (?); Map 1838, 3 chns, 1st cl, by Bland H. Galland, C.E.; construction lines, waterbodies, houses, woods (col), plantations (col), orchards, coastguard stations, foreshore, tithe-free land (blue band).

33/312 Otley (parish) TM 205555
Apt 25.05.1839; 2157a (all); Map 1839, 3 chns, by Benjn Moulton, Woodbridge; waterbodies, houses, woods, windmills (by symbol).

33/313 Oulton or Oldton or Owlton (parish) TM 514940
Apt 22.11.1837; 1971a (1997); Map 1841, 3 chns, 1st cl, by Richd Barnes, Lowestoft; construction lines, waterbodies, river locks.

33/314 Ousden (parish) TL 766583
Apt 14.09.1838; 103a (1200); Map 1839, [3 chns], by W.W. Cawston, Worlington, (tithable parts only); foot/b'way, waterbodies, houses, woods, fences, field boundary ownerships, field gates, roadside waste (col).

33/315 Pakefield (parish) TM 534894
Apt 03.02.1843; 687a (771); Map 1845?, 3 chns, 1st cl, by Richd Barnes, Lowestoft; construction lines, houses, high and low water marks.

33/316 Pakenham (parish) TL 927689
Apt 28.01.1841; 3696a (3696); Map 1840, 6 chns, by Young and Cawston; foot/b'way, waterbodies, houses, woods (col), orchards (col), gardens (col), hedge ownership, field boundary ownerships, field gates, packway, pits, avenue of trees.

33/317 Palgrave (parish) TM 110782
Apt 07.02.1838; 1440a (1474); Map 1837, 3 chns; waterbodies, houses, woods, osiers (by symbol), parkland.

33/318 Parham (parish) TM 310610
Apt 14.03.1839; 2213a (2212); Map 'Working Plan', 1839, 3 chns, 1st cl, in 2 parts, surveyed by Sheldrake and McLachlan, Colchester, (including 30-chn construction line diagram); construction lines, foot/b'way, waterbodies, houses, woods (named), plantations, building names, boundary trees and marks, signposts, greens.

33/319 Peasenhall (parish) TM 348691
Apt 31.12.1840; 1972a (1995); Map 1839?, 4 chns, 1st cl, by B. Hood Galland, C.E., Yoxford; houses, woods, 'M. Chapel', meeting mouse, windmill (by symbol); PRO IR30 has two copies, one with construction lines described as 'Content Plan', and one without which is sealed as first class.

33/320 Pettaugh (parish) TM 168597
Apt 13.07.1839; 795a (all); Map 1839, 3 chns, by Richd and Fredk Fenning; construction lines, waterbodies, houses, windmill (by symbol).

33/321 Pettistree (parish) TM 301546
Apt 09.08.1841; 1767a (1767); Map 3 chns, 1st cl, surveyed by Clinton, Dickson, Purvis and Merry in January 1839; construction lines, waterbodies, houses, woods, plantations, orchards.

33/322 Playford (parish) TM 216476
Apt 25.11.1844; 150a (1219); Map 1846, 6 chns, (tithable parts only in detail); turnpike roads, woods, plantations, tithe-free owner; pictorial church; north pointer is decorated with sketchy inverted fish.

33/323 Polstead (parish) TL 990390
Apt 16.03.1842; 3402a (all); Map 1838, 6 chns, 'Copied from Mr Corby's Survey' by Wm Baker, Woolpit; waterbodies, houses, woods (col), plantations (col), parkland (col), arable (col), grassland (col), orchards (col), gardens (col), fence.

33/324 Poslingford (parish) TL 770490
Apt 12.11.1840; 2438a (2438); Map 1841, 4 chns, 'Compiled from Maps in the possession of various proprietors and corrected and Part Surveyed' by John King and Son, Saffron Walden; waterbodies, woods, osiers (by symbol), parkland, building names, vicarage.

33/325 Preston (parish) TL 940507 [Preston St Mary]
Apt 15.02.1839; 1932a (1931); Map 1838, 3 chns, by George Dring, Long Melford; waterbodies, houses, woods, plantations, orchards; scale-bar is ruler-like.

33/326 Ramsholt (parish) TM 317415
Apt 09.05.1840; 1753a (2107); Map 1840, 4 chns, by Benjn Moulton, Woodbridge; construction lines, waterbodies, houses, woods, osiers (by symbol), plantations, reeds.

33/327 Rattlesden (parish) TL 972582
Apt 10.09.1838; 3254a (3254); Map 6 chns, surveyed 1831 and revised 1839 by Richd Payne; foot/b'way, waterbodies, houses, woods (named),

orchards, hops, gardens, building names, road names, malt office, boundary trees and posts, meeting house, windmill, greens, pasture ('P'); pictorial church.

33/328 Raydon (parish) TM 052355
Apt 30.11.1838; 2335a (2335); Map 1840?, 3 chns; construction lines, waterbodies, houses, woods (named), pit, drains.

33/329 Rede (parish) TL 802562
Apt 21.03.1838; 1224a (all); Map 1839, 3 chns, by W.W. Cawston, Worlington; foot/b'way, waterbodies, houses, woods, stiles; north pointer ends in a hand holding a ring with a spike.

33/330 Redgrave (parish) TM 057766
Apt 10.11.1845; 3353a (3353); Map 1846, 6 chns, in 2 parts; waterbodies, houses, woods (col), parkland, gardens.

33/331 Great Redisham (parish) TM 404855 [Redisham]
Apt 27.04.1842; 734a (733); Map 1840, 3 chns, 1st cl, by Crickmay and Beales, Beccles; construction lines, foot/b'way, waterbodies, houses, woods, plantations, mill mound; meaning of colour bands is unclear.

33/332 Redlingfield (parish) TM 187706
Apt 17.07.1839; 1075a (1075); Map 1839, 3 chns, by John Fisher; waterbodies, houses (by shading), woods, windmill (pictorial).

33/333 Rendham (parish) TM 354654
Apt 31.12.1840; 1687a (1721); Map surveyed in 1840, 4 chns, 1st cl, by Alfred Sharman and J. Campbell; construction lines, waterbodies, houses, defaced boundary.

33/334 Rendlesham (parish) TM 339531
Apt 05.09.1839; 2020a (all); Map 1840, 4 chns, 1st cl, by J. Smy, Saxmundham, for B. Moulton, Woodbridge; construction lines, waterbodies, houses, woods, osiers (by symbol); pink bands are used for some bracing.

33/335 Reydon (parish) TM 494781
Apt 31.07.1841; 2727a (2727); Map 1839, 3 chns, 1st cl, by Lenny and Croft, Bury St Edmunds and Wrentham; construction lines, waterbodies, houses, woods, osiers (by symbol), orchards, heath/moor, fences, field boundary ownerships, field gates, building names, road names, avenue of trees, pit, pound, drains; bridge named.

33/336 Rickinghall Inferior and Rickinghall Superior (district) TM 039742 [Ricklinghall]
Apt 08.09.1840; 3367a (3367); Map 6 chns, in 2 parts, surveyed in 1815 for enclosure and revised 1839 by Richd Payne; waterbodies, houses, woods (col), plantations (col), building names, road names, limekilns and pit (col), parsonage, brick kiln, windmill (pictorial), drains; pictorial church.

33/337 Ringsfield (parish) TM 402872
Apt 08.03.1844; 1667a (1666); Map 1844?, 3 chns, by Geo. Baker and Jno. Crickmay, Bungay and Beccles; waterbodies, houses, woods, pit; pink bands are used for bracing.

33/338 Ringshall (parish) TM 040525
Apt 31.03.1838; 2117a (all); Map 1838, [3 chns], surveyed by W. Ruffell; construction lines, woods (named), landowners (col).

33/339 Risby (parish) TL 798669
Apt 20.11.1839; 2801a (all); Map 1839, 6 chns, by Lenny and Croft, Bury St Edmunds; turnpike roads, toll gate, waterbodies, houses, woods (named), parkland, orchards, gardens, heath/moor, fences, private roads, rectory, chalk pit, pits, nursery (by symbol); pond named.

33/340 Rishangles (parish) TM 164687
Apt 21.03.1846; 719a (718); Map 1847?, 6 chns; foot/b'way, waterbodies, houses.

33/341 Rumburgh (parish) TM 353813
Apt 20.10.1843; 1041a (1468); Map 1842, 3 chns, 1st cl, by Geo. Baker, Bungay, and Jno. Chickmay, Beccles, (tithable parts only in detail); waterbodies, houses, woods.

33/342 Rushbrooke (parish) TL 888618
Apt 26.08.1839; 1060a (1060); Map 1840, 6 chns, litho (by Straker, 118 Bishopsgate, London), by W.S. Grimwade, (includes small manuscript enlargement of detail); foot/b'way, waterbodies, houses, woods (named), plantations, parkland, orchards, gardens, wire fence, chalk pit, dry pit, boundary tree; houses are hand-coloured.

33/343 Rushmere (parish) TM 495875
Apt 22.11.1837; 760a (759); Map 1839?, 3 chns, 1st cl, by Richd Barnes, Lowestoft; construction lines; buildings are shown in outline only, without fill.

33/344 Rushmere St Andrew (parish) TM 192452
Apt 26.02.1845; 2143a (2142); Map 1840, 3 chns, by S.L. Bransby, Ipswich; waterbodies, houses, woods, gardens, windmills (pictorial), pits (col), heath; pictorial church.

33/345 Great Saxham (parish) TL 789638
Apt 13.04.1839; 1429a (all); Map 1840, 4 chns, by Lenny and Croft, Bury St Edmunds; waterbodies, houses, woods, gardens, fences; pictorial church.

33/346 Little Saxham (parish) TL 801637
Apt 17.11.1846; 1307a (all); Map 1843, 6 chns, by Richard Payne, Bury St Edmunds; foot/b'way, waterbodies, houses, woods (col, named), building names, spring, pits (col), churchyard (col), green (col).

33/347 Saxmundham (parish) TM 386630
Apt 02.09.1841; 1102a (1101); Map 1840, 3 chns, by B.H. Galland, C.E.; waterbodies, houses, woods (col), plantations, gardens (col), sand and other pits.

33/348 Saxted (parish) TM 258654 [Saxtead]
Apt 11.07.1838; 1163a (1202); Map 1839?, [4 chns], by Preston; foot/b'way, waterbodies, houses, greens, holdings (col).

33/349 Seamer (parish) TL 999466 [Semer]
Apt 18.06.1838; 1248a (all); Map 1838, 3 chns, in 2 parts, surveyed by W. and A. Ruffell; construction lines, waterbodies, houses, woods, plantations, landowners.

33/350 Shaddingfield (parish) TM 430844 [Shadingfield]
Apt 04.05.1840; 1369a (1369); Map 1839, 3 chns, by Crickmay and Beales, Beccles, Suffolk; construction lines, waterbodies, houses, woods, sand pit, dry pit, arches, pump, rookery, mill, public and private roads, glebe, rookery.

33/351 Shelland (parish) TM 003604 [Not listed]
Apt 05.03.1839; 540a (all); Map 1841, 3 chns, by P. Baker, Woolpit; waterbodies, houses, woods, gardens, roadside waste (col); pictorial church.

33/352 Shelley (parish) TM 019382
Apt 15.06.1841; 928a (928); Map 1838, 3 chns, 'copy', by R. Postans; waterbodies, houses, farmyards (col), woods (col), osiers (by symbol), arable (col), orchards, gardens (col), wooden bridge.

33/353 Shimpling Thorne (parish) TL 863514 [Shimplingthorne]
Apt 14.02.1839; 2698a (2698); Map 1839, 6 chns, by William Browne, Davey Place, Norwich; waterbodies, houses, woods, parkland, orchards, building names, landowners (col), windmill (by symbol).

33/354 Shipmeadow (parish) TM 380898
Apt 27.02.1839; 821a (all); Map 1841?, 6 chns, by Crickmay and Beales, Bungay and Beccles; foot/b'way, waterbodies, woods, grassland (by symbol), pits, common, glebe; pictorial church.

33/355 Shotley (parish) TM 238359
Apt 23.02.1839; 2052a (all); Map 1839, 3 chns, by Benjn Spurling; hill-drawing, waterbodies, houses, woods, osiers (by symbol), orchards, gardens, marsh/bog, field boundary ownerships, windmill (by symbol), martello towers, pits, common, saltings.

33/356 Shottisham (parish) TM 323447
Apt 22.01.1840; 1135a (all); Map 1838, 6 chns, by Bland Hood Galland, C.E., Yoxford; waterbodies, houses, woods, osiers (by symbol), arable (col), grassland (col), field names, mill, hall (in gothic), windmill, glebe, common, field acreages, ownerships (col).

33/357 Sibton (parish) TM 369693
Apt 25.10.1842; 1773a (2861); Map 1839, 4 chns, surveyed by B.H. Galland, C.E., (tithable parts only); waterbodies, houses, woods, plantations, holding boundary ownerships; it is unclear why some fields are tinted pink.

33/358 Snape (parish) TM 400590
Apt 21.08.1846; 2100a (2100); Map 1848?, 3 chns; houses, woods, plantations, embankments, sand pit, post mill, toll gate, windmills (by symbol), commons, drains; unmarked boundary between trees is described.

33/359 Somerleyton (parish) TM 451971
Apt 15.09.1837; 1391a (1410); Map 1843, 3 chns, 1st cl, by Richd Barnes, Lowestoft; construction lines, houses, woods, brickworks, avenue of trees; pictorial church.

33/360 Somersham (parish) TM 084481
Apt 31.07.1839; 1027a (1027); Map 1839, 4 chns, by S.W. Parkes, Ipswich; foot/b'way, waterbodies, houses, woods, orchards, gardens, building names, windmill (by symbol).

33/361 Somerton (parish) TL 812530
Apt 26.05.1841; 1040a (all); Map 1840, 3 chns, surveyed by William Borley, Alpheton; waterbodies, houses, woods, plantations, orchards, pit (col); pictorial church.

33/362 Sotherton (parish) TM 429793
Apt 04.10.1838; 1085a (1085); Map 1838, 3 chns, 1st cl, by Lenny and Croft, Bury St Edmunds; construction lines, foot/b'way, waterbodies, houses, orchards, fences, field boundary ownerships, field gates.

33/363 Sotterley (parish) TM 463847
Apt 31.12.1840; 1593a (1593); Map 1842, 3 chns, 1st cl, by Richd Barnes, Lowestoft; construction lines, houses, stiles; uninhabited buildings are shown in outline only.

33/364 All Saints with St Nicholas, Southelmham (parish) TM 330828 [All Saints South Elmham]
Apt 20.06.1839; 1621a (1600); Map 1839, 4 chns, 1st cl, by Bland H. Galland, C.E.; construction lines, waterbodies, houses, glebe.

33/365 St Cross or St George in Southelmham (parish) TM 300838 [St Cross South Elmham]
Apt 16.01.1840; 1287a (1110); Map 1839, 4 chns, 1st cl, surveyed by B.H. Galland, C.E.; construction lines, waterbodies, houses.

33/366 St James in Southelmham (parish) TM 321811 [St James South Elmham]
Apt 21.10.1840; 1302a (all); Map 1840, 3 chns, 1st cl, by J. Crickmay and G. Baker, Beccles, Suffolk; construction lines, waterbodies, houses; pink bands are used for some bracing.

33/367 St Margaret in Southelmham (parish) TM 313840 [St Margaret South Elmham]
Apt 28.01.1841; 589a (710); Map 1838, 3 chns, 1st cl, by Geo. Baker, Bungay, and Jno. Crickmay, Beccles; construction lines, waterbodies, houses, woods.

33/368 St Michael in Southelmham (parish) TM 342833 [St Michael South Elmham]
Apt 21.05.1846; 825a (930); Map 1842, 3 chns, 1st cl, by W.S. Grimwade, Wethingsett; construction lines, waterbodies, houses, field boundary ownerships, field gates, road names, boundary trees.

33/369 St Peter in Southelmham (parish) TM 335852 [St Peter South Elmham]
Apt 22.01.1840; 572a (all); Map 1839, 4 chns, 1st cl, surveyed by Bland H. Galland; construction lines, waterbodies, houses, ownership boundaries.

33/370 Southolt (parish) TM 200690
Apt 11.07.1838; 798a (798); Map 1839, 6 chns, by H. Preston; waterbodies, houses, greens.

33/371 Southtown or Little Yarmouth with West Town (parish) TG 520070
Apt 11.03.1839; 695a (?); Map 1841, 3 chns, 1st cl, by Pratt and Son, Norwich, and Richard Barnes, Lowestoft; construction lines, waterbodies, houses, field boundary ownerships.

33/372 Southwold (parish) TM 501759
Apt 31.12.1840; 367a (all); Map 1840, 3 chns, in 2 parts, by Lenny and Croft, Bury St Edmunds, (tithable parts only); landowners, windmills (pictorial), brickworks, chapel, glebe.

33/373 Spexhall (parish) TM 381811
Apt 08.11.1837; 1484a (1484); Map 1838, 3 chns, by James Drane, Norwich; foot/b'way, turnpike roads, waterbodies, houses, woods, plantations, orchards, gardens, building names, parsonage, milestones, boundary trees, pit (col), boundary posts.

33/374 Sproughton (parish) TM 124442
Apt 15.07.1837; 2394a (2393); Map 1838?, 3 chns, 'From Compilations and Surveys' by Spencer L. Bransby, Ipswich; construction lines, turnpike roads, waterbodies, houses, farmyards, woods, osiers (by symbol), plantations, parkland, orchards, arable (col), grassland (col), gardens (col), building names, river lock, watermill (by Dawson's symbol), pit (col).

33/375 Stanningfield (parish) TL 880563
Apt 03.03.1838; 1455a (all); Map 1838, 3 chns, surveyed by Richd Payne, Bury St Edmunds; construction lines, foot/b'way, waterbodies, woods (named), plantations, orchards, building names, parsonage, dovecot, greens.

33/376 Stansfield (parish) TL 782525
Apt 26.09.1837; 1989a (all); Map 1840, 6 chns, by Lenny and Croft; waterbodies, houses, woods (named), parkland, orchards, fences, building names, road names, pound, green; bridge named.

33/377 Stanstead (parish) TL 843499
Apt 31.01.1839; 1162a (1162); Map 1838, 3 chns, by George Dring, Melford, Suffolk; waterbodies, houses, woods (col), coppice (col), plantations, arable (col), grassland (col), orchards, gardens (col), field boundary ownerships, building names, parsonage.

33/378 Stanton (parish) TL 968734
Apt 16.04.1839; 3254a (3254); Map 1839, 9 chns, by Henry Calver; waterbodies, houses, woods, osiers (by symbol), orchards, windmills (pictorial); pictorial church; scale bar has two small north pointers at each end.

33/379 Sternfield (parish) TM 393615
Apt 31.12.1840; 1106a (all); Map 1838, 3 chns, by Bland Hood Galland, Civil Engineer, Yoxford; waterbodies, houses, woods (col), plantations (col), parkland, orchards, gardens, rectory, sand pits, hedgerow trees; a fly or bee surmounts the title.

33/380 Stoke Ash (parish) TM 119701
Apt 02.09.1841; 1201a (all); Map 1841, 6 chns, by H. Preston, Worlingworth; waterbodies, houses, woods, osiers (by symbol), plantations, orchards, gardens, windmill (pictorial). Apt omits some field names.

33/381 Stoke juxta Clare (parish) TL 735445 [Stoke by Clare]
Apt 30.10.1839; 2362a (2361); Map 1840, 4 chns, by J. Hasell, Sudbury, Suffolk; foot/b'way, houses, building names, stile, greens; bridges named.

33/382 Stoke by Nayland (parish) TL 987357 [Stoke-by-Nayland]
Apt 26.04.1838; 5278a (5277); Map 1837, 9 chns; waterbodies, houses, woods (col), plantations (col), parkland, arable (col), grassland (col), orchards (col), gardens (col), building names; bridge named; north pointer has crown and plumes. Apt omits land use.

33/383 Stonham Aspall (parish) TM 140600 [Stonham Aspal]
Apt 10.09.1838; 2400a (all); Map 1838, 6 chns; foot/b'way, waterbodies, houses, woods; scale bar has small north pointers at each end; main north pointer has feathery crown.

33/384 Little Stonham (parish) TM 115611 [Little Stoneham]
Apt 09.05.1840; 1194a (all); Map 1839, 6 chns, in 10 parts, by Newton and Woodrow, Norwich, (includes nine 1-chn enlargements of detail); foot/b'way, waterbodies, houses, woods, orchards.

33/385 Stoven (parish) TM 448822
Apt 27.09.1838; 797a (all); Map 1838, 3 chns, 1st cl, by Lenny and Croft; construction lines, turnpike roads, waterbodies, houses, woods, plantations, parkland, orchards, fences, field boundary ownerships, field gates, road names, greens, common (col); scale statement and north pointer are combined.

33/386 West Stow (parish) TL 808732
Apt 12.09.1837; 2927a (2926); Map 1840, 8 chns, by Lenny and Croft, Bury St Edmunds; waterbodies, houses, woods, plantations, parkland, heath/moor, fences, staunch, sluices, hall, rectory, lodges; land tinted yellow is tithable to rector of Wordwell.

33/387 Stowlangtoft (parish) TL 959685
Apt 20.03.1848; 1472a (all); Map 1848, 6 chns, by John Croft, Bury St Edmunds; foot/b'way, waterbodies, houses, plantations, parkland, lawn (col), orchards, gardens, fences, pits. Apt omits field names.

33/388 Stowmarket (parish) TM 046586
Apt 12.09.1840; 1033a (1033); Map 'Working Plan', 1839, 3 chns, 1st cl, in 2 parts, surveyed by Sheldrake and McLachlan, Stowmarket, (tithable parts only in detail; including 15-chn construction line diagram); construction lines, waterbodies, houses, woods, plantations, orchards, hops, road names, vicarage, camping ground, windmills (by symbol), pit, tithe-free areas (col); bridge named; district was surveyed in conjunction with 33/389.

33/389 Stowupland (parish) TM 078598
Apt 27.01.1841; 2841a (2841); Map 'Working Plan', 1839, 3 chns, 1st cl, in 3 parts, by Sheldrake and McLachlan, Stowmarket, (including 15-chn construction line diagram with pictorial church); construction lines, waterbodies, houses, plantations, windmills, paling, tithe-free areas (col), grass in mixed-use fields (by annotation); a pecked boundary is annotated 'pollards'; district was surveyed in conjunction with 33/388.

33/390 Stradbrooke (parish) TM 250740 [Stradbroke]
Apt 08.06.1840; 3702a (all); Map 1841?, [10 chns]; waterbodies, houses, woods, plantations, workhouse.

33/391 Stradishall (parish) TL 742528
Apt 21.01.1839; 1377a (1376); Map 1839, 6 chns, surveyed by J. King and Son, Saffron Walden; waterbodies, houses, woods, building names, rectory, commons.

33/392 Stratford St Andrew (parish) TM 351604
Apt 19.11.1846; 793a (793); Map 3 chns, 1st cl, surveyed in October 1838 by M. Clinton, S. Dickson and J. Purvis, Land Surveyors for J. Smy, C.E.; construction lines, waterbodies, houses, woods (col), pits, drains, holding boundaries (col); pink bands are used for some bracing.

33/393 Stratford St Mary (parish) TM 053347
Apt 31.01.1839; 1432a (1461); Map 1838, 3 chns; waterbodies, woods, orchards. Apt omits land use.

33/394 Stuston (parish) TM 135780
Apt 15.11.1843; 776a (775); Map 1839, 3 chns, surveyed by J. Manning, 64 Bethel St, Norwich; foot/b'way, waterbodies, houses, woods, residual open fields.

33/395 Stutton (parish) TM 145345
Apt 08.05.1844; 2120a (all); Map 1844, 3 chns, by Benjn Spurling, Burgh; waterbodies, houses, woods, parkland, orchards, field boundary ownerships, pits, avenues of trees.

33/396 Sudborne (parish) TM 430530 [Sudbourne]
Apt 22.03.1839; 5349a (5429); Map 1841, 5 chns, 1st cl, surveyed by Bland H. Galland, Civil Engineer; construction lines, waterbodies, houses, woods (col, named), parkland, gardens, high and low water marks, beach, crag pit, embankment, hall, sand pit, disputed boundary, saltings.

33/397 All Saints Sudbury (parish) TL 868411 [Not listed]
Apt 29.11.1845; 39a (all); Map 1846, 3 chns, by J. Hasell, Sudbury; waterbodies, woods, plantations, orchards, gardens, grassland (col), road names, gas works, school; public buildings are hatched, and others are shown in outline only. Apt omits land use.

33/398 St George and St Peter in Sudbury (parish) TL 880420 [Not listed]
Apt 04.09.1840; 745a (?); Map 1840?, 3 chns, by H. Coates, 12 Duke St, Portland Place, London, (tithable parts only in detail); waterbodies, woods, field boundary ownerships, road names, landowners, mill, clay pits; red bands may show tithe ownership.

33/399 Sutton (parish) TM 305465
Apt 15.08.1844; 5971a (all); Map 1844, 8 chns; waterbodies, houses, woods.

33/400 Swefling (parish) TM 342639 [Sweffling]
Apt 07.09.1841; 1120a (all); Map 1839, 4 chns, 1st cl, by B.H. Galland, C.E.; construction lines, waterbodies, houses, woods (col), plantations (col), orchards, gardens (col), glebe, parsonage, churchyard, 'ditch taken away', ownerships (col); meaning of green band is unclear.

33/401 Swilland (parish) TM 194526
Apt 09.07.1839; 952a (951); Map 1839, [3 chns]; by Richard, Frederick and Richard Fenning; construction lines, houses, farmyards, churchyard, windmill (by symbol).

33/402 Sylcham (parish) TM 212783
Apt 31.08.1841; 1603a (1603); Map 1839, 6 chns; foot/b'way, waterbodies, houses, woods, plantations, orchards, gardens, pit, drains.

33/403 Tannington (parish) TM 245675
Apt 26.01.1841; 1602a (1602); Map 1841?, 6 chns; waterbodies, houses, woods (col), green.

33/404 Tattingstone (parish) TM 138372
Apt 28.02.1837; 1637a (all); Map 1837, 3 chns, by Calver and Grimwade; foot/b'way, waterbodies, houses, pits.

33/405 Theberton (parish) TM 432653
Apt 05.06.1838; 1938a (1954); Map 'Revised Plan', 1839, [5 chns]; foot/b'way, waterbodies, houses; pink bands are used for bracing. Apt omits most field names.

33/406 Thelnetham (parish) TM 003768
Apt 20.01.1847; 1774a (all); Map 1846, 6 chns; houses; uninhabited buildings are shown in outline only.

33/407 Thorington (parish) TM 421732
Apt 31.05.1839; 1411a (all); Map 1841, 8 chns, by J. Stigall; waterbodies, houses, woods, plantations.

33/408 Thorndon All Saints (parish) TM 148688 [Thorndon]
Apt 13.06.1839; 2680a (2680); Map surveyed in 1838, 3 chns, by John Hayward; construction lines, waterbodies, houses, woods, windmill (by symbol), glebe, (yellow), 'town land'; north pointer has crown and plumes.

33/409 Great Thornham (parish) TM 102713 [Thornham Magna]
Apt 30.01.1841; 1324a (1324); Map 1844?, 6 chns; waterbodies, houses, gardens; title is upside down to scale and area numbers.

33/410 Little Thornham (parish) TM 106728 [Thornham Parva]
Apt 30.01.1841; 677a (676); Map 1844?, 6 chns; waterbodies, houses.

33/411 Thorpe Morieux (parish) TL 940536
Apt 11.09.1843; 2457a (2457); Map 1843, 3 chns, in 2 parts, surveyed by Ruffell and Sexton; construction lines; buildings are shown in outline only, without fill.

33/412 Thrandeston (parish) TM 118763
Apt 15.02.1845; 1375a (all); Map 1845, 6 chns, by H. Preston; waterbodies, houses, greens, marsh, glebe.

33/413 Great Thurlow (parish) TL 672510
Apt 21.03.1840; 2023a (2023); Map 1839, 3 chns, by W. Ruffell; woods (named).

33/414 Little Thurlow (parish) TL 671511
Apt 21.03.1846; 1382a (all); Map 1846, 4 chns, by John French; foot/b'way, waterbodies, woods; legend explains parish boundaries.

33/415 Thurston (parish) TL 930654
Apt 26.08.1839; 2200a (2200); Map 1840, 3 chns, by P. Baker, Woolpit; waterbodies, houses, woods (col), parkland, grassland (col), orchards, gardens (col), boundary trees, windmill (by symbol), fences.

33/416 Thwaite (parish) TM 115680
Apt 10.05.1839; 832a (all); Map 'Working Plan', surveyed in 1838, 3 chns, 1st cl, by Hayward and Wells; construction lines, waterbodies, houses, woods.

33/417 Timworth (parish) TL 869691
Apt 19.06.1840; 1359a (all); Map 1840, 8 chns, by Lenny and Croft, Bury St Edmunds; foot/b'way, waterbodies, houses, plantations, orchards, field gates, pits.

33/418 Tostock (parish) TL 955638
Apt 04.03.1843; 945a (all); Map 1843, 6 chns, by W.S. Grimwade, Wetheringsett, Suffolk; foot/b'way, waterbodies, houses, woods (col), parkland, orchards, gardens, parsonage, hall, glebe (yellow), churchyard (col), green.

33/419 Trimley St Martin (parish) TM 265368
Apt 30.06.1840; 2138a (2338); Map 1839, 6 chns, by Newton and Woodrow, Norwich; waterbodies, houses, farmyards, orchards, embankment, windmills (pictorial), drains; pictorial church.

33/420 Trimley St Mary (parish) TM 279361
Apt 05.12.1840; 1868a (2208); Map 1839, 6 chns, by Newton and Woodrow, Norwich; waterbodies, houses, woods, embankment, drains, estuary cliffs; pictorial church.

33/421 Troston (parish) TL 896727
Apt 09.11.1841; 1764a (all); Map 1841, 6 chns, by Richard Payne, Bury St Edmunds; waterbodies, houses, woods (col), plantations (col), windmill, pits (col).

33/422 Tuddenham St Martin (parish) TM 183487 [Tuddenham]
Apt 09.10.1838; 1239a (all); Map 1838, 3 chns, by S.L. Bransby, Ipswich; waterbodies, houses, woods (col), orchards, windmill (pictorial), pit (col); pictorial church.

33/423 Tuddenham St Mary (parish) TL 740710 [Tuddenham]
Apt 11.07.1837; 2645a (2644); Map 1837, 3 chns, by Lenny and Croft, Bury St Edmunds; waterbodies, plantations, fences, building names, road names, mill stream, windmill (col), watermill (by Dawson's symbol), rectory, spring (named), green.

33/424 Tunstall (parish) TM 375550
Apt 26.01.1842; 2863a (all); Map 1840, 6 chns, by Pratt and Son, Norwich; waterbodies, houses, woods (named), parkland, gardens, road names, embankment, avenue of trees, pits, tidal zone (col), common; green band may show heath and common; pictorial church.

33/425 Ubbeston (parish) TM 320722
Apt 10.09.1838; 1212a (1212); Map 1839?, 3 chns, by John Stigall, Bram; foot/b'way, waterbodies, houses, woods (col), plantations (col), orchards (col), arable (col), grassland (col), windmill (by symbol), holding boundaries (col).

33/426 Ufford (parish) TM 293523
Apt 04.12.1843; 1157a (1156); Map 1844?, 4 chns, by Benjamin Moulton, Woodbridge; waterbodies, houses, woods, plantations, pits.

33/427 Uggeshall (parish) TM 458808
Apt 04.10.1838; 1474a (1473); Map 1838, 3 chns, 1st cl, by Lenny and Croft, Wrentham; construction lines, waterbodies, houses, woods, plantations, parkland, orchards, fences, field boundary ownerships, field gates, building names, road names, churchyard, rectory, windmill (pictorial), brickworks, stiles, pits; map includes a considerable part of Frostenden (33/174); one field boundary is annotated 'Thrown down'.

33/428 Walberswick (parish) TM 481748
Apt 14.11.1840; 1961a (1960); Map 1841, 8 chns, 'Copied' by Pratt and Son, Norwich; waterbodies, houses, woods, heath/moor, ferry, beach.

33/429 Great Waldingfield (parish) TL 910440
Apt 26.06.1838; 2424a (2423); Map 1838, 3 chns, in 18 parts, by J. Hasell, (some parts at 6 or 8 chns); construction lines; some of the detached parts have location descriptions; buildings are shown without infill; pictorial church.

33/430 Little Waldingfield (parish) TL 930450
Apt 31.05.1839; 1575a (1574); Map 1839, 4 chns, 'Revised' by William Borley, Alpheton; waterbodies, houses, woods, plantations, parkland, orchards, gardens, avenues of trees, pit, private roads (uncoloured).

33/431 Waldringfield (parish) TM 278445
Apt 26.08.1839; 876a (all); Map 1839, 3 chns, by S.L. Bransby, Ipswich; houses, woods; uninhabited buildings are shown in outline only; pictorial church.

33/432 Walpole (parish) TM 371739
Apt 19.11.1846; 1653a (1750); Map 1850?, 6 chns; foot/b'way, waterbodies, houses, woods, boundary trees and milestones, pits, 'Old River'. Apt omits land use and most field names.

33/433 Walsham le Willows (parish) TM 010712 [Walsham Le Willows]
Apt 21.10.1842; 2801a (2800); Map 1842, 6 chns, by Lenny and Croft, Bury St Edmunds; waterbodies, houses, woods, parkland, orchards, road names, signpost (pictorial), windmill (pictorial).

33/434 Walton (parish) TM 292355
Apt 15.01.1845; 1988a (1988); Map 1840, 3 chns, by Benj. Moulton, Woodbridge; construction lines, waterbodies, houses, woods, orchards, drains.

33/435 Wangford (parish) TM 470789
Apt 29.08.1839; 303a (851); Map 1839, 6 chns, by Lenny and Croft, Bury St Edmunds, (tithable parts only); waterbodies, woods, landowners, pit, green, pack way; pictorial church; tithe owner is named in map title.

33/436 Wangford near Brandon (parish) TL 762832 [Wangford]
Apt 24.12.1842; 3263a (3252); Map 1843, 5 chns; waterbodies, houses, woods, lodge (pictorial), warren, breck, fen, carr.

33/437 Wantisden (parish) TM 361527 [Not listed]
Apt 07.08.1845; 2126a (all); Map 1845, 4 chns, 'Copied and Revised from Johnson's Survey' by Benj. Moulton; waterbodies, houses, woods, pit; green band may show tithe ownership.

33/438 Washbrook (parish) TM 107425
Apt 15.05.1838; 1444a (1443); Map surveyed 1837, 3 chns, by Chapman, Son and Webb, Arundel St, Strand; waterbodies, houses, woods, field boundary ownerships.

33/439 Wattisfield (parish) TM 009738
Apt 23.10.1844; 1518a (1517); Map 1839?, 3 chns, surveyed by Henry and Herbert Coates, 12 Duke St, Portland Place, London; waterbodies, houses, plantations, glebe, green; the map appears to have been amended before resubmission in 1847.

33/440 Wattisham (parish) TM 011519
Apt 29.11.1841; 1299a (all); Map 1842?, 3 chns, in 3 parts, surveyed by W. Ruffell; woods (col), landowners, boundary oak, churchyard, ownerships (col, named); one detached portion has been scraped out and redrawn in a new position.

33/441 Little Weltenham (parish) TL 890600 [Little Welnetham]
Apt 13.07.1838; 593a (592); Map 1838, 6 chns, by W.S. Grimwade; foot/b'way, waterbodies, houses, woods, landowners, boundary trees; a note explains that the red line is the parish boundary as agreed with an assistant tithe commissioner.

33/442 Little Wenham (parish) TM 085398
Apt 29.08.1843; 932a (all); Map 1843?, 3 chns, 'Working Plan', surveyed by Sheldrake and McLachlan, Colchester; construction lines, waterbodies, houses, boundary post.

33/443 Wenham Magna (parish) TM 068393 [Great Wenham]
Apt 29.08.1843; 1124a (1123); Map 1843?, 3 chns, surveyed by Sheldrake and McLachlan, Colchester; construction lines, foot/b'way,

waterbodies, fences, boundary posts and trees, sand pit; buildings are shown in outline only.

33/444 Winhaston and Mells (parish and hamlet) TM 402759
Apt 30.09.1839; 2327a (2326); Map 1839, 8 chns, by Pratt and Son; greens.

33/445 Westerfield (parish) TM 176478
Apt 16.05.1839; 1071a (all); Map 1839, [6 chns], 'Corrected from an old Survey' by Benjn Spurling; waterbodies, houses, woods, plantations, field boundary ownerships, pits, windmill (by symbol). Apt omits land use.

33/446 Westhall (parish) TM 412815
Apt 16.05.1841; 2317a (2316); Map 1840, 12 chns, revised by B.H. Galland from a survey of 1812 by R. Barnes; foot/b'way, houses, arable (col), grassland (col), field boundary ownerships, glebe (grey); pictorial church; uninhabited buildings are shown in outline only.

33/447 Westhorpe (parish) TM 042694
Apt 12.06.1839; 1322a (1322); Map 1840?, [6 chns], by Preston, Surveyor; waterbodies, houses, road names, common; uninhabited buildings are shown in outline only.

33/448 Westleton (parish) TM 445685
Apt 25.08.1842; 6103a (6103); Map 1842?, 4 chns, copied 'from B.H. Galland's Map' by J. Stagoll; houses, building names, windmills, drains; bridges named.

33/449 Westley (parish) TL 827647
Apt 15.07.1837; 1217a (all); Map 1837, 3 chns, surveyed for enclosure in 1813 and revised by R. Payne; construction lines, foot/b'way, waterbodies, houses, woods, plantations, orchards, gardens, old churchyard, private road, pit; table lists owners, occupiers, field names, land use and acreages.

33/450 Weston (parish) TM 428870
Apt 26.02.1840; 1551a (1550); Map 1839, 3 chns, by Crickmay and Beales, Beccles; foot/b'way, waterbodies, houses, woods (col), landowners, sand pits, public and private roads.

33/451 Weston Market (parish) TL 989779 [Market Weston]
Apt 25.02.1842; 1078a (1083); Map 1842, 7.5 chns, by Lenny and Croft, Bury St Edmunds; waterbodies, houses, woods (named), parkland, gardens, fences, building names, road names, windmill, pound, rectory.

33/452 Wetherden (parish) TM 011641
Apt 23.08.1845; 1831a (all); Map 1846?, 3 chns, by J. and J. Barnes; construction lines, railway, waterbodies, houses, woods (col), windmill (pictorial), avenue of trees; compass rose and title are multi-coloured.

33/453 Wetheringsett with Brockford (parish) TM 133653
Apt 30.06.1841; 3784a (3783); Map 1840, 4 chns, 1st cl, by B. Moulton, Woodbridge, Suffolk, and J. Smy, Saxmundham, Suffolk; multi-colour bands are used for some bracing.

33/454 Weybread (parish) TM 242809
Apt 16.04.1839; 2477a (2476); Map 1839, 6 chns, by S.W. Parkes, Ipswich; waterbodies, houses, woods, drains. Apt omits most field names.

33/455 Whatfield (parish) TM 025465
Apt 06.12.1843; 1571a (all); Map 1844?, 3 chns, 1st cl, foot/b'way, waterbodies, houses, woods (col), field gates, building names, boundary stones and posts, glebe.

33/456 Great Whelnetham (parish) TL 879592 [Great Welnetham]
Apt 09.09.1842; 1483a (all); Map 1842, 3 chns, by Richard Payne, Bury St Edmunds, Suffolk; construction lines, waterbodies, houses, woods (named), orchards, fences, field boundary ownerships, boundary trees, windmills, turnpike gate, gravel pit (col), parsonage, greens.

33/457 Great Whelnetham (district) TL 830580 [Not listed]
Apt 06.12.1843; 11a (all); Map 1844?, 3 chns; waterbodies.

33/458 Whepstead (parish) TL 832582
Apt 23.02.1843; 2670a (2670); Map 1843, 3 chns, 1st cl, by W.W. Cawston; construction lines, waterbodies, houses, gardens, road names, stone cross; in the churchyard there is a rectangle with 'A.C. 1791' written to it.

33/459 Wherstead (parish) TM 153407
Apt 13.07.1839; 2019a (all); Map 1839, 4 chns, by S.L. Bransby, Ipswich; waterbodies, houses, woods; pictorial church.

33/460 Whitton-cum-Thurlston (parishes) TM 155479
Apt 24.05.1839; 1460a (all); Map 1840, 3 chns, by Benjn Spurling; waterbodies, houses, woods, plantations, field boundary ownerships, boundary trees, stone pit, parish boundary.

33/461 Wickham Market (parish) TM 299559
Apt 30.04.1840; 1175a (all); Map 1842, 3 chns, litho (by Shaw and Son, 137 Fetter Lane, London), 1st cl, in 6 parts, (includes five small manuscript enlargements of detail); houses (by shading), woods, workhouse, mill, churchyard (named in gothic).

33/462 Wickham Skeith (parish) TM 095699
Apt 15.06.1839; 1771a (1770); Map 'A Rough Map', 1840, 3 chns, surveyed in 1823 by John Hayward; waterbodies, woods, green, windmills (pictorial).

33/463 Wickhambrook (parish) TL 750564
Apt 05.02.1840; 4348a (4348); Map 1839, 3 chns, 1st cl, by Tunstall and Hine, 10 Allen Terrace, Kensington; construction lines, waterbodies, houses, woods (col), field boundary ownerships, avenue of trees, mill; legend explains symbols.

33/464 Wilby (parish) TM 242718
Apt 27.05.1838; 1844a (1844); Map not dated, [6 chns]; waterbodies, houses, common, ownerships (col); pictorial church.

33/465 Willisham (parish) TM 071505
Apt 01.11.1839; 927a (all); Map 1839, 3 chns, by S.W. Parkes, Ipswich; waterbodies, houses, woods (col), chalk pit; pink band shows land owned by the tithe owners; pictorial church.

33/466 Willingham (parish) TM 442850
Apt 16.03.1840; 1023a (1023); Map 1841?, 3 chns, 1st cl, by Richd Barnes, Lowestoft; construction lines, foot/b'way; buildings are shown in outline only, without fill.

33/467 Wingfield (parish) TM 229771
Apt 31.10.1840; 2441a (2441); Map 1841?, 6 chns, by W.S. Millard and Son, Norwich; waterbodies, woods, greens; pictorial church.

33/468 Winston (parish) TM 178615
Apt 23.05.1845; 1477a (1476); Map 1846?, 3 chns; green.

33/469 Wissett (parish) TM 365793
Apt 22.01.1841; 2260a (2259); Map 1839, 8 chns, 'Revised' by Bland Hood Galland, C.E.; woods, mill, pit, pound, ownerships (pink); pictorial church.

33/470 Wiston (parish) TL 958335 [Wissington]
Apt 16.04.1839; 1486a (1485); Map 1837, 6 chns; waterbodies, houses, woods, landowners (col); pictorial church. Apt omits land use.

33/471 Withersdale (parish) TM 281804 [Withersdale Street]
Apt 15.02.1840; 880a (880); Map 1839, 3 chns, in 2 parts; construction lines, waterbodies, houses, woods, pits.

33/472 Withersfield (parish) TL 650484
Apt 29.11.1841; 2509a (all); Map 1840, 6 chns, litho (by J.R. Jobbins, 3 Warwick Ct, Holborn), by J. King and Son, Saffron Walden; waterbodies, woods, residual open fields (named), building names, field names, rectory, windmill (pictorial), commons.

33/473 Witnesham (parish) TM 183510
Apt 15.11.1843; 1996a (all); Map 1840, 3 chns, by Benjn Spurling; waterbodies, houses, woods (col), hops (col), pits, windmill (by symbol), field boundary ownership.

33/474 Wixoe (parish) TL 714436
Apt 24.08.1839; 620a (all); Map 1839, 3 chns, surveyed by J. Hasell; waterbodies, houses, woods, osiers (by symbol), plantations, field boundary ownerships, building names, holding boundaries (col); pictorial church.

33/475 Woodbridge (parish) TM 266486
Apt 09.05.1840; 1060a (all); Map surveyed in 1838, 3 chns, by Benjn Moulton; waterbodies, houses, woods, parkland, town hall.

33/476 Woolpit (parish) TL 981619
Apt 18.09.1845; 1878a (1877); Map 1845, 3 chns, surveyed by Baker and Sexton; houses, brickworks, windmill (by symbol), heath, green; uninhabited buildings are shown in outline only, including the church.

33/477 Woolverstone (parish) TM 188382
Apt 07.12.1838; 952a (all); Map 1839, 3 chns, by S.W. Parkes, Ipswich; construction lines, foot/b'way, waterbodies, houses, woods, parkland (named), field boundary ownerships, boundary posts and trees. Apt omits land use.

33/478 Wordwell (parish) TL 832731
Apt 19.06.1840; 2299a (all); Map 1840, 6 chns, by Lenny and Croft, Bury St Edmunds; waterbodies, houses, plantations, parkland, gardens, heath/moor, hall, glebe (yellow), land tithable to another district (pink).

33/479 Worlingham (parish) TM 450900
Apt 04.05.1840; 1632a (all); Map 1840, 6 chns, by Richard Barnes, Lowestoft; woods, plantations, parkland, marsh mill (pictorial), ice house, dove house; pictorial church.

33/480 Worlingworth (parish) TM 230690
Apt 24.07.1837; 2447a (2446); Map 1837, [6 chns], by J. Preston, Worlingworth, Suffolk; foot/b'way, waterbodies, houses, woods, parkland, orchards, gardens, building names, avenue of trees, rectory; colours may show property ownerships.

33/481 Wortham (parish) TM 082783
Apt 13.06.1840; 2727a (all); Map 1838, 6 chns; waterbodies, houses, woods, plantations, parkland, gardens. Apt omits most field names.

33/482 Great Wratting (parish) TL 686486
Apt 10.03.1841; 1330a (all); Map 1840, 6 chns, surveyed by J. King and Son, Saffron Walden; waterbodies, houses, woods, osiers (by symbol), building names, rectory; buildings are named in three different styles of writing.

33/483 Little Wratting (parish) TL 690473
Apt 02.09.1840; 937a (all); Map 1840, 3 chns, by T.A. Melhuish, Barton Mills, Suffolk; construction lines, foot/b'way, waterbodies, houses, woods (named), orchards, fences, building names, parsonage, boundary post, commons, waste; pink bands are used for some bracing.

33/484 Wrentham (parish) TM 491831
Apt 13.06.1839; 2304a (2303); Map 1839, 3 chns, 1st cl, by Lenny and Croft, Bury St Edmunds; construction lines, foot/b'way, turnpike roads, waterbodies, houses, woods (named), parkland, gardens, fences, field gates, building names, road names, rectory, lodge; discontinuous yellow bands may be bracing.

33/485 Wyverstone (parish) TM 036679
Apt 31.01.1839; 1523a (1522); Map 1838, 3 chns, by Josh Manning, Norwich; foot/b'way, waterbodies, houses, woods, parkland, grassland (col), orchards.

33/486 Yaxley (parish) TM 121740
Apt 24.03.1842; 1239a (all); Map 1839, 6 chns, litho, by Joseph Manning, Land Surveyor and Lithographer, 64 Bethel St, Norwich; waterbodies, houses (by shading), woods, parkland; pictorial church.

33/487 Yoxford (parish) TM 391691
Apt 13.06.1839; 2725a (2724); Map 1840, 7 chns, 'revised' by B.H. Galland, C.Engineer, Yoxford, (includes enlargement of village centre at 3.5 chns); foot/b'way, waterbodies, houses, woods, building names, churchyard; uninhabited buildings are shown in outline only.

Surrey

PRO IR29 and IR30 34/1-139

150 tithe districts: 484,766 acres
139 tithe commutations: 433,566 acres
75 voluntary tithe agreements, 64 compulsory tithe awards

Tithe and tithe commutation

In Surrey 93 per cent of tithe districts were subject to payment of tithes in 1836 and sixty-four districts were wholly tithable (Fig. 46). The main reasons for tithe exemption in this county were commutation at the time of enclosure, the merger of tithes in the land, and exemption by prescription. As in Kent and Sussex, all woodland in the Weald was tithe free.

Assistant tithe commissioners and local tithe agents who worked in Surrey are listed in Table 34.1 and the valuers of tithe rent-charge in Table 34.2. A majority of Surrey valuers were resident either in or just outside the county, though a few came from further afield in Hampshire, Kent or Essex. Two valuations were made by Newton and Woodrow of Norwich, who undertook much work in the eastern counties, and one is by William Brown of South Carlton, near Lincoln. Brown valued Gatton in Surrey which was an outlying part of the Monson family estates centred near Lincoln. Surrey is unusual in that seven valuations were carried out by the Tithe Commission in default of a valuation having been lodged within the statutory six months after the confirmation of an agreement or award.

Tithe maps

Some 32 per cent of Surrey's 139 tithe maps are sealed as first class. This proportion is exceeded only by Herefordshire, Kent, Monmouthshire and Sussex. Unusually, there are several first-class maps of urban areas, notably the maps of Croydon, Dorking, and Epsom. The tithe maps of both Epsom and Fetcham were originally prepared for parochial assessment purposes. Construction lines are present on 8 per cent of second-class maps; that of Godalming is a particularly good example of a map which clearly aspired to first-class status but for some reason failed the Tithe Commission's tests. Ten second-class maps are acknowledged copies of earlier surveys, though as seven of these acknowledgements are by one group of map-makers it is reasonable to suppose that copying was much more widespread. It is known, for example, that the tithe map of Lingfield is derived from a map of 1816 and that of Wimbledon from a parochial assessment map of 1838.

Surrey tithe maps are drawn at a variety of scales, ranging from one inch to one and a

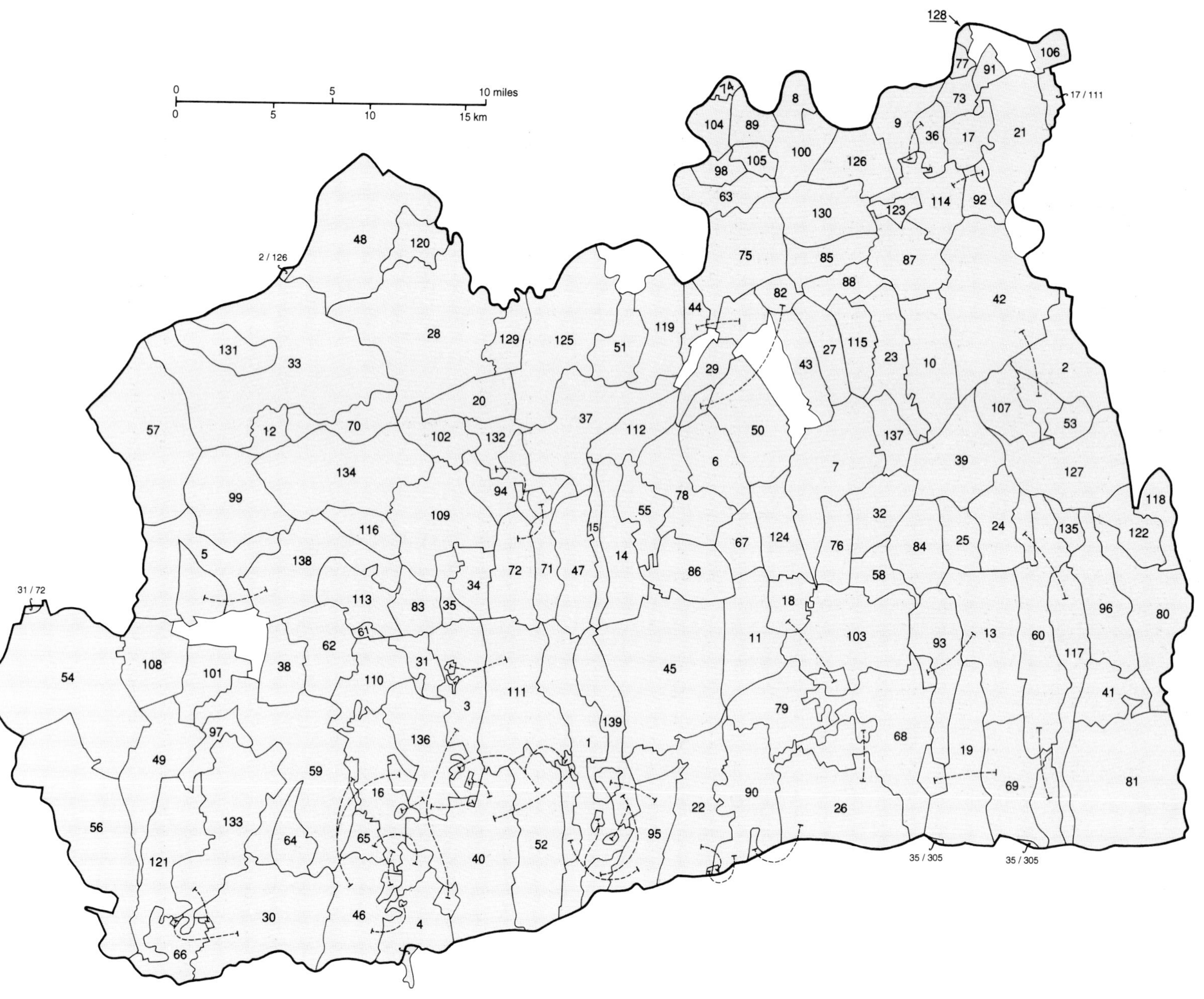

Fig. 46 Surrey: tithe district boundaries.

half chains to one inch to twelve chains. About 68 per cent of the county's tithe maps are in the recommended scale range of one inch to three to four chains.

Although at the time of the tithe surveys Surrey was still very much an agricultural county, the north-eastern part was densely settled and partly industrialised. Oil mills are shown at Wandsworth and the Battersea tithe map portrays the market gardens and a pigeon-shooting ground. Some 71 per cent of Surrey tithe maps show woodland and 14 per cent depict heath and moor but agricultural land uses are poorly recorded. Less than 4 per cent of maps distinguish arable and grassland.

At least 113 Surrey tithe maps in the Public Record Office collection can be attributed to a particular map-maker. The most prolific were the Crawters who worked from Cobham in Surrey and from Holborn in London and produced 18 maps (four with Job Smallpeice of Godalming). The Crawters were more careful than most to acknowledge copying, usually by a standard phrase 'copied from the plans of the several proprietors'. The proximity of London results in a rather larger proportion than usual of attributed maps made by London surveyors (33 per cent).

The quality of Surrey tithe maps is very varied. There are some carefully executed first-class plans but also some which are rather crudely drawn, for example those of Caterham and Sanderstead. Surrey maps are not especially decorated, though a few churches are shown by pictogram, as at Tandridge, and at Egham colourful pictograms depict folly towers.

Table 34.1. *Agreements and awards for commutation of tithes in Surrey*

Assistant commissioner/ local tithe agent	*Number of agreements**	*Number of awards*
John Pickering	29	0
Francis Offley Martin	0	25
Thomas James Tatham	1	19
John Maurice Herbert	0	12
Horace William Meteyard	12	0
F. Browne Browne	7	0
John Mee Mathew	7	0
Thomas Smith Woolley	7	3
Joseph Townsend	4	4
William Heard	3	0
Edward Greathed	1	0
Roger Kynaston	1	0
Tithe Commissioners	0	1

*Computed from the number of extant reports on tithe agreements in the tithe files [PRO IR 18].

Table 34.2. *Tithe valuers and tithe map-makers in Surrey*

Name and address (in Surrey unless indicated)	*Number of districts*	*Acreage*
Tithe valuers		
William Keen, Godalming	22	95,781
John Nash, Reigate	13	53,876
Thomas Crawter, Cobham	9	20,847
George Smallpeice	8	28,492
Tithe Commissioners	7	15,142
James Martin Sanderson, Sunbury, Middlesex	6	13,884
Henry Crawter, Holborn, Middlesex	6	12,867
Charles Osborn, Fareham, Hampshire	5	11,753
Raymond Willshire, Lambeth	5	3,182
Others [35]	58	177,742
Attributed tithe map-makers		
Messrs Crawter, Cobham, and Holborn, London	14	32,214
Edward J. Smith, 25 Parliament Street, London	6	18,958
Richard Dixon, Godalming	5	32,370
Henry Hull, Woking	5	18,682
Bushell and Vine, Fitzroy Square, London	4	21,922
Job Smallpeice, Godalming	4	19,532
Edward F. Neale, Southampton, Hampshire	4	14,015
H. Walter, Windsor, Berkshire	4	13,338
Edward Charles Duncombe, Guildford	4	9,295
Charles Lee, Golden Square, London	4	7,938
Raymond Willshire, Lambeth	4	1,847
Others [39]	75	176,870

Table 34.3. *The tithe maps of Surrey*: scales and classes

Scale in chains/inch	*All maps*		*First Class*		*Second Class*	
	Number	*Acreage*	*Number*	*Acreage*	*Number*	*Acreage*
>3	4	2,765	0	0	4	2,765
3	80	230,793	40	134,970	40	95,823
3.5	1	3,900	0	0	1	3,900
4	14	56,859	4	27,388	10	29,471
4.5, 5, 5.8	3	3,470	0	0	3	3,470
6	24	82,737	0	0	24	82,737
<6	13	53,042	0	0	13	53,042
TOTAL	139	433,566	44	162,358	95	271,208

Table 34.4. *The tithe maps of Surrey: dates*

	1837	*1838*	*1839*	*1840*	*1841*	*1842*	*1843*	*1844*	*1845*	*1846*	*1847*	*1848*	*1849*	*1850*	*>1850*
All maps	4	9	26	17	17	15	16	9	4	3	5	2	3	3	6
1st class	1	4	9	10	2	9	4	1	1	0	2	0	0	0	1
2nd class	3	5	17	7	15	6	12	8	3	3	3	2	3	3	5

Surrey

34/1 Abinger (parish) TQ 118422 [Abinger Hammer]
Apt 25.04.1838; 5547a (5547); Map 1839, 6 chns, 'Compiled from the Original Plans of the General Proprietors' by Job Smallpeice, Godalming, and Thomas Crawter, Cobham; foot/b'way, waterbodies, houses, woods (col), gate posts, stone stile, pasture wood, greens.

34/2 Addington (parish) TQ 370636
Apt 22.09.1837; 3613a (all); Map 1841, 3 chns, 1st cl, by H. Walter; construction lines, hill-drawing, foot/b'way, waterbodies, houses, woods, plantations, hedge ownership, fence ownership, field gates, building names, pits, boundary trees and stones (by symbol); some gates are shown pictorially, others by dots.

34/3 Albury (parish) TQ 055457
Apt 30.04.1838; 4504a (4503); Map 1839, 4 chns, in 2 parts, by H. Walter, Windsor; hill-drawing, foot/b'way, waterbodies, houses, woods, plantations, parkland, hedge ownership, fence ownership, field gates, road names, heaths, commons, furze (by symbol).

34/4 Alfold (parish) (partly in Sussex) TQ 036347
Apt 22.04.1839; 2884a (2883); Map 1840, 3 chns, 1st cl, by Jas Richardson, 12 Pall Mall; construction lines, turnpike roads, toll bar, canal with towpath and locks, lock house, wooden bridges (by symbol), waterbodies, houses, woods, fence ownership, field boundary ownerships, field gates, building names, greens; woods shown.

34/5 Ash and Normandy (tithing in parish of Ash) SU 915523
Apt 29.12.1841; 4768a (all); Map 1843, 4 chns, by J. Streat; construction lines, canal with towpath, houses, woods, plantations, hops, building names, road names, culvert, rectory, workhouse, peat moor, greens; parks are shown by annotation.

34/6 Ashtead (parish) TQ 184584
Apt 20.07.1838; 2516a (all); Map 1839, 9 chns, by Newton and Woodrow, Farnham; foot/b'way, waterbodies, houses, woods (col), parkland (in detail), common; colours may indicate land ownership.

34/7 Banstead (parish) TQ 245585
Apt 26.11.1840; 5518a (all); Map 1841, 12 chns, in 2 parts, by Benjn Badcock, Oxford (including 24-chn scale plan of heath); turnpike roads and gate, woods, parkland, building names, mill, boundary tree, vicarage, internal tithings, heaths.

34/8 Barnes (parish) TQ 224768
Apt 29.11.1837; 936a (all); Map 'Surveyed in 1837', 3 chns; foot/b'way, waterbodies, houses, riverside towpath, suspension bridge, common, green; some pecked boundaries have distances in feet from solid boundaries.

34/9 Battersea (parish) TQ 279760
Apt 31.07.1839; 1614a (all); Map 1838, 3 chns, by Charles Lee, Golden Square, London; railway, foot/b'way, waterbodies, houses, woods, parkland (in detail), orchards, heath/moor, hedge, fence, field boundary ownerships, road names, field names, lodges, windmill, sluice, workhouses, rope walk, corn mill, mill ponds, pigeon shooting ground, internal drainage ditches; gardens, commons, nursery, farm yards, and stock yard shown by annotation. (The map in PRO IR 30 is a copy; original is in PRO IR 77/64.)

34/10 Beddington and Wallington (parish and hamlet in parish of Beddington) TQ 296638
Apt 30.11.1839; 3900a (3909); Map 1840, 3.5 chns, by Messrs Crawter; railway, parkland (in detail, col), heath/moor, fence, toll gate, lodge, chalk pit, pound, snuff mill, mill, greens, demesne, hamlet boundary.

34/11 Betchworth (parish) TQ 206495
Apt 13.07.1840; 3726a (3726); Map 1841, 3 chns, by John Hosmer, 103 Camden Road Villas, Camden Town, London; construction lines, foot/b'way, waterbodies, houses, woods, plantations, field boundary ownerships; a boundary is annotated 'This Division is taken from an old Map of the Manor of Brockham'.

34/12 Bisley (parish) SU 950591
Apt 12.02.1846; 951a (all); Map 1847?, 3 chns; waterbodies, houses, woods, plantations, open fields (named), hedge ownership, fence ownership, building names, road names, pound, well.

34/13 Bletchingley (parish) TQ 333500
Apt 31.12.1840; 5585a (all); Map 1843, 4 chns, 1st cl, in 2 parts, by P. Cassidy; construction lines, hill-drawing, foot/b'way, waterbodies, houses, windmill, lime kiln, mounds or tumuli; public roads are identified by letter; colour bands may indicate ownerships; map has a note: 'The contraction of this sheet towards the extremities is about 5 links on 1000, but in and approaching the centre only 2 $1/_2$ - on acct. of which I have added 1 perch to the acre in the quantities, which is the general contraction throughout the sheet. - Sd. P. Cassidy'. (The map in PRO IR 30 is a copy; original is in PRO IR 77/66.)

34/14 Great Bookham (parish) TQ 136537
Apt 10.10.1839; 3249a (all); Map 1840, 3 chns, 1st cl, by H. Walter; hill-drawing, foot/b'way, waterbodies, houses, woods (named), plantations, marsh/bog, hedge ownership, field boundary ownerships, field gates, building names, boundary posts and trees, mill, school, triangulation stations; park named; meaning of colour band around houses and gardens is unclear.

34/15 Little Bookham (parish) TQ 125539
Apt 26.09.1840; 951a (all); Map 1842, 3 chns, 1st cl; construction lines, waterbodies, houses, woods, field boundary ownerships, boundary trees and marks, rectory, common.

34/16 Bramley (parish) TQ 008412
Apt 22.03.1843; 3973a (4008); Map surveyed 1838-39, 3 chns, by Henry Hull, Bramley, Surrey; construction lines, woods, arable, grassland, orchards, gardens, heath/moor, furze, common, nursery (by symbol), hedge ownership, stone pit, 'Boundary of the Weald of Sussex'; pecked lines in arable fields may denote limit of ploughing or inbound-outbound.

34/17 St Matthew Brixton (district in parish of Saint Mary Lambeth) TQ 315750 [Brixton]
Apt 08.04.1842; 1334a (all); Map 1843, 3 chns; canal, waterbodies, woods, building names, road names, water works, house of correction, green. Apt omits land use.

34/18 Buckland (parish) TQ 225515
Apt 14.02.1846; 1407a (1744); Map 1846, 6 chns, in 2 parts, by Edward Charles Duncombe, Guildford; foot/b'way, waterbodies, mill pond, parsonage, glebe, park, green.

34/19 Burstow (parish) TQ 320432
Apt 25.10.1841; 4718a (4717); Map 1839, 4 chns, by Edward Grantham, Croydon, Surrey; construction lines, foot/b'way, waterbodies, woods (col), field boundary ownerships, building names, road names, stiles, windmill, boundary tree, commons, furze; colours may indicate land ownership; one windmill is shown by a pictogram, another in plan.

34/20 Byfleet (parish) TQ 058611
Apt 02.09.1840; 2068a (2068); Map 1841, 6 chns, in 2 parts, by J.M. Sanderson, Sunbury, Middlesex (tithable parts only in detail; includes 3-chn plan of open fields); railway, foot/b'way, canal and towpath, waterbodies, houses.

34/21 Camberwell St Giles (parish) TQ 342763 [Camberwell]
Apt 12.09.1837; 4342a (4342); Map 1842?, 3 chns, ? by Thomas Bygrave, Clements Inn, Surveyor and Valuer; foot/b'way, canal and towpath, houses, woods, road names, boundary and City posts, boundary stones, asylum, windmill, college, burial ground, chapels, greens, township boundaries; legend explains boundary symbols. (The map in PRO IR 30 is a copy; original is in PRO IR 77/67.)

34/22 Capel (parish) TQ 181410
Apt 29.09.1838; 5523a (5522); Map 1839, 6 chns, 'Compiled from the Original Plans of the General Proprietors' by Job Smallpeice, Godalming, and Thomas Crawter, Cobham; foot/b'way, waterbodies, houses, woods (col), field gates, turnpike gate, greens, commons.

34/23 Carshalton (parish) TQ 276638
Apt 25.11.1847; 2904a (all); Map 1848, 3 chns, by Messrs Crawter, 7 Southampton Buildings, Chancery Lane, and Cobham, Surrey; railway, foot/b'way, waterbodies, houses, woods, plantations, open fields, building names, pound, park; grey bands may indicate land ownership.

34/24 Caterham (parish) TQ 335555
Apt 07.06.1839; 2460a (all); Map 1838, 6 chns, copied by Rushworth

and Jarvis, Saville Row; foot/b'way, turnpike roads, waterbodies, houses, building names, road names, chalk pits, rubbish bank, school, commons, greens.

34/25 Chaldon (parish) TQ 316548
Apt 12.09.1837; 1623a (all); Map 1837, 6 chns; litho (Standidge); foot/b'way, right of way, waterbodies, woods, plantations, gardens, heath/moor, furze (by symbol), hedge ownership, fence ownership, field gates, pit, boundary posts and trees, parsonage, farm names, glebe, common.

34/26 Charlwood (parish) TQ 247414
Apt 18.07.1839; 7000a (all); Map 1842?, 3 chns, 1st cl, in 3 parts, by Edwd F. Neale, Southampton; construction lines, survey base-line, railway, foot/b'way, waterbodies, houses, woods, furze, fence, field gates, building names, parsonage, pond, greens, common (col), county oak; parks, commons and heath shown by annotation; pecked lines within field perimeters could be ploughing margins or evidence of inbound-outbound. (The map in PRO IR 30 is a copy; original is in PRO IR 77/69.)

34/27 Cheam (parish) TQ 246643
Apt 08.09.1840; 1894a (all); Map 1840, 5.8 chns, by Messrs Crawter; hill-drawing, foot/b'way, waterbodies, woods, parkland, field names, chalk pit (by symbol), brickfield (by symbol), common; church is shown pictorially.

34/28 Chertsey (parish) TQ 031649
Apt 11.03.1844; 5468a (10229); Map 1844, 6 chns, (tithable lands only); canal with towpath and locks, waterbodies, houses, tithing boundaries.

34/29 Chessington (parish) TQ 181628
Apt 13.03.1839; 1230a (all); Map 1839, 3 chns; waterbodies, houses, woods (col), plantations, parkland (col), orchards, field gates.

34/30 Chiddingfold (parish) SU 958349
Apt 02.05.1842; 6936a (6936); Map 1843?, 6 chns, in 2 parts, by Richard Dixon, Godalming; waterbodies, houses, woods (col, by Dawson's symbol), plantations (col, by Dawson's symbol), fences, building names, rectory, kennels; legend gives symbols for dwelling houses, out houses, church, mill, rivers, ponds, woods, fir plantations, boundary and commons.

34/31 Chilworth, or St Martha (parish) TQ 032477
Apt 08.02.1847; 1070a (1070); Map 1846, 3 chns, by Keen and Son, 2 Parliament Street, Westminster; foot/b'way, waterbodies (named), houses, woods, marsh/bog, building names, paper mills, boundary road, glasshouses (by symbol).

34/32 Chipstead (parish) TQ 271559
Apt 20.01.1845; 2333a (2333); Map 'Compiled 1838', 6 chns, by Moore and Keatley; railways, foot/b'way, waterbodies, houses, woods (col), plantations, parkland, arable (col), grassland (col), orchards (col), hedge ownership, fence ownership, windmill (by symbol); different symbols are used for the (unnamed) Surrey Iron Railway (a tramway) and the London and Brighton Railway (a 'proper' railway); there is a note that colour bands 'surrounds the various properties' and that where the parish boundary does not follow a fence, it is dotted.

34/33 Chobham (parish) SU 960623
Apt 23.09.1843; 2021a (11536); Map 1845, 3 chns, by Sanderson, Sunbury (tithable parts only); waterbodies, houses.

34/34 East Clandon (parish) TQ 060520
Apt 19.05.1843; 1449a (all); Map 1843?, 3 chns, 1st cl, by Edward J. Smith, 25 Parliament Street; construction lines, foot/b'way, waterbodies, houses, open fields, field boundary ownerships; there is a note that two areas are also included in the map and apportionment of West Horsley.

34/35 West Clandon (parish) TQ 045518
Apt 15.02.1838; 988a (all); Map 1839, 3 chns, 1st cl, by Geo. Doswell, 35 Bermead St, Southampton; construction lines, hill-drawing, foot/b'way, waterbodies, houses, woods, plantations, heath/moor, fence, building names, pound, school, chalk pits (by symbol); parks shown by annotation.

34/36 Clapham (parish) TQ 295749
Apt 26.04.1838; 1233a (1233); Map 1838, 1.5 chns, ? by Thomas Bygrave, Lincoln's Inn, Surveyor and Valuer (tithable parts only); waterbodies, houses, woods (col), common (col), building names, road names, spring, workhouse, boundary marks, schools, chapels, brewery, boundary mereings, tithe-free areas; colour bands may indicate ownerships. (The map in PRO IR 30 is a copy; original is in PRO IR 77/71.)

34/37 Cobham (parish) TQ 114597
Apt 17.06.1848; 519a (5228); Map 1845, 6 chns, by Messrs Crawter, Cobham, Surrey, and Southampton Buildings, Chancery Lane, London, (tithable parts only, tinted); waterbodies, houses, plantations (col).

34/38 Compton (parish) SU 959474
Apt 25.10.1841; 1972a (all); Map 1839, 3 chns, 1st cl, by H. Walter, Windsor; construction lines, hill-drawing, foot/b'way, waterbodies, houses, woods, plantations, hedge ownership, fence ownership, field gates, building names, chalk pits (by symbol), Hog's Back.

34/39 Coulsdon (parish) TQ 312586
Apt 28.02.1837; 4199a (4403); Map 1837, 3 chns; railway, foot/b'way, woods, plantations, open fields; pecked lines in fields could indicate either ploughing margin or inbound-outbound.

34/40 Cranley (parish) TQ 064384 [Cranleigh]
Apt 26.07.1841; 7340a (7340); Map 1842, 8 chns, in 2 parts, by Richard Dixon, Godalming; foot/b'way, canal and towpath, waterbodies, houses, woods, plantations, orchards, common (by symbol), underwood (by symbol), furze (by symbol), heath/moor, fence, building names, rectory; pictorial church.

34/41 Crowhurst (parish) TQ 396471
Apt 26.09.1842; 2082a (2081); Map 1839, 3 chns, by Francis Fuller, Croydon; railway, waterbodies, woods, building names, road names, farm boundaries (col).

34/42 Croydon (parish) TQ 333664
Apt 12.07.1843; 9872a (9821); Map 1838, 3 chns, 1st cl, by W. Roberts, 68 Chancery Lane; railways with stations, foot/b'way, canal with towpath, waterbodies, houses, woods, plantations, parkland, orchards, building names, road names, mill, spa gardens, barracks, gaol, chalk pit (by symbol), town hall, gaol; direction pointer has feathers decoration and 'Ich Dein' motto. (The map in PRO IR 30 is a copy; original is in PRO IR 77/72.)

34/43 Cuddington (parish) TQ 231633 [Not listed]
Apt 31.01.1839; 1837a (1827); Map 1839?, 3 chns, by Edward Neale, Southampton; construction lines, waterbodies, houses, woods, hedge ownership, fence ownership, field gates, building names, boundary stones (by symbol), extra-parochial land, common (col).

34/44 Long Ditton (parish) TQ 174655
Apt 25.11.1841; 2116a (all); Map 1842, 6 chns, by Messrs Crawter, Cobham, and Southampton Buildings, Chancery Lane, London; waterbodies, houses, woods (col), commons.

34/45 Dorking (parish) TQ 164478
Apt 04.12.1841; 10020a (10020); Map 1838, 3 chns, 1st cl, 'Plotted Plan', by Bushell and Vine, 40 Upper Charlotte Street, Fitzroy Square; construction lines, foot/b'way, waterbodies, houses, farmyards (col), woods, plantations, heath/moor, common, building names, road names, pound, mills, lime works (col), castle ruins, rookery, private walk, folly towers, chapel; park and two woods are shown by annotation; pecked lines in fields could indicate either ploughing margin or inbound-outbound. (The map in PRO IR 30 is a copy; original map is in PRO IR 77/74.)

34/46 Dunsfold (parish) TQ 005352 [Dunsfold Green]
Apt 29.07.1847; 4393a (4393); Map surveyed in 1843 and 1844, 4 chns, in 3 parts, by Henry Hull, Woking, Surrey; foot/b'way, waterbodies, houses, canal with lock and towpath.

34/47 Effingham (parish) TQ 115530
Apt 03.06.1839; 3149a (3148); Map 1842, 3 chns, 1st cl, by Michael Fitzgerald; construction lines, foot/b'way, waterbodies, houses, woods, plantations, orchards, field boundary ownerships, building names, boundary trees, turnpike gate, milestones, chalk pits, kiln, commons.

34/48 Egham (parish) SU 992692
Apt 11.05.1842; 6705a (7435); Map 1841, 6 chns, by William Sherborn, Bedfont, Middlesex; waterbodies, woods (col), field boundary ownerships, building names, duck ponds, cascade, race course, grand stand (pictorial), clock tower (pictorial), belvidere (pictorial), greens, manorial boundaries (col); grey bands indicate field boundary ownership.

34/49 Elstead (parish) SU 895425
Apt 04.01.1841; 4119a (all); Map 1839, 3 chns, 1st cl, in 2 parts, by Bushell and Vine; foot/b'way, waterbodies, houses, woods, plantations, hops, building names, road names, commons.

34/50 Epsom (parish) TQ 205605
Apt 21.03.1842; 4389a (4389); Map 'Surveyed by order of the Guardians of the Epsom Union', 1838, 3 chns, 1st cl; foot/b'way, waterbodies, woods, open fields, field boundary ownerships, building names, road names, workhouse, race course, grand stand, greens, warren, manorial divisions (col), parks (by annotation). (The map in PRO IR 30 is a copy; the original is in PRO IR 77/75.)

34/51 Esher (parish) TQ 134639
Apt 06.08.1846; 2080a (all); Map 1847, 3 chns, by Messrs Crawter, Cobham, Surrey, and Southampton Buildings, Chancery Lane; railway, waterbodies, houses, woods (col), turnpike gate.

34/52 Ewhurst (parish) TQ 097391
Apt 28.11.1840; 5483a (5483); Map 1840, 3 chns, 1st cl, in 3 parts, by Frederick E.H. Drayson; construction lines, waterbodies, woods (col); both public roads and public open space are tinted sienna.

34/53 Farleigh (parish) TQ 375607
Apt 15.07.1839; 1060a (all); Map 1840?, [3 chn], by Davies and Hughes, 12 Haymarket; foot/b'way, waterbodies, houses.

34/54 Farnham (parish) SU 850468
Apt 22.10.1840; 10292a (9786); Map 1839, 6 chns, in 2 parts, by William Harding, (part 1 litho by E. Jones, 24 Charlotte Square, Bloomsbury, London, part 2 at 2 chns, manuscript, of the town); foot/b'way, waterbodies, woods, plantations, parks (by annotation), hops (by Dawson's symbol), open fields, building names, road names, commons, workhouse, old brick kilns, abbey ruins, mills. There is a second copy of both parts in PRO IR 77/76, coloured to show extraordinary rent charges.

34/55 Fetcham (parish) TQ 148560
Apt 25.10.1842; 1723a (1723); Map 'Surveyed by order of the Guardians of the Epsom Union', 1839, 3 chns, 1st cl, by Frederick Ross Milton, Greenwich, Kent; construction lines, foot/b'way, houses, field boundary ownerships, building names, road names, glebe (col), kennels; woodland and ponds are shown by annotation.

34/56 Frensham (parish) SU 865395
Apt 26.11.1839; 8692a (8691); Map 1839, 4 chns, 1st cl, by James Harding, Junr, Farnham; construction lines, hill-drawing, foot/b'way, turnpike roads, waterbodies, houses, woods, plantations, parks (by annotation), heath/moor, building names, road names, mills, paper mill, chapel, workhouse, pottery, commons (col), greens, tithing boundary; two large ponds are named in gothic writing; north pointer has Prince of Wales' feathers and 'Ich Deiu' motto.

34/57 Frimley (chapelry or hamlet) SU 889589
Apt 30.05.1842; 7506a (all); Map 1842, 8 chns, by Edward Charles Duncumb, Guildford; railway, turnpike roads, waterbodies, woods, plantations, heath/moor, road names; north pointer has feathers.

34/58 Gatton (parish) TQ 275526
Apt 11.07.1838; 1240a (all); Map 1838, 8 chns, by Henry Chilcott, Croydon; hill-drawing, foot/b'way, waterbodies, houses, woods, arable (col), grassland (col), gardens, suspension bridge. Apt omits land use.

34/59 Godalming (parish) SU 979426
Apt 30.12.1845; 9099a (9098); Map 1841, 3 chns, in 15 parts, by Richard Dixon, Godalming (with town at 1 chn, enlargements of small fields, and 40 chn combined index and construction line diagram); construction lines, railway, canal with towpath and locks, waterbodies, houses, woods, plantations, heath/moor, building names, road names, bay windows, garden steps, tithing boundaries, public ponds (col); internal pillars of church are shown.

34/60 Godstone (parish) TQ 359488
Apt 26.01.1842; 6783a (6783); Map 1840, 4 chns, 1st cl, in 3 parts 'Surveyed by P. Cassidy L.S. ... under the direction of B.H. Galland, C.E.'; railway, waterbodies, houses, woods (col), parkland, gardens, marsh/bog, green (col), building names, brewery, vicarage, lime kiln, flooded area (col); colour bands indicate ownerships.

34/61 Holy Trinity and St Mary, Guildford (parish) TQ 003493 [Not listed]
Apt 10.03.1849; 176a (176); Map 1849, 2 chns, by Edward C. Duncombe, Guildford; canal with towpath and locks, road names, mill pond; colour bands are used to brace groups of built-up closes.

34/62 Guildford, St Nicholas (parish) SU 984486 [Not listed]
Apt 21.05.1841; 2836a (all); Map 1839, 3 chns, 1st cl, in 6 parts, by Henry Adams for C. Witherby, 3 Church Court, Clements Lane, Lombard St, London, Land and Timber Surveyor, (urban parts at 1 chn); construction lines, hill-drawing, foot/b'way, canal with towpath and locks, waterbodies, houses (outside built-up part), woods, plantations, marsh/bog, fence, road names, boundary stones and tree, sheep preserve.

34/63 Ham (parish) TQ 192716
Apt 16.03.1842; 1919a (?); Map 1841, 3 chns, 'Compiled from the Original Plans of the Several Proprietors' by Thomas Crawter, Cobham; waterbodies, houses, woods, open fields, boundary trees, river towpath, boundary stones and posts, park (by annotation), common.

34/64 Hambledon (parish) SU 967386
Apt 02.12.1844; 1557a (all); Map 1845, 7 chns, in 2 parts, by Alfred Mellersh, Guildford; turnpike roads, turnpike gate, milestone, waterbodies, houses, woods (col, named), plantations (col), road names, brick kilns, workhouse, malthouse, common, furze (by symbol).

34/65 Hascombe (parish) TQ 008384
Apt 11.06.1841; 1540a (1539); Map surveyed in 1839 and 1840, 3 chns, by Henry Hull, Bramley, nr Guildford, Surrey; construction lines, waterbodies, houses, woods, plantations, arable, meadow, pasture, furze, shrubbery orchards, gardens, hedge ownership, 'Boundary of the Weald of Sussex', stone pit; all land use is shown by annotation; pecked lines in fields could be evidence either of ploughing margins or of inbound-outbound.

34/66 Haslemere (parish) SU 909330
Apt 25.05.1842; 1877a (1877); Map 1842, 3 chns, by Alfred Mellersh, Godalming, Surrey; waterbodies, houses, woods (col), plantations (col), furze (by symbol), fence, commons.

34/67 Headley (parish) TQ 200542
Apt 16.06.1840; 1630a (all); Map 1841, 6 chns, by Newton and Woodrow, Norwich; foot/b'way, waterbodies, houses, woods (named), building names; pictorial church.

34/68 Horley (parish) TQ 286449
Apt 19.11.1846; 7215a (7215); Map 1848?, 8 chns; railway and station, waterbodies, woods, orchards, building names, kilns, mill, windmill, commons. (The map in PRO IR 30 is a copy; the original is in PRO IR 77/77.)

34/69 Horne (parish) TQ 344428
Apt 30.05.1842; 4532a (all); Map 1841, 3 chns, in 2 parts, by M. Adams; railway, waterbodies, houses, pound; windmills outside district are shown by symbol.

34/70 Horsell (parish) SU 995597
Apt 07.03.1850; 206a (2890); Map 1851?, 6 chns, by Edward Charles Duncombe, Guildford (tithable parts only); canal, building names.

34/71 East Horsley (parish) TQ 099530
Apt 17.09.1846; 1825a (all); Map 1842?, 3 chns, 1st cl, by Edmund J. Smith, 25 Parliament Street; waterbodies, houses, woods (col), plantations, marsh/bog, field gates, building names, boundary trees, chalk pit, glebe.

34/72 West Horsley (parish) TQ 082527
Apt 10.04.1839; 2994a (2993); Map 1839, 3 chns, 1st cl; construction lines, hill-drawing, waterbodies, houses, woods (named), coppices (by symbol), hedge ownership, field boundary ownerships, building names, sheep lays, chalk pit (by symbol), heath, rough pasture (by annotation).

34/73 Kennington (district in parish of St Mary, Lambeth) TQ 307772
Apt 25.06.1842; 853a (969); Map 1843, 3 chns, by Ray Willshire, Gingham's Place, Lambeth; road names, waterworks, commons, green. Apt omits land use.

34/74 Kew (parish) TQ 188773
Apt 31.07.1850; 227a (230); Map 1850, 3 chns, by R. and J. Clutton, 8 Whitehall Place, (tithable parts only); waterbodies, houses, building names, landowners, river towpath.

34/75 Kingston upon Thames (parish) TQ 197689 [Kingston Upon Thames]
Apt 20.06.1839; 4765a (4765); Map 1840, 3 chns, 'Compiled from the Original Plans of the Several Proprietors' by Thomas Crawter; railway, waterbodies, houses, woods (col). (The map in PRO IR 30 is a copy; the original is in PRO IR 77/78.)

34/76 Kingswood (liberty) TQ 251544
Apt 20.03.1844; 1812a (1811); Map 1844, 4 chns; foot/b'way, woods (col).

34/77 Lambeth Church (district in parish of St Mary Lambeth) TQ 309786 [Lambeth]
Apt 25.06.1842; 40a (186); Map 1844, 3 chns, in 25 parts, by Ray Willshire, Gingham's Place, Lambeth (tithable parts only, tinted; includes 24 small plans at 1 inch to 40 feet (1:480)); road names, female orphan asylum, workhouse, river stairs. Apt omits land use.

34/78 Leatherhead (parish) TQ 169567
Apt 02.11.1840; 3507a (all); Map 1841, 3 chns, 1st cl, in 2 parts, by Frederick and Henry Edwin Drayson, Faversham; foot/b'way, waterbodies, building names, prison, turnpike, pound.

34/79 Leigh (parish) TQ 224463
Apt 24.11.1849; 3420a (3719); Map 1851, 3 chns, 1st cl, by Washbourne and Keen, 8 Cannon Row, Westminster; construction lines, foot/b'way, waterbodies, houses, field boundary ownerships, field gates; pecked lines in fields could show ploughing margins or inbound-outbound.

34/80 Limpsfield (parish) TQ 420515
Apt 22.06.1840; 3904a (all); Map 1841, 8 chns, by Richard Dixon, Godalming, Surrey; waterbodies, houses, woods, plantations, heath/moor.

34/81 Lingfield (parish) TQ 404429
Apt 17.05.1845; 9010a (9010); Map 1846?, 9 chns, foot/b'way, waterbodies, woods, road names, mills; scale-bar is graduated with Roman numerals.

34/82 Malden (parish) TQ 216669
Apt 07.06.1839; 1272a (1272); Map 1839, 6 chns, by Nash and Sons, Reigate, Surrey, and 1 Raymond Buildings, Greys Inn Square, London, Land Agents and Surveyors, litho (Standidge); foot/b'way, waterbodies, woods, orchards, gardens, fences; pictorial church.

34/83 Merrow (parish) TQ 030508
Apt 30.11.1838; 1609a (1608); Map 1839?, 3 chns, 1st cl, construction lines, hill-drawing, waterbodies, houses, woods, heath/moor, open fields, field gates, common, pits or quarries (by symbol).

34/84 Merstham (parish) TQ 293546
Apt 28.04.1840; 2535a (all); Map 1839, 8 chns, in 2 parts, 'Copied' by Moore and Son ('village properties' at 3 chns); railway, foot/b'way, turnpike road and gate, waterbodies, houses, woods, parkland, arable (col), grassland (col), orchards, heath/moor, hedge ownership, fence ownership, landowners, boundary trees and posts, limekilns, glebe, 'Parish land'; the London and Brighton Railway is shown in grey without 'rails', the Croydon, Merstham and Godstone Railway (a tramway) by a single line with cross-bars, in red.

34/85 Merton (parish) TQ 242686
Apt 16.12.1843; 1026a (1780); Map 1844, 5 chns, by Messrs Crawter, Cobham, Surrey, and Southampton Buildings, Chancery Lane (tithable parts only); railway, waterbodies, houses.

34/86 Mickleham (parish) TQ 172529
Apt 31.12.1838; 2850a (2849); Map 1839, 3 chns, by Henry Sanderson, Sheffield; hill-drawing, foot/b'way, waterbodies, houses, woods (col, named), plantations, parks (by annotation), open fields (named), building names, chapel ruins, ice house, rectory, mounds, ford, swallow hole, boundary trees, boundary posts, 'fence removed', 'supposed old fence', chalk pit, old quarry, quarries (by symbol), pits (by symbol); some areas outside the district are mapped; there is a note that the average contraction of the paper during plotting was about 5 links in 20 chains [= 1 part in 400].

34/87 Mitcham (parish) TQ 282689
Apt 27.02.1846; 2893a (2893); Map 1847, 3 chns, by Messrs Crawter, Cobham, Surrey, and Southampton Buildings, Chancery Lane, London; railway, foot/b'way, waterbodies, houses, woods, open fields, greens.

34/88 Morden (parish) TQ 251675
Apt 05.08.1837; 1428a (all); Map 1837, [3 chns], 1st cl, by T.J. Tatham, Bedford Place; construction lines, foot/b'way, waterbodies, houses, woods, plantations, orchards, road names, field names, boundary marks.

34/89 Mortlake (parish) TQ 197755
Apt 13.05.1839; 1168a (all); Map surveyed in October 1838, 1st cl, [3 chns], by Frederick S. Pepperstone, 15 Buckingham St, Strand; construction lines, foot/b'way, waterbodies, houses, open fields, fences, field gates, common.

34/90 Newdigate (parish) TQ 209415
Apt 18.06.1840; 4458a (all); Map 1841, 6 chns, 'Compiled from the Original Plans of the Several Proprietors' by Thomas Crawter, Cobham; waterbodies, houses, woods (col).

34/91 St Mary Newington (parish) TQ 324783 [Newington]
Apt 22.09.1848; 151a (624); Map 1850, 3 chns, (tithable parts only); road names, ecclesiastical district boundaries (col); linework for tithe-free parts is in red.

34/92 St Luke, Norwood (district in parish of St Mary Lambeth) TQ 319719 [Not listed]
Apt 08.04.1842; 952a (all); Map 1843?, 3 chns, by Raymon Willshire; waterbodies, woods, building names, road names, house of cemetery, glebe (col).

34/93 Nutfield (parish) TQ 309488
Apt 19.05.1843; 3374a (all); Map 1840?, 3 chns, 1st cl, by Edward Neale, Southampton; construction lines, railway, foot/b'way, waterbodies, houses, woods, common, parks (by annotation), fences, field gates, building names; railway appears to have been added after the rest of the map had been completed.

34/94 Ockham (parish) TQ 077569
Apt 25.04.1838; 2340a (all); Map 1840, 3 chns, 1st cl, in 2 parts, by Edward Jones, 24 Charlotte Street, Bloomsbury, London; construction lines, hill-drawing, waterbodies, woods (named), plantations, gardens, hedges, field gates, building names, commons, milestones, lodges, schools, quarries or pits (by symbol); part 2 is in a different style from part 1, with coloured woods, e.g.

34/95 Ockley (parish) TQ 155394
Apt 28.10.1840; 4286a (4286); Map 1841, 6 chns, 'Compiled from the Original Plans of the Several Propertors' by Job Smallpeice, Godalming and Thomas Crawter, Cobham; hill-drawing, waterbodies, houses, woods (col), stone pit (by symbol), green.

34/96 Oxted (parish) TQ 394515
Apt 27.04.1839; 3627a (all); Map 1839, 3 chns, by Dixon and Maitland, 21 John Square, Bedford Row, London; construction lines, railway, waterbodies, houses, field boundary ownerships.

34/97 Peperharrow (parish) SU 923434 [Peper Harow]
Apt 22.03.1842; 1455a (all); Map 1840, 3 chns, 1st cl, in 2 parts, by Bushell and Vine, 40 Upper Charlotte Street, Fitzroy Square; construction

lines, foot/b'way, waterbodies, houses, woods, building names, conduit, stile, river weirs, bath, common; hills are named.

34/98 Petersham (parish) TQ 189729
Apt 26.08.1850; 550a (660); Map 1851, 4.5 chns, by R. and J. Clutton, Whitehall Place; waterbodies, building names, road names; parks and plantations shown by annotation.

34/99 Pirbright (parish) SU 931557
Apt 11.06.1841; 4580a (4579); Map 1841, 6 chns, in 3 parts, by J. Streat, Ash (including common fields at 3 chns); railway, foot/b'way, canal and locks, waterbodies, houses, woods, plantations, building names, mills, boundary stones (by symbol), heath, green. The map carries a note that it was insured against fire for $50 [about 2.5d per acre] in October 1841.

34/100 Putney (parish) TQ 227742
Apt 18.02.1848; 1420a (all); Map 1849, 3 chns, by Charles Lee, 20 Golden Square; railway with station, waterbodies, woods, plantations, heath/moor, reservoir, commons.

34/101 Puttenham (parish) SU 922468
Apt 16.12.1840; 1897a (1896); Map 1841, 4 chns; waterbodies, houses, woods, plantations, open fields, building names, heath, commons.

34/102 Pyrford (parish) TQ 041590
Apt 08.06.1844; 1869a (1868); Map 1843, 3 chns, 1st cl, by Edmund Jo. Smith, 25 Parliament Street; construction lines, railway, canal with towpath and locks, waterbodies, houses, plantations, field boundary ownerships, building names; colour band indicates tithe-free lands.

34/103 Reigate (parish) TQ 259500
Apt 20.11.1843; 6008a (6008); Map surveyed in December 1842, 3 chns, 1st cl, by John Hosmer, 103 Camden Town Villas, Camden Town, London; construction lines, hill-drawing, railways, foot/b'way, waterbodies, houses, woods, plantations, moat.

34/104 Richmond (parish) TQ 184759
Apt 31.08.1849; 1153a (1230); Map 1851, 4 chns, (tithable parts only); railway and station, foot/b'way, road names, pagoda, lodge, almshouses, Wesleyan Institution, burial ground, workhouse, theatre, ferry, royal boundary, park entrances, park (by annotation).

34/105 Richmond Park (district in parishes of Putney and Mortlake) TQ 205738
Apt 31.05.1850; 970a (all); Map 1851, 2.27 chns, (4.4 inches to 10 chns or 1 inch to 50 yards, 1:1800), in 2 parts, by E. and G.N. Driver, 5 Whitehall, London; waterbodies, houses, woods, individual trees, marsh/bog, building names, landowners, gravel pit, boundary trees and stones, spring, park entrance gates; colour bands show parish boundaries.

34/106 Rotherhithe St Mary (parish) TQ 358795 [Rotherhithe]
Apt 16.04.1844; 386a (886); Map 1844, 2.42 chns (1 inch to 160 feet, 1:1920), by M. Fitzgerald and J. Eivers, 12 Buckingham Street (tithable parts only); railways, canal with towpath, waterbodies, marsh/bog, road names, docks, school, Thames Tunnel entrance, timber pond, boundary stones.

34/107 Sanderstead (parish) TQ 337614
Apt 31.03.1843; 2245a (all); Map 1843?, 6 chns, railway, woods (col), plantations (col); colour bands may indicate ownerships.

34/108 Seale with Tongham (parish and hamlet in parish of Seale) SU 894474
Apt 21.10.1839; 2967a (2967); Map 1839, 4 chns, by James Harding; foot/b'way, turnpike roads, waterbodies, houses, woods, plantations, parkland, hops (by symbol), heath/moor, furze (by symbol), building names, chalk pits; red band indicates tithe-free lands. Compass pointer has feathers decoration and 'Ich Dein' motto.

34/109 Send and Ripley (parish) TQ 041551
Apt 08.06.1844; 5162a (5162); Map 1843, 3 chns, 1st cl, by Edmund J. Smith, 25 Parliament Street; construction lines, foot/b'way, waterbodies, canal with towpath and locks, houses, field boundary ownerships, building names, ford, windmills (by symbol), pond, tithe-free land, copses (by annotation).

34/110 Shalford (parish) TQ 006469
Apt 10.02.1845; 2591a (2590); Map 1842?, 3 chns, 1st cl; construction lines, foot/b'way, canal with towpath and locks, waterbodies, houses (dotted), woods, osiers, plantations, orchards, heath/moor, hedge ownership, fence ownership, field gates, footbridges.

34/111 Shere (parish) TQ 082461
Apt 20.09.1844; 6396a (all); Map 1843?, 3 chns, in 2 parts, by Layton Cooke; foot/b'way, waterbodies, houses, woods (named), plantations, furze, building names, chalk pits (by symbol, col), wayside cross (by symbol), rectory. Apt omits field names.

34/112 Stoke D'Albernon (parish) TQ 145599 [Stoke D'Abernon]
Apt 06.08.1846; 2028a (all); Map 1845, 3 chns, 1st cl, by Joseph Witty for W. Keen, Esq; construction lines, foot/b'way, waterbodies, houses.

34/113 Stoke next Guildford (parish) SU 999511 [Not listed]
Apt 25.02.1842; 2314a (all); Map 1842?, 3 chns, 1st cl; construction lines, waterbodies, houses (dotted), woods, hedge ownership, fence ownership, field gates, workhouse.

34/114 Streatham (parish) TQ 301721
Apt 07.06.1839; 2832a (all); Map 1840?, 3 chns; construction lines, waterbodies, boundary post, common (col). Apt has cropping information. (The map in PRO IR 30 is a copy; the original is in PRO IR 77/80.)

34/115 Sutton (parish) TQ 259647
Apt 20.07.1839; 1804a (all); Map 1840?, 3 chns, 1st cl, by Edward Neale, Southampton; construction lines, waterbodies, houses, woods, fence, field gates, recreation ground.

34/116 Sutton (tithing in parish of Woking) TQ 004544 [Sutton Place]
Apt 04.02.1848; 1483a (?); Map 1849, 6 chns, by William Hull; waterbodies, houses; houses (hatched brown).

34/117 Tandridge (parish) TQ 377487
Apt 17.02.1845; 3887a (all); Map 1841, 3 chns, in 4 parts, by P. Cassidy, London; railway, waterbodies, houses, farmyards (col), woods (col), field gates; pictorial church; red bands may indicate ownership.

34/118 Tatsfield (parish) TQ 422563
Apt 17.05.1839; 1276a (all); Map 1843, 12 chns; hill-drawing, houses, woods, plantations, building names, chalk pit (by symbol), parsonage, greens.

34/119 Thames Ditton (parish) TQ 156649
Apt 29.12.1843; 2865a (2865); Map 1843, 3 chns, by Messrs Crawter, Cobham, Surrey and Southampton Buildings, Chancery Lane; railway, waterbodies, houses, woods (col), open fields.

34/120 Thorpe (parish) TQ 028689
Apt 16.06.1840; 1495a (1495); Map 1840?, 9 chns, (tithable parts only); foot/b'way.

34/121 Thursley (parish) SU 901371
Apt 06.05.1846; 4348a (4348); Map surveyed in 1846-7, 3 chns, 1st cl, by Henry Hull, Woking, Surrey; construction lines, waterbodies, houses, commons.

34/122 Titsey (parish) TQ 410552
Apt 02.05.1839; 1936a (all); Map 1843?, 12 chns; waterbodies, chalk pits (col, sym).

34/123 Tooting Graveney (parish) TQ 276713
Apt 11.11.1846; 562a (all); Map 1847, 3 chns, 1st cl, by Messrs Crawter, Cobham, Surrey and Southampton Buildings, Chancery Lane, London; railway, waterbodies, houses, woods, open fields, boundary stones and post, common.

34/124 Walton-on-the-Hill (parish) TQ 220550 [Walton on the Hill]
Apt 09.01.1840; 2592a (all); Map 'Corrected November 1839', 4 chns, by Robert Vernon, Copthall, Banstead, Surrey; foot/b'way, waterbodies, houses, woods (named), heaths, open fields, building names, race course.

34/125 Walton-on-Thames (parish) TQ 108650
Apt 29.11.1840; 313a (6834); Map 1843, 6 chns, by Messrs Crawter, Cobham, Surrey and Southampton Buildings, Chancery Lane, London, (tithable parts only, tinted); railway, road names.

34/126 All Saints, Wandsworth (parish) TQ 259738 [Wandsworth]
Apt 12.10.1841; 2353a (all); Map 1841, 3 chns, by C. Lee, Golden Square; railways, foot/b'way, waterbodies, woods, open fields (named), common, green, hedge ownership, fence ownership, building names, road names, lodge, cross, asylum, burial grounds, oil mills, mills, reservoir, causeway; park, orchard and garden are shown by annotation. (The map in PRO IR 30 is a copy; the original is in PRO IR 77/82.)

34/127 Warlingham-cum-Chelsham (parishes) TQ 374582 [Warlingham and Chelsham]
Apt 31.12.1842; 5091a (all); Map 1842, 6 chns, by Richard Dixon, Godalming; houses, woods, plantations, orchards, heath/moor, building names, windmill (pictorial), parish boundary; legend explains symbols for dwelling houses, out house, churches, parks, roads, boundary line, woods, fir plantations, commons and orchards. Apt includes cropping information.

34/128 Waterloo St John (district in parish of St Mary Lambeth) TQ 312800 [Not listed]
Apt 16.06.1842; 3a (233); Map 1844, 3 chns, in 14 parts, by Ray Willshire, Wolsingham Place, Lambeth (tithable parts only, with 13 enlargements at 1 inch to 40 feet, 1:480); road names, hospital, female orphan asylum, school. Apt omits land use.

34/129 Weybridge (parish) TQ 076644
Apt 16.12.1843; 878a (1292); Map 1844?, 3 chns, (tithable parts only); railway, waterbodies, houses.

34/130 Wimbledon (parish) TQ 239711
Apt 04.02.1848; 2551a (all); Map 1850, 3 chns, by Charles Lee and John Pickering; railway, waterbodies, woods, plantations, heath/moor.

34/131 Windlesham (parish) SU 926634
Apt 13.09.1841; 1954a (5874); Map 1843, 3 chns, in 2 parts, by J.M. Sanderson, Sunbury, Land and Timber Surveyor (tithable parts only); waterbodies, houses.

34/132 Wisley (parish) TQ 068585
Apt 26.08.1843; 1321a (1321); Map 1842, 3 chns, 1st cl, in 2 parts, by Edmund J. Smith, 25 Parliament Street; construction lines, foot/b'way, waterbodies, houses, field boundary ownerships, building names, woodland (by annotation); one construction line is annotated 'This line is a production of East Horsley Base Line'.

34/133 Witley (parish) SU 935397
Apt 28.11.1843; 6328a (6328); Map 1840, 4 chns, 1st cl, by Bushell and Vine; waterbodies, houses, woods, plantations, parks (by annotation), building names, lodge, mill, 'semephore', brick kilns, chapelry boundary (col), commons.

34/134 Woking (except Sutton) (parish) SU 987572
Apt 13.12.1841; 7332a (all); Map 1840, 3 chns, 1st cl, in 2 parts, by Edward J. Smith, 25 Parliament Street, (includes small enlargement of detail); construction lines, hill-drawing, railways and station, foot/b'way, canal with towpath and locks, waterbodies, houses, woods (col), plantations (col), field gates, building names, paper mills, hotel, boundary tree; some names are picked out in colour; enlargement is 'pointed to' by a 'hand', (with cuff link). (The map in PRO IR 30 is a copy; original is in PRO IR 77/84.)

34/135 Woldingham (parish) TQ 374554
Apt 19.03.1852; 667a (all); Map 1852, 4 chns; hill-drawing, waterbodies, houses, woods, plantations, building names, chalk pits (by symbol).

34/136 Wonersh (parish) TQ 035435
Apt 12.11.1842; 4428a (4427); Map surveyed in 1840-42', 3 chns, 1st cl, by Henry Hull, Bramley, Surrey; construction lines, canal with towpath and footbridge, waterbodies, houses, boundary trees, 'Weald Boundary', heath, commons, greens, gardens (by annotation).

34/137 Woodmansterne (parish) TQ 278600
Apt 12.01.1845; 1590a (all); Map 1844?, 3 chns, 1st cl, by Frederick and Henry E. Drayson; waterbodies, houses, building names, rectory, green.

34/138 Worplesdon (parish) SU 959518
Apt 18.05.1838; 6796a (7140); Map 1839, 3 chns, 1st cl, in 3 parts, by Chitty and Harding, Farnham; construction lines, foot/b'way, canal, waterbodies, houses, woods, plantations, hops, heath/moor, building names, chapels, mills, rectory, semaphore.

34/139 Wotton (parish) TQ 135445
Apt 29.05.1839; 4176a (4176); Map 1839, 6 chns, 'Compiled from the Original Plans of the Several Proprietors' by Job Smallpeice, Godalming and Thomas Crawter, Cobham; waterbodies, houses, woods (col), boundary stile (by symbol), post and tree, folly tower.

Sussex

PRO IR29 and IR30 35/1-306

323 tithe districts: 929,765 acres
306 tithe commutations: 891,267 acres
190 voluntary tithe agreements, 116 compulsory tithe awards

Tithe and tithe commutation

Some tithe was still payable in 95 per cent of Sussex tithe districts but only 69 districts were wholly tithable in 1836 (Fig. 47). The main causes of tithe exemption in Sussex were modus payments in lieu of tithes, the merger of tithes in the land, and exemption by prescription. As in Kent and Surrey, all woods in the Weald were tithe free; this was the largest category of tithe exemption in Sussex and applied in more than half the tithe districts.

Assistant tithe commissioners and local tithe agents who worked in Sussex are listed in Table 35.1. James Hodson of Falmer was the most prolific tithe valuer in Sussex; he worked in forty districts in this county but seems not to have undertaken tithe valuations outside Sussex. Six tithe districts were valued by men based in or near London but all the other valuers give addresses in Sussex or just outside the county.

Thirty-seven (12 per cent) of Sussex tithe apportionments provide both 'in-bound' and 'out-bound' quantities, that is acreages for both the cultivated part of a field and the total including hedges and other unproductive parts.

Tithe maps

The tithe maps of Sussex are above average both in terms of planimetric accuracy and completeness of content. Almost exactly one-third are sealed as first class, a proportion exceeded only in Kent and Monmouthshire. Construction lines are present on 11 per cent of the second-class maps and as in Kent there was evidently a greater amount of new tithe commutation surveying in Sussex than in most other counties.

The peak years of map production in Sussex were 1839-40 but the last Sussex map, that of Battle, was not completed until 1858 and is unusual for a late map as it covers the whole district. By the 1850s most tithe maps portray residual tithable areas in otherwise largely tithe-free districts (Table 35.4).

Sussex tithe maps are drawn at scales varying from one inch to one chain to one inch to ten chains but 70 per cent of maps are in the recommended scale range of one inch to three to four chains (Table 35.3).

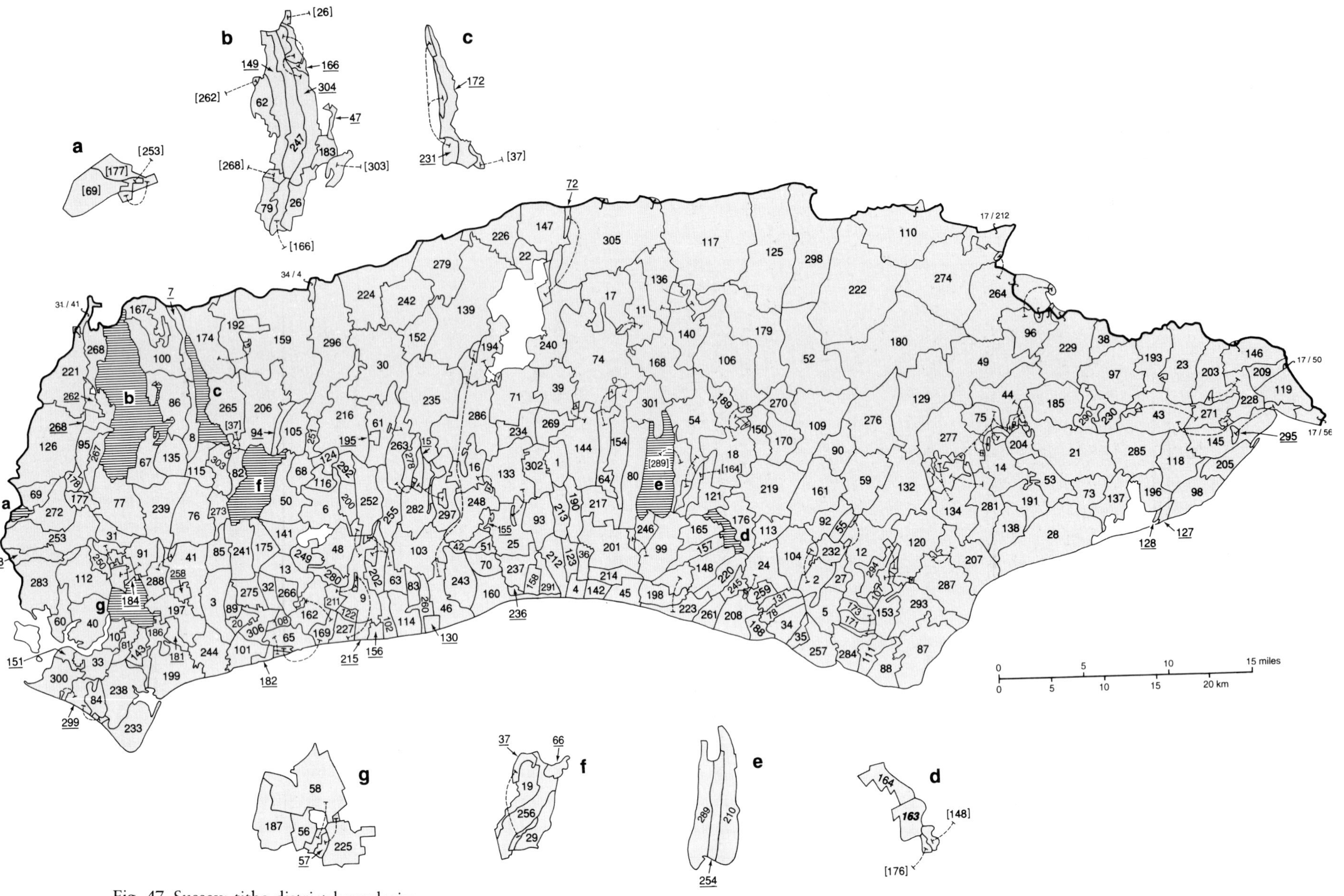

Fig. 47 Sussex: tithe district boundaries.

Agricultural land use in Sussex is rather more thoroughly mapped than in most other counties. About 13 per cent of the county's tithe maps distinguish arable and grass, 21 per cent depict gardens, and 21 per cent map orchards. The depiction of other components of the rural landscape is also rather better than average. Parks are shown on 23 per cent of the maps, 17 per cent distinguish heath and moor, 7.5 per cent map marsh or bog, and woodland appears on 67 per cent of maps. The mapping of field boundaries is also unusually good with field boundary ownership defined on 36 per cent of maps. At Pycombe there is a 'road used on suffrance'; rights of way are not often explicitly defined on tithe maps and this is a most unusual description. At Lindfield there is a priory site reputedly 'quite unknown prior to this survey' and at Brighton only the cowhouses remained tithable and the way that they are mapped results in one of the most idiosyncratic of all tithe maps.

Some 256 Sussex tithe maps in the Public Record Office collection can be attributed to a particular map-maker; the most prolific was William Figg of Lewes who produced thirty-six maps, though some of these are copies of earlier work. An above average number of maps in Sussex (10 per cent) were the work of men from well outside the county, most notably the Draysons of Faversham in Kent who produced seventeen maps. Other surveyors came from as far afield as Frome and Wincanton in Somerset. Sussex tithe maps have more additional ornamentation than those in adjoining counties; about 20 per cent have a decorative border and the ornamentation of map titles, borders, and north pointers includes devices such as Prince of Wales's feathers, scallops and leaves. The map of East Hoathley has a cartouche of flowers and leaves and the Winchelsea tithe map has both a pictorial depiction of navigation aids and a neat vignette of Camber Castle.

Table 35.1. *Agreements and awards for commutation of tithes in Sussex*

Assistant commissioner/ local tithe agent	*Number of agreements**	*Number of awards*
John Farncombe	158	0
Francis Offley Martin	0	45
John Maurice Herbert	0	40
Thomas Smith Woolley	11	17
Joseph Townsend	8	4
Thomas James Tatham	0	9
Charles Osborn	4	0
Job Smallpeice	2	0
A. O. Baker	1	0
James Hodson	1	0
John Pickering	1	0
John Job Rawlinson	0	1
John Smith	1	0
Charles Wilson	1	0

*Computed from the number of extant reports on tithe agreements in the tithe files [PRO IR 18].

Table 35.2. *Tithe valuers and tithe map-makers in Sussex*

Name and address (in Sussex unless indicated)	*Number of districts*	*Acreage*
Tithe valuers		
James Hodson, Falmer	40	136,232
Charles Osborn, Fareham, Hampshire	35	86,509
John Smith, Lewis	32	87,918
Thomas Boniface, Climping	29	57,626
John Farncombe, Brighton	13	29,682
John Stapley, Bognor	13	28,715
Others [65]	144	464,585
Attributed tithe map-makers		
William Figg, Lewes	36	79,541
Frederick and Henry E. Drayson, Faversham, Kent	17	55,891
Henry Salter, Arundel	17	31,336
Edward Fuller, Chichester	16	30,460
Joseph Butler, Chichester	16	29,964
John Adams, Hawkhurst, Kent	15	60,803
John Elliott, Chichester	10	26,061
William Leach, Brighton	10	19,240
Messrs H. and F. Hitchins, Brighton	9	19,845
Others [51]	100	361,120

Table 35.3. *The tithe maps of Sussex: scales and classes*

Scale in chains/inch	*All maps*		*First Class*		*Second Class*	
	Number	*Acreage*	*Number*	*Acreage*	*Number*	*Acreage*
>3	2	92	0	0	2	92
3	188	546,381	98	352,585	90	193,796
4	27	85,082	5	27,830	22	57,252
4.5	3	5,698	0	0	3	5,698
5	21	49,670	0	0	21	49,670
6	54	160,334	0	0	54	160,334
<6	11	44,010	0	0	11	44,010
TOTAL	306	891,267	103	380,415	203	510,852

Table 35.4. *The tithe maps of Sussex: dates*

	<1837	*1837*	*1838*	*1839*	*1840*	*1841*	*1842*	*1843*	*1844*	*1845*	*1846*	*1847*	*1848*	*>1848*
All maps	3	6	19	67	66	38	23	19	12	10	13	12	6	11
1st class	0	0	4	22	27	15	10	8	5	4	1	2	3	2
2nd class*	3	6	15	45	39	23	13	11	7	6	12	10	3	9

*One second-class tithe map of Sussex in the Public Record Office collection is undated.

Sussex

35/1 Albourne (parish) TQ 257164
Apt 08.06.1839; 1749a (1740); Map 1838, 3 chns, by Willm Bishop Harding, surveyor and draughtsman, Frome, Somerset, 'copy' by Willm Duncum, March 1841; construction lines, waterbodies, houses, hedge ownership.

35/2 Alciston (parish) TQ 498054
Apt 20.10.1843; 2079a (2079); Map 1844?, 3 chns, 1st cl, by Willm Figg, Lewes; construction lines, foot/b'way, waterbodies, houses, open fields, building names.

35/3 Aldingbourne (parish) SU 934054
Apt 20.07.1847; 3070a (3069); Map 1846, 6 chns, by E. Fuller, Chichester, (tithable parts only in detail); railway with station, foot/b'way, canal with towpath, waterbodies, houses, woods, plantations, parkland, field gates, road names, landowners, drains, common. Apt has in-bound and out-bound quantities.

35/4 Aldrington (parish) TQ 273050
Apt 29.09.1843; 776a (776); Map 1843, 3 chns, 1st cl, by H. and F. Hitchins; construction lines, waterbodies, coastline. Apt omits land use.

35/5 Alfriston (parish) TQ 509026
Apt 29.06.1842; 2426a (all); Map 1843, 3 chns, 1st cl, by C.F. Humbert, Watford, Herts; construction lines, foot/b'way, waterbodies, houses, building names, road names, windmill (by symbol), chalk pits, drains; bridges named.

35/6 Amberley with Rackham (township and hamlet in parish of Amberley) TQ 039134
Apt 10.12.1846; 2900a (2900); Map 1847, 4.5 chns, in 2 parts, by Joseph Butler, Chichester; foot/b'way, waterbodies, houses, field gates, building names, sewer, boundary trees, chalk pits.

35/7 North Ambersham (tithing in parish of Steep) SU 910284 [Not listed]
Apt 02.07.1847; 1112a (1112); Map 1840, 3 chns, 1st cl, by Fredk and Henry Drayson; construction lines, waterbodies, houses, waste, private roads.

35/8 South Ambersham (tithing in parish of Steep) SU 916210
Apt 02.07.1847; 243a (1506); Map 1848, 3 chns, 1st cl, by William Bridger, Chichester, (tithable parts only); waterbodies, houses, fences.

35/9 Angmering (except Ham and Barcham) (parish) TQ 070060
Apt 01.11.1839; 3096a (?); Map 1839, 3 chns, by Henry Salter, Arundel; hill-drawing, foot/b'way, waterbodies, houses, woods, plantations, marsh/bog, heath/moor, quarries, windmills, lands in other districts (red), lands in Ham and Bargeham (blue).

35/10 Appledram (parish) SU 842024 [Apuldram]
Apt 22.07.1845; 907a (all); Map 1838, 3 chns, by J. Butler, Chichester; hill-drawing, foot/b'way, canal with towpath, waterbodies, houses, sluices, quay, headland, bay, windmill, common; coast features named.

35/11 Ardingley (parish) TQ 339300 [Ardingly]
Apt 11.03.1840; 3818a (3817); Map 1841?, 3 chns, by T.H. Spencer, 3, Everett Street, Russell Square, London; railway, foot/b'way, waterbodies, houses, woods, plantations, orchards, field boundary ownerships, building names, mill, ox-bow.

35/12 Arlington (parish) TQ 546078
Apt 14.02.1843; 5186a (5185); Map 1840, 4 chns, 1st cl, by W. Figg, Lewes; construction lines, waterbodies, houses, woods (named).

35/13 Arundel (parish) TQ 005079
Apt 11.09.1840; 1968a (1968); Map 1841, 3 chns, by Henry Salter, Arundel; waterbodies, houses, woods, plantations, parkland; double lines may be drains.

35/14 Ashburnham (parish) TQ 680150 [Not listed]
Apt 30.09.1840; 3648a (3648); Map 1839, 5 chns, by W.Rider, C.E.; waterbodies, woods (named), gardens, building names, school, almshouses, old park; bridges named; map includes detached parts of other districts. [There is no copy in PRO IR 30; map details are from East Sussex County Record Office PAR 233/21/2.]

35/15 Ashington cum Buncton (parish) TQ 129161
Apt 14.07.1847; 1273a (1273); Map 1847, 3 chns, in 4 parts, by Joseph Butler; foot/b'way, waterbodies, houses, building names, chapel, boundary trees.

35/16 Ashurst (parish) TQ 178157
Apt 07.12.1843; 2356a (2355); Map 1844, 3 chns, 1st cl, by John Wood, Lindfield by Cuckfield, Sussex; construction lines, foot/b'way, waterbodies, houses, woods, orchards, heath/moor, field boundary ownerships, field gates, building names, rectory, common, green.

35/17 Balcombe (parish) TQ 309311
Apt 16.11.1839; 4786a (4786); Map 1840, 3 chns, by H. Walter, Windsor; construction lines, hill-drawing, railway with viaduct, foot/b'way, waterbodies, houses, woods (named), plantations, parkland (named), marsh/bog, heath/moor, hedge ownership, fence ownership, field gates, building names, stone pit or quarry.

35/18 Barcombe (parish) TQ 426168
Apt 11.10.1839; 4984a (4983); Map 1839, 3 chns, 1st cl, by Fredk and Henry Drayson; construction lines, foot/b'way, waterbodies, houses, orchards, hops, field gates, river naviagation channels, boundary trees, paper mill, stiles, waste, green, ox-bow lakes; bridge named.

35/19 Barlton or Barlavington (parish) SU 972165
Apt 10.04.1839; 1175a (1175); Map 1840, 5 chns; waterbodies, houses, farmyards (col), woods (col), plantations (col), parkland (col), arable (col), grassland (col), orchards, hops, gardens (col), marsh/bog, heath/moor, rock outcrops, hedge ownership, fence ownership, quarries.

35/20 Barnham (parish) SU 960035
Apt 20.03.1849; 871a (730); Map 1846, 3 chns, by Thomas Wisdom, South Berstead; railway, foot/b'way, canal with towpath, waterbodies, woods (col). Apt has in-bound and out-bound quantities.

35/21 Battle (parish) TQ 749160
Apt 27.05.1858; 8211a (7880); Map 1859, 3 chns, by J.W. Cole; hill-drawing, railway with station, foot/b'way, turnpike roads, road embankments, toll gate, waterbodies, houses, farmyards, woods (col, named), plantations (col), parkland (named), orchards, building names, road names, abbey, deanery, fishpond, National School, old sand pit, windmills, powder mills, keepers lodge, lodge, maze, boundary posts; part of district boundary is taken from 'Westfield map'; woodland is green and other land is brown.

35/22 Baybush (tithing in parish of Beeding otherwise Seale) TQ 231349 [Not listed]
Apt 19.07.1841; 1525a (?); Map 1846, 3 chns, 1st cl, by I.R. Monkhouse; railway, foot/b'way, occupation roads, waterbodies, houses, woods, parkland, heath/moor, hedge ownership, building names; there is a note that map has been compared with 'the original combined map of Lower Beeding and Bewbush'.

35/23 Beckley (parish) TQ 855238
Apt 08.03.1839; 3526a (5316); Map 1841?, 4 chns; foot/b'way, waterbodies, houses, woods (col), arable (col), grassland (col), orchards, gardens (col), heath/moor, building names, road names, rectory, watermill (by symbol), drains.

35/24 Beddingham (parish) TQ 450065
Apt 22.11.1842; 2919a (2918); Map 1840, 6 chns, by William Figg, Lewes; hill-drawing, waterbodies, houses, woods, orchards, river embankments, drains.

35/25 Beeding (tithing in parish of Beeding) TQ 210104 [Upper Beeding]
Apt 13.12.1843; 3423a (3847); Map 1842, 3 chns, 1st cl, by James and Edmund Smith, Upper Beeding near Steyning, (tithable parts only); construction lines, foot/b'way, waterbodies, open fields, field boundary ownerships, mill; double lines may be drains.

35/26 Bepton (parish) SU 859183
Apt 23.10.1838; 1225a (1224); Map 1838, 3 chns, 1st cl, by Thomas Baker, 55 Vauxhall Street, London; construction lines, foot/b'way, waterbodies, houses (by shading), orchard (by annotation), hedge

ownership, fence ownership, building names, road names, field names, farm names, ruins, rectory, glebe, brickyard, common; some physical features named; pecked lines indicate approximate position of scattered trees and brushwood.

35/27 Berwick (parish) TQ 523054
Apt 16.05.1838; 1097a (all); Map 1840, 4 chns, 1st cl, by Alfred Sharman and John Campbell; construction lines, waterbodies, houses, drains.

35/28 Bexhill (parish) TQ 728087
Apt 08.12.1843; 8000a (8814); Map 1839, 3 chns, 1st cl, by John Adams, Hawkhurst, Kent; construction lines, foot/b'way, canal, waterbodies, houses, woods (by name), field gates, building names, martello towers, high water mark, artificial drainage channels, telegraph (by symbol), green, Hastings municipal boundary. Apt has in-bound and out-bound quantities.

35/29 Bignor (except Buddington) (parish) SU 985141
Apt 09.08.1844; 1146a (?); Map 1843, 6 chns, in 2 parts, by Henry Salter, Arundel; hill-drawing, foot/b'way, waterbodies, houses, woods, plantations, parkland, orchards, open fields, hedge ownership, fence ownership, boundary stones; lengthy note explains position of detached portion.

35/30 Billingshurst (parish) TQ 097261
Apt 22.01.1841; 6758a (6758); Map 1841, 6 chns, by Messrs Crawter, Cobham Surrey and Southampton Buildings, Chancery Lane, London; waterbodies, houses, woods.

35/31 Binderton (parish) SU 842115 [Not listed]
Apt 30.01.1849; 1324a (1790); Map 1847, 3 chns, 1st cl, by John Elliott, Chichester; construction lines, hill-drawing, foot/b'way, waterbodies, houses, woods, plantations, parkland, hedge ownership, fence ownership, field gates.

35/32 Binsted (parish) SU 986062 [Binstead]
Apt 15.08.1840; 1087a (1086); Map 1838, 3 chns, 1st cl, by E. Fuller, Chichester, Sussex; construction lines, foot/b'way, waterbodies, houses, woods, plantations, hedge ownership, fence ownership, field boundary ownerships, field gates, drains; a note says that this copy was deposited in the house of Henry Upton Esq for the inspection of the landowners, Oct 26th 1840.

35/33 Birdham (parish) SU 822001
Apt 26.10.1847; 1808a (1948); Map 1846, 3 chns, by Joseph Butler, Chichester; foot/b'way, canal with towpath, waterbodies, houses, woods (named), open fields, building names, coastline, mill. Apt has in-bound and out-bound quantities.

35/34 Bishopston (parish) TQ 471014 [Bishopstone]
Apt 28.11.1844; 1829a (all); Map 1840, 3 chns, 1st cl, by William Figg, Lewes; construction lines, hill-drawing, foot/b'way, waterbodies, houses, woods, plantations, orchards, marsh/bog, rock outcrops, field gates, building names, tumuli, artificial drainage channels, quarry, stone pits, tide mill, embankments, coastline, beach, mill pond; colour bands may show property ownerships.

35/35 East Blatchington (parish) TQ 483002
Apt 20.11.1843; 756a (821); Map 1844, 3 chns, by William Figg, Lewes; hill-drawing, foot/b'way, waterbodies, houses, woods, building names, beach, coastline, pits, mill, downs.

35/36 West Blatchington (parish) TQ 279075
Apt 07.06.1839; 876a (all); Map 1839, 6 chns, copied from a map made in 1829 by R. Gabb by Wm Leach; foot/b'way, waterbodies, woods, hedge ownership, building names, quarry, dole stones; colours may show land use.

35/37 Bodecton or Burton (parish) SU 970186 [Not listed]
Apt 08.08.1843; 810a (809); Map 1841, 5 chns; waterbodies, farmyards, woods (col, named), plantations (col), arable (col), grassland (col), orchards, gardens (col), heath/moor, hedge ownership, fence ownership, building names, road names, mill, boundary marks, sand or stone pit, common.

35/38 Bodiam (parish) TQ 778261
Apt 07.05.1839; 1597a (1596); Map 1840, 4 chns, by John Barnes and Son, Sandhurst, Kent; foot/b'way, waterbodies, houses, drains, moated castle.

35/39 Bolney (parish) TQ 257231
Apt 05.07.1842; 3547a (3546); Map 1840, 3 chns, 1st cl, by Barber, Bolney, Sussex; waterbodies, houses, woods, plantations, estate boundary hedge ownership, road names, property boundaries.

35/40 Bosham (parish) SU 818038
Apt 01.11.1841; 3194a (all); Map 1839, [?9 chns], in 4 parts, copied from the enclosure map made by Messrs Driver, revised and corrected to 1839 by J. Butler, Chichester, (includes three small enlargements of detail); foot/b'way, waterbodies, houses, farmyards (col), woods (named).

35/41 Boxgrove (parish) SU 911083
Apt 31.01.1839; 3676a (3676); Map 1841, 3 chns, 1st cl, by John Elliott, Chichester; construction lines, foot/b'way, plantations, heath/moor, hedge ownership, fence ownership, field boundary ownerships, field gates, obelisk; map also covers West Hampnet (35/288).

35/42 Bramber (parish) TQ 176098
Apt 14.02.1839; 855a (all); Map 1840?, 3 chns; construction lines, foot/b'way, waterbodies, houses, woods, open fields, field boundary ownerships, field gates; many tithe areas have been renumbered.

35/43 Brede (parish) TQ 828193
Apt 21.03.1846; 4840a (4840); Map 1840, 3 chns, 1st cl, in 3 parts, by J.S. Thomson, Tenterden, Kent, (includes 12-chn index); cons-truction lines, foot/b'way, waterbodies, houses, woods, orchards, fence ownership, field boundary ownerships, field gates, building names, drains; scale bar and compass rose are combined. Apt has in-bound and out-bound quantities.

35/44 Brightling (parish) TQ 689212
Apt 31.10.1839; 4614a (4613); Map 1838, 4 chns, by W. Rider, C.E.; construction lines, waterbodies, woods (named), plantations, parkland (in detail, named), orchards, gardens, open fields, field gates, building names, temple, gardener's house, observatory; bridge named.

35/45 Brighton (parish) TQ 318046
Apt 24.02.1851; 774a (2320); Map 1852, 4 chns, in 70 parts, (tithable parts only; including 69 separate plans at 1 inch to 50 ft (1:600) of cowhouses, which are the only remaining tithable property); railways, railway terminus, goods line, waterbodies, woods, building names, road names, palace, hotels, crescents, race course, race stand, steam saw mills, castle, cemetery, distance in feet of cowhouses to street corners. Apt omits some field names but includes cow population figures.

35/46 Broadwater (parish) TQ 145044
Apt 02.09.1847; 2834a (2560); Map 'Rough Map', 1848, 3 chns, 1st cl, in 2 parts, by Messrs Hide and Patching, Worthing; construction lines, railway with station, foot/b'way, turnpike roads, waterbodies, houses, rock outcrops, field boundary ownerships, building names, road names, farm names, landowners, casino, dispensary, chalk pits, mill, sand or stone pits, rectory, manor house, chapels, crescents, hotels, market, brickyard, high water mark, beach, Coast Guard Station, drains, downs, greens, pasture liable to flooding, town boundary; pleasure grounds, parks, gardens, nursery grounds (with ownerships) and parsonage land shown by annotation; bridge named; built-up parts generalised. (The map in PRO IR 30 is a copy; original is in PRO IR 77/85.)

35/47 Buddington (tithing in parish of Bignor) SU 886235 [Not listed]
Apt 01.03.1841; 173a (?); Map 1840, 3 chns, 1st cl, by Fredk and Henry Drayson; construction lines, houses.

35/48 Burpham (parish) TQ 051095
Apt 09.05.1840; 2723a (all); Map 1840, 4 chns, 'compiled' by Henry Salter, Arundel; hill-drawing, foot/b'way, waterbodies, houses, woods, hedge ownership, drains.

35/49 Burwash (parish) TQ 665244
Apt 18.06.1839; 7321a (7321); Map 1839, 3 chns, 1st cl, by John Adams, Hawkhurst, Kent; construction lines, foot/b'way, waterbodies, houses, field gates, building names, mill, boundary trees, forest land, sand or stone pit, ornamental ground; bridge named; mapmaker notes 'Those parts of the main lines that are ruled in Green have been run out since they were chained first and will be found in the field books - the line

books only contain the Parts ruled in Red'. Apt has in-bound and out-bound quantities.

35/50 Bury (parish) TQ 004142
Apt 18.07.1839; 3418a (3340); Map 1850?, 6 chns, by Henry Salter, Arundel; hill-drawing, foot/b'way, turnpike roads, toll gate, waterbodies, houses, woods, plantations, marsh/bog, heath/moor, chalk pits.

35/51 Buttolphs otherwise Botolphs (parish) TQ 187094
Apt 31.07.1843; 929a (all); Map 1853, 3 chns, by George Blunden, Arundel; hill-drawing, foot/b'way, private roads and drift ways (col), waterbodies, houses, woods, orchards, hedge ownership, fences, building names, drains, sand or stone pits, glebe.

35/52 Buxted (parish) TQ 497249
Apt 26.05.1841; 8944a (8943); Map 1840, 3 chns, 1st cl, by John Adams, Hawkhurst; construction lines, waterbodies, houses, plantations (named), parkland, building names, forest land, gravel pit, rectory, sand or stone pit, common; gates named. Apt has in-bound and out-bound quantities.

35/53 Catsfield (parish) TQ 724137
Apt 18.06.1840; 2944a (2944); Map 1839, 5 chns, by W. Rider, C.E.; waterbodies, woods (named), plantations, parkland (named), building names.

35/54 Chailey (parish) TQ 390200
Apt 26.04.1838; 5889a (5889); Map 1839?, 3 chns, 1st cl, by Fredk and Henry E. Drayson; construction lines, waterbodies, houses, plantations, rock outcrops, building names, windmill (pictorial), shepherds hut, quarries, milestone, commons; hill named.

35/55 Chalvington (parish) TQ 526102
Apt 12.03.1838; 729a (all); Map 1839, 4 chns, by W. Rider, C.E.; waterbodies, woods (named), gardens, building names.

35/56 Chichester, St Bartholomew (parish) SU 855045 [Not listed]
Apt 25.11.1847; 234a (233); Map 1846, 3 chns, by E. Fuller, Chichester; railway, foot/b'way, turnpike roads and gate, canal basin, waterbodies, houses, hedge ownership, fence ownership, field gates, road names, drains, city walls, nursery (by annotation), city liberty boundaries.

35/57 Chichester, St Pancras (part of) (parish) SU 862038 [Not listed]
Apt 16.10.1848; 103a (103); Map 1847, 3 chns, by Joseph Butler, (tithable parts only); railway, foot/b'way, canal with towpath, waterbodies, houses, building names; built-up parts generalised and tinted. Apt has in-bound and out-bound quantities.

35/58 Chichester, St Peter the Great, otherwise the Subdeanery (part of) (parish) SU 859059 [Not listed]
Apt 31.03.1849; 1381a (1321); Map 1847, 3 chns, by Joseph Butler, (tithable parts only); railway, foot/b'way, canal, waterbodies, houses, building names, Cathedral; built-up parts generalised and tinted. Apt has in-bound and out-bound quantities.

35/59 Chiddingly (parish) TQ 549141
Apt 07.10.1839; 4297a (4297); Map 1839, 6 chns, by Richard Lower, Chiddingley near Uckfield, Sussex; waterbodies, woods, building names, mill, greens.

35/60 Chidham (parish) SU 793045
Apt 21.01.1848; 1619a (all); Map 1846, 3 chns, by E. Fuller, Chichester; railway, turnpike roads, waterbodies, houses, woods, plantations, heath/moor, hedge ownership, field gates, building names, road names, coastline, gate houses, milestone, sea bank, ferry. Apt has in-bound and out-bound quantities.

35/61 West Chiltington (except Nytimber) (parish) TQ 095203
Apt 02.07.1839; 3918a (3917); Map 1840, 6 chns, by Messrs Crawter, Cobham, Surrey and Southampton Buildings, London; waterbodies, houses, woods (col), plantations, building names, common.

35/62 Chithurst (parish) SU 837249
Apt 08.09.1840; 1048a (1047); Map 1840, 3 chns, 1st cl, by Fredk and Henry E. Drayson; construction lines, waterbodies, houses, common.

35/63 Clapham (parish) TQ 100068
Apt 31.07.1843; 1794a (all); Map 1844, 6 chns, by Henry Salter, Arundel; waterbodies, houses, woods, plantations, hedge ownership, fence ownership.

35/64 Clayton (parish) TQ 301164
Apt 21.08.1838; 2402a (2462); Map 1841, 3 chns, 1st cl, by Dixon and Maitland, Godalming, Surrey; construction lines (main in red, subsidiary in blue), railway, waterbodies, houses, woods (col), building names, priory, parsonage, mills, common.

35/65 Climping (parish) TQ 005019
Apt 16.12.1843; 1806a (2185); Map 1843, 6 chns, 'compiled' by J.F. Tidey, Littlehampton; foot/b'way, waterbodies, woods, field gates, building names, road names, drains, windmill (pictorial).

35/66 Coates (parish) SU 996178
Apt 08.09.1840; 346a (345); Map 1839, 3 chns, 1st cl, by William Bridger, Petworth, Sussesx; construction lines, waterbodies, houses, open fields, fence ownership.

35/67 Cocking (parish) SU 874176
Apt 07.11.1842; 2603a (2602); Map 1840, 3 chns, 1st cl, by Fredk and Henry Drayson; construction lines, waterbodies, houses, plantations, rock outcrops, building names, quarry, watermill (by symbol), milestone, downs.

35/68 Coldwaltham (parish) TQ 019166
Apt 22.01.1841; 1194a (all); Map 1841, 4 chns, in 2 parts, by J. Butler, Chichester, (includes small enlargement of detail); hill-drawing, foot/b'way, canal, waterbodies, houses, woods (col), plantations (col).

35/69 Compton (parish) SU 774152
Apt 27.09.1841; 1662a (all); Map 1841, 6 chns, by Jas W. Blackman, Fareham; waterbodies, houses, woods, plantations, parkland, building names.

35/70 Coombes (parish) TQ 186078
Apt 25.08.1841; 1293a (1292); Map 1840, 5 chns; hill-drawing, waterbodies, houses, farmyards (col), woods (col), plantations (col), arable (col), grassland (col), gardens (col), heath/moor, rock outcrops, open fields, hedge ownership, drains, quarries, chalk pits; 'Variable' (convertible) lands are shown in brown with green edging.

35/71 Cowfold (parish) TQ 216228
Apt 02.04.1839; 4458a (4458); Map 1840, 3 chns, 1st cl, by Wm Duncum, Reading, Berkshire; construction lines, foot/b'way, waterbodies, houses, hedge ownership, fence ownership; map has large coloured compass rose.

35/72 Crawley (parish) TQ 273374
Apt 16.01.1840; 770a (770); Map 1839, 3 chns, in 3 parts, (including index): North Division by H. Walter, Windsor; South Division 'copied' by J. Plumer, Horsham; construction lines, foot/b'way, waterbodies, houses, woods, plantations, heath/moor, hedge ownership, fence ownership, field gates, building names, road names.

35/73 Crowhurst (parish) TQ 765121
Apt 22.01.1841; 2160a (2160); Map 1840, 3 chns, by W. Rider C.E., Battel; construction lines, waterbodies, houses; double lines may be drains.

35/74 Cuckfield (parish) TQ 297255
Apt 30.11.1843; 11167a (11167); Map 1843, 10 chns, in 2 parts, (includes enlargement of town at 5 chns); railway with tunnel, foot/b'way, waterbodies, houses, woods (named), building names, tan yard, greens, heath common, park.

35/75 Dallington (parish) TQ 663192
Apt 05.07.1842; 2873a (2873); Map 1843, 4 chns, 1st cl, by Thos Hughes; construction lines, waterbodies, houses; scale bar is not figured.

35/76 East Dean (parish) SU 916131
Apt 17.03.1848; 4647a (all); Map 1847, 3 chns, by John Elliott, Chichester; hill-drawing, foot/b'way, waterbodies, houses, woods, hedge ownership, fence ownership, field boundary ownerships, field gates, sand or stone pits, old chalk pit, lime kiln.

35/77 West Dean (parish) SU 849141
Apt 30.01.1849; 4762a (2290); Map 1848, 3 chns, 1st cl, by John Elliott;

hill-drawing, foot/b'way, waterbodies, houses, woods, plantations, parkland, hedge ownership, fences, field gates, allotments, sand or stone pits, quarries; map has note that this copy has been compared with the original and is correct.

35/78 Denton (parish) TQ 464028
Apt 19.04.1839; 1009a (1008); Map 1839, 6.5 chns, by Jno. Budgen; hill-drawing, waterbodies, river embankments, drains, ownership boundaries (col).

35/79 Didling (parish) SU 838187
Apt 15.02.1843; 815a (814); Map 1840, 3 chns, by Henry Hull, Bramley near Guildford, Surrey; foot/b'way, waterbodies, houses, gardens.

35/80 Ditcheling (parish) TQ 328151 [Ditchling]
Apt 24.02.1843; 4184a (4183); Map 1839, 3 chns, 1st cl, by John Wood, Lindfield, Sussex; construction lines, hill-drawing, foot/b'way, waterbodies, woods, orchards, fence ownership, field boundary ownerships, field gates, quarries, tumuli.

35/81 Donnington (parish) SU 851016
Apt 02.12.1842; 1030a (all); Map 1839, 3 chns, by E. Fuller, Chichester; construction lines, foot/b'way, canal with towpath, waterbodies, houses, woods, plantations, hedge ownership, fence ownership, field boundary ownerships, field gates, road names, ornamental ground.

35/82 Duncton (parish) SU 958170
Apt 15.06.1837; 1324a (1324); Map 1837, 5 chns, by William Knight; foot/b'way, waterbodies, houses, farmyards, woods, plantations, arable (col), grassland (col), orchards, gardens, heath/moor, rock outcrops, hedge ownership, fence ownership, field gates, building names, chalk pits, old chalk pits, boundary stones; farm named; mapmaker notes: 'The Boundaries are principally copied from, The Earl of Egremont's Manorial Maps, executed by Crow, and revised and corrected, under the direction of, William Knight'; map has note of its adoption and landowners' signatures.

35/83 Durrington (parish) TQ 118058
Apt 24.05.1839; 891a (891); Map 1839, 3 chns, 'copy' by Hide and Patching, Worthing; waterbodies, houses, farmyards, woods, arable (col), grassland (col), orchards, gardens, heath/moor, rock outcrops, hedge ownership, hedgerow trees, building names, quarry, sand or stone pits, Coate farm boundary, roadside waste (col), stone walls.

35/84 Earnley (parish) SZ 822967
Apt 08.09.1845; 1157a (all); Map 1845, 3 chns, by Alfred Mellersh, Godalming; waterbodies, houses, woods (col), orchards (col), fences, building names, coastline, high water mark, 'horse block', windmill (pictorial), chapel, drains.

35/85 Eartham (parish) SU 939095
Apt 14.02.1839; 1504a (all); Map 1840, 6 chns, 'Enlarged from the Inclosure Map made in 1813, revised and corrected to the present time' by J. Butler, Chichester; hill-drawing, foot/b'way, waterbodies, houses, woods (col), plantations (col), parkland (col), quarry, Roman road.

35/86 Easebourne (parish) SU 899235
Apt 02.07.1847; 1053a (?); Map 1840, 3 chns, 1st cl; waterbodies, woods, building names, 'Cowdry ruins', boundary stones; map has a note that the original map was damaged and so this version has been adopted as the apportionment map.

35/87 Eastbourne (parish) TV 602987
Apt 17.06.1841; 5051a (all); Map 1840-1, 6 chns, in 2 parts, copied 'from a survey by J. Adams' by W. Figg, Lewes, (includes town separately at 3 chns); hill-drawing, waterbodies, houses, woods, parkland, orchards, gardens, marsh/bog, rock outcrops, building names, high water mark, chalk pits or quarries, coastline, cliffs, circular redoubt, downs; coast features named; double lines may be drains.

35/88 Eastdean (parish) TV 562971
Apt 29.08.1844; 2151a (all); Map 1846?, 4 chns; hill-drawing, waterbodies, houses, building names, flagpoles, preventive station, lighthouse, sand or stone pits or quarries, green.

35/89 Eastergate (parish) SU 950051
Apt 06.06.1845; 914a (912); Map 1845, 3 chns, by John Adams, Hawkhurst; railway, foot/b'way, waterbodies, houses, woods, building names. Apt has in-bound and out-bound quantities.

35/90 Easthothly (parish) TQ 525168 [East Hoathley]
Apt 31.07.1839; 2576a (2000); Map 1839, 3 chns, prepared for tithe commutation and parochial assessments by Richard Lower, Chiddingly, Sussex; foot/b'way, waterbodies, houses, woods (by name), field gates, building names, boundary stones, windmill (pictorial), sand or stone pit; red band may show present or former common land, greens and woodland; north pointer is decorated with flowers and leaves, which also enclose mapmaker's name and map date, and is tipped with acorn and oak leaves.

35/91 Eastlavant (parish) SU 869099 [East Lavant]
Apt 22.04.1839; 2884a (all); Map 1840, 3 chns, 1st cl, by John Elliott, Chichester; construction lines, hill-drawing, foot/b'way, waterbodies, houses, hedge ownership, fence ownership, field boundary ownerships, field gates, field name; map also covers Mid Lavant (35/184).

35/92 Eckington otherwise Ripe (parish) TQ 511104
Apt 22.11.1837; 1879a (1120); Map 1839, 6 chns, by Willm Figg, Lewes; waterbodies, houses, woods (named), orchards, fences, building names, mill.

35/93 Edburton (parish) TQ 239116
Apt 31.12.1841; 2651a (2651); Map 1842, 6 chns, by E. and G.N. Driver; hill-drawing, foot/b'way, turnpike roads, waterbodies, houses, farmyards, woods, plantations, osiers, arable (col), grassland (col), orchards, marsh/bog, heath/moor, open fields, hedge ownership, building names, field names, field acreages, lime kiln, quarry, boundary stones, downs.

35/94 Egdean (parish) SU 998207
Apt 29.11.1837; 711a (710); Map 1837, 5 chns, by William Knight; waterbodies, houses, farmyards, woods, arable (col), grassland (col), orchards, gardens, heath/moor, hedge ownership, fence ownership, field gates, towpath, limekiln, drains, common; mapmaker notes 'The Boundaries are principally copied from, The Earl of Egremont's Manorial Maps, executed by Crow, and revised and corrected, under the direction of, William Knight'; map has note of adoption proceedings and landowners' signatures.

35/95 Elsted (parish) SU 815192
Apt 14.02.1843; 1790a (1789); Map 1840, 6 chns, by Henry Hull, Bramley, Surrey; waterbodies, houses, gardens.

35/96 Etchingham (parish) TQ 708270
Apt 08.12.1837; 3751a (3750); Map 1843, 3 chns, in 3 parts, by Thomas Hughes, (including 10-chn location diagram); hill-drawing, waterbodies, houses, woods, plantations, building names, road names, rectory, glebe, sand or stone pits, road embankments, drains. Apt has in-bound and out-bound quantities.

35/97 Ewhurst (parish) TQ 790230 [Ewhurst Green]
Apt 23.03.1844; 5719a (5719); Map 1843, 3 chns, 1st cl, by W. Beck; foot/b'way, turnpike roads, toll houses, waterbodies, houses, woods (col), field boundary ownerships, field gates, building names, road names, pound, mill, green; double lines may be drains; map has note that this copy was compared with the original map and the reference numbers are correct. Apt has in-bound and out-bound quantities.

35/98 Fairlight (parish) TQ 863122
Apt 30.11.1839; 2899a (3309); Map 1839, 3 chns, 1st cl, by John Adams, Hawkhurst; construction lines, canal, waterbodies, houses, rock outcrops, building names, Coastguard stations, coastline, quarry, cliffs, vicarage, boundary stones; bridge named. Apt has in-bound and out-bound quantities.

35/99 Falmer (parish) TQ 356086
Apt 25.05.1838; 4358a (4358); Map 1841, 4 chns, by Willm Figg, Lewes; hill-drawing, waterbodies, houses, plantations, parkland, orchards, gardens, rock outcrops, building names, lodges, stone pit. Apt omits some land use.

35/100 Farnhurst (parish) SU 883273 [Fernhurst]
Apt 30.04.1846; 4776a (4757); Map 1841, 3 chns, 1st cl, by Fredk and Henry E. Drayson, Faversham, Kent; construction lines, foot/b'way, waterbodies, houses, fences, field gates, building names.

35/101 Felpham (parish) SU 964008
Apt 14.06.1844; 2053a (all); Map 1844, 3 chns, by Thomas Wisdom, South Bersted; waterbodies, houses, woods, plantations, coastline, mills, drains.

35/102 Ferring (parish) TQ 094034
Apt 24.02.1840; 935a (all); Map 1837, 3 chns, by Henry Salter; foot/b'way, waterbodies, houses, woods, hedge ownership, field gates, high and low water marks, 'Holy Breadth' lands boundary.

35/103 Findon (parish) TQ 126091
Apt 23.11.1838; 4337a (4336); Map 1839, 3 chns, by Messrs Hide and Patching, 14, High Street, Worthing; waterbodies, houses, field boundary ownerships, building names, obelisk, downs; two areas are 'No Man's Land'.

35/104 West Firle (parish) TQ 479076
Apt 29.09.1843; 3392a (all); Map 1841, 3 chns, 1st cl, by Willm Figg, Lewes; hill-drawing, foot/b'way, waterbodies, houses, woods (named), plantations, parkland (in detail, named), orchards, gardens, marsh/bog, rock outcrops, fences, building names, road names, tower, drains, quarries, parsonage, workhouse, old road.

35/105 Fittleworth (parish) TQ 012202
Apt 02.04.1839; 2368a (2367); Map 1839, 5 chns; foot/b'way, waterbodies, houses, farmyards (col), woods (col), plantations (col), arable (col), grassland (col), orchards (col), gardens (col), heath/moor, open fields, hedge ownership, fences, drains, river towpath, river locks, commons.

35/106 Fletching (parish) TQ 421253
Apt 27.03.1841; 8463a (8463); Map 1840, 3 chns, 1st cl, by Thomas Hughes; construction lines, waterbodies, houses, orchards, gardens (col), field gates, building names, boundary stones, mills, parsonage, limekiln, down, common, forest land; bridges named.

35/107 Folkington (parish) TQ 575049
Apt 31.01.1838; 1521a (1521); Map 1838, 3 chns, by Willm Figg, Lewes; construction lines, hill-drawing, foot/b'way, turnpike roads and gate, waterbodies, woods, fences, field gates, building names, field names, sand or stone pits, quarries, limekiln, common, downs, glebe; arable, grass, garden shown by annotation in some fields.

35/108 Ford (parish) SU 998035
Apt 20.06.1839; 478a (all); Map 1839, 3 chns; hill-drawing, foot/b'way, canal with towpath, locks, wharf, river embankments, drains, waterbodies, houses, woods, fence ownership, field gates, building names, road names

35/109 Framfield (parish) TQ 505194
Apt 31.03.1841; 6382a (6700); Map 1843?, 3 chns; construction lines (in red and blue), waterbodies, houses, woods (col, named), heath/moor, common or waste (col); map has note: 'In all cases where fields are bounded by streams the centre is invariably taken. All shaws not numbered are included in the fields in which they are situate'.

35/110 Frant (parish) TQ 589362
Apt 22.01.1846; 8873a (8872); Map 1846, 10 chns, surveyed in 1802 by Thomas Budgen and revised by E.W. Gilbert, litho (by S. Parmenter, 304, Strand, London); waterbodies, woods, plantations, parkland (named), rock outcrops (named), fences, building names, castle, keepers house, abbey, downs, green. Apt omits some field names.

35/111 Friston (parish) TV 549985
Apt 29.08.1844; 1446a (all); Map 1848, 6 chns, by W. Figg, Lewes; hill-drawing, waterbodies, houses, woods, building names, well, preventive station, flagstaff (pictorial), sand or stone pits, windmill (pictorial), boundary trees.

35/112 Funtington (parish) SU 814073
Apt 07.06.1838; 3635a (all); Map 1839, [8 chns], copied from the en-=closure map by Messrs Driver, revised and corrected by J. Butler, Chichester; foot/b'way, waterbodies, houses, woods (col, named), plantations (col), parkland (col), orchards, gardens, building names, road names, chapel, mills; scale is noted in pencil; map has landowners' signatures of approval.

35/113 Glynde (parish) TQ 456097
Apt 13.06.1839; 1570a (1569); Map 1838, 6 chns, by William Figg, Lewes; hill-drawing, waterbodies, woods (col), parkland (col), arable (col), grassland (col), heath/moor, hedge ownership, fences (pictorial), field gates, building names, boundary trees and posts, sand or stone pit, quarry, drains, downs; bridge and hill named.

35/114 Goring (parish) TQ 109030 [Goring-by-Sea]
Apt 04.08.1843; 1960a (2182); Map 1839, 3 chns, by Henry Salter, Arundel; foot/b'way, waterbodies, houses, woods, parkland, orchards, hedge ownership.

35/115 Graffham (parish) SU 924176
Apt 10.03.1842; 1658a (1658); Map 1841, 6 chns, by Jas W. Blackman, Fareham; waterbodies, woods, heath/moor; hill named.

35/116 Greatham (parish) TQ 037155
Apt 16.03.1837; 770a (769); Map 1838?, 3 chns, by R. Wright, 54, Gt Ormond Street; canal, drains, ownerships (col). District is apportioned by holding; Apt omits land use, but refers to colour-coding of ownerships on the map.

35/117 East Grinstead (parish) TQ 409356
Apt 26.07.1842; 15034a (15071); Map 1841, 6 chns, in 2 parts, (includes town separately at 4.5 chns); hill-drawing, waterbodies, farmyards, woods (col), plantations (col), parkland (named), hops, building names, stone quarry, sand or stone pits, mill, windmill (pictorial), ruins (pictorial), boundary stones and trees. (The map in PRO IR 30 is a copy; original is in PRO IR 77/86.)

35/118 Guestling (parish) TQ 848151 [Guestling Green]
Apt 01.04.1842; 3565a (3564); Map 1843, 3 chns, 1st cl, by John Adams, Hawkhurst; construction lines, foot/b'way, waterbodies, woods (by name), houses, field gates, building names, drains, windmill, green. Apt has in-bound and out-bound quantities.

35/119 East Guldeford (parish) TQ 951214
Apt 18.02.1843; 2816a (2430); Map 1839, 3 chns, by John Adams, Hawkhurst; waterbodies, houses, road names, walls, sewers, shingle banks, Royal Military Road; double lines may be drains. Apt has in-bound and out-bound quantities.

35/120 Hailsham (parish) TQ 597085
Apt 23.03.1842; 5283a (5283); Map 1842, 3 chns, 1st cl, by Thomas Hughes; construction lines, waterbodies, houses, Liberty of Pevensey boundary; double lines are drains; mapmaker notes: 'where drains form the boundaries the centres are the limits of the numbers'.

35/121 Hamsey (parish) TQ 402127
Apt 22.02.1838; 2762a (2761); Map 1840, 6 chns, by William Figg, Lewes; hill-drawing, foot/b'way, waterbodies, houses, woods, plantations, osiers, parkland, orchards, marsh/bog, fences, field gates, drains, river and drainage embankments, nursery ground.

35/122 Ham and Bargham (tithing in parish of Angmering) TQ 058035 [Not listed]
Apt 24.09.1850; 1264a (?); Map 1847, 6 chns, in 2 parts, 'compiled' by Henry Salter, Arundel; railway, foot/b'way, waterbodies, houses, woods, osiers, parkland, marsh/bog, hedge ownership, building names, landowners, sand or stone pit.

35/123 Hangleton (parish) TQ 265080
Apt 21.12.1841; 1159a (all); Map 1841, 5 chns, by Messrs Crawter; hill-drawing, foot/b'way, waterbodies, woods, orchards, building names, sand or stone pits, old lime kiln, downs.

35/124 Hardham (parish) TQ 042175
Apt 21.08.1849; 949a (680); Map 1851, 4 chns; hill-drawing, foot/b'way, canal with tunnel and towpath, waterbodies, houses, woods, orchards, building names, drains.

35/125 Hartfield (parish) TQ 468345
Apt 26.08.1842; 10268a (10267); Map 1842, 3 chns, by Hy and J. Chilcott; construction lines, waterbodies, houses, farmyards, woods, plantations, parkland, hops, fences, field gates, building names, mill, chapel. Apt has in-bound and out-bound quantities.

35/126 Harting (parish) SU 785194 [East and South Harting]
Apt 26.05.1841; 7832a (7832); Map 1840, 6 chns, 'from shorto' by

D. Ayling, Liss, Petersfield; foot/b'way, waterbodies, houses, woods (named), plantations, parkland (in detail, named), building names, mills, garden (by annotation), down, heath.

35/127 Hasting, All Saints (parish) TQ 835104 [Not listed]
Apt 20.09.1838; 366a (461); Map 1839, 3 chns, 1st cl, by John Adams, Hawkhurst; waterbodies, houses, woods, plantations.

35/128 Hastings, St Clement (parish) TQ 828102 [Not listed]
Apt 04.10.1838; 100a (all); Map 1839, 3 chns, 1st cl, by John Adams, Hawkhurst; foot/b'way, waterbodies, houses, woods, plantations, ornamental ground, field gates; north pointer has coronet and Prince of Wales's feathers.

35/129 Heathfield (parish) TQ 604213
Apt 09.03.1842; 7970a (7970); Map 1843?, 3 chns, 1st cl, in 2 parts; waterbodies, houses, woods (named), plantations, parkland (named), building names, stone pits, gravel pits, mills, tower, green.

35/130 Heene (parish) TQ 134027 [Not listed]
Apt 16.05.1839; 417a (546); Map 1838, 3 chns, by Hide and Patching, Worthing; foot/b'way, waterbodies, houses, farmyards (col), arable (col), grassland (col), gardens (col), hedge ownership, fences, mill, ornamental ground; red lines may be walls.

35/131 South Heighton (parish) TQ 462038
Apt 09.03.1842; 923a (all); Map 1841, 3 chns, by W. Figg, Lewes; waterbodies, houses, woods, orchards, gardens, open fields, drains, boundary stones.

35/132 Hellingly (parish) TQ 586131
Apt 02.05.1840; 6015a (6015); Map 1842, 3 chns, 1st cl, ? by H.E. Drayson; construction lines, waterbodies, building names, drains, chapel.

35/133 Henfield (parish) TQ 209157
Apt 29.01.1844; 4492a (4491); Map 1845, 3 chns, by H. and F. Hitchins; hill-drawing, foot/b'way, waterbodies, houses, woods, plantations, parkland, open fields, quarries.

35/134 Herstmonceux (parish) TQ 635114
Apt 08.03.1839; 5039a (5039); Map not dated, 6 chns; waterbodies, woods, plantations, orchards, hops, building names, castle, drains, parsonage, churchyard.

35/135 Heyshott (parish) SU 898181
Apt 24.12.1839; 2171a (2171); Map 1840, 5 chns; hill-drawing, foot/b'way, waterbodies, houses, farmyards (col), woods (col), arable (col), grassland (col), orchards (col), gardens (col), heath/moor, hedge ownership, field gates.

35/136 West Hoathley (parish) TQ 359322 [West Hoathly]
Apt 26.05.1841; 4863a (4863); Map 1841, 3 chns, by Thos Hughes; foot/b'way, waterbodies, houses, woods, plantations, orchards, hops, hedges, building names, watermill (by symbol), mill, windmill, common.

35/137 Hollington (parish) TQ 785119
Apt 07.12.1842; 2479a (2470); Map 1844, 3 chns, by William Campbell, Hastings; construction lines, hill-drawing, waterbodies, houses, road embankments, drains. Apt has in-bound and out-bound quantities.

35/138 Hooe (parish) TQ 685094
Apt 31.10.1839; 2449a (2448); Map 1840?, 3 chns, 1st cl, by Norris and Dickinson, Wincanton; construction lines, foot/b'way, occupation roads, waterbodies, houses, building names, drains, kiln, windmill (by symbol), greens; map border and title have leafy decoration; there is an incomplete table summarising land use.

35/139 Horsham (parish) TQ 178311
Apt 01.02.1844; 10792a (10770); Map 1851?, 3 chns, 1st cl, in 6 parts, (includes 40-chn index); railway with station, waterbodies, houses, woods, plantations, parkland (named), heath/moor, fences, building names, road names, mill pond, mill, county gaol, kiln, green; bridges named. Apt omits some field names.

35/140 Horsted Keynes (parish) TQ 385283
Apt 05.03.1839; 4304a (4304); Map 1842, 3 chns, 1st cl, by John Payte; construction lines, waterbodies, houses, building names, mill.

35/141 Houghton (parish) TQ 003111
Apt 03.03.1848; 15a (1455); Map 1849, 3 chns, 'made for the commutation of tithes' by George Blunden, Arundel, (tithable parts only in detail); waterbodies, houses, woods (named), arable (col), hedge ownership, building names, field names, field acreages, landowners.

35/142 Hove (parish) TQ 291050
Apt 13.12.1841; 713a (872); Map 1839, 5 chns, 'copied' by Wm Leach, Brighton; hill-drawing, railways, foot/b'way, waterbodies, woods, arable (col), grassland (col), gardens, sand or stone pits; pictorial church; built-up parts generalised.

35/143 Hunston (parish) SU 863014
Apt 04.04.1848; 1004a (1003); Map 1847, 3 chns, by E. Fuller, Chichester; foot/b'way, canal with towpath, waterbodies, houses, woods, open fields (named), hedge ownership, fence ownership, field gates, common, boundary stone; bridges and road gates named. Apt has in-bound and out-bound quantities.

35/144 Hurstpierpoint (parish) TQ 282177
Apt 24.03.1842; 5047a (5046); Map 1841, 3 chns, 1st cl, in 2 parts, by Dixon and Maitland, Godalming, Surrey, (includes town sep-arately at 1 chn); construction lines, waterbodies, houses, woods, underwood (green band), building names, mills, watermills.

35/145 Icklesham (parish) TQ 899169
Apt 28.01.1845; 4760a (5700); Map 1845, 3 chns, 1st cl, by Jno. and C. Davie, Rye; foot/b'way, waterbodies, houses, woods (col), fences, drains, coastline, high water mark, sewers, castle, martello tower, Royal Military Canal. Apt has in-bound and out-bound quantities.

35/146 Iden (parish) TQ 920248
Apt 29.08.1843; 2947a (2947); Map 1842, 3 chns, 1st cl, by Thos Hughes; construction lines, canal, waterbodies, houses, drains. Apt has in-bound and out-bound quantities.

35/147 Ifield (parish) TQ 246374
Apt 17.04.1841; 4116a (4116); Map 1839, 3 chns, 1st cl, by H. Walter, Windsor; construction lines, foot/b'way, waterbodies, houses, woods (named), orchards, marsh/bog, hedge ownership, fences, field gates, building names, watermills (by symbol), Quakers' Meeting House, kilns (by symbol), windmill (by symbol), vicarage, mill, drains, moated house, mill ponds, heath, greens; there is a note that part of the parish boundary differs slightly from the map of Charlwood parish, an alteration to the boundary line having been agreed between the two parishes.

35/148 Iford (parish) TQ 398067
Apt 29.06.1842; 2173a (2173); Map 1840, 6 chns, by W. Figg, Lewes; hill-drawing, waterbodies, houses, woods, orchards, open fields, quarries, tumuli, drains.

35/149 Iping (parish) SU 851247
Apt 09.03.1842; 1925a (1925); Map 1840, 3 chns, 1st cl, by Fredk and Henry E. Drayson; construction lines, waterbodies, houses, common.

35/150 Isfield (parish) TQ 451185
Apt 25.08.1841; 1862a (1862); Map 1840, 6 chns, by William Figg, Lewes; waterbodies, houses, woods, parkland, gardens, heath/moor, fences, building names, parsonage; pictorial church.

35/151 West Itchenor (parish) SU 795008
Apt 04.06.1838; 547a (all); Map 1839, 3 chns, by J.Butler, Chichester; foot/b'way, waterbodies, houses, coastline, spit, inlets.

35/152 Itchingfield (parish) TQ 130282
Apt 14.12.1840; 2499a (2470); Map 1839, 3 chns, 1st cl, by H. Walter, Windsor; foot/b'way, waterbodies, houses, woods, hedge ownership, fence ownership, field boundary ownerships, field gates, building names, rectory, green; bridge named; scale is graduated in both chains and in an unspecified unit.

35/153 Jevington (parish) TQ 565020
Apt 08.05.1839; 2099a (2099); Map 1839, 8 chns, by W. Figg, Lewes; turnpike roads, waterbodies, houses, woods, orchards, gardens, open fields, building names, mill, turnpike gate.

35/154 Keymer (parish) TQ 315175
Apt 29.05.1845; 3538a (3538); Map 1845, 3 chns, 1st cl, by Edward Sheridan; railway, waterbodies, houses, windmill; map has note that this copy has been compared with the original and is correct. Apt omits some field names.

35/155 Kings Barns (tithing in parish of Beeding) TQ 189119 [Kings Barn Farm]
Apt 02.04.1840; 425a (all); Map 1839, 3 chns, by H. and F. Hitchins, Brighton; foot/b'way, drains.

35/156 Kingston (near Arundel) (parish) TQ 084020
Apt 26.05.1841; 435a (582); Map 1838, 3 chns, by J.F. Tidey, Littlehampton; construction lines, foot/b'way, waterbodies, farmyards (col), woods, plantations, parkland, gardens (col), field gates, sluice; field boundaries emphasised in colour; border has scallop corners.

35/157 Kingston (near Lewes) (parish) TQ 387080 [Kingston near Lewes]
Apt 03.03.1843; 1653a (1653); Map 1840, 6 chns, by Wm Figg, Lewes; foot/b'way, waterbodies, houses, woods, orchards, gardens, sand or stone pit, drains, mill.

35/158 Kingston by Sea (parish) TQ 226062
Apt 04.05.1847; 800a (all); Map 1845, 1st cl, [3 chns], by H. and F. Hitchins; construction lines, hill-drawing, railway, waterbodies, houses, woods, coastline, sand or stone pit, boundary stones or posts, occupation road.

35/159 Kirdford (parish) TQ 007283
Apt 10.05.1845; 12276a (12275); Map 1841, 4 chns; water-bodies, woods, plantations, parkland, marsh/bog, heath/moor, fences (pictorial), common.

35/160 Lancing (parish) TQ 194051
Apt 26.11.1838; 2402a (3262); Map 1838, 3 chns, 1st cl, 'The Enclosure Plan corrected and the residue of the parish surveyed in 1838', by Messrs Bassett and Co, Southampton Office, Fitzroy Square; hill-drawing, foot/b'way, waterbodies, woods, parkland, building names, landowners, churchyard, chalk pit, beach, coastline, embankment, milestone, drains, copyhold properties; bridge named; north pointer has Prince of Wales's feathers.

35/161 Laughton (parish) TQ 502130
Apt 04.09.1838; 5075a (5075); Map 1840, 4 chns, 1st cl, by W. Figg, Lewes; construction lines, waterbodies, houses, woods, plantations, parkland, heath/moor, field gates, drains; red lines may be walls.

35/162 Leominster or Lyminster (parish) TQ 025048
Apt 26.11.1838; 2668a (2667); Map 1837, 3 chns, by Henry Salter, Arundel; foot/b'way, waterbodies, houses, woods, plantations, heath/moor, hedge ownership, fence ownership, drains; map has note of adoption, with landowners' signatures.

35/163 Lewes, St John the Baptist, Southover (parish) TQ 417092 [Not listed]
Apt 20.10.1843; 26a (?); Map 1844, 1 chns, by Richard Lower, Chiddingly, Sussex, (tithable parts only in detail); houses, woods (col), plantations (col), arable (col), grassland (col), orchards (col), gardens (col), fences, field gates, building names, road names, brewery, pound, crescent, glebe, priory land, ownerships (col); map title has scroll decoration.

35/164 Lewes, St John under the Castle of Lewes (parish) TQ 408107 [Not listed]
Apt 17.01.1844; 1366a (?); Map 1841, 3 chns, by W. Figg; hill-drawing, foot/b'way, waterbodies, houses, woods (named), orchards, gardens, heath/moor, green, rock outcrops, building names, road names, quarries, gaol, paper mill, drains; hill named; built-up parts generalised.

35/165 Lewes, St Peter and St Mary Westout, otherwise St Ann (parish) TQ 390097 [Not listed]
Apt 22.07.1842; 1826a (?); Map 1844?, 3 chns; hill-drawing, waterbodies, houses, woods, plantations, gardens, building names, racecourse, tumulus, mills, ornamental gardens.

35/166 Linch (parish) SU 862276 [Not listed]
Apt 04.07.1848; 428a (1220); Map 1848, 6 chns; woods, plantations.

35/167 Linchmere (parish) SU 878303
Apt 05.06.1846; 2101a (2101); Map 1846, 3 chns, by Alfred Mellersh, Godalming; waterbodies, houses, woods, common.

35/168 Lindfield (parish) TQ 362251
Apt 30.09.1848; 5785a (5776); Map 1845, 3 chns, by H. Drayson; construction lines, railway, canal, waterbodies, houses, building names, mills, site of priory, brickyard, isolated trees, disputed boundary; mapmaker notes that the site of the priory 'was quite unknown prior to this survey'.

35/169 Littlehampton (parish) TQ 035022
Apt 21.05.1841; 1103a (1224); Map 1842?, 3 chns, in 2 parts, 'copy' by J.F. Tidey, Littlehampton; waterbodies, fences, building names, road names, drains, ferry, fort, manor farm lands (col, named); a blank rectangle may have been intended to frame a legend.

35/170 Little Horsted (parish) TQ 473178
Apt 23.02.1839; 2377a (2240); Map 1844?, 3 chns, 1st cl; hill-drawing, foot/b'way, waterbodies, houses, woods, plantations.

35/171 Litlington (parish) TQ 536009
Apt 21.06.1844; 893a (all); Map 1845, 3 chns, by William Figg, Lewes; waterbodies, houses, building names, drains.

35/172 Lodsworth (parish) SU 928244
Apt 10.09.1841; 1806a (1805); Map 1839, 3 chns, 1st cl, by Thomas Baker, 25 Vauxhall Street, London; construction lines, hill-drawing, foot/b'way, canal with towpath, waterbodies, houses (by shading), woods, plantations, parkland, hedge ownership, fence ownership, building names, road names, mills, old saw pit, boundary markers, heathland, commons, greens; hills and bridges named.

35/173 Lullington (parish) TQ 537022 [Not listed]
Apt 29.08.1845; 1162a (all); Map 1843, 7 chns, by Wm Figg, Lewes; waterbodies, houses, building names, drains.

35/174 Lurgashall (parish) SU 932285
Apt 15.07.1841; 4850a (4850); Map 1840, 5 chns; waterbodies, houses, farmyards (col), woods (col), plantations (col), parkland (col), arable (col), grassland (col), orchards (col), gardens (col), heath/moor (col), hedge ownership, fence ownership, greens, commons.

35/175 Madehurst (parish) SU 982101
Apt 31.12.1840; 1871a (1908); Map 1841, 3 chns, 1st cl, by Davis and Hughes, 12, Haymarket; construction lines, turnpike roads and gate, waterbodies, houses, woods (col, named), plantations (col, named), parkland (in detail, named), gardens, fence ownership, field gates, building names, stables, school, lodges, lawns and gardens (by annotation), downs; hills named. Apt gives land use by occupiers rather than by fields.

35/176 South Malling (parish) TQ 431105
Apt 23.10.1844; 189a (2680); Map 1849?, 6 chns, by William Figg, Lewes, (tithable parts only); hill-drawing, foot/b'way, turnpike roads and gate, woods, building names, landowners, paper mill, quarry, drains, sewer, windmill (pictorial), boundary cross, boundary posts, downs, farm names; bridge named.

35/177 East Marden (parish) SU 814145
Apt 08.04.1842; 969a (all); Map 1842, 4 chns, in 2 parts, 'partly surveyed but principally compiled from approved maps' by Edward Fuller, Chichester; foot/b'way, waterbodies, houses, woods, plantations, gardens, field gates, well.

35/178 North Marden (parish) SU 806162
Apt 22.01.1841; 682a (all); Map 1841, 6 chns, by Jas W. Blackman, Fareham; houses, woods, down.

35/179 Maresfield (parish) TQ 456278
Apt 16.10.1840; 5320a (7750); Map 1840, 3 chns, 1st cl, by Fredk and Henry E. Drayson; construction lines, waterbodies, houses, plantations, watermill (by symbol), common, waste.

35/180 Mayfield (parish) TQ 579264
Apt 28.10.1843; 13599a (13604); Map 1844, 4 chns, 1st cl, by Hughes

and Payte; foot/b'way, turnpike roads, waterbodies, houses, building names, mills, turnpike gate, vicarage, windmills, forge.

35/181 Merston (parish) SU 897023
Apt 14.07.1841; 711a (710); Map 1840, 3 chns, by E. Fuller, Chichester; foot/b'way, canal, waterbodies, houses, woods, plantations, gardens, heath/moor, hedge ownership, fence ownership, field gates, building names, road names, canal with towpath, boundary stone; map is signed by landowners, certifying their approval.

35/182 Middleton (parish) SU 982001 [Middleton-on-Sea]
Apt 17.03.1848; 646a (all); Map 1838, 3 chns, 1st cl, by Edwd Fuller, Chichester; construction lines, foot/b'way, waterbodies, houses, woods, ornamental ground, marsh/bog, heath/moor, rock outcrops, hedge ownership, fence ownership, field boundary ownerships, field gates, sluice, flag pole, groynes, low water mark, coastline, shingle beach, foreshore (col). Apt has in-bound and out-bound quantities.

35/183 Midhurst (parish) SU 882218
Apt 15.12.1846; 671a (671); Map 1841, 3 chns, 1st cl, by Henry E. Drayson; construction lines, hill-drawing, waterbodies, houses, woods, hedges, building names, boundary stones, chapels, town hall.

35/184 Midlavant (parish) SU 856085 [Mid Lavant]
Apt 17.03.1849; 1174a (350); Map 1840, 3 chns, 1st cl, by John Elliott, Chichester; foot/b'way, houses, hedge ownership, field boundary ownerships, field gates.

35/185 Mountfield (parish) TQ 734205
Apt 31.10.1839; 3841a (3841); Map 1839, 4 chns, by W. Rider, C.E.; waterbodies, woods (named), plantations (named), parkland (in detail, named), building names, walls (in red).

35/186 North Mundham (parish) SU 873009
Apt 05.08.1848; 1882a (1882); Map 1847, 3 chns, by Joseph Butler; foot/b'way, canal with towpath, waterbodies, houses, fences, building names, wall, windmill. Apt has in-bound and out-bound quantities.

35/187 New Fishborne (parish) SU 842049 [Not listed]
Apt 27.05.1840; 619a (all); Map 1839, 3 chns, by C. Lewis, Havant; foot/b'way, turnpike roads, waterbodies, houses, farmyards, woods, parkland, arable (col), grassland (col), orchards, gardens, marsh/bog, heath/moor, building names, road names, brick yard, mills, mill ponds, coal yards, toll bar, coastline, mud flats, spring, chapel, boundary stones, green lanes (col), mudflats (by symbol), sedges (by annotation), nursery (by annotation), common.

35/188 Newhaven or Meeching (parish) TQ 443011
Apt 09.09.1841; 1000a (1217); Map 1841, 3 chns, surveyed by Norris and Dickinson in 1838 and copied by Willm Figg; hill-drawing, waterbodies, woods, building names, drains, workhouse.

35/189 Newick (parish) TQ 421208
Apt 31.01.1839; 1966a (1866); Map 1839?, 3 chns, 1st cl, by Fredk and Henry E. Drayson; construction lines, foot/b'way, waterbodies, houses, building names, chapel, ox-bow, common.

35/190 Newtimber (parish) TQ 273122 [Not listed]
Apt 09.01.1840; 1693a (1693); Map 1840, 5 chns; hill-drawing, foot/b'way, turnpike roads, waterbodies, houses, farmyards (col), woods (col), plantations (col), parkland (col), arable (col), grassland (col), gardens (col), rock outcrops, hedge ownership, fence ownership, chalk pit, limekiln, toll bars, milestone.

35/191 Ninfield (parish) TQ 704119
Apt 30.06.1841; 2555a (2554); Map 1842?, 6 chns; foot/b'way, waterbodies, woods, orchards, fences, field gates, drains.

35/192 Northchapel (parish) SU 955293
Apt 04.10.1837; 3855a (3854); Map 1839, 5 chns; waterbodies, houses, farmyards (col), woods (col), arable (col), grassland (col), orchards (col), gardens (col), heath/moor (col), hedge ownership, fences, limekiln, green.

35/193 Northiam (parish) TQ 828244
Apt 18.08.1840; 3487a (3486); Map 1842?, 6 chns; waterbodies, woods, drains. Apt omits land use.

35/194 Nuthurst (parish) TQ 188263
Apt 24.06.1845; 3260a (3260); Map 1847?, 3 chns, 1st cl; hill-drawing, foot/b'way, waterbodies, houses, forest land (named), woods (named), plantations, parkland (named), marsh/bog, heath/moor, common, building names, mills, mill ponds, fish ponds, smithy, post office, Wesleyan Chapel, private roads, green lanes; bridges named.

35/195 Nytimber (district in parish of West Chiltington) TQ 086192 [Not listed]
Apt 16.03.1837; 46a (?); Map 1808, 4 chns, (tithable parts tinted); foot/b'way, waterbodies, houses, woods, parkland, gardens, hedge ownership, fence ownership, field gates, building names, landowners, limekilns, windmill (pictorial), private road, common; map is subtitled 'The property of Chas F. Goring Esqr'; parts of adjacent districts are also mapped.

35/196 Ore (parish) TQ 822125
Apt 30.11.1840; 2149a (2149); Map 1842, 3 chns, 1st cl, in 2 parts, by William Figg, Lewes, Sussex, (includes 1.5-chn enlargement of detail); construction lines, hill-drawing, waterbodies, houses, road embankments, mill. Apt omits some field names.

35/197 Oving (parish) SU 904042
Apt 25.03.1840; 2946a (2946); Map 1838, 3 chns, by E. Fuller, Chichester; construction lines, foot/b'way, turnpike roads, toll bar, canal with towpath, waterbodies, houses, woods, plantations, parkland, gardens, open fields and furlongs (named), hedge ownership, fence ownership, field gates, road names, 'St Jame's Post', city liberty boundary, drains, pound; map has landowners' signatures of approval.

35/198 Ovingdean (parish) TQ 356040
Apt 07.11.1839; 1619a (all); Map 1839, 4.5 chns, by Wm Leach, Brighton; hill-drawing, foot/b'way, waterbodies, houses, farmyards (col), woods (col), arable (col), grassland (col), gardens (col), hedges, fences, sand or stone pit, racecourse; pictorial church.

35/199 Pagham (parish) SZ 895993
Apt 13.02.1849; 4096a (?); Map 1847, 6 chns, by E. Fuller, Chichester; foot/b'way, waterbodies, houses, woods, ornamental ground, marsh/bog, heath/moor, allotments, rock outcrops (named), field gates, building names, road names, preventive stations, quay, sluice, walls, high water mark, coastline, groynes (pictorial), sand and mud flats, shingle, signal posts (pictorial), foreshore (col); bridge named. Apt has in-bound and out-bound quantities.

35/200 Parham (parish) TQ 060139 [Not listed]
Apt 14.02.1839; 1264a (1264); Map 1840, 3 chns, 'compiled' by Henry Salter, Arundel; waterbodies, houses, woods, parkland, hedge ownership, downs.

35/201 Patcham (parish) TQ 304090
Apt 16.03.1842; 4398a (4398); Map 1842, 4 chns, by Wm Leach, Brighton; hill-drawing, railway, foot/b'way, waterbodies, houses, woods (col), plantations (col), arable (col), grassland (col), gardens (col), ornamental ground, hedge ownership, fence ownership, tumulus, sand or stone pits or quarries; map is described as a map of the estates of Mrs Elizabeth Rowe and John Paine Esqr, surveyed by Wm Figg in 1811, the remainder surveyed and the whole copied by Wm Leach in 1842.

35/202 Patching (parish) TQ 087082
Apt 17.12.1847; 1748a (1748); Map surveyed in 1838 and commuted in 1847, 6 chns, by Henry Salter, Arundel; hill-drawing, foot/b'way, waterbodies, houses, woods, parkland, hedge ownership, field gates, building names, sand or stone pits; hill named.

35/203 Peasmarsh (parish) TQ 882228
Apt 16.01.1840; 3719a (3718); Map 1840, 3 chns, by Js Parsons, Beckley; turnpike roads, waterbodies, houses, farmyards (col), woods (col), plantations (col), parkland (col), arable (col), grassland (col), orchards (col), hops, gardens (col), building names, drains, ferry, windmill (pictorial), boundary posts, kiln, vicarage land; Dawson's land use symbols are used.

35/204 Penhurst (parish) TQ 698169
Apt 30.06.1840; 1462a (1462); Map 1839, 5 chns, by W. Rider, C.E.; waterbodies, woods, plantations, parkland (named), building names.

35/205 Pett (parish) TQ 895147
Apt 09.07.1844; 1941a (2350); Map 1839, 3 chns, 1st cl, by John Adams, Hawkhurst; construction lines, Royal Military Canal with towpath, waterbodies, houses, woods, building names, martello towers, drains, ordinary high water mark. Apt has in-bound and out-bound quantities.

35/206 Petworth (parish) SU 986224
Apt 13.07.1837; 5983a (5982); Map 1838, 5 chns; hill-drawing, foot/b'way, turnpike roads, toll bar, waterbodies, houses, farmyards (col), woods (col), plantations (col), parkland (col, in detail), arable (col), grassland (col), orchards (col), gardens (col), heath/moor (col), rock outcrops, open fields, hedge ownership, fence ownership, farm names, road names, river towpath, stone pits or quarries, limekilns, common.

35/207 Pevensey (parish) TQ 650067
Apt 07.05.1839; 4352a (4586); Map 1842?, 6 chns, (tinted); foot/b'way, waterbodies, gardens (col), heath/moor, hedges, fences, field gates, building names, castle, martello towers, shingle beach, coastline, drains, sewers, green, 'Old Droveways', glebe (red band); bridge named.

35/208 Piddinghoe (parish) TQ 422021
Apt 18.10.1843; 2377a (all); Map 1840, 7 chns, by William Figg, Lewes; hill-drawing, waterbodies, houses, woods, gardens, rock outcrops, open fields, building names, cliffs, coastline, quarries, drains, ox-bow lakes.

35/209 Playden (parish) TQ 931227
Apt 28.08.1843; 1308a (1308); Map 1842, 3 chns, 1st cl, by Thos Hughes; construction lines, waterbodies, houses, field gates, river locks, drains, mill. Apt has in-bound and out-bound quantities.

35/210 Plompton (parish) TQ 362155 [Plumpton]
Apt 31.05.1839; 2424a (2423); Map 1840, 3 chns, 1st cl, by William Figg, Lewes; construction lines, hill-drawing, foot/b'way, waterbodies, houses, woods, plantations, orchards, marsh/bog, quarry, sand or stone pits, ornamental ground indicated.

35/211 Poling (parish) TQ 045051
Apt 16.06.1838; 911a (923); Map 1837, 3 chns, by Henry Salter, Arundel; construction lines, foot/b'way, waterbodies, houses, woods (named), arable (by annotation), grassland (by annotation), hedge ownership, fence ownership, field gates, building names, field names, landowners, occupiers, brick yard, hundred pound, parsonage, tithe-free land; double lines may be drains; map is signed by landowners, certifying its adoption.

35/212 Portslade (parish) TQ 252078 [Portslade-by-Sea]
Apt 19.06.1841; 1967a (all); Map 1840, 3 chns, 1st cl, in 2 parts, by H.S. Tiffen, Hythe, Kent, (including construction line diagram); construction lines, hill-drawing, railway, foot/b'way, rights of way, waterbodies, houses, woods, parkland, fences, field boundary ownerships, building names, mill, coastline, shingle, low and high water marks, cliffs, quarries; physical features named. Apt has in-bound and out-bound quantities.

35/213 Poynings (parish) TQ 260121
Apt 04.02.1843; 1643a (1643); Map 1840, 6 chns, by E. and G.N. Driver; hill-drawing, foot/b'way, waterbodies, houses, woods (col), arable (col), grassland (col), orchards, hedge ownership, building names, road names, field names, field acreages, milestone, lodge, manor house, mill, spring, Devil's Dyke, 'Poynings butter track', common; physical features named; some fields have cultivation annotations.

35/214 Preston (near Brighton) (parish) TQ 306062
Apt 13.12.1841; 1287a (1286); Map 1839, 3 chns, 'surveyed by H. and F. Hitchins 1838 and copied by Wm Leach, Brighton'; railway, foot/b'way, waterbodies, houses, farmyards (col), woods (col), arable (col), grassland (col), gardens (col), rock outcrops, fences, field gates, chalk pits, windmills (pictorial).

35/215 East Preston (parish) TQ 071021
Apt 26.05.1841; 490a (all); Map 1838, 3 chns, in 2 parts, by J.F. Tidey, Littlehampton; waterbodies, houses, arable (col), grassland (col), field name, brickyard, coastline.

35/216 Pulborough (parish) TQ 059206
Apt 28.02.1839; 6398a (6398); Map 1841, 3 chns, 1st cl, in 2 parts, by Thomas Thurston, Ashford, (including 30-chn construction line diagram); construction lines, hill-drawing, foot/b'way, canal with locks and tow path, waterbodies, houses, woods (col, named), open fields, field boundary ownerships, field gates, building names, road names, field names, boundary markers, moats, rectory, sand or stone pit, lime kilns, brick kilns, wharf, watermill (by symbol), windmill (by symbol), mills, drains, quarries, commons; bridges and hill named; mapmaker notes that the divisions between some of the 'cants' not surviving on the ground, have been copied from an ancient map; red lines may be walls. Apt has in-bound and out-bound quantities.

35/217 Pycombe (parish) TQ 296125 [Pyecombe]
Apt 07.08.1839; 2249a (2249); Map 1838, 4 chns, by E. and G.N Driver; hill-drawing, foot/b'way, waterbodies, houses, farmyards, woods (col), arable (col), grassland (col), gardens (col), heath/moor (col), hedge ownership, fence ownership, field gates, building names, field names, field acreages, landowners, milestone, road cutting, old chalk pits, chalk pits, remains of Roman camp, vicarage, stocks, 'road used on suffrance', ornamental ground; physical features named; where fields do not agree wholly with the colours the mapmaker has tabulated the various land uses, e.g. 39.5 acres pasture, 0.75 acres coppice and 0.75 acres waste.

35/218 Racton (parish) SU 782096 [Not listed]
Apt 03.09.1840; 1180a (1180); Map 1839, 3 chns, by E. Fuller, Chichester; construction lines, hill-drawing, foot/b'way, waterbodies, houses, farmyards, woods, plantations, parkland, hedge ownership, fence ownership, field boundary ownerships, field gates, building names, boundary trees, chalk pit, brick kilns, sand or stone pits, timber yard; farmyards, rickyards, orchards, gardens, copse and plantation are indicated by annotation.

35/219 Ringmer (parish) TQ 456134
Apt 31.08.1843; 5626a (5626); Map 1840, 6 chns, in 2 parts, by Richard Lower, Chiddingly, Sussex, (includes 2-chn enlargement of detail); foot/b'way, turnpike roads, waterbodies, houses, woods, plantations, field gates, building names, road names, lunatic asylum, marl pit, mill, toll gate, windmill, boundary stones, boundary cross, greens.

35/220 Rodmell (parish) TQ 413056
Apt 05.02.1839; 1925a (all); Map 1839, 4 chns: Shine Brooks surveyed by G. Picknall in 1759, Rodmell by W. Figg in 1829 and Northease by W. Figg in 1837, all 'reduced to one scale and copied' by Wm Leach, Brighton; hill-drawing, waterbodies, farmyards, woods, arable (col), grassland (col), water meadow (stippled green), sheep pasture (dark green), orchards, gardens (col), open fields, hedge ownership, fence ownership, field boundary ownerships, drains, stone pits or quarries, windmill (pictorial); pictorial church.

35/221 Rogate (parish) SU 805251
Apt 17.06.1844; 4874a (4873); Map 1843, 6 chns, by Henry E. Drayson, Midhurst, Sussex; waterbodies, building names, common.

35/222 Rotherfield (parish) TQ 546311
Apt 26.02.1839; 14733a (14733); Map 1841, 3 chns, 1st cl, by E. Sheridan; construction lines, waterbodies, houses, building names, windmill (pictorial, named), boundary features, possible modus land boundary.

35/223 Rottingdean (parish) TQ 377029
Apt 16.04.1838; 3147a (all); Map 1839, 3 chns, by Wm Leach, Brighton; hill-drawing, foot/b'way, waterbodies, houses, woods, plantations, gardens, heath/moor, rock outcrops, open fields, hedge ownership, fences, cliffs, coastline, sand or stone pits, windmill (pictorial); meaning of colours is uncertain.

35/224 Rudgwick (parish) TQ 084320
Apt 15.12.1840; 5831a (5830); Map 1841, 3 chns, 1st cl, by Fredk and Henry E. Drayson; canal, waterbodies, building names, mill, windmill (by symbol).

35/225 Rumboldswyke (parish) SU 872037 [Not listed]
Apt 17.03.1848; 646a (645); Map 1844, 3 chns, by J. Butler, Chichester; railway, foot/b'way, canal with towpath, waterbodies, houses, open fields.

35/226 Rusper (parish) TQ 208365
Apt 20.12.1842; 3126a (3126); Map 1839, 3 chns, 1st cl, by H. Walter,

Windsor; foot/b'way, waterbodies, houses, woods, parkland, orchards, heath/moor, hedge ownership, fence ownership, building names, road names, rectory.

35/227 Rustington (parish) TQ 055021
Apt 18.03.1839; 1067a (all); Map 1840?, 3 chns, in 3 parts, by J.F. Tidey, Littlehampton; waterbodies, houses, woods (col), parkland, arable (col), grassland (col), orchards, gardens (col), fences, field gates, road names, field name, windmill (pictorial), coastline; bands emphasise field boundaries.

35/228 Rye (parish) TQ 915212
Apt 30.06.1841; 2314a (2313); Map 1841?, 3 chns; hill-drawing, waterbodies, houses, woods, arable (col), grassland (col), orchards, gardens, heath/moor, building names, ferry, drains, boundary stones, beaches, wharf, martello tower, harbour, cliffs, windmills (pictorial), corporation boundary, road destinations, ornamental ground, military road; built-up parts generalised and tinted.

35/229 Salehurst (parish) TQ 742251
Apt 30.01.1841; 6482a (6481); Map 1840?, 3 chns, 1st cl, by John Adams, Hawkhurst; hill-drawing, foot/b'way, waterbodies, houses, woods (named), plantations, parkland, building names, mill, quarry, drains, nursery ground. Apt has in-bound and out-bound quantities.

35/230 Sedlescomb (parish) TQ 785193 [Sedlescombe]
Apt 06.02.1843; 2049a (2049); Map 1841, 3 chns, 1st cl, by John Adams, Hawkhurst; construction lines, foot/b'way, waterbodies, houses, woods (by name), field gates, building names, brick kiln, churchyard. Apt has in-bound and out-bound quantities.

35/231 Selham (parish) SU 929203
Apt 02.07.1847; 1042a (1042); Map 1840, 3 chns, 1st cl, by Fredk and Henry E. Drayson; construction lines, trig points, waterbodies, houses, boundary stones, waste.

35/232 Selmeston otherwise Simpston (parish) TQ 513076
Apt 15.06.1840; 1591a (1590); Map 1840, 6 chns, in 2 parts, by W. Figg, Lewes; hill-drawing, waterbodies, houses, woods, orchards, gardens, marsh/bog, building names, sand or stone pit.

35/233 Selsey (parish) SZ 860944
Apt 21.05.1841; 3495a (4314); Map 1839, 3 chns, by I.T. Lewis, Fareham; construction lines, foot/b'way, waterbodies, houses, woods, osiers, marsh/bog, hedge ownership, coastline, Selsey Bill, harbour creeks and islands; map is signed by landowners, certifying their approval.

35/234 Shermanbury (parish) TQ 221194 [Not listed]
Apt 31.10.1837; 1911a (1911); Map 1839, 3 chns, 1st cl, by H. and F. Hitchins, Brighton; construction lines, foot/b'way, waterbodies, fences.

35/235 Shipley (parish) TQ 141227
Apt 17.12.1847; 7698a (7698); Map 1849, 3 chns, 1st cl, by I.F. Tidey, Littlehampton; foot/b'way, waterbodies, houses, marsh/bog, building names, boat house, castle, windmill, green.

35/236 New Shoreham (parish) TQ 215052 [Shoreham-by-Sea]
Apt 17.03.1849; 66a (170); Map 1850, 2 chns; railway, houses, road names, mill, drains; built-up parts mostly generalised.

35/237 Old Shoreham (parish) TQ 216073
Apt 22.06.1844; 1867a (all); Map 1850, 4 chns; hill-drawing, railway, waterbodies, houses, woods, building names, river embankments, farm and property boundaries (col), farm names. District is apportioned by holding.

35/238 Sidlesham (parish) SZ 848975
Apt 03.03.1848; 4109a (4109); Map 1846, 6 chns, by E. Fuller, Chichester; foot/b'way, waterbodies, houses, woods, plantations, field gates, road names, drains, ferry, sluice, mill pond, coastline, mud flats, channels, lands liable to tidal inundation; bridge named. Apt has in-bound and out-bound quantities, and summary of land use for holdings and tithe-owners.

35/239 Singleton (parish) SU 886134
Apt 12.05.1848; 4051a (5010); Map 1847, 6 chns, by John Elliott; hill-drawing, foot/b'way, waterbodies, houses, woods, plantations, hedge ownership, fence ownership, field gates, tumulus, sand or stone pits, road embankments, boundary posts, racecourse, forest land. Apt has in-bound and out-bound quantities.

35/240 Slaugham (parish) TQ 256286
Apt 21.04.1842; 5364a (5363); Map 1843?, 3 chns, 1st cl; foot/b'way, waterbodies.

35/241 Slindon (parish) SU 961100
Apt 16.11.1839; 2504a (2504); Map 1840, 4 chns, 'copied' by H. Salter, Arundel; hill-drawing, foot/b'way, waterbodies, houses, woods, plantations, hedge ownership, sand or stone pit.

35/242 Slinfold (parish) TQ 120315
Apt 15.02.1843; 4308a (4330); Map 1845?, 3 chns, 1st cl; construction lines, foot/b'way, waterbodies, woods, parkland, field gates, building names; bridge named.

35/243 Sompting (parish) TQ 163065
Apt 31.10.1840; 2930a (2930); Map 1834, 6 chns, by John Adams junr, Hawkhurst, Kent; foot/b'way, waterbodies, houses, woods (named), parkland, field gates, building names, vicarage, drains, chalk pit and kiln, downs.

35/244 South Bersted (parish) SU 931010
Apt 12.05.1842; 2857a (3008); Map 1842, 3 chns, by Messrs Hitchins and J. Wisdom; foot/b'way, waterbodies, drains.

35/245 Southease (parish) TQ 423048
Apt 12.10.1841; 853a (all); Map 1845, 3 chns, by William Figg, Lewes; waterbodies, houses, woods, drains, green.

35/246 Stanmer (parish) TQ 338101
Apt 15.02.1839; 1347a (?); Map 1840, 4 chns, by William Figg, Lewes; foot/b'way, waterbodies, houses, woods, plantations, parkland, orchards, gardens.

35/247 Stedham (parish) SU 859246
Apt 23.09.1845; 1452a (2249); Map 1846?, 6 chns; waterbodies, marsh, glebe.

35/248 Steyning (parish) TQ 175125
Apt 26.09.1840; 3383a (3383); Map 1841?, 6 chns; waterbodies, building names, landowners, vicarage, drains, common, downs; bridge named.

35/249 South Stoke (parish) TQ 022090
Apt 20.11.1843; 1294a (all); Map 1834, 6 chns, by Henry Salter, Arundel; waterbodies, houses, woods, plantations, parkland (named), hedge ownership, drains, sand or stone pit.

35/250 West Stoke (parish) SU 828087
Apt 06.08.1846; 870a (all); Map 1839, 3 chns, by John Elliott, Chichester; hedge ownership, fence ownership, field gates.

35/251 Stopham (parish) TQ 028194
Apt 16.02.1838; 877a (876); Map 1839, 5 chns; hill-drawing, foot/b'way, waterbodies, houses, farmyards, woods (col), plantations (col), arable (col), grassland (col), orchards (col), gardens (col), heath/moor (col), hedge ownership, fence ownership, parish stone pit, drains, stone pit, common; it is unclear why some woodland is uncoloured.

35/252 Storrington (parish) TQ 080141
Apt 19.06.1840; 3264a (3264); Map 1841, 3 chns, 1st cl, by Messrs H. and F. Hitchins, Brighton; construction lines, waterbodies.

35/253 Stoughton (parish) SU 786107
Apt 12.11.1840; 5423a (all); Map 1840, 6 chns, in 3 parts, by J. Butler, Chichester, (includes 1-chn enlargement of detail); foot/b'way, waterbodies, houses, forest, woods (named), plantations, parkland, building names.

35/254 Street (parish) TQ 351152 [Streat]
Apt 12.02.1838; 1270a (1270); Map 1839, 3 chns, by W. Figg, Lewes; waterbodies, houses, woods, heath/moor, rock outcrops, fences, field gates, building names, quarry, parsonage, common, downs.

35/255 Sullington (parish) TQ 101130
Apt 08.09.1840; 2340a (2340); Map 1840, 3 chns, 1st cl, by H. and F. Hitchins, Brighton; construction lines, foot/b'way, waterbodies.

35/256 Sutton (parish) SU 974151
Apt 03.06.1837; 2062a (2061); Map 1840, 5 chns; foot/b'way, waterbodies, houses, farmyards (col), woods (col), plantations (col), arable (col), grassland (col), orchards (col), gardens (col), open fields, hedge ownership, ornamental gardens.

35/257 Sutton cum Seaford (parish) TV 502990
Apt 23.02.1839; 2351a (?); Map 1839, 3 chns, by Wm Leach, Brighton; foot/b'way, waterbodies, houses, woods (col), plantations (col), arable (col), grassland (col), gardens (col), rock outcrops, hedge ownership, fence ownership, battery, tower, boundary posts, coastline, cliffs, shingle beach, stone pits or quarries, drains; red lines may be walls; bridge and bays named.

35/258 Tangmere (parish) SU 903062
Apt 31.01.1839; 774a (all); Map 1839, 3 chns, 1st cl, by John Elliott, Chichester; construction lines, foot/b'way, waterbodies, houses, hedge ownership, fence ownership, field boundary ownerships, field gates.

35/259 Tarring Neville (parish) TQ 445040
Apt 09.03.1842; 939a (all); Map 1843, 3 chns, 1st cl, by William Figg, Lewes; construction lines, trig points, waterbodies, houses, drains.

35/260 West Tarring (parish) TQ 130043
Apt 10.09.1839; 1194a (1226); Map 1838, 3 chns, by Messrs Hide and Patching, Worthing; hill-drawing, foot/b'way, waterbodies, houses, woods (col), arable (col), grassland (col), hedge ownership, building names, beach, sand or stone pits, parsonage, chalk pit; red lines may be walls; one area is 'No-man's land'.

35/261 Telscombe (parish) TQ 399024
Apt 26.09.1842; 1179a (all); Map 4.5 chns, 'common fields and sheep pasture surveyed by Wm Figg 1811, the remainder surveyed and the whole mapped' in 1842 by Wm Leach; hill-drawing, waterbodies, houses, arable (col), grassland (col), gardens, rock outcrops, open fields, coastline, cliffs, stone pits or quarries; pictorial church; arable is both yellow and pinkish-brown.

35/262 Terwick (parish) SU 823235 [Not listed]
Apt 29.05.1839; 718a (718); Map 1837?, 3 chns, in 2 parts, one part surveyed in 1837 by W.H.H. Shorts, Midhurst; foot/b'way, waterbodies, woods, orchards, gardens, heath/moor, hedge ownership, field gates, boundary stones, common.

35/263 Thakeham (parish) TQ 109180
Apt 12.11.1840; 2980a (2980); Map 1841, 3 chns, 1st cl, by H. and F. Hitchins, Brighton; construction lines, foot/b'way, waterbodies.

35/264 Ticehurst (parish) TQ 679302
Apt 28.07.1840; 8203a (8202); Map 1839, 3 chns, 1st cl, in 2 parts, by John Adams, Hawkhurst, Kent; construction lines, foot/b'way, turnpike roads and gate, waterbodies, houses, woods (named), plantations, parkland (named), orchards, rock outcrops, building names, road names, quarries, boundary posts, old gravel pit, workhouse, gravel pits, mills. Apt has in-bound and out-bound quantities.

35/265 Tillington (parish) SU 951227
Apt 04.10.1837; 3766a (3766); Map prepared 'under the directions of the Tithe Commissioners', 1839, 3 chns, 1st cl, by Thomas Baker, 25, Vauxhall Street, London; construction lines, foot/b'way, waterbodies, houses, open fields, hedge ownership, fence ownership, building names, limekiln, ox-bow lakes, river locks, common.

35/266 Tortington (parish) TQ 005057
Apt 14.04.1841; 1132a (1131); Map 1840, 3 chns, by E. Fuller, Chichester; construction lines, hill-drawing, foot/b'way, waterbodies, houses, woods, plantations, parkland, arable (by annotation), grassland (by annotation), hedge ownership, fence ownership, field boundary ownerships, field gates, building names, old chalk pits, drains, quay, brick yard; some fields are annotated with land use; map has land agent's signature of approval.

35/267 Treyford (parish) SU 824182
Apt 15.02.1843; 1261a (all); Map 1840, 6 chns, by Henry Hull, Bramley, Surrey; foot/b'way, waterbodies, houses, gardens, barrows, wood (by annotation).

35/268 Trotton cum Tuxlith (parish) SU 825254
Apt 10.01.1840; 3877a (3877); Map 1840, 3 chns, 1st cl, by Fredk and Henry E. Drayson; construction lines, waterbodies, houses, building names, common, tithe-free land (red).

35/269 Twineham (parish) TQ 252199
Apt 16.03.1837; 1909a (1908); Map 1839?, 3 chns, 1st cl; construction lines, waterbodies, houses, woods; along district boundary are notes on ownership of grass and 'after grass'. (The map in PRO IR 30 is a copy; original is in PRO IR 77/87.)

35/270 Uckfield (parish) TQ 470211
Apt 10.08.1841; 1717a (1717); Map 1843?, 3 chns; foot/b'way, turnpike roads and gate, waterbodies, houses, woods (col), parkland, building names, workhouse, lodges, kitchen garden, watermill (by symbol), common.

35/271 Udimore (parish) TQ 883190
Apt 20.03.1838; 2221a (2221); Map 1839?, 4 chns; waterbodies, woods, field gates, building names, drains, boundary posts, glebe, poor house; map is subtitled 'The property of Lord George Cavendish now the Earl of Burlington', and appears to have been extensively altered by scraping. Apt omits land use.

35/272 Upmarden (parish) SU 786135 [Up Marden]
Apt 08.03.1843; 2928a (all); Map 1841, 6 chns, 'partly surveyed and partly compiled from approved maps', by Edward Fuller, Chichester; hill-drawing, foot/b'way, waterbodies, houses, woods, parkland, gardens, field gates, building names, semaphore, windmill, quarry, limekiln, downs, windmill (pictorial).

35/273 Upwaltham (parish) SU 941135
Apt 16.11.1837; 1245a (all); Map 1840, 5 chns; hill-drawing, waterbodies, houses, farmyards (col), woods (col), arable (col), grassland (col), orchards (col), gardens (col), hedge ownership.

35/274 Wadhurst (parish) TQ 630320
Apt 30.09.1839; 10148a (10147); Map 1840, 3 chns, by John Budgen; waterbodies, houses, boundary trees.

35/275 Walberton (parish) SU 968059
Apt 17.12.1847; 1723a (all); Map 1846, 6 chns, in 2 parts, by Henry Salter, Arundel; hill-drawing, railway, foot/b'way, waterbodies, houses, woods, hedges, landowners, quarries.

35/276 Waldron (parish) TQ 558195
Apt 29.03.1842; 6218a (6218); Map 1841, 3 chns, 1st cl, by E. Sheridan; construction lines, waterbodies, houses, building names, boundary trees and features, windmills (pictorial, named), woods (by name).

35/277 Warbleton (parish) TQ 629179
Apt 08.11.1837; 5763a (5763); Map 1838, 3 chns, by R. Lower, Chiddingly, and drawn by Mark Anthony Lower; construction lines, foot/b'way, waterbodies, fence ownership, field gates, building names, field names, farm names, landowners, rectory, windmill, mills, pits, watermill, dial post, woods (by name); orchards, gardens and farmyards shown by annotation; an incomplete table of land use has leafy surround; colour bands may show property ownerships or holdings; in tiny lettering on a leaf appears the name 'Mercie Lower'.

35/278 Warminghurst (parish) TQ 120171
Apt 29.03.1848; 84a (1051); Map 1848, 3 chns, in 2 parts, by George Blunden, Littlehampton; foot/b'way, waterbodies, houses, woods, arable (col), grassland (col), heath/moor, hedge ownership, field gates, building names, boundary trees, occupation road.

35/279 Warnham (parish) TQ 151343
Apt 02.11.1840; 4920a (4920); Map 1844, 3 chns, 1st cl, by H. Walter; waterbodies, houses, hedge ownership, building names, mill; bridge named.

35/280 Warningcamp (parish) TQ 043071
Apt 05.03.1840; 920a (?); Map 1839, 3 chns, 1st cl, by Henry Salter, Arundel, Sussex; construction lines, hill-drawing, foot/b'way, water-

bodies, houses, woods, orchards, hedge ownership, field gates, sand or stone pits, quarry, drains, commons.

35/281 Wartling (parish) TQ 666110
Apt 27.12.1839; 4736a (4736); Map 1843?, 6 chns; waterbodies, woods (named), hops, building names, drains. Apt omits some land use.

35/282 Washington (parish) TQ 126132
Apt 23.09.1840; 3163a (3162); Map 1839, 3 chns, by Hide and Patching, Worthing; houses, field boundary ownerships, building names, windmill.

35/283 Westbourn (parish) SU 775072 [Westbourne]
Apt 04.09.1840; 4306a (5091); Map 1840, 3 chns, 1st cl, in 2 parts, by H.S. Tiffen, Hythe, Kent, (including construction line diagram); construction lines, hill-drawing, foot/b'way, canal, waterbodies, houses, marsh/bog, fence ownership, field gates, building names, field names, common, workhouse, coastline, sand or stone pits, chalk pit, kiln, mill, brick kiln, woods, (by annotation); bridge named; there is a note that some boundaries, the marks of which have been lost, are taken from the Enclosure Award. Apt has in-bound and out-bound quantities.

35/284 Westdean (parish) TV 529991
Apt 12.12.1842; 2290a (2464); Map 1840, 6 chns, by Wm Figg, Lewes; hill-drawing, waterbodies, houses, woods, rock outcrops, building names, drains, coastline, cliffs, sand or stone pits, river embankments; bridge named.

35/285 Westfield (parish) TQ 808157
Apt 31.12.1840; 4273a (4272); Map 1841, 3 chns, 1st cl, by John Adams, Hawkhurst; hill-drawing, foot/b'way, waterbodies, houses, woods (named), plantations, parkland, building names, road names, vicarage, mill, marl pit. Apt has in-bound and out-bound quantities.

35/286 West Grinsted (parish) TQ 176205 [West Grinstead]
Apt 10.01.1847; 6658a (6658); Map 1840?, [3 chns], in 4 parts; construction lines, hill-drawing, foot/b'way, river locks, canal with towpath, wharf, waterbodies, houses, woods, plantations, parkland (named), orchards, gardens, hedge ownership, fence ownership, field gates, building names, road names, quarry, sand or stone pits, milestone, greens, common; gardens and rickyard indicated by annotation; some boundaries highlighted in colour; bridge named. (The map in PRO IR 30 is a copy; original is in PRO IR 77/88.)

35/287 Westham (parish) TQ 625046
Apt 22.12.1838; 4531a (4718); Map 1839?, 8 chns; foot/b'way, waterbodies, woods, orchards, hedges, building names, road names, drains, mill, almshouse; bridge named.

35/288 Westhampnett (parish) SU 879074
Apt 26.11.1838; 1899a (all); Map 1842, 3 chns, 1st cl, by John Elliott, Chichester; foot/b'way, waterbodies, parkland, hedge ownership, fence ownership, field boundary ownerships, field gates, boundary posts.

35/289 Westmeston cum Chiltington (parish) TQ 342149
Apt 12.02.1838; 4075a (4075); Map 1841, 3 chns, in 3 parts, by W. Figg, Lewes; construction lines, waterbodies, houses, woods (named), plantations, parkland, orchards, gardens, heath/moor, rock outcrops, fences, field gates, building names, road names, limekiln, quarry, green, sheep down; pictorial church. Apt omits some field names. [The original of 'Part 3' is in PRO IR 77/89.]

35/290 Whatlington (parish) TQ 763193
Apt 22.02.1840; 1256a (1255); Map 1839, 6 chns, by E.B. Green and Richd Tress, litho (by Shaw and Sons, London); waterbodies, woods (named), plantations, field boundary ownerships, road names, field names, mill pond; orchard and hops indicated by annotation.

35/291 South Wick (parish) TQ 244061 [Southwick]
Apt 11.07.1842; 994a (all); Map 1843, 4 chns; railway, foot/b'way, waterbodies, houses, rock outcrops, road names, quarries, low water mark, boundary stones; pictorial church.

35/292 Wiggonholt (parish) TQ 059169
Apt 16.03.1837; 842a (841); Map 1839, 5 chns; hill-drawing, foot/b'way, waterbodies, houses, farmyards, woods (col), plantations (col), arable (col), grassland (col), gardens (col), marsh/bog (col), heath/moor, hedge ownership, fence ownership, drains; map is signed by a land agent, certifying approval.

35/293 Willingdon (parish) TQ 597027
Apt 15.07.1842; 4218a (4259); Map 1843, 9 chns, by W. Figg; hill-drawing, waterbodies, houses, woods, coastline, sand or stone pit or quarry, martello towers. Apt omits some field names and has in-bound and out-bound quantities.

35/294 Wilmington (parish) TQ 552058
Apt 27.04.1838; 1745a (1744); Map 8 chns, 'surveyed by P. Potter, 1801, copied by Wm Leach, 1839', (tithable parts only in detail); waterbodies, woods, orchards, gardens, heath/moor, building names, windmill, common; meaning of colours is unclear. Apt indicates freehold and copyhold lands.

35/295 Winchelsea, St Thomas the Apostle (parish) TQ 905172 [Winchelsea]
Apt 11.03.1842; 826a (1510); Map 1842, 3 chns, by Jas Parsons; woods, heath/moor, road names, harbour channels, sluice, town gates (pictorial), lighthouse (pictorial), beacon (pictorial), flagpole (pictorial), site of tower, high water mark, salt marsh, Royal Military Canal and road, foreshore (col); built-up parts tinted; map is decorated with a wash drawing of Camber Castle.

35/296 Wisborough Green (parish) TQ 050277
Apt 23.06.1842; 8485a (8484); Map 1842, 5 chns; canal with towpath, waterbodies, houses, farmyards (col), woods (col), plantations (col), parkland (col), arable (col), grassland (col), orchards (col), gardens (col), heath/moor (col), hedge ownership, fence ownership, building names, mill, greens, commons; bridge named.

35/297 Wiston (parish) TQ 154141
Apt 31.05.1839; 2865a (2865); Map 1841, 6 chns, by William Figg, Lewes; waterbodies, woods, parkland (named), gardens, heath/moor, rock outcrops, building names, barrow, rectory, chapel, sand or stone pit. Apt omits some field names, and divides acreage column into 'nett' and 'gross' quantities.

35/298 Withyham (parish) TQ 506341
Apt 24.05.1843; 8087a (8086); Map 1842, 3 chns, 1st cl, by E. Sheridan; construction lines, foot/b'way, waterbodies, houses, foot sticks, mill dam.

35/299 East Wittering (parish) SZ 808975
Apt 24.12.1842; 1196a (1505); Map 1842, 3 chns, by Joseph Butler, Chichester; foot/b'way, waterbodies, houses, coastline.

35/300 West Wittering (parish) SZ 786986
Apt 11.02.1848; 2371a (3615); Map 1846, 3 chns, by Joseph Butler, Chichester; foot/b'way, waterbodies, houses, building names, coastline, harbour entrance. Apt has in-bound and out-bound quantities.

35/301 Wivelsfield (parish) TQ 348211
Apt 05.02.1838; 3103a (3103); Map 1842, 3 chns, 1st cl, by John Wood, Lindfield, Sussex; foot/b'way, public roads, 'tenantry roads', waterbodies, building names, tan yard, greens, common; mapmaker notes: 'one perch per acre has been added for contraction, 1841'. Apt omits land use. [In PRO IR 77/90 there is a 'Draft Map', surveyed by Norris and Dickinson, Wincanton, with a similar contraction note to the IR 30 version, but dated 'June 41'.]

35/302 Woodmancote (parish) TQ 237160
Apt 13.04.1839; 2236a (2236); Map 1840, 3 chns, by Tunstall and Hine, 10, Allen Terrace, Kensington; waterbodies, houses, woods (col), field boundary ownerships, boundary trees; legend explains some symbols.

35/303 Woolavington (parish) SU 943170 [Not listed]
Apt 14.09.1841; 2530a (2530); Map 1839, 6 chns, in 4 parts, by J.W. Blackman, Fareham; waterbodies, houses, woods, plantations, parkland, marsh/bog, heath/moor, road names, chalk pit, bound cross, downs; bridge named.

35/304 Woolbeding (parish) SU 872234
Apt 11.04.1839; 2254a (2253); Map 1839, 3 chns, 1st cl, by Thomas Baker, 'according to the Directions of the Tithe Commissioners', 'with the Chain-Lines used in the Survey'; construction lines, foot/b'way, waterbodies, houses (by shading), ornamental ground, hedge ownership, fence ownership, building names, road names, field names, sheepwalks, rectory, green, lime kilns; orchards, coppice, woodland, plantation, common and warren are indicated by annotation.

35/305 Worth (parish) TQ 312367
Apt 12.09.1842; 13251a (13250); Map '1839 and 1840', 3 chns, 1st cl, in 3 parts, by H.S. Merrett; construction lines, railway, foot/b'way, turnpike roads, toll bars, waterbodies, houses, woods (col), parkland (named), grassland, hedges, field boundary ownerships, field gates, building names, boundary stones, mills, mill ponds, kilns, Methodist Chapel, downs (col), forest, heathland, commons, greens, glebe (pink). (The map in PRO IR 30 is a copy; original is in PRO IR 77/91.)

35/306 Yapton (parish) SU 977030
Apt 08.06.1841; 1699a (1699); Map 1839, 3 chns, by E. Fuller, Chichester; construction lines, foot/b'way, canal with towpath, waterbodies, houses, hedge ownership, fence ownership, field gates, road names, drains; meaning of colours is unclear.

Warwickshire

PRO IR29 and IR30 36/1-169

248 tithe districts: 573,288 acres
168 tithe commutations: 284,799 acres
68 voluntary tithe agreements, 100 compulsory awards,
1 corn rent annuity

Tithe and tithe commutation

As Warwickshire is a midland county subject to extensive commutation of tithe in the course of parliamentary enclosure, it is no suprise to find that by 1836 68 per cent of Warwickshire tithe districts by number, but only about 50 per cent of the county by area, remained subject to payment of tithes (Fig. 48). Only forty-six districts were wholly tithable at this date; elsewhere the main causes of tithe exemption were commutation at the time of enclosure, modus payments in lieu of tithes, the merger of tithes in the land, and exemption by prescription.

Assistant tithe commissioners and local tithe agents who worked in Warwickshire are listed in Table 36.1. Warwickshire is somewhat remarkable in that a considerable number of its tithe valuers operated from addresses well outside the county (Table 36.2). In the apportionment of Shilton it is stated that the valuation is by one William Staresmore Marvin, who describes himself as 'Vicar of Shawbury, Salop.'

Tithe maps

Warwickshire conforms to the usual pattern of counties in which much tithe had already been commuted in that only 5 per cent of the county's 168 tithe maps are sealed as first class, and no second-class map carries construction lines. Eighty-one Warwickshire tithe maps in the Public Record Office collection can be attributed to a particular map-maker (Table 36.2). The two numerically most productive map-makers, Stelfox and Oakley, were especially conscientious in acknowledging sources where their maps are based on earlier work. At Pooley the map covers the whole district but only one field remained subject to tithe, a situation strongly suggestive of the re-use of an existing parish map. As in some other counties with much tithe-free land, there were two peaks of map production in Warwickshire: the first and larger was in 1840-43 and a secondary high point occurred in 1848-50 (Table 36.4). Warwickshire tithe maps are drawn at a variety of scales from one inch to 2.5 chains to one inch to 12 chains but only about 30 per cent are in the

Fig. 48 Warwickshire: tithe district boundaries.

recommended scale range of one inch to 3 to 4 chains. The six- and eight-chain scales were much more favoured in Warwickshire (52 per cent of districts).

Apart from woodland (on 66 per cent of maps) and parkland (on 16 per cent) Warwickshire tithe maps are generally uninformative about land use. Industry is shown on 5 per cent of the county's tithe maps and in especial detail at Aston and Birmingham St Thomas. The two most conspicuous Roman roads in the county, Fosse Way and Watling Steet, are almost invariably named. Three maps show windmills pictorially, but apart from a few colourful borders, Warwickshire tithe maps are notably lacking in decorative embellishments.

Table 36.1. *Agreements and awards for commutation of tithes in Warwickshire*

Assistant commissioner/ local tithe agent	*Number of agreements**	*Number of awards*
Thomas Smith Woolley	35	53
Francis Offley Martin	0	34
F. Browne Browne	8	0
John Maurice Herbert	0	8
John Pickering	7	0
Edward Greathed	6	0
William Wakeford Attree	0	5
Roger Kynaston	5	0
Horace William Meteyard	5	0
John Mee Mathew	2	0
William Heard	1	0
Thomas Sudworth	1	0

*Computed from the number of extant reports on tithe agreements in the tithe files [PRO IR 18].

Table 36.2. *Tithe valuers and tithe map-makers in Warwickshire*

Name and address (in Warwickshire unless indicated)	*Number of districts*	*Acreage*
Tithe valuers		
Thomas Holyoake, Little Alne	11	28,143
Richard Stelfox, Allesley	11	20,532
John Harris, Ward End, Birmingham	10	37,254
Joseph Jenaway, Clifton upon Dunsmore	7	4,376
John Dumolo, Dunton House, Curdworth	6	10,354
James Bateman, Emscote, St Nicholas, Warwick	6	9,777
Others [66]	117	174,363
Attributed tithe map-makers		
Richard Stelfox, Allesley	13	21,239
Charles Oakley, Allesley	9	16,182
James Bateman, Emscote, St Nicholas, Warwick	7	11,945
John Moore, Warwick	5	7,940
Joseph Gilbert, Welford, Northamptonshire	5	6,060
Edward Cherry, Wellesbourne	4	5,345
John Dumolo, Dunton House, Curdworth	4	3,152
Others [28]	34	65,217

Table 36.3. *The tithe maps of Warwickshire: scales and classes*

Scale in chains/inch	*All maps*		*First Class*		*Second Class*	
	Number	*Acreage*	*Number*	*Acreage*	*Number*	*Acreage*
>3	1	1,325	0	0	1	1,325
3	40	40,420	8	14,916	32	25,504
4	11	9,008	0	0	11	9,008
5	11	18,126	0	0	11	18,126
5.5	1	1,867	0	0	1	1,867
6	74	133,777	0	0	74	133,777
7, 7.5	4	2,991	0	0	4	2,991
8	14	53,032	0	0	14	53,032
<8	11	24,252	0	0	11	24,252
Not to scale	1	1	0	0	1	1
TOTAL	168	284,799	8	14,916	160	269,883

Table 36.4. *The tithe maps of Warwickshire: dates*

	1838	*1839*	*1840*	*1841*	*1842*	*1843*	*1844*	*1845*	*1846*	*1847*	*1848*	*1849*	*1850*	*1851*	*>1851*
All maps	3	14	17	14	14	17	8	3	9	10	13	14	17	14	1
1st class	0	1	0	1	1	2	0	0	0	2	0	1	0	0	0
2nd class*	3	13	17	13	13	15	8	3	9	8	13	13	17	14	1

*One second-class tithe map of Warwickshire in the Public Record Office collection is undated.

Warwickshire

36/1 Abbots Salford (township in parish of Salford Priors) SP 069499 [Abbot's Salford]
Apt 19.04.1849; 250a (?); Map 1848, 3 chns, by C.F. Cheffins, Southampton Buildings, Holborn (tithable parts only); waterbodies, woods (col), orchard, arable (col), gassland (col).

36/2 Alcester (parish) SP 072588
Apt 12.05.1851; 137a (1530); Map (drawn on Apt) 1853?, 12 chns, (tithable parts only); woods. Apt omits land use.

36/3 Allesley (parish) SP 282812
Apt 02.04.1840; 4156a (4225); Map 1841, 6 chns, litho (Standidge), in 8 parts, by Chas Oakley, Allesley, (including 2 chn enlargement of village, and five 3 chn enlargements of detail); foot/b'way, turnpike roads, waterbodies, woods, parkland, orchard, building names, road names, mill, avenue of trees, green (named).

36/4 Great Alne (parish) SP 116602
Apt 18.07.1839; 1753a (1753); Map 1841?, 3 chns, 1st cl; construction lines, foot/b'way, waterbodies, open fields; area numbers and one farm name are 'upside down' to the title.

36/5 Ansley (parish) SP 290927
Apt 26.01.1844; 2827a (2869); Map 1844?, 6 chns; foot/b'way, waterbodies.

36/6 Anstey (parish) SP 403831 [Ansty]
Apt 29.11.1850; 256a (990); Map 1852?, 6 chns, (tithable parts only); canal; stream named. Apt omits land use.

36/7 Arley (parish) SP 288901
Apt 27.06.1839; 1929a (1929); Map 1840?, 6 chns; foot/b'way, waterbodies.

36/8 Arrow (parish) SP 069561
Apt 13.02.1849; 1947a (all); Map 1847, 3 chns, 1st cl, by King and Nockolds, Saffron Walden and Stansted, Essex, and 'Del. by Simeon John King, Saffron Walden, Essex'; waterbodies, houses, woods (named), parkland (col), building names, rectory, mill, lodge; Ragley Hall gardens are shown by annotation.

36/9 Ashow (parish) SP 314704
Apt 23.03.1839; 1012a (1012); Map 1843?, 9 chns, 'skeleton map', ? by John Moore, Warwick; woods (col), grassland (col).

36/10 Aston juxta Birmingham (parish) SP 110890 [Aston]
Apt 11.12.1845; 13878a (13877); Map 1848, 8 chns, in 5 parts, by William Fowler and Son, (including four 5-chn enlargements of detail); railways and stations, turnpike roads, toll gates, canal with towpath, waterbodies, woods, parkland, orchard, building names, road names, furnace, works, rolling mill, mills, reservoir, water works, barracks, chapels, township boundaries and names; built-up part generalised.

36/11 Atherstone (parish) SP 208513 [Atherstone on Stour]
Apt 26.03.1844; 1064a (1060); Map 1844?, 6 chns; railway, waterbodies, hedge ownership, fence ownership, field gates.

36/12 Austrey (parish) SK 296084
Apt 08.03.1844; 1952a (2097); Map 1840, 6 chns; foot/b'way, occupation roads, waterbodies, woods, fences, road names, mill; pecked boundaries are between ownerships, and dot-dash boundaries are within ownerships.

36/13 Baddesley Clinton (parish) SP 203715
Apt 20.02.1847; 1329a (all); Map 1848, 3 chns, by Washbourne and Keen, 8 Cannon Row, Westminster; foot/b'way, canal with towpath, waterbodies.

36/14 Baddesley Ensor (parish) SP 271982
Apt 28.02.1849; 1020a (1100); Map 1848, 3 chns, by John Dumolo; railway with tunnel, foot/b'way, waterbodies, houses, woods, orchard, collieries, Roman road, boundary stone, windmill (pictorial).

36/15 Baginton (parish) SP 352744
Apt 22.01.1841; 1667a (all); Map 1841, 4 chns, ? by Henry Houghton, Baginton; waterbodies, woods, plantations; the two owners of the district are named in the title. Apt omits land use.

36/16 Barcheston (district) SP 272402
Apt 03.05.1849; 45a (1475); Map 1850, 6 chns; foot/b'way, houses, woods.

36/17 Barston (parish) SP 202791
Apt 18.06.1840; 1867a (1866); Map 1842?, 5.5 chns; foot/b'way, waterbodies, ford.

36/18 Barton on the Heath (parish) SP 257325 [Barton-on-the-Heath]
Apt 27.05.1839; 1164a (all); Map 1839, 3 chns, by C. Oakley, Allesley; foot/b'way, waterbodies, houses, woods, parkland, gardens, osiers.

36/19 Baxterly (parish) SP 272966 [Baxterley]
Apt 12.11.1840; 875a (all); Map 1842?, 6 chns; waterbodies, houses, toll gate, commons.

36/20 Beaudesert (parish) SP 158675
Apt 02.07.1839; 1243a (1285); Map 1839?, 3 chns; hill-drawing, turnpike roads, waterbodies, woods, parkland, pound, freeboard.

36/21 Bedworth (parish) SP 350870
Apt 05.03.1840; 1095a (2157); Map 1840?, 6 chns, in 2 parts, (including 0.5 chn enlargement of detail); canal with towpath, waterbodies, woods (col), parkland, gardens (col), heath/moor (col), fences, landowners, rectory, walls (in red); whole district is numbered, but only the lands tinted light yellow appear in Apt; map has signed statement of adoption for tithe commutation.

36/22 Berkeswell (parish) SP 249788 [Berkswell]
Apt 10.04.1839; 5958a (5958); Map 1841?, 8 chns; waterbodies.

36/23 Bickenhill (parish) SP 193835
Apt 13.07.1837; 3772a (3771); Map 1839, 6 chns, in 2 parts; railway, turnpike roads, canal with towpath, waterbodies, woods, internal divisions (col).

36/24 Bidford (parish) SP 100520 [Bidford-on-Avon]
Apt 04.12.1849; 12a (3240); Map 1852, 3 chns, in 2 parts, (tithable parts only, tinted); flour mills, paper mill, weir, lock; the mills are the only tithable property.

36/25 Billesley (parish) SP 151568
Apt 26.05.1846; 62a (750); Map 1850, 4 chns, (tithable parts only, tinted); foot/b'way, waterbodies, landowners.

36/26 Bilton (parish) SP 490737
Apt 15.06.1839; 2244a (2243); Map 1840, 9 chns, in 4 parts, 'Partly made from a new Survey and the remainder from old Maps', by C. Oakley, (including village at 4 chns and two enlargements of detail); railway, foot/b'way, waterbodies, woods, building names, landowners, toll gate; modus land is not mapped in detail.

36/27 Binton (parish) SP 148544
Apt 31.01.1851; 1a (1260); Map (drawn on Apt) 1852?, no scale, (tithable parts only); landowners.

36/28 St George, Birmingham (parish) SP 068883 [Not listed]
Apt 19.05.1847; 129a (?); Map 1845, 8 chns, (tithable parts only); canal with towpath, road names, schools, hospital, asylum.

36/29 St Thomas, St Martin and All Saints, Birmingham (district) SP 050870 [Not listed]
Apt 19.05.1847; 1444a (all); Map 1845, 6 chns, litho; canal with reservoir and feeder, tunnel, towpath and earthworks, waterbodies, woods, parkland, building names, road names, railway stations, grammar school, theatre, offices, burial ground, cemetery, hospital, Proof House, glass house, lead works, baths, post office, Excise Office, windmill, markets, monument, barracks; built-up part generalised.

36/30 Bishops Itchington (parish) SP 392566 [Bishop's Itchington]
Apt 09.10.1838; 3027a (all); Map 1839, 3 chns, surveyed for tithe apportionment by C. Oakley, Allesley; waterbodies, houses, woods, building names, footbridges.

36/31 Bishops Tachbrooke (parish) SP 310610 [Bishop's Tachbrook]
Apt 06.05.1843; 3467a (all); Map 1843?, 6 chns, in 2 parts, (including small enlargement of detail); foot/b'way, waterbodies, woods, parkland, building names, churchyard, freeboard, charity land, glebe land.

36/32 Bourton on Dunsmore (parish) SP 447715
Apt 19.08.1845; 38a (2520); Map 1846?, 3 chns, ? by T.W. Martin, Dunchurch, (tithable parts only); foot/b'way, waterbodies, houses, woods (col), hedges (col).

36/33 Brailes (parish) SP 312398 [Not listed]
Apt 06.08.1846; 753a (5220); Map 1849, 6 chns, by Davis, Saunders and Hicks, Oxford and Banbury, (tithable parts only); foot/b'way, waterbodies, houses, woods (col), hedge ownership, field gates.

36/34 Brandon and Bretford (district in parish of Wolston) SP 405765
Apt 19.05.1848; 1971a (?); Map 1849?, 6 chns, by John Holbeche, 25 Waterloo St, Birmingham; hill-drawing, railway and embankment, foot/b'way, waterbodies, woods, parkland, pit.

36/35 Brockhurst, Monks Kirby, Street Ashton, Newnham Paddox (including Muswell Leys) and Walton Parva (townships or hamlets in parish of Monks Kirby) SP 480838
Apt 30.11.1839; 3400a (all); Map 1841?, 8 chns; railway, waterbodies, woods (col), Roman road.

36/36 Brownsover (townships or hamlets in parish of Clifton upon Dunsmore) SP 510776
Apt 23.01.1845; 873a (872); Map 1848, 6 chns, 'Chiefly copied from old maps' by Joseph Gilbert; foot/b'way, canal with towpath, charity lands; colour bands and tint show holdings. Apt omits land use.

36/37 Budbrook (parish) SP 252643 [Budbrooke]
Apt 15.05.1841; 3217a (3216); Map 1840, 9 chns, by J. Bateman, Barford; canal with towpath, waterbodies, woods (col), parkland, fence ownership, field boundary ownerships, building names.

36/38 Bulkington (parish) SP 395867
Apt 03.02.1842; 2375a (4510); Map 1843, 6 chns, in 2 parts, by R. Stelfox, Allesley, (including small enlargement of detail); foot/b'way, canal with towpath, waterbodies, woods, building names, landowners, toll gate, windmill (by symbol), hamlet boundaries (col).

36/39 Burmington (parish) SP 273373
Apt 08.07.1842; 808a (all); Map 1844?, 6 chns; foot/b'way, waterbodies, houses, woods, hedge ownership, stiles.

36/40 Butlers Marston (parish) SP 318498
Apt 15.03.1851; 139a (1620); Map 1851?, 4 chns, (tithable parts only); hedge ownership, landowners.

36/41 Caldecote (parish) SP 351945
Apt 22.10.1839; 687a (all); Map 1842, 6 chns; canal with towpath, waterbodies, woods (col).

36/42 Cesters Over (hamlet in parish of Monks Kirby) SP 505820 [Not listed]
Apt 11.05.1843; 1097a (all); Map 1843, 3 chns, by Messrs Tatham and Son, Bedford Place, Russell Sq, London; railway, waterbodies, houses, woods, isolated tree, osiers (by symbol), Roman road.

36/43 Chadshunt (parish, hamlet or chapelry) SP 349530
Apt 23.10.1838; 1335a (all); Map 1839?, 4 chns; foot/b'way, waterbodies, woods (col), parkland, building names, landowners; pictorial church; the owner is named in the title. District is apportioned by holding and fields are not shown.

36/44 Charlcote (parish) SP 269569 [Charlecote]
Apt 15.08.1848; 749a (2190); Map 1849?, 4 chns, ? by Wm Kendall, Kineton, (tithable parts only); waterbodies, houses; pictorial church.

36/45 Chesterton or Great Chesterton (township in parish of Chesterton) SP 351583 [Chesterton]
Apt 18.05.1849; 2386a (all); Map 1849, 6 chns, ? by William Kendall, Kineton; waterbodies, Roman road, church doles (col), windmill (pictorial); pictorial church.

36/46 Church Lawford (parish) SP 449757
Apt 26.03.1849; 1703a (1865); Map 1850?, 6 chns; railway, foot/b'way, waterbodies, woods, glebe.

36/47 Claverdon and Norton Lindsey (parish) SP 212642
Apt 16.04.1838; 4177a (4330); Map 1840, [6 chns], in 4 parts, (including three small enlargements of detail; canal with towpath, waterbodies, woods (col), heath/moor (col), greens (named) commons.

36/48 Clifton (township or hamlet in parish of Clifton upon Dunsmore) SP 534762 [Clifton upon Dunsmore]
Apt 08.03.1845; 1651a (2870); Map 1850?, 5 chns, (tithable parts only); railway, canal, houses.

36/49 Long Compton (parish) SP 288332
Apt 30.06.1849; 112a (3530); Map 1850?, [3 chns], (tithable parts only in detail); waterbodies, woods (col).

36/50 Compton Wyniates (parish) SP 327423 [Compton Wynyates]
Apt 10.06.1848; 997a (997); Map 1848, 6 chns, (tithable parts only); hill-drawing, waterbodies, woods, plantations, gardens, windmill (pictorial), nurseries (by symbol).

36/51 Great Copston or Copston Magna (township or hamlet in parish of Monks Kirby) SP 460880 [Copston Magna]
Apt 07.12.1842; 1125a (all); Map 1843, 6 chns, in 5 parts, copied by J. Gilbert, Welford, (tinted; including four 3-chn enlargements of detail); hill-drawing, foot/b'way, waterbodies, woods (col), road names, landowners, chapel.

36/52 Corley (parish) SP 300854
Apt 27.05.1839; 1375a (all); Map 1840?, 5 chns, surveyed in 1830 by John Dumolo; foot/b'way, waterbodies, woods, field boundary ownerships, road names, stiles; common areas are tinted yellow and other areas are tinted green.

36/53 Cosford (hamlet in parish of Newbold upon Avon) SP 498787
Apt 01.05.1839; 554a (all); Map 1839, 3 chns, by C. Oakley, Allesley; railway, canal with towpath, waterbodies, woods, osiers (by symbol).

36/54 Coughton (parish) SP 083603
Apt 14.02.1839; 232a (1186); Map 1840?, 6 chns, by G.F. Johnson, (tithable parts only); foot/b'way, field gates, ownerships (col); one owner is named in the title.

36/55 Coundon (hamlet) SP 313813
Apt 30.09.1841; 1046a (all); Map 1844?, 6 chns; foot/b'way, waterbodies, houses, woods, pit, greens (named).

36/56 Holy Trinity, Coventry (parish) SP 332805 [Not listed]
Apt 26.05.1846; 1825a (1824); Map 1848, 6 chns, by R. Stelfox, Allesley, (tithable parts only); railways, turnpike roads, toll gates, canal with towpath, waterbodies, building names, road names, vicarage, boundary stones, city boundary, water works, gaol, mill, gasworks, Roman Catholic Chapel, greens, Lammas and Michaelmas lands (col).

36/57 Coventry St Michael and St John the Baptist with Whitley and Calludon (district) SP 337787 [Not listed]
Apt 05.06.1846; 3666a (3665); Map 1847, 8 chns, partly copied from one of 1792, and partly newly surveyed, by R. Stelfox, Allesley, (tithable parts only in detail); railways with station and viaduct, foot/b'way, turnpike roads, toll bars, waterbodies, woods, building names, road names, water works, Roman Catholic Chapel, city boundary, parish boundary (col), mills, coal wharf, house of industry, commons, Lammas lands and Michaelmas lands (col).

36/58 Curdworth (parish) SP 192931
Apt 06.05.1846; 788a (3170); Map 1846, 5 chns, (tithable parts only) foot/b'way, canal with towpath, waterbodies.

36/59 Dordon (township or hamlet in parish of Polesworth) SK 273008
Apt 23.02.1849; 1062a (?); Map 1850?, 10 chns, litho, (tinted and hand-coloured); hill-drawing, railway, canal with towpath, waterbodies, woods (col), stiles. All detail outside the district boundary has been cut away, suggesting that this map is in fact a portion of a map of the whole of the parish of Polesworth.

36/60 Dosthill (district in parish of Kingsbury) SK 217001
Apt 07.08.1839; 669a (?); Map 1840?, 5 chns, by John Dumolo; railway, foot/b'way, waterbodies, woods, osiers, building names.

36/61 Dunchurch (parish) SP 475707
Apt 26.02.1839; 4846a (4846); Map 1840, 6 chns, ? by Joseph Truslove, (tithable parts only in detail); waterbodies, houses, building names, toll gate, vicarage, brick kiln, township boundaries, tenants' names, church and poor lands.

36/62 Easenhall (hamlet in parish of Monks Kirby) SP 461796
Apt 28.11.1840; 1112a (all); Map 1839, 7 chns, in 2 parts, partly copied and partly from a new survey by C. Oakley, (including small enlargement of detail); foot/b'way, waterbodies, canal with towpath, houses, woods, parkland, field boundary ownerships.

36/63 Edgbaston (parish) SP 053847
Apt 31.01.1851; 235a (2545); Map 1851?, 6 chns, (tithable parts only); canal, woods, building names, road names; stream named; border has unusual rounded and extruded corners; north pointer has feathery decoration.

36/64 Elmdon (parish) SP 169826
Apt 20.06.1839; 1127a (1127); Map 1839?, 6 chns; foot/b'way, waterbodies, gardens.

36/65 Exhall (parish) SP 342851
Apt 29.03.1847; 204a (780); Map 1850, 6 chns, in 2 parts, (tithable parts only in detail; open fields also at 3 chns); railway, canal with towpath, waterbodies, woods, open fields.

36/66 Farnborough (parish) SP 439502
Apt 28.01.1841; 1954a (1953); Map surveyed in 1840, 3 chns, by Sanders Pepper; canal with towpath, waterbodies, houses, woods, plantations, parkland, gardens, tithe ownership (col).

36/67 Fillongley (parish) SP 275865
Apt 15.04.1843; 4732a (4731); Map 1844, 6 chns, in 5 parts, by R. Stelfox, Allesley, (including four 3-chn enlargements of detail; village not mapped in detail); foot/b'way, waterbodies, woods, parkland, building names, windmill, vicarage, mills, school, greens.

36/68 Foleshill (parish) SP 347828
Apt 10.07.1841; 1637a (2594); Map 1840?, 8 chns, (tithable parts only); waterbodies, canal with towpath, tithable status (col).

36/69 Frankton (parish) SP 421705
Apt 11.09.1840; 461a (1636); Map 1841, 6 chns, in 2 parts, (tithable parts only); foot/b'way, waterbodies, woods, field boundary ownerships, landowners, rectory, hall.

36/70 Grandbro' (parish) SP 482658
Apt 09.06.1849; 1966a (4100); Map 1849, 3 chns, 1st cl, in 3 parts, by William Phillips, Coventry, (tithable parts only; part 1 is of Woolscot, 1849, 1st class; part 2 is of Calcott, 1851, 6 chns, 2nd class; part 3 is 30-chn index); construction lines, turnpike roads, canal with towpath, waterbodies, houses, hedge ownership, field gates, building names, milestones, mill, initialled boundary stones, modus land; part 2 has woods (col).

36/71 Grendon (parish) SK 291005
Apt 31.07.1848; 2322a (2360); Map 1850, 9 chns, in 2 parts, (part 2 in manuscript, 6 chns), litho (by Fox and Paghe (?), lithographers to the Queen; with hand-colour); hill-drawing, railway, foot/b'way, waterbodies, woods (col), parkland, rectory.

36/72 Hallend and Freazley with Delves and Quarry Hill (townships or hamlets in parish of Polesworth) SP 250999
Apt 17.03.1849; 162a (?); Map 1850, 6 chns, by Lakin and Swinburne, Worcester, (tithable parts only); foot/b'way, waterbodies, woods, fences, building names, landowners, Roman road.

36/73 Hampton, Diddington, Kinwalsey and Balsall (hamlets or townships in parish of Hampton in Arden) SP 190810 [Hampton in Arden]
Apt 14.07.1841; 5133a (?); Map 1842, 6 chns, in 3 parts, (tithable parts only; one part at 8 chns); railways, canal with towpath, waterbodies.

36/74 Hampton Lucy (parish) SP 245578
Apt 06.05.1846; 3050a (all); Map 1846, 8 chns, by Moore, Warwick; foot/b'way, waterbodies, houses, plantations; a wood is shown by name.

36/75 Harborough Magna or Great Harborough (parish) SP 484798
Apt 01.11.1842; 284a (1580); Map surveyed in 1843, 3 chns, 1st cl, in 6 parts, by Josh. Gilbert, Welford, (including two small enlargements of detail); railway, foot/b'way, waterbodies, woods, orchard, gardens, field boundary ownerships, landowners, tithe-free land, fox cover; two incomplete construction lines are shown.

36/76 Haseley (parish) SP 235695
Apt 08.01.1841; 1152a (1152); Map 1841, 6 chns, by J.B.H. Bennett; foot/b'way, turnpike roads, waterbodies, woods (named), plantations, heath/moor, building names, rectory, water mill, dam. Apt has cropping information.

36/77 Hatton (parish) SP 231668
Apt 27.02.1841; 4099a (4099); Map 1841, 6 chns, in 4 parts, ? by Joseph Bennett, Tutbury, Staffs; foot/b'way, turnpike roads, canal with towpath and named bridges, waterbodies, woods (named), building names, parsonage, rectory, mill, school, boundary tree.

36/78 Hillmorton (parish) SP 534739
Apt 22.11.1842; 1268a (3150); Map 1843, 1st cl, [3 chns], in 6 parts, by J. Gilbert, Welford, Northants, (tithable parts only); construction lines, railway, canal with towpath and locks, waterbodies, houses, gardens, field boundary ownerships, turnpike gates, timber yard.

36/79 Honity (parish) SP 245722 [Honiley]
Apt 22.01.1846; 643a (all); Map 1846, 6 chns, ? by John George Jackson, Newbold Lodge, Leamington Priors; foot/b'way, waterbodies, woods, hedge ownership, park bank.

36/80 Honington (parish) SP 271423
Apt 31.07.1844; 103a (2441); Map 1850?, 6 chns, (tithable parts only); foot/b'way, waterbodies, woods (col), landowners.

36/81 Idlicote (parish) SP 288440
Apt 22.12.1842; 1408a (all); Map 1841, 6 chns, 'from a Map made by Henry Clark', by R.C. Gale, Winchester; waterbodies, woods (col).

36/82 Ipsley (parish) SP 058658
Apt 14.04.1841; 2514a (all); Map 1841, 6 chns, by G.M. [?] Cooper, Henley in Arden; turnpike roads, waterbodies, woods.

36/83 Kenilworth (parish) SP 278728
Apt 07.07.1848; 90a (6480); Map 1849, 6 chns, by Moore, Warwick, (tithable parts only); railway, foot/b'way, waterbodies, landowners, awarded road.

36/84 Keresley (hamlet or township in parish of St Michael, Coventry) SP 318835
Apt 19.12.1845; 1059a (1058); Map 1846, 6 chns, in 2 parts, by R. Stelfox, Allesley, (including 3-chn enlargement), litho; foot/b'way, turnpike roads, toll gate, milestone, waterbodies, woods, parkland, orchard, building names, road names, boundary stones and tree, keepers walk, tithe-free and tithe-merged land (col); roads are hand coloured.

36/85 Kingsbury (district in parish of Kingsbury) SP 228962
Apt 24.05.1847; 6592a (?); Map 1849?, 5 chns; railway, canal with towpath, waterbodies, woods (named), building names, landowners, brickyard, toll gates, mills, hamlet or township boundaries (col); a few meadows are named; other colours may show property ownerships.

36/86 Kingston or Chesterton Parva (township in parish of Chesterton) SP 363567 [Not listed]
Apt 18.05.1849; 1172a (all); Map 1849, 8 chns, ? by William Kendall, Kineton; waterbodies, freeboards.

36/87 Knowle (hamlet in parish of Hampton in Arden) SP 185755
Apt 24.12.1839; 3323a (?); Map 1841?, 6 chns, waterbodies, canal with towpath and locks.

36/88 Ladbrooke (parish) SP 420589 [Ladbroke]
Apt 08.02.1838; 1929a (all); Map 1838, [6 chns], 'Made principally from old Maps', by C. Oakley; waterbodies, houses, woods, parkland, rectory, hall. Apt omits land use.

36/89 Lambcote (hamlet in parish of Eatington) SP 268477 [Not listed]
Apt 25.06.1851; 12a (?); Map (drawn on Apt) 1852?, 3 chns, by E. Jackson, (tithable parts only); waterbodies.

36/90 Lapworth (parish) SP 170710
Apt 19.02.1839; 2972a (2971); Map surveyed in 1842, 3 chns, 1st cl, by John Pickering; construction lines, foot/b'way, canal, waterbodies, houses, woods, plantations, field boundary ownerships, boundary stones, windmill, tithe-free land (col).

36/91 Little Lawford (township in parish of Newbold upon Avon) SP 475771
Apt 31.07.1848; 31a (?); Map 1850, 3 chns, (tithable parts only); foot/b'way, waterbodies, woods, plantations.

36/92 Long Lawford (hamlet or township in parish of Newbold upon Avon) SP 468756
Apt 23.01.1845; 1702a (?); Map 1846?, 6 chns, in 3 parts, by C. Oakley, (including village separately at 3 chns); railway, foot/b'way, waterbodies, houses, woods, osiers, orchard, chapel, ford.

36/93 Leamington Hastings (parish) SP 458669
Apt 02.05.1843; 3245a (all); Map 1843, 10 chns; foot/b'way, turnpike roads, canal with towpath, woods, field boundary ownerships, puddle bank.

36/94 Leamington Priors (parish) SP 321653 [Royal Leamington Spa]
Apt 10.03.1852; 121a (1720); Map 1853, 4 chns, by Wm Russell, (tithable parts only); waterbodies, field names. Apt omits most land use.

36/95 Leek Wootton (parish) SP 290690
Apt 24.06.1846; 608a (1860); Map 1847, 7.5 chns, in 2 parts, by James Bateman, Warwick; waterbodies, woods, field boundary ownerships, landowners, modus land (col).

36/96 Lighthorne (parish) SP 337558
Apt 28.08.1840; 2008a (all); Map 1843, 6 chns; waterbodies, Roman road.

36/97 Lillington (parish) SP 328673
Apt 09.10.1838; 1325a (1324); Map 1839?, 8 chns; waterbodies; bridge named.

36/98 Loxley (parish) SP 258523
Apt 17.03.1848; 575a (1620); Map 1847, 3 chns, by E. Cherry; foot/b'way, turnpike roads, waterbodies, houses, woods, plantations, coppice, orchard, field boundary ownerships.

36/99 Maxstoke (parish) SP 229889
Apt 26.05.1846; 1540a (2701); Map 1849?, 5 chns, in 2 parts, (tithable parts only); waterbodies, woods, parkland, mill; bridge named.

36/100 Moreton Morrell (parish) SP 310555
Apt 06.06.1846; 521a (536); Map 1846, 6 chns, by James Bateman, Warwick, (tithable parts only); foot/b'way, waterbodies, woods, arable (col), grassland (col), building names, landowners; owner is named in the title, and adjoining owners are named.

36/101 Newbold and Little Harbro' (township or district in parish of Newbold on Avon) SP 481779 [Newbold on Avon]
Apt 31.07.1848; 644a (?); Map 1850, 4 chns, in 2 parts; railway, canal, houses.

36/102 Newbold Pacey (parish) SP 305578
Apt 09.02.1843; 1825a (1824); Map '1842-3', 3 chns, by E. Cherry, Wellesbourne; foot/b'way, private road, turnpike roads, waterbodies, houses, woods, plantations, gardens, ornamental gardens (col), hedge ownership, fence ownership, building names, road names, field names, landowners, churchyard, freeboard; stream named; gardens and stable yards are shown by annotation.

36/103 Newbold Revel (hamlet in parish of Monks Kirby) SP 443802 [Not listed]
Apt 28.11.1840; 294a (all); Map 1839, 7 chns, partly from old maps and partly from a new survey by C. Oakley; canal with towpath, waterbodies, houses, woods, parkland, field boundary ownerships, hall.

36/104 Newnham Regis (parish) SP 451777 [King's Newnham]
Apt 26.03.1849; 1437a (1418); Map undated, 6 chns; foot/b'way, canal with towpath, waterbodies, woods. Apt omits most land use.

36/105 Newton and Biggen (district in parish of Clifton on Dunsmore) SP 538781
Apt 23.01.1845; 256a (1160); Map 1847, 3 chns, by T.W. Martin, Dunchurch; railway, foot/b'way, waterbodies, fences, field boundary ownerships; scale bar is styled like a ruler with the end broken off.

36/106 Nuneaton (parish) SP 364922
Apt 14.09.1842; 3019a (6112); Map 1842, 6 chns, in 7 parts, by R. Stelfox, Allesley, (tithable parts only; including six small enlargements of detail); foot/b'way, turnpike roads, toll gate, canal with towpath, waterbodies, woods, building names, landowners; woods are tinted if tithe-free, as are other isolated tithe-free areas.

36/107 Nuthurst (township or chapelry in parish of Hampton in Arden) SP 150710 [Not listed]
Apt 16.05.1839; 690a (all); Map 1842?, 6 chns; waterbodies, houses, woods, obelisk (pictorial).

36/108 Offchurch (parish) SP 367656
Apt 31.12.1846; 2273a (all); Map 1848, 8 chns, by James Bateman, Warwick; railway, foot/b'way, canal with towpath, waterbodies, houses, woods, plantations, parkland, fences, Roman and droving roads, freeboard, glebe boundary (green).

36/109 Oversley (township in parish of Arrow) SP 097563 [Oversley Green]
Apt 16.11.1849; 401a (2273); Map 1853?, 6 chns, (tithable parts only); foot/b'way, waterbodies, workhouse; bridges named.

36/110 Great Packington (parish) SP 235840
Apt 19.06.1840; 2451a (2451); Map 1842?, 6 chns; waterbodies, woods, field acreages. Apt omits field names and occupiers.

36/111 Packwood (parish) SP 164734
Apt 14.02.1839; 1656a (all); Map 1840?, [3 chns]; foot/b'way.

36/112 Pailton (hamlet in parish of Monks Kirby) SP 474819
Apt 16.03.1842; 174a (?); Map 1842, 3 chns, in 6 parts, by R. Stelfox, Allesley, (tithable parts only; village at 3 chns, four parts at 4 chns, and 12-chn location map); foot/b'way, waterbodies, woods, parkland, landowners, mill pond.

36/113 Perry Crofts (district in parish of Tamworth) SK 212046
Apt 20.07.1846; 217a (?); Map 1847, 3 chns; foot/b'way, woods, fences, railway station, boundary stones.

36/114 Polesworth (hamlet or township in parish of Polesworth) SK 263019
Apt 23.02.1849; 262a (?); Map 1850, 10 chns, litho, (with hand colour); hill-drawing, foot/b'way, canal with towpath, waterbodies, woods (col), building names, colliery, brickyard, stiles; all detail outside the district boundary has been cut away, suggesting that this map is in fact a portion of a map of the whole of the parish of Polesworth; tithe area numbers have been added in MS.

36/115 Pooley (hamlet or township in parish of Polesworth) SK 255030 [Not listed]
Apt 10.02.1849; 11a (?); Map 1849, 6 chns; canal with towpath, waterbodies, woods; whole district is mapped, and the one tithable field is picked out in yellow.

36/116 Preston Baggot (parish) SP 172658 [Preston Bagot]
Apt 11.03.1839; 1302a (1302); Map 1839, 1st cl, [3 chns], by Nathaniel Lea, 40 Bennetts Hill, Birmingham; construction lines, canal with towpath, waterbodies.

36/117 Princethorpe (township in parish of Stretton on Dunsmore) SP 399707
Apt 28.04.1849; 37a (?); Map 1850?, 3 chns, (tithable parts only, tinted); hedges, landowners.

Apt 28.04.1849; 37a (?); Map 1850?, 3 chns, (tithable parts only, tinted); hedges, landowners.

36/118 Priors Hardwick (parish) SP 463565
Apt 13.08.1846; 649a (1600); Map 1847?, 3 chns, in 2 parts, by George King and James William Johnson, (tithable parts only); foot/b'way, canal with towpath and locks, waterbodies, houses, landowners.

36/119 Priors Marston (parish) SP 489572
Apt 17.11.1846; 127a (3630); Map 1847?, 3 chns, by George King, (tithable parts only); foot/b'way, waterbodies, houses, woods, landowners.

36/120 Radbourne (parish) SP 443571 [Not listed]
Apt 20.03.1849; 1150a (1149); Map 1849?, 3 chns; foot/b'way, turnpike roads, canal with towpath, waterbodies, woods, osiers, fences, field gates, drift road.

36/121 Radford Semele (parish) SP 351636
Apt 22.06.1843; 2094a (2093); Map 1843, 4 chns, by John Moore, Warwick; foot/b'way, private roads, canal with towpath and lock, waterbodies, houses, woods, plantations, field gates, building names, pits.

36/122 Rowington (parish) SP 200680
Apt 02.02.1848; 3424a (3424); Map 1847, 3 chns, 1st cl, by John Walker, Birmingham; railway, foot/b'way, canal with towpath, locks and junction, waterbodies, woods, fences, windmill (by symbol).

36/123 Salford Priors (district in parish of Salford Priors) SP 062522
Apt 14.08.1850; 352a (?); Map 1851?, 6 chns, (tithable parts only, tinted); foot/b'way, turnpike roads, waterbodies, woods, building names, boundary stone, glebe; bridge named.

36/124 Seckington (parish) SK 263069
Apt 03.02.1843; 806a (806); Map 1843, 12 chns; waterbodies, gardens, hedges.

36/125 Sheldon (parish) SP 158862
Apt 07.12.1838; 2514a (2514); Map 1839?, 8 chns; railway, turnpike roads, waterbodies.

36/126 Shilton (parish) SP 404844
Apt 15.11.1843; 433a (1075); Map 1844, 6 chns, by R. Stelfox, Allesley, (tithable parts only in detail); foot/b'way, turnpike roads, canal with towpath, waterbodies, woods, building names.

36/127 Shustoke (parish) SP 230905
Apt 20.03.1839; 3895a (3844); Map 1840?, 6 chns, in 2 parts; waterbodies, fences, heath, commons.

36/128 Snitterfield (parish) SP 216598
Apt 05.02.1840; 1115a (3725); Map 1840?, 6 chns, in 3 parts, (tithable parts only); foot/b'way, waterbodies, woods, fences, landowners.

36/129 Solihull (parish) SP 145795
Apt 29.03.1837; 11296a (11296); Map 1840?, 8 chns, in 2 parts, (town mapped separately at 3 chns); turnpike roads, canal with towpath, waterbodies, reservoir, heath.

36/130 Sow (parish) SP 390810
Apt 18.03.1843; 977a (2505); Map 1843, 7.5 chns, in 2 parts, partly from old maps and partly from a new survey by R. Stelfox, Allesley, (tithable parts only); foot/b'way, canal with towpath, waterbodies, woods, building names, landowners, mill; tithe owners are named, and pink bands show tithe ownerships.

36/131 Spernal (parish) SP 096623 [Spernall]
Apt 14.02.1839; 949a (1090); Map 1842?, 6 chns, (tithable parts only in detail); foot/b'way, waterbodies, woods (named), orchard, glebe. District is apportioned by holding and fields are not shown.

36/132 Stoke (parish) SP 356794 [Not listed]
Apt 27.02.1840; 921a (920); Map 1841, 6 chns, in 2 parts, ? by Richard Stelfox, Allesley, (including small enlargement of detail); foot/b'way, turnpike roads, canal with towpath, waterbodies, woods, osiers.

36/133 Stoneleigh (parish) SP 315755
Apt 24.11.1843; 9908a (9907); Map 1843, 6 chns, (tithable parts only in detail); hill-drawing, foot/b'way, waterbodies, road names, stiles, pits, dams, reservoirs; bridges named; park, heath, common and woodland are shown by annotation. Apt omits land use.

36/134 Stratford on Avon (district in parish of Old Stratford) SP 194552 [Stratford-upon-Avon]
Apt 21.01.1846; 2168a (?); Map 1848, 6 chns, in 5 parts, by James Bateman, Warwick, (tithable parts only in detail; including 12-chn skeleton plan of whole district); railway, foot/b'way, canal with towpath, waterbodies, houses, woods, plantations, parkland, orchard, road names, landowners, lodge, canal.

36/135 Stratton Baskerville (parish) SP 411915 [Stretton Baskerville Village]
Apt 30.09.1851; 1036a (all); Map 1851, 6 chns, by R. Stelfox, Allesley; foot/b'way, canal with towpath, waterbodies, woods, marsh/bog (col), road names, glebe (col); green band shows rent-charge payable to Burton Hastings. Scale bar is ruler-like.

36/136 Stretton on Dunsmoor (parish) SP 419729 [Stretton-on-Dunsmore]
Apt 17.03.1848; 539a (?); Map 1848, 3 chns, by James Wm. Johnson, (tithable parts only); foot/b'way, waterbodies, houses, woods, field boundary ownerships, landowners; scale-bar is ruler-like.

36/137 Stretton on the Fosse (parish) SP 448818 [Stretton-on-Fosse]
Apt 28.03.1837; 820a (1939); Map 1838?, 3 chns, in 3 parts, (tithable parts only); railway, foot/b'way, waterbodies, houses, woods (col), hedge ownership, field names, toll gate, stiles, rickyard, milking yard, field acreages; orchard and coppice are shown by annotation.

36/138 Studley (parish) SP 086651
Apt 27.10.1845; 4262a (4262); Map 1847?, 6 chns; waterbodies, woods, parkland, gardens. Apt omits land use for tithe-free land.

36/139 Sutton Coldfield (parish) SP 130950
Corn rent conversion, 1919; 13030a (?); Map 1895, 9 chns, in 2 parts; waterbodies, woods (named), parkland, bogs (by annotation), building names, canal with towpath and earthworks, guide post (by symbol), dam, rectory, mill, commons, new roads; main map is described as 'Traced at the Board of Agriculture from the Map annexed to the Corn Rent Schedule referred to in the Inclosure Award dated 28th November 1851', and is accompanied by an Ordnance Survey 6-inch (1:10,560) 1st edition composite, showing the ecclesiastical divisions. Apt omits land use.

36/140 Tanworth (parish) SP 127734 [Tanworth-in-Arden]
Apt 21.09.1839; 9400a (9400); Map 1842?, 10 chns, in 2 parts, (town also mapped at ?1.5 chns); canal with towpath and reservoir, waterbodies.

36/141 Thornton (hamlet in parish of Eatington) SP 272504 [Not listed]
Apt 25.06.1851; 411a (?); Map 1851?, 6 chns; woods, barn. Apt omits most land use.

36/142 Ufton (parish) SP 379621
Apt 21.07.1840; 1784a (1920); Map 1844, 6 chns; waterbodies; scale-bar is diced light and dark blue, with grey penumbra.

36/143 Upton (township in parish of Radley) SP 368453
Apt 14.07.1847; 545a (all); Map 1849, 9 chns, by Davis, Saunders and Hicks, Oxford and Banbury; turnpike roads, waterbodies, woods (col), gardens, hedge ownership, barn.

36/144 Walton D'Eville and Walton Mauduit (township or manor in parish of Wellesbourne) SP 291526 [Walton]
Apt 14.05.1840; 2182a (?); Map 1845?, 6 chns; foot/b'way, waterbodies, gardens, footbridge.

36/145 Wappenbury (parish) SP 379699
Apt 30.06.1852; 15a (1550); Map 1852?, 4 chns, in 2 parts, (tithable parts only in detail, tinted); including 80-chn scale location map); woods, field acreages; owner is named in the title.

36/146 Warmington (parish) SP 405482
Apt 27.11.1841; 647a (1750); Map 1841?, 3 chns; foot/b'way, waterbodies, houses, gardens, field gates, stiles, waste.

36/147 Warton (hamlet or township in parish of Polesworth) SK 282038
Apt 10.02.1849; 80a (?); Map 1850?, 6 chns, (tithable parts only). Apt omits land use.

36/148 Warwick, St Mary, and part of St Nicholas (district) SP 279646 [Not listed]
Apt 04.02.1848; 2908a (?); Map 1848, 6 chns, by James Bateman; foot/b'way, canal with towpath, waterbodies, houses, woods, parkland, field boundary ownerships, building names, road names, toll gates, racecourse (col), grand stand, castle, commons, freeboard; built-up part generalised.

36/149 Warwick St Nicholas (district in parish of Warwick St Nicholas) SP 297648 [Not listed]
Apt 04.02.1848; 250a (?); Map 1848, 6 chns, by James Bateman, Warwick, (tithable parts only); canal with aqueduct and towpath, waterbodies, houses, woods, parkland, fences, building names, road names, school, spring.

36/150 Wasperton (parish) SP 278595
Apt 18.05.1841; 1620a (1619); Map '1838-9', 3 chns, by E. Cherry; foot/b'way, waterbodies, houses, woods (named), coppice, orchard, gardens (by annotation), hedge ownership, fence ownership, field boundary ownerships, field gates, building names, field names, landowners, fords, stiles, vicarage, churchyard, wood yard; red band shows tithe-free land; compass pointer has plumes; table gives summary acreages for tithable land.

36/151 Weddington (parish) SP 368938
Apt 26.08.1840; 910a (all); Map 1842, 5 chns; waterbodies, woods, plantations, Roman road.

36/152 Weethley (chapelry or hamlet in parish of Kinworton) SP 053554
Apt 02.11.1839; 628a (all); Map 1846?, 5 chns; woods, county road.

36/153 Welford (parish) (partly in Gloucs) SP 110492 [Welford-on-Avon]
Apt 28.04.1840; 1379a (3550); Map 'compiled from various plans' in 1840, 8 chns, in 2 parts, (tithable parts only); houses, woods, building names, landowners, mill; bridge named.

36/154 Wellesbourne Mountford (township in parish of Wellesbourne) SP 266548
Apt 05.05.1848; 1694a (?); Map 1849, 6 chns, in 2 parts, by Moore, Warwick, (some meadows also at 2.5 chns); foot/b'way, turnpike roads, waterbodies, houses, woods, plantations, parkland.

36/155 Whateley (district in parish of Kingsbury) SP 220992
Apt 12.10.1837; 88a (?); Map 1838?, 5 chns, ? by John Dumoto, (tithable parts only in detail, tinted); foot/b'way, waterbodies, woods (col), landowners.

36/156 Over Whitacre (parish) SP 258914
Apt 24.06.1841; 1375a (1375); Map 1842?, 5 chns; waterbodies.

36/157 Whitchurch (parish) SP 225475 [Not listed]
Apt 02.05.1842; 1936a (1942); Map 1843?, 4 chns; waterbodies, woods (col), open fields, hedge ownership, field gates, hamlet boundaries (col); open fields are numbered in Roman numerals with arabic subdivisions.

36/158 Whitnash (parish) SP 331623
Apt 16.08.1837; 1243a (all); Map 1842?, 3 chns, foot/b'way, waterbodies, open fields; open strips are divided by solid light blue lines. North pointer has plumes.

36/159 Wibtoft (hamlet in parish of Claybrook) SP 477872
Apt 02.04.1845; 848a (?); Map 1843, 6 chns, in 2 parts, by R. Stelfox, Allesley, (including small enlargement of detail); foot/b'way, waterbodies, woods, Roman road, chapel.

36/160 Willington (hamlet in parish of Barcheston) SP 274391
Apt 08.06.1839; 755a (all); Map 1839, 3 chns, by T.C. Banister; foot/b'way, waterbodies, woods, coppice, orchard, hedge ownership, fence ownership, field gates, footbridge; common land is tinted green.

36/161 Wishaw (parish) SP 176950
Apt 28.11.1845; 1197a (all); Map 1846?, 3 chns; foot/b'way, waterbodies, houses, parkland, fences, mill, hall, rectory, haha, greens (named).

36/162 Withybrook (parish) SP 441845
Apt 02.11.1842; 2510a (all); Map 1843, 5 chns, partly copied and partly 'from Actual Survey' by Joseph Gilbert, Welford; foot/b'way, canal with towpath, waterbodies, woods, orchard, gardens, field boundary ownerships, Roman road; Withybrook is tinted green, hamlet of Hopsford is tinted beige; table summarises acreages.

36/163 Great Woolford (parish) SP 250343 [Not listed]
Apt 28.02.1845; 1355a (all); Map 1848?, 8 chns; waterbodies, hedge ownership, field boundary ownerships.

36/164 Little Wolford (hamlet in parish of Great Wolford) SP 266350
Apt 28.03.1842; 1325a (all); Map '1828-9', (1844?), 2.5 chns, by E. Cherry; waterbodies, houses, woods, orchard, heath/moor (col), open fields, hedge ownership, field names, toll gate, quarter boundaries (col), green (col); bridges named.

36/165 Part of Great Wolford in Little Wolford (district in parish of Little Wolford) SP 266350 [Not listed]
Apt 24.04.1850; 30a (all); Map 1850?, 6 chns, (tithable parts only). District is apportioned without acreages or other details for individual owners or holdings.

36/166 Wolston and Marston (hamlet or township in parish of Wolston) SP 424750
Apt 29.09.1849; 949a (?); Map 1851?, 6 chns, (tithable parts only in detail, tinted); railway, foot/b'way, waterbodies, woods, parkland, fences, Roman road. (There are two copies of the map in PRO IR 30, one a cartridge-paper orignal, the other a contemporary traced copy, with a note that it was deposited in the parish.)

36/167 Wolverton or Wolverdington (parish) SP 215614
Apt 17.12.1847; 246a (1320); Map 1849, 4 chns, (tithable parts only); foot/b'way, waterbodies, woods.

36/168 Wolvey (parish) SP 430880
Apt 12.02.1850; 174a (3790); Map 1850, 3 chns, by R. Stelfox, Allesley; foot/b'way, turnpike roads, waterbodies, pinfold, tithe ownerships (col).

36/169 Wootton Wawen or Waves Wootton (parish) SP 142638
Apt 27.07.1840; 8302a (8700); Map 1841?, 6 chns, in 5 parts, by Edw. Cooper, Henley in Arden, (including one part at 4 chns, two at 6chns, and 12-chn index); canal with towpath, waterbodies, woods, barnyard.

Westmorland

PRO IR29 and IR30 37/1-85

98 tithe districts: 500,905 acres
85 tithe commutations: 168,151 acres
37 voluntary tithe agreements, 48 compulsory tithe awards

Tithe and tithe commutation

In 1836 86 per cent of the tithe districts of Westmorland by number but only about 34 per cent of the county by area remained subject to payment of tithes. The discrepancy in these proportions is largely accounted for by extensive areas of upland which were either tithe free or subject to nominal modus payments apportioned on lowland fields. Only five Westmorland districts were wholly subject to tithe at this date (Fig. 49). The main causes of tithe exemption were commutation at the time of enclosure, modus payments in lieu of tithes (in 78 per cent of tithe districts), the merger of tithes in the land, and exemption by prescription. Tithes in the very large parish of Kendal had been commuted by special private act of parliament in 1834.

Assistant tithe commissioners and local tithe agents who worked in Westmorland are listed in Table 37.1. Two of the most prolific valuers of Westmorland tithes came from some distance outside the county (Table 37.2). As in other northern and north-western counties, many Westmorland tithe apportionments contain detailed lists of animal moduses.

Tithe maps

About 5 per cent of the tithe maps of Westmorland are sealed as first class. Construction lines are present on a further five second-class maps and on the map of Stainmoor sightings are given on to a number of Ordnance Survey triangulation stations. By contrast to most counties, there is a dip rather than a peak in map production around 1840; the peak years of map output in Westmorland were 1839 and 1842-43 (Table 37.4).

Westmorland tithe maps are drawn at scales of from one inch to 1.5 chains to one inch to eight chains but over half the maps are in the recommended scale range of one inch to three to four chains. The smallest scale used in this county was the eight-chain, whereas in most northern counties scales as small as fifteen to twenty chains are found in significant numbers.

In common with the general pattern in northern England, Westmorland maps are poor records of land use other than woodland, though as is to be expected in an upland county, a

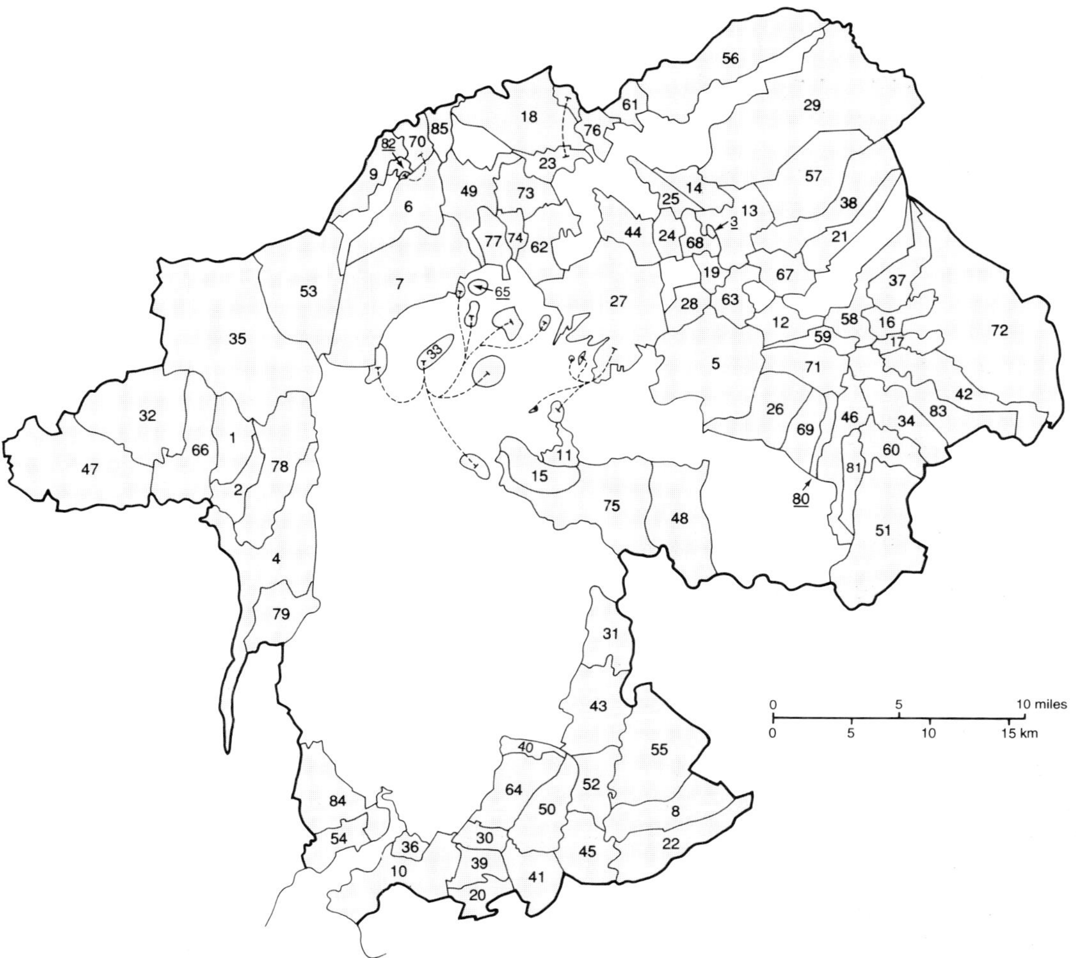

Fig. 49 Westmorland: tithe district boundaries.

high proportion (22 per cent) show some slopes. Indeed the map of Orton is a comprehensive record of local physiography.

Fifty-four Westmorland tithe maps in the Public Record Office collection can be attributed to a particular map-maker. All seem to have been based in or near the county, with the possible exception of James Hay who gives Musselburgh as an address on two of his eight maps (Table 37.2).

Overall, Westmorland tithe maps have a very 'grey' appearance, with roads uncoloured and a lack of red tinting for occupied houses. There is limited use of stamped instead of written names, most notably on the map of Appleby but otherwise there is little decoration on Westmorland tithe maps, though a number have north pointers adorned with feathers or acorns. Some maps around Kirkby Lonsdale are very neatly finished with tree symbols and lettering almost as regular as printing. Conversely, three tithe maps in the north-west of the county rank amongst the most crude of all tithe maps.

Table 37.1. *Agreements and awards for commutation of tithes in Westmorland*

Assistant commissioner/ local tithe agent	*Number of agreements**	*Number of awards*
John Job Rawlinson	16	14
John Strangeways Donaldson Selby	1	17
John Mee Mathew	3	9
Henry Pilkington	11	0
Charles Howard	2	7
Thomas Martin	6	0
Richard Burton Phillipson	3	0
George Wingrove Cooke	1	0

*Computed from the number of extant reports on tithe agreements in the tithe files [PRO IR 18].

Table 37.2. *Tithe valuers and tithe map-makers in Westmorland*

Name and address (in Westmorland unless indicated)	*Number of districts*	*Acreage*
Tithe valuers		
William Talbot, Burton in Kendal	9	20,055
William and Miles Turner, Lyth	9	8,709
James Birrell, Gretna, Dumfriesshire	9	24,759
Sylvanus Miller, Durham	7	15,225
Richard Atkinson, Bassenthwaite Hall, Cumberland	5	6,664
Anthony Battersby Tomlinson, Biggins House	4	5,925
John Graham, Yanwath Hall	4	4,323
Others [26]	47	82,491
Attributed tithe map-makers		
Miles Turner, Lyth	9	10,672
John Watson, Kendal, and M. and J. Turner, Lyth	8	27,194
James Hay, Kirkby Stephen/Musselburgh, Scotland	8	18,008
William Powson, Kirkby Stephen	5	8,879
George Larmer, Carlisle, Cumberland	4	8,365
Others [16]	20	41,245

Table 37.3. *The tithe maps of Westmorland: scales and classes*

Scale in chains/inch	*All maps*		*First Class*		*Second Class*	
	Number	*Acreage*	*Number*	*Acreage*	*Number*	*Acreage*
>3	1	48	0	0	1	48
3	24	47,967	4	12,833	20	35,134
4	24	52,904	0	0	24	52,904
5	1	1,176	0	0	1	1,176
6	26	42,849	0	0	26	42,849
7.5	1	2,023	0	0	1	2,023
8	8	21,184	0	0	8	21,184
TOTAL	85	168,151	4	12,833	81	155,318

Table 37.4. *The tithe maps of Westmorland: dates*

	1838	*1839*	*1840*	*1841*	*1842*	*1843*	*1844*	*1845*	*1846*	*1847*	*1848*	*1849*
All maps	10	14	8	7	12	14	3	10	2	3	0	2
1st class	0	1	2	1	0	0	0	0	0	0	0	0
2nd class	10	13	6	6	12	14	3	10	2	3	0	2

Westmorland

37/1 Ambleside above Stock (township in parish of Grasmere) NY 387071 [Not listed]
Apt 07.12.1838; 192a (1583); Map for 'Corn Rent in lieu of Tithe' 1843?, 6 chns, in 2 parts, (tithable parts only); landowners, school, waterfall. District is apportioned by holding.

37/2 Ambleside below Stock (township in parish of Windermere) NY 390044 [Not listed]
Apt 07.12.1838; 150a (1661); Map for 'Corn Rent in lieu of tithe' 1843?, 6 chns, in 3 parts, (tithable parts only); building names, landowners, toll bar. District is apportioned by holding.

37/3 Appleby (township in parish of St Lawrence, Appleby) NY 683203
Apt 19.04.1843; 48a (48); Map 1843, 1.5 chns, by M. and J. Turner, Lyth; hill-drawing, waterbodies, woods, footbridge (pictorial); most of the smaller letters and figures are stamped. Apt omits most land use.

37/4 Applethwaite (township in parish of Windermere) SD 407994
Apt 30.11.1838; 1585a (6231); Map for 'Corn Rent in lieu of Tithe', 1839?, 6 chns, in 2 parts, (tithable parts only in detail); hill-drawing, woods, building names, landowners, sheepwash, quarries, watering place, Roman road, peat areas. District is apportioned by holding.

37/5 Asby (parish) NY 682118
Apt 23.12.1843; 4096a (8395); Map 3 chns, in 4 parts: Asby Cotsford and Asby Little, by M. and J. Turner, Lyth, near Kendal, 1840; Asby Winderwath by I. Watson Junr, Kendal, 1841; foot/b'way, waterbodies, woods, plantations, open fields, building names, marble mill, township boundaries; it is unclear why some fields are tinted.

37/6 Askham (parish) NY 500220
Apt 07.07.1838; 2298a (4327); Map '1837-8', 6 chns, by J. Bintley, Kendal; woods, open fields, building names, mill; tints indicate lands in Askham and Helton townships. Apt omits land use.

37/7 Bampton (parish) NY 489173
Apt 15.02.1839; 3720a (10390); Map surveyed 1838-9, 3 chns, in 2 parts, by J. Bintley, Kendal; waterbodies, woods (named), plantations, open fields, greens, commons, building names, mill, standing stones (by symbol), lime kiln; pastures and tarns named.

37/8 Barbon (parish) SD 652825
Apt 30.09.1840; 2035a (4204); Map 1841, 8 chns, in 4 parts, (enclosed lands only; including 'homesteads, gardens, etc.' at 4 chns); hill-drawing, foot/b'way, turnpike roads, waterbodies, woods, plantations, heath/moor, building names, parsonage, field acreages.

37/9 High Barton (township in parish of Barton) NY 474242 [Barton]
Apt 11.04.1839; 2168a (5653); Map 'A Reduced Plan', 'Surveyed June 1838', 6 chns; turnpike roads, private road, waterbodies, woods, plantations, building names, ford, quarry, school, mill, boat house; tints show holdings; legend shows turnpike roads as coloured and 'Occupation' roads as uncoloured. Apt omits land use.

37/10 Beetham (township in parish of Beetham) SD 479791
Apt 13.02.1845; 5216a (7101); Map 1839, 4 chns, by J. Tayler; foot/b'way, waterbodies, woods (col, named), open fields, building names, moss, foreshore (col); compass pointer, with elaborate decoration, is printed and stuck on.

37/11 Birbeck Fells (township in parish of Orton) NY 592060 [Not listed]
Apt 05.02.1840; 1732a (?); Map 1840, 3 chns, 1st cl, by Jno. Watson, Kendal; construction lines, woods, plantations, building names, school, ford, well, boundary stones, sheep fold, pinfold, common, stinted pasture. Apt omits land use.

37/12 Bleatarn (township in parish of Warcop) NY 727142
Apt 29.01.1846; 1970a (?); Map 1846, 6 chns, by M. Turner, Lyth; woods, plantations; most lettering is stamped; scale is wrongly stated to be 3 chns.

37/13 Bongate and Langton (township in parish of St Michaels Appleby or Bongate) NY 699207 [Langton]
Apt 19.04.1843; 177a (3261); Map 1845?, 3 chns, by Joseph Richardson, (tithable parts only); footbridge. Apt omits land use.

37/14 Brampton (township in parish of Long Marton) NY 676230
Apt 17.02.1841; 1545a (?); Map 'Original or Working Plan', 1838, 3 chns, by George Larmer, Carlisle; construction lines, hill-drawing, waterbodies, open fields, Roman road, mill, ford, school. Apt omits some land use.

37/15 Bretherdale and part of Fawcett Forest (district in parish of Orton) NY 573047 [Not listed]
Apt 05.02.1840; 2685a (?); Map 1840, 3 chns, 1st cl, by M. and J. Turner, Lyth, near Kendal; construction lines, hill-drawing, woods, plantations, building names, old road, fords, boundary stones, Fawcett Forest boundary; some hill-tops named in gothic writing. Apt omits land use.

37/16 Brough, including Church Brough and Market Brough (township or district in parish of Brough) NY 799146
Apt 12.04.1843; 966a (all); Map 1841, 4 chns, by James Hay; foot/b'way, woods, building names, castle, glebe (col).

37/17 Brough Sowerby (township or district in parish of Brough) NY 803127
Apt 12.04.1843; 1083a (all); Map 1841, 4 chns, by James Hay; woods, building names, fords.

37/18 Brougham (parish) NY 570280
Apt 19.04.1839; 1092a (6040); Map 1839, 6 chns, (tithable parts only); hill-drawing, waterbodies, woods, building names, field boundary ownership, notable tree.

37/19 Burralls (township in parish of St Lawrence Appleby) NY 684177 [Not listed]
Apt 19.04.1843; 689a (689); Map 1843, 3 chns, by M. and J. Turner, Lyth; hill-drawing, foot/b'way, orchards, building names, barns. Apt omits field names.

37/20 Burton (township in parish of Burton in Kendal) SD 532772 [Burton-in-Kendal]
Apt 15.03.1841; 1438a (1437); Map 1842?, 6 chns; foot/b'way, canal, waterbodies, woods, plantations, building names, mill dam.

37/21 Burton (township in parish of Warcop) NY 772203 [Not listed]
Apt 12.01.1846; 1087a (?); Map 1849, 3 chns, by G.H. Bailey, Brough; waterbodies.

37/22 Casterton (parish) SD 653806
Apt 13.05.1843; 4230a (all); Map 1847?, 4 chns; waterbodies, woods, plantations, parkland, building names, boundary marks, county stone.

37/23 Cliburn (parish) NY 587251
Apt 13.01.1843; 475a (1360); Map surveyed in October 1842, 3 chns; woods; district is divided into two estates, one of which is tinted light blue; table lists areas.

37/24 Colby (township in parish of St Lawrence Appleby) NY 657201
Apt 19.04.1843; 919a (919); Map 1845, 3 chns, by M. Turner, Lyth; woods, plantations.

37/25 Crackenthorpe (township in parish of St Michaels Appleby or Bondgate) NY 656229
Apt 19.04.1843; 1341a (1341); Map 1843, 3 chns, by J. Bintley, Kendal; foot/b'way, turnpike roads, toll bar, waterbodies, woods, building names, ford, mill.

37/26 Crosby Garrett (township in parish of Crosby Garrett) NY 718084
Apt 19.04.1843; 2051a (3008); Map 1845, 4 chns, by William Powson, Kirkby Stephen; waterbodies, woods, marsh/bog, building names, mill.

37/27 Crosby Ravensworth (parish) NY 621157
Apt 28.01.1841; 4680a (15024); Map 1842-5, 3 chns, in 6 parts, (tithable parts only: includes 2 parts of 1844-5 at 8 chns by different mapmaker, and 16 chn index); hill-drawing, railway, woods, building names, vicarage, school, well, pillar (by symbol), boundary stones, mill; map is described as of 'The Ancient Land' in the parish.

37/28 Drybeck (township in parish of St Lawrence Appleby) NY 667154
Apt 19.04.1843; 1351a (1351); Map 1842, 3 chns, by Watson and Turner, Kendal; foot/b'way, woods, plantations, orchards, building names, waterfall, ford, mill, footbridge (pictorial).

37/29 Dufton (parish) NY 738284
Apt 19.04.1843; 4406a (18129); Map 1843, 4 chns, in 2 parts, by William Carr, Chalkfoot, near Carlisle; waterbodies, woods, building names, waterfall, mill, rectory; legend explains boundary symbols.

37/30 Farleton (township in parish of Beetham) SD 535810
Apt 29.06.1839; 1176a (1175); Map 1840?, 5 chns, by Hodgson and Watson; hill-drawing, canal with towpath and earthworks, waterbodies, woods (col), building names, lime kilns, sheepfold, ford.

37/31 Firbank (township in parish of Kirkby Lonsdale) SD 616941
Apt 20.02.1841; 1780a (3017); Map 1842, 8 chns, in 4 parts, 'Copied' by A.B. Tomlinson, Biggins, near Kirkby Lonsdale, (tithable parts only; including three 4 chn enlargements of detail); foot/b'way, woods, plantations, building names, school, chapel.

37/32 Grasmere (township in parish of Grasmere) NY 328091
Apt 30.11.1838; 5903a (7615); Map 1843, 6 chns, in 2 parts, (tithable parts only); building names, landowners, toll bar, smithy.

37/33 Hardendale, Mardale, Swindale, Tailbert and Rayside, Thornshap and Keld, Toathman, and Wet Sleddale (district in parish of Shap) NY 510128
Apt 13.06.1842; 938a (?); Map 1842?, 4 chns, (tithable parts only); construction lines, waterbodies, watermill (by symbol), chapel, crags and rock outcrops; 'Shap Abbey' is shown by an ashlar pillar, in perspective; names at the 'top' of the map are upside down; map is very crude in appearance.

37/34 Hartley (parish) NY 799078
Apt 14.05.1844; 2023a (3350); Map 1839, 7.5 chns, by W. Powson; foot/b'way, woods; colours may show land ownership.

37/35 Hartsop and Patterdale (township in parish of Barton) NY 383140
Apt 27.07.1839; 4651a (8314); Map 1839, [6 chns], by George Ladyman; waterbodies, building names, crags (named), glebe (col), township divisions (col); chain distances are given for detached portions. Apt omits land use.

37/36 Haverbrack (parish) SD 489806
Apt 31.03.1838; 655a (923); Map 1839, 4 chns; foot/b'way, woods (col), plantations, parkland, building names, limekiln, warehouse, foreshore (col), common.

37/37 Hillbeck (township or district in parish of Brough) NY 802175
Apt 12.04.1843; 1714a (all); Map 1840, 4 chns, by James Hay; foot/b'way, building names, mill, tower, cross; meaning of tints is unclear.

37/38 Hilton (township in parish of St Michael Appleby or Bongate) NY 762216
Apt 22.02.1840; 1381a (4182); Map 1840?, 4 chns, ? by George Larmer, Carlisle; foot/b'way, waterbodies, open fields, building names, mills; moor and tarn named.

37/39 Holme (township in parish of Burton in Kendal) SD 532792
Apt 15.03.1841; 1617a (1616); Map 1842?, 6 chns; foot/b'way, canal with towpath, waterbodies, woods, plantations, parkland, heath/moor, building names, kiln, boundary stone, mill, field ditches.

37/40 Holmscales (hamlet in parish of Burton in Kendal) SD 567863 [Holmescales]
Apt 23.12.1845; 846a (?); Map 1847?, 3 chns; turnpike roads, woods, plantations, field gates, building names, road names, boundary trees, quarry.

37/41 Hutton Roof (township in parish of Kirkby Lonsdale) SD 566784
Apt 18.05.1843; 2635a (2635); Map 1845?, 6 chns; woods, building names, school.

37/42 Kaber (township in parish of Kirby Stephen) NY 834096
Apt 18.09.1844; 2424a (3962); Map 1841, 4 chns, in 2 parts, by James Hay; foot/b'way, building names.

37/43 Killington (township in parish of Kirkby Lonsdale) SD 606895
Apt 20.02.1841; 4876a (4875); Map 1842?, 8 chns; hill-drawing, foot/b'way, waterbodies, woods, plantations, building names, watering place.

37/44 Kings Meaburn (parish) NY 633206 [King's Meaburn]
Apt 31.05.1841; 2382a (2381); Map 1842, 4 chns, by D.W. Rome, Alston; foot/b'way, occupation roads, open fields, road names, ford, mill.

37/45 Kirkby Lonsdale (township in parish of Kirkby Lonsdale) SD 598800
Apt 16.10.1848; 3099a (3098); Map 1849, 6 chns, corrected and copied by J.W. Wolfenden (?), Kirkby Lonsdale; waterbodies, woods, plantations, building names, free grammar school, ford, pit; built-up part not mapped.

37/46 Kirkby Stephen (township in parish of Kirkby Stephen) NY 763077
Apt 27.08.1842; 1626a (3522); Map 1839, 3 chns, 1st cl, by James Hay, Kirkby Stephen; construction lines, foot/b'way, houses; uncoloured roads may be private; map has summary of areas.

37/47 Langdale (township in parish of Grassmere) NY 288058 [Not listed]
Apt 03.01.1839; 270a (7702); Map for 'Corn Rent in lieu of Tithe' 1843?, 6 chns, (tithable parts only); building names, landowners, school.

37/48 Langdale (township in parish of Orton) NY 659014
Apt 30.09.1844; 6087a (?); Map 1845, 4 chns, by John Watson, Junior, Kendal; foot/b'way, woods, plantations, building names, landowners, boundary stones, smithy, sheep folds, ancient watercourse; physical features and streams named.

37/49 Lowther (parish) NY 534228
Apt 22.09.1837; 1032a (3520); Map 1838, 4 chns, in 5 parts, (tithable parts only in detail; includes 8-chn index); hill-drawing, woods, field boundary ownerships, school, well, limekilns, ford. Apt omits land use.

37/50 Lupton (township in parish of Kirkby Lonsdale) SD 574825
Apt 18.05.1843; 3439a (3439); Map 1845?, 8 chns; waterbodies, woods, plantations, building names, mill, smithy, old pit.

37/51 Mallerstang (township in parish of Kirkby Stephen) NY 784001 [Not listed]
Apt 23.08.1842; 4944a (4944); Map surveyed in 1839, [3 chns], in 2 parts, by John Rook, (tithable parts only); hill-drawing, foot/b'way, occupation road, turnpike roads, toll bar, houses, woods (col, named), gardens (col), hedge ownership, field boundary ownerships, building names, field names, castle ruins and earthworks, pound, waterfall; other colours show property ownerships. Apt omits land use.

37/52 Mansergh (township in parish of Kirkby Lonsdale) SD 603842
Apt 18.05.1843; 2569a (2568); Map 1845?, 4 chns; foot/b'way, waterbodies, woods, plantations, parkland, building names, school, chapel; lettering varies according to building function.

37/53 Martindale (township in parish of Barton) NY 432170
Apt 29.09.1838; 1011a (8060); Map 'taken in September 1838', 4 chns, by Matthew Wilkinson, Rosegill; John Jackson, Martindale; Anthony Wright, Raside, (tithable parts only); commons; map is very crude in appearance.

37/54 Meathop and Ulpha (parish) SD 442813
Apt 27.06.1845; 402a (3561); Map 1845, 6 chns, by M. Turner, Lyth, (tithable parts only in detail); woods, plantations, sea wall; tithe area numbers are stamped. Apt omits land use.

37/55 Middleton (township in parish of Kirkby Lonsdale) SD 643863
Apt 12.07.1842; 3503a (7503); Map 1845?, 8 chns, (of 'the Enclosed Lands'); foot/b'way, waterbodies, woods, coppice, plantations, building names, boundary stone, school, smithy, common.

37/56 Milburn (parish) NY 696316
Apt 19.06.1840; 3122a (5282); Map 'Original Plan', 1838, 4 chns, surveyed by George Larmer, Carlisle; construction lines, foot/b'way, open fields, building names, mill. Apt omits land use.

37/57 Murton (township in parish of St Michael Appleby or Bongate) NY 744238
Apt 05.02.1840; 2317a (5766); Map 1838, 4 chns, surveyed by George Larmer, Carlisle; foot/b'way, building names, mill, school, Methodist chapel.

37/58 Great Musgrave (parish) NY 776169
Apt 04.11.1842; 1824a (4080); Map 1840, 6 chns, in 3 parts, by W. Powson, Kirkby Stephen, (including two 4-chn enlargements); woods.

37/59 Little Musgrave (township in parish of Crosby Garrett) NY 750132
Apt 30.09.1847; 1216a (1216); Map 1839, 6 chns, by William Powson, Kirkby Stephen; foot/b'way, woods (col), plantations (col), gardens (col), field boundary ownerships, building names, common; river bars are tinted; other colours show land ownership; title is in cartouche formed by an uncoloured garland of leaves; compass has acorn pointer.

37/60 Nateby (township in parish of Kirkby Stephen) NY 791060
Apt 23.08.1842; 1069a (2075); Map 1846, 3 chns, by Anthony Clarkson; hill-drawing, woods, plantations, orchards, building names, shaft, ford, limekiln. Acorn adorns north pointer.

37/61 Newbiggin (parish) NY 636286
Apt 20.10.1842; 738a (1184); Map 1843, 4 chns, in 3 parts, by W. Carr, Chalk-foot, near Thursby, Carlisle, (tithable parts only); woods, plantations, building names; streams named; legend explains boundary symbols.

37/62 Newby (parish) NY 578198
Apt 23.04.1839; 2888a (2887); Map 1838, 6 chns, by John Watson, Kendal; foot/b'way, waterbodies, woods, plantations, building names, mill, sepulchre, metal banks.

37/63 Great Ormside (township in parish of Ormside) NY 695157
Apt 19.04.1843; 2056a (?); Map 1845, 3 chns, in 2 parts, by M. Turner, Lyth; woods, plantations, orchards, ford. Apt omits land use for some tithe-free lands.

37/64 Preston Patrick (township in parish of Burton in Kendal) SD 553841 [Not listed]
Apt 04.03.1846; 924a (3580); Map for Corn Rent in lieu of Vicarial tithe, 1847?, 6 chns, (tithable parts only in detail); turnpike roads, canal with towpath, woods, plantations, building names, landowners, Friends' Meeting House, chapel, school. District is apportioned by holding.

37/65 Rosegill (township in parish of Shap) NY 538167 [Not listed]
Apt 21.08.1838; 96a (?); Map 'taken' in June 1840, 4 chns, by Matthew Wilkinson, Rosegill, and Anthony Wright, Raside, (tithable parts only); construction lines.

37/66 Rydall and Loughrigg (township in parish of Grasmere) NY 363063 [Rydal]
Apt 13.11.1838; 149a (5200); Map for 'Corn Rent in lieu of Tithe', 1843?, 6 chns, in 2 parts, (tithable parts only in detail); waterbodies, building names, landowners, boat house.

37/67 Sandford (township in parish of Warcop) NY 727175
Apt 28.06.1844; 224a (?); Map 1844, 3 chns, in 2 parts, by Joseph Richardson, (tithable parts only); woods, building names, landowners. Apt omits land use.

37/68 Scattergate (township in parish of St Lawrence Appleby) NY 674198 [Not listed]
Apt 19.04.1843; 612a (960); Map 1843, 3 chns, by M. and J. Turner, Lyth; hill-drawing, foot/b'way, woods, plantations, castle, moat. Apt omits some land use.

37/69 Smardale (township in parish of Kirkby Stephen) NY 739076
Apt 24.08.1842; 1765a (1735); Map 1839, 8 chns, by W. Powson; woods (col), plantations (col), gardens (col); colour bands indicate land and field boundary ownership. Acorn adorns compass pointer. Apt omits land use.

37/70 Sockbridge (township in parish of Barton) NY 504263
Apt 19.04.1839; 1123a (11818); Map 1840?, 6 chns, in 2 parts, (tithable parts only in detail, tinted); foot/b'way, waterbodies, woods, plantations, gardens, building names, landowners, mill.

37/71 Soulby (township in parish of Kirkby Stephen) NY 743113
Apt 20.04.1841; 2495a (2495); Map 1842?, 8 chns; woods, building names; streams named.

37/72 Stainmoor (township in parish of Brough) NY 855137 [Not listed]
Apt 12.04.1843; 6877a (all); Map 1844, 4 chns, in 2 parts, by James Hay, Musselburg (or Brough); construction lines, building names, toll bar, gate to pasture, old road to London, common (col); Hay's address is Musselburg on part 1 and Brough on part 2; some land is tinted yellow; the reason for this is uncertain; an eastward protrusion is copied elsewhere, and marked 'This may be cut off'; one construction line is annotated 'On the Ordnance Station Mikle Hill', others for other OS stations, and on Middle Fell is 'Three Stations in the Trigonometrical Survey of England are seen from this point'.

37/73 Great Strickland (township in parish of Morland) NY 568232
Apt 25.09.1838; 2265a (2265); Map 1838, 6 chns, by I. Watson, Kendal; foot/b'way, waterbodies, woods, building names, private footpath, mill, lime kilns, cow shed, field houses, tithe barn, fords, boundary tree, public quarry (col).

37/74 Little Strickland (township in parish of Morland) NY 563207
Apt 15.09.1841; 772a (772); Map 1843?, 4 chns; hill-drawing, woods, plantations, field boundary ownerships, building names, quarry (col), mill, school, chapel.

37/75 Tebay (parish) NY 616029
Apt 03.03.1841; 6790a (?); Map 1841, 3 chns, 1st cl, in 2 parts: east of the Lune by John Watson, Kendal; west of the Lune by M. and J. Turner, Lyth, near Kendal; construction lines, woods, building names, boundary stones, marks and mounds, Roman mound, riparian sand bed, screes, quarry. Apt omits land use.

37/76 Temple Sowerby (parish) NY 613268
Apt 19.06.1840; 1177a (1176); Map 'Reduced Plan', surveyed in November 1838, 6 chns, by D. Browne; hill-drawing, foot/b'way, woods, plantations, orchards, gardens, peat moss, building names, tan yard, toll bar, chapel, mill, ford, footbridge; bridges named.

37/77 Thrimby (township in parish of Morland) NY 548200
Apt 29.06.1839; 184a (1506); Map 1839, 4 chns, (tithable parts only); woods, field boundary ownerships, building names.

37/78 Troutbeck (township in parish of Windermere) NY 415055
Apt 26.04.1839; 781a (5322); Map for 'Corn Rent in lieu of tithe', 1841?, 6 chns, in 6 parts, (tithable parts only in detail); hill-drawing, foot/b'way, building names, road names, landowners.

37/79 Undermillbeck (township in parish of Windermere) SD 414959 [Not listed]
Apt 30.11.1838; 1985a (?); Map 1842, 3 chns, in 2 parts, by Watson and Turner, Kendal, (tithable parts only); waterbodies, woods, plantations, parkland, building names, boat houses, ferry pier, hotels, school, rectory, shed. Apt omits land use.

37/80 Waitby (township in parish of Kirkby Stephen) NY 752072
Apt 23.08.1842; 653a (972); Map 1842, 4 chns, by Richard Garth, Hawes, Yorkshire; waterbodies, woods, plantations, orchards, gardens, building names, school house.

37/81 Wharton (township in parish of Kirkby Stephen) NY 767042 [Not listed]
Apt 23.08.1842; 1482a (1483); Map 1839, 3 chns, by James Hay, Musselburgh; ford.

37/82 Low Winder (township in parish of Barton) NY 492250 [Not listed]
Apt 26.04.1839; 298a (298); Map 1843?, 6 chns, (tithable parts only, tinted); woods, building names.

37/83 Winton (township in parish of Kirkby Stephen) NY 814089
Apt 07.10.1842; 1836a (3383); Map 1839, 3 chns, in 2 parts, by James Hay; hill-drawing, waterbodies, woods (col), plantations, rock outcrops, field boundary ownerships, building names, school, hedgerow trees; colour bands indicate land and estate boundary ownerships.

37/84 Witherslack (township in parish of Beetham) SD 442838
Apt 22.02.1845; 1291a (4689); Map 1843, 8 chns, by M. Turner, Lyth, (tithable parts only in detail); waterbodies, building names, road names, mill; bridges named.

37/85 Yanwath and Eamont Bridge (township in parish of Barton) NY 519270
Apt 22.04.1843; 734a (1169); Map 1844?, 6 chns; hill-drawing, foot/b'way, woods, building names, mills, ring earthwork. Apt omits land use.

Wiltshire

PRO IR29 and IR30 38/1-299

336 tithe districts: 880,978 acres
295 tithe commutations: 697,874 acres
185 voluntary tithe agreements, 110 compulsory tithe awards,
4 corn rent annuities

Tithe and tithe commutation

Some tithe was still payable in 88 per cent of Wiltshire tithe districts in 1836 but only 113 districts were wholly subject to tithe (Fig. 50). The main causes of tithe exemption in this county were commutation at the time of enclosure, modus payments in lieu of tithes, and merger of tithes in the land (usually where the landowner and tithe owner were one and the same).

Assistant tithe commissioners and local tithe agents who worked in Wiltshire are listed in Table 38.1. Wiltshire deviates somewhat from the usual pattern of locally based valuers as in eighteen districts tithe rent-charge was valued by men based in or near London; thirteen are by John Iveson of Halliford, Middlesex (Table 38.2).

Tithe maps

About 6 per cent of Wiltshire's 295 tithe maps are sealed as first class and very few (2 per cent) second-class maps carry construction lines. It is thus probably reasonable to infer that a majority of Wiltshire tithe maps derive in part from compilations of earlier maps rather than from entirely new surveys. Map scales employed in this county range from one inch to two chains to one inch to sixteen chains with only 29 per cent of maps in the recommended scale range of one inch to three to four chains.

The depiction of agricultural land use on Wiltshire tithe maps is somewhat better than average as about 14 per cent distinguish arable and grass, 10 per cent depict gardens, 8 per cent map parks, 17 per cent portray orchards, and 56 per cent show woodland. A few maps depict field boundary walls by a 'battlement' effect as at, for example, Great Chalfield and Tockenham. Strip lynchets appear on some maps as at Coombe Bissett, at Westbury the White Horse is shown, but otherwise the careful mapping of antiquities by the Ordnance Survey some years earlier finds no echo on Wiltshire tithe maps.

About a half of Wiltshire tithe maps in the Public Record Office collection can be attributed to a particular map-maker; the most prolific was the partnership of Little and

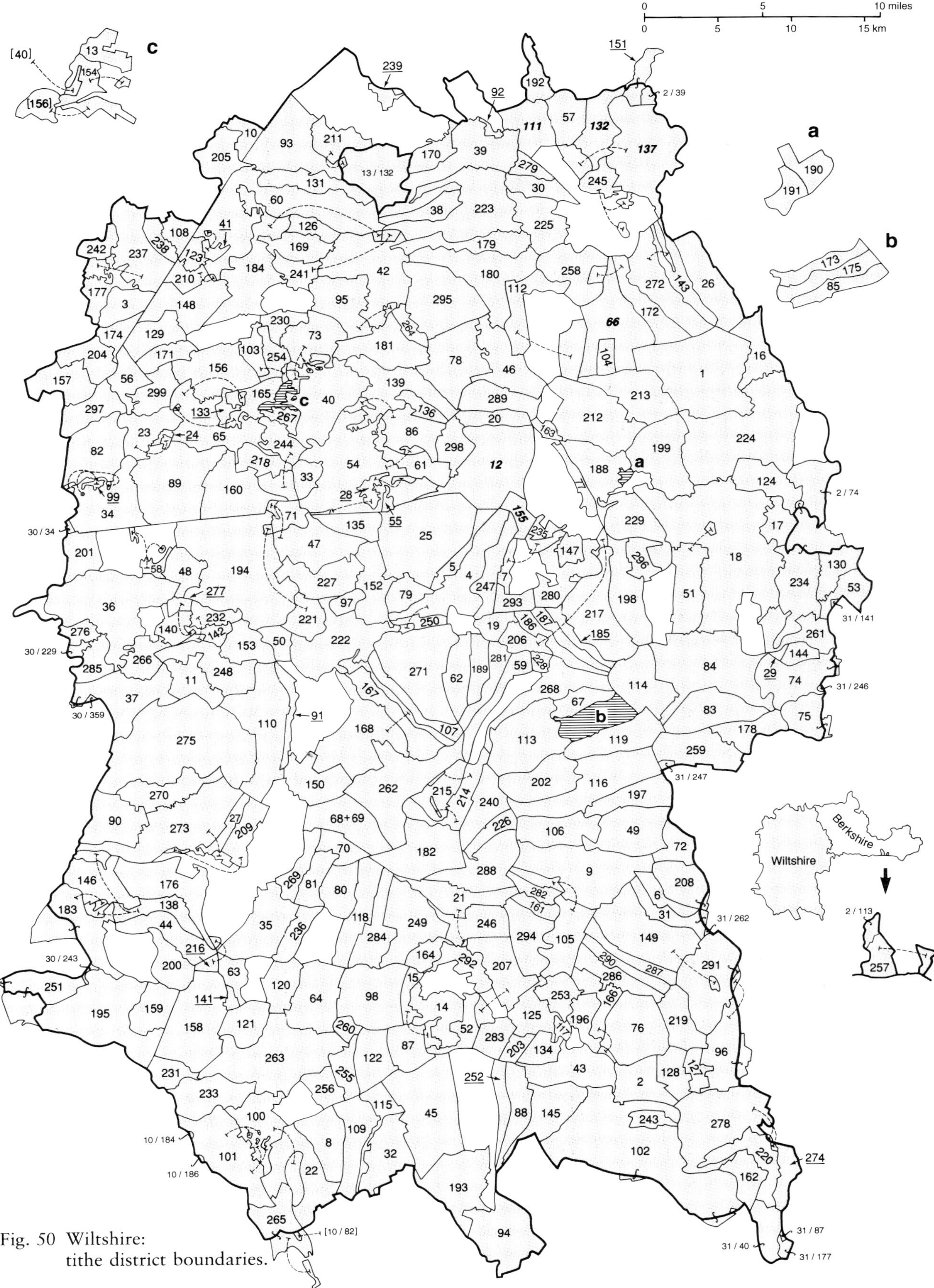

Fig. 50 Wiltshire:
tithe district boundaries.

Weaver of Chippenham who produced thirty-two maps. Their style is neat but otherwise unremarkable as also is the work of James Poole of Sherborne, Dorset (fifteen maps) and Francis Kelsey of Salisbury (thirteen maps).

In general Wiltshire tithe maps are fairly plain and some of those of downland districts have a very bare, empty appearance. There is little decoration to be found and the miniature world map in the compass boss on the map of Box is very much the exception. A unique feature of the tithe map of Warminster made by the surveyors Cruse and Fox and lithographed by Hollway of Bath, is a pasted-on lithograph, by Standidge of London, of a view of the town from the Bath road by T. Cruse. The map of Rowde is an unusual example of a first-class tithe map with full land-use colouring.

Table 38.1. *Agreements and awards for commutation of tithes in Wiltshire*

Assistant commissioner/ local tithe agent	*Number of agreements**	*Number of awards*
George Bolls	144	0
Aneurin Owen	17	98
Charles Pym	12	1
George Wingrove Cooke	0	10
Robert Page	2	0
James Jerwood	2	0
John Johnes	2	0
Thomas Smith Woolley	1	0
Tithe Commissioners	0	1

*Computed from the number of extant reports on tithe agreements in the tithe files [PRO IR 18].

Table 38.2. *Tithe valuers and tithe map-makers in Wiltshire*

Name and address (in Wiltshire unless indicated)	*Number of districts*	*Acreage*
Tithe valuers		
Francis Attwood, The Close, Salisbury	33	85,259
Robert Davis Little, Chippenham	26	39,035
Michael John Festing, Maiden Bradley	13	31,848
John Iveson, Halliford, Middlesex and others	13	27,197
James Combes, Tisbury	12	36,228
Thomas Davis, Warminster	11	24,741
Richard Stratton, Upavon	11	24,507
Daniel Trinder, Cirencester,	10	36,978
Thomas Waters, Stratford sub Castle	10	25,885
Others [71]	156	366,196
Attributed tithe map-makers		
Little and Weaver, Chippenham	32	61,660
James Poole, Sherborne, Dorset	15	42,676
Francis J. Kelsey, Salisbury	14	44,988
Alfred M. May, Marlborough	13	31,475
Daniel Trinder, Cirencester, Gloucestershire	9	31,961
Phillips and Westbury, Andover, Hampshire	7	17,461
Others [32]	65	181,372

Table 38.3. *The tithe maps of Wiltshire: scales and classes*

Scale in chains/inch	*All maps*		*First Class*		*Second Class*	
	Number	*Acreage*	*Number*	*Acreage*	*Number*	*Acreage*
>3	4	530	0	0	4	530
3	60	113,812	18	41,405	42	72,407
3.5	2	182	0	0	2	182
4	24	58,837	0	0	24	58,837
4.5	2	2,016	0	0	2	2,016
6	145	351,820	0	0	145	351,820
6.67, 7, 7.5	3	4,101	0	0	3	4,101
8	28	95,533	0	0	28	95,533
9	17	34,511	0	0	17	34,511
<9	10	36,532	0	0	10	36,532
TOTAL	295	697,874	18	41,405	277	656,469

Table 38.4. *The tithe maps of Wiltshire: dates*

	1837	*1838*	*1839*	*1840*	*1841*	*1842*	*1843*	*1844*	*1845*	*1846*	*1847*	*1848*	*1849*	*1850*	*>1850*
All maps	6	31	67	48	34	22	27	18	9	10	5	8	6	1	3
1st class	2	2	9	2	0	1	0	1	0	0	1	0	0	0	0
2nd class	4	29	58	46	34	21	27	17	9	10	4	8	6	1	3

Wiltshire

38/1 Aldbourn (parish) SU 244762 [Aldbourne]
Apt 26.09.1837; 8496a (8495); Map 1837, 12 chns, '... reduced from 3 Chains', in 2 parts, by T. Duke, Hodson, Marlborough (including 3-chn enlargement of village); foot/b'way, waterbodies, houses, woods (col, by Dawson's symbol), plantations (col), arable (col), grassland (col), heath/moor (col, by Dawson's symbol), building names, road names, field names, toll gate, village pond, cross. Dawson's symbols are used for woods and commons.

38/2 Alderbury (district) SU 190265
Apt 25.11.1847; 2175a (2175); Map 1849?, 4 chns; railway, foot/b'way, waterbodies, houses, woods, parkland, gardens, building names, ford, footbridges (by symbol); names within the district are in gothic writing.

38/3 Alderton (parish) ST 844826
Apt 07.08.1839; 1587a (all); Map 1840, 4 chns, by Little and Weaver, Chippenham, Wilts; waterbodies, houses, open fields.

38/4 Allcannings, Etchilhampton and Fullaway (township in parish of Allcannings) SU 074622 [All Cannings]
Apt 25.03.1839; 4326a (all); Map 1839, 10 chns, in 5 parts, by J.R. Bramble, Devizes, and George Oakley Lucas, Devizes, (Allcannings at 10 chns with village at 3 chns, unsigned, undated; Etchilhampton, 4 chns, unsigned; Fullaway, 3 chns, by Lucas; 10-chn index); construction lines, foot/b'way, waterbodies, houses, woods, plantations, orchards, hedge ownership, monument. Each part is drawn to a different specification.

38/5 Allington (township in parish of Allcannings) SU 081650
Apt 17.09.1839; 1157a (all); Map 1839?, 9 chns; houses.

38/6 Allington (parish) SU 206393
Apt 28.12.1839; 936a (all); Map 1840, 6 chns; houses; some arable and pasture is shown by annotation; colour bands may indicate ownerships or holdings.

38/7 Alton Barnes (parish) SU 109633
Apt 21.06.1839; 1054a (all); Map 1838, 3 chns, in 2 parts, by George Oakley Lucas, Devizes; construction lines, foot/b'way, canal with towpath, waterbodies, houses, woods, orchard.

38/8 Alvediston (parish) ST 974233
Apt 31.12.1842; 2532a (2531); Map 1844, 6 chns; waterbodies, woods; dot-dash boundaries indicate unfenced boundaries between owners, and pecked boundaries indicate divisions within an ownership.

38/9 Amesbury (parish) SU 152416
Apt 02.09.1843; 5891a (5890); Map 1846, 6 chns, by J. and R. Waters, Cranbury Place, Southampton; waterbodies, houses, woods (col), parkland; Stonehenge and the town centre are not mapped in detail.

38/10 Ashley (parish) ST 932945
Apt 17.07.1838; 947a (all); Map 1838, 6 chns; waterbodies, houses, farmyards, woods (col), plantations (col), arable (col), grassland (col), gardens (col).

38/11 West Ashton (tithing in parish of Steeple Ashton) ST 884558
Apt 27.10.1838; 2009a (2040); Map 1840, 6 chns, by Y. and I.P. Sturge; waterbodies, houses, woods, plantations, road names, turnpike; scale-bar is ruler-like.

38/12 Avebury (parish) SU 101704
Apt 22.02.1845; 1070a (4544); Map 1845?, 6 chns, (tithable parts only); waterbodies, houses.

38/13 Avon (parish) ST 954760
Apt 04.08.1842; 157a (156); Map 1842?, 4.5 chns, copied by Little and Weaver, Chippenham; waterbodies, houses.

38/14 Barford St Martin (parish) SU 052324
Apt 30.06.1840; 2237a (2236); Map 1840, 6 chns, by J. Poole, Land and Timber Surveyor, Sherborne, Dorset; houses. Apt is by holding and omits land use.

38/15 Baverstock (parish) SU 028329
Apt 22.05.1839; 1168a (all); Map 1840, 6 chns, by J. Poole, Landsurveyor etc, Sherborne, Dorset; houses; only holding boundaries are shown. Apt omits land use.

38/16 Baydon (district) SU 284777
Apt 15.09.1845; 44a (3060); Map 1848, 3 chns, by Aylwin and May, Marlborough and Newbury; foot/b'way, houses, woods.

38/17 Little Bedwin (parish) SU 295653 [Little Bedwyn]
Apt 24.02.1841; 1037a (4233); Map 1840, 6 chns; canal with towpath, houses, woods, plantations, field names, vicarage. Apt omits land use.

38/18 Great Bedwyn (parish) SU 266640
Apt 24.01.1850; 2608a (10420); Map 1846, 6 chns, by A.M. May, Marlborough (tithable parts only); canal with towpath and locks, waterbodies, woods, plantations, tithing boundaries (col); there is a note, 'The parts coloured show the Boundaries of the different Tithings'.

38/19 Beechingstoke (parish) SU 097589
Apt 25.04.1838; 880a (880); Map 1838, 3 chns, by Robert Davis Little, Chippenham; foot/b'way, houses, woods (col), plantations (col), osiers (by symbol), parkland (col), arable (col), grassland (col), orchards (col), gardens (col), hedge ownership, fence ownership, field gates, building names (in gothic); table gives land ownership and use.

38/20 Berwick Bassett (parish) SU 098735
Apt 01.12.1843; 1388a (1388); Map 1838, 3 chns, 1st cl, by J.R. Bramble, Devizes; construction lines, waterbodies, houses, woods, plantations, gardens, heath/moor, hedge ownership, fence ownership, field names, landowners, milestone, boundary stone, glebe; it is unclear why one group of buildings is coloured blue, unless it is a later addition; the map has a rather rough appearance, suggesting a draft rather than a fair plan.

38/21 Berwick St James (parish) SU 066397
Apt 02.05.1843; 2487a (2487); Map 1843?, 6 chns, in 2 parts; foot/b'way, houses; pictorial church.

38/22 Berwick St John (parish) ST 958215
Apt 30.06.1840; 3669a (3669); Map 1840?, 9 chns, in 5 parts, (including four 3-chn enlargements of detail); houses, woods.

38/23 Slaughterford and Biddlestone St Nicholas (parish) ST 856734
Apt 18.10.1839; 2291a (2291); Map 1839?, 6 chns, in 2 parts; waterbodies, houses; farm named.

38/24 Biddestone St. Peter (parish) ST 866734 [Not listed]
Apt 31.05.1839; 127a (all); Map 1849?, 4 chns, (probably tithable parts only); waterbodies.

38/25 Bishops Cannings, Horton, Bourton and Easton (district in parish of Bishops Cannings) SU 048654
Apt 22.12.1848; 7495a (?); Map 1841, 3 chns, by J.R. Bramble; canal with towpath and swing bridges, waterbodies, houses, woods (col), gardens, road names, Wansdyke, milestones (by symbol), tumuli, township/tithing boundaries (col).

38/26 Bishopstone (parish) SU 252826
Apt 10.09.1838; 4452a (4452); Map 1839, 8 chns, by J. Poole, Sherborne; waterbodies, houses. Apt is by holding and omits land use.

38/27 Bishopstrow (parish) ST 908452
Apt 28.03.1839; 1046a (1045); Map 1839, 7.5 chns, in 3 parts; houses, woods, plantations.

38/28 Blackland (parish) SU 016685
Apt 16.06.1845; 538a (537); Map 1845, 6 chns, by R.D. Little, Chippenham; waterbodies, houses, woods (col), plantations (col), arable (col), grassland (col), orchards, osiers (col).

38/29 Blagden (extra-parochial place) SU 293562 [Not listed]
Apt 06.05.1848; 88a (all); Map 1849?, 3 chns, by Aylwin and May, Marlborough and Newbury; foot/b'way, woods (col).

38/30 Blunsden Saint Andrew (parish) SU 135897 [Blunsdon St Andrew]
Apt 10.01.1838; 1422a (all); Map 1837, 3 chns, 1st cl, by William Bryan Wood, Barnbridge, Chippenham; construction lines, foot/b'way,

waterbodies, houses, woods, plantations, coppice (by symbol), field gates, stiles; 'battlement' effect may indicate walls.

38/31 Boscombe (parish) SU 209381
Apt 12.09.1840; 1693a (1692); Map 1839, 6 chns, in 2 parts, by R.C. Gale, Winchester, (including 3-chn enlargement of common fields); waterbodies, houses, woods (col), Roman road, notable trees and bush, barrow, windmill (pictorial).

38/32 Bower Chalke (parish) SU 011222 [Bowerchalke]
Apt 31.12.1842; 2967a (2966); Map 1843?, 8 chns, by J. Poole, Sherborne, Dorset; houses. Apt is partly by holding and omits land use.

38/33 Bowood (liberty) ST 967698 [Not listed]
Apt 31.12.1845; 969a (969); Map 1847, 4 chns, by R.D. Little, Chippenham, Wilts; waterbodies, houses, woods; writing within the district is in gothic.

38/34 Box (parish) ST 828684
Apt 10.12.1838; 4218a (4217); Map 1839, 3 chns, 1st cl, in 2 parts, by Cotterells and Cooper, Bath; railway with tunnel shafts, water-bodies, houses, building names, quarries, mills, green, diverted road. Underlining of map title has a miniature (1.02 cm. diameter) world map worked in.

38/35 Boyton (parish) ST 932380
Apt 17.05.1839; 3956a (all); Map 1839, 6 chns, in 2 parts; foot/b'way, waterbodies, houses, woods, plantations, parkland, orchards, open fields, linches (hatched), glebe (col); bridge named in gothic writing.

38/36 Bradford (parish) ST 827616 [Bradford-on-Avon]
Apt 05.06.1840; 11311a (11310); Map 1841, 8 chns, in 14 parts, by G.C. Ashmead, Bristol, (including 13 4-chn enlargements of town and 'Common Meads'); canal with towpath and aqueducts, woods, plantations, orchards, open fields, building names; colours indicate tithable status.

38/37 North Bradley (parish) ST 839550
Apt 12.11.1841; 4036a (4036); Map 1843, 3 chns, in 2 parts, by Cruse and Fox, Warminster; foot/b'way, waterbodies, houses, open fields, road names, pound, tithing boundaries; bridges named.

38/38 Bradon (township in parish of Purton) SU 057884 [Not listed]
Apt 16.06.1838; 1478a (all); Map 1839, [?8 chns], 'Copied from an Old Map', by R.D. Little, Chippenham; railway, foot/b'way, houses.

38/39 Braydon and Great and Little Chelworth (hamlet and tithings in parish of Cricklade Saint Sampson) SU 084922 [Chelworth Lower and Upper Greens]
Apt 12.11.1841; 5257a (?); Map 1842, 10 chns, in 3 parts, ? by Daniel Trinder (including enlargement of town); railway, canal with towpath, waterbodies, woods, field boundary ownerships, houses (town only).

38/40 Bremhill (parish) ST 982755
Apt 05.05.1848; 285a (5920); Map 1848, 10 chns, by R.D. Little, Chippenham, Wilts (tithable parts only); canal with towpath, houses, building names (in gothic), mill.

38/41 Bremilham (parish) ST 904859 [Not listed]
Apt 23.11.1838; 433a (433); Map 1839, 6 chns, in 5 parts; waterbodies, woods (col), arable (col), grassland (col), orchards (col), gardens (col), field boundary ownerships.

38/42 Brinkworth (parish) SU 020853
Apt 12.10.1840; 5465a (5464); Map 1842?, 10 chns; railway, canal, tithe-free land (col); map is described as 'of Brinkworth and Grittenham'.

38/43 Britford (parish) SU 146279
Apt 12.01.1839; 3149a (3148); Map 1839?, 3 chns, in 2 parts; foot/b'way, waterbodies, houses, hedge ownership, footbridges, workhouse, water meadow channels (in detail).

38/44 Brixton Deverill (parish) ST 866383
Apt 28.09.1838; 2450a (all); Map 1839, 9 chns; houses, woods, glebe (col).

38/45 Broad Chalke (parish) SU 042250
Apt 31.12.1842; 6905a (6904); Map 1843, 8 chns, by J. Poole, Sherborne, Dorset; houses. Apt is by holding and omits land use.

38/46 Broadhinton, Broadtown, Bynoll and Sandfurlong (district in parish of Broadhinton) SU 108773 [Broad Hinton]
Apt 21.04.1845; 3659a (3659); Map 1846, 6 chns; waterbodies, woods, plantations, building names.

38/47 Bromham (parish) ST 974650
Apt 04.05.1843; 3594a (3593); Map 1845?, 6 chns; foot/b'way, waterbodies, woods, plantations.

38/48 Broughton Gifford (parish) ST 881638
Apt 14.12.1840; 1678a (1677); Map 1841, 6 chns, in 2 parts, (including 3-chn enlargement of field); waterbodies, houses, boundary stones, commons; houses are black, other buildings grey; enlargement of field has chain distances to fix its pecked boundaries; map is described as 'Plan furnished by the Landowners and adopted for the purposes of the Tithe Commutation'.

38/49 Bulford (parish) SU 188442
Apt 27.04.1838; 1714a (3475); Map 1838, [8 chns], (tithable parts only); hill-drawing, waterbodies, houses, plantations, sheep pond; hill named.

38/50 Bulkington (tithing in parish of Keevil) ST 947585
Apt 07.08.1839; 973a (973); Map 1839, 4 chns; waterbodies, houses, orchards, gardens, road names, field names, milestone (by symbol), cross; farm, bridges and two brooks named.

38/51 Burbage (parish) SU 230609
Apt 20.10.1840; 3283a (3283); Map 1843, 6 chns, by A.M. May, Marlborough; canal with towpath, waterbodies, woods (col, named), plantations (col).

38/52 Burcombe (parish) SU 071308
Apt 08.05.1846; 1451a (1450); Map 1847, 6 chns, by J. Poole, Sherborne; foot/b'way, houses, pit.

38/53 Buttermere (parish) SU 344608
Apt 01.11.1839; 1502a (all); Map 1842?, 6 chns; foot/b'way, waterbodies, houses.

38/54 Calne (parish) SU 001705
Apt 11.06.1842; 8079a (8079); Map 8 chns, surveyed in 1827-8 by Thomas Cruse, 'Corrected, Reduced and Published' 1843 by Little and Weaver, Chippenham, litho (by J. Hollway, Bath); waterbodies, houses, woods, plantations, orchards, open fields, building names (in gothic), strip-lynchets (col); buildings, water and lynchets are hand-coloured; built-up part is generalised.

38/55 Calstone Wellington (parish) SU 024676 [Not listed]
Apt 18.11.1844; 309a (all); Map 6 chns, in 5 parts, surveyed by Thomas Cruse in 1830, and 'Corrected and Copied' 1844, by Little and Weaver, Chippenham (with 16-chn scale 'Road or Index Map', 1845); waterbodies, houses, farmyards (col), woods (col), plantations (col), arable (col), grassland (col), orchards (col), gardens (col), hedge ownership, fence ownership.

38/56 Castle Combe (parish) ST 845772
Apt 16.02.1841; 1494a (1494); Map 1841, 6 chns, in 2 parts 'Copied from an Old Map and partly remeasured', by Little and Weaver, Chippenham, (including village at 3-chns); houses.

38/57 Castle Eaton (parish) SU 156947
Apt 01.11.1839; 1957a (all); Map 1840, 6 chns, ? by Daniel Trinder; foot/b'way, waterbodies, houses, arable (col), grassland (col); colour bands show both land use and field boundary ownership.

38/58 Great Chalfield (parish) ST 860635
Apt 30.12.1837; 700a (all); Map 1838, 3 chns, by R.D. Little, Chippenham; foot/b'way, waterbodies, houses, farmyards (col), woods (col), plantations (col), arable (col), grassland (col), orchards (col), gardens (col), hedge ownership, fence ownership, field gates, building names (gothic), stiles; 'battlement' effect may indicate walls.

38/59 Charlton (parish) SU 095535
Apt 27.07.1840; 1706a (1706); Map 1841, 6 chns; houses.

38/60 Charlton, Brokenborough and Westport St Mary (parish) ST 940899
Apt 08.01.1840; 9369a (9368); Map 1840, 10 chns, by Daniel Trinder; waterbodies, woods (col), arable (col), grassland (col), field boundary

ownerships, common; built-up part is generalised; colour bands show both land use and field boundary ownership.

38/61 Cherhill (parish) SU 044702
Apt 28.03.1844; 1818a (1817); Map 1843, 6 chns; waterbodies, houses, woods, plantations, osiers.

38/62 Cheriton and Conoch (parish and chapelry) SU 071554
Apt 28.03.1844; 1859a (1858); Map 1845?, 4.5 chns; foot/b'way, waterbodies, houses, woods, gravel pit, quarry, chapelry boundary.

38/63 Chicklade (parish) ST 910347
Apt 09.03.1838; 1039a (all); Map 1838, 6.67 chns; houses, woods, coppice (by Dawson's symbol).

38/64 Chilmark (parish) ST 966332
Apt 03.01.1840; 3155a (3154); Map 1839, 6 chns, in 2 parts, by J. Poole, Sherborne, Dorset (included detached part at 8 chns); houses, turnpike gate, coppices (named), downs, ox drove.

38/65 Chippenham (district) ST 900730
Apt 02.08.1847; 4412a (?); Map 1848, 6 chns, in 5 parts, by R.D. Little, Chippenham, Wilts (including four 3-chn enlargements of meadows); railway with station, canal with towpath, waterbodies, houses, building names, (in gothic), common; built-up part generalised.

38/66 Chiseldon (parish) SU 186798
Apt 26.12.1843; 1023a (4750); Map 1844, 3 chns, in 3 parts, by T. Dyke, (tithable parts only, one at 4 chns); waterbodies, feeder, reservoir, road names; buildings shown in outline only, without fill; garden shown by annotation.

38/67 East Chisenbury (parish) SU 156533
Apt 25.05.1844; 1363a (?); Map 1856?, 6 chns; houses, woods, open fields, gorse (col).

38/68 Chitterne All Saints (parish) ST 993456 [Chitterne]
Apt 05.03.1840; 353a (4476); Map 1843, 9 chns, by H.G. Buxton, (tithable parts only); road names, landowners. Apt is by holding.

38/69 Chitterne All Saints (parish) ST 993456 [Chitterne]
Corn rent conversion, 1882; 2560a (4476); Map 1882?, 9 chns, in 2 parts (village at 3 chns); school.

38/70 Chitterne St Mary (parish) ST 986438 [Not listed]
Apt 22.10.1841; 1199a (1198); Map 1842, 9 chns; houses, barrow.

38/71 Chittoe (township in parish of Bishops Cannings) ST 957673
Apt 14.09.1848; 8a (1100); Map 1849?, 12 chns, (tithable parts only, tinted); waterbodies, woods, parkland, building names; map also includes tithe-free land; scale-bar is ruler-like.

38/72 Chelderton (parish) SU 221428 [Cholderton]
Apt 11.03.1840; 1662a (all); Map 1841, 6 chns, by Phillips and Westbury, Andover; waterbodies, houses, farmyards (col), woods (col), plantations (col), arable (col), grassland (col), gardens (col), pits (col); farmyards and gardens are both yellow; darker green indicates 'Down'.

38/73 Christian Malford (parish) ST 976798
Apt 05.04.1838; 3105a (3104); Map 1840, 4 chns, 'Copied from Private Maps, Corrected, and in part measured' by Little and Weaver, Chippenham; railway, canal with towpath, houses, turnpike gate, mills, factory, school, chapel, rectory.

38/74 Chute (parish) SU 302542 [Chute Standen]
Apt 12.10.1840; 3181a (3181); Map 1841, 6 chns, by Phillips and Westbury, Andover; foot/b'way, houses, woods, plantations, parkland, building names, road names, cross, windmill (pictorial), parsonage, boundary wells; some hills and downs named.

38/75 East and West Walks of the Forests of Chute and Wakeswood (extra-parochial place) (partly in Hants) SU 311517 [Not listed]
Apt 07.08.1839; 1937a (all); Map 1839, 3 chns, by George Oakley Lucas, Devizes; foot/b'way, waterbodies, houses, woods, hedge ownership, fence ownership.

38/76 Clarendon (liberty) SU 187302 [Not listed]
Apt 18.06.1847; 3278a (all); Map 1849, 9 chns, (tinted); railway, woods (col), landowners; apportionment is by holding, and the map only shows farm boundaries, with acreages and occupiers; this information is duplicated in a table.

38/77 Clatford (tithing in parish of Preshute) SU 156690
Apt 28.11.1840; 982a (?); Map 1840?, 8 chns; houses, woods.

38/78 Cliffe Pypard (parish) SU 075775 [Not listed]
Apt 08.02.1840; 3985a (3985); Map 1843?, 6 chns, by Little and Weaver, Chippenham, Wilts; foot/b'way, waterbodies, houses, building names.

38/79 Coate (parish) SU 036614
Apt 26.06.1848; 1399a (?); Map 1841, 3 chns; canal with towpath, waterbodies, houses.

38/80 Codford St Mary (parish) ST 986406
Apt 08.05.1839; 2124a (all); Map 1839, 6 chns; houses, woods, plantations, osiers (by symbol), orchards, open fields (col, named); hatched strips are downland for which the rent charge 'is apportioned upon those estates that have rights thereon'.

38/81 Codford St Peter (parish) ST 967415
Apt 17.05.1839; 1612a (1611); Map 1840?, [6 chns]; foot/b'way, waterbodies, houses, woods, osiers (by symbol), water meadow channels.

38/82 Colerne (parish) ST 821722
Corn rent conversion, 1875; 3932a (3620); Map 1873, 3 chns, by A.M. May, Marlborough; waterbodies, houses, woods (col, named), plantations, parkland, field gates, building names, chapels, schools, mill, stiles; the style is exactly the same as May was using 30-35 years earlier.

38/83 Collingbourn Ducis (parish) SU 245527 [Collingbourne Ducis]
Apt 19.12.1845; 3382a (all); Map 1844, 6 chns, 'Copied from a plan made by W. Stanley in 1843', by A.M. May, Marlborough; foot/b'way, waterbodies, woods (col), plantations (col); north pointer has Prince of Wales feathers and 'Ich Dien' motto.

38/84 Collingborn Kingston (parish) SU 240559 [Collingbourne Kingston]
Apt 25.09.1843; 7293a (7293); Map 1843, 6 chns, by A.M. May, Marlborough; waterbodies, woods (col), plantations (col), camp, notable pond, windmill, tithing boundaries (col), churchyard (col); dot-dash lines separate lands in the same occupancy; pecked lines separate occupancies; compass star has 'Ich Dien' and Prince of Wales' feathers.

38/85 Comb (tithing in parish of Enford) SU 168516 [Not listed]
Apt 09.02.1843; 181a (?); Map 1843, 3.5 chns, in 2 parts; sheep drove. (There are two identical copies of the map in PRO IR 30.)

38/86 Compton Bassett (parish) SU 038726
Apt 27.10.1838; 2633a (2632); Map 1839, 6 chns, in 2 parts, by Phillips and Westbury, Andover; waterbodies, houses, woods, osiers, parkland, fence ownership, field gates, building names, avenue of trees, pit; colours show tithe ownerships; part 2 has field names and land use annotations.

38/87 Compton Chamberlain (parish) SU 029296 [Compton Chamberlayne]
Apt 08.05.1848; 1872a (all); Map 1848, 6 chns; foot/b'way, waterbodies, fences, field gates, building names, mill, mill hatches, chalk pits, water meadow channels.

38/88 Coombe Bissett (parish) SU 107250
Apt 24.12.1839; 2197a (2196); Map 1840?, 4 chns, by F.J. Kelsey, Salisbury; waterbodies, houses, strip lynchets, Grim's Ditch; scale is stated to be 4 chns, but measuring the scale-bar gives 6 chns, and comparison with Ordnance Survey 6-inch suggests 4 chns is correct.

38/89 Corsham (parish) ST 873702
Apt 20.07.1837; 6499a (6498); Map 1838?, 4 chns, in 4 parts, by F.J. Kelsey, Salisbury; railway, foot/b'way, waterbodies, houses, hedge

ownership, fence ownership, field gates, building names, flights of steps, stiles; lilac tint may indicate lands liable to vicarial tithe only.

38/90 Corsley (parish) ST 828463
Apt 26.11.1841; 22a (2580); Map 1842, 8 chns, 'Extracted from the Map annexed to the Warminster and Corsley Inclosure Award', (tithable parts only); houses.

38/91 Coulston (parish) ST 950530
Apt 21.01.1840; 868a (868); Map 1841, 6 chns; hill-drawing, waterbodies, houses, woods, plantations, road cuttings.

38/92 Cricklade St Mary (parish) SU 101938 [Cricklade]
Apt 21.08.1839; 121a (121); Map 1840, 2 chns; waterbodies, houses, foundry.

38/93 Crudwell, or Crudwell cum Eastcourt or Eastcot (parish) ST 959934
Apt 19.06.1840; 4785a (4780); Map 1841, 6 chns, by Daniel Trinder; waterbodies, houses, arable, grassland, field boundary ownerships, building names; colour bands are used to show land use and field boundary ownership; woodland is treated as grass.

38/94 Damerham South (district) SU 096165 [Damerham]
Apt 31.08.1846; 4564a (all); Map 1841, 8 chns, by Harry Holloway, Ringwood, Hants; foot/b'way, waterbodies, houses, woods (col), heath/moor, furze, building names, road names, mill, boundary stone, toll bar, chalk pit, gravel pit, notable pond, brick kiln, chalk pit (by symbol).

38/95 Dauntsey (parish) ST 997821
Apt 05.11.1846; 1931a (3301); Map 1847, 12 chns; canal; map only shows roads, rivers (named), church and holdings (named), with tithable areas coloured. District is apportioned by holding and fields are not shown.

38/96 West Dean (parish) SU 252283
Apt 21.09.1843; 3452a (3452); Map 1844?, 8 chns; canal, houses; a few outlying buildings are uncoloured.

38/97 St John the Baptist, Devizes (parish) ST 994609 [Not listed]
Apt 31.07.1839; 640a (639); Map 1839, 3 chns, 1st cl, by George Oakley Lucas, Devizes; construction lines, foot/b'way, canal and locks, waterbodies, houses, woods, plantations, orchards, hedge ownership, fence ownership, road names, prison, old bridewell, brewery, market place, town ditch, butchers' shambles; some built-up parts generalised.

38/98 Dinton and Teffont Magna (parish and chapelry) SU 005330
Apt 28.04.1840; 4087a (all); Map 1840, 6 chns, by J. Poole, Sherborne, Dorset; waterbodies, houses. Apt omits land use.

38/99 Ditcheridge or Ditteridge (parish) ST 818698 [Ditteridge]
Apt 02.10.1838; 374a (374); Map 1839, 3 chns, 1st cl, by Cotterells and Cooper, Bath; railway, waterbodies, houses, mill.

38/100 Donhead St Andrew (parish) ST 924246
Apt 22.02.1839; 3541a (3540); Map 1840, 6 chns, in 2 parts, by S. Stephens, Southampton; waterbodies, houses, farmyards (col), woods (col), arable (col), grassland (col), orchards (col), gardens (col); the same colour is used for farmyards and gardens; churchyard is shown by a curious grouping of squares.

38/101 Donhead St Mary (parish) ST 902227
Apt 30.07.1840; 5247a (5247); Map 1841?, 8 chns, in 2 parts; waterbodies, houses, woods, parkland, open fields; pictorial church.

38/102 Downton (parish) SU 189218
Apt 09.03.1838; 13221a (all); Map 1839?, 4 chns, in 4 parts, by F.J. Kelsey, Salisbury (including 10-chn index); foot/b'way, waterbodies, houses, building names, Grims Ditch, right of way, water meadow channels, tithing boundaries (col); the plan of Nunton and Bodenham has a 6-chn scale-bar, and a 3-chn scale statement; comparison with Ordnance Survey 6-inch shows it to be 4-chn.

38/103 Draycot Cerne (parish) ST 933788
Apt 13.04.1839; 1066a (1066); Map 1839, 6 chns, 'Copied from an old Plan' by R.D. Little, Chippenham; waterbodies, houses.

38/104 Draycott Foliatt (parish) SU 178777 [Draycot Foliat]
Apt 09.04.1839; 703a (all); Map 1838, 3 chns, by T. Dyke, Hodson; foot/b'way, waterbodies, houses, farmyards (col), woods (col), plantations (col), arable (col), grassland (col), orchards (col), gardens (col), hedge ownership, water ownerships, well (by symbol), Roman road; there is an 'Explanation' of symbols and colours and also of the letters showing water ownership in the village.

38/105 Durnford (parish) SU 141369 [Not listed]
Apt 13.02.1840; 2622a (3423); Map 1842?, 6 chns, in 2 parts, (tithable parts only); foot/b'way, woods, tumuli, tithing boundaries (col).

38/106 Durrington (parish) SU 136442
Apt 11.06.1839; 2683a (all); Map 1839, 6 chns, 'Copied from the Award Map' by R.C. Gale, Winchester; houses, woods (col), plantations (col); map is dated '1859', but this appears to be an error for '1839'.

38/107 Easterton (tithing or hamlet in parish of Market Lavington) SU 038532
Apt 22.11.1839; 1596a (1596); Map 1839?, 9 chns; waterbodies, houses.

38/108 Easton Grey (parish) ST 881875
Apt 27.11.1838; 1046a (all); Map 1838, 6 chns, by Richard Hall, Cirencester; foot/b'way, waterbodies, houses, woods, plantations, osiers (by symbol), parkland, arable (col), grassland (col), gardens.

38/109 Ebbesborne Wake (parish) ST 991228 [Ebbesbourne Wake]
Apt 20.05.1843; 2762a (2762); Map 1843, 8 chns, by J. Poole, Sherborne, Dorset; houses. Apt omits land use.

38/110 Edington (parish) ST 937525
Apt 23.06.1842; 5705a (all); Map 1843, 6 chns; waterbodies, houses, woods, plantations, open fields, building names, road names, factory, mills, springs, long barrows, soot house, avenue of trees, lime quarry, tithing boundaries. (col), common, down; several 'bottoms' and 'hollows' are named.

38/111 Eisey with Water Eaton (parish) SU 132945 [Not listed]
Apt 31.08.1848; 879a (1840); Map 1849, 6 chns; foot/b'way, canal with towpath, waterbodies, houses, woods, plantations, arable (col), grassland (col), field boundary ownerships, ox-bow lakes; colour bands indicate both land use and field boundary ownership.

38/112 Elcombe, Westlecot, Salthorp and Overtown (district in parish of Wroughton or Ellingdon) SU 117816
Apt 19.10.1843; 3560a (?); Map 1846, 8 chns, by Henry Weaver, Southampton; railway, foot/b'way, turnpike roads, canal with towpath, waterbodies, houses, building names, landowners.

38/113 Enford and Fifield (tithing in parish of Enford) SU 118510
Apt 17.12.1847; 558a (?); Map 1848, 10 chns; tithe-merged land.

38/114 Everleigh (parish) SU 196546
Apt 21.08.1841; 3276a (all); Map 1842, 8 chns; foot/b'way, waterbodies, houses, woods, plantations, windmill, barrow; two different shades of sienna road fill are used. Apt omits most land use.

38/115 Fifield Brabant (parish) SU 009250 [Fifield Bavant]
Apt 18.10.1843; 1146a (1145); Map 1843, 8 chns, by Cruse and Fox; houses.

38/116 Figheldean (parish) SU 165474
Apt 30.07.1839; 5279a (5279); Map 1840?, 6 chns; foot/b'way, houses, woods, open fields.

38/117 Fisherton Anger (parish) SU 136304 [Not shown]
Apt 21.09.1842; 324a (all); Map 1843, 3 chns, in 2 parts, (including built-up part separately at 1 chn); houses, landowners, mill, county gaol, infirmary, inn gardens.

38/118 Fisherton-delamere (parish) SU 001389 [Fisherton de la Mere]
Apt 27.04.1838; 2861a (2861); Map 1838, 6 chns; foot/b'way, waterbodies, houses, plantations, parkland, orchards, heath/moor, linches (hatched), osiers (by symbol), tithing boundaries (col).

38/119 Fittleton (parish) SU 185506
Apt 22.09.1838; 3175a (3185); Map 1839, 9 chns, by William Bryan Wood, Barnbridge, Wilts; foot/b'way, waterbodies, houses, farmyards (col), woods (col), plantations (col), osiers (by symbol), arable (col), grassland (col), orchards (col), gardens (col), hedge ownership, field boundary ownerships; colour bands show both field boundary ownership and land use.

38/120 Fonthill Bishop (parish) ST 942342
Apt 07.03.1838; 1735a (all); Map 1838, 6 chns; houses, woods, plantations, weir.

38/121 Fonthill Gifford (parish) ST 920315
Apt 14.09.1840; 1962a (all); Map 1840?, 6 chns; waterbodies, houses, woods, road tunnel.

38/122 Fovant (parish) SU 005288
Apt 22.05.1839; 2161a (all); Map 1840, 6 chns; houses, woods, pit or quarry, limekilns (by symbol).

38/123 Foxley (parish) ST 891859
Apt 06.03.1841; 751a (all); Map 1844, 8 chns, by John Pyne; foot/b'way, waterbodies, houses, woods (col), arable (col), grassland (col), orchards (col), hedge ownership (col), fence ownership, field gates, Foss Way.

38/124 Froxfield (parish) SU 290688
Apt 25.03.1845; 2214a (2214); Map 1846, 6 chns, by William Bryan Wood, Barnbridge, Chippenham; foot/b'way, canal with towpath, waterbodies, houses, woods, orchards.

38/125 Fugglestone St Peter (parish) SU 117317
Apt 06.06.1840; 1684a (1684); Map 1840, 6 chns, by J. Poole, Sherborne, Dorset; houses. Apt is by holding and omits land use.

38/126 Garsdon (parish) ST 974878
Apt 13.04.1839; 1136a (1136); Map 1839?, 6 chns, by F.J. Kelsey, Salisbury; waterbodies, houses.

38/127 East Grimstead (parish) SU 228272
Apt 12.09.1843; 930a (930); Map 1845, 6 chns; railway, foot/b'way, canal, old canal, waterbodies, houses, woods.

38/128 West Grimstead (parish) SU 212270
Apt 03.10.1837; 1483a (1483); Map 1837?, 4 chns, by F.J. Kelsey, Salisbury; foot/b'way, waterbodies, houses, woods (named), gardens, building names.

38/129 Grittleton (parish) ST 862802
Apt 30.07.1838; 2041a (all); Map 1840, 3 chns, by Little and Weaver, Chippenham; foot/b'way, waterbodies, houses.

38/130 Ham (parish) SU 333626
Apt 18.05.1838; 1606a (all); Map 1839, 6 chns; foot/b'way, private road, waterbodies, woods, hedge ownership, glebe; colour bands show holdings; the width of a bridleway is given.

38/131 Hankerton (parish) ST 977907
Apt 25.02.1841; 2151a (2150); Map 1840, 6 chns, by Daniel Trinder; waterbodies, houses, woods, plantations, arable (col), grassland (col), field boundary ownerships; colour bands show field boundary ownership and arable and grass.

38/132 Hannington (parish) SU 177937
Apt 20.08.1839; 173a (2412); Map 1839, 3 chns, in 2 parts, (tithable parts only); grassland (col).

38/133 Hardenhuish (parish) ST 910748
Apt 05.04.1838; 478a (477); Map 1839, 3 chns, in 3 parts, by R.D. Little, Chippenham; waterbodies, houses, open fields, hedge ownership, fence ownership, field gates.

38/134 West Harnham (parish) SU 124290 [Harnham]
Apt 23.05.1843; 19a (1130); Map 1844?, 6 chns; houses, paper mill, mills.

38/135 Heddington (parish) SU 003663 [Not listed]
Apt 26.05.1841; 1686a (1686); Map 1841, 8 chns, by William Bryan Wood, Barnbridge, Chippenham; waterbodies, houses, woods, arable (col), grassland (col), field boundary ownerships.

38/136 Highway (parish) SU 050741
Apt 30.10.1839; 814a (all); Map 1840, 4 chns, by J. Marmont, Bristol; waterbodies, houses, woods, orchards, open fields.

38/137 Highworth (parish) SU 205921
Apt 19.12.1838; 5017a (10000); Map 1840, [6 chns], in 2 parts, (tithable parts only); railway, foot/b'way, waterbodies, houses, woods, arable, grassland, field boundary ownerships, landowners; field boundary ownership and arable and grass are shown by colour bands.

38/138 Hill Deverill (parish) ST 862400
Apt 07.07.1848; 1846a (all); Map 1848, 6 chns; waterbodies, houses, woods, plantations, reeds or osiers, pit or quarry.

38/139 Hillmarton (parish) SU 032761 [Not listed]
Apt 12.09.1842; 4182a (4182); Map 1841, 6 chns, by Little and Weaver, Chippenham, Wilts; foot/b'way, waterbodies, houses, building names.

38/140 Hilperton (parish) ST 874596
Apt 30.12.1837; 1079a (all); Map 1838, 4 chns; canal with towpath and draw or swing bridges, waterbodies, houses, orchards; river and canal are named in gothic.

38/141 Hindon (parish) ST 908331
Apt 07.04.1843; 213a (212); Map 1844?, 2 chns; waterbodies, houses.

38/142 Hinton (tithing in parish of Steeple Ashton) ST 902590 [Not listed]
Apt 06.01.1842; 704a (all); Map 1842, 3 chns, 1st cl, in 3 parts, by H.G. Buxton, Devizes; construction lines, waterbodies, parsonage, houses, woods, plantations, orchards, foot/b'way, road names, toll gate, road and path ownerships and widths.

38/143 Hinton, or Little Hiniton (parish) SU 230830 [Not listed]
Apt 22.07.1840; 1816a (1815); Map 1839, 6 chns, by R.C. Gale, Winchester; foot/b'way, waterbodies, houses, woods (col), orchards, park gate.

38/144 Hippenscombe (extra-parochial place) SU 307562
Apt 06.05.1848; 829a (all); Map 1848, 3 chns, by Washbourne and Keen, 8 Cannon Row, Westminster; waterbodies, houses.

38/145 Homington (parish) SU 128249
Apt 30.11.1843; 78a (1340); Map 1846?, 8 chns, (tithable parts only); pound.

38/146 Horningsham (parish) ST 815419
Apt 20.09.1845; 2541a (2541); Map 1844, 9 chns, by Cruse and Fox; waterbodies, houses, deer park.

38/147 Huish (parish) SU 149642
Apt 21.01.1840; 754a (all); Map 1841, 6 chns; foot/b'way, waterbodies, woods.

38/148 Hullavington (parish) ST 891824
Apt 25.02.1841; 3121a (3121); Map 1842?, 6 chns, by John Darley, Chippenham; waterbodies, houses, open fields. Tithe-free areas are numbered in Apt but all other details are omitted.

38/149 Idmiston (parish) SU 196367
Apt 30.12.1841; 5521a (5520); Map 1844?, 6 chns, in 4 parts, (including index); houses, open fields, stone pit; base-line is related to Salisbury Cathedral spire.

38/150 Imber (parish) ST 966483
Apt 31.05.1838; 3034a (3033); Map 1838, 6 chns; foot/b'way, waterbodies, houses, woods, plantations, building names (in gothic), hut, windmill (pictorial).

38/151 Inglesham (parish) (partly in Berks) SU 204969
Apt 14.09.1841; 927a (927); Map 1842, 3 chns; waterbodies, farmyards (col), woods, osiers, arable (col), grassland (col), orchards (col); arable, grass and field boundary ownership are shown by colour bands.

38/152 Saint James (parochial chapelry in parish of Bishops Cannings) SU 014619 [Not listed]
Apt 22.12.1848; 2138a (2648); Map 1841, 3 chns, in 2 parts; foot/b'way, canal with towpath, waterbodies, houses, building names, workhouse, park (by annotation), green, borough boundary (col); larger ponds named.

38/153 Keevil (manor) ST 925583
Corn rent conversion, 1864; 2049a (2883); Map 1863, 3 chns; foot/b'way, waterbodies, houses, woods, parkland, road names, manor house, mill, toll gate; bridges named.

38/154 Kelloweys or Calloes (parish) ST 950757 [Not shown]
Apt 31.05.1839; 140a (all); Map 1839, [3 chns], 1st cl, by William Bryan Wood, Barnbridge, Chippenham; construction lines, foot/b'way, waterbodies, houses, hedge ownership, stiles.

38/155 East Kennett or East Kynett (parish) SU 118665
Apt 27.04.1838; 198a (808); Map 1838, 3 chns, (tithable parts only); houses, woods, arable (by symbol), grassland (by symbol), gardens, hedge ownership, field boundary ownerships, landowners.

38/156 Kington St Michael (parish) ST 905775
Apt 14.02.1842; 4136a (4136); Map 1842, 6 chns, in 2 parts, by Little and Weaver, Chippenham, litho (by Hollway, Bath; roads hand-coloured); waterbodies, houses (cross-hatched), woods, orchards, building names, parsonage.

38/157 West Kington (parish) ST 800774
Apt 18.01.1840; 2444a (all); Map 1839, 3 chns, 1st cl, by T. Weaver, Bath; construction lines, waterbodies, houses, Roman road, ford; scale-bar and compass rose are combined, and scale statement is on a banner.

38/158 East Knoyle (parish) ST 884317
Apt 08.12.1838; 5558a (5558); Map 1839, 6 chns; waterbodies, houses, woods, osiers (by symbol), plantations, heath/moor, pit or quarry, lynchets (hatched).

38/159 West Knoyle (parish) ST 854326
Apt 14.08.1839; 1914a (all); Map 1841?, 8 chns; hill-drawing, waterbodies, woods, glebe.

38/160 Lacock (parish) ST 915690
Apt 26.09.1837; 3640a (3639); Map 1838, 3 chns, 'Copied from Old Plans and in part re-measured' by R.D. Little, Chippenham; canal with towpath, waterbodies, houses, woods, building names, road names, mill, vicarage, conduit house, lodges, green, common; bridges named.

38/161 Lake (tithing in parish of Wilsford) SU 121391
Apt 07.07.1847; 791a (?); Map 1847?, 3 chns, 1st cl; construct-ion lines, houses, woods, osiers (by symbol).

38/162 Landford (parish) SU 264198
Apt 16.04.1839; 1690a (all); Map 1839, 6 chns, by F.J. Kelsey, Salisbury; foot/b'way, waterbodies, houses.

38/163 Langdon Wyke or Wykedown and Temple Ruckley (tithing in parish of Preshute) SU 136726 [Not listed]
Apt 03.06.1846; 415a (?); Map 1846, 6 chns, by A.M. May, Marlborough (tinted); waterbodies, houses, plantations, field gates.

38/164 Little Langford (parish) SU 042359
Apt 30.04.1838; 1011a (all); Map 1839, 6 chns; waterbodies, houses, woods.

38/165 Langley Burrell (parish) ST 935756
Apt 31.10.1840; 1726a (1725); Map 1840, 6 chns, in 4 parts, by Little and Weaver, Chippenham, Wilts; railway, waterbodies, houses, toll gate.

38/166 Laverstock (parish) SU 169322
Apt 31.08.1841; 1675a (all); Map 1842?, 6 chns, in 2 parts, (including 1.5 chn enlargement of group of cottages); houses, field names, toll gate.

38/167 East Lavington (tithing in parish of Market Lavington) SU 026529 [Not listed]
Apt 21.01.1840; 3126a (all); Map 1840?, 4 chns, in 3 parts, by F.J. Kelsey, Salisbury, (one part at 16 chns); waterbodies, houses.

38/168 West Lavington (parish) SU 004520
Apt 12.01.1839; 6284a (6283); Map 1840?, 6 chns; waterbodies, houses.

38/169 Lea and Cleverton (parish) ST 965861
Apt 13.04.1840; 1740a (1739); Map 1839, 4 chns, 'Copied from an Old Map' by R.D. Little, Chippenham; waterbodies, houses.

38/170 Leigh (hamlet in parish of Ashton Keynes) SU 062925
Apt 11.06.1840; 1347a (?); Map 1839, 4 chns, by D. Trinder; foot/b'way, waterbodies, houses, arable, grassland, milestone (by symbol), stiles; colour bands show field boundary ownerships and land use; a few buildings are not colour-infilled: this appears to be an oversight.

38/171 Leigh de la Mere (parish) ST 872788 [Leigh Delamere]
Apt 13.04.1840; 1227a (all); Map 1840, 6 chns, by Little and Weaver, Chippenham, Wilts; waterbodies, houses.

38/172 Liddington (parish) SU 204812
Apt 06.06.1840; 1524a (2767); Map 1840, 3 chns, in 4 parts, by T. Dyke, (tithable parts only); foot/b'way, turnpike roads, waterbodies, houses, farmyards, arable, grassland, gardens, hedge ownership, droveways; only part 1 has land use information; uninhabited buildings are uncoloured on parts 2 and 3.

38/173 Littlecot (district or township in parish of Enford) SU 160525 [Littlecott]
Apt 30.06.1840; 719a (?); Map 1839, 6 chns; houses.

38/174 Littleton Drew (parish) ST 837803
Apt 23.11.1838; 971a (971); Map 1841?, 3 chns; waterbodies, houses, toll gate.

38/175 Longstreet (tithing in parish of Enford) SU 165522
Apt 31.12.1842; 498a (?); Map 1843, 6 chns, by Phillips and Westbury, Andover; houses; colours indicate ownerships.

38/176 Longbridge Deverill (parish) ST 861418
Apt 14.03.1838; 4157a (4156); Map 1839?, 9 chns, in 5 parts, (including 36-chn index); waterbodies, houses, tithe-free land (col).

38/177 Luckington (parish) ST 831837
Apt 27.02.1839; 1625a (all); Map 1839, [3 chns], 1st cl; construction lines, foot/b'way, waterbodies, houses, woods, hedge ownership, building names, turnpike, stiles, road cutting, ford, boundary stone, field acreages.

38/178 Ludgarshall (parish) SU 276509 [Ludgershall]
Apt 27.07.1839; 1773a (all); Map 1841, 6 chns, by Phillips and Westbury, Andover; houses, farmyards (col), woods (col), parkland (col), arable (col), grassland (col), gardens (col); coppice named.

38/179 Lydiard Millicent (parish) SU 093858
Apt 11.01.1839; 2321a (all); Map 1839, 6 chns, by Richard Hall, Cirencester; railway, waterbodies, houses, farmyards (col), woods (named), parkland, arable (col), grassland (col), orchards, gardens, field boundary ownerships, manor house, green.

38/180 Lydiard Tregoze (parish) SU 095839
Apt 13.07.1839; 3032a (5142); Map 1840, 6 chns, in 2 parts, 'Copied and corrected' from other plans by Little and Weaver, Chippenham, Wilts, Engineers and Surveyors; railway, canal with towpath, waterbodies, houses, building names, parsonage, brick pits, common.

38/181 Lyneham (parish) SU 026787
Apt 08.03.1845; 160a (3242); Map 1846?, 4 chns, in 3 parts, (tithable parts only); foot/b'way, waterbodies, houses.

38/182 Maddington (parish) SU 052434
Apt 27.03.1841; 3973a (3973); Map 1841, 6 chns, in 3 parts; foot/b'way, waterbodies, houses, open fields.

38/183 Maiden Bradley (parish) (partly in Somerset) ST 798393
Apt 11.08.1840; 4547a (4546); Map 1840, 6 chns; foot/b'way, waterbodies, houses, woods, plantations, orchards; red band may indicate tithe-free area.

38/184 Malmesbury (parish) ST 933844
Apt 27.05.1840; 5333a (5332); Map 1840, 6 chns, in 5 parts, by Daniel Trinder, (including four small enlargements of detail); waterbodies, houses, woods, arable (col), grassland (col), park (annotated), field boundary ownerships, road names; arable, grass and field boundary ownerships are shown by colour bands; built-up part is generalised.

38/185 Manningford Abbots (parish) SU 148579
Apt 12.08.1843; 919a (919); Map 1843, 6 chns; foot/b'way, waterbodies, houses, woods, plantations, osiers (by symbol), gravel pit (col), pond.

38/186 Manningford Bohun (parish) SU 138574 [Manningford Bohune]
Apt 30.07.1839; 1305a (all); Map 1839, 3 chns, by R. C. Gale, Winchester; waterbodies, houses, woods (col), road names, mounds.

38/187 Manningford Bruce (parish) SU 144575
Apt 25.04.1838; 1089a (all); Map 1838, 6 chns, 'Copied from the Award Map with the subsequent alterations' by George Oakley Lucas, Devizes; foot/b'way, waterbodies, houses, woods, plantations, hedge ownership.

38/188 Manton and Elcot (village in parish of Preshute) SU 170697
Apt 21.04.1845; 3227a (?); Map 1843 (title), 1844 (bottom right), 6 chns, in 2 parts, by A.M. May, Marlborough, (including 3-chn enlargement of detail); foot/b'way, waterbodies, houses, woods (col), plantations (col, by Dawson's symbol), osiers (by symbol), building names, workhouse, school, ring earthwork or maze, turnpike gate, road cuttings, tithing boundaries (col), common.

38/189 Marden (parish) SU 085560
Apt 11.06.1839; 1279a (all); Map surveyed 1839, [3 chns], 1st cl; construction lines, houses.

38/190 St Mary Marlborough (parish) SU 191694 [Not listed]
Apt 11.11.1840; 116a (115); Map 1842, 2 chns, by A.M. May, Marlborough; woods, orchards, road names, gas works, town hall, school, green (col), common; built-up part is generalised.

38/191 St Peter Marlborough (parish) SU 187691 [Not listed]
Apt 27.02.1841; 80a (79); Map 1842, 2 chns, by A.M. May, Marlborough; woods, town hall; built-up area is generalised.

38/192 Marston Maisey (parish) SU 134975 [Marston Meysey]
Apt 01.11.1839; 1277a (all); Map 1839, 6 chns, ? by Daniel Trinder, Cirencester; canal with towpath, waterbodies, houses, woods, arable (col), grassland (col), gardens (col), open fields, field boundary ownerships; colour bands shown arable and grass and field boundary ownership.

38/193 Martin (parish) SU 064202
Apt 22.01.1846; 4501a (4501); Map 1841, 8 chns, by Harry Holloway, Ringwood; foot/b'way, waterbodies, houses, woods (col), open fields, building names, road names, barrow, common; pond named.

38/194 Melksham (parish) ST 924637
Apt 28.01.1837; 10893a (12572); Map 1837, 3 chns, in 2 parts, by George Oakley Lucas, Devizes, (part 2, of Seend, by F.J. Kelsey, Salisbury); construction lines, foot/b'way, canal with towpath, locks and swing or draw bridges, waterbodies, houses, woods, plantations, parkland, orchards, hedge ownership, fence ownership, field gates, stiles; some double lines may be walls.

38/195 Mere (parish) ST 819321
Apt 22.06.1848; 7358a (7400); Map 1848, 6 chns, by James Poole, Junior, Sherborne, Dorset; waterbodies, houses.

38/196 Milford, adjoining New Sarum (district) SU 149308 [Milford]
Apt 29.07.1843; 1337a (1336); Map 1844?, 6 chns, in 4 parts, ? by Th. S. Waters (including two enlargements of detail); foot/b'way, houses, woods.

38/197 Milston and Brigmerston (parish) SU 194466
Apt 12.03.1841; 2244a (2243); Map 1841, 6 chns; waterbodies, plantations (col), parkland, orchards, hedges, field names, landowners, milestone, embankment; 'C.E. Rendall, Esqe - Revd. Peter Hall, Rector' appear in title; oak leaf and acorn decorate compass.

38/198 Milton Lilborne (parish) SU 188605 [Milton Lilbourne]
Apt 15.08.1840; 3503a (3502); Map 1842, 6 chns; canal with towpath, waterbodies, woods (named), plantations; hill named.

38/199 Minall or Mildenhall (parish) SU 214704 [Mildenhall]
Apt 22.09.1838; 4025a (4025); Map 1842, 6 chns; woods, plantations, building names, downs; open field named.

38/200 Monkton Deverill (parish) ST 866358
Apt 14.03.1838; 1736a (1735); Map 1839, 9 chns, by Curse and Fox, Warminster; turnpike roads, waterbodies, houses, hedge ownership, tithe-free land (col). Apt omits land use for tithe-free areas.

38/201 Monkton Farleigh (parish) ST 809649
Apt 02.05.1842; 1797a (1796); Map 1846?, 9 chns; waterbodies, houses.

38/202 Netherhaven or Netheravon (parish) SU 127478 [Netheravon]
Corn rent conversion, 1864; 3441a (5160); Map 1903?, 9 chns, litho (by Ordnance Survey), is a copy of enclosure map, 1790; road names, churchyard; plantations named; map has note, 'N.B. This Plan was adopted for the Commutation of Corn Rents 19th May, 1864, to which no Plan is attached'. Apt omits land use.

38/203 Netherhampton (parish) SU 106293
Apt 01.06.1844; 767a (796); Map 1840, 6 chns, by J. Poole, Sherborne, Dorset; houses. Apt omits land use.

38/204 Nettleton (parish) ST 824792
Apt 02.10.1838; 1959a (all); Map 1838, 3 chns; foot/b'way, houses, woods, plantations, arable (col), grassland (col), field boundary ownerships; colour bands show arable, grass and field boundary ownership.

38/205 Long Newnton (parish) ST 909930
Apt 17.07.1838; 2290a (2289); Map 1838, 6 chns; waterbodies, houses; north pointer has a flag attached.

38/206 North Newnton and Hilcott (parish) SU 116578
Apt 20.09.1839; 1353a (1381); Map 1838, 3 chns, in 2 parts, ? by Richard Hall, Cirencester; foot/b'way, waterbodies, houses, woods, plantations, arable (col), grassland (col), field boundary ownerships; colour bands show arable, grass and field boundary ownership.

38/207 South Newton (parish) SU 096347
Apt 19.04.1844; 3371a (3370); Map 1845?, 6 chns; construction (or check) lines (in pencil), turnpike roads, houses, chalk pit, mound; discontinuous streams may be water-meadow channels; rivers named.

38/208 Newton Toney (parish) SU 224402 [Newton Tony]
Apt 18.05.1839; 2365a (2365); Map 1839, 6 chns, by Phillips and Westbury, Andover; foot/b'way, waterbodies, houses, woods (named), plantations (named), parkland, building names, footbridges, parsonage, grotto.

38/209 Norton Bavant (parish) ST 919449
Apt 05.02.1842; 2166a (2165); Map 1841, 8 chns; houses, woods, plantations, orchards.

38/210 Norton Coleparle (parish) ST 888841 [Norton]
Apt 06.06.1840; 1002a (1001); Map 1840, 3 chns, by E. and S. Rich, Didmarton; construction lines, waterbodies, houses; north pointer has a crescent and flag.

38/211 Oaksey (parish) ST 992935
Apt 15.12.1843; 1802a (1802); Map 1843, 6 chns, in 3 parts, by Frederick Webb, Cirencester, (including two 3-chn scale enlargements of detail); railway, foot/b'way, waterbodies, houses.

38/212 Ogbourn St Andrew (parish) SU 166736 [Ogbourne St Andrew]
Apt 22.11.1839; 5349a (all); Map 1842, 6 chns, by Phillips and Westbury, Andover; foot/b'way, turnpike roads, old turnpike road, waterbodies, houses, woods (named), plantations, building names, road names, field names, earthwork, well, pond, dog kennel.

38/213 Ogborne St George (parish) SU 202749 [Ogbourne St George]
Apt 13.12.1843; 3585a (all); Map 1844, 3 chns, 1st cl, by Alfred M. May,

Marlborough; construction lines, waterbodies, houses, woods, plantations, hedge ownership, brick kiln, quarry or pit.

38/214 Orcheston St George (parish) SU 068460 [Not listed]
Apt 11.08.1838; 2363a (2363); Map 1840, 6 chns, by Bramble, Devizes; waterbodies, woods, plantations, building names, field names; farm named.

38/215 Orcheston St Mary (parish) SU 054470 [Not listed]
Apt 30.08.1843; 1738a (1737); Map 1843, 6 chns, by Arthur Dean, 6 New Broad Street, Bank; houses, plantations, mounds, Wansditch, rectory; colours show ownerships.

38/216 Pertwood (parish) ST 895359 [Not listed]
Apt 09.03.1838; 450a (all); Map 1838, 4 chns; waterbodies, houses, woods, plantations.

38/217 Pewsey (parish) SU 162596
Apt 25.04.1838; 4791a (4791); Map 1839, 4 chns, by Thomas Tilbrook; hill-drawing, canal with towpath, waterbodies, houses, woods, plantations, coppice (by symbol), spear bed (by symbol), workhouse, gully, pits.

38/218 Pewsham (extra-parochial place) ST 936708 [Not listed]
Apt 11.01.1839; 1348a (1347); Map 1840, 3 chns, 1st cl; foot/b'way, canal with towpath and lock house, waterbodies, houses, building names, gravel pit.

38/219 Pitton and Farley (parish) SU 217307
Apt 31.07.1839; 2158a (2157); Map 1841?, 6 chns; hill-drawing, foot/b'way, farmyards (col), woods (col), arable (col), grassland (col), orchards (col), gardens (col), road names; pictorial church; coppice named.

38/220 Plaitford (parish) SU 278218
Apt 22.03.1843; 1179a (all); Map 1843?, 6 chns; waterbodies, farmyards (col), woods (col, named), arable (col), grassland (col), orchards (col), gardens (col), common.

38/221 Polshot (parish) ST 967599 [Not found]
Apt 16.06.1837; 1589a (1589); Map 1837, 3 chns, 1st cl, by George Oakley Lucas, Devizes; construction lines, foot/b'way, canal with towpath, waterbodies, houses, orchards, hedge ownership, mills, road cutting.

38/222 Potterne (parish) ST 984578
Apt 30.10.1839; 4957a (4956); Map 1839, 4 chns, enlarged from a 10-chn survey of 1812 by Nicholas Webb, and assumed to be correct except for the 'The Villages and Fields that have been altered', which 'are entirely re-surveyed'; waterbodies, houses, woods, plantations, osiers (by symbol), open fields, building names, road names, common, tithing boundaries (col).

38/223 Purton (parish) SU 094886
Apt 16.06.1838; 6401a (6400); Map 1839, 6 chns, by Richard Hall, Cirencester; railway, foot/b'way, canal with towpath, waterbodies, houses, woods, parkland, arable (col), grassland (col), orchards, gardens, field boundary ownerships, building names, quarry, workhouse; colour bands indicate grass, arable and field boundary ownership.

38/224 Ramsbury (parish) SU 275716
Apt 03.12.1841; 2051a (9742); Map 1842?, 6 chns, in 7 parts, 'on a reduced scale', (tithable parts only); waterbodies, houses, woods.

38/225 Rodbourne Cheney (parish) SU 137874 [Rodbourne]
Apt 17.10.1843; 2653a (2728); Map 1845, 6 chns, by H. Weaver, Surveyor and Engineer, Southampton; railway, foot/b'way, canal with towpath and locks, waterbodies, houses.

38/226 Rollestone (parish) SU 090444
Apt 07.06.1839; 837a (all); Map 1839?, 16 chns, by Charles Marsh Lee; foot/b'way, field names, tumuli.

38/227 Rowde (parish) ST 982622
Apt 16.10.1840; 2665a (2665); Map 1839, 3 chns, 1st cl, by J.R. Bramble, Devizes; construction lines, foot/b'way, canal with flight of locks and towpath, waterbodies, houses, farmyards (col), woods (col), plantations (col), parkland (col), arable (col), grassland (col), orchards (col), gardens, hedge ownership, fence ownership, field gates, building names, road names, landowners, spring, turnpike gates, milestone (with distances), borough boundary (col), road earthworks, field acreages; legend explains land-use tints, and table lists ownership and acreages; hatching may denote lynchets.

38/228 Rushall (parish) SU 128562
Apt 16.11.1842; 2164a (all); Map 1843, 6 chns; foot/b'way, houses, barrow; dot-dash boundaries are used between tithe areas in the same holding, pecked boundaries are used between different holdings.

38/229 Savernake (liberty) SU 197662 [Savernake Forest]
Apt 20.11.1840; 3422a (?); Map 1842, 6 chns, by A.M. May, Marlborough; foot/b'way, canal with towpath, waterbodies, houses, woods (col), plantations (col), osiers (by symbol), building names; map is titled 'Savernake - Great Parks'.

38/230 Seagry (parish) ST 952811 [Not listed]
Apt 18.06.1840; 1014a (all); Map 1840, 6 chns, by F.J. Kelsey, Salisbury; foot/b'way, waterbodies, houses.

38/231 Sedghill (parish) ST 863281
Apt 30.12.1837; 1175a (1175); Map 1838, 3 chns; foot/b'way, waterbodies, woods, plantations, orchards, hedge ownership, fence ownership, field gates.

38/232 Semington (chapelry in parish of Steeple Ashton) ST 902602 [Not listed]
Apt 09.03.1838; 1239a (1238); Map 1837, 4 chns, in 3 parts; canal with towpath, waterbodies, houses, orchards, landowners, building names, chapel; buildings and canal are named in gothic.

38/233 Semley (parish) ST 888267
Apt 25.04.1838; 2946a (2945); Map 1839, 6 chns; waterbodies, houses, woods, commons.

38/234 Shalbourn (parish) (partly in Berks) SU 311628 [Shalbourne]
Apt 19.12.1845; 5356a (?); Map 1843, 6 chns; woods, plantations, brickworks, county boundary.

38/235 Shaw (district in parish of Overton) SU 130654
Apt 21.01.1842; 481a (?); Map 1842, 6 chns; foot/b'way, houses, woods, landowners, Wansdyke.

38/236 Sherrington (parish) ST 954376
Apt 17.05.1839; 1281a (all); Map 1839, [6 chns]; waterbodies, houses, woods, osiers, mound; hatching may indicate lynchets.

38/237 Sherston Magna (parish) ST 850865 [Sherston]
Apt 22.11.1839; 4280a (4280); Map 1839, 3 chns, 1st cl, in 2 parts, by E. and S. Rich, Didmarton, (including 15-chn scale triangulat-ion diagram); construction lines, waterbodies, houses, woods (named), gardens, pits or quarries, road cuttings, ford; north pointer has flag and crescent.

38/238 Sherston Parva or Pinkney (parish) ST 868868 [Pinkney]
Apt 29.08.1842; 951a (950); Map 1843, 4 chns; foot/b'way, waterbodies, houses, farmyards, woods, parkland, arable, grassland, orchards, gardens, field boundary ownerships, Roman road; colour bands show arable, grass and field boundary ownership.

38/239 Shorncote (parish) SU 028968
Apt 11.11.1840; 485a (485); Map 1840, 6 chns, in 2 parts, by Daniel Trinder; foot/b'way, waterbodies, houses, woods (col), arable (col), grassland (col), field boundary ownerships, stiles, common; colour bands indicate arable, grass and field boundary ownership.

38/240 Shrewton (parish) SU 086462
Apt 28.01.1839; 2154a (2178); Map 1840, 6 chns, in 4 parts; foot/b'way, houses.

38/241 Little Somerford (parish) ST 967844
Apt 11.08.1843; 1393a (1392); Map 1847, 4 chns, in 3 parts, (including detached portion at 12-chns); houses, arable, grassland, field boundary ownerships, landowners; colour bands show arable, grass and field boundary ownership. Map is dated 1847 in title, but there is a June 1846 Tithe Commission receipt-stamp.

38/242 Sopworth (parish) ST 829863
Apt 11.08.1838; 1012a (all); Map 1838, 3 chns, 1st cl, by E. and S. Rich, Didmarton; construction lines, waterbodies, houses, boundary trees and stones; legend explains symbols for 'Parish Boundary', 'Number of Chains on line', 'Number of Station'.

38/243 Standlynch (parish) SU 196239 [Not listed]
Apt 07.03.1840; 694a (694); Map 1839?, 9 chns; foot/b'way, houses, woods, parkland.

38/244 Stanley and Nethermore (district in parish of Chippenham) ST 943724
Apt 27.06.1850; 285a (?); Map 1850, 6 chns, by R.D. Little, Chippenham, Wilts, (tithable parts only); foot/b'way, waterbodies, houses.

38/245 Stanton Fitz-Warren (parish) SU 178900 [Stanton Fitzwarren]
Apt 27.07.1843; 1392a (1391); Map 1845?, 6 chns; foot/b'way, canal with towpath, waterbodies, houses.

38/246 Stapleford (parish) SU 079380
Apt 05.06.1840; 2016a (2015); Map 1841?, 7 chns; waterbodies, houses.

38/247 Staunton St Bernard (parish) SU 097630 [Not listed]
Apt 04.09.1845; 1979a (all); Map 1846?, 6 chns; hill-drawing, canal, waterbodies, houses, earthwork.

38/248 Steeple Ashton (tithing in parish of Steeple Ashton) ST 906562
Apt 05.08.1841; 2808a (2808); Map 1841, 6 chns; turnpike roads, waterbodies, houses, woods (named), osiers (by symbol), orchards, gardens, building names, road names, limekiln.

38/249 Steeple Langford (parish) SU 038380
Apt 27.04.1838; 3941a (all); Map 1839?, 6 chns; foot/b'way, open fields; buildings are shown in outline only.

38/250 Stert (tithing in parish of Urchfont) SU 045595
Apt 22.11.1843; 638a (638); Map 1845?, 6 chns, by William Perris; waterbodies, houses, farmyards (col), woods, plantations, arable (col), grassland (col), gardens, open fields, building names, farm names (in gothic); colour bands show arable, grass, farmyards, gardens and field boundary ownership.

38/251 Stourton (parish) (partly in Somerset) ST 766342
Apt 09.04.1839; 3471a (all); Map 1839, [6 chns]; waterbodies, houses, woods, parkland; dash-dot boundaries are between holdings, pecked boundaries are within holdings.

38/252 Stratford Toney or Stratford St Anthony or Stony Stratford (parish) SU 095251 [Stratford Tony]
Apt 14.03.1838; 1174a (all); Map 1839?, 3 chns, ? by F.J. Kelsey, Salisbury; waterbodies, houses, ford, fence.

38/253 Stratford under the Old Castle (parish) SU 135330 [Stratford Sub Castle]
Apt 11.01.1839; 1483a (1483); Map 1839?, 6 chns, ? by F.J. Kelsey, Salisbury; foot/b'way, waterbodies, houses, castle, earthworks.

38/254 Sutton Benger (parish) ST 947784
Apt 07.08.1839; 1173a (1173); Map 1839, 6 chns, by R.D. Little, Chippenham, Wilts; waterbodies, houses, pit.

38/255 Sutton Mandeville (parish) ST 986279
Apt 05.06.1838; 1301a (1300); Map 1839?, 8 chns; waterbodies, houses, woods, orchards.

38/256 Swallowclift (parish) ST 971269 [Swallowcliffe]
Apt 07.04.1843; 1344a (1344); Map 1844?, 6 chns; woods (col).

38/257 Swallowfield (district) SU 719645
Apt 25.02.1841; 2198a (?); Map 1841, 3 chns, in 2 parts, by Hawkes and Son, Reading; waterbodies, houses, woods (named), osiers (by symbol), building names, mills, pound, commons (col).

38/258 Swindon (parish) SU 159837
Apt 20.11.1840; 1532a (3136); Map 1841, 6 chns, by Little and Weaver, Chippenham, Wilts, (tithable parts only); railways, foot/b'way, canal with towpaths, waterbodies, houses, building names (in gothic), quarries, boundary stones.

38/259 North Tedworth (parish) SU 236499 [North Tidworth]
Apt 29.01.1840; 3070a (all); Map 1844?, 4 chns, ? by Thomas Barnes Northeast; arable (col), grassland (col), glebe, avenue of trees; map has an amateurish appearence and is evidently by the same author as South Tedworth, Hants (31/247).

38/260 Teffont Evias (parish) ST 987310
Apt 09.05.1840; 743a (all); Map 1841?, 3 chns; foot/b'way, waterbodies, houses, woods, proposed lake, field acreages.

38/261 Tidcombe (parish) SU 307569
Apt 19.02.1839; 2321a (2321); Map 1843?, 6 chns, by F.J. Kelsey, Salisbury; foot/b'way, waterbodies, houses, linches.

38/262 Tilshead (parish) SU 025479
Apt 01.03.1853; 1a (3990); Map (drawn on Apt) 1853, 3.5 chns; mill (the only tithable property).

38/263 Tisbury (parish) ST 944291
Apt 08.10.1838; 7355a (7355); Map 1839?, 8 chns; waterbodies; pictorial church.

38/264 Tockenham (parish) SU 041800
Apt 20.03.1838; 761a (all); Map 1838, 3 chns, by R.D. Little, Chippenham; foot/b'way, canal with towpath, waterbodies, houses, woods, ash bed (by symbol), parkland, orchards, gardens, hedge ownership, fence ownership, field gates, building names, footbridges (by symbol), ford; 'battlement' effect may indicate yard and garden walls; map includes a terrier.

38/265 Tollard-Royal and Tollard-Farnham (parish and tithing) ST 942170 [Tollard Royal and Tollard Farnham]
Apt 10.09.1838; 2808a (all); Map 1839, 6 chns; hill-drawing, foot/b'way, waterbodies, woods (named), heath/moor, open fields, fences, parsonage, pound, glebe (col), tithing boundaries.

38/266 Trowbridge (parish) ST 851575
Apt 30.06.1837; 2443a (2442); Map 1838, 3 chns, in 3 parts, (tithable parts only); canal with towpath, aqueduct, waterbodies, houses, woods, plantations, orchards, road names, rectory, mills, tithing boundaries; all names are written in gothic.

38/267 Tytherton Lucas (tithing in parish of Chippenham) ST 953741 [Not listed]
Apt 20.07.1838; 607a (all); Map 1838, 3 chns, by R.D. Little, Chippenham; waterbodies, houses, building names; there is a 'reference' to owners, occupiers, land use and acreages.

38/268 Uphaven (parish) SU 132544 [Upavon]
Apt 26.02.1839; 3329a (3329); Map 1838, 9 chns, in 2 parts, by R.C. Gale, Winchester, (includes village at 3 chns); foot/b'way, waterbodies, houses, woods (col), plantations (col), mounds or barrows (by symbol), turnpike gate, milestones, well, tithe-free lands (col); farm names are written across some groups of fields, and some physical features are shown. Apt omits land use.

38/269 Upton Lovell (parish) ST 958424
Apt 30.03.1838; 1399a (all); Map 1838, 6 chns; houses, woods, plantations, osiers (by symbol), orchards, occupation roads, boundary stone, turnpike gate, water meadow channels.

38/270 Upton Scudamore (parish) ST 864476
Apt 27.10.1838; 2503a (2503); Map 1839, 6 chns, in 4 parts; foot/b'way, houses, woods, penciled check-lines.

38/271 Urchfont, Eastcott and Wedhampton (townships or tithings in parish of Urchfont) SU 040564
Apt 14.01.1842; 6235a (6235); Map 1841, 6 chns; waterbodies, houses, woods, plantations, tithing boundaries (col).

38/272 Wanborough (district) SU 215824
Apt 14.11.1843; 385a (4440); Map 1844?, 6 chns, (tithable parts only); foot/b'way, waterbodies, houses, farmyards, woods (col), arable (col), grassland (col), orchards (col).

38/273 Warminster (parish) ST 874455
Apt 28.03.1840; 210a (6370); Map 1840, 9 chns, in 4 parts, by Cruse and Fox, litho (Standidge); hill-drawing, foot/b'way, waterbodies, houses (black), woods, coppice, plantations, open fields, building names, poorhouse, limekiln, hillfort, vicarage, strip lynchets; physical features named; colours show tithe owners; gummed on to the PRO copy is a Standidge lithograph, 'Entrance to Warminster, from the Bath Road', from a drawing by T. Cruse.

38/274 West Wellow (parish) SU 293198
Apt 05.09.1837; 1345a (all); Map 1839?, 6 chns; waterbodies, houses, woods, plantations, fords.

38/275 Westbury (parish) ST 872515
Apt 05.02.1840; 11901a (all); Map 1840, 3 chns, 1st cl, in 7 parts, (parts 5 to 7 litho (Standidge): part 5 is 15 chn index, parts 6 and 7, of built-up parts, at 3 chns), by Cotterells and Cooper, Bath; construction lines, hill-drawing, foot/b'way, waterbodies, houses, woods, plantations, parkland, avenue of trees, orchards, hedge ownership, field gates, field acreages, building names, road names, turnpike gates, gullies, mills, factory, gas works, brick yards, pounds, workhouse, church yard, school, white horse (in plan), hill-fort, spring, stone pits, mound, old moat, township boundary; numerous steep slopes are shown by bold grey hill-drawing; black hill-drawing is used for what appear to be gullies, rills and cuttings; some writing is 'upside down'; parts 6 and 7 show inhabited buildings by hatching.

38/276 Westwood (parish) ST 809593
Apt 26.11.1841; 813a (813); Map 1843, 3 chns; canal with towpath and aqueduct, waterbodies, houses, woods, plantations, orchards, quarry, pits, workhouse, turnpike gate.

38/277 Whaddon (parish) ST 878612
Apt 22.04.1839; 438a (all); Map 1840, 6 chns, foot/b'way, canal with towpath, houses.

38/278 Whiteparish (parish) SU 239238
Apt 14.05.1840; 6285a (6284); Map 1841?, 6 chns, in 2 parts, by F.J. Kelsey, Salisbury; foot/b'way, waterbodies, houses, building names, road names, brick kiln.

38/279 Widhill (manor or tithing in parish of Cricklade St Sampson) SU 127913 [Not listed]
Apt 18.05.1838; 742a (all); Map 1838, 3 chns, by F.J. Kelsey, Salisbury; foot/b'way, waterbodies, houses, gardens, building names.

38/280 Wilcot (parish) SU 145620
Apt 31.05.1839; 2668a (2668); Map 1839, 6 chns, by R.D. Little, Chippenham; foot/b'way, canal with towpath, waterbodies, houses, woods, plantations, parkland, heath/moor, hedge ownership, fence ownership, chalk pit, lynchets (hatched); table below title explains which tithe area numbers belong to which tithing.

38/281 Wilsford (parish) SU 092545
Apt 01.01.1844; 3385a (?); Map 1844?, 6 chns; foot/b'way, houses, osiers (by symbol), drove, chalk pits; title is in scroll frame.

38/282 Wilsford or Wevelsford (district) SU 121403 [Wilsford]
Apt 06.05.1846; 823a (?); Map 1851, 8 chns, 'Copied from a Map made by W. Tabb and Son in 1815', by John Waters, Salisbury; houses, plantations, parkland, building names.

38/283 Wilton (parish) SU 092301
Apt 07.06.1844; 1792a (1791); Map 1844, 6 chns, by J. Poole, Sherborne, Dorset; houses, road names, deer park, hare warren, watermeadow channels; meadow named.

38/284 Wily (parish) SU 009370 [Wylye]
Apt 22.09.1838; 2280a (all); Map 1841, 6 chns, by J. Poole, Sherborne, Dorset; houses, water meadow channels. Apt omits land use.

38/285 Wingfield (parish) ST 818573
Apt 27.03.1839; 1384a (all); Map 1840?, 4 chns, in 3 parts; waterbodies, houses, farmyards, woods (named), plantations, orchards, building names, turnpike gate.

38/286 Winterborne Earls (parish) SU 176339 [Winterbourne Earls]
Apt 16.04.1839; 1664a (all); Map 1839?, 9 chns, ? by F.J. Kelsey, Salisbury; foot/b'way, waterbodies, houses.

38/287 Winterborne Gunner (parish) SU 182350 [Winterbourne Gunner]
Apt 31.08.1840; 1506a (1562); Map 1840, 9 chns, in 2 parts, by M.R. Harris, Salisbury; foot/b'way, houses, woods, open fields, road names, barrow, Roman road.

38/288 Winterborne Stoke (parish) SU 085417 [Winterbourne Stoke]
Apt 20.11.1839; 3420a (3419); Map 1840?, 8 chns; foot/b'way, houses.

38/289 Winterbourne Bassett (parish) SU 102749
Apt 06.10.1840; 2167a (2210); Map 1843, 6 chns, by John Pyne; waterbodies, houses, woods, orchards, hedge ownership, building names.

38/290 Winterborne Dauntsey (parish) SU 177345 [Winterbourne Dauntsey]
Apt 08.02.1842; 1162a (all); Map 1844?, 3 chns, in 2 parts; foot/b'way, waterbodies, houses, woods, open fields, ring fort; detached part is positioned in relation to the main part by a bearing on Salisbury Cathedral spire.

38/291 Winterslow (parish) SU 237334 [Middle Winterslow]
Apt 23.09.1840; 4843a (4843); Map 1841, 8 chns, in 2 parts, by M. Peniston, Salisbury (part 2 at 12 chns); foot/b'way, houses, woods.

38/292 Wishford Magna (parish) SU 072353 [Not listed]
Apt 27.09.1838; 1611a (all); Map 1839, 6 chns, by J. Poole, Sherbourne, Dorset; foot/b'way, houses. Apt omits land use.

38/293 Woodborough (parish) SU 111605
Apt 03.03.1838; 1016a (all); Map 1838, 6 chns; canal with towpath, waterbodies, houses, woods, osiers (by symbol, col).

38/294 Woodford (parish) SU 115368 [Not listed]
Apt 27.12.1839; 2781a (all); Map 1840, 3 chns, by George Hewett, Junior, Elvetham, Hants; woods, field boundary ownerships.

38/295 Wootton Bassett (parish) SU 064821
Apt 23.09.1840; 4778a (4778); Map 1841, 8 chns; railway, canal with locks, waterbodies, woods; village is generalised.

38/296 Wootton Rivers (parish) SU 198631
Apt 15.05.1838; 1180a (1179); Map 1840, 6 chns; canal with towpath, woods.

38/297 North Wraxall (parish) ST 819752
Apt 04.04.1837; 2127a (all); Map 1838, 3 chns, by F.J. Kelsey, Salisbury; foot/b'way, waterbodies, houses.

38/298 Yatesbury (parish) SU 071716
Apt 17.09.1840; 1668a (all); Map 1840, 3 chns, by Little and Weaver, Chippenham, Wilts; waterbodies, houses, open fields, barrow.

38/299 Yatton Keynell (parish) ST 865762
Apt 08.05.1841; 1750a (1749); Map 1842, 3 chns, by Little and Weaver, Chippenham, Wilts; waterbodies, houses.

Worcestershire

PRO IR29 and IR30 39/1-153

208 tithe districts: 478,582 acres
153 tithe commutations: 331,347 acres
82 voluntary tithe agreements, 71 compulsory tithe awards

Tithe and tithe commutation

About three-quarters of Worcestershire tithe districts contained some tithable land in 1836 but only fifty-four districts were wholly subject to tithe (Fig. 51). The main causes of tithe exemption in this county were commutation at the time of enclosure, modus payments in lieu of tithes, the merger of tithes in the land, and exemption by prescription.

Assistant tithe commissioners and local tithe agents who worked in Worcestershire are listed in Table 39.1 and the valuers of tithe rent-charge in Table 39.2. A common characteristic of Worcestershire schedules of tithe apportionment is the recording of intermixed land uses such as 'arable and meadow' and 'arable and rough pasture'. The apportionment for Hartlebury divides the parish into manors, that for Hanbury cites Nash's *History of Worcestershire* as its source for tithe exemptions, and that of Newbold upon Stour records open-field farming in unusual detail.

Tithe maps

Although the eastern part of the county is 'midland', Worcestershire forms part of the concentration of first-class tithe maps centred on Monmouthshire; 31 per cent of the county's 153 maps are sealed as first class. In scale, Worcestershire tithe maps vary from one inch to three chains to one inch to twelve chains with a total of 58 per cent of maps in the recommended scale range of one inch to three to four chains and most of the remainder at the six-chain scale (Table 39.3). Nineteen second-class maps are lithographed, which is a high proportion. Although there were several lithographers in Birmingham, most of these maps were lithographed in London by Standidge.

The land-use record of Worcestershire tithe maps is very poor but, as is often the case in counties with a large number of first-class maps, field boundary ownership is identified on a high proportion (47 per cent) of maps. Industry is recorded on 7 per cent of the county's maps and includes quarrying, forging, brine pits, chemical and brick works, and spinning, paper and snuff mills. On some maps canals are mapped in detail. Unusual details recorded on Worcestershire tithe maps include a police station at Bredicote, a maypole at Kings

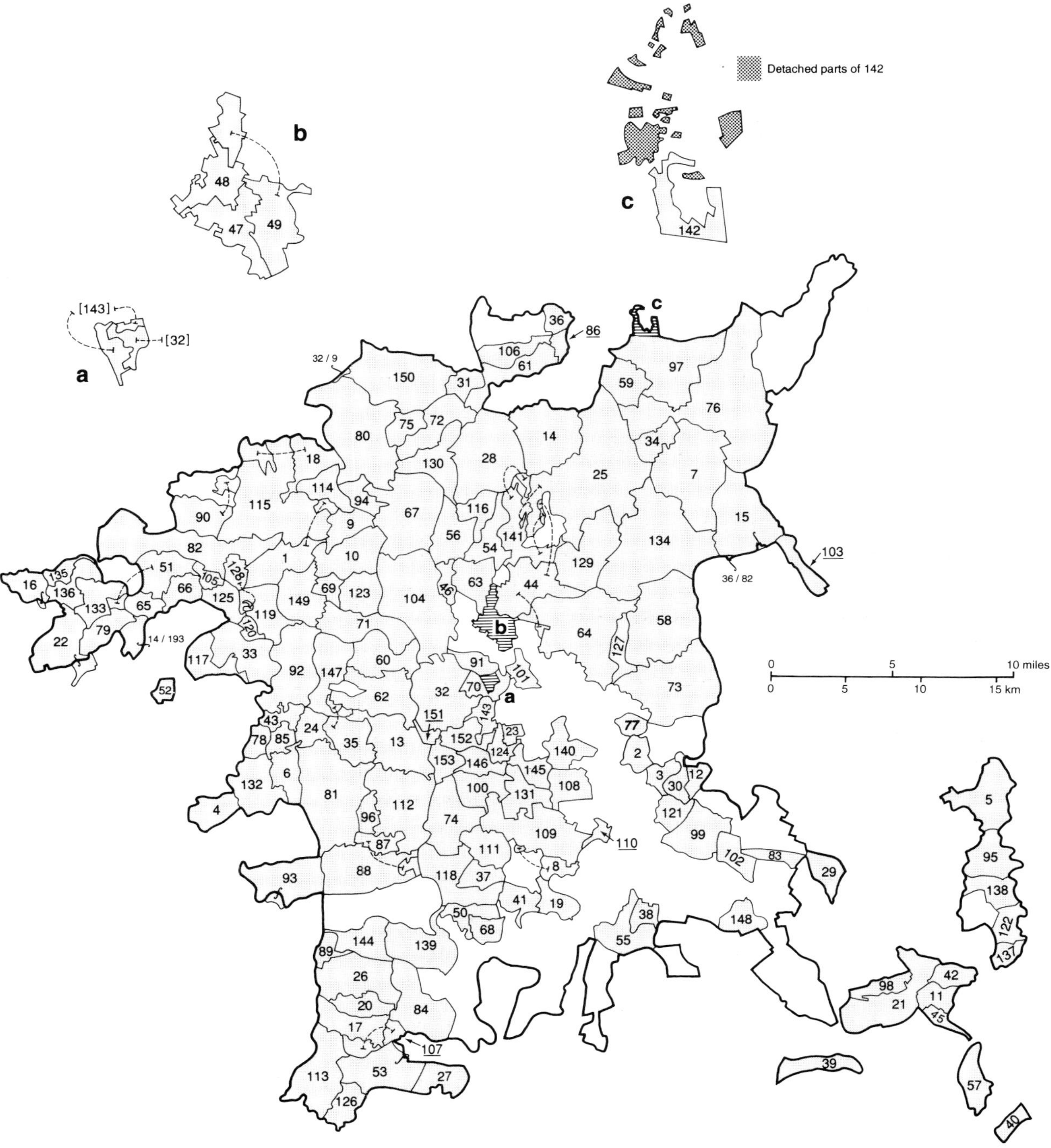

Fig. 51 Worcestershire: tithe district boundaries.

Norton, and a folly at Orleton; at Offenham the ferry and ferryman are pictured. There is little decorative embellishment on Worcestershire tithe maps, though a few have ornamental compass roses.

Some 105 Worcestershire tithe maps in the Public Record Office collection can be attributed to a particular map-maker. As usual, most maps were produced by men resident in or near the county but two were produced by Messrs Crawter of London (Table 39.2).

Table 39.1. *Agreements and awards for commutation of tithes in Worcestershire*

Assistant commissioner/ local tithe agent	*Number of agreements**	*Number of awards*
John Job Rawlinson	0	63
Thomas Hoskins	43	0
Charles Pym	17	0
George Bolls	13	0
N. S. Meryweather	9	0
Aneurin Owen	0	4
John Johnes	1	2
George Wingrove Cooke	0	1
Thomas Smith Woolley	1	0
Tithe Commissioners	0	1

*Computed from the number of extant reports on tithe agreements in the tithe files [PRO IR 18].

Table 39.2. *Tithe valuers and tithe map-makers in Worcestershire*

Name and address (in Worcestershire unless indicated)	*Number of districts*	*Acreage*
Tithe valuers		
Richard Chambers Herbert, Worcester	22	34,663
Jeremiah Mathews, Park Hall, Kidderminster	19	39,497
James Webb, Worcester	14	22,288
Henry Lakin junior, Worcester	11	26,637
William Woodward, Bredons Norton	9	21,238
Thomas Henry Davis, Orleton	8	19,175
Thomas Holyoake, Little Alne, Warwickshire	8	17,434
Others [36]	62	150,415
Attributed tithe map-makers		
James Webb, Worcester	28	45,346
Richard Chambers Herbert, Worcester	27	48,318
Oates and Perrens, Stourbridge	8	22,811
Others [17]	30	84,705

Table 39.3. *The tithe maps of Worcestershire: scales and classes*

Scale in chains/inch	*All maps*		*First Class*		*Second Class*	
	Number	*Acreage*	*Number*	*Acreage*	*Number*	*Acreage*
3	80	150,656	47	95,467	33	55,189
4	9	15,803	1	6,130	8	9,673
5	11	19,674	0	0	11	19,674
6	45	128,560	0	0	45	128,560
<6	8	16,654	0	0	8	16,654
TOTAL	153	331,347	48	101,597	105	229,750

Table 39.4. *The tithe maps of Worcestershire: dates*

	1838	*1839*	*1840*	*1841*	*1842*	*1843*	*1844*	*1845*	*1846*	*1847*	*1848*	*1849*	*>1849*
All maps	18	26	27	17	21	20	7	5	5	1	1	1	3
1st class	6	12	5	8	4	7	1	1	2	1	0	1	0
2nd class*	12	14	22	9	17	13	6	4	3	0	1	0	3

*One second-class tithe map of Worcestershire in the Public Record Office collection is undated.

Worcestershire

39/1 Abberley (parish) SO 750680
Apt 03.11.1842; 2637a (all); Map 1841, 3 chns, 1st cl, in 2 parts, by James Webb, Worcester; construction lines, waterbodies, houses, fences, field boundary ownerships, field gates, building names.

39/2 Abberton (parish) SO 996533
Apt 23.06.1845; 1002a (1001); Map 1842, 6 chns, by R.C. Herbert, Worcester; waterbodies, fences, building names, mill.

39/3 Abbots Lench (hamlet in parish of Fladbury) SP 012518 [Not listed]
Apt 10.06.1841; 870a (all); Map 1843, 4 chns, 'copied from a survey of Wm Hill's' by James Webb, Worcester.

39/4 Acton Beauchamp (parish) SO 698501
Apt 31.08.1840; 1530a (all); Map 1839, 3 chns, by W.H. Apperley, Hereford; construction lines, foot/b'way, waterbodies, houses, woods, fences, field boundary ownerships, field gates, building names, mill, quarry.

39/5 Alderminster (parish) SP 241495
Apt 30.04.1840; 3168a (3167); Map 1842?, 6 chns; railway, waterbodies, houses, woods (col), parkland, hedge ownership, boundary of tithe-free land.

39/6 Alfrick (hamlet in parish of Suckley) SO 748526
Apt 28.03.1838; 1646a (?); Map 1839, 3 chns, 1st cl, by James Webb, Worcester; construction lines, foot/b'way, waterbodies, houses, woods (by name), open fields, fences, field boundary ownerships, field gates, building names, paper mill, chapelry boundary, green; map covers the whole parish of Suckley (see 39/132), but was 'deposited for Alfrick only'.

39/7 Alvechurch (parish) SP 040737
Apt 31.05.1842; 6747a (6747); Map 1843, 6 chns, by John Walker, Birmingham; hill-drawing, railway, foot/b'way, turnpike roads, canal with towpath, reservoirs, embankments, waterbodies, woods, parkland, orchard, park, green.

39/8 St Andrew (chapelry in parish of Pershore) SO 938453 [Not listed]
Apt 25.10.1841; 848a (?); Map 1842, 3 chns; turnpike roads, toll gate, waterbodies, building names, workhouse, woods (by name).

39/9 Kings Areley (parish) SO 794802 [Areley Kings]
Apt 31.07.1839; 1450a (all); Map 1838, 3 chns, by J. Mathews, litho (Standidge); foot/b'way, turnpike roads, waterbodies, woods (named), field acreages, field boundary ownerships, churchyard, common.

39/10 Astley (parish) SO 792680
Apt 17.07.1839; 2958a (all); Map 1840, 6 chns, by Oates and Perrens, Stourbridge, litho (Standidge); foot/b'way, waterbodies, woods (named), rock outcrops, building names, mill.

39/11 Aston (hamlet in parish of Blockley) SP 205358
Apt 13.08.1840; 1144a (?); Map 1842?, 6 chns; waterbodies, houses, woods (col), hedge ownership.

39/12 Atch Lench (hamlet in parish of Church Lench) SP 038512
Apt 17.03.1841; 648a (?); Map 1841, 6 chns, by T. Yells, Bengeworth; woods. Apt omits land use.

39/13 St John in Bedwardine (parish) SO 827843
Apt 09.01.1840; 3775a (3775); Map 1840, 3 chns, 1st cl, by James Webb, Worcester; construction lines, waterbodies, houses, fences, field boundary ownerships, field gates, building names, mills, weir, canal mouth, heath.

39/14 Bellbroughton (parish) SO 942768
Apt 10.01.1840; 4605a (4605); Map 1840, 4 chns, by John Davies; foot/b'way, waterbodies, woods (named), building names, rectory, common.

39/15 Beoley (parish) SP 065705
Apt 29.04.1843; 4480a (4480); Map 1842?, 5 chns; waterbodies; colour bands show 'free board' land, 'demesne' land, land subject to and free from modus.

39/16 Berrington (township in parish of Tenbury) SO 569669
Apt 15.03.1843; 1358a (?); Map 1843, 3 chns, 1st cl, by R.C. Herbert, Worcester; foot/b'way, waterbodies, houses, field boundary ownerships, building names, mill, boundary trees, common, county boundary.

39/17 Berrow (parish) SO 787345
Apt 14.03.1843; 2181a (2180); Map 1844, 3 chns, 1st cl, by R.C. Herbert, Worcester; construction lines, turnpike roads, waterbodies, rock outcrops, open fields, field boundary ownerships, building names, parsonage, sand or stone pits or quarries, green.

39/18 Bewdley (hamlet in parish of Ribbesford) SO 772749
Apt 12.06.1843; 2841a (?); Map 1845, 5 chns, 'copied from a map made by John Walker' and 'revised' by James Webb, Worcester; foot/b'way, waterbodies, building names, snuff mill.

39/19 Birlingham (township in parish of Nafford) SO 932431
Apt 23.12.1841; 43a (1210); Map 1842, 3 chns; foot/b'way, houses, open fields, building names, mill; bridge named.

39/20 Birtsmorton (parish) SO 796359
Apt 19.02.1839; 1268a (1268); Map 1839, 3 chns, 1st cl, by Robert Jones; construction lines, foot/b'way, waterbodies, field boundary ownerships, field gates, building names, rectory, green (col).

39/21 Blockley (hamlet in parish of Blockley) SP 135350
Apt 19.08.1842; 1535a (?); Map 1843, 5 chns, by Messrs Crawter; foot/b'way, waterbodies, woods, building names, stables; village generalised.

39/22 Bockleton (parish) (partly in Herefordshire) SO 591626
Apt 20.10.1841; 3229a (all); Map 1842, 3 chns, 1st cl, by R.C. Herbert, Worcester; construction lines, waterbodies, houses, field boundary ownerships, building names, parsonage, mill, common named.

39/23 Bredicote (parish) SO 905448 [Bredicot]
Apt 10.07.1841; 398a (all); Map 1846, 3 chns, by James Webb, Worcester; railway, foot/b'way, waterbodies, houses, fences, building names, rectory, police station.

39/24 Broadwas (parish) SO 765558
Apt 11.04.1839; 1161a (1160); Map 1839, [3 chns], 1st cl, by Samuel Barnett, St Johns, Worcester; construction lines, turnpike roads, waterbodies, houses, woods, open fields, fences, field boundary ownerships, field gates, green.

39/25 Bromsgrove (parish) SO 970730
Apt 19.02.1839; 10969a (10968); Map 1840, 6 chns; railway, waterbodies, woods, orchards, building names, windmill, workhouse, obelisk, mills, greens.

39/26 Castlemorton (parish) SO 787402
Apt 28.12.1838; 3656a (all); Map 1838, 3 chns, by Arthur Causton, Berkley Street, Gloucester; foot/b'way, waterbodies, houses, woods, plantations, orchards, heath/moor, field boundary ownerships, field gates, avenue of trees, commons and waste lands (col).

39/27 Chaceley (parish) SO 849306
Apt 21.07.1840; 1725a (all); Map 1841, 3 chns, by Josiah Castree, Gloucester; foot/b'way, waterbodies, woods, plantations, osiers, field boundary ownerships, building names.

39/28 Chaddesley Corbett (parish) SO 892750
Apt 17.07.1839; 5914a (5914); Map 1838, 6 chns, litho (Standidge); foot/b'way, waterbodies, woods, building names, road names, school, vicarage, Catholic chapel, mills, spinning mill, forge.

39/29 Church Honeybourne (parish) SP 122441 [Honeybourne]
Apt 01.09.1841; 902a (1312); Map 1842, 4 chns, 'compiled from Old Surveys' by James Webb, Worcester; foot/b'way, waterbodies, houses, fences.

39/30 Church Lench (township in parish of Church Lench) SP 023513
Apt 11.03.1839; 757a (?); Map 1840?, 3 chns; foot/b'way, waterbodies, houses, woods, arable (col), grassland (col), orchards, gardens (col).

39/31 Churchill (parish) SO 874797
Apt 30.07.1839; 924a (924); Map 1840, 6 chns, litho; foot/b'way, turnpike roads, waterbodies, woods, fences, boundary trees.

39/32 Claines (parish) SO 860580
Apt 08.12.1841; 4813a (4813); Map 1843, 3 chns, 1st cl, by Henry Lakin, junr and James Webb, Worcester; construction lines, canal, waterbodies, houses, open fields, fences, field boundary ownerships, building names, field names, gasworks, mills, grandstand, county castle, pound, shire hall, Catholic chapel, greens.

39/33 Clifton-upon-Teme (parish) SO 719616 [Clifton Upon Teme]
Apt 16.01.1845; 2973a (2972); Map 1845, 3 chns, 1st cl, in 2 parts, by James Webb, Worcester; construction lines, foot/b'way, waterbodies, houses, plantations, fences, field boundary ownerships, field gates, building names, castle, vicarage, mill.

39/34 Cofton Hackett, otherwise Coston Hackett (parish) SP 012755
Apt 27.11.1838; 1262a (all); Map 1839, ?12 chns, by John Walker, Birmingham; hill-drawing, railway, waterbodies, woods, plantations, embankment.

39/35 Cotheridge (parish) SO 794550
Apt 30.09.1850; 46a (2202); Map 1851?, 4 chns, (tithable parts only); turnpike roads, building names, road names, milestone.

39/36 Cradley (township in parish of Halesowen) SO 941847
Apt 29.12.1843; 733a (732); Map 1844?, 5 chns, in 2 parts, (includes 2-chn enlargement of open field strips); foot/b'way, waterbodies, woods, open fields, building names, forge, mill.

39/37 Croome D'Abitot (parish) SO 885448
Apt 02.11.1840; 1148a (1148); Map 1840, 6 chns, by R.C. Herbert, Worcester; turnpike roads, tollgate, waterbodies, woods (named), building names, moorland.

39/38 Cropthorne (parish) SO 997318
Apt 24.12.1842; 730a (2000); Map 1844, 3 chns, in 2 parts, 'copied from a survey of G.G. Jones's' by James Webb, Worcester; waterbodies, houses, road names, brick kiln.

39/39 Cutsden (hamlet in parish of Bredon) SP 106308 [Cutsdean]
Apt 08.09.1851; 47a (1578); Map 1852?, 6 chns; foot/b'way, plantations, field names. District is apportioned by holding.

39/40 Daylesford (parish) SP 251263
Apt 12.01.1842; 653a (653); Map 1844, 4 chns; turnpike roads, waterbodies, woods, parkland.

39/41 Defford (chapelry in parish of Pershore) SO 910433
Apt 01.02.1842; 529a (?); Map 1842, 6 chns, by R.C. Herbert, Worcester; railway, viaduct, turnpike roads, waterbodies, open fields, field boundary ownerships, field names, common, common meadows; bridge named.

39/42 Ditchford (hamlet in parish of Blockley) SP 215369
Apt 16.04.1842; 1039a (all); Map 1843?, 3 chns; waterbodies, road names, field acreages. District is apportioned by holding.

39/43 Dodenham (parish) SO 745565 [Doddenham]
Apt 30.12.1840; 916a (all); Map 1841, 3 chns, 1st cl, by James Webb, Worcester; construction lines, waterbodies, houses, fences, field boundary ownerships, field gates, building names.

39/44 Dodderhill (parish) SO 918654
Apt 07.04.1842; 3683a (5450); Map 1843, 3 chns, 1st cl, by R.C. Herbert, Worcester; construction lines, canal, waterbodies, field boundary ownerships, building names, boundary trees, brine pits.

39/45 Dorn (hamlet in parish of Blockley) SP 209339
Apt 19.04.1842; 554a (all); Map 1843?, 6 chns; railway, foot/b'way, waterbodies, woods (col), hedge ownership.

39/46 Doverdale (parish) SO 860660
Apt 17.07.1838; 744a (all); Map 1838, 3 chns, 1st cl, by James Webb, Worcester; construction lines, foot/b'way, waterbodies, houses, fences, field boundary ownerships, field gates, building names, mill, rectory, sand or stone pits, waste.

39/47 St Andrew, Droitwich (parish) SO 893621
Apt 07.07.1838; 541a (all); Map 1839?, 6 chns; foot/b'way, canal, waterbodies, houses, woods, orchards, building names; gardens are shown by annotation.

39/48 St Nicholas, Droitwich (parish) SO 892633
Apt 03.07.1838; 344a (343); Map 1839, 3 chns, by R.C. Herbert, Worcester; turnpike roads, toll gate, canal, waterbodies, woods, fences, field boundary ownerships, building names, road names, mill, workhouse.

39/49 St Peter, Droitwich (parish) SO 902625
Apt 14.11.1840; 699a (698); Map 1840?, 6 chns, by Richd Court, senr, Bewdley, Worcs, land agent and surveyor; foot/b'way, turnpike roads, waterbodies, houses, woods, orchards, fences, building names, mill, free school, mill pool; gardens are shown by annotation.

39/50 Earls Croome (parish) SO 872425 [Earl's Croome]
Apt 23.11.1838; 1142a (1141); Map 1838, 3 chns, 1st cl, by R.C. Herbert, Worcester; construction lines, turnpike roads, toll gate, waterbodies, fences, field boundary ownerships, building names, castle, commons, field acreages.

39/51 Eastham (parish) SO 663680
Apt 28.10.1843; 2367a (3846); Map 1839, 3 chns, 1st cl, in 2 parts, by Lakin and Giles, Worcester; foot/b'way, waterbodies, houses, woods, hedge ownership, fences, field gates, building names, parsonage, boundary trees.

39/52 Edwin Loach (parish) SO 664589 [Edvin Loach]
Apt 06.03.1846; 534a (all); Map 1845, 3 chns; woods, quarry. Apt omits some field names.

39/53 Eldersfield (parish) SO 803317
Apt 18.11.1841; 3307a (3307); Map 1843, 3 chns; waterbodies, houses, open fields (named), field boundary ownerships, field gates, building names, road names, meadows (named), green.

39/54 Elmbridge (chapelry in parish of Dodderhill) SO 892697
Apt 20.11.1841; 1770a (?); Map 1842, 3 chns, 1st cl, by R.C. Herbert, Worcester; construction lines, waterbodies, field boundary ownerships, building names, mill, green.

39/55 Elmley Castle (parish) SO 985407
Apt 09.12.1842; 2057a (2057); Map 1843, 3 chns, by James Webb, Worcester; waterbodies, houses, fences, building names, park (named).

39/56 Elmley Lovett (parish) SO 868694
Apt 30.12.1840; 2381a (2381); Map 1842?, 6 chns, in 2 parts; foot/b'way, turnpike roads, waterbodies, houses, woods (named), parkland, building names, rectory, common, greens.

39/57 Evenlode (parish) SP 223293
Apt 13.04.1839; 194a (1563); Map 1840?, 6 chns; foot/b'way, waterbodies, houses, woods, hedge ownership, field gates, landowners.

39/58 Feckenham (parish) SP 020630
Apt 14.02.1839; 6788a (6787); Map 1840, 6 chns, in 39 parts, (including 37 small sketch plans of small plots and buildings in the parish and a 3-chn enlargement of Feckenham village); foot/b'way, waterbodies, woods, plantations, orchards, field boundary ownerships, building names, road names, mills, windmill, greens.

39/59 Frankley (parish) SO 990800
Apt 15.08.1840; 1901a (1901); Map 1842, 5 chns, litho (Standidge); waterbodies, woods (named), building names.

39/60 Grimley (parish) SO 820602
Apt 23.09.1840; 2459a (2459); Map 1842, 3 chns, turnpike roads, waterbodies, woods (named), open fields (named), fences, building names, lodge, church house, greens.

39/61 Hagley (parish) SO 909805
Apt 07.07.1837; 2363a (2363); Map 1838, 8 chns, by J. Mathews, litho

(Standidge); foot/b'way, waterbodies, woods, plantations, parkland, rock outcrops.

39/62 Hallow (parish) SO 810580
Apt 13.09.1841; 3557a (3556); Map 1839, 3 chns, 1st cl, by Lakin and Giles, Worcester; construction lines, waterbodies, houses, woods, hedge ownership, fences, field boundary ownerships, building names.

39/63 Hampton Lovet (parish) SO 885658 [Hampton Lovett]
Apt 07.07.1838; 1908a (all); Map 1839, 3 chns, by R.C. Herbert, Worcester; turnpike roads, waterbodies, woods (named), fences, field boundary ownerships, building names, rectory.

39/64 Hanbury (parish) SO 956622
Apt 07.07.1838; 7533a (7533); Map 1838, 6 chns, by Richd Court, senr and R.C. Herbert; railway, canal, wharf, waterbodies, woods (named), fences, field boundary ownerships, building names, rectory, greens.

39/65 Hanley Child (chapelry in parish of Eastham) SO 650652
Apt 25.03.1840; 941a (all); Map 1844?, 6 chns; waterbodies, houses, woods, stone pit or quarry, heath.

39/66 Hanley William (parish) SO 673660
Apt 15.07.1839; 1155a (all); Map 1839, 3 chns, 1st cl, by Lakin and Giles, Worcester; foot/b'way, waterbodies, houses, woods, plantations, parkland, rock outcrops, hedge ownership, fences, field gates, building names, boundary trees, quarry, limekiln, heath.

39/67 Hartlebury (parish) SO 838708
Apt 03.07.1838; 5494a (all); Map 1838, 6 chns, by William Price, Ross; foot/b'way, turnpike roads, canal, waterbodies, woods (named), plantations, osiers, parkland, orchards, hops, marsh/bog, building names, road names, ferry, gravel pits, spinning factory, mills, castle, forge, heath, green.

39/68 Hill Croome (parish) SO 885310
Apt 20.03.1839; 982a (982); Map 1838, 3 chns, 1st cl, by R.C. Herbert, Worcester; waterbodies, woods, fences, field boundary ownerships, building names, limekiln.

39/69 Hillhampton (hamlet in parish of Martley) SO 775660
Apt 29.12.1840; 786a (786); Map 1841, 6 chns, by Oates and Perrens, Stourbridge, litho (Standidge); foot/b'way, waterbodies, woods, hops, fences, building names.

39/70 Hindlip (parish) SO 880581
Apt 13.07.1838; 1054a (1054); Map 1838, 3 chns, by James Webb, Worcester; foot/b'way, canal with towpath and locks, waterbodies, houses, woods, arable (col), grassland (col), hedge ownership, fences, field boundary ownerships, field gates, building names, parsonage, private carriage road, green; map has note of adoption proceedings.

39/71 Holt with Little Witley (parochial chapelry) SO 810630
Apt 31.01.1839; 2911a (all); Map 1840?, 6 chns, by Oates and Perren; waterbodies, woods (named), orchards, building names, castle.

39/72 Hurcott and Comberton and land south of River Stour (district in parish of Foreign of Kidderminster) SO 853765
Apt 19.01.1842; 2475a (all); Map 1841, 6 chns, litho (Standidge); hill-drawing, foot/b'way, waterbodies, woods (named), parkland, building names, rolling mill, mill, forge, milestone.

39/73 Inkberrow (parish) SP 020580
Apt 30.01.1840; 6792a (?); Map 1840?, 6 chns; waterbodies, houses, woods, arable (col), grassland (col), glebe (blue).

39/74 Kempsey (parish) SO 862492
Apt 21.06.1841; 3106a (all); Map 1840, 5 chns, by R.C. Herbert, Worcester; construction lines, turnpike roads, waterbodies, woods, open fields, building names, field names, common meadows, greens, commons.

39/75 Kidderminster (borough in parish of Kidderminster) SO 832769
Apt 20.09.1842; 645a (?); Map 1844?, 4 chns; canal, waterbodies, building names; built-up part mostly generalised.

39/76 Kings Norton (parish) SP 065790 [King's Norton]
Apt 28.12.1838; 12133a (12132); Map 1840, 6 chns, in 5 parts, by John Walker, Birmingham, (includes 24-chn index); hill-drawing, railway with cutting, foot/b'way, turnpike roads, toll gates, canal, canal feeder, reservoir, tunnels, waterbodies, woods, plantations, parkland, orchards, field boundary ownerships, field gates, building names, road names, chapels, chemical works, sand or stone pits, quarry, mills, Maypole, greens; map has leafy borders.

39/77 Kington (parish) SO 992553
Apt 26.11.1839; 24a (1000); Map (drawn on Apt) 1848?, 8 chns, (tithable parts only); foot/b'way, plantations, building names, landowners, mill, private roads.

39/78 Knightwick (parish) SO 728551
Apt 30.12.1840; 859a (all); Map 1841, 3 chns, 1st cl, by James Webb, Worcester; construction lines, waterbodies, houses, fences, field boundary ownerships, field gates, building names, rectory.

39/79 Kyre, otherwise Kyre Wyard (parish) SO 629639
Apt 15.07.1839; 1521a (1520); Map 1840, 3 chns, 1st cl, by James Bourn, junr, Cleobury Mortimer; construction lines, waterbodies, houses, woods, plantations.

39/80 Lands west of the River Stour (district in parish of Kidderminster) SO 805765 [Not listed]
Apt 31.01.1851; 155a (?); Map 1851?, 9 chns; turnpike roads, waterbodies, woods (named), building names, racecourse, workhouse, green.

39/81 Leigh (parish) SO 780508
Apt 07.07.1838; 6130a (6129); Map 1839, 4 chns, 1st cl, by R.C. Herbert, Worcester; construction lines, waterbodies, fences, field boundary ownerships, building names, chapel, rectory, mill; green bands surround pasture lands, including some orchards and gardens; meaning of red band is unclear; bridge named; compass rose has floral boss. (The map in PRO IR 30 is a copy; original is in PRO IR 77/92.)

39/82 Lindridge (parish) SO 674698
Apt 20.12.1839; 2481a (6252); Map 1840-43, 3 chns, 1st cl, in 3 parts, by James Webb, Worcester; canal, waterbodies, houses, fences, building names, vicarage, weir, chapel, common.

39/83 South Littleton (parish) SP 092460
Apt 16.10.1840; 841a (841); Map 1839, 3 chns, by N. Izod and R.C. Herbert; foot/b'way, waterbodies, field boundary ownerships, building names.

39/84 Longdon (parish) SO 836354
Apt 11.03.1840; 3904a (all); Map 1840, 3 chns; waterbodies, woods, plantations, open fields (named), building names.

39/85 Lulsley (hamlet in parish of Suckley) SO 742551
Apt 05.10.1838; 846a (all); Map 1839, 3 chns, by James Webb, Worcester; waterbodies, houses, woods, arable (col), grassland (col), building names, chapel.

39/86 Luttley (township in parish of Hales Owen) SO 941829
Apt 31.12.1842; 430a (430); Map 1842, 5 chns, litho (Standidge); foot/b'way, waterbodies, woods, building names, mill, green.

39/87 Madresfield (parish) SO 809474
Apt 15.08.1840; 1193a (1192); Map 1838, 3 chns, 1st cl, in 2 parts, by James Webb, Worcester; construction lines, foot/b'way, waterbodies, houses, woods, fences, field boundary ownerships, field gates.

39/88 Great Malvern (except Newland) (parish) SO 800455
Apt 09.10.1841; 4234a (?); Map 1843, 3 chns, 1st cl, by Henry Lakin, junr, Worcester; construction lines, waterbodies, houses, woods, field boundary ownerships, boundary stones, common; hills named.

39/89 Little Malvern (except land disputed between this parish and Welland) (parish) SO 772403
Apt 02.03.1847; 624a (943); Map 1840, 3 chns, 1st cl, by James Webb, Worcester; construction lines, waterbodies, houses, fences, field boundary ownerships, field gates, pound, boundary marks; hills named.

39/90 Mamble (parish) SO 691714
Apt 09.03.1838; 2658a (2658); Map 1839?, 6 chns, by Bourn and Jones,

Cleobury Mortimer; waterbodies, houses, woods, field gates, building names.

39/91 Martin Hussingtree (parish) SO 882602
Apt 29.12.1840; 909a (908); Map 1840, 3 chns, 1st cl, by Henry Lakin, junr; foot/b'way, canal, waterbodies, houses, woods, fences, field boundary ownerships, field gates, building names, parsonage, green, heath.

39/92 Martley (except Hillhampton) (parish) SO 752600
Apt 13.04.1843; 4339a (all); Map 1840, 6 chns, by Oates and Perrens, Stourbridge, litho (Standidge); waterbodies, woods, rock outcrops, building names, rectory, court house, avenue of trees.

39/93 Mathon (parish) (partly in Hereford) SO 748458
Apt 28.11.1840; 3366a (3366); Map 1840, 3 chns, by Lakin and Giles, Worcester; foot/b'way, waterbodies, houses, woods (named), plantations, orchards, hops, fences, building names, green, tithe-free lands (green), county boundary (yellow).

39/94 Lower Mitton (hamlet in parish of Kidderminster) SO 800721
Apt 01.03.1845; 861a (861); Map 1849?, 3 chns, 1st cl, litho (by R.B. Moody and Co., Lith, 12 Canon St, Birmm.); foot/b'way, canal with basins (in detail), waterbodies, woods, plantations, orchards, fences, building names, road names, school, mill.

39/95 Newbold upon Stour (parish) SP 246453 [Newbold-on-Stour]
Apt 22.07.1840; 2287a (?); Map 1841, 3 chns, in 2 parts, by E. Cherry; railway ('back cutting'), turnpike roads, toll gate, waterbodies, houses, woods (named), orchards, open fields (named in detail, including quarters, furlongs and pieces, with coloured boundaries), hedge ownership, fences, field gates, road names, field names, mills, wharfs, limekilns, commons, green, glebe, churchyard, rickyard, gardens (by annotation); bridge named. Map and Apt together form an unusually detailed record of open field farming.

39/96 Newland (hamlet in parish of Great Malvern) SO 800492
Apt 12.09.1842; 787a (?); Map 1841, 3 chns, 1st cl, by Henry Lakin, junr, Worcester; construction lines, foot/b'way, waterbodies, houses, woods, parkland, orchards, hops, field boundary ownerships, field gates, building names, chapel, green.

39/97 Northfield (parish) SP 030810
Apt 30.07.1839; 5951a (5951); Map 1840, 6 chns, by Oates and Perrens, Stourbridge, litho (Standidge); railway, foot/b'way, turnpike roads, canal, tunnel, waterbodies, woods (named), rock outcrops, building names, pit, mill, castle.

39/98 Northwick (hamlet in parish of Blockley) SP 164365 [Not listed]
Apt 11.07.1842; 853a (?); Map 1843, 5 chns, by Messrs Crawter; foot/b'way, waterbodies, woods, plantations, parkland (named, in detail), gardens, building names, tithe-free land.

39/99 Norton and Lenchwick (parish) SP 035477
Apt 31.01.1845; 2614a (2614); Map 1845, 6 chns, 'compiled from various plans'; turnpike roads and gate, waterbodies; map is signed by landowners or their agents.

39/100 Norton juxta Kempsey (parish) SO 882512 [Norton]
Apt 19.08.1841; 1812a (all); Map 1839, 3 chns, 1st cl, by R.C. Herbert, Worcester; construction lines, railway, turnpike roads, waterbodies, open fields (named), fences, field boundary ownerships, building names, vicarage.

39/101 Oddingley (parish) SO 915590
Apt 16.01.1838; 869a (869); Map 1838, 3 chns, ? surveyed by Jereh Mathews, 'drawn' by Oates and Perren; railway, foot/b'way, canal with towpath, waterbodies, woods, building names; compass rose is combined with the scale bar.

39/102 Offenham (parish) SP 062455
Apt 27.02.1841; 1216a (1215); Map not dated, 3 chns; construction lines, waterbodies, fences, field boundary ownerships, ferry; ferry is shown pictorially, complete with oarsman.

39/103 Oldberrow, otherwise Oldborough (parish) SP 112670
Apt 26.01.1838; 1186a (all); Map 1839?, 6 chns, by Edw. Cooper, junr; waterbodies, woods, plantations, building names, landowners, rectory; a house is named 'Barrels, the Seat of Robt Knight Esqre'; compass rose has leafy boss. Apt omits land use.

39/104 Ombersley (parish) SO 845645
Apt 17.07.1839; 2301a (6962); Map 1840, 6 chns, by R.C. Herbert, Worcester; turnpike roads, waterbodies, building names. Apt omits land use.

39/105 Orleton (hamlet in parish of Eastham) SO 693670
Apt 03.04.1839; 540a (all); Map 1839, 3 chns, 1st cl, by Lakin and Giles, Worcester; hill-drawing, foot/b'way, waterbodies, houses, woods, ashbeds, 'orles', plantations, fences, field boundary ownerships, field gates, building names, folly, chapel, boundary trees.

39/106 Pedmore (parish) SO 911821
Apt 16.02.1842; 1474a (1474); Map 1846, 5 chns, litho (Standidge); turnpike roads, waterbodies, woods, plantations, rock outcrops, fences, building names, sand pit, racecourse, grandstand, quarry, rectory, common.

39/107 Pendock (parish) SO 815341
Apt 17.03.1841; 1163a (all); Map 1840, 3 chns, by R.C. Herbert and Henry Lakin, junr; turnpike roads, waterbodies, fences, field boundary ownerships, building names, road names, rectory.

39/108 Peopleton (parish) SO 949509
Apt 23.12.1841; 1475a (all); Map 1842?, 6 chns; foot/b'way, turnpike roads, houses, hedges, road names, quarry; bridges named.

39/109 Pershore, Holy Cross (parish) SO 940475 [Not listed]
Apt 30.06.1843; 206a (2950); Map 1846, 3 chns, 1st cl, by Herbert and Smith, Worcester; railway, waterbodies, houses, woods (by name), field boundary ownerships, field gates, building names.

39/110 Piddle Wyre (hamlet in parish of Fladbury) SO 967478 [Wyre Piddle]
Apt 04.12.1841; 369a (?); Map 1841, 5 chns; foot/b'way, houses.

39/111 Pirton (parish) SO 888469
Apt 02.11.1840; 1670a (1669); Map 1840, 6 chns, by R.C. Herbert, Worcester; railway, waterbodies, woods (named), fences, building names, rectory.

39/112 Powick (parish) SO 830500
Apt 09.10.1841; 5194a (5194); Map 1846, 3 chns, 1st cl, by Henry Lakin, junr; turnpike roads, toll gates, waterbodies, woods (named), plantations, open fields, field boundary ownerships, building names, field names, milestones, ford, ferry, vicarage, brick kiln, greens, meadows; hills named.

39/113 Redmarley D'Abitott (parish) SO 763313 [Redmarley D'Abitot]
Apt 30.11.1838; 3779a (all); Map 1838, 3 chns, 1st cl, by Henry Lakin, junr, Worcester; foot/b'way, waterbodies, houses, woods, plantations, parkland, orchards, fences, field boundary ownerships, building names, road names, mills, pinfold, boundary stones.

39/114 Ribbesford (parish) SO 779729
Apt 11.07.1839; 1576a (?); Map 1838, 7 chns, by Jereh Mathews; turnpike roads, waterbodies, woods (named), avenues of trees, building names, glebe (green), tithe-free land (pink); compass rose has floral decoration with the north pointer tipped with an acorn and a banner.

39/115 Rock (parish) SO 740720
Apt 14.02.1842; 7754a (7754); Map 1843, 3 chns, 1st cl, by James Bourn, junr, Cleobury Mortimer; construction lines, waterbodies, houses, woods, plantations, ash beds, quarry.

39/116 Rushock (parish) SO 885711
Apt 07.03.1842; 1219a (1218); Map 1840, 6 chns, by Oates and Perrens, Stourbridge, litho (Standidge); foot/b'way, waterbodies, woods, rock outcrops, fences, building names, rectory.

39/117 Lower Sapey, otherwise Sapey Pitchard (parish) SO 687611
Apt 05.03.1842; 1698a (1697); Map 1841, 3 chns, 1st cl, by James Webb,

Worcester; construction lines, waterbodies, houses, fences, field boundary ownerships, field gates, building names.

39/118 Severn Stoke (parish) SO 856440
Apt 31.10.1840; 3270a (3269); Map 1840, 6 chns, by R.C. Herbert, Worcester; foot/b'way, turnpike roads, waterbodies, woods, fences, building names.

39/119 Shelsey Beauchamp (parish) SO 735635 [Shelsley Beauchamp]
Apt 18.03.1843; 2197a (all); Map 1842, 6 chns, in 2 parts, by Oates and Perrens, Stourbridge, (includes two 3-chn enlargements of detail), litho (Standidge); foot/b'way, waterbodies, woods, hops, rock outcrops, fences, building names.

39/120 Shelsey Walsh (parish) SO 721631 [Shelsley Walsh]
Apt 13.12.1842; 469a (all); Map 1842, 6 chns, litho (Standidge); foot/b'way, waterbodies, woods, building names, forge mill.

39/121 Sheriffs Lench (hamlet in parish of Church Lench) SP 020490 [Sheriff's Lench]
Apt 17.03.1841; 1119a (?); Map 1841, 6 chns, by T. Yells, Bengeworth; foot/b'way, waterbodies, woods, plantations, field gates.

39/122 Shipston on Stour (parish) SP 252403 [Shipston-on-Stour]
Apt 09.01.1840; 1198a (all); Map 1841?, 4 chns; foot/b'way, waterbodies, woods, hedge ownership, field gates.

39/123 Shrawley (parish) SO 801651
Apt 15.11.1838; 1877a (1877); Map 1839, 6 chns, litho (Standidge); waterbodies, woods, rock outcrops, building names, rectory, mill; bridges named.

39/124 Spetchley (parish) SO 895540
Apt 15.08.1840; 779a (779); Map 1839, 3 chns, by James Webb, Worcester; railway with station, waterbodies, houses, arable (col), grassland (col), building names.

39/125 Stanford (parish) SO 708652 [Stanford on Teme]
Apt 15.07.1839; 1279a (1278); Map 1839, 3 chns, 1st cl, by James Webb, Worcester; construction lines, foot/b'way, waterbodies, houses, rock outcrops (named), fences, field boundary ownerships, field gates, building names, parsonage; compass rose decorated with vine leaves and grapes.

39/126 Staunton (parish) SO 780290
Apt 12.05.1842; 1448a (all); Map 1843, 6 chns, 'copied from a survey and map by P. Baker and adopted by the land owners' by Josiah Castree, Gloucester; turnpike roads, toll gates, waterbodies, houses, woods, field boundary ownerships, field gates, building names, mills, parsonage.

39/127 Stock and Bradley (chapelry in parish of Fladbury) SO 987619 [Bradley Green]
Apt 17.03.1847; 1143a (all); Map 1841, 3 chns, 1st cl, by R.C. Herbert, Worcester; construction lines, turnpike roads, tollgate, waterbodies, fences, field boundary ownerships, building names.

39/128 Stockton (parish) SO 714674 [Stockton on Teme]
Apt 23.07.1841; 894a (all); Map 1841, 3 chns, 1st cl, by James Webb, Worcester; construction lines, waterbodies, houses, fences, field boundary ownerships, field gates.

39/129 Stoke Prior (parish) SO 968679
Apt 17.12.1845; 3820a (3820); Map 1846, 3 chns, by John Walker, Birmingham; hill-drawing, foot/b'way, railway with station, railway and canal embankments, canal, reservoir, waterbodies, woods, fences, building names, chapel.

39/130 Stone (parish) SO 857745
Apt 15.07.1841; 2450a (2450); Map 1841, 6 chns, by Oates and Perren, Stourbridge, litho (Standidge); foot/b'way, turnpike roads, canal, waterbodies, woods, building names, mill.

39/131 Stoulton (parish) SO 910503
Apt 30.11.1838; 1952a (1952); Map 1839?, 5 chns; waterbodies, houses, farmyards (col), arable (col), grassland (col), gardens (col), hedge ownership, fences, field gates, building names.

39/132 Suckley (except Alfrick and Lulsley) (parish) SO 723519
Apt 28.03.1838; 2694a (all); Map 1839, 3 chns, 1st cl, by James Webb, Worcester; foot/b'way, waterbodies, houses, woods (by name), fences, field boundary ownerships, field gates, building names, green.

39/133 Sutton (hamlet in parish of Tenbury) SO 615660 [Not listed]
Apt 09.10.1841; 1474a (?); Map 1843, 3 chns, by R.C. Herbert, Worcester, (tithable parts only); turnpike roads, waterbodies, houses, fences, field boundary ownerships, building names, mill.

39/134 Tardebigg (parish) SP 007682 [Tardebigge]
Apt 27.11.1839; 8995a (8994); Map 1842?, 12 chns; railway, canal with tunnel, reservoir, floodgates, old wharf, waterbodies, woods (named), parkland, building names, road names, pound, greens; bridge named; pictorial church.

39/135 Tenbury (township) SO 592678 [Tenbury Wells]
Apt 15.03.1843; 702a (?); Map 1843, 3 chns, 1st cl, by R.C. Herbert, Worcester; waterbodies, fences, field boundary ownerships, building names, road names, market place.

39/136 Foreign of Tenbury (township in parish of Tenbury) SO 600673 [Not listed]
Apt 17.03.1843; 1527a (?); Map 1843, 3 chns, 1st cl, by R.C. Herbert, Worcester; waterbodies, woods (by name), fences, field boundary ownerships, building names, mill.

39/137 Tidmington (parish) SP 254385
Apt 01.09.1841; 754a (754); Map 1842?, 4 chns; foot/b'way, turnpike roads, waterbodies, houses, farmyards, woods, coppices (by symbol), avenues of trees, orchards, gardens, hedge ownership, fences, field gates, road names, field names.

39/138 Tredington (parish) SP 249429
Apt 14.11.1840; 2998a (5285); Map 1843, 3 chns, in 3 parts, by J. Allen, Oxford, (one part at 6 chns, ?1846); railway, foot/b'way, turnpike roads, waterbodies, houses, woods (named), open fields (named in gothic, with quarters and furlongs), hedge ownership, field gates, building names, field names, rectory, common. Apt generalises land use.

39/139 Upton upon Severn (parish) SO 831399
Apt 22.02.1840; 3171a (all); Map 1841, 3 chns, 1st cl; construction lines, foot/b'way, turnpike roads, toll bar, waterbodies, houses, woods, open fields, fences, field boundary ownerships, field gates, building names, parsonage, sand or stone pit, heaths, common, green.

39/140 Upton Snodsbury (parish) SO 944540
Apt 25.05.1839; 1662a (1661); Map 1838, 6 chns, 'compiled from surveys taken at different periods' by R.C. Herbert, Worcester; turnpike roads, waterbodies, woods (named), fences, building names, road names.

39/141 Upton Warren (parish) SO 910685
Apt 14.02.1838; 2601a (2600); Map 1839, 6 chns, by Richd Court, senr, Land Agent and Surveyor, Bewdley, Worcs; turnpike roads, waterbodies, houses, woods (col), orchards, building names, rectory, greens. Apt omits land use.

39/142 Warley Wigorn (township in parish of Halesowen) SO 999836 [Not listed]
Apt 16.04.1840; 1452a (?); Map 1844?, 10 chns, in 4 parts, (includes three 3-chn enlargements of detail); waterbodies, woods, open fields.

39/143 Warndon (parish) SO 885565
Apt 10.11.1841; 989a (all); Map 1843, 3 chns, by James Webb, Worcester; foot/b'way, canal, waterbodies, houses, fences, building names, vicarage.

39/144 Welland (except land disputed between this parish and Little Malvern) (parish) SO 797403
Apt 28.03.1840; 1945a (all); Map 1847, 3 chns, 1st cl, by Henry Lakin, Worcester; turnpike roads, waterbodies, houses, woods, open fields (named), fences, field gates, building names, road names, schoolhouse, commons.

39/145 White Ladies Aston (parish) SO 922523
Apt 20.11.1839; 1231a (1230); Map 1838, 3 chns, by James Webb, Worcester; waterbodies, houses, woods, arable (col), grassland (col), fences, building names.

39/146 Whittington (chapelry in parish of Worcester, St Peter the Great) SO 880530
Apt 06.08.1841; 990a (989); Map 1842, 3 chns, 1st cl, by R.C. Herbert; hill-drawing, railway, turnpike roads, waterbodies, field boundary ownerships, building names, chapel, boundary stones, gravel pits.

39/147 Wichenford (parish) SO 780598
Apt 01.12.1838; 2669a (2669); Map 1838, 3 chns, 1st cl, by James Webb, Worcester; construction lines, foot/b'way, waterbodies, houses, woods (named), fences, field boundary ownerships, field gates, building names; green named.

39/148 Wickhamford (parish) SP 067414
Apt 28.12.1843; 827a (1242); Map 1843?, 8 chns; turnpike roads, waterbodies, woods, orchards, gardens, fences, building names; tithable lands are tinted and numbered; pictorial church.

39/149 Great Witley (parish) SO 761650
Apt 14.02.1838; 2634a (2633); Map 1839, 6 chns, litho (Standidge); hill-drawing, waterbodies, woods, plantations, parkland (in detail), orchards, hops, rock outcrops, fences, building names, rectory, sand or stone pit or quarry; hill named.

39/150 Wolverley (parish) SO 840800
Apt 26.11.1839; 5532a (5532); Map 1838, 3 chns, by James Webb, Worcester; foot/b'way, canal, waterbodies, houses, arable (col), grassland (col), fences, pit, castle; compass rose has floral boss.

39/151 Worcester, St Clements (parish) SO 848552 [Not listed]
Apt 28.05.1841; 35a (149); Map 1845, 3 chns, by James Webb, Worcester; construction lines, foot/b'way, waterbodies, houses, fences, field boundary ownerships, field gates, ferry.

39/152 Worcester, St Martin (parish) SO 870547 [Not listed]
Apt 05.06.1839; 1393a (all); Map 1839, 3 chns, 1st cl; construction lines, foot/b'way, canal, waterbodies, houses, woods (by name), fences, field boundary ownerships, field gates, building names, workhouse.

39/153 Worcester, St Peters the Great (parish) SO 860528 [Not listed]
Apt 15.07.1841; 1251a (1252); Map 1842, 3 chns, 1st cl, by R.C. Herbert, Worcester; construction lines, railway, turnpike roads, toll gate, canal, canal basin, waterbodies, field boundary ownerships, building names, road names, boundary stones; green bands may indicate gardens.

York City and Ainsty

PRO IR29 and IR30 40/1-18

36 tithe districts: 47,692 acres
17 tithe commutations: 14,972 acres
7 voluntary tithe agreements, 10 compulsory tithe awards,
1 corn rent annuity

Tithe and tithe apportionments

Yorkshire, the largest ancient county of England and Wales, includes the smallest tithe county recognised by the Tithe Commission, the City and Ainsty of York. In 1847 the Ainsty was merged with the West Riding but by that time much of its tithe commutation was complete and so its continuing existence as a tithe county was assured. Many parishes in the City of York were already exempt from tithe, and the rural portion included districts which were either wholly exempted by commutation at the time of parliamentary enclosure or in which there were modus payments in lieu of tithes (Fig. 52). Assistant tithe commissioners and local tithe agents who worked in the City and Ainsty of York are listed in Table 40.1 and the valuers of its tithe rent-charge in Table 40.2.

Tithe maps

The tithe maps of the City and Ainsty of York are very similar to those in the adjacent parts of the West and North Ridings. None is sealed as first class and the map content is unremarkable. Despite its small size, the county's tithe maps employ seven different scales, ranging from one inch to one chain to one inch to twelve chains. Wilstrop is one of only four Yorkshire maps in the Public Record Office collection to be lithographed; though the whole district was mapped, less than 3 per cent of its area was subject to tithe.

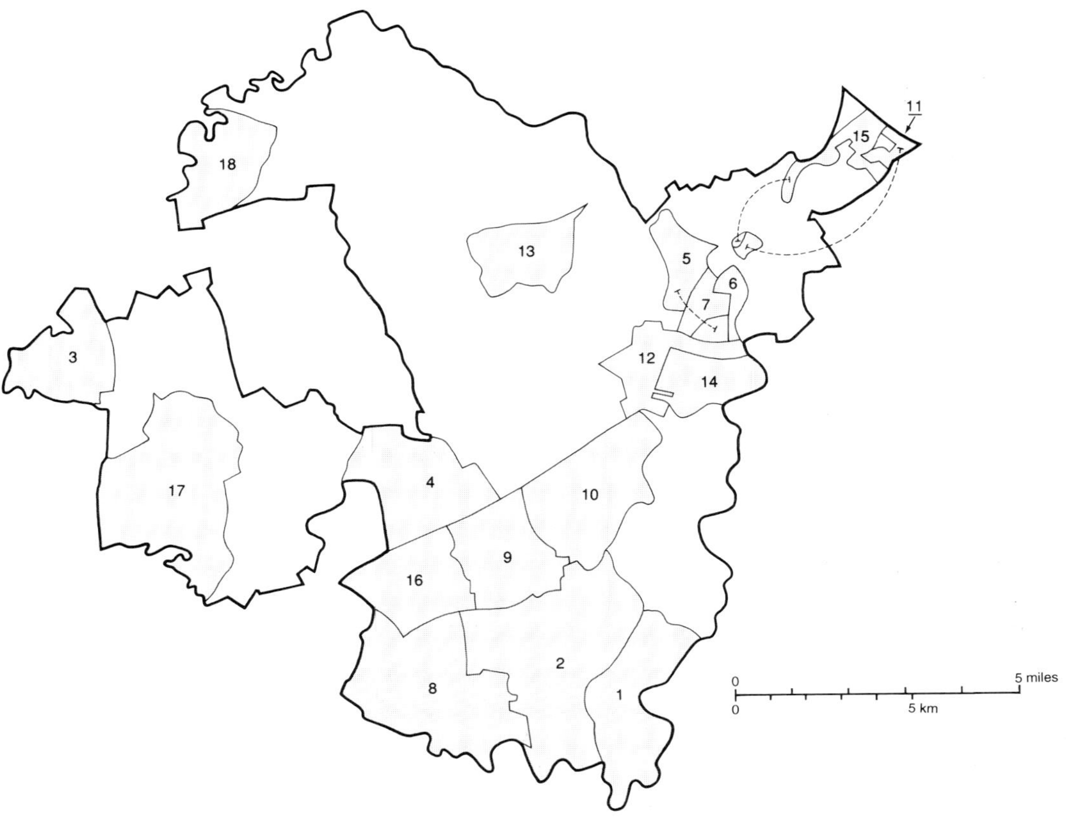

Fig. 52 York City and Ainsty: tithe district boundaries.

Table 40.1. *Agreements and awards for commutation of tithes in York City and Ainsty*

Assistant commissioner/ local tithe agent	*Number of agreements**	*Number of awards*
Charles Howard	7	6
John Job Rawlinson	0	3
John Mee Mathew	0	1

*Computed from the number of extant reports on tithe agreements in the tithe files [PRO IR 18].

Table 40.2. *Tithe valuers and tithe map-makers in York City and Ainsty*

Name and address (all in Yorkshire)	*Number of districts*	*Acreage*
Tithe valuers		
Christopher Paver, Peckfield	3	3,640
Robert Smith, Acaster Malbis	2	1,678
James Bulmer, York	2	1,360
Henry Moiser, Heworth Grange	2	947
Others [8]	8	7,347
Attributed tithe map-makers		
John Humphries, Ripon	2	2,459
Robert Smith, York	2	1,678
Others [6]	6	5,280

Table 40.3. *The tithe maps of York City and Ainsty: scales and classes*

Scale in chains/inch	*All maps*		*First Class*		*Second Class*	
	Number	*Acreage*	*Number*	*Acreage*	*Number*	*Acreage*
>3	1	11	0	0	1	11
3	5	6,280	0	0	5	6,280
4	1	1,390	0	0	1	1,390
4.5	1	546	0	0	1	546
6	6	4,624	0	0	6	4,624
8	2	2,093	0	0	2	2,093
12	1	28	0	0	1	28
TOTAL	17	14,972	0	0	17	14,972

Table 40.4. *The tithe maps of York City and Ainsty: dates*

	1837	*1838*	*1839*	*1840*	*1841*	*1842*	*1843*	*1844*	*1845*	*1846*	*1847*	*1848*	*1849*	*1850*	*1851*
2nd class	1	1	2	0	2	1	1	1	0	3	2	0	1	1	1

York City and Ainsty

40/1 Acaster Seilby (township in parish of Stillingfleet) SE 572417 [Acaster Selby]
Apt 15.09.1838; 1523a (all); Map 1839, 6 chns, in 2 parts, by Tuke and Allanson, York, (includes enlargement of village at 3 chns); foot/b'way, waterbodies, woods, building names, ferry.

40/2 Appleton (township in parish of Bolton Percy) SE 553422 [Appleton Roebuck]
Corn rent conversion, 1926; 1357a (2780); Map 1926, 1:2500, by Ordnance Survey, (tithable parts only); building names, road names, moat. Apt omits occupiers, land use and field names.

40/3 Bickerton (township in parish of Bilton) SE 450506
Apt 25.06.1851; 1024a (1080); Map 1851, 8 chns; waterbodies, Roman road.

40/4 Bilbrough (parish) SE 528468
Apt 24.05.1838; 1390a (1389); Map 1837, 4 chns, by John Humphries; foot/b'way, waterbodies, woods (col), plantations (col), parkland, heath/moor, residual open fields, building names, churchyard, pit, ownerships (col); land of one owner and all tithe-free land are uncoloured.

40/5 St Mary Bishophill the younger (township in parish of St Mary Bishophill the younger) SE 590517 [Not listed]
Apt 26.09.1845; 513a (?) Map 1847, 6 chns, by Thos Holliday; railways, foot/b'way, woods, field boundary ownerships, stiles, city wall and gate.

40/6 St Mary Bishophill the Elder (township in parish of St Mary Bishophill the Elder) SE 602504 [Not listed]
Apt 04.07.1844; 11a (all); Map 1844, 1 chn, by H.R. Spence, York, (tithable parts only in detail); woods, road names, city walls with turrets and gates (named).

40/7 St Mary Bishophill the Elder without the Postern (township in parish of St Mary Bishophill the Elder) SE 596504 [Not listed]
Apt 20.03.1849; 99a (?); Map 1850?, 6 chns, copied by W.J. Ware from a survey made in 1824, (tithable parts only, tinted); foot/b'way, waterbodies, landowners.

40/8 Bolton Percy (township in parish of Bolton Percy) SE 527417
Apt 19.04.1843; 817a (2170); Map 1843, 3 chns, by R. Smith, York, (tithable parts only, tinted); railway, foot/b'way, waterbodies, woods, osiers (by symbol), building names.

40/9 Colton (township in parish of Bolton Percy) SE 545448
Apt 18.04.1845; 1129a (all); Map 1846?, 6 chns, (tinted); railway with occupation crossings, foot/b'way, woods, orchard, gardens.
40/10 Copmanthorpe (township in parish of St Mary Bishophill the younger) SE 563561
Apt 26.09.1837; 1613a (all); Map 1839, [3 chns]; railway, foot/b'way, woods, plantations, stiles. Apt has cropping information.

40/11 St Cuthbert (parish) SE 606518 [Not listed]
Apt 29.04.1845; 546a (all); Map 1846, 4.5 chns, ? by Henry Moiser, Heworth, Yorks N.R., Land Agent; foot/b'way, waterbodies, fence, field boundary ownerships; tithable lands are tinted.

40/12 Dringhouses (township in parishes of Holy Trinity, Micklegate, St Mary Bishophill the elder, and Acomb) SE 580490
Apt 20.08.1839; 752a (751); Map 1842?, 6 chns; turnpike roads, waterbodies, woods, milestone, racecourse.

40/13 Knapton (township in parishes of Acomb and Holy Trinity) SE 557522
Apt 12.10.1841; 861a (all); Map 1841, 3 chns, by R. Smith, York; foot/b'way, woods, orchard, parish boundary.

40/14 Middlethorpe (township in parish of St Mary Bishophill the Elder) SE 594487
Apt 10.09.1838; 608a (all); Map 'made from an Ocular Survey in 1838', [6 chns]; turnpike roads, waterbodies, woods, plantations, orchard, open meadows, building names, road names, race course, gallops, haling road, mileposts, milestone, common.

40/15 St Savior (parish) SE 604521
Apt 05.06.1845; 401a (?); Map 1846, 3 chns, in 2 parts, (tinted); foot/b'way, waterbodies, parkland.

40/16 Steeton (township in parish of Bolton Percy) SE 525443 [Not listed]
Apt 03.06.1846; 1069a (all); Map 1847, 8 chns, ? by John Humphries, Ripon; foot/b'way, waterbodies, woods; colouring of fields is ornamental.

40/17 Wighill (parish) SE 472468
Apt 17.03.1849; 2588a (2588); Map 1849, 3 chns, by William Ellison and William R Bromley; foot/b'way, waterbodies, woods (named), parkland (col), orchard, gardens, building names, green (col), churchyard (col); dikes named.

40/18 Wilstrop (township) SE 488547 [Not listed]
Apt 30.06.1840; 28a (1022); Map 1841?, [12 chns], in 2 parts, litho (by Ingrey and Madeley, 310 Strand, with hand-colour); foot/b'way, woods; the tithable portion is tinted pink.

Yorkshire, East Riding

PRO IR29 and IR30 41/1-209

352 tithe districts: 750,002 acres
209 tithe commutations: 255,113 acres
70 voluntary tithe agreements, 139 compulsory tithe awards

Tithe and tithe commutation

Although geographically a northern county, the tithe survey characteristics of the East Riding of Yorkshire have more in common with Lincolnshire and the midland counties characterised by extensive parliamentary enclosure. In 1836 tithes were still payable in 59 per cent of East Riding tithe districts but enclosure (in a third of tithable districts), modus payments in lieu of tithes (in 30 per cent of districts), the merger of tithes in the land, and exemption by prescription are the main reasons why only 34 per cent of the total area of the East Riding was tithable at this date (Fig. 53).

Assistant tithe commissioners and local tithe agents who worked in the East Riding are listed in Table 41.1. As usual, most valuers of tithe rent-charge lived in or near the county. The employment of a Lincolnshire man to value Burnby is probably due to the fact that much of the tithe district was owned by a Lincolnshire landowner (Table 41.2).

Eight East Riding tithe districts are apportioned by holding and so the tithe apportionments lack information about individual fields; these skeletal schedules of apportionment are matched by seven other tithe apportionments which contain field-by-field cropping information.

Tithe maps

The first-class map coverage of the East Riding is somewhat similar to that of Lincolnshire with maps of this standard extant for less than 5 per cent of tithe districts. Construction lines are present on seven second-class maps but as in other counties it is difficult to gauge the extent to which the tithe maps of the East Riding were compiled from earlier mapping. The specification of the tithe map of Atwick suggests that it is very likely based on an earlier enclosure map. About a third of this tithe district remained tithable after parliamentary enclosure in 1769; the tithe map is at the same scale as the enclosure map (one inch to eight chains) and significantly includes skeletal details of tithe-free lands in the district. At Kilnsea the relationship between the enclosure map of 1840 and the tithe map is

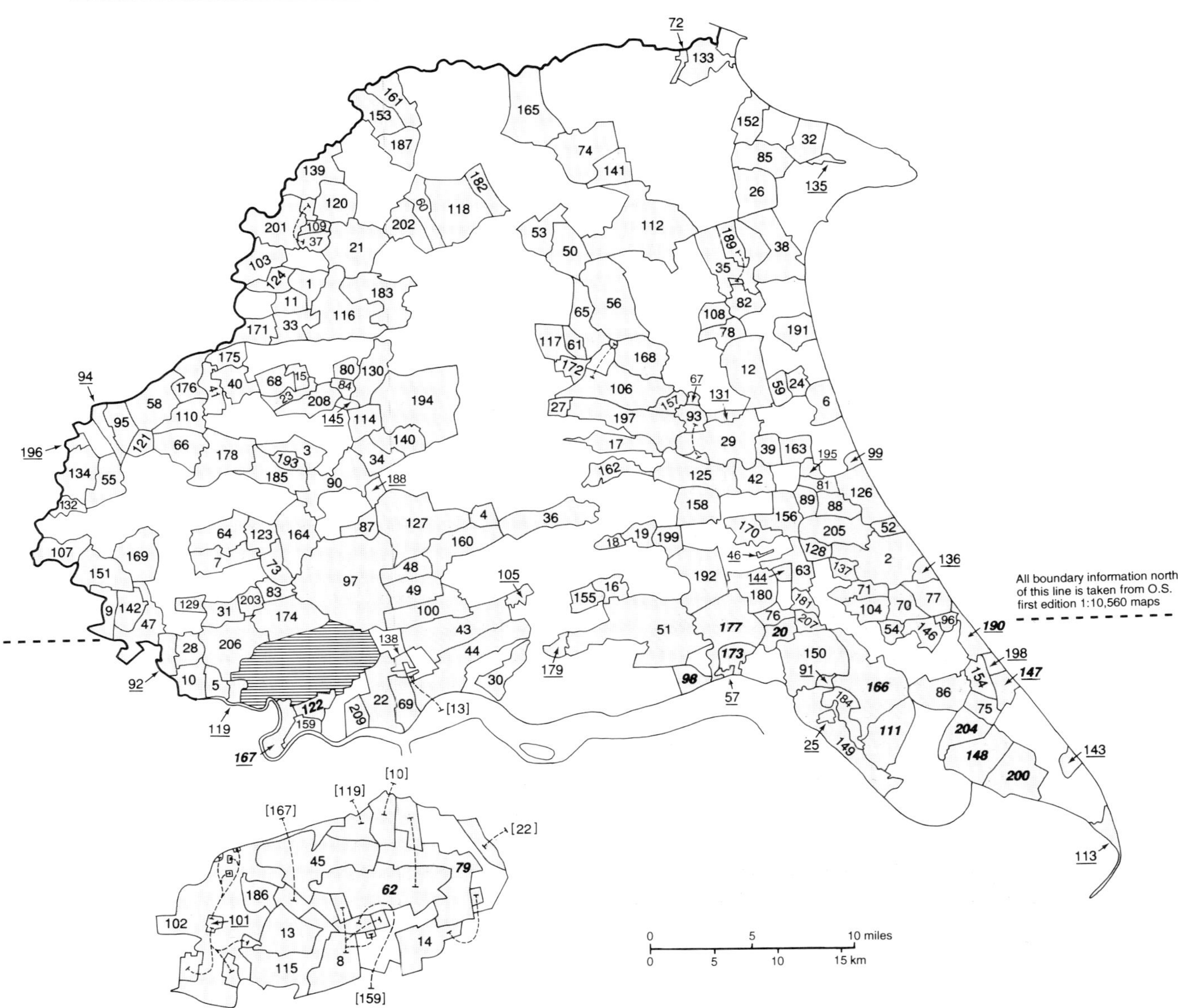

Fig. 53 Yorkshire, East Riding: tithe district boundaries.

less certain. The enclosure map is at eight chains and the tithe map of 1843 is at four chains, though a complete resurvey after so short an interval is rather unlikely.

As usual in counties where much tithe had already been commuted, the output of maps in the East Riding deviated from the national pattern of a single peak around 1839-40. There were three high points in this county: in 1839, 1844 and 1848 (Table 41.4). East Riding tithe maps are drawn at a variety of scales from one inch to two chains to one inch to twenty chains and there are more maps in the East Riding than elsewhere in Yorkshire or in Lincolnshire in the officially recommended scale range of one inch to three to four chains. Indeed, a majority of the county's tithe maps are drawn to these scales.

As guides to land use, East Riding tithe maps are similar to those of the other parts of Yorkshire. Field boundary ownership is indicated on 21 per cent of maps but as elsewhere in Yorkshire there are few maps which distinguish fenced and hedged boundaries.

Map-makers can be identified for 153 East Riding tithe maps in the Public Record Office collection. The most prolific map-maker (as also valuer) was Edward Page of Beverley who made one-sixth of East Riding tithe maps, all characterised by a distinctive, uncoloured and boldly lettered style. The general standard of execution of East Riding maps is better than in the rest of Yorkshire. Apart from wavy-line borders on some of Gregory Page's maps, decorative embellishments are unusual on East Riding tithe maps. A number have scale bars made up like rulers and Ulrome has a snakes-and-eggs decoration in the cartouche. One notable exception to the general rule is the map of South Cliffe which dates from 1775 and was adopted by the landowners without alteration. It has a decorative border and cartouche very different from the general run of East Riding and indeed English and Welsh tithe maps.

Table 41.1. *Agreements and awards for commutation of tithes in Yorkshire, East Riding*

Assistant commissioner/ local tithe agent	*Number of agreements**	*Number of awards*
Charles Howard	43	60
John Job Rawlinson	0	32
George Louis	0	20
Joseph Townsend	2	17
Richard Burton Phillipson	8	0
Robert Hart	6	0
George Wingrove Cooke	0	5
John Mee Mathew	0	4
John Penny	4	0
Henry Pilkington	4	0
John Pickering	2	0
John Story Penleaze	2	0
Charles Pym	1	0
Tithe Commissioners	0	1
Thomas Smith Woolley	1	0

*Computed from the number of extant reports on tithe agreements in the tithe files [PRO IR 18].

Table 41.2. *Tithe valuers and tithe map-makers in Yorkshire, East Riding*

Name and address (all in Yorkshire)	*Number of districts*	*Acreage*
Tithe valuers		
Edward Page, Beverley	24	34,685
Richard Iveson, Hedon	11	18,100
John George Weddall, North Hall, Howden	9	7,126
Leonard Brooke Earnshaw, Hessle	8	8,351
James Dunn, Patrington	8	7,410
Samuel Stephenson, Carlton	7	14,105
George Alderson, York	7	6,278
Daniel Seaton, York	6	7,460
Others [76]	129	151,598
Attributed tithe map-makers		
Edward Page, Beverley	39	55,230
John George Weddall, North Hall, Howden	13	14,732
Richard Iveson, Hedon	10	18,843
Thomas Spenceley, Cottingham	8	16,232
George Alderson, York	8	7,969
Robert Wise, Malton	6	13,307
Francis Carr and ? Holliday, York	6	6,208
Henry R. Spence, Elvington	6	3,676
Others [33]	57	70,696

Table 41.3. *The tithe maps of Yorkshire, East Riding: scales and classes*

Scale in chains/inch	*All maps*		*First Class*		*Second Class*	
	Number	*Acreage*	*Number*	*Acreage*	*Number*	*Acreage*
>3	2	607	0	0	2	607
3	71	95,337	10	18,852	61	76,485
4	44	44,920	0	0	44	44,920
5	4	7,553	0	0	4	7,553
6	50	71,507	0	0	50	71,507
6.67	1	539	0	0	1	539
8	24	21,956	0	0	24	21,956
<8	13	12,694	0	0	13	12,694
TOTAL	209	255,113	10	18,852	199	236,261

Table 41.4. *The tithe maps of Yorkshire, East Riding: dates*

	<1837	*1837*	*1838*	*1839*	*1840*	*1841*	*1842*	*1843*	*1844*	*1845*	*1846*	*1847*	*1848*	*>1848*
All maps	1	3	6	22	15	14	25	16	23	10	14	12	15	32
1st class	0	2	0	2	2	0	1	0	2	1	0	0	0	0
2nd class*	1	1	6	20	13	14	24	16	21	9	14	12	15	32

*One second-class tithe map of the East Riding of Yorkshire in the Public Record Office collection is undated.

Yorkshire, East Riding

41/1 Acklam (township in parish of Acklam) SE 785613
Apt 19.09.1845; 395a (?); Map 1847, 5 chns, by W.J. Ware, (tithable parts only); foot/b'way, woods, quarry. District is partly apportioned by holding, with incomplete owner-occupier information.

41/2 Aldborough, Bewick, Carlton, Fosham, Tansterne and Etherdwick (townships or hamlets in parish of Aldborough) TA 229385 [Aldbrough]
Apt 27.03.1845; 4911a (4911); Map 1840, 3 chns, in 2 parts, surveyed by Edwd Page; foot/b'way, waterbodies, woods, plantations.

41/3 Allerthorpe (township in parish of Thornton cum Allerthorpe) SE 778477
Apt 28.09.1839; 1565a (1565); Map 1840?, 3 chns, surveyed by David Lee; foot/b'way, canal with locks and towpath, woods, parkland, orchards, heath/moor; tithable land and some tithe-free is pink; other tithe-free land, including common, is yellow.

41/4 Arras (hamlet in parish of Market Weighton) SE 922419
Apt 12.03.1841; 875a (?); Map 1846, 4 chns, (tinted); turnpike roads, farmyards (col), woods (col), heath/moor (col), field boundary ownerships, field gates, road names, landowners. Apt omits field names.

41/5 Asselby (township in parish of Howden) SE 717278
Apt 11.11.1841; 387a (1117); Map 1842?, 6 chns, in 2 parts, by J.G. Weddall, North Hall, (tithable parts only); landowners, occupation roads, mill; drain named.

41/6 Atwick in Holderness (parish) TA 187513 [Atwick]
Apt 11.02.1840; 850a (2350); Map 1841?, 8 chns, ? by Edward Page, Beverley, (tithable parts only in detail, banded); foot/b'way, waterbodies, woods, plantations; pictorial church.

41/7 Aughton (parish) SE 722380
Apt 19.04.1842; 761a (4295); Map 1846, 3 chns, ? by Robert Smith; foot/b'way, waterbodies, woods, orchards, gardens, landowners; drain named. Apt omits field names.

41/8 Balkholme (township in parish of Howden) SE 787274
Apt 09.02.1842; 784a (1199); Map 1847, 6 chns, by J.G. Weddall, North Hall, nr Howden; railway, waterbodies, woods, open fields.

41/9 Barlby (township in parish of Hemingbrough) SE 634340
Apt 31.05.1841; 1412a (1411); Map 1842, 3 chns, (tinted); railway, waterbodies, woods, orchards, gardens, open fields (col, named), building names, field names, river embankment, chapel, landing, new road, common (col).

41/10 Barmby on the Marsh (township in parish of Howden) SE 697284
Apt 10.05.1842; 1692a (1711); Map 1842, 6 chns, in 2 parts, (tithable parts only in detail); waterbodies, open fields, field boundary ownerships, ferry, windmill (by symbol), pinfold, woods (by annotation), modus land.

41/11 Barthorpe (township in parish of Acklam) SE 771601 [Not listed]
Apt 19.09.1845; 979a (?); Map 1847, 12 chns; foot/b'way, waterbodies; colouring of fields is ornamental.

41/12 Beeford (township in parish of Beeford) TA 128540
Apt 31.10.1842; 572a (3470); Map 1845?, 4 chns, in 2 parts, ? by Edward Page, Beverley, (tithable parts only; one part at 3 chns); waterbodies, woods, plantations, osiers (by symbol), landowners.

41/13 Belby (township in parish of Howden) SE 770283 [Not listed]
Apt 12.06.1841; 15a (679); Map 1842, 4 chns, in 2 parts, by James Campbell; railway, foot/b'way, canal; tithable parts tinted; acreages are summarised.

41/14 Bellasize (township in parish of Eastrington) SE 814282
Apt 04.11.1844; 607a (1343); Map 1846, 8 chns, by J.G. Weddall, (tithable parts only); railway.

41/15 Bellthorpe (hamlet in parish of Bishop Wilton) SE 781537 [Not listed]
Apt 31.03.1849; 554a (all); Map 1849, 6 chns; foot/b'way, waterbodies.

41/16 Bentley (township in parish of Rowley) TA 024361
Apt 14.03.1838; 1021a (all); Map 1838?, 4 chns, ? by Thomas Donkin, Westow; foot/b'way, waterbodies, woods, pit, landowners; the principal owner's land is coloured yellow. Apt has cropping information.

41/17 Beswick (township) TA 024479
Apt 28.05.1845; 1470a (1593); Map 1846, 3 chns, 'compiled' by Edwd Page; foot/b'way, waterbodies, woods, plantations.

41/18 St Mary, Beverley (parish) TA 021396 [Not listed]
Apt 28.05.1846; 570a (570); Map 1848, 3 chns, 'Compiled' by Edwd Page; foot/b'way, waterbodies, market cross, fish shambles, session house, market place, burial ground, north gate, boundary stones, windmill (pictorial), common pasture; tithe-free land is pink, and apportioned by holding.

41/19 St Nicholas, Beverley (parish) TA 046403 [Not listed]
Apt 28.05.1846; 898a (898); Map 1847, 3 chns, 'compiled' by Edward Page; railway, foot/b'way, waterbodies, woods, road names.

41/20 Bilton (township in parish of Swine) TA 153323
Apt 06.09.1848; 40a (1120); Map 1848, 3 chns, by Geo. Wilkinson, Hull, (tithable parts only); waterbodies, landowners, toll bar, arable (col), grassland (col).

41/21 Birdsall (parish) SE 822643
Apt 12.04.1838; 3973a (all); Map 1838, 8 chns, by Thomas Donkin, Westow; waterbodies, woods, road names, field names, landowners (col), field acreages; gardens, nursery and fox cover are shown by name. Apt has cropping information.

41/22 Blacktoft (parish) SE 843272
Apt 13.03.1838; 3314a (3313); Map 1838, 3 chns, by J.G. Weddall; foot/b'way, canal, waterbodies.

41/23 Bolton (township in parish of Bishops Wilton) SE 773520
Apt 31.05.1841; 904a (all); Map 1841?, 3 chns; foot/b'way, waterbodies, woods, plantations.

41/24 Bonwick (township or district in parish of Skipsea) TA 165529 [Not listed]
Apt 18.01.1840; 746a (745); Map 1841?, 4 chns; woods.

41/25 Boreas Hill (district in parish of Paull) TA 189254
Apt 31.05.1845; 279a (?); Map 1846, 3 chns; waterbodies, woods, parkland.

41/26 Boynton (parish) TA 134690
Apt 17.10.1843; 471a (2690); Map 1845, 8 chns, 'compiled' by E. Page, (tithable parts only in detail); foot/b'way, woods, plantations; pictorial church.

41/27 Bracken (township in parish of Kilnwick) SE 982511
Apt 21.07.1848; 663a (662); Map 1849?, 3 chns, (surveyed by Hy Dodsworth in February 1835; litho by Gibsons, York); waterbodies, houses (black), plantations, orchards, landowners, chalk pit, field acreages, grassland (by annotation); the owner is named in the title; summary acreages are given bottom right. Apt omits field names.

41/28 Brackenholme with Woodhall (township in parish of Hemingbrough) SE 695308
Apt 30.11.1842; 838a (1503); Map 1843, 6 chns, by Joseph Whitle, (tithable parts only); railway, foot/b'way, waterbodies, woods, orchards, building names, embankment, stiles.

41/29 Brands Burton (township in parish of Brands Burton) TA 111484 [Brandesburton]
Apt 20.10.1842; 4563a (all); Map surveyed in 1842, 3 chns, by Edwd Page; hill-drawing, foot/b'way, waterbodies, woods, plantations, parkland, orchards, gardens, pit.

41/30 Brantingham (parish) SE 943293
Apt 18.11.1844; 268a (3632); Map 1844, 4 chns, 'compiled' by Edwd Page, (tithable parts only in detail; includes 12-chn index); waterbodies, woods, plantations.

41/31 Breighton (township in parish of Bubwith) SE 721338
Apt 25.09.1847; 1402a (2030); Map 1848?, 3 chns; foot/b'way, waterbodies, houses, open fields (named), common.

41/32 Buckton (township in parish of Bridlington) TA 175732
Apt 17.10.1843; 89a (2047); Map 1844?, 6 chns, ? by L.B. Earnshaw, Hessle, (tithable parts only in detail); field acreages. District is apportioned by holding; Apt omits most field names.

41/33 Bugthorpe (parish) SE 773579
Apt 30.06.1843; 123a (1990); Map 1843, 8 chns, 'copied from the Plan of the Parish' by W.J. Ware, (tithable parts only, tinted); foot/b'way, waterbodies, woods.

41/34 Burnby (township in parishes of Burnby and Hayton) SE 839465
Apt 18.07.1843; 1668a (all); Map 1849, 9 chns, by Thomas Laughton, Brigg, Lincs; railway, waterbodies, woods (named), building names, chalk pit, springs, rectory, land and tithe ownerships (col), parish boundary. Apt omits land use.

41/35 Burton Agnes and Haisthorpe (townships in parish of Burton Agnes) TA 119621
Apt 18.01.1840; 3852a (3851); Map surveyed in 1840, 6 chns, by E. Page, (includes 12-chn index); foot/b'way, waterbodies, osiers (by symbol), plantations, open fields (named, with balks and field heads named), landowners, stone pit, private roads; drains named; pictorial church.

41/36 North Burton or Cherry Burton (parish) SE 972417 [Cherry Burton]
Apt 28.02.1839; 3362a (all); Map 1840?, 6 chns; foot/b'way, waterbodies, woods, parkland, pits, township boundaries.

41/37 Burythorpe (parish) SE 790648
Apt 19.12.1838; 1226a (1225); Map 1839, 4 chns, by Tuke and Allanson, (tinted); woods.

41/38 Carnaby (parish) TA 155639
Apt 30.06.1849; 214a (2000); Map 1849?, 8 chns, (tithable parts only); waterbodies; pictorial church. Apt omits land use and generalises field names.

41/39 Catfoss (township in parish of Sigglesthorne in Holderness) TA 144472 [Not listed]
Apt 28.12.1838; 1051a (all); Map 1839?, 3 chns, (surveyed in May 1730 by William Brown); woods, field names, field acreages; no buildings or water are shown. Apt omits land use.

41/40 High Catton (township in parish of Catton) SE 730530
Apt 16.05.1843; 404a (1640); Map 1844, 6 chns, by H.R. Spence, York, (tithable parts only); woods, field names, landowners. Apt omits field names.

41/41 Low Catton (township in parish of Catton) SE 712528
Apt 16.05.1843; 81a (2140); Map 1843, 3 chns, by Henry R. Spence, York, (tithable parts only); waterbodies; bridge named.

41/42 Catwick (parish) TA 132450
Apt 17.10.1843; 1a (1650); Map 1844, 8 chns, compiled by Edward Page, (tithable parts only in detail); foot/b'way; pictorial church; only a mill remains tithable, covering 12 perches. Apt omits land use.

41/43 North Cave (parish) SE 903325
Apt 24.11.1841; 3503a (6913); Map 1839, 4 chns, by George Thomas, (tithable parts only in detail); foot/b'way, waterbodies, houses, woods, parkland, road names, stiles, field acreages; drains named; township acreages are summarised.

41/44 South Cave and Bromfleet (townships in parish of South Cave) SE 908304
Apt 30.08.1839; 5466a (6675); Map 1839, 3 chns, in 2 parts, by J.G. Weddall, North Hall; railway, foot/b'way, canal with towpath, waterbodies, plantations, heath/moor.

41/45 Cavil with Partington (township in parish of Eastrington) SE 781307
Apt 19.01.1842; 1203a (1279); Map 1842?, 3 chns; railway, waterbodies, woods, plantations, orchards, gardens, hedge, fence, road names, ownerships (col); legend explains ownership colours.

41/46 Cawood Charity Farm (farm in parish of Swine) TA 142389 [Not listed]
Apt 13.09.1839; 58a (all); Map 1839?, 4 chns, by Geo. Alderson, (tinted); foot/b'way, waterbodies, field boundary ownerships, field acreages, landowners.

41/47 Cliffe cum Land (township in parish of Hemingbrough) SE 664331
Apt 31.05.1841; 2592a (all); Map 1844, 6 chns; railway, foot/b'way, waterbodies, woods, plantations.

41/48 North Cliffe (township in parish of Sancton) SE 862375
Apt 26.08.1848; 4a (1298); Map 1849?, 12 chns, (tithable parts only); canal with towpath, manor house. Apt omits land use.

41/49 South Cliffe (township in parish of North Cave) SE 869357
Apt 26.10.1837; 2025a (all); Map 1775, 4 chns, by P.R. Occlesham; foot/b'way, waterbodies, woods (col), heath/moor, field names, field acreages; pictorial church; colouring of fields is ornamental; legend explains symbols; title is in mirror-frame, with leafy decoration; border has three rows of blocks and arrows; the owner is named in the title; the map appears to be an original of 1775, with an adoption statement pasted to it. Apt omits land use.

41/50 Cottam (township in parish of Langtoft) SE 990637
Apt 18.07.1844; 2540a (all); Map 1843, 8 chns, by L.B. Earnshaw, Hessle; woods; it is unclear why both dot-dash and pecked field boundaries are used.

41/51 Cottingham (parish) TA 044332
Apt 23.01.1838; 9496a (9495); Map 1839, 3 chns, 1st cl, in 2 parts: part 1 by Thos. Spenceley, Cottingham; part 2 surveyed by Geo Wilkinson, Hull in 1838; construction lines, foot/b'way, turnpike roads, toll bar, woods, parkland, gardens, field boundary owner-ships, building names, road names, castle site, stone pits, mill, gravel pit, landing place, ferry, drainage ditches, green; drains named; building names are written in two sizes, according to importance. Apt omits some land use and field names for modus and tithe-free land.

41/52 Little Cowden (parish) TA 237410
Apt 27.05.1851; 500a (all); Map 1852, 3 chns, by Jas. Melrose, York; waterbodies, houses, woods.

41/53 Cowlam (parish) SE 968657 [Not listed]
Apt 18.10.1843; 2036a (2036); Map surveyed in 1844, 3 chns, by Edwd Page, Beverley; foot/b'way, waterbodies, plantations, field boundary ownerships.

41/54 Danthorpe (township in parish of Humbleton) TA 244327
Apt 29.04.1844; 738a (737); Map surveyed October 1844, 3 chns, by L.B. Earnshaw, Hessle; plantations.

41/55 Deighton (township in parish of Escrick) SE 633445
Apt 25.09.1843; 1728a (1947); Map 1844, 6 chns; waterbodies, woods, tithe-free areas.

41/56 Great Driffield and Little Driffield (townships in parish of Great Driffield) TA 023597 [Driffield]
Apt 14.05.1845; 5059a (5058); Map surveyed in 1847, 3 chns, by Edwd Page; railway with station, foot/b'way, canal, waterbodies, plantations; it is unclear why both dot-dash and pecked field boundaries are shown.

41/57 Drypool (township in parish of Drypool) TA 114289 [Not listed]
Apt 30.06.1843; 172a (1156); Map 1851?, 3 chns, (tithable parts only in detail).

41/58 Dunnington (parish) SE 669514
Apt 20.06.1838; 1222a (3199); Map 1839, 3 chns, by Carr and Holliday, (tithable parts only); foot/b'way, waterbodies, woods, building names, stiles.

41/59 Dunnington (township in parish of Beeford) TA 151525
Apt 20.10.1842; 841a (841); Map surveyed 1842, 3 chns, 1st cl, by Edwd Page; foot/b'way, waterbodies, plantations.

41/60 Duggleby (township in parish of Kirkby Grindalyth) SE 877670
Apt 26.06.1844; 1707a (1706); Map surveyed April 1839, 4 chns;

hill-drawing, foot/b'way, waterbodies, houses, woods (col), plantations (col), principal holding boundaries (col).

41/61 East Burn (township in parish of Kirkburn) SE 993563 [Eastburn]
Apt 30.05.1844; 832a (all); Map surveyed in 1846, 3 chns, by Edwd Page; foot/b'way, waterbodies, woods, plantations, orchards.

41/62 Eastrington (township in parish of Eastrington) SE 800298
Apt 15.08.1844; 303a (3580); Map 1845?, 8 chns, (tithable parts only).

41/63 Ellerby (township in parish of Swine) TA 168380 [Not listed]
Apt 22.05.1849; 60a (3470); Map surveyed in 1850, 3 chns, in 4 parts, by Richard Iveson, Hedon, (tithable parts only; includes 12-chn index); waterbodies, field boundary ownerships.

41/64 Ellerton Priory (parish) SE 717401 [Ellerton]
Apt 13.07.1843; 101a (2552); Map 1849?, 6 chns, (tithable parts only, tinted); waterbodies, field boundary ownerships, landowners; tithable buildings are red, and others are grey. Apt omits field names.

41/65 Emswell with Kelleythorpe (township in parish of Driffield) SE 997583
Apt 30.04.1844; 2335a (2376); Map 1842, 6 chns, 'compiled' by Edwd Page; foot/b'way, waterbodies, woods, plantations, heath/moor.

41/66 Elvington (township in parish of Elvington) SE 687479
Apt 13.05.1844; 93a (2256); Map 1849?, 4 chns, (tithable parts only, tinted); landowners.

41/67 Emmotland (township or hamlet in parish of North Frodingham) TA 086517
Apt 23.09.1840; 148a (?); Map 1840, 2 chns, ? by Edward Page, Beverley. Apt omits land use.

41/68 Fangfoss with Spittle (parish) SE 760532
Apt 23.04.1844; 1364a (1364); Map 1845, 6 chns, 'Copied... from Plans and Eye Sketches produced by the landowners' by W.J. Ware; foot/b'way, waterbodies, woods, building names, road names; land shaded pink pays tithe to lay owners as well as to the vicar. Apt omits land use.

41/69 Faxfleet (township in parish of South Cave) SE 861267
Apt 31.07.1844; 1323a (2034); Map 1843, 5 chns, by J.G. Weddall; railway, foot/b'way, canal, building names, brick yard, warping drain, tithe-free land (col); shorter-pecked field boundaries are between ownerships.

41/70 Fitling (township in parish of Humbleton) TA 250350
Apt 21.05.1844; 1504a (1504); Map 1847, 3 chns, by James Dunn; construction lines, foot/b'way, waterbodies, houses, woods (col), orchards (col), gardens (col), field boundary ownerships, stiles.

41/71 Flinton (township in parish of Humbleton) TA 216360
Apt 29.04.1844; 1397a (1397); Map 1844, 3 chns, by Thos. Spenceley, Cottingham, (tinted); construction lines, foot/b'way, waterbodies, woods, gardens, field boundary ownerships, landmark tree, drains (named); scale bar is ruler-like.

41/72 East Flotmanby (hamlet in parish of Folkton) TA 077791 [Not listed]
Apt 13.03.1838; 333a (all); Map 1842?, 8 chns, (tinted); waterbodies, plantations, hedge ownership, landowners; owner is named in the title. District is apportioned by holding, though fields are numbered separately; Apt omits land use.

41/73 Foggathorpe (township in parish of Bubwith) SE 758377
Apt 10.08.1844; 1284a (1284); Map 1842, 6 chns, by Thos Holliday, (tinted); foot/b'way, waterbodies, woods, chapel, stiles.

41/74 Foxholes (parish) TA 005725
Apt 07.06.1838; 2481a (4200); Map 1839, 6 chns, by Henry Scott; waterbodies, woods, well, drain. Apt omits most field names.

41/75 South Frodingham (township in parish of Owthorne) TA 315264 [Not listed]
Apt 06.05.1843; 1190a (1190); Map 1843, 6 chns, by Thos Spenceley, Cottingham, near Hull, (tinted; includes 3-chn enlargement of detail); waterbodies, woods, landowners, hall; scale bar is ruler-like.

41/76 Ganstead (township in parish of Swine) TA 149338
Apt 21.11.1848; 61a (802); Map 1849, 3 chns, (tithable parts only); foot/b'way, waterbodies, woods (col), arable (col), grassland (col), field boundary ownerships, landowners, garden (by annotation,).

41/77 Garton and Grimston (townships in parish of Garton) TA 273354
Apt 23.03.1843; 1787a (1797); Map 1843, 6 chns; waterbodies, woods, plantations, modus land boundary; scale bar is ruler-like.

41/78 Gembling (township in parish of Foston upon the Wolds) TA 110570
Apt 20.07.1843; 22a (1223); Map 1849, 4 chns, by Robt Wise, Malton, (tithable parts only); landowners.

41/79 Gillberdyke (township in parish of Eastrington) SE 827309
Apt 25.05.1844; 474a (570); Map 1845?, 4 chns, by J.G. Weddall, North Hall, Howden, (tithable parts only); waterbodies.

41/80 Great Givendale (township) SE 815541
Apt 11.04.1839; 732a (741); Map 1839?, [20 chns]; foot/b'way, pit; no buildings are shown; meaning of green tint is unclear. District is apportioned by holding; Apt generalises land use and omits field names.

41/81 Goxhill (parish) TA 182445
Apt 29.06.1839; 831a (all); Map 1840, 8 chns, ? by Edward Page, Beverley; hill, waterbodies, woods, glebe, destination pointer; pictorial church.

41/82 Gransmoor (township in parish of Burton Agnes) TA 125597
Apt 16.07.1839; 1234a (all); Map surveyed October 1839, 3 chns, by Wm Ditmas; foot/b'way, waterbodies, plantations, field boundary ownerships, field acreages; the owner is named in the title; yellow band distinguishes land outside district.

41/83 Gribthorpe (township in parish of Bubwith) SE 760356
Apt 16.12.1841; 876a (875); Map 1841, 4 chns, by Henry R. Spence, York; woods.

41/84 Grimthorpe (township in parish of Givendale) SE 814526 [Not listed]
Apt 08.08.1849; 539a (all); Map 1850?, 6.67 chns; foot/b'way, waterbodies, woods (col), field gates, glebe (col), wood pasture; the owner is named in the title.

41/85 Grindale (township in parish of Bridlington) TA 141720
Apt 07.10.1841; 2415a (all); Map surveyed in 1843, 6 chns, by Gregory Page and Henry Scott; waterbodies, field boundary ownerships, destination pointers.

41/86 Halsham (parish) TA 279275
Apt 22.09.1847; 2878a (all); Map 1848, 4 chns, by Richard Iveson, Hedon; waterbodies, field boundary ownerships, drainage ditches.

41/87 Harsewell (parish) SE 828409 [Harswell]
Apt 21.07.1840; 1107a (1106); Map 1840, 6 chns, by John Howgate, Knaresborough, (tinted); foot/b'way, waterbodies, woods, field boundary ownerships; colouring of fields is ornamental.

41/88 Great Hatfield (township in parish of Sigglesthorne in Holderness) TA 198429
Apt 29.06.1839; 940a (939); Map 1840, 10 chns, ? by Edward Page, Beverley; foot/b'way, plantations, heath/moor.

41/89 Little Hatfield (township in parish of Sigglesthorne in Holderness) TA 174432
Apt 29.06.1839; 944a (all); Map 1842?, 4 chns; houses, glebe, field gates; recent and present owner are named, bottom right; buildings are shown by semi-conventional drawings.

41/90 Hayton (parish) SE 804447
Apt 28.05.1838; 1847a (all); Map surveyed in 1837, 3 chns, 1st cl, by

Geo. Alderson, York, (tinted); construction lines, foot/b'way, turnpike roads, waterbodies, houses, woods, mill pool, glebe (col).

41/91 Hedon (parish) TA 189285
Apt 26.08.1848; 312a (1440); Map 1849, 3 chns, by Richard Iveson, Hedon; hill-drawing, waterbodies, haven basin, old haven.

41/92 Hemingbrough (township in parish of Hemingbrough) SE 679305
Apt 31.05.1841; 1095a (all); Map 1841, 6 chns, by Messrs White and Dawson; railway, foot/b'way, waterbodies, woods, orchards, ferry, drain.

41/93 Hempholme (township in parish of Leven) TA 086501
Apt 01.03.1842; 1321a (1320); Map 1842, 4 chns, 'compiled' by Edward Page; woods, plantations, canal with locks and towpath.

41/94 St Lawrence Heslington (township in parish of St Lawrence) SE 631487 [Not listed]
Apt 21.08.1839; 1371a (all); Map 1839, 3 chns, by Carr and Holliday; foot/b'way, waterbodies, woods, open fields (named), hall, windmill.

41/95 St Pauls (township in parish of St Pauls Heslington) SE 641496 [Not listed]
Apt 28.03.1840; 1187a (all); Map 1839, 3 chns, by Carr and Holliday; waterbodies, woods, open fields, pinfold.

41/96 Hilston (parish) TA 286335
Apt 02.07.1846; 549a (548); Map 1846, 3 chns, by James Dunn; construction lines, waterbodies, woods (col), parkland, field boundary ownerships.

41/97 Holme upon Spalding Moor (parish) SE 816367 [Holme-on-Spalding-Moor]
Apt 02.11.1847; 148a (10820); Map 1848?, 4 chns, in 3 parts, (tithable parts only); railway, woods, gardens; tithable buildings are carmine and others are grey; bridge named.

41/98 Holy Trinity, Kingston upon Hull (parish) TA 084284 [Not listed]
Apt 30.06.1843; 459a (1827); Map 1848?, 2 chns, surveyed by Geo. Wilkinson, (tithable parts only); waterbodies, toll bar, old waterworks, botanic gardens, chapel, refuge, college, penitentiary; some tithe-free land is tinted light green, and buildings thereon are dark green; tithable public buildings are grey-brown.

41/99 Hornsea Burton (hamlet or township in parish of Hornsea) TA 210466
Apt 21.05.1844; 401a (?); Map 1845, 6 chns, by Thos Spenceley, Cottingham, (tithable parts only, tinted); waterbodies, woods, landowners; scale-bar is ruler-like.

41/100 Hotham (parish) SE 878341
Apt 29.06.1839; 146a (2670); Map 1840, 4 chns, by E. Page, (tithable parts only, tinted); waterbodies, plantations, parkland, road names, landowners.

41/101 Howden (township in parish of Howden) SE 748286
Apt 17.11.1842; 1803a (?); Map 1844, 6 chns, in 2 parts, by Jas Campbell; railway, foot/b'way, houses (grey), woods, arable (col), grassland (col), orchards, gardens, open fields (named), former open field names, building names, ferry. Apt omits land use for tithe-free land.

41/102 Howden (district in parish of Howden) SE 748295
Apt 28.05.1846; 793a (?); Map 1848?, 6 chns, in 2 parts; railway, waterbodies, woods, field boundary ownerships, building names, former open field names.

41/103 Howsham (township in parish of Scrayingham) SE 750630
Apt 30.11.1838; 2056a (2056); Map 1839, 6 chns; foot/b'way, waterbodies, woods, building names, mill, hauling path, stiles, lodge, field acreages; colours show tithable status; those other than green are modus lands. Apt has some cropping information, but otherwise omits land use, particularly for modus land.

41/104 Humbleton (township in parish of Humbleton) TA 224345
Apt 29.04.1844; 1470a (1469); Map 1845, 3 chns, 1st cl, surveyed by W. Watson; construction lines, foot/b'way, waterbodies, plantations, orchards; scale-bar is ruler-like; village name in title is on sky ground. Apt omits some field names.

41/105 Hunsley (township in parish of Little Weeton) SE 949354 [Not listed]
Apt 10.04.1838; 504a (?); Map 1839?, [4 chns], (tithable parts only); woods, plantations, field acreages. Apt has cropping information.

41/106 Hutton Cranswick (township in parish of Hutton Cranswick) TA 029527
Apt 31.12.1846; 552a (4710); Map 1848, 4 chns, 'compiled' by Edwd Page; railway, woods; pictorial church.

41/107 Kilfield (township in parish of Stillingfleet) SE 597389 [Kelfield]
Apt 17.04.1838; 1729a (all); Map 1839, 6 chns, 'Copied from an Old Plan' by W. Shipton, Land Agent and Surveyor, York, (tinted); waterbodies, houses, woods, parkland, orchards, embankment, holding boundary ownerships.

41/108 Great Kelk (township in parish of Foston) TA 102586
Apt 12.02.1842; 1122a (1131); Map 1841, 4 chns, 'Copied from an Old Plan' by W. Shipton, York; waterbodies, open fields (col, with 'Flatt' numbers), balk.

41/109 Kennythorpe (township in parish of Langton) SE 790660
Apt 10.08.1839; 533a (all); Map 1839, 4 chns, by Tuke and Allanson, (tinted); woods. Apt omits land use and field names.

41/110 Kexby (township in parish of Catton) SE 693505
Apt 16.05.1843; 23a (1751); Map 1848?, 4 chns, (tithable parts only); field names, field acreages, landowners.

41/111 Keyingham (parish) TA 241246
Apt 17.02.1842; 1891a (1890); Map surveyed 1844, 3 chns, in 2 parts, by Richard Iveson, (tithable parts only; one part at 8 chns); construction lines, drains (named).

41/112 Kilham (parish) TA 045658
Apt 24.12.1844; 775a (7660); Map 1846, 4 chns, by Edwd Page, (tithable parts only); foot/b'way, waterbodies, plantations.

41/113 Kilnsea with Spurn (parish) TA 415158
Apt 25.10.1842; 906a (11036); Map 1843?, 4 chns; waterbodies (named), marsh, warren, embankment, lighthouses, coal yard, shed, lifeboat house.

41/114 Kilnwick Percy (parish) SE 830500
Apt 30.04.1838; 1561a (all); Map 1839?, 4 chns; hill-drawing, woods, road names, field names, landowners, hall, parsonage; no other buildings are shown; some physical features named.

41/115 Kilpin (township in parish of Howden) SE 775272
Apt 12.06.1841; 431a (836); Map 1842?, 6 chns, in 2 parts, by John Geo. Weddall, North Hall, (tithable parts only); landowners, ferry.

41/116 Kirbyunderdale (parish) SE 809587 [Kirby Underdale]
Apt 20.03.1838; 5049a (all); Map compiled from maps of 1774, 1800 and 1812, and corrected in November 1837, 8 chns, in 3 parts, by W.J. Ware, (includes one part at 8 chns and 16-chn index); hill-drawing, foot/b'way, waterbodies, woods, parkland, landowners, chalk pit; on part 1 important buildings are red and the rest are hatched.

41/117 Kirkburn (township in parish of Kirkburn) SE 975561
Apt 24.08.1844; 1370a (1369); Map 1846, 4 chns, 'compiled' by Edwd Page; foot/b'way, waterbodies; pictorial church. Apt omits some field names.

41/118 Kirkbygrindalyth, including Mowthorpe (township with hamlet in parish of Kirkbygrindalyth) SE 902675
Apt 09.12.1848; 4487a (4930); Map 1850, 4 chns, by Thomas Buxton, Land Agent and Surveyor, Malton; waterbodies, woods, building names, quarries, glebe.

41/119 Knedlington (township in parish of Howden) SE 731274
Apt 17.02.1842; 181a (668); Map 1842, 3 chns, in 2 parts, by Geo. Alderson, York, (tithable parts only, tinted); orchards, landowners,

ferry; tithable buildings are carmine and others are grey. District is apportioned by holding.

41/120 Langton (township in parish of Langton) SE 807678
Apt 29.06.1844; 2290a (2290); Map 1843, 6 chns, by Robt Wise, Malton; hill-drawing, foot/b'way, waterbodies, woods, osiers (by symbol), parkland, heath/moor (col), field boundary ownerships, racecourse, stand, fishpond, well, quarry, hall, ownerships (col); map date is surrounded by sunburst, and mapmaker's name is on drape between two groups of flowers.

41/121 Langwith (township in parish of Wheldrake) SE 658478 [Not listed]
Apt 28.03.1840; 782a (all); Map 1841, 6 chns, by F. Carr; foot/b'way, waterbodies, woods, heath/moor.

41/122 Laxton (township in parish of Howden) SE 793262
Apt 12.06.1841; 149a (1520); Map not dated, [3 chns], in 3 parts, ? by J.G. Weddall, (tithable parts only; includes index); field boundary ownerships, landowners, green, prominent tree; scale is stated to be 6 chns, but this has been corrected to 3 chns in pencil.

41/123 Laytham (township in parish of Aughton) SE 749403
Apt 30.06.1843; 658a (1365); Map 1846, 10 chns, by Fras Carr, York, (tithable parts only); waterbodies, landowners, right of road.

41/124 Leppington (township in parish of Scrayingham) SE 761615
Apt 13.04.1843; 1163a (all); Map 1843, 6 chns; woods, residual open fields, fords.

41/125 Leven (township in parish of Leven) TA 088457
Apt 01.03.1842; 2041a (3517); Map 1842, 6 chns, compiled by Edward Page, (tithable parts only in detail); foot/b'way, waterbodies, woods, canal with locks and towpath, glebe; pictorial church.

41/126 Mappleton (parish) TA 219437
Apt 28.12.1838; 2450a (all); Map 3 chns, in 4 parts, (includes 9-chn index): Mappleton 'Surveyed Octr. 1839 by R.A. S... [flaked] under the Inspection of Edwd Page'; Rowlston surveyed in 1839 by Geo. Wilkinson, Hull; Great Hatfield, 1840; foot/b'way, waterbodies, plantations, gardens, heath/moor, open fields, field boundary ownerships, field names, hall; the map content varies between the parts.

41/127 Market Weighton with Shipton (district in parish of Market Weighton with Shipton) SE 875412
Apt 06.05.1846; 134a (?); Map 1846, 4 chns, in 5 parts, by W.B. Plummer and W. Thompson, (tithable parts only; including location diagram); built-up part generalised; leaves, mistletoe and banner decorate Plummer's cartouche; Thompson's cartouche is octagonal, and his map has a table of acreages.

41/128 Marton (township in parish of Swine) TA 179392
Apt 28.04.1849; 938a (950); Map surveyed 1849, 3 chns, by Richard Iveson, Hedon, Yorks; waterbodies, field boundary ownerships; scale-bar is ruler-like.

41/129 Menthorpe (township in parish of Skipwith and Hemingbrough) SE 696345
Apt 13.08.1839; 623a (990); Map 1839?, 3 chns, 1st cl, ? by George Alderson, York, (tinted); construction lines, waterbodies, houses, ferry, common (col), tithe-free land.

41/130 Millington (parish) SE 836539
Apt 30.11.1843; 455a (2750); Map 1850, 12 chns, (tithable parts only); waterbodies, woods.

41/131 Moor Town (township in parish of Brands Burton) TA 110503 [Not listed]
Apt 22.12.1842; 498a (all); Map 1845, 4 chns, 'compiled' by E. Page; foot/b'way, waterbodies, plantations, field gates, old moat; bridge and drains named.

41/132 Moreby (township in parish of Stillingfleet) SE 601427 [Not listed]
Apt 31.03.1842; 656a (?); Map 1842, 6 chns, (tinted); foot/b'way, waterbodies, woods, parkland (named), orchards, gardens, open meadows; land awarded in lieu of tithe on ings is tinted beige; dikes named.

41/133 Muston (township in parish of Hunmanby) TA 097798
Apt 07.09.1838; 2226a (all); Map 4 chns, partly surveyed in 1838 by T. Duggleby and Son, Hunmanby; waterbodies, woods, road names, cliff, windmill (pictorial), quarry, lodge, glebe (col), waste (col), moors; drain named; pictorial church. Apt generalises or omits field names.

41/134 Naburn (township) SE 612454
Apt 16.05.1848; 320a (2466); Map 1849, 6 chns, (tithable parts only); waterbodies, woods.

41/135 Newsome Field (district in parish of Bempton or Benton) TA 189716 [Not listed]
Apt 29.06.1840; 304a (all); Map 1841, 4 chns, surveyed by H. Scott; waterbodies, woods, hedge ownership, mill; cartouche is decorated with flowers and thistles at bottom.

41/136 East Newton and Ringborough (township in parish of Aldborough) TA 267374
Apt 28.03.1845; 630a (630); Map surveyed July 1845, 3 chns, by E. Page; construction lines, foot/b'way, waterbodies, plantations, field boundary ownerships.

41/137 West Newton (township in parish of Aldborough) TA 202377
Apt 25.07.1845; 779a (778); Map 1847, 3 chns, surveyed by Richd Iveson, Hedon, Yorks; waterbodies, field boundary ownerships.

41/138 New Village (district) SE 860298
Apt 09.09.1846; 410a (all); Map 1847?, 6 chns, by J.G. Weddall, North Hall, nr Howden, (includes enlargement of village at 3 chns); canal with towpath, waterbodies, woods, orchards.

41/139 Norton (parish) SE 790704
Apt 21.02.1846; 2378a (2679); Map 1848, 4 chns, by Robt Wise, Malton; hill-drawing, railway, foot/b'way, waterbodies, woods, orchards, building names, bone mill, pit, vicarage; sunburst decorates map title. Apt omits field names.

41/140 Nunburnholme (township in parish of Nunburnholme) SE 856483
Apt 18.08.1849; 69a (1480); Map 1850, 8 chns, (tithable parts only, tinted); woods, landowners.

41/141 Octon Grange (district in parish of Thwing) TA 025705
Apt 31.07.1839; 538a (?); Map 1842?, 20 chns; foot/b'way, building names, landowners. Apt omits land use and field names.

41/142 Osgodby (township in parish of Hemingbrough) SE 647343
Apt 31.05.1841; 313a (1524); Map 1841, 9 chns; railway, woods, landowners, tithe-free lands (col).

41/143 Outnewton (township in parish of Easington) TA 382219 [Out Newton]
Apt 25.08.1842; 661a (all); Map 1842, 3 chns; waterbodies, rock outcrops, cliffs.

41/144 Owbrough (hamlet in parish of Swine) TA 155372 [Oubrough]
Apt 15.02.1839; 456a (all); Map surveyed 1839, 3 chns, by Wm Dilmas; waterbodies, plantations, field boundary ownerships.

41/145 Ousthorpe (township in parish of Pocklington) SE 816514 [Not listed]
Apt 06.09.1843; 330a (all); Map 1844, 3 chns; foot/b'way, waterbodies, ford.

41/146 Owstwick (township in parish of Roos and Garton) TA 272325
Apt 13.04.1843; 1331a (1330); Map surveyed in 1840, 3 chns, by Richard Iveson, near Hedon, Yorks; waterbodies, houses, woods, hedge ownership.

41/147 Owthorne (township in parish of Owthorne) TA 332281
Apt 28.04.1843; 241a (1278); Map 1847, 3 chns, by Thos Spenceley,

Cottingham, (tithable parts only, tinted); waterbodies, field boundary ownerships; scale-bar is ruler-like.

41/148 Patrington (parish) TA 312225
Apt 20.03.1843; 184a (4494); Map 1843, 6 chns, (tithable parts only); drain named.

41/149 Paull (district in parish of Paull) TA 202234
Apt 29.09.1849; 4539a (?); Map 1850, 6 chns, by Richard Iveson, Hedon, Yorks; foot/b'way, waterbodies; very few buildings are shown.

41/150 Preston (township in parish of Preston) TA 181305
Apt 05.04.1843; 4980a (5370); Map 1848, 5 chns, surveyed by Richard Iveson, Hedon, Yorks; foot/b'way, waterbodies, foreshore (col), low water mark, drainage ditches.

41/151 Riccall (parish) SE 627375
Apt 23.08.1842; 2055a (3060); Map 1842, 3 chns, ? by George Alderson; foot/b'way, waterbodies, woods, parkland, open fields (col, named), building names, embankment, footbridge, boundary of tithe-free land; enclosed land is tinted green.

41/152 Righton or Reighton (parish) TA 131747
Apt 23.04.1844; 3a (1818); Map 1844, 8 chns, 'compiled' by Gregory Page, (tithable parts only in detail).

41/153 Rillington (township in parish of Rillington) SE 840753
Apt 12.11.1847; 2136a (2460); Map 1848, 4 chns, 'Copied from Divers Maps and Surveys' by R. Wise, Malton; railways with station, foot/b'way, waterbodies, woods, plantations, heath/moor; map date is surrounded by a sunburst. Apt omits field names.

41/154 Rimswell (township in parish of Owthorne) TA 313286
Apt 29.03.1844; 1217a (1216); Map 1844, 3 chns, 1st cl, surveyed by Robert Iveson, Hedon; construction lines, foot/b'way, woods, field boundary ownerships.

41/155 Risby (township in parish of Rowley) TA 003352
Apt 28.02.1839; 964a (all); Map surveyed March 1840, 3 chns, 1st cl, by Edward Page; construction lines, foot/b'way, waterbodies, woods, plantations, heath/moor, field boundary ownerships.

41/156 Rise (parish) TA 156421
Apt 30.04.1838; 1820a (2012); Map 1838?, 8 chns; foot/b'way, woods, gardens, field names, field acreages, landowners (col), footbridge; pictorial church. Apt omits land use.

41/157 Rotsea (township in parish of Hutton Cranswick) TA 071514
Apt 31.12.1846; 784a (783); Map surveyed January 1848, 4 chns, by Edward Page; woods, plantations; dyke named.

41/158 Routh (parish) TA 090427
Apt 27.09.1843; 2383a (all); Map surveyed 1844, 3 chns, by E. Page; waterbodies, woods, parkland, field boundary ownerships, drains.

41/159 Saltmarshe (township in parish of Howden) SE 780244
Apt 15.06.1841; 1050a (1190); Map 1842, 8 chns, in 2 parts, by J.G. Weddall, North Hall; foot/b'way, landowners; tithe-merged land is olive-green.

41/160 Sancton (township in parish of Sancton) SE 904398
Apt 25.10.1842; 1856a (3410); Map 1841, in 2 parts: part 1 surveyed by David Sait for the enclosure commissioners in 1770, 16 chns; part 2 by E. Page, 4 chns; former open field names; no buildings are shown.

41/161 Scampston (township in parish of Rillington) SE 858762
Apt 05.02.1847; 115a (2382); Map 1848?, 6 chns, (tithable parts only); foot/b'way, waterbodies, parkland, landowners; owner is named in the title. District is apportioned by holding.

41/162 Scorborough (parish) TA 025460
Apt 21.07.1840; 1325a (1324); Map 1843, 4 chns, 'compiled' by Edwd Page; foot/b'way, waterbodies, woods, plantations, parkland, orchards, gardens, footbridges.

41/163 Seaton (district in parish of Sigglesthorne) TA 165474
Apt 29.06.1839; 1203a (all); Map 1840, 3 chns, 1st cl, surveyed by E. Page; construction lines, foot/b'way, woods, field boundary ownerships.

41/164 Seaton Ross (parish) SE 778402
Apt 21.10.1850; 765a (3380); Map 1851, 8 chns, by Geo. Alderson, York, (tithable parts only in detail, tinted); waterbodies, woods, landowners; tithable buildings are red and tithe-free are hatched.

41/165 Sherburn (parish) SE 958759
Apt 10.01.1849; 4688a (4630); Map 1850, 6 chns, by Robt Wise, Malton; railway with station, waterbodies, plantations, quarry.

41/166 Skeckling with Burstwick (parish) TA 223287
Apt 17.07.1849; 1235a (5720); Map 1850, 3 chns, in 2 parts surveyed by Rd Iveson, Dock St, Hull, (tithable parts only); construction lines, waterbodies, field boundary ownerships.

41/167 Skelton (township in parish of Howden) SE 767240
Apt 14.09.1841; 257a (1545); Map 1843, 8 chns, by John Geo. Weddall, North Hall, Faxfleet, (tithable parts only); landowners.

41/168 Skerne (parish) TA 046552
Apt 30.11.1847; 178a (2733); Map 1849, 6 chns, 'compiled' by Edwd Page, (tithable parts only in detail); railway, waterbodies, landowners.

41/169 Skipwith (township in parish of Skipwith) SE 657387
Apt 26.01.1840; 1783a (2569); Map 1841, 3 chns, by Geo. Alderson, York, (tinted); foot/b'way, waterbodies, woods, underwood, parkland, orchards, open fields (col, named), field names, hall, footbridge, common (col).

41/170 North Skirlaugh and Rowton and part of Arnold (district in parish of Swine) TA 130411
Apt 12.09.1848; 82a (510); Map surveyed January 1849, 3 chns, by Edward Page, (tithable parts only in detail); foot/b'way, woods, landowners.

41/171 Skirpenbeck (parish) SE 745575
Apt 31.03.1843; 1a (1560); Map 1843, 3 chns, by W.J. Ware, (tithable parts only); parkland, landowners, toll bar.

41/172 Southburn (township in parish of Kirkburn) SE 991544
Apt 24.08.1844; 1022a (1021); Map 1846, 4 chns, 'compiled' by Edwd Page.

41/173 Southcoates or Sudcoates (township in parish of Drypool) TA 119302 [Not listed]
Apt 29.07.1843; 250a (1050); Map 1851, 6 chns, (tithable parts only); waterbodies.

41/174 Spaldington (township in parishes of Bubwith and Aughton) SE 769334
Apt 31.03.1849; 3358a (3170); Map 1851, 12 chns; woods, tithe-free land (col).

41/175 Stamford Bridge East (township in parish of Catton) SE 725553 [Not listed]
Apt 16.05.1843; 1a (680); Map 1844, 3 chns, by Henry R. Spence, York; weir; only the tithable part, a mill, is mapped.

41/176 Stamford Bridge West with Scoreby (township in parish of Catton) SE 696537 [Not listed]
Apt 09.06.1841; 23a (1891); Map 'Outline Plan', 1841, 8 chns, by Henry R. Spence, York, (tithable parts only in detail); woods.

41/177 Sutton and Stoneferry (township in parish of Sutton) TA 114330 [Sutton-on-Hull]
Apt 13.07.1843; 548a (4450); Map 1851, 6 chns, by Abraham Atkinson, Longholme, (tithable parts only).

41/178 Sutton upon Derwent (parish) SE 720470
Apt 06.08.1844; 1070a (3360); Map 1844?, 12 chns; foot/b'way. District is apportioned by owner, only one occupier is named, and fields are not shown.

41/179 Swanland (township in parish of Ferriby) SE 983311

Apt 29.06.1839; 743a (4118); Map 1840, 3 chns, in 3 parts, surveyed by Robt Iveson, 2 Victoria Place, Vincent St, Hull, (tithable parts only); foot/b'way, woods, field boundary ownerships, landowners.

41/180 Swine (township in parish of Swine) TA 135361
Apt 21.11.1848; 51a (2190); Map 1849, 3 chns, by Geo. Wilkinson, Hull, (tithable parts only); foot/b'way, waterbodies, woods, arable (col), grassland (col), field boundary ownerships, landowners, chapel.

41/181 Thirtleby (township in parish of Swine) TA 172349
Apt 15.06.1842; 750a (750); Map 1842, 3 chns, by Thos Spenceley, Cottingham, (tinted); foot/b'way, waterbodies, woods, gardens, field boundary ownerships, tithe-free land (pink), drains (named); scale-bar is ruler-like. Apt omits land use and field names for tithe-merged land.

41/182 Thirkleby (township in parish of Kirbygrindalythe) SE 925689 [Not listed]
Apt 02.02.1843; 1344a (1343); Map 1843, 8 chns, by Thos Buxton, Land Agent and Surveyor, Malton; waterbodies, landowners.

41/183 Thixondale (township in parish of Wharram Percy) SE 846606 [Thixendale]
Apt 21.11.1845; 988a (3697); Map 1846, 6 chns, by Francis Carr, York, (tithable parts only); waterbodies, plantations, landowners. Apt omits field names.

41/184 Thorngumbald (township in parish of Paull in Holderness) TA 204254
Apt 30.03.1849; 1602a (1450); Map 1848, 6 chns, by John Webster, 118 Osborne St, Hull; orchards.

41/185 Thornton (township in parish of Thornton) SE 759454
Apt 05.02.1845; 2291a (2290); Map 1844, 3 chns, by Henry R. Spence, York; foot/b'way, waterbodies, woods, plantations, orchards, canal with locks and towpath.

41/186 Thorpe (township in parish of Howden) SE 760297 [Not listed]
Apt 15.06.1841; 15a (296); Map 1842, 4 chns, by Jas Campbell; arable (col), grassland (col), field acreages, canal with towpath.

41/187 Thorpe Bassett (parish) SE 861729
Apt 25.11.1841; 1793a (all); Map 1842, 3 chns, by Robt Wise, Malton; foot/b'way, waterbodies, woods, plantations, orchards, hedge, building names, pits or quarries; colour bands show owners and field boundary ownership; map date is on sky background.

41/188 Thorpe le Street (township in parish of Nunburnholme) SE 838440
Apt 18.03.1837; 657a (all); Map 1837, 3 chns, 1st cl, by Geo. Alderson, York; foot/b'way, houses, woods (col), osiers (by symbol), parkland, arable (col), grassland (col), gardens (col), field boundary ownerships, field gates, field acreages, glebe. Apt has cropping information.

41/189 Thurnholme (township in parish of Burton Agnes) TA 116644 [Thornholme]
Apt 07.05.1840; 1324a (1324); Map 1841?, 6 chns, in 2 parts, ? by Alfred Simpson; plantations, open fields, road names, landowners; stream named.

41/190 Tunstall (parish) TA 300327
Apt 20.03.1843; 98a (1607); Map 1847, 6 chns, by James Dunn, (tithable parts only); foot/b'way, houses, field boundary ownerships, landowners; pictorial church; link-lines with chain distances show relationship of mapped parts to church.

41/191 Ulrome or Ouram (chapelry in parishes of Barmston and Skipsea) TA 162571
Apt 27.09.1843; 120a (1651); Map 1844?, [8 chns], (tithable parts only in detail, tinted); former open field names, landowners; larger houses and church are shown pictorially; map title is decorated with two brown snakes, coloured triangles, and what appear to be multi-coloured eggs. District is apportioned by holding; Apt generalises land use.

41/192 Waghen (township in parish of Waghen) TA 096372 [Wawne]
Apt 06.06.1846; 3696a (3695); Map 1842, 3 chns, by Edward Page; hill-drawing, foot/b'way, waterbodies, woods, plantations, osiers (by symbol), orchards, gardens, field boundary ownerships, pits.

41/193 Waplington (township) SE 772466 [Not listed]
Apt 15.02.1839; 790a (790); Map 1839?, [4 chns], in 2 parts; only field boundaries and names are shown.

41/194 Warter (parish) SE 872516
Apt 20.04.1844; 1969a (all); Map 1844, 6 chns, by Thos Spenceley, Cottingham, (tithable parts only); waterbodies, woods, field boundary ownerships; scale bar is ruler-like.

41/195 Wassand (district in parish of Sigglesthorne) TA 175459 [Not listed]
Apt 29.06.1839; 506a (?); Map 1840, 4 chns, ? by Edward Page, Beverley; foot/b'way, waterbodies, woods, parkland, reeds.

41/196 Water Fulford (township in parish of Fulford or St Martin Micklegate York) SE 607479 [Fulford]
Apt 23.05.1844; 266a (432); Map 1844, 6 chns, (tithable parts only); foot/b'way, woods.

41/197 Walton (parish) TA 031501
Apt 25.05.1849; 123a (?); Map 1850?, 9 chns, by W. Hodgson, East Ayton, (tithable parts only in detail, tinted); foot/b'way, field acreages. Apt generalises land use.

41/198 Waxholme (township in parish of Owthorne) TA 320301
Apt 13.04.1843; 534a (746); Map 1844, 3 chns, 1st cl, surveyed by Robt Iveson, Hedon; construction lines, foot/b'way, open fields, field boundary ownerships.

41/199 Weel (township in parish of St John Beverley) TA 067399
Apt 27.09.1849; 50a (1150); Map 1851, 4 chns, 'compiled' by Gregory Page, (tithable parts only in detail).

41/200 Welwick (parish) TA 342209
Apt 17.06.1846; 921a (6694); Map 1846?, 8 chns, in 3 parts, by James Dunn, (tithable parts only); foot/b'way, waterbodies, woods, field boundary ownerships, green lane (col).

41/201 Westow (parish) SE 765659
Apt 25.03.1840; 2918a (2917); Map 1841?, 6 chns; foot/b'way, waterbodies, woods, plantations. Apt omits land use.

41/202 Wharram le Street (parish) SE 865660
Apt 12.04.1838; 2001a (all); Map 1838, 4 chns, by Thomas Donkin, Westow; foot/b'way, waterbodies, woods, plantations, building names, field names, landowners (col), field acreages. Apt has cropping information.

41/203 Willitoft (township in parishes of Bubwith and Aughton) SE 741348
Apt 21.01.1843; 855a (all); Map 1847, 5 chns; woods; land tinted yellow and unnumbered is presumably tithe-free.

41/204 Winestead (parish) TA 297242
Apt 12.08.1851; 9a (2570); Map (drawn on Apt) 1852?, 3 chns, by E. Jackson, (tithable parts only); foot/b'way, turnpike roads, waterbodies, woods.

41/205 Withernwick (parish) TA 196408
Apt 11.08.1843; 209a (2600); Map 1844, 8 chns, (tithable parts only).

41/206 Wressle (parish) SE 728311
Apt 09.07.1839; 3705a (all); Map 1839, 6 chns, by M. Durham, Thorne, (tinted); railway, foot/b'way, waterbodies, woods, field boundary ownerships, castle, windmills (by symbol). Apt has cropping information.

41/207 Wyton (township in parish of Swine) TA 176334
Apt 15.06.1842; 788a (all); Map 1842, 3 chns, by Thos Spenceley, Cottingham, (tinted); construction lines, foot/b'way, waterbodies, woods, parkland, gardens, field boundary ownerships, toll bar; drains named; ditches across fields are shown discontinuously; scale-bar is ruler-like.

41/208 Yapham and Meltonby alias Meltonby and Yapham (township in parish of Pocklington) SE 786513
Apt 12.06.1844; 1819a (all); Map 1845, 6 chns, by Thos Holliday; foot/b'way, waterbodies, woods, mill.

41/209 Yokefleet (township in parish of Howden) SE 825253
Apt 22.05.1845; 80a (1597); Map 1847?, 8 chns, in 3 parts, by J.G. Weddall, North Hall, nr Howden, (tithable parts only; includes 80-chn index); woods, building names; drains named.

Yorkshire, North Riding

PRO IR29 and IR30 42/1-421

520 tithe districts: 1,358,379 acres
421 tithe commutations: 789,883 acres
202 voluntary tithe agreements, 219 compulsory tithe awards

Tithe and tithe commutation

In 1836 81 per cent of the tithe districts of the North Riding by number but only about 58 per cent of the county by area were still subject to payment of tithes (Fig. 54). As usual in northern England the main reason for tithe exemption was the payment of a modus in lieu of tithes (in 58 per cent of tithable districts). Commutation of tithes in the course of parliamentary enclosure is the reason for many wholly tithe-free districts and substantially reduced the proportion of tithable land in some 10 per cent of other districts. Other important reasons for tithe exemption in the North Riding were the merger of tithes in the land and exemption by prescription.

Assistant tithe commissioners and local tithe agents who worked in the North Riding of Yorkshire are listed in Table 42.1 and the valuers of tithe rent-charge in Table 42.2. In seventeen districts tithes are apportioned by holding and so the schedules of tithe apportionment lack information on field names and land use.

Tithe maps

Only two North Riding maps, both of small tithe districts, are sealed as first class and construction lines are present on only two second-class maps. Some maps have indications that they were constructed by new surveys as, for example, at Bishopdale where the map-maker Edward Other writes, 'made in November and December 1838.' As in other counties with a number of districts with only small tracts of tithable land, there were two peaks of map production, in 1839 and in 1846-49 (Table 42.4).

The tithe maps of the North Riding are drawn at a variety of scales from one inch to one chain to one inch to sixteen chains; 44 per cent of maps are in the officially recommended scale range of one inch to three to four chains. About 37 per cent of maps are at the six-chain scale and most of the remainder of the county is mapped at the eight-chain scale.

As is common in northern England, the tithe maps of the North Riding are informative about woodland, which is portrayed on 78 per cent of the maps but other land uses are poorly mapped. A marked problem with North Riding maps is that tree symbols are often

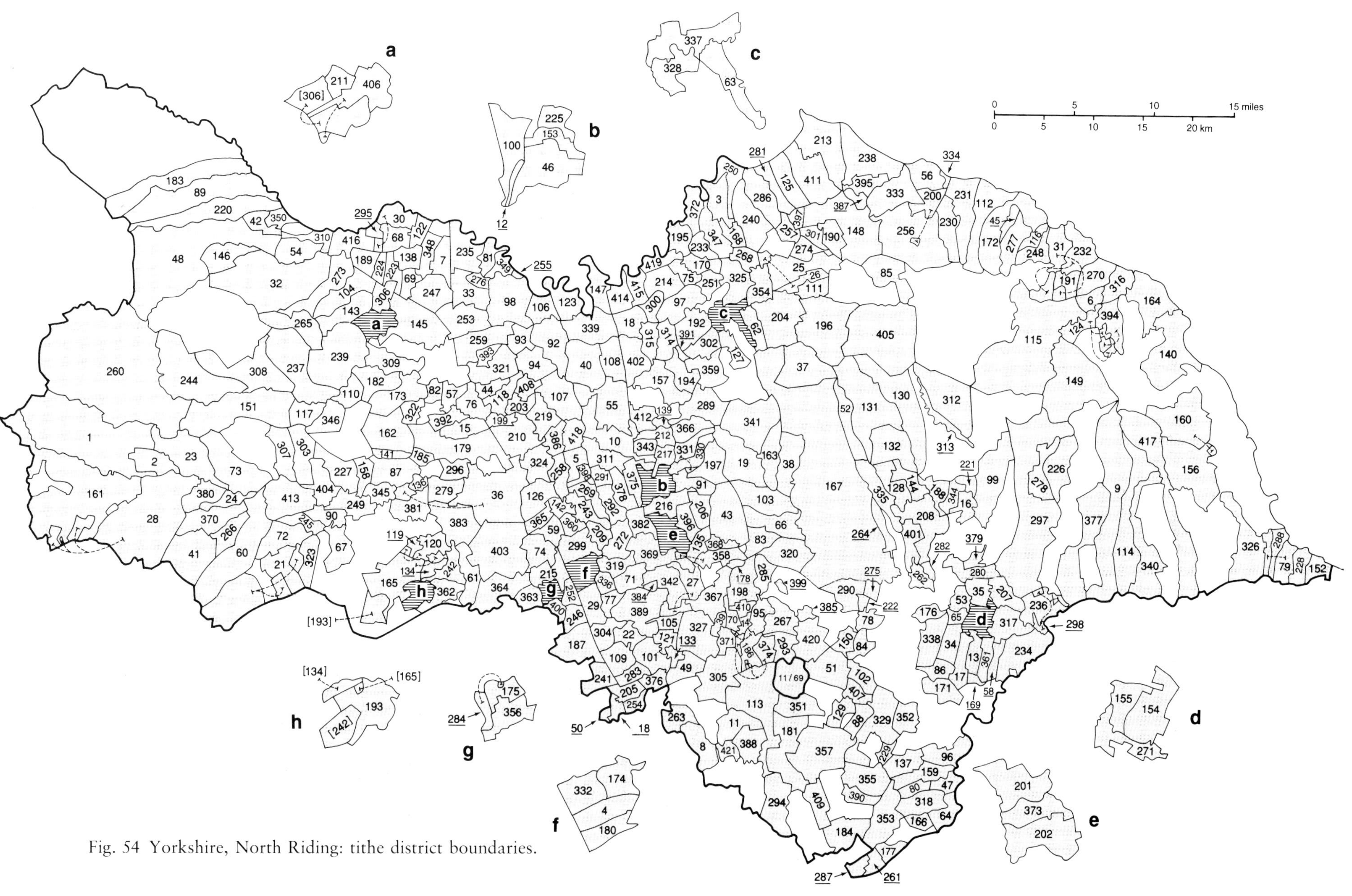

Fig. 54 Yorkshire, North Riding: tithe district boundaries.

drawn such that it is unclear whether woods, plantations, orchards, gardens or heath are intended; reference to the tithe apportionments is not always helpful and it is sometimes necessary to make a judgement depending either on context or by reference to later Ordnance Survey maps. The use of colour to distinguish landed estates or tithable status is common on North Riding tithe maps and at Sexhow the map-maker shows holding boundaries by thickening up the field boundaries, a neat idea rarely if ever encountered elsewhere. Some slopes are shown on about one-sixth of North Riding tithe maps, though it is open to question whether much of this depiction is very effective. At Upleatham, the annotation 'Mudge's pole' is perhaps a relic of Ordnance Survey operations and at Wycliffe a suspension bridge is shown pictorially.

About 81 per cent of North Riding tithe maps in the Public Record Office collection can be attributed to a particular map-maker which is an unusually high proportion (Table 42.2). As well as being numerically the most important tithe valuer in the North Riding, Thomas Bradley of Richmond was also the most prolific map-maker as he was employed in fifty-six districts where he made straightforward maps, often coloured to distinguish landowners. Bradley favoured the six-chain scale, whereas Thomas Dixon of Darlington preferred the four-chain for many of his thirty-one maps. Henry Scott of Oulston produced thirty maps in styles varying from very plain to moderately ornamental, with such features as shadowed trees. Thomas Buxton of Malton was especially careful to note which of his maps are copies and which are original surveys.

A number of North Riding maps have decorated scale bars or titles. Particularly notable are Barningham with sickle, hoe and rake, Hutton le Hole with the title on a scroll with wheatears behind, and Middleton Quernhow with drawing instruments. Such decoration is unusual on northern England tithe maps.

Table 42.1. *Agreements and awards for commutation of tithes in Yorkshire, North Riding*

Assistant commissioner/ local tithe agent	*Number of agreements**	*Number of awards*
Charles Howard	76	109
John Job Rawlinson	14	82
Richard Burton Phillipson	40	0
Thomas Hoskins	31	0
Henry Pilkington	23	0
Robert Hart	10	0
George Wingrove Cooke	0	8
John Mee Mathew	0	8
Joseph Townsend	0	5
John Strangeways Donaldson Selby	4	6
John Story Penleaze	3	0
John Penny	2	0
George Louis	0	1

*Computed from the number of extant reports on tithe agreements in the tithe files [PRO IR 18].

Table 42.2. *Tithe valuers and tithe map-makers in Yorkshire, North Riding*

Name and address (in Yorkshire unless indicated)	*Number of districts*	*Acreage*
Tithe valuers		
Thomas and Christopher Lonsdale, Bradley, Richmond	57	150,212
Thomas Buxton, Malton	19	47,047
Thomas Phillips, Helmsley	17	27,650
Thomas Scott, Oulston	16	28,696
William Simpson, Nunthorpe Hall	15	12,611
Anthony Hall, East Cowton	13	21,069
Henry Scott, Oulston	12	17,377
Thomas Dixon, Darlington, Durham	12	16,966
Daniel Seaton, York	12	10,337
Christopher Lonsdale Bradley, Richmond	10	30,806
Thomas Watson, Northallerton	10	15,582
John Whinfield Parrington, Marton	9	16,271
Henry Trumper, Swinton, Masham	8	14,432
Others [106]	211	380,827
Attributed tithe map-makers		
Thomas Bradley and Son, Richmond, Yorkshire	56	143,584
Thomas Dixon, Darlington, Durham	31	52,518
Henry Scott, Oulston	30	50,757
William Simpson, Pinchingthorpe	29	32,014
Thomas Buxton, Malton	28	69,781
George Peirson, Guisborough	12	23,031
Robert Wise, Malton	11	18,868
Anthony and Robert Reed, Stockton upon Tees, Durham	9	16,079
Walton Alderson, Leyburn	9	14,962
Others [46]	127	386,688

Table 42.3. *The tithe maps of Yorkshire, North Riding: scales and classes*

Scale in chains/inch	*All maps*		*First Class*		*Second Class*	
	Number	*Acreage*	*Number*	*Acreage*	*Number*	*Acreage*
>3	2	20	0	0	2	20
3	58	85,219	2	2,062	56	83,157
3.5	2	2,927	0	0	2	2,927
4	126	202,688	0	0	126	202,688
5	9	22,774	0	0	9	22,774
5.5	1	1,511	0	0	1	1,511
6	155	297,565	0	0	155	297,565
7	1	2,645	0	0	1	2,645
8	48	121,967	0	0	48	121,967
9, 10, 10.67	8	24,572	0	0	8	24,572
12	9	21,384	0	0	9	21,384
16	2	6,611	0	0	2	6,611
TOTAL	421	789,883	2	2,062	419	787,821

Table 42.4. *The tithe maps of Yorkshire, North Riding: dates*

	1837	*1838*	*1839*	*1840*	*1841*	*1842*	*1843*	*1844*	*1845*	*1846*	*1847*	*1848*	*1849*	*>1849*
All maps	6	55	58	32	31	41	22	19	22	19	37	20	30	28
1st class	0	0	0	1	0	0	0	0	0	0	0	0	1	0
2nd class*	6	55	58	31	31	41	22	19	22	19	37	20	29	28

*One second-class tithe map of the North Riding of Yorkshire in the Public Record Office collection is undated.

Yorkshire, North Riding

42/1 High Abbotside (township in parish of Aysgarth) SD 860940 [Not listed]
Apt 09.05.1840; 6215a (11150); Map 1843, 8 chns, in 2 parts, by T. Bradley and Son, Richmond, Yorks, (tithable parts only); hachures, waterbodies, woods, building names, boundary mounds, toll bar, chapel; bridges and tarn named.

42/2 Low Abbotside (township in parish of Aysgarth) SE 022914 [Not listed]
Apt 09.05.1840; 1981a (5080); Map 1843, 6 chns, by T. Bradley and Son, Richmond, Yorks, (tithable parts only); hill-drawing, woods, building names, waterfall.

42/3 Acklam in Cleveland (parish) NZ 480178 [Acklam]
Apt 25.11.1848; 1477a (all); Map 1849, 8 chns; railway, foot/b'way, waterbodies, woods, parkland, building names; bridge named.

42/4 Ainderby Quernhow (township in parish of Pickhill) SE 352808
Apt 02.12.1840; 527a (527); Map 1840, 6 chns, by Thomas Robinson, Ripon; foot/b'way; north pointer has a snake entwined round it, with forked tongue.

42/5 Ainderby Steeple (township in parish of Ainderby Steeple) SE 332922
Apt 05.02.1847; 310a (1138); Map 1847, 3 chns, 'redrawn' by Thomas Dixon, Darlington, (tithable parts only); waterbodies, woods, ownerships (col).

42/6 Aislaby (township in parish of Whitby) NZ 857086
Apt 14.07.1843; 1069a (all); Map 1844, 3 chns, by Robt Wise, Land Agent and Surveyor, Malton; hill-drawing, railway, foot/b'way, waterbodies, woods, parkland, gardens, moor (col), field boundary ownerships, building names, school, quarries (col), weir, Methodist Chapel, rubbish tip (col).

42/7 Aldborough (township in parish of St John Stanwick) NZ 206116 [Aldbrough St John]
Apt 03.05.1845; 1719a (all); Map 1848?, 6 chns, 'Copied' by Thomas Bradley and Sons, Richmond, Yorks; foot/b'way, woods, fence, building names; stream named.

42/8 Aldwark (township in parish of Alne) SE 470640
Apt 21.06.1841; 2214a (2217); Map 1846, 8 chns, by William Pearson, Rymer House, near Thirsk, Yorkshire; foot/b'way, waterbodies, woods, field boundary ownerships, ownerships (col).

42/9 Allerston (parish) SE 890890
Apt 30.07.1846; 10012a (10012); Map 1847, 3 chns: part 1 by Edwd Page; part 2 by Robt Wise, Malton; foot/b'way, waterbodies, woods, plantations, osiers, orchards, field boundary ownership, ling post, 'Panniermen's Road'; physical features named. Apt omits most field names.

42/10 Northallerton (township in parish of Northallerton) SE 372942
Apt 02.08.1842; 3218a (4239); Map 1842, 8 chns, in 3 parts, (including town at 2.5 chns, and open strips at 4 chns); railway, modus land, residual open fields, mill, house of correction, shambles, cross, toll booth, vicarage; colouring of fields is ornamental.

42/11 Alne (township in parish of Alne) SE 503663
Apt 13.11.1844; 2240a (2240); Map 1843, 6 chns, surveyed by Henry Scott, Oulston; railway with station, foot/b'way, waterbodies, woods, plantations, osiers, parkland, arable (col), grassland (col), orchards, heath/moor, field boundary ownerships, toll bar, windmill, mansion, watermill; colour bands show land use and field boundary ownership.

42/12 Alverton or Northallerton Ings (township in parish of Leak) SE 413893 [Not listed]
Apt 05.06.1845; 80a (all); Map 1847, 3 chns, by William Simpson, Nunthorpe, near Stokesley; open fields, boundary marks.

42/13 Amotherby (township in parish of Appleton le Street) SE 750735
Apt 12.11.1844; 1251a (1250); Map 1849, 3 chns, 1st cl; construction lines, foot/b'way, waterbodies, houses, plantations, orchards, quarries, signpost (pictorial), garden (by annotation), moor.

42/14 Angram Grange (township in parish of Coxwold) SE 515762
Apt 19.04.1839; 439a (all); Map 1840, 6 chns, 'copied' by H. Scott; waterbodies, woods (col), ford.

42/15 Appleton (township in parish of Catterick) SE 233952 [East and West Appleton]
Apt 25.11.1841; 1584a (1583); Map 1842, 6 chns, by T. Bradley and Son, Richmond, Yorks; waterbodies, woods, building names; colours indicate owners.

42/16 Appleton le Moors (township in parish of Lastingham) SE 740880 [Appleton-le-Moors]
Apt 15.11.1848; 1281a (2570); Map 1849?, 6 chns, in 3 parts, by Robt Abbey, Hutton; foot/b'way, woods, mill.

42/17 Appleton le Street, including Eastthorpe (township in parish of Appleton le Street) SE 733729 [Appleton-le-Street]
Apt 03.12.1844; 728a (1140); Map surveyed in 1845, 4 chns, in 2 parts, by Thomas Buxton, Malton, (part 2 dated 1846); foot/b'way, waterbodies, woods, osiers (by symbol).

42/18 Appleton upon Wiske (township in parish of Great Smeaton) NZ 395056 [Appleton Wiske]
Apt 02.02.1839; 1827a (1827); Map 1838, 4 chns, partly corrected and partly surveyed by Thos Dixon, Darlington; foot/b'way, waterbodies, woods, arable (col), grassland (col), orchards, hedge ownership, field gates.

42/19 Arden with Ardenside (townships in parish of Hawnby) SE 505925 [Not listed]
Apt 15.08.1845; 6a (4613); Map 1849, 6 chns, by G.B. Lancaster, Harom, (tithable parts only, tinted); hill-drawing, building names.

42/20 Arkleside, Blackrake, Coverhead, Pickle, Swineside and Woodale (hamlets or vills in parish of Coverham) SE 010790
Apt 04.06.1846; 6729a (?); Map 1846, 3 chns, in 2 parts, by William Thornton, Carlton; hill-drawing, woods, building names, sheepfold, boundary stones; a few hills are named.

42/21 Arundel Grange, Bradley, Breckonrigge, Fleesop, Gammersgill, Hindlethwaite and Horsehouse (hamlets or vills in parish of Coverham) SE 050815
Apt 04.06.1846; 1523a (?); Map 1848, 3 chns, by William Thornton, Carlton; houses, ravine.

42/22 Asenby (township in parish of Topcliffe) SE 397750
Apt 13.03.1838; 1131a (1130); Map 1838, 6 chns, by T. Bradley and Son, Richmond; waterbodies, woods, orchards, gardens, residual open fields, building names, mill and weir, waste.

42/23 Askrigg (township in parish of Aysgarth) SD 953921
Apt 30.08.1839; 4742a (4741); Map 1840, 8 chns, in 2 parts, 'made from a Township Plan of the same scale' by Edwd Other, (includes enlargement of village at 3 chns); waterbodies, woods, parkland, building names, boundary marks and stone, well; yellow band shows land tithe-free when in owner's occupation.

42/24 Aysgarth (township in parish of Aysgarth) SD 997881
Apt 31.12.1841; 1174a (1174); Map 1843, 4 chns, by W. Alderson, Leyburn; foot/b'way, houses, woods (col), stiles, ford, heap of boundary stones.

42/25 Great Ayton (township in parish of Ayton) NZ 560110
Apt 12.12.1846; 2919a (3146); Map 1847, 5 chns, by James Biggins; hill-drawing, foot/b'way, woods, parkland, heath/moor, owners of tithe-free land.

42/26 Little Ayton (township in parish of Ayton) NZ 567099
Apt 28.09.1846; 1335a (1334); Map 1847, 4 chns, in 2 parts, by James Biggins; foot/b'way, waterbodies, woods, plantations.

42/27 Bagby (chapelry in parish of Kirkby Knowle) SE 460802
Apt 17.04.1845; 2397a (1795); Map 1847, 8 chns, by Henry Scott, Oulston, near Easingwold; railway, foot/b'way, waterbodies, woods, parkland, field boundary ownerships, lodge, township boundaries (col).

42/28 Bainbridge (township in parish of Aysgarth) SD 913863
Apt 31.12.1841; 14984a (14983); Map 1843, 8 chns, in 6 parts, by T. Bradley and Son, Richmond, Yorks, (includes villages separately at 4 chns); hill-drawing, foot/b'way, waterbodies, woods, building names; lake named.

42/29 Baldersby (township in parish of Topcliffe) SE 360778
Apt 10.09.1838; 1753a (1752); Map 1839, 6 chns, by Henry Scott, (tinted); foot/b'way, woods, heath/moor, field boundary ownerships, building names, Great North Road, stiles, pinfold, tithe-free land (red band).

42/30 Barforth (township in parishes of Gilling and St John Stanwick) NZ 162160 [Not listed]
Apt 19.12.1845; 2004a (2003); Map 1847?, 3 chns, in 3 parts, (including one part at 4 chns and 12-chn index); waterbodies, woods, landowners, chapel ruins, toll bar, quarry, ox-bow, ford.

42/31 Barnby (township in parish of Lythe) NZ 822138 [Not listed]
Apt 22.10.1845; 97a (1435); Map surveyed June 1849, 4 chns, by Thomas Buxton, Malton, (tithable parts only); foot/b'way, well; tithable buildings are carmine, and others are grey.

42/32 Barningham (parish) NZ 045095
Apt 28.01.1841; 10772a (10771); Map 1837-41, 6 chns, in 5 parts, by T. Bradley and Son, Richmond, Yorks, (includes one part at 12 chns, part of Barningham village at 3 chns, and 18-chn index); waterbodies, woods, moor, building names, shooting box, stones, coal shaft, ownerships (col); some hills named; one north pointer is decorated with sickle, hoe and rake, and one part has landowners' signatures, adopting the map.

42/33 Barton (township in parish of Gilling and St John Stanwick) NZ 237083
Apt 06.04.1842; 2423a (?); Map 1839, 4 chns, by Thomas Dixon, Darlington; waterbodies, woods, orchards, heath/moor, mere stones, quarries, ownerships (col).

42/34 Barton le Street (township in parish of Barton le Street) SE 724745 [Barton-le-Street]
Apt 30.04.1844; 1644a (1644); Map 1841, 3 chns, by A. and R. Reed, Stockton upon Tees; foot/b'way, waterbodies, houses, woods, residual open fields, stream bank.

42/35 Great and Little Barugh (townships in parish of Kirby Misperton) SE 753793
Apt 22.12.1841; 1433a (all); Map surveyed in 1842, 4 chns, by Thomas Buxton, Land Agent and Surveyor, Malton; foot/b'way, waterbodies, woods (col), stiles, roadside waste.

42/36 Bedale (parish) SE 260890
Apt 08.02.1838; 8160a (7551); Map 1838, 6 chns, in 5 parts, by T. Bradley and Sons, Richmond, Yorks, and John Humphries, Ripon, Yorks, (tithable parts only in detail; includes 12-chn index); waterbodies, woods, parkland, heath/moor, building names, hospitals, rectory, gashouse, mill, townships (col); some streams named.

42/37 Bilsdale (chapelry in parish of Helmsley) NZ 573013
Apt 04.12.1841; 575a (18971); Map 1842, 8 chns, by William Tuke, Land Agent, York, (tithable parts only); woods, tithe-merged land (green). Apt omits land use.

42/38 Bilsdale West Side (township in parish of Hawnby) SE 560914 [Not listed]
Apt 15.08.1845; 2011a (4014); Map 1847, 8 chns, by Jno. Wright; foot/b'way, woods, field boundary ownerships, building names, quarry, boundary stones (by symbol), moor; streams named.

42/39 Birdforth (township) SE 485762
Apt 27.03.1839; 605a (604); Map 1838, 4 chns; waterbodies, houses, woods.

42/40 Birkby (parish) NZ 351014
Apt 30.06.1840; 3620a (3619); Map 1840?, 8 chns; railway, waterbodies, woods, toll bar, rectory, townships (col).

42/41 Bishopdale (township in parish of Aysgarth) SD 967828
Apt 29.06.1839; 4806a (4805); Map 'made in November and December 1838', 3 chns, by Edwd Other; woods, plantations, building names, principal construction lines.

42/42 Boldron (township in parish of Startforth) NZ 021151
Apt 08.03.1842; 1223a (1222); Map 1841, 3 chns, surveyed by T. Dixon, Darlington; hill-drawing, waterbodies, woods, orchards, building names, quarry, toll bar, well, ownerships (col).

42/43 Boltby (township in parish of Felixkirk) SE 492870
Apt 12.06.1845; 4782a (4782); Map 1847, 6 chns, by W. Pearson, Marderby Grange, nr Thirsk, Yorks; waterbodies, woods, field boundary ownerships, quarries, fords, barrows, glebe (pink), land free of great tithe (blue); some physical features named.

42/44 Bolton upon Swale (township in parish of Catterick) SE 256992 [Bolton-on-Swale]
Apt 28.09.1839; 878a (878); Map 1839, 5 chns, by T. Dixon, Darlington, (tinted); hill-drawing, foot/b'way, orchards. Apt omits land use.

42/45 Borrowby (township in parish of Lythe) NZ 773160
Apt 28.08.1845; 664a (710); Map surveyed July 1846, 4 chns, by Thomas Buxton, Land Agent etc, Malton.

42/46 Borrowby (township in parish of Leake) SE 428893
Apt 31.12.1850; 885a (1280); Map 1851, 4 chns, by William Simpson, Nunthorpe; woods.

42/47 Bossall and Barnby (hamlets in parish of Bossall) SE 723607
Apt 17.10.1843; 943a (1090); Map 1844, 6 chns, 'Reduced and Copied' by W.J. Ware, (tinted); foot/b'way, waterbodies, woods, osiers (by symbol), parkland, orchards, hamlet boundaries.

42/48 Bowes (township in parish of Bowes) NY 950130
Apt 10.03.1849; 2906a (16090); Map 1850, 6 chns, surveyed and drawn by Morley Headlam, (tithable parts only); waterbodies, woods; yellow indicates ownership of certain tithes; it is unclear what pink and green tint mean.

42/49 Brafferton (township in parish of Brafferton) SE 453717
Apt 04.07.1844; 1853a (1920); Map 1843, 8 chns, by James Powell, Knaresbrough, (tinted); railway, foot/b'way, woods, glebe (pink), former common (yellow); bridge named.

42/50 Brampton (hamlet in parish of Kirby on the Moor) SE 372670 [Not listed]
Apt 23.02.1849; 9a (?); Map 1850, 6 chns, by John Humphries, Ripon; waterbodies, woods, field acreage; tithable part is tinted green.

42/51 Brandsby (parish) SE 605717
Apt 01.11.1839; 3046a (all); Map 1840, 8 chns, copied by Henry Scott, (tinted); waterbodies, woods, hall, rectory, churchyard, glebe (pink); one estate is yellow.

42/52 Bransdale West Side (township in parish of Kirkdale) SE 618956 [Not listed]
Apt 17.07.1844; 606a (4965); Map 1845, 6 chns. Apt omits land use.

42/53 Brawby (township in parish of Salton) SE 734787
Apt 06.06.1840; 110a (800); Map surveyed May 1841, 3 chns, by Thomas Buxton, Surveyor and Engineer, Malton, (tithable parts only); foot/b'way, waterbodies, woods (col), field gates, landowners, occupation roads; tithable buildings are carmine and others are hatched.

42/54 Brignall (parish) NZ 063124
Apt 13.07.1838; 2018a (all); Map 1839?, 4 chns, (tinted); waterbodies, woods, dam, slate quarries, glebe (pink), 'holme'; bridge named.

42/55 Brompton (township in parish of Northallerton) SE 376981
Apt 24.02.1841; 3801a (3801); Map 1839, 4 chns, surveyed by T. Dixon, Darlington; railway, foot/b'way, turnpike roads, waterbodies, woods, orchards, ownerships (col).

42/56 Brotton (township in parish of Skelton in Cleveland) NZ 689206
Apt 18.03.1845; 1973a (2291); Map 1845, 6 chns, by George Pierson, nr Guisbrough.

42/57 Brough (township in parish of Catterick) SE 215985 [Not listed]
Apt 31.05.1841; 1082a (1082); Map 1842, 6 chns, by T. Bradley and Son, Richmond, Yorks, (tinted); hill-drawing, foot/b'way, waterbodies, woods, heath/moor, building names, chapel; bridge named.

42/58 Broughton (township in parish of Appleton-le-Street) SE 770729
Apt 31.12.1846; 856a (855); Map surveyed May 1846, 4 chns, by Thomas Buxton, Land Agent and Surveyor, New Malton; foot/b'way, waterbodies, woods, green lane; the title overlies mapped areas.

42/59 Burneston (township in parish of Burneston) SE 318851
Apt 04.09.1838; 1185a (all); Map 1838, 6 chns, by Thomas Bradley and Son, Richmond; waterbodies, houses, woods, Great North Road, ownerships (col); stream named

42/60 Burton cum Walden (township in parish of Aysgarth) SE 004821
Apt 31.12.1841; 4622a (6790); Map 1842, 4 chns, by W. Alderson, Leyburn; hill-drawing, houses, woods (col), field gates, Pear Moor Road, waterfall.

42/61 Burton upon Yore (township in parish of Masham) SE 235810 [High and Low Burton]
Apt 07.05.1838; 782a (2242); Map 1838, 6 chns, (tithable parts only); hill-drawing, foot/b'way, waterbodies, woods, building names, landowners, mill, weir, pit, ownerships (col).

42/62 Great Busby (township in parish of Stokesley) NZ 522056
Apt 28.02.1837; 1368a (1368); Map 1838, 6 chns, by William Simpson, Pinchingthorpe, near Guisborough; hill-drawing, foot/b'way, waterbodies, woods.

42/63 Little Busby (township in parish of Stokesley) NZ 509052 [Not listed]
Apt 28.02.1837; 310a (675); Map 1839?, 4 chns, by H. Sanderson, (tithable parts only); landowners.

42/64 Buttercrambe and Aldby (hamlets in parish of Bossall) SE 725578
Apt 16.01.1844; 1682a (all); Map 1849, 6 chns, surveyed in 1829, and 'Corrected and Copied' by W.J. Ware, (tinted); foot/b'way, waterbodies, woods (col), plantations (col), parkland (col), gardens, river locks, demesne (lilac).

42/65 Butterwick (township in parish of Barton-le-Street) SE 730770
Apt 10.12.1838; 634a (640); Map 1839, 8 chns, by Tuke and Allanson, (tinted).

42/66 Old Byland (parish) SE 545860
Apt 13.06.1846; 228a (2733); Map 1846, 6 chns, by H. Scott, Oulston, (tithable parts only), litho (by G. Smith); foot/b'way, arable (col), grassland (col), building names.

42/67 Caldbergh (district in parish of Coverham) SE 113837
Apt 03.03.1843; 138a (?); Map 1847, 3 chns, by W. Thornton, Carlton, (tithable parts only); foot/b'way; bridge is shown pictorially; north pointer has oak leaf boss.

42/68 Caldwell (township in parish of St John's Stanwick) NZ 160140
Apt 16.01.1849; 11a (2000); Map 1850, 3 chns, ? by J.H. Hutchinson, Grantham, (tithable parts only); woods.

42/69 Carkin (township in parish of Gilling) NZ 172096 [Not listed]
Apt 15.12.1845; 650a (650); Map 1847, 4 chns; foot/b'way, waterbodies, woods, plantations, rock outcrops, building names, quarry, limekiln.

42/70 Carlton Husthwaite (parish) SE 500767
Apt 30.07.1839; 811a (810); Map surveyed in 1840, 3 chns, 1st cl, by G.B. Lancaster, Marderby Grange, nr Thirsk, Yorks; waterbodies, woods.

42/71 Carlton Miniott (township in parish of Thirsk) SE 398807
Apt 08.07.1841; 1533a (all); Map 1842, 6 chns, by H. Scott; railway, waterbodies, houses, woods, plantations, osiers (by symbol), heath/moor, bowrake [freeboard], pink band shows land tithable to Kirby Knowle.

42/72 Carlton Town (township in parish of Coverham) SE 051844 [Carlton]
Apt 28.12.1846; 2717a (?); Map 1847, 4 chns, by W. Thornton; hill-drawing, foot/b'way, houses, woods, limekilns, peat roads, boundary stones, well.

42/73 Caperby cum Thoresby (township in parish of Aysgarth) SD 995915 [Carperby]
Apt 27.07.1839; 4940a (4950); Map 1840, 6 chns, by T. Bradley and Son, Richmond, Yorks; hill-drawing, foot/b'way, water-bodies, woods, residual open fields, ownerships (col), quarry, waterfall, ford, wells, boundary marks; bridge and some physical features named.

42/74 Carthorpe (township in parish of Burneston) SE 302832
Apt 11.07.1838; 2056a (all); Map 1839, 6 chns, by T. Bradley and Son, Richmond; waterbodies, woods, building names, ownerships (col), pit.

42/75 Castleleavington (township in parish of Kirkleavington) NZ 449106 [Not listed]
Apt 23.04.1839; 1029a (1028); Map 1839?, 4 chns; waterbodies, mill.

42/76 Catterick (township in parish of Catterick) SE 240972
Apt 31.05.1841; 1561a (1561); Map 1841, 6 chns, by T. Bradley and Son, Richmond, Yorkshire; hill-drawing, waterbodies, woods, building names, pits, limekilns, ownerships (col); tithe-free land is uncoloured and unnumbered.

42/77 Catton (township in parish of Topcliffe) SE 377783
Apt 27.03.1839; 804a (all); Map 1839, [9 chns], copied by Henry Scott; plantations, heath/moor, field boundary ownerships, ownerships (col).

42/78 Cawton (township in parish of Gilling) SE 631767
Apt 17.02.1838; 1039a (1038); Map 1840, 6 chns, by Thos Hornby, Wombleton; hill-drawing, foot/b'way, waterbodies, woods, plantations, field gates, lime kilns. Apt omits land use.

42/79 Cayton (township in parish of Cayton) TA 060830
Apt 05.11.1846; 2380a (1208); Map 1848, 6 chns, by W. Hodgson, East Ayton; railway, hamlet boundaries, glebe; buildings are shown in outline only, unfilled.

42/80 Claxton (township in parish of Bossall) SE 690601
Apt 08.12.1841; 813a (all); Map 1842, 4 chns; waterbodies, woods.

42/81 Cleasby (parish) NZ 253121
Apt 15.08.1848; 38a (970); Map 1849, 4 chns, (tithable parts only); foot/b'way; 'IW.R' appears at the foot of the title.

42/82 Colburn (township in parish of Catterick) SE 200986
Apt 31.05.1841; 1292a (1318); Map 1842, 6 chns, by T. Bradley and Son, Richmond, Yorkshire; waterbodies, woods, building names, ford, ownerships (col).

42/83 Cold Kirby (parish) SE 532842
Apt 09.04.1847; 1620a (1620); Map 1846, 6 chns, by James Powell; hill-drawing, foot/b'way, waterbodies, woods, building names, road names, dial stone, limekilns, spring, quarry, rubbing house, ownerships (col); dales named.

42/84 Colton or Coulton (township in parish of Hovingham) SE 635740
Apt 30.01.1849; 1067a (1067); Map 1849, 8 chns, by John Humphries, Ripon, (includes 2-chn enlargement of detail); woods, landowners, ownerships (col).

42/85 Commondale (township in parish of Gisborough) NZ 658108
Apt 23.04.1844; 460a (1131); Map 1844, 4 chns, by James Biggins, (tithable parts only); woods.

42/86 Coneysthorpe (township in parish of Barton le Street) SE 717719
Apt 30.04.1844; 1193a (1192); Map 1844, 4 chns, ? by Thomas Buxton; foot/b'way, lake.

42/87 Constable Burton (township in parish of Fingal) SE 162908
Apt 03.07.1847; 2573a (2572); Map 1848, 4 chns, by I. Colling, Hunton; waterbodies, woods (named), parkland (named), gardens, field names, hall, lawn, ford; field acreages have been scraped away.

42/88 Cornborough (township in parish of Sheriff Hutton) SE 631669 [Not listed]
Apt 16.12.1846; 1079a (1082); Map 1847, 6 chns, by Thos Holliday; foot/b'way, waterbodies, stiles; green bands emphasise field boundaries.

42/89 Cotherston (township in parish of Romaldkirk) NY 957178 [Cotherstone]
Apt 19.04.1839; 8228a (8228); Map 1838, 4 chns, by Machell, Carlisle; hill-drawing, foot/b'way, woods, orchards, gardens, rock outcrops, quarries, well, weir, limekiln, boundary stones, old limekiln, sheepfolds, currocks (pictorial), dam, old level and shafts, beilds, stiles; some physical features named; north pointer has acorn tip.

42/90 Coverham (township in parish of Coverham) SE 097864
Apt 18.03.1842; 659a (?); Map 1839, 3 chns, by W. Alderson, Leyburn; hill-drawing, foot/b'way, waterbodies, houses, woods (col), building names, watermills (by Dawson's symbol), stone bridge, sheepfolds, springs, ford, limekiln; areas tinted pink may be tithe-free. Apt omits occupiers, land use and field names for modus lands.

42/91 Cowesby (parish) SE 460900
Apt 03.06.1837; 1167a (1167); Map 1845, 6 chns, 'Revised and drawn by E. Campbell, Buxton, for W. Lancaster Esq. Thirsk'; foot/b'way, woods, plantations, gardens, quarry, boundary stones, mound, moor, field boundary ownership.

42/92 East Cowton (parish) NZ 317038
Apt 02.08.1838; 3311a (3310); Map 1838, 4 chns, 'Corrected and in part Surveyed' by T. Dixon, Darlington; railway, foot/b'way, waterbodies, woods, hedge ownership, ownerships (col), roadside encroachments.

42/93 North Cowton (township in parish of Gilling) NZ 282043
Apt 22.11.1838; 1319a (1321); Map 1838, 6 chns, by T. Bradley and Son, Richmond, Yorks; woods, residual open fields, building names.

42/94 South Cowton (township in parish of Gilling) NZ 299018 [Not listed]
Apt 31.07.1848; 2136a (2136); Map 1849, 8 chns; foot/b'way, waterbodies, woods, parkland, heath/moor, building names, (in three grades of importance), ownerships (col).

42/95 Coxwold (township in parish of Coxwold) SE 530771
Apt 11.04.1839; 1370a (1369); Map 1840, 6 chns, copied by Henry Scott; hill-drawing, waterbodies, woods, field boundary ownerships, school, fords, hospital, kiln, tree in village street.

42/96 Crambe and Barton-le-Willows (township in parish of Crambe) SE 711635
Apt 07.10.1839; 2139a (2138); Map 1840, 6 chns, in 4 parts, by Thos Holliday, York, (includes 3-chn enlargement of detail); foot/b'way, waterbodies, woods (col), field boundary ownerships, hauling path, pinfold. Apt has cropping information.

42/97 Crathorne (parish) NZ 450080
Apt 30.09.1844; 2530a (2530); Map 1842, 4 chns, by T. Dixon, Darlington; foot/b'way, waterbodies, woods, orchards, building names, ownerships (col).

42/98 Croft (township in parish of Croft) NZ 273083 [Croft-on-Tees]
Apt 22.12.1841; 4483a (?); Map 1843, 6 chns, by John Lee, Bishop Auckland; railway, turnpike roads, waterbodies, woods, mill, mill dam, rectory, hotel, terrace, hall, park, spa, saw mill, weigh house; bridge named.

42/99 Cropton (township in parish of Middleton) SE 760900
Apt 30.06.1849; 153a (3810); Map 1852, 3 chns, in 2 parts, by Robert Abbey, Glazedale, (tithable parts only); woods, plantations, landowners.

42/100 Crosby (township in parish of Leake) SE 409907 [Not listed]
Apt 31.12.1850; 742a (1430); Map 1851, 3 chns, by William Simpson, Nunthorpe; woods.

42/101 Cundall with Leckby (townships in parish of Cundall) SE 419728
Apt 19.07.1844; 196a (1905); Map 1844, 8 chns, by James Powell, Knaresbro', (tithable parts only, tinted); foot/b'way, field boundary ownerships.

42/102 Dalby (parish) SE 638709
Apt 30.03.1838; 1298a (all); Map 1838-9, 4 chns, in 2 parts; foot/b'way, waterbodies, woods (col), landowners, spring, field acreages, holding boundaries (col); stream named; one part has a 'sunburst' effect in the title.

42/103 Dale Town and Murton (district in parishes of Hawnby and Murton) SE 536882
Apt 04.09.1845; 1784a (3510); Map 1847, 16 chns; hill-drawing, foot/b'way, woods (named), building names, holding boundaries (col), commons; gills named; tithe-free part is mapped but not numbered. Apt omits land use.

42/104 Dalton (township in parish of Kirkby Ravensworth) NZ 110087
Apt 30.01.1841; 2619a (2619); Map 1842, 6 chns, by T. Bradley and Son, Richmond, Yorks; hill-drawing, foot/b'way, woods, heath/moor, building names, ownerships (col).

42/105 Dalton (township in parish of Topcliffe) SE 438762
Apt 22.07.1841; 1248a (1247); Map 1842, 4 chns; railway; bridge and streams named.

42/106 Dalton on Tees (township in parish of Croft) NZ 308067 [Dalton-on-Tees]
Apt 08.04.1842; 1595a (?); Map 1842, 4 chns, by T. Dixon, Darlington; railway, foot/b'way, waterbodies, woods, orchards, building names, ownerships (col).

42/107 Danby Wiske (township in parish of Danby Wiske) SE 322985
Apt 07.05.1840; 2592a (3247); Map 1841, 8 chns, by T. Bradley and Son, Richmond, Yorks, (tithable parts only); hill-drawing, woods, heath/moor, building names, ownerships (col). District is apportioned by partly holding; Apt only gives occupation information for glebe.

42/108 Deighton (township in parish of Northallerton) NZ 375020
Apt 10.08.1841; 2053a (all); Map 1839, 9 chns; glebe (col). District is apportioned by holding and fields are not shown; Apt generalises land use.

42/109 Dishforth (township in parish of Topcliffe) SE 375725
Apt 30.10.1840; 1714a (1714); Map 1841, 6 chns; foot/b'way, woods, scattered trees, orchards, building names.

42/110 Downholme (township in parish of Downholme) SE 116987
Apt 11.05.1848; 655a (1294); Map 1848, 4 chns, by W. Thornton, Carlton; hill-drawing, woods (col), field gates; hill and beck named; tithe-free areas are shown in pink and, though numbered, do not appear in Apt; compass boss has oak leaf decoration.

42/111 Easby (township in parish of Stokesley) NZ 578090
Apt 21.04.1838; 1128a (1241); Map 1838, 6 chns, by William Simpson, Pinchingthorpe, near Guisbrough, (tithable parts only); foot/b'way, woods, monument, ford.

42/112 Easington (township in parish of Easington) NZ 745165
Apt 27.09.1837; 3600a (3893); Map 1838, 4 chns; foot/b'way, waterbodies, woods (named), plantations (named), building names, alum works, cliffs, boundary stones (pictorial), quarry, staiths, moors, waste (by annotation), gardens (by annotation).

42/113 Easingwold (township in parish of Easingwold) SE 527686
Apt 15.04.1840; 6924a (6923); Map 1841, 6 chns, surveyed by Henry Scott, Oulston; railway, foot/b'way, waterbodies, woods (col), plantations (col), osiers (by symbol), orchards, field boundary ownerships, building names, road names, toll bar, mill; bridge named; map date is surrounded by a sunburst, flowers and leaves.

42/114 Ebberston (parish) SE 900860
Apt 02.01.1844; 906a (6350); Map 1844, 4 chns, in 3 parts, by Thomas

Buxton, Land Agent and Surveyor, Malton; foot/b'way; drains, streams and bridges named.

42/115 Egton (township in parish of Lyth) NZ 800040
Apt 08.07.1841; 1113a (15146); Map surveyed June 1842, 4 chns, in 2 parts, by Thomas Buxton, Land Agent and Surveyor, Malton, (tithable parts only); woods, landowners, market cross; bridge named; tithable buildings are hatched and others are carmine. Apt omits some land use.

42/116 Ellerby (township in parish of Lyth) NZ 800145
Apt 07.05.1840; 739a (739); Map 1840, 4 chns, by William Simpson, Pinchingthorpe, near Guisbrough; woods, cliffs.

42/117 Ellerton Abbey (township in parish of Downholme) SE 070965
Apt 30.09.1846; 26a (1490); Map (drawn on Apt) 1852?, 4 chns, (tithable parts only); abbey ruins.

42/118 Ellerton upon Swale (township in parish of Catterick) SE 266979 [Ellerton]
Apt 19.11.1839; 1609a (1609); Map 1839, 5 chns, by T. Dixon, Darlington, (tinted); foot/b'way, waterbodies, woods, orchards, footbridge, mound.

42/119 Ellingstring (township in parish of Masham) SE 179838
Apt 07.05.1838; 403a (all); Map 1838, 6 chns, ? by Henry Trumper, Swinton, Masham, Yorks; woods, ownerships (col), waste. District is mostly apportioned by holding, with fields omitted; Apt generalises land use.

42/120 High and Low Ellington (township in parish of Masham) SE 198837
Apt 07.05.1838; 1711a (1710); Map 1838, 10 chns, ? by Henry Trumper, Swinton, Masham, Yorks; ownerships (col), woods, ford; stream named. District is apportioned by holding, with fields omitted; Apt generalises land use.

42/121 Elmine cum Crakenhall (township in parish of Topcliffe) SE 433747 [Eldmire]
Apt 22.07.1841; 969a (900); Map 1837, 4 chns; foot/b'way, waterbodies, houses.

42/122 Eppleby (township in parish of Gilling) NZ 183147
Apt 07.07.1847; 1061a (1060); Map 1842, 4 chns, 'Corrected and in part Surveyed' by T. Dixon, Darlington; foot/b'way, woods, building names, ownerships (col).

42/123 Eryholme (township in parish of Gilling) NZ 330080 [Not listed]
Apt 22.09.1847; 2199a (2198); Map 1843, 6 chns; hill-drawing, woods, building names, landowners, Great North Road, holding boundaries (col). District is apportioned by holding and fields are not shown.

42/124 Eskdaleside (township in parish of Whitby) NZ 852062 [Not listed]
Apt 14.07.1843; 3741a (all); Map 1844, 6 chns, surveyed by Robt Wise, Surveyor etc., Malton; railway, foot/b'way, woods, field boundary ownerships, building names, boundary stone, chapels, old alum works, old quarry, moor (col).

42/125 Eston (township in parish of Ormesby) NZ 552193
Apt 28.02.1839; 1920a (all); Map 1839, 6 chns, by William Simpson, Pinchingthorpe, near Guisbrough; woods, churchyard.

42/126 Exelby Leeming and Newton (township in parish of Burneston) SE 308888
Apt 25.02.1840; 2326a (2331); Map 1838, 6 chns, ? by T. Bradley and Son, Richmond, Yorks; foot/b'way, woods, plantations, heath/moor, building names, pit, ownerships (col).

42/127 Faceby (township or chapelry in parish of Whorlton) NZ 498034
Apt 01.05.1845; 7a (1402); Map 1845, 4 chns, by William Simpson, Pinchingthorpe, near Guisborough, (tithable parts only); foot/b'way, landowners, churchyard.

42/128 Fadmoor (township in parish of Kirkby Moorside) SE 669896
Apt 20.04.1847; 1440a (2495); Map 1848, 8 chns, by J.H. Phillips; foot/b'way, woods, field boundary ownerships, stiles. Apt omits land use.

42/129 Farlington (township in parish of Sheriff Hutton) SE 613677
Apt 07.05.1840; 1163a (1163); Map 1841, [4 chns]; foot/b'way, woods (col), tithe-free land (col); stream named.

42/130 Farndale East Side (township in parish of Lastingham) SE 680980 [Not listed]
Apt 07.11.1838; 314a (9103); Map 1839, 4 chns, in 2 parts, by Tuke and Allanson, York, (tithable parts only); woods. Apt omits land use.

42/131 Farndale High Quarter with Bransdale East Side (townships in parish of Kirkby Moorside) SE 640980 [Not listed]
Apt 20.04.1847; 2656a (8950); Map 1848, 8 chns, in 2 parts, by J.H. Phillips, (tithable parts only); woods, field boundary ownerships, building names, mills.

42/132 Farndale Low Quarter (township in parish of Kirby Moorside) SE 662936 [Not listed]
Apt 18.06.1847; 762a (3560); Map 1848, 8 chns, by J.H. Phillips, (tithable parts only); waterbodies, woods, mill.

42/133 Fawdington (township in parish of Cundall) SE 441730
Apt 16.11.1846; 424a (423); Map 1847, 8 chns; foot/b'way, waterbodies, woods, ownerships (col).

42/134 Fearby (township in parish of Masham) SE 196814
Apt 07.05.1838; 852a (853); Map 1838, 8 chns, ? by Henry Trumper, Swinton, Masham, Yorks; woods, building names, ownerships (col). District is mostly apportioned by holding; Apt generalises land use.

42/135 Feliskirk (township in parish of Feliskirk) SE 465841 [Felixkirk]
Apt 20.11.1843; 1171a (all); Map 1845?, 6 chns, in 2 parts, by T. Bradley and Son, Richmond, Yorks, (includes 3-chn enlarge-ment of detail); foot/b'way, waterbodies, woods, building names, ownerships (col).

42/136 Fingal (township in parish of Fingal) SE 183898 [Finghall]
Apt 18.09.1838; 532a (all); Map 1839, 4 chns; woods. Apt omits field names for most glebe, and all land use.

42/137 Flaxton (township in parish of Bossall and Foston) SE 676628
Apt 16.01.1844; 1826a (all); Map surveyed in 1843, 3 chns, in 2 parts, by Thomas Buxton, Land Agent and Surveyor, Malton; foot/b'way, waterbodies, woods (col), building names.

42/138 Forcett (township in parish of Gilling) NZ 173117
Apt 19.12.1845; 1573a (1572); Map 1847, 4 chns; foot/b'way, waterbodies, woods, plantations, parkland, building names, mill, footbridge; hall and church are named in gothic.

42/139 Foxton (township in parish of Kirby Sigston) SE 427958
Apt 29.04.1845; 378a (all); Map 1845, 6 chns, by Wm Alderson, West Lodge, Bedale; foot/b'way, waterbodies, woods (col, named), field boundary ownerships, mill, stiles, ownerships (col), roadside en-croachments; stream named.

42/140 Fylingdales (township in parish of Whitby) NZ 943037 [Not listed]
Apt 14.07.1843; 12865a (all); Map surveyed in 1843, 4 chns, in 5 parts, by Thomas Buxton, Land Agent and Surveyor, Malton, (tithable parts only; includes 20-chn index, 1844); hill-drawing, waterbodies, woods (col), building names, alum rock, old alum works, beacon (pictorial), boundary stones, cross (pictorial), standing stones (pictorial), sheepfold, well; some physical features named; north pointers have plumes.

42/141 Garriston (township in parish of Hawkswell) SE 158924
Apt 10.01.1849; 661a (660); Map 1849, 4 chns, by John Colling, Hunton; plantations, field names.

42/142 Gatenby (township in parish of Burneston) SE 328875
Apt 26.02.1839; 849a (849); Map 1838, 4 chns, by Otley and Lax, Darlington; foot/b'way, occupation roads, waterbodies, woods, orchards, gardens, heath/moor, brickyard.

42/143 Gayles (township in parish of Kirkby Ravensworth) NZ 116067
Apt 31.12.1840; 2461a (2467); Map 1842, 6 chns, by T. Bradley and Son,

Richmond, Yorks; hill-drawing, foot/b'way, woods, heath/moor, building names, quarry, ownerships (col).

42/144 Gillamoor (township in parish of Kirkby Moorside) SE 681901
Apt 20.04.1847; 1403a (2540); Map 1848, 8 chns, by J.H. Phillips; foot/b'way, woods, field boundary ownerships, stiles. Apt omits most land use.

42/145 Gilling (township in parish of Gilling) NZ 177052 [Gilling West]
Apt 24.08.1847; 57a (4440); Map 1851?, 3 chns, in 2 parts, (tithable parts only); woods, field names, landowners, field acreages.

42/146 Gilmonby (township in parish of Bowes) NY 995117
Apt 07.06.1847; 1962a (2244); Map 1847, 8 chns; green (col); no buildings are shown. District is partly apportioned by holding.

42/147 Grisby and Over Dinsdale (townships in parish of Sockburn) NZ 362094 [Not listed]
Apt 08.10.1846; 1986a (all); Map 1847, 6 chns; foot/b'way, waterbodies, woods, heath/moor, building names, ford.

42/148 Gisborough (township in parish of Gisborough) NZ 618158 [Guisborough]
Apt 10.07.1844; 1764a (6120); Map 1845, 3.5 chns, (tithable parts only); waterbodies, houses, woods.

42/149 Goathland (township in parish of Pickering) NZ 847003
Apt 29.01.1845; 10055a (10055); Map surveyed June 1845, 5 chns, by Thomas Buxton, Land Agent and Surveyor, Malton; railway, foot/b'way, waterbodies, boundary stones, cross (by symbol) and mounds; some physical features named.

42/150 Grimstone (township in parish of Gilling) SE 618743 [Not listed]
Apt 30.11.1838; 1009a (1009); Map 1838, 4 chns; hill-drawing, foot/b'way, woods (col), plantations (col), heath/moor, landowners, lime kilns (col), holding boundaries (col), roadside waste (col), field acreages.

42/151 Grinton (township in parish of Grinton) SE 001970
Apt 16.01.1844; 2865a (2934); Map 1841, 6 chns, in 6 parts, by Anthony Clarkson, (tithable parts only; includes five 2-chn enlargements of detail); hill-drawing, foot/b'way, houses, woods, orchards, gardens, heath/moor, building names, hilltop 'Station', mill, vicarage.

42/152 Gristhorpe (township in parish of Filey) TA 093824
Apt 31.03.1847; 49a (1070); Map 1853?, 3 chns, by Wm Hodgson, East Ayton, Land Agent, (tithable parts only); railway, landowners.

42/153 Gueldale (township in parish of Leake) SE 431901 [Not listed]
Apt 31.12.1850; 324a (?); Map 1851, 4 chns, by William Simpson, Nunthorpe; woods.

42/154 Great Habton (township in parish of Kirby Misperton) SE 760769
Apt 22.12.1841; 944a (1700); Map 1849, 6 chns, 'In part surveyed' by R. Wise, Malton; waterbodies, woods, orchards.

42/155 Little Habton (township in parish of Kirbymisperton) SE 749776
Apt 23.11.1841; 434a (444); Map 1842, 4 chns, by William Tuke, Land Agent, York, (tinted); waste.

42/156 Hackness, Suffield cum Everly, Broxa and Silpho (townships in parish of Hackness) SE 970920
Apt 18.11.1846; 250a (4300); Map 1847?, 12 chns, (tithable parts only in detail). Apt omits most land use.

42/157 East Harlsey (parish) SE 427999
Apt 08.07.1846; 673a (2802); Map 1847, 6 chns, in 2 parts, by William Simpson, Nunthorpe, near Stokesley; woods, landowners.

42/158 Harmby (township in parish of Spennithorne) SE 113905
Apt 21.11.1848; 105a (860); Map 1851, 4 chns, by Thomas Whitfield, (tithable parts only); woods, landowners.

42/159 Harton (township in parish of Bossall) SE 694618
Apt 21.04.1841; 1951a (1951); Map 1842, 6 chns, by Thos Holliday, (tinted); foot/b'way, waterbodies, woods, field gates, building names.

42/160 Harwood-dale (township in parish of Hackness) SE 953967 [Harwood Dale]
Apt 22.06.1837; 5512a (all); Map 1838, 12 chns, in 2 parts; woods, grassland (col), heath/moor, landowners, ownership boundaries (col); some buildings and roads may be omitted; legend explains land use depiction and ownership boundaries. District is apportioned by holding and fields are not shown.

42/161 Hawes (township in parish of Aysgarth) SD 860900
Apt 09.01.1840; 16873a (16872); Map 8 chns, surveyed by Thomas Bradley, Richmond, 1820, and corrected to 1840 by John Edwin Oates, York; waterbodies, woods, plantations, building names, waterfalls (named), mill, quarry, toll bar, colliery, boundary marks, commons, pastures, peat moors, ravine; streams and bridge named.

42/162 East and West Hawkswell and Barden (townships in parish of Hawkswell) SE 152947 [East Hauxwell]
Apt 12.01.1849; 2888a (3370); Map 1849, 6 chns, by W. Thornton, Carlton; foot/b'way, waterbodies, woods, plantations, parkland, gardens, obelisk (pictorial), footbridges, townships (col).

42/163 Hawnby (township in parish of Hawnby) SE 540927
Apt 13.08.1845; 2380a (all); Map 1847, 8 chns, (includes enlargement of village at 4 chns); foot/b'way, woods, building names; stream named.

42/164 Hawsker cum Stainsacre (township in parish of Whitby) NZ 918088 [High Hawsker]
Apt 15.07.1843; 3702a (4396); Map surveyed in 1844, 4 chns, ? by Thomas Buxton, Malton, Yorks; cliffs, railway, waterbodies, woods, building names, road names, cross (pictorial), abbey ruins (in detail), mills, workhouse, saw mill, dry dock, chemical works, limekiln, windmill.

42/165 Healey with Suttons (township in parish of Masham) SE 160800
Apt 07.05.1838; 4827a (4827); Map 1839, 16 chns, in 2 parts, ? by Henry Trumper, Swinton, Masham, Yorks; woods, ownerships (col); streams named. District is apportioned by holding and fields are not shown; Apt omits holding acreages.

42/166 Over Helmsley (parish) SE 695568 [Upper Helmsley]
Apt 28.05.1838; 851a (850); Map not dated, [6 chns]; woods (by annotation), common.

42/167 Helmsley, Rievaulx, Sproxton, Pockley, Harom, Beadlam, Bilsdale, Laskill Pasture and Carlton (townships in parish of Helmsley) SE 600910
Apt 23.12.1844; 1501a (25411); Map 1846, 8 chns, in 6 parts, (tithable parts only; one part at 12 chns; includes 2-chn enlargement of detail); foot/b'way, woods, stiles.

42/168 Hemlington (township in parish of Stainton) NZ 499143
Apt 10.02.1849; 1098a (1097); Map 1849, 8 chns, by James Biggins; waterbodies, woods.

42/169 Hildenley (township in parish of Appleton le Street) SE 749709 [Not listed]
Apt 16.11.1844; 22a (270); Map (drawn on Apt) 1849?, 8 chns, (tithable parts only); waterbodies, woods. Apt omits land use.

42/170 Hilton (parish) NZ 465113
Apt 18.08.1840; 1340a (1340); Map 1838, 6 chns; woods, landowners. Apt has cropping information.

42/171 Hinderskelf (parish) SE 711699 [Not listed]
Apt 22.11.1847; 293a (1620); Map 1849, 4 chns, by Robt Wise, Malton, (tithable parts only); foot/b'way, waterbodies, woods (named), parkland, building names, mausoleum, temple, private carriage drive, avenue of trees.

42/172 Hinderwell (parish) NZ 765165
Apt 29.11.1838; 1563a (1990); Map 1853, 6 chns, by T. Bradley and Son, Richmond; foot/b'way, waterbodies, woods, boundary stone, ownerships (col), cliffs.

42/173 Hipswell and St Martin (township and hamlet in parish of Catterick) SE 168988
Apt 23.06.1842; 2536a (2785); Map 1843, 12 chns, by T. Bradley and

Son, Richmond, Yorkshire; foot/b'way, woods, building names, landowners, toll bar, weir, ownerships (col). Most of the district is treated as one large tithe area, with no holding or other details.

42/174 Holme (township in parish of Pickhill) SE 356821
Apt 30.07.1839; 536a (all); Map 1839, 6 chns, by T. Bradley and Son, Richmond, Yorks; woods, building names, ownerships (col).

42/175 Holme cum Howgrave (township in parish of Kirklington) SE 318800
Apt 26.02.1839; 288a (?); Map 1838, 3 chns, by A. and R. Reed, Stockton upon Tees; foot/b'way, waterbodies, boundary stones. Apt has cropping information.

42/176 South Holme (township in parish of Hovingham) SE 702775
Apt 15.02.1840; 363a (777); Map 1839, 4 chns, by Tuke and Allanson, (tithable parts only); woods, landowners (col). Apt omits land use.

42/177 Holtby (parish) SE 667539
Apt 13.06.1838; 875a (1046); Map 1839, 3 chns, by Henry R. Spence; foot/b'way, waterbodies, woods. Apt omits land use.

42/178 Hood Grange (hamlet) SE 506821
Apt 14.10.1846; 311a (all); Map 1847, 5 chns, by Thos Holliday; foot/b'way, waterbodies, woods.

42/179 Hornby (parish) SE 235935
Apt 25.09.1843; 4675a (3713); Map 1844, 8 chns, by T. Bradley and Son, Richmond, Yorks, (tithable parts only in detail, tinted); waterbodies, woods, heath/moor, building names, mill, townships (col).

42/180 Howe (township in parish of Pickhill) SE 352800
Apt 31.08.1842; 385a (all); Map 1842, 6 chns, ? by A. and R. Reed; foot/b'way, woods, Great North Road, ownerships (col).

42/181 Huby (township in parish of Sutton on the Forest) SE 558642
Apt 17.12.1838; 4515a (4515); Map 1838, 4 chns; waterbodies, woods (named), heath/moor, field boundary ownerships, building names, brick yard; legend explains tithe ownership colours. Apt omits some land use.

42/182 Hudswell (township in parish of Catterick) SE 141997
Apt 06.09.1842; 2288a (2831); Map 1843, 6 chns, by T. Bradley and Son, Richmond, Yorks, (tithable parts only in detail); woods, plantations, public quarry, ownerships (col).

42/183 Hunderthwaite (township in parish of Romaldkirk) NY 950195
Apt 29.06.1839; 6300a (6299); Map 1838, 3 chns, by A. and R. Reed, Stockton upon Tees; hill-drawing, woods, plantations, rock outcrops, building names, slate quarry, boundary stones; streams and gills named. Apt has cropping information and also some information on non-agrarian uses, e.g. 'Chandler's Shop'.

42/184 Huntington (township in parish of Huntington) SE 620557
Apt 31.05.1841; 2558a (2557); Map 1841, 4 chns, 'copied' by R. Smith, York; foot/b'way, occupation road, toll bar, waterbodies, woods, river lock, swing bridge; north pointer has feathers. Apt omits land use and field names for modus lands.

42/185 Hunton (township in parish of Patrick Brompton) SE 188922
Apt 03.09.1847; 297a (1830); Map 1848, 6 chns, by T. Bradley and Son, Richmond, (tithable parts only in detail, tinted); heath/moor; land tithable to landowner (pink).

42/186 Husthwaite (township in parish of Husthwaite) SE 518736
Apt 29.06.1839; 1621a (1621); Map 1841, 6 chns, in 2 parts, by H. Scott, (includes enlargement of village at 3 chns); foot/b'way, waterbodies, woods, field boundary ownerships, building names.

42/187 Hutton Conyers (township or extra-parochial district) SE 345741
Apt 17.11.1848; 2140a (4061); Map 1849, 6 chns, in 2 parts, by John Humphries, Ripon, (includes 2-chn enlargement of detail); railway, foot/b'way, waterbodies, woods, ownerships (col).

42/188 Hutton le Hole (township in parish of Lastingham) SE 705895 [Hutton-le-Hole]
Apt 10.08.1839; 1061a (2860); Map 1839?, 6 chns; hill-drawing, woods (col), field boundary ownerships, building names, commons, moor; bridge named; it is unclear what the colours mean; dividers, quill pen and measuring rod surround ruler-style scale bar; map title is on a scroll resting on a pillar, with wheat ears behind.

42/189 Hutton Long Villiers (township in parish of Gilling) NZ 126118 [Not listed]
Apt 31.05.1838; 1241a (?); Map 1839?, 4 chns; woods, pit.

42/190 Hutton Lowcross (township in parish of Gisborough) NZ 597142 [Not listed]
Apt 23.04.1844; 1543a (1573); Map 1845, 5 chns, by George Peirson, Guisbrough.

42/191 Hutton Mulgrave (township in parish of Lythe) NZ 835101
Apt 22.10.1845; 87a (1480); Map surveyed June 1849, 4 chns, by Thomas Buxton, Land Agent and Surveyor, Malton, (tithable parts only); woods; stream named.

42/192 Hutton near Rudby (township in parish of Rudby) NZ 458052 [Hutton Rudby]
Apt 12.06.1838; 2341a (2341); Map 1839, 6 chns, by John Howgate, Knaresborough; hill-drawing, foot/b'way, waterbodies, woods, building names, mill, weir, toll gate, avenue of trees; three different styles of writing are used for building names, perhaps indicating importance; tithable land is pink and tithe-free land is green. Apt has cropping information.

42/193 Ilton cum Pott (township in parish of Masham) SE 190790
Apt 07.05.1838; 2048a (2220); Map 1839, 10.67 chns, in 3 parts, ? by Henry Trumper, Swinton, Masham, Yorks; woods, ownerships (col); stream named. District is apportioned by groups of holdings, and not all occupiers are named; Apt generalises land use.

42/194 Ingleby Arncliffe (parish) NZ 448005
Apt 02.02.1843; 1268a (1875); Map 1843, 4 chns, in 2 parts, 'made from Estate plans upon various scales and degrees of accuracy' by A. and R. Reed, Stockton upon Tees, (tithable parts only in detail; includes 2-chn enlargement of detail); woods, plantations, building names.

42/195 Ingleby Barwick (township in parish of Stainton) NZ 442139 [Not listed]
Apt 10.02.1849; 1505a (?); Map 1849, 3 chns; waterbodies, woods, orchards.

42/196 Ingleby Greenhow (parish) NZ 593053
Apt 19.04.1839; 4694a (7066); Map 1839, 8 chns, (tithable parts only in detail); waterbodies, woods, plantations, landowners. District is apportioned partly by holding; Apt omits land use and field names.

42/197 Kepwick (township) SE 477917
Apt 31.12.1850; 1510a (2520); Map 1851, 4 chns, by William Simpson, Nunthorpe, (tithable parts only); woods, tramroad.

42/198 Kilburn (township in parish of Kilburn) SE 512804
Apt 30.06.1840; 2744a (all); Map 1840, 8 chns, by G.B. Lancaster, Thirsk; foot/b'way, woods, field boundary ownerships; meaning of pink band and green-tinted fields is unclear.

42/199 Killerby (township in parish of Catterick) SE 268960 [Not listed]
Apt 31.05.1841; 39a (712); Map 1843, 6 chns, by T. Bradley and Son, Richmond, Yorks, (tithable parts only); landowners, (col).

42/200 Kilton (township in parish of Skelton in Cleveland) NZ 695175 [Kilton Thorpe]
Apt 30.01.1845; 1636a (1643); Map 1844, 9 chns, by George Pierson, Guisbrough, (tinted).

42/201 North Kilvington and part of Thornton-le-Street (township and part of township in parish of Thornton-le-Street) SE 440860
Apt 15.07.1845; 1191a (all); Map 1845, 6 chns, 'Redrawn' by T. Dixon, Darlington; woods.

42/202 South Kilvington (township in parish of South Kilvington) SE 442841
Apt 16.05.1844; 1052a (all); Map 1846, 6 chns, surveyed by Henry Scott, Oulston, Easingwold, (tinted); foot/b'way, waterbodies, woods, osiers (by symbol), orchards, gardens, field boundary ownerships, building names, rectory, glebe (col).

42/203 Kiplin (township in parish of Catterick) SE 285975
Apt 19.11.1839; 989a (993); Map 1839, 5 chns, by T. Dixon, Darlington, (tinted); foot/b'way, waterbodies, woods, parkland, gardens. Apt omits land use.

42/204 Kirby in Cleveland (parish) NZ 547063 [Kirby]
Apt 20.04.1843; 4716a (all); Map 1842, 6 chns, by James Biggins; foot/b'way, woods, plantations; streams crossing fields are shown discontinuously; no buildings are shown.

42/205 Kirby Hill (township in parish of Kirby on the Hill alias Kirby on the Moor) SE 393697 [Kirkby Hill]
Apt 31.12.1840; 1164a (1164); Map 1842, 8 chns, by J. Powell, Knaresbrough; foot/b'way, waterbodies, building names; tithe-merged land is pink, tithe-free land is yellow, and other land is green.

42/206 Kirbyknowle (parish) SE 468872 [Kirby Knowle]
Apt 28.02.1839; 1556a (all); Map 1838, 6 chns, by T. Bradley and Son, Richmond, Yorks, (tinted); hill-drawing, foot/b'way, waterbodies, woods, plantations, building names, glebe (col).

42/207 Kirby Misperton (township in parish of Kirby Misperton) SE 778793
Apt 04.07.1846; 1740a (1739); Map 1845, 8 chns, by Henry Scott, Land Agent and Surveyor, Oulston, near Easingwold; waterbodies, woods, plantations, parkland, fish pond.

42/208 Kirby Moorside (township in parish of Kirby Moorside) SE 697866 [Kirkbymoorside]
Apt 17.08.1847; 3513a (4136); Map 1848, 8 chns, in 4 parts, by J.H. Phillips, (includes enlargement of town at 4 chns); foot/b'way, woods, field boundary ownerships, stiles, vicarage, pit.

42/209 Kirby Wiske (township in parish of Kirby Wiske) SE 364848
Apt 19.04.1839; 1070a (1089); Map 1840, 6 chns, by T. Bradley and Son, Richmond, Yorks; waterbodies, woods, parkland, building names.

42/210 Kirkby Fleetham (parish) SE 280945
Apt 14.07.1838; 2974a (all); Map 1838, 6 chns, by T. Bradley and Son, Richmond; waterbodies, woods, parkland, Great North Road, ownerships (col).

42/211 Kirkby Ravensworth (township in parish of Kirkby Ravensworth) NZ 135063 [Ravensworth]
Apt 29.10.1840; 218a (all); Map 1841, 6 chns, by T. Bradley and Sons, Richmond, Yorks; woods, ownerships (col).

42/212 Kirkby Sigston (township in parish of Kirkby Sigston) SE 423946 [Kirby Sigston]
Apt 29.04.1845; 1217a (all); Map 1845, 6 chns, by W. Alderson, West Lodge, Bedale; foot/b'way, woods, stiles, toll gate, ownerships (col).

42/213 Kirkleatham (township in parish of Kirkleatham) NZ 590232
Apt 25.02.1840; 72a (5479); Map 1840, 8 chns, by George Pierson, Guisbrough, (tithable parts only); arable (col), grassland (col), gardens, rabbit warren, seashore (col); legend explains land use colours.

42/214 Kirkleavington (township in parish of Kirkleavington) NZ 428097 [Kirklevington]
Apt 28.09.1839; 2161a (all); Map 1839?, 4 chns; foot/b'way, turnpike roads, toll bars, plantations (by annotation), orchard (by annotation).

42/215 Kirklington (township) SE 319811
Apt 14.08.1839; 1910a (1910); Map 1840, 4 chns.

42/216 Knayton with Brawith (township in parish of Leake) SE 437880
Apt 31.12.1850; 1850a (1390); Map 1851, 6 chns, by William Simpson, Nunthorpe; waterbodies, woods.

42/217 Landmouth with Catto (township in parish of Leake) SE 428926 [Not listed]
Apt 31.12.1850; 789a (600); Map 1851, 3 chns, by William Simpson, Nunthorpe; houses, woods.

42/218 Langthorp (township in parish of Kirkby upon the Moor alias Kirkby Hill) SE 380677 [Langthorpe]
Apt 24.11.1841; 556a (556); Map 1842, 6 chns, by John Hustwaite; canal, weir.

42/219 Langton upon Swale (parish) SE 309965 [Great Langton]
Apt 12.06.1837; 1840a (1840); Map 1837, 4 chns, 'Corrected and in part Surveyed' by Thos Dixon, Darlington, (tithable parts only); foot/b'way, farmyards, woods (col), plantations (col), parkland, arable (col), grassland (col), orchards, field boundary ownerships, field acreages.

42/220 Lartington (township in parish of Romaldkirk) NY 973166
Apt 21.03.1841; 4072a (5299); Map 1840, 4 chns, by T. Dixon; hill-drawing, foot/b'way, waterbodies, woods, parkland, marsh/bog, rock outcrops, building names, fish pond, boundary stones, pit, ownerships (col); physical features named.

42/221 Lastingham (township in parish of Lastingham) SE 739902
Apt 15.11.1848; 407a (690); Map 1841, 3 chns, in 3 parts, ? by Robert Abbey, Hutton; foot/b'way, waterbodies, woods, parkland, orchards, stiles, ownerships (col).

42/222 Laysthorpe (township in parish of Stonegrave) SE 633787 [Not listed]
Apt 31.05.1842; 312a (312); Map 'made in 1842', 4 chns, by John Howgate, Knaresbrough, (tinted); foot/b'way, waterbodies, woods, gardens, building names, stiles.

42/223 East Layton (township in parishes of Melsonby and St John Stanwick) NZ 143107
Apt 03.05.1845; 1046a (all); Map 1845, 4 chns, ? by William Lax, Darlington; foot/b'way, waterbodies, woods, plantations, quarry.

42/224 West Layton (township in parish of Gilling) NZ 157107
Apt 29.03.1848; 738a (570); Map 1848, 4 chns, by William Lax, Darlington; foot/b'way, waterbodies, woods, building names, pits.

42/225 Leake (township in parish of Leake) SE 429912
Apt 31.12.1850; 311a (210); Map 1851, 3 chns, by William Simpson, Nunthorpe; woods.

42/226 Levisham (parish) SE 832921
Apt 29.06.1848; 2963a (2962); Map 1847, 6 chns, by Robt Wise, Malton; hill-drawing, railway with station, foot/b'way, waterbodies, woods (col), field boundary ownerships, moor (col), boundary stones, pits, quarry; some physical features named; map date is framed in a sunburst.

42/227 Leyburn (township in parish of Wensley) SE 108912
Apt 23.09.1840; 2401a (2407); Map 1839, 3 chns, by Edwd Other; woods, plantations, building names, walk mill, public quarry; above the scale is a note, 'This Plan is made from two plans at three and six chains to an Inch', and below is a note that lands banded yellow belong to Lord Bolton, and those banded green to the freeholders.

42/228 Libberston (township in parish of Filey) TA 077825 [Lebberston]
Apt 31.03.1847; 8a (1590); Map (drawn on Apt) 1852?, 2.5 chns, (tithable parts only).

42/229 East Lilling (township in parish of Sheriff Hutton) SE 658635
Apt 24.10.1846; 79a (1530); Map 1847, 3 chns, by Fras Carr, York, (tithable parts only); foot/b'way, waterbodies, woods, landowners.

42/230 Liverton (township in parish of Easington) NZ 712155
Apt 27.09.1837; 2394a (2400); Map 1837, 4 chns, 'Enlarged and Copied'

by John Curtis, Snaith; hill-drawing, foot/b'way, woods (named), field names, stiles, mill race, boundary bush (by symbol); some field boundaries, a footpath, and a few field gates are shown in red.

42/231 Lofthouse (parish) NZ 720170 [Loftus]
Apt 27.09.1837; 3384a (3935); Map 1838?, [6 chns], by T. Bradley and Sons, Richmond; foot/b'way, waterbodies, heath/moor, woods, building names, alum works, sea-cliffs, ownerships (col).

42/232 Lythe (township in parish of Lythe) NZ 845130
Apt 22.10.1845; 127a (3904); Map surveyed in June 1849, 4 chns, by Thomas Buxton, Land Agent and Surveyor, Malton, (tithable parts only); foot/b'way, sea ride; tithable buildings are carmine, and others are grey.

42/233 Maltby (township in parish of Stainton) NZ 477146
Apt 10.02.1849; 1088a (1093); Map 1850, 3 chns, by William Simpson, Nunthorpe; woods.

42/234 Old Malton (parish) SE 793737
Apt 29.10.1844; 2955a (3983); Map 1847, 5 chns, by Thomas Buxton, Land Agent and Surveyor, New Malton, (tithable parts only, but including also some land outside the district); waterbodies, woods (col), osiers (by symbol), building names, cattle market, quarry, tithe-free land; bridge named. Apt omits some field names.

42/235 Manfield (parish) NZ 227125
Apt 28.11.1840; 3456a (3455); Map 1841, 6 chns, in 2 parts, by T. Bradley and Son, Richmond, Yorkshire, (includes 2-chn enlargement of detail); hill-drawing, foot/b'way, waterbodies, woods, plantations, building names, ownerships (col), mill; stream named.

42/236 The Marishes (township in parish of Pickering) SE 813781 [High and Low Marishes]
Apt 12.11.1845; 1745a (2289); Map surveyed in 1846, 4 chns, by Thomas Buxton, Land Agent and Surveyor, Malton; foot/b'way, waterbodies, woods; streams crossing fields are shown, tithe-free land (col).

42/237 Marrick (parish) NZ 060010
Apt 30.06.1848; 1695a (5560); Map 1851, 6 chns, ? by T. Bradley and Son, Richmond, Yorks, (tithable parts only in detail); woods, field boundary ownerships, ownerships (col).

42/238 Marsk in Cleveland (parish) NZ 635218 [Marske-by-the-Sea]
Apt 29.08.1845; 606a (?); Map 1846, 8 chns, by George Pierson, Guisbro', (tithable parts only, tinted); residual open fields, landowners.

42/239 Marske (parish) NZ 102021
Apt 16.05.1845; 6558a (6557); Map 1847?, 12 chns; hill-drawing, foot/b'way, woods, building names, boundary stone, obelisk, ownerships (col); stream named. District is apportioned by holding and fields are not shown; Apt generalises land use.

42/240 Marton in Cleveland (parish) NZ 513161 [Marton]
Apt 18.07.1840; 3376a (all); Map 1841, 6 chns, 'made from Estate Plans upon various scales and degrees of accuracy' by A. and R. Reed, Stockton upon Tees; foot/b'way, waterbodies, woods, plantations, orchards, gardens, building names, vicarage; church and a ruin are named in gothic.

42/241 Marton le Moor (township in parishes of Topcliffe and Kirby Hill) SE 370705 [Marton-le-Moor]
Apt 12.09.1838; 1614a (all); Map 1838, 6 chns, by Wm Mafham, Ripon, from a survey of 1789; waterbodies, woods, marsh/bog, Great North Road, parish boundary.

42/242 Masham (township in parish of Masham) SE 216812
Apt 07.05.1838; 2195a (8657); Map 1839, 12 chns, in 2 parts, ? by Henry Trumper, Swinton, Masham, Yorks; waterbodies, woods, ownerships (col); stream named. District is apportioned by holding or owner and fields are not shown; Apt generalises land use.

42/243 Maunby (township in parish of Kirby Wiske) SE 353870
Apt 19.04.1839; 1500a (1500); Map 1840, 6 chns, by T. Bradley and Son, Richmond, Yorkshire; foot/b'way, waterbodies, woods, plantations, orchards, ferry, ownerships (col); stream named.

42/244 Melbecks (township in parish of Grinton) NY 955005 [Not listed]
Apt 16.01.1844; 3151a (10106); Map 1842, 6 chns, in 59 parts, by Anthony Clarkson, (includes 58 2-chn enlargements of detail); foot/b'way, houses, woods, plantations, gardens, building names, chapel.

42/245 Melmerby (township in parish of Coverham) SE 071859
Apt 28.09.1846; 1153a (1153); Map 1847, 4 chns, by Wm Thornton, Carlton; foot/b'way, ford, boundary stones (with markings described); bridge named.

42/246 Melmerby (township in parish of Wath) SE 343767
Apt 30.11.1838; 1109a (all); Map 1839, 6 chns, by T. Bradley and Son, Richmond, Yorks; waterbodies, woods, building names, ownerships (col), Great North Road.

42/247 Melsonby (township in parish of Melsonby) NZ 193088
Apt 09.05.1840; 2670a (all); Map 1840, 6 chns, by T. Bradley and Son, Richmond, Yorks; hill-drawing, foot/b'way, waterbodies, woods, orchards, heath/moor, building names, quarry, ownerships (col).

42/248 Mickleby (township in parish of Lythe) NZ 807130
Apt 22.10.1845; 82a (1340); Map surveyed June 1849, 4 chns, by Thomas Buxton, Land Agent and Surveyor, Malton, (tithable parts only); foot/b'way, waterbodies, building names.

42/249 Middleham (parish) SE 120873
Apt 15.11.1843; 2109a (2108); Map 1839, 3 chns, by A. and R. Reed, Stockton upon Tees; waterbodies, woods, plantations, castle ruins (named in gothic).

42/250 Middlesborough (parish) NZ 496197 [Middlesbrough]
Apt 19.07.1848; 98a (2300); Map 1840, 4 chns, by Matthew Bowser, Thornaby Grange, (tithable parts only); foot/b'way, landowners.

42/251 Middleton upon Leven (township in parish of Rudby) NZ 475095 [Middleton-on-Leven]
Apt 28.02.1839; 1130a (1129); Map 1838, 6 chns, by William Simpson; waterbodies, woods, churchyard.

42/252 Middleton Quernhow (township in parish of Wath) SE 337790
Apt 28.05.1838; 736a (all); Map 1838, 4 chns; foot/b'way, waterbodies, woods (col), orchards, road names, field names, ownerships (col), stiles, well; buildings are shown by small elevation symbols; landowners are named in title, which is in a rectangular frame with ball-and-arrow decoration; dividers, quill pen and pencil surmount the scale bar.

42/253 Middleton-Tyas (township in parish of Middleton-Tyas) NZ 228058 [Middleton Tyas]
Apt 18.03.1841; 3125a (3154); Map 1844?, 6 chns, by T. Bradley and Son, Richmond, Yorkshire; hill-drawing, waterbodies, woods, plantations, building names, ownerships (col), pits.

42/254 Milby (township in parishes of Kirkby on the Moor alias Kirkby Hill, and Aldborough) (partly in Yorks, West Riding) SE 404681
Apt 23.08.1847; 727a (all); Map 1848, 6 chns, in 2 parts, (includes 3-chn enlargement of detail); railway, foot/b'way, canal, woods, parish and riding boundary; colouring of fields is ornamental.

42/255 Monk End (district in parish of Crofton) NZ 279102
Apt 13.12.1843; 111a (all); Map 1843, 3 chns, by William Lax, Darlington; hill-drawing, foot/b'way, woods, parkland, gardens, building names, embankment, school, rectory, mill, mill race, boundary stone; churchyard is shown with black marks, symbolising graves; stream named.

42/256 Moorsom (Great and Little) and Stanghow (township in parish of Skelton) NZ 680150 [Moorsholm]
Apt 30.11.1839; 7075a (6610); Map 1840, 9 chns, by George Peirson, Guisbrough, (tithable parts only in detail); boundary stones (pictorial).

42/257 Morton (township in parish of Ormesby) NZ 552149 [Not listed]
Apt 11.04.1839; 991a (990); Map 1839, 4 chns, by William Simpson, Pinchingthorpe, near Guisbrough; waterbodies, woods.

42/258 Morton upon Swale (township in parish of Ainderby Steeple) SE 324907 [Morton-on-Swale]
Apt 23.09.1840; 1533a (1533); Map 1838, 3 chns, 'Corrected and in part

Surveyed' by T. Dixon, Darlington; foot/b'way, waterbodies, woods, orchards, hedge ownership (col).

42/259 Moulton (township in parish of Middleton-Tyas) NZ 250040
Apt 18.03.1841; 2930a (2954); Map 1841, 6 chns, by T. Bradley and Son, Richmond, Yorks; waterbodies, woods, heath/moor, building names; stream named.

42/260 Muker (township in parish of Grinton) NY 880015
Apt 17.01.1844; 30262a (30262); Map 1841, 6 chns, in 7 parts, by Anthony Clarkson, (tithable parts only; includes six 2-chn enlargements of detail); hill-drawing, foot/b'way, woods, gardens, building names, smithy, common quarries, mines, smelt mills, pits.

42/261 Murton (township in parish of Osbaldwick) SE 651526
Apt 18.05.1843; 824a (1060); Map 1842, 6 chns, (tinted); foot/b'way, field boundary ownerships.

42/262 Muscoates (township in parish of Kirkdale) SE 692808
Apt 17.07.1844; 943a (947); Map 1846, 6 chns; woods.

42/263 Myton on Swale (parish) SE 447668 [Myton-on-Swale]
Apt 30.06.1848; 1575a (1480); Map 1849, 6 chns, by Thos Holliday, (tinted); foot/b'way, waterbodies, woods, parkland, stiles, hall, fords, field boundary ownership.

42/264 Nawton (township in parish of Kirkdale) SE 652848
Apt 17.07.1844; 281a (1260); Map 1845, 6 chns, (tithable parts only in detail); waterbodies, woods; colours, explained in legend, indicate what tithes are payable. Apt omits land use.

42/265 New Forest (township in parish of Kirby Ravensworth) NZ 062052 [Not listed]
Apt 28.05.1838; 2979a (2978); Map 1839, 6 chns, by Thomas Bradley and Son, Richmond; hill-drawing, foot/b'way, woods, field boundary ownerships, building names, shooting box, boundary marks, moor, open pasture, fords; gills named.

42/266 Newbiggin (township in parish of Aysgarth) SD 995848
Apt 29.06.1839; 1704a (2000); Map 1840, 3 chns, by Edwd Other; woods.

42/267 Newbrough (township in parish of Coxwold) SE 551769 [Not listed]
Apt 30.09.1846; 2313a (2313); Map 1846, 6 chns, by H. Scott, Oulston; hill-drawing, waterbodies, woods, plantations, parkland, gardens, field boundary ownerships, building names, holdings (col); hill named.

42/268 Newby (township in parishes of Seamer and Stokesley) NZ 511111
Apt 15.06.1838; 1211a (1211); Map 1839, 6 chns, by William Simpson, Pinchingthorpe, near Guisbrough, (tinted); woods; areas tinted blue only pay rectorial tithes.

42/269 Newby Wiske (township in parish of Kirby Wiske) SE 360888
Apt 19.04.1839; 1395a (1395); Map 1839, 4 chns, 'Corrected and in part Surveyed' by T. Dixon, Darlington; waterbodies, woods, parkland, orchards, building names, ownerships (col), drainage ditches.

42/270 Newholm cum Dunsley (township in parish of Whitby) NZ 861109
Apt 15.07.1843; 2165a (2254); Map 1845, 4 chns, by Robt Wise, Surveyor etc., Malton; woods (col), field boundary ownerships; sunburst and clouds frame date and other details in title.

42/271 Newsham (township in parish of Appleton le Street) SE 746760 [Not listed]
Apt 21.01.1840; 509a (?); Map 1841, 4 chns, 'redrawn' by H. Scott, Oulston; field boundary ownership, ownerships (col).

42/272 Newsham (township in parish of Kirby Wiske) SE 384843
Apt 19.04.1839; 1066a (?); Map 1839, 4 chns, 'Corrected and in part Surveyed' by Thos Dixon, Darlington; railway, foot/b'way, waterbodies, woods, orchards, ownerships (col). Apt omits some field names.

42/273 Newsham (township in parishes of Kirby Hill alias Kirby Ravensworth and Barningham) NZ 090090
Apt 14.11.1840; 3313a (all); Map 1837, 6 chns, by John Humphries, Ripon; woods, building names, landowners, quarries, boundary marks, wells, footbridge; colours may indicate tithable status; map has landowners' signatures, signifying its adoption; rake, pitchfork, sickle and scythe decorate the north pointer.

42/274 Newton (parish) NZ 568130 [Newton under Roseberry]
Apt 08.06.1837; 1163a (?); Map 1838, 3.5 chns, by William Simpson, Pinchingthorpe, near Guisbrough; hill-drawing, foot/b'way, waterbodies, woods, churchyard, quarry, disputed area.

42/275 East Newton (lordship in parish of Stonegrave) SE 642796
Apt 30.07.1839; 591a (591); Map 1839, 4 chns, copied by Henry Scott; foot/b'way, woods, cross (by symbol).

42/276 Newton Morrell (township in parish of Barton) NZ 242096
Apt 24.08.1839; 612a (?); Map 1843, 6 chns; woods.

42/277 Newton Mulgrave (township in parish of Lythe) NZ 777140
Apt 28.08.1845; 2196a (all); Map surveyed July 1846, 4 chns, by Thomas Buxton, Land Agent and Surveyor, Malton.

42/278 Newton upon Rawcliffe (township in parish of Pickering) SE 808908 [Newton-on-Rawcliffe]
Apt 28.12.1843; 2401a (2401); Map surveyed in 1843, 4 chns, in 3 parts, by Thomas Buxton, Land Agent and Surveyor, Malton; railway, waterbodies, woods, road names, mills, spring, diverted stream, moor; stream and 'scarr' named.

42/279 Newton le Willows or Newton in the Willows (township in parishes of Patrick Brompton and Fingal) SE 211891 [Newton-le-Willows]
Apt 14.07.1838; 1797a (1797); Map 1838, 6 chns, by T. Bradley and Son, Richmond, Yorks, (tinted); hill-drawing, woods; land in Fingal is pink; it is unclear what yellow banding indicates.

42/280 Normanby (township in parish of Normanby) SE 744814
Apt 31.01.1839; 1753a (1768); Map 1839, 4 chns, in 2 parts, by Thomas Buxton, Land Surveyor etc, Malton; foot/b'way, waterbodies, woods (col), orchards, landowners; meaning of colour bands is unclear.

42/281 Normanby (township in parish of Ormesby) NZ 540188
Apt 29.06.1839; 1344a (all); Map 1838, 4 chns, by William Simpson, Pinchingthorpe, near Guisbrough; woods.

42/282 Northolme (township in parish of Great Edston) SE 705807 [Not listed]
Apt 10.12.1850; 21a (610); Map 1851, 4 chns; waterbodies, woods, river bank, field boundary ownership; tithable parts are tinted green, with acreages; stream named. Apt omits some field names.

42/283 Norton le Clay (township in parish of Cundal) SE 400710 [Norton-le-Clay]
Apt 31.12.1844; 603a (1023); Map 1847, 6 chns, in 3 parts, by John Humphries, Ripon, (tithable parts only; includes two 1-chn enlargements of detail); foot/b'way, woods, ownerships (col).

42/284 Nunwick-cum-Howgrave (township in parish of Kirklington) SE 309752
Apt 27.02.1839; 118a (748); Map 1838, 3 chns, by A. and R. Reed, Stockton upon Tees; foot/b'way, plantations. Apt has cropping information.

42/285 Oldstead (township in parish of Kilburn) SE 533809
Apt 23.10.1844; 1371a (1379); Map 1846, 6 chns, surveyed by Henry Scott, Oulston; foot/b'way, waterbodies, woods, parkland, field boundary ownerships, ownerships (col), building names, observatory, quarry.

42/286 Ormesby (township in parish of Ormesby) NZ 528180
Apt 08.03.1839; 2769a (2846); Map 1839, 4 chns, by William Simpson, Pinchingthorpe, near Guisbrough; woods, churchyard.

42/287 Osbaldwick (township in parish of Osbaldwick) SE 635522
Apt 31.12.1849; 561a (?); Map 1850, 4 chns, by Fras Carr, York, (tithable parts only); woods.

42/288 Osgodby (township in parish of Cayton) TA 053844
Apt 05.11.1846; 1062a (1375); Map 1848, 6 chns, by W. Hodgson, East Ayton; buildings are shown in outline only, without fill.

42/289 Osmotherley (township in parish of Osmotherley) SE 472977
Apt 02.07.1847; 2011a (all); Map 1848, 4 chns, by T. Dixon, Darlington, (tithable parts only); foot/b'way, waterbodies, woods, building names, quarry, footbridges; scale graduation is '25,30,45'; dot-dash lines divide one ownership.

42/290 Oswaldkirk (parish) SE 618792
Apt 06.09.1838; 2158a (?); Map 3 chns, in 3 parts: Oswaldkirk 1841, surveyed by Henry Scott; Newton Grange 1839, by Tuke and Allanson; waterbodies, woods, field boundary ownerships, ownerships (col), building names, chapel; map content differs between the parts.

42/291 North Otterington (township in parish of North Otterington) SE 365903
Apt 25.11.1841; 771a (782); Map 1842, 4 chns, 'Corrected and in part Surveyed' by T. Dixon, Darlington; railway, waterbodies, woods, plantations, ownerships (col).

42/292 South Otterington (parish) SE 378878
Apt 08.04.1842; 1415a (1414); Map 1842, 4 chns, 'Corrected and in part Surveyed' by T. Dixon, Darlington; railway, waterbodies, woods, plantations, orchards.

42/293 Oulston (township in parish of Coxwold) SE 553739
Apt 29.06.1839; 1503a (1502); Map 1840, 6 chns, copied by H. Scott; hill-drawing, waterbodies, woods (col), field boundary ownership.

42/294 Overton (parish) SE 550587
Apt 05.01.1848; 465a (5163); Map 1848?, 6 chns; railway.

42/295 Ovington (township in parish of Gilling) NZ 135145
Apt 24.05.1838; 496a (530); Map 1839, 4 chns; hill-drawing, foot/b'way, waterbodies, wood (by annotation), field gates, landowners, field acreages, ownerships (col); stream named.

42/296 Patrick Brompton (township in parish of Patrick Brompton) SE 222909
Apt 24.05.1838; 580a (all); Map 1838, 6 chns, by T. Bradley and Son, Richmond; woods, parkland, ford, ownerships (col); streams named.

42/297 Pickering (township in parish of Pickering) SE 810870
Apt 30.04.1838; 14280a (14280); Map 1839, 4 chns, in 5 parts, by Thomas Buxton, Land Surveyor etc, Malton; hill-drawing, railway with passing loop, foot/b'way, houses (incomplete), waterbodies, woods (col), gardens (col), residual open fields, road names, windmill (by symbol), marl pit (col), quarries, springs, limekilns, churchyard, castle yard, cross, beacon hill; drains named; meaning of yellow tint is unclear; colour bands on part 4 show holdings on Duchy of Lancaster estates.

42/298 Pickering (district in parish of Pickering) SE 813761 [Not listed]
Apt 21.03.1848; 802a (?); Map surveyed April 1849, 4 chns, by Thomas Buxton, Land Agent and Surveyor, Malton; railway, waterbodies, building names; streams and bridge named.

42/299 Pickhill with Roxby (township in parish of Pickhill) SE 345835
Apt 08.02.1838; 2131a (all); Map 1838, 6 chns, by T. Bradley and Son, Richmond; waterbodies, woods, plantations, field boundary ownerships, building names, Great North Road, ownerships (col).

42/300 Picton (township in parish of Kirkleavington) NZ 415075
Apt 01.05.1844; 990a (all); Map 1844?, 4 chns, by T. Todd, Yarm; foot/b'way.

42/301 Pinchingthorpe (township in parish of Guisbrough) NZ 579147 [Not listed]
Apt 10.10.1837; 844a (880); Map 1838, 6 chns, by William Simpson, Pinchingthorpe, near Guisbrough; foot/b'way, woods, disputed area.

42/302 Potto (township in parish of Whorlton) NZ 473038
Apt 31.10.1840; 1431a (1442); Map 1840, 4 chns, by William Simpson, Pinchingthorpe, near Guisbrough.

42/303 Preston (township in parish of Wensley) SE 069925 [Preston-under-Scar]
Apt 01.11.1839; 2510a (2509); Map 1839, 4 chns, compiled from 4 and 8 chn plans by Edwd Other; woods, plantations, boundary stones and marks, hall, ownerships (col); stream named.

42/304 Rainton-with-Newby (township in parish of Topcliffe) SE 373753
Apt 30.08.1838; 1511a (1511); Map 1839, 5.5 chns, by Wm Morton, Leeming Lane; foot/b'way, waterbodies, houses, woods, parkland, building names.

42/305 Raskelf (township in parish of Easingwold) SE 485705
Apt 30.06.1840; 4171a (5030); Map 1841, 8 chns, ? by John Humphries, Ripon, Yorks; railway, foot/b'way, waterbodies, woods, moors; colouring of tithable fields is ornamental; sunburst surrounds date in title.

42/306 Ravensworth (township in parish of Kirkby Ravensworth) NZ 146086
Apt 29.10.1840; 2176a (all); Map 1841, 6 chns, by T. Bradley and Son, Richmond, Yorks; waterbodies, woods, building names, ownerships (col).

42/307 Redmire (township in parish of Wensley) SE 052930
Apt 27.03.1843; 2198a (2219); Map 1841, 4 chns, by Edwd Other; waterbodies, woods, plantations, rock outcrops, building names, boundary stones and marks, glebe boundary (red); a note below the title explains that colour bands show Lord Bolton's and the freeholders' lands.

42/308 Reeth (township in parish of Grinton) NZ 015010
Apt 16.01.1844; 5659a (5659); Map 1839, 6 chns, in 4 parts, by Anthony Clarkson, (includes three 3-chn enlargements of detail); hill-drawing, foot/b'way, houses, woods, gardens, building names, lead mines, quarries, slate quarries, adits, limekilns (by symbol), old limekiln, bield walls, ford, corn mill, smithy, boundary marks.

42/309 Richmond (parish) NZ 158018
Apt 30.08.1839; 2341a (2341); Map 1840, 4 chns, by T. Bradley and Son, Richmond, (tithable parts only in detail); hill-drawing, waterbodies, woods, plantations, heath/moor, building names, ownerships (col), castle, weir, mill, paper mill, racecourse, grandstand; built-up part generalised; tithable buildings are hatched, and tithe-free buildings are grey.

42/310 Rokeby (parish) NZ 079139 [Not listed]
Apt 30.11.1838; 1114a (1114); Map 1839?, 6 chns; foot/b'way, woods, parkland, building names; tithable land is pale green and a named tithe-free lordship is pink; glebe is yellow; stream and bridge named.

42/311 Romanby (township and constabulary) SE 373923
Apt 01.08.1842; 2028a (2027); Map 1839, 4 chns, 'Corrected and in part Surveyed' by Thos Dixon, Darlington; foot/b'way, waterbodies, woods, parkland, orchards, holdings (col).

42/312 Rosedale East Side (township in parish of Middleton) SE 715985 [Not listed]
Apt 31.10.1850; 375a (5100); Map 1851, 12 chns, (cultivated parts only); building names; tithable lands are tinted pink and numbered.

42/313 Rosedale Westside (township in parish of Lastingham) SE 708968 [Not listed]
Apt 26.11.1838; 1096a (7900); Map 1840?, 6 chns; foot/b'way, woods (col), landowners, ownerships (col); scale is surmounted by dividers.

42/314 East Rounton (township in parish of Rudby in Cleveland) NZ 432048
Apt 20.11.1846; 1565a (1565); Map 1847?, 4 chns; urn surmounts title. District is apportioned by holding and fields are not shown; Apt generalises land use.

42/315 West Rounton (parish) NZ 414036
Apt 31.05.1838; 1430a (all); Map 1838, 4 chns, 'Corrected and in part Surveyed' by Thos Dixon, Darlington; foot/b'way, waterbodies, woods (col), osiers (by symbol), parkland, arable (col), grassland (col), orchards, hedge ownership, field gates, field acreages.

42/316 Ruswarp and Whitby (townships in parish of Whitby) NZ 886102
Apt 14.07.1843; 1477a (2243); Map 1844, 3 chns, by Thomas Buxton, Land Agent and Surveyor, Malton; railway, building names, windmills, factory, suspension bridge, docks.

42/317 Ryton (township in parish of Kirby Misperton) SE 782763
Apt 22.12.1841; 1998a (2228); Map 1842, 4 chns, in 2 parts, by Robert Wise, Land Surveyor etc, Malton; foot/b'way, waterbodies, woods, osiers (by symbol), orchards, building names, holdings (col); bridge named.

42/318 Sandhutton (township in parish of Bassall) SE 695585 [Sand Hutton]
Apt 31.05.1842; 2186a (all); Map 1842, 12 chns, copied by W.J. Ware, (tinted); waterbodies, woods (col), parkland, heath/moor, ownerships (col).

42/319 Sandhutton (township in parish of Thirsk) SE 386818
Apt 27.11.1841; 1335a (all); Map surveyed in May 1841, 3 chns, by Henry Scott, Oulston; railway, foot/b'way, waterbodies, woods, osiers (by symbol), field boundary ownerships, building names, ownerships (col); map date is framed by sunburst, surrounded by flowers, and mapmaker's name is on a drape.

42/320 Scawton (parish) SE 560830
Apt 13.07.1839; 2757a (2768); Map 1839, 4 chns, by Thos Buxton, Malton; foot/b'way, waterbodies, woods (col); pictorial church. Apt omits some field names.

42/321 Scorton (township in parish of Catterick) NZ 258007
Apt 27.05.1840; 2645a (2645); Map 1839, 7 chns, in 2 parts, ? surveyed by Thomas Dixon and ? drawn by G.B. Lancaster, (tinted; includes enlargement of village at 4 chns); foot/b'way, village green (col).

42/322 Scotton (township in parish of Catterick) SE 178965
Apt 31.05.1841; 966a (1500); Map 1844, 3 chns; woods. Apt omits land use.

42/323 West Scrafton (township in parish of Coverham) SE 075817
Apt 04.06.1846; 645a (all); Map 1849, 3 chns, by W. Thornton, Carlton; foot/b'way, waterbodies, houses, footbridge.

42/324 Scruton (parish) SE 304916
Apt 30.08.1839; 2066a (2066); Map 1839, 4 chns, 'Corrected and in part Surveyed' by Thos Dixon, Darlington; foot/b'way, waterbodies, woods, plantations, parkland, orchards, gardens, nursery, ownerships (col).

42/325 Seamer (township in parish of Seamer) NZ 505095
Apt 21.06.1838; 2611a (2610); Map 1838, 6 chns, by William Simpson, Pinchingthorpe, near Guisbrough, (tithable parts only in detail); foot/b'way, waterbodies, woods, churchyard.

42/326 Seamer (township in parish of Seamer) TA 024846
Apt 08.11.1849; 158a (4540); Map 1850, 12 chns, by Robt Wise, Malton, (tithable parts only in detail, tinted); railways, field boundary ownerships. Apt omits some field names.

42/327 Sessay cum Hutton Sessay (parish) SE 466749
Apt 06.04.1842; 3666a (3666); Map 1838, 4 chns; railway, foot/b'way, woods (named), plantations, avenue of trees, township boundaries; streams named.

42/328 Sexhow (township in parish of Rudby) NZ 486060
Apt 23.11.1838; 499a (501); Map 1838, 8 chns; foot/b'way, waterbodies, woods, plantations, field names; the owner is named in the title; thickened field boundaries may be holding boundaries.

42/329 Sheriff Hutton (township in parish of Sheriff Hutton) SE 650665
Apt 17.12.1847; 918a (4310); Map 1848, 6 chns, in 4 parts, by Thos Holliday, (tithable parts only; includes 50-chn index); waterbodies, woods, field boundary ownerships, building names, lodge.

42/330 Nether Silton (township in parish of Leake) SE 463923
Apt 31.12.1850; 1515a (2610); Map 1851, 5 chns, partly surveyed by Henry Scott; foot/b'way, woods, parkland, orchards, heath/moor, field boundary ownerships, ownerships (col).

42/331 Over Silton (township in parish of Over Silton) SE 455935
Apt 11.04.1839; 1172a (all); Map 1840, 6 chns, redrawn by H. Scott; hill-drawing, waterbodies, woods (col), field boundary ownerships, ownerships (col), boundary stones and marks, quarry, moor (col).

42/332 Sinderby (township in parish of Pickhill) SE 342816
Apt 07.07.1838; 542a (all); Map 1839, 6 chns, by T. Bradley and Son, Richmond, Yorks; woods, Great North Road, ownerships (col).

42/333 Skelton (township in parish of Skelton in Cleveland) NZ 658188
Apt 18.03.1845; 7194a (3830); Map 1846, 9 chns, in 2 parts, by George Peirson, Marske, near Guisbrough, (includes village separately at 3 chns); hill-drawing, woods, heath/moor, seashore.

42/334 Skinningrove (township in parish of Skelton in Cleveland) NZ 711199
Apt 12.03.1846; 172a (171); Map 1846, 3 chns, by George Peirson, Marske, near Guisbrough, (tinted); ford.

42/335 Skiplam (township in parish of Kirkdale) SE 652888
Apt 17.07.1844; 1750a (2760); Map 1845?, 6 chns; waterbodies, woods; note above the scale explains colouring of map by tithable status. Apt omits land use.

42/336 Skipton upon Swale (township in parish of Topcliffe) SE 374800 [Skipton-on-Swale]
Apt 22.07.1840; 828a (827); Map 1842, 4 chns, redrawn by Henry Scott; foot/b'way, waterbodies, woods (col), osiers (by symbol), field boundary ownerships.

42/337 Skutterskelfe (township in parish of Rudby) NZ 493071 [Not listed]
Apt 07.01.1840; 970a (all); Map 1838, 8 chns, by T. Dobbin; waterbodies, woods, plantations, ownership boundary.

42/338 Slingsby (parish) SE 704750
Apt 10.06.1848; 2363a (2363); Map surveyed November 1848, 4 chns, by Thomas Buxton, Land Agent and Surveyor, Malton; waterbodies, shepherd's hut, sheep walk, maypole (by symbol), castle, woods (by annotation); hills and stream named. Apt omits some land use and some field names.

42/339 Great Smeaton (parish) NZ 355051
Apt 20.11.1841; 3316a (all); Map 1843, 6 chns, by William Lax, Darlington; foot/b'way, waterbodies, woods (named), building names, rectory, wells, pump, windmill, tile sheds, turnpike gate, pinfold; churchyard is shown with black dots, symbolising tombstones.

42/340 Snainton (chapelry in parish of Brompton) SE 925835
Apt 05.11.1846; 416a (?); Map 1847, [? 4 chns]; 'Surveyed and Planned by Hornsey and Kendall', (tithable parts only); waterbodies, woods, orchards; stream and drain named.

42/341 Snilesworth (township in parish of Hawnby) SE 520960 [Not listed]
Apt 23.08.1845; 6a (5105); Map 1849?, 6 chns, (tithable parts only); field acreages. Apt omits land use.

42/342 Sowerby (township in parish of Thirsk) SE 435801
Apt 08.02.1842; 2528a (2528); Map 1845, 6 chns, by W. Lancaster, Marderby Grange, Thirsk; railways, foot/b'way, waterbodies, woods, gardens. Apt omits most field names.

42/343 Sowerby under Catcliffe (township in parish of Kirkby Sigston) SE 410935 [Not listed]
Apt 25.04.1845; 799a (all); Map 1845, 6 chns, by Wm Alderson, West Lodge, Bedale; foot/b'way, woods, field boundary ownerships, ownerships (col), stiles.

42/344 Spaunton (township in parish of Lastingham) SE 723887
Apt 15.11.1848; 1289a (1540); Map 1849, 6 chns, surveyed by Robert Wise, Malton; hill-drawing, foot/b'way, waterbodies, woods, disused pits; sunburst surrounds map date.

42/345 Spennithorne (township in parish of Spennithorne) SE 147887
Apt 10.01.1849; 209a (1280); Map 1851?, 6 chns, (tithable parts only); foot/b'way, waterbodies, woods, landowners.

42/346 Stainton (township in parish of Downholme) SE 100960
Apt 18.02.1848; 1851a (1851); Map 1849, 10 chns; waterbodies, flag quarry, boundary marks, peat moor. District is apportioned by holding or owner and fields are not shown; Apt generalises land use.

42/347 Stainton (township in parish of Stainton) NZ 475145
Apt 10.02.1849; 2243a (2820); Map 1849, 8 chns, by James Biggins, Ingleby Greenhow; foot/b'way, waterbodies, woods, parkland.

42/348 Stanwick St John (township) NZ 193125 [Stanwick-St-John]
Apt 03.05.1845; 1363a (?); Map 1847, 6 chns, 'Copied' by Thomas Bradley and Son, Richmond; foot/b'way, waterbodies, woods, plantations, parkland, building names, marl pit.

42/349 Stapleton (township in parishes of Croft and Gilling) NZ 263122
Apt 27.11.1841; 945a (?); Map 1838, 3 chns, by Otley and Lax, Darlington; hill-drawing, foot/b'way, turnpike and township roads, waterbodies, woods, orchards, gardens, heath/moor, field boundary ownerships, building names, toll bar, boat house, boundary marks, ownerships (col), parish boundary; bridge named.

42/350 Startforth (township in parish of Startforth) NZ 043153
Apt 19.04.1839; 939a (938); Map 1839, 3 chns; construction lines, foot/b'way, woods, plantations, well; tithable land is yellow and tithe-free land is pink.

42/351 Stillington (parish) SE 571678
Apt 30.07.1839; 677a (2013); Map 1840, 6 chns, by James Powell, Knaresbro', (tithable parts only in detail); foot/b'way, waterbodies, woods; land in green pays all tithes, land in pink pays small tithes and land in purple pays great tithes.

42/352 Stittenham (township in parish of Sheriff Hutton) SE 682670 [High Stittenham]
Apt 23.12.1846; 1583a (all); Map 1850?, 8 chns; woods, building names. District is apportioned by owner and fields are not shown; Apt generalises land use and only names one occupier.

42/353 Stockton on the Forest (parish) SE 663572
Apt 31.07.1847; 434a (3270); Map 1851?, 8 chns, (tithable parts only); waterbodies, woods, field boundary ownerships, building names, landowners, cross. Apt omits land use.

42/354 Stokesley (township) NZ 527097
Apt 28.02.1837; 1744a (1744); Map surveyed 20 June 1838, 3 chns, by William Simpson, Pinchingthorpe, near Guisbro'; construction lines, woods, field boundary ownerships, tithe-free field (col), mill race; built-up part generalised and tinted.

42/355 Strensall (township in parish of Strensall) SE 680610
Apt 25.05.1849; 1194a (2212); Map 1849, 6 chns, by Fras Carr, York; railway with station and platform, canal with locks, waterbodies, woods, plantations, building names.

42/356 Sutton cum Howgrave (township in parish of Kirklington) SE 320790 [Sutton Howgrave]
Apt 26.02.1839; 591a (660); Map 1838, 3 chns, by A. and R. Reed, Stockton upon Tees; foot/b'way, waterbodies, plantations. Apt has cropping information.

42/357 Sutton on the Forest (township in parish of Sutton on the Forest) SE 600627 [Sutton-on-the-Forest]
Apt 30.11.1846; 2291a (5800); Map 1847, 8 chns, by Fras Carr, York, (tithable parts only); waterbodies, woods, heath/moor, landowners.

42/358 Sutton under Whitestone Cliffe (township in parish of Felixkirk) SE 482828 [Sutton-under-Whitestone-cliffe]
Apt 20.11.1843; 1854a (1854); Map 1846, 6 chns, in 2 parts; foot/b'way, waterbodies, woods, limekilns; land coloured yellow is tithe-free and extra-parochial; land coloured light green is free of great tithe; it is unclear why detached lands are tinted green.

42/359 Swainby (hamlet in parish of Whorlton) NZ 475010
Apt 15.09.1840; 757a (?); Map 1842, 4 chns, by William Simpson, Pinchingthorpe, near Guisbrough; woods.

42/360 Swainby cum Allerthorpe (township in parishes of Pickhill and Burneston) SE 338857 [Not listed]
Apt 26.02.1839; 869a (868); Map 1838, 6 chns, by T. Bradley and Son, Richmond; field boundary ownerships, ford, parish boundary hedge; lands in Pickhill are pink and lands in Burneston are lilac.

42/361 Swinton (township in parish of Appleton le Street) SE 760730
Apt 03.12.1844; 843a (1200); Map 1845, 6 chns, by Charles F. Ash, Malton, (tithable parts only in detail); waterbodies, arable (col), grassland (col), orchards, landowners, field boundary ownership; colour bands show both land use and field boundary ownership.

42/362 Swinton (township in parish of Masham) SE 209789
Apt 07.05.1838; 1614a (1614); Map 1839, 12 chns, ? by Henry Trumper, Swinton, Masham, Yorks; waterbodies, woods, parkland, ownerships (col). District is apportioned by holding or owner and fields are not shown; Apt generalises land use.

42/363 East Tanfield (township in parish of Kirklington) SE 297788
Apt 24.05.1838; 1237a (all); Map 1837, 4 chns, by Thos Robinson, Ripon, from a survey of 1792; houses, woods, plantations, building names

42/364 West Tanfield (parish) SE 265793
Apt 26.09.1837; 3140a (3139); Map 1837, 4 chns, by Thos Robinson, Ripon, from a survey of 1792; waterbodies, woods, plantations, building names, ancient camp, mill, quarry, township boundaries.

42/365 Theakston (township) SE 309863
Apt 21.08.1839; 935a (991); Map 1838, 6 chns, by T. Bradley and Sons, Richmond, Yorks; waterbodies, woods, parkland, ownerships (col).

42/366 Thimbleby (township in parish of Osmotherley) SE 451951 [Not listed]
Apt 07.07.1847; 94a (1670); Map 1848, 4 chns, redrawn by T. Dixon, Darlington, (tithable parts only); woods, building names.

42/367 Thirkleby (parish) SE 482791
Apt 21.09.1842; 2597a (2597); Map 1842-4, 3 chns, in 4 parts, by Henry Scott, Oulston, and William Lancaster, Marderby, Thirsk, (includes 12-chn index); foot/b'way, waterbodies, woods, plantations, parkland, field boundary ownerships, quarry, ownerships (col).

42/368 Thirlby (township in parish of Felixkirk) SE 490840
Apt 29.01.1844; 575a (575); Map 1847, 6 chns; woods, field boundary ownership; land free of great tithe is pink, and modus land is faint yellow.

42/369 Thirsk (district in parish of Thirsk) SE 418828
Apt 21.07.1842; 2947a (all); Map 1843, 4 chns, by Henry Scott, Land Agent etc, Oulston; railway, foot/b'way, waterbodies, woods, plantations, gardens, heath/moor, road names, tool-house, brick works and pond, foundry, tithe barn, mansion; it is unclear what colour bands mean.

42/370 Thoralby (township in parish of Aysgarth) SD 983860
Apt 24.01.1840; 2841a (2840); Map 1841, 4 chns, in 2 parts, by Walton Alderson, Leyburn; hill-drawing, foot/b'way, waterbodies, houses, woods (col), building names, ford, footbridge.

42/371 Thormanby (parish) SE 493744
Apt 11.04.1842; 959a (958); Map 1842, 4 chns.

42/372 Thornaby (township in parish of Stainton) NZ 455165 [Thornaby-on-Tees]
Apt 10.02.1849; 1571a (1230); Map 1850, 3 chns, by William Simpson, Nunthorpe; railway, waterbodies, woods.

42/373 Thornborough (township in parish of South Kilvington) SE 437850 [Not listed]
Apt 13.05.1844; 537a (all); Map 1844, 4 chns, by William Simpson, Pinchingthorpe, near Guisbrough; foot/b'way, glebe.

42/374 Thornton cum Baxby (township in parish of Cuxwold) SE 535735 [Not listed]
Apt 29.06.1839; 1441a (1440); Map 1840, 6 chns, surveyed by Henry Scott; waterbodies, building names, ownerships (col).

42/375 Thornton le Beans (township in parish of North Otterington) SE 399901 [Thornton-le-Beans]
Apt 20.01.1842; 1351a (1351); Map 1842, 4 chns, corrected and partly surveyed by T. Dixon, Darlington; waterbodies, woods, plantations, parkland, building names, avenue of trees, ownerships (col). Apt omits some field names.

42/376 Thornton Briggs (township in parish of Brafferton) SE 421704 [Not listed]
Apt 11.08.1842; 1079a (all); Map 'made' (surveyed?) in 1842, 3 chns, by John Howgate, Knaresbrough, (tinted); foot/b'way, waterbodies, woods, field gates, building names.

42/377 Thornton Dale (parish) SE 850840
Apt 31.08.1846; 1067a (1066); Map surveyed June 1847, 3 chns, by Edwd Page; foot/b'way, waterbodies, woods, orchards, landowners, water engine; stream named.

42/378 Thornton le Moor (township in parish of North Otterington) SE 388898 [Thornton-le-Moor]
Apt 25.11.1841; 1492a (1492); Map 1842, 4 chns, corrected and partly surveyed by T. Dixon, Darlington; railway, foot/b'way, waterbodies, woods, orchards, building names.

42/379 Thornton Risebrough (township in parish of Normanby) SE 749828 [Not listed]
Apt 03.10.1837; 596a (all); Map 1838, 6 chns, copied by Henry Scott; foot/b'way, waterbodies, woods (col), road names, field acreages.

42/380 Thornton Rust (township in parish of Aysgarth) SD 977886
Apt 30.08.1839; 1924a (1923); Map 1840, 3 chns, surveyed by Walton Alderson, Leyburn; hill-drawing, foot/b'way, occupation roads, houses, woods (col), field gates, quarry, limekiln (by symbol), springs, stiles, boundary marks, shooting box, river gravel (col), common.

42/381 Thornton Steward (parish) SE 178872
Apt 10.09.1840; 2079a (2079); Map 1841, 6 chns, by T. Bradley and Son, Richmond, Yorks; foot/b'way, waterbodies, woods, plantations, heath/moor, ownerships (col).

42/382 Thornton-le-Street (district in parish of Thornton-le-Street) SE 406859
Apt 17.05.1845; 1027a (all); Map 1845, 4 chns, redrawn by T. Dixon, Darlington; foot/b'way, waterbodies, woods, plantations, landowners, ownerships (col).

42/383 Thornton Watlass (parish) SE 222858
Apt 28.02.1837; 2623a (3783); Map 1838, 6 chns, ? by T. Bradley and Son, Richmond, Yorks; hill-drawing, waterbodies, woods, parkland, building names, townships (col).

42/384 Thorpe Field (district or hamlet in parish of Thirsk) SE 418798 [Thorpefield]
Apt 22.04.1839; 229a (all); Map 1839, 3 chns, by Thos Robinson, Ripon; railway, waterbodies, houses, field acreages.

42/385 Thorpe le Willows (township in parish of Kilburn) SE 578772 [Not listed]
Apt 31.07.1839; 454a (?); Map 1839, 4 chns.

42/386 Thrintoft (township in parish of Ainderby Steeple) SE 320942
Apt 02.12.1840; 1183a (1183); Map 1838, 4 chns, corrected and partly surveyed by T. Dixon, Darlington; foot/b'way, waterbodies, woods, orchards, hedge ownership, ownerships (col), fords; table summarises acreages.

42/387 Tocketts (township in parish of Guisbrough) NZ 622178 [Not listed]
Apt 14.07.1841; 654a (653); Map 1841, 6 chns, by George Peirson, Guisbrough.

42/388 Tollerton (township in parish of Alne) SE 522647
Apt 13.09.1842; 355a (2340); Map 1843, 8 chns, by Geo. Thomas, Land Surveyor and Valuer, Layerthorpe, York, (tithable parts only in detail); railway, landowners, ownerships (col).

42/389 Topcliffe (township in parish of Topcliffe) SE 405773
Apt 02.02.1838; 4066a (4066); Map 1838?, 3 chns, by Thomas Robinson, Ripon, from a survey of 1819; railway, foot/b'way, waterbodies, houses, woods, building names, toll bar, waste; stream named.

42/390 Towthorpe (township in parishes of Huntington and Strensall) SE 638598
Apt 12.06.1841; 1031a (all); Map 1842, 8 chns; foot/b'way, waterbodies, boundary stone, parish boundary.

42/391 Trenholme (hamlet in parish of Whorlton) NZ 446026 [Not listed]
Apt 12.04.1845; 274a (?); Map 1846, 6 chns, by George Peirson, Marske, near Guisbrough, (tinted); foot/b'way, plantations.

42/392 Tunstall (township in parish of Catterick) SE 213961
Apt 10.11.1841; 1257a (1262); Map 1842, 6 chns, ? by Thomas Bradley and Son, Richmond, Yorks; woods, heath/moor, building names, fords.

42/393 Uckerby (township in parish of Catterick) NZ 249026
Apt 28.05.1841; 751a (756); Map 1841, 6 chns, by T. Bradley and Son, Richmond, Yorks; foot/b'way, woods, ownerships (col).

42/394 Ugglebarnby (township in parish of Whitby) NZ 883063
Apt 14.07.1843; 2218a (all); Map 1844, 6 chns, surveyed by Robt Wise, Malton; railway, plantations (col), heath/moor, field boundary ownerships, building names, alum works, pits, boundary stones, chapel, moors (col, with acreages).

42/395 Upleatham (parish) NZ 632195
Apt 22.07.1841; 1378a (?); Map 1842, 6 chns, by George Peirson, Guisbrough, (tithable parts only); waterbodies, landowners, old church, 'Mudge's Pole'.

42/396 Upsall (township in parish of South Kilvington) SE 452862
Apt 26.01.1846; 1278a (1278); Map 1846, 6 chns, by Henry Scott, Oulston, near Easingwold, litho (by George Smith, Easingwold, with hand colour); woods, field boundary ownerships, building names, pale dike, modus lands (pink).

42/397 Upsil (township in parish of Ormesby) NZ 560160 [Not listed]
Apt 19.04.1839; 497a (660); Map 1839, 4 chns, by William Simpson, Pinchingthorpe, near Guisbrough; foot/b'way, waterbodies, woods.

42/398 Warlaby (township in parish of Ainderby Steeple) SE 349906
Apt 28.12.1846; 12a (751); Map 1847, 2 chns, (tithable parts only); foot/b'way, landowners.

42/399 Wass (township in parish of Kilburn) SE 552799
Apt 13.08.1845; 723a (?); Map 1847, 6 chns, by Thos Holliday; foot/b'way, waterbodies, woods, field boundary ownerships, building names.

42/400 Wath (township in parish of Wath) SE 325775
Apt 07.07.1838; 740a (all); Map 1838, 4 chns, by Thomas Robinson, Jr, Ripon, from a survey of 1792; foot/b'way, waterbodies, houses, woods; a snake is twined round the north pointer.

42/401 Welburn (township in parish of Kirkdale) SE 680842
Apt 24.07.1844; 219a (1582); Map surveyed December 1848, 4 chns, by Thomas Buxton, Land Agent and Surveyor, Malton, (tithable parts only); waterbodies, woods, building names, mill; stream named; tithable buildings are carmine and tithe-free are grey.

42/402 Welbury (parish) NZ 400012
Apt 15.06.1841; 2351a (2569); Map 1841, 3 chns, corrected and partly surveyed by T. Dixon, Darlington; foot/b'way, waterbodies, woods, parkland, orchards, building names, ownerships (col).

42/403 Well (parish) SE 268838
Apt 19.09.1848; 147a (6451); Map 1849, 3 chns, in 2 parts, by Thomas Turnbull, Knaresbrough, (tithable parts only); foot/b'way, woods, field gates, landowners, limekilns.

42/404 Wensley (township in parish of Wensley) SE 085900
Apt 09.05.1840; 1987a (1986); Map 1839, 3 chns, by Edwd Other; waterbodies, woods, plantations; a note below the scale says that the map is made from two plans at 3 and 4 chn scale, and that yellow band shows Lord Bolton's land and green band other owners; it is unclear why both dot-dash and pecked lines between fields are used.

42/405 Westerdale (township in parish of Stokesley) NZ 650040
Apt 21.04.1838; 2569a (15930); Map 1838, 6 chns, in 2 parts, by Thos Holliday, York; foot/b'way, woods, field boundary ownerships, building names, ford, mill, ownerships (col); stream named.

42/406 Whashton (township in parish of Kirkby Ravensworth) NZ 145060
Apt 29.10.1840; 1195a (all); Map 1841, 6 chns, by T. Bradley and Sons, Richmond, Yorks; hill-drawing, waterbodies, woods, plantations, building names, ownerships (col).

42/407 Whenby (parish) SE 630693
Apt 31.01.1839; 989a (1010); Map 1839, 4 chns, by Thos Buxton, Malton; waterbodies, houses, woods (col), roadside waste (col), holding boundaries (col).

42/408 Whitwell (township in parish of Catterick) SE 289993
Apt 31.05.1841; 1079a (1084); Map 1842, 6 chns, by T. Bradley and Son, Richmond, Yorks; woods, orchards, building names, ownerships (col).

42/409 Wigginton (parish) SE 593583
Apt 19.04.1842; 1466a (?); Map 1842, 6 chns, by Francis Carr and Henry R. Spence, York, (tithable parts only in detail); foot/b'way, waterbodies, woods, plantations (col), building names. Apt omits land use for modus lands.

42/410 Wildon Grange (township in parish of Coxwold) SE 511775
Apt 26.02.1839; 691a (692); Map 1842, 4 chns, redrawn by Henry Scott; waterbodies, houses, field boundary ownerships, building names, holding boundaries (col).

42/411 Wilton (parish or chapelry) NZ 580200
Apt 28.12.1843; 454a (6928); Map 1844, 6 chns, by George Peirson, Guisbrough, (tithable parts only); landowners.

42/412 Winton (township in parish of Kirkby Sigston) SE 407965
Apt 29.04.1845; 1348a (all); Map 1845, 3 chns, by W. Alderson, West Lodge, Bedale; waterbodies, woods; part of title is typeset.

42/413 West Witton (township in parish of West Witton) SE 077822
Apt 21.10.1840; 3716a (3715); Map 1840, 8 chns, in 2 parts, made from a parish plan of the same scale by Edwd Other, (includes 4-chn enlargement of detail); waterbodies, woods, plantations, tithe-free land boundary.

42/414 High Worsall (chapelry in parish of Northallerton) NZ 383080
Apt 27.08.1845; 1509a (1511); Map 1847?, 6 chns; farm names. District is apportioned by holding and fields are not shown.

42/415 Low Worsall (township in parish of Kirk Leavington) NZ 399089
Apt 01.05.1844; 1312a (all); Map 1844, 4 chns, 'made from various Estate Plans of various Scales and degrees of Accuracy' by Matthew Bowser, Thornaby Grange; woods, road names, toll bar.

42/416 Wycliffe (parish) NZ 115135
Apt 02.12.1840; 2162a (all); Map 1841, 6 chns; waterbodies, woods, parkland, suspension bridge (pictorial), ownerships (col); streams across fields are shown discontinuously; one stream named.

42/417 Wykeham (parish) SE 953857
Apt 06.05.1848; 2030a (7535); Map 1849, 6 chns, in 5 parts partly surveyed by Robt Wise, Malton, (tithable parts only); hill-drawing, waterbodies, woods, spring, limekiln, chapel, 'how'; stream named; map date is surrounded by sunburst.

42/418 Yafforth (township in parish of Danby-Wiske) SE 327946
Apt 23.02.1843; 1116a (1300); Map 1843, 8 chns, by T. Bradley and Son, Richmond, Yorks, (tithable parts only in detail); woods, building names, ownerships (col).

42/419 Yarm (parish) NZ 420120
Apt 24.06.1837; 1056a (1135); Map 1838, 3 chns, by T. Simpson and Son; waterbodies, woods, road names, churchyard, tithe-free lands (blue); built-up part generalised; legend explains road colourings and boundary depiction.

42/420 Yearsley (township in parish of Coxwold) SE 585747
Apt 11.04.1839; 2765a (all); Map 1840, 6 chns, copied by H. Scott; waterbodies, woods (col), heath/moor, ownerships (col).

42/421 Youlton (township in parish of Alne) SE 498635
Apt 13.09.1842; 780a (780); Map 1843, 4 chns, by James Powell, Knaresbro'; foot/b'way, woods, ownerships (col).

Yorkshire, West Riding

PRO IR29 and IR30 43/1-446

642 tithe districts: 1,723,906 acres
446 tithe commutations: 930,198 acres
182 voluntary tithe agreements, 264 compulsory tithe awards

Tithe and tithe commutation

The West Riding of Yorkshire is both the largest historical county and the largest tithe county but in 1836 only 54 per cent of its area remained subject to payment of tithes (Fig. 55). Only fifty districts (11 per cent) were wholly tithable at this date and as in most counties with a large extent of upland, modus payments in lieu of tithes were the main cause of tithe exemption (in 298 tithe districts). Other important reasons for tithe exemption in the West Riding were commutation at the time of parliamentary enclosure, the merger of tithes in the land, and exemption by prescription. Assistant tithe commissioners and local tithe agents who worked in the West Riding of Yorkshire are listed in Table 43.1 and the valuers of tithe rent-charge in Table 43.2.

Tithe maps

The distribution and proportion of first-class tithe maps in the West Riding is unusual in that less than 6 per cent of tithable districts were mapped to first-class standards but these cover more than 12 per cent of the tithable acreage of the county. First-class maps are mainly of tithe districts in the north west, around Skipton and Settle, where there are some very large townships. Furthermore, in 1842-44 the Ordnance Survey had a Divisional Office at Skipton under an enthusiastic officer, Captain Durnford, which obtained commissions to produce seven first-class tithe maps. Only three West Riding second-class maps have construction lines, though on very few maps is copying explicitly acknowledged. There were two peaks of map production in the West Riding: a first in 1839-40 and a second in 1846-49 (Table 43.4). West Riding tithe maps are drawn at a variety of scales from one inch to one chain to one inch to sixteen chains and 38 per cent of the county is mapped at the recommended scales of one inch to three or four chains. The six-chain scale was the most popular and a significant area was mapped at the eight-chain scale.

As often in 'upland' counties with extensive exemption by modus payments, West Riding tithe maps are poor records of arable and grass which are distinguished on less than 2 per cent of the maps. They are better records of gardens (on 15 per cent), parks (on 21 per cent), orchards (on 7 per cent) and woodland (on 85 per cent). Comparatively few maps distinguish inhabited and uninhabited buildings (8 per cent) and as usual larger urban areas are either generalised or not mapped at all. The mapping of natural ground forms reflects to some extent the upland nature of much of the county and many West Riding tithe maps record weirs and river shoals. At Doncaster the race course is shown in detail, at Goldsborough roadside encroachments are clearly mapped, and at Paythorne a water fountain is shown pictorially. As in Lancashire, Ordnance Survey tithe maps omit all land use but include a wealth of minor details such as stepping stones and cattle troughs, features which were not always depicted on the published six-inch maps and are rarely recorded on private surveyors' tithe maps. Although the Ordnance Survey made little direct contribution to West Riding tithe mapping, its passage through the county is occasionally evident. On the High Hoyland tithe map there is a pencil note made in 1850 which records the settlement of a disputed boundary by the Ordnance Survey and the map of Ossett has a part labelled 'Now in Horbury township by arrangement with the Ordnance Survey.'

About two-thirds of West Riding tithe maps in the Public Record Office collection can be attributed to a particular map-maker. The most prolific was William Wordsworth of Black Gates, near Wakefield who produced twenty-eight rather ordinary looking maps. Richard Birks of Barnsley produced twenty-seven maps, unremarkable save that a few have typeset cartouches and titles. Thomas Robinson and John Humphries of Ripon together produced twenty-two maps, several of which highlight fields by colouring which is purely ornamental, rather than used to highlight land use or ownership. John Greenwood of Gisburn who produced fifteen maps was the brother of Christopher Greenwood the county map-maker and there are stylistic similarities between the two men's work. Greenwood employed two styles, a fundamentally uncoloured one for his second-class work, and a more elaborate one with coloured buildings for his first-class maps. Except that he did not distinguish arable and grassland, Greenwood's tithe maps are close to Dawson's ideal as set out in his 'Instructions' of 1836. Among the more individualistic maps in the county are the thirteen by Sam Swire of Skipton, nearly all of which use grey flecking to show cultivated land. It is possible that Christopher Paver was the maker of a large group of anonymous but related maps of tithe districts where he was employed as the valuer of tithe rent-charge.

On many West Riding tithe maps, particularly those by James Alexander and Makin Durham, the whole of the tithable part of a district is tinted, often in green. Although West Riding tithe maps are not decorative in a collective sense, there are a number of individual exceptions. At Yeadon tree symbols are coloured in a striking mixture of yellow, crimson, green, and blue. Several maps have cartouches, a few have leafy surrounds, and the map of Harewood has a cartouche composed of a fanciful flying creature.

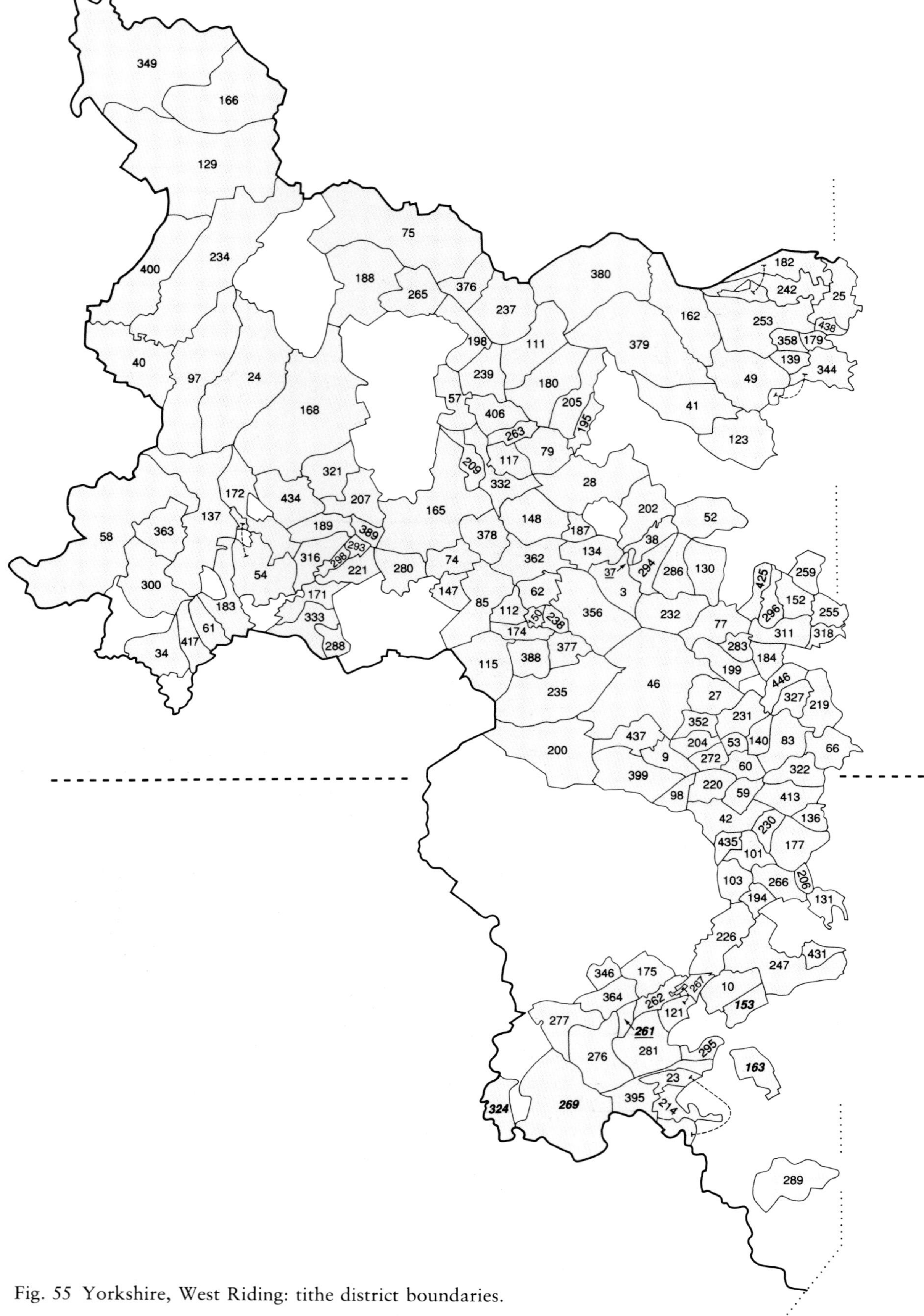

Fig. 55 Yorkshire, West Riding: tithe district boundaries.

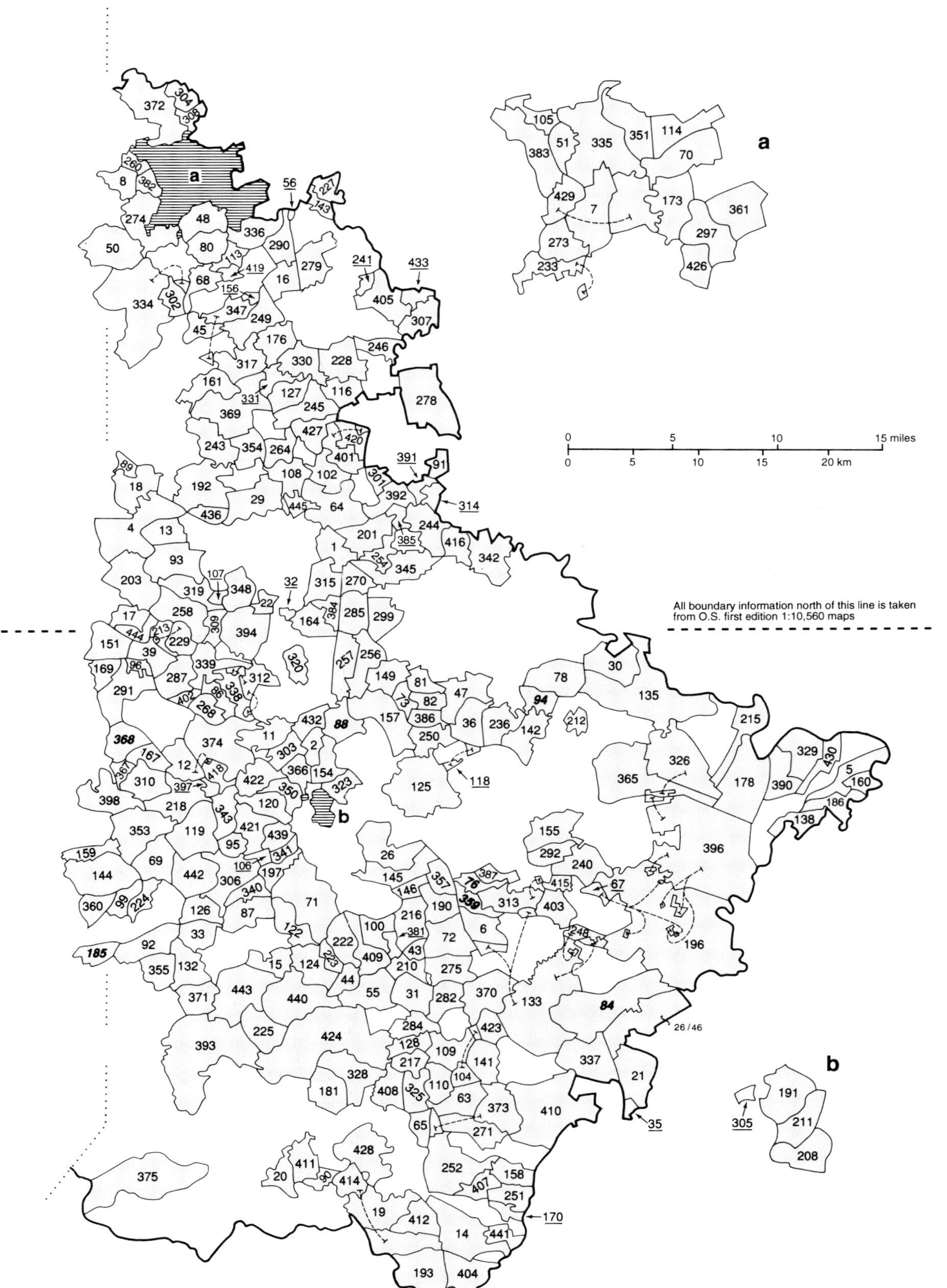

a
b
0 5 10 15 miles
0 5 10 15 20 km
All boundary information north of this line is taken from O.S. first edition 1:10,560 maps

Table 43.1. *Agreements and awards for commutation of tithes in Yorkshire, West Riding*

Assistant commissioner/ local tithe agent	*Number of agreements**	*Number of awards*
Charles Howard	71	98
Richard Burton Phillipson	53	0
Joseph Townsend	0	23
John Pickering	18	0
Thomas Hoskins	16	0
Henry Pilkington	16	0
John Job Rawlinson	7	131
George Wingrove Cooke	0	7
Thomas Martin	6	0
Robert Hart	5	0
Horace William Meteyard	5	0
John Mee Mathew	0	4
John Penny	2	0
Thomas Sudworth	2	0
Thomas Smith Woolley	0	1

*Computed from the number of extant reports on tithe agreements in the tithe files [PRO IR 18].

Table 43.2. *Tithe valuers and tithe map-makers in Yorkshire, West Riding*

Name and address (in Yorkshire unless indicated)	*Number of districts*	*Acreage*
Tithe valuers		
Christopher Paver, Peckfield, Sherburn	39	68,367
William Wordsworth, Black Gates	29	43,907
Richard Birks, Barnsley	19	37,257
Daniel Seaton	19	24,678
Thomas and William Parker, Eastby, Skipton	18	37,354
Ralph Lodge, Bishopdale	16	85,510
William Simpson, Loversall	16	41,025
Thomas Bradley, Richmond	11	48,818
Tithe Commissioners	11	20,879
Thomas Robinson the younger, Ripon	11	15,657
John Humphries	10	11,836
Felix Leach, Brungerley	9	34,076
William Bingley, Ellerslie Lodge, Penistone	8	18,847
Makin Durham, Thorne	8	16,309
Others [100]	222	425,678
Attributed tithe map-makers		
William Wordsworth, Black Gates	28	42,298
Richard Birks, Barnsley	26	50,055
Thomas Robinson, Ripon	16	54,026
John Greenwood, Gisburn	15	54,761
James Alexander, Doncaster	14	31,907
Sam. Swire, Skipton	13	40,826
James Powell, Knaresborough	13	22,214

Table 43.2. *(cont.)*

Name and address (in Yorkshire unless indicated)	*Number of districts*	*Acreage*
Makin Durham, Thorne	9	24,116
John Howgate, Knaresborough	8	9,087
Ordnance Survey	7	15,306
Henry Teal and Sons, Leeds	7	9,510
John Richardson, Dalston, Carlisle, Cumberland	6	9,918
Thomas Ingle, Bradford	6	8,665
John Humphries, Ripon	6	4,664
John Watson junior, Kendal, Westmorland	5	39,683
Thomas Bradley and Sons, Richmond	5	11,768
Joseph Hall, Huddersfield	5	10,714
Richard Petty, Crosshills	5	6,831
Robert Horsman, Wetherby	5	5,038
Others [61]	104	286,994

Table 43.3. *The tithe maps of Yorkshire, West Riding: scales and classes*

Scale in chains/inch	*All maps*		*First Class*		*Second Class*	
	Number	*Acreage*	*Number*	*Acreage*	*Number*	*Acreage*
>3	5	3,417	0	0	5	3,417
3	123	226,137	24	87,496	99	138,641
4	56	123,051	2	27,512	54	95,539
4.5, 5, 5.5	11	11,212	0	0	11	11,212
6	183	340,142	0	0	183	340,142
7, 7.5	4	3,693	0	0	4	3,693
8	38	146,033	0	0	38	146,033
9	15	44,648	0	0	15	44,648
10, 11	2	7,252	0	0	2	7,252
12	8	23,224	0	0	8	23,224
16	1	1,389	0	0	1	1,389
TOTAL	446	930,198	26	115,008	420	815,190

Table 43.4. *The tithe maps of Yorkshire, West Riding: dates*

	1837	*1838*	*1839*	*1840*	*1841*	*1842*	*1843*	*1844*	*1845*	*1846*	*1847*	*1848*	*1849*	*1850*	*>1850*
All maps	3	32	35	47	24	27	38	19	26	47	46	38	28	15	19
1st class	0	7	4	5	0	0	5	3	1	0	0	0	0	1	0
2nd class*	3	25	31	42	24	27	33	16	25	47	46	38	28	14	19

*Two second-class tithe maps of the West Riding of Yorkshire in the Public Record Office collection are undated.

Yorkshire, West Riding

43/1 Aberford (township in parish of Aberford) SE 430383
Apt 02.10.1847; 1537a (1536); Map 1848?, 6 chns; waterbodies, woods, parkland, quarry.

43/2 Ackton (township in parish of Featherstone) SE 410230
Apt 31.12.1841; 935a (934); Map 1843, 6 chns; woods.

43/3 Addingham (township in parish of Addingham) SE 074494
Apt 27.09.1843; 2358a (4293); Map 1843, 3 chns, 1st cl, in 3 parts, by Ordnance Survey, (drawn by Robert Nixon, C.A.); construction lines, trig points, waterbodies, houses, gardens, rock outcrops, fences, building names, pump, trough, well, sandstone quarries, springs, stone, toll bar, ruins, milestones, guide post, Roman road, Roman and other remains, mill pond, cotton factory, worsted factory, tan yard, gasometer (by symbol), schools, various chapels, post office, smithy, Quaker Meeting Ho., footbridge, waterfall, graveyard, tomb; bridges named; some physical features named.

43/4 Addle-cum-Eccup (township in parish of Addle) SE 268403 [Adel]
Apt 28.11.1844; 3020a (4576); Map 'made' April 1848, 8 chns, by James Powell, Knaresborough, (tithable parts only in detail); foot/b'way, waterbodies, woods, reservoirs, churchyard; colours may show property ownerships.

43/5 Adlingfleet (township in parish of Adlingfleet) SE 825205
Apt 23.10.1844; 253a (1680); Map 1846?, 6 chns, in 3 parts, ? by Makin Durham, (includes 24-chn index); tithable lands are tinted.

43/6 Adwick-le-Street (township in parish of Adwick-le-Street) SE 541083 [Adwick le Street]
Apt 16.05.1844; 1624a (all); Map 1844, 6 chns, by J. Alexander, Doncaster, (tinted); foot/b'way, waterbodies, woods, plantations, osiers (by symbol), parkland, orchards, building names, mill, Great North Road, pit (col), glebe (pink).

43/7 Aismunderby with Bondgate (township in parish of Ripon) SE 312686 [Not listed]
Apt 19.11.1839; 1056a (1055); Map 1837, 6 chns, by Thomas Robinson, Junior, Ripon; foot/b'way, canal, waterbodies, houses, woods, parkland, building names, wharf, quarry (col), well.

43/8 Aldfield (township in parish of Ripon) SE 263693
Apt 08.12.1840; 1226a (1225); Map 1838, 3 chns, by William Morton, Hope, Cottage, Leeming Lane; foot/b'way, waterbodies, houses, woods, building names, field acreages.

43/9 Allerton (township in parish of Bradford) SE 113342
Apt 28.02.1849; 1849a (1970); Map 1850, 6 chns, by Josh. Smith, Albion Court, Bradford; hill-drawing, foot/b'way, turnpike roads, waterbodies, woods, gardens, building names, chapels, pit, reservoir, mill, school; hill named; buildings are named in three styles, according to importance.

43/10 Almondbury (township in parish of Almondbury) SE 156138
Apt 18.11.1847; 2512a (2585); Map 1850, 2 chns, by William Ellison, Leeds; hill-drawing, railway, foot/b'way, waterbodies, woods, plantations, building names, mills, stiles, weirs; north pointer has spiky leaves, and star-flower boss.

43/11 Altofts (township in parish of Normanton) SE 380240
Apt 03.04.1839; 1762a (1761); Map 1839, 6 chns, by Henry Teal and Son, Leeds; railways with earthworks, foot/b'way, occupation roads, canal, canal and river towpaths and locks, waterbodies, woods, parkland, building names.

43/12 Alverthorpe (township in parish of Wakefield) SE 311216
Apt 17.06.1845; 1636a (1636); Map 1845, 6 chns, by W. Wordsworth, Black Gates, (tithable parts only in detail); waterbodies, woods, parkland.

43/13 Alwoodley (township in parish of Harewood) SE 298407
Apt 06.06.1845; 33a (1511); Map 1845, 6 chns, by T. Kell, Bramham, (tithable parts only in detail, tinted); streams named. Apt omits land use and field names.

43/14 North and South Anston (townships in parish of Anston) SK 529836
Apt 31.01.1850; 1667a (4490); Map 1850, 6 chns; railway, foot/b'way, canal, waterbodies, woods, building names; colours may show property ownerships.

43/15 Ardsley (township in parish of Darfield) SE 382057
Apt 25.09.1838; 1213a (1212); Map 1839, 6 chns; foot/b'way, turnpike roads, woods (col), mill, poorhouse, pond. Apt omits some land use.

43/16 Arkendale (parish) SE 392613
Apt 09.01.1840; 3325a (?); Map 1841, 6 chns, by Walton Alderson, Leyburn, (tithable parts only); hill-drawing, foot/b'way, houses, woods (col), stiles, sheepfolds, smelt mill.

43/17 Armley (township in parish of Leeds) SE 269337
Apt 21.02.1845; 898a (907); Map 1846, 3 chns; railways, turnpike roads, canal with towpath, waterbodies, woods, building names, road names.

43/18 Arthington (township in parish of Addle) SE 275445
Apt 23.02.1849; 2220a (1780); Map 1849, 3 chns, by T. Newsam, Leeds; hill-drawing, railway with tunnel, viaduct and earthworks, foot/b'way, waterbodies, woods, plantations, osiers (by symbol), parkland, orchards, heath/moor, building names, quarries, stiles, toll bar, mills, weir; colours may show property ownerships.

43/19 Aston cum Aughton (parish) SK 461857
Apt 18.09.1838; 2915a (2915); Map 1838, 9 chns, by Richd. Birks; railway, foot/b'way, waterbodies, woods (col), toll bar.

43/20 Attercliffe with Darnall (townships in parish of Sheffield) SK 383884
Apt 17.05.1850; 1219a (1270); Map 1852, 6 chns; railways, canal, woods, canal with towpath.

43/21 Austerfield (township) SK 660963
Apt 15.08.1839; 2776a (2776); Map 1840, 3 chns, 1st cl, by R. Weightman; construction lines, foot/b'way, woods (by name), field boundary ownerships, quarries.

43/22 Austhorpe (district or township in parish of Whitkirk) SE 375343
Apt 31.07.1839; 609a (660); Map 1839, 3 chns, by Henry Teal and Son; railway, foot/b'way, waterbodies, woods, parkland, orchards, gardens, building names, windmill, old chemical works, glasshouse, ownerships (col).

43/23 Austonley (township in parish of Almondbury) SE 110075
Apt 18.11.1847; 1174a (1760); Map 1851, 4 chns, by Thomas Young, Humshaugh, Hexham; foot/b'way, waterbodies, houses, woods, orchards, building names, mills, reservoir.

43/24 Austwick and Lawkland (townships) SD 775675
Apt 31.10.1851; 9941a (9620); Map 1847, 3 chns, by John Watson, Junr, Kendal; hill-drawing, railway, foot/b'way, woods, plantations, gardens, building names, boundary stones and rocks, mill, school, slate quarry, sheepfold; physical features named; colour bands may be hamlet boundaries; scale bar is on a drape, surmounted by a banner'.

43/25 Azerley (township in parishes of Kirkby Malzeard and Ripon) SE 260740
Apt 21.11.1838; 3862a (3919); Map 1839, 8 chns, by T. Bradley and Son, Richmond; waterbodies, woods, building names; colours may show holdings.

43/26 Badsworth (parish) SE 462142
Apt 30.07.1839; 2620a (3815); Map 1840, 4 chns, in 2 parts; foot/b'way, turnpike roads, waterbodies, woods, parkland, road names, field names, boundary stone.

43/27 Baildon (township in parish of Otley) SE 149399
Apt 05.06.1845; 1723a (all); Map 1846?, 6 chns; foot/b'way, waterbodies, woods, building names, churchyard, mills, green, moor, waste.

43/28 Barden (township in parish of Skipton) SE 053582 [Not listed]
Apt 24.09.1846; 110a (6115); Map 1847, 4 chns, (tithable parts only, tinted); woods, plantations, parkland, field gates, building names, waterfall; 'gill' named.

43/29 Bardsey cum Rigton (township in parish of Bardsey) SE 368434
Apt 28.10.1843; 2746a (2745); Map 1845?, 9 chns, ? by John Howgate; foot/b'way, waterbodies, woods, plantations, building names, mill.

43/30 Barlow (township in parish of Brayton) SE 645288
Apt 05.02.1847; 2279a (2278); Map 1847?, 6 chns; foot/b'way, woods (named), windmill (by symbol), ownerships (col).

43/31 Barnbrough (parish) SE 485031 [Barnburgh]
Apt 30.07.1839; 1900a (1947); Map 1839, 6 chns, in 2 parts, by J. Alexander, Doncaster; hill-drawing, waterbodies, woods (named), orchards, gardens, building names, former open field names, spring, mills, pits; colours may show property ownerships.

43/32 Barrowby (hamlet in parish of Garforth) SE 392335 [Not listed]
Apt 01.12.1841; 231a (all); Map 1842?, 3 chns.

43/33 Barugh (township in parish of Darton) SE 321080
Apt 31.05.1845; 194a (1419); Map 1845, 6 chns, by Richard Birks, (tithable parts only, tinted); foot/b'way, waterbodies, woods, building names, canal with towpath, toll bar.

43/34 Bashall Eaves (township in parish of Mitton) SD 700440
Apt 12.05.1848; 1330a (3640); Map 1845, 6 chns, by P.R. Allanson, York, (tithable parts only); foot/b'way, waterbodies, woods (col), landowners.

43/35 Bawtry (township) SK 655937
Apt 15.08.1839; 244a (all); Map 1840, 3 chns, 1st cl, by Robert Weightman, Torworth; construction lines, waterbodies, field boundary ownerships, gravel pit. Apt omits some field names.

43/36 Beal or Beaghall and Hellingley (townships in parish of Hellington) SE 538247
Apt 15.02.1840; 1758a (1757); Map 1842?, 6 chns, 'Copied' by R. Smith, York; waterbodies, woods, canal with towpath and lock, weir, osiers, tithe-free land, (yellow).

43/37 Beamsley (township in parish of Addingham) SE 082515
Apt 02.02.1843; 308a (all); Map 1843, 4 chns; waterbodies, woods, building names; streams named.

43/38 Beamsley (township in parish of Skipton) SE 100530 [Not listed]
Apt 24.09.1846; 780a (1206); Map 1847, 4 chns, by Richd. Gouthwaite, Lumby; turnpike roads, waterbodies, woods, building names, hospital, chapel, tithe-free land (pink); streams named.

43/39 Beeston (township in parish of Leeds) SE 288308
Apt 23.02.1847; 1487a (1535); Map 1847, 6 chns, by W. Wordsworth, Blackgates; railways, waterbodies, woods.

43/40 Bentham (township in parish of Bentham) SD 685685 [High and Low Bentham]
Apt 30.07.1839; 6241a (7642); Map 1839, 3 chns, 1st cl, in 2 parts: part 1 by M. and J. Turner, Lyth, and part 2 by J. Watson, Kendal, (tithable parts only); foot/b'way, waterbodies, woods, plantations, parkland, orchards, building names, barns, rectory, toll bar, Queen of Fairy's Chair, old quarry, mill; north pointer on part 1 has plumes.

43/41 Bewerley (township in parish of Ripon) SE 130650
Apt 07.11.1838; 5872a (5872); Map 1840, 6 chns, by T. Robinson, Ripon; waterbodies, woods, building names, smelt mill, crag, conspicious stone, moor with acreages; gills named.

43/42 North Bierley (township in parish of Bradford) SE 160290 [Bierley]
Apt 10.01.1849; 3407a (3090); Map 1850, 3 chns, by John Richardson, Carlisle; hill-drawing, railway, foot/b'way, turnpike roads, waterbodies, woods, residual open fields, building names, road names, iron works, pits.

43/43 Bilham (township in parishes of Hooton Pagnell and Barmborough) SE 488065 [Not listed]
Apt 18.08.1849; 541a (518); Map 1850, 4.5 chns, by Messrs Roberts and Wood, Land Agents, 68 Chancery Lane; foot/b'way, waterbodies, woods (named), field gates, building names, occupation road, sand pit, well, parish boundary.

43/44 Billingley (township in parish of Darfield) SE 437042
Apt 30.07.1839; 861a (861); Map 1840, 3 chns; railway, foot/b'way, residual open fields; title has circular surround with oak leaves and acorns.

43/45 Bilton Park (district in parish of Knaresborough) SE 328572 [Not listed]
Apt 29.06.1839; 799a (?); Map 1840, [6 chns]; turnpike roads, houses, road names.

43/46 Bingley (parish) SE 095405
Apt 16.01.1845; 10340a (13892); Map 1845, 6 chns, in 4 parts, (includes enlargement of Bingley town at 3 chns); railway, canal with towpath and locks, woods, building names, boundary marks, knoll; moors and hills named.

43/47 Birkin (township in parish of Birkin) SE 528274
Apt 30.01.1845; 2065a (all); Map 1845, 8 chns; woods.

43/48 Bishop Monkton (township in parish of Ripon) SE 325663
Apt 19.11.1839; 2090a (2089); Map 1837, 6 chns, by Thomas Robinson, Ripon; foot/b'way, waterbodies, woods, ownership boundary; stream named.

43/49 High and Low Bishopside (townships in parish of Ripon) SE 180668
Apt 20.07.1838; 1814a (5813); Map 1838, 6 chns, by John Crookes and Son, Leeds, (tithable parts only); foot/b'way, waterbodies, building names, kiln, smelt house, toll bars, pinfold, mills; buildings are shown in outline only, without infill; gill named.

43/50 Bishop Thornton (township in parish of Ripon) SE 255635
Apt 19.11.1839; 3028a (3027); Map 1838, 6 chns, by Thomas Robinson, Ripon; foot/b'way, waterbodies, woods, building names, mill, Catholic chapel.

43/51 Bishopton (township in parish of Ripon) SE 299711
Apt 25.09.1838; 376a (375); Map 1837, 6 chns, by Thomas Robinson, Ripon; foot/b'way, waterbodies, houses, woods, parkland, mill race, weirs, coach road; stream named.

43/52 Blubberhouses (township in parish of Fewston) SE 150550
Apt 23.01.1845; 52a (3524); Map 1846?, 8 chns, ? by John Howgate, (tithable parts only); landowners.

43/53 Bolton (township in parish of Calverley) SE 168357
Apt 09.12.1846; 705a (736); Map 1847, 3 chns, by W. Wordsworth, Blackgates; canal with towpath and locks, foot/b'way, waterbodies, woods, road embankment.

43/54 Bolton by Bolland (parish) SD 770510 [Bolton-by-Bowland]
Apt 10.01.1840; 5788a (5792); Map 1841?, 10 chns, in 4 parts, by John Greenwood, Gisburn, (includes three 3-chn enlargements of detail); foot/b'way, waterbodies, woods, parkland (col), gardens (col), hedge ownership, field boundary ownerships, holdings (col), building names, lime kiln, mill, chapel, school, cross, glebe, roadside waste (col).

43/55 Bolton upon Dearne with Goldthorpe (parish) SE 453031
Apt 11.07.1837; 2213a (2213); Map 1838?, 6 chns, ? by Richard Birks; foot/b'way, mills, tithe-free land.

43/56 Boroughbridge (township in parish of Aldborough) SE 396667
Apt 12.03.1846; 64a (85); Map 1846, 1 chn; waterbodies, Great North Road.

43/57 Bordley (township or hamlet in parish of Burnsall) SD 938654
Apt 30.09.1844; 2797a (?); Map surveyed in 1841, 3 chns, by John Greenwood, Gisburn; hill-drawing, houses, woods, rock outcrops, stone walls, holding boundary ownerships (col), field gates, hedges, hedgerow trees, building names, well, barn; legend explains symbols.

43/58 Forest of Bowland, Higher Division (township in parish of Slaidburn) SD 650530
Apt 26.09.1843; 18988a (?); Map 1841, 8 chns, by J.R. Alton; foot/b'way,

waterbodies, woods, building names, wells, springs, boundary stones; physical features named.

43/59 Bowling (township in parish of Bradford) SE 141310
Apt 10.01.1849; 1546a (1545); Map 1849, 6 chns, by Thomas Dixon, Bradford, (tinted); hill-drawing, railways, foot/b'way, turnpike roads, toll bar, waterbodies, woods (named), parkland, gardens, building names, road names, iron works, mills, winding engine, pit, mill dam, old mill, reservoirs, schools, chapel, parsonage; churches are named in gothic, as is one school, and chapels in ordinary lettering.

43/60 Bradford (township in parish of Bradford) SE 175335
Apt 22.12.1848; 1584a (1680); Map 1850, 3 chns, ? by John Richardson, Dalston, Cumberland, (tithable parts only in detail); railways and stations, foot/b'way, waterbodies, woods, parkland, gardens, building names, road names, cavalry and infantry barracks, quarries, reservoir, infirmary, toll bar, glazed areas (grey bands), coal pits, back-to-back housing.

43/61 West Bradford (township in parish of Mitton) SD 738462
Apt 18.06.1847; 1932a (1700); Map 1847, 6 chns, 'Constructed from existing plans' by P.R. Allanson, York, (includes enlargement of village at 3 chns); foot/b'way, waterbodies, woods (col), ford.

43/62 Bradleys Both (township in parish of Kildwick) SE 011488 [High and Low Bradley]
Apt 14.04.1841; 1894a (1894); Map 1842, 4 chns, by Sam Swire, Skipton; foot/b'way, turnpike roads, occupation road, canal with towpath, waterbodies, woods, parkland, orchards, field boundary ownerships, field gates, building names, corn mill, quarries, public stone quarry, stiles; grey flecking in fields shows cultivated land; hill named.

43/63 Braithwell (township in parish of Braithwell) SK 531947
Apt 29.01.1840; 1920a (1920); Map 1839, 3 chns, by John Snipe; foot/b'way, waterbodies, houses, woods (col), open fields (named); it is unclear why some fields are tinted pink.

43/64 Bramham (township in parish of Bramham) SE 430422
Apt 16.06.1842; 3972a (all); Map 1843, 6 chns, by William Tuke, (tinted; includes enlargement of village); waterbodies, woods (col), churchyard.

43/65 Bramley (township in parish of Braithwell) SK 495925
Apt 25.03.1840; 984a (all); Map 1842, 3 chns, by John Snipe; foot/b'way, waterbodies, houses, woods (col); it is unclear why some fields are tinted pink.

43/66 Bramley (township in parish of Leeds) SE 243349
Apt 05.05.1845; 2332a (2331); Map 1846, 6 chns; foot/b'way, railway, canal with towpath and lock, waterbodies, woods.

43/67 Sand or South Bramwith (township in parishes of Hatfield and Barnby Dun) SE 629110
Apt 06.02.1842; 479a (all); Map 1843?, 6 chns, in 5 parts, (tinted; includes 27-chn index); foot/b'way, woods, field boundary ownerships.

43/68 Brearton (township in parish of Knaresborough) SE 323612
Apt 29.06.1839; 1394a (1393); Map 1838, 7.5 chns, by James Powell, Knaresborough, (tinted); foot/b'way, waterbodies, woods, residual open fields (named); streams named.

43/69 Bretton West (township or manor in parish of Great Sandal) SE 285135 [West Bretton]
Apt 31.03.1845; 8a (876); Map 1849?, 3 chns, (tithable parts only); foot/b'way, woods (named), field gates.

43/70 Bridge Howick (township in parish of Ripon) SE 347707 [Bridge Hewick]
Apt 27.09.1844; 867a (all); Map 1845, 8 chns, (tinted); foot/b'way, woods, glebe (green).

43/71 Brierley, South Hiendley and Shafton (district in parish of Felkirk) SE 410106
Apt 18.01.1840; 4541a (4540); Map 1840, 8 chns, in 5 parts, ? by Richd Birks, (includes 16-chn index and a small enlargement of detail); foot/b'way, waterbodies, woods (col, named), heath/moor (col), building names, road names, toll bar, quarry; map titles are printed; a 'park' appears only on the index.

43/72 Brodsworth (parish) SE 513074
Apt 06.02.1846; 638a (3170); Map 1847, 12 chns, ? by James Alexander, Doncaster, Yorks, (tinted); foot/b'way, waterbodies, woods (col), parkland, gardens, 'Roman Ridge', pit.

43/73 Brotherton (township in parish of Brotherton) SE 481264
Apt 17.04.1845; 477a (798); Map 1846, 3 chns; railway, foot/b'way, plantations, open fields.

43/74 Broughton (township in parish of Broughton) SD 938518
Apt 02.07.1847; 211a (2109); Map 1847, 3 chns, by Robert Bradley, (tithable parts only); foot/b'way, waterbodies, houses, woods, wells.

43/75 Buckden (township in parish of Arncliffe) SD 895795
Apt 26.03.1841; 13225a (13224); Map 1844?, 4 chns, in 2 parts, ? by Sam Swire, Skipton; hill-drawing, foot/b'way, waterbodies, woods (named), plantations, parkland, orchards, field boundary ownerships, building names, 'Allotments' (col, named), stinted pastures (col, named), deer park, occupation road, turbary, old wall, boundary stones and marks; cultivated land is shown by grey flecking; red lines may be walls; acreages are given for unnumbered areas.

43/76 Burghwallis (township in parish of Burghwallis) SE 536117
Apt 12.11.1849; 35a (?); Map 1851, 9 chns, (tithable parts only); wood (col, with acreage), landowner.

43/77 Burley (township in parish of Otley) SE 157488 [Burley in Wharfedale]
Apt 26.02.1845; 1632a (4037); Map 1847, 5 chns, (tithable parts only); waterbodies, woods, tithe-free lands (pink), modus lands (yellow).

43/78 Burn (township in parish of Brayton) SE 602282
Apt 29.04.1847; 2372a (all); Map 1847?, 4 chns; railway, canal, woods.

43/79 Burnsal with Thorpe Sub Montem (townships in parish of Burnsal) SE 018605 [Burnsall]
Apt 28.12.1848; 1841a (2968); Map 1849, 3 chns, in 3 parts: part 1 by James Scally; parts 2 and 3 by D. McCay; waterbodies, woods (col), plantations (named), mill pond.

43/80 Burton Leonard (parish) SE 333640
Apt 29.08.1845; 1739a (1739); Map 1846, 9 chns; foot/b'way, waterbodies, woods, gardens.

43/81 Burton Salmon (township in parish of Monk Fryston) SE 496277
Apt 31.01.1843; 913a (913); Map 1843, 6 chns; railway, woods.

43/82 Byram cum Poole (township in parish of Brotherton) SE 501262 [Byram-cum-Sutton]
Apt 04.04.1845; 795a (795); Map 1847, 6 chns; waterbodies, woods, hall.

43/83 Calverley with Farsley (township in parish of Calverley) SE 210360
Apt 18.09.1845; 2987a (3500); Map 1846, 6 chns, by W. Wordsworth, Black Gates; railway, canal with towpath, waterbodies, woods, weir, glebe.

43/84 Cantley (parish) SE 635020
Apt 04.05.1847; 20a (5160); Map 1849, 6 chns, by C.A. Parker, Sheffield, (tithable parts only, tinted); railway, woods, building names, road names, Great North Road.

43/85 Carlton (parish) SD 970480 [Carleton]
Apt 05.03.1840; 5117a (5117); Map 1841, 6 chns, in 3 parts, by Sam Swire, Skipton, (includes two 2-chn enlargements of detail); waterbodies, woods, plantations, heath/moor (col, named), building names, footbridge (by Dawson's symbol), boundary marks, limekilns; grey flecking shows cultivated land. Apt omits land use.

43/86 Carlton (hamlet in parish of Rothwell) SE 339271
Apt 26.09.1839; 828a (?); Map 1840, 3 chns, by Richd. Gouthwaite,

Leeds; waggonway, waterbodies, woods, arable (col), grassland (col); scale bar has elaborate diagonal patterning; north pointer has two angels, each blowing a trumpet.

43/87 Carlton (township in parish of Roystone) SE 359097
Apt 31.10.1844; 1117a (1953); Map 1845, 6 chns, by Richd Birks, Barnsley, (tithable parts only in detail); hill-drawing, railway with earthworks, canal with towpath and earthworks, foot/b'way, turnpike roads, waterbodies, woods (named), building names; tithe-free areas tinted.

43/88 Castleford (parish) SE 432248
Apt 04.02.1846; 35a (2040); Map 1846?, 3 chns, (tithable parts only).

43/89 Castley (township in parish of Leathley) SE 264463
Apt 29.01.1844; 528a (527); Map 1848?, 6 chns, by J. Howgate, Knaresborough; railway with earthworks, foot/b'way, woods, ford, mill dam.

43/90 Catcliffe (township in parish of Rotherham) SK 418882
Apt 02.08.1847; 153a (648); Map 1849, 5 chns, by Arthur Dyson, Tinsley, (tithable parts only); woods, road names, landowners.

43/91 Catterton (township in parish of Tadcaster) SE 510455
Apt 31.05.1844; 713a (712); Map 1845?, 4 chns; foot/b'way, waterbodies, woods, orchards, road names, gravel pit, moated site; a table of field names and acreages has been pasted over.

43/92 Cawthorne (parish) SE 283071
Apt 08.02.1848; 191a (3440); Map 1851, 7 chns, in 6 parts, by Richard Birks, (tithable parts only; also includes 24-chn skeleton plan of whole district); waterbodies, woods, building names.

43/93 Chapel Allerton (township in parish of Leeds) SE 303380
Apt 29.10.1844; 2718a (2747); Map 1845?, 3 chns; waterbodies, woods (named), parkland, building names, road names, Methodist chapel.

43/94 Chapel Haddlesey (township in parish of Birkin) SE 588263
Apt 04.05.1838; 191a (1000); Map not dated, 3 chns, (tithable parts only); foot/b'way, canal with towpath, waterbodies, houses (by shading), field gates, road names, landowners, windmill (pictorial); the owner of the township is named in the title.

43/95 Chevet (township in parish of Roystone) SE 248151
Apt 22.07.1844; 826a (all); Map 1847, 12 chns, (tinted); railway with tunnel, foot/b'way, waterbodies, woods, parkland, gardens, building names, lodge, boat house, mill dam.

43/96 Churwell (township in parish of Batley) SE 273296
Apt 22.02.1843; 486a (488); Map surveyed in 1843, 3 chns, by Richd Carter, Halifax, (includes two small enlargements of detail); foot/b'way, waterbodies, woods (named), gardens, coal pits, road earthworks, toll gate, weir, reservoir, pump.

43/97 Clapham with Newby (townships in parish of Clapham) SD 730680
Apt 31.10.1851; 5477a (14720); Map 1847, 3 chns, by John Watson, Jun., Kendal; hill-drawing, railway with station, foot/b'way, waterbodies, woods, plantations, parkland (in detail), gardens, field gates, building names, boundary stones, wells, sheepfolds, pot hole, springs, grotto, boat house, sundial, vicarage, school, sand pit, toll bar, pinfold, old mill, manorial boundary; physical features comprehensively named; the mapping extends into adjacent districts; scale is framed by columns and arch.

43/98 Clayton (township in parish of Bradford) SE 118318
Apt 10.01.1849; 1723a (1610); Map 1849, 6 chns, by Thomas Dixon, Bradford, (tinted); foot/b'way, waterbodies, woods, building names, chapel, school, mills, engine pit, coal pits, old quarry, mill dams; various styles of writing are used for names, according to importance.

43/99 Clayton West (township in parish of High Hoyland) SE 259105
Apt 14.07.1841; 1098a (1098); Map 1842, 6 chns, ? by Richard Birks; foot/b'way, turnpike roads, waterbodies, woods (col, named), building names, quarries, mills, chapels.

43/100 Clayton with Frickley (parish) SE 456083
Apt 05.02.1846; 70a (1640); Map 1847, 6 chns, (tithable parts only, tinted); waterbodies, woods, parkland.

43/101 Cleckheaton (township in parish of Birstal) SE 177258
Apt 29.02.1848; 1685a (1726); Map 1849, 6 chns, by William Ellison, Leeds; railway with station, foot/b'way, waterbodies, woods, building names, toll bar, chapels (by shading).

43/102 Clifford (township in parish of Bramham) SE 426451
Apt 30.06.1842; 1492a (all); Map 1842, 6 chns, ? by Wm Skipton, (includes two 3-chn enlargements of detail); waterbodies, houses, woods, parkland, riverside cliffs.

43/103 Clifton (township in parish of Dewsbury) SE 162241
Apt 17.12.1842; 128a (?); Map 1844, 3 chns, in 2 parts, by J. Marriott, (tithable parts only); railway, foot/b'way, canal, woods, building names, road names, mill, malt kiln, obelisk (pictorial), boundary stones, stiles, holding boundaries (col); tithable buildings are carmine, and other buildings are hatched.

43/104 Clifton Crookhill and Butterbush (district in parish of Conisbrough) SK 522965
Apt 15.08.1839; 840a (all); Map 1840, 6 chns, in 2 parts, by J. Alexander, Doncaster, (tithable parts only); hill-drawing, foot/b'way, waterbodies, woods, parkland, gardens, heath/moor (col), residual open fields (named), building names, landowners, Clifton Beacon and trig station, quarry.

43/105 Clotherholme (township in parish of Ripon) SE 286722 [Not listed]
Apt 25.09.1838; 329a (328); Map 1839, 9 chns, by John Humphries, Ripon, Yorks, (tinted); foot/b'way, woods; above the scale is 'This plan is not required to be tested. John Humphries.'

43/106 Cold-hiendley (township in parish of Felkirk) SE 371141 [Cold Hiendley]
Apt 18.06.1840; 377a (?); Map 1842, 6 chns; railway, foot/b'way, canal with towpath, field names; bridge named; colour bands appear to be ornamental.

43/107 Coldcotes (district or hamlet in parish of Leeds) SE 335352 [Not listed]
Apt 21.02.1845; 221a (?); Map 1845, 3 chns; woods, road names.

43/108 Collingham (parish) SE 395448
Apt 26.06.1848; 2344a (2553); Map 1849, 6 chns, by R. Carr, York; hill-drawing, foot/b'way, waterbodies, woods, parkland, pit.

43/109 Conisbrough (district in parish of Conisbrough) SK 514984
Apt 18.12.1839; 2329a (?); Map 1840, 6 chns, in 3 parts, by J. Alexander; foot/b'way, waterbodies, woods, parkland, gardens, heath/moor (col), open fields (named), building names, landowners, lime works and quarries, castle, limekilns (by symbol), toll bar; enclosed fields are tinted pale green.

43/110 Conisbrough Parks (district in parish of Conisbrough) SK 507961
Apt 14.04.1847; 1331a (?); Map 1848, 6 chns, by J. Alexander, Doncaster, (tinted); foot/b'way, woods, parkland, orchards, field boundary ownership, building names, pit.

43/111 Coniston (hamlet in parish of Burnsal) SE 005695 [Conistone]
Apt 28.12.1848; 5331a (5331); Map 1849, 8 chns, in 3 parts, by John Greenwood, Gisburn, (includes enlargement of village at 3 chns); foot/b'way, waterbodies, building names, sheepfolds, boundary marks, school, wells, barns, old limekiln, stepping stones, watering place, waterfall; buildings have outer shading, but no infill.

43/112 Cononley (township in parish of Kildwick) SD 988472
Apt 27.05.1840; 1432a (1431); Map 1842, 4 chns, by Sam Swire, Skipton; waterbodies, woods, plantations, orchards, gardens, building names; grey flecked lines show cultivated land; hills named; pecked field boundaries are within ownerships, dot-dash field boundaries are between ownerships.

43/113 Copgrove (parish) SE 350632
Apt 02.04.1840; 832a (all); Map 1840, 6 chns, by J. Powell, Knares-

borough, (tinted); foot/b'way, waterbodies, woods, fish pond, glebe (pink).

43/114 Copt Hewick (township in parish of Ripon) SE 345718
Apt 08.07.1841; 627a (626); Map 1841, 9 chns, by J. Humphries, Ripon; foot/b'way, woods (col), heath/moor, residual open fields, holdings (col).

43/115 Cowling (township in parish of Kildwick) SD 961428
Apt 10.01.1846; 3366a (4512); Map 1846, 3 chns, (tinted); woods, building names, mill, former moss; a sketchy cherub surmounts the title.

43/116 Cowthorpe (parish) SE 438518
Apt 04.04.1845; 1323a (1323); Map 1848, 6 chns; woods (named), gardens, heath/moor, weir; glebe (pink) it is unclear what yellow-green tint means.

43/117 Cracoe (township in parish of Burnsall) SD 988602
Apt 21.10.1839; 1877a (2370); Map surveyed in 1840, 3 chns, by Sam Swire; hill-drawing, foot/b'way, woods, plantations, orchards, gardens, heath/moor (col), rock outcrops, field gates, boundary stone and gates, well, springs, limekilns, quarry, turf pits, turf roads, 'Face of Turf graft in 1841', occupation road; cultivated land is shown by grey flecking.

43/118 Cridling Stubbs (township in parish of Womersley) SE 518213
Apt 01.02.1847; 377a (1380); Map 1847, 6 chns, ? surveyed by C. Birks, Barnsley, and drawn by Richard Cuttle; railway, foot/b'way, canal with towpath, wharf, orchards, gardens, road names, limestone quarries.

43/119 Crigglestone (township in parish of Sandal Magna) SE 319161
Apt 17.10.1843; 3057a (3057); Map 1843, 3 chns, ? by Wm Wordsworth; foot/b'way, turnpike roads, waterbodies, woods (named), plantations, parkland, gardens, building names, Methodist Chapel, mill dam, brewery, collieries, tan yard, boat house; bridge named.

43/120 Crofton (parish) SE 375183
Apt 31.01.1844; 1505a (1504); Map 'Corrected 1843', 3 chns; railway and station, foot/b'way, canal with towpath and locks, waterbodies, woods (col), osiers (by symbol), fish pond, windmill, school, quarry, old quarry, hall, toll bar, well.

43/121 South Crosland (township in parish of Almondbury) SE 114128
Apt 18.11.1847; 161a (1560); Map 1848-50, 3 chns, in 2 parts, by Joseph Hall, Huddersfield, (tithable parts only in detail); foot/b'way, waterbodies, rock outcrops, building names, stiles, factory, mills, dyehouse, weir. Apt omits land use.

43/122 Cudworth (township in parish of Roystone) SE 390087
Apt 31.10.1844; 1713a (1712); Map 1845, 6 chns, by Richd Birks, Barnsley; railway with station, foot/b'way, turnpike roads, waterbodies, woods (col), gardens, building names, mill, weir, chapel, old river course.

43/123 Dacre (township in parish of Ripon) SE 174615
Apt 30.06.1843; 5291a (all); Map 1843, 6 chns, by W. Cockett, (includes two enlargements of villages at 3 chns); foot/b'way, woods, boundary stones, sheep wash, weir; common pasture is tinted pale yellow and tithable land is tinted pink; stream named.

43/124 Darfield (township in parish of Darfield) SE 407055
Apt 29.06.1839; 1862a (1862); Map 1839, 6 chns, ? by Richard Birks; foot/b'way, waterbodies, woods (col), building names, mills.

43/125 Darrington (parish) SE 493199
Apt 31.01.1839; 1875a (4820); Map 1840, 8 chns, ? by John Horsley, (tithable parts only in detail); waterbodies, woods, parkland, gardens.

43/126 Darton (township in parish of Darton) SE 322101
Apt 01.06.1844; 271a (1337); Map 1844, 6 chns, by Richd Birks, Barnsley, (tithable parts only in detail, tinted); hillock, foot/b'way, waterbodies, woods, building names, vicarage, mill, quarry, obelisk (pictorial); pictorial church; tithable buildings are grey and tithe-free are black.

43/127 North Deighton (township in parish of Kirk Deighton) SE 395518
Apt 09.02.1839; 1408a (1407); Map 1838, 7 chns, by James Powell, Knaresborough; mound, foot/b'way, turnpike roads, woods, ownerships (col); bridge named.

43/128 Dennaby (township in parish of Mexbrough) SK 480990 [Denaby Main]
Apt 16.10.1839; 1035a (1035); Map 1840, 4 chns, by Wm Bingley; foot/b'way, waterbodies, woods (col), canal, old course of river, locks, ferry, weir; cartouche is decorated with oak leaves and acorns.

43/129 Dent (township in parish of Sedbergh) SD 720850
Apt 12.03.1846; 5629a (23200); Map 1840, 3 chns, 1st cl, by A. Clarkson and R. Garth, Swaledale, N.R., (includes 64-chn index); construction lines, hill-drawing, woods, plantations, building names, river embankments, mills, chapel, Friends Meeting House, ravines; bridge named.

43/130 Denton (township or chapelry in parish of Otley) SE 145505
Apt 05.06.1845; 211a (3100); Map 1848, 4.5 chns, copied from Sir C.H. Ibbetson's plan by Messrs Hayward, Northampton, (tithable parts only); foot/b'way, waterbodies, woods, landowners; streams named.

43/131 Dewsbury (township in parish of Dewsbury) SE 238220
Apt 07.12.1847; 186a (1392); Map 1848, 4 chns, in 2 parts, by J. Marriott, Dewsbury, (tithable parts only); railways, foot/b'way, canal with towpath, woods.

43/132 Dodworth (township in parish of Silkstone) SE 312052
Apt 7.4.1847; 700a (1947); Map 1847, 7 chns, by Richard Birks, Barnsley, (tithable parts only in detail); hill-drawing, foot/b'way, turnpike roads, waterbodies, woods (named), plantations, parkland, building names, ownerships (col), quarries, reservoir, tan yard, furnace, spring, school; pictorial church; tithable buildings are red; other buildings are hatched.

43/133 Doncaster (parish) SE 583029
Apt 11.03.1839; 8586a (6527); Map 1839, 12 chns, in 3 parts, by James Alexander; foot/b'way, waterbodies, woods, plantations, parkland, residual open fields, building names, field names, brick kilns, racecourse (in detail), grandstand, winning post, drains (named), quarries, gas works, sand pit, Deaf and Dumb Institution, toll bar, townships (col, named); built-up part generalised.

43/134 Draughton (township in parish of Skipton) SE 050520
Apt 24.09.1846; 2258a (2257); Map 1847, 3 chns, by Richard Petty, Crosshills; hill-drawing, waterbodies, woods, orchards, field boundary ownerships, building names.

43/135 Drax (parish) SE 668262
Apt 31.03.1838; 6259a (6474); Map 1839?, 9 chns; waterbodies, woods, open fields, building names, road names, tithe-free land (col); scale bar has elaborate arrow patterns and is surmounted by a sketchy eagle; parish name in title is on 'sky' ground.

43/136 Drighlington (township in parish of Birstal) SE 226288
Apt 29.02.1848; 1131a (1130); Map 1848, 6 chns, by W. Wordsworth, Black Gates; waterbodies, woods, road earthworks.

43/137 Easington (township in parish of Slaidburn) SD 735555
Apt 18.01.1843; 9091a (9090); Map 1844, 4 chns, 1st cl, in 2 parts, by A. Halliday, Preston; foot/b'way, woods, building names, boundary stones and marks, school, private roads (uncoloured); some physical features named.

43/138 Eastoft (township in parish of Adlingfleet) SE 792164
Apt 20.07.1839; 1389a (1389); Map '1822' (? copy of 1840), 16 chns, in 3 parts, (includes 8-chn enlargement of detail); landowners, ownerships (col).

43/139 Eavestone (township in parish of Ripon) SE 216682
Apt 30.06.1843; 1120a (1119); Map 1843, 4 chns, by Thomas Robinson, Ripon; waterbodies, woods, crag, boundary marks.

43/140 Eccleshill (township in parish of Bradford) SE 188360
Apt 19.12.1848; 1145a (1070); Map 1850?, 3 chns, by Thomas Ingle, Bradford; railway, canal with towpath, foot/b'way, waterbodies, woods, gardens; some field boundaries have been cancelled or added in red, whereas others were apparently always red, which could indicate walls.

43/141 Edlington (parish) SK 543977 [Not listed]
Apt 12.05.1840; 1728a (1727); Map 1840, 6 chns, by J. Alexander, Doncaster, (tinted); foot/b'way, waterbodies, woods (named), building names, dog monument, well, earthwork, quarry, pit, glebe (pink), common, green. Apt omits land use.

43/142 Egbrough or Egborough (township in parish of Killington) SE 578239 [Low Eggborough]
Apt 22.11.1838; 1901a (1997); Map 1839?, 6 chns, by Geo. Alderson, York, (tinted); foot/b'way, turnpike roads, canal with towpaths, woods; mapmaker's name is damaged.

43/143 Ellenthorpe (township in parish of Aldborough) SE 420672 [Not listed]
Apt 12.03.1846; 589a (all); Map 1846, 4 chns; foot/b'way, waterbodies, woods, orchards, open fields, building names; colours may show property ownerships.

43/144 Elmeley (township in parish of Elmeley) SE 247129 [Emley]
Apt 09.10.1841; 3466a (3465); Map 1842, 6 chns, in 4 parts, ? by Richd Birks, (tithable parts only in detail; including three 3-chn enlargements of residual open fields); waterbodies, woods (col), building names, rectory, quarry, furnace, factory, chapel; modus and tithe-free lands tinted green.

43/145 North Elmsall (township in parish of South Kirby) SE 480125
Apt 22.03.1842; 2072a (2071); Map 1842?, 4 chns, by R. Smith, York; woods, parkland.

43/146 South Elmsall (township in parish of South Kirkby) SE 485115 [South Emsall]
Apt 21.04.1845; 548a (1740); Map 1851, 6 chns, in 2 parts, (tithable parts only, tinted); foot/b'way, woods, building names, road names, former open field names, mill, windmill (pictorial); bridge named; tithable buildings are red, and tithe-free buildings are shown in outline only. Apt omits almost all land use.

43/147 Elslack (township in parish of Broughton) SD 940490
Apt 30.10.1839; 187a (1762); Map 1845, 6 chns, by Thos Kell, Bramham; waterbodies, woods, plantations, building names, mill, disputed common.

43/148 Embsay with Eastby (townships in parish of Skipton) SE 004551
Apt 24.09.1846; 2523a (2522); Map 1847, 3 chns, by James Scalby; foot/b'way, waterbodies, woods, orchards, Methodist Chapels, hall.

43/149 Fairburn (township in parish of Ledsham) SE 467286
Apt 26.06.1839; 1386a (1386); Map 1838, 3 chns; railway, canal with towpath and tunnel entrance, landing, waterbodies, woods, arable (col), grassland (col), field boundary ownerships, building names, plaster pits, quarries.

43/150 Farnhill (township in parish of Kildwick) SE 005466
Apt 28.04.1845; 562a (583); Map 1845, 4 chns, by Sam Swire, Skipton; hill-drawing, canal with towpath, woods (named), plantations, moor, crag, well, boundary stone; cultivated ground is shown by horizontal grey flecking.

43/151 Farnley (township in parish of Leeds) SE 252322
Apt 29.07.1844; 1991a (1990); Map 1844, 6 chns, ? by Wm. Wordsworth; foot/b'way, waterbodies, woods, coal pit.

43/152 Farnley (township in parish of Otley) SE 203476
Apt 05.06.1845; 364a (1822); Map 1848, 3 chns, by Robert Horsman, Wetherby; foot/b'way, woods, chapel, holdings (col).

43/153 Farnley Tyas (township in parish of Almondbury) SE 171133
Apt 18.11.1847; 72a (1623); Map 1849?, 4 chns, (tithable parts only); woods.

43/154 Featherstone (township in parish of Featherstone) SE 421213
Apt 31.12.1841; 1311a (1310); Map 1842, 8 chns; woods.

43/155 Fenwick (township in parish of Campsall) SE 596162
Apt 04.02.1846; 113a (2060); Map 1846, 3 chns, in 2 parts, by Fras. Carr, York, (tithable parts only in detail; includes 12-chn index) waterbodies, woods, landowners.

43/156 Ferrinsby (township in parish of Knaresborough) SE 367598 [Ferrensby]
Apt 26.02.1839; 235a (all); Map 1840?, 6 chns, by J. Howgate, Knaresborough, (tithable parts only, tinted); woods.

43/157 Ferry Fryston (township) SE 470255 [Not listed]
Apt 15.03.1838; 3041a (3040); Map 1840, 6 chns; railway, woods, parkland, residual open fields; pink shows lands in parish of Pontefract; green shows lands exempt from great tithes.

43/158 Firbeck (parish) SK 564885
Apt 09.06.1841; 1258a (all); Map 1842?, 6 chns; foot/b'way, waterbodies, woods.

43/159 Flockton (township in parish of Thornhill) SE 240149
Apt 12.05.1848; 1090a (all); Map 1849?, 3 chns, by Makin Durham, Thorne, (tinted); foot/b'way, waterbodies, woods (col), parkland, gardens (col), rock outcrops, old pits, pit, tunnel, old tunnel, quarries (col), reservoir bank, air pit, chapel, manor house; scale-bar is ruler-like, and frames mapmaker's name, and is surmounted by a banner.

43/160 Fockerby (township in parish of Aldingfleet) SE 839196
Apt 04.07.1844; 794a (804); Map 1846?, 6 chns, in 5 parts, ? by Makin Durham, (tithable parts only, tinted; includes 36-chn index); waterbodies, woods, peat moss.

43/161 Follifoot (township in parish of Spofforth) SE 335530
Apt 22.11.1847; 1781a (1799); Map 1848, 6 chns; railway with tunnel, foot/b'way, waterbodies, woods (col), heath/moor, park; bridge named.

43/162 Fountains Earth (township in parish of Kirkby Malzeard) SE 130720 [Not listed]
Apt 28.08.1838; 2837a (6833); Map 1838, 8 chns, in 2 parts, (including 1-chn enlargement of Lofthouse village); foot/b'way, waterbodies, woods.

43/163 Fulstone (township in parish of Kirkburton) SE 182081
Apt 19.12.1845; 4a (1200); Map (drawn on Apt) 1853?, 4 chns, (tithable parts only). Apt omits land use.

43/164 Garforth (township in parish of Garforth) SE 410330
Apt 18.05.1841; 1457a (1700); Map 1841, 3 chns; railway, woods, tithe-merged land (pink).

43/165 Gargrave (parish) SD 930560
Apt 25.11.1841; 11616a (all); Map surveyed in 1838-9, 3 chns, 1st cl, in 6 parts, by John Greenwood, Gisburn, (includes 30-chn index); construction lines, hill-drawing, foot/b'way, turnpike roads, canal with towpath and locks, waterbodies, houses, woods (named), plantations, parkland, orchards, gardens (by annotation), marsh/bog, open fields, hedge ownership, fence ownership, field boundary ownerships, building names, field names, landowners, chapel, boundary stones, wells, quarries, milestone, old mill, limekiln, saw mill, weighing machine, warehouse, coal stays, lodge, spring, barns, cotes, sheepfold, dog kennel, ice house, pump house, boat house; physical features named; legend explains symbols, including stone walls, stone and foot bridges, hedges with and without trees, 'Bye or Cross Roads', sunk roads, and (using Dawson's symbols) limekilns, smithies, watermills, embankments.

43/166 Garsdale (township in parish of Sedbergh) SD 760920
Apt 20.02.1841; 3600a (8280); Map 1840, 3 chns, 1st cl, in 6 parts, by Anthony Clarkson and Richard Garth, Swaledale, York N.R., (includes three 36-chn indexes); construction lines, hill-drawing, woods, plantations, building names, toll bar, pit, school, Friends Meeting Houses.

43/167 Gawthorpe (township or district in parish of Dewsbury) SE 285225
Apt 30.12.1842; 1132a (?); Map 1843, 6 chns, by W. Wordsworth, Blackgates; waterbodies, woods, heath/moor, building names.

43/168 Giggleswick (parish) SD 815635
Apt 04.11.1844; 18421a (18419); Map 1843, 4 chns, 1st cl, in 11 parts, by Machell and Withers, Carlisle, (includes 30-chn index); construction

lines, hill-drawing, foot/b'way, waterbodies, woods, parkland, rock outcrops, building names, well, boundary tree, stones and marks, limekilns, weir, mills, waterfalls, old mill, dog kennel, school, pinfold, wash fold, old river course; north pointer is decorated with acron and oak leaves.

43/169 Gildersome (township in parish of Batley) SE 247290
Apt 17.09.1849; 971a (1120); Map 1850, 3 chns, by W. Wordsworth, Black Gates; waterbodies, woods, turnpike gate; tithe-free areas are unnumbered.

43/170 Gildingwells (township in parishes of Laughton-en-le-Morthen and St Johns) SK 557854
Apt 31.12.1840; 585a (all); Map 1841?, 3 chns, by Dollond, London; waterbodies; scale bar, superimposed on the compass pointer, is styled and coloured like a ruler.

43/171 Gisburn (township in parish of Gisburn) SD 775545
Apt 29.06.1846; 2029a (all); Map 1847, 6 chns, in 3 parts, by John Greenwood, Gisburn, (includes enlargement of village at 3 chns); foot/b'way, waterbodies, woods, parkland, orchards, gardens, building names, stiles, limekiln, well, lodges, mill, deer house, dog kennels, toll gates, quarries; stream named.

43/172 Gisburn Forest (township in parish of Gisburn) SD 775545
Apt 06.05.1846; 4756a (4756); Map 1846, 6 chns, in 2 parts, by John Greenwood, Gisburn; foot/b'way, waterbodies, building names, mill, chapels, smithy, schools, boundary stone; buildings are shown in outline only; north pointer has plumes.

43/173 Givendale (township in parish of Ripon) SE 342687 [Not listed]
Apt 08.12.1840; 788a (788); Map 1839, 6 chns, by William Morton, Ripon; foot/b'way, waterbodies, houses, woods.

43/174 Glusburn (township in parish of Kildwick) SD 997451
Apt 31.12.1845; 1516a (1516); Map copied from one of 1824 by Samuel Washington, with 'the alterations' to April 1846, 3 chns, by Rich. Petty, Crosshills; hill-drawing, waterbodies, woods, plantations, field boundary ownerships, building names.

43/175 Golcar (township in parish of Huddersfield) SE 090162
Apt 13.08.1849; 1481a (1560); Map 1851?, 4 chns; railway with viaduct and station, canal with towpath and locks, foot/b'way, waterbodies, weirs, quarries.

43/176 Goldsbrough (township in parish of Goldsbrough) SE 386560 [Goldsborough]
Apt 21.12.1846; 1712a (all); Map 1847?, 4 chns, in 2 parts, (includes 2-chn enlargement of detail); railway, foot/b'way, waterbodies, houses, woods (col), osiers (col), parkland, arable (col), grassland (col), gardens (col), boiling spring, fords.

43/177 Gomersal (township in parish of Birstal) SE 210267
Apt 29.02.1848; 3119a (3119); Map 1849, 3 chns, by William Ellison, Leeds; foot/b'way, waterbodies, woods, parkland, orchards, residual open fields, building names, mills, quarry, toll bar, chapels, workhouse.

43/178 Goole (township in parish of Snaith) SE 745197
Apt 02.12.1841; 3768a (4280); Map 1842, 6 chns, (tithable parts only in detail); waterbodies, woods (col), plantations (col), churchyard.

43/179 Grantley (township in parish of Ripon) SE 233700
Apt 31.12.1842; 744a (743); Map 1843, 6 chns, by Thomas Robinson; foot/b'way, waterbodies, houses.

43/180 Grassington (township in parish of Linton) SE 018668
Apt 09.07.1846; 5714a (5714); Map 1846?, 3 chns; foot/b'way, waterbodies, footbridge, hippings, smelt mill, shaft, common, wood (by name).

43/181 Greasbrough (township in parish of Rotherham) SK 421953
Apt 31.07.1847; 144a (2329); Map 1849, 3 chns, by T. Parkinson, Rotherham, (tithable parts only in detail); railway, foot/b'way, waterbodies, building names, toll bar.

43/182 Grewelthorpe (township in parish of Kirkby Malzeard) SE 215765
Apt 30.07.1839; 2096a (3820); Map 1840, 6 chns, in 2 parts, by T. Bradley and Son, Richmond, Yorks, (tithable parts only in detail); waterbodies, woods, building names, well, ownerships (col); two streams named.

43/183 Grindleton (township in parish of Mitton) SD 758482
Apt 28.11.1846; 3734a (3733); Map 1848, 6 chns, in 4 parts, by S.A. Dawson, (includes two 3-chn enlargements of detail); foot/b'way, waterbodies, woods, building names, corn mill.

43/184 Guiseley (township in parish of Guiseley) SE 192428
Apt 18.07.1839; 1525a (1525); Map May and June 1838, 3 chns, 1st cl, by Robt Cooper, York; construction lines, foot/b'way, waterbodies, woods (named), field boundary ownerships, building names, road names, mill, mill dams, stiles, quarries, old quarry, pumps, trough, tan pits, Methodist Chapel, school, rectory, cross, pinfold, old churchyard.

43/185 Gunthwaite (township in parish of Peniston) SE 238065 [Not listed]
Apt 31.07.1850; 79a (1080); Map 1850?, 3 chns, ? by Christopher Soulsby, (tithable parts only); woods, heath/moor.

43/186 Haldenby (township in parish of Adlingfleet) SE 819179 [Not listed]
Apt 28.11.1840; 1399a (1422); Map 1841?, 9 chns, by J.G. Weddall, North Hall; waterbodies, drains (named). Apt omits land use.

43/187 Halton East (township in parish of Skipton) SE 041541
Apt 16.09.1842; 948a (1244); Map surveyed in 1840, 6 chns, in 2 parts, by Sam Swire, Skipton, Yorks, (includes enlargement of village at 3 chns); foot/b'way, woods, parkland; cultivated land is shown by grey flecking.

43/188 Halton Gill (township in parish of Arncliffe) SD 865755
Apt 26.03.1841; 7638a (7367); Map 1842, 3 chns; foot/b'way, woods, field gates, building names, landowners, moors; some streams named.

43/189 Halton West (township in parish of Long Preston) SD 833544
Apt 14.12.1839; 2210a (2209); Map 1839, 6 chns, by Sam Swire; hill-drawing, waterbodies, woods (col), plantations (col), parkland, arable (col), grassland (col), gardens (col), building names, limekiln; hills named; there is a note on the back of the map by George Dudgeon, solicitor, Settle: 'NOT a first class map.'

43/190 Hamphall Stubbs (township in parish of South Kirby) SE 506102 [Hampole]
Apt 27.04.1838; 217a (?); Map 1838, 3 chns, by M. Durham, Thorne; foot/b'way, turnpike roads, woods, field names, landowners, quarry, Little John's Cave and well, pinfold, field acreages; buildings are shown in outline only, without infill.

43/191 West Hardwick (township in parish of Wragby) SE 414187
Apt 30.04.1842; 25a (?); Map 1843, 4 chns, by Rd. Cuttle, (tithable parts only).

43/192 Harewood (township in parish of Harewood) SE 325445
Apt 24.05.1845; 87a (3622); Map 1845?, 4 chns, (tithable parts only); field boundary ownerships, landowners; buildings are shown by small conventional drawings; fences not belonging to tithable lands are coloured red; a table lists field names and acreages; the cartouche is colourful, with a grinning face at the bottom, and possibly represents a fantastic flying creature; the scale, graduated in poles and surmounted by dividers, and compass rose are also colourful.

43/193 Harthill (parish) SK 491809
Apt 20.11.1843; 3442a (2940); Map 1844, 8 chns, ? by Bradley, Richmond; canal with towpath, woods, ownerships (col).

43/194 Hartshead (township in parish of Dewsbury) SE 181222
Apt 12.12.1842; 135a (?); Map 1847, 3 chns, in 2 parts, by J. Marriott, Dewsbury, (tithable parts only); railway, foot/b'way, canal with towpath and locks, woods, building names, recreation ground, stiles.

43/195 Hartlington (township in parish of Burnsall) SE 044630
Apt 12.09.1848; 1352a (1351); Map 1848, 4 chns, by W. Thornton, Carlton; hill-drawing, foot/b'way, waterbodies, houses, woods, stiles; a quill pen appears below the title.

43/196 Hatfield (parish) SE 690080
Apt 07.01.1841; 15683a (21150); Map 1840, 9 chns, in 2 parts, (tithable parts only, tinted; includes 3-chn enlargement of detail); canal with towpath, woods.

43/197 Havercroft (township in parish of Felkirk) SE 384132
Apt 30.11.1839; 918a (?); Map 1840, 6 chns; railway, foot/b'way, canal, waterbodies, quarries.

43/198 Hawkswick (township in parish of Arncliffe) SD 955710
Apt 26.03.1841; 2970a (2970); Map 1841, 3 chns, by James Powell, Knaresborough; foot/b'way, woods, stepping stones; compass boss has a small star.

43/199 Hawksworth (township in parish of Otley) SE 161422
Apt 05.06.1845; 2451a (2451); Map 1848, 5 chns, by Robt Horsman, Wetherby; foot/b'way, waterbodies, woods (named, by Dawson's symbol), gardens (by Dawson's symbol), building names, boundary stones, chapel, moor; meaning of green and purple bands is unclear.

43/200 Haworth (township in parish of Bradford) SE 015355
Apt 28.02.1849; 8170a (10540); Map 1850, 3 chns, 1st cl, in 5 parts, by Horatio Merryweather, Burnley, (includes enlargement of village at 1.5 chns, and redrawing of village at 3 chns); construction lines, trig station (named), foot/b'way, waterbodies, woods, rock outcrops, building names, Methodist and Baptist Chapels, Baptist Sunday School, parsonage, school, grammar school, mills, footbridges, boundary stones (pictorial), old mill, toll bar, stone quarry, pinfold, hamlet boundaries; an unusually large 'pointer' draws attention to the enlarged plan of the village.

43/201 Hazelwood (township in parish of Tadcaster) SE 457401 [Hazel Wood]
Apt 21.11.1848; 29a (2051); Map 1850, 2 chns, (tithable parts only); road names, pump.

43/202 Hazlewood (township in parish of Skipton) SE 094557
Apt 24.09.1846; 141a (2483); Map 1847?, 8 chns, by Richd. Petty, Crosshills, (tithable parts only); hill-drawing, foot/b'way, woods; stream named.

43/203 Headingley cum Burley (township in parish of Leeds) SE 272367
Apt 16.01.1845; 3051a (3058); Map 1846?, 6 chns; railways, waterbodies, woods, parkland, gardens, weirs.

43/204 Heaton (township in parish of Bradford) SE 135355
Apt 22.12.1848; 1297a (1296); Map 1849, 4 chns, by John Richardson, Dalston, Carlisle; railway, foot/b'way, turnpike roads, toll gate, waterbodies, woods, park, building names, road names, mill, bath house, coal pit, quarries, reservoir.

43/205 Hebden (township in parish of Linton) SE 040650
Apt 09.07.1846; 2583a (3583); Map 1843, 3 chns, 1st cl, in 3 parts, by Ordnance Survey; construction lines, trig stations (named), foot/b'way, waterbodies, houses, gardens, rock outcrops (named), building names, moor, troughs, stepping stones, wells, chapels, school, marked stones, foot stick, sluices, shafts, waterfall, limekilns (by symbol), boundary stones, limestone quarry, lead mines (by symbol), cotton factory, corn mill, smithies; streams named.

43/206 Heckmondwike (township in parish of Birstal) SE 218240
Apt 29.02.1848; 663a (663); Map 1848, 3 chns, by W. Wordsworth, Black Gates; railway, waterbodies, woods, orchards, gardens, quarry, school; pecked lines are between ownerships and pecked lines with crossbars are within ownerships.

43/207 Hellifield cum Arnford and Newton (townships in parish of Long Preston) SD 862569
Apt 09.12.1839; 3381a (3381); Map surveyed in 1839, 3 chns, 1st cl, by John Greenwood, Gisburn; hill-drawing, construction lines, foot/b'way, turnpike roads, waterbodies, houses, woods (col), parkland, gardens, marsh/bog (col), rock outcrops, hedge ownership, fence ownership, field boundary ownerships, field gates, building names, field names, landowners, moors, fish pond, boat house, sheepfold, milestone, quarries, wash dam, waterfall, scattered rocks, site of old house, barns, smithy, pinfold, chapels, well, haha, archery target; legend explains symbols, including demesne boundaries, hedges with trees, smithies (by Dawson's symbol), stone, wood and foot bridges, quarries, stone walls and limekilns; bridge named.

43/208 Hessle (township in parish of Wragby) SE 422170
Apt 30.04.1842; 96a (?); Map 1843, 4 chns, by H.J. Morton, Wakefield, (tithable parts only); woods, quarry, common.

43/209 Hetton (township in parish of Burnsall) SE 953602
Apt 21.10.1839; 1712a (?); Map 1839, 6 chns, by Sam Swire; hill-drawing, foot/b'way, waterbodies, woods (col), arable (col), pasture (col), meadow (col), orchards, gardens, heath/moor, road names, field names, watering place, springs, stiles, occupation road; legend explains tints.

43/210 Hickleton (parish) SE 482053
Apt 21.03.1846; 23a (1047); Map 1846, [12 chns], (tithable parts only in detail, tinted); field boundary ownerships, toll bar. Apt omits field names.

43/211 Hill Top (township in parish of Wragby) SE 422177 [Not listed]
Apt 30.04.1842; 44a (?); Map 1843, 4 chns, by H.J. Morton, Wakefield, (tithable parts only); woods.

43/212 Hirst Courtney (township in parish of Birkin) SE 616246
Apt 09.05.1838; 606a (605); Map 1838?, 4 chns; construction lines, foot/b'way, houses, smithy (by Dawson's symbol), stiles.

43/213 Holbeck (township in parish of Leeds) SE 291321
Apt 21.06.1845; 420a (760); Map 1846, 3 chns; railways, foot/b'way, canal with towpath, waterworks, waterbodies, woods, field boundary ownerships, building names, road names, chapels, workhouse, factories, mills, flax mill, foundry, common (col); bridge named.

43/214 Holme (township in parish of Almondsbury) SE 105055
Apt 18.11.1847; 1227a (3990); Map 1851, 4 chns; foot/b'way, waterbodies, houses, woods, plantations, building names, road names, mills.

43/215 Hook (township in parish of Snaith) SE 755245
Apt 31.05.1841; 1741a (all); Map 1843, 6 chns, in 2 parts; canal, waterbodies, woods; pink may show tithe ownership.

43/216 Hooton Pagnell (township in parish of Hooton Pagnell) SE 485085
Apt 15.05.1846; 1968a (1967); Map 1847?, 6 chns, in 11 parts, ? by H.J. Morton, Wakefield, (including ten enlargements of open fields); foot/b'way, waterbodies, woods (col), plantations, parkland, residual open fields (named), quarry, glebe, hamlet boundaries, common.

43/217 Hooton Roberts (parish) SK 483973
Apt 30.07.1839; 1038a (1048); Map 1840, 4 chns, by Wm Bingley; foot/b'way, turnpike roads, waterbodies, woods (col, named), parkland, building names, toll bar, limekiln, quarry, town and turnpike limestone quarries, spring, well, ford, weir, garden (by annotation), rookery (by symbol); oak leaves and acorns surround title; scale-bar has wheat-ear decoration.

43/218 Horbury (township in parish of Wakefield) SE 306190
Apt 13.02.1847; 1183a (1183); Map 1848, 6 chns, in 2 parts, by Joseph Thompson, Leeds, (includes enlargement of Horbury village at 3 chns); railway with tunnel and station, foot/b'way, canal with towpath and locks, waterbodies, woods, osiers (by symbol), parkland, weirs.

43/219 Horsforth (township in parish of Guiseley) SE 238388
Apt 25.09.1839; 2730a (2729); Map 1838, 3 chns, 1st cl, by Robert Cooper; construction lines, foot/b'way, waterbodies, woods (named), parkland, gardens, field boundary ownerships, building names, mills, mill race, mill dams, chimney, quarries, old quarries, old ponds, external stairways, crane, tan pits, toll bar, pumps, troughs, fish pond, sundial, Baptist Chapel.

43/220 Horton (township in parish of Bradford) SE 142319 [Great and Little Horton]
Apt 10.01.1849; 2013a (2070); Map 1851?, 3 chns, by Thomas Ingle,

Bradford; foot/b'way, waterbodies, woods, gardens; churches and public buildings are black, but unnamed on the map.

43/221 Horton (township in parish of Gisburn) SD 862510
Apt 06.05.1846; 2019a (2018); Map 1844, 3 chns, 1st cl, in 2 parts, by Ordnance Survey, (drawn by Patrick Brewer and James Stephenson, Civil Assistants); construction lines, trig points (named), foot/b'way, waterbodies, houses, gardens, marsh, building names, Independent Chapel, water troughs, pumps, wells, draw wells, milestone, milepost, graveyard, stepping stones, old embankment, tithe barn, wooden bridge, saw pit, limestone quarry, limekiln (by symbol), spring; bridges and streams named.

43/222 Great Houghton (township in parish of Darfield) SE 439071
Apt 15.02.1840; 1618a (1637); Map 1840, 4 chns, ? by Richard Birks; foot/b'way, waterbodies, woods (col), heath/moor (col), building names, road names, well; title is stamped.

43/223 Little Houghton (township in parish of Darfield) SE 423058
Apt 30.07.1839; 645a (644); Map 1839?, 6 chns, ? by Richard Birks; railway, foot/b'way, mill.

43/224 High Hoyland (township in parish of High Hoyland) SE 275106
Apt 14.07.1841; 837a (836); Map 1843, 6 chns, by Richard Birks, Barnsley; waterbodies (named), woods (col, named), parkland (named), school, garden house; there is a pencil note dated 1 May 1850 as to the correct boundary, and an Ordnance Survey report thereon.

43/225 Hoyland Swaine (township in parish of Silkstone) SE 370002
Apt 19.06.1845; 204a (1936); Map 1849?, 6 chns, in 4 parts, ? by Richard Birks, (tithable parts only in detail; includes 18-chn index); turnpike roads, woods, quarry.

43/226 Huddersfield (township in parish of Huddersfield) SE 150190
Apt 16.03.1850; 1484a (3950); Map 1851, 4 chns, by John Richardson, Dalston, Cumberland, (tithable parts only); railway with station and tunnel, foot/b'way, turnpike roads, canal with towpath and lock, waterbodies, woods (named), gardens, building names, ancient course of river, weirs, mill, quarries.

43/227 Humberton (township in parishes of Aldborough and Kirkby Hill) SE 425685
Apt 30.06.1848; 1014a (2320); Map 1848, 6 chns, by Thos Holliday; railway with station, foot/b'way, woods (col), field boundary ownerships, building names, river bank, ferry, stiles, riding boundary.

43/228 Hunsingore and Cattall (townships in parish of Hunsingore) SE 436545
Apt 27.09.1850; 2190a (all); Map 1851, 9 chns; hill-drawing, railway, level crossing, foot/b'way, waterbodies, woods, Roman road, tile yard, mill, quarry, township boundaries; Hunsingore is tinted pink and Cattall is tinted yellow.

43/229 Hunslet (township in parish of Leeds) SE 304320
Apt 21.02.1845; 865a (1100); Map 1846, 3 chns; railways with station, foot/b'way, waterbodies, woods, cemetery, weir; public buildings and churches are coloured black, but not named.

43/230 Hunsworth (township in parish of Birstal) SE 186284
Apt 29.02.1848; 1374a (1310); Map 1848, 6 chns, by W. Wordsworth, Black Gates; railway, waterbodies, woods.

43/231 Idle (township in parish of Calverley) SE 173382
Apt 26.09.1845; 2338a (2420); Map 1846, 6 chns, by W. Wordsworth, Black Gates; railway, canal locks and towpath, waterbodies, woods, weir.

43/232 Ilkley (township in parish of Ilkley) SE 112468
Apt 08.05.1846; 1940a (3961); Map 1847?, 3 chns; foot/b'way, waterbodies, houses, woods.

43/233 Ingerthorp (township in parish of Ripon) SE 294662 [Ingerthorpe]
Apt 15.06.1843; 510a (all); Map 1843, 6 chns; foot/b'way, woods, ownerships (col).

43/234 Ingleton (township in parish of Bentham) SD 740760
Apt 30.07.1839; 17859a (17858); Map 1847?, 8 chns, in 2 parts, (includes enlargement of Ingleton village at 4 chns); hill-drawing, foot/b'way, waterbodies, woods, moss, building names, slate quarries, tan yard, colliery, watering place, limekiln, sheepfold, barns, caves, boundary marks, old boundary stones; physical features named.

43/235 Keighley (parish) SE 022400
Apt 28.08.1840; 10356a (10350); Map 1841?, 6 chns, by William Hopkinson; waterbodies, woods, building names, quarries, turbary, moss, common, school, weir; meaning of yellow and green tints is unclear.

43/236 Kellington (township in parish of Kellington) SE 555245
Apt 19.11.1839; 1679a (1679); Map surveyed in 1839, 6 chns, by Henry Teal, junior; foot/b'way, canal with towpath, waterbodies, woods, osiers (by symbol), glebe.

43/237 Kettlewell (township in parish of Kettlewell) SD 980725
Apt 17.09.1846; 5451a (all); Map 1847, 4 chns; foot/b'way, woods, building names, boundary stones, Methodist Chapel, common, parish and township boundaries.

43/238 Kildwick (township in parish of Kildwick) SE 021464
Apt 14.04.1847; 873a (873); Map 1847, 4 chns, by Richard Petty, Crosshills; foot/b'way, canal with towpath, waterbodies, woods, parkland, orchards, gardens, building names, ox-bow lakes, tithe barn, parsonage.

43/239 Kilnsey (township or hamlet in parish of Burnsall) SD 965672
Apt 30.09.1844; 3253a (3253); Map 1845, 4 chns, by Sam Swire; hill-drawing, woods (named), plantations, gardens, rock outcrops, field boundary ownerships, building names, enclosure allotments (named), lodge, occupation roads; cultivated land is shown by grey flecking.

43/240 Kirk Bramwith (parish) SE 622132
Apt 04.02.1843; 1987a (1260); Map 1843, 6 chns, (tinted); woods, field boundary ownerships, river bank.

43/241 Kirkby Hall (township in parish of Little Ouseburn) SE 455607 [Kirby Hall]
Apt 02.06.1846; 413a (411); Map 1846, 8 chns; foot/b'way, waterbodies, woods, field boundary ownerships, hall.

43/242 Kirkby Malzeard (township in parish of Kirkby Malzeard) SE 215745
Apt 30.11.1838; 2560a (3421); Map 1840, 6 chns, by T. Bradley and Son, Richmond, Yorks; foot/b'way, waterbodies, woods, ownerships (col); stream named.

43/243 Kirkby Overblow and Kearby cum Netherby (townships in parish of Kirkby Overblow) SE 334480
Apt 28.12.1838; 3644a (2757); Map in 3 parts, by T. Newsam, Leeds: Kearby 3 chns, surveyed by Jonathan Taylor in 1800 and corrected in 1838; Kirkby 6 chns, 1838, (includes 12-chn index); foot/b'way, woods, building names, road names, former open field names, chapel, waste (zigzag), ravine.

43/244 Kirkby Wharfe, Gairnston and North Milford (township in parish of Kirkby Wharfe) SE 501404
Apt 13.05.1844; 746a (1840); Map 1846, 6 chns, by J.T.W. Bell, Newcastle on Tyne, (tithable parts only in detail); railway, foot/b'way, turnpike roads, toll bar, waterbodies, woods (col), osiers, building names, mill, holdings (col).

43/245 Kirk Deighton and part of Stockeld (district in parish of Kirk Deighton) SE 408505
Apt 17.03.1846; 2319a (2319); Map 1847, 4 chns; railway, waterbodies, woods.

43/246 Kirk Hammerton (township in parish of Kirk Hammerton) SE 465555
Apt 17.02.1847; 54a (996); Map 1848, 3 chns, by E. Micklethwait, Grimsby; railway, foot/b'way, turnpike roads, waterbodies, woods, orchards, field boundary ownerships, ownerships (col), parsonage, hall, boathouse, weir; the whole district is mapped, though only a small part is tithable.

43/247 Kirkheaton (parish) SE 195171
Apt 21.04.1845; 3624a (6468); Map 1845-6, 3 chns, 4-chns and 6-chns, in 8 parts, by W. Wordsworth, Black Gates, (tithable parts only in detail); railway, foot/b'way, waterbodies, woods, parkland, ford, weir, old pits; each main part has a small diagram showing its relationship to the others. Scale bars are ruler-like.

43/248 Kirk Sandall (township in parish of Kirk Sandall) SE 618077
Apt 21.03.1846; 121a (?); Map 1846, 6 chns, (tithable parts only, tinted); waterbodies, river lock, weir, dyke (named).

43/249 Knaresborough (township in parish of Knaresborough) SE 373582
Apt 04.04.1845; 1902a (2838); Map 1846, 8 chns, by J. Howgate, Knaresborough, (tithable parts only; including Knaresborough town separately at 3 chns); foot/b'way, woods, rock outcrops, road names, windmill, churchyard, castle, castle yard and earthworks, moat.

43/250 Knottingley (township in parish of Pontefract) SE 507233
Apt 25.08.1842; 1038a (1344); Map 1843, 3 chns, by R. Smith; foot/b'way, canal with towpath, waterbodies, woods, osiers (by symbol), open fields, windmills (pictorial); built-up part generalised; tithe-free areas are yellow-green.

43/251 Langold and Letwell (townships in parishes of Laughton-en-le-Morthen and St Johns) SK 563866
Apt 31.12.1840; 1301a (all); Map 1841?, 6 chns; waterbodies.

43/252 Laughten-en-le-Morthen (parish) SK 515889 [Laughton en le Morthen]
Apt 05.10.1839; 811a (3545); Map 1840, 8 chns, by J. Alexander, Doncaster, (tithable parts only, tinted); hill-drawing, waterbodies, woods, building names, windmill, quarry.

43/253 Laverton (township in parish of Kirkby Malzeard) SE 195715
Apt 22.11.1838; 2756a (6707); Map 1838, 6 chns, by T. Robinson, Ripon; woods, quarries, post, commons.

43/254 Lead Hall (township in parish of Ryther) SE 461381 [Lead Hall Farm]
Apt 19.12.1845; 17a (900); Map 1847, 3 chns, (tithable parts only); chapel, field acreages. Apt omits land use.

43/255 Leathley (township in parish of Leathley) SE 243465
Apt 29.01.1844; 1569a (1568); Map 1846, 6 chns, by J. Howgate, Knaresborough; foot/b'way, waterbodies, woods, osiers (by symbol), parkland, heath/moor, building names, toll bar, walk mill, weir.

43/256 Ledsham (township in parish of Ledsham) SE 452295
Apt 18.06.1840; 1864a (1864); Map 1840, 6 chns; woods, gardens, glebe (pink), modus lands (green). Apt omits some land use.

43/257 Ledstone (township in parishes of Ledsham and Kippax) SE 435297 [Not listed]
Apt 31.10.1840; 1926a (1926); Map 1840, 6 chns; canal with towpath, waterbodies, woods, parkland, open fields, modus land (green), land exempt from small tithe (pink).

43/258 Leeds (township in parish of Leeds) SE 310338
Apt 16.10.1845; 1750a (2100); Map 1847, 3 chns, (tithable parts only in detail); railways with stations, foot/b'way, canal with towpath and locks, waterbodies, woods, parkland, building names, road names, iron works, weir, toll bar, cemetery, reservoir, barracks, mill, industrial school, house of recovery, moor; bridge named; churches and public buildings are black; only Anglican churches are named.

43/259 Lindley (township in parish of Otley) SE 223501
Apt 05.06.1845; 137a (1499); Map 1848, 4 chns, copied from a plan by J. Teal of 1795 by Robt Horsman, Wetherby, (tithable parts only); woods, building names, springs, boundary stone, mill, mill goyt; bridge named.

43/260 Lindrick (township in parish of Ripon) SE 271709 [Not listed]
Apt 12.07.1838; 721a (721); Map 1838, 6 chns, by Thomas Robinson, Jr, Ripon; foot/b'way, waterbodies, woods, gravel pit.

43/261 Lingards (township in parish of Almondbury) SE 075125 [Not listed]
Apt 18.11.1847; 61a (500); Map 1849?, 3 chns, (tithable parts only); woods.

43/262 Linthwaite (township in parish of Almondbury) SE 098142
Apt 18.11.1847; 1234a (1334); Map 1848, 3 chns, ? by Joseph Hall, Huddersfield, (tinted); hill-drawing, foot/b'way, canal with towpath and locks, waterbodies, building names, mill, quarries, stiles. Apt omits land use.

43/263 Linton (township in parish of Linton) SD 987623
Apt 09.07.1846; 1202a (1201); Map 1843, 3 chns, 1st cl, by Ordnance Survey; construction lines, foot/b'way, waterbodies, houses, gardens, rock outcrops, field gates, building names, worsted mill, trigs (named), steps, footbridge, stepping stones, limestone quarries, limekilns, quarries, coal hole, water troughs, graveyard, hospital [almshouses], rectories, well, gasometer, sluice, draw well; streams named.

43/264 Linton (township in parish of Spofforth) SE 386472
Apt 24.05.1838; 1207a (1214); Map 1838, 3 chns, 'from different Surveys'; foot/b'way, waterbodies, woods, beech tree (pictorial), river embankment, stone quarry.

43/265 Litton (township in parish of Arncliffe) SD 910740
Apt 26.03.1841; 3923a (4400); Map 1843, 3 chns, made for the Poor Law Guardians by Ordnance Survey; houses, rock outcrops, building names, boundary stones, waterfalls, limekilns (by symbol), wells, spring, footstick, saw pit, swallow-holes, signpost, draw well, stocks, water-trough, old lead shaft, waterfall, smith; bridges and some streams named; signpost distances are given.

43/266 Liversedge (township in parish of Birstal) SE 200237
Apt 29.02.1848; 2144a (2144); Map 1848, 6 chns, by W. Wordsworth, Black Gates; railway, waterbodies, woods, quarry.

43/267 Lockwood (township in parish of Almondbury) SE 129153 [Not listed]
Apt 18.11.1847; 805a (804); Map 1848, 2 chns, ? by Joseph Hall, Huddersfield, (tinted); railway, foot/b'way, waterbodies, building names, stiles, weir, canal with towpath and locks, quarries. Apt omits land use.

43/268 Lofthouse (township in parish of Rothwell) SE 330260
Apt 22.12.1838; 1075a (?); Map 1841, 8 chns, in 2 parts, (one part at 4 chns); foot/b'way, road names, quarry.

43/269 Lords Mere (district in parish of Rochdale) SE 023054 [Not listed]
Apt 06.03.1847; 61a (?); Map 1847, 3 chns, in 4 parts, by Thomas Hesslegrave, Dobcross, (tithable parts only); foot/b'way, landowners.

43/270 Lotherton or Lotherton cum Aberford (township in parish of Sherburn) SE 444362
Apt 10.08.1839; 1053a (1052); Map 1840?, 6 chns; common; some fields are annotated 'Fee Simple' and 'Fee Tail'. Apt omits land use.

43/271 Maltby (parish) SK 536921
Apt 04.09.1839; 4518a (4517); Map 1843?, 6 chns, by R. Smith, York; foot/b'way, waterbodies, woods (col), plantations (col), building names, abbey ruins, common, park and green. Apt omits land use for tithe-merged land.

43/272 Manningham (township in parish of Bradford) SE 148342
Apt 22.12.1848; 1296a (1295); Map 1849, 3 chns, by John Richardson, Dalston, near Carlisle; railway, foot/b'way, waterbodies, woods,

building names, road names, mill dam, corn mill, mills, chapels, lodges, carriage road, toll gate, reservoir, quarries.

43/273 Markenfield (township in parish of Ripon) SE 288671 [Not listed]
Apt 27.09.1844; 602a (all); Map 1845, 5 chns, (tinted); foot/b'way, waterbodies, woods, field gates; buildings are shown in outline only, without fill.

43/274 Markington with Wallerthwaite (township in parish of Ripon) SE 272656
Apt 03.08.1844; 3056a (3056); Map 1844, 8 chns; waterbodies, woods, Fountains Abbey, old course of river.

43/275 Marr (parish) SE 516051
Apt 09.09.1844; 1807a (1807); Map 1845, 3 chns, 1st cl, by William Roberts, 68 Chancery Lane; waterbodies, houses, woods, pits, yard, old wall, quarries; scale is in moulded surround.

43/276 Marsden (township in parish of Almondbury) SE 047093
Apt 18.11.1847; 5061a (5061); Map 1848, 6 chns, in 2 parts, by Joseph Hall, Huddersfield, (tinted); foot/b'way, waterbodies, woods, reservoir and dam, weirs, moor. Apt omits land use.

43/277 Marsden (township in parish of Huddersfield) SE 018128
Apt 10.07.1849; 3453a (2050); Map 1850, 6 chns, by Joseph Hall, Huddersfield, (tinted); waterbodies, railway with tunnel, siding and station, quarries, canal with towpath and locks.

43/278 Long Marston (parish) SE 505508
Apt 29.08.1844; 1780a (4281); Map 1845?, 4.5 chns, in 3 parts; foot/b'way, waterbodies, woods, gardens, open fields, landowners, township boundaries; most of the district is tinted green, but it is unclear why part is not; below the title is a note: 'The Red Ink Figures in the Open Land Fields denote the width of the several divisions'.

43/279 Marton and Grafton (townships in parish of Marton cum Grafton) SE 414624
Apt 26.07.1841; 1198a (1198); Map 1841, 6 chns, by James Powell, Knaresbro', (tithable parts only, tinted); foot/b'way, turnpike roads, woods, landowners.

43/280 Martons-both (parish) SD 898509 [East and West Marton]
Apt 29.03.1843; 2786a (2793); Map surveyed in 1840, 3 chns, 1st cl, by John Greenwood, Gisburn; construction lines, foot/b'way, turnpike roads, waterbodies, houses, woods (named), gardens, shrubberies, rock outcrops, hedge ownership, field gates, building names, field names, site of old house, sheepfold, dog kennel, wash dam, quarries, lime kilns, notable tree, barns, churchyard, spas, wells, fish pond, milestones, stack yard, cote, coal stay; legend explains symbols, including symbols for cuttings and embankments, turnpike roads, wooden bridges, walls, hedges with and without trees, limekilns, smithies (by Dawson's symbol) and quarries (with rock-drawing). Apt omits most land use.

43/281 Meltham (township in parish of Almondbury) SE 090100
Apt 18.11.1847; 4526a (4525); Map 1848, 4 chns; hill-drawing, foot/b'way, waterbodies, woods, building names, mills, school; scale bar is coloured in horizontal bands.

43/282 Melton on the Hill (parish) SE 513025 [High Melton]
Apt 31.07.1847; 1464a (1464); Map 1848, 11 chns, by J. Alexander, Doncaster, (tinted); hill-drawing, waterbodies, woods, parkland, field boundary ownerships, building names, mill, mill goit.

43/283 Menstone (township in parish of Otley) SE 170437 [Menston]
Apt 05.06.1845; 1132a (all); Map 1848?, 3 chns, by Robt Horsman; foot/b'way, waterbodies, woods (named), gardens, building names, road names, Wesleyan Chapel, mill; hill named; 'Old Hall' is in gothic.

43/284 Mexbrough (township in parish of Mexbrough) SE 485005 [Mexborough]
Apt 28.02.1839; 1289a (all); Map 1839, 6 chns, by J. Alexander, Doncaster; foot/b'way, canal with embankments, towpath and locks, waterbodies, woods, open fields (named), river embankments, pottery, ferry, ox-bow lake, quarries, motte and bailey, bell-pits; enclosed fields are tinted green.

43/285 Micklefield (township in parish of Sherburn) SE 442332 [Old and New Micklefield]
Apt 10.08.1839; 1755a (1755); Map 1844, 4 chns; railway, waterbodies, woods (col), heath/moor, Roman ridge road, old pit, tithe-merged lands (pink band).

43/286 Middleton (township in parish of Ilkley) SE 115505
Apt 17.03.1846; 2554a (2763); Map 1846, 8 chns, by James Powell, Knaresborough, (tinted); foot/b'way, woods, building names, waste (green), moor.

43/287 Middleton (township in parish of Rothwell) SE 306287
Apt 12.11.1839; 1798a (1797); Map 1840, 4 chns, by Henry Teal and Sons, Leeds; foot/b'way, waterbodies, farmyards, woods.

43/288 Middop or Midhope (township in parish of Gisburn) SD 843448 [Not listed]
Apt 29.06.1846; 1167a (1090); Map 1847, 6 chns, by John Greenwood, Gisburn; foot/b'way, waterbodies, building names, milestone, quarries, spring, barns, limekilns, wells, stiles; buildings are shown in outline only, without fill; north pointer has plumes.

43/289 Midhope (district in parish of Ecclesfield) SK 213977 [Not listed]
Apt 21.03.1846; 3477a (?); Map 1847, 12 chns, ? by Paul Bright, Sheffield, (tithable parts only in detail; includes enlargement of Midhope village at 6 chns); quarry, pike; streams named.

43/290 Minskip (township in parish of Aldborough) SE 390647
Apt 31.12.1840; 1395a (all); Map 1840, 6 chns, by John Howgate, Knaresborough, (tinted); waterbodies, woods.

43/291 Morley (township in parish of Batley) SE 260270
Apt 10.03.1843; 2697a (2698); Map 1843, 3 chns, by W. Wordsworth, Blackgates; waterbodies, woods, plantations, parkland, gardens, building names, well, reservoirs, quarry, mills.

43/292 Moss (township in parish of Campsall) SE 600138
Apt 04.02.1846; 103a (2300); Map 1846, 3 chns, in 5 parts, by Francis Carr, York, (includes 12-chn index); foot/b'way, waterbodies, woods, landowners.

43/293 Nappa (township in parish of Gisburn) SD 860528
Apt 06.05.1846; 578a (all); Map 1844, 3 chns, 1st cl, by Ordnance Survey, (plotted and drawn by J. Stephenson, Civil Assistant); construction lines, trig station (named), waterbodies, houses, building names, milestone, toll bar, limestone quarry, wells, limekiln (by symbol), boundary stone.

43/294 Nesfield with Langbar (township in parish of Ilkley) SE 097509
Apt 16.04.1846; 1202a (2161); Map 1847, 6 chns, by James Powell, Knaresborough, (tinted); foot/b'way, woods, building names, shooting house, boundary stones, well, limekilns (by symbol), weir, ferry, moor (col), roadside wastes (col), slope.

43/295 Netherthong (township in parish of Almondbury) SE 139097
Apt 18.11.1847; 733a (850); Map 1850, 3 chns; foot/b'way, waterbodies, woods, parkland, building names, quarries, mill. Apt omits land use.

43/296 Newall with Clifton (township in parish of Otley) SE 197476
Apt 05.06.1845; 1047a (1473); Map 1847, 5 chns, surveyed 1841 by Ingle and Smith, Bradford, (tithable parts only in detail); foot/b'way, waterbodies, woods, gardens; bridge named.

43/297 Newby with Mulwith (township in parish of Ripon) SE 356677
Apt 31.10.1851; 769a (700); Map 1851, 6 chns, by John Humphries, Ripon; foot/b'way, waterbodies, woods, gardens, heath/moor, hall, ownerships (col).

43/298 Newsholme or Newsome (township in parish of Gisburn) SD 840515
Apt 06.05.1846; 742a (741); Map 1846, 6 chns, by John Greenwood,

Gisburn; foot/b'way, waterbodies, houses, building names, toll bar, limekilns, notable stone, quarries, milestones.

43/299 Newthorpe and Huddleston or Huddleston cum Lumby (township in parish of Sherburn) SE 465330
Apt 16.10.1839; 1532a (2089); Map 1840, 8 chns; foot/b'way, waterbodies, residual open fields. Apt omits land use.

43/300 Newton (township in parish of Slaidburn) SD 690500
Apt 18.01.1843; 5826a (6556); Map surveyed in May 1838, 3 chns, 1st cl, by J.R. Allen and J. Watson, Preston; hill-drawing, foot/b'way, waterbodies, woods, plantations, rock outcrops, ownership boundaries (col), building names, school, Friends Meeting House, Friends burial ground, lead mines, old cop, stepping stones, sheepfold, old quarry; physical features named.

43/301 Newton Kyme (parish) SE 464446
Apt 06.03.1846; 1319a (1050); Map 1846, 6 chns, in 2 parts, (includes village separately at 3 chns); foot/b'way, waterbodies, woods, osiers (by symbol), parkland, avenue of trees; colouring of fields is ornamental.

43/302 Nidd (parish) SE 303598
Apt 25.06.1841; 1014a (1016); Map 1841, 8 chns, by Wm Wordsworth, Blackgates; hill-drawing, waterbodies, woods, landowners, avenue of trees, ownerships (col).

43/303 Normanton (township in parish of Normanton) SE 392223
Apt 30.07.1839; 1175a (1181); Map 1839, 6 chns; railways, waterbodies, woods (col), arable (col), grassland (col), quarry.

43/304 Norton Conyers (township in parish of Wath) SE 315765
Apt 26.02.1839; 985a (985); Map 1839, 6 chns, by J. Humphries, Ripon, Yorks; waterbodies, woods, lodge, hall, stables, garden (by annotation); colouring of fields is ornamental.

43/305 Nostel, including Nostel, Foulby, and part of Huntwick (townships in parish of Wragby) SE 402187
Apt 04.06.1842; 28a (?); Map 1842, 3 chns, by Wm Wordsworth, Blackgates, (tithable parts only); woods.

43/306 Notton (township in parish of Roystone) SE 347125
Apt 18.07.1839; 2596a (2595); Map 1842?, 6 chns; railway, turnpike roads, canal with towpath, waterbodies, woods (named), osiers (by annotation), plantations (by annotation), building names, field names, mill and dam, field acreages; colour bands may show field boundary ownerships. District is apportioned by holding; Apt omits land use.

43/307 Nun Monkton (parish) SE 492578
Apt 30.07.1838; 470a (1692); Map 1838, 4 chns, (tithable parts only, tinted); foot/b'way, woods, building names, road names, mill syke, common.

43/308 Nunwick (township in parish of Ripon) SE 322752
Apt 26.02.1839; 749a (748); Map 1839?, 6 chns, ? by John Humphries, Ripon; foot/b'way, waterbodies, woods, hedges, field boundary ownership, ownerships (col); below the title is 'This Plan is not required to be tested. John Humphries, Valuer'.

43/309 Osmondthorpe, Skelton and Thornes (district or hamlets in parish of Leeds) SE 334324
Apt 20.01.1845; 482a (?); Map 1845, 3 chns; railway, turnpike roads, waterbodies, woods, parkland, building names, road names, weirs, tithe-free areas (col).

43/310 Ossett (township or district in parish of Dewsbury) SE 279201
Apt 02.11.1842; 1864a (?); Map 1843, 6 chns, by W. Wordsworth, Blackgates; railway, waterbodies, woods, spa, quarries, new canal; some cancelled tithe area numbers are annotated 'Now in Horbury Township by arrangement under the Ordnance Survey'.

43/311 Otley (township in parish of Otley) SE 208448
Apt 05.06.1845; 1265a (2233); Map 1847, 5 chns, by Ingle and Smith, Bradford, (surveyed in 1835 by J.B. Ingle; tithable parts only in detail)); foot/b'way, waterbodies, woods, parkland, gardens; a house is annotated 'New erections since 1835'.

43/312 Oulton with Woodlesford (townships in parish of Rothwell) SE 365285
Apt 18.06.1840; 1273a (1278); Map 1840, 3 chns, in 2 parts; railway, turnpike roads, canal, waterbodies, woods, plantations, parkland, building names, river locks, township boundary.

43/313 Owston (township in parish of Owston) SE 560104
Apt 04.08.1842; 1944a (1944); Map 1842, 9 chns, by J. Alexander, Doncaster, (tinted); foot/b'way, waterbodies, woods, plantations, parkland, orchards, gardens, building names, quarries, rows of trees, glebe (pink); bridge and drains named; meaning of yellow tint is unclear.

43/314 Oxton (township in parish of Tadcaster) SE 506430
Apt 28.11.1844; 656a (all); Map 1845, 3 chns, by Henry R. Spence, York; foot/b'way, waterbodies, woods, osiers (by symbol), parkland, building names.

43/315 Parlington (township in parish of Aberford) SE 421359
Apt 02.10.1847; 1724a (1726); Map 1849, 6 chns; ox-bow lake.

43/316 Paythorne (township in parish of Gisburn) SD 822518
Apt 06.05.1846; 2628a (2627); Map 1846-7, 6 chns, in 3 parts, by John Greenwood, Gisburn, (includes 3-chn enlargement of detail); foot/b'way, waterbodies, woods, parkland, building names, fountain (pictorial), limekiln, barn, fishery, weir; buildings are shown in outline only, without infill; one north pointer has plumes; fine pecked lines by river may indicate limit of flooding.

43/317 Plumpton (township in parish of Spofforth) SE 362544 [Not listed]
Apt 25.11.1847; 2071a (2250); Map 1848, 6 chns, (tinted); foot/b'way, waterbodies, woods (col), plantations (col), grassland, gardens, building names, quarries, mill, weirs, toll bars, boundary stones, crag.

43/318 Pool (township in parish of Otley) SE 240448
Apt 05.06.1845; 954a (810); Map 1849, 4 chns, by Robt Horsman; waterbodies, woods, gardens, quarry, toll bar, chapel, mill, hall, weir, walk mill.

43/319 Potternewton (township in parish of Leeds) SE 319358
Apt 21.02.1845; 1657a (1657); Map 1845, 3 chns; turnpike roads, waterbodies, woods, parkland, building names, road names, mills.

43/320 Great and Little Preston (township in parish of Kippax) SE 401294
Apt 29.12.1845; 1004a (all); Map 1846, 4 chns; woods (named).

43/321 Long Preston (township in parish of Long Preston) SD 838597
Apt 09.12.1839; 3534a (3533); Map surveyed 1839, 3 chns, 1st cl, by John Greenwood, Gisburn; construction lines, hill-drawing, foot/b'way, turnpike roads, waterbodies, woods (named), parkland, gardens, rock outcrops, hedges, field boundary ownerships, field gates, building names, road names, field names, drainage banks, barns, sheepfold, smithies, Baptist and Methodist Chapels, vicarage, almshouses, pump houses, mill, wells, stone (pictorial); streams named; legend explains symbols, including turnpike and bye roads, stone and foot bridges, stone walls, rail fences, hedges with and without trees and (by Dawson's symbol) smithies and mills.

43/322 Pudsey (township in parish of Calverley) SE 214330
Apt 12.03.1846; 2342a (2342); Map 1847, 6 chns, by W. Wordsworth, Black Gates; waterbodies, woods, burial ground, quarries.

43/323 Purston Jaglin (township in parish of Featherstone) SE 433198
Apt 15.12.1842; 984a (984); Map 1843, 6 chns; foot/b'way, turnpike roads, toll bar, waterbodies, woods (col), osiers (by symbol, col), parkland, gardens (col), building names, windmill (pictorial).

43/324 Quick Mere (district in parish of Rochdale) SD 973054 [Not listed]
Apt 05.02.1847; 176a (?); Map 1847, 3 chns, by Thomas Hesslegrave, Dobcross, (tithable parts only); railway, foot/b'way, waterbodies, road names.

43/325 Ravenfield (parish) SK 488948
Apt 31.01.1846; 1227a (all); Map 1853, 8 chns; waterbodies, woods. District is partly apportioned by holding; Apt omits land use and field names.

43/326 Rawcliffe (township in parish of Snaith) SE 697216
Apt 23.06.1842; 4410a (4410); Map 1843?, 8 chns, (tinted; includes enlargement of Rawcliffe village at 4 chns); waterbodies, woods, drainage bank, canal with towpath, waste.

43/327 Rawdon (township in parish of Guiseley) SE 213392
Apt 23.01.1837; 1522a (1535); Map November and December 1838, 3 chns, 1st cl, ? by Robert Cooper, Leeds; foot/b'way, waterbodies, woods (named), parkland, lawn (by annotation), orchards (by annotation), plantation (by annotation), garden (by annotation), field boundary ownerships, building names, school, parsonage, Methodist, Baptist and other chapels, Friends Meeting House, boundary stones, toll bar, stiles, fish ponds, trough, mill dam, coal pit, old coal pit, old pit hill, pit hill, post office, lodge, mills, working pits, broken fences, occupation road, stables, common.

43/328 Rawmarsh (parish) SK 440968
Apt 05.02.1845; 211a (2448); Map 1848?, 6 chns, (tithable parts only in detail); foot/b'way, canal with lock and towpath, reservoir, waterbodies, woods, parkland, building names, rectory, pottery, collieries, forge, toll bars, stables, school.

43/329 Reedness (township in parish of Whitgift) SE 793217
Apt 16.06.1845; 1758a (2884); Map 1846, 6 chns, by M. Durham, Thorne, (tinted); waterbodies, woods, open fields (named), waste.

43/330 Great Ribston with Walshford (townships in parish of Hunsingore) SE 405545
Apt 23.02.1849; 7a (1780); Map 1851, 2 chns, (tithable parts only, tinted); turnpike roads, woods, plantations, landowners.

43/331 Little Ribston (township in parish of Spofforth) SE 386533
Apt 18.02.1848; 856a (855); Map 1848, 3 chns; foot/b'way, waterbodies, woods, orchards, gardens, field gates, building names, gravel pit (col), quarry (col), common (col).

43/332 Rilston (township in parish of Burnsall) SD 970586 [Rylstone]
Apt 21.10.1839; 2451a (3050); Map 1840, 6 chns, in 2 parts, by Sam Swire, (including Rilston Moor at 24 chns); hill-drawing, foot/b'way, waterbodies, woods (named), plantations, gardens, building names, field names, field acreages, stiles, spring, coalpits; cultivated ground is shown by blue-grey flecked shading; some physical features named.

43/333 Rimmington (township in parish of Gisburn) SD 817459
Apt 29.06.1846; 3082a (3082); Map 1846, 6 chns, in 5 parts, by John Greenwood, Gisburn, (including one 3-chn and two 2-chn enlargements of detail); crag, foot/b'way, waterbodies, building names, schools, various chapels, limekilns, milestone, well, quarry, pit mouth, chimney (pictorial), smelt mill, mill, old mill dam; bridge named.

43/334 Ripley (parish) SE 280586
Apt 11.04.1839; 1836a (1836); Map 1838, 4 chns, by James Powell, Knaresborough; foot/b'way, turnpike roads, waterbodies, woods, parkland, building names, ownerships (col).

43/335 Ripon (township in parish of Ripon) SE 312712
Apt 20.07.1838; 1445a (all); Map 1839, 6 chns, (includes town separately at 3 chns); waterbodies, woods, Minster, Deanery, cross, canal with locks, mill, house of correction, gaol, weir; bridge named; colouring of fields is ornamental; there is a statement below the title, signed by the three valuers, that the plan is not required to be tested.

43/336 Roecliffe (township in parish of Aldborough) SE 371656
Apt 18.04.1840; 1794a (1794); Map 1840, 8 chns, by Jno. Parlour and Joseph King; waterbodies, woods, road names, drains (named).

43/337 Rossington (parish) SK 623988
Apt 31.05.1838; 3007a (3009); Map 1838, 9 chns, by J. Alexander, Doncaster; foot/b'way, waterbodies, woods (named), plantations, parkland, nursery (by symbol), building names, former open field names, lodge, ownerships (col); bridge named.

43/338 Rothwell cum Royds (district in parish of Rothwell) SE 344271
Apt 24.07.1844; 1456a (1456); Map 1844, 6 chns, in 3 parts, by Richd Gouthwaite, Lumby, (includes enlargement of Rothwell village at 3 chns); railway, turnpike roads, canal with locks and towpath, ox-bow lakes, waterbodies, woods, mills, quarry.

43/339 Rothwell Haigh (township in parish of Rothwell) SE 333297
Apt 07.09.1838; 1730a (1730); Map 1839, 6 chns, by Richd Gouthwaite, Leeds; railway, canal, waterbodies, woods, arable (col), grassland (col), canal towpath.

43/340 Roystone (township in parish of Roystone) SE 359113
Apt 31.10.1844; 1004a (1004); Map 1845?, 4 chns, by Richard Birks, Barnsley; hill-drawing, railway with earthworks, foot/b'way, canal with earthworks and towpath, waterbodies, heath/moor, residual open fields (named), road names, vicarage, churchyard, chapel, tithe-free land (green).

43/341 Ryhill (township in parish of Wragby) SE 389148
Apt 25.10.1842; 583a (582); Map 1843, 6 chns, in 3 parts, by Richard Birks, Barnsley, (includes enlargement of open fields at 3 chns); hill-drawing, foot/b'way, waterbodies, woods, gardens, marsh/bog, heath/moor (col), open fields (named), canal reservoir, quarry, chapel, Gospel Tree; map title is stamped.

43/342 Ryther-cum-Ossendyke (township in parish of Ryther) SE 548382
Apt 10.12.1838; 2655a (2654); Map 1838, 6 chns; foot/b'way, woods (col), ownerships and holdings (col); stream named; north pointer has stylised diadem and feathers. Apt omits some land use.

43/343 Great Sandal (township in parish of Great Sandal) SE 342181 [Sandal]
Apt 08.03.1844; 1529a (1529); Map 1844, 6 chns, by W. Wordsworth, Blackgates; foot/b'way, canal with locks and towpath, waterbodies, woods, parkland, orchards, castle hill, quarries, mill, foundry.

43/344 Sawley (township in parish of Ripon) SE 245675
Apt 08.07.1841; 3203a (3203); Map 1842, 9 chns, in 2 parts, by Thomas Robinson, Richmond; foot/b'way, waterbodies, woods, ownerships (col); stream named.

43/345 Saxton with Scarthingwell (township in parish of Saxton) SE 478379
Apt 11.06.1847; 472a (2662); Map 1848, 6 chns, (tithable parts only, tinted); waterbodies, hall.

43/346 Scammonden (township in parish of Huddersfield) SE 058168
Apt 26.06.1849; 850a (2080); Map 1851, 3 chns, by John Richardson, Dalston, near Carlisle; foot/b'way, waterbodies, woods, building names, mills, quarries, chapels.

43/347 Scriven with Tentergate (township in parish of Knaresborough) SE 351587
Apt 26.02.1839; 1410a (1767); Map 1839, 6 chns, (tithable parts only, tinted); hill-drawing, foot/b'way, waterbodies, woods, building names, mill; tithable buildings are carmine and others are hatched; stone bridge is shown by Dawson's symbol.

43/348 Seacroft (district in parish of Whitkirk) SE 352354
Apt 21.01.1840; 1584a (?); Map 1841, 6 chns, by H. Teal and Son, Leeds; railway, waterbodies, woods, hall, (includes 3-chn enlargement of detail), modus land boundaries (col).

43/349 Sedbergh (township in parish of Sedbergh) SD 670940
Apt 29.06.1839; 7971a (21402); Map 1838-9, 3 chns, 1st cl, in 8 parts: parts 1 to 4 (including 15-chn index) by M. and J. Turner, Lyth, near Kendal; parts 5-7 by John Watson, Kendal; construction lines, foot/b'way, waterbodies, woods, plantations, parkland, building names, entrenchment, barns, cotton mill, toll bar, maltkiln, mills, vicarage, chapels, smithy.

43/350 Sharlston (township in parish of Warmfield) SE 390192
Apt 07.05.1842; 1127a (1126); Map 1839, 3 chns, by W. Wordsworth, Blackgates; waterbodies, woods, heath/moor, residual open fields (named), former open field names, old and new toll houses, old and new engines, spoil heaps, hall, ownerships (col).

43/351 Sharow (township in parish of Ripon) SE 328720
Apt 08.07.1841; 672a (all); Map 1841, 6 chns; foot/b'way, waterbodies, woods, old ox-bow; colouring of fields is ornamental; scale bar is eccentrically graduated, and is styled like a measuring bar, propped up on what could be a tree stump or stone.

43/352 Shipley (township in parish of Bradford) SE 139375
Apt 10.01.1849; 1346a (1140); Map 1849, 3 chns, by Ingle and Smith, Darley St, Bradford, (surveyed by G.T. Lister in 1848); railways with station (in detail) and sidings, foot/b'way, canal with aqueduct, towpath and locks, waterbodies, woods, plantations, gardens, weir, mills, toll bar, gas works, pits.

43/353 Shitlington (township in parish of Thornhill) SE 272161
Apt 04.07.1848; 3409a (3409); Map 1849, 4 chns, by Richard Carr, York; railway, canal with towpath and locks, foot/b'way, waterbodies, woods, plantations, parkland, orchards, building names, quarries.

43/354 Sicklinghall with Woodhall (townships in parish of Kirkby Overblow) SE 362472
Apt 07.02.1838; 1406a (1030); Map 1838, 3 chns, by Thos Trickett; foot/b'way, waterbodies, woods (col, named), parkland, field boundary ownerships, landowners, fish pond, ford, hall, township boundaries, field acreages. Apt omits land use and field names for most modus lands.

43/355 Silkstone (township in parish of Silkstone) SE 290050
Apt 24.06.1845; 1421a (1426); Map 1846, 6 chns, by W. Wordsworth, Blackgates; waggonway, waterbodies, woods, quarry.

43/356 Silsden (township in parish of Kildwick) SE 053468
Apt 25.04.1845; 6896a (6908); Map copied from a plan of May 1836 with alterations to May 1845, 6 chns, in 18 parts, by Horatio Merryweather, Burnley, (includes 17 1-chn enlargements of detail); foot/b'way, canal with towpath, waterbodies, building names, stiles, boundary stones, mill, weir; churches and public buildings are black, but not named; scale bar is styled like a ruler.

43/357 Skelbrooke (township in parish of South Kirby) SE 502122 [Skelbrook]
Apt 21.04.1845; 932a (1687); Map 1848?, 4.5 chns; waterbodies, woods (col), parkland, gardens.

43/358 Skelding (township in parish of Ripon) SE 212701 [Not listed]
Apt 25.10.1842; 965a (965); Map 1843, 6 chns, by Thomas Robinson, Ripon; woods.

43/359 Skellow (township in parish of Owston) SE 531101
Apt 31.07.1839; 412a (982); Map 1840?, [6 chns], (tithable parts only).

43/360 Skelmanthorpe (hamlet or district in parishes of High Hoyland, Emley and Kirkburton) SE 239103
Apt 22.02.1842; 927a (?); Map 1842, 3 chns, ? by Richard Birks; turnpike roads, waterbodies, woods (named), gardens, building names, road names, common, engine, weir, chapel; map title is stamped and gummed on.

43/361 Skelton (township in parish of Ripon) SE 368686
Apt 22.06.1843; 880a (879); Map 1842, 6 chns, by James Powell, Knaresborough; tithe-merged land (col).

43/362 Skipton (township in parish of Skipton) SD 999511
Apt 31.01.1840; 3826a (3826); Map 1843, 4 chns, by Sam Swire, Skipton, (tithable parts only in detail); hill-drawing, railway, canal with towpath, waterbodies, woods (named), plantations, parkland, gardens, field boundary ownerships, field gates, enclosure allotments, building names, public stone quarries, reservoir, ox-bow lake, workhouse, boundary stones, limestone quarries and offices, Catholic Church, old course of river, footbridge; cultivated land is shown by grey flecking; hills named.

43/363 Slaidburn (township in parish of Slaidburn) SD 700540
Apt 18.01.1843; 5184a (5617); Map 1838, 3 chns, 1st cl, by A. Halliday; foot/b'way, waterbodies, woods, parkland, building names, limekilns, weir, pits.

43/364 Slaithwaite (township in parish of Slaithwaite) SE 100142
Apt 30.06.1849; 20a (2320); Map 1851?, 3 chns, (tithable parts only); waterbodies. Apt omits land use.

43/365 Snaith and Cowick (townships in parish of Snaith) SE 660200
Apt 24.01.1840; 5726a (6455); Map 1840, 6 chns, by M. Durham, Thorne, (tinted); foot/b'way, canal, waterbodies, woods, parkland, canal with towpath, river embankment, peat moors.

43/366 Snydale (township in parish of Normanton) SE 400208
Apt 20.08.1839; 1032a (1032); Map 1841, 8 chns, in 2 parts, by Henry Teal and Son, (including open field at 3 chns); waterbodies, woods, plantations, parkland, fence, field names.

43/367 Soothill Nether (township or district in parish of Dewsbury) SE 258214 [Lower Soothill]
Apt 27.12.1842; 545a (?); Map 1843, 3 chns, by W. Wordsworth, Blackgates; foot/b'way, waterbodies, woods, Methodist Chapel; meaning of brown tint is unclear.

43/368 Soothill Upper (township or district in parish of Dewsbury) SE 260238 [Not listed]
Apt 01.02.1847; 151a (?); Map 1849, 6 chns, ? by Richard Birks, (tithable parts only); foot/b'way, woods, occupation road.

43/369 Spofforth (township in parish of Spofforth) SE 349506
Apt 25.11.1847; 5156a (5156); Map 1848, 6 chns; railway with station, waterbodies, woods, gardens, heath/moor, building names, former open field names, quarry, tithe-free areas (pink), estate boundary (pink). Apt omits land use for tithe-free lands.

43/370 Sprotborough (parish) SE 543028 [Sprotbrough]
Apt 15.05.1846; 3866a (3865); Map 1847, 12 chns, by J. Alexander, Doncaster; foot/b'way, waterbodies, woods, plantations, parkland, gardens, building names, quarry, ferries, river locks, townships (col), glebe (col); bridges named. Apt omits land use.

43/371 Stainborough (township in parish of Silkstone) SE 320032 [Not listed]
Apt 28.10.1843; 1693a (1692); Map 1844, 12 chns, by Richard Birks, Barnsley, (tithable parts only in detail); railway, waterbodies, woods (col), parkland, gardens and pleasure ground (by annotation), building names, colliery, mill, menagerie, tower, castle (pictorial), pit, old mill, ownerships (col), tithe-free land (col); map title and decorative border are typeset.

43/372 North Stainley with Steninford (townships in parish of Ripon) SE 295755
Apt 27.05.1840; 4115a (4114); Map 1840, 12 chns, in 3 parts,? by Thomas Robinson, Ripon, (includes two small enlargements of detail); foot/b'way, waterbodies, woods, building names; bridge named; colouring of fields is ornamental.

43/373 Stainton-cum-Hellaby (parish) SK 553937 [Stainton]
Apt 12.08.1840; 2789a (2789); Map 1841, 6 chns, by Paul Bright, Sheffield; waterbodies, woods (col), plantations (col), building names, quarry, tithe-free areas (pink), glebe (yellow); compass boss includes four acorns.

43/374 Stanley cum Wrenthorpe (township in parish of Wakefield) SE 332231
Apt 24.07.1845; 2352a (4345); Map 1846, 6 chns, by W. Wordsworth, Blackgates; railway, waggonways, foot/b'way, waterbodies, woods, canal with towpath, ox-bow lake, pit; tithe-free land is mapped but not numbered.

43/375 Stannington, Storrs and Dungworth (district in parish of Ecclesfield) SK 272888
Apt 21.03.1846; 2881a (?); Map 1846, 8 chns, in 8 parts, (includes seven 3-chn enlargement of detail); hill-drawing, waterbodies, woods,

plantations, building names, cross, Jewish and Quaker Burial Grounds, Unitarian and Methodist Chapel, school, mills, forge, paper mill, corn mill, reservoirs, dams; tithable lands are tinted pink and numbered.

43/376 Starbotton (township in parish of Kettlewell) SD 950750
Apt 17.09.1846; 2948a (2948); Map 1847, 4 chns; foot/b'way, woods, occupation road, boundary stones, wood pasture, parish and township boundaries.

43/377 Steeton with Eastburn (townships in parish of Kildwick) SE 031436
Apt 31.12.1845; 2043a (2043); Map 1846, 3 chns, by Richard Petty, Crosshills; hill-drawing, foot/b'way, waterbodies, woods, plantations, gardens, residual open fields, field boundary ownerships, building names, old ox-bows.

43/378 Sturton with Thorlby (townships in parish of Skipton) SD 965535
Apt 31.01.1840; 2926a (2926); Map 1842, 8 chns, by James Powell, Knaresbrough, (tinted); canal, waterbodies, woods, ox-bow lakes.

43/379 Stone Beck Down (township in parish of Kirkby Malzeard) SE 100700 [Not listed]
Apt 21.08.1838; 12617a (12710); Map 1839, 8 chns, in 2 parts, by T. Robinson, Ripon, (includes village separately at 2 chns); woods, building names, old house, crags, pikes; some physical features named.

43/380 Stone Beck Up (township in parish of Kirkby Malzeard) SE 050755 [Not listed]
Apt 16.08.1838; 13975a (14160); Map 1839, 8 chns, in 2 parts, ? by T. Robinson, Ripon, (includes Middlesmoor village separately at 2 chns); hill-drawing, foot/b'way, woods, building names, limits of enclosed common; gills and streams named.

43/381 Stotfold (township or extra-parochial district) SE 472069
Apt 13.03.1846; 2a (255); Map 1847?, 6 chns, (tithable parts only in detail).

43/382 Studley Royal or Studley Magna (township in parish of Ripon) SE 283693
Apt 07.06.1838; 685a (685); Map 1838, 6 chns, by Thomas Robinson, Ripon; foot/b'way, waterbodies, woods, parkland, gardens, waterfalls, avenue of trees, quarry.

43/383 Studley Parva or Studley Roger (township in parish of Ripon) SE 287710
Apt 12.12.1840; 940a (939); Map 1840, 6 chns; foot/b'way, woods (col); colouring of fields is ornamental.

43/384 Sturton or Sturton Grange (township in parish of Aberford) SE 425335
Apt 02.10.1847; 868a (867); Map 1849, 6 chns; waterbodies, field boundary ownerships, colliery.

43/385 Stutton (township in parish of Tadcaster) SE 481415
Apt 25.04.1843; 559a (all); Map 1843?, 6 chns; foot/b'way, ownership boundaries (col). Apt omits field names.

43/386 Sutton (township in parish of Brotherton) SE 500250 [Not listed]
Apt 04.04.1845; 598a (597); Map 1846, 5.5 chns; woods, parkland.

43/387 Sutton (township in parish of Campsall and Burghwallis) SE 552124
Apt 31.05.1838; 758a (all); Map 1838?, 3 chns, ? by William Shipton, Land Agent, York, (tithable parts only in detail); construction lines, turnpike roads, waterbodies, houses, woods, open fields (named), field boundary ownerships.

43/388 Sutton (township in parish of Kildwick) SE 001432 [Sutton-in-Craven]
Apt 26.06.1840; 2319a (2319); Map 1841, 6 chns, by Sam Swire, Skipton, Yorkshire; foot/b'way, waterbodies, woods, parkland, field boundary ownerships, building names, springs, quarries, reservoir, mill; cultivated land is shown by grey flecked lines. Apt omits land use.

43/389 Swinden (township in parish of Gisburn) SD 869539
Apt 06.05.1846; 1034a (1033); Map 1846, 6 chns, by John Greenwood, Gisburn; foot/b'way, waterbodies, woods, rock outcrops (named), building names, sheepfolds, barns, limekiln, private roads (uncoloured); north pointer has plumes.

43/390 Swinefleet (township in parish of Whitgift) SE 773200
Apt 16.06.1845; 1097a (2445); Map 1846, 6 chns, in 2 parts, ? by Makin Durham, Thorne, (includes enlargement of village at 3 chns); woods (col), open fields (named), river embankment; tithable areas are tinted pink. Apt has some cropping information.

43/391 Tadcaster East (township in parish of Tadcaster) SE 494438
Apt 08.03.1844; 556a (555); Map 1841, 3 chns, by Henry R. Spence, York; foot/b'way, waterbodies, woods, watermill.

43/392 Tadcaster West (township in parish of Tadcaster) SE 472431
Apt 31.12.1844; 1478a (1478); Map 1844, 3 chns, by Henry R. Spence, York; woods, weir, osiers (by symbol).

43/393 Tankersley (parish) SK 325990
Apt 30.07.1839; 8407a (8404); Map 1840, 8 chns; turnpike roads, toll bars, woods (col, named), parkland, building names, landowners, rectory, school, pillar (pictorial), deer houses, well house, mills, forge, iron works, old engine, township boundaries, tithe-free land (green band), ownerships (col). District is apportioned by holding; Apt generalises land use.

43/394 Temple Newsam (district in parish of Whitkirk) SE 335321
Apt 14.10.1845; 3098a (3097); Map 1847, 3 chns, by James McAnulty, Leeds, (tinted); railway, foot/b'way, canal with towpath, waterbodies, woods, plantations, building names, mill, coal pits, dried-up ox-bows, schools, vicarage, milestone, toll bar, chemical works, old vitriol works, pinfold, Methodist Chapel, Wesleyan Chapel.

43/395 Upper Thong (township in parish of Almondbury) SE 080055 [Upperthong]
Apt 18.11.1847; 950a (710); Map 1851, 4 chns, by Thomas Young, Humshaugh, Hexham; foot/b'way, waterbodies, houses, woods, plantations, building names, town hall, reservoir, weir, pencil test lines.

43/396 Thorne (parish) SE 720137
Apt 25.08.1840; 12000a (11900); Map 1840, 8 chns, in 2 parts, by M. Durham, Thorne, (tinted; includes enlargement of Thorne town at 3 chns); turnpike roads, canal with towpath, waterbodies, woods, road names.

43/397 Thornes (township in parish of Wakefield) SE 331197
Apt 13.02.1847; 1517a (1517); Map 1847, 6 chns, in 3 parts, by Joseph Thompson, Leeds, (includes two enlargements of built-up parts at 3 chns); railway, foot/b'way, canal with locks and towpath, waterbodies, woods, osiers (by symbol), parkland, avenues of trees, fences, building names, old ox-bow, mound.

43/398 Thornhill (township in parish of Thornhill) SE 246186
Apt 18.09.1845; 2487a (2487); Map 1846, 6 chns, by Richard Birks, Barnsley; hill-drawing, railway with station, waggonway, canal with towpath and locks, lock house, foot/b'way, waterbodies, woods, parkland, building names, parsonage, weir, glebe (grey); modus lands are tinted by owner, and not mapped in detail; demesne buildings are black and other buildings are hatched. Apt omits land use for modus lands.

43/399 Thornton (township in parish of Bradford) SE 080330
Apt 10.01.1849; 4740a (4390); Map 1849, 6 chns, by Thomas Dixon, Bradford; foot/b'way, turnpike roads, toll bar, waterbodies, woods, building names, mills, schools, reservoir, quarries, chapels, boundary stones, copperas works, factory; map is coloured by hamlets; 'Church' and adjoining schools are named in gothic, and other schools are named in ordinary italic.

43/400 Thornton in Lonsdale (parish) SD 680750
Apt 11.09.1840; 10053a (10052); Map 1841, 6 chns, in 4 parts, by J. Watson, Lancaster, (includes one part at 4 chns, 1840, by Hodgson and Watson, Lancaster, partly resurveyed and partly copied from old plans, and 18-chn index); foot/b'way, turnpike roads, toll gate, woods (col), building names, school, chapel, quarries, sheepfold, watering

place, well, cotton mill, corn mill, spring, caves; legend on 4-chn part explains some symbols.

43/401 Thorp Arch (parish) SE 433464 [Thorpe Arch]
Apt 30.06.1842; 1607a (1607); Map 1842, 9 chns, (including 3-chn enlargement of 'ings'); woods, flint mill, well, ford, hall, weir.

43/402 Thorpe (township in parish of Rothwell) SE 315271 [Thorpe on the Hill]
Apt 29.06.1839; 534a (534); Map 1839, 3 chns, by Wm Wordsworth, Blackgates; foot/b'way, woods, parkland, fences, building names, road names, boundary stone, quarry, ownerships (col); north pointer has plumes.

43/403 Thorpe in Balne (township in parish of Barmby Dun) SE 600100
Apt 09.02.1844; 1507a (1507); Map 1848, 6 chns, by J. Alexander, Doncaster; hill-drawing, waterbodies, woods, osiers (by symbol), building names, embankment, ford, ferry, tithe-free areas (green); bridge named.

43/404 Thorpe Salvin (parish) SK 531807
Apt 31.05.1848; 2198a (2180); Map 1848, 8 chns; railway, waterbodies, woods, building names, canal with towpath, mill.

43/405 Thorpe Underwood (township in parish of Little Ouseburn) SE 470595
Apt 06.05.1846; 2185a (2185); Map 1846, 8 chns; waterbodies, woods, field boundary ownerships.

43/406 Threshfield (township in parish of Linton) SD 970640
Apt 09.07.1846; 2643a (2644); Map 1843, 3 chns, 1st cl, in 2 parts, by Ordnance Survey; construction lines, trig points (named), waterbodies, houses, gardens, rock outcrops, field gates, building names, limestone limekilns (by symbol), quarries, water troughs, cave, draw wells, wells, pound, milestone, school, weir, corn mill, footstick, moor.

43/407 Throapham and Thwaites (townships in parishes of Laughton-en-le-Morthen and St John's) SK 536876
Apt 31.12.1840; 1044a (all); Map 1841, 6 chns; waterbodies, woods (named), building names, common.

43/408 Thrybergh (parish) SK 467953
Apt 30.07.1839; 1623a (1624); Map 1840, 4 chns, by Wm Bingley; foot/b'way, right of bridle road, turnpike roads, waterbodies, woods, parkland, building names, spring, weir, ice house, summer house, stables, kennels, ferry, cross (by symbol), lodge, quarry, old mill, blacking mill; cartouche is decorated with acorns and oak leaves.

43/409 Thurnscoe (parish) SE 459063
Apt 30.07.1839; 1665a (1665); Map 1842, 4 chns, by Edwd Micklethwait, Architect and Surveyor, Barnsley; foot/b'way, waterbodies, woods (named), orchards, building names, road names, rectory, shed; legend explains that tithable land is green, abbey land is pink, glebe is blue and tithe-free land is uncoloured.

43/410 Tickhill (parish) SK 595935
Apt 31.01.1848; 6514a (6514); Map 'made in 1848', 6 chns, by Henry Ellison, Stone, (tithable parts only in detail); foot/b'way, waterbodies, woods, building names, castle yard, quarries, paper mill, tithe-free lands (col) are edged green.

43/411 Tinsley (township in parish of Rotherham) SK 400900
Apt 29.07.1847; 164a (1623); Map 1849, 8 chns, (tithable parts only); wood (named), canal; some isolated fields connected to the rest by a road are mapped at 5 chns; no buildings are shown.

43/412 Todwick (parish) SK 491848
Apt 27.09.1849; 42a (1860); Map 1851?, 6 chns, by Geo. Sanderson, Mansfield, (tithable parts only, tinted); foot/b'way, woods (col), field acreages.

43/413 Tong (township in parish of Birstal) SE 210308
Apt 29.02.1848; 837a (2644); Map 1848, 6 chns, by W. Wordsworth, Black Gates, (tithable parts only); woods, road names.

43/414 Treeton and Wales (township and manor in parish of Treeton) SK 439880
Apt 05.05.1838; 1523a (1573); Map 1838, 6 chns, in 2 parts; railway, canal, woods (col, named), building names, field boundary ownership; meaning of colours is unclear; pecked lines are used within ownerships and dot-dash lines between them.

43/415 Trumfleet (township in parish of Kirk Sandall) SE 602117
Apt 19.12.1840; 473a (all); Map 1841?, 3 chns; foot/b'way, houses, woods; the meaning of the colours is unclear.

43/416 Ulleskelf (township in parish of Kirkby Wharf) SE 521389
Apt 14.11.1843; 1300a (1299); Map 1844, 6 chns, in 4 parts, (including three 3-chn enlargements of detail); railway, woods, parkland, orchards, dyke (named), drains.

43/417 Waddington (township in parish of Mitton) SD 724448
Apt 24.04.1850; 1269a (1800); Map 1851, 6 chns; foot/b'way, waterbodies, woods, parkland, well, churchyard, weir, footbridge; one owner, 'Mr. F. Leach', who is also the tithe valuer, is named; it is unclear why some buildings are black and some are red.

43/418 Wakefield (township in parish of Wakefield) SE 336208
Apt 30.01.1845; 441a (630); Map 1845, 4 chns, by W. Wordsworth, Blackgates, (tithable parts only in detail); railways with station, foot/b'way, waterbodies, woods, gardens, house of correction, gas works, mills, market place; public and prominent buildings are grey; other buildings are hatched.

43/419 Walkingham Hill with Ockany (township in parish of Knaresbrough) SE 350618
Apt 29.06.1839; 423a (422); Map 1839, 8 chns, by James Powell, Knaresborough, Yorks, (tinted); woods, field boundary ownership.

43/420 Walton (parish) SE 446480
Apt 15.06.1841; 965a (1670); Map 1842, 9 chns, by Henry R. Spence, York; waterbodies, woods.

43/421 Walton (township in parish of Sandal Magna) SE 364165
Apt 31.01.1844; 327a (1810); Map 1844, 3 chns, in 2 parts, by W. Wordsworth, Blackgates, (tithable parts only); railway with tunnel mouth and viaduct, canal with towpath and locks, foot/b'way, waterbodies, woods, orchards, gardens, fences.

43/422 Warmfield cum Heath (township in parish of Warmfield) SE 368205
Apt 30.06.1840; 1333a (1492); Map 1840, 6 chns; railway, foot/b'way, waterbodies, woods, open fields, canal with towpath and locks, commons (col), wastes (col); pictorial church; meaning of grey band and of shading on common is unclear.

43/423 Warmsworth (parish) SE 547005
Apt 27.05.1840; 1043a (1042); Map 1838, 6 chns, by J. Alexander, Doncaster; hill-drawing, foot/b'way, turnpike roads, waterbodies, woods, parkland, open fields (named), ferry, mill, quarries, lime kilns, ownerships (col). Apt omits land use.

43/424 Wath upon Dearne (parish) SK 420999 [Wath Upon Dearne]
Apt 20.02.1841; 11818a (10709); Map 1842, 4 chns, in 14 parts, ? by Richard Birks and William Bingley, (including one 3-chn and one 1-chn enlargement of detail and 24-chn index); railway, waggonway, foot/b'way, turnpike roads, canal with locks, earthworks and tunnel, woods, parkland, gardens, heath/moor, building names, road names, quarries, steel works, potteries, iron works, chapels, churchyard, school, vicarage, menagerie, lodges, stables and training ground, pyramid, fish pond, greenhouse, temple; pictorial church.

43/425 Weston (township in parish of Weston) SE 185484
Apt 04.09.1845; 98a (1372); Map 1847, 4 chns, (tithable parts only, tinted); plantations, avenue of trees, field acreages.

43/426 Westwick (township in parish of Ripon) SE 351665
Apt 25.10.1842; 411a (all); Map 1843, 6 chns; foot/b'way, waterbodies, woods, osiers (by symbol), hauling path, locks, weir; compass rose boss has oak leaf decoration.

43/427 Wetherby (township in parish of Spofforth) SE 413487
Apt 24.05.1838; 1571a (1570); Map 1838, 3 chns, 1st cl, by James Powell, Knaresborough, (tinted); foot/b'way, turnpike roads, waterbodies, woods, building names, road names, mill, weir, limestone quarries, gravel hole, cattle market.

43/428 Whiston (township in parish of Whiston and Rotherham) SK 452903
Apt 04.05.1847; 60a (3190); Map 1849, 3 chns, in 2 parts, by T. Parkinson, Rotherham, (tithable parts only); waterbodies, houses, woods, building names, field acreages, field boundary ownerships.

43/429 Whitcliffe with Thorpe (township in parish of Ripon) SE 300690
Apt 18.01.1840; 1205a (all); Map 1839, 8 chns, in 2 parts, by John Humphries, Ripon, (one part at 6 chns); woods, canal with towpath and locks; colouring of fields is ornamental.

43/430 Whitgift (township in parish of Whitgift) SE 812212
Apt 28.05.1845; 1181a (1309); Map 1846, 6 chns, by M. Durham, Thorne, (tithable parts only, tinted); foot/b'way, waterbodies, woods, open fields, river embankment.

43/431 Lower Whitley (township in parish of Thornhill) SE 227171 [Whitley Lower]
Apt 08.04.1846; 1012a (1011); Map 1849, 3 chns, by J. Thompson, Leeds; foot/b'way, woods, plantations, mill.

43/432 Whitwood (township in parish of Featherstone) SE 410252
Apt 14.04.1842; 1046a (1045); Map 1842, 4 chns, by Henry Teal and Son, Leeds; railway, foot/b'way, turnpike roads, waterbodies, woods, orchards, fences, pottery, ox-bow lakes, dam, windmill, mill, toll bar.

43/433 Widdington (township in parish of Little Ouseburn) SE 492596 [Not listed]
Apt 12.03.1846; 41a (650); Map 1846, 8 chns, (tithable parts only); woods.

43/434 Wigglesworth (township in parish of Long Preston) SD 800565
Apt 21.10.1839; 4090a (4089); Map 1840, 6 chns, in 2 parts, by John Greenwood, Gisburn, (includes 3-chn enlargement of detail); foot/b'way, waterbodies, houses, farmyards, woods (col), parkland, common meadow strips, hedge ownership, ownerships (col), field gates, building names, barns, school, tithe barn, pencil test-lines; legend explains symbols, including embankments (by hill-drawing), stone and foot bridges, stone walls, hedges with and without trees, quarries, and (by Dawson's symbols) water mills and smithies.

43/435 Wike (township in parish of Birstal) SE 155267
Apt 29.02.1848; 921a (920); Map 1848, 3 chns; railway, foot/b'way, turnpike roads and gate, waterbodies, woods, building names, road names, public watering place, wells, stiles, chapel, mill; border has black and white lozenge pattern.

43/436 Wike (township in parishes of Harewood and Bardsey) SE 333420
Apt 18.01.1840; 879a (880); Map 1839, 3 chns; woods, residual open fields, field gates, parish boundary.

43/437 Wilsden (township in parish of Bradford) SE 083360
Apt 03.03.1849; 2333a (2450); Map 1850, 6 chns, 'Copied' by E.W. Coen; hill-drawing, foot/b'way, turnpike roads, waterbodies, woods, building names, dam, common.

43/438 Winksley (township in parish of Ripon) SE 247712
Apt 30.06.1843; 703a (703); Map 1844, 3 chns, by T. Robinson; foot/b'way, waterbodies, woods, gardens; stream named.

43/439 Winterset (township in parish of Wragby) SE 384158 [Wintersett]
Apt 31.05.1842; 692a (1052); Map 1843, 6 chns, by Richard Birks, Barnsley; foot/b'way, waterbodies, woods (col), plantations (col), orchards, gardens, reservoir, engine; title is stamped.

43/440 Wombwell (township in parish of Darfield) SE 395027
Apt 18.09.1838; 3521a (3557); Map not dated, 6 chns, ? by Richard Birks; canal, railway, waterbodies, woods (col), building names, mills.

43/441 Woodsetts (township in parish of Anston) SK 554835
Apt 31.01.1850; 808a (?); Map 1850, 6 chns, by Thomas Bradley and Son, Richmond, Yorks; woods, ownerships (col). Apt omits some land use.

43/442 Woolley (township in parish of Roystone) SE 320128
Apt 30.10.1839; 2570a (2569); Map 1842, 6 chns; foot/b'way, waterbodies, woods (named), plantations, parkland, road names, field names, mill, dam, ice house, lodge, holding boundaries (col), field boundary ownerships, field acreages, garden (by annotation).

43/443 Worsbrough (township in parish of Darfield) SE 351030
Apt 22.09.1838; 3594a (3594); Map 1839?, 6 chns, ? by Richard Birks; waggonway, foot/b'way, waterbodies, woods, building names, reservoir, avenue of trees.

43/444 Wortley (township in parish of Leeds) SE 277321
Apt 02.09.1846; 933a (1036); Map 1846, 3 chns; foot/b'way, turnpike roads, toll bar, woods, parkland, road names, old windmill, chapel, workhouse, jail; churches and public buildings are black, and not all are named; gaol is named, but no buildings are shown; hills named.

43/445 Wothersome (township in parish of Bardsey) SE 400425
Apt 12.12.1842; 660a (692); Map 1844, 6 chns, by John Howgate, Knaresborough; waterbodies, woods, building names, quarry.

43/446 Yeadon (township in parish of Guiseley) SE 202406
Apt 23.01.1838; 1648a (1660); Map 1838, 3 chns, by W.J. Jack, Leeds; foot/b'way, waterbodies, woods (col), building names, road names, quarries (col), windmill, Methodist Chapel, burial ground, toll gate, boundary stones, mill, dams, schools, corn mill, weir; it is unclear why certain areas are tinted.

Anglesey

PRO IR29 and IR30 44/1-74

76 tithe districts: 175,846 acres
74 tithe commutations: 165,547 acres
44 voluntary tithe agreements, 30 compulsory tithe awards

Tithe and tithe commutation

All but two of Anglesey's seventy-six tithe districts were subject to payment of tithes in 1836 and thirty-two districts were wholly tithable; the main cause of exemption elsewhere was the payment of a modus in lieu of tithes (Fig. 56).

Assistant tithe commissioners and local tithe agents who worked in Anglesey are listed in Table 44.1 and the valuers of tithe rent-charge in Table 44.2. In fifty-eight tithe districts (78 per cent) tithe was apportioned by holding, the highest proportion in England and Wales. As a result, there is very little information on the acreages, names and land uses of individual fields in the schedules of tithe apportionment. Indeed, Anglesey tithe surveys are the most impoverished of any county in terms of the data which they contain.

Tithe maps

The tithe mapping of Anglesey is dominated by the work of John R. Haslam of Menai Bridge who produced sixty-two maps covering 82 per cent of the county by area. They are maps of austere uniformity, are all at the eight-chain scale, and have a minimal content comprising only roads and holding boundaries. Buildings are either not shown at all or by uncased red blocks. Churches are not rendered in plan but simply located by crosses. Haslam was a former Ordnance Survey employee who had worked on small-scale mapping in Britain and his work often looks like an enlargement of the skeleton of a topographical map; it is certainly in marked contrast to the work of Doull in Kent or Galland in Suffolk who had both worked on the large-scale survey in Ireland and made a substantial contribution to the total of English first-class tithe maps. Neither Haslam nor anyone else made a first-class map in Anglesey. Apart from woodland on twelve maps, there are hardly any indications of land use on Anglesey tithe maps. A few maps have colour bands to indicate ownership boundaries and a few windmills are shown by pictorial symbols.

Although the Anglesey maps are so uninformative, the uniformity of scale and content suggests that a majority, certainly those by Haslam, are the result of new surveys. Haslam's

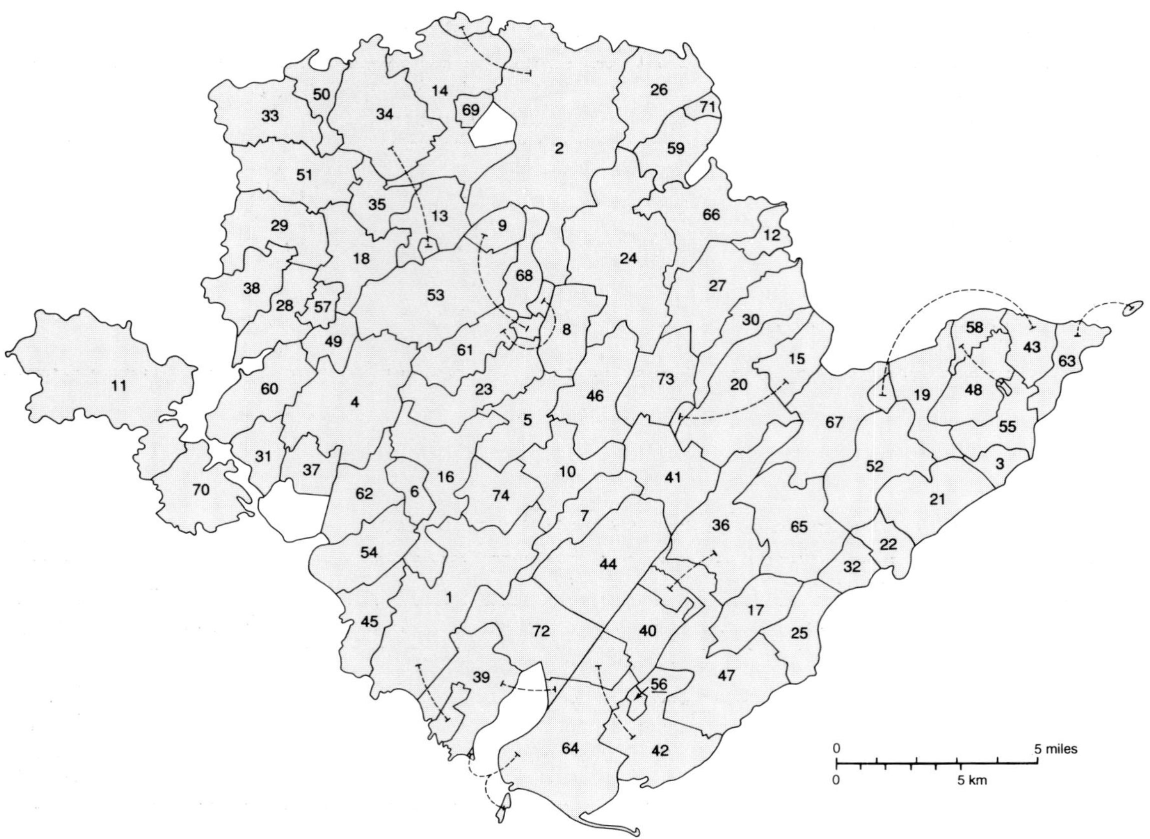

Fig. 56 Anglesey: tithe district boundaries.

maps are almost devoid of decoration, though one has a Greek vase decorating the north pointer and some other map-makers used north pointers decorated with diadems and Prince of Wales's feathers.

Table 44.1. *Agreements and awards for commutation of tithes in Anglesey*

Assistant commissioner/ local tithe agent	*Number of agreements**	*Number of awards*
John Fenton	42	0
Aneurin Owen	13	29
John Pickering	0	1

*Computed from the number of extant reports on tithe agreements in the tithe files [PRO IR 18].

Table 44.2. *Tithe valuers and tithe map-makers in Anglesey*

Name and address (in Anglesey unless indicated)	*Number of districts*	*Acreage*
Tithe valuers		
John R. Haslam, Menai Bridge	62	135,055
William Williams, Holyhead	8	20,337
Others [4]	4	10,155
Attributed tithe map-makers		
John R. Haslam, Menai Bridge	62	136,590
R. Lloyd Ellis, Carnarvon	4	9,221

Table 44.3. *The tithe maps of Anglesey: scales and classes*

Scale in chains/inch	*All maps*		*First Class*		*Second Class*	
	Number	*Acreage*	*Number*	*Acreage*	*Number*	*Acreage*
3	1	166	0	0	1	166
6	3	11,246	0	0	3	11,246
8	69	151,244	0	0	69	151,244
18	1	2,891	0	0	1	2,891
TOTAL	74	165,547	0	0	74	165,547

Table 44.4. *The tithe maps of Anglesey: dates*

	1839	*1840*	*1841*	*1842*	*1843*	*1844*	*1845*	*1846*	*1847*	*1848*	*1849*	*1850*
2nd class	4	12	13	4	6	10	8	7	6	1	0	3

Anglesey

44/1 Aberffraw (parish) SH 370713
Apt 29.12.1843; 6115a (6252); Map 1845?, 8 chns, ? by John R. Haslam; not all roads appear to be shown. District is apportioned by holding and fields are not shown.

44/2 Amlwch (parish) SH 429934
Apt 08.11.1841; 9221a (all); Map 1841?, 8 chns, ? by John R. Haslam; built-up part generalised. District is apportioned by holding and fields are not shown.

44/3 Beaumaris (parish) SH 593760
Apt 11.04.1844; 441a (1220); Map 1845, 8 chns, by John R. Haslam; castle ruins; built-up part not mapped. District is apportioned by holding and fields are not shown.

44/4 Bodedern (parish) SH 345802
Apt 28.11.1840; 4236a (4235); Map 1840, 8 chns; waterbodies; north pointer has diadem, Prince of Wales' feathers and 'Ich Dien'. Apt omits land use and some field names.

44/5 Bodwrog (parish) SH 405787
Apt 12.05.1843; 1814a (all); Map 1843?, 8 chns, ? by John R. Haslam. District is apportioned by holding and fields are not shown.

44/6 Ceirchiog (parish) SH 359758 [Not listed]
Apt 04.05.1844; 613a (613); Map 1845?, 8 chns, ? by John R. Haslam. District is apportioned by holding and fields are not shown.

44/7 Cerrigceinwen (parish) SH 430746
Apt 05.02.1842; 1582a (all); Map 1842?, 8 chns, ? by John R. Haslam. District is apportioned by holding and fields are not shown.

44/8 Coedana (parish) SH 429822
Apt 02.03.1840; 1628a (all); Map 1840?, 8 chns, ? by John R. Haslam. District is apportioned by holding and fields are not shown.

44/9 Gwredog (parochial chapelry) SH 404864
Apt 31.05.1842; 936a (936); Map 1840, 6 chns, by R. Lloyd Ellis, Carnarvon; field boundary ownerships, landowners, holding boundaries (col). District is apportioned by holding; Apt generalises land use.

44/10 Heneglwys (parish) SH 422761
Apt 05.02.1842; 2063a (all); Map 1842?, 8 chns, ? by John R. Haslam; waterbodies. District is apportioned by holding and fields are not shown.

44/11 Holyhead (parish) SH 240810 [Holyhead or Caergybi]
Apt 30.11.1840; 6048a (?); Map 1840, 6 chns; waterbodies, woods, gardens, windmill. Apt omits land use and some field names.

44/12 Llanallgo (parish) SH 505855
Apt 31.10.1845; 659a (659); Map 1846?, 8 chns, ? by John R. Haslam. District is apportioned by holding and fields are not shown.

44/13 Llanbado (parish) SH 377870
Apt 08.07.1841; 1743a (all); Map 1841?, 8 chns, by John R. Haslam; farm names. District is apportioned by holding and fields are not shown.

44/14 Llanbadrig (parish) SH 380920
Apt 15.02.1844; 4098a (4097); Map 1841, 8 chns, by John R. Haslam. District is apportioned by holding and fields are not shown.

44/15 Llanbedrgoch (parish) SH 515805
Apt 30.06.1841; 1486a (all); Map 1841, 8 chns, by John R. Haslam; very few buildings are shown. District is apportioned by holding and fields are not shown.

44/16 Llanbeulan (parish) SH 372755 [Not shown]
Apt 04.05.1844; 2944a (2943); Map 1845?, 8 chns, ? by John R. Haslam; chapel. District is apportioned by holding and fields are not shown.

44/17 Llanddaniel (parish) SH 495702 [Llandaniel Fab]
Apt 13.10.1841; 1680a (1679); Map 1844, 8 chns, ? by John R. Haslam; waterbodies.

44/18 Llanddausaint (parish) SH 345853 [Llanddeusant]
Apt 15.06.1841; 2012a (all); Map 1841?, 8 chns, ? by John R. Haslam; very few buildings are shown. District is apportioned by holding and fields are not shown.

44/19 Llanddona (parish) SH 563793
Apt 04.07.1846; 1918a (?); Map 1847?, 8 chns, ? by John R. Haslam; very few buildings are shown. District is partly apportioned by holding; Apt omits land use.

44/20 Llanddyfnan (parish) SH 490790
Apt 30.06.1841; 3481a (all); Map 1844, 8 chns, by John R. Haslam. Apt omits some field names.

44/21 Llandegfan (parish) SH 571745
Apt 11.04.1844; 2232a (2760); Map 1845?, 8 chns, by John R. Haslam. District is apportioned by holding and fields are not shown.

44/22 Llandesilio (parish) SH 550727 [Not listed]
Apt 02.06.1842; 828a (all); Map 1843?, 8 chns, by John R. Haslam. District is apportioned by holding and fields are not shown.

44/23 Llandrygarn (parish) SH 390797 [Not listed]
Apt 22.02.1840; 2431a (all); Map 1841?, 8 chns, ? by John R. Haslam. District is apportioned by holding and fields are not shown.

44/24 Llandyfrydog and Llanfihangel Trer Beirrd (parish) SH 449853
Apt 23.05.1840; 5390a (all); Map 1840, 8 chns, in 2 parts, by John R. Haslam; windmill (pictorial). District is apportioned by holding and fields are not shown.

44/25 Llanedwen (parish) SH 512692 [Not listed]
Apt 13.10.1841; 1599a (1939); Map 1844, 8 chns, by John R. Haslam; quarry; yellow bands may show property ownerships.

44/26 Llaneilian (district in parish of Llaneilian) SH 468916
Apt 16.02.1847; 1906a (1905); Map 1847?, 8 chns, ? by John R. Haslam; map includes Rhos-y-mynach (44/71), without tithe area numbers. District is apportioned by holding and fields are not shown.

44/27 Llaneugrad (parish) SH 486837 [Not listed]
Apt 26.10.1846; 2695a (2695); Map 1847?, 8 chns, ? by John R. Haslam. District is apportioned by holding and fields are not shown.

44/28 Llanvachraeth (parish) SH 315835 [Llanfachraeth]
Apt 20.08.1845; 1498a (1887); Map 1846?, 8 chns, by John R. Haslam. District is apportioned by holding and fields are not shown.

44/29 Llanfaethly (parish) SH 312871 [Llanfaethlu]
Apt 21.11.1840; 2400a (all); Map 1840, 8 chns, by R. Lloyd Ellis, Carnarvon; plantations, gardens; north pointer has diadem and Prince of Wales' feathers. Apt omits land use and field names.

44/30 Llanfairmathaferneithaf (parish) SH 500822 [Not listed]
Apt 30.06.1841; 1914a (all); Map 1842?, 8 chns, by John R. Haslam; cliffs; colours may show property ownerships. District is apportioned by holding, though some fields are numbered separately; Apt omits land use.

44/31 Llanfairyneubwll (parish) SH 299779
Apt 26.02.1840; 1060a (all); Map 1841?, 8 chns; waterbodies, building names; colours may show property ownerships. Apt omits land use and field names.

44/32 Llanfairpwllgwyngyll (parish) SH 538718
Apt 02.06.1842; 853a (all); Map 1843?, 8 chns, by John R. Haslam. District is apportioned by holding and fields are not shown.

44/33 Llanfairynghornwy (parish) SH 310918
Apt 24.09.1842; 2136a (2135); Map 1841, 8 chns, by John R. Haslam; building names. District is apportioned by holding and fields are not shown.

44/34 Llanfechell (parish) SH 359912
Apt 23.12.1842; 3638a (3637); Map 1843?, 8 chns, ? by John R. Haslam; waterbodies, cliffs; Llanddugwell chapelry is tinted pale green. District is apportioned by holding and fields are not shown.

44/35 Llanfflewyn (parish) SH 353878
Apt 15.06.1841; 1266a (all); Map 1841?, 8 chns, by John R. Haslam; building colouring is problematic. District is apport-ioned by holding and fields are not shown.

44/36 Llanfihangel Esgeifiog and Llanffinan (parish and chapelry) SH 482735 [Not listed]
Apt 27.01.1844; 4156a (4156); Map 1841, 8 chns, in 2 parts, ? by John R. Haslam; foot/b'way, windmill (pictorial). District is apportioned by holding and fields are not shown.

44/37 Llanfihangelynhowyn (parish) SH 320771 [Llanfihangel yn Nhowyn]
Apt 02.03.1840; 1074a (all); Map 1841?, 8 chns; waterbodies (named); colours may show property ownerships. Apt omits land use and field names.

44/38 Llanfwrog (parish) SH 301846
Apt 21.11.1840; 1623a (all); Map 1840, 8 chns, by R. Lloyd Ellis, Carnarvon; waterbodies; north pointer has diadem and Prince of Wales' feathers. Apt omits land use and some field names.

44/39 Llangadwaladr and Llanfeirian or Egwysael (parishes) SH 385689
Apt 12.06.1843; 3489a (4718); Map 1844?, 8 chns, ? by J.R. Haslam; building names; north pointer has Greek-vase decoration. District is apportioned by holding and fields are not shown.

44/40 Llangaffo (parish) SH 451699
Apt 10.10.1839; 1590a (all); Map 1839, 8 chns, by John R. Haslam, Eirianallt, Gwyndy, Anglesey; building names, ownership boundaries (col). District is apportioned by holding and fields are not shown.

44/41 Llangefni (parish) SH 465765
Apt 24.01.1843; 2427a (all); Map 1843?, 8 chns, ? by John R. Haslam. District is apportioned by holding and fields are not shown.

44/42 Llangeinwen (parish) SH 452653 [Not listed]
Apt 05.09.1839; 4488a (5388); Map 1840?, 8 chns, by John R. Haslam, Erianallt; building names, sandbanks (named), ownership boundaries (col). District is apportioned by holding and fields are not shown.

44/43 Llangoed (parish) SH 610807
Apt 09.03.1849; 1344a (1343); Map 1850?, 8 chns, in 2 parts, ? by John R. Haslam. District is apportioned by holding and fields are not shown.

44/44 Llangristiolus (parish) SH 439729
Apt 19.08.1841; 3937a (all); Map 1840, 8 chns, by John R. Haslam; building names, windmill (pictorial), ownership boundaries (col). District is apportioned by holding and fields are not shown.

44/45 Llangwyfan (parish) SH 337709 [Not listed]
Apt 02.11.1839; 1747a (1828); Map 1839, 8 chns, by John R. Haslam, by Gwyndy, Anglesey; field boundary ownerships, building names, boundary stones, ownerships (col), 'Rocks and Sands', 'Rocks below Vegetation'; colour bands may show holdings. District is apportioned by holding and fields are not shown.

44/46 Llangwyllog (parish) SH 436795
Apt 23.07.1847; 913a (2301); Map 1847?, 8 chns, by John R. Haslam. District is apportioned by holding and fields are not shown.

44/47 Llanidan (parish) SH 475680 [Not listed]
Apt 13.10.1841; 4262a (4645); Map 1844?, 6 chns, by R. Lloyd Ellis, Carnarvon.

44/48 Llaniestin (parish) SH 588794 [Not listed]
Apt 09.03.1849; 1664a (1663); Map 1850, 8 chns, by John R. Haslam. District is apportioned by holding and fields are not shown.

44/49 Llanllibio (parish) SH 332822 [Not listed]
Apt 01.12.1843; 827a (826); Map 1846?, 8 chns, ? by John R. Haslam. District is apportioned by holding and fields are not shown.

44/50 Llanrhwydrys (parish) SH 336920 [Not listed]
Apt 21.02.1840; 1144a (all); Map 1839, 8 chns, by John R. Haslam, Eirianallt, Gwyndy, Anglesey; building names, ownership boundaries (col). District is apportioned by holding and fields are not shown.

44/51 Llanrhyddlad (parish) SH 325892
Apt 30.06.1843; 2585a (all); Map 1843?, 8 chns, by John R. Haslam. District is apportioned by holding and fields are not shown.

44/52 Llansadwrn (parish) SH 550760
Apt 13.02.1840; 2891a (2891); Map 1840?, 18 chns; water-bodies, holdings (col). District is apportioned by holding and fields are not shown.

44/53 Llantrisaint (parish) SH 374834 [Llantrisant]
Apt 01.12.1843; 4447a (4447); Map 1844, 8 chns, by John R. Haslam; District is apportioned by holding and fields are not shown.

44/54 Llanvaeloy (parish) SH 342735 [Llanfaelog]
Apt 04.05.1844; 2302a (2732); Map 1845?, 8 chns, by John R. Haslam. District is apportioned by holding and fields are not shown.

44/55 Llanvaes (parish) SH 600777 [Llanfaes]
Apt 23.07.1847; 675a (2297); Map 1847?, 8 chns, ? by John R. Haslam. District is apportioned by holding and fields are not shown.

44/56 Llanvair yn y cymwd (parish) SH 448668 [Not listed]
Apt 13.10.1841; 166a (166); Map 1845?, 3 chns.

44/57 Llanvigael (parish) SH 329835 [Llanfigael]
Apt 15.10.1845; 485a (484); Map 1846, 8 chns, by John R. Haslam. District is apportioned by holding and fields are not shown.

44/58 Llanvihangel din silwy (parish) SH 588815 [Not listed]
Apt 09.03.1849; 833a (833); Map 1850, 8 chns, by John R. Haslam. District is apportioned by holding and fields are not shown.

44/59 Llanwenllwyfo (parish) SH 477895 [Not listed]
Apt 18.04.1843; 1622a (all); Map 1842?, 8 chns, by John R. Haslam; map includes 44/71 Rhos-y-mynach, tinted, but not numbered. District is apportioned by holding and fields are not shown.

44/60 Llanynghenedl (parish) SH 300800
Apt 20.08.1845; 2360a (2965); Map 1846?, 8 chns, by John R. Haslam. District is apportioned by holding and fields are not shown.

44/61 Llechcynvarwy (parish) SH 385815 [Llechcynfarwy]
Apt 01.01.1844; 1965a (1964); Map 1844, 8 chns, by John R. Haslam. District is apportioned by holding and fields are not shown.

44/62 Llechylched (parish) SH 340760 [Not listed]
Apt 04.05.1844; 1783a (1783); Map 1845, 8 chns, by John R. Haslam; old and new churches. District is apportioned by holding and fields are not shown.

44/63 Newborough (parish) SH 420655 [Niwbwrch or Newborough]
Apt 28.02.1845; 4305a (7410); Map 1846, 8 chns, by John R. Haslam; waterbodies. District is apportioned by holding and fields are not shown.

44/64 Penmon (parish) SH 624801
Apt 23.07.1847; 428a (7180); Map 1847, 8 chns, by John R. Haslam; quarry, island. District is apportioned by holding and fields are not shown.

44/65 Penmynydd (parish) SH 519739
Apt 13.09.1843; 3153a (all); Map 1844?, 8 chns, by John R. Haslam; hill-drawing.

44/66 Penrhos Llugwy (parish) SH 487866 [Rhos Lligwy]
Apt 11.10.1845; 350a (2894); Map 1846, 8 chns, by John R. Haslam; few buildings are shown. District is apportioned by holding and fields are not shown.

44/67 Pentraeth (parish) SH 529781
Apt 30.06.1841; 2984a (all); Map 1844?, 8 chns, ? by John R. Haslam.

44/68 Rhodyeidio (parish) SH 411851 [Not listed]
Apt 01.01.1844; 1004a (1003); Map 1844, 8 chns, by John R. Haslam. District is apportioned by holding and fields are not shown.

44/69 Rhosbeirio (parish or parochial chapelry) SH 394914
Apt 10.02.1841; 369a (all); Map 1840, 8 chns, by John R. Haslam;

holding boundaries (col). District is apportioned by holding and fields are not shown.

44/70 Rhoscolyn (parish) SH 273759 [Rhos Mynach]
Apt 23.05.1840; 2195a (all); Map 1841?, 8 chns; waterbodies, plantations, marsh/bog (col), rock outcrops, building names, foreshore sand; colours may show holdings. Apt omits land use.

44/71 Rhos y mynach (district in parishes of Llanwenllwyfo and Llaneilian) SH 487910
Apt 29.03.1848; 494a (493); Map 1848?, 8 chns, by John R. Haslam. District is apportioned by holding and fields are not shown.

44/72 Trefdraeth (parish) SH 410700
Apt 10.02.1841; 3135a (all); Map 1840, 8 chns, by John R. Haslam; coal works, embankment, farm names; colours may show property ownerships. District is apportioned by holding and fields are not shown.

44/73 Tregayan (parish) SH 463800 [Tregaian]
Apt 10.09.1839; 2066a (2066); Map 1839?, 8 chns; waterbodies, mill; very few buildings are shown. District is apportioned by holding and fields are not shown.

44/74 Trewalchmai (parish or chapelry) SH 398754 [Gwalchmai]
Apt 24.02.1840; 1701a (all); Map 1841?, 8 chns, by John R. Haslam; the only building shown is the church. District is apportioned by holding and fields are not shown.

Breconshire

PRO IR29 and IR30 45/1-82

82 tithe districts: 478,096 acres
81 tithe commutations: 428,120 acres
63 voluntary tithe agreements, 18 compulsory tithe awards

Tithe and tithe commutation

All but one of the tithe districts of Breconshire were subject to payment of tithes in 1836 and forty-two were wholly tithable (Fig. 57). The two main causes of tithe exemption in Breconshire were modus payments in lieu of tithes (affecting 31 per cent of districts) and exemption of some woodland (in 27 per cent of districts).

Assistant tithe commissioners and local tithe agents who worked in Breconshire are listed in Table 45.1 and the valuers of tithe rent-charge in Table 45.2. In five districts tithe rent-charge was apportioned by holding and for these districts and for a number of others apportioned by field, property and field names and land-use information are absent from the schedules of apportionment.

Tithe maps

Breconshire is outstanding in Wales in that 12 per cent of its eighty-one tithe maps are sealed as first class (Table 45.3). In the whole of Wales (excluding Monmouthshire) only 2.3 per cent of maps achieved this distinction. No second-class map carries construction lines and it is possible that most of the remainder of the county's maps were compiled from earlier surveys. Indeed, the most prolific map-maker in the county, William Jones of Brecon, often acknowledges this fact. A good example of his style is the map of St Davids, an acknowledged compilation.

Breconshire tithe maps are drawn at a variety of scales from one inch to three chains to one inch to twenty-four chains. About a fifth of all the maps are in the recommended scale range of one inch to three to four chains, but 62 per cent are at the six- or eight-chain scales (Table 45.3). The Public Record Office collection includes both manuscript and lithographed versions of the map of Aberyskir. As usual in upland England and Wales, Breconshire tithe maps are satisfactory as records of woodland (on 78 per cent of the maps) but contain very little information on other land uses.

Breconshire tithe maps are as a whole plain rather than decorative, though six have borders which are more than purely functional. On the map of Llanwithol the scale is set

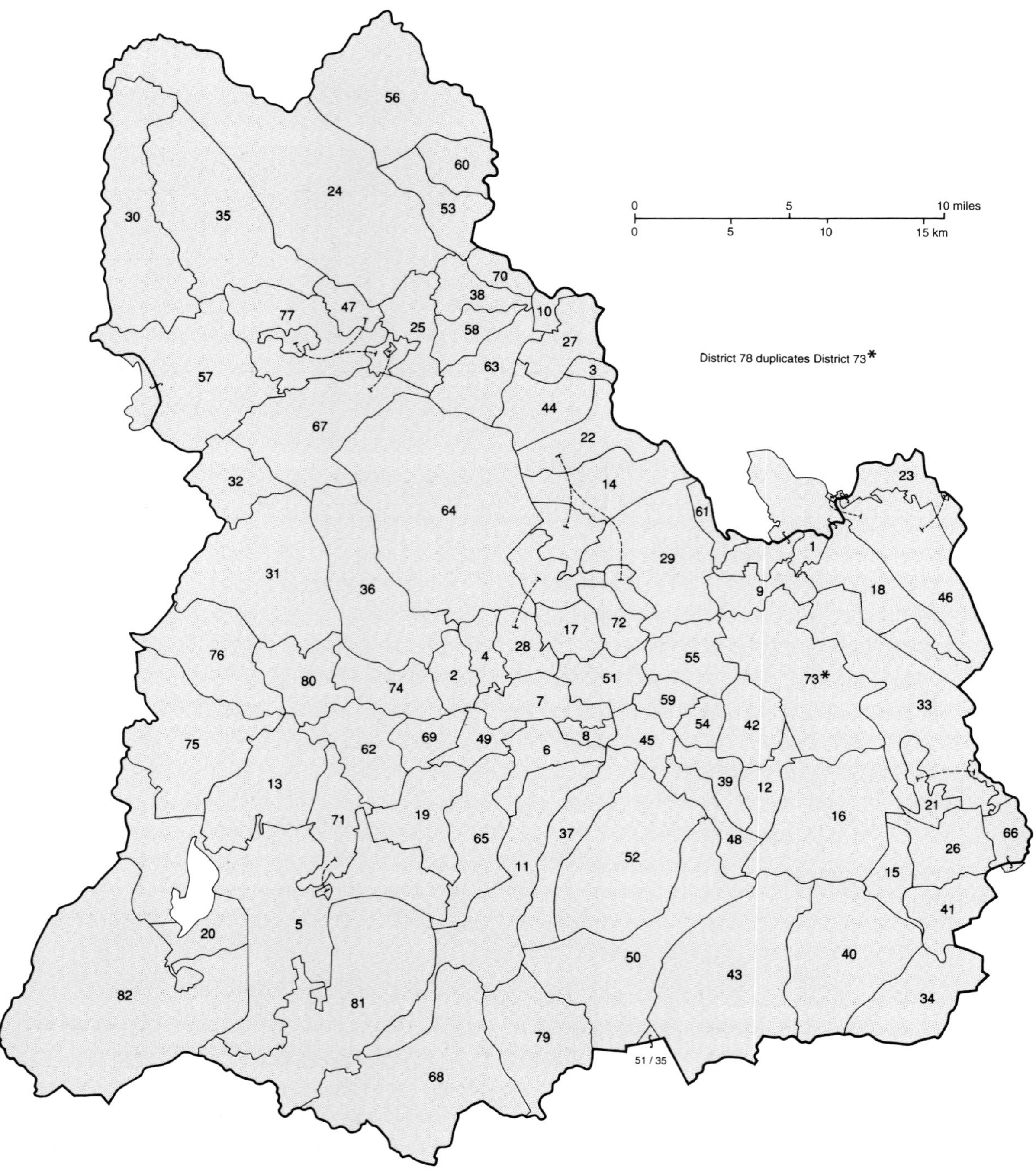

Fig. 57 Breconshire: tithe district boundaries.

into the border and on that of Glyn the direction pointer is a figure of a man in a tall hat with outstretched arms. Rather fewer north pointers have Prince of Wales's feathers than on tithe maps of districts further north in Wales.

Table 45.1. *Agreements and awards for commutation of tithes in Breconshire*

Assistant commissioner/ local tithe agent	*Number of agreements**	*Number of awards*
Thomas Hoskins	52	0
John Johnes	8	15
Aneurin Owen	0	2
Tithe Commissioners	0	1

*Computed from the number of extant reports on tithe agreements in the tithe files [PRO IR 18].

Table 45.2. *Tithe valuers and tithe map-makers in Breconshire*

Name and address (in Breconshire unless indicated)	*Number of districts*	*Acreage*
Tithe valuers		
William Jones, Brecon	20	100,677
Morris Sayce, Kington, Herefordshire	13	79,533
Evan Jones Griffiths, Llandilo, Carmarthenshire	10	27,389
William Powell, Pantycorred	7	44,846
William Fosbrooke, Hereford	7	32,234
Others [13]	24	143,431
Attributed tithe map-makers		
William Jones, Brecon	17	107,701
Morris Sayce, Kington, Herefordshire	14	86,846
Evan Jones Griffiths, Llandilo, Carmarthenshire	14	43,773
Thomas Bate, Brecon	6	34,569
Others [10]	20	114,811

Table 45.3. *The tithe maps of Breconshire: scales and classes*

Scale in chains/inch	*All maps*		*First Class*		*Second Class*	
	Number	*Acreage*	*Number*	*Acreage*	*Number*	*Acreage*
3	12	46,353	9	42,196	3	4,157
4	5	20,836	1	13,909	4	6,927
6	20	50,877	0	0	20	50,877
8	30	181,709	0	0	30	181,709
<8	14	128,345	0	0	14	128,345
TOTAL	81	428,120	10	56,105	71	372,005

Table 45.4. *The tithe maps of Breconshire: dates*

	1837	*1838*	*1839*	*1840*	*1841*	*1842*	*1843*	*1844*	*1845*	*1846*	*1847*	*1848*	*1849*	*1850*
All maps	2	0	13	19	10	12	4	7	3	1	8	1	0	1
1st class	0	0	2	3	0	0	0	1	1	0	3	0	0	0
2nd class	2	0	11	16	10	12	4	6	2	1	5	1	0	1

Breconshire

45/1 Aberllunvey (parish) SO 175377 [Not listed]
Apt 27.08.1849; 605a (626); Map 1850, 6 chns, 'Mapped for J. Iveson Esqr' by Jno. Lewis, Glasbury; waterbodies, houses, woods, field boundary ownerships, building names, smithy, boundary tree, old forge.

45/2 Aberyskir (parish) SN 993312 [Aberyscir]
Apt 29.06.1837; 1918a (1918); Map 1837, 6 chns, by Bate of Brecon, Mineral and Land Surveyor; woods, building names, mill; scale is laid across north pointer, which has plumes; PRO IR 30 also contains a lithographed copy by Standidge of 1838.

45/3 Alltmawr (parish) SO 065475
Apt 27.10.1840; 499a (all); Map 1842, 6 chns, by E.I. Griffiths, Llandilo; waterbodies, woods, gardens.

45/4 Battle (parish) SO 009322
Apt 18.09.1845; 1544a (1544); Map 1847, 3 chns, by Geo. Taylor, Engineering Surveyor etc, Brecon; foot/b'way, waterbodies, woods, plantations, parkland, orchards, building names, kennel, boundary stone, weirs, chapel, glasshouses.

45/5 Great Forest of Brecon (district in parishes of Defynock, Llywell and Ystradfelty) SN 895185 [Not listed]
Apt 27.03.1841; 13948a (?); Map 1842?, 24 chns, in 2 parts, ? by Morris Sayce, (tithable parts only); railway, parish boundaries (col); streams named.

45/6 St Davids (parish) SO 035271 [Not listed]
Apt 05.11.1841; 2790a (2789); Map 1842, 8 chns, 'Compiled' by W. Jones, Brecon; hill-drawing, waterbodies, woods, plantations, building names, gaol, workhouse; green band surrounds 'College Parish', which is mapped but not numbered.

45/7 St John the Evangelist, Upper Division (district in parish of St John the Evangelist) SO 042295 [Not listed]
Apt 18.04.1839; 2932a (2932); Map 1840?, 9 chns, ? by Morris Sayce; hill-drawing, waterbodies, woods, building names, priory, tithe barn, ancient fortress, kennel; 'Map' in title is on 'cloud' background; colours show tithe-free lands; lake named. Apt omits land use and some field names.

45/8 St Mary (chapelry in parish of St John the Evangelist) SO 060280 [Not listed]
Apt 30.08.1838; 706a (705); Map 1839?, 4 chns, compiled by W. Jones, Brecon; railway, canal and towpath, woods, race course, barracks; built-up part generalised.

45/9 Bronllys (parish) SO 150356
Apt 11.03.1839; 2109a (2109); Map 1840?, 4 chns; open fields (residual), weir.

45/10 Builth (parish) SO 040505 [Builth Wells]
Apt 19.11.1840; 713a (712); Map 1842, 3 chns, in 2 parts, by E.J. Griffiths, Llandilo, (town also at 3 chns); hill-drawing, waterbodies, houses, woods, building names, old castle, toll bar.

45/11 Cantreff (parish) SO 025197 [Cantref]
Apt 30.08.1838; 8889a (all); Map 1839, 12 chns, 'Compiled' by W. Jones, Brecon; waterbodies, woods, pound, limekilns, boundary cairns; streams and hills named. Apt omits land use.

45/12 Cathedine (parish) SO 151253
Apt 18.04.1839; 1567a (all); Map 1839, 6 chns, 'Compiled' by W. Jones, High St, Brecon, (tithable parts only); foot/b'way, waterbodies, houses, woods, plantations, gardens, common.

45/13 Cray (district in parish of Defynnock) SN 900250 [Crai]
Apt 22.08.1840; 6975a (?); Map 1840, 8 chns, by Morris Sayce; woods, plantations, building names, site of old house, mill, quarry, turbary. Apt omits some land use and some field names.

45/14 Crickadarn (parish) SO 074400
Apt 21.01.1842; 4331a (4331); Map 1843, 8 chns; foot/b'way, waterbodies, woods, plantations, building names, mill, ring earthworks, common. Apt omits some field names.

45/15 Crickhowell (parish) SO 211208
Apt 27.12.1839; 1942a (all); Map 1844?, 3 chns, 1st cl, by W. Fosbrooke, Hereford; waterbodies, houses, field boundary ownerships, building names, forts, mill, well. Apt omits some land use and some field names.

45/16 St Michael, Cwmdu (parish) SO 180230 [Cwmdu]
Apt 01.09.1843; 10968a (all); Map 1845, 3 chns, 1st cl, in 2 parts, 'Map'd for Mr Wm Jones, Bellevue Place, Brecon' by John Lewis; waterbodies, houses, building names, boundary stones, mounds and trees, vicarage, chapel, springs. Apt omits most field names.

45/17 Garthbrengy (parish) SO 050336
Apt 25.11.1839; 2001a (2001); Map 1840, 6 chns, 'Compiled' by Wm Jones, Brecon; waterbodies, woods, building names, mill, common; north pointer has plumes.

45/18 Glasbury (parish) (partly in Radnorshire) SO 180391
Apt 28.10.1841; 9216a (9216); Map 1844?, 8 chns; waterbodies, houses, woods; a few fences are shown. Apt omits some field names.

45/19 Glyn (district in parish of Defynnock) SN 970240 [Not listed]
Apt 22.08.1840; 4169a (?); Map 1842, 8 chns, ? by Morris Sayce; woods, plantations, building names, chapel; buildings are shown in outline only, without fill; man in hat surmounts the north pointer and points to the four directions. Apt omits a few field names.

45/20 Glyn Tawe (hamlet in parish of Defynnock) SN 850130 [Glyntawe]
Apt 22.08.1840; 2682a (?); Map 1842, 4 chns, by W. and H. Williams, Land and Mineral Surveyors, Swansea; woods, building names. Apt omits land use and some field names.

45/21 Grwynefawr and Grwynefechan (district in parish of Talgarth) SO 236237 [Not listed]
Apt 18.07.1839; 1900a (all); Map 1840?, 3 chns; houses, building names, mill, chapel, holding boundaries (col); some buildings are without fill, and could be ruins. Apt omits some field names.

45/22 Gwenddwr (parish) SO 070440
Apt 17.11.1840; 8262a (8262); Map 1841, 9 chns, in 6 parts, 'Compiled' by William Jones, Bellevue Place, Brecon, (tithable parts only); houses, woods, plantations, orchards. Apt omits a few field names.

45/23 Hay (parish) SO 223407 [Hay-on-Wye]
Apt 21.03.1846; 2602a (all); Map 1847?, 6 chns; railway, building names.

45/24 Llanavanfaur (district in parish of Llanavanfaur) SN 930560 [Llanafan-fawr]
Apt 20.11.1840; 7971a (all); Map 1840, 8 chns, by E.I. Griffiths, Llandilo Fawr, (tithable parts only); woods, holdings (col).

45/25 Llanavanfechan (parish) SN 970500 [Llanfechan]
Apt 20.11.1840; 2283a (all); Map 1840, 6 chns, in 2 parts, by E.J. Griffiths, Llandilofawr, (tithable parts only); woods, plantations, ownerships (col).

45/26 Llanbedr (parish) SO 248215
Apt 28.07.1840; 3832a (all); Map 1839, 3 chns, 1st cl, surveyed for Wm Fosbrooke by L. Carey and M. Smith; construction lines, field boundary ownerships, building names, mill, sheep track, wells, boundary marks; there is a summary of acreages below the title; north pointer is of unusual pattern, with red trimming; some detail outside the district intersecting construction lines is shown. Apt omits a few field names.

45/27 Llanddewi'r Cwm (parish) SO 045487
Apt 01.11.1839; 3102a (3101); Map 1840, 3 chns, 1st cl, by W. Fosbrooke, Hereford; construction lines, hill-drawing, waterbodies, houses, rock outcrops, field boundary ownerships, building names, boundary trees, mill; lake named. Apt omits most field names.

45/28 Llandefailogfach (parish) SO 030329 [Llandefaelog]
Apt 28.10.1840; 4211a (all); Map surveyed February 1839, 8 chns, in 2 parts, by Bate of Brecon; hill-drawing, waterbodies, woods, building names, chapel. Apt omits a few field names.

45/29 Llandefalley (parish) SO 104370 [Llandefalle]
Apt 21.01.1842; 8509a (8509); Map 1843, 6 chns; waterbodies (col), woods, plantations, building names, rectory, mills. Apt has some cropping information, but omits most field names.

45/30 Llandewi Abergwessin (parish) SN 821560 [Not listed]
Apt 27.06.1846; 10511a (10511); Map 1842, 16 chns, by H. Price, L.S., Abergavenny; woods, lead measures, springs, carn, farm names; streams named.

45/31 Llandilofane (parish) SN 890370 [Llandeilo'r Fan]
Apt 21.10.1839; 10491a (10491); Map surveyed 1839, 12 chns, by Bate of Brecon; woods, building names; villages are surrounded by red bands and are not mapped in detail. Apt omits some land use and some field names.

45/32 Llandulas or New Church Hir Abbot (parish) SN 877414 [Tirabad]
Apt 19.01.1847; 3220a (all); Map 1847?, 12 chns, by David Davies; building names. District is apportioned by holding; Apt generalises land use.

45/33 Llanelieu (parish) SO 205325
Apt 21.01.1840; 1537a (all); Map 1842?, 6 chns, (tithable parts only); there is a long note about the location of the detached part. Apt omits most field names.

45/34 Llanelly (parish) SO 230135
Apt 31.10.1839; 5183a (all); Map 1847, 3 chns, 1st cl, by J. and M. Nunan, Abergavenny; construction lines, waterbodies; one built-up part generalised. Apt omits field names.

45/35 Llanfihangel Abergwessin (parish) SN 865560 [Abergwesyn]
Apt 13.01.1841; 6837a (all); Map 1841?, 8 chns, by E.I. Grffiths, Llandilo; waterbodies, houses, woods, plantations, old mound, boundary stones and marks, holdings (col).

45/36 Llanfihangel Nantbran (parish) SN 943353 [Llanfihangel nant Bran]
Apt 17.12.1839; 9161a (9161); Map surveyed 1840, 12 chns, by T. Bate, Brecon, (village also at 4 chns); waterbodies, woods, building names. Apt omits land use.

45/37 Llanfrynach (parish) SO 048232
Apt 02.11.1840; 7127a (7127); Map 1840, 9 chns, in 2 parts, 'Compiled' by William Jones, Brecon, (tithable parts only; one part at 14 chns); canal with towpath, waterbodies, woods, plantations, parkland, orchards, gardens, building names. Apt omits a few field names.

45/38 Llanganten (parish) SO 003514 [Not listed]
Apt 06.05.1846; 2259a (2258); Map 1844, 8 chns, by E.I. Griffiths, Llandilo; waterbodies, woods, plantations, building names. Apt omits a few field names.

45/39 Llangasty tall y llyn (parish) SO 130250 [Llangasty-Talyllyn]
Apt 16.02.1841; 2120a (all); Map 1841?, 9 chns; foot/b'way, waterbodies, woods, plantations, parkland, building names, glebe, common.

45/40 Llangattock (parish) SO 190160
Apt 08.07.1845; 9597a (all); Map 1847?, 3 chns, 1st cl, by J. and M. Nunan, Abergavenny; construction lines, canal, building names, ironworks, workhouse. Apt omits field names.

45/41 Llangenney (parish) SO 244180 [Llangenny]
Apt 12.11.1840; 2784a (all); Map 1839, 3 chns, 1st cl, by W. Fosbrooke, Hereford; construction lines, houses, field boundary ownerships, building names, forge, quarry; some uninhabited buildings have not been tinted; table summarises acreages. Apt omits a few field names.

45/42 Llangorse (parish) SO 144280
Apt 05.02.1842; 2807a (all); Map surveyed 1840, 8 chns, in 2 parts, by T. Bate, Brecon; hill-drawing, railway, waterbodies, woods, building names; lake named. Apt omits a few field names.

45/43 Llangunnider (parish) SO 130140 [Llangynidr]
Apt 02.06.1842; 13909a (all); Map 1840, 4 chns, 1st cl, surveyed for Wm Fosbrooke by L. Carey; hill-drawing, railway, canal with towpath, waterbodies, houses, building names, boundary marks, rectory, iron works, limestone quarries, limekilns, old limekilns. Apt omits some field names.

45/44 Llangynog (parish) SO 023460 [Not listed]
Apt 04.09.1845; 929a (1429); Map 1844, 8 chns, by E.I. Griffiths, Llandilo, (tithable parts only); farmyards, woods, building names; north pointer has Prince of Wales feathers and 'Ich Dien'.

45/45 Llanhamlach (parish) SO 090278
Apt 15.09.1838; 1867a (1867); Map 1839, 6 chns, 'compiled' by Wm Jones, Brecon; hill-drawing, canal with towpath, woods, plantations, orchards, gardens, open fields, pound.

45/46 Llanigon (parish) SO 235365
Apt 18.04.1844; 4456a (all); Map 1845, 6 chns, by William Jones, Belle Vue Place, Brecon; railway, waterbodies, houses, building names. Apt omits field names.

45/47 Llanlleonvel (parish) SN 931509 [Not listed]
Apt 06.05.1846; 2901a (2900); Map 1844, 6 chns, by E.I. Griffiths, Llandilo; woods, plantations, building names, mill; some streams named; mapmaker's name is on streamer knotted around scale bar.

45/48 Llansaintfread (parish) SO 125235 [Llansantffraed]
Apt 19.02.1845; 2248a (all); Map 1845?, 6 chns; waterbodies, houses, woods, plantations, orchards, building names, rectory, tower, stables, ford; title and direction pointer are combined.

45/49 Llanspythid (parish) SO 007279 [Llanspyddid]
Apt 23.10.1838; 1692a (1691); Map 1839?, 8 chns, ? by Morris Sayce; waterbodies, woods, plantations, parkland, building names. Apt omits some field names.

45/50 Llanthetty (parish) SO 160090 [Not listed]
Apt 07.05.1839; 5981a (5980); Map surveyed 1839, 8 chns, in 2 parts, by Bate of Brecon; canal with tunnel, wharf, waterbodies, woods, building names.

45/51 Llanthew (parish) SO 069308
Apt 08.07.1841; 2696a (2695); Map 1841, 6 chns, by William Jones; waterbodies, woods, plantations, building names, old forge, mound, common.

45/52 Llanvigan (parish) SO 085215 [Not listed]
Apt 02.11.1840; 6742a (all); Map 1841, 6 chns, 'Compiled' by Wm Jones, Brecon; canal with towpath, woods, plantations, building names; scale-bar is ruler-like.

45/53 Llanvihangel Brynpabean (district in parish of Llanvilhangel Brynpabean) SN 985565 [Not listed]
Apt 20.11.1840; 3396a (all); Map 1841, 8 chns, by E.J. Griffiths, Llandilo, (tithable parts only); woods. Apt omits some land use.

45/54 Llanvihangel talyllyn (parish) SO 115285 [Llanfihangel Tal-y-llyn]
Apt 03.07.1837; 1233a (1233); Map 1837?, 6 chns, in 6 parts, 'Partly from Old Maps and partly from new Surveys made under the direction of Morris Sayce' (with 5 enlargements of detail, including the village at 1.5 chns); railway, waterbodies, woods, orchard. Apt omits land use.

45/55 Llanvillo (parish) SO 112318 [Llanfilo]
Apt 11.03.1841; 3306a (all); Map 1847?, 3 chns, 1st cl, surveyed by J. Nunan, Abergavenny; construction lines. Apt omits field names.

45/56 Llanwithol (parish) SN 950620 [Llanwrthwl]
Apt 19.01.1847; 18851a (all); Map 1848?, 8 chns, in 3 parts, ? by Morris Sayce; foot/b'way, woods, rock outcrops, building names, footbridge, horse bridge, boundary stones and marks, ferry, mill, chapel, sheds, copper mine, gin, slate quarry, barn, wire bridge; one part extensively duplicates a protrusion; scale is set into border. Apt omits some field names.

45/57 Llanwrytyd (parish) SN 863478 [Llanwrtyd]
Apt 06.05.1846; 11336a (11335); Map 1847, 16 chns, by David Davies; foot/b'way, building names, mill, chapel, mineral spring. Apt omits land use.

45/58 Llanynis (parish) SN 999497 [Not listed]
Apt 11.06.1840; 1850a (all); Map 1840, 6 chns, by E.I. Griffiths, Llandilofawr, (tithable parts only); woods, plantations, holdings (col).

45/59 Llanywern (parish) SO 101290
Apt 31.03.1846; 1430a (all); Map 1847, 4 chns, by John Lewis; waterbodies, houses, woods (col), building names, boundary trees, spring. Apt omits some field names.

45/60 Llysdinam (hamlet in parish of Llanafanfawr) SN 999583
Apt 30.01.1841; 2476a (all); Map 1840, 6 chns, by E.I. Griffiths, Llandilofawr, (tithable parts only); waterbodies, woods, plantations, holdings (col).

45/61 Llyswen (parish) SO 127384
Apt 30.4.1839; 1068a (all); Map 1840, 6 chns, by William Jones, Brecon; waterbodies, woods, plantations, parkland, orchards, gardens, open fields, building names, burying ground; bridge named.

45/62 Maescar (hamlet or parcel in parish of Devynnock) SN 947266
Apt 04.10.1838; 4242a (?); Map 1839?, 8 chns, ? by Morris Sayce; woods, plantations, building names, mill.

45/63 Maesmynis (parish) SO 008472
Apt 18.01.1843; 4013a (all); Map 1843, 8 chns, by E.I. Griffiths, Llandilo; hill-drawing, woods, building names, mills, chapel; north pointer has 'Ich Dien' and Prince of Wales feathers. Apt omits a few field names.

45/64 Merthyr Cynog (parish) SN 980400
Apt 20.02.1840; 21278a (21278); Map 1840, 12 chns, 'Compiled' by Wm Jones, Brecon; waterbodies, woods, plantations, building names, chapel, cairns, ruins, common.

45/65 Modrydd (hamlet in parish of Llanspyddid) SO 004230
Apt 23.10.1838; 4774a (4774); Map 1839, 10 chns, 'Compiled' by Wm Jones, Brecon; hill-drawing, waterbodies, woods, orchard; physical features named.

45/66 Partrishow (parish) SO 275225 [Patrishow]
Apt 10.02.1841; 1482a (all); Map 1840, 3 chns, 1st cl, surveyed for Wm Fosbrooke by L. Carey and T. M'Grane; construction lines, houses, building names, plank across stream, mill, boundary stone. Apt omits some field names.

45/67 Penbuallt (hamlet in parish of Llangammarch) SN 915455 [Not listed]
Apt 22.09.1843; 5423a (5423); Map 1844, 8 chns, by Wm Jones, Llangeitho, Lampeter; woods, building names, mill. Apt omits land use and some field names.

45/68 Penderyn (parish) SN 980090
Apt 27.04.1839; 12765a (12765); Map 1840, 8 chns, 'Compiled' by Wm Jones, Brecon; waterbodies, houses, woods, plantations, building names, boundary stone, cairns, quarries, iron works.

45/69 Penpont (hamlet in parish of Llanspythidd) SN 975277
Apt 13.03.1838; 1971a (1970); Map 1839?, 8 chns, ? by Morris Sayce; waterbodies, woods (col), plantations (col), building names, chapel, common.

45/70 Rhosferrig (hamlet or parcel in parish of Llanfihangel Brynpabean) SO 021521 [Rhosferig]
Apt 13.01.1841; 1320a (1320); Map 1841, 8 chns, by E.J. Griffiths, Llandilo; woods, plantations, suspension bridge (pictorial).

45/71 Senny (hamlet in parish of Devynnock) SN 930235 [Not listed]
Apt 24.08.1840; 3496a (?); Map 1840, 8 chns, ? by Morris Sayce; woods, plantations, hedges, building names, chapel, mill, antiquity. Apt omits land use.

45/72 Talachddu (parish) SO 075335
Apt 28.02.1845; 1819a (all); Map 1846, 6 chns, 'Compiled' by William Jones, Brecon; waterbodies, woods, plantations, orchards, gardens, building names, mill, glebe.

45/73 Talgarth, Trevecca, Pwllyurach and Forest (hamlet or borough in parish of Talgarth) SO 160310
Apt 25.11.1839; 7413a (all); Map 1841?, 8 chns, in 2 parts, surveyed by M. and W. Sayce, (tithable parts only; town also at 4 chns); hill-drawing, waterbodies, woods, heath/moor, building names, chapels, mill, college, common. Apt omits land use and some field names. [See also 45/78.]

45/74 Trallong (parish) SN 955303
Apt 30.01.1840; 3385a (3384); Map 1842?, 8 chns, ? by Morris Sayce; hill-drawing, waterbodies, woods, plantations, gardens, heath/moor, building names, bank, ancient camp, chapel.

45/75 Trayanglaes (hamlet or parcel in parish of Llywell) SN 860272 [Not listed]
Apt 16.04.1839; 10647a (?); Map 1841?, 8 chns, in 2 parts, ? by Morris Sayce; waterbodies, woods, building names, mill, spring, tile quarry, boundary stone. Apt omits land use and some field names.

45/76 Trayanmawr (hamlet or parcel in parish of Llywell) SN 870320 [Not listed]
Apt 16.04.1839; 5892a (?); Map 1841?, 8 chns, ? by Morris Sayce; woods (col), building names, turnpike gate; north pointer has sheep-tail plumes. Apt omits land use and some field names.

45/77 Treflis (hamlet in parish of Llangammarch) SN 920480 [Not listed]
Apt 28.03.1844; 6326a (6325); Map 1843, 8 chns, by E.I. Griffiths, Llandillo; waterbodies, woods, plantations, building names; north pointer has Prince of Wales feathers and 'Ich Dien'. Apt omits a few field names.

45/78 SO 160310 Trevecca
This district is combined with 45/73; there is no map or apt for 45/78.

45/79 Vaynor (parish) SO 035115
Apt 28.09.1841; 6598a (6597); Map 1842, 8 chns, by William Jones, Brecon; hill-drawing, woods, plantations, building names; hill named; north pointer has plumes.

45/80 Ysclydach (hamlet or parcel in parish of Llywell) SN 913308 [Ynys-Clydach]
Apt 10.02.1841; 3848a (?); Map 1842, 8 chns; waterbodies, woods, building names, common. Apt omits land use.

45/81 Ystradfelty (district in parish of Ystradfelty) SN 940123 [Ystradfellte]
Apt 24.06.1840; 14296a (19025); Map 1842, 10 chns, by William Jones, Brecon; waterbodies, woods, plantations, building names, mill, chapel, common; acorn decorates tip of north pointer.

45/82 Ystradgunlais (parish) SN 810140 [Ystradgynlais]
Apt 30.04.1839; 21955a (all); Map 1844, 8 chns, by Wm. J.H. Williams, Swansea; railway, canal with towpath, waterbodies, woods, building names, iron works. Apt omits land use and a few field names.

Cardiganshire

PRO IR29 and IR30 46/1-74

74 tithe districts: 440,630 acres
74 tithe commutations: 432,843 acres
57 voluntary tithe agreements, 17 compulsory tithe awards

Tithe and tithe commutation

All Cardiganshire tithe districts were subject to payment of tithes in 1836 and forty districts were wholly tithable at this date (Fig. 58). Elsewhere, the main causes of exemption were modus payments in lieu of tithes and the exemption of most woodland.

Assistant tithe commissioners and local tithe agents who worked in Cardiganshire are listed in Table 46.1. Tithe valuers from outside the immediate vicinity of the county contributed rather more than usual to this county's valuations of tithe rent-charge. Notable among these are Anthony and Robert Reed of Stockton upon Tees who valued Llanbadarnfawr which is the largest of all Welsh tithe districts, at over 52,000 acres. Six other districts were valued by men based in Herefordshire.

Cardiganshire tithe apportionments are amongst the least useful in the whole country as sources of land-use information and field-names. In nine districts tithe was apportioned by holding with the result that the schedules of tithe apportionment of these districts lack information on fields and a majority of field-by-field schedules of apportionment omit some or all field names and state of cultivation descriptions. The apportionment for Llandyfriog has some cropping information and a few, including Mount, include descriptions of particular grassland types. The apportionment for Llanarth employs an unusual alpha-numeric system to link tithe areas to the particular hamlet to which each belongs.

Tithe maps

Cardiganshire has no first-class maps. No map explicitly acknowledges copying and a few, for example some by George Pugh, are described as 'surveyed'. Samuel Bartley is unusual in announcing 'Second Class Map' in several of his map titles.

The pattern of map scales in Cardiganshire is similar to that employed in Carmarthenshire; only six maps are at the minimum recommended scale of four chains whereas the most favoured scale was the eight-chain (for 63 per cent of the maps). The smallest scale used

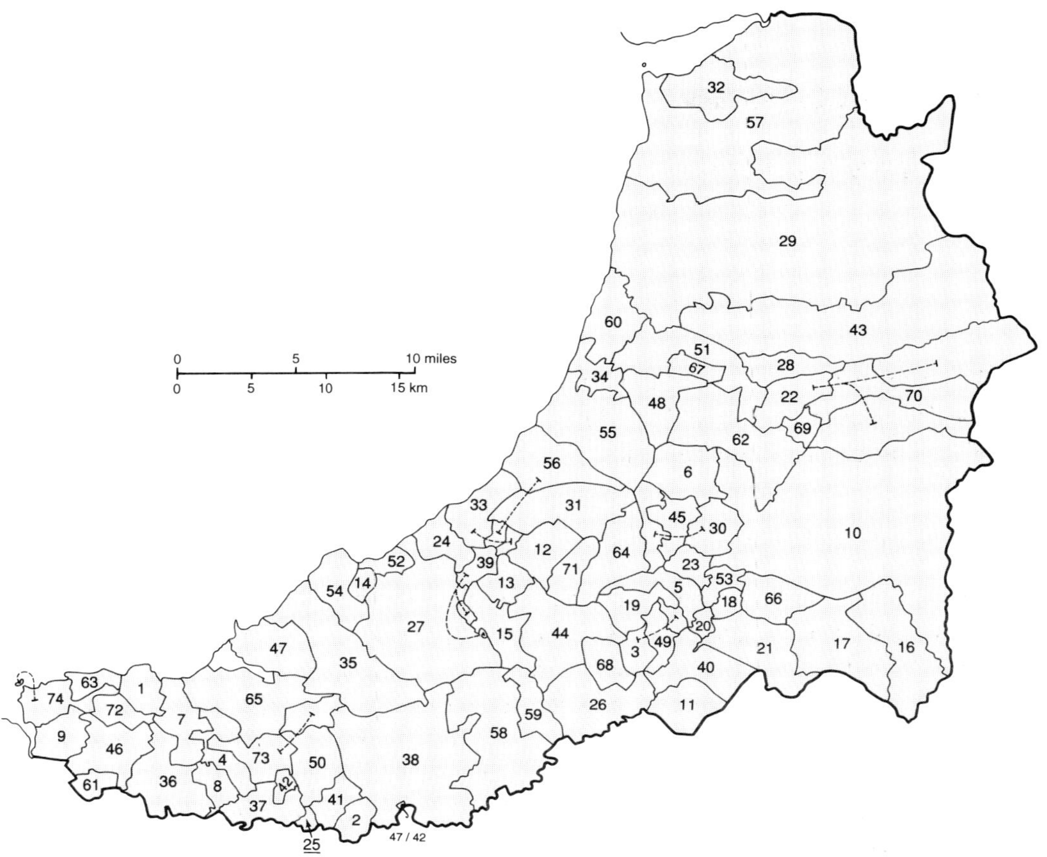

Fig. 58 Cardiganshire: tithe district boundaries.

was one inch to sixteen chains (Table 46.3). The peak of map production was in 1844, much later than nationally (Table 46.4).

Apart from woodland (on 73 per cent of maps), Cardiganshire tithe maps have almost no land-use information. None distinguishes inhabited buildings or provides any information about field boundaries beyond the fact of their existence. A few lead mines and slate quarries are shown.

Fifty-six Cardiganshire tithe maps in the Public Record Office collection can be attributed to a particular map-maker; the most prolific was Owen Lloyd of Cardigan who produced twelve maps which are generally very ordinary except for the careful attention paid to wells and springs. Overall the tithe maps of Cardiganshire are more colourful than are those of Pembrokeshire and Carmarthenshire and the overall standard of execution is much better than in Merionethshire, if hardly remarkable by the standards of English counties. A few north pointers are decorated with plumes or leaves.

Table 46.1. *Agreements and awards for commutation of tithes in Cardiganshire*

Assistant commissioner/ local tithe agent	*Number of agreements**	*Number of awards*
Thomas Hoskins	42	0
John Johnes	11	15
Aneurin Owen	1	2

*Computed from the number of extant reports on tithe agreements in the tithe files [PRO IR 18].

Table 46.2. *Tithe valuers and tithe map-makers in Cardiganshire*

Name and address (in Cardiganshire unless indicated)	*Number of districts*	*Acreage*
Tithe valuers		
John William Rees, Pengarregfawr, Llanilar	11	65,734
Samuel Bartley, Llandefeilog, Carmarthenshire	10	33,214
Alfred Thomas, Carmarthen	8	69,247
Owen Lloyd, Cardigan	8	22,895
Others [19]	37	241,753
Attributed tithe map-makers		
Owen Lloyd, Cardigan	12	29,557
Samuel Bartley, Llandefeilog, Carmarthenshire	9	36,911
George Pugh, Aberystwyth	7	38,955
Edwards and Saunders	6	24,622
Alfred Thomas, Carmarthen	4	57,881
Others [8]	14	76,202

Table 46.3. *The tithe maps of Cardiganshire: scales and classes*

Scale in chains/inch	*All maps*		*First Class*		*Second Class*	
	Number	*Acreage*	*Number*	*Acreage*	*Number*	*Acreage*
4	6	19,634	0	0	6	19,634
5	1	1,228	0	0	1	1,228
6	14	73,995	0	0	14	73,995
7	1	2,868	0	0	1	2,868
8	47	270,069	0	0	47	270,069
<8	5	65,049	0	0	5	65,049
TOTAL	74	432,843	0	0	74	432,843

Table 46.4. *The tithe maps of Cardiganshire: dates*

	1838	*1839*	*1840*	*1841*	*1842*	*1843*	*1844*	*1845*	*1846*	*1847*	*1848*	*1849*
2nd class*	1	6	7	7	9	10	15	3	6	6	2	1

*One second-class tithe map of Cardiganshire in the Public Record Office collection is undated.

Cardiganshire

46/1 Aberporth (parish) SN 244504
Apt 05.04.1838; 2201a (all); Map 1839, 4 chns, 'Second Class Map', by Samuel Bartley, L.S.; building names. Apt omits land use and field names.

46/2 Bangor (parish) SN 389407 [Bangor Teifi]
Apt 30.12.1837; 1392a (all); Map 1841, 8 chns, by Benjamin Lewis; hill-drawing, waterbodies, woods, building names. District is apportioned by holding and fields are not shown.

46/3 Bettws Bledrws (parish) SN 591524 [Bettws Bledrws]
Apt 11.04.1839; 2216a (2216); Map 1844, 8 chns, by Owen Lloyd, Cardigan; waterbodies, woods, plantations, parkland, building names, mill pond, quarry, common; pink band surrounds named estate; north pointer has plumes. Apt omits land use and field names.

46/4 Bettws Evan (parish) SN 302477 [Betws Ifan]
Apt 21.03.1839; 2477a (2640); Map 1841, 8 chns, by W.J. Howell, Valuer and Surveyor, Aberporth, litho (Standidge); woods, gardens, building names. Apt omits land use and field names.

46/5 Bettws Leiki (township in parish of Llandewibrefi) SN 612580 [Capel Bettes Lleucu]
Apt 21.06.1845; 2342a (all); Map 1847?, 8 chns; foot/b'way, waterbodies, woods.

46/6 Blaenpennal (township or chapelry in parish of Llanddewibrefy) SN 625655
Apt 15.08.1842; 4106a (all); Map 1842, 8 chns, by Thos. Hand; hill-drawing, waterbodies, farmyards, woods, building names. Apt omits some field names.

46/7 Blaenporth (parish) SN 268488
Apt 31.10.1837; 3478a (3548); Map 1839, 4 chns, 'Second Class Map', by Samuel Bartley, L.S., Llandefeilog, Carmarthen; waterbodies, woods, building names, mill. Apt omits land use and field names.

46/8 Brongwyn (parish) SN 296438
Apt 06.12.1844; 1621a (1620); Map 1846, 8 chns, by Edward Lloyd; waterbodies, woods, plantations, building names, mill. Apt omits land use and field names.

46/9 St Marys, Cardigan (parish) SN 188476 [Cardigan]
Apt 21.03.1839; 2412a (all); Map 1846, 8 chns, by Owen Lloyd, Cardigan; foot/b'way, waterbodies, woods, building names, limekiln, mill (by Dawson's symbol), mill ponds, high water mark; pink band surrounds tithe-free built-up part. Apt omits field names.

46/10 Caron (parish) SN 740610 [Not listed]
Apt 27.12.1839; 39139a (39138); Map 1842?, 8 chns, in 7 parts, ? by Alfred Thomas, Carmarthen, (town also at 4 chns; 40-chn index); waterbodies, building names, boundary stones and marks, carns, chapel, pound, mill, ring earthwork, sheep cot, ruins, waterfall, spring, common; some streams are named; scale and true and magnetic north pointers are combined; stiff conventional leaves decorate one north pointer. Apt omits land use and some field names.

46/11 Cellan (parish) SN 625483
Apt 04.04.1843; 3645a (3645); Map 1843, 8 chns, 'Mapped' by Edwards and Saunders; building names, common, boundary cairns and bank; bottom right is 'The common measured and mapped by S. Evans, 1844'. Apt omits land use.

46/12 Cilcennin (parish) SN 527601
Apt 22.09.1840; 3406a (all); Map 1843, 8 chns, by Samuel Bartley, L.S., Apportioner; woods, building names. Apt omits land use and field names.

46/13 Cilieayron (parish) SN 500580 [Ciliau Aeron]
Apt 29.06.1839; 1915a (1914); Map 1843, 8 chns, by Samuel Bartley, L.S., Apportioner; waterbodies, woods, building names. Apt omits land use and field names.

46/14 Cydplwyf (hamlet or parcel in parish of Llanina) SN 401580 [Not listed]
Apt 15.07.1837; 793a (?); Map 1839?, 8 chns, ? by Morris Sayce and John Harvey; woods, building names, factory. Apt omits land use.

46/15 Dihewid (parish) SN 497546 [Dihewyd]
Apt 04.11.1844; 3453a (all); Map 1845, 8 chns, 'Mapped' by Edwards and Saunders; waterbodies, woods, building names, factory, boundary stones, spring, district boundary (col), private roads (uncoloured). Apt omits land use and field names.

46/16 Doithie Carnddwr (township in parish of Llanddewibrefi) SN 775525 [Not listed]
Apt 15.08.1840; 7468a (all); Map 1842, 8 chns; boundary stones, carn, rock; colour bands may show holdings. District is apportioned by holding and fields are not shown.

46/17 Doithie Pysgottwr (township in parish of Llanddewibiefi) SN 731524 [Not listed]
Apt 15.08.1840; 7770a (all); Map 1842, 10 chns; waterbodies, boundary marks, holding boundaries (col). District is apportioned by holding and fields are not shown.

46/18 Garth and Ystrad (township in parish of Llanddewibrefy) SN 654559
Apt 18.11.1841; 853a (853); Map 1842, 6 chns, by D.M. Llewellyn; building names; scale lacks figures and is surrounded by drapes, the whole held by an eagle in its talons; stiff conventional leaves decorate north pointer. Apt omits land use.

46/19 Garthele (hamlet in parish of Llanddewibrefi) SN 586559 [Gartheli]
Apt 16.12.1845; 2476a (all); Map undated, [8 chns]; foot/b'way, woods, building names. Apt omits some field names.

46/20 Gogoyan (township in parish of Llanddewibrefi) SN 634544
Apt 21.06.1845; 707a (all); Map 1847?, 4 chns; hill-drawing, waterbodies, woods, building names, holding boundaries (col). Apt omits land use.

46/21 Gorwith (township in parish of Llanddewi brefi) SN 672528 [Not listed]
Apt 07.11.1839; 6604a (all); Map 1842?, 8 chns, in 2 parts, ? by Alfred Thomas, Carmarthen, (village also at 4 chns); building names, springs, ruins, boundary stones and rocks, old wall, lead mine shaft, common. Apt omits land use and some field names.

46/22 Gwnnws (parish) SN 712702 [Not listed]
Apt 04.05.1844; 17959a (all); Map 1847?, 8 chns, in 4 parts, (includes 24-chn index); waterbodies, woods, marsh/bog, building names, level, mine pits, slate quarries, mill, beacon, turbary; streams named.

46/23 Gwynfil (township in parish of Llanddewi brefy) SN 627588 [Not listed]
Apt 21.01.1842; 1522a (1522); Map 1842, 6 chns, 'Drawn' by D.M. Llewellyn; hill-drawing, waterbodies, woods, building names. Apt omits land use.

46/24 Henfriniw (parish) SN 458611 [Not listed]
Apt 29.11.1845; 2141a (all); Map 1846, 4 chns, by Edwards and Saunders; hill-drawing, foot/b'way, waterbodies, woods, rock outcrops, building names, meeting houses, cliffs, timber yard, kilns, quarries, shipwright yard, mill; pink band surrounds Aberaeron town, (tithe-free). Apt omits land use and field names.

46/25 Henllan (parish) SN 356410
Apt 17.10.1839; 387a (387); Map 1844, 4 chns, by Owen Lloyd, Cardigan; woods, plantations, building names, ford, glebe; bridge named. Apt omits field names.

46/26 Lampeter Pont Stephen (parish) SN 562483 [Lampeter]
Apt 15.06.1839; 6204a (6204); Map 1843, 8 chns, by Owen Lloyd, Cardigan; foot/b'way, waterbodies, woods, plantations, orchard, building names, college, mill leat, mill, well, quarries; pink band surrounds town (tithe-free). Apt omits land use and field names.

46/27 Llanarth (parish) SN 442554
Apt 15.07.1837; 15020a (15044); Map 1839?, 12 chns, ? by Morris Sayce and John Harvey; hill-drawing, waterbodies, woods, building names, old camp, cliffs, pound, mills; letter prefixes, explained in legend, indicate to which hamlet each tithe area belongs. Apt omits land use.

46/28 Llanavan (parish) SN 698728 [Llanafan]
Apt 29.07.1843; 2588a (all); Map 1845, 6 chns, surveyed by George Pugh, Aberystwith; hill-drawing, woods, plantations, gardens, building names, mill, boundary stones, site of house, levels, ford, nursery (by flecking), chapel; pecked lines are within and dot-dash lines are between holdings; three styles of writing indicate apparent importance of buildings.

46/29 Llanbadarnfawr (parish) SN 710810 [Llanbadarn Fawr]
Apt 03.03.1843; 52421a (52750); Map 1846, [8 chns]; water-bodies, woods, building names, mines, turf bog, workhouse, fish pond, chapel, township boundaries (col) and names. Apt omits some field names.

46/30 Llanbadarn odyn (parish) SN 646611 [Not listed]
Apt 21.06.1845; 4425a (all); Map 1849?, 8 chns; hill-drawing, waterbodies, woods. Apt omits most field names.

46/31 Llanbadarntrefeglwys (parish) SN 545635 [Not listed]
Apt 20.08.1839; 3907a (all); Map 1843, 8 chns, by Samuel Bartley, L.S., Apportioner; waterbodies, woods, building names. Apt omits land use and field names.

46/32 Llancynfelyn (parish) SN 658925
Apt 06.06.1844; 5022a (6556); Map 1844, 6 chns, by Richd Morgan; woods, plantations, heath/moor, building names, limekilns (by symbol). Apt omits some field names.

46/33 Llanddewy Aberarth (parish) SN 480631 [Aberarth]
Apt 04.04.1839; 3521a (all); Map 1843, 8 chns, in 3 parts, by Samuel Bartley, L.S., Apportioner, (including 3 and 4-chn enlargements of detail); waterbodies, woods, building names, limekilns, workhouse. Apt omits land use and field names.

46/34 Llanddinol (parish) SN 568720 [Llanddeiniol]
Apt 18.04.1839; 1997a (all); Map 1840, 6 chns, surveyed by George Pugh, Machynlleth; hill-drawing, woods, building names, cliffs. Apt omits land use.

46/35 Llandissiliogogo (parish) SN 390520 [Not listed]
Apt 23.04.1841; 10224a (10224); Map 1843?, 8 chns; hill-drawing, woods, rock outcrops, building names, encampment, mill, cliffs, well, meeting house, common. Apt omits land use and field names.

46/36 Llandugwydd (parish) SN 258440 [Llandygwydd]
Apt 04.04.1839; 5595a (5595); Map 1841?, 8 chns, by Samuel Bartley, L.S., Apportioner; waterbodies, woods, building names. Apt omits land use and field names.

46/37 Llandyfriog (parish) SN 330418
Apt 26.08.1839; 2868a (2867); Map 1844?, 7 chns; waterbodies, woods, building names, old river, mill; pink band surrounds (tithe-free) built-up area.

46/38 Llandyssil (parish) SN 440450 [Llandysul]
Apt 31.12.1841; 17556a (17556); Map 1846?, 16 chns, in 2 parts, (includes village at 8 chns); building names, chapel, holding boundaries. Apt omits land use.

46/39 Llanerchayron (parish) SN 483591 [Llanaeron]
Apt 29.06.1839; 1606a (all); Map 1843?, 8 chns; building names, mill. Apt omits land use.

46/40 Llanfairclydogan (parish) SN 628518 [Llanfair Clydogau]
Apt 16.10.1839; 4815a (all); Map 1844, 8 chns, by Owen Lloyd; woods, building names, boundary bush; pecked lines show boundaries within holdings, dot-dash lines boundaries between holdings. Apt omits land use and field names.

46/41 Llanfairorllwyn (parish) SN 379421 [Not listed]
Apt 15.07.1839; 1744a (all); Map 1844, 8 chns, by Owen Lloyd; waterbodies, woods, building names, mill, quarry; pecked lines show boundaries within holdings, dot-dash lines boundaries between holdings. Apt omits field names.

46/42 Llanfairtrefligen (parish) SN 341437 [Not listed]
Apt 20.07.1843; 648a (648); Map 1844, 8 chns, by Owen Lloyd, Cardigan; waterbodies, woods, plantations, tumulus, site of church, spring, glebe. Apt omits land use and field names.

46/43 Llanfihangle y Croddyn (parish) SN 720750 [Llanfihangel-y-Creuddyn]
Apt 25.09.1844; 22553a (all); Map 1847, 9 chns, surveyed by George Pugh, Aberystwith; woods, building names, township boundaries (col); pecked lines show boundaries within holdings, dot-dash lines boundaries between holdings. Apt omits some land use and some field names.

46/44 Llanfihangel Ystrad (parish) SN 535543 [Ystrad Aeron]
Apt 09.02.1839; 5316a (7467); Map 1843?, 8 chns; building names, encampment; colour bands show holdings according to tithe ownership. Apt omits land use.

46/45 Llangeitho (parish) SN 619620
Apt 20.08.1839; 2150a (2150); Map 1838, 10 chns; the only building shown is the church. Apt omits land use.

46/46 Llangoedmore (parish) SN 218460 [Llangoedmor]
Apt 03.03.1838; 4946a (4946); Map 1839?, 8 chns, ? by Morris Sayce; woods, building names, mills; north pointer has plumes. Apt omits land use and some field names.

46/47 Llangrannog (parish) SN 338537 [Llangranog]
Apt 20.10.1840; 4339a (4383); Map 1841, 6 chns, in 3 parts, by W.J. Howell, Valuer and Surveyor, Aberporth, (includes two 4-chn enlargements of detail), litho (Standidge); hill-drawing, woods, gardens, rock outcrops, building names, landowners, cliffs, toll bar, milestone, vicarage; brook named; bearing on 'Baidsey Island' is given. Apt omits land use and some field names.

46/48 Llangrwyddon (parish) SN 609701 [Llangwyryfon]
Apt 16.05.1843; 3847a (all); Map 1844, 6 chns; waterbodies, woods, plantations, ring earthwork; acorn and oakleaves form tip of north pointer.

46/49 Llanguby (parish) SN 609531 [Llangybi]
Apt 12.10.1839; 1809a (all); Map 1844, 8 chns, by Owen Lloyd, Cardigan; woods, plantations, building names, mill pond. Apt omits land use and field names.

46/50 Llangunllo (parish) SN 363451 [Llangynllo]
Apt 04.04.1839; 3650a (3650); Map 1842, 8 chns, by Owen Lloyd, Cardigan; hill-drawing, waterbodies, woods, building names, quarry, springs, mill (by symbol), meeting house. Apt omits land use and field names.

46/51 Llanilar (parish) SN 625750
Apt 30.05.1843; 6403a (all); Map 1844, 8 chns, surveyed by D. Morley Llewelyn, Carmarthen; foot/b'way, waterbodies, woods, gardens, building names, quarries, vicarage, township names. Apt omits a few field names.

46/52 Llanina (parish) SN 416596 [Not listed]
Apt 15.07.1837; 1073a (?); Map 1839?, 8 chns, ? by Morris Sayce and John Harvey; hill-drawing, waterbodies, woods, rock outcrops, building names, cliffs, offshore rocks, quarry; north pointer has plumes. Apt omits land use.

46/53 Llanio (township in parish of Llanddewybrefy) SN 648575 [Not listed]
Apt 21.01.1842; 1228a (all); Map 1845?, 5 chns, by Thomas Hand; woods, orchard, landowners, holdings (col, named). Apt has some cropping information but omits field names.

46/54 Llanllwchaiarn (parish) SN 385575 [Not listed]
Apt 21.03.1846; 3181a (all); Map 1847, 6 chns, by W. Jones, Bellevue, Brecon; hill-drawing, building names, rope walks. Apt omits field names.

46/55 Llanrhystid (parish) SN 575683 [Llanrhystud]
Apt 10.09.1839; 8615a (8770); Map 1841, 8 chns, ? by Alfred Thomas, Carmarthen; building names. Apt omits land use and a few field names.

46/56 Llansaintffraed (parish) SN 534658 [Llansantffraed]
Apt 08.07.1841; 5229a (all); Map 1844, 8 chns, in 3 parts, ? by Thomas Bate, Brecon, (includes part of village at 4 chns); building names, limekilns, turnpike gate, mill, hamlet boundaries and names. Apt omits some field names.

46/57 Llanvihangel Geneurglyn (parish) SN 680900 [Not listed]
Apt 31.10.1845; 30137a (all); Map 1847, 6 chns, in 4 parts, by Richard Morgan, Talybont, (includes 18-chn index); waterbodies, woods, building names, mill, mines, antiquity, cliffs, private roads. Apt omits some field names.

46/58 Llanwenog (parish) SN 492461
Apt 02.03.1843; 10720a (10720); Map 1840, 4 chns, by John Saunders and John Edwards; waterbodies, woods, building names, meeting house, quarry, mill, hamlet boundaries and names. Apt omits land use.

46/59 Llanwnen (parish) SN 520484 [Llanwnnen]
Apt 02.02.1844; 2480a (2480); Map 1844, 8 chns, by John and Thomas Saunders; waterbodies, woods, building names, quarries. Apt omits land use.

46/60 Llanychaiarn (parish) SN 579761 [Llanfarian]
Apt 30.06.1843; 4020a (all); Map 1844, 6 chns, surveyed by George Pugh, Aberystwith; hill-drawing, woods, building names, ring earthwork, cliffs.

46/61 Llechryd (chapelry) SN 206439
Apt 10.10.1839; 943a (943); Map 1840?, 8 chns; woods, building names, mill. Apt omits land use.

46/62 Lledrod (parish) SN 660680
Apt 12.06.1843; 8692a (all); Map 1844, 6 chns, by Richard Morgan, Talybont, Aberystwyth; waterbodies, woods; pecked lines show boundaries within holdings, and dot-dash lines show boundaries between holdings.

46/63 Mount (parish) SN 210517 [Mwnt]
Apt 22.06.1847; 1141a (1142); Map 1848, 8 chns, by Owen Lloyd, Cardigan; hill-drawing, waterbodies, rock outcrops, building names, wells, cliffs, limekilns, springs. Apt omits field names.

46/64 Nantcwnlle (parish) SN 580597 [Not listed]
Apt 11.07.1839; 4603a (all); Map 1843?, 8 chns; building names, holding boundaries. Apt omits land use.

46/65 Pembryn (parish) SN 325500 [Penbryn]
Apt 05.04.1838; 8228a (8347); Map 1841, 8 chns, by Samuel Bartley, L.S., Apportioner; waterbodies, woods, building names, rocks, hamlet boundary; pecked lines show boundaries within, dot-dash lines boundaries between holdings. Apt omits land use and field names.

46/66 Prisk and Carvan (township in parish of Llandewibrefi) SN 690560 [Not listed]
Apt 16.10.1839; 3523a (all); Map 1842?, 8 chns, ? by Alfred Thomas, Carmarthen; waterbodies, building names, boundary stones, carns; streams named. Apt omits land use.

46/67 Rhosdie (parish) SN 637724 [Rhos-y-Garth]
Apt 29.06.1839; 1307a (all); Map 1841, 6 chns, surveyed by George Pugh, Aberystwith; hill-drawing, woods, building names, intrenchment, boundary marks, common. Apt omits land use.

46/68 Silian (parish) SN 567514
Apt 16.12.1845; 2183a (all); Map 1846, 8 chns, by Saunders and Edwards; foot/b'way, common, woods, building names, quarry; pink bands indicate tithe ownership. Apt omits land use and field names.

46/69 Sputty Ystradmeurig (parish) SN 711681 [Ystradmeurig]
Apt 29.06.1839; 945a (all); Map 1843, 6 chns, surveyed by George Pugh, Aberystwyth; hill-drawing, building names, earthwork. Apt omits land use.

46/70 Sputty Ystwyth (parish) SN 774703 [Ysbyty Ystwyth]
Apt 21.01.1842; 5545a (5544); Map 1848, 6 chns, surveyed by George Pugh, Aberystwyth; hill-drawing, foot/b'way, waterbodies, woods, building names, boundary marks, carns (named), level; lakes named. Apt omits land use.

46/71 Trefilan (parish) SN 547587
Apt 13.03.1839; 2202a (2201); Map 1840?, 8 chns; waterbodies, building names, holdings, ownership boundaries (col). Apt omits land use and field names; acreages are only given for holdings, though fields are numbered.

46/72 Tremain (parish) SN 228492
Apt 16.01.1838; 1658a (all); Map 1840, 8 chns, by Owen Lloyd, Cardigan; waterbodies, woods, building names, springs, mill, hamlet boundary. Apt omits land use and field names.

46/73 Troedyraur (parish) SN 318457
Apt 08.11.1837; 4660a (4660); Map 1840, 8 chns, 'Second Class Map', by Samuel Bartley, L.S., Apportioner; waterbodies, woods, building names; pecked lines show boundaries within holdings, and dot-dash lines show boundaries between holdings. Apt omits land use and field names.

46/74 Verwig (parish) SN 180500 [Ferwig]
Apt 17.02.1838; 2873a (3062); Map 1839-40, 8 chns, 'Second Class Map', 'Mapped' by Owen Lloyd, Cardigan; hill-drawing, waterbodies, rock outcrops, building names, cliffs, meeting houses, wells, crugs, harbour, high water mark, spout, limekiln, mill pond, watermill (by symbol), quarry, common. Apt omits land use and field names.

Carmarthenshire

PRO IR29 and IR30 47/1-82

83 tithe districts: 592,659 acres
82 tithe commutations: 547,020 acres
62 voluntary tithe agreements, 20 compulsory tithe awards

Tithe and tithe commutation

All but one tithe district in Carmarthenshire were subject to payment of tithes in 1836 but only sixteen districts were wholly tithable at this date (Fig. 59). As elsewhere in Wales the main causes of tithe exemption were modus payments in lieu of tithes (60 per cent of tithable districts) and the exemption of some woodland.

Assistant tithe commissioners and local tithe agents who worked in Carmarthenshire are listed in Table 47.1 and the valuers of the county's tithe rent-charge are set out in Table 47.2. In eighteen districts tithes are apportioned by holding so that the tithe apportionments of these places contain no record of property names or the land use of fields. This information is also either absent or incomplete for several other districts where tithe was apportioned field-by-field. As in Pembrokeshire, valuers George and Henry Goode distinguish between various types of grassland, such as 'moory mead', 'moory pas[ture]' and 'clover hay'.

Tithe maps

Carmarthenshire resembles most Welsh counties in that not one tithe district was mapped to first-class standards. Indeed, only one map was made at as large a scale as one inch to three chains and only four more are at the smallest officially recommended scale of one inch to four chains. The most popular scale in the county was the eight-chain which was used in 69 per cent of tithe districts, and the smallest scale employed was one inch to sixteen chains (Table 47.3). A few maps acknowledge copying of earlier work but it is impossible to say how widespread this may have been.

Woodland is the land use most often recorded (on 62 per cent of maps) but not one map distinguishes arable, grass, gardens, heath and moor, or marsh and bog, only six depict parkland and only one portrays orchards. Non-agricultural features are also scantily recorded; only six maps distinguish houses from other buildings and only two record foot- and bridleways. An exception amongst Carmarthenshire tithe maps is the enlarged plan of

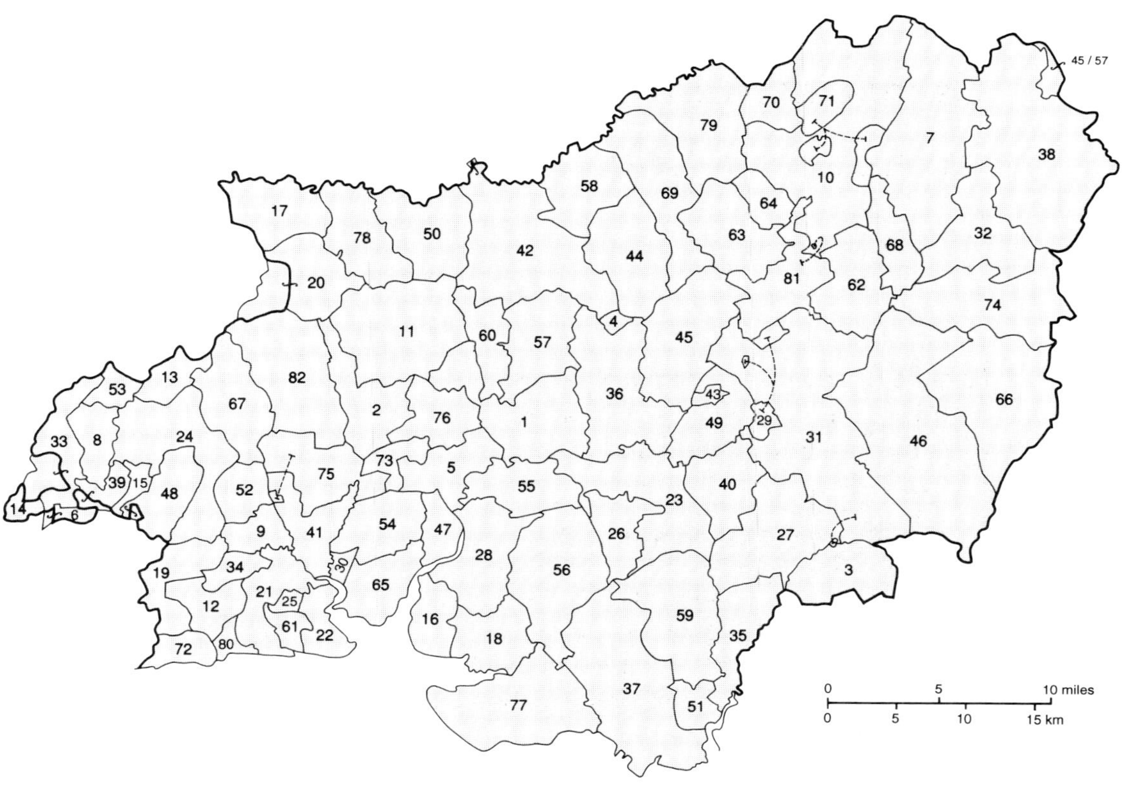

Fig. 59 Carmarthenshire: tithe district boundaries.

Carmarthen itself which maps industrial activity and a number of public buildings including detailed plans of the gaols.

Sixty-four Carmarthenshire maps in the Public Record Office collection can be attributed to a particular map-maker (Table 47.2). As in Glamorganshire and Pembrokeshire, the most prolific of these was the partnership of Harry Goode and Henry Philpott of Haverfordwest. They employ a style similar to their work elsewhere, one which is completely uncoloured and often with a characteristic plain cartouche and an intersecting scale bar and north pointer. Morris Sayce of Kington, Herefordshire, made four tithe maps in Carmarthenshire and was the only map-maker to come from far outside the county. Overall, there is little decorative embellishment on Carmarthenshire tithe maps; that of Brechfa has a coloured north pointer which is unusual in Wales.

Table 47.1. *Agreements and awards for commutation of tithes in Carmarthenshire*

Assistant commissioner/ local tithe agent	*Number of agreements**	*Number of awards*
John Johnes	26	18
Thomas Hoskins	29	0
Aneurin Owen	0	2
Morris Sayce	1	0

*Computed from the number of extant reports on tithe agreements in the tithe files [PRO IR 18].

Table 47.2. *Tithe valuers and tithe map-makers in Carmarthenshire*

Name and address (in Carmarthenshire unless indicated)	*Number of districts*	*Acreage*
Tithe valuers		
George Goode, Croft Cottage, Carmarthen	10	81,010
Harry Phelps Goode, Haverfordwest, Pembrokeshire	9	33,310
William Goode, Llangadock	8	54,497
Morris Sayce, Kington, Herefordshire	7	77,970
Alfred Thomas, Carmarthen	7	27,988
William Morgan, Tanylan, Llansawel	6	50,877
Others [16]	35	221,368
Attributed tithe map-makers		
Goode and Philpott, Haverfordwest, Pembrokeshire	9	33,213
William Morgan, Tanylan, Llansawel	7	60,908
Thomas Hand	5	43,168
Evan John Griffiths, Llandilo	5	35,759
William Goode, Llangadock	5	31,862
Morris Sayce, Kington, Herefordshire	4	36,413
Others [18]	29	196,041

Table 47.3. *The tithe maps of Carmarthenshire: scales and classes*

Scale in chains/inch	*All maps*		*First Class*		*Second Class*	
	Number	*Acreage*	*Number*	*Acreage*	*Number*	*Acreage*
3	1	3,414	0	0	1	3,414
4	4	10,191	0	0	4	10,191
6	9	50,422	0	0	9	50,422
8	57	366,031	0	0	57	366,031
<8	11	116,962	0	0	11	116,962
TOTAL	82	547,020	0	0	82	547,020

Table 47.4. *The tithe maps of Carmarthenshire: dates*

	1837	*1838*	*1839*	*1840*	*1841*	*1842*	*1843*	*1844*	*1845*	*1846*	*1847*	*1848*	*1849*	*1850*
2nd class	1	4	12	20	14	10	5	5	1	5	1	3	0	1

Carmarthenshire

47/1 Abergwile (parish) SN 460230 [Abergwli]
Apt 30.04.1838; 10749a (10748); Map 1840?, 8 chns; waterbodies, woods, building names, chapels. Apt omits land use and some field names.

47/2 Abernant (parish) SN 345235
Apt 28.06.1842; 6321a (6321); Map 1839, 8 chns; woods, building names, mill, common. Apt omits land use.

47/3 Bettws (parish) SN 665115 [Betws]
Apt 17.09.1846; 6466a (6465); Map 1848, 8 chns, by E.I. Griffiths, Llandilo; railway, waterbodies, watermill (by Dawson's symbol).

47/4 Brechfa (parish) SN 515299
Apt 23.09.1845; 530a (530); Map 1847, 4 chns, by Ben. Jones; hill-drawing, waterbodies, woods (col), gardens (col), pound, ownerships (col); pictorial church; direction star is multi-coloured.

47/5 St Peter, Carmarthen (parish) SN 400202 [Carmarthen]
Apt 23.09.1837; 5155a (5155); Map 1838, 6 chns, in 2 parts, (including enlargement of Carmarthen town surveyed by Alfred Thomas, Carmarthen); hill-drawing, waterbodies, woods, rock outcrops, building names, road names, workhouse, town hall, gaols (in detail), monument, graveyards, old priory, chapel, tabernacle, gas works, tin works, brick yards, old quarry, furnace mills, limekiln, old pottery, holding boundaries (col).

47/6 Castelldwyran and Grondre (district in parish of Cilymaenllwyd) (partly in Pembrokeshire) SN 131186 [Not listed]
Apt 20.07.1843; 875a (876); Map 1843, 10 chns, by Goode and Philpott, Haverfordwest; building names, chapel.

47/7 Cilycwm (parish) SN 740430
Apt 30.01.1843; 14579a (all); Map 1844, 16 chns, in 2 parts, by David Davies, (tithable parts only; includes village at 4 chns); woods, building names, mills. District is apportioned by holding and fields are not shown.

47/8 Cillymainllwyd (parish) SN 152234 [Not listed]
Apt 08.12.1837; 3505a (all); Map 1838?, 8 chns, ? by Alfred Thomas, Carmarthen, (tithable parts only in detail; includes village at 4 chns); waterbodies, woods, hedge ownership, building names, footbridges, chapel. Apt omits land use.

47/9 St Clears (parish) SN 261168
Apt 24.04.1838; 2535a (2534); Map 1841?, 4 chns, by Goode and Philpott, Haverfordwest; woods; plain cartouche and scale intersect north pointer.

47/10 Conwil Gaio or Cayo (parish) SN 670430 [Caio]
Apt 23.04.1839; 19076a (35364); Map 1840, 8 chns, ? by William Morgan, Tanylan, Llansawel, Carm.; holding boundaries (col). District is apportioned by holding and fields are not shown.

47/11 Conwill in Elvet (parish) SN 370305 [Cynwyl Elfed]
Apt 21.03.1840; 13153a (13153); Map 1840, 12 chns, surveyed by Samuel Ball, Kidwelly; woods, building names; horizontal shading in some woods may indicate timber woods. District is apportioned by holding, though fields are numbered separately; Apt omits land use and field names.

47/12 Eglwyscummin (parish) SN 222110 [Not listed]
Apt 22.02.1843; 3741a (all); Map 1842?, 8 chns, by Wm Goode, L.S.; hill-drawing, waterbodies, houses, woods, plantations, building names.

47/13 Eglwysfairacherig (chapelry in parish of Henllanamgoed) SN 205275 [Not listed]
Apt 09.08.1843; 2619a (all); Map 1843, 8 chns, by Walter Lloyd; woods, building names, pits. Apt omits land use.

47/14 Egremont (parish) SN 097195 [Llandre Egremont]
Apt 23.04.1844; 1007a (1006); Map 1844, 8 chns, by H.P. Goode and Philpott, Haverfordwest; building names.

47/15 Henllan Amgoed (parish) SN 180200
Apt 27.07.1844; 1052a (all); Map 1846?, 8 chns, ? by Goode and Philpott; woods, building names.

47/16 St Ishmael (parish) SN 371095
Apt 05.02.1840; 3647a (8081); Map 1840, 8 chns, by Thomas Hand; waterbodies, woods, building names, ballast quay, mill, sands. Apt omits land use.

47/17 Kenarth (parish) SN 290390 [Cenarth]
Apt 04.10.1838; 6430a (6429); Map 1839, 8 chns, ? by Morris Sayce; waterbodies, woods, building names, castle, workhouse, salmon leap, mills, chapel of ease; built-up part generalised. Apt omits land use.

47/18 Kidwelly (parish) SN 422074
Apt 30.01.1840; 5170a (5170); Map 1840, 8 chns, surveyed by Samuel Ball, Kidwelly; canal with towpath, waterbodies, woods, parkland, gardens, building names, tin mills, forge, mill, hamlet boundaries (col) and names, foreshore sand and clay; built-up part generalised; north pointer has plumes. District is apportioned by holding, though fields are numbered separately; Apt omits land use and field names.

47/19 Kiffig (parish) SN 198141 [Not listed]
Apt 17.12.1839; 4556a (all); Map 1840?, 12 chns, ? by John Harvey, Haverfordwest; building names, chapel; scale intersects north pointer. Apt omits land use and field names.

47/20 Kilrhedyn (parish) (partly in Pembrokeshire) SN 300348 [Not listed]
Apt 22.07.1840; 7856a (7856); Map 1841, 12 chns, by Samuel Ball, Kidwelly; woods, building names, mill, boundary cairns, college. Apt omits land use.

47/21 Laugharne (parish) SN 262122 [Not listed]
Apt 08.04.1841; 5470a (?); Map 1842?, 6 chns, in 2 parts, ? by Wm Goode, (including 3-chn enlargement of moor); waterbodies, houses, woods, fences, building names, sand dunes.

47/22 Laugharne (township in parish of Laugharne) SN 300100
Apt 31.12.1842; 3414a (?); Map 1846?, 3 chns, in 2 parts, (includes enlargement of town at 2 chns); railway, waterbodies, houses, woods, residual open fields, building names, parsonage, castle remains, burrows; scale intersects north pointer.

47/23 Llanarthney (parish) SN 550180
Apt 19.01.1847; 10995a (10994); Map 1848, 8 chns, by E.J. Griffiths, Llandilo; woods. Apt omits some field names.

47/24 Llanboidy (parish) SN 220240
Apt 14.03.1839; 10667a (10666); Map 1843?, 6 chns, by H.P. Goode and Philpott, Haverfordwest; woods, building names; north pointer has diadem, plumes and (blank) banner. Apt omits some land use.

47/25 Llandawke (parish) SN 280110
Apt 14.12.1839; 589a (613); Map 1840, 6 chns, copied from a map of 1804 by Essex Davies; waterbodies, glebe. District is apportioned by holding and fields are not shown; some roads are apparently omitted.

47/26 Llanddarog (parish) SN 510150
Apt 26.02.1839; 4501a (4501); Map 1846, 6 chns, by Edward Neale, Bridgend; houses. Apt omits some field names.

47/27 Llandebie (parish) SN 620150 [Llandybie]
Apt 31.12.1840; 10710a (10710); Map 1841, 8 chns, by E.I. Griffiths, Llandilo; railway, farmyards, woods. Apt omits some land use and some field names.

47/28 Llandefailog (parish) SN 414133 [Llandyfaelog]
Apt 28.01.1842; 8447a (7320); Map 1844?, 8 chns; building names, mill, hamlet boundaries; plain cartouche is superimposed on north pointer with plumes. Cydplwyf Kidwelly division is apportioned by holding, though fields are individually numbered; elsewhere Apt omits land use and some field names.

47/29 Llandefeysant (parish) SN 612228 [Not listed]
Apt 21.04.1838; 1551a (1551); Map 1839, 8 chns, in 2 parts, by E.I. Griffiths, Llandeilofawr; waterbodies, woods, plantations, parkland, watermill (by Dawson's symbol), holdings (col); crude stylised leaves form arms of direction pointer. Apt omits land use.

47/30 Llandilo Abercowin (parish) SN 315139 [Llandilo-abercowin]
Apt 28.10.1840; 882a (922); Map 1840?, 8 chns; woods, building names, embankment, boundary bushes.

47/31 Llandilo-vawr (parish) SN 650210 [Llandeilo]
Apt 05.04.1838; 25628a (25628); Map 1841?, 12 chns, in 2 parts; railway, waterbodies, woods, building names, mill, poor house, common; built-up part generalised. Apt omits land use and some field names; 'Chapels, Dissenting' have a separate section. The schedule to the agreement notes that as there is no map of the parish the acreages can only be estimateed.

47/32 Llandingat (parish) SN 772348 [Not listed]
Apt 13.03.1839; 8108a (8107); Map 1840, 6 chns, (includes Llandovery town at 1.5 chns); woods, plantations, holdings (col). Apt omits land use.

47/33 Llandisilio (parish) (partly in Pembrokeshire) SN 126239 [Llandissilio]
Apt 26.11.1839; 6468a (all); Map 1840?, 8 chns; waterbodies, woods, building names, mill, ford, footbridge, chapel, county boundary; bridge named. Apt omits land use.

47/34 Llandouror (parish) SN 242140 [Llanddowror]
Apt 21.07.1845; 1783a (1783); Map 1845, 8 chns, by Goode and Philpott, Haverfordwest, (includes village at 3 chns); waterbodies, woods, building names.

47/35 Llanedy (parish) SN 591073 [Llanedi]
Apt 08.09.1841; 5632a (5632); Map 4 chns, 'Mapped by Henry Brodie... August 1842 - Surveyors, David Roberts and William Glasbrook'; railway, waterbodies, building names, colliery, mills, chapel, parsonage. Apt omits land use and field names.

47/36 Llanegwad (parish) SN 515255 [Llanegwad]
Apt 05.12.1839; 12331a (12330); Map 1841?, 8 chns, ? by Morris Sayce; woods (col), building names, mill, Roman camp, boundary stone. Apt omits land use and some field names.

47/37 Llanelly (parish) SN 520040 [Llanelli]
Apt 19.02.1841; 2825a (18075); Map 1842?, 8 chns, (tithable parts only in detail); railway, tramway, canal with towpath, building names. Apt omits land use.

47/38 Llanfairarybryn (parish) SN 810410 [Not listed]
Apt 28.01.1839; 23458a (23457); Map 1841, 12 chns, surveyed by Bate of Brecon; waterbodies, woods, building names, mill. Apt omits most land use.

47/39 Llanfallteg (parish) (partly in Pembrokeshire) SN 157197
Apt 30.08.1843; 1867a (all); Map 1843, 8 chns, 'Drawn' by G.M. Llewellyn, Carmarthen; building names, county boundary.

47/40 Llanfihangel Aberbythych (parish) SN 590185 [Not listed]
Apt 11.03.1839; 6037a (6036); Map 1839, 6 chns, by E.J. Griffiths, Llandilofawr; hill-drawing, waterbodies, houses, woods, plantations, parkland, gardens (col), building names, oxbows, toll bars, quarry, holding boundaries. District is apportioned by holding; Apt omits land use.

47/41 Llanfihangel Aberconrn (parish) SN 305165 [Not listed]
Apt 15.05.1841; 5180a (5180); Map 1842, 9 chns, in 3 parts, by John Lewis, (includes enlargement of two villages at 3 chns); waterbodies, woods, plantations, building names, chapel, smithy, quarry, mill, mill stream, limekiln; pink bands may show tithe ownership and yellow bands may show tithe-free land.

47/42 Llanfihangel ar arth (parish) SN 450360 [Llanfihangel-ar-arth]
Apt 27.04.1841; 15994a (15993); Map 1842?, 8 chns, by Thomas Hand; woods, building names, mill, common. District is apportioned by holding; Apt omits land use.

47/43 Llanfihangelcilyfargen (parish) SN 598266 [Not listed]
Apt 11.07.1839; 517a (516); Map 1839, 8 chns, by John Lewis, (tinted); woods, building names. District is apportioned by holding; Apt omits land use.

47/44 Llanfihangel Rhos-y-Corn (parish) SN 535345 [Not listed]
Apt 28.10.1842; 9012a (9012); Map 8 chns, 'Mapped by Edwards Saunders and B. Jones for B. Jones and J. Saunders, April 1844'; turnpike roads, waterbodies, woods, building names, footbridge, cairns, mill, holding boundaries (col), common. Apt omits land use.

47/45 Llanfynydd (parish) SN 570290
Apt 18.01.1839; 10775a (10744); Map 1840, 8 chns, ? by Morris Sayce; woods, plantations, building names; leaves twine round lance-shaped north pointer. District is apportioned by holding, though fields are numbered separately; Apt omits land use and some field names.

47/46 Llangadock (parish) SN 720220 [Llangadog]
Apt 10.01.1838; 15643a (15642); Map 1839, 8 chns, in 2 parts, by William Goode, (enclosed parts only; includes town at 2 chns); woods, building names, houses (in town only), churchyard (col). Apt omits land use.

47/47 Llangain (parish) SN 386159
Apt 28.04.1841; 695a (2660); Map 1841?, 8 chns, (tithable parts only); building names; scale and north pointers are combined. Apt omits land use.

47/48 Llangan (parish) (partly in Pembrokeshire) SN 203193
Apt 08.04.1839; 4952a (4952); Map 1841?, 8 chns, by Goode and Philpott, Haverfordwest.

47/49 Llangathen (parish) SN 585223
Apt 11.01.1839; 5514a (5513); Map 1839, 8 chns, by William Goode, (tinted); hill-drawing, waterbodies, woods, plantations, gardens, building names, mills, forge (smithy), chapel, ford, poorhouse, kiln, oxbow, old river courses; stream named. Apt omits land use.

47/50 Llangeller (parish) SN 390370
Apt 07.12.1839; 8000a (7999); Map 1839, [9 chns], by Thos Hand; building names, crugs, hamlet boundaries. Apt omits land use and some field names.

47/51 Llangennech (parish) SN 556024
Apt 11.11.1842; 2344a (2394); Map 1843?, 8 chns; hill-drawing, foot/b'way, building names, quay, holding boundaries (col). Apt omits land use.

47/52 Llanginning (parish) SN 252197 [Llangynin]
Apt 27.06.1838; 3270a (3270); Map 1840, 6 chns, by Goode and Philpott, Haverfordwest; scale intersects north pointer.

47/53 Llanglydwen (parish) SN 167272
Apt 27.04.1844; 1825a (1834); Map 1846?, 8 chns, ? by A. Thomas; building names, poorhouse. Apt omits some field names.

47/54 Llangunnog (parish) SN 352162 [Llangynog]
Apt 21.03.1840; 4879a (4879); Map 1840?, 8 chns; building names, farm names, mill, college, tithe-merged land; scale and north pointer are combined. Apt omits land use.

47/55 Llangunnor (parish) SN 465182
Apt 09.06.1841; 5796a (all); Map 1842?, 8 chns; building names. Apt omits land use.

47/56 Llangyndeyrn (parish) SN 465125 [Llangendeirne]
Apt 30.04.1846; 11811a (11810); Map 1848, 8 chns, by E. Blathwayt, Kidwelly; canal with towpath, woods, building names, limekilns, mill, common.

47/57 Llanllawddog (parish) SN 464292
Apt 28.08.1838; 7014a (7013); Map 1842?, 8 chns; woods, building names, mill. Apt omits land use.

47/58 Llanllwny (parish) SN 500400 [Llanllwni]
Apt 15.06.1841; 6625a (6624); Map 1842, 6 chns, by B. Jones; hill-drawing, turnpike roads, private roads (uncoloured), waterbodies, farmyards (col), woods (col), plantations, parkland (col), orchard, gardens (col), tumuli, holding boundaries (col). Apt omits land use.

47/59 Llanon (parish) SN 555085 [Llannon]
Apt 17.07.1841; 11447a (11446); Map 1841, 8 chns, by Thomas Hand;

railway, canal with inclined plane, waterbodies, woods, parkland, building names, iron works, reservoir, mill. Apt omits some field names.

47/60 Llanpumpsant (parish) SN 430290 [Llanpumsaint]
Apt 10.12.1838; 4080a (4079); Map 1839, 8 chns, by Thomas Hand; woods, building names, chapel. Apt omits land use and some field names.

47/61 Llansadurnen (parish) SN 278095
Apt 30.03.1843; 1494a (all); Map 1841, 4 chns, by 'William Goode, Surveyor' and 'Drawn by Jacob Rees'; hill-drawing, waterbodies, plantations, building names, lime kilns and quarries, mill; scale-bar is ruler-like.

47/62 Llansadwrn (parish) SN 685315
Apt 18.01.1839; 7065a (all); Map 1839, 8 chns, by Dl Beynon; woods, plantations, turbary. District is apportioned by holding, though fields are numbered separately; Apt omits land use.

47/63 Llansawel (parish) SN 595365
Apt 12.07.1838; 7168a (7168); Map 1838, 8 chns, by John Bowen and William Morgan; holding boundaries (col). District is apportioned by holding and fields are not shown.

47/64 Llansawel (hamlet of Wen) (parish) SN 625380 [Not listed]
Apt 17.02.1838; 2851a (2851); Map 1838, 8 chns, by John Bowen and William Morgan; holding boundaries (col). District is apportioned by holding and fields are not shown.

47/65 Llanstephan (parish) SN 340112
Apt 05.12.1840; 4289a (6710); Map 1841?, 8 chns, (tithable parts only); building names, limekilns, embankment, castle remains; scale is superimposed on north pointer. Apt omits land use.

47/66 Llanthoysaint (parish) SN 776230 [Llanddeusant]
Apt 22.02.1838; 7307a (?); Map 1841?, 8 chns. Apt omits land use and some field names.

47/67 Llanwinio (parish) SN 245265
Apt 26.06.1848; 7169a (7169); Map 1850?, 8 chns, litho, ? by H.P.Goode; woods, building names. Apt omits some land use.

47/68 Llanwrda (parish) SN 715352
Apt 26.09.1837; 4441a (all); Map 1837, 8 chns, by William Morgan, holding boundaries (col). District is apportioned by holding and fields are not shown.

47/69 Llanybyther (parish) SN 540400 [Llanybydder]
Apt 25.11.1840; 10031a (all); Map 1840, 8 chns, by W. Morgan and B. Jones; chapel, tumuli, vicarage. District is apportioned by holding and fields are not shown.

47/70 Llanycrwys (parish) SN 632452 [Llancrwys]
Apt 04.04.1839; 3379a (3379); Map 1840, 8 chns, ? by William Morgan; holding boundaries (col). District is apportioned by holding and fields are not shown.

47/71 Lower Hamlet and Hamlets of Cwmtwrch and Cwmcothy (hamlet in parish of Conwil Gaio or Cayo) SN 659414 [Not listed]
Apt 16.05.1838; 6421a (6421); Map 1840, 8 chns, ? by William Morgan; holding boundaries (col). District is apportioned by holding and fields are not shown.

47/72 Marros (parish) SN 202086
Apt 14.12.1839; 2174a (all); Map 1840?, 10 chns; building names; north pointer and scale are combined. Apt omits land use.

47/73 Merthyr (parish) SN 354211
Apt 23.11.1838; 2219a (2218); Map 1839, [8 chns]; woods, building names, spring. Apt omits land use.

47/74 Mothvey (parish) SN 775305 [Myddfai]
Apt 15.02.1839; 11914a (11914); Map 1840, 8 chns, by David Davies; hill-drawing, foot/b'way, waterbodies, houses, woods, plantations, parkland, park paling, building names. Apt omits land use.

47/75 Mydrim (parish) SN 300210 [Meidrim]
Apt 09.06.1841; 6906a (6905); Map 1840, 8 chns, in 2 parts, drawn by Walter Lloyd; woods, building names. Apt omits land use.

47/76 Newchurch (parish) SN 390240
Apt 21.06.1844; 4824a (4894); Map 1846?, 8 chns, by Geo. Goode, Surveyor etc, Carmarthen; building names. Apt omits land use.

47/77 Pembrey (parish) SN 425035
Apt 07.06.1839; 14707a (all); Map 1841, 8 chns, by William Hand; canal with towpath, aqueduct, woods, building names, sluice, high water mark, boundary stones, finger post (by symbol), harbour. Apt omits land use.

47/78 Penboyr (parish) SN 345375
Apt 03.05.1838; 6877a (6876); Map 1840, 8 chns, ? by Morris Sayce; woods, building names, cairn, quarry, common. Apt omits land use and some field names.

47/79 Pencarreg (parish) SN 590440
Apt 09.12.1841; 10392a (10392); Map 1841, 8 chns, by William Morgan, John Edwards and John Rees, Land-Surveyors; waterbodies, woods, boundary marks. Apt omits land use.

47/80 Pendine (parish) SN 233086
Apt 14.12.1839; 963a (1578); Map 1842?, 8 chns, ? by John Harvey; limekilns. Apt omits some field names.

47/81 Talley (parish) SN 634317
Apt 28.09.1838; 7168a (7167); Map 1839, 8 chns, by W. Morgan; holding boundaries (col). District is apportioned by holding and fields are not shown.

47/82 Treleach ar Bettws (parish) SN 292276 [Trelech]
Apt 29.08.1845; 11503a (11492); Map 1844, [10 chns], ? by John Lewis, Walter Lloyd, William Pugh; waterbodies, woods, building names, chapels, commons. Apt omits land use.

Carnarvonshire

PRO IR29 and IR30 48/1-69

73 tithe districts: 361,097 acres
69 tithe commutations: 340,472 acres
57 voluntary tithe agreements, 12 compulsory awards

Tithe and tithe commutation

About 94 per cent of the tithe districts of Carnarvonshire were subject to the payment of tithes in 1836 but only one district was wholly tithable (Fig. 60). Moduses in lieu of tithes were paid in 90 per cent of tithable districts.

Assistant tithe commissioners, local tithe agents and the valuers of tithe rent-charge in Carnarvonshire are listed in Tables 48.1 and 48.2. In nineteen districts tithes are apportioned by holding and for these districts the schedules of tithe apportionment contain no information on individual fields. The apportionment for Clynog has a number of unusual land-use descriptions which include 'bog waste', 'fuel ground', and 'waste rock'.

Tithe maps

Carnarvonshire, in common with most Welsh and other counties in which moduses were prevalent, has no first-class maps and only one map with original construction lines. Only three maps are stated to be copies but it is difficult to say how widespread copying may have been.

Carnarvonshire tithe maps are drawn at a variety of scales from one inch to two chains to one inch to thirty-six chains and only 34 per cent are in the recommended scale range of one inch to three to four chains. The most favoured scale in this county was the eight-chain used in 33 per cent of tithe districts (Table 48.3). Llanystymdwy, a parish of 6,500 acres, is mapped at the two-chain scale rarely used outside urban areas. In contrast, the similarly sized parish of Llanvair vechan is mapped at a scale of one inch to thirty-six chains and is the smallest-scale of all English and Welsh tithe maps.

As usual in Wales, the only land use recorded at all widely on Carnarvonshire maps is woodland (on 63 per cent). None shows arable or grass and only five tithe maps distinguish inhabited and uninhabited buildings. The nature of the terrain helps explain the high proportion (30 per cent) of maps which show slopes; several maps portray quarries.

Forty-five Carnarvonshire tithe maps in the Public Record Office collection can be attributed to a particular map-maker, the most prolific of whom was Thomas Davies

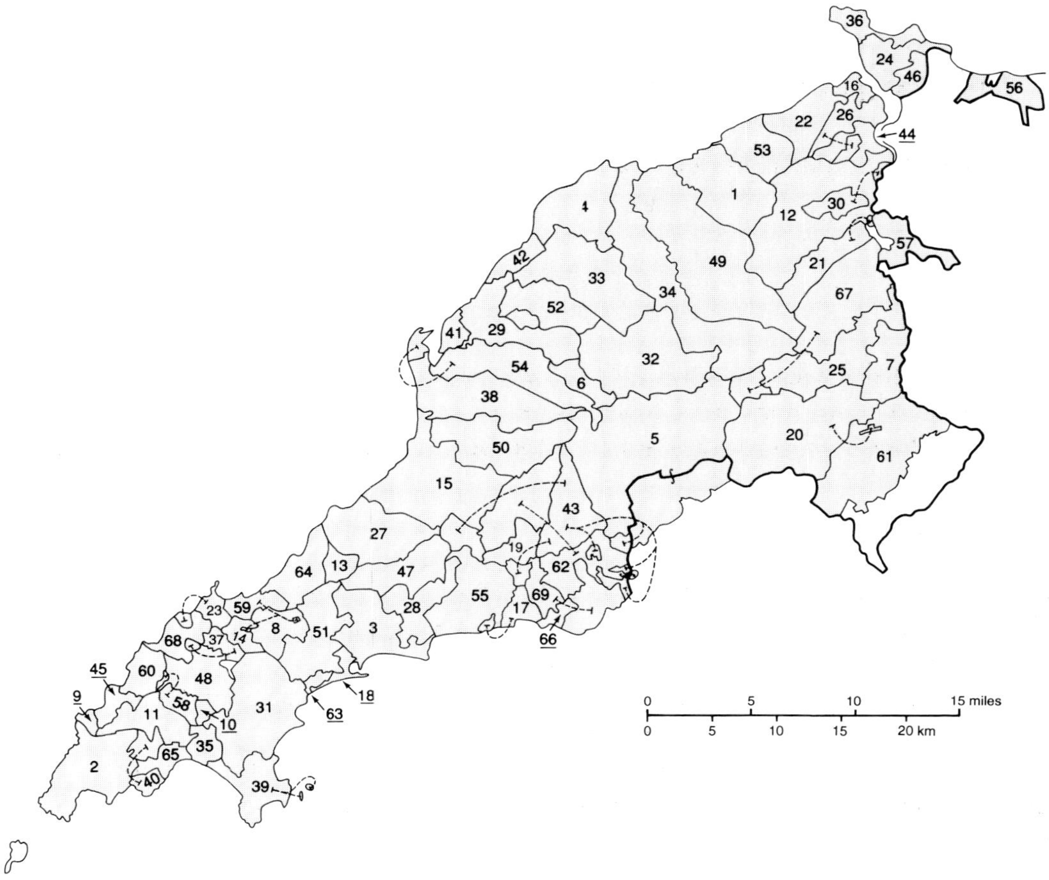

Fig. 60 Carnarvonshire: tithe district boundaries.

Owen of Pwllheli who made thirteen maps. His maps vary in style, some are plain, but others have coloured borders or woodland. Three maps are by James Spooner of Morfa and are characterised by careful execution and very thorough naming of buildings. Although in Wales the dispersed nature of settlement perhaps encouraged map-makers to name buildings to a greater extent than they did in England, Spooner's work is nonetheless outstanding in this respect.

Carnarvonshire maps possess rather more decorative embellishments than do most of those in North Wales; seventeen have decorative borders, sometimes with bird-like corners, and several have north pointers with Prince of Wales's feathers, a diadem, and the motto 'Ich Dien'.

Table 48.1. *Agreements and awards for commutation of tithes in Carnarvonshire*

Assistant commissioner/ local tithe agent	*Number of agreements**	*Number of awards*
John Fenton	50	0
Aneurin Owen	7	12

*Computed from the number of extant reports on tithe agreements in the tithe files [PRO IR 18].

Table 48.2. *Tithe valuers and tithe map-makers in Carnarvonshire*

Name and address (in Carnarvonshire unless indicated)	*Number of districts*	*Acreage*
Tithe valuers		
Edward Edwards, Gwynfryn	25	100,832
Francis Marston, Hopesay, Shropshire	10	80,684
Others [18]	34	158,956
Attributed tithe map-makers		
Thomas Davies Owen, Pwllheli	13	50,647
Henry Kennedy, London and Bangor	8	55,430
R. Lloyd Ellis, Carnarvon	4	50,689
James Spooner and Son	3	21,149
Messrs E. and T. Johnson, Llanrhos	3	6,271
John R. Haslam, Menai Bridge, Anglesey	3	5,321
John Price, Chester/Ruthin	3	4,958
Others [7]	8	38,165

Table 48.3. *The tithe maps of Carnarvonshire: scales and classes*

Scale in chains/inch	*All maps*		*First Class*		*Second Class*	
	Number	*Acreage*	*Number*	*Acreage*	*Number*	*Acreage*
>3	1	6,523	0	0	1	6,523
3	9	49,802	0	0	9	49,802
4	15	56,478	0	0	15	56,478
6	16	50,728	0	0	16	50,728
7.5	1	3,106	0	0	1	3,106
8	23	137,349	0	0	23	137,349
<8	4	36,486	0	0	4	36,486
TOTAL	69	340,472	0	0	69	340,472

Table 48.4. *The tithe maps of Carnarvonshire: dates*

	1839	*1840*	*1841*	*1842*	*1843*	*1844*	*1845*	*1846*	*1847*	*1848*	*1849*
2nd class*	20	18	6	1	3	5	5	1	4	4	1

*One second-class tithe map of Carnarvonshire in the Public Record Office collection is undated.

Carnarvonshire

48/1 Aber (parish) SH 670710 [Abergwyngregyn]
Apt 02.03.1847; 7318a (8833); Map 1848, 6 chns, by Kennedy and Johnson, Bangor; railway, turnpike road (col), waterbodies, woods, heath/moor, school, mill, boundary marks, slate quarry, waterfall, lordship boundary; lake named. District is apportioned by holding, though fields are numbered separately; Apt generalises land use.

48/2 Aberdaron (parish) SH 175280
Apt 19.11.1844; 6904a (7078); Map 1845?, [10 chns]; well. Apt omits field names.

48/3 Abereirch (parish) SH 395380 [Abererch]
Apt 13.05.1844; 5811a (5962); Map 1840, 6 chns; waterbodies, woods; border has stylised-bird corners; north pointer has diadem, plumes and 'Ich Dien'.

48/4 Bangor (parish) SH 562700
Apt 08.11.1840; 6804a (7543); Map 1840?, 3 chns; building names, chapel, Menai Bridge, Cathedral, common (edged green). Apt omits field names.

48/5 Beddgelert (parish) SH 605515
Apt 04.12.1839; 6717a (26716); Map 1840, 16 chns, by R. Lloyd Ellis, Carnarvon; waterbodies, turnpike gate, ownerships (col), holding boundaries (col); physical features named; north pointer has diadem and Prince of Wales feathers; border has 'bird' corners. District is apportioned by holding and fields are not shown.

48/6 Bettwsgarmon (parish) SH 557562 [Betws Garmon]
Apt 31.08.1839; 2760a (2759); Map 1840, 6 chns, by Thos Davies Owen, Pwllheli; building names, holding boundaries; lake named; border has 'bird' corners. District is apportioned by holding and fields are not shown.

48/7 Bettws y Coed (parish) SH 780570 [Betws-y-Coed]
Apt 30.06.1841; 3537a (all); Map 1840, 8 chns, 'Made from Existing Surveys' by Henry Kennedy, 100 Chancery Lane, London; waterbodies, woods, field boundary ownerships, churchyard, turnpike gate, pound, holding boundaries (col); bridge and lakes named. District is apportioned by holding and fields are not shown.

48/8 Bodean or Bodfuan (parish) SH 324384 [Boduan]
Apt 20.10.1840; 2573a (2572); Map 1839, 8 chns, by Thos Davies Owen, Pwllheli; waterbodies, woods (col). Apt omits land use.

48/9 Bodferin (parish) SH 178312 [Not listed]
Apt 05.06.1840; 512a (511); Map 1840, 4 chns.

48/10 Bottwnog (parish) SH 262318 [Botwnnog]
Apt 04.05.1840; 487a (487); Map 1839, 4 chns, by John Price, Chester; waterbodies, farmyards, woods, orchard, building names, chapels, school; mapmaker's name is stamped.

48/11 Bryncroes (parish) SH 220315
Apt 24.11.1840; 3646a (3646); Map 1844, 8 chns, ? by Thos Davies Owen, Pwllheli; waterbodies.

48/12 Caerhun (parish) SH 714692
Apt 24.07.1846; 13403a (13402); Map 1847, 8 chns, by Kennedy and Johnson, Bangor; waterbodies, woods, heath/moor; physical features named. District is apportioned by holding; Apt generalises land use.

48/13 Carngiwch (parish or chapelry) SH 372423 [Carnguwch]
Apt 23.05.1840; 1345a (1344); Map 1839, 6 chns; hill-drawing, waterbodies, building names, fuel ground, mill; north pointer has diadem, Prince of Wales feathers and 'Ich Dien'.

48/14 Ceidio (parish) SH 288380 [Not listed]
Apt 23.03.1846; 1081a (1081); Map 1843?, 4 chns, by Thos Davies Owen, Pwllheli; waterbodies, houses, woods (col), chapel.

48/15 Clynog (parish) SH 452485 [Clynnog Fawr]
Apt 21.09.1843; 11487a (12060); Map 1839, 8 chns; waterbodies, woods (col), plantations, foreshore (col); north pointer has diadem, Prince of Wales feathers and 'Ich Dien'; border has 'bird' corners.

48/16 Conwy (parish) SH 770782
Apt 21.02.1846; 933a (2437); Map 1848?, 8 chns, by John R. Haslam; railway, suspension and tubular bridges, town wall and bastions; built-up part generalised. District is apportioned by holding and fields are not shown.

48/17 Crickieth (parish) SH 506390 [Criccieth]
Apt 04.09.1839; 1569a (1678); Map 1839, 6 chns, by John Price, Chester; hill-drawing, waterbodies, woods (col), plantations (col), building names, slate quarry, turnpike gate, foreshore (col), tithe-free land (col). Apt omits land use.

48/18 Deneio (parish) SH 373351 [Denio]
Apt 23.01.1844; 902a (1278); Map 1846, 3 chns, by Richd Roberts, Carnarvon; hill-drawing, waterbodies, houses, woods, embankment, workhouse; built-up part generalised.

48/19 Dolbenmaen (parish or chapelry) SH 506436
Apt 28.08.1839; 2146a (2145); Map 1844?, 3 chns, by James Spooner and Sons; waterbodies, houses, woods, marsh/bog, hedge ownership, building names (thorough), lodge, boundary stones, rectory, school, mound, waterfalls.

48/20 Dolwyddelen (parish) SH 721521 [Dolwyddelan]
Apt 30.06.1841; 14385a (all); Map 1840, 8 chns, in 2 parts, 'Made from Existing Surveys' by Henry Kennedy, 100 Chancery Lane, London; hill-drawing, waterbodies, field boundary ownerships, building names, slate quarry, castle, crags, farm boundaries; lakes named. District is apportioned by holding and fields are not shown.

48/21 Dolgarog and Ardda (township in parish of Llanbedr y cenin) SH 745658 [Dolgarrog]
Apt 31.08.1846; 3359a (3359); Map 1847, 8 chns, by Messrs Kennedy and Johnson; waterbodies, woods, sheepwalk; lakes named. District is apportioned by holding; Apt generalises land use.

48/22 Dwygyfylchi (parish) SH 730760 [Dygyflchi]
Apt 29.12.1842; 3790a (5794); Map 1839, 3 chns, by Robert Williams; railway, waterbodies, woods, heaps of stones, quarries, stone circle, boundary stones (pictorial), common pasture, township boundaries; hills named.

48/23 Edeyrn (parish) SH 277399 [Edern]
Apt 23.05.1840; 1360a (1380); Map 1840?, 6 chns, in 2 parts, (including 1.5 chn enlargement of detail); waterbodies, cliffs.

48/24 Eglwysrhos (parish) SH 793800 [Llanrhos]
Apt 17.02.1846; 3106a (3735); Map 1840, 7.5 chns, by Messrs E. and T. Johnson, Llanrhos; foot/b'way, waterbodies, woods (col), plantations, marsh/bog, building names, estate boundaries.

48/25 Gwydyr (township in parish of Llanwrst) SH 740560
Apt 31.12.1842; 7621a (7621); Map 1840, 8 chns, by Henry Kennedy, Bangor N. W., and 100 Chancery Lane, London; hill-drawing, waterbodies, plantations, field boundary ownerships, chapel. District is apportioned by holding and fields are not shown.

48/26 Gyfin (parish) SH 769759 [Gyffin]
Apt 31.08.1848; 3556a (3705); Map 1848?, 8 chns, ? by John R. Haslam, Menai bridge, Anglesey. District is apportioned by holding and fields are not shown.

48/27 Llanaelhaiarn (parish) SH 399451 [Llanaelhaearn]
Apt 27.10.1840; 6729a (6698); Map 1839, 8 chns, ? by R.Ellis; hill-drawing, waterbodies, woods, rock outcrops, building names, chapels, foreshore sand and rocks (col); border has 'bird' corners; north pointer has diadem, Prince of Wales feathers and 'Ich Dien'.

48/28 Llanarmon (parish) SH 426392
Apt 10.02.1841; 3753a (3753); Map 1839, 8 chns, by Thos Davies Owen, Pwllheli; hill-drawing, waterbodies, woods (col); north pointer has diadem, Prince of Wales feathers and 'Ich Dien'; border has 'bird' corners.

48/29 Llanbeblig (parish) SH 490620 [Not listed]
Apt 22.04.1841; 6322a (6792); Map not dated, 4 chns; waterbodies, quarry, low water mark, boundary rock; built-up part generalised.

48/30 Llanbedr and Tal y cavn (townships) SH 753693 [Llanbedr-y-cennin]
Apt 17.09.1846; 1551a (1551); Map 1847, 6 chns, by Messrs Kennedy and Johnson; woods, ferry. District is apportioned by holding and fields are not shown; Apt generalises land use.

48/31 Llanbedrog, Llangian and Llanfihangel Bachellaeth (parishes) SH 305320
Apt 18.09.1839; 9583a (10298); Map 1840?, 4 chns, in 3 parts, by Thos Davies Owen, Pwllheli; hill-drawing, waterbodies, woods, plantations, parkland, gardens, cliffs, foreshore; there are variations in style between the parts.

48/32 Llanberris (parish) SH 579599 [Llanberis]
Apt 10.09.1839; 10432a (10431); Map 1839, 8 chns, by R. Lloyd Ellis, Carnarvon; hill-drawing, waterbodies, hotel, castle, sheepwalks, holding boundaries (col); serrated ridges are shown by very conventionalised rows of hill-drawing; lakes named. District is apportioned by holding and fields are not shown.

48/33 Llanddeniolen (parish) SH 560650 [Llanddeiniolen]
Apt 07.06.1839; 9024a (9024); Map 1839, 8 chns, by R. Lloyd Ellis, Carnarvon; railway, waterbodies, woods, building names, ownership boundaries (col), public turbary; physical features named; lakes are named, Llyn Peris and Llyn Padarn being confused.

48/34 Llandegai (parish) SH 620650
Apt 12.12.1840; 8609a (16100); Map 1841, 12 chns, 'Reduced from the original Survey' by John Barrow, (tithable parts only); hill-drawing, railway, waterbodies, woods (col), parkland, fish weirs, slate quarry (col), foreshore (col), low water mark. District is apportioned by holding and fields are not shown.

48/35 Llandegwning (parish) SH 269294
Apt 19.12.1842; 1369a (1488); Map 1839, 3 chns, by Thos Davies Owen, Pwllheli; waterbodies, woods, foreshore (col); border has 'bird' corners.

48/36 Llandudno (parish) SH 781825
Apt 11.10.1845; 1914a (2729); Map 1845?, 4 chns, by Messrs Johnson, Surveyors etc., Llanrhos; building names, waste (col), mines (by symbol).

48/37 Llandudwen (parish) SH 277372
Apt 26.10.1848; 1331a (1331); Map 1849?, 6 chns; waterbodies, woods, holding boundaries (col); not all roads are shown. District is apportioned by holding and fields are not shown; Apt generalises land use.

48/38 Llandwrog (parish) SH 497543
Apt 15.09.1840; 9417a (9516); Map 1841, 4 chns; waterbodies, sands (col).

48/39 Llanengan (parish) SH 300268
Apt 15.09.1840; 3721a (4354); Map 1842?, 8 chns; foreshore (col), cliffs; offshore islands are unnumbered.

48/40 Llanfaelrhys (parish or chapelry) SH 219268
Apt 19.11.1844; 1680a (1679); Map 1840, 6 chns; building names. Apt omits some field names.

48/41 Llanfaglan (parish) SH 465605 [Llanfagan]
Apt 31.08.1839; 1272a (1884); Map 1839, 3 chns, surveyed by Claudius Shaw, Bangor; construction lines; north pointer has plumes and 'Ich Dien'.

48/42 Llanfairisgaer (parish) SH 515660 [Not listed]
Apt 10.10.1839; 1909a (2474); Map 1840, 4 chns, in 2 parts; hill-drawing, woods, building names, ownership boundaries (col), demesne.

48/43 Llanfihangel y Pennant (parish) SH 543453 [Llanfihangel-y-pennant]
Apt 04.12.1839; 8845a (8844); Map 1844?, 3 chns, in 4 parts, by James Spooner and Sons; foot/b'way, waterbodies, houses, woods, gardens, marsh/bog, hedge ownership, building names (very thorough), boundary stones, turbaries (col), lodge, engine house, trials for slate, walled garden, spring, watermill (by Dawson's symbol), sheepfold, chapel, embankment.

48/44 Llangelynin (parish) SH 777740 [Not listed]
Apt 26.02.1846; 1832a (2017); Map 1845?, 8 chns, ? by John R. Haslam, Menai bridge, Anglesey; rock outcrops. District is apportioned by holding and fields are not shown.

48/45 Llangwnadle (parish) SH 194334 [Llangwnadl]
Apt 30.06.1841; 1243a (1243); Map 1841?, 4 chns, in 8 parts, (including seven 3-chn enlargements of detail); building names, boundary stones, construction lines (on enlargements only).

48/46 Llangwstenin (parish) SH 812794
Apt 29.10.1845; 1251a (1314); Map 1845?, 8 chns, by Messrs E. and T. Johnson, Surveyors etc., Llanrhos; woods (col), heath/moor.

48/47 Llangybi (parish) SH 427419
Apt 10.02.1841; 4519a (all); Map 1841?, 6 chns, by Thos Davies Owen, Pwllheli; waterbodies, woods (col).

48/48 Llaniestyn (parish) SH 261348
Apt 24.11.1840; 4256a (4256); Map 1840, 6 chns; hill-drawing, waterbodies, woods (col).

48/49 Llanllechid (parish) SH 656658
Apt 09.01.1840; 10811a (18111); Map 1839, 4 chns, in 3 parts, by R. Edwards; waterbodies, tithe-free land, land 'Now built upon'; buildings are shown in outline only, without fill. District is apportioned by holding and fields are not shown.

48/50 Llanllyfni (parish) SH 490520
Apt 13.09.1839; 7521a (7521); Map 1840, 6 chns, by Thos Davies Owen, Pwllheli; waterbodies; north pointer has diadem, Prince of Wales feathers and 'Ich Dien'; border has 'bird' corners. Apt omits some field names.

48/51 Llannor (parish) SH 353372
Apt 11.06.1840; 5554a (5553); Map 1839, 8 chns; waterbodies, woods (col); border has 'bird' corners.

48/52 Llanrug (parish) SH 539625
Apt 04.06.1839; 4516a (4516); Map 1840, 3 chns, by R. Lloyd Ellis, Carnarvon; hill-drawing, waterbodies, woods, parkland, gardens, building names, quarry; colours may show property ownerships; tree symbols are inverted vis-a-vis writing and title; north pointer has some serpents-tongue decoration.

48/53 Llanvair vechan (parish) SH 698736 [Llanfair fechan]
Apt 07.07.1847; 4256a (6521); Map 1848, 36 chns, by Kennedy and Johnson, Bangor; railway, woods, holding boundaries; some holding boundaries and tree symbols are blue. District is apportioned by holding and fields are not shown; Apt generalises land use.

48/54 Llanwnda (parish) SH 500580
Apt 31.08.1839; 8765a (11459); Map 1841?, 4 chns; railway, waterbodies, beach (col).

48/55 Llanystymdwy (parish) SH 477400 [Llanystumdwy]
Apt 27.09.1841; 6523a (6780); Map 1843?, 2 chns, in 2 parts, by Thos Davies Owen, Pwllheli; woods (col), plantations, sands (col).

48/56 Llysfaen (parish) SH 893776
Apt 23.09.1842; 1560a (all); Map 1839, 6 chns; hill-drawing, woods, building names, commons, telegraph station, ownerships (col), 'Land worn down by the sea'. Apt omits land use.

48/57 Maenau (district in parish of Eglwysvach) SH 798665 [Maenan]
Apt 21.08.1847; 2902a (2902); Map 1847, 8 chns, by John Price, Ruthin; hill-drawing, waterbodies, woods, parkland, fence, boundary stones, sub-township boundaries; colours may indicate moduses; no buildings are shown.

48/58 Meilltyrne (parish) SH 242328 [Meyllteryn]
Apt 04.05.1840; 1519a (1519); Map 1839, 8 chns, by Thomas Davies Owen, Pwllheli; hill-drawing, woods (col), plantations.

48/59 Nefyn (parish) SH 307406
Apt 17.11.1840; 1706a (1816); Map 1839, 4 chns, in 2 parts, (including 2-chn enlargement of the town); hill-drawing, waterbodies, woods (col), rock outcrops, open fields (residual), windmill (pictorial), chapel, cliffs, foreshore, beach (col); border has bird corners; north pointers have diadem, 'Ich Dien' on scroll, and Prince of Wales feathers.

48/60 Penllech (parish or chapelry) SH 220350
Apt 09.05.1840; 2095a (2187); Map 1840?, 6 chns; waterbodies, woods (col), building names, cliffs, beach (col).

48/61 Penmachno (parish) SH 779497
Apt 25.05.1842; 11208a (11208); Map 1839, 8 chns; hill-drawing, foot/b'way, woods, building names, slate quarry, almshouses; colours may show property ownerships.

48/62 Penmorfa (parish) SH 540420
Apt 28.08.1839; 10158a (10157); Map 1844?, 3 chns, in 2 parts, by James Spooner and Sons; foot/b'way, waterbodies, houses, woods, plantations, gardens, turbaries (col), building names (very thorough), shop, quarries, boundary stones, cairn; physical features named; types of quarry are described.

48/63 Penrhos (parish or chapelry) SH 351342
Apt 14.09.1840; 453a (555); Map 1839, 4 chns, by Thos Davies Owen, Pwllheli; embankments.

48/64 Pistyll (parish or chapelry) SH 348428
Apt 31.10.1840; 3811a (3949); Map 1839, 6 chns, by R. Ellis; hill-drawing, rock outcrops, building names, cliffs; north pointer has diadem, Prince of Wales feathers, and 'Ich Dien' on scroll.

48/65 Rhiw (parish) SH 228278
Apt 24.11.1842; 1494a (1653); Map 1844, 4 chns; waterbodies, woods (col), gardens (col), heath/moor.

48/66 Treflys (parish) SH 535380 [Not listed]
Apt 04.09.1839; 781a (999); Map 1840?, 4 chns; hill-drawing, waterbodies, woods (col), building names, cliffs, sand, chapel. Apt omits land use.

48/67 Trefriw and Llanrhychwyn (parish) SH 757620
Apt 18.09.1841; 9577a (9576); Map 1841?, 8 chns, in 3 parts, (including ?64-chn index); waterbodies, woods (col), modus lands (col); lakes named; physical features named. District is apportioned by holding and fields are not shown.

48/68 Tydweiliog (parish or chapelry) SH 240373 [Tudweiliog]
Apt 20.01.1845; 2241a (2241); Map 1845?, 6 chns, by Henry P. Owen, Pwllheli; waterbodies, woods (col), sand (col).

48/69 Ynyscynhaiarn (parish) SH 524400 [Not listed]
Apt 05.09.1842; 5347a (6546); Map 1843?, 8 chns, by Thos Davies Owen, Pwllheli; hill-drawing, waterbodies, woods (col), cliffs, embankments, town green and quay (col), foreshore (col); Tremadoc and Port Madoc are named and carefully mapped.

Denbighshire

PRO IR29 and IR30 49/1-106

107 tithe districts: 442,397 acres
106 tithe commutations: 343,732 acres
92 voluntary tithe agreements, 14 compulsory tithe awards

Tithe and tithe commutation

Although in 1836 all but one of the tithe districts of Denbighshire remained liable to tithe, only about 78 per cent of the county by area was still tithable and in more than two-thirds of districts some land was exempt (Fig. 61). Modus payments in lieu of tithes were the main cause of tithe exemption and applied in 58 per cent of all tithable districts.

Assistant tithe commissioners and local tithe agents who worked in Denbighshire are listed in Table 49.1 and the county's valuers of tithe rent-charge in Table 49.2. In ten districts tithes are apportioned by holding and the schedules of tithe apportionment for these places lack information on the acreage, land use, and names of individual fields and properties. Land use and field names are also incomplete or wholly omitted in some apportionments made on a field-by-field basis. On the other hand, seven apportionments include field-by-field information on arable crops; geographically Denbighshire is on the margins of the Staffordshire/Cheshire concentration of this practice.

Tithe maps

In conformity with other North Wales counties, Denbighshire lacks first-class maps, though original construction lines are present on three second-class maps. It is hard to tell how many maps are the result of original survey and how many are copies, though not one map-maker explicity refers to copying earlier work.

Denbighshire tithe maps are drawn at a variety of scales from one inch to one chain to one inch to 26.67 chains. Exactly one-fifth are in the recommended scale range of one inch to three to four chains and 55 per cent are at scales of one inch to six to eight chains (Table 49.3). As usual in Wales, the tithe maps of Denbighshire are good records of woodland (on 89 per cent of the maps) but poor records of other land use; none shows arable or grass, and only seven depict gardens, 11 per cent show parks (the Chirk map shows the park in detail, including deer sheds), and 10 per cent identify heath and moor. What is probably the only measurement of altitude above sea-level recorded on a tithe map is to be found on the map of Llandegla.

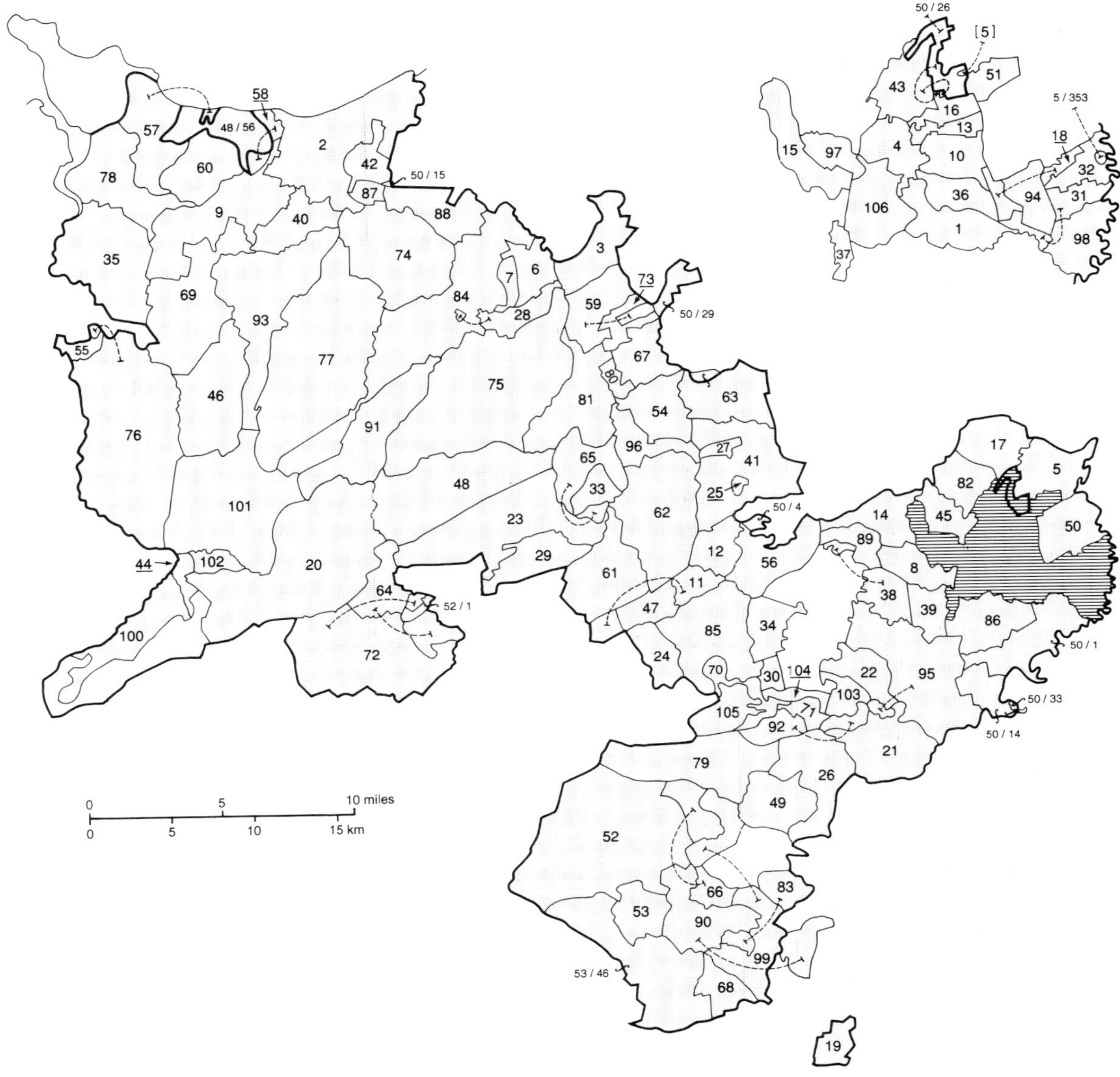

Fig. 61 Denbighshire: tithe district boundaries.

Only forty-five Denbighshire tithe maps in the Public Record Office collection can be attributed to a particular map-maker; the three most prolific were William Lloyd of Wrexham, John Price of Denbigh or Ruthin, and George W. Chaloner. Between them these map-makers produced twenty-three maps, covering 18 per cent of the area of the county, and all characterised by heavy linework. Denbighshire has two of the least impressive of all tithe maps. That of Nantglyn is at a scale of one inch to 26.67 chains and has a corresponding paucity of detail, and that of Gwythrania has a note appended by the tithe commissioners which states that 'this map appears to be a sketch only'. It is very much a sketch map and is one of only three known tithe maps not drawn to scale. The map of Llanbedr Dyffryn Clwyd is exceptional amongst both Denbighshire and Welsh tithe maps generally in that it is brightly coloured. The map of St George employs stamped names, also an unusual feature in Wales.

Table 49.1. *Agreements and awards for commutation of tithes in Denbighshire*

Assistant commissioner/ local tithe agent	*Number of agreements**	*Number of awards*
Aneurin Owen	47	13
John Fenton	43	0
John Johnes	3	0
George Wingrove Cooke	0	1
Charles Pym	1	0

*Computed from the number of extant reports on tithe agreements in the tithe files [PRO IR 18].

Table 49.2. *Tithe valuers and tithe map-makers in Denbighshire*

Name and address (in Denbighshire unless indicated)	*Number of districts*	*Acreage*
Tithe valuers		
John Welch, Berth	19	81,886
Richard Yates, Whittington, Shropshire	9	29,302
Robert Roberts, Tyddyn Issa	8	32,515
Francis Marston, Hopesay, Shropshire	7	31,217
William Lloyd, Wrexham	7	7,938
Issac Porter, Oswestry, Shropshire	6	15,788
Robert Piercy, Chirk	6	11,994
Others [25]	44	133,092
Attributed tithe map-makers		
William Lloyd, Wrexham	9	7,938
John Price, Denbigh/Ruthin	8	39,086
George W. Chaloner	6	16,365
John Roberts, Corwen	3	8,791
Thomas Jenkins	3	7,001
Iassac Porter, Oswestry, Shropshire	2	2,352
Others [12]	18	27,416

Table 49.3. *The tithe maps of Denbighshire: scales and classes*

Scale in chains/inch	*All maps*		*First Class*		*Second Class*	
	Number	*Acreage*	*Number*	*Acreage*	*Number*	*Acreage*
>3	1	202	0	0	1	202
3	9	19,803	0	0	9	19,803
4	12	19,029	0	0	12	19,029
5	9	9,642	0	0	9	9,642
6	38	122,860	0	0	38	122,860
6.5	1	1,224	0	0	1	1,224
8	20	97,948	0	0	20	97,948
<8	15	71,289	0	0	15	71,289
Not to scale	1	1,735	0	0	1	1,735
TOTAL	106	343,732	0	0	106	343,732

Table 49.4 The tithe maps of Denbighshire: dates

	<1837	*1837*	*1838*	*1839*	*1840*	*1841*	*1842*	*1843*	*1844*	*1845*	*1846*	*1847*	*1848*
2nd class	1	0	11	19	14	14	10	11	9	6	3	4	3

Denbighshire

49/1 Abenbury Vawr and Abenbury Vechan (township in parish of Wrexham) (partly in Flint) SJ 360495 [Not listed]
Apt 13.08.1842; 1217a (all); Map 1838, 8.5 chns; waterbodies, woods, county boundary.

49/2 Abergele (parish) SH 945775
Apt 05.05.1840; 8997a (?); Map 1839, 8 chns, by T.G. Cummings; woods, building names, lands allocated to poor. Apt omits some field names.

49/3 Aberwhiler (township in parish of Bodfary) SJ 110700 [Aberwheeler]
Apt 31.12.1842; 3343a (all); Map 1843?, 8 chns; waterbodies, woods, heath/moor (col), ownerships (col); names are stamped.

49/4 Acton (township in parish of Wrexham) SJ 342526
Apt 17.12.1839; 852a (all); Map 1840?, 9 chns, litho; hill-drawing, waterbodies, woods, parkland, building names. Apt has cropping information.

49/5 Allington (except Holt Parks) (township in parish of Gresford) SJ 381569 [Not listed]
Apt 30.10.1843; 3052a (3052); Map 1845?, 6 chns, in 2 parts, (includes 3-chn enlargement of detail); waterbodies, woods, plantations, building names, gravel pit, pinfold, parsonages; bridge named; colours may indicate tithe ownership.

49/6 Bannister Issa (township in parish of Henllan) SJ 070690 [Not listed]
Apt 05.02.1842; 1823a (?); Map 1842?, [8 chns]; woods, field boundary ownerships, building names.

49/7 Bannister Ucha (township in parish of Henllan) SJ 055681 [Not listed]
Apt 05.02.1842; 689a (?); Map 1841, 8 chns; waterbodies, woods, field boundary ownerships, building names, gardens (by annotation). Apt omits some field names.

49/8 Bersham (township in parish of Wrexham) SJ 305505
Apt 12.12.1840; 1899a (all); Map 1841, 6 chns, in 4 parts, (includes three 3-chn enlargements of detail); foot/b'way, waterbodies, woods, building names, quarries, workhouse.

49/9 Bettws-yn-Rhos (parish) SH 888728 [Betwys-yn-rhos]
Apt 08.01.1841; 6262a (6262); Map 1841?, 6 chns; foot/b'way, waterbodies, woods, building names, quarry, parish quarry (col), churchyard (col).

49/10 Breston and Gourton (township in parish of Wrexham) SJ 367519 [Not listed]
Apt 13.08.1842; 845a (all); Map 1841?, 8 chns; foot/b'way, waterbodies, woods, parkland, landowners, boundary stones, township boundaries (col), ownerships (col).

49/11 Boddyn Wyddog and Bryntangor (township or district) SJ 170497 [Bodanwydog]
Apt 19.10.1841; 1549a (?); Map 1845, 13.33 chns, by Jno. Price, Ruthin; woods. District is apportioned by holding and fields are not shown.

49/12 Bodigre yr Abbot and Bodigre yr Tarll (township) SJ 181518 [Not listed]
Apt 29.05.1847; 1875a (?); Map 1848, 8 chns, by John Price, Denbigh; woods, heath/moor, building names, mill, entrenchment.

49/13 Borras Riffre (township in parish of Gresford) SJ 370529 [Not listed]
Apt 20.09.1843; 333a (332); Map 1843, 5 chns, by W. Lloyd, Wrexham; waterbodies, houses, woods, orchard, marsh/bog (col), field boundary ownerships.

49/14 Brymbo (township in parish of Wrexham) SJ 283539
Apt 03.09.1844; 2451a (2451); Map 1839, 4 chns, by Hugh Grainger and G.H. Chaloner; waterbodies, woods, plantations, building names, tollgate. Apt has cropping information.

49/15 Broughton (township in parish of Wrexham) SJ 308520 [Pentre Broughton]
Apt 27.07.1844; 1183a (1183); Map 1839, 4 chns, by Hugh Grainger and Geo. W. Chaloner; waterbodies, woods, building names.

49/16 Burras Hovah (township in parish of Wrexham) SJ 377534 [Not listed]
Apt 17.12.1839; 454a (all); Map 1840, 6 chns, litho; waterbodies, woods. Apt has cropping information.

49/17 Burton (township in parish of Gresford) SJ 350583
Apt 16.01.1844; 2809a (2809); Map 1844?, 6 chns; waterbodies, woods, building names, chapel, wooden bridge; yellow tint indicates tithe ownership.

49/18 Caca Dutton (township in parish of Gresford) SJ 406516 [Not listed]
Apt 30.10.1843; 411a (all); Map 1843, 5 chns, by W. Lloyd, Wrexham; houses, woods, field boundary ownerships.

49/19 Carreghofa (township in parish of Llanymynech) SJ 254208 [Not listed]
Apt 08.09.1837; 1224a (1223); Map 1828, 6.67? chns; canal, aqueduct, waterbodies, woods, quarry, commons; map is dated 1828, and there are no later stamped dates.

49/20 Cerryg-y-drudion (parish) SH 940495 [Cerigydrudion]
Apt 09.04.1847; 7586a (11586); Map 1848?, 8 chns; waterbodies, woods; mountains named. Apt omits land use.

49/21 Chirk (parish) SJ 283398
Apt 08.03.1837; 4636a (4635); Map 1838, 3 chns, in 2 parts; construction lines, hill-drawing, foot/b'way, canal with towpath and tunnel, aqueduct, waterbodies, woods, plantations, parkland, gardens, fence, building names, Offa's Dyke, deer sheds, boundary stones and bushes, forge, township boundaries, field acreages, waste. Apt omits land use.

49/22 Christionydd Kenrick (township in parish of Ruabon) SJ 274441 [Not listed]
Apt 12.10.1844; 2015a (?); Map 1845, 6 chns, (tithable parts only); waterbodies, woods, fence, building names, iron works, foundary, spoil heaps; bridge named.

49/23 Clocaenog (parish) SJ 060540
Apt 14.08.1839; 6672a (6671); Map 1840?, 6 chns, (tithable parts only); foot/b'way, woods, building names.

49/24 Coedrwg (township or district) SJ 150450 [Not listed]
Apt 28.10.1841; 1811a (?); Map 1845, 13.33 chns, in 2 parts, by Jno. Price, Ruthin, (includes 3-chn enlargement of certain fields); common. District is apportioned by holding and no buildings or fields are shown.

49/25 Creigiog is glan (township in parish of Llanarmon yn lal) SJ 194554 [Creigiog-isaf]
Apt 24.05.1847; 202a (?); Map 2 chns, surveyed November 1848 by Hugh Lloyd Jones; hill-drawing, woods, plantations, gardens, building names, vicarage, lime kilns, old fort, mine shaft. Apt omits some land use.

49/26 Crogen Iddon, Crogen Wladis, Cilcochwyn and Erwallo (township in parish of Llangollen) SJ 250380
Apt 02.04.1839; 4705a (?); Map 1839, 6 chns, in 7 parts, (includes three enlargements of detail); waterbodies, woods, building names, pillar, quarry, mill, limekilns, pits, Offas Dyke, boundary marks, springs, old bank; bridge named.

49/27 Cyfnant (township in parish of Llanarmon) SJ 187575 [Not listed]
Apt 31.01.1844; 411a (all); Map 1842?, 8 chns, by J. Overton; woods.

49/28 Denbigh (parish) SJ 060660
Apt 30.06.1840; 1473a (1500); Map 1840?, 4 chns, in 2 parts; foot/b'way, waterbodies, woods, gardens, building names, road names, castle, tower, new church, ruins, turnpike gate, goblin, farmyard, mill, stack yards, tanyard, chapel; built-up part generalised. Apt omits field names.

49/29 Derwen y mal (parish) SJ 071508 [Derwen]
Apt 31.12.1842; 2648a (3912); Map 1841, 6 chns, drawn by Thos Jenkins; woods, building names, common. Apt omits land use.

49/30 Dinbrin (township in parish of Llangollen) SJ 215435 [Not listed]
Apt 12.06.1844; 504a (?); Map 1844, 4 chns; waterbodies, woods, plantations, building names, common.

49/31 Dutton diffaeth (township in parish of Gresford) SJ 410507 [Not listed]
Apt 20.09.1843; 612a (all); Map 1843, 5 chns, in 2 parts, by W. Lloyd, Wrexham; waterbodies, houses, woods, field boundary ownerships.

49/32 Dutton y Brain (township in parish of Gresford) SJ 410512 [Not listed]
Apt 20.09.1843; 587a (all); Map 1843, 5 chns, by W. Lloyd, Wrexham; houses, woods, field boundary ownerships.

49/33 Efenechtyd (parish) SJ 108557
Apt 14.09.1841; 1218a (1217); Map 1839, 4 chns, by Geo. W. Chaloner; woods, building names.

49/34 Eglwys Eagle (township in parish of Llangollen) SJ 215465 [Eglwyseg]
Apt 29.10.1844; 1589a (?); Map 1844, 6 chns; waterbodies, woods, building names; hills named.

49/35 Eglwys-Vach (district in parish of Eglwys-Vach) SH 808702 [Eglwysbach]
Apt 03.08.1843; 7838a (7838); Map 1841, 8 chns, by J. Price, Denbigh; hill-drawing, waterbodies, farmyards (col), woods, parkland, building names, furnaces, vicarage, township boundaries, private roads (green). Apt has some cropping information.

49/36 Erlas (township in parish of Gresford) SJ 367507 [Not listed]
Apt 20.09.1843; 711a (710); Map 1842, 5 chns, by W. Lloyd, Wrexham; waterbodies, woods, parkland, field boundary ownerships, landowners.

49/37 Erthig (township in parish of Gresford) SJ 326487 [Not listed]
Apt 20.09.1843; 284a (284); Map 1843?, 5 chns, by W. Lloyd, Wrexham; waterbodies, woods, plantations, heath/moor, field boundary ownerships.

49/38 Esclusham Above (township in parish of Wrexham) SJ 285490 [Not listed]
Apt 21.05.1845; 2104a (all); Map 1844?, 6 chns; waterbodies, woods.

49/39 Esclusham Below (township in parish of Wrexham) SJ 313480 [Not listed]
Apt 07.06.1844; 1687a (all); Map 1839, 4 chns, in 2 parts, surveyed by Henry P. Hughes; waterbodies, woods, heath/moor, building names.

49/40 Garthowen, Bodrychwin, Cynant, Cyler or Cilin, and Tre'r bont or Dolganner (district in parish of Llanfairtalhaiarn) SH 928715 [Garthewin]
Apt 11.02.1842; 2749a (2749); Map 1839, 3 chns, surveyed by Claudius Shaw, Bangor; construction lines, waterbodies, woods, pit.

49/41 Gelligynnain, Chwelieriog, Alltyymbyd, Benhadlen, Gwaenyf-fynnon, Trevellan, Creigiog Uwchglan and Erryrys (townships in parish of Llanarmon) SJ 191561 [Not listed]
Apt 29.03.1844; 6665a (?); Map 1842?, 8 chns; waterbodies, woods, reservoir; hamlets named.

49/42 St George (township in parish of St George) SH 972753
Apt 16.05.1840; 1501a (?); Map 1839, 8 chns; woods, parkland, building names, ownerships (col); names are stamped.

49/43 Gresford (township in parish of Gresford) SJ 349544
Apt 30.10.1843; 1000a (999); Map 1844, 3 chns, by ? Issac Taylor; waterbodies, woods.

49/44 Gwerni Hywel (district in parish of Corwen) SH 859496 [Not listed]
Apt 27.09.1845; 729a (?); Map 1847, 8 chns; woods, building names, boundary stone, quarry.

49/45 Gwersyllt (township in parish of Gresford) SJ 318538
Apt 20.09.1843; 1655a (1654); Map 1843, 6 chns, by John Price, Denbigh; waterbodies, woods, parkland, fence, building names, Offa's Dyke, engine; north pointer has leaves and acorn. Apt omits some land use.

49/46 Gwytherin (parish) SH 877617
Apt 17.03.1840; 6118a (all); Map 1842?, 8 chns; woods, heath/moor.

49/47 Gwythrania, Tre Llan and Tan y Bedwal (townships or district in parish of Bryn Eglwys) SJ 141476 [Not listed]
Apt 15.06.1841; 1735a (?); Map 1840?, by ? Robert Roberts, and James Owens; holding names, churchyard; no buildings are shown, and the map has a note appended, 'This Map appears to be a Sketch only'; this map is not drawn to scale, the district being compressed from an approximate rectangular shape to a square. District is apportioned by holding and fields are not shown.

49/48 Gwyffylliog (parish) SJ 030560 [Cyffylliog]
Apt 30.11.1841; 4688a (6652); Map 1842, 9 chns, (tithable parts only); woods. Apt has cropping information.

49/49 Hafodgunfawr, Nantgwryd and Talygarth (township in parish of Llangollen) SJ 220360 [Not listed]
Apt 12.09.1838; 1129a (?); Map 1841?, 6 chns, in 6 parts, (tithable parts only; including three 3-chn enlargements of detail); woods, building names, mill, Baptist Chapel, commons, encroachments, township boundaries (col).

49/50 Holt (township in parish of Gresford) SJ 394531
Apt 19.08.1843; 2764a (2763); Map 1843, 6 chns; waterbodies, woods, heath/moor.

49/51 Holt Parks (district in parish of Gresford) SJ 382545 [Not listed]
Apt 14.08.1843; 477a (477); Map 1844?, 6 chns; waterbodies, building names. Apt omits land use.

49/52 Llanarmon Dyffryn Ceiriog (parish) SJ 140330
Apt 14.08.1839; 3432a (6557); Map 1839, 6 chns, in 2 parts, by I. Porter, Oswestry, (tithable parts only); woods, plantations, building names, springs, boundary marks; physical features named.

49/53 Llanarmon mynydd mawr (chapelry) SJ 135287 [Llanarmon Mynydd mawr]
Apt 15.07.1839; 1324a (2590); Map 1840, 6 chns; waterbodies, woods, building names; hill named.

49/54 Llanbedr Dyffryn Clwyd (parish) SJ 148600 [Llanbedr-Dyffryn-Clwyd]
Apt 05.09.1837; 1845a (all); Map 1838?, 6 chns; hill-drawing, waterbodies, woods (col), parkland (col), gardens (col), old road, ownerships (col).

49/55 Llanddoget (parish) SH 793635 [Llanddoged]
Apt 21.11.1837; 759a (758); Map 1841, 3 chns.

49/56 Llandegla (parish) SJ 210502
Apt 14.06.1847; 3391a (3390); Map 1847, 6 chns, by Robert Piercy, Chirk; woods, plantations, building names, quarry, tower, township boundaries (col); tower is 'Shooting Tower', with altitude 1857 feet given; physical features along boundary are named; north pointer has Prince of Wales' feathers.

49/57 Llandrillo-yn-Rhos (parish) SH 840785
Apt 13.10.1846; 4801a (6801); Map 1847, 6 chns, in 5 parts, by ? Richard Yates, (including enlargements of Mochdre village at 1 chn, and Colwyn village at 2 chns); waterbodies, woods, building names, post office, cliffs, chapels, boundary stones and trees, old road, township boundaries, common (col); a detached part of Carnarvonshire is fully mapped.

49/58 Llandulas (parish) SH 908781 [Llanddulas]
Apt 22.02.1843; 531a (716); Map 1839, 6 chns, in 2 parts; railway, woods, building names, vicarage, boundary marks, ownerships (col), beach, old road, 'Great Road from Chester to Holyhead'. Apt omits some field names.

49/59 Llandyrnog (parish) SJ 109659
Apt 20.03.1839; 3223a (all); Map 1838, 4 chns, in 2 parts, by Hugh Grainger; waterbodies, woods, parkland, building names, chapel, mill, smithy, school.

49/60 Llanetian yn Rhos (parish) SH 868750 [Llanelian-yn-Rhos]
Apt 27.03.1841; 3383a (3382); Map 1840, 12 chns; foot/b'way, woods, building names, township boundaries (col), ownership boundaries (col). District is apportioned by holding.

49/61 Llanelidan (parish) SJ 110500
Apt 23.04.1839; 3578a (all); Map 1847?, [16 chns]; woods, churchyard, common. District is apportioned by holding and fields are not shown.

49/62 Llanfair dyffryn Clywd (parish) SJ 150540 [Llanfair Dyffryn Clwyd]
Apt 28.09.1838; 5028a (all); Map 1839?, 9 chns; waterbodies, woods (col), plantations, gardens, heath/moor, hedges. Apt omits some field names.

49/63 Llanferres (parish) SJ 188612
Apt 27.04.1838; 3755a (all); Map 1838?, 8 chns; waterbodies, woods; hill named. Apt omits land use.

49/64 Llanfihangel Glyn y Myfyr (parish) SH 980490 [Llanfihangel Glyn Myfyr]
Apt 23.05.1840; 4203a (4202); Map 1841, 8 chns; waterbodies, woods (col), heath/moor.

49/65 Llanfwrog (parish) SJ 105573
Apt 16.11.1841; 3069a (3068); Map 1839, 4 chns, by G.W. Chaloner; waterbodies, woods, building names; built-up part generalised. Apt omits most land use.

49/66 Llangadwaladr (parish) SJ 182303
Apt 18.07.1839; 2793a (4718); Map 1839, 6 chns; foot/b'way, waterbodies, woods, rock outcrops, building names, boundary stones and marks, springs, footbridges, quarries; lakes named.

49/67 Llanganhafel (parish) SJ 133633 [Llangynhafal]
Apt 28.03.1839; 2364a (all); Map 1838, 3 chns, by Thos Jenkins; hill-drawing, woods, building names, rectory, ownerships (col); hill named.

49/68 Llangedwin (parish) SJ 191241 [Llangedwyn]
Apt 18.07.1839; 1628a (all); Map 1841, 6 chns; waterbodies, woods, building names, quarry, well, mill.

49/69 Llangerniew (parish) SH 862668 [Llangernyw]
Apt 20.10.1838; 7753a (all); Map 1840, 6 chns; woods (col), building names, boundary stones. Apt omits some land use.

49/70 Llangollen Fawr, Llangollen Abbott, Bache, Rhysgog and Cysltle (township in parish of Llangollen) SJ 215419 [Llangollen]
Apt 22.04.1839; 1439a (?); Map 1843?, 3 chns, in 10 parts, (including Llangollen town at 1.5 chns, one township at 6 chns, various enlargements of detail and 18-chn index); woods, fence, building names.

49/71 Llangollen fechan (township in parish of Llangollen) SJ 239412 [Not listed]
Apt 01.09.1838; 528a (?); Map 1838, 4 chns, by I. Porter, Oswestry; construction lines, boundary bushes and tree, waste.

49/72 Llangwm (parish) SH 980450
Apt 26.08.1840; 10589a (10578); Map 1841, 8 chns; waterbodies, woods, gardens, heath/moor.

49/73 Llangwyfan (parish) SJ 122653
Apt 19.09.1840; 1137a (1136); Map 1840?, 4 chns; waterbodies, woods, heath/moor, building names, lodge.

49/74 Llannevydd (parish) SH 985705 [Llannefydd]
Apt 06.11.1841; 7445a (7444); Map 1844, 8 chns, by W.M. Clark; waterbodies, woods, farm names. Apt has cropping information.

49/75 Llanrhaiadr in Cinmerch (parish) SJ 035615 [Llanrhaeadr]
Apt 18.06.1840; 16977a (16976); Map 1841, 13.33 chns, by J. Price; waterbodies, woods, building names, landowners, old vicarage, demesne, turbaries (col), holding names. District is apportioned by holding and fields are not shown.

49/76 Llanrwst (parish) SH 835585
Apt 15.12.1841; 15298a (15297); Map 1839, 9 chns; hill-drawing, woods, building names, chapels, mill, embankment, ownership boundaries (col); bridge named; built-up part generalised.

49/77 Llansannan (parish) SH 940630
Apt 17.09.1839; 14974a (14973); Map 1842?, 6 chns, in 2 parts; waterbodies, woods, marsh/bog, building names, boundary stones, vicarage, mill, physical features named; gardens shown by annotation. Apt omits some field names.

49/78 Llansantffraid Glan Conwy (parish) SH 812748
Apt 21.06.1842; 5021a (5726); Map 1839, 5 chns, by G.H. Chaloner; waterbodies, woods, building names, township boundaries. Apt omits some field names.

49/79 Llansantfraid Glyn Ceiriog (parish) SJ 175375 [Glyn Ceiriog]
Apt 27.04.1838; 2613a (all); Map 1838, 6 chns, by I. Porter, Oswestry; waterbodies, common. PRO has two copies of the map, one very ordinary, the other much more neat.

49/80 Llanychan (parish) SJ 119615 [Not listed]
Apt 30.07.1838; 567a (all); Map 1838?, 4 chns; foot/b'way, waterbodies, woods, gardens (col), building names.

49/81 Llanynys (parish) SJ 100605
Apt 14.12.1841; 4922a (4921); Map 1840, 12 chns, in 2 parts, by 'J.R.', (includes 3-chn enlargement of residual open fields); waterbodies, woods, open fields; map date and maker's name are surrounded by flourish, in which is included a small eye. Apt has cropping information.

49/82 Llay (township in parish of Gresford) SJ 332560
Apt 22.09.1843; 2162a (2161); Map 1842, 6 chns; waterbodies, woods, building names, mill.

49/83 Lledrod and Estynwallen (township in parish of Llansilin) SJ 225305
Apt 20.09.1838; 1717a (?); Map 1838, 6 chns, in 2 parts, by Is. Porter, Oswestry.

49/84 Lleweni, Isar, Lleweni Uchar, Llan, Rhanhir, Rhan Vawr, Parc and Uwch Caeran (townships in parish of Henlan) SJ 008646 [Not listed]
Apt 14.01.1842; 11773a (?); Map 1841?, 8 chns; foot/b'way, waterbodies, woods, parkland, field boundary ownerships, building names. Apt omits some field names.

49/85 Maes yr Uchn, Llandynan, Cymmo Dupart and Cymmo Tryan (townships or district in parish of Llantisilio) SJ 175465
Apt 30.10.1841; 6109a (?); Map 1845, 13.33 chns, in 2 parts, by John Price, (includes 3-chn enlargement of detail); woods, landowners, weir, common (col); no buildings are shown on the main map. District is apportioned by holding and fields are not shown.

49/86 Marchwiel (parish) SJ 350470
Apt 02.02.1841; 3317a (3316); Map 1840, 3 chns, by W. Lloyd, Wrexham; foot/b'way, waterbodies, houses, woods, plantations, building names, wooden bridges (shown by Dawson's symbol).

49/87 Meifod (township in parish of St George) SH 971734 [Not listed]
Apt 18.06.1840; 499a (all); Map 1839, 8 chns; woods, ownerships (col).

49/88 Meriadog and Gwigvair (township in parish of St Asaph) SJ 018718 [Wigfair]
Apt 11.09.1843; 3046a (3046); Map 1846, 3 chns, 'enlarged' by W.M. Clark; woods, building names, township boundaries (col); names are stamped.

49/89 Minera (township in parish of Wrexham) SJ 267526
Apt 21.05.1845; 1352a (all); Map 1844?, 6 chns, by ? Issac Taylor; waterbodies, woods.

49/90 Moelfre, Lloran Ucha, Lloran issa, Rhiwlas issfoel and Sychtyn (townships in parish of Llansilin) SJ 180282
Apt 06.06.1844; 6303a (?); Map 1843, 6 chns, in 3 parts, (tithable parts only); waterbodies, woods, heath/moor, building names, limekilns, boundary marks, quarries.

49/91 Nantglyn (parish) SH 978586
Apt 23.05.1840; 2013a (5600); Map 1840, 26.67 chns; common; the only building shown is the church Apt generalises land use.

49/92 Pengwern (township in parish of Llangollen) SJ 216407 [Not listed]
Apt 18.12.1839; 678a (?); Map 1842?, [6 chns], (tithable parts only); woods, holding boundaries (col); few buildings or roads are shown. District is apportioned by holding and fields are not shown; Apt generalises land use.

49/93 Prysllygoed, Barrog, Melay, Diebach, Petrual, Cornival and Talhaiarn (townships in parish of Llanfairtalhaiarn) SH 900668 [Not listed]
Apt 09.06.1842; 8365a (8365); Map 1842, 6 chns; waterbodies, boundary stones and wall.

49/94 Ridley (township in parish of Gresford) SJ 395402 [Not listed]
Apt 20.09.1843; 670a (669); Map 1844?, 6 chns; waterbodies, building names, school. Apt omits land use.

49/95 Ruabon (district in parish of Ruabon) SJ 305448
Apt 09.11.1844; 8303a (?); Map 1845, 6 chns, in 3 parts, (includes enlargement of village at 3 chns); hill-drawing, waterbodies, houses, woods, parkland, building names, coal works, coal banks, kennels, vicarage, township boundaries.

49/96 Ruthin and Llanchydd (consolidated parishes) SJ 130580
Apt 31.07.1841; 1989a (1989); Map 1839, 4 chns, by Thomas Jenkins; waterbodies, woods, building names, castle, town hall, mill; built-up part generalised.

49/97 Stansty (township in parish of Wrexham) SJ 322521 [Not listed]
Apt 21.06.1844; 565a (565); Map 1842, 5 chns, by W. Lloyd, Wrexham; waterbodies, woods, field boundary ownerships.

49/98 Sutton (township in parish of Gresford) SJ 409488 [Not listed]
Apt 26.09.1843; 1118a (all); Map 1843, 5 chns, by W. Lloyd, Wrexham; waterbodies, houses, woods, field boundary ownerships.

49/99 Sycharth, Priddbwlch, Llansiln, Bodlith and Rhiewlas Uwchfoel (townships in parish of Llansilin) SJ 210290 [Llansilian]
Apt 25.03.1840; 4716a (?); Map 1841, 6 chns, in 2 parts, (tithable parts only); waterbodies, woods, plantations, building names, landowners, vicarage, mill, township boundaries; grey band shows allotments of common under 20 years; bridges named.

49/100 Tir Evan (township in parish of Yspytty) SH 833461 [Ysbyty Ifan]
Apt 24.01.1843; 3054a (all); Map 1840, 12 chns, by Jno. Roberts, Corwen, (tithable parts only); woods.

49/101 Tir yr Abbot isau (district) SH 895545 [Not listed]
Apt 27.09.1845; 11264a (?); Map 1846, 8 chns; waterbodies, holding boundaries (col); lakes named and a few physical features along the boundary are named. District is apportioned by holding and fields are not shown.

49/102 Tre-brys (township in parish of Yspytty) SH 880508 [Not listed]
Apt 24.01.1843; 815a (all); Map 1840, 12 chns, by ? Jno. Roberts, Corwen; woods.

49/103 Trevor Issa (township in parish of Llangollen) SJ 262427 [Trevor]
Apt 12.09.1838; 1134a (?); Map 1838, 6 chns; canal, waterbodies, woods, parkland, building names, common.

49/104 Trevor Ucha (township in parish of Llangollen) SJ 232424 [Trevor Uchaf]
Apt 22.09.1838; 869a (?); Map 1839, 6 chns, (includes enlargement of village at 3 chns) waterbodies, woods, common.

49/105 Vivod (township in parish of Llangollen) SJ 192420
Apt 14.02.1839; 493a (?); Map 1839, 3 chns, (tithable parts only, tinted); hill-drawing, waterbodies, woods, field boundary ownerships, footbridge, common.

49/106 Wrexham Regis and Wrexham Abbot (township in parish of Wrexham) SJ 337501 [Wrexham or Wrecsam]
Apt 31.12.1844; 1272a (1271); Map 1846, 6 chns, by J. Price, Ruthin, (includes town separately at 2 chns); waterbodies, fences, road names, gravel pit.

Flintshire

PRO IR29 and IR30 50/1-43

43 tithe districts: 169,924 acres
43 tithe commutations: 160,391 acres
33 voluntary tithe agreements, 10 compulsory tithe awards

Tithe and tithe commutation

All Flintshire tithe districts contained some tithable land in 1836, though only nine districts were wholly tithable at this date (Fig. 62). As in Denbighshire the main cause of tithe exemption was the payment of a modus in lieu of tithes (in 76 per cent of tithe districts). Assistant tithe commissioners and local tithe agents who worked in Flintshire are listed in Table 50.1. As in other counties in North Wales, a significant contribution to the valuation of tithe rent-charge in Flintshire was made by men from well outside the county, notably John Matthews of Aberystwyth, and Francis Marston from the south of Shropshire (Table 50.2). Tithe was apportioned by holding in only two districts, a low proportion by the standards of North Wales and no fewer than ten (23 per cent) of tithe apportionments have records of crops listed field-by-field, the highest proportion of any county. In a number of other tithe apportionments various types of grassland, such as 'old pasture' and 'mown' (meadow), are distinguished. An unusual entry at Erbistock in the rarely used 'remarks' column of the schedule of apportionment is 'Old pasture until 1840'.

Tithe maps

In common with the rest of North Wales, Flintshire has neither first-class maps nor second-class maps with original survey construction lines. Copying of earlier surveys is acknowledged on three maps, though this practice is likely to have been more widespread.

Flintshire tithe maps are characterised by a general use of small scales; only four maps are drawn at the largest scales used in the county, one inch to four chains, whereas the most favoured scale is the six-chain (56 per cent of tithe districts) and the small scale of one inch to twelve chains was used for four maps (Table 50.3).

As is usual in Wales, woodland is well recorded (on 90 per cent of Flintshire maps) and so is parkland (on 21 per cent) but apart from industry (on six maps, mostly of mining), other land uses do not feature prominently. One map distinguishes arable and grass but none shows field boundary ownership.

Only fourteen Flintshire tithe maps in the Public Record Office collection can be

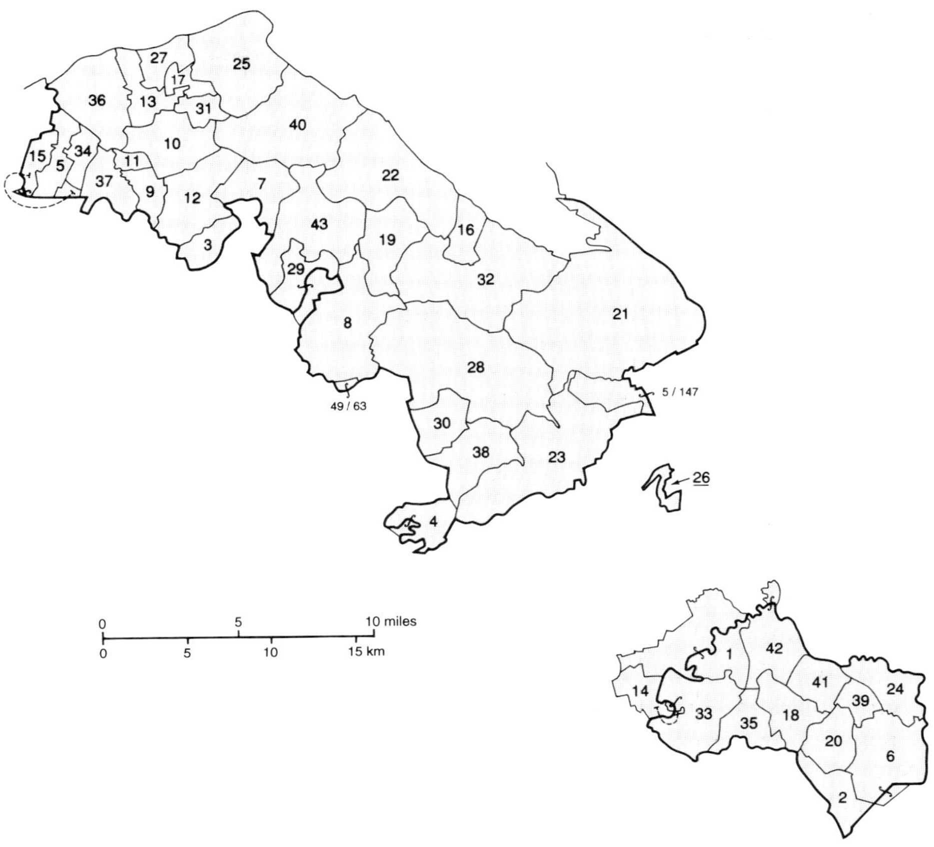

Fig. 62 Flintshire: tithe district boundaries.

attributed to a particular map-maker (Table 50.2). The general standard of execution is unremarkable on the whole. Two maps have stamped lettering, three have decorated borders, and one, Caerwys has a frame around an enlargement of detail drawn to suggest a separate piece of paper pinned on to the map. An above average number of tithe maps in this county are drawn on parchment or vellum, rather than on paper.

Table 50.1. *Agreements and awards for commutation of tithes in Flintshire*

Assistant commissioner/ local tithe agent	*Number of agreements**	*Number of awards*
Aneurin Owen	18	10
John Fenton	8	0
John Johnes	4	0
Charles Pym	1	0

*Computed from the number of extant reports on tithe agreements in the tithe files [PRO IR 18].

Table 50.2. *Tithe valuers and tithe map-makers in Flintshire*

Name and address (in Flintshire unless indicated)	*Number of districts*	*Acreage*
Tithe valuers		
Issac Taylor, Holywell	6	28,235
Thomas Wood Lee, Oak Bank	6	14,523
Robert Piercy, Chirk, Denbighshire	4	12,492
John Matthews, Aberystwyth, Cardiganshire	4	10,774
Francis Marston, Hopesay, Shropshire	4	5,934
Others [14]	19	88,433
Attributed tithe map-makers		
Joseph Fenna	2	10,195
John Price, Chester	2	5,476
Others [10]	10	25,107

Table 50.3. *The tithe maps of Flintshire: scales and classes*

Scale in chains/inch	*All maps*		*First Class*		*Second Class*	
	Number	*Acreage*	*Number*	*Acreage*	*Number*	*Acreage*
4	5	7,196	0	0	5	7,196
6	24	80,794	0	0	24	80,794
8	6	29,964	0	0	6	29,964
9,10	4	30,639	0	0	4	30,639
12	4	11,798	0	0	4	11,798
TOTAL	43	160,391	0	0	43	160,391

Table 50.4. *The tithe maps of Flintshire: dates*

	1838	*1839*	*1840*	*1841*	*1842*	*1843*	*1844*	*1845*	*1846*	*1847*	*1848*	*1849*	*1850*
2nd class	5	12	8	4	2	1	4	2	1	0	0	3	1

Flintshire

50/1 Bangor (parish) (partly in Denbighshire) SJ 372432 [Bangor-is-y-coed]
Apt 12.09.1837; 5796a (5795); Map 1839-40, 6 chns, by Joseph Fenna; waterbodies, woods, building names, river cliff. Apt has cropping information, and omits some field names.

50/2 Bettisfield (township in parish of Hanmer) SJ 461362
Apt 28.01.1839; 2284a (2284); Map 1839?, 6 chns, litho; foot/b'way, canal with towpath, woods, parkland, marsh/bog, building names.

50/3 Bodfary (parish) SJ 097705 [Bodfari]
Apt 14.09.1843; 1449a (1449); Map 1844?, 6 chns; waterbodies, woods, building names, forge, school, lodge. Apt omits some field names.

50/4 Bodiris (township in parish of Llanarmon) (partly in Denbighshire) SJ 225540 [Not listed]
Apt 30.04.1840; 2502a (?); Map 1842, 8 chns; waterbodies, building names, landowners, well; lake named. District is apportioned by holding and fields are not shown.

50/5 Bodlewyddan (township in parish of St Asaph) SJ 001764 [Bodelwyddan]
Apt 27.01.1841; 1676a (1676); Map 1840, 4 chns; waterbodies, woods, parkland, orchard, building names; colours show owners; some lettering is stamped.

50/6 Bronnington (township in parish of Hanmer) SJ 503398 [Bronington]
Apt 28.01.1839; 4851a (4850); Map 1839, 6 chns, corrected by Bate and Timmis; foot/b'way, waterbodies, woods, building names, causeways, pinfold, turbary and moss (by annotation); mere named. Apt has cropping information.

50/7 Caerwys (parish) SJ 123749
Apt 25.11.1848; 2604a (2603); Map 1849, 6 chns, in 2 parts, (including 4-chn enlargement 'Copied from the Survey for the Inclosure made in 1810'); hill-drawing, foot/b'way, waterbodies, woods, paper mill, glebe, gardens (by annotation); tithe-free land is greeny-grey, described in a note bottom left as 'Indian Ink'; enlargement is on 'scroll', with pins at each corner, 'attaching' it to the main map, and has field names. Apt has cropping information.

50/8 Cilcen (parish) SJ 177660 [Cilcain]
Apt 17.12.1839; 6404a (6403); Map 1841?, 8 chns; woods; colour bands may show townships.

50/9 Cil Owain, Bodeugan and Rhyllon (township or district in parish of St Asaph) SJ 057745 [Not listed]
Apt 22.04.1843; 1195a (1195); Map 1845, 6 chns.

50/10 Cwm (parish) SJ 072772
Apt 05.01.1844; 3702a (all); Map 1839, 10 chns; hill-drawing, woods, building names, quarries; colours show ownerships; hills named.

50/11 Cyrchynan (township or district) SJ 046760 [Not listed]
Apt 12.06.1843; 531a (531); Map 1844?, 6 chns, by R. Shone; waterbodies, woods, building names, boundary stone; map is dated 1834, bottom right. Apt omits cropping information.

50/12 Dymerchion or Tremerchion (parish) SJ 082732
Apt 19.06.1840; 3874a (3873); Map 1841, 12 chns, by John Price, Chester; waterbodies, woods. District is apportioned by holding and fields are not shown.

50/13 Dyserth (parish) SJ 057794
Apt 11.06.1839; 1884a (3348); Map 1839, 8 chns; foot/b'way, waterbodies, woods, parkland, heath/moor, common, building names, engine, mill, marsh (by annotation); 'Sea' is in sea-shell-like lettering.

50/14 Erbistock (parish) SJ 348427
Apt 12.10.1844; 1602a (1602); Map 1843, 4 chns, by John Price, Denbigh; waterbodies, houses, woods, parkland, fence, boat house, ferry, watermill (by Dawson's symbol); colours may show owners. North pointer has Prince of Wales feathers and 'Ich Dien'. Apt has cropping information.

50/15 Faenol (township in parish of St Asaph) SH 991764 [Not listed]
Apt 23.09.1840; 1345a (1345); Map 1842?, 4 chns, in 2 parts; waterbodies, woods, parkland, building names; some lettering is stamped; colours show owners.

50/16 Flint (parish) SJ 245713 [Flint or Y Fflint]
Apt 03.10.1837; 1575a (all); Map 1840?, 6 chns; waterbodies, woods, building names, castle, gaol, mill, smelting works; town is generalised and is edged yellow.

50/17 Gwaenysgor (parish) SJ 080810
Apt 01.08.1846; 794a (794); Map 1846, 6 chns; waterbodies, woods, building names, pit; annotation 'Cottages' suggests some buildings are not mapped.

50/18 Halghton (township in parish of Hanmer) SJ 432411 [Not listed]
Apt 28.01.1839; 2314a (2313); Map 1840?, 6 chns; foot/b'way, waterbodies, woods, building names, paper mill, mills. Apt has cropping information.

50/19 Halkin (parish) SJ 200720 [Halkyn]
Apt 13.07.1839; 3141a (all); Map 1840?, 6 chns; woods. Apt omits land use.

50/20 Hanmer (township in parish of Hanmer) SJ 458392
Apt 28.01.1839; 2248a (2247); Map 1840, 6 chns, by Groom and Greening, Woodgate, litho (by J. Bell, Liverpool); waterbodies, woods. Apt has cropping information.

50/21 Hawarden (parish) SJ 316658
Apt 18.12.1839; 16986a (17695); Map 1841, 9 chns, in 5 parts, (including four enlargements of detail); waterbodies, boundary stones, township boundaries (col). Apt omits land use.

50/22 Holywell (parish) SJ 210740
Apt 25.03.1841; 7532a (13382); Map 1841, 8 chns, (tithable parts only); woods, township boundaries (col). Apt omits land use.

50/23 Hope (parish) SJ 297577
Apt 07.02.1849; 9164a (9166); Map 1850, 6 chns, in 3 parts; railway with station, waterbodies, woods, building names, township boundaries (col); meaning of blue band is unclear.

50/24 Iscoyd (township in parish of Malpas) SJ 492426 [Not listed]
Apt 10.09.1838; 2608a (2607); Map 1839?, 12 chns, litho; waterbodies, woods, parkland, building names, chapel, mill, moor, greens; area numbers are MS.

50/25 Llanasa (parish) SJ 110818
Apt 15.06.1839; 5850a (10809); Map 1839, 8 chns, in 2 parts; waterbodies, woods (col), lighthouse, township boundaries (col); border has trefoil-and-mould decoration. Apt omits land use.

50/26 Mayord and Hoseley (township in parish of Gresford) SJ 359552 [Marford]
Apt 20.09.1843; 581a (580); Map 1844, 6 chns, by John Davies, Mollington; waterbodies, woods, arable (col), grassland (col), building names, gravel hole, mills. Apt omits land use.

50/27 Meliden (parish) SJ 066825
Apt 31.05.1839; 1484a (all); Map 1839, 4 chns, by Richard Godwin Dawson; woods, open fields, seashore, mine works.

50/28 Mold (parish) SJ 242630 [Mold or Yr Wyddgrug]
Apt 05.09.1837; 12270a (12270); Map 1839?, 6 chns, in 12 parts, (including 36-chn index); woods, county hall, township boundaries (col). Apt omits land use.

50/29 Nannerch (parish) (partly in Denbighshire) SJ 150686
Apt 28.01.1839; 2792a (2792); Map 1838, 8 chns; hill-drawing, waterbodies, woods, building names, county boundary (col); moels (named). Apt omits land use.

50/30 Nerquis (township in parish of Mold) SJ 230600 [Nercwys]
Apt 03.08.1838; 2281a (2280); Map 1838, 6 chns; waterbodies, woods. Border has trefoil-and-mould decoration. Apt omits land use.

50/31 Newmarket (parish) SJ 090791 [Not listed]
Apt 14.04.1845; 1031a (1031); Map 1844, 6 chns; waterbodies, woods, building names, vicarage, well.

50/32 Northop (parish) SJ 250680
Apt 25.05.1838; 8852a (12366); Map 1839?, 9 chns; waterbodies, woods, parkland, avenues of trees, embankments, township boundaries (col); moel named.

50/33 Overton (parish) SJ 382411
Apt 12.09.1837; 4399a (4398); Map drawn in 1838, [6 chns], by Jos. Fenna; waterbodies, woods, parkland, building names, green (named); bridge named. Apt omits land use.

50/34 Pengwern (township in parish of St Asaph) SJ 017767
Apt 11.11.1840; 1089a (1089); Map 1840, 4 chns, by Geo. W. Chaloner; waterbodies, woods, building names, old river course; green band may show modus lands.

50/35 Penley (township in parish of Ellesmere) SJ 410404
Apt 12.09.1837; 2037a (2036); Map 1838, 12 chns, by Joseph Welch; foot/b'way, waterbodies, woods, building names, mill. Apt has cropping information.

50/36 Rhyddlan (parish) SJ 030797 [Rhuddlan]
Apt 18.07.1839; 4099a (5670); Map 1839, [? 9 chns]; woods, open fields, building names, beach, castle, chapels, vicarage, old river course, timber yard; built-up part generalised; river gravel, gardens and common shown by annotation; colours show ownerships.

50/37 Talar, Brynpolyn, Gwernglevryd and Gwerneigron (district in parish of St Asaph) SJ 032747 [Not listed]
Apt 26.07.1843; 1945a (1945); Map 1845, 6 chns.

50/38 Trythen (township in parish of Mold) SJ 242573 [Treuddyn]
Apt 03.08.1838; 3554a (3554); Map 1839, 6 chns; waterbodies, woods, plantations; moel named. Apt omits land use.

50/39 Tybroughton (township in parish of Hanmer) SJ 466423 [Not listed]
Apt 28.01.1839; 1151a (1150); Map 1839, 6 chns, by Thomas Fenna; foot/b'way, waterbodies, woods. Apt has cropping information.

50/40 Whitford (parish) SJ 140780
Apt 13.10.1846; 7856a (13065); Map 1849?, 6 chns, by I. Jenkins; railway, waterbodies, woods, plantations, parkland, race course, embankment.

50/41 Willington (township in parish of Hanmer) SJ 450428 [Not listed]
Apt 28.01.1839; 1875a (1874); Map 1840?, 6 chns, litho; waterbodies, houses (black), woods. Apt has cropping information.

50/42 Worthenbury (parish) SJ 420460
Apt 13.06.1837; 3279a (all); Map 'Compiled and Corrected' in 1838, 12 chns, by Joseph Gregory; waterbodies, houses, woods, gardens. Apt omits land use.

50/43 Ysgeiviog (parish) SJ 152723 [Ysceifiog]
Apt 06.07.1846; 5905a (5905); Map 1849, 6 chns; waterbodies, woods, racecourse (col), common (col). Apt has some cropping information.

Glamorganshire

PRO IR29 and IR30 51/1-130

137 tithe districts: 518,015 acres
130 tithe commutations: 490,704 acres
46 voluntary tithe agreements, 74 compulsory tithe awards

Tithe and tithe commutation

Almost all Glamorganshire tithe districts were subject to payment of tithes in 1836 and thirty-eight districts were wholly tithable (Fig. 63). The main causes of tithe exemption in this county were modus payments in lieu of tithes (in 52 per cent of tithable districts), exemption by prescription, and the exemption of some woodland.

Assistant tithe commissioners and local tithe agents who worked in Glamorganshire are listed in Table 51.1. As in Pembrokeshire, tithe valuation work in Glamorganshire was dominated by Harry Goode of Haverfordwest who valued 27 per cent of the districts (Table 51.2).

It is quite common for Glamorganshire tithe apportionments to omit some field names and occasionally Welsh terminology is used as, for example 'Ty y gardd' instead of 'Cottage and garden'. As elsewhere in southern Wales, in some Glamorganshire tithe apportionments a number of grassland types such as 'clover hay' and 'moory pasture' are distinguished.

Tithe maps

Glamorganshire is one of four Welsh counties with some first-class mapping (5 per cent of maps) and in addition three second-class maps have construction lines. The main peak of map production was quite late (1840-43) and there was a secondary high point of mapping in 1846.

The scales used for Glamorganshire tithe maps vary from one inch to two chains to one inch to sixteen chains. Some 25 per cent of maps are in the recommended scale range of three to four chains, and map-makers working in the larger districts in the upland northern half of the county favoured the six-chain (43 per cent) and eight-chain scales (29 per cent). Fifteen second-class maps are lithographed (12 per cent) probably due to the influence of the surveyors and lithographers Goode and Philpott who were active in this county (Table 51.3).

As elsewhere in Wales, Glamorganshire tithe maps are fairly good sources of woodland

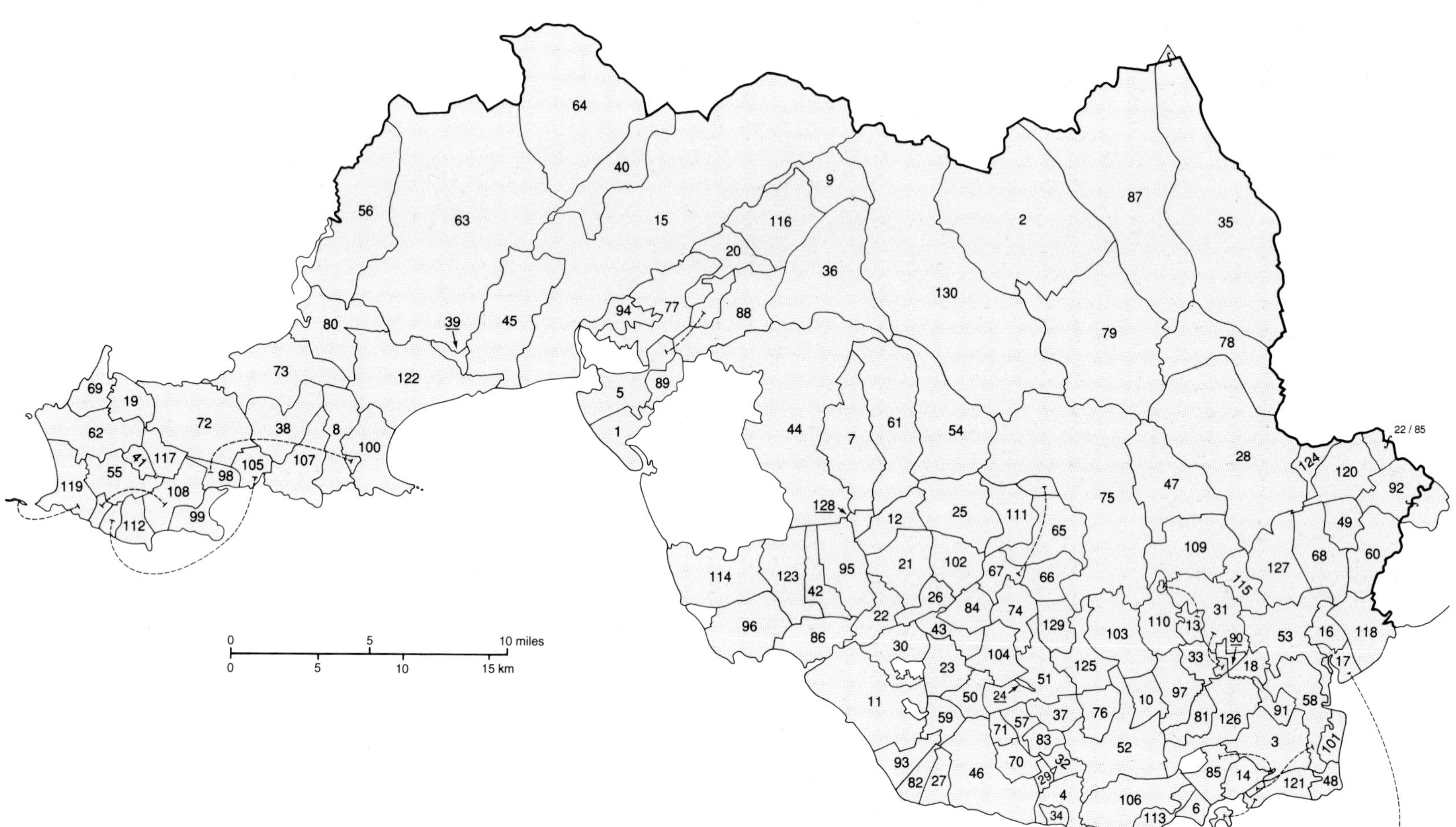

Fig. 63 Glamorganshire: tithe district boundaries.

information (on 58 per cent of maps) but are poor records of agricultural land use. For example, none distinguishes arable or grass, only 5 per cent of maps portray gardens, 7 per cent depict parks, and 10 per cent map orchards. In contrast industrial activity is identified on about one-sixth of the maps. At Aberdare industrial buildings are shown distinctively and on the Langonoyd map individual factory chimneys are mapped. The town of Swansea is portrayed in unusual detail for a tithe map of an urban area. The map of Oystermouth is notable for its portrayal of slopes and landforms.

Some 102 Glamorganshire tithe maps in the Public Record Office collection can be attributed to a particular map-maker. As in Pembrokeshire, the most prolific producers were Harry Goode and Henry Philpott of Haverfordwest, who mapped more than a quarter of Glamorganshire tithe districts. Their maps are usually uncoloured and they produced high-quality lithographs of a number. A few of their maps in the Gower, of which Penrice is a good example, have coloured water and attractive beige wash for slopes and cliffs. Goode and Philpott's maps often have small cartouches for title and author and scale bars and north pointers which intersect each other. The second most prolific map-maker in Glamorganshire was Edward Neale of Bridgend or Southampton who mapped 12 per cent of the county's tithe districts. He was responsible for most of the first-class maps of Glamorganshire. The map of Scully is the best-executed map in the county with exquisite details of foreshore rocks. In contrast the map for Ynysawdre is drawn on the back of the printed notice of tithe apportionment.

Apart from the intersecting cartouches, scale bars and north pointers which were Goode and Philpotts's trade mark, Glamorganshire tithe maps are not generally ornamented. A very high proportion are uncoloured (even for roads and water) whereas just a few north pointers have plumes or other decoration, as for example, a sheaf of corn on the map of Lantwit Lower.

Table 51.1. *Agreements and awards for commutation of tithes in Glamorganshire*

Assistant commissioner/ local tithe agent	*Number of agreements**	*Number of awards*
John Johnes	14	72
Thomas Hoskins	38	0
Aneurin Owen	0	2

*Computed from the number of extant reports on tithe agreements in the tithe files [PRO IR 18].

Table 51.2. *Tithe valuers and tithe map-makers in Glamorganshire*

Name and address (in Glamorganshire unless indicated)	*Number of districts*	*Acreage*
Tithe valuers		
Harry Phelps Goode, Haverfordwest, Pembrokeshire	35	95,800
Evan David, Radyr Court	18	87,679
Edward Neale, Broadland, Laleston*	16	45,583
George Halket, Winskeel, Coity	9	26,153
Thomas Lott Martin	7	42,087
Others [28]	45	193,402
Attributed tithe map-makers		
Goode and Philpott, Haverfordwest, Pembrokeshire	34	68,456
Edward Neale, Laleston/Bridgend*	16	53,165
George Smith Strawson, Cardiff	14	24,947
William Jones, Brecon	12	70,460
Others [19]	26	147,413

*On some Glamorganshire maps and on all his maps of southern England Neale gives his address as Southampton.

Table 51.3. *The tithe maps of Glamorganshire: scales and classes*

Scale in chains/inch	*All maps*		*First Class*		*Second Class*	
	Number	*Acreage*	*Number*	*Acreage*	*Number*	*Acreage*
>3	1	70	0	0	1	70
3	10	19,229	7	14,326	3	4,903
4	23	43,490	0	0	23	43,490
5	1	881	0	0	1	881
6	56	154,566	0	0	56	154,566
8	38	270,293	0	0	38	270,293
<8	1	2,175	0	0	1	2,175
TOTAL	130	490,704	7	14,326	123	476,378

Table 51.4. *The tithe maps of Glamorganshire: dates*

	1838	*1839*	*1840*	*1841*	*1842*	*1843*	*1844*	*1845*	*1846*	*1847*	*1848*	*1849*	*1850*
All maps	2	9	20	23	9	17	6	12	17	8	6	0	1
1st class	0	0	2	2	1	1	0	0	1	0	0	0	0
2nd class	2	9	18	21	8	16	6	12	16	8	6	0	1

Glamorganshire

51/1 Aberavon (parish) SS 753903
Apt 10.09.1841; 1944a (2598); Map 1843?, 4 chns, by L.J. Griffiths; railway, building names, lock, float, weir, old course of river; churches are red and other buildings grey; scale is ruler-like.

51/2 Aberdare (parish) SO 001029
Apt 09.11.1844; 16310a (16310); Map 1846?, 8 chns; construction lines, hill-drawing, railways, waterbodies, woods, plantations, building names, furnace, iron works; industrial buildings are hatched, and other buildings are solid black.

51/3 St Andrews (parish) ST 153708 [St Andrews Major]
Apt 11.08.1840; 3149a (3149); Map 1840, 6 chns, in 2 parts, by G.S. Strawson, (includes enlargement of village at 3 chns); houses, woods, building names, castle, mill stream, commons. Apt omits some field names.

51/4 St Athans (parish) ST 020680 [St Athan]
Apt 03.09.1839; 1486a (1771); Map [6 chns] 1839, by G.S. Strawson; waterbodies, houses, woods, boundary stones. Apt omits some field names.

51/5 Baglan (parish) SS 752922
Apt 10.09.1841; 5240a (6479); Map 1843, 4 chns, by L.J. Griffiths; railway, woods, residual open fields, building names, boundary marks; scale is ruler-like; north pointer has plumes.

51/6 Barry (parish) ST 100672
Apt 26.08.1839; 484a (835); Map 1839?, 4 chns; road names, ruins. District is apportioned by holding; Apt omits land use, and owner and occupier details are generalised.

51/7 Bettws (parish) SS 895895 [Betws]
Apt 30.06.1843; 5086a (5086); Map 1843, 6 chns, by Edwd Neale; building names, grave, hamlet boundary, green, tram road.

51/8 Bishopstone (parish) SS 578902 [Bishopston]
Apt 05.01.1844; 2388a (2387); Map 1844?, 8 chns, in 20 parts, by Fr. Price, Surveyor etc, Norton, (including three 3-chn and sixteen 4-chn enlargements of detail); woods, building names, spring, well, boundary stone, mill stream, kiln, common, glebe, manor boundary.

51/9 Blaengwrach (hamlet in parish of Glyncorrwg) SN 890050 [Not listed]
Apt 04.08.1845; 3033a (all); Map 1846, 6 chns, by Edwd Neale; canal with towpath, waterbodies.

51/10 Bonvilstone (parish) ST 070738 [Bonvilston]
Apt 03.09.1839; 1179a (1178); Map 1841?, 4 chns, ? by Goode and Philpott, Haverfordwest; the meaning of the pink bands is unclear; plain cartouche intersects scale.

51/11 St Brides Major and Wick (parish and chapelry) SS 902741
Apt 12.03.1840; 7123a (7772); Map 1840, 6 chns, in 2 parts; hill-drawing, waterbodies, woods, parkland, building names, foreshore (col), cliffs, beacon (by symbol), common (col). [There is no copy of map in PRO IR 30; information is from Diocesan copy, held by National Library of Wales.]

51/12 St Brides Minor (hamlet in parish of St Brides Minor) SS 930850 [Not listed]
Apt 30.12.1842; 1830a (all); Map 1843, 6 chns, in 2 parts, by E. Neale, Laleston, (includes 3-chn enlargement of detail); common (col); scale is ruler-like.

51/13 St Brides Super Ely (parish) ST 100778 [St Bride's super Ely]
Apt 31.07.1839; 676a (676); Map 1841?, 6 chns, in 2 parts, by Goode and Philpott, Haverfordwest, litho; waterbodies, woods, building names; scale intersects plain cartouche.

51/14 Cadoxton juxta Barry (parish) ST 133687 [Cadoxton]
Apt 29.03.1844; 977a (1028); Map 1840, 6 chns, by G.S. Strawson; houses, woods (col), building names, mill; a ruined house is named in gothic. Apt omits most field names.

51/15 Cadoxton juxta Neath (parish) SN 780010 [Cadoxton-Juxta-Neath]
Apt 26.07.1841; 31157a (32060); Map 1841?, 8 chns, in 3 parts, ? by Morris Sayce, (includes two enlargements of villages at 4 chns); railway, inclined plane, canal with towpath, waterbodies, woods, plantations, building names, Roman road, race course, boundary stone, brewery, mills, collieries, tin works, iron works, copper works, cheadle works, chapels, abbey ruins, hamlet boundaries and names; hills named; north pointer has plumes. Apt omits some field names.

51/16 St John the Baptist, Cardiff (parish) ST 181775 [Not listed]
Apt 31.07.1844; 928a (1493); Map 1845, 6 chns, by G.S. Strawson, Cardiff; railways, building names, workhouse, castle mound, toll gates; built-up part generalised. Apt omits some field names.

51/17 St Mary, Cardiff (parish) ST 190753 [Caerau]
Apt 31.07.1844; 828a (all); Map 1845, 6 chns, in 2 parts, by R.A. Rees; canal, waterbodies, locks, docks, lighthouse. Apt omits field names.

51/18 Cayra (parish) ST 135753
Apt 22.11.1839; 747a (746); Map 1840?, 6 chns, by Goode and Philpott, Haverfordwest, litho; building names.

51/19 Cheriton (parish) SS 461931
Apt 18.03.1846; 1319a (1419); Map 1848?, 4 chns, litho, by H.P. Goode, Surveyor etc, Haverfordwest; waterbodies, woods, building names, well, mill, quarries, salt-marsh, 'slime'. Apt omits some land use.

51/20 Clyne (hamlet in parish of Llantwit juxta Neath) SS 815995
Apt 15.09.1845; 2165a (all); Map 1847?, 8 chns, by William Jones; railway, turnpike roads, canal with towpath, woods, building names, kiln.

51/21 Coity, Higher Hamlet (hamlet in parish of Coity) SS 928818 [Coity]
Apt 19.11.1840; 2912a (2911); Map 1840?, 3 chns, 1st cl, by Edwd Neale, Southampton; construction lines, waterbodies, houses, woods (col), fences, castle, ruins, common, boundary stones; there is a table summarising acreages; map also covers 51/22.

51/22 Coity, Lower Hamlet (hamlet in parish of Coity) SS 907793 [Not listed]
Apt 19.11.1840; 1661a (1660); Map 1841?, 3 chns, 1st cl, in 2 parts, by Edward Neale, Bridgend, (includes Bridgend separately at 1.5 chns); construction lines, waterbodies, houses, fences, market, slaughter house, town hall, chapel, workhouse; on enlargement houses are hatched and other buildings are grey.

51/23 Colwinstone (parish) SS 944760 [Colwinston]
Apt 18.01.1839; 1762a (1760); Map 1841?, 6 chns, by Goode and Philpott, Haverfordwest, litho; pink band divides rectorial and vicarial tithe-areas.

51/24 Cowbridge (parish) SS 994747
Apt 05.02.1841; 70a (96); Map 1843?, 2 chns, surveyed and lithographed by H.P. Goode and Philpott, Haverfordwest; foot/b'way, waterbodies, building names, road names, toll gates, market house, town hall, sheep market.

51/25 Coychurch, Higher Hamlet (hamlet in parish of Coychurch) SS 960850 [Not listed]
Apt 15.05.1841; 3911a (3910); Map 1841?, 3 chns, by Edward Neale, Southampton; construction lines, houses, woods, building names, old chapel, footbridge, factory (with Dawson's watermill symbol), commons; map also covers 51/111.

51/26 Coychurch, Lower Hamlet (hamlet in parish of Coychurch) SS 940798 [Coychurch]
Apt 15.05.1841; 1091a (1090); Map 1841?, 3 chns, 1st cl, by Edwd Neale, Southampton; construction lines, waterbodies, houses, woods, boundary stones (by symbol), chapel, common.

51/27 St Donats (parish) SS 942692
Apt 18.01.1844; 881a (1018); Map 1848?, 5 chns; waterbodies, woods, building names, lime kilns and quarries, smithy, cross, castle, tower, yard, old hedges, glebe, park; pictorial church.

51/28 Eglwsilan (parish) ST 120890 [Not listed]
Apt 31.07.1839; 13619a (13619); Map 1841, 8 chns, 'Compiled' by Wm Jones, Brecon; hill-drawing, railway, canal with towpath, waterbodies, woods, plantations, building names, weir, chain works, furnace, castle, chapel; hills named; scale-bar is ruler-like. Apt omits some field names.

51/29 Eglwysbrewis (parish) ST 007690 [Eglwys-Brewis]
Apt 03.09.1839; 368a (367); Map 1840, 3 chns, by Goode and Philpott, Haverfordwest.

51/30 Ewenny (parish) SS 919773
Apt 26.11.1840; 1975a (1975); Map 1842?, 6 chns, by Goode and Philpott, Haverfordwest, Surveyors and Lithographers, litho; waterbodies, woods. Apt omits some land use.

51/31 St Fagans with Lanilterne (parish with chapelry) ST 117780 [St Fagans and Capel Llanilltern]
Apt 21.08.1839; 3322a (3321); Map 1840, 8 chns, by G.S. Strawson; waterbodies, houses, woods, building names, chapelry boundary. Apt omits field names.

51/32 Flemingstone (parish) ST 018701 [Flemingston]
Apt 21.03.1840; 673a (all); Map 1840, 6 chns, by E. Neale, Southampton; houses.

51/33 St George (parish) ST 102755 [St George's]
Apt 16.12.1842; 1058a (1058); Map 1843, 4 chns, by H.P. Goode and Philpott, Haverfordwest; woods, quarry. Apt omits some field names.

51/34 Gileston (parish) ST 015669
Apt 20.11.1844; 351a (496); Map 1846, 4 chns, by G.S. Strawson, Cardiff; waterbodies, building names, boundary stone. Apt omits some field names.

51/35 Gellygaer (parish) SO 120020 [Gelligaer]
Apt 18.08.1841; 16573a (16573); Map 1842, 8 chns, 'compiled' by William Jones, Brecon, (tithable parts only in detail); railway, waterbodies, woods, plantations, building names, iron works (col), boundary cairn, mill, chapel, engine, pit, common; north pointer has plumes. Apt omits some field names.

51/36 Glyncorrwg (hamlet in parish of Glyncorrwg) SS 877993
Apt 30.11.1844; 8263a (8262); Map 1847, 6 chns; houses, building names.

51/37 St Hilary (parish) ST 015728
Apt 08.06.1838; 1183a (1200); Map 1839, 4 chns, by H.P. Goode and Philpott, Land Agents and Surveyors, Haverfordwest; waterbodies; green band divides vicar's and rector's portions of district; plain cartouche intersects scale and north pointer.

51/38 Ilston (parish) SS 551910
Apt 20.03.1844; 2879a (2879); Map 1846, 4 chns, by William Williams, 5 Gower St, Swansea; waterbodies, woods. Apt omits some field names.

51/39 St John (parish) SS 665948 [Not listed]
Apt 20.11.1844; 431a (431); Map 1847?, 4 chns, by John Williams; waterbodies, canal with locks.

51/40 Kilybebell (parish) SN 753053 [Cilybebyll]
Apt 29.05.1838; 4015a (4014); Map 1840?, 4 chns, by Goode and Philpott, Haverfordwest; plain cartouche intersects scale, which lacks figures; north pointer has diadem and plumes.

51/41 Knelston (parish) SS 461896
Apt 05.01.1844; 538a (all); Map 1845, 6 chns; waterbodies.

51/42 Laleston (parish) SS 866819
Apt 14.12.1840; 1632a (1631); Map 1841?, 6 chns, 'Delineated' by Edward Neale, Bridgend; boundary tree. Apt omits some land use.

51/43 Langan (parish) SS 954777 [Llangan]
Apt 13.04.1840; 1176a (1175); Map 1840?, 3 chns, 1st cl, by Edwd Neale, Southampton; construction lines, waterbodies, houses, common (col).

51/44 Langonoyd (parish) SS 850910 [Llangynwyd]
Apt 21.08.1839; 15462a (15460); Map 1841, 6 chns, by Edward Neale, Bridgend; railway, boundary stones, churchyard, hamlet boundaries and names; pecked lines appear to be within holdings, and dot-dash lines between holdings; unhatched circles on some buildings could be factory chimneys; bridges are shown by 'arch' effect.

51/45 Lansamlet (parish) SS 685975 [Llansamlet]
Apt 22.11.1844; 6736a (all); Map 1846, 4 chns, in 2 parts, (includes 8-chn extension of detail); railway, canal with towpath, waterbodies, woods, high water mark, racecourse; railway is unnamed and seems to be a later addition. Apt omits land use.

51/46 Lantwit Major (parish) SS 970690 [Llantwit Major]
Apt 11.08.1840; 4914a (5298); Map 1842?, 8 chns, by Goode and Philpott, Surveyors and lithographers, Haverfordwest, (includes town separately at 3 chns), litho. Apt omits some field names.

51/47 Lantwit Vardre (parish) ST 085860 [Llantwit Fardre]
Apt 28.03.1844; 5312a (5311); Map 1843, 8 chns, in 3 parts, by J.T. Williams, Glog, near Newbridge, (includes two 4-chn enlargements of detail); railway, woods, plantations, orchards, building names, chapel, rail works, tin works, tramway; hill named. Apt omits field names.

51/48 Lavernock (parish) ST 182686
Apt 27.07.1844; 624a (1014); Map 1845, 3 chns; orchards, gardens, building names. Apt omits most field names.

51/49 Lisfane (parish) ST 190837 [Lisvane]
Apt 12.10.1844; 1339a (1338); Map 1845, 6 chns, ? by G.S. Strawson, Surveyor etc, Cardiff; waterbodies. Apt omits field names.

51/50 Lisworney (parish) SS 961741 [Llysworney]
Apt 10.10.1838; 897a (all); Map 1840?, 6 chns, by Goode and Philpott, Haverfordwest, litho.

51/51 Llanblethian (parish) ST 008750
Apt 22.07.1840; 3149a (3148); Map 1841?, 8 chns, by H.P. Goode and Philpott, Haverfordwest; woods; ruler-like scale intersects compass rose. Apt omits some field names.

51/52 Lancarvan (parish) ST 054712 [Llancarfan]
Apt 18.06.1840; 4967a (4500); Map 1841?, 6 chns, by Goode and Philpott, Haverfordwest; tithe-free hamlet boundary. Apt omits some land use.

51/53 Llandaff (parish) ST 164772 [Llanddewi]
Apt 14.11.1844; 3888a (4352); Map 1846, 8 chns, in 2 parts, (includes town at 4 chns); railway, woods, orchards, race course, intended railway. Apt omits some land use and some field names.

51/54 Landefodog (parish) SS 955905 [Not listed]
Apt 15.08.1840; 6508a (6508); Map 1842, 8 chns, by Edwd Neale; building names, mill, boundary stones.

51/55 Llandewi (parish) SS 450880 [Llanddewi]
Apt 08.09.1841; 1853a (all); Map 1845?, 4 chns; building names.

51/56 Llandilo-tal-y-bont (parish) SN 600035 [Not listed]
Apt 14.12.1840; 7297a (7401); Map 1843?, 8 chns, (tithable parts only in detail); railway, building names, landowners, chapels, forge, mills, boundary cairns, common. Apt has some cropping information, but omits most land use.

51/57 Llandough (parish) SS 992725
Apt 13.06.1846; 683a (all); Map 1843, 4 chns, by William Glasbrook, Penyfedw, nr Moriston; woods, orchards, building names, parsonage, mill.

51/58 Llandough, Cogan and Leckwith (parishes) ST 170730
Apt 15.05.1841; 1303a (all); Map 1841, 8 chns; railway, waterbodies, woods, parish boundaries, common. Apt omits field names.

51/59 Llandow (parish) SS 943730
Apt 03.08.1841; 1087a (all); Map 1841?, 8 chns, by Goode and Philpott, Haverfordwest; waterbodies, woods; plain cartouche intersects north pointer. Apt omits some land use.

51/60 Llanedarne (parish) ST 204810 [Llanedeyrn]
Apt 13.11.1844; 2637a (2636); Map 1846, 6 chns, 'Compiled' by

William Jones; waterbodies, woods, plantations, parkland, orchards, building names, boundary stones, boundary trees (pictorial).

51/61 Llangeinor (parish) SS 920900
Apt 12.12.1843; 6710a (6710); Map 1844?, 6 chns; building names, old beacon (by symbol), boundary stone (by symbol), boundary bank, common (col). Apt omits some field names.

51/62 Llangennith (parish) SS 436915
Apt 18.01.1844; 3080a (all); Map 1845?, 6 chns; hill-drawing, foot/b'way, waterbodies, woods, building names, mill, high water mark, intrenchments, quarry, burrows, heaps of stones, limekiln, glebe (col); colour bands may show tithe ownerships.

51/63 Llangevelach (parish) SN 665025 [Llangyfelach]
Apt 15.12.1838; 27306a (27305); Map 1841?, 8 chns, in 2 parts, (includes enlargement of village at 4 chns); railway, tramways, canal with towpath, waterbodies, woods, parkland, building names, copper works, chemical works, meeting houses, mills, lodges, chapel, machine, level, old river course, commons. Apt omits land use and some field names. (The map in PRO IR 30 is a copy; originals are in PRO IR 77/93 and IR 77/94.)

51/64 Llanguicke (parish) SN 730090 [Not listed]
Apt 02.08.1838; 12550a (12550); Map 1841, 8 chns, by Henry Philpott; railway, canal with towpath, woods, building names, coal works. Apt omits land use and some field names.

51/65 Llanharran (parish) ST 020738 [Llanharan]
Apt 21.11.1845; 3050a (all); Map 1846?, 6 chns, (includes enlargement of village at 3 chns); woods, plantations, parkland, building names. Apt omits some field names.

51/66 Llanharry (parish) ST 011709
Apt 12.06.1843; 1554a (all); Map 1844?, 4 chns; building names, well, mill.

51/67 Llanilid (parish) SS 982715
Apt 30.06.1843; 1574a (all); Map 1844, 6 chns, in 2 parts. Apt omits some field names.

51/68 Llanishen (parish) ST 177818
Apt 12.08.1844; 2916a (2915); Map 1845, 6 chns, 'Compiled' for G.S. Strawson by R.A. Rees; waterbodies, woods, plantations, orchards, gardens, heath/moor, building names, racecourse, tithe-free land. Apt omits field names.

51/69 Llanmadock (parish) SS 445942 [Llanmadoc]
Apt 30.06.1843; 1393a (all); Map 1845?, 8 chns; hill-drawing, waterbodies, houses, woods, marsh/bog (by Dawson's symbol), heath/moor (col), high water mark.

51/70 Llanmaes (parish) SS 988700
Apt 03.11.1843; 1086a (all); Map 1843, 6 chns; waterbodies, houses, road names.

51/71 Llanmihangel (parish) SS 980720
Apt 11.03.1840; 586a (all); Map 1840?, 6 chns; waterbodies, woods, garden; pictorial church.

51/72 Llanrhidian Lower Division (district in parish of Llanrhidian) SS 498922 [Llanrhdian]
Apt 25.03.1847; 8768a (12958); Map 1848?, 8 chns, by H.P. Goode, Surveyor and Lithr, Haverfordwest, litho; foot/b'way, waterbodies, woods, building names, notable rock (pictorial); some physical features named; a 3-chn map accompanies schedule to award in Apt.

51/73 Upper Hamlet of Llanrhidian (hamlet in parish of Llanrhidian) SS 548945 [Not Listed]
Apt 25.03.1847; 5952a (9106); Map 1848?, 8 chns, litho, ? by H.P. Goode, Surveyor and lithographer, Haverfordwest; railway, canal, woods, building names.

51/74 Llansannor (parish) SS 992794
Apt 29.12.1843; 1799a (all); Map 1845?, 6 chns, by H.P. Goode and Philpott, Surveyors etc, H'west; woods, orchards. Apt omits some field names.

51/75 Llantrisaint (parish) ST 040870 [Llantrisant]
Apt 28.03.1840; 16669a (16669); Map 1841, 6 chns, in 3 parts, by Peter Henderson, C.E., (includes enlargements of villages at 3 chns and 2 chns); railway, waterbodies, castle mound. Apt omits most field names.

51/76 Llantrythid (parish) ST 039728
Apt 06.11.1839; 1392a (1391); Map 1840?, 8 chns, by Goode and Philpott, Haverfordwest; plain cartouche, scale and compass rose intersect each other; pecked lines are within holdings and dot-dash lines are between holdings.

51/77 Lantwit Lower (hamlet in parish of Lantwit Juxta Neath) SS 780980 [Not listed]
Apt 25.04.1845; 1266a (4266); Map 1846, 8 chns, by A.R. Wallace; railway, canal with locks and towpath, waterbodies, woods, building names, quarry; sheaf of corn surmounts north pointer. Apt omits some field names.

51/78 Lanvabon (parish) ST 120942 [Llanfabon]
Apt 13.03.1841; 5370a (5369); Map 1842, 8 chns, by William Jones, Brecon; hill-drawing, railway, woods, plantations, building names, mill, tramroads. Apt omits some field names.

51/79 Llanwonno (parish) ST 040948
Apt 27.03.1841; 13014a (13013); Map 1842, 8 chns, in 4 parts, by William Jones, Brecon, (including three 3-chn plans of 'disputed lands'); hill-drawing, railway, woods, plantations, building names, sheepfold, boundary cairns and stones; acorn forms tip of north pointer.

51/80 Loughor (parish and borough) SS 578973
Apt 18.03.1839; 3590a (3999); Map 1841?, 8 chns; railway, canal with towpath, waterbodies, woods, building names, low water mark, chemical works, zinc works, colliery, works, mill, shipping place, smith's shop, castle, castle mound; 'Mynydds' named. District is apportioned by holding, though fields are numbered separately; Apt omits land use and some field names.

51/81 St Lythians (parish) ST 101721 [St Lythans]
Apt 12.06.1838; 1249a (all); Map 1839, 6 chns, by G.S. Strawson, Cardiff. Apt omits land use.

51/82 Marcross (parish) SS 930691
Apt 10.09.1840; 886a (all); Map 1841?, 8 chns, by Goode and Philpott, Haverfordwest; hedges; plain cartouche intersects north pointer. Apt omits some field names.

51/83 St Marychurch (parish) ST 004713 [St Mary Church]
Apt 13.06.1846; 727a (all); Map 1843, 4 chns, by William Glasbrook, Penyfedu, near Moriston; woods (col), building names, mill, sand pit.

51/84 St Mary Hill (parish) SS 962790
Apt 17.03.1843; 1405a (1404); Map 1844?, 8 chns, by H.P. Goode and Philpott, Haverfordwest.

51/85 Merthyr Dovan (parish) ST 112691 [Merthyr Dyfan]
Apt 24.08.1839; 1342a (1396); Map 1840, 6 chns, in 2 parts, by G.S. Strawson, Cardiff; houses, woods, building names, landowners. Apt omits some field names.

51/86 Merthyrmawr (parish) SS 870772 [Merthyr mawr]
Apt 20.03.1844; 2101a (2590); Map 1843, 6 chns; waterbodies, houses, woods, parkland, gardens, pit.

51/87 Merthyr Tidvil (parish) SO 070040 [Merthyr Tydfil]
Apt 11.06.1846; 17745a (17744); Map 1850, 8 chns, in 3 parts, by M. Nunan, (includes two 3-chn enlargements of glebe); railways, canal with towpath, waterbodies, woods, plantations, rock outcrops, building names, wharf, quarry, iron works, works, boundary stones and marks, racecourse, stables, chapel ruins; built-up part generalised; yellow band shows tithe-free areas.

51/88 Michaelstone Higher (hamlet in parish of Michaelstone super Avon) SS 830970 [Not listed]
Apt 18.12.1839; 4121a (4120); Map 1841?, 6 chns, by Goode and Philpott, Haverfordwest; scale is ruler-like and intersects plain cartouche.

51/89 Lower Hamlet of Michaelstone (hamlet in parish of Michaelstone Super Avon) SS 788932 [Not listed]
Apt 13.03.1845; 915a (915); Map 1847, 4 chns, by Adam Murray;

waterbodies, woods, building names, works (col), chimney. Apt omits some field names.

51/90 Michaelstone super Ely (parish) ST 115762 [Michaelston-super-Ely]
Apt 26.02.1839; 299a (all); Map 1839?, 6 chns, lithographed by Goode and Philpott; hedges; plain cartouche and scale intersect north pointer.

51/91 Michaelstone le Pit (parish) ST 150730 [Michaelston-le-Pit]
Apt 30.08.1843; 791a (790); Map 1843?, 6 chns, by H.P. Goode and Philpott, Surveyors and Lithrs, Haverfordwest, litho; waterbodies, woods; north pointer has plumes.

51/92 Michaelstone y Vedw (parish) (partly in Monmouthshire) ST 230850 [Michaelston-y-Fedw]
Apt 18.01.1839; 3434a (all); Map 1839, 6 chns, 'Compiled' by William Jones, Brecon; waterbodies, woods, plantations, parkland, orchards, gardens, building names, rectory, avenues of trees.

51/93 Monknash (parish) SS 921705
Apt 21.07.1838; 1324a (1584); Map 1839, 8 chns, by Goode and Philpott, Haverfordwest; tithe-free land; scale, plain cartouche and north pointer intersect each other.

51/94 Neath (parish) SS 757970
Apt 13.03.1845; 1122a (all); Map 1845, 8 chns, by D. Rees; canal with towpath, waterbodies, woods, building names, chemical works, workhouse, rope walk; built-up part generalised; north pointer has rose-like centre and spiky-leaf pointers; scale-bar is measuring rod in frame.

51/95 Newcastle (parish) SS 890820
Apt 14.12.1840; 2871a (2870); Map 1842, 6 chns, by Edwd Neale; railway, waterbodies, common, tithe-free land (red band). Apt omits some field names.

51/96 Newton Nottage (parish) SS 830782 [Nottage]
Apt 27.06.1846; 3318a (3877); Map 1843, 3 chns, 1st cl, by Thomas Morris, Newport; construction lines, railway with tunnel, waterbodies, houses, building names, wells, harbour, breakwater, steam mill, lodge, windmill, water meadow, common. Apt omits some field names.

51/97 St Nicholas (parish) ST 091741
Apt 19.12.1838; 2105a (2104); Map 1838, 6 chns, in 2 parts, by Goode and Philpott, Haverfordwest, (includes enlargement of village at 3 chns); waterbodies, woods, building names; ruler-like scale intersects north pointer. Apt omits almost all land use.

51/98 Nicholaston (parish) SS 512885
Apt 18.05.1844; 626a (all); Map 1846?, 6 chns, in 2 parts, by H.P. Goode, H'west; hill-drawing, woods, building names, embankment, parsonage.

51/99 Oxwich (parish) SS 495865
Apt 05.01.1844; 1197a (all); Map 1846?, 6 chns, in 2 parts, by H.P. Goode, Haverfordwest, (includes enlargement of part of village at 2 chns); hill-drawing, waterbodies, woods, building names, school, parsonage, lime quarries, glebe.

51/100 Oystermouth (parish) SS 605893
Apt 17.02.1844; 3975a (all); Map 1844?, 8 chns, in 6 parts, by Richard Price, Norton, near Swansea, (includes five 4-chn enlargements of detail); hill-drawing, waterbodies, woods (named), common, rock outcrops, building names, castle, washing lake, lighthouse, cliffs; coast features named. Apt omits some land use.

51/101 Penarth (parish) ST 187711
Apt 30.11.1843; 1142a (1507); Map 1847, 4 chns, ? by G.S. Strawson, Cardiff; building names, field names, wood (by annotation), glebe, coastal rock.

51/102 Pencoed (hamlet in parish of Coychurch) SS 960820
Apt 03.09.1839; 2045a (2045); Map '1837 and 1838', 4 chns, by G.S. Strawson and H.J. Clayton; construction lines, waterbodies, houses, woods, parkland, rock outcrops, building names, limekilns, barn, springs, ruins, colliery, chapel, common (col). Apt omits some land use and some field names.

51/103 Pendoylan (parish) ST 056771
Apt 13.11.1844; 3504a (all); Map 1847?, 6 chns, litho; waterbodies, woods, castle; hill named; pecked lines appear to be within holdings, and dot-dash boundaries appear to be between holdings.

51/104 Penlline (parish) SS 978767 [Penllyn]
Apt 18.01.1839; 1784a (1784); Map 1840?, 8 chns, by Goode and Philpott, Haverfordwest; plain cartouche, scale and north pointer intersect each other.

51/105 Penmaen (parish) SS 529888
Apt 18.05.1844; 1483a (all); Map 1846?, 4 chns, in 2 parts, by William Williams, Swansea; woods. Apt omits some land use and some field names.

51/106 Penmark (parish) ST 062678
Apt 13.08.1840; 3235a (3395); Map 1841, 6 chns, by G.S. Strawson, Cardiff, (includes enlargements of two villages at 3 chns); waterbodies, houses, woods, building names, mills, castle ruins, parsonage. Apt omits land use.

51/107 Pennard (parish) SS 566888
Apt 20.06.1846; 2248a (2292); Map 1848, 6 chns, ? by William Williams, Swansea; waterbodies, woods, building names, castle (pictorial), mill, pits, burrows.

51/108 Penrice (parish) SS 487877
Apt 29.11.1844; 2203a (2248); Map 1846?, 6 chns, in 2 parts, by H.P. Goode, Haverfordwest; hill-drawing, waterbodies, woods, parkland, building names, castle, cliffs, mill; building infill is omitted on part 2. Apt omits some field names.

51/109 Pentyrch (parish) ST 098828
Apt 20.08.1839; 3975a (3975); Map 8 chns, surveyed 1838-9 by Bate of Brecon; hill-drawing, railway, waterbodies, woods (named), rock outcrops, building names, iron furnace, forge; hill named.

51/110 Peterstone super Ely (parish) ST 079779 [Peterston-super-Ely]
Apt 21.04.1845; 2011a (2010); Map 1845?, 8 chns.

51/111 Peterstone super Montem (parish) SS 995845 [Not listed]
Apt 04.05.1841; 2060a (2060); Map 1842?, 3 chns, 1st cl, by Edwd Neale; houses, building names, factory (with Dawson's watermill symbol).

51/112 Port Eynon (parish) SS 459860
Apt 26.11.1844; 1057a (all); Map 1846?, 6 chns, by H.P. Goode, Haverfordwest, (includes village separately at 2 chns); hill-drawing, building names. Apt omits some field names.

51/113 Porthkerry (parish) ST 082667
Apt 11.08.1838; 917a (1131); Map 1839?, 4 chns, 'Compiled from Old Estate Maps by T.Burn...'; road names; mapmaker's name is partly lost. District is apportioned by holding and fields are not shown; no individual acreages are given for occupiers.

51/114 Pyle and Kenfig (parish) SS 811816
Apt 19.12.1845; 4527a (5251); Map 1847, 4 chns, by L.J. Griffith, Ynisygerwn; railway, waterbodies, woods, building names, limekiln, quarries, tithe-free areas (col); some coast features named; ruler-like scale-bar intersects plain cartouche. Apt omits all land use and some field names for tithe-free land.

51/115 Radyr (parish) ST 128803
Apt 30.01.1841; 1530a (1530); Map 1840, 6 chns, by G.S. Strawson, (includes two 3-chn enlargements of detail); railway, waterbodies, ford, tramway. Apt omits field names.

51/116 Resolven (hamlet in parish of Lantwil juxta Neath) SN 855020
Apt 07.12.1841; 4560a (4560); Map 1843, 8 chns, drawn by William Jones; woods (col, named), landowners, machine, levels, mill, waterfall, old furnace, boundary stones and marks, holdings (col, named), tramway; some streams named. District is apportioned by holding and fields are not shown.

51/117 Reynoldston (parish) SS 479898
Apt 23.07.1838; 1048a (1047); Map 1840?, 8 chns; waterbodies, woods, building names, mill. Apt omits land use.

51/118 Roath (parish) ST 200776
Apt 17.09.1839; 2430a (3500); Map 1840, 6 chns, in 2 parts 'compiled' by Wm Jones, (including 3-chn enlargement of Splott Moors); waterbodies, houses, woods, plantations, orchards, gardens, marsh/bog.

51/119 Rossilly (parish) SS 422881 [Rhossili]
Apt 03.07.1845; 1306a (all); Map 1846?, 6 chns, by H.P. Goode, Haverfordwest; hill-drawing, woods, rock outcrops, building names, parsonage, kiln, cliffs; headland named.

51/120 Ruddry (parish) ST 191865 [Rudry]
Apt 11.06.1840; 2640a (2639); Map 1843, 6 chns, by William Jones; woods, plantations, orchards, building names, forge, ruins, common; ruins are shown without infill. Apt omits some field names.

51/121 Sully (parish) ST 150680
Apt 11.03.1840; 2108a (2167); Map 1846, 3 chns, 1st cl, by Jos. Dickinson; construction lines, hill-drawing, foot/b'way, waterbodies, woods, parkland, rock outcrops, field boundary ownerships, building names, landowners, high and low water marks, bathing house, rectory, well, castle ruins, limekilns, old kilns, old mill, mill, sluice, sea bank; a tidal channel is described as 'variable'; coast features are named and mapped in detail.

51/122 Swansea (parish) SS 630940
Apt 17.08.1838; 6350a (9029); Map 1842?, 8 chns, in 2 parts, (includes lithographed enlargement of town at 2 chns); tramroad, canal with wharfs, quays, ferry, waterbodies, woods, building names, road names, hamlet boundaries, reservoir, lookout, town hall, postern, castle, market place, assembly rooms, schools, museum, house of industry, gaol, infirmary, burial ground, chapels, gas works, slaughter houses, pottery, coal and timber yards, quarries, flint mill, mills, patent slip, toll house, ballast heaps, jetty, land for harbour improvements, high and low water marks, sand hills; green bands are used for some bracing. Apt omits land use and some field names.

51/123 Tythegstone (parish) SS 852811 [Tythegston]
Apt 14.12.1840; 2872a (2871); Map 1841, 6 chns, 'Delineated' by Edward Neale. Apt omits land use for tithe-free land.

51/124 Van (hamlet in parish of Bedwas) ST 169873
Apt 07.09.1844; 825a (all); Map 4 chns, surveyed 1846 by Wm Jones; woods, plantations, building names.

51/125 Welsh St Donats (parish) ST 030760
Apt 26.08.1840; 2175a (2175); Map 1841?, 16 chns, by Goode and Philpott, Haverfordwest, litho; waterbodies, woods; plain cartouche, scale and north pointer intersect each other.

51/126 Wenvoe (parish) ST 124720
Apt 24.08.1839; 2852a (2955); Map 1840, 6 chns, by G.S. Strawson; waterbodies, houses, woods, orchards, gardens (col), building names, pound, mill, rectory, wire fence (pictorial), castle. Apt omits field names.

51/127 Whitchurch (parish) ST 147807
Apt 21.07.1840; 3193a (3192); Map 1840, 6 chns, 'Compiled' by Wm Jones; railway, canal with towpath, waterbodies, woods, plantations, orchards, gardens, building names, works, chapel, limekiln, common; coppice and timber woods are shown by Dawson's symbols.

51/128 Ynysawdre (hamlet in parish of St Brides Minor) SS 900845 [Not listed]
Apt 30.12.1842; 387a (all); Map 1843, 6 chns, by E. Neale, Laleston; houses, common; scale is ruler-like; map is drawn on the back of a printed Apt schedule sheet. Apt omits some field names.

51/129 Ystradowen (parish) ST 016781
Apt 08.02.1848; 1495a (all); Map 1848, 6 chns, litho; woods, orchards, boundary stones and marks; some physical features named.

51/130 Ystradyfodwg (parish) SS 960970 [Not listed]
Apt 13.11.1844; 24515a (24515); Map 1847, 8 chns, by J.T. Williams, Glog Pontypridd, Cardiff; hill-drawing, waterbodies, woods, plantations, rock outcrops, building names. Apt omits some land use and some field names.

Merionethshire

PRO IR29 and IR30 52/1-33

34 tithe districts: 429,852 acres
33 tithe commutations: 306,730 acres
23 voluntary tithe agreements, 10 compulsory tithe awards

Tithe and tithe commutation

Although in 1836 all but one of the tithe districts of Merionethshire remained subject to payment of tithes, about 29 per cent of the area of the county was tithe free (Fig. 64). This was mainly due to the fact that tithe was not apportioned on 'mountain' land. Two districts were wholly tithable at this date; in all the others there were modus payments in lieu of some tithes and in over a third of districts woodland was exempt from tithe.

Assistant tithe commissioners and local tithe agents who worked in Merionethshire are listed in Table 52.1 and the valuers of the county's tithe rent-charge in Table 52.2. In almost a third of Merionethshire districts tithe was apportioned by holdings with the result that there are no entries relating to individual land parcels in the schedules of apportionment of these tithe districts. In addition some field-by-field apportionments contain no land-use entries.

Tithe maps

With the possible exception of Anglesey, the tithe surveys of Merionethshire are cartographically the most impoverished of all English and Welsh counties. There are no first-class maps, the largest scale used is one inch to five chains (and that for a very small district) and half the tithable area of the county is mapped at, or less than, one inch to twelve chains. The tithe map of Llanfrothen is a very rough location sketch and is not drawn to scale. Apart from woodland on 42 per cent of maps, almost no land use is recorded and on only one map are inhabited buildings shown. Only six Merionethshire tithe maps in the Public Record Office collection have any indication of authorship; the most prolific map-maker responsible for a group of maps characterised by distinctive borders is anonymous. One positive feature of Merionethshire maps is their decoration; several have north pointers with Prince of Wales's feathers, and two, Pennal and Tywyn, have wheat ear and oak leaf decorated north pointers.

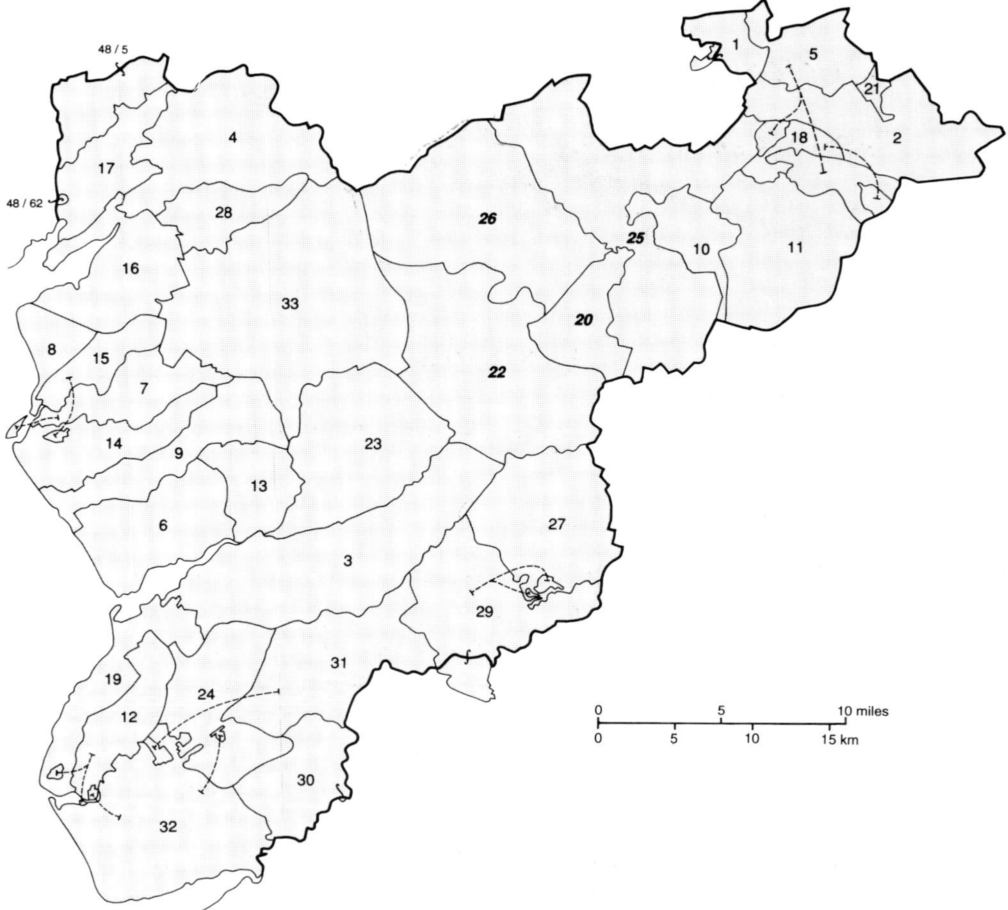

Fig. 64 Merionethshire: tithe district boundaries.

Table 52.1. *Agreements and awards for commutation of tithes in Merionethshire*

Assistant commissioner/ local tithe agent	*Number of agreements**	*Number of awards*
Aneurin Owen	16	10
John Fenton	8	0

*Computed from the number of extant reports on tithe agreements in the tithe files [PRO IR 18].

Table 52.2. *Tithe valuers and tithe map-makers in Merionethshire*

Name and address (in Merionethshire unless indicated)	*Number of districts*	*Acreage*
Tithe valuers		
Thomas Payne, Dolgelly	8	92,550
Walter Powell Jones, Cefn Rug	4	37,001
Richard Humphreys Richards, Llanfair isaf	4	29,965
Others [11]	17	147,214
Attributed tithe map-makers		
Edward Jones, Tynberth, Corwen, Denbighshire	2	15,262
John Roberts, Corwen, Denbighshire	2	11,892
Others [2]	2	4,773

Table 52.3. *The tithe maps of Merionethshire: scales and classes*

Scale in chains/inch	*All maps*		*First Class*		*Second Class*	
	Number	*Acreage*	*Number*	*Acreage*	*Number*	*Acreage*
5	1	694	0	0	1	694
6	7	46,349	0	0	7	46,349
8	8	89,450	0	0	8	89,450
10	2	7,942	0	0	2	7,942
12	10	97,846	0	0	10	97,846
20	3	41,912	0	0	3	41,912
26.6	1	15,182	0	0	1	15,182
Not to scale	1	7,355	0	0	1	7,355
TOTAL	33	306,730	0	0	33	306,730

Table 52.4. *The tithe maps of Merionethshire: dates*

	1839	*1840*	*1841*	*1842*	*1843*	*1844*	*1845*	*1846*	*1847*	*1848*	*1849*
2nd class	1	7	11	7	1	1	2	0	1	0	2

Merionethshire

52/1 Bettws Gwerfil Goch (parish) SJ 022483
Apt 11.02.1842; 2650a (2650); Map 1842?, 8 chns, in 2 parts, (including 4 chn enlargement of detail); woods, gardens, heath/moor. One farm is apportioned by holding.

52/2 Corwen (parish) SJ 090430
Apt 13.05.1839; 8716a (12646); Map 1840, 12 chns; hill-drawing, foot/b'way, waterbodies, woods, plantations, churchyard, mounds. Apt omits land use.

52/3 Dolgelly (parish) SH 766167 [Dolgellau]
Apt 02.06.1838; 25032a (25607); Map 1842?, 20 chns; strand, sand banks; lakes named. District is apportioned by holding and no fields are shown.

52/4 Festiniog (parish) SH 700440 [Ffestiniog]
Apt 08.02.1842; 16456a (16456); Map 1842?, 8 chns; waterbodies, field boundary ownerships, building names, rectory. District is apportioned by holding and no fields are shown. (There is no copy in PRO IR 30; details are from National Library of Wales copy, which itself is partly original and partly a photocopy. The version which supplied the photocopy appears to have been coloured by holdings.)

52/5 Gwyddelwern (parish) SJ 075470
Apt 22.10.1839; 9128a (9127); Map 1842?, 12 chns; waterbodies, woods, plantations, gardens (by annotation).

52/6 Llanaber (parish) SH 640200
Apt 17.09.1839; 11920a (12679); Map 1841, 6 chns; waterbodies, rock outcrops, foreshore and offshore sandbank (col); north pointer has diadem, Prince of Wales feathers and 'Ich Dien'; border has 'bird' corners.

52/7 Llanbedr (parish) SH 633284
Apt 15.08.1840; 7103a (7312); Map 1841, 6 chns; waterbodies; north pointer has diadem, 'Ich Dien', and Prince of Wales feathers; border has 'bird' corners.

52/8 Llandanwg (parish) SH 586316
Apt 30.07.1840; 3610a (4964); Map 1841, 6 chns; waterbodies, castle; north pointer has diadem, 'Ich Dien' and Prince of Wales feathers.

52/9 Llanddwywio (parish) SH 650240 [Llanddwywe]
Apt 09.05.1840; 9009a (9348); Map 1841, 6 chns, in 2 parts; waterbodies; private roads numbered and uncoloured; north pointer has diadem, 'Ich Dien', and Prince of Wales feathers; border has 'Bird' corners.

52/10 Llanderfel (parish) SH 987370 [Llandderfel]
Apt 23.01.1838; 5529a (all); Map 1839, 12 chns, in 3 parts, by J.R. [? John Roberts], Corwen, (enclosed parts only); waterbodies, woods, plantations, heath/moor. Apt omits land use.

52/11 Llandrillo (parish) SJ 050360
Apt 27.10.1840; 6363a (28200); Map 1841, 12 chns, in 2 parts, by John Roberts, Corwen, (including 3-chn enlargement of detail; enclosed parts only); waterbodies, woods, plantations, churchyard.

52/12 Llanegryn (parish) SH 620080
Apt 21.05.1841; 6825a (6819); Map 1842, 8 chns; waterbodies, occupation roads; bridge named; north pointer has diadem, 'Ich Dien', and Prince of Wales feathers; border has 'bird' corners.

52/13 Llanelltyd (parish) SH 705220 [Llaneltyd]
Apt 03.02.1843; 3155a (6736); Map 1845?, 10 chns, (enclosed part only); waterbodies, landowners, tithe-free land (col); lake named; border has decorative corners. District is apportioned by holding, and no fields are shown.

52/14 Llanenddwyn (parish) SH 630255
Apt 09.05.1840; 7117a (7777); Map 1841, 6 chns, waterbodies; north pointer has diadem, 'Ich Dien', and Prince of Wales' feathers.

52/15 Llanfair (parish) SH 613310
Apt 18.12.1839; 5196a (5196); Map 1840, 6 chns; waterbodies; meaning of colour bands is unclear; border has 'bird' corners; north pointer has diadem, Prince of Wales feathers and 'Ich Dien'.

52/16 Llanfihangelytraethau and Llandecwyn (parishes) SH 630370
Apt 18.01.1842; 6736a (14482); Map 1842?, 8 chns, in 3 parts, (including some detail separately at 4 chns); railway, waterbodies, woods, building names, sands, chapels, slate wharf, embankment, parish boundary; colour bands show estates. Apt omits some land use and field names.

52/17 Llanfrothen (parish) SH 625435
Apt 02.05.1840; 7355a (7482); Map 1840, described as 'Sketch Map' of the district, not drawn to scale. District is apportioned by holding (col on map) and no information about fields is given; all acreages in Apt are rounded to nearest acre.

52/18 Llangar (parish) SJ 060423 [Not listed]
Apt 28.09.1838; 2394a (3578); Map 1840?, 6 chns, in 2 parts, by Edwd Jones, Tynberth, near Corwen, (detached part at 16 chns); hill-drawing, waterbodies, woods, plantations, landowners, lime rocks, gravel beds. Apt omits land use.

52/19 Llangelynin (parish) SH 603092 [Llangelynnin]
Apt 20.07.1839; 8559a (11004); Map 1841?, 20 chns; ferry, embankment, tidal flats, common; church is only building shown; colours emphasise holdings. District is apportioned by holding and no fields are shown.

52/20 Llangower (parish) SH 920310
Apt 29.12.1842; 3716a (5600); Map 1844, 12 chns, (enclosed part only); waterbodies, woods, building names, rectory; colours may show ownerships. Apt omits land use.

52/21 Llansanfraid glyn Dyvrdwyn (manor) SJ 103447 [Not listed]
Apt 26.11.1844; 694a (693); Map 1845, 5 chns, by John Price, Ruthin; woods.

52/22 Llanuwchlyn (parish) SH 870270 [Llanuwchllyn]
Apt 31.07.1847; 4079a (12000); Map 1849?, 12 chns, in 5 parts, by Jones, Cynwyd, (four small enlargements of detail; tithable parts only); hill-drawing, waterbodies, woods, building names, common; mountain and lake named; colour bands show ownerships.

52/23 Llanvachraith (parish) SH 770250 [Llanfachreth]
Apt 12.06.1846; 4787a (10000); Map 1847?, 10 chns, in 7 parts, (enclosed parts only; including 32-chn 'Skeleton Map of Roads'); landowners; the skeleton map shows some farms which do not appear on the main map. District is apportioned by holding and no fields are shown.

52/24 Llanvihangel y penant (parish) SH 660090 [Llanfihangel-y-pennant]
Apt 07.06.1838; 8321a (8321); Map 1840?, 20 chns; hill-drawing, building names. District is apportioned by holding and no fields are shown.

52/25 Llanvor and Nantfreur (district) SH 940370 [Llanfor]
Apt 16.11.1847; 20030a (20030); Map 1849, 12 chns, (enclosed parts only); waterbodies, building names, common; meaning of pink tint is unclear. Apt omits land use.

52/26 Llanycil (parish) SH 855365
Apt 19.12.1838; 12868a (12868); Map 1841, 12 chns, in 7 parts, '2nd Class Map' by Edw Jones, Tynberth, Corwen, (enclosed parts only; including six enlargements of detail); hill-drawing, waterbodies, woods, old river course, lakeside gravel; hills, mountain and lake named; inns and pubs at Bala are comprehensively mapped.

52/27 Llanmowddwy (parish) SH 895180 [Llanmawddwy]
Apt 23.12.1842; 15291a (15290); Map 1843, 8 chns; waterbodies. Apt omits land use.

52/28 Maentwrog (parish) SH 700400
Apt 09.05.1840; 5466a (5465); Map 1841, 12 chns; waterbodies, building names, chapels, private road; colours show ownerships and colour bands show holdings. District is apportioned by holding and no fields are shown.

52/29 Mallwyd (parish) (partly in Montgomeryshire) SH 833143
Apt 22.05.1838; 16451a (16450); Map 1841?, 8 chns; houses, slate

quarry, county boundary, holding boundaries (col). Apt is by holding and omits land use.

52/30 Pennal (parish) SH 720040
Apt 02.06.1838; 7462a (7461); Map 1842, 8 chns, (enclosed part only); woods (col); bridge named; tithable buildings are carmine and tithe-free ones are grey; acorn, wheatear, barleyear and oakleaf decorate north pointer. Apt omits land use and some field names.

52/31 Talyllyn (parish) SH 750110 [Tal-y-llyn]
Apt 03.08.1838; 15182a (15182); Map 1840, 26.67 chns; hill-drawing, waterbodies, building names. District is apportioned by holding and fields are not shown.

52/32 Towyn (parish) SH 645005 [Tywyn]
Apt 29.09.1838; 17579a (26372); Map 1841, 8 chns; waterbodies, woods; tithable buildings are carmine and tithe-free buildings are grey; Towyn town is incompletely mapped; gardens at Aberdovey are shown by annotation; green bands may show ownerships; acorn, wheatear, barleyear and oakleaf decorate north pointer. Apt omits land use.

52/33 Trawsfynydd (parish) SH 730350
Apt 18.08.1839; 21951a (21950); Map 1840, 12 chns, (enclosed parts only); hill-drawing, waterbodies, woods, building names, common; lakes named; colours show ownerships. Apt omits land use.

Montgomeryshire

PRO IR 29 and IR30 53/1-75

75 tithe districts: 522,003 acres
75 tithe commutations: 423,997 acres
58 voluntary tithe agreements, 17 compulsory tithe awards

Tithe and tithe commutation

All the tithe districts of Montgomeryshire contained land subject to payment of tithes in 1836 and fourteen districts were wholly tithable (Fig. 65). As in most of Wales, the main cause of tithe exemption (in 73 per cent of districts) was payment of a modus in lieu of tithes, and woodland was exempt in a quarter of the districts. Much of the high mountain land in the county yielded so little that in practice it was treated as if tithe free.

Assistant tithe commissioners and local tithe agents who worked in Montgomeryshire are listed in Table 53.1 and the valuers of tithe rent-charge in Table 53.2. Unusually for Wales, tithe in all Montgomeryshire districts was apportioned field-by-field rather than by holdings. Nevertheless, some tithe apportionments do have blank entries under property names and state of cultivation. In some districts various grassland types are distinguished; the apportionment for Llangadfan notes a particularly wide variety.

Tithe maps

Montgomeryshire is unusual amongst Welsh counties in that two of the seventy-five maps are sealed as first class. No second-class map has construction lines but on only one map is copying acknowledged. Only the two first-class maps are at as large a scale as one inch to three chains; a majority of Montgomeryshire's tithe maps (77 per cent) are at one inch to six chains (Table 53.3).

As usual in Wales, agricultural land use is poorly recorded on the tithe maps. Although 26 per cent of maps show orchards, none depicts arable or grass, though 93 per cent do map woodland which is an unusually high proportion for any county.

Forty-four Montgomeryshire tithe maps in the Public Record Office collection can be attributed to a particular map-maker; as with tithe valuations, the most prolific were Charles Mickleburgh, who produced twenty maps, and William Parry, who produced twelve maps. Mickleburgh's maps are considerably better executed than the average for Wales, with crisp linework and lettering. Parry employs two styles, one plain, and the other with diced and coloured scale bars and coloured woodland. The tithe map of Kerry is

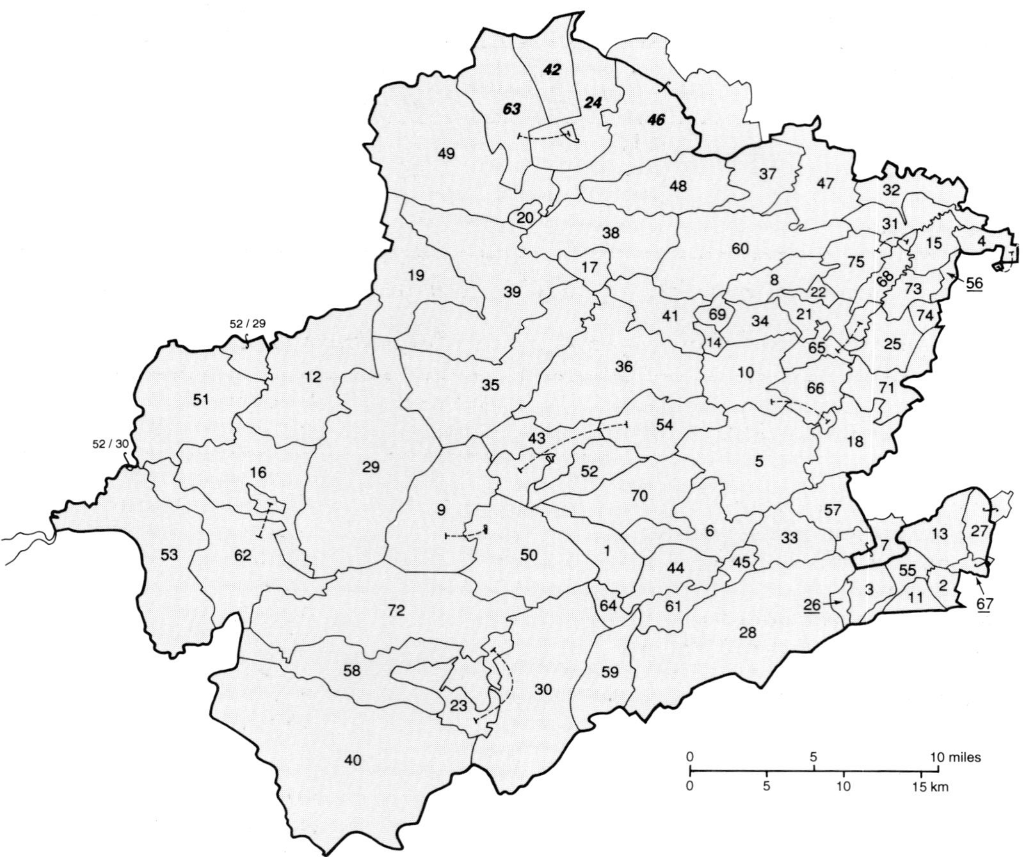

Fig. 65 Montgomeryshire: tithe district boundaries.

one of half a dozen maps in a distinctive style, characterised by bold naming and colouring of townships which are all by the same anonymous map-maker. Notwithstanding the fact that comparatively few surveyors worked in this county, Montgomeryshire tithe maps display a considerable variety of style.

A few Montgomeryshire tithe maps are decorated; that of Darowen has two faces (mermen?) in the north pointer, Mochtre, though a long distance from the sea includes a maritime scene above the scale, and the map of Pool Lower contains a picture of Powis Castle.

Table 53.1. *Agreements and awards for commutation of tithes in Montgomeryshire*

Assistant commissioner/ local tithe agent	*Number of agreements**	*Number of awards*
John Fenton	40	0
Aneurin Owen	17	16
John Johnes	2	0
George Wingrove Cooke	0	1

*Computed from the number of extant reports on tithe agreements in the tithe files [PRO IR 18].

Table 53.2. *Tithe valuers and tithe map-makers in Montgomeryshire*

Name and address (in Montgomeryshire unless indicated)	*Number of districts*	*Acreage*
Tithe valuers		
Charles Mickleburgh, Montgomery	14	73,178
William Parry, Morfodion, Llanidloes	11	105,707
William and John Humphries, Berriew	6	42,309
John Baker, Cefngwifed	5	26,087
Richard Yates, Whittington, Shropshire	4	31,663
Thomas Owen Sturkey, Highgate, Newtown	4	29,997
David Jones, Llanfyllin	4	18,661
Timotheus Burd, Whistone Priory, Shropshire	4	13,664
Others [18]	23	82,731
Attributed tithe map-makers		
Charles Mickleburgh, Montgomery	20	102,623
William Parry, Llanidloes	12	110,276
David Jones, Llanfyllin	5	20,864
Others [5]	7	41,067

Table 53.3. *The tithe maps of Montgomeryshire: scales and classes*

Scale in chains/inch	*All maps*		*First Class*		*Second Class*	
	Number	*Acreage*	*Number*	*Acreage*	*Number*	*Acreage*
3	2	15,151	2	15,151	0	0
6	58	311,321	0	0	58	311,321
8	8	44,278	0	0	8	44,278
9	6	49,690	0	0	6	49,690
12	1	3,557	0	0	1	3,557
TOTAL	75	423,997	2	15,151	73	408,846

Table 53.4. *The tithe maps of Montgomeryshire: dates*

	1838	*1839*	*1840*	*1841*	*1842*	*1843*	*1844*	*1845*	*1846*	*1847*	*1848*	*1849*	*1850*
All maps	2	10	18	8	8	5	1	4	7	3	2	2	5
1st class	0	0	2	0	0	0	0	0	0	0	0	0	0
2nd class	2	10	16	8	8	5	1	4	7	3	2	2	5

Montgomeryshire

53/1 Aberhafesp (parish) SO 061948
Apt 12.10.1839; 4569a (4568); Map 1839, 6 chns, by William Parry, Llanidloes; waterbodies, houses, woods (col), building names, observatory, rectory, turbaries, quarries. Apt omits land use.

53/2 Aston (township in parish of Lydham) SO 290910
Apt 31.01.1845; 1126a (all); Map 1846, 6 chns, by Charles Mickleburgh, Montgomery; foot/b'way, waterbodies, woods, plantations, fences, field boundary ownerships, building names, race course, pit.

53/3 Bacheldre and Hopton Issa (township in parish of Churchstoke) SO 240910
Apt 18.12.1839; 2012a (2012); Map 1839, 6 chns, ? by Charles Mickleburgh, Montgomery; hill-drawing, foot/b'way, waterbodies, woods, plantations, orchards, building names, mill, township boundaries (col); colours may show property ownerships. Apt omits some field names.

53/4 Bausley (township in parish of Alberbury) SJ 334150 [Not listed]
Apt 08.02.1840; 1685a (?); Map 1840, 6 chns, in 2 parts; foot/b'way, waterbodies, woods, plantations, heath/moor, building names, pinfold, mill.

53/5 Berriew (parish) SJ 170010
Apt 07.01.1840; 12010a (12010); Map 1840, 3 chns, 1st cl, in 4 parts, by J.H. Poundley, Kerry, Montgomeryshire; construction lines, hill-drawing, foot/b'way, canal with towpath and aqueduct, waterbodies, houses, woods, plantations, parkland, orchards, building names, toll gate, mill, wells, chapels, quarry, township boundaries. Apt omits most field names.

53/6 Bettws or Bettws Caederven (parish) SO 135962 [Bettws Cedewain]
Apt 19.11.1840; 5305a (5305); Map 1840, 6 chns; canal with towpath, waterbodies, houses, woods (col), plantations, orchards, building names, chapel, site of castle, township boundaries.

53/7 Brompton, Rhiston and Weston Madoc (townships in parish of Churchstoke) (partly in Shropshire) SO 248942
Apt 20.10.1840; 2707a (2707); Map 1839, 6 chns, by Charles Mickleburgh, Montgomery; foot/b'way, waterbodies, houses, woods, plantations, orchards, hedges, field boundary ownerships, building names, township boundaries (col); reason for tinting some fields green or blue is obscure.

53/8 Upper Broniarth and Lower Broniarth (township in parish of Guilsfield) SJ 210135 [Broniarth]
Apt 23.09.1840; 2756a (?); Map 1842, 6 chns, in 2 parts, by Charles Mickleburgh, Montgomery, (including 2-chn enlargement of detail); foot/b'way, waterbodies, woods, plantations, gardens, field boundary ownerships, building names, smithy, public house, pumphouse, old mill, chapels, well, barn, quarries, pound, commons.

53/9 Carno (parish) SN 955978
Apt 31.01.1848; 10983a (10982); Map 1849, 6 chns, by William Parry, Morfodion, Llanidloes; waterbodies, farmyards, woods, building names, township boundaries.

53/10 Castle Caerinion (parish) SJ 167063 [Castle Caerinion]
Apt 08.01.1840; 6540a (6540); Map 1839, 6 chns, in 8 parts, by Charles Mickleburgh, Montgomery, (including enlargement of detail, and two 12-chn indexes); foot/b'way, woods, plantations, orchards, gardens, heath/moor, hedges, field boundary ownerships, building names, chapels, mill, vicarage, pound, township boundaries (col), commons. Apt omits land use.

53/11 Castlewright (township in parish of Mainston) SO 273905 [Not listed]
Apt 24.06.1841; 1333a (1332); Map 1842, [6 chns]; waterbodies, woods, plantations, orchards, building names, chapel, boundary trees, turnpike gate, earthwork.

53/12 Cemmes (parish) SH 870080 [Cemmaes]
Apt 22.05.1838; 6721a (9247); Map 1841, 8 chns, by William Parry, Llanidloes, (tithable parts only); waterbodies, woods, building names, commons, sheepwalk. Apt omits land use.

53/13 Churchstoke and Hurdley (townships in parish of Churchstoke) SO 294950 [Church Stoke]
Apt 23.05.1840; 3586a (3586); Map 1840, 6 chns; hill-drawing, waterbodies, woods, plantations, parkland, orchards, building names, quarry, boundary marks, ancient fort, mill, township boundaries; modus land is tinted blue.

53/14 Coffronydd (township in parish of Pool) SJ 141089 [Cyfronydd]
Apt 22.08.1840; 608a (607); Map 1846, 6 chns, in 2 parts, by Charles Mickleburgh, Montgomery; waterbodies, woods, plantations, building names, mill, smithy; north pointer has diadem, plumes and 'Ich Dien'.

53/15 Criggion (township in parish of Alberbury) SJ 296147
Apt 15.02.1839; 2401a (?); Map 1838, 6 chns, by Samuel H. Ashdown, Uppington, Shrewsbury; foot/b'way, woods, pillar (pictorial), chapel; bridge named.

53/16 Darowen (parish) SH 827007
Apt 19.12.1845; 7913a (10000), (tithable parts only); Map 1846, 8 chns; waterbodies, woods, building names, commons; two faces, possibly of mermen, are incorporated in the north pointer.

53/17 Dolwar (township in parish of Llanfihangel) SJ 062143 [Dolanog]
Apt 07.10.1841; 1430a (?); Map 1840, 6 chns, ? by Charles Mickleburgh, Montgomery; woods, field boundary ownerships, building names, common, encroachments; bridge named.

53/18 Forden (parish) SJ 240019
Apt 27.10.1840; 5271a (5270); Map 1843-4, 6 chns, in 4 parts, by Charles Mickleburgh, Montgomery, (one part at 9 chns; including 12-chn index); foot/b'way, waterbodies, woods, plantations, gardens, hedges, fences, building names, chapel, smithy, lodge, quarry, house of industry, mill, turnpike, Offa's Dyke, finger post (pictorial), boundary stones, township boundaries (col); one north pointer has diadem and plumes. Apt omits land use.

53/19 Garthbeibo (parish) SH 945155 [Not listed]
Apt 25.10.1838; 3743a (7200), (tithable parts only); Map 1841, 6 chns, in 2 parts, by Charles Mickleburgh, Montgomery; waterbodies, woods, plantations, field boundary ownerships, building names, factory, commons.

53/20 Garthbwlch (township in parish of Llanwyddyn) SJ 020182 [Not listed]
Apt 16.07.1850; 762a (?); Map 1850, 6 chns, by William Parry, Llanidloes; woods, building names.

53/21 Gungrogfechan, Trebydan and Garth (townships in parish of Guilsfield) SJ 220105 [Not listed]
Apt 12.12.1840; 2832a (?); Map 1846, 6 chns; canal with towpath, waterbodies, houses, woods, parkland, township boundaries.

53/22 Hendrehen Llan and Trowscoed (district in parish of Guilsfield) SJ 215117 [Not listed]
Apt 14.07.1842; 761a (?); Map 1845, 6 chns; waterbodies, woods, building names.

53/23 Hengynwith-fach, Brithdir, Treflin, and Kilmachallt (townships in parish of Llanidloes) SN 970845 [Not listed]
Apt 30.11.1840; 4605a (all); Map 1840, 6 chns, by William Parry; waterbodies, houses, woods, building names, toll bars, public quarry (col), township boundaries; built-up part generalised.

53/24 Hirnant (parish) SJ 050230
Apt 02.07.1839; 2203a (4000), (tithable parts only); Map 1840, 8 chns, ? by David Jones, Llanfyllin; woods, plantations, heath/moor.

53/25 Hope and Cletterwood (township in parish of Buttington) SJ 261081
Apt 23.09.1840; 3240a (3239); Map 1841, 6 chns, by Charles Mickleburgh, Montgomery; foot/b'way, waterbodies, woods, plantations, building names, parsonage, weirs, quarry, mills, old course of river; bridge named.

53/26 Hopton Ucha (township in parish of Churchstoke) SO 221901 [Hopton Uchaf]
Apt 20.02.1841; 726a (726); Map 1843, 6 chns, by Charles Mickleburgh, Montgomery; hill-drawing, foot/b'way, waterbodies, woods, plantations, hedges, building names, quarries, finger post (pictorial), stiles, pound.

53/27 Hussington or Hyssington (parish) (partly in Shropshire) SO 322958
Apt 14.02.1839; 2409a (2382); Map 1840, 6 chns; hill-drawing, foot/b'way,

woods (col), plantations (col), building names, boundary trees and stones, churchyard, spring, commons.

53/28 Kerry (parish) SO 155890
Apt 30.06.1840; 21430a (21430); Map 1842, 6 chns; waterbodies, houses, woods, plantations, parkland, hedges, building names, mills, township boundaries and names, manor boundary (yellow). Apt omits some field names.

53/29 Llanbrynmair (parish) SH 900030
Apt 20.12.1839; 12470a (19006); Map 1841, 9 chns, by William Parry, Llanidloes; waterbodies, woods, building names, sheepwalks.

53/30 Llandinam (parish) SO 020850
Apt 29.11.1845; 18065a (18064); Map 1847, 6 chns, by William Parry; waterbodies, woods, building names, motte and bailey, mill, township boundaries and names. Apt omits land use and field names.

53/31 Llandrinio (parish) SJ 280175
Apt 20.10.1840; 3833a (3832); Map 1841, 9 chns; waterbodies, woods, orchards, canal with towpath, township boundaries.

53/32 Llandysilio (parish) SJ 273190
Apt 19.02.1839; 3141a (3141); Map 1840, 3 chns, 1st cl, 'Rough Plan' by Groom and Greening, Woodgate, Salop; construction lines, waterbodies, houses, woods, plantations, canal with towpath and aqueduct.

53/33 Llandyssil (parish) SO 190950 [Llandysul]
Apt 12.10.1840; 4071a (4071); Map 1839, 6 chns, 'Compiled principally from Maps produced by the several landowners'; waterbodies, woods, plantations, orchards, building names, churchyard (col), chapel, mills, factory, quarries, nursery (by symbol). Apt has some cropping information.

53/34 Llanerrochwell (township in parish of Guilsfield) SJ 175100 [Llanerchbrochwell]
Apt 23.09.1840; 2649a (?); Map 1841, 6 chns; waterbodies, woods (named), parkland, building names, private roads (uncoloured). Apt omits land use.

53/35 Llanerfyl (parish) SJ 013077
Apt 12.06.1849; 14905a (16255); Map 1850, 6 chns, in 4 parts, by Mickleburgh and Son, Montgomery, (including 18-chn index); foot/b'way, waterbodies, woods, building names, domen, corn mill, township boundaries and names; north pointer has plumes. Apt omits some field names.

53/36 Llanfair (parish) SJ 065055 [Llanfair Caereinion]
Apt 22.04.1839; 16157a (16157); Map 1842, 6 chns, in 11 parts, by Charles Mickleburgh, Montgomery, (including 18-chn index, and two 2-chn enlargements of the town); waterbodies, woods, plantations, parkland, gardens, marsh/bog, heath/moor, hedges, building names, town hall, turnpike gate, chapel, vicarage, quarries, mills (with Dawson's symbol), weir, township boundaries (col), turbaries; bridge named; urn appears at end of one north pointer.

53/37 Llanvechan (parish) SJ 186201 [Llanfechain]
Apt 20.03.1839; 4464a (4462); Map 1839, 6 chns, ? by Issac Porter, Oswestry, Salop; waterbodies, building names, boundary trees and marks, rectory.

53/38 Llanfihangel (district in parish of Llanfihangel) SJ 080170 [Llanfihangel-yng-Ngwynfa]
Apt 12.06.1844; 8364a (?); Map 1847, 6 chns, by David Jones, Llanfyllin, Montgomery; waterbodies, common.

53/39 Llangadfan (parish) SJ 001120
Apt 12.09.1838; 16929a (16929); Map 1840, 6 chns, in 8 parts, by Charles Mickleburgh, Montgomery, (including one part at 16 chns and 24-chn index); foot/b'way, waterbodies, woods, plantations, gardens, hedges, field boundary ownerships, building names, foot bridge, boundary stones, smithies, mill, rectory, lodge, chapel, quarry, turbaries; lakes and some streams and bridges named.

53/40 Llangirrig (parish) SN 910800 [Llangurrig]
Apt 27.12.1843; 11903a (all); Map 1845, 9 chns, ? by William Parry, Llanidloes; woods, building names, boundary marks, common; scale has yellow dicing.

53/41 Llangyniw (parish) SJ 120100 [Llangyniew]
Apt 12.06.1849; 4611a (4513); Map 1850, 6 chns, (including 1.5 chns enlargement of detail); woods (named), plantations, hedges, building names, chapel, mound, pinfold, turnpike, township boundaries (col) and names, turbary; north pointer has plumes and diadem. Apt omits some field names.

53/42 Llangynog (parish) SJ 052262
Apt 17.12.1839; 975a (3223); Map 1840, 8 chns, by David Jones, Llanfyllin, Montgomeryshire, (tithable parts only).

53/43 Llanllugan (parish) SJ 030023
Apt 04.08.1849; 2922a (3945); Map 1850, 6 chns, ? by William Parry, Llanidloes, (tithable parts only); waterbodies, woods, building names, mills, common. Apt omits some field names.

53/44 Llanwchairn (parish) SO 110932 [Llanllwchaiarn]
Apt 14.04.1841; 4427a (4426); Map 1842, 6 chns, in 2 parts, (built-up part also at 3 chns); hill-drawing, foot/b'way, canal with towpath and basin, waterbodies, woods, plantations, orchards, heath/moor, hedges, fences, building names, weir, ford, road earthworks, mill, well, boundary trees, township boundaries and names. Apt omits field names.

53/45 Llanmerewic (parish) SO 158933 [Llanmerewig]
Apt 20.10.1840; 978a (978); Map 1838, 6 chns; waterbodies, woods, plantations, orchards, gardens, hedges, field boundary ownerships, building names, flannel racks, factory, vicarage; colours may show holdings or property ownerships.

53/46 Llanchaiadr yn Mochnant (parish) (partly in Denbighshire) SJ 120260 [Llanrhaeadr-yn-Mochnant]
Apt 15.07.1839; 11267a (23294), (tithable parts only); Map 1841, 6 chns, in 12 parts, (including built-up parts at 3 chns and 30-chn index); hill-drawing, waterbodies, woods, plantations, building names, vicarage, toll bar, market hall, churchyard, smithy, mills, common, township boundaries.

53/47 Llansaintfraid (parish) SJ 220200 [Llansantffraid-ym-Mechn]
Apt 25.10.1838; 7130a (6065); Map 1840?, 8 chns, by S. Groom; waterbodies, woods, township boundaries (col); there is an incomplete tabulation of townships.

53/48 Llanvyllin (parish) SJ 118198 [Llanfyllin]
Apt 21.01.1848; 7924a (7923); Map 1850, 6 chns, by William Parry; waterbodies, woods, building names, workhouse, mound, township boundaries (col) and names.

53/49 Llanwyddyn (parish) SJ 000200 [Llanwddyn]
Apt 19.11.1840; 5429a (?); Map 1846, 6 chns, by David Jones, Llanfyllin, (tithable parts only); foot/b'way, field boundary ownerships, common.

53/50 Llanwnog (parish) SO 015940
Apt 29.11.1845; 10701a (all); Map 1846, 6 chns, in 5 parts, by James King, Oxford, (including Caersws township at 3 chns and 12-chn index); waterbodies, woods, workhouse, township boundaries and names.

53/51 Llanwrin (parish) SH 795065
Apt 15.09.1837; 10352a (10351); Map 1839, 9 chns, in 3 parts, (including two enlargements of detail; tithable parts only); hill-drawing, waterbodies, woods, plantations, building names, common, recent encroachments.

53/52 Llanwyddelan (parish) SJ 052002
Apt 22.05.1843; 3784a (3784); Map 1843, 6 chns; woods, plantations, building names, chapel, vicarage, township boundaries. Apt omits some field names.

53/53 Machynlleth (parish) SN 770960
Apt 31.12.1842; 14861a (14861); Map 1844, 8 chns; waterbodies, woods, plantations, gardens (by annotation); built-up part generalised; tithable buildings are carmine, and tithe-free are grey; streams and lake are named. Apt omits land use and some field names.

53/54 Manavon (parish) SJ 115035 [Manafon]
Apt 19.10.1847; 6635a (6635); Map 1848, 6 chns, in 2 parts; waterbodies, houses, woods, plantations, hedges, building names, rectory, boundary stones, mills, township boundaries and names. Apt omits some field names.

53/55 Mellington (township in parish of Churchstoke) SO 264923
Apt 27.12.1839; 1519a (1519); Map 1842, 6 chns, ? by Charles Mickleburgh, Montgomery; waterbodies, woods, parkland, field boundary ownerships, building names, avenue of trees, Offa's Dyke; north pointer has diadem and plumes.

53/56 Middletown (township in parish of Alberbury) (partly in Shropshire) SJ 305125
Apt 20.03.1848; 737a (?); Map 1849, 6 chns; waterbodies, woods, field boundary ownerships, building names.

53/57 Montgomery (parish) SO 220970 [Montgomery or Trefaldwyn]
Apt 07.11.1838; 3289a (3288); Map 1839, [6 chns], in 2 parts, by C. Mickleburgh, Montgomery, (town also at 2 chns); hill-drawing, foot/b'way, waterbodies, woods, plantations, parkland, orchards, rock outcrops, hedges, fences, field boundary ownerships, building names, intrenchments, ruins of castle, gaol, old town wall, domen, conduit.

53/58 Morvodion, Croeslwybr, Manledd Glynharren and Ystradynodd (township in parish of Llanidloes) SN 910870 [Morfodion]
Apt 29.11.1845; 11186a (11186); Map 1846, 6 chns, by William Parry, Llanidloes; waterbodies, houses, woods, plantations, orchards, building names, township boundaries (col) and names; scale-bar is multi-coloured, with cornucopia flourish. Apt omits some field names.

53/59 Mochtre (parish) SO 065862 [Mochdre]
Apt 15.04.1841; 5026a (5025); Map 1839, 6 chns; foot/b'way, waterbodies, woods, hedges, building names, tomen, boundary trees, wells, vicarage, mill, turbaries, private roads (uncoloured); ship, tower, fisherman, ruin and trees appear in picture above scale; leaves decorate north pointer.

53/60 Nantymeichied, Penniarth, Teirtref, Dyffryn, Main, Cynllyfnog, Ystymeolwyn, Trefnanney, Cwm and Keel (townships in parish of Myfod or Meifod) SJ 160150 [Not listed]
Apt 10.10.1839; 11609a (all); Map 1842, 6 chns, in 11 parts, by Charles Mickleburgh, Montgomery, (including village at 2 chns, and index); waterbodies, woods, plantations, fences, field boundary ownerships, building names, vicarage, mills, smithy, chapels, quarries, turnpike, pound, township boundaries (col); bridge named; index has plumes and diadem on north pointer and is dated 1842. Apt omits land use.

53/61 Newtown (parish) SO 115910 [Newtown or Y Drenewydd]
Apt 16.02.1843; 2736a (2736); Map 1843, 6 chns; waterbodies, woods, plantations, orchards, hedges, fences, building names, toll gate, mound, quarry, factory; churches and public buildings are distinctively hatched but not named. Apt omits some field names.

53/62 Penegoes (parish) SN 830950
Apt 15.09.1837; 6903a (8085), (tithable parts only); Map 1839, 9 chns, in 6 parts, 'Compiled from Surveys made by various Persons', (including 3-chn enlargement of detail; woods, building names, rectory, common; bridge named.

53/63 Pennant (parish) SJ 025265 [Pennant Melangell]
Apt 28.12.1839; 3893a (5000); Map 1842, 8 chns, in 3 parts, by David Jones, Llanfyllin, Montgomery, (tithable parts only); waterbodies; adjoining village churches are shown by coloured conventional drawings.

53/64 Penstrowed (parish) SO 068906
Apt 20.10.1840; 1220a (all); Map 1840, 6 chns, 'Compiled from Old Surveys' by J.M. Poundley, Kerry, Montgomeryshire; houses, woods, plantations, parkland, orchards, hedges, fences, building names, boundary marks, quarry; hill named. Apt omits some land use and some field names.

53/65 Pool, Lower division (divisions in parish of Pool) SJ 220080 [Not listed]
Apt 22.08.1840; 2638a (2637); Map 1840, 6 chns, in 5 parts, by Charles Mickleburgh, Montgomery, (including 12-chn index); canal with towpath and locks, waterbodies, woods, plantations, parkland, orchards, gardens, hedges, field boundary ownerships, building names, turnpike gates, vicarage, mills, quarry, factories, lodge, old road, depot, bowling green, well; index sheet has picture of Powis Castle with seated figure in foreground; one other part has north pointer with plumes. Apt omits land use for tithe-free land.

53/66 Pool, Upper and Middle Divisions (divisions in parish of Pool) SJ 212052 [Not listed]
Apt 22.08.1840; 3557a (3557); Map 1840, 12 chns, in 2 parts, by Charles Mickleburgh, Montgomery, (including 12-chn index); canal with towpath and locks, waterbodies, woods, plantations, parkland, orchards, gardens, building names, dairy, reservoir, kennel, kiln, gasometer, turnpike gates, lime kilns, quarry, chapel. Apt omits land use for tithe-free lands.

53/67 Snead (parish) (partly in Shropshire) SO 310927
Apt 22.05.1843; 582a (644); Map 1841, 8 chns; waterbodies, woods, orchards, building names, mill, churchyard.

53/68 Tirymynech (township in parish of Guilsfield) SJ 260125 [Tirymynach]
Apt 23.09.1840; 1871a (?); Map 1845, 6 chns; canal with towpath and locks, waterbodies, houses, woods, orchards. Apt omits land use for tithe-free lands

53/69 Trefedrid (township in parish of Meifod) SJ 106104 [Tycerrig]
Apt 20.09.1838; 1005a (all); Map 1840, 6 chns; woods, plantations, heath/moor. Apt omits land use.

53/70 Tregynon (parish) SO 090980
Apt 31.12.1841; 6760a (6760); Map 1840, 6 chns; waterbodies, houses, woods, plantations, building names, boundary stones and marks, township boundaries. Apt omits some field names.

53/71 Trelystan, Rhos Goch and Leighton (townships in parish of Worthen) SJ 264058
Apt 30.11.1844; 4229a (4227); Map 1847?, 9 chns; waterbodies, woods, plantations, building names, ring fort, township boundaries.

53/72 Treveglwys (parish) SN 930910 [Trefeglwys]
Apt 07.08.1847; 18166a (18166); Map 1848, 6 chns, by William Parry, Llanidloes; waterbodies, farmyards (col), woods, building names, township boundaries (col) and names; lake named; north pointer has diadem and plumes. Apt omits some land use and some field names.

53/73 Trewern (township in parish of Buttington) SJ 272118
Apt 23.09.1840; 1861a (1860); Map 1840, 6 chns, by Charles Mickleburgh, Montgomery; waterbodies, woods, plantations, orchards, heath/moor, hedges, field boundary ownerships, building names, turnpike gates, chapel; hill named.

53/74 Uppington (township in parish of Alberbury) SJ 285100 [Not listed]
Apt 07.06.1844; 1002a (?); Map 1843, 6 chns; waterbodies, woods; map is drawn with north at the bottom.

53/75 Varchoel, Burgedin and Rhetescyn (townships in parish of Guilsfield) SJ 243139
Apt 23.06.1842; 3594a (?); Map 1845, 6 chns; waterbodies, woods, building names, canal with towpath, township boundaries (col).

Pembrokeshire

PRO IR29 and IR30 54/1-138

147 tithe districts: 390,308 acres
138 tithe commutations: 376,029 acres
102 voluntary tithe agreements, 36 compulsory tithe awards

Tithe and tithe commutation

In 1836 94 per cent of Pembrokeshire tithe districts were subject to payment of tithes but only sixty-four districts (46 per cent) were wholly tithable at this date (Fig. 66). The most important exemption was of woodland in 34 per cent of tithable districts but modus payments in lieu of tithes and the merger of tithes in the land were also significant causes of tithe exemption in Pembrokeshire.

Assistant tithe commissioners and local tithe agents who worked in Pembrokeshire are listed in Table 54.1. As in Glamorganshire, the valuation of tithe rent-charges in Pembrokeshire was dominated by Harry Phelps Goode of Haverfordwest who valued almost exactly a half of the tithable districts. As elsewhere in southern Wales, the dominance of pastoral farming encouraged detailed descriptions of grassland. For example, at Llanrihan classifications include 'moory pas[ture]', 'moor', 'clover hay' and 'moory mead'. On the other hand, many Pembrokeshire apportionments often omit some field names and a number have blank state of cultivation columns.

Tithe maps

Pembrokeshire is similar to most Welsh counties as none of its 138 maps is sealed as first class, nor do any carry construction lines. Only two maps acknowledge copying, though it is to be suspected that Goode and Philpotts's extraordinary output was achieved at least partly by this means. Map scales used in this county range from one inch to three chains to one inch to twelve chains with only 12 per cent of maps in the recommended scale range of one inch to three to four chains. The great majority are at the six-chain (36 per cent) and the eight-chain (46 per cent) scales.

Pembrokeshire tithe maps are poor records of land use; only 42 per cent show woodland and only one or two maps depict gardens, orchards or inhabited buildings. Although every map records field boundaries, none has information on field boundary ownership or type of boundary.

Harry Goode and Henry Philpott of Haverfordwest dominated Pembrokeshire tithe

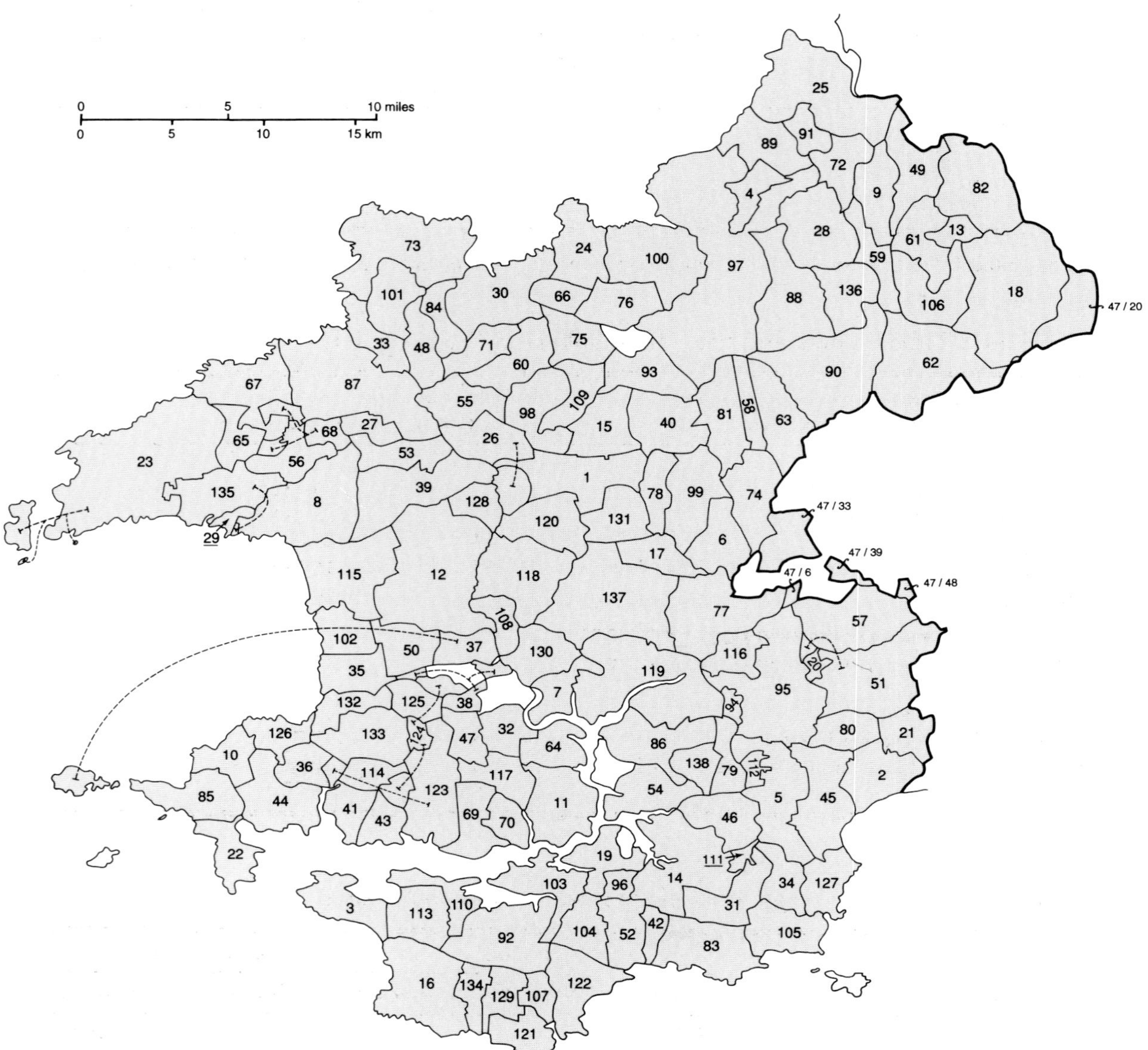

Fig. 66 Pembrokeshire: tithe district boundaries.

surveys and mapped some two-thirds of tithable districts. They eschewed colour, used their trademark of intersecting scale bar, plain cartouche and north pointer on many of their maps, and lithographed twenty-three. John Jones of Pembroke and John Tamlyn of Haverfordwest both employed a very similar style so that the tithe maps of this county have a uniformity of appearance surpassed only by those of Anglesey.

Table 54.1. *Agreements and awards for commutation of tithes in Pembrokeshire*

Assistant commissioner/ local tithe agent	*Number of agreements**	*Number of awards*
John Johnes	37	36
Thomas Hoskins	55	0
John Fenton	1	0
Aneurin Owen	1	0

*Computed from the number of extant reports on tithe agreements in the tithe files [PRO IR 18].

Table 54.2 Tithe valuers and tithe map-makers in Pembrokeshire

Name and address (in Pembrokeshire unless indicated)	*Number of districts*	*Acreage*
Tithe valuers		
Harry Phelps Goode, St Martins, Haverfordwest	81	206,382
John Harvey, Haverfordwest	33	108,271
John Jones, Pembroke	14	30,085
Samuel Bartley, Llandefailog, Carmarthenshire	5	16,989
Others [5]	5	14,302
Attributed tithe map-makers		
Harry Goode and Henry Philpott, Haverfordwest	93	241,398
John Jones, Pembroke	10	19,183
Owen Lloyd, Cardigan	7	19,748
John Tamlyn, Haverfordwest	5	19,767
Samuel Bartley, Llandefailog, Carmarthenshire	5	16,989
Others [4]	9	36,870

Table 54.3. *The tithe maps of Pembrokeshire: scales and classes*

Scale in chains/inch	*All maps*		*First Class*		*Second Class*	
	Number	*Acreage*	*Number*	*Acreage*	*Number*	*Acreage*
3	10	24,901	0	0	10	24,901
4	7	8,179	0	0	7	8,179
6	51	116,654	0	0	51	116,654
8	64	207,933	0	0	64	207,933
<8	6	18,362	0	0	6	18,362
TOTAL	138	376,029	0	0	138	376,029

Table 54.4. *The tithe maps of Pembrokeshire: dates*

	<1837	*1837*	*1838*	*1839*	*1840*	*1841*	*1842*	*1843*	*1844*	*1845*	*1846*	*1847*	*1848*	*1849*
2nd class	1	0	6	27	12	24	15	18	12	10	4	7	1	1

Pembrokeshire

54/1 Ambleston (parish) SN 005256
Apt 18.03.1843; 3957a (all); Map 1844?, 10 chns, by H.P. Goode and Philpott, Lith., Haverfordwest, litho. District is apportioned by holding; Apt omits some field names.

54/2 Amroth (parish) SN 159081
Apt 31.10.1844; 2648a (2878); Map 1845?, 6 chns; waterbodies, building names, mill. Apt omits some field names.

54/3 Angle (parish) SM 869021
Apt 23.11.1841; 2277a (all); Map 1842, 8 chns, by John Harvey.

54/4 Bayvil (parish) SN 108412 [Not listed]
Apt 06.06.1844; 1344a (1344); Map 1845?, 8 chns, ? by H.P. Goode and Philpott, Haverfordwest; woods. Apt omits some field names.

54/5 Begelly cum East Willamston (parish) SN 105066 [East Williamston]
Apt 03.09.1841; 3878a (all); Map 1842?, 3 chns, in 2 parts, by Goode and Philpott, Surveyors and lithographers, Haverfordwest; woods; part 1 is manuscript, unsigned, part 2 is litho, and at 6 chns. Apt omits some land use.

54/6 Bletherstone (parish) SN 075215 [Bletherston]
Apt 21.06.1839; 2367a (2366); Map 1843?, 6 chns, by Goode and Philpott, Haverfordwest.

54/7 Boulston (parish) SM 985135
Apt 05.08.1842; 1663a (1822); Map 1844, 6 chns, by H.P. Goode and Philpott, Haverfordwest, (tithable parts only in detail); woods, building names, quarry.

54/8 Brawdy (parish) SM 849248 [Not listed]
Apt 29.11.1842; 5342a (5401); Map 1844, 8 chns, by H.P. Goode and Philpott, Haverfordwest; woods. Apt omits some field names.

54/9 Bridell (parish) SN 177410
Apt 31.10.1837; 2180a (2179); Map 1839, 8 chns, 'Second Class Map', by Samuel Bartley, L.S.; waterbodies, woods, parkland, building names. Apt omits land use and field names.

54/10 St Brides (parish) SM 809105
Apt 13.06.1839; 1683a (all); Map 1840?, 6 chns, by Goode and Philpott, Haverfordwest; ownership boundaries (col).

54/11 Burton (parish) SM 987067
Apt 24.03.1838; 3415a (3815); Map 1840?, 6 chns; residual open fields. Apt omits land use and some field names.

54/12 Camrose (parish) SM 927203
Apt 17.05.1839; 8129a (8129); Map 1841?, 8 chns, by John Tamlyn, Haverfordwest; scale-bar intersects plain cartouche.

54/13 Capel Colman (chapelry) SN 216384 [Not listed]
Apt 13.03.1846; 770a (all); Map 1848, 8 chns, by Owen Lloyd, Cardigan; waterbodies, farmyards, woods, plantations, parkland, building names, springs, mill. Apt omits land use and some field names.

54/14 Carew (parish) SN 051033
Apt 03.05.1838; 5256a (all); Map 1839?, 6 chns, ? by Goode and Philpott; waterbodies, woods, building names, parsonage; plain cartouche and scale-bar intersect. Apt omits land use.

54/15 Castlebythe (parish) SN 017287
Apt 13.08.1842; 2537a (all); Map 1845?, 8 chns, by H.P. Goode and Philpott, Surveyors etc, H'west, litho; building names. Apt omits some field names.

54/16 Castlemartin (parish) SR 910974
Apt 03.07.1838; 4503a (all); Map 1839?, 8 chns; waterbodies, woods, building names, landowners, springs, chapel, mills, mill streams, rocks; coast features named. Apt omits land use.

54/17 Clarbeston (parish) SN 050210
Apt 11.03.1839; 779a (1588); Map 1839, 8 chns, by Goode and Philpott, Haverfordwest, (tithable parts only in detail), litho; building names; Prince of Wales feathers, diadem and 'Ich Dien' appear, bottom right; plain cartouche, scale-bar and north pointer intersect each other. Apt omits land use.

54/18 Clydey (parish) SN 248355 [Not listed]
Apt 30.11.1839; 8120a (all); Map 1841, 12 chns, surveyed by Samuel Ball, Kidwelly; woods, building names, crug, quarries, common. Apt omits land use and many field names.

54/19 Cosheston (parish) SN 009038
Apt 16.03.1840; 2021a (all); Map 1841, 6 chns, by Jno. Jones; building names, private road; pictorial church.

54/20 Crinow (parish) SN 128143
Apt 31.12.1840; 353a (352); Map 1839, 3 chns, by Goode and Philpott, Haverfordwest; woods; scale-bar intersects north pointer.

54/21 Crunwear (parish) SN 178103 [Not listed]
Apt 25.06.1842; 1690a (all); Map 1843?, 6 chns, by H.P. Goode and Philpott, Surveyors etc, Haverfordwest; building names, quarry, parsonage. Apt omits some field names.

54/22 Dale (parish) SM 806053
Apt 06.03.1847; 1709a (3038); Map 1847?, 8 chns; waterbodies, woods, rock outcrops, building names, lighthouses, cliffs, windmill. Apt omits some field names.

54/23 St Davids (parish) SM 768272
Apt 26.06.1838; 10666a (11185); Map 1840-41, 3 chns, in 4 parts, 'Survey'd and Mapped' by Essex Davies, (includes 12-chn index); hill-drawing, waterbodies, houses, rock outcrops, building names, street names, churchyard, Bishops Palace ruins, watermills (by Dawson's symbol), quarries, cross (by symbol), meeting house, walled garden, sand and shingle, windmill (by symbol).

54/24 Dinas (parish) SN 011389 [Not listed]
Apt 21.05.1841; 2329a (2328); Map 1843?, 6 chns, (tithable parts only).

54/25 St Dogmells (parish) SN 148464 [St Dogmaels]
Apt 28.02.1838; 5985a (6220); Map 1838, 8 chns, '2nd Class Map', by Samuel Bartley, L.S., Llandefeilog, Carmarthen; waterbodies, woods, building names, common, hamlet boundaries (col) and names; church wall is shown by battlement effect; built-up part generalised. Apt omits land use and field names.

54/26 St Dogwells (parish) SM 959275 [Not listed]
Apt 24.06.1846; 3348a (3347); Map 1846, 8 chns, by H.P. Goode, Haverfordwest, (tithable parts only in detail); waterbodies, woods, building names, pit, parsonage.

54/27 St Edrens (parish) SM 894285 [Not listed]
Apt 05.08.1842; 917a (all); Map 1843, 8 chns, by H.P. Goode and Philpott, Haverfordwest; scale-bar intersects north pointer.

54/28 Eglwyswrw (parish) SN 142385
Apt 07.03.1838; 3665a (3664); Map 1841, 8 chns, 'Mapped' by Owen Lloyd, Cardigan; hill-drawing, waterbodies, woods, building names, spring, mill, vicarage, meeting house, avenue of trees, toll house, poor house, mill leat. Apt omits field names.

54/29 St Elvis (parish) SM 821243 [Not listed]
Apt 08.11.1837; 414a (414); Map 1838, 4 chns, by Goode and Philpott; rock outcrops; north pointer intersects scale-bar. Apt omits land use.

54/30 Fishguard (parish) SM 962362
Apt 28.12.1839; 4163a (4208); Map 1843, 3 chns, 'Surveyed' by Essex Davies, and 'Mapped' by Hy. Philpott and T. Tamlyn, Surveyors etc, Haverfordwest; rock outcrops, cliffs.

54/31 St Florence (parish) SN 079014
Apt 18.01.1840; 2491a (2490); Map 1842, 6 chns, by Jno. Jones; building names; pictorial church. Apt omits land use.

54/32 Freystrop (parish) SM 957118
Apt 08.11.1837; 1592a (all); Map 1839?, 6 chns; railway; scale-bar intersects north pointer. Apt omits some field names.

54/33 Granston (parish) SM 903333
Apt 23.01.1839; 1639a (1639); Map 1841, 6 chns, by Goode and Philpott, Haverfordwest, litho (with MS additions); extra-parochial boundary. Apt omits land use and some field names.

54/34 Gumfreston (parish) SN 103022
Apt 11.04.1839; 1645a (all); Map 1840?, 8 chns, by Goode and Philpott, Haverfordwest, litho; scale-bar and plain cartouche intersect.

54/35 Harroldston West (parish) SM 879149 [Haroldston West]
Apt 10.10.1839; 1719a (all); Map 1841, 8 chns, by Goode and Philpott, Haverfordwest, litho; building names; plain cartouche and scale-bar intersect north pointer with plumes.

54/36 Hasguard (parish) SM 850100
Apt 08.07.1841; 1476a (all); Map 1841, 6 chns, by Goode and Philpott, Haverfordwest; waterbodies, woods. Apt omits some land use.

54/37 St Martins (parish) SM 940163 [Not listed]
Apt 13.08.1842; 1956a (all); Map 1842, 6 chns, in 3 parts, by Goode and Philpott, Surveyors and lithographers, Haverfordwest, (tithable parts only in detail; including Skomer Island at 12 chns, and town at 3 chns), litho; hill-drawing, waterbodies, woods, building names, cliffs, chapel; bridges named. Apt omits some land use and some field names.

54/38 St Thomas (parish) SM 941151 [Not listed]
Apt 18.03.1839; 1017a (all); Map 1840?, 4 chns, in 2 parts, by Goode and Philpott, Haverfordwest, (includes enlargement of town at 2 chns); waterbodies, building names, asylum, workhouse, race course, mills, street names; scale-bar intersects plain cartouche.

54/39 Hayscastle (parish) SM 912251
Apt 29.11.1842; 4463a (4462); Map 1844, 8 chns, by H.P. Goode and Philpott, Haverfordwest.

54/40 Henry's Moat (parish) SN 050287
Apt 28.08.1838; 3166a (3166); Map 1840?, 8 chns, ? by John Harvey. Apt omits land use and some field names.

54/41 Herbrainstone (parish) SM 870075 [Herbrandston]
Apt 30.04.1838; 1424a (all); Map 1839, 3 chns, by H.P. Goode and Philpott, Haverfordwest; limekiln.

54/42 Hodgeston (parish) SS 034998
Apt 20.08.1840; 709a (709); Map 1840?, 8 chns; hill-drawing, foot/b'way, waterbodies, woods, springs, limekilns, barn, quarries, old quarries, glebe, waste, orchard (by annotation); one field is annotated 'Very steep'; a 'Wall' is shown with double lines. Apt omits land use.

54/43 Hubberstone (parish) SM 889064 [Hubberston]
Apt 18.06.1839; 1271a (all); Map 1840?, [3 chns], by Goode and Philpott, Haverfordwest; building names, road names, windmill, rectory, observatory, tithe-free land (col). Apt omits most land use.

54/44 St Ishmaels (parish) SM 833078 [St Ishmael's]
Apt 18.03.1839; 3018a (4167); Map 1839, 6 chns, by Goode and Philpott, Haverfordwest, litho; waterbodies, building names. Apt has cropping information, but Apt omits some field names.

54/45 St Issells (parish) SN 132072 [Not listed]
Apt 24.09.1839; 3741a (3830); Map 1842?, 6 chns, by Goode and Philpott, Haverfordwest; railway, woods; scale-bar intersects plain cartouche; the meaning of the pecked and dot-dash lines is unclear. Apt omits some field names.

54/46 Jefferston (parish) SN 072062 [Jeffreyston]
Apt 30.04.1844; 2344a (2343); Map 1845?, 6 chns, by H.P. Goode and Philpott, Surveyors and Lithrs, Haverfordwest, litho; woods, building names, mill. Apt omits land use and some field names.

54/47 Johnstone (parish) SM 935115 [Johnston]
Apt 31.12.1842; 1293a (all); Map 1843?, 6 chns, by Goode and Philpott, Surveyors and lithographers, Haverfordwest, litho; woods, building names. Apt omits some field names.

54/48 Jordanstone (parish) SM 921331 [Jordanston]
Apt 06.02.1843; 1877a (1876); Map 1846, 6 chns, by Essex Davies, Fishguard; woods. Apt omits some land use.

54/49 Kilgerran (parish) SN 196415 [Cilgerran]
Apt 13.07.1838; 2672a (2672); Map 1844, 8 chns, ? by Samuel Bartley, L.S., Apportioner; waterbodies, woods, building names, common. Apt omits land use and field names.

54/50 Lambston (parish) SM 908163
Apt 10.10.1839; 1760a (all); Map 1839, 4 chns, by John Tamlyn, Surveyor, near Haverfordwest; building names, mill. Apt omits some field names.

54/51 Lampeter Velfrey (parish) SN 160140
Apt 21.12.1842; 5667a (5667); Map 1842, 8 chns, by Goode and Philpott, Haverfordwest; woods. Apt omits some field names.

54/52 Lamphey (parish) SS 019995 [Not listed]
Apt 20.11.1839; 1977a (1976); Map 1841?, 6 chns; woods, building names. Apt omits land use.

54/53 St Lawrence (parish) SM 912272
Apt 30.04.1838; 1752a (1751); Map 1839?, 6 chns, ? by Goode and Philpott; waterbodies.

54/54 Lawrenny (parish) SN 031078
Apt 27.01.1842; 2363a (2672); Map 1843, 6 chns, by H.P. Goode and Philpott, Haverfordwest; pill.

54/55 Letterston (parish) SM 940300
Apt 07.03.1838; 2219a (2216); Map 1839, 6 chns, in 2 parts, by Goode and Philpott, Haverfordwest, (includes enlargement of village at 3 chns); waterbodies, common. Apt omits land use and some field names.

54/56 Llandeloy (parish) SM 855275
Apt 09.08.1845; 1844a (1843); Map 1845, 12 chns, by Goode and Philpott, Haverfordwest. Apt omits some land use.

54/57 Llandewi Velfry (parish) SN 150170 [Llandewi Velfrey]
Apt 11.06.1840; 4022a (all); Map 1841?, 8 chns; waterbodies, rock outcrops, building names, parsonage, quarry; scale-bar is combined with pointers showing true and magnetic north.

54/58 Llandilo (parish) SN 099293
Apt 29.06.1839; 1132a (all); Map 1841?, 8 chns, by Goode and Philpott, Haverfordwest; scale-bar intersects plain cartouche.

54/59 Llanfairnantgwynn (parish) SN 169371 [Llanfair-Nant-Gwyn]
Apt 18.04.1837; 1669a (1668); Map 1838, 8 chns, 'Constructed principally from existing maps', by John Tamlyn, Surveyor, near Haverfordwest; waterbodies, woods (col), building names, well, castle. Apt omits land use.

54/60 Llanfair nanty goff (parish) SM 972323 [Not listed]
Apt 30.07.1838; 2597a (2597); Map 1839, 8 chns, 'from existing maps' by John Tamlyn, Surv., near H'west; waterbodies, building names; woods and rocks are shown by annotation; one stream is annotated 'Winter Course'. Apt omits land use.

54/61 Llanfihangel Penbedw (parish) SN 196381 [Penbedw]
Apt 24.04.1837; 2410a (all); Map 1840, 8 chns, 'Mapped' by Owen Lloyd, Cardigan; hill-drawing, waterbodies, woods, plantations, building names, springs, quarry. Apt omits land use and field names.

54/62 Llanfirnach (parish) SN 200310 [Llanfyrnach]
Apt 29.06.1838; 6329a (6328); Map 1844, 8 chns, by Owen Lloyd, Cardigan; waterbodies, woods, building names, mill, meeting house. Apt omits field names.

54/63 Llangolman (parish) SN 115282
Apt 29.06.1839; 2912a (all); Map 1841?, 8 chns, by Goode and Philpott, Haverfordwest; scale-bar intersects north pointer.

54/64 Langum (parish) SM 983103
Apt 28.10.1840; 2025a (2434); Map 1841?, 6 chns, by H.P. Goode and Philpott, Haverfordwest; woods; scale-bar intersects plain cartouche. Apt omits some land use.

54/65 Llanhowell (parish) SM 820280 [Not listed]
Apt 23.08.1845; 1582a (all); Map 1842, 6 chns, by H.P. Goode and Philpott, Haverfordwest; woods, building names. Apt omits some land use.

54/66 Llanllawer (parish) SN 001359 [Not listed]
Apt 13.08.1842; 1203a (1202); Map 1843, 12 chns, by H.P. Goode and Philpott, H'west; woods, building names.

54/67 Llanrian (parish) SM 825315 [Llanrihan]
Apt 31.12.1842; 3683a (all); Map 1844, 6 chns, by H.P. Goode and Philpott, Haverfordwest, litho; building names. Apt omits some field names.

54/68 Llanrithan (parish) SM 871286 [Llanreithan]
Apt 06.07.1838; 1719a (all); Map 1839, 6 chns, by H.P. Goode and Philpott, Land Agents and Surveyors, Haverfordwest; plain cartouche, scale-bar and north pointer intersect each other.

54/69 Llanstadwell, Impropriate District (district in parish of Llanstadwell) SM 938062
Apt 09.12.1848; 2196a (?); Map 1849?, 6 chns, ? by Goode and Philpott, litho; hill-drawing, waterbodies, woods, building names. Apt omits land use and some field names.

54/70 Llanstadwell, third part or portion (district in parish of Llanstadwell) SM 955065
Apt 18.04.1837; 1051a (?); Map 1830, 3 chns, by Goode and Philpott, H'west; waterbodies, Ordnance land.

54/71 Llanstinnan (parish) SM 954331 [Not listed]
Apt 16.06.1846; 1579a (1579); Map 1847?, 6 chns, by H.P. Goode, Haverfordwest; waterbodies, woods, plantations, mill, encampment. Apt omits some field names.

54/72 Llantood (parish) SN 157423
Apt 08.05.1838; 1792a (all); Map 1839, 4 chns, ? by Samuel Bartley, L.S., Apportioner; woods, building names; map is described in title as 'Second Class Map'. Apt omits land use and field names.

54/73 Llanwnda (parish) SM 915395
Apt 17.11.1843; 5612a (all); Map 1845, 6 chns, by T. Tamlyn; building names, sands (col).

54/74 Llanycefn (parish) SN 098239
Apt 20.08.1846; 2685a (2684); Map 1847, 8 chns, by H.P. Goode, Haverfordwest; building names. Apt omits land use and field names.

54/75 Llanychare (parish) SN 008332 [Llanychaer]
Apt 15.02.1842; 2054a (2053); Map 1845?, 12 chns, by H.P. Goode and Philpott, Surveyors etc, Haverfordwest; woods, building names.

54/76 Llanychlwydog (parish) SN 031351 [Not listed]
Apt 28.07.1842; 2283a (2283); Map 1844, 8 chns, surveyed by Hy. Philpott for Goode and Philpott, Haverfordwest; hill-drawing, woods; dot-dash lines are between holdings, and pecked lines are within holdings.

54/77 Llawhaden (parish) SN 076176
Apt 29.06.1839; 4490a (4490); Map 1843?, 8 chns, by H.P. Goode and Philpott, Haverfordwest; woods; scale-bar intersects plain cartouche. Apt omits some land use and some field names.

54/78 Llysyfrane (parish) SN 040245 [Llys-y-fran]
Apt 23.02.1839; 1467a (1466); Map 1839, 6 chns, by Goode and Philpott, Haverfordwest; scale-bar intersects plain cartouche.

54/79 Loveston (parish) SN 077092
Apt 29.03.1841; 1234a (all); Map 1841?, 6 chns, by J. Jones; waterbodies, building names; scale-bar and north pointer are combined. Apt omits land use.

54/80 Ludchurch (parish) SN 141108
Apt 12.11.1839; 1607a (1607); Map 1841?, 4 chns, by H.P. Goode and Philpott, Land Agents and Surveyors, Haverfordwest; waterbodies, building names; plain cartouche intersects scale-bar. Apt omits some land use.

54/81 Maenclochog (parish) SN 085282
Apt 29.06.1839; 2755a (all); Map 1841, 8 chns, in 2 parts, by Goode and Philpott, Haverfordwest, (includes village at 3 chns); scale-bar intersects plain cartouche. Apt omits some field names.

54/82 Manerdivy, including Kilvowir (parish and chapelry) SN 234408 [Manordeifi]
Apt 15.11.1838; 4360a (3506); Map 1842, 8 chns, ? by Samuel Bartley, L.S., Apportioner; woods, building names, chapelry boundary. Apt omits land use and field names.

54/83 Manorbeer (parish) SS 061986 [Manorbier]
Apt 30.01.1840; 3494a (3493); Map 1842?, 8 chns, by Jno. Jones; waterbodies, building names. Apt omits land use.

54/84 Manorowen (parish) SM 935345
Apt 18.04.1837; 1263a (all); Map 1838, [3 chns], by H.P. Goode and Philpott, Haverfordwest; waterbodies, building names, churchyard.

54/85 Marloes (parish) SM 795082
Apt 16.07.1842; 2479a (2478); Map 1843, 6 chns, in 2 parts, by H.P. Goode and Philpott, Haverfordwest, (includes village at 2 chns); woods, building names. Apt omits some field names.

54/86 Martletwy (parish) SN 038107
Apt 20.10.1840; 3352a (3551); Map 1844, 8 chns, by H.P. Goode and Philpott, Surveyors and Lithrs, Haverfordwest, litho; woods, building names. Apt omits some field names.

54/87 Mathry (parish) SM 885315
Apt 21.02.1842; 6992a (6992); Map 1843?, 8 chns, by Goode and Philpott, Surveyors and lithographers, Haverfordwest, litho; waterbodies, building names. Apt omits some field names.

54/88 Meline (parish) SN 129358 [Not listed]
Apt 26.10.1837; 4523a (4523); Map 1841?, 6 chns, by Goode and Philpott, Haverfordwest; scale-bar intersects plain cartouche. Apt omits some land use.

54/89 Moilgrove (parish) SN 120440 [Moylgrove]
Apt 08.03.1847; 2442a (2442); Map 1847, 6 chns, by H.P. Goode, Haverfordwest, (includes enlargement of village at 2 chns); waterbodies, woods, plantations, rock outcrops, building names, cliffs. Apt omits some field names.

54/90 Monachlogddu (parish) SN 145305 [Mynachlogddu]
Apt 03.09.1840; 6167a (6166); Map 1846, 8 chns, by H.P. Goode, H'west; building names, mill, common. Apt omits some field names.

54/91 Monington (parish) SN 137443
Apt 18.08.1837; 1011a (all); Map 1838, 4 chns, 'Mapped' by Owen Lloyd, Cardigan; hill-drawing, foot/b'way, waterbodies, houses, woods, parkland, orchard, gardens, fences, building names, springs, mill pond, mill leat, mill (by symbol), gravel pit, well, kiln, quarry. Apt omits land use.

54/92 Monkton (parish) SR 948998
Apt 31.05.1839; 4270a (4629); Map 1841?, 8 chns, by Goode and Philpott, Haverfordwest; waterbodies, woods; plain cartouche, scale-bar and north pointer intersect each other. Apt omits some field names.

54/93 Morville (parish) SN 044313 [Morvil]
Apt 11.03.1839; 2551a (all); Map 1839, 8 chns, by Goode and Philpott, Haverfordwest; plain cartouche, scale-bar and north pointer intersect each other.

54/94 Mounton (chapelry) SN 081125 [Not listed]
Apt 08.07.1845; 331a (330); Map 1846, 6 chns, by H.P. Goode, H'west; woods, chapel; buildings are shown in outline only, without infill.

54/95 Narberth (parish) SN 105132
Apt 31.12.1840; 6085a (6084); Map 1842?, 8 chns, by Goode and Philpott, Haverfordwest; woods; built-up part generalised; plain cartouche intersects ruler-like scale-bar. Apt omits some field names.

54/96 Nash (parish) SN 018024 [Not listed]
Apt 27.10.1840; 578a (all); Map 1839, 4 chns, by John Jones; lodge, parsonage. Apt omits land use.

54/97 Nevern (parish) SN 090370
Apt 10.09.1840; 14522a (14637); Map 1843, 8 chns, by H.P. Goode and Philpott, Haverfordwest; waterbodies, woods, building names; most

names are in upright writing, but a few less important ones are italic. Apt omits some field names.

54/98 Little Newcastle (parish) SM 979294
Apt 23.10.1844; 2712a (2712); Map 1847?, 8 chns, by H.P. Goode, Haverfordwest; waterbodies, building names, ring-fort.

54/99 New Moat (parish) SN 065245
Apt 23.02.1839; 3102a (3101); Map 1839?, 8 chns, ? by John Harvey; building names, mill; scale-bar intersects north pointer. Apt omits land use.

54/100 Newport (parish) SN 054378
Apt 27.04.1844; 4607a (4711); Map 1845, 8 chns, by H.P. Goode and Philpott, Haverfordwest; woods, building names; built-up part generalised. Apt omits some field names.

54/101 St Nicholas (parish) SM 905360
Apt 23.01.1839; 2142a (all); Map 1841?, 6 chns, by Goode and Philpott, Haverfordwest; building names, boundary stone; scale-bar intersects two small plain cartouches. Apt omits land use.

54/102 Nolton (parish) SM 875173
Apt 26.01.1838; 1505a (all); Map 1839, 6 chns, by Goode and Philpott, Haverfordwest; mill, rill; scale-bar and plain cartouche intersect north pointer, which is decorated with a bird and clouds.

54/103 St Mary Pembroke (parish) SM 989025 [Not listed]
Apt 31.05.1839; 2433a (all); Map 1841, 8 chns, by Goode and Philpott, Haverfordwest; woods, building names, dock; built-up part and docks generalised.

54/104 St Michael, Pembroke (parish) SR 999999 [Not listed]
Apt 31.05.1839; 1818a (all); Map 1841, 8 chns, by Goode and Philpott, Haverfordwest; waterbodies; built-up part generalised; scale-bar and plain cartouche intersect north pointer.

54/105 Penally (parish) SS 104996
Apt 10.07.1841; 2568a (all); Map 1842?, 8 chns, by Goode and Philpott, Surveyors and Lithrs, Haverfordwest, litho; woods, building names, limekilns. Apt omits some field names.

54/106 Penrith, including Castellan (parish and chapelry) SN 205345 [Not listed]
Apt 11.08.1837; 3082a (all); Map 1844, 8 chns, by Owen Lloyd, Cardigan; building names, spring, mill pond; chapelry boundary. Apt omits some field names.

54/107 St Petrox (parish) SR 970965
Apt 17.12.1839; 968a (all); Map 1840?, 8 chns, by John Jones; waterbodies, building names, limekiln; pictorial church. Apt omits land use.

54/108 Prendergast (parish) SM 959176
Apt 13.08.1842; 1105a (1104); Map 1843?, 6 chns, by H.P. Goode and Philpott, Surveyors and lithors, Haverfordwest, litho; waterbodies, woods, building names; built-up part generalised. Apt omits some field names.

54/109 Puncheston (parish) SN 006302
Apt 15.02.1842; 1726a (all); Map 1844, 6 chns, by H.P. Goode and Philpott, Haverfordwest. Apt omits some field names.

54/110 Pwllcrochon (parish) SM 922029 [Pwllcrochan]
Apt 11.04.1839; 1637a (all); Map 1840?, 6 chns, by Goode and Philpott, Haverfordwest; plain cartouche is superimposed on north pointer.

54/111 Redburth (parish) SN 088038
Apt 31.07.1841; 306a (all); Map 1842?, 3 chns, by Goode and Philpott, Surveyors and lithogs, Haverfordwest, litho.

54/112 Reynalton or Reynaldston (parish) SN 090089
Apt 06.02.1843; 526a (all); Map 1843, 3 chns, by H.P. Goode and Philpott, H'west.

54/113 Rhoscrowther (parish) SM 915015
Apt 18.03.1839; 2366a (all); Map 1838, 6 chns, by H.P. Goode and Philpott, Haverfordwest; waterbodies; scale-bar intersects plain cartouche.

54/114 Robeston West (parish) SM 883092
Apt 17.03.1843; 1101a (1100); Map 1843?, 8 chns, by H.P. Goode and Philpott, Surveyors and Liths, Haverfordwest, litho; woods, building names.

54/115 Roch (parish) SM 879207
Apt 08.12.1837; 4419a (4603); Map 1839, 6 chns, by Goode and Philpott, Haverfordwest; waterbodies; scale-bar intersects north pointer; dot-dash lines separate holdings, and pecked lines are within holdings. Apt omits land use and some field names.

54/116 Robeston Wathen (chapelry in parish of Narberth) SN 085155
Apt 27.04.1844; 1388a (1345); Map 1845, 8 chns, ? by Goode and Philpott; waterbodies, woods, building names, mill leat, limekiln, quarry.

54/117 Rosemarket (parish) SM 954088
Apt 31.12.1842; 1759a (1759); Map 1843?, 6 chns, by H.P. Goode and Philpott, Haverfordwest, litho; waterbodies, woods, building names. Apt omits many field names.

54/118 Rudbaxton (parish) SM 970200
Apt 13.08.1842; 4090a (4142); Map 1844, 6 chns, by H.P. Goode and Philpott, Haverfordwest; woods, building names. Apt omits many field names.

54/119 Slebech, Minwere and Newton (parish) SN 033141 [Not listed]
Apt 11.11.1846; 7035a (7164); Map 1847?, 8 chns, in 2 parts, by H.P. Goode, Haverfordwest, (includes Mynwere village at 3 chns); waterbodies, woods, plantations, parkland, building names, belvidere, stables, quarry, pheasantry, meeting house, mill, limekiln, low water mark, parish boundaries, glebe. Apt omits some field names.

54/120 Spittal (parish) SM 988230
Apt 15.03.1838; 2665a (2674); Map 1839, 6 chns, in 2 parts, by Goode and Philpott, Haverfordwest, (includes enlargement of village at 3 chns); scale-bar intersects north pointer. Apt omits land use.

54/121 Stackpole Bosher or Bosherton (parish) SR 962941 [Bosherston]
Apt 20.10.1837; 1566a (all); Map 1839?, 8 chns, ? by John Jones; waterbodies, building names, sands; pictorial church. Apt omits land use.

54/122 Stackpole Elidor or Cheriton (parish) SR 991969
Apt 17.12.1839; 2845a (all); Map 1840?, 8 chns, by John Jones; building names, watermill (by symbol), cliffs, sands; pictorial church. Apt omits land use.

54/123 Stainton (rector's portion) (district in parish of Stainton) SM 918079 [Steynton]
Apt 26.01.1842; 4063a (4406); Map 1842, 8 chns, in 3 parts, by Goode and Philpott, Haverfordwest; built-up part not mapped; woods. Apt omits some land use and some field names.

54/124 Stainton (vicar's portion) (district in parish of Stainton) SM 910115 [Steynton]
Apt 09.06.1842; 1697a (all); Map 1843, 8 chns, by Goode and Philpott, H'west. Apt omits some field names.

54/125 Stainton (district) SM 910136 [Steynton]
Apt 07.10.1839; 1184a (all); Map 1839, [9 chns], by Goode and Philpott, Haverfordwest, litho; building names; scale is stated to be 6 chns, but a pencil note suggests 9 chns, which is confirmed by comparison with OS mapping; dot-dash lines indicate ownerships. Apt omits land use and some field names.

54/126 Talbenny (parish) SM 837116
Apt 21.06.1839; 1425a (all); Map 1839, 6 chns, by Goode and Philpott, Haverfordwest, litho (with names and tree ornament in manuscript); woods, building names; plain cartouche intersects scale-bar and north pointer.

54/127 St Mary's, Tenby (parish) SN 128022 [Tenby]
Apt 12.10.1840; 1983a (2242); Map 1841?, 8 chns, by Goode and Philpott, Haverfordwest, litho; waterbodies, woods, building names, tithe-free areas (col). Apt omits some land use and some field names.

54/128 Great Trefgarn (parish) SM 951239 [Treffgarne]
Apt 11.09.1843; 1206a (all); Map 1847, 8 chns, by Essex Davies; waterbodies, mill, quarries.

54/129 St Twinnels (parish) SR 950967 [St Twynnells]
Apt 30.04.1838; 1358a (all); Map 1839?, 8 chns, ? by John Jones; building names, limekilns, quarry, kiln; pictorial church. Apt omits land use.

54/130 Uzmaston (parish) SM 980159
Apt 07.08.1839; 2071a (all); Map 1841?, 6 chns, by Goode and Philpott, Haverfordwest, litho; building names.

54/131 Walton East (parish) SN 024231
Apt 22.03.1839; 1893a (all); Map 1840, 8 chns, by John Jones; building names, mill (by symbol); pictorial church. Apt omits land use.

54/132 Walton West (parish) SM 871134
Apt 11.08.1841; 1293a (all); Map 1842, 6 chns, by H.P. Goode and Philpott, Haverfordwest. Apt omits some land use and some field names.

54/133 Walwyns Castle (parish) SM 881115 [Walwyn's Castle]
Apt 30.01.1840; 2905a (all); Map 1842?, 6 chns, by Goode and Philpott, Surveyors and lithographers, Haverfordwest; woods, building names. Apt omits some field names.

54/134 Warren (parish) SR 935967
Apt 11.06.1839; 1169a (all); Map 1839?, 8 chns, ? by John Jones; hill-drawing, waterbodies, building names; pictorial church. Apt omits land use.

54/135 Whitechurch in Dewsland (parish) SM 805255 [Whitchurch]
Apt 20.07.1838; 1864a (3138); Map 1839, 6 chns, in 3 parts, by Goode and Philpott, Haverfordwest, (includes Upper and Lower Solva at 3 chns); building names; scale-bar intersects plain cartouche; pecked lines are within holdings, and dot-dash lines are between holdings.

54/136 Whitechurch in Kemes (parish) SN 160352 [Not listed]
Apt 21.03.1839; 2481a (all); Map 1841, 8 chns, by Owen Lloyd, Cardigan; hill-drawing, foot/b'way, waterbodies, woods, rock outcrops, building names, wool factory, meeting houses, smith, boundary stones and marks, mill, spring. Apt omits land use and field names.

54/137 Wiston (parish) SN 015185
Apt 26.04.1838; 7031a (7030); Map 1843?, 8 chns, by Goode and Philpott, Haverfordwest; plain cartouches intersect scale-bar and north pointer.

54/138 Yerbeston (parish) SN 063090
Apt 04.04.1844; 1224a (all); Map 1845, 8 chns, by Goode and Philpott, Haverfordwest. Apt omits some field names.

Radnorshire

PRO IR 29 and IR30 55/1-53

53 tithe districts: 298,303 acres
53 tithe commutations: 231,357 acres
37 voluntary tithe agreements, 16 compulsory tithe awards

Tithe and tithe commutation

Although in 1836 tithes remained payable in every Radnorshire tithe district and all tithes remained payable in thirty-two tithe districts, only 77 per cent of the area of the county was still tithable at this date (Fig. 67). As in much of upland England and Wales this was largely because of modus payments or because all remaining tithe was apportioned on the lower-lying land. In five Radnorshire tithe districts all woodland was tithe free.

Assistant tithe commissioners and local tithe agents who worked in this county are listed in Table 55.1 and the valuers of tithe rent-charge in Table 55.2. Radnorshire is unusual for an upland county as none of its districts is apportioned by holding. However, almost all the schedules of tithe apportionment lack some field names and a few omit land-use information.

Tithe maps

Exceptionally for a Welsh county, a few Radnorshire tithe maps were considered accurate enough to merit sealing as first-class and in addition construction lines are present on two second-class maps. Three maps are acknowledged copies of earlier surveys. Radnorshire tithe maps are drawn at a variety of scales from one inch to 1.5 chains to one inch to 16 chains but only 15 per cent are in the recommended scale range of one inch to 3 to 4 chains (Table 55.3). With the exception of woodland which is portrayed on all but four maps, Radnorshire maps are almost wholly devoid of land-use or field-boundary information.

Morris and William Sayce dominated the tithe survey mapping of Radnorshire as they did the valuation of tithe rent-charge and were responsible for over half the county's maps (Table 55.2). Their maps exhibit minor differences of style but are characterised by grey infill for buildings and grey woodland symbols, the latter sometimes mushroom-shaped. Overall Radnorshire tithe maps are rather better finished than is general for North Wales, though they are very ordinary by English standards.

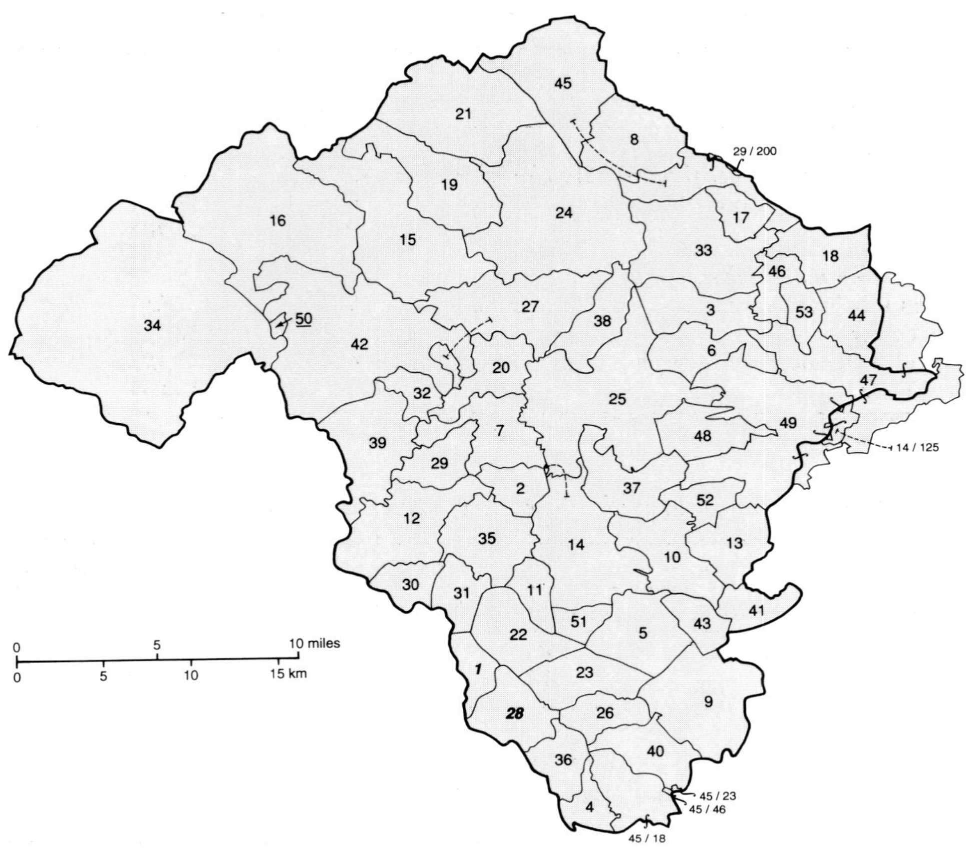

Fig. 67 Radnorshire: tithe district boundaries.

Table 55.1. *Agreements and awards for commutation of tithes in Radnorshire*

Assistant commissioner/ local tithe agent	*Number of agreements**	*Number of awards*
John Johnes	10	14
Thomas Hoskins	20	0
Aneurin Owen	0	2
George Bolls	1	0

*Computed from the number of extant reports on tithe agreements in the tithe files [PRO IR 18].

Table 55.2. *Tithe valuers and tithe map-makers in Radnorshire*

Name and address (in Radnorshire unless indicated)	*Number of districts*	*Acreage*
Tithe valuers		
Morris and William Sayce, Kington, Herefordshire	40	196,401
Charles Fowke, Boughrood	6	17,754
Others [6]	7	17,202
Attributed tithe map-makers		
Morris and William Sayce, Kington, Herefordshire	28	131,057
George Tayler	5	27,119
James and B. Lewis, Cwmscawen	4	13,495
Others [3]	4	10,833

Table 55.3. *The tithe maps of Radnorshire: scales and classes*

Scale in chains/inch	*All maps*		*First Class*		*Second Class*	
	Number	*Acreage*	*Number*	*Acreage*	*Number*	*Acreage*
>3	1	189	0	0	1	189
3	4	10,470	3	6,592	1	3,878
4	4	9,350	2	5,201	2	4,149
6	10	27,204	0	0	10	27,204
8	31	167,469	0	0	31	167,469
<8	3	16,675	0	0	3	16,675
TOTAL	53	231,357	5	11,793	48	219,564

Table 55.4. *The tithe maps of Radnorshire: dates*

	1839	*1840*	*1841*	*1842*	*1843*	*1844*	*1845*	*1846*	*1847*	*1848*
All maps	7	12	6	8	9	3	4	1	0	1
1st class*	1	0	0	0	2	1	0	0	0	0
2nd class*	6	12	6	8	7	2	4	1	0	1

*One first-class tithe map and one second-class tithe map of Radnorshire in the Public Record Office collection are undated.

Radnorshire

55/1 Aberedw (parish) SO 080473
Apt 18.08.1843; 2415a (4300), (tithable parts only); Map 1843?, 8 chns, ? by Geo. Tayler, (includes village at 4 chns); houses, woods, plantations, building names, boundary marks, castell, mill. Apt omits some field names.

55/2 Bettws Disserth (parish) SO 105578 [Bettws]
Apt 05.04.1838; 1885a (1885); Map not dated, 4 chns, 1st cl, ? by Morris and William Sayce; construction lines, woods, building names; some construction lines are noted as unnecessary, but surveyed because of initial uncertainty as to the parish boundary. Apt omits some field names.

55/3 Bleddfa (parish) SO 219682
Apt 12.11.1840; 2198a (2740); Map 1842?, 8 chns, ? by M. and W. Sayce, (tithable parts only); waterbodies, woods, building names, common; north pointer has diadem and plumes.

55/4 Boughrood (parish) SO 139396
Apt 16.05.1839; 1633a (all); Map 1841?, 6 chns. Apt omits some field names.

55/5 Bryngwyn (parish) SO 177495
Apt 11.04.1844; 4537a (all); Map surveyed 1844, 8 chns, by J.G. and B. Lewis; hill-drawing, waterbodies, woods, marsh/bog, building names, mill, boundary crosses and stones, ancient ditch, turbary; two hills named.

55/6 Cascob (parish) (partly in Herefordshire) SO 221660
Apt 16.05.1839; 3124a (2548); Map 1840, 8 chns; woods, plantations, building names, parsonage. Apt omits some field names.

55/7 Cefnllys (parish) SO 100620 [Not listed]
Apt 16.05.1839; 4070a (all); Map 1840?, 8 chns, ? by M. and W. Sayce; waterbodies, woods, plantations, commons, building names, castle ruins, mill; north pointer has plumes. Apt omits a few field names.

55/8 Church (township in parish of Beguildy) SO 182782 [Not listed]
Apt 30.09.1846; 3038a (?); Map 1846, 8 chns, by Geo. Tayler; waterbodies, woods, building names, common, sheepwalk. Apt omits some field names.

55/9 Clirow and Bettws Clirow (parish and hamlet) SO 213453 [Clyro]
Apt 25.05.1838; 7226a (7225); Map 1839?, 8 chns, in 2 parts, (includes enlargement of detail); foot/b'way, waterbodies, woods, plantations, building names, mound, mill, quarries, turbary. Apt omits some field names.

55/10 Colva (parish) SO 190540
Apt 31.08.1837; 2294a (all); Map 1840?, 8 chns, in 2 parts, (tithable parts only); houses, woods, building names.

55/11 Cregrina (parish) SO 115521
Apt 27.03.1838; 1596a (all); Map 1839, 6 chns, ? by M. and W. Sayce, (tithable parts only); woods, plantations, building names, walk mill, boundary trees, common. Apt omits a few field names.

55/12 Disserth (parish) SO 045569
Apt 05.04.1838; 6650a (6650); Map not dated, 8 chns; water-bodies, woods, building names. Apt omits some field names.

55/13 Gladestry (parish) SO 230546
Apt 05.06.1839; 3221a (all); Map 1839, 8 chns, ? by M. and W. Sayce; waterbodies, woods, building names, mill; north pointer has plumes. Apt omits some field names.

55/14 Glascombe (parish) SO 149545 [Glascwm]
Apt 31.08.1837; 6984a (6984); Map 1840?, 8 chns, ? by M. and W. Sayce; waterbodies, woods, building names, mill, boundary marks, common. Apt omits some field names.

55/15 Golon and Cefn Pawl or Upper or Golon Division (divisions in parish of Llanbister or Lambister) SO 050730 [Not listed]
Apt 01.11.1839; 10965a (10965); Map 1842?, 8 chns, ? by M. and W. Sayce; woods, plantations, building names, mill, smithy, sheepwalks; north pointer has crown and plumes.

55/16 Saint Harmon (parish) SN 970770 [St Harmon]
Apt 16.05.1839; 6921a (12000); Map 1840, 12 chns, ? by M. and W. Sayce, (tithable parts only); woods, plantations, building names, mills; brook and hill named. Apt omits land use and a few field names.

55/17 Heyop (parish) SO 240750
Apt 15.07.1842; 1854a (all); Map 1842?, 8 chns, by M. and J.W. Sayce; waterbodies, woods, building names, spring, race course, boundary marks, quarry.

55/18 Knighton (parish) SO 284716 [Knighton or Trefyclawdd]
Apt 19.02.1839; 2461a (all), (tithable parts only); Map 1840?, 9 chns; waterbodies, woods, building names, castle bank, workhouse; bridge named; north pointer has plumes. Apt omits some field names.

55/19 Llananno (parish) SO 070760
Apt 20.10.1840; 4400a (4400); Map 1842?, 8 chns, ? by M. and J.W. Sayce, (tithable parts only); waterbodies, woods (col), building names, mill, common. Apt omits some field names.

55/20 Llanbadarnfawr (parish) SO 090644 [Not listed]
Apt 28.01.1839; 3647a (all); Map 1839?, 8 chns, ? by M. and W. Sayce; waterbodies, woods, building names, parsonage, common; north pointer has plumes. Apt omits some field names.

55/21 Llanbadarn Vynydd (parish) SO 085800 [Llanbadarn Fynydd]
Apt 20.10.1840; 8966a (8965), (tithable parts only); Map 1843?, 8 chns, ? by Geo. Tayler; hill-drawing, woods, plantations, building names, mill, commons.

55/22 Llanbadarn y Garreg (parish) SO 104497 [Llanbadarn-y-garreg]
Apt 27.03.1838; 628a (all); Map 1839, 6 chns, ? by M. and W. Sayce, (tithable parts only); woods, building names, chapel, mill, bank, pound house, common; stream named. Apt omits some field names.

55/23 Llanbedr Painscastle (parish) SO 146467 [Llanbedr and Painscastle]
Apt 14.07.1847; 3878a (all); Map 1848, 3 chns, by Richard Meredith, Hay; construction lines, hill-drawing, foot/b'way, building names, boundary crosses and marks; leaves are twined around the lower part of the north pointer. Apt omits field names.

55/24 Llanbister (parish) SO 138745
Apt 30.01.1841; 14838a (14837); Map 1843?, 8 chns, ? by M. and W. Sayce; waterbodies, woods, plantations, nursery woods, building names, tollgate, commons; north pointer has very large crown and plumes. Apt omits some field names.

55/25 Llandegley (parish) SO 140630
Apt 13.11.1840; 3729a (all); Map 1842, 8 chns, by Geo. Tayler; woods, building names, mill, common; scale is ruler-like. Apt omits some field names.

55/26 Llandewifach (parish) SO 156452 [Not listed]
Apt 22.05.1843; 2297a (all); Map 1843, 6 chns, 'Surveyed and Mapped for C. Fowke, Esqr by J.G. and B. Lewis'; woods (col), building names, tumulus, common. Apt omits some field names.

55/27 Llandewy-Ystradenny (parish) SO 108689 [Llandewi Ystradenni]
Apt 01.11.1839; 8076a (all); Map 1840?, 8 chns, ? by M. and W. Sayce; waterbodies, woods, building names, mill, commons; north pointer has crown and plumes. Apt omits some field names.

55/28 Llandilo Graban (parish) SO 100453 [Llandeilo Graban]
Apt 12.09.1839; 2090a (all); Map 1841?, 6 chns, (tithable parts only); mill (by symbol). Apt omits most field names.

55/29 Llandrindod (parish) SO 067600 [Llandrindod Wells]
Apt 30.09.1840; 2689a (all); Map 1840, 4 chns, 'Compiled and Surveyed' by T. M'Grane and Carey; hill-drawing, waterbodies, houses, woods, heath/moor, building names, glebe, mill, wells, springs, pump house, mill race, common. Apt omits most field names.

55/30 Llanelwedd (parish) SO 044528
Apt 04.09.1845; 2020a (2020); Map 1842, 8 chns, by E.I. Griffiths, Land Agent and Surveyor, Llandilo; waterbodies, woods, building names, turnpike gates, earthwork, boundary stone; mapmaker's name is on streamer draped across scale bar; north pointer has Prince of Wales feathers and 'Ich Dien'. Apt omits some field names.

55/31 Llanfaredd (parish) SO 072522
Apt 18.08.1843; 2246a (all); Map 1843, 8 chns, by E.I. Griffiths, Llandilo; woods, plantations, building names, mill; north pointer has Prince of Wales feathers and 'Ich Dien'. Apt omits some field names.

55/32 Llanfihangele Helygen (chapelry) SO 048642 [Llanfihangel-helygen]
Apt 22.07.1840; 1460a (all); Map 1841, 4 chns; construction lines, waterbodies, woods, plantations, gardens, building names, boundary trees, common. Apt omits a few field names.

55/33 Llangunllo (parish) SO 216720
Apt 15.06.1839; 5627a (all); Map 1842?, 8 chns, in 2 parts, ? by M. and W. Sayce, (tithable parts only; includes village at 4 chns); waterbodies, woods, building names, mill; north pointer has plumes. Apt omits a few field names.

55/34 Llansaintfread Cumtoyddwr (parish) SN 895685 [Llansantffraed-Cwmdeuddwr]
Apt 28.08.1838; 7293a (32000); Map 1840?, 16 chns, in 2 parts, ? by M. and W. Sayce, (tithable parts only; includes village at 2 chns); waterbodies, woods, building names, chapel, factory, mills, lodge; county name in title is on 'cloud' background. Apt omits land use.

55/35 Llansaintfraed in Elvet (parish) SO 091555 [Llansantffraed-in-Elwel]
Apt 30.12.1837; 3316a (4000); Map 1839?, 4 chns, 1st cl, (tithable parts only); construction lines, hill-drawing, waterbodies, woods, building names, chapel, mill, weir, common; one principal construction line is annotated '80 links allowed for acclivity'. Apt omits most field names.

55/36 Llanstephan (parish) SO 125421
Apt 10.03.1841; 2407a (2407); Map 1843?, 6 chns, (tithable parts only). Apt omits most field names.

55/37 Llanfihangel Nantmellan (township in parish of Llanfihangel Nantmellan) SO 172579 [Llanfihangel-Nant-Melan]
Apt 17.05.1842; 4227a (8150); Map 1842?, 8 chns, ? by M. and W. Sayce; waterbodies, woods (col), plantations (col), building names, mill, churchyard, sheepwalk. Apt omits some field names.

55/38 Llanvihangel Rhydithon (parish) SO 165675 [Llanfihangel Rhydithon]
Apt 01.11.1839; 3204a (3204); Map 1840?, 8 chns, in 2 parts, ? by M. and W. Sayce; waterbodies, woods, building names, mill.

55/39 Llanyre (chapelry) SO 030612
Apt 25.11.1840; 5901a (all); Map 1841?, 8 chns, ? by M. and W. Sayce; waterbodies, woods, building names, mills, chapel, commons. Apt omits a few field names.

55/40 Llowes (parish) SO 180425
Apt 30.06.1843; 3319a (all); Map 1844, 6 chns, in 2 parts, 'Surveyed and Mapped for C. Fowke Esqr. by J.G. and B. Lewis'; waterbodies, woods (col), gardens, fence, building names, oxbow. Apt has some cropping information and omits some field names.

55/41 Michaelchurch upon Arrow (parish) SO 241509 [Michaelchurch-on-Arrow]
Apt 01.04.1844; 1336a (all); Map 1845?, 8 chns; houses, woods, plantations, building names, footbridges, quarries.

55/42 Nantmel (parish) SO 012678
Apt 25.11.1840; 16387a (all); Map 1841?, 8 chns, ? by M. and W. Sayce; waterbodies, woods (col), building names, boundary stones, common; north pointer has large crown and plumes; lake named; roads across commons are apparently not mapped. Apt omits land use and some field names.

55/43 Newchurch (parish) SO 210500
Apt 30.10.1844; 1789a (all); Map 1845?, 6 chns, ? by M. and W. Sayce; waterbodies, houses, woods (col), plantations (col), building names, old brook course. Apt omits a few field names.

55/44 Norton (parish) SO 303676
Apt 31.03.1843; 3145a (3144); Map 1843, 3 chns, 1st cl, in 2 parts, by Wm Sayce, Kington; construction lines, waterbodies, houses, woods (named), plantations, building names, Offa's Dyke, boundary marks, weirs, mill, quarries, fishponds; pecked line round village may indicate tithe ownership. Apt omits a few field names.

55/45 Pennant, Medwalledd and Creigbyther (townships in parish of Beguilay) SO 215765 [Not listed]
Apt 27.06.1844; 9071a (?); Map 1843?, 8 chns, in 4 parts, ? by Geo. Tayler, (tithable parts only); woods, plantations, building names. Apt omits some field names.

55/46 Pilleth (parish) SO 258697
Apt 22.04.1843; 1897a (all); Map 1844, 3 chns, 1st cl, by William Sayce, Kington; construction lines, waterbodies, houses, woods, building names, brick kiln. Apt omits some field names.

55/47 Presteign (parish) (partly in Herefordshire) SO 320640 [Presteigne or Llanandras]
Apt 09.08.1844; 10689a (11126); Map 1845, 6 chns, in 2 parts, by Wm Sayce; waterbodies, houses, woods, plantations, building names, road names, old castle, quarries; built-up part generalised. Apt omits some field names.

55/48 New Radnor (parish) SO 215614
Apt 31.01.1845; 3342a (all); Map 1845?, 8 chns, 'Copied from an Old Survey for Mr Fowke' by J.G. and B. Lewis; waterbodies, woods, plantations, building names, castle mound. Apt omits some field names.

55/49 Old Radnor (parish) SO 266610
Apt 03.01.1840; 10060a (10069); Map 1841?, 8 chns, ? by M. and W. Sayce; waterbodies, woods (named), plantations, gardens, building names, chapels, mill, turnpike gate. Apt omits some field names.

55/50 Rhayader ar Gwy (chapelry) SN 972681 [Rhayader]
Apt 22.07.1840; 189a (all); Map 1840?, 1.5 chns, by M. and W. Sayce; waterbodies, woods, market hall; map date is on 'cloud' background; north pointer has crown and plumes; scale is set in border. Apt omits most field names.

55/51 Rhulan (parish) SO 140500 [Rhulen]
Apt 31.08.1837; 756a (all); Map 1839, 6 chns, (tithable parts only); hill-drawing, waterbodies, woods, building names; bridge named. Apt omits some field names.

55/52 Treuern and Gwaithla (township in parish of Llanvihangel Nantmellan) SO 217572
Apt 12.11.1839; 1816a (all); Map 1840?, [8 chns], ? by M. and W. Sayce; waterbodies, woods, building names. Apt omits some field names.

55/53 Whitton (parish) SO 275677
Apt 23.12.1843; 1550a (all); Map 1843, 3 chns, 1st cl, by Wm Sayce, Kington; waterbodies, houses, woods, plantations, gardens, building names, Offa's Dyke, spring, quarries, boundary trees, vicarage, school, common. Apt omits some field names.

The tithe maps of England and Wales: a 'national' survey?

First-class and second-class tithe maps

The Tithe Commutation Act of 1836 was amended in 1837 to establish two classes of tithe maps: first class and second class.[1] This is an essentially legal distinction; first-class maps are legal evidence of all matters which they portray, whereas the Tithe Commission sanctioned second-class maps as evidence of only those facts of direct relevance to tithe commutation. Though such a distinction may be of singular importance to those seeking precise evidence of land parcel boundaries and areas, perhaps for resolving property or rights-of-way disputes, to that overwhelming majority of tithe map users concerned with recovering facts about local topography, economy or society for use in an historical reconstruction, the legal distinction between first-class and second-class maps is largely irrelevant.

The division of the tithe surveys into first- and second-class maps was instituted to overcome difficulties experienced in the first few months of tithe commutation.[2] Clauses 32 and 35 of the 1836 Tithe Commutation Act required that a map be made of each tithe district but also permitted landowners to adopt an existing map if they were satisfied that it was suitable. On the other hand, clause 63 of the Act required the tithe commissioners to certify the accuracy of each adopted tithe map. Problems arose where landowners adopted maps which the Tithe Commission could not certify as accurate; the permissiveness of clauses 32 and 35 conflicted with the statutory requirement of clause 63.

It is quite probable that those who drafted these clauses assumed that certifying the accuracy of a map would be a formality, perhaps just a matter of confirming the veracity of each copy of a map and apportionment, rather than testifying that a map represented correctly all the features that it portrayed.

Lieutenant Robert Kearsley Dawson of the Royal Engineers, a man who had spent most of his professional career with the Ordnance Survey, was appointed an assistant tithe commissioner in 1836 with special responsibility for tithe commutation mapping. In November of that year he set down guidelines for tithe maps which would have ensured that they were accurate enough to serve as legal evidence.[3] Some two months later the first

[1] An Act to Amend an Act for the Commutation of Tithes in England and Wales, 1 Vict. cap. 69; 2 & 3 Vict. cap. 62 extended the amendments to maps accompanying compulsory awards.

[2] R. J. P. Kain and H. C. Prince, *The tithe surveys of England and Wales* (Cambridge, Cambridge University Press, 1985), pp. 69-86.

[3] Extracts from R. K. Dawson's instructions for 'the preparation of plans for the purpose of the Tithe Commutation Act' are reproduced in Kain and Prince, *The tithe surveys of England and Wales*, pp. 83-4.

tithe map was received by the Tithe Commission, tested in Lieutenant Dawson's office, and found to be seriously inaccurate. This map, of the parish of Tonge in Kent, had been adopted by the parish landowners as suitable for tithe commutation purposes and it highlighted the conflict between the freedom of landowners to supply any map they liked and the legal obligation of the tithe commissioners to certify planimetric and topographic accuracy. If the tithe commissioners were forced to reject all maps which failed their tests of total accuracy, then a great deal more new surveying would be necessary which would all add to landowners' costs of tithe commutation. Dawson estimated the cost of copying an existing map at one penny an acre and of new survey to a sufficiently high standard to satisfy the Tithe Commission's requirements at ninepence an acre, so quite large sums of money were at stake.[4]

By the strict exercise of its perceived duty to require absolute accuracy in tithe maps, the Tithe Commission brought the process of tithe commutation to a halt no sooner than it had begun. In essence the Tithe Act was ambiguous in its specification of a tithe map. This problem was compounded further by Dawson's suggestion that the opportunity should be taken of using tithe survey maps as a basis for a 'general survey' of all the land in every parish and township in the country on the model of continental European cadastral surveys.[5]

In April 1837 a select committee of the House of Commons was appointed to review the map requirements of the Tithe Commutation Act. The evidence from witnesses called before the committee concentrated on the question of the freedom of landowners to supply any map they chose and the conflicting obligation of the tithe commissioners to certify its accuracy. The select committee took no evidence on the desirability of a national survey and observed in their report that they did not feel obliged to comment on this matter.

In essence, their proceedings revolved around the views of two persons. The first was William Blamire, member of parliament for Cumberland and then a tithe commissioner. The second was Sir James Graham, another Cumberland member of parliament, who throughout the hearings made no secret of his distaste for any scheme which might increase the costs of tithe commutation to landowners. The select committee, minded very much of the principle of voluntaryism on which the 1836 Act was based, recommended that the Tithe Act be amended to free the tithe commissioners from certifying the accuracy of maps which failed to meet their standards. The Tithe Act Amendment Act of 1837 brought two classes of tithe map into being, the first and second classes, with first-class maps clearly identified by the presence of the Tithe Commission's official seal and a certification of accuracy signed by two tithe commissioners (Fig. 68).[6] The decision as to whether to commission a map to a specification which would enable it to achieve first-class status was entirely a matter for local landowners.

As Fig. 69 shows, first-class maps are very unevenly distributed across the country with particular concentrations in south-west England, in Kent, Surrey and Sussex, in Suffolk, and in Monmouthshire, Herefordshire and Worcestershire, and in Cumberland. The concentration in Cumberland may well be a result of Blamire's influence in the county and

[4] Kain and Prince, *The tithe surveys of England and Wales*, p. 73.

[5] R. J. P. Kain and Elizabeth Baigent, *Cadastral maps in the service of the state: a history of property mapping* (Chicago, Chicago University Press, 1992).

[6] R. J. P. Kain, 'R. K. Dawson's proposal in 1836 for a cadastral survey of England and Wales', *Cartographic Journal*, 12 (1975), 81-8.

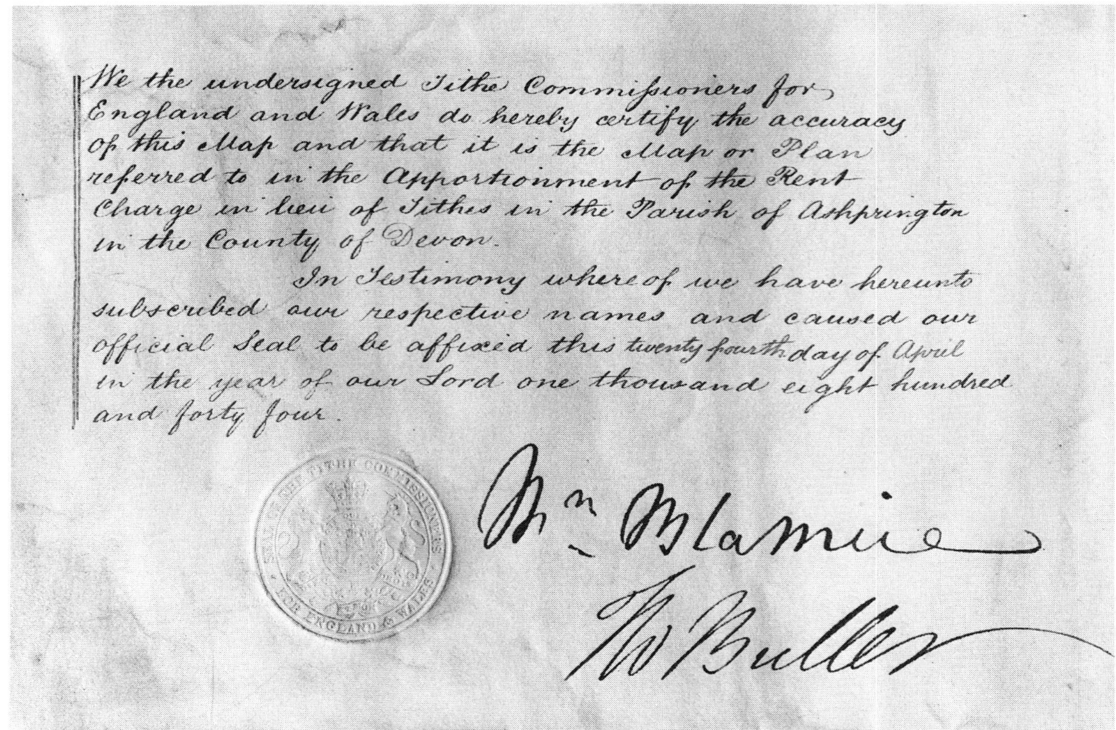

We the undersigned Tithe Commissioners for England and Wales do hereby certify the accuracy of this Map and that it is the Map or Plan referred to in the Apportionment of the Rent Charge in lieu of Tithes in the Parish of Ashprington in the County of Devon.

In Testimony whereof we have hereunto subscribed our respective names and caused our official Seal to be affixed this twenty fourth day of April in the year of our Lord one thousand eight hundred and forty four.

Wm Blamire

TW Buller

Fig. 68 The Tithe Commission's official seal which denotes a first-class map. Photograph reproduced by kind permission of the Archivist, Devon Record Office.

that in Kent is perhaps due to reaction to payment of tithes in kind and a desire to ensure that settlement of the 'tithe question' would indeed be permanent. Elsewhere it is noticeable that there is little first-class mapping in counties characterised either by extensive tithe commutation in association with earlier parliamentary enclosure or in counties where modus payments in lieu of tithe were usual. It is possible that part of the unevenness is also a reflection of successful promotion of the merits of first-class mapping by the map-makers themselves. For example, maps produced by Richard Barnes of Lowestoft, Suffolk and those of the Kent- based surveyors Alexander Doull of Chatham, Frederick and Henry Drayson of Faversham, and Thomas Thurston of Ashford are almost all first class.

Original maps were tested against entries in surveyors' field books in the Tithe Commission's Somerset House offices. Evidence on some maps suggests that the interval between initial receipt of a map and eventual affixing of the first-class seal could be as much as three years in the early 1840s when large numbers of potential first-class plans were produced. This delay fell to as little as a few months by the early 1850s when production of aspiring first-class maps had almost ceased. Unfortunately it is not possible to say how many maps were tested and found sub-standard and how many were never submitted for first-class testing.[7]

[7] Field books were presumably returned to surveyors once testing was complete; none is known to be held by the Public Record Office.

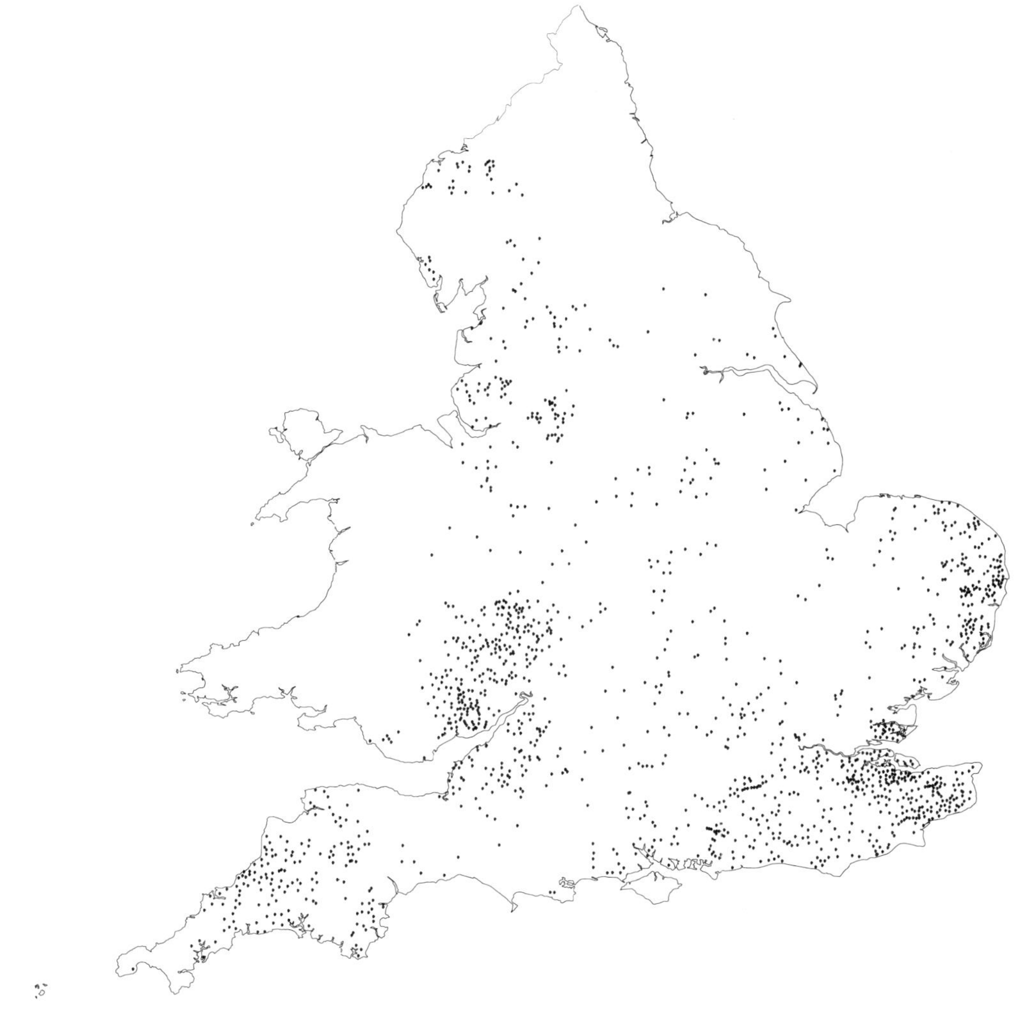

Fig. 69 England and Wales: first-class tithe maps.

Some 1,458 maps (12 per cent of the total) which cover 4,000,131 acres (15 per cent of the tithable area of England and Wales) are sealed as first class, a figure somewhat less than Dawson's own estimate of 2,333 that he made in 1852 as the work of tithe commutation was drawing to a close.[8] First-class maps certainly approach the planimetric accuracy of Ordnance Survey 1:2500 maps produced from 1855 onwards but they do not as a rule equal the comprehensiveness of Ordnance Survey topographic content. However, certain features, such as ponds, inhabited buildings, and field boundary ownership, are distinguished on a higher proportion of first-class than of second-class maps, though as a general rule first-class maps contain less topographic information than do second-class maps.

The finish of first-class maps varies a great deal. Most are very much the 'plain working plans' recommended by R. K. Dawson's instructions for 'the preparation of plans for the

[8] Kain and Prince, *The tithe surveys of England and Wales*, p. 86.

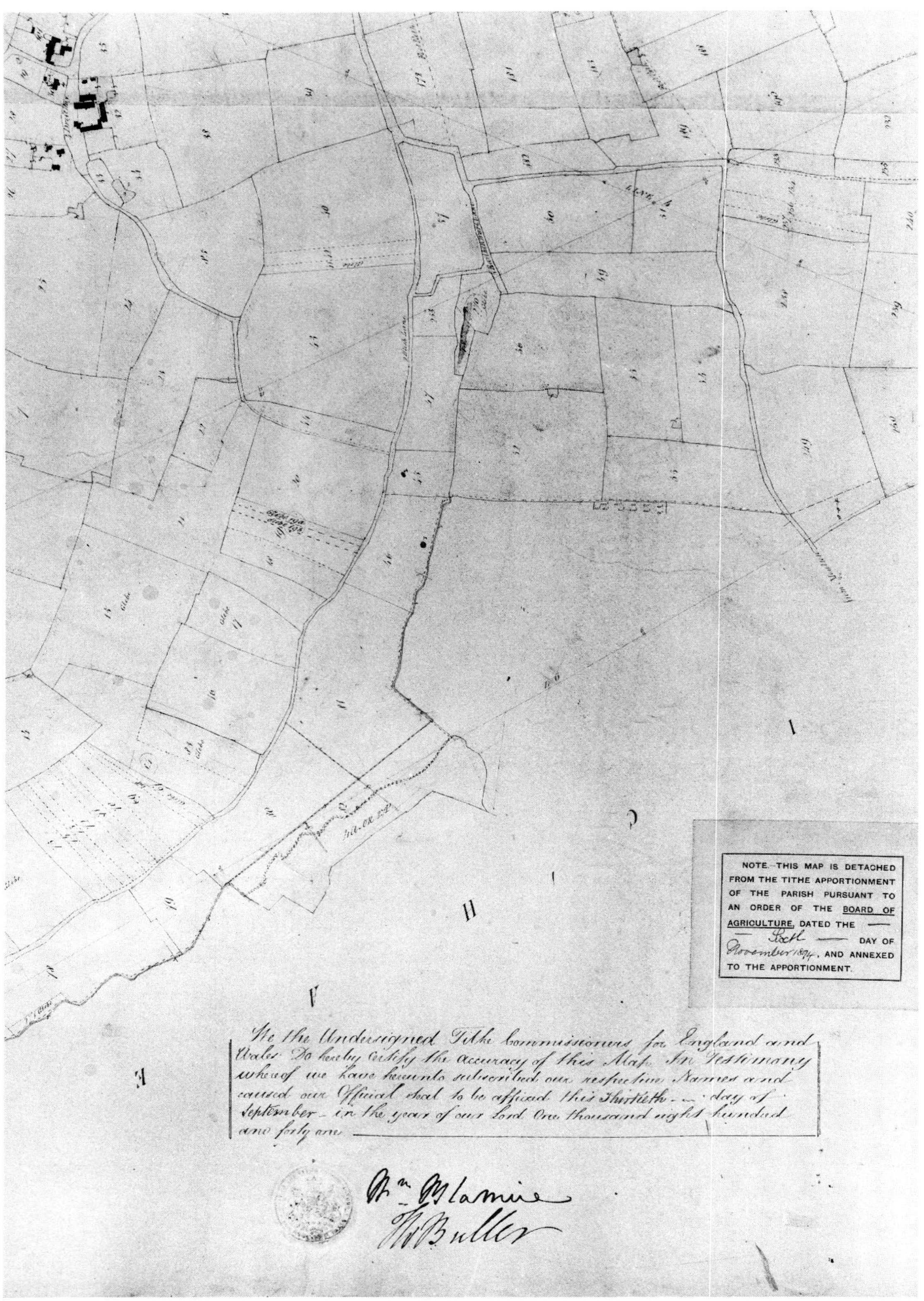

Fig. 70 Wacton, Norfolk, 1840. This version of the tithe map is at one inch to three chains and does not show woodland; compare with Fig. 71. Source: PRO IR30 23/600. Photograph reproduced by kind permission of the Keeper of the Public Record Office.

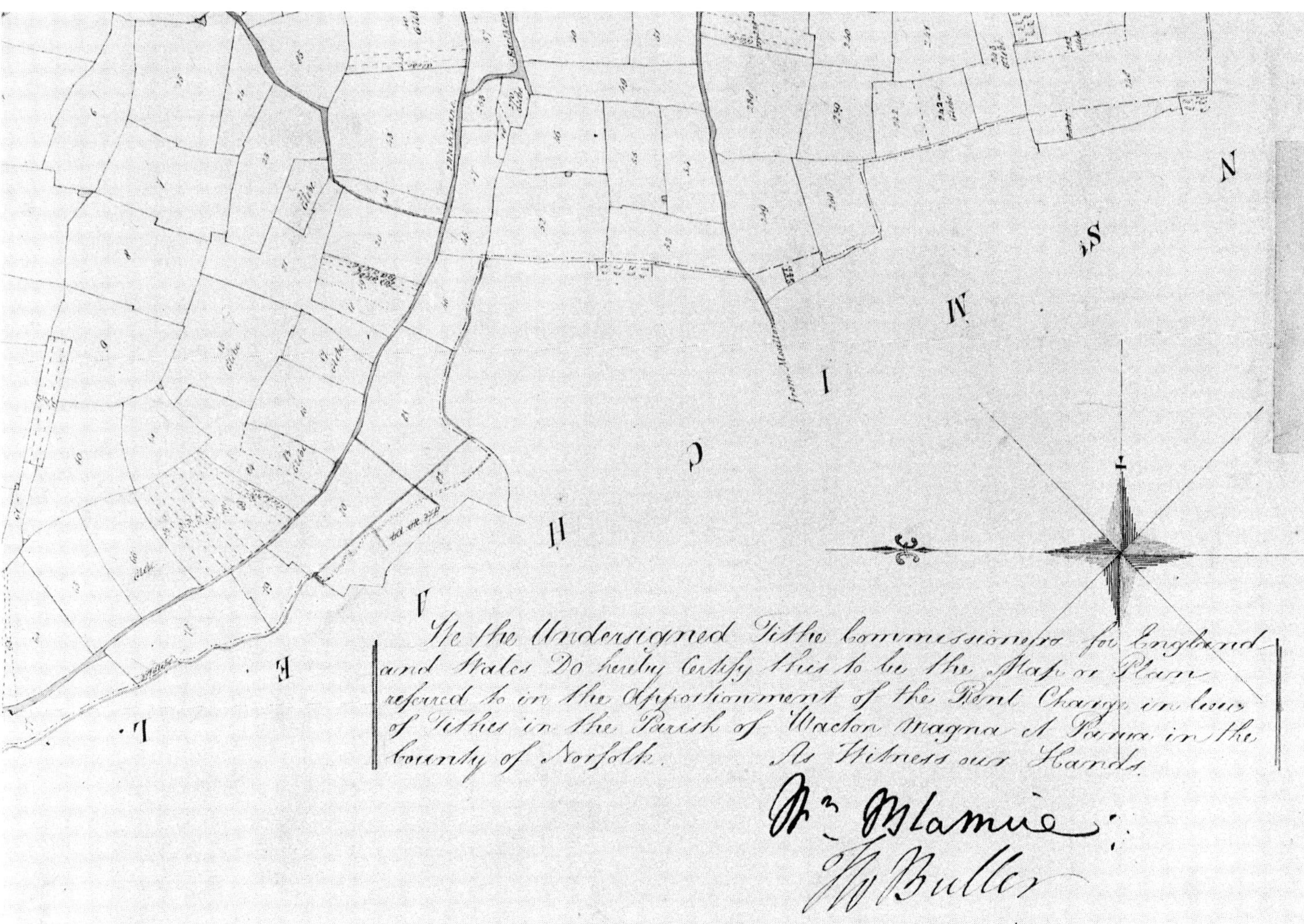

Fig. 71 Wacton, Norfolk: statutory copy of tithe map at one inch to six chains, 1840.

purpose of the Tithe Commutation Act' issued in November 1836.[9] Some are clearly preliminary drafts plotted straight from the field books but equally some, such as those of Kent tithe districts by Alexander Doull or Thomas Thurston, are characterised by a very high standard of finish. A rarety in the Public Record Office collection is a first-class map with colouring to distinguish land use and with symbols which are artistic as well as functional; the map of Skidbrook cum Saltfleet in Lincolnshire is a most notable exception. Sometimes a surveyor furnished a plain 'working plan' for retention by the Tithe Commission and produced a more colourful version containing more topographic detail for local deposit.[10] The Public Record Office collection contains two versions of the tithe maps of a few districts. For example, one map of the parish of Wacton in Norfolk is a first-class, one inch to three chains map and the second is a one inch to six chains reduced copy. The six-chain copy depicts woods which are not identified on the three-chain 'plain working plan' (Figs. 70 and 71). Although many first-class maps in the Public Record Office are copy maps rather than originals, a statement by the map-maker as on the map of West Dean in Sussex that 'I have compared this copy with the original map', is exceptional.

New surveys and maps based on existing surveys

The one-eighth of all tithe maps sealed as first class are almost all new surveys but it is impossible to ascertain how much copying of earlier work there is and how many new surveys there are, among the other 10,327 tithe maps (Fig. 72). This distinction is rarely stated on the maps themselves (Fig. 73) which may mean that the map of Buslingthorpe, Lincolnshire copied from one of 1653, is not necessarily the 'oldest' tithe map of England and Wales (Fig. 74). On the map of Great Hucklow, Derbyshire the surveyor says, 'Note – This Plan is made from the Township Plan, dated 1811 and from sundry Estate Plans upon various scales and degrees of accuracy and is adopted by the Landowners'. Those map-makers who consistently distinguish between copying and original work, such as Thomas Thurston of Ashford, Kent are shining exceptions to the general rule. Even a statement 'surveyed by . . .' in a map title does not necessarily indicate an entirely new tithe map as the survey referred to could have been made many years earlier. Compilation from enclosure maps may reasonably be suspected for those maps of very small areas of residual tithable land in districts where most tithes had been commuted earlier under the terms of an enclosure act (Fig. 75). Copying and revising from an earlier survey is particularly likely in the case of those maps on which the numbering of tithe areas does not begin at '1' and on which the numeration of tithe areas is discontinuous. The inclusion of some tithe free land on a tithe map may also be an indication that the map is a copy but where tithe free land was scattered throughout a tithe district, it may well have been easier to survey the whole district and to sort out afterwards which lands were tithable and which were not (Fig. 76).

The presence of construction lines on a tithe map is not an infallible guide to the fact of a new survey. In his instructions 'for the preparation of plans for the purpose of the Tithe Commutation Act', Dawson said that construction lines were necessary so that a map's accuracy could be tested (Fig. 77). It would, though, be perfectly feasible to re-use an old

[9] Reproduced in Kain and Prince, *The tithe surveys of England and Wales*, pp. 83-4.

[10] R. J. P. Kain and S. A. H. Wilmot, 'Tithe surveys in national and local archives', *Archives*, 20 (1992), 106-17.

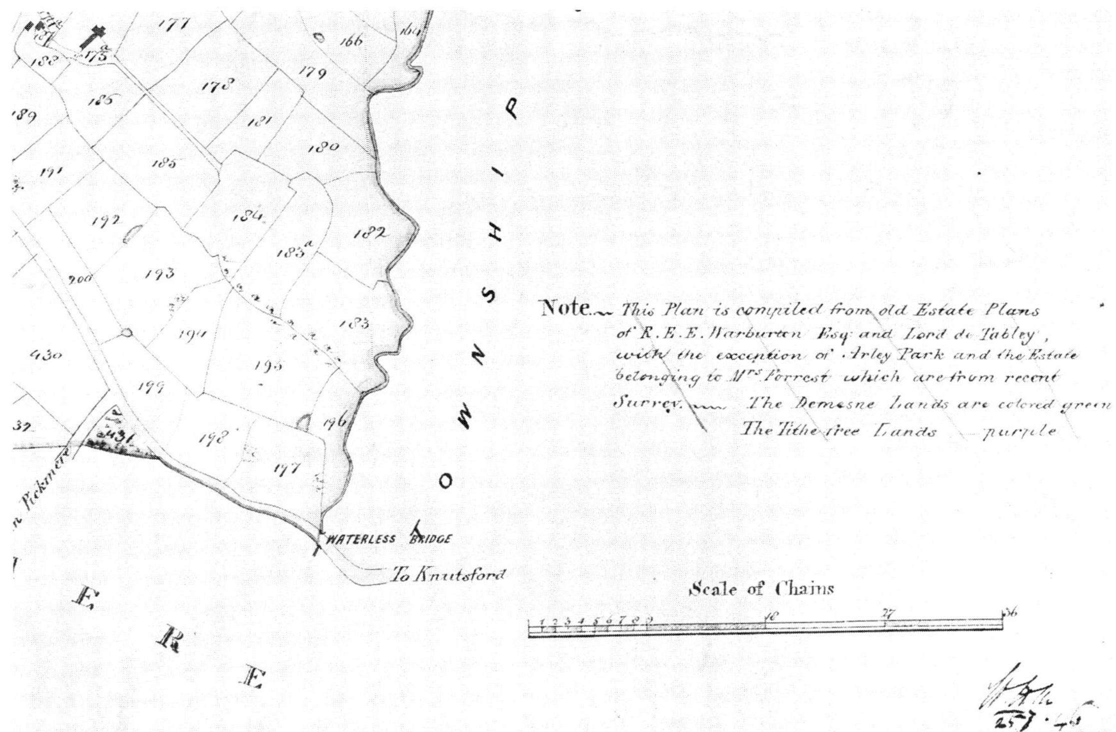

Fig. 72 Aston, Cheshire, 1846. Notes such as this which provide evidence of the provenance of the map data are the exception rather than the rule on tithe maps. Source: PRO IR30 5/25. Photograph reproduced by kind permission of the Keeper of the Public Record Office.

survey by replotting construction lines and measurements from the original field books, if still extant. Indeed, it is possible that a proportion of the 475 second-class maps with construction lines, maps presumably submitted for first-class testing, failed for this reason (Fig. 78). On the first-class map of Alkrington, Lancashire there is clear evidence of this as the surveyor notes, 'the trial lines were run in testing the accuracy of an existing plan and then formed the base lines of the new survey'. Equally, some 18 per cent of first-class tithe maps in the Public Record Office collection do not contain construction lines, though these must have been present on other copies of the maps for them to have been certified as first class.

Construction lines are almost invariably drawn in red but occasionally some or all are in blue. It is unusual for construction lines not to be annotated either with field-book page numbers or chain distances. Unfortunately the red ink in which these are written fades badly over time and it is not always possible to tell what these annotations represent. Occasionally first and second order triangulation stations are noted and very occasionally trigonometrical angles are given; the map of Orford, Suffolk, by Bland H. Galland is a particularly notable example of where this is done. Diagrams showing the layout of the main construction lines were not required but are occasionally found (Fig. 79); most of those on maps in the Public Record Office collection are the work of Thomas Thurston of Ashford, Kent (Figs. 80 and 81). Occasionally construction lines are annotated with

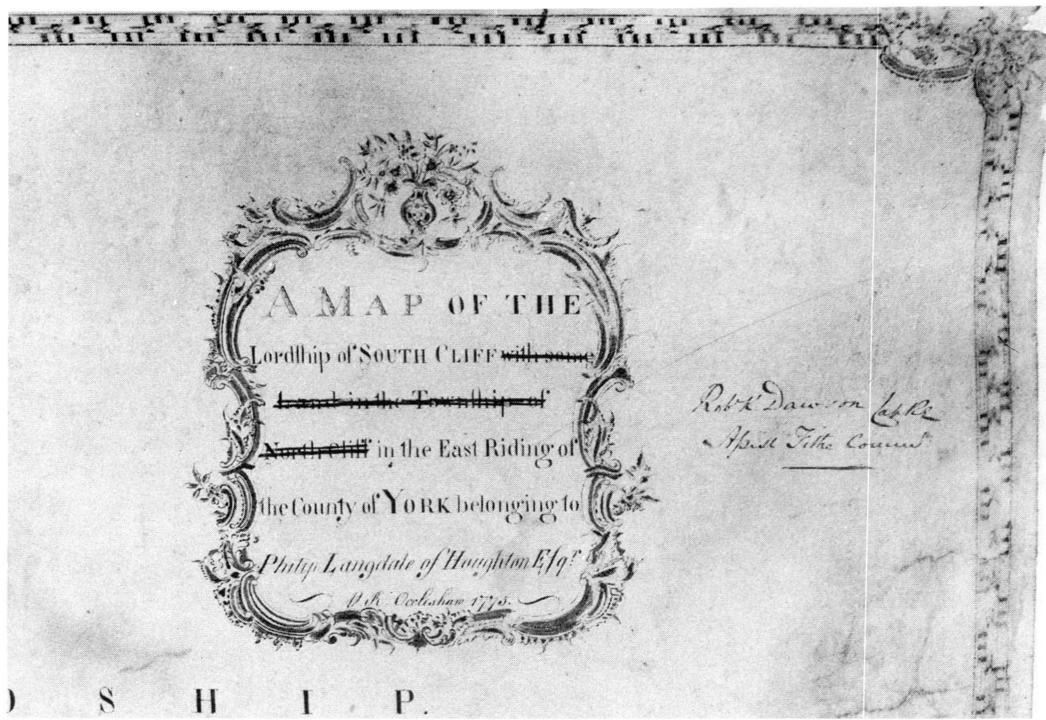

Fig. 73 South Cliffe, East Riding of Yorkshire, 1775. This is the oldest map adopted for tithe commutation in the Public Record Office collection, though it is known that other maps, such as that of Buslingthorpe in Lincolnshire (see Fig. 74) were redrawn from even earlier surveys. The decorated border and cartouche of this eighteenth-century map would be exceptional for a tithe map of the 1840s. Source: PRO IR30 41/49. Photograph reproduced by kind permission of the Keeper of the Public Record Office.

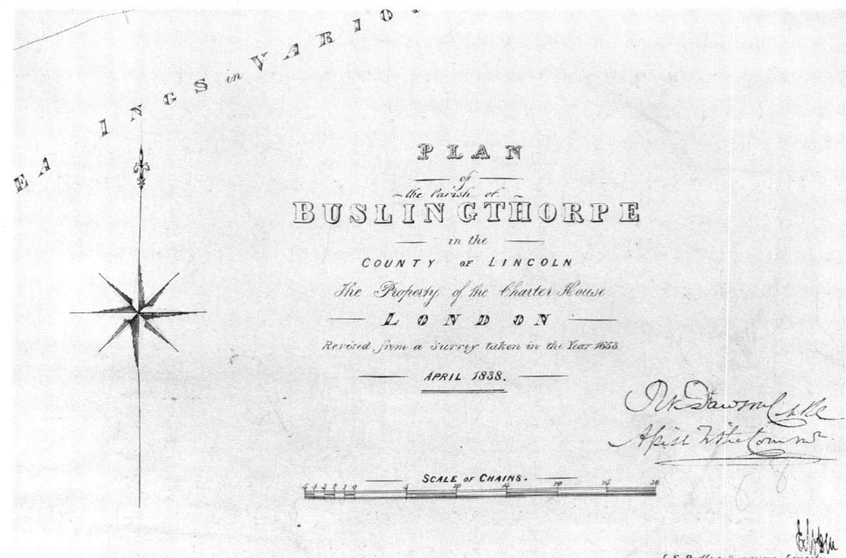

Fig. 74 Buslingthorpe, Lincolnshire, 1838. At first sight this is an unexceptional map but it is derived from the earliest survey (1653) acknowledged on any tithe map in the Public Record Office collection. Source: PRO IR30 20/69. Photograph reproduced by kind permission of the Keeper of the Public Record Office.

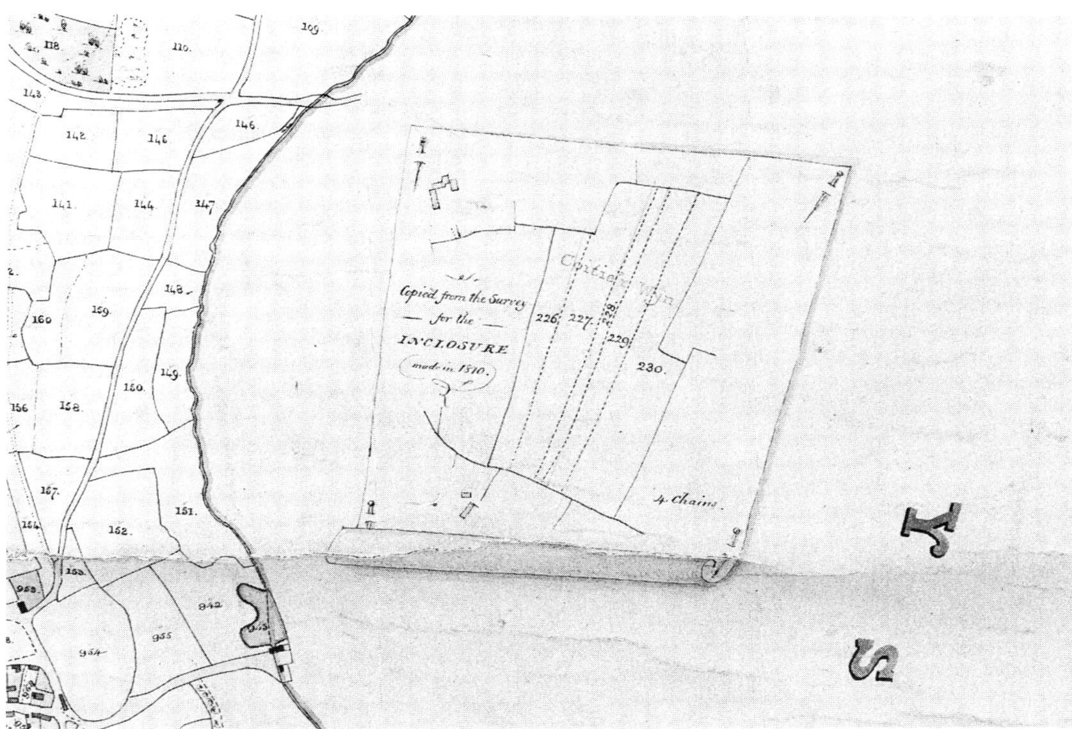

Fig. 75 Caerwys, Flintshire, 1849. Parliamentary enclosure was often accompanied by commutation of tithe and so it is unusual for a tithe map to derive, as does this one, from an enclosure map. Source: PRO IR30 50/7. Photograph reproduced by kind permission of the Keeper of the Public Record Office.

comments, as at Great Mongeham, Kent where the full extension of the lines was not carried out as it was considered too 'dangerous' (Fig. 82).

As the minimum acceptable scale for consideration for first-class status was one inch to 4 chains (1:3168) and as only 5,516 maps (47 per cent) are at this or larger scales, at least 53 per cent of tithe maps were presumably never intended to be other than second class (Figs. 83 and 84). At Holcomb Burnell in Devon, the despairing surveyor, Mr Philp of Exeter, appended a disclaimer to his map to the effect that, 'the Land which this Map represents is nothing scarcely but Hill and Dale, hence many of the lines will not prove to that degree of accuracy which they would if the ground was level'.

Map-makers

Although it is axiomatic that every map must have been made by someone, only 7,767 tithe maps in the Public Record Office collection (66 per cent) have either an explicit statement of authorship or sufficient clues to ascribe them with confidence to a particular map-maker. The pattern of attributed tithe maps varies widely, from over 93 per cent in Pembrokeshire, 89 per cent in Kent and 85 per cent in Cornwall and Devon to no more than 36 per cent in Rutland, 32 per cent in Flintshire and only 18 per cent in Merionethshire. One problem is that map-makers often signed their work in the margin where it is vulnerable to

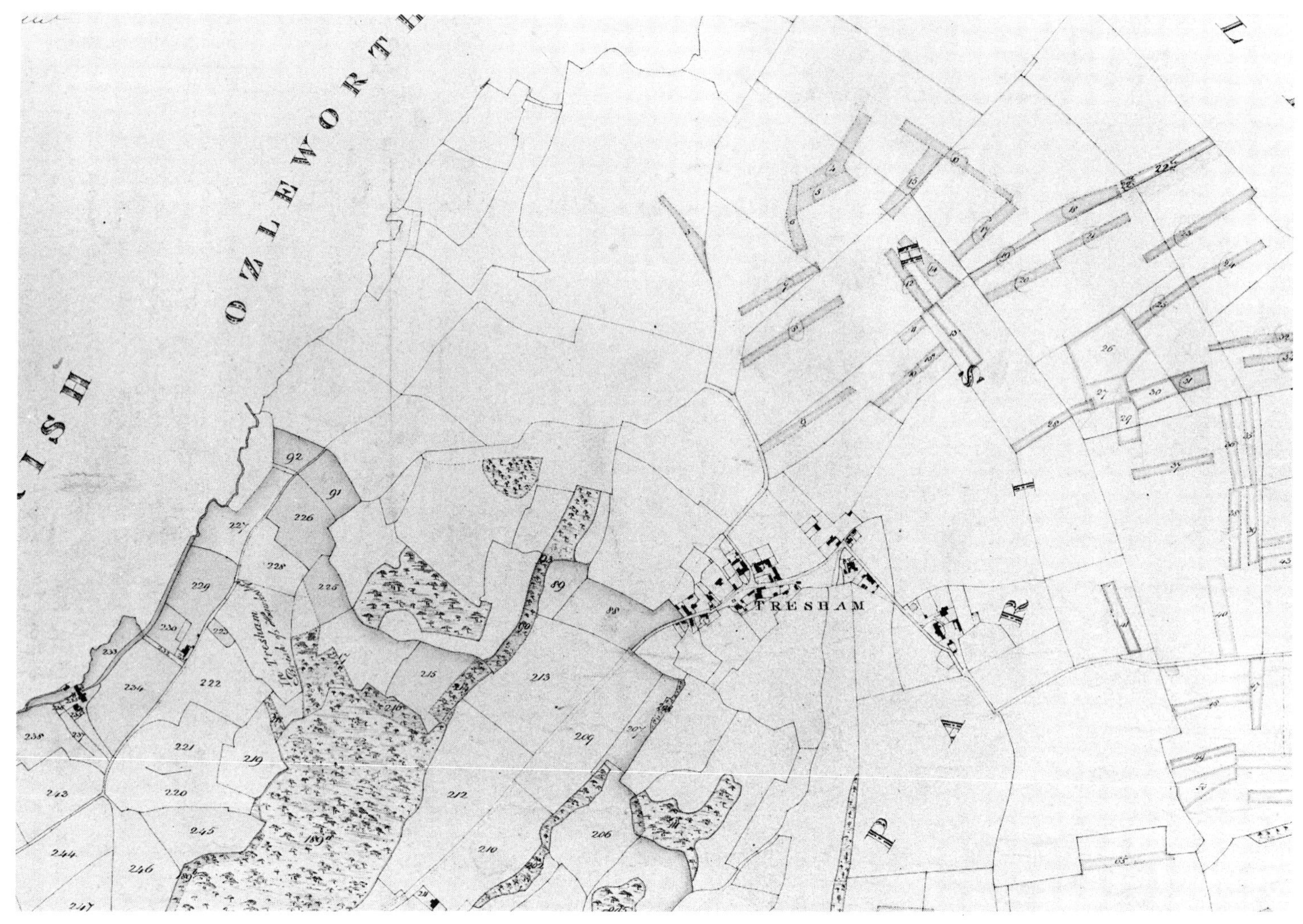

Fig. 76 Alderley, Gloucestershire, 1838. The intermixture of lands tithable to different districts often required skeletal mapping outside a district for locational purposes. Source: PRO IR30 13/4. Photograph reproduced by kind permission of the Keeper of the Public Record Office.

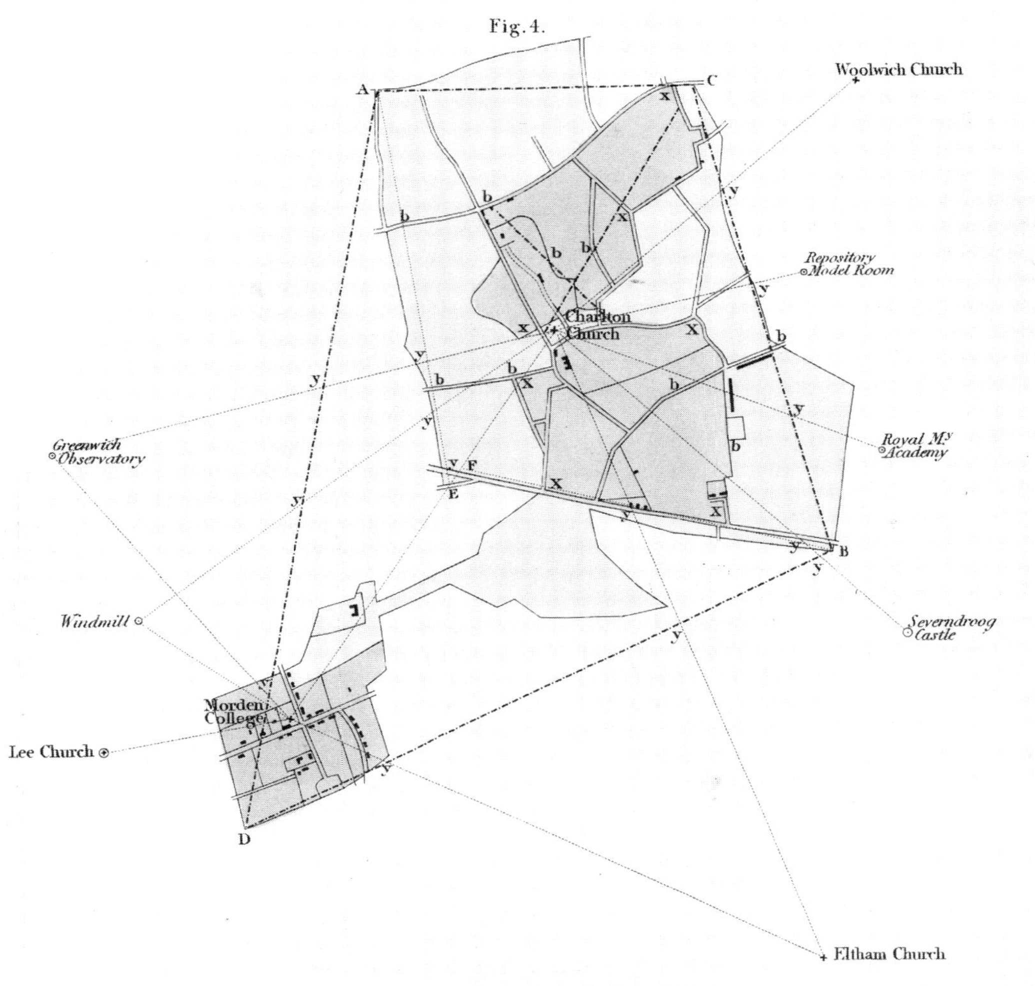

Fig. 77 R. K. Dawson's instructions for setting out tithe map construction lines. This is one of a number of recommendations that he made in his instructions for 'the preparation of plans for the purpose of the Tithe Commutation Act'. Source: 'Copy of papers respecting the proposed survey of lands under the Tithe Act', *British Parliamentary Papers (House of Commons)*, 1837, XLI.

cropping or flaking and there is no doubt that inspection of diocesan copies would enable more tithe maps to be attributed to a named map-maker. For example, Stuart Mason tells us that he has been able to identify the map-makers of a further forty-one Essex tithe maps by reference to diocesan copies in Essex Record Office.

A full list of tithe map-makers known from the Pubic Record Office collection of maps and a county-by-county summary of the work of each is set out in Appendix 3 and the work of the most prolific map-makers in England and Wales is summarised in Appendix 4. These appendices and Fig. 85 which plots the locations of all the tithe districts mapped by the more prolific tithe map-makers demonstrate that a majority of map-makers worked in

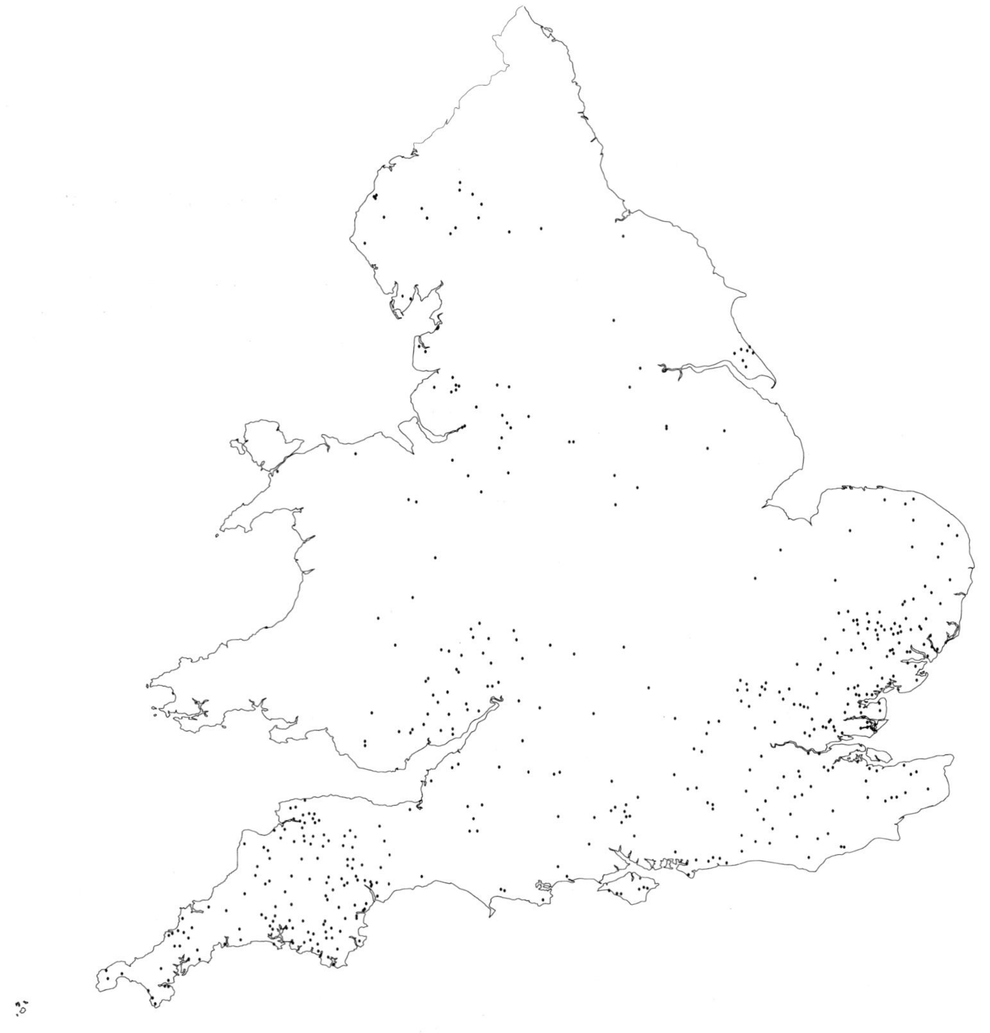

Fig. 78 England and Wales: second-class tithe maps with construction lines.

one county only, that very many made only one tithe map, and that only a small minority of map-makers worked in four or more counties.[11] It was exceptional for any one map-maker to produce many first-class maps.

Some men undertook both survey and valuation work but most first-class maps were made by men who did no tithe valuations and may be presumed to have been specialist land surveyors. Included among the specialists are men who had worked for the Ordnance Survey such as Alexander Doull, Bland H. Galland, John Haslam and John Hosmer.

In those parts of northern England where tithe commutation and the Ordnance Survey six-inch mapping proceeded contemporaneously, the Ordnance Survey was permitted to supply 1:2376 tithe surveys on a repayment basis when invited to do so by landowners.[12]

[11] Kain and Prince, *The tithe surveys of England and Wales*, pp. 56-61.

[12] See the papers in PRO WO 44/702.

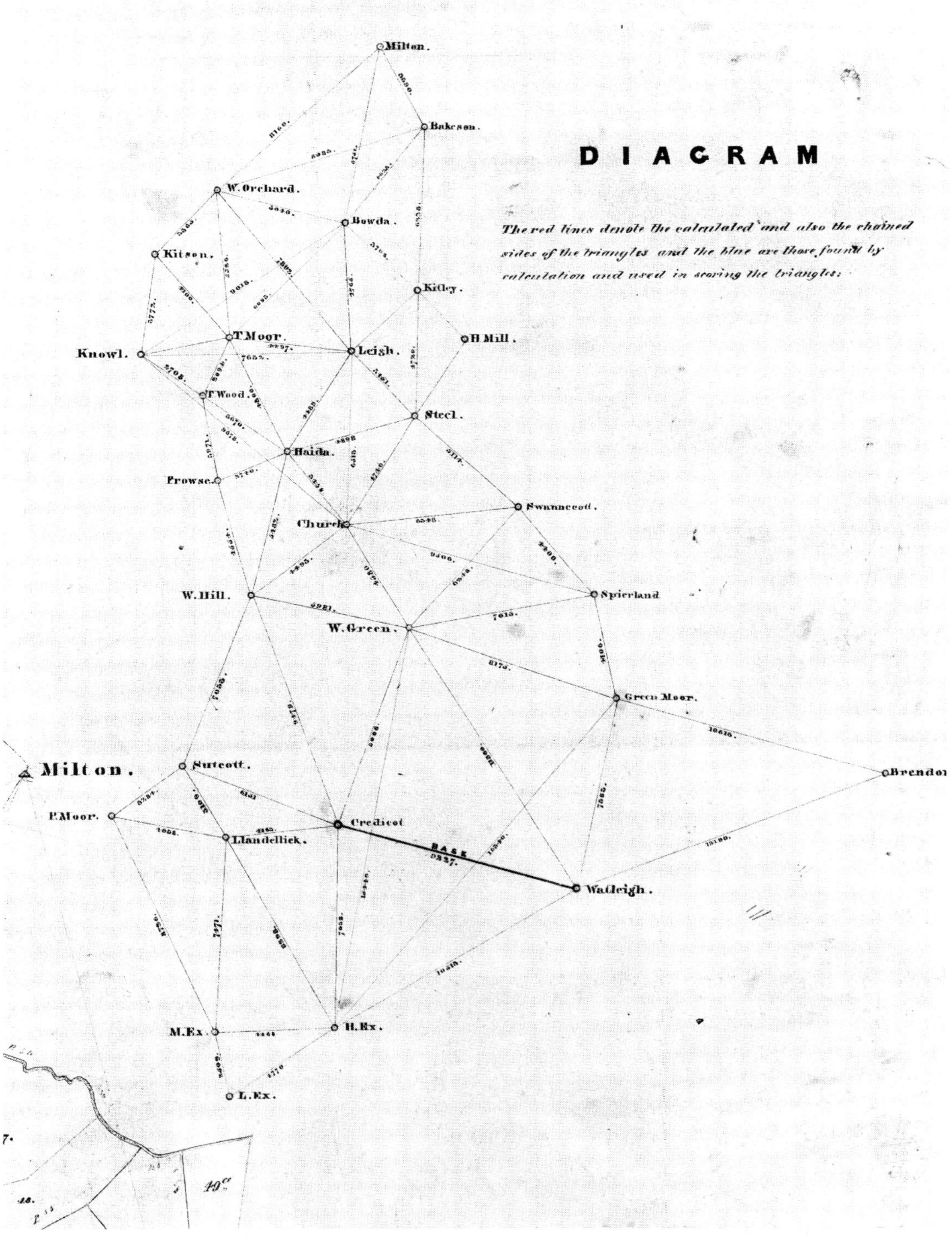

Fig. 79 Week St Mary, Cornwall, 1839. Construction line diagrams are not very common on first-class tithe maps. On the original from which this photograph is taken primary and secondary lines are distinguished by different colours. Source: PRO IR30 6/206. Photograph reproduced by kind permission of the Keeper of the Public Record Office.

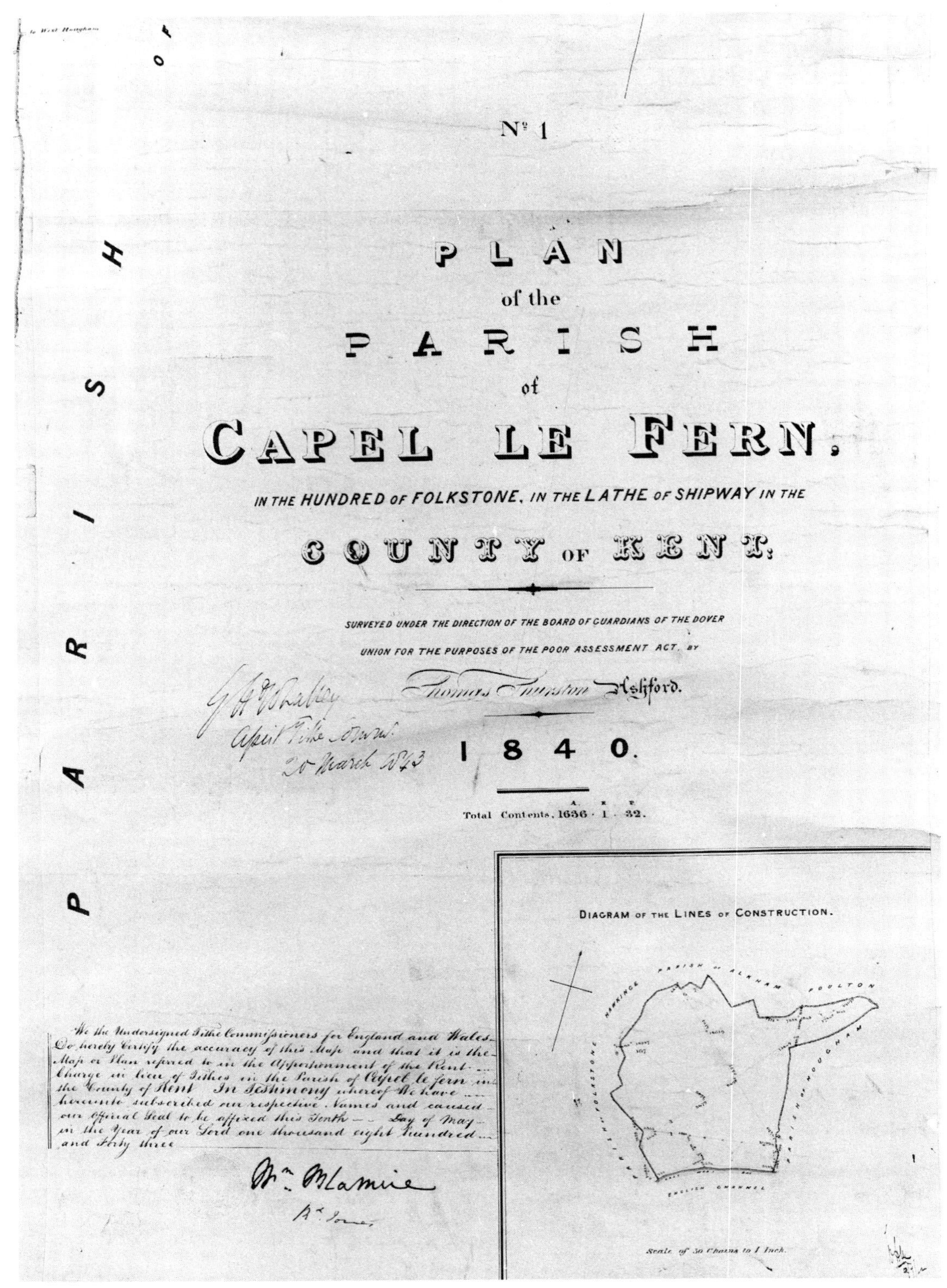

Fig. 80 Capel le Fern, Kent, 1840. This map has two unusual features: it carries a construction line diagram and it claims to be made for Poor Rate Assessment rather than for tithe purposes. It is likely that many more maps served such dual purposes. Source: PRO IR30 17/70. Photograph reproduced by kind permission of the Keeper of the Public Record Office.

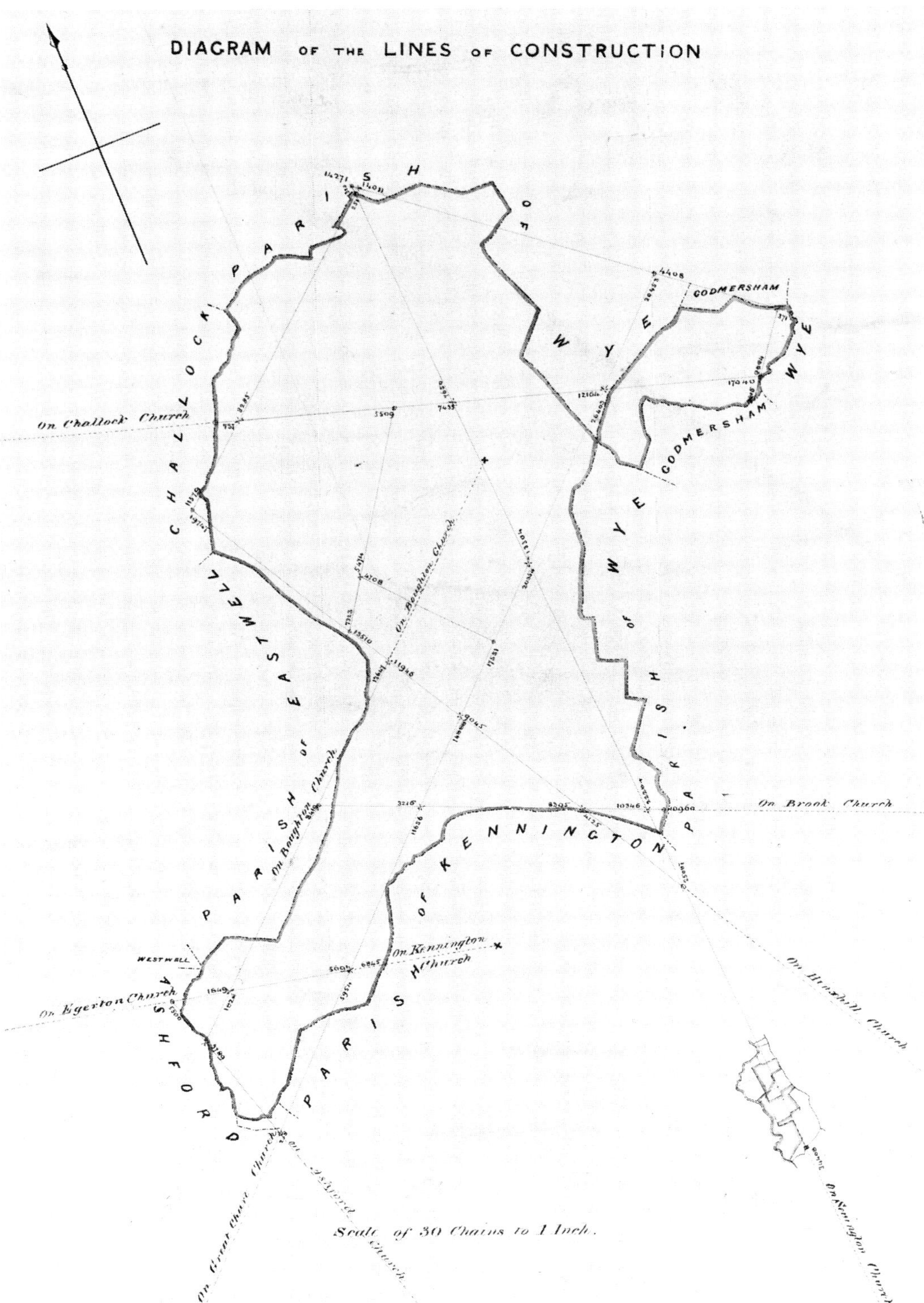

Fig. 81 Boughton Aluph, Kent, 1839. Most of Thomas Thurston's first-class maps include a construction line diagram. Source: PRO IR30 17/40. Photograph reproduced by kind permission of the Keeper of the Public Record Office.

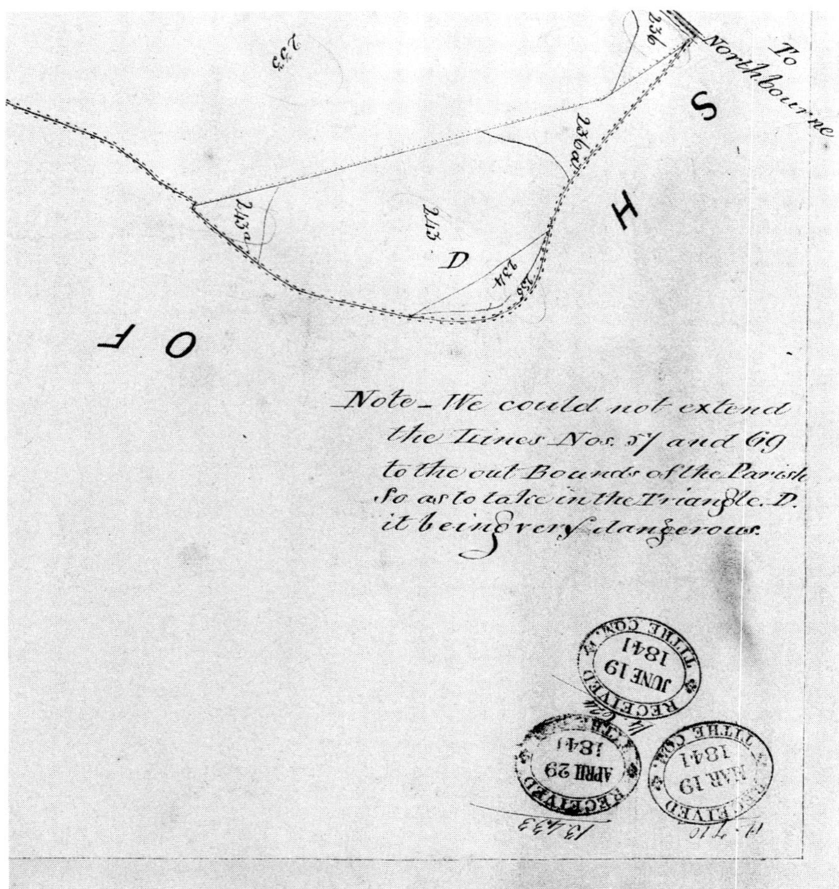

Fig. 82 Great Mongeham, Kent, *circa* 1841. It is not clear whether the 'danger' referred to here was a physical one on the ground or a technical one arising from survey procedure. Source: PRO IR30 17/256. Photograph reproduced by kind permission of the Keeper of the Public Record Office.

Some twenty-eight Lancashire and seven West Riding of Yorkshire tithe maps were produced in this way by the Ordnance Survey (Fig. 85). This was done by replotting at the larger one inch to three chains scale measurements originally made for published Ordnance Survey six inch to a mile maps. Ordnance Survey tithe maps lack the land-use information usual on the six-inch but sometimes include building projections and other minor details not found on Ordnance Survey maps published at the smaller scale. Ordnance Survey tithe maps were accepted as first class without testing. However, an Ordnance Survey map with unofficial annotations of Yealand Conyers, Lancashire on which a railway was added by an independent land surveyor and unofficial copies of Ordnance Survey six-inch mapping at Barton, Lancashire were designated second class (Figs. 86 and 87).

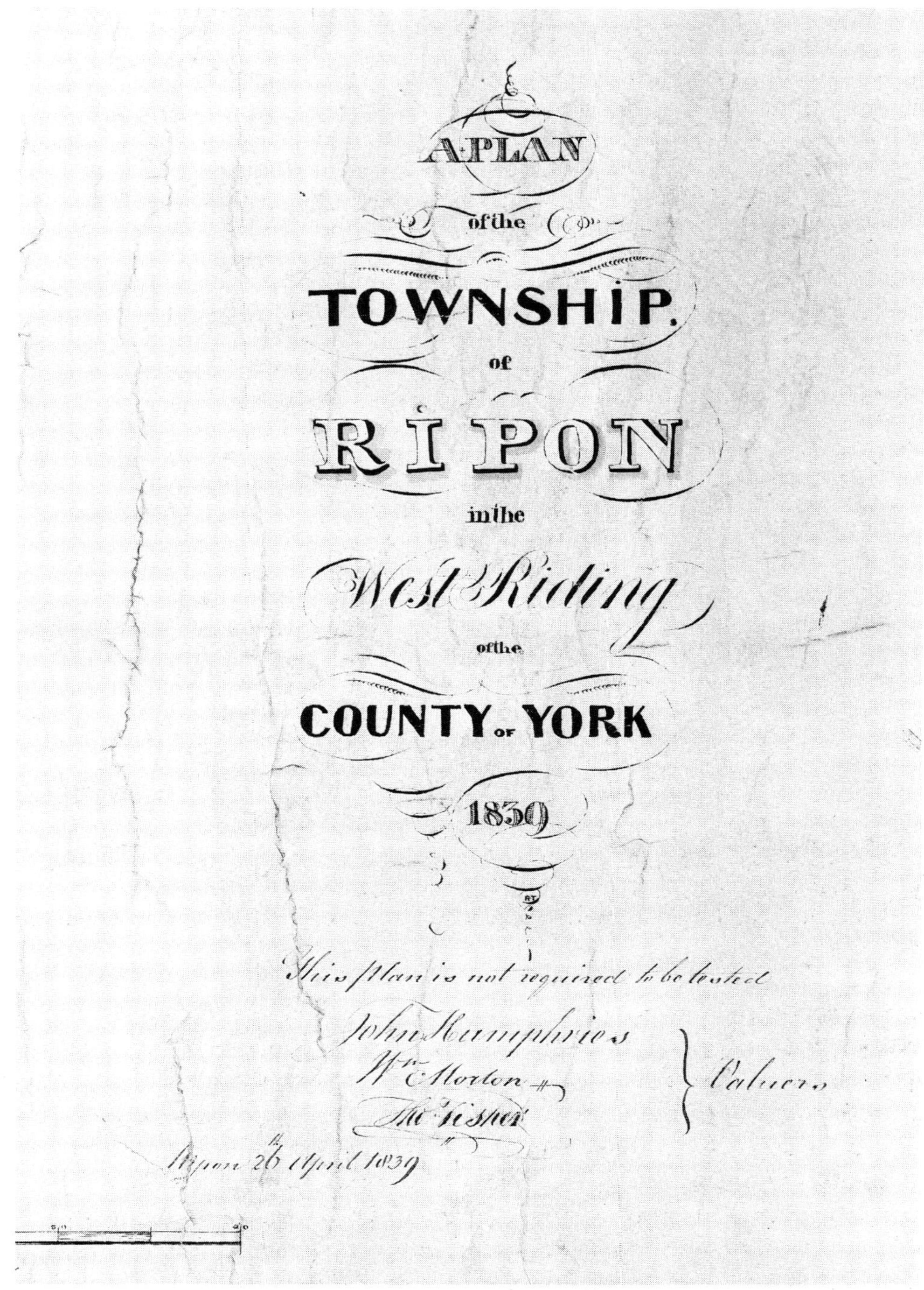

Fig. 83 Ripon, West Riding of Yorkshire, 1839. The statement 'this plan is not required to be tested' indicates that it was not intended to be first class. Source: PRO IR30 43/335. Photograph reproduced by kind permission of the Keeper of the Public Record Office.

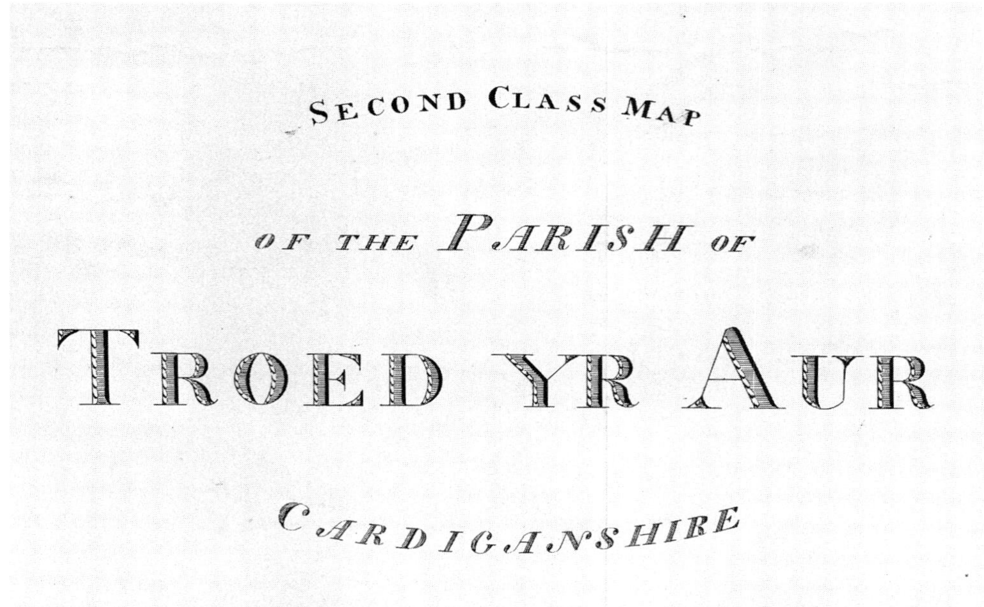

SECOND CLASS MAP
OF THE PARISH OF
TROED YR AUR
CARDIGANSHIRE

Fig. 84 Troed yr Aur, Cardiganshire, 1840. Landowners here had a clear view of the type of map with which they would be satisfied! Source: PRO IR30 46/73. Photograph reproduced by kind permission of the Keeper of the Public Record Office.

Tithe map scales

The overwhelming majority of tithe maps are drawn to scales clearly related to the Gunter's chain of 22 yards in length. The most commonly employed scales are one inch to three chains (1:2376) for 3,722 tithe maps (32 per cent), one inch to four chains (1:3168) for 1,614 tithe maps (14 per cent), one inch to six chains (1:4752) for 3,915 tithe maps (33 per cent), and one inch to eight chains (1:6336) for 1,197 tithe maps (10 per cent). The national distributions of maps drawn at these various scales are plotted on Figs. 88, 89, 90, and 91.

As a general rule counties outside Wales can be divided into those where the predominant scale is the three-chain and those where it is the six-chain. The latter are generally those counties where either much tithe had been commuted before 1836 in association with parliamentary enclosure, or those where the proportion of first-class maps is less than the national average. This generalisation is not seriously disturbed by local peculiarities, such as the use of the five-chain (1:3960) scale in parts of the Midlands or of a scale of one inch to three Cheshire chains of 32 yards (1:3485) for a few tithe maps of Cheshire and Lancashire. In central and northern Wales six-chain or smaller scales are more usual. One of the smallest scale of all tithe maps is that of Nant Glyn, Denbighshire at a scale of 26.67 chains to an inch (Fig. 92).

An advantage of using a larger scale is that it is possible to portray smaller enclosures more accurately but landowners may have feared that any increase in scale would result in a proportionate increase in cost. This was to some extent illusory, particularly if a wholly

Fig. 85 Tithe districts mapped by the Ordnance Survey and the most extensive private map-making practices. A Ordnance Survey; B John R. Haslam of Menai Bridge; C Harry Goode and Henry Philpott of Haverfordwest; D Thomas Thurston of Ashford in Kent; E Lenny and Croft of Bury St Edmunds; F Robert Pratt and Son of Norwich.

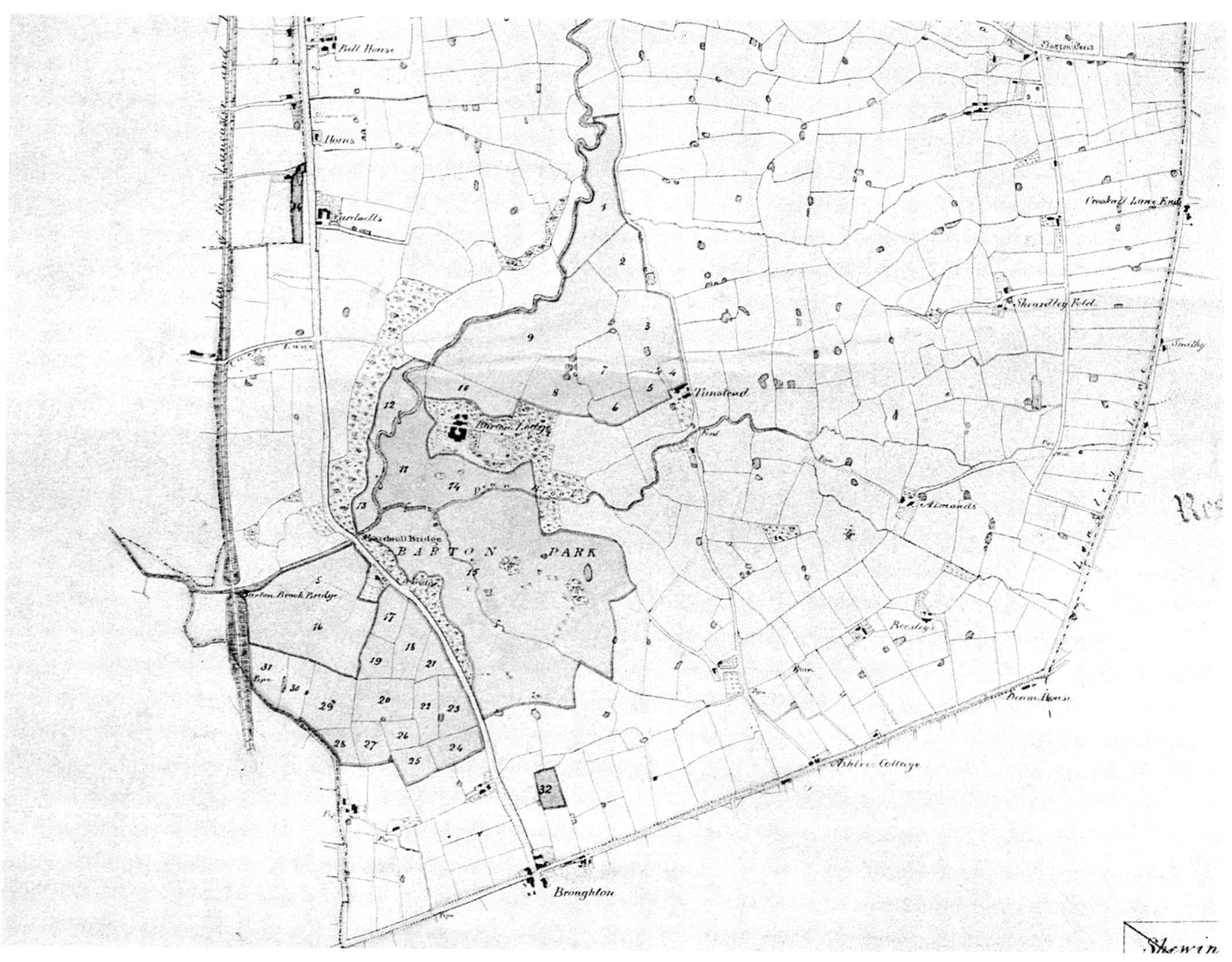

Fig. 86 Barton, Lancashire, 1847. Although it was often alleged at the time that in Lancashire tithe map-makers plagarised from the Ordnance Survey, examples of this practice are rarely encountered. Compare with Fig. 87. Source: PRO IR30 18/26. Photograph reproduced by kind permission of the Keeper of the Public Record Office.

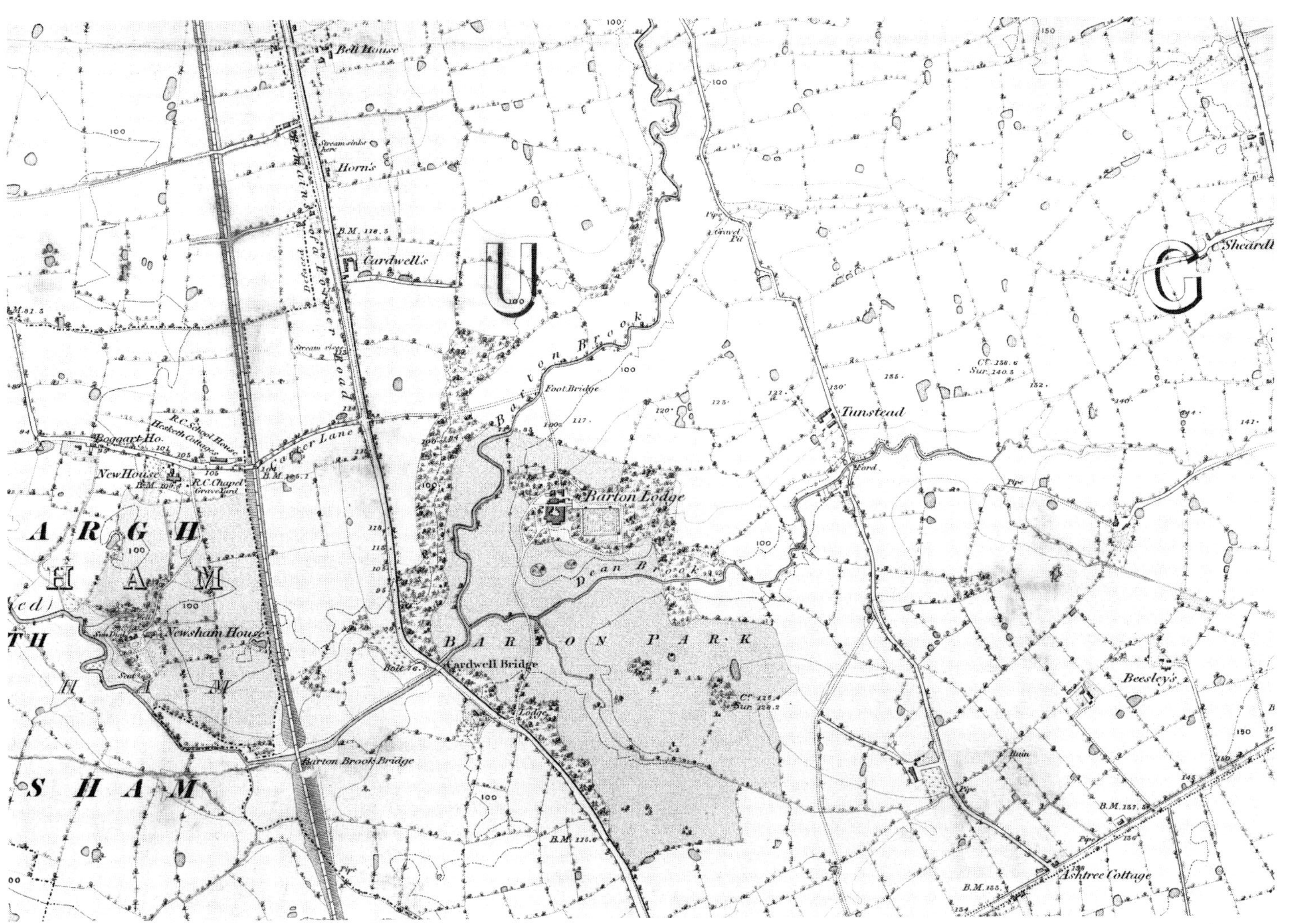

Fig. 87 Extract from Ordnance Survey six-inch map, Lancashire sheet 53, published 1848. Compare with Fig. 86. Source: authors' collection.

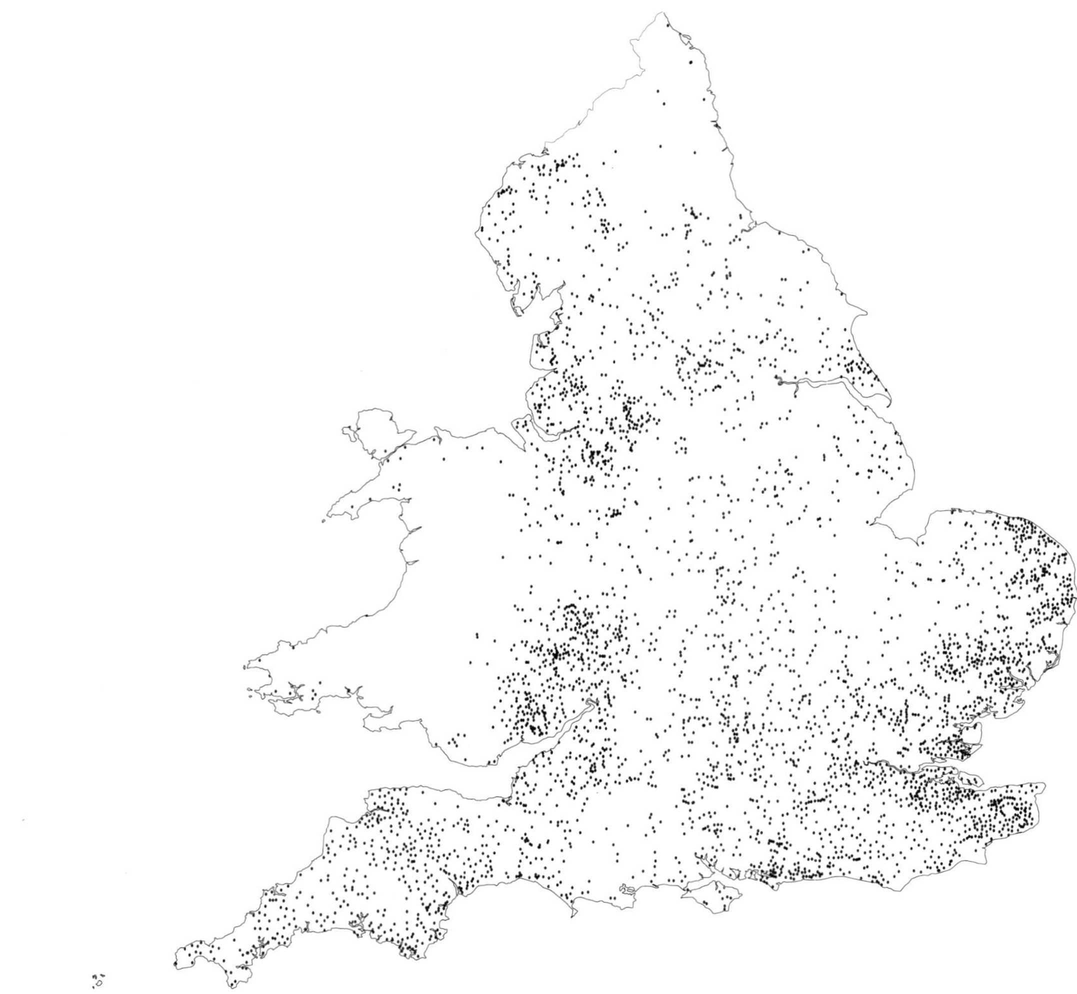

Fig. 88 England and Wales: tithe maps at a scale of one inch to three chains.

new survey was envisaged, as details such as field boundaries and buildings had to be recorded whatever the scale.[13] Use of a smaller scale was certainly more economical if an old map was being copied, as the length of linework to be copied increases as the square of the scale so that doubling the scale would entail four times as much line-drawing. One expedient commonly adopted was to draw the main map of a tithe district at a relatively small scale, say six chains to an inch, and then to provide enlargements of those parts where the cadastral pattern was complex. In tithe districts containing tithable built-up areas, the urban parts are often mapped separately at a larger scale than the main map. Sometimes the use of enlargements is so extensive that one questions whether it would not

[13] This was a powerful Ordnance Survey argument for the use of the 1:2500 rather than the 1:10,560 scale; see Richard Oliver, 'The Ordnance Survey in Great Britain, 1835-1870', Unpublished University of Sussex D.Phil. thesis, 1986, Chapter 5, and especially p. 209.

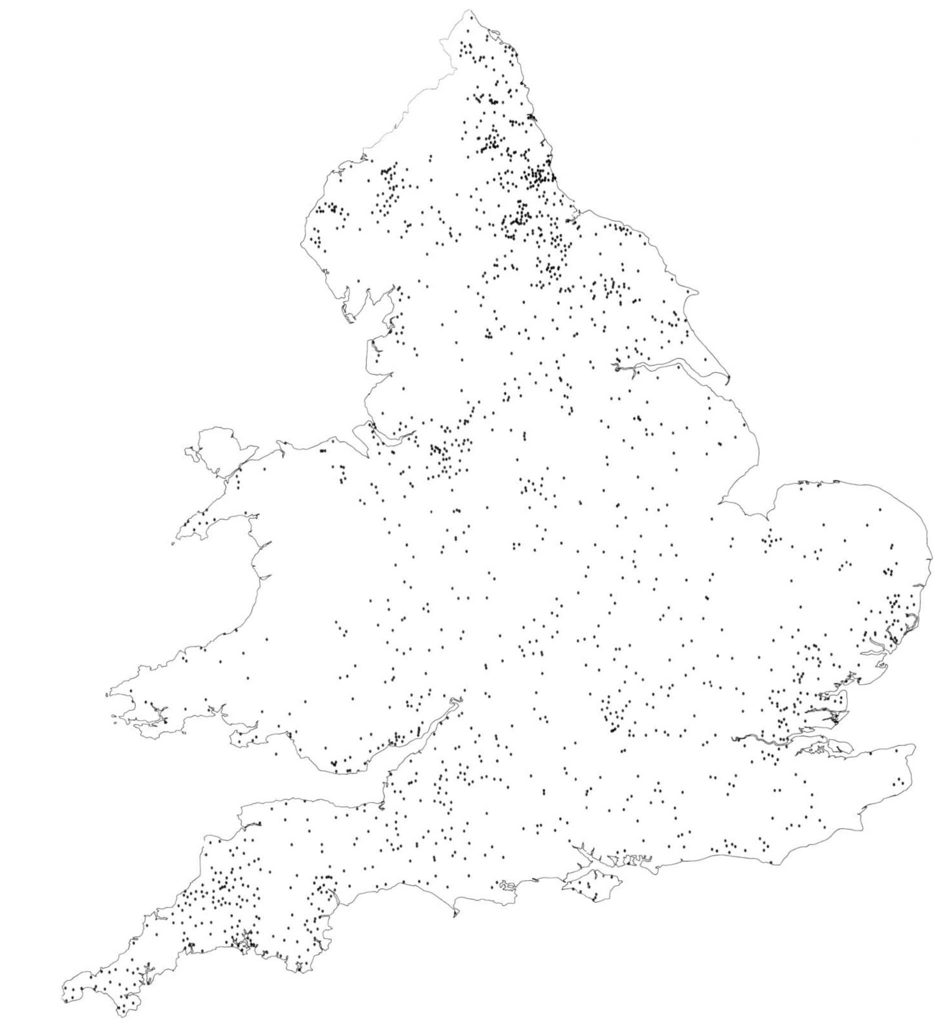

Fig. 89 England and Wales: tithe maps at a scale of one inch to four chains.

have been more judicious to use a larger scale in the first place. An extreme instance of this practice is afforded by the tithe map of Wiveliscombe, Somerset which is a six-chain main map supplemented by no fewer than forty enlargements of detail! A variation met with in districts where only small residual tracts of tithable land remained is the provision of a skeleton map of the whole district, often showing little more than the road network and perhaps the church, accompanied by enlargements of the few tithable lands.

The scale of a particular tithe map is usually indicated by a conventional scale bar, though occasionally the scale is stated in words only. Some maps have both scale bar and scale statement and some omit both; for all but three of these last a scale has been calculated for the county-by-county catalogue entries by comparison with other maps.[14]

[14] The exceptions are PRO IR30 36/27, 49/47 and 52/17, which are sketch maps not drawn to a consistent scale.

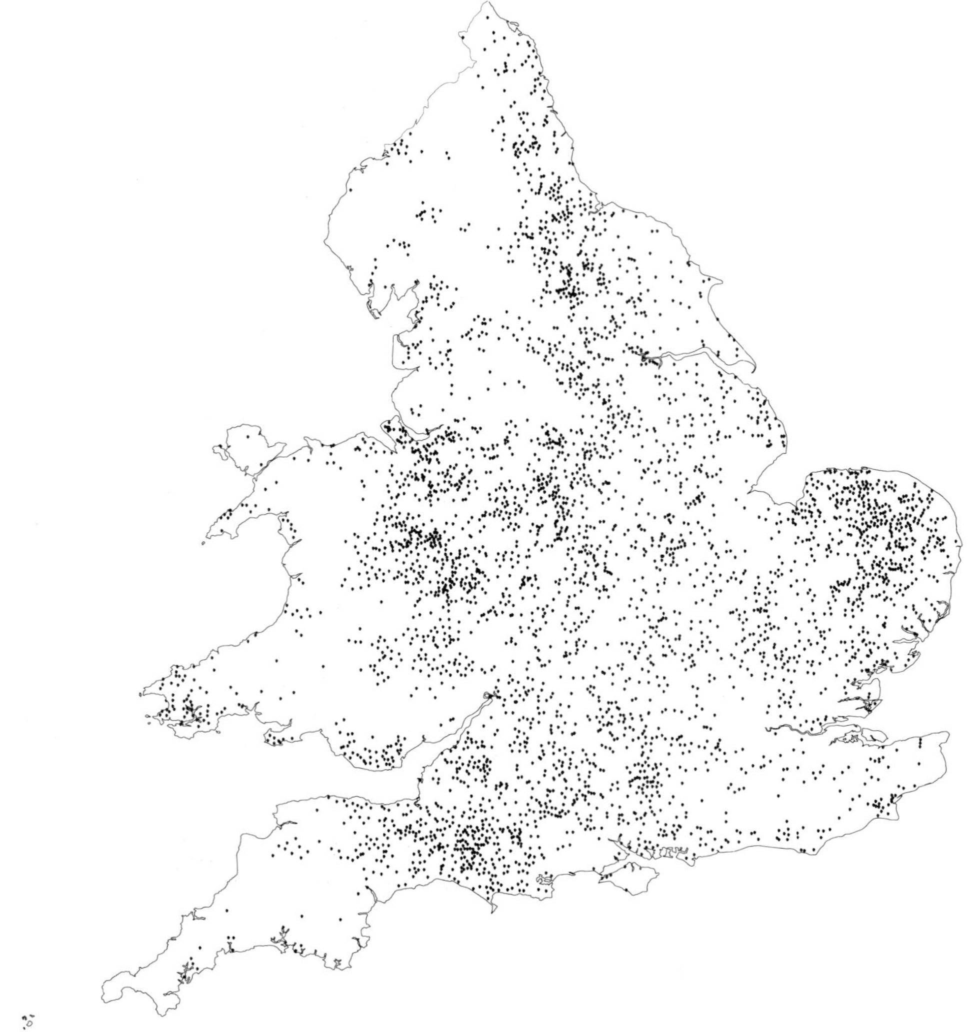

Fig. 90 England and Wales: tithe maps at a scale of one inch to six chains.

Manuscript and printed tithe maps

The overwhelming majority of tithe maps remain in manuscript; only 269 maps in the Public Record Office collection (fewer than 3 per cent) are printed. However, it is known that for a number of tithe districts the Public Record Office tithe map is in manuscript but the diocesan copy is printed and also that the Public Record Office holds both manuscript and printed maps of a few tithe districts (Figs. 93 and 94).[15] Most printed tithe maps are lithographed and most of these were undertaken by Standidge and Co. of 77 Cornhill, London, a leading firm of lithographers much employed for official work at this date. Some

[15] Kain and Wilmot, 'Tithe surveys in national and local archives', pp. 106-17. Where the Public Record Office holds both a manuscript and a printed map of a tithe district we count it as manuscript for statistical purposes.

Fig. 91 England and Wales: tithe maps at scales of one inch to eight chains and smaller scales.

lithography was undertaken by provincial firms and a few map-makers, notably Joseph Manning of Norwich and the partnership of Harry Goode and Henry Philpott of Haverfordwest, Pembrokeshire, offered a combined map-making and lithographing service. Lithographed tithe maps are found in most parts of the country (Fig. 95) but there are notable concentrations in Glamorganshire, Pembrokeshire, Somerset and Worcestershire (99 maps, or about 37 per cent).

There is no single explanation for the printing of this minority of tithe maps; the decision to print was made by local landowners moved by a variety of motives for wanting additional copies. As with printed tithe apportionments, useful comment is impeded by a lack of information as to the relative costs of copying by hand and by printing. In Ireland at about this time the Ordnance Survey considered it as cheap to produce six copies of a map

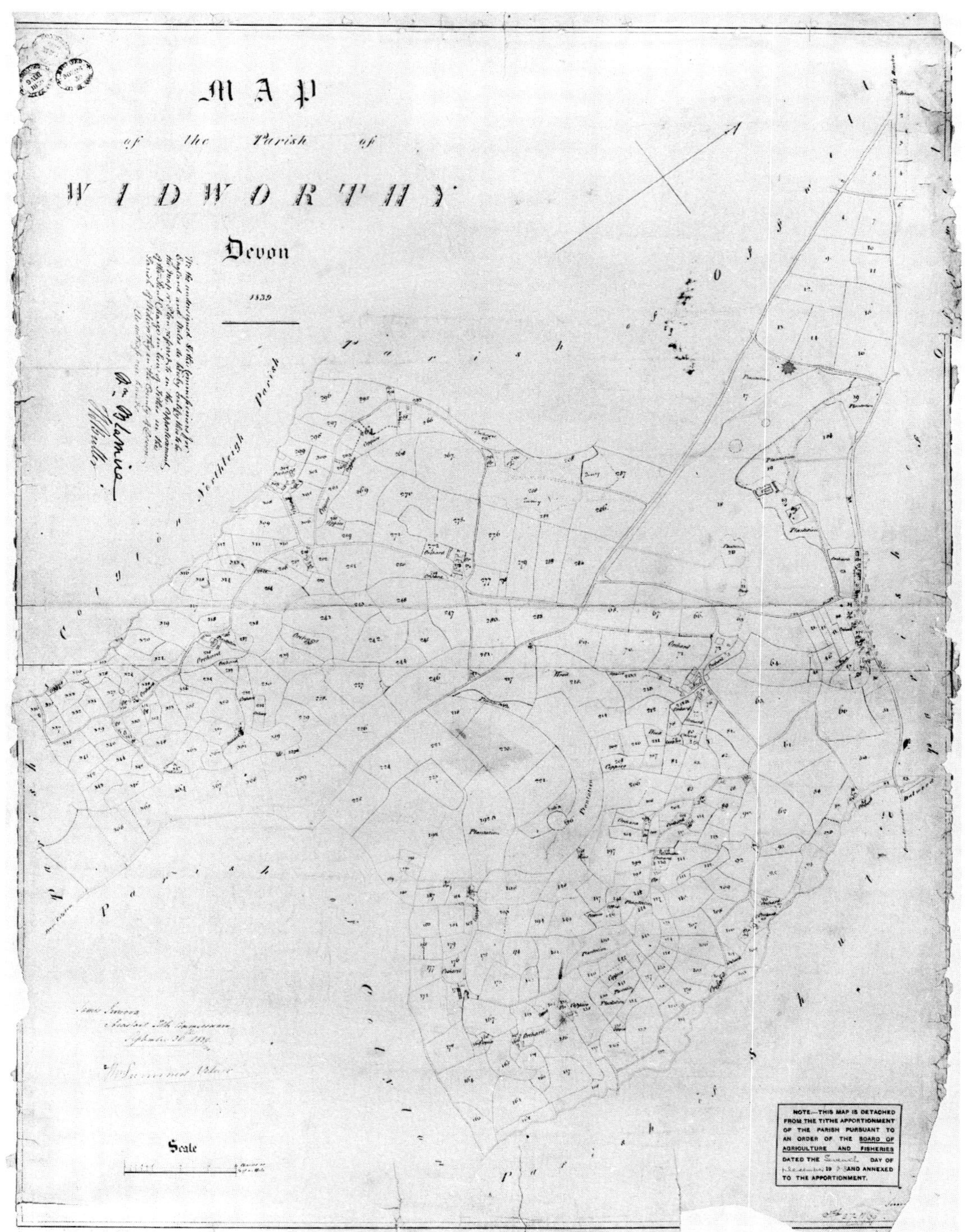

Fig. 92 Widworthy, Devon, 1839. There are two versions of this map in the Public Record Office collection: this one is in manuscript and woodland and orchards are indicated by annotation. Source: PRO IR30 9/450. Photograph reproduced by kind permission of the Keeper of the Public Record Office.

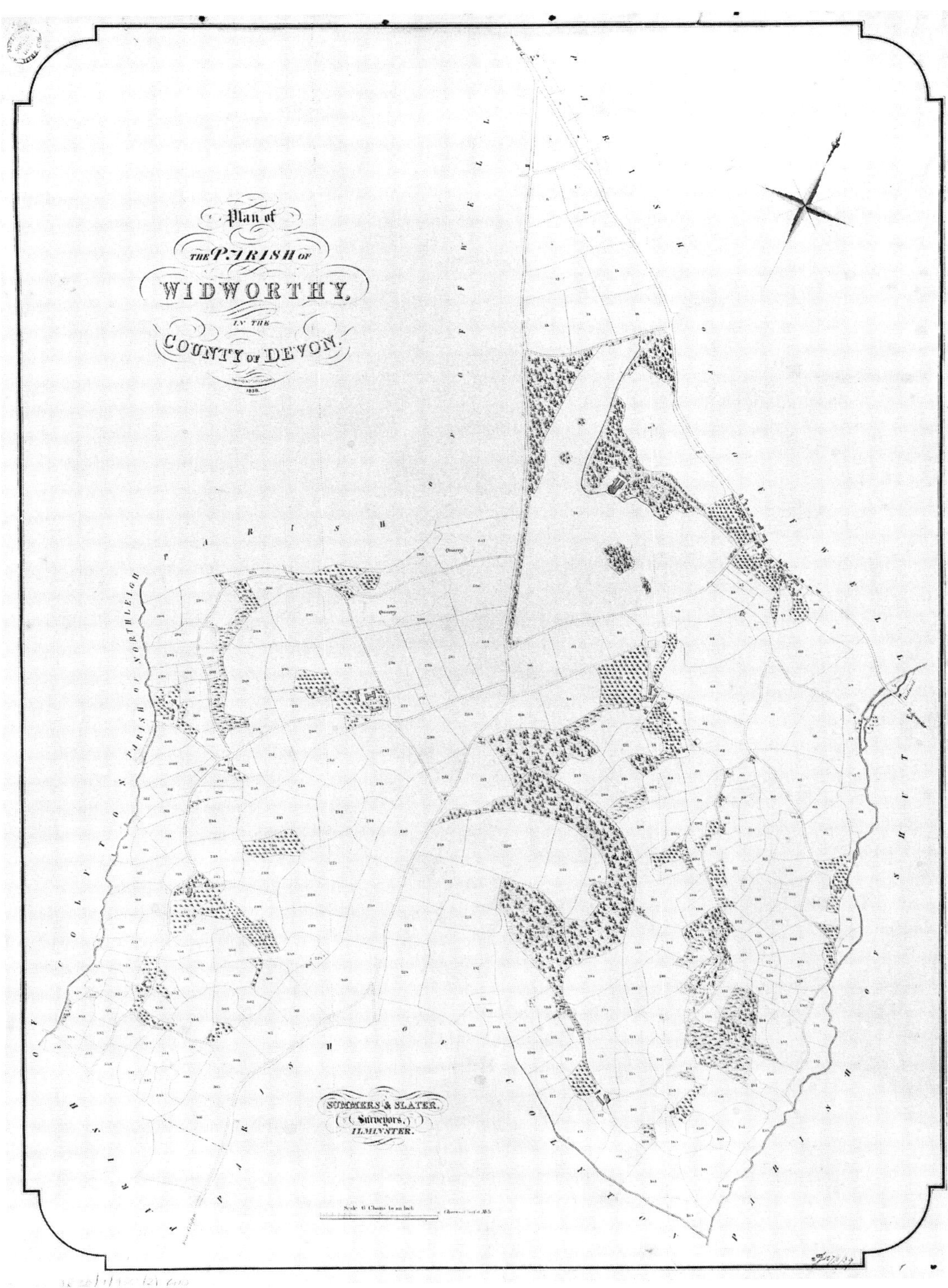

Fig. 93 Widworthy, Devon, 1839. This is a lithographed version of the map illustrated in Fig. 93. It was lithographed by Standidge and Co. of London and has this company's characteristic border with rounded corners. Source: PRO IR30 9/450. Photograph reproduced by kind permission of the Keeper of the Public Record Office.

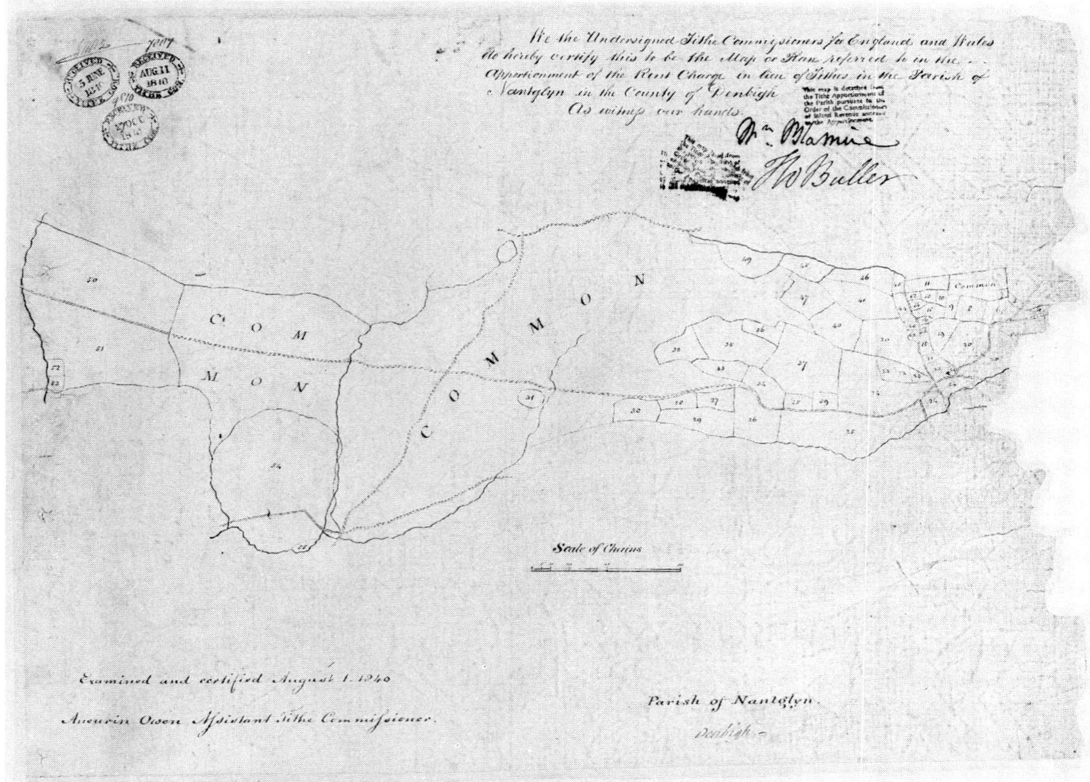

Fig. 94 Nantglyn, Denbighshire, 1840. This is one of the smallest tithe maps, both physically and in scale at one inch to 26.67 chains or 1:21,120. Source: PRO IR30 49/91. Photograph reproduced by kind permission of the Keeper of the Public Record Office.

by engraving on copper as by hand copying.[16] Engraving involved cutting the image into the printing surface and was a much slower process than lithography where the image was drawn on the printing surface, so it is possible that the economic calculation was finely balanced between hand copying and printing the necessary copies of a tithe map.[17] Occasionally landowners presented unaltered existing maps for tithe commutation such as that of South Cliffe in the East Riding of Yorkshire made in 1775 and in these cases lithography would have been a convenient way of producing the extra copies. Lithography could also be useful for making a copy at a smaller scale of an elaborate larger-scale map; it is known, for example, that the diocesan copy of the tithe map of Chirk, Denbighshire is of this type and there are other examples of this practice in Devon.[18] With only two exceptions, all lithographed tithe maps are second-class maps. In a very few instances an

[16] J. H. Andrews, *A paper landscape: the Ordnance Survey in nineteenth-century Ireland*, (Oxford, Oxford University Press, 1975), pp. 65-6.

[17] Some lithographed tithe maps may well have been printed in more than three copies; for example the Public Record Office has two copies of the lithographed map of Chaldon, Surrey, and there are multiple copies of several lithographed tithe maps in the Somerset Record Office. Some of these were formerly in collections of estate papers.

[18] Kain and Wilmot, 'Tithe surveys in national and local archives', p. 111.

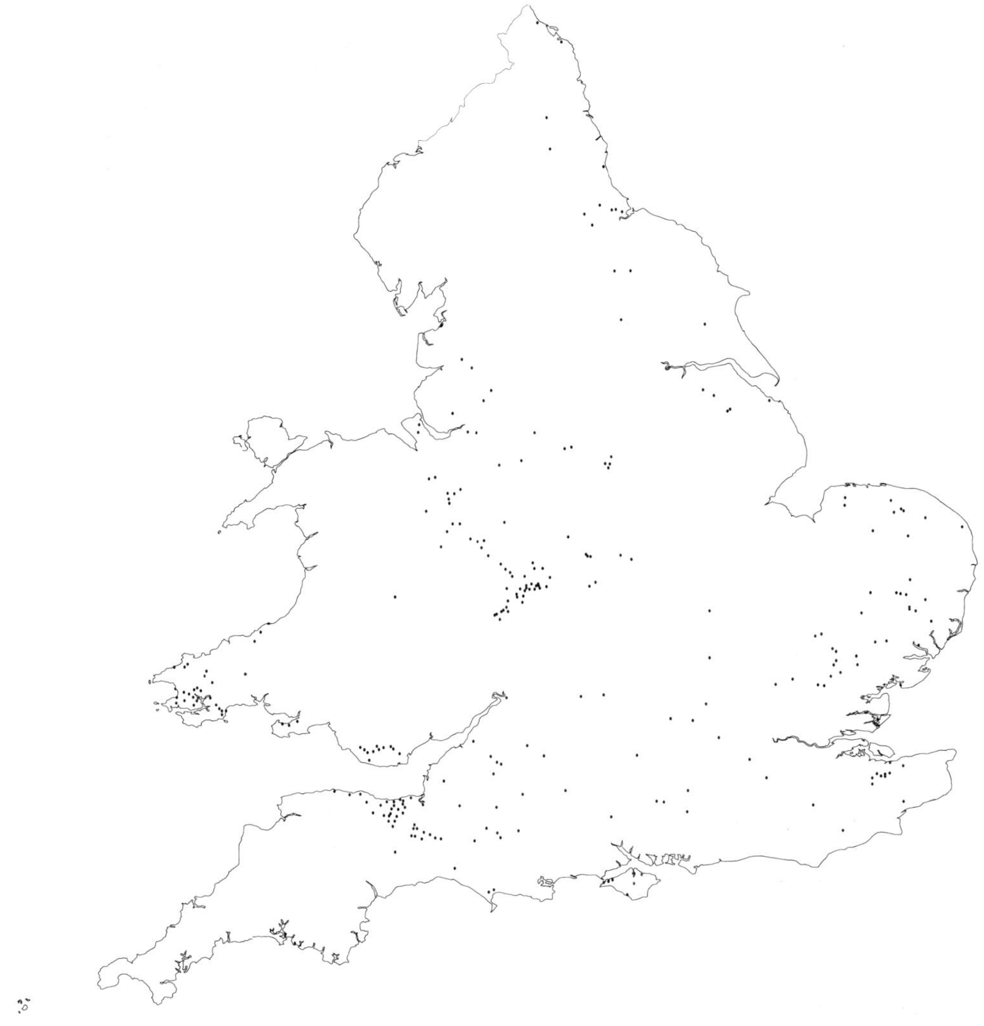

Fig. 95 England and Wales: lithographed tithe maps.

existing lithographed parish map was adopted for tithe commutation as at Polesworth in Warwickshire (Fig. 96).

Although most printed tithe maps were produced by lithography, a small number of Durham and Northumberland maps were engraved on copper. These are of townships owned by Greenwich Hospital Estates and map copies for tithe commutation purposes were presumably either taken from the estate stock, or printed specially.[19] Although the Ordnance Survey commenced publication of its six-inch mapping of Lancashire in 1846, the Public Record Office collection of tithe maps includes only one example of a published

[19] The maps were engraved by J. and C. Walker, a firm which, like Standidge, undertook extensive official work including the engraving of Admiralty charts. There are 'clean' copies of the Greenwich Hospital maps in PRO MPI 162.

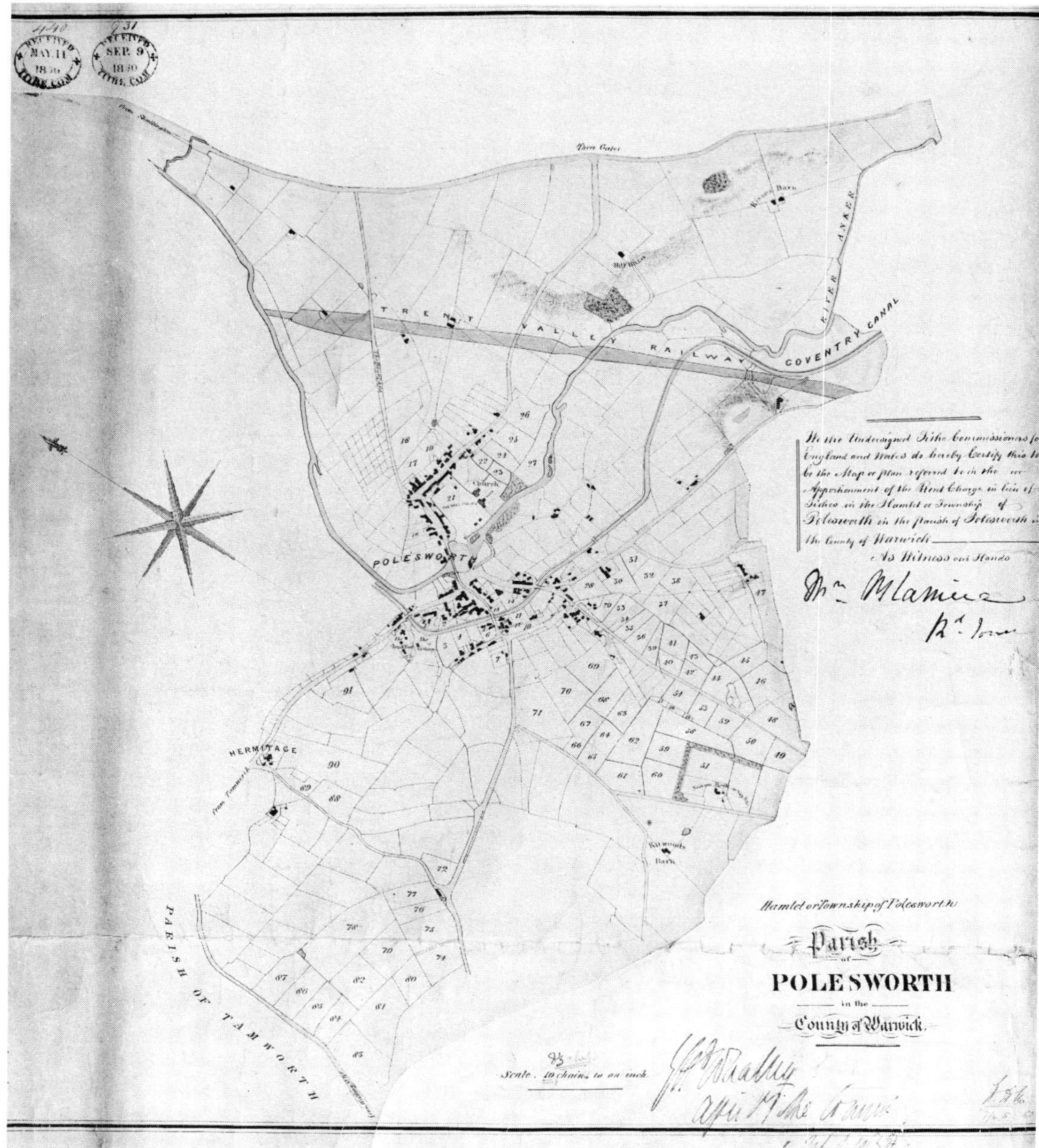

Fig. 96 Polesworth, Warwickshire, 1850. The 'tithe map' of this township is an extract from an existing lithographed map of the whole parish. Source: PRO IR30 36/114. Photograph reproduced by kind permission of the Keeper of the Public Record Office.

Ordnance Survey map adapted for tithe commutation purposes: that of the township of Little Bolton.

Allied to map printing is the use of mechanical aids for lettering and the use of pre-printed cartouches and scale bars. Stamped lettering, the use of individual letters set up in a hand-held stamp to provide an appearance very similar to letterpress, was employed

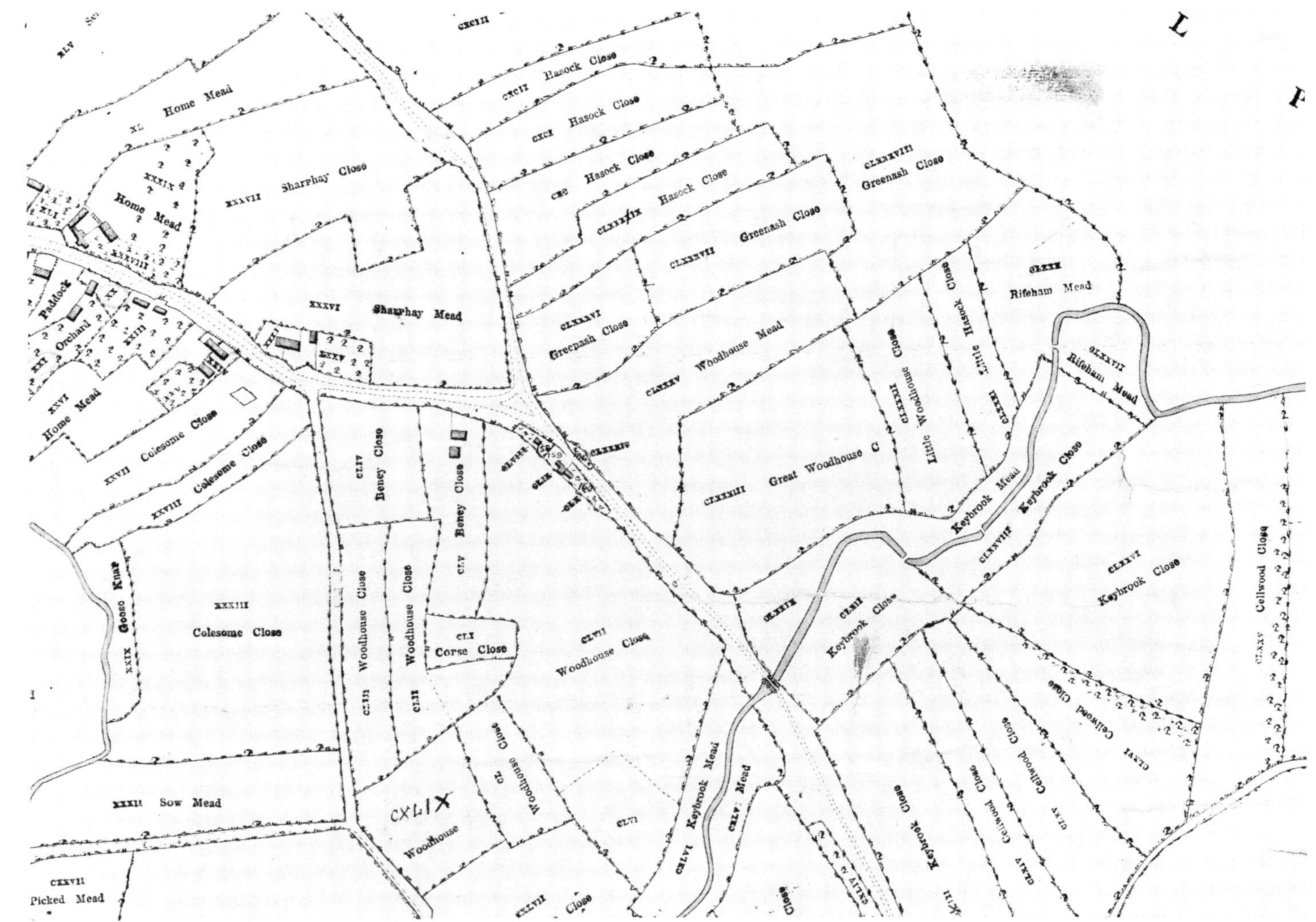

Fig. 97 West Orchard, Dorset, *circa* 1841. This map is unusual in that letters and figures have been stamped rather than written by hand. The use of Roman numerals is also very rare on tithe maps. Source: PRO IR30 10/160. Photograph reproduced by kind permission of the Keeper of the Public Record Office.

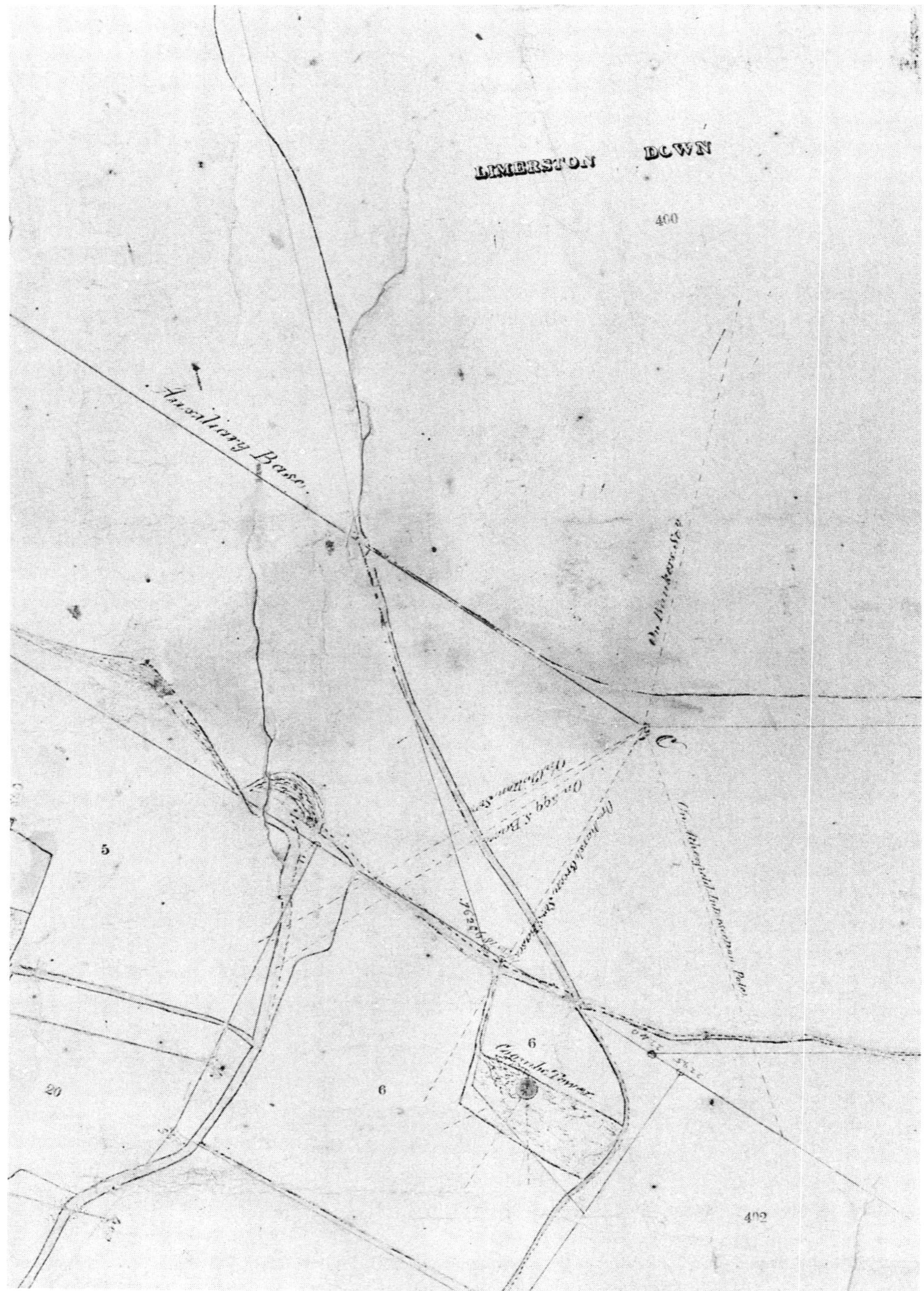

Fig. 98 Brighstone, Hampshire, 1840. On this map both the tithe area numbers and the notes on the construction lines are stamped rather than written. Source: PRO IR30 31/43. Photograph reproduced by kind permission of the Keeper of the Public Record Office.

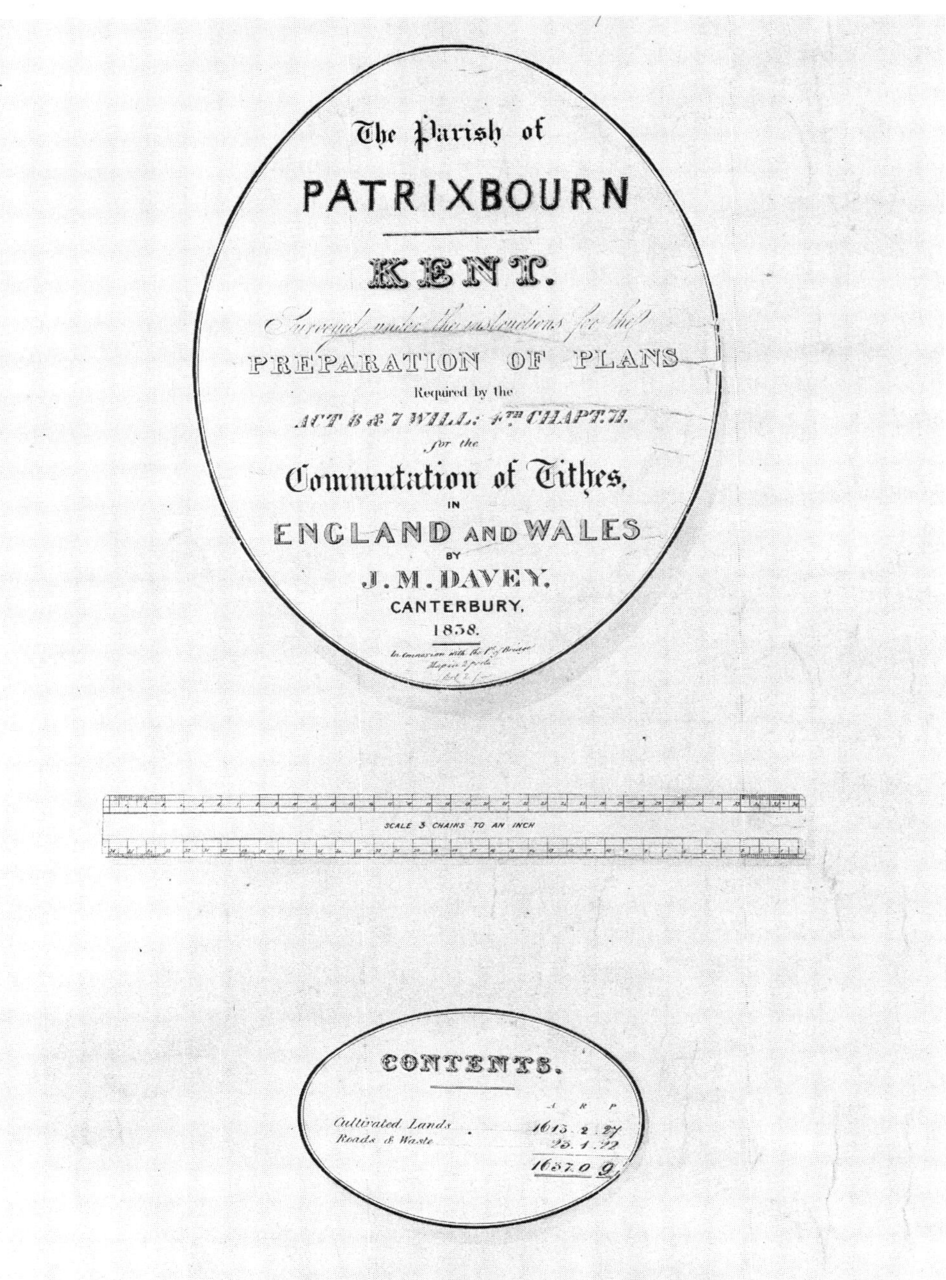

Fig. 99 Bridge and Patrixbourne, Kent, 1838. Few tithe map-makers used preprinted (lithographed) cartouches and scale bars; J. M. Davey of Canterbury was an exception. Source: PRO IR30 17/51. Photograph reproduced by kind permission of the Keeper of the Public Record Office.

by a few tithe map-makers, most notably the Badcocks of Launceston who worked extensively in Devon and Cornwall. Its use is unquestionably a matter of personal choice on the part of an individual map-maker (Figs. 97 and 98). The layout and the intensity of inking of letters is often uneven and this may explain why the method was eschewed by most tithe map-makers. No examples of stencil lettering have been found on a manuscript tithe map, though this technique may have been employed on lithographed maps.[20] Nor have we noticed any instances of the symbols representing land use or vegetation applied by mechanical aid.

A few map-makers did use pre-printed cartouches, notably J. M. Davey in Kent and Richard Birks in the West Riding of Yorkshire. Birks's have plain borders and typed lettering; Davey's are lithographed with somewhat extravagant handwritten lettering. He also used lithographed scale bars (Fig. 99).[21]

The chronology of tithe map production

Most of the tithe maps in the Public Record Office collection have a maker's date but a minority do not and these have been dated in our county-by-county catalogue from the Tithe Commission's receipt stamp. On forty-five maps this stamp is either missing or illegible and so no date can be ascribed. It is exceptional for the date on a map to be specified as that of survey (Fig. 100); in default of an explicit statement it is safest to assume that the dates cited are those of map drafting.

The peak period of tithe map production was in the two years of 1839 and 1840 when 3,682 tithe maps, a little less than a third of the total, were made. After 1840 output fell away steadily so that in the two years 1849 and 1850 only 668 tithe maps were produced, representing 6 per cent of the total by number but less than 4 per cent of the total mapped acreage of England and Wales. By the late 1840s, tithe commutation was complete in a number of counties and most of the remaining work was in districts where only a small amount of tithe remained to be commuted (Figs. 101, 102, 103, and 104). At the beginning of 1863 only five cases were still outstanding: these were Winteringham in Lincolnshire, where a long-running modus dispute was about to be settled; the tiny parish of Llangunnock, Monmouthshire which was overlooked until 1864; Hutton in Lancashire where problems in effecting mergers delayed commutation until 1874; Moulton in Lincolnshire where disputed tithable status of some reclaimed land was complicated by parish boundary uncertainties eventually resolved by a private Act of Parliament so that commutation could be completed in 1880; and a district in Hemingstone parish in Suffolk tithable to Barham which was the last commutation of all in 1883, and which appears to

[20] It may be noted parenthetically that the Ordnance Survey adopted stamped lettering for manuscript plans in the early 1850s but from 1855 until the late 1880s it preferred to use stencilled lettering for printed 1:2500 plans. There was still prejudice against the use of mechanical as opposed to hand-lettering for the best-quality work well into the twentieth century: see H. S. L. Winterbotham, *A key to maps*, (London and Glasgow, Blackie, 1936), pp. 78 and 194. It may also be noted that the numerous altered tithe apportionment maps of the second half of the nineteenth century which appear to have been drawn 'in-house' by the Tithe Commissioners all use hand-lettering.

[21] Pre-printed cartouches were extensively used in Ireland in the eighteenth century; see J. H. Andrews, *Plantation acres*, (Ulster Historical Foundation, 1985), pp. 153-4.

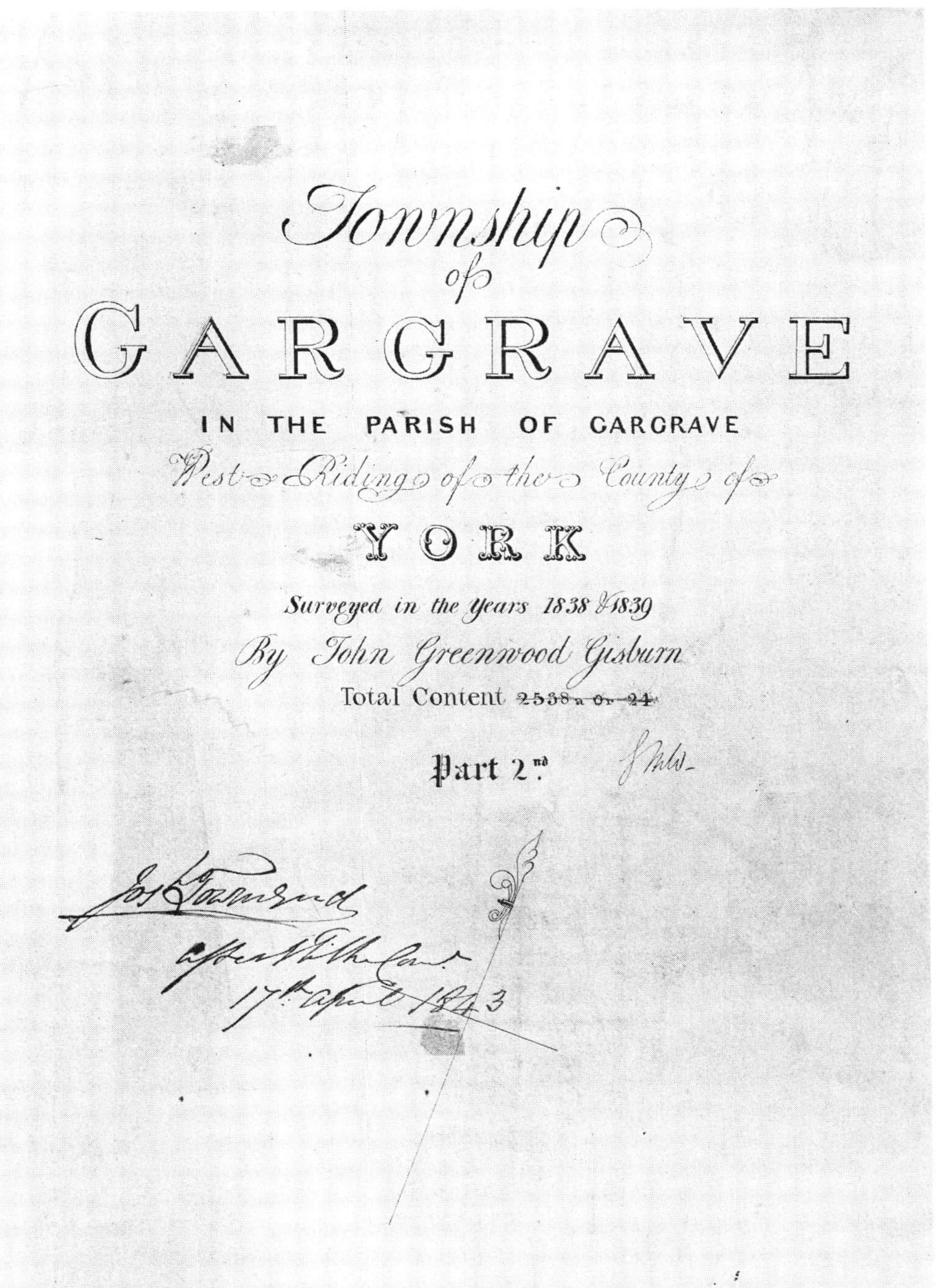

Fig. 100 Gargrave, West Riding of Yorkshire, 1839. It is unusual for tithe maps to state the year(s) in which they were surveyed. Source: PRO IR30 43/165. Photograph reproduced by kind permission of the Keeper of the Public Record Office.

Fig. 101 England and Wales: tithe maps dated 1836-39.

have been overlooked because the Hemingstone tithes were commuted only after those of Barham.[22]

Topographic content of the tithe surveys

Public boundaries

One of the more conspicuous attributes of large-scale Ordnance Survey maps is the careful mapping of public boundaries. Boundary mapping is less obvious on the tithe surveys

[22] See respectively, PRO IR18 5418, 5617, 4113 (though the documents which would probably explain the delay have been weeded from this tithe file), 5415, and 9567 (Barham), 9785 (Hemingstone), and 9786 (Hemingstone, lands tithable to Barham). Unfortunately the last-named file, which might once have contained an explanation of this delay, has been heavily weeded.

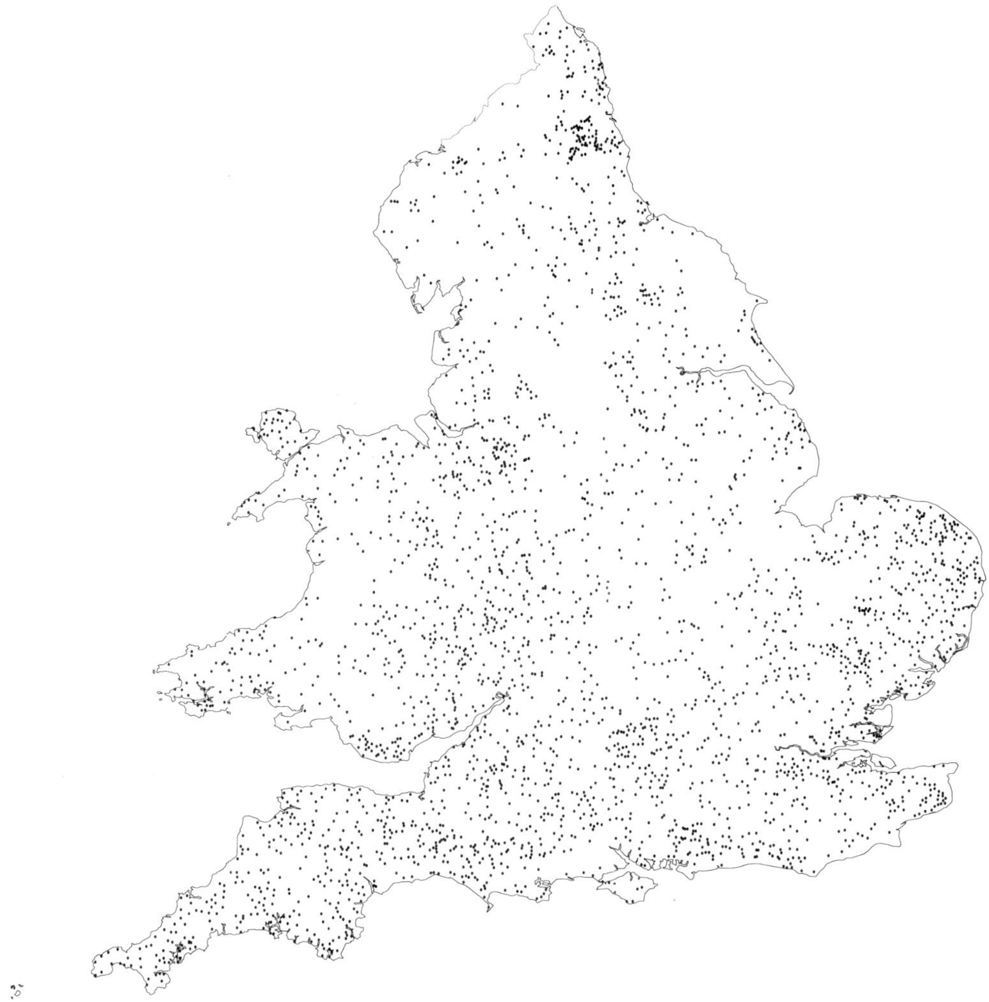

Fig. 102 England and Wales: tithe maps dated 1840-41.

because most tithe districts were single parishes or single townships and so the contribution of the tithe surveys to the national boundary archive is liable to be underestimated. In fact the determination of the outer boundaries of tithe districts was as important as determining the boundaries between tithe areas and a useful by-product of tithe commutation is the mapping of parish and township boundaries (see Appendix 2). In about 180 cases the Tithe Commission was required to intervene to resolve boundary disputes and subsequently the Ordnance Survey made extensive use of tithe maps when preparing its own boundary mapping.[23] Mere trees, boundary stones and other inorganic markers along tithe district boundaries are sometimes shown on tithe maps; the methods used are variously pictorial, symbolic, or by location dot and name.

[23] Sir Henry James (ed.), *Account of the methods and processes . . . of the Ordnance Survey* (London, HMSO, 1875), p. 40.

Fig. 103 England and Wales: tithe maps dated 1842-45.

Roads

As a general rule all roads are shown on tithe maps where they run across or form the boundary of tithable land, although there are occasional exceptions. For example, the tithe map of Warlingham cum Chelsham in Surrey omits a number of public roads and paths which re-appear on the tithe maps of adjoining districts.

Turnpike roads are distinguished on 907 tithe maps, 8 per cent of the total. The proportions are notably above the average in Cheshire, Derbyshire, Durham, Herefordshire, Lancashire, Monmouthshire, Staffordshire, Worcestershire and the West Riding of Yorkshire, which may be partly attributable to the greater density of turnpike roads in the industrialised parts of most of these counties. Turnpike roads are generally indicated on tithe maps either by name or by identification of toll gates; it is rare for turnpikes to be

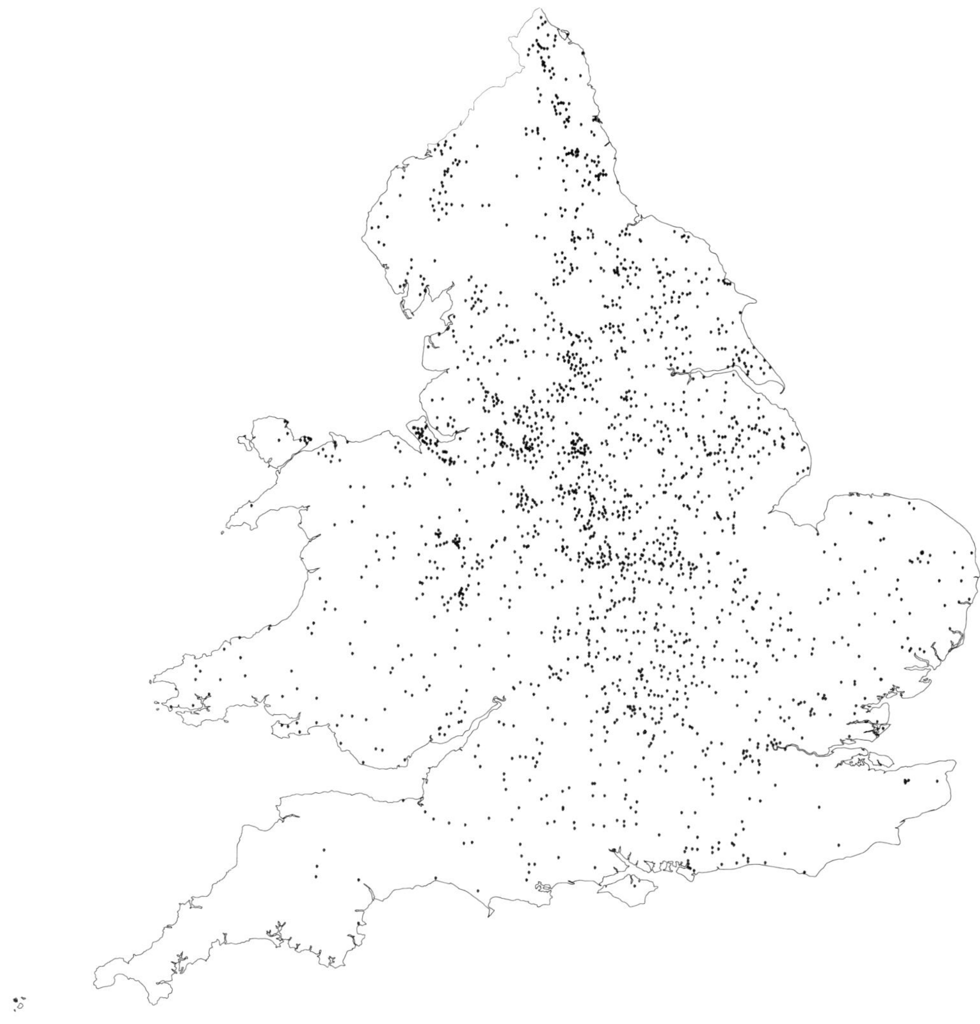

Fig. 104 England and Wales: tithe maps dated 1846-83.

shown by boldened road casing and very rare for distinctive colouring to be employed.

It is very unusual for rights of way to be unequivocally indicated on tithe maps (Figs. 105 and 106); most rights of way which are specified correlate with the practices of individual map-makers, for example Thomas Thurston in Kent (Fig. 107). Also unusual is indication of former rights of way, such as the annotation: 'Site of an ancient Public Carriage Way, Stopped by Order of Magistrates, Confirmed at the General Quarter Sessions', on the map of Statfold, Staffordshire.

The portrayal of roads on tithe maps can be understood only by reference to the prime purpose of the maps themselves. The direct and immediate purpose of tithe maps was to serve as an official record of the boundaries of all *tithe areas* (usually fields or other similar land parcels) on which tithe rent-charge was apportioned in the schedule of tithe apportionment. The portrayal of roads is one matter that is incidental to this prime

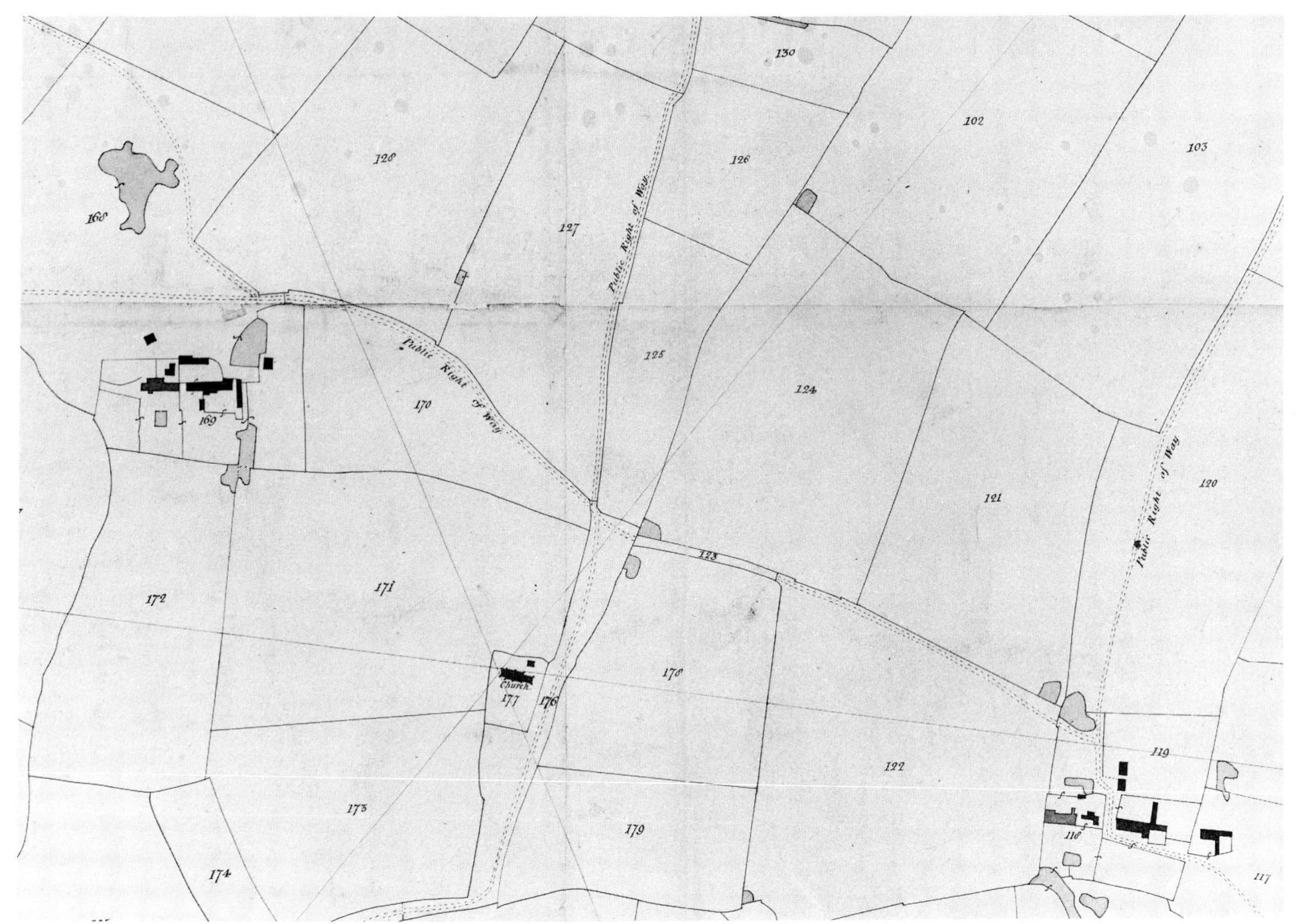

Fig. 105 Linstead Magna, Suffolk, 1842. A detailed record of rights of way as on this map, is exceptional. Source: PRO IR30 33/273. Photograph reproduced by kind permission of the Keeper of the Public Record Office.

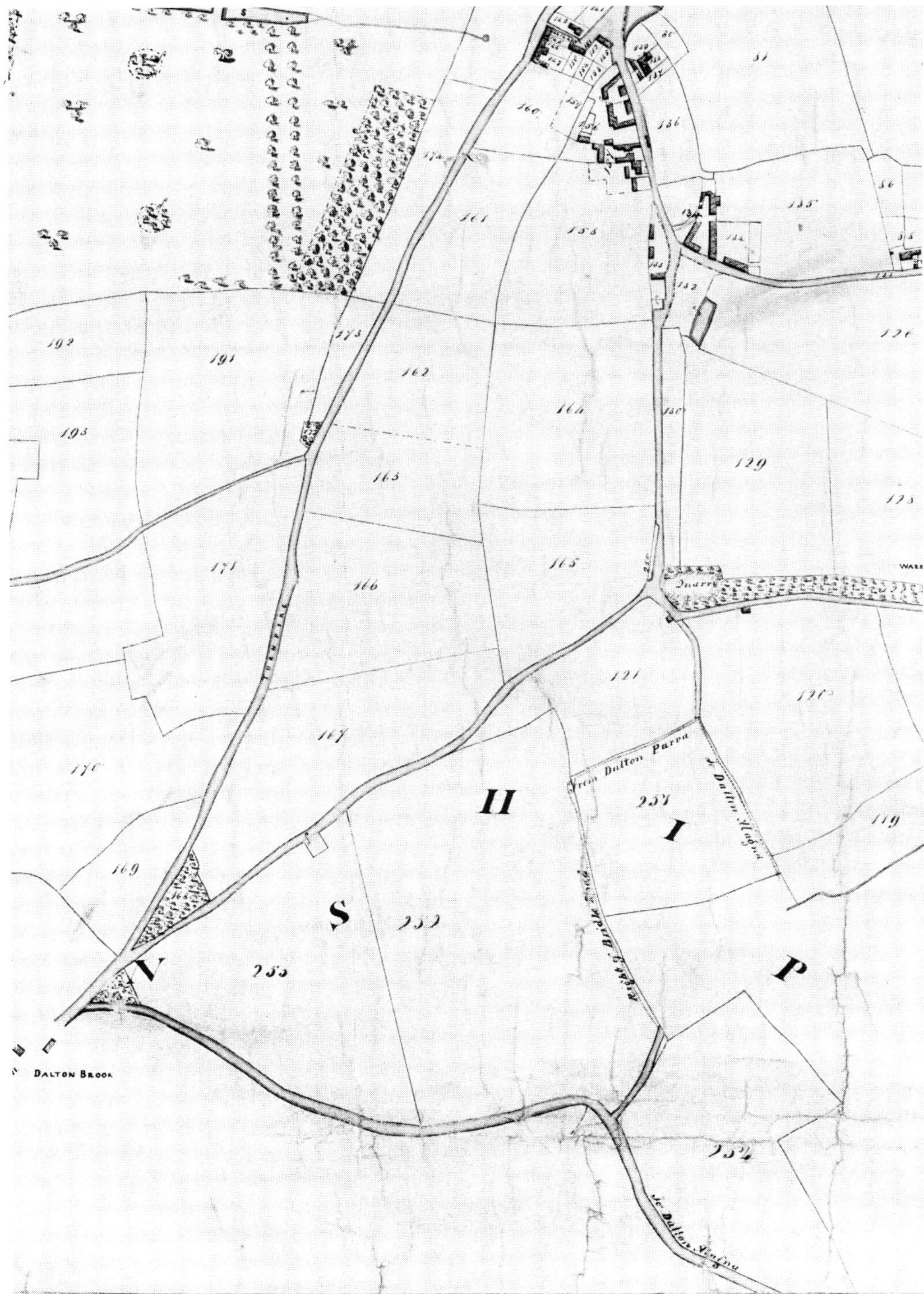

Fig. 106 Thrybergh, West Riding of Yorkshire, 1840. Another example of that minority of tithe maps which specify rights of way. Source: PRO IR30 43/408. Photograph reproduced by kind permission of the Keeper of the Public Record Office.

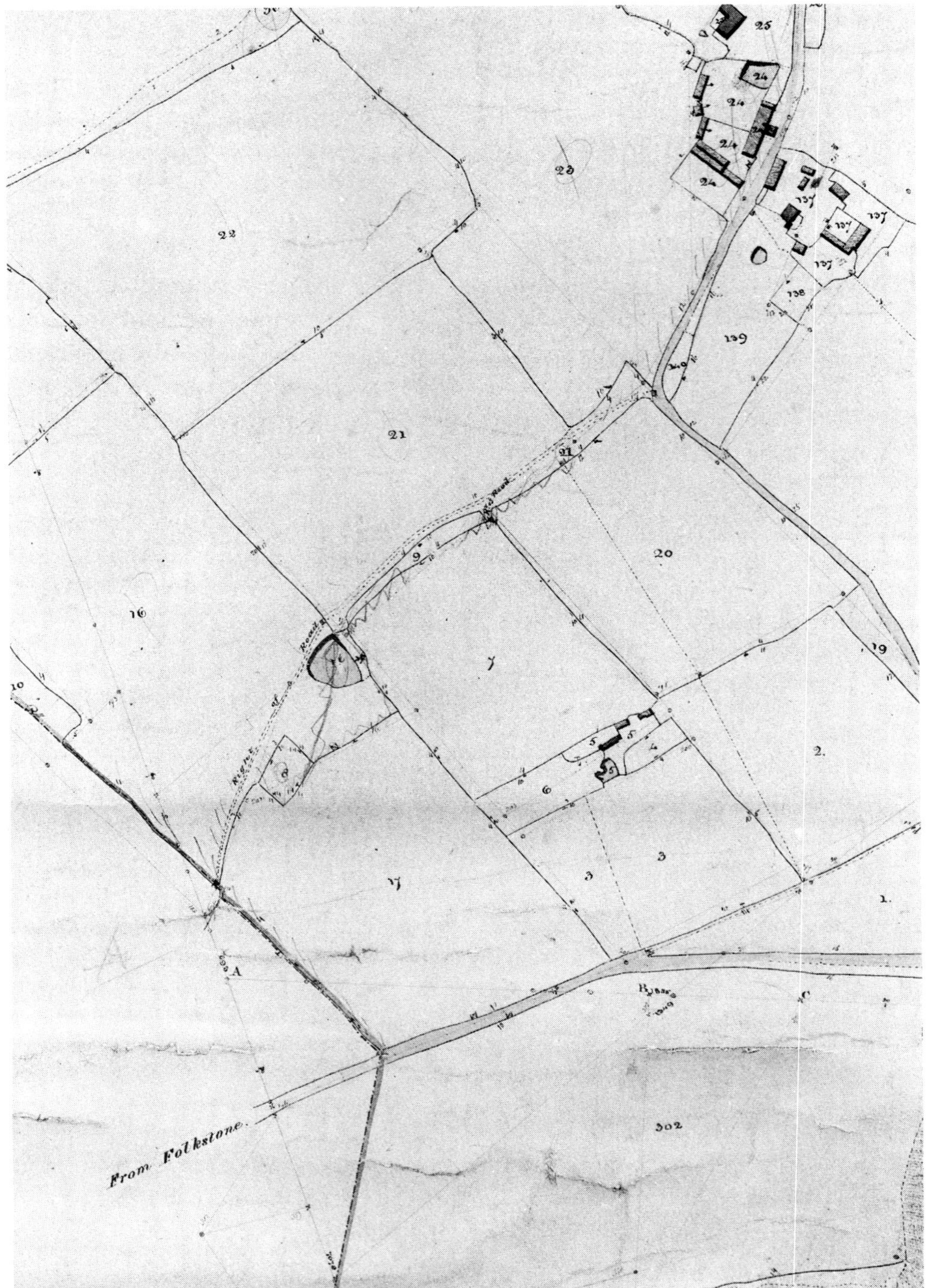

Fig. 107 Capel le Fern, Kent, 1840. This is a typical example of Thomas Thurston's style, and includes two of his characteristic features: rights of way, and small numerals alongside field boundaries. The purpose of these numerals is unknown. Field boundary ownership is shown by 'T' symbols and field gates by pictograms. Source: PRO IR30 17/70. Photograph reproduced by kind permission of the Keeper of the Public Record Office.

purpose of tithe commutation and its associated map record. Roads are shown only because their margins very often constituted a tithe area boundary and also because the official instructions 'for the preparation of plans for the purpose of the Tithe Commutation Act' suggest that surveyors should plot on tithe maps such topographic information 'usually given in estate surveys'.[24] There was, though, no statutory requirement to follow these instructions. In general terms, *no* tithe map provides direct evidence of whether a road *was used* or not, nor the purposes for which it might have been used unless there is annotation to that effect (Figs. 108 and 109).

Some roads on tithe maps are coloured in sienna. A convention on large-scale maps at this time was to colour public highways and to leave private and occupation roads uncoloured, though there was no requirement to make this distinction on tithe maps and, as noted above, very few maps do specify which routes were public rights of way. It is difficult to say how extensive the practice of colouring roads was because lighter shades have faded and cannot be distinguished readily from the colour of the paper. However, colouring of roads does appear to have been relatively uncommon on first-class maps and in Wales. At a local level, the practice varied very much. For example, the tithe map of Alderley parish in Cheshire is in three parts. On the parts relating to Over Alderley and Great Warford every road and path is tinted sienna including unfenced paths braced with and crossing single tithe areas. On the third part of the map, that for Nether Alderley, this practice is not followed and some roads and ways are left white.

Some 1,366 tithe maps, 12 per cent of the total, name some or most roads. There are very few significant deviations from this average figure with the notable exceptions that road names appear on less than 1 per cent of Welsh tithe maps but on nearly 35 per cent of those of Lancashire and 54 per cent of those of Middlesex. The last can be explained by the unusually large number of tithe maps which include built-up areas but the proportion in Lancashire is in marked contrast to that of the adjoining counties which are below the national average. As with the naming of buildings discussed below, it is rare for tithe maps to approach the completeness of Ordnance Survey large-scale maps as far as road names are concerned. Also, the naming of roads on tithe maps is usually highly selective; in Lincolnshire and Warwickshire, for example, it is common for only Roman or other ancient main roads to be named.

Footpaths and bridleways

About 4,400 tithe maps (37 per cent of the total) distinguish footpaths or bridleways from other roads and highways. Sometimes this is done by the use of single or double pecked lines in place of the continuous lines of roads and highways; occasionally they are identified by annotation. It is not, though, always clear whether fine pecked lines are intended to show an unfenced road or a track or path, a problem which also bedevils interpretation of nineteenth-century Ordnance Survey maps.

The national distribution of maps showing footpaths and bridleways is fairly even except that first, very few are shown on Welsh tithe maps, second, that substantially fewer than the average are distinguished on most maps of eastern England, and third, that substantially more than the average are depicted on the maps of some midland and

[24] Kain and Prince, *The tithe surveys of England and Wales*, pp. 80–3.

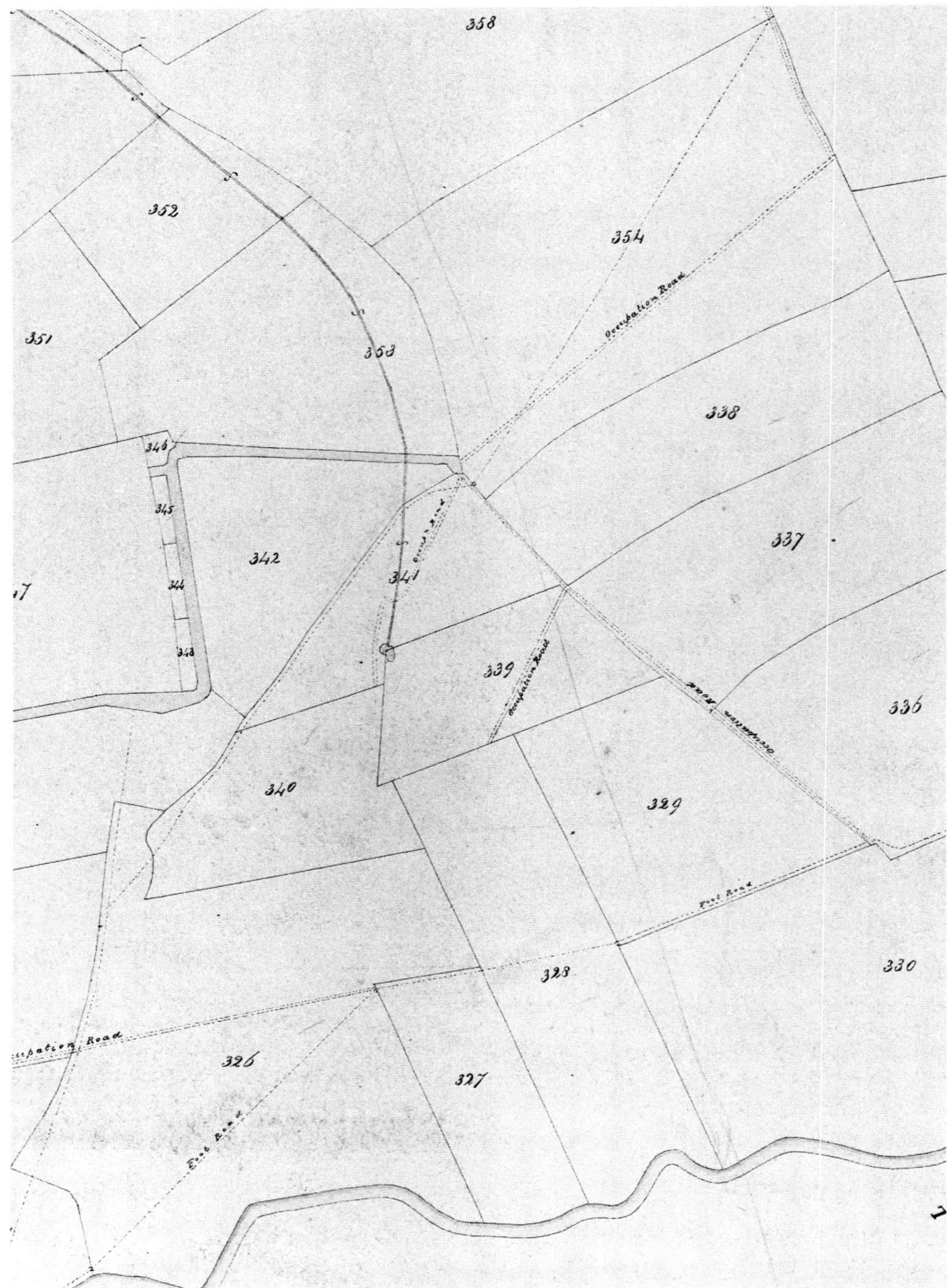

Fig. 108 Barnby in the Willows, Nottinghamshire, 1840. Tithe maps occasionally record occupation roads, as here. Source: PRO IR30 26/7. Photograph reproduced by kind permission of the Keeper of the Public Record Office.

northern counties (they appear on 63 per cent of Leicestershire maps). It is not clear how far these facts reflect the density of footpaths and bridleways in reality and how far it is a product of different surveying and map-drafting practices.

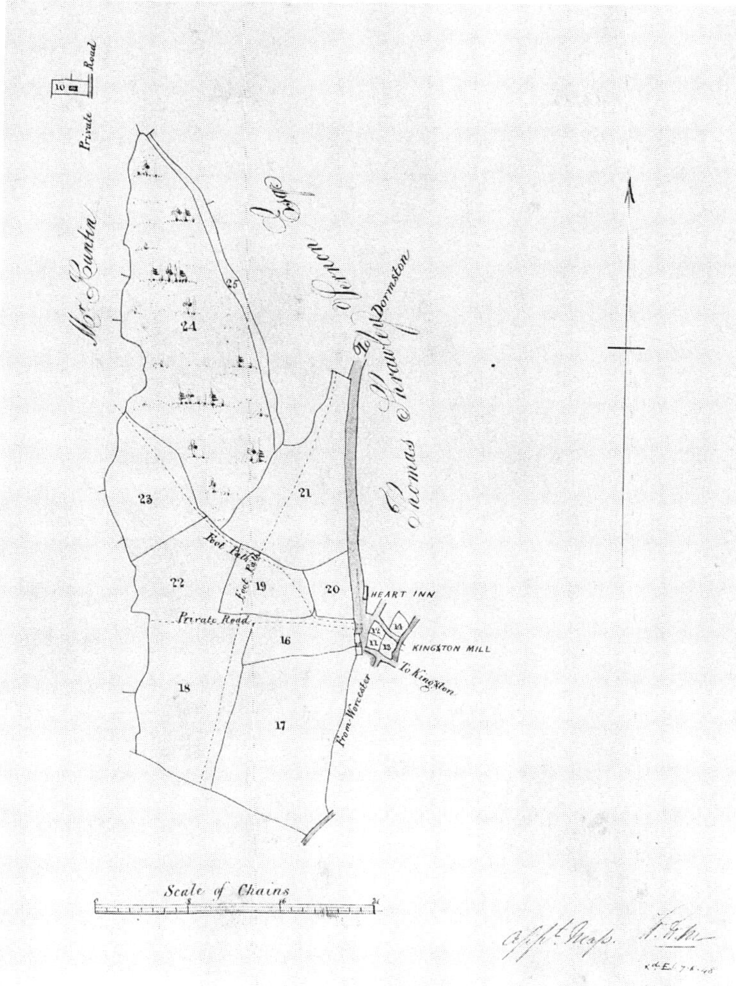

Fig. 109 Kington, Worcestershire, *circa* 1848. Private roads are sometimes distinguished on tithe maps, as here. The numbering of tithe areas is discontinuous and this map may derive from the enclosure map of *circa* 1782 of which no surviving copy is known, Adjoining landowners are named. Source: PRO IR30 39/77. Photograph reproduced by kind permission of the Keeper of the Public Record Office.

Canals and railways

It may be assumed that tithe maps depict all canals which existed at the time of tithe survey and towpaths and locks are usually indicated as well (Figs. 110 and 111). Colliery waggonways, quarry tramways and other industrial railways are usually differentiated from standard gauge railways on tithe maps. Waggonways and tramways are usually shown by a single pair of lines placed much closer together than those representing a road. Main-line railways, like canals, can be assumed to be shown on a tithe map where they existed; apparent omissions, for example at Repham, Lincolnshire, are probably due to maps having been surveyed just before railway construction but drawn up and dated later. Railways are usually shown by the outer fences only and are coloured distinctively, usually red or purple but yellow is sometimes used and green occasionally. Sometimes sleepers are

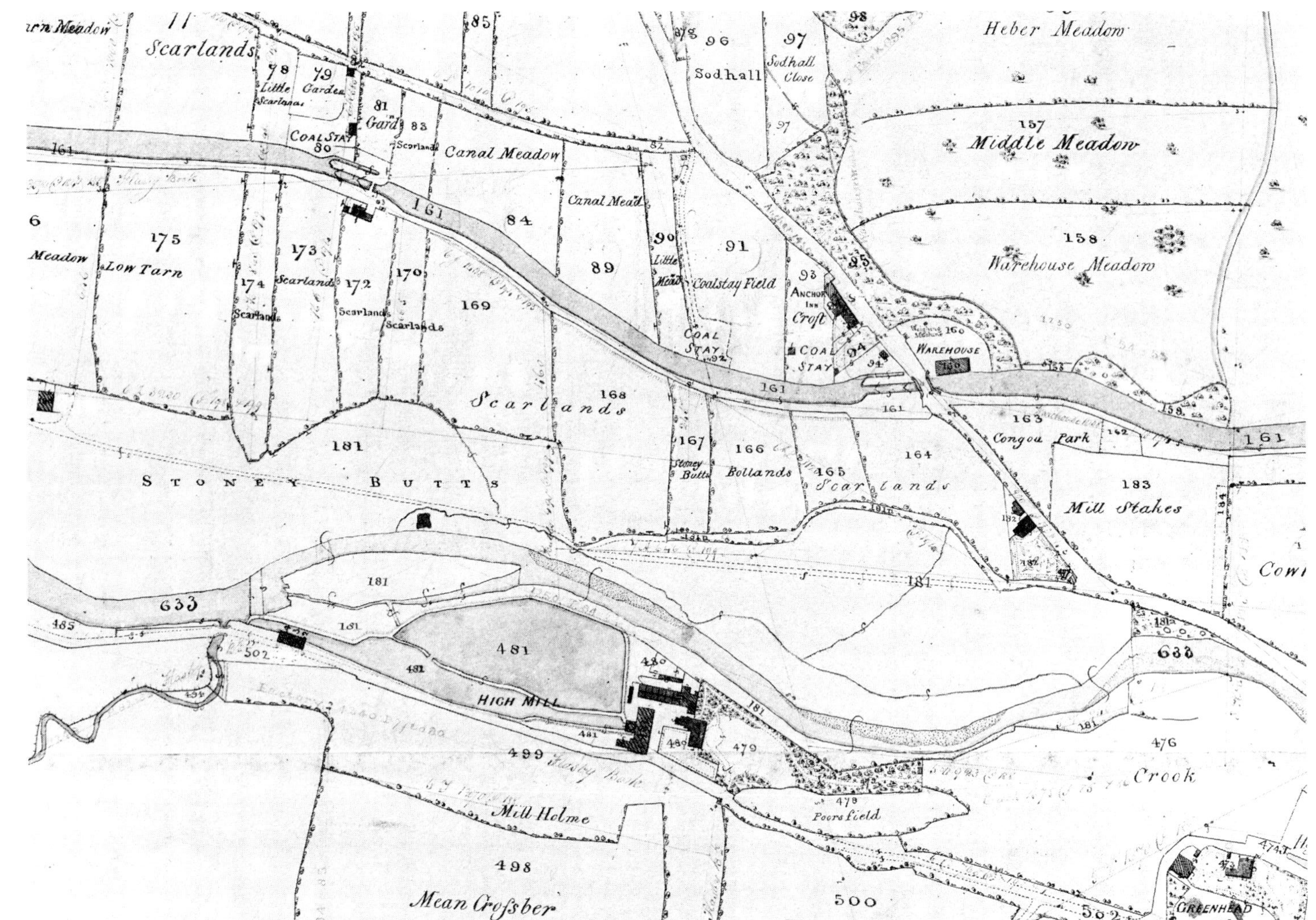

Fig. 110 Gargrave, West Riding of Yorkshire, 1839. The name of Greenwood is usually associated with Christopher, the county map-maker, but his brother John executed a number of very detailed first-class tithe maps. Had all tithe maps approached this standard of completeness then it is questionable whether the Ordnance Survey 1:2500 would ever have been made. Source: PRO IR30 43/165. Photograph reproduced by kind permission of the Keeper of the Public Record Office.

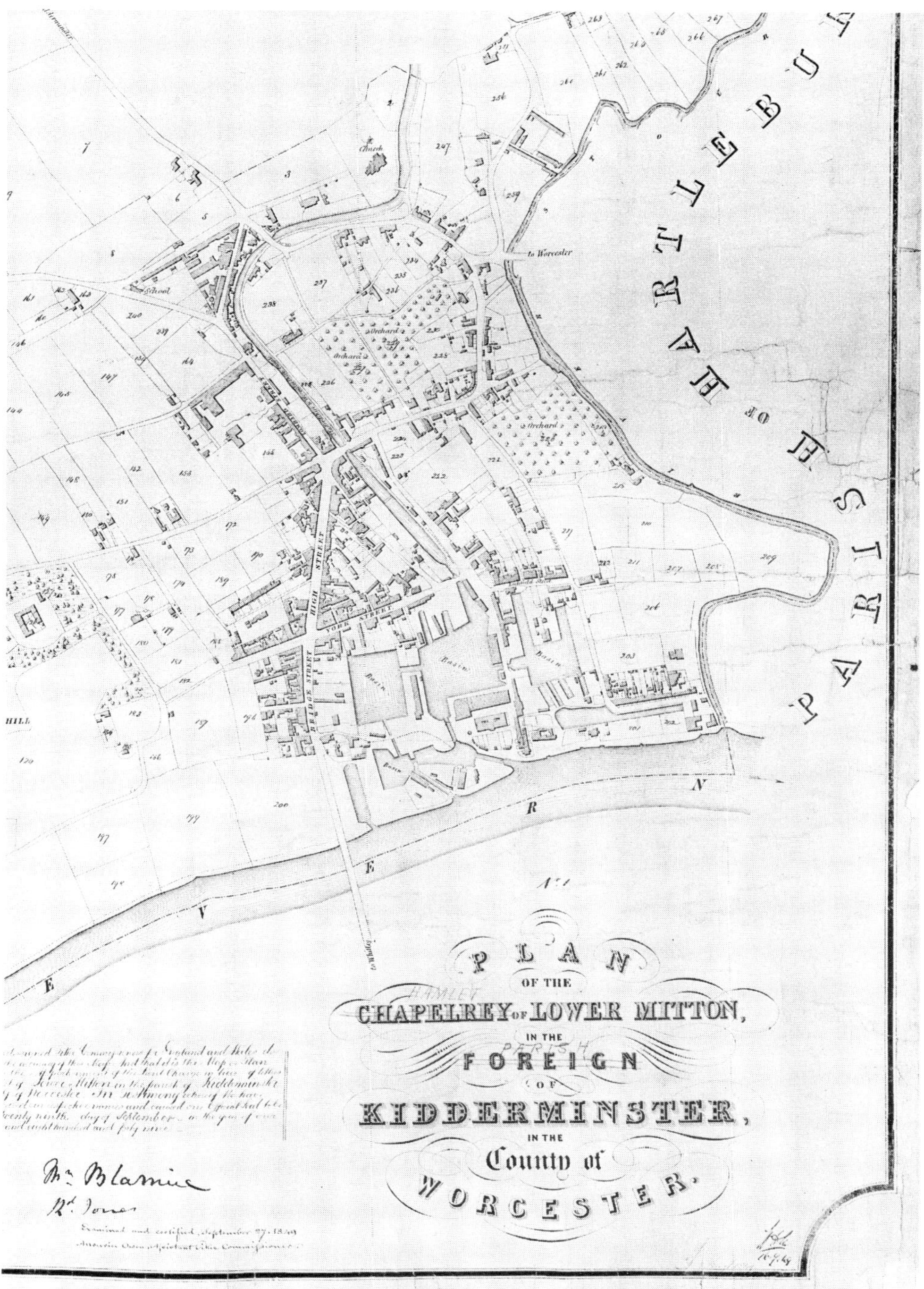

Fig. 111 Lower Mitton, Worcestershire, *circa* 1849. The mapping of canal basins in such detail is uncommon on tithe maps. Source: PRO IR30 39/94. Photograph reproduced by kind permission of the Keeper of the Public Record Office.

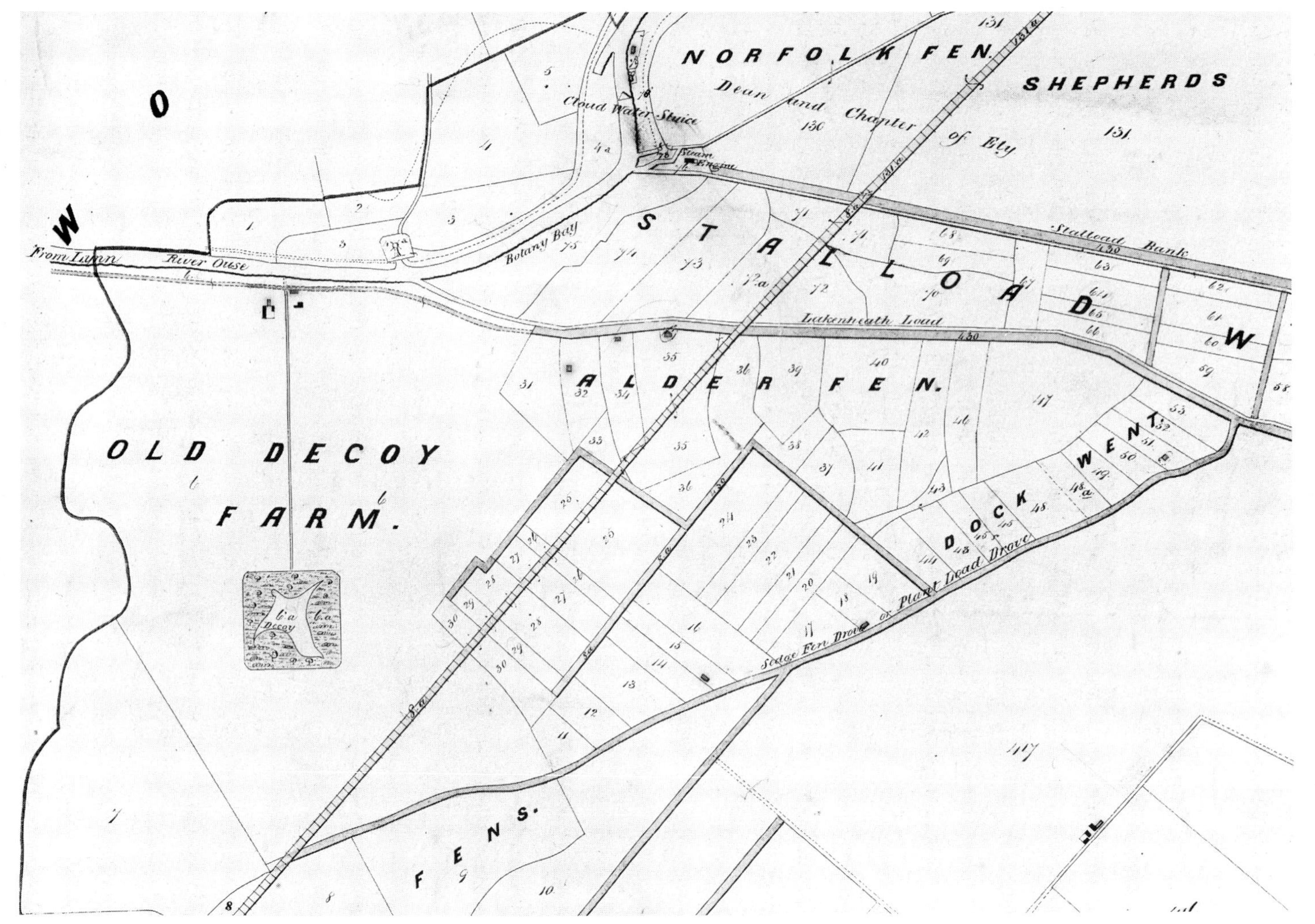

Fig. 112 Lakenheath Fen Lands, Suffolk, 1854. This is a good example of a fenland tithe map which shows drainage features in some detail. The 'sleeper' railway symbol is unusual for a tithe map. Source: PRO IR30 33/264. Photograph reproduced by kind permission of the Keeper of the Public Record Office.

Newcastle are unusual in that they systematically recorded this information. More usually the representation of railway tracks on tithe maps is partial; for example, at Lincoln station the 'running lines' are shown but the platform lines and sidings are not, and at Hammersmith, Middlesex the tithe map shows the track on part only of the West London Railway.

Industry

Industrial land use recorded in the county-by-county catalogue entries includes all non-agricultural and non-residential land uses which can be clearly identified. Thus it includes both heavy industry serving much more than the local economy, such as coal-mining, iron-founding, cotton-milling and engineering, and also those light, local or agriculturally related industries such as brewing, tanning, gas and water works and brick and tile making. Industrial land use is distinguished on 813 tithe maps, some 7 per cent of the whole. The recording of industry tends to reflect the pattern of industrialisation, with significantly higher concentrations than elsewhere in Cornwall (Fig. 113), Glamorganshire, Staffordshire (Fig.114) and England north of a Humber-Mersey line than elsewhere. The greatest density recorded in the tithe surveys is in Lancashire where industrial activity appears on more than a quarter of the county's tithe maps.

In about two-thirds of instances particular industries are described, as for example, 'colliery', 'brewery', 'glass works'; otherwise descriptions are more general, for instance 'factory', or 'quarry'. Clearly the industrial content of tithe maps is partial; these land uses are not recorded in any systematic manner.

Landforms and waterbodies

The main object of the tithe surveys was to record the boundaries of tithe areas; other details were of lesser importance and their inclusion may be as much the result of past practice and of client expectations as of actual distributions. Of all the topographic content found on tithe maps the careful depiction of rock outcrops might be thought the least relevant to the immediate needs of tithe valuation and commutation (Fig. 114). Rock outcrops appear on 409 tithe maps (less than 4 per cent of the total) and their presence appears to be due more to variations in map-making practice than to any systematic reflection of terrain. For example, the mapping of rock outcrops in Cumberland, Derbyshire, Durham and Westmorland is only slightly above the national average, in Wales it is slightly below average, whereas they appear on nearly 10 per cent of maps of Northumberland and Sussex, over 11 per cent of those of Devon, and nearly 29 per cent of those of Cornwall. Some of this variation can be explained by the use of rock symbols to show coastal cliffs but this is not a complete explanation.

Where slopes are portrayed on tithe maps it is usually by hachures (Fig. 115) but occasionally brush-shading is used. It is very rare for tithe maps to show slopes in the kind of detail which is one of the most marked achievements of the Ordnance Survey; the tithe map of Langdale in Orton, Westmorland, is unusual in this regard. Usually the depiction of slopes on tithe maps is restricted to escarpments and other very prominent features and to

Fig. 113 Gwennap, Cornwall, 1839. Although tithe was an agricultural rather than an industrial impost, some tithe maps provide a detailed picture of industry and especially of mining. Source: Cornwall Record Office, Gwennap tithe map. Photograph reproduced by kind permission of the County Archivist, Cornwall Record Office.

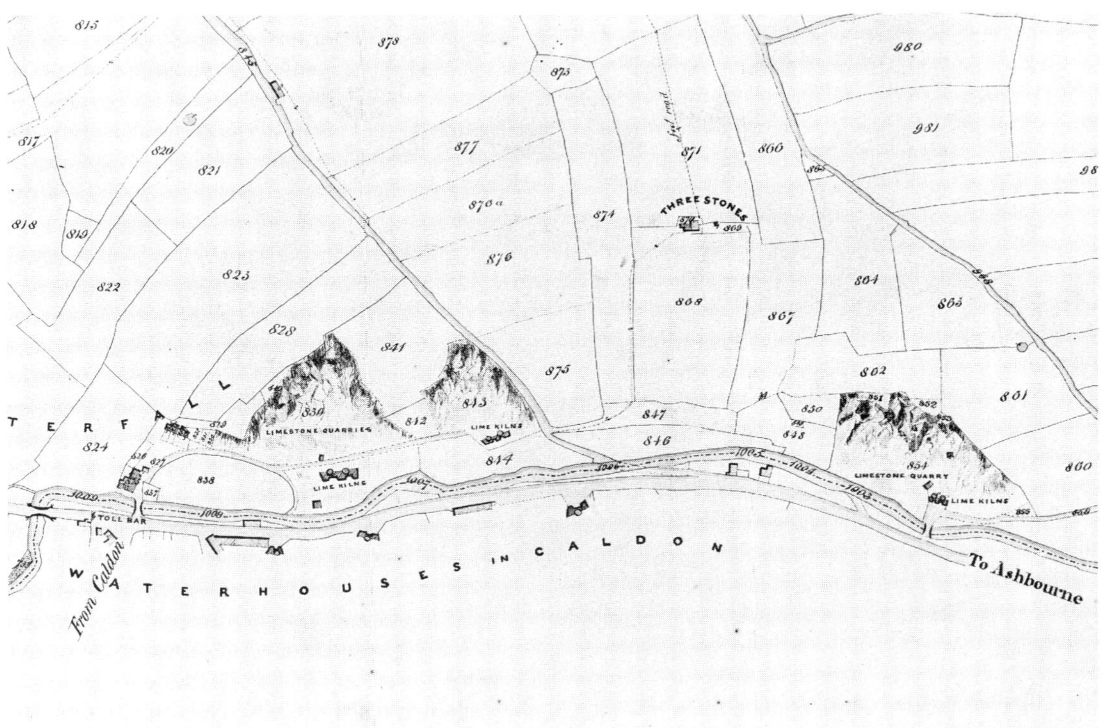

Fig. 114 Waterfall, Staffordshire, 1846. This map is distingushed by particularly fine rock-drawing. Source: PRO IR30 32/223. Photograph reproduced by kind permission of the Keeper of the Public Record Office.

river cliffs. This to some extent explains the discrepancy between the 20 per cent of Northumberland maps and the 34 per cent of County Durham maps which show slopes. On the other hand, the discrepancy between the 13 per cent of Surrey maps and 7 per cent of Kent maps which show slopes by comparison with the 27 per cent of Sussex maps, must presumably be sought in differences in map-making practice. The one and only indication of absolute height on a tithe map is that of a 'shooting tower' on the map of Llandegla, Denbighshire.

Rivers and streams wide enough to be portrayed by double lines are usually shown where they cross or run alongside tithable land. However, field ditches are much less often mapped and small streams and ditches forming field boundaries are not always distinguished from other types of field boundary on tithe maps (Fig. 116).

Foreshore and marine features are rarely recorded on tithe maps. Foreshore was always tithe free and as it was owned usually by the Crown it came neither within the scope of tithe commutation nor of earlier private estate surveys. Consequently, the mapping of the foreshore at Capel le Fern, Kent, illustrated in Fig. 117, is unusual and is probably a reflection of the conscientious approach of its surveyor, Thomas Thurston.

Ponds and lakes are recorded on 8,551 tithe maps, almost three-quarters of the total. They are recorded on a smaller proportion of tithe maps in counties where there is a higher than average proportion of apportionment by holding as in the north-east of England and

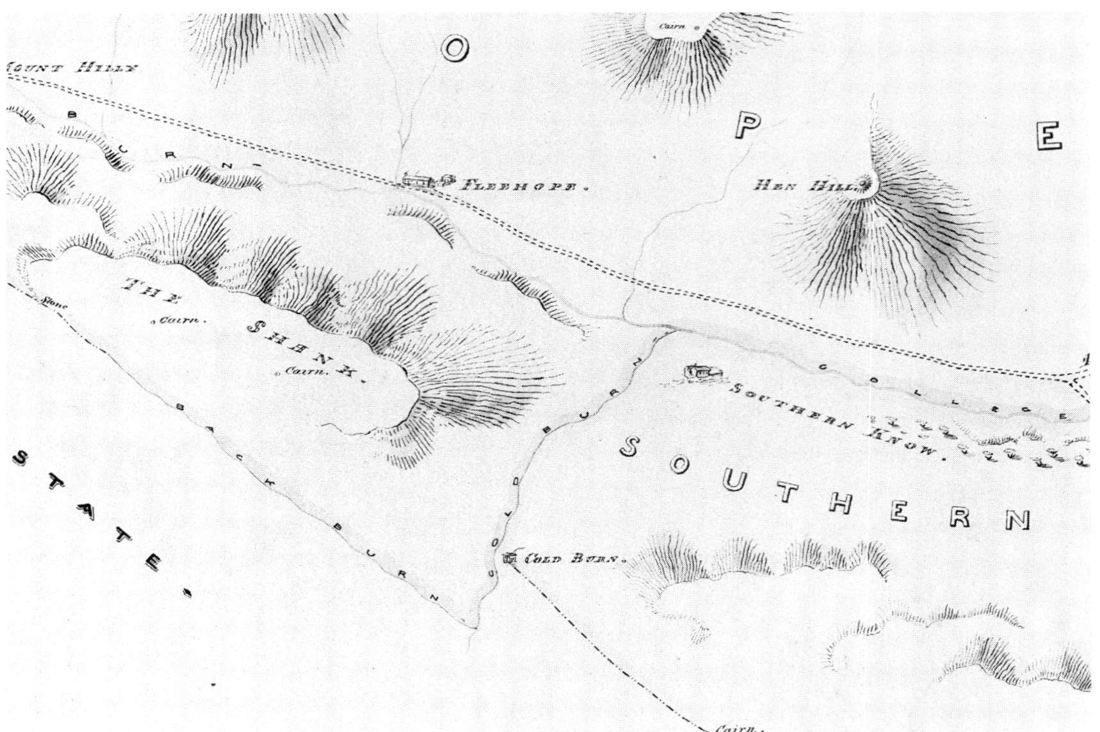

Fig. 115 Grey's Forest, Northumberland, 1845. Tithe maps of upland country sometimes show relief by hachures and this is a particularly good example. The pictograms of buildings are very unusual. Source: PRO IR30 25/201. Photograph reproduced by kind permission of the Keeper of the Public Record Office.

in Wales. Ponds appear, for example, on only 33 per cent of Northumberland maps and 16 per cent of Anglesey maps. Conversely waterbodies are most thoroughly recorded in Hertfordshire and Sussex, in which counties these features appear on over 95 per cent of maps.

Towns and villages

Densely built-up areas were usually tithe free by 1836 and in consequence tithe maps very often generalise or omit the topographic detail of urban areas (Fig. 118). Two notable exceptions are the tithe maps of Whitehaven and Swansea, parts of which are illustrated in Figs. 119 and 120. Small towns with a more open topography including garden areas yielding tithes are more often mapped and villages are almost invariably portrayed in detail (Figs. 121 and 122).

As with the mapping of tithe free agricultural land discussed above, surveyors may well have found it more convenient to survey or copy the whole of a tithe district including any tithe free built-up parts and then to leave the disentangling of tithable land to the valuer. Furthermore tithe maps were sometimes made with the secondary purpose of assessing parochial rates in which case a complete map including the built-up parts of a district was required. A number of tithe maps in Kent, Surrey and elsewhere were originally made for

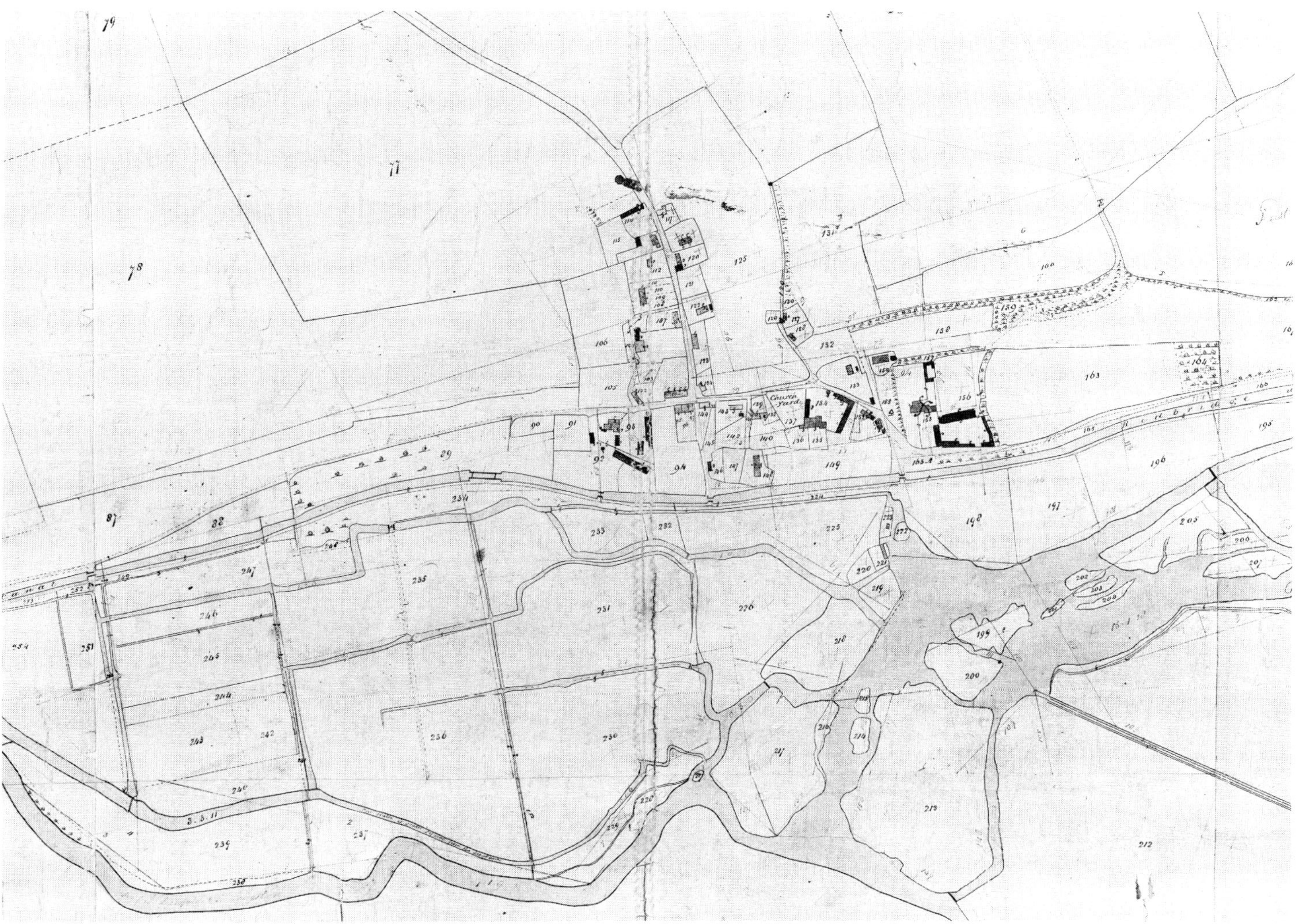

Fig. 116 Leckford, Hampshire, 1840. On the whole, tithe surveys are not very good records of water meadows; this is an exceptional map. Source: PRO IR30 31/159. Photograph reproduced by kind permission of the Keeper of the Public Record Office.

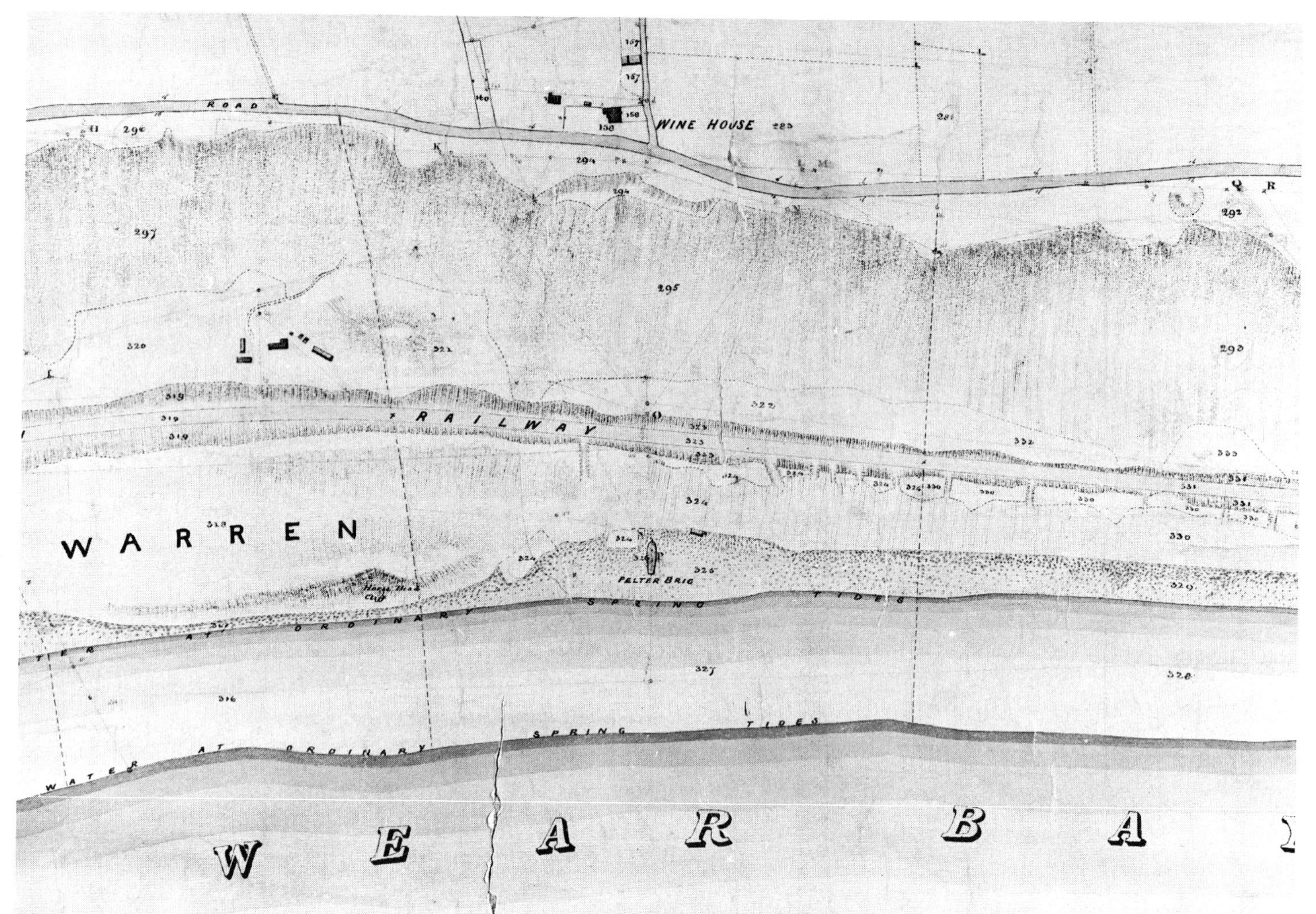

Fig. 117 Capel le Fern, Kent, 1840. This is a first-class map by Thomas Thurston of Ashford which portrays the cliffs, foreshore and a beached ship with great care. Source: PRO IR30 17/70. Photograph reproduced by kind permission of the Keeper of the Public Record Office.

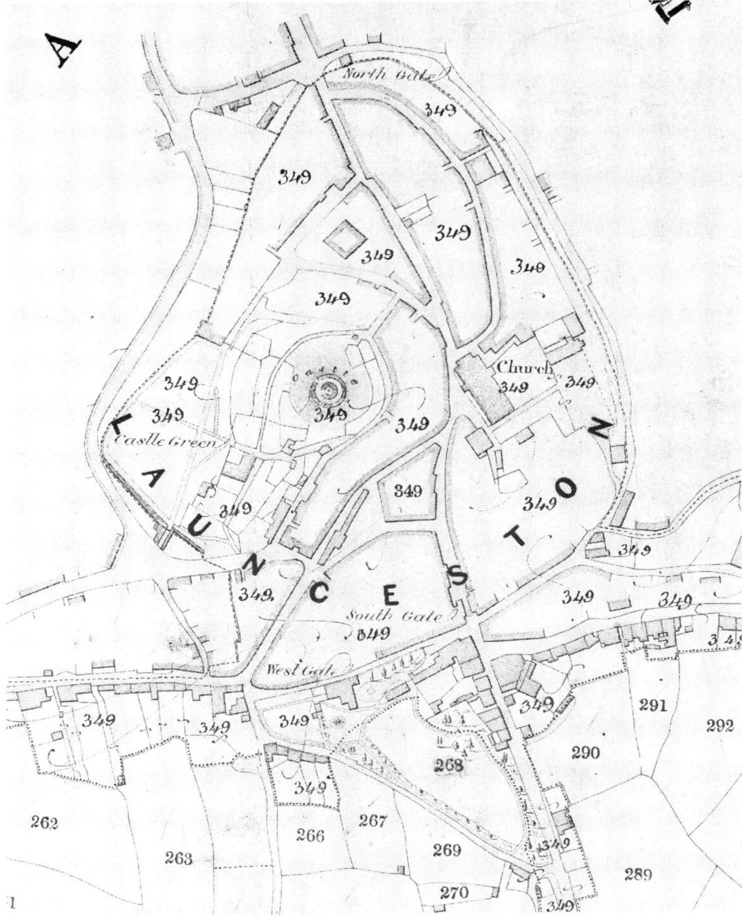

Fig. 118 St Mary Magdalene, Cornwall, 1839. Most urban land was tithe free and usually was not plotted in full detail on tithe maps. Here the entire built-up area of Launceston is surrounded by a dotted line and subsumed within a single tithe area number: '349'. Source: Cornwall Record Office, St Mary Magdalene tithe map. Photograph reproduced by kind permission of the County Archivist, Cornwall Record Office.

rating purposes, and the detailed urban mapping of Newark and Southwell in Nottinghamshire may have been made with a view to such additional uses. Substantially the same persons paid rates as paid tithes and so a dual purpose map could be an attractive financial proposition.

Houses and buildings

Inhabited buildings are distinguished from uninhabited buildings on 4,901 tithe maps (about 42 per cent of the total) but are much more frequently depicted on first-class maps (on more than 76 per cent). Almost all the tithe maps of counties south of a Severn-Wash line show houses in above-average proportion, and vice-versa (Fig. 123). The usual practice is to show houses in red or carmine (occasionally in darker shades, including

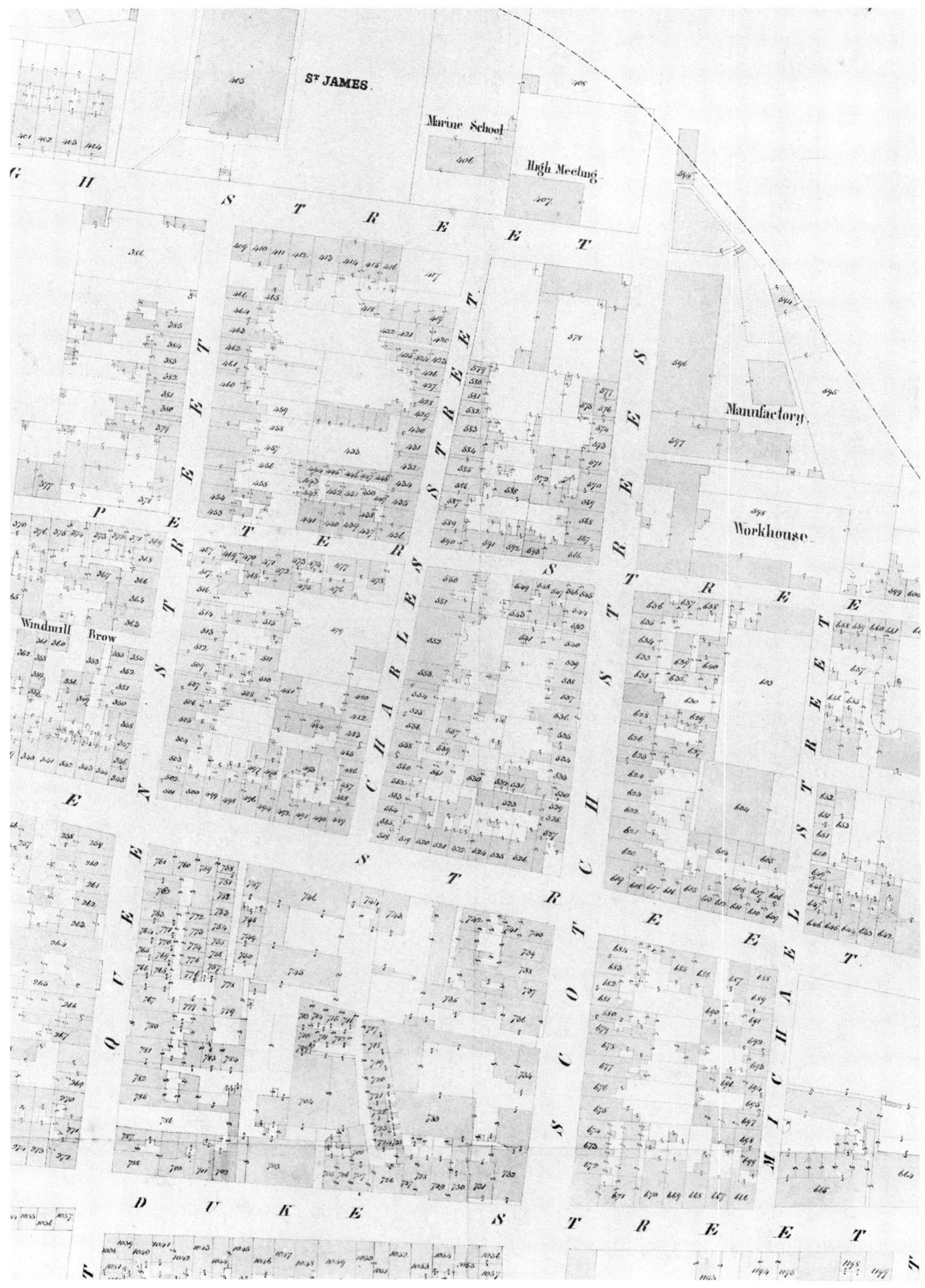

Fig. 119 Whitehaven, Cumberland, 1847. Detailed tithe mapping of urban areas such as this is most unusual. Source: PRO IR30 7/184. Photograph reproduced by kind permission of the Keeper of the Public Record Office.

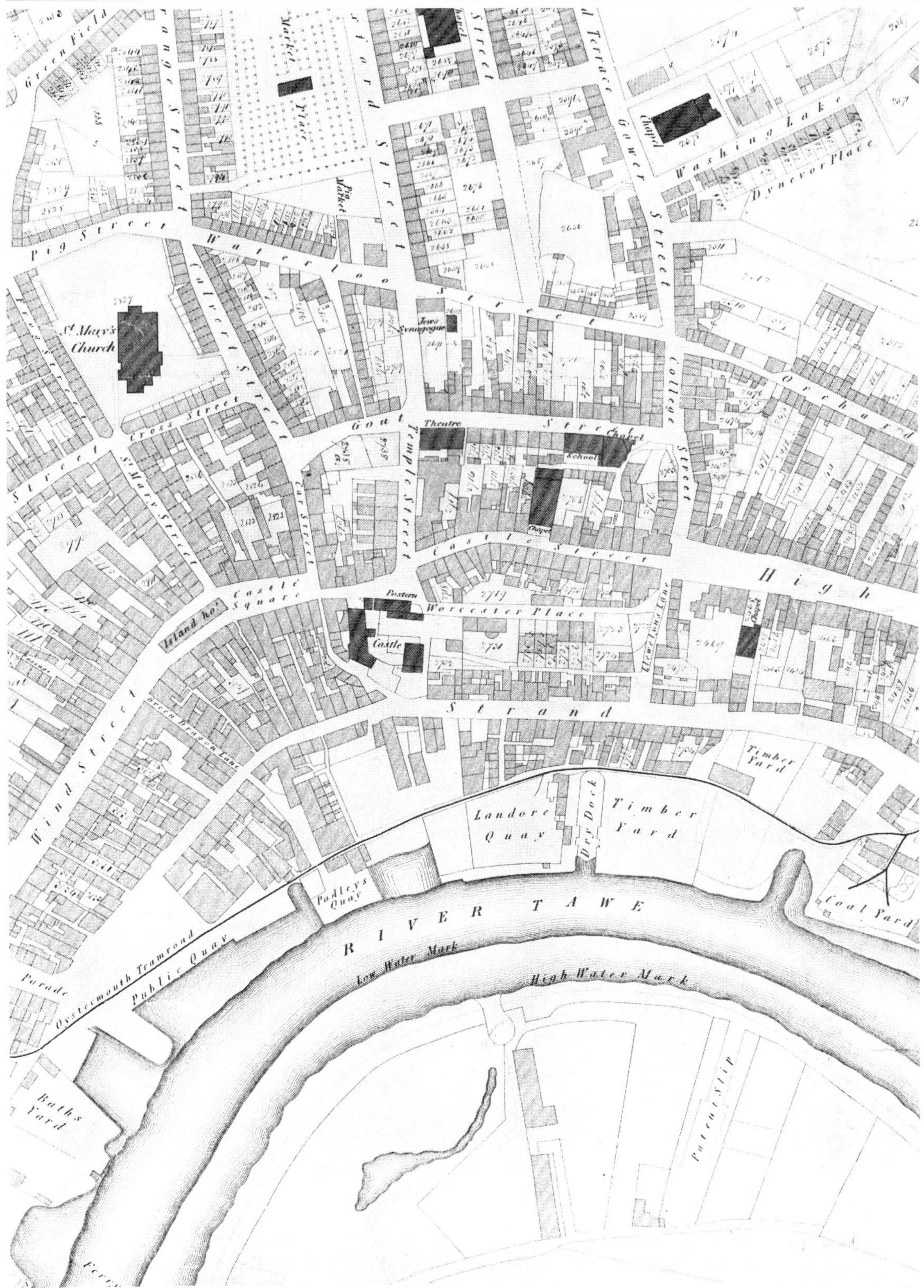

Fig. 120 Swansea, Glamorganshire, *circa* 1842. Another rare example of a tithe map which portrays the urban morphology in exceptional detail. Source: PRO IR30 14/106. Photograph reproduced by kind permission of the Keeper of the Public Record Office.

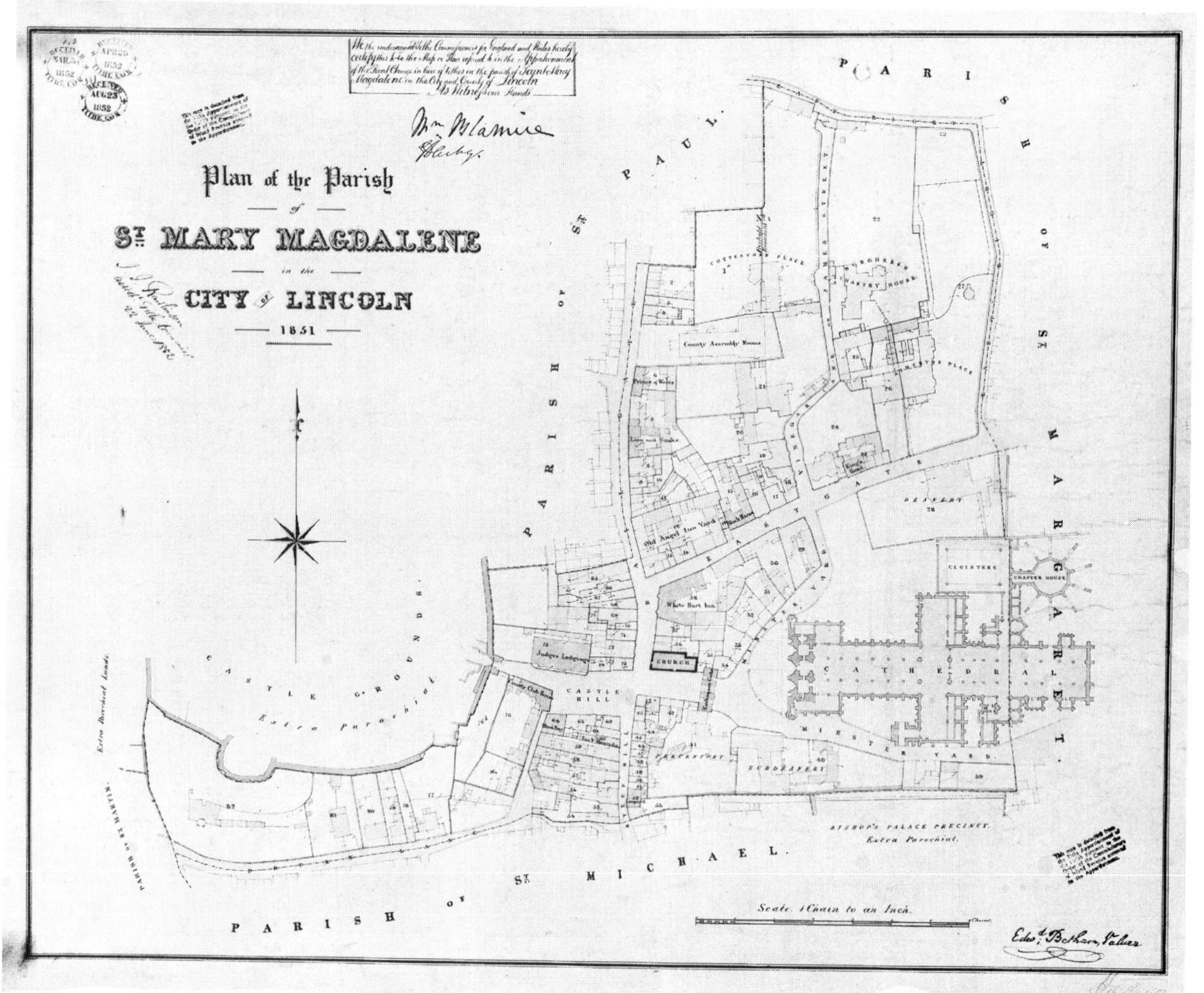

Fig. 121 St Mary Magdalene, Lincoln, 1851. Little urban land was subject to tithe commutation and mapping of this detail and quality which foreshadows that of the Ordnance Survey is rarely encountered on tithe maps. Source: PRO IR30 20/213. Photograph reproduced by kind permission of the Keeper of the Public Record Office.

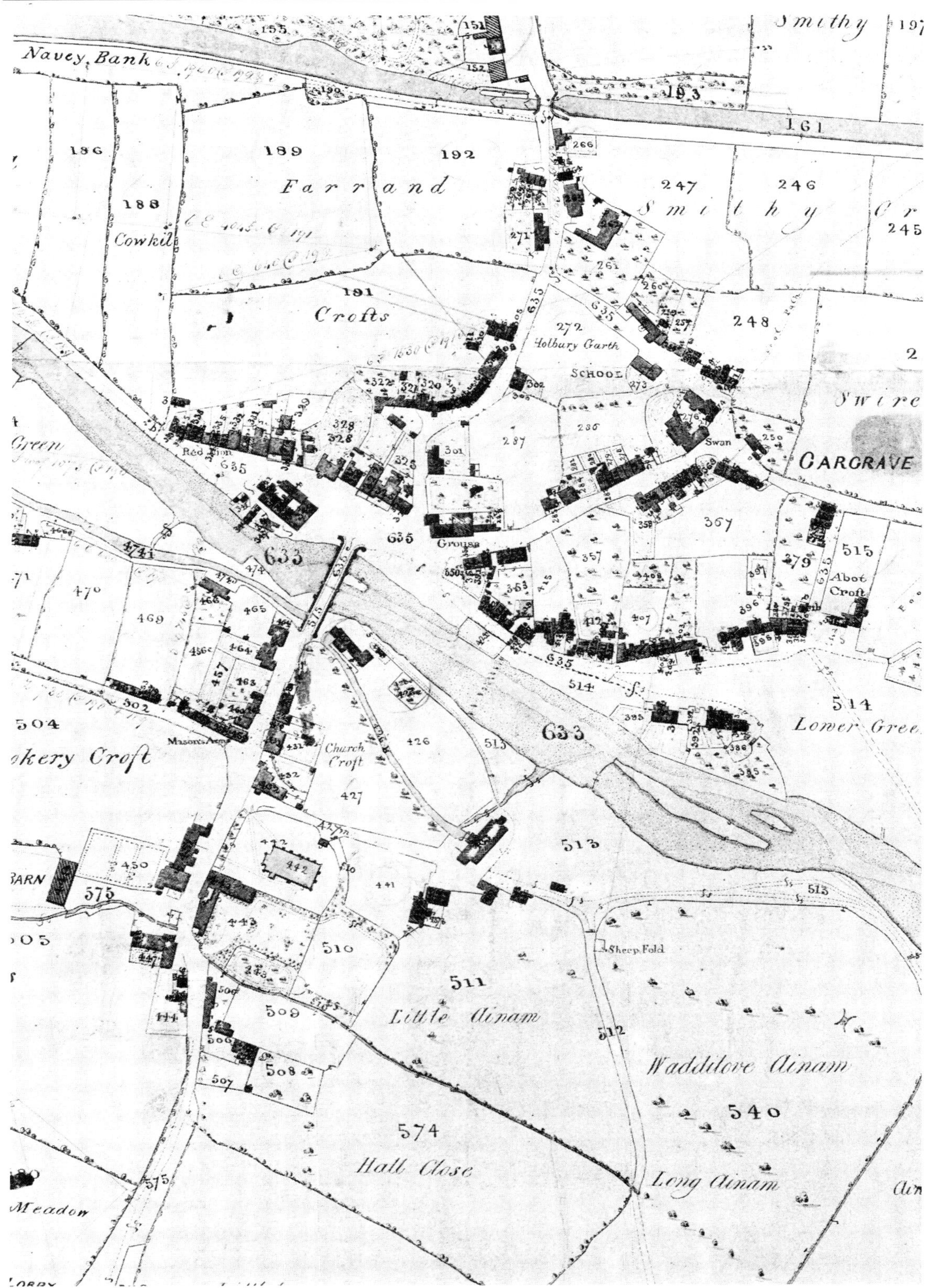

Fig. 122 Gargrave, West Riding of Yorkshire, 1839. John Greenwood's tithe map provides an exact depiction of the village topography. Source: PRO IR30 43/165. Photograph reproduced by kind permission of the Keeper of the Public Record Office.

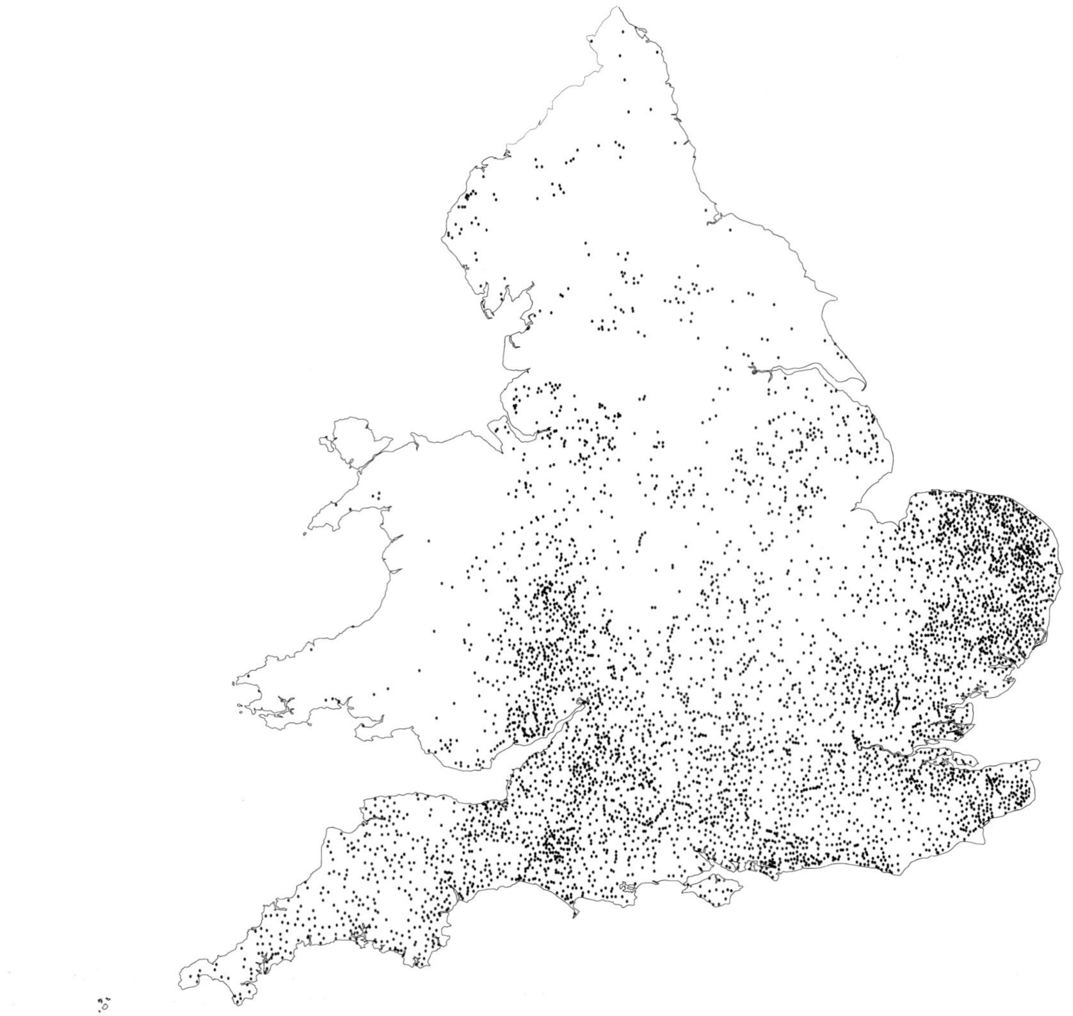

Fig. 123 England and Wales: tithe maps which distinguish houses from other buildings.

brown) and uninhabited buildings in grey, though black hatching or solid black are often employed, as occasionally are purple or blue. The tithe map of Knaresdale, Northumberland is a particularly crude example on which buildings are shown by small open circles (Fig. 124). On lithographed maps uninhabited buildings are often shown by single hatching and inhabited buildings by cross-hatching; alternatives are to single-hatch all buildings and to indicate inhabited houses by adding a dot, or to hatch uninhabited buildings and to show inhabited buildings in solid black. Occasionally, notably in the eastern half of Yorkshire, tithable buildings are coloured red and tithe free buildings identified by another colour; the map of Hull Holy Trinity has tithe free buildings infilled in green (Fig. 125). Stylised building symbols are used on a few tithe maps (Figs. 126 and 127).

On some 5,184 tithe maps (44 per cent of the total) buildings are named. Once again this applies more to first-class maps (56 per cent) than to second-class maps. The number of

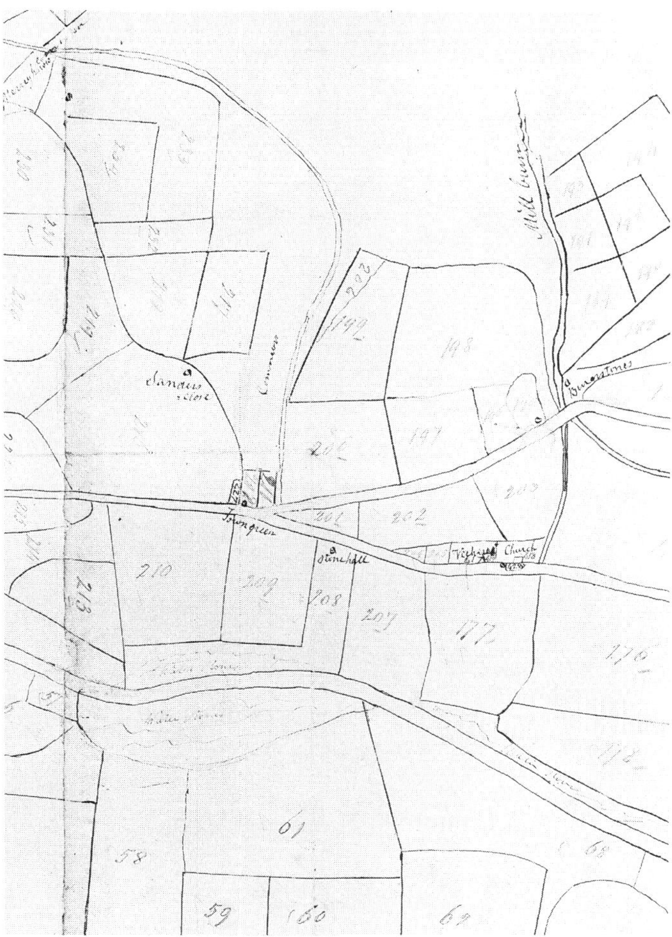

Fig. 124 Knaresdale, Northumberland, *circa* 1838. Few tithe maps show buildings as crudely as does this one by small open circles. Source: PRO IR30 25/284. Photograph reproduced by kind permission of the Keeper of the Public Record Office.

buildings named on a particular tithe map varies greatly, from perhaps just the manor house and one or two other evidently important houses, to other maps on which the density of names approaches that characteristic of later Ordnance Survey maps. Maps with building names tend to be of districts in upland counties with predominantly dispersed rather than nucleated settlement patterns on the one hand, and of counties which were little affected by parliamentary enclosure on the other. The extremes are represented by Rutland with only one map with building names and Radnorshire, with 92 per cent of maps having this information.

Inns and public houses are sometimes named where they are landmarks but in general they are not identified. The very thorough mapping of inns and public houses in Bala, Merionethshire, though routine for an Ordnance Survey large-scale map, is unparalleled for a tithe map. The naming of public buildings such as schools and parsonages varies from map to map but it is quite common for these to be the only buildings named on a map (Fig. 128).

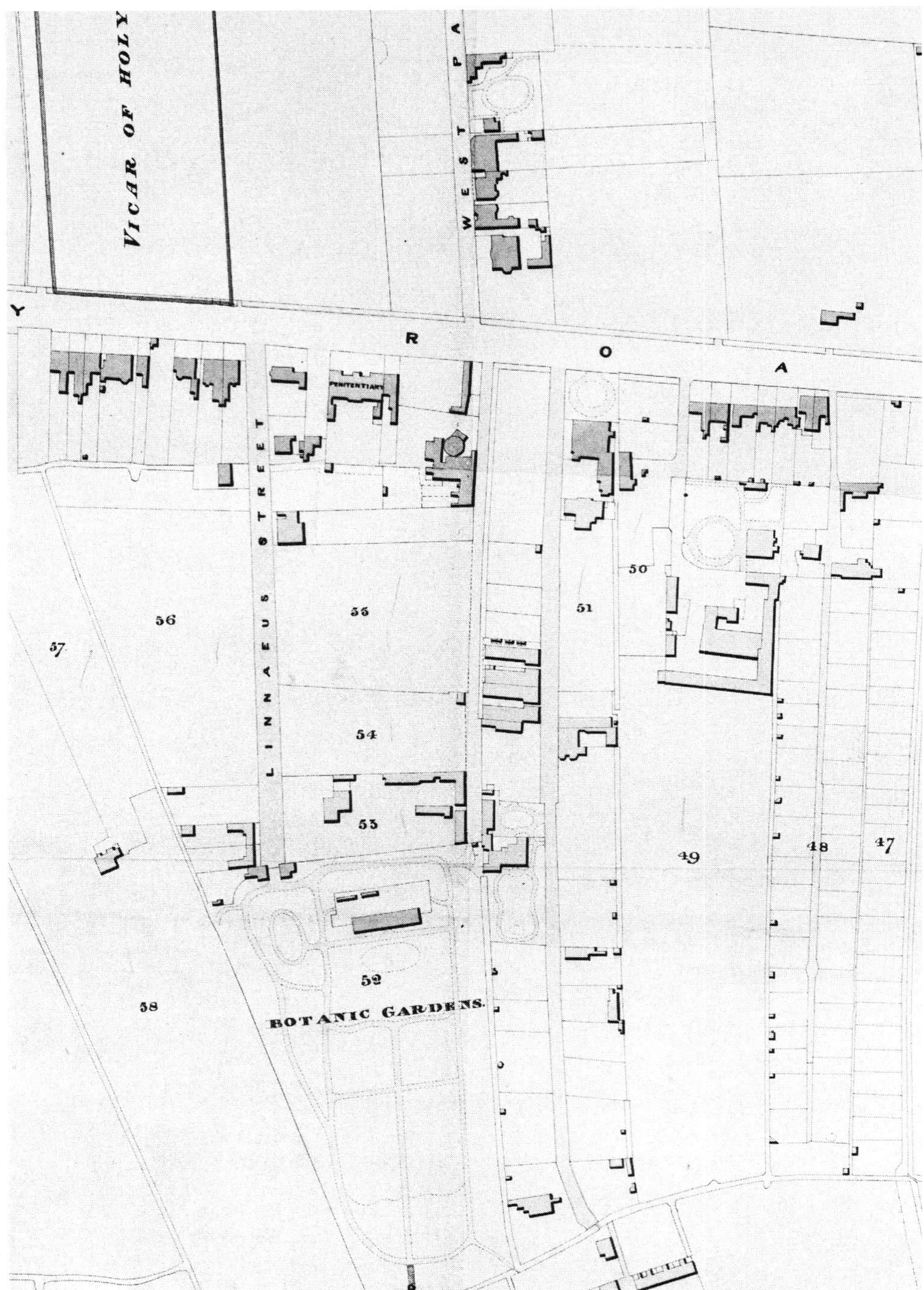

Fig. 125 Holy Trinity, Kingston upon Hull, East Riding of Yorkshire, *circa* 1848. The usual convention on tithe maps is to distinguish inhabited and uninhabited buildings but a variation found on some Yorkshire maps where only part of a district remained subject to tithe was to distinguish tithable and tithe free buildings. On the original map, tithable buildings are coloured carmine and tithe-free ones are green; these appear here as light and dark grey respectively. Source: PRO IR30 41/98. Photograph reproduced by kind permission of the Keeper of the Public Record Office.

Fig. 126 Cocklaw, Northumberland, *circa* 1839. The depiction of buildings in elevation on large-scale maps had largely died out by the 1830s; this is one of only about half a dozen tithe map examples. Source: PRO IR30 25/122. Photograph reproduced by kind permission of the Keeper of the Public Record Office.

Land use

Woodland

Tithe maps show woodland either by tree symbols which vary from hasty pen loops to highly coloured minature works of art, or by green, blue or grey tint, or by a combination of these methods. Tithe maps portray woodland with greater consistency than any other feature; it is depicted on 7,909 maps (67 per cent of the total) and there is relatively little variation from county to county. With the exception of Anglesey where only one map shows woodland, the extremes are represented by Merionethshire (24 per cent of maps) and Montgomeryshire (93 per cent of maps). There seems to be no clear relationship between the depiction of woodland and the nature of terrain or the extent or type of tithable land though, as with other types of land use, a lower proportion of first-class maps (less than 50 per cent) identify woodland which accounts for the under-recording of woodland in Monmouthshire, Herefordshire and Kent, all of which are counties with above average proportions of first-class tithe maps.

Two-thirds of those maps which portray woodland do not distinguish different types; on the remaining third, plantations are distinguished from timber or ancient woods by conventional symbols with usually either a 'conifer' symbol or a 'non-coniferous' symbol

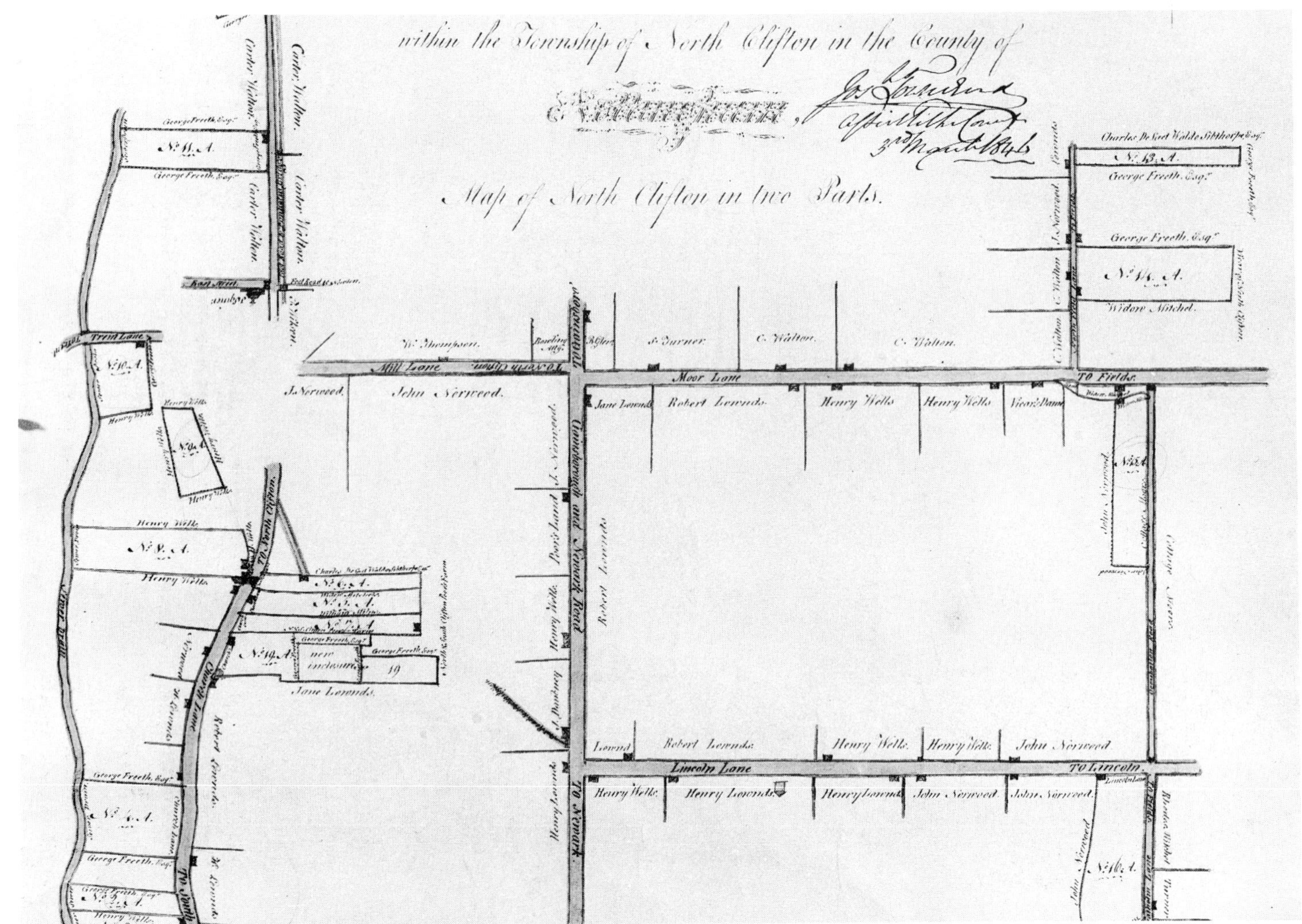

Fig. 127 North Clifton, Nottinghamshire, 1845. There were various solutions to the problem of mapping tithe districts in which only small residual areas remain tithable; this diagramatic, topological approach is unquestionably the most unusual. Source: PRO IR30 26/32. Photograph reproduced by kind permission of the Keeper of the Public Record Office.

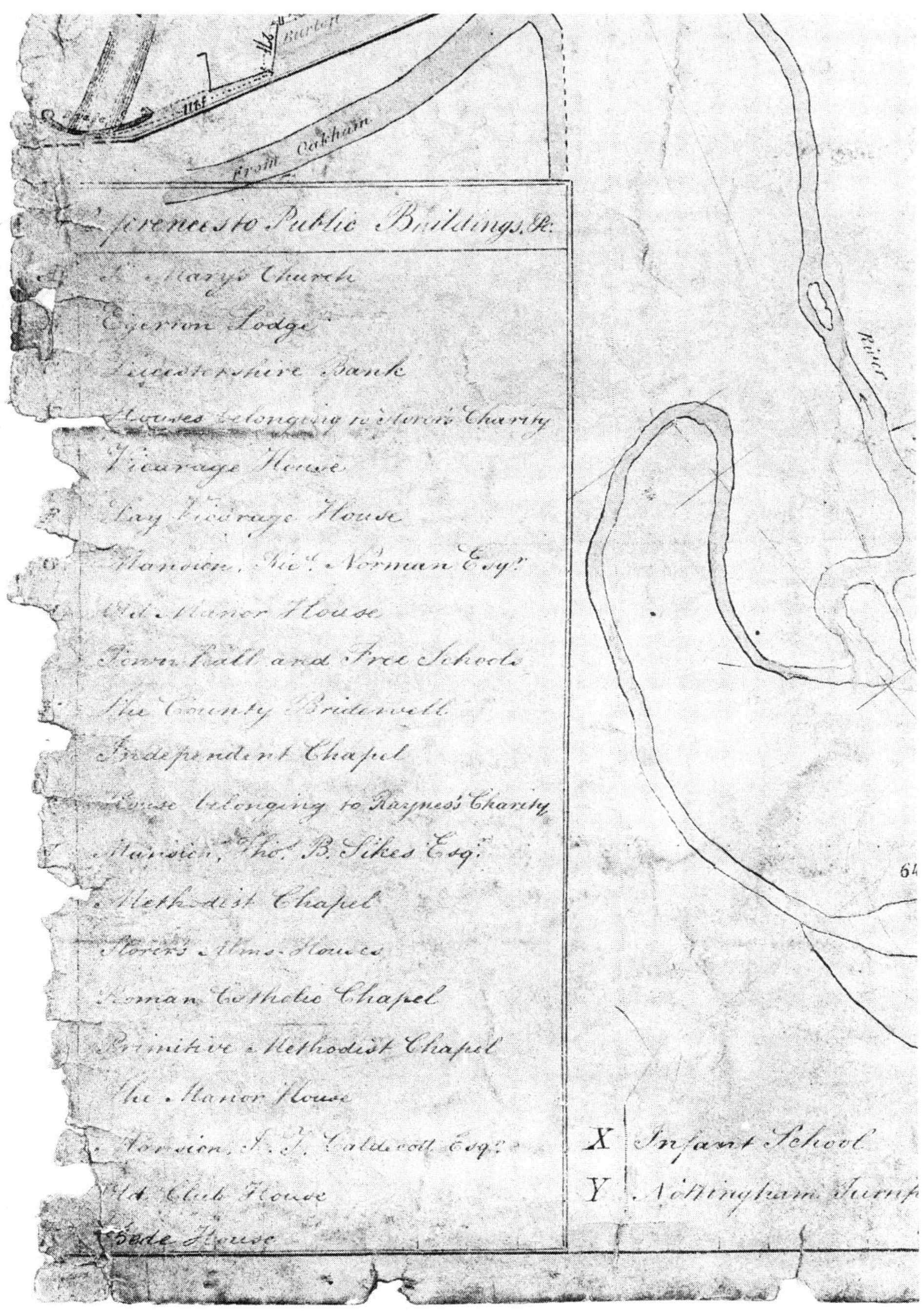

Fig. 128 Melton Mowbray, Leicestershire, 1843. The table which lists public buildings and important private buildings is unique on a tithe map, though very common on published maps of the period. Source: PRO IR30 19/101. Photograph reproduced by kind permission of the Keeper of the Public Record Office.

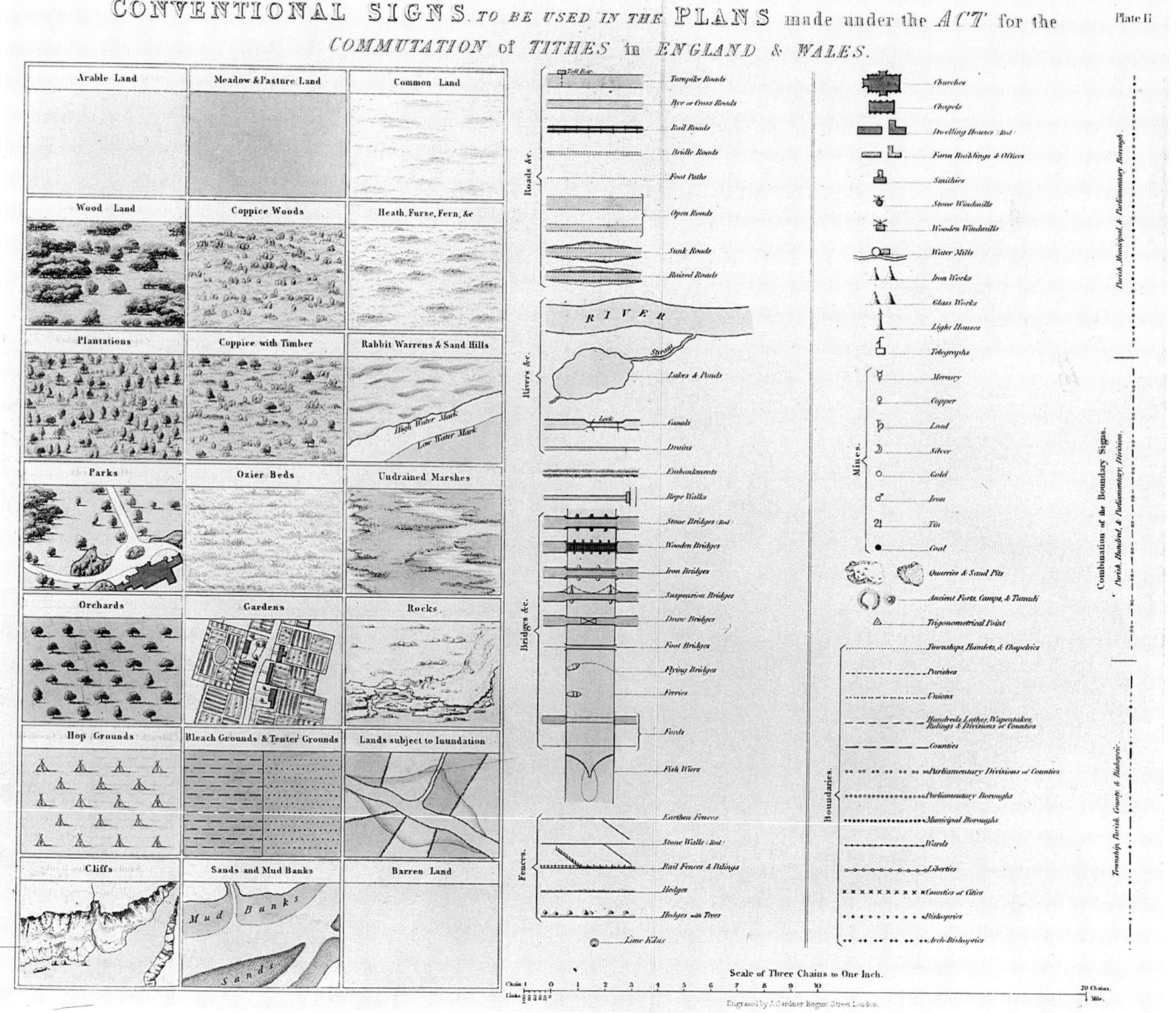

Fig. 129 R. K. Dawson's system of conventional signs for tithe maps. Source: 'Copy of papers respecting the proposed survey of lands under the Tithe Act', *British Parliamentary Papers (House of Commons)*, 1837, XLI.

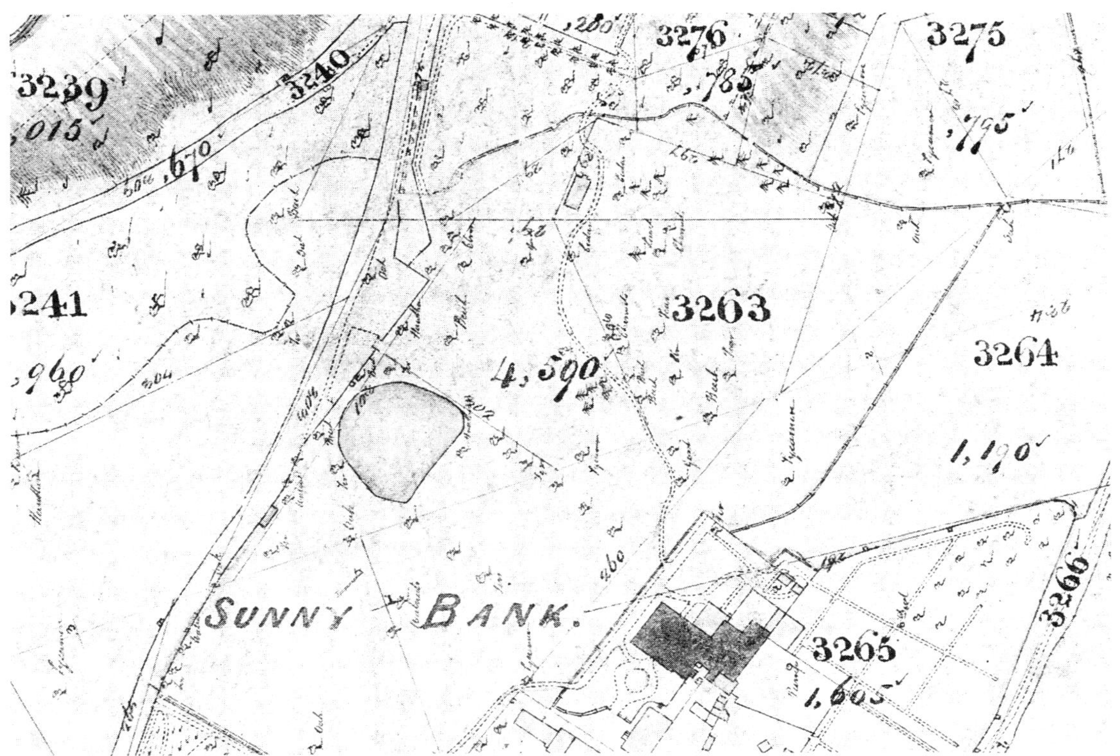

Fig. 130 Madeley, Shropshire, 1848. The record of parkland tree types, in minute writing, is unique to this map. Source: PRO IR30 29/211. Photograph reproduced by kind permission of the Keeper of the Public Record Office.

set in regular patterns to distinguish plantations from other woodland. In his instructions 'for the preparation of plans for the purpose of the Tithe Commutation Act', Robert Kearsley Dawson proposed the separate mapping by symbol of each of timber woods, plantations and coppices (Fig. 129) but very few tithe maps are found with symbols resembling those which he proposed and even fewer distinguish coppice from other types of woodland. Coppice may sometimes be identified by reference to tithe apportionments, though often the state of cultivation columns describe all woodland simply as 'wood'. Osiers are sometimes shown distinctively, often by a symbol which on casual inspection suggests wetland rather than woodland. Some map-makers used a conifer-like symbol for all woodland; this is particularly marked in Suffolk where the worst, but by no means only, culprits were the prolific map-making partnership of Lenny and Croft. Nor is it clear what definition of 'plantation' was used by surveyors or valuers; occasional discrepancies in this respect between map and apportionment are indicative of the problem.

Tithe maps rarely if ever provide a comprehensive record of trees growing in hedgerows but they often identify notable solitary landmark trees. Mere trees along boundaries are occasionally mapped and the particular tree type noted but the identification of tree species in Madeley Park, Shropshire is unique (Fig. 130).

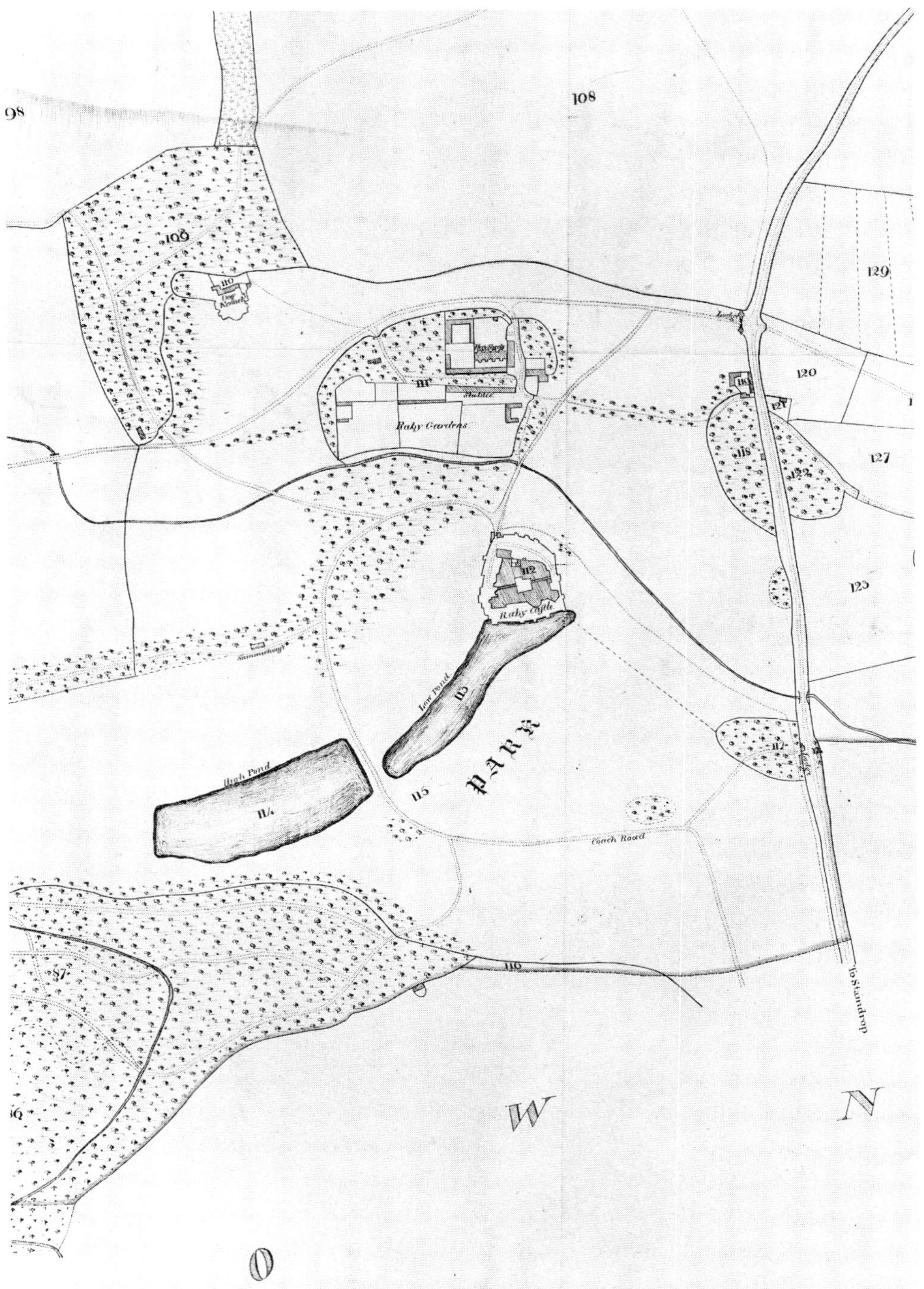

Fig. 131 Raby and Keverstone, Durham, *circa* 1839. This is a good example of parkland depiction on a tithe map. Source: PRO IR30 11/213. Photograph reproduced by kind permission of the Keeper of the Public Record Office.

Parks

The depiction of parks on tithe maps varies very widely from county to county. The two main methods for distinguishing parks from other grass and wood areas are to show them either by distinctive colour (often by a darker green than used to show ordinary grassland) or by symbols representing scattered clumps of trees; how far the latter are conventional or representational is a matter for local investigation (Fig. 131). Parks are distinguished less often on first-class maps but the marked under-representation of parkland on Kent tithe maps cannot be attributed wholly to this cause and rather must reflect local map-makers' practices.

Arable and grass

Arable and grass are distinguished from other land uses on 496 tithe maps or about 4 per cent of the whole. A further eight tithe maps show arable but not grass and another fifty-three distinguish grassland but not arable (Fig. 132). Very few first-class maps record either category, though had Dawson's scheme of November 1836 being carried into execution, every map would have carried this information. The usual method employed on those maps which do distinguish arable and grass is to tint arable land brown and grassland green, though red or pink are occasionally used for arable, and yellow or blue for grass (Figs. 133 and 134). In Gloucestershire and some other counties, land use is distinguished by coloured bands around the edge of fields. On a few tithe maps written annotations in fields are used and sometimes arable land is shown with conventional 'furrows' (Figs. 135 and 136).

Hops were an especially valuable arable crop and hop grounds were subject to extraordinary tithe rent-charges. This special status did not, however, guarantee special cartographic treatment. Where hop grounds are identified on tithe maps it is invariably by a pictorial symbol with a 'twining' core.

It is very unusual for grassland to be divided into meadow and pasture on tithe maps, though this distinction is usually made in tithe apportionment entries.

Orchards

Orchards are shown by regular pictorial symbols on 1,538 tithe maps (13 per cent of the total) but this mapping is only partly related to their geographical distribution. For example, in most Welsh counties few or no orchards are mapped yet they appear on over a quarter of Montgomeryshire tithe maps. Their recording on 33 per cent of Devon maps, 30 per cent of Gloucestershire maps and 37 per cent of Somerset maps can be explained by the importance of the cider industry in the South West but their presence on only 10 per cent of Surrey tithe maps, 17 per cent of those of Kent and less than 9 per cent of those of Essex seems not to reflect their actual distribution. Orchards are rarely recorded in those counties which were subject to extensive parliamentary enclosure which may reflect both the lesser importance of orchards in those counties and the larger proportion of tithe mapping of residual lands in these regions. There are some surprising discrepancies in the mapping of orchards between adjoining counties: orchards appear on over 25 per cent of Suffolk tithe maps but on less than 8 per cent of those of Norfolk.

Fig. 132 England and Wales: tithe maps which distinguish arable and grass.

Gardens

Gardens attached to houses are shown on 920 tithe maps (some 8 per cent of the whole). They are usually shown either by blocks of coloured bands, by abstract geometrical patterns of broken lines, by patterns of minature 'bushes', or by patterns representing stylised paths. Garden mapping varies widely from county to county with no obvious rationale; they are shown, for example, on over 21 per cent of Sussex tithe maps and 14 per cent of those of Kent, but on only 8 per cent of those of Middlesex, 5 per cent of Surrey maps, and 4 per cent of Essex tithe maps. Gardens are less often mapped in counties subject to extensive parliamentary enclosure and in Wales but there are some notable exceptions to this generalisation. In Warwickshire the proportion of maps showing gardens is slightly above the national average and in Montgomeryshire where 11 per cent of maps show gardens, it is markedly higher.

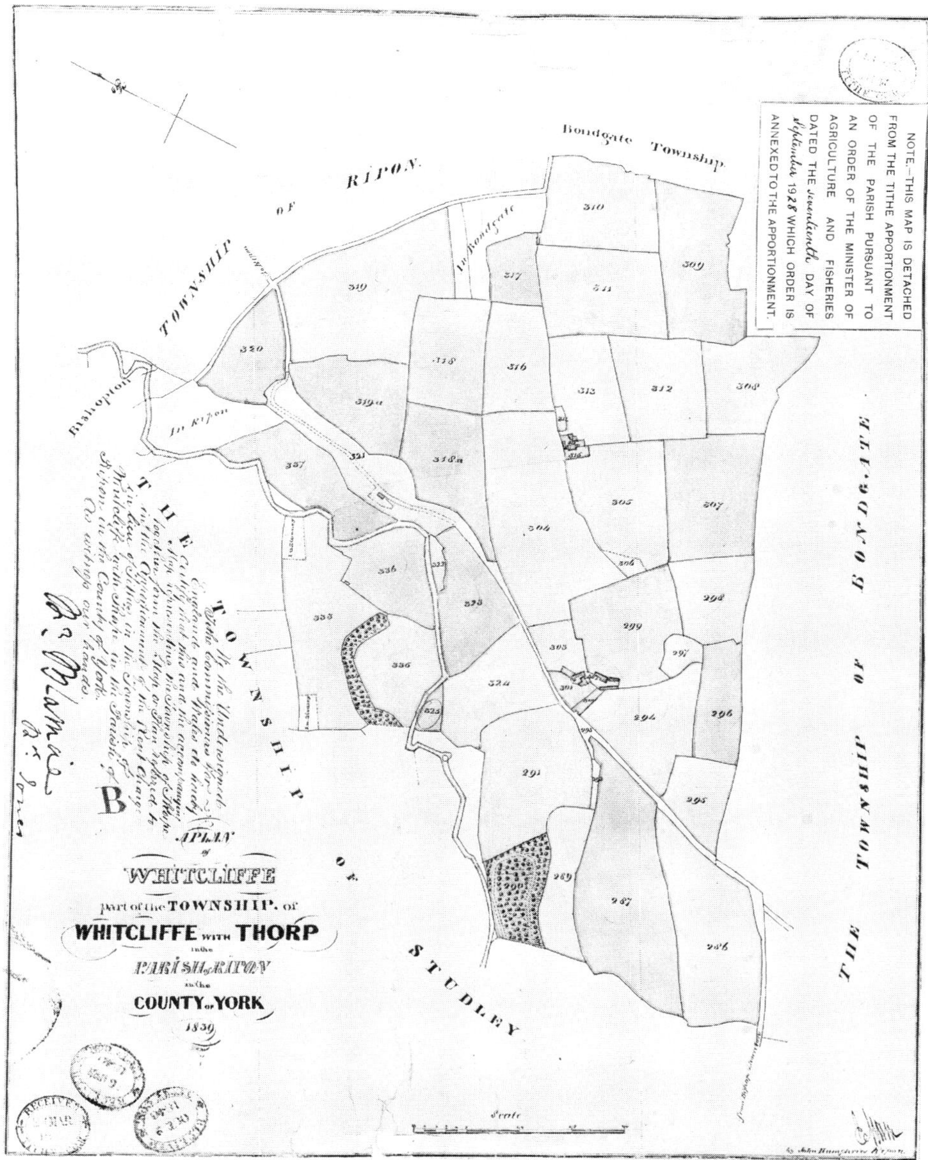

Fig. 133 Whitcliffe with Thorpe, West Riding of Yorkshire, 1839. The differential colouring of fields, discernible even on this black and white reproduction, is ornamental rather than functional and is peculiar to some Yorkshire tithe maps. Source: PRO IR30 43/429. Photograph reproduced by kind permission of the Keeper of the Public Record Office.

Heathland, moorland and waste

The mapping of uncultivated land varies from county to county in a way that has little to do with its actual distribution. In many Welsh and northern counties and in midland 'enclosure' counties these categories of land are rarely if ever recorded on tithe maps. Heaths, moors and wastes are identified on less than 5 per cent of West Riding maps but on more than 6 per cent of Suffolk maps, nearly 17 per cent of those of Sussex, and almost 20

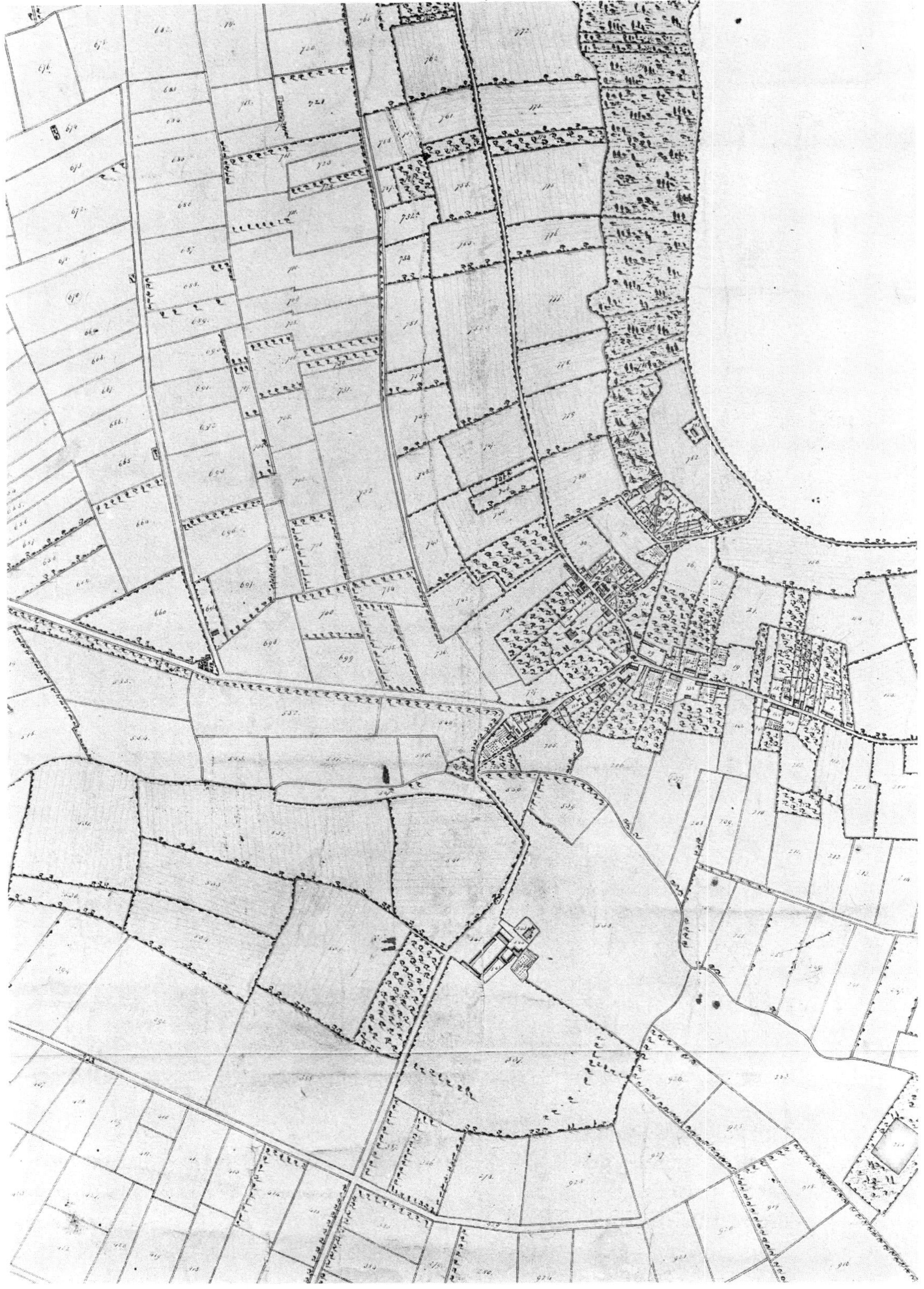

Fig. 134 Aller, Somerset, *circa* 1838. A splendid example of a map with full land use colouring. Source: PRO IR30 30/4. Photograph reproduced by kind permission of the Keeper of the Public Record Office.

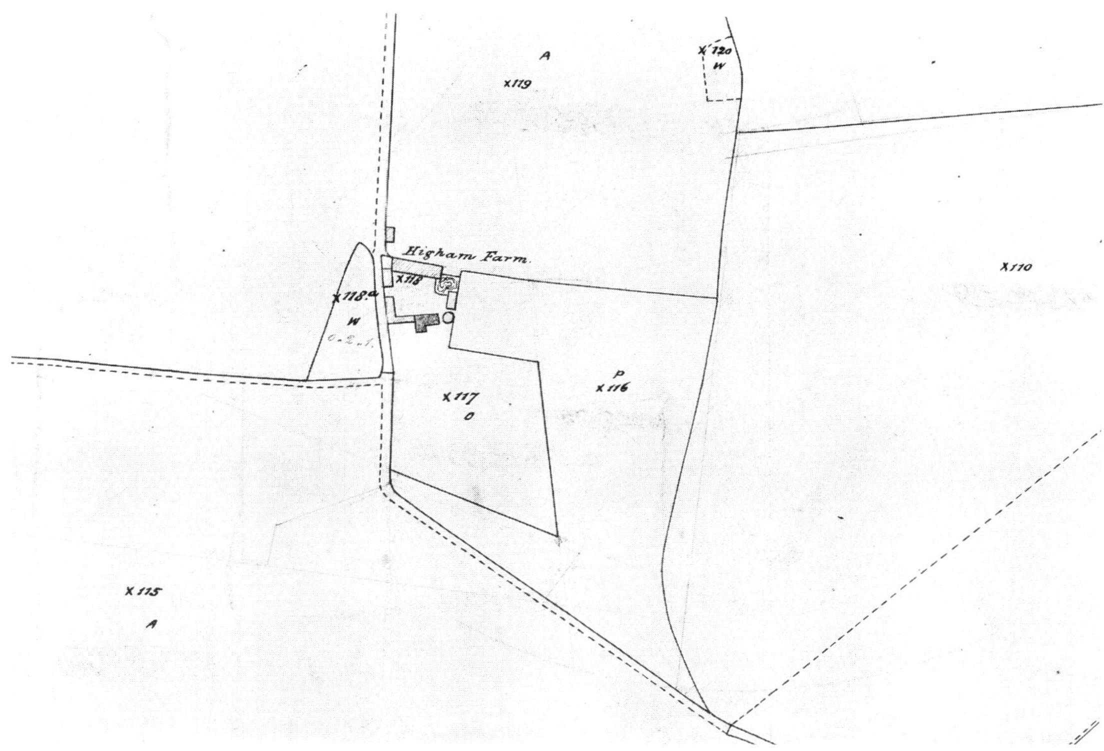

Fig. 135 Bridge and Patrixbourne, Kent, 1838. Arable and pasture are occasionally shown by 'A' and 'P', as here, rather than by use of colour. Source: PRO IR30 17/51. Photograph reproduced by kind permission of the Keeper of the Public Record Office.

per cent of those of Cornwall and Hertfordshire. These land uses are shown usually by a 'tufty' symbol similar to that used by the Ordnance Survey, though sometimes with the addition of colour. In his recommendations of November 1836, Dawson provided separate conventional symbols for common and heathland but these are never employed. He also recommended that rabbit warrens be portrayed distinctively but very few warrens are recorded on tithe maps.

Wetlands

Only 265 tithe maps (less than 3 per cent) distinguish marshes and other wetlands. In some counties no wetlands are recorded at all whereas in Berkshire wetlands appear on 13 per cent of the maps. Whether wetlands are mapped or not on tithe maps clearly relates more to local mapping practice than to the actual distribution of this kind of land. Wetlands are usually shown by either a reedy symbol, somewhat similar to that favoured by the Ordnance Survey, by flecking in black or blue, or by a combination of the two methods.

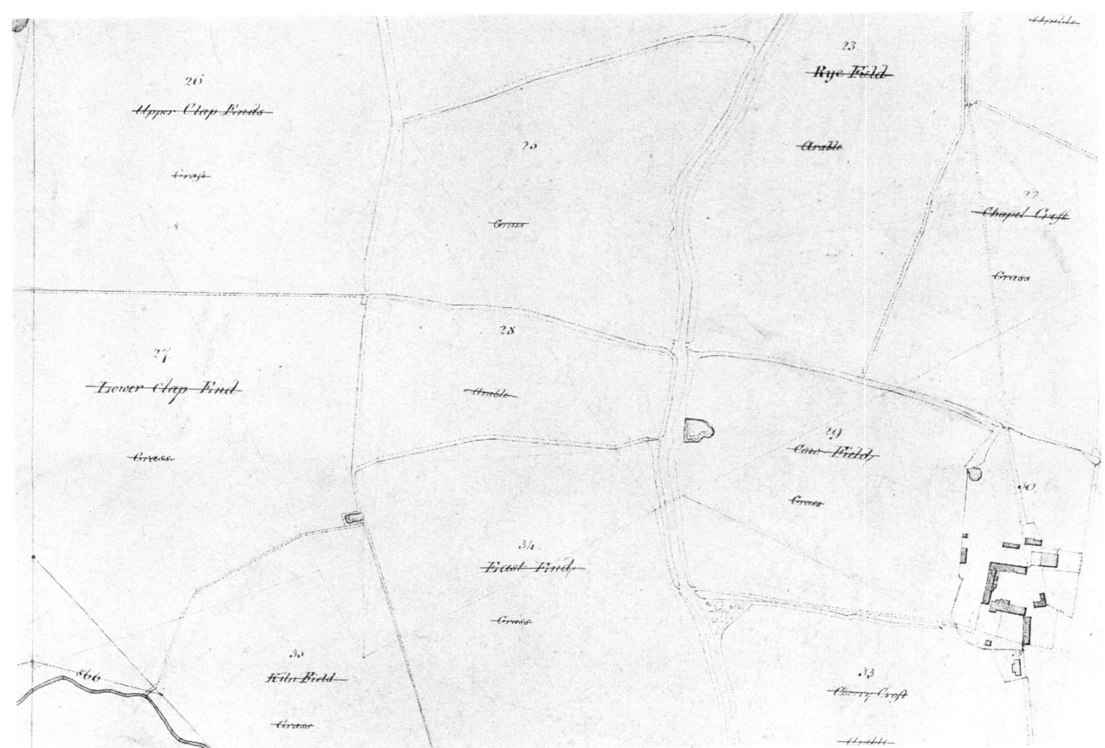

Fig. 136 Folkington, Sussex, 1838. Tithe maps occasionally distinguish land uses by annotation rather than by colour. This map also records field names. Source: PRO IR30 35/107. Photograph reproduced by kind permission of the Keeper of the Public Record Office.

Fields

Open fields

By 1836 the enclosure of open field was very nearly complete and many of the 656 tithe maps which record open fields contain little more than a few residual strips of arable or meadow. The high figure of 44 per cent of Hertfordshire maps which depict open fields is exceptional, as are the Rutland maps of districts where open-field farming was still practised on an extensive scale (Fig. 137). Enclosure subsequent to tithe commutation meant that tithe dues had to be re-apportioned and an altered apportionment and map prepared. Altered apportionment maps of recently enclosed districts provide useful before-and-after comparisons (Fig. 138).

Field boundaries

Tithe maps record several different types of field boundary, including hedges, fences, stone walls (unusually) and earthern banks (very exceptionally), and also field boundary ownership (Fig. 139). However, although 1,648 tithe maps (14 per cent) show hedges or fences, only 364 of those maps (just over 3 per cent of all tithe maps) show both. Some 73 per cent of the 868 tithe maps which show hedges indicate hedge ownership, usually by drawing the hedge symbol on the owner's side of a single line which denotes the field boundary, or by a symbol, usually a 'T', placed in the enclosure to which the field

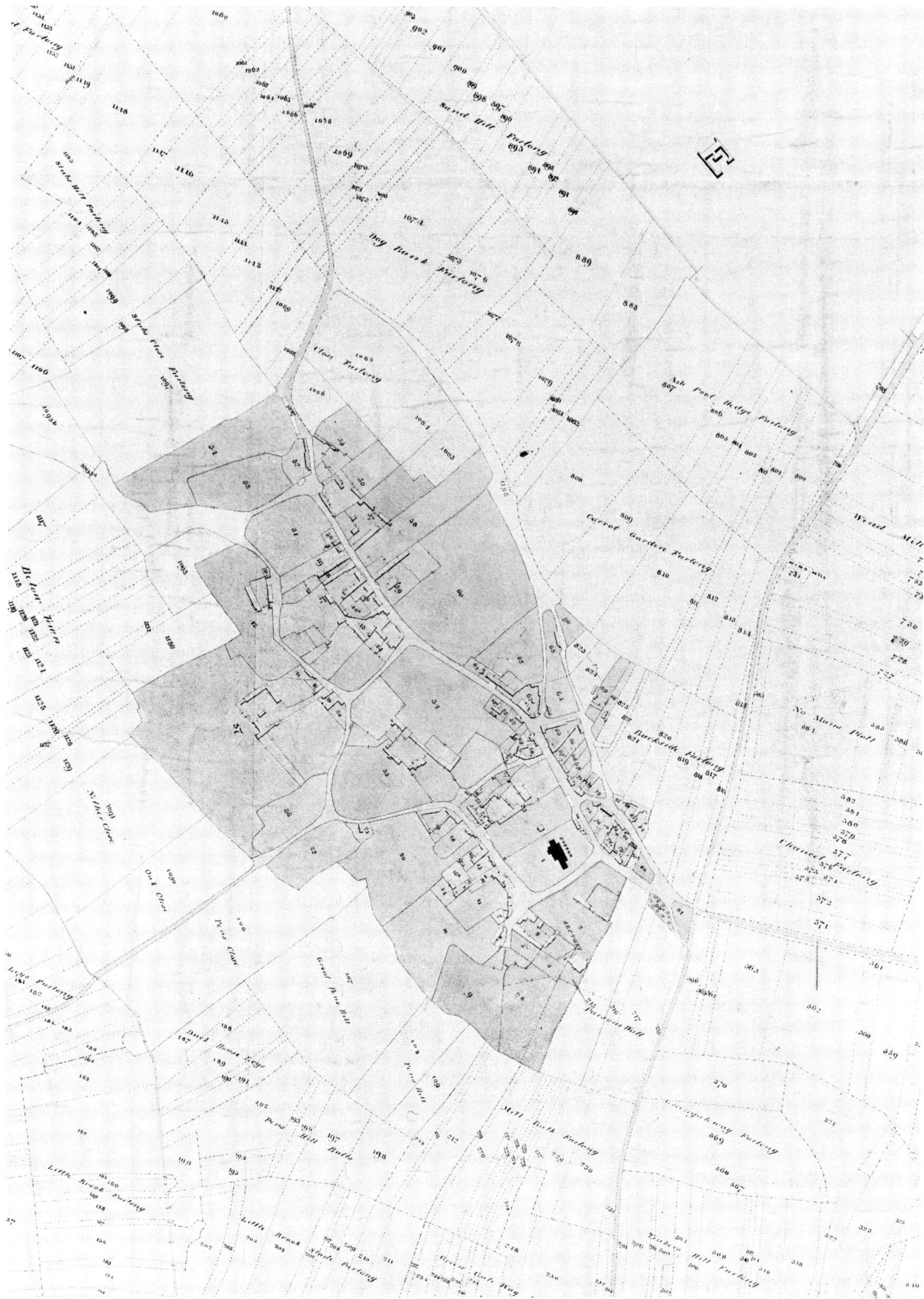

Fig. 137 Seaton, Rutland, 1847. In parts of the English Midlands extensive open-field farming continued long enough to be recorded on tithe maps. This district was wholly reapportioned in 1862 following enclosure: see Fig. 138. Source: PRO IR30 28/27. Photograph reproduced by kind permission of the Keeper of the Public Record Office.

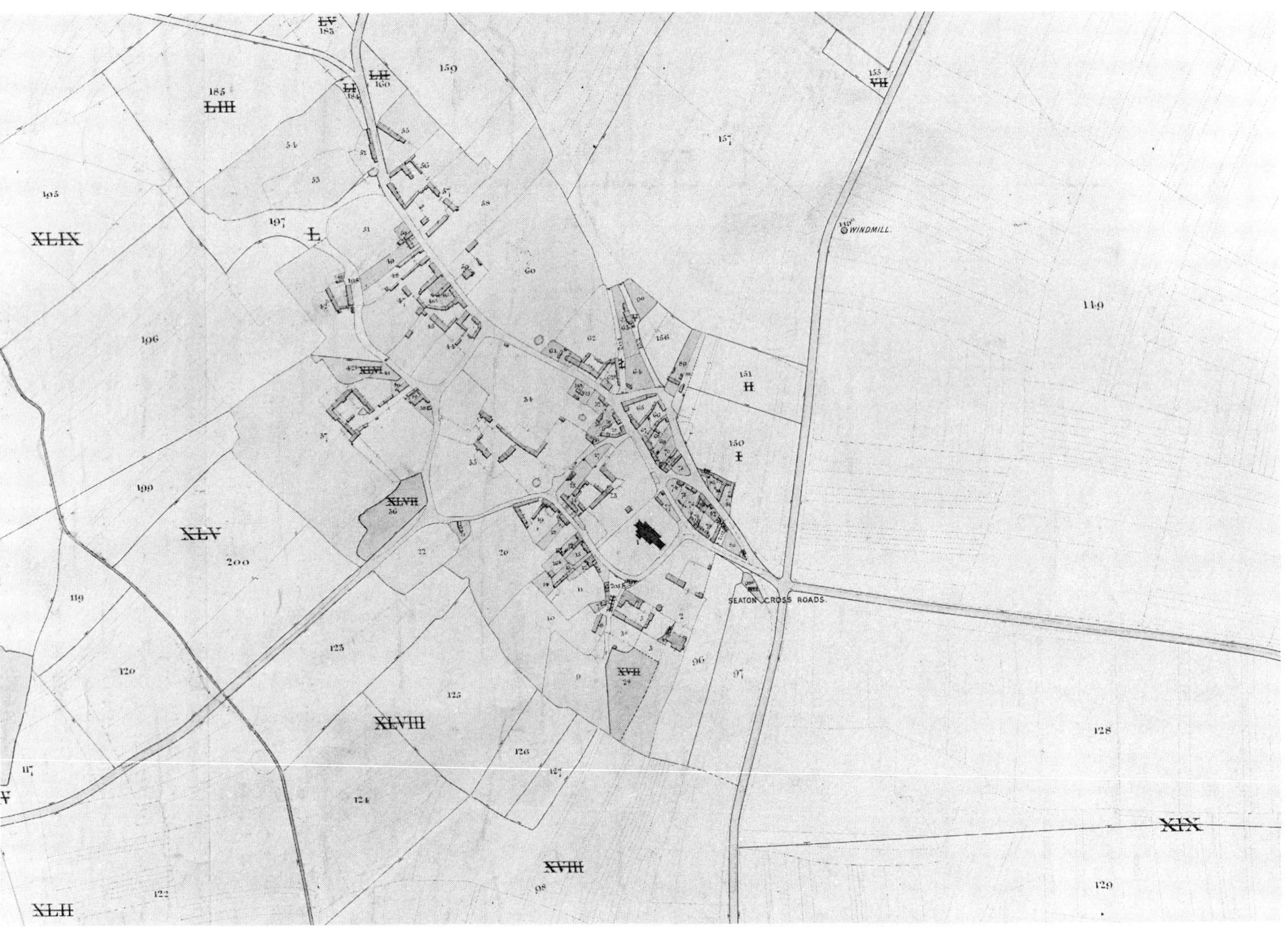

Fig. 138 Seaton, Rutland, altered apportionment map, 1862. This is one of a number of maps prepared for districts where the open fields were enclosed some years after tithe commutation had been effected. Source: PRO IR30 28/27. Photograph reproduced by kind permission of the Keeper of the Public Record Office.

Fig. 139 England and Wales: tithe maps which record the ownership of field boundaries.

boundary belongs, or by similarly placed colour bands. Although rather more tithe maps show fences rather than hedges, only 22 per cent of those maps show fence ownership. Fences are usually shown similarly to hedges, by a symbol on its side. Walls are usually represented by very narrow double lines but occasionally by a 'battlement' effect.

Proportionately more first-class maps record hedges and fences; over 25 per cent show either one or the other, though only just over 6 per cent show both. Very many more first- than second-class maps record field boundary ownership.

Field gates

Field gates are shown on 1,413 tithe maps, 12 per cent of the total. Most counties have a few maps with them (except in Wales, where not a single one is recorded outside Monmouthshire) but there are pronounced concentrations in the south-east of England,

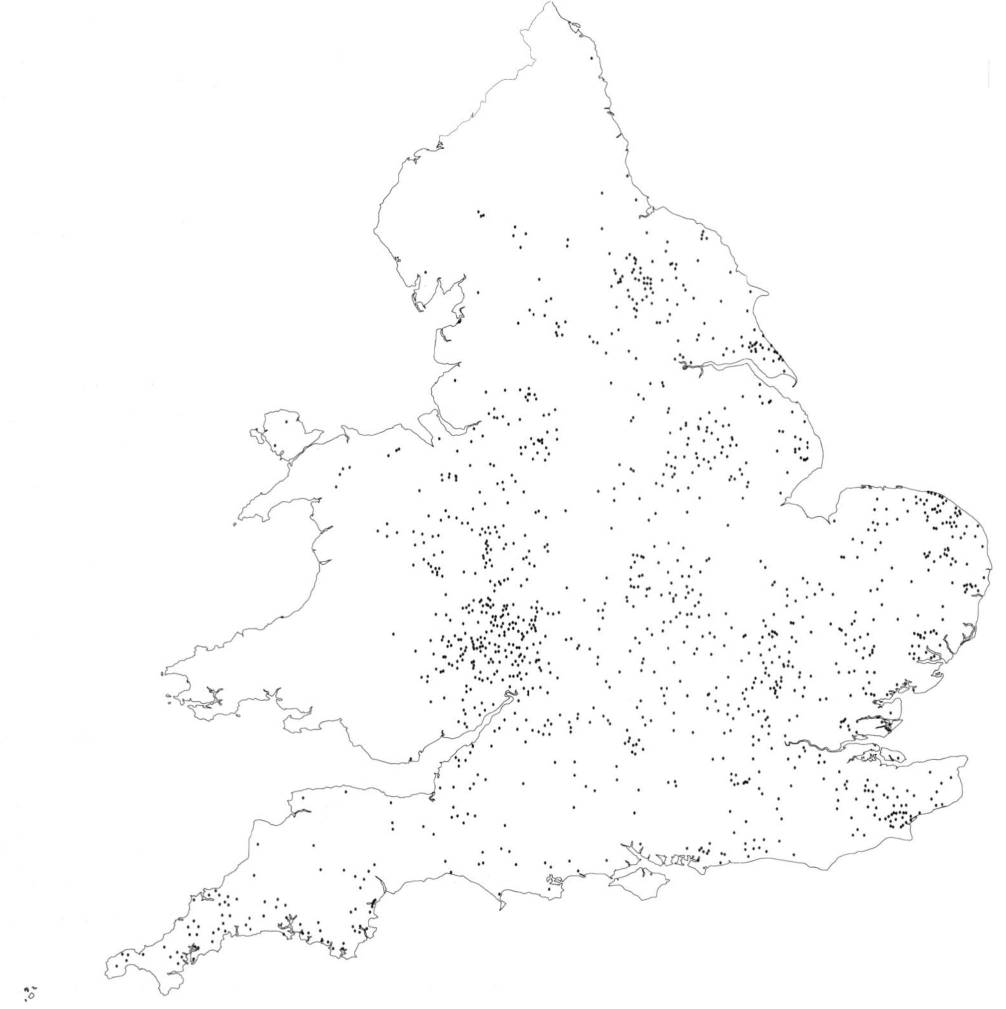

Fig. 140 England and Wales: tithe maps with field names.

Devon, and in Shropshire and most of its adjoining English counties. In both Shropshire and Sussex gates are recorded on 27 per cent of tithe maps; in contrast they are recorded on only 3 per cent of Yorkshire tithe maps. Gates are recorded more often on first-class maps (nearly 26 per cent) than on second-class maps (10 per cent) but there is extensive recording of gates in counties such as Cheshire and Shropshire with below average first-class tithe map cover.

Field names

Field names appear on 549 tithe maps, about 5 per cent of the total. It is very unusual for a tithe map to contain a comprehensive record of field names, though of course this information is usually available in the apportionments. Often the names are of open fields or former open fields and there is an above-average proportion of maps with field names in those counties most affected by parliamentary enclosure. The highest proportion of maps with field names (25 per cent) is in Hertfordshire, whereas hardly any fields are named in Wales and very few are named on the tithe maps of 'upland' English counties (Fig. 140).

Miscellaneous features

The primary purpose of the tithe surveys was to record the boundaries of tithe areas and this intention was expressed most purely in the first-class 'working plans'. Almost everything else – names, land use, ownership information – was inessential and was provided largely as a result of either the particular practice of the private estate mappers recruited to the tithe survey, or because these additional features were already present on existing maps used in so many places as a basis for tithe commutation maps. Indeed, R. K. Dawson recommended that tithe maps should contain 'all the details usually given in estate surveys'.[25] Miscellaneous features which appear on tithe maps as a result of these processes include leisure facilities, archaeological information, village greens, inns and public houses, boundary land marks, the boundaries and naming of estates, and public buildings.

Although cricket grounds and recreation grounds set out under enclosure awards are occasionally depicted, the most common sports facilities recorded on tithe maps are race courses. At Whittington, Staffordshire the grandstand, 'winning chair' and 'betting chair' are identified. Fox-hunting kennels are noted occasionally.

Archaeological information plotted on tithe maps is mainly confined to major earthworks, such as Cadbury Castle in Somerset, the occasional white horse, for example at Westbury, Wiltshire, and castles. The tithe map of Lindfield, Sussex records the site of a priory 'quite unknown prior to this survey'. Occasionally ancient earthworks are shown in plan but not named; for example, some unnamed rings on the original map of Honington, Lincolnshire are described as a Roman camp on an altered apportionment map.

The depiction of boundaries of landed estates and annotations of landowners' names are uncommon on tithe maps. Estate or holding boundaries are shown more often in those parts of the country to the north-west of an Exe–Tees line, probably because of the greater incidence of apportionment by holdings or estates in those parts of the country. Maps such as that of Southwell in Nottinghamshire which indicate types of land tenure field-by-field are very exceptional (Fig. 141). The naming of landowners or estates or farms (as opposed to farm buildings) is in general uncommon but there are two important exceptions. One is the naming and often also the distinctive colouring of glebe, charity or other land with special or tithe-exempt status; the other is naming the landowners surrounding isolated parcels of tithable land detached from the main part of a tithe district or surrounded by tithe free land within a tithe district.

Borders and cartouches

Borders on tithe maps vary from the non-existent, as on the great majority of maps, through plain single lines, colour bands within casings, to abstract or floral patterns. With the proviso that some borders have been partly or completely cropped from the Public

[25] Cited in Kain and Prince, *The tithe surveys of England and Wales*, p. 83.

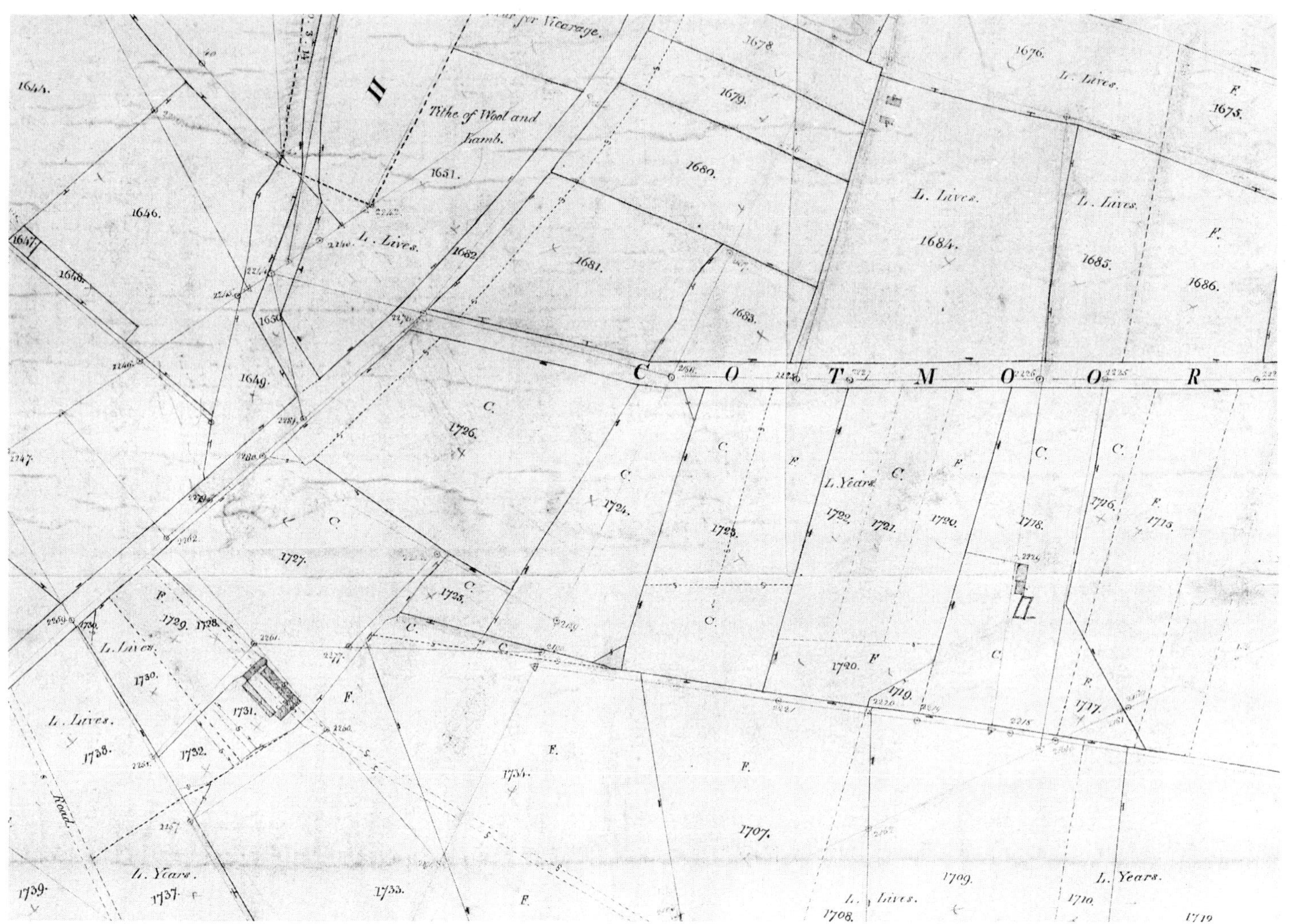

Fig. 141 Southwell, Nottinghamshire, 1840. This first-class map with construction lines is unusual as it indicates land tenure: 'C' for copyhold, 'F' for freehold and 'L' for leasehold. Field boundary ownership is shown by 'T' symbols. Source: PRO IR30 26/112. Photograph reproduced by kind permission of the Keeper of the Public Record Office.

Record Office collection of tithe maps and that more will probably be found on diocesan map copies, decorative borders have been found on 576 tithe maps (5 per cent). Ornamental borders appear on only 2 per cent of first-class maps, a reflection of the 'plain working plan' concept. As with most such matters incidental to the prime purpose of tithe maps, the provision of a decorative border was a matter for the individual map-maker. For example, the above-average numbers in the East Riding of Yorkshire and Staffordshire are due to the practices of Edward Page and J. P. Lofthouse respectively. Page favoured an unusual wavy-line pattern and Lofthouse employed ball and half-quatrefoil decoration suggestive of a ceiling cornice. Tithe maps lithographed by Standidge usually have a plain line border with inset quarter-circular corners.

Cartouches are present on 253 tithe maps, 2 per cent of the total. The majority are fairly plain boxes or shaded circles; those with pictorial or symbolic elements are exceptional and are discussed below. Once again their provision was very much a reflection of individual map-makers' practices; the highest proportion of maps with cartouches, nearly 30 per cent, is in Pembrokeshire where their use is directly attributable to the Goode and Philpott map-making partnership, whose maps also account for most of the cartouches in Carmarthenshire and Glamorganshire.

Legends, explanations and tabulated information

Although late twentieth-century map users are accustomed to maps with legends, mid-nineteenth century map users were not. Until nearly the end of the century the Ordnance Survey confined its explanation of map signs and symbols to information on county index sheets. Users of tithe maps were no better served. One reason for this was that the majority of the symbols used are readily recognisable, for instance, groups of trees signify woodland, blue infill indicates ponds, and roads with boldened casing are more important than those without. More problematic are symbols for boundaries which could not be expressed by pictograms and a minority of tithe maps do carry full explanations of such boundary symbols. Comparatively few tithe maps contain comprehensive legends (Figs. 142, 143, and 144).

A few tithe maps have tables of landowners, occupiers, field acreages, or summaries of land use; these are invariably lightly struck through, suggesting that their presence may be due to adoption and copying of existing maps (Fig. 145). Index diagrams to surveys in several parts are provided on a few maps (Figs. 146 and 147), as are diagrams of districts which were composed of several detached parts (Fig. 148).[26]

Decoration on tithe maps

Decoration on tithe maps can be divided into that which is functional, such as the pictorial representation of windmills and churches which would be mapped anyway in some form, and that which is purely ornamental or symbolic, such as decoration of cartouches.

Extensive areas of colour are used on tithe maps for various purposes as, for example a

[26] In the course of conservation work in the 1930s indexes were prepared for some multi-part tithe maps using the contemporary Ordnance Survey six-inch maps as a base.

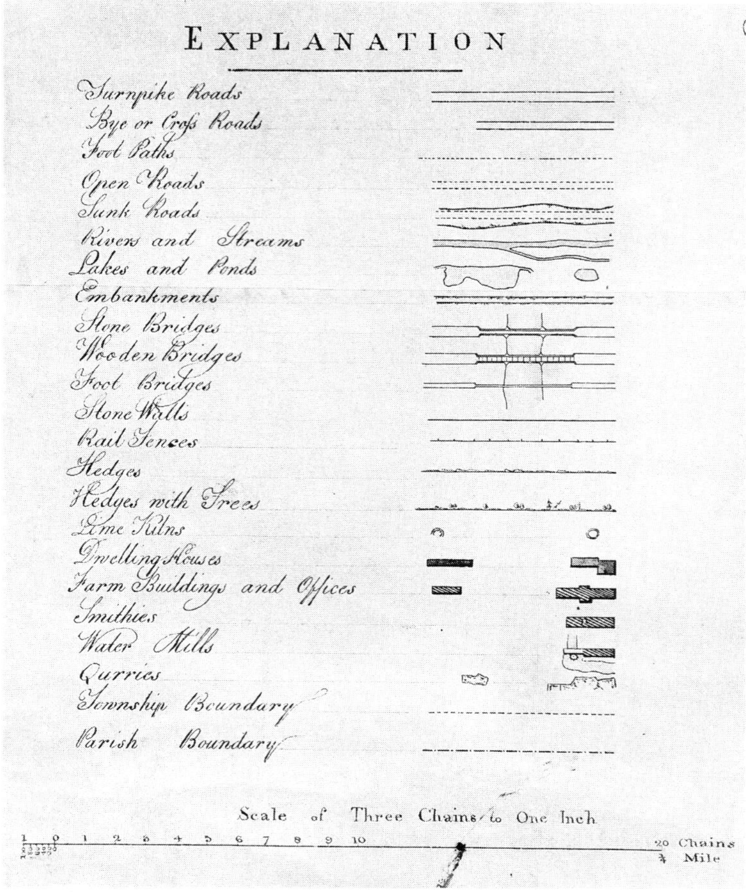

Fig. 142 Gargrave, West Riding of Yorkshire, 1839 by John Greenwood. It is rare for a tithe map to carry such a comprehensive legend as this and to use symbols so closely resembling those recommended by Dawson (cf. Fig. 129). The style of lettering is similar to that used by Christopher Greenwood on his county maps. Source: PRO IR30 43/165. Photograph reproduced by kind permission of the Keeper of the Public Record Office.

ground tint to highlight tithable land in a district (Fig. 149). The use of colour for such purposes is a function of the preferences of individual map-makers. S. Hill and Son of Croft, Lincolnshire, for example, usually tint tithable areas on their second-class maps in green. Such tinting, essentially an aid to legibility, is not found on first-class maps. Colour-tinting is also extensively employed to show lands either wholly exempt from tithe, or else subject to moduses or other special tithing status (Fig. 150).

It is unusual for ordinary buildings to be represented pictorially on tithe maps but in certain parts of England it is common to show windmills and churches pictorially. Sometimes windmills are shown in plan as ordinary buildings with an 'X' added on a stalk to represent the sails, sometimes they are shown by stylised drawings, and occasionally they are drawn realistically as post-mills or tower-mills. Pictorial windmills are particularly common in the eastern counties; they are unusual but not unknown on first-class maps (Fig. 151).

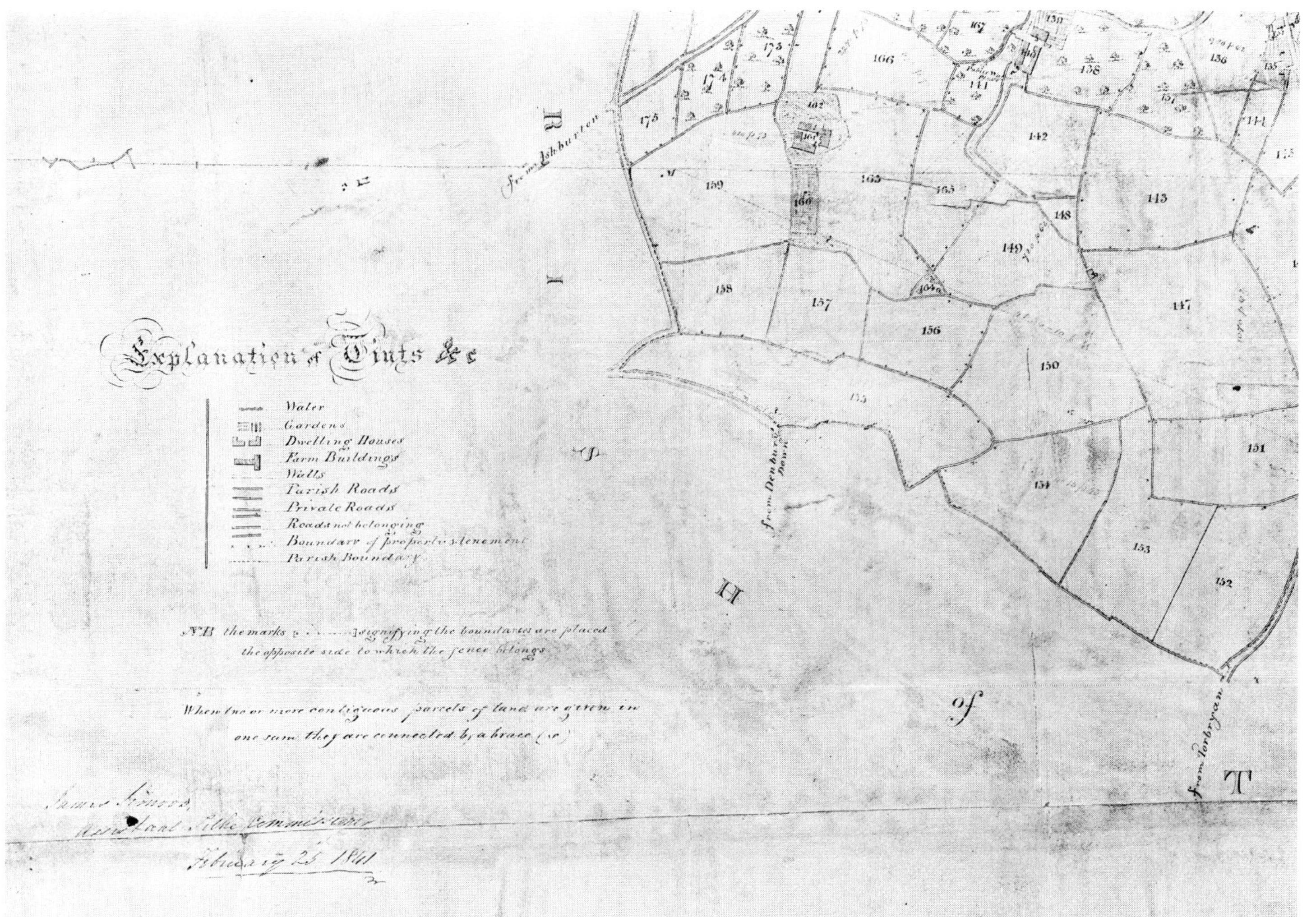

Fig. 143 Denbury, Devon, 1839. Legends explaining conventions are unusual on tithe maps, though for the most part the symbolism used on most tithe maps is self-explanatory. Source: PRO IR30 9/151. Photograph reproduced by kind permission of the Keeper of the Public Record Office.

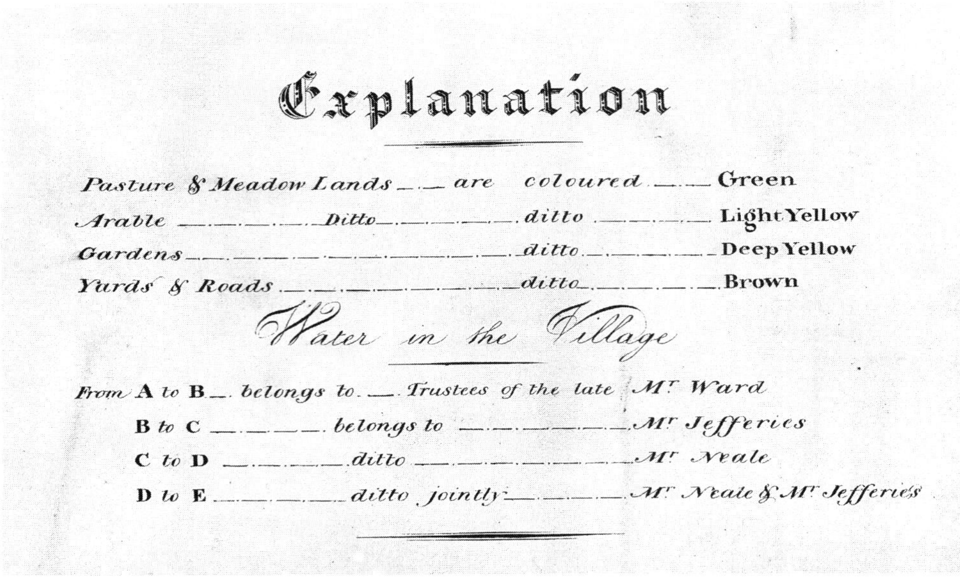

Explanation

Pasture & Meadow Lands ___ are coloured ___ Green
Arable ___ Ditto ___ ditto ___ Light Yellow
Gardens ___ ditto ___ Deep Yellow
Yards & Roads ___ ditto ___ Brown

Water in the Village

From A to B ___ belongs to ___ Trustees of the late Mr Ward
B to C ___ belongs to ___ Mr Jefferies
C to D ___ ditto ___ Mr Neale
D to E ___ ditto jointly ___ Mr Neale & Mr Jefferies

Fig. 144 Draycott Foliatt, Wiltshire, 1838. An explanation of symbols is sometimes found on tithe maps but the notes on water ownership are unique to this map. Source: PRO IR30 38/104. Photograph reproduced by kind permission of the Keeper of the Public Record Office.

Unlike windmills, churches are universal features of the landscape. The usual manner of representing churches on tithe maps is to show them in plan with perhaps distinctive colouring or the addition of a cross. Sometimes they are identified by a cross symbol alone, a practice which is particularly common in Wales.[27] The pictorial representation of churches ranges from stylised portrayals similar to those used on Elizabethan county maps to what appear to be realistic representations. Although scattered examples can be found in most counties, the pictorial representation of churches is mostly concentrated in a broad swathe from Somerset to Norfolk, in which last county the practice reaches its most extreme manifestation with pictorial churches on nearly 29 per cent of the county's tithe maps. Sometimes the churchyard with gravestones is depicted; at Erpingham, Norfolk there are birds overhead and a couple are walking towards the church. As with windmills, pictorial churches are found less often on first-class maps; the example illustrated in Fig. 153 is all the more remarkable for being on a map by Richard Barnes of Lowestoft whose first-class maps are otherwise of unusual austerity. Other buildings are occasionally depicted pictorially, as, for example, a pigeon house at Barwick, Somerset (Fig. 154).

The most common type of purely decorative embellishment on tithe maps is the scale bar drawn as a ruler with chamfered corners. Much less common than embellished scale bars are coloured floral surrounds of map titles, dates on stone slabs resting against broken

[27] This is characteristic of John Haslam's Anglesey maps. Haslam had formerly worked for the Ordnance Survey and he may have inherited the practice from his Ordnance Survey experience.

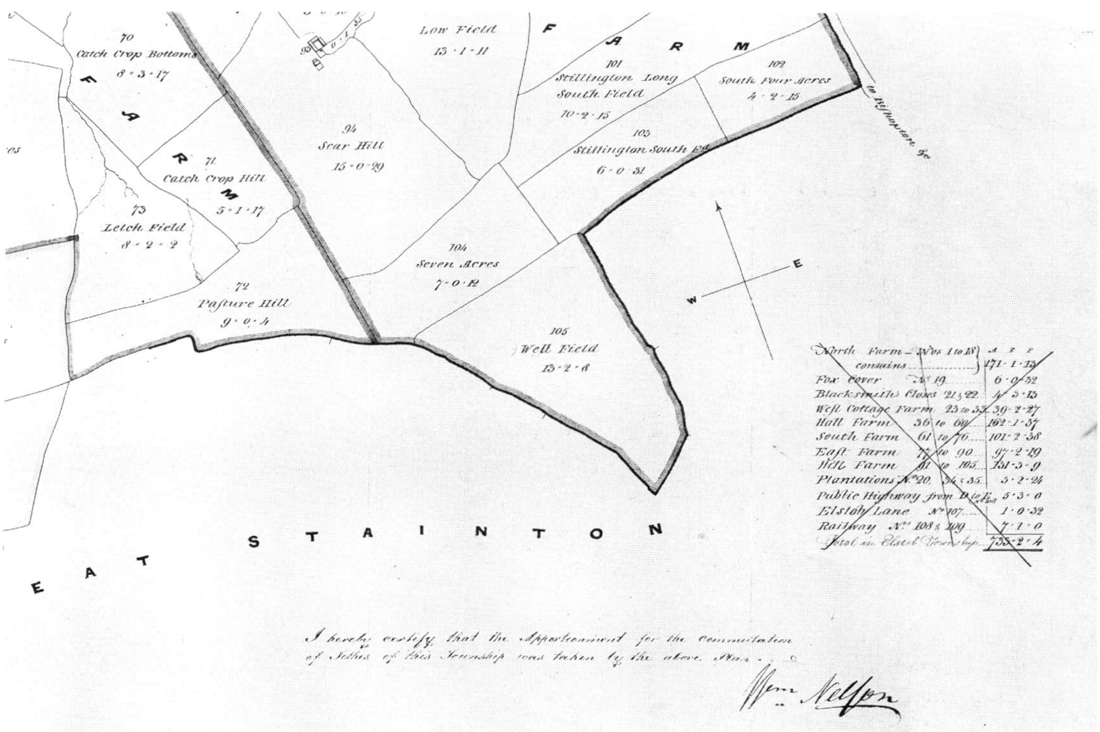

Fig. 145 Elstob, Durham, 1837. Tithe maps occasionally carry tables which list farms and their acreages. Such tables were not favoured by the Tithe Commission and, as on this map, they are usually struck through. Source: PRO IR30 11/89. Photograph reproduced by kind permission of the Keeper of the Public Record Office.

columns or tree trunks, decoration of ordinary scale bars by displays of drawing instruments (encountered in the South West and occasionally elsewhere) or farm implements (a Yorkshire speciality), and drawings of churches or mansions within map titles (Figs. 153, 155, 156, 157, 158, 159, and 160). A few maps of districts in the South West have sea areas decorated with ships (Fig. 161); the small steamship on the map of Eccles, Norfolk (Fig. 162) is exceptional both in its location and in its subject matter. Also a south-western speciality is the recitation of mottoes on tithe maps as, for example, the declaration of 'Union, Peace and Plenty' on the map of Blackawton, Devon.

Though most decoration on tithe maps is ornamental, occasionally it has the function of supplementing the information on the map by providing evidence of the elevation of buildings and other structures. A notable example is Winchelsea Castle in Sussex (Fig. 163).

Altered tithe apportionments and maps

Even before the initial tithe commutation process was completed, it was subjected to detailed amendment in the form of altered tithe apportionments and maps. There were

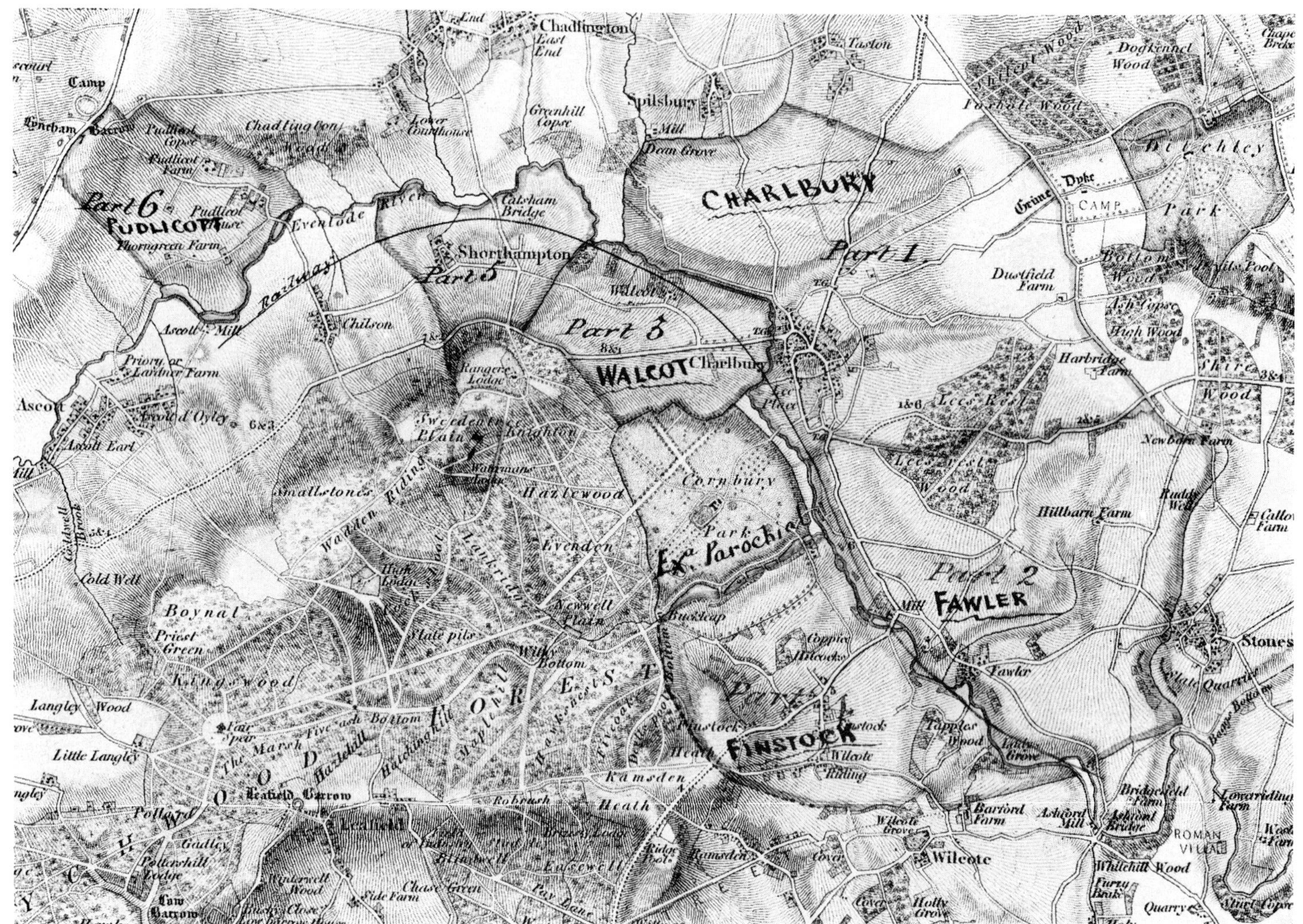

Fig. 146 Charlbury, Oxfordshire, 1848. Although many tithe maps were drawn in several parts, and although by this time much of England and Wales was covered by the Ordnance Survey one-inch Old Series, this is the only instance where a published Ordnance Survey map was used as an index to the various parts of a tithe map. Source: PRO IR30 27/30. Photograph reproduced by kind permission of the Keeper of the Public Record Office.

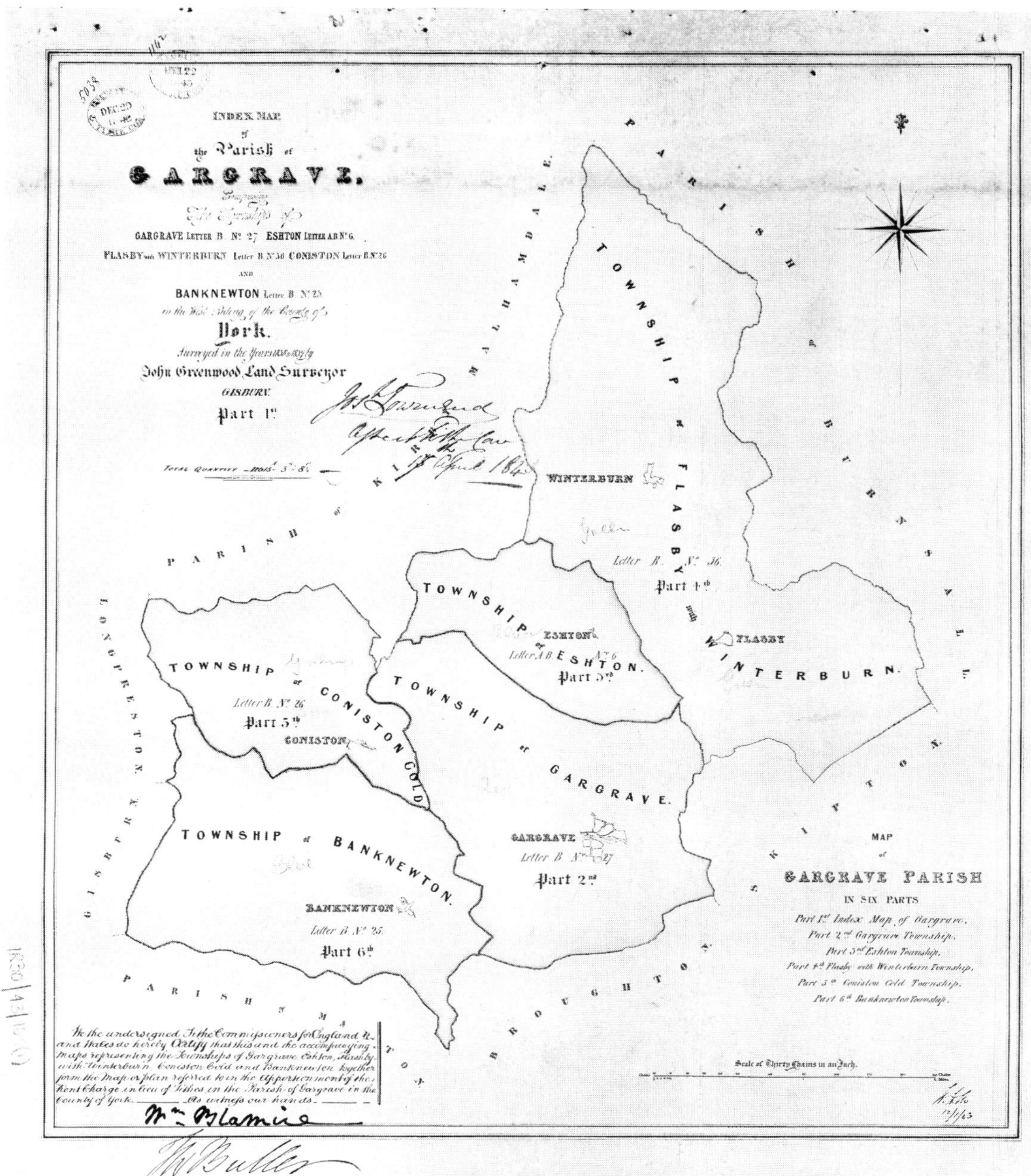

Fig. 147 Gargrave, West Riding of Yorkshire, 1839. Diagrams such as this of the constituent townships within a parish are unusual on tithe maps. Source: PRO IR30 43/165. Photograph reproduced by kind permission of the Keeper of the Public Record Office.

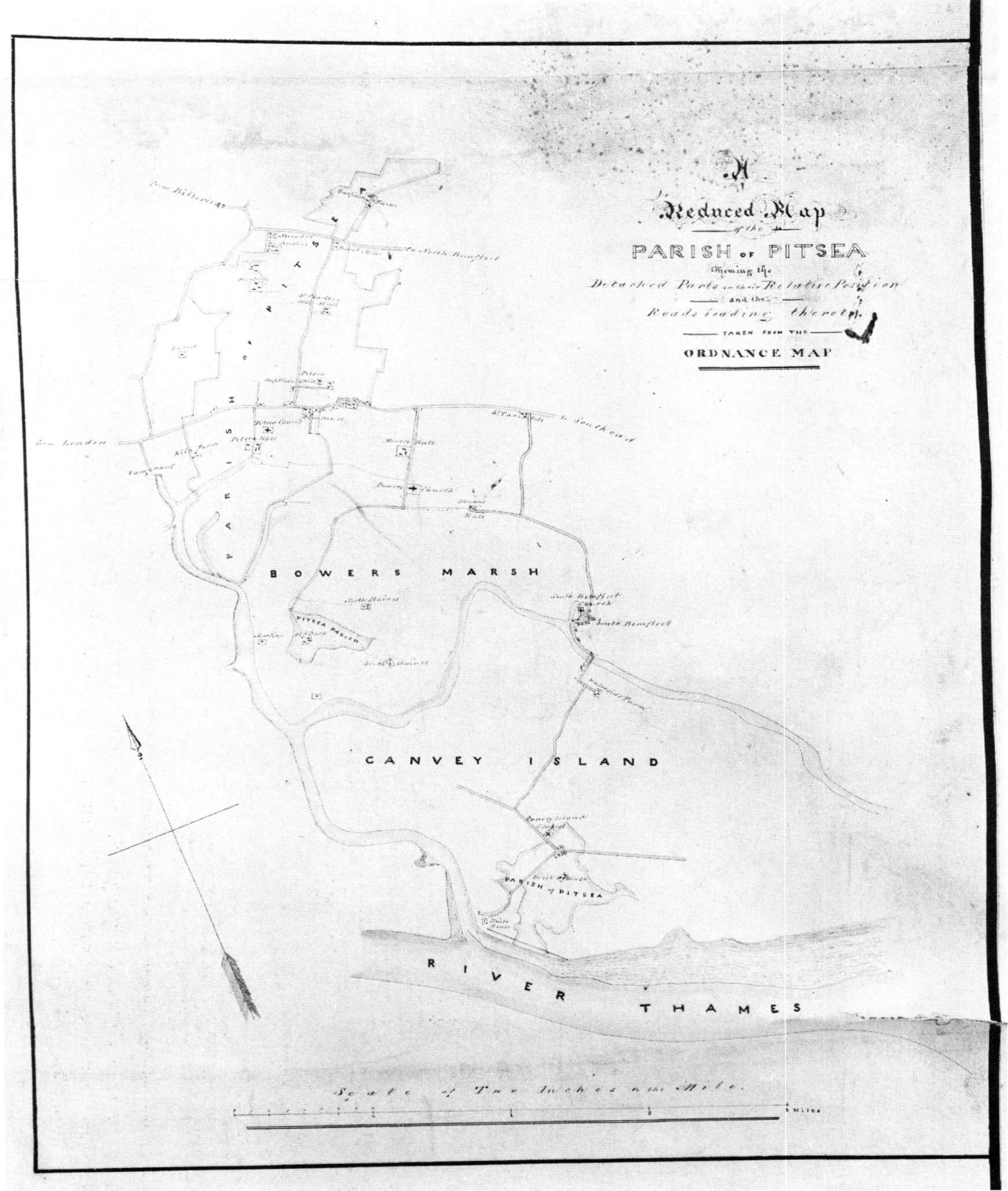

Fig. 148 Pitsea, Essex, 1845. Small index maps are occasionally provided for parishes with scattered detached parts; this one claims to be derived from the Ordnance Survey. Source: PRO IR30 12/264. Photograph reproduced by kind permission of the Keeper of the Public Record Office.

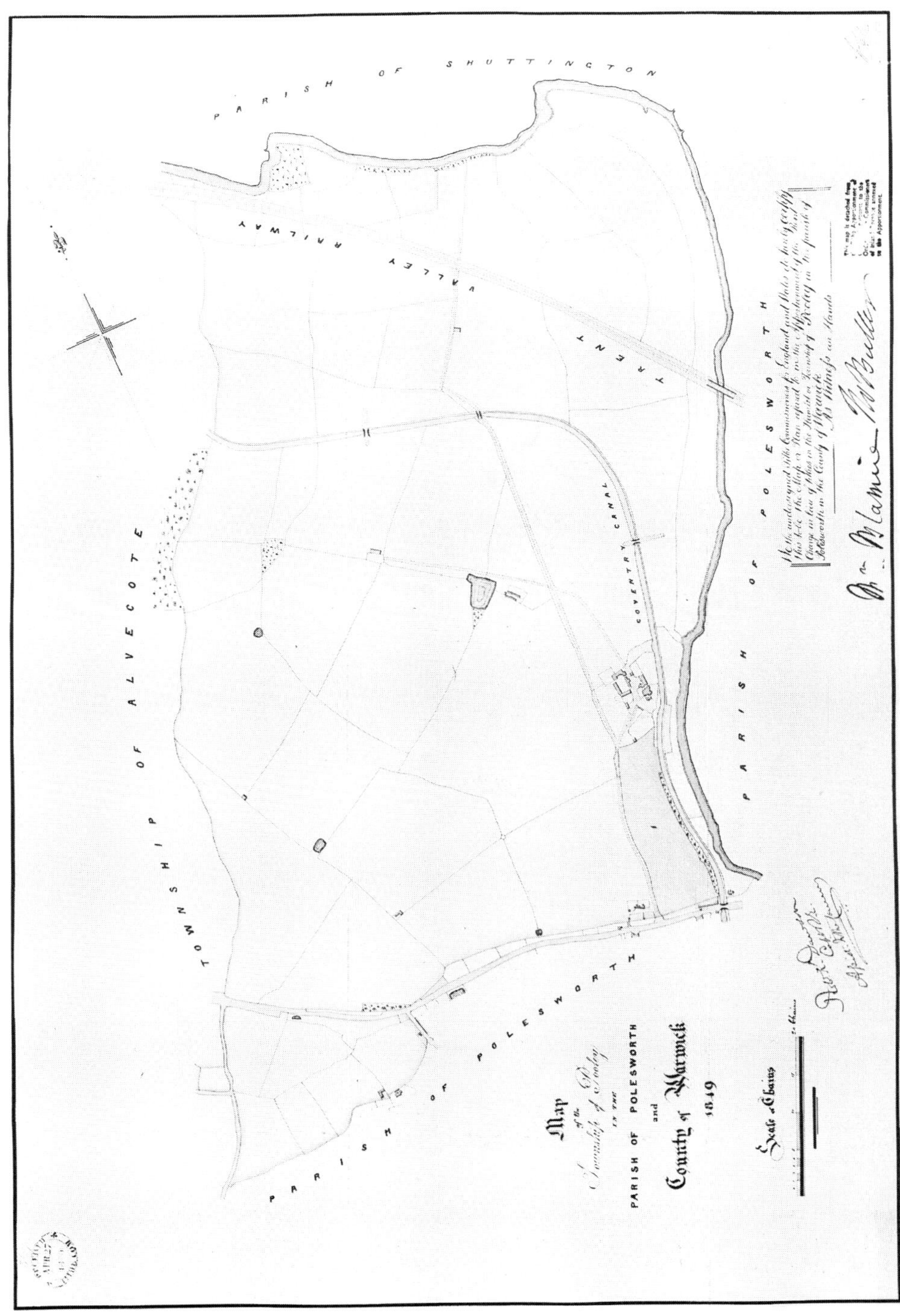

Fig. 149 Pooley, Warwickshire, 1849. Only one (highlighted) field remained tithable but the Pooley tithe map covers the whole tithe district so it is likely that this tithe map is copied from an earlier survey. Source: PRO IR30 36/115. Photograph reproduced by kind permission of the Keeper of the Public Record Office.

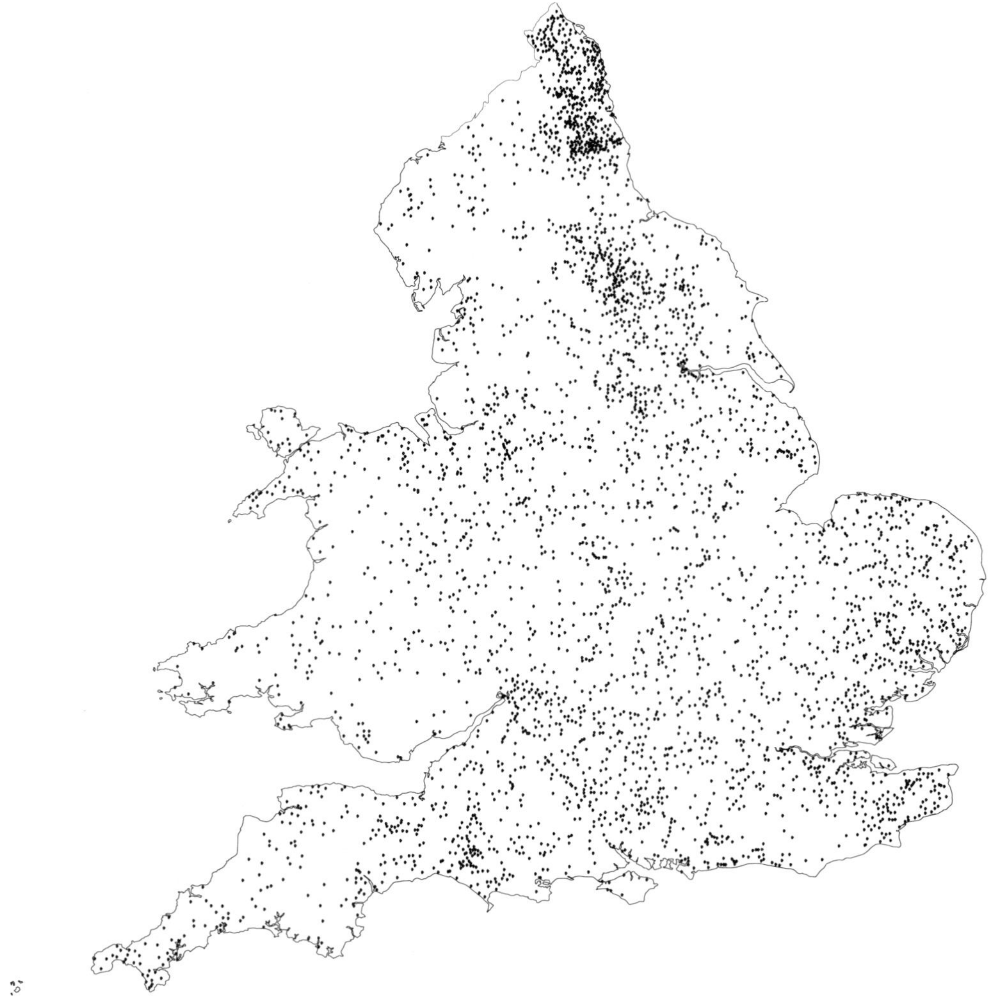

Fig. 150 England and Wales: tithe maps which use colour to distinguish features other than buildings, roads and water.

three main reasons for reapportionment: enclosure or other radical alteration of field boundaries and the landownership cadaster, subdivision of tithe areas for building purposes, and railway construction. Reapportionment might take place on the initiative of either tithe payers or tithe owners; it was not compulsory and, although in practice inevitable when open-field land was redistributed and enclosed, it was by no means an axiomatic consequence of either railway construction or of subdivision prior to suburban building. Altered apportionments are set out in exactly the same way as original apportionments (except that state of cultivation information is usually omitted after *circa* 1870) and they are accompanied by maps, known as altered apportionment maps.

By the 1840s few open-field tithe districts remained and most of these late enclosures were carried out under the General Enclosure Act of 1845 by a unified Copyhold, Tithe and

Fig. 151 Faversham, Kent, *circa* 1842. This careful depiction of Ospringe Mill is of unknown purpose and was omitted when a replacement copy of this map was made in 1915. Source: PRO IR 77/30. Photograph reproduced by kind permission of the Keeper of the Public Record Office.

Inclosure Commission. These enclosure maps are invariably first class but the altered tithe apportionment maps derived from the enclosure maps were always treated as second class.[28]

Reapportionment as a consequence of building development seems to have been much more common in the vicinity of London than elsewhere in the country. Eventually some tithe districts near London were almost wholly reapportioned, though this was usually done piecemeal as estates were successively developed; the reapportionment of a whole district, such as Woldingham, Surrey in 1898, is exceptional.

[28] Compare, for example, the enclosure map of Corringham and Springthorpe in PRO MAF 1/29 with the altered apportionment maps in PRO IR30 20/103, 104 and 302.

Fig. 152 Brauncewell, Lincolnshire, 1845. Decorative drawings such as this are very uncommon on tithe maps of northern and eastern England. Source: PRO IR30 20/56. Photograph reproduced by kind permission of the Keeper of the Public Record Office.

Reapportionment of land affected by railway construction displays little consistency of practice. For example, in the 1900s the Great Western Railway constructed a number of new lines which were accompanied by altered tithe apportionments but no such wholesale reapportionment accompanied the building of the Great Central Railway's London extension in the 1890s or its other new lines a few years later.[29] Altered tithe apportionments generated by railways usually show little other than the boundary of railway property, though some produced by the Bell family in Northumberland in the 1850s after the construction of the railway from Newcastle to Berwick, show track layouts.

The cartography of altered tithe apportionment maps reflects to some extent the parallel development of Ordnance Survey 1:2500 mapping and the concomitant decline of local map-making. Early altered apportionment maps, such as the series produced in the late 1840s along the route of the railway from Norwich to Great Yarmouth in Norfolk, were usually made by local map-makers and cartographically they are little different from original tithe maps (Fig. 164). By the 1870s, the Tithe Commission was producing altered apportionment maps itself in the Commission's 'house style' by re-using original tithe maps as far as possible. Although Ordnance Survey 1:2500 mapping began to appear in 1855 and covered about half of England and Wales by 1880, the Tithe Commission used it very little until the 1890s. From about 1902 onwards the Ordnance Survey added details of an altered apportionment to ordinary sales copies of its 1:2500 mapping (Fig. 165). After 1923, the usual procedure was for the Ordnance Survey to redraw the reapportioned cadaster from its 1:2500 maps (Fig. 166).

[29] See, for example, along the Great Western Railway's Castle Cary to Langport line in Somerset.

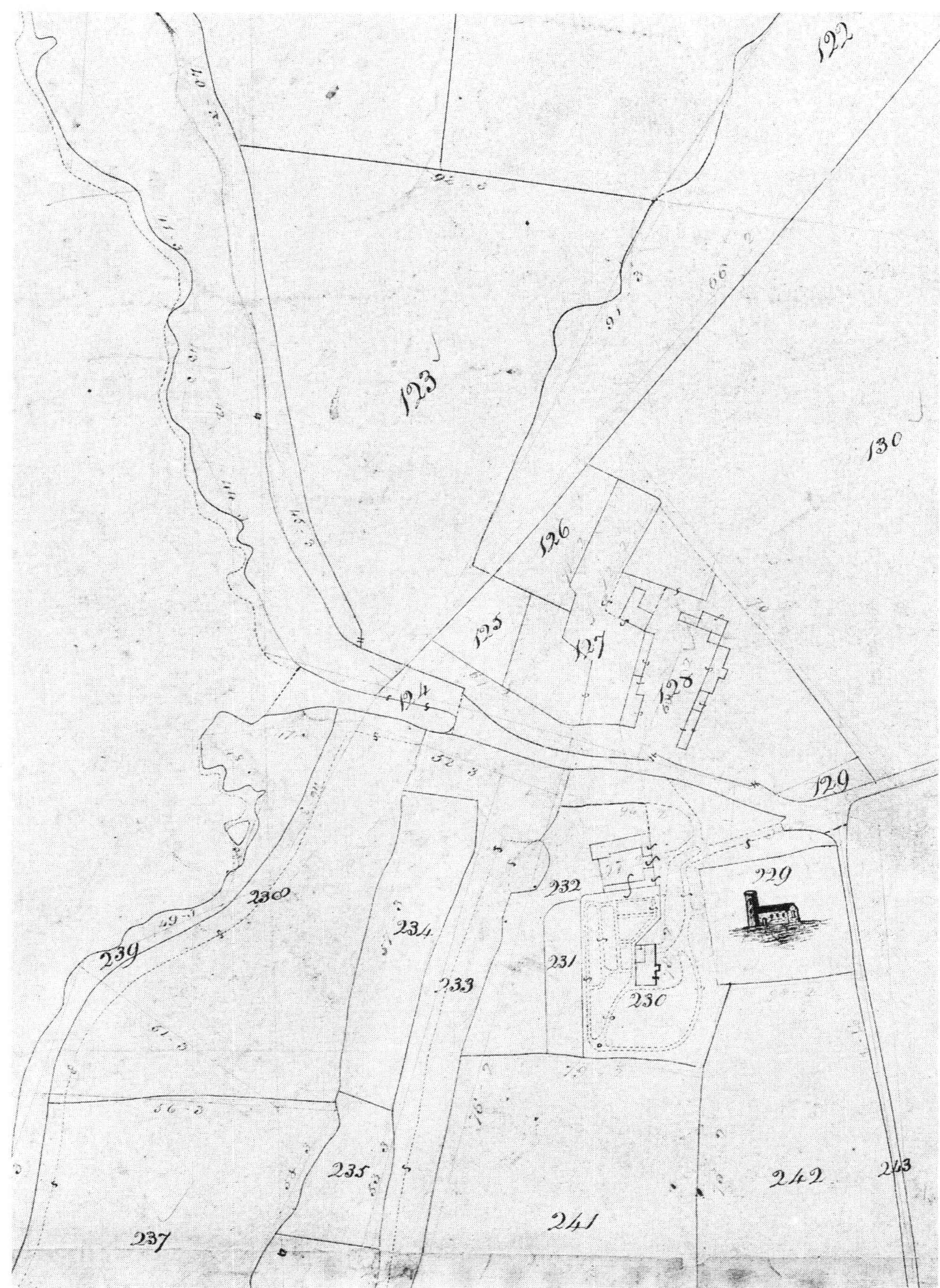

Fig. 153 Burgh Castle, Suffolk, 1842. This map by Richard Barnes of Lowestoft is a good example of the most austere type of first-class map containing as it does little but construction lines, field boundaries, and the outlines of buildings. The pictorial church is exceptional on a first-class map. Source: PRO IR30 33/84. Photograph reproduced by kind permission of the Keeper of the Public Record Office.

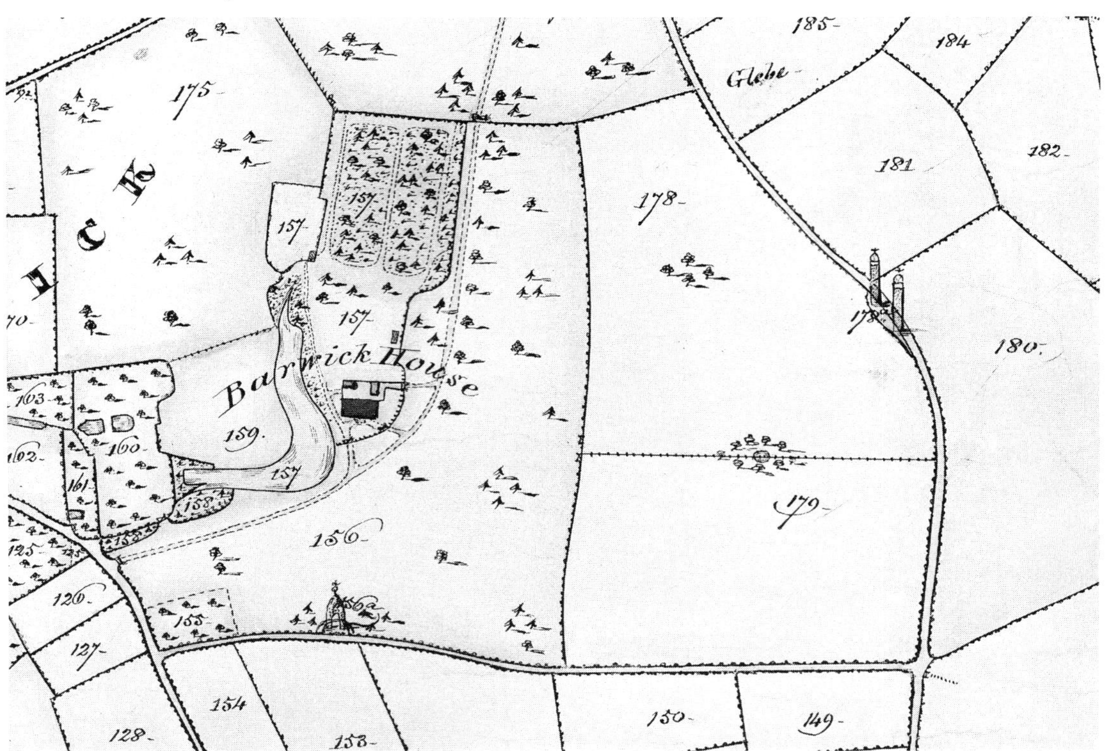

Fig. 154 Barwick, Somerset, 1837. Source: PRO IR30 30/29. The curious pictorial building below '156' is described as a 'pigeon house' in the apportionment; to the left of '180' there are two folly towers. Photograph reproduced by kind permission of the Keeper of the Public Record Office.

Original and statutory copies of tithe maps

The Tithe Commutation Act required an original map and two statutory copies for each tithe district. The original map was supposedly retained by the Tithe Commission, one of the copies was destined for the relevant diocesan office, and the second copy was for the tithe district. Conventional wisdom has it that differences between an original tithe map and the two statutory copies reflect 'nothing more than the extent of variations in mid-nineteenth-century clerical exactitude'.[30] Such a contention finds support in the provisions of the 1836 Tithe Commutation Act and furthermore, if the 1836 statute had been followed to the letter, it would now be the case that the Public Record Office tithe map collection which represents the holdings of the Tithe Commission's London office, would comprise original and amended plans, whereas the maps held in county record offices, derived from diocesan and parish records, would represent statutory copies. Comparison of the original and copy maps of some 650 tithe districts which we have undertaken reveals an archival history both more complex and more interesting than the official blueprint sketched above. Not only do the tithe maps of different places differ in

[30] Kain and Prince, *The tithe surveys of England and Wales*, p. 135.

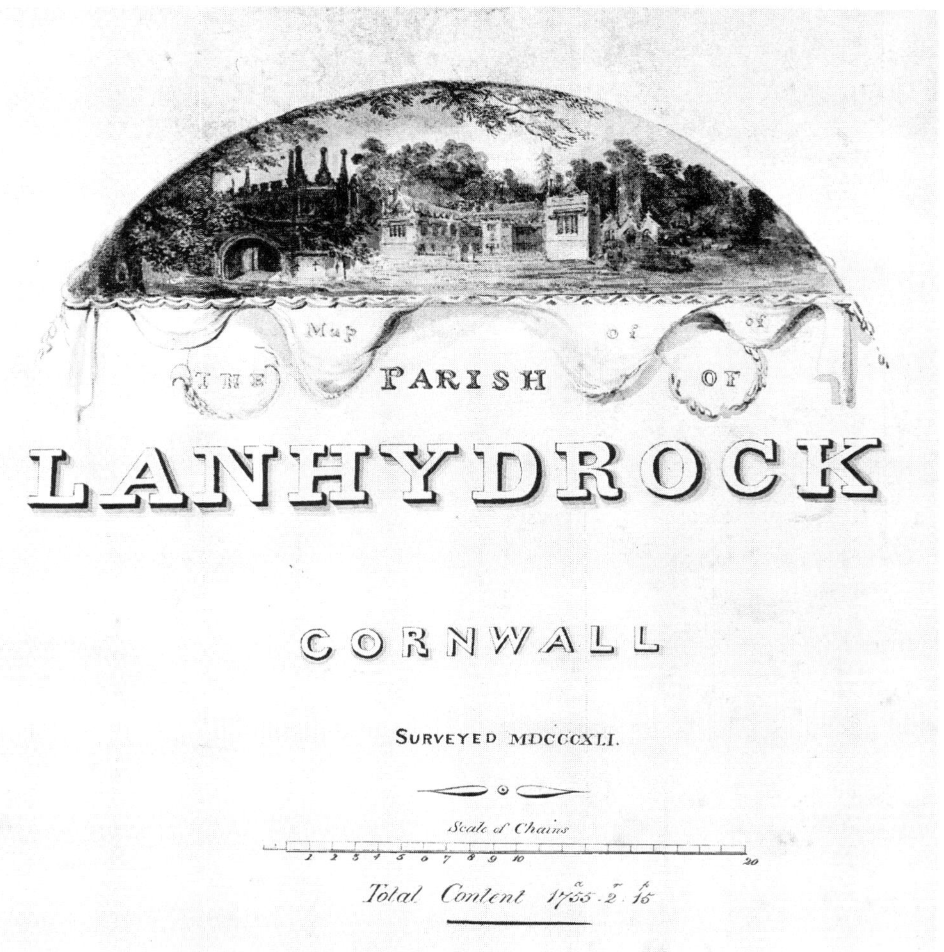

Fig. 155 Lanhydrock, Cornwall, 1841. Decorative cartouches on tithe maps are unusual; elaborately coloured examples are even more rare. Source: PRO IR30 6/96. Photograph reproduced by kind permission of the Keeper of the Public Record Office.

cartographic style and content, but there are also significant differences between the extant examples of tithe maps for the same place.[31]

The assumption that the maps held in the Public Record Office represent the original or amended plans is confirmed by the data available in a majority of cases. However, two pieces of evidence suggest that this is not always the case. First, original maps drawn up for tithe commutation by trigonometrical survey carried triangulation or construction lines. When the statutory copies of these maps were made, construction lines were often omitted. The discovery of twenty-seven cases where construction lines are present on the county record office tithe maps but not on the Public Record Office maps is interesting, for it is consistent with the conclusion that in these instances the diocese retained the original working plan drawn up by the surveyor, and the Public Record Office version is in fact a

[31] This section is based closely on Kain and Wilmot, 'Tithe surveys in national and local archives', pp. 106-17.

Fig. 156 Sithey, Cornwall, 1841. Decoration of this sort is unusual on tithe maps, though more common in the South West than elsewhere. Source: PRO IR30 6/174. Photograph reproduced by kind permission of the Keeper of the Public Record Office.

copy. A rare confirmation of this conclusion is given on the diocesan tithe map for Morthoe parish in Devon, on which the words 'original working plan' form part of the map title (Fig. 167).[32] Further evidence which suggests that county record offices contain some original tithe surveys are the respective dates of diocesan and Public Record Office tithe maps; some county record office maps actually predate the Public Record Office versions.

It is not clear how these original maps escaped the bureaucratic net and found their way into local archives. All versions of the maps of every district should at one stage have been inspected in London, so the error could have been committed centrally in the return of the wrong version to the diocese. Alternatively the original may have been either accidentally or deliberately retained by the landowners and copies sent to London.

The proposition that differences between the Public Record Office and diocesan maps are a result of poor copying is only a partial truth. Many of the differences between the two sets are the outcome of a deliberate choice on the part of local landowners and surveyors to produce a map for local retention at a different scale and degree of detail from that submitted to the London office of the Tithe Commission. In most cases the difference is that the local copy is drawn at a smaller scale than the Public Record Office version, usually one inch to six chains in place of the three-chain scale. The tithe map of Kentisbeare parish in Devon is unusual in that the original three-chain map is held in the Devon Record Office and the reduced scale copy at six chains per inch is held in the Public Record Office collection.[33]

Differences in scale chosen or the degree of accuracy of the local copy also produce discrepancies in the class awarded to the maps of a given tithe district. At Clawton, Halwell, Morchard Bishop and Sampford Spiney in Devon, and Kimpton and Little

[32] Morthoe tithe map, Devon County Record Office, Exeter.
[33] Kentisbeare tithe map, Devon CRO, Exeter and PRO IR30 9/239.

Fig. 157 Tywardreath, Cornwall, *circa* 1839. This is one of a small group of Cornish tithe maps with unusually decorative titles. Source: PRO IR30 6/200. Photograph reproduced by kind permission of the Keeper of the Public Record Office.

Munden in Hertfordshire, the choice of a six-chain scale locally meant that the diocesan copies were deemed second class by the Tithe Commission whereas the original tithe maps for those parishes in the Public Record Office are first-class maps at a scale of three or four chains per inch.[34]

Other discrepancies arising from a deliberate choice on the part of the surveyors to produce two distinct versions for the diocese and the Tithe Commission include differences in the use of colour and decoration. Analysis of Devon tithe maps indicates that, although the majority of the maps exhibit no significant difference (82 per cent), 12 per cent of the tithe maps forming the Public Record Office set are more decorated than the corresponding

[34] Clawton, Halwell (Black Torrington Hundred), Morchard Bishop and Sampford Spiney tithe maps in Devon CRO, Exeter and PRO IR30 9/115; 9/193; 9/293; 9/356. Kimpton and Little Munden tithe maps, Hertfordshire County Record Office, Hertford and PRO IR30 15/59 and 15/70.

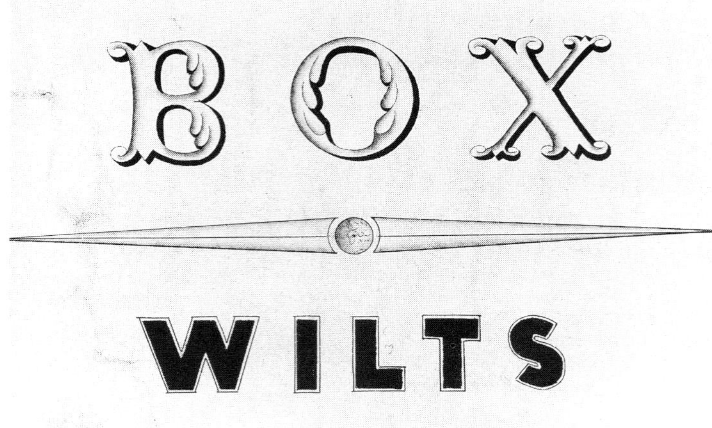

Fig. 158 Box, Wiltshire, 1839. Tithe map decoration can sometimes be very discreet; a small world globe is worked in to the title of this map. Source: PRO IR30 38/34. Photograph reproduced by kind permission of the Keeper of the Public Record Office.

Fig. 159 Holton-le-Moor, Lincolnshire, 1838. Decorated cartouches are particularly rare on tithe maps of eastern England. Source: PRO IR30 20/178. Photograph reproduced by kind permission of the Keeper of the Public Record Office.

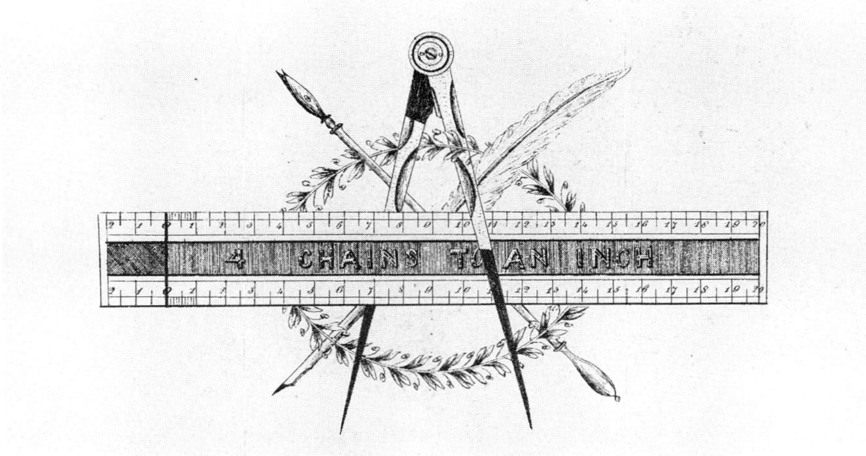

Fig. 160 Bratton Clovelly, Devon, 1845. Displays of drawing instruments are occasionally used to decorate tithe map scales, as are scale bars drawn to resemble rulers. Source: Devon Record Office, Bratton Clovelly tithe map. Photograph reproduced by kind permission of the County Archivist, Devon Record Office.

county record office set and that 6 per cent of Devon's tithe maps are more decorative in the Devon Record Office (diocesan) version. One might have expected that the holdings of the Public Record Office would be less decorated, as a general rule, than the county record office equivalents as the Tithe Commission considered that 'plain working plans' were the most suitable kind of map for a record of tithe commutation. For example, the diocesan tithe maps of the parishes of Dodbrook, Dunkeswell, Sampford Courtney and East Teignmouth in Devon bear striking ornamental features which are not present on the London versions.[35] On the other hand, amongst the tithe maps of Devon, fourteen decorative cartouches which embellish the Public Record Office maps do not appear on the diocesan set in the Devon Record Office.

In short, the assertion that discrepancies between original and copy tithe maps arise from transcription errors oversimplifies and understates the degree of difference. As a general indication of the extent of the variation, for more than 40 per cent of the 650 districts analysed, there is some difference in map content between diocesan and Public Record Office maps. Furthermore, this analysis has been confined to diocesan versions of tithe maps held in county record offices. There is often a third version: the parish tithe map. Parish maps are likely to add a further dimension to the variations in tithe map content which have been discussed here.[36]

[35] Compare tithe maps of Dodbrook, Dunkeswell, Sampford Courtney and East Teignmouth, Devon CRO, Exeter with PRO IR30 9/154; 9/164; 9/354 and 9/402.

[36] For example, the parish version of the tithe map of St Peters in Hertfordshire is more detailed than the corresponding diocesan map: P. Walne, *Catalogue of manuscript maps in the Hertfordshire Record Office* (Hertford: Hertfordshire County Council, 1969).

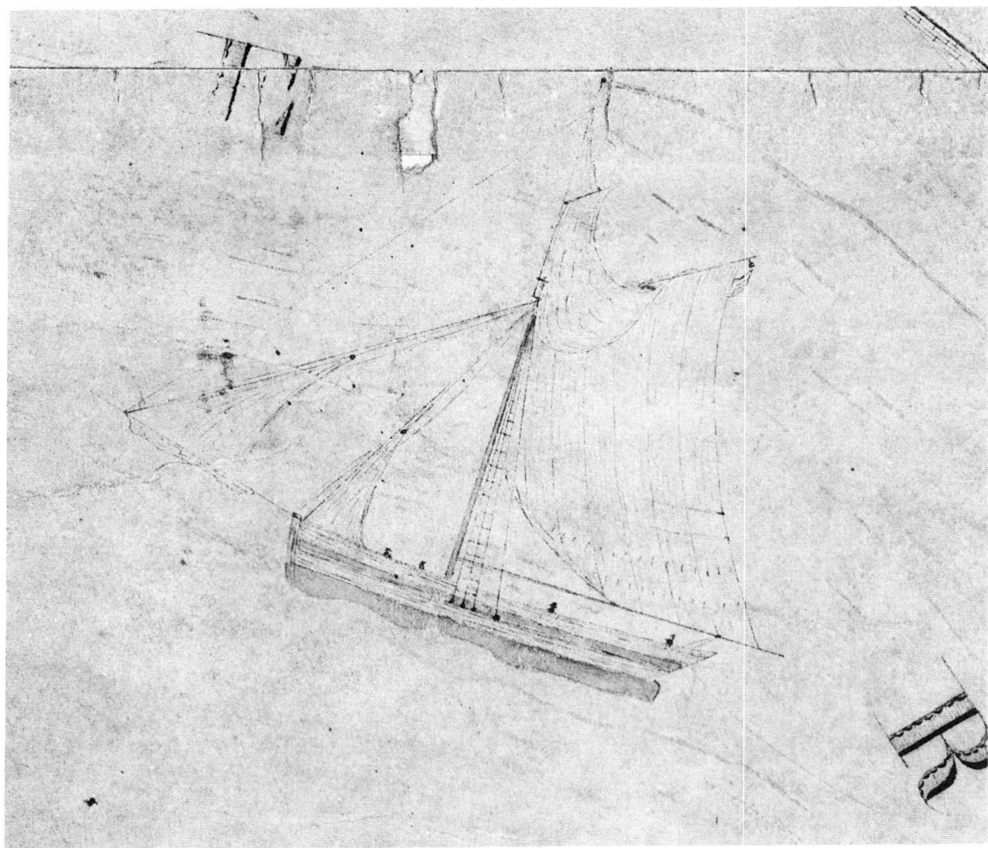

Fig. 161 Northam, Devon, 1839. The decoration of areas of sea with pictures such as this was unusual by this date and is rarely found on tithe maps. Source PRO IR30 9/303. Photograph reproduced by kind permission of the Keeper of the Public Record Office.

A quintessential tithe map?

Our general conclusion derived from the inspection and analysis of every tithe map of England and Wales in the Public Record Office collection is that it is quite illegitimate to speak of a 'typical' tithe map. The most likely single scale to be encountered is six chains to an inch (but 67 per cent are drawn at different scales); very many tithe maps were made in the three years 1839 to 1841 (but about a half are dated other than '*circa* 1840'); a 'typical' tithe map would be the work of a local surveyor (only a few hundred were produced by men working away from their immediate locality); and most tithe maps are second class (only about one in eight are first class). Beyond such basic facts it is unwise to predict from the characteristics of the *corpus* to the characteristics of an individual map. The area that an individual tithe map may cover varies from 74,918 acres at Elsdon, Northumberland to just 0.02 acres at West Wratting in Cambridgeshire (Fig. 168). The cartographic style and standard of execution of tithe maps also vary enormously, from the meticulous neatness of professional map-makers such as those of the Bell partnership (Fig. 169) to very crude

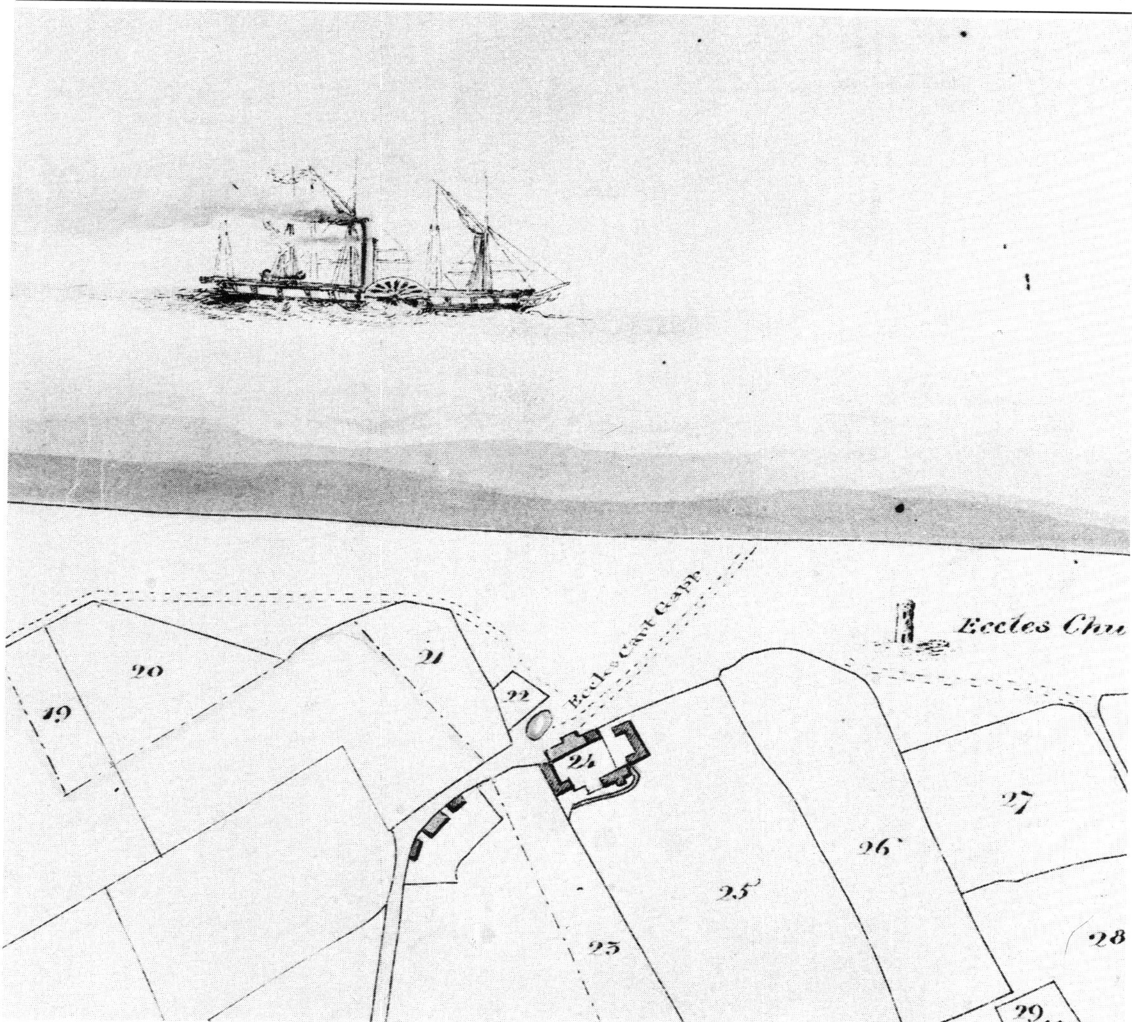

Fig. 162 Eccles next the Sea, Norfolk, 1839. In many ways this is an ordinary second-class tithe map but it has two less common features. Many tithe maps of eastern England show churches pictorially as on this map but sea decoration with ships is much less common and no other tithe map is known to show a steamship. Source: PRO IR30 23/189. Photograph reproduced by kind permission of the Keeper of the Public Record Office.

sketch maps made by often anonymous surveyors (Figs. 170, 171, and 172). The presence or absence of particular items of topographic detail has little to do with the actual distribution of those features but rather reflects individual landowners' and map-makers' perceptions of what a tithe survey should contain. Local tradition of estate cartography was a powerful influence on the nature and content of tithe maps notwithstanding the fact that every tithe map stems from the Tithe Commutation Act of 1836 (amended in 1837) which governed tithe commutation in every parish and township in England and Wales where tithe was still payable. Each of our county-by-county catalogue of tithe maps in the

Fig. 163 Winchelsea, Sussex, 1842. This kind of decorative feature is very rare on tithe maps. Source: PRO IR30 35/295. Photograph reproduced by kind permission of the Keeper of the Public Record Office.

Public Record Office collection, our analyses of these entries county-by-county, and this final national, aggregate analysis and summary, have underscored the essential heterogeneity of tithe maps. Each map was made by a private map-maker commissioned by local landowners. Each tithe map is a unique creation. Though tithe surveys cover three-quarters of England and Wales, tithe maps are individuals and should not be dubbed components of a 'national survey'.

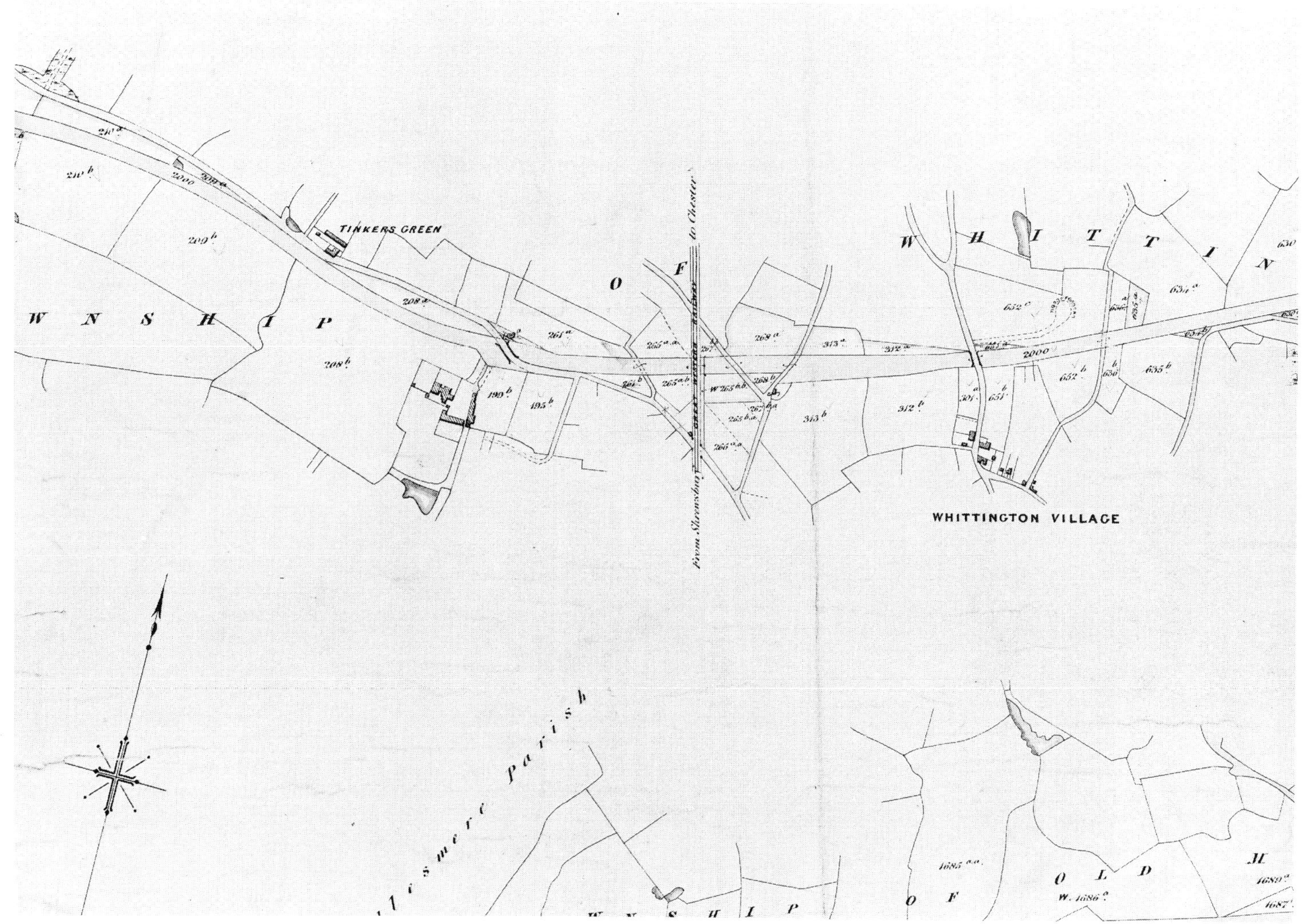

Fig. 164 Whittington, Shropshire, altered apportionment map, 1871. An altered apportionment was necessitated here by railway construction. This comparatively early example of an altered tithe apportionment map was probably prepared by a private map-maker; by the 1880s these maps were usually prepared by the Copyhold, Tithe and Enclosure Commission 'in house'. Source: PRO IR30 29/344. Photograph reproduced by kind permission of the Keeper of the Public Record Office.

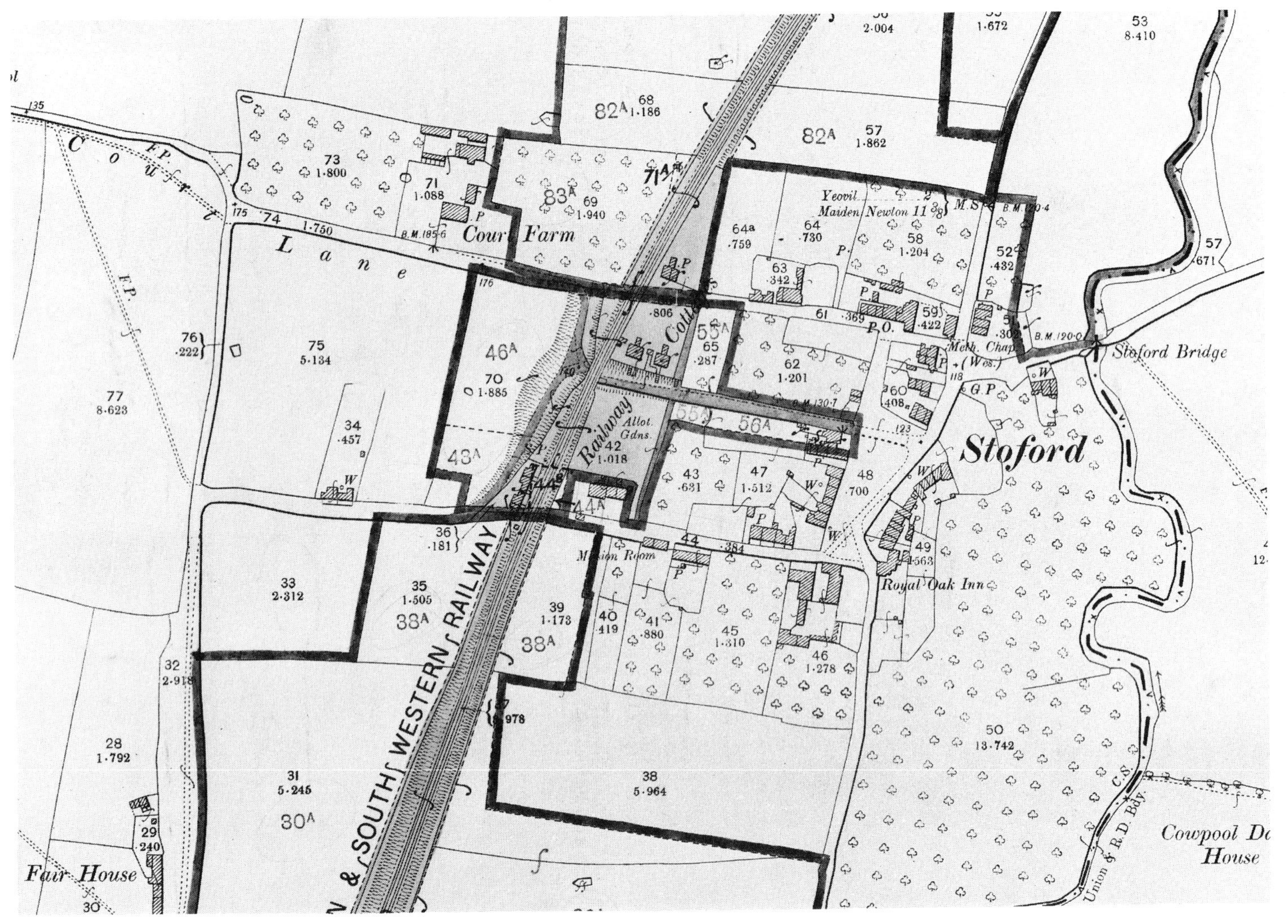

Fig. 165 Barwick, Somerset, altered apportionment map, 1908. This is one of many such altered apportionment maps prepared by the Ordnance Survey in the early twentieth century. The altered apportionment information has been added to an ordinary sales copy of the map. Source: PRO IR30 30/29. Photograph reproduced by kind permission of the Keeper of the Public Record Office.

Fig. 166 Gwythrania, Tre Llan and Tan y Bedwal, Denbighshire, altered apportionment map, 1924. This is an example of the standard Ordnance Survey style for 1:2500 altered apportionment maps prepared from *circa* 1923 onwards. Source: PRO IR30 49/47. Photograph reproduced by kind permission of the Keeper of the Public Record Office.

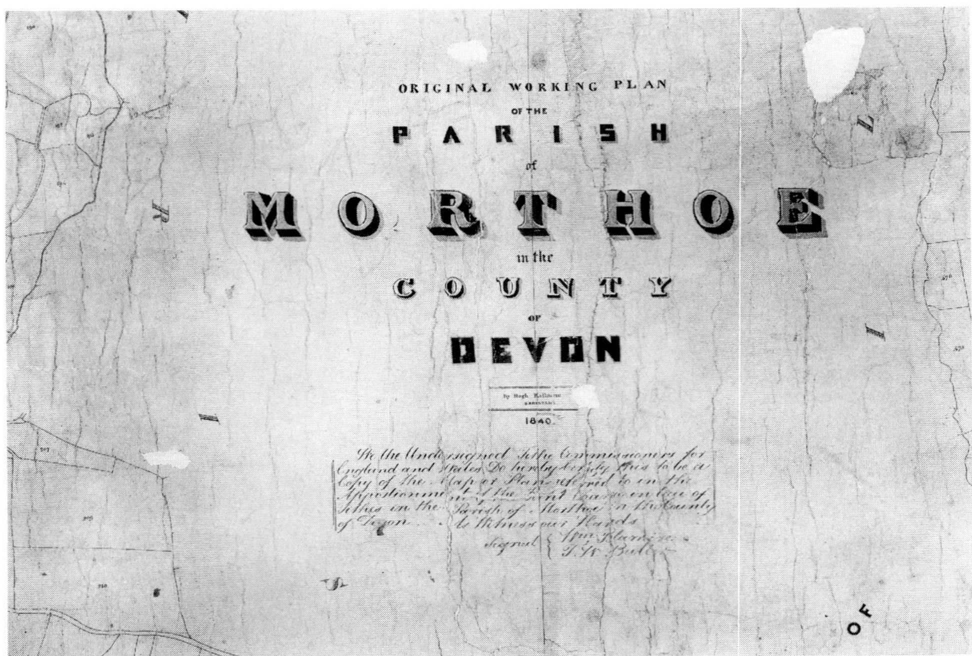

Fig. 167 Morthoe, Devon, tithe map, 1840. This is an original tithe map but one now held in a county record office collection and not the Public Record Office. Photograph by courtesy of Devon Record Office.

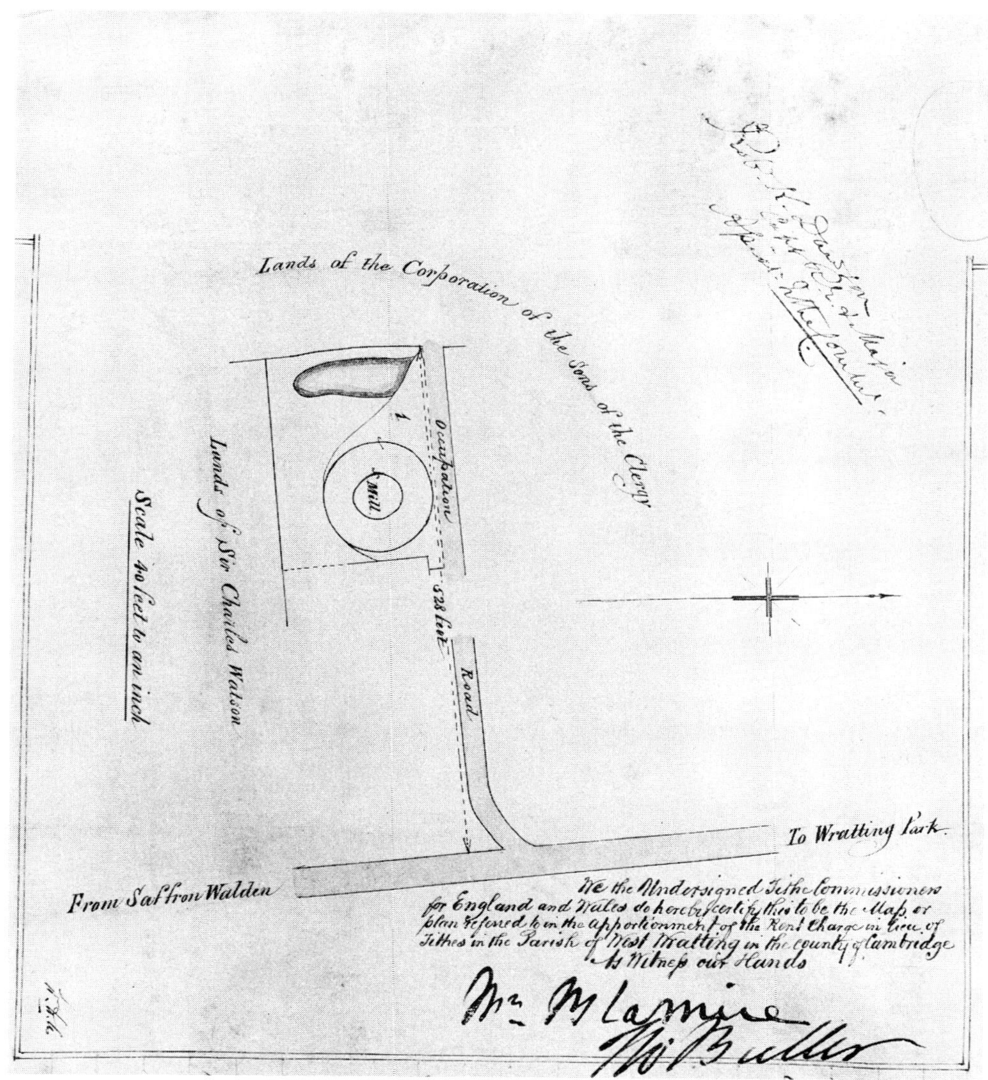

Fig. 168 West Wratting, Cambridgeshire, *circa* 1852. This is the smallest tithe district of all (0.02 acre) and the map is drawn on a page of the tithe apportionment. Source: PRO IR30 4/93. Photograph reproduced by kind permission of the Keeper of the Public Record Office.

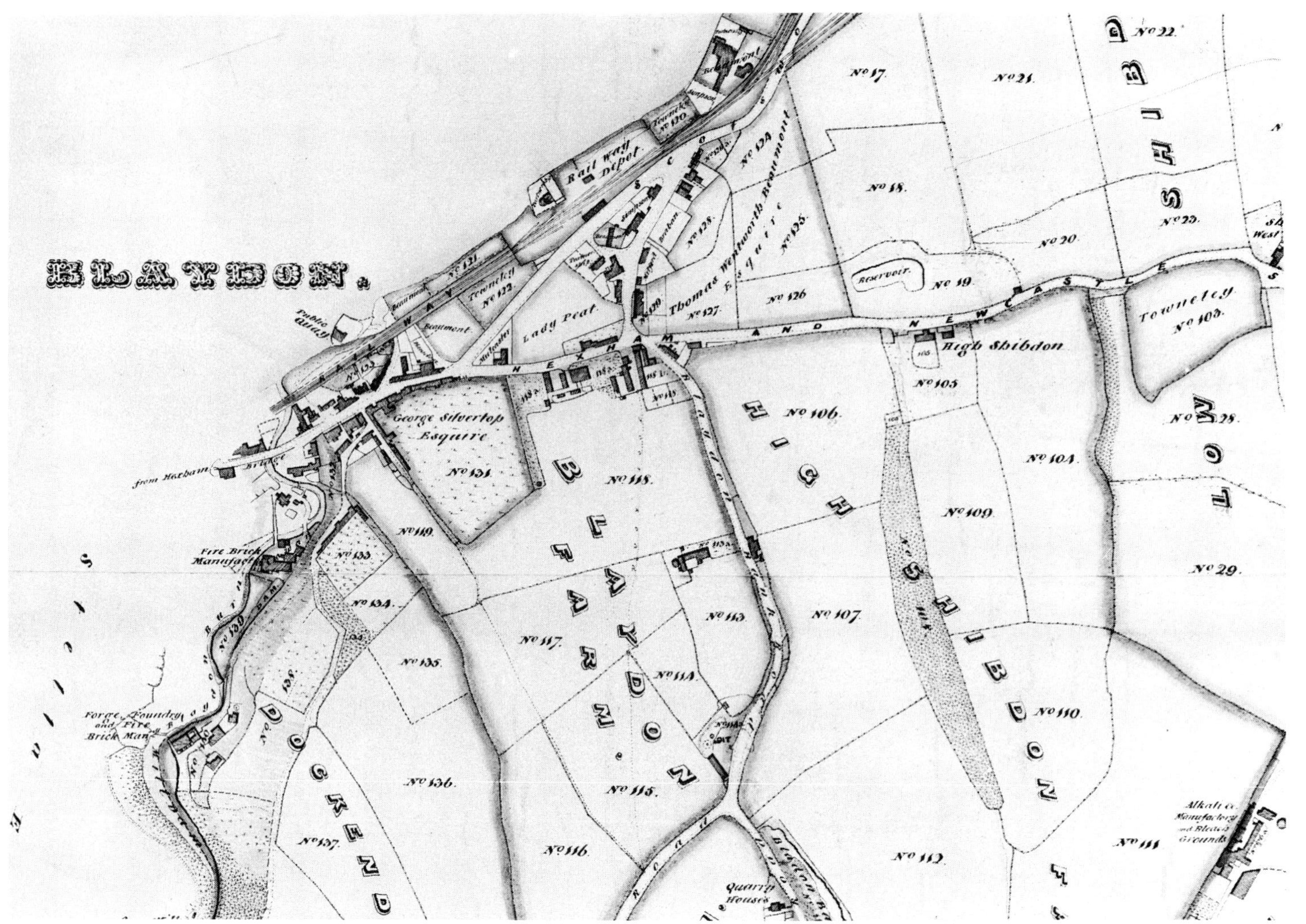

Fig. 169 Winlaton, Durham, 1838. This is a good example of the carefully executed cartographic style of the Bell family of Newcastle. Source: PRO IR30 11/286. Photograph reproduced by kind permission of the Keeper of the Public Record Office.

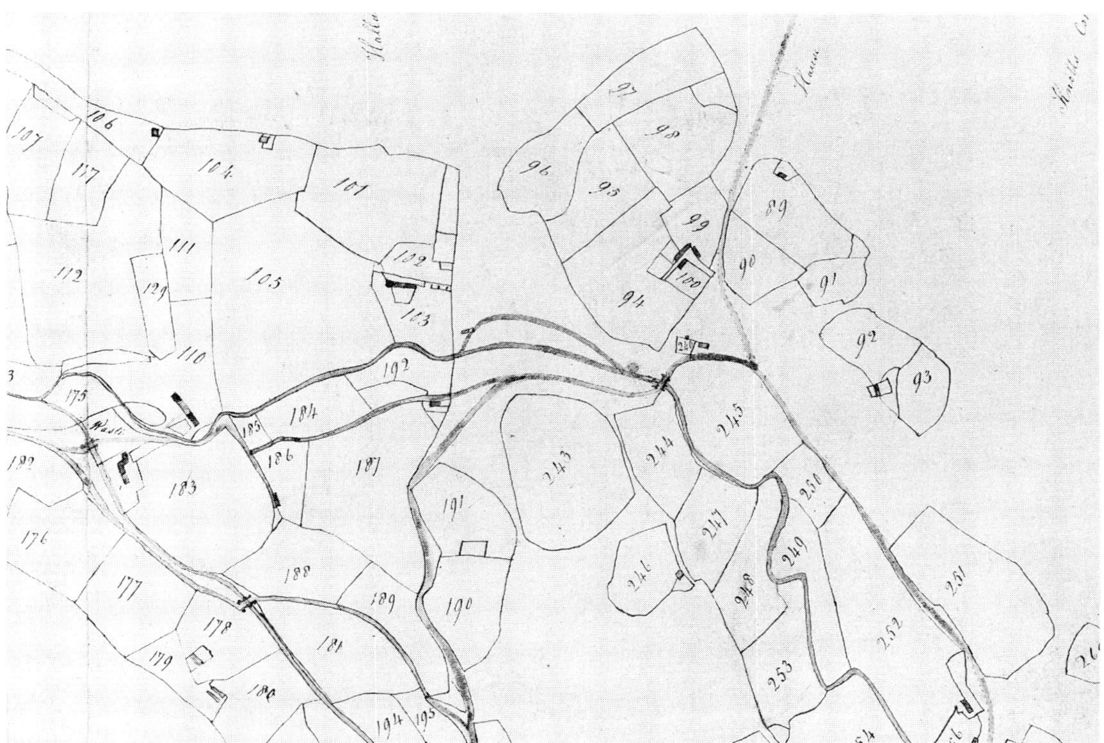

Fig. 170 Martindale, Westmorland, 'taken in September 1838'. This is one of the more crudely executed of tithe maps. Source: PRO IR30 37/53. Photograph reproduced by kind permission of the Keeper of the Public Record Office.

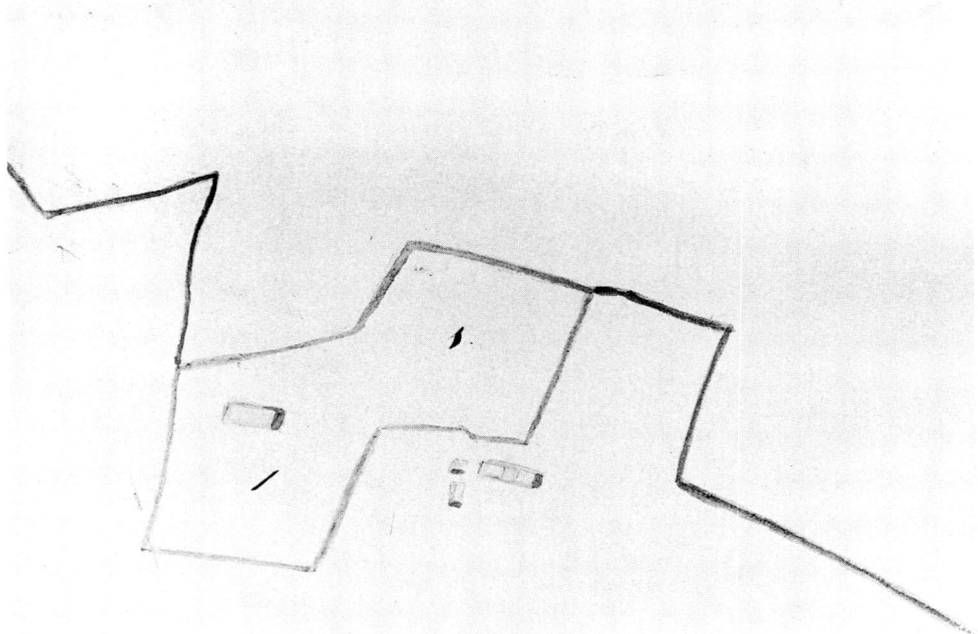

Fig. 171 Titlington, Northumberland, *circa* 1842. Field boundaries are drawn with a brush rather than a pen. This unusual procedure gives an impression of approximation rather than accuracy. Source: PRO IR30 25/434. Photograph reproduced by kind permission of the Keeper of the Public Record Office.

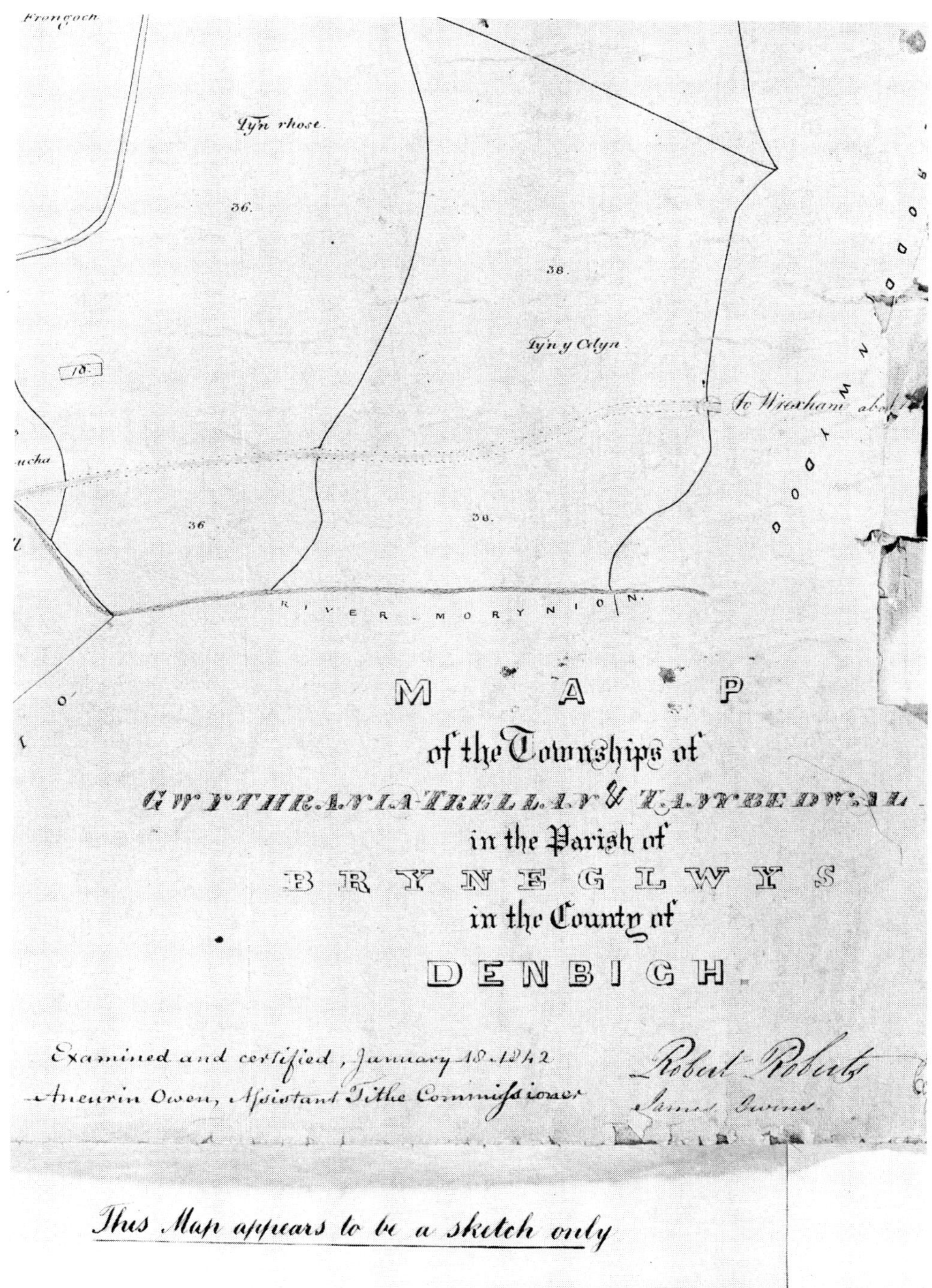

Fig. 172 Gwythrania, Tre Llan and Tan y Bedwal, Denbighshire, *circa* 1840. As the note suggests, this map is a diagram, rather than a scale plan. There are only two other examples of such diagramatic tithe maps. Source: PRO IR30 49/47. Photograph reproduced by kind permission of the Keeper of the Public Record Office.

Appendix 1

Assistant tithe commissioners and local tithe agents of England and Wales: reports on tithe agreements and draft tithe awards

Note: the counties in which a particular commissioner officiated are set out in descending order of the total number of commutations (agreements plus awards) for which he was responsible.

Name	*Total no. of reports*	*Total no. of awards*	*Counties*	*Reports*	*Awards*	*Counties*	*Reports*	*Awards*
George Ashdown	61	–	Shropshire	42	–	Staffordshire	19	–
Richard Atkinson	1	–	Cumberland	1	–			
William Wakeford Attree	–	75	Hampshire	–	19	Warwickshire	–	5
			Buckinghamshire	–	17	Berkshire	–	3
			Hertfordshire	–	13	Essex	–	2
			Huntingdonshire	–	5	Northamptonshire	–	2
			Oxfordshire	–	5	Kent	–	1
A. O. Baker	51	–	Hampshire	46	–	Sussex	1	–
			Kent	4	–			
Arthur Biddell	22	1	Suffolk	21	–	Norfolk	–	1
			Essex	1	–			
George Bolls	327	1	Wiltshire	144	–	Worcestershire	13	–
			Dorset	116	–	Cheshire	–	1
			Gloucestershire	37	–	Radnorshire	1	–
			Herefordshire	16	–			
F. Browne Browne	139	1	Buckinghamshire	19	–	Warwickshire	8	–
			Hampshire	18	–	Northamptonshire	7	–
			Essex	16	–	Surrey	7	–
			Suffolk	13	–	Bedfordshire	4	–
			Berkshire	10	1	Hertfordshire	4	–
			Cambridgeshire	10	–	Middlesex	3	–
			Kent	10	–	Huntingdonshire	1	–
			Oxfordshire	9	–			
John Coldridge	2	1	Devon	2	–	Buckinghamshire	–	1
George Wingrove Cooke	–	259	Shropshire	–	58	Lincolnshire	–	4
			Derbyshire	–	40	Devon	–	3
			Staffordshire	–	33	Gloucestershire	–	3

Name	Total no. of reports	Total no. of awards	Counties	Reports	Awards	Counties	Reports	Awards
George Wingrove Cooke			Leicestershire	–	29	Dorset	–	2
			Nottinghamshire	–	23	Rutland	–	2
			Cheshire	–	12	Denbighshire	–	1
			Wiltshire	–	10	Herefordshire	–	1
			Cumberland	–	8	Lancashire	–	1
			Yorks, North Riding	–	8	Monmouthshire	–	1
			Yorks, West Riding	–	7	Montgomeryshire	–	1
			Somerset	–	5	Westmorland	–	1
			Yorks, East Riding	–	5	Worcestershire	–	1
Henry Dixon	11	–	Essex	7	–	Cambridgeshire	1	–
			Somerset	2	–	Suffolk	1	–
William Downes	11	–	Essex	10	–	Suffolk	1	–
John Farncombe	169	–	Sussex	158	–	Hampshire	9	–
			Kent	2	–			
John Fenton	192	–	Carnarvonshire	50	–	Flintshire	8	–
			Denbighshire	43	–	Merionethshire	8	–
			Anglesey	42	–	Pembrokeshire	1	–
			Montgomeryshire	40	–			
Henry Gilbert	13	–	Kent	17	–			
William Glasson	44	–	Cornwall	44	–			
Edward Greathed	48	–	Hertfordshire	8	–	Lincolnshire	4	–
			Derbyshire	7	–	Essex	3	–
			Rutland	6	–	Bedfordshire	1	–
			Staffordshire	6	–	Middlesex	1	–
			Warwickshire	6	–	Surrey	1	–
			Leicestershire	5	–			
Henry Bertram Gunning	214	–	Norfolk	109	–	Cambridgeshire	17	–
			Suffolk	86	–	Huntingdonshire	2	–
Edward Young Hancock	34	–	Essex	34	–			
Robert Hart	22	–	Yorks, North Riding	10	–	Yorks, West Riding	5	–
			Yorks, East Riding	6	–	Nottinghamshire	1	–
William Heard	175	–	Essex	49	–	Surrey	3	–
			Hertfordshire	37	–	Bedfordshire	2	–
			Suffolk	35	–	Huntingdonshire	2	–
			Norfolk	20	–	Oxfordshire	2	–
			Cambridgeshire	11	–	Middlesex	1	–
			Hampshire	9	–	Warwickshire	1	–
			Berkshire	3	–			
John Maurice Herbert	–	158	Sussex	–	40	Suffolk	–	6
			Cheshire	–	15	Bedfordshire	–	5
			Surrey	–	12	Berkshire	–	5
			Buckinghamshire	–	11	Essex	–	5
			Kent	–	11	Cambridgeshire	–	4
			Middlesex	–	11	Hertfordshire	–	4
			Warwickshire	–	8	Oxfordshire	–	4
			Norfolk	–	7	Hampshire	–	3
			Northamptonshire	–	6	Huntingdonshire	–	2
Thomas P. Hilder	39	–	Kent	39	–			
James Hodsen	1	–	Sussex	1	–			

Name	*Total no. of reports*	*Total no. of awards*	*Counties*	*Reports*	*Awards*	*Counties*	*Reports*	*Awards*
John Holder	173	–	Cheshire	132	–	Shropshire	11	–
			Staffordshire	17	–	Nottinghamshire	1	–
			Derbyshire	12	–			
Thomas Hoskins	538	–	Herefordshire	103	–	Carmarthenshire	29	–
			Monmouthshire	56	–	Gloucestershire	27	–
			Pembrokeshire	55	–	Radnorshire	20	–
			Breconshire	52	–	Yorks, West Riding	16	–
			Worcestershire	43	–	Cheshire	10	–
			Cardiganshire	42	–	Shropshire	9	–
			Glamorganshire	38	–	Staffordshire	5	–
			Yorks, North Riding	31	–	Lincolnshire	2	–
Charles Howard	303	447	Yorks, West Riding	71	109	Cheshire	6	19
			Yorks, North Riding	75	98	Nottinghamshire	2	16
			Yorks, East Riding	43	60	York City & Ainsty	7	6
			Lincolnshire	27	50	Staffordshire	5	5
			Shropshire	8	36	Cumberland	3	7
			Durham	41	–	Westmorland	2	7
			Lancashire	11	17	Rutland	2	–
Anthony Jackson	4	–	Cambridgeshire	3	–	Hertfordshire	1	–
Henry Jemmett	20	–	Oxfordshire	13	–	Buckinghamshire	2	–
			Berkshire	5	–			
James Jerwood	1	214	Devon	122	1	Somerset	7	–
			Cornwall	61	–	Wiltshire	2	–
			Dorset	22	–			
John Johnes	300	132	Glamorganshire	14	72	Breconshire	8	15
			Herefordshire	2	74	Flintshire	4	–
			Pembrokeshire	37	36	Denbighshire	3	–
			Monmouthshire	12	54	Worcestershire	1	2
			Carmarthenshire	26	18	Wiltshire	2	–
			Cardiganshire	11	15	Montgomeryshire	2	–
			Radnorshire	10	14			
Roger Kynaston	207	–	Essex	63	–	Warwickshire	5	–
			Suffolk	49	–	Cambridgeshire	2	–
			Kent	27	–	Middlesex	2	–
			Hampshire	23	–	Staffordshire	2	–
			Berkshire	10	–	Bedfordshire	1	–
			Derbyshire	8	–	Buckinghamshire	1	–
			Norfolk	6	–	Hertfordshire	1	–
			Oxfordshire	6	–	Surrey	1	–
Frederick Leigh	1	75	Devon	73	–	Berkshire	–	1
			Cornwall	2	–			
George Louis	31	310	Devon	3	191	Durham	1	2
			Cornwall	2	90	Somerset	1	–
			Yorks, East Riding	–	20	Leicestershire	–	1
			Dorset	17	2	Nottinghamshire	–	1
			Gloucestershire	4	–	Staffordshire	–	1
			Lincolnshire	3	1	Yorks, North Riding	–	1
Francis Offley Martin	–	282	Sussex	–	45	Norfolk	–	14
			Warwickshire	–	34	Oxfordshire	–	11
			Berkshire	–	25	Hampshire	–	10
			Surrey	–	25	Kent	–	9
			Bedfordshire	–	20	Cambridgeshire	–	7

Name	*Total no. of reports*	*Total no. of awards*	*Counties*	*Reports*	*Awards*	*Counties*	*Reports*	*Awards*
Francis Offley Martin			Huntingdonshire	–	18	Essex	–	6
			Northamptonshire	–	18	Suffolk	–	5
			Buckinghamshire	–	17	Hertfordshire	–	2
			Middlesex	–	16			
Thomas Martin	132	1	Lancashire	82	–	Cumberland	6	–
			Derbyshire	20	–	Westmorland	6	–
			Cheshire	12	1	Yorks, West Riding	6	–
John Mee Mathew	167	108	Essex	45	–	Surrey	7	–
			Yorks, East Riding	4	41	Berkshire	6	1
			Shropshire	9	20	Oxfordshire	5	–
			Cheshire	1	24	Middlesex	4	–
			Staffordshire	16	5	Yorks, West Riding	–	4
			Suffolk	19	–	Buckinghamshire	3	–
			Kent	16	–	Cambridgeshire	3	–
			Hampshire	13	–	Hertfordshire	3	–
			Lincolnshire	–	12	Leicestershire	2	–
			Westmorland	3	9	Warwickshire	2	–
			Norfolk	9	22	Cumberland	1	–
			Derbyshire	–	9	Lancashire	–	1
			Nottinghamshire	5	4	Rutland	–	1
			Yorks, North Riding	–	8			
? Mears	91	–	Norfolk	80	–	Cambridgeshire	4	–
			Suffolk	5	–	Huntingdonshire	2	–
James Drage Merest	232	267	Norfolk	161	154	Essex	1	–
			Suffolk	64	108	Lincolnshire	1	–
			Cambridgeshire	–	5	Shropshire	1	–
			Staffordshire	4	–			
Horace William Meteyard	156	4	Norfolk	42	–	Buckinghamshire	4	–
			Kent	28	–	Derbyshire	4	–
			Suffolk	12	–	Lancashire	1	3
			Surrey	12	–	Middlesex	3	–
			Shropshire	11	–	Oxfordshire	3	–
			Hampshire	9	–	Cambridgeshire	2	–
			Berkshire	7	–	Nottinghamshire	2	–
			Essex	5	–	Cheshire	1	–
			Warwickshire	5	–	Staffordshire	–	1
			Yorks, West Riding	5	–			
N. S. Meryweather	16	–	Worcestershire	9	–	Staffordshire	2	–
			Shropshire	5	–			
John Milner	8	–	Dorset	7	–	Somerset	1	–
John B. Neal	6	–	Durham	3	–	Northumberland	3	–
Thomas Neve	1	–	Kent	1	–			
Charles Osborn	26	–	Hampshire	22	–	Sussex	4	–
Aneurin Owen	145	302	Wiltshire	17	98	Worcestershire	–	4
			Dorset	5	78	Cardiganshire	1	2
			Denbighshire	47	13	Somerset	–	3
			Anglesey	13	29	Monmouthshire	–	3
			Montgomeryshire	17	16	Breconshire	–	2
			Flintshire	18	10	Carmarthenshire	–	2
			Merionethshire	16	10	Glamorganshire	–	2
			Carnarvonshire	7	12	Radnorshire	–	2
			Gloucestershire	–	10	Herefordshire	–	1

Name	*Total no. of reports*	*Total no. of awards*	*Counties*	*Reports*	*Awards*	*Counties*	*Reports*	*Awards*
Aneurin Owen			Devon	2	5	Pembrokeshire	1	–
John Penny	65	1	Lancashire	30	–	Northumberland	2	–
			Cheshire	11	–	Staffordshire	2	–
			Durham	4	–	Yorks, North Riding	2	–
			Lincolnshire	4	–	Yorks, West Riding	2	–
			Shropshire	4	–	Berkshire	1	–
			Yorks, East Riding	4	–			
Robert Page	334	–	Somerset	284	–	Devon	9	–
			Gloucestershire	23	–	Herefordshire	6	–
			Dorset	8	–	Wiltshire	4	–
Thomas Clements Parr	69	–	Berkshire	35	–	Hampshire	6	–
			Oxfordshire	28	–			
John Story Penleaze	18	–	Durham	13	–	Yorks, East Riding	2	–
			Yorks, North Riding	3	–			
John Penny	65	–	Lancashire	30	–	Yorks, East Riding	4	–
			Cheshire	11	–	Northumberland	2	–
			Durham	4	–	Staffordshire	2	–
			Lincolnshire	4	–	Yorks, North Riding	2	–
			Shropshire	4	–	Yorks, West Riding	2	–
Richard Burton Phillipson	340	–	Yorks, West Riding	53	–	Derbyshire	21	–
			Cheshire	43	–	Lincolnshire	15	–
			Yorks, North Riding	40	–	Yorks, East Riding	8	–
			Northumberland	38	–	Nottinghamshire	7	–
			Staffordshire	36	–	Leicestershire	3	–
			Shropshire	30	–	Westmorland	3	–
			Durham	27	–	Rutland	2	–
			Lancashire	24	–	Cumberland	1	–
Thomas Phippard	4	–	Hampshire	3	–	Dorset	1	–
John Pickering	277	1	Lincolnshire	63	–	Cambridgeshire	5	–
			Surrey	29	–	Kent	4	–
			Suffolk	24	–	Northamptonshire	4	–
			Essex	20	–	Rutland	4	–
			Yorks, West Riding	18	–	Buckinghamshire	3	–
			Leicestershire	17	–	Hertfordshire	3	–
			Nottinghamshire	17	–	Huntingdonshire	3	–
			Derbyshire	12	–	Norfolk	3	–
			Shropshire	10	–	Yorks, East Riding	3	–
			Staffordshire	8	–	Oxfordshire	3	–
			Warwickshire	7	–	Anglesey	–	1
			Hampshire	6	–	Middlesex	1	–
			Bedfordshire	5	–	Sussex	1	–
			Berkshire	5	–			
Henry Pilkington	422	–	Northumberland	173	–	Cheshire	8	–
			Durham	101	–	Staffordshire	8	–
			Lancashire	32	–	Essex	5	–
			Yorks, North Riding	23	–	Yorks, East Riding	4	–
			Shropshire	20	–	Northamptonshire	3	–
			Yorks, West Riding	16	–	Leicestershire	2	–
			Cumberland	13	–	Lincolnshire	2	–
			Westmorland	11	–	Derbyshire	1	–
Charles Pym	163	313	Somerset	37	101	Monmouthshire	3	–
			Gloucestershire	31	76	Oxfordshire	2	–
			Worcestershire	17	63	Berkshire	1	–

Name	Total no. of reports	Total no. of awards	Counties	Reports	Awards	Counties	Reports	Awards
Charles Pym			Shropshire	5	28	Denbighshire	1	–
			Staffordshire	2	32	Derbyshire	–	1
			Herefordshire	27	2	Dorset	–	1
			Devon	11	4	Flintshire	1	–
			Wiltshire	12	1	Lincolnshire	1	–
			Cornwall	6	–	Middlesex	1	–
			Essex	4	–	Yorks, East Riding	1	–
			Leicestershire	–	4			
John Job Rawlinson	106	1079	Northumberland	7	133	Westmorland	16	14
			Yorks, West Riding	7	131	Shropshire	–	17
			Cheshire	–	130	Nottinghamshire	3	9
			Lincolnshire	5	113	Rutland	–	9
			Cumberland	24	81	Buckinghamshire	–	3
			Yorks, North Riding	14	82	York City & Ainsty	–	3
			Lancashire	18	73	Dorset	–	1
			Durham	7	85	Herefordshire	–	1
			Derbyshire	4	77	Kent	–	1
			Leicestershire	1	49	Norfolk	–	1
			Yorks, East Riding	–	32	Oxfordshire	–	1
			Staffordshire	–	31	Sussex	–	1
William Richards	1	–	Cornwall	1	–			
Morris Sayer	1	–	Carmarthenshire	1	–			
John S. Donaldson Selby	65	131	Northumberland	51	64	Yorks, North Riding	4	6
			Cumberland	2	33	Durham	5	1
			Westmorland	1	17	Lancashire	1	–
			Cheshire	–	10	Lincolnshire	1	–
Job Smallpeice	2	–	Sussex	2	–			
John Smith	1	–	Sussex	1	–			
Thomas Sudworth	74	–	Cheshire	54	–	Derbyshire	1	–
			Staffordshire	7	–	Lincolnshire	1	–
			Shropshire	5	–	Norfolk	1	–
			Lancashire	2	–	Warwickshire	1	–
			Yorks, West Riding	2	–			
Thomas Sutton	38	–	Norfolk	31	–	Essex	1	–
			Suffolk	6	–			
Gelinger C. Symons	38	–	Shropshire	34	–	Staffordshire	4	–
Thomas James Tatham	8	287	Essex	6	91	Sussex	–	9
			Hampshire	–	63	Middlesex	–	4
			Oxfordshire	–	47	Bedfordshire	–	2
			Berkshire	–	20	Hertfordshire	–	2
			Surrey	1	19	Northamptonshire	–	2
			Kent	–	19	Middlesex	1	–
			Buckinghamshire	–	18	Suffolk	–	1
Joseph Townsend	104	227	Lancashire	–	61	Rutland	1	9
			Yorks, West Riding	–	23	Surrey	4	4
			Derbyshire	–	24	Lincolnshire	1	6
			Nottinghamshire	–	21	Huntingdonshire	5	–
			Hampshire	15	4	Leicestershire	1	4
			Yorks, East Riding	2	17	Shropshire	–	5
			Essex	17	–	Yorks, North Riding	–	5
			Kent	1	15	Cambridgeshire	3	–
			Northumberland	–	15	Staffordshire	–	3

Name	Total no. of reports	Total no. of awards	Counties	Reports	Awards	Counties	Reports	Awards
Joseph Townsend			Buckinghamshire	13	–	Bedfordshire	2	–
			Hertfordshire	13	–	Berkshire	–	2
			Sussex	8	4	Durham	–	1
			Berkshire	10	–	Norfolk	1	–
			Oxfordshire	6	4	Northamptonshire	1	–
Thomas Turner	12	–	Suffolk	7	–	Norfolk	5	–
Charles Warner	4	–	Shropshire	4	–			
John West	33		Northamptonshire	16	–	Buckinghamshire	5	–
			Huntingdonshire	9	–	Bedfordshire	3	–
George Hammond Whalley	–	2	Cornwall	–	2			
Charles Wilson	6	–	Kent	5	–	Sussex	1	–
Thomas Smith Woolley*	258	400	Kent	46	144	Cambridgeshire	6	4
			Warwickshire	26	53	Huntingdonshire	5	4
			Northamptonshire	9	68	Derbyshire	5	3
			Lincolnshire	47	4	Surrey	4	3
			Leicestershire	13	36	Staffordshire	4	2
			Sussex	11	17	Berkshire	4	1
			Nottinghamshire	11	11	Oxfordshire	–	3
			Hertfordshire	7	12	Cheshire	–	1
			Hampshire	10	8	Herefordshire	–	1
			Norfolk	14	1	Middlesex	–	1
			Buckinghamshire	9	5	Wiltshire	1	–
			Suffolk	12	–	Worcestershire	1	–
			Bedfordshire	4	7	Yorks, East Riding	1	–
			Essex	8	2	Yorks, West Riding	–	1
Thomas S. Woolley, junior*	42	–	Lincolnshire	11		Hertfordshire	2	–
			Warwickshire	9	–	Huntingdonshire	2	–
			Oxfordshire	7	–	Bedfordshire	1	–
			Berkshire	5	–	Essex	1	–
			Surrey	3	–	Nottinghamshire	1	–
Tithe Commissioners	–	37	Devon	–	9	Monmouthshire	–	1
			Durham	–	7	Norfolk	–	1
			Staffordshire	–	3	Northamptonshire	–	1
			Suffolk	–	2	Somerset	–	1
			Breconshire	–	1	Surrey	–	1
			Gloucestershire	–	1	Wiltshire	–	1
			Herefordshire	–	1	Worcestershire	–	1
			Kent	–	1	Yorks, East Riding	–	1
			Lincolnshire	–	1			

*It is likely that some of the reports and awards entered under Thomas Smith Woolley were in fact written by his son, Thomas Smith Woolley junior. Entries under the son's name in this table are reports which can be ascribed to him with certainty; he appears not to have been employed by the Tithe Commission before 1840 so only the authorship of the reports and awards post-dating 1840 is in doubt. In the set of tables accompanying the introductions to each county, the reports and awards of the two men are entered under one name.

Appendix 2

Tithe district boundaries on the maps of PRO IR 105 and the Ordnance Survey 'Index to Tithe Survey'

The maps published on the one-inch to one mile scale by the Ordnance Survey and known as the 'Index to Tithe Survey' arose out of the need of the then Registrar General, George Graham, for a map of parish boundaries for the population census.[1] It is unclear exactly when this need was first perceived but it was certainly no later than August 1846 when the secretary of the Poor Law Commission wrote to Graham saying that they would find such a map 'most useful'.[2] Mr Bethune, a Home Office official, wrote in November of the same year: 'I consider it almost impossible to overrate the importance of such a map, the want of which has long been a disgrace to the country, and has been the cause of innumerable difficulties and blunders in carrying out the various measures of social and political reform with which the legislation of late years has been much occupied.' Bethune explained that an opportunity to prepare such a map had been lost when tithe commutation mapping was debated in 1836-37, and that in his present work of establishing districts under the Small Debts Act, he was 'obliged to trust to general recommendations of convenience or inconvenience without accurately knowing what I shall have to recommend.' At the same time, Captain Robert Kearsley Dawson supplied an estimate for the preparation of such a map which included £1,400 for transferring parish boundaries from the tithe surveys to the Ordnance Survey one-inch maps.

The scheme did not advance very quickly; Graham wrote to the Treasury in November 1846 but appears to have been rebuffed. In April 1847 he sought support from Sir Charles Wood who commented that the proposed map could be used for agricultural statistics and highway district purposes. In December 1847 Graham applied to the Treasury for authority to procure a set of Ordnance Survey maps marked up with parish boundaries from Tithe Commission data. The Treasury apparently demurred, as in January 1848 Graham wrote again, saying that whereas an *ad hoc* survey to supply the boundaries would cost as much as £1.4 million, the Ordnance Survey was collecting the information in the north of England in the course of its general mapping and that for elsewhere it could be supplied by the Tithe Commission 'from the most authentic sources' for £2,000.[3]

The Treasury referred the matter to the Tithe Commission which replied optimistically

[1] Unless noted otherwise, this section is based on the papers in PRO T1/5381/16699.

[2] When the commissioners mapped the new Poor Law Unions *circa* 1840 they improvised boundaries on an Ordnance Survey base; these maps survive in the atlas collection of the Royal Geographical Society (IC213 and IC214). Compared with the Index to the Tithe Survey or later Ordnance Survey mapping, the improvised boundaries run in very generalised and fairly straight lines.

[3] In view of the costs quoted by the Ordnance Survey in 1842 for a three-chain full survey of England and Wales (PRO WO 44/702) this seems a gross overestimate.

that the apparent difficulty of joining second-class maps would disappear when information was reduced to the one-inch scale. The tithe surveys contained relatively little urban mapping, though Dawson could supply such information from parliamentary and municipal boundary commission maps.[4] Nor did the Tithe Commission have maps of an estimated 2,000 parishes which were tithe free at the time of tithe commutation. The Treasury seized on this last point as an excuse not to proceed further, citing it in a reply to a letter from the Poor Law Commission. In May 1848 the Poor Law Commission received a further letter from Dawson in which he said that boundaries of some tithe free parishes could be obtained from the maps of adjoining tithable parishes and many of the others could be taken from 'existing plans' obtainable from 'Clerks of the Peace and Surveyors and others with whom I am in almost daily communication.' This persuaded the Treasury and the project was authorised on 18 July 1848.

Tithe map boundaries were plotted in the Tithe Commission's London office on to a set of Ordnance Survey one-inch Old Series maps which was a mixture of sheets supplied probably in October 1836, as far as they had then been published, supplemented by the supply, probably in 1844, of the sheets published during the intervening period.[5] Tithe district boundaries were drawn in red on these maps in the Tithe Commission's office and colour washes applied to highlight districts and to indicate the boundaries of registration districts. This set of maps now forms PRO IR 105.[6]

The maps of IR 105 differ from the published Index to Tithe Survey in a number of respects. First, IR 105 maps omit a few lengths of boundary which appear on the published maps but more often the sheets of IR 105 include lengths of boundary omitted from the published map, probably as a result of clerical error.[7] Second, IR 105 includes some boundaries in parts of the country where tithe surveys were not carried out. These non-tithe boundaries are concentrated in Nottinghamshire and Derbyshire which suggests that they may well have been a trial for supplying boundaries not available from the tithe surveys, a practice subsequently abandoned.[8] Elsewhere boundaries are confined to those derived from tithe maps. Third, in Lancashire and Yorkshire the Tithe Commission plotted the boundaries as it had done elsewhere, but the Ordnance Survey did not engrave this information on the Index to Tithe Survey, preferring instead to use the parish boundary information which it had collected in the course of its six-inch survey of those counties.[9] As a result, the only Index to Tithe Survey coverage of those counties was of those sheets which included parts of adjoining counties and the township boundaries were

[4] 'Maps of the proposed divisions of the counties by Boundary Commissioners in respect to parliamentary representation under the Reform Bill of 1832' by R. K. Dawson in *Reports from Commissioners on the proposed divisions of counties and boundaries of boroughs*, 1832, British Library Map Library, BL Maps 145.c.27(1).

[5] See PRO WO 47/1732, p. 10953, (12 October 1836) and references to maps in PRO IR 105 in Harry Margary, *The Old Series Ordnance Survey*, (Lympne, Harry Margary), volumes VI and VII (1992, 1989).

[6] It should be noted that the copy of Sheet 3 in IR 105 is a copy of the published Index to Tithe Survey, printed in 1862. IR 105 also includes most of the Old Series sheets of northern England published after 1850, though without tithe survey annotations.

[7] See, for example, south-west of Kidlington, Oxfordshire, on Sheet 45 S.W.

[8] Non-tithe-survey-derived boundaries are particularly numerous in the south-west part of Sheet 70 (PRO IR 105/71), but are also to be found in parts of Sheets 71, 72, 81 and 82.

[9] Except for some reason in Sheets 85 and 86, where the rather incomplete Tithe Commission data was used. On Sheet 88 S.W. the parish information was at first (in about 1856) included on the ordinary version, but with the prepration of the Index to the Tithe Survey version *circa* 1863 was henceforth published only on the latter.

not published at the one-inch scale at all.[10] Omitted both from the manuscript compilation preserved in PRO IR 105 and from the published Index to Tithe Survey are the boundaries of a few tithe districts which were mapped in the early 1850s and which indicate that IR 105 was prepared in 1849-50.[11]

By the autumn of 1849 engraving work was under way and by 1853 all the sheets south of the Aberystwyth–Birmingham line and in eastern England had been prepared with boundaries derived from the tithe surveys. For reasons that are not entirely clear, work seems to have come to a standstill until it was revived in the early 1860s. The engraving of the Index to the Tithe Survey was probably completed between 1865 and 1867.[12]

The demand for the Index to Tithe Survey was probably very small. Only four complete sets are known; three of these are legal deposit sets and the fourth was acquired by the Local Government Board.[13] Possibly the longest-used set of these maps was the manuscript model of *circa* 1849-50 now preserved in PRO IR 105. This was still in use in the 1950s when the 'London to Yorkshire Motorway' was added to Sheet 46 in ball-point pen. The set has numerous other, less obviously anachronistic annotations, including notes which appear to refer to tithe redemptions and corn rents, and a few boundaries have been completed in pencil.[14]

As with the tithe surveys themselves, the Index to Tithe Survey was at first an unprecedented achievement and then, as Ordnance Survey mapping developed, increasingly a makeshift no longer based on 'the most authentic sources'. The value to contemporaries of the Index to Tithe Survey as a record of boundaries steadily diminished and then altogether vanished as the publication of the Ordnance Survey one-inch New Series progressed between 1874 and 1896. Many boundaries which the Index to Tithe Survey showed somewhat inexactly (partly due to the shortcomings of the second-class tithe maps and partly due to the planimetric deficiencies of the one-inch Old Series, particularly in southern England), were subsequently mapped much more exactly at the one-inch and at larger scales. However, the Index to Tithe Survey retains the advantage that it shows in compact form many boundaries as they existed before the rationalisations which were effected after 1876.

The maps of tithe districts which accompany our county-by-county catalogue derive mainly from the data on the maps in PRO IR 105. The basic procedure was that these maps were compared with photocopies of the published Index to Tithe Survey; in the great majority of cases the boundaries were in agreement, and where they were not the

[10] They were not published as township boundaries *sensu strictu*. In 1879 the Ordnance Survey decided to treat townships as civil parishes, and as a result the township boundaries appeared, as civil parish boundaries, when the revised one-inch map (New Series, second edition) was published in the late 1890s.

[11] For example, Bassingham, Lincolnshire, (tithe map 1852), and Bole, Nottinghamshire (tithe map 1850), both omitted from Sheet 83, and Thornton Curtis, Lincolnshire, (tithe map 1850), omitted from Sheet 86.

[12] *Catalogue of the maps and plans... of the Ordnance Survey of England and Wales, to 1st May 1865*, (Southampton, Ordnance Survey, 1865; copy in PRO STAT 1/20), p. 8, indicates that at that time sheets 59 N.E., 60 N.W., S.W. and S.E., 61 S.E., 62 (all quarters), 63 N.W., N.E. and S.W., 71 S.W. and S.E., 73 S.W. and 75 S.E. remained to be issued. Most of the sheets of the set now in British Library, Map Library Maps 209.a.1 were printed by 1867.

[13] These are respectively: Bodleian Library (Maps C17.26b), British Library ('green label' set, accessed September 1873), National Library of Scotland (no pressmark), and British Library, Map Library, Maps 209.a.1. One or two sheets are missing from this last and one or two are duplicated.

[14] There are some good examples of these on Sheet 44 (IR 105/45).

discrepancy was investigated by reference to the original tithe maps. In Lancashire and Yorkshire south of the Preston–Hull line the maps in PRO IR 105 supplied boundaries of tithe districts which were never published as such by the Ordnance Survey. As noted above, not all tithe district boundaries were mapped on the Index to the Tithe Survey; for those districts where the boundaries were not mapped for tithe purposes, the deficiency was supplied from the Ordnance Survey six-inch first edition (surveyed 1854-89). Checks on the accuracy of the boundaries thus obtained were made for Lincolnshire, Norfolk, Suffolk and all the Welsh counties (except Monmouthshire) by comparing boundaries already obtained from PRO IR 105 with those on the tithe maps themselves as the latter were examined for encoding.

North of the Preston–Hull line a different procedure was followed. On the strength of a statement by the Ordnance Survey in 1875, it was assumed that tithe district boundaries are the same as those shown on the first edition of the Ordnance Survey six-inch (surveyed between 1841 and 1863 in these counties).[15] These boundaries were copied on to photocopies of the Ordnance Survey one-inch New Series second edition (published 1897-98) and then checked against the Public Record Office class list of tithe districts; boundaries of districts not shown on the Ordnance Survey maps have been obtained from the tithe maps.

[15] Sir Henry James (ed.), *Account of the methods and process... of the Ordnance Survey...* (London, HMSO, 1875), p. 40.

Appendix 3

Tithe map-makers of England and Wales

Appendix 3 lists in alphabetical order the surveyors and map-makers named on the Public Record Office collection of tithe maps. 1,659 map-makers or groups of map-makers are listed here; a considerable number of other maps can be attributed to a particular map-maker by reference to diocesan and parish copies of tithe maps held in county record offices and other local collections.

Data are arranged in the following order:

1 Name of map-maker.
2 Address or addresses (if given) and occupation (if other than, or additional to, 'surveyor' or 'land surveyor').
3 Number of maps that he made in a particular county.
4 Name of that county (in brackets).
5 Total acreage that he mapped in that county.
6 Information on 3-5 are repeated for the other counties in which that map-maker was employed, in alphabetical order of counties.
7 Total number of maps and total acreage mapped, set out in the form: number of maps : acreage.

ABBEY, Robert, Hutton, Yorkshire. 3 (Yorkshire, North Riding) 1,841
ABBOTT, Samuel, Lowdham, Nottinghamshire. 1 (Lincolnshire) 1,298; 1 (Nottinghamshire) 365; TOTAL 2 : 1,663
ADAMS, Charles F., Barkway, Hertfordshire. 5 (Hertfordshire) 8,147
ADAMS, Henry, Clements Lane, London, (Land and Timber Surveyor). 1 (Kent) 3,851; 1 (Surrey) 2,836; TOTAL 2 : 6,657
ADAMS, John, Hawkhurst, Kent. 14 (Kent) 25,697; 15 (Sussex) 60,803; TOTAL 29 : 86,500
ADAMS, John Eastridge, and William Rowden Sanders, Plymouth, Devon. 1 (Devon) 688
ADAMS, Moses, Isleworth, Middlesex. 1 (Surrey) 4,532; 2 (Middlesex) 4,812; TOTAL 3 : 9,344
ADAMS, Moses, Isleworth, Middlesex and Thomas Tyerman, 14 Parliament St, Westminster. 1 (Middlesex) 267
ADAMS, Moses, Isleworth, Middlesex and William Thomas Warren. 1 (Middlesex) 1,684
ADAMS, S. W., Newton Ferrers, Devon. 5 (Devon) 10,524
ADAMS, Thomas, Dartford, Kent. 1 (Kent) 3,588
ADDISON, Thomas junior, Preston, Lancashire. 6 (Lancashire) 13,440
ADIE, George, Rugeley, Staffordshire. 8 (Staffordshire) 33,951
ADNAMS, Henry, Chieveley, Berkshire. 2 (Berkshire) 3,827
ALDERSON, George, York. 8 (Yorkshire, East Riding) 7,969; 1 (Yorkshire, West Riding) 1,901; TOTAL 9 : 9,870
ALDERSON, Walter, Leyburn, Yorkshire. 9 (Yorkshire, North Riding) 14,962; 1 (Yorkshire, West Riding) 3,325; TOTAL 10 : 9,870
ALEXANDER, James, Doncaster, Yorkshire. 2 (Lincolnshire) 768; 14 (Yorkshire, West Riding) 31,907; TOTAL 16 : 32,765
ALGER, C. S., Diss, Norfolk. 5 (Norfolk) 8,205; 1 (Suffolk) 1,458; TOTAL 6 : 9,663
ALLANSON, P. R., York. 2 (Yorkshire, West Riding) 3,262. *See also* William Tuke
ALLEN, Hans W. 7 (Cornwall) 33,852; 2 (Devon) 4,094. TOTAL 9 : 37,946
ALLEN, I. W., West Retford, Nottinghamshire. 1 (Nottinghamshire) 15
ALLEN, J., Oxford. 1 (Worcestershire) 2,998
ALLEN, J. R. 1 (Lancashire) 1,947
ALLEN, J. R. and J. Watson, Preston, Lancashire. 1 (Yorkshire, West Riding) 5,826
ALLEN, Robert J., Durham. 2 (Northumberland) 2,934
ALLERTON, Richard, Strand, London. 1 (Bedfordshire) 3,345; 2 (Herefordshire) 11,085; TOTAL 3 : 14,430
ALLERTON, Richard, James Renshaw and John Doyley. 1 (Middlesex) 612
ALTON, J. R. 1 (Yorkshire, West Riding) 18,988
ANDREW, John, Plympton St Mary, Devon. 7 (Devon) 20,966
ANDREWATHA, John, Truro, Cornwall. 2 (Cornwall) 1,408
ANDREWS, Henry, Modbury and John Grant, Ugborough, Devon. 2 (Devon) 6,125

ANDREWS, William, Ivinghoe, Buckinghamshire. 3 (Buckinghamshire) 6,214
ANSTICE, G., Stockland, Dorset. 1 (Devon) 5; 2 (Dorset) 7,560; TOTAL 3 : 7,565
APPERLEY, William Havard, Hereford. 1 (Gloucestershire) 1,517; 21 (Herefordshire) 36,146 ; 4 (Monmouthshire) 15,677; 1 (Worcestershire) 1,530; TOTAL 27 : 54,870. *See also* William Fosbrooke.
ARDEN, W. *See* Cuming and Hill
ARKLE, Thomas, High Carrick, Northumberland. 5 (Northumberland) 85,253
ARMSTRONG, Robert. 1 (Monmouthshire) 1,864
ARNOLD, George, Dolton, Devon. 3 (Devon) 9,708
ARTHUR, William, Little Bavington, Northumberland. 1 (Northumberland) 513
ASH, Charles Bowker, Eccleshall, Staffordshire. 9 (Staffordshire) 10,044
ASH, Charles F., Malton, Yorkshire. 1 (Yorkshire, North Riding) 843
ASH and Son. 1 (Shropshire) 3,036
ASHDOWN, Samuel H., Uppington, Shropshire. 1 (Cheshire) 685; 1 (Montgomeryshire) 2,401; 30 (Shropshire) 58,106; 2 (Staffordshire) 5,252. TOTAL 34 : 66,444
ASHENDON. *See* Thomas White Collard
ASHMEAD, George Culley, Bristol, Gloucestershire. 8 (Somerset) 15,919; 1 (Wiltshire) 11,311; TOTAL 9 : 27,230
ASHTON, J., Chesterfield. *See* George Unwin
ASQUITH, Richard, Carlisle, Cumberland. 16 (Cumberland) 37,953. *See also* P. Kendall
ATKINSON, Abraham, Langholme, Haxey, Lincolnshire. 1 (Lincolnshire) 4,836; 1 (Yorkshire, West Riding) 548; TOTAL 2 : 5,384
ATKINSON, W., Bassenthwaite, Cumberland. *See* William Hodgson
ATMORE, John, Barford, Norfolk. 1 (Norfolk) 912
ATTY, James Louis, Ashridge, Hertfordshire. 1 (Bedfordshire) 1,738
AYLING, D., Liss, Petersfield, Hampshire. 1 (Hampshire) 3,680; 1 (Sussex) 7,832; TOTAL 2 : 11,512. *See also* George Doswell, (Hampshire, 1)
AYLWIN, William and Alfred M. May, Marlborough, Wiltshire and Newbury, Berkshire. 1 (Hampshire) 2,119

BADCOCK, Benjamin, Oxford. 1 (Surrey) 5,518
BADCOCK, Henry and Robert, Launceston, Cornwall. 12 (Cornwall) 36,559; 16 (Devon) 60,442; TOTAL 28 : 97,001. *See also* John Palmer, Devonport
BAILEY, Charles, Nynehead, Somerset. 1 (Somerset) 324
BAILEY, Charles, Nynehead, Somerset, and Thomas Wright, Tiverton, Devon. 1 (Devon) 3,768
BAILEY, George Henry, Brough, Westmorland. 1 (Westmorland) 1,087
BAILLIE, William, Newbury, Berkshire, (civil engineer). 8 (Berkshire) 28,202; 1 (Hampshire) 476; TOTAL 9 : 28,678
BAKE, Henry, Barton, Lincolnshire. 1 (Lincolnshire) 15
BAKER, A. 1 (Essex) 1,549
BAKER, Charles, Painswick, Gloucestershire. 8 (Gloucestershire) 14,618; 1 (Herefordshire) 1,174; TOTAL 9 : 15,892
BAKER, Charles, Painswick, Gloucestershire and Y. and J.P. Sturge. 1 (Gloucestershire) 6,205
BAKER, George, Bungay, Suffolk. 5 (Norfolk) 10,121
BAKER, George and Jno. Crickmay, Bungay, Suffolk. 11 (Suffolk) 13,511
BAKER, Hughbert, Parliament St, Westminster, Middlesex. 3 (Cornwall) 16,935; 1 (Devon) 3,468; TOTAL 4 : 20,403
BAKER, P., Woolpit, Suffolk. 3 (Suffolk) 3,340
BAKER, Robert, Writtle, Essex. 45 (Essex) 104,053
BAKER and Sexton. 1 (Suffolk) 1,878
BAKER, Thomas, 25 Vauxhall St, London. 4 (Sussex) 8,051
BAKER, William, Oakley, Wimborne, Dorset. 1 (Dorset) 1,032
BAKER, William, Woolpit, Suffolk. 1 (Suffolk) 3,402
BALL, Samuel, Kidwelly, Carmarthenshire. 3 (Carmarthenshire) 26,179; 1 (Pembrokeshire) 8,120; TOTAL 4 : 34,299
BALLMENT, Hugh, Barnstaple, Devon. 13 (Devon) 31,605
BANISTER, T. C. 1 (Warwickshire) 755
BANKS, Robert, Scampton, Lincolnshire. 1 (Lincolnshire) 2,148
BANNERMAN, Alexander, Chorley, Lancashire. 2 (Lancashire) 4,535
BARBER, Bolney, Sussex. 1 (Sussex) 3,547
BARFIELD, Arthur, Great Dunmow, Essex. 1 (Essex) 1,443
BARKER, John. 2 (Cumberland) 801
BARKER, William, Claypole, Lincolnshire. 1 (Lincolnshire) 254
BARNARD, J., Great Dunmow, Essex. 1 (Essex) 600
BARNES, John and Son, Sandhurst, Kent. 1 (Sussex) 1,597
BARNES, John, Buxhall, Suffolk. 6 (Suffolk) 10,833
BARNES, Richard, Lowestoft, Suffolk. 4 (Norfolk) 7,295; 24 (Suffolk) 34,694; TOTAL 28 : 41,989. *See also* Pratt and Son
BARNETT, Samuel, St Johns, Worcester. 1 (Herefordshire) 1,245; 1 (Worcestershire) 1,161; TOTAL 2 : 2,406
BARNICOAT, John Wallis, Falmouth, Cornwall and John J. Gummoe, St Austell, Cornwall. 2 (Cornwall) 6,480. *See also* Richard Carveth
BARROW, John. 1 (Carnarvonshire) 8,609
BARRY, Thomas D. 1 (Monmouthshire) 671
BARTHOLOMEW, Thomas, Langton by Wragby, Lincolnshire. 8 (Lincolnshire) 12,333
BARTHOLOMEW, W., Goltho, near Wragby, Lincolnshire. 1 (Lincolnshire) 253
BARTLEY, Samuel, Llandefeilog, Carmarthenshire. 9 (Cardiganshire) 36,911; 5 (Pembrokeshire) 16,989; TOTAL 14 : 53,900
BARWISE, Joseph, Liverpool, Lancashire. 1 (Lancashire) 1,883
BASSETT, Messrs and Co., Southampton Office, Fitzroy Square. 1 (Sussex) 2,402
BASSETT, S. S. *See* Charles Williams, (Cornwall, 1)
BATE, Charles Harry. 1 (Monmouthshire) 2,228
BATE, Samuel, Knutton, Newcastle-under-Lyme, Staffordshire. 1 (Shropshire) 4,804; 14 (Staffordshire) 8,070; TOTAL 15 : 12,874
BATE, Thomas, Brecon. 6 (Breconshire) 34,569; 1 (Cardiganshire) 5,229; 1 (Carmarthenshire) 23,458; 1 (Glamorganshire) 3,975; 3 (Herefordshire) 7,981; 1 (Monmouthshire) 6,838. TOTAL 13 : 82,050
BATE and Timmis, Whitchurch, Shropshire. 1 (Cheshire) 972; 1 (Flintshire) 4,851; 1 (Shropshire) 14,271. TOTAL 3 : 20,094
BATEMAN, James, Emscote, St Nicholas, Warwick. 7 (Warwickshire) 11,945
BATEMAN, John Frederic, Manchester, Lancashire. 1 (Lancashire) 191
BAUSOR, Paul, Southwell, Nottinghamshire. 1 (Lincolnshire) 2,606; 3 (Nottinghamshire) 4,227; TOTAL 4 : 6,833
BAYLIS, Philip. 1 (Herefordshire) 1,689
BEADEL, James, Witham, Essex. 11 (Essex) 33,887

BEALES, Beccles, Suffolk. *See* Jno. Crickmay
BEARD, T. D. W., Cranbrook, Kent, (architect and surveyor). 1 (Kent) 6,508
BEARDS, Thomas, Avington, Hampshire. 4 (Hampshire) 8,724; 1 (Somerset) 2,344; TOTAL 5 : 11,068
BEARNE, Edward Snelling, Teigngrace, Newton Abbot, Devon. 1 (Devon) 1,330
BEAUCHAMP, John, Wells, Somerset. 1 (Somerset) 3,063
BECK, W. 1 (Sussex) 5,719
BECKETT, Henry, Wolverhampton, Staffordshire. 4 (Staffordshire) 11,636
BECKETT, John, Oulton Farm, Cheshire. 7 (Cheshire) 13,327
BECKETT, Richard T., Oulton Farm, Cheshire. 1 (Cheshire) 938
BELL, John, Gateshead, Durham. 2 (Durham) 4,762
BELL, J. T. W., Newcastle upon Tyne, Northumberland. 2 (Durham) 2,072; 1 (Yorkshire, West Riding) 746; TOTAL 3 : 2,818
BELL, Robert, The Nook, Irthington, Cumberland. 1 (Cumberland) 685
BELL, Thomas and Sons, Newcastle upon Tyne, Northumberland. 16 (Durham) 39,075; 89 (Northumberland) 195,193; TOTAL 105 : 234,268
BELL, William, Manchester, Lancashire. 6 (Lancashire) 9,526
BELL, William, Manchester, Lancashire, and Henry O'Hagan, Blackburn, Lancashire. 2 (Lancashire) 13,912
BELOE, Alfred T. 1 (Somerset) 1,233
BENNET, Francis. 1 (Lincolnshire) 3,480
BENNETT, H. 1 (Dorset) 967
BENNETT, Joseph Bennett Hankin, Tutbury, Staffordshire. 10 (Derbyshire) 7,406; 1 (Nottinghamshire) 2,392; 21 (Staffordshire) 24,595; 2 (Warwickshire) 5,251. TOTAL 34 : 39,644
BENNETT, Thomas Oatley, Bruton, Somerset. 10 (Somerset) 18,122
BENNISON, Christopher, London / Liverpool, Lancashire, (civil engineer and surveyor). 9 (Cornwall) 36,592
BENNISON, Jonathan, Liverpool, Lancashire. 7 (Lancashire) 15,740
BENSON, William, Bury, Lancashire. 5 (Lancashire) 22,245
BENTLEY, William, Owersby, Lincolnshire. 1 (Lincolnshire) 1,436
BERRY, 66 Chancery Lane, London. *See* Newton and Berry
BETHAM, Edward and Son, Lincoln. 5 (Lincolnshire) 1,817
BETHAM, George, Lincoln. 1 (Lincolnshire) 1,261. *See also* James Sandby Padley
BEVAN, Richard and John, Whiteheads Grove. 1 (Essex) 2,951
BEVAN, Richard Dunstanne, Uffculme, Devon. 2 (Devon) 6,123
BEYNON, Daniel, Kidwelly, Carmarthenshire. 1 (Carmarthenshire) 7,065
BIBBY, H., Preston, Lancashire. 2 (Lancashire) 2,845
BIBBY, James Carter, 28 Butlers Court, Fishergate, Preston, Lancashire. 1 (Lancashire) 2,347
BIDWELL, Charles M., Ely, Cambridgeshire. 3 (Cambridgeshire) 11,128; 7 (Huntingdonshire) 24,026; TOTAL 10 : 35,154
BIDWELL, Charles M., Ely, Cambridgeshire, and Charles Mumford, Downham Market, Norfolk. 1 (Cambridgeshire) 21,746
BIDWELL, Charles M., Ely, Cambridgeshire and John Bailey Denton, 9 Grays Inn Square, London. 1 (Cambridgeshire) 13,909
BIGGINS, James, Ingleby Geenhow, Yorkshire. 6 (Yorkshire, North Riding) 12,771
BINGLEY, William, Ellerslie Lodge, Penistone, Yorkshire. 3 (Yorkshire, West Riding) 3,696. *See also* Richard Birks
BINNS and Clifford, Birmingham, (surveyors, lithographers and draftsmen). 1 (Staffordshire) 3,470
BINNS, Jonathan, Lancaster. 3 (Lancashire) 7,009
BINTLEY, J., Kendal, Westmorland. 1 (Lancashire) 2,767; 3 (Westmorland) 7,359; TOTAL 4 : 10,126
BIRCHAM, W. G., Fakenham, Norfolk. 31 (Norfolk) 57,950
BIRD, John J., Boughton Monchelsea, Kent. 1 (Essex) 2,586
BIRD, John Jackson. 1 (Kent) 2,295
BIRD, Thomas. 1 (Essex) 1,776
BIRD, Thomas, 8 Chatham St, Manchester, Lancashire. 2 (Lancashire) 5,593
BIRKET, Charles. 12 (Lancashire) 38,562
BIRKS, C., Barnsley, Yorkshire. 1 (Yorkshire, West Riding) 377
BIRKS, Richard, Barnsley, Yorkshire. 25 (Yorkshire, West Riding) 38,237
BIRKS, Richard, Barnsley, Yorkshire and William Bingley, Ellerslie Lodge, Penistone, Yorkshire. 1 (Yorkshire, West Riding) 11,818
BLACKMAN, James W., Fareham, Hampshire. 4 (Sussex) 6,532; 17 (Hampshire) 62,162; TOTAL 21 : 68,694
BLACKMORE, Messrs, Clayhidon / Churchingford, Devon. 4 (Devon) 15,424; 2 (Somerset) 2,877; TOTAL 6 : 18,301. See *also* Frost and Blackmore
BLAKE, William. *See* Benjamin Herman
BLAKEWAY, W. 1 (Cheshire) 629
BLASHILL, Thomas, Kings Acre, Herefordshire. 4 (Herefordshire) 3,747
BLATHWAYT, Edward, Kidwelly, Carmarthenshire. 1 (Carmarthenshire) 11,811
BLOODWORTH, Charles, Kimbolton, Huntingdonshire. 5 (Huntingdonshire) 1,873
BLOODWORTH, Thomas. 1 (Buckinghamshire) 1,259
BLUNDEN, George Blunden, Arundel, Sussex. 3 (Sussex) 1,028
BLUNDY, T. F. 1 (Lincolnshire) 843
BLYTH, R. T. 1 (Lincolnshire) 2,190
BODY, George S. and John S. Body, St Germans, Cornwall. 2 (Cornwall) 8,548
BODY, William, South Brent, Somerset. 1 (Somerset) 1,719
BODY, William, South Brent, Somerset, and James Peachey Williams. 1 (Somerset) 3,038
BOLTON, J., Ulverston, Lancashire. 1 (Lancashire) 4,016
BONSOR, William, Clipston, Market Harborough, Northamptonshire. 3 (Northamptonshire) 5,100
BOOTH, Allen, Knutton, Staffordshire. 2 (Staffordshire) 14,236
BOOTH, D., Sundridge, Kent. 5 (Kent) 21,469
BOOTH, Robert Stapleton, Wainfleet, Lincolnshire. 1 (Leicestershire) 1,317; 5 (Lincolnshire) 14,685; TOTAL 6 : 16,002
BORLEY, William, Alpheton, Suffolk. 9 (Suffolk) 17,709
BOUCH, Thomas. 4 (Cumberland) 7,639
BOURN, James junior, Cleobury Mortimer, Shropshire. 1 (Herefordshire) 2,078; 6 (Shropshire) 13,463; 3 (Worcestershire) 11,933; TOTAL 10 : 27,474.
BOURNE, John, Newcastle upon Tyne, Northumberland. 19 (Northumberland) 23,530
BOURNE, William. 1 (Lincolnshire) 2,820
BOWEN, John, Glanthames, Llandilofawr, Carmarthenshire, and William Morgan. 2 (Carmarthenshire) 10,019
BOWEN, John, Bocconoc, Cornwall. 3 (Cornwall) 4,310
BOWLER, William A., Colchester, Essex. 1 (Essex) 26

BOWMAN, Edmund, Newcastle upon Tyne, Northumberland. 2 (Durham) 2,213; 29 (Northumberland) 51,949; TOTAL 31: 54,162
BOWRON and Harris. 1 (Essex) 3,050
BOWSER, Matthew, Thornaby Grange, Yorkshire. 1 (Durham) 192; 2 (Yorkshire, North Riding) 1,410; TOTAL 3 : 1,602
BOYCE, G. A., Tiverton, Devon. 4 (Devon) 11,411
BRACKENBURY, Percy William, Wellow House, Ollerton, Nottinghamshire. 1 (Lincolnshire) 2,543; 14 (Nottinghamshire) 34,503; TOTAL 15 : 37,046
BRADDOCK, Joseph. *See* Joseph Broadhurst
BRADFIELD, Thomas, Litcham, Norfolk. 4 (Norfolk) 5,806
BRADLEY, Robert. 1 (Yorkshire, West Riding) 211
BRADLEY, Thomas and Sons, Richmond, Yorkshire. 56 (Yorkshire, North Riding) 143,584; 5 (Yorkshire, West Riding) 11,768; TOTAL 61 : 155,352
BRADSAM, James. *See* Robert Jervis, (Lancashire, 1)
BRADY, Charles Robert, Castle Farm, Stockport, Lancashire. 1 (Cheshire) 659
BRADY, M., 55 Chester St, Kennington Lane, London. 2 (Kent) 3,161
BRADY, M., Brigg, Lincolnshire. 2 (Lincolnshire) 1,774
BRAMBLE, John Roger, Devizes, Wiltshire. 1 (Dorset) 3,407; 4 (Wiltshire) 13,905; TOTAL 5 : 17,312
BRAMBLE, John Roger, Devizes, Wiltshire and George Oakley Lucas, Devizes, Wiltshire. 1 (Wiltshire) 4,326
BRANSBY, John. 1 (Suffolk) 881
BRANSBY, Spencer L., Ipswich, Suffolk. 3 (Essex) 7,511; 1 (Oxfordshire) 1,270; 14 (Suffolk) 24,145; TOTAL 18 : 32,926
BRANSON, Thomas, Norton, Stockton, Shropshire. 1 (Shropshire) 2,184
BRAUND, George, and Henry Hearn, Exeter, Devon. 2 (Cornwall) 6,472; 24 (Devon) 75,617; TOTAL 26 : 82,089
BRAVENDER, John, Cirencester, Gloucestershire. 1 (Berkshire) 345; 1 (Gloucestershire) 1,340; TOTAL 2 : 1,685
BRERETON, Jno., Melton Mowbray, Leicestershire. 1 (Leicestershire) 1,753
BRIDGER, William, Petworth / Chichester, Sussex. 2 (Sussex) 589
BRIGHT, Edmund C., Sheffield, Yorkshire. 1 (Derbyshire) 329
BRIGHT, Paul, Sheffield, Yorkshire. 8 (Derbyshire) 5,381; 2 (Yorkshire, West Riding) 6,266; TOTAL 10 : 11,647.
BRIGHT, W., Admaston, Wellington, Shropshire. 1 (Shropshire) 828; 1 (Staffordshire) 3,298; TOTAL 2 : 4,126
BRITTAIN, C., Liverpool, Lancashire. 5 (Cheshire) 3,285
BROADHURST, Joseph and Joseph Braddock, Bugsworth, Derbyshire. 1 (Derbyshire) 3,806
BROCK, William, Launceston, Cornwall. 1 (Cornwall) 2,487; 1 (Devon) 4,212; TOTAL 2 : 6,699
BRODIE, Henry. 1 (Carmarthenshire) 5,632
BROMLEY, John, Derby. 19 (Derbyshire) 30,225; 7 (Leicestershire) 6,327; 1 (Lincolnshire) 604; 1 (Northamptonshire) 2,281; 3 (Nottinghamshire) 2,507; 4 (Staffordshire) 2,794; TOTAL 35 : 44,738
BROMLEY, Robert, Derby. 15 (Derbyshire) 25,971; 4 (Leicestershire) 6,001; 1 (Nottinghamshire) 2,162; 2 (Staffordshire) 2,797; TOTAL 22 : 36,931
BROMLEY, William R. *See* William Ellison
BROWN, Edward, Newton St Cyres, Devon. 1 (Devon) 1,853
BROWN, J., Oughterside, Cumberland. 1 (Cumberland) 929
BROWN, John, Brislington, Somerset and Jacob Sturge, Bristol, Gloucestershire. 2 (Somerset) 2,925
BROWN, John, Farewell, Staffordshire. 1 (Staffordshire) 1,048
BROWN, J. O. 1 (Bedfordshire) 2,394
BROWN, John T., Norwich, Norfolk. 1 (Norfolk) 3,048. *See also* Joseph Manning
BROWN, Thomas, Maidstone, Kent. 1 (Kent) 3,320
BROWN, T. and T. D. W. Dearn. 1 (Kent) 9,862
BROWN, W., Tonbridge, Kent. 2 (Kent) 21,091
BROWN, William, Tring, Hertfordshire. 15 (Buckinghamshire) 17,563; 1 (Hertfordshire) 2,024; TOTAL 16 : 19,587
BROWN, William Edward, Long Eaton, Derbyshire. 1 (Nottinghamshire) 83
BROWNE, D. 1 (Westmorland) 1,177
BROWNE, E. 4 (Devon) 16,460
BROWNE, J., Norwich, Norfolk. 1 (Norfolk) 1,683
BROWNE, J. O., 8 Furnivals Inn, London. 1 (Hertfordshire) 3,956; 1 (Suffolk) 2,344; TOTAL 2 : 6,300
BROWNE, R. P., Greenwich, Kent. 1 (Kent) 799
BROWNE, William, Norwich, Norfolk, (surveyor and lithographer). 1 (Essex) 3,933; 1 (Huntingdonshire) 3,740; 5 (Norfolk) 10,835; 6 (Suffolk) 11,594; TOTAL 13 : 30,102
BUCKLAND, William T., Wraysbury, Buckinghamshire. 5 (Buckinghamshire) 6,122
BUDD, Francis. 1 (Somerset) 1,526
BUDGEN, John, Tunbridge, Kent. 1 (Kent) 2,373; 3 (Sussex) 11,157; TOTAL 4 : 13,530
BUDGEN, Richard, Abergavenny, Monmouthshire. 1 (Monmouthshire) 385
BULL, John, 16 Tavistock St, Covent Garden, London. 1 (Essex) 1,029
BURCHAM, Charles, Kings Lynn, Norfolk. 10 (Norfolk) 19,421
BURGESS, Thomas, Norton, Runcorn, Cheshire. 3 (Lancashire) 5,520
BURGESS, Thomas, Norton, Runcorn, Cheshire and Richard Owen. 8 (Cheshire) 18,485
BURN..., T. 1 (Glamorganshire) 917
BURTON, Robert, Dunmow / Hatfield Broad Oak. 5 (Essex) 9,403
BURTON, Thomas junior, Langley, Norfolk. 14 (Norfolk) 17,331. *See also* W. G. Jones, Loddon
BURTON, William, Bury, Lancashire. 1 (Lancashire) 2,307
BUSHELL, Henry W., 40 Upper Charlotte St, Fitzroy Square, London. 1 (Devon) 6,595; 1 (Northamptonshire) 1,115; TOTAL 2 : 7,710
BUSHELL, Henry W. and William Charles Vine, London. 2 (Cornwall) 16,599; 4 (Surrey) 21,922; TOTAL 6 : 38,521
BUTLER, Joseph, Chichester, Sussex. 16 (Sussex) 29,964
BUTTERWORTH, Joseph, Manchester, Lancashire. 1 (Lancashire) 956
BUXTON, H. G., Devizes, Wiltshire. 2 (Wiltshire), 1,057
BUXTON, Thomas, Malton, Yorkshire, (surveyor and engineer). 2 (Yorkshire, East Riding) 5,831; 28 (Yorkshire, North Riding) 69,781; TOTAL 30 : 75,612
BYGRAVE, Thomas, Clements Inn, London. 3 (Essex) 7,242; 2 (Surrey) 5,575; TOTAL 5 : 12,817

CALVER, Henry, Diss, Norfolk. 8 (Norfolk) 14,944; 5 (Suffolk) 9,691; TOTAL 13 : 24,635
CAMPELL, E., Buxton, Derbyshire. 1 (Yorkshire, North Riding) 1,167
CAMPBELL, James, Howden, Yorkshire. 3 (Yorkshire, East Riding) 1,833
CAMPBELL, John. *See* Alfred Sharman
CAMPBELL, Thomas A., Nottingham. 1 (Derbyshire) 1,148; 1 (Nottinghamshire) 790; TOTAL 2 : 1,938

CAMPBELL, William, Hastings, Sussex. 1 (Sussex) 2,479
CANNING, George. 1 (Northamptonshire) 1,549
CAREY, L., and others. 3 (Breconshire) 19,223. *See also* T. M'Grane
CARLOS and Fitzgerald, Hanover Chambers, Buckingham St, Adelphi, London. 2 (Cornwall) 12,690; 1 (Essex) 2,241; TOTAL 3 : 14,931
CARR, Francis, York. 4 (Yorkshire, North Riding) 4,125; 2 (Yorkshire, West Riding) 216; TOTAL 6 : 4,431
CARR, Francis and Thomas Holliday, York. 6 (Yorkshire, East Riding) 6,208
CARR, Francis, York, and Henry R. Spence, Elvington, York. 2 (Yorkshire, North Riding) 1,466
CARR, Richard Carr, York. 2 (Yorkshire, West Riding) 5,753
CARR, William, Chalkfoot, Carlisle, Cumberland. 2 (Cumberland) 865; 2 (Westmorland) 5,144; TOTAL 4 : 6,009
CARRINGTON and Robinson, Sevenoaks, Kent. 1 (Kent) 2,765
CARRUTHERS, George. *See* William Hetherington
CARRUTHERS, John Beard, Willsbridge, Bitton, Gloucestershire. 1 (Gloucestershire) 2,589
CARTER, F., W. Thomas and S. Hendy. 2 (Cornwall) 6,785
CARTER, Richard, Halifax, Yorkshire. 1 (Yorkshire, West Riding) 486
CARTWRIGHT, R., 1 Warwick Place, Bedford Row, London. 1 (Norfolk) 751
CARVETH, Richard, St Austell, Cornwall. 1 (Cornwall) 2,632
CARVETH, Richard, and John J. Gummoe, St Austell, Cornwall, and John E. Barnicoat, Falmouth, Cornwall. 1 (Cornwall) 5,935
CASSIDY, P., London. 1 (Berkshire) 2,850; 1 (Gloucestershire) 2,984; 3 (Surrey) 16,255; TOTAL 5 : 22,089
CASTREE, Josiah, Gloucester. 3 (Gloucestershire) 3,962; 2 (Worcestershire) 3,173; TOTAL 5 : 7,135
CATTLIN, F., 39 Ely Place, Holborn, London. 1 (Devon) 5,396
CATTLIN, Frederick F., Danbury, Essex. 1 (Essex) 1,249. *See also* Jonathan Lewis
CAUSTON, Arthur, Berkeley Street / Clarence Street, Gloucester. 1 (Gloucestershire) 439; 1 (Herefordshire) 3,772; 1 (Worcestershire) 3,656; TOTAL 3 : 7,867. *See also* Robert Jackman *and* Thomas Wakeman
CAWLEY, George, Tabley, Knutsford, Cheshire. 24 (Cheshire) 24,007. *See also* James Cawley
CAWLEY, James, Macclesfield / Tabley Superior, Cheshire. 19 (Cheshire) 40,839; 2 (Shropshire) 13,330; TOTAL 21 : 77,256
CAWLEY, James and George Cawley, Tabley Superior, Cheshire. 3 (Cheshire) 4,244
CAWLEY, James and Thomas Dyson Firth, Macclesfield, Cheshire. 14 (Cheshire) 19,544
CAWLEY, James, Tabley Superior, Cheshire, and Thomas Smith, Dunham Massey, Cheshire. 1 (Cheshire) 1,629
CAWSTON, William Westerman, Worlington, Suffolk. 9 (Suffolk) 37,797
CHAFER, William, Yawthorpe, Lincolnshire. 1 (Lincolnshire) 712
CHALONER, George W. 3 (Denbighshire) 9,508; 1 (Flintshire) 1,089; TOTAL 4 : 10,597
CHALONER, George W. and Hugh Grainger. 3 (Denbighshire) 6,857
CHANDLER, W. 1 (Suffolk) 522
CHAPMAN, Thomas. *See* Edward Dowding
CHAPMAN, Thomas, Son, and William Webb, 3 Arundel St, Strand, London. 1 (Berkshire) 1,454; 3 (Essex) 7,238; 1 (Norfolk) 1,362; 2 (Suffolk) 2,399; TOTAL 7 : 12,453
CHAPPLE and Oliver. 1 (Devon) 2,209
CHEESMAN, John, Buckland, Dover, Kent. 7 (Kent) 9,093
CHEFFINS, C. F., Southampton Buildings, Holborn, London. 1 (Warwickshire) 250
CHEFFINS, William, Bishop's Stortford, Hertfordshire. 1 (Essex) 2,533
CHERRY, Edward, Wellesbourne, Warwickshire. 4 (Warwickshire) 5,345; 1 (Worcestershire) 2,287; TOTAL 5 : 7,632
CHILCOTT, Charles, Crowcombe, Somerset. 2 (Somerset) 5,666
CHILCOTT, Henry, Croydon, Surrey. 1 (Surrey) 1,240
CHILCOTT, Henry and J. Chilcott. 1 (Sussex) 10,268
CHITTY, Manwaring, Farnham, Surrey. 5 (Hampshire) 15,312
CHURCHILL, Henry, Aylesbury, Buckinghamshire. 1 (Buckinghamshire) 1,719
CLARK, J. F., Newmarket, Suffolk. 1 (Suffolk) 2,666
CLARK, W. M. 2 (Denbighshire) 10,091
CLARKE, Adam Taylor, Norwich, Norfolk. 11 (Norfolk) 15,321
CLARKE, H. J., Hereford. 2 (Herefordshire) 2,213
CLARKE, Henry. *See* Caleb Cull
CLARKE, John, Higham Cliff, Alfreton, Derbyshire. 5 (Derbyshire) 2,993. *See also* George Unwin
CLARKE, Turner P., Andover, Hampshire. 1 (Hampshire) 5,470
CLARKSON, Anthony. 4 (Yorkshire, North Riding) 41,937; 1 (Westmorland) 1,069; TOTAL 5 : 43,006
CLARKSON, Anthony and Richard Garth, Swaledale, Yorkshire. 2 (Yorkshire, West Riding) 9,229
CLARKSON, J. F. 1 (Lancashire) 1,572
CLARY, John Berry, Reading, Berkshire. 1 (Berkshire) 386; 1 (Oxfordshire) 642; TOTAL 2 : 1,028
CLAYTON, Henry, Ingatestone, Essex. 12 (Essex) 28,851
CLAYTON, H. J. *See* G. S. Strawson
CLAYTON, J. *See* Henry Clayton
CLIFFORD. *See* Binns and Clifford
CLIMIE, D. 1 (Devon) 2,375
CLINTON, Dickson, Purvis and Merry. 1 (Suffolk) 1,767
CLUTTON, Robert and J. Clutton, Whitehall Place, London. 2 (Surrey) 777
CLUTTON, William, 8 Parliament Street, London. 1 (Gloucestershire) 823
COATES, Henry, 12 Duke St, Portland Place, London. 5 (Essex) 5,807; 2 (Suffolk) 2,263; TOTAL 7 : 8,070
COATES, Herbert. *See* Henry Coates.
COBB, Henry, 18 Lincolns Inn Fields, London. 3 (Kent) 4,206
COCHRANE, W. E. 1 (Northumberland) 227
COCKETT, W. 1 (Yorkshire, West Riding) 5,291
COEN, E. W. 1 (Yorkshire, West Riding) 2,333
COKER, Henry. 1 (Suffolk) 1,906
COLDRIDGE, John, Exeter, Devon. 6 (Devon) 11,337
COLE, J. W. 1 (Sussex) 8,211
COLEMAN, E. P., Dover, Kent. 2 (Kent) 1,867
COLES, R. P. 1 (Northamptonshire) 1,471
COLLARD, Thomas White, Canterbury, Kent. 24 (Kent) 54,816. *See also* Thomas Cooper

COLLARD, Thomas White, Canterbury, Kent, and Harry Finnet, Maidstone, Kent. 1 (Kent) 4,391
COLLARD, Thomas White, Canterbury, Kent, and Ashenden or Ashendon. 2 (Kent) 46
COLLING, John, Hunton, Yorkshire. 2 (Yorkshire, North Riding) 2,234
COLLINGWOOD, William Brewster, Denton, Lincolnshire. 1 (Leicestershire) 1,009; 3 (Lincolnshire) 4,226; TOTAL 4 : 5,235
COLLINS, Thomas, Culworth, Northamptonshire. 2 (Northamptonshire) 2,290
COLMAN, Samuel, Norwich, Norfolk. 3 (Norfolk) 3,338
CONROY, George. 1 (Cornwall) 7,894; 1 (Suffolk) 1,638; TOTAL 2 : 9,532
COOKE, Layton, Adelphi, St Martins, London. 1 (Oxfordshire) 359; 1 (Surrey) 6,396; TOTAL 2 : 6,755
COOLING, H. *See* T. Read.
COOM, Henry, Bodmin, Cornwall. 2 (Cornwall) 6,987
COOPER. *See* Cotterells and Cooper
COOPER, Charles, Alverdiscott, Bideford, Devon. 1 (Cornwall) 8,078; 10 (Devon) 31,211; TOTAL 11 : 39,289
COOPER, Edward junior, Henley in Arden, Warwickshire. 1 (Warwickshire) 8,302; 1 (Worcestershire) 1,186; TOTAL 2 : 9,488
COOPER, George and Son, Alverdiscott, Bideford, Devon. 1 (Cornwall) 2,646
COOPER, G. M., Henley in Arden, Warwickshire. 1 (Warwickshire) 2,514
COOPER, Henry. *See* Thomas Cooper
COOPER, Robert, Leeds / York. 3 (Yorkshire, West Riding) 5,777
COOPER, Thomas, Canterbury, Kent. 13 (Kent) 15,703
COOPER, Thomas, Canterbury, Kent and Thomas White Collard, Canterbury, Kent. 1 (Kent) 2,441
COOPER, Thomas, Canterbury, Kent, and Henry Cooper. 2 (Kent) 286
COPE, William S., Milton, Norton in the Moors, Staffordshire. 1 (Cheshire) 1,100
COPLAND, George. 1 (Devon) 3,115
CORBY, Robert, Whitlingham, Norfolk. 3 (Norfolk) 4,277
CORBY, William, Whitlingham, Norfolk. 2 (Norfolk) 1,775
CORFIELD, Edward, Keppel St, Bloomsbury, London. 3 (Essex) 2,872
COTGREAVE, Robert, Eccleston, Cheshire. 3 (Cheshire) 4,232. *See also* Sam. Hughes
COTTERELL, J. H., Bath, Somerset. 1 (Devon) 3,039
COTTERELL, W. F., Bath, Somerset. 1 (Devon) 2,093
COTTERELLS and Cooper, Bath, Somerset. 2 (Gloucestershire) 2,706; 19 (Somerset) 28,553; 3 (Wiltshire) 16,493; TOTAL 24 : 47,752
COTTON, Benjamin S. W., West Pennard, Somerset. 1 (Cornwall) 2,666; 2 (Somerset) 3,916; TOTAL 3 : 6,582
COULSON, I. 2 (Durham) 550; 29 (Northumberland) 125,999; TOTAL 31 : 126,549
COURT, Richard senior, Bewdley, Worcestershire. 2 (Worcestershire) 3,300
COURT, Richard senior, Bewdley, Worcestershire, and Richard Charles Herbert, Worcester. 1 (Worcestershire) 7,533
COURT, S. 3 (Somerset) 7,539
COWELL, Philip James, Thetford, Norfolk. 1 (Norfolk) 2,027
COX, William Collard, Williton, Somerset. 9 (Devon) 33,734; 11 (Somerset) 45,797; TOTAL 20 : 79,531. *See also* Drew and Cox, etc.
CRAIG, John, Lowick, Northumberland. 2 (Northumberland) 2,618
CRAMPTON, John. 1 (Cheshire) 657
CRANER, J. 1 (Derbyshire) 890
CRANSTON, James, Kings Acre, Herefordshire. 6 (Herefordshire) 6,963
CRAWLEY, Charles E., Manchester, Lancashire. 1 (Lancashire) 2,109
CRAWTER, Messrs, Cobham, Surrey and Southampton Blgs, Chancery La, London. 20 (Essex) 71,508; 1 (Hampshire) 1,392; 6 (Hertfordshire) 13,489; 3 (Kent) 4,790; 14 (Surrey) 32,214; 3 (Sussex) 11,835; 2 (Worcestershire) 2,388; TOTAL 49: 137,616
CRAWTER, Thomas, Cobham, Surrey. *See* Job Smallpeice
CREACH, H. C., Ashburton, Devon. 1 (Devon) 2,300
CRICKMAY, Jno. *See also* George Baker
CRICKMAY, Jno. and Beales, Beccles, Suffolk. 5 (Suffolk) 6,346
CRISPIN, Henry junior and Richard Davie Gould. 2 (Cornwall) 10,560
CRISPIN, Henry, Chulmleigh / South Molton, Devon. 13 (Devon) 56,132
CROFT. *See* Lenny and Croft
CROFT, John, Bury St Edmunds, Suffolk. 4 (Suffolk) 5,706
CROMPTON, James. *See* John J. Myres
CRONK, E. E. and G. Cronk, Seal, Sevenoaks, Kent. 2 (Kent) 4,678
CRONK, William, Seal, Kent. 1 (Kent) 1,867
CROOKES, John and Son, Leeds, Yorkshire. 1 (Leicestershire) 1,166; 1 (Yorkshire, West Riding) 1,814; TOTAL 2 : 2,980
CROOME, James, Acton Hall, Berkeley, Gloucestershire. 4 (Gloucestershire) 6,849
CROOME, John. 1 (Gloucestershire) 1,114
CROOME, William, Tewkesbury, Gloucestershire. 3 (Gloucestershire) 3,930; 1 (Herefordshire) 845; TOTAL 4 : 4,775
CROSS, Joseph, Wisbech, Cambridgeshire. 2 (Lincolnshire) 5,656
CROZIER, W. 1 (Northumberland) 1,262
CRUSE and Fox, Warminster, Wiltshire. 1 (Somerset) 6,932; 5 (Wiltshire) 9,669; TOTAL 6 : 16,601
CULL, Caleb. 1 (Gloucestershire) 2,259
CULL, Caleb and Henry Clarke. 1 (Herefordshire) 2,523
CUMING, George, Easton on the Hill, Northamptonshire. 1 (Leicestershire) 340
CUMING, George, Easton on the Hill, Northamptonshire, and William Arden. 1 (Rutland) 1,344
CUMING, George and Hill, Easton on the Hill, Northamptonshire. 1 (Huntingdonshire) 779; 4 (Lincolnshire) 3,327; 3 (Rutland) 3,458; TOTAL 8 : 6,220
CUMING, N., Tavistock, Devon. 1 (Devon) 1,413
CUMMING, Geoffrey, Exeter, Devon. 1 (Somerset) 845
CUMMING, George W., Wickenden, Exeter, Devon. 2 (Devon) 2,564
CUMMINGS, T. G. 1 (Denbighshire) 8,997
CUNDY, Thomas S., Empingham, Rutland. 1 (Rutland) 505
CURTIS, John, Snaith, Yorkshire. 1 (Yorkshire, North Riding) 2,394
CUTMORE, Thomas, Halwell, Totnes, Devon. 9 (Devon) 22,402
CUTTLE, Richard, Ryhill, Wragby, Yorkshire. 1 (Yorkshire, West Riding) 25

DABBS, William, Leicester. 2 (Cheshire) 3,341; 1 (Leicestershire) 1,266; TOTAL 3 : 4,607
DAGLISH, John, St Helens, Lancashire. 5 (Lancashire) 11,156

DALE, John, Woolvercott, Oxfordshire. 2 (Oxfordshire) 1,872
DARBYSHIRE, John and George C. Darbyshire, Brompton, Kent. 5 (Kent) 16,881
DARLEY, John, Chippenham, Wiltshire. 1 (Wiltshire) 3,121
DAVENPORT, George Francis, Oxford. 1 (Oxfordshire) 3,791
DAVENPORT, George Horatio, Knutsford, Cheshire. 7 (Cheshire) 7,036
DAVEY, Fred R., Canterbury, Kent. 2 (Kent) 8,173
DAVEY, J. M., Canterbury, Kent. 11 (Kent) 25,031. *See also* Thomas W. Collard
DAVIE, Jno. and C. Davie, Rye, Sussex. 1 (Sussex) 4,760
DAVIES, David, Froodvale, Conwil Caio, Carmarthenshire. 2 (Breconshire) 14,556; 2 (Carmarthenshire) 26,493; TOTAL 4 : 41,049
DAVIES, Essex, Fishguard, Pembrokeshire. 1 (Carmarthenshire) 589; 3 (Pembrokeshire) 13,759; TOTAL 4 : 14,348
DAVIES, Henry, Kimpton, Hertfordshire. 1 (Bedfordshire) 15,232; 7 (Hertfordshire) 17,710; TOTAL 8 : 32,942
DAVIES, Hewett and Hughes, 12 Haymarket, London. 1 (Surrey) 1,060; 1 (Sussex) 1,871; TOTAL 2 : 2,931
DAVIES, John, Stourbridge, Worcestershire. 1 (Herefordshire) 636; 1 (Shropshire) 1,775; 2 (Staffordshire) 1,274; 1 (Worcestershire) 4,605; TOTAL 5 : 8,290
DAVIES, John, Mollington, Cheshire. 33 (Cheshire) 40,518; 1 (Flintshire) 581; TOTAL 34 : 41,099
DAVIES, William Henry, Abingdon, Berkshire. 3 (Berkshire) 3,799; 3 (Oxfordshire) 6,778; TOTAL 6 : 10,577
DAVIS, Cornelius B., The Hitchen, East Woodhay, Berkshire. 3 (Berkshire) 4,047; 2 (Hampshire) 4,218; TOTAL 5 : 8,265
DAVIS, Richard, Banbury, Oxfordshire. 1 (Berkshire) 2,424; 2 (Buckinghamshire) 6,858; 5 (Northamptonshire) 4,617; TOTAL 8 : 13,979
DAVIS and Saunders, Banbury and Oxford. 3 (Buckinghamshire) 5,039; 4 (Northamptonshire) 1,016; 13 (Oxfordshire) 11,882; TOTAL 20 : 17,937
DAVIS, Saunders and Hicks, Oxford and Banbury, Oxfordshire. 2 (Warwickshire) 1,298
DAVISON, Thomas, Durham. 18 (Durham) 36,738; 1 (Lincolnshire) 1,706; TOTAL 19 : 38,444
DAWE, John, Withycombe Raleigh, Devon. 1 (Devon) 7,563
DAWSON. *See* White and Dawson
DAWSON. *See* Joseph Whitle
DAWSON, Richard Godwin, Llanasa, Flintshire. 1 (Flintshire) 1,484
DAWSON, S. A. 1 (Yorkshire, West Riding) 3,734
DAWSON, William, Exeter, Devon. 11 (Devon) 24,444; 1 (Dorset) 248; TOTAL 12 : 24,692. *See also* Jno. Coldridge
DAY, Charles, Collyweston, Northamptonshire. 2 (Bedfordshire) 2,550; 1 (Huntingdonshire) 714; 2 (Lincolnshire) 1,987; 4 (Northamptonshire) 8,260; 4 (Rutland) 3,829; TOTAL 13 : 17,340
DEAN, Arthur, 6 New Broad St, London. 1 (Wiltshire) 1,738
DEAN, William, Stratford, Essex. 1 (Essex) 4,390
DEARN, T. D. W. *See* T. Brown
DENNETT, John and Son. 2 (Hampshire) 3,863
DENT, Richard, Camden Town, London. 5 (Hampshire) 13,737. *See also* James Bocock Holbrook
DENTON, John Bailey, 9 Grays Inn Square, London. 2 (Bedfordshire) 4,610; 2 (Essex) 3,358; 4 (Hertfordshire) 14,600; TOTAL 8 : 22,568. *See also* Charles M. Bidwell
DEYNS, John Fuller, North Walsham, Norfolk. 4 (Norfolk) 2,990
DIBBIN, F. W., Chiswick, Middlesex. 1 (Berkshire) 4,315
DICKINSON, John, Austerfield, Yorkshire. 2 (Nottinghamshire) 1,014
DICKINSON, Joseph, Dowlais, Glamorganshire. 1 (Glamorganshire) 2,108
DICKINSON, J. N. 1 (Cumberland) 4,399
DICKINSON, W. *See* William Gaythorp and William Hetherington
DICKINSON, T. F. *See* Norris and Dickinson
DICKSON. *See* Clinton, Dickson, Purvis and Merry
DILMAS or DITMAS, William. 2 (Yorkshire, East Riding) 1,690
DIXON, Henry, Oxford. 1 (Berkshire) 1,430; 2 (Buckinghamshire) 4,034; 6 (Oxfordshire) 9,805; TOTAL 9 : 15,269
DIXON, Richard, and Maitland, 21 John St, Bedford Row, London. 2 (Kent) 5,440; 1 (Somerset) 1,791; 1 (Suffolk) 1,665; 1 (Surrey) 3,627; 2 (Sussex) 7,449; TOTAL 7 : 19,972
DIXON, Richard, Furnival's Inn, London. 1 (Hampshire) 3,318; 2 (Somerset) 7,880; 5 (Surrey) 32,370; TOTAL 8 : 43,568
DIXON, Thomas, Bradford, Yorkshire. 3 (Yorkshire, West Riding) 8,009
DIXON, Thomas, Darlington, Durham. 4 (Durham) 6,581; 31 (Yorkshire, North Riding) 52,518; TOTAL 35 : 59,099
DOBBIN, T. 1 (Yorkshire, North Riding) 970
DOBSON, Robert, Preston, Lancashire. 7 (Lancashire) 3,213
DODD, Moses. 2 (Oxfordshire) 6,138
DODD, Moses, 16 New Broad St, London. 1 (Essex) 1,893
DODSWORTH, Henry. 1 (Yorkshire, East Riding) 663
DOE, George. 1 (Devon) 332
DOHERTY, John. 5 (Devon) 13,311; 2 (Dorset) 2,700; TOTAL 7 : 16,011
DOLLOND, London. 1 (Yorkshire, West Riding) 585
DONKIN, Thomas, Westow, Yorkshire. 3 (Yorkshire, East Riding) 6,995
DOSWELL, George, 35 Bermead St, Southampton, Hampshire. 7 (Hampshire) 23,753; 1 (Surrey) 988; TOTAL 8 : 24,741
DOUBELL, Charles. *See* D. A. Nicholson
DOULL, Alexander, Chatham, Kent. 1 (Devon) 10,474; 11 (Essex) 35,913; 31 (Kent) 68,705; TOTAL 43 : 115,092
DOWDING, Edward and Thomas Chapman. 2 (Gloucestershire) 3,922
DOWLING, George, Lowestoft, Suffolk. 1 (Suffolk) 61
DOYLEY, John senior, Belgrave St, New Road, London. 1 (Essex) 2,996
DOYLEY, John. *See* Richard Allerton
DOYLEY, John King, Grays Inn, London. 1 (Hertfordshire) 6,606
DRANE, James, Norwich, Norfolk. 2 (Norfolk) 3,760; 1 (Suffolk) 1,484; TOTAL 3 : 5,244
DRANE, William, Norwich, Norfolk. 25 (Norfolk) 35,986
DRAYSON, Frederick and Henry Edwin Drayson, Faversham, Kent. 1 (Devon) 2,696; 2 (Hampshire) 11,128; 26 (Kent) 54,136; 3 (Surrey) 10,580; 17 (Sussex) 55,891; TOTAL 49 : 134,431
DREDGE, Richard, High Wycombe, Buckinghamshire. 2 (Buckinghamshire) 7,383
DREW, Messrs, and Cox, R. P. Frise, Williton, Somerset. 1 (Devon) 9,188
DREW, John, Peamore, Exeter and Thomas Wright, Tiverton, Devon. 1 (Devon) 1,341
DREWRY, James. 1 (Kent) 1,310
DRING, George, Long Melford, Suffolk. 1 (Essex) 2,125; 3 (Suffolk) 5,924; TOTAL 4 : 8,049

DRIVER, Edward and George Neale Driver, 5 Whitehall, London. 2 (Berkshire) 7,696; 1 (Essex) 57; 1 (Kent) 3,713; 2 (Middlesex) 1,768; 1 (Surrey) 970; 3 (Sussex) 6,543; TOTAL 10 : 20,747
DRURY, George, Ipswich, Suffolk. 1 (Suffolk) 1,922
DUCKWORTH, John, Barnet, Hertfordshire. 1 (Middlesex) 240
DUCKWORTH, John and Edward Taplin, Barnet, Hertfordshire. 2 (Hertfordshire) 4,784
DUGGLEBY, T. and Sons, Hunmanby, Yorkshire. 1 (Yorkshire, East Riding) 2,226
DUMOLO, John, Dunton House, Curdworth, Warwickshire. 4 (Warwickshire) 3,152
DUNCAN, Thomas, Alnwick, Northumberland. 1 (Northumberland) 503
DUNCOMBE, Edward Charles, Guildford, Surrey. 1 (Middlesex) 173; 4 (Surrey) 9,295; TOTAL 5 : 9,468
DUNCUM, William, Reading, Berkshire. 1 (Sussex) 4,458
DUNN, James, Patrington, Yorkshire. 2 (Lincolnshire) 4,165; 4 (Yorkshire, East Riding) 3,072; TOTAL 6 : 7,237
DUNN, Joseph, Hartford, Cheshire. 1 (Cheshire) 1,747
DUREY, George, Great Chart, Kent. 5 (Kent) 16,713
DURHAM, John, Stony Stratford, Buckinghamshire. 8 (Buckinghamshire) 6,990; 14 (Northamptonshire) 13,896; TOTAL 22 : 20,886
DURHAM, Makin, Thorne, Yorkshire. 7 (Lincolnshire) 12,863; 1 (Yorkshire, East Riding) 3,705; 9 (Yorkshire, West Riding) 24,116; TOTAL 17 : 40,684
DURRANT, Edwin, Kings Lynn, Norfolk. 21 (Norfolk) 53,798
DYKE, C. P. 1 (Berkshire) 4,623
DYKE, George Pottow, Christchurch, Hampshire. 1 (Hampshire) 10,605
DYKE, T., Marlborough, Wiltshire. 4 (Wiltshire) 11,746
DYKES, William, Blacktoft Grange, Yorkshire, East Riding. 1 (Staffordshire) 1,489
DYMOCK, Joseph Dymock. 5 (Berkshire) 7,275; 4 (Oxfordshire) 9,509; TOTAL 9 : 16,784
DYMOND, Robert, Exeter, Devon. 11 (Devon) 27,589
DYSON, Arthur, Tinsley, Yorkshire. 1 (Yorkshire, West Riding) 153

EAGLE, J. 1 (Leicestershire) 1,228
EARNSHAW, Leonard Brooks, Hessle, Yorkshire. 3 (Yorkshire, East Riding) 3,367
EASTCOTT, Richard, and Frise, Devonport, Devon. 1 (Devon) 2,770; 3 (Cornwall) 6,203; TOTAL 4 : 8,973
EASTCOTT and Pollgreen. 1 (Cornwall) 9,998
EASTON, George, Oakley, Wimborne, Dorset. 10 (Dorset) 17,842. *See also* John Baverstock Knight
EASTON, John, Bradford or Taunton, Somerset. 1 (Devon) 4,704; 2 (Somerset) 11,391; TOTAL 3 : 16,095
EATON, John, Long Buckenham, Norfolk. 6 (Norfolk) 18,656
EDWARDS, John. *See* William Morgan
EDWARDS, R. 1 (Carnarvonshire) 10,811
EDWARDS and Saunders. 6 (Cardiganshire) 24,622
EDWARDS, Saunders and B. Jones. 1 (Carmarthenshire) 9,012
EIVERS, J. and M. Fitzgerald, 12 Buckingham St, London. 1 (Buckinghamshire) 6,152; 1 (Surrey) 386; TOTAL 2 : 6,538
EIVERS, John, 12 Buckingham St, Adelphi, London. 1 (Middlesex) 219. *See also* Michael Fitzgerald
ELIOT, George Henry, 39 Great Marlborough St, London. 1 (Berkshire) 2,980
ELLIOTT, James. *See* Peter Gillard
ELLIOTT, John. 1 (Somerset) 5,699
ELLIOTT, John, Chichester, Sussex. 10 (Sussex) 26,061
ELLIOTT, Samuel. 8 (Kent) 23,997
ELLIS, Henry, Sampford Peverell, Devon. 1 (Devon) 2,580
ELLIS, H. T., Ipswich, Suffolk. 2 (Suffolk) 3,140
ELLIS, R. 2 (Carnarvonshire) 10,540
ELLIS, R. Lloyd, Carnarvon. 4 (Anglesey) 9,221; 4 (Carnarvonshire) 50,689; TOTAL 8 : 59,910
ELLISON, Henry, Stone, Staffordshire. 1 (Lincolnshire) 84; 1 (Yorkshire, West Riding) 6,514; TOTAL 2 : 6,598
ELLISON, William, Leeds, Yorkshire. 3 (Yorkshire, West Riding) 7,316
ELLISON, William and William R. Bromley. 1 (York City & Ainsty) 2,588
EMPRINGHAM, G. 1 (Lincolnshire) 2,249
ENGALL, George James, Cheltenham, Gloucestershire. 1 (Gloucestershire) 131
ETHEREDGE, Frederick William. 3 (Norfolk) 4,907
EVANS, Charles B. and Christopher Hannan, Helston, Cornwall. 1 (Cornwall) 1,510
EVANS, Charles B. *See also* Jno. King
EVANS, Charles, Ludlow, Shropshire. 1 (Shropshire) 6,200
EVANS, Herbert, Ludlow, Shropshire. 1 (Shropshire) 585
EYES, Edward junior, Liverpool, Lancashire. 3 (Lancashire) 4,212

FAIRBANK, Josiah, Sheffield, Yorkshire. 1 (Derbyshire) 868
FAXTON, J., Attleburgh, Norfolk. 1 (Norfolk) 2,164
FENDICK, William, Watton, Norfolk. 2 (Norfolk) 4,339
FENNA, Joseph. 1 (Cheshire) 801; 2 (Flintshire) 10,195; TOTAL 3 : 10,996
FENNA, Thomas, Cherry Hill, Malpas, Cheshire. 3 (Cheshire) 5,013; 1 (Flintshire) 1,151; 1 (Shropshire) 10,097; TOTAL 5 : 16,261
FENNING, Richard and Frederick Fenning. 6 (Suffolk) 7,193
FENWICK, Thomas, Morpeth, Northumberland. 4 (Northumberland) 3,721
FIDEL, Anthony, Faringdon, Berkshire. 2 (Berkshire) 2,500
FIDEL, James, Oxford. 1 (Oxfordshire) 438
FIELDER, Charles, Sparsholt, Hampshire. 5 (Hampshire) 11,249
FIGG, William, Lewes, Sussex. 36 (Sussex) 79,541
FINNET, Harry. *See* Thomas White Collard
FINNIS, Harry, Leybourne Castle, Maidstone, Kent. 3 (Kent) 7,259
FIRTH, Thomas Dyson, Macclesfield, Cheshire. *See* James Cawley
FISHER, Edward, Little Bowden, Northamptonshire. 1 (Northamptonshire) 53
FISHER, John. 1 (Suffolk) 1,075
FISHWICK, Henry H., Rochdale, Lancashire. 2 (Lancashire) 2,411
FITZGERALD, Michael, Buckingham Street, London. 1 (Buckinghamshire) 1,886; 2 (Cornwall) 2,360; 1 (Devon) 3,152; 2 (Middlesex) 2,475; 1 (Surrey) 3,149; TOTAL 6 : 9,873. *See also* Carlos and Fitzgerald and John Eivers

FLECK, Gabriel. 3 (Essex) 5,506; 2 (Hertfordshire) 1,792; TOTAL 5 : 7,298
FLOWERS, Edward. 2 (Essex) 2,127
FOOKS, William, Sherborne, Dorset. 1 (Dorset) 70
FORDHAM, Elias Pym, Dover, Kent. 1 (Kent) 1,881
FORSHAW, William, Manchester, Lancashire. 3 (Lancashire) 9,055
FORTESCUE, W. H., and Christopher Hannan. 1 (Cornwall) 1,719
FOSBROOKE, William, Hereford. 3 (Breconshire) 7,828; 1 (Gloucestershire) 1,591; 29 (Herefordshire) 65,134; 2 (Shropshire) 604; TOTAL 35 : 75,357
FOSBROOKE, William, Hereford, and William Havard Apperley, Hereford. 3 (Herefordshire) 14,466
FOSBROOKE, William, Hereford, and William Price. 1 (Herefordshire) 5,606
FOWLER, Robert, Birmingham, Warwickshire. 1 (Shropshire) 2,400
FOWLER, William and Son, Birmingham, Warwickshire. 1 (Shropshire) 679; 6 (Staffordshire) 26,145; 1 (Warwickshire) 13,878; TOTAL 8 : 40,702
FOWLER, Louth, Lincolnshire. *See* Maughan, Louth, Lincolnshire
FOWLIE, James. 1 (Hampshire) 10,494
FOX. *See* Cruse and Fox
FRANCIS, William, Great Marlow, Buckinghamshire. 1 (Buckinghamshire) 1,065
FREEBODY, William Y., 7 Furnivals Inn, London. 2 (Oxfordshire) 2,981
FREEMAN, Richard, Wisbech, Cambridgeshire. 3 (Cambridgeshire) 16,386; 2 (Norfolk) 10,374; TOTAL 5 : 26,760
FRENCH, John. 2 (Suffolk) 2,340
FRISE. *See* Richard Eastcott
FRISE, R. P. *See* Drew and Cox
FROST and Blackmore. 1 (Somerset) 404
FRY, Robert, Culmstock, Devon. 1 (Devon) 3,494
FULLER, Edward, Chichester, Sussex. 16 (Sussex) 30,460
FULLER, Francis, Croydon, Surrey. 1 (Kent) 4,646; 1 (Surrey) 2,082; TOTAL 2 : 6,728
FULLER, William Henry, Reading, Berkshire. 8 (Berkshire) 16,408

GABB, Robert, Abergavenny, Monmouthshire. 1 (Monmouthshire) 3,289
GACE, Joseph, Louth, Lincolnshire. 2 (Lincolnshire) 1,375
GALE, Richard C., Winchester, Hampshire. 5 (Dorset) 13,831; 23 (Hampshire) 124,556; 1 (Warwickshire) 1,408; 5 (Wiltshire) 10,826; TOTAL 34 : 150,621
GALLAND, Bland Hood, Yoxford, Suffolk. 1 (Oxfordshire) 1,149; 22 (Suffolk) 41,564; TOTAL 23 : 42,713. *See also* P. Cassidy
GALLAND, Bland Hood, Yoxford, Suffolk and D. Vaughan. 1 (Devon) 7,163
GALLIERS, Richard, Ledbury, Herefordshire. *See* William Sayce
GARLAND. *See* Humphrey and Garland
GARLICK, G. *See* L. Myers
GARLICK, George, Greenalgh, Lancashire. *See* William Gregson
GARNER, George, Wotton-under-Edge, Gloucestershire. 1 (Gloucestershire) 4,881
GARTH, Richard, Hawes, Yorkshire. 1 (Westmorland) 96. *See also* Anthony Clarkson
GASKELL, T. 1 (Lancashire) 280
GAYTHORP, William, Whitehaven, Cumberland. 5 (Cumberland) 11,347
GAZE, Marker, Chester. 2 (Cheshire) 3,230
GEE, Edward. 1 (Lincolnshire) 3,044
GEORGE, Richard B., Rochester, Kent. 4 (Kent) 15,536
GERMON, Jno. *See* George Murphy
GERRARD, Thomas, Kingsley, Cheshire. 2 (Cheshire) 3,017
GIBSON, John, Eggleston, Durham. 1 (Durham) 1,081
GIBSON, Thomas, Robertsbridge, Kent. 1 (Kent) 4,382
GIBSON, W. *See* J. and P. Payte
GILBERT, E. W. 1 (Sussex) 8,873
GILBERT, Joseph, Welford, Northamptonshire. 1 (Leicestershire) 1,408; 4 (Northamptonshire) 4,160; 5 (Warwickshire) 6,060; TOTAL 10 : 11,628
GILBERT, George and Thomas Tayspill, Colchester, Essex. 1 (Buckinghamshire) 1,656; 36 (Essex) 64,028; 3 (Suffolk) 7,946; TOTAL 40 : 73,630
GILBERT, William Henry, Sibertswold, Kent. 1 (Kent) 1,600
GILES. *See* Henry Lakin
GILL, J. *See* J. and P. Payte
GILLARD, Peter, Stokenham and James Elliott, Littlehempstone, Devon. 1 (Devon) 5,928
GINDERS, Jeremiah junior, Ingestre, Staffordshire. 1 (Staffordshire) 2,007
GISBORNE, Edward Sacheverell, Hay, Breconshire. 1 (Gloucestershire) 4,376; 6 (Herefordshire) 15,825; 4 (Monmouthshire) 21,995; TOTAL 11 : 42,196
GISBORNE, Edward Sacheverell, Nottingham. 2 (Nottinghamshire) 1,298
GLASBROOK, William, Penyfedu, Moriston, Glamorganshire. 2 (Glamorganshire) 1,410
GLENISTER, John Rolfe, Tring, Hertfordshire. 1 (Bedfordshire) 4,172; 4 (Buckinghamshire) 3,653; 2 (Hertfordshire) 5,543; TOTAL 7 : 13,368
GLENISTER, William, Norwich, Norfolk. 6 (Norfolk) 10,206
GODMAN, John, St Stephens, St Albans, Hertfordshire. 7 (Hertfordshire) 36,770
GOODACRE. *See* Walker and Goodacre, Leicester
GOODE, George, Carmarthen. 1 (Carmarthenshire) 4,824
GOODE, Harry and Henry Philpott, Haverfordwest, Pembrokeshire. 9 (Carmarthenshire) 33,213; 34 (Glamorganshire) 68,456; 93 (Pembrokeshire) 241,398; TOTAL 136 : 343,067
GOODE, William, Llangadock, Carmarthenshire. 5 (Carmarthenshire) 31,862
GOULD, A. B., (Lieut., Madras Artillery). 1 (Devon) 2,819
GOULD, George junior, Okehampton, Devon. 2 (Devon) 8,949
GOULD, Richard Davie. 1 (Devon) 1,103. *See also* Henry Crispin junior
GOULD, William, Okehampton, Devon. 4 (Devon) 17,829
GOULD, William, and Taperell, Okehampton, Devon. 2 (Devon) 9,383
GOUTHWAITE, Richard, Leeds, Yorkshire. 4 (Yorkshire, West Riding) 4,794
GOWER, Stephen Stock, Ipswich, Suffolk. 1 (Suffolk) 228
GRAHAM, G. H., Woolwich, Kent. 1 (Kent) 1,174
GRAHAM, Robert, Harelaw Slack, Cannobie, Dumfriesshire. 1 (Cumberland) 218
GRAHAM, William and George Graham. 2 (Devon) 9,452
GRAINGER, Hugh. *See* George W. Chaloner

GRANT, John, Ugborough, Devon. 13 (Devon) 36,562. *See also* Henry Andrews
GRANTHAM, Edward, Croydon, Surrey. 1 (Surrey) 4,718
GRATTON, Joseph, Timberfield, Chesterfield, Derbyshire. 11 (Derbyshire) 17,183
GREATOREX, Edward. 1 (Derbyshire) 993
GREAVES, Thomas, Hale, Altrincham, Cheshire. 8 (Cheshire) 12,938
GREEN, E. B. and Richard Tress. 1 (Sussex) 1,256
GREEN, James junior, Manchester, Lancashire. 1 (Lancashire) 5,056
GREENING. *See* Groom and Greening
GREENWELL, John, Darlington, Durham. 1 (Northumberland) 2,255
GREENWOOD, George. 1 (Lancashire) 2,940
GREENWOOD, John, Gisburn, Yorkshire. 15 (Yorkshire, West Riding) 54,761
GREGORY, John, Adderley, Shropshire. 3 (Cheshire) 4,375
GREGORY, Joseph, Worthernbury, Flintshire. 1 (Cheshire) 2,871; 1 (Flintshire) 3,279; TOTAL 2 : 6,150
GREGSON, William, Kirkham, Preston, Lancashire. 1 (Cheshire) 1,073
GREGSON, William, Kirkham, Lancashire, and George Garlick, Greenalgh, Lancashire. 5 (Lancashire) 7,009
GRIFFIN, John, Hemel Hempstead, Hertfordshire. 1 (Bedfordshire) 258; 5 (Hertfordshire) 11,059; TOTAL 6 : 11,317. *See also* John Rolfe Glenister
GRIFFITHS, Evan John, Llandilo Fawr, Carmarthenshire. 14 (Breconshire) 43,773; 5 (Carmarthenshire) 35,759; 2 (Radnorshire) 4,266; TOTAL 21 : 83,798
GRIFFITHS, E. W. 2 (Northumberland) 6,738
GRIFFITHS, Lewis J., Ynisygerwn, Glamorganshire. 3 (Glamorganshire) 11,711
GRIMWADE, W. S., Wetheringsett, Suffolk. 10 (Suffolk) 14,030
GRIST, George, Canterbury, Kent. 3 (Kent) 3,827
GRIST, J. 1 (Kent) 3,319
GROOM and Greening, Woodgate, Shropshire. 1 (Flintshire) 2,248; 2 (Montgomeryshire) 10,271; TOTAL 3 : 12,519
GROOM, Samuel, Wem, Shropshire. 6 (Shropshire) 20,327
GROUNDS, Henry, Cambridge. 1 (Cambridgeshire) 2,376
GROVE, B., Birmingham, Warwickshire. 2 (Derbyshire) 3,623
GUMMOE, John J. *See* John Wallis Barnicoat *and* Richard Carveth

HALE, Henry, Woking, Surrey. 1 (Hampshire) 567
HALE, Robert. 1 (Essex) 4,387
HALE, Robert and Charles Mumford. 1 (Suffolk) 1,571
HALES, Ralph, Cobridge, Staffordshire. 1 (Staffordshire) 1,879
HALL, Joseph, Huddersfield, Yorkshire. 5 (Yorkshire, West Riding) 10,714
HALL, Richard, Cirencester, Gloucestershire. 1 (Berkshire) 1,123; 32 (Gloucestershire) 45,535; 1 (Monmouthshire) 789; 3 (Wiltshire) 9,768; TOTAL 37 : 57,215
HALLIDAY, Andrew, Preston, Lancashire. 15 (Lancashire) 29,371; 2 (Yorkshire, West Riding) 14,175; TOTAL 17 : 43,546
HAM, Ralph, Taunton, Somerset. 7 (Somerset) 11,396
HAMMONDS, George, Adney, Newport, Shropshire. 4 (Shropshire) 8,138
HAMMONDS, R. 1 (Shropshire) 3,465; 1 (Staffordshire) 4,204; TOTAL 2 : 7,669
HAND, Llandenny, Raglan, Monmouthshire. 1 (Monmouthshire) 1,484
HAND, Thomas. 2 (Cardiganshire) 5,334; 5 (Carmarthenshire) 43,168; TOTAL 7 : 48,502
HAND, William. 1 (Carmarthenshire) 14,707
HANDFORD, Nathaniel, Chelsea, Middlesex. 1 (Middlesex) 387
HANNAN, Christopher. *See* Charles B. Evans *and* W. H. Fortescue
HANNING, Joshua, Rosliston, Derbyshire. 1 (Derbyshire) 1,808
HANSON, Joseph, Caldecote, Leicestershire. 1 (Leicestershire) 2,952
HARDING, George, Maer, Newcastle-under-Lyme, Staffordshire. 1 (Cheshire) 1,048; 1 (Warwickshire) 151; TOTAL 2 : 1,199
HARDING, James, Farnham, Surrey. 1 (Hampshire) 740; 3 (Surrey) 18,455; TOTAL 4 : 19,915
HARDING, Samuel, Alpraham, Cheshire. 18 (Cheshire) 24,883
HARDING, Samuel, Willoughbridge Wells, Ashley, Staffordshire. 1 (Staffordshire) 4,717
HARDING, William. 1 (Surrey) 10,292
HARDING, William Bishop, Frome, Somerset. 1 (Sussex) 1,749
HARDWICK, George, Little Gonerby, Lincolnshire. 2 (Lincolnshire) 3,280
HARDWICK, John. 2 (Lincolnshire) 453
HARDY, John, Oxford. 2 (Berkshire) 4,848
HARDY, William, Lincoln. 5 (Lincolnshire) 3,895
HARFORD or HARTFORD, James, Bristol, Gloucestershire. 3 (Norfolk) 4,960
HARKNESS, George, Barnstaple, Devon. 1 (Devon) 6,582
HARKNESS, James McNair and Henry O'Hagan. 2 (Devon) 2,930
HARPER, William. 1 (Lancashire) 2,094
HARRIS, E. 2 (Somerset) 11,247
HARRIS, Francis, Leominster, Herefordshire. 4 (Herefordshire) 8,286
HARRIS, John, Thatcham, Berkshire. 4 (Berkshire) 5,841
HARRIS, J. C. 1 (Essex) 1,077
HARRIS, M. R., Salisbury, Wiltshire. 1 (Wiltshire) 1,506
HARRIS, Samuel John, Leicester. 3 (Leicestershire) 1,069
HARRIS, T. C., Great Bromley, Essex. 1 (Essex) 1,747
HARRIS. *See* Bowron and Harris
HARRISON, William. 1 (Northumberland) 1,131
HARVEY, John, Haverfordwest, Pembrokeshire. 2 (Carmarthenshire) 5,519; 3 (Pembrokeshire) 8,545; TOTAL 5 : 14,064. *See also* Morris Sayce
HARWOOD, Richard, Cambridge. 5 (Cambridgeshire) 5,744
HASELL, James, Sudbury, Suffolk. 7 (Essex) 9,779; 10 (Suffolk) 17,666; TOTAL 17 : 27,445
HASLAM, John R., Menai Bridge, Anglesey. 62 (Anglesey) 136,590; 3 (Carnarvonshire) 5,321; TOTAL 65 : 141,911
HASLETT, J. J. and Michael O'Rourke. 2 (Herefordshire) 6,947
HATCHARD, Thomas, Godmanchester, Huntingdonshire. 1 (Huntingdonshire) 3,719
HAWKES, Francis and Sons, Reading, Berkshire. 7 (Berkshire) 18,675; 1 (Wiltshire) 2,198; TOTAL 8 : 20,873
HAWKES, J. D., Holt, Norfolk. 2 (Norfolk) 4,714

HAWKES, Thomas, Williton, Somerset. 3 (Somerset) 16,705. *See also* Daniel Horwood
HAY, James, Kirkby Stephen, Westmorland, or Musselburgh, Scotland 8 (Westmorland) 18,008
HAYWARD, John, Thorndon, Suffolk. 5 (Suffolk) 8,577
HAYWARD, Richard and Son or Messrs Hayward, Northampton. 2 (Huntingdonshire) 2,545; 4 (Leicestershire) 3,596; 15 (Northamptonshire) 18,524; 2 (Rutland) 904; 1 (Yorkshire, West Riding) 211; TOTAL 24 : 25,780
HEADLAM, Morley. 1 (Yorkshire, North Riding) 2,906
HEARD, Robert, Dulverton, Somerset. 4 (Devon) 10,724
HEARD, William Thomas, St Margarets, Ware / Hitchin, Hertfordshire. 2 (Bedfordshire) 6,281; 2 (Berkshire) 5,848; 1 (Hampshire) 3,300; 1 (Huntingdonshire) 2,349; 4 (Hertfordshire) 3,949; 1 (Northamptonshire) 449; 2 (Oxfordshire) 514; TOTAL 13 : 22,690
HEARLE, R. F., Sherborne, Dorset. 1 (Dorset) 1,004
HEARN, Henry, Exeter, Devon. *See* George Braund
HEATHFIELD, Thomas, Stoodleigh, Devon. 1 (Devon) 761
HEATHMAN, A., Duloe, Cornwall, J. Rutger, Marazion, Cornwall, and R. Henwood, Penzance, Cornwall. 1 (Cornwall) 5,845
HEATON, Charles, Endon, Leek, Staffordshire. 2 (Cheshire) 3,636; 1 (Staffordshire) 1,921; TOTAL 3 : 5,557
HEATON, Edwin, Leek, Staffordshire. 1 (Derbyshire) 643; 1 (Staffordshire) 1,280; TOTAL 2 : 1,923
HEATON, Thomas, Endon, Leek, Staffordshire. 1 (Staffordshire) 1,959
HELLING, James, Lea Wellington, Somerset. 1 (Devon) 3,024
HELLYER, Thomas, Ryde, Isle of Wight. 2 (Hampshire) 17,925
HENDERSON, Peter, (civil engineer). 1 (Glamorganshire) 16,669
HENDY, S. *See* F. Carter
HENWOOD, R., Penzance, Cornwall. 2 (Cornwall) 14,356. *See also* A. Heathman
HERBERT, Richard Chambers, Worcester. 2 (Gloucestershire) 1,846; 2 (Herefordshire) 4,120; 1 (Shropshire) 2,082; 25 (Worcestershire) 46,314; TOTAL 30 : 54,362; *See also* Richard Court and N. Izod
HERBERT, Richard Chambers, Worcester and Henry Lakin junior, Worcester. 1 (Worcestershire) 1,163
HERBERT, William, Worcester. 1 (Herefordshire) 3,550
HERBERT and Smith, Worcester. 1 (Worcestershire) 206
HERMAN, Benjamin, Northam, Devon. 1 (Devon) 2,194
HERMAN, Benjamin and William Blake, Bideford, Devon. 1 (Devon) 5,798
HESSELGRAVE, Thomas, Dobcross, Yorkshire. 2 (Yorkshire, West Riding) 237
HETHERINGTON, George, Willowhill, Kirklinton, Cumberland and George Carruthers. 1 (Cumberland) 216
HETHERINGTON, William, Cockermouth, Cumberland and William Dickinson. 1 (Cumberland) 1,721
HEWETT, George, and E. Hewett, Elvetham, Hampshire. 2 (Hampshire) 15,580
HEWETT, George, Elvetham, Hampshire, and Oxford. 7 (Hampshire) 26,221; 1 (Wiltshire) 2,781; TOTAL 8 : 29,002
HEYDON, Christopher, Shirenewton, Monmouthshire. 2 (Monmouthshire) 817
HEYWARD, Richard. 2 (Derbyshire) 5,852
HICKS. *See* Davis, Saunders and Hicks
HICKSON, John, Worksop, Nottinghamshire. 4 (Nottinghamshire) 9,225
HIDE and Patching, Messrs, Worthing, Sussex. 6 (Sussex) 12,836
HIGGIN, J. V. 1 (Lancashire) 773
HIGGS, William, Burghley, Northamptonshire. 1 (Rutland) 1,682
HILDER, William, Tonbridge, Kent. 1 (Buckinghamshire) 930
HILL. *See* George Cuming
HILL, Samuel and Son, Croft, Lincolnshire. 25 (Lincolnshire) 39,027
HILL, Simon, St Martins, Looe, Cornwall. 1 (Cornwall) 3,069
HILL, Thomas, Ashton-under-Lyne, Cheshire. 4 (Cheshire) 4,743
HILL, William, Cleobury Mortimer, Shropshire. 1 (Shropshire) 1,527
HILLS, John, Billericay, Essex. 8 (Essex) 15,310
HINE. *See* Tunstall and Hine
HITCHEN, Thomas. 1 (Cheshire) 661
HITCHINS, Messrs H. and F., Brighton, Sussex. 1 (Buckinghamshire) 6,616; 9 (Sussex) 19,845; TOTAL 10 : 26,461
HOCKING, E. and J., Tregony, Cornwall. 1 (Cornwall) 3,108
HODGE, Robert. 3 (Cornwall) 19,829
HODGES, Richard, North Petherton, Somerset. 2 (Somerset) 7,860
HODGSON, C. 1 (Cumberland) 90
HODGSON, William. 2 (Cumberland) 4,605
HODGSON, William, East Ayton, Yorkshire. 1 (Yorkshire, East Riding) 123; 3 (Yorkshire, North Riding) 3,491; TOTAL 4 : 3,614
HODGSON and Watson. 1 (Westmorland) 1,176; 2 (Lancashire) 5,222; TOTAL 3 : 6,398. *See also* John Watson junior
HODSELL, William, South Ash, Kent. 5 (Kent) 11,382
HOGGARTH. *See* John Watson junior
HOLBECHE, John, 25 Waterloo St, Birmingham, Warwickshire. 1 (Warwickshire) 1,971; 1 (Staffordshire) 573; TOTAL 2 : 2,544
HOLBROOK, James Bocock, Hendon, Middlesex, and Richard Dent, Camden Town, Middlesex. 1 (Middlesex) 7,832
HOLDEN, Richard, Burnley, Lancashire. 1 (Lancashire) 4,007
HOLLIDAY, Thomas, York. 1 (York City & Ainsty) 513; 2 (Yorkshire, East Riding) 3,103; 8 (Yorkshire, North Riding) 11,265; 1 (Yorkshire, West Riding) 1,014; TOTAL 12 : 15,895. *See also* Francis Carr
HOLLINGSWORTH, D., Hertford. 1 (Hertfordshire) 2,067
HOLLOWAY, Harry, Ringwood, Hampshire. 4 (Dorset) 10,930; 3 (Hampshire) 11,221; 2 (Wiltshire) 9,064; TOTAL 9 : 31,215. *See also* Charles Sharp
HOLLOWAY, Harry, Ringwood, Hampshire and F. P. Webb. 1 (Hampshire) 2,545
HOLTUM, William, Walmer, Kent. 3 (Kent) 3,147
HOLYOAK, Richard, Sharnford, Leicestershire. 1 (Leicestershire) 6
HOPKINS, G. H., Belpher, Derbyshire. 1 (Derbyshire) 1,330
HOPKINSON, William, Keighley, Yorkshire. 1 (Yorkshire, West Riding) 10,356
HORNBY, Thomas, Wombleton, Yorkshire. 1 (Yorkshire, North Riding) 1,039
HORNCASTLE, John, The Yews, Maltby, Yorkshire. 1 (Nottinghamshire) 4,110
HORNIDGE, Thomas, 10 Mitre Court Chambers, Temple, London. 1 (Norfolk) 2,163
HORNSEY, Thomas, Stillingfleet Lodge, Brompton, Yorkshire, and Kendall. 1 (Yorkshire, North Riding) 416
HORSLEY, John, Saxby, Lincolnshire. 1 (Yorkshire, West Riding) 1,875
HORSMAN, Robert, Wetherby, Yorkshire. 5 (Yorkshire, West Riding) 5,038

HORWOOD, Daniel, Bristol, Gloucestershire. 2 (Gloucestershire) 4,386; 4 (Somerset) 9,729; TOTAL 6 : 14,115
HORWOOD, Daniel, Bristol, Gloucestershire and Thomas Hawkes, Williton, Somerset. 1 (Somerset) 3,762
HOSKING or HOSKEN, G. *See* Richard Pentreath
HOSMER, John, Camden Town, London. 1 (Gloucestershire) 6,724; 2 (Surrey) 9,734; TOTAL 3 : 16,458
HOTSON, Richard, Long Stratton, Norfolk. 2 (Norfolk) 2,562
HOUGHTON, Dugdale, Birmingham, Warwickshire. 1 (Shropshire) 1,706
HOUGHTON, Edward, Wells, Norfolk. 3 (Norfolk) 6,488
HOUGHTON, Henry, Baginton, Warwickshire. 1 (Warwickshire) 1,667
HOWARD, Henry, Winchester, Hampshire. 2 (Buckinghamshire) 2,394; 3 (Hampshire) 4,770; TOTAL 5 : 7,164
HOWELL, William Jones, Aberporth, Cardiganshire. 2 (Cardiganshire) 6,816
HOWGATE, John, Knaresborough, Yorkshire. 1 (Yorkshire, East Riding) 1,107; 3 (Yorkshire, North Riding) 3,732; 8 (Yorkshire, West Riding) 9,087; TOTAL 12 : 13,926
HOWSON, T., Blackburn, Lancashire. 1 (Lancashire) 842
HUBBARD, William, Dartford, Kent. 3 (Kent) 5,413
HUDDLESTON, John, Newborough, Northumberland. 4 (Cumberland) 5,687; 1 (Lancashire) 4,694; TOTAL 5 : 10,381. *See also* Thomas Woodmass, Alston, Cumberland
HUDDLESTON, John, Plymstock, Devon. 1 (Devon) 2,903
HUDDLESTON, Messrs, and White, Plymtree, Devon. 1 (Devon) 1,784
HUDSON, George, Woolwich, Kent. 1 (Kent) 1,116
HUDSON, William, Epworth, Lincolnshire. 8 (Lincolnshire) 11,998
HUGHES. *See* Davies and Hughes
HUGHES, Henry P. 1 (Denbighshire) 1,687
HUGHES, Sam, and Robert Cotgreave. 1 (Cheshire) 4,136
HUGHES, Thomas. 8 (Sussex) 43,087
HULL, Henry, Bramley, Surrey. 5 (Surrey) 18,682; 3 (Sussex) 3,866; TOTAL 8 : 22,548
HULL, Thomas. 3 (Lancashire) 6,944
HULL, William. 1 (Surrey) 1,483
HUMBERT, Charles F., Watford, Hertfordshire. 1 (Sussex) 2,426; 1 (Somerset) 2,092; TOTAL 2 : 4,518
HUMPHREY and Garland. 1 (Devon) 3,953
HUMPHRIES, John, Ripon, Yorkshire. 1 (Durham) 3,008; 1 (Lincolnshire) 3,211; 2 (York City & Ainsty) 2,459; 6 (Yorkshire, North Riding) 11,203; 6 (Yorkshire, West Riding) 4,664; TOTAL 16 : 24,545
HUNTER. *See* Miller and Hunter
HUNTLY, William, Dover, Kent. 9 (Kent) 13,805
HURST, George, Canterbury, Kent. 1 (Kent) 1,185
HUSSEY, William, High Wycombe, Buckinghamshire. 2 (Gloucestershire) 1,488
HUSSEY, William and Son, High Wycombe, Buckinghamshire. 6 (Buckinghamshire) 30,504
HUSTHWAITE, John. 1 (Yorkshire, North Riding) 556
HUTCHINSON, John Houseman, Grantham, Lincolnshire. 3 (Lincolnshire) 5,202; 1 (Nottinghamshire) 616; 1 (Yorkshire, North Riding) 11; TOTAL 5 : 5,829
HYDE, Charles and Son, Horsley, Stroud, Gloucestershire. 2 (Gloucestershire) 3,902
HYDE, Henry, Wareham, Dorset, (land surveyor, architect, etc.). 6 (Dorset) 16,566; 3 (Hampshire) 9,911; TOTAL 9 : 26,477

ILETT, Charles. 1 (Somerset) 1,121
ILETT, P. B., Taunton, Somerset. 1 (Somerset) 866
INGLE, Thomas, Bradford, Yorkshire. 2 (Yorkshire, West Riding) 3,158
INGLE, Thomas, Bradford, Yorkshire, and Joseph Smith. 3 (Yorkshire, West Riding) 3,158
IRISH, Thomas B. and A. S. Parker, Winkleigh, Devon. 9 (Devon) 43,101
IVESON, Richard, Hedon, Yorkshire. 1 (Lincolnshire) 1,527; 10 (Yorkshire, East Riding) 18,843; TOTAL 11 : 20,370
IVESON, Robert, Hedon, Yorkshire. 3 (Yorkshire, East Riding) 2,494
IZOD, N. and Richard Chambers Herbert, Worcester. 1 (Worcestershire) 841
IZOD, N. *See also* Henry Lakin

JACK, A. 1 (Middlesex) 1,293
JACK, W. J., Leeds, Yorkshire. 1 (Yorkshire, West Riding) 1,648
JACKMAN, Robert, Gloucestershire. 1 (Gloucestershire) 2,532
JACKMAN, Robert, Gloucestershire and Simon Strode. 1 (Gloucestershire) 8,026 *See also* Thomas Wakeman
JACKSON, E. 1 (Warwickshire) 12
JACKSON, E. 1 (Yorkshire, East Riding) 9
JACKSON, John, Martindale, Westmorland. *See* Matthew Wilkinson
JACKSON, John George, Newbold Lodge, Leamington Priors, Warwickshire. 1 (Warwickshire) 643
JACKSON, Joseph, March, Cambridgeshire. 8 (Cambridgeshire) 58,084; 1 Huntingdonshire. 2,868; 1 (Lincolnshire) 4,646; TOTAL 10 : 65,598
JAGO, Richard Howlett, 74 Great Queen St, Lincolns Inn Fields, London. 1 (Essex) 721
JAMES, Richard, Chideock, Dorset. 7 (Dorset) 14,262
JANE, William, Chepstow, Monmouthshire. 1 (Monmouthshire) 479
JARVIS. *See* Rushworth and Jarvis
JARVIS, William, Kingsbridge, Devon. 6 (Devon) 19,206
JAY, G. R. and W. Ruffell. 5 (Essex) 19,365
JENKINS, I. 1 (Flintshire) 7,856
JENKINS, Thomas. 3 (Denbighshire) 7,001
JENNINGS, Daniel, Carlisle. *See* P. Kendall
JERVIS, Robert, Manchester, Lancashire. 2 (Lancashire) 3,476
JOHNSON. *See* Henry Kennedy
JOHNSON, Messrs E. and T., Llanrhos, Carnarvonshire. 3 (Carnarvonshire) 6,271
JOHNSON, G. F. 1 (Warwickshire) 232
JOHNSON, James William, Stretton on Dunsmore, Warwickshire. 1 (Warwickshire) 539
JOHNSTONE, John, Sandbach, Cheshire. 1 (Cheshire) 2,584
JOLL, William, Plymouth, Devon and George Murphy. 1 (Devon) 6,938

JONES, Benjamin, Gwarallt, Llanllwny, Carmarthenshire. 2 (Carmarthenshire) 7,155. *See also* Edwards, Saunders and B. Jones
JONES, David, Llanfyllin, Montgomeryshire. 5 (Montgomeryshire) 20,864
JONES, Edward, Charlotte St, London. 1 (Surrey) 2,340
JONES, Edward, Tynberth, Corwen, Denbighshire. 2 (Merionethshire) 15,262
JONES, Hugh Lloyd. 1 (Denbighshire) 202
JONES, John, Pembroke. 10 (Pembrokeshire) 19,183
JONES, Joseph, Oswestry, Shropshire. 2 (Shropshire) 3,233
JONES, Robert, Ledbury, Herefordshire. 1 (Gloucestershire) 885; 5 (Herefordshire) 11,200; 1 (Worcestershire) 1,268; TOTAL 7 : 13,353
JONES, W. G., Loddon, Norfolk. 7 (Norfolk) 11,043; 3 (Suffolk) 2,915; TOTAL 10 : 13,958
JONES, W. G., Loddon, Norfolk and T. Burton junior, Langley, Norfolk. 1 (Norfolk) 2,238
JONES, William, Bellevue, Brecon. 17 (Breconshire) 107,701; 1 (Cardiganshire) 3,181; 12 (Glamorganshire) 70,460; 6 (Monmouthshire) 33,190; TOTAL 36 : 214,532
JONES, William, Pontesbury / Broseley, Shropshire. 3 (Shropshire) 1,716
JONES, William, Llangeitho, Lampeter, Cardiganshire. 1 (Breconshire) 5,423
JONES, William, Cradley, Herefordshire. 1 (Herefordshire) 5,967
JONES, Cynwyd, Merionethshire. 1 (Merionethshire) 4,079
JULIAN, George H., Exeter, Devon. 1 (Devon) 1

KEATLEY. *See* Moore and Son
KEEN, I., Dulverton, Somerset. 1 (Somerset) 4,046
KEEN, William, 8 Cannon Row, Westminster, Middlesex. 1 (Oxfordshire) 1,600
KEEN, William and Son, 2 Parliament St, Westminster, Middlesex. 2 (Bedfordshire) 2,508; 3 (Buckinghamshire) 8,752; 1 (Surrey) 1,070; TOTAL 6 : 12,330
KEEN. *See also* Washbourne and Keen
KELL, Thomas, Bramham, Yorkshire. 2 (Yorkshire, West Riding) 220
KELLETT, Robert, Wigan, Lancashire. 5 (Lancashire) 13,348
KELSEY, Francis J., Salisbury, Wiltshire. 2 (Berkshire) 3,711; 1 (Oxfordshire) 1,621; 1 (Somerset) 778; 14 (Wiltshire) 44,988; TOTAL 18 : 51,098
KEMP, W. 1 (Dorset) 475
KENDALL. *See* Thomas Hornsey
KENDALL, P., Whitehaven, Richard Asquith, Carlisle, and Daniel Jennings, Carlisle, Cumberland. 1 (Cumberland) 6,226
KENDALL, William, Kineton, Warwickshire. 1 (Staffordshire) 1,276; 3 (Warwickshire) 4,307; TOTAL 4 : 5,583
KENNEDY, Henry, 100 Chancery Lane, London and Bangor, Carnarvonshire. 3 (Carnarvonshire) 25,653; 3 (Lincolnshire) 7,706; TOTAL 6 : 34,259
KENNEDY, Henry, 100 Chancery Lane, London and Bangor, Carnarvonshire, and Johnson. 5 (Carnarvonshire) 29,887
KENNETT, Thomas, Wye, Kent. 1 (Kent) 663
KETTLE, John, Chipping Campden, Gloucestershire. 2 (Gloucestershire) 327
KIDGER, Joseph, Ashby-de-la-Zouch, Leicestershire. 1 (Leicestershire) 335
KING, Alexander, Nether Stowey, Somerset. 3 (Somerset) 3,593
KING, George, Southam, Warwickshire. 2 (Warwickshire) 776
KING, James, Oxford. 1 (Montgomeryshire) 10,701
KING, Jno., and C. B. Evans. 1 (Cornwall) 7,909
KING, John and Son, Saffron Walden, Essex. 7 (Cambridgeshire) 15,150; 18 (Essex) 40,015; 1 (Huntingdonshire) 3,365; 6 (Suffolk) 13,332; TOTAL 32 : 71,862
KING, John, Winslow, Buckinghamshire. 7 (Buckinghamshire) 7,236
KING, Joseph. *See* J. Parlour
KING and Knockolds, Saffron Walden and Stansted, Essex. 1 (Warwickshire) 1,947
KIRK, Edward. 1 (Derbyshire) 421
KITTOW, Jonathan, North Petherwin, Devon. 7 (Cornwall) 19,589; 6 (Devon) 22,705; TOTAL 13 : 42,294
KNAPP, John, Bradford, Wiltshire. 1 (Somerset) 68
KNIGHT, Humphrey Evans, Puddlehinton, Dorset. 3 (Dorset) 5,261
KNIGHT, James Alexander. 1 (Devon) 797
KNIGHT, John Baverstock, Puddlehinton, Dorset. 17 (Dorset) 38,865
KNIGHT, John Baverstock, Puddlehinton, Dorset, and George Easton. 1 (Dorset) 1,742
KNIGHT, John Baverstock, Puddlehinton, Dorset, and Levi Luckam. 1 (Dorset) 3,818
KNIGHT, John Baverstock, Puddlehinton, Dorset, and John Martin. 1 (Dorset) 2,091
KNIGHT, William, Petworth, Sussex. 2 (Sussex) 2,035
KNIGHTINGALE, James, Kingston, Surrey. 1 (Buckinghamshire) 7,735
KNIGHTINGALE, James, Kingston, Surrey, and James Stratford, Amersham, Buckinghamshire. 1 (Buckinghamshire) 4,718
KNOCKOLDS. *See* King

LACEY, John, Oakham, Rutland. 1 (Rutland) 448
LADYMAN, George. 1 (Westmorland) 4,651
LAING, Charles, 14 Charlotte St, Manchester, Lancashire. 1 (Cheshire) 1,582
LAKIN, Henry, Worcester. 2 (Herefordshire) 5,380
LAKIN, Henry junior, Worcester. 2 (Gloucestershire) 3,523. *See also* Richard C. Herbert
LAKIN, Henry, and Edward Swinburne, Worcester. 1 (Warwickshire) 162
LAMB, George, Derby. 1 (Cheshire) 3,073; 13 (Derbyshire) 17,889; 1 (Leicestershire) 1,510; TOTAL 15 : 22,472
LANCASTER, George Brown, Thirsk, Yorkshire. 1 (Leicestershire) 1,619; 3 (Yorkshire, North Riding) 3,561; TOTAL 4 : 5,180. *See also* Thomas Dixon
LANCASTER, T., Lifton, Devon. 1 (Devon) 5,982
LANCASTER, William, Marderby Grange, Thirsk, Yorkshire. 1 (Yorkshire, North Riding) 2,528. *See also* Henry Scott
LANE, John, Stony Stanton, Hinckley, Leicestershire. 2 (Leicestershire) 3,817
LANGTON, Stephen St Peter, Teeton, Northampton. 1 (Northamptonshire) 81
LANGWITH, Joseph Silvester, Grantham, Lincolnshire. 7 (Lincolnshire) 7,812
LARKER, George, Carlisle, Cumberland. 5 (Cumberland) 9,646; 4 (Westmorland) 8,365; TOTAL 9 : 18,011
LAUGHTON, Thomas, Brigg, Lincolnshire. 2 (Lincolnshire) 541; 1 (Yorkshire, East Riding) 1,668; TOTAL 3 : 2,209
LAURANCE, John, Leicester. 3 (Lancashire) 5,465; 1 (Leicestershire) 811; TOTAL 4 : 6,276
LAVENDER, Thomas, Watford, Hertfordshire. 3 (Hertfordshire) 15,533
LAVERICK, John, Durham. 7 (Durham) 12,433
LAWRENCE, William, South Kelsey, Lincolnshire. 1 (Lincolnshire) 329

LAWSON, John. 1 (Lancashire) 2,309
LAWTON. *See* Taylor and Lawton
LAX, William, Darlington, Durham. 4 (Yorkshire, North Riding) 5,111. *See also* Otley and Lax
LAYCOCK, Frederick James, Lanchester, Durham, (teacher). 3 (Durham) 6,223
LEA, Nathaniel, 40 Bennetts Hill, Birmingham, Warwickshire. 1 (Lancashire) 2,277; 1 (Warwickshire) 1,302; TOTAL 2 : 3,579
LEACH, William, Brighton, Sussex. 10 (Sussex) 19,240
LEDGER, Reuben, Knotty Ash, West Derby, Lancashire. 2 (Lancashire) 1,203. *See also* Henry White
LEE, Charles, Golden Square, London. 3 (Surrey) 4,387
LEE, Charles, Golden Square, London and John Pickering. 1 (Surrey) 2,551
LEE, Charles Marsh, Salisbury, Wiltshire. 1 (Wiltshire) 837
LEE, David. 1 (Yorkshire, East Riding) 1,565
LEE, John, Bishop Auckland, Durham. 10 (Durham) 14,885; 1 (Yorkshire, North Riding) 4,483; TOTAL 11 : 19,368
LEE, Joseph, Redbrook, Flintshire. 1 (Cheshire) 1,219
LEECH, John, Leek, Warwickshire. 1 (Warwickshire) 29
LEHAIR, J., Leverington, Cambridgeshire. 2 (Cambridgeshire) 10,935
LENNY and Croft, Bury St Edmunds, Suffolk. 4 (Cambridgeshire) 47,478; 1 (Hertfordshire) 4,385; 15 (Norfolk) 59,807; 42 (Suffolk) 71,952; TOTAL 62 : 183,712
LENNY, Issac, Norwich, Norfolk. 7 (Norfolk) 9,796
LEWIS, Benjamin, Llanllwy, Carmarthenshire. 1 (Cardiganshire) 1,392
LEWIS, Charles, Havant, Hampshire. 6 (Hampshire) 15,638; 1 (Sussex) 619; TOTAL 7 : 16,251
LEWIS, I. T., Fareham, Hampshire. 1 (Hampshire) 7,389; 1 (Sussex) 3,495; TOTAL 2 : 10,884
LEWIS, James and B. Lewis, Cwmscawen, Radnorshire. 4 (Radnorshire) 13,495
LEWIS, John, Glasbury, Radnorshire. 3 (Breconshire) 13,003
LEWIS, John, (? Treleach, Carmarthenshire). 2 (Carmarthenshire) 5,697
LEWIS, John. *See* Walter Lloyd
LEWIS, John Theophilus and Walker, Southampton, Hampshire. 2 (Hampshire) 4,260
LEWIS, Jonathan and Son, Bobbingworth, Essex. 2 (Essex) 5,631
LEWIS, Jonathan and Son, Bobbingworth, Essex and Frederick F. Cattlin. 1 (Essex) 1,628
LITTLE, Richard Davis, Chippenham, Wiltshire. 2 (Somerset) 1,761
LITTLE and Weaver, Chippenham, Wiltshire, (engineers and surveyors). 2 (Berkshire) 3,892; 32 (Wiltshire) 61,660; TOTAL 34 : 65,552
LLEWELLYN, D. Morley, Carmarthen. 3 (Cardiganshire) 8,778
LLEWELLYN, G. H., Carmarthen. 1 (Carmarthenshire) 1,867
LLOYD, Edward. 1 (Cardiganshire) 1,621
LLOYD, Owen, Cardigan. 12 (Cardiganshire) 29,557; 7 (Pembrokeshire) 19,748; TOTAL 19 : 49,305
LLOYD, Walter, Pantowen, Mydrim, Carmarthenshire. 2 (Carmarthenshire) 9,525
LLOYD, Walter, Pantowen, Mydrim, Carmarthenshire, John Lewis and William Pugh. 1 (Carmarthenshire) 11,503
LLOYD, William, Wrexham, Denbighshire. 9 (Denbighshire) 7,938
LOCK, Thomas junior, Instow, Devon. 4 (Devon) 7,191
LOFTHOUSE, Joseph P., Hopton, Staffordshire. 1 (Cheshire) 2,853; 13 (Staffordshire) 25,006; TOTAL 14 : 27,859
LONG, George and George Taylor, Wolverhampton, Staffordshire. 1 (Gloucestershire) 13,420; 4 (Staffordshire) 4,889; TOTAL 5 : 18,309
LONGHURST, Thomas, Alrewas, Staffordshire. 1 (Derbyshire) 1,277; 1 (Warwickshire) 12; TOTAL 2 : 1,289
LOVAT. 1 (Lancashire) 1,973
LOVELL, Thomas, Huntingdon. 4 (Huntingdonshire) 540
LOWER, Richard, Chiddingly, Sussex. 5 (Sussex) 18,288
LUCAS, George Oakley, Devizes, Wiltshire. 1 (Hampshire) 8,723; 1 (Middlesex) 473; 6 (Wiltshire) 17,202; TOTAL 8 : 26,398. *See also* John Roger Bramble
LUCKHAM, Levi. *See* John Baverstock Knight
LUCKRAFT, M. Warren, W. Reaney and W.T. Warren, Crediton, Devon. 21 (Devon) 81,921
LUCKRAFT, J. P. and Co. 5 (Norfolk) 5,704
LUSBY, John. 1 (Lincolnshire) 477
LUSCOMBE, R., Torquay, Devon. 1 (Devon) 2,939

M'GRANE, T. 1 (Monmouthshire) 828; 2 (Norfolk) 3,681; TOTAL 3 : 4,509
M'GRANE, T. and L. Carey. 1 (Radnorshire) 2,689. *See also* L. Carey
MACHELL, John, Carlisle, Cumberland. 1 (Cumberland) 3,021; 7 (Durham) 36,077; 1 (Yorkshire, North Riding) 8,228; TOTAL 9 : 47,326
MACHELL, John, and Withers, Carlisle, Cumberland. 1 (Yorkshire, West Riding) 18,421
MADDOCK, Thomas, Southport, Lancashire. *See* Henry White
MAGER, Francis W., Louth, Lincolnshire. 1 (Lincolnshire) 2,167
MAITLAND. *See* Dixon and Maitland
MALLAM, Thomas Boyn, Woodfield Lodge, Paddington, Middlesex. 4 (Hertfordshire) 8,270
MALLETT, John, Meeth, Devon. 1 (Devon) 607
MANN and Son, Norwich, Norfolk. 2 (Norfolk) 3,375
MANNING, Joseph, Norwich, Norfolk, (surveyor and lithographer). 17 (Norfolk) 29,555; 11 (Suffolk) 19,777; TOTAL 28 : 49,332
MANNING, Joseph, Norwich, Norfolk, (surveyor and lithographer) and John T. Brown. 4 (Norfolk) 5,465
MANSFORD, Henry, Frome, Somerset. 1 (Somerset) 715
MARLEY, Thomas, Shildon, Durham. 1 (Durham) 928
MARMONT, James, Bristol, Gloucestershire. 4 (Gloucestershire) 6,025; 8 (Somerset) 17,823; 1 (Wiltshire) 814; TOTAL 13 : 24,662. *See also* Cotterells and Cooper
MARRACK, William. *See* Richard Pentreath
MARRIOTT, J., Dewsbury, Yorkshire. 3 (Yorkshire, West Riding) 449
MARTIN, John, Evershot, Dorset. 27 (Dorset) 55,018; 1 (Somerset) 6,925; TOTAL 28 : 61,943. *See also* John Baverstock Knight
MARTIN, T. W., Dunchurch, Warwickshire. 1 (Leicestershire) 625; 1 (Warwickshire) 294; TOTAL 2 : 919
MARTYR, Messrs Richard Smirke, and Wright, Greenwich, Kent. 3 (Kent) 8,015
MASHAM, W., Ripon, Yorkshire. 1 (Yorkshire, North Riding) 1,614
MASON, Issac, Hornacott, Launceston, Cornwall. 2 (Cornwall) 13,994; 1 (Devon) 5,022; TOTAL 3 : 19,016
MASON, Michael J., Foxborough, Essex. 5 (Essex) 9,784
MASSEY, Robert, Birmingham, Warwickshire. 1 (Herefordshire) 2,191
MATHEWS, Jeremiah, Park Hall, Kidderminster, Worcestershire. 1 (Staffordshire) 717; 3 (Worcestershire) 5,389; TOTAL 4 : 6,006

MATHEWS, Jeremiah, Park Hall, Kidderminster, Worcestershire, and Oates and Perren, Stourbridge, Worcestershire. 1 (Worcestershire) 869
MAUD, William, Sherborne, Dorset. 1 (Somerset) 712
MAUGHAN, Jno. 1 (Lancashire) 2,907
MAUGHAN and Fowler, Louth, Lincolnshire. 1 (Lincolnshire) 63
MAWSON, Charles, Warrington, Lancashire. 3 (Lancashire) 6,689
MAY, Alfred M., Marlborough, Wiltshire. 13 (Wiltshire) 31,475. *See also* William Aylwin
MCANULTY, James, Leeds, Yorkshire. 1 (Yorkshire, West Riding) 3,098
MCCALL, George, Bromfield, Cumberland ('G. M. C. '). 1 (Cumberland) 182
MCCAY, D. 2 (Lancashire) 15,352. *See also* James Scally
MCCORMICK, P., Grosmont, Monmouthshire. 3 (Monmouthshire) 13,441
MCDERMOTT, Michael, Ipswich, Suffolk. 2 (Suffolk) 3,135
MCLACHLAN, John, Stowmarket, Suffolk. 1 (Kent) 6,949; 3 (Suffolk) 6,429; TOTAL 4 : 13,378. *See also* Robert E. Sheldrake
MCWILLIAM, Francis. 1 (Nottinghamshire) 1,070
MEAD, Joseph, Northal, Edlesborough, Bedfordshire. 1 (Bedfordshire) 302
MELHUISH, T. A., Barton Mills, Suffolk. 1 (Suffolk) 937
MELLERSH, Alfred, Godalming / Guildford, Surrey. 2 (Surrey) 3,434; 2 (Sussex) 3,258; TOTAL 4 : 6,692
MELLING, Edward George, Winstanley, Wigan, Lancashire. 2 (Lancashire) 5,665
MELROSE, James, York. 1 (Yorkshire, East Riding) 500
MEREDITH, Richard, Hay, Breconshire. 1 (Radnorshire) 3,878
MERRETT, H. S. 1 (Sussex) 13,251
MERRY. *See* Clinton, Dickson, Purvis and Merry
MERRYWEATHER, Horatio, Burnley, Lancashire. 1 (Lancashire) 1,785; 2 (Yorkshire, West Riding) 15,066; TOTAL 3 : 16,851
METCALF, William. 4 (Monmouthshire) 13,398
MEW, Herbert, Canewdon, Essex. *See* Benjamin Pickever Wilme
MICKLEBURGH, Charles, Montgomery. 20 (Montgomeryshire) 102,623; 11 (Shropshire) 32,176; TOTAL 31 : 134,799
MICKLETHWAIT, Edward, Grimsby, Lincolnshire and Barnsley, Yorkshire. 2 (Lincolnshire) 2,368; 2 (Yorkshire, West Riding) 1,719; TOTAL 4 : 4,087
MILES, R. D., Leicester. 1 (Huntingdonshire) 194; 20 (Leicestershire) 26,053; TOTAL 21 : 26,247
MILES, Thomas, Leicester. 1 (Derbyshire) 20; 1 (Huntingdonshire) 42; 6 (Leicestershire) 5,315; 1 (Northamptonshire) 1,782; TOTAL 9 : 7,159
MILLARD, Charles William, Norwich, Norfolk. 1 (Norfolk) 2,527
MILLARD, John, Bristol, Gloucestershire. 1 (Gloucestershire) 2,927; 1 (Somerset) 1,170; TOTAL 2 : 4,097
MILLARD, William Salter and Son, Norwich, Norfolk. 21 (Norfolk) 33,164; 1 (Suffolk) 2,441; TOTAL 22 : 35,605
MILLER and Hunter. 1 (Lancashire) 4,647. *See also* John J. Myres
MILLER, Sylvanus, Durham. 4 (Cumberland) 17,121
MILLINGTON, Edward, Fleet, Lincolnshire. 4 (Lincolnshire) 18,188
MILLS, Edward, Birkenhead, Cheshire. 1 (Cheshire) 43
MILLS, Mansfeldt F. and Smithers, Chesterfield, Derbyshire. 8 (Derbyshire) 5,001
MILNE, James. 1 (Northumberland) 2,048
MILTON, Frederick Ross, Greenwich, Kent. 1 (Surrey) 1,723
MITCHELL, William. 1 (Cumberland) 1,941; 2 (Gloucestershire) 674; TOTAL 3 : 2,615
MOISER, Henry, Heworth, Yorkshire. 1 (York City & Ainsty) 546
MONKHOUSE, I. R. 1 (Sussex) 1,525
MOORE, John, Warwick. 1 (Oxfordshire) 333; 5 (Warwickshire) 7,940; TOTAL 6 : 8,273
MOORE, Richard Coddington, Harmston, Lincolnshire. 12 (Lincolnshire) 19,737
MOORE and Son / Moore and Keatley. 2 (Surrey) 4,868
MOORSHEAD, John, South-hill, Cornwall. 1 (Cornwall) 5,781
MORGAN. *See* Robinson and Morgan
MORGAN, Richard, Talybont, Aberystwyth, Cardiganshire. 3 (Cardiganshire) 43,851
MORGAN, William, Tanylan, Llansawel, Carmarthenshire. 5 (Carmarthenshire) 40,485; *See also* John Bowen
MORGAN, William, Tanylan, Llansawel, Carmarthenshire, John Edwards and John Rees. 1 (Carmarthenshire) 10,392
MORGAN, William, Tanylan, Llansawel, Carmarthenshire and B. Jones. 1 (Carmathenshire) 10,031
MORLEY, William, Corby, Cumberland. 1 (Cumberland) 352
MORRIS, Billingsley, Birmingham, Warwickshire. 1 (Shropshire) 920
MORRIS, C. S., Thetford, Norfolk. 1 (Norfolk) 263
MORRIS, R. *See* Samuel Morris
MORRIS, Samuel, Sutton Cheney, Leicestershire. 1 (Leicestershire) 1,555
MORRIS, Samuel, Sutton Cheney, Leicestershire and William Thorpe. 3 (Leicestershire) 2,899
MORRIS, Samuel, and R. Morris, Sutton Cheney, Leicestershire. 2 (Leicestershire) 3,812
MORRIS, Samuel and R. Morris, Sutton Cheney, Leicestershire, and John Thorpe, Shenton, Leicestershire. 1 (Leicestershire) 1,283
MORRIS, Thomas, Newport, Monmouthshire. 1 (Glamorganshire) 3,318; 37 (Monmouthshire) 81,313; TOTAL 38 : 84,631
MORRIS, William, Bristol, Gloucestershire. 2 (Devon) 19,498; 1 (Somerset) 2,315; TOTAL 3 : 21,813
MORTIMER, W. and Son, Newport, Isle of Wight. 4 (Hampshire) 5,153
MORTON, H. J., Wakefield, Yorkshire. 3 (Yorkshire, West Riding) 2,108
MORTON, John, Studholme, Carlisle, Cumberland. 1 (Northumberland) 4,920
MORTON, John, Woodchester, Gloucestershire. 1 (Berkshire) 999
MORTON, William, Leeming Lane / Ripon, Yorkshire. 1 (Yorkshire, North Riding) 1,511; 2 (Yorkshire, West Riding) 2,014; TOTAL 3 : 2,525
MOSS, George, Crewkerne, Somerset. 1 (Dorset) 902; 5 (Somerset) 9,449; TOTAL 6 : 10,351
MOULTON, Benjamin, Woodbridge, Suffolk. 20 (Suffolk) 35,472
MULLINER, Thomas, 37 Old Broad St, London. 3 (Northamptonshire) 11,088
MUMFORD, Charles, Downham Market, Norfolk. 6 (Norfolk) 14,147. *See also* Charles M. Bidwell *and* Robert Hale
MURPHY, George and Jno. Germon. 1 (Devon) 7,656
MURPHY, George. *See* William Joll
MURRAY, Adam and Son, 35 Craven St, Strand, London. 1 (Glamorganshire) 915; 1 (Rutland) 1,527; TOTAL 2 : 2,442
MURRAY, Robert G. 1 (Buckinghamshire) 52
MUSSON, Francis, Grantham, Lincolnshire. 1 (Lincolnshire) 2,677
MYATT, J., Whitmore, Newcastle, Staffordshire. 1 (Staffordshire) 1,435
MYATT, John, Buerton, Audlem / Congleton, Cheshire. 3 (Cheshire) 3,333
MYERS, L., G. Garlick and I. Reynolds. 1 (Oxfordshire) 2,090

MYLNE, E. W. 1 (Hertfordshire) 2,437
MYRES, John J., Preston, Lancashire. 3 (Lancashire) 9,247
MYRES, John J., Preston, Lancashire, and James Crompton. 1 (Lancashire) 3,102
MYRES, John J., Preston, Lancashire, and Miller and Hunter. 1 (Lancashire) 2,854

NADEN, Joseph, Chesterfield Grange, Shenstone, Staffordshire. 1 (Staffordshire) 8,452
NASH and Sons, Reigate, Surrey and Greys Inn, London. 1 (Surrey) 1,272
NASH, William Thomas, Royston, Hertfordshire. 1 (Hertfordshire) 1,143
NATION, T. 1 (Hampshire) 2,048
NEALE, Charles J., Mansfield, Nottinghamshire. 1 (Derbyshire) 42; 3 (Nottinghamshire) 3,857; TOTAL 4 : 3,899
NEALE, Edward, Southampton, Hampshire, or Laleston / Bridgend, Glamorganshire. 1 (Carmarthenshire) 4,501; 16 (Glamorganshire) 53,165; 1 (Hampshire) 1,804; 4 (Surrey) 14,015; TOTAL 22 : 73,485
NEIGHBOUR, J. and Son, Oxford. 2 (Berkshire) 2,555
NEIGHBOUR, John Edward, Oxford. 20 (Oxfordshire) 28,930
NELSON, William, Alnwick, Northumberland. 1 (Northumberland) 2,604
NEW, G. R., High Wycombe, Buckinghamshire. 1 (Buckinghamshire) 1,353
NEW, Thomas B., Worcester. 1 (Devon) 1,892
NEWBERY, Thomas. 1 (Dorset) 3,271
NEWBY, William Lw., Burrowdale, Cumberland. 1 (Cumberland) 2,998
NEWHAM, William, Kings Lynn, Norfolk. 1 (Norfolk) 4,181
NEWSAM, T., Leeds, Yorkshire. 2 (Yorkshire, West Riding) 5,664
NEWTON and Berry, 66 Chancery Lane, London. 1 (Cambridgeshire) 1,091
NEWTON, Robert. 1 (Somerset) 2,108
NEWTON, Robert and Robert P. Purssey. 1 (Somerset) 5,475
NEWTON and Woodrow, Norwich, Norfolk. 2 (Essex) 4,838; 1 (Kent) 1,654; 39 (Norfolk) 68,897; 9 (Suffolk) 18,202; 2 (Surrey) 4,146; TOTAL 53 : 97,737
NICHOLSON, D. A. and Charles Doubell. 1 (Kent) 5,979
NICHOLSON, Edward, 18 Princess St, Manchester, Lancashire. 3 (Cheshire) 5,622; 4 (Lancashire) 785; TOTAL 7 : 6,407
NIGHTINGALE, Richard, Lyndhurst, Hampshire. 4 (Hampshire) 8,121
NIXON, Robert and James Nixon, Sandy Syke, Longton, and Thomas Smith, Whitebeck, Bewcastle, Cumberland. 1 (Cumberland) 4,929
NOBLE, George Richard, Woodford, Essex. 1 (Essex) 2,004
NOCKOLDS, J. A. or Messrs, and Son, Stansted, Essex. 6 (Essex) 13,043
NOCKOLDS, Arthur, Stansted, Essex. 1 (Hertfordshire) 1,516
NORRIS, William, Exeter, Devon. 6 (Devon) 22,688
NORRIS, W. and T. F. Dickinson, Wincanton, Somerset. 1 (Dorset) 914; 10 (Somerset) 16,851; 1 (Sussex) 2,449; TOTAL 12 : 20,214
NORTHCOTE, George, Barnstaple, Devon. 8 (Devon) 23,890
NORTHEAST, Thomas Barnes, North Tedworth, Wiltshire. 1 (Hampshire) 2,176
NUNAN, James, Abergavenny, Monmouthshire. 1 (Herefordshire) 2,082; 9 (Monmouthshire) 23,237; TOTAL 10 : 25,319
NUNAN, J. and M., Abergavenny, Monmouthshire. 3 (Breconshire) 18,086
NUNAN, M. 1 (Glamorganshire) 17,745

OAKDEN, Charles, Waresley, Huntingdonshire. 2 (Cambridgeshire) 2,717; 2 (Huntingdonshire) 2,591; TOTAL 4 : 5,308
OAKLEY, Charles, Allesley, Warwickshire. 1 (Northamptonshire) 1,866; 9 (Warwickshire) 16,182; TOTAL 10 : 18,048
OATES, Christopher, and Perren, Stourbridge, Worcestershire. 2 (Shropshire) 408; 8 (Worcestershire) 22,811; TOTAL 10 : 23,219. *See also* Jeremiah Mathews
OATES, John Edwin, York. 1 (Yorkshire, North Riding) 16,873
OCCLESHAM, P. R. 1 (Yorkshire, East Riding) 2,025
O'HAGAN, Henry. *See* William Bell, Manchester *and* James M. Harkness
OKELL, Joseph. 1 (Cheshire) 1,137
OLIVER. *See* Chapple and Oliver
OLIVER, James, Beaminster, Dorset. 2 (Dorset) 8,436
OLIVER, Thomas, Newcastle, Northumberland. 3 (Northumberland) 1,988
OLVER, J. S., Falmouth, Cornwall. 7 (Cornwall) 36,738
ORDNANCE SURVEY. 28 (Lancashire) 70,367; 7 (Yorkshire, West Riding) 15,306; TOTAL 35 : 85,673
ORME, Charles Cave John, Louth, Lincolnshire. 33 (Lincolnshire) 54,555
O'ROURKE, Michael. *See* J. J. Haslett
OSBOURNE, George, Elberton, Gloucestershire. 2 (Gloucestershire) 3,169
OTHER, Edward, Stockton on Tees, Durham. 8 (Yorkshire, North Riding) 24,064
OTLEY and William Lax, Darlington, Durham. 13 (Durham) 19,799; 2 (Yorkshire, North Riding) 1,794; TOTAL 15 : 21,593
OVERTON, J. 1 (Denbighshire) 411
OWEN, Henry P., Pwllheli, Carnarvonshire. 1 (Carnarvonshire) 2,241
OWEN, James. *See* Robert Roberts
OWEN, Richard. 3 (Cheshire) 4,246. *See also* Thomas Burgess
OWEN, Thomas Davies, Pwllheli, Carnarvonshire. 13 (Carnarvonshire) 50,647
OWEN, Thomas E., Portsmouth, Hampshire. 1 (Hampshire) 4,924

PADLEY, James Sandby, Lincoln. 13 (Lincolnshire) 18,678
PADLEY, James Sandby, and George Betham, Lincoln. 1 (Nottinghamshire) 1,889
PADLEY, Paul, London. 1 (Kent) 3,908
PAGE, Edward, Beverley, Yorkshire. 39 (Yorkshire, East Riding) 55,230; 2 (Yorkshire, North Riding) 11,079; TOTAL 41 : 66,309
PAGE, Gregory, Beverley, Yorkshire. 2 (Yorkshire, East Riding) 53
PAGE, Gregory, Beverley, Yorkshire, and Henry Scott. 1 (Yorkshire, East Riding) 2,415
PAINTER, William, Stower Provost, Dorset. 2 (Dorset) 2,341
PALIN, John, Christleton, Cheshire. 1 (Cheshire) 1,068
PALMER, Edwin, Stawley, Somerset. 1 (Devon) 1,876; 1 (Somerset) 3,100; TOTAL 2 : 4,976
PALMER, J., Bedford. 1 (Bedfordshire) 880
PALMER, John, Devonport, Devon. 3 (Devon) 16,017
PALMER, Robert G. 1 (Essex) 1,259

PANK, G., Cromer, Norfolk. 1 (Norfolk) 1,740
PARK, George. 1 (Lincolnshire) 745
PARK, Phillip, Preston, Lancashire. 9 (Lancashire) 14,615
PARK, Robert, 8 George St, Euston Square, London. 4 (Devon) 6,144
PARKER, A. S. *See* Thomas B. Irish
PARKER, C. A., Sheffield, Yorkshire. 1 (Yorkshire, West Riding) 20
PARKER, Thomas, Willand, Devon. 1 (Devon) 990
PARKES, S. W., Ipswich, Suffolk. 1 (Essex) 2,551; 10 (Suffolk) 14,209; TOTAL 11 : 16,760
PARKIN, John, Idridgehay, Wirksworth, Derbyshire. 15 (Derbyshire) 22,182; 2 (Staffordshire) 1,812; TOTAL 17 : 23,994
PARKIN, John, New House, Upton, Birkenhead, Cheshire. 1 (Cheshire) 98
PARKIN, John junior, Lostwithiel, Cornwall. 1 (Cornwall) 111
PARKINSON, John, Ley Fields, Rufford, Nottinghamshire. 2 (Lincolnshire) 1,464
PARKINSON, S. 1 (Essex) 1,793
PARKINSON, T., Rotherham, Yorkshire. 2 (Yorkshire, West Riding) 204
PARLOUR, J., Burton Leonard, Yorkshire, and Joseph King. 1 (Yorkshire, West Riding) 1,794
PARRY, William, Llanidloes, Montgomeryshire. 12 (Montgomeryshire) 110,276
PARSON, George, Wellington, Somerset. 1 (Hampshire) 6,677; 1 (Somerset) 5,196; TOTAL 2 : 11,873
PARSONS, James, Beckley, Sussex. 2 (Sussex) 4,545
PATCHING. *See* Hide and Patching
PAVER, John. 1 (Nottinghamshire) 1,704
PAYN, J., Fawlsey, Northamptonshire. 1 (Northamptonshire) 2,332
PAYNE, Richard, Bury St Edmunds, Suffolk. 2 (Norfolk) 7,575; 13 (Suffolk) 23,498; TOTAL 15 : 31,073
PAYTE, John. 1 (Sussex) 4,304
PAYTE, J., P. Payte, J. Gill and W. Gibson. 1 (Kent) 9,685
PEACE, Thomas, Wolverhampton, Staffordshire. 1 (Staffordshire) 1,985
PEACHEY, P., 17 Salisbury Square, London. 1 (Bedfordshire) 2,561
PEACOCK, Thomas, Bishop Auckland, Durham. 1 (Durham) 989
PEACOCK, William, Great Marlow, Buckinghamshire. 1 (Buckinghamshire) 1,305
PEARSON, William, near Thirsk, Yorkshire. 2 (Yorkshire, North Riding) 6,996
PEART, William, Metheringham, Lincolnshire. 1 (Lincolnshire) 9
PEIRSON, George, Guisborough, Yorkshire. 1 (Durham) 748; 12 (Yorkshire, North Riding) 23,031; TOTAL 13 : 23,779
PENISTON, M., Salisbury, Wiltshire. 1 (Wiltshire) 4,843
PENTREATH, Richard, Penzance, Cornwall. 1 (Cornwall) 4,357
PENTREATH, Richard, Penzance, Cornwall, and George Hosking. 2 (Cornwall) 5,456
PENTREATH, Richard, Penzance, Cornwall, William Marrack, and George Hosking. 2 (Cornwall) 7,266

PEPPER, Sanders. 1 (Staffordshire) 332; 1 (Warwickshire) 1,954; TOTAL 2 : 2,286
PEPPERSTONE, Frederick S., Buckingham St, Strand, London. 1 (Surrey) 1,168
PERCY, Edward Thomas, Sherborne, Dorset. 4 (Dorset) 16,317; 1 (Somerset) 1,021; TOTAL 5 : 17,338
PERKINS, S. H., Faversham, Kent. 1 (Kent) 3,576
PERREN. *See* Jeremiah Mathews *and* Christopher Oates
PERRIS, William. 1 (Wiltshire) 638
PETTY, Richard, Crosshills, Yorkshire. 5 (Yorkshire, West Riding) 6,831
PEYTON, Richard, Cooks Court, Carey St, London. 1 (Essex) 2,779; 1 (Kent) 2,608; TOTAL 2 : 5,387
PHILLIPS, J. H. 5 (Yorkshire, North Riding) 9,774
PHILLIPS, Robert B., 78 King William St, London. 1 (Kent) 5,430
PHILLIPS, Thomas and Giles Westbury, Andover, Hampshire. 8 (Berkshire) 20,803; 26 (Hampshire) 67,140; 7 (Wiltshire) 17,461; TOTAL 41 : 105,404
PHILLIPS, William, Coventry, Warwickshire. 2 (Leicestershire) 3,657; 1 (Warwickshire) 1,966; TOTAL 3 : 5,623
PHILP, J., Exeter, Devon. 5 (Devon) 18,034
PHILPOTT, Henry, Haverfordwest, Pembrokeshire. 1 (Glamorganshire) 12,550; 2 (Pembrokeshire) 6,446; TOTAL 3 : 18,996. *See also* Harry Goode
PICKERING and Smith, 14 Whitehall Place, London. 1 (Derbyshire) 16; 1 (Essex) 1,524; TOTAL 2 : 1,540
PICKERING, John Pickering, 2 Derby St, Westminster, Middlesex. 1 (Staffordshire) 901; 1 (Warwickshire) 2,972; TOTAL 2 : 3,873. *See also* Charles Lee
PICKERING, William, Axminster, Devon. 3 (Devon) 5,489; 1 (Dorset) 3,182; TOTAL 4 : 8,671
PIERCY, Robert, Chirk, Denbighshire. 1 (Denbighshire) 3,391
PIGGOT, George, Bolton, Lancashire. 2 (Lancashire) 68
PINK, Richard and Charles Pink, Hambledon, Hampshire. 5 (Hampshire) 9,548
PITT, Walter. 1 (Herefordshire) 697
PLAYER, Thomas Player, Pensford, Somerset. 15 (Somerset) 17,257
PLAYFORD, George F., North Repps, Norfolk. 5 (Norfolk) 3,023
PLUMER, J., Horsham, Sussex. *See* Henry Walter
PLUMLEY, J., Bristol, Gloucestershire. 1 (Gloucestershire) 542
PLUMMER, W. B. 1 (Yorkshire, East Riding) 134
POLGREEN, R., St Germans, Cornwall. 1 (Cornwall) 1,138. *See also* Eastcott and Pollgreen
POOLE, James, Sherborne, Dorset. 1 (Devon) 3,019; 18 (Dorset) 39,810; 11 (Somerset) 18,693; 15 (Wiltshire) 42,676; TOTAL 45 : 104,198
PORTER, Issac, Oswestry, Shropshire. 2 (Denbighshire) 2,352; 1 (Montgomeryshire) 4,464; 5 (Shropshire) 7,088; TOTAL 8 : 13,904
PORTER, Richard Philpott, Nunnery Farm, St Martins, Worcestershire. 1 (Herefordshire) 546
POSTANS, Richard, Shelley, Suffolk. 1 (Suffolk) 928
POSTLETHWAITE, Harry, St Johns Wood, London. 1 (Hampshire) 8,715
POTTER, Peter, Kentish Town, Maidstone, Kent. 1 (Kent) 878
POTTER, Peter junior, Gorway House, Walsall, Staffordshire. 1 (Staffordshire) 2,398
POUNDLEY, J. H., Kerry, Montgomeryshire. 2 (Montgomeryshire) 13,230
POWELL, James, Knaresborough, Yorkshire. 6 (Yorkshire, North Riding) 6,290; 13 (Yorkshire, West Riding) 22,214; TOTAL 19 : 28,504
POWELL, John, Marden, Herefordshire. 1 (Herefordshire) 1,732
POWELL, Joseph, Sutton, Herefordshire. 1 (Herefordshire) 1,002
POWSON, William, Kirby Stephen, Westmorland. 5 (Westmorland) 8,879
PRATT, Robert and Son, Norwich, Norfolk. 59 (Norfolk) 108,709; 7 (Suffolk) 17,378; TOTAL 66 : 126,087
PRESTON. 2 (Suffolk) 2,485

PRESTON, Henry, Worlingworth, Suffolk. 4 (Suffolk) 5,034
PRESTON, J., Worlingworth, Suffolk. 1 (Suffolk) 2,447
PRICE, Francis, Norton, Oystermouth, Glamorganshire. 1 (Glamorganshire) 2,388
PRICE, H., Abergavenny, Monmouthshire. 1 (Breconshire) 10,511; 1 (Monmouthshire) 290; TOTAL 2 : 10,801.
See also J. and M. Nunan
PRICE, John, Chester / Denbigh / Ruthin, Denbighshire. 3 (Carnarvonshire) 4,958; 8 (Denbighshire) 39,086; 2 (Flintshire) 5,476; 1 (Merionethshire) 694; TOTAL 14 : 50,214
PRICE, Richard, Norton, Swansea, Glamorganshire. 1 (Glamorganshire) 3,975
PRICE, William, Ross, Herefordshire. 1 (Gloucestershire) 703; 27 (Herefordshire) 56,653; 1 (Worcestershire) 5,494; TOTAL 29 : 62,850.
See also William Fosbrooke
PRICKETT, George, Highgate and 12 Southampton Buildings, London. 1 (Kent) 4,525
PRUJEAN, John, Clements Inn, London. 1 (Essex) 1,666; 1 (Monmouthshire) 5,167; TOTAL 2 : 6,833.
PUGH, George, Aberystwyth, Cardiganshire. 7 (Cardiganshire) 38,955
PUGH, William. *See* Walter Lloyd
PURCHAS, Robert Nathaniel, Chepstow, Monmouthshire. 1 (Herefordshire) 1,631; 7 (Monmouthshire) 16,291; TOTAL 8 : 17,922
PURSSEY, Robert P., Monksilver, Somerset. 3 (Somerset) 4,944. See also Robert Newton
PURVIS. *See* Clinton, Dickson, Purvis and Merry
PYNE, John. 1 (Middlesex) 1,311; 2 (Wiltshire) 2,918; TOTAL 3 : 4,229

QUESTED, George, Ash near Wingham, Kent. 7 (Kent) 11,866
QUESTED, John, Maidstone, Kent. 3 (Kent) 8,775

'J. R.' 1 (Durham) 1,589
RAINE, I. 2 (Northumberland) 2,957
RANGER, R. A., Tunbridge Wells, Kent. 1 (Kent) 2,062
RAWSON, William, Barton upon Humber, Lincolnshire. 4 (Lincolnshire) 6,194
RAY, Walter J., Great James St, Bedford Row, London. 3 (Essex) 9,082
RAYMOND, John, Shaftesbury, Dorset. 13 (Dorset) 32,686
RAYMOND, William. 1 (Dorset) 1,633
READ, T. and H. Cooling. 1 (Buckinghamshire) 2,139
READWIN, T. A., Wokingham, Berkshire. 1 (Berkshire) 1,515
REANEY, W. *See* Luckraft, Warren *et al.*
REAY, Thomas. 1 (Northumberland) 579
REED, Anthony and Robert Reed, Stockton upon Tees, Durham. 1 (Lancashire) 1,704; 2 (Shropshire) 27,165; 9 (Yorkshire, North Riding) 16,079; TOTAL 12 : 44,948
REED, Benjamin, Old Broad St, London. 1 (Berkshire) 1,298
REED, Joseph junior, Tregathenan, Cornwall. 1 (Cornwall) 5,833
REED, Richard. See Charles Williams
REES, D. 1 (Glamorganshire) 1,122
REES, Jacob. See William Goode
REES, John. See William Morgan
REES, R. A. 2 (Glamorganshire) 3,744
REID. *See* White and Reid
RENSHAW, James, 8 Union Court, Old Broad St, London. 1 (Essex) 764; 4 (Kent) 6,797; TOTAL 5 : 7,561. See also Richard Allerton
REYNOLDS, I. *See* L. Myers
REYNOLDS, Matthew, Old Warden, Bedfordshire. 5 (Bedfordshire) 8,688; 1 (Buckinghamshire), 1,744; 2 (Hertfordshire) 2,558; TOTAL 8 : 12,990
RHODES, S., 2 Bow Churchyard, London. 1 (Kent) 1,412
RICH, E. and Stiles Rich, Didmarton, Gloucestershire. 4 (Gloucestershire) 3,917; 3 (Wiltshire) 6,294; TOTAL 7 : 10,211
RICHARDS, Henry, Abbotts Court Farm, Dorset. 3 (Dorset) 7,756
RICHARDS, William, Tiverton, Devon. 13 (Devon) 46,526; 1 (Dorset) 5,003; TOTAL 14 : 51,529
RICHARDSON, J. 1 (Middlesex) 1,237
RICHARDSON, James, 5 Bickford Place, Kennington, London. 1 (Buckinghamshire) 3,905
RICHARDSON, James, 12 Pall Mall, London. 1 (Surrey) 2,884
RICHARDSON, James, Cambridge. 1 (Hertfordshire) 4,309
RICHARDSON, James, West (Middlesex) Water Works, (surveyor and engineer). 1 (Berkshire) 9,102
RICHARDSON, John, Dalston, Carlisle, Cumberland. 6 (Yorkshire, West Riding) 9,918
RICHARDSON, Joseph, Hoff Row, St Lawrence Appleby, Westmorland. 2 (Westmorland) 401
RIDER, E. 7 (Sussex) 19,398
RISDON, Joseph, Speccott, Merton, Devon. 5 (Devon) 13,436
ROBERTS, J. 1 (Cheshire) 10
ROBERTS, John, Corwen, Denbighshire. 3 (Denbighshire) 8,791; 2 (Merionethshire) 11,892; TOTAL 5 : 20,683
ROBERTS, P., Burnley, Lancashire. 1 (Lancashire) 4,711
ROBERTS, Richard, Carnarvon. 1 (Carnarvonshire) 902
ROBERTS, Robert, Tyddyn Issa, Denbighshire, and James Owen. 1 (Denbighshire) 1,735
ROBERTS, William, 68 Chancery Lane, London. 5 (Kent) 15,018; 1 (Surrey) 9,872; 2 (Yorkshire, West Riding) 2,348; TOTAL 8 : 27,238
ROBINSON, George. 5 (Cumberland) 6,891; 1 (Lancashire) 327; TOTAL 6 : 7,218
ROBINSON, John, Bootle, Cumberland. 3 (Cumberland) 4,456
ROBINSON, John, Keldray, near Ulverston, Lancashire. 6 (Lancashire) 13,962
ROBINSON, Messrs and Morgan, Dublin, (civil engineers). 3 (Cornwall) 9,126; 1 (Devon) 2,595; TOTAL 4 : 11,721
ROBINSON, Murrell R., Otford Castle, Sevenoaks, Kent. 4 (Kent) 6,543. *See also* Carrington and Robinson
ROBINSON, Thomas, Ripon, Yorkshire. 6 (Yorkshire, North Riding) 9,939; 16 (Yorkshire, West Riding) 54,026; TOTAL 22 : 63,965
ROBINSON, William, Hesket-new-market, Cumberland. 5 (Cumberland) 10,775
ROBSON, Andrew. 2 (Northumberland) 1,457
ROBSON, Robert and Matthew Ryle junior. 3 (Durham) 5,442
RODDAM, Jonathan, Stanhope, Durham. 2 (Durham) 21,379
ROE, William, Derby. 1 (Nottinghamshire) 554
ROME, D. W., Alston, Cumberland. 2 (Cumberland) 44,361; 2 (Northumberland) 7,985; 1 (Westmorland) 2,382; TOTAL 5 : 54,728

ROODHAM, Henry. 1 (Durham) 2,169
ROOE, Jno. 1 (Lincolnshire) 5,386
ROOK, John. 1 (Westmorland) 4,944
ROPER, Henry C. junior, Uttoxeter, Staffordshire. 6 (Derbyshire) 3,167
ROTHWELL, William, Winwick, Lancashire. 10 (Lancashire) 20,579
ROTSON, Andrew. 2 (Northumberland) 2,109
ROWE, Abieser, Barnstaple, Devon. 4 (Devon) 17,633
ROWE, John. 1 (Cornwall) 3,907
ROWE, Samuel, Malpas, Cheshire. 1 (Cheshire) 548
RUCE, George. 1 (Cheshire) 744
RUFFELL, G., Brightlingsea, Essex. 1 (Suffolk) 4,462
RUFFELL, W. 2 (Essex) 7,411. *See also* G. R. Jay
RUFFELL, W. and A. Ruffell, Kersey, Suffolk. 17 (Suffolk) 31,513
RUMBALL, John Horner, St Albans, Hertfordshire. 7 (Hertfordshire) 22,871
RUNDLE, John, Hayle, Cornwall. 2 (Cornwall) 7,000
RUSH, Alfred, Messing, Essex. 6 (Essex) 19,758
RUSHWORTH and Jarvis, Saville Row, London. 1 (Surrey) 2,460
RUSSEL, Robert, Brackley, Northamptonshire. 2 (Northamptonshire) 2,632
RUSSELL, William. 1 (Warwickshire) 121
RUTGER, J. H., Marazion, Cornwall. 6 (Cornwall) 17,944; 1 (Devon) 897; TOTAL 7 : 18,841. See also A. Heathman
RYLE, Matthew junior. *See* Robert Robson

'A. R. S. ' 1 (Leicestershire) 903
SALKELD, John, Melmerby, Cumberland. 4 (Cumberland) 7,529
SALKELD, William, Wylie Mar, Hayton, Cumberland. 2 (Cumberland) 123
SALTER, Henry, Arundel, Sussex. 17 (Sussex) 31,336
SALTER and Son, Attleborough, Norfolk. 1 (Norfolk) 87
SAMPLE, William and T. Sample, Matfen, Northumberland. 2 (Northumberland) 1,871
SANDERCOCK, John, and Sons, Altarnun, Cornwall. 8 (Cornwall) 49,317
SANDERS, William Rowden, Plymouth, Devon. *See* John Eastridge Adams
SANDERSON, Charles, Reading, Berkshire. 1 (Berkshire) 682
SANDERSON, George, Mansfield, Nottinghamshire. 2 (Derbyshire) 1,823; 10 (Nottinghamshire) 23,479; 1 (Yorkshire, West Riding) 42; TOTAL 13 : 25,344
SANDERSON, H. 1 (Yorkshire, North Riding) 310
SANDERSON, Henry, Sheffield, Yorkshire. 1 (Surrey) 2,850
SANDERSON, James Martin, Sunbury, Middlesex, (land and timber surveyor). 3 (Hampshire) 11,845; 2 (Middlesex) 2,750; 3 (Surrey) 6,043; TOTAL 8 : 17,890
SANDS, Reepham, Norfolk. 2 (Norfolk) 2,466
SANDS, Alexander. 2 (Norfolk) 2,775
SARSFIELD, Francis Molloy, Birkenhead, Cheshire. 1 (Cheshire) 652
SAUNDERS. *See* Davis and Saunders
SAUNDERS. *See* Edwards, Saunders and B. Jones
SAUNDERS, James, Kirtlington, Oxford. 1 (Northamptonshire) 869; 8 (Oxfordshire) 14,847; TOTAL 9 : 15,716. *See also* Davis and Saunders
SAVILL, John, and Son, Sible Hedingham, Essex. 5 (Essex) 19,484
SAWDYE, Edward and James Taperell, Ashburton, Devon. 4 (Devon) 15,339
SAWYER, Thomas, Hertford. 1 (Hertfordshire) 6,016
SAXBY, William, Edenbridge, Kent. 2 (Kent) 8,525
SAYCE, Morris, Kington, Herefordshire. 14 (Breconshire) 86,846; 4 (Carmarthenshire) 36,413; 4 (Cardiganshire) 21,832; 1 (Glamorganshire) 31,157; TOTAL 23 : 176,248
SAYCE, Morris and William Sayce. 16 (Herefordshire) 39,216; 28 (Radnorshire) 131,057; 1 (Shropshire) 3,724; TOTAL 45 : 173,997
SCALLY, James. 1 (Lancashire) 8,501; 2 (Yorkshire, West Riding) 4,364; TOTAL 3 : 12,865
SCOTT, Henry, Oulston, Yorkshire. 1 (Durham) 2,780; 2 (Yorkshire, East Riding) 2,785; 30 (Yorkshire, North Riding) 50,757; TOTAL 33 : 56,322. *See also* Gregory Page
SCOTT, M. *See* Thomas Sopwith
SEDGWICK, John and Son, Rickmansworth, Hertfordshire. 1 (Hertfordshire) 9,938
SEXTON. *See* Baker and Sexton
SHARMAN, Alfred and John Campbell. 1 (Suffolk) 1,687; 1 (Sussex) 1,097; TOTAL 2 : 2,784
SHARP, Charles, Ringwood, Hampshire. 1 (Hampshire) 7,562
SHARP, Charles, and Harry Holloway, Ringwood, Hampshire. 1 (Hampshire) 10,895
SHARP, Charles, Ringwood, Hampshire and John Waters, Salisbury, Wiltshire. 1 (Hampshire) 9,554
SHAW, Claudius, Bangor, Carnarvonshire. 1 (Carnarvonshire) 1,272; 1 (Denbighshire) 2,749; TOTAL 2 : 4,021
SHAW, John, Derby. 3 (Derbyshire) 662; 1 (Nottinghamshire) 3; TOTAL 4 : 665
SHEARM, Thomas. 1 (Cornwall) 1,010
SHELDRAKE, Robert E., Colchester, Essex. 5 (Essex) 8,987
SHELDRAKE, Robert E. and John McLachlan, Colchester, Essex. 13 (Suffolk) 27,012
SHERBORN, William, Bedfont, Middlesex. 3 (Middlesex) 10,084; 1 (Surrey) 6,705; TOTAL 4 : 16,789
SHERIDAN, Edward. 2 (Kent) 3,549; 4 (Sussex) 32,576; TOTAL 6 : 36,125
SHERINGHAM, William George, Truro, Cornwall. 2 (Cornwall) 4,431
SHIPTON, William, York. 2 (Yorkshire, East Riding) 2,851; 1 (Yorkshire, West Riding) 758; TOTAL 3 : 3,609
SHONE, Richard, St Asaph, Flintshire. 1 (Flintshire) 531
SHORTS, W. H. H., Midhurst, Sussex. 1 (Sussex) 718
SHUTER, W. 4 (Gloucestershire) 5,102
SIBLEY, Buntingford, Hertfordshire. *See* Charles F. Adams
SIMPSON, Alfred, New Malton, Yorkshire. 1 (Yorkshire, East Riding) 1,324
SIMPSON, Frederick, Derby. 2 (Derbyshire) 2,008
SIMPSON, Robert, Alderley, Cheshire. 1 (Cheshire) 597
SIMPSON, Thomas and Son, Nunthorpe, Yorkshire. 1 (Yorkshire, North Riding) 1,056

SIMPSON, William, Pinchingthorpe, Guisborough, Yorkshire. 2 (Durham) 2,298; 29 (Yorkshire, North Riding) 32,014; TOTAL 31 : 34,312
SINGLETON. *See* William Thornbarrow
SKILL, William, Lincoln. 1 (Lincolnshire) 336
SKIPTON, William. 1 (Yorkshire, West Riding) 1,492
SLATER, James, Ilminster, Somerset. *See* William Summers
SMALL and Son, Buckland, Dover, Kent. 10 (Kent) 16,735
SMALLPEICE, Job, Godalming and Thomas Crawter, Cobham, Surrey. 4 (Surrey) 19,532
SMITH. *See* Pickering and Smith, 14 Whitehall Place, London
SMITH. *See* Herbert and Smith
SMITH, Benson. 2 (Lancashire) 3,906
SMITH, Charles junior, Alton, Staffordshire. 4 (Staffordshire) 5,245
SMITH, Edward. 3 (Northumberland) 2,478
SMITH, Edward J., 25 Parliament Street, London. 6 (Surrey) 18,958
SMITH, E. and Son. 4 (Hampshire) 16,287
SMITH, G., Oundle / Market Deeping, Lincolnshire / Stamford, Lincolnshire. 8 (Northamptonshire) 5,546
SMITH, George Alexander. 1 (Hertfordshire) 7,137
SMITH, Graville, Castle Donington, Derbyshire. 1 (Derbyshire) 1,484
SMITH, Henry, Bath, Somerset. 2 (Gloucestershire) 4,689
SMITH, James and Edmund Smith, Upper Beeding, Steyning, Sussex. 1 (Sussex) 3,423
SMITH, Joseph, Albion Court, Bradford, Yorkshire. 1 (Yorkshire, West Riding) 1,849. *See also* Thomas Ingle
SMITH, M. 1 (Herefordshire) 2,433. *See also* L. Carey
SMITH, Parker, Caythorpe, Grantham, Lincolnshire. 1 (Lincolnshire) 191
SMITH, Robert, York. 3 (Lincolnshire) 9,121; 2 (York City & Ainsty) 1,678; 1 (Yorkshire, East Riding) 761; 1 (Yorkshire, North Riding) 2,558; 4 (Yorkshire, West Riding) 9,486; TOTAL 11 : 23,604
SMITH, Thomas, Rugby, Warwickshire. 1 (Northamptonshire) 58
SMITH, Thomas, Dunham Massey, Cheshire. 1 (Cheshire) 1,629. *See also* James Cawley
SMITH, Thomas, Whitebeck, Bewcastle, Cumberland. *See* Robert and James Nixon
SMITHERS and Mills, Chesterfield, Derbyshire. *See* George Unwin (Derbyshire, 1) and Mansfeldt F. Mills
SMY, James, Saxmundham, Suffolk. 13 (Suffolk) 20,459. *See also* Benjamin Moulton, (Suffolk, 1)
SNELL, William, Stonehouse, Devon. 2 (Devon) 2,903
SNIPE, John. 2 (Yorkshire, West Riding) 2,904
SODDREL. 1 (Cumberland) 916
SOPWITH, Thomas and M. Scott, Arcade, Newcastle, Northumberland. 1 (Northumberland) 4,388
SOULSBY, Christopher, Harthill, Rotherham, Yorkshire. 1 (Yorkshire, West Riding) 79
SPENCE, Henry Ramsey, Elvington, York. 1 (York City & Ainsty) 11; 6 (Yorkshire, East Riding) 3,676; 1 (Yorkshire, North Riding) 875; 4 (Yorkshire, West Riding) 3,655; TOTAL 12 : 8,217. *See also* Francis Carr
SPENCELEY, Thomas, Cottingham, Hull, Yorkshire. 2 (Nottinghamshire) 2,381; 8 (Yorkshire, East Riding) 16,232; TOTAL 10 : 18,613
SPENCER, T. H., 3 Everett St, Russell Square, London. 1 (Hampshire) 425; 1 (Sussex) 3,818; TOTAL 2 : 4,243
SPOONER, James and Son, Morfa Lodge, Carnarvonshire. 3 (Carnarvonshire) 21,149
SPURLING, Benjamin, Burgh, Suffolk. 12 (Suffolk) 18,910
SPURLING, John, Shotley, Suffolk. 4 (Suffolk) 8,489
SQUIRE, Jacob and John Williamson (schoolmaster), North Clifton, Nottinghamshire. 1 (Nottinghamshire) 62
STALEY, B., Youlgreave, Bakewell, Derbyshire. 1 (Staffordshire) 3,230
STANWIX, Jonathan, Egremont, Cumberland. 3 (Cumberland) 2,471
STEELE, William, Walton, Cumberland. 1 (Cumberland) 528
STELFOX, Richard, Allesley, Warwickshire. 2 (Cheshire) 2,195; 3 (Leicestershire) 1,335; 1 (Northamptonshire) 1,625; 13 (Warwickshire) 21,239; TOTAL 19 : 26,394
STEPHENS, John and Richard Stephens, Cardinham, Cornwall. 4 (Cornwall) 10,451
STEPHENS, Samuel, 180 High St, Southampton, Hampshire. 1 (Dorset) 1,773; 3 (Hampshire) 14,747; 1 (Wiltshire) 3,541; TOTAL 5 : 20,061
STIGOLL, John, Bramfield / Linstead Parva, Suffolk. 12 (Suffolk) 24,615
STODDART, Andrew, South Shields, Durham. 7 (Durham) 11,534; 1 (Northumberland) 1,202; TOTAL 8 : 12,736
STOKES, George, Hereford. 1 (Herefordshire) 410
STORR, Richard, Cirencester, Gloucestershire. 1 (Gloucestershire) 451
STORY, William, Shrewsbury, Shropshire. 8 (Shropshire) 14,647
STRATFORD, James, Amersham, Buckinghamshire. *See* James Knightingale
STRAWSON, George Smith, Cardiff, Glamorganshire. 14 (Glamorganshire) 24,947
STREAT, J., Ash, Surrey. 1 (Hampshire) 4,144; 2 (Surrey) 9,348; TOTAL 3 : 13,492
STRODE, Simon. *See* Robert Jackman
STUBBS, Oliver, Hinton St George, Somerset. 1 (Herefordshire) 4,872
STUDHOLME, John, Carlisle, Cumberland. 2 (Cumberland) 4,606
STURGE, Jacob. *See* Young Sturge *and* John Brown
STURGE, Young and Jacob Player Sturge, Bristol, Gloucestershire. 14 (Gloucestershire) 39,564; 6 (Somerset) 10,408; 1 (Wiltshire) 2,009; TOTAL 21 : 51,981. *See also* Charles Baker
SUMMERS, William, and James Slater, Ilminster, Somerset. 3 (Devon) 5,688; 1 (Dorset) 1,789; 10 (Somerset) 11,727; TOTAL 14 : 19,204
SURPLICE, Samuel Herrick, Beeston, Nottinghamshire. 1 (Leicestershire) 1,173; 2 (Nottinghamshire) 2,219; TOTAL 3 : 3,392
SURRIDGE, Joseph Smith, Coggeshall, Essex. 9 (Essex) 17,702; 1 (Hertfordshire) 4,701; TOTAL 10 : 22,403
SUTER, Thomas, Exeter, Devon. 1 (Cornwall) 5,877; 1 (Devon) 6,234; TOTAL 2 : 12,111
SWINBURNE, Edward. *See* Henry Lakin
SWIRE, Sam., Skipton, Yorkshire. 13 (Yorkshire, West Riding) 40,826
SYMONDS, Giles, Dorchester, Dorset. 1 (Dorset) 14
SYMONS, Henry, Fancy, Egg Buckland, Devon. 10 (Devon) 29,137
SYMONS, Robert, Truro, Cornwall. 8 (Cornwall) 46,313

'G. T.' 1 (Derbyshire) 7,891
TALBOT, Frederick C., Brocklesby / Caistor, Lincolnshire. 14 (Lincolnshire) 27,266
TALBOT, William, Lane House, Preston Patrick, Burton in Kendal, Westmorland. 1 (Lancashire) 1,115
TALLIS, Richard Poyntell, Darfield, Yorkshire. 1 (Northamptonshire) 9

TAMLYN, John, Haverfordwest, Pembrokeshire. 5 (Pembrokeshire) 19,767. *See also* Henry Philpott
TAPERELL, James, Ashburton, Devon. 4 (Devon) 7,175. *See also* Edward Sawdye
TAPERELL, John. 4 (Dorset) 6,200
TAPERELL. *See* William Gould
TAPLIN, Edward. *See* John Duckworth
TARRY, H. 1 (Leicestershire) 1,357
TATHAM, Messrs T. J. and Son, Bedford Place, Russell Square, London. 1 (Surrey) 1,428; 1 (Warwickshire) 1,097; TOTAL 2 : 2,525
TAYLER, George. 5 (Radnorshire) 27,119; 2 (Shropshire) 1,594; TOTAL 7 : 28,713
TAYLER, J. 1 (Lancashire) 3,738; 1 (Westmorland) 5,216; TOTAL 2 : 8,954
TAYLOR, George, Huddersfield, Yorkshire. 3 (Monmouthshire) 5,584
TAYLOR, George, Wolverhampton, Staffordshire. 1 (Shropshire) 3,424. *See also* George Long
TAYLOR, George, Brecon, (engineering surveyor). 1 (Breconshire) 1,544
TAYLOR, Issac. 2 (Denbighshire) 2,352
TAYLOR, John, Ollerset, Stockport, Cheshire. 3 (Cheshire) 6,223; 4 (Derbyshire) 12,139; TOTAL 7 : 18,362
TAYLOR and Lawton. 1 (Lancashire) 1,272
TAYLOR, Samuel, 30 Cooper Street, Manchester, Lancashire. 1 (Cheshire) 1,561; 1 (Lancashire) 68; TOTAL 2 : 1,629
TAYSPILL, Thomas, Colchester, Essex. *See* George Gilbert
TEAL, Henry and Sons, Leeds, Yorkshire. 7 (Yorkshire, West Riding) 9,510
TEAL, Henry junior, Leeds, Yorkshire. 1 (Lincolnshire) 812
TENCH, Walter, Hereford. 4 (Herefordshire) 9,450; 4 (Shropshire) 8,030; TOTAL 8 : 17,480
THOMAS, Alfred, Carmarthen. 4 (Cardiganshire) 57,881; 3 (Carmarthenshire) 10,485; TOTAL 7 : 88,366.
THOMAS, David. 2 (Monmouthshire) 6,788
THOMAS, George, Layerthorpe, York. 1 (Yorkshire, East Riding) 3,503; 1 (Yorkshire, North Riding) 355; TOTAL 2 : 3,858
THOMAS, Richard, Falmouth, Cornwall. 3 (Cornwall) 7,915
THOMAS, W. *See* F. Carter
THOMPSON, G. M., 9 Grays Inn Square, London. 1 (Buckinghamshire) 599
THOMPSON, John, Newlyn, Cornwall, (Civil Engineer). 9 (Cornwall) 36,006. *See also* Woodmass
THOMPSON, Joseph, Leeds, Yorkshire. 3 (Yorkshire, West Riding) 3,712
THOMPSON, William, Bishop Auckland, Durham. 1 (Durham) 1,175
THOMSON, J. S., Tenterden, Kent. 5 (Kent) 15,249; 1 (Sussex) 4,840; TOTAL 6 : 20,089
THORNBORROW, William, Broughton, Lancashire. 2 (Lancashire) 3,091
THORNTON, Richard, Manchester, Lancashire. 3 (Cheshire) 4,603; 9 (Lancashire) 18,091; TOTAL 12 : 22,694
THORNTON, William, Carlton, Yorkshire. 8 (Yorkshire, North Riding) 16,448; 1 (Yorkshire, West Riding) 1,352; TOTAL 9 : 17,800
THORPE, John, Shenton, Leicestershire. 1 (Leicestershire) 935. *See also* Samuel Morris
THORPE, W. 1 (Leicestershire) 1,320. *See also* Samuel Morris
THURSTON, Thomas, Ashford, Kent. 60 (Kent) 159,713; 1 (Sussex) 6,398; TOTAL 61 : 166,111
TIDEY, J. F., Littlehampton, Sussex. 1 (Hampshire) 282; 6 (Sussex) 12,599; TOTAL 7 : 12,881
TIFFEN, H. S., Hythe, Kent. 1 (Kent) 1,109; 2 (Sussex) 6,273; TOTAL 3 : 7,382
TILBROOK, Thomas, Horningsham, Wiltshire. 1 (Wiltshire) 4,791
TIMMIS. *See* Bate and Timmis
TIMMIS, Richard, Wolverhampton, Staffordshire. 2 (Staffordshire) 1,277
TINKER, F., Hyde, Cheshire. 2 (Lancashire) 2,591
TINKER, Joseph, Hyde, Cheshire. 4 (Cheshire) 4,729
TINKLEY, F., Fakenham, Norfolk. 1 (Norfolk) 2,209
TISDALE, Thomas, Shrewsbury, Shropshire. 2 (Shropshire) 67
TODD, James, Abergavenny, Monmouthshire. 1 (Monmouthshire) 4,229
TODD, T., Yarm, Yorkshire. 1 (Yorkshire, North Riding) 990
TOMLINSON, A. B., Biggins, Kirkby Lonsdale, Westmorland. 1 (Westmorland) 1,780
TOMLINSON, J., Sleaford, Lincolnshire. 1 (Lincolnshire) 1,548
TOOTELL, Joseph, Maidstone, Kent. 1 (Hertfordshire) 2,952; 4 (Kent) 9,557; 4 (Middlesex) 6,739; TOTAL 9 : 19,248
TOPLISS, J., Ticknall, Derbyshire. 1 (Derbyshire) 1,867
TOWNSEND, W. Hicks, Bristol, Gloucestershire. 2 (Gloucestershire) 4,494; 1 (Somerset) 305; TOTAL 3 : 4,799
TREASURE, John, Newport, Shropshire. 1 (Derbyshire) 2,472; 8 (Shropshire) 30,104; 3 (Staffordshire) 15,243; TOTAL 12 : 47,819
TRESS, Richard. *See* E. B. Green
TRESS, William, Finsbury Square, London. 3 (Middlesex) 8,111
TRICKETT, Thomas. 1 (Yorkshire, West Riding) 1,406
TRINDER, Daniel, Cirencester, Gloucestershire. 6 (Berkshire) 15,569; 10 (Gloucestershire) 35,778; 9 (Wiltshire) 31,961; TOTAL 25 : 83,308
TRIPP, C. H. 1 (Kent) 1,651
TROTTER, George, Tunstall, Durham. 3 (Durham) 3,510
TROY, Edmund. *See* Thomas Ward
TRUMPER, Henry, Swinton, Masham, Yorkshire. 7 (Yorkshire, North Riding) 13,690
TRUMPER, James, Southall, Middlesex. 1 (Middlesex) 626
TRUMPER, William, Dorney, Berkshire. 1 (Berkshire) 347
TRUSLOVE, Joseph. 1 (Warwickshire) 4,846
TUCKER, John Millard, Bristol, Gloucestershire. 1 (Gloucestershire) 1,287; 9 (Somerset) 16,307; TOTAL 10 : 17,594
TUCKER, John Thomas, Totnes / Bridgetown, Devon. 3 (Devon) 7,919
TUKE, William, Bradford, Yorkshire. 1 (Yorkshire, West Riding) 3,972
TUKE, William and P. R. Allanson, York. 1 (York City & Ainsty) 1,523; 2 (Yorkshire, East Riding) 1,759; 5 (Yorkshire, North Riding) 2,310; TOTAL 8 : 5,592
TUNSTALL and Hine, 10 Allen Terrace, Kensington, Middlesex. 1 (Suffolk) 4,348; 1 (Sussex) 2,236; TOTAL 2 : 6,584
TURNBALL, Thomas, Knaresborough, Yorkshire. 1 (Yorkshire, North Riding) 147
TURNER, F. L. 1 (Cornwall) 8,997
TURNER, John junior, Durham. 13 (Durham) 31,180
TURNER, Miles, Lyth, Westmorland. 9 (Westmorland) 10,672
TURNER, M. and J. Turner, Lyth, Westmorland. 1 (Cumberland) 2,743. *See also* John Watson
TWEEN, Joseph, Knebworth, Hertfordshire. 1 (Buckinghamshire) 2,665
TYERMAN, Thomas, 14 Parliament St, Westminster, Middlesex. *See* Moses Adams (Middlesex, 1)

TYRES, James, Thrussington, Leicestershire. 2 (Leicestershire) 791

UNDERWOOD, F., Witney, Oxfordshire. 3 (Oxfordshire) 5,882
UNDERWOOD, J., Witney, Oxfordshire. 1 (Oxfordshire) 189
UNWIN, George. 10 (Derbyshire) 39,087
UPTON, William, Raithby, Lincolnshire. 4 (Lincolnshire) 5,742
UTTING, F. J., Wisbech, Cambridgeshire. 1 (Cambridgeshire) 4,792; 1 (Norfolk) 4,656; TOTAL 2 : 9,448
UTTING, James, Kings Lynn, Norfolk. 19 (Norfolk) 40,612. *See also* Edwin Durrant

VALPRY, N. L., Chelmsford, Essex. 1 (Essex) 56
VAUGHAN, D. *See* Bland Hood Galland
VERNON, Robert, Copthall, Banstead, Surrey. 1 (Surrey) 2,592
VERNON, William, Willington, Cheshire. 1 (Cheshire) 366
VICARS, Murray, Exeter, Devon. 3 (Cornwall) 25,060
VINE, William Charles, Lambeth, Surrey. 1 (Berkshire) 10. *See also* Henry W. Bushell
VINES, Uriah Bryant, Newbury, Berkshire. 2 (Berkshire) 7,956

WADMAN, William, Martock, Somerset. 14 (Somerset) 26,734
WAINWRIGHT, Charles, Shepton Mallet, Somerset. 7 (Somerset) 11,063
WAINWRIGHT, Thomas, Manchester, Lancashire. 1 (Cheshire) 5,139; 1 (Lancashire) 1,546; TOTAL 2 : 6,685
WAITE, Haxey, Lincolnshire. 1 (Lincolnshire) 1,812
WAKEMAN, Thomas, Robert Jackman, and Arthur Causton. 1 (Gloucestershire) 1,205
WALKER. *See* John Theophilus Lewis
WALKER, C., Swinford, Northamptonshire. 1 (Northamptonshire) 974
WALKER, J., Maidstone, Kent. 1 (Kent) 947
WALKER, John, Birmingham, Warwickshire. 1 (Warwickshire) 3,424; 4 (Worcestershire) 23,962; TOTAL 5 : 27,386
WALKER, R. H. 2 (Staffordshire) 12,114
WALKER, Wylam. 1 (Northumberland) 4,776
WALKER and Goodacre, Leicester. 4 (Leicestershire) 1,048
WALL, George Young, Durham. 9 (Durham) 16,727
WALLACE, Alfred R., Neath, Glamorganshire. 1 (Glamorganshire) 1,266
WALLACE, W. G. 1 (Bedfordshire) 1,288
WALTER, Henry, Windsor, Berkshire. 3 (Berkshire) 8,080; 2 (Buckinghamshire) 1,437; 4 (Surrey) 13,338; 5 (Sussex) 19,447; TOTAL 14 : 42,302
WALTER, Henry, Windsor, Berkshire, and J. Plumer, Horsham, Sussex. 1 (Sussex) 770
WANKLYN, Phillip Endell, Monmouth. 2 (Monmouthshire) 3,882
WARBURTON, Richard, Flixton, Lancashire. 1 (Lancashire) 974
WARD, Dickinson, Tutbury, Staffordshire. 1 (Derbyshire) 1,688
WARD, Thomas, Bristol, Gloucestershire. 2 (Gloucestershire) 4,188; 3 (Somerset) 6,382; TOTAL 5 : 11,570
WARD, Thomas, Bristol, Gloucestershire and Edmund Troy, Tytherton, Chippenham, Wiltshire. 1 (Gloucestershire) 2,315
WARE, W. J., Skirpenbeck, Yorkshire. 4 (Durham) 9,121; 1 (York City & Ainsty) 99; 5 (Yorkshire, East Riding) 6,932; 3 (Yorkshire, North Riding) 4,801; TOTAL 13 : 20,953
WARMINGTON, Augustus Henry, Honition, Devon. 1 (Devon) 1,747
WARREN, J. F. H., Langport, Somerset. 2 (Somerset) 2,337
WARREN, Michael, Winchester St, Pimlico, London. 1 (Kent) 20
WARREN, M. and W. T. *See* Luckraft, M. Warren, W. Reaney and W.T. Warren
WARREN, William Thomas, Isleworth, Middlesex. 1 (Middlesex) 179
WASHBOURNE and Keen, 8 Cannon Row, Westminster, Middlesex. 1 (Berkshire) 326; 1 (Essex) 6,659; 2 (Northamptonshire) 193; 1 (Oxfordshire) 281; 1 (Surrey) 3,420; 1 (Warwickshire) 1,329; 1 (Wiltshire) 829; TOTAL 8 : 13,037
WATERS, John, Salisbury, Wiltshire. 1 (Hampshire) 61; 1 (Wiltshire) 823; TOTAL 2 : 884. *See also* Charles Sharp
WATERS, J. and R., Cranbury Place, Southampton, Hampshire. 1 (Wiltshire) 5,891
WATERS, Thomas S., Stratford sub Castle, Wiltshire. 1 (Wiltshire) 1,337
WATFORD, Alexander, Cambridge. 8 (Cambridgeshire) 25,823
WATSON, J., Preston, Lancashire. *See* Allen and Watson
WATSON, James, Rothbury, Northumberland. 13 (Northumberland) 32,420
WATSON, John junior, Kendal, Westmorland. 2 (Cumberland) 10,725; 10 (Lancashire) 17,860; 4 (Westmorland) 12,972; 3 (Yorkshire, West Riding) 25,411; TOTAL 19 : 56,968. *See also* Hodgson and Watson, Watson and Hoggarth *and* Watson and Turner
WATSON, John, Kendal, and Hoggarth, Kendal, Westmorland. 2 (Cumberland) 7,439
WATSON, John, Kendal, and M. and J. Turner, Lyth, Westmorland. 1 (Lancashire) 2,085; 4 (Westmorland) 14,422; 2 (Yorkshire, West Riding) 14,212; TOTAL 7 : 20,719. See also Hodgson and Watson
WATSON, R. H., Bolton Park, Cumberland. 1 (Cumberland) 3,876
WATSON, W. 1 (Yorkshire, East Riding) 1,470
WATTS, Edward, Yeovil, Somerset. 1 (Devon) 2,068; 5 (Dorset) 7,168; 10 (Somerset) 14,375; TOTAL 16 : 23,611
WEATHERLEY, Nicholas, Newcastle upon Tyne, Northumberland. 3 (Northumberland) 26,787; 2 (Durham) 4,060; TOTAL 5 : 30,847
WEAVER, Chippenham, Wiltshire. *See* Richard Davis Little and Weaver
WEAVER, Henry, Southampton, Hampshire, (surveyor and engineer). 2 (Wiltshire) 6,213
WEAVER, Thomas, Bath, Somerset. 3 (Gloucestershire) 9,156; 3 (Somerset) 3,808; 1 (Wiltshire) 2,444; TOTAL 7 : 15,408
WEBB, F. P. *See* Harry Holloway
WEBB, Frederick, Cirencester, Gloucestershire. 1 (Wiltshire) 1,802
WEBB, James, Worcester. 1 (Devon) 5,583; 4 (Gloucestershire) 7,203; 12 (Herefordshire) 26,596; 1 (Oxfordshire) 1,770; 1 (Shropshire) 1,386; 28 (Worcestershire) 45,346; TOTAL 47 : 87,884.
WEBB, William. *See* Thomas Chapman
WEBSTER, John, 118 Osborne St, Hull, Yorkshire. 1 (Yorkshire, East Riding) 1,602
WEDDALL, John George, North Hall, Howden, Yorkshire. 1 (Staffordshire) 2,176; 13 (Yorkshire, East Riding) 14,732; 1 (Yorkshire, West Riding) 1,399; TOTAL 15 : 18,307
WEIGHTMAN, Robert, Torworth, Nottinghamshire. 6 (Nottinghamshire) 11,519; 2 (Yorkshire, West Riding) 3,020; TOTAL 8 : 14,539
WELCH, E. J., Whalley, Lancashire. 2 (Lancashire) 88
WELCH, Joseph. 1 (Flintshire) 2,037

WESTBURY, Giles. *See* Thomas Phillips
WHEATCROFT, John, Wirksworth, Derbyshire. 2 (Derbyshire) 2,264
WHITE. *See* Huddleston and White
WHITE, Messrs, and Dawson. 1 (Yorkshire, East Riding) 1,095
WHITE, Henry, Warrington, Lancashire. 28 (Cheshire) 38,465; 6 (Lancashire) 20,244; TOTAL 34 : 58,709
WHITE, Joseph, Mells, Somerset. 2 (Somerset) 2,315
WHITE and Reid. 1 (Monmouthshire) 4,194
WHITEHEAD, Arthur, Chard, Somerset. 4 (Somerset) 8,470
WHITEHEAD, William, Altrincham, Cheshire. 1 (Cheshire) 803
WHITFIELD, Thomas. 1 (Yorkshire, North Riding) 105
WHITLE, Joseph, Whalley, Preston, Lancashire. 1 (Lancashire) 3,677; 1 (Yorkshire, East Riding) 838; TOTAL 2 : 4,515
WHITLE, Joseph, Whalley, Preston, Lancashire and Dawson. 1 (Lancashire) 2,451
WHITLEY, Nicholas, Truro, Cornwall. 6 (Cornwall) 20,470
WHITTEN, William, Wellingborough, Northamptonshire. 2 (Northamptonshire) 288
WHITTET, Richard, Comberton, Cambridgeshire. 1 (Cambridgeshire) 4,066
WIDDICOMBE, John, Ugborough, Devon. 3 (Devon) 3,643
WIGGINS, John, 30 Tavistock Place, London. 1 (Devon) 6,733; 5 (Norfolk) 14,259; TOTAL 6 : 20,992
WILDING, John. 1 (Hertfordshire) 1,453
WILDS, W., Hertford. 2 (Hertfordshire) 1,526
WILKINSON, George, Hull, Yorkshire. 3 (Yorkshire, East Riding) 550
WILKINSON, Matthew, Rosegill and Anthony Wright, Raside, Westmorland. 2 (Westmorland) 1,107
WILLIAMS, (land and mineral surveyor). *See* William J. H. Williams
WILLIAMS, Charles and Richard Reed, Grampound, Cornwall. 4 (Cornwall) 14,475
WILLIAMS, G. P. 1 (Devon) 1,572
WILLIAMS, G. T. 1 (Oxfordshire) 227
WILLIAMS, Henry, 19 Romney Place, Maidstone, Kent. 1 (Kent) 1,420
WILLIAMS, Henry, Newport, Monmouthshire. 2 (Monmouthshire) 2,488
WILLIAMS, James Peachey, Bridgwater, Somerset. 1 (Gloucestershire) 6,217; 9 (Monmouthshire) 12,083; 12 (Somerset) 32,115; TOTAL 22 : 50,415. *See also* William Body
WILLIAMS, John, Bicester, Oxfordshire. 1 (Buckinghamshire) 2,522; 1 (Oxfordshire) 4,308; TOTAL 2 : 6,830
WILLIAMS, John. 1 (Glamorganshire) 431
WILLIAMS, J. T., Glog Pontypridd, Glamorganshire. 2 (Glamorganshire) 29,827
WILLIAMS, Robert. 1 (Carnarvonshire) 3,790
WILLIAMS, William, Swansea, Glamorganshire. 3 (Glamorganshire) 6,160
WILLIAMS, William, Ashford, Kent. 3 (Kent) 3,537
WILLIAMS, William J. H., Swansea, Glamorganshire. 2 (Breconshire) 24,637
WILLIAMSON, John, North Clifton, Nottinghamshire, (schoolmaster). *See* Jacob Squire
WILLIAMSON, S., Wigan, Lancashire. 1 (Lancashire) 2,522
WILLSHIRE, Raymond, Lambeth, Surrey. 4 (Surrey) 1,847
WILME, Benjamin Pickever, Bedford Row, London, and Herbert Mew, Canewdon, Essex. 1 (Essex) 6,310
WILMOT, Edward Woollett, Hulme Walfield, Astbury, Cheshire. 5 (Cheshire) 6,548; 1 (Derbyshire) 1,281; 1 (Lancashire) 170; TOTAL 7 : 7,999
WILSON, W. H., Pilsley, Derbyshire. 2 (Derbyshire) 2,846
WISDOM, Thomas, South Berstead, Sussex. 2 (Sussex) 2,924. *See also* H. and F. Hitchins
WISE, Robert, Malton, Yorkshire. 6 (Yorkshire, East Riding) 13,307; 11 (Yorkshire, North Riding) 18,868; TOTAL 17 : 32,175
WITHERS. *See* John Machell and Withers
WITHERS, Alexander. 1 (Cornwall) 2,458
WITTY, J. 1 (Bedfordshire) 1,021
WITTY, Joseph. 1 (Buckinghamshire) 6,251; 1 (Surrey) 2,082; TOTAL 2 : 9,354
WOLFENDEN, George, Kirkby Lonsdale, Westmorland. 4 (Lancashire) 7,421
WOLFENDEN, J. W., Kirkby Lonsdale, Westmorland. 1 (Westmorland) 3,099
WOOD. *See* William Roberts ((Yorkshire, West Riding), 1)
WOOD, Henry, Brown Lodge, Rochdale, Lancashire. 1 (Lancashire) 2,978
WOOD, Henry Moses, Nottingham. 2 (Lincolnshire) 4,877; 1 (Nottinghamshire) 600; TOTAL 3 : 5,477
WOOD, James, Liverpool, Lancashire. 1 (Lancashire) 1,259
WOOD, John. 1 (Lincolnshire) 1,342
WOOD, John, Lindfield, Sussex. 3 (Sussex) 9,643
WOOD, William Bryan, Barnbridge, Chippenham, Wiltshire. 4 (Berkshire) 20,266; 3 (Gloucestershire) 13,415; 7 (Monmouth-shire) 12,357; 2 (Oxfordshire) 1,011; 5 (Wiltshire) 8,637; TOTAL 21 : 55,686
WOODLAND, W., Ramsgate, Kent. 1 (Kent) 541
WOODMASS, J., Woodmass Thompson & Co., and others, Ivybridge, Devon. 15 (Cornwall) 61,796; 19 (Devon) 68,176; 2 (Dorset) 5,183; TOTAL 36 : 135,155
WOODMASS, J. 1 (Somerset) 1,619
WOODMASS, Thomas, Alston, Cumberland. 6 (Cumberland) 6,394
WOODMASS, Thomas, Alston, Cumberland, and John Huddleston. 1 (Cumberland) 7,313
WOODROW. *See* Newton and Woodrow
WOODS, James, Liverpool, Lancashire. 4 (Lancashire) 4,683
WORDSWORTH, William, Black Gates, Yorkshire. 28 (Yorkshire, West Riding) 42,298
WORRALL, William, Chester. 17 (Cheshire) 12,725
WRIGHT. *See* Richard Smirke Martyr
WRIGHT, Anthony, Raside, Westmorland. *See* Matthew Wilkinson
WRIGHT, Henry Cornelius, Tavistock St, London. 2 (Hampshire) 6,829
WRIGHT, James, Aylsham, Norfolk / Brixton Road, London. 57 (Norfolk) 79,592; 1 (Suffolk) 979; TOTAL 58 : 80,571
WRIGHT, J., Norwich, Norfolk. 1 (Norfolk) 604
WRIGHT, Jno. 1 (Yorkshire, North Riding) 2,011
WRIGHT, John. 1 (Suffolk) 862
WRIGHT, John, Foulsham, Norfolk. 3 (Norfolk) 5,523
WRIGHT, R., 54 Great Ormond St, London. 1 (Sussex) 770

WRIGHT, Robert junior, Norwich, Norfolk. 1 (Huntingdonshire) 1,553
WRIGHT, R. J., Norwich, Norfolk. 1 (Cambridgeshire) 25,856; 1 (Dorset) 593; TOTAL 2 : 26,449
WRIGHT, Thomas, Tiverton, Devon. *See* Charles Bailey *and* John Drew
WRIGHT, W. H. 2 (Lincolnshire) 4,769; 1 (Nottinghamshire) 2,011; TOTAL 3 : 6,780
WYATT, R. and V. H. Wyatt. 1 (Cambridgeshire) 2,528
WYLEY, James, High Onn, Staffordshire. 2 (Staffordshire) 6,712

YATES, Richard, Whittington, Shropshire. 1 (Denbighshire) 4,801; 1 (Shropshire) 795; TOTAL 2 : 5,596
YELLS, T., Bengeworth. 1 (Gloucestershire) 274; 2 (Worcestershire) 1,767; TOTAL 3 : 2,041
YORK, William, Compton Martin, Somerset. 3 (Somerset) 5,908
YOUNG, Frederic, Bicester, Oxfordshire. 1 (Oxfordshire) 2,323
YOUNG, John, Liverpool, Lancashire. 6 (Lancashire) 23,968
YOUNG, Thomas, Humshaugh, Hexham, Northumberland. 2 (Lancashire) 1,906; 2 (Yorkshire, West Riding) 2,124; TOTAL 4 : 4,030
YOUNG, W. H., Mildenhall, Suffolk. 3 (Suffolk) 14,467

Appendix 4

Map-makers who made twenty-five or more tithe maps in England and Wales

Map-maker	*No*	*Acreage*
Harry Goode and Henry Philpott, Haverfordwest, Pembrokeshire	136	343,067
Thomas Bell and Sons, Newcastle upon Tyne, Northumberland	105	234,268
Robert Pratt and Son, Norwich, Norfolk	66	126,087
John R. Haslam, Menai Bridge, Anglesey	65	141,911
Lenny and Croft, Bury St Edmunds, Suffolk	62	183,712
Thomas Thurston, Ashford, Kent	61	166,111
Thomas Bradley and Sons, Richmond, Yorkshire	61	155,352
James Wright, Aylsham, Norfolk	58	80,571
Newton and Woodrow, Norwich, Norfolk	53	97,737
Messrs Crawter, London, Cobham, Surrey, and Cheshunt, Herts	49	137,616
Frederick and Henry Edwin Drayson, Faversham, Kent	49	134,431
James Webb, Worcester	47	87,884
Morris and William Sayce, Kington, Herefordshire	45	173,997
James Poole, Sherborne, Dorset	45	104,198
Alexander Doull, Chatham, Kent	43	115,092
Thomas Phillips and Giles Westbury, Andover, Hampshire	41	105,404
Edward Page, Beverley, Yorkshire	41	66,309
George Gilbert and Thomas Tayspill, Colchester, Essex	40	73,630
James Cawley and others, Macclesfield, Cheshire	39	102,673
William Fosbrooke, Hereford	39	95,429
Thomas Morris, Newport, Monmouthshire	38	84,631
Richard Hall, Cirencester, Gloucestershire	37	57,215
William Jones, Bellevue, Brecon	36	214,532
Woodmass partnership, Ivybridge, Devon	36	135,155
Ordnance Survey	35	85,673
William Figg, Lewes, Sussex	35	79,541
Thomas Dixon, Darlington, Durham	35	59,099
John Bromley, Derby	35	44,738
Richard C. Gale, Winchester, Hampshire	34	150,621
Samuel H. Ashdown, Uppington, Shropshire	34	66,444
Little and Weaver, Chippenham, Wiltshire	34	65,552
Henry White, Warrington, Lancashire	34	58,709
John Davies, Mollington, Cheshire	34	41,099
Joseph Bennett Hankin Bennett, Tutbury, Staffordshire	34	39,644
Richard Chambers Herbert, Worcester	33	57,529
Henry Scott, Oulston, Yorkshire	33	56,322
John King and Son, Saffron Walden, Essex	32	71,862
Charles Mickleburgh, Montgomery	31	134,799
I. Coulson	31	126,549

Map-maker	*No*	*Acreage*
W. G. Bircham, Fakenham, Norfolk	31	57,950
Edward Bowman, Newcastle upon Tyne, Northumberland	31	54,162
William Simpson, Pinchingthorpe, Guisborough, Yorkshire	31	34,312
Thomas Buxton, Malton, Yorkshire	30	75,612
William Price, Ross, Herefordshire	29	62,850
Henry and Robert Badcock, Launceston, Cornwall	28	97,001
John Martin, Evershot, Dorset	28	61,943
Joseph Manning, Norwich, Norfolk	28	49,332
William Wordsworth, Black Gates, Yorkshire	28	42,298
Richard Barnes, Lowestoft, Suffolk	28	41,989
Thomas White Collard, Canterbury, Kent	27	59,253
George Braund and Henry Hearn, Exeter, Devon	26	82,089
Daniel Trinder, Cirencester, Gloucestershire	25	83,308
Richard Birks, Barnsley, Yorkshire	25	38,237

Place-name index

Most tithe districts are either parishes (in southern England and Wales) or townships (in northern England) and are easily identified as their place-names have not changed since the compilation of the tithe surveys. A first objective of this Place-name index is to assist with the identification of that minority of tithe districts the names of which have changed. Entries in upright typeface are the modern forms of changed names as recorded in the *Ordnance Survey gazetteer of Great Britain: all names from the 1:50,000 Landranger map series* (3rd edition, Southampton and London, Ordnance Survey and Macmillan, 1992). These modern names are followed by the respective Public Record Office Class IR29 and IR30 tithe district reference number in the form 'county number'/'district number' as used in our county-by-county tithe survey catalogue.

A further difficulty in determining whether a tithe survey is extant for a particular place is occasioned by the Tithe Commissioners' practice of sometimes combining two or more townships or parishes to constitute a single tithe district. Both the Public Record Office class lists and our own catalogue follow the original Tithe Commission lists and arrange tithe districts in general alphabetic order within counties by the *first* element of such multiple place-names. A second objective of this Place-name index is to list in strict alphabetic order the second and subsequent elements of compound names; these are presented in *italic typeface* followed by the index number of the tithe district of which each is a part.

Abbess Roding, 12/2
The Abbey Demesnes, 13/190
Abbots Bickington, 9/1
Abbots Ripton, 16/1
Abbot's Salford, 36/1
Abbotstone, 31/146
Abenhall, 13/1
Aberarth, 46/33
Abererch, 48/3
Abergwesyn, 45/35
Abergwli, 47/1
Abergwyngregyn, 48/1
Aberwheeler, 49/3
Aberyscir, 45/2
Abinger Hammer, 34/1
Aby, 20/34
Acaster Selby, 40/1
Acklam, 42/3
Acton Pigott, 29/3
Acton Trussell, 32/2
Adbolton, 26/60
Adel, 43/4
Admaston, 29/193
Adney, 29/120
Adwick le Street, 43/6
Agden, 5/2
Aiket Gate, 7/7
Aikton, 7/2
Ailby, 20/4
Ailesworth, 24/28
Ailiston, 30/6

Aisholt, 30/12
Alcumlow, 5/274
Aldborough, 23/2
Aldbourne, 38/1
Aldbrough St John, 42/7
Aldby, 42/64
Aldeburgh, 33/3
Alderley Edge, 5/7
Aldershot, 31/2
Aldershott, 10/3
All Cannings, 38/4
All Saints, Kings Lynn, 23/357
All Saints South Elmham, 33/364
Allendale Town, 25/8
Allerthorpe, 42/360
Allexton, 19/1
Allington, 33/15
Alltyymbyd, 49/41
Alpington, 23/669
Alscott, 29/193
Alsop en le Dale, 8/7
Altarnun, 6/4
Alton, 8/120
Alveton, 32/6
Alwington, 9/9

Alwinton, 25/9
Amaston, 29/273
Amble-by-the-Sea, 25/15
Amblecote, 32/7
Ansford, 30/5
Ansty, 36/6
Anthony, 6/7
Antingham, 23/9
Antingham St Margaret, 23/9
Appleton-le-Moors, 42/16
Appleton-le-Street, 42/17
Appleton Park, 5/17
Appleton Roebuck, 40/2
Appleton Wiske, 42/18
Apuldram, 35/10
Arbury, 18/172
Ardda, 48/22
Ardeley, 15/117
Ardingly, 35/11
Areley Kings, 39/9
Argoed, 29/182
Armathwaite, 7/7
Armeringhall, 23/11
Arnford, 43/207
Arnold, 41/170
Arrowe Hill, 5/19
Ascot, 27/95
Ascott-under-Wychwood, 27/6
Ash, 17/11
Ashansworth, 31/13
Ashby-de-la-Zouch, 19/6
Ashby Parva, 19/4
Ashby St Mary, 23/12
Ashe, 11/97
Ashendon, 3/3
Ashton, 14/80, 18/195
Aspenden, 15/10
Assenden, 27/113
Astbury, 5/287
Asterley, 29/254
Aston, 5/27, 36/10
Aston juxta Mondrum, 5/24
Aston le Walls, 24/6
Aston Subedge, 13/10
Atherstone on Stour, 36/11
Attleborough, 23/20
Atwick, 41/6
Aughton, 43/19
Aulston, 30/6
Awbery Street, 2/130
Aycliffe, 11/6
Aylburton, 13/127
Aylesby, 20/2
Aymestrey, 14/11
Aynho, 24/7
Ayot St Peter, 15/13

Bache, 49/70
Bagber, 10/212
Bagginswood, 29/329
Bagnall, 32/43
Bagot's Bromley, 32/15
Bagthorpe, 23/26
Bailey, 18/3
Bainton, 27/13
Balsall, 36/73
Bamburgh Field, 20/107
Bangor-is-y-coed, 50/1
Bangor Teifi, 46/2
Barden, 42/162
Bare, 18/251
Bargham, 35/122
Barlavington, 35/19
Barnby, 42/47
Barnshaw, 5/178
Barnwell, 4/13
Barrog, 49/93
Barrow Gurney, 30/25
Barton, 37/9
Barton Bendish, 23/48
Barton in the Beans, 19/104
Barton-le-Street, 42/34
Barton-le-Willows, 42/96
Barton-on-the-Heath, 36/18
Barton-under-Needwood, 32/18
Bassaleg, 22/4
Bassingfield, 26/60
Bastwick, 23/443
Baswich, 32/21
Batheaston, 30/33
Baulking, 2/13
Baxby, 42/374
Baxterley, 36/19
Bayford, 30/155
Baylham, 33/30
Beachamwell, 23/47, 23/48
Beachamwell St John, 23/48
Beadlam, 42/167
Beaghall, 43/36
Bearse Common, 13/31
Beau Manor, 19/164
Beauchamp Roding, 12/24
Beauworth, 31/19
Beckering, 20/176
Beckermet, 7/9, 7/10
Bedburn, 11/12
Bedingfield, 33/35
Bedingham Green, 23/51
Bednall, 32/2
Beech Hill, 31/241
Beer, 9/359
Beer Hackett, 10/14
Beere, 30/232
Beesby, 20/171
Beeston, 23/52
Begbroke, 27/14
Bekesbourne, 17/21
Belchamp St Paul, 12/27
Belton, 20/35
Benhadlen, 49/41
Benhall Green, 33/39
Benington, 15/20
Benningworth, 20/37
Benson, 27/15
Benthall, 29/8
Bere Ferrers, 9/31
Berkamsted, 15/22
Berkswell, 36/22
Berners Roding, 12/35
Berringtonlaw, 11/15
Berwick-upon-Tweed, 25/44
Beswick, 18/211
Bethnal Green, 21/40
Betteshanger, 17/26
Bettws, 55/2
Bettws Bledrws, 46/3
Bettws Caederven, 53/6
Bettws Cedewain, 53/6
Bettws Clirow, 55/9
Betws, 47/3, 51/7
Betws Garmon, 48/6
Betws Ifan, 46/4
Betws-y-Coed, 48/7
Betwys-yn-rhos, 49/9
Bevercotes, 26/10
Beverston, 13/23
Bevill's Wood, 16/3
Bewick, 41/2
Bickerstone, 23/33
Bickley, 5/106
Biddick Waterville, 11/16
Biddlestone, 25/48
Biddlestone St Nicholas, 38/23
Bidford-on-Avon, 36/24
Bierley, 43/42
Biggen, 36/105
Bilbrook, 32/24
Bildeston, 33/43
Billinge, 18/30, 18/31
Billingford, 23/424
Billy Row, 11/71
Bilsborrow, 18/32
Bilsdale, 42/167
Binstead, 31/25, 35/32
Bintree, 23/67
Binweston, 29/38
Birch, 12/36
Birch, 29/29
Bircholt Forstal, 17/33
Birkenhead, 18/103
Birtley, 25/53, 25/54
Bishopsbourne, 17/35
Bishop's Castle, 29/39
Bishop's Cleeve, 13/24
Bishops Frome, 14/18
Bishop's Hull, 30/47
Bishop's Itchington, 36/30
Bishop's Nympton, 9/41
Bishop's Stortford, 15/24
Bishop's Sutton, 31/27
Bishop's Tachbrook, 36/31
Bishop's Tawton, 9/42
Bishopston, 51/8

Bishopstone, 35/34
Bishop's Waltham, 31/28
Bispham Green, 18/35
Bittering, 23/71
Black Bourton, 27/26
Blackrake, 42/20
Black Torrington, 9/47
Blakemere, 14/20
Blean, 17/93
Bletchingdon, 27/19
Bletherston, 54/6
Blo' Norton, 23/74
Blunsdon St Andrew, 38/30
Bobington, 32/31
Bodanwydog, 49/11
Bodelwyddan, 50/5
Bodeugan, 50/9
Bodfari, 50/3
Bodfuan, 48/9
Bodlith, 49/99
Bodrychwin, 49/40
Boduan, 48/8
Bold Heath, 18/39
Bolney, 27/70
Bolstone, 14/22
Boltham, 20/47
Bolton-by-Bowland, 43/54
Bolton-le-Sands, 18/40
Bondgate, 43/7
Bondgate in Auckland, 11/20
Bondsmans Mead, 27/38
Boningale, 29/43
Bonsdale, 20/119
Bonvilston, 51/10
Booley, 29/149
Boreatton, 29/29
Bosherston, 54/121
Bostock Green, 5/62
Botolphs, 35/51
Botton, 18/349
Botusfleming, 6/13
Botwnnog, 48/10
Botwyle, 29/65
Boughton Street, 17/41
Bournes, 18/103
Bournmoor, 11/28
Bourton, 38/25
Bourton Meadow, 27/26
Bourton-on-the-Water, 13/28
Bovey Tracy, 9/50
Bow, 21/6
Bowerchalke, 38/32
Bowness-on-Solway, 7/25
Boycott, 29/254
Brackley, 24/16
Bradenham, 23/80, 23/81
Bradford-on-Avon, 38/36
Bradford-on-Tone, 30/53
Bradley, 19/73, 29/125, 39/127, 42/21
Bradley Green, 5/65, 39/127
Bradley in the Moors, 32/43
Bradwall Green, 5/66
Bradwell, 12/48
Bradwell-on-Sea, 12/47
Bramhall, 5/67
Brampton Bryan, 14/25
Brandesburton, 41/29
Brandiston, 23/87
Bransdale East Side, 42/131
Bratton, 29/193
Braunston, 24/18
Brawith, 42/216
Breckonrigge, 42/21
Bredenbury, 14/28
Brent Knoll, 30/59
Brentford, 21/7
Brentingby, 19/166
Brereton Green, 5/69
Bretford, 36/34
Brickendon, 15/6
Bridge Hewick, 43/70
Bridgerule, 9/66
Brierton, 11/33
Brightwalton, 2/24
Brigmerston, 38/197
Brimington, 8/54
Brimpsfield, 13/32
Brithdir, 53/23
Britwell Priory, 27/21
Broadclyst, 9/69
Broad Hinton, 38/46
Broadnymett, 9/72
Broadtown, 38/46
Broadwey, 10/28
Brockford, 33/453
Brockhampton, 13/24
Brockley Green, 33/72
Brockton, 29/297
Brockwear Common, 13/31
Brocton, 32/38
Brokenborough, 38/60
Bromborough, 5/75
Bromley, 21/8
Bromley Hurst, 32/1
Broniarth, 53/8
Bronington, 50/6
Brook, 17/53, 31/45
Brooke, 28/5
Brooksby, 19/23
Brookthorpe, 13/33
Broome, 29/12
Broome, 32/41
Broomfleet, 41/44
Broomhall Green, 5/76
Broomridge, 25/279
Broughton, 3/9
Brownside, 8/56
Broxa, 42/156
Broxbourne, 15/28
Brumby, 20/58
Brympton D'Everey, 30/71
Bryngwyn, 22/12
Brynpolyn, 50/37
Bryntangor, 49/11
Buckland in the Moor, 9/82
Buckland-tout-Saints, 9/83
Buckwood Stubs, 1/10
Budbrooke, 36/37
Bugbrooke, 24/24
Bugsworth, 8/56
Builth Wells, 45/10
Bulkeley, 5/106
Bullinghope, 14/38
Bullock's Hall, 25/83
Bulphan, 12/58
Bulthy, 29/59
Buncton, 35/15
Burcott, 29/193
Bures, 33/81
Burgedin, 53/75
Burgh on Bain, 20/62
Burgh St Margaret, 23/107
Burgh St Margaret, 23/107
Burgh St Mary, 23/107
Burleston, 10/34
Burley, 43/203
Burley in Wharfedale, 43/77
Burnham-on-Crouch, 12/61
Burnham-on-Sea, 30/76
Burnham Overy Town, 23/114
Burnsall, 43/79
Burrough, 19/27
Burston, 32/13
Burstwick, 41/166
Burton, 20/66
Burton-in-Kendal, 37/20
Burton Lazaars, 19/56
Burton Lazars, 19/28
Burwardsley, 5/87
Bury St Edmunds, 33/86
Bushby, 19/149
Butley Town, 5/88
Butterbush, 43/104
Buttery, 29/120
Button Oak, 29/180
Bynoll, 38/46
Byram-cum-Sutton, 43/82
Byshottles, 11/32
Bywell, 25/91, 25/92

Cadeby, 20/380
Cadoxton, 51/14
Caerau, 51/17
Caergybi, 44/11
Caerleon, 22/49
Caio, 47/10
Caister-on-Sea, 23/121
Caistor St Edmund, 23/122
Calceby, 20/246
Calcot, 29/36
Caldecote, 15/32, 16/9
Caldicot, 22/14

Caldwell, 8/51
Callaly, 25/95
Callaughton, 29/45
Callingwood, 32/206
Calloes, 38/154
Calludon, 36/57
Calvington, 29/120
Camberwell, 34/21
Cambois, 11/41
Canford Magna, 10/37, 10/38
Cann, 10/186
Canon Pyon, 14/46
Cantref, 45/11
Capel Bettes Lleucu, 46/5
Capel-le-Ferne, 17/70
Capel St Mary, 33/91
Cardeston, 29/66
Cardigan, 46/9
Cardinham, 6/26
Carleton, 43/85
Carleton St Peter, 23/127·
Carleton St Peter, 23/129
Carlton, 41/2, 42/167
Carlton, 42/72
Carlton Colville, 33/93, 33/94
Carlton-le-Moorland, 20/80
Carlton Scroop, 20/82
Carnguwch, 48/13
Carperby, 42/73
Carvan, 46/66
Castellan, 54/106
Castle Acre, 23/130
Castle Caerinion, 53/10
Castle Pulverbatch, 29/80
Catherston Leweston, 10/40
Cattall, 43/228
Catto, 42/217
Cawood, 18/17
Caynham, 29/63
Caynton, 29/120
Cefn Pawl, 55/15
Cemmaes, 53/12
Cenarth, 47/17
Cerigydrudion, 49/20
Chadwell St Mary, 12/70
Chaighley, 18/3
Chalvey, 3/112
Chapel Chorlton, 32/58
Chappel, 12/71
Chapple, 12/71
Charlton Mackrell, 30/97
Charlton Musgrove, 30/99
Charlton-on-Otmoor, 27/31
Charney, 2/87
Charney Meadow, 27/26
Chawleigh, 9/100
Chedburgh, 33/98
Cheddington, 3/39
Chedington, 10/51
Chelsham, 34/127
Chelson, 9/104
Chelsworth, 33/100
Chelworth Lower Green, 38/39
Chelworth Upper Green, 38/39
Cheriton, 54/122
Cherrington, 29/317
Cherry Burton, 41/36
Chester-le-Street, 11/45
Chesterton Parva, 36/86
Chignall St James, 12/75
Chignall Smealy, 12/76
Child's Ercall, 29/76
Chiltington, 35/289
Chilton Polden, 30/113
Chilworth, 27/95
Chineham, 31/180
Chipping Barnet, 15/17
Chipping Campden, 13/38
Chisfield, 15/46
Chislehurst, 17/87
Chisworth Chunall, 8/53
Chitterne, 38/68, 38/69
Cholderton, 38/72
Chorlton-cum-Hardy, 18/73
Christchurch Twynham, 31/64
Church Brough, 37/16
Church Hougham, 17/188
Church Leigh, 32/138
Church Somershall, 8/191
Church Stoke, 53/13
Church Stowe, 24/116
Churchtown, 18/190
Churton on the Heath, 5/119
Chute Standen, 38/74
Chwelieriog, 49/41
Cilcain, 50/8
Cilcochwyn, 49/26
Cilgerran, 54/49
Ciliau Aeron, 46/13
Cilin, 49/40
Cilybebyll, 51/40
Clapton, 4/23
Clapton-in-Gordano, 30/123
Clapton on the Hill, 13/28
Clare, 27/113
Claxby, 20/87
Claxby, 20/360
Clay Cross, 8/59
Clayton-le-Woods, 18/77
Clee Downton, 29/84
Clee St Margaret, 29/83
Cleestanton, 29/84
Cleobury Mortimer, 29/131
Cletterwood, 53/25
Cleverton, 38/169
Clewer Green, 2/38
Clifton, 43/296
Clifton upon Dunsmore, 36/48
Clifton upon Teme, 39/33
Clopton, 24/32
Clopton Green, 33/107
Close House, 25/266
Closworth, 30/129
Clotton, 5/124
Clowne, 8/61
Cluddley, 29/193
Clynnog Fawr, 48/15
Clyro, 55/9
Clyst Honiton, 9/118
Clyst Hydon, 9/119
Clyst St George, 9/120
Coate, 27/7
Coates, 13/190
Coathill, 7/56
Coatsay Moor, 11/53
Coberley, 13/62
Cockerington St Leonard, 20/98
Cockerton, 11/76
Cockley Cley, 23/141
Codrington, 13/211
Cogan, 51/58
Coggeshall, 12/84
Coggeshall Hamlet, 12/85
Cold Hatton, 29/316
Cold Hiendley, 43/106
Coldmeece, 32/70
Coldwell, 25/118
Colebatch, 29/91
Colebrooke, 9/128
Colepike Hall, 11/57
Colesbourne, 13/53
Collingbourne Ducis, 38/83
Collingbourne Kingston, 38/84
Colston Bassett, 26/35
Colthrop, 2/130
Colwinston, 51/23
Combe Florey, 30/133
Combe Hay, 30/134
Combeinteignhead, 9/130
Combe Martin, 9/132
Comberbach, 5/128
Comberton, 39/72
Combhill, 25/234
Comley, 29/65
Compton, 9/134
Compton Chamberlayne, 38/87
Compton Valence, 10/69
Compton Wynyates, 36/50
Coney Weston, 33/25
Conington, 16/13
Conoch, 38/62
Coppenhall, 5/115
Coppull, 18/83
Coppycrooks, 11/130
Copston Magna, 36/51
Corby Glen, 20/102
Cornhill-on-Tweed, 11/63
Cornival, 49/93
Corringham, 20/103
Cossall, 26/136
Coston, 29/88
Coston Hackett, 39/34
Cothercott, 29/349

Cotherstone, 42/89
Coton, 32/109
Coton Hill, 29/97
Cottesbach, 19/40
Cottisford, 27/39
Cotton, 18/195
Cotton Abbotts, 5/132
Cotwall, 29/123
Coulton, 42/84
Coverhead, 42/20
Cowick, 43/365
Crai, 45/13
Crakenhall, 42/121
Cranleigh, 34/40
Cranmore, 30/148
Cranwich, 23/153
Craswall, 14/56
Creeting All Saints, 33/123
Creeting St Olaves, 33/123
Creigbyther, 55/45
Creigiog-isaf, 49/25
Creigiog Uwchglan, 49/41
Crewe Green, 5/135
Criccieth, 48/17
Cricklade, 38/92
Crixeth, 12/102
Croeslwybr, 53/58
Croft, 18/290, 19/24
Croft-on-Tees, 42/98
Crogen Wladis, 49/26
Crookdene, 25/138
Crookham, 2/130
Cropper, 8/209
Crosby-on-Eden, 7/51
Crosscanonby, 7/52
Crostwick, 23/163
Croxton, 23/226
Cruckmeole, 29/16
Cruckton, 29/254
Crudgington, 29/316
Cubley Common, 8/68
Cuerdley Cross, 18/93
Culgaith, 7/17
Cumberford Coton, 32/233
Cunscough, 18/216
Curridge, 2/43
Curry Rivel, 30/161
Cutsdean, 39/39
Cwm, 53/60
Cwmcarvan, 22/20
Cwmcothy, 47/71
Cwmtwrch, 47/71
Cyffylliog, 49/48
Cyfronydd, 53/14
Cyler, 49/40
Cymmo Dupart, 49/85
Cymmo Tryan, 49/85
Cynant, 49/40
Cynllyfnog, 53/60
Cynwyl Elfed, 47/11
Cynynion, 29/199
Cysltle, 49/70

Dalbury Lees, 8/70
Dalderby, 20/285
Dalton-in-Furness, 18/97
Dalton-on-Tees, 42/106
Damerham, 38/94
Darley Dale, 8/71
Darmsden, 33/21
Darnall, 43/20
Davidstow, 6/41
Dawley Bank, 29/105
Daywell, 29/344
Deenethorpe, 24/43
Delves, 36/72
Denaby Main, 43/128
Denio, 48/18
Denston, 33/133
Deptford, 17/111
Derrythorpe, 20/7
Dersingham, 23/166
Derwen, 49/29
Detling, 17/108
Dexthorpe, 20/360
Diddington, 36/73
Diebach, 49/93
Dihewyd, 46/15
Dillington, 23/170
Dinting, 8/53
Dinton, 3/35
Ditchling, 35/80
Ditteridge, 38/99
Ditton, 29/108
Dodbrooke, 9/154
Doddenham, 39/43
Dolanog, 53/17
Dolganner, 49/40
Dolgarrog, 48/21
Dolgellau, 52/3
Dolphinholme, 18/103
Dolwyddelan, 48/20
Donnington, 2/108, 19/76
Dovaston, 29/182
Downholland Cross, 18/105
Draycot Foliat, 38/104
Draycott, 8/228
Draycott in the Moors, 32/82
Drayton St Leonard, 27/51
Driby, 20/246
Driffield, 41/56
Duckmanton, 8/201
Duddlewick, 29/308
Dukinfield, 5/148
Dungworth, 43/375
Dunham-on-the-Hill, 5/151
Dunholme, 20/117
Dunsden, 27/58
Dunsden Green, 27/58
Dunsfold Green, 34/46
Dunsley, 42/270
Dunstan, 25/158
Duxford, 4/26
Dyffryn, 53/60
Dygyflchi, 48/22

Eamont Bridge, 37/85
Earith, 16/4
Earlham, 23/184
Earl's Croome, 39/50
Earl Stoneham, 33/140
Earnshaw House Farm, 5/154
East Appleton, 42/15
East Barsham, 23/38
Eastburn, 41/61
Eastburn, 43/377
Eastby, 43/148
East Camel, 30/354
East Carleton, 23/129
East Charleton, 9/99
Eastcot, 38/93
Eastcott, 38/271
Eastcourt, 38/93
East Dowlish, 30/170
East Foreign and West Foreign Liberty with the Town Liberty, 29/131
East Harting, 35/126
East Hauxwell, 42/162
East Hoathley, 35/90
East Kynett, 38/155
East Lavant, 35/91
East Marton, 43/280
East Newbiggin, 11/189
East Orchards, 10/100
East Stour, 10/206
East Stourmouth, 17/352
East Stratton, 31/178
Easton, 38/25
Easton-in-Gordano, 30/182
Eastthorpe, 42/17
East Tytherley, 31/258
East Williamston, 54/5
Eaton, 29/117
Eaves, 32/43
Ebbesbourne Wake, 38/109
Ebnal, 29/344
Eccles Road, 23/188
Edern, 48/23
Edgcote, 24/48
Edge, 29/254
Edgerley, 29/182
Edgmond, 29/120
Edjal, 32/44
Edvin Loach, 39/52
Edwardstone, 33/143
Edwyn Ralph, 14/76
Efford, 9/134
Egborough, 43/142
Egerton Green, 5/162
Egwysael, 44/39

Eglwysbach, 49/35
Eglwys-Brewis, 51/29
Eglwyseg, 49/34
Eight Roods, 16/35
Elcot, 38/188
Eldmire, 42/121
Ellastone, 32/90
Ellerdine, 29/274
Ellerton, 41/64, 42/118
Ellisfield, 31/144
Elmley Island, 17/126
Elmstone Hardwicke, 13/82
Elveden, 33/147
Elvet Hill, 11/91
Embleton, 11/88
Emborough, 30/186
Emelden, 11/88
Emley, 43/144
Emneth, 23/409
Enchmarsh, 29/65
Ennerdale Bridge, 7/66
Enson, 32/185
Ercall Magna, 29/123
Erryrys, 49/41
Erwallo, 49/26
Esh, 11/97
Eshott, 25/175
Eskdale, 7/127
Etchilhampton, 38/4
Etherdwick, 41/2
Everly, 42/156
Ewhurst, 31/180
Ewhurst Green, 35/97
Ewyas Harold, 14/79
Eynsford, 17/132
Eyton, 29/8, 29/128
Eyton upon the Weald Moors, 29/124

Fairstead, 12/125
Faringdon, 2/54
Farleigh Hungerford, 30/229
Farlesthorpe, 20/129
Farley, 29/254, 38/219
Farringdon, 10/115
Farsley, 43/83
Farthingstone, 24/53
Far Wilne, 8/183
Farworth, 26/119
Faugh, 7/77
Faulkbourne, 12/129
Fawcett Forest, 37/15
Fawdon, 25/183
Fawkham Green, 17/140
Fawler, 2/80
Fearnhead, 18/252
Felixkirk, 42/135
Felixstowe, 33/156
Felsham, 33/157
Feltwell, 23/204
The fences, 13/31
Fen Drayton, 4/30
Fenby, 20/14
Fenton, 7/77, 16/44
Fenton, 32/32
Fenton Culvert, 32/32
Fenton Vivian, 32/32
Fernhill, 29/344
Fernhurst, 35/100
Ferrensby, 43/156
Ferryhill, 11/102
Ferwig, 46/74
Ffestiniog, 52/4
Fifield, 38/113
Fifield Bavant, 38/115
Filberts, 2/68
Filgrave, 3/110
Fincham, 23/208
Fincham St Martin, 23/208
Finghall, 42/136
Fisherton de la Mere, 38/118
Flamstead, 15/40
Flax Bourton, 30/52
Fleesop, 42/21
Fleggburgh, 23/107
Flemingston, 51/32
Flitteriss Park Farm, 28/11
Flixton, 33/47
Folkingham, 20/127
Ford, 18/234
The Ford, 14/85
Forest, 29/68
Forest, 45/73
The Forest fences, 13/31
Forest of Chute, 38/75
Forest of Wakeswood, 38/75
Fornham St Genoveve or St Genovieve, 33/166
Forton, 18/167
Foscote, 3/46
Fosdyke, 20/5
Fosham, 41/2
Foulby, 43/305
Fowlmere, 4/31
Foxcott, 31/8
Foxhouses, 18/103
Foxley, 24/12
Frankton, 29/344
Freazley, 36/72
Frenchay, 13/88
Frickley, 43/100
Friesthorpe, 20/137
Frinsted, 17/146
Frinton-on-Sea, 12/139
Friston, 20/85
Frith, 11/105
Frome, 30/200
Frome St Quintin, 10/80
Frome Whitfield, 10/77
Froome Bishop, 14/18
Froxfield Green, 31/106
Fulford, 41/196
Fullaway, 38/4
Fulnetby, 20/257

Gairnston, 43/244
Gamelsby, 7/2
Gammersgill, 42/21
Gamston, 26/60
Ganerew, 14/89
Garth, 53/21
Gartheli, 46/19
Garthewin, 49/40
Gatten, 29/300
Gayhurst, 3/48
Gelligaer, 51/35
Gidleigh, 9/186
Gill, 7/121
Gilling West, 42/145
Gillingham, 23/237
Gillingham St Mary, 23/237
Girsby, 20/62
Glascwm, 55/14
Glastonbury, 30/201
Glazebrook, 18/270
Glen Parva, 19/62
Glororoum, 25/353
Glossop, 8/53
Glyn Ceiriog, 49/79
Goat, 7/162
Godwick, 23/581
Golder, 27/113
Goldsborough, 43/176
Goldthorpe, 43/55
Goodnestone, 17/151, 17/152
Gopsall Hall Farm, 19/65
Goring-by-Sea, 35/114
Gorleston-on-Sea, 33/184
Gorran Churchtown, 6/65
Gosford, 27/82
Gourton, 49/10
Grafton, 43/279
Grain, 17/199
Grateley, 31/112
Graveley, 15/46
Grays, 12/145
Great Altcar, 18/11
Great Bittering, 23/56, 23/243
Great Bolas, 29/42
Great Bricett, 33/70
Great Brington, 24/21
Great Chelworth, 38/39
Great Chesterton, 36/45
Great Easton, 12/121
Great Elm, 30/184
Greater Poston, 29/255
Great Hanwood, 29/143
Great Harborough, 36/75
Great Harrowden, 24/66
Great Horton, 43/220
Great Kings Mill Ground, 27/92

Great Langton, 42/219
Great Milton, 27/95
Great Moorsom, 42/256
Great or Far Wilne, 8/183
Great Ravendale, 20/258
Great Stainton, 11/245
Great Swinburne, 25/127
Great Urswick, 18/319
Great Welnetham, 33/456, 33/457
Great Wenham, 33/443
Great Witcombe, 13/220
Great Woolton with Thingwall, 18/223
Greenford, 21/18
Greenhalgh, 18/137
Greenshawhill, 25/273
Greenstead, 12/147
Greensted, 12/146
Gregories, 18/103
Greinton, 30/204
Greywell, 31/114
Grimsby, 20/153
Grimston, 41/77
Grindley, 5/404
Grinshill, 29/138
Grondre, 47/6
Grunty Fen, 4/11
Grwynefechan, 45/21
Guestling Green, 35/118
Guisborough, 42/148
Gunness, 20/155
Gunthorpe, 24/93
Gwaenyffynnon, 49/41
Gwalchmai, 44/74
Gwehelog, 22/29
Gwerneigron, 50/37
Gwernglevryd, 50/37
Gwigvair , 49/88
Gyffin, 48/26

Habergen, 30/232
Hackensall, 18/253
Hackington, 17/165, 17/345
Hackleton, 24/95
Hackness, 42/156
Hackney, 21/19
Hackwell, 12/163
Haconby, 20/156
Hadleigh, 33/51
Haggonfield, 26/109
Haighton Green, 18/142
Hail Weston, 16/24
Hainford, 23/266
Haisthorpe, 41/35
Hale Fen, 4/11
Hales, 32/84
Halkyn, 50/19
Hall Carr, 18/84
Hallgarth, 11/116
Halstead, 12/152
Halston, 29/254
Halton, 3/50
Halwill, 9/193
Hambleden, 3/51
Hamblerice, 31/116
Hampole, 43/190
Hampstead, 21/24
Hampstead Norreys, 2/67
Hampton Bishop, 14/94
Hampton Green, 5/185
Hampton in Arden, 36/73
Hampton Lovett, 39/63
Hamsteels, 11/37
Hanbury Woodend, 32/109
Harbledown, 17/166
Harcourt, 29/27
Hardley Street, 23/258
Hardwick, 23/460
Hardwick, 23/486
Harehope, 25/214
Hargreave, 5/55
Harleston, 23/440
Harnham, 38/134
Haroldston West, 54/35
Harom, 42/167
Harrowden Parva, 24/66
Harswell, 41/87
Hartlaw, 25/233
Hartle, 8/99
Hartley, 25/392
Harwich, 12/159
Harwood Dale, 42/160
Hasland, 8/54
Hatfield, 15/23
Hatfield Broad Oak, 12/160
Haughton, 26/61
Haughton Green, 18/151
Haughton Le Skerne, 11/123
Haunton, 32/68
Havering-atte-Bower, 12/162
Hawkeridge, 2/29
Hay-on-Wye, 45/23
Haynes, 1/23
Hazel, 13/31
Hazel Wood, 43/201
Hazelwood, 8/103
Heap Bridge, 18/154
Heapey, 18/155
Heath, 43/422
Heathwaite, 18/205
Hebburn, 11/150
Heddon-on-the-Wall, 25/240
Hedley on the Hill, 25/242
Helions Bumpstead, 12/59
Hellaby, 43/373
Hellingley, 43/36
Helmington, 11/145
The Hem, 29/338
Hemel Hempstead, 15/50
Hempstead, 12/165
Hempsted, 13/103
Hempston Arundell, 9/202
Hencott, 29/156
Hencott Stye, 29/156
Henley-on-Thames, 27/72
Henlle, 29/344
Henllys, 22/31
Henwick, 2/130
Herbrandston, 54/41
Herringby, 23/527
Heskin Green, 18/163
Heslington, 41/94, 41/95
Hest, 18/289
Hethpool, 25/236
High Bentham, 43/40
High Bickington, 9/206
High Bradley, 43/62
High Bray, 9/207
High Burton, 42/61
High Church, 25/440
Higher Ashton, 9/19
Higher Bebington, 5/43
High Ercall, 29/123
Higher Shurlach, 5/355
High Fields, 26/52
High Halden, 17/159
High Hawsker, 42/164
High Hesket, 7/80
High Highlaws, 25/257
Highley, 29/157
High Marishes, 42/236
High Melton, 43/282
High Moorsley, 11/178
High Newton-by-the-Sea, 25/344
High Ongar, 12/252
High Roding, 12/282
High Stittenham, 42/352
High Urpeth, 11/268
High Wycombe, 3/128, 3/129
Hilcott, 38/206
Hilfield, 10/105
Hill Chorlton, 32/58
Hillesden, 3/58
Hindford, 29/344
Hindlethwaite, 42/21
Hinton, 29/254
Hinton, 29/308
Hinton Martell, 10/107
Hisland, 29/21
Hitchenden, 3/63
Hockliffe, 1/27
Hodden, 25/235
Hoe, 23/301
Holbrook, 8/108
Holburn, 25/260
Holdenhurst, 31/64
Holdgate, 29/161
Holland-on-Sea, 12/173
Holme Fen, 16/27
Holme-on-Spalding-Moor, 41/97
Holme Pierrepont, 26/60
Holt, 29/162

Holton, 33/220
Holveston, 23/59
Holwell, 10/73
Holy Cross, Westgate, 17/61
Holystone, 25/212
Holywell, 25/208
Homer, 29/147
Honeybourne, 39/29
Honeychurch, 9/217
Honiley, 36/79
Hoo, 17/384
Hooke, 10/112
Hoppen, 25/302
Hopton, 29/111, 29/234
Hopton Issa, 53/3
Hopton on Sea, 33/225
Hopton Uchaf, 53/26
Hopwas, 32/233
Horkstow, 20/180
Horringer, 33/227
Horsehouse 42/21
Horsenden, 3/60
Horton, 29/358, 38/25
Horton Green, 5/208
Hortonwood, 29/170
Hoseley, 50/26
Houghton Green, 18/172
Houghton-le-Spring, 11/144
Houghton on the Hill, 23/422
Houghton St Giles, 23/309
Hoveton, 23/310, 23/311
Howgrave, 42/175
Howick Cross, 18/173
Howsham, 20/72
Howtel, 25/269
Hubberston, 54/43
Huddleston, 43/299
Hulcote, 24/47
Hull, 41/98
Hulme Walfield, 5/211
Hulver Street, 33/208
Huntwick, 43/305
Hurdley, 53/13
Hurworth-on-Tees, 11/146
Hyde, 13/156
Hyssington, 53/27
Hythe, 17/192

Ickburgh, 23/315
Icklingham, 33/232, 33/233
Ilketshall St Margaret, 33/239
Illogan, 6/75
Ilmer, 3/65
Ince-in-Makerfield, 18/181
Ingerthorpe, 43/233
Ingoe, 25/272
Ingol, 18/195
Inwood, 29/254
Irby in the Marsh, 20/189
Irby upon Humber, 20/190
Ireby, 7/88
Isar, 49/84
Isle Brewers, 30/237
Isle of Portland, 10/173
Islington, 21/33
Islington, 23/579

Jacobstowe, 9/235
Jeffreyston, 54/46
Johnston, 54/47
Jordanston, 54/48

Kattern, 30/90
Kearby, 43/243
Kearsley, 18/186
Keel, 53/60
Keld, 37/33
Kelfield, 20/71
Kelfield, 41/107
Kellamergh, 18/51
Kelleythorpe, 41/65
Kelsall, 5/220
Kempshott, 31/285
Kempston, 1/30
Kenardington, 17/202
Kenfig, 51/114
Kerdestone, 23/442
Kersall, 18/50
Ketsby, 20/246
Keythorpe, 19/152
Kidbrooke, 17/205
Kidderminster, 39/72, 39/80
Kilbourn, 8/123
Kilgwrrwg, 22/17
Kilmachallt, 53/23
Kilmeston, 31/147
Kilvowir, 54/82
Kinfare, 32/136
Kings Barn Farm, 35/155
King's Bromley, 32/130
Kingskerswell, 9/243
Kings Langley, 15/60
King's Meaburn, 37/44
Kingsmead, 27/38
Kings Mill Ground, 27/92
King's Newnham, 36/104
King's Norton, 19/81, 39/76
King's Nympton, 9/244
King's Somborne, 31/151
King's Stanley, 13/118
Kingston, 17/209, 31/152
Kingston near Lewes, 35/157
Kingston St Mary, 30/249
Kingston upon Thames, 34/75
Kings Worthy, 31/153
Kintbury, 2/81
Kinwalsey, 36/73
Kirby, 24/12
Kirby Bedon, 23/331, 23/332
Kirby Hall, 43/241
Kirby Knowle, 42/206
Kirby-le-Soken, 12/187
Kirby Sigston, 42/212
Kirby Underdale, 41/116
Kirk Hallam, 8/125
Kirkby Hill, 42/205
Kirkby la Thorpe, 20/199
Kirkbymoorside, 42/208
Kirklevington, 42/214
Kirkley, 33/258
Kirstead Green, 23/334
Kitner, 30/157
Kittisford, 30/253
Knawston, 19/85
Knighton, 32/3
Knodishall, 33/261
Knuckshadwell, 29/213
Knutsford, 5/227, 5/228
Kynnersley, 29/183
Kyre Wyard, 39/79
Kyrton, 9/143

Lach Dennis, 5/229
Lache, 5/253
Lake Hurst, 29/338
Lambourn, 2/82
Lampeter, 46/26
Land, 41/47
Landevenny, 22/10
Lane End, 32/144
Langbar, 43/294
Langford, 23/315
Langley, 3/69, 27/85
Langley, 29/243
Langley Sudeley Tenements, 13/190
Langport, 30/257
Langthorpe, 42/218
Langton, 37/13
Langton by Wragby, 20/206
Langtree, 18/294
Lanilterne, 51/31
Lansbury, 16/37
Lanteglos, 6/101
Lappal, 29/189
Larkton, 5/106
Laskill Pasture, 42/167
Latton Bush, 12/197
Laughton, 20/127
Laughton en le Morthen, 43/252
Lawkland, 43/24
Lawling, 12/196
Layer de la Haye, 12/203
Lea, 29/254
Leaden Roding, 12/205
Lead Hall Farm, 43/254
Lebberston, 42/228
Leckby, 42/101
Leckwith, 51/58
Leeming, 42/126

Leesthorpe, 19/115
Leigh Delamere, 38/171
Leigh-on-Sea, 12/207
Leighterton, 13/29
Leighton, 53/71
Leigh upon Mendip, 30/260
Leinthall Starkes, 14/128
Lelant, 6/201
Lenborough, 3/72
Lenchwick, 39/99
Lenton, 20/208, 20/209
Letwell, 43/251
Leveland, 17/15
Levington, 33/297
Lewknor, 27/89
Lexington, 26/74
Leysdown on Sea, 17/223
Lightwood Forest, 32/29
Linby, 26/77
Lindeth, 18/325
Linhope, 25/273
Linshiels, 25/296
Linton, 13/106
Lisvane, 51/49
Litchurch, 8/166
Little Amwell, 15/6
Little Aston, 32/13
Little Barugh, 42/35
Little Bedwyn, 38/17
Little Berkamstead, 15/21
Little Birch, 12/36
Littlebourne, 17/227
Littlebredy, 10/26
Little Bricett, 33/309
Little Burgh, 23/369
Little Chelworth, 38/39
Little Colan, 6/30
Littlecott, 38/173
Little Cowarne, 14/53
Little Driffield, 41/56
Little Faringdon, 2/55
Little Hanwood, 29/16
Little Harbrough, 36/101
Little Harrowden, 24/66
Little Hassall, 5/193
Little Hautbois, 23/337
Littlehempston, 9/202
Little Hiniton, 38/143
Little Hockham, 23/291
Little Horton, 43/220
Little Lumley, 11/163
Little Marsden, 18/212
Little Milton, 27/95
Little Moorsom, 42/256
Little Porringland, 23/312
Little Poston, 29/255
Little Preston, 43/320
Little Rissington, 13/166
Little Rowsley, 8/71
Little Sampford, 12/291
Little Singleton, 18/286
Little Sombourne, 31/151
Little Stoneham, 33/384
Little Thetford, 4/72
Little Urswick, 18/319
Little Usworth, 11/269
Little Warford, 5/256
Little Welnetham, 33/441
Little Wigborough, 12/382
Little Wigston, 19/159
Little Yarmouth, 33/371
Lizard, 6/92
Llan, 49/84
Llanaelhaearn, 48/27
Llanaeron, 46/39
Llanafan, 46/28
Llanafan-fawr, 45/24
Llanandras, 55/47
Llanarmon Mynydd mawr, 49/53
Llanbadarn Fawr, 46/29
Llanbadarn Fynydd, 55/21
Llanbadarn-y-garreg, 55/22
Llanbadoc, 22/39
Llanbeder, 22/40
Llanbedr-Dyffryn-Clwyd, 49/54
Llanbedr-y-cennin, 48/30
Llanberis, 48/32
Llancarfan, 51/52
Llanchydd, 49/96
Llancrwys, 47/70
Llandaniel Fab, 44/17
Llanddeiniol, 46/34
Llanddeiniolen, 48/33
Llandderfel, 52/10
Llanddeusant, 44/18, 47/66
Llanddewi, 51/55
Llanddewi Fach, 22/67
Llanddewi Rhydderch, 22/66
Llanddoged, 49/55
Llanddowror, 47/34
Llanddulas, 49/58
Llanddwywe, 52/9
Llandecwyn, 52/16
Llandefaelog, 45/28
Llandefalle, 45/29
Llandegveth, 22/41
Llandeilo, 47/31
Llandeilo Graban, 55/28
Llandeilo'r Fan, 45/31
Llandewi Velfrey, 54/57
Llandewi Ystradenni, 55/27
Llandilo-abercowin, 47/30
Llandissilio, 47/33
Llandre Egremont, 47/14
Llandrindod Wells, 55/29
Llandybie, 47/27
Llandyfaelog, 47/28
Llandygwydd, 46/36
Llandynan, 49/85
Llandysul, 46/38, 53/33
Llanedeyrn, 51/60
Llanedi, 47/35
Llanegwad, 47/36
Llanelian-yn-Rhos, 49/60
Llanellen, 22/45
Llanelli, 47/37
Llaneltyd, 52/13
Llanerchbrochwell, 53/34
Llanfabon, 51/78
Llanfachraeth, 44/28
Llanfachreth, 52/23
Llanfaelog, 44/54
Llanfaes, 44/55
Llanfaethlu, 44/29
Llanfagan, 48/41
Llanfair Caereinion, 53/36
Llanfair Clydogau, 46/40
Llanfair fechan, 48/53
Llanfair Kilgeddin, 22/74
Llanfair-Nant-Gwyn, 54/59
Llanfair Waterdine, 29/200
Llanfarian, 46/60
Llanfechain, 53/37
Llanfechan, 45/25
Llanfeirian, 44/39
Llanffinan, 44/36
Llanfigael, 44/57
Llanfihangel-ar-arth, 47/42
Llanfihangel Bachellaeth, 48/31
Llanfihangel Glyn Myfyr, 49/64
Llanfihangel-helygen, 55/32
Llanfihangel nant Bran, 45/36
Llanfihangel-Nant-Melan, 55/37
Llanfihangel Rhydithon, 55/38
Llanfihangel Rogiet, 22/77
Llanfihangel Tal-y-llyn, 45/54
Llanfihangel Trer Beirrd, 44/24
Llanfihangel-y-Creuddyn, 46/43
Llanfihangel-yng-Ngwynfa, 53/38
Llanfihangel yn Nhowyn, 44/37
Llanfihangel-y-pennant, 48/43, 52/24
Llanfilo, 45/55
Llanfor, 52/25
Llanfrechfa, 22/81
Llanfyllin, 53/48
Llanfyrnach, 54/62
Llangadog, 47/46
Llangan, 51/43
Llangarron, 14/137
Llangasty-Talyllyn, 45/39
Llangattock-Vibon-Avel, 22/52
Llangedwyn, 49/68
Llangelynnin, 52/19
Llangendeirne, 47/56
Llangenny, 45/41
Llangernyw, 49/69
Llangian, 48/31
Llangoedmor, 46/46
Llangollen, 49/70
Llangollen Abbott, 49/70
Llangovan, 22/55
Llangranog, 46/47

Llangua, 22/37
Llangunnog, 22/56
Llangurrig, 53/40
Llangwm, 22/57
Llangwnadl, 48/45
Llangwyryfon, 46/48
Llangybi, 46/49
Llangyfelach, 51/63
Llangynhafal, 49/67
Llangynidr, 45/43
Llangyniew, 53/41
Llangynin, 47/52
Llangynllo, 46/50
Llangynog, 47/54
Llangynwyd, 51/44
Llanharan, 51/65
Llanhennock, 22/58
Llanilltern, 51/31
Llanllowel, 22/61
Llanllwchaiarn, 53/44
Llanllwni, 47/58
Llanllywel, 22/61
Llanmadoc, 51/69
Llanmartin, 22/62
Llanmawddwy, 52/27
Llanmerewig, 53/45
Llannefydd, 49/74
Llannon, 47/59
Llanpumsaint, 47/60
Llanreithan, 54/68
Llanrhaeadr, 49/75
Llanrhaeadr-yn-Mochnant, 53/46
Llanrhidian, 51/72
Llanrhos, 48/24
Llanrhychwyn, 48/67
Llanrhystud, 46/55
Llanrihan, 54/67
Llansamlet, 51/45
Llansantffraed, 45/48, 46/56
Llansantffraed-Cwmdeuddwr, 55/34
Llansantffraed-in-Elwel, 55/35
Llansantffraid-ym-Mechn, 53/47
Llansilian, 49/99
Llansiln, 49/99
Llanspyddid, 45/49
Llantarnam, 22/78
Llantilio Crossenny, 22/69
Llantilio Pertholey, 22/70
Llantrisant, 44/53, 22/71, 51/75
Llantwit Fardre, 51/47
Llantwit Major, 51/46
Llanuwchllyn, 52/22
Llanvair-Discoed, 22/73
Llanvapley, 22/75
Llanvihangel Crucorney, 22/46
Llanvihangel Gobion, 22/47
Llanvihangel Pontymoel, 22/79
Llanwarne, 14/140
Llanwddyn, 53/49
Llanwnnen, 46/59
Llanwrthwl, 45/56
Llanwrtyd, 45/57
Llanybydder, 47/69
Llanychaer, 54/75
Llanystumdwy, 48/55
Llechcynfarwy, 44/61
Lleweni Uchar, 49/84
Lloran issa, 49/90
Lloran Ucha, 49/90
Llysworney, 51/50
Llys-y-fran, 54/78
Loanend, 11/142
Longbenton, 25/40
Long Bredy, 10/129
Long Crichel, 10/74
Longdon on Tern, 29/204
Longfleet, 10/131
Longframlington, 25/195
Long Lane, 29/193
Longnewton, 11/195
Longstanton, 4/64
Long Stanton All Saints, 4/64
Long Sutton, 20/323
Longtown, 7/105
Loscoe, 8/63
Lotherton cum Aberford, 43/270
Loughrigg, 37/66
Lound, 26/121
Low Bentham, 43/40
Low Bishopside, 43/49
Low Bradley, 43/62
Low Burton, 42/61
The Lowe, 29/175
Low Eggborough, 43/142
Low Ellington, 42/120
Lower Ashton, 9/19
Lower Bebington, 5/44
Lower Benefield, 24/10
Lower Broughton, 29/56
Lower Elkstone, 32/89
The Lower Mean, 13/31
Lower Quinton, 13/162
Lower Soothill, 43/367
Low Hesket, 7/79
Lowlin, 25/30
Low Marishes, 42/236
Low Marnham, 26/81
Low Moorsley, 11/178
Low Newton-by-the-Sea, 25/344
Loxbeare, 9/260
Lubenham, 19/95
Luccombe, 30/269
Ludford, 20/222
Ludgershall, 38/178
Ludworth, 8/53
Luffincott, 9/262
Lullingfield, 29/29
Lullingstaine, 17/232
Lumby, 43/299
Lutton, 20/326
Luxulyan, 6/113
Lyde, 14/176
Lydley, 29/65
Lyminster, 35/162
Lympstone, 9/266
Lynemouth, 25/295
Lynsted, 17/225
Lytchett Minster, 10/136

Mabe Burnthouse, 6/114
Mablethorpe, 20/223
Mablethorpe St Peter, 20/332
Maenan, 48/57
Maesbrook, 29/212
Maesbrook Ucha, 29/182
Maesbury, 29/313
Main, 53/60
Malehurst, 29/254
Maltby, 20/256
Manafon, 53/54
Manledd Glynharren, 53/58
Manningford Bohune, 38/186
Mannington, 23/323
Manorbier, 54/83
Manordeifi, 54/82
Mansell Lacy, 14/149
Mapledurwell, 31/169
Mapleton, 8/139
Mapperton, 10/5
Mardale, 37/33
Marehouse, 29/29
Marford, 50/26
Margaret Roding, 12/221
Marholm, 24/85
Marholme, 24/85
Mariansleigh, 9/275
Market Brough, 37/16
Market Drayton, 29/112
Marketshall, 23/122
Market Weston, 33/451
Markshall, 12/224
Marlow, 3/75
Marsh, 29/346
Marshchapel, 20/227
Marske-by-the-Sea, 42/238
Marston, 20/182, 36/166
Marston Meysey, 38/192
Marston on Dove, 8/141
Martinscroft, 18/346
Martinstown, 10/257
Martleston, 2/88
Marton, 42/240
Marton-le-Moor, 42/241
Mary Tavy, 9/277
Marylebone, 21/39
Maryport, 7/126
Matterdale End, 7/112
Mattishall, 23/366
Mawgan, 6/124
Mawkins, 13/31
Mawsley, 24/55
Medbourne, 19/100

Medlicott, 29/7
Medwalledd, 55/45
Meeching, 35/188
Meidrim, 47/75
Melay, 7/78, 49/93
Mells, 33/444
Meltonby, 42/208
Melton St Mary and All Saints, 23/370
Membris, 24/143
Menston, 43/283
Meole Brace, 29/47
Meols, 5/261
Merry Shield, 25/310
Merthyr Dyfan, 51/85
Merthyr mawr, 51/86
Merthyr Tydfil, 51/87
Mexborough, 43/284
Meyllteryn, 48/58
Meynell Langley, 8/127
Michael Brows, 7/162
Michaelchurch Escley, 14/155
Michaelchurch-on-Arrow, 55/41
Michaelston-le-Pit, 51/91
Michaelston-super-Ely, 51/90
Michaelston-y-Fedw, 51/92
Micheldever, 31/178
Michelmersh, 31/179
Micklethwaite, 7/137
Mid Lavant, 35/184
Middle Herrington, 11/131
Middle Quarter, 18/205
Middlesbrough, 42/250
Middle Winterslow, 38/291
Middleton, 8/147
Middleton, 18/172, 24/38
Middleton-on-Leven, 42/251
Middleton-on-Sea, 35/182
Middleton Scriven, 29/279
Middleton Stoney, 27/93
Middleton Tyas, 42/253
Middlezoy, 30/454
Middridge, 11/172
Midhope, 43/288
Milborne Port, 30/291
Mildenhall, 38/199
Milford on Sea, 31/175
Millmeece, 32/153
Millom Above, 7/117
Milton, 17/251
Milton Abbot, 9/283
Milton Bryan, 1/40
Milton Keynes, 3/80
Milton Lilbourne, 38/198
Milton-under-Wychwood, 27/94
Minstead, 31/177
Minster, 17/253, 17/254
Minterne Magna, 10/150
Minwere, 54/119
Miserden, 13/134
The Moat, 29/298
Moathall, 29/16
Mochdre, 53/59
Monken Hadley, 21/22
Monk Hesleden, 11/174
Monk Sherborne, 31/180
Monks Kirby, 36/35
Monk Soham, 33/293
Moor Crichel, 10/151
Moore, 5/272
Moorgate, 26/16
Moorgreen, 26/84
Moorsholm, 42/256
Moortown, 29/123
Mordon, 11/179
More, 29/224
Moreleigh, 9/296
Moreton, 14/80
Moreton, 32/81
Moreton Jeffries, 14/161
Moreton on Lugg, 14/162
Moreton Pinkney, 24/86
Morfodion, 53/58
Morley St Botolph, 23/377
Morley St Buttolph and Morley St Peter, 23/377
Morningthorpe, 23/382
Morpeth Castle
Morrell, 12/283
Mortehoe, 9/297
Morton Grange Farm, 11/181
Morton-on-Swale, 42/258
Morton Tinmouth, 11/180
Morvil, 54/93
Morwenstow, 6/138
Mossdale, 7/26
Moston, 29/295
Moulton St Mary, 23/380
Mowthorpe, 41/118
Moylgrove, 54/89
Much Hoole, 18/168
Much Wenlock, 29/335
Mucklestone, 32/156
Mulwith, 43/297
Murrah, 7/12
Murton, 42/103
Muswell Leys, 36/35
Mwnt, 46/63
Myddfai, 47/74
Myddle, 29/216
Mylor Churchtown, 6/142
Mynachlogddu, 54/90
Myndtown, 29/220
Mynyddislwyn, 22/96
Myton-on-Swale, 42/263

Nantgwryd, 49/49
Narburgh, 23/387
Naunton, 13/212
Neasham, 11/186
Needham, 33/21
Needingworth, 16/28
Nempnett Thrubwell, 30/304
Nercwys, 50/30
Nesbitt Hall, 11/185
Nescliffe, 29/348
Neston, 5/283
Netheravon, 38/202
Nether Burrow, 18/55
Netherby, 43/243
Nether Heyford, 24/70
Nethermore, 38/244
Nether Pool, 5/427
Nether Wasdale, 7/127
Nether Wyersdale, 18/60
Nevill Holt, 19/73
Newark-on-Trent, 26/87
Newbiggin, 25/333
Newbiggin-by-the-Sea, 25/334
Newbold, 8/54
Newbold on Avon, 36/101
Newbold-on-Stour, 39/95
Newborough, 32/157
Newbourne, 33/302
Newby, 42/304, 43/97
Newchurch, 22/98
New Church Hir Abbot, 45/32
New Hall Hey, 18/84
Newington, 17/266, 34/91
New Micklefield, 43/285
New Milton, 31/176
Newnham, 29/254
Newnham Paddox, 36/35
Newsome, 43/298
Newstead, 20/72
Newton, 5/265, 13/143, 29/364, 42/126, 54/119
Newton, 23/392, 29/14, 43/207
Newton by Toft, 20/239
Newton Heath, 18/227
Newton-le-Willows, 18/228, 42/279
Newton Longville, 3/84
Newton-on-Rawcliffe, 42/278
Newton Reigny, 7/129
Newton St Faith, 23/306
Newton Tony, 38/208
Newton under Roseberry, 42/274
Newtown, 29/29
Newtown Botcheston, 19/106
Niwbwrch, 44/63
Norbury Moor, 5/297
Norham West Mains, 11/197
Normacot, 32/160
Normanby, 20/135
Normanby le Wold, 20/240
Normandy, 34/5
Normanton-on-the-Wolds, 26/88
Northales, 33/119
Northallerton Ings, 42/12
Northalt, 21/42
Northaw, 21/42
North Barsham, 23/39

North Benfleet, 12/29
North Biddick, 11/269
North Cotes, 20/96
North Denchurch, 2/68
Northenden, 5/299
North Hill, 6/145
Northlead, 30/441
North Milford, 43/244
North Owersby, 20/248
North Petherwin, 9/322
North Tidworth, 38/259
North Trewick, 25/442
North Widcombe, 30/459
Northwood, 29/78
Norton, 38/210, 39/100
Norton Canes, 32/161
Norton-in-the-Moors, 32/162
Norton-Juxta-Twycross, 19/109
Norton-le-Clay, 42/283
Norton Lindsey, 36/47
Norton Meadow, 27/26
Norton Sub Hamdon, 30/311
Norton under Cannock, 32/161
Nottage, 51/96
Nunclose, 7/7
Nymet Tracey, 9/51
Nympsfield, 13/145

Oakley, 29/191
The Oaks, 29/254
Oby, 23/13
Occlestone Green, 5/302
Ockany, 43/419
Ocle Pychard, 14/168
Odstone, 19/110
Offerton Green, 5/304
Offord D'Arcy, 16/42
Ogbourne St Andrew, 38/212
Ogbourne St George, 38/213
Old Acres, 11/39
Oldborough, 39/103
Oldcastle, 22/99
Old Catton, 23/134
Oldcotes, 26/91
Old Deanham, 25/143
Old Felton, 25/5
Old Fletton, 16/18
Old Marton, 29/344
Old Micklefield, 43/285
Old Milton, 31/176
Oldton, 33/313
Ollerset, 8/21
Ompton, 26/68
Onslow, 29/16
Orby, 20/244
Ormesby St Michael, 23/406
Orton, 24/105
Osbaldeston, 18/235
Osbaston, 29/123
Oslaston, 8/209
Ossendyke, 43/342
Otby, 20/358
Oubrough, 41/144
Oulton, 32/152
Oultonlowe Green, 5/307
Ouram, 41/191
Out Newton, 41/143
Outwell, 4/27
Over, 13/106
Over Burrow, 18/55
Over Dinsdale, 42/147
Oversley Green, 36/109
Over Stowey, 30/324
Overton, 29/364
Overtown, 38/112
Owermoigne, 10/162
Owlton, 33/313
Owslebury, 31/200
Oxcombe, 20/250
Oxenbold, 29/297

Padfield, 8/53
Paglesham Churchend, 12/256
Paignton, 9/315
Painscastle, 55/23
Palgrave, 23/514
Pallett Wythes, 7/162
Pamber Green, 31/201
Pancrasweek, 9/316
Pangbourne, 2/98
Panson, 29/16
Panteg, 22/100
Papworth Everard, 4/58
Parc, 49/84
Parkhouse, 25/105
Parm, 5/273
Partington, 41/45
Patrishow, 45/66
Patrixbourn, 17/51
Patterdale, 37/35
Patton, 29/248
Pawston, 25/356
Peele, 5/209
Pen-y-clawdd, 22/105
Penbedw, 54/61
Penbryn, 46/65
Penllyn, 51/104
Pennant Melangell, 53/63
Penniarth, 53/60
Pennycross, 9/445
Penrhos, 22/103
Pentre Broughton, 49/15
Pentregaer, 29/199
Peover Heath, 5/319
Peper Harow, 34/97
Perranuthnoe, 6/153
Peterstone Wentlooge, 22/106
Peterston-super-Ely, 51/110
Peter Tavy, 9/321
Petrockstowe, 9/323
Petrual, 49/93
Pexall, 5/200
Pickle, 42/20
Pickstock, 29/120
Pickup Bank, 18/352
Piercebridge, 11/206
Pinkney, 38/238
Pipe Hill, 32/44
Pitchcott, 3/88
Pitney Lortie, 30/338
Pitstone, 3/87
Plealey, 29/16
Plenmeller, 25/359
Ploughley, 2/68
Plumpton, 18/330
Plumpton, 35/210
Plympton, 9/329, 9/330
Pockley, 42/167
Podimore, 30/348
Podymore Milton, 30/348
Polmer, 29/254
Pontesbright, 12/71
Pontesford, 29/254
Pontop, 11/59
Poringland, 23/428
Portslade-by-Sea, 35/212
Postern, 8/187
Pott, 42/193
Potterhanworth, 20/255
Pott Shringley, 5/326
Poultney, 19/102
Poulton, 5/324, 5/325
Poulton-le-Fylde, 18/250
Poyntington, 30/339
Poynton, 29/150
Preese, 18/327
Prescott, 29/128, 29/329
Presteign, 55/47
Preston Bagot, 36/116
Preston Deanery, 24/100
Preston-on-Tees, 11/210
Preston on the Weald Moors, 29/258
Preston St Mary, 33/325
Preston-under-Scar, 42/303
Preston Wynne, 14/179
Priddbwlch, 49/99
Priestcliffe, 8/205
Priors Dean, 31/69
Puddletown, 10/168
Pudleston, 14/180
Pulham St Mary Magdalen, 23/432
Puncknowle, 10/178
Pwllcrochan, 54/110
Pwllyurach, 45/73
Pyecombe, 35/217

Quarry Hill, 36/72
Quedgeley, 13/161
Queen's Arbour, 2/37

Quoisley, 5/252
Quy, 4/66

Rackham, 35/6
Radford, 26/137
Raglan, 22/109
Ramsgate, 17/299
Ratcliffe on Soar, 26/100
Ravensworth, 42/211
Rayside, 37/33
Rayton, 26/94
Reach, 1/24
Redisham, 33/331
Redmarley D'Abitot, 39/113
Redruth, 6/165
Reepham, 20/260, 23/442
Reighton, 41/152
Rhan Vawr, 49/84
Rhanhir, 49/84
Rhayader, 55/50
Rhetescyn, 53/75
Rhiewlas Uuchfoel, 49/99
Rhiston, 53/7
Rhiwlas issfoel, 49/90
Rhosferig, 45/70
Rhos Goch, 53/71
Rhos Lligwy, 44/66
Rhos Mynach, 44/70
Rhossili, 51/119
Rhos-y-Garth, 46/67
Rhuddlan, 50/36
Rhyllon, 50/9
Rhysgog, 49/70
Rickinghall, 33/336
Rievaulx, 42/167
Rigsby, 20/4
Rigton, 43/29
Rimpton, 30/364
Ringborough, 41/136
Ringsash, 9/18
Ringstead, 23/448
Ripe, 35/92
Ripley, 34/109
Risby, 20/266
Ritton, 29/184
Rockland All Saints, 23/449
Rocksavage, 5/122
Rodborough, 13/131
Rodbourne, 38/225
Roggiett, 22/113
Rogiet, 22/113
Rolleston, 19/120
Romford, 12/162, 12/177
Ronton, 32/179
Roomhill, 17/56
Roseacre, 18/311
Roseden, 25/382
Rosliston, 8/176
Ross-on-Wye, 14/184
Roston, 8/154
Rotherhithe, 34/106
Rousden, 9/352
Rowell, 24/105
Rowlestone, 14/185
Rowsley, 8/178
Rowston, 20/265
Rowton, 29/12, 41/170
Roxby, 42/299
Roxham, 23/467
Royal Leamington Spa, 36/94
Ruanlanihorne, 6/167
Ruckley, 29/188
Rudry, 51/120
Runcton Holme, 23/296
Runnington, 30/362
Runston, 22/90
Rusholme, 18/276
Rushton, 5/158
Ruyton-XI-Towns, 29/277
Ryehall, 25/438
Rylstone, 43/332

St Andrews Major, 51/3
St Anthony, 6/6
St Anthony-in-Meneage, 6/5
St Athan, 51/4
St Bride's Netherwent, 22/10
St Brides Wentlooge, 22/11
St Clement, 6/29
St Clether, 6/27
St Comus and Damian in the Blean, 17/165
St Cross South Elmham, 33/365
St Dogmaels, 54/25
St Dunstan, 17/165
St Endellion, 6/47
St Erney, 6/93
St Gennys, 6/59
St George, 30/182
St George in Southelmham, 33/365
St George's, 51/33
St Giles-on-the-Heath, 9/187
St Harmon, 55/16
St Ippollitts, 15/58
St Ishmael's, 54/44
St James South Elmham, 33/366
St John, 15/6
St Just, 6/82
St Keyne, 6/120
St Lawrence, 12/242, 31/158
St Lythans, 51/81
St Margaret Clee, 29/83
St Margarets, 14/153
St Margaret's at Cliffe, 17/241
St Margaret South Elmham, 33/367
St Martha, 34/31
St Martin, 6/120, 6/121
St Martin, 42/173
St Martin's, 29/214
St Mary Church, 51/83
St Marychurch, 9/110
St Mary Hoo, 17/242
St Mary in the Marsh, 17/243
St Mary's, 6/122
St Maughans, 22/91
St Mawgan, 6/125
St Michael Caerhays, 6/133
St Michael Church, 30/287
St Michael South Elmham, 33/368
St Newlyn East, 6/144
St Nicholas in Feltwell, 23/204
St Nicholas, Southelmham, 33/364
St Osyth, 12/73
St Paul's Cray, 17/99
St Paul's Walden, 15/102
St Peters, 17/291
St Peters, Cockley Cley, 23/141
St Peter South Elmham, 33/369
St Sampsons, 6/64
St Stephen, 6/178
St Stephens, 6/176, 6/177, 15/92
St Stephens, 17/165
St Thomas, 9/407
St Thomas in Pensford, 30/384
St Twynnells, 54/129
Salle, 23/470
Salthorp, 38/112
Salwick, 18/79
Sampford Courtenay, 9/354
Sand Hutton, 42/318
Sandair, 7/162
Sandford, 2/154, 13/212
Sandford-on-Thames, 27/119
Sandfurlong, 38/46
Sandhoe, 25/390
Sansaw, 29/86
Sapey Pitchard, 39/117
Sapperton, 13/172
Sarre, 17/148
Sascott, 29/254
Saughall, 5/348
Savernake Forest, 38/229
Saxby, 20/275
Saxby All Saints, 20/276
Saxlingham Nethergate, 23/475
Saxtead, 33/348
Scabgill, 18/103
Scales, 18/229
Scarthingwell, 43/345
Scofton, 26/94
Scole, 23/407
Scoreby, 41/176
Sco Ruston, 23/146
Scothorn, 20/281
Scott Willoughby, 20/283
Scottow, 23/146
Scottow, 23/479
Scrainwood, 25/391
Scrotby, 23/406
Seabridge, 32/65
Seagrims Hill Meadow, 31/282

Sea Palling, 23/416
Seaton House, 25/84
Seavington St Mary, 30/371
Sedgeford, 23/482
Sedlescombe, 35/230
Sedsall, 8/80
Seisdon, 32/215
Selattyn, 29/314
Sellindge, 17/321
Semer, 33/349
Setch or Setchey, 23/460
Sevenoaks, 17/322
Sewstern, 19/125
Seywell, 24/12
Shadingfield, 33/350
Shadymoor, 29/298
Shaftesbury, 10/184, 10/185, 10/186
Shafton, 43/71
Shakerley, 18/314
Shalbourne, 38/234
Shaldon, 9/360
Shalstone, 3/96
Shangton, 19/127
Shapwick, 10/183
Shatton, 8/39
Shaugh Prior, 9/361
Shebbear, 9/362
Sheepy Magna, 19/131
Sheepy Parva, 19/132
Shelsley Beauchamp, 39/119
Shelsley Walsh, 39/120
Shelton, 32/112
Shelvock, 29/285
Shephall, 15/87
Shepherdswell, 17/330
Shepshead, 19/130
Sherfield on Loddon, 31/223
Sheriff's Lench, 39/121
Shifnal, 29/287
Shilling Okeford, 10/188
Shillingford Abbot, 9/368
Shimplingthorne, 33/353
Shipbourne, 17/326
Shipston-on-Stour, 39/122
Shipton, 41/127
Shipton Bellinger, 31/224
Shipton-under-Wychwood, 27/123
Shirwell, 9/367
Shobrooke, 9/369
Shoeburyness, 12/300
Shoreham-by-Sea, 35/236
Shorthill, 29/16
Shotesham, 23/492
Shotisham St Botolph, 23/492
Shotisham St Martin, 23/492
Shotisham St Mary, 23/492
Shotton, 11/160
Shrawardine, 29/8
Shurdington Magna, 13/14
Shuttleworth, 18/320
Sibberscott, 29/16
Silpho, 42/156
Silverstone, 24/110
Simmondley, 8/53
Simonward, 6/19
Simpston, 35/232
Singleton, 18/286
Skelton, 43/309
Skidbrook, 20/291
Skipton-on-Swale, 42/336
Skirwith, 7/17
Sleap, 29/316
Sloothby, 20/366
Smethwick Green, 5/69
Snarestone, 19/136
Snibstone, 19/112
Snitterton, 8/222
Snorscomb, 24/111
Softley, 11/164
Sollers Hope, 14/189
Somershal Herbert, 8/191
Sonning, 2/117
Souldrop, 1/46
South Acre, 23/507
Southam, 13/24
South Anston, 43/14
South Benfleet, 12/30
South Blyth, 25/341
South Bramwith, 43/67
South Brewham, 30/61
Southbrook, 22/108
Southchurch, 12/304
South Emsall, 43/146
South Hamlet, 13/103
South Harting, 35/126
South Hiendley, 43/71
Southrepps, 23/510
South Tidworth, 31/247
South Walsham, 23/606
South Walsham St Mary, 23/606
South Warnborough, 31/232
Southwick, 35/291
Sowerby, 18/182
Spernall, 36/131
Spindleston, 25/353
Spital Hill, 25/412
Spittal, 11/242
Spittle, 25/410, 41/68
Sproston Green, 5/362
Sproxton, 42/167
Spurn, 41/113
Stain, 20/310
Stainsacre, 42/164
Stainton, 43/373
Stalybridge, 5/367
Stamford, 29/120
Standford, 29/120
Stanford, 17/340
Stanford-le-Hope, 12/310
Stanford on Teme, 39/125
Stanghow, 42/256
Stanmore, 21/48
Stanninghall, 23/223
Stanstead, 17/341
Stanstead Abbotts, 15/90
Stanton-by-Dale, 8/193
Stanton Fitzwarren, 38/245
Stanton Long, 29/297
Stanwardine in the Fields, 29/29
Stanwardine in the Wood, 29/29
Stanwick-St-John, 42/348
Staple Fitzpaine, 30/386
Staunton in the Vale, 26/115
Staunton on Arrow, 14/192
Staynall, 18/293
Steely, 11/38
Stelling Minnis, 17/344
Steninford, 43/372
Stenson, 8/218
Steppingly, 1/49
Steynton, 54/125
Stinsford, 10/197
Stob Hill, 25/105
Stobhill, 25/105
Stockeld, 43/245
Stockerston, 19/139
Stockleigh English, 9/380
Stockleigh Pomeroy, 9/381
Stocklinch St Magdalen, 30/391
Stockton-on-Tees, 11/251
Stockton on Teme, 39/128
Stodday, 18/19
Stoke, 30/155, 32/13
Stoke Bishop, 13/214
Stoke Bruerne, 24/114
Stoke by Clare, 33/381
Stoke-by-Nayland, 33/382
Stoke D'Abernon, 34/112
Stoke Lane, 30/400
Stoke St Milborough, 29/84
Stoke Sub Hamdon, 30/401
Stoneferry, 41/177
Stoney Stretton, 29/307
Stonham Aspal, 33/383
Stony Stratford, 38/252
Storrs, 43/375
Stour Provost, 10/208
Stourpaine, 10/204
Stow, 20/25, 20/342
Stow, 20/315
Stow cum Quy, 4/66
Stowe, 29/309
Stowe-by-Chartley, 32/198
Stow Longa, 16/49
Stow Maries, 12/323
Stradbroke, 33/390
Stratford St Anthony, 38/252
Stratford Sub Castle, 38/253
Stratford Tony, 38/252
Stratford-upon-Avon, 36/134
Stratton-on-the-Fosse, 30/405
Streat, 35/254
Streatlam, 11/244

Street Ashton, 36/35
Stretton-on-Dunsmore, 36/136
Stretton-on-Fosse, 36/137
Stubby Lane, 32/81
Stuchbury, 24/118
Studley Magna, 43/382
Studley Roger, 43/383
Sturton Grange, 43/384
Sudbourne, 33/396
Sudbury, 33/397, 33/398
Sudcoates, 41/173
Suffield, 42/156
Sugley, 25/145
Sugnall, 32/202, 32/203
Sulhampstead Abbots, 2/125
Sulhampstead Bannister, 2/125
Sulhampstead Upper End, 2/125
Summerfield, 23/504
Sunninghill, 2/126
Surlingham St Saviour, 23/536
Sutton Bonington, 26/120
Sutton Courtenay, 2/128
Sutton cum St Andrew, 23/115
Sutton Howgrave, 42/356
Sutton-in-Craven, 43/388
Sutton in Holland, 20/323
Sutton Lane Ends, 5/377
Sutton Mallet, 30/410
Sutton Montague, 30/411
Sutton-on-Hull, 41/177
Sutton on Sea, 20/322
Sutton-on-the-Forest, 42/357
Sutton Place, 34/116
Sutton Pointz, 10/176
Suttons, 42/165
Sutton St Edmund, 20/324
Sutton-under-Whitestone-cliffe, 42/358
Sutton Weaver, 5/378
Swainscoe, 32/28
Swalcliffe, 27/134
Swallowcliffe, 38/256
Sweffling, 33/400
Swindale, 37/33
Swineside, 42/20
Swingfield Minnis, 17/363
Swinhope, 20/328
Sychtyn, 49/90
Sydenham Damerel, 9/393
Symondsbury, 10/217

Tailbert, 37/33
Talhaiarn, 49/93
Tal y cavn, 48/30
Talygarth, 49/49
Tal-y-llyn, 52/31
Tamerton Foliot, 9/395
Tansterne, 41/2
Tanworth-in-Arden, 36/140
Tan y Bedwal, 49/47
Tapton, 8/54
Tarbock Green, 18/298
Tardebigge, 39/134
Tarnacre, 18/264
Tarnicar, 18/263
Tarrant Keyneston, 10/222
Tarrant Launceston, 10/223
Tarrant Rushton, 10/218
Tattersett, 23/232
Teffont Magna, 38/98
Teignmouth, 9/402, 9/403
Teirtref, 53/60
Temple Combe or Temple Coombe, 30/1
Temple Normanton, 8/54
Temple Ruckley, 38/163
Tenbury Wells, 39/135
Tenby, 54/127
Tentergate, 43/347
Terrington St Clement, 23/552
Terrington St Johns, 23/552
Thannington, 17/165
Thatcham, 2/130
The Abbey Demesnes, 13/190
The fences, 13/31
The Ford, 14/85
The Forest fences, 13/31
The Hem, 29/338
The Lowe, 29/175
The Lower Mean, 13/31
The Moat, 29/298
The Oaks, 29/254
The Vern, 14/84
Theydon Bois, 12/337
Theydon Garnon, 12/338
Theydon Gernon, 12/338
Thingwall, 5/390
Thingwall, 18/223
Thixendale, 41/183
Thompson's Walls, 25/125
Thoresby, 42/73
Thorlby, 43/378
Thornaby-on-Tees, 42/372
Thornborough, 25/128
Thorndon, 33/408
Thorne Coffin, 30/417
Thornes, 43/309
Thorney Lanes, 32/157
Thornfalcon, 30/418
Thornham Magna, 33/409
Thornham Parva, 33/410
Thornset, 8/21
Thornshap, 37/33
Thornton-le-Beans, 42/375
Thornton-le-Moor, 42/378
Thornton-le-Moors, 5/391
Thornton-le-Street, 42/201
Thorpe, 23/566, 23/567
Thorpe, 33/6, 33/12
Thorpe Abbotts, 23/564
Thorpefield, 42/384
Thorpe le Fallows, 20/340
Thorpe-le-Soken, 12/335
Thorpe on the Hill, 43/402
Thorpe St Andrew, 23/567
Thorpe Sub Montem, 43/79
Thorpe Thewles, 11/258
Throphill, 25/432
Throwleigh, 9/411
Thrupp, 27/82
Thunderley, 12/385
Thurlbear, 30/420
Thurlestone, 9/413
Thurlston, 33/460
Thurne, 23/13
Thurnham, 17/368
Thurning, 23/560
Thwaites, 43/407
Thwaite St Mary, 23/576
Tibbiston, 32/211
Tiln, 26/57
Tilney St Lawrence, 23/579
Tilsop, 29/230
Tirabad, 45/32
Tirymynach, 53/68
Toathman, 37/33
Tollard Farnham, 38/265
Tollard Royal, 38/265
Tongham, 34/108
Torbryan, 9/416
Torquay, 9/417
Torrisholme, 18/251
Tothby, 20/4
Tottington, 18/307, 18/308
Tranmere, 5/403
Trebydan, 53/21
Tredunnock, 22/118
Trefaldwyn, 53/57
Trefardclawdd, 29/199
Trefeglwys, 53/72
Treffgarne, 54/128
Treflin, 53/23
Trefnanney, 53/60
Trefonen, 29/323
Trefyclawdd, 55/18
Tregaian, 44/73
Tregavethan Manor, 6/189
Tre Llan, 49/47
Trelech, 47/82
Trelleck, 22/120
Tremerchion, 50/12
Trepenal, 29/201
Tre'r bont, 49/40
Treuddyn, 50/38
Trevecca, 45/73
Trevellan, 49/41
Trevor, 49/103
Trevor Uchaf, 49/104
Trewen, 6/197
Tre-wyn, 14/41
Trottiscliffe, 17/373
Trowscoed, 53/22

Trowse Millgate, 23/590
Truro, 6/198
Tuddenham, 33/422, 33/423
Tudweiliog, 48/68
Tuxlith, 35/268
Twemlow Green, 5/405
Twerton, 30/430
Twinstead, 12/353
Tyberton, 14/206
Tycerrig, 53/69
Tydd St Giles, 4/74
Tydd St Mary, 20/350
Tythegston, 51/123
Tytherington, 5/398
Tywyn, 52/32

Ugley, 12/312
Ukinton, 5/158
Ulcombe, 17/376
Ulpha, 37/54
Unerigg, 7/64
Upavon, 38/268
Up Holland, 18/317
Up Marden, 35/272
Upper Arley, 32/9
Upper Beeding, 35/25
Upper Bullingham, 14/38
Upper Earnstrey Park, 29/115
Upper Elkstone, 32/89
Upper Heath, 29/154
Upper Helmsley, 42/166
Upper Letcombe, 2/84
Upper or Golon Division, 55/15
Upper Parks, 29/115
Upper Quinton, 13/162
Upperthong, 43/395
Upshire, 12/174
Usworth, 11/269
Uwch Caeran, 49/84

Venn and Vern, 14/84
Vennington, 29/346
The Vern, 14/84
Vernham's Dean, 31/141
Verwood, 10/81

Wacton, 23/600
Waddesdon, 3/113
Wainfleet St Thomas, 20/241
Walcot, 24/112
Walcott, 23/601
Wales, 43/414
Walford, 29/128
Walkerslow, 29/364
Wall, 32/44
Wallerthwaite, 43/274
Wallington, 34/10
Wallop, 29/68
Wallridge, 25/449
Walltown, 25/455
Walshford, 43/330
Waltham, 12/174
Walton, 8/54, 29/25, 29/123
Walton, 18/322, 36/144
Walton-in-Gordano, 30/437
Walton-le-Dale, 18/321
Walton Mauduit, 36/144
Walton on the Hill, 34/124
Walton-on-the-Naze, 12/365
Walton-on-Trent, 8/220
Walton Parva, 36/35
Walwyn's Castle, 54/133
Wampool, 7/2
Wandsworth, 34/126
Wangford, 33/436
Wansford, 24/125
Warham St Mary the Virgin, 23/611
Wasdale, 7/127
Water Eaton, 27/82, 38/111
Waters Upton, 29/328
Wattlesborough, 29/8
Watton at Stone, 15/107
Wavendon, 3/116
Waves Wootton, 36/169
Wawne, 41/192
Waybourne, 23/599
Weare Giffard, 9/439
Wedhampton, 38/271
Weedon Bec, 24/134
Welbatch, 29/343
Welcombe, 9/440
Welford-on-Avon, 36/153
Well, 17/194
Wells, 30/445
Wells-next-the-Sea, 23/621
Welney, 4/76
Welshampton, 29/331
Welton le Wold, 20/361
Wendy, 4/78
Wentnor
Wesham, 18/215
West Appleton, 42/15
Westbourne, 35/283
West Bridgford, 26/20
Westbury-on-Severn, 13/213
Westbury on Trym, 13/214
Westbury-sub-Mendip, 30/447
West Butsfield, 11/38
Westby, 20/29
West Charleton, 9/99
West Chevington, 25/115
West Dowlish, 30/170
West Felton, 29/127
West Fen, 4/11
Westgate, 25/171
West Grinstead, 35/286
West Hackney, 21/20
West Harle, 25/216
West Harptree, 30/448
West Hawkswell, 42/162
West Hoathly, 35/136
West Hougham, 17/188
West Kingsdown, 17/206
Westlaby, 20/365
Westlecot, 38/112
Westleigh, 18/197
West Longridge, 11/162
West Lulworth, 10/248
West Lynn, 23/358
West Marton, 43/280
West Meon, 31/269
West Milton, 10/174
West Newbiggin, 11/189
Westnewton, 25/347
Weston, 29/29, 31/178
Weston, 29/297
Westonbirt, 13/217
Weston Cotton, 29/313
Weston-in-Gordano, 30/451
Weston Madoc, 53/7
Weston-on-the-Green, 27/146
Weston-on-Trent, 32/228
Weston-sub-Edge, 13/218
Weston-super-Mare, 30/452
West Porringland, 23/312
Westport St Mary, 38/60
West Runton, 23/464
West Shefford, 2/110
West Stour, 10/207
West Stourmouth, 17/352
West Stratton, 31/178
West Thorpe, 20/340
West Town, 33/371
West Wretham, 23/663
Wet Sleddale, 37/33
Wettleton, 29/304
Wevelsford, 38/282
Weybourne, 23/599
Wharles, 18/311
Whartons Meadow, 27/92
Whatmore, 29/44
Wheatacre, 23/627
Wheatenhurst, 13/221
Wheathampstead, 15/111
Whitby, 42/316
Whitchurch, 21/49
Whitchurch, 30/194, 54/135
Whitelackington, 30/457
Whitley Bay, 25/471
Whitley Lower, 43/431
Whitney-on-Wye, 14/226
Whittle, 8/21
Whittle-le-Woods, 18/336
Whittlesey St Andrew, 4/83
Wichling, 17/396
Wick, 51/11
Wick St Lawrence, 30/442
Wicken Bonant, 12/377
Wicken Bonhunt, 12/377

Wickham St Paul, 12/378
Wickmore, 23/650
Widcombe, 30/276
Widecombe in the Moor, 9/449
Wigfair, 49/88
Wiggington, 32/233
Wiggonby, 7/2
Wigmore, 29/346
Wigwig, 29/147
Wildsworth, 20/207
Wilksley, 5/145
Willingale, 12/383
Willington Corner, 5/435
Willoughby Waterleys, 19/160
Willstone, 29/65
Wilsey Meadow, 27/92
Wilson, 29/65
Wilton, 23/293
Wimblingswold, 17/270
Winchelsea, 35/295
Windsor, 2/146
Winsley, 29/338
Winson, 13/8
Winston, 11/287
Winterborne Came, 10/256
Winterborne Clenston, 10/249
Winterborne Whitechurch, 10/254
Winterborne Zelston, 10/259
Winterbourne Dauntsey, 38/290
Winterbourne Earls, 38/286
Winterbourne Gunner, 38/287
Winterbourne Stoke, 38/288
Wintersett, 43/439
Winterton-on-Sea, 23/643
Wisbech, 4/90
Wissington, 33/470
Withersdale Street, 33/471
Withington, 5/443
Withycombe Raleigh, 9/454
Witton Bridge, 23/648
Wix Bishop and Wix Ufford, 33/241
Wolferton, 23/656
Wolverdington, 36/167
Wolverton, 31/289
Wolvesnewton, 22/128
Wolviston, 11/292
Womenswold, 17/270
Woodale, 42/20
Woodcoates, 26/49
Wood Dalling, 23/652
Woodend, 24/12
Woodgarston, 31/180
Woodhall, 29/16, 41/28, 43/354
Woodham Ferrers, 12/390
Woodhouse, 32/44
Woodhouse Eaves, 19/164
Woodland, 18/205
Woodlands, 10/113
Woodlesford, 43/312
Woodmancote, 13/24
Woodstock, 27/18
Woodston, 16/59
Woodthorpe, 20/317
Wood Walton, 16/60
Wool, 10/64
Woolaston, 13/229
Woolley, 8/31
Woolstone, 3/124
Woolton, 18/223
Woolverton, 30/359
Wootton Bridge, 31/290
Wootton Fitzpaine, 10/266
Workwell, 23/440
Wormsley, 14/235
Worthing, 23/544
Wotton, 29/21
Wotton-under-Edge, 13/231
Wraysbury, 3/131
Wrayton, 18/217
Wrecsam, 49/106
Wreighill, 25/491
Wrenthorpe, 43/374
Wrentnall, 29/80
Wrexham, 49/106
Wrockwardine, 29/193
Wroot Acres, 20/280
Wychnor, 32/232
Wyddial, 15/112
Wyke, 29/125
Wykedown, 38/163
Wykham Park, 27/149
Wylye, 38/284
Wymeswold, 19/161
Wyre Piddle, 39/110

Yaddlethorpe, 20/46
Yateley, 31/297
Y Drenewydd, 53/61
Yeardsley, 5/423
Yeaton, 29/128
Yetlington, 25/95
Yetminster, 10/55
Y Fflint, 50/16
Ynys-Clydach, 45/80
Yorton, 29/369
Yr Wyddgrug, 50/28
Ysbyty Ifan, 49/100
Ysbyty Ystwyth, 46/70
Ysceifiog, 50/43
Ystrad, 46/18
Ystrad Aeron, 46/44
Ystradfellte, 45/81
Ystradgynlais, 45/82
Ystradmeurig, 46/69
Ystradynodd
Ystymeolwyn, 53/60